Medical Law: Text and Materials

Medical Law: Text and Materials

Ian Kennedy LLM
of the Inner Temple, Barrister.
Professor of Medical Law and Ethics
Head of Department of Laws
and Director, Centre of Medical Law
and Ethics, King's College, London.

Andrew Grubb MA (Cantab)
of the Inner Temple, Barrister.
Law Fellow and Director of Studies in Law
Fitzwilliam College,
Cambridge.

Butterworths
London
1989

United Kingdom	Butterworth & Co (Publishers) Ltd, 88 Kingsway, LONDON WC2B 6AB and 4 Hill Street, EDINBURGH EH2 3JZ
Australia	Butterworths Pty Ltd, SYDNEY, MELBOURNE, BRISBANE, ADELAIDE, PERTH, CANBERRA and HOBART
Canada	Butterworths Canada Ltd, TORONTO and VANCOUVER
Ireland	Butterworth (Ireland) Ltd, DUBLIN
New Zealand	Butterworths of New Zealand Ltd, WELLINGTON and AUCKLAND
Puerto Rico	Equity de Puerto Rico, Inc, HATO REY
Singapore	Malayan Law Journal Pte Ltd, SINGAPORE
USA	Butterworth Legal Publishers, AUSTIN, Texas; BOSTON, Massachusetts; CLEARWATER, Florida (D & S Publishers); ORFORD, New Hampshire (Equity Publishing); ST PAUL, Minnesota; and SEATTLE, Washington

A CIP Catalogue record for this book is available from the British Library.

ISBN 0 406 50041 X

Printed and bound in Great Britain by Mackays of Chatham PLC, Kent

Preface

Medical law is one of the fastest growing areas of legal study. It is also one of the most exciting and challenging since it draws on a wide range of existing legal areas, eg tort law, criminal law, family law, but does so in the context of certain unifying themes and concepts which mark off medical law as a separate field of study. Add to this the fascination and difficulty of the host of problems posed for society by advances in medicine and medical technology, and the importance and attraction of the subject become clear.

It is, furthermore, like any area of law an intensely practical subject. The problems it poses exist as real problems for doctors, nurses, patients, administrators, relatives, indeed for all of us. It is, therefore, a subject in which analysis must point to some sort of workable solution which satisfies the demands of legal reasoning and of the various parties involved, of public policy and private needs.

The last few years have seen a very considerable growth in the number of books concerned with medical law. We offer this book as a further contribution and one designed both to introduce the student to the great range of the subject and to make available to the student and practitioner alike the wealth of material now available in common law jurisdictions. The accompanying text is far more extensive than may be usual in books of materials. The reasons are not hard to find. Where there are materials in English law, they often need careful analysis and explication. And often there simply are no materials such that, if a particular area is to be analysed, it must be by way of text.

We both look back, with the nostalgia which distance lends, to weekly journeys up and down the M11, usually in the rain and often in the fog, and in and out of Cambridge and Liverpool Street stations. The collaboration was great fun. That explains, perhaps, why we took so long to finish the book!

Thanks are due to many people. In particular Pearl Watts typed the whole of the manuscript and earned our eternal gratitude as well as admiration for her endurance and cryptographic skills. Sylvia Seeley was the pillar on which our world rested and, as ever, she was marvellous. We saw off several editors assigned to us, but Butterworths persevered and we thank them. Cathy Barnard, Roy Burrows, Ben Ward and Winnie Yue were enthusiastic and helpful assistants, supported by generous grants from Fitzwilliam College and the University of Cambridge. Josie, AG's dog, was a constant companion but slept through it all. And our respective families suffered and supported us uncomplainingly.

The law is stated as of December 9, 1988.

IK
AG

Table of contents

Acknowledgments

The publishers and authors wish to thank the following for permission to reprint material from the sources indicated:

American Psychiatric Association: Roth, Meisel & Lidz: 'Tests of Competency to Consent to Treatment' (March 1977) American Journal of Psychiatry.

American Society of Law and Medicine: 'A Moment in Human Development; Legal Protection, Ethical Standards and Social Policy on the Selective Non-treatment of Handicapped Neonates' – American Journal of Law and Medicine, Vol 3 no 1 (1988), pp 39–41; Mady: 'Surrogate Mothers: The Legal Issues' (1984) Am J Law & Med 324, pp 332–339; Annas: 'Reconciling Quinlan and Saikewitz' (1984) 4 AJLM 367, p 376.

Association of the British Pharmaceutical Industry: 'Guidelines for Medical Experiments on Non-patient Human Volunteers' (1988), paras 1–12, appendices A–C; 'Guidelines in respect of injuries resulting to patients who are used in drug research' (1983), paras 11.7–11.8.

Australian Government Publishing Service: Law Reform Commission of Australia Report No 7: 'Human Tissue Transplants', pp 22–24, paras 176–178, 245; Human Tissue Act 1982, ss 38(1), 39(1); Senate Select Committee on Human Embryo Experimentation (1985), paras 2.12–2.14, 3.7–3.33, A23–A24.

Baylor Law Review, Vol 27, pp 6–10: Dr Karen Teel: 'The Physician's Dilemma: A Doctor's View: What the Law Should Be'.

Blackwell (Basil) Ltd: The Report to the Committee of Inquiry into Human Fertilisation and Embryology (Cmnd 9314) (1984) (The Warnock Report), paras 2.5, 2.13, 3.3, 3.4, 4.4, 4.7–9, 4.17, 4.19, 4.22, 4.25, 5.1–5, 6.8, 8.10–12, 10.11, 10.12, 11.8, 11.9, 11.11–50, 12.5, 13.13: Mary Warnock: 'A Question of Life', pp 642, 700.

British Institute of International and Comparative Law: Norrie: 'Human Tissue Transplants, Legal Liability in Different Jurisdictions' ICLQ (1985) July, pp 445–446.

British Medical Association: British Medical Journal, (1980) 10th May, CIBA Foundation Study Group on Compensation; British Transplantation Society Committee Report (1975), BMJ, p 257; Gillon: 'Ethics of Fetal Brain Cell Transplants', BMJ (1988) 30th April; Pallis: 'ABC of Brain Stem Death', pp 1–9, 17, 23, 28–32; Diagnosis of Death, Code of Practice (1976), (1976) 2 BMJ 1187–8, (1979) 1 BMJ 332; Tunkel: 'Abortion, How Early, How Late, How Legal?'; BMA Guidelines on Use of Fetal Tissue, The Bulletin, May

1988, p 6; Gillon: 'Philosophical Medical Ethics' (1985); Handbook of Medical Ethics (1984) para 1.6; Dworkin: 'Archives of Diseases in Childhood' (1978), p 445.

Cambridge University Press: J Spencer: 'Tissue Donors, Are They Rescuers or Merely Volunteers?' (1979) CLJ 45 at pp 46–47.

Canada Government Publishing Centre: Keyseringk: 'Sanctity of Life or Quality of Life', study written for the Law Reform Commission of Canada (1979) pp 50–51, 57–60, 70–72; Canadian Criminal Code, s 45; Somerville: 'Consent to Medical Care', Law Reform Commission of Canada Report (1980), pp 96–98.

Canada Law Book Incorporated: Johnson v Wellesley Hospital (1970) 17 DLR (3d) 139, 144–145; Lepp v Hopp 98 DLR (3d) at 470; Kelly v Hazlett 75 DLR (3d) 536, 562–563; Reibl v Hughes 114 DLR (3d) 10–11, 12–13, 15–17, 494–495; White v Turner (1981) 120 DLR (3d) 264, 285; Hopp v Lepp (1980) 112 DLR (3d) 67; Re Superintendant of Family and Child Services and Dawson 145 DLR (3d) 610, 611–612, 620, 622–624; Urbanski v Patel (1978) 84 DLR (3d) 650; Scarborough General Hospital (1980) 110 DLR (3d) 5713; Anderson v Chasney (1949) 4 DLR 71, (1950) 4 DLR 223; Girard v Royal Columbian Hospital (1976) 66 DLR (3d) 676; Zimmer v Ringrose (1981) 124 DLR (3d) 215.

Carswell Company Ltd: Halwiska v University of Saskatchewan (1965) 52 WWR 608, 616; Picard: 'Legal Liability of Doctors and Hospitals in Canada' 2nd Edn (1984), pp 45–46, 141, 143, 146–147, 243–247, 260–261, 308–311, 313–314.

Clarendon Press: Skegg: 'Law, Ethics and Medicine' (1984), pp 30–31, 36–37, 43–46, 51–52, 60–62, 72–73, 79–80, 107–109, 128–131, 135–136, 213–223; Gurry: 'Breach of Confidence' (1985), pp 58–60, 148–149; Whittaker: 'The EEC Directive on Product Liability', Year Book of European Law 1984, pp 257–258.

Columbia Law Review: Robertson: 'Organ Donations by Incompetents and Substituted Judgment Doctrine' 76 Colum L Rev 48 (1976), copyright c.1976 by the Directors of the Columbia Law Review Association Inc. All Rights Reserved. Reprinted by permission.

Croom Helm: Lamb: 'Death, Brain Death and Ethics', pp 11–16.

Darton, Longman & Todd Ltd: The Dictionary of Medical Ethics by AS Duncan, GR Dunstan & RB Welbourn (eds), pp 384–385, published and copyright 1983 by Darton, Longman & Todd Ltd and is used by permisson of the publishers.

DHSS Publications: Conference of the Medical Royal Colleges and their Faculties of the UK, Working Paper Report (Hoffenberg) 'On the Supply of Donor Organs for Transplantation' (1987), p 6; 'Organ Transplantation in Neonates' (1988), paras 4.7.3, 5.1–5.3; 'Advice to Health Ministers on Healthy Volunteer Studies', June 1987, paras 6.1–6.3, 6.14–6.17.

Edinburgh University Press: Meyers: 'The Human Body and the Law', pp 66, 116–117.

Edward Arnold (Publishers) Ltd: Report of Working Party on Living Wills, King's College/Age Concern.

Elsevier: Stone: 'English Law in Relation to AID and Embryo Transfer', in 'Law and Ethics of AID and Embryo Transfer', pp 69–70.

Faber & Faber Ltd: Glanville Williams: 'Sanctity of Life and the Criminal Law', pp 141, 274–275, 286, 289–290.

Foundation Press Incorporated: Williams 104 NW 12; Little v Little (1979) 576 SW (2d) 493; Kaimowitz v Dept of Mental Health for the State of Michegan 42 US LW 2063; Custody of a Minor 393 NE (2d), pp 148–149; Prosser, Wade & Schwartz: 'Cases & Materials on Torts', p 100; Waddington & Waltz: 'Cases on Law and Medicine', pp 139–141, 967, 980–983; Areen, King, Goldberg & Capron: 'Law, Science and Medicine', pp 956–960, 1223–1224.

Frank Cass & Co Ltd: Jackson & Powell: 'Professional Negligence' (2nd edn) (1987), paras 6.38, 6.102; Terry: 'The Malpractice Crisis in the United States, A Dispatch from the Trenches' (1986) 2 Prof Neg 145–150; Dugdale: 'Diverse Reports, Canadian Professional Negligence Cases', 2 Prof Neg (1986) 108 at 109–110.

General Medical Council: GMC Ruling – Transplantation of Non-regenerative Tissue – Standards Committee Item 7, Dec 1985, para 1; GMC 'Blue Book' 1983, para 83 (4); 1985, para 83 (4); 1987, paras 83–85, 9.28, 9.38, 9.68, 9.81.

Gower Publishing Group: McClean & Maher: 'Medicine, Morals and the Law', pp 1–4, 13–15, 64–66; McClean: 'Negligence, A Dagger at the Doctor's Back'; 'Justice, Lord Denning and the Constitution', ed Robson & Wachtmann, p 104.

Hastings Center: Andrews: 'My Body, My Property' Hastings CR (Oct 1986), pp 31–38; Caplan: 'Organ Procurement: It's not in the cards' (1984); Annas: 'From Canada With Love' (Dec 1987), pp 36–39; Capron: 'Anencephalic Donors: Separating the Dead from the Dying' (Feb 1987).

IME Publications Ltd: Bulletin of the Institute of Medical Ethics, February 1986, pp 8–9.

Institute of Law Research and Reform of Alberta: 'Sterilisation Decisions, Minors and Mentally Incompetent Adults' (March 1988), H24–35, paras 9.43–91.

Institute of Medical Ethics Publications Ltd: Kirby: 'Informed Consent, What Does It Mean?', Journal of Medical Ethics 1983, p 70.

Jordan & Sons Ltd: Re P (Minors) (1987) 2 FLR 421; A v C (1985) FLR 445; Re C (a Minor) (1985) FLR 846; Gold v Haringey Health Authority (1987) FLR 137–140.

Journal of Medical Ethics: Skegg: 'The Case for a Statutory Definition of Death', June 1976; Gillon: 'Impaired Autonomy and Rejection of Treatment', JME 1983, Vol 9, no 3, pp 131–132.

King's Fund Publishing and Press Office: Ham, Dingwall et al: 'Medical Negligence, Compensation and Accountability' (1988), pp 8–17, 26–34; Roberts: 'Rights and Wrongs in Medicine', King's College Studies 1986, pp 103–109; Capron: 'A National Commission on Medical Ethics', in 'Health, Rights and Resources' (1988), pp 188–190; Scarman: 'Law and Medical Practice', in 'Medicine in Contemporary Society' (1987), pp 137–138.

Kluwer Publishing: Lanham: 'Transplants and the Human Tissue Act 1961' (1971) 11 Med Sci Law 16, 17–18, 18–20, 21–22; Skegg: 'Human Tissue Act 1961' (1976) 16 Med Sci Law 197–199; Skegg: 'Liability for the Unauthorised Removal of Cadaveric Transplant Materials' (1974) 14 Med Sci Law 53, 55–56; Skegg: (1977) 17 Med Sci Law 123, 124.

Lancet: 'Commercialisation in Transplantation: the Problems and Some Guidelines for Practice', Lancet, 28 Sept 1985, pp 715–716.

Law Book Company: Cane: 'Injuries to Unborn Children' (1977) 51 ALJ 704, 707–708; Fleming: 'Law of Torts' (7th ed) (1987), pp 23, 72, 73, 74–75, 110, 471–472.

Law Society: Pearl & Pearl: 'AIDS – An Overview of the Legal Implications: Liability in Tort (1989) 86 Law Soc Gaz 28.

Lexington Books: Werthman: 'Medical Malpractice Law: How Medicine is Changing the Law', pp 31–32.

Lloyds of London Press Ltd: Wimpey Construction UK Ltd v DV Poole (1984) 2 Lloyds Rep 498.

Longman Professional & Business Communications Division: Clarke v Adams (1950) 94 SJ 599; Landau v Werner (1961) 105 SJ 1008.

McGill Law Journal: Somerville: 'Structuring the Issues in Informed Consent' (1981) 26 McGill LJ 740; Picard: 'The Liability of Hospitals in Common Law Canada' (1981) 26 McGill LJ 997.

Medical Protection Society: 'Consent, Confidentiality, Disclosure of Medical Records', 1988 Medical Protection Society General Consent Form; 'General Practice Complaints Procedure' (1983), paras 3, 13, p 6.

Michegan Law Review Association: Dukeminier: 'Supplying Organs for Transplantation' 68 Mich L Rev, pp 811–866, (April 1970).

MIT Press: Jonsen & Hellegers: 'Conceptual Foundations for an Ethics of Medical Care' (1974) (reprinted in Reiser, Dyck & Curran: 'Ethics in Medicine' (1977); Sisla Bok: 'The Tools of Bio-Ethics' (1976) (reprinted in Reiser, Dyck & Curran); Dyck: 'Ethics and Medicine' (1973) (reprinted in Reiser, Dyck & Curran).

Monash University: 'Law and Medical Experimentation' (1987) 13 Monash Univ LR 189, pp 200, 204, 198–203.

New England Journal of Medicine: Beecher: 'Ethics and Clinical Research' 274 New Eng J Med 1354 (1966).

New Zealand Government Printing Office: Crimes Act 1961, s 61, as amended by Crimes (Amendment) Act 1977, s 2; Crimes Act 1961, as amended in 1977, ss 3, 61A, 182A.

Northern Ireland Legal Quarterly, SLS Legal Publications: Davies: 'Fabricated Man: the Dilemma Posed by Artificial Reproductive Techniques', (1984) 35 NILQ 354, p 365.

Ontario Law Reform Commission: Report on Human Artificial Reproduction and Related Matters (1984), pp 102–104, 106–107, 118–120, 123–130, 153–159, 185–190. © Reprinted with permisson from the Queen's Printer for Ontario.

Oxford University Press: Lockwood: 'Moral Dilemmas in Modern Medicine' (1985), pp 156–169; Singer & Wells: 'New Ways of Making Babies, Reproduction Revolution' (1984), pp 107–108, 114–120; Kuhse & Singer: 'Should the Baby Live?' (1985), pp 18–20; Nicholson: 'Medical Research With Children' (1986), pp 24–26, 119–120, 154; Hare: 'Little Human Guinea Pigs' (in 'Moral Dilemmas in Modern Medicine' ed Lockwood); Beauchamp & Childress: 'Principles of Biomedical Ethics', 2nd edn (1983), pp 66–69; Faden & Beauchamp: 'A History and Theory of Informed Consent' (1986), pp 123, 125, 127–128, 129, 130–131, 132–133, 137–138, 139; Gorovitz: 'Doctor's Dilemmas' (1982), pp 75–79, 83–89, 98–111, 146–150; Institute of Medical Ethics, 'Medical Research With Children' (1986), pp 33–37; Gurry: 'The Law Relating to Breach of Confidence' (1985), pp 58–60, 148–149; Lee: 'Law and Morals', pp 59–60; Eekelaar: 'The Emergence of Children's Rights' (1986) 6 Oxford Journal of Legal Studies 161, pp 180–181; Devlin: 'Samples of Law Making' (1960), pp 83, 95, 103.

Penguin Books Ltd: Scott: 'The Body As Property' (1981), pp 127–134, 136; Brazier: 'Medicine, Patients and the Law', pp 11–12, 53–54, 70, 90, 128–134; Glover: 'Causing Death and Saving Lives', pp 22–26, 29–33.

Pitman Publishing: Whitfield: 'The General Medical Council' (in 'Medical Malpractice' (1980) ed J Leahy Taylor).

Routledge & Keegan Paul: Harris: 'The Value of Life', pp 133–134.

Royal College of Obstetricians & Gynaecologists: Report on Foetal Liability and Clinical Practice, pp 10–15.

Russell Sage Foundation: Katz: 'Experimentation With Human Beings' (1972), pp 292–306.

Shaw & Sons Ltd: Gostin: 'Mental Health Services Law and Practice', para 20.16.

Smith: 'Warnock and After: The Legal and Moral Issues Surrounding Embryo Experimentation', in 'Medicine, Ethics and the Law', ed M Ockleton.

Society For the Right to Die: Handbook of 1985 Living Will Laws, pp 5–7, reprinted with permisson of the Society for the Right to Die, New York.

Stevens & Sons Ltd: Robertson: 'Informed Consent to Medical Treatment' 97

LQR 123–124; Glanville Williams: Current Legal Problems 1958, p 136; Glanville Williams: 'Textbook of Criminal Law' 1st edn, p 237; Glanville Williams: 'Textbook of Criminal Law' 2nd edn, 148–149, 285, 289, 294–301, 378, 579, 589–591, Leng: 'Death and the Criminal Law' 45 MLR 206 at 208–209; Dworkin: 'The Law Relating to Organ Transplantation' MLR Vol 33 July 1970; Matthews: 'Whose Body, People as Property', Current Legal Problems 1983, pp 225–226; Pace: 'Civil Liability for Pre-Natal Injuries' (1977) MLR 141, pp 141–147, 150–153; Montrose: 'Is Negligence an Ethical or Sociological Concept?' (1958) 21 MLR 259; Robertson: 'A New Application for the Rescue Principle' (1980) 96 LQR 19, 20; McClean: 'The Implication of No-Fault Liability for the Medical Profession' (in 'Medicine, Ethics and the Law', ed Freeman), pp 147, 151–158.

St Louis University: Rosencranz & Lavey: 'Treating Patients With Communicable Diseases' (1987) 32 St Louis ULJ 75.

Sweet & Maxwell Ltd: Winfield & Jolowicz on Tort, 12th edn, p 706; Hoggett: 'Mental Health Law', pp 133, 201–203; Keown: 'Miscarriage, A Medico–Legal Analysis' (1984) Crim LR 605, 608–611; Tunkel (1974) Crim LR 461 at 465; Eaton: 'The British Response to Surrogate Motherhood', The Law Teacher Vol 19 (1985), pp 181–185; Eekelaar & Dingwall: 'Some Legal Issues in Obstetric Practice', Journal of Social Welfare (1984), p 258; Finch: 'Health Services Law' (1981), pp 37–39; Price: 'Selective Reduction and Feticide, the Parameters of Abortion' (1988) Crim LR 199; R v Lennox-Wright (1973) Crim LR; R v Bodkin Adams (1957) CLR 365: 'Encyclopaedia of Health Services and Medical Law', ed Jacobs & Davies, paras 1.031–1.044; Jackson & Powell: 'Professional Negligence', 2nd edn, (1987), para 1.10; Stephen: 'Digest of the Criminal Law' (1878), p 145.

Tavistock Publications: Edwards: 'Human Embryo Research: Yes or No', pp 149–150.

UC Davis Law Review: Capron: 'Alternative Birth Technologies: Legal Challenges' (1987) UC Davis LR pp 679, 682, 697–701.

US Government Printing Office: President's Commission for the Study of Ethical Problems in Medicine and Biomedical and Behavioral Research: 'Deciding to Forego Life Sustaining Treatment' (1983), pp 78–81, 82–88, 136–139, 139–141, 217–223; 'Making Health Care Decisions' (1983), pp 31–35, 32, 35–36, 38–40, 52–62, 62–67, 63–68, 68–69, 70–72, 82–88, 136–139, 139–141, 172–173; 'Defining Death' (1981), pp 32, 35–36, 38–40, 62–67, 68–69, 70–72; Regulations on Protection of Human Subjects (1983) 45 CFR 46, 46.102, 46.116.

University of Louisville: Brophy: 'Surrogate Mother Contract Agreement', Journal of Family Law Vol 22, pp 266–288.

University of Minnesota: McCoid: 'A Reappraisal of Liability for Unauthorised Medical Treatment (1957) 41 Minnesota LR 381, pp 422–424.

University of Nebraska: Martyn & Jacobs: 'Legislating Advance Directives for the Terminally Ill, the Living Will and Durable Power of Attorney', 63 Neb L Rev 779, 797–802 (1984).

University of New South Wales Law Journal: Sappideen: 'The Surrogate Mother, A Growing Problem' (1983) 6 UNSWLJ 79, 90–91.

University of Toronto: Dickens: 'Reproduction Law and Medical Consent' 35 Univ Toronto Law J (1985), pp 255–286.

University of Virginia: 'Sale of Human Organs', Virginia Law Rev (1985) Vol 71, 71.1015.

University of Western Ontario: Robertson: 'Overcoming the Causation Hurdle in Informed Consent Cases', University of Western Ontario Law Review (1984) Vol 22, pp 78–80.

Unwin Hyman: Snowden & Mitchell; 'The Artificial Family', pp 16–20.

Victoria Government Publishing Office: Status of Children (Amendment) Act 1984, ss 10A(1), 10D, 10E; Infertility (Medical Procedures) Act 1984, ss 10(1), 11(1), 12(1), 13(1), 14, 30.

Voluntary Licensing Authority: VLA's 3rd Report, April 1988, Keown, annex 5; Report of the Panel Appointed to Hear the Application for a Product License to Market; In Vitro Fertilisation and Embryology, April 1988.

Waller, Professor Louis: an extract from the Cambridge Colloquium, 'Making Law for Laboratory Life in Australia, pp 7–9.

West Publishing Co: Furrow, Jost & Schwartz: 'Health Law' (1987), pp 276–285, 310–315; Black's Law Dictionary (5th Ed) (1979), p 360.

Williams, Professor Glanville: correspondence, 'Times' (1981) 13 August. Wisconsin Law Review: Gelfand: 'Living Will Statutes, the First Decade' (1987) Wisconsin LR 737, pp 740–744, 746–747, 750–753.

Table of statutes

References in this Table to *Statutes* are to Halsbury's Statutes of England (Fourth Edition) showing the volume and page at which the annotated text of an Act may be found.

Page references printed in **bold** type indicate where the section of an Act is set out in part or in full.

List of cases

Page numbers printed in **bold** type indicate where part of the judgment of a case is set out.

Part I

Introduction

Chapter 1

The doctor/patient relationship

The case of *Gillick v West Norfolk and Wisbech Area Health Authority* [1984] 1 All ER 365 per Woolf J; revsd [1985] 1 All ER 533, CA; revsd [1985] 3 All ER 402, HL may serve for us as a good beginning for the study of medical law. This is not necessarily because of what it specifically relates to; rather, it represents an example of modern medical law. It is self-evidently not a case on medical negligence. Medical law is much more than this, though some would have you believe otherwise. *Gillick* shows how medical law is inseparably intertwined with medical ethics. It also shows you that as an area of law, medical law does not respect the traditional compartments with which lawyers have become familiar, such as torts, contracts, criminal law, family law and public law. Instead, medical law cuts across all of these subjects and today must be regarded as a subject in its own right. We maintain that it is a discrete area concerned with the law governing the interactions between doctors and patients and the organisation of health care. There are common issues which permeate all the problems which arise: respect for autonomy, consent, truth-telling, confidentiality, respect for personhood and persons, respect for dignity and respect for justice. All of these ethical issues run throughout the area. Until these common themes are recognised and reflected in legal thinking and analysis, a coherent approach to the emerging problems in medical law will be difficult. There is a need to develop a body of legal doctrine which reflects the coherence of the ethical principles and the analysis derived therefrom: achieving this is our aim.

A case-study in medical law and ethics

In February 1981 the Department of Health and Social Security (DHSS) published the following memorandum of guidance as part of a circular (HSC (IS)32) concerning family planning. The circular 'outlined the arrangements to be made for the organisation and development of a comprehensive family planning service within the national health service' (per Woolf J at 367).

REVISED SECTION G—THE YOUNG

Clinic sessions should be available for people of all ages, but it may be helpful to make separate, less formal arrangements for young people. The staff should be experienced in dealing with young people and their problems. There is widespread concern about counselling and treatment for children under 16. Special care is needed not to undermine parental responsibility and family stability. The Department would therefore hope that in any case where a doctor or other professional worker is approached by a person under the age of 16 for advice in these matters, the doctor, or other professional, will always seek to persuade the child to involve the parent or guardian (or other person *in loco parentis*) at the earliest stage of consultation, and will proceed from the assumption that it would be most unusual to provide advice about contraception without parental consent. It is, however, widely accepted that consultations between doctors and patients are confidential; and the Department recognises the importance which doctors and patients attach to this principle. It is a principle which applies also to the other professions concerned. To abandon this principle for children under 16 might cause some not to seek professional advice at all. They could then be exposed to the immediate risks of pregnancy and of sexually-transmitted disease, as well as other long-term physical, psychological and emotional consequences which are equally a threat to stable family life. This would apply particularly to young people whose parents are, for example, unconcerned, entirely unresponsive, or grossly disturbed. Some of these young people are away from their parents and in the care of local authorities or voluntary organisations standing *in loco parentis*. The Department realises that in such exceptional cases the nature of any counselling must be a matter for the doctor or other professional worker concerned and that the decision whether or not to prescribe contraception must be for the clinical judgment of a doctor.

There followed correspondence between a Mrs Victoria Gillick and the administrator of the Area Health Authority in whose area Mrs Gillick lived.

Concerning the *new* DHSS Guidelines on the contraceptive and abortion treatment of children under both the legal and medical age of consent, *without* the knowledge or consent of the parents, can I please ask you for a written assurance that in no circumstances whatsoever will any of my daughters . . . be given contraceptive or abortion treatment whilst they are under *sixteen*, in any of the Family Planning Clinics under your control, without my prior knowledge, and irrefutable evidence of my consent? Also, should any of them seek advice in them, can I have your assurance that I would be automatically contacted in the interests of my children's safety and welfare? If you are in any doubt about giving me such assurances, can I please ask you to seek legal medical advice.

Yours faithfully
Mrs Victoria Gillick

She received the following reply on 27 January 1981:

Thank you for your letter of 21st January addressed to the Chairman and he has asked me to reply to you on his behalf. I enclose for your information a copy of the official guidance issued in May 1980, together with a copy of a recent press statement made by the Minister of Health on this important matter. You will see that the Minister emphasises that it would be most unusual to provide advice about contraception without parental consent, but it does go on to say that the final decision must be for the doctor's clinical judgment. We would expect our doctors to work within these guidelines but, as the Minister has stated, the final decision in these matters must be one of clinical judgment.

Not satisfied, Mrs Gillick issued proceedings on 5 August 1982 against the Area Health Authority and the DHSS. *Inter alia* she pleaded that:

The said Notice, which has no authority in law, gives advice which is unlawful and wrong and which adversely affects or which may adversely affect the welfare of the Plaintiff's said children, and/or the rights of the Plaintiff as parent and custodian of the said children.

PARTICULARS

The said advice: (a) condones and/or encourages and/or recommends and/or directs the giving of contraceptive or abortion advice to a child below the age of 16, thereby contemplating the fact or the possibility of a criminal offence against such child, namely the offence of unlawful sexual intercourse with an infant; further, it contemplates the barring of the parent and/or custodian of such child from access to information necessary for the proper and effective discharge of his or her duties towards such child, and in particular the duties of supervising the physical and moral welfare of such child; (b) permits and/or advises a doctor to conduct a physical examination on a child below the age of 16 and/or to prescribe and/or administer drugs to such child without the prior knowledge or consent of the said child's parent or guardian; (c) condones and/or encourages and/or connives at unlawful conduct on the part of males over the age of 14 against female children below the age of 16, namely the committing of offences of unlawful sexual intercourse with an infant.

Mrs Gillick asked the court to grant her a declaration in the following terms (on the use of private proceedings when the issues involved were matters of public law, see the discussion of *O'Reilly v Mackman* [1982] 3 All ER 1124 by Lords Scarman and Fraser in *Gillick* and the commentary by Jolowicz [1986] CLJ and Harlow (1986) 49 MLR 768):

> (i) a declaration against the First Defendants and the Second Defendants on a true construction of the said Notice and in the events which have happened, including and in particular the publication and the circulation of the said Notice, that the said Notice has no authority in law and gives advice which is unlawful and wrong, and which adversely affects or which may adversely affect the welfare of the Plaintiff's said children, and/or the rights of the Plaintiff as parent and custodian of the said children, and/or the ability of the Plaintiff properly and effectively to discharge her duties as such parent and custodian; (ii) a declaration against the First Defendants that no doctor or other professional person employed by the First Defendants either in the Family Planning Service or otherwise may give any contraceptive and/or abortion advice and/or treatment to any child of the Plaintiff below the age of 16 without the prior knowledge and/or consent of the said child's parent or guardian.

On 26 July 1983 Woolf J refused Mrs Gillick her declarations. The judge decided that the doctor would not *necessarily* be acting unlawfully in following the guidance. First, he rejected the argument that the doctor would commit a criminal offence either under s 28 of the Sexual Offences Act 1956 of 'caus[ing]' or 'encourag[ing] the commission of unlawful sexual intercourse with . . . a girl under the age of 16 for whom he is responsible' or under the common law as an accessory to the crime committed by a man who had sexual intercourse with the girl. Secondly, the judge rejected the argument that a girl under the age of 16 could never give a valid consent to contraceptive treatment such that the decision should always rest with the girl's parents.

Mrs Gillick appealed to the Court of Appeal which after five days of argument granted Mrs Gillick her two declarations: first, that the notice issued was 'contrary to law', secondly, in the terms of the second declaration sought by Mrs Gillick, subject to an amendment so as to add at the end 'save in case of emergency or with the leave of the court'.

What does the first declaration mean?

Parker LJ: The extent of a parent's rights and duties with respect to the medical treatment of a child

(a) *The statutory background*

Until the Family Law Reform Act 1969, by s 1 of which the age of majority was reduced from 21 to 18, there was no statutory provision with regard to a minor's consent to surgical, medical or dental treatment, but s 8 of that Act provided:

> '(1) The consent of a minor who has attained the age of sixteen years to any surgical, medical or dental treatment which, in the absence of consent, would constitute a trespass to his person, shall be as effective as it would be if he were of full age; and where a minor has by virtue of this section given an effective consent to any treatment it shall not be necessary to obtain any consent for it from his parent or guardian.
>
> (2) In this section "surgical, medical or dental treatment" includes any procedure undertaken for the purposes of diagnosis, and this section applies to any procedure (including, in particular, the administration of an anaesthetic) which is ancillary to any treatment as it applies to that treatment.
>
> (3) Nothing in this section shall be construed as making ineffective any consent which would have been effective if this section had not been enacted.'

The construction of this section is the subject of dispute. For the appellant it is contended that, but for s 8, no consent could be given by a minor, and that the effect of sub-s (1) is to lower the age of consent in the particular case to 16 but that at any lesser age, if consent is required, it can only be given by a parent or guardian.

Subsection (3) is, it is submitted, merely to make it clear that, where a parent's consent has been obtained, it is not made ineffective because a consent from the minor could be or could have been obtained under sub-s (1).

For the respondents, however, it is contended that all that the section was doing was to make it clear (1) that in the case of a person who had attained the age of 16 the doctor had no need to satisfy himself that the minor was of sufficient understanding to give consent and (2) that the purpose of sub-s (3) was merely to ensure that a consent by a minor under 16 which would have been valid prior to the Act could still be relied on.

There is no decided case that, prior to the Act, the consent of a minor under the age of 16 would have been effective and there are many indications that it would not, as I shall in due course show.

Although prior to 1969 there was no statutory provision relating to consent to treatment, the National Health Service (General Medical and Pharmaceutical Services) Regulations 1962, SI 1962/2248, gave to a person who had attained the age of 16 the right to choose his own doctor by providing that until such age the right should be exercised on his behalf by a parent, guardian or other person who had the care of the child, and the Mental Health Act 1959, s 5(2) (which deals with the informal admission of patients requiring treatment for a mental disorder) provides:

'In the case of an infant who has attained the age of sixteen years and is capable of expressing his own wishes, any such arrangements as are mentioned in the foregoing subsection may be made, carried out and determined notwithstanding any right of custody or control vested by law in his parent or guardian.'

This last provision plainly proceeds on the basis that the right of custody or control vested in a parent or guardian carried with it the right to prevent a minor submitting to treatment for mental disorder or admitting himself to a hospital or nursing home therefor and qualifies that right in respect, but only in respect, of minors who have attained the age of 16 years *and* are capable of expressing their own wishes. This as it seems to me is but one aspect of what is inherent in the right to custody or control. In this connection certain provisions of the Children Act 1975 are of some assistance:

'**85.**—(1) In this Act, unless the context otherwise requires, "the parental rights and duties" means, as respects a particular child (whether legitimate or not), all the rights and duties which by law the mother and father have in relation to a legitimate child and his property; and references to a parental right or duty shall be construed accordingly and shall include a right of access and any other element included in a right or duty.

(2) Subject to section 1(2) of the Guardianship Act 1973 (which relates to separation agreements between husband and wife), a person cannot surrender or transfer to another any parental right or duty he has as respects a child . . .'

It will be observed that there is a recognition that the father and mother have both rights and duties in respect of the child himself and his property and that, subject to the specific exception, a person is incapable of surrendering or transferring any parental right or duty. Under this provision therefore a parent cannot opt out of his rights and duties whatever they may be.

Sections 86 and 87(2) then deal with the question of legal custody and actual custody:

'**86.** In this Act, unless the context otherwise requires, "legal custody" means, as respect a child, so much of the parental rights and duties as relate to the person of the child (including the place and manner in which his time is spent) but a person shall not by virtue of having legal custody of a child be entitled to effect or arrange for his emigration from the United Kingdom unless he is a parent or guardian of the child.

87. . . . (2) While a person not having legal custody of a child has actual custody of the child he has the like duties in relation to the child as a custodian would have by virtue of his legal custody . . .'

Thus a legal custodian and actual custodian for so long as the child is in his actual custody has, it is recognised, all the parental rights and duties relating to the person of the child including specifically the place at which and manner in which his time is spent. For the purposes of the 1975 Act a child is, in effect, a minor (see s 107(1)).

On the face of it, if there is a right and duty to determine the place and manner in which a child's time is spent, such right or duty must cover the right and duty completely to control the child subject of course always to the intervention of the court. Indeed there must, it seems to me, be such a right from birth to a fixed age unless whenever, short of majority, a question arises it must be determined, in relation to a particular child and a particular matter, whether he or she is of sufficient understanding to make a responsible and reasonable decision. This alternative appears to me singularly unattractive and impracticable, particularly in the context of medical treatment. If a child seeks medical advice the doctor has first to decide whether to accept him or her as a patient. At this stage, however, unless the child is going to his or her own general practitioner, which in the present context is unlikely, the doctor will know nothing about the child. If he decides to accept the child as a patient then, it is said, there is an inviolable duty of confidence and the parent cannot be informed or his or her consent sought without the child's permission. The doctor is entitled to decide what advice or treatment to administer.

Finally in this section it is necessary to mention s 48 of the Education Act 1944. Subsection (3) places a duty on every local education authority to make arrangements for seeing that comprehensive facilities for free medical treatment should be available to pupils in attendance at every school or county college maintained by it and empowers it to make such arrangements for senior pupils at any other educational establishment maintained by it. Subsection (4) places on every local education authority the further duty to make arrangements for encouraging and assisting pupils to take advantage of such facilities but contains the following proviso:

'Provided that if the parent of any pupil gives to the authority notice that he objects to the pupil availing himself of any medical treatment provided under this section the pupil shall not be encouraged . . . so to do.'

A senior pupil is by s 114 of the 1944 Act a person between the ages of 12 and 19. The age of majority was, at the time, 21.

This provision appears to me a plain recognition of the right of a parent to control the treatment provided for a child up to the age of 19.

Taken together, the statutory provisions in my opinion support the appellant's contentions.

(b) *The case law*

There are two classes of cases to be considered, first those cases which are specifically concerned with medical treatment and second those which are not.

In the first class of case I refer first to *Re D (a minor) (wardship: sterilisation)* [1976] 1 All ER 326, [1976] Fam 185. In that case a child, D, was severely handicapped and, for reasons which do not matter, her parents decided, when she was very young, to seek to have her sterilised when she reached about 18. She reached puberty at the age of 10 and her mother, who had over the years discussed the possibility of sterilisation with a consultant paediatrician, a Dr Gordon, raised the matter with him again. He and the mother agreed that the sterilisation operation should be performed provided that a Miss Duncan, a consultant gynaecologist, also agreed. Miss Duncan, did agree and D was accordingly booked into a hospital in order that a hysterectomy might be performed. The former and present headmasters of D's school, a social worker involved with the family and the plaintiff, Mrs Hamidi, an educational psychologist who had seen D on a number of occasions, disagreed with what was proposed. An attempt was made by them to secure a change of views but this failed. The plaintiff therefore instituted wardship proceedings and sought the ruling of the court as to what should be done. The matter was heard by Heilbron J in chambers but a full judgment was given in open court. There were two issues: (1) whether the wardship should be continued and (2) whether the proposed sterilisation should take place. Heilbron J decided that wardship should continue and that the operation should not take place. As to the first issue the judge said ([1976] 1 All ER 326 at 333, [1976] Fam 185 at 193–194):

'This operation could, if necessary, be delayed or prevented if the child were to remain a ward of court, and as Lord Eldon LC so vividly expressed it in *Wellesley*'s case (1827) 2 Russ 1 at 18, 38 ER 236 at 242: "It has always been the principle of this Court, not to risk the incurring of damage to children which it cannot repair, but rather to prevent the damage being done." I think that is the very type of case where this court should "throw some care around this child", and I propose to continue her wardship which, in my judgment, is appropriate in this case.'

And as to the second:

'In considering this vital matter, I want to make it quite clear that I have well in mind the natural feelings of a parent's heart, and though in wardship proceedings parents' *rights* can be superseded, the court will not do so lightly, and only in pursuance of well-known principles laid down over the years. The exercise of the court's jurisdiction is paternal, and it must be exercised judicially, and the judge must act, as far as *humanly possible*, on the evidence, as a *wise parent would act*.' (My emphasis.)

The first of these passages recognises explicitly that unless the wardship was continued the mother could and would proceed with the proposed operation, and the second that in refusing leave to have the operation performed the court was superseding the parents' rights.

Two further matters require mention before I leave this case. First, Dr Gordon asserted that provided he had the consent of the mother the decision whether the operation should be performed was within his and Miss Duncan's sole clinical judgment. As to this the judge said ([1976] 1 All ER 326 at 335, [1976] Fam 185 at 196):

'I cannot believe, and the evidence does not warrant the view, that a decision to carry out an operation of this nature performed for non-therapeutic purposes on a minor, can be held to be within the doctor's sole clinical judgment.'

It is to be noted that in the present case an even larger claim is asserted, namely on the basis of clinical judgment alone to proceed *without the parents' consent* and contrary to her known wishes and express prohibition.

Second, albeit it may not need stating since there is no dispute, the judge made it quite clear that once a child is a ward of court no important step in the life of that child can be taken without the consent of the court.

It was not seriously contended by counsel for the department that the giving of contraceptive advice and treatment to a girl under 16 would be other than an important step in her life. Assuming that it would be, it follows that, in the case of a ward, a doctor who was approached for contraceptive advice and treatment in the case of such a person would be obliged to inform the court and obtain its consent. Since, in wardship, the court is under a duty to act as a wise parent would act it is submitted that, if there is no wardship, parental consent must be sought in order that he or she should have the opportunity to act wisely. Such contention appears to me to have considerable force.

The next case, *Re P (a minor)* (1982) 80 LGR 301, is a decision of Butler-Sloss J in chambers, reported with her permission. P was aged 15 and had become pregnant for the second time. She was in the care of the local authority. They and P were in favour of an abortion but her parents, whose consent the local authority had, albeit not obliged to do so, properly sought, objected strongly on religious grounds. When they objected, the local authority instituted wardship proceedings. The parents' wishes were overridden but since the child was in care this is not of particular significance. What is of some importance however is that Butler-Sloss J not only ordered that an abortion should take place against the parents' wishes, but ordered further that, with the approval and at the request of the mother, she be fitted thereafter with a suitable internal contraceptive device. As to this the judge said: 'I assume that it is impossible for this Local Authority to monitor her sexual activities and, therefore, contraception appears to be the only alternative.'

Butler-Sloss J stated that, in reaching her conclusions, she had found helpful what had been said by the House of Lords about parental rights and obligations in a case much relied on by counsel for the department, namely *J v C* [1969] 1 All ER 788, [1970] AC 668. That case, however, affords little assistance as to what rights and obligations (or duties) are comprised in parental rights and obligations, for the question was whether s 1 of the Guardianship of Infants Act 1925 (which makes the welfare of the infant the first and paramount consideration in proceedings in which custody or upbringing is in question) applies only to disputes between parents or whether it also applies to disputes between parents and strangers. In so far as parental rights and obligations figured at all it was therefore in relation to the weight to be given to them in reaching a conclusion under the Act as to what was best for the child and not in relation to their extent. The department's reliance on this case is in my opinion misplaced.

Re N (*minors*) (*parental rights*) [1974] 1 All ER 126, [1974] Fam 40 was also relied on but that case also affords no real assistance.

The cases which do in my opinion assist are those cases relating to the age of discretion relied on by the appellant, all of which counsel for the department submits should be disregarded on the ground that they related to custody.

In *R v Howes* (1860) 3 E & E 332, 121 ER 467 the question was whether a father was, by habeas corpus, entitled to recover the custody of a child between 15 and 16 notwithstanding that the child did not desire to be in his custody. Cockburn CJ, giving the judgment of the court on the father's application for the return of the child to his custody, said (3 E & E 332 at 336–337, 121 ER 467 at 468–469):

'Now the cases which have been decided on this subject shew that, although *a father is entitled to the custody of his children till they attain the age of twenty-one, this Court will not grant a habeas corpus to hand a child which is below that age over to its father, provided that it has attained an age of sufficient discretion to enable it to exercise a wise choice for its own interests. The whole question is, what is that age of discretion?* We repudiate utterly, as most dangerous, the notion that any intellectual precocity in an individual female child can hasten the period which appears to have been fixed by statute for the arrival of the age of discretion; for that very precocity, if uncontrolled, might very probably lead to her irreparable injury. The *Legislature has given us a guide, which we may safely follow, in pointing out sixteen as the age up to which the father's right to the custody of his female child is to continue; and short of which such a child has no discretion to consent to leaving him.*' (My emphasis.)

The repudiation of the notion that intellectual precocity can hasten the age at which a minor can be considered to be of sufficient discretion to exercise a wise choice for its own interests and the fixing of a single age is to be noted.

In *Re Agar-Ellis, Agar-Ellis v Lascelles* (1883) 24 Ch D 317 a father put restrictions on his 17-year-old daughter's intercourse with her mother. The girl was at the time a ward of court. Brett MR said (at 326): '. . . the father has the control over the person, education and conduct of his children until they are twenty-one years of age. That is the law.' It had been argued that, because in habeas corpus proceedings a girl of 16 or more would not be delivered up to her father if she was content to remain where she was, this showed that the father's right of custody and control terminated altogether at age 16, but this argument was rejected on the ground that habeas corpus was a special case. Cotton LJ, having quoted the passage from Cockburn CJ set out above, said (at 331):

'Therefore the Lord Chief Justice there most distinctly recognises what, having regard to the Act, I should have thought was beyond dispute, that during infancy and over sixteen the right of the father still continues.'

The Act referred to was the Tenures Abolition Act 1660, s 8 of which gave the father the right to dispose of the custody and tuition of his children up to the age of 21.

The judgment which, however, I find of most assistance is that of Bowen LJ, from which I quote at greater length (at 335–336):

'Now a good deal of this discussion has turned upon the exact limits of parental authority. As far as one can see, some little confusion has been caused by the use in earlier law books of distinctions by which the law now no longer strictly stands.

The strict Common Law gave to the father the guardianship of his children during the age of nurture and until the age of discretion. The limit was fixed at fourteen years in the case of a boy, and sixteen years in the case of a girl; but beyond this, except in the case of the heir apparent, if one is to take the strict terminology of the older law, the father had no actual guardianship except only in the case of the heir apparent, in which case he was guardian by nature till twenty-one. That was what was called guardianship by nature in strict law. But for a great number of years the term "guardian by nature" has not been confined, so far as the father is concerned, to the case of heirs apparent, but has been used on the contrary to denote that sort of guardianship which the ordinary law of nature entrusts to the father till the age of infancy has completely passed and gone. I do not desire to elaborate the matter more than is necessary. The history I think of the term "natural guardianship" and of its extension, more especially in Courts of Equity, to the father's natural custody and to the authority which a father has over his child up to the complete age of twenty-one, will be found in *Hargreave's* note to *Coke* (Co Lit 88b). There is, therefore, a natural paternal jurisdiction between the age of discretion and the age of twenty-one, which the law will recognise. It has not only been recognised by the Common Law and by the Court of Chancery but it has also been recognised by statute. The [Tenures Abolition Act 1660] enables the father by his will to dispose of the custody and tuition of his child or children until they attain the age of twenty-one years. It seems to me to follow that if a father can dispose of the custody and tuition of his children by will until the age of twenty-one, it must be because the law recognises, to some extent, that he has himself an authority over the children till that age is reached. To neglect the natural jurisdiction of the father over the child until the age of twenty-one would be really to set aside the whole course and order of nature, and it seems to me it would disturb the very foundation of family life.'

This case has been subject to some trenchant criticism since, but it makes it perfectly clear that the father had a legal right of custody until 21, the then age of majority, and that that right included a right of control over the person. It also specifies as being established *one* age of discretion for boys and *one* for girls.

The trenchant criticism above referred to appears in *Hewer v Bryant* [1970] 1 QB 357 at 369, [1969] 3 All ER 578 at 582 a case in which the matter for decision was the meaning of the words 'in the custody of a parent' in s 22(2)(b) of the Limitation Act 1939, as amended by the Law Reform (Limitation of Actions, &c.) Act 1954. In that section the court construed the words as covering a case where, as a matter of fact, the minor was in the effective care and control of the parent. There was, however, considerable discussion of the more general aspect of parental rights which is presently of assistance. The trenchant criticism appears in the judgment of Lord Denning MR:

'I would get rid of the rule in *Re Agar-Ellis* and of the suggested exceptions to it. That case was decided in the year 1883. It reflects the attitude of a Victorian parent towards his children. He expected unquestioning obedience to his commands. If a son disobeyed, his father would cut him off with 1s. If a daughter had an illegitimate child, he would turn her out of the house. His power only ceased when the child became 21. I decline to accept a view so much out of date. The common law can, and should, keep pace with the times. It should declare, in conformity with the recent report on the Age of Majority (Report of Committee on Age of Majority (Cmnd 3342)), that the legal right of a parent to the custody of a child ends at the eighteenth birthday; and even up till then, it is a dwindling right which the courts will hesitate to enforce against the wishes of the child, the older he is. It starts with a right of control and ends with little more than advice.'

The more general discussion appears in the judgment of Sachs LJ ([1969] 3 All ER 578 at 584–585, [1970] 1 QB 357 at 372–373) of which I quote only that part of it which says:

'In its wider meaning the word "custody" is used as if it were almost the equivalent of "guardianship" in the fullest sense—whether the guardianship is by nature, by nurture, by testamentary disposition, or by order of a court. (I use the words "fullest sense" because guardianship may be limited to give control only over the person or only over the administration of the assets of an infant.) Adapting the convenient phraseology of counsel, such guardianship embraces a "bundle of rights", or to be more exact, a "bundle of powers", which continue until a male infant attains 21, or a female infant marries. These include power to control education, the choice of religion, and the administration of the infant's property. They include entitlement to veto the issue of a passport and to withhold consent to marriage. They include, also, both the personal power physically to control the infant until the years of discretion and the right (originally only if some property was concerned) to apply to the courts to exercise the powers of the Crown as parens patriae. It is thus clear that somewhat confusingly one of the powers conferred by custody in its wide meaning is custody in its limited meaning, ie, such personal power of physical control as a parent or guardian may have.'

Despite his views concerning *Re Agar Ellis,* Lord Denning MR was clearly of the view that the legal right to custody continues, and should continue, up to but not beyond the child's eighteenth birthday (which it does) albeit that the right was a dwindling one. This it clearly is, if only because a boy of 14 or a girl of 16 can give an adequate consent to being out of its father's custody or in that of another so as to defeat any claim of the father by habeas corpus to have it back. Furthermore, albeit there may remain until 18 a legal right of control, it may, as the child grows older, be necessary for the parents, because physical control is no longer practical, to seek the assistance of the court to buttress and support the legal right.

As to Sach LJ's observation it does not appear to me to matter whether one refers to the parent or guardian having a bundle of powers or a bundle of rights. What is important is the recognition of the wide area in which, subject always to intervention by the court, a parent or guardian is entitled (by the exercise of a power or right) to control a child.

The next in this group of cases which requires mention is *R v D* [1984] AC 778, [1984] 2 All ER 449, where the House of Lords had, in a criminal matter, to consider two certified questions, namely (a) whether the common law offence of kidnapping exists in the case of a child victim under the age of 14 years and (b) whether, in any circumstances, a parent may be convicted of such an offence where the child victim is unmarried and under the age of majority.

Both questions were answered in the affirmative. For present purposes it is only necessary to refer to it by reason of certain comments made by Lord Brandon (with whose speech all other members of the Appellate committee agreed) concerning the Irish case *The People (A-G) v Edge* [1943] IR 115, a case in which the history of the parental right to custody is the subject of exhaustive discussion. With regard to the decision itself he said [1984] AC 778 at 803, [1984] 2 All ER 449 at 455:

'There is, in my view, nothing in *Edge*'s case to show that the Irish Supreme Court was of the opinion that there did not exist any common law offence of kidnapping a child under 14. On the contrary, it is implicit in its decision that it considered that such an offence did exist, but that, in order to establish it, the taking or carrying away of such a child would have to be shown to have been without the consent of the child's parent or other lawful guardian, rather than without the consent of the child himself. It will be necessary to consider later whether this distinction, between a child over 14 and one under 14, accords with the English law of kidnapping.'

He reverted to this matter in these terms ([1984] 2 All ER 449 at 457, [1984] AC 778 at 806):

'In my opinion, to accept that doctrine as applicable under English law would not be consistent with the formulation of the third ingredient of the common law offence of kidnapping which I made earlier on the basis of the wide body of authority to which your Lordships were referred. That third ingredient, as I formulated it earlier, consists of the absence of consent on the part of the person taken or carried away. I see no good reason why, in relation to the kidnapping of a child, it should not in all cases be the absence of the child's consent which is material, whatever its age may be. In the case of a very young child, it would not have the understanding or the intelligence to give its consent, so that absence of consent would be a necessary inference from its age. In the case of an older child, however, it must, I think, be a question of fact for a jury whether the child concerned has sufficient understanding and intelligence to give its consent; if, but only if, the jury considers that a child has these qualities, it must then go on to consider whether it has been proved that the child did not give its consent. While the matter will always be for the jury alone to decide, I should not expect a jury to find at all frequently that a child under 14 had sufficient understanding and intelligence to give its consent. I should add that, while the absence of the consent of the person having custody or care and control of a child is not material to what I have stated to be the third ingredient of the common law offence of kidnapping, the giving of consent by such a person may be very relevant to the fourth such ingredient, in that, depending on all the circumstances, it might well support a defence of lawful excuse.'

Although Lord Brandon is dealing with the criminal law and we are not, the opinion of the Appellate Committee that a child under 14 can in certain circumstances for the purposes of kidnapping give a valid consent may clearly be of significance and requires examination.

By way of preliminary I must, with respect, point out that in *Edge*'s case the age of 14 was considered of significance because in that case the allegedly kidnapped child was a boy and for a boy the age of discretion was 14, whereas in the case of a girl it was 16. The passages which I have quoted must therefore be considered with appropriate amendments to cover the two cases.

Lord Brandon envisages for the purposes of the criminal law three questions: (1) whether the child was so young that absence of consent would be a necessary or legal inference from its age; this he regards as a matter of ruling by the judge although he does not give any guidance as to how young a child must be before any such inference is drawn; (2) whether, if the judge does not rule that absence of consent is presumed, the particular child had at the time sufficient understanding and intelligence to give its consent; a question for the jury; (3) if the jury are satisfied that the particular child had such understanding and intelligence whether they are also satisfied that he or she did not give consent (see [1984] AC 778 at 806, [1984] 2 All ER 449 at 457).

It appears to me that if at some *age* there is a necessary inference that consent is absent that age must be a fixed age even for the purposes of the criminal law. The fixed age might be different for girls and boys but I am unable to see how it can vary as between individual girls and boys. It is apparent that Lord Brandon regarded the age as being below 14 and, since the child concerned was there aged 5, more than 5, but this leaves a nine-year gap which at some time will need to be resolved.

Whatever may be the case with regard to the criminal law and kidnapping however, and clearly very different considerations apply there, it still seems to be the case that consent of the child is no answer to habeas corpus unless the child has attained the age of either 14 or 16 as the case may be.

In relation to other aspects of custody and control there must also be a fixed age in order that parents, children and those dealing with children may know where they stand and what are their powers, rights, duties or obligations. It is difficult to see why any other age than the age of discretion should be applicable and there is nothing in the authorities to point to any lower age.

So far as kidnapping is concerned, if the victim is old enough for consent to be legally possible there can be no objection to an investigation at the trial and a finding of fact by the jury on the two questions mentioned. Indeed such findings would be essential before a person were convicted.

In the field which is presently under consideration however, I regard any such consideration as both impractical and undesirable. A child may be of sufficient understanding and intelligence to give a consent before, or not until after, it has attained whatever may be the fixed age, but if there be no such age then neither parent, child nor strangers will know what their respective positions are. In the present field I would not therefore, unless driven, accept that the position is as the

House of Lords have held it to be for the purposes of a charge of kidnapping. I am not so driven.

It is important to remember that, wherever a child is concerned, the court is in the background in order that, in the event of dispute, it may override, in effect, everyone, in the interests of the child. In the case of medical treatment, contraceptive or otherwise, it cannot exercise its jurisdiction to protect children unless the doctor either seeks the court's ruling himself or informs the parent of what he proposes to do, so that the parent may either consent or himself or herself seek the court's ruling. If the doctor takes either course the parent is necessarily informed. It is however a vital part of the department's case that, save with the child's permission, the parent shall not be told but that the matter must be left to the clinical judgment of the doctor, who may for example have been told, 'If dad knew he'd beat me up'.

Talk of clinical judgment is in my view misplaced. I can see nothing particularly clinical in a decision to fit an interuterine device in a Roman Catholic girl aged 13 on the ground that she wishes to *start* having sexual intercourse with a boyfriend and because attempts with a sheath have been a disastrous failure, even if the girl or boy or both assert that they will otherwise proceed without any contraceptive measures.

The doctor in such circumstances cannot help taking into account his views on the moral, social, religious etc aspects.

I fully appreciate that information to the parent may lead to family trouble and that knowledge that going to the doctor involves disclosure to parents may deter others from seeking advice and treatment with, possibly, highly undesirable or even tragic results. A parent who, for example, had fought hard for the rights which the appellant seeks and had won the battle might thereafter wish that she had never fought it, for it might lead to pregnancy, a backstreet abortion and even death. Such matters are, however, matters for debate elsewhere. If it be the law that until a girl is 16 no one may, save by the intervention of the court, afford advice or treatment without the parent's consent, then that law must be observed until it is altered by the legislature. The common law must, it is true, move with the times or keep up to date whenever it legitimately can but, if, as the law presently stands, the relevant age is 16, then it cannot in my opinion legitimately change that position. Even if the case went to the House of Lords and all the judges were unanimous, the decision would be one of nine men only without the materials on which to act.

I have mentioned the foregoing wider aspects in order that it should be clear that I have not forgotten them. Before passing to another subject I mention one further matter. If a child can, without a parent's knowledge and consent, seek and receive contraceptive advice and treatment, he or she can, logically, also presumably do so in respect of other treatment. There are clearly inherent dangers in this. A mother who, for example, does not know that her child has had some particular injection or is taking some form of drug may, if the child is in an accident and unconscious, assure the doctor that she has not had that injection and is not taking any drugs. This may have serious and possibly fatal consequences. I give this particular example because it is, I hope and believe, free from the strong feelings aroused by the particular advice and treatment here under consideration.

So far as civil law is concerned I have not found anything in any case which supports the view that at *least* up to the age of discretion either a child itself or anyone dealing with the child can lawfully interfere with the parents' rights flowing from custody.

That such rights (and duties) exist cannot be doubted. Nor can it be doubted that up to *some* age no one save the court is entitled to interfere. The only question it seems to me to be determined is what that age is.

Under the common law it appears to me to be plain that, in general, that age is the age of majority so far as outsiders are concerned, albeit that in habeas corpus proceedings someone who has reached the age of discretion may give a consent which will prevent a parent recovering custody and that for the purposes of a defence to a common law charge of kidnapping the consent of someone under the age of discretion may suffice.

I am of opinion that the present law is that, save in so far as changed by statute o:
by such recognised exceptions as marriage or joining the armed forces, the age of
majority prevails. Indeed, if it does not, the jurisdiction of the court which lasts till
the age of majority can be stultified, for decisions can be taken which may be against
the interests of the child without the parents knowing and thus having the
opportunity to resort to the court for its assistance.

The criminal aspects
(a) Statutory provisions
Before Woolf J, consideration of the question of the possible criminal liability of a
doctor providing contraceptive advice and treatment to a girl under 16 was much
canvassed, the appellant contending that a doctor who did so would be committing
an offence under s 28 of the Sexual Offences Act 1956 or aiding and abetting an
offence under s 6 of that Act.

Whether in an individual case a doctor who followed the guidance notes would
commit a criminal offence of either kind must depend on the circumstances. Counsel
for the appellant conceded that in some cases he would not and counsel for the
department conceded that in some cases he would. Both of these concessions were
inescapable. They make it both unnecessary and undesirable to consider the direct
impact of the criminal law on the position of doctors proceeding in accordance with
the notes of guidance. However, the provisions already referred to and other
provisions of the Act remain of importance, as providing a clear indication of public
policy. Furthermore, some assistance is to be found in this connection from other
sections and from both earlier and later statutory history.

Sections 50 and 51 of the Offences against the Person Act 1861 created the
offences of having unlawful carnal knowledge respectively of a girl under the age of
10 years and a girl between the ages of 10 and 12 years. The former offence was a
felony carrying a minimum sentence of 3 years' penal servitude and a maximum of
penal servitude for life or a maximum of two years' imprisonment with or without
hard labour. The latter offence was a misdemeanour carrying a sentence of three
years' penal servitude or imprisonment with or without hard labour for a term not
exceeding two years.

By the Offences against the Person Act 1875 the foregoing sections were repealed
and re-enacted with amendments, (1) substituting the ages of 12 and 13 for the ages
of 10 and 12, (2) raising the minimum term of penal servitude for the graver offence
from three to five years, (3) removing the possible sentence of penal servitude in the
case of the lesser offence and (4) expressly stating in the case of the lesser offence
that it was committed 'whether with or without her consent'. This last specific
provision was presumably because by raising the age, there were being brought
within the criminal law cases in which hitherto consent would have prevented any
offence existing at all.

Ten years later, the Criminal Law Amendment Act 1885 repealed the 1875 Act
and by ss 4 and 5 re-enacted the earlier provision with amendments, (1) raising the
respective ages to 13 and 16, (2) making attempts to commit either of the offences
offences in themselves and (3) providing in the case of the lesser offence the defence
that the person charged had reasonable cause to believe that the girl was of or above
the age of 16 years.

The 1885 Act remained in force until it was repealed by the 1956 Act, the relevant
sections being replaced by ss 5 and 6 of the new Act. Under the new sections the
graver offence remained a felony carrying a maximum sentence of imprisonment
for life and the lesser offence remained a misdemeanour carrying a maximum
sentence of two years' imprisonment. The respective ages remained unchanged.
Attempts were, in both cases, preserved as separate offences in themselves, carrying
maximum sentences of two years' imprisonment in both cases. As before there were
no special defences in respect of the graver offence but in the case of the lesser
offence there were two special defences provided by ss 6(2) and (3), which provided

'(2) Where a marriage is invalid under section two of the Marriage Act, 1949, or
section one of the Age of Marriage Act, 1929 (the wife being a girl under the age
of sixteen), the invalidity does not make the husband guilty of an offence under

this section because he has sexual intercourse with her, if he believes her to be his wife and has reasonable cause for the belief.

(3) A man is not guilty of an offence under this section because he has unlawful sexual intercourse with a girl under the age of sixteen, if he is under the age of twenty-four and has not previously been charged with a like offence, and he believes her to be of the age of sixteen or over and has reasonable cause for the belief. In this subsection, "a like offence" means an offence under this section or an attempt to commit one, or an offence under paragraph (1) of section five of the Criminal Law Amendment Act 1885 (the provision replaced for England and Wales by this section).'

Since 1956 there have been two changes of importance. First by the Indecency with Children Act 1960 the maximum penalty for an attempt to commit the graver offence was increased from two years to seven years. Second, in 1967, as a result of the abolition of the distinction between felony and misdemeanour, certain procedural changes were made. An incidental result of this was that concealment of the graver crime, which previously would itself have constituted a crime, namely misprision of felony, ceased to be a crime.

So far as these two particular offences are concerned it will thus be seen that from 1861 to 1960 Parliament has seen fit, by way of the criminal law, progressively to increase the protection to the young, raising the ages at which their consent would prevent intercourse from being a crime from 12 to 13 to 16 and that, as late as 1960, additional protection was accorded to the under-thirteens by raising the maximum penalty for an offence of attempt from two years to seven years. It will also be seen that in the case of the lesser offence the defence provided by the 1885 Act was severely limited by the 1956 Act.

As to the graver crime, until 1967 anyone who was aware that an offence had been committed would have been under a positive duty to report it to the police or other lawful authority and would have been guilty of a common law offence if he failed to do so. Whether this applied also in the case of contemplated felonies had not been decided when the offence ceased to exist. In *Sykes v DPP* [1962] AC 528, [1961] 3 All ER 33 Lord Denning suggested that there might be exceptions to the general rule, including amongst such possible exceptions a doctor and his patient. He recognised, however, that parent and child was not an exception.

For present purposes the precise limits of the offence are of no importance. What is or may be of some importance however is that the graver crime was, until 1967, considered so serious that there was a public duty to report it.

Other sections of the 1956 Act which have some bearing are (1) s 14, which provides that it is an offence (subject to a special exception) to commit an indecent assault on a woman and also that a girl under 16 'cannot in law give any consent which would prevent an act being assault for the purposes of this section', (2) s 19 which, subject to an exception, makes it an offence to take an unmarried girl under the age of *18* out of the possession of her parent or guardian against *his* will, (3) s 20, which creates the like offence, but without the exception in the case of a girl under 16, and (4) ss 25 and 26, which provide, in the case respectively of girls under 13 and those between 13 and 16, that it is an offence for the owner of premises and certain others to permit the girl to resort to or be on the premises for the purpose of having unlawful sexual intercourse with men or a particular man. The former offence was originally a felony subject to a maximum sentence of life imprisonment. It still is so subject. The latter offence was and is subject to a maximum sentence of two years.

As to s 14, a normal preliminary to contraceptive advice and treatment is a vaginal examination, and some contraceptive devices involve in their fitting that which would, without consent, prima facie be indecent assaults. It may be that a doctor who, without the consent of a woman, examines her vagina for medical purposes commits no indecent assault, but there are clearly strong arguments the other way. In my view a doctor who, for example, examines a ten year old, is at least at risk of prosecution unless he has the consent of a parent and this is so up to the age of 16 when, if the child consents the consent is valid by statute and the offence ceases. Moreover, it has always been the law that for a plain civil trespass to a child a parent had his own right to sue in certain circumstances.

Section 19 affords a parent greater protection than habeas corpus, for in that case, if a girl is 16, she can in that connection give a valid consent. The position with regard to girls under 16 is in like case for both crime and habeas corpus, but between 16 and 18, although habeas corpus will not avail if the child consents, her consent is irrelevant to the crime. However, between 18 and 21, which was the then age of majority, the parent was unprotected either by habeas corpus or by the criminal law. This does not, however, mean that the right to custody ceased at 18, merely that from then on, albeit the child was under age, her consent was valid for criminal and habeas corpus purposes.

Since by ss 25 and 26 anyone who allowed sexual intercourse with a girl under 16 to take place on his premises would commit an offence and, if the girl were under 13, would until 1967 have committed a felony, it would, as it seems to me, be odd to say the least if it was perfectly lawful to take action which would go some way to lessen the inhibitions of a girl under 16 and a man against sexual intercourse by protecting them from any ensuing undesirable consequences.

These sections are the successors of like provisions in the 1885 Act under which a mother was convicted for allowing her 14-year-old illegitimate daughter to have intercourse with a man in their joint home: see *R v Webster* (1885) 16 QBD 134. A mother or father, therefore, clearly has a duty to prevent the act of intercourse where by virtue of ownership of premises she or he can control the situation.

The provisions of the criminal law all appear to me to support the view which I have already expressed. It is true that prior to 1885 the consent of a girl under 16 would prevent intercourse with her being a crime, but since then girls under 16 have been consistently treated as being unable to give consent.

It appears to me that it is wholly incongruous, when the act of intercourse is criminal, when permitting it to take place on one's premises is criminal and when, if the girl were under 13, failing to report an act of intercourse to the police would up to 1967 have been criminal, that either the department or the area health authority should provide facilities which will enable girls under 16 the more readily to commit such acts. It seems to me equally incongruous to assert that doctors have the right to accept the young, down, apparently, to any age, as patients, and to provide them with contraceptive advice and treatment without reference to their parents and even against their known wishes.

It may well be that it would be highly unlikely that, in the case of a girl aged, say, 10, a doctor would do any such thing, but that is in my view irrelevant. The question is simply whether a doctor is entitled to do so or whether in doing so he would infringe the parents' legal rights.

I can find no additional cases on the criminal aspect which assist in relation to the limited area in which for present purposes it is relevant.

In the final analysis the position is in my view as follows. (1) It is clearly established that a parent or guardian has, as such, a parcel of rights in relation to children in his custody. (2) By statute, subject to an exception, such rights can be neither abandoned nor transferred. (3) Such rights include the right to control the manner in which and the place at which the child spends his or her time. (4) Those rights will be enforced by the courts subject to the right of the court to override the parental rights in the interests of the child. (5) There is no authority of any kind to suggest that anyone other than the court can interfere with the parents' rights otherwise than by resort to the courts, or pursuant to specific statutory powers or exceptions. (6) It is clearly recognised that there is some age below which a child is incapable as a matter of law of giving any valid consent or making any valid decision for itself in regard to its custody or upbringing. (7) The authorities indicate that this age is 16 in the case of girls and 14 in the case of boys, at all events for the purposes of habeas corpus. (8) So far as girls are concerned, the provisions of the criminal law show that Parliament has taken the view that the consent of a girl under 16 in the matter of sexual intercourse is a nullity.

In the light of the above, I conclude that as a matter of law a girl under 16 can give no valid consent to anything in the areas under consideration which apart from consent would constitute an assault, whether civil or criminal, and can impose no valid prohibition on a doctor against seeking parental consent.

I conclude further that any doctor who advises a girl under 16 as to contraceptive steps to be taken or affords contraceptive or abortion treatment to such a girl without the knowledge and consent of the parent, save in an emergency which would render consent in any event unnecessary, infringes the legal rights of the parent or guardian. Save in emergency, his proper course is to seek parental consent or apply to the court.

I express no view whether 16 should or should not be the age below which a girl can give no valid consent and make no valid decision in the two fields under consideration. I express only the view that in law it is presently such age.

Eveleigh and Fox LJJ delivered concurring judgments allowing the appeal. The DHSS appealed to the House of Lords. The appeal was allowed by a majority of three to two (Lords Fraser, Scarman and Bridge; Lords Brandon and Templeman dissenting).

Lord Fraser: Three strands of argument are raised by the appeal. These are: (1) whether a girl under the age of 16 has the legal capacity to give valid consent to contraceptive advice and treatment including medical examination; (2) whether giving such advice and treatment to a girl under 16 without her parents' consent infringes the parents' rights; and (3) whether a doctor who gives such advice or treatment to a girl under 16 without her parents' consent incurs criminal liability. I shall consider these strands in order.

1. The legal capacity of a girl under 16 to consent to contraceptive advice, examination and treatment
There are some indications in statutory provisions to which we were referred that a girl under 16 years of age in England and Wales does not have the capacity to give valid consent to contraceptive advice and treatment. If she does not have the capacity, then any physical examination or touching of her body without her parents' consent would be an assault by the examiner. One of these provisions is s 8 of the Family Law Reform Act 1969, which is in the following terms:
'(1) The consent of a minor who has attained the age of sixteen years to any surgical, medical or dental treatment which, in the absent of consent, would constitute a trespass to his person, shall be as effective as it would be if he were of full age; and where a minor has by virtue of this section given an effective consent to any treatment it shall not be necessary to obtain any consent for it from his parent or guardian . . .
(3) Nothing in this section shall be construed as making ineffective any consent which would have been effective if this section had not been enacted.'
The contention on behalf of Mrs Gillick was that sub-s (1) of s 8 shows that, apart from the subsection, the consent of a minor to such treatment would not be effective. But I do not accept that contention because sub-s (3) leaves open the question whether consent by a minor under the age of 16 would have been effective if the section had not been enacted. That question is not answered by the section, and sub-s (1) is, in my opinion, merely for the avoidance of doubt.

Another statutory provision which was referred to in this connection is the National Health Service (General Medical and Pharmaceutical Services) Regulations 1974, SI 1974/160, as amended by the National Health Service (General Medical and Pharmaceutical Services) Amendment Regulations 1975, SI 1975/719. The regulations prescribe the mechanism by which the relationship of doctor and patient under the NHS is created. Contraceptive services, along with maternity medical services, are treated as somewhat apart from other medical services in respect that only a doctor who specially offers to provide contraceptive or maternity medical services is obliged to provide them: see the definition of 'medical care' and 'treatment' in reg 2(1); see also regs 6(1)(a) and 14(2)(a) and Sch 1, para 13. But nothing turns on this fact. Two points in those regulations have a bearing on the present question although, in my opinion, only an indirect bearing. The first is that by reg 14 any 'woman' may apply to a doctor to be accepted by him for the provision of contraceptive services. The word 'woman' is not defined so as to exclude a girl under 16 or under any other age. But reg 32 provides as follows:

'An application to a doctor for inclusion on his list . . . may be made, either—(a) on behalf of any person under 16 years of age, by the mother, or in her absence, the father, or in the absence of both parents the guardian or other adult person who has the care of the child; or (b) on behalf of *any other person who is incapable* of making such an application by a relative or other adult person who has the care of such person . . .'

The words in para (b) which I have emphasised are said, by counsel for Mrs Gillick, to imply that a person under 16 years of age is incapable of applying to a doctor for services and therefore give some support to the argument on behalf of Mrs Gillick. But I do not regard the implication as a strong one because the provision is merely that an application 'may' be made by the mother or other parent or guardian and it applies to the doctor's list for the provision of all ordinary medical services as well as to his list for the provision of contraception services. I do not believe that a person aged 15, who may be living away from home, is incapable of applying on his own behalf for inclusion in the list of a doctor for medical services of an ordinary kind not connected with contraception.

Another provision, in a different branch of medicine, which is said to carry a similar implication is contained in the Mental Health Act 1983, s 131, which provides for informal admission of patients to mental hospitals. It provides by sub-s (2):

'In the case of a minor who has attained the age of 16 years and is capable of expressing his own wishes, any such arrangements as are mentioned in subsection (1) above [for informal admission] may be made, carried out and determined notwithstanding any right of custody or control vested by law in his parent or guardian.'

That provision has only a remote bearing on the present question because there is no doubt that a minor under the age of 16 is in the custody of his or her parents. The question is whether such custody necessarily involves the right to veto contraceptive advice or treatment being given to the girl.

Reference was also made to the Education Act 1944, s 48, which dealt with medical inspection and treatment of pupils at state schools. Section 48(3), which imposed on the local education authority a duty to provide for medical and dental inspection of pupils, was repealed and superseded by the National Health Service Reorganisation Act 1973, s 3 and Sch 5. The 1973 Act in turn was replaced by the National Health Service Act 1977, s 5(1)(a). Section 48(4) of the Education Act 1944, which has not been repealed, imposes a duty on the local education authority to arrange for encouraging pupils to take advantage of any medical treatment so provided, but it includes a proviso in the following terms:

'Provided that if the parent of any pupil gives to the authority notice that he objects to the pupil availing himself of any of the provision [for medical treatment etc] so made the pupil shall not be encouraged . . . so to do.'

I do not regard that provision as throwing light on the present question. It does not prohibit a child under the stipulated age from availing himself of medical treatment or an education authority from providing it for him. If the child, without encouragement from the education authority, 'wishes to avail himself of medical treatment' the section imposes no obstacle in his way. Accordingly, in my opinion, the proviso gives no support to the contention from Mrs Gillick, but on the contrary points in the opposite direction.

The statutory provisions to which I have referred do not differentiate so far as the capacity of a minor under 16 is concerned between contraceptive advice and treatment and other forms of medical advice and treatment. It would, therefore, appear that, if the inference which Mrs Gillick's advisers seek to draw from the provisions is justified, a minor under the age of 16 has no capacity to authorise any kind of medical advice or treatment or examination of his own body. That seems to me so surprising that I cannot accept it in the absence of clear provisions to that effect. It seems to me verging on the absurd to suggest that a girl or a boy aged 15 could not effectively consent, for example, to have a medical examination of some trivial injury to his body or even to have a broken arm set. Of course the consent of the parents should normally be asked, but they may not be immediately available. Provided the patient, whether a boy or a girl, is capable of understanding what is proposed and of expressing his or her own wishes, I see no good reason for holding that he or she lacks the capacity to express them validly and effectively and to authorise the medical man to make the examination or give the treatment which he advises. After all, a minor under the age of 16 can, within certain limits, enter into a contract. He or she can also sue and be sued, and can give evidence on oath. Moreover, a girl under 16 can give sufficiently effective consent to sexual intercourse to lead to the legal result that the man involved does not commit the crime of rape: see *R v Howard* [1965] 3 All ER 684 at 685, [1966] 1 WLR 13 at 15, when Lord Parker CJ said:

'... in the case of a girl under sixteen, the prosecution, in order to prove rape, must prove either that she physically resisted, or if she did not, that her understanding and knowledge were such that she was not in a position to decide whether to consent or resist ... there are many girls under sixteen who know full well what it is all about and can properly consent.'

Accordingly, I am not disposed to hold now, for the first time, that a girl aged less than 16 lacks the power to give valid consent to contraceptive advice or treatment, merely on account of her age.

Out of respect for the comprehensive and fully researched argument submitted by counsel for the DHSS I should notice briefly two old Acts to which he referred, but which do not appear to me to be helpful. One of these is the Act 4 & 5 Ph & M c 8 (abduction (1557)) for punishing 'such as shall take away maidens that be inheritors, being within the age of sixteen years, or that marry them, without consent of their parents'. That Act was evidently passed for the protection of property rather than for protection of the virtue of maidens. It was repealed by the Act 9 Geo 4 c 31 (offences against the person (1828)). We were referred to s 20 of the 1828 Act, but that section was concerned only with punishing abduction of any unmarried girl under the age of 16 and appears to me to have little or no bearing on the present problem.

On this part of the case accordingly I conclude that there is no statutory provision which compels me to hold that a girl under the age of 16 lacks the legal capacity to consent to contraceptive advice, examination and treatment provided that she has sufficient understanding and intelligence to know what they involve. I can deal with the case law more conveniently in what follows.

2. The parents' rights and duties in respect of medical treatment of their child

The amended guidance expressly states that the doctor will proceed from the assumption that it would be 'most unusual' to provide advice about contraception without parental consent. It also refers to certain cases where difficulties might arise if the doctor refused to promise that his advice would remain confidential and it concludes that the department realises that 'in such exceptional cases' the decision whether or not to prescribe contraception must be for the clinical judgment of a doctor. Mrs Gillick's contention that the guidance adversely affects her rights and duties as a parent must, therefore involve the assertion of an absolute right to be informed of and to veto such advice or treatment being given to her daughters even in the 'most unusual' cases which might arise (subject, no doubt, to the qualifications applying to the case of court order or to abandonment of parents' duties).

It was, I think, accepted both by Mrs Gillick and by the DHSS, and in any event I hold, that parental rights to control a child do not exist for the benefit of the parent. They exist for the benefit of the child and they are justified only in so far as they enable the parent to perform his duties towards the child, and towards other children in the family. If necessary, this proposition can be supported by reference to *Blackstone's Commentaries* (1 Bl Com (17th edn, 1830) 452), where he wrote: 'The power of parents over their children is derived from ... their duty.' The proposition is also consistent with the provisions of the Guardianship of Minors Act 1971, s 1, as amended, as follows:

'Where in any proceedings before any court . . . (a) the legal custody or upbringing of a minor . . . is in question, the court, in deciding that question, shall regard the welfare of the minor as the first and paramount consideration, and shall not take into consideration whether from any other point of view the claim of the father in respect of such legal custody, upbringing, administration or application is superior to that of the mother, or the claim of the mother is superior to that of the father.'

From the parents' right and duty of custody flows their right and duty of control of the child, but the fact that custody is its origin throws but little light on the question of the legal extent of control at any particular age. Counsel for Mrs Gillick placed some reliance on the Children Act 1975. Section 85(1) provides that in that Act the expression 'the parental rights and duties' means 'all the rights and duties which by law the mother and father have in relation to a legitimate child and his property', but the subsection does not define the extent of the rights and duties which by law the mother and father have. Section 86 of the Act provides:

'In this Act, unless the context otherwise requires, "legal custody" means, as respects a child, so much of the parental rights and duties as relate to the person of the child (including the place and manner in which his time is spent) . . .'

In the Court of Appeal Parker LJ attached much importance to that section, especially to the words in brackets. He considered that the right relating to the place and manner in which the child's time is spent included the right, as he put it, 'completely to control the child' subject of course always to the intervention of the court. Parker LJ went on thus ([1985] 1 All ER 533 at 540, [1985] 2 WLR 413 at 423):

'Indeed there must, it seems to me, be such a right from birth to a fixed age unless whenever, short of majority, a question arises it must be determined, in relation to a particular child and a particular matter, whether he or she is of sufficient understanding to make a responsible and reasonable decision. This alternative appears to me singularly unattractive and impracticable, particularly in the context of medical treatment.'

My Lords, I have, with the utmost respect, reached a different conclusion from that of Parker LJ. It is, in my view, contrary to the ordinary experience of mankind, at least in Western Europe in the present century, to say that a child or a young person remains in fact under the complete control of his parents until he attains the definite age of majority, now 18 in the United Kingdom, and that on attaining that age he suddenly acquires independence. In practice most wise parents relax their control gradually as the child develops and encourage him or her to beome increasingly independent. Moreover, the degree of parental control actually exercised over a particular child does in practice vary considerably according to his understanding and intelligence and it would, in my opinion, be unrealistic for the courts not to recognise these facts. Social customs change, and the law ought to, and does in fact, have regard to such changes when they are of major importance. An example of such recognition is to be found in the view recently expressed in your Lordships' House by Lord Brandon, with which the other noble and learned Lords who were present agreed, in *R v D* [1984] AC 778 at 806, [1984] 2 All ER 449 at 457. Dealing with the question of whether the consent of a child to being taken away by a stranger would be a good defence to a charge of kidnapping, Lord Brandon said:

'In the case of a very young child, it would not have the understanding or the intelligence to give its consent, so that absence of consent would be a necessary inference from its age. In the case of an older child, however, it must, I think be a question of fact for a jury whether the child concerned has sufficient understanding and intelligence to give its consent; if, but only if, the jury considers that a child has these qualities, it must then go on to consider whether it has been proved that the child did not give its consent. While the matter will always be for the jury alone to decide, I should not expect a jury to find at all frequently that a child under 14 had sufficient understanding and intelligence to give its consent.'

That expression of opinion seems to me entirely contradictory of the view expressed by Cockburn CJ in *R v Howes* (1860) 3 E & E 332 at 336–337, 121 ER 467 at 468–469:

'We repudiate utterly, as most dangerous, the notion that any intellectual precocity in an individual female child can hasten the period which appears to have been fixed by statute for the arrival at the age of discretion; for that very precocity, if uncontrolled, might very probably lead to her irreparable injury. The Legislature has given us a guide, which we may safely follow, in pointing out sixteen as the age up to which the father's right to custody of his female child is to continue; and short of which such a child has no discretion to consent to leaving him.'

The question for decision in that case was different from that in the present, but the view that the child's intellectual ability is irrelevant cannot, in my opinion, now be accepted. It is a question of fact for the judge (or jury) to decide whether a particular child can give effective consent to contraceptive treatment.

In times gone by the father had almost absolute authority over his children until they attained majority. A rather remarkable example of such authority being upheld by the court was *Re Agar-Ellis, Agar-Ellis v Lascelles* (1883) 24 Ch D 317, which was much relied on by the Court of Appeal. The father in that case restricted the communication which his daughter aged 17 was allowed to have with her mother, against whose moral character nothing was alleged, to an extent that would be universally condemned today as quite unreasonable. The case has been much criticised in recent years and, in my opinion, with good reason. In *Hewer v Bryant* [1970] 1 QB 357 at 369, [1969] 3 All ER 578 at 582 Lord Denning MR said:

'I would get rid of the rule in *Re Agar-Ellis* and of the suggested exceptions to it. That case was decided in the year 1883. It reflects the attitude of a Victorian parent towards his children. He expected unquestioning obedience to his commands. If a son disobeyed, his father would cut him off with 1s. If a daughter had an illegitimate child, he would turn her out of the house. His power only ceased when the child became 21. I decline to accept a view so much out of date. The common law can, and should, keep pace with the times. It should declare, in conformity with the recent report on the Age of Majority (Report of the Committee on the Age of Majority (Cmnd 3342) under the chairmanship of Latey J, published in July 1967), that the legal right of a parent to the custody of a child ends at the eighteenth birthday; and even up till then, it is a dwindling right which the courts will hesitate to enforce against the wishes of the child, the older he is. It starts with a right of control and ends with little more than advice.'

I respectfully agree with every word of that and especially with the description of the father's authority as a dwindling right. In *J v C* [1970] AC 668, [1969] 1 All ER 788 Lord Guest and Lord MacDermott referred to the decision in *Re Agar-Ellis* as an example of the almost absolute power asserted by the father over his children before the Supreme Court of Judicature Act 1873 and plainly thought such an assertion was out of place at the present time: see per Lord MacDermott ([1970] AC 668 at 703–704, [1969] 1 All ER 788 at 814–815). In *R v D* [1984] 2 All ER 449, [1984] AC 778 Lord Brandon cited *Re Agar-Ellis* as an example of the older view of a father's authority which his Lordship and the other members of the House rejected. In my opinion, the view of absolute paternal authority continuing until a child attains majority which was applied in *Re Agar-Ellis* is so out of line with present-day views that it should no longer be treated as having any authority. I regard it as a historical curiosity. As Fox LJ pointed out in the Court of Appeal (see [1985] 1 All ER 533 at 554, [1985] 2 WLR 413 at 439), the *Agar-Ellis* cases (1878) 10 Ch D 49, (1883) 24 Ch D 317 seemed to have been regarded as somewhat extreme even in their own day, as they were quickly followed by the Guardianship of Infants Act 1886, which, by s 5, provided that the court may—

'upon the application of the mother of any infant [whether under 16 or not] . . . make such order as it may think fit regarding the custody of such infant and the right of access thereto of either parent, *having regard to the welfare of the infant*, and to the conduct of the parents . . .'

Once the rule of the parents' absolute authority over minor children is abandoned, the solution to the problem in this appeal can no longer be found by referring to rigid parental rights at any particular age. The solution depends on a judgment of what is best for the welfare of the particular child. Nobody doubts, certainly I do not doubt, that in the overwhelming majority of cases the best judges of a child's welfare are his or her parents. Nor do I doubt that any important medical treatment of a child under 16 would normally only be carried out with the parents' approval. That is why it would and should be 'most unusual' for a doctor to advise a child without the knowledge and consent of the parents on contraceptive matters. But, as I have already pointed out, Mrs Gillick has to go further if she is to obtain the first declaration that she seeks. She has to justify the absolute right of veto in a parent. But there may be circumstances in which a doctor is a better judge of the medical advice and treatment which will conduce to a girl's welfare than her parents. It is notorious that children of both sexes are often reluctant to confide in their parents about sexual matters, and the DHSS guidance under consideration shows that to abandon the principle of confidentiality for contraceptive advice to girls under 16 might cause some of them not to seek professional advice at all, with the consequence of exposing them to 'the immediate risks of pregnancy and of sexually-transmitted diseases'. No doubt the risk could be avoided if the patient were to abstain from sexual intercourse, and one of the doctor's responsibilities will be to decide whether a particular patient can reasonably be expected to act on advice to abstain. We were told that in a significant number of cases such abstinence could not reasonably be expected. An example is *Re P (a minor)* (1981) 80 LGR 301, in which Butler-Sloss J ordered that a girl aged 15 who had been pregnant for the second time and who was in the care of a local authority should be fitted with a contraceptive applicance because, as the judge is reported to have said (at 312)—

'I assume that it is impossible for this local authority to monitor her sexual activities, and, therefore, contraception appears to be the only alternative.'

There may well be other cases where the doctor feels that because the girl is under the influence of her sexual partner or for some other reason there is no realistic prospect of her abstaining from intercourse. If that is right it points strongly to the desirability of the doctor being entitled in some cases, in the girl's best interest, to give her contraceptive advice and treatment if necessary without the consent or even the knowledge of her parents. The only practicable course is, in my opinion, to entrust the doctor with a discretion to act in accordance with his view of what is best in the interests of the girl who is his patient. He should, of course, always seek to persuade her to tell her parents that she is seeking contraceptive advice, and the nature of the advice that she receives. At least he should seek to persuade her to agree to the doctor's informing the parents. But there may well be cases, and I think there will be some cases, where the girl refuses either to tell the parents herself or to permit the doctor to do so and in such cases the doctor will, in my opinion, be justified in proceeding without the parents' consent or even knowledge provided he is satisfied on the following matters: (1) that the girl (although under 16 years of age) will understand his advice; (2) that he cannot persuade her to inform her parents or to allow him to inform the parents that she is seeking contraceptive advice; (3) that she is very likely to begin or to continue having sexual intercourse with or without contraceptive treatment; (4) that unless she receives contraceptive advice or treatment her physical or mental health or both are likely to suffer; (5) that her best interests require him to give her contraceptive advice, treatment or both without the parental consent.

That result ought not to be regarded as a licence for doctors to disregard the wishes of parents on this matter whenever they find it convenient to do so. Any doctor who behaves in such a way would, in my opinion, be failing to discharge his professional responsibilities, and I would expect him to be disciplined by his own professional body accordingly. The medical profession have in modern times come to be entrusted with very wide discretionary powers going beyond the strict limits of clinical judgment and, in my opinion, there is nothing strange about entrusting them with this further responsibility which they alone are in a position to discharge satisfactorily.

3. Is a doctor who gives contraceptive advice or treatment to a girl under 16 without her parents' consent likely to incur criminal liability?

The submission was made to Woolf J on behalf of Mrs Gillick that a doctor who provided contraceptive advice and treatment to a girl under 16 without her parents' authority would be committing an offence under s 28 of the Sexual Offences Act 1956 by aiding and abetting the commission of unlawful sexual intercourse. When the case reached the Court of Appeal counsel on both sides conceded that whether a doctor who followed the guidelines would be committing an offence or not would depend on the circumstances. It would depend on the doctor's intentions; this appeal is concerned with doctors who honestly intend to act in the best interests of the girl, and I think it is unlikely that a doctor who gives contraceptive advice or treatment with that intention would commit an offence under s 28. It must be remembered that a girl under 16 who has sexual intercourse does not thereby commit an offence herself, although her partner does: see the Sexual Offences Act 1956, ss 5 and 6. In any event, even if the doctor would be committing an offence, the fact that he had acted with the parents' consent would not exculpate him as Woolf J pointed out ([1984] QB 581 at 595, [1984] 1 All ER 365 at 373). Accordingly, I regard this contention as irrelevant to the question that we have to answer in this appeal. Parker LJ in the Court of Appeal dealt at some length with the provisions of criminal law intended to protect girls under the age of 16 from being seduced, and perhaps also to protect them from their own weakness. Parker LJ expressed his conclusion on this part of the case as follows ([1985] 2 WLR 413 at 435, [1985] 1 All ER 533 at 550):

'It appears to me that it is wholly incongruous, when the act of intercourse is criminal, when permitting it to take place on one's premises is criminal and when, if the girl were under 13, failing to report an act of intercourse to the police would up to 1967 have been criminal, that either the department or the area health authority should provide facilities which would enable girls under 16 the more readily to commit such acts. It seems to me equally incongruous to assert that doctors have the right to accept the young, down, apparently, to any age, as patients, and to provide them with contraceptive advice and treatment without reference to their parents and even against their known wishes.'

My Lords, the first of those two sentences is directed to the question, which is not in issue in this appeal, of whether contraceptive facilities should be available at all under the NHS for girls under 16. I have already explained my reasons for thinking that the legislation does not limit the duty of providing such facilities to women of 16 or more. The second sentence, which does bear directly on the question in the appeal, does not appear to me to follow necessarily from the first and with respect I cannot agree with it. If the doctor complies with the first of the conditions which I have specified, that is to say if he satisfies himself that the girl can understand his advice, there will be no question of his giving contraceptive advice to very young girls.

For those reasons I do not consider that the guidance interferes with the parents' rights.

Lord Scarman concurred on broadly similar lines:

. . . Parental rights clearly do exist, and they do not wholly disappear until the age of majority. Parental rights relate to both the person and the property of the child: custody, care and control of the person and guardianship of the property of the child. But the common law has never treated such rights as sovereign or beyond review and control. Nor has our law ever treated the child as other than a person with capacities and rights recognised by law. The principle of the law, as I shall endeavour to show, is that parental rights are derived from parental duty and exist only so long as they are needed for the protection of the person and property of the child. The principle has been subjected to certain age limits set by statute for certain purposes; and in some cases the courts have declared an age of discretion at which a child acquires before the age of majority the right to make his (or her) own decision. But these limitations in no way undermine the principle of the law, and should not be allowed to obscure it.

... The Court of Appeal favoured a fixed age limit of 16, basing itself on a view of the statute law which I do not share and on its view of the effect of the older case law which for the reasons already given I cannot accept. It sought to justify the limit by the public interest in the law being certain. Certainty is always an advantage in the law, and in some branches of the law it is a necessity. But it brings with it an inflexibility and a rigidity which in some branches of the law can obstruct justice, impede the law's development and stamp on the law the mark of obsolescence where what is needed is the capacity for development. The law relating to parent and child is concerned with the problems of the growth and maturity of the human personality. If the law should impose on the process of 'growing up' fixed limits where nature knows only a continuous process, the price would be artificiality and a lack of realism in an area where the law must be sensitive to human development and social change. If certainty be thought desirable, it is better that the rigid demarcations necessary to achieve it should be laid down by legislation after a full consideration of all the relevant factors than by the courts, confined as they are by the forensic process to the evidence adduced by the parties and to whatever may properly fall within the judicial notice of judges. Unless and until Parliament should think fit to intervene, the courts should establish a principle flexible enough to enable justice to be achieved by its application to the particular circumstances proved by the evidence placed before them.

The underlying principle of the law was exposed by Blackstone and can be seen to have been acknowledged in the case law. It is that parental right yields to the child's right to make his own decisions when he reaches a sufficient understanding and intelligence to be capable of making up his own mind on the matter requiring decision . . .

When applying these conclusions to contraceptive advice and treatment it has to be borne in mind that there is much that has to be understood by a girl under the age of 16 if she is to have legal capacity to consent to such treatment. It is not enough that she should understand the nature of the advice which is being given: she must also have a sufficient maturity to understand what is involved. There are moral and family questions, especially her relationship with her parents; long-term problems associated with the emotional impact of pregnancy and its termination; and there are the risks to health of sexual intercourse at her age, risks which contraception may diminish but cannot eliminate. It follows that a doctor will have to satisfy himself that she is able to appraise these factors before he can safely proceed on the basis that she has at law capacity to consent to contraceptive treatment. And it further follows that ordinarily the proper course will be for him, as the guidance lays down, first to seek to persuade the girl to bring her parents into consultation, and, if she refuses, not to prescribe contraceptive treatment unless he is satisfied that her circumstances are such that he ought to proceed without parental knowledge and consent.

Lord Scarman also rejected Mrs Gillick's arguments based on the criminal law. Like Lord Fraser he adopted the views of Woolf J at first instance. We reproduce here extracts from Woolf J's judgment on this point.

So far as the offence against section 6 of the Sexual Offences Act 1956, is concerned, I accept that a doctor who is misguided enough to provide a girl who is under the age of 16, or a man, with advice and assistance with regard to contraceptive measures with the intention thereby of encouraging them to have sexual intercourse, is an accessory before the fact to an offence contrary to section 6. I stress the words 'with the intention thereby of encouraging them to have sexual intercourse'. However, this, I assume, will not usually be the attitude of a doctor.

There will certainly be some cases, and I hope the majority of cases, where the doctor decides to give the advice and prescribe contraceptives despite the fact he was firmly against unlawful sexual intercourse taking place but felt, nevertheless that he had to prescribe the contraceptives because, whether or not he did so, intercourse would in fact take place, and the provision of contraceptives would, in his view, be in the best interests of the girl in protecting her from an unwanted pregnancy and the risk of a sexually transmitted disease. It is as to whether or not in such a situation the doctor is to be treated as being an accessory, that I have found the greatest difficulty in applying the law.

The judge then referred to the well-known cases of *National Coal Board v Gamble* [1959] 1 QB 11 and *DPP for Northern Ireland v Lynch* [1975] AC 653 and continued:

... three matters have to be borne in mind. First of all, contraceptives do not in themselves directly assist in the commission of the crime of unlawful sexual intercourse. The analogy of providing the motor car for a burglary or providing poison to the murderer, relied on in argument, are not true comparisons. While if the man wears a sheath, there may be said to be a physical difference as to the quality of intercourse, the distinction that I am seeking to draw is clearer where the woman takes the pill or is fitted with an internal device, when the unlawful act will not be affected in any way. The only effect of the provision of the means of contraception is that in some cases it is likely to increase the likelihood of a crime being committed by reducing the inhibitions of the persons concerned to having sexual intercourse because of their fear of conception or the contraction of disease. I therefore see a distinction between the assistance or aiding ... and the act of the doctor in prescribing contraceptives. I would regard the pill prescribed to the woman as not so much 'the instrument for a crime or anything essential to its commission' but a palliative against the consequences of the crime.

The second factor that has to be borne in mind is that the girl herself commits no offence under section 6 since the section is designed to protect her from herself: see *Reg v Tyrrell* [1894] 1 QB 710. This creates problems with regard to relying upon any encouragement by the doctor as making him the accessory to the offence where the girl alone attends the clinic. The well-known case, *R v Bourne* (1952) 36 Cr App Rep 125, has to be distinguished because there, the woman can be said to have committed the offence although she was not criminally responsible because of duress. The doctor, if he is to be an accessory where the woman alone consults him, will only be an accessory if it can be shown that he acted through the innocent agency of the woman, the situation dealt with in *R v Cooper* (1833) 5 C & P 535.

The final point that has to be borne in mind, is that there will be situations where long-term contraceptive measures are taken to protect girls who, sadly, will strike up promiscuous relationships whatever the supervision of those who are responsible for their well-being, the sort of situation that Butler-Sloss J had to deal with in *Re P (a minor)* (1981) 80 LGR 301. In such a situation the doctor will prescribe the measures to be taken purely as a safeguard against the risk that at some time in the future, the girl will form a casual relationship with a man when sexual intercourse will take place. In order to be an accessory, you normally have to know the material circumstances. In such a situation the doctor would know no more than that there was a risk of sexual intercourse taking place at an unidentified place with an unidentified man on an unidentified date—hardly the state of knowledge which is normally associated with an accessory before the fact.

Under this limb of the argument, the conclusion which I have therefore come to is, that while a doctor could, in following the guidance, so encourage unlawful sexual intercourse as to render this conduct criminal, in the majority of situations the probabilities are that a doctor will be able to follow the advice without rendering himself liable to criminal proceedings. Before leaving this limb of the argument, I should make it absolutely clear that the absence of consent of the parents makes no difference to the criminal responsibility of the doctor. If his conduct would be criminal without the parents' consent, it would be equally criminal with their consent.

Lord Bridge concurred with the speeches of both Lords Fraser and Scarman (even though they may not have been in complete agreement!). He devoted most of his speech to the issue of public law, namely the appropriateness of the court's taking jurisdiction in this matter. Lord Bridge did, however, add one very important observation on the issue of criminal law and public policy raised by the case, when he said (at p 428):

> On the issue of public policy, it seems to me that the policy consideration underlying the criminal sanction imposed by statute on men who have intercourse with girls under 16 is the protection of young girls from the untoward consequences of intercourse. Foremost among these must surely be the risk of pregnancy leading either to abortion or the birth of a child to an immature and irresponsible mother. In circumstances where it is apparent that the criminal sanction will not, or is unlikely to, afford the necessary protection it cannot, in my opinion, be contrary to public policy to prescribe contraception as the only effective means of avoiding a wholly undesirable pregnancy.

Lord Brandon dissented from the majority, confining himself entirely to questions of criminal law and public policy.

> **Lord Brandon:** In my opinion the formulation of the question whether such activities can be lawfully carried on without the prior knowledge and consent of the parents of any girl of the age concerned . . . involves the rolling up in one composite question of two quite separate and distinct points of law. The first point of law is whether the three activities to which I have referred can be carried on lawfully in any circumstances whatever. If, on the one hand, the right answer to the first point of law is No, then no second point of law arises for decision. If, on the other hand, the answer to the first question is Yes, then a second point of law arises, namely whether the three activities referred to can only be lawfully carried on with the prior knowledge and consent of the parents of the girl concerned.
>
> The first point of law appears to me to be one of public policy, the answer to which is to be gathered from an examination of the statutory provisions which Parliament has enacted from time to time in relation to men having sexual intercourse with girls either under the age of 13 or between the ages of 13 and 16.
>
> It is, I think, sufficient to begin with the Criminal Law Amendment Act 1885 and then to go on to the Sexual Offences Act 1956, by which the former Act was repealed and largely replaced.
>
> Part I of the 1885 Act, which contained ss 2 to 12, had the cross-heading 'Protection of Women and Girls'. Sections 4 and 5 provided, so far as material:
>
> '**4.** Any person who unlawfully and carnally knows any girl under the age of thirteen years shall be guilty of felony, and being convicted thereof shall be liable at the discretion of the court to be kept in penal servitude for life, or for any term not less than five years, or to be imprisoned for any term not exceeding two years, with or without hard labour . . .
>
> **5.** Any person who—(1.) Unlawfully and carnally knows or attempts to have unlawfully carnal knowledge of any girl being of or above the age of thirteen years and under the age of sixteen years . . . shall be guilty of a misdemeanour, and being convicted thereof shall be liable at the discretion of the court to be imprisoned for any term not exceeding two years, with or without hard labour . . .'
>
> In *R v Tyrrell* [1894] 1 QB 710, [1891–4] All ER Rep 1215 it was held by the Court for Crown Cases Reserved that it was not a criminal offence for a girl between the age of 13 and 16 to aid and abet a man in committing, or to incite him to commit, the misdemeanour of having carnal knowledge of her contrary to s 5 of the Criminal Law Amendment Act 1885 set out above. The ground of this decision was that the 1885 Act had been passed for the purpose of protecting women and girls against themselves: see the judgment of Lord Coleridge CJ ([1894] 1 QB 710 at 712, [1891–4] All ER Rep 1215 at 1215–1216):
>
> The Sexual Offences Act 1956 represents the latest pronouncement of Parliament on these matters. Sections 5 and 6 provide, so far as material:
>
> '**5.** It is a felony for a man to have unlawful sexual intercourse with a girl under the age of thirteen.

6.—(1) It is an offence . . . for a man to have unlawful sexual intercourse with a
girl under the age of sixteen . . .'

Further, by s 37 and Sch 2, the maximum punishment for an offence under s 5 is
imprisonment for life, and that for an offence under s 6 imprisonment for two years.
Since the passing of the 1956 Act the distinction between felonies and misdemeanours
has been abolished. For the purposes of this case, however, nothing turns on this
change of terminology.

My Lords, the inescapable inference from the statutory provisions of the 1885
and 1956 Acts to which I have referred is that Parliament has for the past century
regarded, and still regards today, sexual intercourse between a man and a girl under
16 as a serious criminal offence so far as the man who has such intercourse is
concerned. So far as the girl is concerned, she does not commit any criminal offence,
even if she aids, abets or incites the having of such intercourse. The reason for this,
as explained earlier, is that the relevant statutory provisions have been enacted by
Parliament for the purpose of protecting the girl from herself. The having of such
intercourse is, however, unlawful, and the circumstance that the man is guilty of a
criminal offence, while the girl is not, cannot alter that situation.

On the footing that the having of sexual intercourse by a man with a girl under 16
is an unlawful act, it follows necessarily that for any person to promote, encourage
or facilitate the commission of such an act may itself be a criminal offence, and
must, in any event, be contrary to public policy. Nor can it make any difference that
the person who promotes, encourages or facilitates the commission of such an act is
a parent or a doctor or a social worker.

The question then arises whether the three activities to which I referred earlier
should properly be regarded as, directly or indirectly, promoting, encouraging or
facilitating the having, contrary to public policy, of sexual intercourse between a
man and a girl under 16. In my opinion there can be only one answer to this question,
namely that to give such a girl advice about contraception, to examine her with a
view to her using one or more forms of protection and finally to prescribe
contraceptive treatment for her, necessarily involves promoting, encouraging or
facilitating the having of sexual intercourse, contrary to public policy, by that girl
with a man.

The inhibitions against the having of sexual intercourse between a man and a girl
under 16 are primarily twofold. So far as the man is concerned there is the inhibition
of the criminal law as contained in ss 5 and 6 of the 1956 Act. So far as both are
concerned there is the inhibition arising from the risk of an unwanted pregnancy.
To give the girl contraceptive treatment, following appropriate advice and
examination, is to remove largely the second of these two inhibitions. Such removal
must involve promoting, encouraging or facilitating the having of sexual intercourse
between the girl and the man.

It has been argued that some girls under 16 will have intercourse with a man
whether contraceptive treatement is made available to them or not, and that the
provision of such treatment does not, therefore, promote, encourage or facilitate the
having of such intercourse. In my opinion this argument should be rejected for two
quite separate reasons. The first reason is that the mere fact that a girl under 16
seeks contraceptive advice and treatment, whether of her own accord or at the
suggestion of others, itself indicates that she, and probably also the man with whom
she is having, or contemplating having, sexual intercourse, are conscious of the
inhibition arising from the risk of an unwanted pregnancy. They are conscious of it
and are more likely to indulge their desires if it can be removed. The second reason
is that, if all a girl under 16 needs to do in order to obtain contraceptive treatment is
to threaten that she will go ahead with, or continue, unlawful sexual intercourse
with a man unless she is given such treatment, a situation tantamount to blackmail
will arise which no legal system ought to tolerate. The only answer which the law
should give to such a threat is, 'Wait till you are 16.'

The DHSS has contended that s 5(1) of the National Health Service Act 1977
imposes on it a statutory duty to carry out, in relation to girls under 16 as well as to
older girls or women, the three activities to which I referred earlier. That provision
reads:

'It is the Secretary of State's duty . . . (b) to arrange, to such extent as he considers necessary to meet all reasonable requirements in England and Wales, for the giving of advice on contraception, the medical examination of persons seeking advice on contraception, the treatment of such persons and the supply of contraceptive substances and appliances.'

This provision does not define the 'persons' who are the subject matter of it, nor is there any definition of that expression anywhere else in the Act. In these circumstances it seems to me that a court, in interpreting the provision, must do so in a way which conforms with considerations of public policy rather than in a way which conflicts with them. For the reasons which I have given earlier, I am of the opinion that, in the case of girls under 16, the giving of advice about contraception medical examination with a view to the use of one or other form of contraception, and the prescribing of contraceptive treatment are all contrary to public policy. It follows that I would interpret the expression 'persons' in s 5(1)(b) above as not including girls under 16. Alternatively, I would say that the expression 'all reasonable requirements', which occurs earlier in the provision, cannot be interpreted as including the requirements of a girl under 16 which, if satisfied, will promote, encourage or facilitate unlawful acts of sexual intercourse between a man and her.

My Lords, reference was made in the course of the argument before you to a decision of Butler-Sloss J in *Re P (a minor)* (1981) 80 LGR 301. In that case the judge, in wardship proceedings, ordered that a girl of 15, who had been pregnant for the second time and was in the care of a local authority, should be fitted with a contraceptive appliance because it appeared that it was impossible for the local authority, in whose care she was, to control her sexual conduct. It was contended that this decision was authority for the proposition that, in wardship proceedings at any rate, an order could lawfully be made for the supply and fitting of a contraceptive appliance to a girl under 16.

I do not know what arguments were or were not addressed to Butler-Sloss J in that case, and it is, in any event, unnecessary for your Lordships to decide in these proceedings the limits of the powers of a court exercising wardship jurisdiction. As at present advised, however, I am of opinion, with great respect to Butler-Sloss J, that the order which she made was not one which she could lawfully make.

My Lords, great play was made in the argument before you of the disastrous consequences for a girl under 16 of becoming pregnant as a result of her willingly having unlawful sexual intercourse with a man. I am fully conscious of these considerations, but I do not consider that, if the views which I have so far expressed are right in law, those considerations can alter the position.

It is sometimes said that the age of consent for girls is presently 16. This is, however, an inaccurate way of putting the matter, since, if a man has sexual intercourse with a girl under 16 without her consent, the crime which he thereby commits is that of rape. The right way to put the matter is that 16 is the age of a girl below which a man cannot lawfully have sexual intercourse with her. It was open to Parliament in 1956, when the Sexual Offences Act of that year was passed, and it has remained open to Parliament throughout the 29 years which have since elapsed, to pass legislation providing for some lower age than 16, if it thought fit to do so. Parliament has not thought fit to do so, and I do not consider that it would be right for your Lordships' House, by holding that girls under 16 can lawfully be provided with contraceptive facilities, to undermine or circumvent the criminal law which Parliament has enacted. The criminal law and the civil law should, as it seems to me, march hand in hand on all issues, including that raised in this case, and to allow inconsistency or contradiction between them would, in my view, serve only to discredit the rule of law as a whole.

Since I am of opinion that the first question which I posed earlier, namely whether the provision of contraceptive facilities to girls under 16 was lawful in any circumstances at all, should be answered in the negative, the second question which I posed, relating to the need for prior parental knowledge and consent, does not arise. This is because, on the view which I take of the law, making contraception available to girls under 16 is unlawful, whether their parents know of and consent to it or not.

Lord Templeman also dissented. The principal ground upon which he based his decision was that any girl below the age of 16 was, by the very fact of her youth, incapable of consenting both to sexual intercourse and contraceptive treatment:

I accept also that a doctor may lawfully carry out some forms of treatment with the consent of an infant patient and against the opposition of a parent based on religious or any other grounds. The effect of the consent of the infant depends on the nature of the treatment and the age and understanding of the infant. For example, a doctor with the consent of an intelligent boy or girl of 15 could in my opinion safely remove tonsils or a troublesome appendix. But any decision on the part of a girl to practise sex and contraception requires not only knowledge of the facts of life and of the dangers of pregnancy and disease but also an understanding of the emotional and other consequences to her family, her male partner and to herself. I doubt whether a girl under the age of 16 is capable of a balanced judgment to embark on frequent, regular or casual sexual intercourse fortified by the illusion that medical science can protect her in mind and body and ignoring the danger of leaping from childhood to adulthood without the difficult formative transitional experiences of adolescence. There are many things which a girl under 16 needs to practise but sex is not one of them. Parliament could declare this view to be out of date. But in my opinion the statutory provisions discussed in the speech of my noble and learned friend Lord Fraser and the provisions of s 6 of the Sexual Offences Act 1956 indicate that as the law now stands an unmarried girl under 16 is not competent to decide to practise sex and contraception.

Lord Templeman dealt with the arguments of public policy as follows:

In the present case it is submitted that a doctor may lawfully make a decision on behalf of the girl and in so doing may overrule or ignore the parent who has custody of the girl. It is submitted that a doctor may at the request of a girl under 16 provide contraceptive facilities against the known or assumed wishes of the parent and on terms that the parent shall be kept in ignorance of the treatment. The justification is advanced that, if the girl's request is not met, the girl may persist in sexual intercourse and run the risk of pregnancy. It is not in the interests of a girl under 16 to become pregnant and therefore the doctor may, in her interests, confidentially provide contraceptive facilities unless the doctor can persuade the girl to abstain from sexual intercourse or can persuade her to ensure that precautions are taken by the male participant. The doctor is not bound to provide contraceptive facilities but, it is said, is entitled to do so in the best interests of the girl. The girl must be assured that the doctor will be pledged to secrecy otherwise the girl may not seek advice or treatment but will run all the risks of disease and pregnancy involved in sexual activities without adequate knowledge or mature consideration and preparation. The Department of Health and Social Security (DHSS) memorandum instructs a doctor to seek to persuade the girl to involve the parent but concludes that 'the decision whether or not to prescribe contraception must be for the clinical judgment of a doctor'.

There are several objections to this approach. The first objection is that a doctor, acting without the views of the parent, cannot form a 'clinical' or any other reliable judgment that the best interests of the girl require the provision of contraceptive facilities. The doctor at the family planning clinic only knows that which the girl chooses to tell him. The family doctor may know some of the circumstances of some of the families who form his registered patients but his information may be incomplete or misleading. The doctor who provides contraceptive facilities without the knowledge of the parent deprives the parent of the opportunity to protect the girl from sexual intercourse by persuading and helping her to avoid sexual intercourse or by the exercise of parental power which may prevent sexual intercourse. The parent might be able to bring pressure on a male participant to desist from the commission of the offence of sexual intercourse with a girl under 16. The parent might be able and willing to exercise parental power by removing the family or the girl to a different neighbourhood and environment and away from the danger of sexual intercourse.

The second objection is that a parent will sooner or later find out the truth, probably sooner, and may do so in circumstances which bring about a complete rupture of good relations between members of the family and between the family and the doctor. It is inevitable that, when the parent discovers that the girl is practising sexual intercourse, the girl will in self-justification and in an attempt to reassure the parent reveal that she is relying on contraceptive facilities provided by the doctor in order to avoid pregnancy. The girl and the doctor will be the loser by this revelation.

The third and main objection advanced on behalf of the respondent parent, Mrs Gillick, in this appeal is that the secret provision of contraceptive facilities for a girl under 16 will, it is said, encourage participation by the girl in sexual intercourse and this practice offends basic principles of morality and religion which ought not to be sabotaged in stealth by kind permission of the national health service. The interests of a girl under 16 require her to be protected against sexual intercourse. Such a girl is not sufficiently mature to be allowed to decide to flout the accepted rules of society. The pornographic press and the lascivious film may falsely pretend that sexual intercourse is a form of entertainment available to females on request and to males on demand but the regular, frequent or casual practice of sexual intercourse by a girl or a boy under the age of 16 cannot be beneficial to anybody and may cause harm to character and personality. Before a girl under 16 is supplied with contraceptive facilities, the parent who knows most about the girl and ought to have the most influence with the girl is entitled to exercise parental rights of control, supervision, guidance and advice in order that the girl may, if possible, avoid sexual intercourse until she is older. Contraception should only be considered if and when the combined efforts of parent and doctor fail to prevent the girl from participating in sexual intercourse and there remains only the possibility of protecting the girl against pregnancy resulting from sexual intercourse.

These arguments have provoked great controversy which is not legal in character. Some doctors approve and some doctors disapprove of the idea that a doctor may decide to provide contraception for a girl under 16 without the knowledge of the parent. Some parents agree and some parents disagree with the proposition that the decision must depend on the judgment of the doctor. Those who favour doctor power assert that the failure to provide confidential contraceptive treatment will lead to an increase in pregnancies amongst girls under 16. As a general proposition, this assertion is not supported by evidence in this case, is not susceptible to proof and in my opinion is of doubtful validity. Availability of confidential contraceptive treatment may increase the demand for such treatment. Contraceptive treatment for females usually requires daily discipline in order to be effective and girls under 16 frequently lack that discipline. The total number of pregnancies amongst girls of under 16 may, therefore, be increased and not decreased by the availability of contraceptive treatment. But there is no doubt that an individual girl who is denied the opportunity of confidential contraceptive treatment may invite or succumb to sexual intercourse and thereby become pregnant. Those who favour parental power assert that the availability of confidential contraceptive treatment will increase sexual activity by girls under 16. This argument is also not supported by evidence in the present case and is not susceptible to proof. But it is clear that contraception removes or gives an illusion of removing the possibility of pregnancy and therefore removes restraint on sexual intercourse. Some girls would come under pressure if contraceptive facilities were known to be available and some girls under 16 are susceptible to male domination.

Parliament could decide whether it is better to have more contraception with the possibility of fewer pregnancies and less disease or whether it is better to have less contraception with the possibility of reduced sexual activity by girls under 16. Parliament could ensure that the doctor prevailed over the parent by reducing the age of consent or by expressly authorising a doctor to provide contraceptive facilities for any girl without informing the parent, provided the doctor considered that his actions were for the benefit of the girl. Parliament could, on the other hand, ensure that the parent prevailed over the doctor by forbidding contraceptive treatment for a girl under 16 save by or on the recommendation of the girl's general medical practitioner and with the consent of the parent who has registered the girl as a patient of that general practitioner. Some girls, it is said, might pretend to be over 16 but a doctor in doubt could always require confirmation from the girl's registered medical practitioner.

Lord Templeman went on to decide, however, that, apart from contraception, a doctor could in exceptional circumstances and emergencies lawfully treat a girl under the age of 16 without seeking parental consent.

The aftermath

The General Medical Council (GMC) is charged, *inter alia*, with laying down the standards of good medical conduct which doctors must observe (s 35 of the Medical Act 1983). Failure to comply with these standards can result in a charge of 'serious professional misconduct' and possible disciplinary action may follow (s 36 of the Medical Act 1983).

Prior to Mrs Gillick's action the GMC's guidance in this area, set out in the GMC, *Professional Conduct and Discipline: Fitness to Practice* (August 1983), had stated the following:

> Where a minor requests treatment concerning a pregnancy or contraceptive advice, the doctor should particularly have in mind the need to avoid impairing parental responsibility or family stability. The doctor should assess the patient's degree of parental dependence and seek to persuade the patient to involve the parents (or guardian or other person *in loco parentis*) from the earliest stage of consultation. If the patient refuses to allow a parent to be told, the doctor must observe the rule of professional secrecy in his management of the case.

After the successful appeal to the Court of Appeal, the GMC revised its guidance to take account of the court's decision. The new guidance was as follows (GMC, *Professional Conduct and Discipline: Fitness to Practice* (April 1985)):

> Where a child below the age of 16 requests treatment concerning a pregnancy or contraceptive advice, the doctor must particularly have in mind the need to avoid impairing parental responsibility or family stability. The doctor should seek to persuade the patient to involve the parents (or guardian or other person *in loco parentis*) from the earliest stage of consultation. If the patient refuses to allow a parent's consent to be sought, the doctor should withhold advice or treatment except in an emergency or with the leave of a competent court; but in any event he should observe the rules of professional secrecy.

Following the House of Lords' decision the GMC revised its guidance again to read as follows (GMC, *Professional Conduct and Discipline: Fitness to Practice* (April 1987)):

> 83. Where a child below the age of 16 consults a doctor for advice or treatment, and is not accompanied at the consultation by a parent or a person *in loco parentis*, the doctor must particularly have in mind the need to foster and maintain parental responsibility and family stability. Before offering advice or treatment the doctor should satisfy himself, after careful assessment, that the child has sufficient maturity and understanding to appreciate what is involved. For example, if the request is for treatment for a pregnancy or contraceptive advice, the doctor should satisfy himself that the child has sufficient appreciation of what is involved in relation to his or her

emotional development, family relationships, problems associated with the impact of pregnancy and/or its termination and the potential risks to health of sexual intercourse and certain forms of contraception at an early stage.

84. If the doctor is satisfied of the child's maturity and ability to understand, as set out above, he must nonetheless seek to persuade the child to involve a parent, or another person in loco parentis, in the consultation. If the child nevertheless refuses to allow a parent or such other person to be told, the doctor must decide, in the patient's best medical interests, whether or not to offer advice or treatment. He should however respect the rules of professional confidentiality set out above in the foregoing paragraphs of this section.

85. If the doctor is not so satisfied, he may decide to disclose the information learned from the consultation; but if he does so he should inform the patient accordingly, and his judgment concerning disclosure must always reflect both the patient's best medical interests and the trust the patient places in the doctor.

Questions

(i) Why did the GMC revise its guidance after the Court of Appeal's decision?

(ii) Is the guidance which finally emerged warranted and justified by the decision?

Do you agree with the following comment published in the Bulletin of the Institute of Medical Ethics in February 1986?

[The GMC's] statement was drafted by the Standards Committee of the General Medical Council, with legal advice. It was then amended by a full meeting of the Council. It is a most curious statement, since it is not merely advice to members of the medical profession, but the standard by which the GMC may be called upon to judge their conduct.

It appears that the GMC's advice has been derived from both the concurring and the dissenting judgments delivered by the house of Lords in the *Gillick* case. The conditions at the end of the first paragraph, by which a doctor might satisfy himself of a child's maturity, are taken from Lord Scarman's speech. . . . the GMC followed him fairly closely, but has added a need for the girl to understand the risk of contraception.

The GMC's advice continues by reasserting some of Lord Fraser's five conditions for doctors to comply with if they are to prescribe contraceptives to a minor. But two conditions—that she is very likely to begin or to continue having sexual intercourse with or without contraceptives; and that unless she receives contraceptive advice or treatment her health is likely to suffer—are omitted.

Up to this point the GMC advice has reflected the House of Lords' decision. The next sentence, on confidentiality, is a milder version of previous Blue Book advice. . . . The final sentence of the advice is therefore a major departure both from the GMC's earlier advice on confidentiality and from a principle accepted by doctors ever since Hippocrates. The suggestion that a doctor may call a child immature, because she does not fully understand the risks of contraception, and then inform her parents was inevitably and immediately condemned by the BMA and many other doctors. This part of the GMC's advice appears to have been influenced by the dissenting speech of Lord Templeman: '. . . confidentiality owed to an infant [ie someone under 16] is not breached by disclosure to a parent responsible for that infant if the doctor considers that such disclosure is necessary in the interests of the infant'. But that was not the majority opinion of the House of Lords.

The impression that the GMC wishes to give doctors a free hand to do as they like in this area was not lessened by the President of the GMC pointing out at a press conference that the assessment of a child's maturity was solely a matter of clinical judgment, and was not therefore open to review by the GMC.

Finally, in the light of the decision of the House of Lords the DHSS issued new guidelines (HC (86) 1). The guidelines set out the conditions, based on Lord Fraser's speech, under which doctors may prescribe or advise on contraception

for girls under 16 without informing the parents. The guidelines avoid expressing
any view on the complex issues of confidentiality.

The *Gillick* case is useful to illustrate the scope and nature of medical law
today. First, it shows us the co-existence and interdependence of medical law
and medical ethics. It both emphasises the need to understand the role of these
two disciplines and the often considerable complexities of each of them as
disciplines in their own right. Secondly, the case illuminatingly highlights the
several distinct areas of law which make up the discipline of medical law.
Thirdly, it makes clear that much of medical law (as with most law) reflects and
incorporates considerations of public policy. Let us examine each of these points
in turn.

Medical ethics

Here is not the place to attempt any detailed examination of medical ethics.
There are a number of general works to which the reader is referred, eg
R Veatch *A Theory of Medical Ethics* (1981); H T Engelhardt *The Foundations
of Bioethics* (1986); S J Reiser *Ethics in Medicine* et al (1977); T L Beauchamp
and J F Childress *Principles of Biomedical Ethics* (1983); R Gillon *Philosophical
Medical Ethics* (1986); J Harris *The Value of Life* (1985).

It may be of assistance, however, to offer some introduction to the subject.
This will allow us to return to the *Gillick* case and examine it from the point of
view of medical ethics and medical law and thereby show the relationship
between the two fields of enquiry.

Our first step must be a brief introduction to moral reasoning. Let Jonathan
Glover set the scene, in this extract from his book *Causing Death and Saving
Lives* (1977). In a chapter entitled 'The Scope and Limits of Moral Argument'
he provides the following analysis (pp 22–26):

1 Preliminaries
There is no general agreement how the word 'morality' should be used. Some people
think of morality as a set of rules laid down by God. Others think of it as a set of
socially imposed rules with the function of reducing conflict in society. Others say it
is a set of principles about how we ought to live that apply to everyone impartially,
or which can be defended by appealing to the interests of people in general. These
disagreements are a problem for anyone trying to say what moral beliefs are, but
they will not be discussed here.

The question of what it means to say that a person 'ought' to do something is also
one that will not be raised here. Much recent moral philosophy is devoted to this
difficult problem, which still has no generally accepted solution. But I shall assume
that we all, at *some* level, understand what is meant by saying that someone ought to
do something. Perhaps that is all that the arguments of this book require, beyond
the ruling out of one particularly narrow use of the word 'moral'. On this narrow
view, morality is divorced from what we ought to do. A soldier may say that part of
his morality is the command 'thou shalt not kill', but that moral considerations have
to be subordinated to practical ones, such as the need to defend your country. But,
as the word 'morality' is to be used here, where the soldier thinks that patriotism
ought to take priority over not killing, it is not true that his morality forbids all
killing.

2 Moral disagreements
If a pacifist and a non-pacifist argue about the morality of war, it may be that their
disagreement is essentially factual. The pacifist may say that wars always cause
more misery than they prevent, so that no war is ever justified. The non-pacifist may
agree that no war would be justified if all wars caused more misery than they

prevented, but he may deny that this is true. Evidence, even if only of an inconclusive kind, can be cited in support of one view or the other.

But sometimes moral differences could survive the answering of all relevant factual questions. A pacifist and a non-pacifist might agree that some particular war was likely to cause less misery than it prevented, but still disagree about its morality. The pacifist might say that the reduction of misery does not justify the deliberate taking of human life. If he is asked why he thinks this, he may reply that the sanctity of life is an ultimate belief of his, capable of no further justification. He may then press the non-pacifist to say why he attaches such weight to reducing misery, and the non-pacifist may similarly have to reply that the undesirability of suffering is one of his ultimate beliefs.

Where two people hold different beliefs at the most fundamental level, it may be that no further argument is possible between them. I can defend my view that the avoidance of war is good, because I regard it as only an instrumental good: it is good as a means to things I regard as intrinsically good, such as the avoidance of suffering. But I cannot defend my view that the avoidance of suffering is good. This is just because I think it good in itself, rather than good because it leads to something else that could be cited in its defence.

But it is possible that, in the argument between the pacifist and the non-pacifist, we have not yet reached the level of ultimate principles. The pacifist may claim that killing is always wrong because God has forbidden it. We may then, if we waive questions about how he knows that God exists or what God has forbidden, ask him why he believes that we ought to obey God. Perhaps it will be at this point that no further justification is forthcoming, and we realise that we have finally reached an ultimate belief: in this case that it is intrinsically good to obey God.

Similarly, the non-pacifist may provide reasons why he believes we ought to reduce suffering as much as possible. He may say that people always want to avoid suffering. We may then, if we waive questions about martyrs and masochists, ask him why we ought to satisfy universally held wants. If he can give no further reason, we have discovered something he believes to be intrinsically good.

We can often supply a chain of reasoning when challenged to defend a moral belief about what ought to be done. Any such chain of argument seems either to involve an infinite regress or else to end with an ultimate moral belief. Such a belief is ultimate in that what it tells us to do is not prescribed because it is instrumental to some further good. These ultimate beliefs are like the axioms of a system of geometry: the other beliefs of a moral system are derivable from the axioms, but the axioms themselves cannot be 'proved'.

Many of those who accept John Stuart Mill's claim that 'Questions of ultimate ends are not amenable to direct proof' think that this is sufficient to establish the futility of argument in moral matters. It may seem that, since nothing could count as 'proving' one set of values to be 'true', it is as pointless to argue about morality as it would be to try to persuade someone by argument to prefer one colour to another.

But this is to take too pessimistic a view. Even leaving aside the extent to which argument about facts can be relevant to questions about what ought to be done, there are various fruitful methods of argument about moral beliefs.

One method of arguing against a moral belief is to show that it depends on concepts that are blurred or incoherent. Someone who believes that homosexual acts are wicked because they are unnatural may be open to this kind of argument. If pressed to define 'unnatural' he may find it hard to provide a definition that includes homosexual acts without also including singing at the opera.

Another method of rational moral argument involves the exposure of logical inadequacies. This may take the form of showing that what are taken to be good reasons for holding a belief are not really so. (It is often said that human suffering matters more than animal suffering because we have rationality of a kind or degree that animals lack. But reflection about feeble-minded children may make us question this as a reason for thinking that animal *suffering* is less important.) Or it may take the form of exposing inconsistencies in someone's principles. If you disapprove of all abortions, I may ask you to give a reason. If you reply that to take human life is always wrong, I will ask if you are a complete pacifist. If you hold some non-pacifist views about war, you must either abandon or modify your principle that taking life is always wrong or else change your mind about pacifism. This (very crude) example shows how it is possible to apply legitimate pressure to the moral beliefs of anyone sufficiently rational to be disturbed by inconsistency.

And moral argument has a wider scope than the exposing of inconsistencies within someone's formulated principles. It often takes the form of showing someone that his beliefs have unnoticed consequences that he would find unacceptable. Some general principles used in support of abortion provide an equally good justification for infanticide. Someone who holds such a principle, but who cannot accept the consequent rightness of infanticide, is trapped in an inconsistency. The general principle must be abandoned or modified or else the unpalatable consequence must be accepted. The pattern of argument here is similar to that used to link abortion and pacifism in the previous case. The difference is that there the inconsistency was between two beliefs already formulated and accepted, while here inconsistency is between an accepted principle and a moral response to a question not previously considered.

Moral beliefs can be undermined by our responses to their consequences. But our responses are themselves liable to modification, either by experience or by the development of imagination. Someone who accepts with equanimity that his patriotic principles commit him to supporting certain wars may find this consequence less acceptable if he ever experiences war as a soldier. It is a truism that we are able to accept the rightness of actions or policies often only because of a failure of imagination, and experience of their consequences often greatly changes our responses. Sometimes experience may not be needed. It can be enough to use some imagination, and often films or novels can help us to respond in a more sensitive or imaginative way. Someone who thinks that Stalin's labour camps were an acceptable consequence of a morally legitimate policy may not himself be able to experience such a camp, but the novels of Solzhenitsyn may modify his views about what is acceptable.

Later (pp 29–33) he continues:

4 Why have general moral beliefs?

Sometimes it is said that we can do without general moral beliefs and simply be guided by our intuitive responses. (D H Lawrence has been influential here.) Discussion of morality in general terms can be seen as something stale and second-hand. On this view, insights as to how we should live arise as we develop experimentally a way of life, and the making of generalisations is a derivative task for lovers of taxonomy and the legalistically inclined.

One argument for formulating general moral beliefs is that the alternative is very likely to involve a tacit inconsistency. To take again a crude example, it is characteristic of many people's responses in a political context that they believe that tax increases are a bad thing, but that more money should be spent on schools, hospitals, roads, defence and pensions. There is at least a surface inconsistency in these responses. Only thinking in general terms about priorities, as well as about how to put them into effect, will either remove the inconsistency or show it to be only apparent. (It is striking how many people mess up their lives by not thinking clearly and coherently about what they really value.)

Another argument appeals, not to consistency, but to autonomy. We do not reach adult life with open minds about morality. Whether or not we accept Freud's claims about the way the pressures of family relationships and sexual adjustment mould the super-ego, or Marx's claims about the crucial role of the economic system in determining the moral consciousness of society, only a naïve person could deny the influence of social and personal pressures on moral responses. Many people's responses are simply the result either of childhood conditioning or of the views currently fashionable in their society. The first step away from being manipulated, and towards a more autonomous outlook, is to stand back from a set of responses and to think.

There is also the argument that there may be cases where intuitive reactions cannot be relied on for guidance. Sometimes we suspect that self-interest or emotional disturbance is distorting our responses. Someone asked by a doctor whether or not further efforts should be made to prolong the life of an old relation, painfully ill in a geriatric ward, may not trust his own responses. It may be hard to tell how much they are distorted by the fact that in the event of survival the relation would be a burden, or by fear of guilt if he agrees that treatment should stop. It is helpful, in deciding whether to trust a response, to see whether or not it fits in with general beliefs worked out when free from such pressures.

Sometimes people do not have a single, clear intuitive response by which to be guided. Some babies with gross abnormalities are allowed to die when their lives could be saved. For someone who accepts that this is justified, it may be hard to know where to draw a line. How serious an abnormality makes it better for a person not to live? Many of us have no clear intuitive answer to such a question. If we were doctors or surgeons having to make such choices we would often be quite uncertain what we ought to do. In such cases, we could only fall back on general beliefs about the sorts of factors that ought to be considered. Such beliefs will not always give clear guidance. But for someone who has neither intuitive answers nor any relevant general beliefs, there is no basis whatever on which to decide.

5 Degrees of guidance

There are at least two reasons why general moral beliefs may give inadequate guidance in a particular case. It may be that not all the facts are clear: we may not know how senile the old person will be if he lives, or how much the abnormal baby will come to be able to have a relationship with other people. Another reason is that cases vary so much that beliefs formulated in very general terms may not immediately generate a decision in a complicated situation.

Those who doubt the value of such general beliefs often think that moral beliefs must either be crude and inflexible or else of a cumbersome complexity similar to tax law. But these are not the only alternatives. It is possible to have a moral system whose outlines are sketched in, but whose detailed applications were only worked out in advance where often needed. (A surgeon may give more detailed thought in advance to abortion or euthanasia than to moral questions about censorship.) The more detailed guidance a moral system gives, the more complex it is likely to be. On the other hand, the less it is worked out in detail, the more likely it is to entail unnoticed unacceptable consequences.

6 Is it futile to propose moral beliefs?

It is sometimes said that it is pointless to argue for a set of moral beliefs. It may be claimed that, in morality, any formulated proposal must either reflect a way of life which already has an independent existence or else must be a mere pipe dream. The view that moral proposals must be either superfluous or else powerless seems to underlie some famous remarks made by Hegel. He said:

> One more word about giving instruction as to what the world ought to be. Philosophy in any case always comes on the scene too late to give it. As the thought of the world, it appears only when actuality is already there cut and dried after its process of formation has been completed. The teaching of the concept, which is also history's inescapable lesson, is that it is only when actuality is mature that the ideal first appears over against the real and that the ideal apprehends this same real world in its substance and builds it up for itself into the shape of an intellectual realm. When philosophy paints its grey in grey, then has a shape of life grown old. By philosophy's grey in grey it cannot be rejuvenated but only under-stood. The owl of Minerva spreads its wings only with the falling of the dusk.

It is no doubt true that a person's moral views are influenced by the historical period and by the society in which he lives. But it is possible to develop new beliefs that are not mere reflections of practices already in existence, perhaps as a result of critical thought about existing beliefs and practices. Hegel himself was sceptical of the value of working out such new beliefs. He said:

> Whatever happens, every individual is a child of his time; so philosophy too is its

own time apprehended in thoughts. It is just as absurd to fancy that a philosophy can transcend its contemporary world as it is to fancy that an individual can overleap his own age, jump over Rhodes. If this theory really goes beyond the world as it is and builds an ideal one as it ought to be, that world exists indeed, but only in his own opinions, an insubstantial element where anything you please may, in fancy, be built.

But this scepticism of Hegel's seems to rest on the dubious assumption that new ideas about how the world ought to be cannot influence what in fact happens. And, even if it were true that new moral ideas were generally uninfluential, it would be hard to deny their potential in areas of moral confusion. When certain questions about killing arise, there is no generally agreed doctrine about what ought to be done. In this area especially, it seems unduly pessimistic to suppose that systematic thinking must be powerless to shape conduct. This doctrine of the impotence of ideas rests on one of two beliefs. One is that, in matters of morality, people can never be influenced by each other's beliefs. The other is that our moral beliefs and attitudes never determine what we do. The truth of these claims is more often assumed than argued for.

Gorovitz, in his excellent book *Doctors' Dilemmas* (1982), takes up the theme (pp 75–79):

I once taught a course on moral issues in medicine that had, in the same class, both undergraduate philosophy students and students from the medical school. One day a physician from the university hospital presented to the class a description of a case that was confronting him at the moment—a case that seemed to present only morally troubling choices. The first student called upon to discuss the case launched a sustained inquiry into the facts beyond those in the physician's initial presentation. 'What is the family's economic status? Did you do a bone-marrow analysis?' And so on. The second student took a different approach. 'We want to do the right thing here,' he said. 'And what that is depends on whether or not the consequences of our choice are the only morally relevant considerations.' The first student had scorn for the second student's flight into abstraction. 'This is a real case,' he admonished. 'A decision has to be made. We don't have time for another two thousand years of philosophical speculation, to see if you can resolve what you are still fighting about after the first two thousand years.' And the second student had disdain for the first student's flight into empirical inquiry. 'You seem to think,' he derided, 'that if you just do more tests and surveys and examinations, somehow you'll suddenly discover the right thing to do. But we already know what the issues are in this case; we know enough facts. What we have to decide is what is right, and you're not willing to face that question.'

Both students were right in their criticisms; neither recognised the similarity in their avoidance behavior. Faced with the discomfort of a searingly tragic medical situation, the philosophy student fled to the comfortable refuge of philosophical abstractions. In a parallel way, the medical student plodded along the path of factual inquiry, shielding himself from the challenges of moral inquiry. And the physician pointed out that he had just a few minutes left with the class since he had to return to the hospital to deal with the case.

What the students gradually came to realise—sometimes grudgingly—is that issues of this sort cannot be successfully addressed within the confines of philosophy or within those of medicine. Instead, they require a steady interplay of both practical and theoretical considerations. Only after the two sets of students began each to develop some sense of the other's viewpoint did we begin to make a bit of progress. And so it is with our inquiries here.

Questions about what one ought to do are often questions of a practical sort. For example, whether to use a particular antibiotic, rather than some other one, will be decided on the basis of evidence about the comparative effectiveness of the two drugs for the infection, the patient's tolerance for the drugs, and possibly even questions of supply or cost. Such questions can be exceedingly complex and can sometimes involve conflicts of value that compound their complexity. Sometimes, however, they are straightforward; once one has the relevant facts, it is clear what ought to be done. It is clear, for example, that physicians who intend to reuse syringes should sterilise them between uses. But questions about what ought to be done are not always questions about the most effective path to a desired outcome; instead, they can be questions about what, from a moral point of view, is the right thing to do. Since much of what is philosophically most interesting about medical practice concerns uncertainty about what the morally right thing is to do, I want in this chapter to discuss various aspects of what moral judgments and moral dilemmas are like. After that it should be easier to understand what some of them are like in specifically medical contexts.

For many people, the hard question about morality is how to determine the right thing to do—its being taken for granted that doing the right thing is important. This was the view of Plato, who believed that doing a morally wrong thing was always an error of the understanding, the result of a failure to recognise the right course of action. It was impossible, he thought, to realise that an action was morally right and then to do otherwise. His pupil Aristotle disagreed, thinking it common for people to know what was right and yet to do otherwise. For Aristotle, wrong action could result from weakness of the will—of motivation—even when one knew what one ought to do. The question of the relationship between knowing what is right and wanting to do what is right has occupied philosophers through the ages but will not concern us here. Rather, I take it for granted that we share a concern with acting rightly and that we should therefore proceed directly to an inquiry into what acting rightly requires in the context of clinical medicine. To proceed otherwise would take us far afield because it is difficult at best, and perhaps impossible, to justify a commitment to morality to someone who does not share it. The person who asks, 'Why should I be moral?' is asking a very difficult question—one I will not attempt to answer here.

If we assume, then, that one wants to do what is right, what exactly is such moral behavior? Aristotle, writing about ethics, cautioned that one should not attempt to find more precision in the inquiry than the subject matter will allow. At the outset it is unknown just how much precision that is; I therefore will approach the subject matter of morality by stages, characterising it initially with a fairly rough sketch and subsequently seeking a higher level of precision.

Questions of morality are sometimes identified with questions of law, economics, psychology, or other areas. The connections are real enough, but morality is not simply a matter of these considerations, nor of sociology, prevailing public policy, history, or religion. All these areas may have some bearing on questions of morality; I'm sure that at least most of them do. But they are not the same as morality. This can be shown easily.

Consider first whether the question of what is required by morality is the same as the question of what is required by law. In many cases what the law requires is not completely clear. One common example is a law prohibiting vehicles from the park. Is this intended to exclude the delivery boy on a bicycle? What of the man in a wheelchair? We can clarify the legislation by rewording it to prohibit *motor* vehicles from the park. But then we may find that the man has revised his wheelchair while the legislature was revising the law; he has put a motor on it; it is now a motor vehicle! Further revisions of the law are possible, but the process is cumbersome, slow, costly, and unlikely to succeed. For events in the world unfold in ways that it is impossible ever fully to anticipate, and new situations arise which are neither clearly within nor clearly outside the scope of any given law.

It is far better to recognise the need for interpretation of law, for a process that can take into account such factors as legislative intent, the public interest, precedent, and common sense, as well as the text of the law in question, in determining what does and what does not fall within the scope of that law. Such a process is not morally neutral; turning to the law to solve questions of what to do can require that we confront morally significant questions in trying to understand the law—to which we turned in the hope of finding what is right to do.

Some of the time, however, the law is completely clear. A law absolutely prohibiting abortion under any circumstances would be such a law, unlike a law prohibiting abortion except when the life of the mother is seriously threatened. Even where the law specifies clearly what is required, however, the question of what is right to do remains, and we are compelled to ask whether the law should be broken or challenged by civil disobedience. Take a law strictly forbidding abortion as a case in point. In a state which had enacted such a law, a physician could be asked to abort the pregnancy of a thirteen-year-old victim of rape by an escapee from a state institution for those among the criminally insane who have serious heritable diseases. In such a case the physician would face a moral question—whether to aid the patient despite the law or to obey the law despite the very strong case for aborting the pregnancy.

Notice that I have not said what the physician should do; I have said only that the physician faces a moral question. There is a decision to be made, which different physicians might well make differently. I claim only that it is a significant question to ask what the physician ought to do in such a situation. Yet it is *not* a significant question to ask what the law requires in such a situation; that is a trivial question because the law is completely explicit on the issue. Since one of these two questions is significant, and the other is not, these must be two *different* questions. Thus, to ask what is morally required is to ask a different question from the question of what is legally required. This shows that morality is not simply a question of what the law specifies but is something other than law.

This is not to say that the law is morally irrelevant. On the contrary, the legal facts typically have substantial bearing on our moral deliberations, and should. My point is only that those moral deliberations are sometimes not settled entirely by reference to the law—which shows that whatever morality is, it must be something that is not identical to conformity to law.

A similar argument shows that morality and economics are not identical. Economics often considers questions closely related to moral issues, and it can be tempting to approach a morally troubling situation in economic terms. Production, supply, demand, price, and distribution all are related to questions of social justice, equality, and the satisfaction of human needs and wants. Nonetheless, the economic aspects of a case alone do not entail any moral conclusion about what, all things considered, is right to do. The question of the withdrawal of life-extending treatment—of 'pulling the plug', to use that deplorable colloquialism—is easily resolved on economic grounds in the typical case. It is almost always cheaper, more economically efficient, to 'pull the plug' when a patient's prospects for significant recovery are slight. Yet we cannot help wondering whether doing so is right. And no matter what the answer, the very meaningfulness of the question shows that rightness is something other than economic efficiency alone. So moral judgments are not merely economic judgments.

Similarly, what is psychologically most comfortable or most ennobling, what is sociologically most common, what accords with prevailing public policy, what is in keeping with historical precedent or tradition, and what conforms to the strictures of whatever religious viewpoint, if any, one favors can all be questioned on moral grounds. So the moral dimensions of a situation are not simply the same as the dimensions that fall within the scope of these other areas.

Morality as a domain of judgment is different from any other. To say this, however, is not to explain what does fall within that domain or to deny that morality is closely linked with other areas. The question of what the relationship is between the morality of a situation, on the one hand, and the facts of the situation—that is, the economic, legal, psychological, religious, and other facts—on the other, has been the subject of enduring debate within philosophy. Some writers have held that moral judgments stand entirely apart from judgments of any other sort. But a larger number of writers have believed that moral judgments do depend in some way on the facts of the matter—that while morality may not be *simply* a question of law, economics, psychology, or any other single discipline, the legal, economic, psychological, and other such facts nonetheless together influence what the appropriate moral judgment is in any situation.

Later (pp 83–89) Gorovitz examines the basis of moral reasoning:

Two major traditions in moral philosophy—different viewpoints in thinking about ethical questions—divide over the issue of whether and to what extent the actual or expected consequences of an action determine its moral quality. One tradition includes whose who hold that the moral character of an act depends on its consequences in whole or in part. We call such a position consequentialist. This tradition is exemplified by the utilitarian view of right action, most notably associated with Jeremy Bentham, John Stuart Mill, and a long line of Mill's intellectual descendants. Utilitarianism holds that actions are right if—and only if—they produce the greatest happiness (or utility) for the greatest number of persons. Other views than utilitarianism can be consequentialist, too, however. For example, the erroneous view that those actions are right which maximise beauty in the world, quite apart from the amount of suffering they cause and the amount of happiness or benefit associated with that beauty, would be a consequentialist, but nonutilitarian, theory.

The other major tradition in moral philosophy comprises ethical theories which hold that the moral status of an action is independent of its consequences. This sort of moral theory is exemplified by the views of Immanuel Kant and those who write in his tradition. For Kant, actions are right or wrong independently of the consequences; to be right, an action must have been done from a certain sort of motive. Moral theories that categorise certain classes of action as simply being right or wrong, such as is done by any list of commandments or prescriptions, are also typically nonconsequentialist. Thus, some traditional orthodoxies admonish us to refrain utterly from acts of certain kinds, such as killing, stealing, or lying, on the ground that they are wrong simply by virtue of the kinds of acts that they are. These nonconsequentialist theories are called formalist or deontological theories.

The apparent simplicity of utilitarianism as a moral theory is deceptive. On the surface the theory seems clear and compelling. What could be morally superior to that act which produces more good for more people than any other? But various problems with the theory quickly emerge. First, there are problems internal to the theory—that is, problems in making sense of what it really says. On the one hand, it requires us to maximise the production of happiness; on the other hand, it seems to take distribution into account in speaking of the greatest number. But these two considerations can pull in opposite directions. It may be that in some circumstances we can maximise happiness only by reducing the number of people who are benefited. It is not at all clear how utilitarianism requires us to handle such a situation.

A second internal problem is that of identifying consequences. If the moral character of an action depends on its consequences, it becomes important to know what consequences will flow, or have flown, from each action. But predicting the future is notoriously hard. It is even difficult to tell what is true of the past. If I carelessly give you the wrong medicine and in dealing with the resulting illness, a bright young doctor makes an important discovery that saves many lives, is that discovery one of the consequences of my action? Causal chains are frustratingly resistant to clarification, and it is never easy to be sure what we are talking about when we speak of the consequences of an action. Yet utilitarianism requires us to base our assessment of actions on just such talk.

A third internal problem is that the theory requires us to make comparative judgments about human happiness. Yet it is not obvious that such comparisons can be made in any adequate way. You may exhibit more overt glee than your neighbor, but is it not possible that behind his veneer of restraint he knows a joy that far transcends what prompts your more visible delight? How are we to tell which actions produce the most happiness when it seems impossible to compare one person's happiness with another's?

Despite these problems, utilitarianism has had many defenders, and much of the literature revolves around attempts to fashion a form of utilitarianism that surmounts these difficulties. The more serious challenge to utilitarianism comes from a different direction, however.

The external problems are those that remain once one assumes it possible to understand just what utilitarianism requires and further assumes that it is possible to act in accordance with those requirements. Even then, the charge goes, utilitarianism will not do because it is itself morally unacceptable. Utilitarianism is a theory that defines *right action* as *maximising* action; it places no constraints on the means to that maximisation. It is possible to imagine situations in which the greatest good for the greatest number could be achieved by punishing an innocent man, enslaving a powerless minority, or committing an undetected crime. These actions are wrong despite their consequences, yet the utilitarian is bound to praise them. Thus, utilitarianism is refuted, according to this line of attack.

The utilitarians have fought back with the claim that such criticism misses the mark because it is based on a misunderstanding of the theory it attacks. That misunderstanding, it is claimed, results from taking the principle of utilitarianism to be a principle for evaluating actions when, in fact, it is a principle for evaluating moral guidelines or rules. A moral rule will be accepted, according to this defense of utilitarianism, if its adoption is conducive to producing the greatest happiness for the greatest number. Thus, for utilitarian reasons, we have rules against framing the innocent, enslaving our fellowmen, and committing crimes. So the utilitarian need not endorse such actions after all.

The version of utilitarianism according to which it is individual actions that are to be judged by the utilitarian principle is called, unsurprisingly, *act* utilitarianism. The version according to which actions are judged by rules which are themselves measured against the utilitarian standard is called *rule* utilitarianism. Recent disputes in moral philosophy have focused on the question of whether act utilitarianism and rule utilitarianism are genuinely different—whether one version can escape objections that are telling against the other—and that question remains unresolved. Critics of utilitarianism continue to attack it; its sympathisers continue to devise reformulations of the theory that they hope will be immune to the attacks. But although utilitarianism receives much attention within moral philosophy, it is not the only focus of attention. There are non consequentialist theories as well, contending for prominence.

Plato believed that actions were right if they corresponded to the Good, an ideal that existed independently of any human actions or material objects. The Platonic theory of right action was so obscure and unrelated to actual moral concerns that it was soundly criticised by Aristotle as being irrelevant to human moral deliberation— and therefore deficient as moral philosophy. In Plato's view, rightness was not dependent on the consequences of action; the problem was making sense of what Plato thought it did depend on. (We will consider Aristotle's view of morality later, noting for now merely that he believed the essence of virtue to be rational control of desires, leading to moderation in action.)

Early systems of ethics based on theological beliefs also provide examples of deontological ethical theories. If an action breaks one of the Ten Commandments, there is no question of whether some useful purpose was thereby served; it is a violation, a wrongdoing, simply because a commandment has been broken. Even a theory that had a place within it for consideration of extenuating circumstances would be deontological if it were based on a set of commandments, provided only that the primary basis of moral judgment was conformity to the commandments.

For Kant, the test of an action's morality is the motive from which it springs. Good intentions are not enough, however. To be right, an action must have been done out of a sense of duty, a desire to do the right thing solely because it is right. Further, strict logical conditions limit the choice of actions. Each intentional action conforms to some principle. For example, if I break my promise to you because it is profitable to do so, the principle according to which I am acting allows selective promise breaking. But that cannot be my duty, according to Kant, because of a point of logic. Kant believed that such a principle leads to inconsistency. If I act on such a principle, I must acknowledge the right of anyone else to act on the same principle. But that would mean that people could break their promises whenever there was advantage to be gained by doing so. If that were the case, then there could be no institution of promising; the very possibility of making a promise depends on its being generally understood that one does have an obligation to keep one's promises. In effect, to act on a principle that allows selective promise breaking is to hold that one has no obligation to do what one has an obligation to do. Promise breaking is therefore wrong, always and everywhere, regardless of its consequences.

A second version of Kant's ethical theory—one he claims is equivalent to the first—rests on the principle that one must treat other people always as ends unto themselves and never as means only. If, to continue the example, I break my promise to you for my own profit, I am misusing you, violating your rights for my purposes. I am failing to respect you as an end; I am treating you merely as a means to the furtherance of my own goals. Such action, according to Kant, is always wrong, no matter what the consequences.

This is not to say I cannot justifiably treat others as means. For example, if I want my house painted, I can hire a house painter, He then functions as a means to the achievement of my goal. But he does so freely, acting on pursuit of goals of his own. So I have not treated him as a means only. Rather, I have enlisted his efforts by linking my aspirations with his, respecting his status as an autonomous agent who can freely accept or decline my offer. If I force him to paint the house, however, I have treated him as a means only; I have used him, much as I might use a brush or ladder, violating his dignity as a person.

Kantian morality is austere and unforgiving. It requires strict adherence to principles that draw sharp lines between right and wrong. Duty is clear and simple. Never lie; always keep your promises; never violate the dignity of another. There is no room for explanation of the special circumstances or for suspending a moral rule because of the consequences that will follow if it is not suspended in unusual circumstances.

Unusual circumstances, however, are the stuff of which moral dilemmas are made. I can unwittingly find myself in a situation in which the only way I can keep a promise is by telling a lie. No matter that I should have avoided such situations. What do I do? For the act utilitarian, the answer is easy. I do the thing that maximizes happiness. But Kant gives us no answer at all. He fails to consider the resolution of moral conflict, writing as if the choices we face are like the choice between keeping a promise and breaking it for selfish reasons, rather than the choice between keeping a promise and remaining honest.

Despite such difficulties, Kant has been a moral theorist of towering influence. His resounding defense of the inviolable dignity of each person is a landmark in moral argument; his principle that one must never treat another as a means only, but always as an end unto himself, captures a profound moral insight that lies at the heart of the most powerful objections to consequentialist morality.

Much of the history of moral philosophy deals with the tension between these two basic points of view about the moral importance of consequences and with the attempts on the part of moral theorists to resolve the dispute or strike some sort of plausible balance. Clearly we do have strong temptation to hold the consequences of actions to be relevant to their moral status, and thus, consequentialist moral theories have substantial and sustained appeal. However, they have not become fully dominant precisely because we also believe that there is something morally lacking in an approach that focuses solely on consequences and refuses to acknowledge that certain kinds of actions are simply wrong.

Both consequentialists and nonconsequentialists typically share the view that each person is of equal value as regards that elusive cluster of issues that constitute the subject matter of moral philosophy—right action, moral worth, human rights, justice. Thus, for Mill and the utilitarians, it is the productivity of happiness and the avoidance of pain that count; but everyone's happiness is equally important, and everyone's pain is equally lamentable. And for Kant, moral action must be guided by a principle that one can logically will to be followed by all other persons, without exception. Indeed, it is widely taken to be a criterion of adequacy for any moral theory that it apply equally to all similarly situated persons. Thus, if telling a lie is wrong regardless of the circumstances, it is wrong not merely for you but for me and for anyone else. And if there are some circumstances under which, on utilitarian grounds or any others, it is morally permissible to tell a lie, then it is as permissible for you under those circumstances as it is for me or for anyone else. We thus find endorsement in moral philosophy of the requirement that to be taken seriously as a moral principle, a principle must be applicable equally to all persons as moral agents. That is, what one may do (or is prohibited from doing) all may do (or are prohibited from doing) under circumstances that are similar in morally relevant respects.

This requirement serves to test the moral acceptability of principles concerning how people may, must, or are forbidden to act, and it is essentially a requirement based on a widely shared conviction to the effect that morality allows no bias toward or prejudice against anyone to the advantage or disadvantage of anyone else. Not all theories satisfy this requirement, so it is a requirement that has real force. It rules out, for example, the old notion of perfectionism—the view that what is right is what serves the interests of the finest exemplars of the human species. According to that view, if you have to grind a thousand peasants into the dust to enrich the life of one talented aristocrat, you should grind away. The right course of action is not that which treats people equally or well or maximises happiness; it is that course of action which produces the occasional Bach, Newton, or Picasso—and this because the ultimate good has to do with perfecting the species or upholding some high standard of achievement. Such a position, advocated by Nietzsche, also had proponents among the ancient Greek and the nineteenth-century English aristocracy.

Such theories go against the grain because of their apparent injustice. But clarification of the concept of justice is no less a task than that of clarifying the concept of right action. Indeed, Plato's *Republic*, probably the most famous and important single work in the history of philosophy, takes the concept of justice as its primary focus. The inquiry proceeds by the attempt to discover what the correct definition of the term *just* is. Each definition that is considered is a different theory of justice; an acceptable definition is sought as the culmination of the inquiry, not as a prerequisite to beginning it.

We, too, will be concerned with justice, especially in the delivery of health care. So it behooves us to spend some time considering some competing theories of what justice is. There is no shortage of them. For our purposes, it will suffice to consider three of them in historical order. The first is that held by Mill, for whom justice was a subsidiary moral concept. That is, for Mill, the principles of justice are those guidelines to behavior that we have learned, over the ages, are most important in leading people to act in a utilitarian way. For example, it is unjust to punish an innocent man for a crime we know he did not commit, even if there is some social benefit to be gained by convicting him, and this is a reflection of the fact that respecting the rule that requires us to punish only the guilty will lead to maximising happiness in the long run. Justice, for Mill, is a value that is derivative from the utilitarian principle and hence can never be in conflict with it. The right thing to do will always be just and will always be that which maximises happiness.

Mill's view has been challenged by the observation that there can arise situations in which the action that maximises happiness is plainly unjust. Consider this example. A surgeon has five patients, each of whom faces death because of the failure of a different organ. In each case a transplant would save the patient, but there are no donor organs available. Suddenly the surgeon is called to deal with an emergency—a sixth patient who has been in a serious accident. The surgeon discovers that he can easily save the new patient, whose prospects for complete recovery are excellent, although everyone else erroneously thinks the case is hopeless. But the surgeon realises that if he deliberately fails at the attempt, he can then take the five needed organs from the new patient—who, being unconscious, will never know the difference—and save the lives of all five of the other patients. If we assume that the surgeon can circumvent legal jeopardy, the utilitarian principle plainly seems to require that he perform such action. Yet his doing so seems equally plainly to be an unjust violation of the rights of the new patient. The defender of utilitarianism is faced with two choices: He can argue that this example misrepresents the utilitarian position, or he can accept the example, claiming that the surgeon should indeed take such action, which we only perceive as unjust because of a benighted refusal to embrace utilitarianism as the true moral view. Neither line of defense has been entirely successful—though both have their advocates—and utilitarianism as a theory of justice has failed to win universal endorsement.

(See also J Rawls *A Theory of Justice* (1971) and R Nozick *Anarchy, State and Utopia* (1974).)

Gorovitz then takes us from general principles of moral philosophy into the world of medical ethics (pp 98–111, footnote omitted):

Each new physician is faced with a complicated, often confusing array of decisions about what sort of physician to become. There are two sides to the question—not wholly separable, but distinguishable. One is the question of what the individual is most attracted to as an ideal professional life: Is it a life of medical research, advancing the frontiers; is it neurosurgery, with its high-risk, high-gain intensity; is it the more structured life of the radiologist, who can typically avoid the stress of midnight emergencies every few days; is it the glamour and intellectual dazzle of Park Avenue psychiatry or perhaps the satisfactions of a general practice bringing medical care to a low-income community that previously was isolated from access to good primary care? The other side is the question of what the world needs: Park Avenue may have enough psychiatrists; radiology may be saturated in a way in which geriatric medicine is unlikely ever to be; and the need for rural physicians may be largely unmet. So each medical student faces the prospect of trying to fashion a match between those career paths that constitute the stuff of fondest fantasy and those that give the outside world something it wants and is willing to pay for.

The lucky ones find a good fit easily; for others it is a lifelong struggle. However the choice is made, it will reflect the extent to which the individual is motivated by such factors as income opportunity, on the one hand, and a desire to serve those in need, on the other. Such a choice, and the way in which it is made, will reflect the basic values of the physician at a level that is concerned not so much with what to do in a particular situation as with what sort of person to be over the long run. To a lesser degree, the same sort of reflection of values will occur in the choice of the context of practice—whether it is to be in a health maintenance organisation, a poverty clinic, a carriage trade office in the suburbs, or some other setting. Finally, the way in which the practice is structured—are the offices to be posh, the patients granted credit, the staff provided with good employee benefits?—will be determined in large measure not only by the prevailing conventions of organising a medical practice, not by market conditions alone, but by the tastes and values of the physician whose practice it is, including that physician's sense of how it is appropriate to deal with other human beings.

It would be hard to dispute the claim that these choices are shaped in part by the values of the physician whose choices they are. Nor is it likely that anyone would object to the fact that values play such a role. In medicine, as elsewhere, how one chooses to lead one's life is largely one's right to choose as one will. And whereas we might be moved to praise the young physician who dedicates himself to rural family practice because of a commitment to social justice, we are not thereby denigrating those who are doing cardiac surgery in the metropolis. We might wish for a social policy that would lead a larger number of physicians to choose to help the disadvantaged populations, but we are not likely on that account alone to scorn the physician who pursues a dedication to a somewhat esoteric corner of medical research. Further, if we find that a physician is a mean-spirited, autocratic, unsympathetic employer, we will rightly think ill of the physician for that—not because we believe that the physician's values have no place in shaping professional behavior, but because we have contempt for the values that are manifested in the behavior we discover.

At the level of specific clinical decisions, the situation looks radically different. If a patient with a clearly broken hand enters the office of an orthopedic surgeon, we expect the response to be based solely on the medical possibilities of repairing the hand. (Assume that there are no special problems about payment, simultaneous emergencies competing for the physician's attention, or other extraneous grounds for taking exception to the claim.) The physician in this situation is free to have any sort of attitude at all towards the patient—repugnancy, contempt, dislike, even loathing—so long as those attitudes remain private and do not influence the response to medical need. The hand is broken; the physician can repair the hand; therefore the physician must repair the hand—as well as possible—without regard to personal values that might lead the physician to think ill of the patient or of the patient's values. For instance, the physician may believe that work is crucial to good character, and the patient may be a bum who, although employable, prefers being on the dole; or the physician may be a devout believer in a religion the most effective public critic of which is the patient. It doesn't matter; the physician's personal, nonmedical values have no place here as an influence on medical decisions. That is what I mean here by the claim that clinical decisions should be value-free.

To sharpen the point, imagine the following dialogue. The physician enters, sees the patient, and speaks.

'That's a pretty bad break you've got there. Here, let me have a closer look.'

'Can you fix it all right? Will it heal properly?'

'Oh, I think it could be fixed; I've read the X rays, and I don't see any reason why it couldn't be fixed. But first, just what did you have in mind to do with it, Mr ... uh ... ?'

'Stern. Isaac Stern. I use it in my work.'

'Isaac Stern, the violinist?'

'No, he's a distant relative. I'm Isaac Stern, the pickpocket.'

'Oh, I see. Well, sorry, we don't do pickpocket hands here. Nurse, show Mr Stern out.'

In this episode the physician has values that we might endorse—fine violinists are a benefit to society, pickpockets are not, and the general welfare might even be best served if the pickpocket were not properly treated—but we do not believe that it is proper for the physician to decide whether to set the broken bones on the basis of his own attitude toward what will be done with the hand after it heals. To do so is to import nonmedical values illegitimately into the practice of medicine and thereby to turn medical practice into an instrument for the furtherance of nonmedical aspects of social policy. That is a betrayal of the physician's obligations to cure and to heal and a betrayal of the trust that is bestowed in the granting of the licence to practice medicine. The physician may condemn the pickpocket on moral grounds, but he must set the hand nonetheless.

A second example will be useful. A woman enters a gynecological clinic with a surgically correctable blockage of the fallopian tubes. She has been referred by an *in vitro* fertilisation program on the grounds that her condition is surgically correctable and she is therefore not eligible as a candidate for IVF. The surgeon examines her, decides that her condition can be corrected, and then inquires:

'Ms Mannawollen, you understand that if you have this surgery, you will be able to become pregnant in the normal way?'

'Oh, yes. That's why I want the operation. So I can have a child.'

'Are you married, Ms M.?'

'No, not yet.'

'Then with whom will you have a child?'

'I do have a boyfriend. If it works out, I think we may get married in a year or so.'

'But we really don't know anything about him. Perhaps he is an unsuitable father. Or perhaps you won't actually marry him. Then there's no telling who you will be with next. I'm afraid we can't authorise the corrective surgery yet. We'll have to investigate your case. If we decide that it is a good thing for you to be able to get pregnant, we will do the operation. But if we are not confident that you will bring a wanted child into a wholesome and nurturing environment, then I think we'd best leave you as you are.'

Here, too, we are appalled at the hypothetical physician's attempt to use the provision or denial of medical skills as an instrument for the furtherance of his personal values—and it does not help if we are in sympathy with those values, for what offends is not merely, or not at all, the values themselves but the way in which they are allowed to distort decisions that should be made solely on medical grounds. Again, at the level of clinical practice, medicine should be value-free in the sense that the personal values of the physician should not distort the making of medical decisions.

The examples we have just considered are fiction, toy examples invented to make a point. But the next case is fact. At a major university medical center there is a human fertility clinic; among the services it provides are genetic counseling, fertility testing, artificial insemination, and drug therapy. The process of obtaining artificial insemination involves a number of steps: The applicant's husband is tested to verify sterility, there is psychological counseling to ensure that the couple understands well what is involved in having a child by means of artificial insemination, and only then does treatment proceed. (I refer here to AID, artificial insemination with sperm from a donor—that is, someone other than the husband. Usually, it is not literally donated but is sold to the clinic, often by medical students who are convenient to the clinic, bright, in good health, and in need of extra income. There are also cases where, for special reasons, a woman is inseminated artificially with sperm donated by her husband; this is sometimes done in conjunction with sperm separation techniques that purport—controversially—to be able to increase the odds of having a child of a preselected sex.)

A psychiatrist at the clinic, also trained in gynecology, was involved in interviewing and counseling applicants for AID. Often couples come in together, but in this case a woman came alone. Early in the interview the physician asked her whether her husband had been tested to confirm sterility; she replied, to his surprise, 'I don't have a husband'.

Today that reply might be less startling; a few years ago, at the time of these events, it was new in the experience of the physician. Taken aback, he said, 'I'm not quite sure what to say here. I haven't seen a case of this kind come up before, and I'm just not sure what our clinic's policy would be on inseminating an unmarried woman.'

'I'm not actually—I don't consider myself—an unmarried woman,' she responded. And as the psychiatrist masked his dismay as well as he could, she went on to explain that she considered herself to be married in a stable, long-term lesbian relationship. She and her partner had decided that they wanted a child and that she would bear it. She knew, she said, that she could get herself pregnant in the usual way, but that would involve both a violation of her personal integrity as a committed lesbian and a shameful and deceptive use of some man as an instrument in pursuit of her purposes. Her only honorable course, she pointed out, was AID. The physician's dismay was of a fairly sophisticated sort. At once he knew that any position he took bore risks. If he indicated approval, he might encounter a maelstrom of opposition from his peers in the clinic, some of whom were certain to disapprove of the idea of the clinic's being complicit in such an undertaking. And if he indicated opposition or refusal, for all he knew he might be slapped with some sort of suit on the ground of making discriminatory judgments. There was federal funding in the clinic, and he was unsure just what the limits of the clinic's rights of refusal were. More importantly, he wanted to respond in the way that was right on the merits of the case, but not having thought about such cases at all, he was entirely uncertain what the merits of the case were. Wisely he decided that he needed time to investigate the case and discuss it with others, and he therefore asked the patient to return the following week with her partner to discuss the situation, this being the normal procedure with a typical couple. (It was between these two appointments that I met the physician and heard about the case.)

I have often described this case to classes and audiences, essentially as I have recounted it now. And the question I then ask is whether or not in the final analysis the woman's application should be approved or refused. Always there is dispute; often the response is fairly evenly divided; typically it is heated. You can repeat the exercise easily; gather some friends, present the case, and ask them what their vote would be. But it is the next step that is most important—the provision of the reasons that justify the position that one takes. The positions, and the supporting reasons for them, run the gamut from refusal based on the most virulent sort of opposition to homosexuality to approval based on the view that no consideration is relevant except the clinic's technical ability to provide the service as requested. Neither of these views had any appeal to the physician who faced the case. But most of the other reasons that I have heard people offer on either side did occur to him. And the dialogue that follows can therefore be seen as a recapitulation of the deliberations that raced through his mind as he searched for that initial purpose.

A: The physician's obligation is to serve the patient. It's as simple as that. The patient has a need that the clinic can meet, so the answer has to be yes. Nothing else bears on the case. He's got no right to refuse just because her family situation is one that he sees as odd or unusual or anything else.

B: But giving her AID isn't providing medical treatment to a patient. The physician has no obligation to her, and saying yes wouldn't cure any problem or disease she's got. She's just asking the physician to help her get something she wants, and under the circumstances it's a pretty weird desire at that. Maybe she wants a yacht, too. But the physician has no responsibility to cater to her desires just because it is in the power of the clinic to do it. The AID program was set up as a service to infertile married couples, and there's no reason to extend it to a case like this. He should just say no.

A: But the AID isn't just one thing this woman desires. It's a desire that can be met by a service that this clinic is in the business of providing. The question of cure has nothing to with it; that's as irrelevant in this case as it is in the case of the normal woman in a normal marriage who just has a sterile husband. Nothing gets cured there either. If the clinic will help satisfy the desire for a child in the one case, how can it refuse in the other? There are no good grounds to say no.

B: There are if you think of the child. And you must think of the child. The physician doesn't have to be complicit in bringing a child into an environment like that. Just think of the burdens on that kid—no father and, if that isn't bad enough, somewhere between one and two mothers, depending on how you count. What does he tell the other kids? What kind of model for male-female relationships does he grow up with? If it is a girl, what chance does she have for normal heterosexual development? If it's a boy, what kind of psychological environment are a couple of man-haters going to give him? The physician should say no for the sake of the child, and he's got every right to do so.

A: But you don't know that it would be like that at all. What evidence is there that two women can't raise a child well? Maybe these two can't, and maybe they can. Do you really have a good basis for deciding they can't, or is it just a lot of conventional prejudice that's showing? Because unless you can really make a case that these women would be bad parents, I don't see how you can deny them the chance.

B: Maybe there isn't what you would call hard data. There just aren't enough cases of the right kind about which enough is known. But if you think about it, you can't help seeing that it isn't a wholesome environment. I mean, think about what adoption agencies do. They have a tremendous amount of experience. They aren't going to place a kid in a home like that. They take the question of parental suitability very seriously, and it is well known how hard it can be to get an adoptive child. They know what they are doing, and they would surely vote no on this one.

A: In the first place, adoption agencies are ridiculous. If you aren't some sort of paradigm of wage-earning, churchgoing, middle-class solid citizen, they write you off, no matter how full of love and good sense you are. But if you meet the tests on their little checklists, then it's fine, even if you're really a sleazy tyrant beneath the veneer of respectability. But that isn't even the point. Those agencies are finding homes for kids that already exist. So they can be fussy, especially when they're in a good market situation. But they don't go around saying who can and who can't have kids in the first place. Even if they're right in their views about parental suitability, they don't propose to extend their standards to determine who can have children on their own. I'm not so sure that they would say no for this case, but even if they would, that has nothing to do with the fact that the physician should say yes.

B: But is that right? Or does the argument cut the other way, maybe. There isn't anything more important than the quality of the job that parents do. And you're right, the clinic isn't in the business of curing medical problems. It provides a service that people want, and in that way maybe it is more like a social service agency. Perhaps it should act more like one and start considering parental suitability for all applicants. The lesson of this case may be that the clinic has been entirely too superficial in screening cases. If an applicant is married to a sterile man but is also a drug-addicted prostitute, the clinic should recognise that there's no parental suitability there either and should turn that case down as well.

A: That's wrong. It's wrong on two different grounds. First, it's a start down the path to social control of the worst sort. The clinic judges who gets to have children and who doesn't! But why limit that kind of screening just to the cases that need a fertility clinic? Surely most of the worst parents are physically normal and would never come near the clinic. So if you want to screen to protect potential kids against being born into bad families by preventing their being born at all, you have to screen more broadly. You have to have licenses for people to reproduce. Anybody who gets pregnant without a license is a criminal unless there is an immediate abortion. Maybe only the people with college degrees get to have kids, or the number you get to have depends upon your rank or your politics. That kind of thinking would tear the society apart. But anyway, there's the second reason, and that's much simpler. Everybody has the right to reproduce. To say no is to deny the woman's autonomy with respect to one of the most basic and personal choices that anyone can make.

B: But the point is that most people are not patients at the clinic—you just said so yourself. And that defeats your scare tactic argument about fascism. I'm not proposing anything about a general social policy. I'm talking about how the clinic should respond to the cases that do come to it. They will always be a small minority of the population. I'm suggesting not that the clinic should go out making judgments about the society at large, but that in facing the cases that come to it, it should take all the factors into account, including the interests of the potential children, and then it should have the courage to say no when it concludes that it is a bad situation for a child. It isn't a question of the clinic's deciding what other people do; it *is* a question of the clinic's deciding what the clinic will do. And that is a question of rights, too. A physician should have the right to refuse to do something he judges to be wrong. A devout Catholic physician doesn't have to do abortions, and shouldn't have to—everybody agrees to that on all sides of the abortion debate—and neither should any physician have to inseminate a woman who he's convinced won't be able to provide a decent home for a child.

A: So now we're back to where we started. Even if the physician is convinced a woman won't provide a decent home, what makes that opinion so important? Do they learn in medical school how to test for decent motherhood? That's nothing more than making the physician a moral arbiter without any real basis of expertise. One physician might be homophobic, and the next might be a lesbian herself; but the personal values of the physician have to get set aside, and the nonmedical beliefs do also. The physicians should do what they are trained to do, and that is to provide the services that will help their patients, without trying to fit it all into a larger judgment about the whole social order.

This debate could go on at length, but it is not my intention to pursue it. For the point is not to decide whether the final decision should be to inseminate the woman. It is instead to learn something from the uncertainty that this case generates.

A great many issues arose in the brief debate that represented the physician's uncertainties about how to respond. (If we had pursued the debate, more would likely have arisen.) These issues included the question of the proper function of medical services; the interests of the potential child; the difference between the interests of the actual people who are the subjects of adoption agency activities and the potential, but not actual, people who are the subjects of fertility clinic activities; the extent and nature of the right to reproduce; the possibility of establishing criteria for parental suitability; the right of the providers of medical services to refuse treatment and the question of what it takes to justify such refusal; and the competence of the physician or other clinic staff to make decisions that go beyond the medical factors in the case.

Each of these issues invites extended debate and examination, but extended debate and examination are a luxury that can rarely be afforded in the context of a clinical decision. Indeed, this case is unusual in that it provided the physician an opportunity to defer response for a week, making it possible for him to discuss the case with a variety of people whose advice he could incorporate, as he saw fit, into the decision he finally made. More often, morally challenging situations in medicine require that some decision be made with substantial speed—rarely in a matter of moments, but more commonly on the order of hours or days than on the order of weeks. In such situations, physicians and patients may be well served by having thought about ethical conflict in advance.

The factors that bear on a case like this are of diverse kinds. Some are matters of fact, such as what will actually happen to the child if the woman is inseminated and what the law requires or allows the clinic to do. Other factors are matters of social policy, such as the nature and extent of the right to reproduce. (Would a pregnant woman have a right to take drugs that would cause her child to be a dwarf in order to fulfil a lifelong ambition to be the mother of a circus performer? I ask the question to show that we do believe there should be some limits on the rights of reproduction.) Still other factors are matters neither of empirical fact nor of social policy, but of judgment and value, such as the questions of what counts as parental suitability or how much the potential interests of the possible child should count, as against the actual interests of the actual woman who wants to have a child. Despite these differences in kind among the various facts that arise in the debate, however, one question must be faced with respect to each of them—the question of whether the factor is relevant to the decision at all.

If one believes that a pure consequentialism such as classical act utilitarianism is the correct guide to action, all the factors that are raised will be seen as relevant to the extent that they have bearing on what the consequences of treatment and of refusal would be. In particular, if the child *would* be likely to have an unfortunate childhood, that factor would have to be taken into account. Of course, in such a view, that is because such factors should always be taken into account; there is nothing about this situation that makes the difference. This is not to say that a rule utilitarian would have to believe that decisions about AID should be based on considerations of parental suitability. Instead, a utilitarian might argue that the greatest good for the greatest number will be produced in the long run if considerations of parental suitability are generally not taken into account. But the empirical facts about what will happen in any particular case must always be recognised as *relevant* by the act utilitarian; this might be the one unanticipated case that requires modifying the general policy.

The question of the physician's obligations will be considered in a parallel way. To the extent that honoring an obligation serves the general interest, the utilitarian will say the physician must honor that obligation—but not otherwise. Or the rule utilitarian could argue that it serves the general welfare best for physicians always to honor their obligations, but the holder of such a view would still have to consider in any particular case whether, on the basis of the empirical facts, the particular features of the case justify modification of the general rule about obligations.

Utilitarianism is thus future-oriented; it bases the judgment about what is right to do on considerations of what consequences will follow in the future from each of the various actions under consideration. But it is possible to argue against the utilitarian position, holding that what one ought to do depends more on what has happened in the past or on what is true in the present than on what will happen in the future. If, for example, the clinic has promised its financial backers to provide AID to any applicant who is medically qualified to receive it, there is an obligation based on that past occurrence to approve the application that is pending, no matter what the consequences of such approval might be. It could then be argued that although the financial backers did not have this sort of case in mind and would willingly change the policy for the future, in the present circumstances there is no just basis for refusal. Or one could argue that the woman's right to reproduce is not tempered by any considerations of what the consequences will be if she exercises that right. (This would not by itself entail that the clinic has an obligation to assist her in the exercise of that right. At most, it would entail that the clinic has an obligation not to interfere with her exercise of that right.)

Such critics of a utilitarian position would thus rule out as not relevant a number of the factors that for the utilitarian are central to the case. And in particular, one factor that would not count as morally relevant is the actual outcome for the mother and the child. If refusal results in misery for the woman or a subsequent sense of relief in retrospect that she narrowly averted a moral and personal disaster, or if approval results in the joyful raising of a happy and well-adjusted child or leads to a life of torment for both the mother and the child, these considerations depend on myriad other influences that come into play as the world unfolds and have no bearing on the original decision about what is right to do. For the nonconsequentialist, it isn't the consequences that count, but whether rights have been respected, obligations honored, promises kept. So before the physician who faces the decision can properly assess the factors we have mentioned and then take them into account, he must make a decision about what *sorts* of factors are the morally relevant ones. Only after concluding that a factor is of a sort that should have bearing on the decision can he proceed to give it its proper place in the deliberation. But that will be difficult unless he understands fairly well who, morally speaking, he is. Thus, just as it is important for physicians to be sensitive to the values of their patients, it is also important—and can be comparably difficult—for them to have a sensitive awareness of what their own values are.

Any decision in the case at hand will obviously be determined by a number of considerations, the assessment of which will itself be determined in part by the moral outlook of the physician who must make the decision. No response to this situation can be value-free, for even to decide to treat the woman solely on the ground that she is a medically qualified applicant is to endorse the controversial social policy that such cases should be considered solely on grounds of medical suitability—a position disputed by approximately half of each medical school class that I have asked to consider it.

But this case, it might be argued, provides no evidence that the practice of medicine, more generally, is value-laden. This case is loaded at the outset with the ingredients of ethical debate: sexual preferences, reproductive behavior, illegitimacy, technologically aided conception, parental suitability. This is surely a case the mere appearance of which could reasonably be viewed by the physician as a moral disaster—in the sense that being fraught with conflict, it imposes on him an inescapable necessity of doing something that will provide, at best, the grounds for deep misgivings. Of course, medical education provides no training that will help in a case like this, but this case is just a bit of bad moral luck; one can expect such episodes to be rare enough in the practice of medicine that it is an error to agonise over their apparent intractability. There are two replies to this response, a response I see as self-indulgently comforting. First, it overestimates the rarity of moral conflict. Secondly, it overestimates the importance of rarity.

The case we have just considered does present ethical conflict in a highly visible way. But ethically loaded decisions are part and parcel of medical practice. They arise in the case of the comatose emergency patient who can be resuscitated but who is highly likely to have severe brain damage if revived. They arise in the physician's way of handling his own chronic tardiness. They arise in the use of pain-killing drugs; in the judgments that are made about patient education, informed consent, and patient autonomy; and even in the choice of language that communicates bad news to patients. We have seen cases that illustrate how the making of medical decisions depends on considerations of value as well as on medical factors. The ideal of filtering out the judgmental aspects of such decisions is unrealistic.

Physicians can achieve partial success at limiting their judgments to the areas within which they have expertise, but partial success is all that it will ever be. For the business of medicine is essentially the minding of other people's business, albeit in a limited way. So the physician cannot escape moral dilemmas by deciding to mind his own business—medical decision—while leaving to others the responsibility of minding theirs. Medicine is by its nature intrusive in the lives of its consumers; the providers therefore cannot escape the fact that there are ethical dimensions of nearly all they do. Even when a situation seems wholly uncontroversial—bandage for a scraped knee or an aspirin for a sore throat—the manner in which the case is handled has ethical underpinnings and overtones. And even to do the obvious, uncontroversial thing is to make a choice that affirms and endorses the values that underlie that conventional response. So taking comfort in the prospect of escape from ethical issues on grounds of statistical infrequency provides a thin refuge indeed.

More important, the rarity of ethical dilemmas of a serious sort—whatever the degree of that rarity—should also be of limited comfort. We do not consider a man honest merely because he is mainly honest, stealing only twice a year or only from one corporation. We do not consider a woman courageous although she falters only rarely, when she faces danger. A man is not gentle who beats his wife or children only from time to time, nor is she kindly who is intermittently cruel. Morality is more demanding than that. Even if one were rarely challenged by difficult situations, it would be nonetheless true that the measure of one's character would still depend largely on the way one rose to the occasion when challenge did occur.

The problem of just how demanding the requirements of moral integrity really are is a central one for moral theory. Few would argue in favor of a position so austere as to judge one a moral failure for having made moral errors from time to time. Perfection is elusive in every sphere of life, and just as it is inevitable that physicians will make medical mistakes, provided only that they practice medicine, so, too, will one surely make moral errors, doing what is wrong from time to time, so long as one lives and acts. What is less clear is how closely to moral perfection one should approximate in one's objectives or in the standard one uses for judging oneself. A surgeon must take every surgical error seriously but must not be crippled by discouragement at having erred. Rather, the ability to accept and learn from one's mistakes is a necessary part of success in becoming a surgeon. Similarly, a commitment to acting in an ethical way requires that one be able to accept, learn from, and transcend one's own moral errors and failings. But just how good must one be?

Classical utilitarianism holds that one must act always so as to produce the greatest happiness for the greatest number. Taken literally, this theory seems to require saintliness. For, when we are given almost any action performed in the course of normal everyday life, there seems to be something else one could have chosen to do that would have been more productive of total human happiness. Are you reading a book, mildly enjoying it? You could be working as a volunteer, comforting the dying in a hospital. Did you take an evening off to relax at a movie? You could have been working to relieve hunger among the poor. So an additional problem with utilitarianism is that it seems so demanding as to be incompatible with what we are inclined, even on reflection, to believe is morally required of us.

Other moral theories face similar difficulties, seeming to hold us to standards that are beyond the psychological reach even of people who are generally thought of as exemplars of decency. This may account in part for the appeal that some people find in the moral views that seem (for they are not explicit) to inform Nozick's radical political libertarianism. If a theory asks of you only that you refrain from violating the rights of others, it is relatively easy to comply—easy, at least, compared with what is required by a moral theory that asks us to respect the rights of others and *also* to act in the interests of their welfare. Libertarianism (as a moral theory, not merely as a viewpoint on political organisation) forbids us to violate another person's right to life, for example, but places no burden on us to care about it or to make any effort to sustain it—except as we are committed by contract or other special obligations to do so. (The moral libertarian, of course, *allows* us to be moved to help another by charitable inclinations but cannot consistently require us to do so.) Utilitarianism, on the other hand, is an activist morality, charging us to value the interests of others as we do our own. So the question of how demanding of us a moral theory may properly be turns out to be inseparable from the question of which moral theory most properly merits acceptance.

A moral theory, to be plausible at all, must help us distinguish, from among the things we *might* do, the one (or more) which is right. If a theory about morality—or even a single moral guideline or principle—asks of us that we do what is not possible for us to do, then it can have no bearing on our choices and becomes irrelevant to human behavior. Nor will a theory that fails to distinguish one choice from another among those we face be acceptable; this is the primary failing of what has been called the ethics of love—the theory that admonishes us to do the loving thing without providing us with any way of identifying the one that merits that honorific description. But even theories that seem quite clear in the direction they provide will leave us with substantial uncertainty. Utilitarianism, for example, in calling for the act that maximises happiness, confronts us with the task of making what are sometimes exquisitely difficult assessments of what the consequences of the various options before us will be. This is why, even for the untempered utilitarian, the case of the woman seeking AID is a very difficult one to assess. Still, the utilitarian has a clear sense of what the relevant factors are, and the theory thus shapes and directs moral inquiry for him. And the proponent of an ethics of love would presumably have the moral inquiry shaped in a different way, perhaps with a focus on motivation rather than on outcomes.

If we are given that a moral theory, even when it cannot readily identify what one ought to do, can nonetheless direct one's further explorations by separating out the relevant from the irrelevant considerations, and are given that the practice of medicine involves frequent encounters with the need to make decisions about morally troubling cases, it follows that it would be useful for physicians to have some definitive indication of what the correct moral theory is. But questions of value seem to be precisely those about which we find the greatest dispute, and when we move from a particular disputed case or question of policy to the more basic foundations of moral judgment, we find that the dispute goes right along with us. Controversy about moral matters swirls around us whenever we lift our heads from the daily routine long enough to reflect for even a moment about the moral dilemmas we face. But is the situation hopeless? Can moral philosophy help, or is one in the end cast back entirely one one's own hunches about what to do? And if there is some help to be found, how is that compatible with the diversity of values that we encounter?

Subsequently, Gorovitz responds to his own questions (pp 146–150):

Philosophy can help articulate those new demands and help point the way toward meeting them. It can help us understand the relations between our actions and our aspirations and can teach us to accept as necessary the moral conflict that inevitably arises from the clash between what we want and what the world will yield to us. It can help us identify and understand what we really do value. Moreover, philosophy to some extent can provide a positive moral theory based on the moral content of our pluralistic culture. In sum, it can tell us not, as MacIntyre claims, why we cannot hope for solutions 'in a culture which precisely lacks the means to solve moral problems,' but rather what sorts of solutions we can reasonably hope for. And it can help guide us toward them. Of course, moral philosophy alone cannot provide solutions to moral problems any more than law alone can eliminate legal problems or economics alone can eliminate economic problems. We must always reach beyond philosophy in addressing problems in the world. But we should be wary of reaching without it.

MacIntyre writes that 'what matters most in a period in which human life is tragic is to have the strength to resist false solutions.' No period of human history has been devoid of tragedy; none, I'm sure, ever will be. Human life is always partly tragic, and false solutions should always be resisted. So, too, should false despair. This more optimistic view is shared by Nagel, who acknowledges the inevitability of conflict between moral perspectives, but who then goes on to write:

Does this mean, then, that basic practical conflicts have no solution? The unavailability of a single, reductive method or a clear set of priorities for settling them does not remove the necessity for making decisions in such cases. When faced with conflicting and incommensurable claims we still have to do something—even if it is only to do nothing. And the fact that action must be unitary seems to imply that unless justification is also unitary, nothing can be either right or wrong and all decisions under conflict are arbitrary.

I believe this is wrong, but the alternative is hard to explain. Briefly, I contend that there can be good judgment without total justification, either explicit or implicit. The fact that one cannot say why a certain decision is the correct one, given a particular balance of conflicting reasons, does not mean that the claim to correctness is meaningless. Provided one has taken the process of practical justification as far as it will go in the course of arriving at the conflict, one may be able to proceed without further justification, but without irrationality, either. What makes this possible is *judgment*—essentially the faculty Aristotle described as practical wisdom, which reveals itself over time in individual decisions rather than in the enunciation of general principles. It will not always yield a solution: there are true practical dilemmas that have no solution, and there are also conflicts so complex that judgment cannot operate confidently. But in many cases it can be relied on to take up the slack that remains beyond the limits of explicit rational argument.

Moreover, our pluralistic culture is not as fragmentary as it can appear, and moral guidance can be found to some extent in its hidden coherence. For despite the apparently stark incompatibility among the various moral theories we have glimpsed, they share certain common characteristics that constitute a core of agreement about moral judgment—a common denominator that lies at the heart of our moral outlook despite its diversity. Each theory satisfies the condition that as moral agents all persons are equal and subject to the same fundamental constraints and entitlements that limit moral action for anyone else. This principle of universalisability sets our moral outlook apart from those that endorse hierarchical or caste systems of moral standing. And each of these moral theories is based on a respect for persons—for their rights, interests, and aspirations in different degrees, to be sure—but a respect all the same, that sets our moral outlook apart from those that place the individual in a position of servitude to the interests of a source of value—be it political, theological, or otherwise—that supersedes individual persons in moral importance.

These are independent points about this collection of moral perspectives; a moral theory could satisfy either one alone. That is, a theory could treat all persons alike, but not in a manner that is based on respect for persons. This would be true of a theory for which equality was a basic value, although service to the state was the overriding good to which the rights and interests of individuals, all of them equally, could be sacrificed. Another theory could hold that the source of all value lies in the interests of individual people, although the interests of some people—the more noble and worthy among humankind—are endowed with greater moral importance. Neither of these theories would stand up well under sustained scrutiny. On the contrary, that they each lack one of the two characteristics we are considering would justify their rejection. They serve here only to demonstrate that these two characteristics are genuinely independent and that they are each substantively significant.

These characteristics limit moral choice in the face of conflict. They provide a backdrop that gives our moral outlook a distinguishable stamp. That outlook is not fragmentary in a random way but has a logic that emerges from amidst the pluralism. People are complex, value many things, and do so in ways that distinguish one person from another. Because our deepest commitments are to equality and to respect for persons as moral agents and as the possessors of interests, feelings, and aspirations, we respect a diversity of approaches to closing the gap between what the contending moral theories collectively allow and what in the end one chooses to do. Choice is not entirely unconstrained, for we condemn actions that violate our commitment to equality (such as denying voting rights to the poor) or to respect for persons (such as punishing an innocent man when it would be socially useful, claiming his interests do not count). But the moral common denominators that we can identify still leave unresolved questions about the adjudication of moral conflict.

Faced with such a conflict, an individual must make a choice, and that choice will constitute an exercise of moral judgment. How one responds to such situations is an important ingredient in one's character and personality—a source of diversity in action that we are bound to respect by virtue of our commitment to respect for persons as moral agents. Thus, insofar as respect for persons is a justifiable value, a certain amount of pluralism in ethical perspective is a sign not of moral decay, but of moral progress, of our transcending the strictures of moral hegemony to achieve a respect for persons that allows them the freedom to exercise moral judgment— sometimes well and sometimes perhaps less well—as they pursue their individual objectives and interests. Only when their choices violate the basic commitments to universalisability or to respect for persons can we condemn their actions as definitively and demonstrably wrong. But as their actions unfold over time, some will emerge as having exercised a quality of moral judgment that merits admiration, and others will emerge as self-serving, deceptive, or unfair and will be judged accordingly.

Respect for persons and for equality can take many forms, and bitter conflict as well as searing uncertainty will never be dispelled, especially from an undertaking, like clinical medicine, that is permeated with the need to make decisions that affect human interests so deeply. The more one understands the factors that are relevant to moral choice, the greater the likelihood that one's judgment will bear the test of scrutiny over time. Such understanding is not easily acquired, however, in part because it is so difficult to characterise, but for other reasons also. . . .

At the level of social policy, closure is no easier to attain than at the level of individual decision. It is sometimes achievable, as when there is widespread public agreement about a question that began as controversial. This is close to the case now with respect to fluoridation of the water supply, a practice which is generally accepted but was at one time bitterly opposed by a significant constituency. But at other times closure on the substantive issue in dispute is out of reach. That surely is, and will remain, the case in regard to abortion policy; it is the case, but one day may cease to be so, in the debate about nuclear power. When a moral conflict emerges at the level of public policy, and when closure on the substance of the issue seems impossible, a different sort of closure can be sought, however. Where we all cannot be satisfied with a decision that is made, we can at least try to fashion a process for making it that brings the dispute to rest fairly, having incorporated respectful consideration of the views of all interested parties. Whatever decision results will displease some, but that cannot be avoided when opinion is sharply divided about what the outcome should be. The process can nonetheless gain the respect of the public by ensuring that the judgment in the end is based on a conscientious assessment of the full range of relevant factors.

At the level of individual decisions, however, we search in vain for a procedural analogue. Precisely the difference between a decision faced by an individual and a matter of public or social choice is that there is no collective responsibility or involvement in the individual choice. The physician in the fertility clinic could consult with his colleagues about what to do, and he could call for the formal adoption of a clinic policy toward cases of the sort that he faced, but even prior to that he has to confront, alone, the need to provide an initial response to the woman's request. And in the subsequent deliberations with colleagues, he would still face, alone, the need to determine what his position would be in the ensuing debate about a collective viewpoint. Individual choice thus requires the exercise of moral judgment in a more fundamental way than collective choice. And the only way to ensure that it is based on a full consideration of the morally relevant factors is for the individual who faces the decision to be aware of those factors and disposed to take them respectfully into account.

In the next section we will consider a few specific issues in medicine and health policy. In each case we will explore the way conceptual clarity can lead toward a deeper understanding of the decisions that have to be made, whether it be the physician, the patient, the policymaker, or the citizen who faces the choice. In the penultimate chapter, we will return to our starting point—the behavior of the physician—in order to examine what constitutes being a good doctor and how it can be made more likely that doctors will satisfy the standard I will propose. Although that standard is stated in the context of characterising the good doctor, its ingredients exemplify moral conscientiousness more generally. That chapter may thus be viewed as a discussion of learning to make morally sound choices, whatever the role we fill.

Gorovitz, writing in 1982, is confident about his subject and its subject matter. But medical ethics in any systematic form is a relatively new discipline. Compare the paper written by Jonsen and Hellegers, 'Conceptual Foundations for an Ethics of Medical Care' in 1974 (reprinted in Reiser, Dyck and Curran *Ethics in Medicine* (1977)), in which they seek to sketch out a 'road map' for medical ethics:

I Medical ethics is currently in a muddle. Many questions are asked, but few answers are offered. Many anxieties are aired, but few are assuaged. Worst of all, the diversity of subjects discussed and the variety of arguments propounded makes one wonder whether there is any proper subject matter or proper methodology deserving the name, 'medical ethics'.

During July 1973, when this essay was first conceived, the newspapers carried three major, and many minor, stories about 'medical ethics'. In New York, a respected physician was accused of injecting potassium chloride into his dying cancer patient. In Chicago, the American Medical Association commented on the standards governing the ownership of stock in pharmaceutical companies by individual physicians and by the Association itself. In Aiken, South Carolina, three obstetricians refused, for what they called 'social reasons', to deliver the babies of welfare mothers unless the mothers submitted to sterilisation. All three stories were headlined 'medical ethics'. Euthanasia, financial investments, sterilisation for social reasons: all three concern behavior by physicians, all three pertain, immediately or remotely, to the practice of medicine. This may justify use of 'medical', but what justifies the 'ethics'?

The title of this essay, while rather grandiose, refers to the modest task of stating the propriety of denominating certain sorts of considerations as medical 'ethics' or the 'ethics' of medical care. This essay is designed as a road map for this conference on Health Care and Changing Values. It will, hopefully, provide to its participants the main features of the topography of that ancient realm of the mind called ethics, through which modern medicine must travel.

Popularly, ethics seems to mean any body of prescriptions and prohibitions, do's and don'ts, that people consider to carry uncommon weight in their lives. When their lives are deeply involved in certain activities, ethics can refer to the rules that guide those activities. The *Lexicon* of the Sydenham Society[1] defined 'ethics, medical' as 'the laws of the duties of medical men to the public, to each other and to themselves with regard to the exercise of their profession'. In this purview, euthanasia, financial investments in drugs, and sterilisation for social reasons obviously belong to the family of ethics.

However, ethics, at least for most ethicians, means much more than a body of prescriptions and prohibitions. Ethics means the critical assessment and reconstruction of such bodies in the context of a comprehensive theory of human morality. By 'morality' the present authors mean the actual behavior of human beings, involving judgments, actions, and attitudes, constructed around rationally conceived and effectively based norms whereby that behavior can be judged right or wrong and around values whereby states effected by that behavior are judged good or bad. By 'ethics' the authors mean an academic discipline, a systematic set of propositions that constitute the intellectual instruments for the analysis of morality.

This discipline seeks to elucidate how the norms and values are established and perceived and how the actions are justified. It inquires how one argues and should argue from norms and facts to decisions. It tries to show how values and norms are related to purposes and results. To accomplish such analyses, a theory must be elaborated, within which these elements are comprehensively described and coherently articulated. It provides, when rightly done, not only a descriptive discipline or morality, but a normative one as well, for its analysis purports to reveal the roots of obligation and value appreciation, thereby exposing not how men do *in fact* behave. Ethics, then, is the normative discipline of morality.[2]

An adequate ethics would be a theoretical system capable of suggesting some answers to the sorts of questions arising about morality. The authors believe that since there are at least three sorts of questions, an adequate ethics would consist of at least three principal theories, which we call, in reverence to the traditions of the discipline, the theory of virtue, the theory of duties, and the theory of the common good.

In response to questions like, 'What sort of person can rightly be called a morally good man?', the theory of virtue will expatiate on the character of moral agents, like attitudes, habits, affections, and motives. In response to questions like, 'What ought I to do in this situation?', the theory of action will discuss the nature of action, its objectives, goals, intentions, consequences, and conditions for freedom, and voluntariness. In response to questions like, 'What is the best form of human society?', the theory of common good seeks to understand not the good man alone nor his right actions but the social institutions that make and are made by good men acting rightly.

Medical ethics is, we believe, a species of the genus *Ethics*. It should, then, be constructed out of the three essential theories of ethics. In this essay we contend that, traditionally, medical ethics has dwelt mostly within two of those three theories, namely, the theories of virtue and of duty. Both of these theories, while in need of refurbishing and modernisation, remain indispensable to medical ethics. But the nature of contemporary medicine demands that they be complemented by the third essential theory—the common good. We shall review two traditional forms of medical ethics, indicating their relationship to the classical ethical theories. We shall then state the condition of modern medicine that calls for the theory of the common good. We suggest that this does not merely add an appendix to medical ethics but that it can be the source of a new concept for the discipline that can profoundly affect the more traditional theories of virtue and duty.

II   The term 'medical ethics' is frequently applied to those statements of professional standards that are set forth in 'codes'. There are many such codes, but we shall select the *Ethical Principles of the American Medical Association* as a paradigm. We believe that our analysis applies generally to what is sometimes called 'code ethics'.[3]

The AMA code, adopted in 1847 and revised four times (1903, 1912, 1947, 1955), now consists of ten sections in which such subjects as consultations and precedence, scientific competence, professional courtesy, cooperation with nonphysician health personnel, solicitation of patients, fees, conditions of practice, and confidentiality are treated. Some of these subjects are discussed at length but, for the most part, the principles are succinctly expressed. For example, 'It is unethical . . . for a physician to provide or prescribe unnecessary services or unnecessary ancillary facilities' (Section 4). 'The acceptance of rebates on appliances and prescriptions or of commissions from those who aid in the care of patients is unethical' (Section 7). The preamble states that 'these principles . . . are not immutable laws to govern the physician, for the ethical practitioner needs no such laws; rather they are standards by which he may determine the propriety of his own conduct'. The substance of the code, which comes to 67 pages in its latest edition, consists of these standards that serve to 'standardise' the more common transactions, social and economic, between physicians, between physicians and patients, and between physicians and third parties, such as legal authorities, insurance providers, and the press. We call these standards 'pragmatic directions'.[4]

Interspersed among these pragmatic directions are occasional exhortations to cultivate certain virtues considered proper to the physician. A citation from the Hippocratic literature opens Section 1: The physician 'should be modest, sober, patient, prompt to do his whole duty without anxiety; pious without going so far as superstition, conducting himself with propriety in his profession and in all the acts of his life'. Physicians are expected, notes Section 2, 'in their relationship with patients, with colleagues and with the public, to maintain under God, as they have down the ages, the most inflexible standards of personal honor'. At various points, the virtues of fearlessness, benevolence, patience, and delicacy are recommended. The Preamble notes that, while 'interpretation of these principles by an appropriate authority will be required at times . . . as a rule . . . the physician who is capable, honest, decent, courteous, vigilant, and an observer of the Golden Rule, and who conducts his affairs in the light of his own conscientious interpretation of these principles will find no difficulty in the discharge of his professional obligations'.[5]

Pragmatic standards for common transactions predominate; exhortations to virtue are sparse and, one might cynically say, perfunctory. The predominance of the pragmatic directions has prompted many to refer to the codes as an 'etiquette' rather than an 'ethic'. One of the first codes is *Decorum*, more literally the *Etiquette*, found in the Hippocratic corpus; during the nineteenth century medical codes were frequently called 'etiquettes'. Dr Chauncey Leake[6] writes in the preface to his edition of *Percival's Medical Ethics*, which served as exemplar for the early AMA codes:

> The term 'medical ethics' introduced by Percival is a misnomer. Based on Greek traditions of good taste . . . it refers chiefly to the rules of etiquette developed in the profession to regulate the professional contacts of its members with each other . . . medical etiquette is concerned with the conduct of physicians towards each other and embodies the tenets of professional courtesy. Medical ethics should be concerned with the ultimate consequences of the conduct of physicians toward their individual patients, and toward society as a whole, and it should include consideration of the will and motive behind this conduct.

The concept of etiquette is enticing because it sidesteps the pitfalls of having to define morality. An etiquette is a set of conventional rules, usually quite arbitrary, that reflect behavior in polite society. With obvious repugnance, but impeccable *noblesse oblige*, Lord Chesterfield admonished his son, 'Without hesitation, kiss the Pope's slipper or whatever else the etiquette of that court requires'. An etiquette is hardly susceptible to ethical analysis, for it is seldom possible or profitable to attempt to justify its precepts, which are either simply 'just done' or devised with a clear view to avoiding arguments about precedence, confusion over procedures, etc.

Etiquette is then a set of rules for external behavior that may be presumed to come from an internally virtuous man. Obviously, the external behavior may not reflect the internal man. Yet this is not sufficient to become cynical about the rules of etiquette. At best, they will truly reflect virtue. At worst, they are likely to keep the individual on his *qui vive*.

However, the word 'etiquette' is a misleading description of the codes. They do consist predominantly of pragmatic and arbitrary standards of behavior. But the sparse, almost perfunctory, exhortations to virtue in the modern codes are the faded tokens of their ancestry as ethics. The immediate progenitor of the American codes,

Percival's *Medical Ethics*, is a treatise on the 'Gentleman Physician'. In the eighteenth century, 'gentleman' denoted much more than a polite, gracious, considerate man with *savoir faire*. It was a synonym for the virtuous man. A century earlier, Izaak Walton[7] had written, 'I would rather prove myself a Gentleman, by being learned and humble, valiant and inoffensive, virtuous and communicable than by a found ostentation of riches'. The long tradition of medicine, from the Hippocratic corpus through the Admonita and Epistulae of the Middle Ages, the *Medicus Politicus* of the Renaissance and the eighteenth century treatises on *Duties* and *Character of the Physician* is replete with exhortations to virtues proper to those who would practice medicine. This whole tradition mingles these exhortations with pragmatic directions about bedside manners, consultations, and fees; but the vision of the 'upright man instructed in the art of healing' predominates.

These exhortations to virtue tend to dwindle, almost disappear, in more recent codes. Apparently, they seem to some superfluous, for they belabor the obvious. To others, they seem futile, for they cannot be enforced. Again, they seem vacuous, for they offer no practical guidance for action. Finally, they might seem embarrassing, for they smack of posturing for public consumption.

However, we suggest that these exhortations to virtue constitute the heart of code ethics. Indeed, they are the justification for calling the codes 'ethics' at all. They give to the pragmatic directions a moral substance without which they are, indeed, merely etiquettes. Their disappearance in current codes is not merely a mildly deplorable withering of a charming, but rather quaint, affirmation of the good, the true, and the beautiful. It reflects fundamental uncertainty about the character desired in the person who would practice medicine.

The theory of virtue is a treatise about moral character. It has always been recognised that moral judgments bear not only on the rightness or wrongness of discrete actions but also upon the goodness or badness of rather fixed states of persons who perform actions. Although 'virtue' and 'vice' are words with Victorian tone, great ethicists from Aristotle through Kant to Hartmann have used them to describe rationally intended, effectively rooted attitudes whereby persons consistently seem to incline toward certain sorts of behavior. Terms such as benevolence, honesty, trustworthiness, and sobriety described particular modes of these states of character.[8]

The great ethicists have always noted that while a spectrum of virtues should adorn the good man, particular dispositions were proper to certain roles: courage to the soldier, fairness to the judge, discretion to the ruler. A theory of virtue in medical ethics must explore that disposition most proper to the relationship between physician and patient—trust.

The patient approaching the physician suffers from more than his illness; he suffers from significant social disadvantages. He enters a mysterious domain, where arcane knowledge and rare skills rule. He is nervous, fearful, and perhaps even terrified. He places himself in the hands of a fallible human being. The novelist Kurt Vonnegut writes sardonically in *Goodbye Mr Rosewater*, 'The most exquisite pleasure in the practice of medicine comes from nudging a layman in the direction of terror, then bringing him back to safety again'. The potential for such sadism, which does lie within any physician's power, must be countered by the bond of trust. This bond—or as Paul Ramsay aptly titles it, covenant—arises from more than a contract; it is nourished by the evident trustworthiness of the physician.[9]

Codes do not create virtue. Their pragmatic directions establish certain regularities of procedure that elicit public confidence. But confidence elicited is fulfilled and confirmed only in the personal relationship that Pedro Lain Entralgo[10] calls 'the medical friendship', a delicate alliance that must simultaneously encourage confidence and discourage dependency. The apparent fading of this friendship, under the cold exigencies of scientific skill, technical expertise, harried services, and, frankly, cupidity, has been blamed by many as the major cause of the 'dehumanisation' of care.

In sum, code ethics, as they now exist, might be called the archeological ruins of a doctrine of medical virtue. The codes are, in their present form, collections of pragmatic directions that mark the outer walls of the physician–patient covenant. Their inspiration and the inner confirmation of this covenant require the virtue of trustworthiness. Restoration of exhortations to virtue in the codes would not of course, ensure the actual existence of virtue in physicians. This comes from the manner in which the profession selects and socialises its members from exemplarity, and from exercise. Nonetheless, the theory of virtue in medical ethics requires serious reflection on the virtues proper to the physician and on the obstacles to their realisation in contemporary settings and in contemporary men. Multiplication of codes, regulations, statutes, and standards, particularly if they are expected to be self-enforcing, as are most professional codes, is futile unless those to whom they are addressed comprehend and possess the virtues of the physician.

III Virtue is the inner spirit of morality; action is its outer manifestation. The virtuous physician without skill may be comfort, but cold comfort, to one seeking cure. Medicine is a practical science: theory and experience evoked in clinical decision and action. Medical ethics, then, must be as concerned about the rightness of acts as about the goodness of the agent. A theory of virtue is a necessary, but not sufficient, part of medical ethics.

Ethics provides a second complementary theory, often called theory of duty, that defines the criteria whereby actions are judged right or wrong. It analyses the relationship between intentions and consequences, motivations and circumstances. It studies the conditions of freedom and responsibility underlying imputation of guilt and innocence.

The need for an ethical analysis of actions comprising clinical practice is demonstrated in daily news articles on euthanasia, transplantation, and experimental trials. Serious efforts have been made to provide such an analysis. Jewish medical ethics is predominantly a doctrine of duties. Joseph Fletcher's pioneer work in medical ethics applies utilitarian theory of action to clinical acts. The present authors wish to use as an example the natural law theory of duties as it is found in Roman Catholic medical ethics. A volume on medical ethics in the Catholic tradition contains lengthy discussions of specific clinical actions such as euthanasia, abortion, transplantation, obstetrical techniques, and cosmetic surgery. Pope Pius XII had intense interest in questions of medical ethics and his frequent statements, delivered before distinguished medical societies, lent authoritative tone to the theologians' efforts.[11]

The medical ethics of this tradition is, in a very proper sense, a doctrine of duties. Medical interventions and procedures are analysed in light of an explicitly formulated ethical system of principles and argumentation that can be broadly described as natural law.

The first affirmation of the system is that God has dominion over his creation, the human body, while man is granted a derived dominion over his body that he must exercise in view of the divinely appointed finality of his body and its functions. Because he is ultimately not his own, man has an obligation to preserve his life and health. Any mutilation of his body is an abuse of the derived dominion, unless that mutilation contributes to the good of the whole body. This affirmation, entitled the principle of totality, is the proximate governing principle of Catholic medical ethics.[12]

Other carefully defined principles allow the Catholic moral theologian to thread a precise path through the complexities of medical procedures. The principle of double effect can be invoked when an intervention involves the problem of finding moral justification for both the physical evil of mutilation and some other evil such as the death of a fetus removed in a salpingectomy done for ectopic pregnancy. The distinction between ordinary and extraordinary means of sustaining life, elaborated within the context of the principles of divine dominion and totality, provide to physician and patient thoughtfully defined ethical grounds for making painful ultimate decisions about life and death.[13]

The theory of duty elaborated in Roman Catholic ethics describes an act in terms of (1) the *object*, that is, the objective design of the act and its immediate consequences; (2) the *end*, that is, the intention of the agent; and (3) the *circumstances*, that is, time, place, office, and other relevant concrete conditions of the act. In this approach, all three elements of an act must be right before the act is considered objectively moral. Criteria for evaluating the rightness of the action and its elements are such principles as divine and derived dominion and, more directly, the principle of totality.

In this scheme, a surgical intervention in the case of an ectopic pregnancy, described in terms of its objective, might be called a salpingectomy. The circumstances are advanced erosion of the fallopian tube, the presence of a fetus, and the absence of any therapeutic possibilities other than radical resection. The surgeon intends the removal of the eroding tube and tolerates the inevitable death of the developing fetus. The act would be judged morally right, for in its object, in the intention of the surgeon, and in the given circumstances, it effects the restoration of the integrity of the patient. The abortion is neither intended nor is it the principal objective of the act. It is, in the technical language of this school, an 'indirect' abortion.

The purpose of this description and evaluation of actions is to enable the agent to discern actions that are morally right from those that are morally wrong. Morally right actions must or may be performed. Morally wrong actions must be avoided. Thus, this doctrine of duties contains a doctrine of obligation, grounded in the principle of divine and derived dominion, which distinguishes between obligatory, permissible, and forbidden actions. There is an absolute moral obligation to refrain from morally wrong acts and a conditional moral obligation to perform right acts. The purpose of the theory of duties is to guarantee the moral rectitude of medical intervention. Almost every medical procedure of diagnosis and therapy requires an invasion of the sphere of the patient's physical and psychological independence.

Two points are particularly noteworthy about this example of a theory of duties. First, the principle of totality is defined in terms of the integrity of the *physical* organism of an individual person. Efforts have been made, from time to time, to extend its range to *social* or *interpersonal* totality, but these have never been enthusiastically adopted. Thus, early discussions of homographs, such as renal transplants, tended to disapproval because of the nonbeneficial mutilation of the donor. The suggestion that the bond of charity could thereby be strengthened between donor and recipient won little favor and the transplantation was finally justified on grounds more consonant with traditional doctrine of totality, namely that donation of one of paired organs did not absolutely impair functional integrity. Similarly, attempts to defend contraception by means other than periodic abstinence on the basis that hormonal alteration or tubal ligation would, ultimately, improve the psychological and physical well-being of a woman or benefit the total family situation were met with disfavor. The principle of totality remains tightly linked to physical integrity of single persons, rather than their psychological or social integrity.[14]

This problem has been framed in terms of the traditional Roman Catholic use of the principle of totality. However, it is not a problem unique to that particular form of the theory of duties. Most efforts to formulate a theory of duties, in particular, those influenced by Kantian ethics, have a tendency to thrust the single act or the isolated agent onto center stage and leave the interrelationships of acts and agents in the shadows.

Second, any theory of duties issues prescriptions, prohibitions, and permissions. The physician committed to this moral reasoning must refrain from prohibited interventions. Even though certain concessions are made for unwilling and compelled cooperation in immoral acts, the physician's moral duty is quite clear. Direct abortion, direct sterilisation, positive euthanasia are clearly forbidden. Refusal to perform these actions assures the moral integrity of the physician's conscience. However, from the point of view of those who do not share the physician's conscience, his refusal to perform an act is perceived as denial of a benefit to the petitioner. While any single petitioner might seek that benefit elsewhere, could it be that the conscientiously acting physician, by accumulation of his decisions and by his efforts to effect public policy in favor of his conscience, might impede some public good? And what if all physicians were of identical mind on the issue and all patients of opposite mind?[15]

Both of these problems, the restriction of the principle of totality to the *physical* integrity of single persons and the possibility of disagreement between adherents of this theory of duty and the possible demands of a broader public, suggest that a theory of duties, while necessary, may not be sufficient for adequate ethics. To the extent that such theories concentrate on discreet acts and individual intentions, they neglect the ethical issues arising from the intersection of multiple actions in institutions and society. Thus, an adequate ethics calls for an explicit reflection on the morality of institutions and on the relationship, and possible clash, between social values and individual values. Classical ethics has made such a reflection. It can be conveniently called a theory of the common good.

IV The ethical theories of virtue and of duty are complemented by a theory of the common good. A theory of the common good seeks to elucidate the nature of human communities. These are the institutional forms that human actions create and human virtues sustain and, in their turn, should become the objective conditions nurturing virtue and sustaining action. This theory should treat two principal questions: First, what is the 'common' good or goods? Second, how should they be distributed? The first question inquires about the goods and values that are necessary for individuals and for the society. In the present context, 'health and health care' might be discussed as common goods. This is a crucial discussion for ethics of medical care. However, the second question, properly called the problem of social justice, will be the problem to which we shall attend in the remainder of this paper.[16]

Before considering this problem, it is important to realise that the theory of the common good is not merely a separate third chapter of ethical concepts that should be glanced at from time to time whenever a 'social question' arises. Properly conceived, the theory of the common good is a third dimension in which virtues and actions take on a depth and tone that they do not have in isolation. The very meaning of a virtue or an action depends on its social or institutional setting. For example, lying and deception can be viewed and analysed as a private interaction between two individuals, as in the recent drama *Sleuth*. But when they are considered within the structures of public trust, authority and responsibility that constitute an institution, for example government, quite different issues arise. In what sense, for example, does the problem of National Defense Security morally qualify an act of deception? And, analogously, would a National Health Security be sufficient warrant to deceive patients, or experimental subjects, about the nature of what was being done to them?

It must be clear that considerations of the common good do not *ipso facto* override considerations of individual rectitude of action. Rather, the purpose of the doctrine of the common good is to consider how conflicts may be avoided, reconciled or, more importantly, how the institutional structure can be designed so as to avoid conflict, how to reconcile discord, and how to compensate unjust harm.

There is little or nothing that can be identified as a doctrine of the common good in contemporary ethics of medical care. There is, of course, a conviction on the part of most professionals that they do serve the common good in a significant way. Yet there is, further, a contention on the part of many professionals that the practice of medicine involves significant social injustices. The authors do not intend to argue either conviction or contention. Neither of them, however valid, constitutes a theory of the common good. Such a theory must consist of a comprehensive description of the exigencies of medical care and the institutional forms that serve these exigencies at present. It must propose criteria whereby these institutional forms can be analysed and criticised, not only in terms of the exigencies of care, but in light of certain exigencies of human moral existence. These latter exigencies, when seen in the light of social institutions, have been most clearly expressed by the great ethicists in terms of a doctrine of justice.

Justice, while a virtue, or personal characteristic, of individuals, is above all the 'virtue' of institutions.[17] An institution may be judged ethically 'good' if it exhibits in its organisational structure and in its procedures the characteristics of justice.

The establishment of a just society, for the great ethicists, required not merely the assembling of many just men but the design of social institutions, laws, policies, and economics in which the habits, inclinations, and intentions of just men could be realised in public policy and practice. It is curious that while we often speak of just laws, just courts, just taxes, just contracts, we do not often speak of just medicine.

If, however, justice is pre-eminently the virtue of institutions, our failure to apply the criteria of justice to medicine may result from our failure to recognise that medicine has become, in fact, an institution. Medicine has, in recent years, evolved from a practice, a private technical interaction between two parties, through a profession, a socially coherent, publicly recognised group that defines the conditions under which those private transactions take place, to an institution.[18]

By an institution, we mean a complex interaction of professionals, para-professionals, and the public, on informational, economic, and occupational levels, in identifiable physical environments, whose coordinated decisions and actions have magnified public impact and is recognised culturally and legally as affecting the public welfare in a significant way. Law enforcement, the free market, religion, higher education are institutions in this broad sense.

Just as the free market once consisted of a solo producer exchanging his product for consideration by a single buyer (and still, in essence, consists of that) so the medical transaction once was, and still essentially is, a solo physician diagnosing and treating a single patient. But that essential transaction has gradually been surrounded by the indispensable cooperation of other people, by accessory producers, by physical environments, by customary and legal prescriptions. The face-to-face decisions made in the private transaction have magnified public impact since they now engage the attention of multiple other parties, nurses, druggists, insurance carriers, etc. The coordinated decisions and actions of the institutions have magnified public impact because accepted forms of diagnosis and treatment research, and prevention engage the manufacture of products, the construction of buildings, and the enactment of laws.

Modern medicine, then, is an institution that incorporates a profession that practices a technique and an art. The practice remains, indeed, at the heart of the institution, but it cannot be adequately performed or understood outside of it. Doctrines of virtue and action supply ideals and norms and pragmatic directions for the profession and for the practitioner; a doctrine of the common good must be added to provide an ethics for the institution.

It must be emphasised again that a doctrine of the common good does not supplant the other two modes of ethical analysis. All three doctrines are required for an adequate ethics. The practice of medicine, once conceived as the relief of the suffering of one person by another properly qualified person, was adequately analysed in ethical terms by the two doctrines of virtue and of duty. Today, however, the institutionalisation of practice and professional calls for an institutional ethic. On the other hand, the possibility that misjudgments about the ethical exigencies of virtue and duty might be propagated throughout the institution, still demands a careful ethical scrutiny of quality of individual character and rectitude of single actions.

Institutions are vehicles for the distribution of the benefits and burdens of social life, and it is the function of the principles of justice to determine fair and equitable assignment of rights and duties and fair and equitable distribution of benefits and burdens.[19]

An institution prossesses an identity, an organisation, and resources that enable activities performed by its members to have an extensivity and perpetuity that they otherwise could not have. By extensivity, we mean that activities can have effects on broad contemporary population. By perpetuity, we mean that they can be prolonged in time by affecting future populations. It may be argued that medical actions always factually had effects that fulfilled these definitions of extensivity and perpetuity. However, the development of epidemiology and biostatistics has made the dimensions of this extensivity and perpetuity vividly evident in contemporary medicine.

Only the institutional form provides the exchange of information, the continuity and cooperation, the designation of qualified participants and the utilisation of physical and financial resources to support extensivity and perpetuity. A profession may have an identity based on possession of similar knowledge and techniques and may cooperate to share and assure possession of them, but a professional, as such, did not deliberately utilise information and resources to effect extensivity and perpetuity. Medicine has, in the last 100 years, by virtue of certain scientific and technical accomplishments, evolved from a profession with knowledge of limited effects in time and space to an institution with knowledge of extensive and perpetuated effects.

The most pressing ethical issues of modern medicine arise from the potential for extensivity and perpetuity inherent in its new institutional status. At one time a medical intervention was perceived as a transaction between a physician and a patient. The benefits and the costs were, for the most part, thought to be quite strictly limited to that transaction. Today, benefits and costs are known to be distributed broadly in many ways. Financial costs of medical research and education are borne by an extensive public. Costs of care are borne by insurance purchasers and tax payments. Resource allocation distributes benefits of research to certain afflicted populations at a cost to others. Certain treatment modalities impose burdens on those other than the treated. The effects of certain medical interventions can be perpetuated into future generations, for example, the burden of heredity of certain genetic diseases such as diabetes and hemophilia. Formerly, these patients often did not live long enough to reproduce and hence the defective gene was eliminated from the pool. Techniques for genetic diagnosis and control are directed toward modification of inheritable characteristics.

Where benefits and burdens can be so distributed, the problem of justice arises. Some who will benefit will not bear costs; some who will bear costs will not benefit. When this situation depends not on chance or accident but on planned and conscious decisions about the structure of the institution, it is necessary to ask, 'What justifies the imposition of a burden, a cost, a risk, on any single individual?' Why should one individual benefit at the apparent cost of another? These are the questions at the heart of each of the serious ethical issues of medicine as they are of justice.

The problem of access to medical care is the most obvious field for the application of the concept of justice. This appears to be, on its face, a problem of distributive justice. A subset of this problem is the allocation of scarce resources, such as renal dialysis. However, many other problems that are not usually considered in terms of justice involve deliberate distribution of costs and benefits. Randomised clinical trials, particularly when one of the alternatives is a proven therapeutic agent, involve costs without compensating benefit to certain individuals. An increasing number of therapeutic modalities lay burdens of risk on others than the beneficiaries such as drugs administered to pregnant mothers. In the near future, nuclear-powered artificial hearts— and, perhaps in the further, but real future, DNA therapy through viral agents—will have this effect. The entire realm of genetic control, whether it utilises elimination of births or elimination of defective genomes, raises the question of justice to future generations. Psychosurgery and psychoactive drug therapy, while they may be conceived as interventions beneficial to the individual, have the potential to impose stringent limitations on that individual's freedom from which others may benefit socially, politically, and economically. The classical problem of euthanasia is aggravated by the institutionally supported potential for prolonging dying at great cost, emotional and financial, to survivors.

Finally, the nagging, but ill-defined, problem of dehumanisation of medical care may obtain clarity within the concepts of justice. The great jurisprudent, Georgio del Vecchio, wrote, 'The ideal criteria of justice . . . demand the equal and perfect recognition . . . of the quality or personality in oneself as in all others for all possible interactions among several subjects'.[20] Dehumanisation is, at bottom, unequal and imperfect recognition of the quality of personality, an entity most difficult to quantitate under the criteria required for a just theory of the common good.

Many of the moral problems of medicine appear to be problems of justice. Many of the old problems of medicine, placed in the modern setting, seem to have been transmuted from problems of virtue of duty, into problems of justice. Yet, the theories of justice long familiar to ethics have not been fully mined for their relevance to the moral problems of medicine. The authors are not so naïve as to suppose that the ancient conflicts of individual versus institution and personal duty versus social good will be resolved by yet another invocation of the doctrine of justice. Still, to the extent that considerations of justice contribute to the design of institutions of medicine and to policies governing its practice, many moral problems may be either avoided or ameliorated.

The traditional definition of justice is 'giving to each his due'. The problem of justice is defining what is 'due' to each. This is done, first, by recognising that the 'each' of the definition is both everyman (with a basic humanness shared by all), and the single person, different in ability, merit, and need from all others. Justice thus requires an impartiality resting on the fundamental similarity of all persons and an equity that allows for different treatment justified by different conditions of ability and merit. Effecting justice becomes the continual process of critical scrutiny of the reasons proposed for different treatment of persons. This scrutiny must measure particular considerations against universal characteristics, the claims of ability, merit, and need against the claims of equality of liberty, consideration, and treatment. So stated, the conundrum is not vastly different than the problem of reconciling the age-old precept to give to each according to his need with that of giving to each according to his merit.[21]

The requirements of a theory of justice are not satisfied by the proposition that an act or institution is ethically justified when it produces the 'greater good for the greater number'. This thesis called Utilitarianism, has been much disputed by ethicists and its inherent defects revealed. Nonetheless, it appears to be the dominant ethic for many policymakers in scientific medicine.[22] The problem of the lesser number, disadvantaged for the sake of the greater, remains unsolved.

In medicine, this problem can be particularly pressing, for traditionally medicine has favored the good of individuals, while the law has favored the common good. Today, the realisation of extensivity and perpetuity of modern medicine place many medical interventions directly within the sphere of the common good. Whether the problems thus raised can be 'justly' solved depends on how deeply modern medical practitioners and policymakers reflect on the profound moral dilemmas and theses of the theory of justice. They must refuse to relax those dilemmas either by a facile appeal to the 'inestimable social benefits of medicine', on the one hand, or to the 'inviolable individual rights of patient or practitioner', on the other. Neither assertion can stand alone; both must be comprehended within an adequate theory of justice. Above all, public policy relative to the shape of institutions, the flow of money and people through them, the regulation of their powers, and vigilance over their performance must be devised with the requirements of justice foremost in mind.

Several final points should be made about 'just' medicine. First, the cynical often say, 'Ethics is no more than the simulation of good intentions'. Doctrines of virtue, because virtue can be so easily simulated by scoundrels, are most susceptible to this pessimistic criticism. Doctrines of duty can take refuge in excuses and protestations of ignorance. But doctrines of justice rest on different ground. Their concern is the fair and equitable structure and function of institutions. In this theory of ethics, we are concerned about the institutional forms that set up problems in certain ways and restrict or expand the alternatives for their solution. We do not limit our attention to good intentions alone or to the outcome of single actions. We are concerned about the assignment of rights and duties, the design of offices and tasks, the currents of resources, and support that can best eliminate problems of unfair distribution of burdens and benefits and can best enable virtuous character and right action.

Second, the advent of institutions heralds the appearance of laws. Medicine has always been governed, to a greater or lesser degree, by civil law. Medicine has seldom been happy under that governance. 'Just' medicine raises the menacing threat of medical practice cribbed, cabined, and confined by statute and regulation.

This need not necessarily be the case. Justice and law are not synonymous. A theory of justice is concerned basically with the design of institutions. Institutional design can be created and effected by innumerable agencies other than the state. The profession, related professions and industries, interested and impartial groups, organised and unorganised consumers can, if allowed and enabled, assist in institutional design. However, to the extent that civil law and regulations are advisable, a doctrine of justice is indispensable. It alone can provide the vision of just and equitable distribution that the enacted law should, imperfectly, piecemeal, but steadily, seek to realise. Without a doctrine of just medicine, laws and regulations will be haphazard, aimless, and for this reason frustrating to professional and consumer alike.

In conclusion, then, the thesis of this essay might be restated in terms of an ancient Roman definition of the entire field of ethics: *Honeste vivere, nemini laedere, suum cuique tribuere*—live uprightly, hurt no one, give to each his due. The authors have attempted to state the conceptual foundations for an ethics of medical care under similar titles. It must consist, they maintain, of three essential theories of ethics applied to the unique enterprise of medicine and health care. The theory of virtue concerns those dispositions and qualities that define uprightness of life for those who practice medicine and engage in care. The theory of duties concerns criteria that enable the practitioner to recognise acts that ultimately harm those who seek his help. The theory of justice concerns the establishment of fair and equitable institutions for the practice of medicine and the provision of care. It is the authors' impression that in discussions of medical ethics these questions are often jumbled, that their theoretical bases are unrecognised, and that their intellectual history is unknown. They contend that fruitful progress might be made if future discussions acknowledge the distinction and the interrelation of these three theories of ethics and undertake their careful application to the difficult moral problems of modern medicine. This will make, they hope, for better medicine, for better ethics, and for a better ethics for medical care.

Notes to extract

1. *Lexicon of Medicine and Applied Sciences*. London, The Sydenham Society, 1881–1889.
2. Frankena, W, *Ethics*, Englewood Cliffs, Prentice-Hall, 1963, pp 1–10. Wallace, G, and Walker, A (ed), *The Definition of Morality*. London, Methuen, 1970.
3. *Opinions and Reports of the Judicial Council*. Chicago, American Medical Association, 1969. On the ethical nature of codes, see Veatch, R, Medical ethics: professional or universal? *Harvard Theolog Rev*, 65:531–559, 1972. On the history of the AMA code, see Konold, D, *A History of American Medical Ethics*. Madison, University of Wisconsin, 1962.
4. Our intention is to give an *ethical* analysis of codes. A sociological analysis can be found in Freidson, E, *The Profession of Medicine*. New York, Dodd-Mead, 1970.
5. This echoes an early critique of the AMA code: 'Were the great rule of Christian ethics present to the mind of the physician, "do unto others as ye would that they would should do unto you", there would be but little necessity for societal codes'. Duglison, R, On the present state of medicine in the United States. *Br Foreign Med Rev* 3: 227, 1837.
6. Leake, C, *Percival's Medical Ethics*. Baltimore, Williams & Wilkins, 1927, pp 1–2; Leake, C, Theories of ethics and medical practice. *J Am Med Assoc* 208: 842–847, 1969. On the term 'etiquette', see Jones, W H S, *The Doctor's Oath*. Cambridge, University Press, 1924; and *Ancient medical etiquette, Hippocrates II*. Cambridge, University Press, 1923.
7. *Compleat Angler* 1:3, 1653. See King, L S, *The Medical World of the Eighteenth Century*. Chicago, University of Chicago Press, 1958, p 256.
8. Klubertanz, G, *Habits and Virtues*. New York, Appleton, Century, Crofts, 1965.
9. Ramsey, P, *Patient as Person*. New Haven, Yale University Press, 1970, preface.
10. Lain Entralgo, P, *Doctor and Patient*. New York, McGraw-Hill, 1969.
11. Pius XII, *The Human Body*, Boston, St Paul Press, 1960. See Healy, E, *Medical Ethics*. Chicago, Loyola Press, 1959; Kelly, G, *Medico-Moral Problems*. St Louis

Catholic Hospital Association, 1958; Paquin, J, *Morale et Médecine*. Montreal, L'Immaculée-Conception, 1960.

12. Aquinas, T, *Summa Theologica* II–II, q 65, a1
13. Kelly, G, On the duty of using artificial means to preserve life, *Theolog Stud* 11 : 203–220, 1950; 12 : 550–556, 1951.
14. Nolan, M, Principle of totality in moral theology, *Absolutes in Moral Theology*. Edited by C Curran. Washington, Corpus, 1968; Curran C, *Medicine and Morals*. Washington, Corpus, 1970.
15. This problem is reflected in the debate over the Code of the Catholic Hospital Association. See Catholic hospital ethics: report of the Commission on Ethical Directions for Catholic Hospitals. *Linacre Q* 39, Nov 1972; Brennan J, Quicksands of compromise. Reich, W, Policy vs ethics. McCormick, R, Not what the Catholic hospitals ordered. *Linacre Q* 39, Feb 1972.
16. Our use of the terms 'common good' and 'social justice' may be elucidated by the following: 'Social justice [is] the equal treatment of all persons except as inequality is required by relevant, that is, just-making, considerations . . . it takes equality of treatment to be a *prima facie* requirement of justice, but allows that it may on occasion be overruled by other principles of justice . . . the differences in treatment are not justified simply by arguing that they are conductive to the general good life, but by arguing that they are required for the good lives of the individuals concerned. It is not as if one must first look to see how the general good is best subserved and only then can tell what treatment of individuals is just. Justice entails the presence of equal *prima facie* rights prior to any consideration of utility'. Frankena, W, The concept of social justice, *Social Justice*. Edited by R Brandt, Englewood Cliffs, Prentice-Hall, 1962, pp 13, 15.
17. Rawls, J, *Theory of Justice*. Cambridge, Harvard University Press, 1971, Ch 2.
18. Mechanic, D, *Medical Sociology*. Glencoe, Free Press, 1968, Ch 10–11.
19. Rawls, *op cit*, p 55.
20. del Vecchio, G, *Justice*. Edinburgh, University Press, 1952, p 116.
21. del Vecchio, G, *op cit*; Perelman, C, *Justice*. New York, Random House, 1967; Friedrick, C, Chapman, J. (ed), *Nomos VI: Justice*. New York, Atherton Press, 1963.
22. '. . . the dicta of that school [Utilitarianism] . . . are still used as part of the language of men of science'. Singer, G, Underwood, E A, *A Short History of Medicine*. New York, Oxford Press, 1962, p 208. For critique of Utilitarianism, see, among others, Lyons, D, *Forms and Limits of Utilitarianism*. Oxford, Clarendon Press, 1965.

The concern for basic principles occupied Sisela Bok in 1976 in her well-known essay, 'The Tools of Bioethics' (reprinted in Reiser *et al* (1977)):

I would like to consider, first, some fundamental principles of bioethics and, second, whether bioethics as a discipline possesses workable and rigorous methods whereby these principles can be brought to bear on real and complex human conflicts. Since bioethics is one form of applied ethics, any such questioning of its methodology must also question that of applied ethics in general.

It is especially important to ask these questions now, for today philosophers and social theorists are asked to participate in social choice as they have not been asked since antiquity. At that time, their assistance, while sought by some, was often feared or thought outright disastrous by many. The Roman Senate impatiently decreed in 161 BC, for example, that all philosophers should be banished from the city, along with all teachers of rhetoric. This thought has surely occurred to many policy-makers since.

In part, this impatience is due to the trivialisation which philosophers can bestow upon human predicaments; in part, it is also due to the carelessness of some intellectuals pronouncing on human conflicts from a distance. To a considerable extent, however, the response results from a sense of *threat*—a feeling now experienced by those affected by the social choices in bioethics.

For philosophers, theologians, and social theorists now participate in such choices as what national policy should govern biomedical research on prisoners, or kidney dialysis programs, or fetal research; and their participation cannot help being a threat to those whose scientific and medical activities are at stake. The most natural and immediate response to such a threat is to question the criteria used in the policy choices, the assumptions underlying them, and the methods of arriving at conclusions.

Such questioning is legitimate and crucial. What is *not* legitimate is to hold as many do that outsiders need not worry about the ethics of science and medicine; that these enterprises are somehow value-free; or that any ethical problems which do come up are adequately taken care of within the professions without meddling from the outside.

One of the simplest and best definitions of ethics was put down by Diogenes Laertius in the 3rd century AD.[1] He reported that, for Epicurus,

Ethics deals with things to be sought and things to be avoided, with ways of life and with the 'telos'. (Telos is the chief good or the end of action.)

Ethics, according to such a view, must be taken into account whenever human choice is at stake. Using such a definition, it is clear that there are no more fundamental ethical choices than those which are made in medicine and in science. What *should* we seek through these fields? And what ought we to try to avoid? What ways of life should we encourage? What can doctors choose to do or to avoid to affect our health? And how do their own life-styles affect the care that they provide for others? These questions are at least as central to us all as what happens to our property, our schooling, or our right to vote.

To be blind to moral dimensions of what human beings do to one another is as much of a handicap as to be visually blind or unable to have memories. But it is a more insidious handicap since it is often not recognised as one. Those who are thus deprived stumble through the world of humans unaware that their perception is flawed—and do untold harm to those whose lives they affect. It is in this category that we must place those who insist that there are no ethical considerations in science or in medicine.

The *need* for ethical inquiry, therefore, is great. And the choices made—individually and socially—in the biomedical areas are moral choices at bottom. But the recognition that this is so only sharpens the question of what tools exist for making such choices wisely.

Principles

The principles of bioethics flow together from the health professions and from moral philosophy. They have been expressed through the centuries in codes and oaths and writings by physicians. There are no principles of ethics in medicine which have not also been expressed in moral philosophy. But some general principles of moral philosophy have found more frequent echoes in medicine than others—and some have been almost entirely neglected.

The two fundamental principles of doing good and of not doing harm—of beneficence and of nonmaleficence—are the most immediately relevant to medical practitioners. To preserve life and good health; to ward off illness, pain, and death—these are the perennial tasks of physicians. Their published prayers and oaths[2] express their awareness of needing a very special sense of responsibility in caring for the sick. These principles of helping others and, above all, of not harming them, have found powerful expression at all times in the history of medicine:

Day and night, thou shalt endeavor for the relief of patients with all thy heart and soul. Thou shalt not desert or injure thy patient even for the sake of thy living.[3]

And the ranking of these two principles—the fact that, regardless of what help one brings, one must at the very least not affect patients for the worse—is expressed by Hippocrates in the *Epidemics*:

As to diseases, make a habit of two things—to help, or at least to do no harm.[4]

Because doctors have access to the most intimate concerns of patients, two kinds of harm they might bring to patients have been prohibited in the codes with special urgency: sexual exploitation and breach of confidentiality.[5] Other more general statements have also warned doctors to keep their patients from injustice and from the attention of quacks.

The documents stress the trust and the guild-dictated behavior which should prevail among physicians. They should treat family members of doctors free of charge, regard students as sons, not interfere with one another's practice, and not compete in unseemly ways. Percival's *Medical Ethics*,[6] first published in 1803, is especially vocal on these matters. Percival goes so far as to explain that even a wealthy physician should avoid giving free advice to his affluent patients, because to do so would be an injury to his 'professional brethren'.

These professional courtesies operate to smooth the relationships between physicians. Insofar as they help subdue the inclination to profit from human misery, they serve patients as well as the profession. But insofar as they prevent a physician from interfering with the incompetent or malicious practice of fellow physicians, they obviously do a disservice to patients, by concealing from them what could affect their life and health most profoundly.

The two principles of beneficence and nonmaleficence have nevertheless traditionally been thought to apply mostly to the physician's conduct toward his own patients. But major new conflicts have sprung up recently with the advent of human experimentation and transplantation. For in experiments on human beings, subjects are often placed at some risk of harm or maleficence in order that society or future sufferers from the disease may be benefited. And in transplantation, as of kidneys, one person is being harmed in order to save the life of another. As a result of these developments, the weighing of benefits and harms has taken on a new complexity. How *can* one weigh harm done to some against benefits to others? No matter how hard or how simple, such a process of weighing has been thought by many to constitute the essence of medical decision making. But the simple statement by Amatus,[7] that he had 'never brought about sickness', could no longer be made by most physicians.

Other principles have also been stated in the medical literature—strongly at times, feebly at times; they have even been suppressed or forgotten altogether at times. The principle of equality is most interesting in this respect. Some oaths in antiquity were eloquent on the subject. An inscription on the Sanctuary of Asclepius, for instance, on the south slope of the Acropolis, reads:

he [physician] would be like God: saviour equally of slave, of paupers, of rich men, of princes, and to all a brother.[8]

And a Canon of Medicine, China, Han Dynasty, 200 BC–200 AD, holds that:

He should have bowels of mercy on the sick and pledge himself to relieve suffering among all classes. Aristocrat or commoner, poor or rich, aged or young, beautiful or ugly, enemy or friend, native or foreigner, and educated or uneducated, all are to be treated equally. He should look upon the misery of the patient as if it were his own.

And the oath long thought to have been written by Maimonides[9] states:

Preserve the strength of my body and of my soul that they ever be ready to cheerfully help and support rich and poor, good and bad, enemy as well as friend. In the sufferer let me see only the human being.

By comparison, the *absence* of any thought that the physician should care equally for all is very striking in the Hippocratic Oath,[10] the most widely disseminated oath even today. Nor do the Principles of Ethics of the American Medical Association venture such a notion. The principle of equality, therefore, is only asserted at times, and is absent in today's most commonly used codes in the United States.

The vaster questions of social justice have not, on the whole, been discussed at all in these historical documents. In the past, as now, principles of medical ethics have been primarily principles for *individual* behavior—between health professionals and patients, or between one health professional and another.[11] The increased pressure to consider moral principles governing institutions and societies is beginning to force attention towards questions of medical justice. What is a just allocation of medical resources—among citizens of a community, a state, or even the world? And what roles do equality, beneficence, and nonmaleficence play in such schemes of allocation? These most important of all ethical inquiries are not addressed at all in traditional codes of medical ethics.

Another principle of ethics which is absent in virtually all documents of medical ethics is that of *veracity*—of informing patients truthfully about their condition and prognosis.[12] One of the few who claimed such a principle was Amatus:

If I lie, may I incur the eternal wrath of God and of His angel Raphael, and may nothing in the medical art succeed for me according to my desires.[13]

Other writings either veil this subject in silence, or assume, as Plato stated in the *Republic*,[14] that lies are acceptable from a physician since they are told to us for our own good—as a form of medicine. It is only recently, with the loss in trust and with our awareness of the risks we can run from a false diagnosis, a deceptive prognosis, or treatment we are duped into believing that we need, that the principle of veracity is coming to the forefront.[15] And it is only with the working out of all that informed consent implies and what kind of information it presupposes, that truth-telling and deception are coming to be discussed in a serious way in the health professions.

The absence of concern with veracity reflects in turn the absence of another and more general principle of ethics which is only now being pressed into medical contexts. This is the principle of patient *autonomy*. For while the codes are vocal on the *physician's* liberty, or autonomy in certain respects, they have long been silent on that of the patient. Yet when ethics is defined as an inquiry into human choice and goals, the question of *who chooses* is obviously crucial. This is especially true of choices having to do with illness and health, and, most of all, with what should be done to one's own body.

There are two ways to interfere with legitimate autonomous choices by patients: through overt coercion, and through manipulating the information reaching patients so that they accept what they would not have chosen had they been correctly informed. Both of these forms of assault on autonomy—direct coercion and deception—are especially controversial in medicine because they are undertaken in the name of the *patient's best interest*, and cannot therefore always be discounted. Yet Professor Talcott Parsons has rightly stated that:

The sick person is peculiarly vulnerable to exploitation and at the same time peculiarly handicapped in arriving at a rationally objective appraisal of his situation.[16]

The principle of autonomy, if respected, would lessen this exploitation while increasing the chances for personal appraisal of their predicament by patients.

The major moral principles in medical ethics, of nonmaleficence, beneficence, justice, equality, veracity, and autonomy, therefore, are no different from those debated in ethics more generally. In both domains, the same disagreements come up as to whether one or two of these principles in reality account for all the rest.[17] The same disagreements arise in both about what rights we have with respect to, for example, not being lied to or not being harmed, or about what is a justifiable distribution of resources.

Different theories answer these questions in different ways. Some even claim that ethics can give no answers of this kind. But most theories recognise that ethical principles must at least possess certain formal characteristics. Recently, Baier and Rawls have discussed these characteristics.[18] Three which are crucial are *generality, universality*, and *publicity* (or universal teachability).[19]

To be *general*, a principle should be capable of formulation without recourse to proper names. Thus a principle holding that all that which Mussolini desires is right or good fails to be general in this sense.

A principle which is *universal in application* is one which holds for everyone. Most moral principles are of this kind, but some are not. A form of egoism holding that rules apply to others only, not to oneself, or one's social group, is incapable of living up to this criterion.

Principles which fail on these two grounds usually also fail to comply with the criterion of *publicity*. A principle should be capable of public statement and expression. The same is true, in my opinion, of any application of a moral principle to a concrete situation. Those who argue for and against the extension of the principle of informed consent to experimentation on children ought to be able to do so openly and in advance. Of course, this does not mean that one must always go through such a process. But it should be *possible* to do so.

Such principles of ethics as emerge from a reading of the medical literature do satisfy these criteria. And they provide inspiration and guidance with respect to the humane treatment of patients, the avoidance of harm and unnecessary suffering, and the safeguarding of confidentiality and dignity.

But three major circumstances prevent them from providing the protection for patients which they should ideally inspire. In the first place, as we have seen, certain principles of ethics are nearly nonexistent in writings on *medical* ethics. Secondly, many clear principles of medical ethics are disregarded by a number of practitioners. And thirdly, these principles often conflict in such a way that even those who wish to uphold them are uncertain as to what action to choose.

Complex moral problems

Sometimes there is no disagreement whatsoever, in theory. Every tradition of applied ethics and of medical ethics would condemn those surgeons who deceive patients into thinking they must have operations which they do not need. Similarly, all traditions would condemn those physicians who, employed by industries, examine workers without letting them know that they suffer from illnesses acquired at work. Yet it is well known that innumerable acts of these and other similarly unethical kinds are performed. What is at fault here is not moral reasoning nor the appeal to moral principles. Rather, blame must go to individual callousness and weaknesses in the social structure which permit the pursuit of these practices.

But there are a great many ethical conflicts in medicine where there is no such agreement even in principle, let alone in practice. These are complex conflicts, causing health professionals to divide sharply about what ethical dimensions are at stake. Some of these conflicts arise out of marginal or uncertain aspects of the clear abuses mentioned above. Some have caused bitter disagreement since the beginnings of medicine—how best to care for dying patients, for instance, or whether to allow abortion, or how to distribute scarce medical resources.

Other divisive conflicts confront us now with increasing urgency as a result of modern developments in medical technology and knowledge. Problems posed by the possibility of cloning, or by organ transplantation, or by fetal research or by psychosurgery—these problems all produce genuine disagreement about what *is* best, most beneficial, least harmful, or most conducive to equality.

The moral dilemmas which produce these disagreements share one or more elements of complexity. The information on which choice must be based in these dilemmas is often inadequate, biased, and not of uniform relevance. The individuals involved have divergent, often clashing, interests. And several moral principles are in sharp conflict. Finally, more than one person often claim to be decision makers.

In dilemmas with some or all of these characteristics of complexity, intelligent, well-informed, and well-intentioned persons can sincerely disagree about what should be done. And the disagreement does not spring up in neat categories between holders of different faiths or traditions. It is rather *within* each tradition that suicide or abortion or distribution of health care cause disputes over and over again . . .

We need, therefore, two different strategies for dealing with moral problems in medicine and science. In the clear cases where all theories agree, what is needed is not so much moral reasoning as the mobilisation of public opinion and social change to increase accountability and combat abuse. So long as these are not successful, individuals need also to consider efforts at self-defense, so that they will not be hurt by the abuses in question. But for the more complex problems, we need methods and clarity before we can even reach the point of evaluating social policy, incentives and disincentives, and self-protection. And it is with respect to these complex problems that theologians and philosophers and social theorists have been asked for help with the greatest urgency.

Notes to extract

1. Diogenes Laertius, *Lives of Eminent Philosophers* (Cambridge: Harvard University Press, 1925), vol 2, pp 559–560.

2. See Donald E Konold, 'History of the Codes of Medical Ethics', forthcoming, in the *Encyclopedia of Bioethics*, and M B Etziony, *The Physician's Creed: An Anthology of Medical Prayers, Oaths and Codes of Ethics* (Springfield, I11: Charles C Thomas, 1973).

3. From a Hindu oath of initiation, reproduced in Etziony, *The Physician's Creed*.

4. Hippocrates, *Epidemics*, tr W H S Jones, in *Hippocrates* Vol I. (Note: a more faithful translation would read: 'to help or not to harm'. It may be the interpretation of Hippocrates rather than his own words which has done the ranking.)

5. Every professional relationship gives rise to special kinds of benefits and harms. As a result, some have imagined that medical ethics and legal ethics and other professional ethics are somehow separable from more general principles of morality. There is no need, however, to postulate such separateness. The special harms and benefits can be understood in terms of beneficence, nonmaleficence and other general principles in combination with the specific contracts undertaken in the professional relationship.

6. Thomas Percival, *Medical Ethics* (Oxford: John Henry Parker, 1849).

7. A celebrated Jewish physician who died in 1568 from the plague.

8. The thought that the physician should feel a sense of brotherhood, or kinship, with the patient recurs often in antiquity, in medical and religious texts. It expresses the ideal of *fraternity*, which is an extension, or qualification, of that of equality. The physician can either act as a brother in giving of his expertise to a patient or, more rarely, see himself as brother to all those who suffer, feeling their pain, sharing their lot. To whatever extent this sense of fellow-feeling exists, it stands in sharp contrast to the distant 'professional' manner which is another response to suffering and represents another way of trying to cope. (For a brief discussion of 'fraternity', see J Rawls, *A Theory of Justice* [Cambridge: Harvard University Press, 1971], pp 105–106.)

9. Now attributed to Marcus Herz, and thought to have been published in 1783. See Etziony, *The Physician's Creed*.

10. The Hippocratic Oath makes use of equality only in the limited sense that the physician foreswears sexual advances to those in the household of the sick, be they female or male, free or slave.

11. Much interest has also been accorded questions of medical *etiquette*—governing questions of the appearance of physicians, of grooming and courtesy. See A R Jonsen and A Hellegers, 'Conceptual Foundations for an Ethics of Medical Care', in *Ethics of Health Care*, for an excellent discussion of medical ethics and etiquette in the codes and oaths.

12. Lying *between* health professionals, on the other hand, has always been thought unprincipled. For a thoughtful discussion of the differences between duties that doctors think they owe each other and duties owed to their patients, see William F May, 'Code, Covenant, Contract, or Philanthropy', *Hastings Center Report* 5, 29–38. [footnote omitted.]

13. Reproduced in 'The Ethics of the Practice of Medicine from the Jewish Point of View', Harry Friedenwald, *Johns Hopkins Hospital Bulletin*, August 1917, 256–261.

14. Plato, *Republic* (Cambridge, Harvard University Press, 1930), 389b–d.

15. As literature attests (see, for example, Molière's *Le Médecin Malgré Lui*), patients have always been suspicious of physicians and quacks. But not until this century have these concerns been so consistently voiced and supported by law.

16. Talcott Parsons, *The Social System* (New York: The Free Press, 1951). See pp 436–465 for an analysis of 'the sick role'.

17. Thus W K Frankena, in *Ethics* (Englewood Cliffs: Prentice-Hall, 1973), holds that beneficence and justice (interpreted as equal treatment) are the only principles we need to recognise. G J Warnock, in *The Object of Morality* (London: Methuen, 1971), sees beneficence, nonmaleficence, fairness, and nondeception.

18. K Baier, *The Moral Point of View* (New York: Random House, 1965), Ch VIII; and J Rawls, *A Theory of Justice*, pp 130–136.

19. Rawls and Baier add a fourth—ordering—and a fifth—finality—which will not

be stressed in these pages. *Ordering* requires that the principles adopted make possible an ordering of conflicting claims. This criterion cannot be accepted in empirical dilemmas without a methodology as yet lacking in all theories of ethics. . . . *Finality* requires that reasoning from the principles be conclusive. This, again, is more an ideal than a possible achievement in applied ethics.

Finally, before we leave this general excursus, we should return to two themes which constantly preoccupy the newcomer to medical ethics. They concern the expertise of medical practitioners in medical ethics and the vexed subject of relativism. Arthur Dyck discusses these helpfully in his paper 'Ethics and Medicine' (1973) (reprinted in Reiser *et al* (1977)):

Metaethical questions for medicine

There has been, and there continues to be a strong presumption within the profession of medicine that the profession itself provides the best basis for deciding what is right and wrong in questions of medical research and care. Medical ethics in this view is defined, understood, and practiced by medical professionals. Among medical professionals, those with a doctor's degree in medicine carry the most weight. The proposition that a particular group is best qualified to make and to criticise moral judgments pertaining to their own interests and work is not self-evidently true or false. Whether one believes it to be true or false depends in large measure on one's view of the nature of moral judgments and moral decision-making processes.

Books on medical ethics by specialists in ethics do not uniformly presuppose the special expertise of the medical profession to make moral judgments about medical cases. Joseph Fletcher in *Morals and Medicine* does not presume to be doing medical ethics.[19] Fletcher claims that he is dealing with the ethics of medical care and that in so doing he is not dealing with medical ethics, a term usually used for the rules governing the social conduct and graces of the medical profession: 'Medical ethics is the business of the medical profession, although certainly it has to fall somewhat within the limits of social obligation'.[20] Fletcher recognises that some professionals would give medical ethics as a professional concern a loftier definition. He cites Dr George Jacoby as saying that medical ethics deals with 'the question of the general attitude of the physician toward the patient: to what extent his duty obligates him to intervene in this patient's interest, and what demands the physician has a right and duty to make upon the patient's relatives in regard to obedience and subordination for the purposes of treatment'.[21] Fletcher notes that Dr Jacoby nowhere says anything about the demands the patient has a right and duty to make upon physicians. Fletcher then claims that it is this other perspective, namely the patient's point of view, that he tries to take in examining the morals, principles and values that are at stake in medical care.

Despite Fletcher's distinction between an ethics of medical care and medical ethics as professional ethics, his own book is virtually always referred to as a book in medical ethics. When physicians speak of the book in this way, I think it is because they presume that the issues raised by Fletcher are issues for them as professionals: nothing about medical care is outside the expertise of the physician; certainly nothing about medical care is outside the concern of the physician. When ethicists refer to Fletcher's book as a book in medical ethics, they share the assumption that medical ethics is part of ethics generally and that what distinguishes medical ethics from ethics generally is its concern with the moral questions that arise in and from the practice of medicine.

Thus when Paul Ramsey set out to write a book on patient care entitled *The Patient as Person*, the subtitle is 'Explorations in Medical Ethics'.[22] In the preface to his book, he makes his view of the relation between medical ethics and ethics generally very explicit:

problems of medical ethics . . . are by no means technical problems on which only the expert (in this case, the physician) can have an opinion. They are rather the problems of human beings in situations in which medical care is needed. Birth and death, illness and injury, are not simply events the doctor attends. They are moments in every human life.

... The question, What ought the doctor to do? is only a particular form of the question, What should be done?

... I hold that medical ethics is consonant with the ethics of a wider human community. The former is (however special) only a particular case of the latter. The moral requirements governing the relations of physician to patients and researcher to subjects are only a special case of the moral requirements governing any relations between man and man. Canons of loyalty to patients or to joint adventures in medical research are simply particular manifestations of canons of loyalty of person to person generally.[23]

Ramsey has the utmost respect for the moral sensitivity of physicians. Nevertheless, he is not sanguine that the medical profession and its codes will suffice to guide contemporary medicine through its ethical dilemmas:

In the medical literature there are many articles on ethics which are greatly to be admired. Yet I know that these are not part of the daily fare of medical students, or of members of the profession when they gather together as professionals or even for purposes of conviviality. I do not believe that either the codes of medical ethics or the physicians who have undertaken to comment on them and to give fresh analysis of the physicians' moral decisions will suffice to withstand the omnivorous appetite of scientific research or of a therapeutic technology that has a momentum and a life of its own.

The Nuremberg Code, the Declaration of Helsinki, various 'guidelines' of the American Medical Association, and other 'codes' governing medical practice constitute a sort of 'catechism' in the ethics of the medical profession. These codes exhibit a professional ethics which ministers and theologians and members of other professions can only profoundly respect and admire. Still, a catechism never sufficed. Unless these principles are constantly pondered and enlivened in their application they become dead letters. There is also need that these principles be deepened and sensitised and opened to further humane revision in face of all the ordinary and the newly emerging situations which a doctor confronts—as do we all—in the present day. In this task none of the sources of moral insight, no understanding of the humanity of man or for answering questions of life and death, can rightfully be neglected.[24]

This does not mean that medical ethics is best left to those trained in ethics only. Ramsey argues that physicians can do medical ethics but not without some training in ethics; similarly ethicists need exposure to the fields of medicine to which their ethical reflections are directed. Above all, Ramsey argues that the medical profession should no longer believe that the personal integrity of physicians alone is enough 'to deal with the contemporary quandaries of medical ethics'.[25]

Whereas Ramsey does not become explicit about the metaethical presuppositions that inform his view, a recent essay by Robert Veatch does.[26] This essay argues on theoretical grounds that medical ethics should not be the province of medical practitioners only and that medical decisions cannot be morally justified if they are construed as matters of personal opinion. The fact that these decisions of medical care are made by physicians does not by itself suffice to raise them above the level of personal opinion.

In discussing the relationship between medical ethics and ethics generally, Veatch describes a common debate that occurs between those trained in medicine and those who are not. Veatch cites a case where a woman was diagnosed to be dying from cancer. The medical student who presents the case considers it appropriate to tell the woman gently and diplomatically that although the medical staff will do all that it can to treat her condition, it cannot give her assurances that she will recover. The physician who is the student's supervisor and the other physicians participating in the discussion to which Veatch alludes claimed that as physicians they have a unique ethical duty to do no harm to the patient. The physicians were in agreement that telling the patient she has cancer will harm her and therefore it is wrong to tell her this. Nonphysicians discussing this case disagreed with the physicians regarding the factual question of whether the bad news about cancer would adversely affect the patient and also as to whether the decision ought finally to be based on the principle of not harming or on the principle of truth-telling. What raises the metaethical question here is the claim of the physicians that their understanding of moral norms or principles is unique to the medical profession and should be given priority in medical cases over the judgments of nonprofessionals.

Veatch argues that these physicians were actually claiming that there are specific moral rules applicable in medicine which are valid for physicians qua physicians, and that the general rules and expectations of the larger society may, in specific cases, be justifiably abrogated by them. As Veatch notes, this is an implicit acceptance of a particular metaethical position, namely that of social relativism which argues that to say of an action that it is right or wrong is to say that it is in accord with the mores of one's group. Veatch is quite right in asserting that this metaethical position is not one that ethicists would defend.[27] It is a meaningful question to ask whether anything considered right or wrong by one's group is in fact right or wrong. Indeed, it is a growing consensus in contemporary ethical theory that the peculiarity of moral assertions is precisely that they are assertions that claim to be universalisable.[28]

Notes to extract

19. Boston: Beacon Press, 1960.
20. *Ibid*, p 5.
21. *Ibid*, p 6.
22. New Haven: Yale University Press, 1970.
23. *Ibid*, pp xi–xii.
24. *Ibid*, pp xv–xvi.
25. *Ibid*, p xviii.
26. 'Medical Ethics: Professional or Universal?', *Harvard Theological Review*, Oct, 1972.
27. W K Frankena, *Ethics*, Englewood Cliffs: Prentice-Hall, 1963, pp 92–94, and Bernard Williams, *Morality: An Introduction to Ethics*, New York: Harper and Row, 1972, pp 20–26.
28. W K Frankena, *ibid*, pp 94–96.

Medical ethics and Gillick

How can we analyse *Gillick* in the light of what we have seen generally of medical ethics?

Let us concentrate on two related issues. The first concerns the extent to which a doctor may provide contraceptive advice and treatment to a girl under the age of 16 without obtaining the consent of her parents. The second concerns the extent to which a doctor must respect the confidence of a girl under the age of 16 who seeks contraceptive advice and treatment.

Advice and treatment

1. A doctor has an ethical duty, among other things, to respect the person of his patient. A particularly important feature of this duty is the doctor's duty to respect the autonomy of his patient. Because of the individualist nature of the doctor-patient relationship, this duty to respect autonomy should bind the doctor unless very strong counter-arguments can be advanced.
2. This duty to respect his patient's autonomy means, among other things, that he must ordinarily act in accordance with the wishes of his patient. Consequently, he must obtain (and only act if he has obtained) the consent of his patient to be treated. Equally, he must respect the refusal of his patient.
3. In the context of an adult, it will be presumed that the adult should be regarded as autonomous unless and until the contrary is shown, e g that the adult is mentally incompetent. In the case of a child, there is no such presumption.

4. Having accepted that not all individuals should be regarded as autonomous, it remains to determine by what criteria an individual will be so judged. Only if the individual is regarded as autonomous will the doctor have a duty to respect that person's autonomy *by looking to her* (in the *Gillick* type of case) for consent to advise or treat. If she is not regarded as autonomous, the doctor, if he regards advice or treatment to be called for, has a duty to look elsewhere, eg to her parents, for consent. Parental decisions in these circumstances, taken in the best interests of the child, are part of the process of bringing the child to a stage when she herself can achieve autonomy. To this extent, parents' decisions are properly understood as autonomy-enhancing and not autonomy-reducing.

5. A person generally can be regarded as autonomous when she understands what is involved in a particular decision and the consequences of that decision. Whether a girl in any particular case is so capable must (at least initially) be a question for the doctor.

6. What then is the test of this capacity? Is the girl competent (i) at a certain age—often in this context mooted to be 16—or (ii) when she is capable of understanding what is involved in a decision, whatever her age?

7. If the underlying ethical principle is respect for autonomy, the test of competence must necessarily reflect this. It must take account of the particular circumstances of the particular girl. Position (i) is inflexible: it takes no account of the particular girl's circumstances. Position (ii) avoids this flaw. As a matter of ethical analysis, position (ii) is, therefore, to be preferred.

8. Consequently, a doctor in deciding whether to advise and treat for contraception may act upon and treat as valid the consent of a girl under the age of 16, provided he is satisfied that she has the necessary capacity to be regarded as autonomous, ie she is capable of understanding the nature of the procedure and its consequences. This is subject, of course, to the doctor's prior medical-technical decision that advice and treatment are in the girl's best medical interests.

9. Thus, assuming the primary importance of respect for autonomy, the doctor is entitled to act on the consent of a competent girl, even though she be under the age of 16, regardless of parental consent. But does this not ignore the legitimate interests of others? Do not parents, for example, have rights here which ought to be respected? On a proper analysis, it must be clear that parents have rights only to the extent necessary for them to carry out their duties. And, their primary duty is to bring their child to an enjoyment of autonomy. Once the child is to be regarded as autonomous, to insist that parental wishes should prevail until, for example, the child reaches some arbitrary age such as 16, would, quite obviously, violate the principle of respect for autonomy. Indeed, to give to the parents a right to decide what, if any, contraceptive advice or treatment their competent daughter should receive, simply because she is under the age of 16, would be, in effect, to treat her as the property of her parents.

10. If, on the other hand, the girl is not sufficiently mature to be regarded as autonomous, the doctor cannot, indeed is under a duty not to, rely on any expression of will by the girl. This is, of course, autonomy-enhancing, since by protecting the girl from ill considered decisions, this principle seeks to ensure that she will come to autonomy free from avoidable harm. In such a case, when the girl is immature, as we have seen, it is to the parents that the doctor should ordinarily look.

As you will see this analysis is consistent with the House of Lords decision in *Gillick*. At least, that is, it is consistent with Lord Scarman's speech (with which Lord Bridge agreed); Lord Fraser may have expressed himself slightly differently. Lord Templeman's analysis only differed in so far as he thought a girl under 16 could (or is it should?) never be regarded as capable of acting autonomously in relation to contraceptive advice and treatment, because of the public policy as expressed in the Sexual Offences Act 1956 that a girl is, for her own protection, deemed incapable of consenting to sexual intercourse. As regards other medical treatment he would not disagree with the views of the majority. Lord Brandon decided the case in a different way, but, in the light of his earlier speech in *R v D* [1984] AC 778, there is every reason to believe that, like Lord Templeman, apart from the case of contraceptive advice and treatment his view of the law would be consistent with this ethical analysis.

Confidentiality

The other aspect of the *Gillick* decision which has been more controversial since the decision is the issue of confidentiality. The ethical analysis should go as follows:

1. A doctor covenants with a patient that he will respect the patient's confidences. This is an aspect of the duty to respect autonomy. It reflects the proposition that one feature of autonomy is privacy. Confidences reveal that which is private and, if given on terms that they be kept private (which is a given premise in the doctor/patient relationship) they may not be revealed to anyone without permission or other good reason.
2. Therefore, if on the criteria discussed above, a doctor is satisfied that a girl is to be regarded as autonomous and, therefore, competent to give consent to the contraceptive advice and treatment, he is also under a duty to keep the consultation and any other aspect of his professional relationship with her secret. The girl's medical affairs are confidential, even from her parents.
3. But what if the doctor comes to the conclusion that on the criteria set out the girl is not competent to consent to contraceptive advice or treatment, ie is not to be regarded as autonomous? Certainly, he may not treat the girl on her consent alone (*quaere* may he advise her?). But, must he keep the girl's visit a secret from her parents or must (or just may) he inform them? In an essay discussing the *Gillick* decision 'Law and Medical Practice' in *Medicine in Contemporary Society: King's College Studies 1986–7* (ed P Byrne) at pp 137–8, Lord Scarman stated the following:

> In the case of a child of insufficient understanding, unless he is so satisfied, he cannot treat the girl without her parents' consent. If he says, 'I must tell your parents', she may say, 'Well, please do not. I tell you, you must not do it'. Then he can say, 'Very well, I cannot accept you as a patient'. He is entitled to say that—it may go against the grain—and he would not say it if he thinks, of course, that treatment is necessary. If he does say that, is he under an obligation to tell the parents that the girl has been to see him for advice? He has told her she ought to have their consent, she has refused and he has therefore sent her away without advice. The answer is 'no', because there now emerges another duty of the doctor, to which I have not yet made reference, the duty of respecting the confidence of those who seek his advice, whether they become his patients or not. This girl technically has not become his patient because he has refused to accept her; but the duty of confidence is there and the law would not, I think, require the doctor to break that confidence.

Is this view ethically justified? In our view, it is not for the reasons set out in 4 below.
4. First, it is sometimes argued that a girl may not be competent to consent to contraceptive advice and treatment but may be competent to enter into a doctor/patient relationship entailing a duty of confidentiality. There is a

superficial attraction in this argument. Autonomy, and hence the duty to respect an individual's autonomy, may not be acquired as regards each and every kind of decision at the same time. Understanding increases with maturity. This is undoubtedly correct, and so the argument goes, understanding the notion of privacy and keeping secrets and what is involved in withholding information from a parent may be achieved at a different and earlier stage of maturity than understanding what is involved in contraception.

However, on closer analysis this argument does not help us in this particular context. It is difficult to see how the two aspects of competence can be divorced from one another here. In truth, they stand or fall together. This is clear if you look to the doctor's duty to respect a patient's autonomy. If, as we have seen, in the case of an incompetent girl a doctor *may* most readily act so as to enhance her autonomy (including protecting her from herself and others) by involving the parents, he cannot be under a *duty* not to tell them. There must be cases where it would best serve the interests of an incompetent girl to inform her parents. The doctor may decide not to inform the parents, but if he considers it to be in the girl's best interests, he *may* (and some would say *must*, in this situation) tell them.

Perhaps, Lord Scarman was saying no more than that there is not a *duty* to tell the parents. He cannot be saying that there is no *discretion* to tell the parents.

Our view conforms with the most recent guidance of the GMC. Do you agree with our view or Lord Scarman's? Note the following comments of Lord Templeman in the *Gillick* case:

> No authority compels a doctor to disclose to a parent, otherwise than in the course of litigation, any information obtained as a result of a conversation between the doctor and the infant. On the other hand, in my opinion, confidentiality owed to an infant is not breached by disclosure to a parent responsible for that infant if the doctor considers that such disclosure is necessary in the interests of the infant. A doctor who gave a pledge to a girl under 16 that he would not disclose the fact or content of a conversation would no doubt honour that pledge, but the doctor ought to hesitate before committing himself. A doctor who gave an unconditional pledge of confidentiality to a girl under 16 would, for example, be in a difficult position if the girl then disclosed information which made the doctor suspect that she was being introduced to sexual intercourse by a man who was also introducing her to drugs.

Medical law and Gillick

As regards medical law, the first thing to notice in *Gillick* is the number of traditional areas of law involved; family law, the law of torts, criminal law, administrative law, statutory interpretation and that 'unruly horse', public policy. We have examined the decision in *Gillick* in detail above. Here it will suffice to look at some of the themes of medical law that the case illustrates.

1. The case raised an issue of public law: it concerned a challenge to a DHSS circular and Mrs Gillick's challenge to it, arguably, lay in the realm of public law. Both Lords Fraser and Scarman examined carefully whether Mrs Gillick had, as a consequence, adopted the wrong procedure by using that used in litigation between private individuals. Ultimately, they both determined that she had not. There was no need for her to use the public law procedure for judicial review under RSC Ord 53, although it would have been available to her. The point made here is the potential importance of public law in the regulation of the health service.

2. The case gave rise to a further public law issue arising from the criminal law. Would a doctor be committing a criminal offence as an accessory, should the young girl's partner commit the crime of unlawful sexual intercourse with a girl under the age of 16 (contrary to s 6 of the Sexual Offences Act 1956)? As we shall see throughout this book, the criminal law plays a significant, though often unrecognised part, in medical law in setting the boundaries of permitted practice (for example, in treating the dying through the law of homicide: see Ch 14 *infra*).

3. The case raised several issues of private law. To the medical lawyer, they are all grist for the mill of medical-legal analysis. Some may still view them in terms of traditional civil law compartments. In so doing, however, the interrelatedness of the issues and the consequent need for an analysis which is consistent and coherent may be overlooked. For example, under what, if any, circumstances is the *purported* consent of a girl under the age of 16, *real* consent such that a doctor who touches her in reliance thereon, does not commit the tort of battery (or indeed the crime of battery), a 'tort' point. Further, until a child reaches the age of 16 (in the case of medical treatment) or 18 (in other contexts) is it the parents' exclusive right to act on behalf of their child and in this context to give or withhold consent to contraceptive advice or treatment (a 'family law' point)? (Can there ever, incidentally, be circumstances in which a parent can prevent, by legal order, a child from seeking advice, as opposed to treatment? If so, on what cause of action would such a claim be based?) You will, of course, at once realise that these issues of tort and family law are interlinked.

4. The *Gillick* decision also calls for consideration of the proper role which society and the law have given the doctor. For example, do you think *Gillick* was a case concerned with the situation in which parent and child are in dispute? If so, how can this conflict concerning who decides about treatment be resolved? There are, we would suggest, at least three possible answers, assuming the girl is mature (as defined) the law could:

(i) grant decision-making power to the parents by declaring the child incapable of consenting, despite or regardless of her maturity; or

(ii) grant decision-making power to the child by recognising as legally competent a child who is mature enough to be capable of understanding what is involved; or

(iii) grant decision-making power to the doctor by allowing him to determine what is in the best interests of the child. A variant of this solution would be to combine it with (ii) and say that the child's consent is a *necessary*, but may not be a *sufficient*, condition to permit the doctor to advise and treat. A doctor may on this reasoning still have to seek the parents' consent as well as that of the child, if he is of the view that this is in the child's best interests.

Which of these situations do the judges in *Gillick* adopt?

Notice the following observations of John Eekelaar in his article 'The Emergence of Children's Rights' (1986) 6 OJLS 161, 180–1 (footnotes omitted).

> Both Lord Scarman and Lord Fraser adopted the major premise that once a child had attained sufficient understanding and maturity, he had full capacity to enter legal relationships without the consent of his parents. ... Lord Scarman then concluded that as soon as a child reached this position, any parental right within the relevant area, terminated. The parental right 'yielded' to the child's right. Lord Fraser, however, was less clear about this. In the medical context, he seemed to say that a doctor would only be 'justified' in treating a child without parental consent if this was in the child's best interests, and, as far as contraceptive treatment was concerned, this would normally entail involvement of the parents, although this could be avoided if the child refused to permit it, and the protection of (her) physical

and mental health required such treatment despite lack of parental knowledge and consent. This might mean that, in certain situations, the parental right survives the minor child's acquisition of capacity and, with judicial support, could prevent such a child from acting according to her wishes if her interests demanded such restriction. But an alternative interpretation of the speech is possible. This would permit anyone to deal lawfully with a minor child who had acquired capacity, and restrict the requirement to consult parents (outside exceptional situations) to a rule of good practice applicable only in medical matters and enforceable only through professional discipline. No help is obtained from Lord Bridge, who simply agreed with both Lord Scarman and Lord Fraser. Lord Templeman, who dissented on the issue as far as it related to *contraceptive* treatment, seemed to express a view close to that of Lord Scarman as far as other medical matters were concerned.

In a subsequent case applying *Gillick*, a Canadian court seems to have adopted solution (ii) as being the one approved in *Gillick* (*C v Wren* (1987) 35 DLR (4th) 419 (Alta CA)).

Kerans JA: The suit here is by the parents against the doctor, and not the child. The doctor is not represented but the child has retained counsel and she intervenes.

. . . The ground of appeal is that the learned chambers judge erred in finding that the expectant mother had given informed consent to the proposed surgical procedure.

The law in Alberta is that a surgeon may proceed with a surgical procedure immune from suits for assault if she or he has informed consent from the patient. That test was applied by the learned trial judge, and he found on the evidence before him that this child was capable of giving informed consent and had done so. Without more, that is an end to the matter.

It is argued before us today that informed consent means consent after consideration of issues like the ethics of abortion and the ethics of obligation by children to parents. It may be, as Lord Fraser has said in *Gillick v West Norfolk and Wisbech Area Health Authority*, [1985] 3 All ER 402, that doctors have an ethical obligation in circumstances like this to discuss issues of that sort with young patients. If so, the doctor would account to the College of Physicians and Surgeons for the performance of that obligation. That is not the issue before us today. Rather, the issue is whether these issues relate to the defence of consent to assault. In our view, they do not.

We agree with the learned chambers judge that no serious suggestion exists on the evidence here of a lack of informed consent. Accordingly, there are no grounds to enjoin the doctor from proceeding because there is no suggestion that there will be an illegal assault.

The real issue here relates to an obvious and painful dispute between parent and child about the appropriateness in non-medical terms of the proposed abortion. We express in that respect our sympathy both to the parents and the child for this unfortunate confrontation.

The real thrust of argument before us was that children should obey their parents and the courts should intervene to prevent others from interfering with parental control of those children who are committed to their custody and control. That is not quite the suit that has been brought here today, but we will deal with the issue. Parental rights (and obligations) clearly do exist and they do not wholly disappear until the age of majority. The modern law, however, is that the courts will exercise increasing restraint in that regard as a child grows to and through adolescence. The law and the development of the law in this respect was analysed in detail by Lord Scarman in the *Gillick* case. He analyses the law back to Blackstone and extracts this principle [at p 421]:

> The principle is that parental right or power of control of the person and property of his child exists primarily to enable the parent to discharge his duty of maintenance, protection and education until he reaches such an age as to be able to look after himself and make his own decisions.

He then reviews the application of that principle in cases over the past century, especially in the 'age of discretion' cases. He says [at p 422]:

The 'age of discretion' cases are cases in which a parent or guardian (usually the father) has applied for habeas corpus to secure the return of his child who has left home without his consent. The courts would refuse an order if the child had attained the age of discretion, which came to be regarded as 14 for boys and 16 for girls, and did not wish to return. The principle underlying them was plainly that an order would be refused if the child had sufficient intelligence and understanding to make up his own mind.

He then concludes that the governing rule is [at p 423]:

In the light of the foregoing I would hold that as a matter of law the parental right to determine whether or not their minor child below the age of 16 will have medical treatment terminates if and when the child achieves a sufficient understanding and intelligence to enable him or her to understand fully what is proposed.

We accept that in that context he says that 'understand fully' means understand things like obligation to parents as well as medical matters.

What is the application of the principle in this case? We infer from the circumstances detailed in argument here that this expectant mother and her parents had fully discussed the ethical issues involved and, most regrettably, disagreed. We cannot infer from that disagreement that this expectant mother did not have sufficient intelligence and understanding to make up her own mind. Meanwhile, it is conceded that she is a 'normal intelligent 16 year old'. We infer that she did have sufficient intelligence and understanding to make up her own mind and did so. At her age and level of understanding, the law is that she is to be permitted to do so.

Public policy and Gillick

Perhaps at this point in our study of medical law, a more general point of importance needs to be made. *Gillick* illustrates well the fact that many cases in medical law involve substantial (and often difficult) questions of public policy. In addressing these questions it is an important first step to identify and separate out the issues of fact which shape public policy. As Simon Lee has put it in *Law and Morals* (1986) pp 59–60:

The Gillick saga illustrates that controversies over law and morality often turn on different hunches as to facts and conflicting estimates of consequences. Mrs Gillick, together with Lords Brandon and Templeman, considers that premature sexual activity is best discouraged, and parental involvement is best encouraged, by the law refusing to accept a child's consent as sufficient for the provision of contraceptives.

Others feel that premature sexual activity has to be discouraged by different means, chiefly educational. They believe that the absence of contraceptives will not act as a deterrent. On the contrary, it will merely cause additional problems such as abortion or early motherhood. Moreover, Mrs Gillick's opponents say that a victory for her would have *decreased* parental involvement in the real world. In the vast majority of cases which arose before the litigation, they claim, doctors were able to persuade initially reluctant girls to confide in their parents. Since the Court of Appeal decision, the girls concerned had not given doctors that opportunity.

Once the facts are found, the court decides. It is, of course, trite to observe that most decisions turn on judicial perceptions of what public policy requires. In that respect, *Gillick* is not unusual. What makes it unusual, perhaps, is the highly controversial subject matter of the case which makes it all too obvious that the House of Lords was not merely finding but making law.

Glanville Williams in his article 'The Gillick Saga' (1985) NLJ 1156–8 (footnotes omitted) discusses the questions of public policy raised by the case.

Question of policy

The problem of under-age sexuality raised by this litigation is of large social importance. We live in a society in which frank, indeed crude, carnality receives public acceptance, and is purveyed into the home by television and magazines competing for custom, including magazines encouraging sexual precocity in the young. Parents have largely renounced control over their adolescent children, and the sexes are mixed in the schools. Small wonder that one in eight girls under 16 is now sexually active in Britain. It is said that 10,000 of these girls annually become pregnant, of which number most obtain abortions, but no less than 3,000 become 'schoolgirl mums'.

The resulting question of public policy played a large part in the Gillick saga, not only in the public debate but in the judgments of the courts. No one doubts the high desirability of the parents becoming involved in the discussion of their daughter's sexual problems if this is possible. The difficulty is that so often it is not possible. The girl goes to the doctor because she is not prepared, at any rate at the moment, to confide in her parents; if she knows that he will inform her parents without her consent of her visit to him, or will not help her except on the basis of informing her parents, she is likely not to go to him.

Notwithstanding a deep division of public opinion, consensus exists on important values. There is large agreement on the imprudence of USI (unlawful sexual intercourse) by schoolgirls. The girl should reflect on the fact that she may be getting her companion into trouble. Even if she has had some 'sex education' from her parents or in school, she is likely to be inadequately forewarned against the danger of unintended pregnancy, not to mention the danger of sexually transmitted disease and of the emotional consequences of sexual relations—which cannot be controlled even if the physical consequences can be. Any of these risks, if they eventuate, can be catastrophic for the girl. Schoolgirl pregnancy resulting in childbirth can project the young mother prematurely into adult responsibilities, or at least cause her a severe emotional upset, blight her career prospects, and, in addition, give the unwanted infant a poor start in life.

Of course, all in the pro-Gillick camp were powerfully moved by these considerations. But so were many of the anti-Gillick battalion; so the difference of opinion between the two sides cannot be expressed in these terms.

The pro-Gillick opinion was that to give 'the pill' to schoolgirls would encourage their sexual activity because it would remove its most pronounced 'natural' disadvantage. Lord Brandon, who stated and adopted the Gillick point of view in its purest form, expressed this by saying that both the man and the girl are inhibited by the risk of pregnancy; giving the girl contraceptive treatment largely removes this inhibition. Obviously, there was a measure of truth in the argument, and the Gillick party regarded it as the whole truth. But it was not.

In the first place, the risk of pregnancy was evidently failing to dissuade many girls, as was shown by the number of schoolgirl pregnancies. It seems that the greater number of teenage girls who came to family planning clinics did so after they had started to have intercourse, often, presumably, unprotected. Many sexually active youngsters who did not want to become pregnant were found to be reluctant to seek family planning advice even when it was open to them.

In the second place, the arguments of the Gillick party ignored the important advantage of the opposite course. If schoolgirls who cannot communicate with their parents and who are anxious to avoid pregnancy are allowed to go to a doctor and receive advice with the assurance of confidentiality, there is some possibility that the doctor may be able to persuade them of the wisdom of continence, or at least to talk to their parents about it. It is an established rule of medical ethics, backed by powerful professional sanctions, that doctors must always in such circumstances make an attempt to bring the parents into the picture. And they often succeed. It is said that one third of the girls are persuaded to tell their parents at the first interview, and another third agree later.

Sometimes the doctor fails to persuade the girl, particularly if she has already commenced coition and believes that continuing is her only way of retaining the affection of her admirer. But then the anti-Gillick faction had an additional and more important argument. A policy of forbidding doctors and others to provide contraceptive facilities in confidence would not necessarily prevent (might sometimes be most unlikely to prevent) the girl from continuing with coition, and would make it much more likely that if she did carry on she would conceive. A further argument, which no one used because it would evidently have had no weight, is that refusing advice to the young girl who has become involved with a man without her parents' knowledge sometimes plunges her into deep distress—particularly if she suspects, perhaps wrongly, that she is pregnant.

The argument is sometimes advanced that young girls are not sufficiently responsible to use contraception. Some are not, and do not ask for it; but there is evidence that giving contraceptive assistance does reduce under-age pregnancies. The Department of Health and Social Security first advised in 1974 that contraception should be available to all young people at risk of pregnancy, regardless of age; and the steady fall in the number of under-age pregnancies that has taken place since then is attributed to the new policy. But, the Gillick party say, reducing pregnancies is not the only desideratum. It is also desirable to promote sexual restraint among young people.

Quantifying the risks is beyond our present knowledge. Conceivably, an investigator might discover two communities, in one of which doctors were allowed to provide contraceptives to schoolgirls, and in the other not. He might then compare the rates of schoolgirl (1) coitus and (2) pregnancy in the two communities, in order to determine the extent to which the refusal of contraceptives (1) diminished coitus but (2) increased pregnancies. Of course it would be necessary to eliminate many other factors that might have a bearing on the rates, before a conclusion could be drawn; and even when a valid comparison was made, the investigator would have to find some formula for weighing the social misfortune of sexual precocity against the misfortune of schoolgirl pregnancy. How many schoolgirls are we prepared to countenance in practising coition in order that one school pregnancy may be avoided? There is the further question whether the number we are prepared to accept differs according as the pregnancy in question is (1) medically terminated (so destroying an embryonic human life) or (2) allowed to go to term (so producing a child who is likely to be brought up fatherless, either by an immature and overburdened mother or by adoptive parents or in an institution). How often is it that schoolgirl sex (without resulting pregnancy) affects the girl's happiness in life? We have no firm answers to these questions. They are simplified for those Roman Catholics who totally exclude contemplation of birth control and abortion. (For Mrs Gillick herself, a mother of ten, there was no middle way between unprotected intercourse and total abstention.) According to their beliefs, the choice for their daughters lies between chastity and motherhood, with, at best, only a very perilous middle path. (A doctor, on the Gillick thesis, could not even advise a girl on the rhythm method without her parents' consent.) To say that the daughter of such parents cannot have contraceptive advice without her parents' consent simply says that she cannot have it. But for the large majority in our society, who accept family limitation in its widest sense, the social judgment of what is the best course to take with wayward girls involves imponderables so great as to suggest that the only acceptable policy is to leave concerned adults to do what they can in the individual case. There is no sufficient evidence at present to justify the creation of new legal controls.

The controversial questions of policy involved in Mrs Gillick's campaign show why she preferred, if possible, to enlist the support of the judges rather than that of Parliament. By seeking a declaration as to the 'unlawfulness' of the DHSS memorandum, and therefore of the doctors' behaviour which it encouraged, she avoided all the thorny details of how a restrictive law could be framed: whether it should create a crime or a civil remedy; to whom it should apply; and what exceptions should be allowed. Her counsel argued the case largely in terms of the parent's abstract 'rights' and the child's abstract incapacities, hoping that the court would, by accepting the principles, be moved to pronounce upon the unlawfulness of the conduct objected to, without necessarily considering the specific form of the unlawfulness. In this effort they were notably successful in the Court of Appeal, and very nearly succeeded in the Appellate Committee of the House of Lords.

... The anxiety of the judges—particularly the 'pro-Gillick' judges—to make their decision accord with their notions of policy can be vividly seen in Lord Brandon's dissent. He said that the first point of law was whether the giving of contraceptive advice and assistance to girls under 16 could be carried on lawfully in any circumstances whatever. This question, he said, 'appears to me to be one of public policy'; and he immediately proceeded to discuss it in terms of policy, making the assumption that what was against policy was *ipso facto* against law. This is an astonishing approach. Policy is relevant only in deciding between two 'legally' possible interpretations of the law.

A substantial drawback to judicial attempts to translate policy into law is that the judges do not hear evidence of informed opinion on policy issues, or even of the factual background on which wise judgments are founded. The judges are not only the judges of policy but the witnesses as well. (The judges in the present case made no reference to the fact that the British Medical Association was strongly against the Gillick position; either they did not know the fact, or they thought it immaterial. Nor were they armed with any statistical information on juvenile sexual behaviour.)

... The opinions of Lords Fraser and Scarman, also, showed concern over the social consequences of the decision. They combined a declaration of the doctor's discretion with portentous but slightly ambiguous warnings against its abuse, which seem to have been intended to placate pro-Gillick opinion—though the warnings also had the result of perpetuating a certain degree of confusion. In particular, these two lords set out to consider when a doctor is 'justified' in giving contraceptive advice to a young girl, without always making it clear that what was being referred to was moral justification. For these reasons, the two lords' opinions are particularly likely to be seen by the doctors themselves as Delphic oracles.

Where should such questions be resolved?

One final question remains in the light of this. Are the courts the appropriate forum to resolve questions such as this? Clearly the answer must be 'sometimes'. But, of course, these questions are also for others. Perhaps the most obvious alternative to the courts is Parliament.

As Lord Bridge pointed out in *Gillick* the courts should be cautious about becoming involved in these areas (at p 427):

... the occasions of a departmental non-statutory publication raising, as in that case, a clearly defined issue of law, unclouded by political, social or moral overtones, will be rare. In cases where any proposition of law implicit in a departmental advisory document is interwoven with questions of social and ethical controversy, the court should, in my opinion, exercise its jurisdiction with the utmost restraint, confine itself to deciding whether the proposition of law is erroneous and avoid either expressing ex cathedra opinions in areas of social and ethical controversy in which it has no claim to speak with authority or proffering answers to hypothetical questions of law which do not strictly arise for decision.

If we look to Parliament, it is unlikely that help will be forthcoming. There are as many votes to be lost as won in trying to resolve such charged issues. The delay in dealing with the Warnock Report bears witness to this. If any legislation were to be forthcoming, it would probably be couched in the most general terms and therefore of only limited value to those who must make particular decisions in particular contexts.

Another candidate is the General Medical Council. We have already seen that it has a role to play in providing guidance to the medical profession.

Given the limitations, however, of all the possible institutional methods for responding to the sort of questions we have been considering, is there any better approach? In 1980 in the United States President Carter established the President's Commission for the Study of Ethical Problems in Medicine and Biomedical and Behavioral Research. In the five years of its existence (it was 'defunded' by President Reagan in 1985) the Commission produced sixteen reports which have already become classics. Professor Alex Capron, who was the Executive Director of the Commission, in his article 'A National Commission on Medical Ethics' in *Health, Rights and Resources: King's College Studies* (1988) (ed P Byrne) explains the Commission's functions and evaluates its impact on medical law and ethics in the US (footnotes omitted) (pp 178–190). He does so in the context of an examination of the four model approaches which could be adopted, if it were thought that some sort of commission should, in fact, be set up.

Types of commissions
Ad hoc panels
My first task, then, is to explain what I have in mind as the four types of commissions on medical ethics. The first is the ad hoc panel. This has been, as I understand it, the approach taken here in the United Kingdom, where commissions such as the Warnock committee on alternative methods of human reproduction have functioned successfully. In the United States, too, ad hoc panels have been used; indeed, the first major forays into this general field were of this sort. For example, the Department of Health, Education, and Welfare (DHEW) during the late 1960s and early 1970s established several ad hoc bodies to examine the implications of transplanted and artificial organs, such as the totally implantable artificial heart. I think it is noteworthy that such bodies returned several times to this same topic and yet their recommendations did not seem to have much impact on the activities of the Department nor on the development of public policy generally. The absence of follow-through is a decided risk of ad hoc groups when the topic is not one that can be disposed of in a single legislative or administrative stroke.

In 1972, a journalist uncovered a research project that had been going on for 40 years among black men in rural Alabama. Several hundred men had been involved in this government-sponsored study of untreated syphilis. The study was begun in 1932 prior to the development of effective therapies for syphilis, but it continued up until the time that it was revealed to the public, which was plainly shocked to discover that scientific curiosity had apparently won out over medical care in the treatment of the victims of this disease in the study group. As a consequence, the DHEW established the Tuskegee Syphilis Ad Hoc Advisory Panel made up of distinguished physicians, ethicists, lawyers, and others. Within a few months they issued a report directed both at the particular problems caused by this study and at the larger issue of government regulation of scientific research conducted under government auspices.

It is characteristic of this first type of committee that groups, usually of about a dozen people from medicine, law, economics, ethics, and often a few with prior government service, attempt to reach fairly concrete recommendations and conclusions on a specific subject. Further, such groups are usually staffed by the agency that set them up, which is usually interested in specific fact-finding and recommendations on an immediate problem. Sometimes larger recommendations about the general process may also emerge, as they did from the Tuskegee panel. That body was effective in clarifying most of the facts, though some crucial facts about the degree of intentional deception of the participants were not uncovered. One panel member has now publicly stated that he believes these facts may have been intentionally suppressed and kept from the panel.

Single-subject standing bodies
The broader recommendations of the Tuskegee panel were quickly overshadowed, however, by the creation of another governmental commission in 1974—the National Commission for the Protection of Human Subjects of Biomedical and Behavioral Research. I will use this group to illustrate the second category in my

list—a standing body with authority to study and make recommendations on a narrow field within medical ethics.

The creation of the National Commission had the same provocation as the Tuskegee panel: namely, revelations about human experimentation run amok. In 1972 and 1973 the Congress of the United States took special interest in this subject. In particular, Senator Edward Kennedy, then the chairman of the Senate Health Subcommittee, held hearings on this topic, during which a number of troubling cases, in addition to the Tuskegee study, were disclosed, particularly research in prisons and mental hospitals and research on human fetuses. As a result, provisions were included in the National Research Act of 1974: namely, that each institution conducting federally-supported research with human subjects was required to create an institutional review board (IRB); and an eleven-member commission drawn from medicine, research, law, ethics, and related fields was to be appointed by the Secretary of Health, Education, and Welfare. As a result, the National Commission for the Protection of Human Subjects was appointed by Secretary Caspar W Weinberger on 3 December 1974, and was lodged within the National Institutes of Health, a subdivision of the Department, under the chairmanship of Dr Kenneth Ryan, head of obstetrics and gynecology at Harvard Medical School.

Most of the topics assigned by the National Research Act to the Commission dealt with experiments on humans; in particular, the Commission was instructed to prepare a report within four months on the subject of fetal experiments, to be followed by other reports on psychosurgery and on various groups of experimental subject, such as prisoners, children, and persons institutionalised as mentally disabled. (In addition, the Commission was asked to study the social implications of developments in biomedical research, a rather open-ended topic on which the Commission made little headway compared to its thorough treatment of the topics centrally related to experiments on humans.) To draw together its work and provide guidance to IRBs the Commission also prepared a brief summary report—called the 'Belmont Report' after the federal meeting center at which its conclusions were first debated—in which it set forth several basic principles of bioethics on which it had attempted to base its conclusions.

The staff of the National Commission was a mixed group: some career civil servants, mostly from DHEW, and some outside experts from academic medicine and ethics. In addition, consultants from a wide variety of fields were commissioned to write advisory papers. The Commission held open monthly meetings which included an opportunity for public testimony. In some ways the National Commission seems similar to what I know of the Comité National Consultatif d'Ethique, although the French group has only one annual open meeting, includes government officials, and is much larger in size, consisting of about 35 people.

Broad-based standing bodies

As the National Commission was completing its statutory mandate in 1978, Senator Kennedy recommended raising it to the level of a Presidential Commission to look at issues in human research across the entire federal government. In the House of Representatives, however, the view arose that any successive commission should have a broader mandate, encompassing issues in medical practice as well as in research on human subjects. Through the agreements reached by Senator Kennedy and Representative Paul Rogers, Chairman of the House Health Subcommittee, a provision was attached to a statute passed in 1978 authorising the creation of the President's Commission.

I will use this group to illustrate my third type of governmental bioethics committee. The mandate of such a group is general in nature including potentially all topics in bioethics. The President's Commission was required by its statute to conduct studies of a number of topics—including access to health care, informed consent in treatment as well as in research, genetic screening and counseling, and the definition of death—but the topics could be increased at the request of the President. (President Jimmy Carter, through his Science Advisor, Dr Frank Press, did add a topic—human genetic engineering—to the Commission's mandate.) The topics could also be increased at the option of the Commission itself, and this course was also followed when the Commission chose to add the topic of foregoing life sustaining treatment to its list of studies.

What are the salient characteristics of this third type of commission? Like the National Commission, the President's Commission consisted of eleven members from law, ethics and public affairs, under the chairmanship of Morris B Abrams, a New York lawyer and former President of Brandeis University. Unlike the National Commission, the President's Commission was conceived as a permanent body whose members would serve in groups with staggered terms. Since the Commissioners were not named by the President until the summer of 1979 (and were not sworn in until January 1980), the terms served by the first group of Commissioners expired two years later in the summer of 1981. By the conclusion of the Commission's work, eight of the eleven members were appointees of President Ronald Reagan.

Although the Commission was established in a fashion that contemplated a continuing life (as, for example, the limitation of service to two consecutive four-year terms for any Commissioner), the inclusion of a 'sunset clause' meant that the Commission was scheduled to go out of business in December 1982. The purpose of this clause was to allow the legislature to review the group's work and then, by a simple action, to extend its work. Despite the termination date, I still believe that it makes sense to describe such groups as 'standing committees', both because their lives are of indefinite duration (if the termination date is postponed) and because during the three or four years that the President's Commission functioned, it felt free to range quite widely within the field of bioethics. It is true, nonetheless, that the termination date—with the deadlines it imposed for the completion of reports— was an effective, if somewhat oppressive stimulus for Commissioners and staff alike. It might well be that without this goad, some of the intensity that characterised the Commission would have been lacking. The limited time period also made it sensible to bring in staff from outside government, while a truly permanent body might be more heavily staffed by career civil servants. This is not to condemn such a body as a hopeless bureaucracy, but it has been my experience, especially when part of the subject under scrutiny is the performance of the government itself (as it was in our work), that outsiders are more likely to take a fresh look at an issue and are less likely to temper their findings and recommendations out of a need to be gentle with their fellow civil servants.

Like the National Commission, the President's Commission had to 'do ethics in public', because its work was governed by the Federal Advisory Committee Act which requires that such groups hold their meetings in public unless they make a strong case for the need for specific private sessions. Despite the prediction of some people that sensitive subjects of the sort being dealt with by the President's Commission could not usefully be discussed in public (lest there be a great deal of posturing and pointless rhetoric on all sides) the requirement that the meetings were open to the public did not prove an impediment to the effective functioning of the Commission. Indeed, the requirement seems to me to have had mostly salutary effects. All those who spoke, especially Commissioners and staff members, were mindful of the need for responsible comments and thoughtful deliberations. Further, the fact that a stenographic record was being made of the proceedings encouraged witnesses to aim for a high degree of accuracy and emphasised the importance of pointed comments rather than rambling dissertations. Finally, the fact that the sessions were public served to underline that the subject matter before the Commission was not esoteric but was a matter of concern and interest to all citizens; and their interest was furthered by the general press coverage of many of the meetings, particularly those at which reports and conclusions were set forth.

Another characteristic of the President's Commission—actually one of the most important—was that the Commission had no power to regulate. Its only real power was that of persuasion. In 1978, philosopher Ruth Macklin told the House Committee holding hearings on the bill that established the President's Commission, that to have any clout, the work of a commission must be 'clear and understandable to a concerned public as well as satisfying to those of us who work professionally in the field of biomedical ethics and health policy'. Therefore, the Commission made its minutes widely available to thousands of people across the country who requested to be on its mailing list, and members of the Commission and its staff testified frequently before congressional committees holding hearings on topics germane to the Commission's work and held briefings for Congressional members and their staff. One measure of the effectiveness of the Commission was the frequency with which it was asked to present its work to legislative bodies, as well as the number of times its reports received front-page coverage in the newspapers and were featured on the major news and discussion programmes on radio and television.

Because of the need to persuade, there was a strong drive toward consensus, since a divided body would be unlikely to find its conclusions well respected. Although this may not seem remarkable, it should be remembered that in the eyes of many people the field of bioethics is regarded as highly polarised and subject to political polemics. Yet the only major topic that the Commission chose to avoid was abortion, on which its opinions had not been sought and on which it could add little to the already well-developed medical and ethical arguments on both sides. Otherwise, the Commission tackled many difficult issues. Rather than leading to timid reports, however, the search for consensus actually pushed the Commission's reports further and made them more influential. The Commissioners worked inductively from specific examples to general principles; that is, they moved outward from a common core of agreement to the point where agreement was no longer possible. This form of deliberation helped to show that the sphere of consensus was quite large.

Action-oriented panels
Let me briefly describe the fourth type of governmental group on medical ethics with which we have had experience in the United States, namely a standing body with direct involvement in binding decisions. As a result of the work of the National Commission, new regulations were issued by what is now known as the Department of Health and Human Services in 1978. Among the provisions of these regulations was the requirement that research involving certain highly sensitive groups be approved at a national level by an Ethics Advisory Board (EAB) appointed by the Secretary as well as review and approval by the IRB of the institution at which the research is to be conducted.

The Secretary of the Department of Health, Education, and Welfare, Joseph Califano, established an EAB in 1978. Its first task was to review the acceptability of *in vitro* fertilisation (IVF) because of a protocol submitted by Dr Pierre Soupart of Vanderbilt University. After one year of hearings and commissioned papers, the EAB issued a report in May 1979 recommending that the Secretary permit research on embryos up to two weeks after fertilisation in the laboratory, provided there was to be no implantation of the embryo thereafter. That report has sat on the table for the past eight years without having a definitive response from Secretary Califano or any of his successors, and, ironically, Dr Soupart has since died while waiting for action by the federal government. With the onset of the President's Commission, the EAB was dissolved. Although the President's Commission and EAB had different functions, with no necessary overlap, the EAB did not have the necessary bureaucratic support to continue.

Structure, functions, and accomplishments of the President's Commission
... The work of the President's Commission was carried out by a staff of about 25 people, mostly professionals, with a small support staff. The Commission was housed independently of any government department or agency and was not part of a standing bureaucracy. Most members of the support staff and one senior professional came from careers in government service but all the rest of the staff were outsiders to government. For example, I took leave from the University of Pennsylvania to run the Commission, and other senior staff members, who included a physician, two of the lawyers, two sociologists, an expert in public health, one economist and a succession of philosophers, plus various research assistants, were drawn from academic settings. The Commission met monthly. During the first several years of its work these meetings took the form primarily of hearings at which experts and other interested parties testified on particular topics that were under study by the Commission and were questioned by the Commissioners and senior

staff members. Furthermore, the Commission staff themselves were sometimes in the witness chair, to engage in a dialogue with the Commissioners and attempt to convey the results of their studies and to learn from the Commissioners, in general form, the directions that should be taken by the Commission's reports. Although many of the witnesses were invited—and included the consultants who were writing papers for the Commission—time was always allotted for other experts and members of the general public who wished to appear and make statements.

After the initial phase during which background was provided to the Commissioners, the primary work of the staff was to prepare drafts of the Commission's reports. After these had been reviewed by the Commissioners they were rewritten by the staff. Commissioners who had special expertise in an area under study took a more active hand in the process of revision of these reports. In the end, there was unanimity on all the Commission's ten reports except one, on which there was one dissent. In addition to the ten reports there was one report of the Commission's work in commissioning papers and convening a workshop on *Whistleblowing in Biomedical Research*. The reports were released as finished; the work amounted to 16 volumes because the background papers were published as separate appendix volumes for some of the reports.

Rather than review all of these, I will characterise the results in four ways: (1) laying to rest, (2) the crucible, (3) the watchdog, and (4) the small rock (sometimes called the lightning rod or, less charitably, the dumping ground) but I prefer to think of this last role in Homer's terms when in *The Odyssey*, he says 'a small rock holds back a great wave'.

Laying to rest

The first category is probably best illustrated by the first report the Commission issued in July 1981 on the 'definition' of death. This topic had been a matter of public concern since December 1967 when Dr Christiaan Barnard performed the first human-to-human heart transplant. In 1968 an ad hoc committee at the Harvard Medical School promulgated criteria for diagnosing death in comatose bodies whose breathing was being artificially maintained. By 1980 when the President's Commission began, many states had laws recognising criteria of the type promulgated by the Harvard Committee and there was general medical agreement although no up-to-date guidelines had been agreed upon.

Given the fact that the subject was already well advanced, it seemed to the Commission that the major impediment to its mandate—to consider the advisability of legislation on the subject—was the very multiplicity of statutory proposals that had been made by groups such as the American Medical Association, the American Bar Association, and the National Conference of Commissioners on Uniform State Laws. Most of the legislative 'definitions' had been adopted by states in the early 1970s, but the process had slowed to a trickle, and the few that were legislating tended to write their own bills (with all the confusion and imprecision one would expect) rather than choose among the competing laws. Therefore, the Commission concluded that the best way to avoid simply adding to the multiplicity of proposals was to develop a proposal on which all the major proponents could agree. The result was the Uniform Determination of Death Act (UDDA) which was endorsed by the AMA, the ABA and the NCCUSL, as well as the Commission, when its report *Defining Death* was issued in July 1981. The UDDA has since become law in many states. It recognises that death occurs when there is a total and irreversible cessation of circulatory and respiratory functions, or a total and irreversible cessation of all functions of the brain including the brain stem. Equally important to the provision of a statute was the drafting of a set of medical guidelines by a group of the leading medical experts convened by the Commission. When these guidelines were published in the Journal of the American Medical Association they were hailed as a landmark, and today they provide a reliable statement on medical techniques for determining that death has occurred either on cardiopulmonary or neurological grounds.

To summarise, the 'laying to rest' function of a commission seems to be to develop recommendations for action, in this case for legislation and for professional action, and to bring together a broad coalition of people in the field to insure that the recommendations will be so broadly accepted that the topic will no longer be a matter of division or contention.

The crucible

I refer to the second category as that of the crucible, thinking of it as a place for publicly grinding out conclusions on controversial issues when a consensus is not yet apparent. In the case of the President's Commission, three of its reports probably fall into this category: the one on informed consent, *Making Health Care Decisions*; on 'pulling the plug', *Deciding to Forego Life-Sustaining Treatment*; and on equitable access to health care, *Securing Access to Health Care*. These are all topics which had been approached by divergent groups in the previous decade. The Commission's role here was threefold. First, it had to identify those elements underlying the apparently disparate views expressed in previous discussions. Second, it had to correct misunderstandings or errors, particularly as those were responsible for the divisions in the public debates; and finally, it had to articulate the implications for public policy and ethical behavior in a way that would be broadly acceptable. Plainly these objectives involved the Commission in processes of analysis and synthesis; as such it required more original scholarship than the first ('laying to rest') function because there was less existing agreement. These topics did not in the view of the Commission always lead to recommendations for legislation. In some cases the objective of the Commission was to frame the thinking on the subject of public officials, such as judges and legislators, and to attempt to push the academic experts forward so that the Commission's findings and recommendations could become the starting point for future discussions. This would reduce some of the jagged pieces that had prevented public understanding and the advancement of conclusions.

A good example of this second category was the work of the Commission on patient autonomy, and the necessity for and the means for its preservation in the face of patient incompetence contained in the reports on making health-care decisions and on deciding to forego life-sustaining treatment. These conclusions have been widely influential. For example, in the past year a California Appellate court and the Supreme Court in 'landmark opinions' have placed heavy reliance on the report, *Deciding to Forego Life-Sustaining Treatment*. The weight accorded to this report illustrates that those who perform ethical and social analysis need a clear understanding of the realities of the practice they are scrutinising. Such an understanding was provided for the Commission by its members, its staff and expert consultants who all insisted that the realities be well attended to rather than solely being concerned with ethical or philosophical discourse. A great deal of effort was placed on the clarification of facts as they illuminate issues, such as 'active' versus 'passive' euthanasia—something that can become a matter of heated, but nonetheless rather abstract, discussion until it is grounded in understanding of the realities of hospital practices and nursing home procedures, the means of dealing with pain, and the psychology of physicians and nurses.

Watchdog

The third function of the Commission is well illustrated by its work in the area of federal regulation of human subject research. This is a topic that had been thoroughly studied by our predecessor, the National Commission for the Protection of Human Subjects. The Commission therefore placed particular emphasis on the portion of its mandate to report biennially on the adequacy and uniformity of the federal oversight of research conducted or funded by the government. Although this was perhaps the least exciting topic assigned to the President's Commission, it was very important for several reasons. First, the government's efforts in this area are plainly a matter of great public concern; indeed, the whole process of governmental commissions and study panels in biomedical ethics was begun because of what was perceived as abuses of human subjects in research. Second, since the National Commission had gone out of existence there was a strong possibility that some of its conclusions and recommendations would simply fall between the cracks of the federal bureaucracy if the President's Commission did not vigilantly monitor the response of federal agencies. Third, the National Commission had primarily studied the work of what is now the Department of Health and Human Services, the largest sponsor of research with human subjects, but the President's Commission had a broader mandate. It was to examine research issues throughout the federal government, and one of the principal recommendations in this area in the first biennial report on research in 1981 was that the government should adopt a single set of regulatory requirements for all federally sponsored human subject research to simplify the burdens placed on researchers and the local IRBs.

A small rock

The final function that a standing ethics group can serve is illustrated, I believe, by the work of the President's Commission on a very controversial topic—namely, genetic engineering. In 1980, shortly after the Commission began its work, leaders of the Catholic, Protestant, and Jewish congregations in the United States voiced cries of alarm over the prospect that genetic engineering techniques would be soon extended to human beings. Their concerns, which were addressed to President Carter, led his science advisor to request that the President's Commission add the subject of human genetic engineering to its mandate.

In its report, *Splicing Life*, the Commission took a scientific and a philosophical and religious view of the topic. It attempted to place the concerns in historical context and to show that many forms of manipulation of the genetic basis of human disease were no different from conventional, accepted treatment. But treatment that went beyond the somatic cells to alter the human germ line cells raised moral as well as medical concerns. By the time the Commission had completed its work, a number of newspaper reporters had become interested enough in the topic to write thoughtfully about it for their publications, and the Commission's conclusions were greeted with general support by editorial writers. In three days of Congressional hearings, when the report was issued in November 1982, the conclusions of the Commission were accepted by a wide variety of scientific and ethical experts and by representatives of the religious groups that had initially provoked the study.

Question

Do you think that there is any argument for establishing some kind of Commission in the United Kingdom? If so, what chance do you think there is of its being set up? See Baroness Warnock 'A National Ethics Committee' 297 BMJ 1626 (1988).

Chapter 2

The parties to the relationship

The health care professional

Many providers of health care may become involved in the management of a
patient. Doctors and nurses obviously come to mind and, in most cases, it will
primarily be they who will take care of the patient. But others too may well have
a role to play, for example, physiotherapists, pharmicists, health visitors and,
in the case of pregnant women, midwives. The constitution and regulation of
these various professions are to be found in a complicated collection of primary
and secondary legislation. For our purposes, we will focus our attention
principally on the doctor/patient relationship and, therefore, we will concentrate
on 'Who is a doctor?' and 'Who is a doctor's patient?'. This is not to underplay
the role of other professionals. (The legislation which you should refer to in the
case of these other professions is, for example, the Dentists Act 1984 (dentists);
Pharmacy Act 1954 (chemists); Nurses, Midwives and Health Visitors Act 1979
(nurses etc) and the statutory instruments made thereunder.) A brief summary
of the regulation of the health care professions can be found in the *Encyclopedia
of Health Services and Medical Law* (ed J Jacob and J V Davies) paras 1.031–
1.044.

1–031: Many of the health-care occupations have been recognised by statute. They
are: the doctors' profession now in the Medical Act 1983; the dentists now in the
Dentists Act 1984; the chemists now in the Pharmacy Act 1954; the nurses and
allied professions now in the Nurses, Midwives and Health Visits Act 1979; a
variety of other occupations in the Professions Supplementary to Medicine Act 1960
(speech therapists are outside the Act but some of its forms are applied to them);
the opticians in the Opticians Act 1958; and most recently the suppliers of hearing
aids in the Hearing Aid Council Act 1968.

1–032: The basic function of this type of professional regulation is the maintenance
of registers of practitioners deemed competent. Occasionally, particularly in its
older forms, the Council may be given, or assume, a policing function, *Pharmaceutical
Society of Great Britain v Storkwain Ltd* [1985] 3 All ER 4. Today the structure most
commonly used to achieve this is the establishment of a Council with duties (for
example, to register those who satisfy the 'statutory' criteria) and powers (for
example, to determine the criteria). The efficacy of the registers is supported by the
creation of certain monopolies (which might be shared with specified other groups)
and which are protected by provisions preventing the recovery of fees (or limitations
on the right to take appointments which might yield an income) by the unregistered,
and by the use of the criminal law to protect professional titles. *Younghusband v
Luftig* [1949] 2 KB 354, [1949] 2 All ER 72; *Wilson v Inyang* [1951] 2 KB 799. It is to
be noted that the monopolies of dentists, Dentists Act 1984, s 38 (practice), section
39 (titles), and section 41 (business of dentistry) the monopolies of opticians,
Opticians Act 1958 ss 20–22A, and the monopolies of pharmacists, Medicines Act
1968, are shared with registered medical practitioners.

1–033: It is worth pausing to compare the various schemes. The model, both
historically and today, is that provided under the Medical Acts. The General

Medical Council consists of some ninety members. Fifty are elected by the profession, thirty-four are appointed by the teaching institutions and 'not more than' eleven are nominated by Her Majesty on the advice of the Privy Council. All, except a majority of this eleven, must be 'registered medical practitioners'. (It is the custom to appoint the four Chief Medical Officers for each of the countries of the United Kingdom.) Thus the lay representation on the General Council cannot be greater than six, and the Merrison Report suggested (Committee of Inquiry into the Regulation of the Medical Profession, Cmnd 6018, 1975, para 383) that 'lay' meant non-medical which might include nurses and other health care professionals. Some part of the work of the GMC is conducted by Branch Councils for each of the countries of the United Kingdom. [The membership of the GMC in 1988 was 102; 54 elected, 35 appointed and 13 nominated].

So it is with other professions. The General Dental Council consists of representatives of the 'Dental Authorities', ie the dental schools, together with eighteen elected by the profession and the four Chief Dental Officers for each of the Departments for the countries of the United Kingdom. One dental auxiliary is elected by the Dental Auxiliaries Committee. (A dental auxiliary performs functions in dentistry roughly corresponding to nurses in medicine.) Six persons who are not registered dentists are appointed by the Privy Council. The pattern is largely reflected in the General Optical Council where (Opticians Act 1958 Sched paras 1–5) registered opticians provide eight members, the examining bodies six, the registered medical practitioners six, of whom four are nominated by the Faculty of Ophthalmologists (a part of the Royal College of Surgeons) and two by the Privy Council (one after consultation with the medical profession to represent it and one who shall be engaged in pre-clinical training of doctors). There are six lay members (here 'lay' excludes doctors as well as opticians).

The Pharmaceutical Society of Great Britain is incorporated by Charter from the Crown. It is therefore subjected to the legal rules applicable to such incorporation, *Jenkin v Pharmaceutical Society of Great Britain* [1921] 1 Ch 392 (the 1843 Charter was substantially replaced by the Supplemental Charter of 1953) and its constitution is to be found in its Byelaws. However these Byelaws are themselves subject to the approval of the Privy Council (Pharmacy Act 1954 s 16. Some of the Byelaws grant discretions not subject to the approval of the Privy Council). Its organisational form is thus markedly different from the others. That is, it is closer to the Royal Colleges than other professional councils and boards which are incorporated by statute. The Charter is however recognised by Act of Parliament and in some of its most important functions and powers it is directly comparable to those councils. This form was adopted in both the grant of the Charter (1843) and its first statutory recognition (1852) prior to the first Medical Act (1858). The Council of the Society consists of twenty-one registered pharmaceutical chemists and three persons appointed by the Privy council whose qualifications are not specified.

1–034: This pattern of occupational dominance in the governing councils is repeated in the other statutes regulating the professions. The regulation of nursing and its allied professions is now to be found in the Nurses, Midwives and Health Visitors Act 1979. The professions are governed by the Central Council, committees of the Central Council, National Boards (for each of the countries of the United Kingdom) and committees of the National Boards. The Central Council consists of forty-five members, seven nominated by each of the National Boards and seventeen appointed by the Secretary of State. There is a complex electoral scheme for election to the National Boards, see United Kingdom Central Council for Nurses, Midwives and Health Visitors (Electoral Scheme) Order 1982 (SI 1982 No 1104). Each of the three professions form separate constituencies within the National Boards, and the persons they each may nominate must include, by virtue of the Act, Sched 1, para 1, each profession and also at least one person engaged in the teaching of nurses, midwives or health visiting. The Secretary of State makes appointments, section 1(4), (5) and section 5(4), (5), to both the Central Council and to the National Boards. His appointments are made from practitioners of each of the professions or from registered medical practitioners or persons who have 'such qualifications and experience in education or other fields as . . . will be of value to the Council in the performance of its functions'. The committees of the Central Council and the National Boards include a Midwifery Committee. Further, joint committees between the Central Council and the National Boards may be appointed.

1–035: Somewhat similar provision is to be found in the Professions Supplementary to Medicine Act 1960, although the specific occupations as such are relatively badly represented. Once more there is a Council and Boards for each of the occupations under its wing—they are now chiropodists, dietitians, occupational therapists, physiotherapists, radiographers and remedial gymnasts and orthopists. The Council consists of twenty-three members. Each profession has only one. Of the others six are doctors (appointed variously by the 'English Colleges', ie The Royal Colleges of Physicians, of Surgeons and Obstetricians and Gynaecologists, and the Scottish Corporations). Four persons, of whom only two may be doctors and none can belong to a profession regulated by the Act, are appointed jointly by Secretaries of State. Five other persons are appointed by the Privy Council (and the Secretary of State for Northern Ireland) none of whom may belong to any of the professions or the medical profession. The Boards each contain a majority of practitioners in their respective professions but repeat the general pattern by including doctors. The representative character or the Boards is shown eg in the requirement that the Radiographers Baord shall include both diagnostic and radiotherapeutic radiographers.

1–036: The only exception to the pattern of occupational control is to be found in a possibility under the Hearing Aid Council Act 1968. Under that Act again there is a professional council regulating the occupation of 'dispensers of hearing aids'. It has twelve members, six of whom either are dispensers or employ dispensers. Neither the chairman nor the others can be so engaged but they must have, Sched para 1(3)(*b*), 'specialised medical knowledge of deafness or audiological technical knowledge or who are capable of representing the interests of persons with impaired hearing'. Under this Act therefore there is some chance of a significant consumer representation in the management of the occupation.

1–037: To generalise, the State involvement with the functioning of each of these professional councils is limited to those matters which might involve the use of its wider machinery. Thus the GMC 'may make regulations with respect to the form and keeping of the registers, and the making of entries, alterations and corrections in them'. The only regulations made under this provision which require the approval of the Privy Council are those relating to overseas registration and to restoration to a particular list in the register. The principal significance of these matters is that they concern the level of registration or retention fee which is payable. Other matters do not concern the Privy Council. It is incidentally worth noting that overseas registration does not include those who hold primary European qualifications. Under the 1858 Act, overseas qualifications were not recognised at all, see *Younghusband v Luftig* [1949] 2 KB 354, [1949] 2 All ER 72. The GMC was given power exercisable by order of the Privy Council to recognise such qualifications on a country by country basis by the 1886 Act. The far more flexible provisions were introduced by the 1978 Act. As regards the EEC, domestic policy was overtaken by the First and Second Medical Directives.

1:038: Some of the most important functions of the professional councils are reserved by statute to their Education Committees. In the case of the GMC this committee must be chosen, Medical Act 1983, Sched 1 para 19, (but note also para 25(2) relating to powers of co-option) '. . . as to ensure that the number of appointed members exceeds the number of elected and nominated members . . .', ie teachers of medicine must form the majority. It is possible that no nominated members may be chosen. In accord with the scheme of the 1858 Act, the GMC engages in no teaching or examining. It does however prescribe, section 5, the knowledge skill and standard of proficiency required for registration. It has powers, section 6, to require information as to the requisites for obtaining qualifications and to appoint inspectors at examinations and, section 7, to appoint visitors to medical schools. With the approval of the Privy Council, it may, section 8, add to the list of approved medical schools or, section 9, delete one already there. In order to become fully registered a practitioner must have acquired a pattern of experience prescribed by the Education Committee, sections 5 and 10.

1–039: The change effected by the Medical Act 1969 from clinical experience in 'medicine and surgery' to 'prescribed branches of medicine' reflected a much older recognition of the increases in the specialisation of medicine (See also Opticians Act 1958 s 28 and Professions Supplementary to Medicine Act 1960 s 11.) The doctor acquires it, section 10, at an institution approved by his examining body, but the institution itself is, section 12, subject to visitation by representatives of the Education Committee. Institutional academic freedom is therefore displaced by what is largely the collective academic freedom of the teaching side of the profession as a whole.

1–040: In the other professions there are similar forms for the regulation of education but with the same reservation as before: in education, as in the structure of their councils, the other occupations maintain a dominance but also generally utilise the patronage of doctors. With dentists, all the members of the Education Committee are registered dentists or doctors. As with doctors, the GDC engages in no teaching. That function is carried out by the 'dental authorities' which are defined as 'any medical authority', ie Dentists Act 1984, s 3(3), 'any of the universities or other bodies who choose appointed members of the General Medical Council'. Section 3, and see section 5, authorise the Royal College of Surgeons to continue to hold examinations etc in dentistry.

Again, as with the doctors, the GDC, with the advice, section 2 and Sched 1, of its Education Committee has powers, section 9, regarding the supervision of courses and examinations and, section 10, to appoint visitors and to recommend, section 11, in appropriate cases, that particular degrees or licences in dentistry are not sufficient. The Act maintains a provision, in section 12, which corresponded to one in the old Medical Acts that the General Council shall prevent any degree granting authority from requiring, or preventing, candidates having particular theories. As regards medicine, the Medical Act 1858 s 23 (which became Medical Act 1956 s 14 and was repealed by Medical Act 1978) made similar provision. In both *Allison v General Council of Medical Education and Registration* [1894] 1 QB 750, and *R v General Medical Council ex p Kynaston* [1930] 1 KB 562, it appears that the practitioners fell foul of their professional brethren because of differences in 'theory'. In the one case it was over the use of drug therapy and in the other over the use of tonsillotomy. In neither case did the court appear concerned at any restriction on liberty. They upheld the GMC on grounds relating to the way in which the heterodoxy was expressed. *Allbutt v General Council of Medical Education and Registration* (1889) 23 QBD 400, is perhaps an even stronger case. There the doctor published a book discussing contraception which he sold at a low price. The GMC appear to have taken the view that the price made it available to 'the youth of both sexes to the detriment of public morals' and that was infamous conduct, and see also *Ex p La Mert* (1863) 33 LJ QB 69 4 B & S 582.

1–041: As regards opticians, the Education Committee consists of, Opticians Act 1958 s 17 and its Education Committee Rules 1974 (SI 1974 No 149), one general educationalist, five persons involved in the education of opticians, one in the education of doctors, two ophthalmic surgeons, and two opticians. The GOC has, section 6, powers similar in relation to education to those of the GMC and GDC. It is also so with the Professions Supplementary to Medicine. The Boards (whose corporation is described above but without the statutory formation of an Education Committee) under their Council approve and supervise, sections 4 and 5, courses, qualifications, institutions, and examinations.

1–042: A break in the pattern appears in the Pharmacy Act (and see also Hearing Aid Council Act). True there is provision, in section 4, for the recognition of university degrees in pharmacy but also provision is made, section 3, for the Society itself to conduct examinations. Besides this, the intermediate status of the profession is also illustrated by the Privy Council control of the examiners, section 3(1)(*a*), and the statutory definition of the syllabus, section 3(4). Among other things, it still includes 'the latin language' (although this is no longer insisted on) and excludes 'the theory and practice of medicine, surgery and midwifery'.

1–043: With the nurses and allied professions, the Educational Policy Advisory Committee includes, eight members of the Central Council engaged in teaching nursing, midwifery or health visiting, and four more who can advise on professional education generally. The practice side of the profession is represented by seven specialised nurses (in midwifery, health visiting, district nursing, the nursing of children and of the mentally ill and handicapped, and occupational nursing). The control of education is, as to be expected from both the number of nurses and their variety, more complex: there are eleven Parts of the Register having different educational requirements under The Nurses, Midwives and Health Visitors Rules. Generally, however, the Central Council and the National Boards have similar powers to the other professional councils but their exercise is more formal being contained in a statutory instrument, Nurses, Midwives and Health Visitors Rules Approval Order 1983 (SI 1983 No 873).

1–044: The Privy Council has reserve powers under some of these Acts. Typical of them is the provision as regards doctors, (Medical Act 1983, s 50), which it may use where it considers the GMC or the Education Committee to have failed to secure the prescribed proficiency or do anything which they ought to have done (except appoint visitors to medical schools or to prescribe the period and branches of medicine for the requisite post-clinical experience). There are no corresponding default powers of the Privy Council in the Dentists, the Pharmacy, the Nurses, Midwives and Health Visitors, or the Hearing Aid Council Acts. It does not appear open to the Privy Council to use its default powers merely where it disagrees with the prescriptions of a professional council or its education committee.

One important matter not touched upon in this extract is the *disciplinary* role played by the various regulatory bodies. Since we shall concentrate on doctors, we shall have to return later to consider the role of the General Medical Council in this context (*infra* p 500 et seq). Meanwhile, let us now turn to consider the doctor and patient.

The doctor

Who is a doctor? Anyone can call himself a doctor. Curiously medical practitioners do not ordinarily have doctorates and therefore, the attribution to them of the title 'doctor' is wholly a convention. Thus, when we talk of a doctor we are really concerned with a medical practitioner. The answer to 'who is a doctor?' can be discovered by examining the Medical Act 1983 which is now the governing legislation. As regards a 'fully registered medical practitioner', sections 3 to 5 provide (and notice the role of the Education Committee of the GMC which has already been referred to):

Registration by virtue of primary United Kingdom or primary European qualifications
3. Subject to the provisions of this Act any person who—
> (a) holds one or more primary United Kingdom qualifications and has passed a qualifying examination and satisfies the requirements of this Part of this Act as to experience; or
> (b) being a national of any member State of the Communities, holds one or more primary European qualifications.
is entitled to be registered under this section as a fully registered medical practitioner.

Qualifying examinations and primary United Kingdom qualifications
4.—(1) Subject to the provisions of this Part of this Act, a qualifying examination for the purposes of this Part of this Act is an examination held by any of the bodies or combinations of bodies specified in subsection (2) below for the purpose of granting one or more primary United Kingdom qualifications.

(2) The bodies and combinations of bodies entitled to hold qualifying examinations are—

(a) any of the Universities of Oxford, Cambridge, London, Manchester, Birmingham, Liverpool, Leeds, Sheffield, Newcastle, Bristol, Nottingham, Southampton, Leicester, Wales, Glasgow, Aberdeen, Edinburgh, Dundee or the Queen's University of Belfast or a combination of any two or more of the universities specified in this paragraph;

(b) a combination of the Royal College of Physicians of London and the Royal College of Surgeons of England;

(c) a combination of the Royal College of Physicians of Edinburgh and the Royal College of Surgeons of Edinburgh and the Royal College of Physicians and Surgeons of Glasgow;

(d) the Society of Apothecaries of London;

(e) with the approval and under the directions of the Education Committee, a combination of any two or more of the bodies specified in paragraphs (b), (c) and (d) above.

(3) In this Act 'primary United Kingdom qualification' means any of the following qualifications, namely—

(a) the degree of bachelor of medicine or bachelor of surgery granted by any university in the United Kingdom;

(b) licentiate of the Royal College of Physicians of London or the Royal College of Physicians of Edinburgh or the Royal College of Surgeons of Edinburgh or the Royal College (formerly Royal Faculty) of Physicians and Surgeons of Glasgow;

(c) membership of the Royal College of Surgeons of England;

(d) licentiate in medicine and surgery of the Society of Apothocaries of London.

(4) Any two or more of the universities and other bodies specified in sub-section (3) above may, with the approval and under the directions of the Education Committee, unite or co-operate in conducting examinations held for the purpose of granting primary United Kingdom qualifications.

General functions of the Education Committee in relation to medical education in the United Kingdom

5.—(1) The Education Committee shall have the general function of promoting high standards of medical education and co-ordinating all stages of medical education.

(2) For the purpose of discharging that function the Education Committee shall—

(a) determine the extent of the knowledge and skill which is to be required for the granting of primary United Kingdom qualifications and secure that the instruction given in universities in the United Kingdom to persons studying for such qualifications is sufficient to equip them with knowledge and skill of that extent;

(b) determine the standard of proficiency which is to be required from candidates at qualifying examinations and secure the maintenance of that standard; and

(c) determine patterns of experience which may be recognised as suitable for giving to those engaging in such employment as is mentioned in section 10(2) below general clinical training for the purposes of the practice of their profession.

(3) The determinations of the Education Committee under subsection (2) above shall be embodied in recommendations which may be directed to all or any of the universities or other bodies concerned with medical education.

(4) In this Act—

'the prescribed knowledge and skill' means knowledge and skill of the extent for the time being determined under subsection (2)(a) above and embodied in recommendations under subsection (3) above;

'the prescribed standard of proficiency' means the standard of proficiency for the time being determined under subsection (2)(b) above and embodied in recommendations under subsection (3) above;

'a prescribed pattern of experience' means any pattern of experience for the time being determined under subsection (2)(*c*) above and embodied in recommendations under subsection (3) above.

(The Medical Act also provides for the doctors to have 'provisional' and 'limited' registration as well as 'temporary full' registration: see ss 21–23 and 27.)

Being registered as a 'fully registered medical practitioner' has certain consequences for an individual. The most important, perhaps, is that although the legislation does not prevent a person from practising medicine if his name is not on the medical register, he cannot hold himself out as being a registered medical practitioner. Section 49 of the Medical Act 1983 provides, *inter alia*:

Penalty for pretending to be registered
49.—(1) Subject to subsection (2) below, any person who wilfully and falsely pretends to be or takes or uses the name or title of physician, doctor of medicine, licentiate in medicine and surgery, bachelor of medicine, surgeon, general practitioner or apothecary, or any name, title, addition or description implying that he is registered under any provision of this Act, or that he is recognised by law as a physician or surgeon or licentiate in medicine and surgery or a practitioner in medicine or an apothecary, shall be liable on summary conviction to a fine . . .

On the other hand, being a fully registered medical practitioner confers certain privileges on a doctor. For example, in relation to the recovery of his fees, section 46 of the 1983 Act provides, *inter alia*:

Recovery of fees
46.—(1) Except as provided in subsection (2) below, no person shall be entitled to recover any charge in any court of law for any medical advice or attendance, or for the performance of any operation, or for any medicine which he has both prescribed and supplied unless he proves that he is fully registered.

Similarly, registration allows a doctor to hold certain appointments which he otherwise could not, the most important example being those within the National Health Service. Section 47 provides:

Appointments not to be held except by fully registered practitioners
47.—(1) Subject to subsection (2) below, no person who is not fully registered shall hold any appointment as physician, surgeon or other medical officer—
  (*a*) in the naval, military or air service,
  (*b*) in any hospital or other place for the reception of persons suffering from mental disorder, or in any other hospital, infirmary or dispensary not supported wholly by voluntary contributions,
  (*c*) in any prison, or
  (*d*) in any other public establishment, body or institution, or to any friendly or other society for providing mutual relief in sickness, infirmity or old age.

More generally, being a fully registered medical practitioner confers on a doctor as a matter of public policy the privilege of doing certain things to other people which would otherwise be *prima facie* unlawful. (It is no surprise, therefore, that the law should wish to hold the doctor to account for what he does in the exercise of this privilege).

Registered medical practitioners will usually work either within the NHS, as general practitioners or hospital doctors, or in private practice. These are not mutually exclusive. It is often the case that a particular doctor working in a hospital as a consultant will undertake some private work as well as fulfilling his NHS duties.

(a) THE DOCTOR WITHIN THE NHS

We need to examine here the legal framework within which a registered medical practitioner works as a GP or hospital doctor. We need to consider one general question first: is the legal relationship between a doctor and his patient who is being treated within the NHS contractual in nature? The answer would seem to be no.

A P Bell, in 'The Doctor and the Supply of Goods and Services Act 1982' (1984) 4 LS 175, explains:

> The common law draws an important distinction between treatment under the National Health Service and private treatment. The House of Lords has held[2] that where services are provided pursuant to a statutory obligation there is no contractual relationship, for the element of compulsion is inconsistent with the consensual basis of contract. The fact that the patient makes some payment is irrelevant.[3] Thus, the NHS patient can only sue in tort.

Notes to extract
2. *Pfizer Corpn v Minister of Health* [1965] AC 512.
3. *Ibid*, at 536B, 544G and 552G.

The Royal Commission on Civil Liability and Compensation for Personal Injury chaired by Lord Pearson in their 1978 Report take the same view.

Breach of contract
1313   Private patients may sue their doctors for a breach of contract if inadequate or faulty services have been provided, for example, if a swab has been left in the abdomen after an operation or if blood of the wrong blood group has been used in a transfusion. Under the National Health Service, however, there is no contract between patient and doctor and a plaintiff must rely on an action in tort. But the National Health Service patient is in no worse position than the private patient, because the same considerations determine if there has been a breach of duty whether the case is brought in contract or in tort.

Bell's position represents the orthodox view. The contrary, however, is not completely unarguable, on two bases. First , that the existence of a statutory duty to provide services by A may also serve as consideration for an agreement to provide the same services. The statutory duty may not be inconsistent with a contract based upon valuable consideration by the doctor. Secondly, consideration may actually move from the patient for whom the doctor promises to provide medical services, in that he agrees to have his name entered upon the medical list of the doctor in the knowledge that the doctor will be remunerated by the Family Practitioner Committee. As a consequence, the patient provides good consideration.

(i) The General Practitioner

The legal framework is summarised by Margaret Brazier in her book, *Medicine, Patients and the Law* (1987) pp 242–3.

> The National Health Service Act 1977[1] imposes a duty on district health authorities to make arrangements for general practice in their district. They require '. . . to provide personal medical service for all persons in the district who wish to take advantage of the arrangements'. The actual administration of such medical services is a matter for the local Family Practitioner Committee (FPC). The FPC is crucial to general practice. It administers arrangements for general practice, maintains the medical list of GP's in the area, administers pharmaceutical and other ancillary medical services, and acts as a grievance body for dissatisfied patients. And it is the FPC with whom the general practitioner contracts. The composition of the FPC is

designed to ensure a balance of doctors, representatives of other medical professions and lay people[2].

FPCs are now established by the Health Minister under section 5 of the Health and Social Security Act 1984. He decides which areas a particular FPC will cover, and these do not have to coincide with the administrative areas for district health authorities.

A doctor seeking to enter general practice must apply to have his name entered on the medical list in the area where he wishes to practise. The district health authority will refer his application to a central Medical Practices Committee, who will examine his qualifications and experience.[3] If 'passed' by that Committee,[4] then, save where there is already an excess of doctors in a particular neighbourhood, the doctor's name must be entered on the list. Once on the list the GP enters into a contract with the local FPC to provide general medical services. He may additionally apply to be entered on the obstetric list and provide care for his own maternity patients. The terms of his contract with the FPC are laid down in lengthy and detailed Regulations.[5] These Regulations do not of course create a contract with any individual patient. The GP and his patient within the NHS have no contractual relationship. But the contract between GP and FPC is important to the patient in two respects. First, it provides a detailed framework in which to examine the rights and duties of the doctor towards his NHS patient. Second, the absence of a contract with the GP does not leave the patient without a remedy should his GP prove incompetent or careless. The GP owes him a duty of care just as the hospital doctor does. In any action for negligence the court is likely to look to the obligations undertaken by the doctor as part of his contract with the FPC to determine the scope of the duty owed to the patient.

Notes to extract
1. s 29(1). And see the Health Services Act 1980, s 1(7) and Sched I.
2. See now the Health and Social Security Act 1984, Sched 3.
3. National Health Service Act 1977, s 30(1); Health Services Act 1980, s 1(7) and Sched I.
4. As to experience and qualifications demanded of GPs, they must complete a course of training and apply for a certificate from the Joint Committee on Postgraduate Training for General Practice. Between 1981 and 1985 fewer than 15 out of 7,000 applications were refused; see NHS Vocational Training Regulations 1979, SI 1979 No 1644; 1980 No 1900; 1981 No 1790; 1984 No 215.
5. See the NHS (General Medical and Pharmaceutical Services) Regulations 1974 SI No 160 Sched I as amended by amending regulations SI 1975 No 719; 1976 No 1407; 1980 No 288; 1982 No 1283.

(We will return to the duty of care that a GP owes to his patient later.) Brazier refers to the 'lengthy and detailed' Regulations setting out the terms of the GP's relation wih the FPC. Regulation 3 deals with the FPC and describes the scope of the services which it must administer.

Scope of services
3.—(1) [The services, arrangements for the provision of which, pursuant to section 29 and 41 to 43 of the National Health Service Act 1977, it is, by virtue of section 15 of that Act, the duty of the Committee to administer], shall include—
   (*a*) all necessary and appropriate personal medical services of the type usually provided by general medical practitioners;
   (*b*) the giving by doctors of advice to women on contraception, the medical examination of women seeking such advice, the treatment of such women and the supply to such women of contraceptive substances and appliances (which services are hereinafter referred to as 'contraceptive services'); and
   (*c*) in accordance with and to the extent provided for by these regulations, the provision by doctors of pharmaceutical services.]
(2) The arrangements to which paragraph (1) refers shall incorporate the terms of service.]

Regulation 3 is reflected in the terms of service of the GP which are contained in Schedule 1 to the Regulations and which prescribe the relationship between the FPC and the GP. Paragraph 13 provides:

Service to patients
13. Subject to [paragraphs 3 and 36A], a doctor shall render to his patients all necessary and appropriate personal medical services of the type usually provided by general medical practitioners. He shall do so at his practice premises or, if the condition of the patient so requires elsewhere in his practice area or at the place where the patient was residing when accepted by the doctor, or, if a patient was on the list of a practice declared vacant, when the doctor succeeded to the vacancy, or at some other place where the doctor has agreed to visit and treat him if the patient's condition so requires, and has informed the patient and the Committee accordingly. The doctor shall not be required to visit and treat the patient at any other place. Such services include arrangements for referring patients as necessary to any other services provided under the Health Service Acts and advice to enable them to take advantage of the local authority social services. [This paragraph shall not impose an obligation on the doctor to provide contraceptive services, nor, except in an emergency, maternity medical services unless he had undertaken to provide such services.]

As Brazier points out, a GP must be entered on the FPC's medical list for the area in which he wishes to practice. The Regulations differentiate between general medical services, maternity services and contraceptive services. A GP has a discretion whether to provide the latter two services. As paragraph 13 above indicates, he is obliged to do so only if 'he ha[s] undertaken to provide such services'. In addition to these services, a GP may also provide 'pharmaceutical services' (see Regulations 29B *et seq*).

One further point to notice is that Brazier talks of the 'contract between the GP and the FPC'. Conventional analysis would lead to the conclusion that the relationship is one of a contract of services and not service. In *Wadi v Cornwall and Isles of Scilly Family Practitioner Committee* [1985] ICR 492, however, the Employment Appeal Tribunal curiously held that no contract existed between the GP and the FPC. The basis of the decision was that because the relationship was wholly governed by Regulations which are a creature of statute and impose mandatory terms, the necessary consensual element of a contract was lacking. Do you agree? Is a standard form 'contract' any less of a contract than any other? If the answer is yes, why should it matter that the standard form, in this case, is derived from a statutory instrument?

(ii)   The hospital doctor

Hospital doctors, whether junior or senior, are employed by the relevant health authority under a contract of service. The 1974 Regulations do not apply to them. Their conditions of service are, at least in theory, a matter of agreement between the doctor and the health authority. In practice, they are not. There are two reasons. First, Parliament has laid down some matters, which are no longer open to negotiation, for example, relating to the process of appointment of consultants. Secondly, a hospital doctor's terms of employment are negotiated nationally ('Terms and Conditions of Service of Hospital Medical and Dental Staff (England and Wales)'—the 'red book'). By virtue of certain statutory provisions (which we will see shortly) a doctor may not be employed on less (or indeed more) favourable terms than these. In addition to these statutory provisions, it is likely that the many Government circulars dealing particularly with disciplinary proceedings (eg HM(61)112 and HC(82)13) are either expressly incorporated into the contracts of hospital doctors or would, as a matter of law, be regarded as implied.

This is not the place for a detailed consideration of the terms of the relevant legislation. We will content ourselves with setting out its basic provisions (see more generally, *Disciplining and Dismissing Doctors in the National Health Service* by T Bunbury and A McGregor (1988) *passim*).

Notice also that beyond the general enabling provisions set out here, there are the National Health Service (Appointment of Consultants) Regulations 1982 (SI 1982 No 276). These Regulations lay down, for example, (i) a requirement that a consultant post be advertised (Reg 5); (ii) the constitution of the appointments committee (Reg 6); (iii) rules relating to the selection procedure (Reg 7); (iv) rules relating to who may be appointed (Reg 8).

The National Health Service Act 1977, Schedule 5, paragraph 10 provides:

10. (1) Subject to and in accordance with regulations and such directions as may be given by the Secretary of State, an authority [. . .] may employ such officers as it may determine at such remuneration and on such conditions of service as it may determine; and regulations and directions under this sub-paragraph may contain provision—

(*a*) with respect to the qualifications of persons who may be employed as officers of an authority;

(*b*) requiring an authority to employ, for the purpose of performing prescribed functions of the authority or any other body, officers having prescribed qualifications or experience; and

(*c*) as to the manner in which any officers of an authority are to be appointed.

. . .

(4) Regulations made in pursuance of this paragraph shall not require that all consultants employed by an authority are to be so employed whole-time.

The hospital doctor's conditions of employment are regulated by the National Health Service (Remuneration and Conditions of Service) Regulations 1974 (SI 1974 No 296). Regulation 3 provides:

3.—(1) Subject to paragraph (3) of this regulation, the remuneration of any officer who belongs to a class of officers whose remuneration has been the subject of negotiations by a negotiating body and has been approved by the Secretary of State after considering the result of those negotiations shall be neither more nor less than the remuneration so approved whether or not it is paid out of moneys provided by Parliament.

(2) Subject as aforesaid, where conditions of service, other than conditions with respect to remuneration, of any class of officers have been the subject of negotiations by a negotiating body and have been approved by the Secretary of State after considering the result of those negotiations, the conditions of service of any officer belonging to that class shall include the conditions so approved.

(3) The remuneration or other conditions of service approved under paragraphs (1) and (2) of this regulation may in the case of an individual officer or of officers of a particular description be varied by an authority only as may be provided for by directions given by the Secretary of State.

(b) THE DOCTOR IN PRIVATE PRACTICE

Little need be said here except to note that if the doctor is employed by a private hospital or clinic then his terms and conditions of employment will be a matter of agreement between him and his employer. If, as is likely, the doctor also works within the NHS, certain terms would, however, be unlawful, if they required the doctor to break his contract with the health authority which also employs him. For example, his NHS contract may limit the amount of professional time he spends in private practice. Further, certain terms could be contrary to public policy if, for example, they tend to compromise him in the professional obligations he owes to his patients, whether private or under the NHS. An illustration of this latter example would be if he were required in his contract with a private clinic to refer all patients he sees within the NHS seeking, say, hip replacements to the private clinic. This term would not necessarily allow the doctor to act in the best interests of his patient and would, consequently, be held by a court to be contrary to public policy and hence void.

The patient

It may seem blindingly obvious who are a doctor's patients. However, the relevant law may not be quite as straight forward. As we shall show, the notion of who is a patient *prima facie* turns on the presence of an agreement between a doctor and an individual. But, there is more to it than that. First, an individual may become a doctor's patient without the doctor's explicit consent. This is particularly well illustrated, as we shall see, in the case of a general practitioner working within the NHS. Of course, the majority by his patients will be so with his agreement. Secondly, in the case of those who are unable to comprehend the meaning of being a patient and receiving care (for example, the mentally-ill or young children), the element of consent by *them* will be absent.

Let us now analyse the situations which arise.

(a) THE ADULT PATIENT

(i) In the NHS

1. *Consensual*

With a GP. As we have already noticed, a person will be a GP's patient by virtue of an agreement between them. The first stage involves an application to be included on a GP's medical list. The process whereby a person applies to have his name included on a GP's general medical services list and/or maternity medical services list is set out in Regulations 14 and 23 respectively of the National Health Service (General Medical and Pharmaceutical) Regulations 1974, as amended (amendments in the extracts which follow are indicated by square brackets).

14.—(1) Subject to regulation 18 [see below], application to a doctor for inclusion on his list shall be made by delivering to the doctor a medical card or a form of application signed (in each case) by the applicant or a person authorised on his behalf.

(2) (*a*) A woman may apply to a doctor who has undertaken to provide contraceptive services (whether or not she is included in the list of a doctor for the provision of other personal medical services) to be accepted by him for the provision to her of contraceptive services;

(*b*) such application shall be for the provision of such services for a term of 12 months from the date of acceptance; so however that either the woman or the doctor may terminate the provision to her by him or such services at any time during the term of 12 months;

(*c*) on any such termination or at the end of the term of 12 months whichever first occurs the woman may apply or re-apply to a doctor to be accepted by him for the provision to her of such services and sub-paragraph (*b*) above shall apply to such further application.

18.—(1) A person who—

(*a*) has changed his place of residence from that shown on his medical card, or

(*b*) has obtained in writing on his medical card the consent of the doctor on whose list he is included to transfer to the list of another doctor, or

(*c*) is on the list of a doctor who has obtained the approval of the Committee to a change in the place where he is available for consultation, or

(*d*) having sent his medical card to the Committee, or, if it is not available, applied to the Committee on a form supplied by it for a replacement, has given to the Committee notice in writing of his wish to transfer to the list of another doctor, may . . . apply to a doctor for acceptance on that doctor's list . . .

(3) In any other case [ie not (*d*)] to which paragraph (1) applies a person who applies to and is refused acceptance by another doctor, may apply to the Committee for assignment.

(4) Subject as hereinafter provided, the Committee shall, on the death or on the removal or withdrawal from the medical list of a doctor, [notify the persons on the list of that doctor of the death or on the removal or withdrawal].

(5) A Committee shall inform a doctor as soon as practicable of the removal of a patient from his list on transfer to the list of another doctor.

23.—(1) A woman who, after a doctor has diagnosed that she is pregnant, requires the provision of maternity medical services may arrange for the provision of such services with either—

(*a*) any doctor on the obstetric list, or

(*b*) the doctor on whose list she is included, or

(*c*) any doctor who has under regulation 21(1) [set out below] accepted her as a temporary resident.

(2) A woman who has arranged with a doctor for the provision of maternity medical services may agree with him to terminate that arrangement. In default of such agreement she may apply to the Committee for permission to terminate the arrangement and the Committee after considering the representations if any made by either party and after consulting the Local Medical Committee may terminate the arrangement. Where an arrangement is terminated either under this paragraph or as a result of an application by the doctor under paragraph 12 [set out below] of the terms of service, the woman shall have the right to make a fresh arrangement.

Schedule 1 of the Regulations which sets out, you will recall, the doctor's terms of service provides in paragraph 6:

Acceptance of patients

6.—(1) Subject to sub-paragraph (2), a doctor may agree to accept a person on his list if the person is eligible to be accepted by him.

(2) While a doctor is responsible for treating the patients of another doctor who has given notice of retirement to the Committee or has died, he may not consent to the transfer of any of those patients under regulation 18 to his own list or that of his partner or principal.

(3) When a doctor has agreed to accept a person on his list, he shall within 14 days of receiving it, or as soon thereafter as is practicable, send to the Committee, the medical card or form of application, signed by or on behalf of both the person and the doctor. Where any person is authorised by the doctor to sign the card or form on behalf of that doctor, he shall, in addition to his signature, add the doctor's name.

So, *creation* of the relationship of doctor and patient will usually be consensual. But this is not always the case, as the following examples taken from the 1974 Regulations illustrate.

Assignment by FPC

Assignment of persons to doctors

16.—(1) If a person who is not on the list of any doctor has been refused acceptance by a doctor for inclusion on his list, or if a person who has been refused acceptance by a doctor as a temporary resident, applies to the Committee for assignment to a doctor, his application shall be considered by the Allocation Joint Committee, who shall assign him to and notify accordingly such a doctor as they think fit, having regard to—

(a) the distance between the person's residence and the practice premises of the doctors in the area;

(b) whether within the previous 6 months the person has been removed from the list of any doctor in the area at the request of the doctor; and

(c) such other circumstances, including those concerning the doctors in the area and their practices, as the Allocation Joint Committee think relevant:

Provided that—

(i) a doctor shall not be required to provide contraceptive services for a patient assigned to him under this paragraph, unless pursuant to the provisions of regulation 14(2), he accepts her for the provision of such services;

(ii) a person shall not, without the consent of the Secretary of State, be assigned under this paragraph to a doctor whose list exceeds the maximum permitted by these regulations.]

These provisions are reflected in Schedule 1, paragraph 4(4) (ie, included in the GP's terms of service) which provides:

(4) Where the Committee has notified a doctor that it is applying for the Secretary of State's consent under the proviso to regulation 16(1), the doctor shall give the person proposed for assignment any immediately necessary treatment until the Committee has notified him that—

(a) the Secretary of State has determined that the person shall not be assigned to that doctor; and

(b) either the person has been accepted by, or assigned to, another doctor or another doctor has been notified that an application has been made under the proviso to regulation 16(1) to assign that person to him;

but where the Secretary of State has determined that a person shall not be assigned to a doctor, and the Committee is satisfied, after due enquiry, that the person still wishes to be assigned to a doctor, the Committee shall as soon as practicable request its Allocation Joint Committee to assign that person to another doctor or, as the case may be, seek the Secretary of State's consent to assignment to another doctor under the proviso to regulation 16(1).

Temporary residence. Regulation 21(1) provides:

Arrangements for temporary residents

21.—(1) A person requiring treatment who—

[(a) is not on the list of a doctor providing general medical services in the locality where he is temporarily residing;

(b) normally resides in a school or similar institution in the locality but is temporarily residing at home in that locality;

(c) normally resides at home in the locality but is temporarily residing in any institution in that locality; or]

(d) is moving from place to place and is not for the time being resident in any place;

may apply to any doctor providing services [in the locality] in which he is temporarily residing to be accepted by him as a temporary resident and, subject to paragraph (2) [which defines the meaning of temporary resident], if he is so accepted and is a person mentioned in sub-paragraph (a), (b) or (c) of this paragraph, he shall not be removed from the list of any doctor for which he is already included.

You will notice the words 'may apply' in Regulation 21. Schedule 1, para 4(7) reflects this as regards the doctor.

7. A doctor may accept a person requiring treatment as a temporary resident in accordance with regulation 21 and the provisions of regulation 17 concerning the maximum number of persons he may have on his list shall not restrict him from accepting such a person as a temporary resident.

But, the limits on the need for the doctor's consent are apparent from para 4(3):

(3) If a doctor . . . refuses to accept as a temporary resident a person to whom regulation 21 applies, he shall on request give that person any immediately necessary treatment for one period not exceeding 14 days from the date when that person was refused acceptance or until that person has been accepted by or assigned to another doctor, whichever period is the less.

Emergency. Schedule 1, para 4(1)(*h*) of the 1974 Regulations provides that a doctor's patients will include:

(*h*) persons to whom he may be requested to give treatment which is immediately required owing to an accident or other emergency at any place in his practice area if—
    (i) he is not a doctor to whom paragraph 5 [infirm or elderly doctors] applies, and
    (ii) he is not, at the time of the request, relieved under paragraph 16(2) [reasonable delegation to a deputy] of his obligation to give treatment personally, and
  [(iii) he is available to provide such treatment,
or any persons to whom he may be requested, and he agrees, to give treatment which is immediately required owing to an accident or other emergency at any place in the locality of any Committee on whose medical list he is included, provided, in either case, that there is no doctor who, at the time of the request, is under an obligation otherwise than under this sub-paragraph to give treatment to that person, or there is such a doctor but, after being requested to attend, he is unable to attend and give treatment immediately required;]

Death, retirement, ill health of the doctor. Regulation 19 provides, *inter alia*:

[*Temporary provision of general medical services*
19.—(1) The provisions of this regulation shall apply in relation to the making of arrangements for the temporary provision of general medical services.

(2) Where a doctor ceases to be included on the medical list or his registration in the register is suspended . . . the Committee, after consultation with the Local Medical Committee, may—
  (*a*) make arrangements for the temporary provision of general medical services for that doctor's patients, which arrangements may consist of or include the appointment of one or more doctors to undertake the treatment of such persons;
  (*b*) where a doctor included on a medical list . . . ceases by reason of death to be so included and within 7 days of the date of death any person applies to the Committee in writing on behalf of the estate of that doctor for the appointment of one or more named doctors, appoint one or more of the named doctors to undertake the treatment of the deceased doctor's patients.

(3) The Committee may make such arrangements as it thinks fit for the accommodation and other needs of any doctor appointed under paragraph (2) and, in the case of any doctor appointed under paragraph (2)(*b*), shall where practicable first consult any person who applied to it for the appointment of that doctor.

(4) . . . arrangements under paragraph (2) shall subsist for such period as the Committee may determine, but not beyond the date on which the vacancy is filled or the suspension referred to in paragraph (2) ceases to have effect.

(5) Where it appears to a Committee, after consultation with the Local Medical Committee, that a doctor is incapable of carrying out adequately his obligations under the terms of service because of his physical or mental condition, it may require him to be medically examined.

(6) Where a Committee is satisfied—

(*a*) after receiving from the Local Medical Committee a report under paragraph (9) that because of his physical or mental condition; or

(*b*) that because of continued absence,

a doctor's obligations under the terms of service are not being carried out adequately, it may, after consultation with the Local Medical Committee and with the consent of the Secretary of State, make arrangements for the temporary provision of general medical services for that doctor's patients, which arrangements may consist of or include the appointment of one or more doctors to undertake the treatment of such persons.

(7) ... arrangements under paragraph (6) shall subsist for such period as the Committee may determine, but not, in a case to which paragraph (6)(*a*) applies, beyond the date on which the Committee is satisfied, after consulting the Local Medical Committee, that the doctor is fit to resume his practice.

Schedule 1, para 4(1)(*j*) gives effect to this Regulation, making it clear, as part of the doctor's terms of service, that a doctor's patient shall include:

(*j*) during the period of an appointment under regulation 19, persons whom he has been appointed to treat temporarily:

Non-inclusion on medical list. Schedule 1, para 4(3) provides:

(3) If a doctor refuses to accept for inclusion on his list a person who lives in his practice area and who is not on the list of another doctor practising in that area ... he shall on request give that person any immediately necessary treatment for one period not exceeding 14 days from the date when that person was refused acceptance or until that person has been accepted by or assigned to another doctor, whichever period is the less.

Failure of a person to produce a medical card. Schedule 1, para 4(2) provides:

(2) If a person applies to a doctor for treatment and claims to be on that doctor's list, but fails to produce his medical card on request and the doctor has reasonable doubts about that person's claim, the doctor shall give any necessary treatment and shall be entitled to demand and accept a fee [pursuant to the relevant provisions of Schedule 1].

What of *terminating* the relationship of doctor and patient? Does this depend on the consent of the parties? Schedule 1, paras 10–12 of the 1974 Regulations are the principal provisions dealing with termination of the relationship.

Termination of responsibility for patients

10. A doctor may have any person removed from his list by requiring the Committee so to do and the removal shall take effect on the date of acceptance by, or assignment to, another doctor or on the eighth day after the Committee is so required whichever first occurs, but, if the doctor is at the date when removal would take effect, treating the person otherwise than at intervals of more than 7 days, the doctor shall inform the Committee of the fact and removal shall take effect on the eighth day after the Committee receives notification from him that the patient no longer needs such treatment or upon acceptance by another doctor, whichever first occurs.

11. A doctor desiring to terminate his responsibility for a temporary resident may so inform the Committee; and the date on which his responsibility ceases shall be decided under paragraph 10, as if the temporary resident were a person on his list.

12. A doctor may cease to provide maternity medical services to a woman by agreement with her. In default of agreement the doctor may apply to the Committee for permission to terminate the arrangement and the Committee may terminate the arrangement after considering the representations, if any, made by either party and after consulting the Local Committee. Where a doctor ceases to provide any maternity medical services, he shall inform any woman for whom he has arranged to provide such services that he is ceasing to provide them and that she may make fresh arrangements to receive those services from another doctor.

(See also Regulations 14 and 23 set out *supra* pp 102–3.)

With a hospital doctor When a patient attends a hospital whether as an in-patient or out-patient, at least two distinct legal relationships call for analysis: the relationship between doctor and patient and between the hospital and the patient. (We use the word 'patient' in the context of this second relationship for convenience only. We take the view that a person can only be the patient *stricto sensu* of a doctor, although a hospital may owe him a duty of care under the law of negligence, as we shall see.) Here we are concerned with the relationship between the hospital doctor and the patient.

In the classic (though now dated) work by Lord Nathan, *Medical Negligence* (1957), the underlying explanation of how and why the doctor/patient relationship exists is stated (pp 8 and 10):

> The medical man's duty of care arises then quite independently of any contract with his patient. It is based simply upon the fact that the medical man has undertaken the care and treatment of the patient.

Later Nathan continues:

> It is clear then that the duty of care which is imposed upon the medical man arises quite independently of contract. It is a duty in tort which is based upon the relationship between the medical man and his patient, owing its existence to the fact that the medical man has assumed responsibility for the care, treatment or examination of the patient, as the case may be.

This, in our view, properly reflects the position in English law, as far as it goes, as regards the hospital doctor. Of course, it needs some rather more rigorous analysis. At what point can we determine that the doctor has undertaken the care and treatment of the patient? Put another way, when has the doctor 'assumed responsibility' for the patient? (Let us leave aside for the moment the question whether a doctor/patient relationship may arise by implication in some circumstances, and the difficult question of emergencies.) Consider the process by which a person is normally seen by a hospital doctor. (We shall assume that the patient is an in-patient, but there is no material legal difference if he is an out-patient.)

A patient, emergencies apart, is admitted to an NHS hospital through a formal procedure of reference by a GP and acceptance by a consultant after consultation with the hospital's manager. The admission is to occupy a bed assigned to the relevant consultant within the hospital. The question immediately arises as to the point at which the doctor/patient relationship is created? You will realise immediately that for the medical lawyer the importance of this is to determine when, if at all, a duty is owed by a doctor to a particular person.

Consider the following examples:

Patient 'A' arrives at hospital pursuant to an arrangement to admit him to the care of consultant 'X'. Patient 'A':

1. walks into the hospital and suffers an unexpected heart attack and he requires immediate care;

2. is brought into the hospital by ambulance personnel on a stretcher and he is dropped by them, causing him injury;

3. is placed in a bed in the wrong ward and his condition deteriorates as a consequence;

4. is taken to the ward where the consultant has beds but he receives inappropriate care, e g he is given a meal when he should not have been;

5. asks for assistance during the night. Dr 'Y' who is responsible for consultant 'X's' patients during the night and has just come on duty having been on holiday, and so has never met patient 'A', fails to respond to patient 'A's' request causing patient 'A' harm;

6. suffers a heart attack. Dr 'Z' who is a member of another consultant's team is asked by a nurse to help care for him. Dr 'Z' declines saying that he does not know enough about patient 'A's' medical history.

In formulating answers to the above you should bear in mind:

(a) The admitting consultant's duty may include making all appropriate arrangements for admission to the hospital.

(b) It may not be part of the consultant's duty to be on hand at all times to deal with every eventuality that may arise concerning a person whom it has been agreed to admit under his care.

(c) A consultant as the leader of a team remains responsible for the care of his patient at all times. In fulfulment of this duty he may, of course, from time to time leave the patient in the care of another doctor, but the responsibility remains his.

(d) A hospital may be under a primary duty to exercise all due care as regards anyone to whom it has agreed to provide medical services.

(e) The law does not require a doctor to act as a good samaritan towards any person in the absence of a special relationship based upon an undertaking by the doctor to take care of that person. The conjunction of the presence of an ill person and a doctor in the same ward may not be sufficient to create a special relationship in law when the person has not been accepted as that doctor's patient.

Let us now return to the two additional questions we raised earlier: whether a doctor/patient relationship can arise by implication or because of an emergency.

BY IMPLICATION. An agreement to create the relationship of doctor and patient will be implied between a patient and *any* member of the medical team involved in the clinical management, whether or not the patient is aware of his existence or identity. For example, it is often the practice to require a patient to sign a 'consent form' containing the following words:

> No assurance has been given to me that the operation/treatment will be performed or administered by any particular practitioner (*Consent, Confidentiality, Disclosure of Medical Records* (1988 Medical Protection Society), General Consent Form).

These words became popular after the case of *Michael v Molesworth* (1950) 2 Br Med J 171 in which a successful action was brought by a patient when someone other than the doctor he had expected would carry out the surgery performed the (successful) operation. (Damages of £1 were awarded.) The case concerned a private patient and so was pleaded in contract. Do you think that the same result would be reached in relation to an NHS patient today, even if these words were not included in the consent form? If not, why not? Do you think the court would take account of the fact that a patient in an NHS hospital is aware of limits on resources, both human and material, and of the realities of team care?

What if the member of the team who carries out the treatment is a trainee (see the discussion of *Wilsher, infra* p 400 et seq).

EMERGENCIES. We have already seen the situation of the GP under the 1974 Regulations. What is the position of the hospital doctor? The issue arose in the case of *Barnett v Chelsea and Kensington Committee Hospital Management* [1968] 1 All ER 1068:

Nield J: I turn to consider the nature of the duty which the law imposes on persons in the position of the defendants and their servants and agents. The authorities deal in the main with the duties of doctors, surgeons, consultants, nurses and staff when a person is treated either by a doctor at his surgery or the patient's home or when the patient is treated in or at a hospital. In *Cassidy v Ministry of Health* [1951] 1 All ER 574 at 585, DENNING, LJ, dealt with the duties of hospital authorities and said:

In my opinion, authorities who run a hospital, be they local authorities, government boards, or any other corporation, are in law under the self-same duty as the humblest doctor. Whenever they accept a patient for treatment, they must use reasonable care and skill to cure him of his ailment. The hospital authorities cannot, of course, do it by themselves. They have no ears to listen through the stethoscope, and no hands to hold the knife. They must do it by the staff which they employ, and, if their staff are negligent in giving the treatment, they are just as liable for that negligence as is anyone else who employs others to do his duties for him. Is there any possible difference in law, I ask, can there be, between hospital authorities who accept a patient for treatment and railway or shipping authorities who accept a passenger for carriage? None whatever. Once they undertake the task, they come under a duty to use care in the doing of it, and that is so whether they do it for reward or not.

Here the problem is different and no authority bearing directly on it has been cited to me. It is to determine the duty of those who provide and run a casualty department when a person presents himself at that department complaining of illness or injury and before he is treated and received into the hospital wards. This is not a case of a casualty department which closes its doors and says that no patients can be received. The three watchmen entered the defendants' hospital without hindrance, they made complaints to the nurse who received them and she in turn passed those complaints on to the medical casualty officer, and he sent a message through the nurse purporting to advise the three men. Is there, on these facts, shown to be created a relationship between the three watchmen and the hospital staff such as gives rise to a duty of care in the defendants which they owe to the three men? . . .

In my judgment, there was here such a close and direct relationship between the hospital and the watchmen that there was imposed on the hospital a duty of care which they owed to the watchmen. Thus I have no doubt that Nurse Corbett and Dr Banerjee were under a duty to the deceased to exercise that skill and care which is to be expected of persons in such positions acting reasonably, or, as it is, I think very helpfully, put by the learned author of Winfield on Torts (7th Edn) p 183—

where anyone is engaged in a transaction in which he holds himself out as having professional skill, the law expects him to show the average amount of competence associated with the proper discharge of the duties of that profession or trade or calling, and if he falls short of that and injures someone in consequence, he is not behaving reasonably.

Moreover, the author proceeds to give a warning that the rule must be applied with some care to see that too high a degree of skill is not demanded, and he gives as an example 'a passer-by who renders emergency first-aid after an accident is not required to show the skill of a qualified surgeon'.

You will recall that our concern is to discover the point at which in the law the doctor/patient relationship is created. *Barnett* is usually cited as authority for the proposition that in the case of a person presenting himself at an emergency department of a hospital, the doctor on call has a duty to care for the person on his arrival at the emergency department, ie that a doctor/patient relationship has come into existence by the fact of his presenting himself. Is this too casual a reading of the case? Is it not really a case in the first instance about the primary duty of a hospital to provide emergency medical services, when the hospital has indicated its preparedness to do so by having an emergency department which is open? (For a discussion of the primary duty of a hospital, see *infra* p 373 et seq.) We can test this proposition by imagining the situation in which the receptionist without contacting the medical staff turns Mr Barnett away? Would there be any question there of the doctor on call being in breach of any duty? Surely any question about the creation of the doctor/patient relationship only arises when the doctor is (or ought to be) aware that there is a person presenting himself who apparently requires emergency care?

We have spoken of the hospital having an emergency department open to receive those who need emergency assistance. What if Mr Barnett had, through error, presented himself at the reception desk of the main part of the hospital? Would there be any duty owed to him and who would owe it—the hospital, primarily, or through its servants, or the doctor on emergency call? Would your answer be different if the doctor on emergency call happened to be standing at the desk talking to the receptionist at the particular time?

2. *Non-consensual*

As we have already seen, even though the usual situation is that the doctor and patient have agreed to enter into a relationship, there are exceptions in which Parliament has intervened to assign a patient to a doctor, regardless of the doctor's agreement.

Let us now turn to some more explicit examples of circumstances in which the doctor/patient relationship is non-consensual.

The public health laws

Here, we see individuals who are required to become patients on grounds of public policy. The Public Health (Control of Disease) Act 1984 provides for the medical examination, removal to hospital and detention in hospital of those who are (or are believed to be) suffering from a 'notifiable disease'. Section 10 of the Act defines 'notifiable disease' as meaning cholera, plague, relapsing fever, smallpox and typhus.

Medical examination
35.—(1) If a justice of the peace (acting, if he deems it necessary, ex parte) is satisfied, on a written certificate issued by a registered medical practitioner nominated by the local authority for a district—
  (*a*) that there is reason to believe that some person in the district—
    (i) is or has been suffering from a notifiable disease, or
    (ii) though not suffering from such a disease, is carrying an organism that is capable of causing it, and
  (*b*) that in his own interest, or in the interest of his family, or in the public interest, it is expedient that he should be medically examined, and
  (*c*) that he is not under the treatment of a registered medical practitioner or that the registered medical practitioner who is treating him consents to the making of an order under this section,
the justice may order him to be medically examined by a registered medical practitioner so nominated.
  (2) An order under this section may be combined with a warrant under subsection (3) of section 61 below authorising a registered medical practitioner nominated by the local authority to enter any premises, and for the purposes of that subsection that practitioner shall, if not an officer of the local authority, be treated as one.

(3) In this section, references to a person's being medically examined shall be construed as including references to his being submitted to bacteriological and radiological tests and similar investigations.

Medical examination of group of persons believed to comprise carrier of notifiable disease
36.—(1) If a justice of the peace (acting, if he deems it necessary, ex parte) is satisfied, on a written certificate issued by the proper officer of the local authority for a district—

(*a*) that there is reason to believe that one of a group of persons, though not suffering from a notifiable disease, is carrying an organism that is capable of causing it, and

(*b*) that in the interest of those persons or their families, or in the public interest, it is expedient that those persons should be medically examined,

the justice may order them to be medically examined by a registered medical practitioner nominated by the local authority for that district.

(2) Subsections (2) and (3) of section 35 above apply in relation to subsection (1) above as they apply in relation to subsection (1) of that section.

Removal to hospital of person with notifiable disease
37.—(1) Where a justice of the peace (acting, if he deems it necessary, ex parte) is satisfied, on the application of the local authority, that a person is suffering from a notifiable disease and—

(*a*) that his circumstances are such that proper precautions to prevent the spread of infection cannot be taken, or that such precautions are not being taken, and

(*b*) that serious risk of infection is thereby caused to other persons, and

(*c*) that accommodation for him is available in a suitable hospital vested in the Secretary of State,

the justice may, with the consent of the Area or District Health Authority responsible for the administration of the hospital, order him to be removed to it.

(2) An order under this section may be addressed to such officer of the local authority as the justice may think expedient, and that officer and any officer of the hospital may do all acts necessary for giving effect to the order.

Detention in hospital of person with notifiable disease
38.—(1) Where a justice of the peace (acting, if he deems it necessary, ex parte) in and for the place in which a hospital for infectious diseases is situated is satisfied, on the application of any local authority, that an inmate of the hospital who is suffering from a notifiable disease would not on leaving the hospital be provided with lodging or accommodation in which proper precautions could be taken to prevent the spread of the disease by him, the justice may order him to be detained in the hospital.

(2) An order made under subsection (1) above may direct detention for a period specified in the order, but any justice of the peace acting in and for the same place may extend a period so specified as often as it appears to him to be necessary to do so.

(3) Any person who leaves a hospital contrary to an order made under this section for his detention there shall be liable on summary conviction to a fine not exceeding level 1 on the standard scale, and the court may order him to be taken back to the hospital.

(4) An order under this section may be addressed—

(*a*) in the case of an order for a person's detention, to such officer of the hospital, and

(*b*) in the case of an order made under subsection (3) above, to such officer of the local authority on whose application the order for detention was made,

as the justice may think expedient, and that officer and any officer of the hospital may do all acts necessary for giving effect to the order.

In 1985 the Secretary of State promulgated (pursuant to the 1984 Act) the

Public Health (Infectious Diseases) Regulations 1985 (SI 1985 No 434). Subsequently, these were replaced by the Public Health (Infectious Diseases) Regulations 1988 (SI 1988 No 1546). They provide as follows:

Public health enactments applied to certain diseases
3. There shall apply to the diseases listed in column (1) of Schedule 1 the enactments in the Act listed in column (2) of that Schedule with the modifications specified in column (2).

Schedule 1 of the regulations applies sections 35, 37, 38 (as modified by regulation 5), 43 and 44 of the 1984 Act to acquired immune deficiency syndrome (AIDS). Regulations 5 and 13 provide as follows:

Modification of section 38 of the Act as it is applied to acquired immune deficiency syndrome
5.—(1) In its application to acquired immune deficiency syndrome section 38(1) of the Act shall be modified in accordance with paragraph (2) below.
    (2) The said section 38(1) shall in addition to the circumstances specified in that section apply so that a justice of the peace may on the application of any local authority (acting if he deems it necessary ex parte) make an order for the detention in hospital of an inmate of that hospital suffering from acquired immune deficiency syndrome if the justice is satisfied that on his leaving the hospital proper precautions to prevent the spread of that disease would not be taken by him—
    (*a*) in his lodging or accommodation, or
    (*b*) in other places to which he may be expected to go if not detained in the hospital.

Enforcement and Publication
13(1). These regulations shall be enforced and executed—
    (*a*) in a district, by the local authority for that district, or
    (*b*) in a port health district, by the port health authority for that district so far as these regulations are applicable thereto.

A number of questions arise:

(1) Why are the Regulations couched in terms which apply to AIDS? Does this mean that they do not apply to an individual who is diagnosed as HIV positive but who has not developed AIDS?
(2) If the answer is that the Regulations do not apply to a person diagnosed as HIV postive, does this not mean that the purpose behind Regulation 5(2), modifying s 38 of the Act, may, in part, be defeated?
(3) Why do you think the Secretary of State did not make AIDS a 'notifiable disease'?
(4) Do the 1984 Act or 1988 Regulations allow for the *treatment* of an individual who is detained under them?

Mental health

A further example of a doctor/patient relationship which is non-consensual arises in relation to the mentally disordered. The original justification was represented as being the need to protect the public. Today, although this justification may persist in some cases, the justification advanced is a therapeutic one; the desire to promote, in so far as is possible, the well-being of the mentally disordered patient. This latter justification is certainly so in our first instance, that of civil commitment. It may be less true, however, in other instances.

Compulsory admission to hospital other than through criminal proceedings (Civil Commitment)

MENTAL HEALTH ACT 1983

Admission for assessment

2.—(1) A patient may be admitted to hospital and detained there for the period allowed by subsection (4) below in pursuance of an application (in this Act referred to as 'an application for admission for assessment') made in accordance with subsections (2) and (3) below.

(2) An application for admission for assessment may be made in respect of a patient on the grounds that—

(a) he is suffering from mental disorder of a nature or degree which warrants the detention of the patient in a hospital for assessment (or for assessment followed by medical treatment) for at least a limited period; and

(b) he ought to be so detained in the interests of his own health or safety or with a view to the protection of other persons.

(3) An application for admission for assessment shall be founded on the written recommendations in the prescribed form of two registered medical practitioners, including in each case a statement that in the opinion of the practitioner the condtions set out in subsection (2) above are complied with.

(4) Subject to the provisions of section 29(4) [which provides for the extension of the period of detention in specified circumstances] below, a patient admitted to hospital in pursuance of an application for admission for assessment may be detained for a period not exceeding 28 days beginning with the day on which he is admitted, but shall not be detained after the expiration of that period unless before it has expired he has become liable to be detained by virtue of a subsequent application, order or direction under the following provisions of this Act,

Admission for treatment

3.—(1) A patient may be admitted to a hospital and detained there for the period allowed by the following provisions of this Act in pursuance of an application (in this Act referred to as 'an application for admission for treatment') made in accordance with this section.

(2) An application for admission for treatment may be made in respect of a patient on the grounds that—

(a) he is suffering from mental illness, severe mental impairment, psychopathic disorder or mental impairment and his mental disorder is of a nature or degree which makes it appropriate for him to receive medical treatment in a hospital; and

(b) in the case of psychopathic disorder or mental impairment, such treatment is likely to alleviate or prevent a deterioration of his condition; and

(c) it is necessary for the health or safety of the patient or for the protection of other persons that he should receive such treatment and it cannot be provided unless he is detained under this section.

(3) An application for admission for treatment shall be founded on the written recommendations in the prescribed form of two registered medical practitioners, including in each case a statement that in the opinion of the practitioner the conditions set out in subsection (2) above are complied with; and each such recommendation shall include—

(a) such particulars as may be prescribed of the grounds for that opinion so far as it relates to the conditions set out in paragraphs (a) and (b) of that subsection; and

(b) a statement of the reasons for that opinion so far as it relates to the conditions set out in paragraph (c) of that subsection, specifying whether other methods of dealing with the patient are available and, if so, why they are not appropriate.

Admission for assessment in cases of emergency

4.—(1) In any case of urgent necessity, an application for admission for assessment may be made in respect of a patient in accordance with the following provisions of this section, and any application so made is in this Act referred to as 'an emergency application'.

(2) An emergency application may be made either by an approved social worker or by the nearest relative of the patient; and every such application shall include a statement that it is of urgent necessity for the patient to be admitted and detained under section 2 above, and that compliance with the provisions of this Part of this Act relating to applications under that section would involve undesirable delay.

(3) An emergency application shall be sufficient in the first instance if founded on one of the medical recommendations required by section 2 above, given, if practicable, by a practitioner who has previous acquaintance with the patient and otherwise complying with the requirements of section 12 [which sets out the procedure to be followed in making 'medical recommendations'] below so far as applicable to a single recommendation, and verifying the statement referred to in subsection (2) above.

(4) An emergency application shall cease to have effect on the expiration of a period of 72 hours from the time when the patient is admitted to the hospital unless—

(a) the second medical recommendation required by section 2 above is given and received by the managers within that period; and

(b) that recommendation and the recommendation referred to in subsection (3) above together comply with all the requirements of section 12 below (other than the requirement as to the time of signature of the second recommendation).

(For commentary see L Gostin *Mental Health Services—Law and Practice* (1986) chs 9–11, especially ch 11.)

Compulsory admission to hospital through criminal proceedings

A consideration of this is beyond the scope of this book and we only mention it in passing. For the powers to detain in hospital those convicted of criminal offences, see Part III of the Mental Health Act 1983. An extensive commentary can be found in the standard works on mental health law, eg L Gostin *Mental Health Services—Law and Practice* (1986) ch 15 *passim* and B Hoggett, *Mental Health Law* (2nd ed) (1984) ch 5.

(ii) Private practice

Outside the NHS the doctor/patient relationship arises from a contract made between the parties. The relationship is therefore, a consensual one. While we have seen that there is no contract when treatment takes place within the NHS Lord Templeman pointed out in *Sidaway v Bethlem Royal Hospital Governors and the Maudsley Hospital* [1985] 1 All ER 643 at 665 that: '[t]he relationship between doctor and patient is contractual in origin, the doctor performing services in consideration for fees payable by the patient'. We will see later the extent of a doctor's obligations under a contract to provide private health care. Few cases have dealt with these, but one example is the consideration by the courts of agreements to carry out a sterilisation operation, since such procedures are often undertaken by doctors in private practice: *Thake v Maurice* [1986] 1 All ER 497, CA and *Eyre v Measday* [1986] 1 All ER 488. We shall return to these cases later.

We will not analyse here the content of the contract between the doctor and patient. There are, however, certain general points which arise when the relationship is founded on contract and which must be considered.

1. The existence of a contract does not preclude the existence of duties owed by the doctor to his patient in tort.

2. The parties may expressly agree in the contract that the doctor will owe a duty to the patient which is more onerous than that imposed by the law. However, in the absence of such an express term, the courts will not normally *imply* any terms extending the doctor's duties beyond those that he would owe by virtue of the law of tort in any event.

3. The courts will hold invalid any term in a contract which purports to reduce or remove the doctor's duty in tort (see Unfair Contract Terms Act 1977, s 2).

THE CHILD PATIENT

(i) Within the NHS

Having considered adults as patients, we must now consider children. The relationship of doctor and patient comes into existence when the doctor, for his part, undertakes responsibility for the child and, either the child agrees to be the doctor's patient, having the legal capacity so to do or, if lacking such capacity, another, with the authority to act on behalf of the child enters into the relationship for the child. Ordinarily that other will be *a* parent (see Guardianship Act 1973, s 1), but in certain circumstances others may be acting in loco parentis, for example, a local authority, or the High Court if the child is a ward of court.

It is relatively easy to state these propositions, but consider the following.

A young and immature child finds her way to Dr X's surgery. Dr X asks her what he can do for her. She tells him that she is there without the knowledge of her parents who would not wish her to be there.

  (i) Is the girl the doctor's patient?
 (ii) What consequences flow from a decision that she is his patient?
     (a) May he treat her?
     (b) What legal duty, if any, does he owe her in any event?
     (c) Does an obligation to respect her confidence, including the fact that she wishes the visit to be a secret from her parents, arise?
(iii) What consequences flow from a decision that she is not a patient?
     Can these questions only be answered by determining whether 'patient' is a purely descriptive term, or involves a normative element. If the former, nothing necessarily flows from describing her *factually* as a patient since there still falls to be determined the specific obligation (if any) owed to her. If there is a normative element, then to describe her as a patient necessarily means that certain legal consequences flow from that categorisation, such as, that certain rights vest in the patient and certain duties reside in the doctor. (See, eg the discussion of *Gillick supra* p 74 et seq for a more detailed analysis and consideration of its consequences.)

You will recall the 1974 Regulations concerning GPs and their patients. Can any help be derived from them? Regulation 32 provides as follows:

Exercise of choice of doctor or chemist in certain cases
32. An application to a doctor for inclusion on his list or to a chemist for pharmaceutical services *may* be made, either—
> (*a*) on behalf of any person under 16 years of age, by the mother, or in her absence, the father, or in the absence of both parents the guardian or other adult person who has care of the child; or
> (*b*) on behalf of any other person who is incapable of making such an application by a relative or other adult person who has the care of such person; (our emphasis).

You may not find this all that helpful or illuminating. Does it mean that because a parent '*may*', only a parent can?

The position of the child who is incompetent to enter into a relationship with a doctor is, of course, only an example of the more general problem of when an incompetent person may become a patient.

(ii)   Private practice

If a competent minor were to enter a contract for *private* medical care, would the contract be valid? There is old authority to suggest that 'physick' (i e medical care) is a necessary so that any contract may be binding (*Dale v Copping* (1610) 1 Bulst 39 and *Huggins v Wiseman* (1690) Carth 110). It is a nice question whether a court would hold that medical care is now *as a matter of law* capable of being a necessary, given the existence of a national system of free (or nearly free) health care under the NHS.

(c)   OTHER PERSONS

What other individuals may lack the capacity to become a patient? Such persons might be the mentally ill, the senile and the prisoner. As we have shown, the difficulties arise if there is a normative element in the term 'patient'. We take the view that 'patient' contains a normative element, namely, the need for agreement save in exceptional cases. A person will acquire certain rights as a consequence of this agreement but, of course, to reach an agreement he must be both competent and free to do so. The factor which unites this group of persons is their vulnerability. They may either not understand what it is to have rights (and concomitantly insist upon duties), or they may feel themselves under such duress as to be unable to insist upon their rights, especially the right to refuse to be a patient.

If agreement is the necessary element required to demonstrate that someone has become a patient, and agreement connotes comprehension, understanding and voluntariness, then the uncomprehending mentally ill individual or the prisoner under duress may not in law and ethics be patients, although the *factual* description of patient may be ascribed to them. It would seem to follow from this that, as regards the first group, the uncomprehending, they can only become patients, if at all, through the agency of someone else acting on their behalf. As regards the second group, those who would refuse to be patients but for duress, it would appear that they may not be treated as patients without specific statutory authority and no one may purport to agree on their behalf. (For detailed discussion of these problems, see *infra* ch 4.)

Concluding remark

Some may wonder why we have dealt *in extenso* with what many assume to be a straight-forward matter (eg M Brazier writes as regards the hospital doctor in the NHS that 'a hospital *and all its staff* owe a duty to *patients admitted* for treatment' (our emphasis), *Medicine, Patients and the Law*, at p 70). The reason is obvious quite apart from the intrinsic complexity of the issue. Quite simply, the whole of malpractice law, involving as it does consideration of whether a doctor has complied with the duty owed to his patient, cannot come into play unless and until the existence of a doctor/patient relationship has been established. Only then does a doctor owe a duty of care.

Chapter 3

The legal framework of the doctor/patient relationship

Lord Devlin, over 25 years ago, remarked in his Lloyds Robert Lecture to the Medical Society of London (*Samples of Lawmaking* (1962), 'Medicine and Law' 83, 103):

> Is it not a pleasant tribute to the medical profession that by and large it has been able to manage its relations with its patients on the basis of such an understanding [that conduct be regulated by a general understanding of how decent people ought to behave] and without the aid of lawyers and lawmakers?

Times may well have changed.

For convenience, we will analyse the legal rules governing the doctor/patient relationship as follows: (a) the criminal law; (b) the civil law, particularly, the law of torts and contract. There are, of course, other areas of law which are relevant. For example, if a patient is a child, any analysis could not ignore the principles and rules of family law, eg the notion of acting in the 'child's best interests'. Other relevant areas of law, include, eg public law (see *R v Secretary of State for Health and Social Services, ex p Walker*, (1987) Times, 26 November). In our analysis, the first point to notice, and it is most important, is that there is no regime of legal principles in England which specifically regulate the doctor/patient relationship. This point is good even if the courts when applying, for example, the general principles of the law of negligence, do so in a somewhat different manner in cases involving doctors.

There are one or two exceptions to this general proposition. There exist certain statutory duties or obligations which do specifically apply to the medical profession. Some of these statutory provisions carry with them a penalty for non-compliance. Examples of these can be found in the Misuse of Drugs Act 1971, the Poisons Act 1972 (relating, for instance, to record-keeping), and the Births and Deaths Registration Act 1953 (relating to certification of cause of death). Likewise, many statutory provisions require that, for something to be validly or lawfully done, it must be done by a registered medical practitioner eg section 1(4) of the Human Tissue Act 1961 provides, as regards the removal of tissue for the purposes of transplant:

> (4) No such removal, except of eyes or parts or eyes, shall be effected except by a registered medical practitioner, who must have satisfied himself by personal examination of the body that life is extinct.

Let us now turn to consider what are, perhaps, the more important areas of law relevant to the doctor/patient relationship.

The criminal law

To emphasise what we have already said, there is no special criminal law which is particular to the doctor/patient relationship. In his summing-up to the jury in the case of *R v Arthur* (1981) Times, 6 November—a case in which a consultant paediatrician was charged with the attempted murder of a Down's Syndrome baby—Farquharson J said:

There is no special law in this country that places doctors in a separate category and gives them extra protection over the rest of us . . .

Neither in law is there any special power, facility or licence [*inter alia*] to kill children who are handicapped or seriously disadvantaged in an irreversible way. There is no special law of that kind at all. May I hasten to add—and in the same breath—that none of the eminent practitioners who have come before this court has sought to suggest that there is or should be. They have recognised the limitations which the law has placed upon their profession and, indeed, it is the same as the limitation placed upon everybody else.

Compare s 45 of the Canadian Criminal Code which provides:

Everyone is protected from criminal responsibility for performing a surgical operation upon any person for the benefit of that person if (a) the operation is performed with reasonable care and skill, and (b) it is reasonable to perform the operation, having regard to the state of health of the person at the time the operation is performed and to all the circumstances of the case.

Questions

(i) What can this provision mean, in the light of the common law requirement that a doctor may only touch a patient with his consent? Notice that in New Zealand where s 61 of the Crimes Act 1961 is in identical terms to s 45, the 1961 Act was amended in 1977 (by s 2, Crimes Amendments Act 1977) to add the following:

Further provisions relating to surgical operations
61A.—(1) Every one is protected from criminal responsibility for performing with reasonable care and skill any surgical operation upon any person if the operation is performed with the consent of that person, or of any person lawfully entitled to consent on his behalf to the operation, and for a lawful purpose.

(ii) How do the two New Zealand provisions relate to one another? In the absence of s 61A would the consent of the patient have been necessary? If the answer is yes, is s 61 (and s 45 of the Canadian Code) only a statutory recognition that a doctor may treat (surgically) in an emergency a person who is unable to consent?

(iii) Do you think, therefore, that these statutes add or change anything? Is the law in Canada and New Zealand any different from that which applies in England?

If, then, there is no special criminal law which impinges on the doctor/patient relationship, what does the general criminal law have to say? Let us consider first some statutory provisions and then, secondly, the common law.

(i) STATUTORY

The following are examples of criminal law statutes which could impinge upon the doctor/patient relationship and as a result provide limits to the practice of medicine.

There are certain statutes which regulate touching and other harmful contacts.

OFFENCES AGAINST THE PERSON ACT 1861

Shooting or attempting to shoot, or wounding, with intent to do grievous bodily harm, or to resist apprehension
18. Whosoever shall unlawfully and maliciously by any means whatsoever wound or cause any grievous bodily harm to any person . . . with intent . . . to do some . . . grievous bodily harm to any person, or with intent to resist or prevent the lawful

apprehension or detainer of any person, shall be guilty of felony, and being convicted thereof shall be liable, . . . to be kept in penal servitude for life . . .

Inflicting bodily injury, with or without weapon
20. Whosoever shall unlawfully and maliciously wound or inflict any grievous bodily harm upon any other person, either with or without any weapon or instrument, shall be guilty of a misdemeanour, and being convicted thereof shall be liable . . . to imprisonment for not less than five years.

Assault occasioning bodily harm—Common assault
47. Whosoever shall be convicted upon an indictment of any assault occasioning actual bodily harm shall be liable . . . to be kept in penal servitude . . .; and whosoever shall be convicted upon an indictment for a common assault shall be liable, at the discretion of the court, to be imprisoned for any term not exceeding one year, with or without hard labour.

What would make an intervention by a doctor 'harm' within these sections and what may justify it so that it would not amount to a crime? Lord Devlin (*op cit* at 89) said in 1960:

. . . a surgeon who cuts off a limb may in the strict sense intend to do bodily harm.

Professor Stegg in his book, *Law, Ethics and Medicine* (1984), takes a different view (pp 30–31):

There is one matter which arises in relation to more than one offence, and which it is convenient to deal with at this stage. This is whether a medical procedure which benefits bodily health can be regarded as causing bodily harm. The answer might be thought to be obvious. But some lawyers have assumed that operations which are performed to benefit the health of the patient, and which do in fact do so, nevertheless constitute 'bodily harm'. One reason for this may be that 'bodily harm' has been said to include 'any hurt or injury calculated to interfere with . . . health or comfort'.[3] Many therapeutic medical procedures can be said to 'interfere with health or comfort', and to do so in a manner which is 'more than merely transient and trifling'.[4]

But when, in *R v Donovan*,[5] the Court of Criminal Appeal said that bodily harm includes any hurt or injury calculated to interfere with health or comfort, the court was not concerned with medical procedures. In the later case of *DPP v Smith*,[6] Viscount Kilmuir LC said that he could find no warrant for giving the words 'grievous bodily harm' a meaning 'other than that which the words convey in their ordinary and natural meaning'.[7] The ordinary and natural meaning of bodily harm scarcely includes medical procedures which benefit the bodily health of the person on whom they are performed. Benefit is, after all, the converse of harm. In determining what constitutes bodily harm, a commonsense approach is preferable to one which involves the mechanical application of a definition which was propounded in a context in which medical procedures were not under consideration.[8]

In deciding whether a doctor's conduct is intended to cause, or does cause, bodily harm, it is desirable that the treatment of the patient be considered as a whole. If skin is removed from one part of a person's body, for transplantation to a part which has been burnt, it would be unrealistic to consider the removal of skin on its own. However, there may be a small category of procedures which benefit the patient's health, yet do involve bodily harm. These are procedures which could be regarded as involving physical detriment, but where such detriment is thought to be outweighed by psychological benefit. Examples include some 'sex-change' operations. Whether such procedures amount to bodily harm could depend upon whether 'bodily harm' is taken to include psychological harm which does not have any apparent physical effects.

. . . if it is accepted that bodily harm includes purely psychological harm as well as physical harm, it could be argued that a medical procedure should not be regarded as causing bodily harm if physical detriment is outweighed by psychological benefit.

Notes to extract

[3] *R v Donovan* [1934] 2 KB 498, 509. But see also Stephen, *Digest*, 148 ('bodily injury').

[4] *R v Donovan* [1934] 2 KB 498, 509.

[5] *Ibid* 509. (The court said that, for the purpose of the relevant principle, 'we think that "bodily harm" has its ordinary meaning and includes any hurt or injury calculated to interfere with . . . health or comfort . . .'.)

[6] [1961] AC 290.

[7] *Ibid* 334.

[8] In *R v Hyam* [1975] AC 55, 77C Lord Hailsham said 'It is the absence of intention to kill or *cause grievous bodily harm* which absolves the heart surgeon in the case of the transplant . . .' (emphasis added). Cf Stephen, *Digest*, 148.

However persuasive Professor Skegg's arguments may be, it seems clear that the English courts, on the whole, still regard a surgical procedure as 'harm' which would amount to an offence under the 1861 Act but for the patient's consent to the operation. This must follow from the approach of the Court of Appeal in *A-G's Reference (No 6 of 1980)* [1981] QB 715 which treats surgical procedures as an exception to the criminal law rule that touchings which cause (or are likely to cause) bodily harm may not be validly consented to (see *infra* p 286 *et seq*).

Could it be said that every therapeutic procedure carried out with the consent of a patient will not be an offence under the 1861 Act? Does this just make the word 'therapeutic' carry the burden of analysis? Consider the following legislation.

PROHIBITION OF FEMALE CIRCUMCISION ACT 1985

1. (1) Subject to section 2 below, it shall be an offence for any person—
    (a) to excise, infibulate or otherwise mutilate the whole or any part of the labia majora or labia minora or clitoris of another person; or
    (b) to aid, abet, counsel or procure the performance by another person of any of those acts on that other person's own body.

2. (1) Subsection (1)(a) of section 1 shall not render unlawful the performance of a surgical operation if that operation—
    (a) is necessary for the physical or mental health of the person on whom it is performed and is performed by a registered medical practitioner; or
    (b) is performed on a person who is in any stage of labour or has just given birth and is so performed for purposes connected with that labour or birth by—
       (i) a registered medical practitioner or a registered midwife; or
       (ii) a person undergoing a course of training with a view to becoming a registered medical practitioner or a registered midwife.

    (2) In determining for the purposes of this section whether an operation is necessary for the health of a person, no account shall be taken of the effect on that person of any belief on the part of that or any other person that the operation is required as a matter of custom or ritual.

Questions

(i) Do you think this legislation was strictly necessary given the existence, for example, of the offence under s 18 of the OAPA 1861? (See MacKay, 'Is Female Circumcision Unlawful?' [1983] Criminal Law Review 717 and Lord Hailsham, LC HL Deb Vol 441 col 673, 676–677.)

(ii) Given the discussion above of the meaning of 'harm', does s 2(1) suggest that Professor Skegg's view is wrong, or is the section merely there for the avoidance of doubt?

Further examples of legislation can be found in statutes which touch upon the conduct of a doctor when his patient is pregnant. The Offences Against the Person Act 1861, s 58 provides:

58. Every woman, being with child, who, with intent to procure her own miscarriage, shall unlawfully administer to herself any poison or other noxious thing, or shall unlawfully use any instrument or other means whatsoever with the like intent and whosoever, with intent to procure the miscarriage of any woman, whether she be or not with child, shall unlawfully administer to her or cause to be taken by her any poison or other noxious thing, or shall unlawfully use any instrument or other means whatsoever with the like intent, shall be guilty of an offence, and being convicted thereof shall be liable to imprisonment.

Additionally the Infant Life (Preservation) Act 1929 provides:

1. (1) Subject as hereinafter in this subsection provided, any person who, with intent to destroy the life of a child capable of being born alive, by any wilful act causes a child to die before it has an existence independent of its mother, shall be guilty of felony, to wit, of child destruction, and shall be liable on conviction thereof on indictment to penal servitude for life:

Provided that no person shall be found guilty of an offence under this section unless it is proved that the act which caused the death of the child was not done in good faith for the purpose only of preserving the life of the mother.

(2) For the purposes of this Act, evidence that a woman had at any material time been pregnant for a period of twenty-eight weeks or more shall be prima facie proof that she was at that time pregnant of a child capable of being born alive.

These are the statutes which primarily regulate the carrying out of abortions in England. The Abortion Act 1967 now creates a statutory defence to the offence under s 58 of the 1861 Act, although it has no application to the 1929 Act (see s 5(1) of the 1967 Act). We will return in detail to consider the law relating to abortion in a subsequent chapter (*infra* ch 19). We will see then that the inter-relationship between the statutes has caused some difficulty. Also, we will see that the meaning of 'miscarriage' under s 58 has been a matter of some controversy in determining the legality of the so-called 'morning after pill' (a form of post-coital birth control) and the process known as selective reduction undertaken sometimes during the care of women undergoing *in vitro* fertilisation (see *infra* pp 791–6).

(ii) COMMON LAW

Let us now turn to consider the common law crimes which in principle regulate the legality of a doctor's behaviour.

(a) Assault

There is no reason in principle why a doctor should not be guilty of an assault. If intentionally or recklessly, he puts his patient in fear of the imminent application of force to his person, that, in law, amounts to the crime of assault. There appear to be no cases and, in any event, it must be at best unusual.

(b) Battery

Since any touching done intentionally or recklessly amounts to the crime of battery if done without consent, it is clear that the crime could form an important part of the framework of law governing the doctor/patient relationship. (See generally P D G Skegg, *Law, Ethics and Medicine* pp 32–38.) However, since the same conduct amounts also to the tort of battery and since criminal prosecutions against doctors in connection with their care of patients are most uncommon, it is the *tort* of battery which has until relatively recently served as the basis for regulating the doctor/patient relationship. Now, of course, the tort of negligence has to a large part taken over this role.

For the sake of clarity the following points should be made about *the crime* of battery.

1. As we shall see, there has been judicial disagreement as to whether a touching must be 'hostile' for it to amount to the *tort* of battery (see *infra* pp 172–5). Whatever the outcome of this disagreement may be, the Court of Appeal has held that, for the purposes of the criminal law, 'hostility' is not necessary (*Faulkner v Talbot* [1981] 1 WLR 1528). Therefore, it cannot be said that the crime of battery is irrelevant to medical practice solely because a therapeutic touching by a doctor is not hostile.

2. As a matter of public policy the courts have determined that even some *consensual* touchings may amount to the crime of battery. In *Attorney-General's Reference (No 6 of 1980)* [1981] 2 All ER 1057, Lord Lane CJ, speaking for the court, held:

> We think that it can be taken as a starting point that it is an essential element of an assault that the act is done contrary to the will and without the consent of the victim; and it is doubtless for this reason that the burden lies on the prosecution to negative consent. Ordinarily, then, if the victim consents, the assailant is not guilty.
> . . . The question is: at what point does the public interest require the court to hold otherwise?
> . . . The answer to this question, in our judgment, is that it is not in the public interest that people should try to cause or should cause each other actual bodily harm for no good reason.

However, Lord Lane then went on:

> Nothing which we have said is intended to cast doubt on the accepted legality of properly conducted games and sports, lawful chastisement or correction, *reasonable surgical interference*, dangerous exhibitions etc. These apparent exceptions can be justified as involving the exercise of a legal right, in the case of chastisement or correction, or as needed in the public interest, in the other cases. [Our emphasis.]

Presumably, Lord Lane would include *any* medical intervention, surgical or otherwise, which might otherwise constitute a battery.

In his *Textbook of Criminal Law* (2nd ed 1983) Professor Glanville Williams discusses the implications of this case (pp 589–91):

> . . . the validity of consent to harm is a grey area in the law. It is sufficiently uncertain to have given rise to the opinion[1] that the judges have a commission to pronounce upon the legality of all forms of surgery; and certainly the pronouncement in *A-G's Reference*,[2] conferring the benediction of the judges on 'reasonable surgical interference', seems to confirm that opinion. In practice, of course, the courts would find in favour of such 'interference', if the question ever arose, almost as a matter of routine.
> There have been doubts about sterilisation 'of convenience', ie as a form of birth control.[3] However, medical practice came to accept the operation after counsel advised the BMA that it might be performed without fear of legal repercussions.[4] For some time there was less certainty about castration, which, unlike sterilisation, is a de-sexing operation. It may occasionally be recommended as the only way of obtaining relief from abnormalities in the sexual urge, and in these cases the judges would certainly regard it as lawful. Moreover, the so-called sex-change operation has come to be accepted as lawful.[5] A change from male to pseudo-female sex organs involves castration: the penis and testicles are removed and a pseudo-vagina constructed from the scrotum. Now castration was regarded as a maim at common

law, because it was thought to reduce the will to fight. Yet the male–'female' sex-change is performed openly by reputable surgeons. If the issue were raised, the operation could be supported as conducive to the patient's mental health; and Ormrod J accepted its legality on this ground.[6] Again, no one has ever doubted the legality of the operation of prefrontal leucotomy, which, by severing the frontal lobes of the brain, changes the personality of the patient in certain cases of mental illness. Therapy also gives moral support to some cosmetic surgery, but not all. The justification for padding bosoms, chiselling noses, and restoring hymens lost in pre-marital encounters, is that the patient is pleased and may be socially or maritally advantaged, rather than that the operation is a psychiatric necessity.

A more serious interference with the body is in taking an organ for transplant, such as a kidney. Nevertheless, no serious legal doubts have been expressed about such operations upon adult donors, where a paired organ is surrendered for the benefit of another.[7]

It may be questioned whether the criminal law has any acceptable place in controlling operations performed by qualified practitioners upon adults of sound mind with their consent . . .

In a civil case relating to an operation changing a male to a pseudo-female, Ormrod J said:

There is obviously room for differences of opinion on the ethical aspects of such operations but, if they are undertaken for genuine therapeutic purposes, it is a matter for the decision of the patient and the doctors concerned in his case. The passing of section 1 of the Sexual Offences Act 1967[8] seems to have removed any legal objections which there might have been to such procedures.[9]

There is no reason why the same view should not be taken for all medical procedures, assuming that the patient has capacity to consent. The law would still play a part in determining legal capacity in the case of the young and the mentally abnormal.

If this is so, the only threat presented by the law in respect of operations on the body is to those who are not medically qualified.

Notes to extract
[1] See, eg D W Meyers *The Human Body and the Law* (Edinburgh 1970), *passim*.
[2] § 17.
[3] Williams, *The Sanctity of Life and the Criminal Law* (London 1958) Chap 3; Meyers, *op cit* Chap 1; Bartholomew in 2 Melbourne Univ LRev 77, 397.
[4] [1960] 2 BMJ 1510, 1516. The opinion was reaffirmed by counsel advising the Medical Defence Union: [1966] 1 BMJ 1597. Cf Skegg in [1974] Crim LR 694 n 8.
[5] For earlier doubts see Meyers, *op cit* Chap 3.
[6] See below at n 9.
[7] See Dworkin in 33 MLR 353: Skegg in [1974] Crim LR 33, 698.
[8] Which in general legalised adult homosexual practices.
[9] *Corbett v Corbett (otherwise Ashley)* [1971] P 83 at 99.

In the light of this discussion, do you agree with Professor Skegg when he says (*op cit* p 38) that 'the judges' insistence that there are some applications of force to which consent cannot be given, for the purposes of the offence of battery, should not hinder modern medical practice'?

(c)   Maim

Stephen in his *Digest of the Criminal Law* (1878) defines the crime of maim as follows (p 145):

A maim is bodily harm whereby a man is deprived of the use of any member of his body, or of any sense which he can use in fighting, or by the loss of which he is generally and permanently weakened; but a bodily injury is not a maim merely because it is a disfigurement.

Does this affect the practice of medicine? Professor Skegg in his book argues as follows (pp 43–46):

> In practice, the common law offence of maim has long been supplanted by statutory offences. But it has not been expressly abolished,[72] and a judge has made an extrajudicial statement which suggests that there is at least a theoretical possibility of the offence of maim applying to operations in which a kidney is removed from a healthy living donor, for transplantation into a person who is in need of it.[73] It is therefore desirable to consider the extent to which the offence of maim would apply to medical procedures, and the related issue of whether consent would be effective to prevent liability.
>
> The authorities[74] have long distinguished between acts which permanently disable and weaken a man,[75] rendering him less able in fighting; and acts which simply disfigure. The former are maims, the latter are not. There is no shortage of examples of injuries which fall within one category rather than the other. Over many centuries, it has been agreed that it is a maim to cut off, disable, or weaken an arm or foot. It has also been agreed that it is a maim to deprive a man of an eye, foretooth, or 'those parts, the loss of which in all animals abates their courage'.[76] However, it has also long been accepted that it is not a maim to cut off an ear or nose, as such injuries are said not to affect a man's capacity for fighting.
>
> . . .
>
> Most medical procedures do not permanently disable a person and render that person less able in fighting.[79] They therefore fall outside even the potential scope of any offence of maim.[80] This is as true of the removal of a healthy kidney for transplantation as it is of the removal of a diseased appendix. But even if a medical procedure did come within the potential scope of an offence of maim, it would not follow that a doctor would commit an offence of maim in going ahead with it. Just as the infliction of a maim was sometimes permitted in self-defence,[81] so a maiming operation would not amount to the offence of maim if there was a good reason for it. Hence, even if castration could still be regarded as coming within the potential scope of maim, it would be justified if performed for a therapeutic purpose.[82]
>
> The offence of maim would very rarely apply to any procedure performed in the course of medical practice, even if consent had not been given. But if something was done which did come within the potential scope of maim—as where a member of the armed forces persuaded a friend to cut off his trigger finger for him, in an attempt to obtain a discharge[83]—consent would normally[84] be irrelevant.[85]

Notes to extract

[72] Cf *R v Owen* [1976] 1 WLR 840 (revival of 'the obsolescent offence of embracery': *ibid* 842).

[73] R Ormrod, *op cit*, 9 (cf *Jennings v United States Government* [1982] 3 All ER 104 at 107f–g per Ormrod LJ (DC)). See also Edmund Davies, 'Transplants', 634.

[74] Among the more important accounts of the offence of maim are *Bracton on the Laws and Customs of England* (trans etc S E Thorne), vol ii (1968), 409–10; *Britton* (trans etc F M Nichols, 1865), vol i, 122–3; 1 Co Inst 127a–b, 288a, 3 Co Inst 118 (and also 1 Co Inst 126a–b, 3 Co Inst 62–3); 1 Hawk PC (8th edn), 107–8 (ch XV, ss 1–4); 3 Bl Com 121, 4 Bl Com 205–6; 1 East PC 393, 400–3. See also Stephen, *Digest*, 148–9.

[75] It is often said that the offence of maim does not apply to maiming injuries to any woman, but the rationale of the offence given by some authorities (see eg 1 Co Inst 127a, 4 Bl Com 205) would be consistent with the offence of maim nowadays applying to maiming injuries to at least some women. The view that women were not the subject of maim may have resulted from the fact that women were not required to engage in military service, and the fact that castration has been a standard example of maim. Just as the courts now accept that affrays may be committed in private as well as public places (*R v Button and Swain* [1966] AC 591), so they could take the view that nowadays women as well as men may be the victim of maim.

[76] 4 Bl Com 205; *Russell on Crime* (12th edn, 1964, ed J W C Turner), vol i, 625 (adding a comma after 'animals').
. . .

[79] On the requirement that an injury be permanent for it to constitute a maim, see eg 3 Bl Com 121. See also *R v Jeans* (1844) 1 Car & Kir 539. Even where a medical procedure permanently disabled the patient, and could be regarded as a maim, the doctor would not normally have intended, or been reckless as to, that consequence. On principle, intention or recklessness as to the injury should nowadays be required.
[80] Some medical procedures involve the amputation of limbs which have been specifically mentioned in discussions of maim. However, the amputation of an arm or leg would only come within the potential scope of the offence if it had the effect of permanently disabling the subject in fighting. See 1 Co Inst 288a ('"Maihem" . . . signifieth a corporal Hurt, whereby he loseth a Member, *by reason whereof* he is less able to fight'); 3 Bl Com 121 ('for ever disabled from making so good a defence against future external injuries, *as he otherwise might have done*') (emphasis added). As the injury which led to the amputation would normally have itself disabled the patient, the operation necessitated by that injury should not come within the potential scope of maim.
[81] See 1 East PC 402, which implies other interests may sometimes be balanced against the interest protected by the law of maim. On self-defence and maim, see also 3 Bl Com 121; *Cockcroft v Smith* (1705) 1 Ld Raym 177, 2 Salk 642, 11 Mod 43.
[82] Cf *Corbett v Corbett (otherwise Ashley)* [1971] P 83 at 99A. See generally R B Welbourn, 'Castration' in *Dict Med Ethics*, 49–51. In *Cowburn* [1959] Crim LR 590, Cowburn's counsel asked the Court of Criminal Appeal to assure the prison authorities that it would not be unlawful or contrary to public policy for Cowburn, a sexual psychopath, to be voluntarily castrated while in prison. The judges refused to give such an assurance. However, this should not be interpreted as implying anything as to the legality of such operations. The slightly fuller report in *The Times*, 12 May 1959, makes it very clear that the reason for this refusal was their view that it was not the function of the court to give directions on what takes place in prison.
[83] For an example of this being done, see B Cox, *Civil Liberties in Britain* (1975), 286.
[84] The reason for the qualification is that very exceptionally consent may be relevant in deciding whether a particular medical procedure was, in the circumstances, therapeutic. If the procedure appeared to constitute a maim, the question whether it was therapeutic—and hence whether there was a just cause or excuse for it (cf *Corbett v Corbett* [1971] P 83, 99A)—might in theory be relevant in determining whether it amounted to any offence of maim.
[85] *Wright* (1603) 1 Co Inst 127a–b; see also Bracton, *op cit*, vol ii, p 408. But see generally Williams, *Textbook*, 539–40. (Professor Glanville Williams points out that in *Wright* the parties 'had entered into a conspiracy to defraud the public' and states that 'the brief report does not state whether they were convicted of this conspiracy or of maim'. However, Coke gave his account of the case in the course of his discussion of maim, and stated that 'both of them were indited, fined and ransomed therefore, and that by the opinion of the rest of the Justices, for the cause aforesaid' (1 Co Inst 127b). The 'cause aforesaid' related to the principle underlying the offence of maim. See 1 Co Inst 127a (where the same phrase is used), and also 3 Co Inst 118.) Consent may, of course, affect the liability of the person who is maimed. It was only where the consent had been given that he could be liable. See generally 1 East PC 400–1; 1 Hawk, PC (8th edn) 108; Williams, *Textbook*, 538, 540.

In the light of the Court of Appeal's decision in the *A-G's Reference (No 6 of 1980)*, what (if anything) does the crime of maim add to the crime of battery? Will there be a case where a consent to a touching will be valid for the purposes of the crime of battery but not for the crime of maim?

(d)   Homicide

Taking someone else's life is clearly the most serious of offences. Obviously, talk of homicide has little place in any consideration of the practice of medicine.

There are, however, at least two sets of circumstances which warrant its consideration here. The first is that homicide sets the outer limit of permitted medical practice, serving thereby as a guide to that which society regards as the ultimately impermissible. Secondly, in the case, for example, of the severely handicapped newborn, and of the terminally-ill, a (sometimes) fine line must be drawn between good medical practice, which is both permissible and desirable, and homicide which is neither. Such a line must and can be drawn as we will seek to show subsequently (*infra* chs 12 and 14 respectively) and it is important to demonstrate that this is so.

The two forms of unlawful homicide known to law are, of course, murder and manslaughter. (For definitions of these offences see Glanville Williams, *A Textbook of Criminal Law* (2nd ed), pp 245 *et seq*.) In this century doctors have only been prosecuted on three occasions for the alleged unlawful homicide of a patient in the context of the care of the patient, the prosecution being based on the argument that the regime of care was one intended unlawfully to kill (see *R v Bodkin Adams* [1957] CLR 365; *R v Arthur*, (1981) Times, 2 November and the prosecution of a Dr Carr in Leeds in 1986). We will return in subsequent chapters to deal with the treatment of handicapped neonates and the very ill patient (see chs 12 and 14). But, again let us examine certain general points here.

1. Will the consent of the patient to his being killed provide a defence for the doctor? This, of course, is an example of what is, perhaps unhelpfully, called voluntary euthanasia. Professor Skegg (*op cit* at 128–129) offers the following view:

> Even if the patient pleaded with the doctor to end his life, this would not provide the doctor with a defence in law. And, just as a patient's consent to being killed would not provide a doctor with a defence, nor would the consent of a relative, or anyone else.
>
> The fact that a patient would be very severely handicapped if he were to live, or would find life a burden, does not affect the general principle that it is murder to kill a person by doing some positive act,[28] with the intention of hastening death.[29] There were several statements to this effect in Farquharson J's direction to the jury in *R v Arthur*.[30] He said that it was an important principle in law that 'However serious the case may be; however much the dis-advantage of a mongol or, indeed, any other handicapped child, no doctor has the right to kill it.'[31] There was, he said, no special power, facility, or licence to kill children who are handicapped or seriously disadvantaged in any irreversible way.[32] *R v Arthur* resulted from the death of a newly-born child, but what was said on this matter is equally applicable to other patients.

Notes to extract

[28] Where there is an intentional omission to prolong life, the patient's medical condition is often of crucial importance in determining a doctor's criminal (and civil) liability: see ch 7, esp pp 149–53.

[29] However, in cases of 'mercy killing' by relatives it has become customary to accept a plea of diminished responsibility, and a conviction for manslaughter ensues. See Lawton LJ, 'Mercy Killing: The Judicial Dilemma' (1979) 72 *J Roy Soc Med* 460–1; Roger Leng, 'Mercy Killing and CLRC' (1982) 132 *New LJ* 76–8.

[30] *R v Arthur* (1981) 283 *Br Med J* 1340, [1981] 2 *Lancet* 1101. The pages cited in footnotes ... are to the official transcript of Farquharson J's summing-up to the jury, in the Leicester Crown Court, on 3, 4, and 5 November 1981. Some information about the trial is to be found in *A-G v English* [1983] 1 AC 116 (prosecution for contempt of court, following publication of newspaper article during the trial). Extracts from the summing-up were printed in (1981) 78 *Law Society Gazette* 1341.

31 Transcript, 16F.
32 Transcript, 17A. Farquharson J was directing his comments to the 'doing of an act, a positive act', rather than an omission to do something that would enable a patient to live. See 17D.

2. Will it affect a doctor's liability if that which he did was either in accordance with accepted medical practice within his profession or was done for an exemplary motive?

Discussing the cases of *Adams* and *Arthur*, Skegg argues (pp 129–131):

> In *R v Arthur* Farquharson J said that it was accepted that the doctor had acted from the highest of motives, but directed the jury that 'however noble his motives were
> . . . that is irrelevant to the question of your deciding what his intent was'.33 He said that :34
>> It may be that somebody faced with an ageing relative who was suffering from an incurably painful disease, from the best motive in the world, decides to put a pillow over the poor soul's head so that he or she dies. That would mean that there was then an intent to kill by putting a pillow over the head. The motive, of course, would have been the kindest and the best.
> If a doctor acts with the intention of bringing about the death of a patient, the fact that he was acting to alleviate suffering, or for some other exemplary motive, would not at present provide him with a defence to a charge of murder.35

Later, he continues:

> Even if a doctor acted in compliance with statements on medical ethics propounded by the British Medical Association, or any other organisation, this would not of itself provide a doctor with a defence if he administered a drug—or did any other act39—for the purpose of hastening the death of a patient. In *R v Arthur* Farquharson J commented that it was customary for a profession to agree on rules of conduct for its members but instructed the jury that 'that does not mean that any profession can set out a code of ethics and say that the law must accept it and take notice of it. It may be that in any particular feature the ethic is wrong.'40 He said that 'whatever a profession may evolve as a system of standards of ethics, cannot stand on its own, and cannot survive if it is in conflict with the law'.41 It would therefore be open to a jury to find a doctor guilty of murder even though they believed that he acted in accordance with the ethical standards currently accepted by the medical profession.

Notes to extract
33 Transcript, 26C–D.
34 Transcript, 26D–E.
35 See *R v Hyam* [1975] AC 55 at 73. See generally Williams, *Sanctity*, 283–4.

. . .
39 [footnote omitted].
40 Transcript, 17E–G.
41 Transcript, 82A. But Farquharson J went on to say that he imagined that the jury 'would think long and hard' before concluding that eminent doctors 'have evolved standards which amounted to committing a crime' (Transcript, 82B–C).

The civil law

As regards the civil law, we need specifically to consider the law of contract and of torts, and as a separate matter, because of its particular legal complexity, the law relating to breach of confidence. In real terms, this is the heart of medical law.

(i) CONTRACT

Formation of the contract. Curiously, although the coming into existence of a contract between a doctor and patient is critical, there is little guidance to be found in the law as to when the contract is formed. Given that there must be an offer and acceptance (together with consideration), who is it who offers and who accepts? Is it the patient who offers to pay if the doctor agrees to treat, or the patient who accepts the doctor's offer to treat by agreeing to pay. Do you agree with Picard, in *Legal Liability of Doctors and Hospitals in Canada*, 2nd ed 1984 (at pp 1–2): 'The offer could be found [in law] in the patient's request for treatment and the acceptance in the doctor's commencement of care. Consideration [is] not a problem unless the patient [is] unable to pay. In such circumstances the law of contract [is] held that the patient's submission to treatment [is] sufficient consideration for the doctor's services' (citing *Coggs v Bernard* (1703) 2 Ld Raym 909 and *Banbury v Bank of Montreal* [1918] AC 626)?

The law of contract, however, has limited application in regulating the relationship between doctor and patient in England and Wales because most doctor/patient contracts are within the NHS to which the law of contract does not apply, as we have seen. It is therefore in the context of private practice that the law of contract operates.

(a) Terms

1. *Express terms*

This is entirely a matter of what the parties agree amongst themselves, for example, as to payment or who may carry out a particular procedure. A consent form is an example of an agreement containing express terms (see *Thake v Maurice* [1986] 1 All ER 497 and *Eyre v Measday* [1986] 1 All ER 488).

There are, of course, limits to what the parties may purport to agree through express terms. They cannot, for example, agree to do that which would be regarded as contrary to public policy (see *infra*), nor to waive those obligations implied by law (see *infra*).

2. *Implied terms*

Reasonable care and skill. In two cases in 1986 involving a sterilisation procedure which failed, the Court of Appeal analysed the legal obligations of the doctor to his patient with whom he had contracted to carry out the procedure. In *Eyre v Measday* [1986] 1 All ER 488, Slade LJ said:

> Applying *The Moorcock* principles, I think there is no doubt that the plaintiff would have been entitled reasonably to assume that the defendant was warranting that the operation would be performed with reasonable care and skill. That, I think, would have been the inevitable inference to be drawn, from an objective standpoint, . . . The contract did, in my opinion, include an implied warranty of *that* nature.

Similarly, in the later case of *Thake v Maurice* [1986] 1 All ER 497, Nourse LJ observed:

> The particular concern of this court in *Eyre v Measday* was to decide whether there had been an implied guarantee that the operation would succeed. But the approach of Slade LJ in testing that question objectively is of equal value in a case where it is said that there has been an express guarantee. Valuable too are the observations of Lord Denning MR in *Greaves & Co (Contractors) Ltd v Baynham Meikle & Partners* [1975] 3 All ER 99 at 103–104, [1975] 1 WLR 1095 at 1100 which I now quote in full:

'Apply this to the employment of a professional man. The law does not usually imply a warranty that he will achieve the desired result, but only a term that he will use reasonable care and skill. The surgeon does not warrant that he will cure the patient. Nor does the solicitor warrant that he will win the case.'

Neill LJ in the same case said: 'It is common ground that the defendant contracted to perform a vasectomy operation on Mr Thake and that in the performance of that contract he was subject to the duty implied by law to carry out the operation with reasonable skill and care.'

But notice that Oliver J (as he then was), when talking about the nature of a professional person's obligations, in *Midland Bank v Hett, Stubbs & Kemp* [1979] Ch 384, makes it clear that the implied term that the professional person will use reasonable care and skill is a less than complete description of his obligations.

The classical formulation of the claim in this sort of case as 'damages for negligence and breach of professional duty' tends to be a mesmeric phrase. It concentrates attention on the implied obligation to devote to the client's business that reasonable care and skill to be expected from a normally competent and careful practitioner as if that obligation were not only a compendious, but also an exhaustive, definition of all the duties assumed under the contract created by the retainer and its acceptance. But, of course, it is not. A contract gives rise to a complex of rights and duties of which the duty to exercise reasonable care and skill is but one.

If I employ a carpenter to supply and put up a good quality oak shelf for me, the acceptance by him of that employment involves the assumption of a number of contractual duties. He must supply wood of an adequate quality and it must be oak. He must fix the shelf. And he must carry out the fashioning and fixing with the reasonable care and skill which I am entitled to expect of a skilled craftsman. If he fixes the brackets but fails to supply the shelf or if he supplies and fixes a shelf of unseasoned pine, my complaint against him is not that he has failed to exercise reasonable care and skill in carrying out the work but that he has failed to supply what was contracted for.

Jackson and Powell in *Professional Negligence* (2nd ed 1987) comment on Oliver J's views (para 1.10) (footnotes omitted):

The particular illustration chosen by Oliver J . . . must be used with caution, since the obligations of a carpenter to his employer are generally of a different nature to those owed by a professional man to his client. Nevertheless in every contract between a professional man and his client there will be express or implied terms defining the nature of the engagement. Thus if a surveyor is instructed to produce a report on certain property, there is an express or implied obligation to inspect it. If a surgeon agrees with his patient to perform a particular operation, there may be an implied term that he will 'give the necessary supervision thereafter until the discharge of the patient.' If a solicitor is instructed to effect the grant of an option, there are implied terms that he will draw up the option agreement and effect registration. The importance of specific terms such as these is that a professional man will be liable if he breaks them, quite irrespective of the amount of skill and care which he has exercised.

An example of an implied term other than to exercise care and skill arises, for example, in the case of a doctor fitting a prosthesis. In such a case the question arises as to whether the terms implied by law by virtue of the Supply of Goods and Services Act 1982 as to the fitness for the purpose of the goods supplied or their merchantable quality apply (see generally, Bell (1984) 4 LS 175). Similarly, a contract will have implied into it an obligation to keep the patient's medical information confidential (*Furniss v Fitchett* [1958] NZLR 396).

Guarantee of success. It is one thing for the law to expect a contract to be performed properly, it is quite another to demand of the doctor that he guarantee success unless he has expressly agreed to do so. As Nourse LJ stated in *Thake v Maurice* (*supra*):

> Lord Denning MR thought [in *Greaves v Baynham Meikle & Partners*], and I respectfully agree with him, that a professional man is not usually regarded as warranting that he will achieve the desired result. Indeed, it seems that that would not fit well with the universal warranty of reasonable care and skill, which tends to affirm the inexactness of the science which is professed. I do not intend to go beyond the case of a doctor. Of all sciences medicine is one of the least exact. In my view a doctor cannot be objectively regarded as guaranteeing the success of any operation or treatment unless he says as much in clear and unequivocal terms. The defendant did not do that in the present case.

Courts in other jurisdictions have been prepared to find that a doctor has guaranteed a particular result and when he has failed to achieve it, they have allowed the patient to succeed in an action for breach of contract. Two cases involving cosmetic surgery illustrate this. In *Sullivan v O'Connor* (1973) 296 NE 2d 183, the plaintiff, a professional entertainer, sued the defendant because of the condition of her nose after he had operated. Justice Kaplan described the plaintiff's condition as follows:

> . . . judging from exhibits, the plaintiff's nose had been straight, but long and prominent; the defendant undertook by two operations to reduce its prominence and somewhat to shorten it, thus making it more pleasing in relation to the plaintiff's other features. Actually the plaintiff was obliged to undergo three operations, and her appearance was worsened. Her nose now had a concave line to about the midpoint, at which it became bulbous; viewed frontally, the nose from bridge to midpoint was flattened and broadened, and the two sides of the tip had lost symmetry. This configuration evidently could not be improved by further surgery.

The court allowed the plaintiff to recover for breach of contract. The court went on, however, to warn of the difficulties facing plaintiffs who allege that a doctor guaranteed success:

> It is not hard to see why the courts should be unenthusiastic or skeptical about the contract theory. Considering the uncertainties of medical science and the variations in the physical and psychological conditions of individual patients, doctors can seldom in good faith promise specific results. Therefore it is unlikely that physicians of even average integrity will in fact make such promises. Statements of opinion by the physician with some optimistic coloring are a different thing, and may indeed have therapeutic value. But patients may transform such statements into firm promises in their own minds, especially when they have been disappointed in the event, and testify in that sense to sympathetic juries. If actions for breach of promise can be readily maintained, doctors, so it is said, will be frightened into practicing 'defensive medicine'. On the other hand, if these actions were outlawed, leaving only the possibility of suits for malpractice, there is fear that the public might be exposed to the enticements of charlatans, and confidence in the profession might ultimately be shaken.
>
> . . . The law has taken the middle of the road position of allowing actions based on alleged contract, but insisting on clear proof. Instructions to the jury may well stress this requirement and point to tests of truth, such as the complexity or difficulty of an operation as bearing on the probability that a given result was promised.

In the Canadian case of *LaFleur v Cornelis* (1979) 28 NBR (2d) 569 (New Brunswick), the defendant, a cosmetic surgeon, performed a procedure to reduce the size of the plaintiff's nose. He failed to inform her that there was a 10% risk of scarring. She, in fact, was scarred. In addition to succeeding in an action in negligence, the plaintiff established a breach of contract. Barry J said (at pp 576–7):

A cosmetic surgeon is in a different position than the ordinary physician. He is selling a special service and he is more akin to a businessman. Therefore, this is not the ordinary malpractice case. Normally a doctor contracts to use the best skill he possesses and he is expected to exercise at least the methods ordinarily employed by similarly trained professionals. If he does not do so, he may be guilty of negligence in carrying out his contract, as I have found the defendant was in this case.

In the instant case, that was not the kind of a contract which the defendant entered into with the plaintiff. The latter told the defendant what she wanted, namely, a smaller nose. The defendant drew a sketch on his notes to show the changes he would make if the plaintiff paid him a fee of $600.00. There was no misunderstanding whatever. Both parties were *ad idem* as to what each was to do. The plaintiff paid the fee and the defendant failed to carry out his part of the contract. Negligence is not a factor in a straight breach of contract action. There is no law preventing a doctor from contracting to do that which he is paid to so. I appreciate that usually there is no implied warranty of success, in the absence of special circumstances. In this case, the defendant stated to the plaintiff—'no problem. You will be very happy.' He made an express agreement, which he was not required to, without explaining the risk.

I find that the parties made a contract, and the defendant breached it, leaving the plaintiff with a scarred nose with a minimal deformity.

Questions

(i) In the last case the judge considered cosmetic surgery to be a 'special service' and hence he was prepared to interpret the contract between the parties as including a guarantee that a particular outcome would be achieved. What is so 'special' about cosmetic surgery? Can you think of any other types of medical care in relation to which a similar conclusion could be reached?

(ii) There is a more general point to be made concerning actions in contract brought against doctors. It is generally assumed that (cases of guarantee apart) there is no legal significance in pleading a malpractice action in contract or tort. Is this true? Can a patient who sues her doctor in contract claim damages either for pain and suffering or mental anguish that may be caused to her? (See *Hayes v Dodds* (1988) NLJR 259.) (Notice, that in *LaFleur v Cornelis, supra,* the judge awarded damages for both of these.) Can you think of any other legally significant differences between the two kinds of action which would be relevant here?

(b) Public policy limitations

There are circumstances in which the law will not assist one party to enforce an agreement reached with the other and indeed may forbid on pain of criminal sanction the performance of such an agreement. An example would be an agreement to do that which would amount to maim.

We have already seen the general proposition set out in the context of the criminal law in *A-G's Reference (No 6 of 1980), supra.* While 'reasonable surgical interferences' may not be contrary to public policy, some agreements may embody terms which would, if performed, be contrary to public policy. Consider the following examples:

1. *Arrangements for surrogate motherhood.*

At common law, the position in England was made clear by the courts in *A v C* [1985] FLR 445 (Comyn J and CA). The case concerned an application by a father for access to his illegitimate child. He had paid a woman to conceive the child by artificial insemination and carry it to term. The court denied him access. We will return to the issues raised by surrogacy in a later chapter (ch 8). For our present purposes the words of Comyn J at first instance suffice:

Comyn J: . . . The agreement between the parties I hold as being against public policy. None of them can rely upon it in any way or enforce the agreement in any way. I need only give one of many grounds for saying this, namely that this was a purported contract for the sale and purchase of a child.

In the celebrated New Jersey case of *Baby M* (1988) 537 A 2d 1227, the Supreme Court of New Jersey summed up the public policy considerations as follows:

Wilentz CJ: The surrogacy contract is based on, principles that are directly contrary to the objectives of our laws. It guarantees the separation of a child from its mother; it looks to adoption regardless of suitability; it totally ignores the child; it takes the child from the mother regardless of her wishes and her maternal fitness; and it does all of this, it accomplishes all of its goals, through the use of money.

Beyond that is the pontential degradation of some women that may result from this arrangement. In many cases, of course, surrogacy may bring satisfaction, not only to the infertile couple, but to the surrogate mother herself. The fact, however, that many women may not perceive surrogacy negatively but rather see it as an opportunity does not diminish its potential for devastation to other women.

In sum, the harmful consequences of this surrogacy arrangement appear to us all too palpable. In New Jersey the surrogate mother's agreement to sell her child is void. Its irrevocability infects the entire contract, as does the money that purports to buy it.

(See *infra* p 729 for a detailed analysis of this case.)

In England, Parliament has now to some extent intervened, in the Surrogacy Arrangements Act 1985. To the extent that they are made criminal offences by s 2, surrogacy arrangements are unenforceable as being contrary to public policy.

2.—(1) No person shall on a commercial basis do any of the following acts in the United Kingdom, that is—

(*a*) initiate or take part in any negotiations with a view to the making of a surrogacy arrangement,

(*b*) offer or agree to negotiate the making of a surrogacy arrangement, or

(*c*) compile any information with a view to its use in making, or negotiating the making of, surrogacy arrangements;

and no person shall in the United Kingdom knowingly cause another to do any of those acts on a commercial basis.

(2) A person who contravenes subsection (1) above is guilty of an offence; but it is not a contravention of that subsection—

(*a*) for a woman, with a view to becoming a surrogate mother herself, to do any act mentioned in that subsection or to cause such an act to be done, or

(*b*) for any person, with a view to a surrogate mother carrying a child for him, to do such an act or to cause such an act to be done.

2. *Sale of body fluids and tissue.*

We will consider this issue in detail in the context of donation of tissue and body fluids in a later chapter (ch 13). For now, we refer to the paper by Professor Dukeminier, 'Supplying Organs for Transplantation' (1970) 68 Michigan LR 811, 857–861, in which he addresses the question: 'Is the Sale of a Spare Organ Against Public Policy?' (footnotes omitted).

There are at least four basic positions from which one may approach the problem of organ sale. The first is founded upon an acceptance of the general ethical principle of preservation of life. That principle, simply stated, is that an individual should not endanger his life except for the love of another or in a case such that the danger is an indirect consequence of the activity. This position has deep roots in Judaeo-Christian, and even earlier, teachings that man should not seek his own destruction. Unlike the Eskimos, who encourage suicide by the elderly when they can no longer contribute to the family larder, most western societies have long condemned taking one's own life. In ancient Athens a man who unsuccessfully attempted suicide was punished by the cutting off of his hand. In medieval England a stake was driven through the heart of a man who committed suicide and all his property was forfeited to the crown; Christians who committed suicide could not be buried in consecrated ground. Remnants of this attitude can still be found in laws against abetting and, in some places, attempting suicide.

However, the principle of preserving life does permit some exceptions. Society condones, and even praises, some acts of heroism and self-sacrifice, such as that of the man who gives up his seat in the lifeboat, the passerby who enters a burning building to save the occupants, or the mother who jumps into the rapids to save her child. These are heroic acts motivated by the desire to help others. Under this view, the sole motivation for risking one's life by giving up an organ must be the love of one's fellow man, and a gift of a spare organ to a specific donee is permissible so long as such a motivation exists. Otherwise, allowing the removal of an organ for transplantation is condemned.

Yet if a charitable motive is so important in judging conduct in situations involving a risking of one's life, how can we permit men to risk their lives in driving racing cars, in entering boxing contests, and in pursuing all kinds of paid risky occupations and still object to the paid kidney donor? When confronted with this question many moral theologians draw a line between direct and indirect effects. For race car drivers and others in risky occupations, dying or being functionally impaired is an indirect consequence, which is foreseen as only possible. In the transplantation case, they argue, removal of the organ from the donor is a life-risking procedure which is the necessary means to the end. If, however, the direct-indirect distinction is accepted, the conclusion that it is unethical to pay a man for a kidney to save life, even though the risks to him are small, but ethical to pay a race car driver at the Indianapolis 500 for entertainment, even though the risks to him are great, can hardly be avoided. Such a principle is troubling indeed.

The second position from which the problem of organ sale can be approached may be characterised as one of 'free will'. This position is based upon the principle that a person should be able to do whatever he chooses, so long as he does not harm another. Particular among the young, this position is now much in vogue. It underlines much of the current trend to liberate 'sins', such as private deviate sexual conduct and fornication by the unmarried, from criminal sanction. Undoubtedly this principle has also influenced the judicial decisions which have relaxed old proscriptions against obscenity, and it is the base of the recent decisions holding that statutes requiring motocyclists to wear helmets are unconstitutional since the state may not require a citizen to protect his health alone. As applied to organ sales, the argument would be that an individual has the right to decide for himself whether to sell an organ.

A principal difficulty with this view is that in harming himself a person may harm society; a person who gives or sells a kidney might, if his other kidney fails, have to be maintained by the government on an artificial kidney machine. If he gives or sells other spare organs, the risk that he will disable himself is greater and the resulting harm to society may be substantial. To represent society's interest, a person other than the donor, such as a judge or a physician, must appraise the possible harm to society at large.

A variation of the free-will view is that free will, or informed consent as it is known in medico-legal terminology, should be the ethical criterion, but that a monetary payment for an organ would constitute economic coercion so that the consent would not really represent an act of free will. This is a merely a conclusion, however, and is not a reason. What is really at issue is the determination of criteria by which to measure 'unfair inducement' or 'economic coercion' in situations involving the risking of life. Why is it unfair to induce a man to sell a kidney and not unfair to induce him into the boxing ring or into a coal mine?

The third way of evaluating the propriety of permitting organ sale is not to start from any general ethical rule of human conduct but to narrow the problem to the context of the physician-patient relationship. Professor Paul Freund has pointed out that '[t]he great traditional safeguard in the field of medical experimentation is the disciplined fidelity of the physician to his patient: *primum non nocere*. First of all, do not do injury.' From this viewpoint the basic question is not the donor's motivation or freewill; the issue is whether buying this particular organ from this individual patient is for his welfare. If the principle of totality permits sacrificing a part of the body for the good of the whole—which includes spiritual gain and the avoidance of psychological trauma—it is not difficult to conceive of situations in which a physician could ethically conclude that the sale is for the patient's welfare. Suppose, for example, that a very rich man needs a kidney and the closest tissue match is his sister, who is poor. While the sister is thinking about offering a kidney, her brother lets her know that he will accept it only in exchange for 100,000 dollars—an exchange which may have income and estate tax advantages for him. If the sister decides to sell the kidney, her knowledge of forthcoming remuneration makes it impossible to conclude that she acts solely for spiritual gain, and yet it does not seem unethical to allow her to sell the kidney. Under the principle of totality, the surgeon must conclude that the donor benefits by removal of his kidney. To arrive at that conclusion the surgeon may have to inquire as to how the donor proposes to use any monetary payment and may then have to decide for himself whether the donor will benefit physically or mentally from that particular use.

Finally, the question of organ sale can be probed by disregarding ethical positions and analysing only the consequences of permitting such sales. Sales will have some impact both on the total amount of economic resources which are to be allocated to medicine and on the selection of recipients, but the precise nature of that impact is not clear. The nature of the impact will depend upon the manner in which two distinguishable problems are approached: (1) creating an adequate quantity of organs supplied and (2) selecting the persons to receive them. The quantity of organs supplied could be increased by buying them, and they could then be allocated among recipients by some method other than sale. For example, a third party, such as the government or a hospital, might absorb the cost. But the consequence of the government's purchase of organs for recipients might be that the government's economic resources which are committed to medicine would be used for the purchase of organs rather than for other medical needs. To achieve the best use of the resources available for medical purposes, other ways of securing a satisfactory quantity of organs should first be exhausted. If the cost of buying organs is passed on to the recipient, life-saving resources would be distributed on the basis of ability to pay. The use of wealth as a means of selecting who shall be saved among the dying raises immensely troublesome ethical and legal quandaries.

Under some approaches to the problem the procedure of buying organs may be thought to be impermissible in some or all circumstances. The sounder arguments, however, appear to permit a surgeon to offer remuneration if, acting in accordance with contemporary ethical standards and with the permission of a hospital review committee, he concludes that in a particular case the operation will promote the physical or mental health of the donor. In arriving at that conclusion, the surgeon and the review committee must balance various interests, but the most important is the doctor's duty to his patient.

Do you agree with Professor Dukeminier's conclusion? Do you think an English court would be more likely to reflect the approach of much of the Commonwealth legislation, exemplified in the Human Tissue Act 1982 of the Australian State of Victoria? Sections 38(1) and 39(1) provide as follows:

38. (1) . . . a person shall not sell, or agree to sell, tissue (including his own tissue) or the right to take tissue from his body.

39. (1) . . . a person shall not buy, agree to buy, offer to buy, hold himself out as being willing to buy, or inquire whether a person is willing to sell to the person or another person—
   (*a*) tissue; or

(*b*) the right to take tissue from the body of another person.

Could Dukeminier's view reflect an American preference for 'free enterprise' and 'the market'?

In 1984 the matter was settled at least at the federal level by making commerce in organs a crime, s 301(c)(1) National Organ Transplant Act (42 NSC 274(e)). And see now in the UK the Human Organ Transplants Bill 1989.

3. *Transsexualism.*
David Meyers examines the public policy considerations in *The Human Body and the Law* (1970) at p 66.

> The enquiry is concerned fundamentally with the extent to which an individual's consent will insulate the performing surgeon from criminal liability for the surgical invasion that is repugnant or unjustified to many.
>
> It may eventually be resolved that consent to such operations will only negate their criminality when their purpose is considered to be therapeutic. The question then to be resolved will be: what is therapeutic?
>
> While conversion surgery for transsexuals involves a more severe, more repugnant bodily infringement, it is also sought to be justified on wider, rather atypical therapeutic grounds. The practice is often advocated not so much to ease the torment and suffering of the transsexual as it is to serve as a therapeutic measure to prevent him from harming himself either physically or mentally. The therapeutic effect then of the surgery is indirect, in deterring the patient from subsequently injuring himself. This is an extension of traditional interpretations of therapeutic motive and it remains to be seen whether public policy will accept such an extension in this controversial context.
>
> If full, knowing consent has been given by the patient and medical opinion feels conversion surgery in some degree to be irrefutably indicated, then, it is submitted, the public has no interest in denying the acute transsexual the only means currently known to medical science for relief of his severe, self-endangering condition by threatening the performing surgeon with criminal prosecution.

Sex reassignment operations are now available within the National Health Service. Their legality was probably established by the case of *Corbett v Corbett (otherwise Ashley)* [1970] 2 All ER 33. Although this case concerned the validity of a purported marriage between a man and another who had undergone a sex reassignment operation and so the legality of the operation did not specifically arise, Ormrod J clearly did not regard it as unlawful. He said (at p 43):

> There is, obviously, room for differences of opinion on the ethical aspects of such operations but, if they are undertaken for genuine therapeutic purposes, it is a matter for the decision of the patient and the doctors concerned in his case. The passing of the Sexual Offences Act 1967, s 1, seems to have removed any legal objections which there might have been to such procedures.

His reference to the Sexual Offences Act 1967 is, perhaps, a little curious since this legalises sexual intercourse between consenting male adults over the age of 21. What do you think that he had in mind? Since then, however, public policy, and the legality of the procedure, have never been questioned again (e g *R v Tan* [1983] QB 1053, CA and *Rees v United Kingdom* [1987] 2 FLR 111 (ECtHR)).

Is there any common theme in these examples? Could it be in the concept of treatment? Do you think, therefore, that if a procedure is described as 'treatment', then it will be lawful ie not contrary to public policy? If this is so, who should be the arbiter of what 'treatment' is?

(ii) TORT

As distinct from the law of contract, the law of torts applies so as to regulate all doctor/patient relationships. The two torts which primarily concern us are battery and negligence.

(a) Battery

Professor Fleming in his *Law of Torts* (7th ed 1987) defines a battery (at p 23):

> Of the various forms of trespass to the person the most common is the tort known as battery, which is committed by intentionally bringing about a harmful or offensive contact with the person of another. The action, therefore, serves the dual purpose of affording protection to the individual not only against bodily harm but also against any interference with his person which is offensive to a reasonable sense of honour and dignity. The insult in being touched without consent has been traditionally regarded as sufficient, even though the interference is only trivial and not attended with actual physical harm.

Applying this to the touching of a patient by a doctor, Cardozo J stated in a much quoted passage from *Schloendorff v Society of New York Hospital* (1914) 105 NE 92:

> Every human being of adult years and sound mind has a right to determine what shall be done with his own body; and a surgeon who performs an operation without his patient's consent commits an assault [sc battery], for which he is liable in damages.

There have been relatively few cases in England in which a patient has successfully sued his doctor for battery on the ground that he had not consented to being touched. However, there are one or two examples—*Hamilton v Birmingham RHB* [1969] 2 BMJ 456 (sterilisation without consent during the performance of a Caesarean section); *Michael v Molesworth* [1950] 2 BMJ 171 (operation performed by a different surgeon from the one agreed); *Cull v Royal Surrey County Hospital* [1932] 1 BMJ 1195 (patient consented to an abortion and the doctor carried out a different procedure, a hysterectomy). This does not mean that the tort of battery is unimportant. Its greatest significance lies in the fact that it represents, as Cardozo J pointed out in *Schloendorff*, a statement by the law of the importance of an individual patient's right to determine what should or should not be done to his body. Further proof of this is, of course, the fact that, as regards the tort of battery, the plaintiff need not prove that he has suffered harm so as to recover damages. Harm is assumed, since the tort protects the plaintiff from harm which is symbolic as well as that which results in injury. It is clear that a battery will be committed by a doctor even if he acts only out of what he sees as the best interests of his patient.

Mohr v Williams
104 NW 12 (1905) (Supreme Court of Minnesota)

> Plaintiff consulted defendant, an ear specialist, concerning trouble with her right ear. On examining her, he found a diseased condition of the right ear, and she consented to an operation upon it. When she was unconscious under the anaesthetic, defendant concluded that the condition of the right ear was not serious enough to require an operation; but he found a more serious condition of the left ear, which he decided required an operation. Without reviving the plaintiff to ask her permission, he operated on the left ear. The operation was skilfully performed, and was successful. Plaintiff nevertheless brought an action for battery and succeeded.

Brown J: The last contention of defendant is that the act complained of did not amount to an assault and battery. This is based upon the theory that, as plaintiff's left ear was in fact diseased, in a condition dangerous and threatening to her health, the operation was necessary, and having been skilfully performed at a time when plaintiff had requested a like operation on the other ear, the charge of assault and battery cannot be sustained; that, in view of these conditions, and the claim that there was no negligence on the part of defendant, and an entire absence of any evidence tending to show an evil intent, the court should say, as a matter of law, that no assault and battery was committed, even though she did not consent to the operation. In other words, that the absence of a showing that defendant was actuated by a wrongful intent, or guilty of negligence, relieves the act of defendant from the charge of an unlawful assault and battery.

We are unable to reach that conclusion, though the contention is not without merit. It would seem to follow from what has been said on the other features of the case that the act of defendant amounted at least to a technical assault and battery. If the operation was performed without plaintiff's consent, and the circumstances were not such as to justify its performance without, it was wrongful; and, if it was wrongful, it was unlawful. As remarked in *1 Jaggard on Torts*, 437, every person has a right to complete immunity of his person from physical interference of others, except in so far as contact may be necessary under the general doctrine of privilege; and any unlawful or unauthorised touching of the person of another, except it be in the spirit of pleasantry, constitutes an assault and battery. In the case at bar, as we have already seen, the question whether defendant's act in performing the operation upon plaintiff was authorised was a question for the jury to determine. If it was unauthorised, then it was, within what we have said, unlawful. It was a violent assault, not a mere pleasantry; and, even though no negligence is shown, it was wrongful and unlawful.

(For a similar case in Canada, see *Murray v McMurchy* [1949] 2 DLR 442 (Supreme Court of British Columbia).)

The variety of situations in which a battery action may be brought is explored by Allan McCoid in his seminal article 'A Reappraisal of Liability for Unauthorised Medical Treatment' (1957) 41 Minnesota LR 381, 422–424 (footnotes omitted).

The study of cases involving unauthorised operations or medical treatment indicates the existence of a great diversity of factual situations ranging from a case such as *Schloendorff v Society of New York Hospital*, in which the doctor operated in direct violation of express prohibitions of the patient and the operation resulted in serious physical injury, to cases such as *Mohr v Williams* or *Pratt v Davis*, in which the operation was done without the express consent of the patient but probably caused no serious harm to the patient and in point of fact may have conferred some benefit. Between these two extremes lie cases in which there was only a limitation upon a general scope of consent the violation of which did not seriously injure the patient, as in *Rolater v Strain*, and cases in which there was no express prohibition but substantial harm resulted to the patient from an operation which went beyond the scope of express consent, as in *Wall v Brim* or *Paulsen v Gundersen*. Yet the courts tend to group together all of these diverse fact situations under the category of 'assault and battery' and rely upon any one of the early cases as authority for imposing liability upon the doctor which may differ substantially from the nature and scope of liability in a general malpractice action.

. . .

Traditionally the distinction between an 'assault and battery' and a 'negligent tort' has been drawn on the basis of the existence or nonexistence of 'intent', that state of mind in which the actor acts for the purpose of accomplishing a given consequence or acts with knowledge that such a consequence is substantially certain to occur, although there need be no showing of a hostile or malicious purpose or of an intent to do harm. In all of the cases discussed in this article, the physician knew what he was doing; he knew that he was performing a certain operation or that he was rendering certain treatment affecting the body of the patient. In all but a few of the cases it is to be inferred that he also knew that there was no specific assent to such operation or treatment, and in some of those few the lack of such knowledge was the result of mistake as to the identity of the patient or the identity of a particular portion of the body to be treated, neither of which would constitute a defense. In each of the cases there has been a legal 'harm' in the sense of a physically harmful invasion of the body of the plaintiff-patient or an interference with the patient's personal integrity or right to determine what shall and shall not be done with his body. Following these traditional lines of analysis, one would conclude that except in a very rare case, such as a true emergency, the doctor who acts without the consent of a patient is guilty of an assault and battery.

What appears to distinguish the case of the unauthorised operation from traditional assault and battery cases is the fact that in almost all of the cases, the doctor is acting in relative good faith for the benefit of the patient. It is true that in some cases the results are not in fact beneficial, but the courts have stated repeatedly that doctors are not insurers. The traditional assault and battery, on the other hand, involves a defendant who is acting for the most part out of malice or in a manner which is generally considered as 'anti-social'. And in general the assaulter and batterer is not seeking to confer any benefit upon the plaintiff, even though he may believe, as Dean Prosser has suggested, that he is complimenting the plaintiff by his amatory advances. This leads to the conclusion that there is some basis for separating most of the cases discussed in this paper from the traditional assault and battery. At the same time, there appears to be justification for retaining the 'assault and battery' classification for such situations as occurred in *Bryan v Grace, Wellman v Drake* and *Keen v Coleman*, as well as the 'fraud' cases. Operations, declared to be anti-social in their very nature by statutes making their performance a crime, deserve specialised treatment.

So, the central issue for the medical lawyer here is the legal notion of consent. We will return in some detail to this in chapter 4. For the present, notice the following:

1. A legally valid, or real, consent consists of the following elements:
(a) it is given by a competent person;
(b) it is given voluntarily;
(c) it is an informed consent.

2. As to (a), we have already seen in our discussion of *Gillick* earlier that the legal requirement of competence means that the patient must have the capacity to comprehend certain information relating to the nature, purpose and consequences of the touching. In the case of adults, competence is presumed. By virtue of section 8 of the Family Law Reform Act 1969 this presumption is extended to children aged between 16 and 18 for 'surgical, medical or dental treatment'. There is no such presumption in the case of younger children: that was the context in which *Gillick* was decided.

Some adults will not be presumed competent or, more accurately, the usual presumption will be easily rebutted, for example, when the patient is demented or mentally handicapped.

In the case of those who are *incompetent* to make a particular decision concerning their medical treatment, we shall have to explore later the possibility of *proxy* or *surrogate* consent by another, for example, a parent in the case of a child. Similarly we will explore later the legal rules, if any, concerned with when a doctor may treat an incompetent patient, for example, an unconscious patient requiring treatment in an emergency.

3. As to (b) in 1 above, we will see later that permission *in*voluntarily given, is not in law a valid consent.

4. As to (c), we will explore later in detail the information which a patient must have concerning any proposed treatment, in order to give a valid consent. Further, we will see that the answer to this question also serves as a way of

assisting us to determine whether a failure to disclose information to a patient is a matter for the tort of battery or negligence.

Consider the following cases:

Reibl v Hughes
(1980) 114 DLR (3d) 1 (Can. SC)

Laskin CJ: The tort [of battery] is an intentional one, consisting of an unprivileged and unconsented to invasion of one's bodily security. True enough, it has some advantages for a plaintiff over an action of negligence since it does not require proof of causation and it casts upon the defendant the burden of proving consent to what was done. Again, it does not require the adducing of medical evidence, although it seems to me that if battery is to be available for certain kinds of failure to meet the duty of disclosure there would necessarily have to be some such evidence brought before the Court as an element in determining whether there has been such a failure . . .

The well-known statement of Cardozo J in *Schloendorff v Society of New York Hospital* (1914), 211 NY 125 at 129, 105 NE 92 at 93, that 'every human being of adult years and sound mind has a right to determine what shall be done with his own body; and a surgeon who performs an operation without his patient's consent commits an assault, for which he is liable in damages' cannot be taken beyond the compass of its words to support an action of battery where there has been consent to the very surgical procedure carried out upon a patient but there has been a breach of the duty of disclosure of attendant risks. In my opinion, actions of battery in respect of surgical or other medical treatment should be confined to cases where surgery or treatment has been performed or given to which there has been no consent at all or where, emergency situations aside, surgery or treatment has been performed or given beyond that to which there was consent.

. . .

In situations where the allegation is that attendant risks which should have been disclosed were not communicated to the patient and yet the surgery or other medical treatment carried out was that to which the plaintiff consented (there being no negligence basis of liability for the recommended surgery or treatment to deal with the patient's condition), I do not understand how it can be said that the consent was vitiated by the failure of disclosure so as to make the surgery or other treatment an unprivileged, unconsented to and intentional invasion of the patient's bodily integrity. I can appreciate the temptation to say that the genuineness of consent to medical treatment depends on proper disclosure of the risks which it entails, but in my view, unless there has been misrepresentation or fraud to secure consent to the treatment, a failure to disclose the attendant risks, however serious, should go to negligence rather than to battery. Although such a failure relates to an informed choice of submitting to or refusing recommended and appropriate treatment, it arises as the breach of an anterior duty of due care, comparable in legal obligation to the duty of due care in carrying out the particular treatment to which the patient has consented. It is not a test of the validity of the consent.

You will see from this extract from the leading Canadian case, that the Chief Justice considered that the scope of battery in medical law is restricted. Failure of the doctor to provide information will only in exceptional circumstances mean that the patient has not consented to a particular procedure. It is another matter, as we will see, whether an action in negligence may lie for the non-disclosure.

In England the courts have similarly restricted the availability of the tort of battery in medical law.

Chatterton v Gerson
[1981] QB 432

The plaintiff sought pain relief from the defendant doctor. He injected her intrathecally with phenol solution so as to interrupt the nerve connection to the brain. She alleged that he had not warned her that this might lead to numbness and possible loss of muscle power—the very thing which resulted. She failed in her claim which was pleaded alternatively in battery and in negligence. As to the former, Bristow J said:

In my judgment what the court has to do in each case is to look at all the circumstances and say 'Was there a real consent?' I think justice requires that in order to vitiate the reality of consent there must be a greater failure of communication between doctor and patient than that involved in a breach of duty if the claim is based on negligence. When the claim is based on negligence the plaintiff must prove not only the breach of duty to inform, but that had the duty not been broken she would not have chosen to have the operation. Where the claim is based on trespass to the person, once it is shown that the consent is unreal, then what the plaintiff would have decided if she had been given the information which would have prevented vitiation of the reality of her consent is irrelevant.

In my judgment once the patient is informed in broad terms of the nature of the procedure which is intended, and gives her consent, that consent is real, and the cause of the action on which to base a claim for failure to go into risks and implications is negligence, not trespass. Of course if information is withheld in bad faith, the consent will be vitiated by fraud. Of course if by some accident, as in a case in the 1940s in the Salford Hundred Court where a boy was admitted to hospital for tonsillectomy and due to administrative error was circumcised instead, trespass would be the appropriate cause of action against the doctor, though he was as much the victim of the error as the boy. But in my judgment it would be very much against the interests of justice if actions which are really based on a failure by the doctor to perform his duty adequately to inform were pleaded in trespass.

Similarly in *Hills v Potter* [1984] 1 WLR 641, the plaintiff had not been informed of the risk of paralysis and was left paralysed from the neck down after an operation to effect a cure for a neck deformity. Hirst J said:

As to the claim for assault and battery, the plaintiff's undoubted consent to the operation which was in fact performed negatives any possibility of liability under this head: see *Chatterton v Gerson* [1981] QB 432.

(The plaintiff's claim in negligence also failed.)

The leading English case is *Sidaway v Bethlem Royal Hospital Governors* [1984] 1 All ER 1018, CA; [1985] 1 All ER 643, HL. This case concerned a woman who underwent an operation to relieve pain in her neck and shoulders. The surgeon told her of the possibility of disturbing a nerve root and the consequences of this. However, she alleged that he did not tell her that there was a risk of damaging the spinal cord and the possibly catastrophic consequences if that transpired. In fact, this did occur and the plaintiff sued. She brought her action in negligence, no doubt in light of *Chatterton* and *Hills*. Her action failed, but the Court of Appeal chose to state its view of the scope and application of the tort of battery. In what circumstances, if any, could failure to disclose information give rise to an action in battery? Sir John Donaldson MR said:

Consent
I am wholly satisfied that as a matter of English law a consent is not vitiated by a failure on the part of the doctor to give the patient sufficient information before the consent is given. It is only if the consent is obtained by fraud or by misrepresentation of the nature of what is to be done that it can be said that an apparent consent is not a true consent. This is the position in the criminal law (*R v Clarence* (1888) 22 QBD 23, 43) and the cause of action based upon trespass to the person is closely analogous. I should add that the contrary was not argued upon this appeal.

Dunn LJ said:

The first argument was that unless the patient's consent to the operation was a fully informed consent the performance of the operation would constitute a battery on the patient by the surgeon. This is not the law of England. If there is consent to the nature of the act, then there is no trespass to the person. So in *R v Clarence*, 22 QBD 23, a conviction of rape was quashed where the woman did not know that the prisoner was suffering from a venereal disease which he communicated to her. If she had known, she would not have consented to sexual intercourse, but as she had consented to the act of sexual intercourse, even though without knowledge of the probable risk of infection, there was no rape. On the other hand, in *R v Flattery* (1877) 2 QBD 410 where a doctor had had sexual intercourse with a patient under pretence of performing a surgical operation, his conviction of rape was upheld because the patient had only consented to an operation and not to the act of sexual intercourse. As Bristow J said in *Chatterton v Gerson* [1981] QB 432, 443: 'once the patient is informed in broad terms of the nature of the procedure which is intended, and gives her consent, that consent is real' so that it affords a defence to a battery.

In dismissing Mrs Sidaway's appeal, the House of Lords made no comment on this aspect of the case.

Finally, in *Freeman v Home Office (No 2)* [1984] 1 All ER 1036, Sir John Donaldson MR reiterated his earlier views in *Sidaway*:

> If there was real consent to the treatment, it mattered not whether the doctor was in breach of his duty to give the patient the appropriate information before that consent was given. Real consent provides a complete defence to a claim based on the tort of trespass to the person. Consent would not be real if procured by fraud or misrepresentation but, subject to this and subject to the patient having been informed in broad terms of the nature of the treatment, consent in fact amounts to consent in law.

5. Notice that both Laskin CJ in *Reibl* and Sir John Donaldson MR in both *Sidaway* and *Freeman*, while restricting the scope of battery in medical law, were prepared to recognise a situation in which battery would be relevant, namely when the doctor had practised fraud or misrepresentation. Do you see any differences in the potential scope given to fraud and misrepresentation by the two judges?

6. It is clear that the English courts do not favour the action in battery in the context of medical treatment. In *Hills v Potter* Hirst J said

> I should add that I respectfully agree with Bristow J [in *Chatterton*] in deploring reliance on these torts in medical cases of this kind; the proper cause of action, if any, is negligence.

Lord Scarman expressly agreed with these remarks in *Sidaway* when the case reached the House of Lords. Why should this be so? Consider the following remarks of Justice Mosk in the Californian case of *Cobbs v Grant* (1972) 502 P 2d 1.

> [M]ost jurisdictions have permitted a doctor in an informed consent action to interpose a defense that the disclosure he omitted to make was not required within his medical community. However, expert opinion as to community standard is not required in a battery count, in which the patient must merely prove failure to give informed consent and a mere touching absent consent. Moreover a doctor could be held liable for punitive damages under a battery count, and if held liable for the intentional tort of battery he might not be covered by his malpractice insurance. Comment, 'Informed Consent in Medical Malpractice', 55 Cal L Rev 1396 (1967). Additionally, in some jurisdictions the patient has a longer statute of limitations if he sues in negligence.

Do any or all of these reasons apply in England? In particular, will a doctor's defence organisation act for him, and pay any damages awarded against him, in an action for battery brought against him?

7. The decision of the Court of Appeal in *Wilson v Pringle* [1986] 2 All ER 440 in which it was held that a 'hostile' touching was required for the tort of battery to lie was not applied in the medical case of *T v T* [1988] 1 All ER 613. Wood J said, '[t]he incision made by the surgeon's scalpel need not be and probably is most unlikely to be hostile, but unless a defence or justification is established it must in my judgment fall within the definition of [battery]'.

(b) Negligence

Most legal actions arising from the professional conduct of a doctor in relation to his patient are brought in the tort of negligence. These actions are often referred to as 'medical malpractice' and we deal in detail with them in ch 5. Here we merely seek to outline the basic elements of them.

In order to succeed in an action for medical negligence, a patient must establish the following:
1. That a duty of care was owed by the doctor to the patient.
2. That the doctor was in breach of the appropriate standard of care imposed by the law.
3. That the breach of duty caused the patient harm or injury recognised by law as meriting compensation.
4. That the extent and *quantum* of the loss that has flowed from the breach of duty is recoverable in law.

1. Duty of care

We have already seen in the previous chapter that a doctor owes a duty of care to his patient. In general terms the scope of the doctor's duty will relate to all aspects of his care of the patient, ie diagnosis, treatment, and, as we shall see, advice and counselling. Thus, a legal action concerning a doctor's duty of care may relate, *inter alia*, to a failure to prevent an illness, failure to attend or examine a patient, making a wrong diagnosis, committing an error in the course of treatment or failing to explain properly what a particular treatment involves.

A difficult question concerning the scope of a doctor's (or a hospital's) duty to take care of a patient has arisen in a number of cases alleging the careless supervision of mentally disturbed patients who kill (or attempt to kill) themselves. Picard, in *Legal Liability of Doctors and Hospitals in Canada* (2nd ed 1984 pp 308–311) explores this. As you will see, she treats the question as involving a species of the primary liability of a hospital.

> The hospital may in some cases have a duty to establish procedures to prevent the patient from injuring himself. In a number of cases a patient has leapt from a hospital window and later sued the hospital alleging that there was a duty to provide surveillance and safeguards. In the sole case[69] in which liability was found against the hospital, the patient was a psychiatric patient with suicidal tendencies who fell to his death from a hospital window. He had been transferred to a semi-private room from the psychiatric ward and, according to the evidence, was recognised as being a 'patient to be watched'. The majority of the Supreme Court of Canada wrote no judgment in this important case but adopted that of the dissenting member of the Court of Appeal. The hospital's liability seems to have been both direct and vicarious and it is unfortunate that the Supreme Court of Canada did not take this opportunity to clarify some of the issues in this important area.
>
> In another case[70] that went to the Supreme Court of Canada, the court held that the neurological patient's sudden leap through the window was not foreseeable and could only have been avoided by taking extreme precautions such as using a restraining device or putting the patient at ground level. However, the lower courts[71]

had held that the hospital was negligent by failing to provide constant supervision of this patient who was suffering from 'epilepsy with post-epileptic automatism' and whose 'tendency to irresponsible moving about was well known to all concerned'.[72]

In the third case[73] to go to our highest court the plaintiff was a surgical patient who, following abdominal surgery, became confused, disturbed and suffered from vivid hallucinations. The hospital assigned three special nurses to care for the patient on eight-hour shifts, but during one of the nurse's coffee breaks he went through a window. All parties to the action agreed that there was no direct liability upon the hospital because the procedures and treatment it had set up for the patient's care met the standard of care expected. Furthermore, there was no vicarious liability found because the risk of the patient doing what he did was not foreseeable to the nurse.

In three other cases[74] the hospitals were also exonerated on the basis that the patient's self-inflicted injury was not a foreseeable risk. In all cases where no liability was found the court accepted evidence that there was no sign that the patient needed special surveillance or that the patient was a danger to himself.

A British Colombia case[75] presents a marked contrast to all those discussed because the Court of Appeal accepted a new standard of care described by the trial judge in these terms:[76]

Taking their evidence, [the defendant's experts] as well as that of other witnesses with professional qualifications and experience in this field of expertise, a *clear picture emerges of a drastic change in the medical approach* to the hospitalisation and treatment of mentally confused or disturbed patients over the last three decades. The old 'locked asylum' concept was non-therapeutic and, as one witness put it, resulted in most people incarcerated in such institutions rarely getting out again. Today the emphasis is on therapy rather than imprisonment; and most mental institutions have, in common with EMI, an 'open door' policy with respect to all except the most seriously, or permanently, disturbed patients, with the emphasis on cure and return to the community.

That this system has its risks is clear from the evidence. Patients escape (or 'elope') in numbers which I found astonishing; and suicides are a far from uncommon occurrence, although there is no evidence that the 'open door' policy has increased this risk. As Dr McFarlane put it, *a decision must be made whether to run a prison, or a hospital;* and no hospital, he said, can be made 'totally suicide proof' [emphasis supplied].

After the open door policy was applied as an appropriate standard of care the hospital was held not to be directly or vicariously liable when a patient injured herself in an escape attempt. Mr Justice Craig said the issue was whether it was reasonably foreseeable that *this* patient might jump over the wall of the roof garden in an attempt to escape. Two other aspects of the judgment are worth noting: a subjective test of the patient was accepted and the test used for measuring proximate cause was unusually precise.

While a subjective appraisal of a psychiatric patient would seem patently reasonable, the direction of Canadian jurisprudence has been that it is not necessary to foresee the 'precise concatenation of events: it is enough to fix liability if one can foresee in a general way the class or character of injury which occurred'.[77] Because escapes were common, and by the new standard of care foreseeable, and because there were 'countless ways' escaping patients might be injured, it seems liability would have followed had the accepted test of proximate cause been applied in this case. It remains to be seen whether the 'open door policy' standard and its consequences will be accepted by other courts.[78]

Thus, it would seem that the duty to supervise a patient will arise when the hospital knows or ought to know of the risk of self-injury.[79] However, the hospital is not an insurer against all hazards and would not be liable if the event in which the patient is injured was not foreseeable.

Notes to extract
69 *Villemure v Turcot*, [1973] SCR 716; for an English case where liability was found, see *Selfe v Ilford* (1970) Times, 26 November.

70 *University Hospital Board v Lepine*, [1966] SCR 561.
71 (1965), 53 WWR 513; which varied 50 WWR, 709 (Alta CA).
72 *University Hosp Bd v Lepine supra* n 70 at 570 quoting Farthing J at trial.
73 *Child v Vancouver Gen Hosp supra* n 31.
74 *Stadel v Albertson*, [1954] 2 DLR 328 (Sask CA); *Flynn v Hamilton*, [1950], OWN
224 (CA); *Brandeis v Weldon* (1916), 27 DLR 235 (BCCA).
75 *Worth v Royal Jubilee Hosp* (1980), 4 L Med Q 59 (BCCA).
76 *Id.*
77 *R v Coté* (1974), 51 DLR (3d) 244 at 252 (SCC) (*per* Dickson J) quoted in Linden,
Canadian Tort Law 345 (1982).
78 See Schiffer, *Psychiatry Behind Bars* 154 (1982), where the author *quaeres* how
the 'open door' policy is to be reconciled with the statutory requirement that an
involuntary (and apparently dangerous) patient be supervised and controlled for her
own welfare and the protection of others.
79 See *Foote v Royal Columbian Hosp* (1983), 19 ACWS (2d) 304 (BCCA). The high
risk of a patient suffering a seizure while bathing was held not to have been
'understood' by nurses.

Such actions have been relatively rare in England. Picard refers (in footnote
69) to one, the *Selfe* case. Powell and Jackson, *Professional Negligence* (2nd ed
1987) para 6.102 set the scene of the English case law:

In *Selfe v Ilford & District Hospital Management Committee*[83] the defendants were
held liable for failing properly to supervise a suicidal patient. The patient was put in
a ground floor ward with 26 other patients, three of whom were suicide risks. There
was an unlocked window at the back of his bed. Hinchcliffe J considered that
supervision by an 'absolute minimum' of three nurses was required. There were
three nurses on duty at the material time. However, two had left the ward for various
reasons and the third was attending to a patient. The plaintiff slipped out through
the window and threw himself from a roof, suffering serious injuries. By contrast, in
Thorne v Northern Group Hospital Management Committee[84] the defendants escaped
liability for the suicide of a patient, because they had exercised reasonable care.
Edmund-Davies J accepted that a greater degree of care and supervision was
required in relation to patients who were suicide risks. However, not every suicide
threat was to be taken seriously. It was for the medical staff to decide in each case
whether stricter supervision was called for or whether the threat was merely
hysterical and, as such, could be largely or even entirely ignored.[85]

Notes to extract
83 *The Times*, 26 November, 1970.
84 *The Times*, 6 June, 1964 and (1964) 108 SJ 115.
85 See also the Canadian decision *Stadel v Albertson* [1954] 2 DLR 328: doctors not
put on notice of the patient's suicidal tendencies.

The only appellate decision in England is the decision of the Court of Appeal in
Hyde v Tameside Area Health Authority, (1981) Times, 15 April. The following
extracts are taken from the Lexis transcript.

Lord Denning MR: In this case a man who attempted to commit suicide has been
awarded £200,000 for his injuries. The first award of its kind ever made in this
country. Is it right?
    In February 1972 Eric Hyde tried to kill himself. He was in a ward on the third
floor of the General Hospital at Ashton-under-Lyne. In the middle of the night of
the 7th February, he got out of bed, smashed the window, jumped out, landed on a
parapet and flung himself from there on to the roadway outside. He lay there
unconscious. He was picked up and taken to the emergency department. He came
round and kept saying, 'Let me die. I have got an incurable disease and want to die'.
He was taken into intensive care. He survived. But as a total wreck. He has total
paralysis of the arms, body and legs, and loss of bladder and bowel control. He is

completely helpless. But he has a devoted wife who has looked after him well. He now sues the hospital authorities for negligence. If the hospital authorities are liable, the damages have been agreed at £200,000. The judge has held that the hospital staff fell short of the standard of competence reasonably to be expected of them. He gave judgment for Mr Hyde for £200,000.

What made this man do this thing? It looks as if it was because he had got it into his head that he had cancer and was going to die in the next hour or so. Shortly before he jumped out of the window, he wrote moving letters to his wife and to his mother and father and to his cousin. He left the letters to be opened after his death. But he did not die. And he did not have cancer. Instead he is kept alive by all the aids which medical skill provides nowadays. He is, I fear, a burden to himself and his family and to the community.

What did the hospital staff do wrong?

Having examined the evidence Lord Denning continued:

. . . this patient was under the care of several nurses at one time or another. Some on days. Some on nights. Some in the mornings. Some in the afternoons. All well qualified. All well experienced. Each of them, according to the judge, failed to assess the true significance of his mental distress. Each of them fell into error. But, even so, it was at most an error of judgment of such a kind that each of them, acting with ordinary care, might have made. It was not such an error as amounted to negligence. It was the very sort of error which I had in mind when I said—and I repeat— 'We must say, and say firmly, that, in a professional man, an error of judgment is not negligent'. Not every error of judgment, of course, but only those errors which a reasonably competent professional man, acting with ordinary care, might commit.

Having held that there had been no breach of duty, Lord Denning continued:

The second point is on causation. The judge dealt with it on foreseeability. He said: 'I accept that foreseeability is now firmly restored as the test of causation', that is, foreseeability of damage of the same type or class. We have recently had to consider this in the Borag case (*Compania Financiera v Soleada SA Hamoor Tanker Corpn Inc* [1981] 1 All ER 856, [1981] WLR 274) and *Lamb v London Borough of Camden* [1981] QB 625. Those cases show that foreseeability is not the sole or exclusive test. To my mind the attempt at suicide here was far too remote a consequence to be the subject of damages. It is like the sequence of Benjamin Franklin: 'For want of a nail, the shoe was lost; for want of a shoe the horse was lost; and for want of a horse the rider was lost; and for want of a rider the battle was lost'. So here the sequence is: If the nurses had reported this man's depression to the doctors, then the doctors might have called in a consultant psychiatrist. If a consultant psychiatrist had been called in, he might have ordered some treatment which might have had some effect on the depression. If it did have some effect on the patient's depression, it might have prevented him from attempting to commit suicide. All these consequences might have followed. But I think it wrong that the law should chase consequence upon consequence—possibility upon possibility—right down on a hypothetical line—so as to award damages to a man who attempted to commit suicide. To my mind the damages are far too remote.

Seeing that this is the first case of its kind to come before the Court of Appeal, I would add a few words on public policy. There have been three cases of the kind tried by judges of first instance. None reported but we have been supplied with transcripts. The first was of a woman who committed suicide. It was in 1960 whilst suicide was still a crime. She walked out of hospital, went home two miles and gassed herself. Her husband as her personal representative sued the hospital authorities for negligence. It was tried by Mr Justice Edmund Davies. He found that there was no negligence and dismissed the claim. It was *Thorne v Northern Group Hospital Management Committee*, 5th June, 1964. The second was of a man who attempted to commit suicide. It was in 1970 after it ceased to be a crime. He had been suffering for years from schizophrenia. He stabbed himself in the stomach and was taken to a general hospital. He was transferred to a psychiatric hospital.

He left the ward, went up a fire escape, leaped off, fell many feet to the ground, and was so badly injured that he was paraplegic for life. He sued the hospital for negligence: first, in not stopping him from getting up to the fire escape; and second, for not treating his back injury properly. It was tried by Mr Justice Thesiger. He found that there was no negligence in not stopping him, but he gave him £8,000 for not treating his injury properly. It was *Parker v Kent Area Health Authority*, 28th July, 1978. The third case was of a boy of 18 who attempted to commit suicide but failed. He cut his wrists with a razor blade, walked into the sea, was rescued, and taken to a hospital ward. Some hours later, he got out of bed, crossed the ward, jumped out, fell many feet and was so badly injured that he was paralysed for life from the chest downwards. He sued the hospital for negligence. It was tried by Mr Justice Mustill. He found that there was no negligence and dismissed the claim. It was *Jarrett v Yorkshire Regional Health Authority*, 1st July, 1980.

I accept that in all those three cases the plaintiff was legally-aided. It was a great burden on the hospitals and on the legal aid fund to have to fight the cases at great length, and much expense on doctors, nurses and experts—when they could have been better employed.

In none of those cases was the defence raised of contributory negligence. It would be very unlikely to prevail, seeing that his only negligence was that he did not succeed in killing himself. Nor, I suspect, would there be any defence of *volenti non fit injuria*, seeing that he did not willingly injure himself. He wanted to die.

Before 1961 I cannot think that any such claim would have succeeded. Suicide was then a crime. So was attempted suicide. And no one was allowed to benefit from his own deliberate crime. Nor were his personal representatives, see *Beresford v Royal Insurance* [1938] AC 580. Is it any different now? Under the Suicide Act 1961 suicide is no longer a crime. Nor is attempted suicide. But it is still unlawful. It is contrary to ecclesiastical law which was, and is still, part of the general law of England, see *Mackonochie v Lord Penzance* [1881] 6 AC 424 at 466 by Lord Blackburn. The suicide's body was not buried in the churchyard with Christian rites. You will remember the gravediggers' scene in Hamlet (Act V, sc i, 1):

'Is she to be buried in Christian burial that wilfully seeks her own salvation?'

I know this all sounds very out of date: but it has a useful lesson for us in modern times. I feel it is most unfitting that the personal representatives of a suicide should be able to claim damages in respect of his death. At any rate, when he succeeds in killing himself. And I do not see why he should be in any better position when he does not succeed. By his act—in self-inflicting this grievous injury—he has made himself a burden on the whole community. Our hospital services and our social welfare services have done, and will do, all they can to help him and his family—in the grievous injury that he has inflicted on himself and on them. But I see no justification whatever in his being awarded, in addition, the huge sum of £200,000—because he failed in his attempt. Such a sum will have to be raised, in the long run, by society itself—a sum which it cannot well afford. The policy of law should be to discourage these actions. I would disallow them altogether—at the outset—rather than burden the community with them. Especially when, as this experience shows, they all fail in the end. At any rate, all failed before the trial judges until this one—and this one now fails before us.

I would therefore allow the appeal and find for the defendants.

Watkins LJ agreed that there had been no breach of duty but said nothing on the points of causation or public policy. O'Connor LJ also agreed that there had been no breach of duty and added:

I do not think that the fact that a patient commits suicide or attempts suicide will necessarily break the chain of causation if breach of duty is established against the hospital. It all depends on the circumstances of an individual case. In the present case applying *The Wagon Mound Overseas Tankship (VR) Morts Dock & Engineering Co* [1961] AC 388, [1961] 1 All ER 404 I do not think that the injury sustained by the plaintiff can be connected to the breach of duty suggested against the hospital.

Questions

(i) Is the law in England as Picard *op cit* states it to be in Canada or is it as Lord Denning states it in the *Hyde* case?

(ii) Should the court take the view that a doctor (or a hospital) is under a duty to prevent a patient under his care from killing himself? Are either or both of the following relevant in answering this question: (i) whether the patient is being treated for mental illness; (ii) whether the patient is sufficiently competent to understand the implications of his conduct?

(iii) Do you think that the court should invoke public policy to deny a claim in these cases which might otherwise succeed?

(iv) Do you agree with Lord Denning that the defences of contributory negligence and *volenti non fit injuria* could not be successfully pleaded against a victim of suicide (or attempted suicide)?

2. Breach of duty

In order to determine whether a doctor has breached his duty to his patient, we must first establish the standard of care required of him by the law. Again, we will return to this in ch 5; but here we can briefly summarise the position by looking at the following case.

Sidaway v Bethlem Royal Hospital Governors
[1985] 1 All ER 643

Lord Diplock (at p 657): For the last quarter of a century the test applied in English law whether a doctor has fulfilled his duty of care owed to his patient has been that set out in the summing up to the jury by McNair J in *Bolam v Friern Hospital Management Committee* [1957] 2 All ER 118, [1957] 1 WLR 582. I will call this the *Bolam* test. At any rate, so far as diagnosis and treatment are concerned, the *Bolam* test has twice received the express approval of this House.

The *Bolam* test is far from new; its value is that it brings up to date and re-expresses in the light of modern conditions in which the art of medicine is now practised an ancient rule of common law. . . .

The standard of skill and judgment in the particular area of the art of medicine in which the doctor practised . . . was the standard of ordinary skill and care that could be expected to be shown by a doctor who had successfully completed the training to qualify as a doctor, whether as general practitioner or as consultant in a specialty if he held himself out as practising as such, as the case might be. But, unless the art in which the [professional] claims to have acquired skill and judgment is stagnant so that no improvement in methods or knowledge is sought (and of few is this less true than medicine and surgery over the last half-century), advances in the ability to heal resulting from the volume of research, clinical as well as technological, will present doctors with alternative treatments to adopt and a choice to select that treatment (it may be one of several) that is in their judgment likely at the time to prove most efficacious or ameliorating to the health of each particular patient committed to their care.

Those members of the public who seek medical or surgical aid would be badly served by the adoption of any legal principle that would confine the doctor to some long-established, well-tried method of treatment only, although its past record of success might be small, if he wanted to be confident that he would not run the risk of being held liable in negligence simply because he tried some more modern treatment, and by some unavoidable mischance it failed to heal but did some harm to the patient. This would encourage 'defensive medicine' with a vengeance. The merit of the *Bolam* test is that the criterion of the duty of care owed by a doctor to his patient is whether he has acted in accordance with a practice accepted as proper by a body of responsible and skilled medical opinion. There may be a number of different practices which satisfy this criterion at any particular time. These practices are likely to alter with advances in medical knowledge. Experience shows that, to the great benefit of humankind, they have done so, particularly in the recent past. That is why fatal diseases such as smallpox and tuberculosis have within living memory become virtually extinct in countries where modern medical care is generally available.

The *Bolam* test was explained by Lord Scarman at p 649:

The *Bolam* principle may be formulated as a rule that a doctor is not negligent if he acts in accordance with a practice accepted at the time as proper by a responsible body of medical opinion even though other doctors adopt a different practice. In short, the law imposes the duty of care; but the standard of care is a matter of medical judgment.

Similarly, Lord Bridge stated (at p 660):

Broadly, a doctor's professional functions may be divided into three phases: diagnosis, advice and treatment. In performing his functions of diagnosis and treatment, the standard by which English law measures the doctor's duty of care to his patient is not open to doubt. 'The test is the standard of the ordinary skilled man exercising and professing to have that special skill.' These are the words of McNair J in *Bolam v Friern Hospital Management Committee* [1957] 2 All ER 118 at 121, [1957] 1 WLR 582 at 586, approved by this House in *Whitehouse v Jordan* [1981] 1 All ER 276 at 277, [1981] 1 WLR 246 at 258 per Lord Edmund-Davies and in *Maynard v West Midlands Regional Health Authority* [1985] 1 All ER 635 per Lord Scarman. The test is conveniently referred to as the *Bolam* test. In *Maynard*'s case Lord Scarman, with whose speech the other four members of the Appellate Committee agreed, further cited with approval the words of the Lord President (Clyde) in *Hunter v Hanley* 1955 SLT 213 at 217:

In the realm of diagnosis and treatment there is ample scope for genuine difference of opinion and one man clearly is not negligent merely because his conclusion differs from that of other professional men ... The true test for establishing negligence in diagnosis or treatment on the part of a doctor is whether he has been proved to be guilty of such failure as no doctor of ordinary skill would be guilty of if acting with ordinary care ...

The language of the *Bolam* test clearly requires a different degree of skill from a specialist in his own special field than from a general practitioner. In the field of neuro-surgery it would be necessary to substitute for the Lord President's phrase 'no doctor of ordinary skill', the phrase 'no neuro-surgeon of ordinary skill'. All this is elementary and, in the light of the two recent decisions of this House referred to, firmly established law.

A number of issues arise which we mention here to alert the reader to the complications implicit in what may seem a clear and simple principle of law.

(a) Is it correct to say that compliance with a practice accepted by a body of responsible medical opinion is, in law, inconsistent with a finding of negligence? The above extracts seem to suggest that it is. Yet, as we will see in ch 5, there are several cases which seem to accept that the court has a right to set the legal standard of care even if medical opinion approves of the particular doctor's conduct (eg *F v R* (1983) 33 SASR 189; *Chasney v Anderson* (1950) 4 DLR 223; *Hucks v Coles*, (1968) Times, 9 May). (For a detailed consideration of this, see *infra* p 413–17.)

(b) How can a breach of duty be established? For example, will a departure from an (or the) approved practice within the medical profession amount *ipso facto* to negligence? Can a plaintiff rely on the maxim, applied elsewhere in the law of negligence, of *res ipsa loquitur* (the thing speaks for itself)? (See *infra* p 422 *et seq*.)

(c) You will notice that Lord Bridge in *Sidaway* speaks of the three functions of a doctor: 'diagnosis, advice and treatment'. What we have seen so far in this section is concerned with the first and the last of these. *Sidaway* was, of course, concerned with the second-advice. Does a doctor's duty of care in tort include a duty to advise his patient of the risks involved in a medical procedure and any alternatives to it which are available? If so, what is the standard of care to be applied? The answer to the first of these questions is that there must obviously be some sort of duty to volunteer information. The answer to the second is more problematical. Is the standard of care the same as for treatment and diagnosis? Will compliance with an accepted practice of non-disclosure of a given risk or alternative exonerate a doctor from a finding of breach of duty? Will the doctor owe the same or a greater duty to advise his patient if rather than giving advice he is answering a question put to him by the patient? The detailed consideration of these questions can be found in ch 4. Consider for the moment these short extracts from the *Sidaway* case.

Lord Scarman (pp 654–5): In a medical negligence case where the issue is as to the advice and information given to the patient as to the treatment proposed, the available options and the risk, the court is concerned primarily with a patient's rights. The doctor's duty arises from his patient's rights. If one considers the scope of the doctor's duty by beginning with the right of the patient to make his own decision whether he will or will not undergo the treatment proposed, the right to be informed of significant risk and the doctor's corresponding duty are easy to understand, for the proper implementation of the right requires that the doctor be under a duty to inform his patient of the material risks inherent in the treatment. And it is plainly right that a doctor may avoid liability for failure to warn of a material risk if he can show that he reasonably believed that communications to the patient of the existence of the risk would be detrimental to the health (including, of course, the mental health) of his patient.

. . . The test of materiality is whether in the circumstance of the particular case the court is satisfied that a reasonable person in the patient's position would be likely to attach significance to the risk.

Lord Bridge (p 663): The issue whether non-disclosure in a particular case should be condemned as a breach of the doctor's duty of care is an issue to be decided primarily on the basis of expert medical evidence, applying the *Bolam* test. But I do not see that this approach involves the necessity 'to hand over to the medical profession the entire question of the scope of the duty of disclosure, including the question whether there has been a breach of that duty'. Of course, if there is a conflict of evidence whether a responsible body of medical opinion approves of non-disclosure in a particular case, the judge will have to resolve that conflict. But, even in a case where, as here, no expert witness in the relevant medical field condemns the non-disclosure as being in conflict with accepted and responsible medical practice, I am of opinion that the judge might in certain circumstances come to the conclusion that disclosure of a particular risk was so obviously necessary to an informed choice on the part of the patient that no reasonably prudent medical man would fail to make it. The kind of case I have in mind would be an operation involving a substantial risk of grave adverse consequences, as for example the 10% risk of a stroke from the operation which was the subject of the Canadian case of *Reibl v Hughes* (1980) 114 DLR (3d) In such a case, in the absence of some cogent clinical reason why the patient should not be informed, a doctor, recognising and respecting his patient's right of decision, could hardly fail to appreciate the necessity for an appropriate warning.

Lord Diplock (pp 657–9): This general duty is not subject to dissection into a number of component parts to which different criteria of what satisfy the duty of care apply, such as diagnosis, treatment and advice (including warning of any risks of something going wrong however skilfully the treatment advised is carried out). . . .

My Lords, no convincing reason has in my view been advanced before your Lordships that would justify treating the *Bolam* test as doing anything less than laying down a principle of English law that is comprehensive and applicable to every aspect of the duty of care owed by a doctor to his patient in the exercise of his healing functions as respects that patient. . . .

To decide what risks the existence of which a patient should be voluntarily warned and the terms in which such warning, if any, should be given, having regard to the effect that the warning may have, is as much an exercise of professional skill and judgment as any other part of the doctor's comprehensive duty of care to the individual patient, and expert medical evidence on this matter should be treated in just the same way. The *Bolam* test should be applied.

(Lord Keith agreed with Lord Bridge; Lord Templeman gave a speech also dismissing the plaintiff's appeal.) Did the House of Lords regard the *Bolam* test as being applicable also in cases involving disclosure of information? If not, what test did the judges lay down?

3. Causation

In cases of medical negligence it is often difficult for the plaintiff to prove that the doctor's breach of duty caused the harm or injury he has suffered. There are two components to this legal requirement: first, the plaintiff must show that the harm or injury would not have occurred '*but for*' the doctor's negligence and secondly, that the harm or injury was a *reasonably foreseeable* consequence of the doctor's negligence rather than one which was too remote. The first aspect of causation is illustrated by the case of *Robinson v Post Office* [1974] 2 All ER 737.

Orr LJ: The circumstances of the accident, which took place between 10.00 and 10.30 am on 15th February 1968, were that he slipped when descending the ladder of one of the Post Office's tower wagons and sustained a wound some three inches long on his left shin. It was not in dispute that the cause of his slipping was the presence of oil on the ladder due to leakage of a pump and that the Post Office were liable for such modest damages as would have been attributable to the plaintiff's wound had nothing further supervened, but unfortunately, as a result of the medical treatment given to the plaintiff, very grave consequences supervened, and the contest in the action was as to the Post Office's liability for these consequences.

The plaintiff after his fall was able to carry on working until knocking-off time at 5.30 pm, after which he went to his general practitioner, Dr MacEwan, who saw him just after 6.00 pm and, after examining the wound, ascertaining its circumstances and that it had been caused some $7\frac{1}{2}$ to eight hours before, and enquiring what anti-tetanus injections the plaintiff had previously had, sent him to a chemist for anti-tetanus serum (hereinafter in this judgment referred to as 'ATS') and on his return gave him an injection of the serum. The plaintiff's own evidence was that from then until 24th February he felt perfectly well, was playing with his children, and was only absent from work because of the wound. His mother, however, gave evidence of his suffering, at the earliest three days after the injection, from an irritation which is referred to in the paragraph entitled 'History' in a report dated 23rd April 1968 by the medical registrar at the Ipswich Hospital and was taken by him to have been giant urticaria. On 24th February, nine days after the injection, the plaintiff showed signs of reaction which were not at first thought to be serious but on the following day he became delirious and on 26th February he was admitted to hospital and was on admission unable to speak. It was not in dispute at the trial that the plaintiff had at this time, as a result of the injection, contracted encephalitis, which is a possible, though a rare, consequence of the administration of ATS; and that the brain damage so sustained has been followed by very severe consequences. The plaintiff appeared at first to make a very good recovery but the improvement was short-lived. He had in early 1969, as a direct result of the brain damage, two attacks of an epileptic character and although there have been no further such attacks there is a risk of their recurrence. He is, as the judge found, a very different man from what he would have been if the accident had not befallen him.

... the judge held that it had not in the circumstances been negligent of Dr MacEwan to administer ATS but that he had been negligent in failing to administer a proper test dose. He went on, however, to find as a fact that if a proper test dose had been administered the plaintiff would not have shown any reaction to it and therefore the failure to administer a proper test dose had not caused or materially contributed to the encephalitis; ...

The judge on this evidence found as a fact that, important as the test procedure was, it was not by any means a certain safeguard against reaction in that, even if the proper test dose procedure were observed and no sign of reaction appeared in half an hour, a patient could still react after a full dose was administered, and in such circumstances he considered that, provided the doctor had not been negligent in deciding to inject ATS at all, what followed would be the patient's misfortune and not the doctor's fault, and he went on to find that in the light of the plaintiff's subsequent history it was 'as near certain as anything can be on an issue of this sort that a proper test dose would have made no difference'.

... this matter, in our view, was largely one of common sense and as a matter of common sense we entirely agree with the judge's conclusion that a reaction which did not, after administration of even the full dose, arise on the plaintiff's way home or in his home until at the earliest three days after the injection, was most unlikely to have manifested itself during the period of half an hour for which, if the test had been properly administered, he would have had to wait in the doctor's surgery before a decision was taken to administer the full dose.

The remaining question on this part of the appeal is whether the judge, having made these findings of fact which we hold to have been fully justified, was right in law in holding that Dr MacEwan was not liable in damages to the plaintiff in respect of his negligence in the administration of the test dose, and we have come without any difficulty to the conclusion that he was right in so holding. Counsel for the Post Office, rightly in our judgment, accepted that the question which, on the authority of *Bonnington Castings Ltd v Wardlaw*, the judge had to ask himself for this purpose was whether the doctor's negligence in this respect had caused or materially contributed to the plaintiff's injury, and plainly on the judge's findings it had not. Recent applications of this principle are to be found in *Cummings (or McWilliams) v Sir William Arrol & Co Ltd* and *Wigley v British Vinegars Ltd*, where employers were found to have been in breach of duty in failing to supply safety belts to, in the first case, a steel erector and, in the second, a window cleaner, but it was found in each case that the employee would not have worn the belt if it had been provided, and that on this basis the employers were not liable. A further example, closer to the present facts, of the application of the same principle is *Barnett v Chelsea and Kensington Hospital Management Committee*, where it was held by Nield J that, although a hospital casualty officer had been negligent in failing to see and examine a man, and in failing to admit him to the wards for treatment, the claim failed because, on the evidence, the man would have died of poisoning even if he had been admitted and treated with all due care.

... We would add, before leaving this issue, that it was accepted for the respondents that on them rested the onus of establishing on a balance of probabilities that the negligence of Dr MacEwan in respect of the test dose did not cause or materially contribute to the injury, but in view of the terms of the judge's findings nothing turns on the question of onus.

The precise cause of injury being what it is—difficult to determine—the courts have in the last few years examined the possibility of developing two new legal principles to ease the task of the patient in establishing a claim. In *Wilsher v Essex Area Health Authority* [1986] 3 All ER 801, the Court of Appeal allowed the plaintiff to recover damages for an injury, even though it could not be proved that the doctor's breach of duty caused it, provided it could be shown that the doctor had 'materially increased the risk' of the plaintiff being injured. The House of Lords ([1988] 1 All ER 871), however, reversed the Court of Appeal's decision, rejecting the view that the plaintiff could establish causation merely by showing this. (For a detailed discussion of *Wilsher*, see *infra* pp 385–87, 400–403, 427–36.)

The second possible development arose in *Hotson v East Berkshire Area Health Authority* [1987] 1 All ER 210. The Court of Appeal held that the plaintiff was entitled to recover damages for the 'loss of a chance' of recovering from an injury he had suffered at school, because this chance of recovery had been lost as a result of the doctor's breach of duty. Prior to the careless misdiagnosis by the doctor there had been a 25% chance that the schoolboy would make a full recovery if promptly treated. He was accordingly awarded 25% of the damages he would have recovered had it been shown that 'but for' the doctor's carelessness he would have recovered from the injury. Again, the House of Lords reversed the Court of Appeal's decision ([1987] 2 All ER 909). (For a detailed discussion, see *infra* pp 437–445.)

The second aspect of causation—'reasonable foreseeability' rarely creates any special difficulties in cases of medical negligence. But it can do so. Imagine, for example, that a doctor negligently performs a sterilisation operation on a female patient who subsequently becomes pregnant or that the doctor negligently fails properly to perform an abortion. In both cases, would the mother's decision not to have an abortion (or further abortion) break the chain of causation between the doctor's breach of duty and the mother's injury and loss associated with the subsequent childbirth? (See *Emeh v Kensington and Chelsea Area Health Authority* [1985] 3 All ER 1044, discussed *infra* pp 585–7.)

4. Quantum of damages

What damages may be recovered in an action for medical negligence? The answer to this question is no different in principle from what it would be in any other case of negligence and you are referred to a standard work on torts for a detailed consideration of this question. However, an example may help you obtain an idea of what is involved. Fortunately for us, one of the leading cases is an action for medical negligence, *Lim v Camden Health Authority* [1979] 2 All ER 910.

The plaintiff was admitted to one of the defendant's hospitals for a minor gynaecological operation. Immediately after the operation she suffered a cardiac arrest and irreparable brain damage. The injuries were the result of the admitted breach of duty of one of the defendant's staff. The plaintiff was described by Lord Scarman as a 'wreck of a human being, suffering from extensive and irremediable brain damage, which has left her only intermittently, and then barely, sentient totally dependent of others'. The case illustrates the fact that in England a court may only award damages in the form of a lump sum. There is no provision for *periodical* payments (cf the suggested 'structured settlement' schemes discussed *infra* by Allen "Structured Settlements" (1988) 104 LQR 448). *Lim* also illustrates the two major heads of damages recoverable: (i) non-pecuniary loss e g pain and suffering and loss of amenity, and (ii) pecuniary loss e g lost earnings, any medical expenses and nursing costs. (Footnotes are omitted in the following extract.)

Lord Scarman:

The questions of principle
It will be convenient to take these questions in the order in which I have listed the appellants' main submissions.

(A) *The total of damages (£254,765)*
The submission that the total of the award was excessive was one of the broadest generality. Whether or not he can establish duplication or overlap or any other error in calculating the separate items of the award, counsel for the appellants submitted

that an award of damages, being a 'jury question', must be fair to both sides, and that in a case such as the present a judge should bear in mind (a) comparable cases, (b) the effect of high awards on the level of insurance premiums or, if, as here, the taxpayer foots the bill, on the taxpayer, (c) the availability of care for the victim under the national health service and (d) public policy. Such generalities as that damages must be treated as a jury question and kept in line with public policy I do not find helpful. Their very breadth merely contributes to uncertainty and inconsistency in an area of the law, the history if not the present practice of which is notorious for both vices. Invoking the memory of the days when juries assessed damages for personal injuries does no more than remind us that the modern practice of reasoned awards by judges is a substantial advance on the inscrutable awards of juries. Of course, awards must be fair. But this means no more than that they must be a proper compensation for the injury suffered and the loss sustained. Nor in this case do I find helpful a comparison of one total award with another. In so far as an award consists of 'conventional' items, e g for pain and suffering, comparability with other awards is certainly of value in keeping the law consistent. But pecuniary loss depends on circumstances; and, where (as in the present case) such loss predominates, comparison with total awards in other cases does not help, and may be misleading.

The two specific matters counsel for the appellants mentioned, the burden on the public (through premiums or taxes) and the availability of national health service care, prove on examination to be for the legislator, not the judge. As to the first, the principle of the law is that compensation should as nearly as possible put the party who has suffered in the same position as he would have been in if he had not sustained the wrong (per Lord Blackburn in *Livingstone v Rawyards Coal Co*). There is no room here for considering the consequence of a high award on the wrongdoer or those who finance him. And, if there were room for any such consideration, on what principle, or by what criterion, is the judge to determine the extent to which he is to diminish on this ground the compensation payable?

The second matter, though introduced by counsel for the appellants as part of his general submissions on the total award, is really one, as he recognised, which falls to be considered in assessing the cost of future care. It is convenient, however, to deal with it at this stage. Section 2(4) of the Law Reform (Personal Injuries) Act 1948 provides that in an action for damages for personal injuries there shall be disregarded, in determining the reasonableness of any expenses, the possibility of avoiding those expenses or part of them by taking advantage of facilities available in the national health service. In *Harris v Brights Asphalt Contractors Ltd* Slade J said of the subsection:

I think all [it] means is that, when an injured plaintiff in fact incurs expenses which are reasonable, that expenditure is not to be impeached on the ground that, if he had taken advantage of the facilities available under the National Health Service Act 1946, those reasonable expenses might have been avoided. I do not understand section 2(4) to enact that a plaintiff shall be deemed to be entitled to recover expenses which in fact he will never incur.

In *Cunningham v Harrison* the Court of Appeal expressed the same view, Lawton LJ saying that a defendant can, notwithstanding the statute, submit that the plaintiff will probably not incur such expenses because he will be unable to obtain outside the national health service the domestic and nursing help which he requires.

I agree with Slade J and the Court of Appeal. It has not been suggested that expenses so far incurred in the care and treatment of Dr Lim have been unreasonable. They are, therefore, protected by the subsection. But it is open to serious question whether for the rest of her life it will continue to be possible to obtain for Dr Lim, outside the national health service, the domestic and nursing help she will require. However, Lord Denning MR and Lawton LJ both of whom were parties to the decision in *Cunningham v Harrison*, have proceeded in the instant case on the basis, which the trial judge must also have accepted, that it will be possible and that the expense of doing so is reasonable. In the absence of any evidence to the contrary, I am not prepared to take a different view, though I recognise the force of the case developed in the Pearson report for legislation repealing the subsection.

The attack, therefore, on the total of damages awarded as being excessive, merely by reason of its size, fails. If the appellants are to succeed, they must show that one or more of the component items of the award are wrong.

(B) *The award for pain and suffering and loss of amenities*
Counsel for the appellants recognised, at the outset of his argument, that, if *Wise v Kaye* and *H West & Son Ltd v Shephard* were correctly decided, his first submission (that the sum awarded should be comparable with the small conventional awards in fatal cases for loss of expectation of life) must fail.

My Lords, I think it would be wrong now to reverse by judicial decision the two rules which were laid down by the majority of the House in *H West & Son Ltd v Shephard*, namely (1) that the fact of unconsciousness does not eliminate the actuality of the deprivation of the ordinary experiences and amenities of life (see the formulation used by Lord Morris of Borth-y-Gest) and (2) that, if damages are awarded on a correct basis, it is of no concern to the court to consider any question as to the use that will thereafter be made of the money awarded. The effect of the two cases (*Wise v Kaye* being specifically approved in *H West & Son Ltd v Shephard*) is twofold. First they draw a clear distinction between damages for pain and suffering and damages for loss of amenities. The former depend on the plaintiff's personal awareness of pain, her capacity for suffering. But the latter are awarded for the fact of deprivation, a substantial loss, whether the plaintiff is aware of it or not. Secondly, they establish that the award in *Benham v Gambling* (assessment in fatal cases of damages for loss of expectation of life) is not to be compared with, and has no application to, damages to be awarded to a living plaintiff for loss of amenities.

I do not underrate the formidable logic and good sense of the minority opinions expressed in *Wise v Kaye* and *H West & Son Ltd v Shephard*. The quality of the minority opinions was, however, matched by the equally formidable logic and good sense of the majority opinions. The question on which opinions differed was, in truth, as old and as obstinate as the philosopher's stone itself. A decision having been taken by this House in 1963 (the year *H West & Son Ltd v Shephard* was decided), its reversal would cause widespread injustice, unless it were to be part and parcel of a comprehensive reform of the law. For since 1962 settlements have proceeded on the basis that the rule adopted in *Wise v Kaye* was correct: and judges have had to assess damages on the same basis in contested cases. We are in the area of 'conventional' awards for non-pecuniary loss, where comparability matters. Justice requires that such awards continue to be consistent with the general level accepted by the judges. If the law is to be changed by the reversal of *H West & Son Ltd v Shephard*, it should be done not judicially but legislatively within the context of a comprehensive enactment dealing with all aspects of damages for personal injury.

I now come to the second submission for counsel for the appellants that, even if *H West & Son Ltd v Shephard* be good law, the sum of £20,000 for Dr Lim's pain, suffering and loss of amenities was excessive. The answer to this submission is to be found in one stark but factually correct observation of Bristow J. He said: 'Dr Lim's loss of the amenities of her good and useful life is total.' Accordingly, I think counsel for the appellants' attack on this head of the award fails.

I turn now to consider the respondent's submission that this award was too low. Counsel for the respondent took two points: first, that the judge underestimated Dr Lim's awareness of her condition and her loss; secondly, that bearing in mind the depreciation in the value of money since *Wise v Kaye* and *H West & Son Ltd v Shephard*, an award of £20,000 was out of line with the sums awarded in those, and other, cases. Both Lawton and Browne LJJ were impressed by the first point. There are passages in the evidence which suggest that Dr Lim's awareness of her condition is greater and more sustained than the trial judge found. He relied on the conclusions formed by Dr MacQuaide, a very distinguished doctor, who on six occasions in 1976 examined Dr Lim in Penang. Dr Macquaide found her emotional state to be blank, and that she was completely lacking in volition and spontaneity. He added that her powers of reasoning were impossible to test. I am not prepared to hold that the judge was wrong in his conclusion that 'she is so intellectually impaired that she does not appreciate what has happened to her'.

The second point also fails, in my judgment. An award for pain, suffering and loss of amenities is conventional in the sense that there is no pecuniary guideline which can point the way to a correct assessment. It is, therefore, dependent only in the most general way on the movement in money values. Like awards for loss of expectation of life, there will be a tendency in times of inflation for awards to increase, if only to prevent the conventional becoming the contemptible. The difference between a '*Benham v Gambling* award' and a '*West v Shephard* award' is that, while both are conventional, the second has been held by the House of Lords to be compensation for a substantial loss. As long, therefore as the sum awarded is a substantial sum in the context of current money values, the requirement of the law is met. A sum of £20,000 is, even today, a substantial sum. The judge cannot, therefore, be shown to have erred in principle, and his award must stand.

In making his assessment, the judge assumed his award would bear interest from the date of service of writ. Were it not to bear interest, he would have increased it by the amount of interest it would have carried so that it reflected the situation as it was at trial. Since trial, this House has laid down in *Pickett v British Rail Engineering Ltd* that awards for pain, suffering and loss of amenities should bear interest from date of service of writ. The judge's original figure of £20,000 represents therefore his assessment, in current money values at date of trial, of the plaintiff's loss as at date of service of writ, to which, following *Pickett's* case, one must add the appropriate interest.

For these reasons I think the judge's award of £20,000 and interest for pain, suffering and loss of amenities should be upheld.

(C)   Loss of earnings, and duplication (overlap)

The appellants' submission is brief and simple. In para 8 of their case it was put in three short sentences:

The Plaintiff ought not to have been awarded damages for loss of earnings as well as for loss of amenities and cost of care. The sum awarded for cost of care exceeded her estimated loss of earnings and *covered all her needs*. The additional award of damages for loss of earnings was duplicatory.

As developed in argument, the submission was a twofold one. First, it was submitted that in catastrophic cases 'loss of earnings' does not reflect a real loss. Secondly, if damages are recoverable for loss of earnings, duplication with other heads of damage is to be avoided. The law must, therefore, ensure that no more is recovered for loss of earnings than what the plaintiff, if not injured, would have saved, or reserved for the support of his, or her, dependants. Since there was no evidence to suggest that Dr Lim would have accumulated any surplus income after meeting her working and living expenses, the trial judge's award for loss of earnings was wholly wrong.

The first submission is contrary to an established line of authority which, beginning with *Phillips v London and South Western Rly Co*, has recently received the seal of this House's approval in *Pickett v British Rly Engineering Ltd*. It is also contrary to the principle of the common law that a genuine deprivation (be it pecuniary or non-pecuniary in character) is a proper subject of compensation. The principle was recognised both in *Phillips's* case, where the loss was pecuniary, and in *H West & Son Ltd v Shephard*, where the loss was non-pecuniary.

The second submission is more formidable. Undoubtedly, the courts must be vigilant to avoid not only duplication of damages but the award of a surplus exceeding a true compensation for the plaintiff's deprivation or loss.

The separate items, which together constitute a total award of damages, are interrelated. They are the parts of a whole, which must be fair and reasonable. 'At the end', as Lord Denning MR said in *Taylor v Bristol Omnibus Co Ltd*, 'the judges should look at the total figure in the round, so as to be able to cure any overlapping or other source of error'. In most cases the risk of overlap is not great, nor, where it occurs, is it substantial. Living expenses continue, or progressively increase, for most plaintiffs after injury as they would have done if there had been no injury. But where, as in *Pickett's* case, the plaintiff claims damages for the earnings of his 'lost years', or, as in the present case, the claim is in respect of a lifetime's earnings lost because, though she will live, she cannot earn her living, a real risk arises that the plaintiff may recover, not merely compensation for loss, which is the entitlement given by law, but a surplus greater than could have been achieved if there had been no death or incapacity. Two deductions, therefore, fall to be made from the damages to be awarded. First, as the cases have always recognised, the expenses of earning the income which has been lost. Counsel for the respondent conceded this much. Secondly, the plaintiff's living expenses. This is necessarily a hypothetical figure in the case of a 'lost years' claim, since the plaintiff does not survive to earn the money; and, since there is no cost of care claim (the plaintiff being assumed to be dead), it falls to be deducted from the loss of earnings award. But where, as in the present case, the expectancy of life is not shortened but incapacity exists, there will be a cost of care claim as well as a loss of earnings claim. How should living expenses be assessed and deducted in such a case? One approach, analogous to the method necessarily adopted in 'lost years' cases, would be to attempt an assessment of how much the plaintiff would have spent and on what, always a most speculative exercise. How, for instance, could anyone tell how Dr Lim would have ordered her standard of living, had she been able to pursue her career? Another approach is, however, available in the case of a living plaintiff. In *Shearman v Folland* the Court of Appeal deducted what has been described as the 'domestic element' from the cost of care. Inevitably, a surviving plaintiff has to meet her living expenses. This approach, being on the basis of a future actuality (subject to the uncertainties of life), is far less hypothetical than the former (which, faute de mieux, has to be adopted in 'lost years' cases). It is a simpler, more realistic, calculation and accords more closely with the general principle of the law that the courts in assessing compensation for loss are not concerned either with how the plaintiff would have used the moneys lost or how she (or he) will use the compensation received.

In the present case, my Lords, it is perfectly possible to estimate the domestic element in Dr Lim's cost of care. The estimated figure must, therefore, be deducted in the assessment of her damages for the cost of her care. In the result, Dr Lim will recover in respect of her future loss a capital sum which, after all proper discounts, will represent her loss of earnings, net after allowing for working expenses, and her cost of care, net after deducting the domestic element. A capital sum so assessed will compensate for a genuine loss and for a genuine item of additional expenditure, both of which arise from the injury she has sustained. It will not contain any element of duplication or go beyond compensation into surplus.

A further argument was addressed to your Lordships in the context of duplication. It was urged that there was an overlap between the sum awarded for loss of amenities and that for loss of future earnings. The amenities which Dr Lim has lost, it was submitted, would have had to be provided out of her earnings. If, therefore, she is to be compensated for the former, she should suffer a deduction from her loss of earnings claim. Reliance was placed on the judgment of Diplock LJ in *Fletcher v Autocar & Transporters Ltd*.

The question whether there can be any overlap between damages for non-pecuniary loss and for pecuniary loss does not arise for decision on the facts of this case. As the majority of the Court of Appeal said, the amount of damages awarded to Dr Lim for loss of amenities was a modest sum. It was not assessed by reference to any expensive pleasures or pursuits such as Diplock LJ postulated in *Fletcher's* case. There was, indeed, no evidence to suggest that Dr Lim had, or was likely to develop, any such tastes or pursuits. There is, therefore, no duplication of damages between the two items in this case.

On the point of principle whether damages for non-pecuniary loss can properly be reduced to avoid an overlap with damages for pecuniary loss I express no final opinion. I confess, however, that I doubt the possibility of overlap; and I note that the Pearson Commission considers it wrong in principle to reduce the one by reason of the size of the other.

(D)   *Cost of future care*
Both parties were agreed that damages under this head are recoverable. The major dispute at trial was whether they should be calculated on the basis of Dr Lim being

cared for in Malaysia or England. This dispute had yielded to the pressure of events by the time the appeal reached this House. One question of principle (other than duplication, with which I have already dealt, and the effect of future inflation, with which I deal later) was, however, discussed before your Lordships. Counsel for the appellants contended that the Court of Appeal, when considering the fairness of the award, had erred in its approach, overlooking the rule that damages for cost of care must be assessed on the basis that capital as well as income is to be used in meeting the cost. I doubt whether the criticism is a fair one; but the point underlying it is sound. Such an approach would, of course, be incorrect in principle. It would go beyond compensation for loss: for it would yield at the expected end of the plaintiff's life a surplus, which, if uninjured, she would not have had, namely the untouched capital. The true principle, as counsel for the respondent conceded, is that the estimate of damages under this head must proceed on the basis that resort will be had to capital as well as income to meet the expenditure; in other words, the cost of care, having been assessed, must be met by an award calculated on an annuity basis.

Counsel for the appellant invited the House to infer a departure from this principle, because of the size of the multiplier selected by the judge and upheld by the Court of Appeal. His multiplier of 18 years was, indeed, very high, too high, I would have thought, in the circumstances. However, it matters not, since for reasons to which I have already briefly referred the award for cost of future care has to be reviewed and revised by the House in the light of the fresh evidence adduced during the hearing of the appeal. I shall attempt this review when I come to the detail of the award.

(E)   *Effect of future inflation*

The trial judge said he made allowance for future inflation in the multiplier for cost of future care and in the multiplier for loss of future earnings. The Court of Appeal, in holding that he had made no mistake in principle, relied on a recent decision of this House, *Cookson v Knowles.* In that case Lord Diplock made the comment that future inflation 'is taken care of in a rough and ready way' because the conventional multipliers applied by the judges assume a rate of interest of 4% or 5%, whereas actual rates of interest are much higher. Lord Fraser of Tullybelton added the comment that in 'exceptional cases, where the [assumed] annuity is large enough to attract income tax at a high rate ... it might be appropriate to increase the multiplier, or to allow for future inflation in some other way'. My Lords, I do not read these passages in the speeches in that case of my noble and learned friends as modifying the law in any way. The law appears to me to be now settled that only in exceptional cases, where justice can be shown to require it, will the risk of future inflation be brought into account in the assessment of damages for future loss. Of the several cases to this effect I would cite as of particular importance *Taylor v O'Connor* and *Young v Percival.* It is perhaps incorrect to call this rule a rule of law. It is better described as a sensible rule of practice, a matter of common sense. Lump sum compensation cannot be a perfect compensation for the future. An attempt to build into it a protection against future inflation is seeking after a perfection which is beyond the inherent limitations of the system. While there is wisdom in Lord Reid's comment in *Taylor v O'Connor* that it would be unrealistic to refuse to take inflation into account at all, the better course in the great majority of cases is to disregard it. And this for several reasons. First, it is pure speculation whether inflation will continue at present, or higher, rates, or even disappear. The only sure comment one may make on any financial prediction is that it is as likely to be falsified as to be borne out by the event. Secondly, as Lord Pearson said in *Taylor v O'Connor,* inflation is best left to be be dealt with by investment policy. It is not unrealistic in modern social conditions, nor is it unjust, to assume that the recipient of a large capital sum by way of damages will take advice as to its investment and use. Thirdly, it is inherent in a system of compensation by way of a lump sum immediately payable, and, I would think, just, that the sum be calculated at current money values, leaving the recipient in the same position as others, who have to rely on capital for their support to face the future.

The correct approach should be, therefore, in the first place to assess damages without regard to the risk of future inflation. If it can be demonstrated that, on the particular facts of a case, such an assessment would not result in a fair compensation (bearing in mind the investment opportunity that a lump sum award offers), some increase is permissible. But the victims of tort who receive a lump sum award are entitled to no better protection against inflation than others who have to rely on capital for their future support. To attempt such protection would be to put them into a privileged position at the expense of the tortfeasor, and so to impose on him an excessive burden, which might go far beyond compensation for loss.

(Later cases have put a gloss on some of the issues raised in this case. For example, *Thomas v Wignall* [1987] 1 All ER 1185, *Hodgson v Trapp* [1988] 3 All ER 870, and *Housecroft v Burnett* [1986] 1 All ER 332.)

Perhaps we should notice one further aspect of the general principles of damages applicable in actions for medical negligence. In actions for negligence awards of damages are intended to be compensatory. It follows that exemplary damages should not be awarded so as to punish the defendant doctor even for his egregious behaviour. If the action were in battery, of course, these damages could be awarded, at least in theory, although no such claim seems to have succeeded in England in the context of medical law. Similarly, the courts have made it clear that they will not award 'aggravated damages' in an action for medical negligence.

On this last point, see the case of *Kralj v McGrath*
[1986] 1 All ER 54

Woolf J: This is a case involving a claim for damages by Mr and Mrs Kralj. It is brought against the first defendant, Mr McGrath, who is a consultant obstetrician, and St Teresa's Hospital in Wimbledon . . .

It relates to the manner in which Mrs Kralj was treated during her confinement for the birth of twins on 19 March 1980. The first twin, Thomas, was born perfectly satisfactorily and he is now a healthy and happy young five-year-old. Unfortunately the second twin, Daniel, was born in an extremely debilitated state and he died on 16 May 1980.

There are two separate claims put forward in the proceedings. First of all Mrs Kralj puts forward a claim for the very considerable pain and suffering, loss and damage she suffered as a result of the manner in which she was treated during her labour. The second claim is brought under the Law Reform (Miscellaneous Provisions) Act 1934 on behalf of the estate of Daniel. Liability is admitted by both defendants, and so it is only necessary for me to adjudicate on the question of quantum . . .

In general terms [Professor Huntingford, an expert witness] said that what had happened to Mrs Kralj was, in his view, horrific treatment, completely unacceptable, breaking all the rules made to safeguard the mother and the baby, and he thought that what Mrs Kralj had undergone was an excruciatingly painful experience, and indicated very bad practice, practice which was totally surprising. . . .

The first [principle] and perhaps the one which has the most general application is the argument of counsel for the plaintiffs that aggravated damages should be awarded to Mrs Kralj because the conduct of Mr McGrath in this case was, to use his words, so outrageous. Counsel agrees that to award aggravated damages in this field is novel, and he could refer to no authority which supported directly his contention that such damages are appropriate . . .

It is my view that it would be wholly inappropriate to introduce into claims of this sort, for breach of contract and negligence, the concept of aggravated damages. If it were to apply in this situation of a doctor not treating a patient in accordance with his duty, whether under contract or in tort, then I would consider that it must apply in other situations where a person is under a duty to exercise care. It would be difficult to see why it could not even extend to cases where damages are brought for personal injuries in respect of driving. If the principle is right, a higher award of damages would be appropriate in a case of reckless driving which caused injury than would be appropriate in cases where careless driving caused identical injuries. Such a result seems to me to be wholly inconsistent with the general approach to damages in this area, which is to compensate the plaintiff for the loss that she has actually suffered, so far as it is possible to do so, by the award of monetary compensation and not to treat those damages as being a matter which reflects the degree of negligence or breach of duty of the defendant. I do, however, accept that the effect on a mother who during the course of her labour undergoes unnecessary suffering may be greater if this results not in the birth of a normal child but a child who is in the unfortunate condition that Daniel was here. It would be easier for a mother to forget or adjust to the consequences of that distressing experience if she has the comfort of a normal child. If instead of having the satisfaction in the birth of a normal child she has the distress of the knowledge that that child is disabled, subject to the disabilities that Daniel was, it will be more difficult for her to overcome the consequences and the unnecessary suffering may have a greater impact on her.

What I am saying is no more than that what the court has to do is to judge the effect on the particular plaintiff of what happened to her. If the situation is one where the consequences are such that she feels able to make light of what has happened, then her loss is less than it will be where the situation is one where the impact of what has happened is accentuated because of the additional stress which the mother is undergoing at that time.

(iii) BREACH OF CONFIDENCE

1. Generally

One of the most fundamental *ethical* obligations owed by a doctor to his patient is to respect the confidences of his patient. That this has long been a central premise in our approach to medicine can be seen from the fact that the Hippocratic Oath states:

> Whatsoever things I see or hear concerning the life of men, in my attendance on the sick or even apart therefrom, which ought not to be noised abroad, I will keep silence thereon, counting such things to be as sacred secrets.

Now, for example the British Medical Association's *Handbook of Medical Ethics* (1984), paragraph 1.6 states: 'A doctor must preserve secrecy on all he knows.' But is there a concomitant *legal* obligation? Francis Gurry in *Breach of Confidence* (1985) examines the law relating to breach of confidence (pp 58–60):

> While the jurisdictional basis is fundamental to the breach of confidence action, considerable uncertainty still surrounds it. For this reason, any conclusions drawn about it must necessarily be tentative and devoid of dogmatism. The view offered here is that the courts have relied on principles freely drawn from the fields of contract, equity, and property, and that the liberal use of these principles points to the existence of a *sui generis* action which has, in terms of conventional categories, a composite jurisdictional basis.
>
> The approach adopted by the courts seems to have two dominant characteristics. First, the courts' attitude to juridiction has been a *pragmatic* one. What has mattered, it seems, is the existence of *a* jurisdiction on which to act in the case immediately in hand. Considerations of conceptual neatness have been secondary to this pragmatic question:
>
> > The true question is whether, *under the circumstances of this case*, the Court ought to interpose by injunction, upon the ground of breach of faith or of contract.
> >
> > That the Court has exercised jurisdiction in cases of this nature does not, I think, admit of any question. Different grounds have indeed been assigned for the exercise of that jurisdiction . . . but, upon whatever grounds the jurisdiction is founded, the authorities leave no doubt as to the exercise of it.[1]
>
> Secondly, the courts' approach to the question of jurisdiction has been a *flexible*

one. This flexibility is nowhere better illustrated than in the relationship between contract and equity. Here the courts have been prepared to introduce an obligation of confidence based on implied contract when the independent jurisdiction in equity has cast doubt on their ability to award damages as well as an injunction.[2] Similar flexibility is demonstrated within the scope of contract alone, where the courts have supplemented a limited express term of confidence with a broader obligation based on the implied terms of the contract.[3]

This flexibility indicates that something more basic than jurisdictional source lies at the foundation of the breach of confidence action. This can be found, it is submitted, in the policy which underlies the circumstances in which relief has been granted—the policy of holding confidences sacrosanct. Thus, the broad notion of a confidence existing between two parties has provided, in the language of the American realists, 'a sort of doctrinal bridge'[4] between contract, equity, and property. The confidence arises out of both the circumstances in which information has been disclosed and the nature of the information itself. The circumstances of a disclosure may be such that the confider is placing the confident in a position of trust. If so, either equity or contract will provide a means by which the trust can be honoured. But a disclosure will not betray a confidence if what has been disclosed is common knowledge. It is only when the information is private or 'confidential', when its general publication would reveal something which the confider wishes to keep secret, that the confidence can be regarded as having been reposed by one person in another. Here, the notion of confidence links contract and equity with property, for the courts have recognised that the publication or misuse of confidential information may injure a person either emotionally[5] or materially[6] even though no *immediate* relationship of trust has been broken. By acknowledging a right of property in information of this kind, the courts have been able to grant relief where the defendant has acquired the information by reprehensible means. But, it may be said, how can the acquisition of confidential information by reprehensible means, rather than the abuse of a relationship of confidence created by a limited disclosure, involve a breach of a *confidence*? The answer may lie in the combination of two factors. First, the person who has the confidential information and who guards it secret places a trust in the rest of society by demonstrating that he wishes to preserve an element of himself or his business free from general publicity. Secondly, the acquirer, as a member of society, can be said to breach that confidence or trust because of the means which he has used to gain the information. These means force an unwanted communication of the information on the possessor of the information. The act of resorting to such means on the part of the acquirer indicates that he is aware of the other's desire to preserve the confidentiality of the information in respect of which his means have forced a disclosure.

Notes to extract

[1] *Morison v Moat* (1851) 9 Hare 241 at 255; 68 ER 492 at 498 per Turner V-C (emphasis added).

[2] The *Nichrotherm* case [1957] RPC 207.

[3] *Thomas Marshall (Exporters) Ltd v Guinle* [1978] 2 WLR 116.

[4] L L Fuller, 'American Legal Realism' (1934) 82 *University of Pennsylvania L Rev* 429–62, 441 (emphasis deleted).

[5] *Prince Albert v Strange* (1849) 2 De Gex and Sm 652, 64 ER 293; (on appeal) (1849) 1 Mac & G 25, 41 ER 1171.

[6] *Exchange Telegraph Co v Howard* (1906) 22 TLR 375.

In *A-G v Guardian Newspapers (No 2)* [1988] 3 All ER 545 at 658, Lord Goff summarised the law:

I start with the broad general principle . . . that a duty of confidence arises when confidential information comes to the knowledge of a person (the confidant) in circumstances where he has notice, or is held to have agreed, that the information is confidential, with the effect that it would be just in all the circumstances that he should be precluded from disclosing the information to others. I have used the words 'notice' advisedly, in order to avoid the . . . question of the extent to which actual knowledge is necessary, though I of course understand knowledge to include circumstances where the confidant has deliberately closed his eyes to the obvious. The existence of this broad general principle reflects the fact that there is such a public interest in the maintenance of confidences, that the law will provide remedies for their protection.

I realise that, in the vast majority of cases, in particular those concerned with trade secrets, the duty of confidence will arise from a transaction or relationship between the parties, often a contract, in which event the duty may arise by reason of either an express or an implied term of that contract. It is in such cases as these that the expressions 'confider' and 'confidant' are perhaps most aptly employed. But it is well-settled that a duty of confidence may arise in equity independently of such cases.

2. Doctors

If this is the law generally, how does it relate specifically to doctors? Again, Gurry discusses the relevant law (*op cit* pp 148–9):

> A doctor is under a legal obligation not to disclose confidential information concerning a patient which he learns in the course of his professional practice:
> > [I]n common with other professional men, for instance a priest . . . the doctor is under a duty not to disclose [voluntarily], without the consent of his patient, information which he, the doctor, has gained in his professional capacity . . .[15]
>
> By analogy with the banker's obligation, it would seem that the doctor's duty of non-disclosure applies not only to information acquired directly from the patient, but also to information concerning the patient which the doctor learns from other sources *in his character as the patient's doctor*. Thus, the obligation of secrecy would extend to reports received by a doctor about a patient from medical specialists or from para-medical services.[16]
>
> As is the case with all obligations of confidence, the doctor's duty is not absolute but is subject to the requirement of disclosure under compulsion of law[17] and in the public interest.[18] Furthermore, his obligation can be released with the express or implied consent of the patient.[19]

Notes to extract
[15] *Hunter v Mann* [1974] QB 767 at 772 per Boreham J (with whom Lord Widgery CJ and May J agreed). This proposition was advanced by Counsel, and Boreham J stated that he would accept it with the addition of the word 'voluntarily', which has been inserted in parenthesis in the text above. The doctor's obligation of confidence was also recognised in *Wyatt v Wilson* (1820)—unreported, but cited with approval by Lord Cottenham LC in *Prince Albert v Strange* (1849) 1 Mac & G 25 at 46, 41 ER 1171 at 1179 and Ungoed-Thomas J in *Argyll v Argyll* [1967] Ch 302 at 319; and in *Kitson v Playfair* (1896) Times, 28 March, at 5 per Hawkins J. It also forms part of the ethics of the medical profession—see the Hippocratic Oath:
> Whatever, in connection with my professional practice or not in connection with it, I see or hear in the life of men which ought not to be spoken abroad, I will not divulge, as reckoning that all such should be kept secret,

quoted in W Sanderson and E B A Rayner, *An Introduction to the Law and Tradition of Medical Practice* (London, 1976), 25.
[16] In certain circumstances the information imparted by a doctor to a patient may be confidential also, and the doctor may restrain its misuse by the patient: see *Latham v Stevens* [1913] Macg Cop Cas 83 (1911–16), where the plaintiff doctor obtained an interlocutory injunction to restrain the defendants from using a medical certificate, granted by the doctor to a patient, in an advertisement claiming that the defendants had invented a cure for consumption. According to the report, Sargant J held that the certificate was given to the patient for limited purposes, so that it would be a breach of trust or confidence for the patient or any other person having

knowledge of the circumstances to publish the certificate or the effect thereof as part of an advertisement or otherwise without the medical practitioner's consent.

17 *Hunter v Mann* [1974] QB 767.
18 *Ibid* 772 per Boreham J (with whom Lord Widgery CJ and May J agreed).
19 *Ibid*.

Gurry refers to the obligation of confidence which arises as a matter of common law. There are specific instances where Parliament has chosen to put the obligation into a statutory form because of the particular circumstances involved. For example, the National Health Service (Venereal Diseases) Regulations 1974 (SI 1974 No 29), Regulation 2, provides:

2. Every Regional Health Authority and every [District Health Authority] shall take all necessary steps to secure that any information capable of identifying an individual obtained by officers of the Authority with respect to persons examined or treated for any sexually transmitted disease shall not be disclosed except—
   (*a*) for the purpose of communicating that information to a medical practitioner, or to a person employed under the direction of a medical practitioner in connection with the treatment of persons suffering from such disease or the prevention of the spread thereof, and
   (*b*) for the purpose of such treatment or prevention.

In *X v Y* [1988] 2 All ER 648 these Regulations were considered. The case concerned two doctors who were being treated for AIDS. A national newspaper had acquired knowledge of this from an employee of the health authority responsible for the hospital where the doctors were being treated. The health authority sought, *inter alia*, an injunction to prevent disclosure by the newspaper of the information so acquired. The defendant newspapers argued that disclosure was in the public interest and that, therefore, even if it were a breach of confidence, it was justified. As to the obligation of confidence, Rose J said:

Under the National Health Service (Venereal Diseases) Regulations 1974 the plaintiffs and their servants have a statutory duty to take all necessary steps to secure that any information capable of identifying patients examined or treated for AIDS shall not be disclosed except to a medical practitioner, or a person under his direction, in connection with and for the purpose of treatment, or prevention of the spread, of the disease. Confidentiality is of paramount importance to such patients, including doctors. The plaintiffs take care to ensure it. Their servants are contractually bound to respect it. If it is breached, or if the patients have grounds for believing that it may be or has been breached they will be reluctant to come forward for and to continue with treatment and, in particular, counselling. If the actual or apprehended breach is to the press that reluctance is likely to be very great. If treatment is not provided or continued the individual will be deprived of its benefit and the public are likely to suffer from an increase in the rate of spread of the disease. The preservation of confidentiality is therefore in the public interest.

As to the defendants' argument, about the public interest, Rose J said:

I keep in the forefront of my mind the very important public interest in freedom of the press. And I accept that there is some public interest in knowing that which the defendants seek to publish (in whichever version). But in my judgment those public interests are substantially outweighed when measured against the public interests in relation to loyalty and confidentiality both generally and with particular reference to AIDS patients' hospital records. There has been no misconduct by the plaintiffs. The records of hospital patients, particularly those suffering from this appalling condition should, in my judgment, be as confidential as the courts can properly keep them in order that the plaintiffs may 'be free from suspicion that they are harbouring disloyal employees'. The plaintiffs have 'suffered a grievous wrong in which the defendants became involved . . . with active participation'. The deprivation of the public of the information sought to be published will be of minimal significance if the injunction is granted; for, without it, all the evidence before me shows that a wide-ranging public debate about AIDS generally and about its effect on doctors is taking place among doctors of widely differing views, within and without the BMA, in medical journals and in many newspapers, including the Observer, the Sunday Times and the Daily Express.

There are two points to notice:
1. The case illustrates that the legal obligation of confidence is not absolute. In some circumstances, disclosure may be legally justified (on which, see *infra* p 541 *et seq*).
2. Everyone involved in the case assumed that the 1974 Regulations applied. Is it right to regard having AIDS or being infected with HIV as having a 'sexually transmitted disease' as specified by Regulation 2?

Another statutory example of the obligation of confidence may be found in the Abortion Regulations 1968 (as amended) (SI 1968 No 390).

Restriction on disclosure of information
5. A notice given or any information furnished to the Chief Medical Officer in pursuance of these regulations shall not be disclosed except that disclosure may be made—
   (*a*) for the purposes of carrying out their duties,
      (i) to an officer of the Ministry of Health authorised by the Chief Medical Officer of that Ministry, or
      (ii) to the Registrar General or a member of his staff authorised by him; or
   (*b*) for the purposes of carrying out his duties in relation to offences against the Act or the law relating to abortion, to the Director of Public Prosecutions or a member of his staff authorised by him; or
   (*c*) for the purposes of investigating whether an offence has been committed against the Act or the law relating to abortion, to a police officer not below the rank of superintendent or a person authorised by him; or
   (*d*) for the purposes of criminal proceedings which have begun; or
   (*e*) for the purposes of bona fide scientific research; or
   (*f*) to the practitioner who terminated the pregnancy; or
   (*g*) to a practitioner, with the consent in writing of the woman whose pregnancy was terminated.
or (*h*) when requested by the President of the General Medical Council for the purpose of investigating whether there has been serious professional misconduct by a registered medical practitioner, to the President of the General Medical Council or a member of his staff authorised by him.

But, apart from these statutory examples, what does the common law have to say? As you will see later, there is a dearth of English case law in the context of medical law. Nevertheless, we have no doubt that the law would in principle protect the confidences of a patient. As Nourse LJ stated (*obiter*) in *Goddard v Nationwide Building Society* [1986] 3 All ER 264 at 271:

The equitable jurisdiction is well able to extend, for example, to the grant of an injunction to restrain an unauthorised disclosure of confidential communications between doctor and patient.

The precise legal basis for an action for breach of confidence is, as Gurry pointed out above, unclear. However, it does appear to be clear that, to succeed in an action, it is not necessary to prove damage in the sense that this is understood in an action in the tort of negligence. It is by no means clear, however, whether disclosure of a confidence is sufficient harm in itself, or whether the plaintiff must also show that he has suffered some detriment (*AG v*

Guardian Newspapers No 2 supra, at 649–50, *per* Lord Griffiths, and at 659 *per* Lord Goff).

There is nothing, of course, to stop a plaintiff from basing a claim for breach of confidence on traditional principles of negligence when he has suffered physical harm for which the ordinary rules of negligence would compensate him. A well-known case in New Zealand illustrates this.

Furniss v Fitchett
[1958] NZLR 396

The defendant doctor, at the invitation of the plaintiff's husband wrote the following letter, which he then gave to the husband. The plaintiff (and, indeed, the husband) were patients of the defendant.

Mrs Phyllis C. L. Furniss   21.5.56
32 Mornington Road.
The above has been attending me for some time and during this period I have observed several things:
(1) Deluded that her husband is doping her.
(2) Accuses her husband of cruelty and even occasional violence.
(3) Considers her husband to be insane and states that it is a family failing.
On the basis of above I consider she exhibits symptoms of paranoia and should be given treatment for same if possible. An examination by a Psychiatrist would be needed to fully diagnose her case and its requirements.

Yours faithfully,
A. J. Fitchett.

The husband later used the letter in separation proceedings brought by the plaintiff. This was the first that she knew of its existence. She sued the defendant for breach of confidence.

Barrowclough CJ: The relationship between the plaintiff and the defendant was that of doctor and patient. The doctor knew—he admitted that he knew—that the disclosure to his patient of his opinion as to her mental condition would be harmful to her. He was careful not to tell her directly what that opinion was. Nevertheless, he wrote out and gave to Mrs Furniss's husband a certificate, expressing that opinion. If he ought reasonably to have had in contemplation that Mrs Furniss might be injured physically, though not financially, as the result of his giving that certificate—and that on the evidence is beyond dispute—then it seems clear that he should have regarded her as 'his neighbour' in Lord Atkin's phrase. If she was his neighbour in that sense, he was under a duty to take care to avoid an act which he could reasonably foresee would be likely to injure her—again physically though not financially . . .

On the facts, it is clear that if Mrs Furniss were to be confronted by this certificate, it was likely to do her harm. The certificate was handed to Mr Furniss, who was then living with his wife. Their relations were extremely strained. She regarded him as mentally unsound and as intent on doping or poisoning her. She had not hesitated to make these accusations against him, and it was because of her accusations that he had been brought to the distraught condition in which he found himself when he begged the doctor to give him a certificate. In these circumstances, it seems to me not only likely, but extremely likely, that when the husband was charged by his wife with mental instability, he would be goaded into a 'tu quoque' retort, and that he would disclose to her either the certificate or at all events its contents. That he apparently did not disclose it, and that the certificate remained hidden from Mrs Furniss for a whole year, speaks volumes for the husband's restraint. It is also to be noted that, in giving the certificate to Mr Furniss, the doctor placed no restrictions on its use. It was not even marked 'confidential'. On that evidence I can only conclude that Dr Fitchett ought reasonably to have foreseen that the contents of his certificate were likely to come to his patient's knowledge, and he knew that if they did, they would be likely to injure her in her health.

I do not hold that the doctor ought to have foreseen the precise manner in which the contents of his certificate did in fact come to Mrs Furniss's knowledge; though, I think, that, in the circumstances disclosed by the evidence, he ought to have foreseen that the certificate could be expected to be used in some legal proceedings, in which his patient would be concerned and thus come to her knowledge. It is sufficient to say that, in my view, on the evidence in the special circumstances of this case, Dr Fitchett should have foreseen that his patient would be likely to be injured as the result of his action in giving to her husband such a certificate as he did give, and in giving it to him without placing any restriction on its use. In these circumstances, I am of opinion that, on the principle of *Donoghue v Stevenson* [1932] AC 562, there arose a duty of care on his part. I have not forgotten that the certificate was true and accurate, but I see no reason for limiting the duty to one of care in seeing that it is accurate. The duty must extend also to the exercise of care in deciding whether it should be put in circulation in such a way that it is likely to cause harm to another.

Later, the judge accepted that the legal duty is not absolute:

I have already held in dealing with the first part of the motion that a doctor's duty of care to his patient includes a duty not to give to a third party a certificate as to his patient's condition, if he can reasonably foresee that the certificate might come to the patient's knowledge, and if he can reasonably foresee that that would be likely to cause his patient physical harm. But I cannot think that that duty is so absolute as to permit, in law, not the slightest departure from it. Take the case of a doctor who discovers that his patient entertains delusions in respect of another, and in his disordered state of mind is liable at any moment to cause death or grievous bodily harm to that other. Can it be doubted for one moment that the public interest requires him to report that finding to someone? Take the case of a patient of very tender years or of unsound mind. Common sense and reason demand that some report on such a patient should be made to the patient's parent or other person having control of him. But public interest requires that care should be exercised in deciding what shall be reported and to whom. Publication or communication of the report to other than appropriate persons could still be a breach of the duty owed by the doctor if the patient thereby suffers unnecessary physical harm.

That which will justify a departure from the general rule must depend on what is reasonable professional conduct in the circumstances under consideration in the particular case.

What is it that the doctor knows or learns which he may not pass on to others by virtue of the obligation of confidence? We discuss this in greater detail (*infra* p 540 *et seq*) but at this point it is helpful to notice that there are at least three different situations which call for analysis:

(a) Where the doctor acquires information expressly from the patient or by his own examination or observation of the patient. There can be no doubt that the obligation and confidence attaches to this information.
(b) Where the doctor acquires the information from a third party in circumstances in which the third party knows of the doctor/patient relationship. There would seem to be no reason to distinguish this from (a) above. It may be asserted, however, that there should be some distinction between the doctor acquiring information from another health care professional as distinct from a lay person. We, however, do not subscribe to this view since, in both situations, the doctor receives the information *qua* professional vis à vis the third party.
(c) Where the doctor acquires the information from a third party in circumstances in which the third party is unaware that he is speaking to the patient's doctor. Here, the answer is not so clear. On one view, since the doctor

does not receive the information *qua* professional vis à vis the third party, he has no professional obligation of confidence. The better view, perhaps, is that a court would recognise a duty to respect confidentiality since what lies at the root of the doctor/patient relationship is the patient's trust that the doctor will not reveal any *clinical* information to another without permission and this would extend to all such information however received.

See now, for an explicit recognition of the doctor's obligation of confidence and detailed discussion of its nature and exent, *W. v Edgell* [1989] 1 All ER 1089.

Part II

Medical law: the general part

Chapter 4

Consent

An introduction

Issues of consent in the doctor/patient relationship arise in three main contexts: (i) in the crime of battery; (ii) in the tort of battery; and (iii) in the tort of negligence. In reality, consent or lack of it is only an issue in the civil law of torts. Although theoretically, a doctor who ordinarily acts without obtaining a patient's consent may not only be exposed to liability in tort, but also runs the risk of facing a criminal prosecution for the crime of battery, there is little or no chance that this will actually happen in the context of the ordinary practice of medicine in good faith. Obviously there are many circumstances where a doctor can be guilty of a crime involving lack of consent. For example, he may obtain his patient's consent to intercourse by representing it as a legitimate examination (*R v Williams* [1923] 1 KB 340) or he may fraudulently represent that a particular medical procedure is essential and thereby gain financial reward from a private patient by deception. But these are matters which do not concern us here since our concern is with the ordinary practice of medicine in good faith.

The scope of the crime of battery, should it ever rise, is likely to be held by the courts to be the same as the tort of battery, apart from the fact that the doctor's intention will be relevant in determining whether he has the necessary *mens rea* for the crime.

PDG Skegg, *Law, Ethics and Medicine* (1984) explains, at pages 79–80:

> In criminal cases, the English courts have sometimes shown a willingness to manipulate the concept of consent to permit the conviction of someone whose behaviour was regarded as deserving of punishment.[20] It is not enough that consent was given to a touching of the same physical scope as that which took place.[21] It must also have been to a touching 'of the same nature' as that which took place.[22] Such an approach gives a court considerable room for manœuvre. However, the English courts are likely to be very reluctant to regard a doctor as guilty of a criminal offence simply because, before treating the patient, he gave an inadequate explanation of the treatment, or concealed the risks involved. In the restricted range of cases in which a patient's consent will be regarded as 'unreal', for the purpose of the tort of battery,[23] it will probably also be regarded as 'unreal', for the purpose of the crime of battery and the related statutory offences.[24] But the criminal courts are not likely to go further in making fine distinctions between medical touchings of one 'nature' and another.

Notes to extract

[20] See eg *Burrell v Harmer* (1966) 116 NLJ 1658. (The conduct in question is now proscribed by the Tattooing of Minors Act 1969, s 1.) Cf *R v Clarence* (1888) 22 QBD 23.

[21] The cases are usually argued, and decided, on the basis that fraud going to the nature of the act vitiates consent. But the better analysis is that in such cases there is no consent to the touching in question, because it is different from that to which consent was given (see *R v Clarence* (1888) 22 QBD 23 at 27–8, 34, 44; *Papadimitropoulos v R* (1957) 98 CLR 249 at 260 (rape)).

[22] Two cases in which a patient's consent was held to be ineffective were *R v Rosinki* (1824) 1 Lew CC 11, 1 Mood CC 19, and *R v Case* (1850) 4 Cox CC 220.

[24] But it is clear that consent induced by a fraudulent misrepresentation which does

not go to the nature of the act, or to the identity of the actor, will prevent a touching from constituting the crime of battery. See eg *R v Clarence* (1888) 22 QBD 23, and also *Papadimitropoulos v R* (1957) 98 CLR 249 (rape). A wider range of misrepresentations and failures to disclose may vitiate consent for the purpose of the tort of battery. See *Hegarty v Shine* (1878) 4 LR Ir 288; *Reibl v Hughes* (1980) 114 DLR (3d) 1 at 11 (*dicta*); and, especially, *Chatterton v Gerson* [1981] QB 432 at 443A–B (*dicta*). It might be thought that the power to distinguish between touchings of one 'nature' and another, together with the tort of negligence and the tort of deceit, would be adequate to deal with such cases. But see J G Fleming, *The Law of Torts* (5th edn, 1977), 78–9; *Salmond and Heuston on the Law of Torts* (18th edn, 1981, edd R F V Heuston and R S Chambers), 473; *Winfield and Jolowicz on Tort* (11th edn, 1979, ed W V H Rogers), 662.

As regards the remaining law, which as we have seen is the civil law of torts, the next question which arises is, like the crime of battery, does the tort of battery have any relevance to the practice of medicine in good faith? For if battery has to do with a harmful or offensive touching how can it be said, the argument goes, that a doctor acting in good faith with the entirely proper motive of seeking to help the patient, could ever be judged to be acting in a 'harmful' or 'offensive' way?

Let us take the argument in stages, since this is a matter of critical importance for the future development of medical law.

Stage 1—definition of battery

Battery can be defined as the intentional application of force to the person of another, the force being harmful or offensive, and being without the consent of that other and without lawful excuse.

Stage 2—relation to medical practice

It could be said that of all the ingredients in the definition of battery the one which has central importance in medical practice is that the touching be 'harmful' or 'offensive'. If the argument were to prevail that a doctor acting in good faith with the intention of helping his patient could *never* be judged to be acting in a 'harmful' or 'offensive' way, then the tort of battery would have no relevance. This would have the consequence that considerations of consent would arise only in the tort of negligence since a crucial element in the tort would be missing regardless of consent.

Stage 3—definition of 'harmful' and 'offensive'

In *Wilson v Pringle* [1987] QB 237, [1986] 2 All ER 440, CA Croom-Johnson LJ expressed the view that the words 'harmful' and 'offensive' were better to be understood by the word 'hostile'. This, of course, does not assist the analysis a great deal since it merely substitutes one word for two others. He did, however, offer a clue as to the meaning of 'hostile' by referring to an example of medical practice, although this was not the context of the case. He suggested that a touching was not hostile if it was 'acceptable in the ordinary conduct of everyday life . . .' (at 447). Some may argue that since doctors' touching of patients is entirely acceptable in everyday life, a doctor acting in good faith *never* engages in 'hostile' touching and therefore can *never* be liable in battery. Is this really so?

Stage 4—the difficulties of *Wilson v Pringle*

The first difficulty is a general one: the notion of 'hostility' is unhelpful and indeed has been specifically rejected by the Court of Appeal in a criminal case of battery in 1981 (*Faulkner v Talbot* [1981] 1 WLR 1528 at 1534, per Lane LCJ: 'a battery is an intentional touching of another person without consent of that person and without lawful excuse. It need not necessarily be hostile or rude or aggressive, as some of the cases seem to indicate').

Notwithstanding this, we must still consider the gloss applied to the requirement of 'harmful' or 'offensive' (rather than 'hostile') touching, namely that it consists of that which is 'unacceptable'. This leads us to the second difficulty. The example offered by Croom-Johnson LJ was as follows:

> . . . what legal rule allows a casualty surgeon to perform an urgent operation on an unconscious patient who is brought into hospital. The patient cannot consent, and there may be no next of kin available to do it for him. Hitherto it has been customary to say in such cases that consent is to be implied for what would otherwise be a battery on the unconscious body. It is better simply to say that the surgeon's action is acceptable in the ordinary conduct of everyday life, and not a battery.

The question is whether this particular example of conduct which is not 'harmful' or 'offensive' (at least *prima facie, pace* Croom-Johnson LJ) can be expanded to all situations of good medical practice?

If, as is undoubtedly the case, Croom-Johnson LJ is right in these particular circumstances, it is important to ask why? The answer, it is suggested, lies in the underlying aim of the law in this context and whether that aim is fulfilled in Croom-Johnson LJ's example. The aim must be that the law seeks to protect and preserve people from unwanted touching. The essence of 'harmfulness' and 'offensiveness' lies, therefore, in the *unwanted* nature of the touching. In the case of a patient who is unconscious and whose condition calls for emergency treatment, it would be hard to argue, save in the most unusual circumstances, that the treatment was unwanted. It is otherwise, however, when the patient is not unconscious and is capable of expressing a view as to whether he wishes to be treated or not and has indicated his view expressly or impliedly. In such a case it is suggested that the essence of what is 'harmful' or 'offensive' lies in what the patient wishes. Thus, in this latter case the notion of 'harmfulness' is best understood as being co-terminous with the notion of consent.

Stage 5—the best view

Three situations need to be considered. First, if the patient is unconscious and is in need of emergency treatment, the doctor may treat and not be subject to any action of battery because his conduct is not 'harmful' or 'offensive' since it is 'acceptable' generally by society.

However, consider, secondly, a similar situation where the patient is unconscious but there is no emergency either because the treatment may be postponed until the patient is conscious or because there is no immediate danger to the life or health of the patient. This is a difficult situation for the law to deal with, simply because it cannot easily be stated one way or another whether medical treatment would be regarded by a court as 'acceptable' to society generally. While the views of the medical profession might be regarded as relevant by the court, ultimately it must be the court as the guardian of the patient's bodily integrity to determine the 'acceptability' of any intervention. Probably such intervention would be regarded as 'unacceptable' and, therefore, 'harmful', 'offensive' or 'hostile' and thus *prima facie*, at least, a battery.

The third situation to be considered is where the patient is conscious and competent and has expressed a view that he does not wish to be treated. This refusal would make the medical treatment 'offensive', 'harmful' or 'hostile' since, as we have seen, in this situation these notions are co-terminous with lack of consent. The views of society on what is 'acceptable' (except perhaps for some overriding consideration of public policy (which is a different issue)) would ordinarily be irrelevant and *prima facie* the doctor would commit a battery.

In short, the concern of the tort of battery is with the principle of the respect for autonomy and this is reflected as much in the notion of harm as in the notion of consent. Both are really concerned with the same issue and, therefore, should not be regarded as amounting to discrete requirements for maintaining an action in battery. The unconscious or the incompetent cannot act autonomously; others must act for them and in so doing are constrained by what is 'acceptable" to society generally. The conscious and competent person is *prima facie* entitled in law to make his own decisions, including who should touch him.

The approach of Croom-Johnson LJ was rejected in *T v T* [1988] Fam 52, [1988] 1 All ER 613. The case concerned a 19-year-old girl whose mental handicap made her incompetent to reach decisions concerning her health care. She became pregnant and the doctors concerned considered it to be in her best interests that she undergo an abortion and a sterilisation operation to prevent further pregnancy. Wood J was asked to declare that these medical procedures would not be unlawful even though the patient could not consent. Wood J expressed his initial view as follows:

> In the light of an inability to obtain consent from anyone, a surgeon who performs an operation without his patient's express or implied consent would be liable for trespass to the person, as assault and battery, a tortious remedy.

However, he then dealt with the argument of counsel for the defendants, which was based upon *Wilson v Pringle*:

> The third basis on which these declarations could be made is that the operations would not in fact be tortious acts. This submission was perfectly straightforward and relied on the authority of *Wilson v Pringle* [1987] QB 237, [1986] 2 All ER 440. It is said that in order to constitute trespass to the person the act itself must be intentional and hostile, and that no act of a doctor treating his patient could be said to be hostile.

Having cited Robert Goff LJ's judgment in *Collins v Wilcock* [1984] 3 All ER 374, a criminal case where the defendant was charged with assaulting a police officer in the execution of his duty, Wood J continued:

> The analysis made by Robert Goff LJ in that passage I summarise as follows; there are certain acts of physical contact which fall within a reasonable and generally acceptable band of conduct which may occur in the ordinary course of daily life and which will be the subject of a deemed consent in order to allow that ordinary daily life to continue (the exigencies of daily life) and that physical contact within that reasonable and acceptable band is no battery. However, when the physical act of contact does not fall within that band, there is the *prima facie* case of battery to which a defence or other justification must be raised as in the examples given by Robert Goff LJ, where he referred to the examples such as children being subjected to reasonable punishment (see [1984] 3 All ER 374 at 378, [1984] 1 WLR 1172 at 1178).
>
> It would not seem to me that operative treatments or perhaps in some more serious cases medical treatments in hospitals fall within the phrases 'exigencies of everyday life' or 'the ordinary conduct of daily life'.

Wood J then referred to *Wilson v Pringle* and the requirement of 'hostility' and stated consistently with his initial view:

> In the present case I have found the analysis of Robert Goff LJ to be of greater assistance than the analysis of the Court of Appeal to which I have just referred.

The incision made by the surgeon's scalpel need not be and probably is most unlikely to be hostile, but unless a defence or justification is established it must in my judgment fall within the definition of a trespass to the person.

Thus in the present case I must face the fact that the operative procedures proposed are *prima facie* acts of trespass.

As we shall see later (*infra* p 294 *et seq*), Wood J went on to find a lawful justification for the medical procedures being performed based upon the necessity of treatment, a justification echoed by the House of Lords in *Re F* (May 24, 1989).

Form of consent

(a) EXPRESS

Consent is expressly given by patients, save in exceptional circumstances, when they sign what has become known as a 'consent form'. An example of such a form is that prepared by the Medical Protection Society in its 1988 publication entitled 'Consent, Confidentiality, Disclosure of Medical Records'.

GENERAL CONSENT FORM

I,...................... of.......................................
(name and address of person giving consent)

    *hereby consent to undergo

OR

    *hereby consent to .... undergoing
(name of patient)

the operation/treatment of...
the nature and purpose of which have been explained to me
by Dr/Mr...
I also consent to such further or alternative operative measures or treatment as may be found necessary during the course of the operation or treatment and to the administration of general or other anaesthetics for any of these purposes.

No assurance has been given to me that the operation/treatment will be performed or administered by any particular practitioner.

Date .... Signature ....
                                       Patient/parent/guardian*

I confirm that I have explained the nature and purpose of this operation/treatment to the person(s) who signed the above form of consent.

Date .... Signature ....
                                       Medical Practitioner

*Delete whichever is inapplicable

There is no specific form prescribed by law to which the document must conform. It need only record faithfully that which was agreed between the parties and not contemplate that which is unlawful. Indeed, there is no requirement in law that consent be reduced to writing. The written consent form is merely therefore evidence of what was agreed. Note the words of Bristow J in *Chatterton v Gerson* [1981] 1 All ER 257 at 265:

I should add that getting the patient to sign a pro forma expressing consent to undergo the operation 'the effect and nature of which have been explained to me', as was done here in each case, should be a valuable reminder to everyone of the need for explanation and consent. But it would be no defence to an action based on trespass to the person if no explanation had in fact been given. The consent would have been expressed in form only, not in reality.

At least two points of construction arise from the consent form prepared by the Medical Protection Society.

(1) It refers to consent to 'further or alternative operative measures or treatment as may be found necessary during the course of the operation or treatment'. What are the limits of this consent? Would it, for example cover a procedure not specifically related to the one named and/or not necessary but, in the view of the doctor, one worth doing while the opportunity existed, e g the removal of a large freckle which could cause problems in the future while removing an appendix? Is it enough for the doctor to say that the patient will doubtless thank him for doing it subsequently and thus has given him authority to proceed (the so called 'thank you' theory of medical ethics). (See further, Picard, *Legal Liability of Doctors and Hospitals in Canada* (2nd Edition 1984), pp 43–44.)

(2) It states that 'no assurance has been given to me that the operation/ treatment will be performed or administered by any particular practitioner'. Does this refer to any doctor providing he is suitably qualified? It would seem that the answer is 'Yes'.

(b)   IMPLIED

Consent may not only be expressly given but may be implied from the patient's conduct, words or the circumstances. Note the following from *The Law of Torts*, Fleming (7th Edition) at p 72:

> Consent may be given expressly, as when a patient authorises a surgeon to perform an operation, but it may just as well be implied: Actions often speak louder than words. Holding up one's bare arm to a doctor at a vaccination point is as clear an assent as if it were expressed in words.[25] Similarly, acquiescence by a landowner in the use by the public of a shortcut across his property permits the inference of an implied licence and prevents him from treating such intruders as trespassers until he has made it clear that further entry is prohibited.[26] Participants in games or sports involving a likelihood of bodily contact, such as wrestling or boxing, consent to all the risks ordinarily incidental, though not to undue violence or unfair play.[27] Even silence and inaction may in some circumstances be interpreted as an expression of willingness. Failure to resist or protest indicates consent if a reasonable person who is aware of the consequences and capable of protest or resistance would voice his objection. A girl who is silent to an amorous proposal cannot afterwards capriciously complain of assault.[28]

Notes to extract
[25] *O'Brien v Cunard SS Co* 28 NE 266 (Mass 1891) 'Words or conduct which are reasonably understood by another to be intended as consent constitute apparent consent and are as effective as consent in fact' (*Res 2d* §892(2)). This rule was relevant in *Schweizer v Central Hospital* (1974) 53 DLR (3d) 494 (like *O'Brien*, involving a foreigner).
[26] [footnote omitted].
[27] *Wright v McLean* (1956) 7 DLR (2d) 253; *Reid v Mitchell* (1885) 12 R 1129.
[28] *Aliter*, if no reasonable person would interpret silence as consent, as when the plaintiff stands his ground after being told that he would be punched on the nose.

Note also the words of Knowlton J from the Canadian case of *O'Brien v Cunard SS Co* (referred to in footnote [25] to the quote from Fleming, above):

Knowlton J . . . To sustain the first count, which was for an alleged assault, the plaintiff relied on the fact that the surgeon who was employed by the defendant vaccinated her on ship-board while she was on her passage from Queenstown to Boston. On this branch of the case the question is whether there was any evidence that the surgeon used force upon the plaintiff against her will. In determining whether the act was lawful or unlawful, the surgeon's conduct must be considered in connection with the surrounding circumstances. If the plaintiff's behavior was such as to indicate consent on her part, he was justified in his act, whatever her unexpressed feelings may have been. In determining whether she consented, he could be guided only by her overt acts and the manifestations of her feelings. [Citations] It is undisputed that at Boston there are strict quarantine regulations in regard to the examination of emigrants, to see that they are protected from small-pox by vaccination, and that only those persons who hold a certificate from the medical officer of the steamship, stating that they are so protected, are permitted to land without detention in quarantine, or vaccination by the port physician. It appears that the defendant is accustomed to have its surgeons vaccinate all emigrants who desire it, and who are not protected by previous vaccination, and give them a certificate which is accepted at quarantine as evidence of their protection. Notices of the regulations at quarantine, and of the willingness of the ship's medical officer to vaccinate such as needed vaccination, were posted about the ship in various languages, and on the day when the operation was performed the surgeon had a right to presume that she and the other women who were vaccinated understood the importance and purpose of vaccination for those who bore no marks to show that they were protected. By the plaintiff's testimony, which, in this particular, is undisputed, it appears that about 200 women passengers were assembled below, and she understood from conversation with them that they were to be vaccinated; that she stood about 15 feet from the surgeon, and saw them form in a line, and pass in turn before him; that he 'examined their arms, and, passing some of them by, proceeded to vaccinate those that had no mark;' that she did not hear him say anything to any of them; that upon being passed by they each received a card, and went on deck; that when her turn came she showed him her arm; he looked at it, and said there was no mark, and that she should be vaccinated; that she told him she had been vaccinated before, and it left no mark; 'that he then said nothing; that he should vaccinate her again;' that she held up her arm to be vaccinated; that no one touched her; that she did not tell him she did not want to be vaccinated; and that she took the ticket which he gave her, certifying that he had vaccinated her, and used it at quarantine. She was one of a large number of women who were vaccinated on that occasion, without, so far as appears, a word of objection from any of them. They all indicated by their conduct that they desired to avail themselves of the provisions made for their benefit. There was nothing in the conduct of the plaintiff to indicate to the surgeon that she did not wish to obtain a card which would save her from detention at quarantine, and to be vaccinated, if necessary, for that purpose. Viewing his conduct in the light of the surrounding circumstances, it was lawful; and there was no evidence tending to show that it was not. The ruling of the court on this part of the case was correct. . . .

A purported modern application of the principle can be found in the proposition that any patient who enters a teaching hospital, by that fact alone consents to being used as an object of teaching by a doctor, who is both the patient's doctor and the teacher of medical students.

Consider the validity of this proposition.

Perhaps we ought to notice here the classic problem of how the doctor should respond to a patient who has attempted to commit suicide. It is difficult to argue that the doctor can plead implied consent. It is equally difficult to imagine that the law would expose him to legal liability if he sought to save the patient's life. Consider the arguments the doctor may advance. (See *infra* p 290 *et seq* on public policy, necessity *et al* for the discussion thereof.)

(c) EXCEEDING CONSENT

The following extract is again from *The Law of Torts*, Fleming (7th Edition) at p 73:

Exceeding consent
Consent is no defence, unless it is given to the precise conduct in question, or at least to acts of a substantially similar nature. One who challenges another to a fist fight does not sanction an attack with a knife;[51] boxers and wrestlers agree to violent bodily contact typical of the sport, but not to deliberate foul play.[52] Nor is a surgeon, charged with a particular operation, justified to depart from instructions and perform a different one;[53] the only occasion which would justify his proceeding without prior authority is when it is 'necessary to save the life or preserve the health of the patient'.[54] In other words, here the balance between preservation of life and self-determination is found in authorising medical procedure only when it would be unreasonable, not just inconvenient, to postpone until consent could be sought.[55]

Notes to extract
[51] *Lane v Holloway* [1968] 1 QB 379, CA.
[52] *McNamara v Duncan* (1971) 26 ALR 584 (football); *Agar v Canning* (1965) 54 WWR 302 (hockey).
[53] *Parmley v Parmley* [1945] SCR 635; *Schweizer v Central Hospital* (1974) 53 DLR (3d) 494. It is now customary for surgeons to demand from their patients a general authorisation for any treatment deemed appropriate.
[54] *Marshall v Curry* [1933] 3 DLR 260. The privilege is not confined to medical aid but applies also where, eg, one restrains a mentally disordered person or would-be suicide: *Crimes Act* 1961 (NZ) s 41; *Rest 2d* §62.
[55] Explicitly recognised in *Criminal Code* (Tas) s 51; cf Qld (s 282) and WA (s 259). See Skegg, *A Justification for Medical Procedures Performed Without Consent*, 90 LQR 512 (1977). A doctor may also apparently claim remuneration in quasi-contract for services rendered pursuant to his privilege, by analogy to necessaries supplied to a lunatic: *Matheson v Smiley* [1932] 2 DLR 787.

Note also *Mulloy v Hop Sang* [1935] 1 WWR 714:

Jackson, DCJ: The plaintiff's claim is for professional fees for an operation involving the amputation of the defendant's hand which was badly injured in a motor-car accident. The accident took place near the town of Cardston and the defendant was taken to hospital there. The plaintiff, a physician and surgeon duly qualified to practice, was called to the hospital and the defendant, being a stranger and unacquainted with the plaintiff, asked him to fix up his hand but not to cut it off as he wanted to have it looked after in Lethbridge, his home city. Later on in the operating room the defendant repeated his request that he did not want his hand cut off. The doctor, being more concerned in relieving the suffering of the patient, replied that he would be governed by the conditions found when the anaesthetic had been administered. The defendant said nothing. As the hand was covered by an old piece of cloth and it was necessary to administer an anaesthetic before doing anything, the doctor was not in a position to advise what should be done. On examination he decided an operation was necessary and the hand was amputated. Dr Mulloy said the wounds indicated an operation as the condition of the hand was such that delay would mean blood poisoning with no possibility of saving it. In this he was supported by the two other attending physicians. I am, however, not satisfied that the defendant could not have been rushed to Lethbridge where he evidently wished to consult with a physician whom he knew and relied on. Dr Mulloy took it for granted when the defendant, a Chinaman without much education in English and probably not of any more than average mentality, did not reply or make any objection to his statement that he would be governed by conditions as he found them, that he had full power to go ahead and perform an operation if found necessary. On the other hand, the defendant did not, in my opinion, understand what the doctor meant, and he would most likely have refused to allow the operation if he did. Further, he did not consider it necessary to reply as he had already given explicit instructions.

Under these circumstances I think the plaintiff should have made full explanation and should have endeavoured to get the defendant to consent to an operation, if necessary. It might have been different if the defendant had submitted himself generally to the doctor and had pleaded with him not to perform an operation and the doctor found it necessary to do so afterwards. The defendant's instructions were precedent and went to the root of the employment. The plaintiff did not do the work he was hired to do and must, in my opinion, fail in his action.

Finally, consider *Mohr v Williams* 104 NW 12 (1905) (Supreme Court of Minnesota). For the facts of this case, see *supra* p 137):

Brown J: It is not, however, contended by defendant that under ordinary circumstances consent is unnecessary, but that, under the particular circumstances of this case, consent was implied; that it was an emergency case, such as to authorise the operation without express consent or permission. The medical profession has made signal progress in solving the problems of health and disease, and they may justly point with pride to the advancements made in supplementing nature and correcting deformities, and relieving pain and suffering. The physician impliedly contracts that he possesses, and will exercise in the treatment of patients, skill and learning, and that he will exercise reasonable care and exert his best judgment to bring about favorable results. The methods of treatment are committed almost exclusively to his judgment, but we are aware of no rule or principle of law which would extend to him free license respecting surgical operations. Reasonable latitude must, however, be allowed the physician in a particular case; and we would not lay down any rule which would unreasonably interfere with the exercise of his discretion, or prevent him from taking such measures as his judgment dictated for the welfare of the patient in a case of emergency. If a person should be injured to the extent of rendering him unconscious, and his injuries were of such a nature as to require prompt surgical attention, a physician called to attend him would be justified in applying such medical or surgical treatment as might reasonably be necessary for the preservation of his life or limb, and consent on the part of the injured person would be implied.

And again, if, in the course of an operation to which the patient consented, the physician should discover conditions not anticipated before the operation was commenced, and which, if not removed, would endanger the life or health of the patient, he would, though no express consent was obtained or given, be justified in extending the operation to remove and overcome them. But such is not the case at bar. The diseased condition of plaintiff's left ear was not discovered in the course of an operation on the right, which was authorised, but upon an independent examination of that organ, made after the authorised operation was found unnecessary. Nor is the evidence such as to justify the court in holding, as a matter of law, that it was such an affection [sic] as would result immediately in the serious injury of plaintiff, or such an emergency as to justify proceeding without her consent. She had experienced no particular difficulty with that ear, and the questions as to when its diseased condition would become alarming or fatal, and whether there was an immediate necessity for an operation, were, under the evidence, questions of fact for the jury.

For consideration of the justification or excuse for treatment without consent by virtue of the operation of the doctrine of necessity or privilege, especially eg in the case of an emergency, see *infra* p 290 *et seq*.

The nature of consent

There are three relevant issues which fall to be determined: (1) Did the patient have capacity in law (was the patient competent to give consent?); (2) Was the person giving consent appropriately informed beforehand?; and (3) Was the consent voluntarily given?

Each of these issues may be analysed by reference to the nature and extent of the doctor's duty, ie to inform or to ensure voluntariness and competence.

(a) CAPACITY

(i) What is capacity?

This first question calls for an inquiry into what factors the law regards as important before attaching any significance to any expression of will by the patient. It is a secondary question (which we will consider later) what particular criteria, if any, must be satisfied before the law recognises in the particular case that the abstract notion of capacity has been satisfied.

There may in essence be two alternative approaches to capacity: (1) status; (2) understanding; but traditional scholarship has not always reflected this. The traditional approach has tended to confuse that which goes to the notion of capacity and that which goes to demonstrate its presence in a particular case. This misunderstanding can be found in the otherwise excellent analysis offered by the President's Commission in their 'Making Health Care Decisions' report in 1983, at pp 169–171 (footnotes omitted):

Identification of incapacity
In the light of the presumption that most patients have the capacity to make health care decisions, on what grounds might a person be found to lack such a capacity? Three general criteria have been followed: the outcome of the decision, the status or category of the patient, and the patient's functional ability as a decisionmaker.

The outcome approach—which the Commission expressly rejects—bases a determination of incapacity primarily on the content of a patient's decision. Under this standard, a patient who makes a health care decision that reflects values not widely held or that rejects conventional wisdom about proper health care is found to be incapacitated.

Using the status approach, certain categories of patients have traditionally been deemed incapable of making treatment decisions without regard to their actual capabilities. Some of these categories of patients—such as the unconscious—correspond closely with actual incapacity. But other patients who are presumed to be incapacitated on the basis of their status may actually be capable of making particular health care decisions. Many older children, for example, can make at least some health care decisions, mildly or moderately retarded individuals hold understandable preferences about health care, and the same may be true in varying degrees among psychotic persons.

The third approach to the determination of incapacity focuses on an individual's actual functioning in decisionmaking situations rather than on the individual's status. This approach is particularly germane for children above a certain age (variously described as from seven to mid-teens). For example, rather than considering children under the age of majority incompetent to decide unless they come within one of the exceptions created by the statutory and common law, these patients could be regarded as competent unless shown to lack decisionmaking capacity. Similarly, a senile person may have been declared incompetent by a court and a guardian may have been appointed to manage the person's financial affairs, but the functional standard would not foreclose the need to determine whether the senility also negated the individual's capacity to make health care decisions. What is relevant is whether someone is in fact capable of making a particular decision as judged by the consistency between the person's choice and the individual's underlying values and by the extent to which the choice promotes the individual's well-being as he or she sees it.

The misunderstanding lies in regarding the first 'outcome approach' as being relevant to determining what is capacity. The better view must be that the outcome approach, if it has any significance at all, can only serve as a possible criterion for establishing capacity.

Thus, the debate concerning capacity must revolve around number 2, status and number 3, understanding, and it is to these that we must now turn.

1.   Status

The appropriateness or otherwise of a status approach to capacity can, perhaps, best be judged by reminding ourselves of the very simple question, what are we concerned about here? The answer in short is a patient's expression of will and the question whether that expression of will ought to be respected. The customary answer given is that it ought to be respected in those circumstances where the patient is capable of acting autonomously, ie in exercising self-determination. It is in the words 'autonomy' and 'self-determination' that the key is to be found. These words tell us that the concern of both the law and ethics is with the individual.

It should follow therefore, that any notion of capacity should be individual-orientated. It should not consist in mere membership of a group to whom a general classification or status is applied, regardless of the individual's particular circumstances, save where the clearest reasons of public policy demand. Any notion of capacity which did adopt such an approach would, by so doing, undermine the commitment to individual rights which it is the central concern of law and ethics to advance.

Some of the candidates proposed for the appropriate status are:

Majority

Note the following from Skegg, *Law, Ethics and Medicine*, at pp 51–52 (footnotes omitted):

> The view that at common law all minors are incapable of consenting to medical procedures results from a fundamental misconception of the position of such procedures in relation to the criminal and the civil law. Medical procedures are not in a different category from other bodily touchings. If minors are incapable by reason of their age alone of consenting to medical procedures, it would follow that they were incapable of consenting to other touchings. This would have interesting consequences. There would not have been any need for the Tattooing of Minors Act 1969, for a tattooist who tattooed a minor with only that minor's consent would commit a battery. So, too, would anyone who embraced a girl who had not attained her majority—unless, on one view, the consent of one of her parents had first been obtained. Furthermore, a minor would not be able to give a legally effective consent to a haircut. There is no reason to believe that this is so, and cases have been decided on the assumption that minors can consent to medical touchings, and to other applications of force.

The status approach in the guise of majority was rejected by Addy J in *Johnston v Wellesley Hospital* (1970) 17 DLR (3d) 139 at 144–5 in the Ontario High Court.

Addy J:—The plaintiff sues for damage allegedly caused to the skin on his cheeks and forehead as a result of being treated by the defendant Dr Williams at the outpatient department of the defendant hospital. The treatment was administered in order to remove certain marks, scars and pitting caused by acne.

. . . I can find nothing in any of the old reported cases, except where infants of tender age or young children were involved, where the courts have found that a person under 21 years of age was legally incapable of consenting to medical treatment. If a person under 21 years were unable to consent to medical treatment, he would also be incapable of consenting to other types of bodily interference. A proposition purporting to establish that any bodily interference acquiesced in by a youth of 20 years would nevertheless constitute an assault would be absurd. If such were the case, sexual intercourse with a girl under 21 years would constitute rape.

. . .

I feel that the law on this point is well expressed in the volume on *Medical Negligence* (1957), by Lord Nathan, p 176:

It is suggested that the most satisfactory solution of the problem is to rule that an infant who is capable of appreciating fully the nature and consequences of a particular operation or of particular treatment can give an effective consent thereto, and in such cases the consent of the guardian is unnecessary; but that where the infant is without that capacity, any apparent consent by him or her will be a nullity, the sole right to consent being vested in the guardian.

16 years of age

In 1969, section 8(1) of the Family Law Reform Act made it clear (if it was not clear before) that majority, whether 21, or 18 as it was reduced to by the same Act, was not relevant when determining capacity to consent to medical treatment.

FAMILY LAW REFORM ACT 1969

8. (1) The consent of a minor who has attained the age of sixteen years to any surgical, medical or dental treatment which, in the absence of consent, would constitute a trespass to his person, shall be as effective as it would be if he were of full age; and where a minor has by virtue of this section given an effective consent to any treatment it shall not be necessary to obtain any consent for it from his parent or guardian.

But the section left unclear whether another age, this time the age of 16, had replaced the age of majority. Subsection 3 states:

(3) Nothing in this shall be construed as making ineffective any consent which would have been effective if this section had not been enacted.

The case of *Gillick* [1986] AC 112, [1985] 3 All ER 402 provided the first opportunity for the court to examine the issue. In the Court of Appeal [1985] 1 All ER 533, Fox LJ decided, at pp 550h–551c, that:

In the final analysis the position is in my view as follows. (1) It is clearly established that a parent or guardian has, as such, a parcel of rights in relation to children in his custody. (2) By statute, subject to an exception, such rights can be neither abandoned nor transferred. (3) Such rights include the right to control the manner in which and the place at which the child spends his or her time. (4) Those rights will be enforced by the courts subject to the right of the court to override the parental rights in the interests of the child. (5) There is no authority of any kind to suggest that anyone other than the court can interfere with the parents' rights otherwise than by resort to the courts, or pursuant to specific statutory powers or exceptions. (6) It is clearly recognised that there is some age below which a child is incapable as a matter of law of giving any valid consent or making any valid decision for itself in regard to its custody or upbringing. (7) The authorities indicate that this age is 16 in the case of girls and 14 in the case of boys, at all events for the purposes of habeas corpus. (8) So far as girls are concerned, the provisions of the criminal law show that Parliament has taken the view that the consent of a girl under 16 in the matter of sexual intercourse is a nullity.

In the light of the above, I conclude that as a matter of law a girl under 16 can give no valid consent to anything in the areas under consideration which apart from consent would constitute an assault, whether civil or criminal, and can impose no valid prohibition on a doctor against seeking parental consent.

I conclude further that any doctor who advises a girl under 16 as to contraceptive steps to be taken or affords contraceptive or abortion treatment to such a girl without the knowledge and consent of the parent, save in an emergency which would render consent in any event unnecessary, infringes the legal rights of the parent or guardian. Save in emergency, his proper course is to seek parental consent or apply to the court.

Parker LJ introduced his own requirement by drawing on the alleged common law principle of the 'age of discretion' to guide him in solving the problem posed by s 8(3). This somewhat mysterious principle, thought by some family lawyers to have been buried, was given a brief moment of after-life before being suitably laid to rest again by the House of Lords.

Lord Fraser in *Gillick* (at p 409e–h):

Provided the patient, whether a boy or a girl, is capable of understanding what is proposed, and of expressing his or her own wishes, I see no good reason for holding that he or she lacks the capacity to express them validly and effectively and to authorise the medical man to make the examination or give the treatment which he advises. After all, a minor under the age of 16 can, within certain limits, enter into a contract. He or she can also sue and be sued, and can give evidence on oath. Moreover, a girl under 16 can give sufficiently effective consent to sexual intercourse to lead to the legal result that the man involved does not commit the crime of rape: see *R v Howard* [1965] 3 All ER 684 at 685, [1986] 1 WLR 13 at 15, when Lord Parker CJ said:

... in the case of a girl under sixteen, the prosecution, in order to prove rape, must prove either that she physically resisted, or if she did not, that her understanding and knowledge were such that she was not in a position to decide whether to consent or resist ... there are many girls under sixteen who know full well what it is all about and can properly consent.

Accordingly, I am not disposed to hold now, for the first time, that a girl aged less than 16 lacks the power to give valid consent to contraceptive advice or treatment, merely on account of her age.

Lord Scarman in *Gillick* (at p 421 g–j):

The Court of Appeal favoured a fixed age limit of 16, basing itself on a view of the statute law which I do not share and on its view of the effect of the older case law which for the reasons already given I cannot accept. It sought to justify the limit by the public interest in the law being certain. Certainty is always an advantage in the law, and in some branches of the law it is a necessity. But it brings with it an inflexibility and a rigidity which in some branches of the law can obstruct justice, impede the law's development and stamp on the law the mark of obsolescence where what is needed is the capacity for development. The law relating to parent and child is concerned with the problems of the growth and maturity of the human personality. If the law should impose on the process of 'growing up' fixed limits where nature knows only a continuous process, the price would be artificiality and a lack of realism in an area where the law must be sensitive to human development and social change. If certainty be thought desirable, it is better that the rigid demarcations necessary to achieve it should be laid down by legislation after a full consideration of all the relevant factors than by the courts, confined as they are by the forensic process to the evidence adduced by the parties and to whatever may properly fall within the judicial notice of judges. Unless and until Parliament should think fit to intervene, the courts should establish a principle flexible enough to enable justice to be achieved by its application to the particular circumstances proved by the evidence placed before them.

And at p 422g–j:

The habeas corpus 'age of discretion' cases are also no guide as to the limits which should be accepted today in marking out the bounds of parental right, of a child's capacity to make his or her own decision and of a doctor's duty to his patient. Nevertheless the 'age of discretion' cases are helpful in that they do reveal the judges as accepting that a minor can in law achieve an age of discretion before coming of full age. The 'age of discretion' cases are cases in which a parent or guardian (usually the father) has applied for habeas corpus to secure the return of his child who has left home without his consent. The courts would refuse an order if the child had attained the age of discretion, which came to be regarded as 14 for boys and 16 for girls, and did not wish to return. The principle underlying them was plainly that an order would be refused if the child had sufficient intelligence and understanding to make up his own mind.

The mentally disordered

As explained by Skegg in *Law, Ethics and Medicine* p 56–7:

The fact that a person is suffering from a mental disorder, as defined in the Mental Health Act 1983[44] does not of itself preclude that person from giving a legally effective consent.[45] Whether the person is capable of doing so depends upon whether that person can understand and come to a decision upon what is involved.[46] Most patients in mental hospitals are capable of giving a legally effective consent, including many who are compulsorily detained. Doctors are sometimes free to proceed without consent,[47] but even then a patient will sometimes have the capacity to give a legally effective consent, which would of itself prevent the doctor's conduct from amounting to the tort or crime of battery.[48]

Notes to extract

[44] S 1(2) of the Mental Health Act 1983 provides that 'In this Act "mental disorder" means mental illness, arrested or incomplete development of mind, psychopathic disorder, and any other disorder or disability of mind, and "mentally disordered" shall be construed accordingly'. The terms are used in this sense in this chapter. On the definition of mental disorder, see also Mental Health (Amendment) Act 1982, ss 1–2.

[45] Cf *Bolam v Friern Hospital Management Committee* [1957] 2 All ER 118, [1957] 1 WLR 582 (action in negligence—voluntary patient in mental hospital, suffering from depression—capacity to consent assumed).

[46] Cf *Mason v Mason* [1972] Fam 302, [1972] 3 All ER 315 (Question of whether voluntary mental patient could validly consent to the grant of a decree of divorce under Divorce Reform Act 1969, s 2(1)(d); Sir George Baker P adopted test of whether the person knew and understood at the time what he was doing.) See also Family Law Reform Act 1969, s 21(4); *R v Morgan* [1970] VR 337, 341–2 (capacity of mentally retarded girl to consent to sexual intercourse); *Re Beaney* [1978] 2 All ER 595, [1978] 1 WLR 770 (degree of understanding required for making a contract, or a gift).

[47] [footnote omitted].

[48] But see s 43 of the Mental Health (Amendment) Act 1982, which applies to treatment for mental disorder which involves 'any surgical operation for destroying brain tissue or for destroying the function of brain tissue', and also to 'such other forms of treatment as may be specified for the purposes of this section by regulations made by the Secretary of State'. Except in circumstances specified in s 48 of the Act, such treatment is not to be given to a detained or to a voluntary patient (ss 42, 50) unless the patient has consented to it; three other persons, including a medical practitioner, have certified that the patient 'is capable of understanding the nature, purpose, and likely effects of the treatment in question and has consented to it'; and

the medical practitioner involved in the certification process has certified, after required consultation, that 'having regard to the likelihood of the treatment alleviating or preventing a deterioration of the patient's condition, the treatment should be given'. See also s 44 (forms of treatment of detained patients requiring consent or a second opinion), s 45 (consent etc to a plan of treatment), and s 46 (withdrawal of consent).

In Part IV of the Mental Health Act 1983, which deals with 'Consent to Treatment', it is explicitly recognised that a person suffering from 'mental disorder' may nonetheless have the capacity in law to consent to or refuse treatment for mental disorder if 'the patient is capable of understanding . . .'

MENTAL HEALTH ACT 1983

57 (2) Subject to section 62 below, a patient shall not be given any form of treatment to which this section applies unless he has consented to it and—
   (a) a registered medical practitioner appointed for the purposes of this Part of this Act by the Secretary of State (not being the responsible medical officer) and two other persons appointed for the purposes of this paragraph by the Secretary of State (not being registered medical practitioners) have certified in writing that the patient is capable of understanding the nature, purpose and likely effects of the treatment in question and has consented to it;

58 (3) Subject to section 62 below, a patient shall not be given any form of treatment to which this section applies unless—
   (a) he has consented to that treatment and either the responsible medical officer or a registered medical practitioner appointed for the purposes of this Part of this Act by the Secretary of State has certified in writing that the patient is capable of understanding its nature, purpose and likely effects and has consented to it.

Contrast the position taken in a Michigan circuit court in the well-known case of *Kaimowitz v Michigan Department of Mental Health* 42 USLW 2063 (1973). In that case the court considered whether a person compulsorily detained in a mental hospital could validly consent to take part in a trial involving psychosurgery as a form of treatment. The court held:

To advance scientific knowledge, it is true that doctors may desire to experiment on human beings, but the need for scientific inquiry must be reconciled with the inviolability which our society provides for a person's mind and body. Under a free government, one of a person's greatest rights is the right to inviolability of his person, and it is axiomatic that this right necessarily forbids the physician or surgeon from violating, without permission, the bodily integrity of his patient.

Generally, individuals are allowed free choice about whether to undergo experimental medical procedures. But the State has the power to modify this free choice concerning experimental medical procedures when it cannot be freely given, or when the result would be contrary to public policy. For example, it is obvious that a person may not consent to acts that will constitute murder, manslaughter, or mayhem upon himself. In short, there are times when the State for good reason should withhold a person's ability to consent to certain medical procedures.

We must first look to the competency of the involuntarily detained mental patient to consent. Competency requires the ability of the subject to understand rationally the nature of the procedure, its risks, and other relevant information. The standard governing required disclosure by a doctor is what a reasonable patient needs to know in order to make an intelligent decision. See Waltz and Scheuneman, 'Informed Consent to Therapy', 64 Northwestern Law Review 628 (1969). . . .

Although an involuntarily detained mental patient may have a sufficient IQ to intellectually comprehend his circumstance (in Dr Rodin's experiment, a person was required to have at least an IQ of 80), the very nature of his incarceration diminishes the capacity to consent to psychosurgery. He is particularly vulnerable as a result of his mental condition, the deprivation stemming from involuntary confinement, and the effects of the phenomenon of 'institutionalisation'.

Institutionalisation tends to strip the individual of the support which permits him to maintain his sense of self-worth and the value of his own physical and mental integrity. An involuntarily confined mental patient clearly has diminished capacity for making a decision about irreversible experimental psychosurgery.

Here is a case where the court appears to be using the status approach. The patient was compulsorily detained and mentally disordered. The court appears to be saying that because of that fact he was incapable of giving a valid consent. The court was using this approach to protect the patient from himself. Is this a legitimate approach?

Consider whether you can identify other examples of a status which the courts have regarded as entailing a lack of capacity to consent.

The conclusion must be that as a matter of principle and in the light of the law as stated by Parliament and the House of Lords the status approach to capacity to consent to medical treatment is not the law. This is not to say that in all circumstances a status approach is unjustified. A fixed and certain age may be appropriate as indicating the capacity, eg to vote, enlist in the armed forces or marry. Consider what may be the justification for a fixed age in those circumstances but not in the day to day practice of medicine. Do you accept Lord Scarman's 'flexibility' argument stated above?

2. Understanding

As has been seen, both Lord Fraser and Lord Scarman in their rejection of the status approach in *Gillick* opt for a notion of capacity centred on understanding (see in particular Lord Scarman's reference to *R v D*). This reflects the view expressed by Addy J in *Johnston v Wellesley Hospital* (1970) 17 DLR (3d) 139 at 144–5, and the virtually unanimous view of scholarly commentators (Fleming; Hoggett; Skegg; Ormrod LJ). The only commentator to argue otherwise is A Sammuels in 'The Doctor and the Law' 49 Med-Leg Journal 139 (1981). Unfortunately, however, the news is both good and bad. In *Gillick* the majority in the House of Lords made it clear that capacity is centred on 'understanding'. The words used to express this view, however, pose problems for the future as to what is involved in the concept of understanding.

Lord Fraser: The solution depends on a judgment of what is best for the welfare of the particular child. Nobody doubts, certainly I do not doubt, that in the overwhelming majority of cases the best judges of a child's welfare are his or her parents. Nor do I doubt that any important medical treatment of a child under 16 would normally only be carried out with the parents' approval. That is why it would and should be 'most unusual' for a doctor to advise a child without the knowledge and consent of the parents on contraceptive matters. But, as I have already pointed out, Mrs Gillick has to go further if she is to obtain the first declaration that she seeks. She has to justify the absolute right of veto in a parent. But there may be circumstances in which a doctor is a better judge of the medical advice and treatment which will conduce to a girl's welfare than her parents. It is notorious that children of both sexes are often reluctant to confide in their parents about sexual matters, and the DHSS guidance under consideration shows that to abandon the principle of confidentiality for contraceptive advice to girls under 16 might cause some of them not to seek professional advice at all, with the consequence of exposing them to 'the immediate risks of pregnancy and of sexually-transmitted diseases'. No doubt the risk could be avoided if the patient were to abstain from sexual intercourse, and one of the doctor's responsibilities will be to decide whether a particular patient can reasonably be expected to act on advice to abstain. We were told that in a significant number of cases such abstinence could not reasonably be expected. An example is *Re P (a minor)* (1981) 80 LGR 301, in which Butler-Sloss J ordered that a girl aged 15 who had been pregnant for the second time and who was in the care of a local authority should be fitted with a contraceptive appliance because, as the judge is reported to have said (at 312)—

> I assume that it is impossible for this local authority to monitor her sexual activities, and therefore, contraception appears to be the only alternative. There may well be other cases where the doctor feels that because the girl is under the influence of her sexual partner or for some other reason there is no realistic prospect of her abstaining from intercourse. If that is right it points strongly to the desirability of the doctor being entitled in some cases, in the girl's best interest, to give her contraceptive advice and treatment if necessary without the consent or even the knowledge of her parents. The only practicable course is, in my opinion, to entrust the doctor with a discretion to act in accordance with his view of what is best in the interests of the girl who is his patient. He should, of course, always seek to persuade her to tell her parents that she is seeking contraceptive advice, and the nature of the advice that she receives. At least he should seek to persuade her to agree to the doctor's informing the parents. But there may well be cases, and I think there will be some cases, where the girl refuses either to tell the parents herself or to permit the doctor to do so and in such cases the doctor will, in my opinion, be justified in proceeding without the parents' consent or even knowledge provided he is satisfied on the following matters: (1) that the girl (although under 16 years of age) will understand his advice; (2) that he cannot persuade her to inform her parents or to allow him to inform the parents that she is seeking contraceptive advice; (3) that she is very likely to begin or to continue having sexual intercourse with or without contraceptive treatment; (4) that unless she receives contraceptive advice or treatment her physical or mental health or both are likely to suffer; (5) that her best interests require him to give her contraceptive advice, treatment or both without the parental consent.
>
> That result ought not to be regarded as a licence for doctors to disregard the wishes of parents on this matter whenever they find it convenient to do so. Any doctor who behaves in such a way would, in my opinion, be failing to discharge his professional responsibilities, and I would expect him to be disciplined by his own professional body accordingly. The medical profession have in modern times come to be entrusted with very wide discretionary powers going beyond the strict limits of clinical judgment and, in my opinion, there is nothing strange about entrusting them with this further responsibility which they alone are in a position to discharge satisfactorily.

Lord Scarman at pp 423–424:

In the light of the foregoing I would hold that as a matter of law the parental right to determine whether or not their minor child below the age of 16 will have medical treatment terminates if and when the child achieves a sufficient understanding and intelligence to enable him or her to understand fully what is proposed. It will be a question of fact whether a child seeking advice has sufficient understanding of what is involved to give a consent valid in law. Until the child achieves the capacity to consent, the parental right to make the decision continues save only in exceptional circumstances. Emergency, parental neglect, abandonment of the child or inability to find the parent are examples of exceptional situations justifying the doctor proceeding to treat the child without parental knowledge and consent; but there will arise, no doubt, other exceptional situations in which it will be reasonable for the doctor to proceed without the parent's consent.

When applying these conclusions to contraceptive advice and treatment it has to be borne in mind that there is much that has to be understood by a girl under the age of 16 if she is to have legal capacity to consent to such treatment. It is not enough that she should understand the nature of the advice which is being given: she must also have a sufficient maturity to understand what is involved. There are moral and family questions, especially her relationship with her parents; long-term problems associated with the emotional impact of pregnancy and its termination; and there are the risks to health of sexual intercourse at her age, risks which contraception may diminish but cannot eliminate. It follows that a doctor will have to satisfy himself that she is able to appraise these factors before he can safely proceed on the basis that she has at law capacity to consent to contraceptive treatment. And it further follows that ordinarily the proper course will be for him, as the guidance lays down, first to seek to persuade the girl to bring her parents into consultation, and, if she refuses, not to prescribe contraceptive treatment unless he is satisfied that her circumstances are such that he ought to proceed without parental knowledge and consent.

Like Woolf J, I find illuminating and helpful the judgment of Addy J of the Ontario High Court in *Johnston v Wellesley Hospital* (1970) 17 DLR (3d) 139, a passage from which he quotes in his judgment in this case ([1984] 1 All ER 365 at 374, [1984] QB 581 at 597). The key passage bears repetition (17 DLR (3d) 139 at 144–145):

> But, regardless of modern trend, I can find nothing in any of the old reported cases, except where infants of tender age or young children were involved, where the Courts have found that a person under 21 years of age was legally incapable of consenting to medical treatment. If a person under 21 years were unable to consent to medical treatment, he would also be incapable of consenting to other types of bodily interference. A proposition purporting to establish that any bodily interference acquiesced in by a youth of 20 years would nevertheless constitute an assault would be absurd. If such were the case, sexual intercourse with a girl under 21 years would constitute rape. Until the minimum age of consent to sexual acts was fixed at 14 years by a statute, the Courts often held that infants were capable of consenting at a considerably earlier age than 14 years. I feel that the law on this point is well expressed in the volume on *Medical Negligence* (1957) by Lord Nathan (p 176): 'It is suggested that the most satisfactory solution of the problem is to rule that an infant who is capable of appreciating fully the nature and consequences of a particular operation or of particular treatment can give an effective consent thereto, and in such cases the consent of the guardian is unnecessary; but that where the infant is without that capacity, any apparent consent by him or her will be a nullity, the sole right to consent being vested in the guardian.'

Lord Templeman in his speech does not dissent from this view in general though he makes an exception for contraceptive treatment for young girls:

Lord Templeman at p 432h: I accept also that a doctor may lawfully carry out some forms of treatment with the consent of an infant patient and against the opposition of a parent based on religious or any other grounds. The effect of the consent of the infant depends on the nature of the treatment and the age and understanding of the infant. For example, a doctor with the consent of an intelligent boy or girl of 15 could in my opinion safely remove tonsils or a troublesome appendix.

The problem is as follows: does a test which stipulates that the patient understands mean that the doctor must satisfy himself (a) that the patient *does in fact* understand what is involved, or (b) that the patient is capable generally of understanding though, as it may subsequently transpire, he did not understand in the particular case, or (c) that the patient as a reasonable patient is capable of understanding or would have understood.

Let us assume that (c) can be discounted since it is not concerned with the circumstances of the particular patient which, as we have seen, ought to be the central concern of the law.

As to which of (a) or (b) represents the law the judicial language is equivocal. Consider pp 413c, 414c, per Lord Fraser and (pp 423j, 424b) per Lord Scarman ([1985] 3 All ER). Contrast the following:

> Provided the patient, whether a boy or a girl, is capable of understanding what is proposed, and of expressing his or her own wishes, I see no good reason for holding that he or she lacks the capacity to express them validly and effectively and to authorise the medical man to make the examination or give the treatment which he advises.

(per **Lord Fraser**, p 409e)

> It is that parental right yields to the child's right to make his own decisions when he reaches a sufficient understanding and intelligence to be capable of making up his own mind on the matter requiring decision.

(per **Lord Scarman**, p 422a)

> It follows that a doctor will have to satisfy himself that she is able to appraise these factors before he can safely proceed on the basis that she has at law capacity to consent to contraceptive treatment.

(per **Lord Scarman**, p 424c)
See also the reference by Lord Scarman to *Johnston v Wellesley Hospital* (1970) 17 DLR (3d) 139.

The importance of the distinction between (a) and (b) lies in what the doctor must do to satisfy his legal duty. If (a) is the law, the doctor could be held to be in breach of his duty on proof that his patient did not understand what had been explained. It would be immaterial for the doctor to argue that ordinarily the patient would have understood it or any reasonable patient would have done so.

Conversely if (b) were the law, the doctor would avoid an allegation of breach of duty if this patient would ordinarily have understood even though in the particular circumstances it can be shown that she did not. The better view must be (b), if only because (a) would place far too great a burden upon the doctor.

It must be noted that *Gillick* is relied on here as providing guidance as to the notion of capacity for medical treatment generally. It seems to make clear that capacity means understanding. It is, of course, a case concerning young persons. And, where young persons are involved the court may be saying that capacity to consent, ie understanding, while being a necessary condition *may* not be a sufficient one for justifying any doctor's action based on an expression of will. The law may demand that the doctor's action also be in the best interests of the girl as judged by someone other than the young person, ie the doctor. This would, of course, run counter to the thesis contained in the notion of capacity that it is the legal reflection of the ethical principle of respect for autonomy. It may, however, be that Lord Fraser believes this to be the law: (p 412f) 'Nobody doubts, certainly I do not doubt, that in the overwhelming majority of cases the best judges of a child's welfare are his or her parents'; (p 413a) 'The only practical course is, in my opinion, to entrust the doctor with a discretion to act in accordance with his view of what is best in the interests of the girl who is his patient'. Lord Scarman, however, does not subscribe to this view and it is submitted his view is to be preferred.

One further consequence of deriving the general law from a case concerning young persons is that the level of comprehension called for by the court seems rather high. (See Lord Scarman's reference to 'understanding *fully* what is the purpose of . . .', and his reference to *Johnston v Wellesley Hospital*). The degree of comprehension called for will be examined next. It can be said here, however, that the particular circumstances of *Gillick*, namely young persons and contraception, may call for a higher standard of comprehension than is ordinarily required by law, or possible in practice.

(ii) Establishing capacity

As has been seen, concern about the establishment of capacity arises out of the two propositions: (1) that a doctor ought to respect his patient's autonomy, but (2) he need only do so when the patient who expresses his will is capable of behaving autonomously. It follows that autonomy is, in effect, a status granted by others, in this case, the doctor. It also follows that in granting the status, it is the doctor's assessment of capacity which is crucial. Thus, capacity is a state of affairs granted by the doctor. In determining capacity, the doctor both as a matter of ethics and law must (ie has a duty to) behave with integrity and satisfy himself that the criteria deemed relevant to determine capacity are present in the particular case. The obverse of this proposition is that if these criteria are present, on any objective assessment, the doctor may not (ie is under a duty not to) impose his own views so as to regard the patient as incapable of understanding and thus, of making his own decisions.

What in law are the criteria by reference to which capacity is to be established? It is critical to notice here that when we talk of the doctor making a decision as to capacity, there are in fact *two* stages to the process. The first is the reference to the relevant criteria. As will be made clear, these criteria are not for doctors to determine but are a matter for moral analysis and/or the law. The second stage is the doctor's application of these general criteria. That clearly is a decision for him alone. In theory it would be subject to review but in practice it would be hard to challenge it; hence our insistence upon integrity. Consider the following materials: what criteria do they suggest?

Roth, Meisel and Lidz, "Tests of competency to consent to treatment" (1977) 134 Am J Psychiatry 279:

> The concept of competency, like the concept of dangerousness, is social and legal and not merely psychiatric or medical (1). Law and, at times, psychiatry are concerned with an individual's competency to stand trial, to make a will, and to contract (2–5). The test of competency varies from one context to another. In general, to be considered competent an individual must be able to comprehend the nature of the particular conduct in question and to understand its quality and its consequences (3, 6). For example, in *Dusky v United States* the court held that to be considered competent to stand trial an individual must have 'sufficient present ability to consult with his lawyer with a reasonable degree of rational understanding— and . . . a rational as well as a factual understanding of the proceedings against him' (7). A person may be considered competent for some legal purposes and incompetent for others at the same time (3). An individual is not judged incompetent merely because he or she is mentally ill (6).
>
> There is a dearth of legal guidance illuminating the concept of competency to consent to medical treatment (8–11). Nevertheless, competency plays an important

role in determining the validity of a patient's decision to undergo or forego treatment. The decision of a person who is incompetent does not validly authorise a physician to perform medical treatment (12). Conversely, a physician who withholds treatment from an incompetent patient who refuses treatment may be held liable to that patient if the physician does not take reasonable steps to obtain some other legally valid authorisation for treatment (13).

In psychiatry the entire edifice of involuntary treatment is erected on the supposed incompetency of some people voluntarily to seek and consent to needed treatment (14). In addition, the acceptability of behavior modification for the patient who is considered dangerous (15), the resolution of ethical issues in family planning (ie, sterilisation) (16, 17), and the right to refuse psychoactive medications (18)—to cite only a few of the more prominent examples—turn in part on the concept of competency.

As we explain in our companion paper in this issue of the *Journal* (19), competency is theoretically one of the independent variables that is determinative in part of the legal validity of a patient's consent to or refusal of treatment. There is therefore a need to specify how competency can be determined. Related questions include the following: Who raises the question of competency? When is this question raised? and Who makes the determination? Answers to these questions are beyond the scope of this paper.

The objective of the present inquiry is to make sense of various tests of competency, to analyse their applicability to patients' decisions to accept or refuse psychiatric treatment, and to illustrate the problems of applying these tests by clinical case examples from the consultation service of the Law and Psychiatry Program of Western Psychiatric Institute and Clinic.

In a brief presentation it is impossible to provide any serious linguistic analysis of a number of words that are frequently used in discussions of competency—words such as 'responsible' (20), 'rational' or 'irrational' (21, 22), 'knowing' (23, 24), 'knowingly' (25, p 99), 'understandingly' (24), or 'capable' (26). These words are often used interchangeably without sufficient explanation or clear behavioural referents. Only the rare scholarly article attempts to explain with precision what is meant by such terms (11); judicial decisions or statutes generally do not.

In evaluating tests for competency several criteria should be considered. A useful test for competency is one that, first, can be reliably applied; second, is mutually acceptable or at least comprehensible to physicians, lawyers, and judges; and third, is set at a level capable of striking an acceptable balance between preserving individual autonomy and providing needed medical care. Reliability is enhanced to the extent that a competency test depends on manifest and objectively ascertainable patient behaviour rather than on inferred and probably unknowable mental status (6).

Tests for competency

Several tests for competency have been proposed in the literature; others are readily inferable from judicial commentary. Although there is some overlap, they basically fall into five categories: 1) evidencing a choice, 2) 'reasonable' outcome of choice, 3) choice based on 'rational' reasons, 4) ability to understand, and 5) actual understanding.

Evidencing a choice

This test for competency is set at a very low level and is the most respectful of the autonomy of patient decision-making (10). Under this test the competent patient is one who evidences a preference for or against treatment. This test focuses not on the quality of the patient's decision but on the presence or absence of a decision. This preference may be a yes, a no, or even the desire that the physician make the decision for the patient. Only the patient who does not evidence a preference either verbally or through his or her behaviour is considered incompetent. This test of competency encompasses at a minimum the unconscious patient; in psychiatry it encompasses the mute patient who cannot or will not express an opinion.

Even such arch-defenders of individual autonomy as Szasz have agreed that patients who do not formulate and express a preference as to treatment are incompetent. In answer to a question about the right to intervene against a patient's will, Szasz has stated.

It is quite obvious, and I make this abundantly clear, that I have no objection to medical intervention vis-à-vis persons who are not protesting, . . . [for example,] somebody who is lying in bed catatonic and the mother wants to get him to the hospital and the ambulance shows up and he just lies there. (27)

The following case example illustrates the use of the test of evidencing a choice:

Case 1. A 41-year-old depressed woman was interviewed in the admission unit. She rarely answered yes or no to direct questions. Admission was proposed; she said and did nothing, but looked apprehensive. When asked about admission, she did not sign herself into the hospital, protest, or walk away. She was guided to the inpatient ward by her husband and her doctor after being given the opportunity to walk the other way.

This test may be what one court had in mind when, with respect to sterlilization of residents of state schools, it ruled that even legally incompetent and possibly noncomprehending residents may not be sterilised unless they have formed a genuine desire to undergo the procedure (28).

The guidelines proposed by the US Department of Health, Education and Welfare concerning experimentation with institutionalised mentally ill people also point in this direction by requiring even the legally incompetent person's 'assent to such participation . . . when . . . he has sufficient mental capacity to understand what is proposed and to express an opinion as to his or her participation' (29, at 46.504c). Although this low test of competency does not fully assure patients' understanding of the nature of what they consent to or what they refuse, it is behavioural in orientation and therefore more reliable in application; it also guards against excessive paternalism.

'Reasonable' outcome of choice

This test of competency entails evaluating the patient's capacity to reach the 'reasonable', the 'right', or the 'responsible' decision (10, 30). The emphasis in this test is on outcome rather than on the mere fact of decision or how it has been reached. The patient who fails to make a decision that is roughly congruent with the decision that a 'reasonable' person in like circumstances would make is viewed as incompetent.

This test is probably used more often than might be admitted by both physicians and courts. Judicial decisions to override the desire of patients with certain religious beliefs not to receive blood transfusions may rest in part on the court's view that the patient's decision is not reasonable (31). When life is at stake and a court believes that the patient's decision is unreasonable, the court may focus on even the smallest ambiguity in the patient's thinking to cast doubt on the patient's competency so that it may issue an order that will preserve life or health. For example, one judge issued an order to allow amputation of the leg of an elderly moribund man even though the man had clearly told his daughter before his condition deteriorated not to permit an amputation (32, 33).

Mental health laws that allow for involuntary treatment on the basis of 'need for care and treatment' (34) without requiring a formal adjudication of incompetency in effect use an unstated reasonable outcome test in abridging the patient's common-law right not to be treated without giving his or her consent. These laws are premised on the following syllogism: the patient needs treatment; the patient has not obtained treatment on his or her own initiative; therefore, the patient's decision is incorrect, which means that he or she is incompetent, thus justifying the involuntary imposition of treatment.

The benefits and costs of this test are that social goals and individual health are promoted at considerable expense to personal autonomy. The reasonable outcome test is useful in alerting physicians and courts to the fact that the patient's decision-making process may be, but not necessarily is, awry. Ultimately, because the test rests on the congruence between the patient's decision and that of a reasonable person or that of the physician, it is biased in favour of decisions to accept treatment, even when such decisions are made by people who are incapable of weighing the risks and benefits of treatment. In other words, if patients do not decide the 'wrong' way, the issue of competency will probably not arise.

Choice based on 'rational' reasons

Another test is whether the reasons for the patient's decision are 'rational', that is, whether the patient's decision is due to or is a product of mental illness (10, 22). As in the reasonable outcome test, if the patient decides in favour of treatment the issue of the patient's competency (in this case, whether the decision is the product of mental illness) seldom if ever arises because of the medical profession's bias toward consent to treatment and against refusal of treatment.

In this test the quality of the patient's thinking is what counts. The following case example illustrates the use of the test of rational reasons:

Case 2. A 70-year-old widow who was living alone in a condemned dilapidated house with no heat was brought against her will to the hospital. Her thinking was tangential and fragmented. Although she did not appear to be hallucinating, she seemed delusional. She refused blood tests, saying 'You just want my blood to spread it all over Pittsburgh. No, I'm not giving it'. Her choice was respected. Later in the day, however, when her blood pressure was found to be dangerously elevated (250 over 135 in both arms), blood was withdrawn against her will.

The test of rational reasons, although it has clinical appeal and is probably much in clinical use, poses considerable conceptual problems; as a legal test it is probably defective (10). The problems include the difficulty of distinguishing rational from irrational reasons and drawing inferences of causation between any irrationality believed present and the valence (yes or no) of the patient's decision. Even if the patient's reasons seem irrational, it is not possible to prove that the patient's actual decision making has been the product of such irrationality. The patient's decision might well be the same even if his or her cognitive processes were less impaired. For example, a delusional patient may refuse ECT not because he or she is delusional but because he or she is afraid of it, which is considered a normal reaction. The emphasis on rational reasons can too easily become a global indictment of the competency of mentally disordered individuals, justifying widespread substitute decision making for this group.

The ability to understand

This test—the ability of the patient to understand the risks, benefits, and alternatives to treatment (including no treatment)—is probably the most consistent with the law of informed consent (19). Decision making need not be rational in either process or outcome; unwise choices are permitted. Nevertheless, at a minimum the patient must manifest sufficient ability to understand information about treatment, even if in fact he or she weighs this information differently from the attending physician. What matters in this test is that the patient is able to comprehend the elements that are presumed by law to be a part of treatment decision making. How the patient weighs these elements, values them, or puts them together to reach a decision is not important.

The patient's capacity for understanding may be tested by asking the patient a series of questions concerning risks, benefits, and alternatives to treatment (35). By providing further information or explanation to the patient, the physician may find deficiencies in understanding to be remediable or not (36). The following case examples illustrate the use of the test of the ability to understand:

Case 3. A 28-year-old woman who was unresponsive to medication was approached for consent to ECT. She initially appeared to be unaware of the examiner. Following an explanation of ECT, she responded to the request to explain its purposes and why it was being recommended in her case with the statement, 'Paul McCartney, nothing to zero'. She was shown a consent form for ECT that she signed without reading. Further attempts to educate her were unsuccessful. It was decided not to perform the ECT without seeking court approval.

Case 4. A 44-year-old woman who was diagnosed as having chronic schizophrenia refused amputation of her frostbitten toes. She was nonpsychotic. Although her condition was evaluated psychiatrically as manifesting extreme denial, she understood what was proposed and that there was some risk of infection without surgery. Nevertheless, she declined. She stated, 'You want to take my toes off; I want to keep them'. Her decision was respected. She agreed to return to the hospital if things got worse. A month later she returned, having suffered an auto-amputation of the toes. There was no infection; she was rebandaged and sent home.

Some of the questions raised by this test of competency are, What is to be done if the patient can understand the risks but not the benefits or vice versa? Alternatively, what if the patient views the risks as the benefits? The following case example illustrates this problem:

Case 5. A 49-year-old woman whose understanding of treatment was otherwise intact, when informed that there was a 1 in 3,000 chance of dying from ECT, replied, 'I hope I am the one'.

Furthermore, how potentially sophisticated must understanding be in order that the patient be viewed as competent? There are considerable barriers, conscious and unconscious and intellectual and emotional (37), to understanding proposed treatments. Presumably the potential understanding required is only that which would be manifested by a reasonable person provided with a similar amount of information. A few attempts to rank degrees of understanding have been made (38). However, this matter is highly complex and beyond the scope of the present inquiry. Certainly, at least with respect to nonexperimental treatment, the patient's potential understanding does not have to be perfect or near perfect for him or her to be considered competent, although one court seemed to imply this with respect to experimental psycho-surgery (39). A final problem with this test is that its application depends on unobservable and inferential mental processes rather than on concrete and observable elements of behavior.

Actual understanding

Rather than focusing on competency as a construct or intervening variable in the decision-making process, the test of actual understanding reduces competency to an epiphenomenon of this process (19). The competent patient is by definition one who has provided a knowledgeable consent to treatment. Under this test the physician has an obligation to educate the patient and directly ascertain whether he or she has in fact understood. If not, according to this test the patient may not have provided informed consent (19). Depending on how sophisticated a level of understanding is to be required, this test delineates a potentially high level of competency, one that may be difficult to achieve.

The provisional decision of DHEW to mandate the creation of consent committees to oversee the decisions of experimental subjects (29, at 46.506) implicitly adopts this test, as does the California law requiring the review of patient consent to ECT (40). Controversial as these requirements may be, they require physicians to make reasonable efforts to ascertain that their patients understand what they are told and encourage active patient participation in treatment selection (41).

The practical and conceptual limitations of this test are similar to those of the ability-to-understand test. What constitutes adequate understanding is vague, and deficient understanding may be attributable in whole or in part to physician behavior as well as to the patient's behavior or character. An advantage that this test has over the ability-to-understand test, assuming the necessary level of understanding can be specified a priori, is its greater reliability. Unlike the ability-to-understand test, in which the patient's comprehension of material of a certain complexity is used as the basis for an assumption of comprehension of other material of equivalent complexity (even if this other material is not actually tested), the actual understanding test makes no such assumption. It tests the very issues central to patient decision making about treatment.

Discussion

It has been our experience that competency is presumed as long as the patient modulates his or her behavior, talks in a comprehensible way, remembers what he or she is told, dresses and acts so as to appear to be in meaningful communication with the environment, and has not been declared legally incompetent. In other words, if patients have their wits about them in a layman's sense (19) it is assumed that they will understand what they are told about treatment, including its risks, benefits, and alternatives. This is the equivalent of saying that the legal presumption is one of competency until found otherwise (42). The Pandora's box of the question of whether and to what extent the patient is able to understand or has understood what has been disclosed is therefore never opened.

In effect, the test that is actually applied combines elements of all of the tests described above. However, the circumstances in which competency becomes an issue determine which elements of which tests are stressed and which are underplayed. Although in theory competency is an independent variable that determines whether or not the patient's decision to accept or refuse treatment is to be honored, in practice it seems to be dependent on the interplay of two other variables, the risk/benefit ratio of treatment and the valence of the patient's decision, i e, whether he or she consents to or refuses treatment.

The phrase 'risk/benefit ratio of treatment' is used here in a shorthand way to express the fact that people who determine patient competency make this decision partly on the basis of the risks of the particular treatment being considered and the benefits of that treatment. We do not mean to imply that any formal calculation is made or that any given ratio is determinative of competency. The problems of who decides what is a risk and what is a benefit, the relative weights to be attached to risks and benefits, and who bears the risks and to whom the benefits accrue (eg, the patient, the clinician, society), are beyond the scope of the present inquiry.

Table 1 illustrates the interplay of the valence of the patient's decision and the risk/benefit ratio of treatment. When there is a favorable risk/benefit ratio to the proposed treatment in the opinion of the person determining competency and the patient consents to the treatment, there does not seem to be any reason to stand in the way of administering treatment. To accomplish this, a test employing a low threshold of competency may be applied to find even a marginal patient competent so that his or her decision may be honored (cell A). This is what happens daily when uncomprehending patients are permitted to sign themselves into the hospital. Similarly, when the risk/benefit is favorable and the patient refuses treatment, a test employing a higher threshold of competency may be applied (cell B). Under such a test even a somewhat knowledgeable patient may be found incompetent so that consent may be sought from a substitute decision maker and treatment administered despite the patient's refusal. An example would be the patient withdrawing from alcohol who, although intermittently resistive, is nevertheless administered sedative medication. In both of these cases, in which the risk/benefit ratio is favorable, the bias of physicians, other health professionals, and judges is usually skewed toward providing treatment. Therefore, a test of competency is applied that will permit the treatment to be administered irrespective of the patient's actual or potential understanding.

However, there is a growing reluctance on the part of our society to permit patients to undergo treatments that are extremely risky or for which the benefits are highly speculative. Thus if the risk/benefit ratio is unfavorable or questionable and the patient refuses treatment, a test employing a low threshold of competency may be selected so that the patient will be found competent and his or her refusal honored (cell C). This is what happens in the area of sterilisation of mentally retarded people, in which, at least from the perspective of the retarded individual, the risk/benefit ratio is questionable. On the other hand, when the risk/benefit ratio is unfavorable or questionable and the patient consents to treatment, a test using a higher threshold of competency may be applied (cell D), preventing even some fairly knowledgeable patients from undergoing treatment. The judicial opinion in the well-known *Kaimowitz* psychosurgery case delineated a high test of competency to be employed in that experimental setting (39).

Of course, some grossly impaired patients cannot be determined to be competent under any conceivable test, nor can most normally functioning people be found incompetent merely by selective application of a test of competency. However, within limits and when the patient's competency is not absolutely clear-cut, a test of competency that will achieve the desired medical or social end despite the actual condition of the patient may be selected. We do not imply that this is done maliciously either by physicians or by the courts; rather, we believe that it occurs as a consequence of the strong societal bias in favor of treating treatable patients so long as it does not expose them to serious risks.

Conclusions

The search for a single test of competency is a search for a Holy Grail. Unless it is recognised that there is no magical definition of competency to make decisions about treatment, the search for an acceptable test will never end. 'Getting the words just right' is only part of the problem. In practice, judgments of competency go beyond semantics or straightforward applications of legal rules; such judgments reflect social considerations and societal biases as much as they reflect matters of law and medicine.

References

1. Shah SA: Dangerousness and civil commitment of the mentally ill: some public policy considerations. Am J Psychiatry 132:501–505, 1975
2. Allen RC, Ferster EZ, Weihofen H: Mental Impairment and Legal Incompetency. Englewood Cliffs, NJ, Prentice-Hall, 1968
3. Hardisty JH: Mental illness: a legal fiction. Washington Law Review 48:735–762, 1973
4. Alexander GJ, Szasz TS: From contract to status via psychiatry. Santa Clara Lawyer 13:537–559, 1973
5. Group for the Advancement of Psychiatry Committee on Psychiatry and Law: Misuse of Psychiatry in the Criminal Courts: Competency to Stand Trial. Report 89. New York, GAP, 1974
6. Green MD: Judicial tests of mental incompetency. Missouri Law Review 6:141–165, 1941
7. *Dusky v United States* 362 US 405 (1960) (per curiam)
8. Informed consent and the dying patient. Yale Law Journal 83:1632–1664, 1974
9. Mental competency of patient to consent to surgical operation or treatment. American Law Reports Annotated, Third Series 25:1439–1443, 1969
10. Friedman PR: Legal regulation of applied behavior analysis in mental institutions and prisons. Arizona Law Review 17:39–104, 1975
11. Shapiro MH: Legislating the control of behavior control: autonomy and the coercive use of organic therapies. Southern California Law Review 47:237–356, 1974
12. *Demers v Gerety* 515 P 2d 645 (NM 1973)
13. *Steele v Woods* 327 SW 2d 187 at 198 (Mo 1959)
14. Peszke MA: Is dangerousness an issue for physicians in emergency commitment? Am J Psychiatry 132:825–828, 1975
15. Halleck SL: Legal and ethical aspects of behavior control. Am J Psychiatry 131:381–385, 1974
16. Grunebaum H, Abernethy V: Ethical issues in family planning for hospitalized psychiatric patients. Am J Psychiatry 132:236–240, 1975

TABLE 1
Factors in selection of competency tests

Patient's decision	Risk/benefit ratio of treatment	
	Favorable	Unfavorable or questionable
Consent	Low test of competency (cell A)	High test of competency (cell D)
Refusal	High test of competency (cell B)	Low test of competency (cell C)

17. *Relf v Weinberger* 372 F Supp 1196 (DC 1974)
18. Michels R: The right to refuse psychoactive drugs: case studies in bioethics. Hastings Center Report 3(3):10–11, 1973
19. Meisel A, Roth LH, Lidz CW: Toward a model of the legal doctrine of informed consent. Am J Psychiatry 134:285–289, 1977
20. A Draft Act Governing Hospitalization of the Mentally Ill, revised. US Public Health Service Publication 51. Washington, DC, US Government Printing Office, 1952, pp 6, 26, 27
21. *Re Yetter* 62 D & C 2d 619 at 624 (CP Northampton County, Pa 1973)
22. Stone AA: Mental Health and Law: A System in Transition. US Department of Health, Education, and Welfare Publication 75–176. Rockville, Md, National Institute of Mental Health, 1975, p 68
23. US Department of Health, Education, and Welfare: Protection of human subjects. Federal Register 39:18914–18920, May 30, 1973
24. *Moore v Webb* 345 SW 2d 239 at 243 (Mo 1961)
25. Friedman PR: Legal regulation of applied behavior analysis in mental institutions and prisons. Arizona Law Review 17:39–140, 1975
26. *New York City Health and Hospital Corp v Stein* 335 NYS 2d 461 at 465 (NY 1972)
27. McDonald MC: And things get rough. Psychiatric News, Nov 5, 1975, pp 13–14
28. *Wyatt v Aderholt* 368 F Supp 1383 at 1385 (MD Ala 1974)
29. US Department of Health, Education, and Welfare: Protection of human subjects: proposed policy. Federal Register 39:30647–30657, Aug 23, 1974
30. *United States v George* 239 F Supp 752 (D Conn 1965)
31. Cantor NL: A patient's decision to decline life-saving medical treatment: bodily integrity versus the preservation of life. Rutgers Law Review 26:228–264, 1973
32. Judge OKs amputation of south sider's leg. Pittsburgh Press, June 4, 1975, p 1
33. Amputate order more human than judicial, Larsen says. Pittsburgh Press, June 8, 1975, p 1
34. Developments in the law—civil commitment of the mentally ill. Harvard Law Review 87:1190–1406, 1974
35. Miller R, Willner HS: The two-part consent form. N Engl J Med 290:964–966, 1974
36. Ingelfinger FJ: Informed (but uneducated) consent. N Engl J Med 287: 465–466, 1972
37. Katz J: Experimentation with Human Beings. New York, Russell Sage Foundation, 1972, pp 609–673
38. Olin GB, Olin HS: Informed consent in voluntary mental hospital admissions. Am J Psychiatry 132:938–941, 1975
39. *Kaimowitz v Michigan Department of Mental Health*, Civil Action 73-19434-AW (Wayne County, Mich, Cir Ct 1973)
40. California enacts rigid shock therapy controls. Psychiatric News, Feb 5, 1975, pp 1, 4–7
41. Szasz RS, Hollender MH: The basic models of the doctor-patient relationship. Arch Intern Med 97:585–592, 1956
42. *Lotman v Security Mutual Life Insurance Co* 478 F 2d 868 (3d Cir 1973)

Can you separate in Roth *et al*'s paper analysis of the notion of capacity from comment on the criteria to be adopted in establishing it?

Consider next the President's Commission for The Study of Ethical Problems in Medicine and Biomedical and Behavioral Research—Making Health Care Decisions, at pp 172–173 (footnotes omitted):

Assessments of incapacity

The objective of any assessment of decisional incapacity is to diminish errors of mistakenly preventing competent persons from directing the course of their own treatment or of failing to protect the incapacitated from the harmful effects of their decisions. Health care professionals will probably play a substantial role, if not the entire one, in the initial assessment and the finding may never be reviewed by outside authorities. Nonetheless, since assessment of an individual's capacity is largely a matter of common sense, there is no inherent reason why a health care professional must play this role.

'Decisionmaking incapacity' is not a medical or a psychiatric diagnostic category; it rests on a judgment of the type that an informed layperson might make—that a patient lacks the ability to understand a situation and to make a choice in light of that understanding. Indeed, if a dispute arises or a legal determination of a patient's competence is required, the judge empowered to make the determination will consider the situation not as a medical expert but as a layperson. On the basis of the testimony of health care personnel and others who know the individual well, and possibly from personal observation of the patient, the judge must decide whether the patient is capable of making informed decisions that adequately protect his or her own interests.

Health care professionals are called upon to make these assessments because the question of incapacity to make health care decisions usually arises while a person is under their care. Particularly within institutions such as hospitals, a treating physician often involves colleagues from psychiatry, psychology, and neurology who have ways to accumulate, organise, and analyse information relevant to such assessments. These examinations can yield considerable information about the patient's capabilities. The sources of useful information to be collected include discussions of the situation with relatives and other care-givers, particularly those in close contact with the patient, such as nurses. Ultimately, whether a patient's capabilities are sufficiently limited and the inadequacies sufficiently extensive for the person to be considered incapacitated is a matter for careful judgment in light of the demands of the situation. If the patient improves (or worsens) or if the decision to be made has different consequences, a reassessment of the individual's capacity may be required.

Finally, in any assessment of capacity due care should be paid to the reasons for a particular patient's impaired capacity, not because the reasons play any role in determining whether the patient's judgment is to be honored but because identification of the causes of incapacity may assist in their remedy or removal. The Commission urges that those responsible for assessing capacity not be content with providing an answer to the question of whether or not a particular patient is incapacitated. Rather, in conjunction with the patient's health care team (of which the assessor may be a member), they should to the extent feasible attempt to remove barriers to decisional capacity.

The President's Commission continues at pp 57–62:

Elements of capacity. In the view of the Commission, any determination of the capacity to decide on a course of treatment must relate to the individual abilities of a patient, the requirements of the task at hand, and the consequences likely to flow from the decision. Decisionmaking capacity requires, to greater or lesser degree: (1) possession of a set of values and goals; (2) the ability to communicate and to understand information; and (3) the ability to reason and to deliberate about one's choices.

The first, a framework for comparing options, is needed if the person is to evaluate possible outcomes as good or bad. The framework, and the values that it embodies, must be reasonably stable; that is, the patient must be able to make reasonably consistent choices. Reliance on a patient's decision would be difficult or impossible if the patient's values were so unstable that the patient could not reach or adhere to a choice at least long enough for a course of therapy to be initiated with some prospect of being completed.

The second element includes the ability to give and receive information, as well as the possession of various linguistic and conceptual skills needed for at least a basic understanding of the relevant information. These abilities can be evaluated only as they relate to the task at hand and are not solely cognitive, as they ordinarily include emotive elements. To use them, a person also needs sufficient life experience to appreciate the meaning of potential alternatives: what it would probably be like to undergo various medical procedures, for example, or to live in a new way required by a medical condition or intervention.

Some critics of the doctrine of informed consent have argued that patients simply lack the ability to understand medical information relevant to decisions about their care. Indeed, some empirical studies purport to have demonstrated this by showing that the lay public often does not know the meaning of common medical terms, or by showing that, following an encounter with a physician, patients are unable to report what the physician said about their illness and treatment. Neither type of study establishes the fact that patients cannot understand. The first merely finds that they do not currently know the right definitions of some terms; the second, which usually fails to discover what the physician actually did say, rests its conclusions on an assumption that information was provided that was subsequently not understood. In the Commission's own survey, physicians were asked: 'What percentage of your patients would you say are able to understand most aspects of their treatment and condition if reasonable time and effort are devoted to explanation?' Overall, 48% of physicians reported that 90–100% of their patients could understand and an additional 34% said that 70–89% could understand.

The third element of decisionmaking capacity—reasoning and deliberation— includes the ability to compare the impact of alternative outcomes on personal goals and life plans. Some ability to employ probabilistic reasoning about uncertain outcomes is usually necessary, as well as the ability to give appropriate weight in a present decision to various future outcomes.

Standards for assessing capacity. The actual measurement of these various abilities is by no means simple. Virtually all conscious adults can perform some tasks but not others. In the context of informed consent, what is critical is a patient's capacity to make a specific medical decision. An assessment of an individual's capacity must consider the nature of the particular decisionmaking process in light of these developments: Does the patient possess the ability to understand the relevant facts and alternatives? Is the patient weighing the decision within a framework of values and goals? Is the patient able to reason and deliberate about this information? Can the patient give reasons for the decision, in light of the facts, the alternatives, and the impact of the decision on the patient's own goals and values?

To be sure, a patient may possess these abilities but fail to exercise them well; that is, the decision may be the result of a mistaken understanding of the facts or a defective reasoning process. In such instances, the obligation of the professional is not to declare, on the basis of a 'wrong' decision, that the patient lacks decisionmaking capacity, but rather to work with the patient toward a fuller and more accurate understanding of the facts and a sound reasoning process.

How deficient must a decisionmaking process be to justify the assessment that a patient lacks the capacity to make a particular decision? Since the assessment must balance possibly competing considerations of well-being and self-determination, the prudent course is to take into account the potential consequences of the patient's decision. When the consequences for well-being are substantial, there is a greater need to be certain that the patient possesses the necessary level of capacity. When little turns on the decision, the level of decisionmaking capacity required may be appropriately reduced (even though the constituent elements remain the same) and less scrutiny may be required about whether the patient possesses even the reduced level of capacity. Thus a particular patient may be capable of deciding about a relatively inconsequential medication, but not about the amputation of a gangrenous limb.

This formulation has significant implications. First, it denies that simply by expressing a preference about a treatment decision an individual demonstrates the capacity to make that decision. The 'expressed preference' standard does nothing to preclude the presence of a serious defect or mistake in a patient's reasoning process. Consequently, it cannot ensure that the patient's expressed preference accords with the patient's conception of future well-being. Although it gives what appears to be great deference to self-determination, the expressed preference standard may actually fail to promote the values underlying self-administration, which include the achievement of personal values and goals. For these reasons, the Commission rejects the expressed preference standard for decisions that might compromise the patient's well-being.

The Commission also rejects as the standard of capacity any test that looks solely to the content of the patient's decision. Any standard based on 'objectively correct' decisions would allow a health professional (or other third party) to declare that a patient lacks decisionmaking capacity whenever a decision appears 'wrong', 'irrational', or otherwise incompatible with the evaluator's view of what is best for the patient. Use of such a standard is in sharp conflict with most of the values that support self-determination: it would take the decision away from the patient and place it with another, and it would inadequately reflect the subjective nature of each individual's conception of what's good. Further, its imprecision opens the door to manipulation of health care decisionmaking through selective application.

Logically, just as a patient's disagreement with a health care professional's recommendation does not prove a lack of decisionmaking capacity, concurrence with the recommendation would not establish the patient's capacity. Yet, as testimony before the Commission made clear, coherent adults are seldom said to lack capacity (except, perhaps, in the mental health context) when they acquiesce in the course of treatment recommended by their physicians. (Challenges to patients' capacity are rarer still when family members expressly concur in the decision.) This divergence between theory and reality is less significant than it might appear, however, since neither the self-determination nor the well-being of a patient would usually be advanced by insisting upon an inquiry into the patient's decisionmaking capacity (or lack thereof) when patient, physicians, and family all agree on a course of treatment. Even if the course being adopted might not, in fact, best match the patient's long-term view of his or her own welfare, a declaration of lack of capacity will lead to a substitute making a decision for the patient (which means full self-determination will not occur), yet will rarely result in a different health care decision being made (which means no change in well-being). Substitution of a third party for an acquiescent patient will lead to a different outcome only if the new decisionmaker has a strong commitment to promoting previously expressed values of the patient that differ significantly from those that guided the physician. If, as would usually be the case, the substitute would be a family member or other individual who would defer to the physician's recommendation, there would be little reason to initiate an inquiry into capacity. The existing practice thus seems generally satisfactory.

Questions of patient capacity in decisionmaking typically arise only when a patient chooses a course—often a refusal of treatment—other than the one the health professional finds most reasonable. A practitioner's belief that a decision is not 'reasonable' is the beginning—not the end—of an inquiry into the patient's capacity to decide. If every patient decision that a health professional disagreed with were grounds for a declaration of lack of capacity, self-determination would have little meaning. Even when disagreement occurs, an assessment of the patient's decisionmaking capacity begins with a presumption of such capacity. Nonetheless, a serious disagreement about a decision with substantial consequences for the patient's welfare may appropriately trigger a more careful evaluation. When that process indicates that the patient understands the situation and is capable of reasoning soundly about it, the patient's choice should be accepted. When it does not, further evaluation may be required, and in some instances a determination of lack of capacity will be appropriate.

M A Somerville, in 'Structuring the Issues Informed Consent' 26 McGill LJ 740 at 783–5 (footnotes omitted):

Rationality
Does the law require rationality of the patient's decision as a substantive element of a valid consent?

The first consideration is the relationship between understanding and rationality. If the law requires that the patient apparently understand the required disclosure of information in order to give a valid consent, does this mean that the law is seeking to promote rationality of the patient's decision and, further, if his decision is adjudged irrational, may it be ignored or overridden on this basis?

Even if it is accepted that understanding of the required disclosed information is being mandated in order to promote rationality, it must be asked whether this means rationality of the decision-making process or rationality of the decision itself or both. Although understanding may promote rationality in both of these respects, it is usually only the rationality of the decision outcome that is relevant to the law, and understanding may not be an essential condition for this. It is quite possible for a decision to be judged rational by an objective bystander, when the reasons on which it was based were quite irrational. Moreover, the law's requirement of understanding of information by the patient may be seen as promoting autonomy rather than rationality. In this case, to require rationality either of the patient's decision-making process or its outcome would be to contradict directly the value of self-determination which is being promoted by requiring understanding, because self-determination requires recognition of the competent patient's right, for no matter what reason or on what basis, to determine what shall be done to himself.

It is submitted that the preferable approach is to view understanding as promoting autonomy, rather than rationality. Any legal limits to irrationality of a decision-making process or decision outcome should then be set by declaring the person factually or legally incompetent. Thus, the right to autonomy would mean that the competent patient could make irrational decisions concerning himself without the law overriding such decisions. Further, in order to give proper scope to such a rule, it is necessary to recognise that irrationality of the decision-making process or of decision outcomes does not of itself indicate incompetence, although in some circumstances it may be evidence of this.

The issue of irrationality of the patient's decision was considered in *Kelly v Hazlett*. The defendant surgeon gave evidence that he considered the plaintiff 'irrational', that is, 'irrational from the point of view of not being able to think the way that [he, the doctor] was thinking, which [he] thought was more rational'. The actual irrationality referred to was the patient's decision to undergo the operation only if the cosmetic procedure were included. In the result the Court held that the patient's 'apparent consent' was insufficient to protect the surgeon from liability in negligence on the basis of failure to obtain informed consent. It is not exactly clear how much the irrationality of the patient's decision influenced his holding, but it seems that such irrationality should at least put the physician on notice that the patient's 'decision was not based upon any knowledge or appreciation of the risk', in which case the physician may not rely on the consent as being valid. This case is probably a demonstration of a court looking to the rationality of the patient's decision to indicate both whether the patient had the required understanding of the risks that must be understood in order to give informed consent, and whether the physician had, or ought to have had, knowledge of any lack of understanding on the part of the patient.

In summary, the question of rationality in matters of consent is difficult. To allow (or even more so, require) second-guessing of the patient's decision according to whether that decision is rational may seriously detract from autonomy (which it is the purpose of consent to protect). The more a person's decision deviates from what the person assessing that decision would decide in the same circumstances, and the more serious the consequences of that decision, the more likely it is that the person making the decision will be labelled incompetent and his decision irrational. Rather than judging the rationality of a patient's decision and validating or invalidating consent on that basis, the better solution (which was probably the approach of the Court in *Kelly v Hazlett*) is to adopt understanding by the patient of the information required to be disclosed as the necessary safeguard. Pursuant to such an approach, provided the patient is otherwise judged to be competent, if the physician has no subjective knowledge that the patient lacks understanding and the reasonable physician would have believed that the patient apparently understood the information disclosed, the resulting consent may be relied upon as valid whether or not the patient's decision is considered rational.

In a paternalistic physician-patient relationship, consent was often the *imprima:ur* of the doctor's rational decision-making on the patient's behalf. Under a doctrine of informed consent the aim is to enable the patient to make a decision on his own behalf. A remaining question is how far the physician is justified in carrying out a patient's informed, irrational decisions. The physician is far less likely to be acting within legal or ethical limits when implementing such a decision requires a positive intervention on his part, than when it is a situation in which he must desist from violating the patient's physical or mental integrity against his will. More explicitly, a patient's irrational refusal of treatment should be accorded greater respect than his irrational demand for it.

Consider now the Editorial in 9 Journal of Medical Ethics, p 131, which reads as follows (footnotes omitted):

Impaired autonomy and rejection of treatment
Two important moral principles can, and occasionally do, come into conflict in the context of medical practice: the first is the principle of helping others who are in need (beneficence), presumably the basic moral principle motivating the caring professions; the second is respect for people's autonomy—acknowledgment of their right to make their own deliberated decision within the context of their own life plan and preferences, so far as this does not harm others. Normally, of course, these two principles do not conflict—people consult doctors because they have medical problems which they want the doctors to do their best to abolish or ameliorate. In a minority of cases, however, the patient rejects the course of action proposed by the doctor and the doctor's dilemma is generated.

The polar cases are relatively uncontroversial. Thus when a patient is clearly competent to make his own decisions and rejects his doctor's advice despite understanding it and the anticipated consequences of rejecting it, then a consensus probably exists in favour of respecting the patient's decision. Hence contemporary medical respect for life-threatening decisions by Jehovah's Witnesses to refuse blood transfusions and by hunger strikers to refuse food and medical attention.

At the other pole, when a patient is clearly incompetent to make autonomous decisions it is widely agreed that beneficent decisions must be taken on his or her behalf, overriding, if this seems desirable, the incompetent patient's protests. A young child is operated on for appendicitis even if he refuses most volubly; a severely mentally handicapped patient is treated with antibiotic injections for his meningitis even if he does hate needles. A patient in a severe confusional state is treated against his will when this is judged necessary. All this is relatively uncontroversial. More controversial is who should make the decisions and on what basis, though once again a consensus is apparently emerging that next of kin and/or the patient's loved ones are presumed to be best placed to make such decisions, in the context of medical advice and where possible on the basis of what the patient would decide autonomously, but failing that, on the basis of the patient's best interests. The presumption that the next of kin should decide on behalf of the incompetent patient is always defeasible and if the doctors or others believe that particular decisions are *not* what the patient would have autonomously wished or not in the patient's best interests, and if agreement between them and the relatives is impossible it is open to them to obtain a judicial assessment.

What, however, differentiates the patient who is competent to make his own deliberated decisions and thus is to have his autonomy respected from the patient who is not? The symposium in this issue of the journal and the paper in the *American Journal of Psychiatry* which provoked it analyse this issue of competence (or competency—the final 'y' is sometimes added where the term has a legal connotation) in the context of 'competent but irrational' refusal of electroconvulsive therapy (ECT) as treatment for depression.

The first important point to emerge from the symposium is that information is essential for autonomous and therefore rational decision-making. One cannot reason or deliberate about alternative courses of action if one has no information about them, and as Dr Taylor, a forensic psychiatrist, points out, patients are likely to make irrational decisions if their doctors give them inadequate information. She explains in detail the clinical importance of ensuring that patients are given adequate information, and given it personally and with care. Nonetheless, as Dr Taylor also points out, the amount of information which patients actually retain is often likely to be fairly limited. How much is necessary for competent decision-making by the patient? Dr Culver and his colleagues recommend a 'minimalist' requirement—a patient should be regarded as competent to reject or accept medical treatment if he knows the doctor believes he is ill and in need of treatment, knows the doctor believes the treatment may help his illness and knows he is expected to decide whether or not to have the treatment. The grounds for this minimalism are that others should not make decisions for patients unless 'it is abundantly clear that the patient is simply unable to represent his or her own interests'.

One problem with this requirement is, as Dr Taylor points out, that patients may meet the cognitive standards set by Culver *et al*, manifest impeccable logical reasoning ability, and yet, because of their seriously distorted perception of the world, base much of their reasoning on false premises. If a patient 'knows' that guns are pointing at him wherever he goes it makes good sense for him to run away or hit back—and it makes good sense to pity and scorn the doctor for not being able to see the guns, or hear the voices, and for diagnosing him as a paranoid psychotic. But is that sort of reasoning to be regarded as *competent*? By the minimal criteria of Culver *et al* presumably it may be; and rejection of medication, however irrational it may be, would therefore be accepted. Many, clinicians and non-clinicians alike, would not accept such decisions as being competently made, nor would they want them respected if they led to actions which harmed others or the patient himself. Thus while Culver *et al* are surely right—in the interests of respecting patients' autonomy—to insist on a 'minimalist' criterion for competence to reject treatment it seems necessary to allow that if a patient's perception of reality is *sufficiently* distorted by delusions, illusions and hallucinations, then his competence to reject treatment may properly be questioned even if he meets Culver and his colleagues' criteria.

However, Professor Sherlock is surely right to criticise the Culver criteria on the grounds that they are only cognitive whereas informed consent and rejection require not only adequate information but also what Sherlock calls voluntariness by which he means 'an uncoerced consent'. And Dr Taylor raises similar doubts in relation to common psychiatric conditions in which patients show no sign of being able to make free decisions of any kind: the patient who just does not know what to do; the patient who sits in the corner wringing his hands and saying nothing; the patient who has 'more important things to think about'—all manifest grossly impaired volition (still these days philosophically a fishy concept but an unshakeably real phenomenon to most clinicians). Their cognitive status, however, may be well up to the standards required by Culver *et al* for recognition of competence. Once again it seems sensible to modify their minimalist cognitive criteria by adding a criterion of voluntariness—a requirement that the patient is in a state of mind in which he can make ordinary voluntary decisions.

Here, however, great care is needed—in the interests of justice—to make sure that the criteria for voluntariness required of patients are no more stringent than those required of anyone else in society for his autonomy to be recognised. Sherlock suggests that an irrational refusal to have ECT can *in itself* be grounds for classifying a patient as incompetent. Somewhat contentiously classifying this as a 'phobia' he says that the patient 'is no more free to decide *vis à vis* the dreaded object than he would be were he faced with severe hardship for failure to comply with a command to consent'. This doctrine that the presence of a phobia is sufficient for a patient to be judged incompetent to reject treatment has only to be universalised to be shown to be far too demanding. Thus, according to the doctrine, if a patient consults her psychiatrist about an admitted phobia to do with, say, spiders or flying or open spaces, and the doctor confirms the diagnosis he immediately is justified in deeming her incompetent to decide about her treatment (because she has a phobia) and in instituting against her will any standard treatment he happens to favour.

Voluntariness and autonomy can be greatly impaired in ordinary life without a person's right to make his own decision being overridden; similar minimalist standards should in justice be set for patients. Thus, while recognition should be given to the fact that mental and other illness can on occasion impair the patient's competence to give any sort of voluntary decision (even if he meets the cognitive standards proposed) the mere presence of a psychiatric or other disorder cannot in itself justify an assessment of incompetence to decide on treatment.

Finally, Professor Sherlock's justification of paternalistic intervention to force a depressed patient to have ECT against his will on the grounds that by doing so he would actually be respecting the patient's autonomy by seeking to increase it requires critical consideration. In a recent issue of the journal an editorial criticised Dr Komrad's argument that illness always represented a state of diminished autonomy and that this justified paternalistic medical interventions imposed in order to restore or increase the patient's autonomy by ameliorating the effects of the illness. Professor Sherlock's argument is similar. To respect a patient's irrational decision to refuse ECT is, he writes, to respect only a 'limited autonomy' and it is better to override that decision in the interests of restoring the patient's full autonomy. 'If we do value autonomy we ought to pursue it in its fullest possible form, not in the truncated one-dimensional case of refusal of ECT. If autonomy is a good then I submit that the morally appropriate course of action is to foster the autonomy of patients by relieving to the best of our abilities the impediments to autonomy such as major depression'.

There can be no objection to this when the patient consents. But when such 'relief of impediments' is imposed against the competent patient's will, then this benign paternalism represents, as Lesser points out, a serious threat to personal freedom. Autonomy is not an all or nothing phenomenon. People are autonomous to different degrees, their autonomy varying with time and circumstances. If mere evidence of impairment of autonomy (or even of serious impairment) is to be used to justify compulsory intervention by others in order to increase people's autonomy then all standard concepts of respect for autonomy and respect for individual liberty will have taken on new, and to many, somewhat sinister meanings.

Consider next the following examples of judicial responses. First *Smith v Auckland Hospital Board* [1965] NZLR 191 at 219:

T A Gresson J: An individual patient must, in my view, always retain the right to decline operative investigation or treatment however unreasonable or foolish this may appear in the eyes of his medical advisers.

The issue of capacity did not arise directly in this case but Greeson J's remark appears to be authority for the proposition that capacity is not to be doubted simply on the ground that the decision is unreasonable in the eyes of others.

Secondly, *Hopp v Lepp* (1979) 98 DLR (3d) 464 at 470:

Prowse J: Each patient is entitled to make his own decision even though it may not accord with the decision knowledgeable members of the profession would make. The patient has a right to be wrong. When specific questions are directed to a surgeon he must make a full and fair disclosure in response to them. This duty requires a surgeon to disclose risks which are mere possibilities if the patient's questions reasonably direct the surgeon's attention to risks of that nature and if they are such that the surgeon, in all of the circumstances, could reasonably foresee would affect the patient's decision.

Thirdly, *The Application of President and Directors of Georgetown College, Inc* (1964) 331 F2d 1000 US Court of Appeals, District of Columbia Circuit

J Skelly Wright: Attorneys for Georgetown Hospital applied for an emergency writ at 4:00 pm, September 17, 1963, seeking relief from the action of the United States District Court for the District of Columbia denying the hospital's application for permission to administer blood transfusions to an emergency patient. The application recited that 'Mrs Jesse E Jones is presently a patient at Georgetown University Hospital', 'she is in extremis', according to the attending physician 'blood transfusions are necessary immediately in order to save her life', and 'consent to the administration thereof can be obtained neither from the patient nor her husband'. The patient and her husband based their refusal on their religious beliefs as Jehovah's Witnesses. The order sought provided that the attending physicians 'may' administer such transfusions to Mrs. Jones as might be 'necessary to save her life'. After the proceedings detailed [below], I signed the order at 5:20 pm.

. . .

Mrs. Jones was brought to the hospital by her husband for emergency care, having lost two thirds of her body's blood supply from a ruptured ulcer. She had no personal physician, and relied solely on the hospital staff. She was a total hospital responsibility. It appeared that the patient, age 25, mother of a seven-month-old child, and her husband were both Jehovah's Witnesses, the teachings of which sect, according to their interpretation, prohibited the injection of blood into the body. When death without blood became imminent, the hospital sought the advice of counsel, who applied to the District Court in the name of the hospital for permission to administer blood. Judge Tamm of the District Court denied the application, and counsel immediately applied to me, as a member of the Court of Appeals, for an appropriate writ.

I called the hospital by telephone and spoke with Dr Westura, Chief Medical Resident, who confirmed the representations made by counsel. I thereupon proceeded with counsel to the hospital, where I spoke to Mr Jones, the husband of the patient. He advised me that, on religious grounds, he would not approve a blood transfusion for his wife. He said, however, that if the court ordered the transfusion, the responsibility was not his. . . .

I asked permission of Mr. Jones to see his wife. This he readily granted. Prior to going into the patient's room, I again conferred with Dr Westura and several other doctors assigned to the case. All confirmed that the patient would die without blood and that there was a better than 50 per cent chance of saving her life with it. Unanimously they strongly recommended it. I then went inside the patient's room. Her appearance confirmed the urgency which had been represented to me. I tried to communicate with her, advising her again as to what the doctors had said. The only audible reply I could hear was 'Against my will'. It was obvious that the woman was not in mental condition to make a decision. I was reluctant to press her because of the seriousness of her condition and because I felt that to suggest repeatedly the imminence of death without blood might place a strain on her religious convictions. I asked her whether she would oppose the blood transfusion if the court allowed it. She indicated, as best I could make out, that it would not then be her responsibility.

Finally in *R v Blaue* [1975] 3 All ER 446, at p 450b–d (footnote omitted):

Lawton LJ: Counsel for the appellant . . . submitt[ed] that the jury should have been directed that if they thought the girl's decision not to have a blood transfusion was an unreasonable one, then the chain of causation would have been broken. At once the question arises—reasonable by whose standards? Those of Jehovah's Witnesses? Humanists? Roman Catholics? Protestants of Anglo-Saxon descent? The man on the Clapham omnibus? But he might well be an admirer of Eleazar who suffered death rather than eat the flesh of swine or of Sir Thomas Moore who, unlike nearly all his contemporaries, was unwilling to accept Henry VIII as Head of the Church in England. Those brought up in the Hebraic and Christian traditions would probably be reluctant to accept that these martyrs caused their own deaths.

As was pointed out to counsel for the appellant in the course of argument, two cases, each raising the same issue of reasonableness because of religious beliefs, could produce different verdicts depending on where the cases were tried. A jury drawn from Preston, sometimes said to be the most Catholic town in England, might have different views about martyrdom to one drawn from the inner suburbs of London.

In the US a number of cases have arisen in which elderly patients suffering from circulatory difficulties have developed problems in the lower limbs calling for consideration of amputation. We consider two contrasting cases. *Lane v Candura* 376 NE 2D 1232 (1978) (Appeal Court of Massachusetts) and *State of Tennessee v Northern* 563 SW 2d 197 (1978) (Court of Appeals of Tennessee). Finally, we look at the case of *Re Yetter* 62 D & C 2d 619 (1973) which raised the same issues in the context of other surgery.

Lane v Candura
376 NE 2d 1232 (1978) (footnotes omitted):

This case concerns a 77-year-old widow, Mrs Rosaria Candura, of Arlington, who is presently a patient at the Symmes Hospital in Arlington suffering from gangrene in the right foot and lower leg. Her attending physicians recommended in April that the leg be amputated without delay. After some vacillation, she refused to consent to the operation, and she persists in that refusal. . . .

The principal question arising on the record before us, therefore, is whether Mrs Candura has the legally requisite competence of mind and will to make the choice for herself. . . .

A person is presumed to be competent unless shown by the evidence not to be competent. . . . Such evidence is lacking in this case. We recognise that Dr Kelley, one of two psychiatrists who testified, did state that in his opinion Mrs Candura was incompetent to make a rational choice whether to consent to the operation. His opinion appears to have been based upon (1) his inference from her unwillingness to discuss the problem with him that she was unable to face up to the problem or to understand that her refusal constituted a choice; (2) his characterisation of 'an unwilling[ness], for whatever reason, to consent to life saving treatment . . . as suicidal;' and (3) a possibility, not established by evidence as a reasonable probability, that her mind might be impaired by toxicity caused by the gangrenous condition. His testimony, read closely, and in the context of the questions put to him, indicates that his opinion is not one of incompetency in the legal sense, but rather that her ability to make a rational choice (by which he means the *medically* rational choice) is impaired by the confusion existing in her mind by virtue of her consideration of irrational and emotional factors.

A careful analysis of the evidence in this case, including the superficially conflicting psychiatric testimony, indicates that there is no real conflict as to the underlying facts. Certainly, the evidence presents no issue of credibility. The principal question is whether the facts established by the evidence justify a conclusion of legal incompetence. The panel are unanimous in the opinion that they do not.

The decision of the judge, as well as the opinion of Dr Kelley, predicates the necessity for the appointment of a guardian chiefly on the irrationality (in medical terms) of Mrs Candura's decision to reject the amputation. Until she changed her original decision and withdrew her consent to the amputation, her competence was not questioned. But the irrationality of her decision does not justify a conclusion that Mrs Candura is incompetent in the legal sense. The law protects her right to make her own decision to accept or reject treatment, whether that decision is wise or unwise.
. . .

Similarly, the fact that she has vacillated in her resolve not to submit to the operation does not justify a conclusion that her capacity to make the decision is impaired to the point of legal incompetence. Indeed, her reaction may be readily understandable in the light of her prior surgical experience and the prospect of living the remainder of her life nonambulatory. Senile symptoms, in the abstract, may, of course, justify a finding of incompetence, but the inquiry must be more particular. What is lacking in this case is evidence that Mrs Candura's areas of forgetfulness and confusion cause, or relate in any way to, impairment of her ability to understand that in rejecting the amputation she is, in effect, choosing death over life.

... this case is like *Re Quackenbush*, 156 NJ Super 282, 383 A2d 785 (Morris County Ct 1978), in which an elderly person, although subject (like Mrs Candura) to fluctuations in mental lucidity and to occasional losses of his train of thought, was held to be competent to reject a proposed operation to amputate gangrenous legs because he was capable of appreciating the nature and consequences of his decision.
...

Mrs Candura's decision may be regarded by most as unfortunate, but on the record in this case it is not the uninformed decision of a person incapable of appreciating the nature and consequences of her act. We cannot anticipate whether she will reconsider and will consent to the operation, but we are all of the opinion that the operation may not be forced on her against her will.

In *Lane v Candura*, the court distinguished the earlier case of *Northern* where the court had determined that the patient was incompetent.

State of Tennessee v Northern
563 SW 2d 197 (1978)

Judge Todd: On January 24, 1978, the Tennessee Department of Human Services filed this suit alleging that Mary C Northern was 72 years old, with no available help from relatives; that Miss Northern resided alone under unsatisfactory conditions as a result of which she had been admitted to and was a patient in Nashville General Hospital; that the patient suffered from gangrene of both feet which required the removal of her feet to save her life; that the patient lacked the capacity to appreciate her condition or to consent to necessary surgery.

Attached to the complaint are identical letters from Drs Amos D Tackett and R Benton Adkins which read as follows:

Mrs Mary Northern is a patient under our care at Nashville General Hospital. She has gangrene of both feet probably secondary to frost bite and then thermal burning of the feet. She has developed infection along with the gangrene of her feet. This is placing her life in danger. Mrs Northern does not understand the severity or consequences of her disease process and does not appear to understand that failure to amputate the feet at this time would probably result in her death. It is our recommendation as the physicians in charge of her case, that she undergo amputation of both feet as soon as possible.
...

The judge then turned to consider whether Miss Northern had capacity to refuse the treatment.

... Capacity means mental ability to make a rational decision, which includes the ability to perceive, appreciate all relevant facts and to reach a rational judgment upon such facts.

Capacity is not necessarily synonymous with sanity. A blind person may be perfectly capable of observing the shape of small articles by handling them, but not capable of observing the shape of a cloud in the sky.

A person may have 'capacity' as to some matters and may lack 'capacity' as to others.
...

In the present case, this Court has found the patient to be lucid and apparently of sound mind generally. However, on the subjects of death and amputation of her feet, her comprehension is blocked, blinded or dimmed to the extent that she is incapable of recognising facts which would be obvious to a person of normal perception.

For example, in the presence of this Court, the patient looked at her feet and refused to recognise the obvious fact that the flesh was dead, black, shriveled, rotting and stinking.

The record also discloses that the patient refuses to consider the eventuality of death which is or ought to be obvious in the face of such dire bodily deterioration.

As described by the doctors and observed by this Court, the patient wants to live and keep her dead feet, too, and refuses to consider the impossibility of such a desire. In order to avoid the unpleasant experience of facing death and/or loss of feet, her mind or emotions have resorted to the device of denying the unpleasant reality so that, to the patient, the unpleasant reality does not exist. This is the 'delusion' which renders the patient incapable of making a rational decision as to whether to undergo surgery to save her life or to forego surgery and forfeit her life.

The physicians speak of probabilities of death without amputation as 90 to 95% and the probability of death with surgery as 50–50 (1 in 2). Such probabilities are not facts, but the existence and expression of such opinions are facts which the patient is unwilling or unable to recognise or discuss.

If, as repeatedly stated, this patient could and would give evidence of a comprehension of the facts of her condition and could and would express her unequivocal desire in the face of such comprehended facts, then her decision, however unreasonable to others, would be accepted and honored by the Courts and by her doctors. The difficulty is that she cannot or will not comprehend the facts.

The Court was clearly influenced by Miss Northern's refusal to comprehend the facts of her situation. It is this which seems to have been considered the feature which distinguished the case from the facts of *Lane v Candura*.

In a concurring judgment, Judge Drowota emphasises this important factor in *Northern*:

Drowota J: In the instant case, the Court found that Miss Northern does not have the capacity to decide whether her feet should or should not be amputated. This finding is not based on any belief by this Court that a competent adult should not be permitted to reject lifesaving treatment. It is *not*, as has been argued to us, based on any idea of this Court that any person who refuses treatment we subjectively think a 'normal' or 'rational' person would choose is 'incompetent' merely because of that refusal. It is based on the Court's finding that Miss Northern is unable or unwilling to comprehend even dimly certain very basic *facts*, without which no one, whether elderly lady, doctor, or judge, would be competent to make such a decision. These facts include the appearance of her feet, which are disfigured, coal black, crusty, cracking, oozing, and rancid. Yet, Miss Northern looks at them and insists that nothing is wrong. Also included is the fact that her doctors are of the opinion that her life is in danger, yet she has expressed no understanding of either the gravity or the consequences of her medical condition. Again, this Court respects Miss Northern's right to disagree with medical opinions and advice. Again, if this Court in good faith could find that she perceived as facts that her feet *do* look and smell as they do, and that her doctors *are* telling her that she needs surgery to save her life, we would not interfere with whatever decision she made regardless of how much it conflicted with the substance of her medical advice or with what we ourselves might have chosen. But from our honest evaluation of the facts and evidence of this case, we have been forced to conclude that Miss Northern does not comprehend such basic facts and hence is currently incompetent to decide this particular question. While this finding was made more difficult by Miss Northern's apparent ability to grasp facts not related to the condition of her feet, it is nonetheless correct.

Since Miss Northern was not competent to decide the question of amputation, it fell . . . to this Court to do so. Again, the question for me is what would Miss Northern decide if she understood the facts. The presumption with any person must be that he would want surgery that would increase the chance of life from 5–10% to 50%, unless some statement made or attitude held while the patient was competent contradicts the presumption. No such contradiction exists in Miss Northern's case. Further, the presumption is strengthened, if anything, by Miss Northern's assertions that she does not want to die. Medically, her feet are dead and lost to her whether or not they are amputated. Psychotic effects are likely if surgery is done, but are quite possible even if Miss Northern survives and loses her feet without surgery. Her prognosis is poor either way, but there is a substantially better chance of life if the surgery is performed. In these circumstances, this Court simply could not find that

Miss Northern, if she had a basic understanding of the situation, would not choose the substantially greater chance of life that surgery offers. Our decision has been made accordingly . . .

Contrast the next case.

Re Maida Yetter
62 D & C 2d 619 (1973) (CP Northampton County PA)

Williams J: This matter involves the appointment of a guardian of the person for Maida Yetter, an alleged incompetent, under the Incompetents' Estates Act of February 28, 1956, PL (1955) 1154, as amended, 50 PS §3101, et seq. The petition was filed by Russell C Stauffer, her brother, and a citation issued on May 10, 1973. The citation was served on the alleged incompetent by a deputy sheriff of Lehigh County at Allentown State Hospital, Lehigh County, Pa, on May 15, 1973. A hearing was held on May 30, 1973, as specified in the petition. Present at the hearing were petitioner and his counsel; Dr Ellen Bischoff, a psychiatrist on the staff of the hospital; Mrs Marilou Perhac, a caseworker at the hospital assigned to Mrs Yetter's ward; the alleged incompetent and her counsel. Mrs Yetter is married, although she has been separated from, and has had no contact with, her husband since 1947.

From the petition and the testimony it appears that the primary purpose of the appointment of a guardian of the person is to give consent to the performance of diagnostic and corrective surgery.

Mrs Yetter was committed to Allentown State Hospital in June 1971, by the Courts of Northampton County after hearings held pursuant to section 406 of the Mental Health and Mental Retardation Act of October 20, 1966, Sp Sess, PL 96, 50 PS §4406. Her diagnosis at that time was schizophrenia, chronic undifferentiated. It appears that late in 1972, in connection with a routine physical examination, Mrs Yetter was discovered to have a breast discharge indicating the possible presence of carcinoma. The doctors recommended that a surgical biopsy be performed together with any additional corrective surgery that would be indicated by the pathology of the biopsy. When this recommendation was first discussed with Mrs Yetter in December of 1972 by her caseworker, Mrs Perhac, who has had weekly counseling sessions with Mrs Yetter for more than a year, Mrs Yetter indicated that she would not give her consent to the surgery. Her stated reasons were that she was afraid because of the death of her aunt which followed such surgery and that it was her own body and she did not desire the operation. The caseworker indicated that at this time Mrs Yetter was lucid, rational and appeared to understand that the possible consequences of her refusal included death.

Mr Stauffer, who indicated that he visits his sister regularly, and Dr Bischoff, whose direct contacts with Mrs Yetter have been since March 1973, testified that in the last three or four months it has been impossible to discuss the proposed surgery with Mrs Yetter in that, in addition to expressing fear of the operation, she has become delusional in her reasons for not consenting to surgery. Her tendency to become delusional concerning this problem, although no others, was confirmed by Mrs Perhac. The present delusional nature of Mrs Yetter's reasoning concerning the problem was demonstrated at the hearing when Mrs Yetter, in response to questions by the court and counsel, indicated that the operation would interfere with her genital system, affecting her ability to have babies, and would prohibit a movie career. Mrs Yetter is 60 years of age and without children.

Dr Bischoff testified that Mrs Yetter is oriented as to time, place and her personal environment, and that her present delusions are consistent with the diagnosis and evaluation of her mental illness upon admission to the hospital in 1971. The doctor indicated that, in her opinion, at the present time Mrs Yetter is unable, by reason of her mental illness, to arrive at a considered judgment as to whether to undergo surgery.

Mr Stauffer testified that the aunt referred to by Mrs Yetter, although she underwent a similar operation, died of unrelated causes some 15 years after surgery.

He further indicated that he has been apprised by the physicians of the nature of the proposed procedures and their probable consequences as well as the probable consequences if the procedures are not performed. He indicated that if he is appointed guardian of the person for his sister, he would consent to the surgical procedures recommended.

At the hearing Mrs Yetter was alert, interested and obviously meticulous about her personal appearance. She stated that she was afraid of surgery, that the best course of action for her would be to leave her body alone, that surgery might hasten the spread of the disease and do further harm, and she reiterated her fears due to the death of her aunt. On several occasions during the hearing she interjected the statements that she would die if surgery were performed.

It is clear that mere commitment to a State hospital for treatment of mental illness does not destroy a person's competency or require the appointment of a guardian of the estate or person: Ryman's Case, 139 Pa Superior Ct 212. Mental capacity must be examined on a case by case basis.

In our opinion, the constitutional right of privacy includes the right of a mature competent adult to refuse to accept medical recommendations that may prolong one's life and which, to a third person at least, appear to be in his best interests; in short, that the right of privacy includes a right to die with which the State should not interfere where there are no minor or unborn children and no clear and present danger to public health, welfare or morals. If the person was competent while being presented with the decision and in making the decision which she did, the court should not interfere even though her decision might be considered unwise, foolish or ridiculous.

While many philosophical articles have been published relating to this subject, there are few appellate court decisions and none in Pennsylvania to our knowledge. The cases are collected in an annotation in 9 ALR 3d 1391. Considering other factors which have influenced the various courts, the present case does not involve a patient who sought medical attention from a hospital and then attempted to restrict the institution and physicians from rendering proper medical care. The State hospital as Mrs Yetter's custodian certainly has acted properly in initiating the present proceeding through the patient's brother and cannot be said to have either overridden the patient's wishes or merely allowed her to die for lack of treatment.

The testimony of the caseworker with respect to her conversations with Mrs Yetter in December 1972, convinces us that at that time her refusal was informed, conscious of the consequences and would not have been superseded by this court. The ordinary person's refusal to accept medical advice based upon fear is commonly known and while the refusal may be irrational and foolish to an outside observer, it cannot be said to be incompetent in order to permit the State to override the decision.

The obvious difficulty in this proceeding is that in recent months Mrs Yetter's steadfast refusal has been accompanied by delusions which create doubt that her decision is the product of competent, reasoned judgment. However, she has been consistent in expressing the fear that she would die if surgery were performed. The delusions do not appear to us to be her primary reason for rejecting surgery. Are we then to force her to submit to medical treatment because some of her present reasons for refusal are delusional and the result of mental illness? Should we now overrule her original understanding but irrational decision?

There is no indication that Mrs Yetter's condition is critical or that she is in the waning hours of life, although we recognise the advice of medical experts as to the need for early detection and treatment of cancer symptoms. Upon reflection, balancing the risk involved in our refusal to act in favor of compulsory treatment against giving the greatest possible protection to the individual in furtherance of his own desires, we are unwilling now to overrule Mrs Yetter's original irrational but competent decision.

Since no additional reasons for the appointment of a guardian of the person are presented, we enter the following

ORDER OF COURT

And now, June 6, 1973, the petition for the appointment of a guardian of the person for Maida Yetter, an alleged incompetent, is refused.

Consider finally in our discussion of this point the following Canadian and English decisions: *Kelly v Hazlett*
(1976) 75 DLR (3d) 536 at pp 562–3:

Was there an informed consent?

Morden J: I have found that on July 28th the plaintiff was told that to straighten the crooked elbow would require the breaking of the bone in her arm followed by a period of time in a cast. The risk of stiffness may have been 'mentioned' but certainly no more than that. The matter was then closed by the mutual decision that the ulnar nerve transplant and the joint clean-out only would be performed. On the following day when the plaintiff was under sedation as the result of an injection of 100 mg of pethidine (a matter to which I shall return), and just prior to the intended operation, she demanded of the defendant that he not operate on her unless her crooked elbow was straightened. According to the defendant, and this was his view at that time, she was 'a little more undependable' than she was previously, 'irrational', 'foolish' and 'silly'. In saying 'irrational' the defendant meant 'irrational from the point of view of not being able to think the way I was thinking which, I think, was more rational'. He further elaborated on this. He said: 'I thought that it was rational to be concerned about her paralyzed, weak hand. She was only interested in the appearance of her elbow'. It may thus be seen that the defendant was concerned with her choice of priorities—between curing the paralysis and straightening the arm—and was not so much concerned with the risks of the osteotomy. I repeat his key evidence on his understanding of her state of mind just prior to the signing of the consent to the osteotomy operation:

Q. Did you have any other discussion with her that morning as to the effects of either operation?

A. Well, I think I probably tried to point out to her that she was being foolish and silly and that it wasn't a wise way for her to act, and it was unwise for her to demand something about which she didn't know the consequences, and I sensed that I was not communicating the consequences to her in a way, or I could sense that she was not understanding what I was attempting to communicate with her by words....

If her state of mind was such that at the point of her conversation with the defendant she did not know the basic nature of the operation required to straighten her arm, and it may be noted that all she was asking for was a *result*, not a procedure, and she manifested this lack of knowledge to the defendant, then her apparent consent to the operation, notwithstanding her clear desire for the result, would be ineffective.
. . .

The plaintiff was calm but more irrational than the day before. I do not think that it could be suggested otherwise than that the giving of a consent under such circumstances, at the very least, leaves the validity of the consent open to question (Rozovsky, *Canadian Hospital Law* (1974), p 36, and *Beausoleil v La Communauté des Soeurs de la Charité de la Providence et al* (1964) 53 DLR (2d) 65, [1965] Que QB 37) and that it would be incumbent on the defendant to prove affirmatively that the effect of the sedation probably did not adversely affect the patient's understanding of the basic nature of the contemplated operation. Notwithstanding these frailties in the defendant's position, I do find that, taking the conversation of the day before into account, that the defendant could reasonably have thought that the plaintiff, in asking to have her elbow straightened on July 29th, was aware that this involved the fracturing and resetting of her arm under general anaesthetic. In other words—that the combination of the sedation, and her labile condition, had not blotted the information from her mind respecting the basic nature and character of the operation when she made her demand. In such circumstances he has shown a sufficient consent to avoid liability on the basis of battery.

Johnston v Wellesley
(1970) 17 DLR (3d) 139:

Addy J: There is in my view no necessity for a doctor to explain in detail the actual medical techniques being used as long as the nature of the treatment is fully understood.

Lord Scarman in *Gillick* says, at p 424b:

In the light of the foregoing I would hold that as a matter of law the parental right to determine whether or not their minor child below the age of 16 will have medical treatment terminates if and when the child achieves a sufficient understanding and intelligence to enable him or her to understand fully what is proposed. It will be a question of fact whether a child seeking advice has sufficient understanding of what is involved to give a consent valid in law ... When applying these conclusions to contraceptive advice and treatment it has to be borne in mind that there is much that has to be understood by a girl under the age of 16 if she is to have legal capacity to consent to such treatment. It if not enough that she should understand the nature of the advice which is being given: she must also have a sufficient maturity to understand what is involved. There are moral and family questions, especially her relationship with her parents; long-term problems associated with the emotional impact of pregnancy and its termination; and there are the risks to health of sexual intercourse at her age, risks which contraception may diminish but cannot eliminate.

Lord Templeman in *Sidaway* [1985] 1 All ER 643 at 509B:

If the doctor making a balanced judgment advises the patient to submit to the operation, the patient is entitled to reject that advice for reasons which are rational, or irrational, or for no reason. The duty of the doctor in these circumstances, subject to his overriding duty to have regard to the best interests of the patient, is to provide the patient with information which will enable the patient to make a balanced judgment if the patient chooses to make a balanced judgment.

A number of criteria seem to be suggested by the cases. They include (i) *reasonableness*—that the decision reached be *reasonable* (is this the same as saying that a patient is competent if the outcome of his decision is one with which you agree?); (ii) *rationality*—that the decision arrived at be a rational one: this is an immensely difficult criterion to deploy. Some may argue that we are all entitled to be irrational, see for example decisions about whom we marry, what job we take, which house we buy and which political party we support. Can a distinction be drawn between a decision based upon an irrational belief which stems from a set of values and a life-style which a person has adopted for some long period of time and a decision based upon a temporary delusion or hallucination which a person doesn't ordinarily hold to? Another strand for analysis may be a distinction between a decision based on beliefs which are deemed irrational, for example that having an x-ray is fundamentally immoral and will condemn one to perdition and a decision based upon a set of beliefs which themselves derive from a plain mistake of fact deluded or otherwise, for example a refusal to have an x-ray because x-ray machines transfer messages to your brain.

The criterion of rationality more than any other highlights the clash between respect for autonomy and beneficence which is often at the root of decisions about competence. Of course, to talk of beneficence as being in conflict with respect for autonomy is to a certain extent to beg an important question. One of the major drawbacks in appeals to beneficence is that to urge that one should seek to do good does not answer the questions 'What is good?' and 'Who decides?'. Furthermore, on a closer analysis, respect for autonomy may be the most highly prized form of doing good which would mean that the alleged clash between respect for autonomy and beneficence does not materialise. It would also follow that the guiding principle in determining the criteria of competence ought, therefore, to be respect for autonomy which when applied to the issue of rationality may require that the sort of irrationality involved in *Re Yetter* ought not to be taken as incompetence. The temporary delusion or the intransigent misperception of facts as the basis of decision ought by contrast to be taken as evidence of incompetence.

The criteria suggested also include (iii) *full understanding*—that to be competent the patient has to understand fully. It is not clear whether the judicial statements intend to refer to the criteria of understanding or to the notion that competence means understanding: Lord Scarman, as will have been seen, puts it that the child must achieve a 'sufficient understanding and intelligence to enable him or her to understand fully what is proposed'. This appears to refer to the notion of understanding as being what competence means, ie the ability to understand fully, the word 'fully' qualifying ability rather than understand. This issue has already been dealt with earlier.

If, however, what is meant is that the criterion of understanding so as to demonstrate competence is full understanding, this cannot be right. One obvious reason is that understanding is never full even in the most mature and experienced doctor let alone the patient. Secondly, does *not* an insistence on 'full' understanding as district from understanding echo the distinction made between adequate information and full information, in the context of the duty to inform the patient. Just as the law does not require that the patient be fully informed—an impossible goal—so it can not require that the patient is only competent if he fully understands.

The final criterion to consider is (iv) *mature balanced judgment*—that to be competent the patient must have been put in a position to, and be able to, weigh and balance relevant facts and arguments in relation to the decision to be taken. Discussion of maturity entails two points of importance here.

First, the capacity to understand reflects and is conditioned by the gradual acquisition of maturity of any particular patient. Secondly, it calls for a distinction to be drawn between maturity and wisdom. What the criterion of maturity calls for is not that the patient arrive at a *wise* decision (contrast Williams (1985) New LJ 1179, 1180) but that the decisions be the product of considered reflection.

Secondly, it follows that someone ought not to be judged incompetent based upon the alleged *unwisdom* of their decision since that would be to usher in the 'outcome approach' and reopen the arguments as to who sets the criteria of wisdom. Instead, a patient should be judged competent if the decision is one which is clearly the product of thinking and reflection regardless of its content.

Consider now ss 57, 58 of the Mental Health Act 1983. Do these provisions assist us in the analysis of competence, either at the level of what it means or at the level of establishing its presence?

Treatment requiring consent and a second opinion
57. (1) This section applies to the following forms of medical treatment for mental disorder—
  (a) any surgical operation for destroying brain tissue or for destroying the functioning of brain tissue; and
  (b) such other forms of treatment as may be specified for the purposes of this section by regulations made by the Secretary of State.

(2) Subject to section 62 below, a patient shall not be given any form of treatment to which this section applies unless he has consented to it and—

    (a) a registered medical practitioner appointed for the purposes of this Part of this Act by the Secretary of State (not being the responsible medical officer) and two other persons appointed for the purposes of this paragraph by the Secretary of State (not being registered medical practitioners) have certified in writing that the patient is capable of understanding the nature, purpose and likely effects of the treatment in question and has consented to it; and

    (b) the registered medical practitioner referred to in paragraph (a) above has certified in writing that, having regard to the likelihood of the treatment alleviating or preventing a deterioration of the patient's condition, the treatment should be given.

(3) Before giving a certificate under subsection (2)(b) above the registered medical practitioner concerned shall consult two other persons who have been professionally concerned with the patient's medical treatment, and of those persons one shall be a nurse and the other shall be neither a nurse nor a registered medical practitioner.

(4) Before making any regulations for the purpose of this section the Secretary of State shall consult such bodies as appear to him to be concerned.

Treatment requiring consent or a second opinion
58. (1) This section applies to the following forms of medical treatment for mental disorder—

    (a) such forms of treatment as may be specified for the purposes of this section by regulations made by the Secretary of State;

    (b) the administration of medicine to a patient by any means (not being a form of treatment specified under paragraph (a) above or section 57 above) at any time during a period for which he is liable to be detained as a patient to whom this Part of this Act applies if three months or more have elapsed since the first occasion in that period when medicine was administered to him by any means for his mental disorder.

(2) the Secretary of State may by order vary the length of the period mentioned in subsection (1)(b) above.

(3) Subject to section 62 below, a patient shall not be given any form of treatment to which this section applies unless—

    (a) he has consented to that treatment and either the responsible medical officer or a registered medical practitioner appointed for the purposes of this Part of this Act by the Secretary of State has certified in writing that the patient is capable of understanding its nature, purpose and likely effects and has consented to it; or

    (b) a registered medical practitioner appointed as aforesaid (not being the responsible medical officer) has certified in writing that the patient is not capable of understanding the nature, purpose and likely effects of that treatment or has not consented to it but that, having regard to the likelihood of its alleviating or preventing a deterioration of his condition, the treatment should be given.

(4) Before giving a certificate under subsection (3)(b) above the registered medical practitioner concerned shall consult two other persons who have been professionally concerned with the patient's medical treatment, and of those persons one shall be a nurse and the other shall be neither a nurse nor a registered medical practitioner.

(5) Before making any regulations for the purposes of this section the Secretary of State shall consult such bodies as appear to him to be concerned.

In the light of the preceding discussion, which criterion do you think the law either does or should adopt in determining competence to consent or refuse treatment? Of course, English law being pragmatic in its approach may adopt different criteria in different contexts, for example in criminal cases such as rape, or in the law of probate dealing with capacity to make a will. Our concern is what is the approach to be adopted in decision-making by patients.

Would you agree that the views set out in the President's Commission (*supra* at 197) seem the most plausible?

(iii) Incorrect assessment of capacity

What if a doctor reaches a view concerning a patient's competence that is objectively unjustified on the evidence and then goes on to act on the purported consent of the patient to treat him? What, if any, cause of action would lie against the doctor? For example, what if a doctor in good faith, but wrongly should determine that a young girl had reflected upon and reached a considered decision about contraception?

Obviously if there were an action it is important to establish which action, for example, negligence or battery, since in the latter action a patient would not need to prove, in order to maintain the action, that he had suffered injury as a result of the doctor's conduct. Whichever action can be brought, there is no doubt that any mistake made by the doctor must be reasonable before the law will (if at all) excuse him. An unreasonable mistake would seem to give rise *prima facie* to a negligence action and, in any event, would not excuse the doctor even if battery was relied upon (*Fletcher v Fletcher* (1859) 1 E & E 420).

Let us therefore assume we are only concerned with *reasonable* mistakes. Deciding which action may be brought is by no means simple: the difficulty lies in whether the mistaken view of the doctor is one of fact or of opinion. If, in law, it is a mistake of fact, then on first principles an action in battery would lie since mistake is not ordinarily a defence to such an international tort.

There may be exceptions to this. For example, a policeman making an arrest in the mistaken belief, based on reasonable grounds, that a crime has been committed, would at common law and not by statute be excused. By contrast, the doctor enjoys no such privilege. Do you consider that the law should allow him the same privilege?

Compare the converse position where the doctor decides in good faith that a patient is *incompetent* when this is not the case. Would the law in these circumstances consider the doctor to have committed a battery if he were, for example, purportedly acting in the public interest to prevent some danger which he thought might materialise if the patient were not, for example, restrained or treated (see *The Law of Torts*, Fleming, pp 72–73)? If, by contrast, in law the mistaken view of the doctor as to the patient's understanding is regarded as a matter of *opinion*, assuming the doctor acts in good faith, then the answer may be different. Will the law excuse the doctor from liability in battery when he has formed a judgment which is mistaken, in that the consensus of informed opinion is otherwise, but is reasonable? On grounds of public policy it may be desirable that the law should recognise a privilege in the doctor in these circumstances. It is difficult, however, to accommodate this view within the traditional principles of the law of torts.

(b) INFORMED CONSENT

The aphorism 'informed consent' has entered the language as being synonymous with valid consent. This is, of course, not so and is in fact unhelpful. It gives only a partial view. The requirement that consent be informed is only one, albeit a very important, ingredient of valid consent. Furthermore, the expression informed consent begs all the necessary questions which are the subject of the following section; for example, how informed is informed?

(i)   Battery

1.   *Nature and purpose*

Chatterton v Gerson [1981] 1 All ER 257, at 266:

Bristow J: In my judgment what the court has to do in each case is to look at all the circumstances and say, 'Was there a real consent?' I think justice requires that in order to vitiate the reality of consent there must be a greater failure of communication between doctor and patient than that involved in a breach of duty if the claim is based on negligence. When the claim is based on negligence the plaintiff must prove not only the breach of duty to inform but that had the duty not been broken she would not have chosen to have the operation. Where the claim is based on trespass to the person, once it is shown that the consent is unreal, then what the plaintiff would have decided if she had been given the information which would have prevented vitiation of the reality of her consent is irrelevant.

In my judgment once the patient is informed in broad terms of the nature of the procedure which is intended, and gives her consent, that consent is real, and the cause of the action on which to base a claim for failure to go into risks and implications is negligence, not trespass. Of course, if information is withheld in bad faith, the consent will be vitiated by fraud. Of course, if by some accident, as in a case in the 1940s in the Salford Hundred Court, where a boy was admitted to hospital for tonsillectomy and due to administrative error was circumcised instead, trespass would be the appropriate cause of action against the doctor, though he was as much the victim of the error as the boy. But in my judgment it would be very much against the interests of justice if actions which are really based on a failure by the doctor to perform his duty adequately to inform were pleaded in trespass.

Notice in *Hills v Potter*, Hirst J's approval of *Chatterton* where, in a case in which the plaintiff alleged non-disclosure of a risk of injury inherent in a medical procedure and claimed that non-disclosure gave rise to an action both in battery and negligence, the judge rejected the battery claim stating: 'As to the claim for assault and battery, the plaintiiff's undoubted consent to the operation which was in fact performed negatives any possibility of liability under this head: see *Chatterton v Gerson* [1981] QB 432, [1981] 1 All ER 257. I should add that I respectfully agree with Bristow J in deploring reliance on these torts in medical cases of this kind. The proper cause of action, if any, is negligence.' (See also Lord Scarman's approval of *Hills* and *Chatterton* on this point in *Sidaway* at p 489e).

Since the House of Lords apparent endorsement in *Sidaway* of this view that consent means only consent sufficient to avoid an action in battery, the argument that battery may also lie where the consent is given in ignorance of relevant material facts seems to have no place in English law. Although the law is unlikely to change, the counter view is both intellectually respectable and, in the light of the interests at stake, may be regarded by some as desirable. See M A Somerville, 'Structuring the issues in Informed Consent', (*op cit*) at pp 742–52 (footnotes omitted):

Battery or negligence?
The proper cause of action when a defective consent is alleged may be either battery or negligence. The difference is significant because:
   It will have important bearing on such matters as the incidence of the onus of proof, causation, the importance of expert medical evidence, the significance of medical judgment, proof of damage and, most important, of course, the substantive basis upon which liability may be found.
While each of these factors will not be discussed in detail here, it is necessary to be aware of them.

Common law courts in Canada have taken the traditional approach that the consent that is both necessary and sufficient for avoiding a cause of action in battery in medical cases is consent to 'the basic nature and character of the operation or the procedure'. The difficulty in applying this rule is determining which factors form part of the basic nature and character of an act and which do not. Such determinations have been made by judges on a case-by-case basis, with no more definite guidelines than the rule itself. But some judges have tried to formulate a clearer, more objective rule, which would help determine when non-disclosure of information or failure to obtain consent should give rise to a cause of action in battery.

The situation facing the judges can be represented diagrammatically:

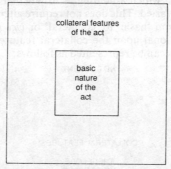

The outer square represents all the consequences or risks to which the patient must consent if liability in tort (battery or negligence) for failure to obtain consent is to be avoided. The inner square represents the factors that make up the basic nature and character of the act of touching. Failure to obtain consent to these factors will give rise to a cause of action in battery. Thus, whether or not battery lies depends on where the inner line is drawn.

That judges will vary in drawing this line, even with respect to the same facts, can be seen by comparing the decision of the majority of the Supreme Court of Canada in *R v Bolduc and Bird* with that of the dissent and that of the Court of Appeal of British Columbia in the same case. Likewise, the judgment of the majority of the Court of Appeal of Ontario in *R v Maurantonio* can be compared with that of the dissent. These are criminal assault (battery) cases, but the rules governing consent in criminal law and in the tort of battery not only have common origins but are directly comparable. Such cases demonstrate that because criminal assault (or

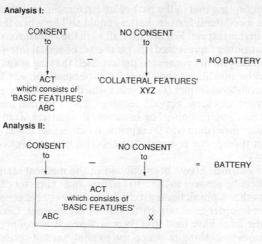

battery) wil not lie if there is consent as to the basic nature and character of the act, liability will depend on whether or not the feature to which consent has *not* been obtained forms part of the act's basic nature and character. Thus, to the extent that there is discretion involved in determining whether or not a particular feature forms part of the basic nature and character of the act ('basic features'), there is discretion as to the imposition of liability. The two possible alternative analyses of any given fact situation that gives rise to this discretion may be represented as above.

From this diagram it can be seen that, depending on whether or not X is held to be a 'collateral feature' or a 'basic feature' of the act alleged to constitute criminal assault or the tort of battery, the necessary consent will or will not be present, respectively, and liability will be determined accordingly.

There is another way in which a holding as to whether or not battery-avoiding consent is present can be varied. This does not require altering the characterisation of a feature of the act from 'basic' to 'collateral' or *vice versa*, but rather makes consent to the act conditional upon the collateral features being as represented. Using the same model this can be represented as follows:

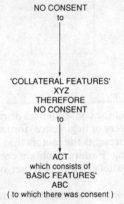

Pursuant to this analysis, it is irrelevant whether X is characterised as a 'basic' or 'collateral' feature, as even if X is a 'collateral' feature, if X is not as represented, the consent will fail to 'flow through' as a valid consent to the act. *R v Williams*, in which the accused, a choir-master, persuaded a young woman that sexual intercourse was therapy for her voice, is probably an example of a court taking such an approach. Depending on the circumstances, whether an act is therapeutic for the patient could be regarded as a 'collateral' feature of the act or could relate to the basic nature of the act. However, accepting that in the particular circumstances characterisation of an act as therapy is a collateral feature, battery could still lie when there is fraud or misrepresentation in this respect. For instance, if, as in the *Williams* case, a collateral feature of an act was not as represented (that is the act of sexual intercourse was not voice therapy), then despite the consent to the act itself (having sexual intercourse), that consent would be invalid, as the Court held, because consent to the act was conditional on the collateral feature (that the act was therapy) being as represented. Although this example may seem very far removed from a normal medical context, it may have important applications. For instance, if a patient were misled to the effect that a particular procedure was therapeutic when in fact it was performed for the purposes of non-therapeutic research, battery-avoiding consent could similarly be vitiated.

How has the law outlined above been applied in the medical relationship? The requirement that there be consent to the basic nature and character of the operation or procedure means that a physician must disclose all inevitable consequences of a proposed procedure in order to obtain battery-avoiding consent. Consequently, all courts faced with the issue have held that there will be a cause of action in battery when a physician does something to which the patient has not consented at all, or which the patient has expressly requested not be done or has refused. Battery could also be established where the physician's act was essentially different in nature from that to which the patient consented. For instance, if the patient was told that the purpose of the operation was to relieve pain, but not told that the consequences would include sterility, any consent given would be invalidated and a cause of action in battery would be available.

Some courts have also held that knowledge of certain risks could be so material to understanding of the basic nature and character of an operation that failure to disclose them would vitiate battery-avoiding consent. In other words, it has been held that not only non-disclosure of inevitable results of a procedure can vitiate battery-avoiding consent, but also non-disclosure of risks of which knowledge was 'essential to an informed decision to undergo the operation'. It is with respect to failures to disclose a risk, as compared with an inevitable consequence, that the Supreme Court of Canada has probably restricted the availability of an action in battery.

It is not easy to decide, from a policy point of view, whether or not a cause of action in battery should be allowed for non-disclosure of certain risks. The argument that it should be allowed is that some risks are so serious that they necessarily relate to the basic nature and character of an operation and, therefore, their non-disclosure should give rise to a battery action. The difficulty is that as only some risks have this effect, how is the line to be drawn between those that do and those that do not? The alternative solution, which may be the position adopted by the Supreme Court of Canada in *Reibl v Hughes*, is that any liability for non-disclosure of a risk can only lie in negligence and not in battery.

[A]ctions of battery in respect of surgical or other medical treatment should be confined to cases where surgery or treatment has been performed or given to which there has been no consent at all or where, emergency situations aside, surgery or treatment has been performed or given beyond that to which there was consent. . . [U]nless there has been misrepresentation or fraud to secure consent to the treatment, a failure to disclose the attendant risks, however serious, should go to negligence rather than to battery. Although such a failure relates to an informed choice of submitting to or refusing recommended and appropriate treatment, it arises as the breach of an anterior duty of due care, comparable in legal obligation to the duty of due care in carrying out the particular treatment to which the patient has consented. It is not a test of the validity of the consent.

That is, non-disclosure of a risk will not give rise to a cause of action in battery except when there has been a 'misrepresentation or fraud to secure consent to . . . treatment'. But what can constitute misrepresentation within this rule, and why does such misrepresentation allow non-disclosure of a risk to give rise to an action in battery, whereas without such misrepresentation it does not?

In exploring these issues it is necessary to determine the basis of the holding of the Supreme Court referred to above. Is it, first, that non-disclosure of a risk does not amount to misrepresentation (although that of an inevitable consequence can); or, second, that information about risks can never relate to the basic nature and character of an operation and thus cannot vitiate battery-avoiding consent; or both propositions; or neither? Presumably, the Court has established the second proposition rather than the first, as it is difficult to draw a distinction between one type of non-disclosure (non-disclosure of inevitable consequences) constituting misrepresentation, and the other (non-disclosure of risks) not doing so. It may be argued that because there is a pre-existing duty to disclose inevitable consequences, but not risks, non-disclosure of inevitable consequences constitutes a misrepresentation, while that of risks does not. But this pre-empts the question to which an answer is sought, that is, just what information is there a duty to disclose so as to avoid an action in battery? Moreover, reliance on a rule that total non-disclosure of a risk does not give rise to a cause of action in battery, because a total non-disclosure cannot constitute misrepresentation, would not exclude a *partial disclosure*. But an approach that recognises partial but not total non-disclosure of risks as misrepresentation would be artificial and could give rise to fortuitous results. Further, the distinction between nonfeasance and misfeasance has no place when there is a pre-existing duty relationship, as there is between physician and patient.

If the Court has not relied on a rule that a non-disclosure is unable to constitute misrepresentation, has it held that the risks of a procedure cannot relate to its basic nature and character? This question can be explored by asking what the situation would be where a significant and serious risk was grossly misrepresented, rather than undisclosed. This could, arguably, give rise to a cause of action in battery within the Court's ruling. However, the fact that misrepresentation of a risk could give rise to a cause of action in battery means, by definition, that the misrepresentation must relate to the basic nature and character of the act. If this is true it shows that the action in battery is not excluded because of the nature of the misrepresentation, that is, because the misrepresentation related to a risk and a risk cannot relate to the basic nature and character of a procedure, but that battery is excluded on some other basis.

If the above analysis is accepted the basis of the Supreme Court's holding is not that total non-disclosure of risks cannot constitute misrepresentation, nor that risks cannot relate to the basic nature and character of a medical procedure. This leaves the question which reveals the key to the basis of the Supreme Court's ruling still unanswered. Why does 'misrepresentation or fraud to secure consent to the treatment' cause non-disclosure of a risk to give rise to a cause of action in battery, where it would not do so if the elements of misrepresentation or fraud were not present?

The true test of whether or not a cause of action in battery will lie for non-disclosure of a risk, provided the risk is serious and sufficiently likely of occurrence to relate to the basic nature and character of the act carried out, depends on the *nature of the physician's conduct with respect to the non-disclosure*. Not only the nature of the undisclosed information is significant, but also the nature of the *failure* to disclose. It is proposed that, if the physician negligently (ie, unintentionally) fails to disclose or misrepresents a risk, he will be liable in negligence. If he intentionally does either of these things the action will also lie in battery, provided that the risk which is not disclosed or is misrepresented is fundamental enough to relate to the basic nature and character of the procedure. Thus the presence or absence of intention with respect to the non-disclosure of a risk which relates to the basic nature and character of an intervention will determine the causes of action available for failure to obtain consent to that risk. By contrast, when the non-disclosure relates to an inevitable consequence of an intervention, intention or lack of it in relation to the non-disclosure is irrelevant to establishing a cause of action in battery. This is true because the intention necessary to support a cause of action for battery arising from an intentional, non-consensual touching of the kind which occurs is present in carrying out the act which has those inevitable consequences, regardless of the presence or absence of intention with respect to the non-disclosure.

Hence, what is being suggested is that the intentional necessary to support an intentional tort will be found in relation to a different element of the tortious act (that is, either the touching or the non-disclosure) depending on whether the failure in obtaining consent relates to failure to inform of risks or of inevitable consequences, but in both cases, the necessary intention may be present.

In relation to determining whether the touching itself was intentional, there is a key concept: the question which must be asked is not simply whether there was consent to a touching, which in most cases there will be, but whether there was consent to touching *of that kind* or *in that manner*. Likewise, it is relevant to ask not only whether there was intention to touch, but whether there was intention to touch *in that manner*. The concept of intention 'to touch in that manner' is broader and more precise than the concept of just touching. It includes the inevitable consequences and purposes of an intervention, as well as the touching itself. Because risks, by definition, may not occur, it is not possible to find the required intention to touch in the manner which results from risks occurring simply by demonstrating their crystallisation. Any proof of intention relates, rather, to the act of non-disclosure of these risks. By contrast, when what occurs is an inevitable consequence of an intervention it can be presumed that this was intended, as in tort a reasonable person is presumed to intend the inevitable consequences of his acts. Consequently, in the latter case, the necessary intention to support intentional touching in that manner and a *prima facie* tort of battery is established by proving the touching, and the only question is whether or not there was sufficient consent.

An objection could be raised here that two different entities are being compared: in one case the question asked is whether or not there is *intentional non-disclosure of information* to which the patient is entitled: that is, is there intentional failure to obtain consent? In the other case the question is whether there is *intentional touching* in a situation where the failure to obtain consent to that touching may have been intentional or unintentional. It is submitted that there is no contradiction between these two approaches. Battery is an intentional tort, which may be established through the intention 'to touch in that manner' or the intentional failure to obtain the necessary consent. It is just that demonstrating the latter is superfluous when it can be shown that there was an intention to touch in a certain manner to which there was no consent.

There is one further problem with the Supreme Court's approach to actions in battery for failure to obtain adequate consent. Some risks are so important that most people would regard them as an essential part of any description of the basic nature and character of a procedure. For instance, the fact that an operation carries a substantial risk of death would cause most persons to characterise that operation as being of a serious nature. Further, can any real distinction be drawn between failure to disclose, for instance, that as a result of an operation a person will certainly be rendered sterile, and failure to disclose that there is a substantial risk of this occurring? It is submitted that the law should not try to draw distinctions that do not accord with generally held views as to what factors constitute the basic nature and character of an act, no matter how conceptually pleasing and easy of application the resulting rule may be.

Thus, with all respect, it is submitted that to the extent that the Supreme Court has limited the availability of an action in battery by stating the law to be that risks do not relate to the basic nature and character of an act and, consequently, their non-disclosure cannot vitiate battery-avoiding consent, the ruling may not be desirable. However, as shown above, the effect of the Supreme Court's ruling on the availability of a battery action will vary, depending on how it is analysed. The analysis suggested accepts the Supreme Court's ruling but minimises its effect of making unavailable a battery action that otherwise would have been available under Canadian common law.

The approach suggested may be summarised as follows: in all cases where lack of consent is alleged, one is arguing either that there was no consent at all to the touching or to touching in that manner. The first question is whether the touching itself and in that manner was intentional. It is highly unlikely that the touching itself will be unintentional, but this is not true of the manner of the touching. The manner of the touching includes two types of consequences: inevitable consequences and risks which eventuate. When the feature of the touching to which it is alleged there was no consent is an inevitable consequence, then there will necessarily have been an *intention* to touch *in that manner*. When, on the other hand, the touching is of that manner because of the crystallisation of a risk, touching *in that manner is unintentional* (unless, possibly, the risk which eventuates was of very high probability, but this case will not be considered here). In the second case, it may initially seem that battery should not lie for non-disclosure of a risk, as the act of which the plaintiff complains—that he was touched in a manner to which he did not consent—was unintentional. However, a second question is relevant: whether the failure to obtain consent was intentional. It is suggested that where it is intentional, and provided the non-disclosure is of a sufficiently serious and probable risk that the risk can be said to form part of the basic nature and character of the intervention, the necessary intention for a cause of action in battery will exist. Such an approach would allow non-disclosure of certain risks because of 'misrepresentation or fraud' to give rise to a cause of action in battery, as the Supreme Court suggests. It would include within the notion of misrepresentation some total non-disclosures; that is, intentional concealment of certain risks would suffice. Thus, only the unintentional non-disclosure of a risk that relates to the basic nature and character of an act would not be actionable in battery. The suggested approach and the correlation of the variables it includes can be demonstrated in the following way:

Non-disclosure:	of inevitable consequence	of 'sufficiently serious and probable' risk
INTENTIONAL	Battery	Battery
UNINTENTIONAL	Battery	Negligence

Defects in consent which do not give rise to a cause of action in battery will be either actionable in negligence (or possibly in contract) or will not be actionable at all. The dividing line between those that are actionable in negligence and those that are not actionable at all is determined by whether or not the physician has breached the standard of care required of him by the law relating to negligence with respect to obtaining the patient's consent. . . .

Finally, it is appropriate here to note that some confusion may be caused because two doctrines 'consent' and 'informed consent' are not distinguished. It is suggested that the word 'consent' be reserved to refer to the substantive entity which must be present to avoid liability in battery and similarly for the term 'informed consent' in relation to negligence. It is proposed that with respect to the substantive content of consent the traditional notion should be retained. This means that consent will be present when there is consent to the basic nature and character of the act. Informed consent is a more extensive concept that also comprehends consent to certain consequences or risks of consequences. But, as further discussion will show, there has not always been consensus as to its requirements. It necessarily includes all elements of the consent doctrine, but the reverse is not true. Thus a physician may have obtained sufficient consent to avoid liability in battery, but not in negligence.

Notwithstanding Somerville's cogent argument, the law in England and Wales undoubtedly reflects a less subtle view of the law expressed by Laskin CJ in *Reibl v Hughes* (1980) 114 DLR (3d) 1 at 10–11:

> In situations where the allegation is that attendant risks which should have been disclosed were not communicated to the patient and yet the surgery or other medical treatment carried out was that to which the plaintiff consented (there being no negligence basis of liability for the recommended surgery or treatment to deal with the patient's condition), I do not understand how it can be said that the consent was vitiated by the failure of disclosure so as to make the surgery or other treatment an unprivileged, unconsented to and intentional invasion of the patient's bodily integrity. I can appreciate the temptation to say that the genuineness of consent to medical treatment depends on proper disclosure of the risks which it entails, but in my view, unless there has been misrepresentation or fraud to secure consent to the treatment, a failure to disclose the attendant risks, however serious, should go to negligence rather than to battery. Although such a failure relates to an informed choice of submitting to or refusing recommended and appropriate treatment, it arises as the breach of an anterior duty of due care, comparable in legal obligation to the duty of due care in carrying out the particular treatment to which the patient has consented. It is not a test of the validity of the consent.

2.   *Fraud, misrepresentation and concealment*

You will notice that Laskin CJ regards fraud and misrepresentation as to facts not concerned with the nature and purpose of the medical procedure as possibly warranting an action in battery; thereby expanding the scope of the tort somewhat. Is this the law of England and Wales?

19th Century criminal law

The two principal cases of *Clarence* and *Flattery* are regarded as authority that fraud (a tortious misrepresentation) cannot serve to vitiate consent unless it is related to the nature and purposes of the act or the identity of the actor. On another view, the question is not whether fraud as to matters going beyond the 'nature and purpose' of the procedure triggers the crime, but rather whether the particular matter in the case is part of the 'nature and purpose' or not, i e 'what are the extent and limits of nature and purpose?'. This often overlooked confusion can be seen in the following extract from Smith and Hogan, *Criminal Law* (6th ed 1988) at pp 435–6 (footnotes omitted):

> . . . in *Flattery* four of the five judges in the Court for Crown Cases Reserved thought that *Barrow* ought to be re-considered; and in *Dee* the Irish Court for Crown Cases Reserved dissented from it and upheld the impersonator's conviction. The *Barrow* line of cases might still be of importance where D obtains intercourse by impersonating some person other than a husband. It is submitted that this should be rape. It is true that, where the husband is impersonated, there is also an error as to the nature of the transaction—it is not marital intercourse but adultery—whereas if D impersonates another, the transaction is both understood to be and is adultery or fornication—but such an error has never been held sufficiently fundamental to found an indictment for rape. Sexual intercourse is, however, a relationship in which personality is supremely important and consent to have intercourse with A is not consent to have intercourse with B. The *Barrow* line of cases is presumably authority against this view but it contained a fundamental inconsistency in that it held that D was guilty of an assault; yet consent should have been equally a defence there as in rape and the cases might be treated, as they were in *Dee*, as depending on the narrow view of rape which was rejected in *Fletcher*.
>
> If D had intercourse with P by impersonating, for example, P's fiancé, it is submitted that *Barrow* should be overruled and D convicted of rape.
>
> Where D, by fraud, deceives the woman as to the nature of the transaction, it is well established that this is rape. So in *Flattery* D was convicted where P submitted to intercourse with him under the impression that he was performing a surgical operation. It is an offence under the Sexual Offences Act 1956, s 3
>
> > for a person to procure a woman, by false pretences or representations, to have sexual intercourse in any part of the world.
>
> It seems probable that this section covers conduct such as that of Flattery but that it also extends to a much wider range of frauds of a much less fundamental character; and it has been held by the Court of Criminal Appeal in *Williams*, a case with substantially the same facts as *Flattery*, that such conduct is still indictable as rape.
>
> Probably any fraud which does not go to the nature of the act or the identity of the man is not sufficient to destroy consent. So misrepresentations by a man as to his wealth, social position or freedom to marry would not render intercourse thereby obtained rape. Even where the woman is induced by fraud to suppose that she is already married to D, her consent to intercourse affords a defence.

The tort cases

Does the law of tort reflect the criminal law? The following extract is from *The Law of Torts*, Fleming (7th Edition 1987), pp 74–75:

> More uncertainty surrounds an intermediate group of situations where the plaintiff is aware of the real nature of the proposed contact but not of its harmful or offensive quality, and the defendant conceals it with knowledge that disclosure would have induced the other to withhold consent.[35] The problem is dramatically raised by an older case[36] of a mistress who sued her lover for infecting her with venereal disease, but lost her claim (based on assault), partly on the ground that there was no legally enforceable duty of disclosure, partly because it was tainted by the meretricious nature of her relationship. However debatable the latter proposition,[37] the former

is open to the most serious doubt. It rests exclusively on decisions which hold that it is not a criminal assault for a husband knowingly to infect his wife, because the mistake relates not to the nature of the connection but merely to its consequences.[38] But the policy favouring acquittal in criminal cases[39] has little weight in civil and should not be decisive in the present context. An assent to bodily contact under a mistake as to its harmful or offensive character ought not to be treated as a genuine consent, if the mistake is known and concealed by the defendant. Thus an action for assault ought to be available to one who permits another to touch him with a piece of metal which, unknown to him but known to the actor, is heavily charged with electricity;[40] or to a woman who consents to intercourse with a man who inveigled her into a bigamous marriage without disclosing that he already had a wife,[41] or to a naive girl who submits to indecent liberties by a physician in the belief that this is a necessary part of the treatment.[42] Such mischief is best deterred by permitting recovery.

Notes to extract
35. *Rest 2d* §55 imposes liability.
36. *Hegarty v Shine* (1878) 4 LR Ir 288. See now Alexander, *Herpes and the Law*, 70 Cornell L Rev 101 (1984).
37. Once emancipated from Victorian morality, is it not sounder policy to discourage conduct like the seducer's rather than penalise the seduced for her easy virtue? But in *Lasher v Kleinberg* 164 Cal Rptr 618 (1980) a man cross-claimed in a paternity suit against the mother for misrepresenting that she was using a contraceptive. It was held that this would encourage unwarranted invasion of privacy.
38. *R v Clarence* (1888) 22 QBD 23 Accord: *Papadimitropoulos v R* (1957) 98 CLR 249 (no 'rape' when woman consented to intercourse under belief, fraudulently induced by the man, that she was married to him; no mistake as to identity of man and character of what he was doing).
39. See Hooper, *Fraud in Assault and Rape*, 3 UBC L Rev 117 (1968).
40. *Rest 2d* §55.
41. In *Garnaut v Rowse* (1941) 43 WALR 29 and *Graham v Saville* [1945] 2 DLR 489 recovery was permitted in actions for deceit, but in *Smythe v Reardon* [1949] QSR 74 the court followed the conventional view that damages in deceit are not at large and dismissed the claim, though suggesting that the plaintiff might have succeeded in an action for assault. The restricted scope of deceit emphasises the need for a remedy in trespass whenever there is an offensive interference unaccompanied by material injury. Anyway, deceit does not lie unless the marriage is invalid: *Said v Said* (1986) 33 DLR (4th) 382 (mere personal characteristics of groom).
42. *Rest 2d* §55, ill 3, 4; based on *De May v Roberts* 9 NW 146 (Mich 1881) (its counterpart: *R v Bolduc and Bird* [1967] SCR 677).

As became clear in the discussion of the criminal law, the real issue may revolve around the different meaning to be attached to the expression, 'nature and purpose', particularly the word 'nature'; is the 'nature' of an act concerned only with a mere description of the mechanics of the touching or does it also take account of what that touching may represent or cause?

In *Hegarty v Shine*, for example, the question at issue was whether an action in battery would lie when a girl was infected with venereal disease following sexual intercourse with the defendant. She consented to sexual intercourse (*quaere* her evidence was that she was asleep at the time) but was unaware of the defendant's diseased condition. Does 'nature' mean the mere sexual connection or must it take account of the circumstances surrounding the sexual connection, ie the disease? If this is not already difficult enough, a further problem concerning the availability of the tort of battery relates to what may be called the extent of the 'fraud exception', ie it is agreed that fraud vitiates consent but fraud as to what and what amounts to fraud?

Bristow J touched on both of these without analysing them in *Chatterton v Gerson* [1981] QB 432, [1981] 1 All ER 257:

> In my judgment once the patient is informed in broad terms of the nature of the procedure which is intended, and gives her consent, that consent is real, and the cause of the action on which to base a claim for failure to go into risks and implications is negligence, not trespass. Of course, if information is withheld in bad faith, the consent will be vitiated by fraud.

As has been seen, the issues were also addressed by Laskin CJ in *Reibl v Hughes* (see above).

Questions

(i) Which of the following is included within the 'fraud exception', deliberate lying, negligent or innocent misrepresentation, conscious concealment?

(ii) Whatever the answer to (i), must the misrepresentation or fraud relate only to the 'nature' and purpose of the procedure or do they extend to other factors which may impinge on the patient's decision?

Professor Picard examines both these issues arising from *Reibl* in *Legal Liability of Doctors and Hospitals in Canada*', at pp 146–147:

> One area of great concern springs from the comments of the Supreme Court of Canada on misrepresentation and fraud. Professor Klar has said that the Chief Justice 'was not clear as to what the misreprsentation or fraud must relate or how it will operate'.[756] Professors Gochnauer and Fleming[757] find an internal inconsistency in the Chief Justice's words and ask whether by them he meant to give an illustration of or an exception to the test for battery. Professor Somerville raises a number of concerns about the step taken by the Supreme Court of Canada and says a basic question is: 'Why does "misrepresentation or fraud to secure consent to the treatment" cause non-disclosure of a risk to give rise to a cause of action in battery, where it would not do so if the elements of misrepresentation or fraud were not present?'[758] She suggests an analysis that minimises the Surpeme Court ruling and its consequence of making a battery unavailable where it would in the past have been available.
>
> At the bottom of the reservations expressed by a number of commentators is the apparent attempt by the Supreme Court of Canada to separate risks and consent. The criticism is strong. As Professor Somerville has summarised it:[759]
>
> > ... it is submitted that to the extent that the Supreme Court has limited the availability of an action in battery by stating the law to be that *risks do not relate to the basic nature and character of an act and, consequently, their non-disclosure cannot vitiate battery-avoiding consent*, the ruling may not be desirable. [emphasis supplied]
>
> Professors Gochnauer and Fleming say:[760]
>
> > The Court's position separating risk and consent is a distortion of our ordinary understanding of the concepts and in a number of cases will defeat our normal, reasonable expectations.
>
> They are critical of the failure of the Supreme Court of Canada to give any policy considerations to justify its position and say:[761]
>
> > By cutting us off from our ordinary intuitions in these matters without setting up signposts of policy the decision fails to clarify wholly the applicability of battery and negligence when there has been a breach of the duty to disclose risks of medical treatment.
>
> The parameters of the new battery action have not yet been fully tested by litigation.[762] Although the number of cases where fraud or 'serious' misrepresentation (such as negligent or fraudulent misrepresentation as contrasted with innocent misrepresentation) will be alleged and proven will likely be few, there may be some confusion in the 'grey' areas. For example, in a case where a person is told he will be given an anaesthetic but is not told this will be done by moving a needle into his

heart would there be misrepresentation?[763] Would there be misrepresentation if a tonsillectomy was described as a minor, routine and safe procedure when for that patient it was not?[764] What about the prescription of tranquilisers for emotional complaints given without a description of the risks of addiction and misuse? Hopefully future judicial review of battery will provide answers if not an assuagement of the critics.

Communication between the health care professional and the patient is the means by which a valid consent to treatment is given. It is also part of the therapy of good medicine. The absence of good communication is the reason for most lawsuits against health care professionals and hospitals.

Notes to extract
756 Klar, 'Developments in Tort Law; The 1980–81 Term' (1982) 3 SCLR 385 at 415.
757 [footnote omitted]
758 . . . Note also that somerville points out that the problem of proper cause of action does not present itself in the same way in Quebec . . ..
759 [footnote omitted].
760 [footnote omitted].
761 [footnote omitted].
762 *See Hankai v York County Hospital* (1981) 9 ACWS (2d) 354 (Ont CA) where a doctor who did a meatotomy without the patient's consent admitted liability.
763 Klar, *Developments in Tort Law: The 1980–81 Term* (1982), 3 SCLR 385 at 415–16 based on *Halushka v University of Saskatchewan* (1965) 52 WWR 608 (Sask CA).
764 See Gochnauer and Fleming, *supra* n 752 at 487–88.

Sir John Donaldson MR in *Sidaway* in the Court of Appeal specifically rejects the view that fraud extends beyond deliberate misrepresentation by adopting *Clarence*. A further consequence of approving *Clarence* must be that he accepts the definition of 'nature' as defined in that case, ie the narrower meaning.

The conclusion as to the current state of English law may be that although there could still be life in the old tort of battery yet, the judges are unlikely to offer it any sustenance. They will probably prefer to develop this area of law through the tort of negligence since it offers both a more flexible legal tool and because, for reasons which we have seen, the tort of battery might be thought to be inappropriate insofar as its language is unsuitable to the everyday practice of medicine.

But a word of caution. As we shall see, the House of Lords in *Sidaway* state clearly that a doctor is not entitled to lie to his patient when a patient seeks information. *Sidaway* was a case which sounded in negligence. Does this follow that the action against the doctor who lies will also sound in negligence or would such deliberate lying or concealment of the truth give rise to a battery action? Cf *Hatcher v Black* (1954) Times, 2 July per Denning LJ and *infra* p 268.

3.　Mistake as to whether patient informed

The patient has relevant information but the doctor thinks otherwise

The key feature here is that the patient's consent is valid if he has the relevant knowledge (ie to give a valid consent, see *supra*) and in the light of that intends to consent. The state of mind of the doctor is irrelevant to this issue. For example, A sees B approach from behind. B intends to surprise A by hitting him on the head with a rolled newspaper. Unknown to B A sees B is a mirror and allows him to do it. A consents to B's touching regardless of B's state of mind.

(a) **The patient does not have the relevant information but the doctor thinks otherwise**

On the face of it, this is the converse of (i) above and the doctor should be liable in battery since the touching of the patient is not consented to even though the doctor thinks it is.

However, an exception to this may be the circumstances where, as Lord Diplock put it in *Sidaway*, 'the patient is estopped from denying that he possessed the relevant information, because he so acted towards the defendant as to lead the latter reasonably to assume the relevant information was known to him'. If Lord Diplock be correct, is there not some tension between his proposition and the requirement of the tort of negligence that the doctor is under a duty to inform a patient, *inter alia*, of the nature and purpose of the treatment? (See *infra* and Picard *op cit*, pp 109–110 on the Canadian law.)

The patient does have the relevant information but does not understand it; the doctor believes the patient does understand it.

A failure to understand something as basic as the 'nature and purpose' of the proposed treatment would ordinarily arise as a consequence of the patient's mental incapacity and falls for consideration in the light of the above discussion.

It could be said to arise where the language used by the doctor was not understood by the patient but in such a case it would not be appropriate to say the patient was informed. At best it would be an example of (a) above.

4. Place of battery in modern medical law

We have already seen (*supra* pp 172–5) that the need for a 'hostile' act has led the English courts in recent years to limit drastically the scope of the tort of battery. There may be costs as well as benefits associated with this development, as Picard points out (*op cit*), at p 141 (footnotes omitted):

> Prior to the decision of the Supreme Court of Canada in *Reibl v Hughes*, a patient could sue in battery or negligence or both where the allegation was that his consent was deficient. The majority of reported cases were brought in battery. However, the action for battery has now been dramatically restricted by the Supreme Court of Canada.
>
> The battery action has definite advantages for the patient over the negligence action. The patient does not have to prove causation or damage, nor does he have to find medical experts to testify. Also, the doctor bears the onus of proving that consent was given to the treatment. The battery action protected the patient against unauthorised touching, whereas the negligence action was the means by which a patient could seek compensation when a duty required of a doctor was carried out in a substandard way and the patient was injured. However, the battery action covering as it also does harmful and offensive bodily contact has a record of being associated with aggressive anti-social behavior and came to be seen in the United States as an inappropriate means of dealing with the problems of consent in the medical context. Thus, the battery action was abandoned for negligence as the proper action where a doctor was the defendant. The Supreme Court of Canada has by its ruling in *Reibl v Hughes* followed the same route. . . .
>
> On appeal Mr Justice Brooke, affected by the American trend, said:
>
> In cases such as this, the notion of battery seems quite inappropriate. In the circumstances when the evidence is consistent only with the fact that the doctor has acted in *good faith and in the interests of the patient*, but in so doing was negligent in failing to make disclosure of a risk inherent in treatment which he recommends and as a result caused his patient loss or damage, the action should properly be in negligence and not in battery. The finding then of battery cannot stand. [emphasis supplied]

Noting Mr Justice Morden's comment that most Canadian cases had proceeded in battery, Brooke JA concluded:

> They are cases where there was an intentional deviation from the consent given, or fraud, or a serious misrepresentation as to procedure and/or risks.

Thus the Ontario Court of Appeal associated the battery action with intentional deviation, fraud, serious misrepresentation and perhaps even with bad faith and selfish interests.

It is interesting to compare this picture of battery with that suggested by an authoritative legal text. Fleming says in speaking of battery:

> The action, therefore, serves the dual purpose of affording protection to the individual not only against bodily harm but also against any interference with his person which is offensive to a reasonable sense of honour and dignity. The insult in being touched without consent has been traditionally regarded as sufficient even though the interference is trivial and not attended with actual physical harm. . . .

And, at p 143:

> Chief Justice Laskin brought battery to its present narrow focus. He said battery should be restricted to situations where:
>
> . . . there has been no consent at all or where, emergency situations aside, surgery or treatment has been performed or given beyond that to which there was consent.
>
> This standard would comprehend cases where there was misrepresentation of the surgery or treatment for which consent was elicited and a different surgical procedure or treatment was carried out . . .
>
> . . . I can appreciate the temptation to say that the genuineness of consent to medical treatment depends on proper disclosure of the risks which it entails, but in my view, *unless there has been misrepresentation or fraud to secure consent to the treatment*, a failure to disclose the attendant risks, however, serious, should go to negligence rather than to battery. Although such a failure relates to an informed choice of submitting to or refusing recommended and appropriate treatment, it arises as the breach of an anterior duty of due care, comparable in legal obligation to the duty of due care in carrying out the particular treatment to which the patient has consented. It is not a test of the validity of the consent. [emphasis supplied].

Note also Robertson, 'Informed Consent to Medical Treatment', 97 LQR, pp 123–124:

> It is submitted that there are two principal reasons for the judicial policy evident in *Chatterton* and *Wells* against trespass claims in informed consent litigation. First, as can be seen from the decisions in *Fowler v Lanning* and *Letang v Cooper*, judicial policy appears to be in favour of restricting claims in battery to situations involving deliberate, hostile acts, a situation which most judges would regard as foreign to the doctor-patient relationship. Coupled with this is the stigma and damage to professional reputation which courts repeatedly emphasise are an inevitable by-product of a successful claim against a doctor. These consequences are probably seen as even more serious in an action for battery than in an action for negligence. The second reason stems from the view expressed in the concluding section of this article, namely, that courts in this country will attempt to restrict the scope of the doctrine of informed consent, principally by means of the requirement of causation, the use of expert evidence as to accepted medical practice, and emphasis on the 'best interests of the patient' principle. Restriction of the doctrine of informed consent in this way would not be possible if it were to be accepted that failure to inform of inherent risks of proposed treatment could ground an action for trespass. As was outlined above, the plaintiff in such an action would not be required to prove, by way of causation, that he would not have consented to the treatment had he been informed of the risks. Similarly, evidence of accepted medical practice has no place in an action for trespass; if failure to disclose a particular risk were to be regarded as vitiating consent, the fact that a reasonable doctor would not have

disclosed the risk cannot absolve the defendant from liability for battery. Finally, although the point is not entirely clear, it would seem that a doctor cannot avoid liability for battery simply on the grounds that he was acting in the best interests of his patient. Thus it can be seen that the three principal ways in which the doctrine of informed consent is likely to be restricted would not be available to a court dealing with a case based in trespass.

For these reasons it is thought that English courts will continue to reject the argument that failure on the part of a doctor to inform his patient of the risks inherent in proposed treatment can give rise to an action for trespass to the person.

(ii) Negligence

1. *Duty to offer information*

Background

A **SOCIAL.** Consider the view of The President's Commission 'Making Health Care Decisions', (see *supra* p 197) at pp 31–35:

The context of consent
The Commission believes that an analysis of 'the ethical and legal implications of requirements for informed consent to ... undergo medical procedure'[50] is best undertaken in the context of a broader examination of relationships between patients and health care professionals in American society. At issue is the definition of the patient-professional relationship, as well as the appropriate role of formal and informal modes of social regulation in shaping it. Clearly, the resolution of these issues requires more than a simple review of the existing law of informed consent. Thus, the remainder of this Report considers patterns of communication between patients and health care professionals and how decisions are made. These inquiries are framed by the Commission's ultimate question about this aspect of its work: how can a fuller, shared understanding by patient and professional of their common enterprise be promoted, so that patients can participate, on an informed basis and to the extent they care to do so, in making decisions about their health care?
Historical development. While the law has proclaimed, if not always given effect to, such propositions as 'Anglo-American law starts with the premise of thorough-going self-determination'[51] and 'each man is considered to be his own master,'[52] recent scholarship has suggested that such sentiments have played little role in traditional health care and are indeed antithetical to the proclaimed norms of the medical profession.[53] Medical skepticism of patients' capacities for self-determination can be traced to the time of Hippocrates:
  Perform [these duties] calmly and adroitly, concealing most things from the patient while you are attending to him. Give necessary orders with cheerfulness and sincerity, turning his attention away from what is being done to him; sometimes reprove sharply and emphatically, and sometimes comfort with solicitude and attention, revealing nothing of the patient's future or present condition.[54]
These attitudes continued to be reflected both in professional codes of ethics and in influential scholarly writings on medical ethics throughout the nineteenth and early twentieth centuries, and indeed survive to this day.[55] Studies of the records of daily medical practice (rather than normative statements of professional ethics) have found distinct 'indigenous medical traditions' of truth-telling and consent-seeking, grounded on the theory that such knowledge 'had demonstrably beneficial effects on most patients' health'.[56] but little evidence exists that such traditions combined in anything like the modern doctrine of informed consent. Nor did they derive from or imply any commitment by the medical profession to patient autonomy. Indeed, when patients' wishes regarding treatment were respected it was largely because providers recognised their limited therapeutic capabilities and the substantial risks accompanying medical interventions (for example, surgery without

antiseptic) as well as the impracticability of forcing treatments on resisting patients.[57]

Contemporary trends. Recent changes in health care practices, as well as broader societal changes in contemporary American life, have led to an intense reexamination of relationships between patients and health care practitioners. Gradually, a new understanding of the proper levels and limits of health care is emerging; from this flow changes in the relative rights and obligations of patients and professionals concerning matters such as disclosures and consent for medical interventions.

Perhaps the most significant single factor in this process is the emergence of the scientific, technological approach to medical care over the course of the past century. The rapidly evolving technical prowess of medicine has, of course, brought with it improved health, greater quality and length of life, and new sources of hope for the ill. This revolution in the capacities of medicine has also had profound effects on the structure of the health care delivery system and on the nature of the patient-professional relationship.

Several of these changes are particularly relevant to informed consent. First, health care is now provided in a vast array of settings, ranging from home visits by traditional family doctors to clinics, health maintenance organisations, and multispecialty group practices, to nursing homes and other long-term or chronic care facilities, to high-technology tertiary care centers. Care is frequently provided by teams of highly specialised professionals whose individual responsibilities may be defined less by the overall needs of the patient than by particular diseases or organs systems. When this occurs there may be no single professional in effective command of the entire care of the patient, no one who knows the patient well and to whom the patient may turn for information, advice, and comfort. In such instances the health care system's increased capacity and determination to overcome a disease or defect may be accompanied by a diminished capacity and inclination to care for the patent in more human terms.[58]

Such situations pose a far more serious threat to patient well-being and autonomy than any formal disclosure of remote risks on informed consent forms could possibly remedy. Indeed, the Commission believes that serious efforts by health care institutions to ensure that patients have one identifiable and reliable source of information concerning their care would do far more to remedy the current ills of the health care system than would legal prescriptions with which compliance can be neither assumed nor enforced.[59]

The expanded potential of medicine has also widened the range of choices about health care. Increasingly, the question is not simply whether to accept a single intervention that is available for a particular condition, but which intervention to choose. Often the alternatives vary markedly in their prospects for success, their intrusiveness, their potential side effects, and their other implications for patients' ability to conduct their lives as they see fit. A determination of what is 'indicated' is thus inextricably intertwined with the needs and values of the particular patient.

These changes in medicine have been accompanied by broader trends in American society and culture that have reinforced their impact. Since the early 1960s there has been an extraordinary emphasis on the rights of citizens to direct the course of their lives, from voting rights to consumer rights. This stress on the individual has been coupled with a skepticism toward claims of specialised expertise and a suspicion of powerful institutions and the 'establishment'. Health care has not escaped its share of criticism in the process.

Some commentators have seen in these trends the basis for a new view of the role of medicine and the nature of the patient-provider relationship:

The traditional paternal model of medicine was premised on trust in the physician's technical competence and moral sensitivity and was characterised by patient dependency and physician control. This model is being replaced gradually by one in which patients are increasingly involved in decisionmaking concerning their own medical care. The rise of consumerism and the associated emergence of 'rights' language in medicine has encouraged some individuals to view medicine as a 'serving' profession and to regard themselves not as patients but as 'medical consumers'. Such medical consumers' sometimes wish to invert the traditional model of medicine and to make the physician a passive agent, a hired technician who practices under the direction and control of his 'client'. However, despite these changes which affect some patients and some physicians, many patients and physicians continue to interact in a fairly traditional, paternalistic physician-patient relationship.[60]

The survey done for the Commission lends support to the conclusion that changes are occurring in the relationship between physicians and patients. Compared with previous studies, the current results demonstrate a clear sense of physicians' responsibilities for making disclosures and reaching mutual decisions.[61] Although the results from the separate surveys of the public and of physicians indicate substantial agreement on these expectations, some lack of congruence remains. Moreover, the observational studies done for the Commission make it apparent that in actual relationships even more divergence occurs between laypeople's and professionals' expectations.

The role of the health care professional thus appears to be in a 'phase of incomplete redefinition', as one Commission witness noted.[62] During this time 'judgments of conscientious persons have become divergent and perplexed' and societal consensus does not exist.[63] No longer are the proper ends and limits of health care commonly understood and broadly accepted; a new concept of health care, characterised by changing expectations and uncertain understanding between patient and practitioner, is evolving. The need to find an appropriate balance of the rights and responsibilities of patients and health care professionals in this time of change has been called 'the critical challenge facing medicine in the coming decades'.[64]

Notes to extract

[50] 42 USC § 300v-1 (a)(1)(A) (1981) the statutory mandate adopted in 1978, under which the Commission examines this issue.

[51] *Natanson v Kline* 186 Kan 393, 350 P2d 1093 (1960).

[52] *Scott v Bradford* 606 P2d 554, 556 (Okla 1980).

[53] See Jay Katz, *Disclosure and Consent in Psychiatric Practice: Mission Impossible?*, in Charles K Hofling, ed, LAW AND ETHICS IN THE PRACTICE OF PSYCHIATRY, Brunner/Mazel, Inc, New York (1980) at 91.

[54] Hippocrates, *Decorum*, in HIPPOCRATES, Harvard University Press, Cambridge, Mass (WHS Jones trans 2d ed 1967), quoted in Katz, *supra* note 46, at 124.

[55] See Katz, *supra* note 53, at 91, 97–100.

[56] Martin S Pernick, *The Patient's Role in Medical Decisionmaking: A Social History of Informed Consent in Medical Therapy* (1981), Appendix E, in Volume Three of this Report.

[57] *Id.*

[58] Dissatisfaction by both patients and some professionals with these depersonalising tendencies of modern medicine is suggested by the renaissance of interest in holistic medicine and the rise of the self-care movement.

[59] The problems of not having one person coordinating care are illustrated in this quote from a patient with leukemia:

I kept fighting through all the fevers and transfusions. I felt I could only survive it by insisting on control. And there would be plenty of chances to test my resolve. The personnel assigned to monitor various functions never coordinated their blood sample requirements on a given day, so they'd come two or three times to leech my tender, collapsing veins. I finally put my foot down.

'You're not going to take more blood,' I shouted. 'You take it once a day. Get together and find out how much you want and for what purpose, and, goddam it, in the absence of an emergency, don't you touch my veins. Also, no one's going to draw blood except the intravenous nurse team,' I said, 'because that's all they do, and they know how to do it.'

I got my way in both instances, thereby saving myself considerable pain.

Morris B Abram, THE DAY IS SHORT, Harcourt Brace Jovanovich, New York (1982) at 209.

[60] Mark Siegler, *Searching for Moral Certainty in Medicine: A Proposal for a New Model of the Doctor-Patient Encounter*, 57 BULL NY ACAD MED 56, 60 (1981).

[61] The legal doctrine of informed consent has been severely criticised by medical professionals for going too far in its requirements for disclosure. Such criticism has diminished substantially in recent years. Furthermore, there is considerable evidence that physicians today actually do disclose a great deal more information to patients than they did 10–20 years ago. See Chapter Four *infra*.

[62] Siegler, *supra* note 60, at 61.

[63] *Id.*

[64] *Id.*

B ETHICAL. Kirby, 9 'Informed consent: what does it mean?' Journal of Medical Ethics 1983, 69 at p 70 (footnotes omitted):

. . . it is important for us to go to the heart of the problem to understand what it is that is behind the notion of 'informed consent'. What is it that theologians, moral philosophers and lawyers are getting at in talking about this patient consent?

Originally, the notion was explained in the legal casebooks as being based upon the need for the patient to be able to 'take courage' as he, or she, faced up to the dire predicament of pre-anaesthetic medicine. In 1767 it was put thus:

It is reasonable that a patient should be told what is about to be done to him, that he may take courage and put himself in such a situation as to enable him to undergo the operation.

Although medicine has come a long way since 1767, the need for patients to take courage and to prepare themselves for medical treatment is still a reality today.

Nowadays, a broader concept is taken as the rationale for informed consent. It is the right of self-determination. A recurrent feature of our civilisation is said to be respect for the autonomy of the individual human being, 'with inherent dignity and value'. Each of us is said ultimately (with rare exceptions) to have the right to control our lives and actions by our own choices, at least to the greatest extent compatible with the rights of others. The fundamental principle underlying consent is said to be a right of self-determination: the principle, or value choice, of autonomy of the person. This fairly general notion is articulated in different ways. It is said to be based on inherent natural rights. It is said to be grounded in a political notion of the importance of the individual. It is claimed to be based upon the right of the patient to 'chart his own destiny' with such information as the health care professional can provide in order that the patient can do so intelligently and with dignity. The principle is not just a legal rule devised by one profession to harass another. It is an ethical principle which is simply reflected in legal rules because our law has been developed by judges sensitive to the practical application of generally held community ethical principles.

A modern interpretation of the principle of informed consent is offered in these terms:

The legal doctrine of informed consent clearly rests upon ethical principles of autonomy and self-determination . . . The ethical need for informed consent in medical practice was a salutory reminder to doctors that their patients were people and not cases and that the patient/doctor relationship needed to be open and honest in recognition of and respect for each patient's autonomy.

Beauchamp & Childress, *Principles of Biomedical Ethics*, (2nd ed 1983) at pp 66–69 offer the following analysis:

Informed consent

The voluntary consent of the human subject is absolutely essential.

This means that the person involved should have the legal capacity to give consent; should be so situated as to be able to exercise free power of choice, without the intervention of any element of force, fraud, deceit, duress, over-reaching, or other ulterior form of constraint or coercion; and should have sufficient knowledge and comprehenion of the subject matter involved as to enable him to make an understanding and enlightened decision. This latter element requires that before the acceptance of an affirmative decision by the experimental subject there should be made known to him the nature, duration, and purpose of the experiment; the methods and means by which it is to be conducted; all inconveniences and hazards reasonably to be expected; and the effects upon his health or person which may possibly come from his participation in the experiment. (*Nuremberg Code*, Rule 1; . . .)

The horrible stores of experimentation in concentration camps led to serious concern about the use of nonconsenting subjects in questionable and sometimes brutal experiments. Since the Nuremberg Trials the issue of informed consent has received more attention than any ethical issue in biomedical research involving human subjects. The Nuremberg Code cited above is one outcome, but controversies about informed consent have also arisen in other quarters. In Anglo-American law, for example, the doctrine of informed consent has gradually emerged from malpractice cases involving nonconsensual touching of the patient's body. Touching competent patients without consent has been found unacceptable in these cases, irrespective of considerations of the quality of care. . . . we shall see how standards for medical *practice* have derived from case law and how standards for *research* have grown from their roots in both the Nuremberg Code and the Declaration of Helsinki.

Functions and justifications of informed consent

In recent years virtually all medical and research codes of ethics have held that physicians must obtain the informed consent of patients before undertaking significant therapeutic or research procedures. These consent measures have been designed largely to protect the autonomy of patients and subjects, but they serve other functions as well. Alexander Capron has helpfully identified several important functions.[5]

1. The promotion of individual autonomy
2. The protection of patients and subjects
3. The avoidance of fraud and duress
4. The encouragement of self-scrutiny by medical professionals
5. The promotion of rational decisions
6. The involvement of the public (in promoting autonomy as a general social value and in controlling biomedical research).

Capron correctly argues that informed consent serves each of these functions. However, both historically and contemporarily, two positions about *function and justification* have dominated the literature. One maintains that the purpose and justification for obtaining informed consent is to protect persons from various risks of harm. Those who subscribe to a justification based on *protection from harm* are inclined to protect patients whether or not it is the patient's choice that leads to an 'unwise' assumption of a risk. The other position sees the purpose and justification for obtaining informed consent as respect for the autonomy of patients, by recognising their rights to know and choose. Those who subscribe to a justification based on *protection of autonomy* are not inclined to protect patients against their choices, on grounds that such constraint would violate their autonomy. The . . . case . . . of a patient (also a physician) who refused further steps to prolong his life, but was resuscitated nonetheless, may well be the result of these two different approaches applied in the clinical setting.

. . . [W]e accept the view that the primary function of informed consent is the protection and promotion of individual autonomy. The communication between a health professional and a patient should prevent ignorance from constraining autonomous choice, whether ignorance is present from a lack of information or a lack of comprehension. Our theory therefore generates requirements of comprehension as well as disclosure. A protection-from-harm justification is based on the principles of nonmaleficence and beneficence, and is put in the most favorable light by legal requirements governing consent. The law of battery protects against intentional bodily invasions where there has been no consent whatever; and the law of negligence holds researchers responsible for inadequate disclosures that might lead to injury.[6] Informed consent provisions thus protect against battery and negligence, and can be justified on this basis in the law. Second-party consent, or consent on behalf of a person given by another, can be similarly justified. Nonetheless, this justification in terms of the principle of nonmaleficence does not seem *fundamental* to moral justifications of first-party consent. While a person's decision may indirectly function to prevent harm, the person may also autonomously choose a greater risk than others would choose for him or her. The principle of autonomy justifies allowing a person this option of accepting increased risk, and we therefore consider the protection of autonomy to be the primary function of informed consent regulations.

A third justification for informed consent is based on the principle of utility: Informed consent requirements will maximally protect and benefit everyone in society, including health professionals, patients, and the institutions of medical practice and research themselves. Rules of consent serve to protect and benefit patients and professionals, to allay public fears (especially about research), to encourage self-scrutiny by physicians and investigators, and to maintain a relation of trust between them. This justification is closely related to Capron's fourth and sixth functions.

Even though justifications based on utility and nonmaleficence are appropriate for some consent requirements, the justifications based on autonomy recognise consent as valid *because* the consenting party is an autonomous person, with all the entitlements that status confers. Neither utility nor nonmaleficence leads to this strong conclusion, for both would justify not seeking consent in some circumstances—utility when it would not maximise the social welfare and nonmaleficence when no apparent harm would result. When informed consent is justified by the principle of autonomy, it is introduced, as Robert Veatch puts it, 'not to facilitate social benefits, but as a check against them',[7] for persons have rights to information and to consent that are independent of such considerations as immediate social utility and risk to patients or subjects.

This view has long-standing appeal in the law, where it is somewhat more fully developed than in writings on moral philosophy. Justice Cardozo's early statement (1914) in behalf of autonomy is well known: 'Every human being of adult years and sound mind has a right to determine what shall be done with his own body; and a surgeon who performs an operation without his patient's consent commits an assault, for which he is liable in damages. ... This is true except in cases of emergency.'[8] An updated, and in some ways even stronger, statement is found in a landmark 1960 case, *Natanson v Kline*, where it is asserted that

Anglo-American law starts with the premise of thoroughgoing self-determination. It follows that each man is considered to be master of his own body, and he may, if he be of sound mind, expressly prohibit the performance of lifesaving surgery, or other medical treatment.[9]

In short, the fact that we would often seek to obtain informed consent, even when it does not maximise immediate social utility and even when subjects and patients are not being protected against risk, indicates that autonomy is the basic justifying principle.

... seriously compromised patients [however] must make vital decisions about treatment in far from ideal contexts for autonomous decisionmaking. In cases where we might fall into error, it seems best to err on the side of ethical conservatism: We should strive not to deny an important medical benefit when a person has not accepted or is incapable of knowledgeably accepting it, even if—after careful examination—we are uncertain about the validity of a consent or refusal. Of course this rule has its limits. The medical benefit might be the wrong choice for other reasons. Like other rules, this one is strictly *prima facie*.

Notes to extract
5. 'Informed Consent in Catastrophic Disease and Treatment', *University of Pennsylvania Law Review* 123 (December 1974): 364–76.

6. Cf Charles Fried, *Medical Experimentation* (New York: American Elsevier, 1974), pp 18ff.
7. Robert M Veatch, 'Three Theories of Informed Consent: Philosophical Foundations and Policy Implications', in National Commission for the Protection of Human Subjects of Biomedical and Behavioral Research, *Appendix to the Belmont Report: Ethical Guidelines for the Protection of Human Subjects of Research*, Volume 1 (Washington: DHEW Publication No (OS) 78–0013, 1978).
8. *Schloendorff v Society of New York Hospitals* 211 NY 125, 127, 129; 105 NE 92, 93 (1914).
9. *Natanson v Kline* 186 Kan 393, 350 P 2d 1093 (1960), rehearing denied, 187 Kan 186, 354 P 2d 670 (1960).

Consider next the view of Carolyn Faulder in *Whose Body Is It?*, (1985), pp 22–31:

Patient consent is a key issue in cases of battery, but agreeing to a procedure is not the same as giving your informed consent. Many patients agree to procedures without understanding what they are about or why they are being asked to agree. These distinctions between forms of consent will be considered more closely in chapter 3. Meanwhile, since informed consent is not a legal right in this country we must examine the moral grounds on which we base our claim to this right and determine whether it can be justified.

Feelings are not enough
The doctrine of informed consent in medical practice arouses strong feelings on all sides. Those who believe that it is a right which cannot be questioned and who base their claim uniquely on the individual's right to self-determination—the principle of autonomy—sometimes refuse to give credence to the very real dilemmas facing doctors in their everyday practice. Many doctors, on the other hand, who base their philosophy of action on their Hippocratic oath . . . to act in the best interests of their patients, will argue that the obligation to seek informed consent is often not necessary, sometimes undesirable and frequently impossible. In short, they do not accept that they have this obligation. They will recount from experience many examples of patients explicitly requesting not to know—'It's up to you doctor, you know best'—and of patients making it clear from the form of their questions that what they are seeking is not the truth but reassurance. The patient who asks, 'I haven't got cancer, have I?' may really be saying 'Don't tell me if I have'. Others will argue that the whole idea of informed consent is a myth. A lay person, so the argument goes, cannot possibly understand the medical implications of her or his condition nor the technical details of the treatment proposed. Knowledge which doctors have acquired through years of training and clinical practice cannot possibly be imparted to someone, however intelligent or well-educated, who does not share the same scientific background. Pushed to its logical conclusion, this argument invariably ends with the statement: 'Look, doctors themselves don't know *everything* about a particular condition so there's no way they can ever "fully" inform the patients'.

I believe we should respect these arguments even while refuting them. We must remember that doctors are at the sharp end of the line. We consult them because we need medical attention and they have the expertise, but sometimes we entertain wholly unreasonable expectations of their omniscience and omnipotence. We expect them to come up with answers which they may not be able to give us and to provide cures which they may not be able to achieve. Doctors, for their part, have been guilty of pandering to these false hopes because it makes their job easier if patients accept their authority without question. Their claim that it is their duty to make decisions on behalf of their patients without involving them more than superficially in the decision-making process has gone unchallenged until recently.

Today, as we know, there is a growing lay opinion, shared by many doctors, that they should present choices to their patients and seek their consent. But if that obligation is to be taken seriously, then we must also accept that in claiming our right to be informed we too will have to shoulder new responsibilities, because rights entail obligations, both on those who claim them and on those from whom they are claimed. And moral rights, to be valid, must be based on principles which are generally accepted as moral.

The five principles

The principle of *autonomy* has already been mentioned several times in passing, and for good reason, because it is the key principle which validates the doctrine of informed consent. Autonomy can be defined as the individual's freedom to decide her or his goals and to act according to those goals. Inherent in this principle is the notion of personal responsibility. Because we believe human beings to be rational we regard them as persons rather than objects or things. A person is a self-determining individual who is able to think about ends, and decide on the means by which she or he intends to fulfil those ends. This same thinking, self-determining person is also a social human being, so the likelihood of her or his being able to take any action in isolation, without either being influenced by social factors or affecting someone somehow, is remote. However, if we take the Kantian line that persons are ends in themselves and should not be used as means by other persons (and it would be difficult to gainsay this view), then we must believe that the principle of autonomy, even if it cannot be the overriding principle on all occasions, is nonetheless extremely important.

Whatever our social philosophy, we all recognise that there are important occasions in our lives when we put ourselves first, that we have a right to do this, and that this right is generally accepted. Illness is one of those times. The body we inhabit is ours and ours alone to decide about, which does not mean that in coming to our decisions we do not consider, and more often than not take, the advice given to us by doctors. We also consider the effects our decisions may have on other people, especially those in a close relation to us. But when all the chips are down we think first and last of ourselves alone. In such circumstances we think of ourselves as being our own ends and we expect others to respect that view of ourselves—just as they expect us to respect them in the same way.

To think of persons as ends in themselves gives them an intrinsic value which demands respect, even if we do not always approve of their actions or the judgments on which they are based. The principle of autonomy does not of itself confer either respectability or morality on the autonomous action and, indeed, many such actions can be highly reprehensible. Nor would any but the most rigid autonomist maintain that human beings must always and at all times act autonomously without any consideration of other people's equal claim to autonomy. Providing we *freely* concede our autonomy to a legitimate authority for specific purposes, as we do in a democratic system, then our fundamental autonomy is preserved.

The notion of what constitutes a legitimate authority is, of course, crucial and should be constantly under review in an alert society. Only lately has this concern been extended to the field of medical ethics. Doctors have always emphasised the importance of authority in their relationship with their patients and based their own claim to clinical autonomy, the right to make decisions on the patient's behalf, on that authority. But do they have a right to assume that patients, in surrendering their bodies to doctors for medical care, have also surrendered their right to self-determination? Surely not, if we accept that the principle of autonomy is a valid moral principle and therefore constant and unable to be 'altered as it alteration finds'. And if we further accept that it is defined in terms of the individual's right to make independent decisions relating to privately determined goals, then we must accept that it applies to all persons in all circumstances unless they consciously resign that right or, for some reason, are unable to exercise it.

Deeply embedded in the principle of autonomy is the concept of 'respect for persons', and one of the ways of expressing that respect is always to assume that they wish to exercise their rights unless they indicate otherwise. In the medical context, that respect between persons for persons is expressed by doctors *enabling* patients to give their informed consent. That, in practical terms, means offering them the opportunity to be informed as much or as little as they require. To do less than that is to deny them their autonomy. But it is equally a denial of autonomy to force unwanted information on those who have clearly indicated, not necessarily verbally, that they do not want it. Respect for persons and for their autonomy implies that we also respect their right *not* to exercise their autonomy in given circumstances or, alternatively, their right to make choices which we may consider to be unwise or irresponsible.

The principle of *veracity* (truthfulness) is, as Sissela Bok discovered when she came to write her penetrating enquiry *Lying, Moral Choice in Public and Private Life*, hardly given a mention in the medical ethical literature. Yet trust, which can only be based on accepting this principle, is an obsessive concern with doctors in their relationship with their patients. Doctors expect their patients to trust them to act always in their best interests, to prescribe only treatments which they consider to be beneficial and to place their skills and their experience at the disposal of their patients. Doctors value their patients' trust, not least because they know that without it their job would be virtually impossible. Sometimes they trade on it. 'My patients do as they are told because they trust me' is often boasted by doctors who, in the following breath, will explain why 'white' lies are sometimes necessary and informed consent is virtually impossible.

'Telling the truth can be dangerously misleading and cause a great deal of unhappiness', one doctor was at pains to explain to me. He cited his experience of telling the mother of an eleven-year-old boy that the child ran a one to two per cent risk of blindness if he was given radiotherapy to get rid of a non-malignant tumour; on the other hand, if it was left untreated it would spread and he would certainly go blind. The child survived the radiotherapy unscathed but the mother ('foolish woman' was the unspoken comment) was tortured by the belief that the child could go blind at any time. Maybe this woman was unduly over-anxious, but it could just be that by now she has been reassured by seeing her son in continuing good health. Our emotions are, in a crisis, usually more powerful influences on our judgement than our reason, as even those who most pride themselves on keeping their cool are obliged to admit, if they are honest. Just how would this same doctor have felt if he had not been frank with her and, by an evil chance, the boy's cure had blinded him? The mother could have accused him, with perfect justification but alas little satisfaction, that he had concealed a vital risk factor from her.

Doctors do not like to confess to their own doubts and worries; indeed they regard such revelations as a sign of weakness, a threat to the patient's morale and a major offence against the canon of trust in the patient-doctor relationship. But who has established this canon of trust? And why is it that trust is almost uniquely discussed in terms of the patient's confidence in the doctor? Seldom do we hear about doctors trusting their patients by, for example, allowing them to see their medical records. Worse still, as we have already noted, the patient's confidence that the information she discloses will be treated as confidential is frequently abused.

Trust between two people, if it is to mean anything, must be reciprocal. They trust each other to observe the same rules of discretion and to respect each other equally as persons, regardless of the differences in their social or material circumstances which may, indeed, be hugely unequal.

A trust is broken when one party to the relationship deceives the other in some way, irrespective of whether the deceived party discovers the deception. But, of course, if we do catch out the trusted person in a lie, then our sense of outrage is acute. We feel we have been duped, manipulated and coerced; we have been deprived of information; we have possibly made choices which we would not have made had we been fully aware of the facts, or, worse still, we have been deprived of choice altogether. In a medical situation none of these feelings does the patient any good, yet such circumstances often arise and, too often, they are blandly ignored by doctors.

In asking their patients to trust them it would seem only fair that doctors should reward that trust by dealing honestly with them. Seeking the informed consent of their patients is part of that honest relationship. Yet there are some doctors who will argue with total sincerity that the only way to preserve that trust is to withhold information or even tell a downright lie. Their justifications for this paradoxical view are examined more fully [elsewhere]. Here we will observe only that the principle of veracity which is widely accepted, even if not always practised, as a moral principle appears to be dispensable in certain medical situations. What we will ultimately question is whether those special circumstances are ever sufficient in themselves to permit doctors the liberty to go against normally accepted standards of trust, especially when we know that often the deception is about a matter of intense concern to the person who is being deceived. This professionally approved licence to lie makes the phrase 'a relationship of mutual trust and respect' so frequently used by doctors to describe their relationship with their patients sound hollow indeed.

The principles of autonomy and veracity are the two most important principles in favour of informed consent. Autonomy is the condition of our claim to be responsible for our own destinies. Veracity, which is the cornerstone of our relationship with others, honours that claim. Next in importance comes the principle of *justice* which acknowledges the claim for patient autonomy by enabling it to be exercised. (The principle of justice also has many other important applications in health care: for example, in resource allocation.)

However we choose to describe the patient-doctor relationship— as a contract, a covenant, or a partnership—it implies that both parties have a duty to treat each other justly. Ideally, doctors should respect the confidence and trust of their patients and seek to meet their personal needs while at the same time balancing the rights of all their other patients to similar attention and care. Ideally, patients should respect the judgement and skills of their doctors and seek to help them by co-operating with treatment procedures and by not making undue demands on them that would prejudice the right of other patients to receive the same attention. If both sides are to meet as equals, as 'joint adventurers in a common cause' as Paul Ramsey, the ethicist, defines the relationship in his book *The Patient as Person*, then the principle of justice requires this equal though different contribution from each of the parties. Implicit in this joint undertaking of equals is the principle of informed consent. If the doctor does not confide in the patient as the patient confides in the doctor, then the relationship is unequal and unjust. To quote Ramsey again, 'Consent expresses or establishes this relationship, and the requirement of consent sustains it'.

Additionally, there are two other principles to consider, especially as they are sometimes invoked by doctors as reasons for *not* seeking informed consent.

The principle of *beneficence* implies the duty to do good. In the negative sense this is interpreted as preventing harm; in the positive sense it means producing benefits of some kind. Doctors understand beneficence as their duty to act in the best interests of their patients, a duty which is hallowed by the Hippocratic tradition and which they have always considered to be their guiding principle of action. I doubt that anyone would wish doctors not to believe in this principle; our trust in them is nourished by knowing that they act according to this belief. But there are some problems about its practice.

Quite simply, who is to decide what are the best interests of the patient? Doctors generally have no hesitation in saying that they must, because their skills and experience give them the advantage of superior knowledge. They understand better than any non-medically qualified person the aetiology (causes) and likely course of the disease they are treating; they appreciate the medical consequences of the decisions they make. And when they do have doubts in a particular case they can draw on the resources of their colleagues. Their patients have put themselves into their hands precisely because they possess these skills and they rely on their doctors to choose the best treatment for them.

Well and good if that is all that constitutes the 'best interests' of a patient. But does it? In real life we well know that there are occasions when something which seems best to one person can be quite the opposite for another. For instance, how often do we read in a newspaper account that someone who has been thrown into deep shock by some traumatic incident, say the loss of her children in a fire, has been put under heavy sedation? To the doctors this may seem like the only proper, compassionate course of action, and maybe for some people it is; for others, however, dulling the agony now may only drive the grief inwards so deeply that the bereaved person never fully recovers.

A woman who lost her husband in a swimming accident had her memory wiped out by three weeks of solid sedation. Because she had not been allowed to live through her desperation at the time, she spent years in a coma of depression, finally expunging the savage guilt she felt only by going on a wild shoplifting spree which ended up in the locked ward of a mental hospital. At last, she was able to unburden herself and find release from the mental torture she had been suffering by being allowed to relive those dreadful last moments when she had pushed off the drowning man clutching at her in order to save herself.

Obviously, we cannot expect doctors to have divine insight about everything relating to their patients' lives, but a story like this illustrates the need for caution in assuming that one solution will suit all and sundry. Real life does not stop in the doctor's waiting room or at the hospital gates. People carry with them in sickness as in health all their personal luggage of hopes, fears, beliefs, experiences, prejudices, expectations and the particular circumstances of their individual existence; becoming a patient does not turn them into a non-person, a 'case' for treatment.

Of course doctors must tell their patients what they think is in their best interests—it would be highly unethical if they did not—but this should not prevent them from seeking also to see things from their patients' perspective. Someone who has already been through a great deal of pain and distress as a result of her disease may reject the idea of further treatment, even though it holds out the hope of living a little longer. What doctors call heroic surgery and we would call dire mutilation, or yet another drastically toxic regime of chemotherapy to hold off encroaching cancer, may simply make that last scrap of life unbearable for the patient. In such circumstances it would be wrong for the doctor to pull rank either by insisting that the treatment was necessary or persuading the patient to accept it by minimising the side effects, especially when we consider how many of these 'wonder treatments' are subsequently discarded.

Fifteen years ago, for example, a woman suffering from breast cancer had been through most of the treatments then available. She knew she was dying and had made all her preparations, but she was persuaded to submit to one more operation—removal of the pituitary gland. This left her face so badly bruised that she put off seeing her children for several days to spare them the shock of her appearance. She saw them only once more before she died. The operation is now recognised to be useless for this particular condition.

If beneficence is left entirely to the subjective judgement of doctors it too easily becomes an excuse for paternalism. But if patients are allowed to exercise their equal right to make subjective judgements on their own behalf and to state what they consider to be their own 'best interests', then it can act as a useful measure for assessing the pros and cons of a particular decision. When doctors apply *only* the principle of beneficence to medical research, and to clinical trials in particular, the interests of the individual patient tend to lose out against the interests of future generations of patients. However, if beneficence is considered *together* with the principle of autonomy then it would seem only proper that the decision as to whether to enter a clinical trial must rest with the patient, not the doctor. As a self-determining person it is in the patient's 'best interest' to make that decision, but of course this is possible only if the doctor enables the patient to give informed consent.

The principle of *nonmaleficence* is the reverse aspect of beneficence: *Primum non nocere* (also attributed to Hippocrates) is a positive principle not to do harm as opposed to merely preventing harm. The distinction is subtle but real and it applies particularly to the doctor's duty to act with due care and avoid negligence. It also assumes a special significance in the context of clinical trials where submitting a new treatment to study under controlled conditions can be justified only if it is believed that it will not produce risks or harms greater than the standard therapy with which it is being compared. The aim of the study is, of course, to discover which treatment produces the most benefits.

Beneficence and maleficence are often balanced against each other to determine conflicting priorities in medical care: how scarce resources should be allocated and which groups of patients have a prior claim to certain services. For example, is the harm some women will suffer because they are not in the decreed age group for breast cancer screening going to be greater than the benefits which will be produced by restricting the service to an identifiable high-risk population? The problem about balancing these claims is the familiar utilitarian difficulty of how exactly you measure the distribution of these aggregated benefits and harms.

When so much is a matter of guesswork, the field is wide open for interested parties in the medical world to fight for their competing claims and forget the most interested party of all—the patient, who is in danger of being cut out as the cuts start biting. We see this happening all the time: a doctor announces that his funds have been slashed so he will no longer be able to carry on his valuable but extremely specialised work for a small group of patients. If the appeal is sufficiently heart-rending—anything to do with children or cancer patients arouses an immediate response, which is guaranteed to be whipped up by media publicity—the doctor is overwhelmed by donations, and the DHSS announces that it has changed its mind and promises to support the work. That probably means that the money allocated for some other equally important but infinitely less glamorous area of health care, like developing aids for the physically handicapped or improving geriatric services, is eaten into, yet again. What is questionable in this kind of situation is not the nature of the work—nobody would want to deny a child its chance to live—but that too often we allow our priorities in health care to be determined by emotional appeal rather than by a cooler appraisal of the total needs of the population.

We, the public, need to be educated together with doctors, researchers *and* the government officials responsible for policy-making in how to make a more just distribution of the resources available. I repeat the point I made earlier in this chapter. Exercising our right to informed consent is important not just for us as individuals but for us as members of a society which professes concern for everyone living in our community. That is why I maintain that although the patient's right to informed consent is by no means the only right in health care it could be the supreme right. To discover whether there are any valid grounds for this assumption we must now examine what *we*, the potential patients, mean by informed consent, its purpose for *us* in the patient-doctor relationship, and how and when we expect to exercise our right to give it, or refuse it.

C LEGAL. Consider first, Faden and Beauchamp, *A History and theory of Informed Consent*, (1986) at pp 123, 125, 127–8, 129, 130–1, 132–3, 137–8, 139 (footnotes omitted):

The Schloendorff case,
In 1914, the eminent Justice Benjamin Cardozo applied the reasoning and precedents of [previous cases] in this celebrated opinion in *Schloendorff* v *Society of New York Hospitals.* In *Schloendorff* the physician had removed a fibroid tumor after the patient had consented to an abdominal examination under anesthesia, but had specifically requested 'no operation'. Ironically, because the case focused on the liability of the defendant hospital for torts committed by surgeons using its facilities, the court neither found a violation of informed consent nor said anything about the information a patient needs in order to exercise the right of self-determination.

Nonetheless, Justice Cardozo's opinion is the most widely quoted in the current informed consent literature, and stands as a classic statement of the patient's right to self-determination: 'Every human being of adult years and sound mind has a right to determine what shall be done with his own body; and a surgeon who performs an operation without his patient's consent commits an assault, for which he is liable in damages'. This brief, eloquent formulation drew considerable attention to the proposition that patients have the right to protect the inviolability of their persons by choosing how they will be treated medically, and that interference with this right may constitute unauthorised bodily invasion—a battery—regardless of the skill with which the treatment was administered and even if it was ultimately beneficial. . . .

1957–1972: Consent becomes informed

After the *Schloendorff* decision, . . . [n]o major advances in the doctrine emerged in the next 40 years, as courts in different jurisdictions took up consent issues and either decided them in battery or disposed of them as matters of malpractice. But the first two decades in the second half of the century evoked a dramatic new development: the evolution of the traditional duty to *obtain consent* into a new, explicit duty to *disclose certain forms of information* and then to obtain consent. This development needed a new term; and so 'informed' was tacked onto 'consent', creating the expression 'informed consent', in the landmark decision in *Salgo* v *Leland Stanford Jr University Board of Trustees* (1957). . . . A few months before the *Salgo* case was decided, a prominent legal commentator had already advocated a choice between battery and negligence theories. In an influential 1957 article, Allan McCoid surveyed the 'unauthorised treatment' decisions to date with the intention of determining 'whether there is a real distinction between "negligent" malpractice and unauthorised treatment or whether the same standard of conduct may be applied in all cases involving improper action on the part of doctors'. Both failure to obtain consent and negligent treatment are improper actions by doctors. Therefore, he reasoned, for reasons of 'consistency of theory and appropriateness of liability', there should be a single basis of liability in all 'malpractice' cases. He found that courts seemed to apply the battery theory of liability in most cases where the procedure consented to differed from the operation performed. Some courts, however, applied negligence law for consistency—especially when, as was common, the unauthorised treatment claim was joined with a negligent treatment claim—or, more often, because negligence theory afforded the plaintiff a longer time in which to bring suit (that is, a longer statute of limitations). McCoid's own reasons for choosing negligence were more philosophical than the courts'. He argued that even though the requirements for battery were met in unauthorised treatment cases, physicians merit special legal treatment because they generally act in good faith for the benefit of their patients.

Informed consent cases that were decided after *Salgo* and that applied the battery theory exhibited an ability equal to that of the negligence theory to address difficult and important consent issues. Nonetheless, the perception grew in most courts that battery was unsuitable and should rarely be used—a perception that may owe more to McCoid's influence than to that of any other commentator or court. The shift in law to liability based on negligence can perhaps be traced as directly to his work as to the opinions in the courts. . . . Two opinions by the Kansas Supreme Court in the case of *Natanson* v *Kline* (1960) must be said to have pioneered the negligence theory in informed consent cases.

. . . *Natanson* held that mere consent of the patient does not shield the physician from negligence even if the medical performance is good. The medical practice can be flawless, but if injury results from a known risk inherent in the procedure that is undisclosed to the patient, the physician may be liable. This notion was new to malpractice, even though the battery theory had always held that flawlessly administered unauthorised treatment could give rise to liability.

Battery and negligence appeared after *Natanson* as virtually identical in their disclosure requirements for informed consent: The procedure's nature, consequences, and risks, as well as its alternatives, all had to be transmitted. The significant difference lay in the disclosure standards: 'Mere consent' was found insufficient in *Natanson* because the patient was not informed of collateral hazards that any 'reasonable medical practitioner' would disclose, a standard that implicitly permits discretion paralleling the physician discretion in *Salgo*. By contrast, we have seen that the post-*Salgo* battery decisions chose a layperson's reasonableness standard to measure the necessary disclosure.

Three 1972 negligence decisions steered a zigzag course between these extremes and came to be regarded as landmarks. These cases were *Canterbury* v *Spence* and two decisions that closely followed *Canterbury* both chronologically and ideologically: *Cobbs* v *Grant* and *Wilkinson* v *Vesey*. This trilogy of decisions led many to believe that the professional practice standard of disclosure would quickly be replaced by the patient-centered reasonable person standard. This trend was considered by some courts and commentators to be the promise and potential glory of a flourishing new doctrine of informed consent based on full protection of the self-determination right. But the promise and glory quickly faded: The professional practice disclosure standard was not displaced in American informed consent law. These three decisions established but an important *minority* trend in American courts.

These three decisions thus followed the contemporary trend, begun in the early cases and firmly established after *Salgo*, of requiring disclosure of diagnosis, prognosis with and without treatment, proposed treatments, risks inherent in the treatment, and alternative treatments and their risks. However, as we have seen, there were now some important differences between the *Natanson* line of negligence cases and this new trilogy. The 1972 decisions combined features of negligence and battery theories into a new approach that attempted a fairer balance than is present in the *Natanson* line of cases between, on the one hand, the right of self-determination of patients and, on the other hand, the exigencies and demands of the physician-patient relationship and the complexities of the legal setting. . . . After *Canterbury*, little of historical significance emerged in the next decade in the courts regarding informed consent, with the exception of *Truman* v *Thomas* (1980). *Truman* was decided in California, by the court that had decided *Cobbs* v *Grant* in 1972. The court in *Truman* permitted the children of a woman who died from cervical cancer to sue her doctor for failing to disclose the risks of not undergoing the Pap smear test, which she had repeatedly refused. Although her physician (and the minority of the court) argued that the duty to disclose applies only to procedures to which patients *consent*, and not to those they refuse, the court quoted *Cobbs*, which held that the patient must be apprised of 'the risks of a decision *not* to undergo the treatment' as well as the 'risks inherent in the procedure . . . and the probability of a successful outcome of the treatment'.

This point is legally and historically important because it is incompatible with the battery theory of liability, as traditionally understood. There is no battery without an unauthorised bodily intrusion, or 'touching'. A disclosure requirement based on battery theory alone must have as its goal the authorisation of interventions that would otherwise be instances of battery. Even when earlier battery decisions acknowledged the patient's right to *decide*—rather than the right merely to be free from unauthorised physical invasions—the choices in the cases had always been to consent to physical invasions. In *Truman* the court was envisioning no such invasion in requiring that refusals be informed.

Regardless of the nature of battery liability, however, the understanding of self-determination espoused by the early battery consent cases seemed even then to be more fundamental, to move beyond this basic physical requirement. For example, the *Mohr* court focused on the deliberative process, rather than solely on which of Mrs Mohr's ears received surgery. But because by definition battery is about physical integrity, battery theory cannot recognise the importance and value of the patient's decision about medical treatment unless it is a decision permitting bodily invasion. This appears to be the only unassailable limitation on the use of battery theory for informed consent . . . .. Negligence law, as *Truman* has shown, can acknowledge the value of the patient's right to decide even if the decision is one to forego some invasion. The end result of *Truman*'s reasoning was to reinforce the strength of the self-determination justification for informed consent by protecting a right to decide that is not compromised by this limitation of legal theory. It also pointed to the need for a theory of informed consent that is independent of the constraints of the battery/ negligence distinction.

Landmark decisions

(A) USA. Canterbury v Spence 464 F 2d 772 (1972) at 781–783, 783–785, 786–788, 788–789 (footnotes omitted):

Robinson J: The context in which the duty of risk-disclosure arises is invariably the occasion for decision as to whether a particular treatment procedure is to be undertaken. To the physician, whose training enables a self-satisfying evaluation, the answer may seem clear, but it is the prerogative of the patient, not the physician, to determine for himself the direction in which his interests seem to lie. To enable the patient to chart his course understandably, some familiarity with the therapeutic alternatives and their hazards becomes essential.

A reasonable revelation in these respects is not only a necessity but, as we see it, is as much a matter of the physician's duty. It is a duty to warn of the dangers lurking in the proposed treatment, and that is surely a facet of due care. It is, too, a duty to impart information which the patient has every right to expect. The patient's reliance upon the physician is a trust of the kind which traditionally has exacted obligations beyond those associated with arms-length transactions. His dependence upon the physician for information affecting his well-being, in terms of contemplated treatment, is well-nigh abject. As earlier noted, long before the instant litigation arose, courts had recognised that the physician had the responsibility of satisfying the vital informational needs of the patient. More recently, we ourselves have found 'in the fiducial qualities of [the physician-patient] relationship the physician's duty to reveal to the patient that which in his best interests it is important that he should know'. We now find, as a part of the physician's overall obligation to the patient, a similar duty of reasonable disclosure of the choices with respect to proposed therapy and the dangers inherently and potentially involved.

This disclosure requirement, on analysis, reflects much more of a change in doctrinal emphasis than a substantive addition to malpractice law. It is well established that the physician must seek and secure his patient's consent before commencing an operation or other course of treatment. It is also clear that the consent, to be efficacious, must be free from imposition upon the patient. It is the settled rule that therapy not authorised by the patient may amount to a tort—a common law battery—by the physician. And it is evident that it is normally impossible to obtain a consent worthy of the name unless the physician first elucidates the options and the perils for the patient's edification. Thus the physician has long borne a duty, on pain of liability for unauthorised treatment, to make adequate disclosure to the patient. The evolution of the obligation to communicate for the patient's benefit as well as the physician's protection has hardly involved an extraordinary restructuring of the law.

There are, in our view, formidable obstacles to acceptance of the notion that the physician's obligation to disclose is either germinated or limited by medical practice. To begin with, the reality of any discernible custom reflecting a professional concensus on communication of option and risk information to patients is open to serious doubt. We sense the danger that what in fact is no custom at all may be taken as an affirmative custom to maintain silence, and that physician-witnesses to the so-called custom may state merely their personal opinions as to what they or others would do under given conditions. We cannot gloss over the inconsistency between reliance on a general practice respecting divulgence and, on the other hand, realisation that the myriad of variables among patients makes each case so different that its omission can rationally be justified only by the effect of its individual circumstances. Nor can we ignore the fact that to bind the disclosure obligation to medical usage is to arrogate the decision on revelation to the physician alone. Respect for the patient's right of self-determination on particular therapy demands a standard set by law for physicians rather than one which physicians may or may not impose upon themselves.

More fundamentally, the majority rule overlooks the graduation of reasonable-care demands in Anglo-American jurisprudence and the position of professional custom in the hierarchy. The caliber of the performance exacted by the reasonable-care standard varies between the professional and non-professional worlds, and so also the role of professional custom. 'With but few exceptions', we recently declared, 'society demands that everyone under a duty to use care observe minimally a general standard'. 'Familiarly expressed judicially', we added, 'the yardstick is that degree of care which a reasonably prudent person would have exercised under the same or similar circumstances'. 'Beyond this,' however, we emphasised, 'the law requires those engaging in activities requiring unique knowledge and ability to give a performance commensurate with the undertaking'. Thus physicians treating the sick must perform at higher levels than non-physicians in order to meet the reasonable care standard in its special application to physicians—'that degree of care and skill ordinarily exercised by the profession in [the physician's] own or similar localities'. And practices adopted by the profession have indispensable value as evidence tending to establish just what that degree of care and skill is.

We have admonished, however, that '[t]he special medical standards are but adaptions of the general standard to a group who are required to act as reasonable men possessing their medical talents presumably would'. There is, by the same token, no basis for operation of the special medical standard where the physician's activity does not bring his medical knowledge and skills peculiarly into play. And where the challenge to the physician's conduct is not to be gauged by the special standard, it follows that medical custom cannot furnish the test of its propriety, whatever its relevance under the proper test may be. The decision to unveil the patient's condition and the chances as to remediation, as we shall see, is oft times a non-medical judgment and, if so, is a decision outside the ambit of the special standard. Where that is the situation, professional custom hardly furnishes the legal criterion for measuring the physician's responsibility to reasonably inform his patient of the options and the hazards as to treatment. . . .

Prevailing medical practice, we have maintained, has evidentiary value in determinations as to what the specific criteria measuring challenged professional conduct are and whether they have been met, but does not itself define the standard. That has been our position in treatment cases, where the physician's performance is ordinarily to be adjudicated by the special medical standard of due care. We see no logic in a different rule for nondisclosure cases, where the governing standard is much more largely divorced from professional considerations. And surely in nondisclosure cases the fact-finder is not invariably functioning in an area of such technical complexity that it must be bound to medical custom as an inexorable application of the community standard of reasonable care.

Thus we distinguished, for purposes of duty to disclose, the special- and general-standard aspects of the physician-patient relationship. When medical judgment enters the picture and for that reason the special standard controls, prevailing medical practice must be given its just due. In all other instances, however, the general standard exacting ordinary care applies, and that standard is set by law. In sum, the physician's duty to disclose is governed by the same legal principles applicable to others in comparable situations, with modifications only to the extent that medical judgment enters the picture. We hold that the standard measuring performance of that duty by physicians, as by others, is conduct which is reasonable under the circumstances.

Once the circumstances give rise to a duty on the physician's part to inform his patient, the next inquiry is the scope of the disclosure the physician is legally obliged to make. The courts have frequently confronted this problem but no uniform standard defining the adequacy of the divulgence emerges from the decisions. Some have said 'full' disclosure, a norm we are unwilling to adopt literally. It seems obviously prohibitive and unrealistic to expect physicians to discuss with their patients every risk of proposed treatment—no matter how small or remote—and generally unnecessary from the patient's viewpoint as well. Indeed, the cases speaking in terms of 'full' disclosure appear to envision something less than total disclosure, leaving unanswered the question of just how much.

The larger number of courts, as might be expected, have applied tests framed with reference to prevailing fashion within the medical profession. Some have measured the disclosure by 'good medical practice', others by what a reasonable practitioner would have bared under the circumstances, and still others by what medical custom in the community would demand. We have explored this rather considerable body of law but are unprepared to follow it. The duty to disclose, we have reasoned, arises from phenomena apart from medical custom and practice. The latter, we think, should no more establish the scope of the duty than its existence. Any definition of scope in terms purely of a professional standard is at odds with the patient's prerogative to decide on projected therapy himself. That prerogative, we have said, is at the very foundation of the duty to disclose, and both the patient's right to know and the physician's correlative obligation to tell him are diluted to the extent that its compass is dictated by the medical profession.

In our view, the patient's right of self-decision shapes the boundaries of the duty to reveal. That right can be effectively exercised only if the patient possesses enough information to enable an intelligent choice. The scope of the physician's communications to the patient, then, must be measured by the patient's need, and that need is the information material to the decision. Thus the test for determining whether a particular peril must be divulged is its materiality to the patient's decision: all risks potentially affecting the decision must be unmasked. And to safeguard the patient's interest in achieving his own determination on treatment, the law must itself set the standard for adequate disclosure.

Optimally for the patient, exposure of a risk would be mandatory whenever the patient would deem it significant to his decision, either singly or in combination with other risks. Such a requirement, however, would summon the physician to second-guess the patient, whose ideas on materiality could hardly be known to the physician. That would make an undue demand upon medical practitioners, whose conduct, like that of others, is to be measured in terms of reasonableness. Consonantly with orthodox negligence doctrine, the physician's liability for nondisclosure is to be determined on the basis of foresight, not hindsight; no less than any other aspect of negligence, the issue on nondisclosure must be approached from the viewpoint of the reasonableness of the physician's divulgence in terms of what he knows or should know to be the patient's informational needs. If, but only if, the fact-finder can say that the physician's communication was unreasonably inadequate is an imposition of liability legally or morally justified.

Of necessity, the content of the disclosure rests in the first instance with the physician. Ordinarily it is only he who is in position to identify particular dangers; always he must make a judgment, in terms of materiality, as to whether and to what extent revelation to the patient is called for. He cannot know with complete exactitude what the patient would consider important to his decision, but on the basis of his medical training and experience he can sense how the average, reasonable patient expectably would react. Indeed, with knowledge of, or ability to learn, his patient's background and current condition, he is in a position superior to that of most others—attorneys, for example—who are called upon to make judgments on pain of liability in damages for unreasonable miscalculation.

From these considerations we derive the breadth of the disclosure of risks legally to be required. The scope of the standard is not subjective as to either the physician or the patient; it remains objective with due regard for the patient's informational needs and with suitable leeway for the physician's situation. In broad outline, we agree that '[a] risk is thus material when a reasonable person, in what the physician knows or should know to be the patient's position, would be likely to attach significance to the risk or cluster of risks in deciding whether or not to forego the proposed therapy'.

The topics importantly demanding a communication of information are the inherent and potential hazards of the proposed treatment, the alternatives to that treatment, if any, and the results likely if the patient remains untreated. The factors contributing significance to the dangerousness of a medical technique are, of course, the incidence of injury and the degree of the harm threatened. A very small chance of death or serious disablement may well be significant; a potential disability which dramatically outweighs the potential benefit of the therapy or the detriments of the existing malady may summons discussion with the patient.

There is no bright line separating the significant from the insignificant; the answer in any case must abide a rule of reason. Some dangers—infection, for example—are inherent in any operation; there is no obligation to communicate those of which persons of average sophistication are aware. Even more clearly, the physician bears no responsibility for discussion of hazards the patient has already discovered, or those having no apparent materiality to patients' decision on therapy. The disclosure doctrine, like others marking lines between permissible and impermissible behavior in medical practice, is in essence a requirement of conduct prudent under the circumstances. Whenever non-disclosure of particular risk information is open to debate by reasonable-minded men, the issue is for the finder of the facts.

Two exceptions to the general rule of disclosure have been noted by the courts. Each is in the nature of a physician's privilege not to disclose, and the reasoning underlying them is appealing. Each, indeed, is but a recognition that, as important as is the patient's right to know, it is greatly outweighed by the magnitudinous circumstances giving rise to the privilege. The first comes into play when the patient is unconscious or otherwise incapable of consenting, and harm from a failure to treat is imminent and outweighs any harm threatened by the proposed treatment. When a genuine emergency of that sort arises, it is settled that the impracticality of conferring with the patient dispenses with need for it. Even in situations of that character the physician should, as current law requires, attempt to secure a relative's consent if possible. But if time is too short to accommodate discussion, obviously the physician should proceed with the treatment.

The second exception obtains when risk-disclosure poses such a threat of detriment to the patient as to become unfeasible or contraindicated from a medical point of view. It is recognised that patients occasionally become so ill or emotionally distraught on disclosure as to foreclose a rational decision, or complicate or hinder the treatment, or perhaps even pose psychological damage to the patient. Where that is so, the cases have generally held that the physician is armed with a privilege to keep the information from the patient, and we think it clear that portents of that type may justify the physician in action he deems medically warranted. The critical inquiry is whether the physician responded to a sound medical judgment that communication of the risk information would present a threat to the patient's well-being.

The physician's privilege to withhold information for therapeutic reasons must be carefully circumscribed, however, for otherwise it might devour the disclosure rule itself. The privilege does not accept the paternalistic notion that the physician may remain silent simply because divulgence might prompt the patient to forego therapy the physician feels the patient really needs. That attitude presumes instability or perversity for even the normal patient, and runs counter to the foundation principle that the patient should and ordinarily can make the choice for himself. Nor does the privilege contemplate operation save where the patient's reaction to risk information, as reasonably foreseen by the physician, is menacing. And even in a situation of that kind, disclosure to a close relative with a view to securing consent to the proposed treatment may be the only alternative open to the physician.

Although this is the first and best known statement in any jurisdiction in the United States on the duty to disclose in negligence, it must be remembered that it is still only a minority of jurisdictions which adopt this view. For a full account see Louisell & Williams *Medical Malpractice* (1982).

(B)   CANADA.

Reibl v Hughes (1980) 114 DLR (3d), 1 at pp 12–13:

Laskin CJC: I think the Ontario Court of Appeal went too far, when dealing with the standard of disclosure of risks, in saying, as it did in the passage of its reasons just quoted, that 'the manner in which the nature and degree of risk is explained to a particular patient is better left to the judgment of the doctor in dealing with the man before him'. Of course, it can be tested by expert medical evidence but that too is not determinative. The patient may have expressed certain concerns to the doctor and the latter is obliged to meet them in a reasonable way. What the doctor knows or should know that the particular patient deems relevant to a decision whether to undergo prescribed treatment goes equally to his duty of disclosure as do the material risks recognised as a matter of required medical knowledge.

It is important to examine this issue in greater detail. The Ontario Court of Appeal appears to have adopted a professional medical standard, not only for determining what are the material risks that should be disclosed but also, and concurrently, for determining whether there has been a breach of the duty of disclosure. This was also the approach of the trial Judge, notwithstanding that on the facts he found against the defendant. (Indeed, the trial Judge seems also to have overstated the duty of disclosure. The Court of Appeal, in contrast, seems to have understated it. Generally, the failure to mention statistics should not affect the duty to inform nor be a factor in deciding whether the duty has been breached.) To allow expert medical evidence to determine what risks are material and, hence, should be disclosed and, correlatively, what risks are not material is to hand over to the medical profession the entire question of the scope of the duty of disclosure, including the question whether there has been a breach of that duty. Expert medical evidence is, of course, relevant to findings as to the risks that reside in or are a result of recommended surgery or other treatment. It will also have a bearing on their materiality but this is not a question that is to be concluded on the basis of the expert medical evidence alone. The issue under consideration is a different issue from that involved where the question is whether the doctor carried out his professional activities by applicable professional standards. What is under consideration here is the patient's right to know what risks are involved in undergoing or foregoing certain surgery or other treatment.

The materiality of non-disclosure of certain risks to an informed decision is a matter for the trier of fact, a matter on which there would, in all likelihood, be medical evidence but also other evidence, including evidence from the patient or from members of his family. It is, of course, possible that a particular patient may waive aside any question of risks and be quite prepared to submit to the surgery or treatment, whatever they be. Such a situation presents no difficulty. Again, it may be the case that a particular patient may, because of emotional factors, be unable to cope with facts relevant to recommended surgery or treatment and the doctor may, in such a case, be justified in withholding or generalising information as to which he would otherwise be required to be more specific.

(C) ENGLAND. 1. *Hills v Potter* [1984] 1 WLR 641 at 652–3:

Hirst J: Before I state my conclusions as to the law, I think it is important to note that the appellation 'doctrine of informed consent', which has come to be used to categorise the principles laid down in these North American cases, may be misleading if it is interpreted as signifying a class of duty dependent on acceptance of these cases. For it is quite clear from the English cases cited above that on any view English law does require the surgeon to supply to the patient information to enable the plaintiff to decide whether or not to undergo the operation. This accords with the practice of all the surgical experts in the case; and also, of course, that of the first defendant himself. The distinctive features of the doctrine as laid down in the Canadian and United States cases relate to the amount of information required and, perhaps more importantly, the standard by which the surgeon's conduct is to be judged.

My conclusions are as follows: 1. In my judgment, McNair J in *Bolam v Friern Barnet Hospital Management Committee* [1957] 1 WLR 582 applied the medical standard to advice prior to an operation, as well as to diagnosis and to treatment. This standard is clearly applied without differentiation to all three aspects of the case which McNair J described as 'the three major points': see pp 586–587, 590.

The fact that the plaintiff was mentally sick did not affect the legal principle, but might of course affect its application to the facts of the particular case, as McNair J himself said, at p 590.

2. Although the House of Lords in *Maynard v West Midlands Regional Health Authority* [1984] 1 WLR 634, did not specifically affirm McNair J in relation to advice as such, the general and unqualified approval given to *Bolam's* case in the House of Lords makes it quite impossible for me to depart from McNair J's decision, especially as it has been applied to advice in the other three first instance cases which I have cited. Indeed I respectfully agree with, and would have thought it right to follow, these first instance cases even without the authoritative guidance contained in *Maynard's* case, which they preceded. I for my part doubt whether the distinction in the medical context between advice on the one hand and diagnosis and treatment on the other is really so clear or so stark as Mr Stone forcefully submitted.

3. I therefore reject Mr Stone's argument that I should apply the standard laid down in the Canadian and cited United States cases, and I hold that the proper standard is the medical standard in accordance with *Bolam v Friern Hospital Management Committee* [1957] 1 WLR 582 and the other first instance cases.

4. This, of course, does not mean that I treat the decisions of the Supreme Court of Canada and the cited United States cases with other than the utmost respect. But in my judgment the principles there laid down could only be incorporated in English law as a result of the decision of an appellate court, which would have to balance the considerations canvassed so cogently in the Canadian and United States judgments against the very formidable problems and potential liabilities which would undoubtedly confront medical men if these principles were applied here. It is common knowledge that the extent of these problems and potential liabilities has caused serious anxiety in the United States, whence the principles laid down in the Canadian decisions are derived (see for example the discussion of this topic in the article '*Informed consent to medical treatment*' by Gerald Robertson in 97 LQR 102, particularly at paragraph (*c*) at p 108). I am bound to say that if the point were free from authority I should be very reluctant indeed to apply the Canadian and United States principles here.

I do not accept Mr Stone's argument that by adopting the *Bolam* principle, the court in effect abdicates its power of decision to the doctors. In every case the court must be satisfied that the standard contended for on their behalf accords with that upheld by a substantial body of medical opinion, and that this body of medical opinion is both respectable and responsible, and experienced in this particular field of medicine.

Sidaway v Board of Governors of the Bethlem Royal Hospital [1985] AC 871, [1985] 1 All ER 643.

Facts: The plaintiff, who had suffered recurrent pain in her neck, right shoulder and arms, underwent an operation in 1974 which was performed by a senior neuro-surgeon at the first defendant's hospital. The operation, even if performed with proper care and skill, carried an inherent, material risk, which was put at between one and two per cent, of damage to the spinal column and the nerve roots. The risk of damage to the spinal column was substantially less than to a nerve root but the consequences were much more serious. In consequence of the operation the plaintiff was severely disabled. Her monetary loss was assessed at £67,500.

The plaintiff claimed damages for negligence against the hospital and the executors of the deceased surgeon, the second defendants. She relied solely on the alleged failure of the surgeon to disclose or explain to her the risks inherent in, or special to, the operation which he had advised. Skinner J found that the surgeon did not tell the plaintiff that it was an operation of choice rather than necessity; that whilst he had told her of the possibility of disturbing a nerve root and the consequences, he did not refer to the danger of damage to the spinal cord; that in refraining from informing her of those two factors he was following a practice which in 1974 would have been accepted as proper by a responsible body of skilled and experienced neuro-surgeons; and applying the test formulated in *Bolam v Friern Barnet Management Committee* [1957] 1 WLR 582 that the standard of care was that of the ordinary skilled man exercising and professing to have that special skill and that a doctor was not negligent if he acted in accordance with the practice accepted at the time as proper by a responsible body of medical opinion, notwithstanding that other doctors adopted different practices, the judge dismissed the plaintiff's claim. The Court of Appeal affirmed Skinner J's decision.

The majority view was given by Lords Bridge, Templeman and Keith.

Lord Bridge [at pp 501–505]: Broadly, a doctor's professional functions may be divided into three phases: diagnosis, advice and treatment. In performing his functions of diagnosis and treatment, the standard by which English law measures the doctor's duty of care to his patient is not open to doubt. 'The test is the standard of the ordinary skilled man exercising and professing to have that special skill.' These are the words of McNair J in *Bolam v Friern Hospital Management Committee* [1957] 1 WLR 582 at 586, approved by this House in *Whitehouse v Jordan* [1981] 1 WLR 246 at 258, *per* Lord Edmund-Davies and in *Maynard v West Midlands Regional Health Authority* [1984] 1 WLR 634 at 638 *per* Lord Scarman. The test is conveniently referred to as the *Bolam* test. In *Maynard's* case, Lord Scarman, with whose speech the other four members of the Appellate Committee agreed, further cited with approval, at 638 the words of Lord President Clyde in *Hunter v Hanley*, 1955 SLT 213 at 217:

> In the realm of diagnosis and treatment there is ample scope for genuine difference of opinion and one man clearly is not negligent merely because his conclusion differs from that of other professional men . . . The true test for establishing negligence in diagnosis or treatment on the part of a doctor is whether he has been proved to be guilty of such failure as no doctor of ordinary skill would be guilty of if acting with ordinary care . . .

The language of the *Bolam* test clearly requires a different degree of skill from a specialist in his own special field than from a general practitioner. In the field of neuro-surgery it would be necessary to substitute for Lord President Clyde's phrase 'no doctor of ordinary skill,' the phrase 'no neuro-surgeon of ordinary skill'. All this is elementary and, in the light of the two recent decisions of this House referred to, firmly established law.

The important question which this appeal raises is whether the law imposes any, and if so what, different criterion as the measure of the medical man's duty of care to his patient when giving advice with respect to a proposed course of treatment. It is clearly right to recognise that a conscious adult patient of sound mind is entitled to decide for himself whether or not he will submit to a particular course of treatment proposed by the doctor, most significantly surgical treatment under general anaesthesia. This entitlement is the foundation of the doctrine of 'informed consent' which has led in certain American jurisdictions to decisions, and in the Supreme Court of Canada, to dicta, on which the appellant relies, which would oust the *Bolam* test and substitute an 'objective' test of a doctor's duty to advise the patient of the advantages and disadvantages of undergoing the treatment proposed and more particularly to advise the patient of the risks involved.

There are, it appears to me, at least theoretically, two extreme positions which could be taken. It could be argued that, if the patient's consent is to be fully informed, the doctor must specifically warn him of *all* risks involved in the treatment offered, unless he has some sound clinical reason not to do so. Logically, this would seem to be the extreme to which a truly objective criterion of the doctor's duty would lead. Yet this position finds no support from any authority, to which we have been referred, in any jurisdiction. It seems to be generally accepted that there is no need to warn of the risks inherent in all surgery under general anaesthesia. This is variously explained on the ground that the patient may be expected to be aware of such risks or that they are relatively remote. If the law is to impose on the medical profession a duty to warn of risks to secure 'informed consent' independently of accepted medical opinion of what is appropriate, neither of these explanations for confining the duty to special as opposed to general surgical risks seems to me wholly convincing.

At the other extreme it could be argued that, once the doctor has decided what treatment is, on balance of advantages and disadvantages, in the patient's best interest, he should not alarm the patient by volunteering a warning of any risk involved, however grave and substantial, unless specifically asked by the patient. I cannot believe that contemporary medical opinion would support this view, which would effectively exclude the patient's right to decide in the very type of case where it is most important that he should be in a position to exercise that right and, perhaps even more significantly, to seek a second opinion as to whether he should submit himself to the significant risk which has been drawn to his attention. I should perhaps add at this point, although the issue does not strictly arise in this appeal, that, when questioned specifically by a patient of apparently sound mind about risks involved in a particular treatment proposed, the doctor's duty must, in my opinion, be to answer both truthfully and as fully as the questioner requires.

The decision mainly relied on to establish a criterion of the doctor's duty to disclose the risks inherent in a proposed treatment which is prescribed by the law and can be applied independently of any medical opinion or practice is that of the District of Columbia Circuit Court of Appeals in *Canterbury v Spence*, 464 F 2d 772. The judgment of the Court (Wright, Leventhal and Robinson JJ), delivered by Robinson J, expounds the view that an objective criterion of what is a sufficient disclosure of risk is necessary to ensure that the patient is enabled to make an intelligent decision and cannot be left to be determined by the doctors. He said, at 784:

Respect for the patient's right of self-determination on particular therapy demands a standard set by law for physicians rather than one which physicians may or may not impose upon themselves.

In an attempt to define the objective criterion it is said, at 787, that 'the issue on non-disclosure must be approached from the viewpoint of the reasonableness of the physician's informational needs.' A risk is required to be disclosed 'when a reasonable person, in what the physician knows or should know to be the patient's position, would be likely to attach significance to the risk or cluster of risks in deciding whether or not to forego the proposed therapy': 464 F 2d 772 at 787. The judgment adds, at 788: 'Whenever non-disclosure of particular risk information is open to debate by reasonable-minded men, the issue is for the finder of facts'.

The court naturally recognises exceptions from the duty laid down in the case of an unconscious patient, an immediate emergency, or a case where the doctor can establish that disclosure would be harmful to the patient.

Expert medical evidence will be needed to indicate the nature and extent of the risks and benefits involved in the treatment (and presumably of any alternative course). But the court affirms, at 792: 'Experts are unnecessary to a showing of the materiality of a risk to a patient's decision on treatment, or to the reasonably, expectable effect of risk disclosure on the decision'. In English law, if this doctrine were adopted, expert medical opinion as to whether a particular risk should or should not have been disclosed would presumably be inadmissible in evidence.

I recognise the logical force of the *Canterbury* doctrine, proceeding from the premise that the patient's right to make his own decision must at all costs be safeguarded against the kind of medical paternalism which assumes that 'doctor knows best'. But, with all respect, I regard the doctrine as quite impractical in application for three principal reasons. First, it gives insufficient weight to the realities of the doctor/patient relationship. A very wide variety of factors must enter into a doctor's clinical judgment not only as to what treatment is appropriate for a particular patient, but also as to how best to communicate to the patient the significant factors necessary to enable the patient to make an informed decision whether to undergo the treatment. The doctor cannot set out to educate the patient to his own standard of medical knowledge of all the relevant factors involved. He may take the view, certainly with some patients, that the very fact of his volunteering, without being asked, information of some remote risk involved in the treatment proposed, even though he describes it as remote, may lead to that risk assuming an undue significance in the patient's calculations. Secondly, it would seem to me quite unrealistic in any medical negligence action to confine the expert medical evidence to an explanation of the primary medical factors involved and to deny the court the benefit of evidence of medical opinion and practice on the particular issue of disclosure which is under consideration. Thirdly, the objective test which *Canterbury* propounds seems to me to be so imprecise as to be almost meaningless. If it is to be left to individual judges to decide for themselves what 'a reasonable person in the patient's position' would consider a risk of sufficient significance that he should be told about it, the outcome of litigation in this field is likely to be quite unpredictable.

I note with interest from a learned article entitled 'Informed Consent to Medical Treatment' by Mr Gerald Robertson, Lecturer in Law, University of Leicester (1981) 97 LQR 102, 108, that only a minority of states in the United States of America have chosen to follow *Canterbury* and that since 1975 'there has been a growing tendency for individual States to enact legislation which severely curtails the operation of the doctrine of informed consent'. I should also add that I find particularly cogent and convincing the reasons given for declining to follow *Canterbury* by the Supreme Court of Virginia in *Bly v Rhoads* 222 SE 2d 783 (1976).

Having rejected the *Canterbury* doctrine as a solution to the problem of safeguarding the patient's right to decide whether he will undergo a particular treatment advised by his doctor, the question remains whether that right is sufficiently safeguarded by the application of the *Bolam* test without qualification to the determination of the question what risks inherent in a proposed treatment should be disclosed. The case against a simple application of the *Bolam* test is cogently stated by Laskin CJC, giving the judgment of the Supreme Court of Canada in *Reibl v Hughes* (1980) 114 DLR (3d) 1 at 13:

> To allow expert medical evidence to determine what risks are material and, hence, should be disclosed and, correlatively, what risks are not material is to hand over to the medical profession the entire question of the scope of the duty of disclosure, including the question whether there has been a breach of that duty. Expert medical evidence is, of course, relevant to findings as to the risks that reside in or are a result of recommended surgery or other treatment. It will also have a bearing on their materiality but this is not a question that is to be concluded on the basis of the expert medical evidence alone. The issue under consideration is a different issue from that involved where the question is whether the doctor carried out his professional activities by applicable professional standards. What is under consideration here is the patient's right to know what risks are involved in undergoing or foregoing certain surgery or other treatment.

I fully appreciate the force of this reasoning, but can only accept it subject to the important qualification that a decision what degree of disclosure of risks is best calculated to assist a particular patient to make a rational choice as to whether or not to undergo a particular treatment must primarily be a matter or clinical judgment. It would follow from this that the issue whether non-disclosure in a particular case should be condemned as a breach of the doctor's duty of care is an issue to be decided primarily on the basis of expert medical evidence, applying the *Bolam* test. But I do not see that this approach involves the necessity 'to hand over to the medical profession the entire question of the scope of the duty of disclosure, including the question whether there has been a breach of that duty'. Of course, if there is a conflict of evidence as to whether a responsible body of medical opinion approves of non-disclosure in a particular case, the judge will have to resolve that conflict. But even in a case where, as here, no expert witness in the relevant medical field condemns the non-disclosure as being in conflict with accepted and responsible medical practice, I am of opinion that the judge might in certain circumstances come to the conclusion that disclosure of a particular risk was so obviously necessary to an informed choice on the part of the patient that no reasonably prudent medical man would fail to make it. The kind of case I have in mind would be an operation involving a substantial risk of grave adverse consequences, as, for example, the ten per cent risk of a stroke from the operation which was the subject of the Canadian case of *Reibl v Hughes* (1980) 114 DLR (3d) 1. In such a case, in the absence of some cogent clinical reason why the patient should not be informed, a doctor, recognising and respecting his patient's right of decision, could hardly fail to appreciate the necessity for an appropriate warning.

In the instant case I can see no reasonable ground on which the judge could properly reject the conclusion to which the unchallenged medical evidence led in the application of the *Bolam* test. The trial judge's assessment of the risk at one to two per cent covered both nerve root and spinal cord damage and covered a spectrum of possible ill effects 'ranging from the mild to the catastrophic'. In so far as it is possible and appropriate to measure such risks in percentage terms—some of the expert medical witnesses called expressed a marked and understandable reluctance to do so—the risk of damage to the spinal cord of such severity as the appellant in fact suffered was, it would appear, certainly less than one per cent. But there is no yardstick either in the judge's findings or in the evidence to measure what fraction of one per cent that risk represented. In these circumstances, the appellant's expert witness's agreement that the non-disclosure complained of accorded with a practice accepted as proper by a responsible body of neuro-surgical opinion afforded the respondents a complete defence to the appellant's claim.

Lord Templeman [at pp 506G–509]: In my opinion a simple and general explanation of the nature of the operation should have been sufficient to alert Mrs Sidaway to the fact that a major operation was to be performed and to the possibility that something might go wrong at or near the site of the spinal cord or the site of the nerve root causing serious injury. If, as the judge held, Mr Falconer probably referred expressly to the possibility of damage to a nerve root and to the consequences of such damage, this warning could only have reinforced the possibility of something going wrong in the course of a delicate operation performed in a vital area with resultant damage. In view of the fact that Mr Falconer recommended the operation, Mrs Sidaway must have been told or could have assumed that Mr Falconer considered that the possibilities of damage were sufficiently remote to be ignored. Mrs Sidaway could have asked questions. If she had done so, she could and should have been informed that there was an aggregate risk of between one per cent and two per cent risk of some damage either to the spinal cord or to a nerve root resulting in injury which might vary from irritation to paralysis. But to my mind this further information would only have reinforced the obvious, with the assurance that the maximum risk of damage, slight or serious, did not exceed two per cent. Mr Falconer may reasonably have taken the view that Mrs Sidaway might be confused, frightened or misled by more detailed information which she was unable to evaluate at a time when she was suffering from stress, pain and anxiety. A patient may prefer that the doctor should not thrust too much detail at the patient. We do not know how Mr Falconer explained the operation to Mrs Sidaway and we do not know the reasons for the terms in which he couched his explanation.

On the assumption that Mr Falconer explained that it was necessary to remove bone and free a nerve root from pressure near the spinal cord, it seems to me that the possibility of damage to a nerve root or to the spinal cord was obvious. The operation was skilfully performed but by mishap the remote risk of damage to the spinal cord unfortunately caused the disability from which Mrs Sidaway is now suffering. However much sympathy may be felt for Mrs Sidaway and however much in hindsight the operation may be regretted by her, the question now is whether Mr Falconer was negligent in the explanation which he gave.

In my opinion if a patient knows that a major operation may entail serious consequences, the patient cannot complain of lack of information unless the patient asks in vain for more information or unless there is some danger which by its nature or magnitude or for some other reason requires to be separately taken into account by the patient in order to reach a balanced judgment in deciding whether or not to submit to the operation. To make Mr Falconer liable for damages for negligence, in not expressly drawing Mrs Sidaway's attention to the risk of damage to the spinal cord and its consequences, Mrs Sidaway must show and fails to show that Mr Falconer was not entitled to assume, in the absence of questions from Mrs Sidaway, that his explanation of the nature of the operation was sufficient to alert Mrs Sidaway to the general danger of unavoidable and serious damage inherent in the operation but sufficiently remote to justify the operation. There is no reason to think that Mr Falconer was aware that, as Mrs Sidaway deposed, a specific warning and assessment of the risk of spinal cord damage would have influenced Mrs Sidaway to decline the operation although the general explanation which she was given resulted in her consenting to the operation.

There is no doubt that a doctor ought to draw the attention of a patient to a danger which may be special in kind or magnitude or special to the patient. In *Reibl v Hughes* (1980) 114 DLR (3d) 1, a surgeon advised an operation on the brain to avoid a threatened stroke. The surgeon knew or ought to have known that there was a four per cent chance that the operation might cause death and a ten per cent chance that the operation might precipitate the very stroke which the operation was designed to prevent. The patient ought to have been informed of these specific risks in order to be able to form a balanced judgment in deciding whether or not to submit to the operation.

When a patient complains of lack of information, the court must decide whether the patient has suffered harm from a general danger inherent in the operation or from some special danger. In the case of a general danger the court must decide whether the information afforded to the patient was sufficient to alert the patient to the possibility of serious harm of the kind in fact suffered. If the practice of the medical profession is to make express mention of a particular kind of danger, the court will have no difficulty in coming to the conclusion that the doctor ought to have referred expressly to this danger as a special danger unless the doctor can give reasons to justify the form or absence of warning adopted by him. Where the practice of the medical profession is divided or does not include express mention, it will be for the court to determine whether the harm suffered is an example of a general danger inherent in the nature of the operation and if so whether the explanation afforded to the patient was sufficient to alert the patient to the general dangers of which the harm suffered is an example. If a doctor conscientiously endeavours to explain the arguments for and against a major operation and the possibilities of benefiting and the dangers, the court will be slow to conclude that the doctor has been guilty of a breach of duty owed to the patient merely because the doctor omits some specific item of information. It is for the court to decide, after hearing the doctor's explanation, whether the doctor has in fact been guilty of a breach of duty with regard to information.

A doctor offers a patient diagnosis, advice and treatment. The objectives, sometimes conflicting, sometimes unattainable, of the doctor's services are the prolongation of life, the restoration of the patient to full physical and mental health and the alleviation of pain. Where there are dangers that treatment may produce results, direct or indirect, which are harmful to the patient, those dangers must be weighed by the doctor before he recommends the treatment. The patient is entitled to consider and reject the recommended treatment and for that purpose to understand the doctor's advice and the possibility of harm resulting from the treatment.

I do not subscribe to the theory that the patient is entitled to know everything nor to the theory that the doctor is entitled to decide everything. The relationship between doctor and patient is contractual in origin, the doctor performing services in consideration for fees payable by the patient. The doctor, obedient to the high standards set by the medical profession impliedly contracts to act at all times in the best interests of the patient. No doctor in his senses would impliedly contract at the same time to give to the patient all the information available to the doctor as a result of the doctor's training and experience and as a result of the doctor's diagnosis of the patient. An obligation to give a patient all the information available to the doctor would often be inconsistent with the doctor's contractual obligation to have regard to the patient's best interests. Some information might confuse, other information might alarm a particular patient. Whenever the occasion arises for the doctor to tell the patient the results of the doctor's diagnosis, the possible methods of treatment and the advantages and disadvantages of the recommended treatment, the doctor must decide in the light of his training and experience and in the light of his knowledge of the patient what should be said and how it should be said. At the same time the doctor is not entitled to make the final decision with regard to treatment which may have disadvantages or dangers. Where the patient's health and future are at stake, the patient must make the final decision. The patient is free to decide whether or not to submit to treatment recommended by the doctor and therefore the doctor impliedly contracts to provide information which is adequate to enable the patient to reach a balanced judgment, subject always to the doctor's own obligation to say and do nothing which the doctor is satisfied will be harmful to the patient. When the doctor himself is considering the possibility of a major operation the doctor is able, with his medical training, with his knowledge of the patient's medical history and with his objective position to make a balanced judgment as to whether the operation should be performed or not. If the doctor making a balanced judgment advises the patient to submit to the operation, the patient is entitled to reject that advice for reasons which are rational, or irrational, or for no reason. The duty of the doctor in these circumstances, subject to his overriding duty to have regard to the best interests of the patient, is to provide the patient with information which will enable the patient to make a balanced judgment if the patient chooses to make a balanced judgment. A patient may make an unbalanced judgment because he is deprived of adequate information. A patient may also make an unbalanced judgment if he is provided with too much information and is made aware of possibilities which he is not capable of assessing because of his lack of medical training, his prejudices or his personality. Thus the provision of too much information may prejudice the attainment of the objective of restoring the patient's health. The obligation of the doctor to have regard to the best interests of the patient but at the same time to make available to the patient sufficient information to enable the patient to reach a balanced judgment if he chooses to do so has not altered because those obligations have ceased or may have ceased to be contractual and become a matter of duty of care. In order to make a balanced judgment if he chooses to do so, the patient needs to be aware of the general dangers and of any special dangers in each case without exaggeration or concealment. At the end of the day, the doctor, bearing in mind the best interests of the patient and bearing in mind the patient's right of information which will enable the patient to make a balanced judgment must decide what information should be given to the patient and in what terms that information should be couched. The court will award damages against the doctor if the court is satisfied that the doctor blundered and that the patient was deprived of information which was necessary for the purposes I have outlined. In the present case on the judge's findings I am satisfied that adequate information was made available to Mrs Sidaway and that the appeal should therefore be dismissed.

Lord Keith concurred with Lord Bridge. By contrast, Lord Diplock, while concurring in the result, differed significantly in his analysis of the doctor's duty to disclose.

Lord Diplock [at pp 498–9]: The merit of the *Bolam* test is that the criterion of the duty of care owed by a doctor to his patient is whether he has acted in accordance with a practice accepted as proper by a body of responsible and skilled medical opinion. There may be a number of different practices which are likely to alter with advances in medical knowledge. Experience shows that, to the great benefit of human kind, they have done so, particularly in the recent past. That is why fatal diseases such as smallpox and tuberculosis have within living memory become virtually extinct in countries where modern medical care is generally available.

In English jurisprudence the doctor's relationship with his patient which gives rise to the normal duty of care to exercise his skill and judgment to improve the patient's health in any particular respect in which the patient has sought his aid, has hitherto been treated as single comprehensive duty covering all the ways in which a doctor is called upon to exercise his skill and judgment in the improvement of the physical or mental condition of the patient for which his services either as a general practitioner or specialist have been engaged. This general duty is not subject to dissection into a number of component parts to which different criteria of what satisfy the duty of care apply, such as diagnosis, treatment, advice (including warning of any risks of something going wrong however skilfully the treatment advised is carried out.) The *Bolam* case itself embraced failure to advise the patient of the risk involved in the electric shock treatment as one of the allegations of negligence against the surgeon as well as negligence in the actual carrying out of treatment in which that risk did result in injury to the patient. The same criteria were applied to both these aspects of the surgeon's duty of care. In modern medicine and surgery such dissection of the various things a doctor had to do in the exercise of his whole duty of care owed to his patient is neither legally meaningful nor medically practicable. Diagnosis itself may involve exploratory surgery, the insertion of drugs by injection (or vaccination) involves intrusion upon the body of the patient and oral treatment by drugs although it involves no physical intrusion by the doctor on the patient's body may in the case of particular patients involve serious and unforeseen risks.

My Lords, no convincing reason has in my view been advanced before your Lordships that would justify treating the *Bolam* test as doing anything less than laying down a principle of English law that is comprehensive and applicable to every aspect of the duty of care owed by a doctor to his patient in the exercise of his healing functions as respects that patient.

Lord Scarman also differed markedly from the majority in his analysis.

Lord Scarman [at pp 488, 490–492, 492, 493–496]: The right of 'self-determination'— the description applied by some to what is no more and no less than the right of a patient to determine for himself whether he will or will not accept the doctor's advice—is vividly illustrated where the treatment recommended is surgery. A doctor who operates without the consent of his patient is, save in cases of emergency or mental disability, guilty of the civil wrong of trespass to the person: he is also guilty of the criminal offence of assault. The existence of the patient's right to make his own decision, which may be seen as a basic human right protected by the common law, is the reason why a doctrine embodying a right of the patient to be informed of the risks of surgical treatment has been developed in some jurisdictions in the USA and has found favour with the Supreme Court of Canada. Known as the 'doctrine of informed consent', it amounts to this: where there is a 'real' or a 'material' risk inherent in the proposed operation (however competently and skilfully performed) the question whether and to what extent a patient should be warned before he gives his consent is to be answered not by reference to medical practice but by accepting as a matter of law that, subject to all proper exceptions (of which the court, not the profession, is the judge), a patient has a right to be informed of the risks inherent in the treatment which is proposed. The profession, it is said, should not be judge in its own cause: or, less emotively but more correctly, the courts should not allow medical opinion as to what is best for the patient to override the patient's right to decide for himself whether he will submit to the treatment offered him. It will be necessary for the House to consider in this appeal what is involved in the doctine and whether it, or any modification of it, has any place in English law.

Unless statute has intervened to restrict the range of judge-made law, the common law enables the judges, when faced with a situation where a right recognised by law is not adequately protected, either to extend existing principles to cover the situation or to apply an existing remedy to redress the injustice. There is here no novelty: but merely the application of the principle ubi jus ibi remedium. If, therefore, the failure to warn a patient of the risks inherent in the operation which is recommended does constitute a failure to respect the patient's right to make his own decision, I can see no reason in principle why, if the risk materialises and injury or damage is caused, the law should not recognise and enforce a right in the patient to compensation by way of damages.

For the reasons already given, the *Bolam* principle does not cover the situation. The facts of this very case expose its limitation. Mr Falconer lacked neither care for his patient's health and well-being nor professional skill in the advice and treatment which he offered. But did he overlook or disregard his patient's right to determine for herself whether or not to have the operation? Did he fail to provide her with the information necessary for her to make a prudent decision? There is, in truth, no evidence to answer these questions. Mrs Sidaway's evidence was not accepted: and Mr Falconer was dead. Assume, however, that he did overlook this aspect of his patient's situation. Since neither his advice nor his treatment could be faulted on the *Bolam* test, his patient may have been deprived of the opportunity to exercise her right of decision in the light of information which she, had she received it, might reasonably have considered to be of importance in making up her mind. On the *Bolam* view of the law, therefore, even if she established that she was so deprived by the lack of a warning, she would have no remedy in negligence unless she could also prove that there was no competent and respected body of medical opinion which was in favour of no warning. Moreover, the tort of trespass to the person would not provide her with a remedy: for Mrs Sidaway did consent to the operation. Her complaint is that her consent resulted from ignorance of a risk, known by the doctor but not made known by him to her, inherent in the operation. Nor would the law of contract offer her a sure way forward. Medical treatment, as in her case, is frequently given today under arrangements outside the control of the law of contract.

One point is clear, however. If failure to warn of risk is actionable in English law, it must be because it is in the circumstances a breach of the doctor's duty of care: in other words, the doctor must be shown to be negligent. English law has not accepted a 'no-fault' basis for the liability of a doctor to compensate a patient for injury arising in the course of medical treatment. If, however, the *Bolam* principle is to be applied to the exclusion of any other test to advice and warning, there will be cases in which a patient who suffers injury though ignorance of a risk known to the doctor has no remedy. Is there any difficulty in holding that the doctor's duty of care is sufficiently extensive to afford a patient in that situation a remedy, if as a result she suffers injury or damage? I think not. The root principle of common law negligence is to 'take reasonable care to avoid acts or omissions which you can reasonably foresee would be likely to injure your neighbour': *Donoghue v Stevenson* [1932] AC 562 at 580 *per* Lord Atkin. If it be recognised that a doctor's duty of care extends not only to the health and well-being of his patient but also to a proper respect for his patient's rights, the duty to warn can be seen to be a part of the doctor's duty of care.

It is, I suggest, a sound and reasonable proposition that the doctor should be required to exercise care in respecting the patient's right of decision. He must acknowledge that in very many cases factors other than the purely medical will play a significant part in his patient's decision-making process. The doctor's concern is with health and the relief of pain. These are the medical objectives. But a patient may well have in mind circumstances, objectives, and values which he may reasonably not make known to the doctor but which may lead him to a different decision from that suggested by a purely medical opinion. The doctor's duty can be seen, therefore, to be one which requires him not only to advise as to medical treatment but also to provide his patient with the information needed to enable the patient to consider and balance the medical advantages and risks alongside other relevant matters, such as, for example, his family, business or social responsibilities of which the doctor may be only partially, if at all, informed.

I conclude, therefore, that there is room in our law for a legal duty to warn a patient of the risks inherent in the treatment proposed, and that, if such a duty be held to exist, its proper place is as an aspect of the duty of care owed by the doctor to his patient. I turn, therefore, to consider whether a duty to warn does exist in our law and, if it does, its proper formulation and the conditions and exceptions to which it must be subject.

Some American courts have recognised such a duty. They have seen it as arising from the patient's right to know of material risks, which itself is seen to arise from the patient's right to decide for himself whether or not to submit to the medical treatment proposed. This is the doctrine of informed consent, to which I have already briefly referred. . . .

There can be little doubt that policy explains the divergence of view. The proliferation of medical malpractice suits in the USA has led some courts and some legislatures to curtail or even to reject the operation of the doctrine in an endeavour to restrict the liability of the doctor and so discourage the practice of 'defensive medicine'—by which is meant the practice of doctors advising and undertaking the treatment which they think is legally safe even though they may believe that it is not the best for their patient.

The danger of defensive medicine developing in this country clearly exists—though the absence of the lawyer's 'contingency fee' (a percentage of the damages for him as his fee if he wins the case but nothing if he loses) may make it more remote. However that may be, in matters of civil wrong or tort, courts are concerned with legal principle: if policy problems emerge, they are best left to the legislature: *McLoughlin v O'Brian* [1983] 1 AC 410. . . .

In my judgment the merit of the propositions enunciated in *Canterbury v Spence* 464 F 2d 772 is that without excluding medical evidence they set a standard and formulate a test of the doctor's duty the effect of which is that the court determines the scope of the duty and decides whether the doctor has acted in breach of his duty. This result is achieved first by emphasis on the patient's 'right of self-determination' and secondly by the 'prudent patient' test. If the doctor omits to warn where the risk is such that in the court's view a prudent person in the patient's situation would have regarded it as significant, the doctor is liable.

The *Canterbury* propositions do indeed attach great importance to medical evidence, though judgment is for the court. First, medical evidence is needed in determining whether the risk is material, ie one which the doctor should make known to his patient. The two aspects of the risk, namely the degree of likelihood of it occurring and the seriousness of the possible injury if it should occur, can in most, if not all, cases be assessed only with the help of medical evidence. And secondly, medical evidence would be needed to assist the court in determining whether the doctor was justified on his assessment of his patient in withholding the warning.

My Lords, I think the *Canterbury* propositions reflect a legal truth which too much judicial reliance on medical judgment tends to obscure. In a medical negligence case where the issue is as to the advice and information given to the patient as to the treatment proposed, the available options, and the risk, the court is concerned primarily with a patient's right. The doctor's duty arises from his patient's rights. If one considers the scope of the doctor's duty by beginning with the right of the patient to make his own decision whether he will or will not undergo the treatment proposed, the right to be informed of significant risk and the doctor's corresponding duty are easy to understand: for the proper implementation of the right requires that the doctor be under a duty to inform his patient of the material risks inherent in the treatment. And it is plainly right that a doctor may avoid liability for failure to warn of a material risk if he can show that he reasonably believed that communication to the patient of the existence of the risk would be detrimental to the health (including, of course, the mental health) of his patient.

Ideally, the court should ask itself whether in the particular circumstances the risk was such that this particular patient would think it significant if he was told it existed. I would think that, as a matter of ethics, this is the test of the doctor's duty. The law, however, operates not in Utopia but in the world as it is: and such an inquiry would prove in practice to be frustrated by the subjectivity of its aim and purpose. The law can, however, do the next best thing, and require the court to answer the question, what would a reasonably prudent patient think significant if in the situation of this patient. The 'prudent patient' cannot, however, always provide the answer for the obvious reason that he is a norm (like the man on the Clapham omnibus), not a real person: and certainly not the patient himself. Hence there is the need that the doctor should have the opportunity of proving that he reasonably believed that disclosure of the risk would be damaging to his patient or contrary to his best interest. This is what the Americans call the doctor's 'therapeutic privilege'. Its true analysis is that it is a defence available to the doctor which, if he invokes it, he must prove. On both the test and the defence medical evidence will, of course, be of great importance.

The 'prudent patient' test calls for medical evidence. The materiality of the risk is a question for the court to decide upon all the evidence. Many factors call for consideration. The two critically important medical factors are the degree of probability of the risk materialising and the seriousness of possible injury, if it does. Medical evidence will be necessary so that the court may assess the degree of probability and the seriousness of possible injury. Another medical factor, upon which expert evidence will also be required, is the character of the risk. In the event of an operation is the risk common to all surgery, eg sepsis, cardiac arrest, and the other risks associated with surgery and the administration of an anaesthetic? Or is it specific to the particular operation under consideration? With the worldwide development and use of surgical treatment in modern times the court may well take the view that a reasonable person in the patient's situation would be unlikely to attach significance to the general risks; but it is not difficult to foresee circumstances particular to a patient in which even the general risks of surgery should be the subject of a warning by his doctor: eg a heart or lung or blood condition. Special risks inherent in a recommended operational procedure are more likely to be material. The risk of partial paralysis, as in this case where the purpose of the operation was not to save life but merely to relieve pain, illustrates the sort of question which may face first the doctor and later the court. Clearly medical evidence will be of the utmost importance in determining whether such a risk is material: but the question for the court is ultimately legal, not medical in character.

If the doctor admits or the court finds that on the prudent patient test he should have disclosed the risk, he has available the defence that he reasonably believed it to be against the best interest of his patient to disclose it. Here also medical evidence, including the evidence of the doctor himself, will be vital. The doctor himself will normally be an essential witness: and the reasonableness of his assessment may well need the support of independent medical testimony.

My conclusion as to the law is therefore this. To the extent that I have indicated I think that English law must recognise a duty of the doctor to warn his patient of risk inherent in the treatment which he is proposing: ᵳnd especially so, if the treatment be surgery. The critical limitation is that the duty is confined to material risk. The test of materiality is whether in the circumstances of the particular case the court is satisfied tʰat a reasonable person in the patient's position would be likely to attach significance to the risk. Even if the risk be material, the doctor will not be liable if upon a reasonable assessment of his patient's condition he takes the view that a warning would be detrimental to his patient's health.

Applying these principles to the present case, I ask first: has the appellant shown the risk of damage to the spinal cord to have been a material risk? The risk was slight—less than one per cent—but, if it were to materialise, it could result in severe injury. It was for the appellant, as plaintiff, to establish that the risk was so great that the doctor should have appreciated that it would be considered a significant factor by a prudent patient in the appellant's situation deciding whether or not to have the operation. The medical evidence even of Mr. Uttley, the appellant's expert witness, gets nowhere near establishing the materiality of the risk in the sense just outlined. It is, of course, possible that Mr Uttley's evidence was not directed to anything other than negligence in the *Bolam* sense. If so, the appellant, who now relies on the principle of informed consent, must accept the consequences: it was up to her to prove such a case, if she were seeking to establish it. Further, we do not know Mr Falconer's assessment of his patient. It is possible that, had he lived, he could have enlightened the court on much that would have been relevant. After an anxious consideration of the evidence I do not find it possible to say that it has been proved that Mr Falconer failed in his duty when he omitted—as we must assume that he did—to warn his patient of the risk of injury to the spinal cord.

At the end of the day, therefore, the substitution of the *Canterbury*, 464 F. 2d 772 propositions for the *Bolam* [1957] 1 WLR 582 test of duty and breach of duty does not avail the appellant because the evidence does not enable her to prove that Mr Falconer was in breach of his duty when he omitted the warning. Lack of evidence was always her difficulty; and it remains so, even though, contrary to the submission of the respondents, the law, in my view, recognises a right of a patient of sound understanding to be warned of material risks save in the exceptional circumstances to which I have referred. Accordingly, I would dismiss the appeal.

Understanding Sidaway

A. THE ISSUES

(a) Bolam or more?

If Lord Diplock's speech is regarded as out of line with prevailing views of medical law and its more recent developments—as it must—it is to the majority's view that we must look to determine whether the test adopted in *Bolam* for diagnosis, prognosis and treatment also applies as regards information and advice. If it does, the legal standard for disclosure is to be wholly determined by reference to the standard of the reasonable doctor which turns upon what is an acceptable level of disclosure to *a* (notice, not 'the') responsible body of medical practitioners.

The key words are those of Lord Bridge:

> . . . the issue whether non-disclosure in a particular case should be condemned as a breach of the doctor's duty of care is an issue to be decided primarily on the basis of expert medical evidence, applying the *Bolam* test.

What can Lord Bridge mean by the qualifying adverb 'primarily'? Can it be the same as 'rightly'? Sir John Donaldson MR said in the Court of Appeal in *Sidaway*:

> . . . I think that, in an appropriate case, a judge would be entitled to reject a unanimous medical view if he were satisfied that it was manifestly wrong and that the doctors must have been misdirecting themselves as to their duty in law.
>
> Another way of expressing my view of the test is to add just one qualifying word (which I have emphasised) to the law as Skinner J summarised it so that it would read:
>
> The duty is fulfilled if the doctor acts in accordance with a practice *rightly* accepted as proper by a body of skilled and experienced medical men.

If so, what do either or both of them mean by their words? Lord Templeman distances himself from *Bolam* when he states that:

> At the end of the day, the doctor, bearing in mind the best interests of the patient and bearing in mind the patient's right of information which will enable the patient to make a balanced judgment must decide what information should be given to the patient and in what terms that information should be couched. The court will award damages against the doctor if the court is satisfied that the doctor blundered and that the patient was deprived of information which was necessary for the purposes I have outlined.

Presumably a doctor 'blunders' when he does not behave 'rightly', ie the rule is a matter of law and not medical practice. If *Bolam simpliciter* does not represent the law of England this must mean that the views of the medical profession are not conclusive on disclosure. (This is not to say they are not relevant.) Is it possible to be more specific about what, in the view of the majority, the law looks for, to determine whether or not a doctor has complied with his legal obligation of disclosure?

(b)   What more?

There are two indications.

(i)   *'Substantial risk of grave adverse consequence'.* Lord Bridge considered that the court might regard as negligent non-disclosure in accordance with accepted medical practice if in the court's opinion: 'disclosure of a particular risk was so obviously necessary to an informed choice on the part of the patient that no reasonably prudent medical man would fail to make it'. His Lordship gave the example of an operation involving a substantial risk of grave adverse consequences, citing the 10% risk of a stroke in *Reibl v Hughes.* What can 'substantial' mean here? If it is to be regarded in terms of percentage of risks this must carry with it certain difficulties for the law's development. It has at least two drawbacks. The first is that it represents what is really a normative exercise (of what *ought* to be disclosed) as if it were an empirical matter. The danger is that this will suggest that the law's approach is a simplistic and arithmetic one, merely concerned with expert evidence on percentages.

The second objection lies in the danger that reference to percentage risks will merely provoke disagreements among experts as to what is the precise percentage in any particular case. Furthermore, it leaves undecided what percentage is the percentage beyond which a risk is regarded as substantial. Would the law not run the risk of having experts give evidence (hand on heart) that a particular risk has only a $3\frac{1}{2}\%$ chance of occurring if 4% had become the magic legal limit? A court would have no criteria by which to chose amongst conflicting expert views. The consequence could be that in effect the law would be handed back to the medical profession through experts.

In any event, discussion of the size of risk in isolation overlooks the fact that in matters of risk calculation it is not only whether a risk exists but of what happens if the risk eventuates which are relevant in determining whether a patient is prepared to run that risk. For example, if an operation may bring benefits but carries a high risk of causing a long term irritating rash, the patient may decide to run that risk whereas he may not decide to run what is represented as a low risk of having a permanent limp as a consequence of the same operation. It is all well and good to refer to 'grave adverse consequences'. The above example tends to suggest that the only judge of what is 'grave' or 'adverse' can be the patient.

(ii)   *General and special risks.* Lord Templeman draws a distinction between risks that are *general* and ones which are *special.* The *former* ordinarily would be known to the patient and no duty to disclose would arise. The latter may call for specific mention by the doctor. Lord Templeman seems to derive this distinction from the Canadian cases. In so doing, however, it is submitted, with respect, he may have read them in a way which others would not. The Canadian cases, particularly *Reibl v Hughes* and *White v Turner* are concerned with 'material risks': 'materiality' depending on what a reasonable patient would want to know. The distinction between 'general' and 'special' risks may be relevant to 'materiality' but is not determinative of it. For, ordinarily, a 'general' risk would not be 'material' because the 'reasonable patient' would be presumed to know it. By contrast, a 'special' risk may be 'material' but need not be. Thus, to categorise a risk as 'general' or 'special' is only tangentially relevant to the question of whether the doctor must disclose it.

White v Turner (1981)
120 DLR (3d) 269 at 284 Notice the analysis of Linden J in per Linden J:

Linden J: The meaning of 'material risks' and 'unusual or special risks' should now be considered. In my view, *material* risks are significant risks that pose a real threat to the patient's life, health or comfort. In considering whether a risk is material or immaterial, one must balance the severity of the potential result and the likelihood of its occurring. Even if there is only a small chance of serious injury of death, the risk may be considered material. On the other hand, if there is a significant chance of slight injury this too may be held to be material. As always in negligence law, what is a material risk will have to depend on the specific facts of each case.

As for 'unusual or special risks', these are those that are not ordinary, common, everyday matters. These are risks that are somewhat extraordinary, uncommon and not encountered every day, but they are known to occur occasionally. Though rare occurrences, because of their unusual or special character, the Supreme Court has declared that they should be described to a reasonable patient, even though they may not be 'material'. There may, of course, be an overlap between 'material risks' and 'unusual or special risks'. If a special or unusual risk is quite dangerous and fairly frequently encountered, it could be classified as a material risk. But even if it is not very dangerous or common, an unusual or special risk must be disclosed.

Even if it be the case that Lord Templeman has re-interpreted Canadian law, the distinction he draws is at least for the time being part of English law. It must therefore be asked what are 'general' and 'special' risks in law? One tenable distinction (though as we have seen *prima facie* irrelevant to the issue of 'materiality') could be that a 'general' risk is one that attends all medical procedures, eg risks from anaesthesia in operations. The reasonable patient would, in law, be expected to be aware of these. On this theory the doctor would not be under a specific duty to volunteer information, though he may do if especially questioned (cf Lord Scarman *infra*).

A 'special' risk, on the other hand, would be one inherent in the particular procedure either because of the nature of the procedure itself or because of *some* particular circumstances of the patient. This is the Canadian view. Is it Lord Templeman's? It may be his view. But even if it is, the distinction is unhelpful unless understood in the context of 'materiality' and the 'reasonable patient' which, as we shall see, Lord Templeman appears to reject.

The difficulty is, however, that what Lord Templeman says, suggests it isn't his view.

When a patient complains of lack of information, the court must decide whether the patient has suffered harm from a general danger inherent in the operation or from some special danger.

It is difficult to know how there can be a 'general danger' inherent in the operation as distinct from all operations. Indeed, on the basis of the words used by Lord Templeman the distinction between 'general' and 'special' becomes a distinction without a difference.

The important question then becomes, what is a 'special risk', because whatever else Lord Templeman means he seems to suggest that there may be a duty to disclose such a risk. He defines a special risk as one which may be 'special in kind or magnitude or special to the patient'. The reference to 'kind' or 'magnitude' does not seem to take us very far. This is because it is at least arguable that the only judge of what is special to the patient can be the patient himself ultimately. This would mean that Lord Templeman is embracing a legal rule which requires that the doctor must disclose that which the specific patient would need to know, a position expressed nowhere except in Oklahoma and rejected elsewhere in the judgment of Lord Templeman, ie a test going beyond the 'reasonable patient', which again Lord Templeman purports to reject in another part of his judgment. The meaning attributed to 'special to the patient' is further rendered imprecise by Lord Templeman's reference to *Reibl v Hughes* and the recourse to percentage risks. Percentage risks may be helpful as regards to 'magnitude' but seem to offer no assistance, without more, in determining whether the risk is 'special to the patient'.

The conclusion must be that Lord Templeman either embraces a test based upon what the particular patient would wish to know (though he rejects this) or his judgment suffers a degree of internal inconsistency.

(c)   *Lord Scarman*

The majority view opted for a duty of disclosure which, while rejecting the *Bolam* test *simpliciter*, leaves the exact nature of the duty somewhat obscure. Lord Scarman declares his commitment to 'the right of his patient to determine for himself whether he will or will not accept the doctor's advice concerning any proposed medical procedure'. This commitment could have led Lord Scarman to opt for either of two positions concerning the legal duty to disclose: the 'reasonable patient' test or the 'particular patient' test. As for the latter, as we have seen Lord Scarman concedes its validity in theory but regards it as Utopian. It may also be logically impossible to satisfy as a test since it may contemplate an infinite regression of question, answer and subsequent question:

Dr: 'So that is what happens. Is there anything else you need to know?'
Patient: 'I don't know, is there any more I can know?'
Dr: 'Yes, the following happens . . . now is there anything else you would like to know?'
Patient: 'I'm not sure, is there anything else you can tell me?'

Lord Scarman therefore opted for the 'reasonable or prudent patient test' as 'the next best thing' to give effect to the patient's right to self-determination. Crucial for the 'reasonable or prudent patient' test in all the jurisdictions in which it has been adopted is the notion of 'materiality', since it is only these risks which the doctor must disclose.

How does Lord Scarman define what risks are material? He states 'the test of materiality is whether in the circumstances of the particular case the court is satisfied that a reasonable person in the patient's position would be likely to attach significance to the risk'. As we have seen, Lord Scarman states that this 'is a question for the court to decide upon all the evidence'. Notice that Lord Scarman rejects the distinction between 'general' and 'special' risks as being relevant to 'materiality'. He states:

> With the worldwide development and use of surgical treatment in modern times the court may well take the view that a reasonable person in the patient's situation would be unlikely to attach significance to the general risks; but it is not difficult to foresee circumstances particular to a patient in which even the general risks of surgery should be the subject of a warning by his doctor, eg a heart or lung or blood condition. Special risks inherent in a recommended operational procedure are more likely to be material.

In keeping with all judicial statements which adopt the 'reasonable patient' test, Lord Scarman seeks to make it clear that the law does not make the duty to disclose absolute, but leaves the doctor with some discretion. This discretion has become known as the 'therapeutic privilege'. He states:

> Even if the risk be material, the doctor will not be liable if upon a reasonable assessment of his patient's condition he takes the view that a warning would be detrimental to his patient's health.

Two points must be made: the first is to ask whether in the result the 'reasonable patient' test plus 'therapeutic privilege' is the same as the test advanced by Lord Bridge. The answer must be that it is not the same. The difference lies in the fact that under Lord Scarman's (and the North American) view, the doctor has a *prima facie* duty to disclose, and must justify non-disclosure by reference to medical evidence concening the particular patient's circumstances.

Thus, it is for the doctor to advance and prove this justification. More significantly for general understanding of the *Sidaway* case, it means that the doctor may not excuse non-disclosure simply by stating that the patient fell into a *class* of patient to none of whom *a responsible body* of medical opinion would have disclosed the information as to risks. *Bolam simpliciter* would suggest such expcrt evidence would be conclusive (see Lord Diplock). The majority opinion would suggest that such evidence would not suffice if it referred to a class of patients only. It would have to be what a body of informed opinion would support should be disclosed to the patient in question and then, such evidence would only be of *primary* relevance and not determinative of breach of duty.

Lord Scarman would appear to reject the relevance of evidence referring to the patient as a member of a particular *class* of patient, and any reliance upon what a responsible body of medical opinion might have done. He states:

> . . . it is plainly right that a doctor may avoid liability for failure to warn of a material risk if he can show that he reasonably believed that communication to the patient of the existence of the risk would be detrimental to the health (including, of course, the mental health) of his patient.

The second point which arises concerns the potential implications of adopting the justification of therapeutic privilege. It needs tight control, otherwise, as the President's Commission argues in 'Making Health Care Decisions' (*op cit*) (pp 95–96):

> The obvious danger with such an exception is the ease with which it can swallow the rule, thereby legitimating wholesale noncompliance with the general obligation of disclosure.[35] Accordingly, some courts and commentators hold that the scope of therapeutic privilege should be severely circumscribed, and that, at the least, the privilege should not apply in situations when the potential harm to the patient from full disclosure would result not from the disclosure itself, but from a treatment decision the practitioner fears the patient might make as a result of the information disclosed.[36] More plausible claims of therapeutic privilege might involve ccrtain disclosures to patients previously known to be suicidal or those susceptible to serious physiological effect of stress, and in situations where there is strong reason to believe that a particular disclosure is likely to result in serious self-destructive behavior that could not be justified in terms of the patient's own long-term values and goals.
>
> Despite all the anecdotes about patients who committed suicide, suffered heart attacks, or plunged into prolonged depression upon being told 'bad news', little documentation exists for claims that informing patients is more dangerous to their health than not informing them, particularly when the informing is done in a sensitive and tactful fashion. On the contrary, as discussed further below, there is much to suggest that therapeutic privilege has been vastly overused as an excuse for not informing patients of facts they are entitled to know. In light of the values at stake, the burden of justification should fall upon those who allege that the informing process is dangerous to patient health, and information should be withheld on therapeutic grounds only when the harm of its disclosure is both highly probable and seriously disproportionate to the affront to self-determination.

Notes to extract
[35] 'The privilege does not accept the paternalistic notion that the physician may remain silent simply because divulgence might prompt the patient to forego therapy the physician feels the patient really needs'. *Canterbury v Spence* 464 F 2d 772, 789 (DCCir 1972). As is true of much of the *Canterbury* case, this language is taken from John R Waltz and Thomas W Scheuneman, *Informed Consent to Therapy*, 62 Nw

UL REV 628, 642 (1970). Other courts have not been as restrictive in their formulation of the privilege; '[A] physician may withhold disclosure of information regarding any untoward consequences of a treatment where full disclosure will be detrimental to the patient's total care and best interest'. *Nishi v Hartwell* 52 Haw 188, 191, 473 P 2d 116, 119 (1970).

MUCH ADO ABOUT NOTHING

The plaintiff may establish a breach of a duty properly to inform but will only succeed in the action if he can also show that the breach of duty caused him some injury. It would appear that injury here must mean more than a sense of grievance at not being told or misinformed. It must mean physical injury or nervous shock as understood in the law of torts (economic loss would be recoverable but would usually arise as a consequence of the physical injury of which complaint has already been made).

Some would say that the need to prove causation makes much of the heart-searching over the duty to inform irrelevant, since the patient may win the argument over the duty to inform yet lose the action because he cannot show causation. This is because it may be hard for him to say that if he were a 'reasonable person' he would still have refused the treatment concerned even with knowledge of the material (but undisclosed) risks, since evidence will have been given by doctors that the treatment involved was, all things being equal, medically desirable.

The question is, of course, whether the test of causation is based upon what the 'reasonable patient' would have consented to had he been properly informed or what the 'particular patient' would have consented to if informed. That the test for the duty to inform may be the 'reasonable patient' standard in some jurisdictions and edging towards it in English law, does not necessarily mean that causation should also be governed by a criterion of reasonableness.

The only English case in point is *Chatterton v Gerson* in which Bristow J appears to have adopted (*obiter*) a subjective test of causation. He appears to have regarded as relevant what she, the patient would have decided. As it happens, however, even in the face of her evidence as to what she felt she would have done, the judge determined that she would have consented because she was 'a lady desperate for pain relief'. Is this approach no more than using the 'reasonable patient' test as a yardstick by which to assess the particular patient's evidence? If this is so, does it not mean that the plaintiff faces a considerable difficulty in succeeding in his action even if he can show a breach of duty to inform?

Consider *Reibl v Hughes* (1980)
114 DLR (3d) 1

Laskin CJC: In saying that the test is based on the decision that a reasonable person in the patient's position would have made, I should make it clear that the patient's particular concerns must also be reasonably based; otherwise, there would be more subjectivity than would be warranted under an objective test. Thus, for example, fears which are not related to the material risks which should have been but were not disclosed would not be causative factors. However, economic considerations could reasonably go to causation where, for example, the loss of an eye as a result of non-disclosure of a material risk brings about the loss of a job for which good eyesight is required. In short, although account must be taken of a patient's particular position, a position which will vary with the patient, it must be objectively assessed in terms of reasonableness.

However, a vexing problem raised by the objective standard is whether causation could ever be established if the surgeon has recommended surgery which is warranted by the patient's condition. Can it be said that a reasonable person in the patient's position, to whom proper disclosure of attendant risks has been made, would decide against the surgery, that is, against the surgeon's recommendation that it be undergone? The objective standard of what a reasonable person in the patient's position would do would seem to put a premium on the surgeon's assessment of the relative need for the surgery and on supporting medical evidence of that need. Could it be reasonably refused? Brooke JA appeared to be sensitive to this problem by suggesting a combined objective-subjective test.

I doubt that this will solve the problem. It could hardly be expected that the patient who is suing would admit that he would have agreed to have the surgery, even knowing all the accompanying risks. His suit would indicate that, having suffered serious disablement because of the surgery, he is convinced that he would not have permitted it if there had been proper disclosure of the risks, balanced by the risks of refusing the surgery. Yet, to apply a subjective test to causation would, correlatively, put a premium on hindsight, even more of a premium than would be put on medical evidence in assessing causation by an objective standard.

I think it is the safer course on the issue of causation to consider objectively how far the balance in the risks of surgery or no surgery is in favour of undergoing surgery. The failure of proper disclosure pro and con becomes therefore very material. And so too are any special considerations affecting the particular patient. For example, the patient may have asked specific questions which were either brushed aside or were not fully answered or were answered wrongly. In the present case, the anticipation of a full pension would be a special consideration, and, while it would have to be viewed objectively, it emerges from the patient's particular circumstances. So too, other aspects of the objective standard would have to be geared to what the average prudent person, the reasonable person in the patient's particular position, would agree to or not agree to, if all material and special risks of going ahead with the surgery or foregoing it were made known to him. Far from making the patient's own testimony irrelevant, it is essential to his case that he put his own position forward.

The adoption of an objective standard does not mean that the issue of causation is completely in the hands of the surgeon. Merely because medical evidence establishes the reasonableness of a recommended operation does not mean that a reasonable person in the patient's position would necessarily agree to it, if proper disclosure had been made of the risks attendant upon it, balanced by those against it. The patient's particular situation and the degree to which the risks of surgery or no surgery are balanced would reduce the force, on an objective appraisal, of the surgeon's recommendation. Admittedly, if the risk of foregoing the surgery would be considerably graver to a patient than the risks attendant upon it, the objective standard would favour exoneration of the surgeon who has not made the required disclosure. Since liability rests only in negligence, in a failure to disclose material risks, the issue of causation would be in the patient's hands on a subjective test, and would, if his evidence was accepted, result inevitably in liability unless, of course, there was a finding that there was no breach of the duty of disclosure. In my view, therefore, the objective standard is the preferable one on the issue of causation.

Dugdale in discussing the Canadian cases since *Reibl* illustrates the difficulty faced by plaintiffs where the 'reasonable patient' test is used for causation. Diverse Reports: Canadian Professional Negligence Cases' 2 *Professional Negligence*, 108 at pp 109–10, he writes:

Causation
To prove causation the patient must show that *but for* the breach of duty there would have been no loss, in other words, that but for the lack of warning there would have been no treatment of the kind proposed and no resulting stroke etc. In *Reibl* Laskin CJ held that this issue of causation had to be tested objectively: a patient has to prove not that he personally, subjectively would have declined the treatment if properly warned, but that a reasonable patient in his position would not have

proceeded with the treatment if fully informed. What would the reasonable patient have chosen to do in the *Casey* situation, if advised of the 2 per cent voice risk and of the 30 per cent risk of suffering a future stroke were the operation to be declined? In all three cases [*Reibl, Casey* and *Ferguson*] it was clear that without the treatment the patient would be running much higher risks of illness or death than he was in undergoing the treatment. The reasonable patient in that situation will obviously opt for the treatment even if fully warned. It was for that reason that the patients lost in the three cases considered. Indeed, it may be doubted whether a subjective test would have made much difference in these cases: in both *Ferguson* and *Casey* the court noted the confidence of the patient in his surgeon and concluded that the surgeon's advice would have been followed in any event.

Does this suggest that where the recommended treatment is reasonable, causation will always prevent recovery for a failure to warn of the risks? That only where there is an unreasonable recommendation will causation and liability be established—in which case might not the liability be more simply based on the negligent selection of the treatment? That this is the consequence of the *Reibl* approach to causation was denied by Laskin CJ. 'Merely because medical evidence establishes the reasonableness of a recommended operation does not mean that a reasonable person in the patient's position would necessarily agree to it, if proper disclosure had been made of the risks attendant upon it ... the patient's particular situation and the degree to which the risks of surgery or no surgery are balanced would reduce the force, on an objective appraisal, of the surgeon's recommendation'. However, he went on to add a qualification: 'the patient's particular concerns must be reasonably based ... thus for example, fears which are not related to the material risks would not be causative factors. However, economic considerations could reasonably go to causation where, for example, the loss of an eye as a result of non-disclosure of a material risk brings about the loss of a job for which good eyesight is required.'

Despite Laskin's denial that 'the adoption of an objective standard (means) that the issue of causation is completely in the hands of the surgeon' ie a surgeon reasonably recommending treatment would be able to show that a full warning would not have influenced a reasonable patient, one is left with the feeling that this will normally be the case unless the treatment is purely elective. It is not surprising that it is in this category of case where the Canadian courts have found causation to be established.

The leading elective treatment case is perhaps *White v Turner*, the case concerning breast reduction surgery. Linden J had no doubt that a reasonable person in the position of the patient, if she were warned of the possible scarring 'would probably not have undergone the operation, except perhaps in rare circumstances'. As Linden noted 'after all, she did live most of her life with large breasts and managed quite well'. Arguments along these lines are likely to be applicable in many cosmetic surgery cases. It is also arguable that the doctor's advice may be less influential in the elective surgery case.

When the English courts have to determine the test of causation it is likely that they will follow the approach adopted in Canada, notwithstanding Dugdale's strictures. It is possible, however, that the issues are more subtle than Dugdale allows. There may be two questions for the court, as we suggested in the discussion of *Chatterton* above: (i) What is the correct test of causation? (ii) How is that to be established: what evidentiary burden should be cast upon the patient? The court may adopt a subjective test of causation but may demand that in seeking to establish that he would not have consented, the plaintiff must meet a standard of evidence which incorporates an element of reasonableness. Note the following from Robertson, 'Overcoming the causation hurdle in informal consent cases', 22 *University of Western Ontario Law Review* (1984), at pp 78–80 (footnotes omitted):

Re-examining the objective test
One way of resolving this [the dilemma of causation] ... is to re-examine the objective test of causation as it is enunciated in *Reibl*, rather than as it is interpreted

in later cases. The first point to note is that Laskin CJC was clearly of the view that the test which he was propounding was a test of causation; he did not intend to discard causation as a necessary requirement in informed consent cases. This observation may appear trite, but it is nonetheless significant. Its significance lies in the fact that *the objective test is not in itself a test of causation*. Establishing that a reasonable person would have declined the treatment does not, *per se*, provide a causal link between the defendant's negligence and the plaintiff's injury. It merely establishes that a reasonable person, if properly informed, would not have suffered injury; it does not, in itself, lead to the conclusion that the plaintiff, if properly informed, would not have suffered injury.

The only way in which the objective test can operate as a test of causation is if there is added to it the presumption that the plaintiff would have acted in the same way as a reasonable person. By applying this presumption, a causal link is established between the defendant's negligence and the plaintiff's injury. Moreover, for the objective test to apply as the sole test of causation in informed consent cases, this presumption must be regarded as irrebuttable. Thus, evidence that the plaintiff, if properly informed, would still have agreed to the treatment, even though a reasonable person would not have done so, must be regarded as irrelevant. To hold otherwise would be to apply a subjective test of causation, that is, determining causation by evidence of what the plaintiff himself would have done if properly informed.

However, it is extremely unlikely that a court would permit a plaintiff to succeed in this type of situation. As will be discussed below, one of the reasons which Laskin CJC gave for adopting the objective standard was to ensure that plaintiffs would not succeed if their conduct would have been unreasonable in the circumstances. In view of this, it would be inconsistent with *Reibl* for a court to find in the plaintiff's favour if it considered that the plaintiff, if properly informed, would have acted unreasonably and agreed to the treatment.

One of two possible conclusions may be drawn from this. The first is that the plaintiff must satisfy *two* tests of causation in informed consent cases: a subjective one and an objective one. It is submitted, however, that the preferable conclusion is that the objective test is not operating as a test of causation. Rather, it is performing primarily an evidentiary function in that it provides a test of the credibility and reliability of the plaintiff's own testimony that he would have declined the treatment if he had been informed of the risks. The objective standard shields the defendant from the plaintiff's 'hindsight and bitterness' by considering his evidence objectively. In this way the court is better able to decide whether the plaintiff would truly have declined the treatment if properly informed.

The objective test performs a second function, namely, that of disposing of unreasonable claims. It creates an additional requirement of reasonable conduct by insisting that, even if the plaintiff would have decided to forego the treatment had he known of the risks, liability can be imposed only if that decision would have been a reasonable one in the circumstances. This second function of the objective test is explained by Linden J in *White v Turner* as follows:

> the requirement is not unlike the need for proof of reasonable reliance in actions for deceit and negligent misrepresentation. In those types of cases, our Courts have avoided assisting gullible fools, who rely on every bit of silly advice they receive.... Consequently, a patient, who says he would have foregone life-saving treatment because it might have caused a rash or a headache, cannot recover on the basis of inadequate disclosure, even if he is believed, because a reasonable patient would have gone ahead.

In summary, it is submitted that the objective test enunciated in *Reibl* was not intended to operate as a test of causation. It was intended to complement the subjective test of causation by performing an evidentiary function and by screening out claims which are based on the plaintiff's own unreasonable conduct. If this submission is correct, it follows that to satisfy the objective test the plaintiff does not have to establish that a reasonable man *would have* declined the treatment. Instead, it is sufficient if the plaintiff establishes that his decision to forego the treatment would have been reasonable in the sense that it is a decision in which a reasonable man might well have reached in similar circumstances. In this way it will be possible for a plaintiff to succeed in establishing causation even if the court concludes that the pros and cons with regard to the proposed treatment are so evenly balanced that a reasonable person might equally have decided for or against undergoing that treatment.

B.   WAIVER

The question here is whether a patient may (expressly or impliedly) absolve a doctor from his duty to inform, assuming the situation to be one in which this duty *prima facie* exists. The answer is probably sometimes but not always. Regrettably it is difficult to be much more precise than this. Note the following from the President's Commission (supra) 'Making Health Care Decisions', (supra) p. 94, (footnote omitted):

> The modest attention paid to the fourth exception—waiver—in the courts and scholarly literature is regrettable given its interesting relationship to the value of self-determination that underlies the doctrine of informed consent. ... self-determination encompasses both the moral right to formal control over a decision and the ideal of active participation in the decisionmaking process. Although these two senses of self-determination often go hand in hand, sometimes they do not, as in the case of a waiver, when a patient asks not to be informed of certain matters and/or delegates decisional authority to another person.
>
> The impact of the waiver exception is that if a waiver is properly obtained the patient remains the ultimate decisionmaker, but the content of his decision is shifted from the decisional level to the metadecisional level—from the equivalent of 'I want this treatment (or that treatment or no treatment)' to 'I don't want any information about the treatment'.
>
> The legal requirements for effective waiver in the context of informed consent have never been clearly articulated by the courts. There is substantial reason to believe that the courts would respect waivers of certain information (for example, the disclosure of particular risks) or the delegation of certain decisions to others. Yet it is questionable whether patients should be permitted to waive the professional's obligation to disclose fundamental information about the nature and implications of certain procedures (such as, 'when you wake up, you will learn that your limb has been amputated' or 'that you are irreversibly sterile'). In the absence of explicit legal guidance, health care professionals should be quite circumspect about allowing or disallowing, encouraging or discouraging, a patient's use of waiver.

Obviously the court must be satisfied that there was in truth a waiver in that the doctor was prepared to inform and the patient willingly declined. The suggestion is that there is a public policy limitation as to what may be waived. Can you see a parallel with the law's limitation on what may be consented to?

2.   Duty to respond to questions

Generally

Hatcher v Black
(1954) Times, 2 July

> Mrs Hatcher was a lady who occasionally broadcast for the BBC. She went into St Bartholomew's Hospital suffering from a toxic thyroid gland. An operation was advised. She asked if there was any risk to her voice. She was reassured by the doctors. The operation was performed. In the course of it, the nerve was so badly damaged that she could not speak properly. She could not broadcast again.

Since Mrs Hatcher had asked her doctor whether there was any risk to her voice, Denning LJ asked:

Denning LJ: What should the doctor tell his patient? Mr Tuckwell admitted that on the evening before the operation he told the plaintiff that there was no risk to her voice, when he knew that there was some slight risk, but that he did it for her own good because it was of vital importance that she should not worry. In short, he told a lie, but he did it because he thought in the circumstances it was justifiable. If this were a court of morals, that would raise a nice question on which moralists and theologians have differed for centuries. Some hold that it is never permissible to tell a lie even for a just cause: a good end, they say, does not justify a bad means. You must not do a little wrong in order to do a great right. Others, however, hold that it is permissible, if the justification is strong enough, and they point to the stratagems used in war to deceive the enemy. This, however, is not a court of morals but a court of law, and the law leaves this question of morals to the conscience of the doctor himself—though I may perhaps remark that if doctors have too easy a conscience on this matter they may in time lose the confidence of the patient, which is the basis of all good medicine. But so far as the law is concerned, it does not condemn the doctor when he only does that which many a wise and good doctor so placed would do. It only condemns him when he falls short of the accepted standards of a great profession; in short, when he is deserving of censure. No one of the doctors that have been called before you has suggested that Mr Tuckwell did wrong. All agree that it was a matter for his own judgment. They did not condemn him; nor should we.

Probably, the law now takes a different view. In the *Sidaway* case it was stated (*obiter*) that the doctor has a duty both to answer questions and to do so truthfully.

Lord Bridge: when questioned specifically by a patient of apparently sound mind about risks involved in a particular treatment proposed, the doctor's duty must, in my opinion, be to answer both truthfully and as fully as the questioner requires.

Lords Diplock and Templeman concurred. Notice that Lord Bridge recognises the touchstone of the duty as being to answer '*fully*'. What does 'fully' mean?

For a long time the leading case was *Smith v Auckland Hospital Board* [1965] NZLR 191:

The appellant had entered the respondent board's hospital at Green Lane, Auckland, for an examination, and, if necessary, for surgical treatment for a suspected aortic aneurism. In the course of the proper preliminary investigations he was subjected to a procedure known as aortography, wherein a catheter is inserted into the femoral artery and guided upwards through the arterial passage towards the aorta, into which ultimately an opaque fluid is injected through the catheter, enabling the aorta to be outlined satisfactorily for the purposes of X-ray photography. In the course of this procedure the appellant suffered a surgical mishap through the catheter accidently dislodging a plaque of atheromatous material from the interior wall of the artery. A condition of clotting supervened, and notwithstanding all due efforts by the surgeons, the appellant's right leg degenerated into a gangrenous condition, and ultimately had to be amputated below the knee. Negligence was pleaded in a number of respects, but the jury found for the defence on all the issues of negligence alleged in respect of the conduct of the aortogram procedure on the part of the operating radiographer or any member of his team. But it was also alleged that, the risk of the mishap being a reasonably foreseeable one, albeit in only a low percentage of cases, it should have been the subject of a warning to the patient in the circumstances of this case; for the appellant gave evidence, which was uncontradicted, that he had made a specific inquiry as to the risk involved in the procedure, and alleged that the answer given was equivalent to an assurance that there was none. It was contended on his behalf that these facts gave rise to a cause of action in negligence, and an issue was put to the jury accordingly in these terms:

Was the defendant by its servants or agents negligent so as to involve the plaintiff in the loss of his leg in ... (d), failing to inform the plaintiff adequately of the risks of conducting a femoral aortogram upon him?

to which the jury answered 'Yes'.

Woodhouse J, on an application by the respondent for judgment for the defendant *non obstante veredicto*, upheld the respondent's submissions, and gave judgment for it notwithstanding the jury's finding, holding that there was no evidence on which the jury could find any breach of duty, and alternatively that, even if there had been such evidence, the answer given by the surgeon could not reasonably be found causative of the damage suffered by the appellant. Both these conclusions were attacked in the appeal.

TA Gresson J in the New Zealand Court of Appeal examined what the duty of the doctor was when asked the question 'is there any risk?' His Lordship said:

> In these circumstances either a refusal to answer at all, which would have carried its own clear implications, or a suggested reference back to Mr Barratt-Boyes, or an honest and reasonably complete and accurate answer was required, and the circumstances did not warrant—as they sometimes may do—a *suppressio veri*. ... Here again the distinction lies in the fact that Mr Windsor did not reply to the appellant's question in accordance with what other competent medical men stated was their practice in a similar situation. After all, it was the appellant's prerogative to decide for himself whether he would submit to the proposed procedures, and this placed the doctor under a duty to give a careful and reasonably accurate reply to the appellant's direct inquiry as to the risk involved.

Two comments can be made. First, that TA Gresson J considers that the duty is, in part, at least, determined by reference to the practice of reasonable doctors and secondly, that this might allow for a range of answers from the *wholly* truthful to the partially truthful to the somewhat deceptive to the '*suppressio veri*'. In the Canadian case of *Hopp v Lepp* (1980) 112 DLR (3d) 67, Laskin CJ found otherwise.

> Apart from situations of this kind, a surgeon need not go into every conceivable detail of a proposed operation so long as he describes its nature, unless the patient asks specific questions not by way of merely general inquiry, and, if so, those questions must be answered, although they invite answers to merely possible risks. If no specific questions are put as to possible risks, the surgeon is under no obligation (although he may do so) to tell the patient that there are possible risks since there are such risks in any operation. It becomes a question of fact of how specific are any questions that are put.

Hopp v Lepp may be reconciled with *Smith* on the basis that in *Smith* the question asked was a '*general*' question and not a '*specific*' one. *Hopp v Lepp* would suggest that where the question is *specific* the doctor has no discretion but to answer and tell the truth. It could be said, therefore, that 'fully' (per Lord Bridge) must mean what Laskin CJ sets out in *Hopp* when the question *is specific*. But can 'fully' be what Gresson J states when the question is a general one? Given that Gresson J contemplates '*suppressio veri*', it would appear not. It may be, therefore, that Lord Bridge's definition of the doctor's duty must be understood as applying to all cases where it is clear to the doctor that the patient is expressly seeking information. *How* the doctor will respond will depend upon the content of the question. A hard and fast distinction between general and specific questions is consequently unhelpful.

If the law be that the doctor must respond and respond truthfully then *prima facie* this would not be an area in which the doctrine of 'therapeutic privilege' would apply. Is this so? There is some suggestion that a doctor may be justified in withholding information (or perhaps not to tell the truth) when to do so could reasonably be regarded as injurious to his patient's health.

Lee v South West Thames Regional Health Authority
[1985] 2 All ER 385 at 389–90:

Sir John Donaldson MR: The recent decision of the House of Lords in *Sidaway v Bethlem Royal Hospital Governors* [1985] AC 871, [1985] 1 All ER 643 affirms that a doctor is under a duty to answer his patient's questions as to the treatment proposed. . . . This duty is subject to the exercise of clinical judgment as to the terms in which the information is given and the extent to which, in the patient's interests, information should be withheld.

Is this either analytically or ethically justifiable? The most recent case dealing with the issue is *Blyth v Bloomsbury Health Authority* (1985) Times, 24 May, reported in on appeal (1987) Times, 11 February:

Kerr LJ: This is an appeal by the defendant health authority against part of a judgment given by Mr Justice Leonard on 23rd May 1985 after a trial lasting some 10 days. The action had been brought by the plaintiff, Mrs Blyth, against . . . the health authority on the ground that negligent advice or information had been given to the plaintiff in December 1978 by a member of staff of University College Hospital ('UCH') in relation to a contraceptive drug called Depo-Provera, which was then injected and had allegedly caused the plaintiff unpleasant side effects after her discharge from the hospital.

The plaintiff, Mrs Blyth, qualified as a nurse in New Zealand. She came here in 1973 and began to take a contraceptive called Minilyn, which caused her considerable problems. It was a combined pill, containing oestrogen and progesterone, and she subsequently gave it up.

She returned to New Zealand in 1975 to nurse her mother, who was unfortunately ill with cancer and died in November of that year. In 1976 she married and returned here; and in 1977 she began to work as a health worker in Hackney. In 1978 she became pregnant, and in May of that year she was referred to UCH for ante-natal care.

In that connection she saw a Miss Aileen Dickins, a consultant at UCH, who gave evidence at this trial. It was then established that she had no, or insufficient, immunity to rubella, but fortunately this had no adverse effects on the subsequent history.

However, two consequences followed. First, although it was of course too late to vaccinate her against rubella at that stage of her pregnancy, it was necessary to do so after the birth of her baby in order to protect her and the baby against the risk of infection. Secondly, since the vaccine could itself cause adverse symptoms to a foetus if she were to become pregnant again within three months, it was necessary that she should have some contraceptive protection during this period, since that was certainly her wish.

The general practice at UCH in that regard at that time was to use Depo-Provera for this purpose in many cases unless there were countervailing factors, or the patient did not want it. The judge found that since 1975, when the drug was introduced, it had been administered to about 100 patients a year.

In the result, when Mrs Blyth was admitted to UCH in December 1978 for the birth of her baby, she received (i) a vaccination against rubella and (ii) an injection of the contraceptive Depo-Provera, which was designed to provide her with contraceptive cover for three months. Depo-Provera was a progesterone-only contraceptive and it was therefore thought that it would not have the same adverse consequences for her as the Minilyn which she had used for some years previously.

It is important to bear in mind throughout that there is no complaint in this case about the prescription or administration of the rubella vaccine; nor of the prescription or administration of the Depo-Provera. An allegation to that effect about the latter drug was abandoned at the beginning of the trial.

The remaining complaints of the plaintiff can be summarised as follows: (1) She was insufficiently informed and advised about the possible side effects of Depo-Provera when she was in hospital, and the hospital staff was negligent in that respect. That is the issue raised on this appeal. (2) If she had been informed about the possible side effects more fully than she was, she would not have agreed to have the Depo-Provera injection. This was found by the judge and is not contested. (3) She suffered from manifold side effects, allegedly due to Depo-Provera, for which she claimed damages. All her allegations in that connection were rejected, with the exception of bleeding and menstrual irregularity. The judge held that on the balance of probability these consequences could be attributed to Depo-Provera for some time after her discharge, but that they had certainly disappeared by February 1980, and on one view by July 1979.

An appeal against the award of £3,500 general damages having been abandoned, we are therefore now only concerned with the first of the three issues which I have mentioned. . . .

I must turn to certain parts of the pleadings. The amended statement of claim included the following paragraphs 6 to 9:

'6. The Plaintiff agreed to have the said drug after being assured by Dr Burt, a member of the staff of the said hospital:

(a) that the only known side effects of Depo-Provera were occasional spotting and one or two irregular periods;
(b) that all effects contraceptive and otherwise ceased after 3/4 months;
(c) that the drug would not affect breast feeding or pass through to the baby.

7. The said assurances were wrong and inaccurate in the following respects:

(a) The known side effects of Depo-Provera included menstrual irregularity, bodyweight changes, mood changes, depression of sexual drive and changes to nails and hair, such side effects lasting for up to a year.
(b) It was known that Depo-Provera would be likely to pass in the milk but it was unknown what effect this would be likely to have on the baby.

8. The Plaintiff would not have agreed to administration of the said drug if she had been told of the possible side effects.
9. As a result of the said drug the Plaintiff suffered menstrual irregularity, mood changes, loss of sexual drive, exzema, galacthorrea'—that is, over-production of milk—'loss of sleep, loss of weight and hormonal changes including changes in her skin colour and texture, loss of hair, change in hair colour and reduced resistance to infection.'

As will be seen, virtually all of these allegations were rejected by the judge. The only symptoms which he accepted she had after discharge were irregular bleeding and menstruation.

In the particulars of negligence the plaintiff included an allegation that the defendants were negligent by '(iv) failing to answer the Plaintiff's enquiries concerning Depo-Provera accurately and of failing to obtain answers to her questions before attempting to give her the said assurances about the said drug'.

She was asked to supply further and better particulars of that allegation, as to the enquiries she had made, to whom they were addressed and full particulars of the answers that were given and that should have been given, and her reply was as follows:

'The Plaintiff informed the Certified Midwife, Sister Nixon, and a Staff Midwife that she was not prepared to have an injection of Depo-Provera until she had discussed the possible consequences of such an injection with a Specialist. The First defendants arranged for Dr Burt to see the Plaintiff. The Plaintiff was able to put various questions to Dr Burt. The relevant questions and answers given by Dr Burt are recorded in the Plaintiff's diary, see under (b) below.'

Then it gives the questions and answers as recorded by the plaintiff in her diary, as follows:

'1. What is in the drug? A. Progesterone only.
2. Are there any side effects? A. Only occasional spotting.'

and then she was asked: 'Does it affect breast feeding? Does it pass in the milk? Does it have an effect on the baby? Are there are known reactions or upsets in any one at all?' All those questions were answered with the word 'No'. 'How long does it take for all effects to wear off: (a) completely, (b) contraceptive, (c) side?', and the answer is: 'All effects completely over within three months.' Then: 'Does it upset periods? (A) Not after three to four months. How does Depo-Provera work in and on the body? (A) Prevention of ovulation.'

There was added: 'The plaintiff should have been told of the known possible side effects of the said drug'.

That alleged record of questions and answers in the plaintiff's diary was rejected by the judge. . . . he said this at p 26D:

'For reasons which are inherent in the passages I have cited, it seems to me important to consider whether the plaintiff asked the nursing and medical staff for information and advice about the drug or not. The plaintiff says that she asked the questions which are set out in her diary. The entry is headed "For Tony"— that is her husband—"tonight, re: DP"—and an abbreviation for "contraceptive". In conjunction with the question as to whether the drug would affect breast-feeding the plaintiff has written in brackets "(intend 6/12"—that is six months— "at least)". I find an artificial flavour to those two entries, particularly the first, if all of the writing, with minor possible exceptions, was done at the same time as the plaintiff maintains. As I have already indicated, I do not regard it as in any way probable that Dr (Burt) would have answered the question in the form "Any known reactions, upsets in anyone at all" with a simple negative. Moreover, I do not believe that a person with the plaintiff's professional training would in fact ask such a question. I therefore doubt the accuracy of the plaintiff's evidence as to how precisely the document came to be written. If she had really been writing the answers, or most of them, down at the time, I think that fact would have been sufficiently unusual to stick in Dr (Burt's) memory, but it does not.'

That speaks for itself.

In an earlier part of his judgment he found the following facts about the discussions concerning Depo-Provera between the plaintiff and, first, Sister Nixon, and thereafter Dr Burt. At p 10C the judge said:

'Sister Nixon is an experienced midwifery sister. I accept her evidence that she would not have witheld information about the tike reading if she had been asked'—that was a reference to the degree of immunity to rubella.

'It was she, of course, who administered both injections. She told me that it was her practice to tell the patient the possible side effects of Depo-Provera. She would have warned of spotting or irregular bleeding which might be light or heavy. If the patient had expressed concern about the injection, it would have been noted in the record and the vaccination would not have been carried out. If the patient requested further advice that would have been recorded and the appropriate arrangements made. The usual practice was to give the vaccine and the Depo-Provera consecutively. As in this case they were administered with an interval of two days the explanation might well be that the plaintiff had been offered the contraceptive injection, for example, by Dr Beatles but was not happy about it initially. Having seen Sister Nixon in the witness box, I am satisfied that she would not have tried to over-persuade the plaintiff into accepting the injection when she did not want it.'

He then turns at p 10H to the important discussion about Depo-Provera which the plaintiff had with Dr Burt:

'Dr Burt was practising in 1978 under her maiden name of Burt. She had qualified in 1974 and was fully registered in July 1975. She had obtained the Diploma of Child Health in 1977, and in 1981, of course subsequently to the events with which this case is concerned, she obtained her Membership of the Royal College of Obstetricians and Gynaecologists by examination. Membership is the senior qualification by examination given by the college. In 1978 Dr (Burt) was reading for that examination. She had previously held senior house office posts before becoming a senior house officer in obstetrics and gynaecology at University

College Hospital on 1st December. It was in the context of this case that she first came across the use of Depo-Provera as a contraceptive, though she had some experience of it in the treatment of cancer. Although she has some memory of a patient who may have been the plaintiff, Dr (Burt) had to accept that she has no memory of events connected with her seeing the plaintiff, apart from what the record contains. This shows that she prescribed the Depo-Provera on 23rd December—that was the Saturday shortly before Christmas. She was then responsible for the obstetric wards and on call for the labour ward and the gynaecological emergencies. Her purpose in seeing the plaintiff was to check her condition prior to discharge. She thinks it was in the course of writing up her notes that she saw that the vaccine had been prescribed and, therefore, appreciated the need for advice that contraceptive action should be taken. The discharge sheet has a section which is headed "Contraception". It contains provision for recording whether advice has been requested or offered. That provision has not been used, but the doctor has simply recorded "Depo-Provera to cover rubella vaccination". She thought that her suggesting Depo-Provera came about because the sister said that it was often used in these circumstances. She would have referred to the data sheet compendium for the proper dosage and in order to see whether there was any other information which she ought to know. The compendium is a book which contains the manufacturers' information about various drugs. At this time the only relevant comment on side effects relating to a single (injection) was as follows: "Clincially Depo-Provera is well tolerated. No significant untoward effects have been reported". However, because of her reading, particularly in preparation for her membership examination, Dr (Burt) was aware that there might be a problem with irregular bleeding. It was her evidence that she would have told the patient of the need for contraception and would have discussed alternative methods. She would have described Depo-Provera as effective, and convenient, and having the appropriate duration of protection, that is to say, 90 days. She would have said that it was in common use at the hospital. She would have warned that there might be the problem of irregular bleeding. She would not, she says, have used the word "spotting" which is attributed to her by the plaintiff. She would have told the plaintiff that the drug was generally acceptable and had no serious or significant side effects. She might have added that progesterone was less associated with side effects than oestrogen and that it would have no adverse effects on the baby. If she had been asked the question postulated by the plaintiff "Are there any known reactions or upsets in anyone at all?" she would have replied that there might be reactions of which she was not aware, and her answer would have been that she did not know. It was the plaintiff's evidence that she prepared a number of questions before she was seen by the doctor. They were recorded in a diary in which she wrote, at any rate, most of the answers as they were given. Dr (Burt) has no memory of this. The doctor accepted that the delay between the prescribing of the vaccine and the Depo-Provera suggests that there may have been some discussion about the latter. She also accepted that she may have been told that the plaintiff wanted to discuss the drug. She agreed that she would have conveyed the impression to the plaintiff that there were no significant side effects other than bleeding.'

The judgment contains no adverse conclusion of any kind concerning Dr Burt, or about her discussion with the plaintiff. Furthermore, none of the medical witnesses criticised her conduct or the information which she gave, as summarised in this account by the judge, other than Professor Huntingford, whose evidence was not accepted as to what was known and required to be disclosed about Depo-Provera in December 1978. On the contrary, the effect of the evidence of all three doctors called by the defendants was to approve the conduct of Dr Burt on the basis of her evidence, which the judge clearly accepted, ie Miss Dickins, Dr Law and an independent highly qualified expert, Dame Josephine Barnes. The judge also clearly accepted the evidence of all these witnesses, and I shall be returning to some short passages in that connection later on.

In effect, therefore, Dr Burt was absolved from any allegation of negligence—

indeed, as appears hereafter, not only by the judge but also by counsel for the plaintiff. Nevertheless, somewhat surprisingly in the circumstances, the judge concluded that the defendants had been negligent. . . . I must refer to some passages in the speeches in the House of Lords in *Sidaway*, on which the judge relied. . . . there were . . . a number of remarks, *obiter* in their context, on the duty to reply to questions. For present purposes I need only refer to two passages. At p 895B Lord Diplock mentioned the natural tendency of many people to want to decide for themselves whether anything should be done to their bodies and whether or not to consent to any treatment which might be advised. In that connection he said:

'No doubt if the plaintiff in fact manifested this attitude by means of questioning, the doctor would tell him whatever it was the patient wanted to know.'

Lord Bridge, with whom Lord Keith agreed, said at p 898B:

'I should perhaps add at this point, although the issue does not strictly arise on this appeal, that, when questioned specifically by a patient of apparently sound mind about risks involved in a particular treatment proposed, a doctor's duty must, in my opinion, be to answer both truthfully and as fully as the question requires.'

The judge referred to these passages and to another passage in the speech of Lord Bridge before dealing with the questions and answers which appear in the plaintiff's diary, to which I have already referred.

Kerr LJ cited further the judgment of Mr Justice Leonard, and continued:

(1) It confirms, as I have already mentioned, that the judge absolved Dr Burt from all blame; indeed, he appears to have commended her conduct.

(2) The judge does not find anywhere what enquiries the plaintiff in fact made about Depo-Provera, let alone that she made any specific enquiry. On the contrary, he had already rejected her evidence that she made the specific enquiries recorded in her diary and in the pleading. All that he said in that connection was that it was more probable than not that she asked for some information and advice, and that she had expressed some sort of reservation about Depo-Provera and had made some form of request for reassurances about it. That, so far as it goes, is of course a finding which the defendants accept, as they must, and it is fully in accordance with the probabilities on the rest of the evidence.

(3) On that assumption, what were the defendants obliged to tell the plaintiff in response, and did they fail in their duty in that regard? In that connection it must be borne in mind that there was no medical evidence on which the judge could properly conclude that the defendants had been negligent by not having given any more information to the plaintiff than what she was told by Dr Burt.

(4) In my view the judge overstated the position on the evidence when he said, at p 28C:

'As Miss Dickins said in evidence, if the patient is making a specific enquiry, it would be right to tell her the whole picture.'

The expression 'the full picture' was used by counsel in his cross-examination of Miss Dickins. Her assent to it, at the end of a question occupying nearly eight lines, cannot properly be divorced from the context of her evidence as a whole, and I set out later on the judge's own summary of it.

(5) In the passage which I have read the judge referred to 'such information as is available to the hospital'; and to the retrieval of information 'from the files'. What he appears to have had in mind was information, case studies, statistics and other literature which had been collated by Dr Law as part of a piece of research of her own, but which was also available for consultation by others; and he may also have had this in mind when he referred twice to 'the full picture'. . . .

For present purposes it is sufficient to take the judge's summary of their evidence, though in my view its effect was a good deal stronger and more favourable to the defendants than the summary suggests.

In relation to Miss Dickins, the judge said at p 20:

'Miss Dickins, who was the consultant obstetrician and gynaecologist in charge of the plaintiff from the time of her referral, preceding Daniel's birth, described

Depo-Provera as being "convenient and useful for suitable patients who needed to be without anxiety about becoming pregnant for a period of three months". Presented with a summary of the answers said to have been by Dr Burt' —and I interpolate 'according to Dr Burt's account of the interview (which the judge accepted) and not according to what the plaintiff claims to have recorded in her diary'—
'she was of the opinion that they contained sufficient information for the patient, in the light of the material which was available in 1978. In her view there was no need to mention the other symptoms which were rare, though she thought that it would be necessary to mention them now because of the public discussion. It was common practice to tell the patient about irregular bleeding, but not the minor side effects. However, she added that, if the patient made a specific enquiry, then it would be proper to tell her the full picture.'
I have already dealt with the point made again in the last sentence.

Then in relation to Dame Josephine Barnes, the judge said:
'(She) is an obstetrician and gynaecologist of formidable reputation. In addition to her academic and institutional distinctions she is a consultant to the Charing Cross and Elizabeth Garrett-Anderson Hospitals. She regards Depo-Provera as useful in certain applications, including cases in which a woman has been vaccinated against rubella and, therefore, needs to avoid pregnancy for three months. Her evidence was that in 1978 all that was known was that the main side effect of the drug was irregular bleeding. The patient should have been told about it: it was probably unnecessary to warn her of other comparatively trivial side effects of which complaint had been made.'

(6) In the light of these comments I conclude that the judge was in error in holding that there was any obligation to pass on to the plaintiff all the information available to the hospital; that is to say in this case the information contained in Dr Law's files. That conclusion could not properly be based upon the evidence. As regards the judge's repeated reference to the need to give a full picture in answer to a specific enquiry, it must be borne in mind, apart from the other matters already mentioned in that regard, that no specific enquiry was found to have been made in this case.

Secondly, I think the judge's conclusions equally cannot properly be based on the remarks of Lord Diplock and Lord Bridge in *Sidaway*. The question of what a plaintiff should be told in answer to a general enquiry cannot be divorced from the *Bolam* test, any more than when no such enquiry is made. In both cases the answer must depend upon the circumstances, the nature of the enquiry, the nature of the information which is available, its reliability, relevance, the condition of the patient, and so forth. Any medical evidence directed to what would be the proper answer in the light of responsible medical opinion and practice—that is to say, the *Bolam* test—must in my view equally be placed in the balance in cases where the patient makes some enquiry, in order to decide whether the response was negligent or not.

In that connection, apart from what was said by Lords Diplock and Bridge, I would also draw attention to the speech of Lord Templeman at p 903D onwards, which suggests to me that the *Bolam* test is all-pervasive in this context. Indeed I am not convinced that the *Bolam* test is irrelevant even in relation to the question of what answers are properly to be given to specific enquiries, or that Lord Diplock or Lord Bridge intended to hold otherwise. It seems to me that there may always be grey areas, with differences of opinion, as to what are the proper answers to be given to any enquiry, even a specific one, in the particular circumstances of any case. However, on the evidence in the present case this point does not arise, since no specific enquiry was found to have been made.

(7) Accordingly, I conclude that the judge erred in finding negligence in relation to what the plaintiff was not told by Dr Burt, whether he relied on the medical evidence or on the *obiter* remarks in *Sidaway*, or both. . . .

Neil LJ: I do not understand that in the decision of the House of Lords in *Sidaway v Board of Governors of the Bethlem Royal Hospital* [1985] AC 871, [1985] 1 All ER 643, in the passages to which my Lord has already drawn attention that Lord Diplock or

Lord Bridge were laying down any rule of law to the effect that where questions are asked by a patient, or doubts are expressed, a doctor is under an obligation to put the patient in possession of all the information on the subject which may be available in the files of a consultant, who may have made a special study of the subject. The amount of information to be given must depend upon the circumstances, and as a general proposition it is governed by what is called the *Bolam* test. In 1978 irregular bleeding was the side-effect which was known and recognised. The plaintiff was told about it. In my judgment it was not established, either by means of evidence of some usual system, which broke down in this particular, or by the application of some rule of law, that the plaintiff would, or should, have been put in possession of the material, or the bulk of the material, then in Dr Law's files.

With the utmost respect to the judge, I think he fell into error. Accordingly, I too would allow this appeal.

C. VOLUNTARINESS

See first *Winfield & Jolowicz on Tort* (12th ed (1984)) p 706 (footnote omitted):

The consent must be freely given
The main point to notice here is that 'a man cannot be said to be truly "willing" unless he is in a position to choose freely, and freedom of choice predicates, not only full knowledge of the circumstances on which the exercise of choice is conditional, so that he may be able to choose wisely, but the absence of any feeling of constraint so that nothing shall interefere with the freedom of his will.'

See also the President's Commission 'Making Health Care Decisions', (*supra*) at pp 63–68 (footnotes omitted):

Voluntariness in decisionmaking
. . . The patient's participation in the decisionmaking process and ultimate decision regarding care must be voluntary. A choice that has been coerced, or that resulted from serious manipulation of a person's ability to make an intelligent and informed decision, is not the person's own free choice. This has long been recognised in law: a consent forced by threats or induced by fraud or misrepresentation is legally viewed as no consent at all. From the perspective of ethics, a consent that is substantially involuntary does not provide moral authorisation for treatment because it does not respect the patient's dignity and may not reflect the aims of the patient.

Of course, the facts of disease and the limited capabilities of medicine often constrict the choices available to patient and physician alike. In that sense, the condition of illness itself is sometimes spoken of as 'coercive' or involuntary. But the fact that no available alternative may be desirable in itself, and that the preferred course is, at best, only the least bad among a bad lot, does not render a choice coerced in the sense employed here. No change in human behavior or institutional structure could remove this limitation. Such constraints are merely facts of life that should not be regarded as making a patient's choice involuntary.

Voluntariness is best regarded as a matter of degree, rather than as a quality that is wholly present or absent in particular cases. Forced treatment—the embodiment of coercive, involuntary action—appears to be rare in the American health care system. Health care professionals do, however, make limited intrusions on voluntary choice through subtle, or even overt, manipulations of patients' wills when they believe that patients would otherwise make incorrect decisions.

Forced treatment. The most overt forms of involuntariness in health care settings involve interventions forced on patients without their consent (and sometimes over their express objection) and those based on coerced consent. Although rare in mainstream American health care, such situations do arise in certain special settings, and therefore require brief discussion. Society currently legitimates certain forced medical interventions to serve important social goals such as promoting the public health (with, for example, compulsory vaccination laws), enforcing the criminal law (removing bullets needed as evidence for criminal prosecutions), or otherwise promotiɲg the well-being of others (sedating uncontrollable inmates of mental institutions on an emergency basis, for example, to protect other inmates or staff).

Although it is typically not viewed as forced treatment, a good deal of routine care in hospitals, nursing homes, and other health care settings is provided (usually by health professionals such as nurses) without explicit and voluntary consent by patients. The expectation on the part of professionals is that patients, once in such a setting, will simply go along with such routine care. However, the Commission's study of treatment refusals found that in a hospital setting it was the routine tests that were most likely to be refused. At least some patients expected that participation was voluntary and refused tests and medications ordered without their knowledge until adequate information was provided about the nature, purpose, and risks of these undertakings. Lack of information in such cases may not only preclude voluntary participation but also raise questions about a patient's rationality, and hence competence.

When a situation offers the patient an opportunity to refuse care, then patient compliance or acquiescence may be viewed as implicit consent. But when the tacit communication accompanying such care is that there is no choice for the patient to make, and compliance is expected and enforced (at least in the absence of vigorous objections), the treatment can be properly termed 'forced'. The following conversation between a nurse and a patient regarding postoperative care, obtained in one of the Commission's observational studies, illustrates forced treatment that follows routinely from another decision (surgery) that was made voluntarily.

Nurse: Did they mention anything about a tube through your nose?

Patient: Yes, I'm gonna have a tube in my nose.

Nurse: You're going to have the tube down for a couple of days or longer. It depends. So you're going to NPO, nothing by mouth, and also you're going to have IV fluid.

Patient: I know. For three or four days they told me that already. I don't like it, though.

Nurse: You don't have any choice.

Patient: Yes, I don't have any choice, I know.

Nurse: Like it or not, you don't have any choice. (laughter) After you come back, we'll ask you to do a lot of coughing and deep breathing to exercise your lungs.

Patient: Oh, we'll see how I feel.

Nurse: (Emphasis) No matter how you feel, you have to do that!

The interview ended a few minutes later with the patient still disputing whether he was going to cooperate with the postoperative care.

Coerced treatment. Unlike forced treatment, for which no consent is given, coerced treatment proceeds on the basis of a consent that was not freely given. As used in this sense, a patient's decision is coerced when the person is credibly threatened by another individual, either explicitly or by implication, with unwanted and avoidable consequences unless the patient accedes to the specified course of action. Concern about coercion is accordingly greatest when a disproportion in power or other significant inequality between a patient and another individual lends credibility to the threat of harm and when the perceived interests of the individuals diverge.

The disparity in power between patient and health care professional may be slight or substantial, depending on the nature of the patient's illness, the institutional setting, the personalities of the individuals involved, and several other factors. In nonemergency settings, a patient typically can change practitioners or simply forego treatment, thus avoiding the potential for coercion. Further, although health care professionals do have interests distinct from and sometimes in conflict with those of their patients, strong social and professional norms usually ensure that priority is accorded to patients' welfare. To be sure, coercion can be exercised with benevolent motives if practitioner and patient differ in their assessments of how the patient's welfare is best served. Nonetheless, there is little reason to believe that blatant forms of coercion are a problem in mainstream American health care. When isolated instances of abuse do arise, the law provides suitable remedies.

A patient's family and other concerned persons may often play a useful role in the decisionmaking process. Sometimes, however, they may try to coerce a particular decision, either because of what they perceive to be in the patient's best interests or because of a desire to advance their own interests. In such instances, since the health care professional's first loyalty is to the patient, he or she should attempt to enhance the patient's ability to make a voluntary, uncoerced decision and to overcome any coercive pressures.

Manipulation. Blatant coercion may be of so little concern in professional-patient relationships because, as physicians so often proclaim, it is so easy for health professionals to elicit a desired decision through more subtle means. Indeed, some physicians are critical of the legal requirement for informed consent on the grounds that it must be mere window dressing since 'patients will, if they trust their doctor, accede to almost any request he cares to make'. On some occasions, to be sure, this result can be achieved by rational persuasion, since the professional presumably has good reasons for preferring a recommended course of action. But the tone of such critics suggests they have something else in mind: an ability to package and present the facts in a way that leaves the patient with no real choice. Such conduct, capitalising on disparities in knowledge, position, and influence, is manipulative in character and impairs the voluntariness of the patient's choice.

Manipulation has more and less extreme forms. At one end of the spectrum is behavior amounting to misrepresentation or fraud. Of particular concern in health care contexts is the withholding or distortion of information in order to affect the patient's beliefs and decisions. The patient might not be told about alternatives to the recommended course of action, for example, or the risks or other negative characteristics of the recommended treatment might be minimised. Such behavior is justly criticised on two grounds: first, that it interferes with the patient's voluntary choice (and thus negates consent) and, second, that it interferes with the patient's ability to make an informed decision. At the other end of the spectrum are far more subtle instances: a professional's careful choice of words or nuances of tone and emphasis might present the situation in a manner calculated to heighten the appeal of a particular course of action.

It is well known that the way information is presented can powerfully affect the recipient's response to it. The tone of voice and other aspects of the practitioner's manner of presentation can indicate whether a risk of a particular kind with a particular incidence should be considered serious. Information can be emphasised or played down without altering the content. And it can be framed in a way that affects the listener—for example, 'this procedure succeeds most of the time' versus 'this procedure has a 40 percent failure rate'. Health professionals who are aware of the effects of such minor variations can choose their language with care; if, during discussions with a patient, they sense any unintended or confused impressions being created they can adjust their presentation of information accordingly.

Because many patients are often fearful and unequal to their physicians in status, knowledge, and power, they may be particularly susceptible to manipulations of this type. Health care professionals should, therefore, present information in a form that fosters understanding. Patients should be helped to understand the prognosis for their situation and the implications of different courses of treatment. The difficult distinction, both in theory and in practice, is between acceptable forms of informing, discussion, and rational persuasion on the one hand, and objectionable forms of influence or manipulation on the other.

Since voluntariness is one of the foundation stones of . . . consent, professionals have a high ethical obligation to avoid coercion and manipulation of their patients. The law penalises those who ignore the requirements of consent or who directly coerce it. But it can do little about subtle manipulations without incurring severe disruptions of private relationships by intrusive policing, and so the duty is best thought of primarily in ethical terms.

The President's Commission may be correct in theory but the English cases do not go so far. See, for instance, Skegg, *Law, Ethics and Medicine* p 95:

Free consent

Writers on medical law sometimes state that consent must be 'freely given'. Discussion of this matter has often been confused by the assumption that principles concerning consent are the same in all contexts, and that because a very limited amount of pressure will render inoperative an employee's assumption of risk, the same amount of pressure will vitiate a patient's consent to medical treatment. The fallacy of the transplanted category[98] has, in the words of W W Cook, 'all the tenacity of original sin and must constantly be guarded against'.[99] Here, too, it is wrong to assume that the law of battery and the law of negligence will necessarily adopt an identical approach. Different areas of the law have different requirements, and conduct which suffices in one area may not suffice in another.

A. Tort and crime of battery

There are two ways in which an apparent consent may be held to be ineffective, for the purpose of the crime or tort of battery. If there is neither express assent nor express dissent, a court may draw a distinction between consent and submission.[1] In this context submission is equated with acquiescence, the absence of dissent, so that although 'every consent involves a submission . . . it by no means follows, that a mere submission requires a consent.[2] Mere submission is often indicative of consent,[3] but where it is shown that the person acquiesced because he did not realise what was involved,[4] or—less important in this context—for fear of the consequences of refusal,[5] the courts may find that the person did not consent. Although the distinction has more often been acted upon in criminal than in civil cases, there is no good reason why it should not be made with the tort, as well as the crime, of battery.[6]

The other means of dealing with cases where what could be regarded as consent was exacted under great pressure, is to invoke the principle that physical violence or threats of physical violence vitiate consent.[7] But it is clear that lesser forms of pressure will not of themselves vitiate consent.[8]

Consent is no less effective when it is unwillingly or reluctantly given; few patients would consent to major surgery if it were not for the force of surrounding circumstances, and the knowledge that health or even life may be in jeopardy if they do not consent. Financial inducements to consent to even non-therapeutic procedures would not vitiate consent.[9] Nor would the fact that the alternative to giving consent was a term of imprisonment,[10] or that there were psychological and social pressures to consent to, for example, the removal of a kidney for transplantation to a relative.[11]

B. Tort of negligence

There has been very little consideration of the amount of pressure a doctor may properly bring to bear on a patient, to induce him to consent, or of the circumstances in which a doctor may be obliged to shield a patient from undue pressure to consent. Nevertheless, it is possible to go a little beyond the mere statement that the doctor must do what any reasonable doctor would do in the circumstances.

A doctor will sometimes be justified in going to great lengths to persuade a patient to undergo a procedure which is in the best interests of the patient's health. With an unduly apprehensive patient, it might sometimes be bad medical practice not to do so.[12] But where the procedure is not intended for the benefit of a patient's health there is a stronger possibility of a doctor being in breach of his duty of care if he brings great pressure to bear on a patient, to induce him to consent. He may also be in breach of his duty of care if he does not attempt to shield his patient from undesirable pressures originating elsewhere. Official statements and codes on the subject of non-therapeutic experimentation often stress the need to obtain a 'free consent' or to prevent 'undue influence' being brought to bear on a patient.[13] These statements and codes could be admitted as evidence of the required standard of care in such cases.[14]

Notes to extract

[98] The expression is taken from the title of the illuminating discussion of the issue by M Hancock in (1959) 37 *Canadian Bar Review* 535–75.

[99] W W Cook, *The Logical and Legal Bases of the Conflict of Laws* (1942), 159.

[1] See eg *R v Case* (1850) 4 Cox CC 220 at 223; *R v Wollaston* (1872) 12 Cox CC 180 at 182. See also *R v Olugbajo* [1982] QB 320 at 332 (rape).

[2] *R v Day* (1841) 9 C & P 722 at 724 (emphasis omitted), quoted with approval in *R v Olugbajo* [1982] 1 QB 320 at 332.

[3] *R v Sinclair* (1867) 13 Cox CC 28 at 29 ('such absence of resistance as would reasonably imply consent'). See also *R v Day* (1841) 9 C & P 722 at 724.

[4] See eg *R v Rosinski* (1824) 1 Mood 19, 1 Lew CC 11; *R v Case* (1850) 4 Cox CC 220; *R v Sinclair* (1867) 13 Cox CC 28; *R v Lock* (1872) LR 2 CCR 10, 13; *Burrell v Harmer* (1966) 116 *NLJ* 1658. See also *R v Williams* [1923] 1 KB 340.

[5] *R v Day* (1841) 9 C & P 722 at 724; *R v Woodhurst* (1870) 12 Cox CC 443 at 444.

[6] The distinction was acted upon in *Agnew v Jobson* (1877) 13 Cox CC 625 (tort), but not in *Latter v Braddell* (1881) 50 LJQB 448. In so far as the latter case suggests that something less than consent may be sufficient, it should not be followed. At one time a touching may have amounted to a battery only if it was 'against the will', rather than 'without the will' (ie 'without consent'), but nowadays the expression 'against the will' is generally treated as a synonym for 'without consent'.

[7] *Latter v Braddell* (1881) 50 LJQB 448.

[8] *Latter v Braddell* (1881) 50 LJQB 448 (non-therapeutic medical examination); *Li Hong Mi v A-G* (1918) 13 HKLR 6 at 44. Cf *Conn v David Spencer Ltd* [1930] 1 DLR 805 (false imprisonment).

[9] In *Halushka v University of Saskatchewan* (1965) 53 DLR (2d) 436 financial considerations had induced the student to consent to the experimental procedures. But it was not suggested that this vitiated his consent. For a discussion of this issue in relation to the analogous crime of rape, see *R v Arnold* [1947] 2 DLR 438. Cf *R v McCoy* [1953] 2 SA 4; *State v Volschenk* [1968] 2 PH, H283.

[10] In *R v Severn* (1979) *Daily Telegraph*, 25 April, p 21 (news report), a sex offender agreed to have a drug implanted into his thigh, rather than undergo a further term of imprisonment. There was reason to believe that the drug would control his libido. It was said that the implant would also make his breasts grow, but that these could be cut off later. (Consent to a specimen of blood being taken for testing is effective, even though consent would not have been given were it not for the fact that the consequence of refusal would be prosecution under the Road Traffic Act 1972, s 8(7) (substituted by Transport Act 1981, s 25(3), Sch 8)).

[11] R Ormrod, 'Medical Ethics' [1968] 2 *Br Med J* 7, 9–10. See also *R v Landry* (1935) 64 CCC 104.

[12] But see *Wells v Surrey Area Health Authority* (1978) *Times*, 29 July, p 3 (news report), which resulted from a woman being sterilised during the course of a Caesarean operation to bring about the birth of her third child. The patient was a Roman Catholic, who at the time of the operation was 35 years of age. She subsequently 'bitterly regretted the sterilisation'. The possibility of sterilisation was first raised when she was already in labour and 'in some state of exhaustion'. Croom-Johnson J held that the patient understood the implications of the operation when she consented to it, and therefore dismissed her claim for 'assault'. But he awarded her damages of £3,000 on the ground that the hospital had been negligent in failing to give her proper advice about the operation. He urged the need for good counselling before taking 'this big and important step in a woman's life'. (See also 'Contraception by Female Sterilisation' (1980) 280 *Br Med J* 1154, 1155.)

[13] See eg 'Responsibility in Investigations on Human Subjects', *Report of the Medical Research Council for the Year 1962–1963* (Cmnd 2382; 1964), 21, 23 (Statement by the Medical Research Council); 'Experimental Research on Human Beings' [1963] 2 *Br Med J* Suppl 57 (Statement approved by Annual Representative Meeting of British Medical Association); 'Code of Ethics of the World Medical Association' [1964] 2 *Br Med J* 177 ('Declaration of Helsinki'); 'Recommendations Guiding Medical Doctors in Biomedical Research Involving Human Subjects' [1976] 1 *Medical Journal of Australia* 206–7.

[14] *Furniss v Fitchett* [1958] NZLR 396 at 405. See also *Qualcast (Wolverhampton) Ltd v Haynes* [1959] AC 743 at 759.

Latter v Braddell
(1881) 50 LJQB 488:

Facts: The plaintiff's mistress requested a doctor to examine the plaintiff, who was a domestic servant, in order to ascertain whether she was pregnant. The plaintiff objected to the examination, but undressed by the doctor's orders, and submitted to be examined. The doctor examined her, and ascertained that she was not pregnant. He used no violence or threats and did nothing more than was necessary for the examination. The mistress was not present.

The plaintiff sued her master and mistress and the doctor for assault. At the trial the Judge directed a verdict for the master and mistress, and the jury found a verdict for the doctor:

Held (affirming the order of the Common Pleas Division), that there was no evidence against the master and mistress, that the verdict in favour of the doctor was right, and that a rule for a new trial was rightly discharged.

The plaintiff appealed.

Bramwell LJ: I am of opinion that Mr Justice Lindley was right; in fact, I may almost say that he was more than right, for it seems to me that he might have directed a verdict for the defendant, Dr Sutcliffe; but if there was any evidence, his direction to the jury was right, and their finding was right, although it may be a practical hardship. Very likely the plaintiff thought the defendants had a right to have her examined; but the truth is, she submitted to it, and it is impossible to say the jury were wrong in finding that she submitted. She may have submitted under an erroneous notion of law, but it was not through fear of violence. It seems to follow that if the verdict for Dr Sutcliffe was right the other defendants are entitled to a verdict. I think Mr Justice Lindley was right in telling the jury that there was no evidence against Captain and Mrs Braddell. There could only be evidence against them if the plaintiff submitted through fear of violence, and if what was done was done by their order.

Baggallay LJ: I am of the same opinion. The argument for the plaintiff is on the ground of misdirection in withdrawing the case against Captain and Mrs Braddell from the jury, and on the ground that the verdict in favour of Dr Sutcliffe was against the weight of evidence. I think the verdict as to Dr Sutcliffe was right. As to Mrs Braddell I am not satisfied that she did more than tell Dr Sutcliffe to do what might be necessary and proper. Order XXXIX rule 3 would be fatal to the appeal, for no wrong was occasioned, even if there was misdirection.

Brett LJ: I am of opinion that Mr Justice Lindley was right. The doctor could only be liable if he did what he did without the consent or submission of the plaintiff; and Captain and Mrs Braddell could only be liable if they authorised the doctor to do what he did, and he did it, without such consent or submission. I think there was no evidence against Captain and Mrs Braddell. As to the doctor, there might be a case against him, though there was not a case against the other defendants. Then, was there any case for the jury as against Dr Sutcliffe? I think Mr Justice Lindley would have been justified in withdrawing the case from the jury. To make out an assault by Dr Sutcliffe, the plaintiff must shew that he used violence, or that she had reasonable cause to believe that he was threatening violence. I think the law laid down in the judgment of Mr Justice Lindley in the Court below is correct. Even if there was any evidence against Dr Sutcliffe I think there was no misdirection; and if the verdict as to him was right the withdrawal from the jury of the case against Captain and Mrs Braddell was immaterial, because, if Dr Sutcliffe did not assault the plaintiff, it does not matter if they authorised him.

The judgment was affirmed.

Is it still the law that violence or the fear of violence must be shown? Would the case be decided in the same way now?

Freeman v Home Office (No 2)
[1984] QB 524, [1983] 1 All ER 1036, CA:

Facts: By writ of 15 October 1979 the plaintiff, David Freeman, who at all material times was serving a sentence of life imprisonment at HM Prison, Wakefield, claimed damages for assault and for battery and for trespass to the person by the administration to him of certain drugs, namely Stelazin and/or Modecate and/or Serenace by or under the direction of Dr Cedric Melville Xavier, the servant or agent of the defendants, the Home Office and/or certain prison officers at HM Prison, Wakefield, being also servants or agents of the defendants, between in or about September 1972 and in or about December 1972 against the plaintiff's will and/or without his consent. By paragraph 4 of the statement of claim it was alleged that the plaintiff had not consented to the administration of the drugs or any of them and had 'actively resisted it, but was overcome forcibly by the said medical officer and/or prison officers'.

Stephen Brown LJ: Mr Blom-Cooper submits not only should the judge have inferred the absence of consent by reference to the documentary evidence but, furthermore, that it is impossible within the prison context as between a prisoner and a prison medical officer for free and voluntary consent to exist, at least, he added, in the absence of any written consent form. The prison medical officer is not merely a doctor, he is, submits Mr Blom-Cooper, a prison officer within the meaning of the Prison Rules and accordingly is a person who can influence a prisoner's life and his prospects of release on licence. There must inevitably be an atmosphere of constraint upon an inmate in such circumstances. He cited the well-known passage from the judgment of Scott LJ in *Bowater v Rowley Regis Corpn* [1944] KB 476 at 479:

With regard to the doctrine 'volenti non fit injuria' I would add one reflection of a general kind. That general maxim has to be applied with specially careful regard to the varying facts of human affairs and human nature in any particular case just because it is concerned with the intangible factors of mind and will. For the purpose of the rule, if it be a rule, a man cannot be said to be truly 'willing' unless he is in a position to choose freely, and freedom of choice predicates, not only full knowledge of the circumstances on which the exercise of choice is conditioned, so that he may be able to choose wisely, but the absence from his mind of any feeling of constraint so that nothing shall interfere with the freedom of his will.

He also cited the American case of *Kaimowitz v Michigan Department of Mental Health* (unreported) (1973) Cir Ct Wayne Co, Mich the decision of a circuit court in the County of Michigan in 1973 which is the subject of a learned article: *Law, Psychiatry and the Mental Health System* (1974), by Alexander Brooks, p 902. The judgment appears in the course of the article. The case concerned an inmate of a state hospital who had been committed to that institution as a criminal sexual psychopath and had signed what was termed an 'informed consent form' to become an experimental subject for experimental surgery and he later withdrew his consent. The court had to consider the nature of a legally adequate 'informed consent'. Although Mr Blom-Cooper recognised that having regard to recent authority 'informed consent' as such does not apply to the law of this country, he nevertheless placed reliance upon a passage of the judgment which appears at p 914 of the article:

We turn now to the third element of an informed consent, that of voluntariness. It is obvious that the most important thing to a large number of involuntarily detained mental patients incarcerated for an unknown length of time, is freedom.

The Nuremberg standards require that the experimental subjects be so situated as to exercise free power of choice without the intervention of any element of force, fraud, deceit, duress, overreaching, or other ulterior form of constraint or coercion. It is impossible for an involuntarily detained mental patient to be free of ulterior forms of restraint or coercion when his very release from the institution may depend upon his co-operating with the institutional authorities and giving consent to experimental surgery.

At p 915:

Involuntarily confined mental patients live in an inherently coercive institutional environment. Indirect and subtle psychological coercion has profound effect upon the patient population. Involuntarily confined patients cannot reason as equals with the doctors and administrators over whether they should undergo psychosurgery. They are not able to voluntarily give informed consent because of the inherent inequality in their position.

Mr Blom-Cooper seeks to apply those considerations and that reasoning to the position of the plaintiff in this present case, and he argues that in fact a valid free and voluntary consent cannot be given by a person such as the plaintiff, who is in prison, to a prison medical officer who is an officer of the prison having a disciplinary role in relation to him. Mr Blom-Cooper also drew the court's attention to the statutory provisions of the Mental Health Act 1983 which relate to detained and voluntary patients. The provisions are to be found in sections 57 and 58 of the Act and relate to the question of consent and impose certain statutory safeguards which have to be fulfilled. He submits that a prisoner like the plaintiff is in a similar situation and accordingly that the court should bear in mind such safeguards in considering whether consent is established.

It was Mr Blom-Cooper's intention to argue additionally that even if contrary to his submission a prisoner can give a legally valid consent to treatment by a prison medical officer, such consent must be 'informed consent'. Having regard to the decision of this court in *Sidaway v Board of Governors of the Bethlem Royal Hospital and the Maudsley Hospital* [1984] QB 493, [1984] 1 All ER 1018, in respect of which judgment was delivered on 23 February 1984, it is not open to him to argue that 'informed consent' is a consideration which can be entertained by the courts of this country. Nevertheless, he submitted to the court that in psychiatric treatment the test of consent should be that which is required by sections 57 and 58 of the Mental Health Act 1983.

Although the circumstances and the facts giving rise to the allegations made in this action afford an opportunity for interesting matters of principle and policy to be raised and considered, nevertheless I find myself in complete agreement with the trial judge that the sole issue raised at the trial, that is to say whether the plaintiff had consented to the administration of the drugs injected into his body, was essentially one of fact. The judge considered with care all the evidence, both oral and documentary, and it is clear from his careful judgment that he took into account the various submissions which Mr Blom-Cooper made as to the nature and effect of the documentary evidence and the setting in which the events occurred. The judge said [1984] 2 WLR 130 at 145c–d:

> The right approach, in my judgment, is to say that where, in a prison setting, a doctor has the power to influence a prisoner's situation and prospects a court must be alive to the risk that what may appear, on the face of it, to be real consent is not in fact so. I have borne that in mind throughout the case.

Essentially, however, the matter is one of fact. The judge made the positive finding that the plaintiff consented. He rejected Mr Blom-Cooper's submission that the plaintiff was entitled to judgment because he was incapable in law of giving his consent to the treatment by Dr Xavier in question. In my judgment he was right so to do. There was ample evidence to justify his finding of fact and accordingly the decision to which he came. It is not for this court to consider and decide this appeal upon the basis of an alternative and hypothetical set of facts and circumstances.

I would dismiss this appeal.

Do you agree with the decison reached by the court? Do you think an appeal to the European Commission on Human Rights would be fruitful, referring to Article X?

Let us repeat the approach of the court in *Kaimowitz v Michigan Department of Mental Health* 42 USLW 2063 (1973):

> We turn now to the third element of an informed consent, that of voluntariness. It is

obvious that the most important thing to a large number of involuntarily detained mental patients incacerated for an unknown length of time, is freedom.

The Nuremberg standards require that the experimental subjects be so situated as to exercise free power of choice without the intervention of any element of force, fraud, deceit, duress, overreaching, or other *ulterior form of constraint or coercion*. It is impossible for an involuntarily detained mental patient to be free of ulterior forms of restraint or coercion when his very release from the institution may depend upon his cooperating with the institutional authorities and giving consent to experimental surgery.

As pointed out in the testimony in this case, John Doe consented to this psychosurgery partly because of his effort to show the doctors in the hospital that he was a cooperative patient. Even Dr Yudashkin, in his testimony, pointed out that involuntarily confined patients tend to tell their doctors what the patient thinks these people want to hear.

The inherently coercive atmosphere to which the involuntarily detained mental patient is subjected has bearing upon the voluntariness of his consent.

Involuntarily confined mental patients live in an inherently coercive institutional environment. Indirect and subtle psychological coercion has profound effect upon the patient population. Involuntarily confined patients cannot reason as equals with the doctors and administrators over whether they should undergo psychosurgery. They are not able to voluntarily give informed consent because of the inherent inequality in their position.[23, 24]

Notes to extract

23. It should be emphasised that once John Doe was released in this case and returned to the community he withdrew all consent to the performance of the proposed experiment. His withdrawal of consent under these circumstances should be compared with his response on January 12, 1973, to questions placed to him by Prof. Slovenko, one of the members of the Human Rights Committee. These answers are part of exhibit 22 and were given after extensive publicity about this case, and while John Doe was in Lafayette Clinic waiting the implantation of depth electrodes. The significant questions and answers are as follows:

1. Would you seek psychosurgery if you were not confined in an institution?
   A. Yes, if after testing this showed it would be of help.
2. Do you believe that psychosurgery is a way to obtain your release from the institution?
   A. No, but it would be a step in obtaining my release. It is like any other therapy or program to help persons to function again.
3. Would you seek psychosurgery if there were other ways to obtain your release?
   A. Yes, if psychosurgery were the only means of helping my physical problem after a period of testing.

24. . . . Prof. Paul Freund of the Harvard Law School has expressed the following opinion: 'I suggest . . . that [prison] experiments should not involve any promise of parole or of commutation of sentence; this would be what is called in the law of confessions undue influence or duress through promise of reward, which can be as effective in overbearing the will as threats of harm. Nor should there be a pressure to conform within the prison generated by the pattern of rejecting parole applications of those who do not participate . . .' P. A. Freund, 'Ethical Problems in Human Experimentation,' New England Journal of Medicine, Volume 273 (1965) pages 687–92.

Do you accept the conclusion reached in *Kaimowitz* or is this an unnecessarily paternalistic view?

Limits on consent

Skegg, *Law, Ethics and Medicine*, p 32 writes:

Crime of battery
Medical procedures which involve bodily touchings come within the potential scope of the crime of battery[12] (known more popularly as assault).[13] But the absence of legally effective consent is an essential element of the offence.[14] If legally effective consent has been given, the medical touching will not constitute the offence of battery. If legally effective consent has not been given, and the doctor is aware of that fact, then even a therapeutic medical touching will amount to the offence of battery, except where a statutory or common law justification is available to the doctor.

Although the absence of consent has been said to be an essential element of the offence of battery, judges have insisted that there are some 'applications of force'[15] to which legally effective consent cannot be given, for the purpose of the offence of battery. The leading cases which supported the existence of such a category were concerned with issues as far removed from medical practice as prize fights,[16] and flagellation for the purpose of sexual gratification.[17] Nevertheless, some of the approaches expounded in these cases had some bearing on medical procedures, and various writers examined the application of these cases to medical practice.[18] But the importance of these cases has been diminished by the *A-G's Reference (No 6 of 1980)*.[19] The opinion of the Court of Appeal on this reference[20] is likely to be the starting-point for any future consideration of this matter in the courts.[21]

The Court of Appeal (which for convenience used the word 'assault' as including 'battery'[22]) started with the proposition that 'ordinarily an act consented to will not constitute an assault'. The court asked 'at what point does the public interest require the court to hold otherwise?' and gave the answer 'that it is not in the public interest that people should try to cause, or should cause, each other actual bodily harm for no good reason'.[23] In such cases, it was said, consent is not effective to prevent liability being incurred.

The phrase 'for no good reason' is important. The Court of Appeal did not say that it was not possible to give a legally effective consent to any application of force which was intended to cause, or which did cause, 'actual bodily harm'.[24] The court said:[25]

Nothing which we have said is intended to cast doubt upon the accepted legality of properly conducted games and sports, lawful chastisement or correction, reasonable surgical interference, dangerous exhibitions, etc. These apparent exceptions can be justified as involving the exercise of a legal right, in the case of chastisement or correction, or as needed in the public interest, in the other cases.

Although the approach adopted by the Court of Appeal prohibits a wide range of consensual contacts,[26] the court's opinion should not lead to difficulties in relation to medical practice.

Many touchings which occur in the course of medical practice do not involve 'any hurt or injury calculated to interfere with health or comfort'. In these cases, consent can prevent liability in battery, even if there is 'no good reason' for the touching. Surgery, and some other medical procedures, could be said to involve 'hurt or injury calculated to interfere with health or comfort' in a manner which is 'more than merely transient and trifling'. As has already been suggested, conduct which benefits bodily health should not be regarded as causing bodily harm. But even if it were regarded as causing bodily harm, there could be absolutely no doubt that it was possible to give a legally effective consent to such procedures.[27] There is clearly a good reason for them.

Sometimes medical procedures which were intended to benefit the patient will fail in their object, and will cause what is undoubtedly bodily harm. If an application of force was not intended to cause bodily harm, and the person responsible did not take an unjustifiable risk as to the causing of bodily harm, then the undesired consequence should not render ineffective consent which would otherwise have been effective.[28] In the course of medical practice there is often good reason to attempt to benefit a patient's health, even though there is a risk of harm resulting.[29] Here, too, consent will undoubtedly prevent liability being incurred.

Some medical procedures are not intended to benefit the person on whom they are performed.[30] Indeed, sometimes a procedure is performed on a person in the knowledge that it will certainly be to that person's bodily detriment. This is the case when a kidney is removed from a healthy person, for transplantation into someone who is in need of it. The operation is a major one, and is not without risks.[31] But it is not unreasonably dangerous, and the probable benefit to the recipient far outweighs the probable detriment to the donor. Hence, if called upon to deal with a case in which a kidney had been removed from a consenting adult, for transplantation into someone in need of it, the courts may confidently be expected to take the view that the operation did not amount to the offence of battery.[32] Even though the operation causes serious bodily harm, there is clearly a good reason for it. There is also a good reason for some non-therapeutic medical experimentation, even if it may cause bodily harm.[33]

Where judges regard an activity as socially acceptable they are unlikely to question the reasons for it. In the *A-G's Reference (No 6 of 1980)* the court spoke of the 'accepted legality' of properly conducted games and sports, of dangerous exhibitions, and of 'reasonable surgical interference'. The need for these 'apparent exceptions' only arises where an application of force is intended to cause, or does in fact cause, bodily harm. As the Court of Appeal was prepared to accept that dangerous exhibitions are needed in the public interest, it would be extraordinary if a later court took a restrictive view of the scope of permissible medical interventions. A court is not likely to inquire closely into whether there are good reasons for a particular intervention. There is no danger of a court attempting to decide whether there were good reasons for removing a kidney from a living donor, instead of keeping the patient on dialysis in the hope that a suitable cadaver kidney would become available. And there is now very little danger of a court seeking to manipulate the offence of battery so as to prevent individuals reaching their own decisions about whether to be sterilised,[34] or undergo cosmetic surgery.[35] Opinions vary as to the desirability of such operations in particular circumstances.[36] But it is doubtful whether judges would regard these operations as sufficiently against the public interest to warrant their being regarded as constituting the offence of battery, despite the presence of consent.[37]

Were a patient to consent to having his limbs amputated, for no good reason, his consent would not prevent the amputation from amounting to the offence of battery. But the judges' insistence that there are some applications of force to which consent cannot be given, for the purpose of the offence of battery, should not hinder modern medical practice.

Notes to extract
[12] The touching need not be 'hostile' or 'aggressive' for it to amount to the offence of battery: see *Faulkner v Talbot* [1981] 1 WLR 1528 at 1534.
[13] In the context of the criminal law, the term 'assault' has long been used to encompass battery, or as a synonym for battery, even though assault and battery are distinct crimes at common law. The reason why this sensible usage has not been adopted in this book is that writers on the law of torts often distinguish between the tort of assault and the tort of battery . . . It is therefore simpler to refer to the crime and the tort of battery, rather than to speak of the crime of assault and the tort of battery (or trespass to the person—which includes both the tort of assault and the tort of battery).
[14] *Fagan v Metropolitan Police Comr* [1969] 1 QB 439 at 444E; *A-G's Reference (No 6 of 1980)* [1981] QB 715 at 718D–E. There is therefore no need to regard medical touchings as batteries (or assaults) licensed by consent. Such an approach is comparable to one which regards consensual sexual intercourse as rape licensed by consent. Although the absence of consent has long been considered an essential element of the offence (see eg *R v Martin* (1840) 9 C & P 213 at 215, 217; *R v Guthrie*

(1870) LR 1 CCR 241 at 243; *R v Lock* (1872) LR 2 CCR 10 at 13; *R v Wollaston* (1872) 12 Cox CC 180 at 182), the judgments in *R v Coney* (1882) 8 QBD 534 and *R v Donovan* [1934] 2 KB 498 have been seen by some to require a reformulation. But these cases can be subsumed within the traditional formulation by speaking of the absence of 'legally effective' consent. There is a hint of this approach in the judgment of Hawkins J in *R v Coney* (1882) 8 QBD 534 at 553. See also *A-G's Reference (No 6 of 1980)* [1981] QB 718D–E, cf 719A.

[15] Even the lightest touch is regarded as an 'application of force', for the purpose of the crime and tort of battery.

[16] *R v Coney* (1882) 8 QBD 534. On prize-fights, see generally L L M Minty, 'Unlawful Wounding; Will Consent Make it Legal?' (1956) 24 *Med-Leg J* 54, 55–8; see also Note (1912) 28 *LQR* 125.

[17] *R v Donovan* [1934] 2 KB 498. *Archbold's Pleading, Evidence and Practice in Criminal Cases* (41st edn, 1982, ed S Mitchell), para 20–124, cites *Donovan* in support of the proposition that 'Consent is no defence where severe blows are given for the purpose of gratifying perverted sexual passion', and goes on to state that it was 'followed in *R v Lawson* May 25 1936, CCA where the law is reviewed'. Enquiries at the Bar Library, the Criminal Appeals Office, and the Public Record Office reveal that no report of the judgments in *R v Lawson* has been retained. A very brief note in *The Times*, 26 May 1936, indicates that the appellants had been convicted of indecent assault, and that the Court of Criminal Appeal (Lord Hewart CJ, du Parcq and Singleton JJ) allowed the appeals, and quashed the convictions. There is no mention of the facts or law.

[18] The present writer discussed the matter in 'Medical Procedures and the Crime of Battery' [1974] *Crim LR* 693–700. For a subsequent examination of these cases, see Adrian Lynch, 'Criminal Liability for Transmitting Disease' [1978] *Crim LR* 612–25.

[19] [1981] QB 715. The reference was made under s 36 of the Criminal Justice Act 1972. Lord Lane CJ read the opinion of the court. The other two judges were Phillips J and Drake J.

[20] The court was asked to give its opinion on the following point of law: 'Where two persons fight (otherwise than in the course of sport) in a public place can it be a defence for one of those persons to a charge of assault arising out of the fight that the other consented to fight?' The answer of the court was 'No, but not, as the reference implies, because the fight occurred in a public place, but because, wherever it occurred, the participants would have been guilty of assault, subject to self-defence, if, as we understand was the case, they intended to and/or did cause actual bodily harm.' ([1981] QB 719E–F.)

[21] The court stated that 'the diversity of view expressed in the previous decisions . . . make some selection and a partly new approach necessary' ([1981] QB 719A).

[22] [1981] QB 718D.

[23] *Ibid* 719. The opinion continued: 'Minor struggles are another matter. So, in our judgment, it is immaterial whether the act occurs in private or in public; it is an assault if actual bodily harm is intended and/or caused. This means that most fights will be unlawful regardless of consent.'

[24] The court did not define 'actual bodily harm', but as *R v Donovan* was one of the few cases cited by counsel, and discussed in the opinion, it may be assumed that they used 'actual bodily harm' to refer to what was described as 'bodily harm' in *R v Donovan*. (It is difficult to conceive of bodily harm which is not 'actual': see generally Williams, *Textbook*, 154.) The words used to describe 'bodily harm' in *R v Donovan* were very similar indeed to those used of 'actual bodily harm' in the then-current edition of *Archbold's Pleading, Evidence and Practice in Criminal Cases*; see 28th edn, 1931, edd R E Ross and T R F Butler, p 953. In this discussion 'bodily harm' will be used as a synonym for 'actual bodily harm'.

[25] [1981] QB 719E.

[26] The court appears to have been aware that its formulation applied to an unnecessarily wide range of contacts, for the opinion concluded with the statement 'We would not wish our opinion on the point to be the signal for unnecessary prosecutions.'

[27] See eg Stephen, *Digest*, 148; *Bravery v Bravery* [1954] 1 WLR 1169 at 1180; *Corbett v Corbett (otherwise Ashley)* [1971] P 83 at 99; *R v Hyam* [1975] AC 55 at 74, 77.

[28] But see the 'answer' in *A-G's Reference (No 6 of 1980)*, quoted in n 20 above. The reference to 'and/or' in that answer is unsatisfactory. The 'good reason' qualification may be particularly important in cases where bodily harm is caused unintentionally.

[29] See eg *R v Hyam* [1975] AC 55 at 74, 77–8.

[30] In *Bravery v Bravery* [1954] 1 WLR 1169 at 1180, Denning LJ accepted that there was a just cause for sterilisation to prevent the transmission of a hereditary disease.

[31] See R G Simmons *et al, Gift of Life* (1977), 165–75; A B Cosimi, 'The Donor and Donor Nephrectomy', in *Kidney Transplantation* (1979, ed P J Morris), 69, 71, 73–8; Editorial, 'Living Related Kidney Donors' [1982] 2 *Lancet* 696.

[32] Edmund Davies, 'Transplants', 634. See also R Ormrod, 'Medical Ethics' [1968] 2 *Br Med J* 7, 9–10; *Urbanski v Patel* (1978) 84 DLR (3d) 650 esp 651, 670–1.

[33] For a case arising out of non-therapeutic experimentation, see *Halushka v University of Saskatchewan* (1965) 53 DLR (2d) 436. The 'good reason' could be found either in the possibility of an eventual benefit to the health of others (and, sometimes, the subject), or in the advancement of knowledge as an end in itself. See also Bernard Häring, *Medical Ethics* (1972), 214–15.

[34] In *Bravery v Bravery* [1954] 1 WLR 1169 at 1180, an appeal from the dismissal of a petition for divorce on grounds of cruelty, Denning LJ expressed the view that 'where a sterilisation operation is done so as to enable a man to have the pleasure of sexual intercourse, without shouldering the responsibilities attaching to it' the operation 'is illegal, even though the man consents to it'. However, Sir Raymond Evershed MR and Hodson LJ dissociated themselves from these observations: see *ibid*. 1175. For a critique of Denning LJ's reasons, see G W Bartholemew, 'Legal Implications of Voluntary Sterilisation Operations' (1959) 2 *Melbourne University Law Review* 77, 93–4; and see also, now, Editorial, 'Vasectomy Reversal' [1980] 2 *Lancet* 625–6. Sterilisation is now a widely-accepted method of birth control, and s 1 of the National Health Service (Family Planning) Amendment Act 1972 provides for voluntary vasectomy services to be provided by local health authorities in England and Wales on the same basis as contraception services under s 1 of the National Health Service (Family Planning) Act 1967. *Halsbury* (vol xi, para 23 n 8) is surely correct in stating that nowadays the legality of such operations 'cannot be doubted'. See also eg *R v Miskimmin* 1974 *Times*, 15 June, p 3 (news report); *Re D (A Minor) (Wardship: Sterilisation)* [1976] Fam 185 at 196; *Wells v Surrey Area Health Authority*, (1978) *Times*, 29 July, p 3 (news report); *Cataford v Moreau* (1978) 114 DLR (3d) 585; *Re Eve* (1981) 115 DLR (3d) 282.

[35] For a Canadian view, see *Petty v MacKay* (1979) 10 CCLT 85. See also Stephen, *Digest*, 149 n 3; *White v Turner* (1981) 120 DLR (3d) 269.

[36] *Quaere*, in what circumstances such operations could properly be regarded as causing bodily harm. These operations are sometimes performed for therapeutic purposes. Given some broad definitions of 'health' (see generally Daniel Callahan, 'The WHO Definition of Health' (1973) 1 *Hastings Center Studies* 77–87), many of these operations could be regarded as for the benefit of the health of the patient.

[37] See generally P D G Skegg, 'Medical Procedures and the Crime of Battery' [1974] *Crim LR* at 699–700. In *R v Coney* (1882) 8 QBD 534 at 549 Stephen J said: 'The principle as to consent seems to me to be this: When one person is indicted for inflicting personal injury upon another, the consent of the person who sustains the injury is no defence to the person who inflicts the injury, if the injury is of such a nature, or is inflicted under such circumstances, that its infliction is injurious to the public as well as to the person injured.' In his *Digest of the Criminal Law* Stephen had expressed a different view, and in the two subsequent editions of the *Digest* which he prepared he left unchanged the statement that 'Every one has a right to consent to the infliction upon himself of bodily harm not amounting to a maim.' (For a fuller account, see P D G Skegg, *op cit*, 699, n 38.) Professor Glanville Williams has used passages from Stephen's *Digest* to support a restrictive interpretation of his judgment in *R v Coney* (see Williams, *Textbook*, 541). But the

fact that Stephen did not amend these passages could be regarded as demonstrating that he recognised that the approach he propounded in *R v Coney* did not receive the support of the majority of the judges in that case. (Professor Glanville Williams states that when Stephen J spoke in *R v Coney* of an injury injurious to the public 'he must have meant an injury that was either (1) a maim or dangerous to life or (2) inflicted in circumstances likely to produce a breach of the peace (the former prize-fight)'. But in *R v Coney* Stephen J said that it was 'against the public interest that the lives *and the health* of the combatants should be endangered by blows' (8 QBD 549; emphasis added). An injury may affect health even though it is not a maim or dangerous to life.)

One of the few explicit judicial references to the limits imposed on consent by public policy in the context of medical law is to be found in *Corbett v Corbett (otherwise Ashley) (No 2)* [1971] P 110, [1970] 2 All ER 654, *per* Ormrod J. He states somewhat delphically: 'If an operation for the re-assignment of a transsexual is undertaken for genuine therapeutic purposes, it is a matter for the decision of the patient and the doctors concerned in his case'. Is this too vague a criterion? Does it leave the determination of public policy to doctors rather than courts in that the words 'therapeutic' and 'non-therapeutic' may not entirely be free of value judgments?

Consent by others

The issue of consent by others arises in circumstances in which the patient is incompetent to make his own decision. This will be discussed below. We will also consider the capacity of parents, spouses, relatives and the court to consent to (or refuse) treatment on behalf of others.

(a) TREATING WITHOUT CONSENT: THE INCOMPETENT

The incompetent include those who fail to meet the criteria discussed above— *supra* p 186 *et seq*—in relation to *Gillick*, because they lack the capacity to consent in law by reason of lack of understanding; those who by reason of mental illness are equally lacking in understanding and those who are unconscious such that they cannot at that moment make their wishes known.

(i) Public policy

1. Under common law. Is there any common law justification for treating an incompetent patient without consent? The following extracts show that there is, although the precise scope of a doctor's power (right?) to intervene is, as you will see, somewhat unclear.

Wilson v Pringle
Notice first [1986] 1 WLR 1 CA, p 447 [1986] 2 All ER 440 at p 447, [1987] QB 237 at p 252

Croom-Johnson LJ referred to the earlier case of *Collins v Wilcock* [1984] 3 All ER 374, [1984] 1 WLR 1172 where Robert Goff LJ examined the situations in which certain touchings without consent might be lawful.

Croom-Johnson J: Robert Goff LJ draws the so-called 'defences' to an action for trespass to the person (of which consent, self-defence, ejecting a trespasser, exercising parental authority, and statutory authority are some examples) under one umbrella of 'a general exception embracing all physical contact which is generally acceptable in the ordinary conduct of daily life'. It provides a solution to the old problem of what legal rule allows a casualty surgeon to perform an urgent operation on an unconscious patient who is brought into hospital. The patient cannot consent . . . Hitherto it has been customary to say in such cases that consent is to be implied for what would otherwise be a battery on the unconscious body. It is better simply to say that the surgeon's action is acceptable in the ordinary conduct of everyday life, and not a battery.

In discussing the hypothetical example of the treatment of an incompetent child, Lord Templeman stated in *Gillick* that:

I accept that if there is no time to obtain a decision from the court, a doctor may safely carry out treatment in an emergency if the doctor believes the treatment to be vital to the survival or health of an infant and notwithstanding the opposition of a parent or the impossibility of alerting the parent before the treatment is carried out. In such a case the doctor must have the courage of his convictions that the treatment is necessary and urgent in the interests of the patient and the court will, if necessary, approve after the event treatment which the court would have authorised in advance, even if the treatment proves to be unsuccessful.

When Lord Templeman refers to the interests of the patients, does he mean the *health* interests of the patient?

The law relating to treatment without consent in England is often described by analogy with the Canadian common law: Ellen Picard explains the Canadian law in her textbook *Legal Liability of Doctors and Hospitals in Canada (op cit)* (pp 45–46):

Emergencies
A person may be unable to give consent due to unconsciousness or extreme illness. In such circumstances a doctor is justified in proceeding without the patient's consent, subject to a number of restrictions.[28]

While the legal basis for substituting the doctor's decision for that of the patient has been debated by academics,[29] Canadian judges have taken a realistic approach. Refusing to strain the law to find consent, the courts have recognised that sometimes a doctor may proceed without consent.[30]

A few important Canadian cases illustrate the limits of this emergency doctrine.

In *Marshall v Curry*,[31] the doctor discovered a grossly diseased testicle in the course of a hernia repair operation. He removed the testicle, firstly because it was necessary for the hernia repair, and secondly because he judged it potentially gangrenous and therefore a menace to the patient's life and health. Because the patient was under general anaesthetic, the doctor proceeded without consent, and subsequently was sued for battery.[32] Prior to this case it had been held that in emergencies, the doctor became the patient's representative with authority to give his consent on the patient's behalf. Here the court refused to employ this reasoning and instead justified the doctor's action in emergency circumstances on 'the higher ground of duty'.[33] The Chief Justice of Nova Scotia said that 'where a great emergency which could not be anticipated arises' a doctor can act without consent 'in order to save the life or preserve the health of the patient'.[34] The action against the doctor was dismissed.

However, in *Murray v McMurchy*,[35] a doctor who tied a patient's fallopian tubes because he had discovered fibroid tumours in the uterine wall during a Caesarian section, and was concerned about the hazards of a second pregnancy, was held liable. The trial judge found that while it was convenient to carry out the procedure at that time, there was no evidence that the tumours were an immediate danger to the patient's life or health.

Similarly, in *Parmley v Parmley and Yule*,[36] in which a patient requested the removal of two teeth and the defendant dentist extracted all of her upper teeth because he found advanced tooth decay and pyorrhea in the gums, the court held the dentist liable. Again there was no evidence of emergency and thus no basis for proceeding without consent. However, an important *obiter* comment was made in the case:[37]

There are times under circumstances of emergency when both doctors and dentists must exercise their professional skill and ability without the consent which is required in the ordinary case. Upon such occasions *great latitude may be given to the doctor or dentist*. [emphasis supplied]

A reconciliation of these cases leads to the principle that consent is unnecessary only where the procedure or treatment is required in order to save life or preserve health. Consent is required on all other occasions and it is no answer for the doctor to say that it was more convenient to perform the unauthorised procedure at that time or that he believed it was then that the patient would have wanted it done.[38]

In short, our Canadian courts differentiate between a procedure that is 'necessary' and one that is 'convenient'.

Notes on extract
[28] See *Reibl v Hughes* (1980) 14 CCLT 1 at 13 (SCC) where Laskin CJ said that 'actions of battery in respect of surgical or other medical treatment should be confined to cases where surgery or treatment has been performed or given to which there has been no consent at all or where, *emergency situations aside*, surgery or treatment has been performed or given beyond that to which there is consent'. [emphasis supplied.]

[29] For an excellent discussion. *See* Skegg, *A Justification for Medical Procedures Performed Without Consent*, [1974] 90 LQ Rev 512; see also Rodgers-Magnet. *The Right to Emergency Medical Assistance in the Province of Quebec* (1980), 40 R du B 373 at 411.

[30] *Marshall v Curry supra* n 19; Note that in some provinces the nurse or doctor who renders emergency care without expecting compensation where facilities are inadequate must be grossly negligent before she or he would be liable. See Emergency Medical Aid Act, RSA 1980, c E-9; Emergency Medical Aid Act, SN 1971, No 15, s 3; Emergency Medical Aid Act, RSS 1978, c E-8, s 3; Medical Act, SNS 1969, c 15, s 38.

[31] *Id.*

[32] Note that negligence was alleged in the pleadings but not proceeded with at trial. *Id* at 263.

[33] *Id* at 275.

[34] *Id* at 275. *But see Boase v Paul* [1931] 1 DLR 562; affd [1931] 4 DLR 435 (Ont CA).

[35] [1949] 2 DLR 442 (BCSC).

[36] [1945] 4 DLR 81 (SCC).

[37] *Id* at 89. See also Skegg, *supra* n 29.

[38] In *Murray v McMurchy supra* n 35, a witness testified that 97 per cent of patients would be annoyed if the additional procedure of removing the tumours had not been taken.

Except for the situation dealt with by Lord Templeman, in each of the others the patient was incompetent because he was unconscious. But this is only one way in which incompetence may occur as we have seen. Perhaps more difficult problems exist if the patient is not unconscious but suffers from some mental incapacity that renders him incompetent to make decisions concerning his health care.

In the following extracts from *Mental Health Services Law and Practice*, (1986) Professor Gostin of Harvard and Professor Hoggett investigate the existence and scope of the justification in this kind of situation.

20.16 Necessity: treatment in the absence of consent
A doctor will, in certain circumstances, be justified in providing treatment or in medically or physically restraining a person . . . without consent. The legal ground upon which such a justification is normally based is the agency of necessity, but the language of consent has also been used; consent in certain circumstances is 'implied' or 'presumed' or can be assumed will be obtained in 'future'. The justification is not subject to tidy or definitive legal characterisation, but is merely a number of disparate judicial responses to specific factual circumstances. Plainly, a life saving medical procedure may be performed where a person cannot provide the requisite consent (eg by reason of unconsciousness) and is not known to object to the performance of the procedure. There are, however, variations on this same set of

facts where the application of the common law is less clear. If the patient, though now incompetent, was known to have an objection to the treatment, the preferred view is that the doctor would not be justified in proceeding. It is helpful to distinguish between short term and permanent incompetency. If the person's incompetency is transient (eg from anaesthetic, sedation, intoxication or temporary unconsciousness) there would not be a justification for doing everything which the doctor judged was beneficial to the patient. The Canadian position would be likely to be adopted where treatments which are 'necessary', ie 'unreasonable to postpone', are distinguished from those which are merely 'convenient'; the former may be performed where the patient is temporarily unable to give consent, while the latter may not. As a general principle, treatment which is given to a patient while temporarily incompetent should be the minimum amount necessary; any treatment which could reasonably be postponed until the patient regained competency should not be given.

20.16.1 Treating a permanently incompetent patient

A much more difficult and important question arises as to the extent of the doctor's powers and duties to treat a non-volitional or otherwise incompetent patient where there is no reasonable likelihood that the person will regain competency. This is a major problem within the mental health services for there are many informal patients who are incompetent to give consent to medical or psychiatric treatment needed for their health and wellbeing—for example, patients who are severely mentally ill, severely mentally handicapped or elderly and confused. Situations arise where highly vulnerable, isolated and withdrawn patients require beneficial medical treatment (such as the removal of a cataract) to which they cannot give consent. There are no English cases to provide guidance. However, it is suggested that, if there is no reasonable likelihood of the patient regaining competency, any treatment which is clearly for the medical benefit of the patient could be given under the doctrine of necessity. Here, treatments which are clearly appropriate, not merely urgently necessary, could be given. It would be difficult to conceive that a court would deny the right of an incompetent patient to the same kind of appropriate medical and dental treatment as competent patients can expect to receive.

There are several qualifications to this principle which can be offered. The doctor should proceed only if there is complete agreement on the need for the treatment. He is also advised to obtain the consent of the nearest relative, although this has no validity in law. If the treatment is for *mental disorder*, the patient should be treated as if he were *temporarily* incompetent; treatment should be administered only if *urgently necessary*—(ie it would significantly affect the patient's health if postponed).

Hoggett in *Mental Health Law* (1984), pp 201–203, writes:

Necessity
But are there any circumstances in which the common law permits intervention without the patient's consent and beyond what is immediately required to *prevent* his doing harm (once again, we must bear in mind the [Mental Health] Act's restrictions on the use of some treatments in some cases)? There are two circumstances in which this question is of vital importance to mental hospital staff. The first is the informal patient who lacks even the low degree of capacity needed for a 'real' consent and is not 'disposed to do mischief to himself or others'. Can nothing be done without 'sectioning' him? As the DHSS (1978) point out, in such cases an absence of dissent cannot be taken as the presence of consent. But a major object of the 1959 Act was to do away with the need to 'section' patients such as the severely mentally handicapped, or the elderly severely mentally infirm. Indeed . . . under the 1983 Act some of these cannot be 'sectioned' long term at all. The other example is the attempted suicide. As suicide is no longer a crime, can he be prevented from carrying out his intention even if he is not 'insane' within the meaning of the common law power to restrain? And if he has succeeded in poisoning or otherwise attacking himself, can steps be taken to save his life against his will and without sectioning him? Indeed, as we shall see later, sectioning will not help where the treatment required is for physical rather than mental disorder.

There are undoubtedly some cases where the common law justifies measures for which no consent has been given, but the underlying principle is not easy to determine. The best example is the unconscious road accident victim. We have no 'good Samaritan' laws making it unlawful to refuse to help him, but it is obviously lawful to intervene without his consent. A less obvious example is the patient who has consented to one operation, during which it is discovered that further treatment is urgently required. The doctor has a duty to prevent his patient coming to harm and the patient might well complain if he suffered as a result of the doctor's failure to act. Once again, we may be sure that the doctor will not be liable if he carries on with something which it would be unreasonable, as opposed to merely inconvenient, to postpone (compare the Canadian cases of *Marshall v Curry* (1933) 3 DLR 260 and *Murray v McMurchy* (1949) 2 DLR 442).

But is the reason for these decisions the patient's implied consent? The patient may indignantly repudiate that suggestion when he comes round, but still the doctor will not be liable (see *Beatty v Cullingworth*, British Medical Journal, November 21, 1896, p 1525). Or is the reason that the treatment was immediately necessary to save the patient's life or perhaps a serious deterioration in his health? Taken to its logical conclusion, such a doctrine would allow us to overrule the protests of any patient, sane or insane, who wished to decline such treatment (for example, the Jehovah's witness who had conscientious objections to a life-saving blood transfusion; or the elderly person who no longer wished for massive surgical attempts to prolong life).

The most we can be absolutely sure of is this. The doctor may proceed where the treatment is 'necessary', in the sense that the patient may die or suffer serious harm if it is postponed until he can be consulted, but only where it is reasonable to assume that the patient would have consented, in other words where he is not known to object. We may also be tolerably certain that the law would not condemn intervention which is absolutely necessary to save the patient's life in some cases where he is known to object. This must be true of the attempted suicide, where in any event it is possible to argue that he did not genuinely wish to succeed, but it is far less obviously true of the known Jehovah's witness who requires a blood transfusion. In all these cases, however, even if there is a technical battery, no jury is likely to convict, and there could be no substantial damages for 'wrongful life'.

But we cannot be sure how much further these principles will carry us, particularly in relation to patients who are permanently incapable of giving or withholding their consent. The hospital may, and indeed must, do what is necessary to sustain life and prevent their coming to serious harm. But does the law permit more substantial intervention? Skegg (1974) has suggested that 'if the patient is likely to be permanently incapable of consenting ... a doctor should be justified in doing whatever good medical practice dictates should be done in the patient's interests'. This is extremely doubtful. It would extend the range of treatments involved, reasoning that it would be unreasonable to postpone them until the patient can be consulted because he can never be consulted. It also assumes that if the patient is incapable of giving a valid consent, his active protests (of which he may very well still be capable) can be overruled. The obvious problem example is a proposed abortion for a severely handicapped woman.

(The example of Professor Hoggett's based upon a Jehovah's Witness who is given a blood transfusion whilst unconscious arose in the Ontario case of *Malette v Shulman* (21 December 1987, unreported) where the defendant ignored a clear written instruction not to transfuse the plaintiff. The plaintiff successfully sued the doctor in battery and recovered $20,000 (Canadian).)

You will note that Professor Gostin suggests that in the case of a patient who has 'no reasonable likelihood of ... regaining competency, any treatment which is clearly for the medical benefit of the patient could be given under the doctrine of necessity'. In *T v T* [1988] Fam 52, [1988] 1 All ER 613, Wood J was faced with a patient in just this situation:

The first defendant celebrated her 19th birthday in the spring of this year. She was born with severe mental handicap. Her parents were divorced some 10 years ago when her mother, the plaintiff, was granted her sole custody.

On 16 June 1987, despite the excellent care of all those around her, the first defendant was found to be pregnant. A subsequent scan revealed a foetus of about 11 weeks. Termination of this pregnancy is recommended by the doctors, and whilst this procedure is being carried out sterilisation is also considered to be in her best interests. Her mother supports these views, as does her social worker. However, the doctors, quite understandably, are unwilling to operate unless protected by an order of the court.

It is necessary to give a picture of life in this home. It is indeed tragic. Looking after her daughter is, for this mother, a full time occupation. Until 1980 she had her own mother to help her. Since then she has received help from friends and from a social care worker.

The first defendant's powers of communication are extremely limited; she does use a few words, but only her mother can really understand them. As a result of this she becomes very frustrated and demands constant supervision and stimulation. She is doubly incontinent and requires changing six to eight times a day. She suffers quite badly from epilepsy (grand mal) and is on a heavy prescription of drugs. She was very attached to her grandmother and had no comprehension of her death. This coincided with the onset of menstruation, itself a traumatic experience, as she has no understanding of the physical workings of her body. From the time of her grandmother's death there has been a marked deterioration in her condition and behaviour. She has become generally unco-operative and destructive for no apparent reason: as an instance, she chews her clothes. Her mother is convinced that the first defendant has no maternal instincts, although she is very possessive of toys and books. She plays with dolls and teddy bears, but only in a rough and destructive manner. She chews the ears off her teddy bears and tries to unpick the stitches and pull out the stuffing. Her dolls are invariably thrown around and she cannot hold anything or concentrate on any matter for any amount of time. Her mother takes the view that she will be totally incapable of understanding the birth of a baby or caring for that child.

In May 1984 the plaintiff mother could cope no more, and the first defendant was admitted to hospital for assessment by a consultant psychiatrist. He found her very disturbed, very destructive and with little or no sense of danger. At the age of 13 she had been assessed to have a mental age of 2.9 years, and he doubted whether she had progressed since then. Her IQ in his opinion was less than 30. She is totally dependent on others, and he did not think that she would have any comprehension of pregnancy or of what was happening to her physically, and in his view also she would be incapable of providing any care for a child. Having examined the family history he thought that there was a small chance of genetic contribution to her mental handicap and therefore possible that the foetus would be handicapped also . . .

In the light of an inability to obtain consent from anyone, a surgeon who performs an operation without his patient's express or implied consent would be liable for trespass to the person—an assault and battery—a tortious remedy. It is important to remember that necessary medical and surgical treatment for mental disorder is covered by the Mental Health Act 1983. I am here dealing with the defendant's physical health in the light of her mental disability. I pose myself the question: is there any basis upon which the court can declare such an assault to be justified?

The first possible approach is to say that in some, if not many cases, there would be an implied consent by the patient to the carrying out of those procedures which the surgeon, without negligence, considers necessary or desirable in the interest of his patient's health. However, on the facts of the present case this could not in my judgment be an appropriate approach, as this patient could never in fact consent. Secondly, the basis of the declaration might be said to be one of necessity. I do not find the use of that word to be sufficiently precise as a test of what the courts would consider to be a justification for the operative procedures anticipated in the present case.

I prefer to approach the problem in this way. This defendant is never going to be able to consent—we are not dealing with a temporary inability such as a person under an anaesthetic, I compare the Canadian cases *Marshall v Curry* (1933) 3 DLR 260 and *Murray v McMurchy* (1949) 2 DLR 442, and there is no one in a position to consent. A medical adviser must therefore consider what decisions should be reached in the best interests of his patient's health. What does medical practice demand?

I use the word 'demand' because I envisage a situation where based upon good medical practice there are really no two views of what course is for the best. Upon the facts of this case I accept the medical evidence that not only would it be contrary to the defendant's best interests to postpone these proposed procedures, but it is positively in her best interests to proceed with due despatch.

It might be argued that the sterilisation could reasonably be postponed for further consideration, and indeed, that was my own first reaction, but after hearing argument I am quite satisfied that the risks to the defendant of a second operation, coupled with the doubts whether it could in fact be achieved in the light of her strength and inability to understand, are such as to be unacceptable, and I have no doubt that her best interests demand that all appropriate procedures to this end are carried out at the same time as the termination.

The third basis upon which these declarations could be made is that the operations would not in fact be tortious acts. This submission was perfectly straightforward and relied upon the authority of *Wilson v Pringle* [1987] QB 237. It is said that in order to constitute trespass to the person the act itself must be intentional and hostile, and that no act of a doctor treating his patient could be said to be hostile.

That was a case where the plaintiff, a schoolboy aged 13, alleged that he had been assaulted by another of the same age, as a result of which he had fallen to the ground and sustained quite serious injuries. The plaintiff took the unusual step of issuing a summons for summary judgment under RSC, Ord 14. It was dismissed by the district registrar, but allowed by the judge in chambers on appeal. The Court of Appeal allowed the appeal giving unconditional leave to defend and remarking: 'It will be apparent that there is a number of questions which must be investigated in evidence'. However, the court went further than was necessary for that decision and sought to analyse what needed to be proved in an action for trespass to the person and to give general guidance.

The court in its judgment cited a number of the earlier cases but the most detailed consideration was given to *Collins v Wilcock* [1984] 1 WLR 1172. In that case a woman police officer had tried to question a woman whom she suspected to be soliciting contrary to the Street Offences Act 1959. That woman walked away and was followed by the officer, who took hold of her arm in order to restrain her.

The passage relied on in the judgment of the Court of Appeal in *Wilson v Pringle* [1987] QB 237, which was the judgment of the court, is, at pp 252–253:

> In our view, the authorities lead one to the conclusion that in a battery there must be an intentional touching or contact in one form or another of the plaintiff by the defendant. That touching must be proved to be a hostile touching. That still leaves unanswered the question 'when is a touching to be called hostile?' Hostility cannot be equated with ill-will or malevolence. It cannot be governed by the obvious intention shown in acts like punching, stabbing or shooting. It cannot be solely governed by an expressed intention, although that may be strong evidence. But the element of hostility, in the sense in which it is now to be considered, must be a question of fact for the tribunal of fact. It may be imported from the circumstances.

In my judgment this is, with respect, rather too simplistic a view of *Collins v Wilcock* [1984] 3 All ER 374, [1984] 1 WLR 1172.

Wood J cited extensively Goff LJ's judgment in the above case, and continued:

The analysis made by Robert Goff LJ in that passage I summarise as follows. There are certain acts of physical contact which fall within a reasonable and generally acceptable band of conduct which may occur in the ordinary course of daily life and which will be the subject of a deemed consent in order to allow that ordinary daily life to continue (the exigencies of daily life) and that physical contact within that reasonable and acceptable band is no battery. However, when the physical act of contact does not fall within that band, there is the *prima facie* case of battery to which a defence or other justification must be raised as in the examples given by Robert Goff LJ, at p 1177, where he referred to the examples such as children being subjected to reasonable punishment. It would not seem to me that operative treatments or perhaps in some more serious cases medical treatments in hospital fall within the phrases 'exigencies of everyday life' or 'the ordinary conduct of daily life'. . . .

In the present case I have found the analysis of Robert Goff LJ to be of greater assistance than the analysis of the Court of Appeal to which I have just referred. The incision made by the surgeon's scalpel need not be and probably is most unlikely to be hostile, but unless a defence or justification is established it must in my judgment fall within the definition of a trespass to the person.

Thus in the present case I must face the fact that the operative procedures proposed are *prima facie* acts of trespass. It would be wholly unrealistic on the facts of this case to think in terms of any implied consent.

I am convinced, as are all the lay and professional persons involved in this case, that it is in the best interests of the first defendant that these procedures should be carried through and I have made the declarations which were sought. I am content to rely upon the principle that in these exceptional circumstances where there is no provision in law for consent to be given and therefore there is no one who can give the consent, and where the patient is suffering from such mental abnormality as never to be able to give such consent, a medical adviser is justified in taking such steps as good medical practice 'demands' in the sense that I have set it out above and on that basis it is that I have made the declaration sought.

As we saw earlier, Wood J rejects the idiosyncratic view of the Court of Appeal in *Wilson v Pringle* that a touching must be 'hostile' which, in this context, would lead to the conclusion that no touching for medical treatment by a doctor could be a battery even in the absence of consent. This was a brave stance for a first instance judge to take. More importantly for our present concerns, Wood J approaches the issues along very similar lines to those suggested by Professor Gostin in the extract above. Beneficial treatment must be lawful.

Questions

(i) Do you see any problems with this approach?
(ii) Were the sterilisation and abortion operations properly regarded as treatment in this case? Notice that Wood J does not suggest that *any* medical treatment would be lawful. Instead, he limits lawful treatment to that which 'medical practice demands' which he explains as medical treatment where there are 'no two views of what course is for the best'.
(iii) Do you think this is an effective limitation on a doctor's power to treat a permanently incompetent adult?
(iv) Is this a rejection of the *Bolam* approach adopted by the courts in cases of medical negligence where two or more professional views are accepted?

2. By statute.

The Mental Health Act 1983, s 63 reads as follows:

Treatment not requiring consent

63. The consent of a patient shall not be required for any medical treatment given to him for the mental disorder from which he is suffering, not being treatment falling within section 57 or 58 above, if the treatment is given by or under the direction of the responsible medical officer.

Notice that treatment is limited to medical treatment 'for the mental disorder from which he is suffering' and is limited to patients 'liable to be detained' under the MHA 1983 (see *T v T* [1988] 1 All ER 613 at p 617, [1988] Fam 52 at p 57, per Wood J). Subject to the exceptions in s 56, sections 57 and 58 refer to certain forms of treatment which require the consent of the patient and (in the case of s 57 and s 58) a second opinion in addition to that of the responsible medical officer or other registered medical practitioner responsible for the care of the patient. The second opinion must state that the patient cannot understand what is proposed or has not consented to it *and* that the treatment is medically indicated.

The Mental Health Act 1983 also includes provisions which represent a statutory example of the doctrine of necessity. Section 62 provides that:

Urgent treatment
62. (1) Sections 57 and 58 above shall not apply to any treatment—
  (a) which is immediately necessary to save the patient's life; or
  (b) which (not being irreversible) is immediately necessary to prevent a serious deterioration in his condition; or
  (c) which (not being irreversible) is immediately necessary to alleviate serious suffering by the patient; or
  (d) which (not being irreversible or hazardous) is immediately necessary and represents the minimum inteference necessary to prevent the patient from behaving violently or being a danger to himself or to others.
  (2) Sections 60 and 61(3) above shall not preclude the continuation of any treatment or of treatment under any plan pending compliance with section 57 or 58 above if the responsible medical officer considers that the discontinuance of the treatment or of treatment under the plan would cause serious suffering to the patient.
  (3) For the purposes of this section treatment is irreversible if it has unfavourable irreversible physical or psychological consequences and hazardous if it entails significant physical hazard.

Note also the following:

NATIONAL ASSISTANCE ACT (1948)

Removal to suitable premises of persons in need of care and attention
47. (1) The following provisions of this section shall have effect for the purposes of securing the necessary care and attention for persons who—
  (a) are suffering from grave chronic disease or, being aged, infirm or physically incapacitated, are living in insanitary conditions, and
  (b) are unable to devote to themselves, and are not receiving from other persons, proper care and attention.
  (2) If the medical officer of health certifies in writing to the appropriate authority that he is satisfied after thorough inquiry and consideration that in the interests of any such person as aforesaid residing in the area of the authority, or for preventing injury to the health of, or serious nuisance to, other persons, it is necessary to remove any such person as aforesaid from the premises in which he is residing, the appropriate authority may apply to a court of summary jurisdiction having jurisdiction in the place where the premises are situated for an order under the next following subsection.
  (3) On any such application the court may, if satisfied on oral evidence of the allegations in the certificate, and that it is expedient so to do, order the removal of the person to whom the application relates, by such officer of the appropriate authority, as may be specified in the order, to a suitable hospital or other place in, or within convenient distance of, the area of the appropriate authority, and his detention and maintenance therein;
  Provided that the court shall not order the removal of a person to any premises, unless either the person managing the premises has been heard in the proceedings or seven clear days' notice has been given to him of the intended application and of the time and place at which it is proposed to be made.
  (4) An order under the last foregoing subsection may be made so as to authorise

a person's detention for any period not exceeding three months, and the court may from time to time by order extend that period for such further period, not exceeding three months, as the court may determine.

(5) An order under subsection (3) of this section may be varied by an order of the court so as to substitute for the place referred to in that subsection such other suitable place in, or within convenient distance of, the area of the appropriate authority as the court may determine, so however that the proviso to the said subsection (3) shall with the necessary modification apply to any proceedings under this subsection.

(6) At any time after the expiration of six clear weeks from the making of an order under subsection (3) or (4) of this section an applicaton may be made to the court by or on behalf of the person in respect of whom the order was made, and on any such application the court may, if in the circumstances it appears expedient so to do, revoke the order.

(7) No application under this section shall be entertained by the court unless, seven clear days before the making of the application, notice has been given of the intended application and of the time and place at which it is proposed to be made—
(a) where the application is for an order under subsection (3) or (4) of this section, to the person in respect of whom the application is made or to some person in charge of him;
(b) where the application is for the revocation of such an order, to the medical officer of health.

(8) Where in pursuance of an order under this section a person is maintained neither in hospital accommodation provided by the Minister of Health under the [National Health Service Act 1977] or by the Secretary of State under the National Health Service (Scotland) [Act 1978], nor in premises where accommodation is provided by, or by arrangement with, a local authority under Part III of this Act, the cost of his maintenance shall be borne by the appropriate authority.

(9) Any expenditure incurred under the last foregoing subsection shall be recoverable from the person maintained or from any person who for the purposes of this Act is liable to maintain that person; and any expenditure incurred by virtue of this section in connection with the maintenance of a person in premises where accommodation is provided under Part III of this Act shall be recoverable in like manner as expenditure incurred in providing accommodation under the said Part III.

(10) [*Repealed for England and Wales by the National Health Service Reorganisation Act 1973, s 57, Sched 5.*]

(11) Any person who wilfully disobeys, or obstructs the execution of, an order under this section shall be guilty of an offence and liable on summary conviction to a fine not exceeding ten pounds.

(12) For the purposes of this section, the appropriate authorities shall be the councils of [districts and London boroughs and the Common Council of the City London][. . .], and in Scotland the councils of [regions and islands areas].

(13) The foregoing provisions of this section shall have effect in substitution for any provisions for the like purposes contained in, or having effect under, any public general or local Act passed before the passing of this Act:
Provided that nothing in this subsection shall be construed as affecting any enactment providing for the removal to, or detention in, hospital of persons suffering from notifiable or infectious diseases.

(14) Any notice under this section may be served by post.

The first question is, does s 47 extend to the *incompetent* person? Secondly, does s 47 allow for medical treatment of a person coming within s 47?

Hoggett writes in *Mental Health Law*, at p 133:

What does an order allow?
The Acts are by no means clear about what may be done with the person once he has been removed. Section 47(1) of the 1948 Act declares that the purpose of the provisions is to secure 'the necessary care and attention' for the people concerned; and section 47(3) provides that the court may order their removal to the hospital or

home, and their 'detention and maintenance therein'. It seems that the [amending] 1951 Act was expressly passed because a doctor had been unable to persuade a person with a broken leg to go to hospital for treatment. Yet the Acts say nothing about imposing medical treatment, as opposed to care, attention and maintenance, without the patient's consent. In this they are very like the Mental Health Act 1959, which seems to have assumed that getting the patient to hospital was the only problem: what happened once he was there could safely be left to the clinical judgment of the doctors. Nowadays, however, we are very much less inclined to read such powers into statutes which do not expressly contain them . . . and it would be most unwise to go beyond the limits of what is permitted by these Acts and by the common law.

(ii) Proxies

1. Parents. A parent who enjoys parental power over a child, or another acting in *loco parentis* such as a local authority, may consent to medical treatment on behalf of that child at least until majority where the child is *incompetent* (see *supra*).

This proposition is implicit in the *Gillick* case. Lord Scarman tells us:

I would hold that as a matter of law the parental right to determine whether or not their minor child below the age of 16 will have medical treatment terminates if and when the child achieves a sufficient understanding and intelligence to enable him or her to understand fully what is proposed. It will be a question of fact whether a child seeking advice has sufficient understanding of what is involved to give a consent valid in law. Until the child achieves the capacity to consent, the parental right to make the decision continues.

However, the law imposes limitations upon the parental authority to consent or withhold consent to medical treatment. Probably, it is sufficient in general terms to say that the parents must act 'in the best interests' of their child, although as we shall see (*infra* p 336 *et seq*) 'in the best interests' may not be a wholly accurate statement of the appropriate legal yard-stick. *Re B* illustrates both the principle that a parent has the authority to act as proxy and also shows that the decision taken falls to be measured by the court in wardship against the criterion of the child's best interest.

Re B (a minor)
[1981] 1 WLR 1421:

Templeman LJ: This morning the judge was asked to decide whether to continue his order that the operation should be performed or whether to revoke that order, and the position now is stark. The evidence, as I have said, is that if this little girl does not have this operation she will die within a matter of days. If she has the operation there is a possibility that she will suffer heart trouble as a result and that she may die within two or three months. But if she has the operation and it is successful, she has Down's syndrome, she is mongoloid, and the present evidence is that her life expectancy is short, about 20 to 30 years.

The parents say that no one can tell what will be the life of a mongoloid child who survives during that 20 or 30 years, but one thing is certain. She will be very handicapped mentally and physically and no one can expect that she will have anything like a normal existence. They make that point not because of the difficulties which will be occasioned to them but in the child's interest. This is not a case in which the court is concerned with whether arrangements could or could not be made for the care of this child, if she lives, during the next 20 or 30 years; the local authority is confident that the parents having for good reason decided that it is in the child's best interests that the operation should not be performed, nevertheless good adoption arrangements could be made and that in so far as any mongol child can be provided with a happy life then such a happy life can be provided.

The question which this court has to determine is whether it is in the interests of this child to be allowed to die within the next week or to have the operation in which case if she lives she will be a mongoloid child, but no one can say to what extent her mental or physical defects will be apparent. No one can say whether she will suffer or whether she will be happy in part. On the one hand the probability is that she will not be a cabbage as it is called when people's faculties are entirely destroyed. On the other hand it is certain that she will be very severely mentally and physically handicapped.

On behalf of the parents Mr Gray has submitted very movingly, if I may say so, that this is a case where nature had made its own arrangements to terminate a life which would not be fruitful and nature should not be interfered with. He has also submitted that in this kind of decision the views of responsible and caring parents, as these are, should be respected, and that their decision that it is better for the child to be allowed to die should be respected. Fortunately or unfortunately, in this particular case the decision no longer lies with the parents or with the doctors, but lies with the court. It is a decision which of course must be made in the light of the evidence and views expressed by the parents and the doctors, but at the end of the day it devolves on this court in this particular instance to decide whether the life of this child is demonstrably going to be so awful that in effect the child must be condemned to die, or whether the life of this child is still so imponderable that it would be wrong for her to be condemned to die. There may be cases, I know not, of severe proved damage where the future is so certain and where the life of the child is so bound to be full of pain and suffering that the court might be driven to a different conclusion, but in the present case the choice which lies before the court is this: whether to allow an operation to take place which may result in the child living for 20 or 30 years as a mongoloid or whether (and I think this must be brutally the result) to terminate the life of a mongoloid child because she also has an intestinal complaint. Faced with that choice I have no doubt that it is the duty of this court to decide that the child must live. The judge was much affected by the reasons given by the parents and came to the conclusion that their wishes ought to be respected. In my judgment he erred in that the duty of the court is to decide whether it is in the interests of the child that an operation should take place. The evidence in this case only goes to show that if the operation takes place and is successful then the child may live the normal span of a mongoloid child with the handicaps and defects and life of a mongol child, and it is not for this court to say that life of that description ought to be extinguished.

Accordingly the appeal must be allowed and the local authority must be authorised themselves to authorise and direct the operation to be carried out on the little girl.

Dunn LJ: I agree, and as we are differing from the view expressed by the judge I would say a few words of my own. I have great sympathy for the parents in the agonising decision to which they came. As they put it themselves, 'God or nature has given the child a way out'. But the child now being a ward of court, although due weight must be given to the decision of the parents which everybody accepts was an entirely responsible one, doing what they considered was the best, the fact of the matter is that this court now has to make the decision. It cannot hide behind the decision of the parents or the decision of the doctors; and in making the decision this court's first and paramount consideration is the welfare of this unhappy little baby.

This echoes the well-known words of Justice Holmes in the Supreme Court of the United States of America in *Prince v Massachusetts* 321 US 158, 170 (1944), the case of a Jehovah's Witness child in need of a blood transfusion to which the parents refused their consent. Authorising the transfusion Holmes J stated: 'Parents may be free to become martyrs themselves, but it does not follow that they are free in identical circumstances to make martyrs of their children before they have reached the age of full and legal discretion when they can make the choices for themselves'. It is as well to notice further the statutory limit on the parents' power to decide a child's best interests, see s 1 of the Children and Young Persons Act 1933.

So far we have been concerned with therapeutic procedures. Do the same principles apply in the case of non-therapeutic procedures? If the principle is that parents may only consent to that which is in the best interests of the child, it would appear at first sight that the answer must be no. This is because it seems hard to argue that interventions not intended as treatment can ever be in the best interests of the child since they must inevitably carry some risk of harm. Of course, this calls for a closer examination of how the terms 'therapeutic' and 'non-therapeutic' have been interpreted and how the courts apply the best interests test.

Therapeutic v non-therapeutic. Ordinarily we think that the key feature of therapy is that it is intended to benefit the patient. Of course, this leaves open the meaning of 'benefit' and whether something can be beneficial although involving some detriment if the former outweighs the latter.

There is little or no English case law on this, but the American cases may be instructive.

Strunk v Strunk
445 SW 2d 145 (Ky App 1969)

Osborne J: The facts of the case are as follows: Arthur L Strunk, 54 years of age, and Ava Strunk, 52 years of age, of Williamstown, Kentucky, are the parents of two sons. Tommy Strunk is 28 years of age, married, an employee of the Penn State Railroad and a part-time student at the University of Cincinnati. Tommy is now suffering from chronic glomerulus nephritis, a fatal kidney disease. He is now being kept alive by frequent treatment on an artificial kidney, a procedure which cannot be continued much longer.

Jerry Strunk is 27 years of age, incompetent, and through proper legal proceedings has been committed to the Frankfort State Hospital and School, which is a state institution maintained for the feeble-minded. He has an IQ of approximately 35, which corresponds with the mental age of approximately six years. He is further handicapped by a speech defect, which makes it difficult for him to communicate with persons who are not well acquainted with him. When it was determined that Tommy, in order to survive, would have to have a kidney the doctors considered the possibility of using a kidney from a cadaver if and when one became available or one from a live donor if this could be made available. The entire family, his mother, father and a number of collateral relatives were tested. Because of incompatibility of blood type or tissue none were [sic] medically acceptable as live donors. As a last resort, Jerry was tested and found to be highly acceptable. This immediately presented the legal problem as to what, if anything, could be done by the family, especially the mother and the father to procure a transplant from Jerry to Tommy. The mother as a committee petitioned the county court for authority to proceed with the operation. The court found that the operation was necessary, that under the peculiar circumstances of this case it would not only be beneficial to Tommy but also beneficial to Jerry because Jerry was greatly dependent upon Tommy, emotionally and psychologically, and that his well-being would be jeopardised more severely by the loss of his brother than by the removal of a kidney.

A psychiatrist, in attendance to Jerry, who testified in the case, stated in his opinion the death of Tommy under these circumstances would have 'an extremely traumatic effect upon him' (Jerry).

The Department of Mental Health of this Commonwealth has entered the case as *amicus curiae* and on the basis of its evaluation of the seriousness of the operation as opposed to the traumatic effect upon Jerry as a result of the loss of Tommy, recommended to the court that Jerry be permitted to undergo the surgery. Its recommendations are as follows:

It is difficult for the mental defective to establish a firm sense of identity with another person and the acquisition of this necessary identity is dependent upon a person whom one can conveniently accept as a model and who at the same time is sufficiently flexible to allow the defective to detach himself with reassurances of continuity. His need to be social is not so much the necessity of a formal and mechanical contact with other human beings as it is the necessity of a close intimacy with other men, the desirability of a real community of feeling, an urgent need for a unity of understanding. Purely mechanical and formal contact with other men does not offer any treatment for the behavior of a mental defective; only those who are able to communicate intimately are of value to hospital treatment in these cases. And this generally is a member of the family.

In view of this knowledge, we now have particular interest in this case. Jerry Strunk, a mental defective, has emotions and reactions on a scale comparable to that of a normal person. He identifies with his brother Tom; Tom is his model, his tie with his family. Tom's life is vital to the continuity of Jerry's improvement at Franfort State Hospital and School. The testimony of the hospital representative reflected the importance to Jerry of his visits with his family and the constant inquiries Jerry made about Tom's coming to see him. Jerry is aware he plays a role in the relief of this tension. We the Department of Mental Health must take all possible steps to prevent the occurrence of any guilt feelings Jerry would have if Tom were to die.

The necessity of Tom's life to Jerry's treatment and eventual rehabilitation is clearer in view of the fact that Tom is his only living sibling and at the death of their parents, now in their fifties, Jerry will have no concerned, intimate communication so necessary to his stability and optimal functioning.

The evidence shows that at the present level of medical knowledge, it is quite remote that Tom would be able to survive several cadaver transplants. Tom has a much better chance of survival if the kidney transplant from Jerry takes place.

Upon this appeal we are faced with the fact that all members of the immediate family have recommended the transplant. The Department of Mental Health has likewise made its recommendation. The county court has given its approval. The circuit court has found that it would be to the best interest of the ward of the state that the procedure be carried out. Throughout the legal proceedings, Jerry has been represented by a guardian *ad litem*, who has continually questioned the power of the state to authorise the removal of an organ from the body of an incompetent who is a ward of the state. We are fully cognisant of the fact that the question before us is unique. Insofar as we have been able to learn, no similar set of facts has come before the highest court of any of the states of this nation or the federal courts. The English courts have apparently taken a broad view of the inherent power of the equity courts with regard to incompetents. *Ex p Whitbread* (1816) 2 Mer 99, 35 ER 878, LC holds that courts of equity have the inherent power to make provisions for a needy brother out of the estate of an incompetent. This was first followed in this country in New York, *Re Willoughby, a Lunatic* 11 Paige 257 (NY 1844). The inherent rule in these cases is that the chancellor has the power to deal with the estate of the incompetent in the same manner as the incompetent would if he had his faculties. This rule has been extended to cover not only matters of property but also to cover the personal affairs of the incompetent. . . .

The right to act for the incompetent in all cases has become recognised in this country as the doctrine of substituted judgment and is broad enough not only to cover property but also to cover all matters touching on the well-being of the ward. The doctrine has been recognised in American courts since 1844.

Review of our case law leads us to believe that the power given to a committee under KRS 387.230 would not extend so far as to allow a committee to subject his ward to the serious surgical techniques here under consideration unless the life of his ward be in jeopardy. Nor do we believe the powers delegated to the county court by virtue of the above statutes would reach so far as to permit the procedure which we are dealing with here.

We are of the opinion that a chancery court does have sufficient inherent power to authorise the operation. The circuit court having found that the operative procedures in this instance are to the best interest of Jerry Strunk and this finding having been based upon substantial evidence, we are of the opinion the judgment should be affirmed. We do not deem it significant that this case reached the circuit court by way of appeal as opposed to a direct proceeding in that court.

Steinfeld J (dissenting): Apparently because of my indelible recollection of a government which, to the everlasting shame of its citizens, embarked on a program of genocide and experimentation with human bodies I have been more troubled in reaching a decision in this case than in any other. My sympathies and emotions are torn between a compassion to aid an ailing young man and a duty to fully protect unfortunate members of society.

The opinion of the majority is predicated upon the authority of an equity court to speak for one who cannot speak for himself. However, it is my opinion that in considering such right in this instance we must first look to the power and authority vested in the committee, the appellee herein. KRS 387.060 and KRS 387.230 do nothing more than give the committee the power to take custody of the incompetent and the possession, care and management of his property. Courts have restricted the activities of the committee to that which is for the best interest of the incompetent. *Harding's Adm'r v Harding's Ex'n* 140 Ky 277, 130 SW 1098 (1910); *Miller v Keown* 176 Ky 117, 195 SW 430 (1912) and 3 ALR 3d 18. The authority and duty have been to protect and maintain the ward, to secure that to which he is entitled and preserve that which he has. *Ramsay's Ex'r v Ramsey* 243 Ky 202, 47 SW 2d 1059 (1932); *Aaronson v State of New York* 34 Misc 2d 827, 229 NYS 2d 550, 557 (1962) and *Young v State* 32 Misc 2d 965, 225 NYS 2d 549 (1962). The wishes of the members of the family or the desires of the guardian to be helpful to the apparent objects of the ward's bounty have not been a criterion. 'A curator or guardian cannot dispose of his ward's property by donation, even though authorised to do so by the court on advice of a family meeting, unless a gift by the guardian is authorised by statute.' 44 CJS Insane Persons §81, p 191.

Two Kentucky cases decided many years ago reveal judicial policy. In *WT Sistrunk & Co v Navarra's Committee* 268 Ky 753, 105 SW 2d 1039 (1937), this court held that a committee was without right to continue a business which the incompetent had operated prior to his having been declared a person of unsound mind. More analogous is *Baker v Thomas* 272 Ky 605, 114 SW 2d 1113 (1938), in which a man and woman had lived together out of wedlock. Two children were born to them. After the man was adjudged incompetent, his committee, acting for him, together with his paramour, instituted proceedings to adopt the two children. In rejecting the application and refusing to speak for the incompetent the opinion stated:

The statute does not contemplate that the committee of a lunatic may exercise any other power than to have the possession, care, and management of the lunatic's or incompetent's estate. No authority is given by any statute to which our attention has been called, or that we have been by careful research able to locate, giving the committee of a lunatic or an incompetent authority to petition any court for the adoption of a person or persons as heirs capable of the inheritance of his or her estate.

The same result was reached in *Re Bourgeois* 144 La 501, 80 So 673 (1919), in which the husband of an incompetent wife sought to change the beneficiary of her insurance policy so that her children would receive the proceeds. *Grady v Dashiell* 24 Wash 2d 272, 163 P 2d 922 (1945), stands for the proposition that a loan to the ward's adult insolvent son made at a time when it was thought that the ward was incurably insane constituted an improper depletion of the ward's estate.

The majority opinion is predicated upon the finding of the circuit court that there will be psychological benefits to the ward but points out that the incompetent has the mentality of a six-year-old child. It is common knowledge beyond dispute that the loss of a close relative or a friend to a six-year-old child is not of major impact. Opinions concerning psychological trauma are at best most nebulous. Furthermore, there are no guarantees that the transplant will become a surgical success, it being well known that body rejection of transplanted organs is frequent. The life of the incompetent is not in danger, but the surgical procedure advocated creates some peril.

It is written in *Prince v Massachusetts* 321 US 158, 64 S Ct 438, 88 L Ed 645 (1944), that 'Parents may be free to become martyrs themselves. But it does not follow they are free, in identical circumstances, to make martyrs of their children before they have reached the age of full and legal discretion when they can make that choice for themselves.' The ability to fully understand and consent is a prerequisite to the donation of a part of the human body. Cf *Bonner v Moran* 75 US App DC 156, 126 F2d 121, 139 ALR 1366 (1941), in which a fifteen-year-old infant's consent to removal of a skin patch for the benefit of another was held legally ineffective.

Unquestionably the attitudes and attempts of the committee and members of the family of the two young men whose critical problems now confront us are commendable, natural and beyond reproach. However, they refer us to nothing indicating that they are privileged to authorise the removal of one of the kidneys of the incompetent for the purpose of donation, and they cite no statutory or other authority vesting such right in the courts. The proof shows that less compatible donors are available and that the kidney of a cadaver could be used, although the odds of operational success are not as great in such case as they would be with the fully compatible donor brother.

I am unwilling to hold that the gates should be open to permit the removal of an organ from an incompetent for transplant, at least until such time as it is conclusively demonstrated that it will be of significant benefit to the incompetent. The evidence here does not rise to that pinnacle. To hold that committees, guardians or courts have such awesome power even in the persuasive case before us, could establish legal precedent, the dire result of which we cannot fathom. Regretfully I must say no.

Are you persuaded by the language of the majority in *Strunk*, or do you prefer the dissent? Subsequently, some American courts have favoured the view advanced by the dissent. Those two cases are *in re Pescinski* (1975) 226 NE 2d 180 (Wiscons in Supreme Court) and *in re Richardson* (1973) 284 So 2d 185 (Louisiana Court of Appeal). For convenience they are set out in the following decision from Texas. You will, of course, notice that ultimately the Texas Court applies *Strunk*.

Little v Little
(1979) 576 SW 2d 493, Court of Civil Appeals of Texas

Cadena, Chief Justice: Anne Little, who has been adjudged incompetent, appeals through her attorney *ad litem* from an order of the probate court of Guadalupe County authorising her mother and guardian, Margaret Little, to consent to a surgical procedure involving the removal of a kidney from Anne's body for the purpose of transplanting such kidney into the body of Anne's younger brother, Stephen, who is suffering from endstage renal disease.

On August 8, 1978, Anne, then aged 14, was declared to be of unsound mind and her mother, appellee here, was appointed guardian of the person and of the estate of Anne. . . . One week later, on August 15, 1978, the guardian filed this application for an order authorising the transplant operation. The guardian, after alleging the nature of Stephen's illness and the fact that a kidney transplant is the only acceptable medical alternative to continued dialysis treatment for Stephen, pointed out that Anne is the only living related donor with acceptable matching characteristics and that permitting Anne to donate her kidney to her brother would be in Anne's best interest and would result in 'great and tangible' benefits to her. The guardian added that the operation would present no threat to Anne's life and that 'to the best of her ability and comprehension' Anne desires to donate her kidney to her brother and would do so if she were competent to make such decision.

The general rule in this State is that a minor cannot consent to medical or surgical treatment. No claim is here made that this case comes within the statutory exceptions to this rule. See Tex Fam Code Ann § 35.03 (Vernon 1975). Persons adjudged to be mentally incompetent share the same disability to consent to medical or surgical treatment. Parents whose parental rights have not been terminated and managing conservators of minors are authorised to consent to medical and surgical treatment of minors. The guardian of a mentally incompetent person has the same powers and duties as does the managing conservator of a minor. . . . Significantly, however, for our purposes, this power of parents, managing conservators and guardians to consent to surgical intrusions upon the person of the minor or ward is limited to the power to consent to medical 'treatment'. . . . Even ascribing to the word 'treatment' its broadest definition, it is, nevertheless, limited to 'the steps taken to effect a cure of an injury or disease . . . including examination and diagnosis as well as application of remedies'. *Black's Law Dictionary* 1673 (rev 4th ed 1968).

We cannot accept the guardian's argument that a donor nephrectomy constitutes medical treatment for the donor. In this case the ward's mental incompetency results from the fact that she suffers from Down's Syndrome, often called 'mongolism', . . . [T]he guardian does not contend that removal of a kidney is a medically acceptable method of curing or treating Down's Syndrome, . . . We think it is clear that the medical procedure authorised by the probate court in this case constitutes 'treatment' of the ward's brother, Stephen, and that the proposed medical procedure has as its purpose curing, remedying or ameliorating the condition of the proposed donee of the ward's kidney. The fact that the proposed surgical procedure cannot be classified as medical treatment of the ward in this case is made apparent by the medical testimony that a donor nephrectomy is medically acceptable, generally, only if the donor is in good health. All of the testimony in this case stresses the fact that the ward is being considered as a donor only because she is in good health and there are no signs of the upper respiratory problems and hypertension frequently associated with mongolism.

Judicial approval for intra-family transplants from incompetent donors has been granted in most cases. Robertson, *Organ Donations by Incompetents and the Substituted Judgments Doctrine*, 76 Colum L Rev 48, 53 (1976). In at least two cases, however, courts have refused to authorise transplants from incompetent donors. *Lausier v Pescinski* 67 Wis 2d 4, 226 NW 2d 180 (1975); *Re Richardson* 284 So 2d 185 (La Ct App), cert denied 284 So 2d 338 (La 1973). In *Lausier* the court justified its refusal to authorise a transplant by noting the absence of specific statutory authority and calling attention to Wisconsin decisions denying the power of a guardian to make gifts from the estate of his ward. However, the following language in the opinion is, perhaps, significant:

An incompetent particularly should have his own interests protected. Certainly no advantage should be taken of him. In the absence of real consent on his part, and in a situation where no benefit to him has been established, we fail to find any authority for the county court, or this court, to approve this operation.

. . . The lone dissenter brushed aside 'benefit' to the incompetent as 'pretty thin soup on which to base a decision as to whether or not the donee is to be permitted to live', but would have permitted the transplant by applying the substituted judgment doctrine's standard which would make the decision turn on what the donor would do if he were competent, concluding that in all probability the incompetent would consent because for him 'it would be a short period of discomfort which would not affect his ability either to enjoy life or his longevity'. The dissenter did not choose to explain how ignoring benefits to the incompetent while speculating as to the choice the donor would make if competent would result in a 'thicker soup'.

In *Richardson*, the Louisiana court, in refusing to authorise the operation, pointed out that the facts in *Strunk*, 'particularly the conclusion relative to the "best interest" of the incompetent, are not similar to the facts in the instant case . . .' The court also pointed out that under Louisiana law a guardian is prohibited from making any donations of the ward's property.

Since our law affords him unqualified protection against intrusion into a comparatively mere property right, it is inconceivable to us that it affords less protection to a minor's right to be free in his person from bodily intrusion to the extent of loss of an organ unless such loss be in the best interest of the minor.

The court then noted that such statement and its conclusion were 'restricted to the facts of the present case'.

We do not assert that the evidence in this case is sufficient to establish that Anne has the mental capacity to fully understand the concept of death. The suggestion, accepted in *Strunk*, that an incompetent potential donor would be subjected to feelings of guilt if his sibling died because the transplant did not take place may also, perhaps, be taken with a grain of salt. But the testimony in this case conclusively establishes the existence of a close relationship between Anne and Stephen, a genuine concern by each for the welfare of the other and, at the very least, an awareness by Anne of the nature of Stephen's plight and an awareness of the fact that she is in a position to ameliorate Stephen's burden. Assuming that Anne is incapable of understanding the nature of death, there is ample evidence to the effect that she understands the concept of absence and that she is unhappy on the occasions when Stephen must leave home for hours when he journeys to San Antonio for dialysis. It may be conceded that the state of development of the behavioral arts is such that the testimony of psychiatrists and psychologists must still be classified as speculative, but, as of today, that has not been accepted as justifying a judicial rejection of the value of such testimony. . . .

Nor is it fair to say that the evidence concerning 'psychological' benefits to Anne consists merely of testimony as to the prevention of detrimental effects which she may suffer if Stephen dies. The testimony is not limited to the prevention of sadness. There is uncontradicted testimony relating to increased happiness. Studies of persons who have donated kidneys reveal resulting positive benefits such as heightened self-esteem, enhanced status in the family, renewed meaning in life, and other positive feelings including transcendental or peak experiences flowing from their gift of life to another. The record before us indicates that Anne is capable of experiencing such an increase in personal welfare from donating her kidney.

The Medical experts who testified in this case conceded that Anne would experience pain and discomfort, but they all referred to it as minimal, and there is evidence that Anne has a high pain threshold. There is however, the possibility that Anne, because of her limited intellectual development, may be less able to understand the transplant procedures or to adapt to the unfamiliar surroundings of a hospital, so that her ordeal may be more burdensome than that of a normal adult. We must assume that all of these possibilities were carefully weighed by the trial judge, who had the opportunity to observe Anne and to hear her unsworn answers to questions, some of which were suggested by the court.

The circumstances of this case may be fairly summarised as follows:

(1) The parents and guardian of Anne consent to the kidney donation by Anne;

(2) Although Anne's statement that she was willing to donate her kidney to her brother cannot be realistically viewed as a knowing consent, there is no evidence indicating that she has been subjected to family pressure and the trial judge took the precaution, at the close of the testimony and before he announced his decision, of requesting and obtaining a physical and psychological evaluation of Anne;

(3) The evidence establishes that without a transplant Stephen will, at the very least, suffere severe and progressive deterioration, and that there are no medically preferable alternatives to a kidney transplant for Stephen;

(4) The dangers of the operation are minimal. Since she is in good health, the risks to Anne are small, and there is evidence that she will not suffer psychological harm;

(5) The evidence establishes that neither long-term dialysis nor a cadaver transplant or transplant from other living donors is medically acceptable;

(6) Stephen will probably benefit substantially from the transplant, and the risks to him from the operation, including long-term risks, are medically acceptable;

(7) The trial court's decision to authorise the operation was made only after a full judicial proceeding in which the interests of Anne were championed by an attorney *ad litem*, appointed by the court. The attorney *ad litem* has assumed an adversarial role, asserting the child's interest in not being a donor and vigorously

questioning the power of the court to authorise the operation. This is not a case where the attorney *ad litem* assumed a purely passive role, participating in the hearing merely to rubber-stamp the guardian's decision while giving to the proceedings the outward appearance of compliance with due process requirements.

Given the presence of all the factors and circumstances outlined above, and limiting our decision to such facts and circumstances, we conclude that the trial court did not exceed its authority by authorising the participation of Anne in the kidney transplant as a donor, since there is strong evidence to the effect that she will receive substantial psychological benefits from such participation. Nothing in this opinion is to be construed as being applicable to a situation where the proposed donee is not a parent or sibling of the incompetent.

We consider it proper and judicious to suggest that the problem of organ donations by incompetents can be more effectively addressed by the legislature, whose members can promulgate standards based on expert medical, psychiatric and psychological information, as well as testimony and experience of social workers which is not readily available to the judiciary. While we believe that the limited nature of our decision in this case will prevent the exploitation of minors and mental incompetents, we acknowledge that legislators are better qualified to conduct the necessary investigations which will yield a system of rules to adequately protect minors and other incompetents from exploitation without denying them such benefits as competent adults may derive from the organ-donating experience.

The judgment of the trial court is affirmed.

Which view do you think would prevail in England? Skegg in *Law, Ethics and Medicine*, writes at p 61 (footnotes omitted):

In dealing with cases such as these, it is necessary to weigh the likelihood of being able to save the potential recipient's life by making use of the proposed donor's organ or tissue; the likelihood of being able to achieve the same end by making use of some alternative source or treatment; the likely and the possible consequences to the proposed donor's health if the potential recipient dies; and the likely and the possible consequences to the donor's health if the organ or tissue is removed for transplantation. English courts would be free to balance the considerations in the same way as some American courts have done, but it would be unwise to assume that they would necessarily hold such operations to be for the donor's benefit. In such cases, the approach of an English court might be the same as that of one of the judges who dissented in the Kentucky case. He did not rule out altogether the possibility of the removal of an organ or tissue being for the benefit of a donor, but he said that in the case in question the opinions concerning psychological trauma were 'at best most nebulous'. He was influenced by the fact that there was no guarantee that the transplant would be a success, and that, whereas the life of the proposed donor was not at present in danger, the removal of a kidney would create some peril.

As you will see the American cases fudge the distinction between therapeutic and non-therapeutic so as to legitimise the contemplated intervention. *Strunk* must be the 'high water mark' of this approach. Do you think a clear line can be drawn between therapeutic and non-therapeutic? Does the distinction turn on an analysis of what benefit if any accrues to the child? Skegg, *op cit*, considers the arguments (footnotes omitted) at pp 60, 62:

More difficult are some of those instances in which the procedure may be said to be to the detriment of one aspect of a minor's health, although for the benefit of another aspect. . . .

The concept of benefit to the minor is not restricted to benefit to the minor's health. For example, the taking of a blood sample for forensic purposes may be in a minor's best interests, even though it is not shown to benefit his health. Financial benefit may outweigh any possible detriment to health. This raises interesting possibilities with non-therapeutic experimentation as well as with transplantation.

Suppose blood from a minor with a rare blood group was urgently required for transfusion. It could be argued that the removal of a quantity of his blood would be for his benefit if, in consideration for the removal, a substantial sum of money was paid into a bank account opened in the minor's name. Judges might find it difficult not to accept this approach if no substantial pain, discomfort, risk, or detriment to health was involved. However, where any of these factors is present, English judges may be expected to be most reluctant to accept the notion that any sum of money fully compensates for, say, the loss of an organ or of non-regenerative tissue. Otherwise, it would be possible to argue that the removal of a kidney was for the minor's benefit, merely because there had been paid into his bank account a sum in excess of that which he would receive in a personal injury claim for the loss of the organ, and for the associated discomfort and inconvenience.

Are we not here in the realm of non-therapeutic procedures, since otherwise the word 'benefit' seems to lack real substance as regards the individual child in question? We will see this difficulty arising particularly acutely in the case of sterilisations shortly.

Non-therapeutic.

We now turn to consider the circumstances, if any, in which a parent may validly authorise a non-therapeutic procedure upon her child.

Bonner v Moran
75 US App DC 156, 126 F 2d 121 (US Court of Appeals for DC) (1941)

Groner CJ: The facts are these. Appellant, a colored boy residing in Washington city, was at the time of the events about to be stated fifteen years of age. His cousin, Clara Howard, who lived in North Carolina, had been so severely burned that she had become a hopeless cripple. She was brought to Washington by her aunt, who was also the aunt of appellant, and taken to the charity clinic in the Episcopal Hospital, where she was seen by appellee, a physician specialising in plastic surgery. Appellee advised that a skin graft would help her, provided the blood of the donor matched. After a number of unsuccessful efforts to match her blood, the aunt persuaded appellant, then a student in junior high school, to go with her to the hospital for the purpose of having a blood test. His blood matched, and the aunt telephoned appellee, who came to the hospital and performed the first operation on appellant's side. His mother, with whom he lived, was ill at the time and knew nothing about the arrangement.

After the operation, appellant returned home and while there advised his mother that he was going back to the hospital to have his side 'fixed up.' Instead, he remained and in the subsequent operations a tube of flesh was cut and formed from his arm pit to his waist line, and at the proper time one end of the tube was attached to his cousin in the effort to accomplish her relief. The result was unsatisfactory, because of improper circulation of the blood through the tube. Accordingly, the tube was severed, after appellant had lost a considerable amount of blood and himself required transfusions. The tube of flesh was later removed and appellant was released from the hospital. From beginning to end, he was there nearly two months . . . in all such cases the basic consideration is whether the proposed operation is for the benefit of the child and is done with a purpose of saving his life or limb. The circumstances in the instant case are wholly without the compass of any of these exceptions. Here the operation was entirely for the benefit of another and involved sacrifice on the part of the infant of fully two months of schooling, in addition to serious physical pain and possible results affecting his future life. This immature colored boy was subjected several times to treatment involving anesthesia, blood letting, and the removal of skin from his body, with at least some permanent marks of disfigurement.

The English case which serves as a point of departure is the case in the House of Lords of *S v S* [1970] 3 All ER 107 at 110, 111–112, HL:

Lord Reid: The Official Solicitor argues on behalf of these children that no blood test of any child ought ever to be ordered unless it can be shown to be in the interest of the child that there should be a test . . .

I must now examine the present legal position with regard to blood tests. There is no doubt that a person of full age and capacity cannot be ordered to undergo a blood test against his will. In my view, the reason is not that he ought to be required to furnish evidence which may tell against him. By discovery of documents and in other ways the law often does this. The real reason is that English law goes to great lengths to protect a person of full age and capacity from interference with his personal liberty. We have too often seen freedom disappear in other countries not only by coups d'état but by gradual erosion; and often it is the first step that counts. So it would be unwise to make even minor concessions. It is true that the matter is regarded differently in the United States. We were referred to a number of State enactments authorising the courts to order adults to submit to blood tests. They may feel that this is safe because of their geographical position, size, power or resources or because they have a written Constitution. But here Parliament has clearly endorsed our view by the provision of s 21(1) of the 1969 Act.

But the position is very different with regard to young children. It is a legal wrong to use constraint on an adult beyond what is authorised by statute or ancient common law powers connected with crime and the like. But it is not and could not be a legal wrong for a parent or person authorised by him to use constraint to his young child provided it is not cruel or excessive. There are differences of opinion as to the age beyond which it is unwise to use constraint, but that cannot apply to infants or young children. So it seems to me to be impossible to deny that a parent can lawfully require that his young child should submit to a blood test. And if the parent can require that, why not the court? There is here no overriding requirement of public policy as there is with an adult.

I shall not refer in detail to the authorities. They were all discussed at some length in argument. But I venture to think that there has been some error in applying to this subject principles and authorities which deal with the custody of children. There the question is simple, though a decision may be very difficult—to whom shall the custody be entrusted? There is no competing question of general public interest, and it has long been well recognised that the paramount question is what is in the best interests of the child. But here there is or may be a conflict between the interests of the child and the general requirements of justice. Justice requires that available evidence should not be suppressed but it may be against the interests of the child to produce it.

The argument, as I understand it, is that a court can only order a blood test of a child in the exercise of the old Chancery jurisdiction acting on behalf of the Sovereign as parens patriae, and that when exercising that jurisdiction a court must act solely in the interests of the child disregarding all more general considerations. I greatly doubt that line of argument. Every court in any litigation must see that the interests of a child are not neglected. I am not at all certain that it is accurate to say that a court orders a blood test. What happens is that by appointing guardians ad litem and by a *Practice Direction* of the Probate Divorce and Admiralty Division of 21st October 1968, the court prevents parents who retain care and control of their children from exercising their right to have blood tests. Then, when an order for a test is sought the true position appears to me to be that the court is being asked to lift this ban. I do not see why any special jurisdiction is necessary either to impose the ban or lift it, and if, in defiance of the ban, a parent should have his child's blood tested, he might incur penalties, but, if it is the law that evidence is admissible though obtained by unlawful means, the court could not refuse to receive the result of such a test in evidence. No case has yet occurred in which a court has ordered a blood test to be carried out against the will of the parent who has the care and control of the child, and I am not at all certain that it would be proper to do that or that it will be possible to do that after Part III of the 1969 Act comes into operation.

But even if one accepts the view that in ordering, directing or permitting a blood test the court should go no further than a reasonable parent would go, surely a reasonable parent would have some regard to the general public interest and would not refuse a blood test unless he thought that would clearly be against the interests of the child? I cannot assume that in the present cases the husbands are acting in selfish disregard of these children's interests in asking for blood tests.

Lord MacDermott [at pp 115, 118]: *3. Must the court, before exercising its jurisdiction to order a blood test to be taken of an infant, be satisfied that it is in the best interests of the infant that it should do so?*

The duty of the High Court as respects the affairs and welfare of infants falls into two broad categories. There is, first of all, the duty to *protect* the infant, particularly when engaged or involved in litigation. This duty is of a general nature and derives from the Court of Chancery and to some extent also, I believe, from the common law courts which were merged along with the Court of Chancery in the High Court of Justice by the Act of 1873. It recognises that the infant, as one not sui juris may stand in need of aid. He must not be allowed to suffer because of his incapacity. But the aim is to ensure that he gets his rights rather than to place him above the law and make his rights superior to those of others, I shall refer to this duty and the powers of the court relative thereto as the 'protective jurisdiction'. Exercising it the court will be alert to see that the infant is separately represented where his interest so requires, and to change his next friend or guardian *ad litem* if not acting with due diligence and in a proper manner. Other examples of the protective jurisdiction are—the payment into court and investment of moneys recovered by an infant in litigation, the appointment of the Official Solicitor to act on his behalf in matters of special difficulty, and the approval of compromises and settlements entered into on the infant's behalf.

. . .

In exercising what I have called the ancillary jurisdiction in relation to infants the court must also observe and, if need be, exercise its protective jurisdiction. For instance, if the court were satisfied that—as might possibly be the case on rare occasions—a blood test would prejudicially affect the health of the infant it would, no doubt, exercise its discretion against ordering the test. And, again, if the court had reason to believe that the application for a blood test was of a fishing nature, designed for some ulterior motive to call in question the legitimacy, otherwise unimpeached, of a child who had enjoyed a legitimate status, it may well be that the court, acting under its protective rather than its ancillary jurisdiction, would be justified in refusing the application. I need not, however, pursue such instances as they do not arise on these appeals. The point to be made is that the protective jurisdiction, if of the nature I have described, would not ordinarily afford ground for refusing a blood test merely because it might, in revealing the truth, prove the infant's illegitimacy in duly constituted paternity proceedings.

What can we learn from this case? First, non-therapeutic interventions may be lawful. Secondly, these include interventions which are not to preserve or protect the immediate *health* interests of the child since the case concerns establishment of paternity. Thirdly, the intervention must, however, be of benefit to the child or putting it another way: 'is it in the child's interests?'. (Note the shift from 'best interests' to 'interests'.) Fourthly, we are still left with determining the precise extent of those interventions which a court will recognise as being of benefit.

May we not be entering the world of *Strunk v Strunk* again? Will the English courts follow the *Strunk* reasoning and discover a benefit which may be more assumed than real? Alternatively, will they state that trivial or slight interventions such as those associated with blood tests may be lawful where there is some readily identifiable, though non-medical, benefit but withdraw from authorising interventions of a more serious nature, particularly where the benefits are less clearly clear?

The sterilisation cases serve as poignant testimony to the difficulty this question poses.

Re D

[1976] 1 All ER 326, [1976] Fam 185

Heilbron J:

The child

D is a girl who was born in Sheffield on 29th November 1963. Sadly soon after her birth she was found to be handicapped, in that she was mentally backward, she suffered from epilepsy and her physical development began to advance at an exceptional rate. D was, and still is, under the care of her general practitioner and of the consultant paediatrician attached to the Sheffield Northern General Hospital, Dr Gordon. Dr Gordon has always taken a most compassionate and concerned interest in his patient, her serious condition and the consequent problems which beset the child, the mother and the rest of her family.

D was born into a family consisting of father, mother and two other daughters. Her father died on 15th October 1971 leaving a mother who has, therefore, over the past four years had to bring up this family alone in extraordinarily difficult circumstances, described by one doctor as appalling, living as they do in grossly overcrowded conditions in a house with only two bedrooms and no inside bathroom or toilet. Mrs B and D sleep together in one bed. Mrs B, who is now 51 years of age, works part-time as a cleaner, and she is, in my judgment, an excellent, caring and devoted mother, whose life has been, and still is, beset with tremendous difficulties, many of which cannot readily be appreciated by those who have not had to deal with the problems which she has so courageously faced. She is not only a very hard-working woman, whose home was described as spotless, but she impressed everyone with her qualities of sincerity and commonsense.

Eventually a firm diagnosis of D's condition was made. She was found to be suffering from a syndrome which comprised a somewhat unusual group of congenital abnormalities. Dr Sotos was the Argentinian doctor whose name was attached to this syndrome, and it is now known as Sotos Syndrome. Its cause is obscure, but it may include some or all of the following signs and symptoms, namely, accelerated growth during infancy, epilepsy, generalised clumsiness, an unusual facial appearance, behaviour problems including emotional instability, certain aggressive tendencies, some impairment of mental function which could result in dull intelligence or possibly more serious mental retardation. D suffered from these signs and symptoms but she was not considered to be as seriously retarded as some children suffering from mental handicaps.

When she was about 4½ years of age, Dr Gordon wrote to the school's medical officer drawing his attention to D's disabilities and asking him to see her, as she would require special education. I refer to this letter because it is an example of the normal and advantageous co-operation between the various professions, persons and agencies concerned with the welfare of children which now exists in this country.

D was in due course sent to a school which was thought to be appropriate. She did not, however, do very well, partly because she exhibited a number of serious behaviour problems, including hostility and a certain amount of violence towards some other children. She was accordingly referred by the school's medical officer to a consultant child psychiatrist, Dr T, to consider her transfer to a more suitable school, and when, in August 1973, D was examined by this psychiatrist, it is important to point out that he concluded that she was quite capable of discussing with him her difficulties and unhappiness at school, but Dr T considered that Mrs B did not fully appreciate the true nature of D's handicap, and as a result somewhat over-protected her. There was other evidence to the same effect and I accept that conclusion; I do not, however, feel it is in any way a ground for criticising Mrs B. To be over-zealous in looking after a handicapped child is a very understandable attitude from a very devoted mother.

D was duly transferred in October 1973 to a school which specialises in work with children who have learning difficulties and associated behavioural problems. The move was a success. I pause to pay my tribute to the dedication and devotion to his pupils of Mr Y, the present headmaster. I entirely agree with counsel for the Official Solicitor that Mr Y was wise, understanding, outstanding in his sphere and completely detached. I unreservedly accept his evidence, which was an entirely objective appraisal of D's progress.

Mrs Hamidi, the plaintiff, who is an experienced, trained and qualified educational psychologist, attached to the local authority educational department, also gave evidence. As an educational psychologist she observes, tests and assesses the social, behavioural and academic skills of various children in order to assist them to fulfil their potential at school, and in general, and to that end she not only had case conferences with D's teachers in regard to her behaviour problems, her emotional and general development, so as to help her to avoid her clumsiness and to improve her general academic performance, but she developed a personal relationship with her, and observed, interviewed and assessed her on the results of standard psychological tests.

From the evidence of Mr Y and Mrs Hamidi it appears that D has an intelligence quotient of about 80—an indication of a dull normal intelligence range. I am satisfied on their evidence that she has a fair academic standard, and her reading, language and conversational skills are reasonably good. She can write but with some difficulty and not very well. She has the understanding of a child of about nine to $9\frac{1}{2}$ years of age.

Mr Y and Mrs Hamidi asserted that her clumsiness has lessened and that she was now able to ride a bicycle, swim and dress herself —albeit slowly. Her interests, which included worship of a well-known 'pop star', were those of a normal girl of her age, and although even at school there were still instances of bad behaviour, she was not a severe management problem, and her behaviour was, and still is, improving.

The evidence of Dr Snodgrass, a consultant paediatrician and senior lecturer in child health called on behalf of the plaintiff, Mrs Hamidi, confirmed that her clumsiness is likely to lessen, and her behaviour to continue to improve. Mrs B was convinced, however, that D was seriously mentally retarded, and she maintained that there was no real improvement in D's behaviour or ability to care for herself, and although in her affidavit, she stated: 'At home D behaves resonably well', in evidence she gave a number of instances of D's difficulties and behaviour problems.

I can appreciate Mrs B's reluctance to accept the school's assessment. I am sure, like many children, D tends to behave better at school than at home or when out with her mother and sisters, when she can be a very real problem and sometimes a very serious embarrassment.

Dr Gordon, relying to some extent on what Mrs B told him, but also on his own assessment of his patient, thought her behaviour had deteriorated, and that she was and would always remain so substantially handicapped, as to be unable either to care for, or maintain herself, or to look after any children she might have.

I am satisfied, and I find, that this young girl has shown marked improvement in her academic skills, in her social competence and in her behaviour problems, which improvement unfortunately neither the mother nor Dr Gordon could accept.

Mr Y, contrary to Dr Gordon's view, maintained that it was unrealistic to be dogmatic about D's future chances of employment, whether or not she would be capable of looking after a family, or her future role in society. The effect of the other medical evidence also supports Mr Y's views on this aspect of D's future and I am satisfied that it would indeed be premature to make such predictions in the case of this 11 year old girl.

I have referred to D's present and future behaviour, social attitudes and academic attainments in some detail, in deference to the substantial body of evidence presented to me, although in the context of this case they are only one aspect of a considerably larger problem, namely whether this child should undergo an operation for sterilisation.

The background to the decision to operate

When Mrs B first realised that she had given birth to a handicapped child, she recalled with deep concern that, many years before, she had lived near a family who had the misfortune to have three mentally retarded children, and their plight and their troubled lives had deeply affected her. She and her husband not unnaturally were extremely worried about D's future, as at that time they thought D could never improve, and so even when D was a very young child they decided that when she reached the age of about 18 they would take the necessary steps to prevent her from having any children, and would apply to have her sterilised. From the decision made in those early days Mrs B has never resiled, and she has in consequence, over the years, had several discussions about this operation with Dr Gordon.

When D reached puberty by the age of ten Mrs B's concern increased, and so she discussed the operation once again with Dr Gordon on 7th January 1975. Mrs B said, and I accept, that when she reiterated to Dr Gordon that she would like D sterilised when she was older, the doctor said: 'We can do it now.' This is indeed confirmed by the doctor in his affidavit when he says that rather than wait any longer the decision should be taken then. Mrs B agreed that the operation should be performed. She was very worried lest D might be seduced and possibly give birth to a baby, which might also be abnormal. She had always believed that D would not, or should not, marry and in any event would be incapable of bringing up a child. Her anxieties are genuine and understandable.

Dr Gordon took the view that there was a real risk that D might give birth to an abnormal foetus. I have already referred to some of his other anxieties. As to the possibility of producing an abnormal child, the evidence of Dr Snodgrass and Dr Newton, the well-known consultant psychiatrist called on behalf of the Official Solicitor, confirmed that there was, as Dr Gordon stated, an increased risk of such an eventuality. On the other hand, they pointed out that no one with this particular syndrome had ever been known to have a baby, and it is not therefore possible to make any precise predictions whether or not they are able to do so.

At that consultation in January Dr Gordon, with Mrs B's agreement, came to a decision provided that Miss Duncan, the consultant gynaecologist, who is a senior lecturer and gynaecologist to the Sheffield and Northern General Hospital, to whom he referred, concurred in his recommendation the operation should be performed. Miss Duncan saw and interviewed both D and Mrs B on 17th February 1975, but she did not examine the child, and I think there is little doubt that Miss Duncan did not give very much independent consideration to the wider implications of this operation, but was content in large measure to rely on Dr Gordon's recommendation and assessment of the situation. She did, however, agree to perform the sterilisation, namely a hysterectomy, and I am satisfied that D was booked to enter hospital on 4th May for that operation to be carried out on 6th May. No one else was consulted prior to that decision. It is surprising that Dr T, the child psychiatrist, was not, for, prior to the date of the recommendation, he had on a number of occasions interviewed and examined the child, and his views, as Dr Gordon later agreed in evidence, must have been of considerable importance in evaluating the numerous problems, medical, social, educational and psychiatric, which such a vital decision involved.

Dr Gordon maintains, however, that his recommendation was one which was based on clinical judgment as a doctor, and that he and the gynaecologist should be the sole judges whether or not it should be performed, provided of course that they had the parent's consent.

Despite Dr Gordon's assertion that his decision should be upheld because it was based on his clinical judgment, he nevertheless, in putting forward his grounds for recommending this operation, stated that such reasons or such grounds were of a twofold character, ie that they were both medical and social. The medical reasons included the possibility that she might give birth to an abnormal child, that her epilepsy might cause her to harm a child, and that the only satisfactory method of birth control was this operation. The social reasons included his opinion that D would be unable in the future to maintain herself save in a sheltered environment, her inability due to epilepsy and other handicaps to cope with a family if she were to marry, without substantial support, the deterioration in her behaviour for which he said there was no known method of improvement and the possibility that she might have to enter an institution as he alleged for social or criminal reasons in the future.

Certain persons concerned with D's welfare, however, took a different view. They were the former and present headmaster of her school, Mrs Hamidi and the social worker involved with the family. They believed that an operation for sterilisation in the case of a minor, particularly a girl of 11, being irreversible and permanent, was a matter of grave concern, and so on 26th March Mrs Hamidi wrote on their behalf and on her own to the senior school medical officer, pointing out in detail the conflict between Mrs B and the school and the welfare services in regard to D's attainments and their concern in regard to the proposed operation, which they pointed out could affect the whole of her future.

On 21st April there was a meeting between Dr Gordon and those professionals working with the child and her family, at which Dr Gordon's social and behavioural reasons for performing this operation were seriously challenged. Dr Gordon, however, refused to acknowledge that these views could possibly be wrong or exaggerated or premature. I think Dr Gordon, whose sincerity cannot be challenged, was persuaded by his emotional involvement with Mrs B's considerable problems and anxieties, and his strong personal views in favour of sterilisation—as he stated in his affidavit, 'Sterilisation is now an emotive word, and we must try to change its image'—to form a less than detached opinion in regard to a number of matters which were not in my view in reality matters of clinical judgment, but which were concerned, to a large extent, with grounds which were other than medical. I feel it is a pity that he was not prepared to accept that others, whose duties, training and skills were directed to the assessment and amelioration of many of these problems, had much to contribute in the formulation of a decision of this gravity.

In my judgment Dr Gordon's views as to D's present and future social and behavioural problems were somewhat exaggerated and mistaken. I think in this area his views were clouded by his resentment at what he considered unjustified interference.

In the event Dr Gordon did not accept the alternative views, and he and Miss Duncan refused to defer the operation despite the grave implications for the child. Mrs Hamidi and the others, therefore, wrote to the area administrator of the health authority requesting an urgent and independent review of this decision. The area administrator consulted the local authority's specialist in community medicine (child health) and he later replied saying that she had made a very careful appraisal of the case, but could not interfere. Mrs Hamidi and her colleagues, however, were not daunted and they thereupon consulted solicitors, and in due course these proceedings got under way. It is only right that I should pay tribute to their courage, persistence and humane concern for this young girl . . .

The type of operation proposed is one which involves the deprivation of a basic human right, namely the right of a woman to reproduce, and therefore it would, if performed on a woman for non-therapeutic reasons and without her consent, be a violation of such right . . .

This operation could, if necessary, be delayed or prevented if the child were to remain a ward of court, and as Lord Eldon LC so vividly expressed it in *Wellesley's* case: 'It has always been the principle of this Court, not to risk the incurring of damage to children which it cannot repair, but rather to prevent the damage being done.'

I think that is the very type of case where this court should 'throw some care around this child', and I propose to continue her wardship which, in my judgment, is appropriate in this case.

Dr Gordon's reason for wishing this operation to be performed was, of course, to prevent D ever having a child. He recognised, as did Mrs B, that there are other methods of achieving that objective, but his view was that D could not satisfactorily manage any form of contraception. Mrs B was concerned lest D might be seduced and become pregnant. She too was against all forms of contraception.

A good deal of evidence was directed to ascertaining whether Mrs B's fears were soundly based or not. The answer is in the nature of things somewhat speculative, but it was common ground that D had as yet shown no interest in the opposite sex, and that her opportunities for promiscuity, if she became so minded, were virtually non-existent, as her mother never leaves her side and she is never allowed out alone.

Much of the evidence, which I found convincing, was to the effect that it was premature even to consider contraception, except possibly to allay the mother's fears.

Mrs B's genuine concern, however, cannot be disregarded. A body of evidence was produced, therefore, to indicate the advantages and disadvantages of various forms of contraception. I shall not, however, burden this judgment with any detailed examination of it, save to say that I do not accept on the evidence Dr Gordon's contention that this young girl, if and when the time arrived, would not be a suitable subject for one of the various methods described by the doctors. I think it is only necessary to refer to the fact that Miss Duncan herself stated in evidence that if Mrs B had been willing to accept one of the methods of contraception, she would have advised one before sterilisation, and I entirely accept Professor Huntingford's evidence that there were certainly two methods, either one of which could be safely and satisfactorily used. I think it was a pity that both Dr Gordon and Mrs B were so reluctant to accept this possibility, or even the alternative of abortion, if, unhappily, it ever proved necessary, rather than the proposed use of such an irrevocable procedure.

It was common ground that D had sufficient intellectual capacity to marry, in the future of course, and that many people of a like kind are capable of, and do so. Dr Gordon agreed that this being so, she and her future husband would then be the persons most concerned in any question of sterilisation, and such an operation might have a serious and material bearing on a future marriage and its consequences.

The purpose of performing this operation is permanently to prevent the possibility of reproduction. The evidence of Professor Huntingford, consultant and professor of obstetrics and gynaecology at the University of London and at St Bartholomew's Hospital and the London Hospital Medical Colleges, was that in his view such an operation was normally only appropriate for a woman who consented to it, possibly at the conclusion of child-bearing, and then only after careful and anxious consideration by her and her husband of many factors and, what is most important, with full knowledge of all its implications.

Professor Huntingford, Dr Snodgrass and Dr Newton were all agreed that such an operation was not medically indicated in this case, and should not be performed. Dr Snodgrass said he was firmly of the view that it was wrong to perform this operation on an 11 year old, on the pretext that it would benefit her in the future. Dr Newton said:

In my opinion sterilisation of a child before the age of consent can only be justified if it is the treatment for some present or inevitable disease. In this case, sterilisation is not a treatment for any of the signs or symptoms of Sotos Syndrome, from which she suffers. I am totally against this operation being performed on D.'

Professor Huntingford stated: 'In my considered opinion it will not be in the best interests of the ward to be sterilised having regard to her age and all other relevant factors.' He had never ever heard of a child of this age being sterilised. Dr Snodgrass, with his great experience of handicapped children of all types, had never known anyone suffering from epilepsy to be sterilised for that reason, nor would he consider recommending such an operation, even if a child was mentally retarded. D was only one of at least a hundred thousand people of a similar degree of dull normal intelligence. If it ever became necessary he would, he said, be prepared to recommend abortion, not sterilisation. Dr Gordon, however, maintained that, provided the parent or parents consented, the decision was one made pursuant to the exercise of his clinical judgment, and that no interference could be tolerated in his clinical freedom.

The other consultants did not agree. Their opinion was that a decision to sterilise a child was not entirely within a doctor's clinical judgment, save only when sterilisation was the treatment of choice for some disease, as, for instance, when in order to treat a child and to ensure her direct physical well-being, it might be necessary to perform a hysterectomy to remove a malignant uterus. Whilst the side effect of such an operation would be to sterilise, the operation would be performed solely for therapeutic purposes. I entirely accept their opinions. I cannot believe, and the evidence does not warrant the view, that a decision to carry out an operation of this nature performed for non-therapeutic purposes on a minor, can be held to be within the doctor's sole clinical judgment.

It is quite clear that once a child is a ward of court, no important step in the life of that child can be taken without the consent of the court, and I cannot conceive of a more important step than that which was proposed in this case.

A review of the whole of the evidence leads me to the conclusion that in a case of a child of 11 years of age, where the evidence shows that her mental and physical condition and attainments have already improved, and where her future prospects are as yet unpredictable, where the evidence also shows that she is unable as yet to understand and appreciate the implications of this operation and could not give a valid or informed consent, but the likelihood is that in later years she will be able to make her own choice, where, I believe, the frustration and resentment of realising (as she would one day) what had happened, could be devastating, an operation of this nature is, in my view, contra-indicated.

For these, and for the other reasons to which I have adverted, I have come to the conclusion that this operation is neither medically indicated nor necessary, and that it would not be in D's best interests for it to be performed.

Questions

Notice the following points that arise from *Re D* and which may be signposts to the direction a future court may take.

1. Heilbron J refers to 'the deprivation of a basic human right, namely the right of a woman to reproduce'. Are we in the realms of human rights here and if so what distinguishes this from *S v S*? If we are, what if any effect does their involvement have on the decision arrived at? Do they, for example, 'trump' all other claims? (See *Re Eve*, *infra*.)

Further, if we are considering human rights, what is the human right in play here? Is there a basic human right to reproduce or are the human rights those of privacy and freedom from bodily interference (see eg Article 2 and 8 of the European Convention of Human Rights)?

2. Heilbron J describes sterilisation as 'non-therapeutic'. Is there a distinction to be drawn between purely contraceptive sterilisation and sterilisation as a response to an existing or immediate health problem? If so, would you consider management of personal hygiene in the same way as treatment for a malignant tumour where the operation necessarily involves sterilisation?

3. Heilbron J formed the view that in the case before her it was proper to wait until such time that the girl might become competent to give or withhold consent to a sterilisation operation herself. Does this mean that if the girl could never be competent Heilbron J would have authorised the operation? If so, how does this square with her reference to 'basic human rights'? Does it mean she contemplates sterilisation as being a lawful option even where it is non-therapeutic and purely contraceptive as a 'last resort'?

4. If Heilbron J does indeed contemplate that sterilisation could be lawful, what meaning could be given to the notion of benefit to the child which lies at the heart of the 'best interests' test? If it be 'benefit', widely defined beyond purely medical benefit (as it must), what are the limits, what are the criteria which set those limits and who determines these? If the court is to set the limits, can it do more than leave the decision ultimately to the good sense of the doctors and parents acting together? Is this satisfactory? Or is this a matter which Parliament should resolve, since Parliament can either outlaw non-therapeutic sterilisation completely or set more careful guidelines, to be observed before any operation may lawfully be carried out?

Compare the approaches adopted in the Supreme Court of Canada and the House of Lords in the following two cases.

Re Eve
(1986) 2 SCR 388: (1981) 115 DLR (3d) 283 (Supreme Court of Canada).

La Forest J:

Background,

When Eve was a child, she lived with her mother and attended various local schools. When she became twenty-one, her mother sent her to a school for retarded adults in another community. There she stayed with relatives during the week, returning to her mother's home on weekends. At this school, Eve struck up a close friendship with a male student: in fact, they talked of marriage. He too is retarded, though somewhat less so than Eve. However, the situation was identified by the school authorities who talked to the male student and brought the matter to an end.

The situation naturally troubled Mrs E. Eve was usually under her supervision or that of someone else, but this was not always the case. She was attracted and attractive to men and Mrs E feared she might quite possibly and innocently become pregnant. Mrs E was concerned about the emotional effect that a pregnancy and subsequent birth might have on her daughter. Eve, she felt, could not adequately cope with the duties of a mother and the responsibility would fall on Mrs E. This would understandably cause her great difficulty; she is a widow and was then approaching sixty. That is why she decided Eve should be sterilised.

Eve's condition is more fully described by McQuaid J as follows:

The evidence established that Eve is 24 years of age, and suffers what is described as extreme expressive aphasia. She is unquestionably at least mildly to moderately retarded. She has some learning skills, but only to a limited level. She is described as being a pleasant and affectionate person who, physically, is an adult person, quite capable of being attracted to, as well as attractive to, the opposite sex. While she might be able to carry out the mechanical duties of a mother, under supervision, she is incapable of being a mother in any other sense. Apart from being able to recognise the fact of a family unit, as consisting of a father, a mother, and children residing in the same home, she would have no concept of the idea of marriage, or indeed, the consequential relationship between, intercourse, pregnancy and birth.

Expressive aphasia was described as a condition in which the patient is unable to communicate outwardly thoughts or concepts which she might have perceived. Particularly in the case of a person suffering from any degree of retardation, the result is that even an expert such as a psychiatrist is unable to determine with any degree of certainty if, in fact, those thoughts or concepts have actually been perceived, or whether understanding of them does exist. Little appears to be known of the cause of this condition, and even less of its remedy. In the case of Eve, this condition has been diagnosed as extreme.

From the evidence, he further concluded:

[t]hat Eve is not capable of informed consent, that her moderate retardation is generally stable, that her condition is probably non-inheritable, that she is incapable of effective alternative means of contraception, that the psychological or emotional effect of the proposed operation would probably be minimal, and that the probable incidence of pregnancy is impossible to predict.

General considerations

Before entering into a consideration of the specific issues before this Court, it may be useful to restate the general issue briefly. The Court is asked to consent, on behalf of Eve, to sterilisation since she, though an adult, is unable to do so herself. Sterilisation by means of a tubal ligation is usually irreversible. And hysterectomy, the operation authorised by the Appeal Division, is not only irreversible; it is major surgery. Eve's sterilisation is not being sought to treat any medical condition. Its purposes are admittedly non-therapeutic. One such purpose is to deprive Eve of the capacity to become pregnant so as to save her from the possible trauma of giving birth and from the resultant obligations of a parent, a task the evidence indicates she is not capable of fulfilling. As to this, it should be noted that there is no evidence that giving birth would be more difficult for Eve than for any other woman. A second purpose of the sterilisation is to relieve Mrs E of anxiety about the possibility of Eve's becoming pregnant and of having to care for any child Eve might bear.

The *parens patriae* jurisdiction is, as I have said, founded on necessity, namely the need to act for the protection of those who cannot care for themselves. The courts have frequently stated that it is to be exercised in the 'best interest' of the protected person, or again, for his or her 'benefit' or 'welfare'.

The situations under which it can be exercised are legion; the jurisdiction cannot be defined in that sense. As Lord MacDermott put it in *J v C* [1970] AC 668, at 703, the authorities are not consistent and there are many twists and turns, but they have inexorably 'moved towards a broader discretion, under the impact of changing social conditions and the weight of opinion . . .' In other words, the categories under which the jurisdiction can be exercised are never closed. Thus I agree with Latey J in *Re X*, ([1975] 1 All ER 697), at 699, that the jurisdiction is of a very broad nature, and that it can be invoked in such matters as custody, protection of property, health problems, religious upbringing and protection against harmful associations. This list, as he notes, is not exhaustive.

What is more, as the passage from *Chambers* cited by Latey J underlines, a court may act not only on the ground that injury to person or property has occurred, but also on the ground that such injury is apprehended. I might add that the jurisdiction is a carefully guarded one. The courts will not readily assume that it has been removed by legislation where a necessity arises to protect a person who cannot protect himself.

I have no doubt that the jurisdiction may be used to authorise the performance of a surgical operation that is necessary to the health of a person, as indeed it already has been in Great Britain and this country. And by health, I mean mental as well as physical health. In the United States, the courts have used the *parens patriae* jurisdiction on behalf of a mentally incompetent to authorise chemotherapy and amputation, and I have little doubt that in a proper case our courts should do the same. Many of these instances are related in *Strunk v Strunk* 445 SW 2d 145 (Ky 1969), where the court went to the length of permitting a kidney transplant between brothers. Whether the courts in this country should go that far, or as in *Quinlan*, permit the removal of life-sustaining equipment, I leave to later disposition.

Though the scope or sphere of operation of the *parens patriae* jurisdiction may be unlimited, it by no means follows that the discretion to exercise it is unlimited. It must be exercised in accordance with its underlying principle. Simply put, the discretion is to do what is necessary for the protection of the person for whose benefit it is exercised; see the passages from the reasons of Sir John Pennycuick in *Re X* at 706–07, and Heilbron J in *Re D* at 332, cited earlier. The discretion is to be exercised for the benefit of that person, not for that of others. It is a discretion, too, that must at all times be exercised with great caution, a caution that must be redoubled as the seriousness of the matter increases. This is particularly so in cases where a court might be tempted to act because failure to do so would risk imposing an obviously heavy burden on some other individual.

There are other reasons for approaching an application for sterilisation of a mentally incompetent person with the utmost caution. To begin with, the decision involves values in an area where our social history clouds our vision and encourages many to perceive the mentally handicapped as somewhat less than human. This attitude has been aided and abetted by now discredited eugenic theories whose influence was felt in this country as well as the United States. Two provinces, Alberta and British Columbia, once had statutes providing for the sterilisation of mental defectives; *The Sexual Sterilisation Act*, RSA 1970, c 341, repealed by SA 1972, c 87; *Sexual Sterilization Act*, RSBC 1960, c 353, s 5(1), repealed by SBC 1973, c 79.

Moreover, the implications of sterilisation are always serious. As we have been reminded, it removes from a person the great privilege of giving birth, and is for practical purposes irreversible. If achieved by means of a hysterectomy, the procedure approved by the Appeal Division, it is not only irreversible; it is major surgery. Here, it is well to recall Lord Eldon's admonition in *Wellesley*'s case, *supra*, at 2 Russ p 18, 38 ER p 242, that 'it has always been the principle of this Court, not to risk the incurring of damage to children which it cannot repair, but rather to prevent the damage being done'. Though this comment was addressed to children, who were the subject matter of the application, it aptly describes the attitude that should always be present in exercising a right on behalf of a person who is unable to do so.

Another factor merits attention. Unlike most surgical procedures, sterilisation is not one that is ordinarily performed for the purpose of medical treatment. The Law Reform Commission of Canada tells us this in *Sterilisation*, Working Paper 24 (1979), a publication to which I shall frequently refer as providing a convenient summary of much of the work in the field. It says at p 3:

Sterilisation as a medical procedure is distinct, because except in rare cases, if the operation is not performed, the *physical* health of the person involved is not in danger, necessity or emergency not normally being factors in the decision to undertake the procedure. In addition to its being elective it is for all intents and purposes irreversible.

As well, there is considerable evidence that nonconsensual sterilisation has a significant negative psychological impact on the mentally handicapped; see *Sterilisation, supra*, at pp 49–52. The Commission has this to say at p 50:

It has been found that, like anyone else, the mentally handicapped have individually varying reactions to sterilisation. Sex and parenthood hold the same significance for them as for other people and their misconceptions and misunderstandings are also similar. Rosen maintains that the removal of an individual's procreative powers is a matter of major importance and that no amount of *reforming zeal* can remove the significance of sterilisation and its effect on the individual psyche.

In a study by Sabagh and Edgerton, it was found that sterilised mentally retarded persons tend to perceive sterilisation as a symbol of *reduced* or *degraded* status. Their attempts to *pass for normal* were hindered by negative self perceptions and resulted in withdrawal and isolation rather than striving to conform . . .

The psychological impact of sterilisation is likely to be particularly damaging in cases where it is a result of coercion and when the mentally handicapped have had no children.

In the present case, there is no evidence to indicate that failure to perform the operation would have any detrimental effect on Eve's physical or mental health. The purposes of the operation, as far as Eve's welfare is concerned, are to protect her from possible trauma in giving birth and from the assumed difficulties she would have in fulfilling her duties as a parent. As well, one must assume from the fact that hysterectomy was ordered, that the operation was intended to relieve her of the hygienic tasks associated with menstruation. Another purpose is to relieve Mrs E of the anxiety that Eve might become pregnant, and give birth to a child, the responsibility for whom would probably fall on Mrs E.

I shall dispose of the latter purpose first. One may sympathise with Mrs E. To use Heilbron J's phrase, it is easy to understand the natural feelings of a parent's heart. But the *parens patriae* jurisdiction cannot be used for her benefit. Its exercise is confined to doing what is necessary for the benefit and protection of persons under disability like Eve. And a court, as I previously mentioned, must exercise great caution to avoid being misled by this all too human mixture of emotions and motives. So we are left to consider whether the purposes underlying the operation are necessarily for Eve's benefit and protection.

The justifications advanced are the ones commonly proposed in support of non-therapeutic sterilisation (see *Sterilisation, passim*). Many are demonstrably weak. The Commission dismisses the argument about the trauma of birth by observing at p 60:

For this argument to be held valid would require that it could be demonstrated that the stress of delivery was greater in the case of mentally handicapped persons than it is for others. Considering the generally known wide range of post-partum response would likely render this a difficult cause to prove.

The argument relating to fitness as a parent involves many value-loaded questions.

Studies conclude that mentally incompetent parents show as much fondness and concern for their children as other people; see *Sterilisation, supra*, p 33 et seq, 63–64. Many, it is true, may have difficulty in coping, particularly with the financial burdens involved. But this issue does not relate to the benefit of the incompetent; it is a social problem, and one, moreover, that is not limited to incompetents. Above all it is not an issue that comes within the limited powers of the courts, under the *parens patriae* jurisdiction, to do what is necessary for the benefit of persons who are unable to care for themselves. Indeed, there are human rights considerations that should make a court extremely hesitant about attempting to solve a social problem like this by this means. It is worth noting that in dealing with such issues, provincial sterilisation boards have revealed serious differences in their attitudes as between men and women, the poor and the rich, and people of different ethnic backgrounds; see *Sterilisation, supra*, at p 44.

As far as the hygienic problems are concerned, the following view of the Law Reform Commission (at p 34) is obviously sound:

... if a person requires a great deal of assistance in managing their own menstruation, they are also likely to require assistance with urinary and fecal control, problems which are much more troublesome in terms of personal hygiene.

Apart from this, the drastic measure of subjecting a person to a hysterectomy for this purpose is clearly excessive.

The grave intrusion on a person's rights and the certain physical damage that ensues from non-therapeutic sterilisation with consent, when compared to the highly questionable advantages that can result from it, have persuaded me that it can never safely be determined that such a procedure is for the benefit of that person. Accordingly, the procedure should never be authorised for non-therapeutic purposes under the *parens patriae* jurisdiction.

To begin with, it is difficult to imagine a case in which non-therapeutic sterilisation could possibly be of benefit to the person on behalf of whom a court purports to act, let alone one in which that procedure is necessary in his or her best interest. And how are we to weigh the best interests of a person in this troublesome area, keeping in mind that an error is irreversible? Unlike other cases involving the use of the *parens patriae* jurisdiction, an error cannot be corrected by the subsequent exercise of judicial discretion. That being so, one need only recall Lord Eldon's remark, *supra*, that 'it has always been the principle of this Court, not to risk damage to children which it cannot repair' to conclude that non-therapeutic sterilisation may not be authorised in the exercise of the *parens patriae* jurisdiction. McQuaid J was, therefore, right in concluding that he had no authority or jurisdiction to grant the application.

Nature or the advances of science may, at least in a measure, free Eve of the incapacity from which she suffers. Such a possibility should give the courts pause in extending their power to care for individuals to such irreversible action as we are called upon to take here. The irreversible and serious intrusion on the basic rights of the individual is simply too great to allow a court to act on the basis of possible advantages which, from the standpoint of the individual, are highly debatable. Judges are generally ill-informed about many of the factors relevant to a wise decision in this difficult area. They generally know little of mental illness, of techniques of contraception or their efficacy. And, however well presented a case may be, it can only partially inform. If sterilisation of the mentally incompetent is to be adopted as desirable for general social purposes, the legislature is the appropriate body to do so. It is in a position to inform itself and it is attuned to the feelings of the public in making policy in this sensitive area. The actions of the legislature will then, of course, be subject to the scrutiny of the courts under the *Canadian Charter of Rights and Freedoms* and otherwise.

Many of the factors I have referred to as showing that the best interests test is simply not a sufficiently precise or workable tool to permit the *parens patriae* power to be used in situations like the present are referred to in *Re Eberhardy's Guardianship*, [307 NW 2d 881 (1981)]. Speaking for the court in that case, Heffernan J had this to say, at p 894:

Under the present state of the law, the only guideline available to circuit courts faced with this problem appears to be the 'best interests' of the person to be sterilised. This is a test that has been used for a number of years in this jurisdiction and elsewhere in the determination of the custody of children and their placement—in some circumstances placement in a controlled environment . . . No one who has dealt with this standard has expressed complete satisfaction with it. It is not an objective test, and it is not intended to be. The substantial workability of the test rests upon the informed fact-finding and the wise exercise of discretion by trial courts engendered by long experience with the standard. Importantly, however, most determinations made in the best interests of a child or of an incompetent person are not irreversible; and although a wrong decision may be damaging indeed, there is an opportunity for a certain amount of empiricism in the correction of errors of discretion. Errors of judgment or revisions of decisions by courts and social workers can, in part at least, be rectified when new facts or second thoughts prevail. And, of course, alleged errors of discretion in exercising the 'best interest' standard are subject to appellate review. Sterilisation as it is now understood by medical science is, however, substantially irreversible.

Heffernan J also alluded to the limited capacity of judges to deal adequately with a problem that has such general social overtones in the following passage, at p 895:
What these facts demonstrate is that courts, even by taking judicial notice of medical treatises, know very little of the techniques or efficacy of contraceptive methods or of thwarting the ability to procreate by methods short of sterilisation. While courts are always dependent upon the opinions of expert witnesses, it would appear that the exercise of judicial discretion unguided by well thought-out policy determinations reflecting the interest of society, as well as of the person to be sterilised, are hazardous indeed. Moreover, all seriously mentally retarded persons may not *ipso facto* be incapable of giving birth without serious trauma, and some may be good parents. Also, there has been a discernible and laudable tendency to 'mainstream' the developmentally disabled and retarded. A properly thought out public policy on sterilisation or alternative contraceptive methods could well facilitate the entry of these persons into a more nearly normal relationship with society. But again this is a problem that ought to be addressed by the legislature on the basis of fact-finding and the opinions of experts.
The foregoing, of course, leave out of consideration therapeutic sterilisation and where the line is to be drawn between therapeutic and non-therapeutic sterilisation. On this issue, I simply repeat that the utmost caution must be exercised commensurate with the seriousness of the procedure. Marginal justifications must be weighed against what is in every case a grave intrusion on the physical and mental integrity of the person.
It will be apparent that my views closely conform to those expressed by Heilbron J in *Re D, supra*. She was speaking of an infant, but her remarks are equally applicable to an adult. The importance of maintaining the physical integrity of a human being ranks high in our scale of values, particularly as it affects the privilege of giving life. I cannot agree that a court can deprive a woman of that privilege for purely social or other non-therapeutic purposes without her consent. The fact that others may suffer inconvenience or hardship from failure to do so cannot be taken into account. The Crown's *parens patriae* jurisdiction exists for the benefit of those who cannot help themselves, not to relieve those who may have the burden of caring for them.
I should perhaps add, as Heilbron J does, that sterilisation may, on occasion, be necessary as an adjunct to treatment of a serious malady, but I would underline that this, of course, does not allow for subterfuge or for treatment of some marginal medical problem. Heilbron J was referring, as I am, to cases where such treatment is necessary in dealing with a serious condition. The recent British Columbia case of *Re K,* [(1985) 19 DLR (4th) 255], is at best dangerously close to the limits of the permissible.
. . . However, [counsel] also argued that there is what he called a fundamental right to free procreative choice. Not only, he asserted, is there a fundamental right

to bear children; there is as well a fundamental right to choose not to have children and to implement that choice by means of contraception. Starting from the American courts' approach to the due process clause in the United States Constitution, he appears to base this argument on s 7 of the *Charter*. But assuming for the moment that liberty as used in s 7 protects rights of this kind (a matter I refrain from entering into), counsel's contention seems to me to go beyond the kind of protection s 7 was intended to afford. All s 7 does is to give a remedy to protect individuals against laws or other state action that deprive them of liberty. It has no application here.

Another *Charter* related argument must be considered. In response to the appellant's argument that a court-ordered sterilisation of a mentally incompetent person, by depriving that person of the right to procreate, would constitute an infringement of that person's rights to liberty and security of the person under s 7 of the *Canadian Charter of Rights and Freedoms*, counsel for the respondent countered by relying on that person's right to equality under s 15(1) of the *Charter*, saying 'that the most appropriate method of ensuring the mentally incompetent their right to equal protection under s 15(1) is to provide the mentally incompetent with a means to obtain non-therapeutic sterilisations, which adequately protects their interests through appropriate judicial safeguards'. A somewhat more explicit argument along the same lines was made by counsel for the Public Trustee of Manitoba. His position was stated as follows:

> It is submitted that in the case of a mentally incompetent adult, denial of the right to have his or her case presented by a guardian *ad litem* to a Court possessing jurisdiction to give or refuse substituted consent to a non-therapeutic procedure such as sterilisation, would be tantamount to a denial to that person of equal protection and equal benefit of the law. Such a denial would constitute discrimination on the basis of mental disability, which discrimination is prohibited by Section 15 of *The Canadian Charter of Rights and Freedoms*.

Section 15 of the *Charter* was not in force when these proceedings commenced but, this aside, these arguments appear flawed. They raise in different form an issue already dealt with, i e, that the decision made by a court on an application to consent to the sterilisation of an incompetent is somehow that of the incompetent. More troubling is that the issue is, of course, not raised by the incompetent, but by a third party.

The court undoubtedly has the right and duty to protect those who are unable to take care of themselves, and in doing so it has a wide discretion to do what it considers to be in their best interests. But this function must not, in my view, be transformed so as to create a duty obliging the court, at the behest of a third party, to make a choice between the two alleged constitutional rights—the right to procreate or not to procreate—simply because the individual is unable to make that choice. All the more so since, in the case of non-therapeutic sterilisation as we saw, the choice is one the courts cannot safely exercise.

Other issues

In light of the conclusions I have reached, it is unnecessary for me to deal with the *Charter* issues raised by the appellant and some of the interveners. It is equally unnecessary to comment at length on some of the subsidiary issues such as the burden of proof required to warrant an order of sterilisation and the precautions that judges should, in the interests of justice, take in dealing with applications for such orders. These do not arise because of the view I have taken of the approach the courts should adopt in dealing with applications for non-therapeutic sterilisation. Since these issues may arise in cases involving applications for sterilisation for therapeutic purposes, however, I will venture a few words about them. Since, barring emergency situations, a surgical procedure without consent ordinarily constitutes battery, it will be obvious that the onus of proving the need for the procedure is on those who seek to have it performed. And that burden, though a civil one, must be commensurate with the seriousness of the measure proposed. In conducting these procedures, it is obvious that a court must proceed with extreme caution; otherwise as MacDonald J noted, it would open the way for abuse of the mentally incompetent. In particular, in any such proceedings, it is essential that the mentally incompetent have independent representation.

Notice that Eve was not a minor but was an incompetent adult. The Supreme Court determined that, nevertheless, it had jurisdiction akin to wardship derived from the Crown's *parens patriae* prerogative power (on which *infra*).

You will have noticed the reference to the earlier decision of the Court of Appeal of British Columbia in *Re K and Public Trustee* (1985) 19 DLR (4th) 255 in La Forest J's judgment. The Supreme Court regarded this case as illustrating the difference between a therapeutic sterilisation and the non-therapeutic sterilisation in *Re Eve*.

> More germane for the present purposes is the recent case of *Re K and Public Trustee* (1985) 19 DLR (4th) 255, where the Court of Appeal of British Columbia ordered that a hysterectomy be performed on a seriously retarded child on the ground that the operation was therapeutic. The most serious factor considered by the court was the child's alleged aversion to blood, which it was feared would seriously affect her when her menstrual period began. It should be observed, and the fact was underscored by the judges in that case, that *Re K and Public Trustee* raised a quite different issue from that in the present case. As Anderson JA put it at p 275: 'I say now, as forcefully as I can, this case cannot and must not be regarded as a precedent to be followed in cases involving sterilisation of mentally disabled persons for contraceptive purposes'.

Do you consider that the facts of *Eve* and *Re K* illustrate satisfactorily the distinction between a therapeutic and a non-therapeutic sterilisation?

Re B (a minor)
[1987] 2 All ER 206 (House of Lords).

Facts: A local authority had the care of a mentally handicapped and epileptic 17-year-old girl who had a mental age of five or six. She had no understanding of the connection between sexual intercourse and pregnancy and birth, and would not be able to cope with birth nor care for a child of her own. She was not capable of consenting to marriage. She was, however, exhibiting the normal sexual drive and inclinations for someone of her physical age. There was expert evidence that it was vital that she should not be permitted to become pregnant and that certain contraceptive drugs would react with drugs administered to control her mental instability and epilepsy. There was further evidence that it would be difficult, if not impossible, to place her on a course of oral contraceptive pills. The local authority, which had no wish to institutionalise her, applied to the court for her to be made a ward of court and for leave to be given for her to undergo a sterilisation operation. The application was supported by the minor's mother. The Official Solicitor, acting as the minor's guardian *ad litem*, did not support the application. The judge granted the application, and an appeal by the Official Solicitor was dismissed by the Court of Appeal. The Official Solicitor appealed to the House of Lords.

> **Lord Hailsham of St Marylebone LC:** There is no doubt that, in the exercise of its wardship jurisdiction, the first and paramount consideration is the well-being, welfare or interests (each expression occasionally used, but each, for this purpose, synonymous) of the human being concerned, that is the ward herself or himself. In this case I believe it to be the only consideration involved. In particular there is no issue of public policy other than the application of the above principle which can conceivably be taken into account, least of all (since the opposite appears to have been considered in some quarters) any question of eugenics. The ward has never conceived and is not pregnant. No question therefore arises as to the morality or legality of an abortion.

The ward in the present case is of the mental age of five or six. She speaks only in sentences limited to one or two words. Although her condition is controlled by a drug, she is epileptic. She does not understand and cannot learn the causal connection between intercourse and pregnancy and the birth of children. She would be incapable of giving a valid consent to contracting a marriage. She would not understand, or be capable of easily supporting, the inconveniences and pains of pregnancy. As she menstruates irregularly, pregnancy would be difficult to detect or diagnose in time to terminate it easily. Were she to carry a child to full term she would not understand what was happening to her, she would be likely to panic, and would probably have to be delivered by Caesarian section, but, owing to her emotional state, and the fact that she has a high pain threshold she would be quite likely to pick at the operational wound and tear it open. In any event, she would be 'terrified, distressed and extremely violent' during normal labour. She has no maternal instincts and is not likely to develop any. She does not desire children, and, if she bore a child, would be unable to care for it.

In these circumstances her mother, and the local authority under whose care she is by virtue of a care order, advised by the social worker who knows her, a gynaecologist, and a paediatrician, consider it vital that she should not become pregnant, and in any case she would not be able to give informed consent to any act of sexual intercourse and would thus be a danger to others. Notwithstanding this, she has all the physical sexual drive and inclinations of a physically mature young woman of 17, which is in fact what she is. In addition, she has already shown that she is vulnerable to sexual approaches, she has already once been found in a compromising situation in a bathroom, and there is significant danger of pregnancy resulting from casual sexual intercourse. To incarcerate her or reduce such liberty as she is able to enjoy would be gravely detrimental to the amenity and quality of her life, and the only alternative to sterilisation seriously canvassed before the court is an oral contraceptive to be taken daily for the rest of her life whilst fertile, which has only a 40% chance of establishing an acceptable regime, and has serious potential side effects. In addition, according to the evidence, it would not be possible in the light of her swings of mood and considerable physical strength to ensure the administration of the necessary daily dose. As her social worker put it, 'if she [the ward] is . . . in one of her moods . . . there is no way' she would try to give her a pill.

In these circumstances, Bush J and the Court of Appeal both decided that the only viable option was sterilisation by occlusion of the Fallopian tubes (not hysterectomy). Apart from its probably irreversible nature, the detrimental effects are likely to be minimal. For my part, I do not myself see how either Bush J or the Court of Appeal could sensibly have come to any other possible conclusion applying as they did as their first and paramount consideration the correct criterion of the welfare of the ward.

The ward becomes of age (18) on 20 May next. There seems some doubt whether some residual *parens patriae* jurisdiction remains in the High Court after majority (cf Hoggett *Mental Health Law* (2nd edn, 1984) p 203 and 8 Halsburys Laws (4th edn) para 901, note 6). I do not take this into account. It is clearly to the interest of the ward that this matter be decided now and without further delay. We should be no wiser in 12 months' time than we are now and it would be doubtful then what legal courses would be open in the circumstances.

We were invited to consider the decision of Heilbron J in *Re D (a minor) (wardship: sterilisation)* [1976] 1 All ER 326 at 332, [1976] Fam 185 at 193, when the judge rightly referred to the irreversible nature of such an operation and the deprivation, which it involves, of a basic human right, namely the right of a woman to reproduce. But this right is only such when reproduction is the result of informed choice of which this ward is incapable. I have no doubt whatsoever that that case was correctly decided, but I venture to suggest that no one would be more astonished than that wise, experienced and learned judge herself if we were to apply these proper considerations to the extreme and quite different facts of the present case.

We were also properly referred to the Canadian case of *Re Eve* (1986) 31 DLR (4th) 1. But whilst I find La Forest J's history of the *parens patriae* jurisdiction of the

Crown (at 14–21) extremely helpful, I find, with great respect, his conclusion (at 32) that the procedure of sterilisation 'should *never* be authorised for non-therapeutic purposes' (my emphasis) totally unconvincing and in startling contradiction to the welfare principle which should be the first and paramount consideration in wardship cases. Moreover, for the purposes of the present appeal I find the distinction he purports to draw between 'therapeutic' and 'non-therapeutic' purposes of this operation in relation to the facts of the present case above as totally meaningless, and, if meaningful, quite irrelevant to the correct application of the welfare principle. To talk of the 'basic right' to reproduce of an individual who is not capable of knowing the causal connection between intercourse and childbirth, the nature of pregnancy, what is involved in delivery, unable to form maternal instincts or to care for a child appears to me wholly to part company with reality.

In the event, I am quite sure that the courts below had jurisdiction, and applied the right criterion for the right reasons, after careful consideration of all the evidential material before them.

Lord Bridge of Harwich: It is unfortunate that so much of the public comment on the decision should have been based on erroneous or, at best, incomplete appreciation of the facts and on mistaken assumptions as to the grounds on which the decision proceeded. I can only join with others of your Lordships in emphasising that this case has nothing whatever to do with eugenic theory or with any attempt to lighten the burden which must fall on those who have the care of the ward. It is concerned, and concerned only, with the question of what will promote the welfare and serve the best interests of the ward.

There is no reason to doubt that the Canadian decision in *Re Eve* was correct on its own facts. La Forest J, delivering the judgment of the Supreme Court, emphasised (at 9) that 'there is no evidence that giving birth would be more difficult for Eve than for any other woman'. The supposed conflict between the views of the Supreme Court in Canada and of the Court of Appeal in England arises from the passage where it is said (31 DLR (4th) 1 at 32):

> The grave intrusion on a person's rights and the certain physical damage that ensues from non-therapeutic sterilisation without consent, when compared to the highly questionable advantages that can result from it, have persuaded me that it can never safely be determined that such a procedure is for the benefit of that person. Accordingly, the procedure should never be authorised for non-therapeutic purposes under the *parens patriae* jurisdiction.

This sweeping generalisation seems to me, with respect, to be entirely unhelpful. To say that the court can never authorise sterilisation of a ward as being in her best interests would be patently wrong. To say that it can only do so if the operation is 'therapeutic' as opposed to 'non-therapeutic' is to divert attention from the true issue, which is whether the operation is in the ward's best interest, and remove it to an area of arid semantic debate as to where the line is to be drawn between 'therapeutic' and 'non-therapeutic' treatment.

In *Re D (a minor) (wardship: sterilisation)* [1976] 1 All ER 326 at 332, [1976] Fam 185 at 193 Heilbron J correctly described the right of a woman to reproduce as a basic human right. The Supreme Court of Canada in *Re Eve* (1986) 31 DLR (4th) 1 at 5 refer, equally aptly, to 'the great privilege of giving birth'. The sad fact in the instant case is that the mental and physical handicaps under which the ward suffers effectively render her incapable of ever exercising that right or enjoying that privilege. It is clear beyond argument that for her pregnancy would be an unmitigated disaster. The only question is how she may best be protected against it. The evidence proves overwhelmingly that the right answer is by a simple operation for occlusion of the Fallopian tubes and that, quite apart from the question whether the court would have power to authorise such an operation after her eighteenth birthday, the operation should now be performed without further delay. I find it difficult to understand how anybody examining the facts humanely, compassionately and objectively could reach any other conclusion.

Lord Oliver of Aylmerton: My Lords, none of us is likely to forget that we live in a century which, as a matter of relatively recent history, has witnessed experiments carried out in the name of eugenics or for the purpose of population control, so that the very word 'sterilisation' has come to carry emotive overtones. It is important at the very outset, therefore, to emphasise as strongly as it is possible to do so, that this appeal has nothing whatever to do with eugenics. It is concerned with one primary consideration and one alone, namely the welfare and best interest of this young woman, an interest which is conditioned by the imperative necessity of ensuring, for her own safety and welfare, that she does not become pregnant. . . .

What prompted the application to the court was the consciousness on the part of her mother and officers of the council responsible for her care that she was beginning to show recognisable signs of sexual awareness and sexual drive exemplified by provocative approaches to male members of the staff and other residents and by touching herself in the genital area. There was thus brought to their attention the obvious risk of pregnancy and the desirability of taking urgent and effective contraceptive measures. Although at present she is subject to effective supervision, her degree of incapacity is not such that it would be thought right that she should, effectively, be institutionalised all her life. The current approach to persons of her degree of incapacity is to allow them as much freedom as is consistent with their own safety and that of other people and although the likelihood is that she will, for the foreseeable future, continue to live at the residential institution, she visits her mother and her siblings at weekends and will, inevitably, be much less susceptible to supervision when she goes to an adult training centre. At the same time the risks involved in her becoming pregnant are formidable. The evidence of Dr Berney is that there is no prospect of her being capable of forming a long-term adult relationship, such as marriage, which is within the capacity of some less mentally handicapped persons. She has displayed no maternal feelings and indeed has an antipathy to small children. Such skills as she has been able to develop are limited to those necessary for caring for herself at the simplest level and there is no prospect of her being capable of raising or caring for a child of her own. If she did give birth to a child it would be essential that it be taken from her for fostering or adoption although her attitude towards children is such that this would not cause her distress. So far as her awareness of her own sexuality is concerned, she has, as has already been mentioned, been taught to manage for herself the necessary hygienic mechanics of menstruation, but it has not been possible to teach her about sexuality in any abstract form. She understands the link between pregnancy and a baby but is unaware of sexual intercourse and its relationship to pregnancy. It is not feasible to discuss contraception with her and even if there should come a time when she becomes capable of understanding the need for contraception, there is no likelihood of her being able to develop the capacity to weigh up the merits of different types of contraception or to make an informed choice in the matter. Should she become pregnant, it would be desirable that the pregnancy should be terminated, but because of her obesity and the irregularity of her periods there is an obvious danger that her condition might not be noticed until it was too late for an abortion to take place safely. On the other hand, the risks if she were permitted to go to full term are serious, for although it is Dr Berney's opinion that she would tolerate the condition of pregnancy without undue distress, the process of delivery would be likely to be traumatic and would cause her to panic. Normal delivery would be likely to require heavy sedation, which would be injurious to the child, so that it might be more appropriate to deliver her by Caesarean section. If this course were adopted, however, past experience of her reaction to injuries suggests that it would be very difficult to prevent her from repeatedly opening up the wound and thus preventing the healing of the post-operative scar. It was against this background and in the light of the increasing freedom which must be allowed her as she grows older and the consequent difficulty of maintaining effective supervision that those having the care of the minor concluded that it was essential in her interests that effective contraceptive measures be taken. Almost all drugs appear to have a bad effect on her and the view was formed, in which her mother concurred, that the only appropriate course offering complete protection was for her to undergo sterilisation by occluding the fallopian tubes, a relatively minor operation carrying a very small degree of risk to the patient, a very high degree of protection and minimal side effects. There is, however, no possibility that the minor, even if of full age, would herself have the mental capacity to consent to such an operation. Hence the application to the court.

The necessity for the course proposed has been exhaustively considered by the Official Solicitor on the minor's behalf and there have been obtained two very careful and detailed reports from Dr Berney who is a consultant in child and adolescent psychiatry, and Mr Barron, a consultant of obstetrics and gynaecology to the Newcastle Health Authority. Both agree on the absolute necessity of taking effective contraceptive measures and the report of Mr Barron, in particular, contains a detailed consideration of the various options. It is unnecessary for present purposes to dilate on the numerous possible courses which have been considered. Her limited intelligence effectively rules out mechanical methods while at the same time the way in which certain contraceptive drugs are likely to react with anti-convulsant drugs administered for her epileptic condition severely limits the available choices. In the end it emerges as common ground that the only alternative to sterilisation which even merits consideration is the administration daily in pill form of the drug progestogen supplemented for the present, at any rate, by the danazol which she is presently taking. This involves a number of disadvantages and uncertainties. In the first place, it involves a regular and uninterrupted course which must be pursued over the whole of the minor's reproductive life of some 30 years or so. Secondly, it involves a *daily* dosage, a matter which has given great concern to those having the care of the minor. Miss Ford, the social worker most closely connected with her, was of the opinion that if the minor was in one of her violent moods there was no possible way in which the pill could be administered. Thirdly, the side effects of the drug over a long term are not yet known. Possibilities canvassed in the course of the evidence of Dr Lowry, the consultant paediatrician at Sunderland District General Hospital, were weight-gain, nausea, headaches and depression. But fourthly, and perhaps even more importantly, the effectiveness of this course is entirely speculative. The matter can perhaps best be summed up in the answer given by Mr Barron when he was asked in examination-in-chief for an assessment of the prospects of achieving a satisfactory contraceptive regime by way of pill. He said:

It would be very speculative because you have a problem here of a girl who is obese who is still quite young, who has all kinds of problems like, for example, taking anti-convulsant therapy for epilepsy, which affect the manner of working certainly of oestrogens, all of which make her a particularly difficult person in whom to perform a normal judgment. Therefore, I think that we might find a successful modus vivendi, but it is difficult to be certain. I think it is perhaps—if you want a kind of guess, I would say that we have a 30 to 40% chance of getting some formulation that would be successful. But of course it would have to be taken for a very long time.

In answer to a further question he surmised that an experimental period of 12 to 18 months might be required.

Here then is the dilemma. The vulnerability of this young woman, her need for protection, and the potentially frightening consequences of her becoming pregnant are not in doubt. Of the two possible courses, the one proposed is safe, but irreversible, the other speculative, possibly damaging and requiring discipline over a period of many years from one of the most limited intellectual capacity. Equally it is not in doubt that this young woman is not capable and never will be capable herself of consenting to undergo a sterilisation operation. Can the court and should the court, in the exercise of its wardship jurisdiction, give on her behalf that consent which she is incapable of giving and which, objectively considered, it is clearly in her interests to give?

My Lords, I have thought it right to set out in some detail the background of fact in which this appeal has come before your Lordships' House because it is, in my judgment, essential to appreciate, in considering the welfare of this young woman which it is the duty of the court to protect, the degree of her vulnerability, the urgency of the the need to take protective measures and the impossibility of her ever being able at this age or any later age either to consent to any form of operative treatment or to exercise for herself the right of making any informed decision in matters which, in the case of a person less heavily handicapped, would rightly be thought to be matters purely of personal and subjective choice.

My Lords, the arguments advanced against the adoption of the expedient of a sterilisation operation are based almost entirely (and, indeed, understandably so) on its irreversible nature. It was observed by Dillon LJ in the Court of Appeal that the jurisdiction in wardship proceedings to authorise such an operation is one which should be exercised only in the last resort and with that I respectfully agree. What is submitted is that, in concluding as it did that the instant case was one in which, as the last resort, that jurisdiction ought to be exercised, the Court of Appeal was in error and had not given sufficient weight to the alternative course of experimentation with the progesteron pill. That submission has been reinforced before your Lordships by a further submission not made in either court below that there lies in the court an inherent jurisdiction in the case of a mentally handicapped subject of any age to sanction, as *parens patriae*, an operation such as that proposed whenever it should be considered necessary. Thus, it is argued, some of the urgency is taken out of the case, for a further application can be mounted at any time should alternative methods of contraception prove ineffective. My Lords, speaking for myself, I should be reluctant to express any view regarding the correctness of this submission without very much fuller argument than it has been possible for counsel in the time available to present to your Lordships. But in fact I do not consider that in the instant case the point is of more than of academic interest for I am, for my part, prepared to assume for present purposes that the *parens patriae* jurisdiction continues into full age. Making that assumption, I remain wholly unpersuaded that the Court of Appeal failed to give full weight to the alternative proposed or that it erred in any way in the conclusion to which it came. It was faced, as your Lordships are faced, with the necessity of deciding here and now what is the right course in the best interests of the ward. The danger to which she is exposed and the speculative nature of the alternative proposed are such that, on any footing, the risk is not one which should properly be taken by the court. For my part I have not been left in any doubt that Bush J and the Court of Appeal rightly concluded that there was no practicable alternative to sterilisation and that the authority sought by the council should be given without further delay.

Your Lordships' attention has, quite properly, been directed to the decision of Heilbron J in *Re D (a minor) (wardship: sterilisation)* [1976] 1 All ER 326, [1976] Fam 185, a case very different from the instant case, where the evidence indicated that the ward was of an intellectual capacity to marry and would in the future be able to make her own choice. In those circumstances Heilbron J declined to sanction an operation which involved depriving her of her right to reproduce. That, if I may say so respectfully, was plainly a right decision. But the right to reproduce is of value only if accompanied by the ability to make a choice and in the instant case there is no question of the minor ever being able to make such a choice or indeed to appreciate the need to make one. All the evidence indicates that she will never desire a child and that reproduction would in fact be positively harmful to her. Something was sought to be made of the description of the operation for which authority was sought in *Re D* as 'non-therapeutic', using the word 'therapeutic' as connoting the treatment of some malfunction or disease. The description was, no doubt, apt enough in that case, but I do not, for my part, find the distinction between 'therapeutic' and 'non-therapeutic' measures helpful in the context of the instant case, for it seems to me entirely immaterial whether measures undertaken for the protection against future and foreseeable injury are properly described as 'therapeutic'. The primary and paramount question is only whether they are for the welfare and benefit of this particular young woman situate as she is situate in this case.

Your Lordships have also been referred to *Re Eve* (1986) 31 DLR (4th) 1, a decision of the Supreme Court of Canada which contains an extremely instructive judgment of La Forest J in which he considered the extent of the *parens patriae* jurisdiction over mentally handicapped persons. His conclusion was that sterilisation should never be authorised for non-therapeutic purposes under the *parens patriae* jurisdiction. If in that conclusion the expression 'non-therapeutic' was intended to exclude measures taken for the necessary protection from future harm of the person over whom the jurisdiction is exercisable, then I respectfully dissent from it for it seems to me to contradict what is the sole and paramount criterion for the exercise of the jurisdiction, viz the welfare and benefit of the ward. La Forest J observed (at 32–33):

> If sterilisation of the mentally incompetent is to be adopted as desirable for general social purposes, the legislature is the appropriate body to do so.

With that I respectfully agree but I desire to emphasise once again that this case is not about sterilisation for social purposes; it is not about eugenics, it is not about the convenience of those whose task it is to care for the ward or the anxieties of her family; and it involves no general principle of public policy. It is about what is in the best interests of this unfortunate young woman and how best she can be given the protection which is essential to her future well-being so that she may lead as full a life as her intellectual capacity allows. That is and must be the paramount consideration as was rightly appreciated by Bush J and by the Court of Appeal. They came to what, in my judgment, was the only possible conclusion in the interests of the minor. I would accordingly dismiss the appeal.

For a discussion of alternative approaches that a court might adopt in relation to authorising sterilisation operations upon incompetent minors and adults, see *infra* Ch 7.

Questions

(i) What meanings did La Forest J give to the terms 'therapeutic' and 'non-therapeutic' medical procedures? Do you agree with him?

(ii) Did the House of Lords in *re B* misunderstand his distinction?

(iii) Had La Forest J been a judge in *re B*, would he have dissented? How would the judges in *re B* have decided *re Eve*?

(iv) Is it a relevant criterion for a parent (or the court), in deciding whether to consent to a medical procedure upon a child, that the procedure is not therapeutic?

2. *Spouses and relatives.*

Skegg puts the issue well and supplies what, in our view, is a correct statement of English law in his book *Law, Ethics and Medicine*, at pp 72, 73:

> It is sometimes stated or assumed that, where a patient is incapable of consenting, an effective consent may be given by his spouse, or by some near relative. Unfortunately, those who hold this view do not indicate the grounds on which it is based. . . .
>
> The better view is that there is no general doctrine whereby a spouse or near relative is empowered to give a legally effective consent to medical procedures to be carried out on an adult.[13] Of course, doctors are sometimes justified in proceeding without the consent of the patient. But this is not because the consent of others justifies a doctor in proceeding without the patient's consent, but because in the circumstances the doctor is justified in proceeding despite the absence of legally effective consent.[14]

Notes to extract

[13] For extrajudicial statements in support of this view, see Devlin, *Samples* [*of Lawmaking* (1962)], 86; N O'Bryan, [[1] The Consent of the Patient to Surgical and Medical Procedures (1961) 8 Proc of Medico-Legal Soc of Victoria 138], 151.

[14] Nevertheless, it is sometimes desirable for a doctor to obtain the agreement of a spouse, or a near relative, to his treating a patient without the patient's consent. Although such agreement does not affect the doctor's legal power to proceed without consent, it reduces any danger there might be of his being prosecuted or sued for doing so.

Sometimes the contrary claim is made in America. However, those who make it have difficulty in pointing to authority in support. They sometimes find refuge in the dictum of *Canterbury v Spence* 464 F 2d 772 at 789 (1972) of Judge Robinson: 'even in situations of that character where the patient is unconscious or otherwise incapable of consenting the physician should, as current law requires, attempt to secure a relative's consent if possible'. The authority cited to support this proposition is *Bonner v Moran* 126 F 2d 121 at 122–23 (1941), but this is a case of parent consenting on behalf of a child.

The same mistaken reasoning can be seen in the judgment of Croom-Johnson LJ in *Wilson v Pringle*, where he assumes that in the case of an unconscious patient, who is, therefore, unable to consent, the next-of-kin may validly consent on the patient's behalf. But, like the other judges before him, he cites no authority for this assumption.

Sometimes, in the case of mentally ill patients, a spouse or relative may be appointed a guardian under the Mental Health Act 1983. In *T v T (supra)*, Wood J considered whether a guardian could consent to medical treatment. You will remember that the case concerned a 19 year old incompetent woman whom it was thought should undergo an abortion and a sterilisation operation in her own best interests.

Wood J: . . . I pose myself the question—is there anyone who can consent on behalf of this defendant? It is submitted that the answer is 'No'.

This defendant is clearly suffering from a mental disorder within section 1 of the Mental Health Act 1983, and I therefore turn to the possibility of a guardianship application and an order under section 7. The procedure for such an application can be cumberous, and it was not suggested that an application *ex parte* on notice, as in the present case, could properly be made. The effect of a guardianship application is set out in section 8 where the relevant words read:
Where a guardianship application, duly made . . . is accepted by that authority, the application shall, subject to regulations made by the Secretary of State, confer on the authority or person named in the application as guardian, to the exclusion of any other person . . . (*b*) the power to require the patient to attend at places and times so specified for the purpose of medical treatment, occupation, education or training.
Section 145 of the Mental Health Act 1983, which is the definition section, provides: '"medical treatment" includes nursing, and also includes care, habilitation and rehabilitation under medical supervision'.
Section 8 replaces section 34(1) of the Mental Health Act of 1959, where subsection (1) reads, materially:
Where a guardianship application, duly made under the foregoing provisions of this Act and forwarded to the local authority within the period allowed by subsection (2) of this section, is accepted by that authority, the application shall . . . confer on the authority or person therein named as guardian, to the exclusion of any other person—and here is the important point—all such powers as would be exercisable by them or him in relation to the patient if they or he were the father of the patient and the patient were under the age of 14 years.
The wording of section 8 of the Mental Health Act 1983 will be seen to be much more restricted than the wider powers of the guardian under section 34 of the Act of 1959. One important effect is to remove the guardian's implicit power to consent to treatment on behalf of the patient. In my judgment there is no power to consent to the present operation to be found in section 8 of the Mental Health Act 1983, and indeed, on a construction of the statute as a whole I am satisfied that medical treatment in this context means psychiatric treatment.

3. The Court: Wardship. Many of the cases already set out (*Re D*; *Re B* (1981); *S v S*) illustrate the existence and scope of the court's power in wardship proceedings to authorise or refuse medical treatment on children.

Under s 41 of the Supreme Court Act 1981, the wardship jurisdiction comes to an end when the child ceases to be a minor, ie at 18 (Family Law Reform Act

1969, s 1). The wardship jurisdiction is of significance for medical law because of the general principle that 'once a child is a ward of court, no important step in the life of that child, can be taken without the consent of the court . . .' (*per* Heilbron J in *Re D*). Few, if any, forms of medical treatment could therefore be properly embarked upon where the child is a ward without first seeking the authorisation of the court.

What is the precise power which the court exercises? It is sometimes said (somewhat carelessly) that a court *orders* that a specific form of treatment be carried out. It may be better analytically to describe the court's power as one of *authorisation* only. For example, Templeman LJ stated that: '. . . the local authority must be authorised themselves to authorise and direct the operation to be carried out . . .', (*Re B (a minor)* (1981)).

This is because first, courts do not make orders which they cannot supervise and secondly, in the context of medical treatment the last word must remain with the doctor. As Somerville put it in her article, 'Refusal of Medical Treatment in "Captive" Circumstances', 63 (1985) Canadian Bar Review 59 at 89:

> Consequently, if the treating physician thought that treatment were contra-indicated, because, for instance, the circumstances had suddenly changed (and there was no negligence involved in holding such an opinion, in that a reasonable and competent physician in the same circumstances could be of the same opinion), the physician would not only have no duty to treat, but would have a duty not to treat, breach of which would constitute medical negligence or malpractice.

Of course, a court may order treatment if what they are really saying is that the child should not be neglected and, for example, left to die, but should receive that treatment which doctors admit would otherwise be appropriate, but which some say should not as a matter of moral principle (rather than medical practice) be delivered in the instant case. (See, for example, the Canadian case *Re Superintendent of Family and Child Service and Dawson* (1983) 145 DLR (3d) 610, but compare *Re B* [1981]. Both these cases are discussed *infra* Ch 12.)

A further area of concern is the position the court sees itself in. Is the court in wardship merely acting: 'as supreme parent of the child, [so that it] must exercise that jurisdiction in the manner in which a wise, affectionate and careful parent would act for the welfare of the child' (per Lord Esher MR in *R v Gyngall* [1893] 2 QB 232 at 241)? If so, does the court have power to authorise (or to withhold authority for) medical treatment which would be outside the parents powers? (See *Re B* [1987] 2 All ER 206 per Dunn LJ, *supra*.) Can it be that since some parents are not always 'wise, affectionate and careful' some decisions must *ex abundante cautalae* be for the court to reach, e g non-therapeutic sterilisation as in *Re B* [1987]?

Finally, in making any decision, the criteria the court uses are those which the law expects a parent to use namely 'best interests' and all that this implies. One school of thought in modern family law would place greater limits than the English cases contemplate on the power of the court since the court is seen as potentially usurping the proper exercise of autonomy by parents; see Goldstein, Freud and Solmit, *Beyond the Best Interests of the Child* (1973) and *Before the Best Interests of the Child* (1980). For a discussion of this in the context of medical decision-making, see B Dickens (1981) 97 LQR 462).

As parens patriae. It is clear that the court's protective wardship jurisdiction comes to an end when a child reaches majority. Until recently, it was thought that thereafter the court had no power to authorise medical treatment on an incompetent adult, however beneficial or necessary the treatment might be (see *Re B* [1987] 2 All ER 206 at 210, CA, *per* Dillon LJ). However, in the Canadian case of *Re Eve*, the Supreme Court 'rediscovered' the Crown's ancient prerogative jurisdiction (originally vested in the Lord Chancellor) over 'lunatics, idiots and others of unsound mind'. La Forest J set out the history of the *parens patriae* jurisdiction.

Re Eve
[1986] 2 SCR 388 (Supreme Court of Canada)

La Forest J: The origin of the Crown's *parens patriae* jurisdiction over the mentally incompetent, Sir Henry Theobald tells us, is lost in the mists of antiquity; see H Theobald, *The Law Relating to Lunacy* (1924). *De Prerogativa Regis*, an instrument regarded as a statute that dates from the thirteenth or early fourteenth century, recognised and restricted it, but did not create it. Theobald speculates that 'the most probable theory [of its origin] is that either by general assent or by some statute, now lost, the care of persons of unsound mind was by Edw I taken from the feudal lords, who would naturally take possession of the land of a tenant unable to perform his feudal duties'; see Theobald, *supra*, p 1.

In the 1540's, the *parens patriae* jurisdiction was transferred from officials in the royal household to the Court of Wards and Liveries, where it remained until that court was wound up in 1660. Thereafter the Crown exercised its jurisdiction through the Lord Chancellor to whom by letters patent under the Sign Manual it granted the care and custody of the persons and the estates of persons of unsound mind so found by inquisition, i e, an examination to determine soundness or unsoundness of mind.

Wardship of children had a quite separate origin as a property right arising out of the feudal system of tenures. The original purpose of the wardship jurisdiction was to protect the rights of the guardian rather than of the ward. Until 1660 this jurisdiction was also administered by the Court of Wards and Liveries which had been created for the purpose.

When tenures and the Court of Wards were abolished, the concept of wardship should, in theory, have disappeared. It was kept alive, however, by the Court of Chancery, which justified it as an aspect of its *parens patriae* jurisdiction; see, for example, *Cary v Bertie* (1696) 2 Vern 333 at 342, 23 ER 814 at 818; *Morgan v Dillon* (1724) 9 Mod Rep 135 at 139, 88 ER 361 at 364. In time wardship became substantively and procedurally assimilated to the *parens patriae* jurisdiction, lost its connection with property, and became purely protective in nature. Wardship thus is merely a device by means of which Chancery exercises its *parens patriae* jurisdiction over children. Today the care of children constitutes the bulk of the courts' work involving the exercise of the *parens patriae* jurisdiction.

It follows from what I have said that the wardship cases constitute a solid guide to the exercise of the *parens patriae* power even in the case of adults . . . But proof of incompetence must, of course, be made.

This marks a difference between wardship and *parens patriae* jurisdiction over adults. In the case of children, Chancery has a custodial jurisdiction as well, and thus has inherent jurisdiction to make them its wards; this is not so of adult mentally incompetent persons (see *Beall v Smith* (1873) 9 Ch App 85 at 92). Since, however, the Chancellor had been vested by letters patent under the Sign Manual with power to exercise the Crown's *parens patriae* jurisdiction for the protection of persons so found by inquisition, this difference between the two procedures has no importance for present purposes.

By the early part of the nineteenth century, the work arising out of the Lord Chancellor's jurisdiction became more than one judge could handle and the Chancery Court was reorganised and the work assigned to several justices including the Master of the Rolls. In 1852 (by 15 & 16 Vict, c 87, s 15 (UK)) the jurisdiction of the Chancellor regarding the 'Custody of the Persons and Estates of Persons found idiot, lunatic or of unsound Mind, was authorised to be exercised by anyone for the time being entrusted by virtue of the Sign Manual.

Since historically the law respecting the mentally incompetent has been almost exclusively focused on their estates, the law on guardianship of their persons is 'pitifully unclear with respect to some basic issues'; see P McLaughlin, *Guardianship of the Person* (Downsview 1979), p 35. Despite this vagueness, however, it seems clear that the *parens patriae* jurisdiction was never limited solely to the management and care of the estate of a mentally retarded or defective person. As early as 1603, Sir Edward Coke in *Beverley's Case* (1604) 4 Co Rep 123 b at 126 a, 126 b, 76 ER 1118 at 1124, stated that 'in the case of an idiot or fool natural, for whom there is no expectation, but that he, during his life, will remain without discretion and use of reason, the law has given the custody of *him*, and all that he has, to the King' (emphasis added). Later at the bottom of the page he adds:

2. Although the state. says, *custodiam terrarum*, yet the King shall have as well the custody of the body, and of their goods and chattels, as of the lands and other hereditaments, and as well those which he has by purchase, as those which he has as heirs by the common law.

At 4 Co Rep p 126 b, 76 ER 1125, he cites Fitzherbert's *Natura brevium* to the same effect. Theobald (*supra*, pp 7–8, 362) appears to be quite right when he tells us that the Crown's prerogative 'has never been limited by definition'. The Crown has an inherent jurisdiction to do what is for the benefit of the incompetent. Its limits (or scope) have not, and cannot, be defined. . . .

It was argued before us, however, that there was no precedent where the Lord Chancellor had exercised the *parens patriae* jurisdiction to order medical procedures of any kind. As to this, I would say that lack of precedent in earlier times is scarcely surprising having regard to the state of medical science at the time. Nonetheless, it seems clear from *Wellesley v Wellesley, supra*, that the situations in which the courts can act where it is necessary to do so for the protection of mental incompetents and children have never been, and indeed cannot, be defined. I have already referred to the remarks of Lord Redesdale. To these may be added those of Lord Manners who, at Bli pp 142–43 and 1085, respectively, expressed the view that 'It is . . . impossible to say what are the limits of that jurisdiction; every case must depend upon its own circumstances'.

Even if *Eve* is correct that it was part of English common law (and it seems to have been), the important question for the English lawyer is whether it remains part of *English* law after the mental health legislation of the twentieth century? This issue was, of course, not relevant, nor discussed in *Eve*. The legislation does not expressly remove the power of the courts which was delegated to the Lord Chancellor and the judges of the court of Chancery. Instead, the argument must be that since the legislation vests that part of the *parens patriae* power dealing with the 'property and other affairs' of the incompetent in the Court of Protection, the remaining power over the 'person' has impliedly been taken away. It is unclear as yet, at least until an appellate court addresses this question, whether this argument is correct; but it does seem to be in direct conflict with the usual approach of constitutional law to see the prerogative as only taken away expressly or by *necessary* implication. Arguably, it does not seem to have occurred here (see now *re F* (1989) discussed in *postscript* to Ch 7).

Even if the power remains, the last delegation to the judges was revoked in 1960 and the Mental Health Act 1959 became law. A new delegation of the Crown's power to the judges would be necessary today (see *re F* (1989) *infra* Ch 7).

In *Re B* the House of Lords left the existence of the *parens patriae* power unresolved because its existence was irrelevant to the case. In *T v T* [1988] Fam 52, [1988] 1 All ER 613, however, Wood J, relying on Halsbury's Laws of England, determined that he did not have the power to authorise an abortion and a sterilisation operation on an incompetent mentally retarded 19-year-old woman.

Wood J: Anyone reading the facts of this case will be aware of their marked similarity to those of *In Re B (A Minor) (Wardship: Sterilisation)* [1987] 2 WLR 1213. That was a decision of the House of Lords. The girl in that case was 17 years of age and it was therefore possible to take proceedings in wardship, a course unfortunately not open to the parties in the present case. Were it so I would respectfully adopt the words of Lord Bridge of Harwich when in referring to the consent given by the courts below to the proposed operation he said, at p 147: 'I find it difficult to understand how anybody examining the facts humanely, compassionately and objectively could reach any other conclusion'.

That is the course that I would wish to follow and the only way in which I could properly do so is if some residual *parens patriae* jurisdiction remains in the High Court after majority. This possibility was referred to by Lord Hailsham of St Marylebone LC, at p 1215: 'There seems some doubt as to whether some residual *parens patriae* jurisdiction remains in the High Court after majority'. Then he referred to *Hoggett, Mental Health Law,* 2nd ed (1984), p 203, and *Halsbury's Laws of England,* 4th ed, vol 8 (1974), p 588, para 901, note 6. Later in his speech he referred to the Canadian case of *In Re Eve* (1986) 31 DLR (4th) 1, where a history of the *parens patriae* jurisdiction of the Crown is set out.

I turn to the paragraph referred to by Lord Hailsham in *Halsbury's Laws of England,* vol 8, p 588. That is dealing with Crown prerogatives, and it reads:

> The care and commitment of the custody of the persons and estates of mentally disordered persons, which belong to the Crown at common law from very early times, and was invariably delegated to the Lord Chancellor by warrant under the sign manual, is now entirely governed by statute.

It is to be found in note 5 that the last warrant was revoked in 1960, and it reads 'See London Gazette 11 November 1960'. It will be remembered, of course, that it was the Mental Health Act 1959 which gave the power of consent to the guardian, which is omitted from the Act of 1983.

The facts of this case illustrate the usefulness and indeed, may I respectfully suggest, the necessity for a residual jurisdiction even when codification purports to cover every eventuality. The simplest remedy would be to issue a fresh warrant restoring this common law jurisdiction. However, this matter was one of urgency and examining the law within the time available I agree with the submission that . . . the court as *parens patriae* has [no] power to give consent, and that therefore the submission is well founded.

It is interesting to observe that the argument that the 1959 Act had impliedly put the prerogative into abeyance was rejected by Wood J when he determined that the power of the Court of Protection over mental patients did not extend to authorising medical treatment.

Part VII of the Act is headed 'Management of Property and Affairs of Patient', Section 95 gives the appointed judge the power to make orders 'with respect to the property and affairs of a patient'. This phrase was considered by Ungoed-Thomas J in *In Re W (EEM)* [1971] Ch 123. In that case the Official Solicitor issued a summons before the nominated judge for authority to prosecute a suit for divorce on behalf of a patient. The facts are not relevant for the present purposes, but Ungoed-Thomas J said, at p 143:

> So my conclusion is, in particular with regard to legal proceedings, including divorce proceedings, that the Court of Protection is not limited in its jurisdiction to dealing with a patient's property or financial affairs, nor limited to dealing with such other matters as may be within its jurisdiction in their property or financial aspects, but that it has exclusive jurisdiction over all the property and all the affairs in all their aspects; *but not to the management or care of the patient's person."*
> (My emphasis.)

It follows that there seem to be no provisions within the Mental Health Act 1983 which assist in the present circumstances.

Perhaps one final observation: you will have noticed from the earlier extract of *T v T* that the guardianship provisions which existed from 1959 until their repeal and replacement in 1982 (now the 1983 Act) did allow a guardian to consent to medical treatment. Therefore, there was during this period no lacuna in respect of the incompetent adult within the Mental Health Act (but, of course, there was as regards the incompetent adult outside the Act). The *parens patriae* power might, therefore, have been said to be impliedly repealed. Does it make any difference that the provision no longer exists? Could it be argued that the 1982 amendments have revived the *parens patriae* power? (See the discussion of the relevant principles in de Smith, *Constitutional and Administrative Law* (5th ed 1985), pp 144–5 and *R v Secretary of State for the Home Dept, ex p Northumbria Police Authority* [1989] QB 26, [1988] 1 All ER 556, CA and see *re F* (1989) postscript to Ch 7.)

4.   *'Best interests' and 'substituted judgment' tests.*

You will have noticed in the cases dealing with the power of proxies to consent on behalf of an incompetent person, discussions about the appropriate test for the parent, relative or court to apply in making a decision. Should the proxy act in the 'best interests' of the incompetent or reach a 'substituted judgment'? The issue has arisen in a number of contexts which we will return to later—such as, sterilisation, organ donation and the dying patient.

In its report on 'Sterilisation Decisions: Minors and Mentally Incompetent Adults' in March 1988, the Institute of Law Research and Reform of Alberta described the first of these tests as follows:

> (1) 'Best interests' test
> 9.31   The 'best interests' test is the test traditionally used for making decisions on behalf of another. It is the test used by the courts in the exercise of their *parens patriae* jurisdiction, and it is the basis for decision making by parents and guardians.
> 9.32   The test is not easily defined. It combines the objectivity of a reasonable person with the subjectivity of the circumstances of the particular individual for whom the decision is being made. Considerable discretion is left with the decision maker.

It is this test with which English law is most familiar. We have seen its application in cases where the proxy was an adult (*Gillick v West Norfolk and Wisbech Area Health Authority*) or where the proxy was the court (*Re B* (1981), and *Re B* (1987). In essence this test is *objective*.

However, it has been argued that a proxy would act more consistently with the aim of enhancing the patient's autonomy if the law required that he or she (or the court) act in accordance with the 'substituted judgment' test. The Alberta Report describes this test as follows (footnotes omitted):

> (2)   'Substituted judgment' test
> 9.35   The 'substituted judgment' test has been employed by some American courts in recent years as an alternative to the best interests test. Under the substituted judgment test the decision is to be the one that would be made by the mentally incompetent person if she were mentally competent. The test requires the application of the subjective values of the individual insofar as they can be known. To apply it, an attempt must be made to ascertain the mentally incompetent person's actual preference for or against such matters as sterilisation, other means of contraception and parenthood.
> 9.36   The substituted judgment test was developed in terminal illness cases involving decisions about the use or removal of life support systems. The Supreme Judicial Court of Massachusetts used it as the basis for a sterilisation decision in the case of *Re Moe*. This court found that the substituted judgment test best protects the mentally *incompetent* person by recognising the dignity, worth and integrity of the person and affording him the same personal rights and choices that are afforded to persons in the mainstream of society.

You will notice that the Report refers to the application of this 'substituted judgment' test in cases of terminally ill patients and sterilisation decisions. We will return to this case law in these contexts later (*infra* Ch 14 and Ch 7 respectively). For the present, it is sufficient to examine the two tests and determine which, if either, is legally more appropriate.

In his article 'Law and Medical Experimentation' (1987) 13 Monash University Law Review 189,200, Professor Gerald Dworkin comments on the 'substituted judgment' test:

Another concept which is creeping into American case-law in contrast to the traditional 'best interests' approach to proxy consent is that of 'substituted judgment'. The proxy, or court, does not attempt to decide what is in the 'best interests' of the patient, but rather what decision would be made by the individual if he were competent. The court 'dons the mental mantle of the incompetent and substitutes itself as nearly as possible for the individual in the decision-making process'.[46] It is one of those strange doctrines which was used in England in the early nineteenth century in connection with the administration of the estates of incompetent persons,[47] forgotten, and then rediscovered recently by American courts. It has been raised in cases involving incompetent persons to help establish whether, for example, to consent to the withdrawal of life support systems or to certain unusual or controversial types of medical treatment, such as shock therapy or psychosurgery.[48]

It is a controversial concept, not the least because of the inherent difficulties of attempting to assess what an incompetent patient would have decided were he competent, whether that assessment should be subjective or objective and, if objective, how it can really differ from a 'best interests' approach.

Notes to extract
46. *Superintendent of Belchertown State School v Saikewicz* 370 NE 2d 417 (1977).
47. *Ex p Whitbread* (1816) 2 Mer 99, 35 ER 878.
48. H W Classen, 'The Doctrine of Substituted Judgment in its Medicolegal Context' (1985) 31 *Med Trial Technique Q* 451.

The origins of the test and some of its difficulties are also discussed by John Robertson in his article 'Organ Donations By Incompetents and the Substituted Judgment Doctrine' (1976) 76 Columbia LR 48 at 57–59,

Under the substituted judgment doctrine—at least since the 1816 case of *Ex p Whitebread*[51]—courts have authorised gifts from the incompetent's estate to persons to whom the incompetent owes no duty of support.[52] The substituted judgment doctrine requires the court to 'don the mental mantle of the incompetent'[53] and to 'substitute itself as nearly as may be for the incompetent, and to act upon the same motives and considerations as would have moved her'.[54] Motives of charity and altruism,[55] self-interest,[56] and even the desire to minimise estate taxes[57] have all been imputed to an incompetent on this basis. To determine whether the incompetent, if sane, would have made a gift, the courts look to several factors that would move one in the incompetent's situation—the needs of the donee, the relationship to the incompetent, the degree of intimacy both before and during incompetency, the ward's past expressions or manifestations of concern or gift-giving, the present and future requirements of the incompetent himself, the extent of others' dependency upon him, and the size and condition of the estate—'giving to these and any other pertinent matters such weight as the incompetent, if sane, probably would have given'.[58]

The decisions have had little difficulty squaring the concept with a duty to act in the best interests of the incompetent. The justifications asserted include benefit to the incompetent,[59] his likely ratification of the imputed choice upon recovery,[60] or the satisfaction of intentions and patterns of conduct commenced before the period of incompetency.[61] A notion of respect for persons has been implicit in the doctrine: it is in the incompetent's best interests to be treated as nearly as possible as the person he would be if his incompetence had never occurred. As an early commentator on the doctrine put it:

Acting for the general welfare and advantage of a person does not mean merely supplying his or her physical wants or investing his or her money wisely. It is as much to the general advantage and welfare of a mother, for example, that the health of her children be preserved and that they be cared for in sickness, as it is that she herself be provided with a proper means of support.[62]

1. *The Standards*. Although the substituted judgment doctrine is recognised in most American and British jurisdictions either in judicial[63] or statutory[64] form, there is wide variation in the facts and circumstances upon which courts find that an incompetent, if competent, would make a gift. The varying results reveal internal tensions which limit the scope of the substituted judgment doctrine in the estate area and its applicability to other situations. The main tension stems from attempting to discern what in fact the incompetent would have done, if competent. The courts invariably focus on the desires and preferences which the incompetent would have had if he never had become incompetent, or if he had, if he recovered and essentially retained his pre-incompetency preference schedule. But there is an alternative approach. The courts could ask what a person in the incompetent's situation would do if he had legal capacity; that is, the courts could act to maximise the present subjective interests of the incompetent.[65]

Notes to extract
51. *Ex p Whitbread, a Lunatic* (1816) 2 Mer Rep 99.
52. See *Re Guardianship of Brice* 233 Iowa 183, 8 NW 2d 576 (1943); *Re Buckley's Estate* 330 Mich 102, 47 NW 2d 33 (1951). The formulations of the doctrine vary. See eg *March v Scott* 2 NJS 240, 63 A 2d 275 (1949) (if 'he could consent'); *Re Johnson* 111 NJ Eq 268, 162 A 96 (NJ Chan 1932) (if 'he had the capacity to act'); *Citizens' State Bank v Shanklin* 174 Mo App 639, 161 SW 341 (1913) (if 'he had been of right mind').
Sometimes the rule is more specifically articulated to refer to what the incompetent would have done if suddenly cured. *Kemp v Arnold* 234 Mo App 154, 113 SW 2d 143 (1938). Other formulations do the reverse and look to the choice he would make if 'he had remained in possession of his faculties', *Re Heeney, a Lunatic* 2 Barb Ch Rep 326 (1847).
53. *Re Carson* 39 Misc 2d 544, 241 NYS 2d 288, 289 (Ulster County Ct 1962).
54. *City Bank v McGowan* 323 US 594, 599 (1944).
55. *Re Flagler, an Incompetent Person*, 248 NY 415, 162 NE 471 (1928); see Note, *Insane Persons: Allowance From Surplus Income of Incompetent for third persons to Whom No Legal Duty is Owing*, 14 CORNELL LQ 89 (1928).
56. *Ex p Whitbread* 2 Mer Rep 99 (1816).
57. *Re Dupont* 41 Del Ch 300, 194 A 2d 309 (1963).
58. *Re Brice* 233 Iowa 183, 187, 8 NW 2d 576, 579 (1943); *Re Fleming's Estate* 173 Misc 851, 19 NYS 2d 234 (Kings County Ct 1940).
59. *Ex p Whitbread* (1816) 2 Mer Rep 99; *Re Evans* (1882) 21 Ch D 297 CA; *Re Darling* (1888) LR 39 Ch D 208 CA.
60. See, eg *Re The Earl of Carysfort* (1840) Cr & Ph 76, 41 ER 418, LC; *Re Thomas, a Lunatic*, 2 Ph 169 (1846).
61. [footnote omitted].
62. Carrington, *The Application of Lunatics' Estates for the Benefit of Dependent Relations*, 2 VA L REV 204, 204–05 (1914).
63. The doctrine was first recognised in the United States in *Re Willoughby, a Lunatic*, 11 Paige 257 (NY 1844), which affirmed the Chancellor's power to support from a lunatic's surplus income one not next-of-kin to whom the lunatic had no legal obligation of support if the Chancellor was satisfied 'beyond all reasonable doubt, that the lunatic himself would have so provided if he had been of sound mind'. *Id*. at 259–60. See also *Re Heeney*, 2 Barb Ch 326 (1847). Several other jurisdictions followed New York in recognising substituted judgment as a equity power. See *Hambleton's Appeal*, 102 Pa 50 (1883); *Re DeNissen's Guardianship*, 197 Wash 265, 275, 84 P 2d 1024, 1028 (1938); *Sheneman v Manring*, 152 Kan 780, 783–84, 107 P 2d 741, 744 (1940). But the doctrine has not been recognised in states in which the probate and other courts charged with the care and management of incompetents had only limited statutory powers and no general equitable jurisdiction. See *Re Guardianship of Estate of Neal*, 406 SW 2d 496 (Tex Civ App 1966); *Kelly v Scott*, 215 Md 530, 137 A 2d 704 (1958); *Lewis v Moody*, 149 Tenn 687, 261 SW 673 (1924).

64. The statutes fall into two classes. One form permits the guardian or the court to make gifts to family, immediate relatives, or specified relatives if the estate is ample enough, without further inquiry as to how the incompetent would have acted. See, *eg*, NJSA 3A:20–4. These statutes depart from the underlying basis of common law substituted judgment. They require no showing of legal obligation to the recipient, prior contact, or, most significantly, circumstances suggesting that the incompetent would have made the gift if competent.

The other class of statutes is more directly in keeping with the purposes of substituted judgment. They allow gifts to designated relatives only if the circumstances show that the incompetent if competent would have made the gift. See, eg, CAL PROBATE CODE §1558 (West 1954).

65. [footnote omitted].

In principle, we would suggest that the 'substituted judgment' test is the correct one. Professor Robertson (*supra*) justifies the substituted judgment test in the following ways at pp 63–68.

If a person because of age or mental disability cannot select or communicate his preferences, respect for persons requires that the integrity of the person still be maintained. As stated by Rawls, maintaining the integrity of the person means that we act toward him 'as we have reason to believe [he] would choose for [himself] if [he] were [capable] of reason and deciding rationally'.[88] It does not provide a license to impute to him preferences he never had or to ignore previous preferences.

Paternalistic decisions are to be guided by the individual's own settled preferences and interests insofar as they are not irrational, or failing a knowledge of these, by the theory of primary goods.[89]

If preferences are unknown, we must act with respect to the preferences a reasonable, competent person in the incompetent's situation would have.

There are several reasons for treating incompetents in this way. One is that if the person recovered or became competent, and was informed of our actions, he would be most likely to ratify a decision that attempted to ascertain and do that which from the circumstances it appeared that he would have wanted done.[90] For such an attempt would continue to regard him, even during his incapacity, as an individual with free choice and moral dignity, and not as someone whose preferences no longer mattered. Even if we were mistaken in ascertaining his preferences, the person could still agree that he had been fairly treated, if we had a good reason for thinking he would have made the choices imputed to him.

In addition, if a person were to decide in advance how he would want to be treated if he lost his rational faculties, he would be likely to choose a scheme that, to the extent possible, approximated what he would do if rational.[91] His moral worth is recognised since he is treated as the person he was, that is, as a person with the final ends and beliefs he previously expressed.[92]. Moreover, since incompetents are treated as persons in other important respects,[93] consistency requires that, when questions arise concerning their treatment in particular situations, they also be treated as persons with wants and preferences. By failing to treat them as we treat competent persons, in similar situations, ascertaining and respecting their lawful choices, we might undercut respect for the incompetent persons in other situations, and eventually diminish respect for all persons.

In most situations respect for the person of incompetents will result in actions which benefit or are in the best interest of the incompetent. A competent person will ordinarily satisfy his wants and preferences. To the extent that the benefits rule advances the incompetent's previously expressed preferences, or procures him more of the primary goods[94] if his preferences are unknown, there is a firm basis for ascribing to him choices which yield a net benefit.

If the incompetent's apparent best interests conflict with the choice he would make if competent, respect for persons requires that his imputed choice have priority. Thus, the fact that a Jehovah's Witness is unconscious does not justify transfusing blood to save his life, if he has previously made it clear that under no circumstances would he want a transfusion and he would not be required to accept a transfusion if conscious.[95] Nor should an unconscious person be maintained on an artificial life-support system contrary to previously expressed preference if he would have been permitted to refuse treatment when conscious. By a parity of reasoning, the absence of benefit to the incompetent should not prevent an intervention when a choice in favor of the intervention can be imputed to the incompetent. In short, if respect for persons dictates honoring the wishes of competents even when their objective interests are impaired, a like rule should apply to incompetents.

One objection to this approach might be that it is absurd to treat an incompetent as he would choose to be treated if he were competent, when he is not competent, perhaps never has been, and may never be. The actual situation of the incompetent diverges from how he is treated or regarded under the substituted judgment doctrine. But it is precisely such a divergence that respect for persons requires and which generally confers benefits on the incompetent. Eliminating this divergence would mean that we treat the incompetent in all respects as a non-thinking, non-choosing, irrational being—in short, as a non-person.

A more substantial problem is specifying precisely what it means to 'choose as the incompetent would, if competent'. It could mean what the person would have chosen if he had never become incompetent—if he had remained in possession of his faculties. But what if the incompetency is congenital, or the person is a child? Alternatively, it could mean the choice made by the incompetent if his incompetency were suddenly lifted for a moment, only to have the clouds of unreason later descend. Or it could mean the person's choice if he were permanently to recover competency. This latter interpretation would be appropriate in the situation of children who will develop the faculty of reason or persons temporarily psychotic; but not in that of the retarded, the senile, or the chronically insane. Proper application of the substituted judgment test depends on specifying the precise characteristics of the situation into which competency is projected when the court substitutes its judgment for that of the incompetent.

If respect for persons means that we accede to a person's choice of ends and means, respect for incompetent persons requires that they be similarly treated. It must be determined what choices a competent person with the characteristics, tastes, preferences, history and prospects of the incompetent would make to maximise his interests or wants–both those he presently has and those he is likely to have in the future. These characteristics might include present incompetency, a period of previous incompetency, and the possibility of future incompetency. His interests or wants will thus vary with the length of the incompetency; his preferences as an incompetent; the identity and preferences established before becoming incompetent; and the likelihood of regaining competency. A competent person with the characteristics of this incompetent cannot very well maximise satisfaction of his preferences if he ignores factors such as present incompetency and future institutionalisation which will determine present and future preferences as an incompetent. To assign the incompetent characteristics as if he had never become incompetent would be to misdescribe him. The divergence between the wants thus assigned him and his actual wants is, in fact, of greater significance than the divergence between his actually being incompetent and the treatment of him as competent for the purposes of the substituted judgment doctrine. The latter divergence merely enables us to respect and honor the wants of the incompetent by treating him like a competent person who would try to maximise his wants. The former distorts what his wants are and thus risks abusing his person by never recognising or satisfying his wants. It acts not to advance his interests, but to advance the interests of a person who superficially resembles the incompetent.

The extent to which the preferences to be maximised depend on recognition of present, past and future incompetency will of course vary with particular situations. A 30-year-old man experiencing a transient psychosis has reasonable prospects of resuming his former social role upon recovery and thus of maintaining his prior preferences. To maximise his wants during his incompetency we must take into account the fact that previous preferences will soon be reasserted. The fact of incompetency alters some of his present wants, but it does not allow us to ignore altogether his past preferences.

Suppose, however, that the prognosis for recovery of the 30-year-old man is nil. He faces an indefinite future of incompetency and institutionalisation, in which he will be unable to advance his own interests as an incompetent. The fact of future incompetency has significantly altered his situation and thus his present interests. If he had been an avid mountain-climber while competent and would be likely to continue this sport upon recovery, it would be pertinent to whether a kidney transplant, which would limit such activity, should occur. But the fact that a kidney transplant would interfere with his climbing would not be relevant if he had no chance of climbing again. Choosing for him on the basis of a set of preferences which would exist only if he were competent would thus be inappropriate. Respect for persons only demands that we make the best and most reasonable choice for a person given his wants and preferences in the circumstances he is presently and likely to be in, and not the circumstances in which we, if omnipotent, would like to place him.

A third situation is that of a child or a person with a long history of incompetency who will attain competency in the future. This case resembles the first, in that the incompetent's preferences must take account of future competency, but differs from the first two situations in that no preferences have been established during a prior period of competency. The interests to be maximised include the incompetent's existing tastes and preferences and the tastes and preferences the person is likely to have in the future when competent. Since the latter are unknowable, it would be in his interest to preserve maximum flexibility.

The fourth situation is that of one who has only a brief history of competency or none at all and no expectation of competency in the future. Severely mentally retarded persons and persons who become incurably insane or incur brain damage at an early age, *inter alia*, fall into this category. To respect the dignity and integrity of such a person the task of substituted judgment will be to ascertain his actual interests and preferences, which will be circumscribed by his present and future incompetency.

In each of these situations the wants or interests of a person in the incompetent's situation will include his present wants in the state of incompetency. But how do we ascertain the wants of an incompetent? Should they be granted any validity at all? If the incompetent lacks the capacity to communicate his preferences in the ways that people ordinarily do, it may be more difficult or perhaps impossible to know them. If he somehow communicates preferences, his very incompetency means that his preferences are not necessarily to be honored. But it would be erroneous to conclude that none of the expressed wants of incompetents should be satisfied. Incompetency encompasses several types of mental impairment, including the inability to have certain wants, the possession of bizarre wants, or the inability to choose among or satisfy conflicting preferences. Thus some expressed wants, if they appear irrational and indicative of his incompetency (such as a desire to fly) need not be honored. Expressed wants not in this category, however, should be satisfied.[96] Clearly, they define, in part, his interests, of which respect for persons must take account.

Respect for persons, as argued above, requires that previously expressed preferences, or preferences we think the incompetent has or would have, should also be honored. What if a past preference conflicts with a present preference? The present preference should be honored if so doing will have a favorable or trivial impact on the attainment of other wants, present or future, attributed to the incompetent. Present preferences should not be respected if they will foreclose achieving other expressed wants or wants the incompetent would be presumed to have if competent.[97] Overriding a present want in order to satisfy an imputed want is justified especially if it permits the satisfaction of other present wants.[98] Substituted judgment thus combines subjective and objective elements. The subjective elements are the present tastes and preferences of the incompetent and those which he might have if competent, if he has a reasonable chance of becoming so. The objective aspect is the determination of what a reasonable person with the characteristics and present and future wants of the incompetent would choose to maximise his interests.

Notes to extract

88. J Rawls, [*A theory of Justice* (1971)], at 209.
89. *Id*. at 249.
90. *Id*.
91. Dworkin, *Paternalism*, in Morality and the Law 119–22 (Wasserstrom ed 1971).
92. In Rawlsian terms, one would focus on what a person would choose in the 'original position'—the hypothetical pre-societal situation in which individuals confront the world and their realities from behind a veil of ignorance, knowing only the general laws of psychology, economics and the like, but nothing about their own characteristics, preferences or interests. See J Rawls, *supra* note [88], at 249–50.

A person in the original position will want to insure himself against the possibility that his powers will be undeveloped or that they will not be able rationally to advance his interests. *Id*. at 249. For this purpose he will adopt principles 'to protect [himself] against the weakness and infirmities of [his] reason and will in society'. *Id*. Since one would want to guarantee the integrity of his person and his final ends and beliefs, he would authorise others to act on his behalf and to do what he would do for himself if he were rational, when he became incapable of looking after his own good. *Id*. at 249–50. Paternalistic decisions are then to be guided by the individual's own settled preferences and interests so long as they are not irrational, or, lacking knowledge of these, by the theory of primary goods; we act for him as we would act for ourselves from the standpoint of the original position. *Ib*. at 249.

93. E g, they are protected by the criminal law.
94. Primary goods are 'things that every rational man is presumed to want. These goods normally have a use whatever a person's rational plan of life'. J Rawls *supra* note [88], at 62. Examples are rights and liberties, powers and opportunities, income and wealth (social primary goods), and health and vigor, intelligence and imagination (nature primary goods).
95. *Re Brooks*, 32 Ill 2d 361, 205 NE 2d 435 (1965). *Contra, JFK Memorial Hospital v Heston*, 58 NJ 576, 279 A 2d 670 (1971).
96. Thus respect for persons requires that to the extent feasible we permit an incompetent to watch television 16 hours a day, engorge himself on ice cream, or to satisfy preferences which are not irrational, up to the point of injury to others. Respect for persons does not require that an incompetent be permitted to mutilate himself. For a rationale of this position, see J Rawls, *supra* note [88], and Shapiro, *Legislating the Control of Behavior Control: Autonomy and the Coercive Use of Organic Therapies*, 47 SO CAL L. REV 237, 276–96 (1974).
97. Thus an incompetent need not be allowed to injure himself by banging his head against a wall.
98. Although treating an incompetent as a person capable of altruism on the basis of evidence that he would so choose if competent seems questionable because he cannot, while incompetent, realise any of the satisfactions of altruism, so treating him might still lead to a greater willingness of society to satisfy his actual present wants.

Professor Robertson identifies a number of situations where a court might be asked to apply a substituted judgment test. Do you agree that they are all appropriate for its application? We consider that the court will be most frequently faced with three types of situation. In our view, the substituted judgment test is only appropriate in the last of these. In the first two the test would be inappropriate:

1. the incompetent child or baby;
2. the incompetent adult who has never been competent to express his wishes and preferences;

3. the incompetent adult who was once competent to express his wishes and preferences.

The difficulties faced by a court or other proxy in applying the substituted judgment test in situations 1 and 2 was recognised in the Alberta Report (*op cit*):

9.37 The obvious difficulty with the application of the substituted judgment standard relates to persons who have been mentally incompetent from birth and who may therefore never have been able to express their values or desires. It may also be difficult to determine the values and desires of a person who was once competent but has been made incompetent by a supervening injury or disease.

Consequently, in *Re Eve*, the Supreme Court of Canada rejected the application of the test to Eve who had been incompetent from birth. The reasoning would also apply in the case of an incompetent child. La Forest J said:

Counsel for the respondent strongly contended, however, that the Court should adopt the substituted judgment test recently developed by a number of state courts in the United States. That test, he submitted, is to be preferred to the best interests test because it places a higher value on the individuality of the mentally incompetent person. It affords that person the same right, he contended, as a competent person to choose whether to procreate or not.

There is an obvious logical lapse in this argument. . . . it is obviously fiction to suggest that a decision so made is that of the mental incompetent, however much the court may try to put itself in her place. What the incompetent would do if she or he could make the choice is simply a matter of speculation. The sophistry embodied in the argument favouring substituted judgment has been fully revealed in *Eberhardy, supra*, at p 893 where in discussing *Grady, supra*, the court stated:

The fault we find in the New Jersey case is the *ratio decidendi* of first concluding, correctly we believe, that the right to sterilisation is a personal choice, but then equating a decision made by others with the choice of the person to be sterilised. It clearly is not a personal choice, and no amount of legal legerdemain can make it so.

. . .

We conclude the question is not choice because it is sophistry to refer to it as such, but rather the question is whether there is a method by which others, acting in behalf of the person's best interests and in the interests, such as they may be, of the state, can exercise the decision. Any governmentally sanctioned (or ordered) procedure to sterilise a person who is incapable of giving consent must be denominated for what it is, that is, the state's intrusion into the determination of whether or not a person who makes no choice shall be allowed to procreate.

It would seem, therefore, that the court (or other proxy) should only use the substituted judgment test if the patient has, at one time, been competent. This approach to closely correlate to one of the leading American cases concerning treatment of the ill and dying (see *in Re Conroy, infra*, Ch 14). It excludes from consideration, therefore, virtually every sterilisation case, every incompetent child case and many cases of organ donation. Do the cases we have set out earlier reflect this?

The following decision illustrates the application of the substituted judgment test in the case of an incompetent patient whose religious beliefs suggested that she would have refused treatment had she been competent.

Re Lucille Boyd
403 A 2d 744 (DC Cir 1979) [footnotes omitted]

Ferren Associate Judge: This appeal presents one question: whether—in a nonemergency situation—the court may authorise a hospital to administer psychotropic drugs to a patient adjudicated mentally ill and incompetent, when that patient, before her illness and incompetency, had rejected any use of medication on religious grounds.

. . . She contends that the court, in deciding whether to force medical treatment on an unwilling incompetent, should apply the 'substituted judgment' rule; ie the court should attempt to ascertain, as nearly as possible, the choice which that individual would make if competent. It follows, according to appellant, that if an individual has clearly expressed a religious objection to medical treatment immediately prior to incompetency, that objection must control the trial court's decision.

. . .

As appellant has pointed out, in nonemergency situations a number of courts have adopted the 'substituted judgment' approach. The court, as surrogate for the incompetent, is to determine as best it can what choice that individual, if competent, would make with respect to medical procedures. . . . . We believe this approach is sound, whether religious preference or other factors are involved, for it is the only way to pay full respect to the individuality and dignity of a person who has expressed clear, deeply felt, even sacred preferences while competent, but no longer has the capacity to decide. The Supreme Judicial Court of Massachusetts recently developed this rationale in *Superintendent of Belchertown State School v Saikewicz*, 373 Mass —, —, 370 NE 2d 417, 428 (1977):

The 'best interests' of an incompetent person are not necessarily served by imposing on such persons results not mandated as to competent persons similarly situated. It does not advance the interest of the State or the ward to treat the ward as a person of lesser status or dignity than others. . . . Nor do statistical factors indicating that a majority of competent persons similarly situated choose treatment resolve the issue. The significant decisions of life are more complex than statistical determinations. Individual choice is determined not by the vote of the majority but by the complexities of the singular situation viewed from the unique perspective of the person called on to make the decision. To presume that the incompetent person must always be subjected to what many rational and intelligent persons may decline is to downgrade the status of the incompetent person by placing a lesser value on his intrinsic human worth and vitality.

Obviously, in attempting to make such a subjective evaluation, in contrast with an objective, 'reasonable person' analysis, the court will be engaging, at best, in approximation; any imputation of a preference to an incompetent person will, to some extent, be fictional. But that inherent limitation does not make the 'substituted judgment' analysis less valid than one which purports to be wholly objective, for *any* analysis presupposes the court's judgment as to what a human being would decide for oneself under the circumstances. There is no reason to believe that the court's use of a hypothetical, reasonable person as the model for its decision is preferable to an approach which attempts, however imperfectly, to account for the particular qualities of mind and preference known about the individual before the court. . . . .

With this said, we should underscore that inevitably the substituted judgment approach, because of its obvious limitations, will result in a synthesis of (1) factors known to be true about the incompetent and (2) other considerations which necessarily suggest themselves when the court cannot be sure about an incompetent's actual wishes. Thus, in trying to decide what choice the individual would make if competent, the court is not precluded from filling the gaps in its knowledge about the incompetent by taking into account what most persons are likely to do in a similar situation. See *Saikewicz, supra*, 373 Mass at —, 370 NE 2d at 430; . . . .

C. We turn now, in greater detail, to how the court should construct the 'substituted judgment' synthesis, particularly as it attempts to account for religious views. With respect to a situation in which an individual's life itself is not at stake, we conclude that (a) when an individual, prior to incompetence, has objected, absolutely, to medical care on religious grounds, (b) the evidence demonstrates a strong adherence to the tenets of that faith, and (c) there is no countervailing evidence of vacillation, the court should conclude that the individual would reject medical treatment. . . .

More specifically, as to the previously-expressed objection itself, several factors are important: whether the objection, if religious, is a recognisable, established one, such as the well-known views of a Jehovah's Witness or Christian Scientist; whether the individual has acted upon these views in ways that demonstrate they have been deeply felt; and whether these views have been long held, perhaps as a matter of family tradition, or if more recently adopted, have been the result of demonstrable experience, such as a religious conversion, which would justify a court's conclusion that the views are unequivocal.

Second, the possibility of detrimental side effects may be especially relevant in a case, such as this, concerning psychotropic drugs. Materials filed with the trial court indicate that such medication may produce side effects which commonly motivate even competent patients to reject their use on nonreligious, as well as religious, grounds. see *Rennie v Klein*, 462 F Supp 1131 (DNJ 1978).

Third, the likelihood of cure or improvement with or without treatment is likely to have a bearing on one's decision. It may be, as we stated in *Osborne, supra* at 374, that absent a conviction as strong as Mr Osborne's when life is threatened and can only be saved with prompt medical assistance, one's 'instinct for survival' may overtake a lifelong conviction that medical care is wrong. But when life cannot be saved—when death is not far off in any event—a patient may be less likely to accept treatment merely to prolong life, see *Quinlan, supra*, especially when the treatment is likely to cause severe pain. See *Saikewicz, supra*. It follows that where the prospect of imminent death is a marginal or nonexistent factor, as in Mrs Boyd's case, there may be even less incentive for one to compromise religious or other principles to accept medication.

. . . it does not appear that the court gave sufficient consideration, under the 'substituted judgment' concept, to Mrs Boyd's previously expressed religious views. . . . the court should inquire whether the hospital still seeks authorisation for psychotropic medication. If it does, the court should then take the 'substituted judgment' approach by attempting to determine what course of action Mrs Boyd would choose now. If the court decides that Mrs Boyd would reject psychotropic drugs on religious grounds if presently competent and fully aware of her situation, it must refuse to authorise such treatment unless the government can demonstrate that a particular, 'compelling state interest' would justify overriding Mrs Boyd's putative choice. . . .

Questions

Do you agree with the court's analysis that this was a case of substituted judgment?

Do you think there is a difference between the situation:

(a) where the court (as proxy) is determining what treatment the patient *did* want; and

(b) where the court (as proxy) is determining what treatment the patient *would* have wanted?

In (a) the views of the patient are clear. In (b) they are not so clear and the court (or other proxy) is attempting to do the best it can to make a decision on behalf of the patient. Is not situation (a) one where the proxy is merely reflecting the patient's actual (albeit earlier) decision reached when competent? Arguably only (b) is a situation where substituted judgment is called for. (See our discussion of *Re Conroy, infra* Ch 14; in particular the 'subjective' and 'limited objective' tests developed in that case.)

(b)   TREATING WITHOUT CONSENT: THE COMPETENT

(i)   As a matter of public policy

1.   Under the common law

The traditional view must be that if a person is competent he may refuse treatment and it would then be unlawful to attempt to treat him because this would amount to the tort of battery and a crime. It would appear to follow that there is no public policy justifying the treatment of the competent against their wishes. This may, however, be easier to accept where the person is obviously competent and/or his condition is not one which is life (?limb) threatening. There is, however, a tendency in all of us, and perhaps more so in doctors, to want to treat even though the person refusing is apparently competent, when it is clear that the person's life is threatened or there is very grave risk to his health. How has the law responded to this? In the few cases which follow you may detect a tendency in the courts to avoid attacking the principle of the inviolability of the person head on and instead choosing, by and large, to cast doubt on the competence of the person whose *decision* is in question. This has the purported merit of preserving the principle while acting beneficiently towards the individual. If, however, it constitutes an improper manipulation of the concept of competence it does the law no credit. It is fair to say that in some cases the court has confronted the principle head on and you may care to consider whether the principle is justified.

The force-feeding cases.

Leigh v Gladstone
(1909) 26 TLR 139 (King's Bench Divisional Court)

> This was an action claiming damages for assault and for an injunction to restrain a repetition of the acts complained of, brought by Mrs Marie Leigh against the Right Hon Herbert Gladstone, MP (the Home Secretary), Captain Percy Green, Governor of Winson-green Prison, Birmingham, and Dr Ernest Haslar Helby, the Medical Officer of the same prison. The defence was that the acts complained of were necessary in order to save the plaintiff's life, and that the *minimum* of force necessary was used. The matter arose out of the forcible feeding in prison of the plaintiff, who had been convicted of resisting the police and disturbing a meeting held by Mr Asquith, in connexion with the woman's franchise movement.
>
>   . . . It was the duty, both under the rules and apart from the rules, of the officials to preserve the health and lives of the prisoners, who were in the custody of the Crown. If they forcibly fed the plaintiff when it was not necessary, the defendants ought to pay damages. The plaintiff did not complain—and it did her credit—of any undue violence being used towards her. The medical evidence was that at the time she was first fed it had become dangerous to allow her to abstain from food any longer.

You may think that this is a product of its time and its circumstances, namely suffragettes seeking to gain the vote in the early part of the twentieth century. Even if its authority is restricted to those who are imprisoned, it can be doubted whether it still represents the law (see 877 HC Debs Col 451, 17 July 1974). A recent Canadian case has added its weight to the general disapproval of *Leigh v Gladstone*. In *A-G of British Columbia v Astaforoff* [1983] 6 WWR 322, Bouck J (at first instance), in factual circumstances similar to *Leigh* held that:

> As I see it, my responsibility is to decide whether, under the particular circumstances of this case, there is a legal duty cast upon the province to force-feed the respondent

against her will in order to prevent her from committing suicide. If there is this duty, then should I make the order compelling the prison officials to carry it out?

I am aware of the responsibility of the court to preserve the sanctity of life. It is a moral as well as a legal duty. However, in the circumstances of this case the facts are against the motion of the Attorney General for Canada. The prisoner has a long history of fasting. Her health is very poor. There is the danger that she might die by the applying of the procedure necessary to get nutrients into the stomach. She is free to leave the prison, but chooses to remain there and starve herself to death. Given these facts, I cannot find that it is reasonable that the Attorney General for British Columbia and the prison authorities under his direction should force-feed her in order to prevent her suicide.

If she becomes unconscious or incapable of making a rational decision, that is another matter. Then she will be unable to make a free choice. But while she is lucid no law compels the provincial officers to apply force to her against her will.

On appeal, the British Columbia Court of Appeal ([1984] 4 WWR 385), in upholding Bouck J, found that there was no duty to feed the prisoner. The court left open, however, whether there was a power to treat such that in any subsequent action brought by the prisoner, there might have been a defence justifying the intervention. Do you agree that such a justification should exist in law?

The neglect cases. The duty to treat postulated in *Leigh v Gladstone* seems to have surfaced in *R v Stone* [1977] QB 354, [1977] 2 All ER 341, CA a case of neglect. In his book, *Law, Ethics and Medicine*, p 113–114 Professor Skegg comments on this case:

> The deceased, who lived with the defendants, suffered from anorexia nervosa. She made it clear that she did not want any medical assistance, and there was no reason to believe that she would have consented to medical treatment. The jury found that the defendants had assumed a duty of care for the deceased, and that a failure to fulfil this duty resulted in the death.[66] In upholding the conviction for manslaughter, the Court of Appeal appears to have assumed that it was open to the defendants, or to a doctor, to disregard the wishes of the 'victim'. But in this and the other prosecutions there does not appear to have been any consideration of what a coroner once spoke of as 'an absolute principle that a person of full age and consciousness is entitled to refuse treatment by a doctor'.[67]
>
> It does not follow from the fact that a doctor, or anyone else, is under a duty to provide medical treatment (or food) that there is an entitlement—much less, an obligation—to administer that treatment (or food) irrespective of the views of the patient. The doctor who was responsible for the victim in *R v Blaue* undoubtedly owed her a duty of care, and in the circumstances would have been in breach of that duty if he had not given her the opportunity of having a blood transfusion. But there was no suggestion that he was therefore obliged, or even permitted, to administer it without consent.

Notes to extract
[66] It is undoubtedly desirable that a doctor be summoned in these circumstances, both to provide independent evidence that the deceased was refusing medical treatment, and to ensure that the patient is informed of the treatment which is available, and the consequences if it is not administered. In some cases there will be a statutory power to take some action: see eg National Assistance Act 1948, s 47 (the operation of which is discussed by J A M Gray, 'Section 47' (1981) 7 *Journal of Medical Ethics* 146–9). But unless it is clear that, had a doctor been summoned, the patient would have consented to life-saving treatment, or that such treatment could lawfully have been imposed in the absence of consent, a failure to summon a doctor should not give rise to liability in homicide.

[67] *The Times*, 6 January 1967, p 10. See also N O'Bryan (a Judge of the Supreme Court of Victoria), 'The Consent of the Patient to Surgical and Medical Procedures' (1961) 8 *Proceedings of the Medico-Legal Society of Victoria* 138; Stephen, *Digest*, 148; *Stoffberg v Elliot* [1923] CPD 148; *Masny v Carter-Halls-Aldinger Co* [1929] 3 WWR 741 at 745. In *R v Smith* [1979] *Crim LR* 251 Griffiths J did at least recognise that the wishes of the deceased might be relevant. But he left it to the jury 'to balance the weight that it is right to give to his wife's wish to avoid calling in a doctor against her capacity to make rational decisions', and added 'if she does not appear too ill it may be reasonable to abide by her wishes. On the other hand, if she appeared desperately ill then whatever she may say it may be right to override.' See [1979] *Crim LR* 252–3.

Suicide cases

Skegg in *Law, Ethics and Medicine* again explains these decisions as follows, p 110–13:

> In all but the most exceptional circumstances, a doctor may not carry out treatment involving the bodily touching of a patient who is capable of consenting, if the patient's consent has not been sought, or if the patient has refused to give consent. The fact that, without the treatment, the patient's health will suffer will not of itself justify a doctor in overriding the patient's refusal. Indeed, in many circumstances, even the certainty that the patient will die if treatment is not given will not justify a doctor in proceeding without consent.
>
> However, there is at least one exception to the general rule that consent is required. Where someone has done something in an apparent attempt to kill himself,[50] doctors will often be justified in taking action to avert the consequences of that action. Prior to the abolition of the offence of suicide,[51] there was no difficulty in explaining the legal basis for a doctor acting to prevent a person from attempting to commit suicide, or to avoid death resulting from such an attempt. Suicide was a felony, so the doctor was simply exercising the general liberty to prevent a felony.[52] Doctors were not only free to prevent someone from committing suicide; they were sometimes under a duty to do so.[53] However, since the enactment of the Suicide Act 1961 it has continued to be accepted that doctors are sometimes free—sometimes, indeed, under a duty[54]—to prevent patients from committing suicide.
>
> In some cases, the person who has apparently attempted to commit suicide will be suffering from a mental disorder which prevents the giving or withholding of consent. But in many cases the person will have a sufficient understanding to give, or withhold, consent.[55] This is so, even though the act will often result from a passing impulse or temporary depression, rather than from a rational and fixed decision. If restrained and given assistance, the majority are glad that their action did not result in death.[56] Hence, even if it is accepted that a person should not be prevented from carrying out a calm or a reasoned decision to terminate his own life,[57] there is an overwhelming case for intervention where there is reason to believe that, if given help, the person will be glad he did not kill, or seriously injure, himself. Doctors are constantly intervening in these circumstances and there can be little doubt that, were their conduct to be questioned, the courts would hold it justified.[58]
>
> Where the need for life-saving treatment does not result from any act of the patient taken with a view to ending his own life,[59] it is normally accepted that a doctor is bound by the patient's refusal of consent. Hence in *R v Blaue*,[60] where the assailant's victim was a Jehovah's Witness who refused to consent to the blood transfusion that was necessary to save her life, there was no suggestion that the doctor would have been justified in overriding her refusal of consent. In one case a patient recovered nominal damages from a doctor who performed a life-saving operation on her, despite her refusal of consent.[61] Such conduct would often amount to a criminal assault, and there would be the possibility of obtaining an injunction restraining further treatment.

Notes to extract
[50] What is said of such cases should also be applicable to those cases where the need for treatment results from an act of some other person, done in compliance with a

suicide pact. S 3 of the Criminal Law Act 1967 could provide a basis for intervention in the latter circumstances.

[51] Suicide Act 1961, s 1.

[52] See *R v Duffy* [1967] 1 QB 63 at 67.

[53] See *Thorne v Northern Group Hospital Management Committee* (1964) 108 Sol Jo 484, (1964) *Times*, 6 June. The death which gave rise to this litigation occurred in 1960, when suicide was still an offence. But the reports do not suggest that the duty of care and supervision was in any way dependent on that fact.

[54] *Selfe v Ilford and District Hospital Management Committee* (1970) 114 Sol Jo 935, (1970) *Times*, 26 November, [1970] 4 *Br Med J* 754. In *Hyde v Tameside Area Health Authority,* (1981) *Times,* 16 April, [1981] 1 *Lancet* 1062, (1981) 282 *Br Med J* 1716–17, the plaintiff had attempted to commit suicide while a patient in hospital. He became a tetraplegic in consequence of the attempt, and Anthony Lincoln J awarded him damages of £200,000. The Court of Appeal allowed the defendant's appeal, Lord Denning MR, Watkins LJ, and O'Connor LJ, all agreeing that on the evidence no breach of duty had been established. No member of the court suggested that there was never a duty to prevent suicide, although Lord Denning MR was of the view that on grounds of public policy the personal representatives of someone who had committed suicide, or the person himself if his attempt does not succeed, should not be permitted to claim damages. The other members of the court did not express such a view. See also *Hôpital Notre-Dame v Dame Villemure* [1970] Que SC 538 revsd; *sub nom Villemure v L'Hopital Notre-Dame* (1972) 31 DLR (3d) 454; *Haines v Bellissimo* (1977) 82 DLR (3d) 215.

[55] If the patient agreed to treatment, it would invariably be accepted that he was capable of giving a legally effective consent. On suicide and attempted suicide, see generally *Suicidology* (1976, ed E S Shneidman); H G Morgan, *Death Wishes?* (1979); W H Trethowan, 'Suicide and Attempted Suicide' [1979] 2 *Br Med J* 319–20.

[56] This is true of many survivors of serious suicide attempts, as well as of para-suicides. See R Fox, 'Attempted Suicide' and 'Suicide' in *Dict Med Ethics* at 31 and 425, respectively.

[57] The Suicide Act 1961 did not provide a legally-protected right to kill oneself, but it would now be open to a court to adopt the view that there is such a right, in at least some circumstances. However in *Hyde v Tameside Area Health Authority* (see n 54) Lord Denning MR was of the view that, although suicide was no longer a crime, it was still 'unlawful'. Some means of committing suicide certainly involve a crime: see eg *Bryan v Mott* (1975) 62 Cr App Rep 71 (cf *R v Norton* [1977] Crim LR 478); *R v Criminal Injuries Compensation Board, ex p Clowes* [1977] 3 All ER 854; *R v Criminal Injuries Compensation Board, ex p Parsons,* (1982) *Times,* 25 November, CA (Offences against the Person Act 1861, s 34); and see also Homicide Act 1957, s 4. *Quaere,* whether suicide, or attempted suicide, infringes s 18 of the Offences against the Person Act 1861 (or any common law offence of maim). S 18 makes it an offence 'unlawfully and maliciously' to cause grievous bodily harm 'to any person' (with intent to do some grievous bodily harm 'to any person'), whereas adjoining offences are phrased in terms of 'any other person' (see ss 20, 23, 24). (But see *R v Arthur* [1968] 1 QB 810, esp 813. Cf. *R v Pardoe* (1894) 17 Cox CC 715. On the greater including the lesser, see eg *R v Woodburne and Coke* (1722) 16 St Tr 53 at 81.) Even where suicide does involve the commission of a crime, it does not follow that there is always a statutory right to prevent it: s 3 of the Criminal Law Act 1967 permits only the use of such force 'as is reasonable in the circumstances' in the prevention of crime.

[58] Cf Viscount Kilmuir LC in (1961) 229 Parl Deb HL 544. See also cases cited in nn 53, 54 above; G Zellick, 'The Forcible Feeding of Prisoners: An Examination of the Legality of Enforced Therapy' [1976] *Public Law* 153, 171–2; Williams, *Textbook* [of Criminal Law (1978)], 570–1.

[59] Whatever may once have been the case, a consideration of this matter is not assisted by an examination of the extent to which the refusal of life-saving treatment would have amounted to the felony of suicide. The considerations which are relevant

when a Jehovah's Witness refuses a blood transfusion necessary to save life, or a patient decides he would rather die at home instead of undergoing major surgery which could prolong his life for a few months, are very different from those which arise with most attempted suicides.

[60] [1975] 1 WLR 1411. Blaue was the assailant who was convicted of manslaughter, but acquitted of murder by reason of his diminished responsibility.
[61] *Anon*, noted in D J A Kerr, *Forensic Medicine* (1935), 71.

Is Professor Skegg right in asserting that a doctor is '. . . under a duty . . . to prevent patients from committing suicide . . .'? Unless his proposition is limited to the incompetent, does he not then contradict himself when he goes on to say:

If, from the fact that a doctor had a duty of care to a patient, it followed that he was entitled to administer necessary treatment without consent, the right to refuse treatment would be severely curtailed. Although some cases appear to have proceeded on the assumption that there is such an entitlement, the courts are unlikely to adopt expressly so undesirable a doctrine. For the most part doctors should not administer even life-saving treatment if the patient refuses consent and no one else is authorised to give it.[68]

Note to extract
[68] See generally I Kennedy, 'The Legal Effect of Requests by the Terminally ill and Aged not to receive further Treatment from Doctors' [1976] *Crim LR* 217–32. three possible exceptions are discussed, but rejected, in P D G Skegg, *op cit*, 526–9.

The latter view of Professor Skegg is borne out by the American case law.

Bouvia v Superior Court
225 Cal Rptr 297 (1986) (California Court of Appeals) (footnotes omitted).

Associate Justice Beach: . . . Petitioner is a 28-year-old woman. Since birth she has been afflicted with and suffered from severe cerebral palsy. She is quadriplegic. She is now a patient at a public hospital maintained by one of the real parties in interest, the County of Los Angeles. Other parties are physicians, nurses and the medical and support staff employed by the County of Los Angeles. Petitioner's physical handicaps of palsy and quadriplegia have progressed to the point where she is completely bedridden. Except for a few fingers of one hand and some slight head and facial movements, she is immobile. She is physically helpless and wholly unable to care for herself. She is totally dependent upon others for all of her needs. These include feeding, washing, cleaning, toileting, turning, and helping her with elimination and other bodily functions. She cannot stand or sit upright in bed or in a wheelchair. She lies flat in bed and must do so the rest of her life. She suffers also from degenerative and severely crippling arthritis. She is in continual pain. Another tube permanently attached to her chest automatically injects her with periodic doses of morphine which relieves some, but not all of her physical pain and discomfort.

She is intelligent, very mentally competent. She earned a college degree. She was married but her husband has left her. She suffered a miscarriage. She lived with her parents until her father told her that they could no longer care for her. She has stayed intermittently with friends and at public facilities. A search for a permanent place to live where she might receive the constant care which she needs has been unsuccessful. She is without financial means to support herself and, therefore, must accept public assistance for medical and other care.

She has on several occasions expressed the desire to die. In 1983 she sought the right to be cared for in a public hospital in Riverside County while she intentionally 'starved herself to death'. A court in that county denied her judicial assistance to accomplish that goal. She later abandoned an appeal from that ruling. Thereafter, friends took her to several different facilities, both public and private, arriving finally at her present location. Efforts by the staff of real party in interest County of Los Angeles and its social workers to find her an apartment of her own with publicly paid live-in help or regular visiting nurses to care for her, or some other suitable facility have proved fruitless.

Petitioner must be spoon fed in order to eat. Her present medical and dietary staff have determined that she is not consuming a sufficient amount of nutrients. Petitioner stops eating when she feels she cannot orally swallow more, without nausea and vomiting. As she cannot now retain solids, she is fed soft liquid-like food. Because of her previously announced resolve to starve herself, the medical staff feared her weight loss might reach a life-threatening level. Her weight since admission to real parties' facility seems to hover between 65 and 70 pounds. Accordingly, they inserted the subject tube against her will and contrary to her express written instructions.

. . . a patient has the right to refuse *any* medical treatment, even that which may save or prolong her life. (*Barber v Superior Court* 147 Cal App 3d 1006, 195 Cal Rptr 484 (1983); *Bartling v Superior Court* 163 Cal App 3d 186, 209 Cal Rptr 220 (1984).) In our view the foregoing authorities are dispositive of the case at bench. Nonetheless, the county and its medical staff contend that for reasons unique to this case, Elizabeth Bouvia may not exercise the right available to others. Accordingly, we again briefly discuss the rule in the light of real parties' contentions.

The right to refuse medical treatment is basic and fundamental. It is recognised as a part of the right of privacy protected by both the state and federal constitutions. (Calif Const, art I, § 1; *Griswold v Connecticut* 381 US 479, 484, 85 S Ct 1678, 1681, 14 L Ed 2d 510 (1965); *Bartling v Superior Court, supra*, 163 Cal App 3d 186, 209 Cal Rptr 220.) Its exercise requires no one's approval. It is not merely one vote subject to being overridden by medical opinion.

In *Barber v Superior Court, supra*, 147 Cal App 3d 1006, 195 Cal Rptr 484, we considered this same issue although in a different context. Writing on behalf of this division, Justice Compton thoroughly analysed and reviewed the issue of withdrawal of life-support systems beginning with the seminal case of *Quinlan* 355 A 2d 647, *cert den* 429 US 922, 97 S Ct 319, 50 LEd 2d 289, (NJ 1976) and continuing on to the then recent enactment of the California Natural Death Act (Health & Saf Code. §§ 7185–7195). His opinion clearly and repeatedly stresses the fundamental underpinning of its conclusion, ie, the patient's right to decide: 147 Cal App 3d at page 1015, 195 Cal Rptr 484. 'In this state a clearly recognised legal right to control one's own medical treatment predated the Natural Death Act. A long line of cases, approved by the Supreme Court in *Cobbs v Grant* 8 Cal 3d 229 [104 Cal Rptr 505, 502 P 2d 1 (1972)] . . . have held that where a doctor performs treatment in the absence of an informed consent, there is an actionable battery. The obvious corollary to this principle is that *a competent adult patient has the legal right to refuse medical treatment*' (emphasis added); 147 Cal App 3d at page 1019, 195 Cal Rptr 484, '[T]he *patient's interests and desires are the key* ingredients of the decision-making process' (emphasis added); at page 1020, 195 Cal Rptr 484, 'Given the general standards for determining when there is a duty to provide medical treatment of debatable value, the question still remains as to who should make these vital decisions. Clearly, the medical diagnoses and prognoses must be determined by the treating and consulting physicians under the generally accepted standards of medical practice in the community and, *whenever possible, the patient himself should then be the ultimate decisionmaker*' (emphasis added); at page 1021, 195 Cal Rptr 484, 'The authorities are in agreement that any surrogate, court appointed or otherwise, ought to be guided in his or her decisions first by his knowledge of *the patient's own desires* and feelings, to the extent that they were expressed before the patient became incompetent'. (Emphasis added.)

Bartling v Superior Court, supra, 163 Cal App 3d 186, 209 Cal Rptr 220, was factually much like the case at bench. Although not totally identical in all respects, the issue there centered on the same question here present: ie, 'May the patient refuse even life continuing treatment?' Justice Hastings, writing for another division of this court, explained: 'In this case we are called upon to decide whether a competent adult patient, with serious illnesses which are probably incurable but have not been diagnosed as terminal, has the right, over the objection of his physicians and the hospital, to have life-support equipment disconnected despite the fact that withdrawal of such devices will surely hasten his death'. (At p 189, 209

Cal Rptr 220.) '(1) Mr Bartling's illnesses were serious but not terminal, and had not been diagnosed as such; (2) although Mr Bartling was attached to a respirator to facilitate breathing, he was not in a vegetative state and was not comatose; and (3) Mr Bartling was competent in the legal sense. [¶] . . . The court below concluded that as long as there was some potential for restoring Mr. Bartling to a "cognitive, sapient life," it would not be appropriate to issue an injunction in this case. [¶] We conclude that the trial court was incorrect when it held that the right to have life-support equipment disconnected was limited to comatose, terminally ill patients, or representatives acting on their behalf.' (at p 193, 209 Cal Rptr 220.)

The description of Mr Bartling's condition fits that of Elizabeth Bouvia. The holding of that case applies here and compels real parties to respect her decision even though she is not 'terminally' ill. The trilogy of *Cobbs v Grant, supra* 8 Cal 3d 229, 104 Cal Rptr 505, 502 P 2d 1, *Barber v Superior Court, supra*, 147 Cal App 3d 1006, 195 Cal Rptr 484, and *Bartling v Superior Court, supra*, 163 Cal App 3d 186, 209 Cal Rptr 220, with their thorough explanation and discussion, are authority enough and in reality provides a complete answer to the position and assertions of real parties' medical personnel.

But if additional persuasion be needed, there is ample. As indicated by the discussion in *Bartling* and *Barber*, substantial and respectable authority throughout the country recognises the right which petitioner seeks to exercise. Indeed, it is neither radical nor startlingly new.

. . .

Further recognition that this right is paramount to even medical recommendation, is evidenced by several declarations of public and professional policy which were noted in both the *Barber* and *Bartling* cases.

For example, addressing one part of the problem, California passed the 'Natural Death Act', Health and Safety Code sections 7185 et seq. Although addressed to terminally ill patients, the significance of this legislation is its expression as state policy 'that adult persons have the fundamental right to control the decisions relating to the rendering of their own medical care . . .' (Health & Saf Code, § 7186.) Section 7188 provides the method whereby an adult person may execute a directive for the withholding or withdrawal of life-sustaining procedures. Recognition of the right of other persons who may not be terminally ill and may wish to give other forms of direction concerning their medical care is expressed in section 7193: 'Nothing in this chapter shall impair or supersede any legal right or legal responsibility which any person may have to effect the withholding or withdrawal of life-sustaining procedures in any lawful manner. In such respect the provisions of this chapter are cumulative'.

Moreover, as the *Bartling* decision holds, there is no practical or logical reason to limit the exercise of this right to 'terminal' patients. The right to refuse treatment does not need the sanction or approval by any legislative act, directing how and when it shall be exercised.

In large measure the courts have sought to protect and insulate medical providers from criminal and tort liability. (Eg, *Barber v Superior Court, supra*, 147 Cal App 3d 1006, 195 Cal Rptr 484.) The California Natural Death Act also illustrates this approach. Nonetheless, as indicated it too recognises, even if inferentially, the existence of the right, even in a non-terminal patient, which overrides the concern for protecting the medical profession.

This right is again reflected in the statute concerning execution of a power of attorney for health care (Civ Code, § 2500), which states in pertinent part: 'Notwithstanding this document, you have the right to make medical and other health care decisions for yourself so long as you can give informed consent with respect to the particular decision. In addition, no treatment may be given to you over your objection at the time. . . .'

A recent Presidential Commission for the Study of Ethical Problems in Medicine and Biomedical and Behavioral Research concluded in part: 'The voluntary choice of a competent and informed patient should determine whether or not life-sustaining therapy will be undertaken, just as such choices provide the basis for other decisions about medical treatment. Health care institutions and professionals should try to enhance patients' abilities to make decisions on their own behalf and to promote understanding of the available treatment options. . . . Health care professionals serve patients best by maintaining a presumption in favor of sustaining life, while recognising that competent patients are entitled to choose to forego any treatments, including those that sustain life'. (*Deciding to Forego Life-Sustaining Treatment*, at pp 3, 5 (US Govt Printing Office 1983) (Report of the President's Commission for the Study of Ethical Problems in Medicine and Biomedical and Behavioral Research).)

. . .

We do not believe that all of the foregoing case law and statements of policy and statutory recognition are mere lip service to a fictitious right. As noted in *Bartling* 'We do not doubt the sincerity of [the hospital and medical personnel's] moral and ethical beliefs, or their sincere belief in the position they have taken in this case. However, if the right of the patient to self-determination as to his own medical treatment is to have any meaning at all, it must be paramount to the interests of the patient's hospital and doctors. . . . The right of a competent adult patient to refuse medical treatment is a constitutionally guaranteed right which must not be abridged'. (Fn omitted, 163 Cal App 3d at p 195, 209 Cal Rptr 220.)

It is indisputable that petitioner is mentally competent. She is not comatose. She is quite intelligent, alert and understands the risks involved.

. . .

Here, if force fed, petitioner faces 15 to 20 years of a painful existence, endurable only by the constant administrations of morphine. Her condition is irreversible. There is no cure for her palsy or arthritis. Petitioner would have to be fed, cleaned, turned, bedded, toileted by others for 15 to 20 years! Although alert, bright, sensitive, perhaps even brave and feisty, she must lie immobile, unable to exist except through physical acts of others. Her mind and spirit may be free to take great flights but she herself is imprisoned and must lie physically helpless subject to the ignominy, embarrassment, humiliation and dehumanising aspects created by her helplessness. We do not believe it is the policy of this State that all and every life must be preserved against the will of the sufferer. It is incongruous, if not monstrous, for medical practitioners to assert their right to preserve a life that someone else must live, or, more accurately, endure, for '15 to 20 years'. We cannot conceive it to be the policy of this State to inflict such an ordeal upon anyone.

It is, therefore, immaterial that the removal of the nasogastric tube will hasten or cause Bouvia's eventual death. Being competent she has the right to live out the remainder of her natural life in dignity and peace. It is precisely the aim and purpose of the many decisions upholding the withdrawal of life-support systems to accord and provide as large a measure of dignity, respect and comfort as possible to every patient for the remainder of his days, whatever be their number. This goal is not to hasten death, though its earlier arrival may be an expected and understood likelihood.

Real parties assert that what petitioner really wants is to 'commit suicide' by starvation at their facility. The trial court in its statement of decision said:

It is fairly clear from the evidence and the court cannot close its eyes to the fact that [petitioner] during her stay in defendant hospital, and for some time prior thereto, has formed an intent to die. She has voiced this desire to a member of the staff of defendant hospital. She claims, however, she does not wish to commit suicide. On the evidence, this is but a semantic distinction. The reasonable inference to be drawn from the evidence is that [petitioner] in defendant facility has purposefully engaged in a selective rejection of medical treatment and nutritional intake to accomplish her objective and accept only treatment which gives her some degree of comfort pending her demise. Stated another way, [petitioner's] refusal of medical treatment and nutritional intake is motivated not by a *bona fide* exercise of her right of privacy but by a desire to terminate her life. . . . [¶] Here [petitioner] wishes to pursue her objective to die by the use of public facilities with staff standing by to furnish her medical treatment to which she consents and to refrain from that which she refuses.

Overlooking the fact that a desire to terminate one's life is probably the ultimate exercise of one's right to privacy, we find no substantial evidence to support the court's conclusion. Even if petitioner had the specific intent to commit suicide in 1983, while at Riverside, she did not carry out that plan. Then she apparently had the ability without artificial aids, to consume sufficient nutrients to sustain herself, now she does not. That is to say, the trial court here made the following express finding, 'Plaintiff, when she chooses, can orally ingest food by masticating "finger food" *though additional nutritional intake is required intravenously and by nasogastric tube. . . .*' (emphasis added.) As a consequence of her changed condition, it is clear she has now merely resigned herself to accept an earlier death, if necessary, rather than live by feedings forced upon her by means of nasogastric tube. Her decision to allow nature to take its course is not equivalent to an election to commit suicide with real parties aiding and abetting therein. (*Bartling v Superior Court, supra,* 163 Cal App 3d 186, 209 Cal Rptr 220; *Lane v Candura, supra,* 376 NE 2d 1232.)

Moreover, the trial court seriously erred by basing its decision on the 'motives' behind Elizabeth Bouvia's decision to exercise her rights. If a right exists, it matters not what 'motivates' its exercise. We find nothing in the law to suggest the right to refuse medical treatment may be exercised only if the patient's *motives* meet someone else's approval. It certainly is not illegal or immoral to prefer a natural, albeit sooner, death than a drugged life attached to a mechanical device.

It is not necessary to here define or dwell at length upon what constitutes suicide. Our Supreme Court dealt with the matter in the case of *Re Joseph G* 34 Cal 3d 429, 194 Cal Rptr 163, 667 P 2d 1176 (1983), wherein declaring that the State has an interest in preserving and recognising the sanctity of life, it observed that it is a crime to aid suicide. But it is significant that the instances and the means there discussed all involved affirmative, assertive, proximate, direct conduct such as furnishing a gun, poison, knife, or other instrumentality or usable means by which another could physically and immediately inflict some death producing injury upon himself. Such situations are far different than the mere presence of a doctor during the exercise of his patient's constitutional rights.

This is the teaching of *Bartling* and *Barber.* No criminal or civil liability attaches to honoring a competent, informed patient's refusal of medical service.

We do not purport to establish what will constitute proper medical practice in all other cases or even other aspects of the care to be provided . . . petitioner. We hold only that her right to refuse medical treatment even of the life-sustaining variety, entitles her to the immediate removal of the nasogastric tube that has been involuntarily inserted into her body. The hospital and medical staff are still free to perform a substantial, if not the greater part of their duty, ie, that of trying to alleviate Bouvia's pain and suffering.

Elizabeth Bouvia was competent to refuse treatment. The court accepted that she had both a constitutional and common law right to refuse treatment. This has been clearly restated by the New Jersey Supreme Court in two recent decisions: *Re Conroy* 486 A 2d 1209 (1985) and *Re Farrell* 529 A 2d 404 (1987) discussed *infra* Ch 14. Notice the following about the *Bouvia* case: (1) Bouvia was not dying or terminally ill when she refused artificial nutrition and hydration; (2) artificial nutrition and hydration were regarded by the California Court of Appeals as indistinguishable from medical treatment or intervention; (3) the court rejected the view that Elizabeth Bouvia intended to kill herself and hence commit suicide.

Questions

Do you think the court was justified in making the findings in (2) and (3) on the facts of the case? would it, in your opinion, make any difference if the court did not view artificial hydration and nutrition as medical treatment? What if the court had decided, as the trial judge had done, that Bouvia was trying to kill herself?

Other interests. The *Bouvia* decision illustrates that the right to refuse medical treatment may not be absolute. The United States courts have accepted this and recognised 4 interests which may potentially outweigh the patient's right. The New Jersey Supreme Court identified these in the important case of *Re Conroy* 486 A 2d 1209 (1985). The facts of this case be found elsewhere (*infra* Ch 14).

Schrieber J: Whether based on common-law doctrines or on constitutional theory, the right to decline life-sustaining medical treatment is not absolute. In some cases, it may yield to countervailing societal interests in sustaining the person's life. Courts and commentators have commonly identified four state interests that may limit a person's right to refuse medical treatment: preserving life, preventing suicide, safeguarding the integrity of the medical profession, and protecting innocent third parties. *See, eg, Satz v Perlmutter, supra, 362 So* 2d at 162; *Re Spring*, 380 *Mass* 629, 640, 405 *NE* 2d 115, 123 (1980); *Comr of Correction v Myers*, 379 *Mass* 255, 261, 399 *NE* 2d 452, 456 (1979); *Saikewicz, supra*, 373 *Mass* at 728, 370 *NE* 2d at 425; *Re Torres*, 357 *NW* 2d 332, 339 (Minn 1984); *Re Colyer*, 99 *Wash* 2d 114, 121, 660 *P* 2d 738, 743 (1983); *President's Commission Report, supra*, at 31–32; Note, '*Re Storar:* The Right to Die and Incompetent Patients," 43 *U Pitt L Rev* 1087, 1092 (1982).

The state's interest in preserving life is commonly considered the most significant of the four state interests. *See, eg, Spring, supra*, 380 *Mass* at 633, 405 *NE* 2d at 119; *Saikewicz, supra*, 373 *Mass* at 740, 370 *NE* 2d at 425; *President's Commission Report, supra*, at 32. It may be seen as embracing two separate but related concerns: an interest in preserving the life of the particular patient, and an interest in preserving the sanctity of all life. Cantor, '*Quinlan*, Privacy, and the Handling of Incompetent Dying Patients,' 30 *Rutgers L Rev* 239, 249 (1977); *see* Annas, 'In re Quinlan: Legal Comfort for Doctors,' *Hastings Center Rep*, June 1976, at 29.

While both of these state interests in life are certainly strong, in themselves they will usually not foreclose a competent person from declining life-sustaining medical treatment for himself. This is because the life that the state is seeking to protect in such a situation is the life of the same person who has competently decided to forego the medical intervention; it is not some other actual or potential life that cannot adequately protect itself. *Cf Roe v Wade, supra*, 410 *US* 113, 93 *S Ct* 705, 35 *L Ed* 2d 147 (authorising state restrictions or proscriptions of woman's right to abortion in final trimester of pregnancy to protect viable fetal life); *State v Perricone*, 37 *NJ* 463, 181 *A* 2d 751, *cert* denied, 371 *US* 890, 83 *S Ct* 189, 9 *L Ed* 2d 124 (1962) (affirming trial court's appointment of guardian with authority to consent to blood transfusion for infant over parents' religious objections); *Muhlenberg Hosp v Patterson*, 128 *NJ Super* 498, 320 *A* 2d 518 (Law Div 1974) (authorising blood transfusion to save infant's life over parents' religious objections).

In cases that do not involve the protection of the actual or potential life of someone other than the decisionmaker, the state's indirect and abstract interest in preserving the life of the competent patient generally gives way to the patient's much stronger personal interest in directing the course of his own life. *See, eg, Quackenbush, supra*, 156 *NJ Super* at 290, 383 *A* 2d 785; Cantor, *supra*, 30 *Rutgers L Rev* at 249–50. Indeed, insofar as the 'sanctity of individual free choice and self-determination [are] fundamental constituents of life,' the value of life may be lessened rather than increased 'by the failure to allow a competent human being the right of choice'. *Saikewicz, supra*, 373 *Mass* at 742, 370 *NE* 2d at 426; *see also* Cantor, *supra*, 30 *Rutgers L Rev* at 250 ('Government tolerance of the choice to resist treatment reflects concern for individual self-determination, bodily integrity, and avoidance of suffering, rather than a depreciation of life's value.').

It may be contended that in conjunction with its general interest in preserving life, this state has a particular legislative policy of preventing suicide. *See NJSA* 30:4–26.3a (subjecting any person who attempts suicide to temporary hospitalisation when the person's behavior suggests the existence of mental illness and constitutes a peril to life, person, or property); see also NJSA 2C:11–6 ('A person who purposely aids another to commit suicide is guilty of a crime of the second degree if his conduct causes such suicide or an attempted suicide, and otherwise of a crime of the fourth degree.') This state interest in protecting people from direct and purposeful self-destruction is motivated by, if not encompassed within, the state's more basic interest in preserving life. Thus, it is questionable whether it is a distinct state interest worthy of independent consideration.

In any event, declining life-sustaining medical treatment may not properly be viewed as an attempt to commit suicide. Refusing medical intervention merely allows the disease to take its natural course; if death were eventually to occur, it would be the result, primarily, of the underlying disease, and not the result of a self-inflicted injury. See *Satz v Perlmutter, supra,* 362 *So* 2d at 162; *Saikewicz, supra,* 373 *Mass* at 743 n 11, 370 *NE* 2d at 426 n 11; *Colyer, supra,* 99 *Wash* 2d at 121, 660 *P* 2d at 743; *see also President's Commission Report, supra,* at 38 (summarising case law on the subject). But cf *Caulk,* NH 480 *A* 2d 93, 96–97 (1984) (stating that attempt of an otherwise healthy prisoner to starve himself to death because he preferred death to life in prison was tantamount to attempted suicide, and that the state, to prevent such suicide, could force him to eat). In addition, people who refuse life-sustaining medical treatment may not harbor a specific intent to die, *Saikewicz, supra,* 373 *Mass* at 743, n 11, 370 *NE* 2d at 426 n 11; rather, they may fervently wish to live, but to do so free of unwanted medical technology, surgery, or drugs, and without protracted suffering, see *Satz v Perlmutter, supra,* 362 *So* 2d at 162–63 ("The testimony of Mr Perlmutter . . . is that he really wants to live, but [to] do so, God and Mother Nature willing, under his own power.').

Recognising the right of a terminally ill person to reject medical treatment respects that person's intent, not to die, but to suspend medical intervention at a point consonant with the 'individual's view respecting a personally preferred manner of concluding life." Note, 'The Tragic Choice: Termination of Care for Patients in a Permanent Vegetative State', 51 *NYUL Rev* 285, 310 (1976). The difference is between self-infliction or self-destruction and self-determination. See Byrn, 'Compulsory Lifesaving Treatment for the Competent Adult', 44 *Fordham L Rev* 1, 16–23 (1975). To the extent that our decision in *John F Kennedy Memorial Hosp v Heston,* 58 *NJ* 576, 581–82, 279 *A* 2d 670 (1971), implies the contrary, we now overrule it.

The third state interest that is frequently asserted as a limitation on a competent patient's right to refuse medical treatment is the interest in safeguarding the integrity of the medical profession. This interest, like the interest in preventing suicide, is not particularly threatened by permitting competent patients to refuse life-sustaining medical treatment. Medical ethics do not require medical intervention in disease at all costs. As long ago as 1624, Francis Bacon wrote, 'I esteem it the office of a physician not only to restore health, but to mitigate pain and dolours; and not only when such mitigation may conduce to recovery, but when it may serve to make a fair and easy passage'. *F Bacon, New Atlantis, quoted in* Mannes, 'Euthanasia vs The Right to Life', 27 *Baylor L Rev* 68, 69 (1975). More recently, we wrote in *Quinlan, supra,* 70 *NJ* at 47, 355 *A* 2d 647, that modern-day 'physicians distinguish between curing the ill and comforting and easing the dying; that they refuse to treat the curable as if they were dying or ought to die, and that they have sometimes refused to treat the hopeless and dying as if they were curable'. Indeed, recent surveys have suggested that a majority of practising doctors now approve of passive euthanasia and believe that it is being practised by members of the profession. See sources cited in *Storar, supra NY* 2d at 385–386 n 3, 420 *NE* 2d at 75–76 n 3, 438 *NYS* 2d at 277–78 n 3 (Jones, J, dissenting), and in Collester, 'Death, Dying and the Law: A Prosecutorial View of the *Quinlan* Case', 30 *Rutgers L Rev* 304, n 3, 312 & n 27.

Moreover, even if doctors were exhorted to attempt to cure or sustain their patients under all circumstances, that moral and professional imperative, at least in cases of patients who were clearly competent, presumably would not require doctors to go beyond advising the patient of the risks of foregoing treatment and urging the patient to accept the medical intervention. *Storar, supra,* 52 *NY* 2d at 377, 420 *NE* 2d at 71, 438 *NYS* 2d at 273; see *Colyer, supra,* 99 *Wash* 2d at 121–23, 660 *P* 2d at 743–44, citing *Saikewicz, supra,* 373 *Mass* at 743–44, 370 *NE* 2d at 417. If the patient rejected the doctor's advice, the onus of that decision would rest on the patient, not the doctor. Indeed, if the patient's right to informed consent is to have any meaning at all, it must be accorded respect even when it conflicts with the advice of the doctor or the values of the medical profession as a whole.

The fourth asserted state interest in overriding a patient's decision about his medical treatment is the interest in protecting innocent third parties who may be harmed by the patient's treatment decision. When the patient's exercise of his free choice could adversely and directly affect the health, safety, or security of others, the patient's right of self-determination must frequently give way. Thus, for example, courts have required competent adults to undergo medical procedures against their will if necessary to protect the public health, *Jacobson v Massachusetts,* 197 *US* 11, 25 *S Ct* 358, 49 *L Ed* 643 (1905) (recognising enforceability of compulsory smallpox vaccination law); to prevent a serious risk to prison security, *Myers, supra,* 379 *Mass* at 263, 265, 399 *NE* 2d at 457, 458 (compelling prisoner with kidney disease to submit to dialysis over his protest rather than acquiescing in his demand to be transferred to a lower-security prison); *accord Caulk, supra,* 480 *A* 2d at 96; or to prevent the emotional and financial abandonment of the patient's minor children, *Application of President & Directors of Georgetown College, Inc,* 331 *F* 2d 1000, 1008 (DC Cir), *cert* denied, 377 *US* 978, 84 *S Ct* 1883, 12 *L Ed* 2d 746 (1964) (ordering mother of seven-month-old infant to submit to blood transfusion over her religious objections because of the mother's 'responsibility to the community to care for her infant'); *Holmes v Silver Cross Hosp,* 340 *F Supp* 125, 130 (ND Ill 1972) (indicating that patient's status as father of minor child might justify authorising blood transfusion to save his life despite his religious objections).

On balance, the right to self-determination ordinarily outweighs any countervailing state interests, and competent persons generally are permitted to refuse medical treatment, even at the risk of death. Most of the cases that have held otherwise, unless they involved the interest in protecting innocent third parties, have concerned the patient's competency to make a rational and considered choice of treatment. See Annot, 93 *ALR* 3d 67, at 80–85 (1979) ('Patient's Right to Refuse Treatment Allegedly Necessary to Sustain Life'). For example, in *Heston, supra,* 58 *NJ* 576, 279 *A* 2d 670, this Court approved a blood transfusion to save the life of a twenty-two-year-old Jehovah's Witness who had been severely injured and was rushed to the hospital for treatment, despite the fact that a tenet of her faith forbade blood transfusions. The evidence indicated that she was in shock on admittance to the hospital and was then or soon became disoriented and incoherent. Part of the Court's rationale was that hospitals, upon which patients' care is thrust, 'exist to aid the sick and the injured', *id* 58 *NJ* at 582, 279 *A* 2d 670, and that it is difficult for them to assess a patient's intent in an emergency and to determine whether a desire to refuse treatment is firmly and competently held, *id* 58 *NJ* at 581, 582, 279 *A* 2d 670. Similarly, courts in other states have authorised blood transfusions over the objections of Jehovah's Witnesses when the patient's opposition to the treatment was expressed in equivocal terms. *Compare Georgetown College, supra,* 331 F 2d at 1006–07 (authorising transfusion to save life of patient who said that for religious reasons she would not consent to the transfusion, but who seemed to indicate that she would not oppose the transfusion if court ordered it since it would not then be her responsibility), *and United States v George,* 239 *F Supp* 752, 753 (D Conn 1965) (transfusion was authorised for patient who told court that he would not agree to the transfusion, but volunteered that if the court ordered it he would not resist in any way since it would be the court's will and not his), *with Re Osborne,* 294 *A* 2d 372, 374, 375 (DC 1972) (stating that guardian should not be appointed to consent to transfusion on behalf of man who told court that he would be deprived of 'everlasting life' if compelled by a court to submit to the transfusion, and who explained, 'it is between me and Jehovah; not the courts . . . I'm willing to take my chances. My faith is that strong.').

We have already seen that the Court of Appeals in *Bouvia*, on the facts of that case, rejected the application of the second of these interests—namely of preventing suicide. The reasoning of Schrieber J is closely analogous. Of the remaining three interests perhaps the protection of innocent third parties is the most worthwhile studying and it has produced, as *Conroy* shows, a number of cases. We have already looked at the *Georgetown College* case (*supra* at p 204). This case may be interpreted as one where, at best, the patient's views were equivocal and, at worst, she was incompetent. However, three further decisions merit examination. In each a medical procedure was ordered by a court upon a competent patient against their wishes. In each the justification was to save the life of the pregnant patient's unborn child.

Raleigh Fitkin–Paul Morgan Memorial Hospital v Anderson 201 A 2d 537 (1964) (New Jersey Supreme Court)

Per curiam: The plaintiff hospital brought an action in the Chancery Division of the Superior Court seeking authority to administer blood transfusions to the defendant Willimina Anderson in the event that such transfusions should be necessary to save her life and the life of her unborn child. The child is quick, the pregnancy being beyond the 32nd week. Mrs Anderson had notified the hospital that she did not wish blood transfusions for the reason that they would be contrary to her religious conviction as a Jehovah's Witness. The evidence establishes a probability that at some point in the pregnancy Mrs Anderson will haemorrhage severely and that both she and the unborn child will die unless a blood transfusion is administered.

The trial court held that the judiciary could not thus intervene in the case of an adult or with respect to an unborn child. Because of the likely emergency we directed immediate argument of the hospital's appeal. At the argument we were advised that Mrs Anderson left the hospital yesterday against the advice of the attending physician and the hospital. It is doubtful whether the hospital has a remaining interest but the parties request the court to determine the issues and since it is likely that the matter would arise again at the instance of an interested party we have decided to do so.

In *State v Perricone*, 37 NJ 463, 181 A 2d 751 (1962), we held that the State's concern for the welfare of an infant justified blood transfusions notwithstanding the objection of its parents who were also Jehovah's Witnesses, and in *Smith v Brennan*, 31 NJ 353, 157 A 2d 497 (1960), we held that a child could sue for injuries negligently inflicted upon it prior to birth. We are satisfied that the unborn child is entitled to the law's protection and that an appropriate order should be made to insure blood transfusions to the mother in the event that they are necessary in the opinion of the physician in charge at the time.

We have no difficulty in so deciding with respect to the infant child. The more difficult question is whether an adult may be compelled to submit to such medical procedures when necessary to save his life. Here we think it is unnecessary to decide that question in broad terms because the welfare of the child and the mother are so intertwined and inseparable that it would be impracticable to attempt to distinguish between them with respect to the sundry factual patterns which may develop. The blood transfusions (including transfusions made necessary by the delivery) may be administered if necessary to save her life or the life of her child, as the physician in charge at the time may determine.

The intervention in this case, a blood transfusion, was intrusive but not as intrusive as in the next case:

Jefferson v Griffin Spalding County Hospital Authority 274 SE 2d 457 (1981) (Supreme Court of Georgia)

Per curiam: On Thursday, January 22, 1981, the Griffin Spalding County Hospital Authority petitioned the Superior Court of Butts County, as a court of equity, for an order authorising it to perform a caesarean section and any necessary blood transfusions upon the defendant, an out-patient resident of Butts County, in the event she presented herself to the hospital for delivery of her unborn child, which was due on or about Monday, January 26. The superior court conducted an emergency hearing on Thursday, January 22, and entered the following order:

This petition and rule nisi were filed and served on defendant today. When the Court convened at the appointed hour, defendant did not appear, in spite of the fact that both she and her husband had notice of the hearing.

Defendant is in the thirty-ninth week of pregnancy. In the past few weeks she has presented herself to Griffin Spalding County Hospital for pre-natal care. The examining physician has found and defendant has been advised that she has a complete placenta previa; that the afterbirth is between the baby and the birth canal; that it is virtually impossible that this condition will correct itself prior to delivery; and that it is a 99% certainty that the child cannot survive natural childbirth (vaginal delivery). The chances of defendant surviving vaginal delivery are not better than 50%.

The examining physician is of the opinion that a delivery by caesarean section prior to labor beginning would have an almost 100% chance of preserving the life of the child, along with that of defendant.

On the basis of religious beliefs, defendant has advised the Hospital that she does not need surgical removal of the child and will not submit to it. Further, she refuses to take any transfusion of blood.

The Hospital is required by its own policies to treat any patient seeking emergency treatment. It seeks authority of the Court to administer medical treatment to defendant to save the life of herself and her unborn child.

The child is, as a matter of fact, viable and fully capable of sustaining life independent of the mother (defendant). The issue is whether this unborn child has any legal right to the protection of the Court.

. . .

Because the life of defendant and of the unborn child are, at the moment, inseparable, the Court deems it appropriate to infringe upon the wishes of the mother to the extent it is necessary to give the child an opportunity to live.

Accordingly, the plaintiff hospitals are hereby authorised to administer to defendant all medical procedures deemed necessary by the attending physician to preserve the life of defendant's unborn child. This authority shall be effective only if defendant voluntarily seeks admission to either of plaintiff's hospitals for the emergency delivery of the child.

The Court has been requested to order defendant to submit to surgery before the natural childbirth process (labor) begins. The Court is reluctant to grant this request and does not do so at this time. However, should some agency of the State seek such relief through intervention in this suit or in a separate proceeding, the Court will promptly consider such request.

On Friday, January 23, the Georgia Department of Human Resources, acting through the Butts County Department of Family and Children Services, petitioned the Juvenile Court of Butts County for temporary custody of the unborn child, alleging that the child was a deprived child without proper parental care necessary for his or her physical health . . . and praying for an order requiring the mother to submit to a caesarean section. After appointing counsel for the parents and for the child, the court conducted a joint hearing in both the superior court and juvenile court cases and entered the following order on the afternoon of January 23:

This action in the Superior Court of Butts County was heard and decided yesterday, January 22, 1981.

This morning, the Georgia Department of Human Resources, acting through the Butts County Department of Family and Children Services, filed a complaint in the Juvenile Court of Butts County alleging deprivation and seeking temporary custody of Jessie Mae Jefferson's unborn child.

Because of the unusual nature of the relief sought in these cases and because the Juvenile Court of Butts County may not have the authority needed effectively to grant the relief sought, the Court consolidates these cases and renders the following judgment both as a Juvenile Court and under the broad powers of the Superior Court of Butts County. The Court readopts its findings contained in the Order dated January 22, 1981.

At the proceeding held today, Jessie Mae Jefferson and her husband, John W Jefferson were present and represented by counsel, Hugh Glidewell, Jr. Richard Milam, Attorney at Law, represented the interests of the unborn child.

Based on the evidence presented, the Court finds that Jessie Mae Jefferson is due to begin labor at any moment. There is a 99 to 100 percent certainty that the unborn child will die if she attempts to have the child by vaginal delivery. There is a 99 to 100 percent chance that the child will live if the baby is delivered by Caesarean section prior to the beginning of labor. There is a 50 percent chance that Mrs Jefferson herself will die if vaginal delivery is attempted. There is an almost 100 percent chance that Mrs Jefferson will survive if a delivery by Caesarean section is done prior to the beginning of labor. The Court finds that as a matter of fact the child is a human being fully capable of sustaining life independent of the mother.

Mrs Jefferson and her husband have refused and continue to refuse to give consent to a Caesarean section. This refusal is based entirely on the religious beliefs of Mr and Mrs Jefferson. They are of the view that the Lord has healed her body and that whatever happens to the child will be the Lord's will.

Based on these findings, the Court concludes and finds as a matter of law that this child is a viable human being and entitled to the protection of the Juvenile Court Code of Georgia. The Court concludes that this child is without the proper parental care and subsistence necessary for his or her physical life and health.

Temporary custody of the unborn child is hereby granted to the State of Georgia Department of Human Resources and the Butts County Department of Family and Children Services. The Department shall have full authority to make all decisions, including giving consent to the surgical delivery appertaining to the birth of this child. The temporary custody of the Department shall terminate when the child has been successfully brought from its mother's body into the world or until the child dies, whichever shall happen.

Because of the unique nature of these cases, the powers of the Superior Court of Butts County are invoked and the defendant, Jessie Mae Jefferson, is hereby Ordered to submit to a sonogram (ultrasound) at the Griffin Spalding County Hospital or some other place which may be chosen by her where such procedure can be given. Should said sonogram indicate to the attending physician that the complete placenta privia is still blocking the child's passage into this world, Jessie Mae Jefferson, is Ordered to submit to a Caesarean section and related procedures considered necessary by the attending physician to sustain the life of this child.

The Court finds that the State has an interest in the life of this unborn, living human being. The Court finds that the intrusion involved into the life of Jessie Mae Jefferson and her husband, John W Jefferson, is outweighed by the duty of the State to protect a living, unborn human being from meeting his or her death before being given the opportunity to live.

This Order shall be effective at 10:00 a.m. on Saturday, January 24, 1981, unless a stay is granted by the Supreme Court of Georgia or some other Court having the authority to stay an Order of this Court.

The parent filed their motion for stay in this court at about 5:30 p.m. on January 23 . . . [T]his court entered the following order on the evening of January 23:

It is ordered that the Motion for Stay filed in this matter is hereby denied. The trial court's orders are effective immediately . . .

Motion for stay denied.

Hill, Presiding Justice: The power of a court to order a competent adult to submit to surgery is exceedingly limited. Indeed, until this unique case arose, I would have thought such power to be nonexistent. Research shows that the courts generally have held that a competent adult has the right to refuse necessary lifesaving surgery and medical treatment (ie, has the right to die) where no state interest other than saving the life of the patient is involved. . . .

On the other hand, one court has held that an expectant mother in the last weeks of pregnancy lacks the right to refuse necessary life saving surgery and medical treatment where the life of the unborn child is at stake. *Raleigh Fitkin-Paul Morgan Memorial Hospital v Anderson*, [42 NJ 421, 201 A 2d 537, cert den 377 US 985, 84 SCt 1894, 12 LEd 2d 1032 (1964)]; see also *Re Melideo*, 88 Misc 2d 974, 390 NYS 2d 523 (1976); *Re Yetter*, 62 Pa D&C 2d 619, 623 (1973).

The Supreme Court has recognised that the state has an interest in protecting the lives of unborn, viable children (viability usually occurring at about 7 months, or 28 weeks). . . .

The mother here was in her last week of normal pregnancy (the 39th week). She had diligently sought parental care for her child and herself, except for her refusal to consent to a caesarean section. She was due to deliver on Monday, January 26, and the medical testimony showed that the birth could occur at any time within 2 weeks of that date. . . .

In denying the stay of the trial court's order and thereby clearing the way for immediate reexamination by sonogram and probably for surgery, we weighed the right of the mother to practice her religion and to refuse surgery on herself, against her unborn child's right to live. We found in favor of her child's right to live.

Justice Smith agreed and added:

. . . In the instant case, it appears that there is no less burdensome alternative for preserving the life of a fully developed fetus than requiring its mother to undergo surgery against her religious convictions. Such an intrusion by the state would be extraordinary, presenting some medical risk to both the mother and the fetus. However, the state's compelling interest in preserving the life of this fetus is beyond dispute. Moreover, the medical evidence indicates that the risk to the fetus *and* the mother presented by a Caesarean section would be minimal, whereas, in the absence of surgery, the fetus would almost certainly die and the mother's chance of survival would be no better than 50 per cent. Under these circumstances, I must conclude that the trial court's order is not violative of the First Amendment, notwithstanding that it may require the mother to submit to surgery against her religious beliefs. See *Raleigh Fitkin-Paul Memorial Hospital v Anderson, supra*; see also *Green v Green*, 448 Pa 338, 292 A 2d 387 (1972).

The *Jefferson* case involved a Caesarian section in circumstances where the court found that it involved little or no risk to mother and child whilst to do nothing would mean the probable death of the fetus and, perhaps, the mother. Do you think the court would (and should) reach the same conclusion if the Caesarian section would not clearly prevent the death of the fetus or if the mother's life was not threatened? What if the procedure itself would be detrimental to the mother's health? The District of Columbia Court of Appeals *in Re AC* (1988) 533 A 2d 611—did order a Caesarian section in this situation:

Associate Judge Nebeker: AC was diagnosed with leukemia when she was thirteen years old. As part of her treatment, she underwent a number of major surgical procedures, therapy, and chemotherapy. When she was twenty-seven years old, after her cancer had been in remission for three years, AC married. At the time she became pregnant, she had not undergone chemotherapy for more than a year. In her fifteenth week of pregnancy, she was referred to the hospital's high-risk pregnancy clinic.

When AC was approximately twenty-five weeks pregnant, she went to her regularly scheduled prenatal visit complaining of shortness of breath and some pain in her back. Her physicians subsequently discovered that she had a tumor mass in her lung which was most likely a metastatic oxygenic carcinoma. She was admitted to the hospital on June 11 and her prognosis was terminal.

On June 15, during AC's twenty-sixth week of pregnancy, AC, her physicians, her mother, and her husband discussed the possibility of providing AC with radiation therapy or chemotherapy to relieve her pain and to continue her pregnancy. Her physicians believed that her unborn child's chances of viability would be greatly increased if it were delivered when it had reached twenty-eight weeks gestational age. By June 16, the date on which the hospital sought the declaratory order in the Superior Court, AC had been heavily sedated so that she could continue to breathe. Her condition was declining, and the attending medical staff concluded that passive treatment was appropriate because the mother would not survive and the child's chances of survival were grim. The hospital administration then decided to test this decision in the Superior Court.

. . .

The fundamental right to bodily integrity encompasses an adult's right to refuse medical treatment, even if the refusal will result in death.

. . .

The state's interest in protecting innocent third parties from an adult's decision to refuse medical treatment, however, may override the interest in bodily integrity. . . . Courts have used this reasoning to hold that parents may not withhold life-saving treatment from their children because of the parents' religious beliefs.

. . .

Some jurisdictions have held that the doctrine is equally applicable to unborn children. See, e g, *Jefferson, supra; Raleigh Fitkin-Paul Morgan Memorial Hospital v Anderson*, 42 NJ 421, 201 A 2d 537 (court appoints guardian for fetus and orders guardian to consent to blood transfusions, over mother's objections, as necessary to save the lives of the mother and the fetus), *cert denied*, 377 US 985 (1964); *Re Jamaica Hospital*, 128 Misc 2d 1006, 491 NYS 2d 898 (Sup Ct 1985) (court appoints physician as guardian of unborn child and orders him to do all that is necessary to save the life of an 18-week-old fetus, including administering blood transfusions to the mother over her objection); *Crouse Irving Memorial Hospital, Inc v Paddock*, 127 Misc 2d 101, 485 NYS 2d 443 (Sup Ct 1985) (court orders pregnant woman to receive blood transfusions to protect the welfare of the fetus that was to be prematurely delivered). But see *Taft v Taft*, 388 Mass 331, —, 446 NE 2d 395, 397 (1983) (court vacates judgment of Probate Court ordering woman in her fourth month of pregnancy to undergo 'purse string' operation to prevent miscarriage, holding that the record in the case did not show 'circumstances so compelling as to justify curtailing the wife's constitutional rights').

There is a significant difference, however, between a court authorising medical treatment for a child already born and a child who is yet unborn, although the state has compelling interests in protecting the life and health of both children and viable unborn children. See *Roe, supra*, 410 US at 163; *Prince, supra*, 321 US at 165. Where birth has occurred, the medical treatment does not infringe on the mother's right to bodily integrity. With an unborn child, the state's interest in preserving the health of the child may run squarely against the mother's interest in her bodily integrity.

It can be argued that the state may not infringe upon the mother's right to bodily integrity to protect the life or health of her unborn child unless to do so will not significantly affect the health of the mother and unless the child has a significant chance of being born alive. Performing Caesarean sections will, in most instances, have an effect on the condition of the mother. That effect may be temporary in otherwise normal patients. The surgery presents a number of common complications, including infection, hemorrhage, gastric aspiration of the stomach contents, and postoperative embolism. 4C Gray, *Attorney's Textbook of Medicine*, 308.50 (3d ed 1987). It also produces considerable discomfort. In some cases, the surgery will result in the mother's death.[5]

Even though we recognise these considerations, we think they should not have been dispositive here. The Caesarean section would not significantly affect AC's condition because she had, at best, two days left of sedated life; the complications arising from the surgery would not significantly alter that prognosis. The child, on the other hand, had a chance of surviving delivery, despite the possibility that it would be born handicapped. Accordingly, we concluded that the trial judge did not err in subordinating AC's right against bodily intrusion to the interests of the unborn child and the state, and hence we denied the motion for stay.

Note to extract
5. The death rate of women upon whom Caesarean sections have been performed is between 0.1 percent and 1 percent, significantly higher than the death rate of women who have delivered their babies vaginally. *Id.*

[Subsequently, the DC Court of Appeals ordered a rehearing of the case before the full court of DC Court of Appeals ((1988) 539 A 2d 203). The decision of the full court has not yet been handed down.] These cases raise a number of questions for the English medical lawyer.

Questions

(i) Would an English court concede that there may be circumstances in which a refusal of treatment by a competent patient could be overridden?
(ii) If so, would this exception to the general rule be restricted to situations where the refusal would probably lead to the death of the patient (or possibly another)? (See *Malette v Shulman* (1988) 63 OR (2d) 243 (Ontario High Court) damages of $20,000 awarded for transfusing an unconscious Jehovah's Witness against her clearly expressed pre-incompetence wishes.)
(iii) Would an English court acknowledge that the life of a third party which was at risk or was certain to end if the patient's refusal was respected might be a sufficient interest to override the refusal?
(iv) If it were a sufficient interest, as in the *Jefferson* and *AC* cases, because the third party was a foetus, how could the court act? Would a court wish to resolve the conflict between the mother's interest in her bodily integrity and the unborn child's interest in life.

In *Re F (in utero)* [1988] Fam 122, [1988] 2 All ER 193, the Court of Appeal rejected the view that an unborn child could be made a ward of court. Primarily, this was because the court accepted the earlier cases of *C v S* [1988] QB 135, [1987] 1 All ER 1230 and *Paton v British Pregnancy Advisory Service Trustees* [1979] QB 276, [1978] 2 All ER 987, which had held that an unborn child has no legal existence until it is physically independent of its mother (ie it has been born): on which, see *infra* Ch 9.

However, the court also accepted the overwhelming practical problems that might arise if wardship were available because of a possible conflict between mother and unborn child.

Balcombe LJ: Approaching the question as one of principle, in my judgment there is no jurisdiction to make an unborn child a ward of court. Since an unborn child has, *ex hypothesi*, no existence independent of its mother, the only purpose of extending the jurisdiction to include a foetus is to enable the mother's actions to be controlled. Indeed, that is the purpose of the present application. In the articles already cited Lowe gives examples of how this might operate in practice:

It would mean, for example, that the mother would be unable to leave the jurisdiction without the court's consent. The court being charged to protect the foetus's welfare would surely have to order the mother to stop smoking, imbibing alcohol and indeed any activity which might be hazardous to the child. Taking it to the extreme were the court to be faced with saving the baby's life or the mother's it would surely have to protect the baby's.

Another possibility is that the court might be asked to order that the baby be delivered by Caesarian section. (In this connection see Fortin—'Legal Protection for the Unborn Child' (1988) 51 MLR 81 and the US cases cited in note 16; in particular *Jefferson v Griffin Spalding Co Hospital Authority* 274 SE 2d 457 (1981).)

Whilst I do not accept that the priorities mentioned in the last sentence of the passage cited above are necessarily correct, it would be intolerable to place a judge in the position of having to make such a decision without any guidance as to the principles upon which his decision should be based. If the law is to be extended in this manner, so as to impose control over the mother of an unborn child where such control may be necessary for the benefit of that child, then under our system of Parliamentary democracy it is for Parliament to decide whether such controls can be imposed and, if so, subject to what limitations or conditions. Thus, under the Mental Health Act 1983, to which we were also referred, there are elaborate provisions to ensure that persons suffering from mental disorder or other similar conditions are not compulsorily admitted to hospital for assessment or treatment without proper safeguards: see sections 2, 3 and 4 of that Act. If Parliament were to think it appropriate that a pregnant woman should be subject to controls for the benefit of her unborn child, then doubtless it will stipulate the circumstances in which such controls may be applied and the safeguards appropriate for the mother's protection. In such a sensitive field, affecting as it does the liberty of the individual, it is not for the judiciary to extend the law.

Is this not indicative of an approach which would suggest that *Jefferson* and *AC* would not be applied in England? Balcombe LJ refers to the intervention of Parliament as being necessary for there to be an intrusion into the competent patient's bodily integrity. It is to examples of this that we now turn.

2. Statutes

eg 1. Mental Health Act 1983.

As regards this Act, two preliminary points must be noticed when the question is raised concerning the treatment of competent persons without their consent. First, not all those who are 'liable to be detained' (and who are subject to detention) under the Act, are by that reason alone incompetent. Secondly, it is clear from the Act that if indeed treatment can be given without consent, it can only under the Act be treatment for the relevant mental disorder, and not for other conditions requiring medical treatment.

Section 63 of the Act allows any treatment, not being within ss 57 and 58, to be given without the consent of the patient. Presumably, this envisages the giving of treatment against the refusal of even a competent patient. Section 63 of the Mental Health Act 1983 reads:

Treatment not requiring consent
63 The consent of a patient shall not be required for any medical treatment given to him for the mental disorder from which he is suffering, not being treatment falling within section 57 or 58 above, if the treatment is given by or under the direction of the responsible medical officer.

Section 57 (dealing with psychosurgery, is not relevant here since it does require consent) need not detain us. By section 58, however, treatment in the form of the long-term administration of medicine, that is beyond three months, on electro-convulsive therapy, may be administered either with the consent of the patient or—importantly for our purposes here—without consent (presumably again in the face of dissent) in the following circumstances:

58 (3) Subject to section 62 below, a patient shall not be given any form of treatment to which this section applies unless—
. . .
  (b) a registered medical practitioner appointed as aforesaid (not being the responsible medical officer) has certified in writing that the patient is not capable of understanding the nature, purpose and likely effects of that

treatment or has not consented to it but that, having regard to the likelihood of its alleviating or preventing a deterioration of his condition, the treatment should be given.

eg 2.   Public Health (Control of Diseases) Act 1984.

As its name suggests, this Act is concerned with the control of disease rather than with treatment. It is concerned primarily with the interests of the public who are not ill rather than with any particular person who may be ill. Section 37 provides as follows:

Removal to hospital of person with notifiable disease

37—(1) Where a justice of the peace (acting, if he deems it necessary, *ex parte*) is satisfied, on the application of the local authority, that a person is suffering from a notifiable disease and—

   (a) that his circumstances are such that proper precautions to prevent the spread of infection cannot be taken, or that such precautions are not being taken, and

   (b) that serious risk of infection is thereby caused to other persons, and

   (c) that accommodation for him is available in a suitable hospital vested in the Secretary of State.

the justice may, with the consent of the Area or District Health Authority responsible for the administration of the hospital, order him to be removed to it.

(2) An order under this section may be addressed to such officer of the local authority as the justice may think expedient, and that officer and any officer of the hospital may do all acts necessary for giving effect to the order.

Similarly, s 38 provides power to detain someone already in hospital and suffering from a notifiable disease, if on leaving the hospital they would not have accommodation in which proper precautions could be taken to prevent the spread of the disease. (Notifiable diseases are cholera, plague, relapsing fever, smallpox and typhus: s 10.)

You will notice that s 37 does not specifically authorise treatment without consent. Would you agree that such a power to treat without consent must be expressly given since such power would override the basic principles of the common law having to do with the inviolability of the person? Is your view affected by s 13?

Regulations for control of certain diseases

13.—(1) Subject to the provisions of this section, the Secretary of State may, as respects the whole or any part of England and Wales, including coastal waters, make regulations—

   (a) with a view to the treatment of persons affected with any epidemic, endemic or infectious disease and for preventing the spread of such diseases,

    . . .

Would Regulations that provided for compulsory treatment in purported exercise of powers granted by this section be *ultra vires*?

The Act also makes provision for the *examination* of any person 'found in [a common lodging-house] with a view to ascertaining whether he is suffering, or has recently suffered, from a notifiable disease' (s 40). The section is restricted to granting a power to *examine*; could this be reasonably interpreted as authorising *treatment* without consent? There are other examples where the law authorises a doctor to carry out examinations.

NATIONAL HEALTH SERVICE ACT 1977

5—(1) It is the Secretary of State's duty—

   (a) to provide for the medical and dental inspection at appropriate intervals of pupils in attendance at schools maintained by local education authorities and for the medical and dental treatment of such pupils,

Does this provision contemplate compulsory treatment?

Recently Regulations were promulgated by the Secretary of State under the Public Health (Control of Diseases) Act 1984 so as to apply ss 37 to those suffering from AIDS as if it were a notifiable disease. (now Public Health (Infectious Diseases) Regulations 1988, SI 1988 No 1546.)

The same question arises here as we saw earlier: does this authorise compulsory treatment of the person suffering from AIDS? This particular provision is curious in at least two respects. First, it refers to those only suffering from 'AIDS' and not to those HIV infected. If a police power under the Public Health Regulations were needed it is rather odd that it does not extend to the person who poses a greater threat than the actual sufferer from AIDS, ie the still healthy HIV infected person. Secondly, the provision may be a response to hysteria since the threat possessed by AIDS to public health is of a different order calling for different responses.

eg 3.   National Assistance Act 1948, s 47.

Removal to suitable premises of persons in need of care and attention
47—(1) The following provisions of this section shall have effect for the purposes of securing the necessary care and attention for persons who—
   (a) are suffering from grave chronic disease or, being aged, infirm or physically incapacitated, are living in insanitary conditions, and
   (b) are unable to devote to themselves, and are not receiving from other persons, proper care and attention.
   (2) If the medical officer of health certifies in writing to the appropriate authority that he is satisfied after thorough inquiry and consideration that in the interests of any such person as aforesaid residing in the area of the authority, or for preventing injury to the health of, or serious nuisance to, other persons, it is necessary to remove any such person as aforesaid from the premises in which he is residing, the appropriate authority may apply to a court of summary jurisdiction having jurisdiction in the place where the premises are situated for an order under the next following subsection.
   (3) On any such application the court may, if satisfied on oral evidence of the allegations in the certificate, and that it is expedient so to do, order the removal of the person to whom the application relates, by such officer of the appropriate authority, as may be specified in the order, to a suitable hospital or other place in, or within convenient distance of, the area of the appropriate authority, and his detention and maintenance therein;
   Provided that the court shall not order the removal of a person to any premises, unless either the person managing the premises has been heard in the proceedings or seven clear days' notice has been given to him of the intended application and of the time and place at which it is proposed to be made.
   (4) An order under the last foregoing subsection may be made so as to authorise a person's detention for any period not exceeding three months, and the court may from time to time by order extend that period for such further period, not exceeding three months, as the court may determine.

Again, does the statute authorise the treatment of a person to whom the section has been applied, without that person's consent?

(ii)   Proxies

The issue here is whether, in law, a parent may give valid consent to treatment (or refuse it) against the wishes of a competent child. As a matter of legal principle the analysis must be concerned with whether the doctor who treats the child may avoid a claim in battery at the suit of the child by pointing to the purported consent of the parent.

Since *Gillick* the prevailing view must be that on reaching maturity (and consequently the competence to decide), the power of the parent to decide on behalf of the child lapses. It has been suggested extra judicially by Sir Roger Ormrod that a different view may be arrived at if the child is a ward of court. In his article 'A Lawyer Looks at Medical Ethics' (1978) 46 Med-Leg J 18, 26, he states:

> Teenagers will have definite views of their own, which are entitled to reasonable respect, although there may be situations where it is justifiable to impose adult views upon them. They may refuse transfusion or operation on religious or cultural grounds and it may be wrong to override such a refusal if to do so would gravely distress the patient or complicate his future in some way.

Questions

(i) Do you think that this still (if it ever did) represents the law?
(ii) How could such a view be justified, particularly if a court in wardship has only the powers of a parent?

Chapter 5

Medical malpractice

An introduction

The background to actions for medical malpractice is explained by Margaret Brazier in *Medicine, Patients and the Law* (pp 53–54).

[The patient] . . . may feel that he has not been fully consulted or properly counselled about the nature and risks of the treatment. He may have agreed to treatment and ended up worse, not better. Consequently a patient may seek compensation from the courts. Or he may simply want an investigation of what went wrong, and to ensure that his experience is not suffered by others.

The law relating to medical errors, commonly described as medical malpractice, operates on two basic principles. (1) The patient must agree to treatment. (2) Treatment must be carried out with proper skill and care on the part of all members of the medical profession involved. Any doctor who operated on or injected, or even touched an adult patient against his will, might commit a battery, a trespass against the patient's person. [We dealt with this in deatil in Chapter 4.] A doctor who was shown to have exercised inadequate care of his patient, to have fallen below the required standard of competence, would be liable to compensate the patient for any harm he caused him in the tort of negligence.

In short, to obtain compensation the patient must show that the doctor was at fault. And if he sues for negligence he must show that the doctor's 'fault' caused him injury. Three overwhelming problems are inherent in these two simple statements.

First, how do courts staffed by lawyer-judges determine when a doctor is at fault? . . . The judges in England defer in the most part to the views of the doctors. Unlike their American brethren, English judges will rarely challenge the accepted views of the medical profession. Establishing what that view is may cause the court some difficulty though. Each side is free to call its own experts and a clash of eminent medical opinion is not unusual.

Second, as liability, and the patient's right to compensation, is dependent on a finding of fault, doctors naturally feel that a judgment against them is a body blow to their career and their reputation. Yet a moment's reflection will remind the reader of all the mistakes he has made in his own job. A solicitor overlooking a vital piece of advice in a conference with a client can telephone the client and put things right when he has a chance to check what he has done. A carpenter can have a second go at fixing a door or a cupboard. An overworked, overstrained doctor may commit a momentary error which is irreversible. He is still a good doctor despite one mistake.

Finally, the doctor's fault must be shown to have caused the patient harm. In general, whether a patient is treated within the NHS or privately, the doctor only undertakes to do his best. He does not guarantee a cure. The patient will have a legal remedy only if he can show that the doctor's carelessness or lack of skill caused him injury that he would not otherwise have suffered. So if I contract an infection and am prescribed antibiotics that a competent doctor would have appreciated were inappropriate for me or my condition, I will be able to sue the doctor only if I can show either (1) that the antibiotic prescribed caused me harm unrelated to my original sickness, for example brought me out in a violent allergy, or (2) that the absence of appropriate treatment significantly delayed my recovery. And in both cases I must prove that had the doctor acted properly the harm to me would have been avoided.

We saw in Chapter 3 that to maintain an action in negligence the plaintiff must establish (i) that the doctor owed him a duty of care, (ii) that the duty was breached, (iii) that he suffered harm caused by that breach. Let us remind ourselves of the basic elements of a case in medical negligence by looking at a decision which acquired some notoriety:

Whitehouse v Jordan
[1981] 1 All ER 267 (House of Lords)
The facts are set out in the speech of Lord Wilberforce.

Lord Wilberforce: My Lords, Stuart Whitehouse is a boy now aged ten; he was born on 7th January 1970, with severe brain damage. In these circumstances, tragic for him and for his mother, this action has been brought, by his mother as next friend, in which he claims that the damage to his brain was caused by the professional negligence of Mr J A Jordan who was senior registrar at the hospital at Birmingham where the birth took place. There were originally also claims against Professor McLaren, the consultant in charge of the maternity unit to which Mr Jordan belonged, and also against the hospital on its own account. But these have disappeared and the hospital, more exactly the West Midlands Regional Health Authority, remains in the case only as vicariously responsible for any liability which may be established against Mr Jordan.

A large number of claims have been made since the event most of which have now been eliminated or withdrawn. The negligence ultimately charged against Mr Jordan is that in the course of carrying out a 'trial of forceps delivery', he pulled too long and too strongly on the child's head, thereby causing the brain damage. The trial judge, after a trial of 11 days in which eminent medical experts were called on each side, and numerous issues were canvassed, reached the conclusion which he expressed in a most careful judgment, that the plaintiff had made good his case: he awarded £100,000 damages. His decision was reversed by a majority of the Court of Appeal (Lord Denning MR and Lawton LJ, Donaldson LJ dissenting) ([1980] 1 All ER 650) which refused leave to appeal to this House. Leave was, however, granted by an Appeal Committee. The essential and very difficult question therefore has to be faced whether, on a pure question of fact, the Court of Appeal was justified in reversing the decision of the trial judge.

Mr Jordan was at the time a senior registrar, of near consultant status, esteemed by his professional colleagues. There is no question but that he brought the utmost care to bear on Mrs Whitehouse's labour and delivery. If he was negligent at all, this consisted in a departure, in an anxious situation, from a standard accepted by the profession at the time. Put very briefly, it was said to lie in continuing traction with the forceps after an obstruction had been encountered so that the baby's head 'impacted'. I shall not explain this word at this stage. It is obvious that the error, if error there was, lay centrally in the area of the exercise of expert judgment and experienced operation. Mr Jordan was a member of the obstetrical unit at the hospital headed by Professor McLaren, which had a high reputation; Professor McLaren himself was a distinguished obstetrician, unfortunately ill at the time of the birth.

Mrs Whitehouse was accepted as 30 years of age; this was her first baby. She was small, only 4ft 10½in in height. She was a difficult, nervous and at times aggressive patient. She was unable, or refused, to agree to vaginal examination during her pregnancy, or to have a lateral X-ray taken, though urged to do so by Professor McLaren. These processes would have helped to discover the exact shape of the pelvis. It is fair to say that when Mr Jordan came on the scene he was not greatly handicapped by this, because Mrs Whitehouse was at that time under epidural anaesthetic, and he was able to examine her vaginally. However, he had not the advantage of accurate measurements of the pelvis or of the ischial spines. . . . The mother was seen by a number of doctors in the course of her pregnancy including Professor McLaren and Mr Jordan. I do not think that any criticism can be made of what they did. She was identified clearly as likely to be a difficult case; on 31st

December 1969 Professor McLaren recorded that he thought the outlet was tight and that a trial of labour would be needed. This means that labour would be permitted to start and to proceed under close supervision in order to see whether the head could, with safety, proceed down the birth canal.

Mrs Whitehouse was admitted to the hospital at 0200 hrs on 6th January 1970, her membranes having ruptured shortly before. The vertex was recorded as engaged at 0230, and this was confirmed by Mr Kelly, of consultant status, at 1000 hrs. He noted 'fair sized baby'.

So at this point we have a small woman, anxious and distressed, awaiting a baby, for her on the large side, with the head in a favourable position and engaged in the pelvis; noted as being probably a case for 'trial of labour'. At 1130 she was given an epidural anaesthetic which would prevent her from feeling pain and probably from sensation below the waist.

At 1830 she was seen by Dr Skinner. He examined her vaginally and abdominally. He reported 'vertex engaged, fetal heart satisfactory . . . pelvis seems adequate'.

Now comes the period critical for this case. At 2330 Mr Jordan, who was not on duty, came to talk to Dr Skinner. On his radio communicator the latter was told that Mrs Whitehouse was fully dilated. Dr Skinner thought that this was the case for a more senior man than he, and Mr Jordan agreed to go; he saw her at 2330 and examined her abdominally and vaginally. He read the notes on the case, which, as the above summary shows, informed him precisely of what he had to deal with; a difficult case calling for great care.

He made a detailed note which I need not copy in full. It gave all the necessary medical details. Against 'pelvis' he wrote 'small gynaecoid' (ie of appropriate female shape) and then 'Normal delivery out of the question'.

He decided to embark on a trial of forceps and did so at 2345. The full expression for this is 'trial of forceps delivery' which, as the evidence showed beyond doubt, means the operator tries to see whether with the use of forceps a delivery per vaginam is possible. This involves two things, first tentative and delicate handling at least at the start; second the necessity of continuously reviewing progress with the obligation to stop traction if it appears that the delivery per vaginam cannot be proceeded with without risk. Then delivery will take place by Caesarian section.

Two things must be said at this stage. First, though for the plaintiff it was at one time otherwise contended, the decision to try for vaginal delivery rather than go at once to a Caesarian section was unquestionably the right and correct procedure, in order to avoid if possible the risk to the mother inevitably involved in section. Secondly, for the plaintiff an attempt was made to draw a line between trial of forceps, on the one hand, and delivery by forceps on the other hand, and to make a case that Mr Jordan was, unjustifiably, proceeding to the latter. This, to my mind, completely failed. There is no such clear-cut distinction. A trial of forceps (delivery) is what it says: it is an attempt at delivery accompanied by the two special conditions I have mentioned. There can be no doubt that this is what Mr Jordan was attempting. I take what happened from his notes. Under 'summary of reasons for operation' he wrote: 'Trial of forceps under epidural anaesthetic. Lower segment Caesarian section under GA'. Then:

(1) Forceps begun at 23 45, 6 1 70. Head rotated to OA [occiput anterior] with Kiellands—no problem. [Kiellands is a kind of forceps used by some operators to rotate the head. This procedure was correct]. A very tight fit. No episiotomy [cutting of the perineum]. After pulling with 5 or 6 contractions, it was obvious that vaginal delivery would be too traumatic—so Caesarian section.'

He then recorded the Caesarian which everyone agrees was impeccably performed in two minutes. He noted 'no apparent (vaginal) trauma'. To complete the history, the baby, extracted apparently unharmed, was handed over to the paediatricians, found apnoeic, and made to breathe after 35 minutes, by which time irretrievable brain damage had occurred.

Here, with one possible exception, is a record of a birth carried out with all correct procedures, with, as unhappily occurs in the best managed hospitals and the best medical care, tragic results. The possible exception lies in the reference in Mr

Jordan's own report to 'pulling with 5 or 6 contractions'. Did Mr Jordan pass the limits of professional competence either in continuing traction too long, or in pulling too hard? That is the whole issue.

Lord Edmund-Davies in his speech, identified the issues.

The principal questions calling for decision are: (a) in what manner did Mr Jordan use the forceps? and (b) was that manner consistent with the degree of skill which a member of his profession is required by law to exercise? Surprising though it is at this late stage in the development of the law of negligence, counsel for Mr Jordan persisted in submitting that his client should be completely exculpated were the answer to question (b), 'Well, at the worst he was guilty of an error of clinical judgment'.

We can learn many things from *Whitehouse*, not least is that cases of medical negligence exemplify, *par excellence*, the proposition that cases turn on facts as well as law. Indeed, proving the facts alleged is often the greatest hurdle faced by any plaintiff, whatever the law may be. *Whitehouse* also illustrates two further issues which continue to challenge lawyers and courts: the wholly legal problem of defining what a doctor's duty consists of and the question, which mixes law and fact, of how to establish whether a doctor was in breach of his duty in any particular set of circumstances. *Whitehouse* does not illustrate what we shall identify as a further major hurdle in establishing the liability of a doctor—the proof of causation, ie that the conduct of the doctor caused the harm complained of. We shall return to these two issues shortly. For the present, let us turn to the first element of an action in medical negligence—the existence of a duty to take care.

An action for medical negligence

1. DUTY OF CARE

(a) A doctor

Brazier observes that: '[a] patient claiming against his doctor . . . usually has no difficulty in establishing that the defendant owes him a duty of care'. (*Medicine, Patients and the Law*) The precise point at which a duty to take care comes into being may not be as easy as Brazier suggests, as our discussion in Chapter 2 illustrates.

Nevertheless, in general terms the essence of the duty is an undertaking by the doctor towards his patient. As Lord Hewart CJ said in *R v Bateman* (1925) 94 LJKB 791, CCA (a case of manslaughter brought against a doctor):

If a person holds himself out as possessing special skill and knowledge, and he is consulted, as possessing such skill and knowledge, by or on behalf of a patient, he owes a duty to the patient to use due caution in undertaking the treatment. If he accepts the responsibility and undertakes the treatment and the patient submits to his direction and treatment accordingly, he owes a duty to the patient to use diligence, care, knowledge, skill and caution in administering the treatment. No contractual relation is necessary, nor is it necessary that the service be rendered for reward.

This, of course, assumes something which already exists, namely that the individual has already become the doctor's patient (see Chapter 2 above).

As regards the NHS, the relationship of doctor and patient in the case of a GP is dealt with in the 1974 Regulations. Doctors who work within NHS hospitals do not come within these Regulations. Consequently, the creation of the doctor-patient relationship is wholly a matter for the common law, i e the existence or otherwise of an undertaking to take care. The common law position is illustrated by *Barnett v Chelsea and Kensington Hospital Management Committee* [1969] 1 QB 428, [1968] 1 All ER 1068.

Nield J: At about 5 am on Jan 1, 1966, three night watchmen drank some tea. Soon afterwards all three men started vomiting. At about 8 am the men walked to the casualty department of the defendants' hospital, which was open. One of them, the deceased, when he was in the room in the hospital, lay on some armless chairs. He appeared ill. Another of the men told the nurse that they had been vomiting after drinking tea. The nurse telephoned the casualty officer, a doctor, to tell him of the men's complaint. The casualty officer, who was himself unwell, did not see them, but said that they should go home and call in their own doctors. The men went away, and the deceased died some hours later from what was found to be arsenical poisoning. Cases of arsenical poisoning were rare, and, even if the deceased had been examined and admitted to the hospital and treated, there was little or no chance that the only effective antidote would have been administered to him before the time at which he died.

I turn to consider the nature of the duty which the law imposes on persons in the position of the defendants and their servants and agents. The authorities deal in the main with the duties of doctors, surgeons, consultants, nurses and staff when a person is treated either by a doctor at his surgery or the patient's home or when the patient is treated in or at a hospital. In *Cassidy v Ministry of Health*, Denning, LJ, dealt with the duties of hospital authorities and said:

> In my opinion, authorities who run a hospital, be they local authorities, government boards, or any other corporation, are in law under the self-same duty as the humblest doctor. Whenever they accept a patient for treatment, they must use reasonable care and skill to cure him of his ailment. The hospital authorities cannot, of course, do it by themselves. They have no ears to listen through the stethoscope, and no hands to hold the knife. They must do it by the staff which they employ, and, if their staff are negligent in giving the treatment, they are just as liable for that negligence as is anyone else who employs others to do his duties for him. Is there any possible difference in law, I ask, can there be, between hospital authorities who accept a patient for treatment and railway or shipping authorities who accept a passenger for carriage? None whatever. Once they undertake the task, they come under a duty to use care in the doing of it, and that is so whether they do it for reward or not.

Here the problem is different and no authority bearing directly on it has been cited to me. It is to determine the duty of those who provide and run a casualty department when a person presents himself at that department complaining of illness or injury and before he is treated and received into the hospital wards. This is not a case of a casualty department which closes its doors and says that no patients can be received. The three watchmen entered the defendants' hospital without hindrance, they made complaints to the nurse who received them and she in turn passed those complaints on to the medical casualty officer, and he sent a message through the nurse purporting to advise the three men. Is there, on these facts, shown to be created a relationship between the three watchmen and the hospital staff such as gives rise to a duty of care in the defendants which they owe to the three men?

. . . In my judgment, there was here such a close and direct relationship between the hospital and the watchmen that there was imposed on the hospital a duty of care which they owed to the watchmen. Thus I have no doubt that Nurse Corbett and Dr Banerjee were under a duty to the deceased to exercise that skill and care which is to be expected of persons in such positions acting reasonably, or, as it is, I think very helpfully, put by the learned author of Winfield on Torts (7th Edn) p 183—

> where anyone is engaged in a transaction in which he holds himself out as having professional skill, the law expects him to show the average amount of competence associated with the proper discharge of the duties of that profession or trade or

calling, and if he falls short of that and injures someone in consequence, he is not behaving reasonably.

Moreover, the author proceeds to give a warning that the rule must be applied with some care to see that too high a degree of skill is not demanded, and he gives as an example 'a passer-by who renders emergency first-aid after an accident is not required to show the skill of a qualified surgeon'.

The judge went on to find the doctor in breach of his duty in failing to examine and treat the deceased. His widow, nevertheless, lost her action because she could not show that this breach *caused* his death (see *infra* p 426).

As we have already seen, *Barnett* can be understood as a case concerned with a hospital's primary duty. The judge, nevertheless, deals with the case, at least in part, as one concerned with the doctor's duty of care (see his reference to Nurse Corbett and Doctor Banerjee at the end of the judgment set out).

(b) Health authority

(i) Primary liability

Picard, 'The Liability of Hospitals in Common Law Canada' (1981) 26 McGill LJ 997, 997—1010.

The earliest hospitals were charitable institutions and protected as such by the courts.[1] They were sustained by endowments and voluntary contributions, which were encouraged in England by the creation of the charitable trust.[2] In order to function hospitals had to purchase supplies of food and equipment, and hire persons to care for the patient and operate the physical plant. Provision was eventually made for some patients to pay for their accommodation.[3] Thus, of necessity, hospitals entered into legal relationships and became accountable under contracts, and by 1907 it was clear that a hospital was liable for the negligence of its employees.[4] But it was also held that a hospital could not be liable for the negligence of employees such as nurses or doctors in the execution of their professional duties, as opposed to administrative functions. The rationale for this limitation was that the hospital neither directed nor controlled the exercise of professional judgment.

In the *Hillyer* case the English Court of Appeal concluded that a hospital undertook certain duties toward a patient:

The governors of a public hospital, by their admission of the patient to enjoy in the hospital the gratuitous benefit of its care, do, I think, undertake that the patient whilst there shall be treated only by experts, whether surgeons, physicians or nurses, of whose professional competence the governors have taken reasonable care to assure themselves; and, further, that those experts shall have at their disposal, for the care and treatment of the patient, fit and proper apparatus and appliances.[5]

Thus, approximately seventy-five years ago, a patient had some recourse against a hospital: in contract, depending on the terms thereof, or in tort, if the hospital had breached its duty to select competent staff and to supply proper equipment, or by vicarious liability, subject to the restriction in the *Hillyer* case.

. . .

The first hospital patients were the cast-offs of society. The middle and upper classes were treated in their own homes by doctors who called on them there and they were cared for by servants and family. It was only the indigent who went to the hospitals, and the hospital and doctor provided their services gratuitously to such patients. A patient injured by either would have had an extremely difficult time pursuing any compensation through legal action.[20] An action in contract might well have failed for lack of intention, uncertainty of terms or lack of consideration.[21] An action in tort might have been brought in trespass to the person but consent could have been implied rather easily.[22] It was the negligence action of the mid-nineteenth century which first brought an opportunity for a patient to demand, in a court of law, that a hospital be held accountable for its actions. But the scope of such an action was quickly restricted by the courts, as outlined earlier. The two main bases for the liability of a hospital, namely a direct duty of care and vicarious liability, were carefully controlled so as to afford hospitals maximum immunity to the suits of patients.

The situation of the modern patient is very different. Today the hospital is the primary institution for health care [in Canada]. It is in the modern hospital that a patient can receive the best health care available because that is where the skill, knowledge and judgment of health-care professionals may be combined with modern medical equipment and technology. Today a patient comes to hospital not seeking charity, but highly skilled medical treatment and he might well have had his name on a waiting-list before being admitted!

... the greatest contrast between patients of the earlier hospitals and of the modern hospital lies in the legal relationships formed with the hospital. Any legal relationship the early patient had with a hospital was tenuous and if it gave rise to legal obligations the courts interpreted them restrictively.[24] The modern patient has strong, well-defined legal relationships with his hospital.

... His relationship, in fact, with a hospital is that of being a patient *of the hospital* and it gives rise to certain duties owed to him by the institution.[26] The hospital must not violate his right to be free from unauthorised touching, nor injure him by carrying out its duties in a sub-standard manner. The doctor-patient relationship likewise gives rise to certain duties but it is crucial to any analysis of the patient's position to remember that, while these duties of hospital and doctor may be concomitant, each set of duties is based on a separate and distinct relationship.

...

The earliest duty of care held to be owed by a hospital to a patient was to select competent staff in order that patients would be attended by skilled persons. At first this duty was very narrowly interpreted. A hospital had only to ascertain that its professionals were qualified and competent. This seemed to be the scope of its direct or personal or corporate duty of care.[59]

...

The scope of the direct duty was expanded, first to include the instruction and supervision of personnel employed by the hospital and then to the provision of the systems and organisation to co-ordinate these activities so that the patient received reasonable care.[61] Since a patient is treated in a physical plant with equipment and medical tools, it is not surprising that hospitals were also given a direct duty to provide and maintain proper facilities and equipment.[62]

There is some authority for the existence of other duties but often it is not clear whether the court was basing the hospital's accountability on grounds of direct liability or vicarious liability. These include a duty to establish procedures to prevent patients from harming themselves or being injured by other patients.[63] There are some older cases from which it might be concluded that a hospital has a duty to set up aseptic procedures and to protect patients and even visitors from infection.[64]

Though in theory it is possible for further duties to be created, a review of the cases[65] reveals that the courts have been most cautious when contrasted with their attitude respecting negligence law in general.[66]

In summary, the precedents support these possible direct duties of a hospital to a patient:

    a) to select competent and qualified employees
    b) to instruct and supervise them
    c) to provide proper facilities and equipment
    d) to establish systems necessary to the safe operation of the hospital.[67]

Since the other components of tort law apply, the hospital has to carry out these duties as competently as the reasonable hospital in the circumstances and, even if found sub-standard, would have to be found to have caused the patient's injuries before liability would result. All of the protection of tort law normally available to defendants is available to the hospital.[68]

The quality of the duties owed by a hospital has led to their sometimes being referred to as 'non-delegable'.[69] This has the significant effect of making the employer of an independent contractor strictly liable for any negligence of the contractor in carrying out the duty of care which was the employer's but which he had contracted or delegated to the independent contractor. This is an exception to the general rule that an employer is not liable for the negligence of an independent contractor employed by him.

. . . Fleming[81] discusses the kinds of cases where non-delegable duties have been found and notes that the list is 'long and diverse' extending from dangerous situations, hazardous substances, fire, lateral support for land, maintenance of premises abutting a highway to instances where the duty would normally be to use reasonable care but where the designation of the duty as non-delegable assures that care will be taken (provision of a safe system of work, compliance with statutory safety standards, responsibilities of occupiers of land to certain others and of hospitals to care for their patients).

Notes to extract

[1] The derivation of 'hospital' from *hospitalis*, in Latin meaning 'a place for guests', is of some etymological interest: see the *Oxford English Dictionary*.

[2] 43 Eliz 1, c 4: see Speller, *The Law Relating to Hospitals and Kindred Institutions*, 4th ed (1978), 3.

[3] *Ibid*, 101.

[4] *Hillyer v Governors of St Bartholomew's Hospital* [1909] 2 KB 820 CA.

[5] *Ibid*, 829.

. . .

[20] See Picard, *supra*, note 17 [*Legal Liability of Doctors and Hospitals in Canada* (1978)], 17–24.

[21] *Ibid*, 51–8.

[22] See *Latter v Braddell* (1881) 50 LJQB 448 CA.

. . .

[24] [*Hillyer v The Governors of St Bartholomew's Hospital* [1909] 2 KB 820].

. . .

[26] See Hamson, 'The Liability of Hospitals for Negligence' in *The Law in Action* (1954) 19, 26–7.

. . .

[59] While the three terms are synonymous and refer to the 'normal' duty of care, all are used by various authors who wish to be understood as differentiating this from vicarious liability.

. . .

[61] [Picard, *op cit*], 251–9. The duty to provide organisation could be expanded to include the provision of medical treatment by doctors who are not employees: see Nathan, *supra*, note 44 [*Medical Negligence* (1957)], 144.

[62] *Picard, supra*, note 17, 259–61.

[63] *Ibid*, 257–8.

[64] *Ibid*, 257: see Nathan, *supra*, note 44, 103.

[65] See generally Picard, *supra*, note 17, 248–61.

[66] Linden, *supra*, note 46 [*Canadian Tort Law*, 2nd ed (1977)], 264.

[67] See Picard, *supra*, note 17, 251–6; Rozovsky, *supra*, note 12 [*Canadian Hospital Law* (1979)], 16–7.

[68] Picard, *supra*, note 17, 169–95.

[69] *Yepremian v Scarborough General Hospital, supra*, note 31; *Gold v Essex County Council* [1942] 2 KB 293, 297 CA *per* Lord Greene, MR; *Cassidy v Minister of Health* [1951] 2 KB 343 at 359 *per* Denning LJ; see also Nathan, *supra*, note 44, 123, 129, 132.

. . .

[81] Fleming, [*The Law of Torts*, 5th ed (1977)] 378; citations to relevant case law may be found therein.

The issue of primary liability of the hospital authority received considerable attention in the immediate aftermath of the creation of the NHS.

Cassidy v Ministry of Health
[1951] 2 KB 343, [1951] 1 All ER 574, CA

The plaintiff entered hospital for an operation on his left hand. At the end of post-operative treatment his hand was made worse. He sued the Minister responsible for the hospital. The Court of Appeal allowed an appeal by the plaintiff and held the hospital authority liable.

Denning LJ: If a man goes to a doctor because he is ill, no one doubts that the doctor must exercise reasonable care and skill in his treatment of him: and that is so whether the doctor is paid for his services or not. But if the doctor is unable to treat the man himself and sends him to hospital, are not the hospital authorities then under a duty of care in their treatment of him? I think they are. Clearly, if he is a paying patient, paying them directly for their treatment of him, they must take reasonable care of him; and why should it make any difference if he does not pay them directly, but only indirectly through the rates which he pays to the local authority or through insurance contributions which he makes in order to get the treatment? I see no difference at all. Even if he is so poor that he can pay nothing, and the hospital treats him out of charity, still the hospital authorities are under a duty to take reasonable care of him just as the doctor is who treats him without asking a fee. In my opinion authorities who run a hospital, be they local authorities, government boards, or any other corporation, are in law under the self same duty as the humblest doctor; whenever they accept a patient for treatment, they must use reasonable care and skill to cure him of his ailment. The hospital authorities cannot, of course, do it by themselves: they have no ears to listen through the stethoscope, and no hands to hold the surgeon's knife. They must do it by the staff which they employ; and if their staff are negligent in giving the treatment, they are just as liable for that negligence as is anyone else who employs others to do his duties for him. What possible difference in law, I ask, can there be between hospital authorities who accept a patient for treatment, and railway or shipping authorities who accept a passenger for carriage? None whatever. Once they undertake the task, they come under a duty to use care in the doing of it, and that is so whether they do it for reward or not.

. . . Where the doctor or surgeon, be he a consultant or not, is employed and paid, not by the patient but by the hospital authorities, I am of opinion that the hospital authorities are liable for his negligence in treating the patient. It does not depend on whether the contract under which he was employed was a contract of service or a contract for services. That is a fine distinction which is sometimes of importance; but not in cases such as the present, where the hospital authorities are themselves under a duty to use care in treating the patient.

I take it to be clear law, as well as good sense, that, where a person is himself under a duty to use care, he cannot get rid of his responsibility by delegating the performance of it to someone else, no matter whether the delegation be to a servant under a contract of service or to an independent contractor under a contract for services.

. . .

It is unfortunate that the principle which I have enunciated was not drawn to the attention of the court in *Gold's* case, but that was my fault, because I was counsel in the case. It was plain there that, if the radiographer was employed under a contract of service, the hospital authorities were liable for his negligence; and I contented myself with showing that he was, citing even workmen's compensation cases for the purpose. This was a bad example, for I see that workmen's compensation cases figured prominently in the later case of *Collins v Hertfordshire County Council*. Hence the courts have drifted almost unconsciously into the error of making the liability of hospital authorities depend on whether the negligent person was employed under a contract of service or a contract for services. The judgment of Lord Greene, MR, in *Gold's* case, however, gives no countenance to this error. He made the liability depend on what was the obligation which rested on the hospital authorities. He showed that hospital authorities were under an obligation to use reasonable care in treatment; see especially what he said at p 304 of his judgment: whence it follows, on the authorities I have just cited, that they cannot get rid of that obligation by delegating it to someone else, not even to a doctor or surgeon under contract for services. If these authorities had been put before Hilbery J, in *Collins'* case I think he would in all probability have found the hospital authorities liable, not only for the negligence of the resident medical officer Miss Knight, but also for that of the part-time paid surgeon Mr. Hunt. Hilbery J, clearly thought that the hospital authorities ought to be liable for the surgeon, but only decided otherwise because of the test of contract of service, which he felt bound to apply. Once that is out of the way, their liability is clear.

. . .

Turning now to the facts in this case, this is the position: the hospital authorities accepted the plaintiff as a patient for treatment, and it was their duty to treat him with reasonable care. They selected, employed, and paid all the surgeons and nurses who looked after him. He had no say in their selection at all. If those surgeons and nurses did not treat him with proper care and skill, then the hospital authorities must answer for it, for it means that they themselves did not perform their duty to him. I decline to enter into the question whether any of the surgeons were employed only under a contract for services, as distinct from a contract of service. The evidence is meagre enough in all conscience on that point. But the liability of the hospital authorities should not, and does not, depend on nice considerations of that sort. The plaintiff knew nothing of the terms on which they employed their staff: all he knew was that he was treated in the hospital by people whom the hospital authorities appointed; and the hospital authorities must be answerable for the way in which he was treated.

(Somervell and Singleton LJJ held the hospital authority to be liable on the basis of vicarious liability.)

Roe v Minister of Health
[1954] 2 QB 66, [1954] 2 All ER 131, CA

Denning LJ: No one can be unmoved by the disaster which has befallen these two unfortunate men. They were both working men before they went into the Chesterfield Hospital in October, 1947. Both were insured contributors to the hospital, paying a small sum each week, in return for which they were entitled to be admitted for treatment when they were ill. Each of them was operated on in the hospital for a minor trouble, one for something wrong with a cartilage in his knee, the other for a hydrocele. The operations were both on the same day, October 13, 1947. Each of them was given a spinal anaesthetic by a visiting anaesthetist, Dr Graham. Each of them has in consequence been paralysed from the waist down.

The judge has said that those facts do not speak for themselves, but I think that they do. They certainly call for an explanation. Each of these men is entitled to say to the hospital: 'While I was in your hands something has been done to me which has wrecked my life. Please explain how it has come to pass'. The reason why the judge took a different view was because he thought that the hospital authorities could disclaim responsibility for the anaesthetist, Dr Graham: and, as it might be his fault and not theirs, the hospital authorities were not called upon to give an explanation. I think that that reasoning is wrong. In the first place, I think that the hospital authorities are responsible for the whole of their staff, not only for the nurses and doctors, but also for the anaesthetists and the surgeons. It does not matter whether they are permanent or temporary, resident or visiting, whole-time or part-time. The hospital authorities are responsible for all of them. The reason is because, even if they are not servants, they are the agents of the hospital to give the treatment. The only exception is the case of consultants or anaesthetists selected and employed by the patient himself. I went into the matter with some care in *Cassidy v Ministry of Health* and I adhere to all I there said.

Morris LJ: . . . In *Gold v Essex County Council* Lord Greene MR pointed out that in cases of this nature the first task is to discover the extent of the obligation assumed by the person whom it is sought to be made liable. He added: 'Once this is discovered, it follows of necessity that the person accused of a breach of the obligation cannot escape liability because he has employed another person, whether a servant or agent, to discharge it on his behalf, and this is equally true whether or not the obligation involves the use of skill'. In the present cases the judge held that both plaintiffs were contributors for hospital and surgical treatment under a contributory scheme run by the hospital, so that they made some contributions which were received by the hospital for their treatment. The exact details of the scheme which the hospital had run were not before us and they might not have added materially to the facts proved. While the requisite standard of care does not vary according as to whether treatment is gratuitous or on payment, the existence of arrangements entitling the plaintiffs to expect certain treatment might be a relevant factor when considering the extent of the obligation assumed by the hospital.

In his judgment in *Gold v Essex County Council* Lord Greene analysed the position of the various persons in the 'organisation' of the hospital to which the plaintiff in that case resorted for free advice and treatment. He said: 'The position of the nurses again . . . if the nature of their employment, both as to its terms and as to the work performed, is what it usually is in such institutions I cannot myself see any sufficient ground for saying that the defendants do not undertake towards the patient the obligation of nursing him as distinct from the obligation of providing a skilful nurse'. This passage conveniently demonstrates a contrast. A hospital might assume the obligation of nursing: it might on the other hand merely assume the obligation of providing a skilful nurse. But the question as to what obligation a hospital has assumed becomes, as it seems to me, ultimately a question of fact to be decided having regard to the particular circumstances of each particular case: the ascertainment of the fact may require in some cases inference or deduction from proved or known facts. In the present case we are concerned only with the position of Dr Graham in 1947 in this voluntary hospital.

The general position in regard to nurses would appear to be reasonably uniform and clear. In *Gold's* case Lord Greene said: 'Nursing, it appears to me, is just what the patient is entitled to expect from the institution, and the relationship of the nurses to the institution supports the inference that they are engaged to nurse the patients. In the case of a nursing home conducted for profit, a patient would be surprised to be told that the home does not undertake to nurse him. In the case of a voluntary hospital with the usual nursing staff his just expectation would surely be the same. The idea that in the case of a voluntary hospital the only obligation which the hospital undertakes to perform by its nursing staff is not the essential work of nursing but only so-called administrative work appears to me, with all respect to those who have thought otherwise, not merely unworkable in practice but contrary to the plain sense of the position'. On the principles so clearly enunciated the court in that case held that the hospital had assumed the obligation of treating a patient who sought treatment by Grenz rays and of giving the treatment by the hand of a competent radiographer. That was the natural and reasonable inference to be drawn from the way in which those running the hospital conducted their affairs and from the nature of the engagement of the radiographer.

If a patient in 1947 entered a voluntary hospital for an operation it might be that if the operation was to be performed by a visiting surgeon the hospital would not undertake, so far as concerned the actual surgery itself, to do more than to make the necessary arrangements to secure the services of a skilled and competent surgeon. The facts and features of each particular case would require investigation. But a hospital might in any event have undertaken to provide all the necessary facilities and equipment for the operation and the obligation of nursing and also the obligation of anaesthetising a patient for his operation. The question in the present case is whether the hospital undertook these obligations. In my judgment they did. There can be no doubt that they undertook to nurse the plaintiffs and to provide the necessary facilities and equipment for the operations. I think they further undertook to anaesthetise the plaintiffs. The arrangements made between the hospital and Dr Pooler and Dr Graham, together with the arrangements by which a resident anaesthetist was employed, had the result that the hospital provided a constantly available anaesthetic service to cover all types of cases.

It is true that Dr Pooler and Dr Graham could arrange between themselves as to when they would respectively be on duty at the hospital: and each was free to do private work. But these facts do not negative the view, to which all the circumstances point, that the hospital was assuming the obligation of anaesthetising the plaintiffs for their operations. I consider that the anaesthetists were members of the 'organisation' of the hospital: they were members of the staff engaged by the hospital to do what the hospital itself was undertaking to do. The work which Dr Graham was employed by the hospital to do was work of a highly skilled and specialised nature, but this fact does not avoid the application of the rule of 'respondeat superior'. If Dr Graham was negligent in doing his work I consider that the hospital would be just as responsible as were the defendants in *Gold v Essex County Council* for the negligence of the radiographer or as were the defendants in *Cassidy v Ministry of Health*. I have approached the present case, therefore, on the basis that the defendants would be liable if the plaintiffs' injuries were caused by the negligence either of Dr Graham or by the negligence of someone on the staff who was concerned with the operation or the preparation for it. On this basis, if negligence could be established against one or more of those for whom the hospital was responsible, it would not matter if the plaintiffs could not point to the exact person or persons who had been negligent.

The Court of Appeal (including Somervell LJ) held that the plaintiffs had failed to establish that the defendants had been careless.

What precise guidance do these cases provide as to (a) the existence of a primary duty and, if so, (b) its scope?

Was it necessary for the courts to answer these questions? Arguably as most medical staff joined the NHS in one way or another the courts were able to fix the hospital with liability vicariously and did not need to pursue the issue of primary liability (see infra p 391 *et seq*).

The English law was considered in 1980 by the Ontario Court of Appeal in *Yepremian v Scarborough General Hospital* (1980) 110 DLR (3d) 513, in reaching a view on the legal principles governing the primary duty of hospitals in Canada. The court was divided.

The facts are set out in the headnote.

The plaintiff suffered a cardiac arrest with resultant brain damage at defendant hospital following the commencement of treatment for a diagnosed diabetic condition. The plaintiff had come home from work on a week-end feeling unwell. He was vomiting and had increased frequency of urination and increased frequency of drinking. The family doctor being away, his family took the plaintiff to see G, a physician, who had obtained his degree in medicine a year earlier, and was working in research, but who filled in on some week-ends as a doctor's replacement. G diagnosed tonsillitis, gave a prescription, and said it was unnecessary to take the plaintiff to a hospital. Later that night at home, the plaintiff began to hyperventilate and his family took him to the emergency department of the defendant hospital, where C, a general practitioner with hospital privileges, was on duty, C did not order a urinalysis and made no diagnosis, other than noting plaintiff's hyperventilation on the emergency record. Following two telephone calls to R, the internist on call and an endocrinologist, the plaintiff was admitted to the intensive care unit of the hospital. Eleven hours later, as a result of a nurse's observations, a diagnosis of diabetes was made. The plaintiff was immediately started on insulin. He continued to hyperventilate and remained unconscious or semi-conscious until he suffered the cardiac arrest about 12 hours later.

The majority view was expressed by Arrup JA and MacKinnon ACJO (Morden JA delivered a concurring judgment).

Arrup JA: Beyond doubt a patient admitted to a hospital expects to receive not only accommodation, food and competent nursing care but also competent medical care. The question still remains: does the hospital undertake to provide that medical care, or does it undertake to select competent doctors who will provide it?

...

The trial Judge has founded liability upon a breach of the hospital's *own* duty— not that of any employed doctor, or of a doctor chosen by it to be on its staff, but an independent duty of its own, which is breached if there is a failure by a specialist on its staff to use reasonable skill and competence in the treatment of a patient in the hospital under his care. I agree that unless there exists in law a 'non-delegable duty of care' owed by the hospital to the patient, the hospital is not liable in this case.

No Court in Canada has even found before that such a duty exists, and with great respect to the trial Judge, I am not persuaded by his reasons that there is such a duty. I am not dismissing those reasons perfunctorily, nor intended to denigrate them, when I say that he seems to me to be saying, in substance, 'In all the circumstances, the hospital *ought* to be liable.' In my view, if the criterion is to be what is fair and reasonable, it would be fair and reasonable that the highly-skilled doctor whose negligence caused the damage should be called upon to pay for it. As the trial Judge did, I must put out of my mind that the plaintiffs chose not to sue him.

I agree with the trial Judge (and have said this earlier in my reasons) that the Yepremians had every right to expect that a large public hospital like Scarborough General would provide whatever was required to treat seriously ill or injured people, but I do not think it follows that the public is entitled to add the further expectation: 'and if any doctor on the medical staff makes a negligent mistake, the hospital will pay for it'.

Rather, I think, a member of the public who knows the facts is entitled to expect that the hospital has picked its medical staff with great care, has checked out the credentials of every applicant, has caused the existing staff to make a recommendation in every individual case, makes no appointment for longer than one year at a time, and reviews the performance of its staff at regular intervals. Putting it in layman's language, a prospective patient or his family who knew none of the facts, would think: 'If I go to Scarborough General, I'll get a good doctor.'

The background facts of this case, including the absence of any choice by the Yepremians as to the doctor in emergency or as to the internist called in, are quite consistent with my statement of what they could reasonably expect to be available. There being no finding that Dr Rosen was unqualified or incompetent, nor that there was anything other than careful consideration and good judgment on the part of the hospital before appointing him to the staff, the hospital fully discharged its obligation to provide competent internal medicine services to Tony Yepremian following his admission to the hospital.

... Great care must be exercised in considering the English cases. The interrelationships of the State, the medical profession, the hospitals and their patients have developed along different lines from those in Ontario. This note of caution was injected by Aylesworth, J.A., in *Aynsley v. Toronto General Hospital* [1969] 2 OR 829 at 844, 7 DLR (3d) 193 at 208; affd [1972] SCR 435 *sub nom Trustees of Toronto General Hospital v Matthews* 25 DLR (3d) 241, where he said that '[T]he introduction into England of nationalised medicine probably has greatly altered the factual situation in that country ...'. ...

(The judge then referred to several Canadian cases and *Roe, Cassidy, Gold* and *Hillyer* and continued:)

I refer back to my note of caution in applying the English cases. What, in the Canadian context, constitutes the 'permanent staff'? What did Morris, LJ, mean by 'members of the "organisation" of the hospital'? As long ago as 1966, Professor Allen Linden (now Linden, J) considered whether the English authorities should be adopted in Canada, in the light of 'different attitudes and practices' in Canada, and suggested that because of such differences, the reception of 'the English rule' might not be justified: see 'Changing Patterns of Hospital Liability in Canada', 5 *Alta L*

Rev 212 at p 217 (1966–67). *Clerk & Lindsell on Torts*, 14th ed (1975) [at p 131], in discussing the modern tendency in England to treat the question of the hospital's liability as raising questions of primary as well as vicarious liability, refers to the duty imposed upon the Minister of Health by s 3 of the *National Health Service Act, 1946* to provide 'medical, nursing or other services required at or for the purposes of hospitals' and 'the services of specialists'. No similar duty has been imposed upon Ontario hospitals by the *Public Hospitals Act*, with respect to the services of specialists or other medical practitioners.

The Government exercises a substantial degree of control over public hospitals, through Regulations and especially through the hospitals' finances. If liability is to be imposed upon hospitals for the negligence of its medical staff, including specialists, not employed by the hospitals, whether directly or by imposing a statutory duty to provide such services, it should be the function of the Legislature, as a policy question, to decide whether and under what conditions such liability is to attach.

MacKinnon ACJO: It was pressed upon us, and I think properly, that the medical profession and hospitals have ordered their professional lives and practices in a particular way in this Province for many years. The practice of medicine and the operation of hospitals have been conducted on the understanding and belief that the law established and supported the independence of the medical profession, in the manner in which they practised, free from the control and direction of hospital boards, unless they were servants or employees (as those words are commonly understood) of the hospital. The Courts hitherto have supported this view.

No matter how much our sympathies may be engaged in a particular case, in my view to reverse the long-standing experience and law would be to enter into a matter of policy, the consequence of such entry being unexamined and unknown to us, and which requires public debate and consideration. I do not view the issue as a novel one—quite the contrary. It is an issue which, if changes were to be effected, would now require the legislative intervention based on a consideration of all the ramifications of such change, particularly its effect on public institutions and on a profession which has cherished its independence. To alter the legal position now by judicial legislation would not, in my view, be appropriate.

The present legal situation, even though one might conclude it would be 'better' or 'fairer' or 'more logical' to fix hospitals with responsibility for the negligence of doctors who are carrying out their medical duties by virtue of having been granted 'hospital privileges', does not, of course, prevent injured parties from suing the negligent doctors. If that had been done in the instant case the Court would not, I am sure, have been faced with the task of seeking to establish a new principle by destroying an old one and declaring a liability relationship based on facts and circumstances that have long existed in this Province and which have hitherto been otherwise interpreted.

The minority view was expressed by Blair and Houlden JJA.

Blair JA: . . . It is . . . well established that the hospital is liable to a patient directly for failure to provide what, in other areas of tort liability, would be called a 'safe system'. Thus a hospital is liable for injury to the patient from inadequate or improperly maintained equipment: *Vuchar v Trustees of Toronto General Hospital* [1937] OR 71, [1937] 1 DLR 298 CA; for failure to provide proper measures for protecting a disturbed person from injuring himself or other patients: *Lepine v University Hospital Board* (1964) 50 DLR (2d) 225, 50 WWR 709 and 765*n* (Alta SC) [varied 54 DLR (2d) 340, 53 WWR 513 and 704; revsd [1966] SCR 561, 57 DLR (2d) 701, 57 WWR 5], and *Wellesley Hospital v Lawson* [1978] 1 SCR 893, 76 DLR (3d) 688, 15 NR 271; for failure to provide sufficient personnel to permit rotation of nurses without danger to patients, as exemplified in the 'coffee-break' cases: *Laidlaw v Lions Gate Hospital* (1969) 8 DLR (3d) 730, 70 WWR 727 (BCSC); *Krujelis v Esdale* (1971) 25 DLR (3d) 557, [1972] 2 WWR 495 (BCSC). In some cases, the line is blurred between injury caused by the failure of the hospital to provide proper equipment or organisation and injury caused by the negligence of employees; none the less, the principle of direct liability is well established by the authorities. It is particularly demonstrated by the common law principle, accepted in *Hillyer's* case and elaborated by statute, that a hospital is responsible for the proper selection of qualified doctors to serve on its staff.

. . . [The hospital] contends that its responsibility to the patient is simply to ensure the provision of medical services by properly-qualified doctors without accepting any responsibility to the patient for the manner in which doctors perform those services.

In the view I take of this case, nothing substantial turns on the manner in which the hospital originally selects and, on an ongoing basis, reviews the competence of its medical staff. The *Public Hospitals Act*, RSO 1970, c 378, s 41, contemplates that this important function will be performed by the medical staff itself, through the medical advisory committee and the chiefs of the various services. Further, it is unnecessary to decide whether the Hospital has any opportunity to control the quality of medical services provided by the medical staff or whether, by its practices and requirements, it causes the medical staff to surrender some independence to the Hospital. Whatever the relationship between the Hospital and its medical staff, the Hospital itself remains responsible for the proper operation of the Hospital system and the related functions of record-keeping and the effective transmission of information within the institution. However the system operates, the Hospital, in the final analysis. is responsible for it and must accept liability in the event of its failure.

. . .

Two questions arise in determining whether in this case the Hospital was under a duty to provide non-negligent medical treatment. The first is whether a hospital *could* have undertaken such a duty. The second is whether it *did*. In my view, both questions must be answered in the affirmative.

The theory upon which such direct liability is founded appears from the judgments of the English Court of Appeal in the famous trilogy of cases: *Gold v Essex County Council* [1942] 2 KB 293; *Cassidy v Ministry of Health* [1951] 2 KB 343, [1951] 1 All ER 574, and *Roe v Minister of Health* [1954] 2 QB 66, [1954] 2 All ER 131.

(The judge then examined these cases and continued:)

The effect of *Gold* and *Cassidy* was finally to displace the rule in *Hillyer's* case and make hospitals vicariously liable for the negligence of doctors employed by them. That this is the *ratio decidendi* derived from the majority judgments in both cases is beyond dispute. The principle deducible from the opinions of the Court of Appeal in *Roe* is less clear. What is important in the present case is not the rule of vicarious liability which these cases establish but the other views on liability expressed by the Judges. Their dicta have been examined meticulously as if they were scriptural texts in the careful arguments addressed to us. Two opposing arguments are based on them.

The respondents argue that the broad basis of liability propounded by Lord Greene in *Gold* and Lord Denning in *Cassidy* and *Roe* supports the judgment of Holland, J. The appellants contend that the opinion expressed by several Judges that the position of consultants is different from that of employed doctors precludes any action based on the negligence of Dr Rosen, who was a non-salaried member of the medical staff. It is conceded that these expressions of opinion were not necessary to the decision in any of these cases and neither issue was decided by them. It is necessary now to consider the degree to which the principles expressed in these dicta can apply in this case.

There is a clear line linking the views of Lord Greene in *Gold* and those of Lord Denning in *Cassidy*, and Lord Denning and Morris, LJ, in *Roe*. Taken together they constitute a developing and yet unified approach to the question of a hospital's obligations. Lord Greene in *Gold* considered that the extent of the obligation undertaken by the hospital had to be determined on the basis of the facts in each case. Lord Denning in *Cassidy* and *Roe* went further and endeavoured to lay down a general principle of law imposing a duty of care on the hospital except where the patient was served by his own doctor. Morris, LJ, in *Roe* preferred Lord Greene's approach and as Lord Nathan in *Medical Negligence* states at p 132:

> ... he clearly indicated that in his view the exact extent of a hospital's obligations can only be decided by considering the circumstances of each particular case in which the question arises.

In my opinion Lord Nathan, *op. cit.*, correctly concluded that the effect of these decisions is to establish that in some cases a hospital can undertake a direct duty to provide treatment to patients. His conclusion is stated at pp 132–3 as follows:

> In these circumstances it can be stated with some confidence that the weight of modern authority favours the view that a hospital authority by receiving a patient undertakes a personal obligation or duty towards that patient, for the breach of which it cannot escape liability by saying that it employed competent persons to discharge the obligation or duty on its behalf; but that the exact extent of the duty is a question of fact in each particular case. This of course leaves unsolved the question, by what criteria is the extent of the obligation or duty to be determined? An examination of the decided cases shows that amongst the relevant considerations for this purpose may be the status of the hospital, the nature of the arrangements it makes for the provision of staff, and the relationship between the hospital and the patient. It will be seen, however, that in past cases the Courts have been inclined to impose uniform obligations upon hospitals, regardless of any differences in status and irrespective of whether the patient in question paid for his treatment or not; so it may well be that the exact consideration of circumstances prescribed by Lord Greene and Morris LJ, will lead to the same generalised conclusion as that contended for by Denning LJ.

Fleming, *The Law of Torts*, 5th ed (1977), states the same proposition more emphatically at the conclusion of the description of erosion of the rule in *Hillyer's* case at pp 361–2:

> Thus hospitals became successively liable for the negligence of their nurses, resident medical officers, radiographers, and even part-time anaesthetists and special consultants. The uncontrollability of such professionals in the performance of their tasks no longer precludes recovery, so long as they are part of the hospital organisation and not employed by the patient himself. Indeed, according to a view which has lately gained increasing support, the distinction between servants and independent contractors may really be irrelevant in this context, because a hospital by receiving a patient assumes a non-delegable, personal duty to ensure that he receives careful treatment at the hands of such staff as it provides, including even visiting specialists and other independent consultants.

This broader basis for direct liability of hospitals is acknowledged in other decisions which have been expressed in more conventional language. I have already referred to the judgments of Somervell and Morris, LJJ, in *Roe's* case where with the greatest of difficulty they dealt with the anaesthetists 'as if' they were employees. The language of Morris LJ [at p 91], provides a parallel for the present case in that he described the anaesthetists as 'members of the "organisation" of the hospital: they were members of the staff engaged by the hospital to do what the hospital itself was undertaking to do'.

. . .

No case binding on this Court has held that hospitals are liable only for negligence of doctors employed by them. Some reservations have been expressed in the English cases, as I have noted, about a hospital's liability for the negligence of doctors variously described as visiting surgeons or consultants. There is no evidence before this Court that such positions in English hospitals are comparable to the positions of the medical staff in Ontario hospitals, and counsel were unable to assist us in this matter. However, assuming that the positions are roughly comparable, it is still the case that the reservations expressed in the English cases are mere *obiter dicta*. They do not preclude this Court from considering whether the Hospital may be liable for the negligence of a member of its medical staff. Because of this Lord Nathan's comments on the liability of visiting consultants are illuminating. He said at pp 143–4:

If the liability of hospitals for the negligence of their staff were in truth a purely vicarious liability, there would, of course, be a great deal to be said for the view that they could escape liability for the negligence of visiting surgeons, for such surgeons might well fall within the category of 'independent contractors' and not within that of servants; although it should be observed that the fact that a person has only a part-time appointment is not necessarily incompatible with his being a servant. But if it is accepted that the liability of a hospital is a personal liability depending upon the extent of the obligation undertaken by the hospital towards the patient, it is surely difficult to come to any other conclusion than that the hospital's obligation extends to treating the patient by the hands of the staff comprised in its organisation, including visiting surgeons and physicians.

In the circumstances of this case, it is the relationship between the patient and the Hospital which is paramount in ascertaining the extent of the Hospital's duty. (In other cases, the relationship between the doctor and the hospital may be more important.)

. . .

The recognition of a direct duty of hospitals to provide non-negligent medical treatment reflects the reality of the relationship between hospitals and the public in contemporary society. This direct duty arises from profound changes in social structures and public attitudes relating to medical services and the concomitant changes in the function of hospitals in providing them. It is obvious that as a result of these changes the role of hospitals in the delivery of medical services has expanded. The public increasingly relies on hospitals to provide medical treatment and, in particular, on emergency services. Hospitals to a growing extent hold out to the public that they provide such treatment and such services.

At the outset of my review of the hospital's duty in tort I asked whether the Hospital *could* have undertaken a direct duty to provide medical treatment, and whether in the circumstances of this case it *did*. From the foregoing I conclude that the common law does recognise that hospitals *can* in certain circumstances be directly liable to patients for the negligent performance of medical services, as held by Holland J. As Lords Greene, Morris and Nathan have observed, whether and to what extent a hospital assumes a direct duty depends upon the circumstances of the particular case. I am of the opinion that in the circumstances of this case the Hospital *is* liable. It is unnecessary to refer again to the facts which I have quoted from the judgment of Holland J. In the emergency, the Hospital provided, as it held itself out to do, the only means of obtaining medical care for Tony. His life was placed completely in the Hospital's hands. He and his family relied entirely on the Hospital to use its resources of equipment and skilled, but anonymous, personnel to restore his health. With the greatest of respect for those who hold the contrary view, I believe that, in the circumstances of this case, the Hospital's obligation to Tony could not be limited merely to placing a qualified doctor at his disposal. The hospital assumed and would be expected to assume complete responsibility for Tony's treatment.

Houlden JA: . . . The functions performed by general hospitals can be divided into two classifications, and I believe these classifications can be used to determine the duty of care owed by a hospital to a patient. . . .

First, a general hospital may function as a place where medical care facilities are provided for the use of a physician and his patient. The patient comes to the hospital because his physician has decided that the hospital's facilities are needed for the proper care and treatment of the patient. This use of the hospital is made possible by an arrangement between the hospital and the physician by which the physician is granted hospital privileges. Where a hospital functions as merely the provider of medical care facilities, then, as the trial Judge pointed out, a hospital is not responsible for the negligence of the physician. The present case does not, of course, come within this classification.

Second, a general hospital may function as a place where a person in need of treatment goes to obtain treatment. Here the role of the hospital is that of an institution where medical treatment is made available to those who require it. The present case falls in this second classification. Tony Yepremian was brought to the Scarborough General Hospital because he was in need of treatment. Does a hospital in these circumstances have the duty to provide proper medical care to a patient? In my judgment, it does.

. . .

The provision of a wide range of medical services is . . . an integral and essential part of the operation of a modern, general hospital. This is so regardless of the way in which the hospital has structured its relationship with the professional personnel who provide those services. While the negligent act may be committed by a particular individual, that act is part of the over-all medical care provided by the hospital. It is medical care that is sought by the patient; and it is proper medical care that should be provided. The primary responsibility for the provision of this medical care is, in my opinion, that of the hospital, and the hospital cannot delegate that responsibility to others so as to relieve itself of liability.

I would therefore define the duty of care of a general hospital . . . in this way: Where a person goes to a general hospital to obtain treatment and the hospital accepts him as a patient, the hospital has a non-delegable duty to use reasonable care and skill in treating him. This duty will, of course, be carried out by the members of the hospital's staff, and if breached, the hospital will be liable to the patient even though the physician who committed the negligent act was not an employee of the hospital and even though the hospital used all due care in granting hospital privileges to the physician.

It was submitted by counsel for the hospital that the creation of such a duty will require hospitals, in order to protect themselves from liability, to supervise and scrutinize the practice of medicine by physicians. In turn, this could interfere with the independence of physicians, as well as inhibit innovation and experimentation. Progress in medical science and the provision of novel and imaginative medical services would be retarded. I find these submissions unpersuasive. I see no reason why, with diligent effort, tolerance, and compromise, these problems, if they arise, cannot be solved. However, the issue in this case is not the finding of a solution for these problems, but who should bear the responsibility for the negligent treatment that was given to Tony Yepremian. In my opinion, the hospital must bear that responsibility.

Questions

(i) Which of these positions do you find more persuasive?
(ii) Whichever view you accept does it help you to determine when the duty arises?

In 1986, however, the Court of Appeal was asked to consider an argument based upon a breach of a health authority's primary duty.

Wilsher v Essex Area Health Authority

[1987] QB 730, [1986] 3 All ER 801. The facts are taken from the headnote:

The plaintiff was an infant child who was born prematurely suffering from various illnesses, including oxygen deficiency. His prospects of survival were considered to be poor and he was placed in the 24-hour special care baby unit at the hospital where he was born. The unit was staffed by a medical team, consisting of two consultants, a senior registrar, several junior doctors and trained nurses. While the plaintiff was in the unit a junior and inexperienced doctor monitoring the oxygen in the plaintiff's bloodstream mistakenly inserted a catheter into a vein rather than an artery but then asked the senior registrar to check what he had done. The registrar failed to see the mistake and some hours later, when replacing the catheter, did exactly the same thing himself. In both instances the catheter monitor failed to register correctly the amount of oxygen in the plaintiff's blood, with the result that the plaintiff was given excess oxygen. The plaintiff subsequently brought an action against the health authority claiming damages and alleging that the excess oxygen in his bloodstream had caused an incurable condition of the retina resulting in near blindness. At the trial of the action the judge awarded the plaintiff £116,199.

In dismissing the appeal, the judges in the Court of Appeal had the following to say on the issue of a health authority's primary duty of care:

Mustill LJ: There is, however, a quite different proposition which might have been advanced, namely that the defendants are directly liable for any adverse consequences of the episode. For example, it might have been said that the defendants owed a duty to ensure that the special baby care unit functioned according to the standard reasonably to be expected of such a unit. This approach would not require any consideration of the extent to which the individual doctors measured up to the standards demanded of them as individuals, but would focus attention on the performance of the unit as a whole. A rather different form of the argument might have been advanced on the following lines. Although the catheter, with its monitor and sampling facility, is a valuable instrument, it will yield misleading and potentially dangerous results if the head is in the wrong place. The defendants therefore owed a duty, if they were to use the catheter on patients entrusted to their care, to ensure that those who were to operate the device knew how to detect when it was wrongly placed, and on their own evidence the junior doctors did not know this. Finally, it might have been said that, if the junior doctors did not have sufficient skill or experience to provide the special care demanded by such a premature baby, the defendants were at fault in appointing them to the posts which they held.

If the nature of the plaintiff's cause of action had been a live issue on this appeal, it would have been necessary to look with care at the developing line of authority on liability for medical negligence. For counsel for the defendants asserted roundly that no health authority ever had been, or in principle ever could be, under any such direct liability as suggested, except perhaps in the case of a person being appointed to a post for which he is not qualified. In the event, however, counsel for the plaintiff explicitly disclaimed on the plaintiff's behalf any intention to put forward a case of direct liability. The trial had been conducted throughout, he made clear, exclusively on the basis of vicarious liability. It is therefore unnecessary to express any opinion on the validity in law of a claim on the alternative basis

While Mustill LJ thought it was unnecessary to decide the question, as you will see, Browne-Wilkinson V-C took the view that the case could not be properly analysed without deciding this point.

Glidewell LJ agreed with the Vice-Chancellor stating:

I agree with Sir Nicolas Browne-Wilkinson V-C that there seems to be no reason in principle why, in a suitable case different on its facts from this, a hospital management committee should not be held directly liable in negligence for failing to provide sufficient qualified and competent medical staff.

Sir Nicolas Browne-Wilkinson V-C said:

. . . I agree with the comments of Mustill LJ as to the confusion which has been caused in this case both by the pleading and by the argument below which blurred the distinction between the vicarious liability of the health authority for the negligence of its doctors and the direct liability of the health authority for negligently failing to provide skilled treatment of the kind that it was offering to the public. In my judgment, a health authority which so conducts its hospital that it fails to provide doctors of sufficient skill and experience to give the treatment offered at the hospital may be directly liable in negligence to the patient. Although we were told in argument that no case has ever been decided on this ground and that it is not the practice to formulate claims in this way, I can see no reason why, in principle, the health authority should not be so liable if its organisation is at fault: see *McDermid v Nash Dredging and Reclamation Co Ltd* [1986] 2 All ER 676 esp at 684–685, [1986] QB 965 esp at 978–979 (reported since the conclusion of the argument).

Browne-Wilkinson V-C did not shrink from referring to the consequences which would flow from the acceptance of the view he advanced.

Claims against a health authority that it has itself been directly negligent, as opposed to vicariously liable for the negligence of its doctors, will, of course, raise awkward questions. To what extent should the authority be held liable if (eg in the use of junior housemen) it is only adopting a practice hallowed by tradition? Should the authority be liable if it demonstrates that, due to the financial stringency under which it operates, it cannot afford to fill the posts with those possessing the necessary experience? But, in my judgment, the law should not be distorted by making findings of personal fault against individual doctors who are, in truth, not at fault in order to avoid such questions. To do so would be to cloud the real issues which arise. In the modern world with its technological refinements, is it sensible to persist in making compensation for those who suffer from shortcomings in technologically advanced treatment depend on proof of fault, a process which the present case illustrates can consume years in time and huge sums of money in costs? Given limited resources, what balance is to be struck in the allocation of such resources between compensating those whose treatment is not wholly successful and the provision of required treatment for the world at large? These are questions for Parliament, not the courts. But I do not think the courts will do society a favour by distorting the existing law so as to conceal the real social questions which arise.

Questions

(i) What is the nature of the health authority's primary duty? Is it (a) to ensure that proper facilities exist, whether medical staff or services, to provide appropriate care; or (b) to ensure that appropriate care is provided; or (c) both of these?
(See also, *Albrighton v Royal Prince Albert Hospital* [1980] 2 NSWLR 542 (CA of NSW) and *Kondis v State Transport Authority* (1984) 154 CLR 672 (Aust HC).)
(ii) Whatever the nature of the duty, when does it arise? A theoretically satisfying answer may be that it arises on the patient's admission. What does this mean in factual terms?
(iii) Is a hospital or clinic outside the NHS in a similar position? Does it not depend on what the institution holds itself out as offering?
(iv) The problems foreseen by Browne-Wilkinson V-C in *Wilsher*, if the direct liability of a health authority is accepted, have already manifested themselves in three cases concerned with the allocation of resources within the health service. These cases were public law cases involving challenges to the Secretary of State for Social Services or a health authority alleging the misuse of their statutory powers. Each case, however, is instructive for us as to whether a court would embroil itself in the sorts of issue Browne-Wilkinson V-C mentions. The first case, *R v Secretary of State for Social Services, ex p Hincks* (18 March 1980, unreported), CA is discussed by John Finch in his *Health Services Law* (1981) at pp 37–39.

On January 15, 1979, four patients commenced legal proceedings against Mr David Ennals, the then Secretary of State for Social Services, alleging that he had failed in his duty to provide an efficient and comprehensive Health Service. In the case of *R v Secretary of State for Social Services, ex p Hincks* (1979), the people making the complaint were orthopaedic patients at a hospital in Birmingham who had waited for treatment for periods longer than was medically advisable. The protracted wait was caused by a shortage of facilities which arose, in part, from a decision not to build a new block on the hospital on grounds of cost. They brought a complaint against the Secretary of State, the regional health authority and the area health authority and applied for declarations that these were in breach of their duty under section 1 of the National Health Service Act 1977, and of the duty under section 3 to provide the accommodation, facilities and services appropriate to the health care which it is the authorities' obligation to provide.

The objectives of this action were threefold: first, to ask the judge to rule whether patients had a legal right to bring such proceedings; second, and if so, that a declaration be made by the court that the named authorities had failed in their statutory duty; and thirdly, if the authorities had so failed, to obtain an order to compel them to perform their duties, and to obtain an award of damages against the Secretary of State and the authorities in respect of the pain and suffering caused by the long wait, the orthopaedic patients having suffered considerably during the time complained of.

The four patients failed in their objectives. While the judge, Mr Justice Wien, said in giving his decision on the case that he sympathised with the pain and distress which the patients had experienced, he continued: 'I have come to the conclusion that it is impossible to pinpoint anywhere a breach of statutory duty on the part of the Secretary of State. . . . It all turns on the question of financial resources. If the money is not there then the services cannot be met in one particular place'. He said that it was for Parliament to decide how much money should be allowed to the National Health Service, and for the Minister (or Secretary of State) to decide how much should go to the regions and health authority areas. The Act says that the Secretary of State's duty is to provide services in respect of his statutory health care obligations 'to such extent as he considers necessary', and the judge pointed out that this formula gives the Secretary of State a clear discretion as to how financial resources are to be used.

The court could only interfere if the Secretary of State had acted so as to frustrate the policy of the Act, or as no reasonable minister could have acted. No such breach had been shown in the present case. Nor, even if such a breach of the statutory obligations had been proved, does the Act give the right to sue for damages in respect of pain and suffering experienced by individual patients. So here was an example of a duty which certainly exists and which represents an obligation of immense social importance. But owing to the court's attitude to this duty, its nature must be distinguished from that of the duty of care which is owed as between individuals and the breach of which, by lack of proper care, is a vital step on the way to a remedy by way of monetary damages.

The Court of Appeal's view
An appeal from this decision was taken to the Court of Appeal (Civil Division) in April 1980, but again the plaintiffs fell at the first fence in that no right of action was held to exist on the part of an individual aggrieved patient to sue for a declaration and damages in respect of protracted pain and suffering alleged to have been caused as a direct result of a failure to provide fuller services within the Health Service. As frequently happens in grey areas of legal regulation the case turned in part on the Court's construction of the word 'reasonable' in section 3 of the 1977 Act. . . .

Lord Denning, the Master of the Rolls and [the then] senior judge of the Court of Appeal, was content to say that the Minister could be considered to have failed in his statutory duty only if his exercise of discretion was so thoroughly unreasonable that no reasonable Minister could have reached it. However, a more convincing reason was given by Lord Justice Bridge, himself once the senior Treasury Counsel and thus highly cognisant of the workings of governmental finance.

It had been argued on behalf of the four patients that nothing in the statutory definition of the Secretary of State's duty to provide facilities and services mentioned any constraint on the limits of this duty based on the requirements of longer-term government financial planning; and that, if the Secretary of State's duty had been intended to be so limited, the statute would have expressly included such a proviso. Lord Justice Bridge rejected this argument, which he admitted was an attractive one, saying that it went too far. If no limits in respect of longer-term financial planning were to be read into public statutory duties such as this one we should be faced with the economics of a bottomless (or at least ever-deepening) pit. The argument put forward on the patients' behalf is even more difficult to accept as a realistic claim when it is realised that the further the medical and technological advances go in the direction of an even more comprehensive patient care, the greater would be the financial burden placed on the Secretary of State if he were to avoid a dereliction of his statutory duty under the National Health Service Act.

No further case of this type seems to have been brought until *Re Walker's Application* (1987) Times, 26 November. The case concerned a baby who suffered from a 'hole in the heart'. The health authority was unable to carry out an operation to correct this because it lacked sufficient resources. The baby's mother claimed that this was unlawful and sought an order from the court that the operation be performed. MacPherson J dismissed the case ((1987) Times, 26 November). The baby's mother appealed.

Sir John Donaldson MR [taken from the Lexis transcript]: It is not for this court, or indeed any court, to substitute its own judgment for the judgment of those who are responsible for the allocation of resources. This court could only intervene where it was satisfied that there was a *prima facie* case, not only of failing to allocate resources in the way in which others would think that resources should be allocated, but of a failure to allocate resources to an extent which was Wednesbury (*Associated Provincial Picture Houses v Wednesbury Corpn* [1948] 1 KB 223) unreasonable, if one likes to use the lawyers' jargon, or, in simpler words, which involves a breach of a public law duty. Even then, of course, the court has to exercise a judicial discretion. It has to take account of all the circumstances of the particular case with which it is concerned.

Taking account of the evidence which has been put before us and all the circumstances, it seems to me that this would be an inappropriate case in which to give leave. If other circumstances arose in this case or another case it might be different, because the jurisdiction does exist. But we have to remember, as I think I have already indicated, that if the court is prepared to grant leave in all or even most cases where patients are, from their point of view, very reasonably disturbed at what is going on, we should ourselves be using up National Health Service resources by requiring the authority to stop doing the work for which they were appointed and to meet the complaints of their patients. It is a very delicate balance. As I have made clear and as Mr Bailey has made clear, the jurisdiction does exist. But it has to be used extremely sparingly.

Nicholls LJ and Caulfield J agreed with Sir John Donaldson MR in dismissing the mother's appeal.

It was accepted in the *Walker* case that there was no immediate danger to the baby in waiting. Would it have made any difference if this had been so? Consider the factually similar case of *R v Central Birmingham Health Authority, ex p Collier* (6 January 1988, unreported).

Stephen Brown LJ [taken from the Lexis transcript]: Mr Demello [counsel for the applicant] has sought to distinguish the factual situation in this case by submitting that here, on the evidence of Mr Collier's affidavit, there is an immediate danger to health. I am not sure that I can accept that the affidavit establishes that fact. We have no medical evidence before us, but, even assuming that it does establish that there is immediate danger to health, it seems to me that the legal principles to be applied do not differ from the case of *Re Walker*. This court is in no position to judge the allocation of resources by this particular health authority. Mr Demello recognises that there is no hint of criticism, let alone of complaint, of any action on the part of the surgeon, or any other doctor at the hospital. There is no complaint of bad faith by the health authority. It is not suggested that they are in any way dragging their feet. Mr Demello asserts that, on the basis of what he would say is 'general knowledge', there is a lack of sufficient resources to enable every bed to be in use at the hospital; but there is no suggestion here that the hospital authority has behaved in a way which is deserving of condemnation or criticism. What is suggested is that somehow more resources should be made available to enable the hospital authorities to ensure that the treatment is immediately given.

Of course this is a hearing before a court. This is not the forum in which a court can properly express opinions upon the way in which national resources are allocated or distributed. [There] may be very good reasons why the resources in this case do not allow all the beds in the hospital to be used at this particular time. We have no evidence of that, and indeed, as the Master of the Rolls has said [in the *Walker* case], it is not for this court, or any court, to substitute its own judgment for the judgment of those who are responsible for the allocation of resources.

From the legal point of view, in the absence of any evidence which could begin to show that there was a failure to allocate resources in this instance in circumstances which would make it unreasonable in the Wednesbury sense to make those resources available, there can be no arguable case. I am bound to say that, whilst I have for my part every sympathy with the position of Mr Collier and his family and can understand their pressing anxiety in the case of their little boy, it does seem to me unfortunate that this procedure has been adopted. It is wholly misconceived in my view. The courts of this country cannot arrange the lists in the hospital, and, if [there] is [no] evidence that they are not being arranged properly due to some unreasonableness in the Wednesbury sense on the part of the authority, the courts cannot, and should not, be asked to intervene.

Having regard to the very recent decision of *Re Walker* it seems to me unfortunate that the step has been taken of bringing the matter before a court again. It may be that it is hoped that the publicity will assist in bringing pressure to bear upon the hospital; I do not know. This court cannot be concerned with matters of that kind. But simply upon the basis—which is a purely legal basis—that the matter comes before this court I can see no ground upon which the application can be granted.

Neill and Ralph Gibson LJJ agreed.

Do these cases give any encouragement to a plaintiff in a negligence action where the essence of his claim that the health authority was in breach of its primary duty of care involves questions of resource allocation within the NHS? (v) The cases we have discussed above are concerned with a duty of care owed by a health authority at common law. Do you think that breach of the following statutory provisions might give rise to an action for damages for breach of statutory duty?

National Health Service Act 1977, s 3(1) provides:

3.—(1) It is the Secretary of State's duty to provide throughout England and Wales, to such extent as he considers necessary to meet all reasonable requirements—
  (a) hospital accommodation;
  (b) other accommodation for the purpose of any service provided under this Act;
  (c) medical, dental, nursing and ambulance services;
  (d) such other facilities for the care of expectant and nursing mothers and young children as he considers are appropriate as part of the health service;
  (e) such facilities for the prevention of illness, the care of persons suffering from illness and the after-care of persons who have suffered from illness as he considers are appropriate as part of the health service;
  (f) such other services as are required for the diagnosis and treatment of illness.

In turn, this duty is delegated to the health authorities created by the legislation. Paragraph 15(1) of Schedule 5 to the Act makes it quite clear that for failure to perform the duty under s 3 it is they and not the Secretary of State who must be sued.

15.—(1) An authority shall, notwithstanding that it is exercising any function on behalf of the Secretary of State or another authority, be entitled to enforce any rights acquired in the exercise of that function, and be liable in respect of any liabilities incurred (including liabilities in tort) in the exercise of that function, in all respects as if it were acting as a principal.

Proceedings for the enforcement of such rights and liabilities shall be brought, and brought only, by or, as the case may be, against the authority in question in its own name.

There is some suggestion in the case law that an action would lie (*Yepremian v Scarborough General Hospital* (1981) 110 DLR (3d) 513 at 564 *per* Blair JA relying on *Razzel v Snowball* [1954] 3 All ER 429, [1954] 1 WLR 1382 and Nathan, *Medical Negligence* (1957) p 144 *et seq*). The better view is that s 3(1) only imposes a duty amenable to control in public law through the judicial review procedure under RSC Order 53. In any event, even if such an action for damages could be brought, there would have to be proved a breach of duty ie that the Secretary of State or the health authority's conduct was *ultra vires*.

As we have seen, this might be difficult.

(ii) Vicarious liability

Ellen Picard in 'The Liability of Hospitals in Common Law Canada' (1981) 26 McGill LJ 997, 1016–17, explains the background to vicarious liability in the context of a hospital (footnotes omitted).

> An alternative basis for the liability of a hospital is based on the doctrine of *respondeat superior*. It is an older and more settled area of law in regard to hospitals than that of direct, or personal or corporate duty. All of the principles of the law of vicarious liability are applied to hospitals, but therein lies the problem. Those principles, set up for masters and servants, shop keepers and clerks, do not fit the hospital and its professional staff. But most courts doggedly try to stretch the old garments to fit the new flesh. The concept that was the material measurement of vicarious liability, the control test, no longer covers modern hospital-doctor relationships.
>
> . . .
>
> But control of that type is most uncommon today. Indeed almost from the moment the control test went into service its deficiencies were obvious. There is a strong consensus among authorities that it is in respect of its application to professional persons that the control test has broken down. An employer of a professional such as a doctor may know nothing about the practice of medicine. He is not only not in a position to control the doctor but if he attempts to do so will find that the employee has exercised his own form of control over the situation and quit.
>
> . . . It seems the control test is not providing a credible, reliable measure of when there should be a shift in bearing the loss from the professional who has caused the negligence to the institution responsible for entering into a relationship with him in order to carry out its functions. Put succinctly, the hospital (X) is achieving many of its ends through professionals (Y). In terms of the 'rough justice' sought to be achieved through the concept of vicarious liability, when should X (a hospital and in law a reasonable person) be held accountable for the negligence of Y (a professional)? Surely the answer is when Y is an integral part of X and is making it possible for X to fulfill its duties and obligations. This theory for determining whether liability should be borne by X has been given a name: the organization test. Fleming has described the organization test as asking whether Y's work was subject to coordinated control as to the *when* and the *where* rather than the *how*.]

How has the case law accommodated these views? Picard describes the development of the law in her book, *Legal Liability of Doctors and Hospitals in Canada* (2nd ed 1984), pp 313–314:

> In 1906 an English[104] court held that a hospital was not vicariously liable for the negligence of a doctor who was an employee because it did not have control over him in his professional activities. Similarly, in a famous English case, *Hillyer v St Bartholomew's Hospital*,[105] the court held that a hospital's responsibilities were to ensure that the persons giving medical care were competent and had proper

apparatus and appliances. It would be vicariously liable for negligent acts of professionals while exercising their 'ministerial or administrative duties', but not while they were carrying out professional duties, the reason for the distinction being the perceived absence of control of the employer over those professional activities. It is worth noting that it was also held that in any case at the critical time the nurses were under the control of the operator surgeon. This *obiter* comment lives on, seemingly full of potential never realized.[106]

Thus, a hospital was for many years not liable for doctor-employees or for any negligence nurse-employees committed in carrying out their professional duties. Its main responsibility was to select personnel carefully. Eventually, however, in 1942 in *Gold v Essex County Council*,[107] this strange split in responsibility was discarded as being 'unworkable and contrary to common sense'. The negligence involved was that of a radiology technician but the position was held to be the same as that of the nurse. Whatever confusion remained was removed in *Cassidy v Ministry of Health*[108] where the hospital was held liable for the negligence of a house surgeon employed as part of the permanent staff. The *Hillyer* decision was reviewed and restricted to its facts. Denning LJ said:[109]

> Relieved thus of *Hillyer's* case, this court is free to consider the question on principle, and this leads inexorably to the result that, when hospital authorities undertake to treat a patient and themselves select and appoint and employ the professional men and women who are to give the treatment, they are responsible for the negligence of those persons in failing to give proper treatment, no matter whether they are doctors, surgeons, nurses, or anyone else. Once hospital authorities are held reponsible for the nurses and radiographers, as they have been in *Gold's* case, I can see no possible reason why they should not also be responsible for the house surgeons and resident medical officers on their permanent staff.

Denning LJ pointed out that it is employers who choose and can dismiss employees and this power is the reason that they should be held vicariously liable even where they cannot for various reasons control the employee.[110] Furthermore, the old control test had become somewhat of an anachronism and it was apparent that one of the policy reasons for restricting the liability of hospitals, that of protecting the privately supported or charity hospital, was no longer present as state-supported hospitals became more common. Thus the questions became whether the person's work was an integral part of the hospital organisation and whether the patient employed him.[111] As will be seen, the last question may have come to be paramount.[112] In the last English case in the chain, *Roe v Minister of Health*,[113] the English Court of Appeal went a step further by holding that a hospital would be liable for a part-time anaesthetist employed and paid by the hospital as a member of the permanent staff but who also carried on a private practice.

Notes to extract

104 *Evans v Liverpool Corpn* ([1906] 1 KB 160).
105 [1909] 2 KB 820, CA.
106 [footnote omitted].
107 [1942] 2 KB 293, CA; see also *Logan v Waitaki Hospital Board* [1935] NZLR 385 (SC).
108 [1951] 1 All ER 574, CA.
109 *Id* at 586.
110 [footnote omitted].
111 Fleming, *The Law of Torts* 345 (6th edn 1983); see also Goodhart, *Hospitals and Trained Nurses* (1938), 54 LQ Rev 553.
112 See discussion of the case of *Yepremian v Scarborough General Hospital infra*.
113 [1954] 2 QB 66, CA.

There appears to be no doubt that anyone who is a member of the medical staff of a hospital, whether part-time or full time, will be judged to be an employee so as to render the health authority (whether District or Regional) vicariously liable for their torts. Some uncertainty was initially expressed after the creation of the NHS of the consultant's position. *Razzel v Snowball* [1954] 3 All ER 429, [1954] 1 WLR 1382 is often cited as putting the matter beyond doubt. In that case Denning LJ observed

> Counsel for the plaintiff pressed us with some observations in the cases concerning consultants. He said that the defendant was a part time consultant, and that a consultant was in a different position from the staff of the hospital. I think that counsel for the defendant gave the correct answer when he said that, whatever may have been the position of a consultant in former times, nowadays, since the National Health Service Act, 1946, the term 'consultant' does not denote a particular relationship between a doctor and a hospital. It is simply a title denoting his place in the hierarchy of the hospital staff. He is a senior member of the staff, and is just as much a member of the staff as the house surgeon is. Whether he is called specialist or consultant makes no difference.

In fact, the case turned on whether a consultant in carrying out treatment was the agent of the Minister, fulfilling the Minister's statutory duty under, what was then, section 3 of the National Health Service Act 1946. Despite this rather unusual feature, the *dictum* of Denning LJ remains helpful.

Since it is in the nature of vicarious liability that the doctor is also liable, the patient's success in obtaining compensation could, in theory, depend on which party was sued. For this reason there was introduced by the Ministry of Health circular HM (54) 32, which provides as follows:

> *Summary:* The present policy of taking legal action to secure contributions from doctors in respect of whose negligence successful claims may be brought against hospital authorities is to be modified. In future, where any doctor who may be liable is a member of a Defence Society and that body accepts responsibility for him, any payment made to the plaintiff is to be apportioned between the doctor(s) and the hospital authority as agreed privately between them or, in default of agreement, in equal shares.

> 1. As Boards and Committees are aware, it has been the Minister's policy (see paragraph 6 of RHB(49)128/HMC(49)108/BG(49)113 that where proceedings are brought against a hospital authority and/or a doctor employed by them for alleged negligence by the doctor the authority should not undertake the defence of the doctor and that if it is sought to make them liable for negligent acts of a doctor employed by them, they should normally take such steps as are open to them under the Law Reform (Married Women and Tortfeasors) Act 1935, [now the Civil Liability (Contribution) Act 1978] to obtain a contribution from him in respect of damages which may be recovered. It has been represented to the Minister that this policy may tend to prejudice that successful conduct of the defence which is in the interest of doctor and hospital authority alike. The Minister has therefore reviewed the position in consultation with representatives of the profession and the Defence Societies and has agreed with them the revised procedure set out in this memorandum.

> 2. Actions may be brought against the hospital authority alone, or against one or more members of their medical staff alone, or against the hospital authority and a member or members of the medical staff jointly. The arrangements set out in the two succeeding paragraphs will apply to all three classes of action so far as regards medical practitioners who are to be defended by the Medical Defence Union or the Medical Protection Society or the Medical and Dental Defence Union of Scotland. As regards medical practitioners not so defended the arrangements hitherto in force should continue even in actions in which the new arrangements are being applied to other parties defended as above.

3. Where both the hospital authority and one or more hospital doctors are cited by the plaintiff as defendants, the following arrangements will apply:

(1) Any defendant may, on notifying the other(s), decide to settle the case out of Court at any stage in the proceedings, but if he does so, he must accept sole liability for payment of the whole sum for which the case is settled; but each defendant shall pay his own costs.

(2) If the defendants decide to explore the possibility of settlement out of Court (and a settlement is ultimately effected), the payment made to the plaintiff shall be borne between the defendants agreed to be liable in such proportion as they may agree between themselves or, in default of agreement on the proportions, in equal shares.

(3) If the defendants agree to defend the action in Court the procedure should be as follows:

   (a) the defendants should try to agree before the action comes to Court on the proportion in which any damages and costs which may be awarded to the plaintiff shall be borne between them;

   (b) if this proves impossible, the defendants should try to reach such agreement after the trial of the action;

   (c) failing agreement under (a) or (b) the damages and costs awarded to the plaintiff shall be borne in equal shares between such defendants as are held liable.

(4) In exceptional circumstances where some important legal or professional principle is involved, any defendant may give notice to the other before delivery of defence by either party that sub-paragraphs (1)–(3) above shall not apply; and the normal legal processes will then be open to all defendants.

4. Where either the hospital authority alone or a hospital doctor alone is cited as defendant in the action, the defendant will have complete discretion whether to fight the action or to attempt to settle it out of Court. The hospital or the doctor solely cited shall not take legal action to obtain a contribution from the other, nor cite the other unless requested so to do when the request shall be conceded forthwith. The Defence Societies recognise, however, that there will be cases where, although one of their members has not been cited, they might properly be asked to make a contribution towards any payment made by the hospital authority to the plaintiff, because the action or inaction of the practitioner in question was a material factor in the negligence complained of. Conversely, in actions in which a hospital doctor alone is cited, there may be circumstances in which the Defence Society asks the hospital authority to make a similar contribution. In either case the procedure should follow the principles set out in paragraph 3(2) and (3) above, as if the party not cited were a defendant.

5. The success of the new arrangements set out above clearly depends on mutual confidence between the defendants and a fully co-operative attitude on the part of both parties from the beginning, and hospital authorities are urged to bear this in mind. There should be full consultation at the request of either party in the formulation of the defence. In any case where, in accordance with paragraph 4, there is a possibility of a contribution being requested from a hospital authority or a doctor who has not been cited, full information about the incident and the possibility of such a request should be exchanged at the earliest opportunity, which normally should be as soon as the Statement of Claim has been delivered, and in event not later than delivery of Defence.

6. The principles of paragraph 5 of RHB(49)128/HMC(49)108/BG(49)113 (which require hospital authorities to obtain the Minister's prior authority to settling any case out of Court for a sum exceeding £500 plus costs and also to consult the Minister on cases raising certain major legal issues) continue to apply. Where, however, in a case to be settled out of Court, the sum to be paid is apportioned between a hospital authority and one or more members of its medical staff, the Minister's authority need be obtained only where the sum apportioned to the hospital authority (not the total sum) exceeds £500. . . . [note this figure is currently £100,000]

7. It has been the normal practice of the Defence Societies to claim the protection of Section 21 of the Limitation Act, 1939, [now Limitation Act 1980] where action is not commenced within one year of the occurrence of the cause of action. Hospital authorities should, as hitherto, not plead this section except with the Minister's prior approval. No liability under paragraphs 3 or 4 for any damages or costs, other than his own costs, should be regarded as falling on any doctor where the hospital authority or the Minister is satisfied that exemption from liability could be successfully claimed under Section 21.

8. The provisions of this circular should be applied to all proceedings, which are commenced on or after the 1st day of April, 1954, and also if it is agreed by, or on behalf of, the hospital authority and the doctor or doctors concerned, to any proceedings which are pending on that date and in which judgment has not been given.

On closer examination do you think the reason for introducing the circular was to help plaintiffs or to reduce defendants' costs by ensuring that one party only need be put to the expense of defending the action safe in the knowledge that the other party would make an agreed contribution to any damages awarded?

In fact, as the scheme is worked, health authorities will only agree to make *any* contribution if satisfied that the fault is not *wholly* that of the doctor. So, a health authority, even if the only party sued, would be likely to seek a contribution from a doctor (in reality his protection society) of up to 100% depending upon the relative faults of the health authority and the doctor. Any such claim by the health authority would not be based upon any informal agreement between it and the protection societies but would be founded in the law of contribution. The circular merely provides a mechanism adjusting compensation between the health authority and the doctor without having the need to resort to legal action. [But note the Government's recent proposal to accept 'crown indemnity' for doctors employed by the NHS. See (1989) Lancet, 8 April at 795. If implemented this would result in health authorities and not the defence organisations paying damages awards made against hospital doctors.]

2. STANDARD OF CARE

(a) Generally

Bolam v Friern Hospital Management Committee
[1957] 2 All ER 118, [1957] 1 WLR 582

Facts: The plaintiff contended that the defendants were vicariously liable for the carelessness of a doctor who administered electro-convulsive therapy to the plaintiff without administering a relaxant drug or without restraining the convulsive movements of the plaintiff by manual control (save for his lower jaw). The plaintiff suffered a fractured jaw as a consequence. He brought an action against the defendants in negligence.

McNair J directed the jury (pp 121–2):
. . .
Before I turn to that, I must explain what in law we mean by 'negligence'. In the ordinary case which does not involve any special skill, negligence in law means this: Some failure to do some act which a reasonable man in the circumstances would do, or doing some act which a reasonable man in the circumstances would not do; and if that failure or doing of that act results in injury, then there is a cause of action. How do you test whether this act or failure is negligent? In an ordinary case it is generally said, that you judge that by the action of the man in the street. He is the

ordinary man. In one case it has been said that you judge it by the conduct of the man on the top of a Clapham omnibus. He is the ordinary man. But where you get a situation which involves the use of some special skill or competence, then the test whether there has been negligence or not is not the test of the man on the top of a Clapham omnibus, because he has not got this special skill. The test is the standard of the ordinary skilled man exercising and professing to have that special skill. A man need not possess the highest expert skill at the risk of being found negligent. It is well-established law that it is sufficient if he exercises the ordinary skill of an ordinary competent man exercising that particular art. I do not think that I quarrel much with any of the submissions in law which have been put before you by counsel. Counsel for the plaintiff put it in this way, that in the case of a medical man negligence means failure to act in accordance with the standards of reasonably competent medical men at the time. That is a perfectly accurate statement, as long as it is remembered that there may be one or more perfectly proper standards; and if a medical man conforms with one of those proper standards then he is not negligent. Counsel for the plaintiff was also right, in my judgment, in saying that a mere personal belief that a particular technique is best is no defence unless that belief is based on reasonable grounds. That again is unexceptionable. But the emphasis which is laid by counsel for the defendants is on this aspect of negligence: He submitted to you that the real question on which you have to make up your mind on each of the three major points to be considered is whether the defendants, in acting in the way in which they did, were acting in accordance with a practice of competent respected professional opinion. Counsel for the defendants submitted that if you are satisfied that they were acting in accordance with a practice of a competent body of professional opinion, then it would be wrong for you to hold that negligence was established. I referred, before I started these observations, to a statement which is contained in a recent Scottish case, *Hunter v Hanley* ([1955] SLT 213 at p 217), which dealt with medical matters, where the Lord President (Lord Clyde) said this:

> In the realm of diagnosis and treatment there is ample scope for genuine difference of opinion, and one man clearly is not negligent merely because his conclusion differs from that of other professional men, nor because he has displayed less skill or knowledge than others would have shown. The true test for establishing negligence in diagnosis or treatment on the part of a doctor is whether he has been proved to be guilty of such failure as no doctor of ordinary skill would be guilty of if acting with ordinary care.

If that statement of the true test is qualified by the words 'in all the circumstances', counsel for the plaintiff would not seek to say that that expression of opinion does not accord with English law. It is just a question of expression. I myself would prefer to put it this way: A doctor is not guilty of negligence if he has acted in accordance with a practice accepted as proper by a responsible body of medical men skilled in that particular art. I do not think there is much difference in sense. It is just a different way of expressing the same thought. Putting it the other way round, a doctor is not negligent, if he is acting in accordance with such a practice, merely because there is a body of opinion that takes a contrary view. At the same time, that does not mean that a medical man can obstinately and pig-headedly carry on with some old technique if it has been proved to be contrary to what is really substantially the whole of informed medical opinion. Otherwise you might get men today saying: 'I don't believe in anaesthetics. I don't believe in antiseptics. I am going to continue to do my surgery in the way it was done in the eighteenth century'. That clearly would be wrong.

The jury returned a verdict for the defendants.

Bolam was applied in *Whitehouse v Jordan* [1981] 1 All ER 267, [1981] 1 WLR 246 the case we saw at the outset of this chapter. Lord Edmund-Davies stated (pp 276–7):

> The principal questions calling for decision are: (a) in what manner did Mr Jordan use the forceps? and (b) was that manner consistent with the degree of skill which a

member of his profession is required by law to exercise? Surprising though it is at this late stage in the development of the law of negligence, counsel for Mr Jordan persisted in submitting that his client should be completely exculpated were the answer to question (b), 'Well, at the worst he was guilty of an error of clinical judgment'. My Lords, it is high time that the unacceptability of such an answer be finally exposed. To say that a surgeon committed an error of clinical judgment is wholly ambiguous, for, while some such errors may be completely consistent with the due exercise of professional skill, other acts or omissions in the course of exercising 'clinical judgment' may be so glaringly below proper standards as to make a finding of negligence inevitable. Indeed, I should have regarded this as a truism were it not that, despite the exposure of the 'false antithesis' by Donaldson LJ in his dissenting judgment in the Court of Appeal, counsel for the defendants adhered to it before your Lordships.

But doctors and surgeons fall into no special category, and, to avoid any future disputation of a similar kind, I would have it accepted that the true doctrine was enunciated, and by no means for the first time, by McNair J in *Bolam v Friern Hospital Management Committee* [1957] 2 All ER 118 at 121, [1957] 1 WLR 582 at 586 in the following words, which were applied by the Privy Council in *Chin Keow v Government of Malaysia* [1967] 1 WLR 813:

... where you get a situation which involves the use of some special skill or competence, then the test as to whether there has been negligence or not is not the test of the man on the top of a Clapham omnibus because he has not got this special skill. The test is the standard of the ordinary skilled man exercising and professing to have that special skill.'

If a surgeon fails to measure up to that standard in *any* respect ('clinical judgment' or otherwise), he has been negligent and should be so adjudged.

The House of Lords returned again to the topic and re-iterated the *Bolam* view in *Sidaway*. We referred to this *in extenso* in chapter 4 and here we need to refer again to Lord Bridge's speech (p 660):

Broadly, a doctor's professional functions may be divided into three phases: diagnosis, advice and treatment. In performing his functions of diagnosis and treatment, the standard by which English law measures the doctor's duty of care to his patient is not open to doubt. 'The test is the standard of the ordinary skilled man exercising and professing to have that special skill.' These are the words of McNair J in *Bolam v Friern Hospital Management Committee* [1957] 2 All ER 118 at 121, [1957] 1 WLR 582 at 586, approved by this House in *Whitehouse v Jordan* [1981] 1 All ER 276 at 277, [1981] 1 WLR 246 at 258 per Lord Edmund-Davies and in *Maynard v West Midlands Regional Health Authority* [1985] 1 All ER 635 per Lord Scarman. The test is conveniently referred to as the *Bolam* test. In *Maynard*'s case Lord Scarman, with whose speech the other four members of the Appellate Committee agreed, further cited with approval the words of the Lord President (Clyde) in *Hunter v Hanley* 1955 SLT 213 at 217:

In the realm of diagnosis and treatment there is ample scope for genuine difference of opinion and one man clearly is not negligent merely because his conclusion differs from that of other professional men ... The true test for establishing negligence in diagnosis or treatment on the part of a doctor is whether he has been proved to be guilty of such failure as no doctor of ordinary skill would be guilty of if acting with ordinary care ...

The language of the *Bolam* test clearly requires a different degree of skill from a specialist in his own special field than from a general practitioner. In the field of neuro-surgery it would be necessary to substitute for the Lord President's phrase 'no doctor of ordinary skill', the phrase 'no neuro-surgeon of ordinary skill'. All this is elementary and, in the light of the two recent decisions of this House referred to, firmly established law.

Who then sets the standard? Notice Lord Scarman's comment in *Sidaway* (p 649):

The *Bolam* principle may be formulated as a rule that a doctor is not negligent if he acts in accordance with a practice accepted at the time as proper by a responsible body of medical opinion even though other doctors adopt a different practice. In short, the law imposes the duty of care; but the standard of care is a matter of medical judgment.

We should note in passing the brief life-span of the 'false antithesis' between an error of judgment and an error amounting to a failure to exercise due care and skill. This was conceived by Lord Denning and given a brief moment in the light as Sheila Maclean writes in 'Negligence—A Dagger at the Doctor's Back?' in *Justice, Lord Denning and the Constitution* (ed P Robson and P Watchman), at p 104 (footnotes omitted):

In the case of *Roe v Minister of Health* he said:
    ... we should be doing a disservice to the community at large if we were to impose liability on hospitals and doctors for everything that happens to go wrong ... We must insist on due care for the patient at every point, but we must not condemn as negligent that which is only misadventure.
Again in the case of *Hatcher v Black* he pointed out the risks of holding doctors liable in these circumstances and suggested that to do so would mean that:
    ... a doctor examining a patient, or a surgeon operating at a table, instead of getting on with his work, would be forever looking over his shoulder to see if someone was coming up with a dagger—for an action for negligence against a doctor is for him like unto a dagger.
The interests of the community then are seen by Lord Denning not as being the facilitation of compensation in the event of damage as a result of medical intervention, but rather as being that medical practice should be interfered with as little as possible.

Lord Denning returned to his creation in *Whitehouse v Jordan* [1980] 1 All ER 650 at 658:

We must say, and say firmly, that, in a professional man, an error of judgment is not negligent. To test it, I would suggest that you ask the average competent and careful practitioner: 'Is this the sort of mistake that you yourself might have made?' If he says: 'Yes, even doing the best I could, it might have happened to me', then it is not negligent. In saying this, I am only reaffirming what I said in *Hatcher v Black* (a case I tried myself), *Roe v Ministry of Health* and *Hucks v Cole*.

Donaldson LJ (as he then was) disagreed; at 662 he said:

It is said that the judge lost sight of the fact that the plaintiff had to establish negligence. The basis of this submission was in part that he nowhere referred to 'errors of clinical judgment' and contrasted such errors with negligence. I can understand the omission, because it is a false antithesis. If a doctor fails to exercise the skill which he has or claims to have, he is in breach of his duty of care. He is negligent. But if he exercised that skill to the full, but nevertheless takes what, with hindsight, can be shown to be the wrong course, he is not negligent and is liable to no one, much though he may regret having done so. Both are errors of clinical judgment. The judge was solely concerned with whether or not the defendant's actions were negligent. If they were not, it was irrelevant whether or not they constituted an error of clinical judgment. The question which Bush J [the trial judge] asked himself was whether there had been any failure by the defendant 'to exercise the standard of skill expected from the ordinary competent specialist having regard to the experience and expertise which that specialist holds himself out as possessing', and added the proviso that 'the skill and expertise which we are considering is that applying in 1969–70'. In my judgment, that was not only the correct question, it was the only relevant question.

Lord Fraser delivered the death-blow in the House of Lords ([1981] 1 All ER 267 at 281:

Referring to medical men, Lord Denning MR said ([1980] 1 All ER 650 at 658): 'If they are to be found liable [sc for negligence] whenever they do not effect a cure, or whenever anything untoward happens, it would do a great disservice to the profession itself.' That is undoubtedly correct, but he went on to say this: 'We must say, and say firmly, that, in a professional man an error of judgment is not negligent.' Having regard to the context, I think that Lord Denning MR must have meant to say that an error of judgment 'is not *necessarily* negligent'. But in my respectful opinion, the statement as it stands is not an accurate statement of the law. Merely to describe something as an error of judgment tells us nothing about whether it is negligent or not. The true position is that an error of judgment may, or may not, be negligent; it depends on the nature of the error. If it is one that would not have been made by a reasonably competent professional man professing to have the standard and type of skill that the defendant held himself out as having, and acting with ordinary care, then it is negligent. If, on the other hand, it is an error that a man, acting with ordinary care, might have made, then it is not negligence.

What if the doctor is a specialist? When a doctor holds himself out as being a specialist the standard of care expected by the law was set out by Lord Scarman in *Maynard v West Midlands Regional Health Authority* [1985] 1 All ER 635 at 638: 'I would only add that a doctor who professes to exercise a special skill must exercise the ordinary skill of his speciality.'

What if the doctor is a novice? The well-known Canadian tort scholar, Allan Linden in *Canadian Tort Law* (3rd ed), discusses this issue (p 140).

Although it has toughened its general standard for specialists, tort law has not diluted it for inexperienced doctors. Hence, a 'novice surgeon' who had not performed a particular operation before was made liable when he severed a nerve.[320] Nor are interns given any special dispensation if they present themselves as being fully qualified. In *Vancouver General Hospital v Fraser*,[321] two interns licenced to practice within the confines of a hospital wrongly read some X-rays of a car accident victim who came to their hospital, talked to his family doctor and then sent him away. The patient later died as a result of complications from a broken neck, which their examination had failed to detect. Their employer, the hospital, was held vicariously liable for their blunder. Mr Justice Rand based his decision on the fact that the interns' conduct was cloaked with 'all the ritual and paraphernalia of medical science'. An intern had to be 'more than a mere untutored communicant between [the family doctor] and the patient'.[322] He must exercise the 'undertaken degree of skill and that cannot be less than the ordinary skill of a junior doctor'. One of the most vital things he must have is an 'appreciation of his own limitations'. By failing to notify a radiologist who was on call at the hospital and by relying on their own imperfect knowledge, they acted negligently.

Notes to extract
[320] *McKeachie v Alvarez* (1970) 17 DLR (3d) 87 at 100 (BC) (*per* Wilson J); see also *Challand v Bell* (1959) 18 DLR (2d) 150 (Alta); *Walker v Bedard* [1945] OWN 120 at 124.
[321] [1952] 2 SCR 36.
[322] *Ibid*, at p 46.

Has Rand J in the case referred to answered the question posed? What does 'the ordinary skill of a junior doctor mean'? Does it mean the skill (sic) of a novice or some minimum standard of competence which even a junior doctor must have for the particular job involved?

Perhaps, the appropriate rule of English law can be derived from the case of *Nettleship v Weston* [1971] 2 QB 691, [1971] 3 All ER 591, CA. The case concerned a learner-driver who mounted the kerb in a car and damaged a lamp-post. Her instructor also suffered injuries. Lord Denning MR said (at p 586):

The responsibility of the learner-driver towards persons on or near the highway
Mrs Weston is clearly liable for the damage to the lamp-post. In the civil law if a driver goes off the road on to the pavement and injures a pedestrian, or damages

property, he is *prima facie* liable. Likewise if he goes on to the wrong side of the road. It is no answer for him to say: 'I was a learner-driver under instruction. I was doing my best and could not help it.' The civil law permits no such excuse. It requires of him the same standard of care as any other driver. 'It eliminates the personal equation and is independent of the idiosyncrasies of the particular person whose conduct is in question': see *Glasgow Corpn v Muir per* Lord Macmillan. The learner-driver may be doing his best, but his incompetent best is not good enough. He must drive in as good a manner as a driver of skill, experience and care, who is sound in wind and limb, who makes no errors of judgment, has good eyesight and hearing, and is free from any infirmity: see *Richley v Faull* and *Watson v Thomas S Whitney & Co Ltd*.

Salmon LJ added (at p 589):

I also agree that a learner-driver is responsible and owes a duty in civil law towards persons on or near the highway to drive with the same degree of skill and care as that of the reasonably competent and experienced driver. The duty in civil law springs from the relationship which the driver, by driving on the highway, has created between himself and persons likely to suffer damage by his bad driving. . . .

Any driver normally owes exactly the same duty to a passenger in his car as he does to the general public, namely to drive with reasonable care and skill in all the relevant circumstances. As a rule, the driver's personal idiosyncrasy is not a relevant circumstance. In the absence of a special relationship what is reasonable care and skill is measured by the standard of competence usually achieved by the ordinary driver.

Megaw LJ agreed.

The Court of Appeal is saying, in essence, that as a matter of public policy the law must set a standard for the benefit of all below which everyone engaging in risk-creating behaviour may not fall. Thus, a junior doctor would be held to that minimum level of competence necessary for the safety and proper treatment of a patient regardless of his actual level of competence or experience.

The Court of Appeal has settled the question as regards English law in *Wilsher v Essex Area Health Authority* [1987] QB 730, [1986] 3 All ER 801. We have already seen the facts of this case set out *supra* at p 385–6.

Mustill LJ [at pp 812–3]: I now turn to the real content of the standard of care. Three propositions were advanced, the first by junior counsel for the plaintiff. It may, I think, be fairly described as setting a 'team' standard of care, whereby each of the persons who formed the staff of the unit held themselves out as capable of undertaking the specialised procedures which that unit set out to perform.

I acknowledge the force of this submission, so far as it calls for recognition of the position which the person said to be negligent held within this specialised unit. But, in so far as the proposition differs from the last of those referred to below, I must dissent, for it is faced with a dilemma. If he seeks to attribute to each individual member of the team a duty to live up to the standards demanded of the unit as a whole, it cannot be right, for it would expose a student nurse to an action in negligence for a failure to possess the skill and experience of a consultant. If, on the other hand, it seeks to fix a standard for the performance of the unit as a whole, this is simply a reformulation of the direct theory of liability which leading counsel for the plaintiff has explicitly disclaimed.

The second proposition (advanced on behalf of the defendants) directs attention to the personal position of the individual member of the staff about whom the complaint is made. What is expected of him is as much as, but no more than, can reasonably be required of a person having his formal qualifications and practical experience. If correct, this proposition entails that the standard of care which the patient is entitled to demand will vary according to the chance of recruitment and rostering. The patient's right to complain of faulty treatment will be more limited if he has been entrusted to the care of a doctor who is a complete novice in the particular field (unless perhaps he can point to some fault of supervision in a person further up the hierarchy) than if he has been in the hands of a doctor who has already spent months on the same ward, and his prospects of holding the health authority vicariously liable for the consequences of any mistreatment will be correspondingly reduced.

To my mind, this notion of a duty tailored to the actor, rather than to the act which he elects to perform, has no place in the law of tort. Indeed, the defendants did not contend that it could be justified by any reported authority on the general law of tort. Instead, it was suggested that the medical profession is a special case. Public hospital medicine has always been organised so that young doctors and nurses learn on the job. If the hospitals abstained from using inexperienced people, they could not staff their wards and theatres, and the junior staff could never learn. The longer-term interests of patients as a whole are best served by maintaining the present system, even if this may diminish the legal rights of the individual patient, for, after all, medicine is about curing, not litigation.

I acknowledge the appeal of this argument, and recognise that a young hospital doctor who must get onto the wards in order to qualify without necessarily being able to decide what kind of patient he is going to meet is not in the same position as another professional man who has a real choice whether or not to practise in a particular field. Nevertheless, I cannot accept that there should be a special rule for doctors in public hospitals; I emphasise *public*, since presumably those employed in private hospitals would be in a different category. Doctors are not the only people who gain their experience, not only from lectures or from watching others perform, but from tackling live clients or customers, and no case was cited to us which suggested that any such variable duty of care was imposed on others in a similar position. To my mind, it would be a false step to subordinate the legitimate expectation of the patient that he will receive from each person concerned with his care a degree of skill appropriate to the task which he undertakes to an understandable wish to minimise the psychological and financial pressures on hard-pressed young doctors.

For my part, I prefer the third of the propositions which have been canvassed. This relates the duty of care, not to the individual, but to the post which he occupies. I would differentiate 'post' from 'rank' or 'status'. In a case such as the present, the standard is not just that of the averagely competent and well-informed junior houseman (or whatever the position of the doctor) but of such a person who fills a post in a unit offering a highly specialised service. But, even so, it must be recognised that different posts make different demands. If it is borne in mind that the structure of hospital medicine envisages that the lower ranks will be occupied by those of whom it would be wrong to expect too much, the risk of abuse by litigious patients can be mitigated, if not entirely eliminated.

Glidewell LJ agreed and added (at p 831):

In my view, the law requires the trainee or learner to be judged by the same standard as his more experienced colleagues. If it did not, inexperience would frequently be urged as a defence to an action for professional negligence.

If this test appears unduly harsh in relation to the inexperienced, I should add that, in my view, the inexperienced doctor called on to exercise a specialist skill will, as part of that skill, seek the advice and help of his superiors when he does or may need it. If he does seek such help, he will often have satisfied the test, even though he may himself have made a mistake.

Sir Nicolas Browne-Wilkinson V-C dissented.

In English law, liability for personal injury requires a finding of personal fault (eg negligence) against someone. In cases of vicarious liability such as this, there must have been personal fault by the employee or agent of the defendant for whom the defendant is held vicariously liable. Therefore, even though no claim is made against the individual doctor, the liability of the defendant health authority is dependent on a finding of personal fault by one or more of the individual doctors. The general standard of care required of a doctor is that he would exercise the skill of a skilled doctor in the treatment which he has taken on himself to offer.

Such being the general standard of care required of a doctor, it is normally no answer for him to say the treatment he gave was of a specialist or technical nature in which he was inexperienced. In such a case, the fault of the doctor lies in embarking on giving treatment which he could not skilfully offer: he should not have undertaken the treatment but should have referred the patient to someone possessing the necessary skills.

But the position of the houseman in his first year after qualifying or of someone (like Dr Wiles in this case) who has just started in a specialist field in order to gain the necessary skill in that field is not capable of such analysis. The houseman has to take up his post in order to gain full professional qualification; anyone who, like Dr Wiles, wishes to obtain specialist skills has to learn those skills by taking a post in a specialist unit. In my judgment, such doctors cannot in fairness be said to be at fault if, at the start of their time, they lack the very skills which they are seeking to acquire.

In my judgment, if the standard of care required of such a doctor is that he should have the skill required of the post he occupies, the young houseman or the doctor seeking to obtain specialist skills in a special unit would be held liable for shortcomings in the treatment without any personal fault on his part at all. Of course, such a doctor would be negligent if he undertook treatment for which he knows he lacks the necessary experience and skill. But one of the chief hazards of inexperience is that one does not always know the risks which exist. In my judgment, so long as the English law rests liability on personal fault, a doctor who has properly accepted a post in a hospital in order to gain necessary experience should only be held liable for acts or omissions which a careful doctor with his qualifications and experience would not have done or omitted. It follows that, in my view, the health authority could not be held vicariously liable (and I stress the word *vicariously*) for the acts of such a learner who has come up to those standards, notwithstanding that the post he held required greater experience than he in fact possessed.

Does the mere reference to the 'post' help? Is not Mustill LJ, with respect, confused by not really talking about a doctor with minimum competence for the task? Could not Mustill LJ have decided the case on the basis that the doctor should never have carried out the procedure complained of because he lacked a minimum competence? Is the analysis of the Vice-Chancellor any more helpful?

Given the law is as the majority have stated it, how can the law accommodate the needs of public policy that a doctor learns at least part of the job through work experience? Does not the answer lie in supervision? If a doctor lacks a minimum competence to carry out a particular procedure but it is proper for him to be present, eg as a learner, then whatever he does must be done under the supervision of the experienced doctor. The negligence, if any, will now be that of the experienced doctor for failure adequately to supervise (this is what Glidewell LJ decided in *Wilsher*, as we have seen).

What of the situation, however, where the inexperienced doctor does not realise his own incompetence and so does not seek supervision? You will recall the words of the Vice-Chancellor in *Wilsher* '. . . one of the chief hazards of inexperience is that one does not always know the risks which exist'. Does *reasonable* supervision contemplate *constant* supervision or something else? If it be the former will the experienced doctor *necessarily* be liable? This cannot, in our view, be the law. As a matter of public policy it is recognised that the medical profession, like any other profession, can only acquire some knowledge and skill by taking independent responsibility albeit within the context of overall supervision by the more experienced.

This does leave unanswered the point raised by the Vice-Chancellor: 'the rights of a patient entering hospital will depend on the experience of the doctor who treats him'. This may somewhat overstate the case but certainly there is a problem here. One answer is the Vice-Chancellor's recourse to the primary liability of the hospital. Another answer is to recall the law relating to consent and consider what information the patient ought to be told so as to make any consent valid.

Linden (*op cit*) in discussing the Canadian law asks the question 'Whether a lower standard of care would be acceptable if an intern junior doctor identified himself as such to the patient?' In effect, Linden is asking whether a patient may by agreement lower the standard of care otherwise imposed by law. In *Nettleship v Weston* there was a difference of opinion. Lord Denning stated, at pp 586–7 (footnotes omitted):

> *The responsibility of the learner-driver towards passengers in the car*
> Mrs Weston took her son with her in the car. We do not know his age. He may have been 21 and have known that his mother was learning to drive. He was not injured. But if he had been injured, would he have had a cause of action? I take it to be clear that, if a driver has a passenger in the car, he owes a duty of care to him. But what is the standard of care required of the driver? Is it a lower standard than he or she owes towards a pedestrian on the pavement? I should have thought not. But, suppose that the driver has never driven a car before, or has taken too much to drink, or has poor eyesight or hearing; and, furthermore, that the passenger *knows* it and yet accepts a lift from him. Does that make any difference? Dixon J thought it did. In *Insurance Comr v Joyce* he said:
>
> > If a man accepts a lift from a car-driver whom he *knows* to have lost a limb or an eye or to be deaf, he cannot complain if he does not exhibit the skill and competence of a driver who suffers from no defect . . . If he knowingly accepts the voluntary services of a driver affected by drink, he cannot complain of improper driving caused by his condition, because it involves no breach of duty.
>
> That view of Dixon J seems to have been followed in South Australia, see *Walker v Turton-Sainsbury*, but in the Supreme Court of Canada Rand J did not agree with it: see *Carr and General Insurance Corpn Ltd v Seymour and Maloney*.
> We have all the greatest respect for Sir Owen Dixon, but for once I cannot agree with him. The driver owes a duty of care to every passenger in the car, just as he does to every pedestrian on the road; and he must attain the same standard of care in respect of each.

Megaw LJ agreed on this point. Salmon LJ, however, disagreed (p 589):

> . . . [T]here may be special facts creating a special relationship which displaces this standard or even negatives any duty, although the onus would certainly be on the driver to establish such facts. With minor reservations I respectfully agree with and adopt the reasoning and conclusions of Sir Owen Dixon in his judgment in *Insurance Comr v Joyce*. I do not however agree that the mere fact that the driver has, to the knowledge of his passenger, lost a limb or an eye or is deaf can affect the duty which he owes the passenger to drive safely. It is well known that many drivers suffering from such disabilities drive with no less skill and competence than the ordinary man. The position, however, is totally different when, to the knowledge of the passenger, the driver is so drunk as to be incapable of driving safely. Quite apart from being negligent, a passenger who accepts a lift in such circumstances clearly cannot expect the driver to drive other than dangerously.
> The duty of care springs from relationship. The special relationship which the passenger has created by accepting a lift in the circumstances postulated surely cannot entitle him to expect the driver to discharge a duty of care or skill which ex hypothesi the passenger knows the driver is incapable of discharging. Accordingly in such circumstances, no duty is owed by the driver to the passenger to drive safely
> . . .

Questions

(i) In the context of medical treatment which view better states the law? Do you think a relevant factor may be a court's unwillingness to accept that agreement by the patient was really *voluntary* rather than reached under the duress of the circumstances?

Two parallel questions also ought to be asked:

(ii) What standard of care would the law expect of a doctor (a) who, unknown to the patient, had particular expertise beyond that normally found? and (b) who professed greater expertise to the patient than in fact he had?

Would the answers to these questions take as a starting point the proposition that a professional will be held to the standard of care he possesses or professes in excess of the minimum standard required by law if this is what he claims to have?

But, note the case of *Wimpey Construction UK Ltd v Poole* [1984] 2 Lloyd's Rep 499.

Facts: The plaintiffs constructed a quay wall. Cracks occurred in the structure and repairs were effected. The plaintiffs claimed the costs under a professional indemnity insurance policy with the defendant in respect of 'any omission, error or negligent act in respect of design or specification of work'. The issue arose whether the plaintiffs were in breach of their duty.

Webster J: [Counsel] on behalf of Wimpeys sought to put two glosses on the [*Bolam*] test for the purposes of this case. The first is that, as he submits, the test is not 'the standard of the ordinary skilled man exercising and professing to have that special skill' if the client deliberately obtains and pays for someone with specially high skills.

Mr Justice Megarry, as he then was, considered but did not decide the question in the *Duchess of Argyll v Beuselinck* [1972] 2 Lloyd's Rep 172, a claim of negligence against a solicitor. At pp 183–184 he said:

... One question that arose during the argument was that of the standard of care required of a solicitor; and although Counsel did their best to assist me, the question remained obscure. It was common ground that, at any rate in normal cases, an action for negligence by a solicitor is an action in contract: see *Groom v Crocker* [1939] 1 KB 194. At one stage, Mr Arnold asserted that this was of importance only in regard to limitation; but I think that later he accepted that this was too restricted a view. I can see that in actions in tort, the standard of care to be applied will normally be that of the reasonable man: those lacking in care and skill fail to observe the standards of the reasonable man at their peril, and the unusually careful and highly skilled are not held liable for falling below their own high standards if they nevertheless do all that a reasonable man would have done. But to say that in tort the standard of care is uniform does not necessarily carry the point in circumstances where the action is for a breach of an implied duty of care in a contract whereby a client retains a solicitor. No doubt the inexperienced solicitor is liable if he fails to attain the standard of a reasonably competent solicitor. But if the client employs a solicitor of high standard and great experience, will an action for negligence fail if it appears that the solicitor did not exercise the care and skill to be expected of him, though he did not fall below the standard of a reasonably competent solicitor? If the client engages an expert, and doubtless expects to pay commensurate fees, is he not entitled to expect something more than the standard of the reasonably competent? I am speaking not merely of those expert in a particular branch of the law, as contrasted with a general practitioner, but also of those of long experience and great skill as contrasted with those practising in the same field of the law but being of a more ordinary calibre and having less experience. The essence of the contract of retainer, it may be said, is that the client is retaining the particular solicitor or firm in question, and he is therefore entitled to expect from that solicitor or firm a standard of care and skill commensurate with the skill and experience which that solicitor or firm has. The

An action for medical negligence 405

uniform standard of care postulated for the world at large in tort hardly seems appropriate when the duty is not one imposed by the law of tort but arises from a contractual obligation existing between the client and the particular solicitor or firm in question. If, as is usual, the retainer contains no express term as to the solicitor's duty of care, and the matter rests upon an implied term, what is that term in the case of a solicitor of long experience or specialist skill? Is it that he will put at his client's disposal the care and skill of an average solicitor, or the care and skill that he has? I may say that Mr Arnold advanced no contention that it was the latter standard that was to be applied; but I wish to make it clear that I have not overlooked the point, which one day may require further consideration.

According to the researches of Counsel has not yet received further consideration. Mr Justice Oliver, as he then was, referred to the *Duchess of Argyll*'s case in *Midland Bank Trust Co Ltd v Hett, Stubbs and Kemp* [1979] Ch 384 at 403, but without, apparently, modifying the conventional test and for my part, if the question be material, I feel constrained by the clear words of the test as expressed by Mr Justice McNair, and by the approval of that test without qualification by the Privy Council and the House of Lords, to treat it as unqualified. Since the hearing ended I have considered the judgment of Mr Justice Kilner Brown in *Greaves & Co (Contractors) Ltd v Baynham Meikle & Partners* [1975] 1 Lloyd's Rep 31, [1974] 1 WLR 1261 where a similar point was considered. The decision in that case, however, rested on 'special circumstances' (see pp 35 and 1269 C–D) and is not, in my view, inconsistent with the conclusion I have reached.

(b) Compliance with approved practice

The central question can be shortly stated: who sets the legal standard of care with which doctors must comply? Is it, as you would ordinarily expect, the law; or is it the medical profession? If it be the latter, this would mean that the medical profession would not only be offering evidence of good practice (a factual matter) but also determining what doctors ought to do (a legal matter).

The prevailing view, certainly in the medical profession and perhaps in the courts, is that it is indeed the medical profession which sets the legal standard. Let us now see how this has come about. We must first set out the state of the existing law.

(i) The case law

Cases in which there is only one professional practice.
In *Marshall v Lindsey County Council* [1935] 1 KB 516 at 539–40 Maugham LJ said:

> The practice of the Home in not refusing fresh patients after a single case of puerperal sepsis had occurred, taking, however, the recognised sterilization precautions, is in accordance with the universal practice of maternity homes and hospitals throughout England. The Ministry of Health is in constant communication with the authorities in charge of maternity homes and hospitals. It has held many inquiries and has issued a number of reports and leaflets in connection with the problem of reducing maternal mortality. It is not suggested that the Ministry has ever proposed the drastic step which the jury appear to favour. In these circumstances I am of opinion that the defendant Council, assuming their responsibility for the acts of the medical officers and nursing staff, have acted in accordance with the recognised practice and are therefore free from liability on the ground of negligence. This is a matter of great importance in relation to the powers of juries. An act cannot, in my opinion, be held to be due to a want of reasonable care if it is in accordance with the general practice of mankind. What is reasonable in a world not wholly composed of wise men and women must depend on what people presumed to be reasonable constantly do. Many illustrations might be given and I will take one from the evidence given in this action. A jury could not, in my opinion, properly hold it to be negligent in a doctor or a midwife to perform his or her duties in a

confinement without mask and gloves, even though some experts gave evidence that in their opinion that was a wise precaution. Such an omission may become negligent if, and only if, at some future date it becomes the general custom to take such a precaution among skilled practitioners.

. . . I do not doubt the general truth . . . that a defendant charged with negligence can clear himself if he shows that he has acted in accord with general and approved practice.

Does it enter the mind of the court that the fact that there is unanimity in the profession may not entail the conclusion that this unanimously approved practice is legally appropriate as being *reasonable*? In other words why cannot a judgment of reasonableness be made by anyone other than a doctor?

Maugham LJ referred to the earlier case in the Privy Council of *Vancouver General Hospital v McDaniel* [1934] 152 LT 56. The plaintiff contracted smallpox while being treated in hospital for diphtheria. The Privy Council held that the defendants were not negligent because the expert evidence showed that the hospital's procedures for treating smallpox and preventing other patients catching it were in accordance with the general practice in Canada and the USA. Lord Alness said it was: 'difficult to affirm that negligence on the part of the [defendants] is proved. A defendant charged with negligence can clear his feet it he shows that he has acted in accordance with general and approved practice.'.

Maugham LJ's *dictum* was approved by the House of Lords in *Whiteford v Hunter* [1950] WN 553 at 554 (*per* Lord Porter).

Cases in which there are two schools of thought.
Maynard v West Midlands Regional Health Authority [1985] 1 All ER 635:

Lord Scarman: My Lords, the question in this appeal is whether a physician and a surgeon, working together in the treatment of their patient, were guilty of an error of professional judgment of such a character as to constitute a breach of their duty of care towards her. The negligence alleged against each, or one or other, of them is that contrary to the strong medical indications which should have led them to diagnose tuberculosis they held back from a firm diagnosis and decided that she should undergo the diagnostic operation, mediastinoscopy. It was an operation which carried certain risks, even when correctly performed, as it is admitted that it was in this case. One of the risks, namely damage to the left laryngeal recurrent nerve, did, as the judge has found and the respondent authority now accepts, unfortunately materialise with resulting paralysis of the left vocal chord. Comyn J, the trial judge, held that the two doctors were negligent. The Court of Appeal (Cumming-Bruce LJ and Sir Stanley Rees, Dunn LJ dissenting) held that they were not. The only issue for the House is whether the two medical men, Dr Ross who was the consultant physician and Mr Stephenson the surgeon, were guilty of an error of judgment amounting to a breach of their duty of care to their patient. Both accept that the refusal to make a firm diagnosis until they had available the findings of the diagnostic operation was one for which they were jointly responsible.

The issue is essentially one of fact; but there remains the possibility, which it will be necessary to examine closely, that the judge, although directing himself correctly as to the law, failed to apply it correctly when he came to draw the inferences on which his conclusion of negligence was based. Should this possibility be established as the true interpretation to be put on his judgment, he would, of course, be guilty of an error of law.

. . .

The only . . . question of law in the appeal is as to the nature of the duty owed by a doctor to his patient.

. . .

The present case may be classified as one of clinical judgment. Two distinguished consultants, a physician and a surgeon experienced in the treatment of chest diseases, formed a judgment as to what was, in their opinion, in the best interests of their patient. They recognised that tuberculosis was the most likely diagnosis. But in their opinion, there was an unusual factor, viz swollen glands in the mediastinum unaccompanied by any evidence of lesion in the lungs. Hodgkin's disease, carcinoma, and sarcoidosis were, therefore, possibilities. The danger they thought was Hodgkin's disease; though unlikely, it was, if present, a killer (as treatment was understood in 1970) unless remedial steps were taken in its early stage. They therefore decided on mediastinoscopy, an operative procedure which would provide them with a biopsy from the swollen gland which could be subjected to immediate microscopic examination. It is said that the evidence of tuberculosis was so strong that it was unreasonable and wrong to defer diagnosis and to put their patient to the risks of the operation. The case against them is not mistake or carelessness in performing the operation, which it is admitted was properly carried out, but an error of judgment in requiring the operation to be undertaken.

A case which is based on an allegation that a fully considered decision of two consultants in the field of their special skill was negligent clearly presents certain difficulties of proof. It is not enough to show that there is a body of competent professional opinion which considers that theirs was a wrong decision, if there also exists a body of professional opinion, equally competent, which supports the decision as reasonable in the circumstances. It is not enough to show that subsequent events show that the operation need never have been performed, if at the time the decision to operate was taken it was reasonable in the sense that a responsible body of medical opinion would have accepted it as proper. I do not think that the words of the Lord President (Clyde) in *Hunter v Hanley* 1955 SLT 213 at 217 can be bettered:

In the realm of diagnosis and treatment there is ample scope for genuine difference of opinion and one man clearly is not negligent merely because his conclusion differs from that of other professional men ... The true test for establishing negligence in diagnosis or treatment on the part of a doctor is whether he has been proved to be guilty of such failure as no doctor of ordinary skill would be guilty of if acting with ordinary care ...

... The judge accepted not only the expertise of all the medical witnesses called before him but also their truthfulness and honesty. But he found Dr Hugh-Jones 'an outstanding witness; clear, definite, logical and persuasive'. The judge continued:

I have weighed his evidence against that of the distinguished contrary experts. I do not intend or wish to take away from their distinction by holding that in the particular circumstances of this particular case I prefer his opinions and his evidence to theirs.

My Lords ... I have to say that a judge's 'preference' for one body of distinguished professional opinion to another also professionally distinguished is not sufficient to establish negligence in a practitioner whose actions have received the seal of approval of those whose opinions, truthfully expressed, honestly held, were not preferred. If this was the real reason for the judge's finding, he erred in law even though elsewhere in his judgment he stated the law correctly. For in the realm of diagnosis and treatment negligence is not established by preferring one respectable body of professional opinion to another. Failure to exercise the ordinary skill of a doctor (in the appropriate speciality, if he be a specialist) is necessary.

This case merely reflects the approach of NcNair J in *Bolam* (which we have already seen) where he said (at p 122C):

A doctor is not guilty of negligence if he has acted in accordance with a practice accepted as proper by a responsible body of medical men skilled in that particular art.

... Putting it the other way round, a doctor is not negligent, if he is acting in accordance with such a practice, merely because there is a body of opinion that takes a contrary view.

A little later, however, McNair J said something you might find rather curious (p 122D–E):

Before I deal with the details of the case, it is right to say this, that it is not essential for you to decide which of two practices is the better practice, as long as you accept that what Dr Allfrey did was in accordance with a practice accepted by responsible persons; but if the result of the evidence is that you are satisfied that this practice is better than the practice spoken of on the other side, then it is a stronger case.

Does this not suggest that it is ultimately for the jury to decide (and not for the judge) whether the doctor's conduct is reasonable? How can these statements be reconciled?

(ii) Comment on the case law

What seems to have happened is that the House of Lords in *Maynard* and also, as we will see, *Sidaway* have elevated to the status of an unquestionable proposition of law derived from *Bolam* that professional practice *will not* be reviewed by the courts.

In the *Sidaway* case Lord Scarman made this quite clear: 'The *Bolam* principle may be formulated as a rule that a doctor is not negligent if he acts in accordance with a practice accepted at the time as proper by a responsible body of medical opinion even though other doctors adopt a different practice. In short, the law imposes the duty of care: but the standard of care is a matter of medical judgement.'.

Two questions arise:
1. Is this good law?
2. Is this law good?

Is this good law? Consider the non-medical cases first:
Cavanagh v Ulster Weaving Co Ltd
[1960] AC 145, [1959] 2 All ER 745, HL. (The facts are taken from the headnote.)

> The appellant, a labourer employed by the respondents, was carrying a bucket of cement weighing some three stones down a roof ladder laid flat against the slated aspect of a slanting roof. He put the bucket down on a plank before starting to descend the ladder facing forwards. Having placed his feet in a position on the second or third rung of the ladder from the top, he had to turn to pick up the bucket and in so doing he slipped and fell some six feet against a sloping glass roof opposite him and injured himself. There was no handrail with which he could support himself with one hand as he descended the ladder with the bucket in the other hand, nor was there any protection to save him from the glass in the opposite roof if he should slip. He was wearing rubber boots which had been provided by the respondents in view of an accumulation of water in the gully between the slanting roofs along which he had to proceed after descending the ladder. In an action by the appellant against the respondents for damages for personal injuries, there was evidence that the rubber boots were two sizes larger than they should have been for a man with feet the size of the appellant's. An expert witness for the respondents was asked in relation to the system adopted for the carrying of cement on the roof, how far 'this set up' was in accord with good practice, and he testified it was perfectly in accord with good practice. His evidence was uncontradicted. A submission on behalf of the respondents that there was no evidence of negligence to go to the jury was disallowed. The jury found that the respondents had been negligent.

The Court of Appeal allowed an appeal by the respondents. The House of Lords unanimously allowed the appellant's further appeal. Viscount Simonds said:

> The evidence given by the expert called for the defence in regard to what was called 'the set up', which was not seriously or perhaps at all challenged, was of very great weight, but I cannot say that it was so conclusive as to require the learned trial judge to withdraw the case from the jury. There were other matters also which they were entitled to take into consideration, and it was for them to determine whether, in all

the circumstances, the respondents had taken reasonable care. I do not think that the learned judges of the Court of Appeal were justified in concluding that reasonable men might not find the verdict which this jury found. If I may respectfully say so, I think that the error of the majority of the court lay in treating as conclusive evidence which is not conclusive however great its weight, particularly where it has to be weighed against other evidence.

As to the evidence of practice, Lord Tucker said (footnotes omitted):

> My Lords, I have already expressed my views on the value of this kind of evidence in *Morris v West Hartlepool Steam Navigation Co, Ltd* ([1956] 1 All ER 385 at 400) which I need not repeat, but it was not necessary for me in that case to refer to the language of Lord Dunedin in *Morton v William Dixon, Ltd*. I would, however, desire to express my agreement with what was said by my noble and learned friend, Lord Cohen, in *Morris's* case where, after reviewing what had been said on this subject in *Paris v Stepney Borough Council* ([1951] 1 All ER 42), and considering the language used by Parker LJ, in the case under consideration, he said ([1956] 1 All ER at 402):
>> I think that the effect of their Lordships' observations is that, when the court finds a clearly established practice 'in like circumstances', the practice weighs heavily in the scale on the side of the defendant and the burden of establishing negligence, which the plaintiff has to discharge, is a heavy one.
> . . .
> My Lords, I would respectfully accept the statement of the law on this subject in the present case by the Lord Chief Justice (Lord MacDermott)
> . . .

He said that, where positive evidence is adduced for the defendant that an employer has not omitted to do anything that is commonly done by other persons in like circumstances,

> Such a fact is clearly relevant, and once it is established, it is my opinion that a finding by the jury that it was folly in the [respondents] to neglect to provide something else, cannot be justified.

In *Thompson v Smiths Shiprepairers (North Shields) Ltd* [1984] QB 405, [1984] 1 All ER 881, the plaintiffs worked in shipbuilding yards for many years. They were exposed to excessive noise which, they alleged, affected their hearing. In an action for negligence brought against their employers, the trial judge, Mustill J (as he then was) considered the relevance of industrial practice in determining whether the employers were in breach of their duty to the plaintiffs.

> The plaintiffs allege that the defendants were negligent in the following respects: (i) in failing to recognise the existence of high levels of noise in their shipyards, and the fact that such noise created a risk of irreversible damage to hearing; (ii) in failing to provide any or sufficient ear protection devices, or to give the necessary advice and encouragement for the wearing of such devices as were provided; (iii) in failing to investigate and take advice on the noise levels in their yards; (iv) in failing to reduce the noise created by work in their yards; (v) in failing to organise the layout and timing of the work so as to minimise the effect of noise. In the first instance I will concentrate on items (i) and (ii), since these are by far the most substantial.
>   There was general agreement that the principles to be applied when weighing up allegations of this kind are correctly set out in the following passage from the judgment of Swanwick J in *Stokes v GKN (Bolts and Nuts) Ltd* [1968] 1 WLR 1776 at 1783:
>> From these authorities I deduce the principles, that the overall test is still the conduct of the reasonable and prudent employer, taking positive thought for the safety of his workers in the light of what he knows or ought to know; where there is a recognised and general practice which has been followed for a substantial period in similar circumstances without mishap, he is entitled to follow it, unless in the light of common sense or newer knowledge, it is clearly bad; but, where there is developing knowledge, he must keep reasonably abreast of it and not be

too slow to apply it; and where he has in fact greater than average knowledge of the risks, he may be thereby obliged to take more than the average or standard precautions. He must weigh up the risk in terms of the likelihood of injury occurring and the potential consequences if it does; and he must balance against this the probable effectiveness of the precautions that can be taken to meet it and the expense and inconvenience they involve. If he is found to have fallen below the standard to be properly expected of a reasonable and prudent employer in these respects, he is negligent.

I shall direct myself in accordance with this succinct and helpful statement of the law, and will make only one additional comment. In the passage just cited, Swanwick J drew a distinction between a recognised practice followed without mishap, and one which in the light of common sense or increased knowledge is clearly bad. The distinction is indeed valid and sufficient for many cases. The two categories are not, however, exhaustive, as the present actions demonstrate. The practice of leaving employees unprotected against excessive noise had never been followed 'without mishap'. Yet even the plaintiffs have not suggested that it was 'clearly bad', in the sense of creating a potential liability in negligence, at any time before the mid-1930s. Between the two extremes is a type of risk which is regarded at any given time (although not necessarily later) as an inescapable feature of the industry. The employer is not liable for the consequences of such risks, although subsequent changes in social awareness, or improvements in knowledge and technology, may transfer the risk into the category of those against which the employer can and should take care. It is unnecessary, and perhaps impossible, to give a comprehensive formula for identifying the line between the acceptable and the unacceptable. Nevertheless, the line does exist, and was clearly recognised in *Morris v West Hartlepool Steam Navigation Co Ltd* [1956] 1 All ER 385, [1956] AC 552. The speeches in that case show, not that one employer is exonerated simply by proving that other employers are just as negligent, but that the standard of what is negligent is influenced, although not decisively, by the practice in the industry as a whole. In my judgment, this principle applies not only where the breach of duty is said to consist of a failure to take precautions known to be available as a means of combating a known danger, but also where the omission involves an absence of initiative in seeking out knowledge of facts which are not in themselves obvious. The employer must keep up to date, but the court must be slow to blame him for not ploughing a lone furrow.

(The judge held that, on the facts, the defendants were not careless in respect of exposure to noise before 1963 but were thereafter.)

Even in professional negligence cases, compliance with approved practice has not been considered conclusive in determining whether a breach of duty has occurred.

In *Edward Wong Finance Co Ltd v Johnson, Stokes and Master* [1984] AC 296, the Privy Council held that the defendant solicitors were careless even though they had complied with the 'normal customary conveyancing practice in Hong Kong'. The Privy Council approved the dissenting judgment of Li JA in the Hong Kong Court of Appeal, which was as follows:

The test for negligence or otherwise in this case means whether a reasonable, diligent and competent solicitor could foresee in January 1976 that damage could result by adopting the Hong Kong practice of completion. . . . Applying this test to the present case I find Miss Leung, as a solicitor when adopting the Hong Kong practice for completion in January 1976 complied with the general practice which had been practised for years without ill result of the form of damage as in this case flowing from it. That goes a long way to show that she was not negligent. However, that is not conclusive. The further question to be asked is: could she foresee the risk or ill result at the material time as an ordinary, reasonable prudent person? I am afraid the answer must be in the affirmative. As a solicitor, even in January 1976, she should know that her client, the plaintiff, would not obtain what it lent its money for unless and until the vendor had executed the assignment and delivered the title deeds. If she parted with the money without such delivery she did not receive what her client had paid for apart from an undertaking or a promise by a fellow member of her profession. As a reasonable person of ordinary prudence she should or ought to have foreseen the risk of parting with the money before obtaining the property one bought in any ordinary transaction. It was not her skill that was put to test. It was her common sense, her prudence of any ordinary person that is put to test. The so called Hong Kong practice has an inherent risk in the ordinary sense. The fact that practically all her fellow solicitors adopted this practice is not conclusive evidence that it is prudent ... acting in accordance with the general practice she took a foreseeable risk for her client while there was no necessity to do so. The fact that other solicitors did the same did not make the risk less apparent or unreal.

Why should the court approach a medical case any differently?

What appears to have happened is that because technical matters are involved, on which expert evidence is needed, courts have regarded the issue of the standard of care as itself a technical matter for the profession. This is, of course, to fail to distinguish between what *is* ordinarily done and what *should* be done. As regards the latter, the court may in certain circumstances have something to say as the guardian of the interests of society, as the cases above show.

Consider now cases involving medical practice both in England and the Commonwealth.

F v R
(1983) 33 SASR 189 (Supreme Court of South Australia)

Facts: A married woman was advised to have a tubal ligation operation to sterilise her when she desired to have no further children. Although the operation was competently performed, the procedure naturally reversed itself sometime later and the plaintiff became pregnant. She brought an action in negligence against the doctor who had advised her for failing to warn her of the less than 1% failure rate. Evidence was given that this was in conformity with a responsible body of medical opinion. The Supreme Court held that the defendant had not been careless. The judges had the following to say on the relevance of evidence of professional practice (footnotes omitted):

King CJ: In answering that question [whether the doctor is in breach of his duty] much assistance will be derived from evidence as to the practice obtaining in the medical profession. I am unable to accept, however, that such evidence can be decisive in all circumstances: *Goode v Nash*. There is great force in the following passage from the judgment of the Supreme Court of Canada in *Reibl v Hughes*:

To allow expert medical evidence to determine what risks are material and, hence, should be disclosed and, correlatively, what risks are not material is to hand over to the medical profession the entire question of the scope of the duty of disclosure, including the question whether there has been a breach of that duty. Expert medical evidence is, of course, relevant to findings as to the risks that reside in or are a result of recommended surgery or other treatment. It will also have a bearing on their materiality but this is not a question that is to be concluded on the basis of the expert medical evidence alone. The issue under consideration is a different issue from that involved where the question is whether the doctor carried out his professional activities by applicable professional standards. What is under consideration here is the patient's right to know what risks are involved in undergoing or foregoing certain surgery or other treatment.

In many cases an approved professional practice as to disclosure will be decisive. But professions may adopt unreasonable practices. Practices may develop in professions, particularly as to disclosure, not because they serve the interests of the clients, but because they protect the interests or convenience of members of the profession. The court has an obligation to scrutinize professional practices to ensure that they accord with the standard of reasonableness imposed by the law. A practice as to disclosure approved and adopted by a profession or a section of it may be in many cases the determining consideration as to what is reasonable. On the facts of a particular case the answer to the question whether the defendant's conduct conformed to approved professional practice may decide the issue of negligence, and the test has been posed in such terms in a number of cases. The ultimate question, however, is not whether the defendant's conduct accords with the practices of his profession or some part of it, but whether it conforms to the standard of reasonable care demanded by the law. That is a question for the Court and the duty of deciding it cannot be delegated to any profession or group in the community.

. . . It is for the Court to decide what a careful and responsible doctor would explain to the patient in the circumstances, and I do not regard as decisive the opinions of the medical witnesses on the point or the existence of a practice of non-disclosure in a section of the profession. If the Court thought that that practice involved a failure to exercise reasonable care towards the patient, I would regard it as its duty to give effect to that view. Indeed I am of opinion that the better practice, and that which accords best with the rights and interests of the patient, is that adopted by those doctors who do warn of the possibility, however slight, of subsequent pregnancy. But that is not to say that in following the non-disclosure practice, the appellant was in breach of her duty of care to the patient. In the totality of the circumstances which I have discussed, and bearing in mind that the appellant was acting in pursuance of a considered judgment as to what was in the best interests of her patient and of a practice followed by a substantial part, probably the greater part, of those medical practitioners practising in this area of medical practice, I consider that her failure to volunteer the information as to the possibility of future pregnancy was not in breach of the legal duty of care.

Bollen J added the following remarks.

Mr Perry's [Counsel for the doctor] answer was that the responsible body of medical opinion should prevail over the view of the Court. That would mean that there was no room for the opinion of the Court on vital issues. The Court's function would be limited to ascertaining that there was a responsible body of medical opinion and deciding whether the surgeon had followed it.

Many cases require the calling of expert evidence. These experts frequently express opinions on matters within their field. Sometimes they speak of what is usually done in any activity within that field. Why is the evidence received? It is received to guide or help the court. A court cannot be expected to know the correct procedure for performing a surgical operation. The Court cannot be expected to know why a manufacturer should guard against metal fatigue. A court cannot be expected to know how to mix chemicals. And so on. Expert evidence will assist the Court. But in the end it is the Court which must say whether there was a duty owed and a breach of it. The Court will have been guided and assisted by the expert evidence. It will not produce an answer merely at the dictation of the expert evidence. It will afford great weight to the expert evidence. Sometimes its decision will be the same as it would have been had it accepted dictation. But the Court does not merely follow expert evidence slavishly to a decision. The Court considers and weighs up all admissible evidence which it has received. If the Court did merely follow the path apparently pointed by expert evidence with no critical consideration of it and the other evidence, it would abdicate its duty to decide, on the evidence, whether in law a duty existed and had not been discharged. Acceptance of Mr Perry's first submission could amount to abdication here.

. . . I can find nothing in *Bolam v Friern Hospital Management Committee* which justifies any suggestion that evidence of the practice obtaining in the medical profession is automatically decisive of any issue in an action against a surgeon for damages in negligence. Sometimes that evidence will be decisive, sometimes not. It is least likely to be decisive when the allegation is of a failure to warn or to heed complaints of pain i e where no information about the method of procedure or basis of diagnosis is required.

... I respectfully think that some of the cases in England have concentrated rather too heavily on the practice of the medical profession.

Admittedly, this was a case on disclosure of risks inherent in a medical procedure. You will recall the difference of opinion about the relevance of professional practice in cases of disclosure of information exemplified in the *Sidaway* case.

We saw that the majority of the House of Lords in *Sidaway* were not wholly content to import the *Bolam* principle into this area of the law. In the Court of Appeal in *Sidaway*, Sir John Donaldson MR (at p 1028) seemed anxious to point out that *Bolam* had been misunderstood. To him, what doctors do is only to be regarded as lawful provided the law considers what they do to be *right*.

I accept the view expressed by Laskin CJC [in *Reibl v Hughes*] that the definition of the duty of care is not to be handed over to the medical or any other profession. The definition of the duty of care is a matter for the law and the courts. They cannot stand idly by if the profession, by an excess of paternalism, denies its patients a real choice. In a word, the law will not permit the medical profession to play God.

Thus, while I accept the *Bolam* test as the primary test of liability for failing to disclose sufficient information to the patient to enable that patient to exercise his right of choice whether or not to accept the advice proffered by his doctor, I do so subject to an important caveat. This is that the profession, or that section of it which is relied on by the defendant doctor as setting the requisite standard of care, is discharging the duty of disclosure as I have defined it. This, incidentally, accords with the approach of Parliament, which, in s 1(5) of the Congenital Disability (Civil Liability) Act 1976, enacted that—

The defendant is not answerable . . . if he took reasonable care having *due regard* to then received professional opinion applicable . . . but this does not mean that he is answerable only because he departed from received opinion.

'Due regard' involves an exercise of judgment, *inter alia*, whether 'received professional opinion' is engaged in the same exercise as the law. This qualification is analogous to that which has been asserted in the context of treating a trade practice as evidencing the proper standard of care in *Cavanagh v Ulster Weaving Co Ltd* [1959] 2 All ER 745, [1960] AC 145 and in *Morris v West Hartlepool Steam Navigation Co Ltd* [1956] 1 All ER 385, [1956] AC 552 and would be equally infrequently relevant.

. . . I think that, in an appropriate case, a judge would be entitled to reject a unanimous medical view if he were satisfied that it was manifestly wrong and that the doctors must have been misdirecting themselves as to their duty in law.

Another way of expressing my view of the test is to add just one qualifying word (which I have emphasised) to the law as Skinner J summarised it, so that it would read:

The duty is fulfilled if the doctor acts in accordance with a practice *rightly* accepted as proper by a body of skilled and experienced medical men.

But even in circumstances of diagnosis and treatment (rather than disclosure) in which it has been assumed that *Bolam* applies, a number of Commonwealth cases flatly reject this view. Consider the decision of the Court of Appeal of Manitoba in *Anderson v Chasney* (1949) 4 DLR 71; affd *sub nom Chasney v Anderson* (1950) 4 DLR 223 (SCC). McPherson CJM said:

The question left for consideration is: Was the doctor negligent in the care of the child after the operation had been completed? It was submitted that the expert testimony given, clearly relieved him of all negligence and that the expert testimony had to be accepted on that point. I cannot agree with that argument. Where there is other evidence in contradiction of the opinion of the expert testimony, which can be understood by a layman, those facts can be taken into consideration. In 48 Corp Jur, p 1151, it is stated: 'Expert evidence is not required, however, where the results of the treatment are of such character as to warrant the inference of want of care from the testimony of laymen or in the light of the knowledge and experience of the jurors themselves'.

And in *Mehigan v Sheehan* 51 Atl Rep (2d) 632 (1947): 'Expert testimony is not necessary for proof of negligence in nontechnical matters or matters of which an ordinary person may be expected to have knowledge'. [headnote]

While the method in which the operation was performed may be purely a matter of technical evidence, the fact that a sponge was left in a position where it was or was not dangerous is one which the ordinary man is competent to consider in arriving at a decision as to whether or not there was negligence.

Coyne JA said:

Dr Chasney defends on the ground that it has not been his practice, and that it is not the usual practice of operators in the hospital in question and of some operators elsewhere, to take these precautions. But he took a chance in neglecting them. Whether to adopt them or not, he says, is a matter of surgical skill and experience and the general practice of practitioners is conclusive. This, however, was not peculiarly a matter of such skill and experience. His counsel argued that if a general practice of surgeons is followed, negligence cannot be attributed, and that expert evidence is conclusive. But if that were correct the expert witnesses would, in effect, be the jury to try the question of negligence. That question, however, must continue to be one for the petit jury empanelled to try the case, if it is a jury case, and for the Court where it is not. The experts remain witnesses to give their expert opinions in assistance of the jury or the Court to determine whether there was negligence or not. The opinions of the experts are not conclusive. But when an operation itself is a complicated and critical one, and acquaintance with anatomy, physiology or other subjects of expert medical knowledge, skill and experience are essential, jury or Court may not be justified in disregarding such opinions and reaching conclusions based on views contrary to those of the experts. That is not the case here. Effective antecedent precautions were not taken and ordinary experience of jurymen or Court is sufficient to enable them to pass upon the question whether such conduct constituted negligence. In my opinion it is clearly so in this case.

...

Whether or not it is negligence to omit to use sponges with ties or to have a count kept is not a matter which requires an expert to decide; it is not special surgical skill that is in question. Such skill is not necessary to answer the question. The point involved is negligence or no negligence. It is not a matter here which requires an expert to decide. General practice of the defendant and some others does not constitute a complete defence. It is some evidence to be taken into consideration on the question of negligence but it is not conclusive on Court or jury. If it were a defence conclusive on jury or Court, a group of operators by adopting some practice could legislate themselves out of liability for negligence to the public by adopting or continuing what was an obviously negligent practice, even though a simple precaution, plainly capable of obviating danger which sometimes might result in death, was well known. A defence based on general practice among surgeons cannot be sustained by evidence of general practice among the surgeons of one hospital in Winnipeg when Dr Chasney admits that it is the practice in the Winnipeg General Hospital to do otherwise, although, as he says, he did not know that at the time of the operation. If a practitioner refuses to take an obvious precaution, he cannot exonerate himself by showing that others also neglect to take it.

...

To return to the case against the doctor: It is true, of course, that Maugham LJ has said that 'an act cannot . . . be held to be due to a want of reasonable care if it is in accordance with the *general practice of mankind* . . . A defendant charged with negligence can clear himself if he shows that he has acted in accord with general and *approved* practice' (The italics are mine.): Maugham LJ, dissenting, in *Marshall*

v Lindsey County Council [1935] 1 KB 516 at 540. The decision of the majority of the
Court was affirmed in [1937] AC 97, [1936] 2 All ER 1076, but with no reference to
the observation quoted above, which is irrelevant to the decision of either Court.

A number of authorities have been cited to us including the case of *Mahon v
Osborne* [1939] 1 All ER 535 at 557, where MacKinnon LJ says that the jury 'must
take the standard of care and diligence of a surgeon from those who could alone,
from their expert knowledge, inform them of it'. This was treated as a universal rule
and relied on by counsel for Dr Chasney to support a principle that as to the
precautions which should be taken in connection with an operation, which is not a
matter of practice and experience of lay persons, the Court or jury must be informed
by proper expert evidence of general surgical practice and must accept such practice
if followed by the defendant, as conclusive against negligence on his part. No such
rule and principle is to be found in the judgment of the other members of the Court
and obviously the statement of MacKinnon LJ was directed to the circumstances of
the particular case then before the Court. All that the case actually decides is that
relevant and material evidence of two surgeons was not properly and adequately
placed before the jury by the trial Judge; that the defendant was thereby prejudiced
and, therefore, that there should be a new trial. Scott and MacKinnon LJJ concurred
in this. If the Court had been of the opinion that the jury were bound to follow the
expert evidence, the Court would have had to allow the appeal and dismiss the
action. The circumstances of that case are entirely and fundamentally different from
the case before us.

Two interpretations may be possible. One, that when the issue at stake,
though technical, is not so technical that a court cannot understand it, then the
court may have a view. But when, however, the issue at stake is sufficiently
technical to be beyond the competence of the court, the court has no alternative
but to follow the expert evidence. The other interpretation is that the court may
always impose its view of what is the proper standard of care regardless of the
technical complexity of the particular issue at stake. Which of these views is
reflected in the rarely cited English case of *Hucks v Cole* (1968) 112 Sol Jo 483,
CA (Lord Denning MR, Diplock and Sachs LJJ)?

Facts: A doctor failed to treat a patient with penicillin and injury resulted when
septicaemia occurred. The trial judge held the doctor liable in negligence. His
appeal was dismissed by the Court of Appeal.

We set out here an extract from the judgment of Sachs LJ in the transcript of
the case.

In the present case Dr Cole knew on the 15th October that the septic places from
which the plaintiff was suffering had been infected by streptococcus pyogenes; that
for this streptococcus in this patient penicillin was bacteriocidal whereas tetracycline,
which was being administered, was not; and that penicillin could easily and
inexpensively be administered before the onset occurred. It was not administered
and the onset occurred: if it had been administered the onset would not have
occurred. Thus (unless there was some good cause for not administering it) the onset
was due to a lacuna between what could easily have been done and what was in fact
done. According to the defence, that lacuna was consistent with and indeed accorded
with the reasonable practice of other responsible doctors with obstetric experience.

When the evidence shows that a lacuna in professional practice exists by which
risks of grave danger are knowingly taken, then, however small the risks, the Courts
must anxiously examine that lacuna—particularly if the risks can be easily and
inexpensively avoided. If the Court finds, on an analysis of the reasons given for not
taking those precautions that, in the light of current professional knowledge, there
is no proper basis for the lacuna, and that it is definitely not reasonable that those
risks should have been taken, its function is to state that fact and where necessary
to state that it constitutes negligence. In such a case the practice will no doubt
thereafter be altered to the benefit of patients.

On such occasions the fact that other practitioners would have done the same thing as the defendant practitioner is a very weighty matter to be put in the scales on his behalf; but it is not, as Mr Webster readily conceded, conclusive. The Court must be vigilant to see whether the reasons given for putting a patient at risk are valid in the light of any well-known advance in medical knowledge, or whether they stem from a residual adherence to out-of-date ideas—a tendency which in the present case may well have affected the views of at any rate one of the defendant's witnesses, who, at a considerable age, seemed not to have any particular respect for laboratory results.

. . .

Despite the fact that the risk could have been avoided by adopting a course that was easy, efficient, and inexpensive, and which would have entailed only minimal chances of disadvantages to the patient, the evidence of the four defence experts to the effect that they and other responsible members of the medical profession would have taken the same risk in the same circumstances has naturally caused me to hesitate considerably on two points. Firstly, whether the failure of the defendant to turn over to penicillin treatment during the relevant period was unreasonable. On this, however, I was in the end fully satisfied that in the light of the admissions made by the defendant himself and by his witnesses—quite apart from Dr May's very cogent evidence—that failure to do this was not merely wrong but clearly unreasonable. The reasons given by the four experts do not to my mind stand up to analysis.

It is in this connection perhaps as well at this stage to mention one other point. The fact that great discoveries have been made which by their unremitting use so far eliminate dangers that the modern practitioner is unlikely ever to see the effects of these dangers is no reason for failing to be unremitting in their use even when the risks have become very small. It is not to my mind in point for a practitioner to say, as Dr Cole said (Day 5, page 20) and as Dr June Smith appeared to say (Day 6, page 32) that if he had previously actually seen how dire the effects were of not taking the relevant precaution he would have taken it, but his experience had not up till then led him to see such results. (The potential irrelevance of the rarity or remoteness of the risk, when the maturing of the risk may be disastrous, is incidentally illustrated in *Chin Keow*'s case [1967] 1 WLR 813, PC.)

Secondly, as to whether, in the light of such evidence as to what other responsible medical practitioners would have done, it can be said that even if the defendant's error was unreasonable, it was [not] negligence in relation to the position as regards practice at that particular date. On this second point it is to be noted that this is not apparently a case of 'two schools of thought', (see the speech of Lord Goddard in *Chapman v Rix*, on the 21st December, 1960, at page 11): it appears more to be a case of doctors who said in one form or another that they would have acted or might have acted in the same way as the defendant did, for reasons which on examination do not really stand up to analysis.

Dr Cole knowingly took an easily avoidable risk which elementary teaching had instructed him to avoid; and the fact that others say they would have done the same neither ought to nor can in the present case excuse him in an action for negligence however sympathetic one may be to him. Moreover, in so far as the evidence shows the existence of a lacuna of the type to which reference was made earlier in this judgment, that lacuna was, in view of the magnitude of the dangers involved, so unreasonable that as between doctor and patient it cannot be relied upon to excuse the former in an action for negligence.

Lord Denning and Diplock LJ agreed that the defendant was in breach of his duty to the plaintiff. Another English case which it is sometimes said gives short shrift to the principle, later enshrined in *Bolam*, is *Clarke v Adams* (1950) 94 Sol Jo 599 (Slade J).

The plaintiff was treated by the defendant, a physiotherapist, for fibrositic condition of the left heel. He suffered injury by burning which resulted in his having to have the leg amputated below the knee, and brought this action for damages. Before applying the treatment the defendant gave the plaintiff this warning: 'When

I turn on the machine I want you to experience a comfortable warmth and nothing more; if you do, I want you to tell me.' Evidence was given by the chief examiner for the Chartered Society of Physiotherapy that that warning was an entirely proper one. Slade J, said that clearly in physiotherapy the co-operation of the patient was vital. The instrument used was dangerous because burns caused by it could lead to serious consequences. It was extremely unlikely that the defendant, a skilled physiotherapist, on being told by the plaintiff that he was undergoing such pain that he could not bear it, would take no precautions. There was no evidence that the apparatus used was defective. The sole question left was therefore whether the warning given by the defendant, said to be an entirely proper one, was sufficient. There must in such circumstances as the present be a warning of danger as it would appear to a hypothetically reasonable person. Would the words used here warn such a person that his safety depended on his informing the defendant the moment he felt more than comfortable warmth? The warning must be couched in terms which made it abundantly clear that it was a warning of danger. He was not satisfied that this warning, although the very warning which the defendant had been taught to give, was adequate, and on that ground the plaintiff was entitled to recover.

Notice, finally, the view of Professor Fleming in the 7th edition of his book *The Law of Torts* (1988), p 110 (footnotes omitted):

Common practice plays its most conspicuous role in medical negligence actions. Conscious at once of the layman's ignorance of medical science and apprehensive of the impact of jury bias on a peculiarly vulnerable profession, courts have resorted to the safeguard of insisting that negligence in diagnosis and treatment (including disclosure of risks) cannot ordinarily be established without the aid of expert testimony or in the teeth of conformity with accepted medical practice. However there is no categorical rule. Thus an accepted practice is open to censure by a jury (nor expert testimony required) at any rate in matters not involving diagnostic or clinical skills, on which an ordinary person may presume to pass judgment sensibly, like omission to inform the patient of risks, failure to remove a sponge, an explosion set-off by an admixture of ether vapour and oxygen or injury to a patient's body outside the area of treatment.

Is this law good? Is there not a fundamental problem underlying the approach of McNair J in *Bolam* and followed thereafter? Is not the standard of care a *prescriptive* question rather than merely descriptive? Being prescriptive, is it not unusual for the court to allow a particular group (in this case the medical profession) to prescribe what the law is?

Professor Montrose with characteristic acumen saw the difficulties raised by *Bolam* immediately as can be seen from his article 'Is Negligence an Ethical or a Sociological Concept?' (1958) 21 MLR 259 (footnotes omitted).

Ever since *Blyth v Birmingham Waterworks* it has been usual to state the standard for negligence by reference to the 'reasonable man', or the 'prudent and reasonable man', the terms used by Baron Alderson in his judgment. Sometimes mention is made of the 'ordinary' man, the 'man on the Clapham omnibus', but hitherto conduct has not been exonerated from being considered negligent merely because it is of the kind ordinarily done by ordinary people. A motorist is not excused because he shows that he acted in accordance with the common practice of motorists. The question of negligence is one of what *ought* to be done in the circumstances, not what *is* done in similar circumstances by most people or even by all people. In so far as negligence is concerned with what ought to be done, it may be called an ethical concept: in so far as it is concerned with what is done, with practice, it may be said to be a sociological concept.

   ... [The view of McNair J in *Bolam*] that conformity with practice cannot be negligent stems from a failure to heed the warning of Stallybrass that the 'imagery' of the 'man in the street' may be misleading. McNair J explained the law of negligence to the jury in these terms: 'In the ordinary case which does not involve any special skill negligence in law means this: Some failure to do some act which a reasonable man in the street would do, or doing some act which a reasonable man in the circumstances would not do: and if that failure or the doing of that act results in injury, then there is a cause of action. How do you test whether this failure or cause of action is negligent? In an ordinary case it is generally said that you judge that by the action of the man in the street. He is the ordinary man. In one case it has been said that you judge it by the conduct of the man on the top of a Clapham omnibus. He is the ordinary man.' But the suggested test, though useful as a guide in many cases, is not a universal test: it omits the important qualification stressed by Stallybrass: 'The "man in the street" does not always show the care of a reasonably prudent man in the circumstances.' From the premises of McNair J it does indeed follow that in 'a situation which involves the use of some special skill or competence', and where there are diverse practices followed by those possessed of that skill, then conformity with one of those practices cannot be negligence. But the qualification which has to be added to the premises has to be added also to the conclusion. It is for the court to say whether the ordinary behaviour of the man in the street, or the ordinary practice of those possessed of 'special skill or competence', is reasonable and prudent.

It is, perhaps, going too far to say that McNair J has entirely omitted the possibility of consideration of a recognised practice as negligence. In the passages already quoted there do occur the epithets 'proper' and 'reasonable', which may refer to objective qualifications and not to subjective beliefs of those following the practice. This attitude appears more clearly in another passage: 'I do not think that I quarrel much with any of the submissions in law which have been put before you by counsel. Counsel for the plaintiff put it in this way, that in the case of a medical man negligence means failure to act in accordance with the standards of reasonably competent medical men at the time. That is a perfectly accurate statement, as long as it is remembered that there may be one or more perfectly proper standards; and if a medical man conforms with one of those proper standards then he is not negligent.' Moreover, in his survey of the evidence McNair J referred throughout to the objective reasons for holding that the practice of the defendants was reasonable. He discussed the evidence which had been given of the mortality risk from the use of relaxant drugs, and of the danger of fracture from the use of manual control.

Though it is submitted that the doctrine that mere conformity with practice is legally well established, analysis is required in order that its limits and value may be ascertained. In the first place it is important to distinguish between average practices and average standards, between what the ordinary man does and what the ordinary man thinks ought to be done. His practice is not a necessary determinant of his ethics. *Video meliora proboque, deteriora sequor* applies to peasants and poets. Chorley contends for the view that negligence in motoring cases should be determined by 'that which is regarded as reasonable by motorists generally': this is very different from a statistical average of the conduct of motorists. In the next place, we should consider a distinction suggested by the dictum of Lord Wright in *Lloyds Bank v E B Savory & Co* [[1933] AC 201]. It will be recalled that he considered a banking practice for failure to provide against a risk. The distinction now to be examined is that between failure to provide against a risk, a fault of omission, and inefficiency in the technique employed to deal with a risk. The failure may be in connection with a known risk, or a risk which ought to have been known. It is true that Lord Wright referred only to risks 'fully known to those experienced in the business of banking', but that limitation arises from the facts of the case. It is surely negligent not to provide against risks which ought to have been known. The fact that it was not appreciated by men experienced in the particular province is, of course, strong evidence that it could not reasonably be expected to have been known and guarded against, but not conclusive evidence. Experts may blind themselves by expertise. The courts should protect the citizen against risks which professional men and others may ignore. A doctor in his enthusiasm for a new cure may not properly appreciate the dangers of his treatment: a trade unionist in his concern for less exhausting labour by his colleagues may not properly appreciate the dangers to others from his easier practice. It is sound ethics and good law for a court, judge or jury to condemn a professional practice which does not provide precautions against risks known to the profession or which the court judges ought to have been known. But when the question arises of whether precautions in fact taken are adequate then different considerations may arise. If the practice adopted is one which is designed by those with skill and competence in the particular province to deal with a risk, is it then good law for the court to bring its own judgment to bear on the matter? Frankfurter J, in a case concerned with 'matters of geography and geology and physics and engineering', pointed out that the court had no expertise in these matters. Chorley likewise points out that in motoring cases, where the question is one of precautions to be taken against the well-known risks of collisions, a court does not as such possess expertise in driving, even though 'the learned trial judge is an experienced motorist'. [(1938) 2 MLR 69.] Perhaps the attitude of McNair J in *Bolam's* case may be 'explained' as being concerned with the adequacy of precautions designed by those with skill and competence to safeguard against a realised risk. The case for the defence was that free movement of the limbs was the best precaution against injury. It is uniformity with a practice consisting in a technique of precautions against risks which eliminates negligence. We are, however, far from judicial recognition of a distinction between failure to provide against a risk, and adequacy of precautions. The most that can be said is that *Bolam's* case is consistent with the distinction.

Why do you think the courts have adopted the *Bolam* approach? One answer might be in the fact that the court is so often presented with an issue of apparent technical complexity. Finding it difficult to determine what is done and hearing evidence of what *is* done tends to depend upon particular facts of each case, the court has tended to elide the distinct issue of what *ought* to be done with its decision of what *is* done.

Take a simple case. Dr X testifies, supported by his witnesses, that he would never carry out a particular procedure when presented with facts 'P'. The plaintiff, supported by his witnesses, says the procedure should have been carried out when facts 'P' were present.

The issue for the court, in essence, is to untangle the reasons offered by the differing medical experts, rather than be concerned superficially with the description of their practice. The reasons offered may relate to, for example, the consequences of carrying (or not carrying) out the procedure, the risks and benefits associated with it, the qualify of information to be gained as against any risk or benefit, the cost in terms of manpower or other expenditure of scarce resources. All of these questions, you will see, are questions of values and not technical-medical issues at all.

Being questions of value, in all other circumstances they would be properly regarded as for the court. Why is this not the case here?

Another reason for the existing state of the law may be the expressed concern of the courts to avoid what has been called the American disease of malpractice litigation resulting in 'defensive medicine'. In *Whitehouse v Jordan* (*supra*), Lord Denning MR described 'defensive medicine' thus (at p 658):

Take heed of what has happened in the United States. 'Medical malpractice' cases there are very worrying, especially as they are tried by juries who have sympathy for the patient and none for the doctor, who is insured. The damages are colossal. The doctors insure but the premiums become very high: and these have to be passed on in fees to the patients. Experienced practitioners are known to have refused to treat patients for fear of being accused of negligence. Young men are even deterred from entering the profession because of the risks involved. In the interests of all, we must avoid such consequences in England.

(See also Lawton LJ at p 659.)

In the *Sidaway* case (*supra*), Lord Scarman offered the following description (at p 653):

> The prolification of medical malpractice suits in the United States of America has led some courts and some legislatures to curtail or even to reject the operation of the doctrine in an endeavour to restrict the liability of the doctor and so discourage the practice of 'defensive medicine', by which is meant the practice of doctors advising and undertaking the treatment which they think is legally safe even though they may believe that it is not the best for their patient.
>
> The danger of defensive medicine developing in this country clearly exists, though the absence of the lawyer's 'contingency fee' (a percentage of the damages for him as his fee if he wins the case but nothing if he loses) may make it more remote. However that may be, in matters of civil wrong or tort courts are concerned with legal principle; if policy problems emerge, they are best left to the legislature: see *McLoughlin v O'Brian* [1982] 2 All ER 298, [1983] 1 AC 410.

(See also, when *Sidaway* was before the Court of Appeal [1984] 1 All ER 1018, Dunn LJ at 1031; Browne-Wilkinson LJ at 1035.)

We shall examine in greater detail the notion of defensive medicine shortly. It will suffice here to remind ourselves that what is meant by the notion is that the state of the law and the consequent fear of litigation cause (or may cause) doctors to carry out procedures which are not called for as a matter of good medical practice but are done *ex abundante cautela*. Whatever the validity of this as a theory (and you can see that not all judges would give it credence), there is little doubt that it is widely perceived to be a real risk. We shall notice that it may be theoretically incoherent. If the law requires doctors to do only *that which other doctors deem reasonable*, where is the need for defensive medicine? But the notion persists (for a fuller discussion, see *infra* pp 466–474).

(c) Departure from approved practice

Is this necessarily a breach of duty? See *Hunter v Hanley* 1955 SC 200 (Court of Sess). (The following facts are taken from the headnote.)

> In an action of damages against a doctor, the pursuer, who had suffered injury as a result of the breaking of a hypodermic needle while she was receiving an injection, alleged that the accident had been caused by the fault and negligence of the defender in failing to exercise the standard of care and competence which it was his duty to display in giving the injection. At the trial the presiding Judge directed the jury in the course of his charge that the test to be applied was whether there had been such a departure from the normal and usual practice of general practitioners as could reasonably be described as gross negligence. The jury having returned a verdict for the defender, the pursuer enrolled a motion for a new trial on the ground of misdirection.

The Court of Session ordered a new trial. Lord President Clyde said:

> It follows from what I have said that in regard to allegations of deviation from ordinary professional practice—and this is the matter with which the present note is concerned—such a deviation is not necessarily evidence of negligence. Indeed it would be disastrous if this were so, for all inducement to progress in medical science would then be destroyed. Even a substantial deviation from normal practice may be warranted by the particular circumstances. To establish liability by a doctor where deviation from normal practice is alleged, three facts require to be established. First of all it must be proved that there is a usual and normal practice; secondly it must be proved that the defender has not adopted that practice; and thirdly (and this is of crucial importance) it must be established that the course the doctor adopted is one which no professional man of ordinary skill would have taken if he had been acting with ordinary care. There is clearly a heavy onus on a pursuer to establish

these three facts, and without all three his case will fail. If this is the test, then it matters nothing how far or how little he deviates from the ordinary practice. For the extent of deviation is not the test. The deviation must be of a kind which satisfies the third of the requirements just stated.

Notice Lord Clyde's third requirement and his use of the word 'established'. Does this mean that it is for the *court* to determine whether the deviation was justified, or is it a matter on which *doctors'* evidence is conclusive?

Note the comment in support of this view of Sellers LJ in *Landau v Werner* (1961) 105 Sol Jo 1008, CA, that: 'a doctor might not be negligent if he tried a new technique but that if he did he must justify it before the court . . . Success was the best justification for unusual and unestablished treatment.' (See also *Holland v Devitt and Moore Nautical College Ltd* (1960) Times, 4 March, per Streatfield J.)

Consider the early heart transplant operations: Were they a 'success' even though the patients died, and if not, was the doctor in breach of his duty to his patient?

What is the legal effect of deviating from approved practice?

Clark v MacLennan
[1983] 1 All ER 416.

Facts: The plaintiff, who was about to give birth to her first child, was admitted to a hospital administered by the second defendants, a health authority. The baby was delivered on 11 June 1975. Soon after the birth the plaintiff began to suffer from stress incontinence, a not uncommon post-natal condition whereby normal bladder control was lost when the sufferer was subjected to mild physical stress. The plaintiff's disability was particularly acute and after conventional treatment failed to bring about an improvement the first defendant, a gynaecologist, performed an anterior colporrhaphy operation on 10 July 1975. It was normal practice among gynaecologists not to perform such an operation until at least three months after birth so as to ensure its success and to prevent the risk of haemorrhage. The operation was not successful and after it was performed haemorrhage occurred causing the repair to break down. Two further anterior colporrhaphy operations were necessary, and they were carried out on 16 January 1976 and in October 1979. Neither was successful with the result that the stress incontinence from which the plaintiff suffered became a permanent disability. She brought an action for damages claiming that the defendants had been negligent in the care and treatment administered to her.

Peter Pain J said:

Where however there is but one orthodox course of treatment and [the doctor] chooses to depart from that, his position is different. It is not enough for him to say as to his decision simply that it was based on his clinical judgment. One has to inquire whether he took all proper factors into account which he knew or should have known, and whether his departure from the orthodox course can be justified on the basis of these factors.

The burden of proof lies on the plaintiff. To succeed she must show, first, that there was a breach of duty and, second, that her damage flowed from that breach. It is against the second defendants that her attack is principally directed.

. . .

On the basis of this authority [*McGhee v National Coal Board* [1972] 3 All ER 1008, [1973] 1 WLR 1, HL], counsel for the plaintiff contended that, if the plaintiff could show (1) that there was a general practice not to perform an anterior colporrhaphy until at least three months after birth, (2) that one of the reasons for this practice was to protect the patient from the risk of haemorrhage and a breakdown of the repair, (3) that an operation was performed within four weeks and (4) that haemorrhage occurred and the repair broke down, then the burden of showing that he was not in breach of duty shifted to the defendants.

It must be correct on the basis of *McGhee* to say that the burden shifts so far as damages are concerned. But does the burden shift so far as the duty is concerned? Must the medical practitioner justify his departure from the usual practice?

It is very difficult to draw a distinction between the damage and the duty where the duty arises only because of a need to guard against the damage. In *McGhee's* case it was accepted that there was a breach of duty. In the present case the question of whether there was a breach remains in issue.

It seems to me that it follows from *McGhee* that where there is a situation in which a general duty of care arises and there is a failure to take a precaution, and that very damage occurs against which the precaution is designed to be a protection, then the burden lies on the defendant to show that he was not in breach of duty as well as to show that the damage did not result from his breach of duty.

Applying this, the judge found that the defendants had not discharged this burden and he entered judgment for the plaintiff.

Mustill LJ in the Court of Appeal in *Wilsher v Essex Area Health Authority* [1986] 3 All ER 801 at 815, has cast doubt on the validity of Peter Pain J's analysis.

If I may say so, the summary of the evidence contained in the judgment in *Clark v MacLennan* has certainly persuaded me that, as a decision on the facts, the case is unimpeachable. Moreover, although the judge indicated that he proposed to decide the case on burden of proof (at 425), this could be understood as an example of the forensic commonplace that, where one party has, in the course of the trial, hit the ball into the other's court, it is for that other to return it. But the prominence given in the judgment to *McGhee* and the citation from *Clark* in the present case suggest that the judge may have set out to assert a wider proposition, to the effect that in certain kinds of case of which *Clark* and the present action form examples, there is a general burden of proof on the defendant. If this is so, then I must respectfully say that I find nothing in . . . general principle to support it.

When the case reached the House of Lords [1988] 1 All ER 871, it was emphatically affirmed that *McGhee* did not have the effect of shifting the burden of proof (per Lord Bridge at p 879, set out *infra* pp 427–436).

What, however, is Mustill LJ deciding here? Undoubtedly the legal burden of proof does not shift, but is Mustill LJ conceding that the burden of adducing evidence has shifted in that once the plaintiff has established an approved practice and deviation therefrom he *may*, but not necessarily *must*, win unless the defendant brings evidence in reply. If this is so, how is this consistent with the view of Lord Clyde in *Hunter v Hanley* above that the plaintiff must not only establish deviation but that this amounts to a breach of duty?

Can it be said that it is always the case that any departure from accepted practice is *ipso facto* innovative therapy? Or, is there a middle ground? (For innovative therapy, see *infra* Ch 11.)

3. PROOF

As we have seen, the *Bolam* test looks to the standards of the medical profession in setting the legal standard of care required of a doctor.

It would seem to follow therefore, that to prove his case the plaintiff must adduce medical evidence sufficient to satisfy the burden of proof. Is this always the case? Would, for example, a plaintiff be non-suited if he demonstrated that his doctor had removed the wrong leg, but did not bring forward medical evidence to suggest that this was not accepted medical practice?

An exception, at least in theory, is *res ipsa loquitur*. Professor Picard in *Legal*

Liability of Doctors and Hospitals in Canada (1984), pp 260–1, sets the scene (footnotes omitted):

> There has been judicial recognition in negligence cases of the hardship on the plaintiff who is attempting to prove negligence when he knows only that an accident has happened and that he was injured. In many instances the details of the accident are known only to the defendant, but sometimes the mere fact that an accident happened will itself give rise to a presumption of negligence on the part of the defendant because the event is such that it would be unlikely to occur unless there had been negligence. The accident 'speaks of negligence'; hence the term used for this circumstance: *res ipsa loquitur*, 'the thing speaks for itself'.
>
> Variously described as a rule, principle, doctrine and maxim, *res ipsa loquitur* is applied in Canada as part of the law of circumstantial evidence and has been called 'one of the great mysteries of tort law'.
>
> As with much of the law, the essentials of *res ipsa loquitur* are easy to state, but its application is complicated. The doctrine will only apply when:
> 1) there is no evidence as to how or why the accident occurred;
> 2) the accident is such that it would not occur without negligence; and
> 3) the defendant is proven to have been in control of or linked to the situation either personally or vicariously.

The courts within the common law system have been largely reluctant to accept that *res ipsa loquitur* has much, if any, place in medical law.

Girard v Royal Columbian Hospital
(1976) 66 DLR (3d) 676 (British Columbia Supreme Court)

Andrews J, in dismissing the plaintiff's claim, stated:

> ... [T]he plaintiff underwent an operation at the Royal Columbian Hospital in New Westminster, British Columbia, which is described as being a left femoral popliteal saphenous vein by-pass graft. Shortly after the operation he noticed a weakness in both legs—more on the left than the right. Although there was no further surgical intervention he was in and out of rehabilitative centres for about a year until his condition stabilised to its present one, which consists of a permanent paralysis of the lower limbs accompanied by partial bladder and bowel deficiency and complete impotence. He is ambulatory by using two canes and is constantly uncomfortable from either sitting or standing for any extended period of time and from the loss of some control of both his bladder and bowel.
>
> ...

As to the doctrine of *res ipsa loquitur* which had been relied upon by the plaintiff, he said:

> The human body is not a container filled with a material whose performance can be predictably charted and analysed. It cannot be equated with a box of chewing tobacco or a soft drink. Thus, while permissible inferences may be drawn as to the normal behaviour of these types of commodities the same kind of reasoning does not necessarily apply to a human being. Because of this medical science has not yet reached the stage where the law ought to presume that a patient must come out of an operation as well or better than he went into it. From my interpretation of the medical evidence the kind of injury suffered by the plaintiff could have occurred without negligence on anyone's part. Since I cannot infer there was negligence on the part of the defendant doctors the maxim of *res ipsa loquitur* does not apply.

Lord Denning reflected this view in his judgment in *Whitehouse v Jordan* [1980] 1 All ER 650 at 657–8:

Lord Denning: The key sentence of the judge was this:

> In getting it wedged or stuck, or unwedged or unstuck, Mr Jordan caused asphyxia

which in turn caused the cerebral palsy. In this respect Mr Jordan fell below the very high standard of professional competence that the law requires of him.

The first sentence suggests that, *because* the baby suffered damage, *therefore* Mr Jordan was at fault. In other words *res ipsa loquitur*. That would be an error. In a high-risk case, damage during birth is quite possible, even though all care is used. No inference of negligence should be drawn from it.

(Note also Denning LJ's remarks in *Roe v Minister of Health* [1954] 2 QB 66 at 80.)

This is not to say that *res ipsa* will never be applied in medical cases, but merely to say that it will be exceptional. Curiously, it is Lord Denning's judgment in *Cassidy v Minister of Health* [1951] 2 KB 343, [1951] 1 All ER 574, which is regarded as the *locus classicus* on the application of *res ipsa loquitur* in medical law.

Denning LJ: If the plaintiff had to prove that some particular doctor or nurse was negligent, he would not be able to do it. But he was not put to that impossible task: he says, 'I went into the hospital to be cured of two stiff fingers. I have come out with four stiff fingers, and my hand is useless. That should not have happened if due care had been used. Explain it, if you can'. I am quite clearly of opinion that that raises a *prima facie* case against the hospital authorities: see *per* Goddard LJ, in *Mahon v Osborne*. They have nowhere explained how it could happen without negligence. They have busied themselves in saying that this or that member of their staff was not negligent. But they have called not a single person to say that the injuries were consistent with due care on the part of all the members of their staff. They called some of the people who actually treated the man, namely Dr Fahrni, Dr Ronaldson, and Sister Hall, each of whom protested that he was careful in his part; but they did not call any expert at all, to say that this might happen despite all care. They have not therefore displaced the *prima facie* case against them and are liable in damages to the plaintiff.

The other well-known case, referred to by Denning LJ in *Cassidy* (and the fact that there are so few cases tells its own story) is *Mahon v Osborne* [1939] 2 KB 14, [1939] 1 All ER 535, CA. The facts (taken from the headnote) were as follows:

The appellant, the resident surgeon, performed an abdominal operation with the help of an anaesthetist, a theatre sister and two nurses. The operation was admittedly a difficult one, and, at its conclusion, the usual count of the swabs which had been used was made, when the surgeon was informed that the count was correct. It was found, as a result of a further operation about 2 months later, that one swab had been left under the part of the liver which is close to the stomach. The patient died, and it was common ground that his death was due to the leaving of the swab in the abdomen. The system in use at the hospital of checking the count of the swabs was fully described in evidence, and was held to be satisfactory. In an action brought by the mother of the deceased against the surgeon for damages for negligence in the performance of the operation, the plaintiff contended that the doctrine of *res ipsa loquitur* was applicable to the circumstances.

The Court of Appeal allowed the doctor's appeal against the trial judge's award of damages. In the course of his judgment Scott LJ said:

It is difficult to see how the principle of *res ipsa loquitur* can apply generally to actions for negligence against a surgeon for leaving a swab in a patient, even if in certain circumstances the presumption may arise. If it applied generally, plaintiff's counsel, having, by a couple of answers to interrogatories, proved that the defendant performed the operation and that a swab was left in, would be entitled to ask for judgment, unless evidence describing the operation was given by the defendant. Some positive evidence of neglect of duty is surely needed. It may be that a full description of the actual operation will disclose facts sufficiently indicative of want of skill or care to entitle a jury to find neglect of duty to the patient. It may be that expert evidence in addition will be requisite. To treat the maxim as applying in every case where a swab is left in the patient seems to me an error of law. The very essence of the rule, when applied to an action for negligence, is that, upon the mere fact of the event happening, for example, an injury to the plaintiff, there arise two presumptions of fact, (i) that the event was caused by a breach by somebody of the duty of care towards the plaintiff, and (ii) that the defendant was that somebody. The presumption of fact arises only because it is an inference which the reasonable man, knowing the facts, would naturally draw, and that is, in most cases, for two reasons, (i) that the control over the happening of such an event rested solely with the defendant, and (ii) that in the ordinary experience of mankind such an event does not happen unless the person in control has failed to exercise due care.

Beyond issues of proof which arise in all litigation there are two additional points which are worth noting in the context of allegations of negligence in medical law.

The first point is made by Jackson and Powell, *Professional Negligence* (2nd ed 1987) para 6.38:

Very often there is no 'general and approved practice' or specific school of thought by reference to which the defendant's conduct can either be justified or condemned as negligent. The question is simply whether, in all the circumstances of the particular case, the mistake made by the defendant was negligent. In this situation the obvious way that an expert witness can assist the court on the issue of negligence (ie the second of the two stages discussed above) is by saying what he would have done in the particular circumstances and/or what he believes other medical practitioners would have done. In *Midland Bank v Hett Stubbs and Kemp*[40] (a claim for solicitors' negligence) Oliver J has expressed the view that such evidence is inadmissible.[41] However, in solicitors' negligence cases the court is able to form its own independent opinion as to the reasonableness or skilfulness of the defendant's conduct on the basis of counsel's submissions alone—a task which is usually impossible in medical negligence cases. It is therefore submitted that the *dictum* of Oliver J referred to above is inapplicable in medical negligence cases. Certainly, in practice, evidence from expert witnesses as to what they would have done, or what they believe other medical practitioners would have done, in the particular circumstances is received and acted upon by the court.

Notes to extract
[40] [1979] Ch 384.
[41] *Ibid* at p 402B–D: 'I must say that I doubt the value, or even the admissibility, of this sort of evidence. . . . Clearly, if there is some practice in a particular profession, some accepted standard of conduct which is laid down by a professional institute or sanctioned by common usage, evidence of that can and ought to be received. But evidence which really amounts to no more than an expression of opinion by a particular practitioner of what he thinks he would have done had he been placed, hypothetically and without the benefit of hindsight, in the position of the defendants, is of little assistance to the court.'

The authors may accurately state what the courts do as a matter of practice but is Oliver J not right as a matter of law?

The second point is one of concern to many doctors. They feel they may well run the risk of being judged in their conduct by reference to the evidence of the most eminent practitioner in the particular field in question. This they feel is unfair. The standards of the centre of excellence or of the teaching hospital should not, they argue, be the standards against which those who do not have the benefit of working in such a centre should be judged (note the remarks of Donnelly J in the Supreme Court of Ontario in the case of *Malette v Shulman* (1988) 47 DLR (4th) 18).

4. CAUSATION

It is one thing to show that the defendant doctor owed the plaintiff a duty which was breached and that the plaintiff has been harmed, it is quite another thing to establish that the breach *caused* the harm. But this is what the law requires.

(a) Factual

Barnett v Chelsea and Kensington Hospital Management Committee
[1969] 1 QB 428, [1968] 1 All ER 1068

The facts of this case are set out *supra* p 372. You will recall that the deceased died from arsenic poisoning which was undetected by the hospital he attended because he was not examined.

> **Nield J:** It remains to consider whether it is shown that the deceased's death was caused by this negligence or whether, as the defendants have said, the deceased must have died in any event. In his concluding submission counsel for the plaintiff submitted that Dr Banerjee should have examined the deceased and, had he done so, he would have caused tests to be made which would have indicated the treatment required and that, since the defendants were at fault in these respects, therefore the onus of proof passed to the defendants to show that the appropriate treatment would have failed, and authorities were cited to me. I find myself unable to accept this argument and I am of the view that the onus of proof remains on the plaintiff, and I have in mind (without quoting it) the decision quoted by counsel for the defendants in *Bonnington Castings Ltd v Wardlaw*. However, were it otherwise and the onus did pass to the defendants, then I would find that they have discharged it, as I would proceed to show.
>
> There has been put before me a timetable which, I think, is of much importance. The deceased attended at the casualty department at 8 5 or 8 10 am. If Dr Banerjee had got up and dressed and come to see the three men and examined them and decided to admit them, the deceased (and Dr Lockett agreed with this) could not have been in bed in a ward before 11 am. I accept Dr Goulding's evidence that an intravenous drip would not have been set up before 12 noon, and if potassium loss was suspected it could not have been discovered until 12 30. Dr Lockett, dealing with this, said 'If [the deceased] had not been treated until after 12 noon the chances of survival were not good'.
>
> Without going in detail into the considerable volume of technical evidence which has been put before me, it seems to me to be the case that when death results from arsenical poisoning it is brought about by two conditions; on the one hand dehydration and on the other disturbance of the enzyme processes. If the principal condition is one of enzyme disturbance—as I am of the view that it was here—then the only method of treatment which is likely to succeed is the use of the specific antidote which is commonly called BAL. Dr Goulding said this in the course of his evidence:
>
>> The only way to deal with this is to use the specific BAL. I see no reasonable prospect of the deceased being given BAL below the time at which he died,
>
> and at a later point in his evidence:
>
>> I feel that even if fluid loss had been discovered death would have been caused by the enzyme disturbance. Death might have occurred later.
>
> I regard that evidence as very moderate, and that it might be a true assessment of the situation to say that there was no chance of BAL being administered before the death of the deceased.
>
> For these reasons, I find that the plaintiff has failed to establish, on the grounds of probability, that the defendants' negligence caused the death of the deceased.

Barnett was a case where the evidence was clear. In most cases of medical negligence the evidence of the cause of the plaintiff's harm will be, at best, unclear—either intrinsically so or because of the preparedness of experts so to testify.

In such circumstances is it any part of the role of the court to assist the plaintiff to establish causation by, for example, adopting a less stringent test of causation than is ordinarily employed? The House of Lords had the opportunity to develop the law in this way in *Wilsher v Essex Area Health Authority* [1988] 1 All ER 871 but, as you will see, chose not to do so.

Lord Bridge of Harwich: My Lords, the infant plaintiff was born nearly three months prematurely on 15 December 1978. He weighed only 1,200g. In the first few weeks of life he suffered from most of the afflictions which beset premature babies. He passed through a series of crises and very nearly died. The greatest danger which faces the very premature baby, on account of the imperfect function of incompletely developed lungs, is death of brain damage from failure of the oxygen supply to the brain. That Martin not only survived but also now retains unimpaired brain function is due both to the remarkable advances of medical science and technology in this field in comparatively recent years and to the treatment he received in the special baby care unit of the Princess Alexandra Hospital, Harlow.

Tragically, however, he succumbed to another well-known hazard of prematurity. He suffers from retrolental fibroplasia (RLF), an incurable condition of the retina which, in his case has caused total blindness in one eye and severely impaired vision in the other. He sued the Essex Area Health Authority (the authority), who are responsible for the Princess Alexandra Hospital, Harlow, on the ground that his RLF was caused by an excess of oxygen tension in his bloodstream in the early weeks attributable to a want of proper skill and care in the management of his oxygen supply. The action was heard by Peter Pain J and the trial lasted 20 days. In addition to the evidence of the medical and nursing staff at the hospital, the judge heard expert evidence from two paediatricians and two ophthalmologists called for the plaintiff and from three paediatricians and one ophthalmologist called for the authority. All were highly qualified and distinguished experts in their respective fields. In addition, no less than 24 articles from medical journals about RLF covering 129 foolscap pages of print were put in evidence.

The allegations of negligence against the authority related to two quite distinct phases of Martin's treatment. The first concerned the first 38 hours after his birth. In order to monitor the partial pressure of oxygen (Po_2) in the arterial blood of a premature baby, it is standard practice to pass a catheter through the umbilical artery into the aorta. This enables the Po_2 to be measured in two ways. At the tip of the catheter is an electronic sensor connected to a monitor outside the body which, if correctly calibrated, should give an accurate reading of the Po_2. In addition, an aperture in the catheter close to the sensor enables samples of blood to be taken for conventional blood analysis at regular intervals to check and, if necessary, adjust the monitor's calibration. Again it is standard practice to check the location of the sensor by X-ray after the catheter has been inserted. In Martin's case the catheter was inserted by mistake into a vein instead of an artery so that the sensor and the sampling aperture were wrongly located in the heart instead of the aorta. This meant that they would sample a mixture of arterial and venous blood instead of pure arterial blood, which would consequently give a false reading of the level of Po_2 in the arterial blood. The house officer and the registrar who were on duty at the material time and who saw the X-ray which was taken both failed to notice the mistake. The judge held this failure to amount to negligence for which the authority were liable. The plaintiff's case in relation to this first allegation of negligence was that the misplaced catheter gave readings of Po_2 well below the true level of Po_2 in the arterial blood which led to excessive administration of oxygen in an attempt to raise the Po_2 level and that in consequence the true Po_2 level was excessively high for a substantial period until the mislocation of the catheter was realised at 8 o'clock on the morning of 17 December 1978.

A second phase of Martin's treatment alleged to have been negligent was between

20 December 1978 and 23 January 1979. Between these dates it was alleged that there were five distinct periods of differing duration when the medical and nursing staff responsible for Martin's care were in breach of duty in allowing the level of Po_2 in his arterial blood to remain above the accepted level of safety. The judge found that four of these five periods of exposure to an unduly high level of Po_2 were due to the authority's negligence.

In making his finding of negligence in relation to each of the periods of raised Po_2 levels except the first attributable to the misplaced catheter, the judge relied on a principle of law which he thought was laid down by this House in *McGhee v National Coal Board* [197. ᵖ 3 All ER 1008, [1973] 1 WLR 1 and which he had stated in his own earlier decis. ᵒn in *Clark v MacLennan* [1983] 1 All ER 416 at 427 in the following terms:

> It seems to me that it follows from *McGhee* that where there is a situation in which a general duty of care arises and there is a failure to take a precaution, and that very damage occurs against which the precaution is designed to be a protection, then the burden lies on the defendant to show that he was not in breach of duty as well as to show that the damage did not result from his breach of duty.

The judge thought that this proposition of law derived support from the decision at first instance of Mustill J in *Thompson v Smiths Shiprepairers (North Shields) Ltd* [1984] 1 All ER 881, [1984] QB 405. He held that the authority had failed to prove on a balance of probabilities either that they were not negligent or that their negligence did not cause or materially contribute to Martin's RLF. He therefore held them liable in damages and gave judgment for the plaintiff for £116,119·14.

The Court of Appeal (Sir Nicolas Browne-Wilkinson V-C, Mustill and Glidewell LJJ) affirmed this judgment by a majority, the Vice-Chancellor dissenting (see [1986] 3 All ER 801, [1987] 1 QB 730). It gave leave on terms to the authority to appeal to this House. A number of issues were argued in the Court of Appeal. It unanimously affirmed the finding of negligence against the authority, though by marginally different processes of reasoning, on the ground of the authority's vicarious liability for the registrar's failure to observe from the X-ray that the first catheter inserted into Martin's umbilicus was located in a vein not in an artery. It unanimously reversed the judge's finding of negligence in relation to the later periods when the level of Po_2 in Martin's blood was raised on the ground that he had misdirected himself in holding that the burden of proof was reversed so that it lay on the authority to show that they were not negligent. On examination of the evidence the Court of Appeal found that no negligence was established in relation to these later periods. No issue arises in the present appeal to your Lordships' House in respect of either of these conclusions on liability and nothing more need be said about them. The crucial issue which now arises and on which the Court of Appeal was divided is whether the judgment can be affirmed on the ground that any raised level of Po_2 in Martin's arterial blood before 8 o'clock on the morning of 17 December 1978 consequent on misplacement of the catheter caused or materially contributed to Martin's RLF.

My Lords, I understand that all your Lordships agree that this appeal has to be allowed and that the inevitable consequence of this is that the outstanding issue of causation must, unless the parties can reach agreement, be retried by another judge. In these circumstances, for obvious reasons, it is undesirable that I should go into the highly complex and technical evidence on which the issue depends any further than is strictly necessary to explain why, in common with all your Lordships, I feel ineluctably driven to the unpalatable conclusion that it is not open to the House to resolve the issue one way or the other, so that a question depending on the consequence of an event occurring in the first two days of Martin's life will now have to be investigated all over again when Martin is nearly ten years old. On the other hand, the appeal raises a question of law as to the proper approach to issues of causation which is of great importance and of particular concern in medical negligence cases. This must be fully considered.

There was in the voluminous expert evidence given at the trial an irreconcilable conflict of opinion as to the cause of Martin's RLF. It was common ground that a sufficiently high level of Po_2 in the arterial blood of a very premature baby, if maintained for a sufficiently long period of time, can have a toxic effect on the immature blood vessels in the retina leading to a condition which may either regress or develop into RLF. It was equally common ground, however, that RLF may occur in premature babies who have survived without any artificial administration of oxygen and that there is evidence to indicate a correlation between RLF and a number of other conditions from which premature babies commonly suffer (eg apnoea, hypercarbia, intraventricular haemorrhage, patent ductus arteriosus, all conditions which afflicted Martin) although no causal mechanisms linking these conditions with the development of RLF have been positively identified. However, what, if any, part artificial administration of oxygen causing an unduly high level of Po_2 in Martin's arterial blood played in the causation of Martin's RLF was radically in dispute between the experts. There was certainly evidence led in support of the plaintiff's case that high levels of Po_2 in general and, more particularly, the level of Po_2 maintained when the misplaced catheter was giving misleadingly low readings of the level in the arterial blood were probably at least a contributory cause of Martin's RLF. If the judge had directed himself that it was for the plaintiff to discharge the onus of proving causation on a balance of probabilities and had indicated his acceptance of this evidence in preference to the contrary evidence led for the authority, a finding in favour of the plaintiff would have been unassailable. That is why it is conceded by counsel for the authority that the most he can ask for, if his appeal succeeds, is an order for retrial of the causation issue. However, the burden of the relevant expert evidence led for the authority, to summarise it in very general terms, was to the effect that any excessive administration of oxygen which resulted from the misplacement of the catheter did not result in the Po_2 in the arterial blood being raised to a sufficiently high level for a sufficient length of time to have been capable of playing any part in the causation of Martin's RLF. One of the difficulties is that, underlying this conflict of medical opinion, there was not only a profound difference of view about the aetiology and causation of RLF in general but also a substantial difference as to the inferences which were to be drawn from the primary facts, as ascertained from the clinical notes about Martin's condition and treatment at the material time and amplified by the oral evidence of Dr Wiles, the senior house officer in charge, as to what the actual levels of Po_2 in Martin's arterial blood were likely to have been during a critical period between 10 pm on 16 December when Martin was first being administered pure oxygen through a ventilator and 8 am the next morning when, after discovery of the mistake about the catheter, the level of oxygen administration was immediately reduced.

Having found the authority negligent in relation to the five periods when the Po_2 level was unduly high, the judge added: 'There is no dispute that this materially increased the risk of RLF.' This statement, it is now accepted, was a misunderstanding of the evidence. Whilst it was common ground that one of the objects of monitoring and controlling the Po_2 level in the arterial blood of a premature baby in 1978 was to avoid or reduce the risk of RLF, it was certainly not accepted by the defence that any of the levels to which Martin was subjected were sufficient in degree or duration to have involved any material increase in that risk. This misunderstanding was one of the factors which led the judge to the conclusion that Martin had established a prima facie case on the issues of causation. He then said:

> But it is open to the defendants on the facts of this case to show that they are not liable for this negligence because on the balance of probability this exposure did not cause Martin's RLF.

It was on this premise that the judge examined the issue of causation. In a judgment which runs to 68 pages of transcript, only $2\frac{1}{2}$ pages are devoted to this issue. The judge repeatedly emphasised that the onus was on the authority, saying at one point:

> For the purpose of this action I need go no further than to consider whether the breaches have probably made no substantial contribution to the plaintiff's condition.

And, again, a little later on: 'So I have to consider whether the exposure that occurred probably did no harm.'

After a brief reference to the evidence of one of the plaintiff's witnesses and one of the authority's witnesses whose answers were based on an assumption of fact which he was invited to make, the judge expressed his conclusion in the following passage:

On the basis of this evidence I find that the defendants fail to show that the first and third periods of exposure did not do any damage; *indeed, the probability is that they did*. As to the second, fourth and fifth periods the position is more doubtful. The trouble is the lack of data. The blood gas readings were not sufficiently frequent to enable us to assess whether the excessively high readings were a peak or whether they indicate a longer period; indeed, it is possible that the true figure went higher. The defendants, in my view, have failed to show that these periods did not cause or materially contribute to Martin's RLF. (My emphasis.)

Counsel for the plaintiff, seeking to uphold the judgment in Martin's favour, naturally relied heavily on the words I have emphasised in this passage and pointed to the contrast between the judge's view, thereby expressed, of the causative effect of what is now the only relevant period of exposure calling for consideration and his doubts about the effect of three of the four later periods. He urged your Lordships to read this as an indication by the judge that, if he had held the onus to lie on the plaintiff, he would have found it discharged on a balance of probabilities. The Court of Appeal did not feel able to accede to a similar submission and I agree with it. As Mustill LJ pointed out ([1986] 3 All ER 801 at 823, [1987] QB 730 at 763), the judge expressed no preference for the plaintiff's experts on this point. Moreover, it is inconceivable that this very careful judge, if he had directed himself that the burden of proof lay on the plaintiff, would not have subjected the complex and conflicting evidence to a thorough scrutiny and analysis before committing himself to an orthodox finding of causation in the plaintiff's favour.

Both parties accepted that the conflict of evidence was of such a nature that it could not properly be resolved by your Lordships simply reading the transcript. Indeed, we were not asked to examine the totality of the voluminous medical evidence. Just as counsel for the authority accepted that it was not open to the House to dismiss the plaintiff's claim, so counsel for the plaintiff accepted that, if he failed in the submission which I have examined and rejected in the foregoing paragraph, he could not invite the House to make an independent finding in the plaintiff's favour on the simple basis that the expert evidence on a balance of probabilities affirmatively established causation.

The Court of Appeal, although it felt unable to resolve the primary conflict in the expert evidence as to the causation of Martin's RLF, did make a finding that the levels of Po_2 which Martin experienced in consequence of the misplacement of the catheter were of a kind capable of causing RLF. Mustill LJ expressed his anxiety whether 'by making a further finding on an issue where there was a sharp conflict between the expert witnesses, we are not going too far in the effort to avoid a retrial' (see [1986] 3 All ER 801 at 825, [1987] QB 730 at 766). But he concluded that it was 'legitimate, after reading and rereading the evidence,' to make this finding based on 'the weight of the expert evidence'. This finding by the Court of Appeal is challenged by counsel for the authority as one which it was not open to it to make. I must return to this later. But assuming, as I do for the present, that the finding was properly made, it carried the plaintiff's case no further than to establish that oxygen administered to Martin as a consequence of the negligent failure to detect the misplacement of the catheter was one of a number of possible causes of Martin's RLF.

Mustill LJ subjected the speeches in *McGhee v National Coal Board* [1972] 3 All ER 1008, [1973] 1 WLR 1 to a careful scrutiny and analysis and concluded that they established a principle of law which he expressed in the following terms ([1986] 3 All ER 801 at 829, [1987] QB 730 at 771–772):

If it is an established fact that conduct of a particular kind creates a risk that injury will be caused to another or increases an existing risk that injury will ensue, and if the two parties stand in such a relationship that the one party owes a duty not to conduct himself in that way, and if the first party does conduct himself in that way, and if the other party does suffer injury of the kind to which the risk related, then the first party is taken to have caused the injury by his breach of duty, even though the existence and extent of the contribution made by the breach cannot be ascertained.

Applying this principle to the finding that the authority's negligence was one of the possible causes of Martin's RLF, he held that this was sufficient to enable the court to conclude that the negligence was 'taken to have caused the injury'. Glidewell LJ reached the same conclusion by substantially the same process of reasoning. Sir Nicolas Browne-Wilkinson V-C took the opposite view.

The starting point for any consideration of the relevant law of causation is the decision of this House in *Bonnington Castings Ltd v Wardlaw* [1956] 1 All ER 615, [1956] AC 613. This was the case of a pursuer who, in the course of his employment by the defenders, contracted pneumoconiosis over a period of years by the inhalation of invisible particles of silica dust from two sources. One of these (pneumatic hammers) was an 'innocent' source, in the sense that the pursuer could not complain that his exposure to it involved any breach of duty on the part of his employers. The other source (swing grinders), however, arose from a breach of statutory duty by the employer. Delivering the leading speech in the House Lord Reid said ([1956] 1 All ER 615 at 617–618, [1956] AC 613 at 619–620):

The Lord Ordinary and the majority of the First Division have dealt with this case on the footing that there was an onus on the defenders, the appellants, to prove that the dust from the swing grinders did not cause the respondent's disease. This view was based on a passage in the judgment of the Court of Appeal in *Vyner v Waldenberg Bros Ltd* ([1945] 2 All ER 547 at 549, [1946] KB 50 at 55) *per* Scott LJ: 'If there is a definite breach of a safety provision imposed on the occupier of a factory, and a workman is injured in a way which could result from the breach, the onus of proof shifts on to the employer to show that the breach was not the cause. We think that that principle lies at the very basis of statutory rules of absolute duty' . . . Of course the onus was on the defendants to prove delegation (if that was an answer) and to prove contributory negligence, and it may be that that is what the Court of Appeal has in mind. But the passage which I have cited appears to go beyond that and, in so far as it does so, I am of opinion that it is erroneous. It would seem obvious in principle that a pursuer or plaintiff must prove not only negligence or breach of duty but also that such fault caused, or materially contributed to, his injury, and there is ample authority for that proposition both in Scotland and in England. I can find neither reason nor authority for the rule being different where there is breach of a statutory duty. The fact that Parliament imposes a duty for the protection of employees has been held to entitle an employee to sue if he is injured as a result of a breach of that duty, but it would be going a great deal further to hold that it can be inferred from the enactment of a duty that Parliament intended that any employee suffering injury can sue his employer merely because there was a breach of duty and it is shown to be possible that his injury may have been caused by it. In my judgment, the employee must, in all cases, prove his case by the ordinary standard of proof in civil actions; he must make it appear at least that, on a balance of probabilities, the breach of duty caused, or materially contributed to, his injury.

Lord Tucker said of Scott LJ's dictum in *Vyner v Waldenberg Bros Ltd*:

. . . I think it is desirable that your Lordships should take this opportunity to state in plain terms that no such onus exists unless the statute or statutory regulation expressly or impliedly so provides, as in several instances it does. No distinction can be drawn between actions for common law negligence and actions for breach of statutory duty in this respect. In both, the plaintiff or pursuer must prove (a) breach of duty, and (b) that such breach caused the injury complained of (see *Wakelin* v *London & South Western Ry Co* (1886) 12 App Cas 41, and *Caswell* v

Powell Duffryn Associated Collieries, Ltd [1939] 3 All ER 722, [1940] AC 152). In each case, it will depend on the particular facts proved, and the proper inferences to be drawn therefrom, whether the respondent has sufficiently discharged the onus that lies on him.

(See [1956] 1 All ER 615 at 621, [1956] AC 613 at 624–625.)

Lord Keith said ([1956] 1 All ER 615 at 621, [1956] AC 613 at 625):

> The onus is on the respondent [the pursuer] to prove his case, and I see no reason to depart from this elementary principle by invoking certain rules of onus said to be based on a correspondence between the injury suffered and the evil guarded against by some statutory regulation. I think most, if not all, of the cases which professed to lay down or to recognise some such rule could have been decided as they were on simple rules of evidence, and I agree that *Vyner* v *Waldenberg Bros Ltd* ([1945] 2 All ER 547, [1946] KB 50), in so far as it professed to enunciate a principle of law inverting the onus of proof, cannot be supported.

Viscount Simonds and Lord Somervell agreed.

Their Lordships concluded, however, from the evidence that the inhalation of dust to which the pursuer was exposed by the defender's breach of statutory duty had made a material contribution to his pneumoconiosis which was sufficient to discharge the onus on the pursuer of proving that his damage was caused by the defenders' tort.

A year later the decision in *Nicholson v Atlas Steel Foundry and Engineering Co Ltd* [1957] 1 All ER 776, [1957] 1 WLR 613 followed the decision in *Bonnington Castings Ltd v Wardlaw* and held, in another case of pneumoconiosis, that the employers were liable for the employee's disease arising from the inhalation of dust from two sources, one 'innocent' the other 'guilty', on facts virtually indistinguishable from those in *Bonnington Castings Ltd v Wardlaw*.

In *McGhee v National Coal Board* [1972] 3 All ER 1008, [1973] 1 WLR 1 the pursuer worked in a brick kiln in hot and dusty conditions in which brick dust adhered to his sweaty skin. No breach of duty by his employers, the defenders, was established in respect of his working conditions. However, the employers were held to be at fault in failing to provide adequate washing facilities which resulted in the pursuer having to bicycle home after work with his body still caked in brick dust. The pursuer contracted dermatitis and the evidence that this was caused by the brick dust was accepted. Brick dust adhering to the skin was a recognised cause of industrial dermatitis and the provision of showers to remove it after work was a usual precaution to minimise the risk of the disease. The precise mechanism of causation of the disease however, was not known and the furthest the doctors called for the pursuer were able to go was to say that the provision of showers would have materially reduced the risk of dermatitis. They were unable to say that it would probably have prevented the disease.

The pursuer failed before the Lord Ordinary and the First Division of the Court of Session on the ground that he had not discharged the burden of proof of causation. He succeeded on appeal to the House of Lords. Much of the academic discussion to which this decision has given rise has focused on the speech of Lord Wilberforce, particularly on two paragraphs. He said ([1972] 3 All ER 1008 at 1012, [1973] 1 WLR 1 at 6):

> But the question remains whether a pursuer must necessarily fail if, after he has shown a breach of duty, involving an increase of risk of disease, he cannot positively prove that this increase of risk caused or materially contributed to the disease while his employers cannot positively prove the contrary. In this intermediate case there is an appearance of logic in the view that the pursuer, on whom the onus lies, should fail—a logic which dictated the judgments below. The question is whether we should be satisfied in factual situations like the present, with this logical approach. In my opinion, there are further considerations of importance. First, it is a sound principle that where a person has, by breach of duty of care, created a risk, and injury occurs within the area of that risk, the loss should be borne by him *unless he shows that it had some other cause.* Secondly, from

the evidential point of view, one may ask, why should a man who is able to show that his employer should have taken certain precautions, because without them there is a risk, or an added risk, of injury or disease, and who in fact sustains exactly that injury or disease, have to assume the burden of proving more: namely, that it was the addition to the risk, caused by the breach of duty, which caused or materially contributed to the injury? In many cases of which the present is typical, this is impossible to prove, just because honest medical opinion cannot segregate the causes of an illness between compound causes. And if one asks which of the parties, the workman or the employers should suffer from this inherent evidential difficulty, the answer as a matter of policy or justice should be that it is the creator of the risk who, ex hypothesi, must be taken to have foreseen the possibility of damage, who should bear its consequences. (My emphasis.)

He then referred to *Bonnington Castings Ltd v Wardlaw* and *Nicholson v Atlas Steel Foundry and Engineering Co Ltd* and added ([1972] 3 All ER 1008 at 1013, [1973] 1 WLR 1 at 7):

The present factual situation has its differences: the default here consisted not in adding a material quantity to the accumulation of injurious particles but by failure to take a step which materially increased the risk that the dust already present would cause injury. And I must say that, at least in the present case, to bridge the evidential gap by inference seems to me something of a fiction, since it was precisely this inference which the medical expert declined to make. But I find in the cases quoted an analogy which suggests the conclusion that, *in the absence of proof that the culpable condition had, in the result, no effect*, the employers should be liable for an injury, squarely within the risk which they created and that they, not the pursuer, should suffer the consequence of the impossibility, foreseeably inherent in the nature of his injury, of segregating the precise consequence of their default. (My emphasis.)

My Lords, it seems to me that both these paragraphs, particularly in the words I have emphasised, amount to saying that, in the circumstances, the burden of proof of causation is reversed and thereby to run counter to the unanimous and emphatic opinions expressed in *Bonnington Castings Ltd v Wardlaw* [1956] 1 All ER 615, [1956] AC 613 to the contrary effect. I find no support in any of the other speeches for the view that the burden of proof is reversed and, in this respect, I think Lord Wilberforce's reasoning must be regarded as expressing a minority opinion.

A distinction is, of course, apparent between the facts of *Bonnington Castings Ltd v Wardlaw*, where the 'innocent' and 'guilty' silica dust particles which together caused the pursuer's lung disease were inhaled concurrently and the facts of *McGhee v National Coal Board* where the 'innocent' and 'guilty' brick dust was present on the pursuer's body for consecutive periods. In the one case the concurrent inhalation of 'innocent' and 'guilty' dust must both have contributed to the cause of the disease. In the other case the consecutive periods when 'innocent' and 'guilty' brick dust was present on the pursuer's body may both have contributed to the cause of the disease or, theoretically at least, one or other may have been the sole cause. But where the layman is told by the doctors that the longer the brick dust remains on the body, the greater the risk of dermatitis, although the doctors cannot identify the process of causation scientifically, there seems to be nothing irrational in drawing the inference, as a matter of common sense, that the consecutive periods when brick dust remained on the body probably contributed cumulatively to the causation of the dermatitis. I believe that a process of inferential reasoning on these general lines underlies the decision of the majority in *McGhee*'s case.

In support of this view, I refer to the following passages. Lord Reid said ([1972] 3 All ER 1008 at 1010, [1973] 1 WLR 1 at 3–4):

The medical witnesses are in substantial agreement. Dermatitis can be caused, and this dermatitis was caused, by repeated minute abrasion of the outer horny layer of the skin followed by some injury to or change in the underlying cells, the precise nature of which has not yet been discovered by medical science. If a man sweats profusely for a considerable time the outer layer of his skin is softened and easily injured. If he is then working in a cloud of abrasive brick dust, as this man was, the particles of dust will adhere to his skin in considerable quantity and exertion will cause them to injure the horny layer and expose to injury or infection the tender cells below. Then in some way not yet understood dermatitis may result. If the skin is not thoroughly washed as soon as the man ceases work that process can continue at least for some considerable time. This man had to continue exerting himself after work by bicycling home while still caked with sweat and grime, so he would be liable to further injury until he could wash himself thoroughly. Washing is the only practicable method of removing the danger of further injury. The effect of such abrasion of the skin is cumulative in the sense that the longer a subject is exposed to injury the greater the chance of his developing dermatitis: it is for that reason that immediate washing is well recognised as a proper precaution.

He concluded ([1972] 3 All ER 1008 at 1011, [1973] 1 WLR 1 at 4–5):

The medical evidence is to the effect that the fact that the man had to cycle home caked with grime and sweat added materially to the risk that this disease might develop. It does not and could not explain just why that is so. But experience shews that it is so. Plainly that must be because what happens while the man remains unwashed can have a causative effect, although just how the cause operates is uncertain. I cannot accept the view expressed in the Inner House that once the man left the brick kiln he left behind the causes which made him liable to develop dermatitis. That seems to me quite inconsistent with a proper interpretation of the medical evidence. Nor can I accept the distinction drawn by the Lord Ordinary between materially increasing the risk that the disease will occur and making a material contribution to its occurrence. There may be some logical ground for such a distinction where our knowledge of all the material factors is complete. But it has often been said that the legal concept of causation is not based on logic or philosophy. It is based on the practical way in which the ordinary man's mind works in the every-day affairs of life. From a broad and practical viewpoint I can see no substantial difference between saying that what the respondents did materially increased the risk of injury to the appellant and saying that what the respondents did made a material contribution to his injury.

Lord Simon said ([1972] 3 All ER 1008 at 1014, [1973] 1 WLR 1 at 8):

But *Bonnington Castings Ltd v Wardlaw* and *Nicholson v Atlas Steel Foundry & Engineering Co Ltd* establish, in my view, that where an injury is caused by two (or more) factors operating cumulatively, one (or more) of which factors is a breach of duty and one (or more) is not so, in such a way that it is impossible to ascertain the proportion in which the factors were effective in producing the injury or which factor was decisive, the law does not require a pursuer or plaintiff to prove the impossible, but holds that he is entitled to damages for the injury if he proves on a balance of probabilities that the breach or breaches of duty contributed substantially to causing the injury. If such factors so operate cumulatively, it is, in my judgment, immaterial whether they do so concurrently or successively.

Lord Kilbrandon said ([1972] 3 All ER 1008 at 1016, [1973] 1 WLR 1 at 10):

In the present case, the appellant's body was vulnerable, while he was bicycling home, to the dirt which had been deposited on it during his working hours. It would not have been if he had had a shower. If showers had been provided he would have used them. It is admittedly more probable that disease will be contracted if a shower is not taken. In these circumstances I cannot accept the argument that nevertheless it is not more probable than not that, if the duty to provide a shower had been neglected, he would not have contracted the disease. The appellant has, after all, only to satisfy the court of a probability, not to demonstrate an irrefragable chain of causation, which in a case of dermatitis, in the present state of medical knowledge, he could probably never do.

Lord Salmon said ([1972] 3 All ER 1008 at 1017, [1973] 1 WLR 1 at 11–12):

I, of course, accept that the burden rests on the appellant, to prove, on a balance of probabilities, a causal connection between his injury and the respondents' negligence. It is not necessary, however, to prove that the respondents' negligence was the only cause of injury. A factor, by itself, may not be sufficient to cause injury but if, with other factors, it materially contributes to causing injury, it is clearly a cause of injury. Everything in the present case depends on what constitutes a cause. I venture to repeat what I said in *Alphacell Ltd v Woodward* [1972] 2 All ER 475 at 489–490, [1972] AC 824 at 847: 'The nature of causation has been discussed by many eminent philosophers and also by a number of learned judges in the past. I consider, however, that what or who has caused a certain event to occur is essentially a practical question of fact which can best be answered by ordinary common sense rather than abstract metaphysical theory'. In the circumstances of the present case it seems to me unrealistic and contrary to ordinary common sense to hold that the negligence which materially increased the risk of injury did not materially contribute to causing the injury.

Then, after referring to *Bonnington Castings Ltd v Wardlaw* and *Nicholson v Atlas Steel Foundry and Engineering Co Ltd* he added ([1972] 3 All ER 1008 at 1018, [1973] 1 WLR 1 at 12–13):

I do not find the attempts to distinguish those authorities from the present case at all convincing. In the circumstances of the present case, the possibility of a distinction existing between (a) having materially increased the risk of contracting the disease, and (b) having materially contributed to causing the disease may no doubt be a fruitful source of interesting academic discussions between students of philosophy. Such a distinction is, however, far too unreal to be recognised by the common law.

The conclusion I draw from these passages is that *McGhee v National Coal Board* laid down no new principle of law whatever. On the contrary, it affirmed the principle that the onus of proving causation lies on the pursuer or plaintiff. Adopting a robust and pragmatic approach to the undisputed primary facts of the case, the majority concluded that it was a legitimate inference of fact that the defenders' negligence had materially contributed to the pursuer's injury. The decision, in my opinion, is of no greater significance than that and the attempt to extract from it some esoteric principle which in some way modifies, as a matter of law, the nature of the burden of proof of causation which a plaintiff or pursuer must discharge once he has established a relevant breach of duty is a fruitless one.

In the Court of Appeal in the instant case Sir Nicolas Browne-Wilkinson V-C, being in a minority, expressed his view on causation with understandable caution. But I am quite unable to find any fault with the following passage in his dissenting judgment ([1986] 3 All ER 801 at 834–835, [1987] QB 730 at 779):

To apply the principle in *McGhee v National Coal Board* [1972] 3 All ER 1008, [1973] 1 WLR 1 to the present case would constitute an extension of that principle. In *McGhee* there was no doubt that the pursuer's dermatitis was physically caused by brick dust; the only question was whether the continued presence of such brick dust on the pursuer's skin after the time when he should have been provided with a shower caused or materially contributed to the dermatitis which he contracted. There was only one possible agent which could have caused the dermatitis, viz brick dust, and there was no doubt that the dermatitis from which he suffered was caused by that brick dust. In the present case the question is different. There are a number of different agents which could have caused the RLF. Excess oxygen was one of them. The defendants failed to take reasonable precautions to prevent one of the possible causative agents (e g excess oxygen) from causing RLF. But no one can tell in this case whether excess oxygen did or did not cause or contribute to the RLF suffered by the plaintiff. The plaintiff's RLF may have been caused by some completely different agent or agents, e g hypercarbia, intraventricular haemorrhage, apnoea or patent ductus arteriosus. In addition to oxygen, each of those conditions has been implicated as a possible cause of RLF. This baby suffered from each of those conditions at various times in the first two months of his life. There is no satisfactory evidence that excess oxygen is more likely than any of those other four candidates to have caused RLF in this baby. To my mind, the occurrence of RLF following a failure to take a necessary precaution to prevent excess oxygen causing RLF provides no evidence and raises no presumption that it was excess oxygen rather than one or more of the four other possible agents which caused or contributed to RLF in this case. The position, to my mind, is wholly different from that in *McGhee*, where there was only one candidate (brick dust) which could have caused the dermatitis, and the failure to take a precaution against brick dust causing dermatitis was followed by dermatitis caused by brick dust. In such a case, I can see the common sense, if not the logic, of holding that, in the absence of any other evidence, the failure to take the precaution caused or contributed to the dermatitis. To the extent that certain members of the House of Lords decided the question on inferences from evidence or presumptions, I do not consider that the present case falls within their reasoning. A failure to take preventive measures against one out of five possible causes is no evidence as to which of those five caused the injury.

Since, on this view, the appeal must, in any event, be allowed, it is not strictly necessary to decide whether it was open to the Court of Appeal to resolve one of the conflicts between the experts which the judge left unresolved and to find that the oxygen administered to Martin in consequence of the misleading Po_2 levels derived from the misplaced catheter was capable of having caused or materially contributed to his RLF. I very well understand the anxiety of the majority to avoid the necessity for ordering a retrial if that was at all possible. But, having accepted, as your Lordships and counsel have had to accept, that the primary conflict of opinion between the experts whether excessive oxygen in the first two days of life probably did cause or materially contribute to Martin's RLF cannot be resolved by reading the transcript, I doubt, with all respect, if the Court of Appeal was entitled to try to resolve the secondary conflict whether it could have done so. Where expert witnesses are radically at issue about complex technical questions within their own field and are examined and cross-examined at length about their conflicting theories, I believe that the judge's advantage in seeing them and hearing them is scarcely less important than when he has to resolve some conflict of primary fact between lay witnesses in purely mundane matters. So here, in the absence of relevant findings of fact by the judge, there was really no alternative to a retrial. At all events, the judge who retries the issue of causation should approach it with an entirely open mind uninfluenced by any view of the facts bearing on causation expressed in the Court of Appeal.

To have to order a retrial is a highly unsatisfactory result and one cannot help feeling the profoundest sympathy for Martin and his family that the outcome is once again in doubt and that this litigation may have to drag on. Many may feel that such a result serves only to highlight the shortcomings of a system in which the victim of some grievous misfortune will recover substantial compensation or none at all according to the unpredictable hazards of the forensic process. But, whether we like it or not, the law, which only Parliament can change, requires proof of fault causing damage as the basis of liability in tort. We should do society nothing but disservice if we made the forensic process still more unpredictable and hazardous by distorting the law to accommodate the exigencies of what may seem hard cases.

Leave to appeal was given by the Court of Appeal on terms that the authority should not seek an order for costs in this House or for variation of the orders for costs in the courts below. For the reasons I have indicated I would allow the appeal, set aside the order of the Court of Appeal save as to costs and order retrial of the issue whether the negligence of the authority, as found by the Court of Appeal, caused or materially contributed to the plaintiff's RLF.

(Lords Fraser, Lowry, Griffiths and Ackner agreed.)

Questions

(i) What assistance, if any, does *McGhee* give to a plaintiff after *Wilsher*?
(ii) What will the plaintiff have to do to make the trial judge, who re-hears the case, find in his favour?

In *Hotson v East Berkshire Area Health Authority* [1987] AC 750, [1987] 2 All ER 909, the House of Lords had to deal with a related problem. The plaintiff was unable to establish, on a balance of probabilities, that the defendants' failure to treat him promptly in breach of duty would have alleviated the injuries he suffered from as a result of falling out of a tree. The trial judge, Simon Brown J, found that there had always been a 75% chance that the injuries would have resulted in his disabilities in any event, but that due to the defendants' carelessness, this had become a 100% certainty. Therefore, even though the plaintiff could not show that 'but for' the defendants' carelessness he would be injury free, he could establish that he had lost a 25% chance of avoiding his eventually permanent injuries. The issue in *Hotson* was whether this could found a claim for damages in the tort of negligence. The trial judge ([1985] 3 All ER 167) and the Court of Appeal ([1987] 1 All ER 210) held that it could. The House of Lords seems to have disagreed.

Lord Bridge of Harwich: My Lords, the respondent plaintiff is now 23 years of age. On 26 April 1977, as a schoolboy of 13, whilst playing in the school lunch hour he climbed a tree to which a rope was attached, lost his hold on the rope and fell some 12 feet to the ground. He sustained an acute traumatic fracture of the left femoral epiphysis. Within hours he was taken to St Luke's Hospital, Maidenhead, for which the appellant health authority (the authority) was responsible. Members of the hospital staff examined him, but failed to diagnose the injury and he was sent home. For five days he was in severe pain. On 1 May 1977 he was taken to the hospital once more and this time X-rays of his hip yielded the correct diagnosis. He was put on immediate traction, treated as an emergency case and transferred to the Heatherwood Hospital where, on the following day, he was operated on by manipulation and reduction of the fracture and pinning of the joint. In the event the plaintiff suffered an avascular necrosis of the epiphysis. The femoral epiphysis is a layer of cartilage separating the bony head from the bony neck of the femur in a growing body. Avascular necrosis results from a failure of the blood supply to the epiphysis and causes deformity in the maturing head of the femur. This in turn involves a greater or lesser degree of disability of the hip joint with a virtual certainty that it will in due course be aggravated by osteoarthritis developing within the joint.

The plaintiff sued the authority, who admitted negligence in failing to diagnose the injury on 26 April 1977. Simon Brown J, in a judgment delivered on 15 March 1985, sub nom *Hotson v Fitzgerald* [1985] 3 All ER 167, [1985] 1 WLR 1036, awarded £150 damages for the pain suffered by the plaintiff from 26 April to 1 May 1977 which he would have been spared by prompt diagnosis and treatment. This element of the damages is not in dispute. The authority denied liability for any other element of damages. The judge expressed his findings of fact as follows ([1985] 3 All ER 167 at 171, [1985] 1 WLR 1036 at 1040–1041):

1. Even had the defendants correctly diagnosed and treated the plaintiff on 26 April there is a high probability, which I assess as a 75% risk, that the plaintiff's injury would have followed the same course as it in fact has, ie he would have developed avascular necrosis of the whole femoral head with all the same adverse consequences as have already ensued and with all the same adverse future prospects. 2. That 75% risk was translated by the defendants' admitted breach of duty into inevitability. Putting it the other way, the defendants' delay in diagnosis denied the plaintiff the 25% chance that, given immediate treatment, avascular necrosis would not have developed. 3. Had avascular necrosis not developed, the plaintiff would have made a very nearly full recovery. 4. The reason why the delay sealed the plaintiff's fate was because it followed the pressure caused by haemarthrosis (the bleeding of ruptured blood vessels into the joint) to compress and thus block the intact but distorted remaining vessels with the result that even had the fall left intact sufficient vessels to keep the epiphysis alive (which, as finding no 1 makes plain, I think possible but improbable) such vessels would have become occluded and ineffective for this purpose.

On the basis of these findings he held, as a matter of law, that the plaintiff was entitled to damages for the loss of the 25% chance that, if the injury had been promptly diagnosed and treated, it would not have resulted in avascular necrosis of the epiphysis and the plaintiff would have made a very nearly full recovery. He proceeded to assess the damages attributable to the consequences of the avascular necrosis at £46,000. Discounting this by 75%, he awarded the plaintiff £11,500 for the lost chance of recovery. The authority's appeal against this element in the award of damages was dismissed by the Court of Appeal (Sir John Donaldson MR, Dillon and Croom-Johnson LJJ) ([1987] 1 All ER 210, [1987] 2 WLR 287). The authority now appeal by leave of your Lordships' House.

. . .

In analysing the issue of law arising from his findings the judge said ([1985] 3 All ER 167 at 175, [1985] 1 WLR 1036 at 1043–1044):

In the end the problem comes down to one of classification. Is this on true analysis a case where the plaintiff is concerned to establish causative negligence or is it rather a case where the real question is the proper quantum of damage? Clearly the case hovers near the border. Its proper solution in my judgment depends on categorising it correctly between the two. If the issue is one of causation then the defendants succeed since the plaintiff will have failed to prove his claim on the balance of probabilities. He will be lacking an essential ingredient of his cause of action. If, however, the issue is one of quantification then the plaintiff succeeds because it is trite law that the quantum of a recognised head of damage must be evaluated according to the chances of the loss occurring.

He reached the conclusion that the question was one f quantification and thus arrived at his award to the plaintiff of one quarter of the damages appropriate to compensate him for the consequences of the avascular necrosis.

It is here, with respect, that I part company with the judge. The plaintiff's claim was for damages for physical injury and consequential loss alleged to have been caused by the authority's breach of their duty of care. In some cases, perhaps particularly medical negligence cases, causation may be so shrouded in mystery that the court can only measure statistical chances. But that was not so here. On the evidence there was a clear conflict as to what had caused the avascular necrosis. The authority's evidence was that the sole cause was the original traumatic injury to the hip. The plaintiff's evidence, at its highest, was that the delay in treatment was a material contributory cause. This was a conflict, like any other about some relevant past event, which the judge could not avoid resolving on a balance of probabilities. Unless the plaintiff proved on a balance of probabilities that the delayed treatment was at least a material contributory cause of the avascular necrosis he failed on the issue of causation and no question of quantification could arise. But the judge's findings of fact, as stated in the numbered paragraphs (1) and (4) which I have set out earlier in this opinion, are unmistakably to the effect that on a balance of probabilities the injury caused by the plaintiff's fall left insufficient blood vessels intact to keep the epiphysis alive. This amounts to a finding of fact that the fall was the sole cause of the avascular necrosis.

The upshot is that the appeal must be allowed on the narrow ground that the plaintiff failed to establish a cause of action in respect of the avascular necrosis and its consequences. Your Lordships were invited to approach the appeal more broadly and to decide whether, in a claim for damages for personal injury, it can ever be appropriate, where the cause of the injury is unascertainable and all the plaintiff can show is a statistical chance which is less than even that, but for the defendant's breach of duty, he would not have suffered the injury, to award him a proportionate fraction of the full damages appropriate to compensate for the injury as the measure of damages for the lost chance.

There is a superficially attractive analogy between the principle applied in such cases as *Chaplin v Hicks* [1911] 2 KB 786, [1911–13] All ER Rep 224 (award of damages for breach of contract assessed by reference to the lost chance of securing valuable employment if the contract had been performed) and *Kitchen v Royal Air Forces Association* [1958] 2 All ER 241, [1958] 1 WLR 563 (damages for solicitors' negligence assessed by reference to the lost chance of prosecuting a successful civil action) and the principle of awarding damages for the lost chance of avoiding personal injury or, in medical negligence cases, for the lost chance of a better medical result which might have been achieved by prompt diagnosis and correct treatment. I think there are formidable difficulties in the way of accepting the analogy. But I do not see this appeal as a suitable occasion for reaching a settled conclusion as to whether the analogy can ever be applied.

As I have said, there was in this case an inescapable issue of causation first to be resolved. But if the plaintiff had proved on a balance of probabilities that the authority's negligent failure to diagnose and treat his injury promptly had materially contributed to the development of avascular necrosis, I know of no principle of English law which would have entitled the authority to a discount from the full measure of damage to reflect the chance that, even given prompt treatment, avascular necrosis might well still have developed. The decisions of this House in *Bonnington Castings Ltd v Wardlaw* [1956] 1 All ER 615, [1956] AC 613 and *McGhee v National Coal Board* [1972] 3 All ER 1008, [1973] 1 WLR 1 give no support to such a view.

I would allow the appeal.

As you will see, Lord Bridge allowed the appeal on a 'narrow ground'. Lords Brandon, Mackay, Ackner and Goff agreed with this conclusion.

Lord Bridge left open the issue of whether the plaintiff could have recovered had he established a lost chance of recovery. Lord Mackay in his speech examined this issue in some depth though, again, without reaching any conclusion.

Lord Mackay: . . . I consider that it would be unwise in the present case to lay it down as a rule that a plaintiff could never succeed by proving loss of a chance in a medical negligence case. In *McGhee v National Coal Board* [1972] 3 All ER 1008, [1973] 1 WLR 1 this House held that where it was proved that the failure to provide washing facilities for the pursuer at the end of his shift had materially increased the risk that he would contract dermatitis it was proper to hold that the failure to provide such facilities was a cause to a material extent of his contracting dermatitis and thus entitled him to damages from his employers for their negligent failure measured by his loss resulting from dermatitis. Material increase of the risk of contraction of dermatitis is equivalent to material decrease in the chance of escaping dermatitis. Although no precise figures could be given in that case for the purpose of illustration and comparison with this case one might, for example, say that it was established that of 100 people working under the same conditions as the pursuer and without facilities for washing at the end of their shift 70 contracted dermatitis: of 100 people working in the same conditions as the pursuer when washing facilities were provided for them at the end of the shift 30 contracted dermatitis. Assuming nothing more were known about the matter than that, the decision of this House may be taken as holding that in the circumstances of that case it was reasonable to infer that there was a relationship between contraction of dermatitis in these conditions and the absence of washing facilities and therefore it was reasonable to hold that absence of washing facilities was likely to have made a material contribution to the causation of the dermatitis. Although neither party in the present appeal placed particular reliance on the decision in *McGhee* since it was recognised that *McGhee* is far removed on its facts from the circumstances of the present appeal your Lordships were also informed that cases are likely soon to come before the House in which the decision in *McGhee* will be subjected to close analysis. Obviously in approaching the matter on the basis adopted in *McGhee* much will depend on what is known of the reasons for the differences in the figures which I have used to illustrate the position. In these circumstances I think it unwise to do more than say that unless and until this House departs from the decision in *McGhee* your Lordships cannot affirm the proposition that in no circumstances can evidence of loss of a chance resulting from the breach of a duty of care found a successful claim of damages, although there was no suggestion that the House regarded such a chance as an asset in any sense.

By agreement of the parties we were supplied with a list of American authorities relevant to the questions arising in this appeal, although they were not examined in detail. Of the cases referred to, the one that I have found most interesting and instructive is *Herskovits v Group Health Cooperative of Puget Sound* 664 P 2d 474 (1983), a decision of the Supreme Court of Washington en banc. In this case the claim arose in respect of Mr Herskovits's death. He was seen at Group Health Hospital at a time when he was suffering from a tumour but this was not diagnosed on first examination. The medical evidence available suggested that at that stage, assuming the tumour was a stage 1 tumour, the chance of survival for more than five years was 39%. When he was treated later the tumour was a stage 2 tumour and the chance of surviving more than five years was 25%. The defendant moved for summary judgment on the basis that, taking the most favourable view of the evidence that was possible, the case could not succeed. The Superior Court of King County granted the motion. This decision was reversed by a majority on appeal to the Supreme Court. The first judgment for the majority in the Supreme Court was delivered by Dore J. Early in his judgment he read from the American Law Institute's Restatement of the Law, Second, Torts 2d (1965) vol 2, § 323, which is in these terms:

One who undertakes, gratuitously or for consideration, to render services to another which he should recognize as necessary for the protection of the other's person or things, is subject to liability to the other for physical harm resulting from his failure to exercise reasonable care to perform his undertaking, if (a) his failure to exercise such care increases the risk of such harm . . .

After noting that the Supreme Court of Washington had not faced the issue of whether, under this paragraph, proof that the defendant's conduct had increased the risk of death by decreasing the chances of survival was sufficient to take the issue of proximate cause to the jury he said (664 P 2d 474 at 476):

Some courts in other jurisdictions have allowed the proximate cause issue to go to the jury on this type of proof . . . These courts emphasized the fact that defendants' conduct deprived the decedent of a 'significant' chance to survive or recover, rather than requiring proof that with absolute certainty the defendants' conduct caused the physical injury. The underlying reason is that it is not for the wrongdoer, who put the possibility of recovery beyond realisation, to say afterward that the result was inevitable . . . Other jurisdictions have rejected this approach, generally holding that unless the plaintiff is able to show that it was *more likely than not* that the harm was caused by the defendant's negligence, proof of a decreased chance of survival is not enough to take the proximate cause question to the jury . . . These courts have concluded that the defendant should not be liable where the decedent more than likely would have died anyway. (Dore J's emphasis.)

To the question whether the plaintiff should be allowed, in the case before him, to proceed to a jury he returned an affirmative answer, and gave as the reason (at 477):

To decide otherwise would be a blanket release from liability for doctors and hospitals any time there was less than a 50 percent chance of survival, regardless of how flagrant the negligence.

In support of this reasoning he referred to *Hamil v Bashline* 481 Pa 256 (1978), a decision of the Pennsylvania Supreme Court, and said:

The *Hamil* court distinguished the facts of that case from the general tort case in which a plaintiff alleges that a defendant's act or omission set in motion a force which resulted in harm. In the typical tort case, the 'but for' test, requiring proof that damages or death probably would not have occurred 'but for' the negligent conduct of the defendant, is appropriate. In *Hamil* and the instant case, however, the defendant's act or omission failed in a *duty* to protect against harm from *another source*. Thus, as the *Hamil* court noted, the fact finder is put in the position of having to consider not only what *did* occur, but also what *might have* occurred. (Dore J's emphasis.)

He goes on to quote from *Hamil's* case 481 Pa 256 at 271:

Such cases by their very nature elude the degree of certainty one would prefer and upon which the law normally insists before a person may be held liable. Nevertheless, in order that an actor is not completely insulated because of uncertainties as to the consequence of his negligent conduct, Section 323(a) [of the Restatement of the Law, Second, Torts 2d] tacitly acknowledges this difficulty and permits the issue to go to the jury upon a less than normal threshold of proof.

He goes on to refer to another decision, namely *Hicks v US* 368 F 2d 626 at 632 (1966), as containing a succinct statement of the relevant doctrine, which he quotes (664 P 2d 474 at 478):

Rarely is it possible to demonstrate to an absolute certainty what would have happened in circumstances that the wrongdoer did not allow to come to pass. The law does not in the existing circumstances require the plaintiff to show to a *certainty* that the patient would have lived had she been hospitalized and operated on promptly. (Judge Sobeloff's emphasis.)

He refers also to a general observation in the Supreme Court of the United States dealing with a contention similar to that argued before him by the doctors and the hospital. In *Lavender v Kurn* 327 US 645 at 653 (1946) the Supreme Court said:

It is no answer to say that the jury's verdict involved speculation and conjecture. Whenever facts are in dispute or the evidence is such that fair-minded men may draw different inferences, a measure of speculation and conjecture is required on the part of those whose duty it is to settle the dispute by choosing what seems to them to be the most reasonable inference.

He therefore concluded that the evidence available which showed at maximum a reduction in the 39% chance of five years' survival to a 25% chance of five years' survival was sufficient to allow the case to go to the jury on the basis that the jury would be entitled to infer from that evidence that the delay in treatment was a proximate cause of the decedent's death (see 664 P 2d 474 at 479). He pointed out, however, that causing reduction of the opportunity to recover (also described as a loss of chance) by one's negligence did not necessitate a total recovery against the negligent party for all damages caused by the victim's death. He held that damages should be awarded to the injured party and his family based only on damages caused directly by premature death, such as lost earnings and additional medical expenses and the like.

The approach of Dore J bears some resemblance to the approach taken by some members of this House in *McGhee v National Coal Board* [1972] 3 All ER 1008, [1973] 1 WLR 1 and by Lord Guthrie in *Kenyon v Bell* 1953 SC 125. Brachtenbach J dissented. He warned against the danger of using statistics as a basis on which to prove proximate cause and indicated that it was necessary at the minimum to produce evidence connecting the statistics to the facts of the case. He gave an interesting illustration of a town in which there were only two cab companies, one with three blue cabs and the other with one yellow cab. If a person was knocked down by a cab whose colour had not been observed it would be wrong to suggest that there was a 75% chance that the victim was run down by a blue cab and that accordingly it was more probable than not that the cab that ran him down was blue and therefore that the company running the blue cabs would be responsible for negligence in the running down. He pointed out that before any inference that it was a blue cab would be appropriate further facts would be required as, for example, that a blue cab had been seen in the immediate vicinity at the time of the accident or that a blue cab had been found with a large dent in the very part of the cab which had struck the victim. He concluded that the evidence available was not sufficient to justify the case going to the jury and noted (664 P 2d 474 at 491):

The apparent harshness of this conclusion cannot be overlooked. The combination of the loss of a loved one to cancer and a doctor's negligence in diagnosis seems to compel a finding of liability. Nonetheless, justice must be dealt with an even hand. To hold a defendant liable without proof that his actions *caused* plaintiff harm would open up untold abuses of the litigation system. (Brachtenbach J's emphasis.)

Pearson J agreed that the appeal should be allowed but did not agree with the reasoning by which that result was supported by Dore J. Pearson J, after examining the authorities and an academic article, stated that he was persuaded that a middle course between the reasoning of Dore and Brachtenbach JJ was correct and concluded 'that the best resolution of the issue before us is to recognise the loss of a less than even chance as an actionable injury' (at 487).

He recognised that this also required that the damage payable be determined by the application of that chance expressed as a percentage to the damages that would be payable on establishing full liability.

I have selected references to the view expressed by the judges who took part in this decision to illustrate the variety of views open in this difficult area of the law. These confirm me in the view that it would not be right in the present case to affirm the general proposition for which counsel for the authority contended. On the other hand, none of the views canvassed in *Herskovits*'s case would lead to the plaintiff succeeding in the present case since the judge's findings in fact mean that the sole cause of the plaintiff's avascular necrosis was the injury he sustained in the original fall, and that implies, as I have said, that when he arrived at the authority's hospital for the first time he had no chance of avoiding it. Accordingly, the subsequent negligence of the authority did not cause him the loss of such a chance.

Lord Mackay referred to the relevance of the *McGhee* case to the issue in *Hotson*. One of his reasons for not rejecting outright the plaintiff's argument concerning the recovery of damages for 'loss of a chance' was that the *McGhee* decision in recognising that damages could be recovered, where the plaintiff was able to show that the defendant had 'materially increased the risk' of injuring him, might imply that 'loss of a chance' of avoiding an injury was entitled to compensation in the tort of negligence. What do you think he would decide today in the light of the House of Lords' treatment of *McGhee* in the *Wilsher* case?

Consider the following:

(i) The Court of Appeal did accept the plaintiff's argument that he had lost a 25% chance of recovery from his injury and that this sounded in damages. Sir John Donaldson MR considered whether it was desirable to accept the plaintiff's argument (pp 215–7):

As a matter of common sense, it is unjust that there should be no liability for failure to treat a patient, simply because the chances of a successful cure by that treatment were less than 50%. Nor, by the same token, can it be just that, if the chances of a successful cure only marginally exceed 50%, the doctor or his employer should be liable to the same extent as if the treatment could be guaranteed to cure. If this is the law, it is high time that it was changed, assuming that this court has power to do so.

Equally I am quite unable to detect any rational basis for a state of the law, if such it be, whereby in identical circumstances Dr A who treats a patient under the national health service, and whose liability therefore falls to be determined in accordance with the law of tort, should be in a different position from Dr B who treats a patient outside the service, and whose liability therefore falls to be determined in accordance with the law of contract, assuming, of course, that the contract is in terms which impose on him neither more nor less than the tortious duty.

The answer I think lies in examining precisely what the plaintiff has to allege and prove. First, he has to prove a duty. This is no problem in this case, since it is admitted. But for that admission, it would have been necessary to establish the duty, the necessary factual basis being proved on the balance of probabilities. I say that because there is no room in either justice or law for holding a defendant liable on the basis that he *may* have been subject to a duty. Either he was or he was not. Second, the plaintiff has to prove a breach of that duty. Here again there is no problem, since the failure to treat the plaintiff properly on the occasion of his first visit to the hospital admittedly constituted a breach of that duty. But, if this breach had had to be established, any necessary facts would have had to have been proved on the balance of probabilities. Again I say this because there is no room in justice or law for holding a defendant liable on the basis that there is a significant possibility, not amounting to a probability, that he was in breach of his duty. Third, in the case of tort but not of contract, the plaintiff has to prove some loss or damage and must do so on the balance of probabilities. It is this third requirement which requires further analysis. Hereafter, for simplicity, I will refer to 'loss or damage' simply as 'loss'.

The distinction between what must be proved in contract and what must be proved in tort in order to establish a cause of action may be regrettable, but it does not lie within the power of this court to do anything about it. In any event, it is not usually of practical importance, save perhaps in the context of limitation, where the loss necessary to complete the cause of action in tort occurs a significant time after the breach of duty. Even in contract, if more than a bare right of action is to be established, the plaintiff must prove a loss of substance and, once again, this must be proved on the balance of probabilities. Having identified and proved that loss, the loss has then to be valued. Identification and valuation are distinct and separate processes, but, pace *McGhee*'s case, it is for the plaintiff to prove both the identified loss and its value and to do so in each case on the balance of probabilities.

In the instant case the plaintiff has no difficulty in identifying the loss on which he relies. It has been described by the judge as 'a substantially increased risk that avascular necrosis would develop and long term disability result' (see [1985] 3 All ER 167 at 171, [1985] 1 WLR 1036 at 1040) and in argument as 'the chance of avoiding avascular necrosis and its consequences'. I think it is the use of the latter description, with its reference to *chances*, which has complicated what is essentially a simple claim. I say that because the use of the word 'chance' imports probabilities and opens the way to the argument put forward by the defendants. I also think that it is inaccurate, because it elides the identification of the loss with the valuation of that loss, and they are distinct processes.

In my judgment the essence of the plaintiff's claim is that he has lost any *benefit* which he would have derived if, on the occasion of his first visit to the hospital, he had received the treatment which he in fact received on the occasion of his second visit. This loss of benefit is, of course, admitted, since it flows inexorably from the admission of negligence. Furthermore, it is admitted that it had some value, namely that earlier treatment would have reduced the period over which the plaintiff would have been in pain. Whether it had any further value was in issue. However, if it had been necessary to prove that earlier treatment constituted any benefit, this would have had to have been done on the balance of probabilities.

. . .

It has been said times without number that the categories of negligence are never closed and, subject to the rules relating to remoteness of damage, which are not material in the instant case, I can see no reason why the categories of loss should be closed either.

Dillon LJ added this (p 219):

Medicine does not deal only in certainties. In that, no doubt, medicine is not unique, but there are very many cases in which the patient who goes to a doctor has only a chance, be it greater or less, of being cured of his ailment, or only a chance of avoiding a further deterioration in his condition. If counsel is right, and the chance is lost through a negligent failure of the doctor to examine the patient properly or to diagnose correctly, with the result that the treatment which alone might have saved the patient is not undertaken, the patient will have no remedy unless he can show that the chance of the treatment, if undertaken, proving successful was more than 50%. That to my mind is contrary to common sense.

Do you agree with this analysis?

The defendants argued in the Court of Appeal that a number of anomalies would result if the plaintiff could recover. Sir John Donaldson MR dealt with them as follows (pp 217–8):

(a)   Damages for a lost chance or increased risk will be recoverable in all negligence actions

By this I think counsel meant that proportionate awards of damages will be recoverable in all negligence actions. Not so. Usually the duty will not confer on the plaintiff the benefit of a chance, but of a certainty. And, even when it confers a chance, breach of that duty will only lead to a proportionate award where it is impossible to determine what would have been the consequences of the plaintiff being given that chance, although possible to determine the likelihood of particular consequences. Take the case of a solicitor who fails to advise his client that the property which he is about to purchase is subject to a right of way. If the client had been told, he would or he would not have gone ahead with the transaction. That would have been *his* choice, not the choice of fate. Ascertaining what his choice would have been is possible, whereas the prospects for a cure of a particular patient are sometimes not. The damages recoverable by the solicitor's client would therefore be all or nothing, depending on whether he could prove, on the balance of probabilities, that he would have abandoned the transaction.

(b)   Time will start to run when a chance is lost or a risk is increased, not when physical injury is sustained

This is no more anomalous than the difference between limitation where the claim is founded in contract and where it is founded in tort. In any event, it is not a case of the cause of action being brought forward in point of time. All that is involved is that different causes of action may have different starting points when calculating periods of limitation.

(c)   Plaintiffs who are deprived of a chance of recovery or exposed to a chance of injury will have a right of action even if they remain uninjured in the event

This may be correct, but it is not of practical consequence, since the loss suffered will be nil and, at best, only nominal damages will be recoverable.

(d)   Where there is a negligent failure to diagnose and treat in a way which would have given a 25% increased chance of survival, the patient would recover damages subject to a 75% discount, but his dependants would obtain no award under the Fatal Accidents Act 1976 because they could not prove that the negligence caused the death

This may be regarded as an anomaly, but it stems from the wording of the statute: 'If death is caused by any wrongful act, neglect or default . . .' I do not regard this anomaly, if such it be, as throwing any light on the problem with which we are concerned.

Do you find Lord Donaldson's dismissal of these arguments convincing?

(ii) Do you think the plaintiff's argument in *Hotson* confused 'statistical chances' (which are by definition abstract) and a real chance personal to the plaintiff himself?

Consider the following extract from the judgment of Croom-Johnson LJ in the Court of Appeal in *Hotson* (p 223):

In his closing speech, the plaintiff's counsel said:
    It is our submission, first of all, that the loss of a chance, even a less than 50% chance, is enough to found a claim for damages in tort . . . damage is proved by proving on the balance of probabilities the loss of a 25% chance.
Put simply that way, the proposition is unsustainable. If it is proved statistically that 25% of the population have a chance of recovery from a certain injury and 75% do not, it does not mean that someone who suffers that injury and who does not recover from it has lost a 25% chance. He may have lost nothing at all. What he has to do is prove that he was one of the 25% and that his loss was caused by the defendant's negligence. To be a figure in a statistic does not by itself give him a cause of action. If the plaintiff succeeds in proving that he was one of the 25% and that the defendant

took away that chance, the logical result would be to award him 100% of his damages and not only a quarter, but that might be left for consideration if and when it arises. In this case the plaintiff was only asking for a quarter.

Even the judge at one point in his judgment said ([1985] 3 All ER 167 at 178, [1985] 1 WLR 1086 at 1047):

> The defendants' breach of duty here (a) denied the plaintiff the 25% chance of escaping, and thus (b) *may have caused* the very disability which occurred. (My emphasis.)

In the end he decided that the 25/75% split in the chances was something which went to quantification of damages and not to causation.

The role of the 25/75% split as no more than part of the evidentiary material going to proof of liability seems to have been largely lost sight of.

Is this not the better analysis of chances? Once the court resolves whether the plaintiff was one of the 75 who do not recover or one of the 25 who do, it resolves whether the plaintiff has established, on a balance of probabilities, whether the defendant caused the injuries. Is it not untenable to talk of lost chances other than at the statistical level? Remember that the House of Lords in *Hotson* state that a judge must try and resolve the issue of causation of the injury one way or the other. Do you think, therefore, that the 'loss of a chance' argument was a 'red herring' in the *Hotson* case emerging from the unusual finding of fact by the trial judge which confused statistical chances with the actual effects of the defendants' breach of duty on the plaintiff.

(iii) If you agree with this argument, do you think there is a case in which the plaintiff can *only* show that he has lost a chance of avoiding an injury?

(iv) Does not the discussion of 'loss of a chance' resort to labelling rather than analysis? Is not the real question how difficult or easy the courts are prepared to make the plaintiff's task in proving causation? A court could, of course, allow a plaintiff to succeed merely by pointing to statistical probability without more. By demanding more, as in *Hotson*, the plaintiff is forced to fulfil a burden of proof which involves demonstrating precisely that which he cannot, namely particular facts. Lord Mackay's observations in *Hotson* are instructive.

Referring to the judgment of Brachtenbach J in the Washington Supreme Court decision of *Herskovits*, Lord Mackay said:

> He gave an interesting illustration of a town in which there were only two cab companies, one with three blue cabs and the other with one yellow cab. If a person was knocked down by a cab whose colour had not been observed it would be wrong to suggest that there was a 75% chance that the victim was run down by a blue cab and that accordingly it was more probable than not that the cab that ran him down was blue and therefore that the company running the blue cabs would be responsible for negligence in the running down. He pointed out that before any inference that it was a blue cab would be appropriate further facts would be required as, for example, that a blue cab had been seen in the immediate vicinity at the time of the accident or that a blue cab had been found with a large dent in the very part of the cab which had struck the victim.

Lord Mackay may be right that 'it would be wrong ... therefore that the company ... would be responsible for negligence'. But are the other two propositions wrong in the sentence beginning 'If a person ...'? Does not Lord MacKay's use of the word 'therefore' indicate that he is moving into the realm of policy.

(b) Legal

Medical negligence cases are no different in attracting the traditional analysis adumbrated by the Privy Council in the *Wagon Mound* [1961] AC 388, [1961] 1

All ER 404. Clearly, issues of foreseeability or remoteness (or whatever term of policy is used) can arise. For example, in *Emeh v Kensington and Chelsea and Westminster Area Health Authority* [1985] QB 1012, [1984] 3 All ER 1044, the Court had to make a policy decision as to whether a woman can properly be expected by the court to undergo an abortion rather than bear an 'unwanted child'. (See discussion *infra* Ch 10.)

5. DEFENCES

Largely *this* is a matter falling within the general law of torts. We notice here only a few points which are of interest to the medical lawyer.

(a) Contributory negligence

Professor Picard discusses this topic in her book *Legal Liability of Doctors and Hospitals in Canada* (1984 2nd ed), pp 243–247:

> A patient has certain duties toward the doctor and to himself. In carrying out these duties he is expected to meet the standard of care of a reasonable patient. If he does not and the breach of this standard is the factual and proximate cause of his injuries he is contributorily negligent, and his compensation will be reduced accordingly.[107] Of course, if his injury is due exclusively to his own negligence his action will be dismissed.[108]
>
> ...
>
> A simple example of how apportionment legislation works follows. Assume a doctor is found to be negligent in his treatment of the patient, who is found to be contributorily negligent for failing to follow the doctor's instructions. If the judge assessed the patient's damages at $10,000 and apportioned liability as 60 per cent to the doctor and 40 per cent to the plaintiff, the result would be that the patient would recover $6,000.
>
> While contributory negligence has been discussed in a handful of Canadian cases, there are only two from British Columbia and one from Quebec where it seems to have been applied.[112] Theoretically the law and practice in a medical negligence case should be the same as in any other negligence case and the decision to find contributory negligence has been 'quite frequent'[113] in the ordinary negligence action. One explanation for its rare application in medical negligence cases might be that the seemingly unequal position of the parties, in that the plaintiff patient may have been ill, submissive, or incapable of acting in his own best interests, has led the courts to set the standard of care that patients must meet for their own care at *an unreasonably low level* [our emphasis]. As patients strive for a more equal role in their medical care and for taking aggressive steps in their own treatment, it is predictable and just that there will be more patients found to be contributorily negligent with a consequential reduction in the compensation that they will receive.[114]
>
> In the older British Columbia case[115] a patient was held to be two-thirds to blame for the blindness she suffered and her doctor, a dermatologist, one-third to blame. (Thus she would get $26,666 of the $80,000 assessed as damages.) She had consulted the dermatologist for a facial skin disorder and he prescribed a drug known as chloroquine or Aralen® which she took for approximately six months under prescription. Because she was a medical receptionist she was able to obtain the drug from a drug salesman at one-half the price and without a prescription and for seven months she took the drug on this basis. At that time the dermatologist who had been alerted to the possible serious side effects of the drug to vision had all patients whom he had treated with it see an ophthalmologist. Unfortunately, he did not read carefully enough the resulting report on the plaintiff because it would have alerted him to the patient's unorthodox practice. Thereafter for two more years the patient obtained the drug from the salesman and when this man retired she went back to

the defendant and was prescribed the drug for at least a further eight months. The trial judge found that at no time was the patient warned of the danger of the prolonged use of the drug but also that the defendant did not have actual knowledge of her continuous use of it either. The evidence indicated that her eyes would not have been damaged had her consumption been limited to the prescriptions.

The patient's negligence was found to lie in obtaining prescription drugs from an unorthodox source, using them on a prolonged basis, and not consulting her doctor. She had failed to meet the standard expected of a reasonable patient and was the major cause of her own injury. The doctor's negligence was based on his failure to carefully peruse the ophthalmologist's report and his failure to discern from 'corneal changes' in that report the probability of recent consumption of the drug. This was obviously a clear case for the application of the contributory negligence rules. In fact, it is even arguable that, like the dental patient who nearly bled to death before obtaining medical assistance, [116] this patient was the sole cause of her injury. The standard of care expected of the reasonable patient is tied to the degree of knowledge with respect to medical matters possessed by the layman. Just as the reasonable person is taken to know that loss of a large volume of blood will seriously endanger his health, he ought also to be attributed with the knowledge that obtaining and consuming prescription drugs without medical supervision is risky. However, the fact remains that the plaintiff in this case was given no warning as to the danger of this particular drug and, in fact, after what she would believe was a satisfactory ophthalmological examination, may have had reason to believe that the drug was safe.

In the Quebec case, [117] the evidence of the doctor and patient was in substantial conflict, but the higher courts were not prepared to disturb the trial judge's holding that the patient was contributorily negligent. The doctor was held negligent for failing to diagnose a fracture of the head of the femur, but the patient did not get further medical treatment for over three months and her claim was reduced by one quarter. Unlike the patient in the British Columbia case, who was active in her own treatment, this patient was passive: she failed to seek treatment. The difference in conduct is reflected in the amount by which each patient's compensation was reduced.

There is an unusual case from British Columbia[118] where the employer of the doctors, a hockey club, was successful in reducing its liability by 20 per cent because of the contributory negligence of a hockey player who failed to seek further medical care from the team doctors or consult his own doctor when serious symptoms persisted.

But, as Picard goes on to point out, it may not be easy to show that a patient was contributorily negligent.

The defence was pursued without success in three other Canadian cases. In *Foote v Royal Columbian Hospital*[119] a doctor was found liable for failing to alert hospital staff to the risk that an epileptic patient whose medication he had changed might have a seizure at any time. During an unsupervised bath the 15-year-old did have a seizure and suffered injuries. The doctor alleged that she should be found contributorily negligent. The trial judge disagreed but said, *obiter*, that had he been convinced that the patient had understood instructions not to bath unsupervised, he would have held her contributorily negligent to the extent of 50 per cent. A man playing touch football broke a lens in his glasses and injured his eye. The optometrist and lens manufacturer whom he sued pleaded contributory negligence, but the trial judge held that this had not been proven by the defendants.[120] In *Bernier v Sisters of Service*[121] the patient was admitted to hospital for an appendectomy. While recovering from the anaesthetic she received second and third degree burns to her feet from hot water bottles placed in her bed. The hospital was found liable for the negligence of the nurses who did not test the temperature and placed them without orders. It was argued that the patient was contributorily negligent in failing to call for help, in failing to disclose an earlier bout of frostbite to her feet and in leaving the hospital early against medical advice. All were rejected by the trial judge. He was of the opinion that the injury occurred to the patient while she was still anaesthetized and that it was not unreasonable to fail to disclose having frozen her feet upon entering hospital for an appendectomy. Furthermore, her leaving hospital had not aggravated her injuries. All in all this patient had acted as a reasonable patient. It is possible to see, however, that a patient who fails to disclose a material fact to a hospital or doctor might be found contributorily negligent,[122] as might a patient who leaves hospital without notice or against medical advice and as a consequence suffers greater injuries.[123]

Other conduct by a patient that might bring a finding of contributory negligence[124] would include failure to return for treatment,[125] to seek treatment,[126] to co-operate during treatment,[127] or to follow instructions.[128] However, to date, in support there are primarily only *obiter* comments in case law from both inside and outside Canada. It remains to be seen whether the new vitality of the patient's role in his own health care will result in the law requiring a higher standard of him.

Notes to extract

[107] Linden [*Canadian Tort Law* (1982)] at 463. Note that the duty of every plaintiff to mitigate his damages refers to conduct *after* the accident. Fleming, *Law of Torts* 226 (1982). See *Savoie v Bouchard* (1982), 23 CCLT 83 (NBQB); affd unreported Sept 19 1983 No 8/83/CA (NBCA). *Poulin v Health Sciences Centre* (1982) 18 Man R (2d) 274 (QB); see also *Strickland v St John's* (1983) 41 Nfld & PEIR 219 (Nfld DC).

[108] Meredith [*Medical Liability of Doctors and Hospitals* (1956)] at 88. Note that the defence of *volenti non fit injuria* seems inappropriate in a medical negligence case. See *Linden supra* n 8 at 501. See also *Savoie v Bouchard* (1982), 23 CCLT 83 (NBQB). For instances of the defence in the US see Louisell and Williams, *Medical Malpractice*, Matthew Bender, New York (1983), at 238. In England, see *Emeh v Kensington*, Times, 21 December (1982).

...

[112] Note that in *Osburn v Mohindra* (1980) 29 NBR (2d) 340 (QB), the defendants, a doctor and the hospital, were held liable in proportions of 75 per cent and 25 per cent *of 75 per cent* respectively. The reason for the plaintiff's recovery being reduced by 25 per cent was not discussed.

[113] Klar, *Contributory Negligence and Contribution Between Tortfeasors* in *Studies in Canadian Tort Law* 146 (2d ed Klar 1977).

[114] Note that it has been suggested that it may not be wise from a tactical point of view to plead this defence but, instead, to take the position that the patient was the sole cause of his own injuries. Louisell and Williams, *supra* n 110 at 249–50.

[115] *Crossman v Stewart* (1977) 5 CCLT 45 (BCSC); see also *Molnar v Conway* unreported 22 June 1978 No 114193 (Alta SC).

[116] *Murrin v Janes* [1949] 4 DLR 403 (Nfld SC).

[117] *Hôpital Notre-Dame de l'Espérance v Laurent* [1978] 1 SCR 605; affirming [1974] CA 543 (Que).

[118] *Robitaille v Vancouver Hockey Club Ltd* (1979) 19 BCLR 158 (SC); varied as to exemplary damages [1981] 3 WWR 481 (CA). For a comment see Balbi, *Liability of Sports Physicians* (1984), ALR.

[119] (1982), 38 BCLR 222 (SC); affd 19 ACWS (2d) 304 (CA).

[120] *Dunsmore v Deshield* (1977), 80 DLR (3d) 386 (Sask QB).

[121] [1948] 1 WWR 113 (Alta SC). Note that the plea of last-clear-chance or ultimate negligence by the defendant against the plaintiff was denied as well; for a comment see Howell, *Case Comment* (1978–79), 43 Sask L Rev 149.

[122] *Kouri, supra* n 109 at 50; *Nykiforuk v Lockwood* [1941] 1 WWR 327 (Sask DC); *Guimond v Laberge* (1956) 4 DLR (2d) 559 (Ont CA); *Leadbetter v Brand* (1980) 37 NSR (2d) 581 (SC); *Ehler v Smith* (1978) 29 NSR (2d) 309 (SC); see also Chapter 3.

[123] Meredith, *supra* . . . at 156; *Worth v Royal Jubilee Hospital* (1980) 4 L Med Q 59 (BCCA).

[124] Kouri, *supra* n 109.

[125] See *Moore v Large* (1932) 46 BCR 179 at 183 (CA); *Hôpital Notre-Dame de l'Espérance v Laurent supra* n 109.

[126] *Robitaille v Vancouver Hockey Club Ltd* (1979) 19 BCLR 158 (SC); varied as to exemplary damages [1981] 3 WWR 481 (CA). See *Hampton v Macadam* (1912) 22 WLR 31 at 35 (Sask). See also *McDaniel v Vancouver Gen Hospital supra* n 28.
[127] *Antoniuk v Smith* [1930] 2 WWR 721 at 734 (Alta CA).
[128] *Marshall v Rodgers* [1943] 2 WWR 545 at 554 (BCCA), where failure to be vaccinated for smallpox was advanced but not seriously pressed.

Do you agree with Picard's use of the words 'unreasonably low level'?

One issue which preoccupies some doctors is, what is called in medical journals, 'patient non-compliance'. This is intended to refer to situations in which a patient may not follow the instructions given by his doctor, eg as regards taking a prescribed medicine. Would a court, in your view, regard this as contributory negligence? Would there be any scope here for the application of the doctrine in American products liability of 'foreseeable misuse' of a product when it is known that patients frequently depart from the instructions in prescriptions?

Consider the following two American cases.

Martineau v Nelson
247 NW 2d 409 (1976) (Supreme Court of Minnesota) (footnotes omitted)

Kelly J: A single issue is dispositive of the appeal: Was the jury's finding of 50% contributory negligence supported by the evidence?

Plaintiffs argue that the issue of contributory negligence was improperly submitted to the jury and that its finding on that issue is not supported by the evidence. This is a case of first impression on the issue of contributory negligence in a sterilisation case. While there have been several reported decisions dealing with actions for malpractice in performing sterilisation operations, including an early Minnesota case sustaining a demurrer to a complaint on a deceit theory, the bulk of the sterilisation cases deal with the burden of proof under theories of negligence and breach of warranty and the problem of provable damages.

Contributory negligence has been recognised as a defence in a number of malpractice cases in other jurisdictions. The defence has been recognised in cases in which the patient has (1) failed to follow the doctor's or nurse's instructions; or (2) refused suggested treatment; or (3) given the doctor false, incomplete, or misleading information concerning symptoms. This court expressly recognised the defence in 1970 in upholding a general verdict for defendant doctor following the submission of his negligence and plaintiff's contributory negligence. In that case, plaintiff had submitted misleading and inaccurate information about her employment status to the doctor and had no telephone, making it difficult for him to contact her regarding the positive result of her Pap smear test. *Ray v Wagner* 286 Minn 354, 176 NW 2d 101 (1970).

Both courts and text writers have emphasised, however, that the availability of a contributory negligence defence in a malpractice case is limited because of the disparity in medical knowledge between the patient and his doctor and because of the patient's right to rely on the doctor's knowledge and skill in the course of medical treatment. Thus, it has been held that it is not contributory negligence to follow the doctor's instructions or to fail to consult another physician when the patient has no reason to believe his pain is caused by the doctor's negligence. It has also been suggested that the patient's neglect of his own health after negligent treatment may be a factor in reducing damages, but should not bar all recovery. . . .

The relevant issue in this case, which must be considered in light of the record and the authorities just discussed, is whether and to what extent plaintiffs may be charged with acting unreasonably in the face of certain statements and advice of defendant doctors. Confronted with the results of a pathological test showing the removal of a segment of an artery [instead of the intended Fallopian tube], and with equivocation on the part of her doctors as to the success of the operation and the necessity of further procedures, plaintiff wife might have acted unreasonably in failing to at least attempt to persuade her husband to have a vasectomy or, in the absence of vasectomy, in failing to continue a regimen of birth control. The record, however, provides only the barest minimum support for these inferences of negligence. The record does not clearly reveal what plaintiff wife did or did not tell her husband about her conference with the doctors. Furthermore, there is no clear evidence of what birth control methods plaintiff did or did not use after the conference and up to the time the child David was conceived.

The evidence of plaintiff husband's contributory fault is plainly insufficient. The only evidence as to his conduct is that he concluded that his wife could not become pregnant and he elected not to have a vasectomy. There is no evidence that he received any advice directly from the doctors nor any evidence that he acted unreasonably in arriving at his conclusion. Moreover, we think that the law of contributory fault should not compel a 32-year-old husband, who might possibly remarry and later change his mind regarding more children, to undergo sterilisation because of a surgeon's negligence.

From our evaluation of the evidence, we have concluded that there must be a new trial for two reasons. First, since we have concluded that plaintiff husband could not have been guilty of any negligence, and since the jury was asked to apportion negligence to husband and wife together, we cannot be certain to what extent the jury relied on erroneous theories as to the husband's negligence in making its apportionment. Second, while there may be some evidence of negligence on the part of plaintiff wife and while the apportionment of such negligence is normally within the province of the jury, we think the 50–50 apportionment in this case is plainly contrary to the weight of the evidence.

We are confronted in this case with the initial failure of the surgeon to properly perform a tubal ligation, coupled with the equivocal statements of the doctors to plaintiff wife regarding the result (ie, both doctors say her tubes are blocked, one encourages vasectomy, the other encourages further procedures if plaintiffs would feel uneasy about marital relations), and plaintiffs' reaction in electing not to pursue further procedures. Neither doctor apparently discussed with plaintiff wife the risks of pregnancy notwithstanding the operation or directly informed her that she could become pregnant again. Under these circumstances, plaintiffs cannot be held equally negligent with the surgeon because the subject matter of their negligence is the interpretation of medical matters about which the doctors owed a greater duty to them than plaintiffs owed to themselves. The superior knowledge and skill of the physicians in this case should have been reflected in straightforward, complete, and accurate information and advice to their patient. That patient should not be denied recovery because she could not sift from their equivocation this kind of information and advice.

For the reasons stated above, we have concluded that there must be a new trial against both defendants on the issues of their negligence, of the contributory negligence of plaintiff wife, and of damages.

Schliesman v Fisher
158 Cal Rptr 527 (1979) (California Court of Appeals)

Stephens JA: Robert Fisher, MD and Leonard Lewis, MD (hereinafter appellants) had treated George Schliesman (hereinafter respondent) since 1969 for various medical problems, including diabetes mellitus, arterio-sclerotic heart disease, peripheral vascular disease, gout, hypertension and distal extremity ulcerations. The diabetes was generally controlled with the administration of Orinase in spite of the fact that respondent was approximately 100 pounds overweight and did not adhere to his prescribed diet. The recurrent ulcerations on his feet were treated with antibiotics, hot soaks, and elevation of the affected extremity.

From November 19 to 22, 1972, respondent was hospitalised for congestive heart failure. At this time, Dr Fisher discontinued the Orinase, instituted a diabetic diet and recounselled respondent regarding the importance of diet as the preferred means of controlling his diabetes. Dr Fisher's decision to discontinue the Orinase was based upon a recent medical study linking Orinase to increased incidences of heart disease in diabetics. When respondent was seen for follow-up care on December 5, 1972, Dr Fisher felt that the cardiac risks associated with Orinase were sufficiently severe to justify keeping respondent off the medication in spite of elevated blood sugars. Further, Dr Fisher's experience with respondent had been such that he felt that respondent was not responsible enough to be given insulin. Respondent's failure to follow medical advice regarding adherence to his diabetic diet and the need for his discontinuance of beer drinking, together with his tendency to periodically stop taking his medication, led Dr Fisher to believe that respondent was sufficiently unreliable to be prescribed insulin for control of his diabetes, since misuse of that drug could cause rather immediate and life-threatening consequences.

Dr Fisher next saw respondent on December 18, 1972, regarding pain and inflammation of his left foot. The evidence is in conflict as to whether the foot was merely inflamed or had already ulcerated at the time of this examination. The usual antibiotic treatment, hot soaks and elevation were prescribed. Two days later, December 20, 1972, respondent presented at the Santa Monica Emergency Room with a draining ulcer on his left foot. Since the emergency room attending physician could reach neither Dr Fisher nor Dr Lewis by phone, respondent was given a tetanus shot and sent home. When respondent reached Dr Lewis a few hours later, immediate arrangements were made for hospitalisation. Once hospitalised, respondent was treated with a broad-spectrum antibiotic, Erythromycin. Orinase was reinstituted, culture and sensitivity tests were ordered to determine the organism that was causing the infection, and a general surgical consultation requested.

It was subsequently discovered that the plaintiff's foot was dead. The plaintiff's leg was amputated below the knee.

Appellants' first contention on appeal is that the trial court erred when it refused to give a proffered instruction for the defence on contributory negligence. For the reasons stated below, we are in agreement with appellants. Here, while the great bulk of testimony was aimed at establishing or refuting that the appellants' care of respondent fell below the applicable standard for medical care, there was still substantial evidence from which the jury could have found that respondent was himself negligent in failing to follow the orders of his physicians regarding diet, weight reduction and medications and that such negligence proximately contributed to the ultimate loss of his leg.

Robert Uller MD, testified for appellants. He is a physician who specialises primarily in endocrinology, with approximately 40% or more of his practice dealing with diabetic patients. Dr Uller testified that patients like respondent, who are 'adult-onset diabetics', are generally obese individuals whose pancreas manufactures a relatively normal amount of insulin, but because of the increased body weight, the amount is insufficient for that individual and the individual's blood sugar is correspondingly high. Further, he testified that a reduction in weight is the best treatment for such patients, as it results in a drop in the level of blood sugar, which can then be further controlled by diet. Speaking of respondent specifically, he said: 'In this particular problem the patient is his own worst enemy because you can only tell him what diet to follow, and the big problem here to date with the blood sugars by and large has been obesity. 290 pounds and six-foot-two, 280 pounds in a six-foot-two individual, that's about 100 pounds above ideal body weight for man of, say, large boned structures, six-foot-two individual, so if the individual would follow the diet, you know, the blood sugars would be no problem'. Further, Dr Uller testified that the fact that respondent responded extremely well to insulin therapy while hospitalized was an indication that his diabetes would respond well if he were to follow the recommended diabetic diet. In fact, the hospital records revealed that respondent had to be taken off of insulin after three days because of a suspected insulin reaction. Dr Uller attributed this response to the fact that while hospitalized, respondent was forced to adhere to the diet prescribed by his physicians, which brought his blood sugars close to the normal range. Administering insulin, then, had the effect of producing an overabundance of insulin in respondent's system. This effect, Dr Uller testified, pointed to the fact that respondent's diabetes would have responded adequately to diet if respondent would have followed his doctors' orders in this regard.

Respondent contends that there is nothing in the record to indicate that there is a direct relationship between the control of diabetes or lack thereof, and the incidence of infection leading ultimately to gangrene and amputation. The testimony of his own experts, however, contradicts this assertion. Gerard F Smith, MD, testified on behalf of respondent. In the course of that testimony he stated: 'Diabetics are more prone to ulcerations, and develop infection because of their high blood sugar. High blood sugar is a media for bacteria to grow. Therefore, if the sugar is out of control and the area to this leg is impaired, we have two factors working: One, we got a good culture media of the existing blood that is there for the bacteria to grow on; Two, we have sugar that is markedly out of control, both of which will cause increased infection.' Also testifying for respondent, Saul Lieb, MD, testified: 'Infection in the presence of diabetes will spread if the treatment of diabetes is not undertaken.'

We note that the foregoing testimony was aimed primarily at the notion that Dr Lewis should not have taken respondent off the Orinase. However, such testimony also provides a foundation from which the jury could have inferred, when coupled with the prior testimony of Dr Uller, that an out-of-control diabetic whose blood sugars are elevated is more likely to get an infection such as the one that invaded respondent's foot and that such an infection will be much more difficult to treat and cure as a result of the out-of-control diabetes. That respondent's diabetes could have been controlled by weight reduction and proper diet is a significant fact. While respondent sought to place the blame for his diabetes being out of control on Dr Lewis for discontinuing the Orinase, it was a fact of some significance to be weighed by the jury that respondent could himself have brought his diabetes under control with diet and weight reduction and was, in fact, counselled by his doctors repeatedly to do so. The failure of the trial court to allow an instruction of contributory negligence took this consideration from the jury and denied appellants jury trial on an essential defense.

(b) Voluntary assumption of risk

In the general law of torts this, in effect, means that the plaintiff has agreed to waive the duty owed by the defendant to observe the required standard of care. It need not be an express agreement although the courts are very reluctant to imply such an agreement, particularly since the Law Reform (Contributory Negligence) Act 1945.

You will recall Professor Picard's reference to the lack of equality of power between the parties in a doctor/patient relationship in her discussion of contributory negligence. Does not this point apply with even greater force here, so as to suggest that a court would not find a patient had voluntarily waived the doctor's duty save in the most exceptional circumstances? Indeed, do you think a court would find that, as a matter of public policy, a patient should *never* be held to have waived a doctor's duty in the context of medical treatment?

(c) Other defences

We do not rehearse here other defences to actions for medical negligence. Perhaps, the most important would be the defence of limitation of action to be found in the Limitation Act 1980. You are referred to the standard books on the law of torts. We content ourselves with the following summary offered by Margaret Brazier in *Medicine, Patients and the Law* (1987) at p 90:

A patient contemplating an action for medical negligence must act relatively promptly. The general rule is that all actions for personal injuries must be brought within three years of the infliction of the relevant injury. This is known as the limitation period and is laid down in the Limitation Act 1980. A writ must be served on the doctor or hospital authority no later than three years from the date of the alleged negligence. But sections 11 and 14 of the 1980 Act provide that where the patient originally either (1) was unaware that he had suffered significant injury, or (2) did not know about the negligence which could have caused his injury, the three-year period only begins to run from the time when he did discover, or reasonably should have discovered, the relevant facts. Where the patient knew all the relevant facts, but was ignorant of his legal remedy, the three-year limitation period runs from the time when he was or should have been aware of the facts.

All is not quite lost for the patient who delays beyond three years or who is ignorant of the law. A judge may still allow him to start an action later. Section 33 of the 1980 Act gives to the court a discretion to override the three-year limitation period where in all the circumstances it is fair to all parties to do so. The courts will examine the effect of allowing the action to go forward on both parties, taking into account, among other things, the effect of delay on the cogency of the evidence, the conduct of the parties, and the advice sought by and given to the patient by his lawyers and medical advisers. The three-year (or longer) limitation period applies only to *starting* legal proceedings. Once started, an action may drag on for years before it is settled or finally decided.

Reforming the current law on malpractice

The Pearson Report (Royal Commission on *Civil Liability and Compensation for Personal Injury*) in 1978 (Cmnd 7054) made a number of somewhat modest (and some would say disappointing recommendations about negligence in the context of medical practice (paras 1325–1371).

Criticisms of the present compensation provisions

1325 Criticisms of the present compensation provisions fall into two parts. First, there are those which relate to the difficulty of making claims following negligent treatment. Secondly, there are those concerning the lack of provision for medical accidents.

Proving negligence

1326 The proportion of successful claims for damages in tort is much lower for medical negligence than for all negligence cases. Some payment is made in 30–40 per cent of claims compared with 86 per cent of all personal injury claims.

1327 We received a good deal of evidence about the difficulty of proving negligence. It was said that it was not always possible to obtain the necessary information on which to base a claim. The patient might not know what had happened and he might have difficulty in obtaining the services of a medical expert to assist him. When a doctor was accused of negligence, his colleagues might naturally be reluctant to give evidence. The medical records might not contain all the details of the case, leaving ample scope for different interpretations by witnesses for and against.

1328 One of our number, who attended a Council of Europe colloquy on the civil liability of physicians, held in Lyons in June 1975, reported that most of the doctors and lawyers there agreed that information should be more readily available to the patient's advisers.

1329 In England and Wales, on an order for discovery, the court may direct disclosure to the applicant or his solicitors. The courts have taken the line that, normally, disclosure would be only to a nominated medical adviser of the applicant. In Northern Ireland, the courts have decided that disclosure may be made to the applicant. This is also the position in Scotland.

1330 Any patient may approach the Health Service Commissioners for investigation of his complaint, but the Commissioners are expressly prevented from investigating a claim in respect of which the person aggrieved has or had a remedy in law (unless it would not be reasonable to expect him to resort to it) or in respect of any action taken solely in consequence of the exercise of clinical judgment.

Medical accidents

1331   We have so far discussed the evidence we received about negligence. But there are many more cases where individuals suffer injury which was not due to negligence. We received a good deal of evidence that the position here was unsatisfactory.

1332   The Royal College of Physicians instanced, 'the possible sequelae of coronary arteriograms, kidney biopsies or amniocenteses'. Injury or death might be associated with, 'the development of hypersensitivity to a drug or antibacterial substance that was properly prescribed'. Dr White Franklin pointed out that a patient who stopped breathing under properly administered and controlled anaesthesia might die or recover with faculties grossly impaired.

1333   Some of these patients (or their dependants) would receive social security benefit, but many would receive no cash benefit of any kind.

What should be done?

1334   Our evidence showed that there was considerable dissatisfaction with the present position and some unease about the future.

1335   We considered various ways of compensating medical accidents with or without negligence. We look first at tort, where liability at present is based on negligence, and consider the possibility either of reversing the burden of proof or of imposing strict liability. Then we go on to examine the possibility of a no-fault scheme which would cover medical accidents irrespective of negligence.

Tort compensation

Reversed burden of proof

1336   Some witnesses suggested that, if the burden of proof were reversed, the patient's difficulties in obtaining and presenting his evidence would be largely overcome. It was said that doctors were in a better position to prove absence of negligence than patients were to establish liability. At the Council of Europe colloquy, however, although it was agreed that the patient was at a disadvantage when he sought to establish a claim, serious doubts were expressed on the desirability of making a radical change in the burden of proof. We share these doubts. We think that there might well be a large increase in claims, and although many would be groundless, each one would have to be investigated and answered. The result would almost certainly be an increase in defensive medicine.

Strict liability

1337   We also considered whether strict liability should be introduced. Whilst this would avoid the difficulties of proving or disproving negligence, there would remain the difficulty of proving that the injury was a medical accident, that is to say that it would not have occurred in any event. It would be necessary to define the area to be covered. For example, the foreseeable result of medical treatment such as amputation of a limb in a case of gangrene would not be included. The problems in defining the scope of medical injuries to be included would be the same as those we consider later in connection with the possibility of introducing a no-fault scheme.

1338   Even if it were possible to limit the scope satisfactorily, the imposition of strict liability, as with reversing the burden of proof, might well lead to an increase in defensive medicine. It would tend to imply rigid standards of professional skill beyond those which the present law requires to be exhibited, and beyond those which (in our view) can fairly be expected. We decided not to recommend that strict liability should be introduced. . . .

The negligence action

1342   In most of the evidence from the medical profession it was urged that tort should be retained. It was argued that, even if some other system were introduced, the tort action based on negligence should continue alongside. Liability was one of the means whereby doctors could show their sense of responsibility and, therefore, justly claim professional freedom. If tortious liability were abolished, there could be some attempt to control doctors' clinical practice to prevent mistakes for which compensation would have to be paid by some central agency. It was said that this could lead to a bureaucratic restriction of medicine and a brake on progress. It was further argued that the traditions of the profession were not sufficient in themselves to prevent all lapses which, though small in number, might have disastrous effects. Some penalty helped to preserve the patient's opportunity to express disapproval and obtain redress.

1343 We record these views as put to us, although some of us feel that they are unsound and at the least overstated. We also feel bound to ask whether the growth of insurance cover does not mitigate the effect claimed for the value of the tort action. On this point, the Medical Defence Union said that, although they paid the compensation, their investigation into the circumstances brought home to the doctor the part he had played and encouraged a sense of personal responsibility. We add the comment that the cases that come to court must often be those in which the Union advises the doctor to contest the claim because he has a good defence, whereas the much smaller number of cases of gross negligence must usually be settled out of court. The system, therefore, would appear to expose to publicity those doctors whose behaviour is on the face of it the least reprehensible.

1344 Nevertheless, in spite of the doubts we express about the particular arguments put to us by the medical profession for the retention of the tort action, it is clear that there would have to be a good case for exempting any profession from legal liabilities which apply to others, and we do not regard the special circumstances of medical injury as constituting such a case.

1345 We were impressed by the difficulties facing a patient who wishes to establish a case, but we doubt if the confidentiality of medical records adds significantly to the plaintiff's difficulties in view of the powers of the courts to order disclosure.

1346 Although the powers of the Health Service Commissioners are restricted to some extent, we note with interest the possibility of change following a report published in November 1977 by the Select Committee on the Parliamentary Commissioner for Administration (HC45) about an independent review of hospital complaints in the National Health Service. The Committee considers that there should be a simple straightforward system for handling complaints in every hospital with emphasis on listening carefully to the patient's or relative's concern and dealing with it promptly. When the complainant is not satisfied he should be able to pursue the matter with the district Administrator. For the most serious cases the Secretaries of State should continue to set up inquiries under the relevant Acts. All other cases not resolved by this procedure should be referable to the Health Service Commissioner, including complaints concerning clinical judgment.

1347 **We recommend** that, subject to our recommendation on volunteers for medical research or clinical trials, the basis of liability in tort for medical injuries should continue to be negligence.

No-fault compensation

1348 Changes made to improve the prospects of getting compensation in the cases of negligence could have no effect on the very much greater number of medical accidents where nobody is at fault.

1349 The employment of new techniques and the development of medical science have increased the ability of the doctor to attempt the treatment of severe diseases and to effect a cure, but at the same time have widened the area in which medical accidents may occur. This trend of greater risks for greater gain is likely to continue.

1350 An operation may have unexpected consequences. Blood products may be used which contain viruses the presence of which could not be foreseen. There are now 3,000 drugs in common use and 10,000 listed drug interactions, both detrimental and beneficial. More will doubtless be discovered.

1351 Many of our witnesses urged us to recommend the introduction of a scheme of no-fault compensation for medical accidents. Dr White Franklin said that negligence should not be the key to any form of monetary compensation. A circuit judge suggested that subsistence level compensation would be appropriate for a medical injury which did not involve negligence. The Royal College of Psychiatrists suggested that over the whole field of personal injury, compensation should not be tied to fault or negligence and should be based on the need of the individual and his family.

1352   Most of our witnesses saw a no-fault scheme as an addition to tort. It was put to us that such a scheme would often overcome the difficulties of proving negligence; and that a special scheme for medical injuries would be justified because of the reliance of the patient on the doctor to preserve his health and perhaps his life.

Overseas experience

1353   No-fault schemes which cover medical accidents have recently been introduced in New Zealand and Sweden. In Volume Three . . . we give a detailed description of the provisions; in this chapter we touch only on some relevant features.

1354   New Zealand's accident compensation scheme covers medical, surgical, dental and first aid misadventure. In an appraisal of the first two years' operation of the scheme, Professor Geoffrey Palmer refers to the Accident Compensation Commission's 'restrictive interpretation' of 'medical misadventure' which 'seems concerned to avoid sliding down the slippery slope and compensating illness or death every time medical treatment fails'. This means that in many cases the claimant is left only with recourse to the common law. The view that the Accident Compensation Commission is treading carefully in this difficult area is supported by reported decisions of the Commission.

1355   The Patient Insurance Scheme in Sweden provides no-fault compensation which is based on the rules for the assessment of tort damages. This includes provision for loss of earnings, necessary medical expenses not covered by social insurance, and non-pecuniary loss. The scheme is financed by the Government and by the county councils who are responsible for the hospitals and for public health facilities. Liability is limited to 20 million kronor (about £3 million) for each incident involving injury and there is an overall limitation of 60 million kronor (about £8½ million) for such injuries in the whole country in one year. This is about £1 a head of the population.

1356   Payments under the scheme are relatively modest because they supplement existing social insurance payments which cover virtually all the adult population, including housewives. Social insurance sickness benefit is 90 per cent of earnings with an earnings ceiling of over £10,000 a year. The Patient Insurance Scheme makes up the payments to 100 per cent. Under industrial agreements, benefit for work accidents is made up to 100 per cent and this further reduces the scope for the payments under the Patient Insurance Scheme. Of the compensation paid during the first year only 12½ per cent was for loss of income.

1357   The scheme covers injury or illness which has occurred as a direct consequence of examination, medication, treatment or any other similar procedure, and does not constitute a natural or probable consequence of an act justified from a medical point of view. Mental illness is not covered unless it results from bodily injury. Injuries resulting from risks which are justified in order to avoid a threat to life or of permanent disability or would have occurred regardless of the treatment are also excluded.

1358   The Swedish scheme is administered by the main insurance companies. The amount of compensation is settled in the same way as tort awards. Disputed claims and questions of principle are referred to a panel consisting of a chairman and one member appointed by the government, two members appointed by county councils and two by insurance companies. Specialist medical advice is available. Only 50 cases have been referred to the panel in the first 23 months of the scheme. The advice of the panel has been accepted in every case. There has been no need to use the arbitration machinery under the Swedish Arbitration Act.

1359   The Swedish and New Zealand schemes cater for relatively small populations, so that it is possible to ensure consistency in decisions by dealing with all difficult or borderline cases centrally. Both schemes have been in operation for a short time and claims will take some time to build up. It will be a few years yet before a useful appraisal can be made.

A no-fault scheme for the United Kingdom?

1360 In considering the possibility of a no-fault scheme for this country we looked first at the question of cost. There are two aspects: the overall cost of any scheme; and the machinery for financing it.

1361 It is difficult to be precise about cost. Minor injuries and complications of treatment could reasonably be excluded as in Sweden, where there has to be some incapacity for work for more than 14 days. If there were as many as 10,000 cases a year, and benefits were provided on the same lines as in our suggested work and road schemes, the total additional cost of compensation over the existing form of compensation would be about £6 million a year. Some addition would have to be made for the cost of administration. This could well be substantial. Judging by the Swedish experience there would be a least two claims for every one that was successful.

1362 We think that it would be appropriate to finance any such scheme through the National Health Service. But the question of what to do about medical accidents in private practice would raise difficulties. Although it might be argued that many doctors have both National Health Service and private patients, that private doctors use National Health Service facilities and that all taxpayers contribute to the National Health Service, nevertheless we think that it is out of the question that a no-fault scheme provided by public funds should cover injuries received in the course of private treatment. There might be other ways of solving the problem. For example, such injuries could be covered by private no-fault insurance, or it might be possible to provide no-fault compensation through a levy on the subscription to medical defence societies. But in view of the decision we come to, as explained below, not to recommend a no-fault scheme because of other even more compelling considerations, we have not worked out in any detail possible ways of meeting this particular difficulty over finance.

1363 Any attempt to devise a no-fault scheme would also run into the problem of whether, and if so, how, treatment given by the 'paramedical' professions should be covered. Most of those in such professions, for example, nurses and physiotherapists, work with or mainly under the direction of doctors or dentists; but there would remain the problem of treatment not given by a medical team, for example chiropody. Outside the National Health Service, there would be the further problem whether other practices, such as osteopathy, should be covered.

Establishing causation

1364 The main difficulty in the way of a no-fault scheme is how to establish causation, since the cause of many injuries cannot be identified. The Medical Research Council said that while future research was likely to establish more causal relationships it would also reveal increasingly complex interactions which would heighten the problems of proving causation in the individual case.

1365 Even with our definition of medical injury we were forced to conclude that in practice there would be difficulty in distinguishing medical accident from the natural progression of a disease or injury, and from a foreseeable side effect of treatment. It is quite normal for a patient not to recover completely for several weeks or months after a major operation; for complications to ensue after operations; and for a patient to find that the drugs prescribed cause serious side effects.

1366 How should words like 'expected' or 'foreseeable' be interpreted? Even rare side effects such as vaccine damage not caused by negligence are often foreseeable in the sense that they are well known to medical science. If such injuries were to be included in a no-fault scheme, where would the line be drawn between them and the accepted risks of treatment? If they were to be excluded, the scheme would do little more than convert the negligence test of tort into a statutory formula, thereby making it easier for the victims of negligence to obtain compensation, but doing nothing for those suffering medical injury from other causes.

1367 In establishing causation, who should take the decision? We envisage that a no-fault scheme would be the responsibility of DHSS. The use of its adjudication procedure, however, would either place more burdens on the medical manpower available, or would put the onus of making the initial decision on the shoulders of junior officials who have neither the experience nor the training to determine these issues.

1368   To establish causation would involve deciding whether the condition was the result of the treatment and, if so, whether it was a result that might have been expected. This would have to be disentangled from the conditions resulting from the progress of the disease or advancing age or from some other purely fortuitous circumstances.

1369   It is easy to distinguish the completely unexpected result from that which was expected. The grey areas in between pose serious difficulties in knowing where to draw the line.

Conclusions on no-fault compensation

1370   We concluded that we could not recommend the introduction of a no-fault scheme for medical accidents in the United Kingdom. Some of us found this was a difficult decision and thought the arguments were finely balanced. All of us appreciate that circumstances may change, and that our conclusions may have to be reviewed in the future.

1371   **We recommend** that a no-fault scheme for medical accidents should not be introduced at present; but that the progress of no-fault compensation for medical accidents in New Zealand and Sweden should be studied and assessed, so that the experience can be drawn upon, if, because of changing circumstances, a decision is taken to introduce a no-fault scheme for medical accidents in this country.

'No-fault', here, does not mean strict liability (as technically it should) but a system in which compensation is awarded not only without the need to prove fault (though there may be other threshold requirements) but, *more importantly*, without the need to have recourse to litigation to claim compensation.

Ten years on Ham, Dingwall *et al* in their magisterial short paper *Medical Negligence: Compensation and Accountability* (1988) wrote (pp 8–15):

The position today

In the decade that has passed since the Pearson Commission reported, the position in relation to medical negligence has changed significantly. The number of successful claims has risen (see below) and there have been increases in the damages awarded by the courts. These developments have given rise to fears that the UK might be following the example of the USA and may be about to experience a malpractice crisis.

In response, the defence societies have increased their subscription rates substantially. As Table 3 shows, subscription rates rose from £40 in 1978 to £1,080 in 1988. The increase in subscription rates was 71 per cent in 1987 and 87 per cent in 1988. This has created particular difficulties for junior doctors. Although

Table 3. Defence Society Subscription Rates 1978–88

Year	Rate £	Annual Increase %
1988	1,080	87
1987	576	71
1986	336	17
1985	288	17
1984	264	35
1983	195	44
1982	135	13
1981	120	26
1980	95	36
1979	70	75
1978	40	—

concessionary rates are available to newly qualified doctors (see Table 4) and those on limited incomes, a junior doctor is required to pay the full rate seven years after qualifying. Until the introduction of new arrangements following the 1988 pay award (see below), this meant that subscription rates could amount to the equivalent of a month's salary. As a result of these pressures, the medical profession has reconsidered its position and has called for a review of existing arrangements.

Table 4. 1988 Defence Society Subscription Rates

	£
Full rate	1,080
Concessionary rates available to members who join within three months of qualification	
1st year	180
2nd year	240
3rd year	396
4th year	492
5th year	600
6th year	744
Non-clinical membership	132
Limited income concessionary rates	
Income ceiling of £6,230	360
Income between £6,231 and £12,460	720

† Subscription rates from January 1 1988 for the Medical Protection Society and the Medical Defence Union

At the same time, health authorities have expressed their concern at the impact of increasing awards on cash limited budgets. As well as the cost of awards themselves, health authorities are worried that the threat of legal action will lead to more defensive medicine. By increasing the use of diagnostic tests and procedures, and by producing greater caution on the part of doctors, it is feared that defensive medicine will add to the pressure on health authority spending, particularly in the acute hospital services.

In parallel with the concern of health authorities and the medical profession, organisations representing patients and their relatives have drawn attention to the shortcomings of the tort system. . . .

First, there is the lengthy and expensive procedure involved in pursuing a claim for damages. This means that cases are often brought only by the rich or those able to obtain legal aid. Cases take a considerable time to work their way through the courts: the average time for settling a claim is four years.

Second, the legal process is by definition adversarial. As such, it may cause doctors and health authorities to close ranks and not offer an adequate explanation to patients and their relatives when things go wrong. In addition, the legal process may itself be distressing in providing a constant reminder of painful or unhappy events.

Third, the emphasis on establishing fault and cause and effect in injury cases turns the tort system into a lottery. Compensation is based not on need but on the ability to prove that somebody was at fault. The rules of the legal process which put the burden of proof on those bringing a claim may create significant difficulties for plaintiffs. As a consequence, similar cases of injury may be compensated quite differently. For example, a child suffering brain damage after contracting encephalitis will receive no compensation, a child suffering brain damage as a result of vaccine damage will receive £20,000, and a child suffering brain damage following traumatic birth delivery may receive hundreds of thousands of pounds compensation. . . .

Fourth, only a small proportion of people suffering medical injuries are compensated through the tort system. This may mean that the losses incurred as a result of injury are inadequately compensated, although other sources of compensation are available.

Underlying these criticisms is a concern that the arrangements for maintaining high standards of medical practice and holding doctors to account for unacceptable standards of practice are inadequate. Action for the Victims of Medical Accidents (AVMA), established in 1982, has highlighted these issues, and has argued for much greater openness and accountability on the part of the medical profession in dealing with the consequences of accidents. One of the points emphasised by AVMA is that most people who suffer medical injuries are not seeking compensation but want an explanation of what went wrong. An adequate system for dealing with injuries needs to provide for this as well as to offer financial compensation.

Before considering these points more fully, it is worth noting a number of other criticisms levelled at the tort system as it applies to medical injury cases. These are:

● those making a claim may find it difficult to obtain the services of a solicitor with relevant expertise
● there may be difficulty in obtaining the services of doctors willing to act as expert witnesses for patients
● the legal process causes distress and expense to doctors and health authorities as well as to patients
● the availability of legal aid may result in legal action being initiated in inappropriate cases, that is cases where those making a claim have little chance of success. . . .

It is against this background that alternatives to existing arrangements have again come under scrutiny. One widely canvassed option is a no-fault compensation scheme. This has found favour with the British Medical Association (BMA) and the Association of CHCs in England and Wales (ACHCEW). Other possibilities include the introduction of differential premiums for doctors to reflect the risks involved in their work; shifting the cost of providing compensation to the NHS . . . reforming the tort law to overcome some of the shortcomings identified; providing more support to medical injury cases through the social security system; and extending first party insurance cover.

The view of AVMA is that a change in the existing arrangements is required but it is not clear what that change should be. The view of the Government is that the case for change remains not proven . . .

To shed more light on this debate, we now consider in more detail the available evidence on the present system and assess whether there is indeed a case for reform. . . .

Before accepting too readily the claim that the UK is experiencing a malpractice crisis, it is important to review the available evidence to establish whether this claim is justified. Ideally, this evidence would include:

● trends in the number of medical accidents occurring expressed as a proportion of patients treated
● trends in the number of medical accidents which result from negligence
● trends in the number of claims made expressed as a proportion of patients treated
● trends in the number of successful claims made expressed as a proportion of patients treated
● trends in damages awarded, including total damages awarded each year, the size of the biggest award and the size of the mean award

In practice, only some of this information is available. It is not possible to identify either the number of accidents occurring or the number of accidents which result from negligence because this information is not collected routinely. Information is available on claims and damages through the defence societies. The Medical Protection Society (MPS) has published some information on trends in awards (Figures 1 and 2) and has informed us that the number of claims received by the Society increased from around 1,000 in 1983 to over 2,000 in 1987 (personal communication). Similar trends are reported by the Medical Defence Union (MDU): the frequency of claims paid more than doubled between 1984 and 1987, and the average value of damages awarded also doubled in the same period (personal communication). The MDU has published a graph (Figure 3) showing changes in the highest sum awarded in medical negligence cases. More detailed data are not made public because the societies consider that this information is commercially sensitive and might be used by insurance companies seeking to enter the medical insurance market.

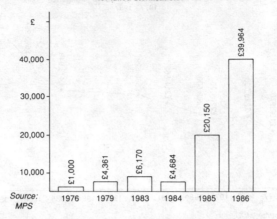

Figure 1 Maximum awards paid by the Medical Protection Society
for failed sterilisation

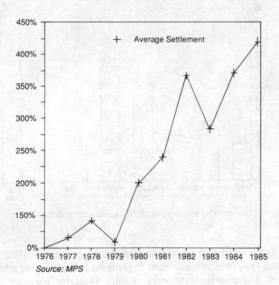

Figure 2 Average costs of settlements. Percentage increase from
January 1976

Health authorities also collect information on claims and damages but again this
has not been fully analysed and published. The DHSS only receives information
from health authorities on awards over £100,000 and the Department is currently
seeking to improve the quality of this information. The DHSS also collates
information on the total payments for losses and compensation made by health
authorities. In 1986–7 a total of £9.3 million was paid out by health authorities
(Hansard, 24 November, 1987, col. 162) but this covers a range of cases including
compensation for unfair dismissals and losses due to theft. There is no information
held centrally on the proportion of these payments spent on compensation for
medical negligence (DHSS, personal communication).

In view of the limited information held by the DHSS, we approached RHA legal
advisers for assistance and received detailed replies from six regions. The experience
of claims opened in these regions in the most recent available year is shown in
Figure 4, together with the US rate for 1984. The variation within the UK is

**Figure 3 Highest sum awarded in medical negligence cases
1977 - 1987**

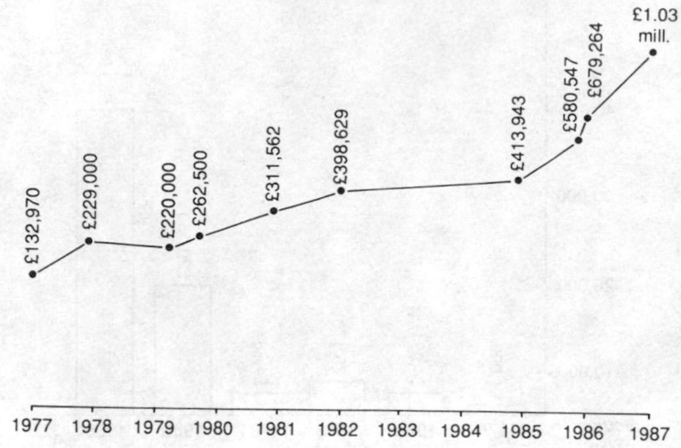

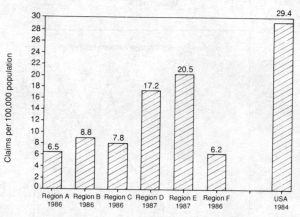

£132,970 £229,000 £220,000 £262,500 £311,562 £398,629 £413,943 £580,547 £679,264 £1.03 mill.

1977 1978 1979 1980 1981 1982 1983 1984 1985 1986 1987

Source: MDU

Figure 4 Annual Claim Rates: Selected English Regions and USA

Claims per 100,000 population

Region A 1986	6.5	
Region B 1986	8.8	
Region C 1986	7.8	
Region D 1987	17.2	
Region E 1987	20.5	
Region F 1986	6.2	
USA 1984	29.4	

Sources: RHA solicitors and US General Accounting Office

striking: most regions had an annual rate of around 8 claims per 100,000 population between 1986 and 1987, but two adjacent regions had annual rates which were more than double this. Time-series data were readily available for only two of the six regions. Figure 5 shows that Region E has always tended to have a high rate of claiming. As the Figure demonstrates, there is a clear upward trend in the number of claims since 1979/80, but with some indication of a levelling off in 1988.

It is difficult to go beyond these global figures to examine the experience of authorities in managing claims and to identify their specific origins. The most useful published data can be found in a study of 100 cases taken at random from the files of the West Midlands RHA ... An audit of these cases found that at the end of three years, 73 actions had been withdrawn, 12 settled out of court and 1 lost in court. Fourteen cases were pending and the authors estimated that nine of these fourteen cases were likely to reach court.

In the context of the Pearson Commission's data, these figures do not suggest that the proportion of claims which are successful is increasing. Indeed the rate at which claims are abandoned would appear to have increased. On the other hand, it would

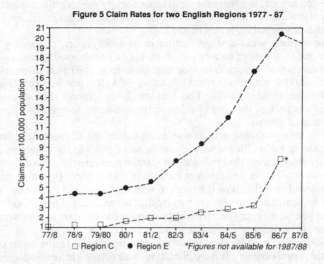

Figure 5 Claim Rates for two English Regions 1977 - 87

appear that the proportion of claims going to court or likely to go to court is increasing.

Evidence we have obtained from another health authority confirms that the rate at which claims are abandoned has increased. In this authority, 75 per cent of claims were abandoned in the 1980s compared with around 50 per cent in the 1970s. There is no evidence from this authority that the severity of the claimants' injuries has reduced over time. However, the higher proportion of claims which are abandoned may mean that some claims are being pursued on weaker grounds than they were previously.

The claims experience of this health authority also revealed some interesting patterns in relation to the nature and sources of medical negligence claims. Most claims resulted from temporary injuries, with conditions like iatrogenic infections, fractures caused by mishandling or lack of supervision, and missed diagnosis of fractures being typical. There is some evidence that claim-provoking incidents in hospitals are most likely to occur on the wards rather than in the operating theatre. Moreover, claims arising from events in operating theatres seem rather more likely to be abandoned. All specialties attract claims, although some attract more claims than others. High risk specialties appear to be obstetrics and gynaecology, anaesthetics, accident and emergency, orthopaedics and neurosurgery.

The evidence from the West Midlands and elsewhere points to a picture in which there is a diversity of claims, many of which arise from relatively minor injuries, with little indication of any systematic variation in the incidence of claim-provoking occurrences. This diversity is reflected in a wide distribution of settlement amounts around a fairly modest average figure. In 1986 prices, the average settlement over the years 1981–86 would appear to be in the region of £15,000 with a standard deviation of £27,000. In addition, health authorities incur legal costs, even where cases are eventually abandoned. Again in 1986 prices, the legal costs of one authority varied between a mean of £210 for abandoned cases, through £1,200 in cases where some payment was made, to £3,000 in cases which were successfully defended in court. Where the authority was required to pay the plaintiff's costs as part of a settlement or award, the mean payment was £2,000.

The impact of subscriptions on the medical profession

As we have noted, a major cause of current concern with compensation arrangements is the impact of increases in defence society subscription rates on the medical profession. In considering this issue, it is worth noting that general practitioners' subscriptions are fully reimbursed by the Government as expenses. As far as hospital doctors are concerned, the increase in defence society subscriptions was taken into account by the Review Body on Doctors' and Dentists' Remuneration in making recommendations on salary levels in 1987.

The Review Body went a stage further in its 1988 report, proposing that two-thirds of the medical rate of subscriptions should be reimbursed as an expense to all whole-time employed practitioners or part-time employed practitioners working wholly for the NHS, with effect from 1 January 1988 (Review Body on Doctors' and Dentists' Remuneration, 1988). The Review Body argued that doctors should continue to bear part of the cost of subscriptions in order to maintain involvement in the handling of claims.

The aim of this proposal, which was accepted by the Government, was to put doctors employed by health authorities on the same basis as they were in 1986. The Review Body emphasised that this was an interim measure that should apply until a better long-term solution had been achieved. In effect, then, the full costs of GPs' subscriptions and two-thirds of the costs of subscriptions paid by doctors employed whole-time by health authorities are met by the Government. This is likely to relieve much of the pressure from the medical profession for change, at an overall cost to the taxpayer of the order of £50 million in England alone.

The subscriptions paid by doctors should also be viewed in the context of those paid by other professions. It is difficult to make straightforward comparisons between professional indemnity insurance in medicine and that available to other professions because of the prevalence of risk-rating and variations in the amount of cover offered. Risk-rating means that the premium charged is weighted by reference to factors like the nature of the business handled, its location and the insured's previous claims record. In a profession serving a private clientele, variations in risk can be expressed as variation in charges to clients. In the NHS, they would either lead to variations in residual income which produced recruitment problems in high-risk specialties, or, more probably, pressure for differential rewards through the Review Body systems. The result would almost certainly be far more costly to administer. Since almost all medical and dental premiums are ultimately paid by the NHS, there seems little to be gained from such a change.

The rates actually paid by doctors appear to be towards the lower end of the range of professional liability premiums. A telephone survey of insurers revealed the following:

Lawyers
Solicitors are required to pay into a mutual fund administered by the Law Society according to a complex scale varying from a minimum of 3.3 per cent of gross fee income below £30,000 in total for a practice to 0.1 per cent of gross fee income above £220,000 per partner, weighted to reflect the ratio between partners and assistant or unqualified staff and the nature of the work being undertaken. This buys £500,000 of cover for each and every claim. Larger practices dealing with high value commercial work obtain top-up cover on the commercial market.

The Bar set up its own mutual fund from 1 April 1988. This groups barristers into four categories depending upon the mix between civil and criminal work in their practice. The fund's directors expect to develop more sophisticated risk-rating in future years. The lowest contribution, for a barrister mainly engaged in criminal work, is 0.3 per cent of gross fee income with a minimum of £20 and a maximum of £390. The highest contributions, from barristers engaged mainly in civil work, are 0.7 per cent of gross fee income up to a maximum of £910 per annum. Coverage is offered in five bands, depending upon the premium paid, from £250,000 up to £2 million for each and every claim. £1 million of cover on this basis would cost between £300 and £499. Practitioners may raise their cover by voluntarily increasing their premium. Leading counsel handling tax cases would need to top up their cover in the insurance market to as much as £10 million but it is unlikely that anyone would pay more than one per cent of their gross fee income.

Financial services
Chartered accountants do not as yet have compulsory insurance although this is under active discussion within their institute. About 60 per cent of them, mostly in

small firms, with an average of 3 partners, are covered under the institute's policy with a commercial insurer. The minimum coverage allowed is 3 times annual gross fees or 30 times the gross income from the largest single source, whichever is greater. The lower limit is fixed at £50,000 for a 1986/7 premium of £385. The maximum currently available under the scheme is £1 million. All coverage is on an aggregate basis. Premiums paid vary between 1 and 3 per cent of a practice's gross fee income depending upon size and claims history. The 'Big Eight' international firms have set up their own mutual fund. In this sector, the highest premiums appear to be paid by insurance brokers where they can go up to 20 per cent of gross income.

Construction

About 40 per cent of architects are not insured at all, either by deliberate choice or as a result of falling behind with premiums during the recent recession in their industry. There is also a particular uncertainty about the position of architects employed in the public sector who do not normally carry their own insurance but whose employers, mostly local authorities, have not accepted liability on their behalf. Those who are insured are mostly covered by a scheme administered by the RIBA.

Current premium rates vary between 4 and 15 per cent of a practice's gross fee income with a minimum of £1,000 per partner. The average is about 7 per cent or around £14,300 per annum at 1987 prices. Rates are influenced by the nature of the business, claims experience and the amount of cover required. Most insured practices carry between £150,000 and £250,000 for each and every claim. Cover of £1 million would cost a typical practice about £80,000 per annum at current rates. Again, the largest firms have formed their own mutual scheme to cover their high-value work.

Chartered engineers pay upwards of £1,000 per head for £250,000 aggregate cover in the commercial market. Much depends on the nature and location of their work, so that anything involving a risky material like water or high value like oil rig design might lead to premiums of up to 8 or 9 per cent of a partner's gross income.

Other health professions

Veterinary surgeons are covered by a defence fund very similar in its operation to the medical defence societies, except that premiums are related to cover, with each practitioner determining his or her own needs. The minimum cover is £50,000 for each and every claim which costs £102 per annum. Practitioners involved in high value work such as racehorses or major intensive husbandry may seek up to £4 million worth of cover at a cost of £2,500 per annum. The package includes £750,000 for incidental injury to humans irrespective of the indemnity selected for liability in respect of animals.

Most independent retail pharmacists are covered by the Chemists' Defence Association which provides up to £3 million in respect of each and every claim. The premium forms part of their annual subscription to the National Pharmaceutical Association, currently £225 plus VAT, and it is not possible to disaggregate this component. The larger chains, such as Boots and some Co-operative societies, make their own arrangements for employed pharmacists. NHS-employed pharmacists are covered by a policy arranged at Lloyd's by the Pharmaceutical Society which covers them for £500,000 aggregate at an annual premium of £32.50.

The great variation in the nature of the cover provided and the methods of calculating premiums make it difficult to translate these figures into direct comparisons with the rates paid by doctors. If, however, we were to attempt an estimate of what a typical professional would pay for £1 million cover on each and every claim, which is broadly the benefit offered by the defence societies, then we would come up with a figure in the range of £1,500 to £5,000, with at least some paying a good deal more and a few paying rather less. This compares with the 1988 subscription of £1,080 for defence society membership and makes the new arrangements with two-thirds reimbursement to doctors working exclusively for the NHS appear a positive bargain.

As a proportion of income a registrar will pay about 2.75 per cent of gross salary once the concessionary rate for junior doctors expires after six years in practice and a senior consultant with an A plus award will pay about 0.5 per cent of gross NHS salary. Again, both seem to be at the lower end of the range for professionals. Insofar as there is a continuing problem, it would seem to be one of equity between practitioners at different stages in their careers with different earning capacities. There are ways of dealing with this short of a fundamental reform of the tort system. A BMA Working Party, for example, has suggested that the concessionary rate might be available for twelve years after qualification with a consequent increase in the full rate subscription to increase the element of cross-subsidy.

Defensive medicine

A further cause of concern is that the increased likelihood of litigation will result in more defensive medicine. This claim is made regularly by the BMA and the defence societies. The argument most frequently articulated is that rather than risk legal action doctors will err on the side of caution by requesting additional diagnostic tests which may be clinically unnecessary. Lord Pitt recently summarised this argument:

> If doctors are to face these awards of severe damages they have to make sure of their defence. You are always better off in the witness box if you can say that you have done all the tests that are considered necessary . . . That means that one is wasting resources. We must therefore face the fact that if we are going to pursue the course that we are now pursuing we shall find an increase in defensive medicine with an alarming waste of resources (*Hansard, House of Lords, 10 November 1987, cols 1350–51*).

In fact, there is little hard evidence that defensive medicine is on the increase. A comprehensive American review of medical malpractice questioned the claim that doctors in the United States were becoming more defensive and noted that if more tests were carried out there could well be benefits for patients. . . . It is also worth reiterating that in the eyes of the law standards of reasonable care in practice are defined by doctors. There is therefore no obligation on doctors to carry out tests and procedures other than those considered reasonable by the profession.

Against this, Harvey and Roberts (1987) have questioned whether doctors will see this as providing them with sufficient protection. These authors maintain that even where clinical guidelines exist doctors may still judge that tests are needed as a defence against possible litigation. However, Kennedy (1987) argues that what is required is for doctors to be better informed of the legal position and to not feel constrained to practise in a way that is inappropriate. Similarly, Carson (1982) has maintained that changes in clinical practice involving reductions in the use of tests need not increase legal liability if the changes are discussed within the profession and receive the support of a responsible body of doctors. These arguments apply not only to tests but also to other areas of clinical practice, such as obstetrics, where it has been suggested that defensive medicine is also on the increase.

One of the most widely cited examples of defensive practice is the rise in caesarean section rates. This is, however, a phenomenon experienced by many countries with very different patterns of litigation (see Figure 6). The trend seems to be much better explained by other factors. These include changes in the perceived risk/benefit ratio following improvements in anaesthetic technology; changing clinical indications; the preference for conducting further deliveries by repeat caesarean; time management benefits for doctors and patients; and, for a time in the US, greater reimbursement for caesarean sections. Many of these factors are reflected in the rising British rates, independently of any concern over the risk of litigation. . . .

Explanations

Various explanations have been proposed for the growth over the last decade in litigation arising from medical accidents. . . . [W]e do not think it is plausible simply to attribute the increase in litigation to a direct copying of American experience. Three other types of explanation have been put forward: a real increase in negligence; easier access to legal representation; and a change in the propensity of patients to sue following an adverse outcome.

Figure 6 Caesarean rates for selected countries 1970 - 84

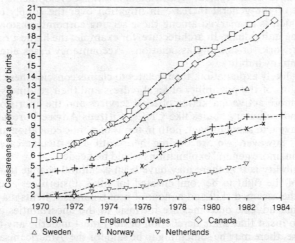

Caesareans as a percentage of births

□ USA   + England and Wales   ◇ Canada

△ Sweden   X Norway   ▽ Netherlands

Derived from Macfarlane and Mugford (1986).

It is really quite impossible to determine whether rates of medical error have changed in the last ten years. Litigation rates are affected by so many factors that they cannot be treated as a reliable proxy for actual medical behaviour. However, the timing of the increase and the lag between events and claims tend to discount the suggestion that the recent squeeze on the real resources available to the NHS has put excessive pressure on staff and caused higher rates of error. The rates began to rise in relation to incidents occurring in the mid 1970s which predate the most acute stringency in health service resources, although it is not impossible that this is a factor in the recent acceleration of the trend.

A more important observation, though, is that this phenomenon is not unique to the medical profession. Almost without exception, other professions' liability insurers report a similar trend over a similar time scale. In the case of architects, for example, there was one claim for every 7 policies in 1979 and 7 for every 10 in 1987. Claims against veterinary surgeons doubled between 1981 and 1987. The real value of paid and reserved claims against accountants increased by 82 per cent between 1979 and 1984. It seems highly improbable that all professionals have simultaneously become more prone to error.

There have certainly been important changes in the market for legal services since 1979. A number of medical commentators, as well as insurers for retail pharmacists and veterinary surgeons, have argued that legal aid has become more freely available and that this has encouraged a proliferation of trivial claims. The statistical basis for this latter statement is uncertain. In the case of medicine, it is certainly not substantiated by any of the figures currently available to us.

What is clear is that the capital and income limits for civil legal aid have consistently lagged behind inflation in the last ten years and the proportion of the population eligible for assistance has decreased. It is possible that the changing nature of the market for legal services, especially the growth of specialisation among solicitors, has improved the presentation of applications so that more are likely to be granted. It is also likely that the liberalisation of access to clinical records in recent years has increased the willingness of Legal Aid Committees to support the initial stages of an action because they know that information will be available at a reasonable cost. They can then take a considered decision on whether the action is worth supporting further.

Both of these developments would tend to facilitate more claims from a smaller pool of eligible claimants. This might be experienced by defendants as a growth in 'trivial' claims because many of them will inevitably prove insubstantial once the documents have been studied. Again, though, these developments must be put in the context of the general increase in litigation over the supply of professional services, which is as marked among those serving corporate customers as among those serving individuals. In architecture, for example, the highest risk of litigation arises from work for housing associations. Accountancy cases almost invariably involve company liability.

The most likely explanation, then, relates to claims consciousness, the awareness among victims of the possibility of legal redress and their readiness to pursue this route. The more active marketing of legal services and the efforts of a number of statutory and voluntary bodies like CHCs, Citizens Advice Bureaux and AVMA may well have had some impact, both in terms of public education and of practical support. If, however, we are dealing here with a particular case of a general phenomenon, more general explanations would be needed.

One possibility is that there may have been a cultural change towards a greater insistence of the right to be compensated for life's misfortunes and an increased distrust of the assumed skill and honour of professionals. Clients may be less ready to accept that adverse outcomes are intrinsic to the uncertainties of professional work and to insist that some dereliction of duty must underlie any failure. In this limited sense, there may be something to be said for the 'Americanisation' thesis.

Taking up the theme of defensive medicine, Nicolas Terry offers the following striking and illuminating comment from an America perspective in 'The Malpractice Crisis in the United States: A Dispatch from the Trenches' (1986) 2 Professional Negligence 145–150 (footnotes omitted).

The crisis drama—an exposition of the characters

The health care industry. The principal characters in our cast here are, unsurprisingly, the doctors and the hospitals. The former point to massive increases in their malpractice insurance rates and their inability to see as many patients as they would like because of legal rules, enthusiastically embraced by flocks of vulture-like lawyers, making them order batteries of unnecessary tests; forcing them to practise what they refer to as 'defensive medicine'.

The hospitals, on the other hand, see themselves viewed as the ultimate 'deep pocket', liable not only for their employees' negligence but as the victims of the rule of joint and several liability. They argue that, almost invariably, they will be joined as co-defendants in a suit brought against, for example, a non-employee doctor and subsequently will be faced with a disproportionate share of the award when the doctor proves to be underinsured. Bearing the brunt of the malpractice crisis, the hospitals feel they have no choice but to pass the costs along to the public in the form of rapidly escalating health care cost.

In short, not only are the health care providers faced with massive increases in insurance premiums but also difficulty in finding coverage. Primary coverage frequently is written by the providers' 'captive' insurers (for example, physician-owned non-profit companies). Health care providers are still dependent, however, on the traditional insurance industry for much of the excess and reinsurance coverage they require.

Much of the available statistical information supports the arguments and accusations emanating from the health industry. The number of claims per doctor has increased. Malpractice premiums are multiplying. There are increasing reports of multimillion awards; so called 'jumbo' awards. Newspaper reports continually highlight seemingly bizarre verdicts.

Overall the health industry has been able to paint a very credible 'crisis' picture. Avaricious lawyers are filing more and more law suits. Some of these are frivolous, unmeritorious claims which the doctors and their insurers have to settle because of high defence costs and the income the defendant-doctor would lose if he became embroiled in the lengthy pre-trial and trial processes. Other claims filed may have more merit but plaintiffs' attorneys, apparently unchecked by the Judges, are persuading juries to return massive, unrealistic awards.

As a result, medical care becomes more expensive because of the resulting costs of high insurance, defensive medicine and of physicians abandoning high-risk areas of practice. These higher costs are being passed onto the consumer; a consumer who finds an already expensive health care delivery system becoming less and less accessible. It is this scenario, expertly conveyed to legislatures by health industry lobbying efforts, that has led to the increasing diminution of the malpractice victim's legal rights through statutory 'reforms' of malpractice law.

The health industry scenario, however, is not without its critics. First, all the talk of 'crisis' tends to ignore one possible reason for the rise in malpractice claims—that there may be an increase in the amount of substandard medical care being foisted upon the American public. This argument may be considered from two perspectives; first, from the patient's point of view; second from the doctor's. The former we can place under a general heading of consumer expectations. The last two decades have shown a declining public respect for the medical (and, for that matter) legal profession. Arrogance, flagrant pandering to self-interest and (at least in the United States) high salaries have tended to change the public's perception of the role of the professional. In brief one who attempts to perpetuate the idea that he can cure the ills of the world should not be surprised by a consumer complaint when a cure not only is not forthcoming but the consumer ends up worse than before. If the consumer perceives the medical (or legal) professional as being no better than a corporate raider or an executive hanging from a golden parachute, is he not more likely to complain about disappointing service?

What of the doctor's perspective? Ask one about his negligent colleagues and you will get a two part retort. First, most doctors are not negligent in the eyes of their peers; rather they are labelled 'negligent' by a legal system that permits judgments to be rendered in unmeritorious suits brought by greedy, ungrateful patients. Second, there may be a few 'bad apples' in the medical profession; they are usually physicians, however, whose incompetence results from drug or alcohol abuse. The doctor will say, 'Trust us and our self-regulatory peer review system and we will root them out'.

Let us leave the impaired physicians, however, and look to the incompetent one. Let us examine those occasions of incompetence that the AMA tells us the law is being too hard on—those doctors that make the 'honest mistakes' (or, as Lord Denning MR, put it in *Whitehouse v Jordan* [1980] 1 All ER 650 at 658, those 'errors of judgment')—how do those honest mistakes occur?

Consider, just for the sake of argument, that a doctor, like any good rational maximiser, will attempt to capitalise on his education and opportunities by stressing volume in his practice. Maybe he will decide to see, say, 25 patients in a day rather than 20. Is it possible that seeing those five extra patients a day opens up the possibility of an 'honest mistake'. How does the doctor react to his decision to see those extra patients a day? He (possibly) knows that by doing so he will be externalising the 'honest mistake' risks to his patients. He (probably) knows that his externalised risk could boomerang back onto him by way of a malpractice judgment. So parallel to externalising his 'mistake' risk to his patients, he needs to externalise his own financial (or liability) risk.

His solution is to externalise that malpractice liability risk to an insurance company. If the insurance company cannot externalise its own risks, it will turn back on its insured with higher premiums. These the doctor cannot or will not externalise to his patients in the form of higher fees. One alternative would be to reduce the number of patients he sees per day, thereby reducing the number of 'honest mistakes' for which he will be responsible. This, however, he is not prepared to do. Therefore he seeks to substitute his externalisation of financial risk of 'malpractice' with a modified externalisation of the malpractice liability risk itself; by persuading legislatures to roll back patient rights to recover for his negligence.

The second part of our alternate 'world view' and the second flaw in the health care providers' position concern their continual reference to jumbo jury awards. A figure often cited in newspaper reports is that the average US malpractice award is now $962,258. It has been pointed out that this statement is misleading for several reasons. First, when this number has been compared to previous years' figures, it has not been adjusted to reflect increases in the consumer price index. Second this data used to arrive at this figure has concerned jury *awards*. It has not taken into account either (usually lower) settlements or the fact that some of these awards may have been later reduced by the trial Judge or successfully appealed. Third the data used has not included cases where the jury had found for the defendant, ie, awarded $0.00 to the plaintiff; yet less than one half of jury cases result in a plaintiff verdict. Finally, it should be noted that, of the $1 million awards made, about 70 per cent are in cases involving permanent paralysis, permanent brain damage, death or multiple amputations.

The third major criticism that may be levelled at the health care provider crisis scenario concerns the industry's complaints with regard to spiralling malpractice insurance premiums. It seems clear that within the past decade, the average malpractice premium has doubled. Yet what is the real level of increase when these figures have been adjusted for inflation? An even more telling statistic concerns the relationship of malpractice premiums to the income of doctors. One report has asserted that, in the same 1976–84 period in which average premiums almost doubled ($4,700 in 1976 to $8,400 in 1984) as a percentage of doctors' gross incomes, the premiums actually *declined*, from 4.4 per cent to 4.2 per cent (*Time* 24 February 1986 at p 60).

The fourth set of doubts that has risen with regard to the health care providers' position concerns the relationship between rising insurance premiums and increases in health care costs generally. This issue should not be underestimated, because it has created for the health industry lobbyists one of their most potent arguments. For the sake of discussion let us accept that jury awards are increasing at a massive rate; further let us accept that those increases are reflected in increased malpractice insurance premiums. What effect do those increases have on the cost of health care?

One analysis of that relationship has concluded that, 'not only do malpractice insurance costs form a trifling percentage of medical costs, but historically medical costs have risen irrespective of malpractice legislation and a decline in insurance premiums'. That same report has suggested that, since health care in the United States is such big business—in fact the nation's third largest industry—with large profits there for the taking, that this has attracted the large corporations into the health care industry leading to over-complex care, over-spending and overcharging.

Certainly, those reports as to the size of the industry are supportable. For example, last year the nation's largest hospital management chain (The Hospital Corporation of America) and the largest distributor of hospital supplies (The American Hospital Supply Corporation) merged to form a combine valued at $6.6 billion, one of the largest non-oil industry mergers in history. Indeed, profit-making chains now own 10 per cent of all US hospitals.

At the same time as the profit motive has become established in the United States medical system, so such profits are being jeopardised by outside forces. Both the federal government with its 'Medicare' plan (about 30 million disabled or elderly Americans qualify for Medicare) and private health insurers such as Blue Cross and Blue Shield are shifting to what is known as the 'prospective payment' system. Under this system, health care providers will no longer be reimbursed for the actual cost of a patient's care. Rather, set fees will be paid on a per-patient basis or on a per-patient, per-general type of medical problem basis. The health care industry will be faced with an interesting option: 'if a hospital spends less on a patient than the fixed amount, it makes money. If it spends more, it must absorb the loss . . . The incentive is to get the patient in and out of the hospital as quickly as possible' (*US News & World Report*, 14 April 1986 at p 60).

The Bar. A visitor to the United States quickly will become familiar with an incessant barrage of advertising in both print and broadcast media. That first reaction to sheer volume of advertising will be followed, almost immediately, by dismay at its prevailing blandness. For the medical or legal professional, a third reaction will not be long delayed. How can there be all these hideously distasteful commercials for doctors and lawyers? The simple answer is that the Supreme Court has dismantled most of the legal controls on truthful, non-misleading professional advertising. According to the Supreme Court, 'Truthful advertising related to lawful activities is entitled to the protections of the First Amendment'. *Re RMJ* 455 US 191, 203 (1982). As such, State Bar Associations and State Supreme Courts are now powerless to regulate lawyer advertising. Certainly many members of the plaintiffs' malpractice bar have not been slow to grasp this opportunity. Such rank commercialism may also be serving to lower the esteem that the medical profession and the public once held for the bar.

Because the malpractice liability system in the United States is financed by the contingency fees system, the lawyer's personal, financial interest in the size of the award leaves him particularly open to criticism. Before the contingency fee system is dismissed as an award-inflating disaster designed to encourage 'ambulance-chasing' consider the alternatives. In general, the United States has no (civil) legal aid system. Does the English legal aid system offer an improvement? Or may it too be criticised? First, for effectively restricting representation to the very poor. Second, for filtering out all but the 'safest' claims through local legal aid screening committees?

When the president of the plaintiffs' bar in the United States says, 'We represent the people that are the injured victims of society', is that merely an expression of avaricious self-interest or an honest evaluation of the lawyer's unique role in defending the rights of an otherwise unrepresented constituency?

The insurance industry. Of course, at the heart of the malpractice system-insurance industry interface is risk-externalisation. You don't need a PhD in economics to understand externalisation of risks—you merely have to understand gambling on an American football game.

The bettor (or mug) goes to the bookie. The bookie takes his bet and gives odds designed so that whoever wins he will pay out the same amount of cash. In other words, the bookie—in an ideal situation—does not gamble; he goes for an even play. How, therefore, do bookies get rich? Through the 'juice'—this is their percentage that they levy on the winning bet. Now if a bookie finds that one side of his equation, despite his odds-making, is getting too heavy he needs to externalise his loss—he will 'lay it off' to another bookie.

Insurance companies operate in much the same way. They take a bet (a premium) on a game (a liability risk) and if the bettor's number comes up (if he is found liable) they pay off the winnings (the claim). Like bookies, (wise) insurers do not try to make their profit on any win-loss (premium-claim) differential. Indeed, just like bookies, they will lay-off (reinsure) any worrisome differential. Rather they make their profit on the 'juice'. For the insurance industry the 'juice' is not any percentage of winning bets, but rather the use of the premium money from the time it is paid to the time a claim (if any) is paid. In other words, the insurer's 'juice' is his investment income from collected premiums.

What has led to the insurers increasing their premiums by such large amounts? March 1986 saw the insurance industry launch a $6.5 million advertising campaign to persuade the public that those premium increases were the result of a 'lawsuit' crisis—the fault of the tort system. One of the catchphrases incorporated into such advertisements is 'The Lawsuit Crisis. We All Pay The Price'. Perhaps one explanation for this new insurance industry campaign is that some commentators have begun to speculate that the malpractice 'crisis' is not the fault of plaintiffs, or even lawyers or doctors:—but a 'non-crisis' manufactured by the insurance industry to protect its excessive profits.

Three reasons may be put forward to explain this insurance 'non-crisis'. First, insurance companies say that they have increased their premiums because of their losses. But insurers have a somewhat novel concept of 'loss'. When they cite 'losses', insurers cite their 'underwriting losses'. The property-casualty insurance industry has quoted a $21.4 billion underwriting loss for 1984 and estimated a $25.2 billion loss for 1985. But these are not actual losses. Rather they show the gap between premium dollars received in a given year when compared to the claim dollars predicted to be paid out in future years.

The second problem with 'underwriting losses' is that they do not take into account the insurer's future investment profits on the collected premiums prior to the payment of predicted claims. Take for example that estimated underwriting loss for 1985 of $25.2 billion when contrasted with the income of the property-casualty industry for 1985 (including investment income) of $32.8 billion, and an increase of $13 billion in net worth for the same period.

Such an analysis of the current crisis poses an important question leading to a third contradiction to the insurers' cry of 'torts crisis'. If this explanation of the insurance industry's practices is accurate, why do these insurance crises occur only occasionally. As Davies has pointed out (PN 1 (1985) p 169), the answer lies in low interest rates. During the late 1970s interest rates were high. Therefore, the insurance industry was able to record very high investment returns on its premiums prior to paying out any claims. High profits generated increased interest in writing policies by insurers to acquire investment income, and hence increased competition between insurers. As has been noted, 'These underwriting losses appear to be largely a result of coverage written in the late 1970s and early 1980s which may have been underpriced due to the industry's desire to obtain premium income to invest at the then prevailing high interest rates'. As the market went 'soft', so panic-stricken insurers either pulled out of markets or looked for areas where they could recoup their previous discounts quickly. The result—insurers increased medical malpractice premiums and orchestrated a 'crisis' scenario designed to focus the public's, the health industry's and the legislatures' anger upon the lawyers.

The judiciary. At the root of health care and insurance industry complaints about substantive malpractice doctrine has been the law's doctrinal growth through the last two decades and its potential for further, pro-plaintiff development. Concerns have been voiced that malpractice will follow in the footsteps of products liability. Whereas English products law became comatose in 1932 (although resuscitation is imminent courtesy of DIR 85/374/EEC, [1985] OJ L210/29), American law had not forgotten the lessons of doctrinal growth learned in the nineteenth century. Both systems had started with rules of non-liability for negligent manufacturers, *Winterbottom v Wright* (1842) 152 ER 402; *Loop v Litchfield* 42 NY 2d 251 (1842); and had progressed by way of an exponential growth of exceptional cases to the imposition of a negligence based risk-shifting system, *Donoghue v Stevenson* [1932] AC 562; *Macpherson v Buick* 111 NE 1050 (NY 1916). American law alone, was to repeat that cycle in the twentieth century; its culmination being the adoption of a strict products liability system. *Greenman v Yuba Power Products Inc* 377 P 2d 897 (Cal 1963), Restatement (Second) of Torts § 402A (1965).

Any products liability/malpractice parallel at first sight seems somewhat strained. After all, the basic principles of health care provider liability under the Anglo-American malpractice law were established as early as the latter part of the eighteenth century. *Slater v Baker and Stapleton* (1767) 95 ER 860, concerned allegations of negligence in the treatment of a broken leg. Specifically that the defendants, an apothecary and the then chief surgeon at St Bartholomew's Hospital, had rebroken the leg and, utilising some experimental *deus ex machina*, had attempted to straighten it through extension rather than by compression. In affirming the jury's verdict for the plaintiff, the Court stated:

> For anything that appears to the Court, this was the first experiment made with this new instrument; and if it was, it was a rash action, and he who acts rashly acts ignorantly: and although the defendants in general may be as skilful in their respective professions as any two gentlemen in England, yet the Court cannot help saying, that in this particular case they have acted ignorantly and unskilfully, contrary to the known rule and usage of surgeons (at 863).

From 1767, therefore, it has been clear, first, that the general principles of our judicial negligence-based regulatory system will apply to the medical malpractice claim. Second, neither the *bona fide* nor impeccable reputation of the defendant will immunise him from liability. Third, medical malpractice falls into a subset of negligence cases which make use of a custom standard requiring expert testimony to be considered by the trier of fact.

Twenty-seven years later, in the first reported American malpractice case, *Cross v Guthery* 2 Root 90 (Conn 1794), the Supreme Court of Connecticut apparently reached a similar conclusion. Therein a plaintiff prevailed with his allegation that his wife had died following a mastectomy 'performed . . . in the most unskillful, ignorant and cruel manner, contrary to all the well-known rules and principles of practice in such cases . . .' (at 91).

That professional standard of care-expert testimony nexus may have been established what seems to the modern torts lawyer eons ago. Nevertheless, in the United States, striking doctrinal changes have occurred since then. First, many jurisdictions have dismembered the old locality rule by which the custom prevailing in the profession had been established by reference to the standard of care existing in the defendant's locality or in a similar locality. See *Small v Howard* 128 Mass 131 (1880). The purpose of this rule was to encourage the 'small town practitioner' by immunising him from the (presumed) higher standards expected of the 'large city practitioner'. The locality rule effectively limited the number of treatment risks that would be reallocated by denying the plaintiff access to a large number of potential, non-local, expert witnesses. The first step taken to ameliorate the harshness of the locality rule was achieved by recharacterising the function of 'locality' as limited to an inquiry into 'available medical resources' to just one of the 'circumstances' to be taken into account by the trier of fact. See, eg, *Brune v Belinkoff* 235 NE 2d 793 at 798 (Mass 1968) 1. Final dismemberment has occurred in those jurisdictions that have replaced such a 'local' test with an explicit 'national' standard of care. See, eg, *Hall v Hilbun* 466 So 2d 856 (Miss 1985). Obviously, in increasing the pool of experts available for the plaintiff, such a national standard leads to a higher proportion of medical treatment risks being reallocated.

If the growth of medical malpractice doctrine relating to the standard of care was to parallel, albeit in its own conservative way, that of products liability so also would malpractice law mirror products liability's reallocation of the traditional burden of proof. Through increasingly imaginative use of the *res ipsa loquitur* doctrine, plaintiffs have been able to get more marginal claims to the jury. See, eg, *Quintal v Laurel Grove Hosp* 397 P 2d 161 (Cal 1964). Specifically, cases involving patient-incurred risks which resulted in claims which were marginal due to evidentiary problems relating to either standard of care or causation issues. Furthermore, some Courts began to flirt with non-custom based standards of care. See, eg, *Darling v Charleston Community Mem Hosp* 211 NE 2d 253 (Ill 1965).

In addition to modifications to the standard of care came an increase in the breadth of the duty of care owed by health care providers. Many of these broader duties have concerned the supply of information to patients. Examples that come to mind are the informed consent and the so-called 'wrongful life' disclosure duties. Of course, one could analyse these doctrinal changes as being a function of increased judicial interest in the concept of patient autonomy in medical decision-making. An alternative view, however, could be that the Courts were attempting to provide compensation for medical risks which had occurred despite the absence of any active provider malpractice. Still further expansions of the duty of care have occurred; involving, for example a duty to warn non-patients of the vicious propensities of patients. See, eg, *Tarasoff v Regents of the University of California* 551 P 2d 334 (Cal 1976) or a failure to report to the authorities a case of suspected child abuse, *Landeros v Flood* 551 P 2d 389 (Cal 1976). In passing, one might note that these last two expansive duties appear to have the worrisome effect of redistributing *non-medical* risks (for example, non-health care provider violence) through the *medical* malpractice insurance system.

It was hardly surprising, with these developments creating apparent exceptions to the traditional malpractice rule of custom-based negligence liability—exceptions almost as numerous as had appeared in the products liability context—that some Judges began to show enthusiasm for the introduction of a strict liability regime for malpractice. See, eg, *Johnson v Sears, Roebuck & Co* 355 F Supp 1065 at 1067 (ED. Wis 1973); *Clark v Gibbons* 426 P 2d 525 at 535 (Cal 1967) (Tobriner J, concurring); *Helling v Carey* 519 P 2d 981 at 984 (Wash 1974) (Utter J, concurring).

At this point, however, the products-malpractice parallel breaks down. In malpractice law there was to be no breakthrough case replacing a rule of negligence (non-strict) liability and its attendant exceptions and extensions with a strict liability regime. At least two reasons may be advanced to explain this absence of judicial climax. First, it is conceptually and practically difficult to fashion a strict liability doctrine for medical care risks. In products liability the Judges solved this problem, first, by constructively presuming foresight of the risk of harm, and second, by (conceptually) shifting their judgmental focus from the conduct of the manufacturer to the condition of the product. The condition of the product was (practically) judged by setting up tests for 'defectiveness' which depend either upon an examination of objective 'consumer expectations' as to the safety of the product (see, eg, *Vincer v Esther Williams All Aluminium Swimming Pool Co* 230 NW 2d 794 (Wis 1975)) or upon the subjection of the product to a risk-benefit analysis in the light of (usually expert) testimony as to feasible economic alternatives (see, eg, *Barker v Lull Engineering Co* 573 P 2d 443 at 457–58 (Cal 1978)).

Second, as the American Judges were poised to make the breakthrough in the mid-1970s they were faced with the first cries of 'crisis! crisis!' This was to be the time for judicial conservation so as not to incure the wrath of state legislators.
...

Conclusion

It would be convenient to conclude that the malpractice crisis in the United States is a minor skirmish which will leave no lasting impression on our torts system. Yet, from that day in 1770 when Shepherd threw his squib into the market square at Milborne Port and watched it bounce around until it exploded near Scott, *Scott v Shepherd* (1773) 96 ER 525, perhaps we have been moving inextricably towards a general torts crisis.

Following closely behind the malpractice crisis are reports of a products liability crisis, a local government liability crisis, a school liability crisis and a toxic waste crisis. Again the stated reason is spiralling insurance premiums. Legislators who give in to the medical malpractice doomsayers no doubt will follow by dismantling most of the other legal protections that we have developed for injured plaintiffs.

With specific regard to medical malpractice reform, the current American buzzword is 'compromise'. A belief that if the lawyers and doctors can get together they can work out a solution. Occasionally this can work. Generally, however, such compromises ignore victims' rights and eschew the tighter regulation of insurance companies. Also, their proponents underestimate the staunch individualism and jealously guarded independence of the legal and medical professions. At this time the battle if anything, is intensifying.

Against this background, Ham, Dingwall *et al, op cit*, consider the case for reform (pp 26–34).

Nevertheless, our analysis has demonstrated that tort law is deficient in a number of respects. In relation to the two main objectives of the law—compensating people injured as a result of negligence, and deterring doctors from acting negligently—the following shortcomings have been identified:

● the procedures involved in pursuing a claim for damages are lengthy and expensive for patients, doctors and health authorities
● only a small proportion of people suffering medically-related injuries obtain compensation
● the emphasis on establishing fault and cause and effect turns the tort system into a lottery: similar cases of injury giving rise to similar needs are compensated totally differently according to the circumstances surrounding their cause and the completeness of the evidence.

● those making a claim may find it difficult to obtain the services of a solicitor with relevant expertise and of doctors willing to act as expert witnesses
● the legal process is adversarial and causes those involved to close ranks. Consequently, patients and their relatives are often not given adequate explanations or apologies when things do go wrong and doctors may be distressed by the apparent hostility and ingratitude of their patients
● the deterrent effect of the law is weakened by the availability of insurance coverage.

We have also emphasised the weaknesses of other arrangements for maintaining high standards of medical practice. These include the variable interest shown by doctors in medical audit and peer review, and the limitations of complaints and disciplinary procedures as mechanisms for ensuring professional accountability. Our analysis has demonstrated that the tort system is one element in a package of measures by which the medical profession is held accountable to the public. Any proposals for reform must consider the law's role in ensuring accountability and promoting high standards while recognising its shortcomings as a means of providing compensation.

Against this background, we now consider the range of policy instruments which are, in theory, available to those contemplating reform. Some of these instruments are concerned primarily to deter negligence, while others aim to provide compensation. The instruments may be used singly or in combination. We begin by outlining options for deterring doctors from acting negligently, and then consider methods of providing compensation. In the first part of the chapter, the menu of options is described briefly, and this is followed by more detailed analysis of those options which in our view merit most serious discussion.

Deterrence

There are three main options for deterring doctors from acting negligently. These are legal liability, regulation backed by statute and self-regulation.

Legal liability

Legal liability for medical accidents can take a number of forms. Doctors can be held strictly liable for all the adverse consequences resulting from medical treatment, or only for the adverse consequences resulting from their negligence. Those held liable can be either individual practitioners or groups of individuals acting collectively. Figure 7 sets out the possibilities.

Figure 7 Deterrence through liability rules

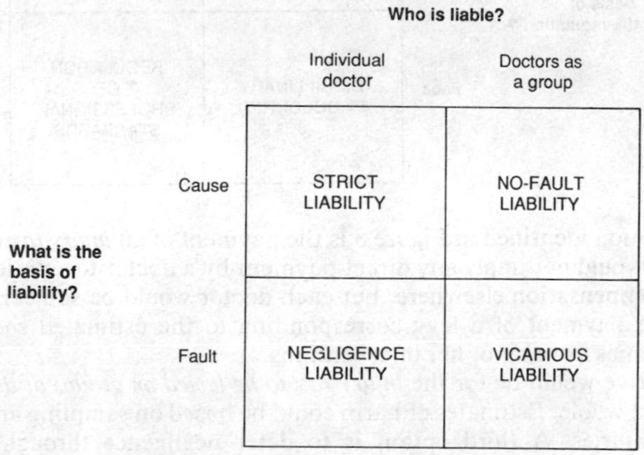

Who is liable?

	Individual doctor	Doctors as a group
Cause	STRICT LIABILITY	NO-FAULT LIABILITY
Fault	NEGLIGENCE LIABILITY	VICARIOUS LIABILITY

What is the basis of liability?

Strict liability exists when individual doctors are held responsible to patients for all the adverse outcomes of medical treatment. *No-fault liability* imposes liability on doctors as a group. The group might be the whole profession or only those doctors involved in the treatment which gave rise to the adverse outcome. *Negligence liability* is the current rule. Under this rule, only those doctors whose standard of care is deemed inadequate by the courts are held liable for the adverse consequences of their actions. The NHS already assumes *vicarious liability* for most of its employees. Under this liability rule the fault of an individual employee renders the employer liable for the adverse consequences resulting from the employee's actions.

All these possibilities can in theory create appropriate incentives for doctors to avoid injuring patients, although in practice the incentives may not operate effectively. Moreover, it is, in principle, possible for patients to contract with individual doctors, hospitals or health authorities in order to agree on a different set of incentives to take care, although again the practical problems of this option may be considerable.

One other possibility should be mentioned, namely that there should be *no liability*. This would shift the entire responsibility to the patient to take his or her own measures to ensure the safety of the care received.

Regulation backed by statute

A second approach to deterrence is to give a regulatory body the power to monitor the adverse consequences of medical intervention. Such a body would receive reports of medical accidents, which would be required by law, and would determine appropriate action to be taken. This would include the power to levy a fine or injury tax. A body of this kind might develop out of the General Medical Council and would combine its regulatory role with oversight of registration and medical education. If this option were to be pursued, there would be a need to ensure that the regulatory body were genuinely independent and accountable to Parliament. This approach relies on a structure of incentives similar to those generated by the various liability rule options discussed above. Figure 8 illustrates the possibilities.

Figure 8 Deterrence through regulation

		Who is regulated?	
		Individual doctor	Doctors as a group
What is the basis of the regulation?	Cause	INJURY TAX ON INDIVIDUAL	INJURY TAX ON GROUP
	Fault	DISCIPLINARY PROCEDURES	REGULATION OF PROFESSIONAL STANDARDS

The first option identified in Figure 8 is the payment of an *injury tax by individual doctors*. This would not imply any direct payment by a doctor to a patient. Patients could seek compensation elsewhere, but each doctor would be subject to a regular audit and the payment of a levy corresponding to the estimated social costs of adverse outcomes from his or her interventions.

An alternative would be for the *injury tax to be levied on groups of doctors* or the profession as a whole. Estimates of harm could be based on sampling and aggregate analysis of injuries. A third option is to deter negligence through *disciplinary procedures*, as happens at present. This requires an agreed procedure for investigating complaints and imposing penalties on individual doctors. Penalties might be either professional or financial but need not be linked to the losses of individual patients.

Finally, the option of *group regulation* might be considered. Rather than having an independent regulatory agency involved with the review of individual doctors, the profession as a whole might be set specific standards of safety and effectiveness and left to develop its own systems of control. The effective sanction here is the risk of losing the privileges of the occupation's protected position in the delivery of health care. The incentive is the concern of colleagues to protect the profession's reputation and maintain public confidence.

Self regulation

A third approach to deterrence avoids using either the civil or criminal law to impose financial incentives on doctors and instead relies on market-based incentives. Even where no one is held liable, there may be powerful incentives in a market situation for providers to maintain standards, simply as a way of ensuring commercial viability. In the NHS the incentives operate differently, relying more on the concern of the professions and health authorities to protect and improve their reputations. This is again an important element of the present system, although it does not always operate effectively.

Compensation

There are three main options for compensating those injured in medical accidents. These are liability insurance, first-party insurance and social security.

Liability insurance

Any system of legal liability could provide compensation for patients selected by the liability rules as long as those held responsible have the means to pay the damages awarded. Effectively this implies that arrangements must exist for the pooling of liabilities through insurance. Of course, under a system of group liability, it is possible that some groups will be large enough to bear their own liability losses without insuring. For smaller groups and individuals, third-party liability insurance is a necessary adjunct to civil liability if the latter is to be an effective means of providing compensation.

First-party insurance

If doctors are not held legally responsible for the adverse consequences resulting from medical treatment, either because it is held that no one should be liable, or because only those accidents caused by negligence are compensated, then the burden of loss arising outside the liability system falls directly on the injured patients. Those at risk may therefore choose to insure against the prospective losses, either directly, by means of an income replacement or medical expenses policy with an insurance company, or indirectly, by means of a negotiated sick pay scheme through which employers meet such losses up to a maximum as part of a wages and conditions package. The payments under such schemes are made without necessary reference to the fault or causation of any other party.

Social security

Each of the above insurance options for spreading losses could be made compulsory by a government which was concerned about the possibility of uncompensated losses. Alternatively, government could itself provide social insurance financed out of employee contributions, general taxation, and/or specific levies on goods and services. Entitlement to benefits under such a scheme could be based on the fact of a disability, and not on its cause. In addition, injured patients may be treated and cared for through the further provision of public health care and social services. Effectively, this would be a system of compensation in kind.

Whatever form of compensation is provided, there always remains, in principle, the opportunity for individuals or groups of individuals to contract with each other in order to arrive at an alternative arrangement. For example, patients could agree to waive their rights to compensation through the courts in return for lower cost treatment. Equally, individuals covered by a social insurance fund may be permitted to contract-out in order to obtain preferable cover under a private insurance policy. In practice, however, people may be barred from restricting their coverage beyond a certain point or from completely opting out of compulsory contributions to a common insurance pool because of possible adverse selection problems.

The agenda for reform

Given the range of options available, it is possible to pursue the objectives of compensation and deterrence separately. As an illustration, doctors could be deterred from acting negligently through regulation by an independent agency with the power to levy an injury tax, while compensation could be provided by first-party or social insurance. However, separating the objectives in this way may be inefficient, in that it undervalues the role of the patient in providing information about negligence. This option may also deprive the patient of the satisfaction of securing an improvement in the circumstances which led to his or her injury and it reduces the opportunities available to victims to obtain psychological redress. Although the effectiveness of the tort system in serving these purposes should not be exaggerated, this element of the system may well be significant in some cases in helping to resolve events through the public attribution or exoneration of responsibility for harm.

The medical litigation system in the UK combines negligence liability and disciplinary procedures initiated by complaints with third-party liability insurance for doctors and self-insurance for health authorities. This system gives the individual patient a key role in the process of deterring negligence and obtaining compensation. However, as we have emphasised, the system has a number of shortcomings.

Many of the other options we have identified also have shortcomings. To give some examples, an injury tax levied on individual doctors would be cumbersome and costly to administer; disciplinary procedures may be ineffective as a form of deterrence if they are invoked only in the most serious cases; and self-regulation depends for its effectiveness on a strong commitment by health authorities and doctors to promote high standards through medical audit and quality assurance programmes. This commitment may not always be present.

Market-oriented solutions such as no liability and voluntary first-party insurance place an unreasonable burden on the patient in terms of assessing the quality of the services available. In extreme cases, the patient may be dead before the inadequacy of the care becomes apparent. This may deter others, but is little consolation to the victim. The marked imbalance in information between patients and doctors is thus a major weakness of market-oriented options.

What then are the policy options which deserve serious consideration in reviewing how the shortcomings of existing arrangements might be overcome? In our view three options merit further analysis. These are:

● the modification of the tort law system and the strengthening of professional accountability
● the introduction of a no-fault compensation scheme, and
● the abandonment of the tort system in favour of providing compensation through social security.

We have selected these options for analysis as they represent different points on the agenda of change facing policy makers. Modifying the existing system and strengthening professional accountability involve incremental reforms, many of which could be introduced at little or no cost. There are obvious attractions in this option to a government committed to tight control of public expenditure. Furthermore, in view of the government's stated position that the case for major reform remains not proven, it may be through a series of minor changes that the best prospects for improvement lie.

No-fault compensation, as we have noted, is an option favoured by a number of organisations active in the field of medical negligence, including the BMA and ACHCEW. There is also relevant overseas experience on which to draw and from which to learn . . . If there should be a further increase in the number of legal claims against doctors and in the size of court awards, the feasibility of this option may come under closer scrutiny. There is therefore merit in assessing the costs of introducing such a scheme in the UK and the measures that would need to be taken to strengthen professional accountability in the context of no-fault compensation.

Abolishing the tort system in favour of providing compensation through social security—our third option—is a fundamental change which is best viewed as a long-term possibility. Nevertheless, it is an option that deserves analysis, if only to highlight the important part played by social security in supporting those suffering injuries. The issue of income support for disabled people is a major area of analysis in its own right, and in this chapter we are able only to illustrate its potential role in the case of medical negligence.

Changing the existing system

Changes to the existing system fall into three categories. These are increasing access to the courts, transferring negligence liability from individual doctors to health authorities while at the same time strengthening the accountability of doctors, and introducing differential insurance premiums for doctors. We now consider each in turn.

Increasing access to the courts

One set of reforms would seek to increase access to the legal system so that patients could more easily obtain compensation and more cases would result. Specific proposals have recently been put forward by the Citizens Action Compensation Campaign and by the report of the Review Body on Civil Justice to the Lord Chancellor. Both express sympathy for the development of contingency fees in Britain and the Civil Justice Review also discusses at length methods by which legal proceedings could be accelerated.

Our view is that contingency fees and the acceleration of legal proceedings are of limited relevance to medical negligence cases. While it is understandable that both litigants and legal personnel are frustrated by delay in establishing liability and determining compensation, its causes are poorly understood. The pace of litigation towards trial or settlement is determined largely by the plaintiff's solicitor. It may be slowed down in order to establish exactly how serious someone's injuries are so as to calculate what would be an appropriate level of compensation. It may be necessary to wait until a victim can be examined by one of the relatively small number of doctors who are skilled in the preparation of expert evidence for civil cases. If the findings are uncertain or the clinical evaluation is contentious, further time may elapse before other specialists can accommodate the patient. Once a case is prepared, a solicitor may wish to have it presented by a specialist barrister who is fully aware of the complexities of the area. In short, there may be good reasons for delay.

Contingency fees have attracted attention as a possible private alternative to legal aid. In fact, their main virtue is that they substitute the judgment of individual solicitors for the monopoly of the local legal aid committee. The American evidence shows that contingency fees are far from representing a poor person's route to justice. Lawyers will not take on cases unless the certainty of winning and the likely profits are sufficient to justify the risk. Thus, they will take relatively low-value cases arising from road traffic accidents, which are cheap to run and have a highly predictable outcome: they are reluctant to take low-value cases in other areas, including medical malpractice, because the return is insufficient to cover their costs. Moreover, medical malpractice is seen as a particularly risky area, because of the intrinsic uncertainty of causation, so that the lawyer has a strong incentive to reject all but those cases on which his own medical advisers give him strong support. The comparative irrelevance of contingency fees in the British context can be seen from the limited use of speculative actions in Scotland. These are not pure contingency, in that lawyers are only allowed to charge on the basis of the work they have done rather than taking a percentage of the eventual recovery, but they are conditional on the outcome of the case.

A more important consideration is that cases should be handled by solicitors skilled in medical negligence work. Plaintiffs are particularly vulnerable because medical litigation is classically conducted by local law firms with limited knowledge and experience in complex personal injury work. They are opposed by a small group of highly specialised firms with great experience of representing defendants. The real requirement is for a means of identifying and certifying solicitors who are competent to handle such cases on behalf of plaintiffs. AVMA and a number of community health councils have developed panels of solicitors to whom they steer cases and whose effectiveness they attempt to monitor. AVMA has devoted particular effort to the development of a monitoring system in an attempt to improve the effectiveness of their panel members. It would be open to the Law Society to build on these initiatives, as they have done with practitioners in child care and mental health law.

If this change were to be fully effective, it would have to be accompanied by a number of other modifications to the present system. One would be greater publicity for legal services in general, either by encouraging solicitors' own marketing of their services or through the development of schemes like the Law Society's Accident Legal Advice Service (ALAS) initiative which has tried to heighten public awareness of the possibility of claiming for damages. These initiatives might be accompanied by a liberalisation of the rules governing the advertising of legal services to enable members of the public to identify more easily solicitors accredited in medical negligence work and to be better informed about the benefits of approaching a specialist.

It would also be desirable to modify the present rules on fee-splitting, so that generalist, High Street firms had a greater incentive to pass complex cases on to practices with a more appropriate level of skills in return for an introduction fee or a proportion of the eventual profit on a successful case. Some attention would have to be given too to the access barriers represented by the current means testing on civil legal aid. At present, the rewards are too low to encourage specialist firms to develop medical negligence work and the eligibility levels are so restricted as to prevent a considerable section of the population from obtaining redress.

If access to legal aid were made easier, an increase in the rate at which claims are made and pursued would be likely to occur. This might accentuate some of the problems of predicting the financial burden for health authorities. One way of responding would be to pool the risks on a national or regional basis, creating in effect an internal insurance scheme as already happens in some places.

Transferring liability to health authorities and strengthening accountability
A second possible change to the existing system would be to transfer negligence liability from individual doctors to health authorities and family practitioner committees. This would put doctors on the same basis as most other NHS staff, with their employer assuming vicarious liability. Such a change would certainly imply a more active role for health authorities and family practitioner committees in promoting high standards of clinical practice and reducing mistakes. . . . Interest in medical audit in the NHS has been uneven, and there are grounds for arguing that a more systematic and rigorous approach is needed.

Health authorities could give a lead by requiring doctors at the appropriate level (firm, department, group practice) to demonstrate that they routinely review the quality of their work. The recent report of the Confidential Enquiry into Perioperative Deaths . . . recommended that clinicians should assess themselves regularly and that surgeons and anaesthetists should actively audit their results. This recommendation applies with equal force to other branches of medicine.

There is increasing evidence that doctors themselves recognise the importance of audit, both as a form of continuing education and as a means of avoiding mistakes. Thus, several of the royal colleges have taken the initiative recently to encourage doctors systematically to assess their work and to discuss their results with colleagues. Equally, at the local level, a number of enthusiastic individuals have demonstrated what can be achieved when doctors set aside time to gather information about their practice and analyse differences in approach. It should be possible to build on this experience in the future to ensure that audit develops with the support of the profession.

There may also be lessons to learn from developments in the United States in risk management, in particular in encouraging reports of adverse events. Drug reactions, for example, are already monitored by the Yellow Card scheme. Hospitals might introduce similar arrangements for the reporting of surgical or other incidents on a confidential basis, rather in the same way as airline pilots are encouraged to report near misses. One incentive for this might be to impose a collective responsibility on the medical and nursing team for the care of a patient.

Modern health care depends so much on the contribution of a number of specialists in different aspects of any particular case that it is questionable whether the concept of individual liability remains entirely appropriate. If one person makes a mistake which others ignore or cover up, then, at least morally, they would seem to be just as responsible for the adverse outcome. An example might be of a surgeon who commits an error during a common procedure. It is argued by risk managers in the United States that anaesthetists and the theatre nurses should feel an obligation to challenge the surgeon as he makes the mistake and to record their dissent if he persists. If they do not, they should be equally vulnerable at law and to professional sanctions. The medical profession, however, see this as a recipe for clinical anarchy. Individual liability, it is claimed, is the proper corollary of clinical autonomy.

As well as strengthening arrangements for medical audit in these and other ways, changes could be made to both disciplinary procedures and complaints procedures to ensure that doctors are held accountable for their clinical competence. In the case of disciplinary procedures, the GMC currently investigates cases of serious professional misconduct but other cases do not fall within its remit. Furthermore, as we have noted, the GMC's procedures are professionally dominated. Proposals are currently under discussion designed to enable the Council to consider less serious examples of misconduct, and this would mean that a wider range of cases could be investigated. But more radical change, involving the setting up of procedures similar to those that exist in Sweden . . ., may be needed if the public is to be reassured that disciplinary procedures are adequate for their purpose.

At the local level, disciplinary procedures against hospital doctors concerning matters of professional competence are set out in circular HM(61)112 and involve an investigation by a panel under a legally qualified chairman. These procedures have been criticised as complex, expensive and lengthy, and their operation is under review by the DHSS and the medical profession. This review provides a timely opportunity for change to be introduced to ensure that adequate arrangements are in place for handling all cases where concern about professional conduct and competence arises, not just those involving the most serious consequences.

Turning to complaints procedures, . . . the existing complaints machinery is complex, fragmented and slow. A case can be made for improving this machinery independently of concern about medical negligence. A starting point would be to implement the proposals of the Davies Committee on hospital complaints. It is in this area that complaints procedures are most open to criticism, particularly as far as complaints about clinical judgment are concerned. If the Committee's proposals for independent investigating panels were implemented it would become easier for patients and their relatives to pursue complaints about clinical matters and to have confidence that these complaints would be thoroughly and rapidly investigated. This in turn might reduce the number of legal claims brought by patients seeking an explanation of what went wrong rather than financial compensation.

In the longer term, the aim should be to simplify the complaints procedures to establish one point of contact whatever the nature of the complaint (clinical or non-clinical; hospital, community health services or family practitioner services) and to guarantee that those hearing complaints are genuinely independent.

Differential premiums for doctors
A third way of reforming the existing system, and an alternative to the transfer of negligence liability to health authorities, would be to change the incentive structure facing doctors by introducing differential insurance premiums. . . . Such risk-rating is common in professional liability insurance and is applied to doctors in the United States. Where professional services are privately provided, there may be some merit in this arrangement. Differential risks can be reflected in differential fees so that there is no direct impact on recruitment to specialties. Doctors can be left with comparable post-premium incomes, or at least, incomes which vary only sufficiently to adjust for the non-pecuniary penalties of a high risk of litigation. Both patients

and doctors are given appropriate indications of the hazards associated with different areas of medicine and an incentive either to safe practice or careful selection of doctor.

In the NHS, however, doctors are paid on a uniform scale. Individual effort and initiative are rewarded to an extent by merit awards or list sizes but there are no systematic differences between specialties in terms of the basic income available from NHS practice. In the absence of any variation, it is hard to imagine that recruitment to high-risk specialties would remain unaffected by differential premiums. Moreover, for practitioners working full time for the NHS, the introduction of such premiums would involve little more than an accounting exercise as the government would bear the major share of the cost through its policy of reimbursing two-thirds of the cost of defence society subscriptions.

The one exception to this argument concerns those doctors combining NHS work with private practice. The potential awards to a victim of negligent private treatment are larger than those to NHS patients because private patients would be able to obtain damages based on the assumption of future private care, whereas this might be disputable for NHS patients. It is debatable whether the NHS should in effect cross-subsidise private practice, although whether this happens in practice is difficult to estimate. In global terms, any subsidy is unlikely to be large, and is in any case roughly corrected by the recently announced arrangements which confine reimbursement of the major portion of defence society subscriptions to those doctors working exclusively for the NHS. It is also possible that the risks of private practice are less because of the different case-mix in that sector. Nevertheless, it remains possible that the public payments may be slightly larger than they would be if private medical practice formed a separate pool for insurance purposes.

Moving to no-fault

The term no-fault compensation refers, strictly, to all schemes which abandon the rule that an injured patient has to show that someone was negligent in order to obtain redress. However, there is an important distinction between those schemes which still require patients to identify an individual responsible for their condition and those which do not. The former, of which Sweden and New Zealand are examples, share with the negligence system the advantage of being able to make constructive use of the desire of injured patients to obtain redress. Adverse outcomes can be attributed to individual doctors and, at least potentially, used as a basis for promoting high standards. Those schemes which sever the link between victims and the agents of their injuries must find alternative ways of achieving this objective.

The extent to which this is a serious problem depends on the ability of individual doctors to avoid accidents. If it is believed that accidents are better understood as a result of organisational failures, rather than personal mistakes, then the attribution of responsibility to individuals is unnecessary. All that is needed is sufficient information to demonstrate that the patient's injury arose from medical treatment together with a means of referring that information to the appropriate manager or health authorities. Information on claims for compensation might be fed back to those responsible for service delivery at the local level and be used in national reviews to alert all care providers to common problems.

Whether a no-fault scheme is based on proof of individualised causation or not, there is likely to be a need for some form of risk-spreading. Health authorities are large enough to self-insure, although the unpredictable impact of awards at a time of scarce resources suggests that this may not be the most efficient means of managing their budgets. There may therefore be a case for pooling risks on a regional or national basis, as happens in Sweden. If causation is placed on an individual basis, then doctors would need to continue to obtain some form of insurance and this could be provided by a consortium of the defence societies.

The potential cost of a no-fault scheme varies greatly according to the assumptions that are made about the rate of claiming and the size of awards. At present, there are roughly ten claims relating to hospital treatment per 100,000 population in England each year. Approximately three of these claims are compensated and the average award is around £15,000. The total cost of the system, including both damages payments and legal expenses, is estimated to be £75 million, of which £65 million is attributed to the NHS, either directly or through the cost of subscriptions to the defence societies out of NHS employees' income.

The Swedish scheme generates about 60 claims per 100,000 population from all health care contacts, although, in practice, almost all of these seem to relate to hospital treatment. Fifty per cent of these claims receive compensation, averaging £3,200 at current exchange rates. If we assume that a Swedish style system were introduced in the UK, at the same rates of claiming and payment, the estimated cost for England alone would be of the order of £50 million per year (see Table 8). This would appear to represent a substantial saving.

Table 8. Estimated costs of a no-fault compensation scheme

A. CURRENT SYSTEM (ENGLAND 1988)	£ mill	B. SWEDISH STYLE NO-FAULT SYSTEM	£ mill
Estimated health authority costs:	15	Estimated cost if Swedish system replicated	50
Assumptions: claim rate = 10 per 100,000 population abandonment rate = 70% average settlement = £15,000 administrative costs = 30% defence society contribution = 50%		**Assumptions:** claim rate = 60 per 100,000 population abandonment rate = 50% average settlement = £3,200 administrative costs = 15%	
Estimated defence society costs*:	60	Estimated cost with average settlement £15,000	235
		Estimated cost with average settlement £7,500	117
Assumptions: income generated from doctors practising in England based on a) subscription rates for 1988 as in MPS/MDU annual reports b) breakdown of medical manpower in England as published by DHSS			
Total	75	*This includes a sum for legal and administrative costs other than those related to negligence cases.*	

However, given the more limited nature of the British social security system compared with Sweden, it would also represent a substantial degree of under compensation. As we noted earlier, the Swedish scheme is designed to top-up other payments in recognition of the pain and suffering involved, and is not the sole source of income replacement or service purchase. If a similarly accessible scheme were introduced in England, the lower barriers to access might allow the rate of claims to rise to Swedish levels. If these claims were compensated at current English rates, the overall cost would rise to £235 million per year. On the other hand, one might expect that the average payment per claim would fall, since an increase in the number of claimants is likely to be associated with a reduction in the average severity of claims. In this case, £235 million should be treated as an upper limit. If the average payment per claim were halved, the cost would be around £117 million per year. While this is certainly well above the present cost of tort litigation, it might be thought that the price were justifiable if the shortcomings of the tort system we have identified were overcome.

For this to happen, it would be important to learn from the experience of New Zealand and Sweden. In particular, careful consideration would need to be given to:

● the definition of accidents to be included in the scheme
● the procedures to be used to prevent accidents, to monitor standards of care, and to encourage rehabilitation
● the importance of ensuring equity in the treatment of accident victims and the sick and disabled
● the means by which doctors would be held accountable and patients would receive an explanation of why an accident happened.

In relation to the last of these points, our proposals for reforming the existing system by extending medical audit and strengthening complaints and disciplinary procedures (see above) would have equal relevance under a no-fault scheme.

The issue of equity of treatment for accident victims and the sick and disabled is more complex. As recent developments in New Zealand have demonstrated, the establishment of special schemes for accident compensation can create distinctions which are difficult to defend. It is for this reason that proposals are now under discussion to reduce the benefits available to accident victims in New Zealand. One of the aims of these proposals is to enable the sick and disabled to be eligible for the same benefits as people injured during accidents. In Sweden, this issue is handled through the social security system which provides a generous level of benefits on the basis of need, with accident compensation supplementing these benefits. This suggests that a further radical option for reform is to introduce a general disability income. We now consider this in more detail.

A general disability income

The replacement of tort by social security is both radical and potentially expensive. As such, it is probably best viewed as a long-term possibility. The advantage of a general disability income is that individuals would receive support on the basis of the fact that their injury and its consequences, and would have to establish neither fault nor cause. The payment of benefits periodically rather than as a lump-sum would also remove much of the present uncertainty about whether a sum of money would be adequate to meet future expenses, and would also permit a continuing review of the victim's circumstances.

The principal advantages of social security as a means of providing compensation lie in its relative accessibility and simplicity. As a result, a large number of beneficiaries can be compensated at a low level of administrative expense. However, these advantages are the product of a generalised, rule-based approach to deciding the appropriate amount of compensation. Benefits may be payable in relation to a schedule of impairments, and/or proof of incapacity for work, without any specific tailoring of payments to the individual's circumstances, as happens under tort law.

The generosity of the social security system is constrained by the extent to which the payment of benefits affects the recipients' recovery, and, where relevant, their return to work. This is a particular concern when disability benefits are payable to those who are permanently, but partially, disabled, and who therefore retain some capacity to work. Designing a set of rules governing the determination of benefits without penalising the decision to return to work for this group of claimants is a task of considerable difficulty. . . .

Two possible solutions are to make awards conditional upon the severity of impairment alone, or to make the assessments irreversible or lump-sum. Either way, this would ensure that subsequent decisions to return to work would not result in a withdrawal of benefit. However, this kind of solution would exaggerate still further the inequities between different types of claimants noted above. The New Zeland approach to this problem has been to limit income replacement to 80 per cent of previous earnings, and to give the Accident Compensation Corporation additional responsibilities for rehabilitation. It is difficult to ascertain the extent to which this has been successful. . . . Clearly, the adoption of a general disability income scheme would not avoid difficult choices between equity and efficiency of the kind which bedevil the tort system.

Moreover, if this option were pursued, a considerable weight would be thrown on the adequacy of other arrangements for monitoring medical standards. Again, this brings into play our proposals earlier . . . [see *infra* at p 498] for extending medical audit, and strengthening complaints and disciplinary procedures. As the New Zealand experience has demonstrated, agreement must be reached on how to deter malpractice before radical changes are introduced.

Conclusion

Faced with these options, how should policy makers proceed? In our view there is a good case for reform, because of the considerable shortcomings of the existing arrangements. On the other hand, it is hard to argue strongly for any particular policy option on the basis of present information. Nevertheless, we can broadly summarise the policy choices in relation to both compensation and deterrence.

It is far from clear that the possibilities have been exhausted for improving the tort system as a means of obtaining compensation. As we noted earlier . . . there are a number of ways in which the system could be changed. In summary, the key measures worth pursuing are:

● providing potential claimants with a means of identifying solicitors with appropriate skills in medical negligence cases
● giving greater publicity to legal services through advertising and other means in order to increase public awareness of the general possibilities of claiming for damages
● modifying fee-splitting arrangements among lawyers to create greater incentives for solicitors to pass on cases to specialists
● making access to legal aid easier, and
● developing a system to enable health authorities to pool their risks in order to cope with a larger number of successful claims.

While these changes would overcome some of the weaknesses of the present system, there would still be a basic inequality between defendants, represented by a small group of experienced and specialised lawyers, and plaintiffs, represented by a dispersed, heterogeneous group of lawyers with infrequent involvement in medical negligence cases. It would also remain difficult to prove fault given the intrinsic uncertainties of human biology and medical technology. In the longer term, then, the inadequacies of the tort system as a method of compensation seem likely to encourage its replacement by a more equitable alternative. If a general disability income is ruled out on grounds of expense, serious consideration could be given to the development of a no-fault scheme.

A no-fault scheme would overcome many of the shortcomings we have identified in the present system: the expense and time involved in pursuing a tort claim; the strong element of lottery; the small proportion of injured patients who receive compensation; and the adversarial nature of the legal process. But . . . neither the Swedish nor the New Zealand schemes offers a model which could be imported directly into the United Kingdom. Each has developed under a particular set of institutional conditions which are not reproduced here. Both also illustrate some of the inherent problems of no-fault schemes, such as the question of equity between people disabled as a result of different sorts of mishap and the means by which claims can be mobilised and screened.

The New Zealand experience also demonstrates the greatest weakness of no-fault schemes, namely the reduction in whatever deterrent effect the tort system may exert. The tort system has the unique feature of presenting the victim of negligence with a financial incentive to pursue a claim against the person believed to be responsible. But, given the difficulties of pursuing claims and the intervening effect of insurance, this is inadequate by itself as a method of preventing accidents.

For this reason, consideration needs to be given to a range of other policy options designed to encourage high quality medical care. In the short term, the most promising options worth pursuing are those which aim to strengthen professional accountability. As we have emphasised throughout this Paper, regardless of whether or not a system of no-fault compensation is introduced, a strong case can be made for improving complaints procedures, reforming the procedures used to discipline doctors, and encouraging the extension of medical audit. To summarise the discussion earlier in this chapter, this would involve:

● developing arrangements for medical audit by requiring doctors to demonstrate that they routinely review the quality of their work and by introducing procedures for the reporting of surgical and other incidents on a confidential basis
● extending and simplifying disciplinary procedures against doctors. This applies both to the GMC's procedures and to the procedures followed by health authorities. The aim should be to ensure that adequate arrangements are in place for handling all cases where concern about professional conduct and competence arise, not just those involving the most serious consequences
● implementing the recommendations of the Davies Committee on hospital complaints in order to establish independent investigating panels to examine complaints about clinical matters.

At the same time, careful consideration should be given to two further changes for implementation in the longer term. These are:

● the introduction of procedures for disciplining doctors based on Sweden's Medical Responsibility Board and involving significant lay participation, and
● the reform of complaints procedures to establish one point of contact whatever the nature of the complaint and to guarantee that those hearing complaints are genuinely independent.

If implemented, these measures would help to deter doctors from acting negligently and would assist patients and their relatives to obtain an adequate explanation when things go wrong.

In conclusion, further research would help to clarify the policy choices we have mapped, but even more important is a political commitment to consider carefully ways in which improvements can be brought about to the benefit of all those involved with medical negligence. Above all, what is now required is an informed debate of the issues and the options, a debate which recognises the need both to provide compensation and to promote deterrence.

You will notice that Ham, Dingwall *et al* refer to the Swedish system. For a detailed account of this system, see the paper by Carl Oldertz in *Compensation for Personal Injury in Sweden and other Countries* (1988), pp 51–78.

For a description of the New Zealand Scheme now consolidated in the Accident Compensation Act 1982, see The Pearson Commission (*op cit*) Volume 3 (pp 191–200) and see the discussion of the Scheme by McLean 'The Implications of No-Fault Liability for the Medical Profession', in *Medicine, Ethics and the Law* (1988) ed M D A Freeman, pp 151–158.

Finally, it is worthwhile to notice the parallel developments in the United States, which reflect the same concerns. The reforms have concentrated on changes within (some would say tinkering with), the existing tort system. They have been designed to strike at the heart of the problems associated with the perceived medical malpractice crisis in America. Consider the following extract from Furrow, Johnson, Jost and Schwartz, *Health Law* (1988) (pp 276–285 and 310–315).

IMPROVING THE LITIGATION PROCESS

Starting in the 1970's, in response to the crisis they perceived, states enacted tort reform legislation. The preamble to the California Medical Injury Compensation Reform Act is a typical statement of the legislative perceptions of the crisis:

The Legislature finds and declares that there is a major health care crisis in the State of California attributable to skyrocketing malpractice premium costs and resulting in a potential breakdown of the health delivery system, severe hardships for the medically indigent, a denial of access for the economically marginal, and depletion of physicians such as to substantially worsen the quality of health care available to citizens of this state.

Tort reform measures were intended by their proponents to reduce either the frequency of malpractice litigation or the size of the settlement or judgment. These measures can be subdivided into four groups:

— those affecting the filing of malpractice claims;
— those limiting the award recoverable by the plaintiff;
— those altering the plaintiff's burden of proof through changes in evidence rules and legal doctrine;
— those changing the role of the courts, usually in the direction of substitution of an alternative forum.

This section will outline the nature of these reforms, consider briefly some of the judicial responses to challenges brought against these reforms, and review several comprehensive reform proposals.

For a useful discussion of the spectrum of reform, see Abraham, 'Medical Malpractice Reform: A Preliminary Analysis', 36 Maryland L Rev 490 (1977).

1. The Nature of Tort Reform

a. *Reducing the filing of claims*

If the frequency of litigation is lowered, it is reasonable to assume that insurance companies will have to pay out at a lower rate, which in turn should lower premiums. Several reforms are intended to either bar certain claims that could previously have been brought, or create disincentives for the bringing of suits.

(1) Shortened statutes of limitations. Over forty states have now modified their statutes of limitations, in response to the criticism that long statutes of repose complicate insurance prediction of claims and result in uncertainty in portfolio management. Historically, the time period for a medical injury was tolled, or began to run, when the injury was discovered. This created the 'long tail' problem. States reduced the time period, typically by requiring that claims be brought within a short time, for example within two years of the injury or one year of the time that the injury should have been discovered with due diligence. . . .

(2) Controlling legal fees. More than twenty states have regulated attorney fees in a variety of ways, including establishing rigid contingency fee structures or requiring judicial review of the 'reasonableness' of the fees. See generally the discussion by the majority and the dissent in *Roa v Lodi Medical Group* 37 Cal 3d 920, 211 Cal Rptr 77, 695 P 2d 164 (1985). The intended effect of these statutes was to make lawyers more selective in screening out nonmeritorious claims, thus eliminating excessive litigation. The evidence as to this claim is presented by Chief Justice Bird in *Roa*. Danzon found that contingent fees tend to result in equalising plaintiff attorney compensation to that of the defence bar (whose income is not controlled), and that controls reduce not only lawyers' income, but also plaintiff compensation. Danzon, [*Medical Malpractice: Theory, Practice and Public Policy* (1985)] at 198.

(3) Payment of costs for frivolous claims. Under such a statute or court rule, when the malpractice claimant is found to have acted frivolously in suing, he must reimburse the provider for reasonable legal fees, witness fees, and court costs. See American Medical Association Special Task Force on Professional Liability and Insurance, Professional Liability in the 80's, Report II, American Medical Association, (updated as of July 1985) at p 23.

b. *Limiting the plaintiff's award*

If the previous reforms hoped to cut down on the number of cases in court, the next category hoped to reduce the overall size of the award.

(1) Elimination of the ad damnum clause. This clause, as part of the initial pleading, states the total monetary claim requested by the plaintiff, an amount presumably inflated beyond the level of actual damages suffered. It is feared that such claims expose the defendant to harmful pretrial publicity, damage his reputation, and

induce juries to make larger awards than the evidence supports. Thirty-two states have legislated to eliminate the ad damnum clause.

(2) Periodic payments. Provisions, now in effect in 18 states, allow or require a court to convert awards for future losses from a single lump sum payment to periodic payments over the period of the patient's disability or life. Such a mode of payment is intended to eliminate a windfall payment to heirs if the injured party dies.

(3) Collateral source rule modifications. The collateral source rule has operated to prevent the trier of fact from learning about other sources of compensation (such as medical insurance) which the plaintiff might possess. The rule arguably permits double recovery. The modifications have either required the court to inform juries about payments from other sources to the patient, or to offset against the award some or all of the amount of payment from other sources. Seventeen states have modified this rule.

(4) Limits on liability. The most powerful reform in actually reducing the size of malpractice awards has been a dollar limit, or cap, on awards. Caps may take several forms:

— a limit on the amount of recovery of general damages, typically pain and suffering;
— a maximum recoverable per case, including all damges;
— a cap on provider liability, through a patient compensation fund which sets a limit on the amount any provider can be liable in any lawsuit. Indiana has a $500,000 limit per claim, Nebraska $1 million, South Dakota a limit of $500,000 for general damages, California $250,000 on recovery for noneconomic damages, including pain and suffering.

c. Altering the plaintiff's burden of proof

Several reforms have altered evidentiary rules or legal doctrine in the direction of increasing the plaintiff's burden of proof.

(1) Res ipsa loquitur. RIL was judicially expanded during the 70's by a number of state courts, creating an inference of negligence (or in three states a presumption) even where expert testimony was needed to establish the 'obviousness' of the defendant's negligence. . . . Doctors objected that they were forced to shoulder a defense burden for some patient harms that were not the result of their negligence. Ten states now have barred the use of the doctrine or limited its operation.

(2) Expert witness rules. . . . the plaintiff is normally required to present expert medical testimony as to the standard of care, the defendant's deviation from it, causation, and damages. Some states have now adopted specific requirements that plaintiff experts be qualified in the particular specialty at issue, or devote a large percent of their practice to the specialty. The intent of these reforms is to reduce the ability of the plaintiff to use a so-called 'hired-gun', a forensic doctor who has never practiced, or no longer practices, in the area of the defendant physician.

(3) Standards of care. The standard of care has evolved from a locality rule to a national standard in most states, not only as to specialists, but also as to general practitioners. Some states have refined the standard by statute to specify the particular locality (local, similar, state) which governs the litigation.

d. Changing the judicial role

The role of the jury as trier of fact has been perceived by critics of the tort system as introducing bias against defendants and causing delay in compensating plaintiffs. Some argue that development of either screening or alternative dispute resolution devices (ADR's) will speed resolution of cases and screen out frivolous claims more effectively than common law litigation. These reforms are important, because they set up a complicated parallel track for disputes which reduces the judicial role.

(1) Pretrial screening devices. Twenty-five states have now put screening panels into place. These panels are intended to rule on the merits of the case before it can proceed to trial and to speed settlement of cases by pricing them in advance of trial. Screening panel laws vary significantly from state to state, but usually require that all cases be heard by the panel before the plaintiff is entitled to trial. A plaintiff is

not prevented from filing suit after a panel's negative finding, but the panel's decision is admissible as evidence at trial. The panels range in size from three to seven members, and often have a judge or a lay person, at least one lawyer, and one or more health care providers from the defendant's specialty or type of institution. The panel conducts an informal hearing in which it hears testimony and reviews evidence. The finding of the panel may cover both liability and the size of the award.

Proponents have contended that such panels are less formal and less time consuming, and therefore less expensive as a way of resolving claims. Better informed panel members, including health care professionals, may also lead to more accurate decisions than a lay jury would achieve. See generally Institute of Medicine, Beyond Malpractice: Compensation for Medical Injuries, National Academy of Sciences, 33 (1978); GAO Report at 133; Carlin, Medical Malpractice Pre-trial Screening Panels: A Review of the Evidence, Intergovernment Health Policy Project 15 (1980).

The concerns as to the panels are that they will delay dispute resolution, will favor the provider, and will be ignored unless their use is mandatory.

(2) Arbitration. While screening panels supplement jury trials, arbitration is intended to replace them. Thirteen states have laws promoting arbitration of malpractice disputes. The expected advantages of arbitration include reduced complexity in fact-finding, lower cost, fairer results, greater access for smaller claims, and a reduced burden on the courts. See GAO Report at 139–40; American Arbitration Association, Arbitration—Alternative to Malpractice Suits, 5 (1975); Ladimer, Solomon, and Mulvihill, 'Experience in Medical Malpractice Arbitration', 2 J Legal Med 443 (1981). None of the state statutes requires compulsory arbitration. Like screening panels, the arbitration process uses a panel to resolve the dispute after an informal presentation of evidence. The panel typically consists of a doctor, a lawyer and a layperson or retired judge. The arbitration panel, however, uses members trained in dispute resolution and has the authority to make a final ruling as to both provider liability and damages. The process is initiated only when there is an agreement between the patient and the health care provider to arbitrate any claims.

The authors then set out an example of legislative intervention in this area:

THE COLUMBIA MEDICAL MALPRACTICE JUSTICE ACT OF 1986

Section 1.

No health care liability claim may be commenced unless the action is filed within two years from the occurrence of the breach or tort or from the date the health care treatment that is the subject of the claim is completed; provided that minors under the age of 12 shall have until their 14th birthday in which to file or have filed on their behalf, the claim.

Section 2.

(1) In an action for damages alleging medical malpractice against a person or party, damages for noneconomic loss which exceeds $225,000.00 shall not be awarded unless 1 or more of the following circumstances exist:
  (a) There has been a death.
  (b) There has been an intentional tort.
  (c) A foreign object was wrongfully left in the body of the patient.
  (d) The injury involves the reproductive system of the patient.
  (e) The discovery of the existence of the claim was prevented by the fraudulent conduct of a health care provider.
  (f) A limb or organ of the patient was wrongfully removed.
  (g) The patient has lost a vital bodily function.
(2) In awarding damages in an action alleging medical malpractice, the trier of the fact shall itemise damages into economic and noneconomic damages.
(3) 'Noneconomic loss' means damages or loss due to pain, suffering, inconvenience, physical impairment, physical disfigurement, or other noneconomic loss.

(4) Subsection (1) of this section does not apply to the amount of damages awarded on a health care liability claim for the expenses of necessary medical, hospital, and custodial care received before judgment or required in the future for treatment of the injury.

(5) In any action on a health care liability claim that is tried by a jury in any court in this state, the following shall be included in the court's written instructions to the jurors: Do not consider, discuss, nor speculate whether or not liability, if any, on the part of any party is or is not subject to any limit under applicable law.

Section 3.

In any malpractice action in which the plaintiff seeks to recover for the cost of medical care, custodial care or rehabilitation services, loss of earnings or other economic loss, evidence shall be admissible for consideration by the court to establish that any such past or future cost or expense was or will, with reasonable certainty, be replaced or indemnified, in whole or in part, from any collateral source such as insurance, social security, workers' compensation or employee benefit programs. If the court finds that any such cost or expense was or will, with reasonable certainty, be replaced or indemnified from any collateral source, it shall reduce the amount of the award by such finding, minus an amount equal to the premiums paid by the plaintiff for such benefits for the two-year period immediately preceding the accrual of such action and minus an amount equal to the projected future cost to the plaintiff of maintaining such benefits.

Section 4.

(1) An action alleging medical malpractice shall be mediated pursuant to subsection (4).

(2) The judge to whom an action alleging medical malpractice is assigned or the chief judge shall refer the action to mediation by written order not less than 91 days after the filing of the answer or answers.

(3) An action referred to mediation pursuant to subsection (1) shall be heard by a mediation panel selected pursuant to subsection (4).

(4) A mediation panel shall be composed of 5 voting members, 3 of whom shall be licensed attorneys, one of whom shall be a licensed or registered health care provider selected by the defendant or defendants and one of whom shall be a licensed or registered health care provider selected by the plaintiff or plaintiffs. If a defendant is a specialist, the health care provider members of the panel shall specialise in the same or a related, relevant area of health care as the defendant.

(5) Except as otherwise provided in subsection (1), the procedure for selecting mediation panel members and their qualifications shall be as prescribed by the court rules or local court rules.

(6) A judge may be selected as a member of a mediation panel, but may not preside at the trial of any action in which he or she served as a mediator.

(7) In the case of multiple injuries to members of a single family, the plaintiffs may elect to treat the action as involving one claim, with the payment of one fee and rendering of one lump sum award to be accepted or rejected. If such an election is not made, a separate fee shall be paid for each plaintiff, and the mediation panel shall then make separate awards for each claim, which may be individually accepted or rejected.

(8) At least 7 days before the mediation hearing date, each party shall submit to the mediation clerk five copies of the documents pertaining to the issues to be mediated and five copies of a concise brief or summary setting forth that party's factual or legal position on issues presented by the action. In addition, one copy of each shall be served, on each attorney of record.

(9) A party has the right, but is not required, to attend a mediation hearing. If scars, disfigurement, or other unusual conditions exist, they may be demonstrated to the mediation panel by a personal appearance; however, testimony shall not be taken or permitted of any party.

(10) The rules of evidence shall not apply before the mediation panel. Factual

information having a bearing on damages or liability shall be supported by documentary evidence, if possible.

(11) Oral presentation shall be limited to 15 minutes per side unless multiple parties or unusual circumstances warrant additional time. The mediation panel may request information on applicable insurance policy limits and may inquire about settlement negotiations, unless a party objects. Following deliberation, the mediation panel shall render an evaluation, to which a majority of the panel must agree.

(12) Statements by the attorneys and the briefs or summaries are not admissible in any subsequent court or evidentiary proceeding.

(13) If a party has rejected an evaluation and the action proceeds to trial, that party shall pay the opposing party's actual costs unless the verdict is more favorable to the rejecting party than the mediation evaluation. However, if the opposing party has also rejected the evaluation, that party is entitled to costs only if the verdict is more favorable to that party than the mediation evaluation.

(14) For the purpose of subsection (13), a verdict shall be adjusted by adding to it assessable costs and interest on the amount of the verdict from the filing of the complaint to the date of the mediation evaluation. After this adjustment, the verdict is considered more favorable to a defendant if it is more than 10% below the evaluation, and is considered more favorable to the plaintiff if it is more than 10% above the evaluation.

(15) For the purpose of this section, actual costs include those costs taxable in any civil action and a reasonable attorney fee as determined by the trial judge for services necessitated by the rejection of the mediation evaluation.

(16) Costs shall not be awarded if the mediation award was not unanimous.

Section 5.

In an action alleging medical malpractice, if the defendant is a specialist, a person shall not give expert testimony on the appropriate standard of care unless the person is or was a physician licensed to practice medicine or osteopathic medicine and surgery or a dentist licensed to practice dentistry in this or another state and meets both of the following criteria:

(1) Specialises, or specialised at the time of the occurrence which is the basis for the action, in the same specialty or a related, relevant area of medicine or osteopathic medicine and surgery or dentistry as the specialist who is the defendant in the medical malpractice action.

(2) Devotes, or devoted at the time of the occurrence which is the basis for the action, a substantial portion of his or her professional time to the active clinical practice of medicine or osteopathic medicine and surgery or the active clinical practice of dentistry, or to the instruction of students in an accredited medical school, osteopathic medical school, or dental school in the same specialty or a related, relevant area of health care as the specialist who is the defendant in the medical malpractice action.

Section 6.

In order to determine what judgment is to be entered on a verdict in an action to recover damages for dental or medical malpractice under this article, the court shall proceed as follows:

(1) The court shall apply to the findings of past and future damages any applicable rules of law, including set-offs, credits, comparative negligence, additurs, and remittiturs, in calculating the respective amounts of past and future damages claimants are entitled to recover and defendants are obligated to pay.

(2) The court shall enter judgment in lump sum for past damages, for future damages not in excess of two hundred fifty thousand dollars, and for any damages, fees or costs payable in lump sum or otherwise under subsection (3). For the purposes of this section, any lump sum payment of a portion of future damages shall be deemed to include the elements of future damages in the same proportion as such elements comprise of the total award for future damages as determined by the trier of fact.

(3) With respect to awards of future damages in excess of two hundred fifty

thousand dollars in an action to recover damages for dental or medical malpractice, the court shall enter judgment as follows:

After making any adjustments prescribed by this subsection and subsection (2), the court shall enter a judgment for the amount of the present value of an annuity contract that will provide for the payment of the remaining amounts of future damages in periodic instalments.

Section 7.

(1) Notwithstanding any inconsistent judicial rule, a contingent fee in a medical malpractice action shall not exceed the amount of compensation provided for in the following schedule:

30 per cent of the first $250,000 of the sum recovered;
25 percent of the next $250,000 of the sum recovered;
20 percent of the next $500,000 of the sum recovered;
15 percent of the next $250,000 of the sum recovered;
10 percent of any amount over $1,250,000 of the sum recovered.

(2) In the event that claimant's or plaintiff's attorney believes in good faith that the fee schedule set forth in subsection (1) of this section, because of extraordinary circumstances, will not give him adequate compensation, application for greater compensation may be made upon affidavit with written notice and an opportunity to be heard to the claimant or plaintiff and other persons holding liens or assignments on the recovery.

The authors then turn to consider the effects of the reforms in the USA:

THE EFFECTS OF REFORM: A PRELIMINARY ASSESSMENT
The reforms of the tort system were enacted with the expectation that liability insurance premiums could be lowered, or at least stabilised, by a reduction in the frequency of malpractice suits and the severity of awards in such suits. It has proved difficult to assess the impact of the reforms, but several studies have identified some measurable impact. The GAO Report of 1985 surveyed six interest groups as to the effect of existing reforms. No consensus was found in their results, although a majority of providers felt that caps has a major impact on the severity of judgments, and a majority of consumers felt that screening panels had a major impact on decreasing the time to close claims. GAO Malpractice Reports, supra.

Four studies have evaluated the effects of the reforms of the mid-1970's. The first used data from claims closed in 1974 and 1976 to examine the disposition of claims, and to measure the impact of collateral source rule modification, contingent fee limits, and caps. Danzon and Lillard, Settlement Out of Court: The Disposition of Medical Malpractice Claims, 12 J Leg Studies 345 (1983). The conclusions were as follows:

—collateral source rule modifications reduced awards by a slight percentage;
—limits on awards, which included caps, ad damnum elimination and periodic payments, reduced potential verdicts by 42% and settlements by 34%;
—contingency fee limits reduced settlements by 9% and the percentage of cases litigated to verdict by 1.5%; it reduced the number of cases dropped by 5%.

The authors conceded that these were tentative results, displaying only short term effects.

A second study looked at the effect of post-1975 reforms on the frequency of claims per capita, the amount per claim paid, and the claim cost per capita, using data from closed claims from 1975 to 1978 by all insurers writing malpractice premiums of a million dollars or more in any year since 1970. Danzon, The Frequency and Severity of Medical Malpractice Claims (1982). Its conclusions were:

—states with caps on awards had awards 19% lower two years after the effective date of the statutes;
—states with contingency fee limits had a somewhat lower amount paid per claim and total claim cost;
—states eliminating the ad damnum had lower total claim costs; there was otherwise no effect on the frequency or amount paid per claim;

—states requiring collateral source offset had 50% lower awards two years after the statute's effective date, but states admitting evidence of collateral sources without required offset displayed no significant effect;

—several reforms displayed no significant effects, including pretrial screening panels, arbitration, res ipsa loquitur or informed consent limitations, and periodic payments.

The third study evaluated the effect of several reforms on the levels and rates of change in insurance premiums paid from 1974 through 1978 by general practitioners, ophthalmologists, and orthopedic surgeons. Sloan, State Responses to the Malpractice Insurance 'Crisis' of the 1970's: An Empirical Assessment, 9 J Health Pol, Pol, and Law 629 (1985). Reforms studied included caps on liability, limits on provider payments to plaintiffs, patient compensation funds, limits on res ipsa loquitur, shortened statutes of limitations, informed consent modifications, contingency fee restrictions, collateral source modifications, ad damnum elimination, imposition of a locality rule, screening panels, arbitration, joint underwriting associations, and health care mutual insurance companies. The reforms therefore included both tort system modification and insurance modification. The conclusions: only screening panels displayed a statistically significant connection to lower malpractice insurance premiums. Sloan concluded that there was '. . . no indication that individual state legislative actions, or actions taken collectively, had their intended effects on premiums'. Sloan, *supra* at 629.

A fourth study by Patricia Danzon updated her earlier studies, based upon analysis of claims nationally over the decade 1975 to 1984, for 49 states in some years, based on data from insurance companies that insured approximately 100,000 physicians. Danzon, The Frequency and Severity of Medical Malpractice Claims: New Evidence, 49 Law & Contemp Probs 57 (1986). Her conclusions are:

—the severity of claims rose twice as fast as the Consumer Price Index, a fact related to the fact that health care prices rose faster than consumer prices generally;

—claim severity continues to be higher in urbanised states, consistent with earlier studies, and is also higher in states 'with a high ratio of surgical specialists relative to medical specialists,' *Id* at 76;

—severity is less in states with larger elderly populations, a fact related to the low wage loss of the elderly and the low potential for damages in a tort suit;

—no correlation was found between the number of lawyers per capita and claim severity;

—the newer data was consistent with earlier findings as to the impact of tort reforms. Statutory caps reduced average severity by 23%. Collateral source offsets appeared to reduce awards by a range of 11 to 18%. Arbitration reduced claim severity by 20%, compared to states without such statutory arbitration. Screening panels did not have a consistent effect in reducing claims severity.

Several studies looked at single reforms, such as panels or arbitration. A 1980 study of screening panels concluded that the panels were effective in disposing of claims before trial, resulting in a significant percentage of claims being dropped or settled after a panel hearing, from a high of 88% of claims disposed of after a panel decision in New Jersey to a low of 38% disposed of in Virginia. Carlin, Medical Malpractice Pre-Trial Screening Panels: A Review of the Evidence, 29, 31 (1980). The very threat of a panel hearing seemed to promote early disposition of claims in some states. The panels in some states also processed claims more quickly than conventional litigation. However, some states were having problems that impaired panel operation. In particular, panels were rarely used where their use was voluntary. Carlin at 32, 37, 39.

A study by the Florida Medical Association in 1985 found that the results of panels were mixed, with some states using panels effectively and others experiencing case backlogs and administrative problems. The authors concluded that panel effectiveness was unproven, and that other court efforts such as a special malpractice court, or other procedural reforms, might be more effective. Florida Medical Association, *Medical Malpractice Policy Guidebook* 188 (1985). Studies by several states of their panels have not been encouraging. New Jersey and New York both recommend that a mandatory screening approach be dropped in favor of some form of voluntary system, such as optional mediation. See *Perna v Pirozzi*, 92 NJ 446, 457–59, 457 A 2d 431, 437 (1983) (presenting findings of a committee appointed by the New Jersey Supreme Court to evaluate New Jersey's panel system); see also Ad Hoc Committee on Medical Malpractice Panels, described in Bower, 'Malpractice Panels and Questions of Fact', 14 Trial LQ 4 (1982). An Arizona study found several problems with the Arizona panels, concluding that (1) settlements increased and claims filed decreased between 1976 and 1978 (the good news); but (the bad news) (2) neither the frequency or level of recovery by claimants was affected; (3) the time to process the malpractice case was lengthened by the panel system; (4) the panel system aggravated problems of difficulty and expense in handling cases, from the lawyers' and panel members' perspectives; (5) the panel hearings took longer than expected. See National Center for State Courts, Medical Liability Review Panels in Arizona: An Evaluation (1980); Spece, The Case Against (Arizona) Medical Malpractice Panels, 63 U Det L Rev 7 (1985).

The *Morris* case [*Morris v Metriyakool* 344 NW 2d 736 (1984)] raised the common law and constitutional arguments against arbitration. Michigan has a developed arbitration framework, requiring hospital to offer arbitration agreements to patients prior to treatment, although the agreements are voluntary on the patient's part. Procedures governing the arbitration are elaborate, and the arbitration is binding on the parties. See Saunders, The Quest for Balance: Public Policy and Due Process in Medical Malpractice Arbitration Agreements, 23 Harv J Leg 267, 271–72 (1986); Terry, The Technical and Conceptual Flaws of Medical Malpractice Arbitration, 30 St Louis UL Journal 571 (1986). A study of the Michigan experience concluded that:

—time between patient injury and claim closing was shorter for claims filed in court and claims filed with arbitration (39.1 versus 41.1 months);

—expenses of defense of claims were lower for arbitration than court claims ($3,652 versus $3,914);

—the median indemnity payment for arbitration claims was less than court claims ($1,000 versus $1,875).

Applied Social Research, Inc, *Evaluation: State of Michigan Medical Malpractice Arbitration Program—Summary Report* 5, 6, 12 (October 1984).

A California study looking at a group of Los Angeles area hospitals participating in an arbitration experiment found that hospitals employing voluntary arbitration had 63% fewer claims; closed claims 22% faster; and realised net savings on closed claims of 62%—41% for loss payments and 21% for investigation and defense costs, as compared to those hospitals not employing voluntary arbitration. Heintz, Medical Malpractice Arbitration: A Viable Alternative, 34 Arbitration Journal 18 (1979). Another California based study reached different conclusions, finding that the total amounts of indemnity paid per incident in arbitration and in court were not different; and that although the time from injury to closing the claim was shorter for arbitration, arbitrated cases tended to involve fewer defendants and involve less severe injuries. Ladimer, Solomon, and Mulvihill, Experience In Medical Malpractice Arbitration, 2 J Leg Med 448–450 (1981).

What do these widely varying, and often conflicting results, mean for the future of reform of the tort system? The results reflect to some extent the nature of the study, and the relative novelty of the reforms such as panels or arbitration. Time will tell whether procedural reforms, requiring an elaborate administrative structure, will mature and prove effective. But any ultimate conclusions as to the merits and nature of reform still depend upon the goals sought for the system. . . . Some of the reforms, such as caps and collateral source offset, appear to have slowed the growth of awards in some states. The growth in malpractice awards, however, seems to be exceeding the annual inflation rate. Some reforms, such as statutes of repose, are likely to reduce claims filings over the longer term. The claims-made insurance policy and mutual insurance companies may also be a more efficient way of allocating risk and protecting insurance availability. The question remains, however:

is the conventional, fault-based litigation system worth keeping for medical accidents? In the next section, several no-fault proposals are presented as potential candidates to replace the current system. As a prelude to your evaluation of systemic reforms, consider the closing comments of Danzon, in *Medical Malpractice: Theory, Practice, and Public Policy* 225–227 (1985):

> In conclusion, the fault-based system is worth retaining if the benefits, in terms of injuries deterred, exceed the costs of litigating over fault and other associated costs, such as defensive medicine. Unfortunately, a full cost-benefit evaluation is impossible because we cannot measure the number of injuries that are prevented as a result of the additional care exercised by medical providers in response to the threat of liability. But we can make a very rough calculation of the benefits, in terms of injury reduction, that would be required to offset the additional costs of operating the tort system, rather than simply compensating victims through first-party insurance and forgoing all aim at deterrence. To make this calculation, let us assume initially that both tort and first-party programs fully compensate victims, and that 80 cents of every health insurance premium dollar reaches the patient as compensation, compared to only 40 cents of every malpractice insurance premium dollar. Thus the 40 cents spent litigating to assign fault through the malpractice system is an additional cost worth incurring only if it results in at least equivalent deterrence benefits. In other words, if the tort system deters at least one injury of comparable severity for every injury currently compensated, the deterrence benefits outweigh the additional costs of the liability system.
>
> We do not know how many injuries are actually deterred, but we can estimate the percentage reduction in the rate of negligent injury that is required. Using the 1974 estimate that 1 in 10 incidents of negligence leads to a claim and 1 in 25 receives compensation, only a 4 percent reduction in the rate of negligent injury is required to justify the costs of the tort system. If the rate of compensation per negligent injury is currently, say, twice as high as it was in 1974, then an 8 percent reduction in the rate of negligent injury would be required. Similarly if the tort system entails significant costs other than the litigation costs considered so far—such as defensive medicine, public costs of operating the courts, time and psychic costs of litigation to patients and providers—then the deterrence benefits would have to be higher. On the other hand, to the extent that the compensation received by victims through tort understates their willingness to pay for injury prevention, the deterrence necessary to justify the system is less.
>
> This rough calculation suggests that if the number of negligent injuries is, generously, 20 percent lower than it otherwise would be because of the incentives for care created by the malpractice system, the system is worth retaining, despite its costs. But this is not grounds for inaction. The malpractice system could be made more cost-effective for purposes of both deterrence and compensation, through reforms such as the restructuring of awards, freedom of private contract, redefinition of the standard of care, and short statutes of repose. These reforms would represent a radical change in traditional tort law and raise the obvious question of why medical malpractice should be singled out for special treatment. My answer would be that it should not; that—where relevant—these reforms should also apply to other areas of tort law, in particular to product liability. Unless such changes are enacted, the growing frustration over the more visible costs of the tort system may lead us to abandon entirely what is potentially a valuable system of quality control.

For a general discussion of the deterrent value of malpractice suits, see Bovbjerg, 'Medical Malpractice on Trial: Quality of Care is the Important Standard,' 49 Law & Contemp. Probs. 321 (1986).

In the light of the above, consider the following:

(i)   The British Medical Association (BMA) at the end of 1987 produced a Working Paper on 'No-fault Compensation' which recorded its Damascene conversion to the cause of a 'no-fault system'.

McLean in 'No-Fault Liability and Medical Responsibility' in *Medicine,*

Ethics and the Law (1988, ed M D A Freeman), comments (p 147) (footnotes omitted):

> In their evidence to the Royal Commission on Civil Liability and Compensation for Personal Injury (Pearson Commission) the medical profession's representations indicated their general hostility to modification or alteration of the basis of liability for personal injury. However much the fault based action may be criticised, the medical profession believed it to be 'one of the means whereby doctors could show their sense of responsibility and, therefore, justly claim professional freedom'. Thus, their view was that—even if a change in the basis of liability was to be considered— the fault based system should continue to be an option. Not only were they concerned that professional freedom would be curtailed by an alteration in liability, but they also feared that such a state run system would permit of intrusion into and bureaucratisation of medical practice. It is fair to say that the Pearson Commission was not overly impressed by such claims, but they nonetheless did not recommend changes to the basis of liability.
>
> Increasingly, however, under headlines such as 'How to Remove Financial Insult from Injury' the press report a change of attitude amongst the medical profession. Now, it would appear, the arguments which so failed to impress the Pearson Commission, also fail to impress the medical profession itself. The BMA is becoming a strong supporter of a no fault system. The question to be posed, therefore, is what is it that has brought about such a dramatic change in attitude?.

What do you think the answer is to the question she poses?

Arnold Simanowitz in 'Medical Accidents: The Problem and The Challenge' in *Medicine in Contemporary Society: King's College Studies 1986–7* (ed P Byrne), provides *an* answer (pp 120–1) (footnotes omitted).

> . . . I do not believe that the number of accidents taking place, proportionate to the number of patients treated, has increased (although the truth of the matter is that there are no statistics available which could demonstrate this or the contrary). It is simply that, thanks in part to the activity of AVMA [Action for the Victims of Medical Accidents], the public has become more aware of its right to complain about inferior medical attention and to seek compensation for negligence from health carers in the same way as it does from any other body or person that is guilty of negligence. As a result, doctors, to quote Dr Maurice Burroughs, the Chairman of the BMA working party, 'are increasingly worried about the rising number of complaints and negligence claims against them' and we often hear how anxious they are about the steep rise in their insurance premiums which in 1986 were increased to £576 a year. In other words, to the cynic it may seem that the impetus for the scheme on the part of the BMA comes primarily not because of concern for the patient but because of concern for the position of their members. This is hardly the best basis for the introduction of 'no fault' compensation.
>
> It is more surprising that the community health councils should have become involved in this aspect of the problem of medical accidents. They, as much as AVMA, will be aware that the vast majority of the victims of medical accidents do not initially seek financial compensation but want an explanation for what went wrong, sympathetic treatment and, if appropriate, an apology. They, as much as AVMA, will be aware how much the attitude of the health carers, when an accident takes place, is the cause of the distress to victims and their families; they as much as AVMA will be aware of the lack of accountability of doctors insofar as accidents are concerned. These major problems will not be solved by a 'no fault' compensation system. Indeed, the last mentioned will be exacerbated, not cured, by the introduction of such a system. It seems that they have made the same mistake as doctors, if for different reasons. They have assumed that the urgent problems which beset the issue of medical accidents can only be overcome by a 'no fault' system and without further investigation have decided to push for it.
>
> There are, in my view, a number of major reasons why the BMA and patients' organisations such as ACHCEW are putting all their energies into pressing for a 'no

fault' compensation scheme. One is the lack of information about the problem of medical accidents itself. It is quite extraordinary that two responsible bodies should be proposing a complex and expensive solution to a problem when they do not have the faintest idea what the size and nature of that problem is. Nobody knows how many medical accidents occur in Britain each year, what their distribution is, or what the nature of the accidents are. The DHSS refuses to keep statistics of medical accidents separately from ordinary accidents (see the reply from the Solicitor General to John Tilley MP, 7th May 1981: 'I regret that this information is not collected and could not be made available except at unacceptable expense'). There is no obligation on health authorities to keep or pool statistics. Even the doctors' defence organisations, the Medical Defence Union, the Medical and Dental Defence Union of Scotland and the Medical Protection Society, who do at least have statistics of doctors who consult them when they believe that they may have been involved in an accident, refuse to publish even that only partly helpful figure. The *British Medical Journal* in a recent editorial recognised that there is a need in Britain for a formal study of how many people are injured by medical treatment.

Do you agree with this answer?

(ii)   The response of the government has been to reject all calls for change in the existing legal system (see Ham, 'Medical negligence claims: the irresistible case for reform' (1988) Independent, 24 November).

(iii)   Under the existing system of compensation through litigation do you think that any of the objectives which litigation is alleged to meet are in fact met? ie:

(a) that the plaintiff-patient has a real prospect of compensation when suffering a medical mishap;
(b) that any compensation is adequate;
(c) that the public interest is served by ensuring that doctors are held to account, and that the best possible standards of care are maintained;
(d) that a particular doctor who is guilty of blameworthy conduct is effectively disciplined.

As regards (d), remember that the more egregious the conduct, the more likely it is that the case will be settled out of court. Remember also who pays the compensation given that a doctor will be a member of a defence organisation.

Interestingly, in 1989 one defence association introduced differential rates of cover to reflect, albeit in a rough and ready way, the relative risks of different types of medical practice (see Ham, Dingwall *et al, op cit*).

As we have already seen (Ham, Dingwall *et al, supra*) a further twist is added by the fact that the premiums of GPs in the NHS are refunded by the relevant FPC. As regards hospital doctors within the NHS, two-thirds of the premium is paid to them as an allowance, in addition to their salary. While rejecting change in the legal structure for dealing with medical malpractice actions, the Government intends to introduce 'Crown indemnity' for hospital doctors employed within the NHS. If implemented, henceforth, health authorities will pay all damage claims arising from the negligence of their doctor-employees. It is hoped this will simplify claims procedures with resulting reductions in costs and increased efficiency.

Do you think this end will be achieved? Do you think doctors will be better represented by their employers than by their defence organisations, which will now have a much more limited role in medical malpractice actions?

(iv)   Note the appearance in May 1988 of another player on the scene, The Citizen Action Compensation Campaign (CACC) under the Presidency of Lord Scarman. This group added its voice to calls for change, in the light of the unsatisfactory outcome of litigation concerned with the drug, Opren (see, for example, *Davies v Eli Lilly & Co* [1987] 3 All ER 94, [1987] 1 WLR 1136). CACC's objectives can be summarised as the following:

(i) to improve levels of compensation;
(ii) to ensure people are not prevented from seeking compensation for personal injury by prohibitive costs;
(iii) to make Legal Aid more widely available;
(iv) to consider the introduction of a limited form of contingency fees;
(v) to ensure a speedier resolution of cases involving large numbers of victims.

(For a general study of the efficiency of litigation see the *Report of the Review Body on Civil Justice* (Cmnd 394) 1988, and for personal injury litigation see especially chapter 7.)

Accountability outside the tort system

Suing doctors is, of course, only one means for seeking to ensure that the public interest is served and doctors are held accountable. Ham, Dingwall *et al* (*op cit*) discuss the other means of achieving professional accountability in their 1988 paper (pp 16–17):

> ..., the issue of accountability lies at the heart of the criticisms voiced against tort law by organisations representing patients and their relatives. The argument advanced by these organisations is that doctors are accountable to patients only in a weak sense and that changes are needed to ensure that adequate explanations are given when things go wrong and that appropriate action is taken against the doctors concerned.
>
> There are various ways of ensuring accountability apart from through the courts. The two most important are professional self-regulation and procedures for holding doctors to account to the public or the public's representatives. The UK has traditionally relied most heavily on self-regulation. Like all professional groups, doctors have argued that responsibility for setting and maintaining standards should lie with the profession. We have noted already that what is defined as reasonable care in a legal context is determined by doctors, and more generally doctors take it upon themselves to ensure that the quality of care provided is satisfactory. The medical defence societies contribute to this through their educational activities. These activities take a number of forms: published reports warning doctors of the risks associated with different aspects of clinical practice; films and tape/slide programmes; and seminars and lectures given by staff of the societies. The aim of these activities is to warn doctors of well-known pitfalls and to improve standards of care.

> *Medical audit*
>
> To the extent that the profession actively monitors standards it does so on an informal basis by means of medical audit and peer review. This involves doctors regularly assessing their practice in discussion with colleagues. In the main, initiatives for audit in the UK have been organised locally by the doctors in a hospital department or the general practitioners in a group practice. In addition, there are examples of more formal mechanisms which are part of a national interest in audit. These include the Health Advisory Service, the National Development Team for Mentally Handicapped People, the Confidential Enquiry into Maternal Deaths, and the Confidential Enquiry into Peri-operative Deaths. All of these mechanisms involve an element of independent professional assessment of standards.
>
> Despite the interest shown in audit both locally and nationally, Sir Raymond Hoffenberg ... has argued that the medical profession has shown considerable

resistance to the concept of audit. Hoffenberg contends that the profession should welcome greater scrutiny of clinical competence, for only in this way will public confidence be maintained and the threat of external regulation avoided.

The General Medical Council

The accountability of doctors to the public is discharged principally through the various procedures that exist for handling complaints. Doctors are closely involved in these procedures, most obviously in the case of the GMC. The GMC is an independent statutory body charged with maintaining a register of doctors, overseeing medical education, and handling disciplinary matters. The GMC is made up mainly of doctors and it investigates allegations of serious professional misconduct. Approximately 1,000 complaints are handled each year and these arise from criminal convictions as well as from the public and the professions. The complaints considered by the GMC include matters of professional etiquette such as advertising and the abuse of personal relationships with patients (for example, entering into a sexual relationship) as well as the neglect by doctors of their professional responsibilities to patients. It is this last category of complaints that includes examples of medical negligence.

Complaints are carefully screened and in the vast majority of cases the Council decides that no question of serious professional misconduct arises and hence no action is taken. Investigation of the remaining cases may result in a letter of advice or admonition to the doctor concerned, or reference to the professional conduct committee. This committee considers approximately five per cent of all cases received by the Council. Approximately one-third of these cases concern the professional responsibilities and clinical competence of doctors. The committee operates like a court and can impose a range of penalties, including in extreme cases striking a doctor off the register. A recent analysis of the work of the GMC concluded that, in comparison with Sweden and the United States, the Council's disciplinary procedures exhibited 'an extraordinary degree of control' . . . by doctors themselves of professional conduct.

Complaints

Apart from the GMC, separate arrangements exist for handling complaints in the hospital and community health services and the family practitioner services. The detail of these arrangements is complex but the basic principles are as follows. In the case of family practitioner services, complaints about breach of contract are heard by service committees of family practitioner committees. These usually comprise three lay members, three medical members and a lay chairman. A complaint normally has to be made within eight weeks of the event which gave rise to it (soon to be extended to 13 weeks). The remit of service committees is limited to breach of terms of service and excludes criticism of a doctor's manner or matters such as the efficiency of appointments systems.

In a study conducted in the early 1970s, Klein found that the most common types of complaint concerned failure to treat a patient in an emergency, failure to provide a proper surgery, failure of deputising services, and improper demands for fees. Complaints involving the clinical judgment of GPs were also considered by service committees but these were in a minority. In the case of complaints about clinical judgment, Klein found that service committees relied heavily on the assessment of their medical members in determining whether doctors were in breach of their duty to provide proper and necessary treatment.

It is worth noting that the number of formal complaints against family practitioners, including GPs, is small: in 1983, 1,313 complaints were investigated in England and practitioners were found to be in breach of their contracts in 341 cases (26 per cent). In the same year, there were around 190 million consultations with family doctors and 30 million courses of dental treatment. . . .

Complaints concerning hospital and community health services are investigated by health authorities following procedures set out in circular HC(88)37. Again, the number of written complaints received is small: 25,336 in relation to hospital services in 1985 in England, or around 3.5 complaints for every 1,000 in-patient and day cases. In the same year, 3,649 written complaints were received concerning community services (DHSS, personal communication).

Complaints about clinical judgment

Special procedures exist for handling hospital complaints in which issues of clinical judgment arise. These procedures involve the consultant in charge of the case initially investigating the complaint and seeking to satisfy the complainant. If this fails, the complaint is referred to the regional medical officer who may ask for an independent professional review to be conducted by two senior doctors. This is invoked in the case of serious complaints only and is intended as an alternative to legal action. A review conducted by regional medical officers early in 1984 . . . indicated that the officers involved believed they were providing a useful service to complainants but various proposals were made for speeding up and improving the procedures.

The procedures for handling complaints concerning clinical judgment are particularly relevant to our interests. This is because a major concern of the commitees and organisations that have analysed these procedures in recent years has been to create a system which satisfies complainants who have the option of taking a case to court but who choose not to do so. It can be argued that if an adequate system can be devised for handling complaints concerning clinical judgments then patients and their relatives will be less likely to pursue a legal remedy. Against this, organisations representing the medical profession have argued that the option of taking a case to court should preclude other methods of independent review.

In addressing this question, the Davies Committee (1973) proposed the establishment of investigating panels of professional and lay members to conduct investigations into hospital complaints concerning clinical judgment. This proposal was not acceptable to the profession and was not implemented. A different stance was taken by the Select Committee on the Parliamentary Commissioner for Administration (1977) which argued that the Health Services Commissioner or Ombudsman should be empowered to look into clinical complaints as well as other complaints incapable of being resolved by a health authority. This too was unacceptable to the profession.

Following lengthy negotiations, the government secured the agreement of doctors to introduce in 1981 the procedures described above. These procedures place responsibility for investigating complaints about clinical judgment firmly in the hands of the profession and do not provide for the sort of lay and independent involvement envisaged by the Davies Committee and the Select Committee. The reason for this is the reluctance of the profession to relinquish control over the handling of complaints. This reluctance stems from the perceived threat to clinical freedom and the risk of double jeopardy if patients decide to go to court after using the independent review process. In fact, the evidence suggests that few complainants do initiate legal action following independent professional reviews. An analysis of complaints dealt with in this way between 1981 and 1983 found that in only 3 out of 94 completed inquiries was a civil action for damages started. . . .

The Health Service Commissioner

The only other source of redress available to patients is the Health Services Commissioner. However, the Commissioner's remit is limited to complaints concerning injustice or hardship suffered by members of the public as a result of a failure in a service provided by a health authority or a failure of an authority to provide a service which it was its duty to provide. Cases outside the Commissioner's jurisdiction include those involving clinical judgment and cases where legal action is proposed. As Table 5 shows, there has been a steady increase in the number of complaints received by the Commissioner but many of these complaints are either rejected or referred back. The largest category of rejected cases (30 per cent in 1986–7) are those involving clinical judgment.

**Table 5. Health Service Commissioner Analysis of Activity
1977–1986. England**

Year	Complaints Received	Rejected or Discontinued	Referred Back	Results Reports Issued
1977/78	494	267	59	94
1978/79	590	426	67	101
1979/80	484	334	58	90
1980/81	556	398	83	98
1081/82	586	419	95	89
1982/83	658	460	96	101
1983/84	770	520	145	96
1984/85	711	387	195	104
1985/86	807	407	238	116

Source: DHSS 1986

Let us now turn to examine some of these mechanisms referred to by Ham, Dingwall *et al* in greater detail.

1. THE GENERAL MEDICAL COUNCIL

First we must concern ourselves with what is perhaps the most important procedure dealing with complaints and discipline that exists. The General Medical Council has, as we have seen, disciplinary powers over all registered medical practitioners.

The General Medical Council's powers are set out in section 36 of the Medical Act 1983.

36.—(1) Where a fully registered person—
  (a) is found by the Professional Conduct Committee to have been convicted in the British Islands of a criminal offence, whether while so registered or not; or
  (b) is judged by the Professional Conduct Committee to have been guilty of serious professional misconduct, whether while so registered or not;
the Committee may, if they think fit, direct—
    (i) that his name shall be erased from the register;
    (ii) that his registration in the register shall be suspended (that is to say, shall not have effect) during such period not exceeding twelve months as may be specified in the direction; or
    (iii) that his registration shall be conditional on his compliance, during such period not exceeding three years as may be specified in the direction, with such requirements so specified as the Committee think fit to impose for the protection of members of the public or in his interests.

It will be seen that the GMC's powers in this regard are performed by the Professional Conduct Committee (PCC). In the so-called 'blue book' (Professional Conduct and Discipline: Fitness to Practice), the GMC explains the position of the PCC and the procedure at hearings before it (paragraphs 9–28):

9. The Professional Conduct Committee is elected annually by the Council and consists of 29 members, of whom only ten sit on any case. Of the 29 members, 18 are elected members of the Council and three are lay members. The Committee normally sits in public and its procedure is closely akin to that of a court of law. Witnesses may be subpoenaed and evidence is given on oath. Doctors who appear before the Committee may be, and usually are, legally represented.
10. The Preliminary Proceedings Committee consists of 11 members, and is also elected annually. It sits in private and on the basis of written evidence and

submissions determines which cases should be referred for inquiry by the Professional Conduct Committee. . . .

11. The Professional Conduct and Preliminary Proceedings Committees are advised on questions of law by a Legal Assessor, who is usually a Queen's Counsel and must be a barrister, advocate or solicitor of not less than ten years' standing.

Rules of procedure
12. The proceedings of the Professional Conduct and Preliminary Proceedings Committees are governed by rules of procedure made by the Council after consultation with representative medical organisations, and approved by the Privy Council. The current rules were made in 1980 and are printed by HM Stationery Office as Statutory Instrument 1980 No. 858. Other rules govern the functions of the Legal Assessor and the procedure for appeals to the Judicial Committee of the Privy Council.

Proceedings: the preliminary stages
13. Cases giving rise to proceedings by the Preliminary Proceedings Committee or the Professional Conduct Committee are of two kinds—those arising from a conviction of a doctor in the courts and those where a doctor is alleged to have done something which amounts to serious professional misconduct. In either kind of case the Council acts only when relevant matters have been brought to its notice.
14. Convictions of doctors are normally reported to the Council by the police. Unless the conviction is of a minor motoring or other trivial offence it is normally referred to the Preliminary Proceedings Committee.
15. Information or complaints concerning behaviour which may be regarded as serious professional misconduct reach the Council from a number of sources. Frequently they concern matters which have already been investigated through some other procedure—for example a Medical Service Committee, or a Committee of Inquiry in the hospital service. Information or complaints received from individual doctors or members of the public, as distinct from public authorities, must be supported by evidence of the facts alleged in the form of one or more sworn statements (statutory declarations made in a prescribed form before a Commissioner for Oaths or a Justice of the Peace).
16. Every complaint or item of information received is scrutinised meticulously. Only a very small proportion are both found to relate to matters which could be regarded as raising a question of serious professional misconduct and also supported, or capable of being supported, by adequate evidence. Where it appears from the allegations made that a question of serious professional misconduct may arise but the evidence initially received is insufficient or does not comply with the Rules, the Council's Solicitor may be asked to make inquiries to establish the facts. A decision whether action shall be taken on an allegation of serious professional misconduct is then taken by the President or by another member of the Council appointed for the purpose. If it appears to the President that the matter is trivial, or irrelevant to the question of serious professional misconduct, he will normally decide that it shall proceed no further. In a case where it is decided to proceed with allegations of serious professional misconduct, the doctor is informed of the allegations made against him and is invited to submit a written explanation. If the doctor responds to this invitation his explanation, which may include evidence in answer to the allegations, is then placed before the Preliminary Proceedings Committee when it considers the case.

Powers of the Preliminary Proceedings Committee: warning letters and letters of advice
17. After considering a case of conviction or of alleged serious professional misconduct the Preliminary Proceedings Committee may decide either:

(a) to refer the case to the Professional Conduct Committee for inquiry; or
(b) to send the doctor a letter; or
(c) to take no further action.

18. Many cases considered by the Preliminary Proceedings Committee are disposed of by a warning letter or a letter of advice—for example cases where a doctor has been convicted for the first time of driving a motor car when under the

influence of drink, or of shoplifting, or cases where a doctor's professional conduct appears to have fallen below the proper standard but not to have been so serious as to necessitate a public inquiry.

20. If on considering a conviction, or allegations of serious professional misconduct, it appears to the Preliminary Proceedings Committee that the doctor may be suffering from a physical or mental condition which seriously impairs his fitness to practise, the Committee may refer the case to the Health Committee instead of the Professional Conduct Committee.

20. If the Preliminary Proceedings Committee decides to refer a case either to the Professional Conduct Committee or to the Health Committee, it may make an order for the interim suspension of the doctor's registration or for interim conditional registration if it is satisfied that this is necessary for the protection of members of the public or is in the doctor's own interests. Such orders may be made for a period not exceeding two months and are intended to be effective only until the case has been considered by the Professional Conduct Committee or by the Health Committee. No such order can be made unless the doctor has been offered an opportunity of appearing before the Preliminary Proceedings Committee and being heard on the question whether such an order should be made. For this purpose the doctor may be legally represented.

Inquiries before the Professional Conduct Committee

21. As already mentioned, the Professional Conduct Committee is bound to accept the fact that a doctor has been convicted as conclusive evidence that he was guilty of the offence of which he was convicted. Provided therefore that a doctor admits a conviction, proceedings in cases of conviction are concerned only to establish the gravity of the offence and to take due account of any mitigating circumstances. In cases of conduct however the allegations, unless admitted by the doctor, must be *strictly proved by evidence*, and the doctor is free to dispute and rebut the evidence called. If facts alleged in a conduct charge are found by the Committee to have been proved, the Committee must subsequently determine whether, in relation to those facts, the doctor has been guilty of serious professional misconduct. Before taking a final decision the Committee invites the doctor or his legal representative to call attention to any mitigating circumstances and to produce testimonials or other evidence as to character. The Committee takes account of the previous history of the doctor.

22. The primary concerns of the Professional Conduct Committee are to protect the public and to uphold the reputation of the medical profession. Subject to these overriding considerations, the Committee will consider what is in the best interests of the doctor himself. If in the course of an inquiry it appears to the Committee that a doctor's fitness to practise may be seriously impaired by reason of his physical or mental condition, the Committee may refer that question to the Health Committee for determination. If the Health Committee finds that it is so impaired, the Professional Conduct Committee will then take no further action in the case.

Powers of the Professional Conduct Committee at the conclusion of an inquiry

23. At the conclusion of an inquiry in which a doctor has been proved to have been convicted of a criminal offence, or judged to have been guilty of serious professional misconduct, the Professional Conduct Committee must decide on one of the following courses:

(a) to conclude the case;

(b) to postpone its determination;

(c) to direct that the doctor's registration be conditional on his compliance, for a period not exceeding three years, with such requirements as the Committee may think fit to impose for the protection of members of the public or in his interests;

(d) to direct that the doctor's registration shall be suspended for a period not exceeding 12 months; or

(e) to direct the erasure of the doctor's name from the Register.

Postponement of determination

24. In any case where the Committee's determination is postponed, the doctor's name remains on the Register during the period of postponement. When postponing

its determination to a later meeting the Committee normally intimates that the doctor will be expected before his next appearance to furnish the names of professional colleagues and other persons of standing to whom the Council may apply for information, to be given in confidence, concerning his conduct since the previous hearing. The replies received from these referees, together with any other evidence as to the doctor's conduct, are then taken into account when the Committee resumes consideration of the case. If the information is satisfactory, the case will then normally be concluded. If however the evidence is not satisfactory, the determination may be postponed for a further period, or the Committee may direct suspension or erasure or may impose conditions on the doctor's registration.

Conditional registration
25.   Examples of conditions which may be imposed are that the doctor should not engage in specified branches of medical practice, or that he should practise only in a particular appointment or under supervision. Another is that he should not prescribe or possess controlled drugs. Another is that he should take specified steps to remedy evident deficiencies in his knowledge, clinical skills, professional attitudes and/or abilities to manage or communicate.
26.   When a doctor's registration has for a period been subject to conditions the Committee may, on resuming consideration of his case, revoke the direction for conditional registration, or revoke or vary any of the conditions, or it may extend the original period of conditional registration. If a doctor is judged by the Professional Conduct Committee to have failed to comply with any of the conditions of his registration, the Committee may direct either suspension of his registration or erasure.

Suspension of registration
27.   If a doctor's registration is suspended, the doctor ceases to be entitled to practise as a registered medical practitioner during that period. When a doctor's registration has been suspended the Committee may, after notifying the doctor, resume consideration of his case before the end of the period of suspension. At that time, if the Committee thinks fit, it may extend the original period of suspension or order erasure or impose conditional registration. Before resuming consideration of the case in such circumstances the Committee may, as when postponing its determination, ask the doctor to give the names of referees from whom information may be sought as to his conduct in the interval. This information will be taken into account when the Committee resumes consideration of the case.

Erasure
28.   Whereas suspension can be ordered only for a specified period, a direction to erase remains effective unless and until the doctor makes a successful application for the restoration of his name to the Register. Such an application cannot be made until at least ten months have elapsed since the original order took effect.

If the PCC directs that a doctor's name should be erased or that his registration should be suspended or made subject to conditions, then the doctor has a right of appeal to the Judicial Committee of the Privy Council, by virtue of section 40 of the 1983 Act. (The detail of the procedure before the PCC is complex and the reader is referred to the appropriate statutory instrument—the General Medical Council Preliminary Proceedings Committee and Professional Conduct Committee (Procedure) Rules of Council 1980 (SI 1980 No 858).)

The GMC acts upon complaints or information from a variety of sources. These are helpfully set out by Adrian Whitfield QC in his paper 'The General Medical Council' in *Medical Malpractice* (1980, ed J Leahy Taylor).

1.   The police are under instruction to report to the Registrar of the GMC convictions of doctors, 'particularly those involving violence, indecency, dishonesty, drink or drugs' (statement by Secretary of State for Home Department, 14 June 1973).
2.   A general practitioner who, following NHS statutory proceedings, is prevented from acting as a principal GP anywhere within the NHS will also be reported by the DHSS.

3. The GMC may be informed of breaches of general practitioners' terms of service within the NHS in a limited number of serious cases.

4. In relation to hospital doctors, the Hospital Memorandum HM(61)37 provides that:

> In order that the statutory bodies responsible for professional discipline may be aware of convictions in the Courts leading to the dismissal or resignation of members of the professions concerned, the Minister asks that in every case the Hospital Authority should send a factual report of the charges and sentence to the Disciplinary Body. . . . A Hospital Authority is of course still free to report to the appropriate body the facts of any other dismissal or resignation where, in the Authority's view, these facts should be made known to the body even though there has been no conviction in the Courts. It is for the professional body concerned itself to decide what action, if any, to take on a report.

In practice, few cases reach the GMC from Hospital Authorities.

5. Complaints may be received from the Home Office or other Official Body, eg in relation to the issue of prescriptions for drugs otherwise than in the course of bona fide treatment.

6. Other doctors may complain, eg of advertisement or canvassing.

7. Patients may complain, eg of sexual misconduct.

8. Newspaper reports—'investigative journalism' included—are also noted by the GMC.

In past years the GMC was unwilling to act save upon a conviction or a complaint supported by all necessary evidence. It is still the case that evidence in support of a private complaint is often prepared for presentation by the complainant's private solicitor. But nowadays the GMC frequently goes to trouble and expense in trying to amass evidence itself.

The central requirements under s 36 before action may be taken against a doctor are that, either (i) he has been convicted of a criminal offence, or (ii) that he has been found guilty of 'serious professional misconduct'.

Little need be said about (i) except that the offence need not be directly connected with the doctor's profession. In paragraph 49 of the 'blue book', the GMC states:

> 49. The public reputation of the medical profession requires that every member should observe proper standards of personal behaviour, not only in his professional activities but at all times. This is the reason why a doctor's conviction of a criminal offence may lead to disciplinary proceedings even if the offence is not directly connected with the doctor's profession. In particular, three areas of personal behaviour can be identified which may occasion disciplinary proceedings:
>
> — Personal misuse or abuse of alcohol or other drugs
> — Dishonest behaviour
> — Indecent or violent behaviour.

(a) 'Serious professional misconduct'

The more difficult part of the definition of the GMC's disciplinary powers is that relating to 'serious professional misconduct'. This phrase was first introduced by the Medical Act 1969. Prior to that, the phrase used was 'infamous conduct in a professional respect'. The change in phraseology was not intended, however, to alter the GMC's jurisdiction. Instead, it was intended to explain the jurisdiction in modern terminology, by reference to the way 'infamous conduct in a professional respect' had been interpreted by the courts.

In *Allinson v General Council of Medical Education* [1894] 1 QB 750 Lord Esher MR stated:

> If it be shown that a medical man, in the pursuit of his profession, has done something with respect to it which would be reasonably regarded as disgraceful or dishonourable by his professional brethren of good repute and competency, then it

is open to the General Medical Council to say that he has been guilty of 'infamous conduct in a professional respect'. The question is not merely whether what a medical man has done would be an infamous thing for anybody else to do, but whether it is infamous for a medical man to do it. An act done by a medical man may be infamous though it would not be infamous if done by anybody else, but to bring such an act within s 29 of the Medical Act 1858, it must also be shown to have been infamous 'in a professional respect'. There may be some acts which, although not infamous if done by any other person, yet if done by a medical man in relation to his profession, that is, with regard either to his patients or to his professional brethren, may be fairly considered as 'infamous conduct in a professional respect'. Such acts would, I think, come within s 29.

Lopes and Davey LJJ expressly agreed.

Adopting terminology reminiscent of s 36 of the 1983 Act, Scruttons LJ, in *R v General Council of Medical Education and Registration of the United Kingdom* [1930] 1 KB 562 at 569, stated that the GMC's jurisdiction extended to 'serious misconduct judged according to the rules, written or unwritten, governing the profession'. As we have seen, the GMC takes the view that this may arise in relation to a doctor's conduct other than in relation to conduct connected with his professional duties. This seems to be borne out by the case of *Marten v Royal College of Veterinary Surgeons' Disciplinary Committee* [1966] 1 QB 1, [1965] 1 All ER 949. This case concerned a practising veterinary surgeon who owned a farm. During the winter months a number of cattle died on his farm from husk. He was charged before the Disciplinary Committee of the Council of the Royal College of Veterinary Surgeons with, *inter alia*, conduct disgraceful to a man in a professional respect, in that he failed to provide adequate nursing for sick animals in his care and that he allowed conditions to exist on his farm which were likely to bring disgrace on the veterinary profession. He was found guilty and he appealed to the court.

Lord Parker CJ said:

The second way, however, in which counsel puts the case is this: that conduct, however disgraceful, cannot be conduct disgraceful to a man in a professional respect unless at the time he is actively practising in that profession or acting in pursuit of his profession. To return to the facts of this case, he says that in all these matters the appellant was not acting as a veterinary surgeon, he was acting merely as a farmer, and that what he did in effect had nothing to do with his profession.

Lord Parker CJ then cited Lord Esher MR's judgment in the *Allinson* case and continued:

Counsel for the appellant says that as a matter of law a professional man's conduct cannot be said to be disgraceful to him in a professional respect unless it was done 'in pursuit of his profession', and he would add that 'in pursuit of his profession' meant 'in the course of the practice of the profession'. For my part I see no valid ground for limiting the words in the manner suggested. If, of course, the conduct complained of is equally reprehensible in any one, whether a professional man or not, as for example, conduct constituting some traffic offence, that conduct would not come within the expression. If the conduct, however, though reprehensible in anyone is in the case of the professional man so much more reprehensible as to be defined as disgraceful, it seems to me that it may, depending on the circumstances, amount to conduct disgraceful to him in a professional respect in the sense that it tends to bring disgrace on the profession which he practises. It seems to me, though I do not put this forward in any sense as a definition, that the conception of conduct which is disgraceful to a man in his professional capacity is conduct disgraceful to him as reflecting on his profession, or, in the present case, conduct disgraceful to him as a practising veterinary surgeon. Looked at in that way, which I think is the correct way, there was here abundant evidence on which the Disciplinary Committee could come to the conclusion that the conduct was disgraceful to the appellant in a professional capacity. At any rate, bearing in mind that this court, as has been said many times, is loath to interfere with the findings of a Disciplinary Committee on such a matter as this, I could not myself possibly interfere.

However, in a case concerned with 'serious professional misconduct' alleged against a dentist (see s 27 of the Dentists Act 1984) the Privy Council, in 1987, doubted the relevance of the pre-1969 case law in interpreting the modern statutory provisions.

In *Doughty v General Dental Council* [1988] AC 164, [1987] 3 All ER 843 Lord Mackay of Clashfern said:

This is an appeal from a decision of the Professional Conduct Committee of the General Dental Council on 12 March 1987 that the appellant had been guilty of serious professional misconduct in relation to three charges and that his name should be erased from the Dentists Register. The three charges in question were:

That being a registered dentist: (1) Between 10th January and 26th October 1984 you accepted 19 patients, whose names and addresses are shown on List 'A' [which is attached to the charge] for dental treatment as National Health Service patients, and thereafter provided them with dental treatment in the course of which, having obtained radiographs of these patients, you: (a) Failed to retain those radiographs for a reasonable period of time after completion of the treatment; (b) Failed to submit those radiographs to the Dental Estimates Board when required to do so by a letter from the Board dated 27th November, 1984. (2) Between 5th June and 16th November, 1984, you accepted 6 patients, whose names and addresses are shown on List 'B' [which is attached to the charge] for dental treatment as National Health Service patients and thereafter provided them with dental treatment in the course of which you failed to exercise a proper degree of skill and attention. (3) Between 21st August and 5th October, 1984, you accepted 4 patients, whose names and addresses are shown on List 'C' [which is attached to the charge] for dental treatment as National Health Service patients, and thereafter provided them with dental treatment in the course of which you failed satisfactorily to complete the treatment required by the patients . . . And that in relation to the facts alleged in each of the above charges you have been guilty of serious professional misconduct.

. . . The committee announced their decision in the following terms:

In relation to the facts alleged in head 1 of the charge which have been admitted, the Committee finds that you have been guilty of serious professional misconduct. In relation to the facts alleged against you in charge 2 in respect of the five remaining patients and in charge 3 in respect of the three remaining patients, the Committee finds that you have been guilty of serious professional misconduct.

The committee directed that the appellant's name be erased from the Dentists Register.

. . .

The next point taken by counsel for the appellant was that in order to prove charges 2 and 3 it was necessary to show that the opinion held by the appellant in relation to the treatment was not honestly held by him and could not honestly be held by a dentist. This submission was founded principally on the observations of Lord Jenkins when giving the judgment of this Board in *Felix v General Dental Council* [1960] 2 All ER 391 at 400, [1960] AC 704 at 721:

With respect to the treatment alleged to have been unnecessary, the evidence (as their Lordships have already observed) showed that, according to the appellant, he honestly believed it to be necessary (or likely to be found necessary) while the dentists who disagreed with him did not claim that the opinion expressed by the appellant was one which no dentist could honestly hold. In this state of the evidence, their Lordships think it would be wrong to impute to the Disciplinary Committee an implied finding to the effect that the appellant did not honestly hold that opinion. An honestly held opinion, even if wrong, in their Lordships' view plainly cannot amount to infamous or disgraceful conduct.

Counsel for the council submitted that the evidence was sufficient to entitle the committee both to hold the facts alleged in charges 2 and 3 proved so far as they had done so and also to hold that those facts constituted serious professional misconduct.

In consideration the applicability of Lord Jenkins' observations to the circumstances of the present appeal, it has to be noted that Lord Jenkins was speaking of a case in which dishonesty was very much the issue and in the context of the statutory provision which was the basis of the proceedings in *Felix v General Dental Council*, namely s 25 of the Dentists Act 1957. So far as relevant it was in these terms:

(1) A registered dentist who either before or after registration . . . (*b*) has been guilty of any infamous or disgraceful conduct in a professional respect, shall be liable to have his name erased from the register . . .

At that time this was the only penalty available in respect of such conduct. The Dentists Act 1983, s 15(1), provided:

For section 25(1) of the [1957] Act (erasure from register for crime or infamous conduct) there shall be substituted—'(1) A registered dentist who (whether before or after registration) . . . (*b*) has been guilty of serious professional misconduct, shall be liable to have his name erased from the register, or to have his registration in it suspended, in accordance with section 26(3) of this Act . . .'

The suspension referred to is suspension for such period not exceeding 12 months as may be specified in the committee's determination. Counsel for the appellant suggests that this change in language was not intended to effect a change in substance. In *R v General Council of Medical Education and Registration of the UK* [1930] 1 KB 562 at 569, referring to the statutory provision there applicable, namely 'infamous conduct in a professional respect', Scrutton LJ said:

It is a great pity that the word 'infamous' is used to describe the conduct of a medical practitioner who advertises. As in the case of the Bar so in the medical profession advertising is serious misconduct in a professional respect and that is all that is meant by the phrase 'infamous conduct'; it means no more than serious misconduct judged according to the rules written or unwritten governing the profession.

In the General Medical Council's booklet entitled *Professional Conduct and Discipline: Fitness to Practice* (1985) the council stated: 'In proposing the substitution of the expression "serious professional misconduct" for the phrase "infamous conduct in a professional respect" the Council intended that the phrases should have the same significance.'

Their Lordships readily accept that what was infamous or disgraceful conduct in a professional respect would also constitute serious professional misconduct but they consider that it would not be right to require the council to establish now that the conduct complained of was infamous or disgraceful and therefore not right to apply the criteria which Lord Jenkins derived from the dictionary definitions of these words which he quoted in *Felix v General Dental Council*. Their Lordships consider it relevant, in reaching a conclusion on whether Parliament intended by the change of wording to make a change of substance, to notice that in addition to this change and in close conjunction with it the additional and much less severe penalty of suspension for a period not exceeding 12 months was provided. Further, in terms of s 1(2) of the Dentists Act 1984, which is the statute presently applicable, 'It shall be the general concern of the Council to promote high standards of dental education at all its stages and high standards of professional conduct among dentists . . .' In the light of these considerations, in their Lordships' view what is now required is that the council should establish conduct connected with his profession in which the dentist concerned has fallen short, by omission or commission, of the standards of conduct expected among dentists and that such falling short as is established should be serious. On an appeal to this Board, the Board has the responsibility of deciding whether the committee were entitled to take the view that the evidence established that there had been a falling short of these standards and were also entitled to take the view that such falling short as was established was serious.

In the present case the three charges of serious professional misconduct of which the appellant has been found guilty do not impute any dishonesty on his part. It was not suggested that he was carrying out unnecessary treatments for the purpose of enhancing his remuneration. What was suggested was that, judged by proper professional standards in the light of the objective facts about the individual patients that were presented in evidence to the committee, the dental treatments criticised as unnecessary would be treatments that no dentist of reasonable skill exercising reasonable care would carry out. It was for the committee with their expertise in this matter to judge as between the witnesses called by the council and the appellant, who had every opportunity to give his own reasons and explanations for what he did, and to judge whether the allegation was made out subject to the matter already dealt with in relation to charge 3. The point taken by counsel for the appellant at this stage of his submission was pressed primarily in relation to the criticisms of the appellant's treatment as unnecessary. With regard to the other criticisms it appears to their Lordships that the failures admitted in relation to charge 1 and admitted in part and proved to a further extent in relation to charge 2 and proved in relation to charge 3 amounted to professional misconduct. Whether the misconduct was serious depended on a number of factors, for example in relation to charge 1 on the number of patients in respect of whom the failure occurred and the importance of preserving the record for the well being of the patient and as a basis for decision on future treatment of the patient. In relation to charges 2 and 3 the seriousness of the conduct depended on the appreciation of such factors as the number of patients involved, the number of treatments criticised in relation to each patient and particularly in relation to unsatisfactory treatments, and the nature and extent of the failure to complete the treatment properly. On all of these matters the committee were particularly well qualified to reach a view and their Lordships see no reason to disagree with their findings.

Lord Mackay proposes a two-stage test, requiring the PCC to ask itself two questions:
1. Did the doctor's conduct fall short, by act or omission, of the standards of conduct expected among doctors? If yes, then:
2. Was this falling short 'serious'?
Question 1 relates to a finding of 'professional misconduct' and question 2 relates to a finding that it is 'serious'. How does Lord Mackay's approach differ from that adopted by a court in an action for medical negligence? This is a very important question because the GMC could well be urged in the future to consider cases of medical negligence as being within its jurisdiction. The GMC itself takes the following view in paragraph 38 of its 'blue book'.

38.   The Council is concerned with errors in diagnosis or treatment, and with the kind of matters which give rise to action in the civil courts for negligence, only when the doctor's conduct in the case has involved such a disregard of his professional responsibility to patients or such a neglect of his professional duties as to raise a question of serious professional misconduct . . .

The GMC thus distinguishes between misconduct which is merely negligent (and not within its jurisdiction) and misconduct which is both negligent and serious (which is within its jurisdiction). Do you think this reflects Lord Mackay's approach?

Clearly, there must be cases of negligence which do amount to 'serious professional misconduct'. The GMC, also in paragraph 38 of its 'blue book', gives an illustration.

. . . A question of serious professional misconduct may also arise from a complaint or information about the conduct of a doctor which suggests that he has endangered the welfare of patients by persisting in unsupervised practice of a branch of medicine in which he does not have the appropriate knowledge and skill and has not acquired the experience which is necessary.

However, do paragraph 38 and the opinion of Lord Mackay in *Doughty* support the view that medical negligence will *necessarily* amount to 'serious professional misconduct'? The distinction was emphasised in an earlier decision of the Privy Council not mentioned by Lord Mackay in *Doughty*, namely: *McEniff v General Dental Council* [1980] 1 All ER 461, [1980] 1 WLR 328.

Facts: The defendant, a dentist, was found guilty of 'infamous or disgraceful conduct in a professional respect' (s 25 of the Dentists Act 1957) and his name was erased from the register. He had allowed unqualified members of his staff to insert fillings after he had drilled his patients' teeth. He appealed, arguing that the legal assessor had wrongly advised the Disciplinary Committee to the GDC in law. The legal assessor had said:

> As far as what constitutes infamous or disgraceful conduct is concerned, to which both advocates have referred, for me the words of Scrutton LJ of *serious* misconduct in a professional respect mean quite plainly that it is for the committee, applying their own knowledge and experience, to decide what is the appropriate standard each practitioner should adhere to, not a special standard greater than is ordinarily to be expected, but the ordinary standard of the profession. I think I have said very little that is in any way new to any member of the committee, but having regard to the submissions made to you I thought I ought at least to say what I have said.

Was this wrong in law? Lord Edmund-Davies on behalf of the Privy Council said:

> These observations have been criticised as wrong in law in that they failed to draw a distinction between mere negligent conduct and infamous or disgraceful conduct. The submission is that there was a misdirection, in that, although in his opening remarks counsel for the General Dental Council had made passing reference to *Felix v General Dental Council*, the legal assessor failed to remind the disciplinary committee of an important passage in the speech of Lord Jenkins, who, in delivering the judgment of this Board in that case, said:
>
> > Granted that ... the full derogatory force of the adjectives 'infamous' and 'disgraceful' in s 25 of the Act of 1957 must be qualified by the consideration that what is being judged is the conduct of a dentist in a professional respect, which falls to be judged in relation to the accepted ethical standards of his profession, it appears to their Lordships that these two adjectives nevertheless remain as terms denoting *conduct deserving of the strongest reprobation*, and, indeed, so heinous as to merit, when proved, the extreme professional penalty of striking-off. (Emphasis mine.)
>
> Although the facts in *Felix v General Dental Council* were quite unlike those of the present case, these observations are of compelling significance. For it has respectfully to be said that although prolonged veneration of the oft-quoted words of Lopes LJ has clothed them with an authority approaching that of a statute, they are not particularly illuminating. It is for this reason that their Lordships regard Lord Jenkins' exposition as so valuable that, without going so far as to say that his words should invariably be cited in every disciplinary case, they think that to do so would be a commendable course. But having said that, it has to be added that the committee in the instant case were duly reminded of decisions which have long been approved of by this Board as accurately stating the relevant law. And their Lordships have in mind in this context the following observations of Lord Guest in *Sivarajah v General Medical Council*:
>
> > The committee are masters both of the law and of the facts. Thus what might amount to a misdirection in law by a judge to a jury at a criminal trial does not necessarily invalidate the committee's decision. The question is whether it can 'fairly be thought to have been of sufficient significance to the result to invalidate the Committee's decision'.
>
> In their Lordships' judgment, it cannot be said that the advice tendered by the legal assessor in this case contained such a defect, and the first ground of criticism must therefore be rejected.

Notice, in *McEniff*, which was a case concerned with the statute which pre-dated the Dentists Act 1984, that the Privy Council expressly approved Lord Jenkins' approach in *Felix* (contrast Lord Mackay in *Doughty*). Do you think that Lord Mackay may have overemphasised the 'dishonesty' requirement in Lord Jenkins' speech? (See, for example, the view of Lord Parker CJ in *Marten v Royal College of Veterinary Surgeons' Disciplinary Committee* [1965] 1 All ER 949 at 951.)

Mr David Bolt, a surgeon (and a frequent chairman of the PCC) offered an explanation in a lecture to the Medico-Legal Society in 1986, 'Dealing With Errors of Clinical Judgment' (1986) 54 Medico-Legal J 220, 229–30.

> If you go back to the 1979 Blue Book you will find that it says:
>> The General Medical Council is not concerned with errors of diagnosis or treatment.
>
> That was a very clear position. However, if you take the 1985 Book, you will find that it is now saying something slightly different. It is saying:
>> The Council is concerned with errors in diagnosis or treatment and with the kind of matters which give rise to action in the Civil Courts for negligence, only when the doctor's conduct in the case has involved such a disregard of his professional responsibility to patients or such a neglect of his professional duties as to raise a question of serious professional misconduct.
>
> I do not want to labour it too much, but from the same page perhaps I could just read you the little list of the things that the General Medical Council reminds doctors that the public now are entitled to expect from registered medical practitioners. They include 'Conscientious assessment of the history, symptoms and signs of a patient's condition. Sufficiently thorough professional attention, examination and, where necessary, diagnostic investigation. Competent and considerate professional management. Appropriate and prompt action upon evidence suggesting the existence of a condition requiring urgent medical intervention and readiness, where circumstances so warrant, to consult appropriate professional colleagues'.
>
> That, taken altogether, is a fairly strong statement of what the General Medical Council expects of doctors in this context. It is fair, I think, to say that it is a field which is only just developing, because the terms that I have read to you have not been in the Blue Book for more than a short time. The difficulty that we have in looking at cases is that if what you are looking at is an isolated event in the career of an otherwise estimable doctor, it would seem to me very wrong and stupid that the profession should be seeking to take major action on that account. If, on the other hand, what you are looking at seems to you to be just a particular event in, shall we say, a pattern of practice which is casual and unconcerned and careless and generally inferior and shabby, then the Professional Conduct Committee may feel that this merits more substantial action.
>
> It is always very difficult to know what form such action should take. Obviously, if you think that all you are looking at is a failure of understanding of a limited field of medicine, then imposing some kind of condition which would lead to a better understanding of that field upon the doctor's freedom to practise may be justified. But if you are looking at, shall we say, a general standard of practice, it is really terribly difficult. You do not necessarily improve the standard of a doctor's practice by taking him out of the practice altogether. This is why very often, let us say, it is seen by the public that the Professional Conduct Committee acts less strongly than might be justified.

(b) Types of conduct amounting to serious professional misconduct

What types of conduct are capable of being 'serious professional misconduct'? The GMC's 'blue book' (Part II) provides some guidance. The following are listed:

(i)   Neglect or disregard of personal responsibilities to patients for their care and treatment.

This seems to include the 'serious' cases of medical negligence and improper delegations of duties to others to which we have referred.

(ii)   Abuse of professional privileges or skills.

This includes unlawfully prescribing controlled drugs, issuing medical certificates and performing abortions. It also includes breaches of medical confidentiality, the exercise of undue influence on patients and sexual relationships with patients.

(iii)   Personal behaviour which is derogatory to the reputation of the medical profession.

This includes personal misuse or abuse of alcohol or drugs, dishonest behaviour and indecent or violent behaviour.

(iv)   Self-promotion, advertising and canvassing.

These, of course, are only illustrations because as paragraph 68 of the 'blue book' reminds us:

> [I]t must be emphasised that the categories of misconduct described in Part II cannot be regarded as exhaustive. Any abuse by a doctor of any of the privileges and the opportunities afforded to him, or any grave dereliction of professional duty or serious breach of medical ethics, may give rise to a charge of serious professional misconduct.

Do you think that the GMC's powers are sufficiently wide?

What role should the Privy Council (on appeal from the PCC) play in setting *legal* limits to the conduct which is capable of being 'serious professional misconduct'? In considering this question, notice the following observations made by the Privy Council in appeals from the PCC.

In *McCoan v General Medical Council* [1964] 3 All ER 143, [1964] 1 WLR 1107 the Privy Council was concerned with a doctor who had been erased from the register following a finding of 'infamous or disgraceful conduct in a professional respect' after he had carried on a sexual relationship with one of his patients. Lord Upjohn said:

> One of the most fundamental duties of a medical adviser, recognised for as long as the profession has been in existence, is that a doctor must never permit his professional relationship with a patient to deteriorate into an association which would be described by responsible medical opinion as improper. It is for this reason that the Medical Acts have always entrusted the supervision of the medical advisers' conduct to a committee of the profession, for they know and appreciate better than anyone else the standards which responsible medical opinion demands of its own profession. Sexual intercourse with a patient has always been regarded as a most serious breach of the proper relationship between doctor and patient and their lordships do not see how the finding of the committee, on the facts of this case, that the appellant was guilty of infamous conduct in a professional respect can be successfully challenged before their lordships.

Similarly, in *Tamesby v General Medical Council* (20 July 1970, unreported) the Privy Council was concerned with a doctor who was found guilty and whose name was erased from the register because he had advertised abortion services. Lord Pearson said: '[i]n a matter of this kind the decision of the Disciplinary Committee, composed of members of the same profession, must carry weight'.

It seems clear, therefore, that the Privy Council is reluctant to interfere with a finding of 'serious professional misconduct' by the PCC. Only if it can be shown that something has clearly gone wrong at the hearing, whether in the legal principles adopted (or as applied to the facts), or in the procedure itself, will the Privy Council intervene.

Brazier, in *Medicine, Patients and the Law* (pp 11–12), is moved to observe that 'there is a widespread suspicion that doctors who fail their patients are let off lightly'. She then calls for a re-evaluation of the traditional approach of the GMC.

> At the heart of the dilemma lies the notion that it is not negligence, nor an isolated failure in caring, that constitutes serious misconduct. The doctor's action or inaction must bring the profession into disrepute. Hence the emphasis the Council places on adultery and alcoholism. The Council should respond to public feeling. In 1987 the doctor who fails to visit a dying child, brushes off a sick patient as neurotic or neglects the elderly brings greater dishonour to medicine than the occasional adulterer.

Do you agree that a doctor who ordinarily is competent, but behaves in an incompetent manner in an isolated incident should be exposed to a procedure which could result in his being prevented from practising medicine? On the other hand is an action in negligence sufficient to meet the needs of the aggrieved patient and protect the public interest, both in holding the doctor to account and seeking to ensure that mistakes are not made again, particularly bearing in mind the observations made earlier about actions in negligence?

In view of the doubts these questions raise, it has been proposed that the GMC's powers should not be restricted to 'serious professional misconduct'. In 1983, Nigel Spearing MP introduced the Medical Act 1983 (Amendment) Bill to widen the powers of the GMC. It provided:

> **1.** Section 36 of the Medical Act 1983 shall have effect with the addition of the following new subsection—
> '(10) Where a fully registered person is judged by the Professional Conduct Committee to have behaved in a manner which cannot be regarded as acceptable professional conduct the Committee may, if they think fit, direct that the registration shall be made conditional in accordance with the foregoing subsection of this section.'

The Bill would have removed one barrier which some argue makes it undesirable for the GMC to consider merely negligent conduct, namely that, under the current legislation, the doctor faces (potentially at least) the severe sanction of having his name erased from the register. The argument behind the Bill was that if the GMC had only the lesser sanction available to it, that of making the doctor's registration 'conditional', it could then take jurisdiction over conduct that was itself less serious without the inappropriate threat of erasure being present.

The Bill never became law. The GMC resisted its enactment and set up a Working Party in 1984 under the chairmanship of Sir Douglas Black. The Working Party set out the GMC's objections in paragraph 6 of its report.

> (a) The amendment could result in confusion and injustice because it would allow the lesser offence of unacceptable conduct to carry a more severe penalty than may be imposed in cases of the greater offence of serious professional misconduct.
> (b) Enactment of the Bill would create judicial difficulty. It would be impracticable for the PCC to maintain a consistent and fair distinction between the lesser and greater offences. The single criterion of serious professional misconduct is well understood as conduct which a doctor's colleagues would regard as disgraceful or dishonourable.
> (c) The formal creation of a new, lesser offence would inevitably encourage defence lawyers to urge the PCC to find that the proven facts amounted to unacceptable rather than serious professional misconduct. Experience has shown that the

arguments of defence lawyers can be cogent and persuasive. As case law accrued, the standards maintained by the GMC could be eroded, to the detriment of the public interest.

(d) The Bill is unnecessary. Mr Spearing suggested use of conditional registration to require a doctor to reappear at a later date citing referees from whom the Committee can obtain confidential reports on the doctor's conduct in the interval. The PCC already has the power to achieve that end by postponing its finding whether a doctor is guilty of serious professional misconduct until a resumed hearing when further evidence about the doctor's conduct in the interim is heard, although this power is rarely used.

Enactment of the Bill would therefore be detrimental to the disciplinary procedure of the Council and it would inevitably result in a much greater proportion of cases being referred for formal inquiry.

The outcome of the GMC's deliberations was an amendment to the 'blue book' contained in what is now paragraph 36. We have already seen this quoted by Mr David Bolt earlier but we repeat it here because of its importance.

36. The public are entitled to expect that a registered medical practitioner will afford and maintain a good standard of medical care. This includes:

    (*a*) conscientious assessment of the history, symptoms and signs of a patient's condition;

    (*b*) sufficiently thorough professional attention, examination and, where necessary, diagnostic investigation;

    (*c*) competent and considerate professional management;

    (*d*) appropriate and prompt action upon evidence suggesting the existence of a condition requiring urgent medical intervention; and

    (*e*) readiness, where the circumstances so warrant, to consult appropriate professional colleagues.

Brazier, *op cit*, comments on these developments (pp 12–13):

. . . [T]he guidelines still beg the question as to when departure from the standards set constitutes *serious* misconduct. No solid guidance by way of illustrative example is given to answer criticism that the GMC is too ready to find there has been misconduct, and admonish the doctor, rather than categorising his conduct as serious; and unless serious misconduct is proved the GMC has no power to take any positive steps to punish the doctor and/or protect other patients.

The GMC has responded to public concern. It has acted on a number of malpractices, notably unsafe prescribing practices. And doctors who failed to warn the parents of a child who died of the dangers of the surgery agreed to were suspended swiftly. Have they yet done enough?

What is your answer to Brazier's concluding question?

(Notice that in May 1987 the GMC set up a Working Party to consider 'Disciplinary Procedure in Relation to Allegations of Failure to Provide a Good Standard of Medical Care'.)

2.   COMPLAINTS AGAINST GENERAL PRACTITIONERS WITHIN THE NHS

General practitioners are, of course, subject to the disciplinary jurisdiction of the GMC. However, most complaints brought against a GP are not made to the GMC. Instead, they are investigated within the framework of procedures set up by the National Health Service (Service Committees and Tribunal) Regulations 1974 (SI 1974 No 455). Under these procedures, complaints are investigated and dealt with by the Family Practitioner Committee (FPC). In fact, the FPC's functions are performed by a sub-committee known as the

Medical Service Committee (MSC). The main features of the procedures can be summarised as follows.

1. A complaint must relate to a breach by the GP of his terms of service as laid down in the National Health Service (General Medical and Pharmaceutical Services) Regulations 1974, Schedule 1 (SI 1974 No 160). We have already seen some of these statutory provisions earlier. A complaint may relate to a breach of any of the paragraphs. In practice, complaints commonly centre around breaches of paragraphs 3 and 13 (see *General Practice Complaints Procedure* (1983), published by the Medical Protection Society), which read as follows:

> 3. Where a decision whether any, and if so what, action is to be taken under these terms of service requires the exercise of professional judgment, a doctor shall in reaching that decision not be expected to exercise a higher degree of skill, knowledge and care than general practitioners as a class may reasonably be expected to exercise.

> 13. Subject to paragraph 3, a doctor shall render to his patients all necessary and appropriate medical services of the type usually provided by general medical practitioners. He shall do so at his practice premises or, if the condition of the patient so requires, elsewhere in his practice area or at the place where the patient was residing when accepted by the doctor or, if a patient was on the list of a practice declared vacant, when the doctor succeeded to the vacancy, or at some other place where the doctor has agreed to visit and treat him if the patient's condition so requires, and has informed the patient and the Committee accordingly. The doctor shall not be required to visit and treat the patient at any other place. Such services include arrangements for referring patients as necessary to any other services provided under the Health Service Acts and advice to enable them to take advantage of the local authority social services. Except in an emergency, this paragraph shall not impose an obligation on the doctor to provide maternity medical services unless he has undertaken to do so.

These paragraphs embody a duty competently to treat and diagnose patients (ic in accordance with the *Bolam* test) and an obligation relating to visiting them. A breach of this latter obligation is a common type of complaint.

2. A complaint may be made by the FPC itself. Usually, however, the complainant is the GP's patient or someone authorised to act on his behalf. In the case of those who are incapable of bringing a complaint through old age, sickness or infirmity, or if the patient is under 18, anyone may bring the complaint.

3. A complaint must be made within eight weeks of the event giving rise to the complaint and it must set out the substance of the matter which is to be investigated (regulation 4). Late complaints may be considered if the failure to comply with the time limits is due to illness or other reasonable cause and the consent of the GP or the Secretary of State is obtained (regulation 5).

4. A complaint must be in writing (regulation 4). When made a complaint will be investigated either by the informal procedure or the more formal procedure.

5. The informal procedure arose out of an agreement between the medical profession and the DHSS. It is not contained within the Regulations. The procedure aims at conciliation. It does not permit any sanctions to be taken against the GP. Indeed, there can be no finding that he has been in breach of his terms of service. The procedure involves the appointment of an individual (usually a lay member of the FPC) to conciliate between the parties.

6. The formal procedure is more common. The procedure is set out in Schedule 1 to the 1974 Regulations. A preliminary filtering of complaints is carried out by the Chairman of the MSC. If he considers there is no case to answer and has given the complainant an opportunity to comment, the complaint will simply be referred to the MSC for report to the FPC and it will be dismissed. In its

publication, *General Practice Complaints Procedure*, the Medical Protection Society points out that it is at this stage that many complaints fail. The Society gives a common example (p 6):

> . . . [I]t is not part of the Terms of Service that one must be polite to a patient and if a complaint merely raises an allegation of bad manners or rudeness on the doctor's part then whatever anyone may think about it the allegation is not one for investigation by a MSC.

(Note: do you think it should be?)

7.   If there are reasonable grounds for believing that there is a case to answer, then written comments are sought from the doctor and further comments from the complainant. The Chairman of the MSC may decide that an oral hearing is unnecessary and the complaint will be brought before the MSC who will report their conclusions to the FPC to make a decision on the basis of the findings of fact by the MSC.

8.   If an oral hearing is considered necessary, both the doctor and patient may appear. Both may be assisted in the presentation of their case by another person, but a lawyer may not *conduct* the case on their behalf (regulation 7).

9.   The hearing is in private (regulation 8). The MSC reports to the FPC who may, amongst other things, do one of the following (regulation 10):

Where no breach of the terms of service is found, dismiss the complaint.

Where a breach is found,
(i)   limit the number of the doctor's patients;
(ii)   recommend to the Secretary of State:
    (a) that the doctor be warned to comply with the terms of service more closely in the future;
    (b) that a sum be withheld from the doctor's remuneration;
    (c) that any expenses reasonably and necessarily incurred by the patient be paid by the doctor.
(iii) recommend to the special tribunal set up under s 46 of the NHS Act 1977 that the continued inclusion of the doctor on the medical list would be prejudicial to the efficiency of the NHS's general medical services.

If the FPC does not act as recommended by the MSC, then reasons must be given.

10.   An appeal lies to the Secretary of State at the suit of either party against an adverse decision (regulation 11), or a doctor may, if the FPC has recommended withholding remuneration, make representations (which is not an appeal) to the Secretary of State (regulation 11(3)). The appeal is heard (if an oral hearing is considered necessary) in private by a panel consisting of an officer of the DHSS and up to three others one of whom must be (or must have been) a GP himself and the chairman will be a lawyer (regulation 12). At this hearing, the parties may be represented by lawyers. An oral hearing may not be dispensed with by the Secretary of State unless the FPC's decision was merely to warn the doctor or recommend to the special tribunal that his name be removed from the medical list. In all other cases, the doctor may demand an oral hearing (regulation 12(1)).

11.   If the FPC or the Secretary of State (on appeal) believes that the GP's conduct may amount to 'serious professional misconduct', then they refer the matter to the GMC.

12.   Both the FPC and the Secretary of State in exercising their functions under the 1974 Regulations are performing functions amenable to control by public law. Consequently, if a patient (or indeed a doctor) can establish that

they have misconstrued the Regulations (ie acted illegally), failed to act fairly (ie procedural impropriety) or acted unreasonably (ie irrationally) then a successful application for judicial review may be made to the High Court. This is so even though the decision of the Secretary of State is stated to be 'final and conclusive' (regulation 12(9); *R v Medical Appeal Tribunal, ex p Gilmore* [1957] 1 QB 574). It is, however, possible that a court might require an individual who was aggrieved by a decision of the FPC to exercise his right of appeal to the Secretary of State before the court would countenance judicial review proceedings. As with all such applications, the court is concerned only with the lawfulness of the FPC or Secretary of State's conduct or decision. It is not entitled to consider the merits of their decisions.

The detailed procedure of these hearings under the 1974 Regulations is beyond the scope of our book. Reference should be made to the 1974 Regulations and the Schedules thereto. Also the Medical Protection Society's book, referred to above, contains a helpful account.

The FPC complaints system is not without its critics. Brazier, *op cit*, comments (p 253):

> It seems loaded in the doctor's favour. The service committee will have at least three doctor members. Their privacy is guaranteed. The sanction of publicity only operates when a doctor suffers the ultimate penalty of removal from the list. It is alleged that the Family Practitioner Committees take a restrictive view of their powers, refusing to adjudicate on matters of clinical judgment. But striking the correct balance between patient and doctor is far from easy. Publicity in the early stages is not necessarily the answer. Perfectly innocent and conscientious doctors would suffer the 'no smoke without fire' syndrome. Legal aid and representation for patients would assist the less articulate. But where would the money come from? The heart of the problem lies perhaps in the many functions entrusted to the FPC. It is essentially an administrative body, a sort of unelected NHS local council. Its utility lies in improving the general working of the service, checking on deputising services, handling of night calls and so on. Whether such a multi-purpose body is the correct forum to investigate individual complaints needs further consideration by the government, the profession and patients.

The Government, aware of these arguments, produced in August 1986 a consultation document, *Family Practitioner Services: Complaints Investigation Procedures.* Subsequently, in its White Paper, *Promoting Better Health* (November 1987), the Government proposed a number of changes. The more important are as follows:

(i) to make the informal procedures adopted by some FPCs available in all cases;
(ii) to allow oral complaints;
(iii) to extend the time limits from eight to 13 weeks for lodging a complaint;
(iv) to ensure that in any hearing MSCs have equal numbers of lay and professional members;
(v) to give MSCs power to seek further particulars of the grounds for a complaint where thought necessary;
(vi) to give patients the right to be represented by a trade union official or Community Health Council representative.

3. COMPLAINTS AGAINST HOSPITAL DOCTORS WITHIN THE NHS

The 1974 Regulations and the procedures they lay down do not apply to hospital doctors. Complaints and disciplinary procedures are mainly derived either from the contract between the doctor and his employing health authority or from Government circulars.

The first matter to note is that there is as yet no statutory complaints procedure available to an aggrieved hospital patient. However, the Hospital Complaints Act 1985 contemplates that health authorities must introduce and publicise complaints procedures.

Section 1(1) provides:

1.—(1) It shall be the duty of the Secretary of State to give to each health authority in England and Wales and to each Health Board in Scotland such directions under section 17 of the National Health Service Act 1977 or section 2(5) of the National Health Service (Scotland) Act 1978 (directions as to exercise of functions) as appear to him necessary for the purpose of securing that, as respects each hospital for the management of which that authority or Board is responsible—

    (a) such arrangements are made for dealing with complaints made by or on behalf of persons who are or have been patients at that hospital; and

    (b) such steps are taken for publicising the arrangements so made,

as (in each case) are specified or described in the directions.

At present, however, the system of hospital complaints may be considered under two headings: (a) those not relating to the exercise of clinical judgment by a doctor; and (b) those which do relate to clinical judgment.

(a) Complaints not relating to clinical judgment

(i) Government circulars

HM (66) 15 issued by the DHSS in 1966 laid down a procedure for investigating these complaints. These provisions were amplified (but not replaced) in 1981 by HC (81) 5 as a result of the recommendations of a Committee, set up by the DHSS and chaired by Sir Michael Davies, on Hospital Complaints Procedures which reported in 1973. HC (81) 5 provides:

PART I—COMMUNICATIONS AND COMPLAINTS

Handling of minor criticisms

4.   Many matters that trouble patients can be dealt with as they arise. For example, minor criticisms about waiting time in an out-patient department, about meals or some aspect of nursing care on the ward, or some misunderstanding about arrangements for nursing services at a patient's home, can often be cleared up to the patient's satisfaction on the spot. Any comment or misgivings voiced by patients, even those which appear trivial, should be listened to sympathetically. It will frequently be possible for the member of staff to whom these are expressed, or the person in charge at the time, to provide an acceptable answer or explanation there and then. Where remedial action has been or is to be taken, its nature should be explained to the complainant. Most minor criticisms are dealt with in this way and, where this is so, and the complainant has expressed himself satisfied, no record of the matter need be kept at ward or department level, unless for any reason the member of staff who handles the complaint and sees the complainant feels that it would be desirable to do so.

Procedure for reporting complaints

5.   A formal complaint, which may be written or oral, is one which the complainant wishes to have investigated by senior staff and on which he wishes to have either a written reply from the authority or an oral explanation from the senior member of staff concerned. If a patient wants to make a formal complaint (where there may be any doubt, he should be asked) the following action should be taken (but see Paragraph 6 below where he wishes to complain in writing to the health authority):

i.   nurses and other non-medical staff should report the matter to the ward sister (or charge nurse, or equivalent person in a hospital department) who will inform the appropriate senior officer and tell the patient this has been done. Any clinical aspects of the complaint should be referred by the senior officer to the consultant concerned. In any case the senior officer should inform the consultant of *all* formal complaints about the treatment and care of patients in his charge.

ii.   medical and dental staff should report the matter to the consultant concerned, telling the patient that they are doing so.

PART II—INVESTIGATING PATIENTS' COMPLAINTS (OTHER THAN THOSE RELATING TO THE EXERCISE OF CLINICAL JUDGMENT BY HOSPITAL MEDICAL AND DENTAL STAFF)

(Note: This part is intended for all senior staff who may be expected to investigate complaints made by patients or on their behalf.)

Main principles

7.   The investigation of formal complaints is the responsibility of senior staff. Staff at ward sister (and equivalent) level or below, and junior medical and dental staff, should not be expected to investigate and reply to formal complaints although they may be asked to assist in an investigation by the senior member of staff responsible.

8.   The following should apply to the investigation of *all* complaints:

i.   All complaints should be investigated thoroughly and fairly and as quickly as circumstances permit. It should be remembered that the unsatisfactory handling of a complaint may become the cause of further complaint.

ii.   A member of staff investigating a complaint should keep the complainant and any persons complained about fully and promptiy informed of reasons for unavoidable delay in resolving the issue.

iii.   Any member of staff involved in a complaint should be fully informed of any allegations at the outset and given an opportunity to reply. He should be advised of his right to seek the help and advice of his professional association or trade union before commenting on a complaint.

9.   Legal advice should always be sought (preferably from the legal adviser to the regional health authority) when dealing with complaints which may lead to litigation. In particular, advice should be sought on matters to be investigated and in what form, so as to minimise the risk of prejudicing any civil proceedings. Legal proceedings or the likelihood of legal proceedings should not deter the authority from undertaking any immediate investigation that may be necessary, eg to uncover faults in procedures and prevent a recurrence.

. . .

Oral complaints

11.   A senior member of staff to whom a complaint is referred in accordance with Part I of this Memorandum should consider whether he may be able to resolve it by discussion with the complainant. He should make a note of any such discussion and its outcome, even if the complainant appears satisfied (in case the complaint is subsequently taken further). The note should be retained with the patient's records.

12.   If discussion fails to resolve the matter to the complainant's satisfaction, or if the senior member of staff concerned considers that the complaint is one that should be put into writing, then

either i.   the complainant should be advised to send a written complaint to the Area or District Health Authority at . . . . (address)

or ii.   *if the complainant is not willing or able to send a written complaint but wishes the matter to be pursued*, the senior member of staff dealing with the matter should arrange for a record of the complaint to be made and for the complainant to sign it. A complainant should be given a copy of any statement he is asked to sign. The complaint should then be dealt with in accordance with the principles set out in the following paragraphs.

Written complaints to the authority

13. Investigation of complaints made in writing to the authority should be co-ordinated by the district administrator (or other senior officer designated by the authority). The Chairman (or other designated member of the authority) should be informed in good time of any complaints that the authority under local arrangements has decided may require to be considered by the authority itself.

14. All complaints should be referred to the appropriate senior member(s) of staff (eg consultant, nursing officer, or head of department concerned) for investigation and report. The principles set out in Paragraph 8 above should be followed in all investigations.

Action following investigation

15. Following an investigation, any action to be taken and the reply to the complainant should be agreed between the district administrator (or other senior designated officer) and senior member(s) of staff concerned: if such agreement cannot be reached, the matter should be referred to the district management team who should agree a reply or refer the matter to the authority.

16. The reply should be sent by the district administrator on behalf of the authority unless a departure from this practice has been agreed by the authority and set out clearly in standing instructions. Where complaints raise matters of serious concern, the Chairman of the authority may on occasion wish to reply to them personally. The reply should explain any action taken or recommended or explain why no action is appropriate. It should be sympathetic in tone and avoid technical terms which the complainant may not understand. All members of staff involved in the complaint should be informed of the outcome.

17. If the complainant remains dissatisfied he should be advised to refer the complaint to the Health Service Commissioner unless the matter is clearly outside the Commissioner's jurisdiction.

We will return to the role of the Health Service Commissioner shortly. You will notice that, in effect, a four stage process is envisaged. First, minor complaints may be dealt with by a member of staff discussing the problem informally with the patient. Secondly, more serious complaints or minor ones concerning which the patient is not satisfied and wishes to persist with formally are investigated by a senior member of staff. Thirdly, a patient who is still not satisfied may then take his complaint to the relevant Regional Health Authority. Fourthly, if the patient remains unsatisfied he may make a complaint to the Health Service Commissioner.

Circular HM(66)15 contains a further procedure in paragraph 7(iii)(b) which allows for the appointment of an independent person or committee in very serious cases. Paragraph 7(iii)(b) provides:

... [I]n the small number of cases which are so serious that they cannot be dealt with satisfactorily in this way, ... the investigation should be referred for independent enquiry. Action to refer such cases should be taken by the Board of Governors or the Regional Hospital Board concerned on a reference from the Hospital Management Committee. The general rule should be that an independent lawyer or other competent person from outside the hospital service should conduct the enquiry, or preside over a small committee set up for the purpose, whose membership should be independent of the authority concerned and should include a person or persons competent to advise on any professional or technical matters. The complainant and any persons who are the subject of the complaint should have an opportunity of being present throughout the hearing, and of cross-examining witnesses, and should be allowed to make their own arrangements to be legally represented if they so wish.

(ii)   The Health Service Commissioner

We have referred above to the Health Service Commissioner (HSC). This office was created by (and the functions of the HSC are set out in) Part V of the National Health Service Act 1977. The HSC's functions are contained particularly in s 115:

115. A Commissioner may investigate—
 (a) an alleged failure in a service provided by a relevant body, or
 (b) an alleged failure of such a body to provide a service which it was a function of the body to provide, or
 (c) any other action taken by or on behalf of such a body,
in a case where a complaint is duly made by or on behalf of any person that he *has sustained injustice or hardship in consequence of the failure or in consequence of maladministration* connected with the other action.
 This section is subject to sections 110 and 113 above and section 116 below. (Our emphasis.)

(A 'relevant body' is defined in s 109 so as to include a Regional or District Health Authority and a Family Practitioner Committee.)
 Certain matters are beyond the jurisdiction of the HSC:

116.—(1) Except as hereafter provided, a Commissioner shall not conduct an investigation under this Part of this Act in respect of any of the following matters—
 (a) any action in respect of which the person aggrieved has or had a right of appeal, reference or review to or before a tribunal constituted by or under any enactment or by virtue of Her Majesty's prerogative, or
 (b) any action in respect of which the person aggrieved has or had a remedy by way of proceedings in any court of law,
but a Commissioner may conduct an investigation notwithstanding that the person aggrieved has or had such a right or remedy, if satisfied that in the particular circumstances it is not reasonable to expect him to resort or have resorted to it.
 (2) Without prejudice to subsection (1) above—
 (a) a Commissioner shall not conduct an investigation under this Part in respect of any such action as is described in Part II of Schedule 13 to this Act; and
 (b) nothing in sections 110, 113 and 115 above shall be construed as authorising such an investigation in respect of action taken in connection with any general medical services, general dental services, general ophthalmic services or pharmaceutical services by a person providing the services.

Schedule 13, Part II of the Act (referred to in s 116(2)(a)) also contains important exclusions. Paragraph 19 reads:

19. The following matters are not subject to investigation by the Health Service Commissioner for England or the Health Service Commissioner for Wales—
 (1) Action taken in connection with the diagnosis of illness or the care or treatment of a patient, being action which, in the opinion of the Commissioner in question, was taken solely in consequence of the exercise of clinical judgment, whether formed by the person taking the action or any other person.
 (2) Action taken by a Family Practitioner Committee in the exercise of its functions under the National Health Service (Service Committees and Tribunal) Regulations 1974, or any instrument amending or replacing those regulations.
 (3) Action taken in respect of appointments or removals, pay, discipline, superannuation or other personnel matters in relation to service under this Act.
 (4) Action taken in matters relating to contractual or other commercial transactions, other than in matters arising from arrangements between a relevant body and another body which is not a relevant body for the provision of services for patients by that other body; and in determining what matters arise from such arrangements there shall be disregarded any arrangements for the provision of services at an establishment maintained by a Minister of the Crown for patients who are mainly members of the armed forces of the Crown.
 (5) Action which has been, or is, the subject of an inquiry under section 84 above.

So, you can see that there are several important exclusions. They include cases in which the patient has a remedy in a court of law (unless it would not be reasonable to expect the patient to pursue this remedy), GPs' dealings with their patients, any action concerned with the diagnosis of illness or the care or treatment of a patient which involved the exercise of clinical judgment, and the performance of the FPC's functions under the 1974 Service Regulations.

Further, s 113 provides:

113.—(1) In determining whether to initiate, continue or discontinue an investigation under this Part of this Act, a Commissioner shall, subject to section 110 above and sections 115 and 116 below, act in accordance with his own discretion.

(2) Any question whether a complaint is duly made to a Commissioner under this Part shall be determined by the Commissioner.

It is doubtful whether this provision would exclude judicial review proceedings if the HSC misconstrued any part of the statutory provisions setting up his jurisdiction to investigate complaints. But, s 113 does suggest that the courts might regard certain issues, for example whether it is reasonable to expect a patient to sue, as a discretionary matter for the HSC, with the consequential effect of greatly curtailing the court's power of review.

Who may complain? Section 111 provides:

111.—(1) A complaint under this Part of this Act may be made by any individual, or by any body of persons whether incorporated or not, . . .

(2) Where the person by whom a complaint might have been made under the preceding provisions of this Part has died, or is for any reason unable to act for himself, the complaint may be made—

(a) by his personal representative, or

(b) by a member of his family, or

(c) by some body or individual suitable to represent him,

but, except as aforesaid and as provided by section 117 below, a complaint shall not be entertained under this Part unless made by the person aggrieved himself.

The Health Authority may also refer a complaint to the Commissioner if it was received by them from a person who alleges maladministration (section 117).

How is a complaint made? Section 114 provides:

114.—(1) A Commissioner—

(a) shall not entertain a complaint under this Part of this Act unless it is made in writing to him by or on behalf of the person aggrieved not later than one year from the day on which the person aggrieved first had notice of the matters alleged in the complaint, but

(b) may conduct an investigation pursuant to a complaint not made within that period if he considers it reasonable to do so.

Prior to investigating a complaint the Act (s 112) requires the HSC to:

(a) . . . satisfy himself that the complaint has been brought by or on behalf of the person aggrieved to the notice of the relevant body in question, and that that body had been afforded a reasonable opportunity to investigate and reply to the complaint, but

(b) a Commissioner shall disregard the provisions of paragraph (*a*) in relation to a complaint made by an officer of the relevant body in question on behalf of the person aggrieved if the officer is authorised by virtue of section 111(2) above to make the complaint and the Commissioner is satisfied that in the particular circumstances those provisions ought to be disregarded.

The procedure to be followed in any investigation is set out in Part I of Schedule 13 of the NHS Act 1977. Brazier, *op cit*, describes the investigation process (pp 128–9) (footnotes omitted).

His powers of inquiry are extensive. He and his staff investigate in private. They will contact all hospital staff involved with a complaint and seek their comments. The Commissioner has complete control of the investigation. If co-operation from hospital staff or administrators is not forthcoming, the production of records and documents may be ordered and staff may be compelled to testify to the Commissioner. Exceptionally evidence can be taken on oath, but this has happened only once so far to my knowledge. In that case the preliminary evidence from the parties had been totally irreconcilable. The Commissioner regretted this occasion. Successive Commissioners pride themselves on good relations with health service staff, rendering resort to powers of compulsion unnecessary.

On completion of an investigation the Commissioner reports to the complainant, the health authority, and any individual against whom allegations were made. The report will contain a decision as to whether the complaint was justified and recommend a remedy. In 1984–5 47 per cent of complaints investigated were found to be justified. The most common remedy is an apology from the authority and the staff member involved. Increasingly he recommends too that the DHSS and health authorities make changes in practice to avoid a recurrence of similar complaints. For example, in 1984–5 on the initiative of the Commissioner steps were taken to review procedures for writing to GPs on the patient's discharge, to improve communication with relatives and to improve monitoring of complaints procedures. Very occasionally the Commissioner may additionally recommend the making of an *ex gratia* cash payment to a patient by way of compensation. These are usually small sums, arising from cases where maladministration has resulted in loss of patients' property or unnecessary expenses. The Commissioner does not regard it as his function to grant monetary compensation for pain and hardship suffered by patients.

Two points arise for comment. First, what is the staple diet of the HSC? Secondly, since many instances of maladministration might result in litigation, how does the HSC interpret his power to investigate a complaint notwithstanding this possibility?

As to the first, again Brazier, *op cit*, describes his work (pp 129–31) (footnotes omitted).

Certain sorts of complaints recur. Waiting lists, lack of communication by medical staff, inadequate liaison with GPs, delay in attendance by doctors, and unsatisfactory supervision of the elderly and vulnerable appear again and again. Maternity and geriatric care seem to generate a disproportionate number of complaints. Rudeness, lack of sympathy and even in extreme cases allegations of assault by staff cause the Commissioner much concern.

The Annual Report for 1984–5 identifies six topics which have caused the Commissioner particular concern. They are (1) care and supervision of the elderly and handicapped, (2) contents and use of medical records, (3) delay in doctors attending patients, (4) arrangements made for discharge from hospital, (5) recording and investigation of alleged assaults, and (6) the initial handling of complaints by hospitals.

. . . Other complaints related to failures to record information about patients, especially when it came from the patient himself. . . .

Two other topics of 1984–5, delay in doctors attending and inadequate arrangements for discharge, again have a common and disturbing cause. . . .

The concerns of the Commissioner in 1984–5 echo familiar themes from the previous eleven years. Other areas which have generated complaints of particular importance include failing to tell patients of their right to object to the presence of medical students, inadequate explanations when obtaining consent to surgery, failing to listen to the patient, and many others in a catalogue illustrating the importance to the patient of being treated as an intelligent individual. Other complaints arise from sheer mismanagement. Dentures get lost. Special diets are ignored, and so on. A number of disquiets arise from the lack of resources. Waiting lists for hip replacements have been investigated by the Commissioner several times.

As to the second point, the HSC has taken a relatively relaxed view. He has investigated cases in which lack of consent or negligence have been the issue. Sometimes, he has agreed to investigate if the patient has undertaken not to pursue any legal action. But, since this is not legally binding, the patient may still pursue a claim in law. If he does so, of course, the patient will have the benefit of the investigatory process of the HSC and his findings. Do you think it is within the HSC's powers to investigate a complaint, given the terms of s 116, in this sort of case? How could his decision to investigate be challenged and by whom?

(b)   Complaints relating to clinical judgment

Until 1981, there was no DHSS circular which dealt with a complaints procedure in cases in which *clinical judgment* was an issue. HC(81)15 Part III now deals with this. It sets up a procedure which has three stages. Stage 1 involves an informal process to be conducted by the consultant in charge of the patient's case. Stage 2 involves a more formal process, if the patient remains dissatisfied. Again, the consultant is involved but so also is the Regional Medical Officer. Stage 3 sets up a review procedure whereby 'second opinions' are obtained from two independent consultants in active practice in the relevant speciality, nominated by the Joint Consultants Committe. HC(81)5 provides as follows (footnotes omitted):

First stage
18. As explained in Paragraph 5 of Part I, a complaint may initially be made, and dealt with, orally or in writing. Complaints concerning clinical matters may be made direct to the consultant concerned, or to a health authority or one of its officers. In either case it is the responsibility of the consultant in charge of the patient to look into the clinical aspects of the complaint. This must be the first step in handling the complaint at the *first stage*.
19. If another member of the medical staff is involved, the consultant should discuss the complaint with the doctor concerned, at the outset and at all later stages in this procedure. It may be helpful to discuss the complaint with the patient's general practitioner. The consultant should try to resolve the complaint within a few days preferably by offering to see the complainant to discuss the matter and seek to resolve his anxieties. If there is any delay, he should get in touch with the complainant and explain the reason. When the consultant sees the complainant, he should make a brief, strictly factual, record in the hospital notes.
20. Where a complaint is made which involves hospital medical staff other than consultants, the consultant in charge of the patient and the doctor concerned should both be involved in the handling of the complaint at all stages.
21. If the consultant feels the risk of legal action is significant, he should at once bring the matter to the notice of the district administrator. Where there are non-clinical aspects to a complaint made direct to a consultant, the consultant should inform the district administrator, who will arrange for these aspects of the complaint to be considered by an appropriate member of staff.
22. Where a complaint which has a clinical element is made to the authority or one of its officers, the district administrator should show the complaint to the consultant concerned and refer the clinical aspects to him.
23. The normal practice will be for the district administrator to send a written reply

to the complainant on behalf of the authority. Any reference to clinical matters in the reply, whether interim or final, should be agreed by the consultant concerned. Sometimes it may be appropriate to confine this to mentioning that the clinical aspects had been discussed between the consultant and the complainant. On occasion, the consultant may wish to send the complainant a written reply direct covering the clinical aspects.

Second stage
24. Where a complainant is dissatisfied with the reply he has received at the first stage, he may renew his complaint either to the authority, one of its administrators or to the consultant. In any case, if he has not so far put his complaint in writing, he should now be asked to do so before his complaint is considered further. The next step, *in this second stage*, is for the Regional Medical Officer (RMO) to be at once informed; this should be done by the consultant, informing the district administrator that he has done so. The RMO will discuss the matter with the consultant.
25. At this point, the consultant may indicate to the RMO that he also wishes to discuss the matter with his professional colleagues. After these discussions, he may consider that a further talk with the complainant might resolve the complaint. If this fails, or if the consultant feels that such a meeting would serve no useful purpose, the RMO should discuss with the consultant the value of offering to the complainant the procedure—outlined more fully below—whereby the RMO would arrange for two independent consultants to see the complainant jointly to discuss the problem. If in the light of his discussion with the consultant and—where necessary—the complainant, the RMO considers it appropriate, the procedure of the *third stage* should be set in motion.

Third stage—independent professional review
26. The procedure at the third stage is intended to deal with complaints which are of a substantial nature, but which are not prima facie (and in the light of legal advice where appropriate) likely to be the subject of more formal action either by the health authority or through the courts. The procedure is intended for use in suitable instances as an alternative to the inquiry procedures provided in HM(66)15, though these will remain available for use when necessary. It would not be appropriate if legal powers such as subpoena seem likely to be required. Nor is it intended that the new procedure should be invoked for complaints of a trivial nature.
27. Arrangements should be made by the RMO for all aspects of the case to be considered by two independent consultants in active practice in the appropriate speciality or specialities. They should be nominated by the Joint Consultants Committee. At least one should be a doctor working in a comparable hospital in another Region. These 'second opinions' should have the opportunity to read all the clinical records. They should discuss the case with the consultant concerned and any other member of the medical staff involved as well as with the complainant. The meeting between the two independent consultants and the complainant should be in the nature of a medical consultation. The consultant who had been in charge of the patient at the time of the event giving rise to the complaint should not be present at the meeting, but should be available if required. The complainant should if he wishes, be accompanied by a relative or personal friend and might wish to ask the general practitioner to be present.
28. 'Second opinions' should discuss the clinical aspects of the problem fully with the complainant. In cases in which it is their view that the clinical judgment of the medical staff concerned has been exercised responsibly, they should endeavour to resolve the complainant's anxieties. The view they have reached and the outcome of the discussion with the complainant should be reported to the RMO on a confidential basis.
29. In other cases the 'second opinions' might feel that discussion with the medical staff concerned would avoid similar problems arising in the future, when they had held such a discussion they would inform the complainant and would explain to him, as far as appropriate, how it was hoped to overcome the problems which had been identified. They should not provide a detailed report for the complainant but

they should report the action they had taken to the RMO. The 'second opinions' would also consider whether there were any other circumstances which had contributed to the problems in the case and on which they could usefully make recommendations, which they would include in their report to the RMO. These might include matters requiring action by the health authority, for example the workload carried by the medical or nursing staff.

30. In exceptional cases it may appear to the 'second opinions', at any stage of an investigation, that the particular case is not appropriate to the second opinions procedure and that the complaint would be best pursued by alternative means. In this event they should report to the RMO accordingly.

Concluding action by the health authority

31. The district administrator will, on completion of the review by the 'second opinions', write formally to the complainant on behalf of the authority, with a copy to the consultant. The district administrator will, where appropriate, explain any action the authority has taken as a result of the complaint but, where clinical matters are concerned, he will follow the RMO's advice regarding the comment which would be appropriate. So far as the authority is concerned the matter will remain confidential unless previous or subsequent publicity makes it essential for the authority to reply publicly, in which case comment on clinical matters will be confined to the terms of the district administrator's letter.

Beyond this procedure, there is no other way outside recourse to the courts in which the patient may pursue his complaint. The HSC's jurisdiction, as we have seen, specifically excludes any case involving a complaint about 'clinical judgment' (Schedule 13, Part III, NHS Act 1977).

Questions

(i)   Does the 'second opinions' procedure provide a satisfactory remedy to an aggrieved patient? David Bolt in his lecture to the Medico-Legal Society, *op cit*, said (at p 224): 'How well it works, I really do not know. I hear very conflicting reports from various sources as to what its success rate is.'

(ii)   Should the HSC's jurisdiction be extended to cover cases involving 'clinical judgment'? Note the following comments of the HSC in his 1979–80 Report.

I am particularly concerned about the difficulties which appear to me to be inherent in a parallel jurisdiction betwen my office and the courts with respect to medical negligence. There is an obvious danger that if my jurisdiction were to be extended to include clinical judgment then a person dissatisfied with some aspect of the medical treatment he has received might take advantage of my office to obtain a 'free' investigation into the merits of a possible case against a Health Authority. If I issue a report in his favour, this report might then be used as the basis for obtaining legal aid for a subsequent action and generally as a means of bringing pressure to bear. While I would see this, in itself, as an abuse, unintended by Parliament, of the service I provide, there is the further—and, in my view, more fundamental—danger that if such an action were subsequently decided against the plaintiff, perhaps on different evidence, the standing of my reports, and hence of my office as a whole, might be diminished. Conversely, if the courts decided for the plaintiff, there might be the equally undesirable suspicion that my report had somehow prejudiced the trial against the Health Service and its employees. And, last, but not least, the co-operation and frankness which I enjoy in my investigations might be seriously lessened if NHS staff thought that my reports might somehow be used to found legal actions against them.

The solution, which has been considerably canvassed elsewhere, might be to offer aggrieved persons a statutory choice: to complain to me, or to take legal action—but not both. I believe this would be acceptable to the great majority of people, since in many of the cases I see the aggrieved person is genuinely not wanting money but a simple, factual explanation of some unexpected death or complication and an assurance that an attempt will be made to prevent a recurrence.

Even if the other serious problems associated with the proposal to extend my jurisdiction to include actions stemming solely from clinical judgment were to be solved, I would regard it as essential to provide also for the matters raised in the preceding paragraphs. And I would still wish to retain, in matters of clinical judgment, my discretion not to investigate a case if, in all the circumstances, I did not think it desirable or useful to do so.

Do you agree? The current HSC has not expressed a view.

(iii) Can a satisfactory distinction be drawn between cases that involve 'clinical judgment' and those that do not? Brazier discusses some examples of decisions taken by the HSC (*op cit*, at pp 133–4) (footnotes omitted):

Narrowly and literally interpreted, this limitation could have put senior doctors at least beyond the Commissioner's reach. Successive Commissioners have declined to follow that path. In the case . . . of the woman with epilepsy sterilised without her consent, the consultant first raised the 'defence' of clinical judgment. The Commissioner's finding that the consultant's decision was not founded on any decision that sterilisation was necessary for her health enabled him to continue his investigation. In 1979–80 a complaint by a woman who had undergone mastectomy and was refused a breast prosthetic on the NHS was investigated. The consultant argued that he never authorised prosthetics, that they were unnecessary and purely cosmetic. The Commissioner rejected his claim that the decision was arrived at in the exercise of clinical judgment. It had nothing to do with treating the complainant's illness; it was not a medical decision. The Commissioner condemned the refusal. One final example: a consultant genuinely concerned with the accessibility of records and X-rays refused to honour an appointment with a patient when the X-rays and records failed to be delivered. He would not even remove the plaster on his leg. The Commissioner found the doctor at fault. His concern for proper access to records was commendable. He may have been in the right in his dispute with the administration but he did not treat that patient properly. Nor could he claim that he acted in the exercise of clinical judgment. His course of action was not related to the care of the patient before him.

Despite the Commissioner's activism in restricting clinical judgment to its proper sphere, strictly medical decisions on the treatment of the individual patient, the exemption of clinical judgment still causes concern. Drawing the line is very difficult. The Commissioner is, as we have seen, unhappy about arrangements for discharge. He cannot, however, question the original medical decision that the patient is fit for discharge. The case of the elderly lady discharged after having been scalded and after a fall exemplifies his problem. The essence of that complaint would seem to be whether she should have been discharged at all.

(iv) Should the HSC be able to impose legally enforceable penalties on those found guilty of maladministration?

(v) Does the procedure laid down in HM(61)112 have any purpose to serve in resolving patients' complaints? The procedure set out in this circular was used in the cause celebre involving Mrs Wendy Savage in 1985. The circular provides for a very formal, court-like procedure. It involves the examination of allegations by an employing health authority of 'serious' professional incompetence or misconduct against a hospital doctor. It is a disciplinary procedure, one possible consequence of which is dismissal. The hearing takes place before an independent panel (usually of three), with a legally qualified chairman, who hear evidence and make a report to the health authority.

4.   COMPLAINTS AGAINST DOCTORS IN PRIVATE PRACTICE

All registered medical practitioners, whether in private practice or within the NHS are subject to the disciplinary jurisdiction of the GMC. Apart from this, however, there is no other formal mechanism other than the tort system thereby doctors in private practice may be held accountable.

Chapter 6

Medical records and confidence

When someone becomes a patient, there arises a *prima facie* obligation in the doctor to keep secret information disclosed to the doctor as part of the medical consultation. As an ethical precept this is as old as Hippocrates, if not older. As a legal precept it has long been assumed to be the case despite the paucity of legal authority (for a discussion of this, see Chapter 3).

The legal position is described by Francis Gurry in his book *Breach of Confidence* (at pp 148–9 footnotes ommitted).

> A doctor is under a legal obligation not to disclose confidential information concerning a patient which he learns in the course of his professional practice:
>
> > [I]n common with other professional men, for instance a priest . . . the doctor is under a duty not to disclose [voluntarily], without the consent of his patient, information which he, the doctor, has gained in his professional capacity . . . [*Hunter v Mann* [1974] 1 QB 767 at 772 *per* Borham J].[15]
>
> By analogy with the banker's obligation, it would seem that the doctor's duty of non-disclosure applies not only to information acquired directly from the patient, but also to information concerning the patient which the doctor learns from other sources *in his character as the patient's doctor*. Thus, the obligation of secrecy would extend to reports received by a doctor about a patient from medical specialists or from para-medical services.[16]
>
> As is the case with all obligations of confidence, the doctor's duty is not absolute but is subject to the requirement of disclosure under compulsion of law[17] and in the public interest.[18] Furthermore, his obligation can be released with the express or implied consent of the patient.

Notes to extract

[15] *Hunter v Mann* [1974] QB 767 at 7/2 per Boreham J. (with whom Lord Widgery CJ and May J. agreed). This proposition was advanced by Counsel, and Boreham J. stated that he would accept it with the addition of the word 'voluntarily', which has been inserted in parenthesis in the text above. The doctor's obligation of confidence was also recognized in *Wyatt v Wilson* (1820)—unreported, but cited with approval by Lord Cottenham LC in *Prince Albert v Strange* (1849) 1 Mac & G 25 at 46, 41 ER 1171 at 1179 and Ungoed-Thomas J. in *Argyll v Argyll* [1967] 1 Ch 302 at 319; and in *Kitson v Playfair*, (1896) *Times* 28 March, at 5 per Hawkins J. It also forms part of the ethics of the medical profession—see the Hippocratic Oath:

> Whatever, in connection with my professional practice or not in connection with it, I see or hear in the life of men which ought not to be spoken abroad, I will not divulge, as reckoning that all such should be kept secret,

quoted in W. Sanderson and E. B. A. Rayner, *An Introduction to the Law and Tradition of Medical Practice* (London, 1976), 25.

[16] In certain circumstances the information imparted by a doctor to a patient may be confidential also, and the doctor may restrain its misuse by the patient: see *Latham v Stevens* [1913] Macg Cop Cas 83 (1911–16), where the plaintiff doctor obtained an interlocutory injunction to restrain the defendants from using a medical certificate, granted by the doctor to a patient, in an advertisement claiming that the defendants had invented a cure for consumption. According to the report, Sargant J. held that the certificate was given to the patient for limited purposes, so that it would be a breach of trust or confidence for the patient or any other person having

knowledge of the circumstances to publish the certificate or the effect thereof as part of an advertisement or otherwise without the medical practitioner's consent.

[17] *Hunter v Mann* [1974] 1 QB 767.

[18] Ibid. 772 per Boreham J. (with whom Lord Widgery CJ and May J. agreed).

As has been seen, the essence of the obligation is that the doctor may not ordinarily disclose that which has been revealed to him and that which he *learns* in the context of a doctor/patient relationship.

Confidence, therefore, is the control of (and access to) information. It is this proposition which we shall analyse here.

Access by patient to medical records

It is important to draw a distinction between access to the document or other record containing the medical information and access to the information itself.

(a)   ACCESS TO THE DOCUMENT

If it could be said that the medical record containing the information belonged in law to the patient, then clearly the patient would be entitled to call for the medical record whenever he wished. In whom, therefore, is the ownership of a medical record vested? In our view, this *prima facie* turns on who owns the paper being used.

(i)   Private patient

1.   Paper belonging to the clinic, hospital or other institution

If the patient's contract is with the doctor then the question who owns the document depends initially on the contract (if any) made, not between the patient and the doctor, but between the doctor and the clinic or institution. For in the absence of any agreement between them whereby ownership of the document is given up by the clinic or institution to the doctor (such that the doctor could then transfer it on himself), the ownership must remain vested in the clinic or institution. If the doctor is made the owner (or as agent may transfer ownership) then whether he does this or not depends upon the relationship between the doctor and the patient (see (2) below).

If, on the other hand, the patient's contract is with the clinic or institution, then ultimate ownership will turn on the terms of the agreement between the parties. Ordinarily, of course, there will be no express term. So, what, if any, term will be implied? There is no clear law on this. It is likely that a court would imply a term to the effect that ownership remained in the clinic or institution, save that the patient should be entitled to possession where this is necessary for his continued health care, eg on a change of doctor or when he seeks a second opinion.

2.   Paper belonging to the doctor

What, however, if the doctor uses his own paper? Where the contract is made between the patient and the clinic or institution, subject to any agreement between the doctor and the clinic or institution, the paper probably belongs to the doctor.

Where the contract is made between the patient and the doctor, ownership depends upon the express or implied terms of that contract. Ordinarily, again, there will be no express term, in which case what term would a court imply? Ordinarily it must be that the court would imply the one seen above, namely that ownership vests, this time, in the doctor subject to a right of possession by the patient in certain circumstances, such as those described above.

(ii) NHS patient

1. *The general practitioner*

Medical records by GPs are said by Margaret Brazier to be 'made on forms . . . supplied by the Family Practitioner Committee and stated expressly to remain their property' (*Medicine, Patients and the Law*, at 46).

2. *Hospital doctor*

Medical records created in NHS hospitals are said by Brazier (*op cit*) to be made 'on NHS property' (presumably paper belonging to the relevant health authority). Then, she continues, '. . . additionally, as hospital doctors, unlike general practitioners, are employees of the health authority, records made by them in the course of their employment belong in law to their employer'. Do you agree with this?

Do you not think that this second argument confuses precisely what she seeks to separate, namely the paper and the information on it, since it is only the *latter* which is acquired during employment? Even so, on a property argument, medical records in this situation clearly belong to the relevant health authority.

One final point concerning access to the document. The Access to Medical Reports Act 1988 came into force on January 1, 1989. It applies to both private and NHS patients. The Act does not give a patient a general right of access to his medical records. Instead, in certain circumstances it establishes a right of access by an individual to *medical reports* sought from that individual doctor for employment or insurance purposes. If the doctor does not have 'responsibility for the clinical care of the individual' (s 2(1)) because he is not the individual's GP then the provisions of the Act do not apply.

The Act deals both with access to (and control of) these medical reports. We deal with 'control' later. The provisions of the Act are complex and we offer here merely a summary.

When an employer (or potential employer) or insurance company seeks a medical report on an individual, it must obtain that individual's consent to seek the report (s 3(1)). As a condition to granting consent, an individual may require that he be given access to the medical report prior to its supply to the employer or insurance company (s 4(1)). Even if he does not impose this condition, an individual may seek access prior to supply by giving the doctor notice (s 3(3)) or, if supply has already occurred, the individual is entitled to access for up to six months thereafter (s 5). Under the Act, 'access' means inspection of a copy of the medical report or obtaining such a copy (ss 6(4) and s(3)). In the latter case, the individual may be charged a reasonable fee (ss 4(4) and 6(3)).

An individual's right of access is not absolute. Section 7 of the Act provides for *three* situations where a doctor will be excused from granting access: (i) where, in the doctor's opinion, disclosure would be 'likely to cause serious harm to the physical or mental health of the individual or others' (s 7(11)); (ii) where disclosure would indicate the intentions of the doctor in respect of the individual (s 7(1)); and (iii) where disclosure would be likely to reveal information about another or identify another who had supplied information to the doctor unless that other had consented or was a doctor in whose care the individual had been (s 7(2)). Each of these situations may prevent an individual obtaining access to the whole or part of the medical record. The exemption is potentially a considerable restriction on the right of access. However, if the doctor seeks to exempt the whole of the medical report from access, then s 7(4) enjoins him from supplying it to the employer or insurance company without the individual's consent.

Finally, s 8 allows an individual to make an application to the county court for an order requiring compliance with the terms of the Act, if the individual is being wrongly refused access.

(b)   ACCESS TO THE INFORMATION

(i)   At common law

Generally, the common law has not recognised a right in the patient to have access to the information in medical records about himself. What this means is that the common law has not recognised a cause of action. This may be because, to do so, ie to order the owner of a medical record to surrender that record to the extent of allowing others to see what is in that record, would represent a curtailment of the right of ownership previously recognised. For, if ownership in this context means a right to property good against everyone, it might contradict this right to allow another to call for the record so as to be able to examine it.

The courts have, however, carved out some exceptions to this general principle. There seem to be three exceptions, but they would appear to be of limited application to doctors and their patients.

The first is illustrated by the decision of the House of Lords in *Secretary of State for Defence v Guardian Newspaper* [1985] AC 339, [1984] 3 All ER 601, but is restricted to obtaining access to documents or copies thereof *by the owner* and, therefore, is irrelevant here. The second derives from the case of *Norwich Pharmacal v Customs and Excise Comrs* [1974] AC 133, [1973] 2 All ER 943. This case permits someone to discover the identity of a wrongdoer by requiring a third party who has information relevant to the wrongdoer, to disgorge it. Conceivably, this could be of use in a medical-legal context where, for example, a patient wishes to obtain the identity of an attending doctor whom the patient wishes to sue and whose name is recorded in notes, but who is otherwise unknown to the patient. The third, based on *C v C* [1946] 1 All ER 562, actually concerned a doctor and his patient.

C v C [1946] 1 All ER 562

Lewis J: The circumstances which gave rise to this application are as follows: The respondent, a short time after marriage, exhibited symptoms which caused her to go to a venereal disease clinic where, on Feb 28, 1945, it was found she was suffering from a venereal disease in a communicable state. On this being discovered the petitioner went to the clinic and was examined, observed and treated by the same doctor who had examined and was treating the respondent. After some time it was found that there was no evidence whatever that the petitioner was suffering from this disease in any form. The respondent was not told that the disease from which she was in fact suffering was in a communicable form or, if it was, on Feb 28, in a communicable form, how long it had been in that form. On Aug 3, 1945, divorce proceedings having been instituted, the doctor was asked, *inter alia*, by the respondent to state particulars of her illness and if it was possible to say the approximate date of the commencement of that illness. Except to say that secondary syphilis was the disease, the doctor did not answer the respondent's request for the further information, which was vital to her and her advisers for the purpose of the defence of the proceedings. On or about Feb 27, 1946, a questionnaire consisting of six questions was sent to the doctor signed personally by the petitioner and the respondent, with the approval of the solicitors for both parties, asking for information as to the condition of the respondent, information which was vital to the parties to have for the proposed presentation of their respective cases. If those questions had been answered in one way the petitioner would have failed in proving what it was necessary to prove, if he was to succeed, and the respondent would have been able successfully to defend the case. To put it another way, the petitioner would have been unable to prove his case and the success of the respondent would have been a foregone conclusion. The doctor refused to give the information, stating that he would, if subpoenaed, give his evidence in court. He appeared in court and gave evidence and answered all questions put to him, and no sort of suggestion was made or could be made as to his good faith.

The question which arises out of these circumstances is: Is a doctor, when asked by his patient to give him or her particulars of his or her condition and illness to be used in a court of law, when those particulars are vital to the success or failure of the case, entitled to refuse and in effect to say: "Go on with your case in the dark and I will tell you in court when I am subpoenaed what my conclusions are"? In the present case the patient asked the doctor to give her this information and asked him also to give the petitioner that same information, with the object of their being placed in a position which would enable them to know whether or not the petitioner had a case against the respondent; in other words, to assist the course of justice. It is, of course, of the greatest importance from every point of view that proper secrecy should be observed in connection with venereal disease clinics, and that nothing should be done to diminish their efficiency or to infringe the confidential relationship existing between doctor and patient. But, in my opinion, those considerations do not justify a doctor in refusing to divulge confidential information to a patient or to any named person or persons when asked by the patient so to do. In the circumstances of this case the information should have been given, and in all cases where the circumstances are similar the doctor is not guilty of any breach of confidence in giving the information asked for.

Putting aside the situation in *C v C* where litigation is pending, is a doctor under a more general obligation to disclose to his patient information pertaining to the condition of the patient's health when the doctor has contributed to that condition? The Court of Appeal has hinted at such an obligation in *Lee v South West Thames Regional Health Authority* [1985] 2 All ER 385 at 389. Sir John Donaldson MR said:

It should never be forgotten that we are here concerned with a hospital-patient relationship. The recent decision of the House of Lords in *Sidaway v Bethlem Royal Hospital Governors* [1985] 1 All ER 643, [1985] 2 WLR 480 affirms that a doctor is under a duty to answer his patient's questions as to the treatment proposed. We see no reason why there should not be a similar duty in relation to hospital staff. This duty is subject to the exercise of clinical judgment as to the terms in which the information is given and the extent to which, in the patient's interests, information should be withheld. Why, we ask ourselves, is the position any different if the patient asks what treatment he has in fact had? Let us suppose that a blood transfusion is in contemplation. The patient asks what is involved. He is told that a quantity of blood from a donor will be introduced into his system. He may ask about the risk of AIDS and so forth and will be entitled to straight answers. He consents. Suppose that, by accident, he is given a quantity of air as well as blood and suffers serious ill effects. Is he not entitled to ask what treatment he in fact received, and is the doctor and hospital authority not obliged to tell him, 'in the event you did not only get a blood transfusion. You also got an air transfusion'? Why is the duty different before the treatment from what it is afterwards?

If the duty is the same, then if the patient is refused information to which he is entitled, it must be for consideration whether he could not bring an action for breach of contract claiming specific performance of the duty to inform. In other words, whether the patient could not bring an action for discovery, albeit on a novel basis.

We consider that some thought should be given to what is the duty of disclosure owed by a doctor and a hospital to a patient after treatment, but that is not an issue in this appeal.

Mustill LJ agreed.

Notice also, *Naylor v Preston Area Health Authority* [1987] 2 All ER 353, [1987] 1 WLR 958 where Sir John Donaldson repeated this view (at p 360).

I personally think that in professional negligence cases, and in particular in medical negligence cases, there is a duty of candour resting on the professional man. This is recognised by the legal professions in their ethical rules requiring their members to refer the client to other advisers, if it appears that the client has a valid claim for negligence. This also appears to be recognised by the Medical Defence Union, whose view is that 'the patient is entitled to a prompt, sympathetic and above all truthful account of what has occurred' (*Journal of the MDU* (1986) vol 2, no 2, p 2). It was also the view (admittedly *obiter*) of myself and Mustill LJ, as expressed in our judgment in *Lee v South West Thames Regional Health Authority* [1985] 2 All ER 385 at 389–390, [1985] 1 WLR 845 at 850. In this context I was disturbed to be told during the argument of the present appeals that the view was held in some quarters that whilst the duty of candid disclosure, to which we there referred, might give rise to a contractual implied term and so benefit private fee-paying patients, it did not translate into a legal or equitable right for the benefit of national health service patients. This I would entirely repudiate. In my judgment, still admittedly and regretfully *obiter*, it is but one aspect of the general duty of care, arising out of the patient/medical practitioner or hospital authority relationship and gives rise to rights both in contract and in tort. It is also in my judgment, not *obiter*, a factor to be taken into account when exercising the jurisdiction under Ord 38 with which we are concerned.

Do you think courts in the future will adopt this approach, bearing in mind Sir John Donaldson admitted that he was 'riding [his] personal hobby-horse or, if you like, flying a kite' ((1985) 53 Medico-Legal Journal 148, 157)?

(ii) Under statute

Under the Data Protection Act 1984, any person (the 'data subject') who has reason to believe that personal data about him is held by another (the 'data user') in circumstances where the information is electronically stored, for example on a computer disc or tape, may apply to the data user to discover whether information is held and, if so, to obtain access to the information (s 21(1)). Section 21(4)(b) provides:

(4) A data user shall not be obliged to comply with a request under this section—
. . .
(b) if he cannot comply with the request without disclosing information relating to another individual who can be identified from that information, unless he is satisfied that the other individual has consented to the disclosure of the information to the person making the request.

Section 21(5) expands upon this.

(5) In paragraph (b) of subsection (4) above the reference to information relating to another individual includes a reference to information identifying that individual as the source of the information sought by the request; and that paragraph shall not be construed as excusing a data user from supplying so much of the information sought by the request as can be supplied without disclosing the identity of the other individual concerned, whether by the omission of names or other identifying particulars or otherwise.

By virtue of s 29(1), however, the Secretary of State promulgated in 1987 the Data Protection (Subject Access Modification) (Health) Order 1987 (SI 1987 No 1903), to modify as s 29(1) puts it, 'the subject access provisions, in relation to, personal data consisting of information as to the physical or mental health of the data subject'. In short, a separate regime was established in the case of health professionals (as defined in the Schedule to the Order). The general exceptions in s 21 are superseded by Regulations 3 and 4 of the Order. These provide that:

3.—(1) This Order applies to personal data consisting of information as to the physical or mental health of the data subject if—

(a) the data are held by a health professional; or
(b) the data are held by a person other than a health professional but the information constituting the data was first recorded by or on behalf of a health professional.

(2) This Order is without prejudice to any exemption from the subject access provisions contained in any provision of the Act or of any Order made under the Act.

4.—(1) The subject access provisions shall not have effect in relation to any personal data to which this Order applies in any case where either of the requirements specified in paragraph (2) below is satisfied with respect to the information constituting the data and the obligations contained in paragraph (5) below are complied with by the data user.

(2) The requirements referred to in paragraph (1) above are that the application of the subject access provisions—

(a) would be likely to cause serious harm to the physical or mental health of the data subject; or
(b) would be likely to disclose to the data subject the identity of another individual (who has not consented to the disclosure of the information) either as a person to whom the information or part of it relates or as the source of the information or enable that identity to be deduced by the data subject either from the information itself or from a combination of that information and other information which the data subject has or is likely to have.

(3) Paragraph (2) above shall not be construed as excusing a data user—

(a) from supplying the information sought by the request for subject access where the only individual whose identity is likely to be disclosed or deduced as mentioned in sub-paragraph (b) thereof is a health professional who has been involved in the care of the data subject and the information relates to him or he supplied the information in his capacity as a health professional; or
(b) from supplying so much of the information sought by the request as can be supplied without causing serious harm as mentioned in sub-paragraph (a) thereof or enabling the identity of another individual to be disclosed or deduced as mentioned in sub-paragraph (b) thereof, whether by the omission of names or other particulars or otherwise.

(4) In relation to data to which this Order applies, section 21 of the Act shall have effect as if subsections (4)(b) and (5) were omitted and as if the reference in subsection (6) to the consent referred to in the said section 21(4)(b) were a reference to the consent referred to in paragraph (2)(b) above.

(5) A data user who is not a health professional shall not supply information constituting data to which this Order applies in response to a request under section 21 and shall not withhold any such information on the ground that one of the requirements specified in paragraph (2) above is satisfied with respect to the information unless the data user has first consulted the person who appears to the data user to be the appropriate health professional on the question whether either or both of those requirements is or are so satisfied.

(6) In paragraph (5) above "the appropriate health professional" means—

(a) the medical practitioner or dental practitioner who is currently or was most recently responsible for the clinical care of the data subject in connection with the matters to which the information which is the subject of the request relates; or

(b) where there is more than one such practitioner, the practitioner who is the most suitable to advise on the matters to which the information which is the subject of the request relates; or

(c) where there is no practitioner available falling within sub-paragraph (a) or (b) above, a health professional who has the necessary experience and qualifications to advise on the matters to which the information which is the subject of the request relates.

(7) Section 21(8) of the Act shall have effect, in relation to data to which this Order applies, as if the reference therein to a contravention of the foregoing provisions of that section included a reference to a contravention of the provisions contained in this Article.

The Explanatory Note to the Order indicates its intent:

This Order provides for the partial exemption from the provisions of the Data Protection Act 1984 which confer rights on data subjects to gain access to data held about them ('the subject access provisions') of data relating to the physical or mental health of the data subject held by any data user where the data are held by a health professional or the information constituting the data was first recorded by or on behalf of a health professional. Schedule 1 to the Order lists the persons who are · health professionals for the purposes of the Order.

The subject access provisions are disapplied only where to supply the data subject with particulars of the information constituting the data would be likely to cause serious harm to his physical or mental health or lead to the identification of another person (other than a health professional who has been involved in the care of the data subject). Before deciding whether either of those criteria is met (and, accordingly, whether to grant or withhold subject access) a data user who is not a health professional is obliged by the Order to consult the medical practitioner or dental practitioner responsible for the clinical care of the data subject or, if there is more than one, the most suitable available medical or dental practitioner or if there is none available a health professional who has the necessary experience and qualifications to advise on the matters to which the information which is requested relates.

How may a patient challenge the propriety of withholding information where the doctor alleges that the terms of this Order apply? The patient has two hurdles to overcome. First, he must know and demonstrate that there is additional information to that which has been revealed. Secondly, he must show that the doctor has acted unlawfully in exercising the statutory discretion in judicial review proceedings. The second is what the patient is interested in, but he may have the gravest difficulty in reaching this stage because of his need to overcome the first hurdle. In the absence of obvious deletions, how will he know? Would the mere threat of litigation (by judicial review) persuade the court to order discovery? If so, would this not defeat the purpose of the exemption in the first place? If not, what effective safeguard does a patient have? Would the court even grant leave to bring judicial review proceedings if faced with a bare assertion of 'I think information has been withheld'?

Are there any limits on those data subjects who can request access? Two specific categories are worthy of note. First there is the 'mentally disordered' who, presumably, though the subject of data may be unable through mental impairment to comply with the formal procedure to obtain access. Section 21(9) specifically addresses this problem. It provides:

(9) The Secretary of State may by order provide for enabling a request under this section to be made on behalf of any individual who is incapable by reason of mental disorder of managing his own affairs.

Presumably the request for access may only be made by a person who otherwise has authority in law to manage the affairs of the person in question under the Mental Health Act 1983. Consequently, s 29(1) seems not to contemplate that the Secretary of State may authorise by Order *anyone* to apply for access. Any such order might be amenable to challenge by judicial review on the ground that it is *ultra vires*. Given our view below, that legal competence to make a request for access under s 21 is simple, i e the 'data subject' must merely be able to complete the request form and appreciate what the making of a request entails, the phrase management of 'affairs' in s 21(9), therefore, must be understood as referring only to an incapacity to do this. (For a similar approach in the context of the Enduring Powers of Attorney Act 1985, see *Re K* [1988] Ch 310, [1988] 1 All ER 358.) The powers of comprehension of a mentally disordered individual will, therefore, have to be very considerably affected before s 21(9) (and any Regulations made under it) will be applicable to him.

Let us consider, secondly, the case of the child who is a patient. In the absence of any specific statutory provision, as is found in s 21(9), the right of access to data is regulated by the general s 21.

21.—(1) Subject to the provisions of this section, an individual shall be entitled—
   (a) to be informed by any data user whether the data held by him include personal data of which that individual is the data subject; and
   (b) to be supplied by any data user with a copy of the information constituting any such personal data held by him;
and where any of the information referred to in paragraph (b) above is expressed in terms which are not intelligible without explanation the information shall be accompanied by an explanation of those terms.

(2) A data user shall not be obliged to supply any information under subsection (1) above except in response to a request in writing and on payment of such fee (not exceeding the prescribed maximum) as he may require; but a request for information under both paragraphs of that subsection shall be treated as a single request and a request for information under paragraph (a) shall, in the absence of any indication to the contrary, be treated as extending also to information under paragraph (b).

(3) In the case of a data user having entries in the register in respect of data held for different purposes a separate request must be made and a separate fee paid under this section in respect of the data to which each entry relates.

. . .

[(4)](a) unless he is supplied with such information as he may reasonably require in order to satisfy himself as to the identity of the person making the request and to locate the information which he seeks; and

These provisions make it clear that it is only the 'data subject' who is entitled to be informed (on request) whether personal data concerning him is held by a 'data user', and only he who can subsequently be supplied with this data. Furthermore, it would appear that the formalities necessary to exercise the right of access consist only of making the relevant request in writing and paying the appropriate fee (s 21(2)). Therefore, it would follow that when the 'data subject' is a child, providing he is capable of making a request in writing accompanied by the fee, the 'data user' is obliged to respond to that request and provide the information.

The question may be raised whether a parent has a right of access to information relating to his or her child? In the above circumstances, there would be no such right, since the 'data subject' is the child, and the child is competent in his own right to make a request. It would be otherwise if the child had authorised a parent to make a relevant request. The parent would then be acting as the agent of the 'data subject'.

On the other hand, if the child were not competent to make the relevant request in writing, would a parent then have a right of access to any information? It would appear that under s 21 no such right exists since the parent is not the 'data subject'. If this were the end of the matter the legal position would be unfortunate since in those very cases in which a parent may legitimately need to obtain information about his child so as to carry out his parental obligations, the Act would prevent him from doing so. The situation is saved, however, by realising that the Act sharply distinguishes between the right of access by the 'data subject' and the power of the 'data user' to disclose. Nothing in the right of access provisions prevents the 'data user' from disclosing information to others (quite apart from the statutory exceptions), provided that the 'data user' has named those others in the classes of potential recipients of information at the time he registered under the Act as a 'data user' (see ss 4(3)(d) and 5(2)(d)). Thus, if the 'data user' has included parents among those to whom he may wish to disclose information, he could be at liberty to disclose to a parent the information (see *infra* on the power to disclose). However, notice that when the discretion to disclose to a parent is contemplated by the 'data user', it is probably the case that the 'data user' must divulge all necessary and relevant information to enable the parent to make a considered decision. The fear that the information could harm the 'data subject', were it to be disclosed to him, would not of itself serve as a reason for refusing to disclose to the parent.

(iii) In the course of litigation

Apart from the Data Protection Act (which only applies to electronically stored information), the common law, as we have seen, confers no right of access upon a patient to his medical records. A proposal to amend the law so as to give a right of access to manually recorded medical records—contained in the Access to Personal Files Bill 1987—failed to become law.

Therefore, the only way a patient may gain access to his medical records is if he contemplates litigation or has already commenced it. Sections 33 and 34 of the Supreme Court Act 1981 provide as follows:

Powers of High Court exercisable before commencement of action
33.—(1) On the application of any person in accordance with rules of court, the High Court shall, in such circumstances as may be specified in the rules, have power to make an order providing for any one or more of the following matters, that is to say—
   (a) the inspection, photographing, preservation, custody and detention of property which appears to the court to be property which may become the subject-matter of subsequent proceedings in the High Court, or as to which any question may arise in any such proceedings; and
   (b) the taking of samples of any such property as is mentioned in paragraph (*a*), and the carrying out of any experiment on or with any such property.
   (2) On the application, in accordance with rules of court, of a person who appears to the High Court to be likely to be a party to subsequent proceedings in that court in which a claim in respect of personal injuries to a person, or in respect of a person's death, is likely to be made, the High Court shall, in such circumstances as may be specified in the rules, have power to order a person who appears to the court to be likely to be a party to the proceedings and to be likely to have or to have had in his possession, custody or power any documents which are relevant to an issue arising or likely to arise out of that claim—
   (a) to disclose whether those documents are in his possession, custody or power; and

(b) to produce such of those documents as are in his possession, custody or power to the applicant or, on such conditions as may be specified in the order—

(i) to the applicant's legal advisers; or

(ii) to the applicant's legal advisers and any medical or other professional adviser of the applicant; or

(iii) if the applicant has no legal adviser, to any medical or other professional adviser of the applicant.

Power of High Court to order disclosure of documents, inspection of property etc in proceedings for personal injuries or death

34.—(1) This section applies to any proceedings in the High Court in which a claim is made in respect of personal injuries to a person, or in respect of a person's death.

(2) On the application, in accordance with rules of court, of a party to any proceedings to which this section applies, the High Court shall, in such circumstances as may be specified in the rules, have power to order a person who is not a party to the proceedings and who appears to the court to be likely to have in his possession, custody or power any documents which are relevant to an issue arising out of the said claim—

(a) to disclose whether those documents are in his possession, custody or power; and

(b) to produce such of those documents as are in his possession, custody or power to the applicant or, on such conditions as may be specified in the order—

(i) to the applicant's legal advisers; or

(ii) to the applicant's legal advisers and any medical or other professional adviser of the applicant; or

(iii) if the applicant has no legal adviser, to any medical or other professional adviser of the applicant.

(3) On the application, in accordance with rules of court, of a party to any proceedings to which this section applies, the High Court shall, in such circumstances as may be specified in the rules, have power to make an order providing for any one or more of the following matters, that is to say—

(a) the inspection, photographing, preservation, custody and detention of property which is not the property of, or in the possession of, any party to the proceedings but which is the subject-matter of the proceedings or as to which any question arises in the proceedings;

(b) the taking of samples of any such property as is mentioned in paragraph (a) and the carrying out of any experiment on or with any such property.

(4) The preceding provisions of this section are without prejudice to the exercise by the High Court of any power to make orders which is exercisable apart from those provisions.

Brazier, in her book *Medicine, Patients and the Law*, comments on these provisions as follows:

The effect of section 33 of the 1981 Act is this. A patient may apply for a court order requiring the doctor or the authority whom he plans to sue to disclose any records or notes likely to be relevant in forthcoming proceedings. Section 34 goes further. The court may order a person *not* a party to proceedings to produce relevant documents. So if the patient has started proceedings against the doctor but believes that the hospital authority or clinic holds notes of value to his claim, the authority or clinic can be made to hand over the notes. This will help the private patient in a dilemma as to whether he should properly proceed against doctor or hospital. And it may of course lead to the hospital being brought into the proceedings.

Once legislation compelling disclosure of documents was enacted, hospitals and medical protection societies reluctantly became prepared to hand over documents voluntarily. They feared a spate of fishing expeditions by aggrieved patients. But they preferred to disclose records to the patient's medical adviser alone, and not to the patient or his lawyers. Indeed, they sought to argue that this was the limit of their obligation. The House of Lords disagreed [*McIvor v Southern Health and Social*

Services Board [1978] 2 All ER 625]. Under the 1970 statute [now replaced by the 1981 Act], they said, the patient himself was entitled to see the documents produced. Pleas that patients would be unduly distressed and fail to understand medical data cut little ice with their Lordships. The 1981 Act is less favourable to patients. A court may limit disclosure to (a) the patient's legal advisers, or (b) the patient's legal and medical advisers, or (c) if the patient has no legal adviser, to his 'medical or other professional adviser'. It is up to the court to decide whether the patient sees the records. But as long as he has retained a lawyer, his la·/yer must be permitted to examine the documents. Hospitals and medical protection societies offering voluntary disclosure often still try to keep records even from the patient's lawyers. Lawyers in the medico-legal field advise against accepting such an offer: a lawyer may spot relevant material in support of a claim which even the most experienced medical advisers could miss.

Three final matters on disclosure need a mention. First, the intention to bring proceedings and the likelihood that they will go ahead must be real before the court will order disclosure. The patient must have some solid ground for thinking he has a claim. He cannot use an application for disclosure as a 'fishing expedition' on the off-chance that some evidence of negligence will come to light [*Dunning v Board of Governors, United Liverpool Hospitals* [1973] 2 All ER 454]. Doctors are advised to say nothing and disclose no records without consulting their protection society. The protection society will require evidence of a bona fide claim before advising disclosure, and a court asked to compel production will not be satisfied with less.

Control by the patient of his medical records

Turning now from the question of access by a patient, the matter for consideration here is the extent to which the patient may control information about him contained in his medical records so as to prevent others learning of it without his authority.

A number of arguments may be deployed as the basis for preserving the secrecy of the patient's information. Some of these arguments, as we shall see, are more valid than others.

(a) OWNERSHIP

Does the patient own his medical record and so, by virtue of this, have a right to control its contents? We have seen that the ownership will be vested in the patient only in the rarest of cases. Thus, this argument leads nowhere.

We have already considered the access provisions of the Access to Medical Reports Act 1988. The Act also gives an individual a limited right to control a medical report created for employment or insurance purposes. Although the Act is not strictly concerned with rights derived from ownership, it is convenient to deal with it here. First, an employer, or insurance company must obtain an individual's consent prior to seeking a medical report upon the individual (s 3(1)). The Act seems to confer an absolute right upon an individual to refuse his consent to this.

The more usual case will be, however, that the individual does consent to the application for the report if he realistically wants the job, promotion or insurance policy that he seeks. Then, the Act contemplates two situations: *conditional* and *unconditional* consent.

First, the individual (as we saw earlier in this chapter), may consent to the making of the application *on condition* that he is granted access to the report. If access has to be granted under the Act (ie the report or the relevant part of it does not fall within the exemption provisions of s 7) then the medical report cannot be supplied to the employer or insurance company without the individual's consent once the individual has obtained access to the report (s 5(1)). Again, the individual's right to refuse consent seems absolute.

However, instead of refusing consent to the supply of the report the individual is entitled, as a condition of his consent, to request that the doctor 'amend any part of the report which the individual considers to be incorrect or misleading' (s 5(2)).

Thereafter, the doctor may only supply the report to the employer or insurance company if (i) he accedes to this request (s 5(2)(a)) or (ii) he attaches to the report a statement by the individual concerning the part of the report which the doctor has refused to amend (s 5(2)(b)).

Secondly, the individual may give his consent to the making of the application for the report *unconditionally*. As we saw earlier, he may still, prior to its supply, notify the doctor that he wishes to have access to the report. Supply of the report is then subject to the same restrictions as if the consent had been initially conditional.

If, however, the individual's unconditional consent remains unchanged, the Act confers upon him no right to control the supply or content of the medical report. In other words, requiring (and obtaining) access to a report is, under the Act, a necessary condition to exercising any control over the supply or content of the report.

(b) CONFIDENCE

(i) The obligation

A right to control based upon the fact that the medical information was imparted in confidence is a much more soundly based argument. We have already analysed the legal basis upon which an obligation of confidence may be grounded and the circumstances under which it arises (*supra* Ch 3). Despite the absence of specific legal authority, we have already taken the view that there can be no doubt that an obligation of confidence is owed by a doctor to his patient (for a recent affirmation of this, as if it were beyond a peradventure, see *Goddard v Nationwide Building Society* [1986] 3 All ER 264 at 271, *per* Nourse LJ). Consequently, *prima facie* a patent may by injunction enjoin a doctor from any threatened disclosure of information.

The underlying moral obligation to respect confidence has, of course, always been a cornerstone of medical ethics. (For a recent statement, see the General Medical Council's *Professional Conduct and Discipline: Fitness to Practice* (April 1987), para 80.)

(ii) Modifications of the obligation

We have in mind, here, circumstances where the law permits or requires disclosure of information about a patient without his consent and even in face of his refusal.

1. Waiver

The GMC's *Professional Conduct and Discipline: Fitness to Practice* (April 1987), para 81, states:

81. The circumstances where exceptions to the rule may be permitted are as follows:

(a) If the patient or his legal adviser gives written and valid consent, information to which the consent refers may be disclosed.

This proposition also states the law, save that it is, of course, a common fallacy to stipulate the need for writing thereby confusing *proof* with *legal validity*.

Although waiver is often regarded as an exception to the obligation of confidence, in fact it is not. It is merely a recognition by the patient that the doctor is no longer under an obligation to keep the confidence—it defeats the *existence* of the obligation. (See eg Hirst J in *Fraser v Thames Television Ltd* [1983] 2 All ER 101 at 122: 'Counsel for the plaintiffs accepts that ... the communication ... in the spring or summer of 1974 was legitimate, since it was done with the plaintiffs' consent.')

Consent to disclose is an example of waiver which would usually be *express*. Waiver may also be *implied*. A common example of the latter is when the patient is in the care of more than one person. In such a case the patient may be assumed to consent to all medical and nursing members of the team being informed so as to properly carry out their respective obligations. The members of the 'team' who receive the information receive it in confidence.

It is a continually vexing question whether information should be imparted to those members of the team who do not belong to a profession with a strictly enforced professional code and who may not preserve records under the same circumstances of confidentiality and yet may have a legitimate interest, eg social workers, occupational therapists etc. It may be that the practical needs involved in the management of a patient would lead a court to say that a doctor has a discretion to disclose to all those professionals who also need to know so as properly to serve the medical needs of the patient. Such a discretion must necessarily be exercised with caution.

2. Statutory

There are a number of statutory provisions which create exceptions to or modifications of the obligation of confidentiality. Consider the following examples.

eg 1: The Abortion Regulations 1968 (SI 1968 No 390 as amended)

Restriction on disclosure of information
5. A notice given or any information furnished to a Chief Medical Officer in pursuance of these regulations shall not be disclosed except that disclosure may be made—

    (a) for the purposes of carrying out their duties,
        (i) to an officer of the Department of Health and Social Security authorised by the Chief Medical Officer of that Department, or to an officer of the Welsh Office authorised by the Chief Medical Officer of that Office, as the case may be, or
        (ii) to the Registrar General or a member of his staff authorised by him; or
    (b) for the purposes of carrying out his duties in relation to offences against the Act or the law relating to abortion, to the Director of Public Prosecutions or a member of his staff authorised by him; or
    (c) for the purposes of investigating whether an offence has been committed against the Act or the law relating to abortion, to a police officer not below the rank of superintendent or a person authorised by him; or
    (d) for the purposes of criminal proceedings which have begun; or
    (e) for the purposes of bona fide scientific research; or
    (f) to the practitioner who terminated the pregnancy; or
    (g) to a practitioner, with the consent in writing of the woman whose pregnancy was terminated; or

(h) when requested by the President of the General Medical Council for the purpose of investigating whether there has been serious professional misconduct by a registered medical practitioner, to the President of the General Medical Council or a member of his staff authorised by him.

e g 2: Public Health (Infectious Diseases) Act 1984

Notifiable diseases

10. In this Act, 'notifiable disease' means any of the following diseases—
(a) cholera;
(b) plague;
(c) relapsing fever;
(d) smallpox; and
(e) typhus.

Cases of notifiable disease and food poisoning to be reported

11.—(1) If a registered medical practitioner becomes aware, or suspects, that a patient whom he is attending within the district of a local authority is suffering from a notifiable disease or from food poisoning, he shall, unless he believes, and has reasonable grounds for believing, that some other registered medical practitioner has complied with this subsection with respect to the patient. forthwith send to the proper officer of the local authority for that district a certificate stating—
(a) the name, age and sex of the patient and the address of the premises where the patient is,
(b) the disease or, as the case may be, particulars of the poisoning from which the patient is, or is suspected to be, suffering and the date, or approximate date, of its onset, and
(c) if the premises are a hospital, the day on which the patient was admitted, the address of the premises from which he came there and whether or not, in the opinion of the person giving the certificate, the disease or poisoning from which the patient is, or is suspected to be, suffering was contracted in the hospital.

. . .

(4) A person who fails to comply with an obligation imposed on him by subsection (1) above shall be liable on summary conviction to a fine not exceeding level 1 on the standard scale.

e g 3: An interesting provision is the National Health Service (Veneral Diseases) Regulations 1974 (SI 1974 No 29) which provides:

2. Every Regional Health Authority and every [District Health Authority] shall take all necessary steps to secure that any information capable of identifying an individual obtained by officers of the Authority with respect to persons examined or treated for any sexually transmitted disease shall not be disclosed except—
(a) for the purpose of communicating that information to a medical practitioner, or to a person employed under the direction of a medical practitioner in connection with the treatment of persons suffering from such disease or the prevention of the spread thereof, and
(b) for the purpose of such treatment or prevention.

This Regulation was introduced so as to give statutory emphasis to the obligation of confidence in this area of medical practice. The reasons are obvious: thus, the circumstances under which disclosure can be made are carefully circumscribed. It could be argued that the wording of the provision is such as to allow a patient's GP to be informed by those working in a Genito-Urinary Clinic without the consent of, and even in the face of the refusal of, the patient.

This has particular significance in the context of AIDS, where some have argued for the right of the GP to be informed of a patient's HIV status, allegedly in the interests of the patient so as to ensure any future care is medically optimal but, in the case of some doctors at least, in their own perceived interests. Would such routine disclosure be justified either because (a) it is necessary for the prevention of the spread of the disease; or (b) it is necessary for the treatment of the patient? Bear in mind when answering this that the notion of *treatment* entails the need for the patient's consent which itself entails agreement to share information about his condition. Can regulation 2(b) have any application, therefore, in the absence of the patient's agreement, to the transfer of the information to his GP?

A small, but important, point to notice is that the obligation of confidence under the Regulations applies when the disease is 'sexually transmitted'. If this is so, a patient who is HIV positive will need to look to the common law for protection of his confidence if he became infected by some other means as, for example, if he is a haemophiliac or has otherwise become HIV positive as a result of an infected blood donation.

e g 4: Data Protection Act 1984

Some may argue that the disclosure provisions of this Act (DPA) amount to an exception to the obligation of confidence between a doctor and his patient. As we saw earlier in this chapter, in the discussion concerning the patient access provision under the Act, s 17 permits a doctor to disclose information concerning a data subject to those listed as potential recipients under s 4(3) at the time of registration. However, the doctor's power or liberty to disclose must be understood as necessarily fettered by any common law obligation of confidence. It follows, therefore, that the 1984 Act makes it unlawful for a data user to disclose data to a person or body not listed at the time of registration.

Some may argue that if, apart from the 1984 Act, the person under the obligation of confidence may by statute or common law disclose the information to another person, the 1984 Act does not make this unlawful. For example, a doctor may in accordance with the Abortion Regulations (*supra*) notify a person or body as specified by regulation 5 without that person or body having been registered as a potential recipient by the data user. This argument can only be based upon s 34(5) of the DPA.

> (5) Personal data are exempt from the non-disclosure provisions in any case in which the disclosure is—
>
> (a) *required by* or under any enactment, by any rule of law or by the order of a court; or . . . (Our emphasis.)

Is the argument correct? Does s 34(5) only apply when the person *prima facie* under the obligation of confidence is under a legal *duty* to disclose.

One other exemption from the non-disclosure provisions may be of interest in the context of medical law. Section 34(8) of the DPA reads as follows:

> (8) Personal data are exempt from the non-disclosure provisions in any case in which the disclosure is urgently required for preventing injury or other damage to the health of any person or persons; and in proceedings against any person for contravening a provision mentioned in section 26(3)(*a*) above it shall be a defence to prove that he had reasonable grounds for believing that the disclosure in question was urgently required for that purpose.

Since, as we have argued, in this context the DPA has to be read in the light of any common law obligation of confidence, do you think that the common law would reflect this statutory exemption (see *infra*)?

e g 5: Police and Criminal Evidence Act 1984

Special provisions as to access
9.—(1) A constable may obtain access to excluded material . . . for the purposes of

a criminal investigation by making an application under Schedule 1 below and in accordance with that Schedule [sc to a circuit judge].

Meaning of 'excluded material'

11.—(1) Subject to the following provisions of this section, in this Act 'excluded material' means—

  (a) personal records which a person has acquired or created in the course of any trade, business, profession or other occupation or for the purposes of any paid or unpaid office and which he holds in confidence;

  (b) human tissue or tissue fluid which has been taken for the purposes of diagnosis or medical treatment and which a person holds in confidence;

  . . .

  (2) A person holds material other than journalistic material in confidence for the purposes of this section if he holds it subject—

  (a) to an express or implied undertaking to hold it in confidence or

  (b) to a restriction on disclosure or an obligation of secrecy contained in any enactment, including an enactment contained in an Act passed after this Act.

Meaning of 'personal records'

12. In this Part of this Act 'personal records' means documentary and other records concerning an individual (whether living or dead) who can be identified from them, and relating—

  (a) to his physical or mental health;

  (b) to spiritual counselling or assistance given or to be given to him;

  (c) to counselling or assistance given or to be given to him, for the purposes of his personal welfare, by any voluntary organisation or by any individual who—

   (i) by reason of his office or occupation has responsibilities for his personal welfare; or

   (ii) by reason of an order of a court, has responsibilities for his supervision.

These provisions apply to medical records, human tissue or tissue fluid, taken for the purposes of diagnostic or medical treatment. In so far as the 'excluded material' comes within the ambit of the DPA 1984, ie it exists in the form of computerised records, the non-disclosure provisions of the DPA will not apply since an order of the circuit judge under Schedule 1 of PACE will bring disclosure within the exemption in s 34(5) of the DPA (see *supra*).

3. Public interest

Lion Laboratories Ltd v Evans
[1984] 2 All ER 417, CA.

Griffiths LJ (at 432): The first question to be determined is whether there exists a defence of public interest to actions for breach of confidentiality and copyright, and, if so, whether it is limited to situations in which there has been serious wrongdoing by the plaintiffs, the so-called 'iniquity' rule.

I am quite satisfied that the defence of public interest is now well established in actions for breach of confidence and, although there is less authority on the point, that it also extends to breach of copyright: see by way of example *Fraser v Evans* [1969] 1 All ER 8, [1969] 1 QB 349; *Hubbard v Vosper* [1972] 1 All ER 1023, [1972] 2 QB 84; *Woodward v Hutchins* [1977] 2 All ER 751, [1977] 1 WLR 760 and *British Steel Corpn v Granada Television Ltd* [1981] 1 All ER 417, [1981] AC 1096.

I can see no sensible reason why this defence should be limited to cases in which there has been wrongdoing on the part of the plaintiffs. I believe that the so-called iniquity rule evolved because in most cases where the facts justified a publication in breach of confidence the plaintiff had behaved so disgracefully or criminally that it was judged in the public interest that his behaviour should be exposed. No doubt it is in such circumstances that the defence will usually arise, but it is not difficult to think of instances where, although there has been no wrongdoing on the part of the plaintiff, it may be vital in the public interest to publish a part of his confidential information. Stephenson LJ has given such an example in the course of his judgment.

Clearly this is potentially a very widely drawn modification to the obligation of confidence. If interpreted too widely, it might swallow up the obligation. What guidance do the cases give to the doctor on when it is in the public interest to disclose confidential information? Lord Wilberforce was anxious to make clear that: 'there is a wide difference between what is interesting to the public and what it is in the public interest to make known'. (*British Steel Corpn v Granada Television Ltd* [1981] 1 All ER 417 at 455.) You may think that this does not take us much further. The GMC's 'blue book', paragraph 81(g), takes us a little further:

> (g) Rarely, disclosure may be justified on the ground that it is in the public interest which, in certain circumstances such as, for example, investigation by the police of a grave or very serious crime, might override the doctor's duty to maintain his patient's confidence.

Notice also the case of *X v Y, supra* p 163, in which Rose J held that it was not in the public interest for a newspaper to disclose to its readers the names of two doctors who were infected with HIV.

In *W v Egdell* [1989] 1 All ER 1089 (Scott J), a psychiatrist disclosed a medical report he had prepared for a detained prisoner under the Mental Health Act 1983 to the hospital where he was detained and the Home Secretary. The court held that this was lawful, balancing the individual's interest in confidentiality against the public's interest in disclosure. The public interest justified the disclosure because of the dangerous nature of the patient and the Home Secretary's need to know this information in exercising his statutory powers under the 1983 Act.

Taking up the GMC's example, it may be helpful to approach it in two stages. First, would the doctor as a matter of law be justified in informing the police of disclosures made to him by a patient that a serious crime, for example of violence, was about to be committed? Or does the justification only apply when the fact of a crime having been committed is disclosed to him? If the answer is that the doctor would be justified in one or both of those circumstances, a second question arises. Does the doctor have a discretion to inform others (more precisely the relevant authorities or the intended victim), or is he under a duty to do so?

In California, the Supreme Court held that in certain circumstances, a doctor could be under a duty to disclose confidential information.

Tarasoff v Regents of the University of California
(1976) 131 Cal Rptr 14 (California Supreme Court) (footnotes omitted)

Tobriner Justice: On October 27, 1969, Prosenjit Poddar killed Tatiana Tarasoff. Plaintiffs, Tatiana's parents, allege that two months earlier Poddar confided his intention to kill Tatiana to Dr Lawrence Moore, a psychologist employed by the Cowell Memorial Hospital at the University of California at Berkeley. They allege that on Moore's request, the campus police briefly detained Poddar, but released him when he appeared rational. They further claim that Dr Harvey Powelson, Moore's superior, then directed that no further action be taken to detain Poddar. No one warned plaintiffs of Tatiana's peril. . . .

Plaintiffs' complaints predicate liability on two grounds: defendants' failure to warn plaintiffs of the impending danger and their failure to bring about Poddar's confinement. . . . Defendants, in turn, assert that they owed no duty of reasonable care to Tatiana. . . . We shall explain that defendant therapists cannot escape liability merely because Tatiana herself was not their patient. When a therapist determines, or pursuant to the standards of his profession should determine, that his patient presents a serious danger of violence to another, he incurs an obligation to use reasonable care to protect the intended victim against such danger. The discharge of this duty may require the therapist to take one or more of various steps, depending upon the nature of the case. Thus it may call for him to warn the intended victim or others likely to apprise the victim of the danger, to notify the police, or to take whatever other steps are reasonably necessary under the circumstances.

In the case at bar, plaintiffs admit that defendant therapists notified the police, but argue on appeal that the therapists failed to exercise reasonable care to protect Tatiana in that they did not confine Poddar and did not warn Tatiana or others likely to apprise her of the danger. . . .

2. Plaintiffs can state a cause of action against defendant therapists for negligent failure to protect Tatiana

The second cause of action can be amended to allege that Tatiana's death proximately resulted from defendants' negligent failure to warn Tatiana or others likely to apprise her of her danger. Plaintiffs contend that as amended, such allegations of negligence and proximate causation, with resulting damages, establish a cause of action. Defendants, however, contend that in the circumstances of the present case they owed no duty of care to Tatiana or her parents and that, in the absence of such duty, they were free to act in careless disregard of Tatiana's life and safety.

In analysing this issue, we bear in mind that legal duties are not discoverable facts of nature, but merely conclusory expressions that, in cases of a particular type, liability should be imposed for damage done. As stated in *Dillon v Legg* 68 Cal 2d 728, 734, 69 Cal Rptr 72, 76, 441 P 2d 912, 916 (1968): 'The assertion that liability must . . . be denied because defendant bears no 'duty' to plaintiff 'begs the essential question—whether the plaintiff's interests are entitled to legal protection against the defendant's conduct . . . [Duty] is not sacrosanct in itself, but only an expression of the sum total of those considerations of policy which lead the law to say that the particular plaintiff is entitled to protection.' (Prosser, Law of Torts [3d ed 1964] at pp 332–333.)'

In the landmark case of *Rowland v Christian* 69 Cal 2d 108, 70 Cal Rptr 97, 443 P 2d 561 (1968), Justice Peters recognised that liability should be imposed 'for an injury occasioned to another by his want of ordinary care or skill' as expressed in section 1714 of the Civil Code. Thus, Justice Peters, quoting from *Heaven v Pender* (1883) 11 QBD 503 at 509 stated: '"whenever one person is by circumstances placed in such a position with regard to another . . . that if he did not use ordinary care and skill in his own conduct . . . he would cause danger of injury to the person or property of the other, a duty arises to use ordinary care and skill to avoid such danger."'

We depart from 'this fundamental principle' only upon the 'balancing of a number of considerations'; major ones 'are the foreseeability of harm to the plaintiff, the degree of certainty that the plaintiff suffered injury, the closeness of the connection between the defendant's conduct and the injury suffered, the moral blame attached to the defendant's conduct, the policy of preventing future harm, the extent of the burden to the defendant and consequences to the community of imposing a duty to exercise care with resulting liability for breach, and the availability, cost and prevalence of insurance for the risk involved.'

The most important of these considerations in establishing duty is foreseeability. As a general principle, a 'defendant owes a duty of care to all persons who are foreseeably endangered by his conduct, with respect to all risks which make the conduct unreasonably dangerous.' (*Rodriguez v Bethlehem Steel Corp* 12 Cal 3d 382, 399, 115 Cal Rptr 765, 776, 525 P 2d 669, 680 (1974); *Dillon v Legg, supra*, 68 Cal 2d 728, 739, 69 Cal Rptr 72, 441 P 2d 912; *Weirum v RKO General, Inc* 15 Cal 3d 40, 123 Cal Rptr 468, 539 P 2d 36 (1975); see Civ Code, § 1714.) As we shall explain, however, when the avoidance of foreseeable harm requires a defendant to control the conduct of another person, or to warn of such conduct, the common law has traditionally imposed liability only if the defendant bears some special relationship to the dangerous person or to the potential victim. Since the relationship between a therapist and his patient satisfies this requirement, we need not here decide whether foreseeability alone is sufficient to create a duty to exercise reasonable care to protect a potential victim of another's conduct.

Although, as we have stated above, under the common law, as a general rule, one person owes no duty to control the conduct of another (*Richards v Stanley* 43 Cal 2d 60, 65, 271 P 2d 23 (1954); *Wright v Arcade School Dist* 230 Cal App 2d 272, 277, 40 Cal Rptr 812 (1964); Rest 2d Torts (1965) § 315), nor to warn those endangered by such conduct (Rest 2d Torts, *supra*, § 314, com c; Prosser, Law of Torts (4th ed 1971) § 56, p 341), the courts have carved out an exception to this rule in cases in which the defendant stands in some special relationship to either the person whose conduct needs to be controlled or in a relationship to the foreseeable victim of that conduct (see Rest 2d Torts, *supra*, §§ 315–320). Applying this exception to the present case, we note that a relationship of defendant therapists to either Tatiana or Poddar will suffice to establish a duty of care; as explained in section 315 of the Restatement Second of Torts, a duty of care may arise from either '(a) a special relation ... between the actor and the third person which imposes a duty upon the actor to control the third person's conduct, or (b) a special relation ... between the actor and the other which gives to the other a right of protection.'

Although plaintiffs' pleadings assert no special relation between Tatiana and defendant therapists, they establish as between Poddar and defendant therapists the special relation that arises between a patient and his doctor or psychotherapist. Such a relationship may support affirmative duties for the benefit of third persons. Thus, for example, a hospital must exercise reasonable care to control the behavior of a patient which may endanger other persons. A doctor must also warn a patient if the patient's condition or medication renders certain conduct, such as driving a car, dangerous to others.

Although the California decisions that recognise this duty have involved cases in which the defendant stood in a special relationship *both* to the victim and to the person whose conduct created the danger, we do not think that the duty should logically be constricted to such situations. Decisions of other jurisdictions hold that the single relationship of a doctor to his patient is sufficient to support the duty to exercise reasonable care to protect others against dangers emanating from the patient's illness. The courts hold that a doctor is liable to persons infected by his patient if he negligently fails to diagnose a contagious disease (*Hofmann v Blackmon* 241 So 2d 752 (Fla App 1970)), or, having diagnosed the illness, fails to warn members of the patient's family (*Wojcik v Aluminium Co of America* 18 Misc 2d 740, 183 NYS 2d 351, 357–358 (1959); *Davis v Rodman* 147 Ark 385, 227 SW 612 (1921); *Skillings v Allen* 143 Minn 323, 173 NW 663 (1919); see also *Jones v Stanko* (1928) 118 Ohio St 147, 160 NE 456).

Since it involved a dangerous mental patient, the decision in *Merchants National Bank & Trust Co of Fargo v United States* 272 F Supp 409 (DND 1967) comes closer to the issue. The Veterans Administration arranged for the patient to work on a local farm, but did not inform the farmer of the man's background. The farmer consequently permitted the patient to come and go freely during nonworking hours; the patient borrowed a car, drove to his wife's residence and killed her. Notwithstanding the lack of any 'special relationship' between the Veterans Administration and the wife, the court found the Veterans Administration liable for the wrongful death of the wife.

In their summary of the relevant rulings Fleming and Maximov conclude that the 'case law should dispel any notion that to impose on the therapists a duty to take precautions for the safety of persons threatened by a patient, where due care so requires, is in any way opposed to contemporary ground rules on the duty relationship. On the contrary, there now seems to be sufficient authority to support the conclusion that by entering into a doctor-patient relationship the therapist becomes sufficiently involved to assume some responsibility for the safety, not only of the patient himself, but also of any third person whom the doctor knows to be threatened by the patient.' (Fleming & Maximov, *The Patient or His Victim: The Therapist's Dilemma* (1974) 62 Cal L Rev 1025, 1030.) ...

We recognise the public interest in supporting effective treatment of mental illness and in protecting the rights of patients to privacy (see *Re Liftschutz, supra*, 2 Cal 3d at 432, 85 Cal Rptr 829, 467 P 2d 557), and the consequent public importance of safeguarding the confidential character of psychotherapeutic communication. Against this interest, however, we must weigh the public interest in safety from violent assault. The Legislature has undertaken the difficult task of balancing the countervailing concerns. In Evidence Code section 1014, it established a broad rule of privilege to protect confidential communications between patient and psychotherapist. In Evidence Code section 1024, the Legislature created a specific and limited exception to the psychotherapist-patient privilege: 'There is no privilege . . . if the psychotherapist has reasonable cause to believe that the patient is in such mental or emotional condition as to be dangerous to himself or to the person or property of another and that disclosure of the communication is necessary to prevent the threatened danger.'

We realise that the open and confidential character of psychotherapeutic dialogue encourages patients to express threats of violence, few of which are ever executed. Certainly a therapist should not be encouraged routinely to reveal such threats; such disclosures could seriously disrupt the patient's relationship with his therapist and with the persons threatened. To the contrary, the therapist's obligations to his patient require that he not disclose a confidence unless such disclosure is necessary to avert danger to others, and even then that he do so discreetly, and in a fashion that would preserve the privacy of his patient to the fullest extent compatible with the prevention of the threatened danger. (See Fleming & Maximov, *The Patient or His Victim: The Therapist's Dilemma* (1974) 62 Cal L Rev 1025, 1065–1066).

The revelation of a communication under the above circumstances is not a breach of trust or a violation of professional ethics; as stated in the Principles of Medical Ethics of the American Medical Association (1957), section 9: 'A physician may not reveal the confidence entrusted to him in the course of medical attendance . . . *unless he is required to do so by law or unless it becomes necessary in order to protect the welfare of the individual or of the community*.' (Emphasis added.) We conclude that the public policy favoring protection of the confidential character of patient-psychotherapist communications must yield to the extent to which disclosure is essential to avert danger to others. The protective privilege ends where the public peril begins.

Our current crowded and computerised society compels the interdependence of its members. In this risk-infected society we can hardly tolerate the further exposure to danger that would result from a concealed knowledge of the therapist that his patient was lethal. If the exercise of reasonable care to protect the threatened victim requires the therapist to warn the endangered party or those who can reasonably be expected to notify him, we see no sufficient societal interest that would protect and justify concealment. The containment of such risks lies in the public interest. For the foregoing reasons, we find that plaintiffs' complaints can be amended to state a cause of action against defendants Moore, Powelson, Gold, and Yandell and against the Regents as their employer, for breach of a duty to exercise reasonable care to protect Tatiana.

Questions

(i) Do you think an English court would follow this decision? Does *W v Egdell (supra)* provide any support?

(ii) If so, what, if any, limits would the court set to the scope of the doctor's duty? Rosencranz and Lavey 'Treating Patients with Communicable Diseases: Limiting Liability for Physicians and Safeguarding the Public Health' (1987) 32 St Louis ULJ 75, 86–87 (footnotes omitted) considers this:

. . . [I]n *Thompson v County of Alameda* [614 P 2d 728 (1980)], the California Supreme Court seemingly limited the scope of the *Tarasoff* duty, holding that no duty to warn existed when a patient with violent propensities, who had made threats of violence to young children in the community, was released from confinement. The court distinguished *Tarasoff*, stating that the earlier case involved a 'known and specifically foreseeable and identifiable victim of the patient's threats'. The *Thompson* court concluded that a person has no duty to warn the police or the parents of threatened children in the community when 'plaintiff's decedent was a member of a large amorphous public group of potential targets'. Similarly, other courts have limited the duty to warn to readily identifiable victims.

(iii) Given the difficulties in determining 'dangerousness', how dangerous must the patient be before the duty in *Tarasoff*, if accepted in England at all, would arise?

(iv) Consider the following: X is diagnosed by Dr A as carrying the human immunodeficiency virus (HIV) which causes AIDS. What are Dr A's legal obligations in these situations:

(a) X is married and Dr A knows X's wife is now at risk of infection (X's wife may also be a patient of Dr A);

(b) as in (a) except X is not married but lives with his partner;

(c) X is not married and does not have a stable relationship with another person at this time, although Dr A knows that X is sexually active.

In considering your responses, give some thought to the distinction between imposing a *duty* upon Dr A to inform others of X's conditon and a *power* to do so.

Also, do you think it should make any difference if Dr A discusses with X the possibility of his transmitting the infection to others and X agrees to inform his sexual partners but, as it turns out, he does not and the infection is transmitted?

(See Hermann and Gagliano 'AIDS, Therapeutic Confidentiality, and Warning Third Parties' (1989) 48 Maryland LR 55.)

Part III

Medical law in action

A : The beginning of life

Chapter 7

Contraception

Non-surgical methods

1. GENERALLY

The forms of contraception considered here are, the condom, the intra-uterine device (IUD), long-acting injectable contraceptives (Depo-provera), and the female contraceptive pill (the pill). Apart from the condom, these require the involvement of doctors to prescribe or fit them. A threshold question is whether these amount to medical treatment.

Lord Scarman in *Gillick* [1985] 3 All ER 402 at 418, said:

> If, as is clear in the light of s 5 of the National Health Service Act 1977 (re-enacting earlier legislation) and s 41 of the National Health Service (Scotland) Act 1978, contraceptive medical treatment is recognised as a legitimate and beneficial treatment in cases in which it is medically indicated.

Section 5(1)(b) of the National Health Service Act 1977 imposes a duty upon the Secretary of State:

> to arrange, to such extent as he considers necessary to meet all reasonable requirements in England and Wales, for the giving of advice on contraception, the medical examination of persons seeking advice on contraception, the treatment of such persons and the supply of contraceptive substances and appliances.

Lord Fraser, in *Gillick op cit* at 407, pointed out:

> These, and other, provisions show that Parliament regarded 'advice' and 'treatment' on contraception and the supply of appliances for contraception as essentially medical matters. So they are, but they may also raise moral and social questions on which many people feel deeply, and in that respect they differ from ordinary medical advice and treatment.

This being so, are there special limitations on the provision of this form of treatment, if otherwise, as Lord Scarman said, it is 'medically indicated'? As a matter of law, does contraceptive treatment differ, as Lord Fraser put it, 'from ordinary medical treatment'?

Our answer would be that if there is any limitation this would only be in the case of children but not if the patient is an adult. The solution will depend upon a precise analysis of Lord Fraser's speech in *Gillick*.

If contraceptive treatment is medically indicated, ie there are sound medical-technical reasons for resort to it and no medical counter-indications, and it is recognised as 'treatment' by Parliament, ordinarily its legality should simply be a matter of valid consent being given. One reading of *Gillick* would have it that consent is not only a necessary, but is also *the* sufficient, condition for the doctor to treat. But, as we have seen (see *supra* Ch 4) another reading of *Gillick* suggests however, that for Lord Fraser, consent though necessary, is not a sufficient condition for this particular form of treatment to be lawful. Lord Fraser, as we saw, may be saying that as a matter of public policy, a doctor must consider whether the treatment is in the best interests of his consenting patient before proceeding: 'The only practicable course is, in my opinion, to entrust the doctor with a discretion to act in accordance with his view of what is best in the interests of the girl who is his patient.' (at 413)

The other apparently special cases involve contraceptive treatment for the mentally ill and handicapped. In our view, these only raise issues of capacity to consent and are not, as a matter of law, special in any other way. It may be otherwise, of course, if, for example, the pill or long-acting injectable contraception were actually being given for reasons of managing personal hygiene rather than contraception. This would raise questions as to the propriety of the action and whether it amounted to treatment. It cannot be treatment, of course, if it is done for the interests of others.

As the Panel of Persons appointed by the Licensing Authority to Hear the Application For a Product Licence to Market the Drug Depo-Provera as a long-term contraceptive stated in their Report (paragraphs 5.4, 5.6):

> There was considerable discussion before us on the issue of consent. We believe that the use of a drug that is long acting and with common and often unpleasant side effects is only acceptable if informed consent is obtained from the recipient. Some potential recipients would, of course, be able to understand and weigh the issues involved and give valid consent to treatment. A number of witnesses told us that these would include some of the mentally ill and mentally handicapped in institutional care, and the socially disadvantaged or socially maladapted in the community, provided that proper counselling was given to them. We believe, however, that for a number of reasons it will be difficult for many potential recipients to give informed consent. This is due to such factors as the lack of time available for explanation and counselling by medical and nursing staff, the lack of training and skills in such counselling among doctors not specialising in family planning, patients not being given information on which to make a decision, the inability of patients to understand and weigh the issues, whether through lack of intelligence, general inadequacy, mental handicap, psychiatric illness or through language difficulties, or because they are unable or unwilling to question or challenge the doctor's guidance.

> It would only be in very exceptional circumstances that patients who were unable to give real consent would be given the drug. The type of situation that we have in mind is that mentioned by Dr Rona McClean in her written evidence, where the patient is mentally handicapped to such a degree that she cannot give consent to any type of medical treatment. In such circumstances the doctor concerned should apply the same criteria to treatment with Depo-Provera as would be applied when considering any form of medical treatment.

One form of non-surgical contraception which poses special legal problems is that form known as post-coital birth control. This is more properly called contragestation rather than contraception. Section 58 of the Offences Against the Person Act 1861 provides:

> **58.**—Every woman, being with child, who, with intent to procure her own miscarriage, shall unlawfully administer to herself any poison or other noxious thing, or shall unlawfully use any instrument or other means whatsoever with the like intent and whosoever, with intent to procure the miscarriage of any woman, whether she be or not with child, shall unlawfully administer to her or cause to be taken by her any poison or other noxious thing, or shall unlawfully use any instrument or other means whatsoever with the like intent, shall be guilty of an offence, and being convicted thereof shall be liable to imprisonment.

(Note also s 59 dealing with the 'supply' and procurement of poison and instruments 'with intent to procure a miscarriage'.)

The Abortion Act 1967, s 1 reads as follows:

1.—(1) Subject to the provisions of this section, a person shall not be guilty of an offence under the law relating to abortion when a pregnancy is terminated by a registered medical practitioner if two registered medical practitioners are of the opinion, formed in good faith—

(a) that the continuance of the pregnancy would involve risk to the life of the pregnant woman, or of injury to the physical or mental health of the pregnant woman or any existing children of her family, greater than if the pregnancy were terminated; or

(b) that there is a substantial risk that if the child were born it would suffer from such physical or mental abnormalities as to be seriously handicapped.

Is a doctor who prescribes post-coital birth control (a double dose regime of a combination of oestrogen and progestrogen hormones), sometimes known as the 'morning after' pill, guilty of an offence under s 58 unless he complies with the terms of the 1967 Act? The central question is when, as a matter of law, can a person be said to act 'with intent to procure a miscarriage'? In turn this requires us to understand the meaning of the word 'miscarriage' in ss 58 and 59. Needless to say, there is no definition offered in English law either in statute or in case law.

One view, advanced is that a 'miscarriage' is procured whenever a fertilised egg is destroyed or expelled from the body whether or not it had been implanted in the uterus. If this view were correct, it would mean that any intervention after conception done with the intention of 'procuring a miscarriage' as so defined, would amount to an offence under the Offences Against the Person Act 1861. It may be interesting, however, to notice the authority and arguments on which this view is based.

Keown writes as follows in 'Miscarriage: A Medico-Legal Analysis' [1984] Criminal Law Review 608–611:

(b) Judicial authority
In addition to the guidance afforded by the actual wording of the abortion provisions, the construction of 'miscarriage' has arisen in several reported cases. These cases, drawn from India, Victoria, and the United States, are of persuasive value on account of the similarity between section 58 and the statutory provisions with which they deal. They point unanimously to an unrestricted construction of 'miscarriage.'

The leading Indian case on the question is *Ademma*,[28] decided by the Court of Appeal at Madras. The defendant was charged under section 312 of the Indian Penal Code 1860 with procuring her own miscarriage.[29] The evidence showed that she had only been pregnant for about a month and that all that came away was a mass of blood. The Sessions Judge ruled that she had not been 'with child' within the meaning of the section. He observed:[30] 'There was nothing which could be called even a rudimentary foetus or child'.[30] Accordingly, Ademma was acquitted. The Court of Appeal, however, consisting of Muttusámi Ayyar and Brandt JJ, ordered a re-trial, holding that the offence could be committed from conception onward:

The term 'miscarriage' is not defined in the Penal Code. In its popular sense it is synonymous with abortion, and consists in the expulsion of the embryo or foetus, ie the immature product of conception. The stage to which pregnancy has advanced and the form which the ovum or embryo may have assumed are immaterial.[31]

The court continued:

Section 312 requires proof that the woman is 'with child,' but it is enough if the fact of pregnancy and the intended expulsion of the immature contents of the uterus are established. The words 'with child' mean pregnant, and it is not necessary to show that 'quickening,' ie perception by the mother of the movements of the foetus, has taken place, or that the embryo has assumed a foetal form.[32] Although the defendant had been pregnant for one month and implantation had, therefore, already occurred somewhere, the broad basis of the court's decision affords sound authority for the legal irrelevance of implantation.[33]

The meaning of 'miscarriage' was also considered by an Australian court in *Trim*.[34] There, the defendant was charged with the murder of one Edna Freeman. The Crown alleged that death had resulted from the defendant's use of a syringe with intent to procure Freeman's miscarriage, and secured a conviction for manslaughter. Trim appealed, contending *inter alia* that the judge had been guilty of a misdirection by ruling that the use of the syringe with intent to evacuate the uterus was an offence under section 62 of the Crimes Act 1928 (the section corresponding to section 58) even if the foetus was believed to be dead. By a majority, the Full Court of the Supreme Court of Victoria dismissed the appeal. Martin J delivered the majority judgment. He observed that, as section 62 did not require proof of pregnancy, 'one, and perhaps the chief, evil which the Legislature wished to prevent was the possibility of harm being done to the woman'.[35] In construing 'miscarriage' broadly enough to prohibit the attempt to expel even a dead foetus, he remarked: 'In popular use the word "abortion" frequently is used as synonymous with "miscarriage," and the presence of the heading, "Attempts to procure abortion," to sections 62 and 63 suggests that the Legislature intended the word "miscarriage" in those sections to cover "abortion"'.[36] He continued: 'In *Webster's Dictionary* appears the following comprehensive definition of 'Abortion': 'Act of giving premature birth; specifically, the expulsion of the human fetus prematurely, particularly at any time before it is viable, or capable of sustaining life; miscarriage'.[37] Martin J then adverted to the restricted definition of 'miscarriage' as abortion between the 'quickening' of the foetus—around the fourth month of pregnancy—and the point of its viability. However, he concluded that just as the word 'birth' in section 64 of the Crimes Act had been broadly interpreted to include even stillbirth, 'The word "miscarriage" should be given no restricted meaning in sections 61 and 62, as one reason for all three sections is the safeguarding of the health of a woman who is or may be with child.'[38] In support of this unrestricted construction, Martin J cited the sixth edition of *Taylor's Principles and Practice of Medical Jurisprudence*, which declared in relation to section 58:

> the statute only uses the word 'miscarriage,' including in that term comprehensively the emptying of a pregnant uterus at any time of conception, ignoring altogether the technical terms abortion, miscarriage, premature confinement, which are merely convenient descriptive words for medical men.[39]

By using such a popular term, it added, the law 'intends thereby to mean the contents of a gravid uterus, whether such contents be well or ill-formed, living or dead, moles, or any other result of conception . . .'[40] Martin J did not regard this definition as authoritative in relation to section 62, but conceded:

> it does convey the sense in which that word is there used, as, by reason of the heading in the material section, and the apparent purpose of the legislation, I consider it is wide enough to include abortion which, in the same work (vol II, p 141) is defined as 'an untimely emptying of a uterus which contains the products of a conception'.[41]

A further source of judicial authority supporting an unrestricted interpretation of 'miscarriage' takes the form of a long and substantial line of case law from the United States, which establishes that 'miscarriage' and 'abortion' are legally synonymous and refer to the expulsion of the products of conception at any period of pregnancy. As early as 1850, the Supreme Court of Pennsylvania stated: 'Miscarriage, both in law and philology, means the bringing forth the foetus before it is perfectly formed and capable of living . . . The word abortion is synonymous and equivalent to miscarriage, in its primary meaning'.[42] The court's statement of the law has been consistently supported by the courts of other states.[43]

Notes to extract
[28] [1886] ILR IX Mad 369.

[29] Section 312 provided, *inter alia*: 'Whoever voluntarily causes a woman with child to miscarry, shall ... be punished with imprisonment ... or with a fine, or with both. . . .'

[30] [1886] ILR IX Mad 369, 370.

[31] *Ibid*.

[32] *Ibid*.

[33] Broad language also characterises a *dictum* of Thomson CJ in a Malaysian case of 1958. Commenting upon the Malaysian equivalent to s 312, he said: 'it is quite clear that the expression "causes a woman with child to miscarry" means to cause her to lose from the womb prematurely the *products of conception* and that therefore there can be no offence under the section unless there are *products of conception.*' *Munah binti Ali v Public Prosecutor* (1958) 24 MLR 159 at 160 (CA) (emphasis supplied).

[34] [1943] VLR 109.

[35] 115.

[36] *Ibid*.

[37] *Ibid*.

[38] 116.

[39] (6th ed, 1910, ed F Smith), vol II, p 142, it should be noted that the word 'uterus' is not here used with anatomical precision: at p 178 of the same volume it is stressed that the law applies equally to extra-uterine pregnancies. See also text at note 53, *infra*.

[40] *Ibid* at p 178. (At p 44, 'conception' is defined as 'the union of sperm and germ.') Similarly, as early as 1844, Taylor had written: 'In a popular sense (and here a *popular* appears to have been purposely selected in preference to a professional term,) miscarriage signifies the violent expulsion not merely of a child, but of moles, hydatids and other diseased growths, or even of coagula of blood': *op cit* note 1, *supra*, p 597 (original emphasis).

[41] [1943] VLR 109 at 116. The dissenting judge, Macfarlan J, advanced an equally liberal interpretation of 'miscarriage' by emphasising the word's connotation of failure. He said, at 112, that s 62 merely required: 'an intent to cause in the case of the woman in question the event of birth, carriage or bearing which would take place in the ordinary course of nature to go amiss—go wrong or fail.'

In *Smith*, MacNaghten J ruled that the intention to remove a dead foetus did not constitute an intention to procure miscarriage on the ground that the rationale of the law was the protection of foetal life (reported in Taylor's *Principles and Practice of Medical Jurisprudence* (11th ed, 1957, eds S Smith and K Simpson), vol II, p 99. Although the outcome of *Smith's* case is preferable, it is submitted that a sounder basis for the ruling would have been that 'miscarriage,' in its ordinary sense, does not include the removal of a dead foetus.

[42] *Mills v Commonwealth* (1850) 13 Pa (1 Harris) 630 at 632. The court added: 'The moment the womb is instinct with embryo life, and gestation has begun, the crime may be perpetrated': *ibid*.

[43] See, eg *Wells v New Eng Mut Life Ins Co of Boston, Mass* 43 A 126 (SC Penn) (1899); *People v Rankin* 74 P 2d 71 (1937) (SC Calif); *Hall v People* 201 P 2d 382 (1948) (SC Col); *Scott v State* 117 A 2d 831 (1955) (SC Del). For further discussion, see Meloy, 'Pre-implantation Fertility Control and the Abortion Laws' (1964) 41 Chicago-Kent LR 183, who concludes at p 206: 'The broad language of statutes and cases would suggest that to use the pre-implantation means on a pregnant woman would be unlawful.' See also King, 'The "Morning-After Pill" and Other Pre-implantation Birth-Control Methods and the Law' (1967) 46 Oregon LR 211, who concludes at p 217: 'Since the function of the pre-implantation means [of] fertility control is to interrupt pregnancy, their use would no doubt violate abortion statutes which do not require pregnancy as an element of the offense; this would be especially true of the use of the 'morning-after' pill taken in the belief that conception may have occurred ... A woman using an intra-uterine device would also violate this type of abortion statute, because, after inserted (*sic*), the intent to destroy any produce of conception will always be present.'

Tunkel ([1974] CLR 461) seeks to provide a further basis for this position by relying on a sentence in Professor Williams's *Sanctity of Life and the Criminal Law*, published in 1958.

> At present both English law and the law of the great majority of the United States regard any interference with pregnancy, however early it may take place, as criminal, unless for therapeutic reasons. The foetus is a human life to be protected by the criminal law from the moment when the ovum is fertilised.

Relying on this, Tunkel argues, at p 465:

> . . . [T]he use of the word 'miscarriage' has always been understood to include any fatal interference with the fertilised ovum: . . . To hold otherwise would, in effect, give a sort of free-for-all moratorium of a week or more after intercourse during which every sort of abortionist could ply his craft with impunity. The law may permit the douching of the vagina soon after intercourse, but that seems the limit of allowable postcoital prevention.

Do you find these arguments persuasive? In particular, do you think that they are relevant to the discussion concerning the difference between 'pre-implantation' and 'implantation'? Do they not, instead, appear to be more concerned with the difference between 'conception' and 'quickening', particularly in the light of the fact that the nineteenth century authorities were unaware of the detail of the physiological processes involved between conception and birth, save in the most general terms?

Furthermore, it should be added that Professor Williams, when he gave his mind to this particular point, wrote (*Textbook of Criminal Law* 2nd ed 1983, p 294):

> **Where exactly is the line drawn between contraception and abortion?**
> Formerly it was thought that the vital point of time was fertilisation, the fusion of spermatozoon and ovum, but it is now realised (although the point has not come before the courts) that this position is not maintainable, and that conception for legal purposes must be dated at earliest from implantation.
>
> The legislation is unspecific. The abortion section does not expressly refer to conception; it speaks merely of a 'miscarriage'. There is, therefore, nothing to prevent the courts interpreting the word 'miscarriage' in a way that takes account of customary and approved birth control practices.

As Williams goes on to point out, to hold the view advanced earlier carries the further consequence that the fitting of an intra-uterine device, sometimes known as the 'coil' (IUD) would also be governed by the Abortion Act and be unlawful. For, it cannot be doubted that a doctor who fits an IUD does so with knowledge that intercourse may take place and, in those circumstances, his intention will be to prevent the intercourse resulting in the implantation of a fertilised egg in the uterus. (There is also evidence that an IUD when fitted may prevent fertilisation, but clearly if done with this intention such a practice could never be unlawful under the 1861 Act. It is, however, questionable whether the two intentions could be separable.)

Surely Professor Williams is correct in writing (*op cit*, pp 294–5) that:

> . . . [N]o one who uses or fits IUDs supposes that they are illegal or are governed by the Abortion Act. The only way to uphold the legality of present medical practice, to make IUDs contraceptives and not abortifacients, is to say that for legal purposes conception is not complete until implantation.

Williams goes on to reach the same view concerning post-coital birth control by use of the 'morning after' pill when he concludes that 'the legal argument (concerning IUDs and 'morning after' pills) is that the word 'miscarriage' in s 58 means the miscarriage of an implanted blastocyst'.

The alternative view, as reflected in Professor Williams's conclusion, was accepted by the (then) Attorney-General in a written answer to the House of Commons in May 1983 (42 Part Deb HC 238 at 239).

> The sole question for resolution therefore is whether the prevention of implantation constitutes the procuring of a miscarriage within the meaning of sections 58 to 59 of the Offences against the Person Act 1861. The principles relating to interpretation of statutes require that the words of a statute be given the meaning which they bore at the time the statute was passed. Further, since the words were used in a general statute, they are *prima facie* presumed to be used in their popular, ordinary or natural sense.
>
> In this context it is important to bear in mind that a failure to implant is something which may occur in the manner described above or quite spontaneously. Indeed in a significant proportion of cases the fertilised ovum is lost either prior to implantation or at the next menstruation. It is clear that, used in its ordinary sense, the word "miscarriage" is not apt to describe a failure to implant—whether spontaneous or not. Likewise, the phrase "procure a miscarriage" cannot be construed to include the prevention of implantation. Whatever the state of medical knowledge in the 19th century, the ordinary use of the word "miscarriage" related to interference at a stage of pre-natal development later than implantation.
>
> In the light of the above I have come to the conclusion that this form of post-coital treatment does not constitute a criminal offence within either sections 58 or 59 of the Offences against the Person Act 1861.

Besides removing doubts about the legality of fitting IUDs, this view of the 'morning after' pill also can be said to conform with a commonsense understanding of the word 'miscarriage'. To 'miscarry' clearly entails that something has been 'carried'. It would be unusual to say that a woman is carrying anything when all that has transpired is that an egg has been fertilised and is travelling through her body. It would accord with commonsense and be quite natural to describe her as carrying something once a fertilised egg is implanted in her uterus.

It follows, therefore, on this interpretation that the 'morning after' pill may be prescribed up to the point at which medical evidence establishes that implantation is likely to occur, which seems to any anywhere between five and ten days after intercourse has taken place.

An example of this commonsense view being adopted by legislation can be found in the 1977 amendment to the Crimes Act 1961 of New Zealand in s 182A:

> **3. Miscarriage defined**—The principal Act is hereby amended by inserting, after section 182, the following section:
>
> '**182A.** For the purposes of sections 183 to 187 of this Act the term 'miscarriage' means—
> (a) The destruction or death of an embryo or fetus after implantation; or
> (b) The premature expulsion or removal of an embryo or fetus after implantation, otherwise than for the purpose of inducing the birth of a fetus believed to be viable or removing a fetus that has died.'

2. LIABILITY FOR DEFECTIVE CONTRACEPTIVE DRUGS AND APPLIANCES

(a) At common law

Under the English common law any allegation that an English contraceptive drug or appliance was defective would sound in negligence. There are three ways in which a contraceptive drug or appliance could be defective, namely: (i) that it was carelessly manufactured so as to expose the user to an unreasonable risk of harm; (ii) that it was badly designed so as to expose the user to an unreasonable risk of harm; and (iii) that it was unaccompanied by appropriate warnings or directions so as to make it not reasonably safe for the user.

(i)   Manufacture

There would appear to be no special problems of law relating to contraceptives. They are treated as any other product in that liability depends upon proof that the manufacturer has failed to exercise reasonable care and skill. He must take reasonable steps to ensure that his manufacturing process is such that the product would meet the appropriate standard of safety, quality and efficacy.

In the case of contraceptives, it is likely that the law also requires the manufacturer to demonstrate that he has taken all reasonable steps to establish an adequate system of post-market surveillance and recall (by, for example recording batch numbers and being able to locate to whom batches were supplied).

(ii)   Design

Similarly, contraceptives are regarded in law as the same as other products as to the reasonableness of their design. Manufacturers, as a consequence, will be expected to have carried out all reasonable research, eg on animals and through clinical trials, and to have taken account of all scientific knowledge available through reasonable endeavour at the time of deciding upon their design. This entails keeping abreast of, what is often called, the 'state of the art' (see *infra* under the Consumer Protection Act 1987). It follows that what was said in (i) above about recall and surveillance applies here.

(iii)   Warnings and directions

A product may be adequately manufactured and designed and still be defective if, in the circumstances, a court would decide that it should be accompanied by appropriate warnings and directions for use.

Warnings. The common law is as stated by Robins JA in the Ontario Court of Appeal in *Buchan v Ortho Pharmaceuticals (Canada) Ltd* (1986) 54 OR (2d) 92 at 100:

> As a matter of common law, it is well settled that a manufacturer of a product has a duty to warn consumers of dangers inherent in the use of its product of which it knows or has reason to know.

Later, Robins JA explained the scope of this duty.

> In determining whether a drug manufacturer's warnings satisfy the duty to make adequate and timely warning to the medical profession of any dangerous side-effects produced by its drugs of which it knows, or has reason to know, certain factors must be borne in mind. A manufacturer of prescription drugs occupies the position of an expert in the field; this requires that it be under a continuing duty to keep abreast of scientific developments pertaining to its product through research, adverse reaction reports, scientific literature and other available methods. When additional dangerous or potentially dangerous side-effects from the drug's use are discovered, the manufacturer must make all reasonable efforts to communicate the information to prescribing physicians. Unless doctors have current, accurate and complete information about a drug's risks, their ability to exercise the fully informed medical judgment necessary for the proper performance of their vital role in prescribing drugs for patients may be reduced or impaired.
>
> Whether a particular warning is adequate will depend on what is reasonable in the circumstances. But the fact that a drug is ordinarily safe and effective and the

danger may be rare or involve only a small percentage of users does not necessarily relieve the manufacturer of the duty to warn. While a low probability of injury or a small class of endangered users are factors to be taken into account in determining what is reasonable, these factors must be balanced against such considerations as the nature of the drug, the necessity for taking it, and the magnitude of the increased danger to the individual consumer. Similarly, where medical evidence exists which tends to show a serious danger inherent in the use of a drug, the manufacturer is not entitled to ignore or discount that information in its warning solely because it finds it to be unconvincing; the manufacturer is obliged to be forthright and to tell the whole story. The extent of the warning and the steps to be taken to bring the warning home to physicians should be commensurate with the potential danger—the graver the danger, the higher the duty.

A reading of Ortho US's warnings to physicians makes it manifest that Ortho was aware or should have been aware of the association between oral contraceptive use and stroke. Moreover, the expert testimony and the exhibits in this case disclose an abundance of published information in medical and scientific journals prior to and at the time the plaintiff was prescribed Ortho-Novum which linked the use of oral contraceptives with stroke. Ortho US provided American physicians with data from and the conclusions of the studies in Britain and the United States, and warned of the risk of cerebral damage posed by the pill. Yet, in Canada, Ortho chose not to provide physicians with any similar warning. Why the medical profession in this country, and, through it, consumers in this country, should be given a less explicit and meaningful warning by the Canadian manufacturer of the same drug is a question that has not been answered. Be that as it may, I think it evident that Ortho failed to give the medical profession warnings commensurate with its knowledge of the dangers inherent in the use of Ortho-Novum; more specifically, it breached its duty to warn of the risk of stroke associated with the use of Ortho-Novum.

Earlier he had said:

The guiding principle of liability underlying the present law of products liability in this country was formulated by Lord Atkin in his classic statement in *M'Alister (or Donoghue) v Stevenson* [1932] AC 562 at 599, HL:

. . . a manufacturer of products, which he sells in such a form as to show that he intends them to reach the ultimate consumer in the form in which they left him with no reasonable possibility of intermediate examination, and with the knowledge that the absence of reasonable care in the preparation or putting up of the products will result in an injury to the consumer's life or property, owes a duty to the consumer to take that reasonable care.

This statement has been the source of subsequent developments in products liability law based on negligence. The *rationale* is that one who brings himself into a relation with others through an activity which foreseeably exposes them to danger if proper care is not observed must exercise reasonable care to safeguard them from that danger. It can now be taken as a legal truism that the duty of reasonable care which lies at the foundation of the law of negligence commonly comprehends a duty to warn of danger, the breach of which will, when it is the cause of injury, give rise to liability: see, generally, Fleming, *The Law of Torts*, 6th ed (1983), at p 459 ff, and Linden *Canadian Tort Law*, 3rd edn (1982), at p 563 ff.

Once a duty to warn is recognised, it is manifest that the warning must be adequate, It should be communicated clearly and understandably in a manner calculated to inform the user of the nature of the risk and the extent of the danger; it should be in terms commensurate with the gravity of the potential hazard, and it should not be neutralised or negated by collateral efforts on the part of the manufacturer. The nature and extent of any given warning will depend on what is reasonable having regard to all the facts and circumstances relevant to the product in question.

The general principle to be applied in determining the degree of explicitness required in a warning was enunciated by the Supreme Court of Canada, speaking through Laskin J., in *Lambert v Lastoplex Chemicals Co Ltd* [1972] SCR 569 at 574–5, 25 DLR (3d) 121 at 125, as follows:

Where manufactured products are put on the market for ultimate purchase and use by the general public and carry danger (in this case, by reason of high inflammability), although put to the use for which they are intended, *the manufacturer, knowing of their hazardous nature, has a duty to specify the attendant dangers, which it must be taken to appreciate in a detail not known to the ordinary consumer or user.* A general warning, as for example, that the product is inflammable, will not suffice where the likelihood of fire may be increased according to the surroundings in which it may reasonably be expected that the product will be used. *The required explicitness of the warning will, of course, vary with the danger likely to be encountered in the ordinary use of the product.*

(Emphasis added.)

The duty is a continuous one requiring that the manufacturer warn, not only of dangers known at the time of sale, but also of dangers discovered after the product has been sold and delivered. In the words of Ritchie J., speaking for the majority of the Supreme Court of Canada in *Rivtow Marine Ltd v Washington Iron Works* [1974] SCR 1189 at 1200, 40 DLR (3d) 530 at 536, [1973] 6 WWR 692:

. . . the knowledge of the danger involved in the continued use of these cranes for the purpose for which they were designed carried with it a duty to warn those to whom the cranes had been supplied, and this duty arose at the moment when the respondents or either of them became seized with the knowledge.

Ordinarily, the warnings must be addressed directly to the person likely to be injured. It is not, however, necessary that that be done in every case. Where, for example, the product is a highly technical one that is intended or expected to be used only under the supervision of experts, a warning to the experts will suffice: *Murphy v St. Catharines General Hospital* [1964] 1 OR 239, 41 DLR (2d) (HCJ). Similarly, a warning to the ultimate user may not be necessary where intermediate examination is anticipated or the intervention of a learned intermediary is understood. As the English Court of Appeal pointed out in *Holmes v Ashford* [1950] 2 All ER 76 at 80:

In the present case . . . it must have been in the contemplation of the manufacturers supplying these goods to hairdressers that hairdressers may be expected to interpose their judgment and reason whether they are going to use a hair dye or not. In my view, if they give a warning which, if read by a hairdresser, is sufficient to intimate to him the potential dangers of the substance with which he is going to deal, that is all that can be expected of them. I think it would be unreasonable and impossible to expect that they should give warning in such form that it must come to the knowledge of the particular customer who is going to be treated. Counsel for the plaintiff says they must take reasonable steps to see that it will come to the notice of any customer. I cannot contemplate any steps which could be calculated to bring a matter of this kind to the knowledge of any person who is treated with the preparation. The most that can be expected of the manufacturer of goods of this kind is to see that the hairdresser is sufficiently warned.

There are surprisingly few reported decisions in Canada or in the United Kingdom involving a drug manufacturer's duty to warn with respect to either over-the-counter or prescription drugs. On the other hand, there is a considerable body of case-law in the United States in which the subject is exhaustively and authoritatively discussed. Counsel, in their very thorough presentations, made reference to many of these decisions in support of their respective positions. In my view, they are pertinent to the issues in this appeal and instructive. American jurisprudence dealing with products liability based on negligence, it may be remembered, is rooted in the same fundamental philosophy and is based on the same general principles of negligence as our law since *M'Alister (or Donoghue) v Stevenson*: see *Prosser and Keeton on Torts*, 5th ed (1984), at p 677 ff. I might add that the plaintiff, as an alternative ground for relief, sought recovery on a theory of strict liability. However, on the view I take of the case, I consider it unnecessary to discuss the imposition of liability on that basis.

In the present state of human knowledge, many drugs are clearly incapable of being made totally safe for their intended or ordinary use even though they have been properly manufactured and are not impure or defective. Notwithstanding a medically recognizable risk, their marketing may be justified by their utility. Apart from any regulatory scheme under the *Food and Drugs Act*, the general rule at common law is that the manufacturer of such drugs, like the manufacturer of other products, has a duty to provide consumers with adequate warning of the potentially harmful side-effects that the manufacturer knows or has reason to know may be produced by the drug. There is, however, an important exception to that general rule. In the case of prescription drugs, the duty of manufacturers to warn consumers is discharged if the manufacturer provides prescribing physicians, rather than consumers, with adequate warning of the potential danger.

This exception, which has come to be known in the United States as the "learned intermediary" rule, adopts an approach sinilar to that taken in cases involving intermediate inspection or intervening cause under the rule in *M'Alister (or Donoghue) v. Stevenson*. The *rationale* for the exception is that prescription drugs are more likely to be complex medicines, esoteric in formula and varied in effect and, by definition, are available only by prescription. the prescribing physician is in a position to take into account the propensities of the drug and the susceptibilities of his patient. He has the duty of informing himself of the benefits and potential dangers of any medication he prescribes, and of exercising his independent judgment as a medical expert based on his knowledge of the patient and the product. In taking the drug, the patient is expected to, and it can be presumed does, place primary reliance on his doctor's judgment. In this relationship, the prescribing physician is said to act as a learned intermediary between the manufacturer and the ultimate consumer. Thus, while the general rule is that manufacturers of drugs have a duty to warn users of known dangers in the use of their products, manufacturers of prescription drugs, because of the intervention of the learned intermediary, have a duty to warn only prescribing physicians: *Reyes v Wyeth Laboratories* 498 F 2d 1264 (1974); *certiorari* denied 419 US 1096; *Terhune v A H Robins Co* 577 P 2d 975 (1978) (Wash); *Sterling Drug, Inc v Cornish* 370 f 2d 82 (1966); *McEwen v Ortho Pharmaceutical Corp* 528 P 2d 522 (1974) (Or).

There are no decisions dealing specifically with oral contraceptives in this country or in England. In most of the jurisdictions in the United States in which the question has been considered, the learned intermediary rule has been adhered to, and manufacturers of oral contraceptives have accordingly been held under a duty to warn only prescribing physicians of the risks associated with their product. Very recently, however, several state courts have concluded that oral contraceptives bear characteristics which render them vastly different from other prescription drugs and which demand that manufacturers be required to warn users directly of risks associated with their use. The reasoning which prompted these courts to hold the learned intermediary rule inapplicable to birth control pills is clearly articulated in the decision of the Supreme Judicial Court of Massachusetts in *MacDonald v Ortho Pharmaceutical Corp* 475 NE 2d 65 (1985) (Mass); *Certiorari* denied 106 S Ct 250.

In that case, which, like this one, involved a stroke found to have been caused by the ingestion of Ortho-Novum, the majority (4:1) of the court, *per* Abrams J, said at 70:

> The oral contraceptive thus stands apart from other prescription drugs in light of the heightened participation of patients in decisions relating to use of 'the pill'; the substantial risks affiliated with the product's use; the feasibility of direct warnings by the manufacturers to the user; the limited participation of the physician (annual prescriptions); and the possibility that oral communications between physicians and consumers may be insufficient or too scanty standing alone fully to apprise consumers of the product's dangers at the time the initial selection of a contraceptive method is made as well as at subsequent points when alternative methods may be considered. *We conclude that the manufacturer of oral contraceptives is not justified in relying on warnings to the medical profession to satisfy its common law duty to warn, and that the manufacturer's obligation encompasses a*

duty to warn the ultimate user. Thus, the manufacturer's duty is to provide to the consumer written warnings conveying reasonable notice of the nature, gravity, and likelihood of known or knowable side effects, and advising the consumer to seek fuller explanation from the prescribing physician or other doctor of any such information of concern to the consumer.

(Emphasis added.) See also: *Re Certified Questions* 358 NW 2d 873 (Mich) (1984); *Odgers v Ortho Pharmaceutical Corpn* 609 F Supp 867 (DC Mich) (1985); *Stephens v G D Searle & Co* 602 F Supp 379 (Mich) (1985); *Lukaszewicz v Ortho Pharmaceutical Corpn* 510 F Supp 961 (Wis) (1981).

Later Robins JA said:

I think it axiomatic that a drug manufacturer who seeks to rely on the intervention of prescribing physicians under the learned intermediary doctrine to except itself from the general common law duty to warn consumers directly must actually warn prescribing physicians. The duty, in my opinion, is one that cannot be delegated. I shall consider the warning as it relates specifically to the plaintiff's physician later, but as a general proposition, a manufacturer cannot justify a failure to warn by claiming that physicians were in a position to learn of the risks inherent in its products through other sources. The manufacturer's duty to warn continues notwithstanding that the information may be otherwise available. In this regard, I respectfully agree with the apt observations of Linden J in *Davidson v Connaught Laboratories* (1980) 14 CCLT 251 (Ont HCJ) at 276:

A drug company cannot rely upon doctors to read all the scientific literature outlining the specific dangers involved in the many drugs they have to administer each day. They are busy people, administering to the needs of the injured and the sick. They have little time for deep research into the medical literature. They rely on the drug companies to supply them with the necessary data. With very little effort the defendant company could have included in the material that it gave to the doctors, who were administering the injections, all the necessary facts. They did not. Even though these severe reactions were 'extremely rare', I think it would have been advisable for the company to have presented the figures that were available, or at least to have referred the doctors to publications where those figures could be learned. Once they have the figures, then the doctors can properly assess the situation and decide whether they will recommend the vaccine or not, and how much information about the risks they should give to their patients. The doctors, however, should have as full information as is reasonable in the circumstances.

See also *Mahr v G D Searle & Co* 390 NE 2d 1214 (1979) (Ill); *Brochu v Ortho Pharmaceutical Corpn* 642 F 2d 652 (1981).

. . .

Before leaving this case, I would return to the question of whether a manufacturer of oral contraceptives is under a duty at common law to warn consumers directly. In doing so, I am not unmindful to the fact that anything I may say at this stage is not necessary to my decision. In deference, however, to the thorough arguments presented on the issue, I make these brief comments.

I do not quarrel with the general proposition advanced by the defendant that where prescription drugs are concerned, the manufacturer's duty to warn is limited to an obligation to warn prescribing physicians of potential dangers that may result from the drug's use. This special standard represents an understandable and sensible exception to the well-recognised common law principle of tort liability that the manufacturer of a product has a duty to warn users of dangers inherent in the use of the product. The question here comes down to whether the *rationale* which is relied on to support this exception with respect to prescription drugs generally can be justified in the case of oral contraceptives.

There can be little doubt that oral contraceptives have presented society with problems unique in the history of human therapeutics. At no time have so many people taken such potent drugs voluntarily over such a protracted time for an objective other than the control of disease. This has introduced a novel element in the doctor-patient relationship. As the advisory committee pointed out, 'in prescribing these drugs, the doctor is usually acting neither to treat nor to prevent a disease. He is prescribing for socioeconomic reasons'. Furthermore, unlike the selection of an appropriate drug for the treatment of illness or injury where patient involvement is typically minimal or non-existent, consumer demand for oral contraceptives prompts their use more often than doctors' advice. The decision to use the pill is one in which consumers are actively involved; more frequently than not, they have made the decision before visiting a doctor to obtain a prescription.

For these reasons, as well as those stated in *MacDonald v Ortho Pharmaceutical Corp* 475 NE 2d 65 (1985), which I quoted earlier, I am of the view that oral contraceptives bear characteristics distinguishing them from most therapeutic, diagnostic and curative prescription drugs. The *rationale* underlying the learned intermediary rule, in my opinion, does not hold up in the case of oral contraceptives. Manufacturers of this drug should be obliged to satisfy the general common law duty to warn the ultimate consumer as well as prescribing physicians. To require this would not be to impose any real burden on drug manufacturers or to unduly interfere with the doctor-patient relationship as it exists with regard to the prescription of this drug. What is more, appropriate warnings conveying reasonable notice of the nature, gravity and likelihood of known or knowable side-effects and advising the consumer to seek further explanation from her doctor of any information of concern to her, would promote the desirable objective of ensuring that women are fully apprised of the information needed to balance the benefits and risks of this form of birth control and to make informed and intelligent decisions in consultation with their doctors on whether to use or continue to use oral contraceptives.

Directions. It is often overlooked that in addition to a duty to warn, a manufacturer may also be under a duty to give adequate directions on how properly to use a product. This is particularly important in the case of the contraceptives (eg frequency dosage etc). Furthermore, that which has been said about the 'learned intermediary' in the context of warnings, applies in the case of directions.

Thus, in conclusion, to be reasonably safe, a contraceptive drug or appliance must be competently manufactured and designed and accompanied by such warnings and directions so as to make foreseeable users reasonably safe. As Fleming points out in his book, *The Law of Torts* (7th Edition), pp 471–2:

A warning would not be sufficient unless it is given to a competent person and adequate to acquaint him fully with the dangerous properties of the substance so that he can himself adopt suitable precautions to prevent it from becoming a source of injury to himself and others.

(b) Consumer Protection Act 1987

The 1987 Act imposes strict liability upon a producer (as defined) of a contraceptive drug or appliance if it is defective (as defined). Section 3(1) states:

3.—(1) Subject to the following provisions of this section, there is a defect in a product for the purposes of this Part if the safety of the product is not such as persons generally are entitled to expect; and for those purposes 'safety', in relation to a product, shall include safety with respect to products comprised in that product and safety in the context of risks of damage to property, as well as in the context of risks of death or personal injury.

This is elaborated in s 3(2).

(2) In determining for the purposes of subsection (1) above what persons generally are entitled to expect in relation to a product all the circumstances shall be taken into account, including—
   (a) the manner in which, and purposes for which, the product has been marketed, its get-up, the use of any mark in relation to the product and any instructions for, or warnings with respect to, doing or refraining from doing anything with or in relation to the product;

(b) what might reasonably be expected to be done with or in relation to the product; and

(c) the time when the product was supplied by its producer to another;

and nothing in this section shall require a defect to be inferred from the fact alone that the safety of a product which is supplied after that time is greater than the safety of the product in question.

Following the pattern previously adopted, the product can be said to be defective in respect of its manufacture or design, or because it is not safe having regard to any instructions or warnings (or the absence thereof).

Although represented as strict liability, are the statutory provisions concerning 'warnings' and 'instructions' (or directions) most properly understood as imposing liability only for negligent warnings or failures to warn etc? Do you think the reasoning in the next case, concerned with negligence liability, would be equally appropriate if a court were interpreting s 3?

McEwen v Ortho Pharmaceutical Corpn
528 P 2d 522 (1974) (Supreme Court of Oregon) (footnotes omitted)

Howell, Justice:

I.   Defendants' duty to warn plaintiff's doctors

There is no question here of any defect in the manufacture of defendants' oral contraceptives, nor of their efficacy when taken as prescribed. It is well settled, however, that the manufacturer of ethical drugs bears the additional duty of making timely and adequate warnings to the medical profession of any dangerous side effects produced by its drugs of which it knows, or has reason to know. E g *Sterling Drug Inc v Cornish* 370 F 2d 82 (8th Cir 1966); *Parke-Davies & Co v Stromsodt* 411 F 2d 1390 (8th Cir 1969); *Stevens v Parke, Davies & Co* 9 Cal 3d 51, 107 Cal Rptr 45, 507 P 2d 653 (1973); *Love v Wolf* 226 Cal App 2d 378, 38 Cal Rptr 183 (1964) *Krug v Sterling Drug Inc* 416 SW 2d 143 (Mo Sup Ct 1967); see 2 Restatement (Second) of Torts 300, § 388 (1965).

The duty of the ethical drug manufacturer to warn is limited to those dangers which the manufacturer knows, or has reason to know, are inherent in the use of its drug. However, the drug manufacturer is treated as an expert in its particular field, and is under a 'continuous duty ... to keep abreast of scientific developments touching upon the manufacturer's product and to notify the medical profession of any additional side effects discovered from its use'. *Schenebeck v Sterling Drug Inc* 423 F 2d 919, 922 (8th Cir 1970); *accord O'Hare v Merck & Co* 381 F 2d 286, 291 (8th Cir 1967). The drug manufacturer's duty to warn is, therefore, commensurate not only with its actual knowledge gained from research and adverse reaction reports but also with its constructive knowledge as measured by scientific literature and other available means of communication.

Although the duty of the ethical drug manufacturer is to warn the doctor, rather than the patient, the manufacturer is directly liable to the patient for a breach of such duty. See *Schenebeck v Sterling Drug, Inc, supra*; *Love v Wolf, supra*. The manufacturer's compliance with this duty enables the prescribing physician to balance the risk of possible harm against the benefits to be gained by the patient's use of that drug. Moreover, as observed by the court in *Sterling Drug, Inc v Cornish, supra* 370 F 2d at 85:

... [T]he purchaser's doctor is a learned intermediary between the purchaser and the manufacturer. If the doctor is properly warned of the possibility of a side effect in some patients, and is advised of the symptoms normally accompanying the side effect, there is an excellent chance that injury to the patient can be avoided. This is particularly true if the injury takes place slowly . . .."

Although the ethical drug manufacturer's duty to warn has been discussed most often with reference to the prescribing physician, the above reasoning applies with equal force to the treating physician. It is especially important that the treating doctor receive the manufacturer's warnings where it is impossible to predict in advance whether a particular patient is apt to suffer adverse effects from a drug, since the treating doctor may be more likely to observe the actual symptoms of the drug's untoward consequences. If the prescribing physician is entitled to make an informed choice in deciding whether the patient should begin taking a prescription drug, it follows that a treating physician should have the same information in making his decision as to whether the patient should stop taking that drug.

The duty of the ethical drug manufacturer to warn extends, then, to all members of the medical profession who come into contact with the patient in a decision-making capacity. To satisfy this duty, the manufacturer must utilize methods of warning which will be reasonably effective, taking into account both the seriousness of the drug's adverse effects and the difficulties inherent in bringing such information to the attention of a group as large and diverse as the medical profession. See *Sterling Drug, Inc v Yarrow,* 408 F 2d 978 (8th Cir. 1969). The warning should be sufficient to apprise the general practitioner as well as the "unusually sophisticated medical man" of the dangerous propensities of the drug. *Parke-Davies & Co v Stromsodt,* 411 F 2d 1390, 1400 (8th Cir 1969). In short, "it is incumbent upon the manufacturer to bring the warning home to the doctor." Rheingold, *Products Liability—The Ethical Drug Manufacturer's Liability,* 18 Rutgers UL Rev 947, 993 (1964).

It has been suggested, however, that the manufacturer of a prescription drug should be under no duty to warn the medical profession that its product is dangerous when used by certain allergic or hypersensitive users. It is unreasonable, so the argument runs, to impose upon the manufacturer a duty to warn doctors of dangers threatening a statistically insignificant number of users. We find this argument unpersuasive.

In the field of negligence the duty to warn is limited to those dangerous propensities of the drug of which the manufacturer knows, or has reason to know. If allergic reactions are harder to anticipate, this should be taken into account in evaluating the manufacturer's knowledge. It must be remembered that the negligence liability of the ethical drug manufacturer is restricted to those dangers which *are* foreseeable.

Furthermore, to simply conclude that it is unreasonable to impose liability where the known danger threatens only a statistically small percentage of the drug's users is to beg the very question of negligence. The size of the class of endangered persons is one—albeit only one—of the factors to be considered in deciding whether the manufacturer's warnings were, in fact, reasonable.

The ethical drug manufacturer is, then, subject to a duty to warn the medical profession of untoward effects which the manufacturer knows, or has reason to know, are inherent in the use of its drug. *Sterling Drug, Inc v Cornish,* supra 370 F 2d 82; *Parke-Davies & Co v Stromsodt, supra* 411 F 2d 1390; *Basko v Sterling Drug, Inc,* 416 F 2d 417 (2d Cir, 1969); *Love v Wolf, supra* 226 Cal. App. 2d 378, 38 Cal Rptr. 183; *Krug v Sterling Drug, Inc, supra* 416 SW 2d 143; cf *Davis v Wyeth Laboratories, Inc,* 399 F 2d 121 (9th Cir 1968). See also *Wright v Carter Products, Inc,* 244 F 2d 53 (2nd Cir 1957); *Hungerholt v Land O'Lakes Creameries, Inc,* 209 F Supp 177 (D Minn 1962), aff'd, 319 F 2d 352 (8th Cir 1963); *Gerkin v Brown & Sehler Co,* 177 Mich 45, 143 NW 48 (1913). But see *Winthrop Laboratories Division of Sterling Drug, Inc v Crocker* 502 SW 2d 850 (Tex Civ App 1973).

Even in California, where product liability has been taken further than in most jurisdictions, as recently as 1985 the California Court of Appeals has held, in *Kearl v Lederle Laboratories* 218 Cal Rptr 453 (1985), that strict product liability and negligence might not differ in the context of adequate warnings.

Sabraw, Associate Judge (at 465–467):

B. Warning defect

1. Background

Professor Wade has stated that "[a] warning can prevent a product from being characterized as unreasonably dangerous [ie, defective] in two types of situations:

(1) the product produces a danger that can be avoided by the user if he is alerted to it and instructed how to avoid it, and (2) the product creates a danger that cannot be eliminated, but its utility is so great that it may be marketed without subjecting the manufacturer to liability, provided the user is made aware of the danger and is given the opportunity to make an informed decision whether to expose himself to it." (Wade, *supra*, 58 NYUL Rev at p 745; see also Twerski *et al, The Use and Abuse of Warnings in Products Liability—Design Defect Litigation Comes of Age* (1976) 61 Cornell) L Rev 495, 517–521.' In the present case we are concerned with the second type of warning.

As an initial matter we question the commonly assumed and often asserted proposition that in products liability cases failure to warn or inadequacy of a warning may be a basis for imposition of *strict liability*. A review of the cases discloses that the analysis called for in this situation is not based on strict liability, but negligence.

... the characteristic that distinguishes strict liability from negligence is proof of actual or constructive knowledge of risk: In a negligence action we focus on the defendant's conduct and require plaintiff to show defendant acted unreasonably in light of a known or constructively known risk. In strict liability actions, on the other hand, we focus on not on the reasonableness of a defendant's conduct but on the product, and we either ignore the question of a manufacturer's actual or constructive knowledge of risk (as in a "consumer expectations" design defect case) or we in effect impute to the manufacturer defendant current scientific knowledge of the risk caused by his product (as in a risk/benefit design defect balancing case). (See, eg, Comment, *The Failure to Warn Defect: Strict Liability of the Prescription Drug Manufacturer in California* (1983) 17 US FL Rev 743, 755.) But in all warning cases— even if the plaintiff or the court claims to analyze failure to warn or inadequacy of warning in the context of a strict products liability claim—the tests actually applied condition imposition of liability on the defendant is having actually or constructively known of the risk that triggers the warning. (*Eg, Carmichael v Reitz, supra*, 17 Cal App 3d 958, 988, 95 Cal Rpter 381; *Christofferson v Kaiser Foundation Hospitals, supra*, 15 Cal App 3d 75, 79–80, 92 Cal Rptr 825; *Oakes v EI Du Pont de Nemours & Co, Inc* 272 Cal App 2d 645, 650–651, 77 Cal Rptr 709, (1969); *Toole v Richardson-Merrell, Inc, supra*, 251 Cal App 2d 689, 709–710, 60 Cal Rptr 398; *Dunn v Lederle Laboratories, supra*, 328 NW 2d 576, 580; *Woodill v Parke Davies & Co, supra*, 402 NE 2d 194, 197–198, and cases cited; *Petty v United States, supra*, 740 F 2d 1428, 1432; *Reyes v Wyeth Laboratories, supra*, 498 F 2d 1264, 1274–1275; *Basko v Sterling Drug, Inc, supra*, 416 F 2d 417, 426; *Sterling Drug, Inc v Yarrow*, 408 F 2d 978, 992–993 (8th Cir 1969); *Davis v Wyeth Laboratories, supra*, 399 F 2d 121, 129; Kidwell, *The Duty to Warn: A Description of the Model of Decision* (1975) 53 Texas L Rev 1375, 1377–1378; Note, *supra*, 48 Fordham L Rev at pp 745–750; Prosser & Keeton on Torts (5th ed 1984) § 99, at p 697; see also Comment, *Strict Liability and the Tortious Failure to Warn* (1984) 11 Northern Kentucky L Rev 409, 419–422 [criticizing but recognizing the present result].)[16]

Just as liability for failure to warn of product risk is based on negligence, the adequacy of a warning is also judged under a reasonableness standard—even if the claim is made under the rubric of a strict products liability "defect". (*Sterling Drug, Inc v Yarrow, supra*, 408 F 2d 978, 992–993; *Feldman v Lederle Laboratories, supra*, 479 A 2d 374, 386 ["negligence and strict liability in warning cases may be deemed to be functional equivalents"]; *Dunn v Lederle Laboratories, supra*, 328 NW 2d 576, 580; Franklin & Mais, *supra*, 65 Cal. LRev at 762, and cases cited in fn 33; Note, *supra*, 32 DePaul L Rev at 254, fn 29; Kidwell, *supra*, 53 Texas L Rev at pp 1378–1379; Prosser & Keeton, *supra*, § 99, at p 697; but see Noel, *Products Defective Because of Inadequate Directions or Warnings* (1969) 23 Sw LJ 256, 267–272.)[17] As recent federal court of appeals decisions have held, an adequate warning in mass inoculation cases (as distinguished from other products or prescription drug cases) requires that vaccinees be directly informed in clear and simple terms by the drug manufacturer[18] of (1) the reasonably foreseeable risk inherent in the products; (2) reasonably available alternative products and the reasonably foreseeable risks posed by such alternatives; and perhaps—in appropriate cases—(3) the reasonably foreseeable results of remaining untreated. (*Petty v United States, supra,* 740 F 2d 1428 at 1436, 1437 [adequacy of swine flu vaccine warnings]; *Unthank v United States* 732 F 2d 1517 at 1521 (10th Cir 1984) [same]; Comment, *Informed Consent to Immunization: The Risks and Benefits of Individual Autonomy* (1977) 65 Cal L Rev 1286, 1295–1299, 1307–1311; see also *Cobbs v Grant* 8 Cal 3d 299, 241–245, 104 Cal Rptr 505, 502 P 2d 1 (1972); cf, Britain, *Product Honesty is the Best Policy: A Comparison of Doctors' and Manufacturers' Duty to Disclose Drug Risks and the Importance of Consumer Expectations in Determining Product Defect* (1984) 79 Nw UL Rev 342.

Notes to extract
16. The contrary and minority rule, advocated by the Chief Justice in her dissent in *Finn v GD Searle & Co, supra,* 35 Cal 3d 691, 723–724, 200 Cal Rptr, 870, 677 P 2d 1147 (see also Comment, *supra,* 17 USFL Rev 743; Comment, *supra,* 23 Duquesne L Rev 199), was recently stated in *Beshada v Johns-Manville Products Corp* 90 NJ 191, 447 A 2d 539 (1982). *Beshada* was immediately subjected to intense scholarly criticism (eg, Page, *Generic Product Risks: The Case Against Comment K and for Strict Tort Liability* (1983) 58 NYUL Rev 853, 877–82; Schwartz, *The Post-Sale Duty to Warn: Two Unfortunate Forks in the Road to a Reasonable Doctrine* (1983) 58 NYUL Rev 892, 901–05; Wade, *supra,* 58 NYUL Rev at pp 754–756; Comment, *Requiring Omniscience: The Duty to Warn of Scientifically Undiscoverable Product Defects* (1983) 71 Geo LJ 1635; Comment, *Beshada v Johns Manville Products Corp: Adding Uncertainty to Injury* (1983) 35 Rutgers L Rev 982), and was effectively and unanimously overruled by the same court two years later in a prescription drug case. (*Feldman v Lederle Laboratories, supra,* 479 A 2d 374, 387–388.)
17. This is true despite the fact that in some cases it may be helpful for the trial court to instruct the jury to consider particular factors in determining the reasonable need for, or adequacy of, a warning. Thus in *Cavers v Cushman Motor Sales, Inc* 95 Cal App 3d 338, 157 Cal Rptr 142 (1979), the court stated that "[i]n assisting the [jurors'] determination of whether the absence of a warning makes a product defective, the trial court should focus their attention on such relevant considerations as the normal expectations of the consumer as to how the product will perform, degrees of simplicity or complication in the operation or use of the product, the nature and magnitude of danger to which the user is exposed, the likelihood of injury, and the feasibility and beneficial effect of including a warning." (*Id,* at pp 347 348, 157 Cal Rptr 142.) Contrary to dicta in *Finn v G D Searle & Co, supra,* 35 Cal 3d 691, 700, 702, 200 Cal Rptr 870, 677 P 2d 1147, and the *Finn* dissent's suggestion at page 724, 200 Cal Rptr 870, 677 P 2d 1147, nothing in *Cavers* suggests, nor was it intended to imply, that failure to warn can or should be subject to an analysis different from negligence simply because it happens to be alleged as a basis of a product defect. *Cavers* simply attempts to give the jury guidance in determining the reasonableness of a warning or the reasonable need for a warning in a typical products liability case.
18. Defendant maintains that because OPV is technically a prescription drug, and because plaintiff consulted a doctor about two weeks before consenting to the vaccine, it had no duty to warn any vaccinee directly. Although this is the law with regard to most prescription drugs (see *Carmichael v Reitz, supra,* 17 Cal App 3d 958, 989 95 Cal Rptr 381; but see *MacDonald v Ortho Pharmaceutical Corpn* (1985) 394 Mass 131, 475 NE 2d 65, 68 [manufacturer's duty to warn consumer regarding dangers posed by oral contraceptive]), this rule is not followed in cases such as this, in which the drug is dispensed at a clinic without close supervision by a prescribing physician. (*Reyes v Wyeth Laboratories, supra,* 498 F 2d 1264, 1275–1278; *Cunningham v Charles Pfizer & Co, supra,* 532 P 2d 1377, 1381; *Petty v United States, supra,* 740 F 2d 1428, 1439–1440; Comment, *Pharmaceutical Manufacturers and Consumer-Directed Information—Enhancing the Safety of Prescription Drug Use* (1984) 34 Catholic UL Rev 117, 122–137.)

The continued relevance of negligence in the new regime of strict liability in the UK is not limited to warnings. It extends also to alleged defects in design.

Section 4(1)(e) provides that:

4.—(1) In any civil proceedings by virtue of this Part against any person ('the person proceeded against') in respect of a defect in a product it shall be a defence for him to show—

. . .

(e) that the state of scientific and technical knowledge at the relevant time was not such that a producer of products of the same description as the product in question might be expected to have discovered the defect if it had existed in his products while they were under his control;

This was a provision available to member states in derogation from the EEC Directive on Product Liability (85/374) which, in its original form adopted a narrower view of 'state of the art' as a defence thereby more properly reflecting the principle of strict liability (see article 7(e)).

If negligence theory requires a manufacturer to utilise technology that was available at the time of manufacture or to warn of risks which were known (or should have been) at that time, a theory of strict products liability could require more. Complying with the state of the art at the time of manufacture might not suffice to excuse him in design defect cases. Warning only about risks that were known (or knowable) also might not be sufficient. Strict liability could require, for example, that a manufacturer warn about even *un*knowable risks and perhaps (though less likely) that he be liable even though he complied with the state of the art. As Lord Scarman stated in the course of a debate in the House of Lords: '[i]f you introduce the 'state of the art' defence, you are really introducing negligence or fault by the back door'. (414 HL Deb col 1427). The recent case in New Jersey of *Feldman v Lederle Laboratories* serves as a good example of the application of negligence thinking, both to 'state of the art' and design defects and warnings in the context of pharmaceutical products.

Feldman v Lederle Laboratories
479 A 2d 374 (1984)

Schreiber J: (at 385–9) When the strict liability defect consists of an improper design or warning, reasonableness of the defendant's conduct is a factor in determining liability. See *Suter, supra*, 81 *NJ* at 171, 406 *A* 2d 140; *Cepeda, supra*, 76 *NJ* at 171–72, 386 *A*.2d 816; *Torsiello v Whitehall Laboratories*, 165 *NJ Super* 311, 320 n, 2, 398 *A* 2d 132 (App Div), certif denied, 81 *NJ* 50, 404 *A* 2d 1150 (1979). The question in strict liability design-defect and warning cases is whether, assuming that the manufacturer knew of the defect in the product, he acted in a reasonably prudent manner in marketing the product or in providing the warnings given. Thus, once the defendant's knowledge of the defect is imputed, strict liability analysis becomes almost identical to negligence analysis in its focus on the reasonableness of the defendant's conduct. In *Cepeda, supra*, 76 *NJ* at 172, 386 *A* 2d 816, and *Suter, supra*, 81 *NJ* at 171, 406 *A* 2d 140, we quoted approvingly Prosser's treatise on torts: 'Since proper design is a matter of reasonable fitness, the strict liability adds little or nothing to negligence on the part of the manufacturer . . . .' *W Prosser, Law of Torts* 659 n 72 (4th ed 1971).

Generally, the state of the art in design defect cases and available knowledge in defect warning situations are relevant factors in measuring reasonableness of conduct. Thus in *Suter, supra*, we explained that other than assuming that the manufacturer knew of the harmful propensity of the product, the jury could consider "the technological feasibility of manufacturing a product whose design would have prevented or avoided the accident, given the known state of the art.' *Id* at 172, 406 *A* 2d 140. We observed that 'the state of the art refers not only to the common practice and standards in the industry but also to the other design alternatives within practical and technological limits at the time of distribution.' *Id*. Moreover, in *O-Brien, supra*, we again referred to the state of the art as an appropriate factor to be considered by the jury to determine whether feasible alternatives existed when the product was marketed. 94 *NJ* at 183–84, 463 *A* 2d 298.

Similarly, as to warnings, generally conduct should be measured by knowledge at the time the manufacturer distributed the product. Did the defendant know, or should he have known, of the danger, given the scientific, technological, and other information available when the product was distributed; or, in other words, did he have actual or constructive knowledge of the danger? The *Restatement, supra*, has adopted this test in comment j to section 402A, which reads in pertinent part as follows:

> *Directions or warning.* In order to prevent the product from being unreasonably dangerous, the seller may be required to give directions or warning, on the container, as to its use. . . . Where the product contains an ingredient . . . whose danger is not generally known, or if known is one which the consumer would reasonably not expect to find in the product the seller is required to give warning against it, *if he has knowledge, or by the application of reasonable, developed human skill and foresight should have knowledge*, of the presence of the ingredient and the danger. [Emphasis added.]

Under this standard negligence and strict liability in warning cases may be deemed to be functional equivalents. See *Sterling Drug Inc v Yarrow*, 408 *F* 2d 978, 992 (8th Cir 1969); *Chambers v G D Searle & Co*, 441 *F Supp* 377, 380 (D Md 1975), aff'd *per curiam*, 567 *F* 2d 269 (4th Cir 1977); *Incollingo v Ewing*, 444 *Pa* 263, 285 n 8, 282 *A* 2d 206, 220 n 8 (1971); 2 *Interagency Task Force on Product Liability, US Dep't of Commerce, Product Liability: Legal Study* 67–68 (1977). Constructive knowledge embraces knowledge that should have been known based on information that was reasonably available or obtainable and should have alerted a reasonably prudent person to act. Put another way, would a person of reasonable intelligence or of the superior expertise of the defendant charged with such knowledge conclude that defendant should have alerted the consuming public? See *Restatement, supra* § 12(2).

Further, a manufacturer is held to the standard of an expert in the field. *Karjala v Johns-Manville Prods Corpn*, 523 *F* 2d 155, 159 (8th Cir 1975); see *Garst v General Motors Corpn*, 207 *Kan* 2, 20, 484 *P* 2d 47, 61 (1971); *Micallef v Miehle Co*, 39 *NY* 2d 376, 386, 358 *NE* 2d 571, 578, 384 *NYS* 2d 115, 121 (1976). A manufacturer should keep abreast of scientific advances. Harper and James, in their treatise on torts, explained that a manufacturer is held to the skill of an expert in that particular business and to an expert's knowledge of the arts, materials and processes. Thus he must keep reasonably abreast of scientific knowledge and discoveries touching his product and of techniques and devices used by practical men in his field. He may also be required to make tests to determine the propensities and dangers of his product. [2 *F. Harper & F. James, The Law of Torts* § 28.4 (1956) (footnotes omitted).] See 2 *R Hursch & H Bailey, American Law of Products Liability* 153–54 (2d ed 1974). Were the available scientific data or other pertinent information such as to "give rise to a reasonable inference that the danger is likely to exist;? Wade (1938), *supra*, at 749. Implicit in the requirement that such a manufacturer is held to the standard applicable to experts in the field is the notion that at least in some fields, such as those impacting on public health, a manufacturer may be expected to be informed and affirmatively to seek out information concerning the public's use of its own product.

Furthermore, a reasonably prudent manufacturer will be deemed to know of reliable information generally available or reasonably obtainable in the industry or in the particular field involved. Such information need not be limited to that furnished by experts in the field, but may also include material provided by others. Thus, for example, if a substantial number of doctors or consumers had complained to a drug manufacturer of an untoward effect of a drug, that would have constituted sufficient information requiring an appropriate warning. See *Hoffman v Sterling Drug, Inc*, 485 *F* 2d 132, 146 (3d Cir 1973) (in judgment for plaintiff alleging negligence and strict products liability in failure-to-warn case against prescription drug manufacturer of Aralen, court found jury question whether defendants used foresight appropriate to their enterprise in view of the number of letters from physicians reporting visual injury in patients using Aralen and subsequent medical literature); *Skill v Martinez*, 91 *FRD* 498, 514 (DNJ 1981), affd on other grounds, 677 *F* 2d 368 (3d Cir 1982) (jury finding in products liability action for plaintiff upheld because 'sufficient knowledge' existed, in the form of articles on preliminary findings by two leading researchers in the field, of danger inherent in taking birth-control pill while smoking to warrant drug manufacturer's giving proper warning); *Hamilton v Hardy*, 37 *Colo App* 375, 385, 549 *P* 2d 1099, 1108 (1976) (under strict liability theory, manufacturer of prescription drugs must warn of dangers and risks, whether or not a causal relationship between use of product and various attendant injuries has been definitively established at the time of the warning); *McKee v Moore*, 648 *P* 2d 21, 24 (Okla 1982) (duty to warn requiries prescription drug manufacturer to maintain current information 'gleaned from research, adverse reaction reports, scientific literature and other available methods') (footnote omitted); 39 Fed Reg 33,230–31 (1974) (FDA requires warnings on drug labels 'when there is significant medical evidence of a possible health hazard, without waiting for a causal relationship to be established by definitive studies which, in some instances, may not be feasible or would take many years').

This test does not conflict with the assumption made in strict liability design defect and warning cases that the defendant knew of the dangerous propensity of the product, if the knowledge that is assumed is reasonably knowable in the sense of actual or constructive knowledge. A warning that a product may have an unknowable danger warns one of nothing. Neither *Depeda* nor *Suter* stated that the manufacturer would be deemed to know of the dangerous propensity of the chattel when the danger was unknowable. See *Ferrigno v Eli Lilly and Co*, 175 *NJ Super* 551, 576, 420 *A*2d 1305 (Law Div. 1980). In our opinion *Beshada, supra*, would not demand a contrary conclusion in the typical design defect or warning case. If *Beshada* were deemed to hold generally or in all cases, particularly with respect to a situation like the present one involving drugs vital to health, that in a warning context knowledge of the unknowable is irrelevant in determining the applicability of strict liability, we would not agree. Many commentators have criticised this aspect of the *Beshada* reasoning and the public policies on which it is based. See e g, Page, 'Generic Product Risks: The Case Against Comment K and for Strict Tort Liability.' 58 *NYUL Rev* 853, 877–82 (1983); Schwartz, 'The Post-Sale Duty to Warn: Two Unfortunate Forks in the Road to a Reasonable Doctrine', 58 *NYUL Rev* 892, 901–05 (1983): Wade (1983), *supra*, at 754–56; Comment, 'Requiring Omniscience: The Duty to Warn of Scientifically Undiscoverable Product Defects," 71 *Geo LJ* 1635 (1983); Comment, '*Beshada v Johns Manville Products Corp:* Adding Uncertainty to Injury', 35 *Rutgers L Rev* 982, 1008–15 (1983); Note, 'Products Liability—Strict Liability in Tort—State-of-the-Art Defense Inapplicable in Design Defect Cases', 13 *Seton Hall L Rev* 625 (1983). But see *Hayes v Ariens Co,* 391 *Mass* 407, 413, 462 *NE* 2d 273, 277–78 (1984) (citing *Beshada* with approval for the proposition that in strict liability the seller 'is presumed to have been informed at the time of sale of all risks whether or not he actually knew or reasonably should have known of them'). The rationale of *Beshada* is not applicable to this case. We do not overrule *Beshada*, but restrict *Beshada* to the circumstances giving rise to its holding. See e g, *Friedman v Podell*, 21 *NJ* 100, 105, 121 *A* 2d 17 (1956); *Konrad v Anheuser-Busch, Inc,* 48 *NJ Super* 386, 388, 137 *A* 2d 633 (Law Div 1958) ('Cases state principles but decide facts, and it is only the decision on the facts that is binding precedent.'). We note, in passing, that, although not argued and determined in *Beshada*, there were or may have been data and other information generally available, aside from scientific knowledge, that arguably could have alerted the manufacturer at an early stage in the distribution of its product to the dangers associated with its use.

In strict liability warning cases, unlike negligence cases, however, the defendant should properly bear the burden of proving that the information was not reasonably available or obtainable and that it therefore lacked actual or constructive knowledge of the defect. Wade (1983), *supra*, at 760–61; see Pollock, 'Liability of a Blood Bank or Hospital for a Hepatitis Associated Blood Transfusion in New Jersey', 2 *Seton Hall L Rev* 47, 60 (1970) ('burden of proof that hepatitis is not detectable and unremovable should rest on the defendant' blood bank or hospital). The defendant is in a superior position to know the technological material or data in the particular field or specialty. The defendant is the expert, often performing self-testing. It is the defendant that injected the product in the stream of commerce for its economic gain. As a matter of policy the burden of proving the status of knowledge in the field at the time of distribution is properly placed on the defendant. See *State v Toscano*,

74 *NJ* 421, 443, 378 *A* 2d 755 (1977) (shifting burden to criminal defendant of proving duress); *Anderson v Somberg*, 67 *NJ* 291, 300–02, 338 *A* 2d 1 (*per* Pashman, J, with two Justices concurring and one Justice concurring in the result) (placing burden of persuasion on multiple defendants in malpractice action where plaintiff was not in a position to identify the responsible party), *cert.* denied, 423 *US* 929, 96 *S Ct* 279, 46 *L Ed* 2d 258 (1975); *cf Griggs v Bertram* 88 *NJ* 347, 365–68, 443 *A* 2d 163 (1982) (in insurance case, shifting to settlor insured burden of going forward, but not of persuasion, on question of whether a settlement was made in good faith); *NOPCO Chem Div v Blau-Knox Co*, 59 *NJ* 274, 284–85, 281 *A* 2d 793 (1971) (shifting burden of production to defendants where machine damaged in transit but buyer did not know which carrier or bailee had damaged it).

One other aspect with respect to warnings based on subsequently obtained knowledge should be considered. Communication of the new warning should unquestionably be given to prescribing physicians as soon as reasonably feasible. Although a manufacturer may not have actual or constructive knowledge of a danger so as to impose upon it a duty to warn, subsequently acquired knowledge, both actual and constructive, also may obligate the manufacturer to take reasonable steps to notify purchasers and consumers of the newly-discovered danger. Compare *Bacardi v Holzman*, 182 *NJ Super* 422, 425, 442 *A* 2d 617 (App Div 1981) (holding that '[t]he manufacturer has no duty to prepare a warning for the consumer when, under all circumstances, the product only comes into the consumer's hands after it is prescribed by the physician'), *with Lukaszewicz v Ortho Pharmaceutical Corp*, 510 *F Supp* 961 (E D Wis 1981) (manufacturer of oral contraceptive had duty under strict liability to warn patients directly of possible side effects where FDA regulation mandated such warning and Wisconsin law made a violation of such a regulation negligence *per se*) *and Pharmaceutical Mfrs Ass'n v Food and Drug Administration*, 484 *F Supp* 1179, 1182 (D Del), aff'd *per curiam*, 634 *F* 2d 106 (3d Cir 1980) (upholding FDA regulation requiring direct warning to consumers of prescription drugs containing estrogens because Congress, in enacting the Food, Drug, and Cosmetic Act, 'intended patients using prescription drugs, as well as those using over-the-counter drugs, to receive' material facts directly).

The timeliness of the warning issue is obliquely present in this case. It is possible that Dr Feldman already had Declomycin on hand when defendant became aware of Declomycin's side effect. If that state of affairs existed, defendant would have had an obligation to warn doctors and others promptly. This most assuredly would include those to whom defendant had already furnished the product. See *Schenebeck v Sterling Drug, Inc*, 423 *F* 2d 919, 922 (8th Cir 1970); *Basko, supra*, 416 *F* 2d at 426. See generally Note 'The Manufacturer's Duty to Notify of Subsequent Safety Improvements', 33 *Stan L Rev* 1087 (1981). The extent and nature of post-distribution warnings may vary depending on the circumstances but in the context of this case, the defendant at a minimum would have had a duty of advising physicians, including plaintiff's father, whom it had directly solicited to use Declomycin.

The trial court charged the jury that the manufacturer of a drug has the obligation to warn if he knew or should have known of the need to issue such a warning. In determining whether defendant should have known of the danger, it referred the jury to the circumstances, relating particularly to the state of knowledge, as evidenced by the literature, in the scientific community. However, upon the retrial the charge should also include the principle expressed herein that a reasonably prudent drug manufacturer should be deemed to know of reasonably obtainable and available reliable information.[7] In addition, we now place the burden of proving the lack of knowledge on the defendant.

[See also the California Supreme Court decision in *Brown v Superior Court* (1988) 751 P 2d 470 adopting a negligence theory for defects in pharmaceuticals whether based upon design or failure to warn]

An explanation of the 'state of the art' defence has been given by one commentator as follows (Simon Whittaker, 'The EEC Directive on Product Liability', Yearbook of European Law 1985, pp 257–8; footnotes omitted):

What then is 'the state of scientific or technical knowledge'? Knowledge is a relative concept, particularly in a scientific context. Does a manufacturer have to be informed of the latest research, the most up-to-date techniques to avail himself of the defence? Where there is disagreement as to particular facts, their interpretation, or the effectiveness of a particular testing procedure, how can the manufacturer decide which is the view which counts as 'the state of knowledge' for the purposes of the Directive? Obviously, he cannot be expected to act on conjecture; on the other hand, he should keep up to date with recent (and perhaps, generally accepted) developments.

Moreover, it is submitted that the '*state* of the scientific knowledge' should be interpreted to include both present and 'constructive' knowledge. A situation covered by 'present knowledge' would be where a drug could not be tested for a certain effect, because there was no reason to believe that it *could* have such an effect. Similarly, a producer would not be liable for impurities in his product, such as a virus in blood products, which could not be detected at the time of putting it into circulation. However, the 'state of knowledge' in some areas may be best described as ignorance. Can a producer hide behind this ignorance when, knowing he is ignorant of potential risks of a product, he fails to research into and find new techniques of investigation before putting the product into circulation? The House of Lords has recently held the designer of a radio-mast liable in negligence for failing to investigate the possible risks of its revolutionary design, even though quite basic facts as to the effects of ice and wind on such a mast had never been researched. The burden of further research on the designer had to be weighed against the risk of serious injury or damage if a fault developed. It would indeed be bizarre if the defence of Article 7(e) were interpreted in such a way that liability under the Directive was narrower than in negligence. This unattractive result may be avoided if the 'state of knowledge' is understood to include 'constructive knowledge', ie what the producer *ought* to have known at the relevant time. But the introduction of a notion like 'constructive knowledge' makes obvious that inclusion of the 'state of the art' defence of Article 7(e) entails discussion of the same considerations as are involved in establishing negligence.

Surgical methods

1. CONSENSUAL

(a) Legality

Can an individual give a valid consent to a surgical operation for sterilisation (vasectomy-male; tubal ligation—female)?

Bravery v Bravery [1954] 1 WLR 1169 CA

Denning LJ: (at 1180) An ordinary surgical operation, which is done for the sake of a man's health, with his consent, is, of course, perfectly lawful because there is just cause for it. But when there is no just cause or excuse for an operation, it is unlawful, even though the man consents to it.

. . . Likewise with a sterilisation operation. When it is done with the man's consent for a just cause, it is quite lawful; as, for instance, when it is done to prevent the transmission of an hereditary disease. But when it is done without just cause or excuse, it is unlawful, even though the man consents to it. Take a case where a sterilisation operation is done so as to enable a man to have the pleasure of sexual intercourse, without shouldering the responsibilities attaching to it. The operation then is plainly injurious to the public interest. It is degrading to the man himself. It is injurious to his wife and to any woman whom he may marry, to say nothing of the way it opens to licentiousness; and, unlike contraceptives, it allows no room for a change of mind on either side.

However, his view probably did not represent the law even in 1954.

Hodson LJ: In our view these observations are wholly inapplicable to operations for sterilisation as such, and we are not prepared to hold in the present case that such operations must be regarded as injurious to the public interest.

In the circumstances of the present case and for the reasons we have given, we are unable to accept the conclusion of Denning LJ at the end of his judgment.

Sir Raymond Evershed MR agreed with Hodson LJ.

Today, there can be no doubt that such operations are lawful and cannot be said to be contrary to public policy since sterilisation for contraceptive purposes is recognised as 'just cause'. If confirmation be needed, Parliament has provided for vasectomy operations to be carried out within the NHS, see the NHS Act 1977, s 5(b):

It is the Secretary of State's duty . . .
   (b) to arrange, to such extent as he considers necessary to meet all reasonable requirements in England and Wales, for the giving of advice on contraception, the medical examination of persons seeking advice on contraception, the treatment of such persons and the supply of contraceptive substances and appliances.

Other jurisdictions have reached similar views, eg Canada (*Cataford v Moreau* (1978) 114 DLR (3d) 585), and in New Zealand s 61A of the Crimes Act 1961 provides that:

61. Surgical operations—Every one is protected from criminal responsibility for performing with reasonable care and skill any surgical operation upon any person for his benefit, if the performance of the operation was reasonable, having regard to the patient's state at the time and to all the circumstances of the case.

(b) Limits

Does the law require not only the consent of the person to be sterilised, but also of some other person in a close relationship to them, for example their spouse or parents?

Spouse or partner

At one time, it was common for consent forms to require the 'agreement' of a spouse to a sterilisation operation. The following general consent form was recommended by the Medical Protection Society for all surgical procedures, including sterilisations, until 1988.

CONSENT FORM

I.   I, ... of . . . .
          (name and address of person giving consent)

     *hereby consent to undergo
OR   *hereby consent to . . . . undergoing
                              (name of patient)

     the operation/treatment of . . . .

     the nature and purpose of which have been explained to me

     by Dr/Mr . . . .
     I also consent to such further or alternative operative measures or treatment as may be found necessary during the course of the operation or treatment and to the administration of general or other anaesthetics for any of these purposes.

     No assurance has been given to me that the operation/treatment will be preformed or administered by any particular practitioner

     Date . . . .   Signature . . . .

II. I, husband/wife,* of the above-named patient, hereby confirm my consent to the above.†

Date .... Signature of spouse ....

III. I confirm that I have explained the nature and purpose of this operation/treatment to the person(s) who signed the above form of consent.

Date .... Signature ....

                                          Physician/Surgeon*

*Delete whichever inapplicable.

†It is recommended that if the patient be married and the procedure likely to affect sexual or reproductive functions, the signature of the spouse should also, when reasonably possible, be obtained.

Notice that such forms called for the 'agreement' of the spouse and not his consent. What did this mean as a matter of law? Was this a provision aimed more at maintaining good domestic relations rather than meeting any legal requirement? Could it have been a valid legal limitation on a spouse's capacity to be sterilised? If so, it would mean, uniquely, that in this area of medical treatment an adult competent person does not have the right to self-determination nor is entitled to confidentiality. Furthermore, it suggests that a spouse who opposed the sterilisation could apply for an injunction if it were thought that the procedure would be carried out without his consent. If a person may not obtain an injunction to prevent a spouse from having an abortion (*Paton v British Pregnancy Advisory Service* [1979] QB 276, [1978] 2 All ER 987), it must be the case that *a fortiori* no action could lie to prevent sterilisation. Thus, it is at best highly doubtful that any requirement of spousal consent has any force in law: it is another matter that sterilisation gained without the knowledge or consent of a spouse may serve as evidence of 'irretrievable breakdown' for the purpose of divorce. However, there would seem to be no legal remedy available to a person who is refused a sterilisation operation without the consent of the spouse; short, perhaps, of instituting proceedings before the General Medical Council.

Support for the proposition that this reflects the common law can be found in the Oklahoma case of *Murray v Vandevander* 522 P 2d 302, which unlike the well-known case of *Planned Parenthood of Missouri v Danforth* 428 US 52 (1976) and its progeny does not rely on constitutional law arguments.

In the case of consensual surgical sterilisation, the same considerations apply concerning the role of parents and doctors and the capacity of children as were discussed in our analysis of *Gillick* (supra Ch 4) and its application to contraception.

Box J: The question presented on appeal is whether a husband can recover from a physician and hospital for damage to a marital relationship resulting from an operation on the wife, consented to by her. It is the opinion of this court that such recovery was rightfully denied by the trial court.

... The natural right of a married woman to her health is not qualified by requiring that she have the consent of her husband in order to receive surgical care from a physician. . . .

We have found no authority and plaintiff has cited none which holds that the husband has a right to a childbearing wife as an incident to their marriage. We are neither prepared to create a right in a husband to have a fertile wife nor to allow recovery for damage to such a right. We find that the right of a person who is capable of competent consent to control his own body is paramount.

There is no allegation in the petition that plaintiff's wife was of diminished capacity or otherwise incapable of consent. There was no necessity for the physician in the instant case to obtain the consent of the plaintiff. No duty was breached by performance of the operation without consent of the husband of the patient.

The defence organisations acknowledge that there is no obligation to obtain the consent of the spouse (eg Medical Protection Society, *Consent Confidentiality, Disclosure of Medical Records* (1988), p 7). The MPS's suggested consent form now does not require a doctor to obtain a spouse's consent (*ibid*, at p 15).

Parent or guardian

In the case of consensual surgical sterilisation, the same considerations apply concerning the role of parents and doctors and the capacity of children as were discussed in our analysis of *Gillick* (*supra* Ch 4) and its application to contraception.

(c) Liability for failed sterilisations

(i) Generally

We consider here the question whether parents may bring an action alleging ʾhat a sterilisation operation has failed and as a consequence they have suffered avoidable harm in that a child has been born and must be raised or that a woman has conceived but decided to undergo an abortion.

We do not consider here the possibility of the child born in these circumstances bringing an action—sometimes called a 'wrongful life' action. In fact, this is a far more complicated issue than is often represented and we return to it in detail later (*infra* Ch 10). For the moment, it is sufficient to note that the action that the child would bring would be one in which the child argued that it was born when it should not have been born and it may arise in three situations: (i) where the child is born disabled (ie with a physical or mental disability); (ii) where the child is born disadvantaged in some way, though not disabled, ie being stigmatised by being illegitimate or black; or (iii) where the child is born neither disabled nor disadvantaged but wishes to assert that though healthy he should not have been born at all.

At common law no action lay in situation (i), (*McKay*). In any event, Parliament put the point beyond doubt in the Congenital Disabilities (Civil Liability) Act 1976, s 1(2)(b), which replaced the common law after 22 July 1976 (s 4(5)).

As regards (ii), the English courts have not been asked to decide this issue but they would most likely reject any claim, as has occurred in the United States (*Zepeda v Zepeda* 19O NE 2d 849 and *Williams v NY State* 18 NY 2d 481). Both situations (ii) and (iii) fall outside the 1976 Act which is limited to cases of 'disability'.

Moreover, as regards situation (iii) the argument that, if no claim at common law could be brought for (i) and no claim for the 'lesser injury' in (ii) could be brought, *a fortiori* the argument must be even stronger for situation (iii). Thus, there is not (nor, arguably, should there be) an action at the suit of a child, born as a result of failed sterilisation. But what of the claim by the parents?

(ii) An action in contract

Most doctors ordinarily treat patients within the NHS and in that case no contract arises between them. Sterilisation, being elective surgery, is quite commonly practised outside the NHS in circumstances where a contract *will* arise. As in any action in contract, the ability of a party to recover in any action depends upon the terms of the contract.

Those advising doctors will undoubtedly take their lead from two recent cases and so draft their terms that it would be most unlikely that an action could sound in contract if it could not sound in tort. The two cases are *Thake v Maurice* and *Eyre v Measday*. Both raise the issue of what the doctor contracts to do, in particular, whether there is a guarantee of sterility.

Eyre v Measday
[1986] 1 All ER, 488 CA

Slade LJ: It is, I think, common ground that the relevant contract between the parties in the present case was embodied as to part in the oral conversations which took place between the plaintiff and her husband and the defendant at the defendant's consulting rooms, and as to the other part in the written form of consent signed by the plaintiff, which referred to the explanation of the operation which had been given in that conversation. It is also common ground, I think, that, in order to ascertain what was the nature and what were the terms of that contract, this court has to apply an objective rather than a subjective test. The test thus does not depend on what either the plaintiff or the defendant *thought* were the terms of the contract in her or his own mind. It depends on what the court objectively considers that the words used by the respective parties must be reasonably taken to have meant. It would, therefore, be of no assistance to the defendant to say that he did not intend to enter into a contract which absolutely guaranteed the plaintiff's future sterility. It would likewise be of no assistance to the plaintiff to say that she firmly believed that she was being offered a contract of this nature.

I now turn to the first of the two principal issues which I have indicated. At the start of his argument for the plaintiff counsel indicated that his primary ground of appeal would be that the effect of the contract between the plaintiff and the defendant was one by which the defendant contracted to render the plaintiff absolutely sterile. That, of course, was the effect of Peter Pain J's decision on the particular facts of *Thake v Maurice*. Nevertheless, on the facts of this case, I, for my part, find this contention quite impossible to sustain. It seems to me quite clear from the evidence which we have as to the conversation which took place between the plaintiff and her husband and the defendant at the defendant's consulting rooms that he explained to them that the operation which he would propose to perform on the plaintiff was an operation by way of *laparoscopic sterilisation* and that that was the method he intended to adopt and no other. Equally, that was the nature of the operation to which the plaintiff herself agreed, as is shown by the form of consent which she signed. The contract was, to my mind, plainly a contract by the defendant to perform that particular operation.

The matter may be tested in this way. Suppose that when the plaintiff had been under anaesthetic the defendant had formed the view that an even more effective way of sterilising her would be to perform a hysterectomy and had carried out that operation, the plaintiff would, of course, have had the strongest grounds for complaint. She could have said:

> I did not give you a general discretion to perform such operation as you saw fit for the purpose of sterilising me. I gave my consent to one particular form of operation. That was the operation I asked you to do and that was the operation you agreed to do.

In the end, as I understood him, counsel for the plaintiff did not feel able to press his argument on the first issue very strongly. The nature of the contract was, in my view, indubitably one to perform a laparoscopic sterilisation.

That, however, is by no means the end of the matter. The question still arises: did the defendant give either an express warranty or an implied warranty to the effect that the result of the operation when performed would be to leave the plaintiff absolutely sterile? In response to our inquiry counsel for the plaintiff helpfully listed the two particular passages in the evidence on which he relied for the purpose of asserting that there was an *express* warranty. The first was a passage where, in the course of examination by her counsel, the plaintiff said:

> We went to the consulting rooms and we saw Mr Measday and we discussed sterilisation. He told us the method that he used for sterilising was the clip. He told us once I had had it done it was irreversible.

Counsel for the plaintiff also relied on a passage in which the plaintiff was asked in chief:

> *Q.* Did he show you a clip? *A.* He showed us a clip and he also showed us the diagram and told us where the the clips would go on the tubes. He said once I had the operation done there was no turning back, I could not have it reversed.

Counsel for the plaintiff referred us to para 2 of the defence in the action which read as follows:

On the 30th October 1978 the Plaintiff consulted the Defendant about an operation of sterilisation. The Defendant examined her and agreed to carry out the operation and advised her that it must be regarded as a permanent procedure. He did not warn the Plaintiff of the slight risk of failure, nor did he guarantee success.

There was thus a specific admission in the defence that the defendant advised the plaintiff that it must be 'regarded as a permanent procedure'.

In the light of these various representations or statements by the defendant, counsel for the plaintiff submitted that it was being expressly represented to the plaintiff that the effect of the operation would be to render her sterile absolutely and for ever. I, for my part, cannot accept that submission. There has been some discussion in the course of argument on the meaning of the phrase 'irreversible' and as to the relevance of the statement, undoubtedly made by the defendant to the plaintiff, that the proposed operation must be regarded as being irreversible. However, I take the reference to irreversibility as simply meaning that the operative procedure in question is incapable of being reversed, that what is about to be done cannot be undone. I do not think it can reasonably be construed as a representation that the operation is bound to achieve its acknowledged object, which is a different matter altogether. For my part, I cannot spell out any such express warranty as is asserted from the particular passages in the evidence and in the pleadings relied on by counsel for the plaintiff to support it, or from any other parts of the evidence.

The test to be applied by the court in considering whether a term can or cannot properly be implied in a contract is that embodied in what is frequently called the doctrine of *The Moorcock* (1889) 14 PD 64, [1886–90] All ER Rep 530. It is conveniently set out in 9 Halsbury's Laws (4th edn) para 355:

A term can only be implied if it is necessary in the business sense to give efficacy to the contract; that is if it is such a term that it can confidently be said that if at the time the contract was being negotiated someone had said to the parties, 'What will happen in such a case', they would both have replied, 'Of course, so and so will happen; we did not trouble to say that; it is too clear.'

Counsel for the plaintiff, in the light of the passage in cross-examination which I have just read and in the light of all the other background of the case to which I have referred, submitted that if someone had said to the parties, 'Is it intended that the defendant should warrant that the operation will render the plaintiff absolutely sterile?', the answer of both parties must have been, 'Yes.' This, he submitted, is really the only possible inference from what had been said on both sides in the defendant's consulting rooms. He particularly drew attention to the question that he had put to the defendant, 'Would it have been reasonable for her to have gone away from your consulting rooms thinking that she would be sterilised and that would be the end of the matter?', to which the defendant had replied, 'Yes, it would.' Counsel for the plaintiff submitted that the defendant himself was thus acknowledging that the reasonable inference would have been as he suggested.

Applying *The Moorcock* principles, I think there is no doubt that the plaintiff would have been entitled reasonably to assume that the defendant was warranting that the operation would be performed with reasonable care and skill. That, I think, would have been the inevitable inference to be drawn, from an objective standpoint, from the relevant discussion between the parties. The contract did, in my opinion, include an implied warranty of that nature. However, that inference on its own does not enable the plaintiff to succeed in the present case. She has to go further. She has to suggest, and it is suggested on her behalf, that the defendant, by necessary implication, committed himself to an unqualified guarantee as to the success of the particular operation proposed, in achieving its purpose of sterilising her, even though he were to exercise all due care and skill in performing it. The suggestion is that the guarantee went beyond due care and skill and extended to an unqualified warranty that the plaintiff would be absolutely sterile.

On the facts of the present case, I do not think that any intelligent lay bystander (let alone another medical man), on hearing the discussion which took place between the defendant and the other two parties, could have reasonably drawn the inference that the defendant was intending to give any warranty of this nature. It is true that in cross-examination he admitted that it would have been reasonable for the plaintiff to have gone away from his consulting rooms thinking that she would be sterilised. He did not, however, admit that it would have been reasonable for her to have left his consulting rooms thinking that he had given her a *guarantee* that after the operation she would be absolutely sterile; this, I think, is the really relevant point. She has to say that this would have been the reasonable inference from what he said to her and from what she and her husband said to him. But, in my opinion, in the absence of any express warranty, the court should be slow to imply against a medical man an unqualified warranty as to the results of an intended operation, for the very simple reason that, objectively speaking, it is most unlikely that a responsible medical man would intend to give a warranty of this nature. Of course, objectively speaking, it is likely that he would give a guarantee that he would do what he had undertaken to do with reasonable care and skill; but it is quite another matter to say that he has committed himself to the extent suggested in the present case.

Do you accept the analysis of Slade LJ, particularly this discussion of the word 'irreversible' and his application of the *Moorcock* principle? The contract arguments were further explored in the next case concerned, this time, with a male sterilisation.

Thake v Maurice
[1986] QB 644, [1986] 1 All ER 497, CA

Neill LJ: It is common ground that the defendant contracted to perform a vasectomy operation on Mr Thake and that in the performance of that contract he was subject to the duty implied by law to carry out the operation with reasonable skill and care. The question for consideration is whether in the circumstances of the instant case the defendant further undertook that he would render Mr Thake permanently sterile by means of this operation.

On behalf of the plaintiffs it is conceded that the defendant never used the word 'guarantee' in relation to the outcome of the operation, but is submitted that what the defendant said and did at the consultation on or about 25 September 1975 would have led a reasonable person in the position of the plaintiffs to the conclusion that the defendant was giving a firm promise that the operation would lead to permanent sterility.

It is not in dispute that the task of the court is to seek to determine objectively what conclusion a reasonable person would have reached having regard to (a) the words used by the defendant, (b) the demonstration which he gave and (c) the form which Mr and Mrs Thake were asked to sign.

Counsel for the plaintiffs placed particular reliance on the following matters: (1) that on more than one occasion the defendant explained to the plaintiffs that the effect of the operation was 'irreversible', subject to the remote possibility of later surgical intervention, and counsel pointed out that this explanation was reinforced by the statement in the form: 'I understand that the effect of the operation is irreversible'; (2) that the defendant agreed in evidence that the word 'irreversible' would have been understood by the plaintiffs as meaning 'irreversible by God or man'; (3) that the demonstration which the defendant gave with his hands and arms and the sketch which he drew would have led the plaintiffs to believe that, because a piece of the vas was to be severed and the severed ends were to be turned back, there was no possibility whatever of the channels being reunited unless some further surgery took place; (4) that the defendant stated that two sperm tests were required to ensure that the operation was successful; this statement would have strengthened the impression given to his listeners that the operation when completed would render the patient sterile.

. . . For my part, however, I remain unpersuaded. It seems to me that it is essential to consider the events of 25 September 1975 and the words which the defendant used against the background of a surgeon's consulting room. It is the common experience of mankind that the results of medical treatment are to some extent unpredictable and that any treatment may be affected by the special characteristics of the particular patient. It has been well said that 'the dynamics of the human body of each individual are themselves individual'.

I accept that there may be cases where, because of the claims made by a surgeon or physician for his method of treatment, the court is driven to the conclusion that the result of the treatment is guaranteed or warranted. But in the present case I do not regard the statements made by the defendant as to the effect of his treatment as passing beyond the realm of expectation and assumption. It seems to me that what he said was spoken partly by way of warning and partly by way of what is sometimes called 'therapeutic reassurance'.

Both the plaintiffs and the defendant expected that sterility would be the result of the operation and the defendant appreciated that that was the plaintiffs' expectation. This does not mean, however, that a reasonable person would have understood the defendant to be giving a binding promise that the operation would achieve its purpose or that the defendant was going further than to give an assurance that he expected and believed that it would have the desired result. Furthermore, I do not consider that a reasonable person would have expected a responsible medical man to be intending to give a guarantee. Medicine, though a highly skilled profession, is not, and is not generally regarded as being, an exact science. The reasonable man would have expected the defendant to exercise all the proper skill and care of a surgeon in that speciality; he would not in my view have expected the defendant to give a guarantee of 100% success.

Accordingly, though I am satisfied that a reasonable person would have left the consulting room thinking that Mr Thake would be sterilised by the vasectomy operation, such a person would not have left thinking that the defendant had given a *guarantee* that Mr Thake would be absolutely sterile.

Nourse LJ: The function of the court in ascertaining, objectively, the meaning of words used by contracting parties is one of everyday occurrence. But it is often exceedingly difficult to discharge it where the subjective understandings and intentions of the parties are clear and opposed. Here the plaintiffs understood that Mr Thake would be permanently sterile. The defendant himself recognised that they would have been left with that impression. On the other hand, he did not intend, and on the state of his knowledge he could not have intended, to guarantee that that would be the case. Both the understanding and tne intention appear to them, as individuals, to have been entirely reasonable, but an objective interpretation must choose between them. In the end the question seems to be reduced to one of determining the extent of the knowledge which is to be attributed to the reasonable person standing in the position of the plaintiffs. Would he have known that the success of the operation, either because it depended on the healing of human tissue, or because in medical science all things, or nearly all things, are uncertain, could not be guaranteed? If he would, the defendant's words could only have been reasonably understood as forecasts of an almost certain, but nevertheless uncertain, outcome and his visual demonstrations as no more than explanations of how the operation would be done. He could not be taken to have given a guarantee of its success.

I do not suppose that a reasonable person standing in the position of the plaintiffs would have known that a vasectomy is an operation whose success depends on a healing of human tissue which cannot be guaranteed. To suppose that would be to credit him with an omniscience beyond all reason. But it does seem to me to be reasonable to credit him with the more general knowledge that in medical science all things, or nearly all things, are uncertain. That knowledge is part of the general experience of mankind, and in my view it makes no difference whether what has to be considered is some form of medical or surgical treatment or the excision, apparently final, of a section of the vas. Doubtless the general experience of mankind will acknowledge the certainty that a limb, once amputated, has gone forever. Such has been the observation from time immemorial of a species to whom the spectacle of war and suffering is commonplace. But where an operation is of modern origin, its effects untried over several generations, would a reasonable person, confronted even with the words and demonstrations of the defendant in this case, believe that there was not one chance in ten thousand that the object would not be achieved? I do not think that he would.

Are you persuaded by Nourse LJ's reasoning? Does it coincide with the approach to contract law ordinarily adopted by the courts? Consider the dissenting view of Kerr LJ:

On this appeal it was common ground that the court's task was to determine objectively the terms of the contract whereby the defendant offered and agreed to operate on the male plaintiff. What would a reasonable person in the position of Mr and Mrs Thake have concluded in that regard? Was it merely that the defendant would perform a vasectomy operation subject to the duty implied by law that he would do so with reasonable skill and care? Or was it that the defendant would perform this operation so as to render Mr Thake permanently sterile? Counsel for the defendant submitted that, even if the latter was the correct objective construction of the terms of the offer made by the defendant, it was nevertheless not so understood by Mr and Mrs Thake. He said that this was merely what they believed would be the result of the operation, not what they believed the defendant had undertaken to do, and he relied on the decision of this court in *Allied Marine Transport Ltd v Vale do Rio Doce Navegacao SA, The Leonidas D* [1985] 2 All ER 796 at 804–805, [1985] 1 WLR 925 at 935–986. But in my view no such further question arises here, since it is plain on the evidence that Mr and Mrs Thake intended that Mr Thake should be rendered permanently sterile and believed that this is what the defendant had agreed to do. No submission on these lines was made below, and it would clearly have been rejected by the judge. The only issue is as to the objective interpretation of the offer made by the defendant once he had agreed to perform the operation.

On this issue I have reached the same conclusion as the judge. Having regard to everything that passed between the defendant and the plaintiffs at the meeting, coupled with the absence of any warning that Mr Thake might somehow again become fertile after two successful sperm tests, it seems to me that the plaintiffs could not reasonably have concluded anything other than that his agreement to perform the operation meant that, subject to two successful sperm tests, he had undertaken to render Mr Thake permanently sterile. In my view this follows from an objective analysis of the undisputed evidence of what passed between the parties, and it was also what the plaintiffs understood and intended to be the effect of the contract with the defendant.

The considerations which lead me to this conclusion can be summarised as follows. First, we are here dealing with something in the nature of an amputation, not treatment of an injury or disease with inevitably uncertain results. The nature of the operation was the removal of parts of the channels through which sperm had to pass to the outside in such a way that the channels could not reunite. This was vividly demonstrated to the plaintiffs by the defendant pulling apart his arms and fists and turning back his wrists, as well as by a sketch. The defendant repeatedly and carefully explained that the effect of the operation was final, as the plaintiffs said again and again in their evidence, subject only to a remote possibility of surgical reversal, and that was the only warning which the defendant impressed on them. Subject to this and the two sperm tests of which the plaintiffs were told, designed to make sure that the operation had in fact been successful, I cannot see that one can place any interpretation on what the defendant said and did other than that he undertook to render Mr Thake permanently sterile by means of the operation. Nor can I see anything in the transcripts of the evidence which leads to any other conclusion, and the defendant himself agreed that in the context of the discussion as a whole, the word 'irreversible' would have been understood by the plaintiffs as meaning 'irreversible by God or man'. On the evidence in this case the position is quite different, in my view, from what was in the mind of Lord Denning MR in *Greaves & Co (Contractors) Ltd v Baynham Meikle & Partners* [1975] 3 All ER 99 at 103–104, [1975] 1 WLR 1095 at 1100 when he said: 'The surgeon does not warrant that he will cure the patient.' That was said in the context of treatment or an operation designed to cure, not in the context of anything in the nature of an amputation. The facts of the present case are obviously extremely unusual, but I do not see why the judge's and my conclusion on these unusual facts should be viewed by surgeons with alarm, as mentioned by the judge. If the defendant had given his usual warning, the objective analysis of what he conveyed would have been quite different.

Do you think that the terms of the MPS's recommended consent form would make the argument of the plaintiffs in *Eyre* and *Thake* even more difficult? As set out in its handbook the form provides, *inter alia*, that:

I have been told that the intention of the operation is to render me sterile and incapable of further parenthood. I understand that there is a possibility that I may not become or remain sterile.

(iii) Negligence

The cause of action. We do not consider here the cause of action arising from the negligent performance of the operation since no special problems arise. What is a distinct and important point here is the nature of the doctor's duty as it relates to the information that the law requires him to give the patient. This calls for a specific application of the general principles set out in *Sidaway*, discussed earlier.

The first case after *Sidaway* in which the point arose was *Thake v Maurice*, which we have already seen. The Court of Appeal in *Thake* determined the issue of negligence (in contract and tort) on the basis of an admission by the defendant that he normally warned patients that there was a slight risk of late-recanalisation in a vasectomy. The issue for the court was one of fact, namely whether he had followed his own practice. Thus, as Kerr LJ remarked:

Accordingly, unlike the situations considered in *Bolam v Friern Hospital Management Committee* and *Sidaway v Bethlem Royal Hospital Governors* in the present case there was nothing to be placed in the balance against the need for the warning which the defendant himself recognised in his evidence. He was a general surgeon with high professional qualifications whose competence was not in question, and I think that the plaintiffs were entitled to rely on his evidence just as if it had been given by an independent expert with the same qualifications. Since there is nothing to be placed against it, I consider that the judge was entitled to conclude, as he did, that the plaintiffs had established an inadvertent breach of duty on the part of the defendant sufficient to amount to negligence both in contract and in tort.

The more usual situation where the doctor has not warned arose in the following case.

Gold v Haringey Health Authority
[1986] 1 FLR 125 (QBD)

Schiemann J [at 137–140]: In the light of the totality of the evidence I conclude:

1. At no stage was Mrs Gold warned clearly that the tubal clipping operation had a failure rate and at no stage was vasectomy mentioned.

2. That when Mrs Gold saw Miss Witt on 24 July she had not come to a firm decision as to what contraceptive measures the couple intended to take in the future. At that meeting Mrs Gold in substance asked Miss Witt how she could avoid having more children and Miss Witt advised female sterilisation without mentioning alternatives.

3. That in a non-contraceptive context, for instance if there had been a therapeutic reason for sterilising Mrs Gold, there was a responsible body of medical opinion which would not, unasked, have mentioned the fact that the operation involved an element of risk.

4. That in the context of someone seeking contraceptive advice there was such a body of medical opinion which would not, unasked, have mentioned that the failure rate of a *post partum* sterilisation operation was several times as high as the ultimate failure rate of a vasectomy.

5. That in the context of someone seeking contraceptive advice there was no such body of medical opinion which would have failed to mention that there was a risk of failure of the *post partum* sterilisation, or that vasectomy was an option, or to make inquiries of the domestic situation of the party seeking advice.

6. That there was no such body of medical opinion which would have regarded the morning of the operation as a permissible time for the first giving of this information.

7. That had Miss Witt on 24 July, or Dr Plummer on 14 August, mentioned that there was a failure rate inherent in the female sterilisation operation, Mrs Gold would have asked further questions and given the information that her husband was content to have a vasectomy, I think it probable that she would have been told that vasectomies had as good, if not better, chance of success, that her husband could be treated as an outpatient, and that she would be able to leave the hospital shortly after the birth rather than wait for the sterilisation operation and its associated extra healing time before she could be discharged. I have little doubt that in those circumstances she would not have agreed to the female sterilisation operation.

8. I am satisfied that – in the absence of any specific medical contraindication of which there was no suggestion in the evidence – in the circumstances Mr Gold would have been vasectomised.

I conclude that it was negligent not to inform Mrs Gold of the failure rate of female sterilisations and that this negligence resulted in Mrs Gold's agreement to adopt that method of contraception and to adopt no other.

Although I have made a distinction in the foregoing findings as to the medical practice between the therapeutic and the contraceptive contexts, it is fair to say that the evidence was not crystal clear on this point and I go on to consider whether I would still have found negligence even had I been satisfied that there was a responsible body of medical opinion which, in a contraceptive counselling context, would have acted as I have found the hospital doctors did act.

Mr Miller argued that on that basis I would be bound by *Sidaway v Board of Governors to the Bethlem Royal Hospital and the Maudsley Hospital* [1985] AC 871 to dismiss the plaintiff's case. I do not agree with him. Let me explain why.

Sidaway was a case where the House of Lords unanimously upheld the trial judge's finding that Mrs Sidaway was not entitled to recover damages against the employers of a neuro-surgeon who had carried out an operation on her without negligence, but whose operation had in fact resulted in very severe injuries. Although unanimous in their conclusion the routes employed by their Lordships to arrive at their common destination varied.

The facts were by no means clear in that case but were held to be:

1. That Mrs Sidaway was in pain which was progressively worsening.

2. That she wanted to see the surgeon who had treated her before.

3. That he recommended a particular operation and was not negligent in so doing.

4. That he delivered a warning of one risk inherent in the operation but not of the particular eventuality which caused the damage.

5. That Mrs Sidaway had not established that the risk was so great that the doctor should have appreciated that it would be considered a significant factor by a prudent patient in Mrs Sidaway's situation in deciding to have the operation.

Lord Scarman found against her on the basis that the burden of proof was on her and that she had to establish that which I have set out in the last recital of fact and that she had failed to establish it. Lord Templeman found against her on the basis that she must have known that the operation carried a risk of serious injury and that there was no obligation on the surgeon to spell matters out further. Lord Diplock found against her on the basis that there was a responsible body of medical opinion which considered that a warning of the type that had undoubtedly been given was adequate and that this was determinative of the appeal. Lords Bridge and Keith found against her on the basis that what degree of disclosure should be made in a particular case was primarily a matter of clinical judgment and where a particular clinical judgment was under attack it was for the plaintiff to show that there was no doctor of ordinary skill acting with ordinary care who would have acted as the defendant acted. Mrs Sidaway, they held, had not shown that.

It is quite clear from the facts of that case, the opening sentence of the respondents' submissions, and from the tenor of the speeches that that case was decided in a therapeutic context. It is also clear that all their Lordships proceeded from the assumption that some warning ought to be given, although it is fair to add that in the circumstances of that case, where some warning had in fact been given, it was easy to proceed from that assumption.

The argument in that case was largely concerned with whether the doctrine of informed consent as it has been developed across the Atlantic should take root here. The majority were clearly of the view that the doctrine of informed consent does not fit into our concept of negligence.

I do not think that I in this case am essentially concerned with this at all. I am concerned with a situation where a woman asks for advice as to methods of contraception and is told that sterilisation is right for her without being told of other options and without being given the information that there is a risk of failure. In that context I consider that as a matter of law I am free to hold that the question whether or no vasectomy should be mentioned as an option, and whether or no the person giving advice should mention that there is a risk that a female sterilisation operation will not achieve the desired result, and whether or no the relative risks of vasectomy and female sterilisation should be disclosed to the person seeking advice, is to be determined not exclusively by reference to the current state of responsible and competent professional opinion and practice at the time, though both are of course relevant considerations, but by the court's view as to whether the person giving advice – who may be a hospital doctor, a general practitioner or a counsellor at a family planning clinic, or a health visitor – acted negligently. I accept that it was the view of the majority of the House of Lords that in the therapeutic context of that case the duty to give advice was subject to the same test as the duty to diagnose and treat, and that this test, known as the *Bolam* test after an earlier case, was that a doctor is not negligent if he acts in accordance with a practice accepted as proper by a responsible body of medical opinion even though other doctors adopt a different practice. This test is different from the one generally applied in actions in respect of negligent advice. I see nothing in the reasons given for adopting the *Bolam* test in the sort of circumstances under consideration in *Sidaway* which compels me to widen the application of this exceptional rule so as to cause it to apply to contraceptive counselling. It is common ground that there is no express decision on this point.

In my judgment, the hospital doctors faced with Mrs Gold, a perfectly normal sensible woman with no particular psychiatric social or medical problems, were under a duty to mention that the operation might not succeed in its aim and to mention other methods of contraception. I can think of no reason why she should not have had these things mentioned to her and none were seriously suggested in the evidence. Indeed, the hospital doctors both agreed that they would in the normal course of events have mentioned those things. The fact that, in the event, I have found that they inadvertently omitted to, does not detract from their evidence on this point.

In those circumstances I find the defendants negligent in not warning of a failure rate and in not mentioning vasectomy.

The Court of Appeal was not impressed with the basis of Schiemann J's judgment (see [1987] 2 All ER 888 at 890).

Lloyd LJ: How then . . . did it come about that the Judge found the defendants guilty of negligence, when he accepted that there was a substantial body of responsible medical opinion in 1979 who would not have given any warning? The answer is that he drew a distinction between advice or warning in a therapeutic context and advice or warning in a contraceptive context.

Why then did the Judge think that it would be an extension of the *Bolam* test to apply it in the present case? The reason can only have been that which I have already mentioned, namely, the distinction between therapeutic and non-therapeutic advice. . . . But I remain unconvinced. In the first place the line between therapeutic and non-therapeutic medicine is elusive. A plastic surgeon carrying out a skin graft is presumably engaged in therapeutic surgery; but what if he is carrying out a face-lift, or some other cosmetic operation? [Counsel for the plaintiff] found it hard to say.

In the second place, a distinction between advice given in a therapeutic and non-therapeutic context would be a departure from the principle on which the *Bolam* test is itself grounded. The principle does not depend on the context in which any act is performed, or any advice given. It depends on a man professing skill or competence in a field beyond that possessed by the man on the Clapham omnibus. If the giving of contraceptive advice required no special skill, then I could see an argument that the *Bolam* test should not apply. But that was not, and could not have been, suggested. The fact (if it be the fact) that giving contraceptive advice involves a different sort of skill and competence from carrying out a surgical operation, does not mean that the *Bolam* test ceases to be applicable. It is clear from Lord Diplock's speech in *Sidaway* that a doctor's duty of care in relation to diagnosis, treatment and advice, whether the doctor be a specialist or general practitioner, is not to be dissected into its component parts. To dissect a doctor's advice into that given in a therapeutic context and that given in a contraceptive context would be to go against the whole thrust of the decision of the majority of the House of Lords in that case. So I would reject [Counsel for the plaintiff's] argument under this head, and hold that the learned Judge was not free, as he thought, to form his own view of what warning and information ought to have been given, irrespective of any body of responsible medical opinion to the contrary.

The Court of Appeal also rejected the second ground upon which Schiemann J found for the plaintiff (see finding (5) *supra* in Schiemann J's judgment).

There was therefore only one open to the evidence, namely, that there was a body of responsible medical opinion which would not have given any warning as to the failure of female sterilisation, and the possible alternatives, in the circumstances in which the defendants actually found themselves. So I would not accept the second of the two grounds on which the Judge decided against the defendants.

Do you think the distinction between therapeutic and non-therapeutic medical procedures rejected by the Court of Appeal can (a) be sustained, and (b) if it can, whether the duty owed by the doctor should be different for each of them? (Note the subsequent rejection of the workability of the distinction in another context by House of Lords in *Re B* [1987] *infra*.)

What justification can there be for not disclosing information when the proposed procedure is one of a number of possible alternatives and the patient is perfectly healthy? Furthermore, what justification can there be for excusing a doctor from disclosing alternative available procedures? Is not the validity of consent in law a matter dependent not only upon risks but also the recital of alternatives? Schiemann J thought so (see finding 7, *supra*). Lloyd LJ did not, relying as he does only on the speech of Lord Diplock in *Sidaway*, which is a curious choice in the light of Lord Scarman's extrajudicial comment in 1986 that: 'we can ignore Lord Diplock's opinion, as he was in a minority of one . . .'.

Nature of the damage. In any action the plaintiff must show that the harm he complains of is of a type which the law recognises as remediable. Here, it is critically important to identify precisely the harm complained of. What is the plaintiff in the context of failed sterilisation complaining of? Becoming pregnant, inducing pregnancy, giving birth, having a child to support, having the economic burden of a child to support? If the plaintiff is the father alone, only some are, of course, relevant.

The exact nature of the harm conditions the response a court may make to the claim—ie is it physical injury or economic loss—since different legal consequences (such as limitation periods and the nature of the duty owed to the plaintiff in law) may apply.

Although this is central to a proper analytical understanding of the cause of action, the courts seem to have preferred to ignore the analytical point and assumed that some remedy ought to be available without being troubled too greatly about the precise basis of the cause of action (cf the 'wrongful life' cases, *infra*). By so doing, it may well be that the courts are merely avoiding, for the moment, the inevitable task of analysis for which there will one day be a call.

What the courts have done, so far, is to subsume this issue into the question of remoteness of damage, thereby confusing the question of whether the harm suffered is legally recognised harm with the question of whether the harm actually suffered (*ex hypothesi* legally recognised harm) should be legally compensated.

Factual causation. In any action based upon a failure to warn, the plaintiff must show that 'but for' the breach of duty (the failure to warn) the patient would not have consented to treatment. Is the legal test subjective or objective? The weakness of the former is clearly that it smacks of *Cobbs v Grant* (1972) 8 Cal 3d 229 20:20 vision. The weakness of the latter is that it may not reflect what the particular patient may have chosen.

In England, the courts have never confronted squarely the issue of which test is correct. What authority there is, however, adopts a subjective test, see *Chatterton v Gerson* [1981] QB 432, [1981] 1 All ER 257. As we saw earlier, it may well be that the courts will follow the lead of *Chatterton v Gerson*, but in applying the subjective test will try out the cogency of the plaintiff's evidence by reference to an evidential requirement of reasonableness.

Consider how a court would respond to the following three situations in the light of the above.

(1) The doctor negligently fails to disclose the small risk of reversal inherent in the sterilisation operation and the plaintiff claims that he or she would not have consented to this procedure had the information been known.

(2) The doctor negligently fails to disclose as above, but the plaintiff alleges that if she had known of the risk of failure she would have been better placed to realise she was pregnant and so seek an abortion which she did not because she did not know. Would it be relevant at what stage of the pregnancy she ought to have realised her condition had she been informed (these were the facts of *Thake v Maurice*)?

(3) The doctor negligently fails to disclose the availability of an alternative procedure which statistically has a lower failure rate than the one proposed (these were the facts of *Gold v Haringey Health Authority*, as found by Schiemann J at first instance).

Legal causation. Will the doctor be held legally responsible for the consequences of a child's birth where a course of action (such as an abortion or the possibility of putting the child up for adoption) was open to the parents but was not followed?

Emeh v Kensington and Chelsea and Westminster Area Health Authority [1985] QB 1012, [1984] 3 All ER 1044, CA

> **Slade LJ:** The judge, in saying that her failure to obtain an abortion was so unreasonable as to eclipse the defendants' wrongdoing, was, I think, really saying that the defendants had the right to expect that, if they had not performed the operation properly, she would procure an abortion even if she did not become aware of its existence until nearly 20 weeks of her pregnancy had elapsed.
>
> I do not, for my part, think that the defendants had the right to expect any such thing. By their own negligence, they faced her with the very dilemma which she had sought to avoid by having herself sterilised.

For the reasons which I have attempted to give, I think that they could, and should, have reasonably foreseen that if, as a consequence of the negligent performance of the operation, she would find herself pregnant again, particularly after some months of pregnancy, she might well decide to keep the child. Indeed, for my part I would go even a little further. Save in the most exceptional circumstances, I cannot think it right that the court should ever declare it unreasonable for a woman to decline to have an abortion, in a case where there is no evidence that there were any medical or psychiatric grounds for terminating the particular pregnancy. And no such evidence has been drawn to our attention relating to this particular pregnancy of the plaintiff in the present case.

What is Slade LJ saying? Does he appear to shift his ground somewhat towards the end of the extract? Waller LJ's view was as follows:

Can it be said that the plaintiff's conduct was so unreasonable as to eclipse the defendants' wrongdoing? In *McKew v Holland & Hannen & Cubitts (Scotland) Ltd* [1969] 3 All ER 1621 at 1624 Lord Reid, dealing with rather different facts but in considering an argument concerning the chain of causation, said:
  But I think it right to say a word about the argument that the fact that the appellant made to jump when he felt himself falling is conclusive against him. When his leg gave way the appellant was in a very difficult situation. He had to decide what to do in a fraction of a second. He may have come to a wrong decision; he probably did. But if the chain of causation had not been broken before this by his putting himself in a position where he might be confronted with an emergency, I do not think that he would put himself out of court by acting wrongly in the emergency unless his action was so utterly unreasonable that even on the spur of the moment no ordinary man would have been so foolish as to do what he did.
That speech of Lord Reid was concurred in by Lord Guest and Lord Upjohn.
So the degree of unreasonable conduct which is required is, on Lord Reid's view, very high. In my opinion, on the findings of the judge, even as they were, I would be disposed to say that this conduct on the part of the plaintiff was not so unreasonable as to eclipse the defendants' wrongdoing. But when there is taken into account, first of all, the judge's misunderstanding of the earlier part of the plaintiff's evidence concerning dates, when she was in fact entirely truthful, and, secondly, when one sees no reference was paid by the judge to the difference between a 20-week pregnancy and an 8-week pregnancy, it would seem that, when the plaintiff decided to have the baby and, having made that decision, she then decided to sue the defendants, her conduct could not be described as utterly unreasonable. Especially when one bears in mind that she had an argument with her husband about it, he apparently wanted her to have an abortion (and the judge accepted that evidence) that makes her decision all the more understandable.
I would therefore come to the conclusion that that finding of the judge, namely her failure to undergo an abortion was so unreasonable as to eclipse the defendants' wrongdoing, is incorrect, and that the plea of *novus actus*, or the failure to take steps to minimise the damage (in whatever way the matter is put), fails.

Purchas LJ stated:

For my part, however, I would respectfully agree with what has fallen from Slade LJ, that it would be intolerable if a defendant, admittedly by his own admission standing charged with negligence of a professional character and having, through that negligence, placed the plaintiff in a position in which a choice or decision had to be made, was able closely to analyse that decision so as to show that it might not have been the right choice, and could thereby escape his liability.
I find it unacceptable that the court should be invited to consider critically in the context of a defence of *novus actus interveniens* the decision of a mother to terminate or not her pregnancy which has been caused by the defendants' negligence. I am satisfied that taking the features of this case as highly as one can against the plaintiff, namely that on 19 January she knew or had reason to suspect she was pregnant, her

decision cannot be questioned. Although the judge put her term of pregnancy at as short a period as 16½ weeks, it must be recalled that from the notes of her general practitioner he recorded and communicated to her a pregnancy period of 18 to 20 weeks. The judge, in coming to his conclusion on a break in the chain of causation, studied the professional evidence of Sir John Dewhurst, and considered the risks and inconvenience and discomfort of a further operation, matters which would not have been in the mind of the plaintiff at all in fact, and discounted her evidence, which he quoted in his judgment and then found not to be established because of his view of the motive of the plaintiff. Those were matters which, in my judgment, were not relevant to the decision within the objective test which the judge had taken from the textbook. They are decisions whether or not the plaintiff might have acted reasonably or not, in mitigation of damage, but in my judgment they certainly have no relevance to the more formal decision whether or not the chain of causation has been broken or at all.

Do you detect a difference of emphasis between these judges?

Public policy and damages. Do you think that a parent should receive compensation when a healthy baby is born?

In the cases where this has been considered the courts have taken differing views.

Udale v Bloomsbury Area Health Authority
[1983] 2 All ER 522

Jupp J (at 529–532): Counsel for the defendants challenges these three heads of damage. He submits that as a matter of public policy damages should not be awarded for the birth of a normal, happy, healthy and, as it happens to be in this case, a much loved child. Whilst damages might be claimed if the child was handicapped or deformed, a normal child, says counsel, should as a matter of public policy be regarded as loved and wanted. I pause to emphasise that any decision of mine is not intended to deal one way or the other with an abnormal child. It would be intolerable, he says, if a child ever learned that a court had publicly declared him so unwanted that medical men were paying for his upbringing because their negligence brought him into the world. Our society, the argument runs, is founded on the basic unit of the family and assumes that children are the natural and desirable consequence of marriage and that the child's subsistence is a benefit alike to the child, the parents, the family and to society as a whole. In short, the law must assume that children are a blessing. It is pointed out that to allow claims against doctors to include the cost of bringing up a child would affect medical decisions which they might have to make whilst the child is being carried in the mother's womb. He refers to the judgment of Ackner LJ in *McKay v Essex Area Health Authority* [1982] 2 All ER 771 at 786, [1982] QB 1166 at 1187, where the Lord Justice cites the Law Commission's Report on Injuries to Unborn Children (Law Com no 60, August 1974; Cmnd 5709) para 89:

Such a cause of action, if it existed, would place an almost intolerable burden on medical advisers in their socially and morally exacting role. The danger that doctors would be under subconscious pressures to advise abortions in doubtful cases through fear of an action of damages, is, we think, a real one.

Counsel for the defendants also submits that it would be invidious to weigh up the benefit of having a child against the cost of bringing it up, and that to give, in effect, a free child to some parents would be invidious. If this kind of damage is recoverable, a court would have to quantify in money the blessings and benefit of having a child and set that sum against the capital cost of the child's upbringing and award the difference if the latter exceeded the former. Plaintiff mothers might be tempted to pretend to a lack of affection for their offspring which ought not to be encouraged.

Finally, counsel for the defendants points to the material advantages that are on the side of having a child. Financial support or assistance, especially perhaps from a son, can be a considerable help to parents in their old age. Daughters often give help with housework, shopping, laundry and the like to their ageing parents. Parents can make a claim in suitable cases under the Fatal Accidents Act 1976 in the event of the child being killed and their losing that support.

In so far as these submissions are based on the *difficulty* of assessing the benefits of parenthood, I do not think they can be right. There is ample authority that courts must, as best they can, assess imponderables of all sorts and value them in money terms. Courts often have to find a figure to represent possible financial and other material benefit, however remote, and also immaterial matters of gain and loss, including emotional matters. But, in so far as it is said it is far more satisfactory for reasons of public policy that such damages should be irrecoverable, the submission has to be examined carefully. There is ample authority, in my judgment, showing that the courts have approached damages in this way: see 12 Halsbury's Laws (4th edn) para 1133. In particular I was referred to passages in *Spartan Steel and Alloys Ltd v Martin & Co (Contractors) Ltd* [1972] 3 All ER 557 at 562, [1973] 1 QB 27 at 37 per Lord Denning MR, *McLoughlin v O'Brian* [1982] 2 All ER 298 at 303, 308–309, [1983] AC 410 at 420, 427 per Lord Wilberforce and Lord Edmund-Davies. It is not necessary to quote these passages. They make it clear that considerations of public policy may have to be applied. The question is only whether there are such considerations, and whether they are so powerful that they should be applied in this particular case. Only last year, the Court of Appeal in *McKay v Essex Area Health Authority* [1982] 2 All ER 771, [1982] QB 1166 rejected a claim based on the birth of a child as being contrary to public policy. It was a case akin, to some extent at least, to the present case and I shall refer to it later.

Counsel have discovered the transcripts of two cases very similar to the present case where the question of public policy could have arisen but, as it turned out, did not fall to be decided. The first is *Emeh v Kensington, Chelsea and Fulham Area Health Authority* (1983) Times, 3 January, a decision of Park J. It was a mother's claim for damages for an operation for sterilisation, which failed through negligence. Park J found as a fact that, after about $16\frac{1}{2}$ weeks of pregnancy, the plaintiff deliberately chose to allow the pregnancy to continue because she wanted to bear another child, and she therefore refused an abortion which she would have been quite prepared to have if her intention had been otherwise. This limited the damages to those $16\frac{1}{2}$ weeks or so. There was a claim for the cost of maintaining the child which was countered by a submission that such a claim would be against public policy. After a brief reference to the authorities, Park J said:

It is not necessary for me to express any view on this part of the claim. If it were held not to be contrary to public policy, the amount to which the plaintiff would be entitled can be calculated from the agreed figures without much difficulty.

That case, accordingly, does not afford the answer.

The second case is *Sciuriaga v Powell* [1980] CA Transcript 597. The claim was for damages in respect of an abortion which failed to remove the fetus owing to the negligence of the defendant doctor. In the result, a perfectly healthy little boy was born to the plaintiff. Damages were awarded under four heads: (1) plaintiff's loss of earnings up to the date of the trial; (2) plaintiff's future loss of earning capacity; (3) impairment of the plaintiff's marriage prospects; and (4) her pain and distress. It is to be observed that the modest sum of £750 was awarded under this last head. The court was not invited to, and did not, consider any question of public policy and there was no claim for the cost of the child's upbringing. However in saying that he had ignored policy considerations, Waller LJ said:

In doing so I must not be taken as assenting to the view that they would be irrelevant in every case . . . I quite see that the incidence of pregnancy and the necessity for Caesarian birth would properly form items of damage for the failure of the operation and, indeed, in this case one of the heads of damage covers this, but, once a woman has given birth to a healthy child without harm to her and the fears of the doctors have been shown to be unfounded, I would not regard it as unarguable in another case that thereafter no more damage would arise.

So, the question at least remains open. In *McKay v Essex Area Health Authority* [1982] 2 All ER 771, [1982] QB 1166 a mother and her child both claimed as plaintiffs because the child had been born with deformities. Her mother had been in contact in early pregnancy with German measles. One of the child's claims for damages was based on the negligence of the doctors in allowing her, in those circumstances, to be born at all. If they had advised properly, her mother would have had an abortion. The Court of Appeal struck out that claim as disclosing no reasonable cause of action; it did so on the grounds of public policy. The court made no adjudication on the mother's claim to the like effect, except to allow it to proceed to trial. Accordingly, although the case demonstrates quite clearly that considerations of public policy do apply to cases of this type, it does not indicate what considerations govern a claim by a mother (as opposed to one by the child itself) for the birth of her child, nor whether those considerations are sufficient to disallow the claim.

Of the policy considerations mentioned in the judgment, some clearly do not apply to the present case, for example, the impossibility which impressed each member of the court (not the difficulty, be it observed, but the impossibility) of comparing life with nothingness or non-existence: *illuc unde negant redire quemquam*. How could a judge compare his experience of life and set it against his ignorance of death? However, some considerations mentioned in *McKay*'s case may be relevant here. (1) The objection that the courts would be open to claims for maintenance by children against doctors who negligently allowed them to be born. (2) The extra burden this would impose on the medical profession and the danger that doctors would be under subconscious pressure to advise abortions for fear of actions for damages. (3) The social implications in the potential disruption of family life and the bitterness it would cause between parent and child. (4) The sanctity of human life which the law must regard as such that failure to prevent it should not be recognised as a cause of action. In other words, the law will not allow an action based on negligence which caused, or at least allowed, a human life to come into being. (5) There should be rejoicing, not dismay, that the surgeon's mistake bestowed the gift of life on the child.

Mrs Udale's claim does not match the claim which the Court of Appeal disallowed in that case. However, the considerations of public policy there put forward are impressive and are relevant to this case. Together with some of the submissions made by counsel for the defendants, they persuade me to the view that on the grounds of public policy the plaintiff's claims in this case, in so far as they are based on negligence which allowed David Udale to come into this world alive, should not be allowed.

The considerations that particularly impress me are the following. (1) It is highly undesirable that any child should learn that a court has publicly declared his life or birth to be a mistake, a disaster even, and that he or she is unwanted or rejected. Such pronouncements would disrupt families and weaken the structure of society. (2) A plaintiff such as Mrs Udale would get little or no damages because her love and care for her child and her joy, ultimately, at his birth would be set off against and might cancel out the inconvenience and financial disadvantages which naturally accompany parenthood. By contrast, a plaintiff who nurtures bitterness in her heart and refuses to let her maternal instincts take over would be entitled to large damages. In short virtue would go unrewarded; unnatural rejection of womanhood and motherhood would be generously compensated. This, in my judgment, cannot be just. (3) Medical men would be under subconscious pressure to encourage abortions in order to avoid claims for medical negligence which would arise if the child were allowed to be born. (4) It has been the assumption of our culture for time immemorial that a child coming into the world, even if, as some say, 'the world is a vale of tears', is a blessing and an occasion for rejoicing.

I am reinforced in the second of these considerations by the fact that, if I had to award damages to Mrs Udale under the disputed heads, I would have to regard the financial disadvantages as offset by her gratitude for the gift of a boy after four girls. Accordingly, in my judgment, the last three heads of damage are irrecoverable. In that event, counsel for the defendants submits that the plaintiff's damages cease at the birth. I do not accept that submission altogether. It seems to me that it is legitimate, without detracting from the above principles of public policy, to have some regard to the disturbance to the family finances which the unexpected pregnancy causes. One may look at the cost of the layette and the sudden necessity of having to find more ample accommodation in assessing the damages for the unwanted pregnancy, without regarding the child as unwanted. One has to bear in mind here that the child has, up until the age of 4 years 2 months, in fact lived in that house without the extension. It has not of course been built. Accordingly, in my view, it is proper to increase the award of damages with this in mind when awarding general damages for the pain, suffering, inconvenience, anxiety and the like, mentioned at the beginning of this judgment. I do so by awarding the sum of £8,000 for these matters together.

Contrast the view of Peter Pain J in *Thake v Maurice* [1984] 2 All ER 513

Peter Pain J: In approaching this problem I firmly put sentiment on one side. A healthy baby is so lovely a creature that I can well understand the reaction of one who asks: how could its birth possibly give rise to an action for damages? But every baby has a belly to be filled and a body to be clothed. The law relating to damages is concerned with reparation in money terms and this is what is needed for the maintenance of a baby.

I have to have regard to the policy of the state as it expresses itself in legislation and in social provision. I must consider this in the light of modern developments. By 1975 family planning was generally practised. Abortion had been legalised over a wide field. Vasectomy was one of the methods of family planning which was not only legal but was available under the national health service. It seems to me to follow from this that it was generally recognised that the birth of a healthy baby is not always a blessing. It is a blessing when the baby is to be born to the happy family life which we would all like a baby to have. Many people hold that that end can be best achieved by restricting natural fertility.

The policy of the state, as I see it, is to provide the widest freedom of choice. It makes available to the public the means of planning their families or planning to have no family. If plans go awry, it provides for the possibility of abortion. But there is no pressure on couples either to have children or not to have children or to have only a limited number of children. Even the one-parent family, whether that exists through choice or through misfortune, is given substantial assistance.

Against that background I ask myself whether the reasons advanced by Jupp J are so compelling that I ought to follow his decision. I do not think they are and, in deference to his careful reasoning, I will consider them one by one.

I do not think that if I award damages here it will lead little Samantha to feel rejection. She is surrounded by a happy, albeit somewhat poverty-stricken, family life. It is this that must make her feel wanted and not rejected. She may learn in years to come that her conception was unwanted. But there is nothing exceptional about this. What matters to a child is how it is received when it enters life. It so often happens that parents reconcile themselves to an unwelcome conception and accept the child with joy. If Samantha is as bright as her father thinks, by the time she comes to consider this judgment (if she ever does) she will, I think, welcome it as a means of having made life somewhat easier for her family.

Next I have to consider the difficulty in setting off the joy of Samantha against the financial disadvantages that her parents would undergo. If I adopt the public policy which Jupp J favours then virtue will indeed go unrewarded. Every credit is due to the plaintiffs for the way in which they have welcomed Samantha into the family. The method of set-off presents difficulties but, once again, I think it can be solved by looking at the hard cash involved and ignoring the intangibles. Both plaintiffs suffered great distress on learning of Mrs Thake's pregnancy. Mrs Thake underwent pain and discomfort in the course of her labour, although it was not particularly difficult. As a result of these sufferings they had a healthy child. But the fact that she has been such a joy to them is largely of their own making. If they had been reluctant to accept her and grudging in the sacrifices they had to make for her support, then they might have had little joy. As I see it, the birth of a healthy child should be set off against their disappointment and the labour pains so that they cancel each other out. The joy they have for Samantha is largely of their own making in the way they have met their difficulties. The claim for Samantha's support and for the costs of the birth remain.

If the principle of public policy applies it should apply throughout and there should be no award in respect of the birth. The injustice of this course was apparent to Jupp J who said ([1983] 2 All ER 522 at 531–532, [1983] 1 WLR 1098 at 1109–1110):

> It seems to me that it is legitimate, without detracting from the above principles of public policy, to have some regard to the disturbance to the family finances which the unexpected pregnancy causes. One may look at the cost of the layette and the sudden necessity of having to find more ample accommodation in assessing the damages for the unwanted pregnancy, without regarding the child as unwanted. One has to bear in mind here that the child has, up until the age of 4 years 2 months, in fact lived in that house without the extension. It has not of course been built. Accordingly, in my view, it is proper to increase the award of damages with this in mind when awarding general damages for the pain, suffering, inconvenience, anxiety and the like, mentioned at the beginning of this judgment.

I do not see the logical basis of this approach.

The third reason advanced hardly applies here since there was no possiblity of an abortion. But, in view of the divisions within the medical profession, I think it has little force. The decision whether to abort or not will usually rest with an obstetrician, who may well be quite independent of the medical man who faces a possible charge of negligence.

As to the fourth ground, for the reasons I have already given I do not accept that it is part of our culture that the birth of a healthy child is always a blessing. It may have been the assumption in the past. I feel quite satisfied that it is not the assumption today.

I entirely accept that the reasons put forward by Jupp J may be valid considerations in the assessment of damages in a particular case. But I feel that to erect them into a rule of public policy applicable to all cases would work great injustice, as it would here. I therefore prefer to follow Watkins J in [*Sciuriaga v Powell*].

The Court of Appeal subsequently preferred the view of Peter Pain J. In *Emeh v Kensington, Chelsea and Westminster Area Health Authority* Waller LJ said:

> The next case to which we were referred was *Udale v Bloomsbury Area Health Authority* [1983] 2 All ER 522, [1983] 1 WLR 1098, a decision of Jupp J in a case where the plaintiff had had a sterilisation operation but had thereafter become pregnant and the sterilisation operation had failed by reason of the negligence of the surgeon. So the question was one of damage. Jupp J gave very careful consideration to the question of public policy. I do not propose to quote his reasons; it is sufficient to say that he came to the conclusion that there were policy objections to the award of damages in relation to the upkeep of the child concerned after birth. He thought there were social implications; he thought that the sanctity of human life had to be considered, and the risk of the child becoming aware that he was so unwanted that damages were being paid by doctors for his maintenance, and so on.
>
> The next case to which we were referred was *Thake v Maurice* [1984] 2 All ER 513, a decision of Peter Pain J. That case concerned an operation of vasectomy on a railway worker who had five children. He and his wife had decided that they should have no more, so the operation was performed on him but then his wife became pregnant again. However, I should say at this stage that in this case, as in the *Udale* case, when the child arrived, the parents were absolutely delighted and were very happy with it. However, in the *Thake* case the reason for the vasectomy operation was because there were five children of the family already, and from the point of view of cost it would be difficult if they had another child. Peter Pain J considered very carefully the matters referred to by Jupp J in the *Udale* case, and he came to the conclusion that he was not prepared to lay down any public policy objections to the claim which was being made.
>
> I do not find the arguments in favour of the public policy objection convincing. If

public policy prevents a recovery of damages, then there might be an incentive on the part of some to have late abortions. On the other hand, damages can be awarded which may in some cases be an encouragement and help to bring up an unplanned child. I see unfortunate comparisons which can be made between the case of a child where the mother receives damages, and a case of another child whose mother does not, as being something which is unfortunate, but which is something which cannot be helped.

Lastly, our attention was drawn to *McLoughlin v O'Brian* [1982] 2 All ER 298, [1983] 1 AC 410, and to the words of Lord Scarman and also Lord Edmund Davies, which seem to be apposite to the decision which we have to make in this case. In that case the House of Lords was concerned with the possibility of a claim for damages for nervous shock by a plaintiff whose family had been injured in a motor accident. She was told of the accident some two hours after it had happened by a neighbour, and she alleged that the impact of what she heard and saw caused her severe shock. The argument was raised that she was out of the range of foreseeability. Lord Scarman said ([1982] 2 All ER 298 at 310, [1983] 1 AC 410 at 430):

The distinguishing feature of the common law is this judicial development and formulation of principle. Policy considerations will have to be weighed; but the objective of the judges is the formulation of principle. And, if principle inexorably requires a decision which entails a degree of policy risk, the court's function is to adjudicate according to principle, leaving policy curtailment to the judgment of Parliament. Here lies the true role of the two law-making institutions in our constitution. By concentrating on principle the judges can keep the common law alive, flexible and consistent, and can keep the legal system clear of policy problems which neither they, nor the forensic process which it is their duty to operate, are equipped to resolve. If principle leads to results which are thought to be socially unacceptable, Parliament can legislate to draw a line or map out a new path.

In my judgment the court should not be too ready to lay down lines of public policy; and I would reject the argument in this case that public policy requires that damages should be confined in the way in which it has been submitted.

The other judges in the Court of Appeal agreed.

Slade LJ: As to public policy, counsel for the defendants naturally referred us to, and relied strongly on, the decision of Jupp J in *Udale v Bloomsbury Area Health Authority* [1983] 2 All ER 522, [1983] 1 WLR 1098. In that case Jupp J held that it was contrary to public policy that damages should be recoverable arising from the cost of the coming into the world of a healthy, normal child. Counsel for the defendants did not feel able to go so far as to submit that there was any principle of public policy which prevented damages from being recoverable for the cost of the birth of a child who was not normal. Nevertheless, in reliance on the *Udale* principle, he submitted that, if we were to reject his principal argument, then, in assessing the measure of damages, the cost of raising a normal child should be deducted from the cost of raising the little girl in the present case.

I do not think that this submission is well founded. Following *mutatis mutandis* the same reasoning as Watkins J at first instance in *Sciuriaga v Powell* (1979) 123 SJ 406, the operation performed on the plaintiff in this case was in accordance with the law; not everyone may approve of that law, but it is the law. So if a woman wishes to be sterilised, and in a legal way causes herself to be operated on for that purpose, I can, for my part, see no reason why, under public policy, she should not recover such financial damage as she can prove she has sustained by the surgeon's negligent failure to perform the operation properly, whether or not the child is healthy.

Jupp J, in his very careful judgment in the *Udale* case, gave a number of reasons for reaching a contrary conclusion, in the case of a normal healthy child, but Peter Pain J, in an equally careful judgment, gave his answers to all of Jupp J's points in the later case of *Thake v Maurice* [1984] 2 All ER 513. In this context I think I need only say that, with great respect to both these judges, I, for my part, prefer the reasoning of Peter Pain J on these particular points; I respectfully agree with what Waller LJ has said in this context.

Purchas LJ: I see no reason for the courts to introduce into the perfectly ordinary, straightforward rules of recovery of damages, whether they are damages flowing from a breach of contract or from tort, some qualification to reflect special social positions. If something has to be done in that respect, as Waller LJ cited from the speech of Lord Scarman in *McLoughlin v O'Brian* [1982] 2 All ER 298 at 310, [1983] 1 AC 410 at 430, then that is a matter which falls more properly within the purview of Parliament. The ordinary rules of remoteness of damage, once the question of a break in the causation has been disposed of, can apply equally well to cases of this sort. Where the arrival of the child has mitigating features, such as those referred to in the judgment to which I have just referred, then, in the ordinary assessment of damages, there will be an appropriate diminution in the damages awarded.

Do you agree with the Court of Appeal? Notice how Lloyd LJ in *Gold v Haringey Health Authority* (*supra*) chose to refer to the observations of Ognall J in the unreported case of *Jones v Berkshire Area Health Authority*.

Before relating the history of the matter, I wish to make one point clear. We are not in this case called on to decide whether it is desirable or not that a plaintiff should be able to claim damages for the birth of a healthy child, and a child which, in this particular case, the plaintiff and her husband are now delighted to have. In *Jones v Berkshire Area Health Authority* (2 July 1986, unreported), another unwanted pregnancy case, Ognall J said:

I pause only to observe that, speaking purely personally, it remains a matter of surprise to me that the law acknowledges an entitlement in a mother to claim damages for the blessing of a healthy child. Certain it is that those who are afflicted with a handicapped child or who long desperately to have a child at all and are denied that good fortune would regard an award for this sort of contingency with a measure of astonishment. But there it is: that is the law.

Many would no doubt agree with the observation. But the desirability of permitting such a claim does not concern us here. At one time there was a conflict of decisions at first instance whether it was against public policy to allow a plaintiff to recover damages for the birth of a healthy child. But that conflict has been resolved, so far as this court is concerned, by the unanimous decision of this court in *Emeh v Kensington and Chelsea and Westminster Area Health Authority* [1984] 3 All ER 1044, [1985] QB 1012. So in the present appeal we are concerned solely with the question whether the plaintiff has established negligence against the defendants by reason of their failure to warn the plaintiff that the operation might not succeed.

Notice also the point made by Purchas LJ in *Emeh* that the court should take account of mitigating features arising out of the birth of the child in calculating the plaintiff's damages. In *Thake*, Peter Pain J cancelled out the plaintiff's damages for pain and suffering because of the corresponding joy as a consequence of the birth of the baby. The Court of Appeal disagreed.

The cross-appeal on damages

Kerr LJ [pp 1050–1051]: The judge awarded damages to the plaintiffs under certain heads in agreed amounts, but he declined to make any award for the plaintiffs' distress when they knew that Mrs Thake would have to have another child, nor for the discomfort, pain and suffering which she had to undergo, though fortunately it was not a difficult pregnancy or delivery. He awarded agreed damages for the cost of the layette and of Samantha's upkeep to the age of 17 in a total of £6,677 and an agreed sum of £2,000 to Mrs Thake for loss of earnings during this period, plus agreed interest in the sum of £1,000, making a total of £9,677. The plaintiffs now cross-appeal against his refusal to make any award for what I can refer to in short as pain and suffering. He gave his reasons for this conclusion as follows ([1984] 2 All ER 513 at 526–527, [1985] 2 WLR 215 at 231):

> Next I have to consider the difficulty in setting off the joy of Samantha against the financial disadvantages that her parents would undergo . . . Every credit is due to the plaintiffs for the way in which they have welcomed Samantha into the family. The method of set-off presents difficulties but, once again, I think it can be solved by looking at the hard cash involved and ignoring the intangibles. Both plaintiffs suffered great distress on learning of Mrs Thake's pregnancy. Mrs Thake underwent pain and discomfort in the course of her labour, although it was not particularly difficult. As a result of these sufferings they had a healthy child. But the fact that she has been such a joy to them is largely of their own making. If they had been reluctant to accept her and grudging in the sacrifices they had to make for her support, then they might have had little joy. As I see it, the birth of a healthy child should be set off against their disappointment and the labour pains so that they cancel each other out. The joy they have for Samantha is largely of their own making in the way they have met their difficulties.

On behalf of the plaintiffs it was accepted that credit would have to be given, in effect by way of a set-off, for the happiness which the plaintiffs ultimately derived from having Samantha as a healthy child. Their counsel accepted that neither of the plaintiffs, in particular Mrs Thake, could therefore claim anything for the time and trouble which would have to be devoted to her care and upbringing, and he pointed out that no such claim had been made. But he contested that the relief and joy which they felt after Samantha had been born should be set off so as to extinguish any claim for their earlier distress, and the pain and suffering of Mrs Thake before and during the birth. I would uphold this submission. The joy of having Samantha should in my view be set off against the time, trouble and care which is inevitably involved in her upbringing. The plaintiffs have rightly made no claim for this. But the pre-natal distress, pain and suffering in my view stand on a separate footing, and I think that it would be wrong to apply this set-off to this head of claim as well, in effect twice over, bearing in mind that the claim for pain and suffering was otherwise unchallenged. One can perhaps take the analogy of a defendant who sustains some injury and suffers distress because of the risk that he may become paralysed. If he then fortunately and happily makes a full recovery, his ultimate well-being will of course be reflected in a low award of damages. But his relief and joy at the outcome cannot properly be used as a basis for reducing, let alone extinguishing, an appropriate award for his initial pain and suffering. This conclusion also appears to me to be in line with such authority as there is on this point. In his judgment in *Emeh v Kensington and Chelsea and Westminster Area Health Authority* [1984] 3 All ER 1044 at 1056, [1985] QB 1012 at 1028 Purchas LJ approved the following passage from a decision of the Supreme Court of Minnesota in *Sherlock v Stillwater Clinic* (1977) 260 NW 2d 169 at 170–171:

> We hold that in cases such as this an action for 'wrongful conception' may be maintained, and that compensatory damages may be recovered by the parents of the unplanned child. These damages may include all prenatal and postnatal medical expenses; the mother's pain and suffering during pregnancy and delivery, and loss of consortium. Additionally, the parents may recover the reasonable costs of rearing the unplanned child subject to offsetting the value of the child's aid, comfort and society during the parents' life expectancy.

It was submitted on behalf of the defendant that, once it is accepted that a set-off must be made, it does not matter against which head of claim it is applied, and I recognise that the passage quoted above is by no means conclusive in the plaintiffs' favour on this aspect. Nevertheless, for the reasons already given, I respectfully differ from the judge that the claim for ante-natal pain and suffering should be extinguished by the happiness of the post-natal events. The joy of parents at the birth of a healthy child, though with the consequent time and trouble which need to be devoted to its upbringing, are both virtually impossible to assess in terms of money. It is therefore right that in law they should be treated as cancelling each other out. But awards of damages for pain and suffering are an everyday feature of our law, and it was not suggested on behalf of the defendant that such damages are irrecoverable in principle for the discomfort and pain of pregnancy and delivery when these occur normally and without adverse incidents. Accordingly, I would uphold the plaintiffs' claim under this head and allow the cross-appeal.

Does that mean that the courts do regard birth as a legally recognised harm?

Once the courts allowed actions for failed sterilisations then the damages claims were bound to increase in size. The leading cases show the beginning of this trend. In *Benarr v Kettering Health Authority* [1988] NLJR 179, Hodgson J awarded a father damages to educate his child, who was born after a failed vasectomy, at private school (about £19,500).

2. WITHOUT CONSENT OF THE PERSON

(a) minor

As we have seen, minority in itself does not connote incapacity to consent to ordinary medical treatment. Is this also true of a minor purporting to consent to surgical sterilisation? In the absence of any law directly in point, a court may adopt one of three approaches; first, that there is nothing so different about sterilisation to take it outside the general rule which we have already seen in Chapter 4. This approach would mean that a minor who was able to comprehend what was involved, and this may be an onerous burden to discharge, would be competent to consent. Secondly, a court could find that the particular circumstances of sterilisation, especially that it is, in practice, irreversible, and the concomitant public policy implications mean that the minor's consent is *a necessary* but *not sufficient* condition for the treatment. Thirdly, a court could state that a minor was by virtue of minority alone incapable ever of understanding, and thereby giving a valid consent to sterilisation. Notice these last two possible views of the law do not mean, as we shall see, that sterilisation of minors is unlawful. They merely address the question of who may consent.

Which of these views represents the law?

When a minor is incompetent who, if anyone, may in law authorise or consent to sterilisation? This, and other questions, fell to be considered by the House of Lords in *Re B*. Ordinarily, the law would look to the parent. Is this so here?

Re B (a minor)
[1987] 2 All ER 206

Lord Templeman: My Lords, for the reasons given by my noble and learned friends the Lord Chancellor and Lord Oliver I would dismiss this appeal but wish to add a few additional observations.

In my opinion sterilisation of a girl under 18 should only be carried out with the leave of a High Court judge. A doctor performing a sterilisation operation with the consent of the parents might still be liable in criminal, civil or professional proceedings. A court exercising the wardship jurisdiction emanating from the Crown is the only authority which is empowered to authorise such a drastic step as sterilisation after a full and informed investigation. The girl will be represented by the Official Solicitor or some other appropriate guardian; the parents will be made parties if they wish to appear and where appropriate the local authority will also appear. Expert evidence will be adduced setting out the reasons for the application, the history, conditions, circumstances and foreseeable future of the girl, the risks and consequences of pregnancy, the risks and consequences of sterilisation, the practicability of alternative precautions against pregnancy and any other relevant information. The judge may order additional evidence to be obtained. In my opinion, a decision should only be made by a High Court judge. In the Family Division a judge is selected for his or her experience, ability and compassion. No one has suggested a more satisfactory tribunal or a more satisfactory method of reaching a decision which vitally concerns an individual but also involves principles of law, ethics and medical practice. Applications for sterilisation will be rare. Sometimes the judge will conclude that a sufficiently overwhelming case has not been established to justify interference with the fundamental right of a girl to bear a child; this was the case in *Re D (a minor) (wardship: sterilisation)* [1976] 1 All ER 326, [1976] Fam 185. But in the present case the judge was satisfied that it would be cruel to expose the girl to an unacceptable risk of pregnancy which could only be obviated by sterilisation in order to prevent child bearing and childbirth in circumstances of uncomprehending fear and pain and risk of physical injury. In such a case the judge was under a duty and had the courage to authorise sterilisation.

If the court in wardship is acting as a 'wise and prudent parent' (*R v Gyngall* [1893] 2 QB 232 at 241–242, *per* Esher MR) why cannot a parent *sua sponte* authorise a sterilisation? Notice no other Law Lord expressly commented upon this point.

Under what circumstances will the court authorise sterilisation in the exercise of its wardship jurisdiction? As we have seen (*supra* Ch 4), the test the English courts adopt is the test of the 'best interests' of the child; notice again *Re B*:

Lord Hailsham LC (at 212): There is no doubt that, in the exercise of its wardship jurisdiction, the first and paramount consideration is the well-being, welfare or interests (each expression occasionally used, but each, for this purpose, synonymous) of the human being concerned, that is the ward herself or himself. In this case I believe it to be the only consideration involved. In particular there is no issue of public policy other than the application of the above principle which can conceivably be taken into account, least of all (since the opposite appears to have been considered in some quarters) any question of eugenics. The ward has never conceived and is not pregnant. No question therefore arises as to the morality or legality of an abortion.

Are there, in fact, two distinct ways of determining 'best interests'? The first, and narrower, approach may be that ordinarily adopted by the English family law which tends to invite a court to form a judgment based upon the particular case before it. This approach tends to eschew regard for any general principle governing the care of all children. Furthermore, and this may be a jurisprudential flaw, it tends to treat normative issues as if they were issues of fact. Facts do not suggest what *ought* to be done; it is the values and policies by reference to which these facts are evaluated which perform this function.

The second, and wider approach, neglected (or rejected) by the English courts, is that which would import into 'best interests' human rights issues—in this case the rights of the child. This was the approach, as we saw earlier, by the Canadian Supreme Court in *Re Eve*, curiously without reference to the Canadian Charter of Rights and Freedoms.

Which approach do you think is more sensitive to the interests of all the parties concerned? What, if any, relevance does the European Convention on Human Rights have, particularly articles 2, 3, 8 and 12?

(b) An adult

We are concerned here with the question of whether sterilisation may be authorised by someone other than the person where that person is an incompetent adult. The traditional view has been that in the absence of any explicit statutory authority, no-one has authority to consent to the medical treatment of another. Reference has been made to the doctrine of emergency or necessity so as to inject some commonsense in the law (*supra* Ch 4).

As we have seen, in *Re Eve* the Canadian Supreme Court held that as a matter of English common law, the court as *parens patriae* could authorise medical treatment including therapeutic sterilisation in the case of an adult. *Eve* relied on such cases as *Wellesley v Duke of Beaufort* (1827) 2 Russ 1 at 20, where Lord Eldon said: '[the jurisdiction] belongs to the King as *parens patriae*, having the care of those who are not able to take care of themselves, and is founded on the obvious necessity that the law should place somewhere the care of individuals who cannot take care of themselves'.

However, in *Re Eve*, the court rejected the view that a 'non-therapeutic' sterilisation could be authorised by the court because, in the words of La Forest J:

> The grave intrusion on a person's rights and certain physical damage that ensues from non-therapeutic sterilisation without consent, when compared to the highly questionable advantages that can result from it, have persuaded me that it can never safely be determined that such a procedure is for the benefit of that person. Accordingly, the procedure should never be authorised for non-therapeutic purposes under the *parens patriae* jurisdiction.
>
> To begin with, it is difficult to imagine a case in which non-therapeutic sterilisation could possibly be of benefit to the person on behalf of whom a court purports to act, let alone one in which that procedure is necessary in his or her best interest.

However, this is not the English law. If there be any power in anyone to authorise the sterilisation of an adult incompetent, it would seem sensible to assume that the circumstances under which the authorisation may be given are the same as those which apply in the case of a minor. As we have seen in *Re B*, the House of Lords adopted what we describe above as the 'first and narrower' approach based upon *ad hoc* decisions looking to the facts of an individual case. Although not a *parens patriae* case, *T v T* required the court to determine when a sterilisation operation on an adult would be lawful without his or her consent. As Wood J put it, what had to be considered was 'what decisions would be in the best interests of the patient's health'. What significance would you attach to Wood J's use of the word 'health'? Is this any different from the test adopted and applied by the House of Lords in *Re B*? If it is, should the test differ as between a minor or an adult, or has one court fallen into error?

In any event, Wood J recognises the possibility of there being an alternative way of resolving this issue. The method of reasoning seems to be that a touching without consent amounts *prima facie* to a battery, but that there may be a public policy justification for the touching. Traditionally, as we saw earlier, this has been called 'necessity' or some other suitably malleable expression. In *T v T* [1988] Fam 52, [1988] 1 All ER 613, Wood J said:

> I prefer to approach the problem in this way. This defendant is never going to be able to consent (we are not dealing with a temporary inability such as a person under an anaesthetic, and I compare the Canadian cases *Marshall v Curry* [1933] 3 DLR 260 and *Murray v McMurchy* [1949] 2 DLR 442) and there is no one in a position to consent. A medical adviser must therefore consider what decisions should be reached in the best interests of his patient's health. What does medical practice

demand? I use the word 'demand' because I envisage a situation where based on good medical practice there are really no two views of what course is for the best. On the facts of this case I accept the medical evidence that not only would it be contrary to the defendant's best interests to postpone these proposed procedures, but it is positively in her best interests to proceed with due dispatch.

It might be argued that the sterilisation could reasonably be postponed for further consideration and indeed that was my own first reaction, but after hearing the argument I am quite satisfied that the risks to the defendant of a second operation, coupled with the doubts whether it could in fact be achieved in the light of her strength and inability to understand, are such as to be unacceptable, and I have no doubt that her best interests demand that all appropriate procedures to this end are carried out at the same time as the termination.

Is Wood J saying that the justification is (a) merely an example of the general notion of 'necessity', relevant here because of the exceptional circumstances of the case, or (b) is derived from the potentially wider proposition that a touching of someone incapable of consenting is always lawful solely on the basis of its being in accordance with what 'good medical practice demands'? (see now *re F* (1989) Times, 25 May *infra*).

Furthermore, just as the European Convention on Human Rights may be relevant in the case of minors, may it not also be applicable in the case of incompetent adults?

Earlier, in the general discussion concerning the power of the court (and, in the case of minor patients, of parents) to consent to medical procedures, we saw the contrasting approaches adopted by the Canadian Supreme Court in *Re Eve* and the House of Lords in *Re B*. Perhaps the most significant issue left untouched by the Law Lords in *Re B* is the possibility that the court should articulate guidelines both for itself and (providing Lord Templeman is wrong) for parents in determining when a sterilisation operation is in an incompetent individual's best interests. The American courts have long had to consider the problems faced in these situations. We may be able to learn something from their approach. However, as with almost any legal problem, different results and approaches can be found in the various American jurisdictions. A helpful summary can be found in the discussion document issued by the Institute of Law Research and Reform of Alberta in its Report 'Sterilisation Decisions: Minors and Mentally Incompetent Adults' (March 1988) [footnotes omitted].

H24. Courts that have assumed the authority to make sterilisation decisions have proceeded cautiously in its exercise. They have applied one of two alternative tests. The first test involves the determination of whether sterilisation is in the individual's 'best interests'. The second test involves making the decision the minor or mentally incompetent adult would have made in the circumstances if he had been competent to make the decision. It is called the exercise of 'substituted judgment'. The application of the best interests test is more usual.

1. **Best interests (including clear and convincing evidence standard)**
H25. Under the best interests test, the authority to consent is approached not as a personification of the mentally incompetent person but as 'a convergence of attitudes and policies held by society'. 'Benefit' is defined by society rather than the individual.

H26. The courts administering the best interests test view the power over procreation as an 'intensely personal right' and 'take great care to ensure that the rights of mentally incompetent persons are jealously guarded'. The cases demonstrate their deep concern to protect mentally incompetent persons from the 'physical and emotional consequences of the sterilisation, and the irreversible, unalterable and permanent nature of the operation'.

H27. Some courts have imposed a 'clear and convincing evidence' standard of proof that sterilisation is in the best interests of the minor or mentally incompetent adult. This standard of proof is higher than the normal civil standard of a preponderance of the evidence and is a burden usually imposed when the state seeks to interfere with individual rights. If the proponent of the sterilisation does not meet the higher standard, the court will not authorise the sterilisation. The effect is to raise a strong presumption that sterilisation is not in the best interests of mentally disabled persons. The higher standard of proof has been applied where the court recognised that the exercise by the court of its power is intended to compensate for a mentally incompetent person's inability to exercise her constitutional right of privacy over procreation. Courts using it emphasise the principle of the inviolability of the person more than the principle of personal autonomy.

H28. In assessing the mentally incompetent persons's best interests, different courts have specified different factors to consider in their best interests tests. The factors include that the person:

1. is incompetent to understand reproduction or contraception and make a sterilisation decision;
2. is unlikely to become competent;
3. is incompetent to make a sterilisation decision (this is particularly important for minors and young adults);
4. is physically capable of reproduction;
5. is likely to be sexually active or exposed to sexual contact;
6. might experience physical or psychological trauma from pregnancy, childbirth or sterilisation;
7. is incapable of caring for a child either alone or with a spouse.

Other factors are that:

1. less drastic methods of birth control are not feasible;
2. less intrusive sterilisation procedures are not available;
3. sterilisation is advisable at this time, contrasted to a future date;
4. scientific advances that will make less drastic contraceptive methods available or improve the person's condition are not foreseeable;
5. those requesting the operation are not seeking it for their own or the public's convenience;
6. sterilisation is medically necessary to preserve the person's life or physical or mental health.

2. Substituted judgment

H29. The Massachusetts Supreme Judicial Court rejected the best interests test and requirement of clear and convincing evidence proof for sterilisation decisions. The fundamental issue, it said, was whether 'the state [sought] to impose a solution on an incompetent based on external criteria, or ... to protect and implement the individual's personal rights and integrity'. The higher standard of proof was appropriate when the state interfered with a person's liberty, not when the individual sought to exercise his or her liberty.

H30. The court decided that the substituted judgment test best promoted the interests of the individual. Substituted judgment is a test that had previously been applied to decisions concerning the cessation of mechanical or chemical life supports for terminally ill persons and organ donations and transplants from mentally incompetent persons. The court '"dons the mental mantle of the incompetent" and substitutes itself as nearly as possible for the individual in the decision-making process'. The court heeds the wishes and values of the mentally incompetent person and decides as he would decide if he were competent. In this way his right of free choice and dignity as an individual are maintained.

H31. The court is to exercise the utmost care in reviewing all the evidence presented. That is to say, the judicial proceeding must be thorough. It must consider, but not be concerned solely with, the following factors:

(1) whether the individual lacks the capacity to make a decision regarding sterilisation;
(2) whether sterilisation entails the least intrusive invasion of the incompetent;

(3) the medical necessity, if any, for sterilisation;

(4) the nature and extent of the disability and whether the incompetent could care for a child;

(5) whether science is on the threshold of an advance in treatment of the disability;

(6) the likelihood of sexual activity;

(7) the possibility of health risks, or psychological damage; and

(8) the religious beliefs and special circumstances of the incompetent.

H32. Where the mentally incompetent person's actual interests and preferences can be garnered from evidence of his experiences and expressions while competent or behaviour while incompetent, the substituted judgment test gives him as nearly as possible the same right to self-determination as a mentally competent person. It concurrently provides a forum for the assertion of the rights of the mentally incompetent person, satisfies the goal of equal protection of the right of procreative choice, and protects against parental or government abuses.

H33. On the other hand, it may be difficult to ascertain the actual desires and preferences of a severely mentally disabled person for sterilisation, other means of contraception or parenthood, especially if the condition has existed from birth or early childhood. It may also be difficult to avoid abuse of the mentally incompetent person: the test is not as predictable as that of clear and convincing evidence of best interests or medical necessity.

3. Procedural safeguards

H34. The tests and factors described above provide personal (substantive law) safeguards for the rights of minors and mentally incompetent adults both from improper bodily violation and for the exercise of their right of privacy. The decisions also provide procedural safeguards. These include: adequate notice (to the parties) of the proceedings; the appointment by the court of an independent guardian *ad litem* who would fully represent the interests of the mentally incompetent person at a full judicial hearing (the guardian *ad litem* should have full opportunity to present proof and cross-examine witnesses and ensure an adversarial proceeding so that both sides of each issue are presented) independent medical, psychological and social evaluations by competent professionals who may be appointed by the court; a personal interview by the court with the person for the purpose of forming an impression of competence; and right of appeal.

H35. The sterilisation decision is for the court: 'It must be the court's judgment, and not just the parents' good faith decision, that substitutes for the incompetent's consent'. Parents or guardians may bring the sterilisation proceedings on behalf of the minor or mentally incompetent adult and the court may authorise them to satisfy the procedural requirements of consent: 'We do not mean that the trial judge must sign the consent form. Procedurally, the trial court should designate a guardian with authority to consent, as was done here. We only wish to point out the reality that the substance of the consent comes from the court rather than the guardian personally'.

You will see that the American courts have not always adopted a 'best interests' test but have instead relied upon a 'substituted judgment' test. As we saw earlier, the 'substituted judgment' test has not been used in England and, indeed, in the case of those who have never been competent to express any wishes, it is difficult to apply (*Re Eve, supra*). The Institute in its Report recommended that certain substantive guidelines should be enshrined in legislation (footnotes omitted).

Factors judge to consider

(1) Elective sterilisation

9.43   It is our view that the legislation should include a mandatory list of factors for the judge to consider in applying the best interests test. We so recommend for a number of reasons. One is that, as the Supreme Court stated in the *Eve* judgment, judges—and the same could be said of lawyers—are not experts on sterilisation. In the words of the Supreme Court:

> Judges are generally ill-informed about many of the factors relevant to a wise decision in this difficult area. They generally know little of mental illness, of techniques of contraception or their efficacy.

Another is that the mixture of medical, genetic and social factors present for consideration complicates the job of the substitute decision maker. A third is that cases are known to have been decided under the Dependent Adults Act without adequate evidence (eg in one case, a sterilisation was ordered of a person whose condition would have made him sterile already).

9.44 The list we have developed is a conglomerate, built from a variety of sources including the Canadian cases of *Re Eve* (in particular the judgment of McDonald J on the appeal to the Prince Edward Island Supreme Court sitting *in banco*) and *Re K* and American cases like *Re Grady*. It includes the factors we will now discuss.

(a) Wishes of person to be sterilised
9.45 A person who is not competent to consent nevertheless may signal preferences or wishes that should be considered (eg, the repeated plea of 'no more babies', or the exhibition of violent aggression toward young children). A person may have expressed wishes before the onset of a disabling condition. Giving consideration to the wishes of the person would foster our third principle of reform. That principle is that the law should respect the dignity, welfare and total development of the minor or mentally incompetent adult for whom sterilisation is being considered.

9.46 The *Eve* judgment suggests that the wishes of the mentally incompetent person do not hold weight. A passage is quoted from the judgment of Mrs Justice Heilbron in the English case of *Re D (A Minor)*. It is to the effect that any answer given by a mentally incompetent person on the matter of sterilisation, or any purported consent, would be valueless. However, we think that insofar as they can be known, the wishes, concerns, religious beliefs or other values and special circumstances of the person to be sterilised should be considered.

(b) Mental condition
9.47 Mental incompetence is a prerequisite to a substitute sterilisation decision. But the relevance of mental condition does not end with this finding. Where there is a reasonable likelihood that the person to be sterilised will become competent to make the decision within a suitable time in the future, an elective sterilisation ordinarily should not be authorised. In such a situation it would be proper for the judge to refuse to make an order. In sum, we recommend the nature and anticipated duration of the disabling condition should be a factor to be considered.

(c) Physical capacity to reproduce
9.48 It would be pointless and wrong to perform a sterilisation on a person who is not capable of natural insemination or pregnancy (eg, males with Down's Syndrome have not been known to reproduce, but a few affected females have had children). Therefore, the physical capacity of the person to reproduce should be a factor for the judge to consider. However, because fertility is difficult to prove, we recommend that a presumption of fertility should be raised if the medical evidence indicates normal development of sexual organs and the evidence does not otherwise raise doubts about fertility.

(d) Engagement in sexual activity
9.49 The likelihood that the person will be sexually active is another factor that should be considered. In ordinary circumstances it would be excessive to sterilise a person where the likelihood is slight. Nor do we think that a sterilisation should be performed to protect a person from possible sexual exploitation or abuse. The emphasis in such cases should be *not* on the curtailment of the choices available to the potential victim but on the curtailment of the undesirable behaviour by the perpetrator of the exploitation or abuse. Sterilisation should not be used as a substitute for proper protection of mentally disabled persons from sexual abuse.

(e) Risks to physical health
9.50   We recommend that the clinical risks to the physical health of the person of undergoing or foregoing the sterilisation should be weighed as a fourth factor, just as they would be in the case of a mentally competent adult making her own decision.

(f) Risks to mental health
9.51   The clinical risks to the mental health of the person of undergoing or foregoing the sterilisation should also be weighed. We have presented examples of traumatic or psychological risks associated with pregnancy and delivery. The possible psychological effect of foregoing a sterilisation should therefore be considered. Studies show that sterilisation may engender a feeling of regret over the loss of the capacity to reproduce. It follows that the traumatic or psychological risks associated with undergoing a sterilisation likewise should be considered.

(g) Alternatives to sterilisation
9.52   The availability and medical advisability of alternative means of medical treatment or contraception should be included as a factor for consideration. As a general rule, a sterilisation should not be performed if a less restrictive means of medical treatment or contraception is available and feasible under the particular circumstances.

(h) Likelihood of marriage
9.53   Childbearing and rearing are normal incidents of marriage. Therefore we are of the view that the chances of the person for marriage in the future should be included as a factor.

(i) Risk of disability in child
9.54   Couples in the general population may seek genetic counselling to help them family planning. Where genetic considerations peculiar to a couple make it likely that their child will be born with a physical or mental disability, genetic counselling enables them to consider whether they would be able to cope satisfactorily. We think it likewise should be possible to consider evidence of genetic peculiarities in deciding whether a sterilisation should be performed on a person who is not competent to consent.

(j) Ability to care for a child
9.55   Another factor that should be considered is the ability of the person to care for a child at the time of the application and any likely changes in that ability in the future.

(k) Other available care
9.56   Consideration should also be given to the care that may be available for prospective offspring (eg, the help of a spouse, or a parent or other relative).

(l) Effect on caregivers
9.57   We recommend that the likely effect of undergoing or foregoing the proposed sterilisation on the ability of those who care for the person to provide required care should be a factor, but looked at only from the perspective of the person for whom sterilisation is being considered. For example, would the person have to be moved to another residence because the burden of supervision without sterilisation would be more than family caregivers are able to handle? Would the move or the sterilisation best serve her interests?

(m) Opportunities for satisfying human interaction
9.58   Satisfying human interaction may be experienced not only as a parent in the family setting, but also while working outside the home, enjoying a recreational activity, taking a bus, talking to a store clerk, engaging in normal sexual relations without fear of pregnancy, or participating in other ordinary daily life events. For some persons the opportunities for satisfying human interaction may be impaired rather than enhanced by the demands of childbearing and rearing. We therefore recommend that the likely effect of the decision on the opportunities the person will have for satisfying human interaction should be a factor.

(n) Wishes of family

9.59   The wishes, concerns, religious beliefs or other values of the family or other interested person may affect the interests of the person to be sterilised. To the extent that they do, they should be considered by the judge.

(o) Any other relevant matter

9.60   The list of factors that we have specified, although extensive, is not exhaustive. We recommend that the judge should be able to give the matter the widest consideration possible. The last factor in the list should therefore direct the judge to consider any other matter that he considers relevant. The matter might be evidence that science or medicine is on the threshold of a breakthrough which could offer alternative and less drastic procedures for contraception. The matter might have to do with the advisability of performing a sterilisation now rather than in the future— while sterilisation should not be postponed until unwanted pregnancy occurs, neither should a sterilisation be authorised before it has become clearly advisable. (Under our recommended legislation the denial of an application at one point in time would not preclude the making of a subsequent application in changed circumstances.)

(2) Hysterectomy for menstrual management

9.61   Several of the factors listed for the judge to consider when the issue is elective sterilisation are also relevant when the issue is hysterectomy for menstrual management. Such factors include: the mental condition of the woman to be sterilised; the risks to her physical health with or without the hysterectomy; the risks to her mental health with or without the hysterectomy; the alternative methods of menstrual management that are reasonably available; the effect of undergoing or foregoing the hysterectomy on the ability of those who care for the woman to provide the required care; the likely effect of undergoing or foregoing the hysterectomy on the woman's opportunities to experience satisfying human interactions; the wishes, concerns, religious beliefs and other values of the woman on whom it is proposed to perform the hysterectomy; the wishes, concerns, religious beliefs and other values of her family or other interested persons; and any other relevant matter, such as whether the decision should be made at the time of the application or postponed to a later date (eg, the trial judge in *Re K* thought that the decision should wait until menstruation occurred and the anticipated reaction to menstrual blood was validated in fact).

9.62   Other factors are not directly relevant to the issue of hysterectomy for menstrual management. They include: the physical capacity of the woman to reproduce; the likelihood that she will engage in sexual activity; the likelihood that she will marry; the risk of disability in offspring; her ability to care for a child who might be born; and other care available for such a child.

9.63   We recommend that the legislation should require the judge to consider the factors in the list for an elective sterilisation that are relevant to the decision to perform a hysterectomy for menstrual management. The legislation should specify that a hysterectomy should not be ordered unless it is less drastic than the alternative methods reasonably available to control menstrual flow. The long term use of the injectable hormonal contraceptive Depo-provera, for example, suppresses menstrual bleeding, rendering it either irregular or absent for months. For this reason, it may be seen to have an advantage for menstrual management. The advantage, however, should be weighed against the possibility of an undetermined carcinogenic effect and the risks and side effects associated with oestrogen that endure for the life of the injection.

(3) Availability of evidence

9.64   Our recommendations place a duty on the judge to consider the factors listed before making an order authorising the performance of an elective sterilisation or a hysterectomy for menstrual management. There may be situations where evidence on a factor is either not available at all or not readily available. In such a situation the judge should be able to make an order in the absence of evidence. We recommend that he be authorised to do so where he is satisfied that evidence cannot reasonably be obtained.

I. Method of sterilisation

9.65   For the most part, the choice of surgical operation or other medical procedure to be used for a sterilisation is a matter to be governed by medical factors and evidence in the individual case. The choice will vary with the condition of the mentally incompetent person and the state of medical science at the time.

9.66   In our opinion, the least injurious or intrusive means of accomplishing the purpose should be used. Unless the medical evidence to the contrary is very persuasive it would be wrong, for example, to use hysterectomy for contraception. We therefore recommend that the legislation should include a section prohibiting the performance of an elective sterilisation by hysterectomy unless the judge, by order, expressly so authorises.

In addition, the Report identifies a number of *procedural* safeguards (pp 124–132) which should be afforded an incompetent individual before a sterilisation operation is performed. At the heart of these safeguards is the need to obtain a court order (remember Lord Templeman's view in *Re B*). Perhaps the most important other safeguards recommended are (1) independent representation and (2) the need for expert evidence of the incompetent's condition, prognosis and needs.

Representation of person to be sterilised
9.76   The provision of independent representation is, we think, a matter of fundamental importance to any reform of the law in this area. Recent American cases provide for the appointment of an independent person, called a guardian *ad litem*, to protect the interests of the person with respect to whom an application is made before the court. The function they see for the guardian *ad litem* is to present proof, cross-examine and otherwise zealously represent the interests of the mentally disabled person. The Supreme Court of Canada judgment in the *Eve* case makes 'independent representation' a requirement.

9.77   We recommend that a lawyer should be appointed to represent the interests of the person with respect to whom an application is brought, that the appointment should be made by a judge, and that it should be mandatory. The lawyer appointed should be competent to deal with the medical, legal, social and ethical issues involved. The lawyer's role would be to make sure that the procedures laid down are followed and that full information regarding the issues of competence, sterilisation, the alternatives and other matters set out in the list of factors for the judge to consider is presented so that the judge can be satisfied that his order is in the person's best interests.

9.78   To facilitate the appointment, the application should include a request for the direction of a judge with respect to the appointment of a lawyer to represent the interests of the person who is the subject of the application.

. . .

Evaluation of person to be sterilised
9.85   A comprehensive evaluation of the condition and circumstances of the person to be sterilised is central to the fair determination of the application.

9.86   Recent American cases hold that the evidence before the court should include independent evaluations of the person to be sterilised made by expert qualified professionals. The requirement has been supported in some Canadian judgments as well. On the Prince Edward Island appeal in *Re Eve*, for example, MacDonald J stated:

> The Court should receive advice based on comprehensive medical, psychological and social evaluation of the individual. It would be desirable that the individual be examined by a paediatrician or internist depending on age; a gynaecologist, urologist or general surgeon and a psychiatrist.

In *Re K*, Wood J of the British Columbia Supreme Court added educational to medical, psychological and psychiatric evidence.

9.87 It is our view that expert evidence should be introduced on an application under our proposed legislation. The evidence would assist the judge to determine the person's mental competence or incompetence and to weigh the advantages and disadvantages of the proposed sterilisation. We make three recommendations in this regard.

9.88 Our first recommendation is that the applicant should be required to file the reports of a physician *and* a psychologist in support of an application for an order authorising a sterilisation.

The main purpose of the physician's report would be to provide a medical opinion about the person's physical and mental health and the risks to that health with or without sterilisation. The main purpose of the psychologist's report would be to provide an expert opinion about the person's mental condition and the psychological consequences to the person of undergoing or foregoing the proposed sterilisation. The reports should be served with the notice of the application.

9.89 We have intentionally chosen not to name a particular medical specialty. A physician is likely to be readily available whereas a gynaecologist, psychiatrist or paediatrician may not be. The report of a specialist could always be obtained where appropriate.

9.90 Our second recommendation is that the lawyer appointed to represent the person's interests should be at liberty to apply to a judge for directions with respect to matters arising in the proceedings, including the engagement of experts to conduct independent evaluations and provide evidence. The lawyer should also be able to obtain directions for the payment of costs incurred in engaging experts and otherwise representing the person's interests.

9.91 Our third recommendation, which we discuss in the next section, is that where the judge has doubt as to whether an order should be made, he should have the power to conduct an investigation into the facts.

Questions

(i) To what extent are these two sets of safeguards part of English law already?

(ii) To the extent that they may not be, should they be?

Postscript

In *Re F* (1989), 25 May, the House of Lords considered the power of the court, if any, to authorise a sterilisation operation on an incompetent adult woman. F was 36 and suffered from a permanent severe mental disability. She had the verbal capacity of a child of two and the general mental capacity of a child of four or five. She was a patient at a mental hospital and had formed a sexual relationship with another patient. The doctors took the view that she would not be able to understand pregnancy, labour and delivery and that she could not cope with caring for a baby. Pregnancy, it was thought, would be 'disastrous' for her psychiatrically. Sterilisation was the only practicable form of contraception. F's mother applied on her behalf for a declaration that sterilisation was lawful even though F could not consent. The House of Lords granted the declaration. The decision confirms, in most respects, the approach of Wood J in *T v T* which we have already considered, but not without some significant differences. The decision can only be summarised and commented on by us briefly here.

The House of Lords held that:

(i) the court has no power derived from the Royal Prerogative as *parens patriae* to authorise a medical procedure of any kind upon an incompetent adult. In addition, the statutory provisions of the Mental Health Act 1983 do not confer on the court any power to authorise a medical procedure.

(ii) the court may, however, in appropriate circumstances grant a declaration that a medical procedure, specifically a sterilisation operation, will be lawful notwithstanding the absence of the individual's consent due to his or her incompetence.

(iii) the court will grant such a declaration because treatment which is in the 'best interests' of a patient is justified under the common law on grounds of public policy (*per* Lord Brandon) or because of the principle of necessity (*per* Lord Goff), when the patient is incompetent. A doctor may even have a duty (*per* Lord Brandon) to administer treatment in such circumstances.

(iv) a patient's 'best interests' are to be determined by applying the *Bolam* test—ie, that the sterilisation is considered desirable by a 'competent body of relevant medical opinion.'

(v) it is desirable that an application to the court should be made in order to obtain 'an independent, objective and authoritative view on the lawfulness of the procedure in the particular circumstances.'

(vi) an application should be made to the Family Division, normally by those responsible for the care of the patient and those intending to carry out the procedure. The patient should always be a party and should be represented by the Official Solicitor.

Several brief comments need to be made on this case.

First as regards (i) above, while it is now clear that the judges no longer have any *parens patriae* power, it is not clear precisely why this is so. Lord Goff appears to follow the reasoning that appealed to Wood J in *T v T* that the revocation of the Royal Warrant in 1960 has removed the power. Lord Brandon, on the other hand, may be going further because his argument may well be that the enactment of the Mental Health Act 1959 abrogated (quaere placed in abeyance?) the prerogative power. Which of these do you think is correct?

Secondly, the clear recognition of a common law justification for treating incompetent patients is to be welcomed. Its precise scope remains uncertain and its application to sterilisation procedures is troubling. These problems arise from the formulations of the common law justification offered by the judges. The common thread is that the procedure must be in the patient's 'best interests.' Here, we see a formulation similar to that used in 'proxy' consent situations when parents or the court act in relation to a child.

The inherent uncertainty of 'best interests' has already been noted. In the situation contemplated by the court the 'proxy' is, however, the doctor wishing to perform the sterilisation operation. How is he to determine where the woman's 'best interests' lie? *Re F* is far from clear. Lord Brandon at one point states that treatment will only be in an individual's best interests 'if it is carried out in order either to save [the individual's life], or to ensure improvement or prevent deterioration in [his] physical or mental health.' Similarly, Lord Goff talks of action taken by a doctor 'to preserve the life, health or well-being of another.' Both of these views would restrict 'best interests' to 'best *medical* interests.' However, it is far from certain that the judges intended this restriction. Indeed, on the facts of *Re F* it would seem hard to justify the procedure if this were the law. It is worth noting that the court did not address the merits of the particular case because it was conceded that the sterilisation was in F's 'best interests.' The case merely concerned the proper legal procedure for authorising the operation.

Thirdly, the court has diluted Wood J's requirement that the procedure be 'demanded.' Compliance with the *Bolam* test will do. Professional opinion would seem, therefore, to be decisive of an individual's 'best interests.' Only if the court limits the criteria upon which such medical opinion must be based will any significant control be exercised over the doctors' 'medical' judgment. The limitations expressed by Lord Brandon and Lord Goff would, to an extent, enable the court to have this significant involvement.

Fourthly, the court does not *require* the involvement of the judiciary prior to a sterilisation operation. As with any proxy, the doctor may act lawfully without first resorting to the court providing the medical procedure is in the patient's 'best interests.' Nevertheless, the judges in *Re F* thought that the court's involvement was highly desirable in cases where sterilisation is proposed. Of course, in other medical procedures the court will rarely be asked to authorise the procedure. The doctor will usually act, without challenge, as he is permitted to do by the common law justification (long accepted but) now specifically stated by the court in *Re F*. Lord Griffith alone went further and held that a sterilisation operation would be lawful *only if* the court's authorisation was granted.

Involvement of the court is to be encouraged in the case of sterilisation procedures. It allows an independent review of a decision to perform a medical procedure which, for many, is regarded as falling outside the category of usual therapeutic medical procedures. The involvement of the court provides the individual with substantive and procedural protection.

Note. We do not consider here the question of sterilisation of prisoners or inmates of other institutions for punitive or rehabilitative purposes. This does not fall within the ambit of medical treatment even though a medical practitioner is involved.

Chapter 8

Facilitating conception

Recent technological developments designed to aid infertile couples in having a baby have raised many problems for medical law and ethics. AID, embryo donation, egg donation and surrogacy each raise important issues for us to consider. Perhaps first, we should look at the different situations which might arise.

The complexities of some of the issues to be considered are well illustrated by the following table set out in Professor Bernard Dickens' article, 'Reproduction Law and Medical Consent' (1985) 35 Toronto Law Journal 255 at 280:

Table of reproductive options

Sperm	Ovum	Uterus	Means of conception	Intended child custody	Explanation
H	W	W	natural	H and W	normal conception
H	W	W	AI	H and W	AI by husband
H	W	W	IVF	H and W	IVF
D	W	W	AI/IVF	H and W	conception by sperm donor
H	D	W	IVF or IV + F and ET	H and W	conception by ovum donor
H	Dl	Dl	AI	H and W	'SM' and SPA by W
H	W	D	any and ET	H and W	SM and SPA by W
H	Dl	D2	any and ET	H and W	ovum donation, SM and SPA by W
D	W	D	any and ET	H and W	SM of W's ovum and adoption
D	D	W	any and ET	H and W	W bears (unrelated) child and SPA by H
D	Dl	Dl	any	H and W	adoption
D	Dl	D2	any and ET	H and W	adoption
F	M	M	any	F and M	child of the union
F	Dl	Dl	any	F	father has child
D	M	M	any	M	mother has child
F	Dl	D2	any and ET	F	father has true surrogate child
D	M	D	any and ET	M	mother has true surrogate child
D	Dl	D2	any and ET	D2	true surrogate has child
D	Dl	Dl	any	third party	adoption
D	Dl	D2	any and ET	third party	adoption
H	W	W	posthumous AI/IVF	W	widow has child
H	W	D	posthumous IVF/IV + F and ET	W	widow has true surrogate child
H	W	D	posthumous IVF and ET	H	widower has true surrogate child

H	= husband (legal or common law)	F	= single father
W	= wife (legal or common law)	M	= single genetic mother
D	= donor of sperm, ovum, or uterine service	SPA	= step-parent adoption
AI	= artificial insemination	IVF	= *in vitro* fertilisation
ET	= embryo transplantation	IV+F	= *in vivo* fertilisation (by AI) and flushing
'SM'	= so-called surrogate motherhood		
SM	= surrogate motherhood	any	= natural conception, AI, IVF, or IV+F

A slightly different scheme is offered by Professor Capron in 'Alternative Birth Technologies: Legal Challenges' (1987) 20 UC Davis Law Review 679, 682:

Reproductive possibilities

No	Name of Method	Genetic Source	Fertilization	Gestation	Social Parents
1	Traditional Reproduction	X_M & Y_M	Natural	M	M & M
2	Artificial Insemination, Husband	X_M & Y_M	AI	M	M & M
3	Test Tube Baby	X_M & Y_M	IVF	M	M & M
4	Artificial Insemination, Donor	X_M & Y_D	AI	M	M & M
5A	Donated Egg	X_D & Y_M	IVF	M	M & M
5B	Transferred Egg	X_D & Y_M	AI with embryo flushing	M	M & M
6	Surrogate Motherhood	X_D & Y_M	AI	D	M & M
7A	Test Tube Baby in Rented Womb	X_M & Y_M	IVF	D	M & M
7B	Transfer to Rented Womb	X_M & Y_M	Natural or AI w/embryo flushing	D	M & M
8	Postnatal Adoption	X_D & Y_D	Natural, AI, or IVF	D	M & M
9	Substitute Father	X_M & Y_D	IVF	M	M & M
10	Brave New World	X_1 & Y_2	IVF or Natural/AI/ w/embryo flushing	3	4 & 5

Abbreviations: X = female, Y = male, AI = artificial insemination, IVF = *in vitro* fertilization, D = donor, M = member of married couple

Artificial Insemination by a Donor (AID) or a Husband (AIH)

The practice and the implications of AID and AIH are explored by R Snowden and G D Mitchell in *The Artificial Family* (1983), pp 16–20.

The procedure of artificial insemination by donor is a simple one. Semen is collected by the donor masturbating into a container which is delivered as quickly as possible to the AI practitioner either for immediate use, or for freezing and storage. Freezing the semen is complex in that it requires semen to be mixed with a cryoprotective medium containing precise amounts of glycerol, egg yolk, fructose and dilute sodium citrate. The mixing process is very carefully undertaken, the resulting mixture being divided into a number of ampoules which, after labelling, are stored in liquid nitrogen. A careful procedure is also followed in thawing the frozen semen when it is required for use. Insemination using fresh or previously frozen semen is undertaken at what is considered the optimal time in the women's menstrual cycle; that is, near the time of ovulation. This is usually ascertained by asking the women concerned to keep an accurate menstrual calendar and basal body temperature record. Using a simple plastic syringe a small amount of semen is deposited high in the vagina near the cervix or sometimes directly into the cervical canal.

It is estimated that approximately 10 per cent of marriages are infertile, and that the husband's infertility is responsible in about one-third of these couples. This indicates an incidence of about 16,000 marriages a year which will be infertile because of the husband. The Peel Report estimated that some 10 per cent of these couples (1,600) may consider AID at sometime during their marriage. AID may also provide a means of producing a healthy family for those couples where the husband suffers from a hereditary disease. Now that a genetic counselling service is offered by the national health service, it is a possible for more couples to avoid the birth of an abnormal child and it is likely that some of these couples will wish to avail themselves of AID. Couples who are unable to enlarge their families because of rhesus factor incompatibility may also make recourse to AID. Another source of AID request is from those in second marriages where the husband has previously undergone voluntary sterilisation. During the past decade the demand for AID has been accelerated by the fall in availability of babies for adoption. Despite the increasing demand for, and acceptance of AID, there is still very little known about the consequences of the procedure. This is, no doubt, mainly due to the atmosphere of secrecy which has always surrounded the practice.

Although AID is not in itself an illegal practice, it leads to a situation where the legal position is far from clear. As the law stands, an AID child is illegitimate and the birth registration entry for such a child should either have the name of the donor, the words 'father not known', or a blank space left where the father's name should be recorded. But almost invariably a husband enters his own name as the father of the child and in doing so he is in contravention of the Registration Act of 1965, unless he is under the impression (rightly or wrongly) that there is a genuine possibility he may be the father. It is partly for this reason that couples undergoing AID are often advised not to abstain from sexual intercourse during the period of artificial insemination. No court in this country has, so far, considered the legitimacy of a child believed to be the product of AID and, moreover, it is thought that any court would presume a child born within a marriage to be the child of the husband and wife unless evidence to the contrary was produced. However, among those seeking AID almost all do so because of the known sterility of the husband. It would seem that in order to deal with the legal difficulties of legitimising the AID child's status, the child's parents, that is, the AID mother and her husband, have embarked on a subterfuge leading in most cases to illegal behaviour. To confer legitimate status on AID children might resolve the legal confusion but our reflections on such a change indicate that there are complexities which may lead to even greater legal, and social, confusions, for it is not only married couples or even heterosexual couples who seek AID. Nevertheless, members of the legal profession are currently considering the implications of conferring legitimate status on AID children within the whole context of the categories of legal status for children who are brought up as members of a family.

One possible solution is for the AID couple, the mother and her husband, to adopt the AID child, but this course of action merely adds to the confusion. The adoption procedures to be followed would appear absurd in such a case and, perhaps more important for the couple, there would be in existence a birth certificate declaring their adoption of the child.

Even the donor does not escape from this legal uncertainty, for it has been suggested that if the identity of a donor becomes known, he could be held responsible for the maintenance of the child or children he has helped to create and on his death his estate could be divided between the offspring he has, perhaps unknowingly, produced. It is interesting to note in this connection that legal advisers to those providing an AID service suggest that consent forms relating to AID provision should be signed by the donor as well as by the couple concerned.

Attempts have been made in other countries to resolve the legal dilemmas associated with AID but no consistent pattern has emegered. Olive Stone, writing in 1973, pointed out that in Switzerland AID is illegal, it being held to be incompatible with marriage, and a child born by AID can be disowned. In France the AID child is held to be legitimate unless an application is made by a woman's husband against affiliation, but such a denial must be made within six months of the child's birth. Portuguese law explicitly declares AID to be insufficient by itself in a dispute about affiliation. . . . In Poland there is no legal notion of legitimacy; a child born within a family is held to be child of both parents unless within six months the man denies he is the parent.

The problem surrounding the legal situation is that it induces deception and illegality in an attempt to circumvent the implications of its enforcement. This deception is often not discouraged by those acting as advisers to the AID couple. Indeed some would say that the deception is being supported and encouraged by many of these advisers who are also those providing the AID service. Falsification of records is taking place and to ignore this fact is to be party to a deceit in relation to the AID child and to society as a whole. Perhaps we should spend our energies in dealing constructively with the difficulties presented by AID rather than in trying to find ways of maintaining secrecy and the subterfuge this entails.

Merely changing the law will have little effect on the real issues surrounding AID, for the AID process is not just a legal issue. Of far more importance are the social implications of the practice. The difficulties in openly stating that a child born to a wife is also not her husband's are of such a psychological and social depth that they act as powerful incentives for the mother's husband to declare he is the AID child's father. It is hardly surprising that what evidence there is points to this being an almost universal practice.

Since the first public debates about the practice of artificial insemination by donor there have been repeated calls for assessment of the psychological and social effects of the practice. These are usually seen as affecting the quality of the relationships within the family. But the social consequences of AID are far wider than those related directly to the AID family itself—the mother, her husband, the AID child and possibly other children of the couple. In this chapter and those which follow an examination is to be made of the social and personal issues involved from two different but overlapping points of view: first, the effect upon the members of the family directly involved and those associated with them in the AID process, and secondly, the way in which the AID family as a unit is related to other close relatives, more distant relatives, friends and neighbours. How members of the AID family view themselves and each other will be affected very strongly by how they believe their relatives and friends would react to their situation. Why individuals see themselves and the others in the way they do may be related more to the influence of the wider group than we often recognise.

There are usually four people directly concerned in the AID process. These are the mother, her husband, the donor and the AI practitioner. There may be others, the family doctor, a close friend or relative, for example, but these four can be said to be the central figures participating in the actual process of producing a child by AID. It is also true to say that the husband is the only one of these four who does not necessarily have to play an active part. He is usually seen as a bystander who may be actively providing encouragement and support during the process but his role is not an essential one for the successful production of an AID child. The result of the collaboration between the mother, the donor and the AI practitioner, if success has been achieved, is the AID child. The AID child has not been listed as a participant in the AID process for the obvious reason that being the product of the process the child is not a participant in the careful planning, the detailed discussions and the inconvenient and sometimes embarrassing procedures that have to be followed in getting sperm from a healthy donor united with an ovum of a healthy woman who desires to be a mother.

It cannot seriously be argued now that AID or AIH is unlawful. As we will see (*infra* at p 624), as regards legitimacy English law has changed since Snowden and Mitchell were writing in 1983.

The Report to the Committee of Inquiry into 'Human Fertilisation and Embryology' (Cmnd 9314) (1984) chaired by Baroness Warnock, considered the position in England (footnotes omitted).

Attitudes to AID

4.7 The first formal public comment on AID in this country came with the publication of the Archbishop of Canterbury's report on artificial insemination in 1948. The Archbishop himself was highly critical of the practice of AID, though not of AIH, recommending that it should be made a criminal offence. However no action was taken in this direction. In 1960 the Feversham Committee, set up by the Government to consider AI, reported; it considered that AIH was an acceptable form of treatment for some couples, but believed that the majority within both society and the medical profession was opposed to the practice of AID. It concluded that AID was an undesirable practice, strongly to be discouraged. Since 1960 the practice of AID has continued to grow. In 1968, the then Minister for Health decided that AIH and AID should be available within the NHS if recommended on medical grounds. The increase in requests for information about AID and where it was provided led the British Medical Association to set up a panel in 1971 under the chairmanship of Sir John Peel to look into the medical aspects of human artificial insemination. This panel reported in 1973 and recommended that, for the small proportion of couples for whom AID would be appropriate, the practice should be available within the NHS at accredited centres. No action was taken to establish a system of accreditation.

4.8 In the decade since the Peel panel reported the trend of increasing acceptability and demand for AID has continued. In 1982, the latest year for which figures are available, the Royal College of Obstetricians and Gynaecologists knew of over 1000 pregnancies conceived and at least 780 live births following AID in this country. This is undoubtedly an under-estimate. But we were not able to find detailed information about AID services. NHS centres are not required to identify themselves in any of the returns that health authorities make to the Health Departments, though there are several centres where AID is provided under NHS auspices which are well-established and whose existence is widely known. In addition there is a number of private centres, particularly in London, providing AID and the British Pregnancy Advisory Service offers AID at some of its pregnancy advice bureaux, located throughout the country.

The present position

4.9 Under existing law neither AIH nor AID is unlawful. A child born to a married couple as a result of AIH is the legitimate child of that couple.

Though the practice itself may be lawful there are nonetheless particular problems arising from the practice which still give rise to legal difficulties.

(i) ANONYMITY OF DONOR

Consider the Warnock Report, paras 4.19–4.22 (*op cit*)

4.19 It is the practice of some clinics in the USA to provide detailed descriptions of donors, and to permit couples to exercise choice as to the donor they would prefer. In the evidence there was some support for the use of such descriptions. It is argued that they would provide information and reassurance for the parents and, at a later date, for the child. They might also be of benefit to the donor, as an indication that he is valued for his own sake. A detailed description also offers some choice to the woman who is to have the child, and lack of such choice can be said to diminish the importance of the woman's right to choose the father of her child.

4.20 The contrary view, also expressed in the evidence, is that detailed donor profiles would introduce the donor as a person in his own right. It is also argued that the use of profiles devalues the child who may seem to be wanted only if certain specifications are met, and this may become a source of disappointment to the parents if their expectations are unfulfilled.

4.21 As a matter of principle we do not wish to encourage the possibility of prospective parents seeking donors with specific characteristics by the use of whose semen they hope to give birth to a particular type of child. We do not therefore want detailed descriptions of donors to be used as a basis for choice, but we believe that the couple should be given sufficient relevant information for their reassurance. This should include some basic facts about the donor, such as his ethnic group and his genetic health. A small minority of the Inquiry, while supporting the principle set out above, and without compromising the principle of anonymity, consider that a gradual move towards making more detailed descriptions of the donor available to prospective parents, if requested, could be beneficial to the practice of AID, provided this was accompanied by appropriate counselling. **We recommend that on reaching the age of eighteen the child should have access to the basic information about the donor's ethnic origin and genetic health and that legislation be enacted to provide the right of access to this.** This legislation should not be retrospective.

4.22 We were agreed that there is a need to maintain the absolute anonymity of the donor, though we recognise that in privately arranged donation, for example between brothers, a different situation would of course apply; such domestic arrangements, however, fall outside any general regulation. Anonymity would give legal protection to the donor but it would also have the effect of minimising the invasion of the third party into the family. Without anonymity, men would, it is argued, be less likely to become donors in view of the risk that they might subsequently be identified and forced to accept parental responsibility for an AID child, by payment of maintenance or otherwise. Clearly in view of our recommendation (4.17) that the AID child should for all purposes be treated as the legitimate child of the couple who have benefited from successful treatment, the donor should have no responsibilities towards the child. . . . We recognise that one consequence of this provision would be that AID children, even if informed about the circumstances of their conception would never be entitled to know the identity of their genetic fathers.

The Ontario Law Reform Commission's Report on 'Human Artificial Reproduction and Related Matters' (1984), pp 185–190 (footnotes omitted), discusses the issues of information and anonymity of donors.

In chapter 3, we noted that a system of linkage in medical records—permitting doctors to link donors to recipients and, thereby, to their offspring—may be of critical importance where medical or genetic information is required, either in an emergency or otherwise. An artificially conceived child may be born with some disability directly related to the medical or genetic characteristics of the donor. In such a case, treatment of the child may require access to health information concerning the donor and the donor's family medical history. Or vital medical information—for example, affecting future decisions concerning reproduction— may come to light and should be communicated to the donor or to his or her other children. Only a system of linkage can ensure the provision of the requisite medical information to the appropriate persons.

Many of the bodies that have considered the question of medical records in the context of artificial conception have concerned themselves with matters relating to linkage. Generally, there has been a predisposition in favour of maintaining a system of linkage, in some cases to facilitate the provision of necessary medical information to one party or another, in other cases to facilitate access to basic information concerning a donor's ethnic origin and genetic health.

The Commission understands that, as a matter of practice, most doctors do in fact keep records that link donors to recipients, while at the same time preserving their anonymity. We wish to express our endorsement of the present general practice of anonymously linking donors to recipients in medical records. Indeed, we think that the matter ought to be taken one step further. While we do not believe that furtherance of this practice, in an attmept to make it universal, should be promoted by statutory enactment, we do recommend that, pursuant to the power given to the Council of the College of Physicians and Surgeons of Ontario under section 50 of the *Health Disciplines Act*, the Council should make regulations that would establish a system of record keeping permitting doctors to link gamete donors with recipients. However, again in light of our subsequent proposals, we wish to underscore our concern lest the actual identity of the donor be divulged. Accordingly, we recommend that anonymity concerning the identity of all parties involved in artificial conception—the donor, the recipient, her spouse or partner (if any), and the child—should be preserved in the medical records.

The preceding recommendation, it should be emphasised, is concerned exclusively with the preservation of the anonymity of the parties among themselves. However, as we have indicated, it may be necessary for a doctor (but not recipients or children) to trace donors after children have been born using their gametes. To repeat, the most important reason for such tracing would be to discover relevant genetic or other information from the donor in order to treat the artificially conceived child or to convey relevant genetic information to the donor or, perhaps, to his or her other biological children.

The Commission recommends that, where a genetic or transmissible defect or disease in a donor or a donor's child becomes known to a doctor, the doctor should be under a duty, imposed by regulations governing the medical profession, to make all reasonable efforts to report all relevant information to any person whose health and welfare the doctor reasonably believes may be affected by it. Sanctions for the failure to abide by such a regulation should lie in potential civil liability in negligence and in the 'professional misconduct' regulations under the *Health Disciplines Act*, rather than in a specific new penalty.

A third matter to which special attention should be given concerns whether practitioners engaged in an artificial conception practice should be legally obligated to follow up the results of any procedure, for example by attempting to ascertain whether conception has taken place and, if so, whether any child who is born suffers from the kinds of genetic or other defect or disease to which reference was made earlier. This issue, then, is intimately related to the preceding one respecting the doctor's duty to report defects in artificially conceived children to others.

Although a system of follow up is obviously desirable, as a practical matter it is often impossible or impracticable for the artificial conception practitioner to obtain information about any subsequent conception and birth. To ensure secrecy, at least at this stage, the recipient woman who has conceived artificially usually leaves the services of that practitioner for her own doctor, who may be unknown to the artificial conception practitioner. The latter may simply assume that the woman has become pregnant or has given up the attempt, and that, if she has conceived, she will be seeing her own doctor henceforward.

The Commission does not believe that it is feasible to go beyond present practice, which in some, but not all, cases may well involve some follow up after artificial conception procedures have been used. Accordingly, we recommend that there should be no positive duty on artificial conception practitioners to take steps to ascertain whether conception and birth have taken place or to ascertain the medical status of any child. However, should it be thought necessary or desirable to deal more formally with this matter, we recommend that any legal obligation to follow up the outcome of artificial conception treatment should be incorporated in the regulations governing the medical profession under the *Health Disciplines Act*.

A final matter relating to medical records in the context of artificial conception concerns access to such records by recipients, their husbands or partners (if any), donors, and artificially conceived children. A subsidiary, albeit no less critically important, question is, assuming access, whether disclosure should be limited to non-identifying information contained in the records, or whether the identity of the parties should be revealable, and, if so, under what circumstances. With respect to the latter question, it bears repeating that earlier we recommended anonymity in the general context of linkage. The issue here is whether an exception should be made for any of the persons involved, particularly the child.

Before we deal specifically with access to medical records, we wish to raise the critical threshold question concerning whether a child should be told of his biological origins. Unfortunately, the answer to this question depends, in part, on interpretations of data that vary significantly and, indeed, on data that has not been gathered to the satisfaction of social scientists, even from the analogous and more accessible field of adoption. The social and psychological ramifications of disclosure are simply not clear; one cannot accurately predict the implications in individual cases.

With respect to the issue of disclosure, we agree in principle with the view expressed in a Report of the Royal College of Obstetricians and Gynaecologists in the United Kingdom that 'the decision to disclose to the child the nature of its parentage should at the present time remain with the "legal" parents'. The decision, we believe, does not lend itself any more to legislative resolution in the artificial conception context than it does in the adoption context, where disclosure of status is not mandated by statute or otherwise, but is left to the legal parents, or, in some cases, others. Each family situation is different, so that a general hypothesis—that, for example, secrecy is deceitful and fundamentally unhealthy—while perhaps reasonable and compelling in the abstract, cannot be translated into a meaningful statutory directive. To counsel common sense, bearing in mind all the circumstances of each case, such as the child's age and temperament, is likely all that can usefully be done concerning this particular matter.

Returning to the separate question of access to medical records, . . . [t]he reports that have canvassed the issue of disclosure have generally favoured anonymity respecting the identity of the parties, although not respecting medical or other related information. The Warnock Committee recommended a relatively open system, for it was of the view that, 'on reaching the age of eighteen the child should have access to the basic information about the donor's ethnic origin and genetic health and that legislation be enacted to provide the right of access to this'.

With respect to the question of access to medical records after a child has, in fact, discovered that he or she was artificially conceived, a minority of the Commission considers that specific legislation is justifiable. These Commissioners would recommend that children born of donated gametes and their legal parents should be entitled to access to all but personally identifying information respecting the donors. A single Commissioner would also grant donors access to nonidentifying information concerning the women and children affected by their donations.

The majority of the Commission, however, does not wish to go this far in respect of access to medical records. They do not believe that legislation could be adequately drafted to take into account the very different needs and emotional makeup of the children in question. In some cases, disclosure of all relevant, nonidentifying information contained in the doctor's record may be appropriate and desirable, while, in other situations, disclosure of some of the information may be more harmful than silence. Accordingly, by a majority, the Commission recommends that the decision concerning access to medical records by the parties involved—the woman, her husband or partner (if any), the child, and the donor—should be left to individual members of the medical profession. However, under no circumstances should any doctor or other person disclose information that could in any way identify the parties involved.

Does the fact that an adopted child may now discover the identity of his natural parents (Adoption Act 1976, s 51) tip the balance of the argument against the recommendation of the Ontario Commission? (Note the negative conclusion expressed in the Government White Paper 'Human Fertilisation and Embryology: A Framework for Legislation' (Cmnd 259 November 1987), paras 81–84).

Until there is legislation, what does the common law provide in, for example, the following situations:

1. A child seeks in an appropriate action to gain discovery of the relevant records which will identify the donor who is his natural father.
2. The doctor or sperm bank now learns that a sperm donor is suffering from (or carries) a genetically transmissible disease which has not affected the child born but may affect its child or that a child born as a result of a sperm donation has a genetic disability which is not manifest in the donor? (*Note:* if the hospital's (or doctor's or sperm bank's) records involve the electronic storage of

information, the provisions of the Data Protection Act 1984 apply. As we have seen (*supra* Ch 6), a data subject (the donor) may see the data stored about him from the data user (the hospital etc). Furthermore, the data user has a discretion to disclose information to those it lists on the register as potential receivers of the information. Given the context of the donation and the agreement of anonymity, any discretion to disclose would, however, be necessarily fettered by the law on confidentiality.)

(ii) CONSENT

Clearly the donor must consent to the donation of his sperm. The issue we are concerned with is whether the husband of the woman to be inseminated must consent. This question is properly understood as reflecting a concern for the consequences of undergoing insemination without spousal consent since, as we have seen, a consent to the procedure itself need only be given by the woman herself. The common law actions for loss of services or consortium have been abolished by statute (the Law Reform (Miscellaneous Provisions) Act 1970, ss 4, 5 and the Administration of Justice Act 1982, s 2).

Two issues remain: first, whether undergoing AID constitutes adultery; secondly, whether it may constitute evidence of irretrievable breakdown of marriage so as to constitute a ground of divorce based upon 'unreasonable behaviour'.

The law is discussed by Olive Stone in 'English law in relation to AID and Embryo Transfer', published in Ciba Foundation Symposium No 12 *Law and Ethics of AID and Embryo Transfer*, pp 69–70.

> There is no legal requirement that if the woman is married her husband should consent. If he does not do so, it is clear that the treatment does not amount to adultery by the wife.[2] Adultery involves sexual intercourse between two persons, at least one of whom is married, but who are not married to each other. Sexual intercourse for this purpose must involve some penetration, however slight, of the female by the male organ.[3] It seems probable, however, that if a wife underwent such treatment without her husband's consent and he objected, considered that the marriage had broken down irretrievably and petitioned for divorce, it might be held that she had behaved in such a way that he could not reasonably be expected to live with her[4] and his petition be granted.

Notes to extract

[2] The Scottish Court of Session so held in *Maclennan v Maclennan* 1958 SLT 12, and the decision is generally accepted as good law in England also. In the United States, the Illinois Court held in *Doornbos v Doornbos* 12 Ill App 2d 473, 139 NE 2d (1956), in a divorce case, that a child born as the result of AID was not a legitimate child and that the use of AID constituted adultery. An appeal was dismissed. In the unreported case of *Hock v Hock* (1945) an Illinois court held that artificial insemination did not establish adultery as ground for divorce. There was a similar decision in Ontario in 1921: *Oxford v Oxford* (1921) 58 DLR 251.

[3] *Dennis v Dennis* [1955] P 153.

[4] Under the Divorce Reform Act 1969, s 2(1)(b). Both the Royal Commission on Human Artificial Insemination, in Cmd 9678 para 90, and the Departmental Committee on the same subject in Cmnd 1105 paras 114–117, recommended that artificial insemination of the wife without the husband's consent should be a ground for divorce. The radical amendment of the grounds for divorce operative after 1970 have made such a specific provision unnecessary.

Consider, now, the case referred to by Olive Stone.

Maclennan v Maclennan
[1958] SC 105 (Court of Session, Scotland)

Lord Wheatly: There are manifestly grave moral, ethical, social and personal considerations involved in the practice of artificial insemination in its various forms which will no doubt be fully deployed elsewhere. It is almost trite to say that a married woman who, without the consent of her husband, has the seed of a male donor injected into her person by mechanical means in order to procreate a child who would not be a child of the marriage has committed a grave and heinous breach of the contract of marriage. The question for my determination, however, is not the moral culpability of such an act but is whether such an act constitutes adultery in its legal meaning. A wife or a husband could commit an act of gross indecency with a member of the opposite sex which would be a complete violation of the marital relationship, but which could not be classified as adultery. It would indeed be easy, according to one's personal viewpoint, to allow oneself to be influenced by the moral, ethical, social and personal considerations to which I have referred and to reach a conclusion based on these considerations, but this problem which I am called upon to solve must be decided by the objective standard of legal principles as these have been developed and must be confined to the narrow issue of whether this form of insemination constitutes adultery in the eyes of the law. If it is not adultery, although a grave breach of the marriage contract, that is a matter for the legislature if it be thought that a separate legal remedy should be provided.

In determining whether the marital offence (which I opine it to be whatever view one takes of its nature) of being impregnated by the seed of another man without the husband's consent constitutes adultery in its legal sense, one naturally seeks a solution from the definitions of 'adultery' in the works of our leading legal writers or in reported decisions. Some of our great legal writers however do not even seek to define it, while others, in referring to it, use terms which are more descriptive than definitive. This may be due to the fact that in earlier days when life was regulated by the natural rather than the scientific order of things, people knew what was meant by adultery and what its concomitants were. Where, however, attempts were made to describe adultery if not to provide an exhaustive definition of it, the idea of *conjunctio corporum* seems to be an inherent concomitant—a conception of the process which incidentally can likewise be found in the book of Deuteronomy, the writings of St Paul and the works of the Canonists. The idea that adultery might be committed by a woman alone in the privacy of her bedroom aided and abetted only by a syringe containing semen was one with which the earlier jurists had no occasion to wrestle. Certainly this form of perpetuation of the species does not conform to the common conception of adultery.

. . . While the primary purpose of sexual intercourse is procreation, in the eyes of the law surrender of the reproductive organs is not necessary to consummate the act of intercourse. Expedients may be used by the parties to secure birth prevention or the woman may have previously undergone an operation by which her reproductive organs were removed, or they may have ceased to function from natural causes and yet the conjunction of the sexual organs involving at least some degree of penetration would constitute intercourse and, in the circumstances under consideration, adultery. Thus impregnation *per se* cannot be a test of adultery, since in the eyes of the law the act of intercourse can be consummated without impregnation either as a result of natural causes or by the parties resorting to artificial expedients (cf *Baxter v Baxter* [1948] AC 274). It would seem, therefore, that in determining such questions as consummation of marriage or adultery, the law looks at the act and not the result . . . As there can be penetration without emission (which would be adultery) and emission following penetration with fertilisation (which would likewise be adultery) it seems to me that these factors are merely incidentals or accidentals of the adulterous act, which consists of the mutual surrender of the bodies and is evidenced by the degree of familiarity thereby occasioned, which is a complete transgression and violation of the contract of marriage. Whether such a degree of familiarity would require to be established by evidence of some degree of penetration, as recent English decisions seem to suggest, or whether it could be established by evidence of something less as Lord Dunedin contemplated, does not seem to me to be of vital importance in the present issue, since whatever view is taken there is involved in both cases the mutual surrender of the bodies to each other for the purposes of carnal gratification in breach of marital obligations.

. . .[I]t seems possible to derive . . . the following propositions, according at least to the law of England.

1. For adultery to be committed there must be the two parties physically present and engaging in the sexual act at the same time.

2. To constitute the sexual act there must be an act of union involving some degree of penetration of the female organ by the male organ.

3. It is not a necessary concomitant of adultery that male seed should be deposited in the female's ovum.

4. The placing of the male seed in the female ovum need not necessarily result from the sexual act, and if it does not, but is placed there by some other means, there is no sexual intercourse.

I appreciate that the second of these findings does not square with Lord Dunedin's *obiter dictum* in *Russell*, which seems to conflict with the decision of Pilcher J, in *Clark* (*supra*), but even on Lord Dunedin's standard, the physical presence of the male organ and its close proximity and juxtaposition to the female organ seem to me to be essential ingredients of the act.

I can find nothing to persuade me that the law of Scotland is not the same as the law of England so far as the legal propositions above enunciated are concerned (although non-consummation of the marriage is not a ground of nullity in the law of Scotland) and in my opinion these propositions are equally valid in our law. To me they seem to consist with the traditional Scottish views on adultery which I have canvassed *supra*. Just as artificial insemination extracts procreation entirely from the nexus of human relationships in or outside of marriage, so does the extraction of the nexus of human relationship from the act of procreation remove artificial insemination from the classification of sexual intercourse. If my views be correct, then it follows logically that artificial insemination by a donor without the consent of the husband is not adultery as the law interprets that term. The only case cited to me wherein a contrary view was reached was the unreported American case of *Doornbos v Doornbos*, which was a declaratory form of action unknown to our procedure. Not having had the benefit of the judgment on which the decision was based, I cannot comment on it, but for the reasons which I have given I must express the view that the decision is one which cannot be followed or supported in our law. It is perhaps not inappropriate however to consider the implications of the contrary view. If artificial insemination by a donor without the husband's consent is to be deemed adultery, the first question which seems to call for a decision is whether the donor whose seed has been used has himself been guilty of adultery. If the answer is in the affirmative, the further question arises, at what point of time has he done so? If it be at the point when the seed is extracted from his body, certain interesting considerations would arise. I gather that seed to obtained can be retained for a considerable time before being used, and in some cases it may not be used at all. If the donor's seed is taken merely to lie *in retentis*, it surely cannot be adultery if that seed is never used. Thus, if his adultery is to be deemed to take place at the time of the parting with the seed, it can only be an adultery subject to defeasance in the event of the seed not being used. Such a statement need only be stated for its absurdity to be manifested. If, on the other hand, his adultery is deemed to take place when the seed is injected into the woman's ovum, this latter act may take place after his death, and in that case the woman's conduct would constitute not only adultery but necrophilism. Such a proposition seems to me to be equally absurd. The third alternative is that the whole process should be regarded as an act of adultery, but as this might in certain cases result in the act covering a period of say two years, and be committed partly during the lifetime and partly after the death of the donor, I cannot distinguish between the absurdity of such a proposition and the absurdity of the other alternatives. Senior counsel for the pursuer appreciated the illogicality and absurdity of these consequences of the proposition that the donor had committed adultery and accepted that he had not. This then forced him to argue that the wife could commit adultery by herself. One need not consider the interesting point whether the administrator could be said to commit adultery, because the administrator might be a woman or the seed might be self injected by the wife herself operating the syringe. The idea that a woman is committing adultery when alone in the privacy of her bedroom she injects into her ovum by means of a syringe the seed of a man who she does not know and has never seen is one which I am afraid I cannot accept. Unilateral adultery is possible, as in the case of a married man who ravishes a woman not his wife, but self-adultery is a conception as yet unknown to the law. The argument of pursuer's counsel was that adultery meant the introduction of a foreign element into the marital relationship. That, however, seems to me to beg the question, because what has still to be determined is what is the foreign element? For the reasons which I have already explained, that foreign element is the physical contact with an alien and unlawful sexual organ, and without that element there cannot be what the law regards as adultery. The introduction of a spurious element into the family, with all its consequences, may be the result of such conduct, but is not a necessary result, and it is by the means and not by the result that this issue is to be judged. If artificial insemination by a donor were to be regarded as adultery, then I opine the view that it would be adultery whether the seed germinated or not, and yet in the latter case there would be no resultant adulteration of the strain. At the root of the argument for the pursuer was the proposition that impregnation is at the basis of adultery, and it was argued that the view of the English judges that there must be penetration indicated that there must be the possibility of insemination. Whatever the moral and ethical aspects of that argument may be, the Courts have now accepted that adultery can take place when the possibility of insemination has been excluded either by natural causes or artificial expedients, and so that argument must fail.

It accordingly follows, in my opinion, that artificial insemination by a donor does not constitute adultery according to our law.

There is no reported case in English law which holds that a woman who undergoes AID without her husband's consent thereby acts in such a way for there to be a finding of 'unreasonable behaviour'. There is no reason to believe, however, that this is other than a matter of fact for the divorce court to adjudicate upon.

(iii) CONTROL

The situation raised here is the extent to which the donor may exercise control over sperm which he has donated.

(a) The living donor

If a person donates sperm and received a sum of money in return as is the normal practice, the first question to answer is whether the donation constitutes a gift or a contract. In turn, this requires us to determine (1) the parties' intentions—whether to contract or make a gift, and (2) whether, as a matter of law, whatever the intention, it is permissible to make a contract for the donation of semen.

These issues, in large part, are the same as those affecting all donations of body tissues and fluids, eg organs for transplant, and we will return to the latter in more detail (*infra*, ch 13). It may, however, be helpful to notice certain points here.

Dickens, in *Medico-Legal Aspects of Family Law* (pp 16–18), commenting on the law in Canada, states that:

> ... Provincial laws derived from the Uniform Human Tissue Act preclude sales

of body materials, whether tissue or non-tissue,[82] other than blood.[83] Section 10 of The Human Tissue Gift Act of Ontario,[84] for instance, provides that:

No person shall buy, sell or otherwise deal in, directly or indirectly, for a valuable consideration . . . any body or part or parts thereof other than blood or a blood constituent, for therapeutic purposes, medical education or scientific research, and any such dealing is invalid as being contrary to public policy.[85]

Since AID is for neither education nor research, this raises the question of whether it serves a therapeutic purpose. The question may arise when resort to AID is because of the woman's physical abnormality, but this is not usually the case; and if it is, and the woman is married, AIH may obviate the question of remunerating a donor. The question of payment arises more particularly, however, in the usual case, when the woman is physically normal and in adequately good health but her husband is sterile, or her social circumstances are such that she has no suitable male partner with whom to conceive a child. Pregnancy may be considered to serve a woman's emotional rather than physical needs. Indeed, the experience places her under increasing physical stress, and possibly mental stress as well, depending upon her own personality and the circumstances of the pregnancy. Similarly, notwithstanding the possibly over-compensating sense of self-fulfilment and satisfactions of parenthood, infant-care and rearing of a child to a point of personal and economic independence impose stresses, borne over many years.

If lack of opportunity for childbearing has a damaging effect upon a woman, it will be of psychological origin, whether expressed psychologically or psychosomatically. Injury through psychological stress or psychosomatic disorder is, of course, entitled to relief, but whether through AID or orthodox procedures to treat an unhealthy condition of mind and/or body is a matter of social rather than purely medical judgment. Since it is a bioethical imperative that persons not be treated as things, it may be unethical to prescribe and facilitate a child's birth as a therapeutic service to the mother. A growing fetus is not an anti-depressant substance, and a baby is not a placebo or token to the mother of her womanly prowess.

Where childlessness, or a strong desire for another child, does not impair a woman's mental or physical health, artificial assistance of pregnancy and motherhood may appear cosmetic in that it provides an elevated sense of fulfilment and an enhancement of human experience. Ranking AID as a cosmetic procedure, and therefore lawful as commerce, may be offensive to cultural standards, however, in that it equates achieving human conception to such relatively trivial practices as selling human hair for wig-making, and it disregards the family unit. This collectivity may be amenable to therapy, since the concept of therapy may have a social and emotional dimension. More pedantically, moreover, provincial health insurance schemes tend not to cover cosmetic procedures, but may include AID as a listed item in their fee schedules.[86]

If AID donation is for a therapeutic procedure, it may still not offend Human Tissue Gift Act provisions, however, so far as the immediate donor is concerned. In the New York case of *Perlmutter v Beth David Hospital*,[87] blood-donation was held to involve not a sale but a service, with the result that implied consumer warranties as to fitness for purpose and merchantability were held inapplicable. An Illinois decision of 1970 rejected this conclusion,[88] but by 1975 legislatures of 43 states had codified the *Perlmutter* principle, recognising that 'When service predominates, the transfer of personal property is but an incidental feature of the transaction'.[89] The basis of the principle is that the public interest requires encouragement of the existence of blood banks by offering the protection that they should be legally liable only for their actual errors, and not be held to the strict standard applicable to products liability. This is reinforced by the consideration that, although blood for transfusion may be indetectably hepatitis-infected so as to be unavoidably unsafe, it is not unreasonably dangerous.[90]

It may be contended on analogy that semen donation is a service as opposed to a commodity transaction, and accordingly that remuneration is not contrary to public policy. The presence of the sales-service dichotomy has been doubted in Canadian law, so that services may be governed by tests relevant to sales, but concessions to blood donation may be considered appropriate. Waddams, for instance, while doubting recognition of the distinction, has observed that 'there may be considerations of social policy that would justify the exemption of medical practitioners from the scope of strict liability'.[91] The social policy supporting the abundant supply of transfusable blood does not necessarily apply equally, however, to semen for insemination. The present state of supply in Canada may nevertheless be rationalised by considering the individual donor to be rendering a service, for which reasonable remuneration is proper, but that commercial sperm banks[92] would be trading in a commodity, in violation of public policy expressed in legislation. For commercial banks to operate in Canadian provinces, therefore, provisions such as s 10 of The Human Tissue Gift Act of Ontario would need to be suitably amended. Amendment to permit sales of semen would not affect the question, however, of whether such an undertaking would be bound by or immune from products liability laws; indeed, the status of blood suppliers remains unestablished in Canada.[93]

Notes to extract

[82] Semen is not 'tissue', which by definition 'includes an organ, but does not include any skin, bone, blood, blood constituent or other tissue that is replaceable by natural processes of repair'; see The Human Tissue Gift Act, 1971, SO 1971 c 83, s 1(c).

[83] [footnote omitted].

[84] *Supra*, n 82. Comparable legislation has been enacted in Alberta, British Columbia, Newfoundland, Northwest Territories and Nova Scotia.

[85] In Quebec the law appears more accommodating. Article 20 of the Civil Code, as amended by SQ 1971, c 84, allows sale of more than blood, providing that 'The alienation must be gratuitous unless its object is a part of the body susceptible of regeneration'; see W F Bowker, 'Experimentation on humans and gifts of tissue: Articles 20–23 of the Civil Code" (1973), 19 McGill LJ 161.

[86] [footnote omitted].

[87] 123 NE 2d 792 (1954) (NYCA).

[88] *Cunningham v MacNeal Memorial Hospital* 266 NE 2d 897 (1970) (Ill SC).

[89] *Supra* n 87, at p 794.

[90] See *McMichael v American Red Cross* 532 SW 2d 7 (1975) (Ky CA).

[91] Stephen Waddams, 'Implied warranties and products liability' (1973), *Special Lectures, Law Society of Upper Canada*, 159, at p 164.

[92] Which appear not to operate as such in Canada; banks exist for storing frozen semen, however, as insurance to men undergoing vasectomy, and for those taking employment with risk of genetic hazard, such as from irradiation.

[93] The British Columbia Royal Commission in its Ninth Report on Family and Children's Law, *Artificial Insemination* (1975), observed that 'It would seem possible at least that the contractual implied warranties might apply to *commercial* sperm banks but that hospitals and physicians would only be liable in tort for negligence'; at p 24. An objection to this proposal is that, while provincial health plans may include AID services, most medical practitioners in this field act primarily outside such plans, regarding the procedure as a private commercial enterprise rather than as a community health service.

Putting aside the specific terms of the legislation mentioned above, do you think that English law takes the same view?

Dickens was anxious to draw a distinction between a contract for sale and a contract for services for two reasons: first, because a contract for sale might be (subject to the meaning of 'tissue') contrary to public policy; secondly, because of the more onerous terms as to 'fitness for purpose' and 'merchantable quality' which would be implied by operation of law in a contract for sale, at least according to American jurisprudence and perhaps in Canadian law at the time Dickens was writing. In English law, however, the distinction does not have these consequences. The same public policy will attach to both and by legislation the same terms will be implied.

What is important for our purposes, therefore, is whether a court would choose to interpret the transaction as a contract at all. If the court considered the transaction as a contract, clearly it would follow that the court would be drawn into considerations more appropriate to consumer contracts, eg matters of merchantable quality and fitness for purpose and the appropriate remedies for breach. It may be that a court would prefer to avoid the consequences of this analysis. If, however, the court did so choose despite what we have said, matters of control over the disposal of the semen would be determined by the express terms of the agreement (if any). For example, a donor, on this reasoning, could direct that the sperm be used for the insemination of a specific person. Beyond this, the court is likely to hold that the donor has abandoned control: then disposal is a matter for the donee. Consider the following American case.

Venner v State

(1976) 354 A 2d 483 (Court of Special Appeals of Maryland) at 498 (footnotes omitted)

> **Powers J** (at 498): It could not be said that a person has no property right in wastes or other materials which were once a part of or contained within his body, but which normally are discarded after their separation from the body. It is not unknown for a person to assert a continuing right of ownership, dominion, or control, for good reason or for no reason, over such things as excrement, fluid waste, secretions, hair, fingernails, toenails, blood, and organs or other parts of the body, whether their separation from the body is intentional, accidental, or merely the result of normal body functions.
>
> But it is all but universal human custom and human experience that such things are discarded—in a legal sense, abandoned—by the person from whom they emanate, either 'on the spot', or, if social delicacy requires it, at a place or in a manner designed to cause the least offense to others.
>
> By the force of social custom, we hold that when a person does nothing and says nothing to indicate an intent to assert his right of ownership, possession, or control over such material, the only rational inference is that he intends to abandon the material. When one places, or permits others to place waste material from his body into the stream of ultimate disposition as waste, he has abandoned whatever legal right he theretofore had to protect it from prying eyes or acquisitive hands.

If, as we think is more likely, a court would wish to avoid the consequences flowing from the contract analysis, it could adopt the alternative analysis which would be to intepret the transaction as a gift. Any money would, on this view, be seen as an *ex gratia* payment.

If it be a gift, it could be a gift subject to express conditions as to disposal, or alternatively it could be a gift without conditions so as to amount to a surrender of control to the donee. If it were a gift subject to conditions then failure to comply with them would carry the ordinary legal consequence that right of control would revert to the donor or damages *in lieu* thereof could be claimed.

(b) The posthumous donation

Consider the following French case:

Parpalaix v CECOS and Fédération Française des Centres d'Etude et de Conservation du Sperme

> It has been duly ascertained by the Court that:
> Alain Parpalaix, while cohabiting with Corinne Richard, developed cancer of the testicles. On being warned by his doctor that the treatment he was to undergo might cause sterility, on 7 December 1981 he deposited an amount of sperm taken for the purpose with the CECOS [Centre d'Etude et de Conservation du Sperme].
>
> In the course of the years 1982 and 1983 he underwent various forms of treatment, and died on 25 December 1983, after contracting marriage with Corinne Richard on 23 December of the same year.

His widow and his parents are asking the CECOS, which is refusing their request, to hand over the sperm for the inseminating of Corinne Parpalaix.

On the scope of the problem brought before the court
The ambit of the question to be resolved by the Court should be determined. The case concerns purely the handing-over to the widow of the [sc flasks] containing the sperm preserved by the CECOS.

The question of the actual insemination, should the request be granted, is purely a matter of conscience for the widow herself and for her doctor, who is bound by the rules of professional etiquette.

Similarly, the question of the parentage of the child, should it be born, has not at the present time to be considered by this court.

On the interpretation of the wishes of Alain Parpalaix and of the CECOS respectively:
The various statements made in the giving of evidence, especially those of Pierre and Danielle Richard, the parents of Corinne Parpalaix, the attitude of Alain Parpalaix, who, during his illness and with the approval of his common-law wife, took steps to preserve his chances of procreating—an attitude solemnly ratified two days prior to his death by a civil and religious marriage—and the taking of sides, as parties to the present proceedings, by Alain Parpalaix's parents, who were in a position to know their son's true intentions, provide a body of evidence and presumptions which unambiguously demonstrate the express desire of Corinne Parpalaix's husband for his consort to be the mother of a child of his and hers, whether conceived in his lifetime or after his death.

It clearly emerges, at the same time, that the CECOS, since it has neither proved nor claimed that it warned Alain Parpalaix of its objection to the handing-over of his sperm after his death, tacitly approved his intention.

A characteristic feature in this connection is the change of attitude on the part of this association, which did not begin to warn 'donors' of its doctrine in the matter until two years after it had accepted Alain Parpalaix's sperm. . . .

It clearly emerges that the agreement of 7 December 1971 was a specific contract involving for the CECOS the obligation to preserve the sperm and restore it to the donor or to hand it over to the person for whom it was intended.

On the legality of the said contract
Neither the preservation or re-delivery of the sperm of a deceased husband nor the insemination of his widow are prohibited or even provided for by any legislation or regulation.

Moreover, they are not an infringement of natural law, since one of the aims of marriage is procreation. . . .

On these various grounds the Court has decided that the request should be granted.

How would the English common law respond to such a case? The analysis needs to proceed in stages. Two issues need to be addressed. First, will an agreement between a donor and hospital that a named person should be inseminated with the donor's sperm after the donor's death, be effective to transfer the property in the sperm to the hospital. Secondly, if it is effective to do this, will the hospital be bound by the condition that the hospital inseminate a named third party with the sperm? Perhaps a threshold question is whether sperm is property capable of being transferred? As we shall see this issue has perplexed some legal commentators (*infra* ch 13). For our purposes here, we can accept that body products, such as blood or sperm, once separated from the body and reduced into someone's control are capable of being owned (see, for example, *R v Welsh* [1974] RTR 478, CA and *R v Rothery* [1976] RTR 550, CA).

1. Passing of property
The answer to this question must depend upon whether the agreement is a valid

will. Analytically, if anything, this agreement can only be a purported testamentary disposition since it seeks to take effect only after the donor's death. Consequently, it would *only* be valid if it complies with the terms of the Wills Act 1837. Ordinarily (unless careful legal advice were taken), this would mean that such an agreement would be invalid because the formal requirements, such as the need for writing and compliance with the witness provisions, would be absent.

2. The binding effect of a condition

This issue will only arise if the agreement is a *will*. If it is, any conditions would bind the hospital (unless they disclaimed the gift) and the donation would analytically be seen as a conditional gift defeasible on failure to comply with the condition as to the sperm's disposal, so that if the condition is not complied with the sperm will form part of the deceased's residual estate. In practice, this would mean that the named person could not compel the hospital to comply with the condition. If the hospital did not wish to inseminate the named person, the property in the sperm might, in the usual case, pass as part of the residual estate (in the usual case again to the spouse). Thereafter, it would be the spouse's property to dispose of as she wished but this would be of little avail since she could not require the doctor to inseminate her. Whatever the law may say about compliance with a posthumous condition to inseminate a wife, there are profoundly difficult moral considerations to be borne in mind. As the Warnock Committee stated, in para 4.4, in the context of AIH (artificial insemination by a husband), and therefore *a fortiori* in the context of AID:

> 4.4 The majority of views expressed to us however, saw AIH as an accepted form of treatment, where clinically indicated. We ourselves see no moral objection to its practice. We believe that where there is the intention to bring about the birth of a child and this takes place within the context of a stable relationship, such intervention is acceptable. It is simply a means of bringing together the sperm and egg of a husband and wife so that fertilisation can take place *in vivo*. Nevertheless we have grave misgivings about AIH in one type of situation. A man who has placed semen in a semen bank may die and his widow may then seek to be inseminated. . . . This may give rise to profound psychological problems for the child and the mother.

In the French case the court decided that the spouse's action against the sperm bank (CECOS) should succeed to the extent that the sperm be delivered up to her.

> The Court, at a public sitting, passing judgment after duly hearing both sides and with the possibility of appeal,

> Dismisses any proceedings against the Fédération Française des Centres d'Etude et de Conservation du Sperme,
>   States that as of the date at which the present judgment becomes final the CECOS shall be under the obligation to deliver to the doctor chosen by Corinne Parpalaix, on being so requested once only and at the date appointed by the said doctor within the succeeding month, the total amount of sperm deposited with it by Alain Parpalaix;
>   States that failing any request made under the said conditions within a period of six months as of the said date the CECOS shall be under the obligation to destroy the sperm in its possession;
>   States that neither enforcement of Article 700 of the New Code of Civil Procedure nor *ad interim* execution of the judgment is called for; . . .

(For the Government's response to this problem in relation to posthumous donation of gametes generally, see paras 59–60 of the 1987 White Paper, set out *infra* p 691.)

(iv) STATUS

Paragraphs 4.9 and 4.17 of the Warnock Report state:

4.9 Under existing law neither AIH nor AID is unlawful. A child born to a married couple as a result of AIH is the legitimate child of that couple. . . . A child born as a result of AID, on the other hand, is illegitimate, and so is liable to suffer all the disadvantages associated with that status. In theory the husband of the woman who bears an AID child has no parental rights and duties in law with regard to that child; these in principle lie with the donor, who could be made liable to pay maintenance, and who could apply to a court for access or custody.

4.17 There is a number of principles which we suggest must underlie the practice of AID. The English Law Commission recommended that the law should be reformed to remove all the legal disadvantages of illegitimacy so far as they affect the illegitimate child. Thus there would be no legal distinction between legitimate and illegitimate children. Both parents would have equal rights unless and until a court ordered otherwise. The Commission further recommended that when a married woman had received AID treatment with her husband's consent, the husband, rather than the donor should, for all legal purposes, be regarded as the father of a child conceived by AID. We unanimously agree and accordingly **recommend that the AID child should in law be treated as the legitimate child of its mother and her husband where they have both consented to the treatment.** This will require legislation.

As regards the requirement of the husband's consent to AID, the Committee went on to recommend that:

4.24 In the case of married couples we considered whether the law needed to impose requirements as to the form in which the husband's consent should be given. **We recommend, following the English Law Commission, that it should be presumed that the husband has consented to AID, unless the contrary is proved.** The legal status of the AID child should not have to depend on proof of consent to treatment or on the existence of a document evidencing consent. In other words, the burden of proof should rest on the husband to show he has not consented. However, we appreciate that where it is shown that the husband has not consented, the effect of our recommendation (see 4.22) that the donor should have no parental rights and duties in relation to the AID child will mean that in the eyes of the law the child will have no father. We regard this as inescapable, and the same situation will arise where AID is provided to an unmarried woman. The law will be recognising what in many cases is already the *de facto* situation.

The recommendations of the Warnock Committee and the Law Commission concerning the status of the child were enacted in the Family Law Reform Act 1987. Section 27 provides:

27.—(1) Where after the coming into force of this section a child is born in England and Wales as the result of the artificial insemination of a woman who—

(a) was at the time of the insemination a party to a marriage (being a marriage which had not at that time been dissolved or annulled); and

(b) was artificially inseminated with the semen of some person other than the other party to that marriage.

then, unless it is proved to the satisfaction of any court by which the matter has to be determined that the other party to that marriage did not consent to the insemination, the child shall be treated in law as the child of the parties to that marriage and shall not be treated as the child of any person other than the parties to that marriage.

(2) Any reference in this section to a marriage includes a reference to a void marriage if at the time of the insemination resulting in the birth of the child both or either of the parties reasonably believed that the marriage was valid; and for the purposes of this section it shall be presumed, unless the contrary is shown, that one of the parties so believed at that time that the marriage was valid.

(3) Nothing in this section shall affect the succession to any dignity or title of honour or render any person capable of succeeding to or transmitting a right to succeed to any such dignity or title.

(v) REGISTRATION

The Warnock Report, para 4.25, states (footnote omitted):

4.25 As matters stand at present there is a temptation for the couple to conceal the true situation when a child is conceived as a result of AID, in order to hide the fact that the husband is infertile and to avoid unfavourable reactions among relatives and friends. Therefore the couple may, in registering the birth, state that the husband is the father, thus committing an offence. Where the mother is married and the husband consents to AID (4.17) **we recommend that the law should be changed so as to permit the husband to be registered as the father.** We are fully aware that this can be criticised as legislating for a fiction since the husband of a woman who has conceived by AID will not be the genetic father of the child and the register of births has always been envisaged as a true genetic record. Nevertheless it would in our view be consistent with the husband's assuming all parental rights and duties with regard to the child. However we are of the view that consideration should be given as a matter of urgency to making it possible for the parents in registering the birth to add 'by donation' after the man's name.

Commenting upon this, the DHSS in its consultation paper entitled 'Legislation on Human Infertility Services and Embryo Research', in December 1986 (Cm 83), stated (para 30):

30. There was little support in the response to the Warnock Report for the proposal for an optional 'by donation' annotation of the birth register. It was recognised that the child must have a birth certificate which concealed the facts about his conception, but there was a strongly held view that the legal father should be allowed to enter his name on the birth register only if the entry could be linked by the Registrar General with a central record of AID births (which could be a responsibility of a statutory licensing body). This was thought to be essential:

(a) to maintain the integrity and reliability of the birth register as a record of biological fact;

(b) to ensure the child's right of access, as an adult, to an accurate record of the biological facts of his birth, and to the information about the donor held on the central record;

(c) to give an AID child who wished to marry the opportunity to ensure that there was no prohibited relationship with the intended spouse (but this would be possible only if the donor's name were recorded on the central record).

A link with a central record would enable the Registrar General to deal more effectively with applications for a correction to a birth entry in the case of an AID child.

(In the subsequent White Paper of November 1987 'Human Fertilisation and Embryology: A framework for legislation' (Cmnd 259), the Government has indicated that one of the functions of the Statutory Licensing Authority (SLA) will be to store such information about 'donation birth' (paras 79–90). It is proposed to give an adult a right to such information (para 83) but that this will be kept under review (para 84).)

For the present we should ask: has the problem of registration gone away in the case of a husband who consents to AID as a result of section 27 of the Family Law Reform Act 1987?

(vi) LIABILITY IN TORT

(a) The donor

If the donor knows (or ought to know) that he is suffering from some transmissible disability which routine testing will not discover and, nonetheless, he donates sperm so as to earn money, is he liable for any subsequent harm suffered by the child? The Congenital Disabilities (Civil Liability) Act 1976, s 1, provides:

> **1.**—(1) If a child is born disabled as the result of such an occurrence before its birth as is mentioned in subsection (2) below, and a person (other than the child's own mother) is under this section answerable to the child in respect of the occurrence, the child's disabilities are to be regarded as damage resulting from the wrongful act of that person and actionable accordingly at the suit of the child.
> (2) An occurrence to which this section applies is one which—
> (a) affected either parent of the child in his or her ability to have a normal, healthy child; or
> (b) affected the mother during her pregnancy, or affected her or the child in the course of its birth, so that the child is born with disabilities which would not otherwise have been present.
> . . .
> (4) In the case of an occurrence preceding the time of conception, the defendant is not answerable to the child if at that time either or both of the parents knew the risk of their child being born disabled (that is to say, the particular risk created by the occurrence); but should it be the child's father who is the defendant, this subsection does not apply if he knew of the risk and the mother did not.

Does s 1(2) (which replaces the common law: see s 4(5)) cover this situation? What is the 'occurrence' required by s 1(2)? If so, does the defence in s 1(4) apply where the defendant is also the father? If it does, will s 1(4) apply where the donor *ought* to know of his condition? Would there be any action at common law by the mother for any nervous shock or other physical injury or financial loss she might suffer?

(b) The doctor or sperm bank

1. Negligence

If the sperm is stored or any screening for defects is performed carelessly then, the same arguments concerning liability under the 1976 Act discussed above would again need to be resolved. Equally, any action at the suit of the mother for nervous shock etc would be the same.

2. Products liability

The Consumer Protection Act 1987, Part II, creates liability without proof of fault where a defective product (as defined in s 3) causes physical injury to another (sections 2 and 5(1)) see *supra* at pp 563–4. Ordinarily, a child born with a handicap resulting from defective sperm would have no action because under

English law the unborn child lacks legal personality. However, s 6(3) of the Act states, *inter alia*:

Section 1 of the Congenital Disabilities (Civil Liability) Act 1976 shall have effect for the purposes of this Part as if—

(a) a person were answerable to a child in respect of an occurrence caused wholly or partly by a defect in a product if he is or has been liable under section 2 above in respect of any effect of the occurrence on a parent of the child, or would be so liable if the occurrence caused a parent of the child to suffer damage; . . .

Do you think this section would allow a child to sue in the circumstances envisaged? Has a child born handicapped suffered damage (s 5(1))?

Would the mother of a child born handicapped as a consequence of defective sperm have an action? The following issues would have to be resolved in her favour: (i) whether sperm is 'a product'; (ii) whether the doctor or sperm bank, although a 'supplier' (s 2(3)), is a producer within the terms of the Act (s 1(2)); (iii) whether any damage which the woman suffers is recognised under the Act as compensatable; (iv) whether the doctor or sperm bank could take advantage of the so called 'state of the art' defence in s 4(1)(e) if the transmissible defect could not have been detected; and (v) whether the doctor or a sperm bank could have a defence under s 4(1)(c) because there is no supply of sperm 'in the course of a business'. (On (i), consider the US cases of *Cunningham v MacNeil Memorial Hospital* 266 NE 2d 897 (1970) (blood a 'product'). Cf *Fisher v Sibley Memorial Hospital* 403 A 2d 1130 (1979) (blood a 'service') and note *Two Rivers Co v Curtiss Breeding Service* 624 F 2d 1242 (1980) (bull semen a 'product'). On (ii), if the doctor or blood bank is only a 'supplier' then they may escape liability by identifying *their* supplier (s 2(3)). Presumably, this would be the donor; how does this fit in with the usual practice of anonymity? On (iii), consider the terms of s 5(1) and (2).)

3. Counselling

It has been suggested by those commenting on the practice of AID that it should not be carried out unless accompanied by appropriate counselling of the woman and her partner. Consider the Warnock Report, paras 3.3 and 3.4:

3.3 A second issue concerns the counselling, advice, information and discussion that should be available for those who seek treatment for infertility. Many of the problems which may arise in the course of treatment, whether this treatment ends in the birth of a child or not, are complex and they need to be given careful consideration over a period of time. We therefore believe that counselling should be available for infertile couples and for donors. In particular the task of the doctor and the counsellor must be to ensure that couples and donors fully understand the implications of what they are embarking on, what rights and duties they may have, and where they may expect to experience difficulties.

3.4 The counselling that we envisage is essentially non-directional. It is aimed at helping individuals to understand their situation and to make their own decisions about what steps should be taken next. Counselling need not necessarily take place at the hospital, though this may be the most convenient location. It should be carried out in a neutral atmosphere and involve a skilled, fully trained counsellor. **We recommend that counselling should be available to all infertile couples and third parties at any stage of the treatment, both as an integral part of National Health Service provision and in the private sector.** We recognise that there may not be sufficient counsellors trained in this field at present, but we feel it is possible for counsellors trained in other fields to adapt their skills to deal with infertility. Specialised further training and funding for those attending such courses will need to be made available.

We look to training bodies in social work and counselling to give guidance on these training needs and how they should be met.

What, if any, action would lie, and at the suit of whom, if no counselling was provided or if it was carelessly carried out? The importance of the matter was recognised in the DHSS Consultation Paper (1986) in paragraph 25, but it is still a matter for debate whether specific legal provision will be made.

25. Strong views were expressed in some responses to the Warnock Report on the need to have specific regard in the provision of infertility services to the welfare of the child who might be born as a result of AID or other treatments. To that end counselling was seen as an essential element in the provision of infertility services so as, for example, to ensure that prospective parents could be helped to understand the implications of available treatments and the issues which they would need to confront later regarding the child's understanding of his origins. The Government accepts that couples should receive counselling and would be glad to have further **views on the development of such services and whether counselling should be a statutory requirement.**

Subsequently, in the White Paper published in November 1987 (Cmnd 259), para 77, the Government concluded:

. . . that centres offering licensed treatments should be required to make counselling available to all couples who are considering such treatments. Counselling should be distinct from discussions with a doctor of any medical treatment he proposes and should be carried out by somebody different, preferably a qualified counsellor. The SLA will be under a statutory obligation to take into account the quality of these counselling services, as well as counselling for donors, when considering whether to grant a licence. Where children born following gamete or embryo donation seek information about their origins, the Government proposes that the SLA should have a statutory obligation to ensure that counselling is made available to them. (The extent and quality of these services will need to be reviewed to take account of any changes of policy on such matters as access to information about the donor.)

(*Note:* the legislation in the state of Victoria in Australia places a specific duty upon the doctor carrying out the medical procedures to ensure that the man and woman have been counselled and that further counselling will be available after the procedure has been performed: Infertility (Medical Procedures) Act 1984, ss 10–13. We will return to this Act later.)

(vii)   Eligibility for Treatment

What, if any, should be the criteria for determining eligibility for infertility treatment? This question arises here in the context of AID when medical assistance is sought but it arises more acutely in IVF treatment which we will discuss shortly. The following extracts from reports of Government bodies in the United Kingdom and Canada deal with this question in the context of infertility treatments generally. First, consider the Warnock Report (paras 2.5–2.13, footnote omitted):

2.5 It is sometimes suggested that infertility treatment should be available only to married couples, in the interests of any child that may be born as a result. While we are vitally aware of the need to protect these interests, we are not prepared to recommend that access to treatment should be based exclusively on the legal status of marriage.

2.6 In discussing treatment for infertility, this report takes the term *couple* to mean a heterosexual couple living together in a stable relationship, whether married or not. We use the words *husband* and *wife* to denote a relationship, not a legal status (except where the context makes differentiation necessary, for example in relation to legitimacy).

2.7 In the evidence, concern was expressed that infertility treatment may be provided for couples without due regard for the interests of any child that may be born as a result. For example the couple may have a previous conviction for child abuse. It has been argued that the greater the degree of intervention in the creation of a child, the more responsibility must be taken for that child. However the evidence also drew attention to the absence of any restrictions on procreation by fertile couples, whatever their circumstances. Indeed, some of the evidence referred to the fact that Articles 8 and 12 of the European Convention on Human Rights guarantee a respect for family life and the right to found a family. It has been argued that these provisions create a right to take full advantage of the techniques which are available to alleviate infertility.

2.8 There are other considerations which many believe should be taken into account. For example, a woman may seek treatment when she has herself, at an earlier stage, been sterilised at her own request. Perhaps because of a new marriage, she now very much wants children. The question may be raised whether, if she has children, albeit from another marriage, she should be eligible for infertility treatment. Again, a woman who has had a child may subsequently become infertile. Opinions may be divided about whether she should be eligible for treatment.

2.9 Furthermore, the various techniques for assisted reproduction offer not only a remedy for infertility, but also offer the fertile single woman or lesbian couple the chance of parenthood without the direct involvement of a male partner. To judge from the evidence, many believe that the interests of the child dictate that it should be born into a home where there is a loving, stable, heterosexual relationship and that, therefore, the *deliberate* creation of a child for a woman who is not a partner in such a relationship is morally wrong. On the other side some expressed the view that a single woman or lesbian couple have a right under the European Convention to have children even though those children may have no legal father. It is further argued that it is already accepted that a single person, whether man or woman, can in certain circumstances provide a suitable environment for a child, since the existence of single adoptive parents is specifically provided for in the Children Act 1975.

2.10 In the same way that a single woman may believe she has a right to motherhood, so a single man may feel he has a right to fatherhood. Though the feminist position is perhaps more frequently publicised, we were told of a group of single, mainly homosexual, men who were campaigning for the right to bring up a child. Their primary aim at present is to obtain in practice equal rights in the adoption field, but they are also well aware of the potential of surrogacy for providing a single man with a child that is genetically his. There have been cases in other countries of surrogacy in such circumstances. It can be argued that as a matter of sex equality if single women are not totally barred from parenthood, then neither should single men be so barred.

2.11 We have considered these arguments, but, nevertheless, we believe that as a general rule it is better for children to be born into a two-parent family, with both father and mother, although we recognise that it is impossible to predict with any certainty how lasting such a relationship will be.

2.12 We have considered very carefully whether there are circumstances where it is inappropriate for treatment which is solely for the alleviation of infertility to be provided. In general we hold that everyone should be entitled to seek expert advice and appropriate investigation. This will usually involve referral to a consultant. However, at the present time services for the treatment of infertility are in short supply, both for initial referral and investigation and for the more specialised treatments considered in this report. In this situation of scarcity some individuals will have a more compelling case for treatment than others. In the circumstances medical practitioners will, clearly, use their clinical judgment as to the priority of the individual case bearing in mind such considerations as the patient's age, the duration of infertility and the likelihood that treatment will be successful. So far this is not contentious. However, notwithstanding our view that every patient is entitled to advice and investigation of his or her infertility, we can foresee occasions where the consultant may, after discussion with professional health and social work colleagues, consider that there are valid reasons why infertility treatment would not be in the best interests of the patient, the child that may be born following treatment, or the patient's immediate family.

2.13 This question of eligibility for treatment is a very difficult one, and we believe that hard and fast rules are not applicable to its solution. We recognise that this will place a heavy burden of responsibility on the individual consultant who must make social judgments that go beyond the purely medical, in the types of case we have discussed. We considered whether it was possible for us to set out the wider social criteria that consultants, together with their professional colleagues, should use in deciding whether infertility treatment should be provided for a particular patient. We decided it was not possible to draw up comprehensive criteria that would be sensitive to the circumstances of every case. We recognise however that individual practitioners are on occasions going to decline to treat a particular patient and **we recommend that in cases where consultants decline to provide treatment they should always give the patient a full explanation of the reasons**. This would at least ensure that patients were not kept in ignorance of the reason for refusal, and would be able to exercise their right to seek a second opinion.

The Ontario Law Reform Commission's Report on 'Human Artificial Reproduction and Related Matters' deals with this issue also at pp 153–9; (footnotes omitted):

(i)   Criteria for assessment: marital status and other matters

One of the most controversial issues respecting the new reproductive technologies concerns eligibility to participate in an artificial insemination or IVF programme, and, more specifically, the question of marital status. In the reports canvassed by the Commission, in the submissions made to us, and in the literature, this critical, threshold issue has been hotly and inconclusively debated. The debate has centred on matters of ethics, religion, private morality, public good, and social policy; it has focused on the importance of the family and marriage as the bedrock of society; and it has ultimately concerned itself, as we believe it must, with different perceptions of what constitutes the best interests of children conceived by artificial means.

Much of the public discussion of, and antipathy to, artificial reproduction is based on the apprehension that 'unsuitable' persons may use the new technologies to become parents. Many who, reluctantly or otherwise, accept or acknowledge that virtually no legal controls can be applied to curb reproduction among 'unsuitable' persons who are fertile argue that artificial conception services should not be made available to such persons: in a sense, since the means of control are available in the latter case, such means should therefore be used. Others have rejected this type of intervention in the context of eligibility, stressing the alleged right of individual reproductive autonomy and the conceptual anomaly of controlling parents using artificial conception while ignoring parents who conceive naturally.

The paramountcy of the interests of the artificially conceived child helps us to put the issue of eligibility in what we believe to be its proper, child-oriented perspective, a perspective reinforced by the Terms of Reference of this Report and by the obvious public interest in the welfare of children. Since we are firmly of the opinion that our proposals for reform must be animated by our perception of the best interests of artificially conceived children, it follows that we do not view the matter of eligibility as predominantly or essentially applicant-oriented, pertaining primarily to the gratification of the potential participants. While we have endorsed the role of artificial conception in order to alleviate the effects of infertility or genetic impairment in such persons, this is not tantamount to an unrestricted acceptance of the right of *all* infertile or genetically impaired persons to participate in an artificial conception programme. Artificially conceived children, and the public, would not be well served by such an unfettered right.

The Commission has canvassed this matter generally in chapter 4, rejecting what it called the 'private ordering' approach to artificial conception in favour of a modified state regulatory approach. We noted that some persons are emotionally ill-equipped to understand or cope with the unique problems of engaging in an artificial conception programme and of bearing and rearing the resulting child, especially where donor gametes are involved. Our general conclusion that the law must impose a degree of regulation in the unique case of artificial conception—regulation that is neither desirable nor practicable in the case of natural reproduction—is particularly apposite when considering the specific issue of eligibility for participation in an artificial conception programme. It is at this initial juncture that the state is able to intervene in a manner that will ensure, as much as possible, that the future child will be born into, and reared in, a satisfactory home environment. Any subsequent state intervention that might take place—if, for example, the child is declared to be 'in need of protection'—is clearly not unimportant, but operates only at a later stage, on an *ad hoc* basis, and in rather extreme cases.

Having concluded, then, that the matter of eligibility must not be left simply to the dictates of persons seeking artificial conception services, it remains for us to set forth the range of alternatives and, finally, the standards or criteria to which we subscribe, bearing in mind that our analysis of the options and our final decision must be viewed from the perspective of the best interests of artificially conceived children.

The Commission recognises, of course, that what may be called 'suitability for parenthood' is an amorphous social and psychological concept, fluctuating from time to time. Yet, notwithstanding the fluidity and ambiguity of the concept, it is noteworthy that most of the reports canvassed by the Commission deal expressly or implicitly with the subject and offer (or, frequently, assume) certain conclusions. The critical issue in respect of 'suitability for parenthood' relates to the question whether a participant in an artificial conception procedure must be legally married, or at least living in some sort of stable relationship, or whether she may be single and not involved in any type of union. The question whether marriage ought to be a precondition to eligibility raises, in turn, a further question, dealt with in chapter 3 of this Report, namely, whether legislation imposing such a requirement would, for example, violate the provisions of the *Canadian Charter of Rights and Freedoms* or the Ontario *Human Rights Code, 1981*. We do not intend to review the contending arguments here, except to note that discrimination based on marital status is prohibited. Indeed, it was precisely for this reason—the perceived conflict with provincial human rights legislation if all but married women were precluded from undergoing artificial insemination—that the majority of the Law Reform Commission of Saskatchewan recommended that, for the time being at least, the law should not prescribe criteria for the selection of recipients.

Most of the other bodies that have turned their attention to the question of marital status have either emphasised that a two parent family is preferable or have ignored the standing of single women, although the British Columbia Royal Commission on Family and Children's Law would not eliminate anyone from consideration 'just because of her marital status', and the Royal College of Obstetricians and Gynaecologists in the United Kingdom would not rule out IVF for single women, notwithstanding its 'grave reservations'.

With respect to the status of unmarried, cohabiting, couples, most of the legislation described in the Appendix to this Report implicitly countenances access by such persons to artificial conception services, but almost all the legislation actually deals with the question only in the context of the status of the child, access to services is, therefore, assumed. Only the Victoria *Interim Report* appears to have suggested that unmarried couples should be precluded from participation, although, even here, the Report did leave the door open for possible participation in the future. Unfortunately, this critical issue was not canvassed in the later Report. However, it bears mentioning that the Victoria *Infertility (Medical Procedures) Act 1984*, provides, with respect to eligibility, that a married woman includes a woman who is 'living with a man as his wife on a *bona fide* domestic basis although not married to him'. In addition, it is made clear that a single woman is not eligible for treatment.

The Commission is acutely aware of the controversy that surrounds the vital question of eligibility. Indeed, the absence of a clear public consensus on this issue is reflected in the views expressed by individual members of the Commission. However, a majority of the Commission has come to the conclusion that, while participation in an artificial conception programme should not be a right given to every infertile or genetically diseased person or couple wishing to have a child, eligibility for participation should not be restricted to married couples or, indeed, even to couples.

As we have said, such a restriction would appear to contravene human rights legislation applicable in this Province. Moreover, any *a priori* exclusions based simply on membership in a particular group (such as married persons) would automatically eliminate from consideration single persons or unmarried couples who, by any standard, would make suitable parents.

A majority of the Commission believes that there are many variables that must be considered, including the home environment, the physical and mental health of the prospective parent or parents, their emotional reaction to artificial conception and its real or potential frustrations, the marital status of the parties and, where married or in a *de facto* relationship, the stability of the union.

Accordingly, a majority of the Commission recommends that stable single women and stable men and women in stable marital or nonmarital unions should be eligible to participate in an artificial conception programme. We wish to emphasise that implementation of this proposal would not entitle any person, whether married or not, to artificial conception services. Rather, the proposal deals first with eligibility, affording equal opportunity to all persons to apply for consideration for services, and, secondly, with their stability, focusing on the human factors involved, and not on the matter of status.

Our proposal is intended, therefore, to permit participation in an artificial conception programme only by those persons who, we believe, are likely to offer a proper home environment for the child. While we have left the door open to single women to apply, we do not envisage either a rash of applications by such women, nor a substantial change in the number of single women artificially inseminated. Indeed, it is our view that, as a general rule, the welfare of children is better served when they are reared in a two parent family. We expect that this belief, which mirrors the perception of most child psychiatrists, social workers, and other knowledgeable professionals, as well as that of the general community, will continue to be reflected in the practice of most artificial conception practitioners.

In order to ensure that the gravity of the eligibility criteria to be addressed by artificial conception practitioners will be fully appreciated by them, we wish to offer a further proposal. In chapter 4, we considered various institutional means that are available to regulate a particular activity, such as legislation, the courts, or the medical profession itself. In the case of the criteria for determining participation in an artificial conception programme, we have already stated our view that the matter ought not to be left to individual physicians. Accordingly, we recommend that the proposed criteria for participation in an artificial conception programme should be set out in regulations made under the *Health Disciplines Act*.

The importance of eligibility to the new reproductive techniques was recognised in the 1986 DHSS Consultation Paper, in para 26:

26. Some have proposed that, to protect the welfare of an unborn child, couples wishing to receive AID or egg or embryo donations (ie where any child born would not be genetically the child of one or both parents) should be subject by law to a formal procedure designed to assess their suitability as parents, as is the case when couples wish to adopt. There would be problems in drawing a line between these treatments and the many other forms of infertility and sub-fertility treatments, eg those using drugs or surgery. However, **the Government would also be glad to have comments on this proposal.**

In the 1987 White Paper, the Government rejected the idea of a formal statutory procedure to assess suitability. Instead, the SLA would be required to take account of centres' procedures for deciding whether to offer treatment, when deciding whether to grant a licence (para 78). It would seem that some centres adopt the same criteria in practice as are used to assess the suitability of couples to adopt (*R v Ethical Committee of St Mary's Hospital (Manchester), ex p H* [1988] 1 FLR 512).

In vitro fertilisation (IVF)

(i) THE TECHNIQUE

The Warnock Report (paras 5.1–5.5) describes the medical and scientific techniques.

In vitro fertilisation

5.1 Unlike AID, *in vitro* fertilisation (IVF) is very much a new development. Of those women who are infertile a small proportion can produce healthy eggs but, although they have a normal uterus, have damaged or diseased fallopian tubes which prevent the egg passing from the ovary to the uterus. A certain proportion of these women can be helped by tubal surgery. Until IVF became a reality, the possibility of achieving a pregnancy for women with tubal problems was not great. IVF may be appropriate perhaps for 5% of infertile couples. Recently claims have been made for IVF as a treatment for other forms of infertility including its use in the treatment of oligospermia[1] and unexplained infertility.

5.2 The concept of IVF is simple. A ripe human egg is extracted from the ovary, shortly before it would have been released naturally. Next, the egg is mixed with the semen of the husband or partner, so that fertilisation can occur. The fertilised egg, once it has started to divide, is then transferred back to the mother's uterus. In practice the technique for recovery of the eggs, their culture outside the mother's body, and the transfer of the developing embryo to the uterus has to be carried out under very carefully controlled conditions. The development of laparoscopic[2] techniques during the 1960s made the collection of the egg, in cases where the ovaries were accessible, relatively easy. (Another technique for egg recovery based on ultrasound identification[3] has now been developed.) It was not particularly difficult to fertilise the human egg *in vitro*. The real difficulty related to the implantation of the embryo in the uterus after transfer. A pregnancy achieved in this way must not only survive the normal hazards of implantation of *in vivo* conception, but also the additional problems of IVF and embryo transfer. More is now known about how best to replicate the natural sequence of events, but undoubtedly achieving a successful implantation is still the most uncertain part of the procedure.

5.3 Because of these difficulties it is common practice to transfer more than one embryo to the potential mother whenever possible, and for this reason several eggs need to be recovered. This is achieved by artificial stimulation, known as superovulation, of the woman's ovaries to ensure that she produces several eggs in one cycle. After an appropriate course of drugs, as many ripe eggs as are accessible are harvested just before the time of ovulation. Each egg is then mixed with semen to achieve fertilisation. Assuming there is no abnormality in the semen, the success rate of fertilisation is usually at least 75%. Some embryos may however show signs of poor or abnormal development; when the time comes to transfer the embryos to the woman it may be that there is only one embryo suitable for transfer, or there may be several.

5.4 The case for transferring more than one embryo is that this should give the woman a better chance of achieving a pregnancy. There is also an argument that if two or more embryos are transferred each helps the other towards implantation. However, if too many embryos are transferred and they all implant this may result in a multiple pregnancy with all the added risks of such a pregnancy including the risks of miscarriage, premature delivery and resulting immaturity at birth. There are differences of opinion about how many embryos should be transferred, given these risks. This is a field where constant reassessment is needed as new evidence becomes available. We have considered arguments that a limit should be imposed on the total number of embryos that should be transferred on each occasion, but we believe that in each individual case the number of embryos to be transferred must be a matter of clinical judgment on the part of the practitioner responsible for the woman's care. This responsibility should be made clear in the consent form. In addition to the technical arguments we have outlined, a practitioner must also give very serious consideration to the social problems for the family that may follow the birth of more than twins, problems that may affect the continuing health and wellbeing of the mother in looking after the children and may adversely affect the children themselves.

5.5 Despite the technical difficulties of IVF, at the time we write, there have been some hundreds of such births throughout the world. These births continue to exercise considerable fascination. At the same time, this public interest creates, in itself, difficulties, adding to the pressure on doctors practising in this field who are not only trying to provide a new treatment for their patients, but are also constantly working in the public

Notes to extract

[1] Oligospermia is the term used to describe semen in which the number of sperm present is reduced or markedly reduced compared with the number of sperm present in normal semen.

[2] The laparoscope is an optical surgical instrument which is used to inspect the internal abdominal and pelvic organs so that minor surgical procedures can be performed including the recovery of one or more eggs from those ovarian follicles that are ripe. Laparoscopy usually requires a general anaesthetic but does not usually involve an overnight stay in hospital.

[3] Ultrasound can now be used to identify the position of a ripe follicle containing an egg. A needle is then passed through the woman's abdominal wall and other organs and is guided to the follicle by use of ultrasound. The egg is then withdrawn through the needle. This technique can be used under local anaesthetic and can be used to recover more than one egg at a time.

In the Government's 1987 White Paper (Annex A, para 10) the following procedures are described which have been developed since the Warnock Report.

10. Since the Warnock Report was published various new treatment methods have been developed, which involve techniques for egg and sperm preparation similar to those used in IVF, but which do not require the creation of human embryos outside the body. These include GIFT (Gamete Intra-Fallopian Transfer); POST (Peritoneal Oocyte and Sperm Transfer) and VISPER (Vaginal Intra-Peritoneal Sperm Transfer). The first two of these involve collecting eggs from a woman's ovary and sperm from a man (usually the husband) and putting them directly into the woman's fallopian tubes (GIFT) or peritoneum (POST). In the last (VISPER) sperm only are placed directly into the woman's peritoneal cavity. None of these methods are suitable forms of treatment where a woman's fallopian tubes are blocked or missing—one of the prime indications for the use of IVF treatment.

(ii) REGULATION

Should the provision of infertility services be regulated? If the answer to this is yes, how, and to what extent, should there be regulation? Should it be a matter of licensing; should the criminal law (and its sanctions) be utilised? Should the regulation emanate from the State or should it be voluntary? These fundamental questions are considered in the materials which follow. First, let us consider the Warnock Report (paras 13.1–13.9).

13.1 Public concern about the techniques we have discussed needs to be reflected in public policy. We believe that all the techniques require active regulation and monitoring, even though, as we realise, such restrictions may be regarded by some as infringing clinical or academic freedom. It is not our intention to interfere with the duty of the doctor to exercise clinical judgment in treating patients. Indeed we accept and expect the doctor to be the person who makes the final decision about whether a treatment is likely to succeed, and whether it should be used. Similarly we accept that scientists must not be unduly restricted in pursuing their research interests especially when this may produce direct therapeutic benefits.

13.2 But doctors and scientists work within the moral and legal framework determined by society. They do not and should not depart radically from that framework. Our intention is that activities which have evolved in an unstructured and unmonitored way should be placed on a properly organised basis, within a framework broadly acceptable to society. The interests of those directly concerned, as well as those of society in general, demand that certain legal and ethical safeguards should be applied.

13.3 The protection of the public, which we see as the primary objective of regulation, demands the existence of an authority independent of Government, health authorities, or research institutions. The authority should be specifically charged with the responsibility to regulate and monitor practice in relation to those sensitive areas which raise fundamental ethical questions. **We therefore recommend the establishment of a new statutory licensing authority to regulate both research and those infertility services which we have recommended should be subject to control.**

13.4 Although we do not see it as our function to specify the precise size and detailed composition of the new body, there are some general points which we would like to make. The new body will need access to expert medical and scientific advice. We could therefore envisage a significant representation of scientific and medical interests among the membership. It would also need to have members experienced in the organisation and provision of services. However, this is not exclusively, or even primarily, a medical or scientific body. It is concerned essentially with broader matters and with the protection of the public interest. If the public is to have confidence that this is an independent body, which is not to be unduly influenced by sectional interests, its membership must be wide-ranging and in particular the lay interests should be well represented. **We recommend that there should be substantial lay representation on the statutory authority to regulate research and infertility services and that the chairman must be a lay person.**

Functions of the new body

13.5 We envisage the new body having two distinct functions, one advisory and one executive. We believe it should issue general guidance, to those working in the field, on good practice in infertility service provision and on the types of research which, without prejudice to its view of any individual project, it finds broadly ethically acceptable. It should also offer advice to Government on specific issues as they arise, and be available for Ministers to consult for specific guidance. As part of its responsibility to protect the public interest, it should publish and present to Parliament, an Annual Report, setting out the facilities for infertility treatment currently licensed and the research currently in progress, its purpose and scope, including an indication of the number of embryos being used, and their type, so that this knowledge may be publicly available.

13.6 Its executive function would be twofold: to grant licences to those wishing to offer the kinds of infertility treatment we have discussed, whether in the NHS or in the private sector; and to grant licences to researchers wishing to work with human gametes and embryos. The licensing body would be supported by an inspectorate, who would undertake regular inspections of premises where such work was carried out, to ensure that licence holders were keeping to the terms of their licences and meeting the prescribed conditions. We do not see it as our function to specify in detail the criteria for granting a licence but there are certain controls which we believe should be imposed. These are discussed in the paragraphs that follow.

Licensing of infertility services

13.7 **We recommend that all practitioners offering the services that we have**

recommended should only be provided under licence, and all premises used as part of any such provision, including the provision of fresh semen and banks for the storage of frozen human eggs, semen and embryos should be licensed by the licensing body.

13.8 Licensed infertility services should be run by a qualified medical practitioner with appropriately qualified supporting staff and adequate facilities. We have given some thought to whether there is a need for special training for infertility services, but have concluded that training, as in other spheres of medicine, should be the responsibility of the appropriate professional bodies. The existence of screening arrangements sufficient to meet a centrally determined standard must be one of the criteria for granting a licence. Once donors have been selected there must be satisfactory arrangements for handling of semen and eggs to ensure that the quality of both is satisfactory and remains so. Any frozen semen or eggs must be properly identifiable throughout the time they are stored, so that there is no danger of confusion. The licensing body should therefore concern itself with these aspects of quality control.

13.9 We would also like the licensing body to consider what follow-up of children born as a result of the new techniques may be needed. We recognise that there are those who believe that any systematic follow-up or research studies would be unduly intrusive, since they would mark out the children and families as in some way different. On the other hand it is argued that only through such studies will it be possible to assess the long-term consequences, both physical, psychological and developmental of the use of these techniques. It is further argued that it is particularly important as a reassurance to prospective parents, to confirm the present understanding that there are no additional risks of abnormality from their use. There is also the question as to whether, as a basis for such follow-up studies, there should be a centrally maintained record of all births. Such a register would enable children on reaching their majority to check whether they were born as a result of any of the new techniques and to discover the information to which they are entitled . . . We recognise the difficulties in establishing such a register, in terms of ensuring completeness, and in relation to confidentiality; for these reasons we have not seen it as part of our remit to make firm proposals. Nonetheless, we see the whole area of follow-up activity as in need of urgent consideration and **recommend that the licensing body be asked to consider the need for follow-up studies of children born as a result of the new techniques, including consideration of the need for a centrally maintained register of such births.**

At present in England there exists a Voluntary Licensing Authority (VLA) set up, as a consequence of the Warnock Report, in 1985 by the Medical Research Council and the Royal College of Obstetricians and Gynaecologists. In its annual reports it has described the process of visitation of establishments and the approval or otherwise of practices followed. (See, most recently: 'The Fourth Report of the Voluntary Licensing Authority For Human *In Vitro* Fertilisation and Embryology' (April 1989).)

The Terms of Reference of the VLA are as follows:

1. To approve a Code of Practice for research in human embryology and for related medical procedures in the treatment of infertility; and to amend the Code from time to time in the light of consultation and experience.
2. To invite all centres, scientists and clinicians engaged in pre-embryo research or developmental practice in *in vitro* fertilisation, GIFT or other such procedures to submit work for approval and licence.
3. To visit each centre before the grant of licence and to return for review visits as necessary.
4. To report to the Medical Research Council and to the Royal College of Obstetricians and Gynaecologists.
5. To publish information on centres and work approved and not approved.
6. To contribute as expedient to the relevant public debate and legislative process.

In pursuance of these, the VLA has issued the following guidelines for clinical practice and research involving IVF procedures. Failure to abide by the guidelines would lead to a centre being refused approval and licence by the VLA or losing a licence it already held.

The effect of this would be two-fold. First, funding would be impossible from the MRC or, possibly, any other body. Secondly, the centre would be perceived by the community (both lay and professional) as not playing by the accepted rules. This occurred in the case of the Humana Hospital Wellington, London which for a time refused to abide by Guideline 12 introduced in 1987 and the VLA withdrew the centre's licence. Even though the centre was privately funded it nonetheless agreed to abide by the guideline and its licence was reinstated.

Guidelines

(1) Scientifically sound research involving experiments on the processes and products of *in vitro* fertilisation between gametes is ethically acceptable, subject to certain provisions detailed in Sections 2–10 below.

(2) Any application made to the Authority must give reasons why information cannot be obtained from studies of species other than the human.

(3) The aim of the research must be clearly defined and relevant to clinical problems such as the diagnosis and treatment of infertility or of genetic disorders, or for the development of safe and more effective contraceptive measures.

(4) Pre-embryos resulting from or used in research should not be transferred to the uterus, except in the course of clinical research studies designed to enhance the possibility of establishing a successful pregnancy in a particular individual.

(5) Suitable signed consent to research involving human ova and sperm should be obtained in every case from the donors; sperm from sperm banks should not be used unless permission for its use in research has been obtained from the donor. Approval for each project must be obtained from the local ethical committee prior to seeking approval from the VLA.

(6) When human ova have been obtained and fertilised *in vitro* for a therapeutic purpose and are no longer required for that purpose it would be ethical to use them for soundly based research provided that the signed consent of both donors was obtained, subject to the same approval as in the preceding section.

(7) Human ova fertilised with human sperm should not be cultured *in vitro* for more than 14 days excluding any period of storage at low temperature (see Section 8) and should not be stored for use in research other than that for which local ethical committee and VLA approval has been obtained.

(8) Where a pre-embryo has been preserved at low temperature, whether donated for research purposes at the time of preservation or subsequently, it may continue to be grown to the equivalent of 14 days' normal development provided that approval has first been obtained from the local ethical committee and the VLA. Storage of individual pre-embryos at low temperature should be reviewed after two years and the maximum storage time should be ten years.

(9) The means of disposal of the pre-embryo must be carefully considered before the start of each project. At the end of a study steps must be taken to stop development of the pre-embryo and the appropriate disposal must be considered in discussion with the local ethical committee and details given to the VLA. The means of disposal will depend on the nature of the particular study that the pre-embryo has been used for. In view of the scarcity of the material, it would be inappropriate to discard any pre-embryo without thorough examination.

(10) Studies on the penetration of animal eggs by human sperm are valuable in providing information on the penetration ability and chromosomal complement of sperm from subfertile men and are considered ethically acceptable provided that development does not proceed beyond the early cleavage stage.

(11) The clinical use of ova stored at low temperatures, involving subsequent *in vitro* fertilisation should not proceed to transfer to the uterus until such time as scientific evidence is available as to the safety of the procedure.

(12) Consideration must be given to ensuring that whilst a woman has the best chance of achieving a pregnancy the risk of a large multiple pregnancy occurring are minimised. For this reason whether IVF or GIFT procedures are used either jointly or separately no more than three eggs or pre-embryos should be transferred in any one cycle, unless there are exceptional clinical reasons when up to four may be replaced per cycle.

(13) The following general considerations must be taken into account when establishing clinical facilities where *in vitro* fertilisation or GIFT is carried out:

(a) each centre must have access to an ethical committee, and no procedure should be undertaken without the knowledge and consent of the ethical committee,

(b) detailed records must be kept along the lines recommended in the Warnock Committee Report, and should include details of the children born as a result of *in vitro* fertilisation; the records should be readily available for examination by duly authorised staff and for collation on a national basis for a follow-up study,

(c) where the director either does not have accredited consultant status, or the equivalent, or is a non-clinical full clinical responsibility must be assumed by a Consultant Advisor who takes an active role in overseeing the centre's treatment protocols and emergency procedures; all other medical, nursing and technical staff must have appropriate experience and training,

(d) specialist medical, surgical and nursing facilities appropriate for the specific techniques used for the treatment must be available,

(e) arrangements for emergency treatment must be made,

(f) there must be adequate arrangements, where appropriate, for the transfer of gametes and pre-embryos between clinical facilities and the laboratory,

(g) centres should have appropriate counselling facilities with access to properly trained independent counselling staff,

(h) whenever donor gametes are to be used both donors and recipients should be tested for hepatitis B and HIV antibodies,

(i) donor sperm should be obtained only from a bank where all appropriate screening tests are undertaken including those recommended by the DHSS AIDS Booklet 4 *AIDS and Artificial Insemination—Guidance for Doctors and AI Clinics* (CMO (86) 12),

(j) egg donors should remain anonymous and for this reason donation for clinical purposes from any **known person including** should be avoided,

(k) **the use of close relatives for IVF surrogacy should be avoided.**

(14) The following general considerations must be taken into account when establishing laboratory facilities where *in vitro* fertilisation is carried out:

(a) each centre must have access to an ethical committee . . .

(b) detailed records must be kept and should be readily available for examination by duly authorised staff,

(c) laboratory staff must have appropriate experience and training in the techniques being used,

(d) laboratory conditions must be of a high standard (e g good culture facilities, facilities for microscopic examination, appropriate incubators and training in 'non touch' techniques),

(e) where gametes and pre-embryos are cultured and stored there must be a very high standard of security and of record keeping and labelling.

So much for the present, the DHSS in its Consultation Paper in 1986 (para 23), suggested for the future three options A, B and C, as follows:

23. There are of course other models for the control of infertility services in addition to the statutory licensing authority (Option A) [the Warnock proposal]. The two most obvious are:

Option B   direct control of certain treatments by a Secretary of State. This approach has been the basis of the Unborn Children (Protection) Bills presented to Parliament . . . In essence the functions of the statutory licensing authority would be carried out by the Secretary of State and his or her Department.

Option C   to rely on voluntary professional self-regulation. The Royal College of Obstetricians and Gynaecologists advises its members at present about the principles which should govern the provision of AID. IVF services are licensed by the VLA. This approach would not of course encompass those who did not belong to the relevant professional body.

Subsequently, in the 1987 White Paper the Government opted for Option A and set out the terms of reference and powers of the proposed independent Statutory Licensing Authority (SLA) 9paras 10–27).

10.   A substantial majority of those responding to the consultation document on this point favoured an independent Statutory Licensing Authority. This included many (for example the Catholic Bishops' Joint Committee on Bio-Ethical Issues) who had strong reservations about the desirability of some of the practices it would control and also the VLA itself. It has always regarded its own work as of a temporary nature and favours the establishment of a statutory authority.

11.   The Government has therefore concluded that an independent Statutory Licensing Authority (SLA) should be established as set out in more detail below.

12.   **Throughout the White Paper, references to the SLA's role in research on human embryos have been included to make clear what the position would be should Parliament decide to permit such research on a limited basis. Their presence does not, of course, in any way seek to pre-empt that decision, and the references have therefore been placed in square brackets.**

13.   The Government accepts the basic principle underlying the Warnock Report recommendations—namely the need 'to regulate and monitor practice in relation to those sensitive areas which raise fundamental ethical questions'. This is taken to go beyond just those medical or professional ethical questions relating to the safety or efficacy of certain clinical practices, to wider ethical issues such as are raised by the artificial creation of life outside the body or use of donated gametes. The SLA will therefore exercise its functions in the following areas:

— any [research or] treatment involving human embryos created in vitro, or procured from the womb of a woman (eg by lavage)
— treatments involving the use of a donated gametes (eg AID) or donated embryos
— the storage, in an arrested state of development, of human gametes or embryos for use at a later stage. (This is currently achieved by freezing using cryo-preservatives.)
— the use of diagnostic tests which involve the penetration by human sperm of an animal ovum . . .

14.   Those new treatment techniques such as GIFT (gamete intra-fallopian transfer . . .) which have developed since the Warnock Report was published will therefore come within the regulatory control of the SLA where they involve the use of gametes donated by a third party. To ensure that the legislation is flexible enough to deal with as yet unforeseen treatment developments which may raise new ethical issues, the Bill will contain powers to make regulations (subject to the affirmative resolution procedure) to add to or subtract from the range of matters coming within the regulatory scope of the SLA.

15.   The SLA will have the following functions:

— to license those providing infertility services involving treatment techniques outlined above. (This will include IVF, AID and egg/embryo donation).
— to license the storage of human embryos and gametes
— to license the diagnostic use of techniques involving the penetration of a non-human ovum by human sperm
[— to license research projects involving the use of human embryos]
— to advise Ministers on medical and scientific developments in the fields of

infertility [and human embryo research]; and such other matters as Ministers may request

— to collect data on facilities available for the provision of those infertility treatments it regulates; data on the volume of activity with regard to those treatments; and data on research currently in progress using human gametes [or embryos]

— to prepare reports on its activities which would be sent to Ministers and laid before Parliament

— to provide guidance to the field on good practice in the areas for which it is responsible. (All or part of this may be included in a Code of Practice which the SLA will be required to draw up, and which will be laid before Parliament.)

— to maintain a register of information about gamete/embryo donors which would be accessible to children born of donor gamete/embryo techniques, and to the Registrars General, as provided for in legislation.

16.   The chairman and members of the SLA will be appointed for a fixed renewable term by the Secretary of State for Social Services in consultation with other Ministers, and after such other consultation as he considers appropriate. He will also have power to terminate appointments in certain circumstances. The Bill will provide that the chairman must be lay—that is to say neither a qualified medical practitioner; nor a scientist involved in work using human gametes or embryos. The membership of the Authority will be of a size determined by the Secretary of State (probably around 15 to 20). The Bill will provide that at least half the members should be lay, and at least one third doctors or scientists with experience of relevant work.

17.   Members will not be appointed on a representational basis, but the Secretary of State will aim to arrive at a membership with a wide and balanced mix of views and experience (including the fields of law, nursing, social work, philosophy and religion as well as medicine and science). It is also important that consumer interests are represented and that there is a reasonable balance between men and women.

18.   Provision will be made for contributing towards the costs of the SLA from public funds, although it will be expected to meet a large proportion of its expenditure from fees collected in connection with its licensing activity.

19.   The SLA will appoint its own staff, including suitably qualified professional staff to assist in its licensing work; and other administrative and support staff. It will be able to establish such advisory sub-committees as it requires to enable it to carry out its functions, and to appoint to them people who are not members of the SLA but have relevant knowledge and experience.

LICENSING POWERS

20.   The Warnock Committee recommended that the SLA should license all practitioners offering regulated infertility services (ie services using treatment techniques coming within the SLA's remit), and all premises used in the provision of such services or for storage of gametes or embryos. The Government accepts the importance of adequate control by the SLA of both practitioners and premises, but there is a need, too, to avoid creating a cumbersome bureaucracy. Furthermore the division of responsibilities between practitioners and those in charge of premises is not clear cut. Satisfactory storage arrangements for example will depend both on the facilities available at the premises and on procedures established by the clinician to ensure accurate labelling of stored gametes and embryos. The key point is that licence holders should have a clear understanding of their responsibilities and should be in a position to ensure that services are provided in accordance with the terms of the licence.

21.   The Government has therefore concluded that the SLA should grant licences for each programme of regulated infertility services. The licence will be held by the person, normally a clinician, in charge of the programme and relate to the provision of services under his direction on specified premises. Separate licences would be required where a clinician offers services on more than one site or where a number of clinicians offer separate programmes on a single site. The SLA will also have

power to grant licences to individuals responsible for the storage of gametes or embryos in facilities where no clinical services are offered [or research carried out] (eg sperm banks). Licences will be granted subject to conditions specified by the SLA and the licence holder will be responsible for ensuring all conditions are met. Licences would be granted for five years, or shorter periods in individual cases at the discretion of the SLA, and could be renewed on expiry.

22.   The Government does not intend to specify in legislation the detailed criteria which should be applied in granting licences. However, there are some key matters which should in all cases be considered before a licence is granted.

23.   The SLA will therefore be required to have regard, in granting licences, to the experience and qualifications of the applicant and his staff, and the adequacy of the proposed premises; arrangements for record-keeping; screening and assessment procedures; and arrangements for storage and disposal of gametes and embryos. The SLA will need to be satisfied that, in his approach to the selection of patients for treatment using one of the regulated treatment methods, the licence holder gives due consideration to alternative treatment methods. The SLA will also be required to satisfy itself that the potential licence holder is in a position to ensure that conditions attached to the licence are fulfilled, and to visit premises before granting a licence.

24.   In connection with its licensing function the SLA will have powers to determine the form in which applications should be made and the information which should be submitted; to charge fees subject to the approval of the Secretary of State; to inspect premises and facilities used in the provision of regulated infertility services; and to carry out any investigations which it considers necessary. Powers of entry will be provided for authorised staff of the SLA, enabling them to enter premises where they have reasonable grounds to believe a criminal offence has been committed; and to carry out inspections and remove material from the premises.

25.   Decisions about licence applications will be taken by the Authority itself on the advice of its officers. The SLA will have powers to vary, revoke, suspend or review any licence if it reasonably believes the conditions of the licence have been breached, or false information has been given by the licence holder; or at the holder's request. It will be required, if it intends to exercise these powers or to refuse a licence, to give notice to the licence holder concerned who will have the right to make representations to the authority. There will also be provision for appeals against the decisions of the SLA, probably to an independent panel appointed by Ministers. In cases of urgency the SLA will be empowered to suspend a licence for up to three months by giving notice to the holder.

26.   The SLA will have a duty to draw up a Code of Practice on the provision of regulated infertility services, which would be laid before Parliament. The Code might include guidelines for screening of donors; obtaining consent from patients and donors; use of stored gametes and embryos; counselling; and appropriate training and experience for medical and nursing staff. Failure to comply with the Code without reasonable excuse would be a ground for variation or revocation of a licence.

27.   The Government accepts that a mandatory licensing system needs to be backed up by effective sanctions. It will be a criminal offence to bring into existence, use or store a human embryo outside the body without an appropriate licence from the SLA. Similarly, it will be forbidden to use gametes donated by a third party to create, by artificial means, an embryo inside the body (eg using techniques such as AID or GIFT) without an appropriate licence from the SLA. It will also be a criminal offence for a person knowingly to furnish false or misleading information for the purpose of obtaining, or assisting another person in obtaining, a licence.

In the State of Victoria in Australia there already exists a complex statutory framework. As Professor Waller writes in in 'Making Law for Laboratory Life in Australia' (cited *infra* p 684), the Infertility (Medical Procedures) Act 1984:

 ... establishes a comprehensive framework for the regulation of *in vitro* fertilisation procedures. It does so by providing that such procedures, in every instance, may only be carried out in a hospital approved by the Minister of Health, may only be carried out in respect of a married couple, and may only be done when the couple has already had infertility treatment for twelve months beforehand, and has received approved counselling about the procedure. The provisions relating to the giving, the recording and the withdrawal of consent, especially in relation to the donation of gametes, are sensitively and carefully drawn and accompany those provisions stipulating the establishment of meticulous record keeping procedures in approved hospitals. These are, in their turn, the sources of the information which must be transmitted for storage in the Central Register.

. . . it contains several provisions regulating donor insemination. It restricts the practice to doctors or persons within approved hospitals. It prescribes counselling for the couple. It requires doctors who perform AID to keep records. Where a live birth results, the doctor shall provide details of the birth, and of the sperm donor involved, to the Health Department.

The Government's White Paper raises the issue of the criminal law. Do you think the Warnock Report adequately addresses this question? What role ought the criminal law to play? Mary Warnock in her book *A Question of Life* (Introductory Chapter) considers this issue:

The relation between morality and the law has been a central issue in jurisprudence for very many years. There is a distinction between the way we approached this issue in the two parts of our report, that concerned with the treatment of infertility and that concerned with research. If the question is what measures to remedy infertility should be permitted in this country, the problem may be put in the following form: Why should the law intervene to prevent people using whatever methods are possible to enable them to have children? Why should not everybody be entitled to whatever is currently the best and most efficient treatment for infertility? The issues here are quite closely parallel to the issues raised in the 1960s by the Wolfenden Report on homosexuality between consenting males. Ought the law to intervene to make such conduct criminal or ought it not? The famous view of Lord Devlin (*The Enforcement of Morals*, Oxford, 1959) was that where there is a consensus of opinion against a certain practice among members of the general public (exemplified by the notorious 'man on the Clapham omnibus') then the law must intervene to prevent conduct which is repellent to that public. A shared moral view, Lord Devlin argued, was the cement that bound society together. If such shared views were not reflected in law, if law did not enforce what society held to be morally right and wrong, then society itself would disintegrate. A society is characterised by a shared moral view; without it there would be no society. Therefore to act against such a shared view would be tantamount to treason. The law could no more permit acts contrary to the shared morality than it could permit treason.

The drawback with Devlin's view is that, increasingly, we are compelled to accept that 'common morality' is a myth. There is no agreed set of principles which everyone, or the majority, or any representative person, believes to be absolutely binding, and especially is this so in areas of moral concern which are radically and genuinely new. We saw that the concept of a 'rule' breaks down, in novel and hitherto unthought-of cases, and the notion that there is a consensus morality in such cases is equally untenable. The question must be recast: In situations where people disagree with each other as to the rights and wrongs of a specific form of behaviour, how do we decide whether or not the law is to intervene?

H L A Hart (*Law, Liberty and Morality*, Oxford, 1963) identified two moral problems, one 'primary' and the other 'critical'. At the first level the question is whether a certain practice (homosexual acts between consenting males, or AID) is morally right or wrong; at the second level the question is whether, if the law intervened on this matter, the infringement of liberty involved would itself be morally right or wrong. If we consider a case that concerned the Inquiry, the case of AID, it is plain that moral opinions about it vary through the whole spectrum, from those who think it absolutely wrong (like members of the Jewish Community, who think that it is 'bringing orphans into the world', and therefore necessarily wrong) through those who are doubtful, because of the possible risk to AID children, to those who regard it as an absolute right that anyone should have access to AID, whether they are married or single, hetero- or homosexual.

Furthermore, any law enacted to render AID a criminal offence, besides going against the moral views of a fair number of the community, would involve, in itself, a disagreeable intrusiveness, for AID is something that can relatively easily be carried out at home, without any medical intervention. For a law to be enforceable, there would need to be a band of snoopers or people ready to pry into the private lives of others, which might well itself constitute a moral wrong.

Similarly, in the controversial matter of surrogate mothers, the Inquiry agreed unanimously that they disapproved of the practice (largely because of possible consequences for the child); but they also agreed that it could not be prevented by law, because of the intrusiveness of any law that would be enforceable. The Inquiry therefore concentrated on how surrogacy for commercial purposes might be checked, leaving on one side the question whether surrogacy was intrinsically morally right or wrong. We might all of us have answered the primary moral question in a way which made surrogacy wrong. This did not pre-empt the answer to the second-order moral question, Should the law be invoked to stop surrogacy? We all agreed that it would be morally wrong to envisage a law which would intrusively curtail human freedom, and which would in addition be impossible to enforce (how could the law tell whether the child whom Abraham claimed as his own was born to Sara, or to a servant girl who happened to be more fertile?) The Inquiry, then, while unanimously answering the first-order question negatively, holding that surrogacy was wrong, nevertheless held that legislation should not be invoked to prevent it. We did however by a majority recommend that the commercial use of surrogacy arrangements, as a way of making money for an agency, could and should be made a criminal offence. For not only was the wrongness of surrogacy compounded by its being exploited for money, but also a law against agencies would not be intrusive into the private lives of those who were actually engaged in setting up a family.

. . . in some cases it was necessary to distinguish the issue of moral right or wrong, as we saw it, from a further, also moral question, whether it would be right to enforce a moral view, even if such a view were agreed. There was, however, a more testing kind of question, infinitely more important, in my opinion. This was the question of research using human embryos. . . . No-one felt inclined to argue that the decision whether or not to embark on research with the use of human embryos was a matter of personal conscience, as they might in the case of AID, surrogacy, or, for that matter, homosexuality between adults. Everyone agreed that this was a matter on which there must be legislation, and that whether and to what extent embryos should be used must be a decision for the law.

The reason for this uncertainty, for the distinction, that is, between what might be thought a private matter and one which was *necessarily* public was somewhat obscure. Nor did the Inquiry draw the distinction explicitly or clearly. But the grounds for it are something like this: research is largely publicly funded. Therefore society, from whom ultimately funding comes, is entitled to know, and even to some extent to control, what research methods are used. . . . There is a strong feeling that certain possible experiments and research should be subject to criminal law and made a criminal offence, wherever undertaken. . . .

All members of the Committee wanted the criminal law to be invoked in this matter.

Do you think Baroness Warnock satisfactorily distinguishes between invocation of the law and the *criminal* law? The use of the criminal law as a regulatory mechanism in this area is considered by Professor A T H Smith in 'Warnock and After: The Legal and Moral Issues Surrounding Embryo Experimentation' in *Medicine, Ethics and Law* (ed M Ockelton), (Proceedings of the Association of Legal and Social Philosophy Thirteenth Annual Conference 1986); footnotes omitted:

The criminal law is one of society's bluntest instruments; it is the institution that society employs to inflict deliberate harm on its members. It would seem to me to follow that it should be employed only when its use is unmistakably called for.

. . .

On the use of the criminal law, Dame Mary observes that 'everyone [on the Committee] agreed that whether and to what extent embryos should be used must be a matter for law'. But there are respectable arguments for the view that, even if there are to be rules, they need not necessarily be criminal in character. It seems to me that the Committee has failed to distinguish clearly (or at all) between the regulatory and condemnatory functions of the law. Dame Mary argues that embryo experimentation should be brought within the ambit of the criminal law as follows:

> Society feels, albeit obscurely, that its members, especially the helpless, such as children and the very old, must be protected against possible exploitation by enthusiastic scientists; and embryos are brought into the category of those deserving protection, just as animals are. This is a matter of public, and widely shared, *sentiment* (italics original).

. . . The precise extent to which it is proper to use the criminal law to reinforce 'public' morality is of course, a very familiar debate, and many think that Professor H L A Hart (and before him John Stuart Mill) had the better of it. It is surprising, to say the least, to find one version of it being adduced in such a conclusory way.

A detailed examination of the issues and a proposal for regulation can be found in the Report of the Ontario Law Reform Commission (*op cit*) which we have already seen above (pp 102–3; 1014; 106–7; 118–30; footnotes omitted):

> In this chapter, the Commission has set forth the extent to which the common law, existing statutory and regulatory provisions, and professional rules of conduct may bear on the use and consequences of the new reproductive technologies in Ontario. At the outset, we cautioned that the 'law' in this area is, in a sense, astigmatic—in the main, ignoring or inadvertently applying to the various legal issues arising from the growth of artificial conception services. While the relatively recent advent of these services goes some distance to explain the present state of affairs, the novelty of at least some of the procedures is rapidly diminishing. As a consequence, hitherto reasonable explanations for the dearth of law in the area of artificial conception are beginning to wear thin.
>
> The Commission is quite aware . . . that the fact that legislation does not speak directly to a certain matter is not, in itself, a damning criticism necessitating immediate remedial action. Silence may well reflect continuing, deep-seated controversy, so that there may be a justifiable wish to permit the law to develop without legislative fetters. Even inadvertent solutions may be equitable responses— a manifestation of the capacity of the legal regime, created to deal with one set of circumstances, to grow and flourish in a new milieu.
>
> On the other hand, the Commission is acutely conscious of the pervasive notion in many circles that the dictates of medical science, when followed to their logical extremes, will lead inexorably to horrors hitherto characterised as fantasy or science fiction. The spectre of cloning, wholly 'test tube' babies, genetic engineering and manipulation—these and other fears frequently feed the view that the only proper response of the law in this area is prohibition and criminalisation.
>
> While, like others, we are seriously concerned about the nature and implications of certain types of medical and other related research and experimentation, we do not subscribe to this rather cataclysmic, certainly pessimistic, view. The automatic invocation of 'logical extremes' and 'worst case scenarios' is not, of course, unique to the present context. But, as a precept for action, these arguments must be viewed with extreme caution; they ought not to animate the proper reaction of the law to all developments in the field of medicine. Keeping pace with new and beneficial scientific advances does not thereby make the law an accomplice with regard to those facets of science unacceptable to the community. The law need not meekly trim its sails to accommodate such unwanted developments. Law and law reform comprehend more than merely wholesale endorsement or outright prohibition; as a manifestation of the perceived needs and wishes of the community, they can also, for example, limit or actively facilitate, encourage, or discourage certain kinds of

activity to one degree or another. The Commission's reaction to, and perception of, the present law and its adequacy, insofar as it relates to the new reproductive technologies, largely mirrors this more flexible approach to what we believe to be the proper role of the law in this area.

Some issues are of such fundamental importance to parents, children, and third parties that they no longer ought to be left to the uncertainties and vicissitudes of evolutionary legal development. Perhaps the most obvious example concerns the status of an artificially conceived child. Leaving aside the contentious issue of surrogate motherhood, should the law expressly acknowledge the social reality of a child conceived with the use of donor gametes, so that the social parents are recognised in law as the only parents? Or should the gamete donor, the biological parent, who is almost invariably, but not always, anonymous, be treated in law as a parent, with all the rights and responsibilities attendant upon such a role? Should the rules respecting birth registration further acknowledge the social realities and reflect the intentions and expectations of all the parties? Is society well served by legislation that basically ignores artificial conception in this context and even, occasionally, encourages subterfuge and prompts individuals to evade the strictures of the law, for example, by registering children to suit their own predilections? . . .

In relation to these technologies, the vision of the present law is uncomfortably out of focus; indeed, it simply has been overtaken by events. To a significant degree, the existing legal regime cannot escape the confines of the natural reproduction mould. And the search for doctrine that is even remotely relevant to the many serious, complex questions raised in the context of artificial conception involves arduous and generally fruitless legal circumnavigation around frequently foreign principles. It is this uncertainty in the legal implications of various activities— particularly, but not exclusively, in relation to status, parentage, and surrogate motherhood—that pervades the law and practice relating to the use of the new reproductive technologies. A broad cross-section of society, from lawyers to doctors, social workers, ethicists, and others, has decried the absence of clear legal rules to guide the actions of all persons participating, or wishing to participate, in artificial conception programmes. Accordingly, we believe that the law must be re-examined and refashioned. It must reflect the benefits of the new technologies and the reasonable hopes of infertile men and women, while at the same time guarding against those excesses perceived to be injurious to the fabric of society. . . . we are constrained to caution against any wholesale abandonment of the view that the law may, and should, act as a progressive, normative guide, not simply a reflection of present community standards. When we consider state intervention in the case of the new reproductive technologies, we may view the issue, at least in part, as a privacy matter. And when the law deals with matters of personal privacy, it frequently swings its pendulum in favour of individual interests. This issue of personal privacy is critical to our study, and any wish on the part of a segment of society to constrict or limit the ability of individuals to choose whatever method they wish to bring a child into the family, and to regularise their relationship with that child, must be balanced against the human costs attending such intervention. The law may reflect the community's level of tolerance; but it may also stretch or fashion it in the interests of a worthy goal.

For the purpose of our conceptual analysis in this chapter, we shall differentiate between two fundamental approaches to reform, representing the two extreme points on what is clearly a continuum. One basic approach we shall term the 'private ordering' approach, where the legal regime is designed to give effect to the intentions of the parties. The other basic approach we shall call the 'state regulation' approach, where the free choice of the parties does not determine what they may do or the consequences of their actions, but where the state actively intervenes to set mandatory normative standards of conduct. With the latter approach, there are certain ancillary matters that must be addressed. For example, how should the state attempt to persuade people to comply with the rules of behaviour to which adherence is deemed essential?

It bears mentioning here that the so-called private ordering model—exemplified, for example, in the case of one's choice to conceive children by natural reproduction—does not necessarily eschew legislative initiatives. Statutory provisions may indeed be required to give effect to, or preclude interference with, the wishes of individuals. This type of legislation differs from that contemplated by the state intervention approach in its essentially facultative animus: it does not, in effect, tell people what to do or not to do, but serves to facilitate their activities where necessary.

We also wish to note that the two basic approaches set forth in this chapter represent conceptual paradigms of how the law might deal with reproductive choices and their consequences. Accordingly, they each provide a theoretical model against which we may measure the kind of legal regime that ought to govern our conduct. However, a consideration of these general approaches is but one stage in the development of our proposals for reform: it is necessary to determine whether this macroscopic approach to law reform—where all aspects of the subject matter are governed by the same broad conceptual approach—is appropriate in the context of artificial conception. Indeed, it may become clear that the special characteristics of the various artificial reproduction technologies, or certain facets of these technologies, must be dealt with differently. In other words, the legal regime governing such matters need not necessarily be uniform and all-embracing; rather, a more flexible approach, sensitive to the requirements of different aspects of the problem in different ways, may be desirable. Such a hybrid approach may, then, marry aspects of the private ordering and state regulation approaches, and even leave room for common law evolution and for the development of normative guidelines outside the Legislature. . . .

In chapter 3 of this Report, the Commission came to the conclusion that the law must take special cognisance of the new artificial conception technologies. In the present chapter, we have examined two main conceptual approaches to law reform in this area, the state regulation approach and the private ordering approach.

When attempting to assess which of the two approaches ought to be adopted in the case of artificial reproduction—or, indeed, whether some hybrid approach is preferable—the models of natural reproduction and adoption immediately spring to mind. More specifically, we inevitably come face to face with a general, fundamental question: should the law treat artificial reproduction differently than the manner in which it treats natural reproduction, at least insofar as the decision to conceive a child is concerned? If the private ordering approach is eschewed in favour of the state regulation approach in the case of artificial reproduction, on what basis is such a determination to be made? . . .

However, while no one can legitimately assume to speak for all segments of the community on so controversial a topic as artificial reproduction, the Commission can attempt to give serious consideration to the conflicting views presented to us directly or gleaned from the increasingly voluminous literature. Our proposals for reform, then, are based on our perception of prevailing community standards, however amorphous they may appear to be, and our view of what members of the community appear to want or be willing to tolerate. Without slavishly and uncritically adopting such standards, they do serve to indicate how members of society believe we ought to be governed. We cannot simply ignore prevailing views, in a sense placing ourselves above the community, enlightening it concerning the 'best' ordering of society. In the area of human conception, whether natural or artificial, it would be presumptuous to take such licence.

Having regard to the considerations just described, we have come to the conclusion that the law must impose a degree of intervention in the case of artificial conception that is neither desirable nor possible in the case of natural reproduction. The wishes of the parties—particularly, the desire of the prospective social parents to have a child—are, in fact, only one of many considerations that should affect the determination of the nature of the new legal regime. Given the implications of artificial conception for persons other than the prospective parents, we strongly believe that 'private ordering' cannot be the sole governing factor. In our view, there are sound philosophical and practical reasons for embracing, at least in some areas, an approach that does not give free rein to the wishes of the parties. . . .

Having concluded that, under certain circumstances, the state ought to intervene in respect of artificial conception in the interest of broader societal values, several subsidiary, but no less critical, questions arise. For example, to what extent and in respect of what activities, if any, should such intervention take the form of either outright prohibition or regulation? If regulation is desirable in respect of any or all of the activities in question, how should the guiding norms be set, and who should set and apply them?

(a) Prohibition or regulation?

We turn first to consider the two forms by which limits may be placed on an individual's private activities, namely, prohibition and regulation. It should first be made clear that the law need not necessarily adopt only one of these two interventionist means. While clearly a wholesale prohibition respecting the use of artificial conception services would leave nothing to regulate, it is entirely reasonable to envisage a legal regime in which some aspects of the new technologies are prohibited, some are strictly controlled, and some are the subject of minimal regulation.

For example, one might wish to prohibit minors from donating ova for use in IVF programmes because extraction of ova may involve surgical intrusion and because a woman's complement of ova is finite. One might believe it essential to prohibit all forms of what may be termed 'genetic engineering', but countenance research at approved or licensed research centres that have ethical review committees to oversee such activities. Or some latitude might be tolerated in respect of payment of semen donors of their reasonable expenses.

The list of possible permutations and combinations involving prohibition and regulation could easily be expanded. But the essential point is that our perception of the different facets of the subject matter should not be static or rigid; we must be open to the suggestion that a hybrid regime, in which a spectrum of responses, from total prohibition to slight regulation, may be both desirable and possible.

The determination of where specific activities ought to be placed on this spectrum—and not left to the unfettered discretion of individuals—is influenced by several more or less obvious factors. As we indicated in the Introduction to this chapter, matters of logic almost inevitably mix with basic human fears and emotions to produce in each of us a sense of what we may be willing or able to tolerate. The spectre of cloning or experimental genetic manipulation may well be anathema to almost everyone in the community, so that a doctrinaire stance—outright prohibition—may be palatable. But, in other areas, consensus may be difficult, even impossible, to achieve. For example, there has been a continuing debate concerning whether adopted children ought to be entitled to have access to information respecting their natural parents, a debate that arises as well in the context of artificial conception where 'anonymous' donor gametes are used. Rational reasons favouring disclosure vie with concerns respecting the possible emotional reactions of the various parties. And so, insofar as adoption law in Ontario is concerned, we have moved slowly away from an extreme posture of secrecy to a regulated access regime.

Aside from assessing the necessity for, or desirability of, either prohibition or some type of regulation based on the particular attributes of each activity, it must be borne in mind that complete prohibition or strict regulation, however justifiable in the abstract, may produce evasion, especially by the desperate or more affluent, who may seek to obtain services in more accommodating jurisdictions. And such violation of the law may well be seen as legitimate in the eyes of the majority or a substantial minority of the population.

But the danger of evasion as such is not the only problem respecting strict punitive measures directed at certain activities. For example, given the relative simplicity of the artificial insemination procedure, its prohibition or strict control may encourage laypersons to perform the insemination on themselves and others, without medical supervision. In other words, this type of artificial reproduction may be driven underground, away from physicians who have the requisite skills and knowledge to prevent or remedy any medical complications that may arise in the recipient or child.

In the case of surrogate motherhood, it is clear that key medical, legal, and other services are available—and have been delivered, to our knowledge, on at least one occasion—outside Ontario to Ontario residents, largely because of the perceived, and correct, view that surrogate motherhood agreements are not enforceable in this Province. Again, attempted suppression does not necessarily result in the elimination of the activity, but may create more perils than anticipated. Indeed, one of the dangers of any prohibition of artificial conception is that it may prejudicially affect children conceived in this fashion. We have already seen that the present law deals only inadvertently with such critical issues as the legal status of an artificially conceived child.

There are, then, important human and other costs of prohibition that must be weighed in the balance before seeking to render a particular practice illegal, even though it may be deemed not to be worthy of any active protection. As in the case of our choice between state regulation and private ordering as a general approach to law reform in this area, these factors have led us to the conclusion that a hybrid regime is both necessary and desirable. Such a regime most adequately reflects the complexity of the subject and the differing norms that, we believe, ought to govern different aspects of each of the new technologies.

(b)   The instruments of regulation

Assuming the adoption of a regulatory approach, at least for some purposes, a second set of issues concerns the particular instruments of regulation. Who should set the requisite standards, how should they be set, and who should apply them? Again, there are several alternative approaches to the resolution of these questions.

The establishment of norms governing conduct may be left to the Legislature, by means of legislation, to the courts, through the development of common law principles, to governmental or other tribunals, to professional bodies, such as the College of Physicians and Surgeons of Ontario, or to a combination of such institutions. In some cases, a statute or regulation may set a standard to be applied by the medical profession itself. In other cases, legislation may be monitored and interpreted by an administrative body or by the courts. Again, there is no universal rule; the particular combination selected in respect of the establishment and application of normative guides depends on several factors, including the type of the particular activity in question and the nature and extent of the control sought.

Regulation need not, of course, take the form of formal, written norms emanating from some body specifically charged with developing applicable guidelines, for example, the Legislature or even the College of Physicians and Surgeons of Ontario (by means of rules of professional conduct). Regulation of conduct may take place incrementally, through the medium of the courts. The courts, utilising existing common law or developing new rules, may either interpret or add glosses on legislation or written guidelines from some other source, or may deal with controversial issues in respect of which there is no universal social policy or consensus and, hence, no "legislated" philosophy.

Courts may, for example, exercise a valuable role in determining such issues as the standard of care that is to be applied by practitioners of artificial conception, and whether institutions such as clinics and hospitals, through their infertility units, bear responsibility for their practitioners' negligence. The advantage of leaving such matters to judicial development is that such development will occur within a generalised jurisprudence, and not be, without justification, distinctive or anomalous to artificial conception.

Further, regarding the establishment of the requisite standard of care, court decisions in some cases may reflect developments in the state of the reproductive art as they occur, unfettered by a legislated or regulated framework that may become based upon outmoded techniques or discredited practices. This may be particularly important, since artificial conception technologies are still evolving and many variations in clinical practice exist, the relative advantages of which have yet to be determined by properly conducted studies. A legislated scheme that embodies any particular practice may give undue preference to a procedure that proves to be no better than others and possibly worse, and may inhibit development of superior alternatives. Courts may well compel the raising of standards by finding that the existing practice—for example, on screening gamete donors for adverse genetic traits or venereal infection—does not satisfy legal requirements respecting the standard of care.

It has been observed that "[t]he most ethically and politically controversial aspect of IVF is the status of the embryo'. A legislated solution to this controversy would be of far-reaching effect, and would have implications for many areas of the law. A judicial approach would define the fact situations in which a particular judicial decision is to apply, and the purposes for which a given solution is designed. Judicial explanation, which itself may undergo several reinterpretations, may be preferable to the structured and traditional language of legislation to say within what limits a particular resolution is to operate.

However, a difficulty with entrusting matters to the courts is that, in some cases, they may adhere to precedents that are not related to advances in artificial conception technologies. Judgments may continue to embody public policy perceptions conditioned by the supposition that conception results only from sexual intercourse, or, perhaps at some future time, that artificial conception results only from artificial insemination or IVF, or a particular mode of artificial conception. The early disposition to equate AID with adultery shows how judicial attitudes, while perhaps understandable in one era, may become and remain part of the problem in another era, which legislation may be required to resolve. Courts may take strict and limiting views, for instance, regarding the inheritance rights of a child not genealogically related to a testator, such as the parent of a husband whose wife had the child by AID, when the testator made a bequest to the husband and the 'heirs of his body'.

There is, however, a dynamic interaction between legislation and judicial attitudes, since courts tend to note the thrust of legislative initiatives, and often take leads from them. If legislation were enacted specifically to accommodate all or certain types of artificial conception, for instance, it might be unlikely that the courts would regard agreements made in furtherance of such particular conceptions as void as against public policy. Courts may, of course, decline to admit a new kind of claim, on the ground that the matter raises a significant issue of public policy that should be tackled by the Legislature before a solution is incorporated into the law by the courts; and they may similarly feel that private arrangements regarding sensitive areas, such as surrogate motherhood agreements, should be approved by an Act of the Legislature rather than by a court. Once generally accommodating legislation has been passed, however, the courts may find such legislation to be an expression of public acceptance or tolerance in which they may find inspiration and direction.

It is never certain, on the other hand, that courts will follow the lead of legislation, or interpret, apply, or extend its provisions in a collaborative way. Judges may hesitate to go further than recent legislation, reasoning that, had the Legislature intended its scheme to embrace an additional step, it would have so provided, and that its failure so to provide is evidence of a contrary intention. For avoidance of doubt, legislation may have to be drafted comprehensively in order to address foreseeable areas of possible application. Oversights and issues beyond anticipation may then have to be left to the courts, but the legislative design may, in principle, aim to be all-embracing, as a self-contained and definitive code.

Alternatively, it may not be necessary to resolve every detail in order to achieve legislation that is sufficiently comprehensive to address a given issue. Depending on the particular issue, minimal legislation may be enacted, fashioning the critical skeleton of a new policy, but leaving the developed form to be supplied by an emerging jurisprudence. Legislation also may properly be structured in order to anticipate and accommodate further developments in related case law, without seeking to affect its direction. If the case law fails to develop, or follows an unsatisfactory direction, the Legislature always retains its residual power to supplement or supersede judgments.

In the same way that certain matters may be left to be resolved by the courts, other matters may best be resolved according to medical professional ethics, bearing in mind that the practice of medicine may include artificial conception and, accordingly, that such a practice may be undertaken only by doctors or persons under their supervision or direction.

We have seen that the Legislature has granted the College of Physicians and Surgeons of Ontario wide powers of self-government. Among other things, the College may regulate the practice of medicine and establish standards of knowledge, skill, qualification, and practice among members. In addition, the College may set ethical standards for doctors.

Having regard to the fact that the statutory mandate of the College is exercised 'in order that the public interest may be served and protected', it is not surprising that persons who are authorised to practise medicine by the College are subject to compulsory discipline for professional misconduct. 'Professional misconduct' is defined in regulations made under the *Health Disciplines Act*, primarily in collaboration with the provincial Ministry of Health. The list of activities constituting professional misconduct tends to be specific, but a residual category exists for 'conduct or an act relevant to the practice of medicine that, having regard to all the circumstances, would reasonably be regarded by members as disgraceful, dishonourable or unprofessional'.

The College of Physicians and Surgeons of Ontario conscientiously consults with those whom it regulates and with the wider community beyond, in the process of formulating its ethical position on various matters, and it is open to public and media comment and ministerial influence. It may strike committees to address particular issues and may involve non-professionals in its deliberations and recommendations. Accordingly, it may reflect an ethical consensus with considerable credibility, although it may be expected that the opinions of the professionals it regulates, who are also strongly represented on the governing council, will be heard with special clarity.

The College periodically updates its principles of ethical practice, and contributes to public education and discussion concerning such principles. It attempts to respond to past events and to anticipate future possibilities, so that practitioners generally are offered guidance when they contemplate innovative practices. Further, unlike courts of law, the College will accommodate requests from doctors for *ad hoc* ethical rulings based upon hypotheses and anticipated scenarios. Its familiarity with the realities of practice and its access to scientific and technical data may afford its judgments a conviction that more abstract theorising may lack.

Contributions to the debate on the ethics of professional practice may come through initiatives of many organisations other than the provincial College. The views of responsible bodies, such as the Medical Research Council, may be of significance regarding, for example, research concerning the use of gametes and embryos. Moreover, the reports of governmental agencies or professional bodies in Canada and around the world can be expected to be seriously considered. Professional ethical principles may, therefore, be informed by a variety of national and international considerations that may influence perceptions of what provincial ethical practice requires. Inasmuch as the ethical assessments of the College of Physicians and Surgeons of Ontario may draw from the same body of knowledge that would be relevant to the design of statutes or regulations, such assessments may serve equally to control conduct within the medical profession, and may even enjoy the greater confidence and sympathetic compliance of individual physicians.

Accordingly, it is possible to leave some matters unaddressed by statute, to be determined by authorised practitioners acting under professional guidance. Practitioners are accountable both through the courts, for the injuries they wrongfully cause to individuals they have a legal duty to protect, and through their professional disciplinary councils, for breach of ethical rules, professional misconduct, or falling below the established standards of their profession. Further, while legislation may be introduced to govern such activities as research, it may be equally appropriate, and perhaps preferable, to confine sensitive research, such as research on embryos, to special centres that maintain credible ethical screening of research proposals through institutional review boards, and that undertake departmental and other monitoring of clinical and research practices.

An advantage of this approach to the control of individual medical practice is that it would utilise existing personnel, institutions, and established mechanisms, whereas new regulatory legislation might require a policing and enforcement service that might be less than comprehensive, costly, and poorly received among professionals conscious of their responsibilities. By the same token, some may argue that professionals are generally too socially conservative, health professionals in particular having been suspected of undue paternalism in pursuing patients' perceived interests rather than patients' expressed wishes. These and other advantages and disadvantages that attach to the control of artificial conception through medical and related professional guidelines must be balanced against the advantages and disadvantages of seeking control through express legislation.

In light of the Commission's philosophy and previous conclusions respecting the appropriate approach to law reform in the case of the new reproductive technologies and respecting the nature of the limits that should be placed on an individual's private actions, it should come as no surprise that, in the present context, we once again eschew a dogmatic approach that would require uniform treatment to be provided in all cases. We believe that some matters—clearly those that involve outright prohibition of certain activities—necessitate statutory control. Other matters, setting out procedural details or licensure requirements, may be left to the regulations. And yet further matters, involving essentially medical judgment or involving ethical issues relating to the conduct of physicians, may be determined by the medical profession, either formally or informally. In all, or most, of these cases, recourse may well be had to the courts to interpret legislation or relevant codes of ethics or professional conduct.

As we have seen, the Government produced a White Paper in November 1987 advocating a statutory licensing system based upon a Statutory Licensing Authority. Legislation is, therefore, probably inevitable. As yet, however, no legislation has been introduced by the Government.

(iii) LEGAL ISSUES

While it is true that many of the *moral* arguments identified in the Warnock Report still give rise for concern for some people, IVF as a medical procedure to alleviate infertility poses few *legal* problems. Instead, it is some of the more involved forms of IVF (such as egg and embryo donation) and the procedures connected with IVF, the aim of which is to develop it further for an understanding of infertility generally (such as embryo experimentation), which pose the legal problems.

(a) IVF (simpliciter)

By this, we mean IVF as, for example, defined in section 10(1) of the Victorian statute in Australia, the Infertility (Medical Procedures) Act 1984 as:

> ... the procedure of implanting in the womb of a woman an embryo derived from an ovum produced by her and fertilised outside her body by semen produced by her husband.

Providing both partners consent and the procedure is not performed negligently, the procedure would appear to give rise to no legal complications particular to the procedure.

(b) IVF (sperm donation)

By this we mean, IVF as, for example, defined in section 11(1) of the same Victorian Infertility (Medical Procedures) Act 1984 as:

... the procedure of implanting in the womb of a woman an embryo derived from an ovum produced by her and fertilised outside her body by semen produced by a man other than her husband.

Does this raise the same issue as AID namely, who in law is to be regarded as the father? Has section 27 of the Family Law Reform Act 1987 (*supra* at p 624) resolved this? (*Note*: the point is specifically dealt with in the equivalent Victorian legislation in Australia which covers 'artificial insemination or the implantation of an embryo in the body of a woman' where the sperm has been donated. The Status of Children (Amendment) Act 1984 amending the Status of Children Act 1974 provides as follows:

10D. (1) A reference in this section to a procedure is a reference to the procedure of implanting in the womb of a woman an embryo derived from an ovum produced by her and fertilised outside her body by semen produced by a man other than her husband.

(2) Where a married woman, in accordance with the consent of her husband, has undergone a procedure as a result of which she has become pregnant—
  (a) the husband shall be presumed, for all purposes, to have produced the semen used for the fertilisation of the ovum used in the procedure and to be the father of any child born as the result of the pregnancy; and
  (b) the man who produced the semen used for the fertilisation of the ovum used in the procedure shall, for all purposes, be presumed not to have produced that semen and not to be the father of any child born as the result of the pregnancy.

(3) A presumption of law that arises by virtue of subsection (2)—
  (a) is irrebuttable; and
  (b) prevails over any conflicting presumption that arises by virtue of section 8 or 10.

(4) In any proceedings in which the operation of subsection (2) is relevant, a husband's consent to the carrying out of a procedure in respect of his wife shall be presumed but that presumption is rebuttable.

(c) IVF (egg donation)

By this we mean IVF defined as, for example, in section 12(1) of the (Victorian) Infertility (Medical Procedures) Act 1984, as:

... the procedure of implanting in the womb of a woman (in this section called 'the patient') an embryo derived from an ovum produced by another woman (in this section called 'the donor') and fertilised outside the body of the patient and outside the body of the donor by semen produced by the husband of the patient.

The problem here is, who in law is the mother? A number of options present themselves.

1.   The AID analogy

One solution is to draw an analogy with AID. This view would regard the woman who donated the egg as the mother of the resulting child in law, just as the man who donated the sperm would, under the common law, be the father.

2.   The Warnock view

The Warnock Report, para 6.8 reads as follows:

6.8 Egg donation produces for the first time circumstances in which the genetic mother (the woman who donates the egg), is a different person from the woman who gives birth to the child, the carrying mother. The law has never, till now, had to face this problem. There are inevitably going to be instances where the stark issue arises of who is the mother. In order to achieve some certainty in this situation it is our view that where a woman donates an egg for transfer to another the donation should be treated as absolute and that, like a male donor she should have no rights or duties with regard to any resulting child. **We recommend that legislation should provide that when a child is born to a woman following donation of another's egg the woman giving birth should, for all purposes, be regarded in law as the mother of that child, and that the egg donor should have no rights or obligations in respect of the child.** We also consider that as with AID . . . , if the parents so wish, the mother's name may be followed in the birth register by the words 'by donation'.

3. The Government's responses

The DHSS Consultation Paper in 1986, at first sight, endorses the Warnock view. Nevertheless, it goes on to state that 'views are invited'. Does this mean that the AID option is still alive? Subsequently, in the 1987 White Paper, the Government accepted the Warnock view. Legislation would make it clear that the 'carrying mother' was the child's mother and that the donor had no parental rights (para 88).

4. Victorian law in Australia

The Status of Children (Amendment) Act 1984 amending the principal Act of 1974 provides as follows:

10E (1) A reference in this section to a procedure is a reference to the procedure of implanting in the womb of a woman an embryo derived from an ovum produced by another woman, being an ovum that has been fertilised by—
(a) semen produced by the husband of the first-mentioned woman; or
(b) semen produced by a man other than the husband of the first-mentioned woman.

(2) Where a married woman, in accordance with the consent of her husband, has undergone a procedure as a result of which she has become pregnant
(a) the married woman shall be presumed, for all purposes, to have become pregnant as a result of the fertilisation of an ovum produced by her and to be the mother of any child born as the result of the pregnancy;
(b) the woman who produced the ovum from which the embryo used in the procedure was derived shall be presumed, for all purposes, not to be the mother of any child born as a result of the pregnancy;
(c) where the semen used for the fertilisation of the ovum from which the embryo used in the procedure was derived was produced by the husband of the married woman, the husband shall be presumed, for all purposes, to be the father of any child born as the result of the pregnancy; and
. . .
(4) In any proceedings in which the operation of subsection (2) is relevant, a husband's consent to the carrying out of a procedure in respect of his wife shall be presumed but that presumption is rebuttable.

Perhaps for the first time reading the Victorian legislation draws our attention to a distinction that is not clearly made elsewhere. This is the distinction between egg donation to a woman who is married and to one who is unmarried. In part the legislation and Warnock recognise the problem and provide a partial solution by regarding the unmarried woman in a stable relationship with a man as if she were married. The Status of Children (Amendment) Act 1984 amending the principal Act of 1974, provides:

10A (1) A reference in this Part to a married woman includes a reference to a woman who is living with a man as his wife on a *bona fide* domestic basis although not married to him.

This, however, leaves unsolved the problem of who is the mother when there is egg donation to the unmarried woman who is not living in a stable relationship with a man. The Victorian legislation solves the problem by making it an offence to carry out such a procedure on this class of unmarried women. Would such legislation be desirable in England? If it were not passed what would be the response of English law to the case of the unmarried woman who had no stable relationship with a man and underwent a procedure involving egg donation (even if this is unlikely as a matter of fact)? It cannot be the law that neither the donor of the ovum nor the woman who bore the child is the mother. This, however, would be the result if the response of the law to AID (in s 27 of the 1987 Act) was exactly mirrored here.

Thus, the commonsense view must be that the gestational mother is the mother for all legal purposes. Do we need legislation for this? Is it not ironic that traditionally we have regarded the donation of sperm as more of a transaction involving a commodity than egg donation. Yet, the sperm donor (prior to s 27 of the 1987 Act) theoretically was still in law regarded as having obligations, while the egg donor appears to be free of them.

(d)   IVF (embryo donation)

By this we mean, IVF, as defined, for example, in section 13(1) of the Infertility (Medical Procedures) Act 1984 as:

> . . . the procedure of implanting in the womb of a woman (in this section called 'the patient') an embryo derived from an ovum produced by another woman (in this section called 'the donor') and fertilised outside the body of the patient and outside the body of the donor by semen produced by a man other than the husband of the patient.

We choose to define embryo donation in this way so as properly to distinguish it from egg donation. The difference lies in the identity of the donor of the sperm and is made so as to allow for more careful analysis. By contrast, Warnock tends to use the two terms interchangeably while purporting to regard them as being different. The Warnock Committee approved 'in general' of embryo donation within the licensing system it recommended.

The two issues we need to consider are; who, in law, is the father and who, in law, is the mother of the child produced as a consequence of embryo donation?

1.   Who is the father?

For the married couple, as we have seen, as a matter of law, section 27 of the 1987 Act would seem to make the husband the father. This accords with the recommendations of the Warnock Committee in para 7.6 of the Report in the Victorian Legislation this point is put beyond doubt (Status of Children (Amendment) Act 1984 s 10E):

> 10E(2) (d)   where the semen used for fertilisation of the ovum from which the embryo used in the procedure was derived was produced by a man other than the husband of the married woman—
>> (i)   the husband shall be presumed, for all purposes, to have produced the semen and to be the father of any child born as the result of the pregnancy; and
>> (ii)   the man who produced the semen shall be presumed, for all purposes, not to have produced that semen and not to be the father of any child born as a result of the pregnancy.

For the unmarried couple we have seen that the Victorian solution is to regard them as if they were married if their relationship is a stable one. In English law, however, no such solution is possible without legislation and so under the common law the sperm donor would be the father even though he would be unidentifiable as a matter of fact. This would also be the legal analysis in Victoria if the procedure was carried out on an unmarried woman not in a stable relationship with a man.

2. Who is the mother?

The question of who, in law, is the mother of any child produced as a result of embryo donation involves precisely the same considerations as those set out above in relation to ova donation. The Warnock Committee recommended that the gestational mother should for all purposes in law be the mother, whether or not she is married. Again the Victorian legislation (Status of Children (Amendment) Act 1984) puts this beyond doubt in s 10E(2)(*a*) and (*b*) (see *infra* p 653). The Government in the 1987 White Paper proposes that legislation should make the 'carrying mother' the child's mother (as in egg donation) (para 88). Donors would be stripped of any parental rights they might otherwise have (*ibid*).

(iv) STATUS OF THE EMBRYO

The status of the embryo, as a matter of ethics, is fundamental to some of the issues we have already considered as it is to those that follow. The claims to protection that an embryo may make upon us clearly condition how we should respond to problems such as embryo donation, storage, disposition and the use of embryos for research purposes. If there be no law at present which clearly stipulates the status of an embryo, and if there be need for such law, any proposed law should reflect the conclusions of the ethical analysis of the status of the embryo.

(a) Is there any law?

The Warnock Report provides the following summary (paras 11.16—11.17):

11.16 We examined the current position of the *in vivo* embryo in law. The human embryo *per se* has no legal status. It is not, under law in the United Kingdom accorded the same status as a child or an adult, and the law does not treat the human embryo as having a right to life. However, there are certain statutory provisions that give some level of protection in various respects. The effect of the Offences Against the Person Act 1861, together with the Abortion Act 1967 (in Scotland the common law as amended by the Abortion Act 1967), is such that abortion is a criminal offence save in the circumstances provided for by the legislation. The Infant Life (Preservation) Act 1929 (which does not apply in Scotland) has as its purpose the protection of the life of a child capable of being born alive. Under civil law in England and Wales the Congenital Disabilities (Civil Liability) Act 1976 allows, in limited circumstances, damages to be recovered where an embryo or foetus has been injured *in utero* through the negligence of some third person. It is thus accorded a kind of retrospective status where it is born deformed or damaged as a result of injury. This Act does not apply in Scotland or Northern Ireland. The legal position at common law is thought to be similar in Scotland, although the law has yet to be tested. Thus, at present the law provides a measure of protection for the embryo *in vivo*. . . .

11.17 Although, therefore, the law provides a measure of protection for the human embryo *in vivo* it is clear that the human embryo under our definition of the term (1.4) is not, under the present law in the UK accorded the same status as a living child or an adult,

Do you agree with the above analysis? Do the provisions cited confer *protection* on the embryo? Professor Glanville Williams in his *Textbook of Criminal Law* (2nd ed 1983) in a footnote, at page 290, states the following:

> Suppose that a doctor, having fertilised an ovum in a test tube (*in vitro* in medical parlance), in order to produce a 'test-tube baby', finds that it will no longer be required, and throws it/him/her away. Is this murder? The embryo has not been 'born', but it has an existence independent of the mother, biologically it is alive, but is not legally alive if the law makes heart-beat the test! The sensible solution is to say that the embryo has not reached a sufficient stage of development to be 'a reasonable creature' within the law of homicide.

Perhaps the important word in the last sentence is 'sensible'. Professor Williams seems to be saying that it is unlikely that a judge would direct a jury in the world we live in, to return a verdict of murder on an admission by a doctor that he has destroyed a two cell embryo. We agree. [In *R v Tait* (1989) Times, 26 April, the Court of Appeal held that a five month old fetus could not be regarded in law as 'another person' for the purposes of section 16 of the offences against the Person Act 1861, making it an offence to make a threat, 'intending that [a person] would fear it would be carried out, to kill . . . a third person.' *A fortiori*, an embryo would not be a person for the purposes of the law of homicide.]

The only occasion on which the issue has been raised before a court is in the *Del Zio* case.

Del Zio v The Presbyterian Hospital

(US District Court for the Southern District of New York, 1978 (footnotes omitted)).

Stewart, District Judge: Plaintiffs, husband and wife, allege in their complaint that the defendants wrongfully caused plaintiff Mrs Del Zio severe emotional distress and tortiously damaged or converted personal property of plaintiffs. Plaintiff Dr Del Zio claims damages for loss of services and severe emotional distress. Defendants, who generally deny the allegations, are Presbyterian Hospital ('Presbyterian'), Dr Raymond L Vande Wiele ('Vande Wiele') and Trustee of Columbia University ('Columbia'). . . . Defendants have moved pursuant to Rule 50(b) of the Federal Rules of Civil Procedure to set aside the verdict for plaintiffs or for a new trial.

Most of the facts are undisputed. Mrs Del Zio had a child by a prior husband in 1963 and Dr Del Zio had two children by a prior marriage. The Del Zios, after their marriage in 1968, unsuccessfully tried to have children. In 1970, Mrs Del Zio learned that her fallopian tubes were blocked and Dr William Sweeney of New York Hospital, her physician, performed an operation to remove the blockage. It appeared to be successful, Mrs Del Zio became pregnant in October, 1970, but suffered a miscarriage in December, 1970. Two further operations on her fallopian tubes were performed by Dr Sweeney in 1971 and in 1972, each of which were unsuccessful.

In 1972, Dr Sweeney advised Mrs Del Zio of a procedure known as in vitro fertilisation, which would in effect by-pass her fallopian tubes. The procedure would involve preparing a culture which would include ova removed from Mrs Del Zio and semen obtained from Dr Del Zio and placing the culture in a test tube which would then be placed in an incubator to accomplish fertilisation. Thereafter, the fertilised ova would be reimplanted into Mrs Del Zio's uterus and, if all went well, she would become pregnant. Although the procedure had been successfully accomplished in animals, there was not known to be any prior successful attempt in man and Dr Sweeney so advised the Del Zios. He also advised the Del Zios that Dr Landrum Shettles of defendant Presbyterian Hospital who was experienced in the field of in vitro fertilisation would participate in the procedure. Dr Shettles was an attending obstetrician-gynecologist at Presbyterian and associate professor of clinical obstetrics and gynecology at College of Physicians and Surgeons of defendant Columbia; Dr Vande Wiele was his immediate supervisor in both capacities. The Del Zios decided to undergo the procedure and gave Dr Sweeney their consent.

On September 12, 1973, after a substantial period of preparation, the procedure was undertaken. Dr Sweeney removed the ova at New York Hospital, the ova was taken to Presbyterian Hospital where Dr Shettles obtained semen from Dr Del Zio, prepared the culture and placed it in an incubator (owned by defendant Columbia) at Presbyterian where it was to remain for four days.

The following day, September 13, 1973, defendant Vande Wiele learned of the test tube and its contents, ordered it removed from the incubator and brought to his office, and then had it placed in a deep freeze. These actions effectively terminated the procedure and destroyed the culture. At the time, Dr Vande Wiele was Chairman of the Department of Obstetrics and Gynecology at Columbia and Chief of the Obstetrical and Gynecological Service at Presbyterian. At the time Dr Vande Wiele gave instructions to remove the test tube and before it was brought to his office, he called Dr Tapley, then Acting Dean of the College of Physicians and Surgeons, the medical school of defendant Columbia, and Mr Alvin Binkert President and chief executive of Presbyterian. He advised each of them of what he was doing and each concurred that the procedure or experiment should be stopped. All of these events occurred between about eight and nine o'clock in the morning of September 13. Thereafter, Dr Vande Wiele called Dr Shettles and told him to come to his office at two o'clock in the afternoon. At that time, when Dr Shettles arrived in his office, Dr Vande Wiele informed Dr Shettles of the actions he had taken and the latter thereafter notified Sweeney.

Dr Sweeney testified that, because of the numerous operations on Mrs Del Zio's abdomen, he would not after the September 1973 operation perform any further such operations unless it were a matter of life or death and that he believed the 1973 operation was her last chance to become pregnant. After that operation, there was evidence that Mrs Del Zio suffered and continues to suffer substantial mental distress and that she was treated by a psychiatrist on a number of occasions over an extensive period of time. There was also evidence that Dr Del Zio had suffered emotional distress.

Our charge contained the following instructions:

As I mentioned, the first theory under which the plaintiffs claim is intentional infliction of emotional distress. One who intentionally or recklessly conducts himself toward another person in a manner so shocking and outrageous that it exceeds all bounds of decency, such person is liable to such other person for any resulting severe mental distress and consequential expenses.
...

The charge further stated, substantially as requested, the contentions of the parties as to this claim in considerable detail . . .

. . . [T]he plaintiffs contend that the conduct of Dr Vande Wiele in terminating the procedure without considering alternatives and without first informing Dr Shettles, Dr Sweeney or the plaintiffs constitutes extreme and outrageous conduct.

The plaintiffs further contend that absent an emergency and they contend that no emergency existed here, a medical procedure being performed in a hospital upon a patient by her physician at her express request and with her fully informed consent may not be terminated by a doctor at another institution unless that doctor first informs her physician of his intention and permits the patient's physician to exercise such alternatives that may be available to him to avoid termination of the procedure.

Plaintiffs further contend that it is no defense that the termination of the procedure may have appeared to be justified to the intervening doctor. Plaintiffs further contend that Dr Vende Wiele had a duty to inform Dr Shettles or Dr Sweeney of his intention to terminate the procedure. And to permit either of them to remove the culture from Columbia University to another place in order to avoid the termination.

The defendants . . . contend that Dr Vande Wiele's actions were reasonable and justified in light of his responsibilities as Chairman of the Department of Obstetrics and Gynecology at Columbia University and as Chief of Services of Obstetrics and Gynecology at Presbyterian Hospital. His obligation to insure that the proper standards of medical care prevailed in both the hospital and the university and his obligations as a physician [*sic*].

Further, the defendants contend that the in vitro experiment presented a substantial possibility of danger to the patient.

The defendants further contend the experiment represented an unwarranted practice which posed danger to any human life resulting from such experimentation and that the state of the art of *in vitro* fertilisation in September, 1973 offered no assurance against possible malformation and damage to any life resulting from such procedure.

The defendants further contend that Dr Vande Wiele knew that the procedure had not been cleared by any committees and review boards whose purpose at the hospital and the university was to adequately review proposed human experimentation. As such, the defendants contend that the Del Zio experiment was in violation of the rules of the Department of Obstetrics and Gynecology protecting subjects of human experimentation and insuring that such experiments are conducted in conformity with the highest standards of medical practice and in addition, was in violation of the assurance filed by the College of Physicians and Surgeons with the Department of Health, Education and Welfare promising that the University would comply with its guidelines concerning experimentation on human beings.

The defendants further contend that the experiment was carried out by individuals who had no competence to carry out such procedure and whose scientific methods were not sufficient in that there was no adequate protocol or notes which could insure proper review. And the defendants also contend that Dr Vande Wiele's supervisor at the hospital and the university specifically ordered that the experiments be stopped.

In assessing the reasonableness of the medical judgment exercised by Dr Vande Wiele, you may consider his duties and responsibilities as a physician and as Chairman of the Department of Obstetrics and Gynecology of Columbia and as Chief of the Obstetrical and Gynecological Service of Presbyterian and his medical judgment as to the procedures as reflected in the contentions I have just outlined, and the state of accepted medical knowledge and published medical literature, but only, as I have told you, that [which] in fact was available on or before September 13, 1973. You may not consider the articles published after September 1973 in considering whether Dr Vande Wiele acted reasonably in 1973.

As you may recall, there were certain articles admitted on post-1973 medical knowledge. I am sure you will remember what I told you, that these were admitted solely on the issue of whether the procedure followed by Dr Shettles and Dr Sweeney in 1973, in September, were scientifically sound, and cannot be considered by you in assessing the reasonableness of the medical judgment exercised at that time by Dr Vande Wiele.

With respect to the conversion theory, the jury was instructed:

> Now the second claim, conversion of property, broadly stated, one who, without authority, intentionally exercises control over the property of another and thereby interferes with the other's right of possession, is guilty of conversion and liable for the value of the property.
>
> . . .
>
> At the outset of their deliberations, the jury requested and were given copies of the charge.

After deliberating approximately 13 hours, the jury found for the plaintiffs on the first claim and awarded Mrs Del Zio 'the amount of $50,000 to be awarded in the amount of $12,500 from Presbyterian Hospital, $12,500 from Columbia University and $25,000 from Dr Raymond L Vande Wiele'. As to Dr Del Zio on this claim, the jury awarded him $3.00, one dollar from each defendant. The jury found for the defendants on the conversion claim.

Defendants have moved pursuant to Rule 50(b) of the Federal Rules of Civil Procedure, for judgment notwithstanding the verdict or for a new trial. The following arguments are made in support of these motions:

> 1. No reasonable juror could find that the defendants' conduct was 'so extreme, outrageous and shocking that it exceeded all reasonable bounds of decency'.
>
> 2. The verdict in favor of defendants on the cause of action for conversion is inconsistent with the verdict in favor of plaintiffs on the cause of action for intentional infliction of emotional distress.
>
> . . .

In addition, defendant Presbyterian contends that the verdict should be set aside because the defendants were prejudiced by adverse publicity, and because of the doctrine of *respondeat superior*. In opposition, plaintiffs ask that the motions be denied.

As to defendant's first contention, there was sufficient credible evidence from which the jury could reasonably find that plaintiffs had met their burden of establishing each of the three elements of the intentional tort cause of action. Even if the jury concluded that Dr Vande Wiele was justified in directing that the experiment not be continued in his hospital, his decision to destroy the contents of the test tube without giving Mrs Del Zio's physician any prior notice, or an opportunity to remove the test tube to some other location, or to consider other alternatives, could reasonably support under all the circumstances a finding by the jury of the kind of deliberate, shocking and reckless conduct required under New York law. The jury might well have also taken into account the evidence tending to indicate that Dr Vande Wiele and Dr Shettles (both of whom testified at length) had sharply conflicting personalities and the evidence that on several occasions Dr Vande Wiele chose to admonish Dr Shettles about his professional conduct, admonitions which Dr Shettles believed to be unjustified. From these circumstances the jury could have found that Dr Vande Wiele had some antipathy, at least, towards his subordinate, Dr Shettles.

Although the defendants were not aware of the precise identity of the plaintiffs, they knew that a particular man and woman were involved in the procedure. It is undisputed that the defendants intended to stop the procedure and that this was done deliberately and without notice; thus, the jury could reasonably have concluded that the defendants acted 'with utter disregard' of the substantial certainty that severe emotional distress would follow from the decision to destroy the contents of the test tube and that the defendants' actions were the proximate cause of the emotional distress which plaintiffs suffered.

The principal objection raised by defendants to the charge on the claim of intentional tort was our refusal to charge as one of the elements that the procedure or experiment have a 'reasonable probability or reasonable substantial possibility of success'. We have found no support in New York cases for defendants' position on this contention. The gist of the tort is conduct deliberately undertaken which predictably caused severe emotional distress. To be sure, if the experiment indisputably and demonstrably had no chance of success and this was known and understood by the plaintiffs, it would seem that the plaintiffs might not be entitled to recover. That was not the situation here. The jury could reasonably find from the medical evidence, the successful animal experiments and the evidence of a successful 'dry run' in 1972, that there was more than an insignificant or remote possibility of success and that plaintiffs and Dr Sweeney were reasonably justified in having an expectation that the experiment might work. The subsequent successful human in vitro fertilisation, implantation and pregnancy accomplished by Drs Steptoe and Edwards in England in 1975 confirm this. We think the high degree of likelihood of success which the defendants['] requested charge on liability would require was inappropriate and improper.

As to the asserted inconsistency between the verdicts on intentional tort and on conversion, they are entirely consistent under the charge. The jury could reasonably have found liability on the conversion claim, but rendered a verdict for defendants on the basis that the amount of damage for conversion was too speculative to be determinable. . . .

Finally, Presbyterian argues that the defendants were prejudiced by adverse publicity. . . . In denying the application, [for an adjournment] we had in mind the following considerations:

3. The likelihood and, indeed, virtual certainty that the attendant publicity would be just as extensive if the trial were postponed another two or three months.

Moreover, in the voir dire of the jury panel, particular attention was paid to the possibility that individuals might have been infected by the publicity. We found no indication that this had happened.

When the media announced the birth of the 'test tube baby' in England on July 26, defendants asked only that the jury be instructed that that event had nothing to do with the case on trial. With the consent of all parties, the jury was instructed as follows:

In that connection I also want to mention that there have been some events in the last—well, overnight, and I suspect that it is very likely that some of you, if not all of you, are aware of what I am talking about. Of course I am talking about the fact that a baby was born in England. I want you to be aware, as I think you already are, that that event has nothing to do with this case, is totally unrelated to the issues in this case. It is not evidence in this case, and it will have nothing to do with your consideration of the evidence in this case, or in your deliberations after the evidence is all in. It is an unrelated event which you may not consider in any way with respect to the issues in this case which are, as I say, totally unrelated.

Moreover, we instructed counsel that no evidence with respect thereto should be offered or would be received. Consequently, except for the above admonition there was no mention of the English episode in the presence of the jury. The jury was also instructed by us constantly, almost every day throughout the five-week trial, that they were to pay no attention to publicity about the case. We have no reason to think that the jury's verdict was tainted by the publicity and we think the amount awarded to plaintiffs supports our view.

We conclude that the verdict was fair; reasonable and lawful.

Although the jury did not award any damages in the action in conversion, can it be implied from this case that the embryo was regarded as property since the judge allowed the claims in conversion to go to the jury? Is it the case that English law regards the embryo as a chattel? If the idea of the embryo being a chattel in law is unappealing both as a matter of legal analysis and ethically, is there any other position that the law could take? It may be helpful to approach this in two stages: first, the ethical arguments, and secondly, the appropriate legal response to these.

In 1984 in Melbourne, Australia the question arose as to what should be done with two embryos which had been frozen at the request of Mr and Mrs Rios following IVF procedures using donor sperm. If the first implantation with Mrs Rios failed it had been planned to use one of the stored embryos. The Rios were, however, killed in an airplane crash in Chile before this could be done.

The Waller Committee (the Victorian equivalent of the Warnock Committee) was asked to advise on the disposition of the embryos. Having initially advised that they should be destroyed, the Committee subsequently changed its mind and proposed that the embryo be removed from storage and set aside, likening this to 'the removal of life support systems from a terminally-ill person. Life is allowed to end'.

The Victorian Government took a different view, however. Section 14 of the Infertility (Medical Procedures) Act 1984 provides that, in a case such as the Rios where there is no recommendation by the parents at the time of the storage:

> ... the Minister shall direct the designated officer of the approved hospital where the embryo is stored to ensure that the embryo is made available for use in a relevant procedure.

What does this tell us about the status of the embryo in law? (For a discussion of the *Rios* case, see G P Smith, 'Australia's Frozen Orphan Embryos: A Medical, Legal and Ethical Dilemma', (1985) 24 J Fam L 27. For a general discussion see *infra* pp 688–692.)

(b)   What are the moral arguments?

Although the status of the embryo arises as a moral question in all aspects of IVF, it is particularly in the context of research on embryos that the debate has taken place. The following materials examine the arguments for us.

The Warnock Report, paras 11.8–11.18 (footnotes omitted) provides a good starting point:

11.8 It was the development of IVF that, for the first time, gave rise to the possibility that human embryos might be brought into existence which might have no chance to implant because they were not transferred to a uterus and hence no chance to be born as human beings. This inevitably led to an examination of the moral rights of the embryo.

11.9 Some people hold that if an embyro is human and alive, it follows that it should not be deprived of a chance for development, and therefore it should not be used for research. They would give moral approval to IVF if, and only if, each embryo produced were to be transferred to a uterus. Others, while in no way denying that human embryos are alive, (and they would concede that eggs and sperm are also alive), hold that embryos are not yet human persons and that if it could be decided when an embryo becomes a person, it could also be decided when it might, or might not, be permissible for research to be undertaken. Although the questions of when life or personhood begin appear to be questions of fact susceptible of straightforward answers, we hold that the answers to such questions in fact are complex amalgams of factual and moral judgements. Instead of trying to answer these questions directly we have therefore gone straight to the question of *how it is right to treat the human embryo.* We have considered what status ought to be accorded to the human embryo, and the answer we give must necessarily be in terms of ethical or moral principles.

Arguments against the use of human embryos

11.11 It is obvious that the central objection to the use of human embryos as research subjects is a fundamental objection, based on moral principles. Put simply, the main argument is that the use of human embryos for research is morally wrong because of the very fact that they are human, and much of the evidence submitted to us strongly supports this. The human embryo is seen as having the same status as a child or an adult, by virtue of its potential for human life. The right to life is held to be the fundamental human right, and the taking of human life on this view is always abhorrent. To take the life of the innocent is an especial moral outrage. The first consequence of this line of argument is that, since an embryo used as a research subject would have no prospect of fulfilling its potential for life, such research should not be permitted.

11.12 Everyone agrees that it is completely unacceptable to make use of a child or an adult as the subject of a research procedure which may cause harm or death. For people who hold the views outlined in 11.11, research on embryos would fall under the same principle. They proceed to argue that since it is unethical to carry out any research, harmful or otherwise, on humans without first obtaining their informed consent, it must be equally unacceptable to carry out research on a human embryo, which by its very nature, cannot give consent.

11.13 In addition to the arguments outlined above, and well represented in the evidence, many people feel an instinctive opposition to research which they see as tampering with the creation of human life. There is widely felt concern at the possibility of unscrupulous scientists meddling with the process of reproduction in order to create hybrids, or to indulge theories of selective breeding and eugenic selection.

11.14 Those who are firmly opposed to research on human embryos recognise that a ban on their use may reduce the volume not only of pure research but also research in potentially beneficial areas, such as the detection and prevention of inherited disorders, or the alleviation of infertility, and that in some areas such a ban would halt research completely. However they argue that the moral principle outweighs any such possible benefits.

Arguments for the use of human embryos

11.15 The evidence showed that the views of those who support the use of human embryos as research subjects cover a wide range. At one end is the proposition that it is only to *human persons* that respect must be accorded. A human embryo cannot be thought of as a person, or even as a potential person. It is simply a collection of cells which, unless it implants in a human uterine environment, has no potential for development. There is no reason therefore to accord these cells any protected status. If useful results can be obtained from research on embryos, then such research should be permitted. We found that the more generally held position, however, is that though the human embryo is entitled to some added measure of respect beyond that accorded to other animal subjects, that respect cannot be absolute, and may be weighed against the benefits arising from research. Although many research studies in embryology and developmental biology can be carried out on animal subjects, and it is possible in many cases to extrapolate these results and findings to man, in certain situations there is no substitute for the use of human embryos. This particularly applies to the study of disorders occurring only in humans, such as Down's syndrome, or for research into the processes of human fertilisation, or perhaps into the specific effect of drugs or toxic substances on human tissue.

. . . [W]e were agreed that the embryo of the human species ought to have a special status and that no one should undertake research on human embryos the purposes of which could be achieved by the use of other animals or in some other way. . . .

11.18 That protection should exist does not entail that this protection may not be waived in certain specific circumstances. Having examined the evidence presented to us about the types of research which might be carried out on human embryos produced *in vitro*, the majority of us hold that such research should not be totally prohibited. We do not want to see a situation in which human embryos are frivolously or unnecessarily used in research but we are bound to take account of the fact that the advances in the treatment of infertility, which we have discussed in the earlier part of this report, could not have taken place without such research; and that continued research is essential, if advances in treatment and medical knowledge are to continue. A majority of us therefore agreed that research on human embryos should continue. Nevertheless, because of the special status that we accord to the human embryo, such research must be subject to stringent controls and monitoring. Moreover, we would not want any handling or transportation of human embryos *in vitro* to fall outside these controls

Are you convinced by the arguments of Warnock? Not everyone is. First, consider the following extract taken from John Harris in *The Value of Life*, pp 133–134 (footnotes omitted):

The main conclusion of Warnock as it affects the arguments of this chapter is that 'the embryo of the human species should be afforded some protection in law' and that the protection it should be afforded should be first, that anyone handling or doing research on embryos should be licensed (such unlicensed work to be a criminal offence); and second, that such handling, research and experimentation as is licensed should not be permitted beyond fourteen days after fertilisation.

Now the Warnock Committee deliberately declines to address the question of whether or not the embryo is a person and what it might mean to claim that an individual is a person, and moves directly to the question of '*how it is right to treat the human embryo*'. This is in a sense just an evasion because, for example, the discussion of the concept of the person developed in this book just is, among other things, a discussion of how it is right to treat the human embryo. However, Warnock makes no serious attempt to discuss how it is right to treat the human embryo. Only two considerations play any part at all in the conclusions at which the Warnock Committee arrives. The first is that apparently overwhelming consideration that 'some precise decision must be taken, in order to allay public anxiety'. And the second is the objection to all research on human embryos, never refuted or even argued against in Warnock, that the human embryo is a potential human being.

The only positive reason given by Warnock for setting the limit on research at fourteen days is that it is at this point that the primitive streak occurs and this is 'the latest stage at which identical twins occur' and hence is the first point at which it is clear that the number of potential human beings present are either one or more than one. However, this point must be irrelevant in any event. For if the potentiality argument is sound, then human potential is present as much before the development of the primitive streak as afterwards. The development of the primitive streak does not affect the fact that the potential for one or more human beings exists, it just makes clear how many potential human beings are present. And of course if, as I argued earlier, the potentiality argument is unsound, then some other reasons must be adduced for protecting the human embryo, and these Warnock never provides.

So, if the potentiality argument is good, it is good against all non-actualisation of human potential and it is an argument against research on the embryo at any stage and against research on human eggs and sperm separately if they could be combined. It is also an argument in favour of unlimited and maximal procreation. If, on the other hand, it is not good then we are left without any account of 'how it is right to treat the human embryo' or rather without any justification for the account that Warnock gives. What is thus needed and what Warnock declines to give is some account of just what it is that is so valuable about adult human beings and other persons and of how and to what extent the features that make us valuable are present in the embryo. Without such an account we have no reason to think it is wrong to treat the embryo in any way that avoids suffering. When we know that research on the human embryo might save the lives of actual human persons, children and adults (which beings Warnock admits to be more valuable than embryos) we are owed some account of what justifies the prevention of such research. And to this end Warnock offers absolutely nothing that could be of an importance comparable to the good moral reasons for doing the research.

Next, consider the somewhat lengthier discourse offered by Michael Lockwood in, 'The Warnock Report: A Philosophical Appraisal', in *Moral Dilemmas in Modern Medicine* (ed M Lockwood), pp 156–169:

Embryo research

Many would suppose that the key question, when one is considering the ethics of scientific research using live human embryos, is 'Is the embryo a human being?' or perhaps 'Is it a person?'—'When does human (or personal) life begin?' The thought, here, is that we have reasonably clear and agreed-upon views about what is and is not morally permissible, in the way of research, when dealing with individuals that are indisputably human beings or persons. Many of the things, perhaps all, that scientists are interested in doing to human embryos, for research purposes, would be universally regarded as unacceptable, if done to a child, say, or indeed to any other innocent human being without his or her consent. So if we knew at what stage the embryo becomes a human being or person, we should know that beyond that point, at any rate, the proposed research was morally impermissible.

The parallel might be challenged, of course, even by someone who was convinced that to experiment on a human embryo, at any stage in its development, is indeed to experiment on a human being. The early embryo, unlike a child, cannot suffer; and if it is not in any case going to be transferred to a womb, one might claim that it does not stand to lose by any physical injury done to it in the course of research. Nevertheless, it could be argued that if one really is dealing with a human being then experimenting on the human embryo constitutes a blatant violation of the Kantian principle that one should never treat a human being merely as a means to an end, but always as an end in itself: in short, it might be thought to be a morally unacceptable form of exploitation.

A further point is this. The death of an innocent human being is, other things being equal, something to be avoided. Thus it must be wrong, *prima facie*, to allow an embryo to develop beyond the point at which a human life begins, in circumstances in which that life is bound then to be prematurely extinguished. In keeping a human embryo alive in the laboratory beyond a certain point—whether for the purposes of experimentation or merely of observation is immaterial—the scientist would be doing just that. This may prompt the ingenious retort that almost anyone who has a child is indirectly bringing about the death of an innocent human being—since the child will, after all, one day die. But of course the point here is that the child's eventual death, regrettable though it is (Tom Nagel has remarked that 'a bad end is in store for us all'[3]), may reasonably be expected to be more than compensated for by the worthwhile life that precedes it. This can hardly be said of the death of an embryo in the laboratory.

For both these reasons, then, the question when human life begins, when we are dealing with a human being or person, might seem to be crucial here. But is it? One philosophical lesson that Mary Warnock would appear to have impressed successfully upon her fellow Committee members—so much so that it is staunchly asserted, not only in the majority Report, but also in a minority Expression of Dissent—is this: Questions such as 'When does life begin?', 'When does a human being come into existence?', and 'When does the embryo or foetus become a person?' are not straightforwardly factual questions at all. Roman Catholics, for example, who, taking the orthodox Vatican line, insist that what begins at conception is 'the life not of a potential human being but of a human being with potential'[4] are not making a purely factual claim—something which can, say, be tested empirically. No, what they are saying already covertly embodies a moral judgment, to the effect that the human embryo and foetus ought to be accorded the same degree of moral respect as we would accord to mature members of the human species. And the same, *mutatis mutandis*, would go for any other assertion as to when human (or personal) life begins: such claims are morally loaded. Hence they cannot, without circularity, be appealed to in order to help settle the question of what is or is not morally acceptable conduct in relation to the human embryo. One is best advised simply to set aside such pseudo-factual questions, and get on with trying to answer directly the straightforwardly evaluative question of how human embryos should be treated.

Regarding the matter in this light, so the argument continues, there are several things that can plausibly be said. First, the human embryo is at least a potential human being (in a sense of 'potential' that neither entails nor excludes 'actual'). That in itself ought, morally, to count for something. On this basis, the Report recommends 'that the embryo of the human species should be afforded some protection in law'.[5] Moreover, the further developed the embryo is, the further along the path to being incontrovertibly a human being, the weightier this claim for moral protection becomes. If I understand it correctly, the Report sees the human embryo as, in moral terms, occupying an initial segment of a continuous spectrum that has beings that are undeniably human beings or persons at the other end; the degree of moral respect owed to the developing embryo and foetus is, roughly speaking, a direct function of its level of development. Even very early human embryos are thus not, according to this view, morally negligible. Granted that even the very early embryo, since it has the potential for human life, is deserving of some moral consideration, there are, of course, other considerations too. The advancement of human knowledge, both in terms of the benefits to humankind that can be expected to result from it, and perhaps also in terms of its intrinsic worth, is a consideration that likewise deserves to be given moral weight. In thinking about the ethics of research on human embryos, these two sorts of consideration therefore have to be weighed against each other.

Some people, while accepting that the framework just sketched is an appropriate one for thinking about the issue, may nevertheless feel that the moral protection deserved by the human embryo in virtue of its potential for human life outweighs considerations about advancing scientific knowledge right from the outset, so that research on live human embryos ought never to be permitted. That is precisely the view put forward in one Expression of Dissent.[6] Others—and this is the majority view expressed in the Report—will think that at a sufficiently early stage the balance of considerations is in favour of allowing some research to be carried out: serious research, that is, research that has the potential for making a substantial contribution to scientific knowledge. Inevitably, however, as we consider embryos at more and more advanced stages of development, the scales will at some point tip the other way: the protection of the embryo then comes to be the paramount consideration, and a point is reached beyond which research ought no longer to be permitted.

Putting things this way, of course, there is no reason to suppose that the point at which the scales tip will be the same for every piece of research that someone might have in mind; the greater the value of the research, the later in embryonic development it might be thought right to permit it to take place (always supposing that the research required embryos at that advanced a stage of development). Realistically, however, it would be neither practical nor satisfactory to try to decide these matters on a case-by-case basis. Nor, in matters such as this, where sensitivity to human life itself is at stake, can we leave it to the discretion of scientists or research-ethics committees, however well-intentioned they might be. The possibilities of abuse are too great. If understandable public anxiety on these matters is to be allayed, one must simply draw a rigid line somewhere and make sure that nobody is allowed to cross it. The Report is insistent on the need for 'barriers'.[7]

Precisely where the line is drawn, given that embryonic development is an essentially continuous process, is, the Report concedes, bound to be to some extent arbitrary, in the light of the above considerations. However, there is something to be said for choosing fourteen days as the cut-off point, seeing that this is just before the point of formation of the 'primitive streak' which later becomes the spinal cord. It is generally believed that division of the embryo, to produce identical twins, triplets, or whatever, is impossible beyond that point. Before then, as Mary Warnock put it in a recent interview, 'the embryo hasn't yet decided how many people it is going to be'. There is thus a sense in which we are not yet dealing with a fully determinate individual.

This I take to be the line of argument that issues in the following key proposals:

We accordingly recommend that no live human embryo derived from in vitro fertilisation, whether frozen or unfrozen, may be kept alive, if not transferred to a woman, beyond fourteen days after fertilisation, nor may it be used as a research subject beyond fourteen days after fertilisation. This fourteen day period does not include any time during which the embryo may have been frozen. We further recommend that it shall be a criminal offence to handle or to use as a research subject any live human embryo derived from in vitro fertilisation beyond that limit.[8]

I have done my best to present this line of thought in as sympathetic and persuasive a way as I can—making explicit, in the process, things which I take to be implicit in the Report itself. But I am bound to say that the argument seems to me to be philosophically flawed. In the first place, while it is perfectly true that terms such as 'life', 'person', and 'human being' are very often, in this context, used in a way that is morally question-begging, it is not clear to me that they have to be used in this way; or (which some would take to be the second horn of the philosophical dilemma here) that if they are not so used such terms then become simply irrelevant to deciding the moral issue. More of that in a moment.

I am, secondly, unconvinced that any moral significance should be attached to primitive-streak formation, even granted that this represents the last moment at which embryonic division can occur. To be sure, there is a venerable tradition, both in philosophy and theology, that human beings are, as a matter of logical necessity, indivisible. (This was argued, for example, by both Descartes and Leibniz.[9] Descartes, indeed, took this supposed indivisibility as a proof of mind–body dualism: since the body clearly is divisible, it followed, he thought, that he was distinct from his body.[10] If the pre-fifteen-day embryo is divisible and persons are not, then it may seem to follow that, before fifteen days at any rate, there is no human being associated with the embryo.

Strictly, of course, this does not follow; embryonic division might be correlated with the coming into existence, in association with one of the two halves, of a new human being altogether. Or, if it is thought an objection to this that it introduces a gratuitous asymmetry into what is ostensibly a symmetrical process, perhaps the original human being is destroyed by the division and supplanted by two new ones. We may waive this point. (The question of how many souls are implicated in the division of an embryo is the sort of thing that would commend itself to someone who is becoming bored with the problem of how many angels can stand on the head of a pin.)

A far more serious objection to the argument is that its premiss seems likely to be false. For there is considerable evidence that human beings are divisible, not only as a matter of logical possibility (that it is logically impossible for human beings to divide was never a very plausible claim), but as a matter of fact. In saying this, I have in mind the celebrated 'split brain' experiments of Sperry and others,[11] in which strikingly dissociated behaviour has been evoked in patients with a severed corpus callosum, the bridge of tissue that normally joins the two hemispheres of the brain. In experimental situations in which it is contrived that different information passes into the two hemispheres, such patients behave in a way that has led Sperry himself and several other workers in the field to conclude that the two hemispheres of their brains are associated with distinct streams of consciousness. (Nor is such behaviour confined to such artificially devised situations: in one famous case, the patient's right hand would embrace his wife, while the left attempted to push her away!) Sperry's own interpretation of the evidence is, admittedly, not universally accepted; but it would seem perverse, in the face of these phenomena, to maintain that human beings are essentially indivisible.[12] Even if, as some have claimed, the behavioural dissociation in 'split-brain' patients is not quite total, it could almost certainly be made so by severing fibres lower down. So divisibility is, I suggest, a red herring here: if very early embryos are to be regarded as non-human beings by virtue of their divisibility, then so, probably, should I be.

That, in any case, is by the way. The heart of the issue lies in the questions whether the potentiality for human (or personal) life inherent in the human embryo really does, as the Warnock Report assumes, confer on it any moral standing and whether one really can, if one is to do justice to this issue, avoid confronting the question when human life begins. I believe that the answer to both questions is 'No'. I have argued this at length in Chapter 1 and am reluctant to repeat myself. Briefly, however, the key points seem to me to be these. First, talk of potentiality is crucially ambiguous in this context. A child may think of himself as a potential astronaut, star footballer, or (in an earlier generation) engine-driver. Here to be a potential X is potentially to be an X: the child, in the unlikely event of his actually becoming an astronaut, say, is the very same individual as that future astronaut.

If, at a given stage of embryonic development, we could say, in this sense, that we had a potential person—something that (assuming that it will develop into a being with the capacity for reflective self-consciousness, rational thought, and so forth) can be regarded as the very same individual as that future being—then it is clear why one should suppose that this conferred on it a certain moral standing. Given that the attributes that mark us off from other animals are ones which, on the whole, we think of ourselves as being very fortunate to possess, we can see that it is very much in the interests of a being with the potential to develop them and to enjoy the kind of life that they make possible, that this potentiality be allowed to come to fruition. Correspondingly, then, it is clear why one should think it wrong to kill a being with such potential, and by extension, wrong to bring into existence an individual with such potential in circumstances where the potential was not going to be realised. This, it could plausibly be argued, is the kind of interest that confers a moral claim—and thus an interest which should (other things being equal) both be respected, when we encounter it, and not be brought into being when it cannot be fulfilled.

This last point is important. If it could be shown that to bring into existence a human embryo was, in the sense just defined, to bring into existence a potential person, then it would, in these terms, make good sense to regard the deliberate creation of human embryos for the purposes of research as being ethically more problematic than the use of 'spare' embryos that were a by-product of *in vitro* fertilisation that was aimed at treating infertility. (The recommendation, by two members of the Warnock Committee not opposed to human-embryo research as such, that the former practice should be banned thus has a certain logic to it.[13]) By the same token, of course, it would then be rational to prefer techniques that did not generate such spare embryos in the first place, and to prefer those that produced less to those that produced more.

Everything here hinges, however, on the later person actually having existed at the earlier time, albeit bereft of self-awareness and the capacity for reasoned thought and action. That is why the question of when human life begins is crucial and inescapable here. It seems to me that the popular conception, according to which this is the central issue, is correct; and the Warnock Report, and Mary Warnock herself, are quite wrong to reject it. So also, I believe, are they wrong to assume that the question when human life begins has to embody a moral decision. Ultimately, the question of when human life begins must hinge on what constitutes the identity of the kind of beings that we essentially are—which is what I take 'human being' to signify, in common parlance. How far back does my identity extend? What is the earliest point at which there existed something identical with me now? (Not qualitatively, of course, but identical in the sense of the very same individual.) This problem of the identity of human beings is notoriously difficult, philosophically; but it has not generally been thought to turn on any matter of moral decision (which is not to say that no matter of moral decision, given suitable moral premises, can turn on it).

What our identity actually does consist in, as I argued in Chapter 1, partly on philosophical and partly on scientific grounds, is a structural continuity within the brain, specifically within the midbrain and cerebral hemispheres, of those neural structures that underlie continuities of memory, personality, and disposition to thought, feeling, and action. I shall not, however, repeat here the arguments for this conclusion. Suffice it to say that, if I am right, then one is not, in the human embryo of two weeks, confronted with a human being, or even a potential human being, much less a potential person—if by that one means something that has the potential actually itself to be a human being or person. (For the two-week-old embryo does not even have a brain.) So if it is that thought that gives rise to moral qualms in relation to embryo research then such qualms may be dismissed as groundless.

There is, to be sure, another sense in which the embryo clearly is a potential person: it has the potential to give rise to a person. Some people might imagine that this should count for something. But I can see no reason why it should. I strongly suspect, moreover, that it is only their failure to distinguish clearly this weaker sort of potentiality from the stronger kind just discussed that has led people to think that way. Indeed, if it did count for something, then human sperm and ova ought also to have some moral claim on us. It seems to me that those who argue on the basis of this latter, weak sense of potentiality, where to be a potential X is not potentially to be an X, are insufficiently embarrassed by this apparent consequence of their views. It is true, of course, that sperm has to fertilise ovum before development can begin; but why should the separateness of the components be thought to make any difference? (I am reminded of what is popularly supposed to be the case in regard to the atom bomb that the Israelis steadfastly deny that they possess; it has been suggested that they have built and tested the components, but have deliberately refrained from making the final assembly, thus rendering their claim not to have built a nuclear weapon strictly true. But of course if what concerns us is the potentiality for an atomic explosion, that is neither here nor there: the components have that potentiality even in their unassembled state, given that they can readily be assembled.)

What is the practical upshot of all this? I understand that there is not the remotest possibility of the brain structures that (according to the view I favour) are a *sine qua non* of human existence having developed even at six weeks, which is when the embryonic stage of development technically gives way to the foetal stage. Contrast the fact that it is not, at present, possible to keep human embryos alive in the laboratory for more than about ten days. So huge, at present, is the gap between what current technology can accomplish in the way of keeping human embryos alive in the laboratory and the earliest point (perhaps eight to ten weeks) at which the brain might have developed to the extent of being able to support some minimal degree of genuinely mental function—the earliest point, for example, at which it might conceivably be able to suffer—that one might think there was no immediate practical need to legislate a cut-off point on embryo research at all. This is probably true, if one is thinking merely of embryos reared *in vitro*. But of course there is also the problem of regulating research on live *aborted* embryos and foetuses. Although this, strictly speaking, lay outside the Warnock Committee's terms of reference, it is clearly a matter on which legislation is called for; and it would (as the Warnock Report points out[14]) create a curious legal anomaly if the law relating to research on live human embryos and foetuses were to discriminate on the basis of their origin. In any case, the Warnock Committee was clearly expected to set a time limit on human-embryo research, and would doubtless have been considered to be shirking its responsibilities had it failed to do so.

The Report does, in fact, consider the possibility of taking as the cut-off point the onset of 'functional activity' in the central nervous system, remarking, however, that 'in the present state of knowledge the onset of central nervous system functional activity could not be used to define accurately the limit to research, because the timing is not known'.[15] True; but that is no reason for dismissing this as a criterion, if such functional activity is what really counts here. The thing to do, in that case, would be to choose the latest point at which the experts are agreed that such functional activity must be absent.

A working party of the Council for Science and Society, commissioned to deliberate the same range of issues as the Warnock Committee, adopted essentially this approach in their own report—and suggested that six weeks might, from this point of view, be an appropriate limit.[16] I suspect that this may be unduly cautious— and, in any case, functional activity *per se* is not what is crucial, from the point of view I advocate, so much as mental activity. (There is much that goes on in the central nervous system, or even the brain—the mediation of reflexes, for example, and temperature regulation—that has nothing to do with mind.) Nevertheless, six weeks has something to be said for it; setting that as a limit would, as we have seen, be tantamount to saying that research on human embryos was permissible, but research on human foetuses was not. It is sufficiently early, I would have thought, to allay public concern significantly (not, of course, that of supporters of LIFE or the Society for the Protection of the Unborn Child—but then nothing short of a total ban on such research would satisfy them);[17] but sufficiently late not to constrain any research project that would, for the foreseeable future, be technically feasible anyway.

Some might object that, even if there is nothing intrinsically wrong with experimenting on human embryos up to six weeks, to allow experiments that late would be to take a substantial step along what is potentially a very dangerous path. In short, switching to the more familiar metaphor, the proposal is vulnerable to a 'slippery-slope' argument. I believe such an objection to be unfounded in this case (though it isn't exactly a philosophical issue whether it is or not). About the best protection one can have against a slippery slope is to have an enforced limit with a clear point that almost everyone is capable of appreciating. I suggest that a limit, of six weeks say, explained in terms of a 'brain life' criterion, fulfils those conditions. Of course, if that were seen to be the point of the limit, and scientific research subsequently demonstrated that (given the underlying rationale) it was far too early, there might well be pressure from the scientific community to extend it a bit. But that would hardly matter. Anyone could see that the rationale behind the limit would not sanction experimenting on a foetus at a later stage, when it was, say, capable of experiencing pain. Any pressure in that direction, therefore, would have to have quite a different source.

From a purely practical standpoint, fourteen days may well turn out to have been a particularly unfortunate choice of cut-off point, since it is just before the process of differentiation gets under way—the process whereby the cells begin to assume the distinct characters appropriate to skin cells, liver cells, nerve cells and so forth. So far, we have been talking merely of the use of live human embryos for the purposes of scientific research. But they may also turn out to have considerable therapeutic potential. Scandinavian scientists have been experimenting with the use of foetal dopamine-producing cells to treat artificially induced Parkinson's disease in rats. The results have been very promising. Mature dopamine cells, though not rejected, simply do not function in their new setting; but cells taken from live foetuses do. Once the process of differentiation has begun, it may well prove possible to produce from the so-called stem cells that are the ancestors of the cell lines characteristic of various kinds of tissue, all kinds of cell cultures for therapeutic purposes, of which dopamine-producing cells (for those suffering from Parkinson's disease) would be merely one example. It has also been suggested, for instance, that diabetes might be cured by the injection into the pancreas of embryo-derived insulin-producing cells. (Problems of rejection are far less in the case of cells taken from embryos or foetuses.)[18] This is all somewhat speculative; but it would seem to me a tragedy if, as a society, we were to deny people suffering from crippling diseases the possibility of a cure, because we had set the limit on keeping embryos alive in the laboratory at fourteen days, rather than, say, twenty. Admittedly, however, this is said from a philosophical standpoint according to which qualms about the moral status of such embryos are, in any case, totally baseless. It is not intended to sway those who, believing (as I do not) that twenty-day-old human embryos are human beings (or at any rate quasi-human beings), not unreasonably feel that whatever advantages might come from experimenting on or otherwise manipulating them in the laboratory would be purchased at too high a moral price.

There is one other observation in the Report regarding embryo research which seems to me deserving of remark: 'We were agreed' it says 'that the embryo of the human species ought to have a special status and no one should undertake research on human embryos the purposes of which could be achieved by the use of animals or in some other way.'[19] From my point of view there is nothing intrinsically wrong with experimenting on human embryos, given that there is no intention of reimplanting them, and therefore no particular point, ethically speaking, in looking for alternatives. But what I find disturbing here is the suggestion that it would be morally preferable to use live animals. Perhaps all that is meant is that it would be preferable to use animal embryos. If, however, what is meant is that it would be preferable to use mature animals, animals that are aware and capable of suffering, then I recoil at the suggestion. I should have thought that, from any sane point of view, it was far preferable to experiment on a near-microscopic blob of unfeeling protoplasm than a feeling, caring being, albeit of a different species. Indeed, where pain and suffering are concerned, I fail to see what species has to do with it. Suffering of a given intensity is, as far as I can see, no less to be regretted or avoided if it happens to a dog than if it happens to a don. Mary Warnock herself has responded, in a reply to an article by John Harris,[20] to possible charges, in this connection, of 'speciesism' (to use Richard Ryder's infelicitous but convenient term):

> It is part of our humanity that we should regard fellow members of the species as in a special relation to ourselves . . . I do not . . . regard a preference for humanity as 'arbitrary', nor do I see it as standing in need of any other justification than that we ourselves are human.[21]

But why could not the white racist argue, in parallel fashion, that he did not see his preference for whites as standing in need of any other justification than that he himself is white? Perhaps Mary Warnock means that morally we ought to feel a special loyalty to members of our own species, just as we would to members of our own family. But this is scarcely a very promising analogy. Family loyalty is based on social ties, not (or at any rate not merely) biological ones. If, on the other hand, it is a question of identification, then I am bound to say that I identify far more strongly with a laboratory rabbit that, like me, sees, feels, and suffers and has a brain, than with a primitive, insensate, and indeed literally brainless clump of cells.

In a sense, of course, all this has been said from a rather narrowly rationalistic standpoint. This is, however, an area where people have strong sentiments and anxieties. The Report declares, in no uncertain terms, that it felt 'bound to take very seriously the feelings expressed in the evidence'.[22] The question thus arises of just how much weight one should give, in this sort of matter, to public sentiment, even if one considers it to be irrational.

Notes to extract
3 Thomas Nagel, 'Death', in *Mortal Questions* (Cambridge: Cambridge University Press, 1979), p 10.
4 *Abortion and the Right to Life: A joint statement of the Catholic Archbishops of Great Britain* (Abbots Langley, Herts: Catholic Information Services, 1980), para 12.
5 Warnock Report, 11.17.

6 Ibid, Expression of Dissent: B. Use of Human Embryos in Research, pp 90–3.

7 Ibid, Foreword, pp 2–3.

8 Ibid, 11.22.

9 Remarks to the effect that minds are indivisible are to be found in many places in Leibniz's writings, eg in *A New System of the Nature and the Communication of Substances* (1695), paras 4 and 11, in L E Loemaker (ed), *G W Leibniz: Philosophical Papers and Letters*, 2nd ed (Dordrecht, 1969), pp 454 and 456.

10 René Descartes, *Meditations on First Philosophy*, 2nd ed (1642), reprinted in Elizabeth Anscombe and Peter Thomas Geach (eds), *Descartes, Philosophical Writings* (London: Nelson, 1964), Sixth Meditation, p 121. Kant criticises Descartes's argument in his *Critique of Pure Reason*, 2nd ed, 416n. There is an excellent discussion of this issue in Jonathan Bennett, *Kant's Dialectic* (Cambridge: Cambridge University Press, 1974), pp 85–7.

11 See R W Sperry, 'Hemisphere Deconnection and Unity in Conscious Awareness', in *American Psychologist*, XIII (1968), pp 723–33. Further references may be found in Thomas Nagel's 'Brain Bisection and the Unity of Consciousness', in his *Mortal Questions*, op cit (see n 3 above), pp 146–64.

12 For philosophical discussion of the implications of these experiments, see the article by Thomas Nagel referred to in n 11 above and also Derek Parfit, *Reasons and Persons* (Oxford: Oxford University Press, 1984), pp 244–66. Parfit assumes that Sperry's interpretation is correct; Nagel questions it, and suggests that the unity of consciousness may not be an all-or-nothing affair. Nagel thinks that the experimental evidence that Sperry cites is to some extent counteracted by the fact that, in most normal circumstances, the behaviour of 'split-brain' subjects seems perfectly integrated. This is indeed a striking fact; it is one that has caused some workers in the field to speculate that the two hemispheres of the brain may be associated with distinct streams of consciousness even in normal people! From this point of view, the reason why the two hemispheres co-operate so well, even when the corpus callosum is severed, is that they have had a lifetime of practice. That speculation aside, I should have thought that the behavioural integration was sufficiently explained (a) by the fact that the two hemispheres are receiving consistent, if not identical, information and (b) by the fact that the two hemispheres are highly motivated towards co-operation. It is interesting, in connection with the latter point, that Donald and Valerie MacKay found recently that they were quite unable, with 'split-brain' subjects, to get the two hemispheres to compete against each other in a simple game: each hemisphere would constantly try to help the other (D M and Valerie MacKay, 'Explicit dialogue between left and right half-systems of split brains', *Nature*, 295 (1982), pp 690–1.) Finally, even in normal circumstances, there are sometimes dramatic (and rather eerie) instances, in 'split-brain' subjects, of dissociation. One I have already mentioned (that of the wife and the husband's hands); in another case a woman complained that she would decide which dress she wanted to wear, but when she went to the wardrobe, her left hand would reach out and take a different one.

13 See Warnock Report, Expression of Dissent: C. Use of Human Embryos in Research, p 94, and also 11.25–11.30.

14 Warnock Report, 11.18.

15 Ibid, 11.20.

16 Council for Science and Society, *Human Procreation: ethical aspects of the new techniques*, Report of a Working Party (Oxford: Oxford University Press, 1984), pp 53–4.

17 A poll carried out recently by MORI for the Order of Christian Unity showed that 34 per cent of people interviewed would be in favour of allowing experiments on human embryos to continue up to the point at which the embryo was capable of feeling pain. Seeing that just over 50 per cent wanted a complete ban on such experiments, and there was presumably a fair number of 'don't knows', this suggests that a substantial majority of those who were in favour of allowing such experiments at all would approve of a six week cut-off point. (See Andrew Veitch, 'Human embryo research "should be forbidden"', *Guardian*, 28 September 1984, p 6, col 1.)

But no doubt some would argue that, given that public opinion is divided, one ought to compromise between this and a total ban by choosing some earlier time limit. It appears to have been on some such basis as this that the Council for Science and Society Working Party ended up recommending a fourteen-day time limit, just like the Warnock Committee. See *Human Procreation*, op cit (see n 16 above), p 82.

18 The likely impact on human-embryo research of passing into law the Warnock Committee's recommendations is assessed in a recent article by Omar Sattaur, 'New conception threatened by old morality', *New Scientist*, 103, No 1423 (27 September 1984), pp 12–17. The therapeutic possibilities are briefly surveyed in Robert Edwards and Patrick Steptoe, *A Matter of Life* (London: Sphere Books, 1981), pp 213–15.

19 Warnock Report, 11.17.

20 See John Harris, 'In Vitro Fertilisation: The Ethical Issues I', *Philosophical Quarterly*, 33 (1983), p 224.

21 Mary Warnock, 'In Vitro Fertilisation: The Ethical Issues II', *Philosophical Quarterly*, 33 (1983), pp 241–2.

22 Warnock Report, Foreword, p 2.

So, we can see that different view points may be held on the merits of the Warnock Committee's analysis (to which we will return later) and its conclusions. Not surprisingly, the many committees throughout the world that have enquired into the new infertility techniques have addressed the moral issues. The analysis of the Federal Senate Select Committee on *Human Embryo Experimentation in Australia* (1984) is particularly impressive (paras 3.7–3.33; footnotes omitted):

3.7 If, as is the view of the Committee, the embryo may be properly described as genetically new human life organised as a distinct entity oriented towards further development, then the stance and behaviour proper to adopt towards it would include not frustrating a process which commands respect because its thrust is towards the further development of a biologically individuated member of the human species.

3.8 Points and stages in the development of the embryo (viz, fertilisation and establishment of genetic identity, implantation, appearance of the primitive streak and neural groove, cerebral and organic development, consciousness, pain awareness and viability) are significant *because* they are critical stages in development. Their significance lies precisely in their being stages.

3.9 The Committee notes that birth of a live human being is a marker event of definitive significance in the legal recognition of a human being as a 'person' entitled to have rights vindicated in legal process. But, the Committee is of the view that no one event succeeding fertilisation is such that it can bear the weight that some would attach to it so that the embryo prior to that chosen marker event might not be accorded the respect practically due to it by way of protecting its development to a succeeding stage.

3.10 Various distinguished committees, scientists and philosophers have indicated that the community should accept various marker events as being definitive.

3.11 Thus the Warnock Report considered that: 'One reference point in the development of the human individual is the formation of the primitive streak. Most authorities put this at about 15 days after fertilisation. This marks the beginning of individual development of the embryo. Taking such a time limit is consonant with the views of those who favour the end of the implantation stage as a limit.'

3.12 The Waller Committee considered that the marker event was: '. . . beyond the stage of implantation, which is completed 14 days after fertilisation. It is after this stage that the primitive streak is formed, and differentiation of the embryo is clearly evident.'

3.13 The NH & MRC chose the stage when implantation in the wall of the uterus would normally occur. Dr Jansen stated in evidence to the Committee that the NH & MRC had chosen implantation as the marker event because: 'At that time the embryonic disc has not differentiated into various parts that could be called parts of an embryo. . . . That is the biological reason why we chose the term implantation: Because it was identifiably on the safe side at which embryonic development reaches a point where an embryo forms in accepted meanings of the term.'

3.14 In passing, the Committee notes that if any justification of destructive non-therapeutic experimentation were attempted, it would appear to make more sense if such experimentation were undertaken *after* the possibility of a future *in utero* has passed and when cells have differentiated, providing material for a wider range of experimental procedures. Indeed the Committee received evidence that an abundance of cells for experimentation related to medical problems, such as thalassaemia and Down's Syndrome, are available in human beings after birth and there is no need to obtain such material from the early embryo.

3.15 On behalf of the MREC, Professor Richard Lovell stated: 'It was put to us that when implantation is complete it is a definable landmark in the development of the foetus. It is now in place—it is talking to its mother, I think the phrase was used—in a sort of way that means that it is latched on in there. It is a biological landmark. It can now go ahead.' In contrast, Professor Lejeune stated: 'There is no special landmark that we could use to tell us that there is a change in the status of the embryo—to use good English—but there are only stages of its development.'

3.16 Dr Alan Trounson, Director of the Centre for Early Human Development at Monash University, in evidence before the Committee, describing the marker events chosen by the Warnock and Waller Committees, said: 'I do not see that there is a magical change between day 13 and day 14. It just happens to be an arbitrary time. At that time the embryonic shield is definitely visible there. I would accept that that is a reasonable time.' Thus for Dr Trounson it was not such a significant time as to preclude his coming back and arguing '. . . with any committee if suddenly we get the answer to the whole of cancer or the whole of every debilitating disease by studying 200 28-day embryos. I would be prepared to put that to the appropriate ethics committee—Federal or whatever—and allow it to make a decision on it.'

3.17 The Warnock Committee wrote:

While, as we have seen, the timing of the different stages of development is critical, once the process has begun, *there is no particular part of the developmental process that is more important than another*; all are part of a continuous process, and unless each stage takes place normally, at the correct time, and in the correct sequence, further development will cease. Thus biologically there is no one single identifiable stage in the development of the embryo beyond which the *in vitro* embryo should not be kept alive. However we agreed that this was an area in which some precise decision must be taken, in order to allay public anxiety. (Committee's emphasis.)

3.18 In this situation prudence dictates that, until the contrary is demonstrated 'beyond reasonable doubt' (to use an expression well-known in our community), the embryo of the human species should be regarded as if it were a human subject for the purposes of biomedical ethics.

3.19 The Committee is not precluding the possibility of such a marker event being so made out with the degree of certainty indicated, but it advises the Senate that no such compelling evidence is forthcoming at the time of preparing this Report.

3.20 Most concede that in the development of early human life a stage is reached (whatever it may be) when it would be improper to carry out destructive non-therapeutic experimentation. In considering the various labels which are applied to the entity preceding that stage the Committee was very conscious of the point made by Professor Margaret Somerville, who appeared in a private capacity but whose expertise is in the field of medical jurisprudence: 'One good legal reason for choosing such an event is to differentiate and dis-identify one group of human cells (embryos) from another group of cells (the rest of us) in order to ensure that precedents set with respect to embryos do not apply to us . . . In short, we must ensure that our differential treatment of human entities is inherently justified and not just a result of extrinsic labels that we attach for the purpose of legitimating certain conduct.'

3.21 The Committee advises the Senate that it was not persuaded of the inherent ethical validity of the marker event authoritatively put forward in Australia, ie the time of the implantation process chosen by the NH & MRC on the advice of the

MREC and promulgated in Supplementary Note 4. The Committee could see nothing which marked it as other than a significant event in a continuum of development until birth.

3.22 The Committee concludes that the respect due to the embryo from the process of fertilisation onwards requires its protection from destructive non-therapeutic experimentation understood in the sense outlined above. The Committee recommends that the principle protecting the embryo from destructive non-therapeutic experimentation be adopted by the Senate in its consideration of this matter.

3.23 In doing so it must be noted that the Committee has not attempted to attribute the status of '*person*' to the embryo in either its philosophical or legal senses. It does not intend to pronounce on this question, nor to canvass the issue of whether the law should treat an embryo as a person within its criminal, tortious, property and other rules. The law does not regard the embryo or fetus as a person for the purpose of successfully vindicating rights until that entity has been born alive. However, there is recognition that damage, caused either with criminal intent or in a tortious sense, can be sustained by an embryo or fetus and in relation to that damage liability may attach to an accused or defendant after the birth of the disabled person. The Committee can see no reason why a person born alive, having been generated by the process of IVF and ET, would not enjoy the same legal rights at that stage.

3.24 However, the Committee is advocating the *protective role of the law for an embryo*, such that obligations are cast on persons not to knowingly frustrate its development by destructive non-therapeutic experimentation. As pointed out by Professor Somerville, there may be a third category between tissue and legal person which the law can erect for certain protective purposes and in relation to which obligations can be imposed on others. How society should embody this protection in its legal arrangements will be dealt with later.

'Spare' and 'specially created' embryos

3.25 Even if the Committee's recommendation were not to be accepted, Australian society would still need to consider whether such experimentation should be able to be carried out on all available embryos, or only on those specifically created for that purpose, or only on those created with a general intention that they be transferred to a uterus but which are surplus to the requirements of a particular IVF program.

3.26 The NH & MRC has never made a distinction between 'spare' and 'specially created' human embryos. Other committees have seen moral distinctions between the two. Thus the majority in the Waller Committee were of the view that experiments could be undertaken on spare embryos (given the other ethical constraints of consent of gamete donors, etc) but not on embryos created specifically for that purpose.

3.27 The reasoning for not experimenting on specially created embryos is best exemplified in the Waller Committee Report:

From a moral perspective, it may be said that, regardless of the particular level of respect which different sections of the community would accord an embryo, this individual and genetically unique human entity may not be formed solely and from the outset to be used as a means for any other human purpose, however laudable. Where the formation occurs in the course of an IVF procedure for the treatment of infertility, the reasons which lead to the embryo's existence are not 'means to an end' ones.

3.28 However, it was not self evident to all witnesses that this was the ethically preferable course. Thus Dr Barbara Burton, who represented the Infertility Federation of Australasia stated in evidence: '. . . we feel that it is perhaps ethically preferable for embryos to be created specifically for research purposes rather than using spare embryos generated in IVF programs, and infertile couples would prefer to see all spare embryos frozen for use in a later treatment cycle . . .'.

3.29 In contrast, Professor Douglas Saunders, Chairman of the Infertility Unit of Royal North Shore Hospital, NSW, explained to the Committee that, although the Hospital Institutional Ethics Committee (IEC) had granted permission to create embryos for specific non-therapeutic experiments (to verify ova-freezing techniques), he was unwilling to do so because the need for embryos for transfer to patients was considered to be greater than the need to experiment. In evidence he explained:

> We have created an embryo. We have 50 couples on a waiting list wanting frozen embryos and we have got to discard those embryos. That is one ethical issue that I find difficult. The other is getting patient recruitment. The difficulty is getting women who are happy to have their tubes tied on an irregular day, not the day that they might have found convenient, in order to get mature oocytes in order to do research.

3.30 The Committee agrees with and adopts the Waller Committee's recommendation that experimentation not be permitted on embryos created specifically for the purpose. However, even if the Committee were to agree, in theory, with the use of *spare* embryos for destructive non-therapeutic experimentation (and it does not) it is the view of the Committee that it would be most imprudent of the community to consider that such a distinction could be easily maintained in practice. As stated in a dissent to the Warnock Report: 'There would be a strong temptation for doctors to harvest more embryos than strictly required for the immediate therapeutic purpose in order to provide "spare embryos". "Spare" would become a euphemism.' As Dr Robyn Rowland, who appeared before the Committee in a private capacity but who was a member of the Asche Committee, said in evidence: 'I am concerned about the possibility of spare embryos because I see the rationale creeping in that you just superovulate women a little more and you end up with excess embryos and then you have them for experimentation.'

3.31 Further, it was pointed out by Dr Robert Jansen that:

> It is a fallacy to distinguish between surplus embryos and specially created embryos in terms of embryo research . . . any intelligent administrator of an IVF program can, by minor changes in his ordinary clinical way of going about things, change the number of embryos that are fertilised. So in practice there would be no purpose at all in enshrining in legislation a difference between surplus and specially created embryos.

3.32 The Reverend W J Uren, Director of the Goody Centre for Bioethics in Western Australia, argued there should be no distinction between 'normal', 'spare' and 'specially created' embryos, but he did so from a different perspective: 'These distinctions . . . of themselves generate no moral reasons for differences of treatment. Rather they invite reflection whether the processes by which surplus embryos are generated and embryos are produced specifically for experimental purposes are morally justifiable. . . . the appeal to this difference between embryos as a criterion for justifying morally difference of treatment is highly suspect.'

3.33 The Committee finds any supposed distinction between so called 'spare' embryos and those created specifically for experimental purposes to be ethically unsound . . . , and practically most unlikely to be maintained. It therefore recommends that no destructive non-therapeutic experimentation be permitted based on any such distinction.

The Government's response to the status of the embryo and the connected issue of what, if any, research should be permitted was as follows. First, the DHSS Consultation Paper in December 1986, paras 45–58 (footnotes omitted):

45. The Warnock Report's recommendations and the Private Members' Bills on research involving human embryos have stimulated considerable debate both on the principle of allowing any such research and the definition of circumstances in which it might be permissible. Public opinion is sharply divided and the debate has demonstrated the depth and sincerity of the opposing views. The Government has recognised this diversity in framing the proposals below to ensure that these views are fully debated.

46. The majority view of the Warnock Committee was that research should be permitted in certain circumstances and within carefully defined controls. They recommended that:

(a) the embryo of the human species should be afforded some protection in law;

(*b*) any unauthorised use of an *in vitro* embryo should in itself constitute a criminal offence;

(*c*) the statutory licensing authority should license research conducted on human embryos *in vitro*;

(*d*) research might be carried out on any embryo resulting from IVF, whatever its provenance, up to end of the fourteenth day after fertilisation but subject to all other restrictions as may be imposed by the licensing body.

47. The Warnock Committee's Report highlights the diversity of views about human embryo research. Two of the three expressions of dissent in the Report were about this subject. Three members of the Committee recommended that no experimentation should be permitted because of the potential of the embryo to become a human person. Four other members of the Committee drew a distinction between the use of 'spare' embryos, produced during attempts at IVF, for research and the deliberate creation of embryos, perhaps from donor gametes, purely for the purpose of research. That group thought that the former was acceptable, but not the latter.

48. *Suggested benefits of research.* Those who favoured the continuation of controlled research involving human embryos have suggested that the continuation of this research is very important because it offers a number of benefits which could not be obtained in any other way. The suggested benefits fall into four main categories:

(*a*) improving the treatment of infertility;

(*b*) gaining further knowledge about factors leading to congenital disease;

(*c*) developing more effective forms of contraception;

(*d*) detecting gene or chromosome abnormalities before implantation.

It is argued that the development of IVF to date has only been possible because of research on human embryos and that further work is needed to improve the success rate of the technique. This could involve investigation of better methods of maturing embryos *in vitro* and storing both gametes and embryos. It is also suggested that human embryo research is necessary to gain deeper insights into male infertility and to allow the full evaluation of the effects of new types of superovulatory drugs on the large number of eggs produced as a result of taking them. A further possibility is that research on the human embryo *in vitro* would allow the development of fuller knowledge of the process of implantation, so increasing the overall success rate of IVF. It would also throw some light on the reasons for chromosomal errors arising during sperm and egg development or at fertilisation; half the miscarriages which occur during the first three months of pregnancy take place for this reason.

49. It is argued that the greatest potential benefits of research involving human embryos lie in the prevention of congenital disorders. Studies of eggs, sperm and early embryos may lead to ways of preventing some chromosomal abnormalities developing. Also, in the future, those who support research envisage the development of techniques including embryo biopsy which might allow the very early detection of embryos which had single gene or chromosome defects which would result in seriously abnormal babies. In the UK some 7000 babies a year (about 1 per cent of all babies) are born with an obvious single gene inherited defect. Preimplantation 'diagnosis' could ultimately result in some fall in that number.

50. It is also suggested that greater knowledge of the physiological processes involved in conception might lead to the development of more efficient forms of contraception. One possibility is that research might assist the development of a contraceptive vaccine.

51. Those who support embryo research would not generally accept the proposition that the embryo should, from the point of conception, be regarded as having the same full human status as a child. Thus they would say that moral arguments based on that premise are misplaced. They would also say that research which could help to alleviate human suffering and handicap has its own moral imperative and justification.

52. *Arguments against research*. Those who are opposed to any research involving human embryos argue that embryos from the point of conception have the same human status as that of a child or an adult. It would thus be improper to conduct research on them which would lead to their eventual destruction. The embryo should be seen as fully human because of its potential for human life, the right to life being the most fundamental of all human rights. It is therefore held that research which leads to the destruction of an embryo is tantamount to murder as the embryo does not have the opportunity to fulfil its potential.

53. It is also suggested that research should only be carried out on a human embryo where it could benefit from it. Such research would enhance the potential of the embryo for development to possible birth. In any event, by its very nature an embryo cannot give consent to any kind of procedure. The latter argument again rests on a belief that the human embryo is entitled to full human status.

54. Some have argued that the suggested benefits of research on human embryos are in fact illusory and that no worthwhile research on hereditary disease could be carried out within the 14-day time limit suggested by the Warnock Report as the embryo would not have developed sufficiently to allow such research to be carried out. For some, a 14-day limit would be the 'thin end of the wedge'; scientists could always argue later for raising it as new research possibilities emerged. It is also argued that animal studies could reveal much of the information which is sought in research on human embryos and that infertility treatment could develop without the need for research involving embryos.

55. *Other views*. The response to this section of the Report does not, however, fall completely into two diametrically opposed positions. There is a range of views about what forms of research might be permitted and how it ought to be controlled. Some have endorsed the views of four members of the Warnock Committee who accepted research involving 'spare' embryos but not research on embryos created from gametes donated for that purpose. Others have pointed out that so few 'spare' embryos are available that confining research to them would severely restrict what research might achieve. Whilst most of those who are in favour of some degree of human embryo research support the 14-day proposed time limit, others suggest this may need to be reviewed at some stage in the future in the light of research which could actually be carried out.

56. The overwhelming majority of those who have responded to the Warnock Report are agreed that the present situation in which there are no statutory controls on research involving embryos is unsatisfactory. Those who argue against research propose that a total or near total ban should be imposed. Those in favour state that the present uncertain legal situation deters researchers from setting up worthwhile projects. Supporters of the principle of research are, in the main, in favour of the regulatory controls suggested by the Warnock Report.

57. The Government recognises that deeply-held moral beliefs help to determine attitudes towards the question of embryo research and that many people feel great disquiet with the present situation in which research involving human embryos can proceed under professional codes of ethics, but without statutory control.

58. The Government has taken a position of neutrality during the Parliamentary and public debates on this issue that have followed the publication of the Warnock Report. In doing so, it is following a long-standing tradition of allowing Members of Parliament a free vote on issues that are ultimately ones for MPs' decision on grounds of conscience.

Secondly, in its 1987 White Paper, the Government proposed two alternative clauses that should be put before Parliament in the Bill (para 30):

30. The Government therefore proposes that the alternative draft clauses which will be made available to Parliament should be along the following lines:

Prohibiting research   It will be a criminal offence to carry out any procedures on a human embryo other than those aimed at preparing the embryo for transfer to the uterus of a woman; or those carried out to ascertain the suitability of that embryo for the intended transfer.

Permitting research Except as part of a project specifically licensed by the SLA, it will be a criminal offence to carry out any procedures on a human embryo other than those aimed at preparing the embryo for transfer to the uterus of a woman or those carried out to ascertain the suitability of that embryo for the intended transfer.

The legislation would make clear that these provisions would not prevent the storage of embryos with the intention of using them for future transfer (if suitable) to a woman; nor allowing embryos to perish where they were not to be transferred (eg because an abnormality had been detected).

Clearly, the former would prevent all research. If the latter clause was accepted by Parliament, the White Paper proposed (para 35):

35. If research is permitted, there is general agreement that it must be under strict control. In this eventuality, the Government proposes that procedures, other than those to prepare an embryo (or assess its suitability) for transfer, should be permitted only as part of a programme of work specified in a project licence issued by the SLA. The licence would be linked to a specific project whose aim must be clearly stated, and would run for a maximum of two years. The SLA would be able to grant licences only if it was satisfied that the aim of the project was to bring about advances in diagnostic or therapeutic techniques, or in fertility control; that it was scientifically valid; and that the applicant had given adequate consideration to the feasibility of achieving the aims of the project without the use of human embryos. It would be a condition of every licence that no restricted procedure should be carried out on an embryo without the signed consent of the donors of the embryo (or donors of the gametes used to create the embryo).

While viewing the regulation of research, if the latter clause were accepted by Parliament, as primarily a matter for the SLA, the Government proposed legislation to limit the SLA's power to license research in two areas: (1) beyond 14 days of development, and (2) in relation to certain kinds of research. As regards (1), paragraphs 33 and 34 of the White Paper stated:

... If research is permitted under licence, the Government accepts that an upper time limit must be set in law beyond which no research is permitted. There is broad agreement among those who supported the Warnock recommendations that the arguments advanced for choosing the appearance of the primitive streak as this limit were sensible. If research is permitted under licence from the SLA, the Government therefore proposes that the Authority will not be able to give a licence for the use of embryos beyond fourteen days or after the appearance of the primitive streak, whichever is the earlier. Use beyond this time would therefore be a criminal offence.

34. The period will be measured as fourteen completed days from the time at which egg and sperm are placed together for fertilisation (excluding periods of storage in an arrested state of development). Licence holders will be required to make a record of this time.

As regards (2), the White Paper continued (paras 36–42):

36. Many people are particularly concerned about the ethical implications of possible future developments in research involving human embryos. The Warnock Committee discussed such possibilities (some purely speculative), including

ectogenesis (maintaining an embryo *in vitro* for progressively longer periods); cloning; and techniques aimed at modifying the genetic constitution of an embryo. It considered that any developments in these fields were precluded by the controls it had proposed, but recommended that the SLA should promulgate guidance on research which would be unlikely to be considered ethically acceptable in any circumstances and would not be licensed. The Government believes that it should go beyond this recommendation and proposes that the legislation should clearly prohibit all such activities, but with a power for Parliament itself, by affirmative resolution, to make exceptions to these prohibitions if new developments made that appropriate.

37. One of the greatest causes of public disquiet has been the perceived possibility that newly developed techniques will allow the artificial creation of human beings with certain pre-determined characteristics through modification of an early embryo's genetic structure. The technical prospects for achieving this are in fact extremely remote, even if anyone wished to undertake such work. Nevertheless, it is a procedure which society would clearly regard as ethically unacceptable, and the Bill will prohibit it.

38. Similar concerns arise from fears that it will one day be possible to produce artificially two or more genetically identical individuals by nucleus substitution (sometimes known as cloning). The Warnock Report (paragraphs 12.11 and 12.14) described techniques by which such results might theoretically be achieved, although there is no knowledge of such work being carried out artificially with human embryos. The Bill will make such practices a criminal offence.

39. The Bill will also contain provisions prohibiting the transfer of a human embryo to the uterus (or any other part) of another species and vice versa; and prohibiting any procedures involving the fusion of cells of a human embryo with cells of the embryo of another species to produce a chimera. It must be stressed that neither of these procedures have been known to be attempted using human genetic material in this country.

40. Finally the Bill will make provision for additions to the list of prohibited research techniques to be made by regulations.

41. The consultation document sought further views on whether trans-species fertilisation involving human gametes should be subject to regulatory control as the Warnock Committee had recommended. At present, the only use of this technique known to the Government is the so-called 'hamster test'. This test involves attempting to penetrate a hamster egg with human sperm to investigate the quality of the latter. It is considered a useful diagnostic test which, if successful, may mean that the man is able to father a child in certain circumstances. A hamster egg fertilised by human sperm appears to be biologically unable to develop beyond the two-cell stage. For the purposes of the test, however, it need not even reach the stage of cell division. Many feel trans-species fertilisation should be banned altogether because of an abhorrence at the idea of hybrid development, while others—not only those with a direct professional interest—support the Warnock Committee's view.

42. As there is universal agreement about the need to prevent the creation of hybrids using gametes (if this were ever to be attempted), the Bill will specify that no licence may permit the fertilisation of a human egg with the sperm of another species. Any attempt to do this would be a breach of the conditions of licence and would therefore be a criminal offence. It would also be an offence to fertilise the egg of another species with human sperm except under licence from the SLA. Licences may be given for use of this technique only in connection with the assessment or diagnosis of sub-fertility before the completion of the fertilisation process. This will be deemed to be completed when the two-cell stage is reached. In other words, anyone who allows development once the first cell division has occurred will be in breach of the law.

Notice the differing view expressed by the New South Wales Law Commission in their Discussion Paper of 1986, taking issue with the Federal Senate Report (*op cit* at p 671) on the definition of 'embryo' and whether it is supportable in the light of the current medical knowledge (paras 8.33–8.36) (footnotes omitted):

8.33 The crucial conclusion of the committee's majority was that an Australia-wide statutory prohibition of most research on IVF 'embryos' (specially defined by the majority) should be introduced with criminal penalties. The foundation of this conclusion, and of the majority's entire report is the special definition of 'embryos':

> . . . the embryo may be properly described as genetically new human life organised as a distinct entity oriented towards further development.

The majority emphasises the importance to its report of its own definition by 'adopting the usage "embryo" to describe the fertilised ovum and succeeding stages up to the observation of human form'. This statement followed a lengthy physiological discussion of the processes of fertilisation and a careful analysis of the use and meaning of the word 'embryo'. It is, however, significant that nowhere in the discussion and analysis is there any reference to the differences between an ovum fertilised by the IVF process and one fertilised by sexual intercourse, although the differences are obliquely referred to at the end of the majority's report. . . .

8.34 Having defined 'embryo' as described above the majority report then concluded without further analysis or argument, that

> . . . the stance and behaviour proper to adopt towards it would include not frustrating a process which commands respect because its thrust is towards the further development of a biologically individuated member of the human species.

We believe that this conclusion may be properly described as a 'value judgment' or a 'moral judgment'.

8.35 For reasons which we now set out below, we are of the opinion that the majority report's definition of 'embryo' is defective because at the least it is ambiguous.

8.36 The majority state in their paragraph 2.21 that their usage of the word 'embryo' is meant to refer to, or 'speak of genetically new human life organised as a distinct entity oriented towards further development'. They also state in paragraph 2.21 that they use the word 'embryo' to describe the fertilised ovum and succeeding stages up to the observation of human form'.

The Commission has been advised that the phrase 'genetically new human life' accurately describes the ripening ovum of every human female of childbearing age at the time of meiosis during her menstrual cycle. Meiosis is a biological event when the ripening ovum sheds 23 of its 46 chromosomes in natural preparation for the possibility of fertilisation. The ovum, by this natural process becomes not only a unique human cell but reorganises itself genetically and acquires a gene structure that is not the same as that of the other cells of the woman in whose body it occurs. The gene structure of the ovum is a 'mix' of the male and female genes that make up the woman's body, and the cell at that point is unique. Its uniqueness is further illustrated by the fact that its gene structure is also different from that of every other ovum or oocyte in the woman's body. The procedure of parthenogenesis can be and has been applied to human ova, causing them to develop without the use of sperm at all, in the same way as the fertilised ovum, up to the 8-cell stage at least.

We are not here concerned with the morality or ethics of parthenogenesis. Our concern is to demonstrate that other living human tissue than the fertilised human egg answers the description 'genetically new human life organised as a distinct entity oriented towards further development'. It follows that an unfertilised human ovum that has been stimulated parthenogenetically is also covered precisely by the majority report's definition of embryo. However, such an ovum is neither an embryo nor a fertilised ovum in any normally understood sense. Indeed, the majority report cites with approval statements that reject the suggestion that either ovum or sperm should be in any way equated with an embryo.

We are further advised that, conversely, there are human tissues that answer the majority's definition of 'embryo' but can never become an embryo (in the normal, medical sense), fetus or human person. For example, tissues, described scientifically as embryonic stem cells and terato-carcinoma cells, are developed in laboratories and are used for research. Their further development involves a disorganised differentiation into types of human somatic cells such as teeth, muscle and skin, but cannot form a human person. However, they answer the description 'genetically new human life organised as a distinct entity oriented towards further development'.

Who, if anyone, do you you think has the better of the moral arguments? Do you think the Government's position (which is likely to be enshrined in legislation) is (1) morally justifiable and (2) one upon which there would be a consensus view in English society?

(c) The 'pre-embryo' saga

It is important to notice a controversy that has developed since the Warnock Report, concerning the correct description of the entity under consideration and its relevance to the moral arguments. The notion of the 'pre-embryo' has been suggested. We can see the beginnings of this debate in the material of the Australian report we have just seen. The Australian Senate Select Committee on *Human Embryo Experimentation in Australia* (*op cit*) comment as follows (footnotes omitted):

> 2.12 The Committee is aware that the UK Voluntary Licensing Authority (VLA) has adopted the term 'pre-embryo' to refer to the cluster of 'cells' observable prior to the emergence of the primitive streak at about 14 to 16 days after fertilisation. The VLA writes:
>
>> Much thought and discussion was devoted to the appropriate term to be used for the early stages of cell division following fertilisation. This was important since 'embryo' is not the correct term for this stage in development, although it has been widely used. The cluster of cells that develops following fertilisation does not always form an embryo and when it does, only a small portion of the entire cluster is involved. The embryo forms about 14–16 days after fertilisation, and it is then clearly destined to become a fetus. To describe the entire initial cell cluster, members preferred the term 'pre-embryo', as it was hoped that this term would be more easily understood than the equally correct term 'conceptus' or 'zygote'.
>
> 2.13 Some scientists would query whether 'degradation' rather than 'non-formation' of an embryo may not be a better description of the possible failure of development noted by the VLA. This Committee merely notes that point, but wishes to concentrate on the debate among scientists, and rejection by many lay people of the use of the term 'pre-embryo'.
>
> David Davies, former editor of the science journal 'Nature' and member of the Warnock Committee of Inquiry into Human Fertilisation and Embryology, writes:
>
>> . . . I am reasonably sure that at least in our discussions the word 'pre-embryo' was never used. Certainly we were all well aware that the human embryo for the first two weeks of its existence, and even more, bears no visual resemblance whatever to the later embryonic and fetal stages, but I can recall no efforts either within or from outside the Committee to redefine the early stages as not an embryo. Within the past year, however, the word 'pre-embryo' has been creeping in.
>> . . .
>>
>> If research on embryos were an uncontentious matter, and if scientists were generally of the opinion that the new terminology helped their understanding, nobody would have many qualms at the name change. But those who are introducing 'pre-embryo' into the vocabulary know full well that the research is indeed contentious and that fundamental issues have yet to be resolved. They complain, with justification, when embryos are described as 'unborn children' in hostile parliamentary bills, but they are themselves manipulating words to polarise an ethical discussion.
>
> 2.14 Without endorsing Davies' suggestion that a term such as 'pre-embryo' has been deliberately devised to base an argument on an apparently simple description, nevertheless the Committee is aware of the warning put to it by Professor Margaret Somerville that definitions operate in this context as behaviour-governing terms rather than apparently descriptive terms.

Significantly, Professor Edwards (a pioneer in the area) is not persuaded of the helpfulness of the distinction. In *Human Embryo Research: Yes or No?*—a report of a meeting held under the auspi[...]dation (pp 149–150) we see the following interchange:

Embryo or pre-embryo?

Clothier: The expression pre-em[...] y suggested by Dr Penelope Leach, who is also a mem[...] .ary Licensing Authority. The connotation in the minds [...] .c is that the embryo already has recognisable human charac[...] whereas what we were talking about could not be said to have hu[...] characteristics. 'Conceptus' connotes the creation of a new life in being, so we arrived at 'pre-embryo'. It would be useful to know what you think of this word.

Maddox: I think it is a cosmetic trick.

McLaren: There is ambiguity in the way scientists use the term 'embryo', . . . we are not justified in continuing to use the term embryo in both senses. We are not talking about cosmetics but about clarity.

Maddox: In the past three years the general public has heard so much about embryos that if scientists now try to say that pre-embryos are what you are concerned with, people would be rather offended. In public discussion it seems to me proper to use the term in two senses without differentiating.

Edwards: The embryo means something much later to doctors than it does to scientists. I am not sure what scientists or doctors would think about 'pre-embryo', but many would question it. In a sense, of course, it is almost an abbreviation of 'preimplantation embryo'. Why can't we stick to the terms we have used for many years, such as preimplantation embryos, morulae, blastocysts, and implanted embryos? This is my opinion, but if a new term clarifies matters, it should perhaps be considered seriously.

Clothier: We all thought that 'pre-embryo' did clarify matters.

Do you agree?

(d) The jurisprudential flaw

Let us now return to the major theme of this section—the moral status of the embryo—and offer some criticisms of the Warnock approach. Does the Report contain a jurisprudential flaw? In considering what action is taken on the recommendations of the Warnock Report account must also be taken of what may be a jurisprudential flaw in the reasoning concerning research of embryos.

In the Warnock Report, para 11.17, it is stated that: 'we were agreed that the embryo of the human species ought to have a special status'. One way in which the Warnock Committee sought to apply the notion of 'special status' was in para 10.11:

10.11 Until now the law has never had to consider the existence of embryos outside the mother's uterus. The existence of such embryos raises potentially difficult problems as to ownership. The concept of ownership of human embryos seems to us to be undesirable. **We recommend that legislation be enacted to ensure there is no right of ownership in a human embryo.**

Is this approach consistent with the Warnock Committee's subsequently held views on the following matters?

eg 1: *Storage*

Para 10.11 Nevertheless, the couple who have stored an embryo for their use should be recognised as having rights to the use and disposal of the embryo, although these rights ought to be subject to limitation. The precise nature of that limitation will obviously require careful consideration. We hope the couple will recognise that they have a responsibility to make a firm decision as to the disposal and use of the embryo.

e g 2 : *Sale*

13.13 There is one further area where we see a role for a licensing body. It has been suggested that if the demand for human gametes and embryos, for either treatment or for research, increased, there could be a risk of commercial exploitation and of an export and import trade. We would see this as undesirable. On the other hand we can foresee situations where the supply of human gametes or embryos might reasonably involve some commercial transaction, for example if a licensed semen bank was asked to supply specimens to a distant part of the country which would involve them in considerable costs of transportation, we see no reason why they should not seek reimbursement of expenses. Thus a complete prohibition on the purchase or sale of such material would be inappropriate. A balance has to be struck and therefore **we recommend that the sale or purchase of human gametes or embryos should be permitted only under licence from, and subject to, conditions prescribed by the licensing body and therefore unauthorised sale or purchase should be made a criminal offence.**

e g 4 : *Disposal*

10.12 We consider that the position that may arise in the event of the death of one or both of a couple who have stored an embryo should be clarified. **We therefore recommend that when one of a couple dies the right to use or dispose of any embryo stored by that couple should pass to the survivor.** We make this recommendation notwithstanding our reservations about the possibility of posthumous pregnancies. **We recommend that if both die that right should pass to the storage authority.**

e g 5 : *Drugs testing*

12.5 It has been suggested that human embryos could be used to test the effects of newly developed drugs or other substances that may possibly be toxic or cause abnormalities. This is an area that causes deep concern because of the possibility of mass production of *in vitro* embryos, perhaps on a commercial basis, for these purposes. We feel very strongly that the routine testing of drugs on human embryos is not an acceptable area of research because this would require the manufacture of large numbers of embryos. We concluded however that there may be very particular circumstances where the testing of such substances on a very small scale may be justifiable.

What **special** status does an embryo have if it may be the object of research during the first fourteen days of gestation and thereafter destroyed? What is ownership if it is not the right to control, including to dispose of by sale, or otherwise?

(e)   Some unresolved issues relating to control and disposal

1.   Chattels or persons

The law seems to permit two models of analysis: that the embryo is either *a chattel* or *a person*. Neither of these models is necessarily an absolutist one, for example, there are some chattels where even the owner's right to dispose of or destroy may be limited by law (for example, animals may not be cruelly destroyed; there are limitations on the disposal of firearms or the possession and use of controlled drugs). Equally, a foetus's claim to continue to survive, even late in gestation, *may* be subordinated to the claim of its mother to exercise control over her own body.

The first model, that the embryo is a chattel, was clearly unattractive to every official body that has reported on embryo research. But does it represent existing law? Regarding it as a chattel makes more sense of the recommendations of the Warnock Committee concerning sale and disposition and of the recommendation in para 11.24 that:

11.24 We are satisfied that 'spare' embryos may be used as subjects for research; **and we recommend accordingly a need to obtain *consent* to the method of use or disposal of spare embryos. We recommend that as a matter of good practice no research should be carried out on a spare embryo without the informed consent of the couple from whom that embryo was generated, whenever this is possible.**

Why require the 'informed consent' of the donors unless to do otherwise would be to infringe some property right of theirs? (Note the *Del Zio* case discussed *supra* p 656).

The second model, that the embryo is a legal person, may be attractive to some but is difficult to substantiate on the existing law. If it were a legal person then clearly in the absence of the competing interest of someone else, as in the case of abortion, it could not be destroyed. Nor could it be sold and the parents would have no authority to give consent to anything which was not in the embryo's 'best interests' which would clearly exclude a non-therapeutic destructive experiment.

Warnock appears, therefore, to have been right in recognising the need for legislation to establish the status of the embryo, although any such legislation would need to avoid the errors into which Warnock may have fallen. The only legislation so far advanced in the UK has been the two Bills under the sponsorship of Enoch Powell MP and Ken Hargreaves MP. These would outlaw all embryo experimentation (it would seem, *therapeutic* as well as non-therapeutic experiments?).

The Unborn Children Protection Bill, introduced by Enoch Powell was in the following terms:

1.—(1) Except with the authority of the Secretary of State under this Act, no person shall—
    (a) procure the fertilisation of a human ovum *in vitro* (that is to say, elsewhere than in the body of a woman), or
    (b) have in his possession a human embryo produced by *in vitro* fertilisation.
(2) The Secretary of State's authority—
    (a) shall be given expressly for the purpose of enabling a named woman to bear a child by means of embryo insertion, and not for any other purpose,
    (b) shall be given in writing and only when applied for, in the prescribed form, by two registered medical practitioners, and
    (c) shall specify—
        (i) the persons by whom, or under whose directions, the procedures of *in vitro* fertilisation and embryo insertion are authorised to be carried out,
        (ii) the place or places where any such procedure is to be carried out, and
        (iii) the persons who may, in pursuance of the authority, have possession or control of embryos produced by such fertilisation.
. . .
  (6) There shall be paid, on or in connection with applications for the Secretary of State's authority under this Act, such fees as may be prescribed; and the fees shall be fixed, so far as practicable, with a view to defraying administration costs arising under this Act.

Compare the legislation in Victoria, the first jurisdiction to legislate on the matter. The Infertility (Medical Procedures) Act 1984 stipulates that embryos may only be formed for the purpose of using them in an IVF procedure. Thus, it outlaws the deliberate creation of embryos for the purpose of experimentation. It goes on to provide that any experiments which are carried out on *excess* (or spare) embryos may only be lawfully done with the approval of the Standing Review and Advisory Committee on infertility set up under s 29 of the Act. To act otherwise is made a serious criminal offence with a maximum penalty of four years imprisonment.

Recourse to detailed legislation may seem superficially attractive but as any lawyer knows to pass laws is not necessarily to make problems go away. For instance, in his paper delivered at the UKNCCL Colloquium on Reproductive Medicine held at Cambridge in September 1987 entitled 'Making Law for Laboratory Life in Australia', Professor Waller writes that:

> The Victorian Standing Review and Advisory Committee considered an experimental procedure submitted for its attention by one Victorian research group. This involved the fertilisation of previously frozen oocytes, to be followed by chromosomal analysis of eight cell embryos in order to determine whether chromosomal damage occurred as a result of the freezing process. The Act, in section 6(8) specifically states that
>
> > Nothing in this Act prevents or inhibits the carrying out in an approved hospital of research on, and the development of techniques for, freezing or otherwise storing ova removed from the body of a woman.
>
> Five members of the Committee decided that the experiment could not be approved since it clearly contemplated the fertilisation of ova for a purpose other than implantation of the resultant embryos. This, they stated, was prohibited by section 6(5). The remaining three members considered that, because of the impact of section 6(8), and in the overall interests of promoting the alleviation of infertility, the experiment could be approved. In its advice to the Minister, the Committee conveyed both the majority's and the minority's view. . . .
>
> Subsequently, the Committee considered a further application from the same research group. In that experiment, single sperm would be inserted by microinjection into oocytes, with chromosomal analysis of the male and female pronuclei being undertaken before syngamy, or fusion, of the separate male and female components. Fusion would be prevented from occurring, as part of the experimental procedure. Syngamy has been defined as that time in the process of fertilisation when the chromosomes derived from both pronuclei align themselves on the mitotic spindle. Thereafter, the first cell division occurs. On this occasion, the Committee divided equally. Four members concluded that the proposed experiment was one upon embryos, and thus prohibited by the words of section 6(5). They interpreted the expression an 'embryo' to mean what was formed when the sperm penetrated the oocyte. Four members decided that the proposed experiment was not one involving embryos, because the process of fertilisation would be halted before syngamy or fusion, and the establishment of a 'genetically unique human entity.' As a result of this division of opinion on the language of the Act, and because of the Committee's unanimous view that the experiment proposed was of great importance, since it might lead to the development of a treatment to alleviate certain kinds of male infertility, it proposed to the Minister of Health that the Act should be amended, so that that experiment, and others like it, may be considered for approval by the Committee. The amended legislation would authorise the Committee to consider, and approve if it thought fit, experiments on fertilised ova before syngamy had occurred, where the gametes were donated by persons being treated in an IVF programme, and the experiment was designed 'to produce information or establish knowledge indicating procedures' that may lead to the establishment of pregnancies in women in IVF programmes. A Bill to give effect to that recommendation was introduced into the Victorian Legislative Council in April 1987, and [became law in December as the Infertility (Medical Procedures) (Amendment) Act 1987.]

Section 4 provides:

> (1) In section 6 of the Principal Act, for sub-section (5) substitute—
> '(5) Where ova are removed from the body of a woman, a person shall not cause or permit fertilisation of any of those ova to commence outside the body of the woman except—
> > (a) for the purposes of the implantation of embryos derived from those ova in the

womb of that woman or another woman in a relevant procedure in accordance with this Act; or

(*b*) for the purposes of a procedure to which section 9A applies that is approved and carried out in accordance with that section.

Penalty: 100 penalty units or imprisonment for four years.'.

(2) After section 9 of the Principal Act insert—

Research on process of fertilisation before syngamy.

'9A. (1) A procedure to which this section applies is an experimental procedure involving the fertilisation of a human ovum from the point of sperm penetration prior to but not including the point of syngamy.

Do you think the Victorian legislation is more consistent with a 'chattel' or 'persons' analysis of the status of the embryo?

2. Storage and Cryopreservation

A particular problem with control and disposal has arisen with the development of cryopreservation of embryos. As the Australian Senate Committee's Report (*supra*) states (footnotes omitted):

A.23 Embryo freezing was developed by the Monash research group so that embryos surplus to those needed for immediate transfer could be retained for transfer in future cycles, thus reducing the need for repeated laparoscopies. A further advantage of embryo freezing is that all embryos resulting from a treatment cycle may be preserved should conditions inadvertently become unsuitable for their immediate transfer (eg uterine bleeding). In addition, abnormalities in the development of the uterus lining, as a result of superovulatory drugs, may reduce the likelihood of successful implantation, and freezing allows their transfer in a subsequent, normal cycle.

A.24 Not all embryos survive the freeze/thawing process. On average, about 50 to 60 per cent do so. However, those which fertilise and result in pregnancy are much fewer. For example, in a study of 314 embryos frozen at Queen Victoria Medical Centre, 197 survived thawing but only 14 pregnancies resulted (seven per cent). Of these only seven came to term (including one set of twins), thus of the original number frozen only 2.2 per cent resulted in a live birth.

A number of legal problems may arise from the procedures described in this Report. Let us consider the situations where an embryo is damaged or destroyed in the course of one of the procedures. Can the parents, or a child who is subsequently born handicapped, bring an action in the tort of negligence? (For a detailed discussion of actions for negligence arising out of the birth of healthy and handicapped children, see Chs 7 and 10.)

An action at the suit of the parents There are a number of possible factual situations which could give rise to liability.

A. LACK OF CARE IN THE PROCESS OF FREEZING WHICH DESTROYS THE EMBRYO

Accepting that the parents could on traditional tort principles establish negligent or careless conduct, the central issue for us here is what interest of theirs do the parents allege has been invaded?

If the embryo, which has been destroyed is regarded in law as a chattel, then their claim will be for invasion of a property interest. It would be for the court to assess the damages which may include emotional distress (see the *Del Zio* claim, *supra*). If, however, the embryo be regarded as a legal person, then the interest of the parents can only be in their own reaction to the embryo's destruction.

At present, the law only recognises such an action based upon careless conduct if nervous shock (and not *mere* distress) is suffered as defined by the courts in cases such as *McLoughlin v O'Brian* [1983] 1 AC 410, [1982] 2 All ER 298. Thus, no claim exists for the loss of the embryo *per se*.

The same analysis would follow if the embryo is destroyed in the thawing process. Equally, this would be true if the embryo were destroyed during the process of implantation. If the mother suffered physical harm, of course, damages could be recovered for this also.

B. LACK OF CARE—DAMAGING THE EMBRYO

If, instead of being destroyed the embryo is damaged, then the following fact situations could arise. Fist, what if the damage is diagnosed *in utero* and the mother undergoes an abortion?

By the time such diagnosis could be carried out, the embryo would, of course, have matured to be a foetus. No difficulty particular to this situation presents itself here. Damages could be recoverable by the mother for the pain and suffering and anxiety for undergoing the abortion and for carrying the foetus to the extent that it resulted in discomfort. As regards damages for the loss of the foetus itself, there is some legal doubt. The courts have awarded damages for a mother for the still-birth of her child (e g *Bagley v North Herts Health Authority* [1986] NLJ Rep 1014). Would the court extend liability even further backwards and allow recovery where the loss is a consequence of an abortion, remembering, of course, that it was the mother's decision to undergo the abortion?

In approaching the answer to this problem, what has happened to the argument that the embryo could be regarded as a chattel in law? Why does the argument appear to be forgotten once the embryo is implanted and begins to mature? Once this has happened, the *person* argument seems to be accepted without question.

Secondly, what if the damage is diagnosed *in utero* but the mother does not abort or, alternatively, if the damage is not discovered until birth. In both these situations, the parents will have a handicapped child for whom to care. Does the mother's decision not to have an abortion have any relevance for her claim? The threshold point must be that there cannot be in law a duty upon a mother to abort a child when she discovers that her foetus is (or may be) disabled in some way. Nor should her decision not to abort the foetus serve to reduce the damages she can recover from an otherwise culpable defendant, save in the most exceptional circumstances.

In *Emeh v Kensington and Chelsea and Westminster Area Health Authority* [1984] 3 All ER 1044, the Court of Appeal was concerned with a case where a negligently performed sterilisation operation had led to the plaintiff giving birth to an unwanted child. One of the points raised was that the mother's decision not to undergo an abortion once she realised she was pregnant prevented her recovering damages. The Court of Appeal firmly rejected this.

> **Slade LJ:** I am quite prepared to infer that she made a conscious decision not to have the pregnancy terminated a second time, but have no doubt that in the circumstances a large number of mixed motives would have influenced her in reaching this decision.
>
> The judge, in saying that her failure to obtain an abortion was so unreasonable as to eclipse the defendants' wrongdoing, was, I think, really saying that the defendants had the right to expect that, if they had not performed the operation properly, she would procure an abortion even if she did not become aware of its existence until nearly 20 weeks of her pregnancy had elapsed.
>
> I do not, for my part, think that the defendants had the right to expect any such thing. By their own negligence, they faced her with the very dilemma which she had sought to avoid by having herself sterilised.
>
> For the reasons which I have attempted to give, I think that they could, and

should, have reasonably foreseen that if, as a consequence of the negligent performance of the operation, she would find herself pregnant again, particularly after some months of pregnancy, she might well decide to keep the child. Indeed, for my part I would go even a little further. Save in the most exceptional circumstances, I cannot think it right that the court should ever declare it unreasonable for a woman to decline to have an abortion, in a case where there is no evidence that there were any medical or psychiatric grounds for terminating the particular pregnancy. And no such evidence has been drawn to our attention relating to this particular pregnancy of the plaintiff in the present case.

For these reasons, and the further reasons given by Waller LJ, I respectfully disagree with the judge's conclusion that the plaintiff's failure to have an abortion broke the chain of causation.

Not surprisingly, there is no English case where a parent has brought such a claim. It is factually different from the cases involving 'wrongful birth' which have been brought, ie where an action is brought by the parents on the birth of their child alleging that had they been advised of the foetus's condition, the birth would have been avoided by an abortion (on which, see *infra* Ch 10). Here, unlike that 'wrongful birth' situation, the defendant will have *caused the damage* to the child and not merely failed to give the parents the right to prevent birth.

Thus, for the parents to have an action they must point to some harm recognised by the tort of negligence as giving rise to liability. What harm can they point to?

There are *three* possibilities.

Physical harm: The mother could point to the harm suffered as a consequence of giving birth. This would allow the parents to claim for their resulting distress. A claim for the expenditure associated with the upkeep of the child (*quaere*, whether this should be limited to *additional* costs due to the child's disability), may be more difficult to justify analytically because of the need to establish that this is not too remote a consequence from the physical harm. The court would have to be persuaded that costs arising from the upkeep of the child are sufficiently intimately associated with the trauma of childbirth so as to be regarded as reasonably foreseeable. If the remedy is contingent upon the trauma of giving birth only the mother as parent could have a claim.

Nervous shock and distress: Providing that a parent can identify that he or she has suffered that kind of harm recognised by the law as 'nervous shock', there would be no impediment to bringing an action under this head. Of course, the problem surrounding a claim for upkeep costs arises once again, as we saw above.

Economic loss: It could be argued that the *only* loss suffered by the parents (especially the father) in the situation with which we are concerned is economic loss unrelated to any physical harm. The courts have not so categorised the loss suffered; undoubtedly this is because of their general reluctance to allow such claims in all but exceptional circumstances. If the courts did regard the harm as economic loss, could it be said that the relationship between the defendant and the parents is sufficiently close to give rise to a duty *not* negligently to inflict upon the parents the financial burdens of a handicapped child?

An action at the suit of the child

We should only concern ourselves with the situation where a child is born. If the child dies *in utero* English law recognises no action at the suit of the child. If, however, through the negligence of another, the child is harmed whether before or during implantation (even though the harm only demonstrates itself subsequently) the question arises as to whether the child, being born alive, may maintain a cause of action.

CONGENITAL DISABILITIES (CIVIL LIABILITY) ACT 1976

1.—(1) If a child is born disabled as the result of such an occurrence before its birth as is mentioned in subsection (2) below, and a person (other than the child's own mother) is under this section answerable to the child in respect of the occurrence, the child's disabilities are to be regarded as damage resulting from the wrongful act of that person and actionable accordingly at the suit of the child.

(2) An occurrence to which this section applies is one which—
  (a) affected either parent of the child in his or her ability to have a normal, healthy child; or
  (b) affected the mother during her pregnancy, or affected her or the child in the course of its birth, so that the child is born with disabilities which would not otherwise have been present.

Can the definition of an 'occurrence' giving rise to liability in subsection (2) be interpreted to cover the situation where an embryo is harmed before or duing implantation?

Consider the view of Iwan Davies in 'Fabricated Man: The Dilemma posed by Artificial Reproductive Techniques' (1984) 35 NILQ 354, 365:

> ... But it is difficult to see how the Act can apply to a negligently performed IVF procedure since this occurs *'en ventre sa eprouvette'* and as Winfield and Jolowicz[73] point out the provision of an 'occurrence before conception' covers the case of negligent injury to the mother's reproductive system *before* conception.[74] In no way can it be said that IVF affects the parents' ability to have a normal healthy child since presumably without IVF no such occurrence would have been possible.[75]

Notes to extract
73 *Winfield and Jolowicz on Tort* (11th edn, 1979), 643.
74 There may be instances where tortious conduct may so affect a parent or ovum as unavoidably to harm a subsequently conceived child, eg, where the ova are damaged *in utero*.
75 If the doctor fails to carry out genetic screening of ova or sperm, the damage to any resulting child might find a basis under the 1976 Act since the doctor will owe a duty of care to the mother. The difficulty, of course, will be proving negligence since no uniform guidelines have been laid down. Even if a standard practice emerges, the Congenital Disabilities (Civil Liability) Act 1976, s 5 expressly states that a doctor will not be liable to any subsequent child because he deviated from the normal practice unless the deviation is in itself unreasonable.

3. Sale

We have seen the approach of the Warnock Committee whereby the sale of human embryos is contemplated as permissible provided certain conditions are met. This, of course, says nothing about the state of existing law save to imply that sale is at present lawful since the recommendation is made that the sale be subject to criminal sanction if other than in the prescribed form. Is this assumption of the Committee correct? The first question must be whether the law regards the embryo as a chattel or a person, which we discussed above. Even if it be regarded as a chattel it is still necessary to consider whether public policy would make it a chattel *extra commercio*. To designate it as such would, of course, only mean that any purported sale would be invalid. In the absence of any specific statutory provision it cannot be certain that any such sale would be a criminal offence. (For a discussion of the sale of human tissue and organs, see Ch 13 *infra*.)

4. Disposal on or after the death of the genetic parents

The Warnock Committee's view on this was as follows:

> 10.12 We consider that the position that may arise in the event of the death of one

or both of a couple who have stored an embryo should be clarified. **We therefore recommend that when one of a couple dies the right to use or dipose of any embryo stored by that couple should pass to the survivor.** We make this recommendation notwithstanding our reservations about the possibility of posthumous pregnancies. **We recommend that if both die that right should pass to the storage authority.**

Does not reference in Warnock to 'the right to use or dispose' of the embryo and talk of indicating 'wishes about the use' of it, suggest that the embryo is regarded as a chattel? Several consequences flow from regarding it as such. For example, (i) the embryo could be the object of a testamentary disposition, or (ii) disposal could include destruction and will do so if there is disagreement over the embryo's future. In the case of the *Rios* embryos, the Victorian Committee in their second advice seemed to equivocate. You will recall that they recommended that the embryos should not be destroyed but should be put aside and left to die.

In 'Making Law for Laboratory Life in Australia' (*supra*), pp 7–9, Professor Louis Waller discusses the Committee's decisions.

The final Report of the Victorian IVF Committee contained a number of recommendations on the cryopreservation and the disposition of laboratory embryos. While a majority of the Committee decided that embryo freezing and storage should be permitted, it unanimously postulated a careful regime to ensure the safety of any embryos so treated, and their disposition if they were not to be removed for transfer to the woman whose ova had been used. This might occur because an immediate transfer of an embryo from that cohort had been successful, or because subsequently accident, death or dissolution of the marriage supervened. While the Committee did 'not regard the couple whose embryo is stored as owning or having dominion over that embryo', it did 'consider that the couple whose gametes are used to form the embryo in the context of an IVF programme should be recognised as having rights which are in some ways analogous to those recognised in parents of a child after its birth. . . . [T]hose rights are not absolute, just as the rights of parents are limited by the rights and interests of the child, and by the larger concerns of the community in which they all live'. In light of these conclusions, the Committee recommended that the couple could not sell or casually dispose of the embryo. After receiving comprehensive information and expert counselling, they might either agree to donation to another infertile couple, or to research or experimental work in connexion with an IVF programme, or that the storage of the frozen embryo should cease. Mindful of the case of the Rios embryos, labelled as the 'orphan embryos' in the international publicity which followed the report that the woman whose ova had been used in their formation had died, with her husband, in an air crash, the Committee proposed that the couple should be required to determine a conditional disposition before storage began. In the event that such a conditional determination was not made—as in Mrs Rios's case—the Committee recommended that the embryo be removed from storage and set aside. That was likened to 'the removal of life-support systems from a mortally ill person. Life is allowed to end'.

The Infertility (Medical Procedures) Act 1984 does not incorporate extensive provisions on cryopreservation. The powers given the Minister, in section 7(3) of the Act, to prescribe terms and conditions for hospitals which are approved to carry out IVF procedures, and the power to make regulations under section 32 of the Act, allow for the development of a system for the control of freezing and storage. But section 14, inserted as one of the several amendments to the Bill which were introduced by the Opposition parties and accepted by the Government, provides that, in a case such as the Rios's, 'the Minister shall direct the designated officer of the approved hospital where the embryo is stored to ensure that [it] is made available for use in [an IVF procedure]'; that is, as a donor embryo. This is the one provision in the legislation where the IVF Committee's recommendation is not wholly or substantially reflected.

Do you think the Victorian Committee's view is any more satisfactory than that of Warnock in resolving the issue of whether the embryo is a chattel or not? Which position, in your view, is reflected in section 14 of the Infertility (Medical Procedures) Act 1984?

The Government's White Paper of November 1987 recognises the difficulty of storage and disposal of such embryos and that the problem should be resolved by making the donor's wishes determinative (paras 51–60).

In its White Paper, the Government rejected the view that the 'storage authority' should have the right of use or disposal of stored embryos (paras 51 and 58). Instead, the donor's wishes should be paramount and only if the donor's consent is obtained may they be used otherwise. Legislation would give effect to this.

51. . . . The Government . . . has concluded that the law should be based on the clear principle that the donor's wishes are paramount during the period in which embryos or gametes may be stored; and that after the expiry of this period, they may only be used by the licence holder for other purposes if the donor's consent has been given to this.

52. The Warnock Committee recommended that embryos should not be stored for longer than 10 years because of current ignorance about the effects of long-term storage, and because of the legal and ethical complications that could arise. They set no maximum limit for gamete storage, but recommended that there should be 5-yearly reviews of both gamete and embryo deposits.

53. The Government accepts that regular reviews are important, and regards this as a matter on which the SLA should give guidance. It accepts that a maximum time-limit should be set for storage of embryos, and indeed of gametes, too. It shares the disquiet felt by many at the implications of long-term storage, while accepting the arguments in favour of allowing some storage period, for example for couples who have had one successful IVF pregnancy and wish to have a second child without the need for further egg recovery and the uncertainty attached to creating new embryos. The Government is not persuaded that it is necessary for this purpose to store embryos for as long as 10 years, and indeed it feels that any benefits this could conceivably bring are outweighed by the increased complexity of the legal and ethical problems which result.

54. The Bill will therefore provide that embryos may be stored for a maximum of 5 years, or such lesser time as the SLA determines. Gametes may be stored for a maximum of 10 years. A power will be included for the Secretary of State to reduce these time limits by regulations.

55. The complexities connected with storage underline the importance of ensuring that, when couples embark on IVF treatment, or when gametes are being donated, the individuals involved have given their consent to the uses to which their gametes or embryos will be put.

56. The Bill will provide that gametes or embryos may only be stored with the signed consent of the donors; and may be used only by the licence holder responsible for storage for the purposes specified in that consent (eg for therapeutic treatment, [or for research]). Those giving consent should be provided with information about the techniques for which their gametes/embryos might be used and about the legal implications of their decision. As a matter of good practice counselling should also be available to them.

57. Donors would have the right to vary or withdraw their consent before the gametes/embryos were used, but the onus would be on them to notify any change to the licence holder. A licence holder receiving notice of such a change will have a duty to inform any other licence holder to whom he has supplied the donor's gametes. (This situation might arise, for example, if a sperm bank supplied sperm to one or more treatment centres.) In the absence of any notification to the contrary, or notification of death, the licence holder must assume that the original consent still holds, and must act accordingly during the storage period. When this ends, he may only use or dispose of the embryo or gametes in accordance with the specified

wishes of the donors. If these are not clear, the embryo or gametes should be removed from storage and left to perish.

58. As far as embryos are concerned, these may not be implanted into another woman, [nor used for research], nor destroyed (prior to the expiry of the storage time limit), in the absence of the consent of **both** donors. If there is disagreement between the donors the licence holder will need to keep the embryo in storage until the end of the storage period, after which time, if there is still no agreement, the embryo should be left to perish.

59. The situation might arise where a husband dies while an embryo is in storage, and his widow asks for this to be transferred to her (or to be inseminated with her husband's stored sperm after his death). The Government recognises that many people are uneasy about this practice, and indeed the Warnock Committee felt it should be actively discouraged. The Government has considered the option of legislating to prevent such situations arising by, for example, providing that stored embryos must be destroyed on the death of one partner. (It would not be ethically acceptable, in the Government's view, to use them for [research or] implantation in another woman without the consent of the donors.) On the other hand, if both husband and widow wished to have the embryo transferred, and they were adequately counselled and aware of the implications on the status of any resulting child (which would not be regarded in law as a child of the marriage), the Government does not feel at present that this should be prohibited by law, although, obviously, it is not a practice which should receive active encouragement.

60. The Bill will provide that the partners should, at the time they give their consent to the storage of embryos or gametes, indicate their wishes about the use of these by their partners should they die. A husband can, for example, indicate whether he is content for his widow to have the embryo implanted; and a woman can indicate whether she is content, should her husband wish, for the embryo to be implanted in another woman after her death. If there is no agreement, then, on the death of one partner, the embryo should be left to perish. (As far as inheritance is concerned, children born in such circumstances will have no rights in law to claim on the estate of the deceased father unless he has made specific provision for this in his will. The same applies to children born of AIH after the father's death.) However, decisions about implanting an embryo in such circumstances should not be taken precipitately, nor without adequate counselling, and this is an aspect on which the SLA will, it is expected, give guidance to those wishing to operate storage facilities.

Does this approach differ from the Australian response to stored embryos as, for example, in the *Rios* case? Is the view that the donors' wishes should be adhered to by the storage authority consistent with any conclusion other than that embryos are chattels?

You will see in paragraph 56 that the Government indicates that prior to storage the written consent of the donors should be obtained and their wishes about use and disposal of the embryo set out. Consequently, the donors' wishes would determine the fate of the embryo. The VLA in its 4th Report in 1989 set out a specimen agreement for those undergoing IVF treatment. *Inter alia*, it contains the following clauses. (How, if at all, do its terms differ from the Government's proposals?)

4. (a) We request that any pre-embryos which are not replaced should, at the discretion of the medical staff, be preserved by freezing or other methods and stored for a period of not more than two years from the date of fertilisation.
(b) We understand that if before the period of two years has expired we wish any pre-embryos to be preserved for a further period, the Centre will be prepared, at our request, to consider such further period of preservation on terms to be negotiated.
(c) We understand that, if we so wish, any suitable pre-embryos so stored may be used for replacement (but only in the above-named woman) and at the discretion of

the medical and scientific staff. We further understand that no assurance can be given that any such pre-embryos will survive or be suitable for replacement.

(d) We agree that no stored pre-embryo shall be removed from the custody of the medical and scientific staff of the Centre without the written consent of both of us (or the survivor), such consent to be given within 28 days before such replacement or removal.

(e) We agree that after the period of two years (or such extension as may be agreed) has expired the Hospital or Centre (subject to the general terms of this agreement) may dispose of the stored pre-embryos at their discretion either by:

    (i) donation to another individual determined by the clinician in charge,

    (ii) destroying by approved methods.

5. We accept that decisions as to the suitability and number of pre-embryos for replacement, at any time and whether frozen or not, will be at the absolute sole discretion of the medical and scientific staff of the Centre, subject to the Guidelines of the ILA.

6. We do not consent to the transfer of any pre-embryo so produced into a woman other than the above-named woman.

Questions

(i) To what extent does *this* agreement make the wishes of the donors paramount?

(ii) What would happen if the donors of the male and female gametes that comprise the embryo disagree?

In the event of an embryo being transferred to its genetic mother after the death of its genetic father or, alternatively, after the death of both and the transfer is to another, questions of inheritance by the resulting child arise. The Warnock Committee recommended that:

10.14 On the question of inheritance and succession we hold that the order in which fertilisation *in vitro* took place should not alter the principle that the first born among siblings in a multiple pregnancy is deemed to be the eldest. The same principle should apply to embryos that have been stored. **We recommend, therefore, that for the purposes of establishing primogeniture the date and time of birth, and not the date of fertilisation, shall be the determining factor.**

10.15 With regard to the possibility of a frozen embryo being transferred to the mother after the death of the father we consider that a similar situation to that which we have recommended in the case of posthumous AIH should apply (see 10.9). **We therefore recommend that legislation be introduced to provide that any child born following IVF, using an embryo that had been frozen and stored, who was not *in utero* at the date of the death of the father shall be disregarded for the purposes of succession to and inheritance from the latter.**

Can the English law adapt to accommodate this without specific statutory provision? (In its White Paper, the Government intends to follow the Warnock proposal; see para 60, *supra* p 691.)

5. Research

We draw no distinction here between the words *research* and *experimentation*. We are concerned with activities calculated to discover or add to knowledge. Such activities may be by intervention or observation. Here we are largely concerned with interventions. We would draw the distinction between *therapeutic* and *non-therapeutic* research. The distinction lies ultimately in the intention of the person engaged in the activity (see the discussion in Ch 11). As regards *therapeutic* research, namely that research which aims to benefit the embryo or enhance its prospects of continued survival, we see no particular legal issues. As regards *non-therapeutic* research, however, the legal issue of whether the embryo is a chattel or a person assumes perhaps the greatest significance in this context of research and experimentation. In the cases of non-therapeutic research which will be destructive of the embryo or will result in the embryo being so damaged as to make it improper to implant it because of the consequential disabilities it could suffer if able to survive to full term, virtually all national reports recommend that the consent of the donors of the gametes should be obtained. For example, the Warnock Committee stated (para 11.24):

> 11.24 We are satisfied that 'spare' embryos may be used as subjects for research; **and we recommend accordingly a need to obtain *consent* to the method of use or disposal of spare embryos. We recommend that as a matter of good practice no research should be carried out on a spare embryo without the informed consent of the couple for whom that embryo was generated, whenever this is possible.**

Why does the Warnock Committee stress the need for consent? Leaving aside matters of good taste and the preservation of good relations between institutions and donors of gametes, is there any *legal* relevance in the calls for consent? Consider, once again, the 'chattel' and 'person' models describing the status of the embryo.

If the embryo be a *chattel* then clearly consent is usually required before someone may deal in any way (including harm) with another's chattels. If consent is given it is usually sufficient to render the conduct lawful. There are minor exceptions to this proposition, eg the harming of one's dog or the destruction of a tree subject to a preservation order. But these are statutory in origin. Without a similar specific provision for embryos which protects them from harm, then consent would be necessary and therefore reference to it has legal relevance. But, it is a central premis of the Warnock Report that an embryo of 'the human species ought to have a special status' (para 11.17). It is hard to argue that regarding the embryo as a chattel amounts to this.

If the embryo is a *person* then the need for consent to research is at odds with traditional legal principles. As we have seen, a parent or guardian may ordinarily only consent to that which is in the 'best interests' or, at least, 'not against the interests' of a child (see Ch 4). The same principle would appear to apply to embryos if they are to be regarded in law as persons. This being so, it would be unlawful for the donors of the gametes which combine to produce the embryo to consent to the embryos' destruction. It could not possibly be in its interest, and it is, in fact, against the embryos' interests.(It would be deemed to have interests if in law it were regarded as a person, including the interest in survival.) Consequently, the recommendation that consent be sought amounts to a jurisprudential flaw. It amplifies, however, the inconsistency in the official reports over the precise status to attribute to the embryo (see the discussion of 'jurisprudential flaw', *supra* p 681).

If non-therapeutic research is taken to include mere observation of the embryo without any accompanying harm to it, this could be validly consented to and this would be consistent with the principle set out above since no harm to the embryo is intended.

Surrogacy

(i) INTRODUCTION

In this section we examine the law as it pertains to surrogate motherhood, a modern practice which as Singer and Wells in *New Ways of Making Babies: Reproduction Revolution* (1984) (pp 107–108) point out, has historical precedents:

> ... there is nothing new about the basic idea of surrogate motherhood. It is even in the Bible. The sixteenth chapter of Genesis tells the following story about Abraham and his wife Sarah (who have, at this stage, not yet been given the new names they

receive from God after he makes his convenant with Abraham, and hence are referred to by their original names of Abram and Sarai):

Abram's wife Sarai had borne him no children. Now she had an Egyptian slave-girl whose name was Hagar, and she said to Abram, 'You see that the Lord has not allowed me to bear a child. Take my slave-girl; perhaps I shall found a family through her.' Abram agreed to what his wife said, so Sarai, Abram's wife, brought her slave-girl, Hagar the Egyptian, and gave her to her husband Abram as a wife . . . He lay with Hagar and she conceived . . .

The Warnock Committee offered an answer to the question 'what is surrogacy?' (paras 8.1–8.3):

8.1 Surrogacy is the practice whereby one woman carries a child for another with the intention that the child should be handed over after birth. The use of artificial insemination and the recent development of *in vitro* fertilisation have eliminated the necessity for sexual intercourse in order to establish a surrogate pregnancy. Surrogacy can take a number of forms. The commissioning mother may be the genetic mother, in that she provides the egg, or she may make no contribution to the establishment of the pregnancy. The genetic father may be the husband of the commissioning mother, or of the carrying mother; or he may be an anonymous donor. There are thus many possible combinations of persons who are relevant to the child's conception, birth and early environment. Of these various forms perhaps the most likely are surrogacy involving artificial insemination, where the carrying mother is the genetic mother inseminated with semen from the male partner of the commissioning couple, and surrogacy using *in vitro* fertilisation where both egg and semen come from the commissioning couple, and the resultant embryo is transferred to and implants in the carrying mother.

8.2 There are certain circumstances in which surrogacy would be an option for the alleviation of infertility. Examples are where a woman has a severe pelvic disease which cannot be remedied surgically, or has no uterus. The practice might also be used to help those women who have suffered repeated miscarriages. There are also perhaps circumstances where the genetic mother, although not infertile, could benefit from the pregnancy being carried by another woman. An example is where the genetic mother is fit to care for a child after it is born, but suffers from a condition making pregnancy medically undesirable.

8.3 If surrogacy takes place it generally involves some payment to the carrying mother. Payment may vary between reimbursement of expenses, and a substantial fee. There may, however, be some instances where no money is involved, for example, where one sister carries the pregnancy for another.

The Victorian legislation provides an example of a statutory definition in the Infertility (Medical Procedures) Act 1984, s 30(1) which provides:

30. (1) In this section, a reference to a woman who acts or agrees with another person or other persons to act, as a surrogate mother is a reference to a woman who has entered into, or enters into, a contract, agreement or arrangement with that other person or those other persons, whether formal or informal, and whether or not for payment or reward under which the woman agrees—

(*a*) to become pregnant, or to seek or attempt to become pregnant, with the intention that a child born as the result of the pregnancy become and be treated, whether by adoption, agreement or otherwise, as the child of that other person or of those other persons; or

(*b*) being pregnant, that a child born as the result of the pregnancy become and be treated, whether by adoption, agreement or otherwise, as the child of that other person or those other persons.

(ii) THE ISSUES

The modern practice of surrogacy is thought to raise the following problems. The Warnock Committee summarised the arguments as follows (paras 8.10–8.12):

8.10 There are strongly held objections to the concept of surrogacy, and it seems from the evidence submitted to us that the weight of public opinion is against the practice. The objections turn essentially on the view that to introduce a third party into the process of procreation which should be confined to the loving partnership between two people, is an attack on the value of the marital relationship . . . Further, the intrusion is worse than in the case of AID, since the contribution of the carrying mother is greater, more intimate and personal, than the contribution of a semen donor. It is also argued that it is inconsistent with human dignity that a woman should use her uterus for financial profit and treat it as an incubator for someone else's child. The objection is not diminished, indeed it is strengthened, where the woman entered an agreement to conceive a child, with the sole purpose of handing the child over to the commissioning couple after birth.

8.11 Again, it is argued that the relationship between mother and child is itself distorted by surrogacy. For in such an arrangement a woman deliberately allows herself to become pregnant with the intention of giving up the child to which she will give birth, and this is the wrong way to approach pregnancy. It is also potentially damaging to the child, whose bonds with the carrying mother, regardless of genetic connections, are held to be strong, and whose welfare must be considered to be of paramount importance. Further it is felt that a surrogacy agreement is degrading to the child who is to be the outcome of it, since, for all practical purposes, the child will have been bought for money.

8.12 It is also argued that since there are some risks attached to pregnancy, no woman ought to be asked to undertake pregnancy for another, in order to earn money. Nor, it is argued should a woman be forced by legal sanctions to part with a child, to which she has recently given birth, against her will.

More fully, the arguments are put by Singer and Wells in *The Reproduction Revolution, supra* (pp 114–120) (footnotes omitted):

Objections to surrogacy

Surrogate motherhood is one of the few applications of IVF of which the general public disapproves. That, at least, is the finding of the 1982 Morgan Gallup Poll in Australia and in Britain. After people had answered questions about more straightforward uses of IVF, they were told the following:

The fertilised egg from one married couple could be put into *another* woman, who would then become pregnant. She would *give the baby back* to the couple after it was born.

More than 70 per cent of the sample in each country said they had heard about this procedure. They were then asked:

Do you think this sort of test-tube baby treatment for married couples to have a child by *another* woman should be *allowed*, or *not*?

In Australia, 32 per cent thought it should be allowed, but 44 per cent thought it should not be. In Britain only 20 per cent thought it should be allowed, with a solid majority of 55 per cent against allowing it. In both countries around a quarter of respondents either had no opinion, or said that they needed to know more, or that the answer depended on other factors.

The poll data does not tell us why so many people thought that full surrogate motherhood should not be allowed. The response is a contrast to the more approving reaction we noted in the previous chapter to the question about the donation of fertilised eggs—or 'pre-natal adoption'. One reason for this different response might be that people do not like the idea of a woman having to 'give back' a baby to whom she has given birth. We shall see in a moment that there is some reason for concern about this aspect of surrogate motherhood. But there is also a crucial difference in the way the two questions were put, which makes the answers not strictly comparable. When people were asked about the donation of fertilised eggs, they were told that the eggs were to be given to another married couple 'so that they can have a child'. The clear implication is that the married couple to whom the eggs are given could not have a child by any other method. In the question asked about surrogate motherhood there was no such implication. Respondents therefore may not have had the plight of the childless couple in mind when they answered. It was open to them to interpret the question as one about a married couple who could have children by the normal method but find it more convenient to use a surrogate. If some respondents did interpret the question in this way, the negative response is easily explained.

No doubt a significant number of people do oppose surrogate motherhood even for couples who cannot otherwise have children. Some may think of it as unnatural, and for that reason wrong. . . . We will simply repeat our conclusion that the naturalness or unnaturalness of a new procedure is not the real issue: the crucial question is whether the procedure is likely to do more good than harm.

Here opponents of surrogacy will point to the horrendous legal tangles that could arise with full surrogacy. Some of these tangles have already arisen among the relatively small number of partial surrogacy arrangements made so far. Although partial surrogacy differs in some relevant respects from full surrogacy, the problems that have arisen with partial surrogacy are at present the best guide to the likely problems of full surrogacy.

Noel Keane, the American lawyer who helped Stefan and Nadia arrange their partial surrogacy contract, has written a book, *The Surrogate Mother*, describing his work in this new field. Keane credits himself with the path-breaking legal work that has made partial surrogacy a reality for many infertile couples. There is no doubt about his enthusiasm for surrogacy. 'Surrogate parenting', he tells us, 'is an idea whose time is coming . . . I think it will replace adoption.' The book itself, Keane says, 'is my legal brief on behalf of a controversial cause to make surrogate motherhood a common reality in the years ahead'.

Given Keane's advocacy of the cause, some sections of *The Surrogate Mother* are alarming. Perhaps most dramatic is the story of Bill and Bridget. In fairness to Keane, it has to be said that the case was one of his early ones. It began in 1977, before he quite knew what he was getting into; nevertheless it illustrates some possible pitfalls of surrogacy.

Bill and Bridget were an infertile couple. Keane put them in touch with Diane. Diane had seen a television talk show in which Keane appeared with another infertile couple and their pregnant partial surrogate. After the show, Diane had phoned offering to help a couple to have a child. She was a thirty-one-year-old divorcee, living in Tennessee with a two-year-old son: when interviewed she seemed a good mother and responsible parent. At that time Keane had not discovered that Kentucky State law allowed the payment of a fee to surrogate mothers, so Diane was told that nothing could be paid except expenses. She signed an agreement to that effect.

Diane soon became pregnant with Bill's child. Then things began to go wrong. She asked Bill and Bridget for money to travel to Boston to visit her mother. They sent her the money. She said she had been robbed of expense money they had sent her. They sent her another cheque. Then her car needed repairs, she had extra medical expenses . . . and so on. Often when she phoned asking for money, she sounded drunk or stoned on drugs. Sometimes she threatened to kill herself unless she got more money. Bill and Bridget did not dare call her bluff. Shortly before the baby was due, Diane demanded $3,000 to pay for a computer course she planned to take. Bill and Bridget paid. In all, they calculated that they sent Diane more than $12,000.

Finally, two weeks before the due date, Diane phoned to say that she was in jail on a drunk-driving charge, and needed bail money. Bill and Bridget flew to Tennessee to stay with Diane and try to prevent anything else going wrong before she had the baby. That is when they found that Diane's 'roommate', Vicky, was really her lover. In despair Bridget turned on her husband. 'Bill', she screamed, 'do you realise that the woman you got pregnant is not only an alcoholic and drug addict but also a lesbian!'

Amazingly, the story has a happy ending. Diane gave birth to a boy, below normal weight and suffering from drug withdrawal symptoms; but after five days in hospital Bill, Jr was healthy enough to go home with his father and his new mother. Diane tried for some time to extract more money by threatening to hold up the adoption proceeding; but when this threat failed to have any effect, she moved interstate without leaving any forwarding address. At the time of writing Keane described the child as 'in legal limbo', but Bill and Bridget were so happy with 'their' child that they told Keane: 'He has made it all worthwhile.'

Two other bizarre Keane stories ended less happily. The first, related in *The Surrogate Mother*, concerns John and Lorelei, a married Connecticut couple unable to have children. The usual story, except that in this case the infertility was not unexpected: Lorelei was a transsexual. Until the age of twenty-one, she had been male. For Keane, this was no obstacle. He took the couple on as his clients. They found Rita, a divorced Californian mother of three who said she was interested in being a surrogate mother 'for humanitarian reasons'. Rita became pregnant, and then asked for $7,500. Keane advised John and Lorelei that they would be breaking the law if they paid; in any case they could not afford to pay. They refused. Rita wrote back: 'I have decided to keep my baby, and the deal is off.'

The baby, a boy, was born in April 1981. Keane brought a custody suit on behalf of John. Blood tests showed with 99 per cent probability that he was the father. Before the case came to court, however, it became apparent that Lorelei's transsexualism would come out into the open and probably damage their already slim chances of success. In a vain attempt to avoid publicity, John and Lorelei decided to give up the legal battle for custody.

Our final Keane disaster is not taken from the pages of his book. It was, however, anticipated by a prescient quotation in the book, taken from an editorial in the *Detroit News*. Writing of the possible legal dilemmas of the new method of motherhood, the editorial asked:

What happens if the proxy mother gives birth to a defective child and the couple refuses to adopt it? Can the surrogate mother sue the father for damages arising from pregnancy? How can the husband be sure he is indeed the father of his 'investment', short of isolating the surrogate from other male contacts?

Keane did not answer these questions in *The Surrogate Mother*. Soon after the book appeared, however, he found himself unable to avoid them.

Late in 1981 Judy Stiver, a Michigan housewife, noticed an advertisement in a local paper. It was one placed regularly by Keane, and it sought women willing to become surrogate mothers for a fee. Judy and her husband, Ray, had a two-year-old daughter, and going through pregnancy again seemed a good way to earn some extra cash. 'We wanted the money to pay some bills and take a vacation', she explained later to a reporter.

Through Keane, Judy Stiver met Alexander and Nadia Malahoff, of New York. She agreed to be impregnated with Alexander Malahoff's sperm and to abstain from sexual intercourse until the baby was conceived. In return, Malahoff agreed to take the baby and pay Mrs Stiver $10,000. All went well until the baby was born, when it was discovered that he suffered from microcephaly, a condition in which the head is abnormally small, and the child often turns out to be mentally retarded.

At first the child was not expected to live: when it became apparent that he would, Malahoff claimed that the baby's blood tests showed that he could not have been the father. Accordingly he refused to accept the baby, and to pay Judy Stiver the agreed fee. At first the Stivers also refused to take the baby, saying that they had come to accept that the baby would be taken from Mrs Stiver, and they did not want another child. When further court-ordered blood tests confirmed that Alexander Malahoff was not the father, however, the Stivers finally agreed to keep the baby.

Many people would consider these episodes provide sufficient grounds for prohibiting surrogacy, whether partial or full. Once we mess around with conventional arrangements for bearing and rearing children, there is no end to the complications that can arise. The result is distress for all concerned.

To those who argue that couples and would-be surrogates have the right to make their own private contractual arrangements in matters that concern no one else, the opponents of surrogacy could reply that in surrogacy contracts someone else is always affected: the child. Society has a right, they would claim, to prohibit such arrangements in order to prevent children being born in undesirable circumstances. They might add that the childless couple are usually too desperate to take proper steps to ensure that a woman offering to act as a surrogate really is a fit and proper person for that purpose. The story of Bill and Bridget suggests this; and Lorelei told Keane that when Rita offered to act as surrogate, 'we were so excited we would have taken someone with purple skin from Mozambique'.

Discussion
We have seen that when A and B have a surrogate motherhood contract with C, at least four things are liable to go wrong:

(1) C might have contracted to refrain from taking alcohol or drugs, but might do it anyway.
(2) C might, during pregnancy, attempt to extort payment, or additional payment beyond any agreed fee, from A and B. To do this she might threaten to have an abortion, or to keep the baby.
(3) C might decide, once the baby is born, that she wishes to keep it, in spite of her contract to give it to A and B.
(4) A and B might decide, once the baby is born, that they do not wish to accept it, perhaps because it is born with a handicap, perhaps because they do not believe it is their genetic child.

No doubt there are many other complications that could arise, but these instances are enough to indicate where surrogacy can lead.

No one denies that surrogacy can cause problems—least of all Keane, who has to be given credit for having openly displayed the troubles some of his clients found themselves in. Keane does not, of course, believe that the problems are a reason for prohibiting surrogacy. He would point to the cases like that of Stefan and Nadia, in which a surrogacy agreement went smoothly, leaving a couple ecstatic over the fulfilment of their otherwise impossible dream of having a child, and a surrogate mother happy with her fee, or perhaps even simply happy with the knowledge that she has helped to bring to others the joy of parenthood. Stefan and Nadia are, Keane could add, more typical than Bill and Bridget, John and Lorelei or the Malahoffs.

In *The Surrogate Mother* Keane gave an account of his first nine cases. If we take this as a sample, then the cases of Bill and Bridget and of John and Lorelei were the two most tangled of these nine. Even so, one of these two had a happy ending. So would it have been right to prevent eight couples having the child they wanted, just in order to save John and Lorelei's disappointment?

Shelley Roberts summarises her detailed consideration of the issues as follows in her paper 'Warnock and Surrogate Motherhood: sentiment or argument', in *Rights and Wrongs in Medicine* (1986, ed P Byrne) at p 103:

Arguments against surrogacy: a review
Having explored some of the objections to surrogacy raised in the Warnock committee's report, several points emerge as particularly problematical. Specifically, these are:

1. that paid surrogacy may be exploitative of the women concerned in that the amount of money offered may overcome the normal, expected refusal to submit to such an onerous invasion of their private lives;
2. that it may be against public policy to permit the transfer of money in respect of the use of the woman's body, in particular her womb;
3. that surrogacy violates the principles of maternal responsibility;
4. that it entails the use of children as means rather than regarding them as ends in themselves;
5. that it may potentially cause distress to children who are witnesses of the process.

Taken together, these points certainly appear to provide sufficient justification for imposing restrictions of at least some sort on surrogacy. Thus, it is suggested that, in general terms, the Warnock committee's negative response to surrogacy was quite appropriate. The difficulty, however, with the proposals outlined in the report is that they do not seem to meet the specific problems identified as arising in surrogacy. If we consider, for example, that, as has been suggested, the exchange of money for the use of a bodily organ is contrary to public policy, then the appropriate solution would seem to be a ban on all paid surrogacy. If we also believe that it is impermissible for a woman to conceive a child for the purpose of giving it away, this suggests that all surrogacy, paid or voluntary, should be prohibited. And, if another major area of concern is the welfare of children born to surrogate mothers, then, if the practice is to continue in any fashion, it must be regulated so as to ensure that welfare. None of these conclusions was reached by the Warnock committee.

The recommendations proposed in the report and adopted in the Government's bill introduced in 1985 attack, instead, only that which is superficially distasteful about surrogate motherhood. The effect of the provisions would be to reduce the volume of surrogacy transactions but sweep the remainder out of sight, where the real problems would be beyond society's ability to respond to or to remedy.

To the extent that these arguments are valid how should the law respond? [For a sympathetic view of surrogacy see, L Andrews *Between Strangers* (1989)].

(iii) POSSIBLE RESPONSES

The Warnock Committee's view, which Roberts refers to in the above extract, was as follows (footnotes omitted):

8.17 The question of surrogacy presented us with some of the most difficult problems we encountered. The evidence submitted to us contained a range of strongly held views and this was reflected in our own views. The moral and social objections to surrogacy have weighed heavily with us. In the first place we are all agreed that surrogacy for convenience alone, that is, where a woman is physically capable of bearing a child but does not wish to undergo pregnancy, is totally ethically unacceptable. Even in compelling medical circumstances the danger of exploitation of one human being by another appears to the majority of us far to outweigh the potential benefits, in almost every case. That people should treat others as a means to their own ends, however desirable the consequences, must always be liable to moral objection. Such treatment of one person by another becomes positively exploitative when financial interests are involved. It is therefore with the commercial exploitation of surrogacy that we have been primarily, but by no means exclusively, concerned.

8.18 We have considered whether the criminal law should have any part to play in the control of surrogacy and have concluded that it should. We recognise that there is a serious risk of commercial exploitation of surrogacy and that this would be difficult to prevent without the assistance of the criminal law. We have considered whether a limited, non-profit making surrogacy service, subject to licensing and inspection, could have any useful part to play but the majority agreed that the existence of such a service would in itself encourage the growth of surrogacy. **We recommend that legislation be introduced to render criminal the creation or the operation in the United Kingdom of agencies whose purposes include the recruitment of women for surrogate pregnancy or making arrangements for individuals or couples who wish to utilise the services of a carrying mother; such legislation should be wide enough to include both profit and non-profit making organisations. We further recommend that the legislation be sufficiently wide to render criminally liable the actions of professionals and others who knowingly assist in the establishment of a surrogate pregnancy.**

8.19 We do not envisage that this legislation would render private persons entering into surrogacy arrangements liable to criminal prosecution, as we are anxious to avoid children being born to mothers subject to the taint of criminality. We nonetheless recognise that there will continue to be privately arranged surrogacy agreements. While we consider that most, if not all, surrogacy arrangements would be legally unenforceable in any of their terms, we feel that the position should be put beyond any possible doubt in law. **We recommend that it be provided by statute that all surrogacy agreements are illegal contracts and therefore unenforceable in the courts.**

8.20 We are conscious that surrogacy like egg and embryo donation may raise the question as to whether the genetic or the carrying mother is the true mother. Our recommendations in 6.8 and 7.6 cover cases where eggs or embryos have been donated. There remains however the possible case where the egg or embryo has not been donated but has been provided by the commissioning mother or parents with the intention that they should being up the resultant child. If our recommendation in 8.18 is accepted, such cases are unlikely to occur because of the probability that the practitioner administering the treatment would be committing an offence. However, for the avoidance of doubt, we consider that the legislation proposed in 6.8 and 7.6 [ie making the gestational mother the legal mother] should be sufficiently widely drawn to cover any such case. If experience shows that this gives rise to an injustice for children who live with their genetic mother rather than the mother who bore them then in our view the remedy is to make the adoption laws more flexible so as to enable the genetic mother to adopt.

In the introduction to her book *A Question of Life*, Baroness Warnock writes (at p xii):

> Similarly, in the controversial matter of surrogate mothers, the Inquiry agreed unanimously that they disapproved of the practice (largely because of possible consequences for the child); but they also agreed that it could not be prevented by law, because of the intrusiveness of any law that would be enforceable. The Inquiry therefore concentrated on how surrogacy for commercial purposes might be checked, leaving on one side the question whether surrogacy was intrinsically morally right or wrong. We might all of us have answered the primary moral question in a way which made surrogacy wrong. This did not pre-empt the answer to the second-order moral question, Should the law be invoked to stop surrogacy? We all agreed that it would be morally wrong to envisage a law which would intrusively curtail human freedom, and which would in addition be impossible to enforce (how could the law tell whether the child whom Abraham claimed as his own was born to Sara, or to a servant girl who happened to be more fertile?) The Inquiry, then, while unanimously answering the first-order question negatively, holding that surrogacy was wrong, nevertheless held that legislation should not be invoked to prevent it. We did however by a majority recommend that the commercial use of surrogacy arrangements, as a way of making money for an agency, could and should be made a criminal offence. For not only was the wrongness of surrogacy compounded by its being exploited for money, but also a law against agencies would not be intrusive into the private lives of those who were actually engaged in setting up a family.

We find helpful the distinction that Baroness Warnock draws between what is morally permissible and the extent to which the law should respond to the immoral.(We are puzzled by the apparent misunderstanding of the Committee's conclusions which, as we have seen, would outlaw *all* agencies whether profit-making or not.)

Several possible responses of the law are set out by Shelley Roberts (*op cit*), at pp 104–109 (footnotes omitted):

ALTERNATIVE SOLUTIONS

A. Total prohibition

How, then, *ought* the issue of surrogacy to be settled? If we are convinced by the argument that no one should be permitted deliberately to avoid her maternal responsibilities, either for love or money, then the obvious solution is to attempt to devise a method of preventing all surrogacy transactions.

This, of course, raises tremendous practical difficulties. First, it is quite possible that couples may be sufficiently determined to have children by surrogacy that they will opt for the practice regardless of whether or not it is prohibited. Secondly, if the law were to make all surrogacy criminally unlawful, it could find itself hindered in the detection and regulation of possible harms and abuses that might result from 'underground' surrogacy. In addition, secrecy in and outside the family about the nature of a child's provenance could well undermine the stability of the families concerned and, consequently, of society.

Finally, the enforcement of laws against surrogacy, given the intimate nature of the arrangements, would be both difficult and possibly counter-productive. What sanctions could be imposed on transgressors? Fines would be unlikely to deter those intent upon paying huge sums of money for a child. If we imprison his parents for conceiving him, it will be the child who will suffer most. Similarly, his position will be jeopardised if we insist he stays with a mother who does not want him, or publicly declare him illegitimate, or refuse to allow the only family that claims him as theirs to have legal recognition as his parents. Thus, it seems that the most obvious response to the problems of surrogate motherhood may be impractical.

B. Licensing and regulation

If indeed it would not be plausible to seek to outlaw surrogacy, then thought must be given to practical methods by which surrogacy could be regulated. How could the most detrimental features of the practice be avoided? One method might be to regulate surrogate transactions by imposing a licensing scheme for agencies, requiring various forms of mandatory screening and counselling for participants.

There are serious problems with this approach. The most obvious is that government interference in, or control of, surrogacy would imply a legitimisation of the practice and perhaps act to encourage participants. If surrogacy clinics were established and licensed, it seems likely that the publicity would increase the popularity of surrogacy as a means of overcoming childlessness. If, however, it is accepted that there are serious problems inherent in surrogacy *per se*, then it is arguable that government ought to discourage rather than encourage the practice. The most serious objections to surrogacy will not be removed even if the process as a whole is subject to close scrutiny, and it would seem wrong to spend sums of public money on the licensing of an activity that has been judged to be contrary to public policy. Thus, it appears that the only legitimate form of regulation would be one which sought to eliminate aspects of surrogacy found to be particularly problematical.

C. Prohibition of commercial surrogacy
1. The role of intermediaries

The solution adopted by the Warnock committee and incorporated into the government's bill is to curtail surrogacy by imposing restrictions on the participation of intermediaries. No person or organisation is to initiate, take part in negotiations or compile information for use in surrogacy arrangements if such is done 'on a commercial basis' (that is, in return for payment to the intermediary).

The prohibition of commercial agencies would certainly limit the growth in the number of surrogate transactions. It would also specifically overcome the sort of abuse seen in the 'stud farms' previously described. One suspects, however, that the measure is designed more to cover up what the public finds distasteful about surrogacy (profit-hungry agencies) than to counteract any ill effects the practice may have upon its participants and on society at large. The more sensational possibilities for exploitation aside, there seems little difference, as regards most of surrogacy's problems, between a commercial agency and a volunteer one, between a transaction mediated by an agency and one conducted privately.

One of the distinctly counterproductive features of the move to curtail intermediaries recommended by the Warnock committee and found in the bill is the effective exclusion of professionals such as doctors and solicitors from surrogacy arrangements. If no person is permitted, in exchange for payment, to compile information in respect of a surrogate arrangement, then couples and prospective surrogates would not, for example, be able to consult their physicians for genetic testing. If no one may take part in the negotiations, then solicitors would not be allowed to assist in facilitating the legal adoption of children born to surrogates.

A prohibition on professional assistance adds to, rather than detracts from, the difficulties associated with surrogacy. It prevents couples from seeking advice that may either lead them to decide against surrogacy or help them to proceed in the way least prejudicial to the interests of all concerned, especially the child. Without in any way encouraging surrogacy, the availability of professional assistance could point towards an informal screening process and allow the resulting child to be properly incorporated into the family that will be caring for him.

On both sides of the Atlantic, professional bodies have already begun to prohibit their members from any form of active recruiting of surrogates. This might be the most sensible way in which to regulate the participation of doctors, solicitors, psychologists and others in the surrogacy process and would be preferable to excluding them completely.

2.   The role of surrogates

Both the Warnock committee and the drafters of the Government's bill recognised that one of the principal problems involved in surrogacy was its commercial aspect. It is suggested, however, that they approached the problem in the wrong way. Instead of seeking to prohibit payment to those assisting in surrogacy arrangements, they should have concentrated on the prohibition of payment to surrogates themselves. Although this solution would not resolve all the fundamental objections to surrogacy, it may be the practical alternative best suited to the protection of those concerned and of society in general.

The result of such a prohibition would probably be to limit the participants in surrogacy arrangements to friends or relatives of the couple seeking a child. Few women would voluntarily bear a child for a stranger. If there were to be an additional ban on advertising, as proposed in section 3 of the bill, then strangers could not ordinarily become involved.

Such a limitation of surrogacy to voluntary arrangements may resolve beneficially a number of the problems associated with surrogacy. First, volunteers would be much less likely to be victims of financial coercion. Equally, they would be unlikely to exploit the couples involved. It is of course arguable that the emotional pressure exerted by a relative or friend could be considerable. However, emotional pressure to perform voluntarily a lawful act is not the sort of duress that is sufficiently severe as to involve sanctions of law.

Secondly, if we refer back to the criteria for organ donations, voluntary womb-leasing ought to fit within the 'approved' category, in that it is the sort of disposition that was thought to be permissible if offered as a donation, but probably contrary to public policy if done in exchange for money. Paid surrogacy, of course, would have been against public policy, according to this test.

A third issue was the disruption of the marriage of the commissioning couple by the surrogate. There is no doubt that the presence of a friend or relative as a 'third party' to the marriage may present a considerable amount of tension. Morally, however, it may be less problematical than a similar intrusion by a stranger. If ties of blood or affection bind the commissioning parents and surrogate, they suggest that the second woman already has a link with the marriage. If anyone could be deemed appropriate as a substitute for the wife, then perhaps it is someone closely related or connected to her and to the family.

The final and perhaps most serious difficulty with surrogacy was the effect of the process upon the children concerned and upon our notions of childhood. At an individual level, the insistence that surrogate transactions be unpaid might well reduce the likelihood of the agreement dissolving into a dispute detrimental to the child. The involvement of friends would result in an arrangement where participants would be inclined to understand and care about each other's interests in the process. An additional benefit is a sort of built-in screening mechanism. A woman who is acting out of love rather than money and who deals directly with the commissioning father is much more likely to ask herself whether or not he is a suitable parent and similarly to consider the prospective mother.

It has been argued, of course, that it is not fair to ask a woman to go through the hardship of a surrogate pregnancy without compensating her for the pain, inconvenience and time. Surely, the better question is whether it is fair to *ask* a woman to undergo a pregnancy for someone else *at all*, and the answer is clearly 'no'. Only if a friend, out of love or compassion, *offers* herself in such a way can the offer be tolerated as a gift of self. The surest way to limit surrogacy to the cases most likely to proceed smoothly is to require an exceptional altruism in the surrogate mother.

However, by allowing even voluntary surrogacy, it is hard to avoid the allegations that surrogacy is equivalent to constructive abandonment and entails the use of a child as the means to an end. The elimination of paid surrogacy would, of course, improve the situation somewhat. The absence of a formal contract and exchange of 'goods' for money would eliminate some of the factors leading to a child-as-product mentality. Although problems could arise either as the result of over-solicitous interference from a surrogate who was a close relative or friend, or confusion for the child as to which woman was his real mother, children might still find it easier to comprehend the idea of 'auntie helping mummy' than of a business transaction between strangers. And it is arguable that a woman who knows the family well into which her child will be adopted, or is herself a member of that family, is committing a less reprehensible act than one who gives her infant to strangers. Nevertheless, the basic philosophical objections remain and nothing short of total prohibition, dismissed as impractical, could remove them. The continuing existence of such problems must serve as a reminder that the scheme proposed here is simply a way in which some forms of surrogacy may be tolerated and not an endorsement of a process which remains fundamentally at odds with public policy.

Given the complexities of the issues arising and the nature of the interests involved, it is inevitable that the law will be involved in some shape or form and to some or other extent. The question then becomes what form that law should take.

One option could be to leave matters to *ad hoc* resolution by the courts as they arise. Alternatively some regulatory scheme could be devised which aims to deal comprehensively with the subject. The latter approach appears to have near universal support. This does not, of course, determine the content of the legal regulation. Professor Alexander Capron, however, adopts an interesting stance urging a minimalist approach through legislation, thereafter relying on traditional family law to achieve the necessary regulation; 'Alternative Birth Technologies: Legal Challenges' (1987) 20 U C Davis LR 697–701:

Is legislation desirable?

Should we remedy this problem by legislating a framework for surrogate contracts? On the one hand, to do so may well increase the frequency of such arrangements—not a salutary development in my view. On the other hand, the primary interest in protection of the offspring is not well-served by the absence of a statutorily established system. What ought such a statute encompass? At a minimum, I would suggest the following.

First, careful medical screening should be performed for all participants in 'surrogacy' to prevent avoidable illness. Granted, this does not exist for ordinary reproduction—but, then, surrogacy is not ordinary. The result may well be achieved through the threat of sanctions on the professionals (physicians, social workers, lawyers, etc) who superintend the arrangements; their failure to screen could be a basis for liability. The risk of eugenic controls being exercised by the state places this aspect of a statute into a difficult balancing act, but the interest in protecting the child is strong enough to compel a hard effort to find a solution that stops short of state control of reproduction.

Second, surrogacy should be regarded as a form of prenatal adoption of the child of one parent by the other parent and provisions for state supervision, including confidential recordkeeping, should parallel those applicable to postnatal adoption. The harder question is whether standards of 'fitness' ought to be applied to the couples; it may be enough to achieve this indirectly through medical supervision. There may, of course, be some issues that cannot be well resolved by the law but must be left to the development of social norms. For example, should the procedure be limited to infertile couples and those with medical reason (genetic or gestational risks) for not reproducing themselves? Rather than trying to develop clear rules on what qualifies as sufficient 'infertility' or 'medical contraindication,' it may be sufficient to leave the question to physicians and potential surrogates: 'Is this couple's problem serious enough to warrant surrogacy?'

Third, and perhaps most important, the parties to the contract should each be bound by their normal parental obligations of care and support, regardless of the breach or alleged breach of the contract by the party. The Malahoff case indicates the potential for abandonment of the child if the parties are free to regard the situation as one of a contract for delivery of a product.

All of the suggestions made thus far aim to protect the interest of the child, which I view as the primary aim of public policy in this field. Other provisions in a statute would expand on this goal, while also attempting to promote additional values.

Fourth, the law should provide that the child is the legal child of the surrogate mother. This was the position of the Warnock Committee in England in 1984.[49] Such a legal rule would do three things. First, it would reinforce the child's interest in having a legally responsible mother at birth. Second, it would place the surrogate in the same position as other women who decide to allow a child to be adopted, which includes having the right to change her mind within a specified time period. Third, it would also discourage surrogacy by exposing the biological father to the risk that he might end up with a financial obligation to the child but without any guarantee of other paternal rights (which would lodge instead with the surrogate's husband).

The rule I suggest regarding maternity raises the more difficult issues of the presumption of paternity. Under the law in the thirty or so states with AID statutes, a child born after AID is presumed to be the legal offspring of her husband if he has consented to the insemination.[50] Applying that rule to surrogacy would make the child the legal offspring of the surrogate's husband if he consents, or would open the physician (and others) to suit if the husband 'non-consented' and later became dissatisfied with the situation. A Michigan decision declining to allow the paternity act to be used to declare prenatally the paternal status of a contracting father was revised on appeal,[51] while a Kentucky court declined to allow a 'mere affidavit' to rebut the presumption of the paternity of the surrogate's husband.[52]

A fifth control that a statute might exercise would be to regulate the amount of payment made. Obviously, such agreements are notoriously difficult to supervise. The major risk that a person runs in going outside the terms permitted in the regulation is the same risk as already exists—namely, holding an unenforceable contract—and that has not deterred hundreds of people so far. Moreover, besides difficulties of enforcement, the question arises, which way should the regulation tend—to hold down payments to the level of actual out-of-pocket expenses (including life and health insurance premiums), which would lead to surrogacy only by true altruists, or to push the price up to a level commensurate with the values of the service and the time and effort involved? The latter would doubtlessly lead to a flood of eager surrogates, but without at least some control, more cases are likely to arise like the one now being litigated in San Diego, in which a Mexican woman is trying to retain custody of the child she bore under a surrogate contract for $1500.[53]

Suppose that the legal regulations adopted are seen as disadvantaging surrogacy compared to AID. Is this unfair discrimination because it treats couples differently based on male versus female infertility? I do not believe that the claimed objection based on 'procreative freedom'[54] is persuasive, for several reasons. First, there is a substantial difference between the role of the 'donor' in AID (merely contributing the germinal material, which is obtained in a risk-free procedure) and the 'donor' in a surrogate contract (who not only contributes the germinal material but carries the child for nine months and gives birth to it).[55] These differences—in time, in risk, in attachment,[56] and in effects on fetal development—implicate the values of well-being and of exploitation set forth earlier. Second, the legal rule in question—that a child born to a woman is legally hers until she gives the child up for adoption—is facially neutral between the situations of AID and surrogacy. In both instances, it vests parental rights and obligations in the woman who is inseminated and her husband. Third, the analogy between AID and surrogate motherhood is inexact; the correct analogue to AID is egg donation . . . In that case, the 'adoptive mother,' who gestates the donated egg (fertilised by the sperm of her husband or another donor) would be the legal mother.[57]

The development of alternative birth technologies is seemingly pushing back the limits of human biology, and in the process sorely testing the limits of human law. The *Baby M* case in New Jersey reminds us of these limits, since it involves at its core the interest of a child who is not a party to the contract. My sense is that, in the absence of a statute that clearly establishes the rules I have recommended in this essay, the *Baby M* court should rule on grounds of the child's 'best interests' in a custodial sense, not on the basis of the contract. Moreover, in so ruling there must be no presumption that wealth or social class is determinative. As the California Supreme Court recently ruled, in a custody dispute over an out-of-wedlock child whose father was seeking custody based on the greater financial means and better home environment he and his new wife could offer compared with the child's working (and still unwed) mother, 'the purpose of child support awards is to ensure that the [parent] otherwise best fit for custody receives adequate funds,' and not to use the poorer parent's position as a ground for denying custody.[58] At the heart of best interests—or 'beyond' it[59]—is stability and continuity for the child.[60] In the *Baby M* case, that consideration could lead custody to be awarded to Dr Stern and his wife (who have had primary custody of most of the child's first year), even if the physician who performed the insemination were now to announce that he had used semen from a man other than Dr Stern.

Notes to extract
[49] *Report of the Committee of Inquiry Into Human Fertilisation and Embryology*, London, Department of Health and Social Security, July, 1984.
[50] Ala Code § 26–17–21 (1986); Alaska Stat § 25.20.045 (1983); Ark Stat Ann § 61–141(c) (1971); Cal Civ Code § 7005 (West 1983); Colo Rev Stat § 19–6–106 (1986); Conn Gen Stat §§ 45–69f to 69n (1985); Fla Stat Ann § 742.11 (West Supp 1984); Ga Code Ann §§ 74–101.1, 74–9904 (Supp 1984); Idaho Code § 39–5401 to 39–5407 (Supp 1984); Ill Ann Stat ch 40 § 1453 (Smith-Hurd Supp 1987); Kan Stat Ann §§ 23–128 to 23–130 (1981); La Rev Stat Ann 188 (West Supp 1984); Md Est & Trusts Code Ann § 1–206(b) (1974); and Md Gen Prov Code § 20–214 (1982); Mich Comp Laws Ann § 333.2824 (1980) and § 700.111 (1980); Minn Stat Ann § 257.56 (West 1982); Mont Rev Code Ann § 40–6–106 (1985); Nev Rev Stat § 126.061 (1986); NJ Stat Ann § 9:17–44 (West Supp 1986); NM Stat Ann § 40–11–6 (1986); NY Dom Rel Law § 73 (McKinney 1977); NC Gen Stat § 49A–1 (1984); Okla Stat Ann tit 10, §§ 551–553 (West Supp 1987); Or Rev State §§ 109.239, 109.243, 109.247, 677.355, 677.360, 677.365, 677.370 (1985); Tenn Code Ann § 53–446 (Supp 1983); Tex Fam Code Ann § 12.03 (Vernon 1975); Va Code § 64.1–7.1 (1980); Wash Rev Code Ann § 26.26.050 (1986); Wis Stat Ann § 767.47(9) (West 1985), § 891.40 (West Supp 1982–1983); Wyo Stat § 14–2–103 (1978).
[51] *Sykowski v Appleyard*, 420 Mich 367, 362 NW 2d 211 (1985) (per curiam), *modifying* 122 Mich App 506, 333 NW 2d 90 (1983).
[52] *Re Baby Girl*, No 83 AD (Jefferson Cir Ct, 6th Div, March 8, 1983).
[53] Scott, *Pair Duped Her on Surrogate Mother Pact, Woman Tells Court*, LA Times, Feb 20, 1987, § I at 22, col 1.
[54] See, eg, Robertson, *Embryos, Families and Procreative Liberty: The Legal Structure of the New Reproduction*, 59 S Cal L Rev 939 (1986).
[55] See Elias & Annas, *Social Policy Considerations in Noncoital Reproduction*, 255 JAMA 62 (1986).
[56] The Ethics Committee of Britain's Royal College of Obstetricians and Gynaecologists recommended against the use of surrogates because women cannot predict the distress they will experience when they have to relinquish a child. Royal

College of Obstetricians and Gynaecologists, Report of the RCOG Ethics Committee on In Vitro Fertilisation and Embryo Replacement or Transfer § 7.3 (1983).

[57] In its discussion draft of a statute on the Status of Children of the New Biology, the drafting committee of the National Conference of Commissioners on Uniform State Laws defines a mother as 'the woman who gives birth to a child . . . whether or not she is the genetic parent' (Sec 3). However, it also offers an optional Section 7 under which a couple who has arranged for a surrogate to bear them a child can establish a binding legal relationship with the child even before its birth, even to the point of being listed on the birth certificate as the legal parents, though information on the true biological parents would be kept confidentially by the court that had reviewed the case and approved the prenatal adoption.

[58] *Burchard v Garay*, 42 Cal 3d 531, 536, 724 P 2d 486, 488, 229 Cal Rptr 800, 802 (1986).

[59] See J Goldstein, A Freud & A Solnit, Beyond the Best Interests of the Child (1973).

[60] See *Re Marriage of Carney*, 24 Cal 3d 725, 730–31, 598 P 2d 36, 37–38, 157 Cal Rptr 383, 384–85 (1979).

In its 1987 White Paper, the Government has indicated that, in addition to the Surrogate Arrangements Act 1985, it intends to legislate further on some issues relating to surrogacy but not others. Finally, the White Paper concludes that the need for legislative intervention will be kept under scrutiny by the SLA. The White Paper indicates that there seems to be little agreement on these matters in England (paras 65–75).

65. Although the Warnock Committee considered that most surrogacy arrangements would in any case be unenforceable in the Courts in any of their terms, it recommended that legislation should put the position beyond doubt. Current legislation (s 85(3) of the Children Act 1975—which applies only to England and Wales) already provides that a person cannot surrender or transfer parental rights or duties to another person. Consequently, an agreement made by a surrogate mother to hand over a baby is not enforceable in the English Courts. But legislation could be introduced to put the issue beyond doubt throughout the UK, making it clear that sums paid to a surrogate mother could not be recovered by the commissioning parents; and that the surrogate mother could not recover expenses she had incurred if the commissioning parents changed their minds about the agreement.

66. The consultation document invited views on whether a non-commercial surrogacy service should be permitted to develop, under strict controls, or whether it should be prohibited by law as a majority of the Warnock Committee recommended. Some respondents considered that there was a role for such a service (as had two members of the Warnock Committee). It argued that in a very few cases surrogacy may be an acceptable solution to a couple's childlessness; and that, since surrogacy will always continue to be practised, whatever the rights or wrongs, it is in the best interests of all concerned—particularly the unborn child—that there should be proper counselling and assessment of the arrangements proposed.

67. Those who supported the majority view of the Warnock Committee, on the other hand, argue that the existence of a non-commercial service would encourage the growth of surrogacy and would sanction a situation in which the interests of the child can never be guaranteed. A further consideration is that if surrogacy were permitted under licence on a non-commercial basis it might be difficult to avoid criminalising individuals who made their arrangements outside this structure. Such criminalisation is felt by many to be against the child's best interests.

68. The Warnock Report recommended that, in addition to the operation of commercial or non-commercial surrogacy agencies, the actions of professionals and others who knowingly assist in the establishment of a surrogate pregnancy should also be rendered criminally liable. The Report did not envisage that legislation would make individuals entering into private surrogacy arrangements with each other liable to criminal prosecution, and the Committee was anxious that children born as a result of such arrangements should not be subject to the taint of criminality.

69. In response to the consultation document, there was a marked division of opinion on whether legislation should prohibit private surrogacy arrangements of this kind especially if they involved payment of a fee and/or expenses to the surrogate mother. It would, in practice, be virtually impossible to enforce such legislation, although of course any surrogate pregnancy which was brought about as a result of one of the methods of treatment regulated by the SLA (eg AID) would be subject to the controls outlined elsewhere in the White Paper.

70. There was also a division of opinion about how far liability in respect of unlawful surrogacy arrangements should extend. Under the 1985 Act only third parties are liable. The surrogate mother and commissioning parents remain free from prosecution even when the arrangement is on a commercial basis. This situation is supported by those who argue that, in the best interests of the child, those immediately involved should not be criminalised. Some feel, however, that liability should extend to anyone making financial gain from the arrangement, while others consider that all parties, including the commissioning parents and surrogate mother, should be criminally liable if they take part in an unlawful arrangement at all.

71. No clear view emerged, either, on whether it should be a criminal offence for a doctor, lawyer or other professional knowingly to assist in establishing a surrogate pregnancy. There is, however, a strong body of opinion opposed to any measures which might prevent the surrogate mother from obtaining proper professional care and advice during her pregnancy. (It should be noted, too, that any professional person who took part in negotiations for a commercial surrogacy arrangement would already be guilty of an offence under existing law.)

72. While there is widespread agreement about the problems surrogacy poses, there is no consensus about the most constructive role legislation might play in dealing with it. It is widely accepted that the interests of the child are paramount, but there is no agreement about whether these are best served by prohibiting surrogacy altogether or allowing it to take place in strictly controlled circumstances.

73. The Government has concluded that legislation should not give any encouragement to the parties of surrogacy arranged privately or on a non-commercial basis. The Bill will contain no provision for licensing non-commercial surrogacy services and will make it clear that any contract drawn up as part of a surrogacy arrangement will be unenforceable, in all its aspects, in the UK Courts. The Government does not however consider that it is appropriate, nor necessarily in the child's best interests, to bring the practice of surrogacy–other than the operation of commercial agencies—within the scope of the criminal law and the Bill will not add to the criminal sanctions contained in the 1985 Act.

74. A clearer view on these complex issues may emerge in the light of developments and the Government believes it is important that the position should be kept under review. This is a task for which the SLA, as an independent body with a balance of lay and specialist views, is well suited. The Government therefore proposes to ask the SLA to look at the position as regards the practice of surrogacy in this country and report to Ministers as requested. It is hoped that this will enable Parliament to review the situation from time to time on the basis of informed and considered advice.

75. As far as future legislative action is concerned, the Bill will contain a provision (already described in paragraph 14) empowering the Secretary of State to lay regulations extending the scope of activities controlled by the SLA. This could be used if, in the light of future developments, it were concluded that, for example, non-commercial surrogacy services should be brought within the framework of the law.

(iv) ENGLISH LAW

(a) The validity of the agreement

1. The criminal law

Is the agreement unlawful *in limine* as constituting a crime? There are at least three possibilities.

First, the parties' agreement may constitute a conspiracy to corrupt public morals or outrage public decency. No English case has addressed this question. Arguably, the fact that a number of surrogacy arrangements have been widely publicised and been the object of litigation without prompting any intervention by the DPP is, at least, *prima facie* evidence that the agreement would not amount to a criminal conspiracy in England. Further, it has sometimes been urged that the fulfilment of a surrogacy arrangement amounts to the crime of 'baby selling'. However, it seems clear that no such crime is known to the common law. 'Baby selling' (the handing over of a child for money) is treated merely at common law as conduct *contra bonos mores*. It is a separate question whether the agreement should be so regarded. We would suggest that it should not.

Secondly, an offence may be committed under the Adoption Act 1958 (as amended), section 50 (see also the Adoption Act 1976, s 28):

> (1) Subject to the provisions of this section, it shall not be lawful to make or give to any person any payment or reward for or in consideration of—
>
> > (*a*) the adoption by that person of a [child];
> >
> > (*b*) the grant by that person of [any agreement or consent] required in connection with the adoption of a [child];
> >
> > (*c*) the transfer by that person of the [actual custody] of a [child] with a view to the adoption of the [child]; or
> >
> > (*d*) the making by that person of any arrangements for the adoption of a [child].

The section was interpreted in the following case.

\ *Re Adoption Application (Payment for Adoption)*
[1987] Fam 81, [1987] 2 All ER 826

Latey J: Mr and Mrs A apply to adopt a little child, now aged 2 years and 4 months. The child's mother (whom I shall call 'the mother') is Mrs B. The child was conceived as a result of a surrogacy arrangement, as it is described, between Mr and Mrs A and Mrs B and her husband, Mr B. As a result of that arrangement Mr A and Mrs B had sexual intercourse on a few occasions and in due course the child was conceived. It was in no sense a love affair. It was physical congress with the sole purpose of procreating a child. As soon as there was conception intercourse ceased.

What led up to this arrangement was this: Mr and Mrs A are a devoted couple. To complete and fulfil their union they dearly wanted a child. For medical reasons Mrs A was and is unable to have a baby. They did everything they could with medical help and advice, including surgery, to overcome this but to no avail. They then tried to adopt a child both in this country and abroad, again to no avail. As to this country, the principal reason given was their ages. This is surprising. At that time Mr A was barely 40, and Mrs A in her mid-30s, well within the normal age of parenthood, I would have thought. Another and subsidiary reason may have been that it was their second marriage, each having been divorced. But there is no doubt that their marriage is solid and stable, especially now that they have the baby, or toddler as it now is.

Then they heard a radio programme, and Mrs A saw a television programme, about surrogacy. They saw it as their last chance.

In the meanwhile, Mr and Mrs B had two children of their own. They decided at that time to have no more (though recently they have had a third child). Mrs B is one who enjoys pregnancy despite sickness and backache. She too heard, saw and read about surrogacy. She was deeply and genuinely moved about the plight of childless couples. There is no question about her sincerity about this. After much thought she decided to embark on this path. She discussed it with her husband, who was not, at first, enthusiastic but acquiesced and later supported her.

She put an advertisement in a magazine. Mr and Mrs A saw it and answered it. They met and the arrangement was made. Finance entered into it and this aspect of it is at the heart of whether an adoption order can be made in this case and, if it can be, whether it should be made. This is because of the terms of certain statutory enactments which I will come to shortly.

The mother, Mrs B, was in full-time employment. She and her husband's joint income enabled them and their children to live in comfort. If she became pregnant it would mean giving up her job and earnings. It would mean incurring other expenses. She had responses from other couples—one couple in particular who offered a very large sum of money. This was not what she wanted.

She agreed with Mr and Mrs A to act as a surrogate mother because as she says:

I wanted to help a childless couple. My own children are very precious to me and I sympathised greatly with any couple who were unable to have children of their own, so much so that I was willing to have another pregnancy in order to give someone else that joy.

She wanted a couple with whom she could be friendly, empathise, have a rapport. She and Mr and Mrs A found each other and she declined the others, including the couple offering the very large sum.

The two couples agreed a global sum of £10,000. The mother says:

The money represented only my loss of earnings, expenses in connection with the pregnancy, and emotional and physical factors. I emphasise that I did not go into the arrangements for commercial reasons, nor did I accept the money to hand [the child] over. I would have done that in any event. In fact, overall, I was marginally worse off. This does not bother me since my motive was not financial.

In his report the child's guardian ad litem says:

The mother does *not* appear to have been primarily motivated in entering into the arrangements by financial considerations. She appears to have felt strongly that through a surrogacy arrangement she could offer an important service to a childless couple and to have regarded the money mainly as the equivalent of compensation for loss of earnings while pregnant. . . . Her interest in surrogacy the mother attributes to a particular pleasure she has in having babies and a great sympathy for women who are unable to experience the joy of having and caring for a baby. The public discussions and debates she heard about this subject struck a special chord for her, thus her initiative in advertising herself.

I have heard the mother speak about this in her evidence. I am left in no doubt that it is the plain, unvarnished truth.

Mr and Mrs A paid £1,000 when she was some months pregnant, and £4,000 shortly after the baby was born. The balance of £5,000 was due some months later, but the mother refused to accept it. This was because she and a professional writer as co-author wrote a book: 'Surrogate Mother. One Woman's Story', from which she made money. That book has been put in as part of the material in this case. It was written pseudonymously and with care to conceal the identity of the child and those connected with the child. I have tried to do the same in this judgment. In the interest of the child nothing must be published which might point to the child's identity with serious consequences to the child later in life, if it were publicly known. Mr and Mrs A's close circle know the facts. They accept and love the child. Mr and Mrs A are very intelligent people who adore the child. They have already worked out what and when they are going to tell the child, and done so admirably, as it seems to me. But for any public publicity to happen about this child as it grows up would certainly damage its emotional development and might be disastrous.

If the word 'commercial' has any bearing on what has to be decided in this case and if it connotes a profit or financial reward element there was nothing commercial in what happened. There was no written contract or agreement; no lawyers were consulted until after the baby was born. The arrangement was one of trust which was fully honoured on both sides.

The rest of the history can be told briefly. The child was born in hospital with Mrs A present at the birth and Mr A joining them almost immediately. Two days later the mother and child went to Mr and Mrs A's home. The four of them spent a week together. The mother went back to her own home. Mr and Mrs A and the child have been together since. The child has thrived. The three of them have been and are supremely happy. The mother and Mr and Mrs A have kept in contact. The mother and Mr B have had a third child. They are closer than they ever have been.

The first question, therefore, is whether in the present case there has been 'any payment or reward' within the meaning of section 50 of the Adoption Act 1958— 'for adoption,' to put it conveniently albeit imprecisely. This is a question of fact to be decided on the evidence. Mr and Mrs A and Mrs B have all given evidence. All are transparently honest. They did not make notes. They did not take legal advice. Not surprisingly, their recollection of the precise sequence of events and what was discussed and when is not clear. What does come out strongly is that what was wanted was a baby and that Mr and Mrs A should have it from birth to care for and bring up. And that it was upon this that they were all concentrating. It was only after the payments had been made and the baby was born that any of them began to turn their minds in any real sense to adoption and the legalities.

In my judgment there was no payment or reward within the meaning of section 50(1) of the Adoption Act 1958.

Do you agree with Latey J's interpretation of s 50 and its application to the facts? Was Latey J right to have regard to the intention of the surrogate mother in entering into the agreement? Are you persuaded by Latey J's view that the agreement was not 'commercial'? Even if it wasn't do you think this is relevant?

Contrast the view of the New Jersey Supreme Court on hearing the appeal in the *Baby M* case ((1988) 537 A 2d 1227) (discussed at first instance by Capron, *supra*).

Wilentz CJ: Our law prohibits paying or accepting money in connection with any placement of a child for adoption. . . . Excepted are fees of an approved agency (which must be a non-profit entity) and certain expenses in connection with childbirth.

Considerable care was taken in this case to structure the surrogacy arrangement so as not to violate this prohibition. The arrangement was structured as follows: the adopting parent, Mrs Stern, was not a party to the surrogacy contract; the money paid to Mrs Whitehead was stated to be for her services—not for the adoption; the sole purpose of the contract was stated as being that 'of giving a child to William Stern, its natural and biological father'; the money was purported to be 'compensation for services and expenses and in no way . . . a fee for termination of parental rights or a payment in exchange for consent to surrender a child for adoption'; the fee to the Infertility Center ($7,500) was stated to be for legal representation, advice, administrative work, and other 'services'. Nevertheless, it seems clear that the money was paid and accepted in connection with an adoption.

The Infertility Center's major role was first as a 'finder' of the surrogate mother whose child was to be adopted, and second as the arranger of all proceedings that led to the adoption. Its role as adoption finder is demonstrated by the provision requiring Mr Stern to pay another $7,500 if he uses Mary Beth Whitehead again as a surrogate, and by ICNY's agreement to 'coordinate arrangements for the adoption of the child by the wife'. The surrogacy agreement requires Mrs Whitehead to surrender Baby M for the purposes of adoption. The agreement notes that Mr *and* Mrs Stern wanted to have a child, and provides that the child be 'placed' with Mrs Stern in the event Mr Stern dies before the child is born. The payment of the $10,000 occurs only on surrender of custody of the child and 'completion of the duties and obligations' of Mrs Whitehead, including termination of her parental rights to facilitate adoption by Mrs Stern. As for the contention that the Sterns are paying only for services and not for an adoption, we need note only that they would pay nothing in the event the child died before the fourth month of pregnancy, and only $1,000 if the child were stillborn, even though the 'services' had been fully rendered. Additionally, one of Mrs Whitehead's estimated costs, to be assumed by Mr Stern, was an 'Adoption Fee', presumably for Mrs Whitehead's incidental costs in connection with the adoption.

Mr Stern knew he was paying for the adoption of a child; Mrs Whitehead knew she was accepting money so that a child might be adopted; the Infertility Center knew that it was being paid for assisting in the adoption of a child. The actions of all three worked to frustrate the goals of the statute. It strains credulity to claim that these arrangements, touted by those in the surrogacy business as an attractive alternative to the usual route leading to an adoption, really amount to something other than a private placement adoption for money.

Do you find the views of the New Jersey court more persuasive than those of Latey J in *Re Adoption Application*? It should be noted that section 50(3) of the Adoption Act 1958 provides: 'This section does not apply . . . to any payment or reward authorised by the court to which an application for an adoption order in respect of a child is made.'

In *Re Adoption Application*, Latey J held that 'authorised by the court' covered not only authorisation in advance of making a payment but could also cover retrospective authorisation after it had been made. Latey J (at p 36) acknowledged that otherwise:

> . . . It would mean, for example, that any payment, however modest and however innocently made, would bar an adoption and do so however much the welfare of the child cried aloud for adoption with all the security and legal rights and status it carried with it: and that, be it said, within the framework of legislation whose first concern is promoting the welfare of the children concerned.
>
> I do not believe that Parliament ever intended to produce such a result (not, anticipating, has it done so in my judgment). The result it intended to produce is wise and humane. It produced a balance by setting its face against trafficking in children, on the one hand, but recognising that there may be transactions which are venial and should not prohibit adoption, on the other hand.

In applying s 50(3) and making the adoption order in favour of the commissioning parents, the judge said:

> It follows that in each case the court has a discretion whether or not to authorise any payment or reward which has already been made or may be contemplated in the future. In exercising that discretion the court would no doubt balance all the circumstances of the case with the welfare of the child as first consideration against what [Counsel for the guardian *ad litem*] well described as the degree of taint of the transaction for which authorisation is asked.

Questions

(i) Do you think that Latey J was correct to hold that authorisation could include subsequent ratification by a court? How would you view this if you were advising a client?

(ii) If ratification can be made by the court, should not the grounds for so doing be made clear by Latey J? But, if the judge had made them clear would they not, in fact, be contrary to the spirit of the Adoption Act 1958?

(iii) Thirdly, could it be argued that to enter the agreement is a criminal offence by virtue of the Surrogacy Arrangements Act 1985?

1.—(1) The following provisions shall have effect for the interpretation of this Act.

(2) 'Surrogate mother' means a woman who carries a child in pursuance of an arrangement—

 (a) made before she began to carry the child, and

 (b) made with a view to any child carried in pursuance of it being handed over to, and the parental rights being exercised (so far as practicable) by, another person or other persons.

(3) An arrangement is a surrogacy arrangement if, were a woman to whom the arrangement relates to carry a child in pursuance of it, she would be a surrogate mother.

(4) In determining whether an arrangement is made with such a view as is mentioned in subsection (2) above regard may be had to the circumstances as a whole (and, in particular, where there is a promise or understanding that any payment will or may be made to the woman or for her benefit in respect of the carrying of any child in pursuance of the arrangement, to that promise or understanding).

(5) An arrangement may be regarded as made with such a view though subject to conditions relating to the handing over of any child.

(6) A woman who carries a child is to be treated for the purposes of subsection (2)(a) above as beginning to carry it at the time of the insemination or, as the case may be, embryo insertion that results in her carrying the child.

(7) 'Body of persons' means a body of persons corporate or unincorporate.

(8) 'Payment' means payment in money or money's worth.

(9) This Act applies to arrangements whether or not they are lawful and whether or not they are enforceable by or against any of the persons making them.

2.—(1) No person shall on a commercial basis do any of the following acts in the United Kingdom, that is—

(a) initiate or take part in any negotiations with a view to the making of a surrogacy arrangement,

(b) offer or agree to negotiate the making of a surrogacy arrangement, or

(c) compile any information with a view to its use in making, or negotiating the making of, surrogacy arrangements;

and no person shall in the United Kingdom knowingly cause another to do any of those acts on a commercial basis.

(2) A person who contravenes subsection (1) above is guilty of an offence;
. . .

(3) For the purposes of this section, a person does an act on a commercial basis (subject to subsection (4) below) if—

(a) any payment is at any time received by himself or another in respect of it, or

(b) he does it with a view to any payment being received by himself or another in respect of making, or negotiating or facilitating the making of, any surrogacy arrangement.

In this subsection 'payment' does not include payment to or for the benefit of a surrogate mother or prospective surrogate mother.

However, the surrogate mother and the commissioning parents are excluded from the effect of these provisions. Subsection 2(2) also says:

. . . but it is not a contravention of that subsection [ie s 2(1)]—

(a) for a woman, with a view to becoming a surrogate mother herself, to do any act mentioned in that subsection or to cause such an act to be done, or

(b) for any person, with a view to a surrogate mother carrying a child for him, to do such an act or to cause such an act to be done.

Furthermore, the 1985 Act only applies to 'commercial' arrangements. To what extent do these provisions apply to professionals involved in surrogacy arrangements, for example doctors and lawyers?

There is, curiously, one potential exception to both these exclusionary rules contained in s 2(2). Section 3 of the 1985 Act reads (in part):

3.—(2) Where a newspaper or periodical containing an advertisement to which this section applies [ie offering to be, or looking for, a surrogate mother] is published in the United Kingdom, any proprietor, editor or publisher of the newspaper or periodical is guilty of an offence.

(3) Where an advertisement to which this section applies is conveyed by means of a telecommunication system so as to be seen or heard (or both) in the United Kingdom, any person who in the United Kingdom causes it to be so conveyed knowing it to contain such an indication as is mentioned in subsection (1) above is guilty of an offence.

(4) A person who publishes or causes to be published in the United Kingdom an advertisement to which this section applies (not being an advertisement contained in a newspaper or periodical or conveyed by means of a telecommunication system) is guilty of an offence.

Do you think these provisions could apply to the surrogate mother or the commissioning parents? Notice that the surrogate mother placed an advertisement in a magazine in *Re Adoption Application* but the facts arose before the 1985 Act came into effect.

Notice that section 30 of the Victorian Infertility (Medical Procedures) Act 1984 clearly makes it an offence even for the parties to the agreement.

S 30(2) A person shall not—
- (a) publish, or cause to be published, a statement or an advertisement, notice or other document that—
    - (i) is intended or likely to induce a person to agree to act as a surrogate mother;
    - (ii) seeks or purports to seek a woman who is willing to agree to act as a surrogate mother; or
    - (iii) states or implies that a woman is willing to agree to act as a surrogate mother;
- (b) make, give or receive, or agree to make, give or receive, a payment or reward for or in consideration of the making of a contract, agreement or arrangement under which a woman agrees to act as a surrogate mother; or
- (c) receive or agree to receive a payment or reward in consideration for acting, or agreeing to act, as a surrogate mother.

If it be criminal to enter into the surrogacy arrangement, what effect would this have in law on the validity of the agreement? The answer must be that such an agreement would be illegal and, as such, could have no legal effect of any kind.

2. Civil law

Is the agreement void on grounds of public policy or, if not, unenforceable? There is no English authority directly in point. But, there are four English cases which have considered surrogacy agreements (*A v C* [1985] FLR 445 (FD and CA); *Re C (a Minor)* [1985] FLR 846; *Re Adoption Application (supra)*; *Re P (Minors) (Wardship: surrogacy)* [1987] 2 FLR 421). In each of them the court has been asked to determine who should have custody of the child. This being so, the court has had recourse to a traditional family law analysis and has based its decision on what is in the 'best interests' of the child (save in the adoption case, but where, in essence, the same principles guided Latey J in exercising his discretion). This has meant that the court has not had to determine the matter of the validity of the surrogacy agreement, for as Sir John Arnold P put it in *Re P (Minors) (supra)*: 'whatever the exact nature of the agreement was, the wardship jurisdiction is not one which is, or is ever, regulated by contract'.

Nonetheless, in two cases (*A v C (supra)* and *Re P (supra)*) the court has offered its view on the validity of surrogacy agreements. In *Re P*, Sir John Arnold P said:

... One possible view about that matter is that there is, or may in certain circumstances be, an a element concerning the surrogacy agreement which is repellent to proper ideas about the procreation of children, so as to make any such agreement one which should be rejected by the law as being contrary to public policy. It is not necessary in this case, for the reasons which I have indicated, to come to any conclusion upon that point. The existence of the agreement is relevant to this extent, that plainly one of the factors which has to be taken into account in determining where the welfare of the children lies, is the factor of the character of the rival custodians who were put forward for consideration and it might be that the willingness of those persons to enter into a surrogacy agreement would reflect upon their moral outlook so adversely as to disqualify them as potential custodians at all, but I do not think that that factor enters into the present case.

In *A v C*, at first instance ([1985] FLR 445), Comyn J stated:

> ... The agreement between the parties I hold as being against public policy. None of them can rely upon it in any way or enforce the agreement in any way. I need only give one of many grounds for saying this, namely that this was a purported contract for the sale and purchase of a child.

In the Court of Appeal ([1985] FLR 453), Ormrod LJ described the arrangement as 'most extraordinary and irresponsible, bizarre and unnatural' and 'a sordid commercial bargain'. He concluded that the arrangement was 'a wholly artificial situation from the very beginning which should never have happened and which no responsible adult should ever have allowed to happen'. Cumming-Bruce LJ described the arrangement in similar terms, '... a kind of baby-farming operation of a wholly distasteful and lamentable kind'; and 'a guilty bargain which should never have been made'; and a 'lamentable commercial transaction'. Stamp LJ confined his judgment to one sentence but could not resist describing the arrangement as 'this ugly little drama'.

In these cases the courts were not specifically considering the validity of the surrogacy agreements and the remarks are, therefore, no more than judicial comment. How would a court approach this issue if it had to face it squarely? Would the court in such a situation not endorse the view of Comyn J at first instance in *A v C* that 'the agreement ... I hold as being against public policy. None of them can rely upon it any way or [sc] enforce the agreement in any way'? Comyn J gives as 'one of the many grounds for saying this ... that this was a purported contract for the sale and purchase of a child'. Do you agree, particularly in the light of the subsequent decision of Latey J in *Re Adoption Application*? Upon what other grounds could a court reach the same conclusion as Comyn J?

In the New Jersey case of *Baby M* 537 A 2d 1227 (1988), the New Jersey Supreme Court examined the validity of a surrogacy contract (footnotes omitted).

> **Wilentz CJ:** In this matter the Court is asked to determine the validity of a contract that purports to provide a new way of bringing children into a family. For a fee of $10,000, a woman agrees to be artificially inseminated with the semen of another woman's husband; she is to conceive a child, carry it to term, and after its birth surrender it to the natural father and his wife. The intent of the contract is that the child's natural mother will thereafter be forever separated from her child. The wife is to adopt the child, and she and the natural father are to be regarded as its parents for all purposes. The contract providing for this is called a 'surrogacy contract', the natural mother inappropriately called the 'surrogate mother'.
>
> ...
>
> **Facts:** In February 1985, William Stern and Mary Beth Whitehead entered into a surrogacy contract. It recited that Stern's wife, Elizabeth, was infertile, that they wanted a child, and that Mrs Whitehead was willing to provide that child as the mother with Mr Stern as the father.

The contract provided that through artificial insemination using Mr Stern's sperm, Mrs Whitehead would become pregnant, carry the child to term, bear it, deliver it to the Sterns, and thereafter do whatever was necessary to terminate her maternal rights so that Mrs Stern could thereafter adopt the child. Mrs Whitehead's husband, Richard, was also a party to the contract; Mrs Stern was not. Mr Whitehead promised to do all acts necessary to rebut the presumption of paternity under the Parentage Act. *NJSA* 9:17–43a(1), –44a. Although Mrs Stern was not a party to the surrogacy agreement, the contract gave her sole custody of the child in the event of Mr Stern's death. Mrs Stern's status as a nonparty to the surrogate parenting agreement presumably was to avoid the application of the baby-selling statute to this arrangement. *NJSA* 9:3–54.

Mr Stern, on his part, agreed to attempt the artifical insemination and to pay Mrs Whitehead $10,000 after the child's birth, on its delivery to him. In a separate contract, Mr Stern agreed to pay $7,500 to the Infertility Center of New York ('ICNY'). The Center's advertising campaigns solicit surrogate mothers and encourage infertile couples to consider surrogacy. ICNY arranged for the surrogacy contract by bringing the parties together, explaining the process to them, furnishing the contractual form, and providing legal counsel.

... After several artificial inseminations over a period of months, Mrs Whitehead became pregnant. The pregnancy was uneventful and on March 28, 1986, Baby M was born.

The court then examined the legislation of New Jersey in relation to (1) the prohibition of adoption for money; (2) the termination of parental rights; and (3) the surrender of custody and consent to adopt. The court concluded that the surrogacy agreement was in direct conflict with the legislation and hence was invalid and unenforceable. The court then went on to consider public policy considerations:

... The contract's basic premise, that the natural parents can decide in advance of birth which one is to have custody of the child, bears no relationship to the settled law that the child's best interests shall determine custody.

. . .

The surrogacy contract guarantees permanent separation of the child from one of its natural parents. Our policy, however, has long been that to the extent possible, children should remain with and be brought up by both of their natural parents. . . . This is not simply some theoretical ideal that in practice has no meaning. The impact of failure to follow that policy is nowhere better shown than in the results of this surrogacy contract. A child, instead of starting off its life with as much peace and security as possible, finds itself immediately in a tug-of-war between contending mother and father.

The surrogacy contract violates the policy of this State that the rights of natural parents are equal concerning their child, the father's right no greater than the mother's. . . . The whole purpose and effect of the surrogacy contract was to give the father the exclusive right to the child by destroying the rights of the mother.

The policies expressed in our comprehensive laws governing consent to the surrender of a child . . . stand in stark contrast to the surrogacy contract and what it implies. Here there is no counseling, independent or otherwise, of the natural mother, no evaluation, no warning.

The only legal advice Mary Beth Whitehead received regarding the surrogacy contract was provided in connection with the contract that she previously entered into with another couple. Mrs Whitehead's lawyer was referred to her by the Infertility Center, with which he had an agreement to act as counsel for surrogate candidates. His services consisted of spending one hour going through the contract with the Whiteheads, section by section, and answering their questions. Mrs Whitehead received no further legal advice prior to signing the contract with the Sterns.

Mrs Whitehead was examined and psychologically evaluated, but if it was for her benefit, the record does not disclose that fact. The Sterns regarded the evaluation as important, particularly in connection with the question of whether she would change her mind. Yet they never asked to see it, and were content with the assumption that the Infertility Center had made an evaluation and had concluded that there was no danger that the surrogate mother would change her mind. From Mrs Whitehead's point of view, all that she learned from the evaluation was that 'she had passed.' It is apparent that the profit motive got the better of the Infertility Center. Although the evaluation was made, it was not put to any use, and understandably so, for the psychologist warned that Mrs Whitehead demonstrated certain traits that might make surrender of the child difficult and that there should be further inquiry into this issue in connection with her surrogacy. To inquire further, however, might have jeopardised the Infertility Center's fee. The record indicates that neither Mrs Whitehead nor the Sterns were ever told of this fact, a fact that might have ended their surrogacy arrangement.

Under the contract, the natural mother is irrevocably committed before she knows the strength of her bond with her child. She never makes a totally voluntary, informed decision, for quite clearly any decision prior to the baby's birth is, in the most important sense, uninformed, and any decision after that, compelled by a pre-existing contractual commitment, the threat of a lawsuit, and the inducement of a $10,000 payment, is less than totally voluntary. Her interests are of little concern to those who controlled this transaction.

Although the interest of the natural father and adoptive mother is certainly the predominant interest, realistically the *only* interest served, even they are left with less than what public policy requires. They know little about the natural mother, her genetic makeup, and her psychological and medical history. Moreover, not even a superficial attempt is made to determine their awareness of their responsibilities as parents.

Worst of all, however, is the contract's total disregard of the best interests of the child. There is not the slightest suggestion that an inquiry will be made at any time to determine the fitness of the Sterns as custodial parents, of Mrs Stern as an adoptive parent, their superiority to Mrs Whitehead, or the effect on the child of not living with her natural mother.

This is the sale of a child, or, at the very least, the sale of a mother's right to her child, the only mitigating factor being that one of the purchasers is the father. Almost every evil that prompted the prohibition on the payment of money in connection with adoptions exists here.

The differences between an adoption and a surrogacy contract should be noted, since it is asserted that the use of money in connection with surrogacy does not pose the risks found where money buys an adoption. Katz 'Surrogate Motherhood and the Baby-Selling Laws', 20 *Colum JL & Soc Probs* 1 (1986).

First, and perhaps most important, all parties concede that it is unlikely that surrogacy will survive without money. Despite the alleged selfless motivation of surrogate mothers, if there is no payment, there will be no surrogates, or very few. That conclusion contrasts with adoption; for obvious reasons, there remains a steady supply, albeit insufficient, despite the prohibitions against payment. The adoption itself, relieving the natural mother of the financial burden of supporting an infant, is in some sense the equivalent of payment.

Second, the use of money in adoptions does not *produce* the problem—conception occurs, and usually the birth itself, before illicit funds are offered. With surrogacy, the 'problem' if one views it as such, consisting of the purchase of a woman's procreative capacity, at the risk of her life, is caused by and originates with the offer of money.

Third, with the law prohibiting the use of money in connection with adoptions, the built-in financial pressure of the unwanted pregnancy and the consequent support obligation do not lead the mother to the highest paying, ill-suited, adoptive parents. She is just as well-off surrendering the child to an approved agency. In surrogacy, the highest bidders will presumably become the adoptive parents regardless of suitability, so long as payment of money is permitted.

Fourth, the mother's consent to surrender her child in adoptions is revocable, even after surrender of the child, unless it be to an approved agency, where by regulation there are protections against an ill-advised surrender. In surrogacy, consent occurs so early that no amount of advice would satisfy the potential mother's need, yet the consent is irrevocable.

The main difference, that the unwanted pregnancy is unintended while the situation of the surrogate mother is voluntary and intended, is really not significant. Initially, it produces stronger reactions of sympathy for the mother whose pregnancy was unwanted than for the surrogate mother, who 'went into this with her eyes wide open'. On reflection, however, it appears that the essential evil is the same, taking advantage of a woman's circumstances (the unwanted pregnancy or the need for money) in order to take away her child, the difference being one of degree.

In the scheme contemplated by the surrogacy contract in this case, a middleman, propelled by profit, promotes the sale. Whatever idealism may have motivated any of the participants, the profit motive predominates, permeates, and ultimately governs the transaction. The demand for children is great and the supply small. The availability of contraception, abortion, and the greater willingness of single mothers to bring up their children has led to a shortage of babies offered for adoption . . . The situation is ripe for the entry of the middleman who will bring some equilibrium into the market by increasing the supply through the use of money.

Intimated, but disputed, is the assertion that surrogacy will be used for the benefit of the rich at the expense of the poor. See e g Radin 'Market Inalienability', 100 *Harv L Rev* 1849, 1930 (1987). In response it is noted that the Sterns are not rich and the Whiteheads not poor. Nevertheless, it is clear to us that it is unlikely that surrogate mothers will be as proportionately numerous among those women in the top twenty percent income bracket as among those in the bottom twenty percent. *Ibid*. Put differently, we doubt that infertile couples in the low-income bracket will find upper income surrogates.

In any event, even in this case one would not pretend that disparate wealth does not play a part simply because the contrast is not the dramatic 'rich versus poor'. At the time of the trial, the Whitehead's net assets were probably negative—Mrs Whitehead's own sister was foreclosing on a second mortgage. Their income derived from Mr Whitehead's labors. Mrs Whitehead is a homemaker, having previously held part-time jobs. The Sterns are both professionals, she a medical doctor, he a biochemist. Their combined income when both were working was about $89,500 a year and their assets sufficient to pay for the surrogacy contract arrangements.

The point is made that Mrs Whitehead *agreed* to the surrogacy arrangement, supposedly fully understanding the consequences. Putting aside the issue of how compelling her need for money may have been, and how significant her understanding of the consequences, we suggest that her consent is irrelevant. There are, in a civilised society, some things that money cannot buy. In America, we decided long ago that merely because conduct purchased by money was 'voluntary' did not mean that it was good or beyond regulation and prohibition. *West Coast Hotel Co v Parrish*, 300 *US* 379, 57 *SCt* 578, 81 *L Ed* 703 (1937). Employers can no longer buy labor at the lowest price they can bargain for, even though that labor is 'voluntary', 29 *USC* § 206 (1982), or buy women's labor for less money than paid to men for the same job, 29 *USC* § 206(d), or purchase the agreement of children to perform oppressive labor, 29 *USC* § 212, or purchase the agreement of workers to subject themselves to unsafe or unhealthful working conditions, 29 *USC* §§ 651 to 678. (Occupational Safety and Health Act of 1970). There are, in short, values that society deems more important than granting to wealth whatever it can buy, be it labor, love or life. Whether this principle recommends prohibition of surrogacy, which presumably sometimes results in great satisfaction to all of the parties, is not for us to say. We note here only that, under existing law, the fact that Mrs Whitehead 'agreed' to the arrangement is not dispositive.

The long-term effects of surrogacy contracts are not known, but feared—the impact on the child who learns her life was bought, that she is the offspring of someone who gave birth to her only to obtain money; the impact on the natural mother as the full weight of her isolation is felt along with the full reality of the sale of her body and her child; the impact on the natural father and adoptive mother once they realise the consequences of their conduct. Literature in related areas suggests these are substantial considerations, although, given the newness of surrogacy, there is little information. . . .

The surrogacy contract is based on principles that are directly contrary to the objectives of our laws. It guarantees the separation of a child from its mother; it looks to adoption regardless of suitability; it totally ignores the child; it takes the child from the mother regardless of her wishes and her maternal fitness; and it does all of this, it accomplishes all of its goals, through the use of money.

Beyond that is the potential degradation of some women that may result from this arrangement. In many cases, of course, surrogacy may bring satisfaction, not only to the infertile couple, but to the surrogate mother herself. The fact, however, that many women may not perceive surrogacy negatively but rather see it as an opportunity does not diminish its potential for devastation to other women.

In sum, the harmful consequences of this surrogacy arrangement appear to us all too palpable. In New Jersey the surrogate mother's agreement to sell her child is void. Its irrevocability infects the entire contract, as does the money that purports to buy it.

It is clear that the public policy, identified by the New Jersey Supreme Court, reflects English public policy (e g *A v C, supra*). (As we shall see later, the court eventually applying a 'best interests' test awarded custody to Mr and Mrs Stern, the commissioning parents.)

If the courts were not to regard the contract as failing *in limine*, would they enforce its terms? Carolyn Sappideen raises the issues generally in 'The Surrogate Mother—A Growing Problem' (1983) 6 UNSWLR 79 at 90–91:

. . . [I]f those contracts were enforceable, difficult problems would arise on breach of contract. Independently of the issue of public policy, a court of equity will not specifically enforce contracts for personal services.[79] Two reasons may be given for this rule; the first is that contracts which require constant supervision will not be enforced and secondly, that a court will not order performance of contracts requiring special confidence and trust. A court of law can, however, enforce the contract by awarding damages for breach of contract. Examples will be given to illustrate inherent difficulties.

(a) Breach by the surrogate
The surrogate may breach the contract (depending on its terms) in a variety of ways, for example smoking, drinking during pregnancy, terminating the pregnancy by abortion, or refusal to hand over custody of the baby.[80] Taking the first examples, smoking and drinking during pregnancy—would this breach allow the couple to treat the contract as at an end? Should the contract provide that the breach of any of its terms renders the contract voidable by the innocent party? Would a fraudulent misrepresentation that the surrogate did not smoke or drink allow the innocent party to rescind? If the innocent party reaffirmed the contract and sued for damages, what would be the damages? For example, how could damage be measured and proved if all that could be shown was that the surrogate had had one cigarette, or one drink?[81] If the surrogate terminated the pregnancy what damages could be recovered by the couple? Presumably all that could be obtained here would be damages for emotional distress suffered as flowing naturally from the breach.[82]

(b) Breach by the couple
Depending on the terms of the contract, breaches could include failure to pay, failure to take custody of the child, or failure to provide health insurance or to adopt the child. If the couple refused to take custody of the child, would the surrogate be able to recover the cost of upkeep for the child until aged eighteen, or would the surrogate be obliged to mitigate her loss by placing the child for adoption?[83]

Notes to extract

79 *Lumley v Wagner* (1852) I De GM & G, 604; *Page One Records Ltd v Britton (t/a the Troggs)* [1967] 3 All ER 822.

80 Contracts may provide that the surrogate must return all monies and expenses paid if she does not surrender the child, see N. P. Keane and D. L. Breo, [*The Surrogate Mother* (1981)] 269. *Cf* Adoption of Children Act (1965) (NSW) s 57.

81 There could be difficulty in deciding the cause of many congenital defects; a handicap arising genetically could be mistakenly attributed to exposure to drugs or trauma during pregnancy, R G Edwards. 'The Problem of Compensation for Antenatal Injuries' (1973) 246 *Nature* 54–55.

82 In a suit based on contract the general rule has been that there can be no recovery for non-economic loss. For a good summary of the general rule and exceptions, see G H Treitel, *The Law of Contract* (5th ed 1979) 687–97.

83 The duty arises to act reasonably in mitigation—but what is reasonable where a woman agrees to hand over a child, *cf Sherlock v Stillwater Clinic* 260 NW 2d 169 (1978).

(See also B Cohen, 'Surrogate Mothers: Whose Baby Is It?' 2 (1984) 10 Am J Law Med 243, 257–264.)

The typical terms of a surrogacy contract can be seen in the New Jersey case of *Baby M* 537 A 2d 1227 (1988) (*supra*). The contract referred to, and set out below, is that used by the Infertility Center of New York (ICNY), the senior executive of which is the attorney, Noel Keane, regarded as the leading exponent of surrogacy arrangements in the United States.

SURROGATE PARENTING AGREEMENT

THIS AGREEMENT is made this   day of   , 19   by and between MARY BETH WHITEHEAD, a married woman (herein referred to as 'Surrogate'), RICHARD WHITEHEAD, her husband (herein referred to as 'Husband'), and WILLIAM STERN (herein referred to as 'Natural Father').

Recitals

THIS AGREEMENT is made with reference to the following facts:

(1) WILLIAM STERN, Natural Father, is an individual over the age of eighteen (18) years who is desirous of entering into this Agreement.

(2) The sole purpose of this Agreement is to enable WILLIAM STERN and his infertile wife to have a child which is biologically related to WILLIAM STERN.

(3) MARY BETH WHITEHEAD, Surrogate, and RICHARD WHITEHEAD, her husband, are over the age of eighteen (18) years and desirous of entering into this Agreement in consideration of the following:

NOW THEREFORE, in consideration of the mutual promises contained herein and the intentions of being legally bound hereby, the parties agree as follows:

1. MARY BETH WHITEHEAD, Surrogate, represents that she is capable of conceiving children. MARY BETH WHITEHEAD understands and agrees that in the best interest of the child, she will not form or attempt to form a parent-child relationship with any child or children she may conceive, carry to term and give birth to, pursuant to the provisions of this Agreement, and shall freely surrender custody to WILLIAM STERN, Natural Father, immediately upon birth of the child; and terminate all parental rights to said child pursuant to this Agreement.

2. MARY BETH WHITEHEAD, Surrogate, and RICHARD WHITEHEAD, her husband, have been married since 12/2/73, and RICHARD WHITEHEAD is in agreement with the purposes, intents and provisions of this Agreement and acknowledges that his wife, MARY BETH WHITEHEAD, Surrogate, shall be artificially inseminated pursuant to the provisions of this Agreement. RICHARD WHITEHEAD agrees that in the best interest of the child, he will not form or attempt to form a parent-child relationship with any child or children MARY BETH WHITEHEAD, Surrogate, may conceive by artificial insemination as described herein, and agrees to freely and readily surrender immediate custody of the child to WILLIAM STERN, Natural Father; and terminate his parental rights;

RICHARD WHITEHEAD further acknowledges he will do all acts necessary to rebut the presumption of paternity of any offspring conceived and born pursuant to aforementioned agreement as provided by law, including blood testing and/or HLA testing.

3. WILLIAM STERN, Natural Father, does hereby enter into this written contractual Agreement with MARY BETH WHITEHEAD, Surrogate, where MARY BETH WHITEHEAD shall be artificially inseminated with the semen of WILLIAM STERN by a physician. MARY BETH WHITEHEAD, Surrogate, upon becoming pregnant, acknowledges that she will carry said embryo/fetus(s) until delivery. MARY BETH WHITEHEAD, Surrogate, and RICHARD WHITE-HEAD, her husband, agree that they will cooperate with any background investigation into the Surrogate's medical, family and personal history and warrants the information to be accurate to the best of their knowledge. MARY BETH WHITEHEAD, Surrogate, and RICHARD WHITEHEAD, her husband, agree to surrender custody of the child to WILLIAM STERN, Natural Father, immediately upon birth, acknowledging that it is the intent of this Agreement in the best interests of the child to do so; as well as institute and cooperate in proceedings to terminate their respective parental rights to said child, and sign any and all necessary affidavits, documents, and the like, in order to further the intent and purposes of this Agreement. It is understood by MARY BETH WHITEHEAD, and RICHARD WHITEHEAD, that the child to be conceived is being done so for the sole purpose of giving said child to WILLIAM STERN, its natural and biological father. MARY BETH WHITEHEAD and RICHARD WHITEHEAD agree to sign all necessary affidavits prior to and after the birth of the child and voluntarily participate in any paternity proceedings necessary to have WILLIAM STERN'S name entered on said child's birth certificate as the natural or biological father.

4. That the consideration for this Agreement, which is compensation for services and expenses, and in no way is to be construed as a fee for termination of parental rights or a payment in exchange for a consent to surrender the child for adoption, in addition to other provisions contained herein, shall be as follows:

(A) $10,000 shall be paid to MARY BETH WHITEHEAD, Surrogate, upon surrender of custody to WILLIAM STERN, the natural and biological father of the child born pursuant to the provisions of this Agreement for surrogate services and expenses in carrying out her obligations under this Agreement;

(B) The consideration to be paid to MARY BETH WHITEHEAD, Surrogate, shall be deposited with the Infertility Center of New York (hereafter ICNY), the representative of WILLIAM STERN, at the time of the signing of this Agreement, and held in escrow until completion of the duties and obligations of MARY BETH WHITEHEAD, Surrogate, (see Exhibit 'A' for a copy of the Escrow Agreement), as herein described.

(C) WILLIAM STERN, Natural Father, shall pay the expenses incurred by MARY BETH WHITEHEAD, Surrogate, pursuant to her pregnancy, more specifically defined as follows:

(1) All medical, hospitalisation, and pharmaceutical, laboratory and therapy expenses incurred as a result of MARY BETH WHITEHEAD'S pregnancy, not covered or allowed by her present health and major medical insurance, including all extraordinary medical expenses and all reasonable expenses for treatment of any emotional or mental conditions or problems related to said pregnancy, but in no case shall any such expenses be paid or reimbursed after a period of six (6) months have elapsed since the date of the termination of the pregnancy, and this Agreement specifically excludes any expenses for lost wages or other non-itemised incidentals (see Exhibit 'B') related to said pregnancy.

(2) WILLIAM STERN, Natural Father, shall not be responsible for any latent medical expenses occurring six (6) weeks subsequent to the birth of the child, unless the medical problem or abnormality incident thereto was known and treated by a physician prior to the expiration of said six (6) week period and in written notice of

the same sent to ICNY. as representative of WILLIAM STERN by certified mail, return receipt requested, advising of this treatment.

(3) WILLIAM STERN, Natural Father, shall be responsible for the total costs of all paternity testing. Such paternity testing may, at the option of WILLIAM STERN, Natural Father, be required prior to release of the surrogate fee from escrow. In the event WILLIAM STERN, Natural Father, is conclusively determined not to be the biological father of the child as a result of an HLA test, this Agreement will be deemed breached and MARY BETH WHITEHEAD, Surrogate, shall not be entitled to any fee. WILLIAM STERN, Natural Father, shall be entitled to reimbursement of all medical and related expenses from MARY BETH WHITE-HEAD, Surrogate, and RICHARD WHITEHEAD, her husband.

(4) MARY BETH WHITEHEAD'S reasonable travel expenses incurred at the request of WILLIAM STERN, pursuant to this Agreement.

5. MARY BETH WHITEHEAD, Surrogate, and RICHARD WHITEHEAD, her husband, understand and agree to assume all risks, including the risk of death, which are incidental to conception, pregnancy, childbirth, including but not limited to, postpartum complications. A copy of said possible risks and/or complications is attached hereto and made a part hereof (see Exhibit 'C').

6. MARY BETH WHITEHEAD, Surrogate, and RICHARD WHITEHEAD, her husband, hereby agree to undergo psychiatric evaluation by JOAN EINWOH-NER, a psychiatrist as designated by WILLIAM STERN or an agent thereof. WILLIAM STERN shall pay for the cost of said psychiatric evaluation. MARY BETH WHITEHEAD and RICHARD WHITEHEAD shall sign, prior to their evaluations, a medical release permitting dissemination of the report prepared as a result of said psychiatric evaluations to ICNY or WILLIAM STERN and his wife.

7. MARY BETH WHITEHEAD, Surrogate, and RICHARD WHITEHEAD, her husband, hereby agree that it is the exclusive and sole right of WILLIAM STERN, Natural Father, to name said child.

8. 'Child' as referred to in this Agreement shall include all children born simultaneously pursuant to the inseminations contemplated herein.

9. In the event of the death of WILLIAM STERN, prior or subsequent to the birth of said child, it is hereby understood and agreed by MARY BETH WHITEHEAD, Surrogate, and RICHARD WHITEHEAD, her husband, that the child will be placed in the custody of WILLIAM STERN'S wife.

10. In the event that the child is miscarried prior to the fifth (5th) month of pregnancy, no compensation, as enumerated in paragraph 4(A), shall be paid to MARY BETH WHITEHEAD, Surrogate. However, the expenses enumerated in paragraph 4(C) shall be paid or reimbursed to MARY BETH WHITEHEAD, Surrogate. In the event the child is miscarried, dies or is stillborn subsequent to the fourth (4th) month of pregnancy and said child does not survive, the Surrogate shall receive $1,000.00 in lieu of the compensation enumerated in paragraph 4(A). In the event of a miscarriage or stillbirth as described above, this Agreement shall terminate and neither MARY BETH WHITEHEAD, Surrogate, nor WILLIAM STERN, Natural Father, shall be under any further obligation under this Agreement.

11. MARY BETH WHITEHEAD, Surrogate, and WILLIAM STERN, Natural Father, shall have undergone complete physical and genetic evaluation, under the direction and supervision of a licensed physician, to determine whether the physical health and well-being of each is satisfactory. Said physical examination shall include testing for venereal diseases, specifically including but not limited to, syphilis, herpes and gonorrhea. Said venereal diseases testing shall be done prior to, but not limited to, each series of inseminations.

12. In the event that pregnancy has not occurred within a reasonable time, in the opinion of WILLIAM STERN, Natural Father, this Agreement shall terminate by written notice to MARY BETH WHITEHEAD, Surrogate, at the residence provided to the ICNY by the Surrogate, from ICNY, as representative of WILLIAM STERN, Natural Father.

13. MARY BETH WHITEHEAD, Surrogate, agrees that she will not abort the child once conceived except, if in the professional medical opinion of the

inseminating physician, such action is necessary for the physical health of MARY BETH WHITEHEAD or the child has been determined by said physician to be physiologically abnormal. MARY BETH WHITEHEAD further agrees, upon the request of said physician to undergo amniocentesis (see Exhibit 'D') or similar tests to detect genetic and congenital defects. In the event said test reveals that the fetus is genetically or congenitally abnormal, MARY BETH WHITEHEAD, Surrogate, agrees to abort the fetus upon demand of WILLIAM STERN, Natural Father, in which event, the fee paid to the Surrogate will be in accordance to Paragraph 10. If MARY BETH WHITEHEAD refuses to abort the fetus upon demand of WILLIAM STERN, his obligations as stated in this Agreement shall cease forthwith, except as to obligations of paternity imposed by statute.

14. Despite the provisions of Paragraph 13, WILLIAM STERN, Natural Father, recognises that some genetic and congenital abnormalities may not be detected by amniocentesis or other tests, and therefore, if proven to be the biological father of the child, assumes the legal responsibility for any child who may possess genetic or congenital abnormalities. (See Exhibits 'E' and 'F'.)

15. MARY BETH WHITEHEAD, Surrogate, further agrees to adhere to all medical instructions given to her by the inseminating physician as well as her independent obstetrician. MARY BETH WHITEHEAD also agrees not to smoke cigarettes, drink alcoholic beverages, use illegal drugs, or take non-prescription medications or prescribed medications without written consent from her physician. MARY BETH WHITEHEAD agrees to follow a prenatal medical examination schedule to consist of no fewer visits than: one visit per month during the first seven (7) months of pregnancy, two visits (each to occur at two-week intervals) during the eighth and ninth month of pregnancy.

16. MARY BETH WHITEHEAD, Surrogate, agrees to cause RICHARD WHITEHEAD, her husband, to execute a refusal of consent form as annexed hereto as Exhibit 'G'.

17. Each party acknowledges that he or she fully understands this Agreement and its legal effect, and that they are signing the name freely and voluntarily and that neither party has any reason to believe that the other(s) did not freely and voluntarily execute said Agreement.

18. In the event any of the provisions of this Agreement are deemed to be invalid or unenforceable, the same shall be deemed severable from the remainder of this Agreement and shall not cause the invalidity or unenforceability of the remainder of this Agreement. If such provision shall be deemed invalid due to its scope or breadth, then said provision shall be deemed valid to the extent of the scope or breadth permitted by law.

19. The original of this Agreement, upon execution, shall be retained by the Infertility Center of New York, with photocopies being distributed to MARY BETH WHITEHEAD, Surrogate and WILLIAM STERN, Natural Father, having the same legal effect as the original.

WILLIAM STERN   DATE
Natural Father

STATE OF
                    SS.:
COUNTY OF

On the   day of   , 19   , before me personally came WILLIAM STERN, known to me, and to me known, to be the individual described in the foregoing instrument and he acknowledged to me that he executed the same as his free and voluntary act.

                                                     NOTARY PUBLIC

Enforcement of the detailed terms of this contract was not the issue in *Baby M*.

However, central to the case was whether the court could enforce the obligation to terminate the parental rights of the surrogate and transfer custody to the natural father, Mr Stern. For the reasons we have seen, the court held this contract to be unenforceable. Equally, the court (as we shall see) held that the transfer of custody to the commissioning parents could only be enforced in so far as this was in the baby's 'best interests'.

Specific questions which arise from contracts such as these are addressed in Theresa Mady's article 'Surrogate Mothers: The Legal Issues' (1981) 7 Am J Law Med 324, 332–339. Although some of the discussion concerns uniquely American law, the analysis (and suggested approach) remains of great interest. In this article the following abbreviations are adopted: $S=$ surrogate mother; $H=$ commissioning male; $W=$ commissioning female.

B. Guidelines for contract provisions and goals

Given that the surrogate mother arrangement is legal, parties still must determine what terms they can include that will be judicially enforced in a written contract. Although the parties' written agreement may be persuasive to a court in establishing their intent, courts are not bound to enforce provisions which are contrary to public policy. Clearly, public policy concerns permeate the surrogate mother arrangement, especially where the interests of an unborn child are at stake. In addition, attempts to contract to specifically enforce personal services are not necessarily binding, for parties cannot divest a court of law of its power to grant relief.[45]

1. Rights and liabilities of S

The rights and liabilities of the surrogate mother stem from two basic promises that she makes to H and W. First, S promises to be inseminated with H's semen and carry the child to term. This includes the assurance that she will seek the necessary medical attention to maintain and ensure the health and safety of the fetus. Second, S promises to surrender to H and W all rights in the child. If S is married,[46] this second promise may become complicated if her husband wishes to retain custody of the child.

The law presumes that a child born to a married woman is the child of the woman and her husband.[47] Since this presumption is rebuttable, S and her husband should state explicitly that they will make no claim to the child; without this statement the intention of the parties may be undercut.[48] Such a provision would help eliminate emotional strain and probable litigation, and would avoid harming the child by involving it in custody proceedings.

If S breaches by not adhering to one or both of these promises, courts will have difficulty devising appropriate remedies. The proper remedy will depend on the type of breach. Three major possibilities for breach arise: S may wish to abort the child, S may negligently cause harm to the fetus, or S may refuse to give up the child after birth

If S desires to abort for any reason, within certain constitutional limits,[49] it is unclear whether she can be legally prevented from so doing. The United States Supreme Court has held that the right to decide to abort is one of constitutional dimension which cannot be limited by the exercise of state law unless pursuant to a compelling state interest.[50] The Court has also held that a woman may decide to abort irrespective of her husband's consent.[51] If a husband cannot veto his wife's decision to abort, it is unclear whether H and W, who are merely in a contractual relationship with S, can impose their will. However, some constitutional rights can be waived prior to their exercise.[52] It is unclear whether all constitutional rights can be irrevocably waived.[53] It has never been decided which category encompasses the right to choose to abort. If S cannot irrevocably waive her right to choose to have an abortion, she will retain this right. If S aborts the fetus, however, she breaches by destroying the essence of the contract. Classical contract remedies do not allow recovery for the emotional upset which H and W would inevitably suffer.[54] Restitution for expenses already paid may be the only viable recourse. Although a tort action for infliction of emotional distress[55] might more appropriately compensate

H and *W*, few jurisdictions have accepted this cause of action.[56] In addition, wrongful death actions may not presently extend to abortion of a fetus.[57]

The second type of breach can occur if *S* negligently causes harm to the fetus, abrogating the promise to provide proper care during pregnancy. In this event, *H* and *W* have two possible avenues of recovery: an action for breach of the terms of the contract, or a tort action based on negligence.[58] Both actions would require *H* and *W* to prove essentially the same elements, although the likelihood of equitable relief rather than damages increases when predicated on the contract action. In either case, *H* and *W* would have to demonstrate that the contract imposed a duty on *S*, whether explicit or implied, to maintain an adequate level of care during pregnancy. If the contract makes explicit the level of care *S* will undertake, including the activities she must forego, then the extent of her duty will be clear. In the absence of specific terms in the contract, the standard of necessary medical attention that *S* must observe would be the same that a reasonable pregnant woman in the circumstances would receive.[59] The range of activities undertaken by reasonable women during pregnancy is expansive, and proving that any given activity falls outside this range would be difficult. Since this duty is not easily defined in the abstract, parties would be well advised to include an explicit statement in the contract, in order to eliminate ambiguities and needless legal complications.

After establishing a duty and breach of that duty, *H* and *W* must prove that the breach proximately caused or will cause the alleged specific injury in order to succeed under either a tort or contract theory. Proof of proximate cause, however, may be difficult because tracing the origin of a congenital defect in a particular child back to a particular source may be impossible.[60] For example, alcohol or caffeine consumption may cause birth defects,[61] but demonstrating that any specific birth defect resulted from such consumption is difficult. Thus, any suit for breach of that duty to provide adequate care will have to overcome this serious obstacle.

Once *H* and *W* establish the elements of a cause of action, two forms of relief are available. In most legal actions, courts assess the injury to the plaintiff and direct the defendant to pay the plaintiff money damages. When payment of money damages is inadequate, because either the harm is not clearly quantifiable,[62] or the underlying basis of the suit depends upon something so unique that money cannot replace it or compensate the plaintiff,[63] courts are willing to prescribe equitable relief: to enjoin the defendant from doing an act or to do an act. Injunction, however, is considered an extraordinary remedy and will not ensue absent a showing that the legal remedy is inadequate.[64]

Obtaining either equitable or legal relief will be difficult, however, since the real purpose of the promise to receive proper care is to protect the welfare of the unborn child. Retrospective legal relief, obtained after a child is born deformed, for instance, clearly is inadequate since money damages will not cure the deformity. Perhaps *H* and *W* can include a liquidated damages clause in the contract,[65] which would provide a specific measure of damages in the event of a specific breach. Yet, courts often strike down liquidated damages as penalties.[66] Thus the damage remedy contains inherent weaknesses that make resort to it unsatisfactory. Given the uncertainties of the equitable remedy, however, the damage remedy may be the only viable means of enforcing this agreement. If *S*'s negligence results in a miscarriage, money damages will be the only possible remedy. Damages are as difficult to determine as if *S* had aborted the fetus, leaving restitution for expenses paid as the only quantifiable measure. Of course, if *H* and *W* are unable to prove negligence on the part of *S*, they would be obligated to pay for the services rendered up to this point. The clearer the contract is concerning the measure of damages, the more likely courts will be to award them.

In the event that *H* and *W* discover, during the term of *S*'s pregnancy, that she has been remiss in obtaining the appropriate level of medical attention, they can request a court to order her compliance. Showing the inadequacy of the legal remedy should not be difficult. Certainly the health and well-being of a child is so unique that a court, if possible, will employ its equity powers to further that end.[67] The problem with injunctions, however, lies in administering orders that direct a woman to receive medical care or to refrain from a certain diet. Courts historically have been reluctant to enjoin parties where the resultant order demands close personal supervision or personal services.[68] Thus, even though the remedy at law would be inadequate, courts may require that alternative, due to the problems inherent in administering equitable orders.

In sum, neither remedy for breach of this promise seems satisfactory. Although injunctive relief is more desirable, it may be judicially unacceptable. In that event only the damage remedy would remain. Damages, however, would be difficult to quantify. In addition, the difficulty in proving proximate cause increases when H and W must demonstrate that a particular activity caused a particular defect. This additional burden will not exist in the case of prospective relief, for H and W will only have to show either that it was prohibited in the terms of the contract, or that it may cause birth defects and that a reasonably prudent pregnant woman would not take the risk. In light of these burdens on H and W, the possibility exists that this promise to obtain adequate medical care, although important to the purpose of the contract, may be wholly unenforceable.

The third way that S can breach the contract is by refusing to give up the child after birth.[69] Monetary damages for H and W in this event do not suffice since the whole purpose of the agreement was to provide them with what they could not otherwise obtain, a child of their own. Since in many cases they are willing to pay money to obtain that child, giving them money as damages would be wholly inadequate. In addition there is no ethically acceptable standard by which a jury can measure the worth of the child.[70] Specific performance, that is, forcing S to surrender the child to H and W, is an equally tenuous alternative. Courts have manifested an extreme reluctance to intervene in domestic relationships.[71] Although S is not a part of the family consisting of H and W, and therefore S, H and W do not comprise a domestic relationship, it seems unlikely that a court would force a woman to give up a child she carried merely on the basis of a contract. Therefore H and W would have to obtain relief in a custody suit where a court would determine the best interests of the child. If the custody suit did not prove favorable for H and W, there would be little recourse. Restitution for expenses incurred by H and W provides the only clear-cut compensable contractual damage.[72]

2. Rights and liabilities of H *and* W

As consideration for the promise of S, H and W promise to pay to S the financial costs of pregnancy and medical care,[73] and to accept the child after birth. Sometimes they also agree to pay S an additional fee for her services. Since H and W have a keen interest in providing good care during pregnancy, presumably they will pay these expenses. However, if H and W breach their promises to pay the costs of pregnancy or to pay the fee to S, recovery would be fairly straightforward, since these expenses either will be delineated in the contract, or easily ascertained by assessing the costs of medical care. If H and W refuse to accept the child after birth, problems will occur in determining the appropriate remedy, similar to those that occur when S refuses to give up the child. Specific performance is unlikely since a court would not force H and W to accept an unwanted child, thereby jeopardizing the child's best interests.

In this instance, S could sue for child support payments. Just as an unwed mother may sue the father of the child for support,[74] S should be able to sue H in the event that he refuses custody. Since S reasonably relied on H and W's promise, she should not have to incur the expenses of bringing up a child that she believed would not be in her custody after its birth. On the other hand, if S wishes to retain custody of the child, she should not be coerced into putting up the child for adoption, despite the rationale of mitigating damages[75] or because she cannot afford to provide adequately for the child. In either case, the father, H, should be estopped from denying responsibility. It should be noted, however, that in the typical artificial insemination case a donor of semen usually does not incur liability for child support unless the donor was the donee's husband.[76] However, regarding the surrogate mother arrangement, H not only recognises that he is the genetic father but also contracts to accept the child and become the father in all respects. The same policy considerations, therefore, which demand insulating the donor from liability in artificial insemination cases do not apply in the surrogate mother cases. In order to make resolution of this issue easier, the contract should include a provision for payment of child support in the event that this sort of breach occurs.

If neither family wants to retain custody of the child, S is free to offer the child for adoption.[77] Perhaps H and W must bear the costs of adoption, but this amount is likely to be small, given the high demand for adoptable babies.[78] The likelihood that either S or H and W will refuse to accept the child increases if the child is born with a deformity or a handicap.[79] Screening procedures should minimise this possibility,[80] and exclude those couples not willing to accept a deformed or handicapped child. Attempting to eliminate these couples at the outset decreases the likelihood of such a problem subsequently arising. In the event, however, that the child is unadoptable, the legal responsibility for care of the child should rest with H and W.

Notes to extract

[45] The remedy at law (ie, monetary damages) must be inadequate before specific performance will be granted. See H McClintock, Handbook of the Principles of Equity § 60 (2nd ed 1948).

[46] This Note contends that S need not be married and discusses the role of S's husband, if she is married, only with respect to her husband's role in screening. If S's husband wholeheartedly consents to the procedure then their marriage should not present a problem. In the absence of consent it would be better for all the parties if S were not married so as to prevent additional complications. The final determination, however, is not a legal one. Rather, the determination will be made by the parties or by a medical screener, if legislation proposed in this Note is passed. . . .

[47] [Footnote omitted.]

[48] Silvoso, *Artificial Insemination: A Legislative Remedy*, 3 W St UL Rev 48, 64 (1975), discusses relinquishment of custody rights in the context of artificial insemination cases.

[49] *Roe v Wade*, 410 US 113 (1973). The Court held that in the first trimester the abortion decision must be left to the medical judgment of the pregnant woman's attending physician. In the stage subsequent to the approximate end of the first trimester, the state may regulate the abortion procedure in ways that are reasonably related to maternal health. After viability the state may regulate or proscribe abortions except where necessary for the preservation of the mother's life or health. *Id* at 164. Tuchler, *Man-Made Man and the Law*, 22 St Louis UL Rev 310, 316 (1978) suggests that not only will S's right to decide to abort be protected by a privacy right, but that it also may be protected by the prohibition against involuntary servitude in the thirteenth amendment to the United States Constitution.

[50] For instance, the Court held in *HL v Matheson*, 101 S Ct 1164 at 1166 (1981) that parental notification may be required before a minor can have an abortion in order to serve the important state interest of family integrity.

[51] *Planned Parenthood of Missouri v Danforth*, 428 US 52 at 69 (1976).

[52] For example, the right to a jury trial may be waived. *Northwest Airlines, Inc v Air Line Pilots Ass'n*, 373 F 2d 136 (8th Cir 1967) (right to trial by jury in suits at common law may be waived); *State v Jelks*, 105 Ariz 175, 461 P 2d 473 (1969) (right to trial by jury in criminal cases may be waived where accused is aware of the right and voluntarily relinquishes it).

[53] For example, the freedom of religion may be waived but the waiver is not irrevocable. See *Thomas v Ind Employment Security Div*, 101 S Ct 1425 (1981) (waiver of religious freedom subsequently can be revoked in employment situation); *Sherbert v Verner*, 374 US 398 (1963).

[54] Erickson, ['Contracts to Bear a Child' (1978) 66 Cal LR 611] at 620 suggests that '[a] remedy in damages should adequately protect the contract parents'. However, while this may be true in classical theory with respect to monetary harm, this does not take into account emotional harm which is likely to be the more significant damage.

[55] *Meyer v Nottger*, 241 NW 2d 911 at 918 (Iowa 1976) (action for intentional infliction of emotional distress was allowed because it included allegation of outrageous conduct by the defendant); *Samms v Eccles*, 11 Utah 2d 289 at 293, 358 P 2d 344 at 347 (1961) (an action may be based upon intentional conduct which any reasonable person would have known would cause emotional distress).

[56] For example, the cause of action was expressly denied in *Wallace v Shoreham Hotel Corpn*, 49 A 2d 81 at 84 (DC Mun Ct App 1946) ('The law does not, and doubtless should not, impose a general duty of care to avoid causing mental distress.' Quoted in *Clark v Associated Retail Credit Men*, 105 F 2d 62 at 66 (DC Cir 1939)). See also, W. Prosser, The Law of Torts § 12 (4th ed 1971).

[57] The case law does not clearly support or reject a wrongful death action for a fetus. For cases supporting such a cause of action, see, e g, *Simmons v Howard Univ*, 323 F Supp 529 (DDC 1971); *Eich v Gulf Shores*, 293 Ala 95, 300 So 2d 354 (1974). For cases dismissing the cause of action, see, e g, *Kilmer v Hicks*, 22 Ariz App 552, 529 P 2d 706 (1974); *Olejniczak v Whitten*, 605 SW 2d 142 (Mo App 1980).

[58] In addition, the child may be able to sue *S* for personal harm suffered due to *S*'s failure to provide proper care during pregnancy. Such suits, however, would be highly speculative, and perhaps totally precluded, if the identity of *S* is not revealed to the child. . . . However, if the case does arise, the child could sue for a breach of promise to provide adequate care to the fetus during pregnancy under a third party beneficiary theory. A third party beneficiary is one for whose benefit two other parties make a contract. See generally, J Calamari & J Perillo, [*The Law of Contracts*, (2nd edn 1977)] at §§ 17-1–17-11; for a discussion of third party beneficiaries in this context see Tuchler, *supra* note 49, at 317. The child is an intended third party beneficiary to the contract between *S, H* and *W*. Therefore in order to recover, the child would have to show that *S*'s engaging in potentially harmful activity constitutes a breach and that, in turn, this activity caused the defect.

The child might also attempt to sue under a tort theory of negligence by demonstrating that *S* owed a duty of care, breached that duty and that harm resulted. See Restatement (Second) of Torts § 281 (1965). The doctrine of intrafamilial immunity, however, could be interposed as a defense to any suit by the child against *S*, the genetic mother. For a definition of the doctrine of intrafamilial immunity, see *Hewlett v George, Ex'r of Ragsdale*, 68 Miss 703 at 711, 9 So 885 at 887 (1891) ('So long as the parent is under an obligation to care for, guide or control and the child is under a reciprocal obligation to aid and comfort and obey, no such action as this can be maintained'). However, at least one commentator suggests that even genetic parents should be liable for prenatal injuries if their actions fall below the standard for reasonably prudent parents. Simon, *Parental Liability for Prenatal Injury*, 14 Colum LJ & Soc Prob 47 (1978). Arguably, this immunity does not even apply since the doctrine of intrafamilial immunity arose to protect family harmony. See *Chaffin v Chaffin*, 239 Or 374 at 381, 397 P 2d 771 at 774 (1964) (wide discretion with respect to support and discipline should be allowed to prevent discord). Realistically, however, suits by the child against the surrogate mother would be unlikely to succeed due to their speculative nature.

[59] While it may be difficult to ascertain what care the 'reasonable pregnant woman' would receive, the test of what is customary is often used to determine whether behavior falls below an acceptable standard. *Denning Warehouse Co v Widener*, 172 F 2d 910 at 913 (10th Cir 1949) (custom tends to show what a reasonably prudent man would do under similar circumstances); *Helweg v Chesapeake & Potomac Telephone Co*, 110 F 2d 546 at 548 (DC Cir 1940) (evidence of customary use, while not conclusive, is relevant). See generally Morris, *Custom and Negligence*, 42 Colum L Rev 1147 (1942).

[60] For a discussion of this problem in regard to *in vitro* fertilisation, see Cohen, *The 'Brave New Baby' and the Law: Fashioning Remedies for the Victims of* In Vitro *Fertilisation*, 4 Am JL & Med 319, 333 (1978).

[61] See Brown, *Ethanol Embryotoxicity: Direct Effects on Mammalian Embryos* In Vitro, 206 Science 573 (Nov 2, 1979), for a discussion of the toxic effects of alcohol on the fetus. See *Caffeine Watching*, NY Times, June 1, 1978, at 41, col 3, which discusses effects of caffeine on the fetus, such as cleft palate and heart trouble.

[62] *Curtice Bros Co v Catts*, 72 NJ Eq 831, 66 A 935 (1907) (specific performance granted because damages could not be adequately measured).

[63] Annot, 90 Am St Rep 634, 648 (1903) ('[I]f a contract stipulates for special, unique, or extraordinary personal services or acts, or where the services to be rendered are purely intellectual, or are peculiar or individual in their character, the court will grant an injunction in aid of specific performance by restraining the breach of the negative covenant.'). The commentator goes on to say, however, that this standard may be inadequate since it is highly discretionary. See *Pusey v Pusey* (1684) 1 Vern 273.

[64] See note 62 *supra*.

[65] Liquidated damages clauses are used, in certain conditions, to determine in advance what damages will be assessed in the event of a breach. See generally Macneil, *Power of Contract and Agreed Remedies*, 47 Cornell LQ 495 (1962).

[66] Generally, a clause will be considered a penalty if the sum stipulated is not a reasonable pre-estimate of the probable loss. See C McCormick, Cases and Materials on Damages §§ 148–149 (2nd ed 1952).

[67] See, eg, *Ex p Buck* 291 Ala 689 at 693, 287 So 2d 441, 445 (1973) ('[t]he equity courts in this state are always open for the protection of minors . . . and any pleading which shows on its face that the welfare of an infant requires an order with respect to its custody or support is sufficient to invoke this jurisdiction'); *Gardner v Rothman*, 370 Mass 79 at 80, 345 NE 2d 370 at 372 (1976) (jurisdiction of equity courts '. . . extends to the persons and estates of infants, and is not restricted to legitimate children'); *Rabuse v Rabuse*, 304 Minn 460 at 463, 231 NW 2d 493 at 495 (1975) (the '. . . general equitable power [to protect infants] obviously includes the right to make provisions for the custody and maintenance of minor children').

[68] *Morris v Peckham*, 51 Conn 128 (1883) (court did not order specific performance in a partnership contract since it held that it had no power to enforce the decree); *De Rivafinoli v Corsetti*, 4 Paige Ch 264 (NY 1883) (court did not order a singer's specific performance since it held that it would be too difficult to determine whether or not defendant had adequately performed); *Lumley v Wagner*, (1852) 42 ER 687 (court indirectly enforced contract by restraining defendant from working for competitor).

[69] A case was in the California courts in which a surrogate mother refused to give up the child. Newsweek, Apr 6, 1981, at 83. The surrogate mother won an out-of-court settlement permitting her to keep custody of the child. Morrow, *Surrogate Mother Gets Custody of Fought-Over Child*, LA Daily J, June 5, 1981, at 1, col 2.

[70] See Moore, *Wrongful Birth—The Problem of Damage Computation*, 48 UMKC L Rev 1 (1979). An analogy can be made to determining damages in the wrongful birth cases, where contraception fails due to the doctor's alleged negligence. Moore suggests that damages with respect to, for example, child-rearing, are speculative.

[71] *Dockery v Hamner*, 281 Ala 343 at 345, 202 So 2d 550 at 551 (1967) ('The relationship of parent and child is confidential.').

[72] See generally Comment, *Restitution: Concept and Terms*, 19 Hastings LJ 1167 (1968).

[73] Humphreys, ['Lawmaking and Science: A Practical Look at *in vitro* Fertilization and Embryo Transfer' (1979) Det CL Rev 429], at 449 n 106 suggests that this may cause a change in health insurance rates and types of coverages.

[74] *Gomez v Perez*, 409 US 535 (1973) (in suit by unwed mother against father for child support, Court held that the father must pay support where state statute required support for legitimate children).

[75] There is a general duty to mitigate damages. This duty requires those injured to take steps to prevent further accumulation of losses after breach by the other party is confirmed. *Clark v Marsiglia*, 1 Denio 317 (NY 1845). The duty to mitigate only requires that the injured party take reasonable steps to mitigate damages. It would be unreasonable to require *S* to put the child up for adoption in order to mitigate damages. See J Calamari & J Perillo, *supra* note [58], at § 14–15.

[76] See, eg, Cal Civ Code § 7005(b) (West Supp 1981); Colo Rev Stat § 19-6-106 (2) (1978). The donor also will most likely remain anonymous.

[77] If *S* gives birth to twins, *H* and *W* are obligated to accept both children and this should be clearly stated in the contract. One can decrease the chances of twins being born by screening out those potential surrogate mothers whose genetic history shows a propensity towards having twins.

[78] Questions of who is responsible for putting the child up for adoption can be resolved by assuming that the child is the legitimate child of *H* and *W*, thereby placing any financial burden for placing the child for adoption on *H* and *W*, ...

[79] Possibly through prenatal testing, *S*, *H* and *W* could discover that the child will be born deformed. *H* and *W* may want *S* to have an abortion at this point. However, *H* and *W* may not be able to force *S* to abort the fetus and remain contractually obligated to accept the baby. See notes 49–51 *supra* and accompanying text.

[80] [Footnote omitted.]

On the specific issue of abortion Eaton writes in his article 'The British Response to Surrogate Motherhood' (1985) Law Teacher 163, 181–182 (footnotes omitted):

> ... Under the current law of abortion, it is difficult to imagine a court ordering a woman in the early stages of pregnancy to carry and give birth to a child she did not want to deliver. The rationale that gives rise to a right to terminate a pregnancy is quite similar to that frequently invoked to deny specific performance. The abortion cases emphasise the uniquely personal nature and the serious consequences of the decision to bear a child. An order prohibiting an abortion would therefore demand the performance of the most personal of services and could impose a severe hardship on the surrogate. Thus specific performance of an agreement restricting abortion is unlikely.
>
> The aggrieved couple is probably limited to the conventional tort and contract remedy of damages. ... Damages for breach of contract appears a more promising avenue of redress. The couple certainly would be entitled to restitution for sums already paid. However, this is a small amount compared with the enormous disappointment and distress the abortion is likely to have caused. The general rule that contract damages do not compensate for non-pecuniary losses is subject to an increasing number of exceptions. Courts have awarded damages for mental distress when such damages were within the contemplation of the parties as a foreseeable consequence of the breach of contract. There are few situations where mental distress is more clearly foreseeable than when a woman breaches her promise not to abort a man's child.
>
> All in all, the commissioning couple should recognise the precarious position they occupy with regard to enforcing contractual provisions regulating pre-natal conduct. Specific performance is probably not a viable option. Damages for breach of contract remains a theoretical, though inadequate, remedy. Money is simply no substitute for a healthy child. The extent to which money damages is a remedy at all depends on the uncertain solvency of the surrogate.

(b) Legal responses to surrogacy

1. Custody of child

As we have seen, the determination of who should have custody of the child is not a matter for the parties to agree amongst themselves. As Sir John Arnold P put it in *Re P (supra)*.

> ...[T]he court's duty is to decide the case, taking into account as the first and paramount consideration, the welfare of the child or children concerned and if that consideration leads the court to override any agreement that there may be in the matter, then that the court is fully entitled to do.

In the *Baby M* case, the New Jersey Supreme Court approached custody in a similar way. Wilentz CJ said:

Having decided that the surrogacy contract is illegal and unenforceable, we now must decide the custody question without regard to the provisions of the surrogacy contract that would give Mr Stern sole and permanent custody. (That does not mean that the existence of the contract and the circumstances under which it was entered may not be considered to the extent deemed relevant to the child's best interests.) With the surrogacy contract disposed of, the legal framework becomes a dispute between two couples over the custody of a child produced by the artificial insemination of one couple's wife by the other's husband. . . . The applicable rule given these circumstances is clear: the child's best interests determine custody.

We note again that the trial court's reasons for determining what were the child's best interests were somewhat different from ours. It concluded that the surrogacy contract was valid, but that it could not grant specific performance unless to do so was in the child's best interests. The approach was that of a Chancery judge, unwilling to give extraordinary remedies unless they well served the most important interests, in this case, the interests of the child. While substantively indistinguishable from our approach to the question of best interests, the purpose of the inquiry was not the usual purpose of determining custody, but of determining a contractual remedy.

. . . The question of custody in this case, as in practically all cases, assumes the fitness of both parents, and no serious contention is made in this case that either is unfit. The issue here is which life would be better *for Baby M, one with primary custody in the Whiteheads or one with primary custody in the Sterns.*

The circumstances of this custody dispute are unusual and they have provoked some unusual contentions. The Whiteheads claim that even if the child's best interests would be served by our awarding custody to the Sterns, we should not do so, since that will encourage surrogacy contracts—contracts claimed by the Whiteheads, and we agree, to be violative of important legislatively-stated public policies. Their position is that in order that surrogacy contracts be deterred, custody should remain in the surrogate mother unless she is unfit, regardless of the best interests of the child. We disagree. Our declaration that this surrogacy contract is unenforceable and illegal is sufficient to deter similar agreements. We need not sacrifice the child's interests in order to make that point sharper. . . . Some of Mrs Whitehead's alleged character failings, as testified to by experts and concurred in by the trial court, were demonstrated by her actions brought on by the custody crisis. For instance in order to demonstrate her impulsiveness, those experts stressed the Whitehead's flight to Florida with Baby M; to show her willingness to use her children for her own aims, they noted the telephone threats to kill Baby M and to accuse Mr Stern of sexual abuse of her daughter; in order to show Mrs Whitehead's manipulativeness, they pointed to her threat to kill herself; and in order to show her unsettled family life, they noted the innumerable moves from one hotel or motel to another in Florida. Furthermore, the argument continues, one of the most important factors, whether mentioned or not, in favor of custody in the Sterns is their continuing custody during the litigation, now having lasted for one-and-a-half years. The Whiteheads' conclusion is that had the trial court not given initial custody to the Sterns during the litigation, Mrs Whitehead not only would have demonstrated her perfectly acceptable personality—the general tenor of the opinion of experts was that her personality problems surfaced primarily in crises—but would also have been able to prove better her parental skills along with an even stronger bond than may now exist between her and Baby M. Had she not been limited to custody for four months, she could have proved all of these things much more persuasively through almost two years of custody.

The argument has considerable force. It is of course possible that the trial court was wrong in its initial award of custody. It is also possible that such error, if that is what it was, may have affected the outcome. We disagree with the premise, however, that in determining custody a court should decide what the child's best interests *would be* if some hypothetical state of facts had existed. Rather, we must look to what those best interests *are, today,* even if some of the facts may have resulted in part from legal error. The child's interests come first:... The custody decision must be based on all circumstances, on everything that *actually* has occurred, on everything that is relevant to the child's best interests. Those circumstances include the trip to Florida, the telephone calls and threats, the substantial period of successful custody with the Sterns, and all other relevant circumstances....

There were eleven experts who testified concerning the child's best interests, either directly or in connection with matters related to that issue. Our reading of the record persuades us that the trial court's decision awarding custody to the Sterns (technically to Mr Stern) should be affirmed...

Our custody conclusion is based on strongly persuasive testimony contrasting both the family life of the Whiteheads and the Sterns and the personalities and characters of the individuals. The stability of the Whitehead family life was doubtful at the time of trial. Their finances were in serious trouble (foreclosure by Mrs Whitehead's sister on a second mortgage was in process). Mr Whitehead's employment, though relatively steady, was always at risk because of his alcoholism, a condition that he seems not to have been able to confront effectively. Mrs Whitehead had not worked for quite some time, her last two employments having been part-time. One of the Whiteheads' positive attributes was their ability to bring up two children, and apparently well, even in so vulnerable a household. Yet substantial question was raised even about that aspect of their home life. The expert testimony contained criticism of Mrs Whitehead's handling of her son's educational difficulties. Certain of the experts noted that Mrs Whitehead perceived herself as omnipotent and omniscient concerning her children. She knew what they were thinking, what they wanted, and she spoke for them. As to Melissa, Mrs Whitehead expressed the view that she alone knew what that child's cries and sounds meant. Her inconsistent stories about various things engendered grave doubts about her ability to explain honestly and sensitively to Baby M—and at the right time—the nature of her origin. Although faith in professional counseling is not a *sine qua non* of parenting, several experts believed that Mrs Whitehead's contempt for professional help, especially professional psychological help, coincided with her feelings of omnipotence in a way that could be devastating to a child who most likely will need such help. In short, while love and affection there would be, Baby M's life with the Whiteheads promised to be too closely controlled by Mrs Whitehead. The prospects for wholesome, independent psychological growth and development would be at serious risk.

The Sterns have no other children, but all indications are that their household and their personalities promise a much more likely foundation for Melissa to grow and thrive. There *is* a track record of sorts—during the one-and-a-half years of custody Baby M has done very well, and the relationship between both Mr and Mrs Stern and the baby has become very strong. The household is stable, and likely to remain so. Their finances are more than adequate, their circle of friends supportive, and their marriage happy. Most important, they are loving, giving, nurturing, and open-minded people. They have demonstrated the wish and ability to nurture and protect Melissa, yet at the same time to encourage her independence. Their lack of experience is more than made up for by a willingness to learn and to listen, a willingness that is enhanced by their professional training, especially Mrs Stern's experience as a pediatrician. They are honest; they can recognise error, deal with it, and learn from it. They will try to determine rationally the best way to cope with problems in their relationship with Melissa. When the time comes to tell her about her origins, they will probably have found a means of doing so that accords with the best interests of Baby M. All in all, Melissa's future appears solid, happy, and promising with them.

Based on all of this we have concluded, independent of the trial court's identical conclusion, that Melissa's best interests call for custody in the Sterns....

It seems to us that given her predicament, Mrs Whitehead was rather harshly judged—both by the trial court and by some of the experts. She was guilty of a breach of contract, and indeed, she did break a very important promise, but we think it is expecting something well beyond normal human capabilities to suggest that this mother should have parted with her newly born infant without a struggle. Other than survival, what stronger force is there? We do not know of, and cannot conceive of, any other case where a perfectly fit mother was expected to surrender her newly born infant, perhaps forever, and was then told she was a bad mother because she did not. We know of no authority suggesting that the moral quality of her act in those circumstances should be judged by referring to a contract made before she became pregnant. We do not countenance, and would never countenance, violating a court order as Mrs Whitehead did, even a court order that is wrong; but her resistance to an order that she surrender her infant, possibly forever, merits a measure of understanding. We do not find it so clear that her efforts to keep her infant, when measured against the Sterns' efforts to take her away, make one, rather than the other, the wrongdoer. The Sterns suffered, but so did she. And if we go beyond suffering to an evaluation of the human stakes involved in the struggle, how much weight should be given to her nine months of pregnancy, the labor of childbirth, the risk to her life, compared to the payment of money, the anticipation of a child and the donation of sperm?

There has emerged a portrait of Mrs Whitehead, exposing her children to the media, engaging in negotiations to sell a book, granting interviews that seemed helpful to her, whether hurtful to Baby M or not, that suggests a selfish, grasping woman ready to sacrifice the interests of Baby M and her other children for fame and wealth. That portrait is a half-truth, for while it may accurately reflect what ultimately occurred, its implication, that this is what Mary Beth Whitehead wanted, is totally inaccurate, at least insofar as the record before us is concerned. There is not one word in that record to support a claim that had she been allowed to continue her possession of her newly born infant, Mrs Whitehead would have ever been heard of again: not one word in the record suggests that her change of mind and her subsequent fight for her child was motivated by anything other than love—whatever complex underlying psychological motivations may have existed.

We have a further concern regarding the trial court's emphasis on the Sterns' interest in Melissa's education as compared to the Whiteheads'. That this difference is a legitimate factor to be considered we have no doubt. But it should not be overlooked that a best-interests test is designed to create not a new member of the intelligentsia but rather a well-integrated person who might reasonably be expected to be happy with life. "Best interests" does not contain within it any idealised lifestyle; the question boils down to a judgment, consisting of many factors, about the likely future happiness of a human being, *Fantony v Fantony, supra,* 21 *NJ* at 536, 122 *A* 2d 593. Stability, love, family happiness, tolerance, and, ultimately support of independence—all rank much higher in predicting future happiness than the likelihood of a college education. We do not mean to suggest that the trial court would disagree. We simply want to dispel any possible misunderstanding on the issue.

Even allowing for these differences, the facts, the experts' opinions, and the trial court's analysis of both argue strongly in favour of custody in the Sterns. Mary Beth Whitehead's family life, into which Baby M would be placed, was anything but secure—the quality Melissa needs most. And today it may be even less so. Furthermore, the evidence and expert opinion based on it reveal personality characteristics, mentioned above, that might threaten the child's best development. The Sterns promise a secure home, with an understanding relationship that allows nurturing and independent growth to develop together.

The court awarded custody to Mr and Mrs Stern.

Given this judicial attitude to the relevance of terms of the surrogacy agreement to the court's decision, it follows that determination of custody will be made according to the traditional principles of family law having to do with the 'best interests' of the child. Surrogacy arrangements can pose particularly difficult questions concerning 'best interests' in at least three situations:

First, where the parties are agreed that custody should vest in the commissioning parents but the court may choose to disregard the terms of the agreement and place the child in the custody of another (*Re C (a Minor)* [1985] FLR 846 and *Re Adoption Application* [1987] Fam 81 [1987] 2 All ER 826).

Re C (a Minor) concerned what was said to be the first commercial surrogacy agreement in England. The surrogate mother was Kim Coton and the case aroused enormous public interest in the early part of 1985. The case resulted in Parliament enacting the Surrogate Arrangements Act 1985 which, as we have seen, makes it a criminal offence to operate a commercial surrogacy agency. *Re C* illustrates that even where all the parties to the agreement are content with who should have custody, the court in the exercise of its wardship jurisdiction must make the ultimate decision, based on its perception of the child's 'best-interests'. The case also illustrates the judiciary's uneasiness with the publication of the names of the parties involved—in this case at least the surrogate mother was already well-known—and, as we shall see, the judge made an order restraining the press from discovering or publishing the names of the parties.

Latey J: The baby's father is Mr A, as I will describe him. He and his wife, Mrs A, are in their 30s and have been married for several years. Mr A is fertile. Mrs A has a congenital defect which prevents her from ever having children. Both dearly wanted a baby. In their home country adoption is slow and a child is usually aged 4 to 5 at adoption. They wanted a baby to bring up from birth. They made inquiries.

In 1983 the father contacted an agency in America and entered into a contract whereby he paid a sum of money and the agency undertook to find a surrogate mother to bear his child. She also would be paid. In England there is a similar agency. A surrogate mother was found.

In 1984 the father came to England, by arrangement, for the sole purpose of providing seminal fluid for insemination of the surrogate mother. It was so arranged that he provided his semen to a qualified nurse and it was introduced into the mother. The father and the mother did not meet and have not met. The insemination was successful, resulting in conception.

The agreement was that the baby on birth was to be handed over to the father and his wife, Mr and Mrs A, to be theirs to care for and bring up.

The father and his wife came to this country in anticipation of the birth and on Friday, 4 January, the baby was born. On the same day the local authority, the London Borough of Barnet, obtained a place of safety order. The baby remained at the hospital, cared for by the nurses.

On Tuesday, 8 January 1985 the father issued a wardship summons. On the same evening there was a hearing before me, when the father was represented by counsel and solicitors, and the London Borough of Barnet was represented by counsel and its legal department. The father and his wife were present.

At that time the social services department had already carried out a good deal of its inquiries, but still had some to complete. It was a fairly lengthy hearing and I made interim orders and directions.

The social services department thought that they could conclude their inquiries by Friday last and I directed that the matter be restored for hearing on that day. They did complete their inquiries and the matter was heard on Friday last.

The inquiries which were deposed to in evidence, were very full and covered every relevant matter. They established that the father, Mr A, is the natural father of the baby; that the natural mother has voluntarily relinquished all parental rights in the child; and that she in fact left the baby in hospital some hours after birth and has not seen her since. The evidence deals in the fullest details with Mr and Mrs A and their health, living and family circumstances and their suitability as parents, about which I will say a little more in a moment.

In the result, the local authority supports to the full the application that the baby be given into the care and upbringing of Mr and Mrs A.

First and foremost, and at the heart of the prerogative jurisdiction in wardship, is what is best for the child or children concerned. That and nothing else. Plainly, the methods used to produce a child as this baby has been, and the commercial aspects of it, raise difficult and delicate problems of ethics, morality and social desirability. These problems are under active consideration elsewhere.

Are they relevant in arriving at a decision on what now and, so far as one can tell, in the future is best for this child? If they are relevant, it is incumbent on the court to do its best to evaluate and balance them.

In my judgment, however, they are not relevant. The baby is here. All that matters is what is best for her now that she is here and not how she arrived. If it be said (though it has not been said during these hearings) that because the father and his wife entered into these arrangements it is some indication of their unsuitability as parents. I should reject any such suggestion. If what they did was wrong (and I am not saying that it was), they did it in total innocence.

It follows that the moral, ethical and social considerations are for others and not for this court in its wardship jurisdiction.

So, what is best for this baby? Her natural mother does not ask for her. Should she go into Mr and Mrs A's care and be brought up by them? Or should some other arrangement be made for her, such as long-term fostering with or without adoption as an end?

The factors can be briefly stated. Mr A is the baby's father and he wants her, as does his wife. The baby's mother does not want her. Mr and Mrs A are a couple in their 30s. They are devoted to each other. They are both professional people, highly qualified. They have a very nice home in the country and another in a town. Materially they can give the baby a very good upbringing. But, far more importantly, they are both excellently equipped to meet the baby's emotional needs. They are most warm, caring, sensible people, as well as highly intelligent. When the time comes to answer the child's questions, they will be able to do so with professional advice if they feel they need it. Looking at this child's well-being, physical and emotional, who better to have her care? No one.

Accordingly, the orders which I made on Friday evening are that the wardship will continue until further order; the care and control of the baby is committed to Mr and Mrs A until further order; on their undertaking to return the child to the jurisdiction if the court should so order (an unlikely contingency in this case) there is leave for them to take her to live outside the jurisdiction. There are further orders that RSC Ord 63, r 4 shall not apply, and that no one may search for, inspect or take a copy of any of the documents filed in these proceedings without leave of the court; and an order to similar effect regarding the documents in the possession of the social services department, again without leave of the court.

I also approved arrangements for the immediate handover of the baby to Mr and Mrs A. These were worked out with the object, amongst others, of avoiding the identification of Mr and Mrs A.

. . .

Finally, I issued a specific order that there must be no disclosure or publicity which *might* (and I stress that word) lead to the identification of Mr and Mrs A. The reasons for this are or should be self-evident. Is this baby to grow into childhood, adolescence and adulthood with the finger pointed at her as 'This is the girl who . . .?' It is unthinkable that it should be so. Were it otherwise the injury to her mental and emotional health might be grave indeed. The wardship continues and with it that specific order. Any breach of it would be a very serious contempt.

It is inconceivable that leave ever will be given to publish the identities of Mr and Mrs A. That being so, it would be kind and compassionate to discontinue any inquiries which may be on foot and leave this couple to bring up their child in peace and quietness of mind.

Secondly, difficulties are also posed where the parties are agreed that, because it has transpired that the child has been born disabled, neither party should be obliged to have custody.

This problem is not resolved merely by saying 'parental rights' are inalienable, even though this is true (Children Act 1975, s 85(2)). This begs the question who the parents are or should be? The court will determine who should have custody on the 'best interests' approach. In doing so, the court will clearly have regard to the fact that the child is unwanted by the parties to the agreement. It may well be in such a case that the child's best interests lie elsewhere than living with any of the parties to the agreement. Adoption or long-term fostering to third parties may be the most likely outcome in this sort of case.

Thirdly, difficulties may arise, where the surrogate mother refuses to surrender the custody of the child to the commissioning couple, as in the following cases: *A v C* (custody to surrogate); *Baby M* (custody to commissioning parents); *Re P (Minors)* (custody to surrogate).

This situation looks the most difficult to resolve since there is a 'tug of war' between the parties to the agreement for the custody of the child. A judicial determination of what are the child's best interests will not necessarily result in any particular party to the agreement obtaining custody. The attitude of Comyn J and the Court of Appeal in *A v C*—which can only be described as open antagonism towards the commissioning father—might not be so likely now.

The American case of *Baby M*, which we have already seen in some detail, illustrates how the court can perceive the child's best interests as lying with the commissioning parents and not with the surrogate who is the natural mother of the child. Even so, this will not always be the case as *Re P (minors)* [1987] 2 FLR 421 illustrates. The facts of the case, taken from the headnote, were as follows:

> A woman offered her services as a surrogate mother to a married professional man who donated sperm by artificial insemination and agreed to pay a lump sum to adopt the child. During her pregnancy she began to have misgivings about giving up the child and when she had given birth to twins in October 1986 her disinclination hardened increasingly. After a period of indecision, and despite her concern and regret about disappointing the father and his wife, she decided to keep the children. She and the father independently approached the local authority who applied to the court to make the children wards of court and to deal with the matter. By the date of the hearing the twins had been cared for by their mother for 5 months.

Having indicated that in determining who should have custody of the twins, their welfare was the 'first and paramount consideration', Sir John Arnold P continued:

> What then are the factors which the court should take into account? I have already mentioned on the side of Mrs P the matters which weigh heavily in the balance are the fact of her maternity, that she bore the children and carried them for the term of their gestation and that ever since she has conferred upon them the maternal care which they have enjoyed and has done so successfully. The key social worker in the case who has given evidence testifies to the satisfactory nature of the care which Mrs P has conferred upon the children and this assessment is specifically accepted by Mr B as being an accurate one. I start, therefore, from the position that these babies have bonded with their mother in a state of domestic care by her of a satisfactory nature and I now turn to the factors which are said to outweigh those advantages, so as to guide the court upon the proper exercise of the balancing function to the conclusion that the children ought to be taken away from Mrs P, and passed over, under suitable arrangements, to Mr and Mrs B. They are principally as follows. It is said, and said quite correctly, that the shape of the B family is the better shape of a family in which these children might be brought up, because it contains a father as well as a mother and that is undoubtedly true. Next, it is said that the material circumstances of the B family are such that they exhibit a far larger degree of affluence than can be demonstrated by Mrs P. That, also, is undoubtedly true.

Then it is said that the intellectual quality of the environment of the B's home and the stimulus which would be afforded to these babies, if they were to grow up in that home, would be greater than the corresponding features in the home of Mrs P. That is not a matter which has been extensively investigated, but I suspect that that is probably true. Certainly, the combined effect of the lack of affluence on the part of Mrs P and some lack of resilience to the disadvantages which that implies has been testified in the correspondence to the extent that I find Mrs P saying that shortage of resources leads to her sitting at home with little E and overeating, because she has no ability from a financial point of view to undertake anything more resourceful than that. Then it is said that the religious comfort and support which the B's derive from their Church is greater than anything of that sort available to Mrs P. How far that is true, I simply do not know. I do know that the B's are practising Christians and do derive advantages from that circumstance, but nobody asked Mrs P about this and I am not disposed to assume that she lacks that sort of comfort and support in the absence of any investigation by way of cross-examination to lay the foundations for such a conclusion. Then it is said, and there is something in this, that the problems which might arise from the circumstance that these children who are, of course, congenitally derived from the semen of Mr B and bear traces of Mr B's Asiatic origin would be more easily understood and discussed and reconciled in the household of Mr and Mrs B, a household with an Asiatic ethnic background than they would be if they arose in relation to these children while they were situated in the home of Mrs P, which is in an English village and which has no non-English connections. Obviously that is expressed contingently as a factor, although there is no means by which the court can measure the likelihood or otherwise of the contingency which has regard to racial discrimination. The situation in which Mrs P lives is not, as it seems to me, likely to breed that sort of intolerance. She lives in a smallish country community, large in terms of a village but small in terms of a town, where there is very little penetration by any immigrant citizens, which does not seem to me to be a community in which racial discrimination is very likely, but it is a factor which contingently at least may have some importance.

Those are the particular matters which are put forward as counterweights to the advantages to which Mrs P can point, and additionally there is the matter to which I have already referred, that it is said that in the letter of mid-November 1986, Mrs P was, herself, recognising that the balance of advantage, which the court is required to consider for the reason that I have indicated, operated in favour of the solution of placing the children with the B's and taking them away from Mrs P, but I do not think that that last factor is of substantial importance. At the time when that letter was written there was, as independent evidence testifies, a prevalent state of things in which Mrs P was suffering from post natal-depression, or at least post-natal stress, so that her expressions of opinion were not likely to have been very reliable at that time. Secondly, any such opinion was expressed at a stage when the children were 1 month old and might not be valid in the circumstance such as now prevails. They are 5 months old and have consistently been looked after by their mother during that 5 months' period and, thirdly, the court is not only not bound, although it might be influenced, by such an expression of opinion, but is required in the due exercise of the jurisdiction to come to its own conclusion upon that topic.

As regards the other factors, they are, in the aggregate, weighty, but I do not think, having given my very best effort to the evaluation of the case dispassionately on both sides, that they ought to be taken to outweigh the advantages to these children of preserving the link with the mother to whom they are bonded and who has, as is amply testified, exercised over them a satisfactory level of maternal care, and accordingly it is, I think, the duty of the court to award the care and control of these babies to their mother.

One final point requires notice. Although *A v C* began as a dispute about custody of a child, eventually the commissioning father's claim was for access alone. This the Court of Appeal rejected. Ormrod LJ said (at 458):

I can see absolutely no advantage to this child in continuing to be in contact with the father, except possibly a financial advantage to which I attach no significance whatever, in this case. If the father is to continue to turn up in the mother's house or to keep meeting her somewhere to take over this child, or to meet some member of her family to take over the child and return the child, the whole of this sordid story will be revived weekly or monthly as the case may be. The mother's position will be handicapped, and the handicapping of her position handicaps the child.

Cumming-Bruce LJ said (at 460–1):

In my view, the effect of the access ordered by the judge must, inevitably be to introduce such a disruptive factor into the mother's emotional life that it is bound to have an adverse effect upon the boy. The boy's interest in this case is identified with the mother's interest, and the boy must be given a mother free from the threat of repeated confrontation with a man with whom she has never had any sort of relationship at all, save one of sordid pecuniary advantage. In my view, any advantage that the father could confer on the child is wholly outbalanced and obviously outbalanced by the disadvantage to the child of being brought up by the mother, who is subject to such a dangerous and persistent reminder of an episode in her life which, though she will never forget it, must be kept as completely in the background as possible.

It is interesting to note that in the *Baby M* case where by contrast, custody was awarded to the commissioning parents, the Supreme Court of New Jersey remitted the issue of access by the surrogate mother, Mary Beth Whitehead, to the trial court. The court observed:

We have decided that Mrs Whitehead is entitled to visitation at some point, and that question is not open to the trial court on this remand. The trial court will determine what kind of visitation shall be granted to her, with or without conditions, and when and under what circumstances it should commence. . . .

While probably unlikely, we do not deem it unthinkable that, the major issues having been resolved, the parties' undoubted love for this child might result in a good faith attempt to work out the visitation themselves, in the best interests of their child.

Questions

(i) Do you agree with the approach, in principle, of the New Jersey Supreme Court or the English Court of Appeal?

(ii) Is it consistent for the New Jersey Supreme Court to find that the natural mother should not have custody but that she should be entitled to access?

2. Legitimacy

As regards the legitimacy of a child born as a result of a surrogacy arrangement, the conclusions reached earlier in the context of AID, egg donation and embryo donation would appear to apply here also. In an attempt, *inter alia*, to put the matter of who is the mother of a child born as a consequence of a surrogate arrangement beyond doubt, the Surrogacy Arrangements (Amendment) Bill 1986 was proposed. Clause 2 of the Bill provided that 'a child born to a surrogate mother . . . shall for all purposes in law be regarded as the child of that mother . . .' Is this not the law in any event?

Questions

(i) What do you think is the effect of s 27 of the Family Law Reform Act 1987 if the surrogate mother's husband consents to her being artificially inseminated? Notice the terms of the *Baby M* contract set out *supra* at p 719.

Section 27 provides:

> **27.** (1) Where after the coming into force of this section a child is born in England and Wales as the result of the artificial insemination of a woman who—
>   (a) was at the time of the insemination a party to a marriage (being a marriage which had not at that time been dissolved or annulled); and
>   (b) was artificially inseminated with the semen of some person other than the other party to that marriage.
>
> then, unless it is proved to the satisfaction of any court by which the matter has to be determined that the other party to that marriage did not consent to the insemination, the child shall be treated in law as the child of the parties to that marriage and shall not be treated as the child of any person other than the parties to that marriage.

(ii) Does this mean the surrogate and her husband are the parents of the child for all purposes? What if:

(a) the surrogate and her partner are not married; or

(b) the surrogate pregnancy results from sexual intercourse with the commissioning male; or

(c) the surrogate agreement signed by the surrogate's husband recites that he does not consent to the artificial insemination of his wife?

Chapter 9

Abortion

Historical background

Consider the following extract from Dickens: *Abortion and the Law* (1966), pp 20–28 (footnotes omitted).

The position at common law

'... [B]ecause the offence was of ecclesiastical cognisance ... the writings of authorities on English criminal law have few references to abortion. The protection the Common Law afforded to human life certainly extended to the unborn child but whether abortion (ie after quickening) amounted to homicide or a lesser offence is not clear beyond doubt from the authorities, and possibly altered at different periods. Bracton, writing in the early part of the thirteenth century said that abortion after animation was homicide. Furthermore, George Crabbe alleges this to have been the position long before; 'If, in Bracton's time, anyone struck a pregnant woman so as to cause abortion, it was homicide, after the foetus was formed. This appears to have been the law in the time of the Saxons'.

An epitome of Bracton, written near the end of the thirteenth century by Fleta is more explicit. His chapter 'De Homicidio' asserts 'He, too, in strictness is a homicide who has pressed upon a pregnant woman or has given her poison or has struck her in order to procure an abortion or to prevent conception, if the foetus was already formed and quickened, and similarly he who has given or accepted poison with the intention of preventing procreation or conception. A woman also commits homicide if, by a potion or the like, she destroys a quickened child in her womb'.

Later authorities, however, do not follow this view, and Coke while quoting Bracton and mentioning Fleta, nevertheless denies homicide. 'If a woman be quick with childe (sic), and by a Potion or otherwise Killeth it in her wombe; or if a man beat her whereby the child (sic) dieth in her body, and she is delivered of a dead childe, this is a great misprision, and no murder; but if the childe be borne alive, and dieth of the Potion, battery or other cause, this is murder: for in law it is accounted a reasonable creature, in *rerum natura*, when it is born alive.'

Coke then demonstrates that a man is accessory to murder who counsels a pregnant woman to kill the child when it is born and continues, 'and yet at the time of the commandment, or counsel, no murder could be committed of the childe in *utero matris*.'

The consequence of this 'great misprision' is not described, but Hawkins wrote in 1716 that the procuring of the abortion of a quick child amounts to a Common Law misdemeanour and is murder if the child is born alive but dies in consequence of its premature birth, or of the means employed.

Blackstone, in his *Commentaries on the Laws of England* (1765) suggests that manslaughter was a possible interpretation of Bracton's characterisation of abortion. He wrote 'Life ... begins in contemplation of law as soon as an infant is able to stir in the mother's womb. For if a woman is quick with child, and by a potion or otherwise, killeth it in her womb; or if any one beat her, whereby the child dieth in her body, and she is delivered of a dead child; this, though not murder, was by the antient (sic) law homicide or manslaughter (Bracton). But Sir Edward Coke doth not look upon this offence in quite so atrocious a light, but merely as a heinous misdemenor.'

That Blackstone should translate as 'a heinous misdemenor' what Coke earlier called 'a great misprision' may suggest the contemporary evaluation of the crime of abortion, as the law of misprision was well known to Blackstone. In his *Commentaries* he wrote 'Misprisions . . . are, in the acceptation of our law, generally understood to be all such high offences as are under the degree of capital, but nearly bordering thereon'. His rejection of this word to describe Coke's view suggests that while the ancient law regarded abortion as homicide or manslaughter, the contemporary view was that it was not a capital offence, nor even close thereto. After classifying misprisions into negative and positive, the latter consisting in the commission of something which ought not to be done, he continued 'Misprisions, which are merely positive, are generally denominated contempts, or high misdemeanors' and are usually punishable with fines and imprisonment.

Blackstone does not adopt the modern division of crimes into felonies and misdemeanours, but draws the distinction 'A crime or misdemeanor, is an act committed, or omitted, in violation of a public law, either forbidding or commanding it. The general definition comprehends both crimes and misdemeanors; which, properly speaking, are mere synonymous terms; though, common usage, the word "crimes" is made to denote such offences as are of a deeper and more atrocious dye; while smaller faults, and omissions of less consequence, are comprised under the gentler name of "misdemeanors" only'.

The *Commentaries on the Laws of England* were written by Blackstone for the lay public, and one may suppose that they were intended to be read according to the common usage, by which misdemeanours were 'smaller faults, and omissions of less consequence'.

Nevertheless, even accepting that in Coke's period (1552–1634) abortion was an offence bordering on the capital, it would probably not have been prosecuted in the Common Law courts, as the ecclesiastical courts retained a criminal jurisdiction, and abortion was generally regarded as their province. However, the Reformation in the mid-sixteenth century challenged this jurisdiction, and in 1641, during the political turmoil immediately before the Civil War, Parliament abolished the senior ecclesiastical courts, the Court of High Commission and the Court of Delegates, and these took into abolition with them the whole system of ecclesiastical courts. In these new circumstances, the Common Law courts would have dealt with the crime of abortion, giving the Common Law an impetus to develop its own principles, but at the Restoration in 1661 the ordinary ecclesiastical courts were re-established, and much of their old criminal jurisdiction revived, in theory. However, in fact, this was becoming increasingly diminished by the growing practice of making ecclesiastical offences statutory felonies, which took them into the Common Law courts. Moreover even where offences were not so removed from the ecclesiastical courts, the Common Law was generating its own concurrent growth, and it was not until 1803 that procuring abortion was made a statutory felony.

Blackstone in 1765 treated it as a Common Law misdemeanour, and support for this is provided in Chitty's *Criminal Law* (1816) which provides precedents from an indictment both under the 1803 Act and under the Common Law, where drawing on a case of 1802 EF is charged in the third count of the indictment with 'unlawfully . . . giving and administering to AE, . . . pregnant with child divers other . . . dangerous pills . . . with a wicked intent to cause and procure the said AE to miscarry . . .' However, references to the procuring of abortion as a crime at Common Law before it became a statutory offence in 1803 are not numerous, and are fairly late in date.

D. Statutory provisions

It appears that before 1803 the crime of abortion was a Common Law misdemeanour capable of commission by the pregnant woman herself and by other persons on her, but in either case only provided that the stage of 'quickening' had been reached. There are scanty records of the crime, because it was mainly regarded as a matter for the ecclesiastical courts and even where prosecuted in the Common Law courts it would be a rare case, as most abortion is committed before the stage of quickening has been reached (a widely accepted time being fourteen weeks after conception).

Lord Ellenborough's Act, receiving the Royal assent on June 24th 1803, for the first time placed the offence of criminal abortion on a statutory basis. Explaining that 'certain . . . heinous Offences, committed with Intent to destroy the Lives of his Majesty's Subjects by Poison, or with Intent to procure the miscarriage of Women . . . have been of late also frequently committed; but no adequate Means have been hitherto provided for the Prevention and Punishment of such Offences', it provides in section 1 'That if any Person or Persons . . . shall wilfully, maliciously, and unlawfully administer to, or cause to be administered to or taken by any of his Majesty's Subjects, any deadly Poison, or other noxious and destructive Substance or Thing, with Intent . . . thereby to cause and procure the Miscarriage of any Woman then being quick with child . . . then and in every such case the Person or Persons so offending, their Counsellors, Aiders, and Abbettors, knowing of and privy to such Offence, shall be and are hereby declared to be Felons, and shall suffer Death'.

Although this section created a capital offence, introducing a more severe penalty than was available for the Common Law misdemeanour, it did not substantially alter the legal definition. Indeed it may have been more restricted, as it dealt only with the abortion of women quick with child, procured by use of 'poison, or other noxious and destructive substance or thing'. By the *ejusdem generis* rule of construction, 'thing' may have excluded instruments or manipulations or exercises.

There was no specific reference to a woman procuring her own abortion, but the words of the section probably included such a case, and the statute was directed to the punishment of such an offence, which was consistent with the position at Common Law. Nevertheless the infrequent prosecution of offenders prevented the matter from being clarified beyond doubt, and it may have been that where a woman procured her own abortion by another, she would be charged as an aider and abettor to that other's offence, or still be liable for the Common Law misdemeanour.

The great innovation of the 1803 Act was in section 2; abortion before quickening became a crime for the first time, and was a felony, although not punished as severely as abortion after quickening. The practical significance of this provision was widespread, as nearly all women who procure their own abortion do so in the early months of pregnancy, before quickening.

Section 2 provides 'And whereas it may sometimes happen that Poison or some other noxious and destructive Substance or Thing may be given, or other means used, with Intent to procure Miscarriage or Abortion where the Woman may not be quick with Child at the Time, or it may not be proved that the Woman was quick with Child, be it therefore further enacted, that if any Person or Persons . . . shall willfully and maliciously administer to, or cause to be administered to, or taken by any Woman, any Medicines, Drug, or other Substance or Thing whatsoever, or shall use or employ, or cause or procure to be used or employed, any Instrument or other Means whatsoever, with Intent thereby to cause or procure the Miscarriage of any Woman not being, or not being proved to be, quick with Child at the time of administering such Things or using such Means', that this shall be felonious, and punishable with fine, imprisonment, whipping or transportation for up to fourteen years.

This section is of interest for two main reasons. First, it adopts the ecclesiastical distinction between the *embryo formatus* and the *embryo informatus*, capital punishment being reserved only for the abortion of the former. Second, this is the only occasion upon which a statute has actually used the word 'abortion'. Other references here and in future statutes, are to 'miscarriage', and one may conclude from the fact that this section is the only one to contain the word, and also the first to deal with the termination of pregnancy before quickening, that the legislature assumed that termination before quickening was probably called 'abortion', and termination after quickening was described as 'procuring a miscarriage'. This linguistic distinction does not appear in Lord Lansdowne's Act of 1828.

This Act, repealing the 1803 Act, preserved the ecclesiastical distinction, and provided in section 8 'That if any Person, with Intent to procure the Miscarriage of any Woman then being quick with Child, unlawfully and maliciously shall administer to her, or cause to be taken by her, any Poison or other noxious Thing, or shall use any Instrument or other Means whatever with the like Intent, every such Offender, and every Person counselling, aiding or abetting such Offender, shall be guilty of Felony, and being convicted thereof, shall suffer Death as a Felon; and if any person, with Intent to procure the Miscarriage of any Woman not being or not being proved to be, then quick with Child, unlawfully and maliciously shall administer to her, or cause to be taken by her, any Medicine or other Thing, or shall use any Instrument or other Means whatever with the like Intent, every such Offender, and every Person counselling, aiding or abetting such Offender, shall be guilty of Felony.' The punishment was imprisonment, transportation or whipping.

The 1828 Act is no more explicit than the 1803 Act on the question of whether an unaided woman procuring, or attempting to procure her own abortion, is covered by the Act, but the same presumption of inclusion may be made, although the uncertainty must be recognised. No authority has suggested her exclusion, and apart from introducing slightly more lenient punishments for abortion before quickening, the 1828 Act made little change to the statutory position. In any event a woman could be indicted as an accessory before the fact to an abortion committed upon herself, and to an operation performed upon her with like intent before quickening.

The words 'any Woman not being, or not being proved to be, then quick with Child' in the Acts of 1803 and 1828, probably relate to the method of determining the state of pregnancy, i e to see if the embryo was *formatus* or *informatus*. The same method was adopted where a woman liable to sentence of death for any offence pleaded her pregnancy as a reason why sentence should not be passed upon her in accordance with law. A Jury of Matrons was sworn in, composed of twelve married women then present in court, and these examined the woman to see if she was 'quick with Child'. Medical aid could be sought to ensure a true verdict, but it appears that women were reluctant to sit; before the court announced that a Jury of Matrons was to be empanelled the doors of the court were locked, to prevent them from leaving. Their reluctance may have been justified in that it may not have been clear at the time just what they were deciding.

If a woman has quickened, the position and the consequences are clear; but if she has been found not to be quick with child, this may be because her pregnancy is not sufficiently advanced, or because she is not pregnant. This latter condition could have affected the position.

In *R v Scudder* [(1828) 1 Mood 216], a case under section 2 of the 1803 Act, but equally applicable to section 13 of the 1828 Act, which used identical words, i e, 'any woman not being, or not being proved to be, quick with child', it was held a complete answer to an indictment for abortion before quickening, to show that the woman was not pregnant. This judgment was, however, at variance with *R v Phillips* [(1811) 3 Camp 76], where Lawrence J said 'It is immaterial whether . . . or not it (savin) was capable of procuring abortion, or even whether the woman was actually with child; if the prisoner believed at the time that it would procure abortion, and administered it with that intent, the case is within the Statute.' This judgment is consistent with the words of the Acts of 1803 and 1828, but interprets simply a division between women who have quickened and those who have not, without distinguishing whether the latter are pregnant or not. This lack of distinction assimilates the *embryo informatus* to the absence of any embryo at all, which is inconsistent with the theological conditioning of the law.

The Offences Against the Person Act, 1837 did not adopt the distinction between women quick or not quick with child, and therefore the case of *R v Wycherley* [(1838) 8 C & P 262] can reveal an issue of exclusively academic interest. In this case, where a surgeon was aiding a Jury of Matrons after a verdict of guilty of murder Gurney B distinguished for him ' "Quick with Child" is having conceived. "With quick Child" is when the child has quickened.' Applying this definition to the Acts of 1803 and 1828, it could be said that the capital offence was committed in the case of a pregnant woman, the less serious offence relating to a woman who was not pregnant. In terms of medical knowledge the critical distinction is between pregnancy and non-pregnancy, and this legal division might therefore have been rational. 'Quickening' is merely a change in the position of the uterus, and is not evidence of animate life coming to the foetus, which might justify the greater protection provided by the greater punishment.

The Offences Against the Person Act, 1837 not only abandoned the distinction between the *embryo formatus* and the *embyro informatus* in applying its sanction, but did not distinguish a pregnant woman from one who was not. It provided in section 6 'That whosoever, with Intent to procure the Miscarriage of any Woman, shall unlawfully administer to her or cause to be taken by her any Poison or other noxious Thing, or shall unlawfully use any Instrument or other Means whatsoever with the like Intent, shall be guilty of Felony.' The punishment was transportation or imprisonment, this being one of Lord John Russell's reform measures abolishing the death sentence.

There was still no express reference to a woman who procured her own abortion, but there was no doubt that the Act was intended and understood to include her within its ambit. An early draft of the section had distinguished the position of such a woman from that of another person charged with procuring her abortion, in whose case there was a requirement of proof of pregnancy. Lord Lyndhurst's criticisms of this requirement prevailed to omit this from the final draft.

One may consider the use of the word 'unlawfully' at this stage in the development of the law relating to abortion. The 1803 Act used the expression 'wilfully, maliciously, and unlawfully' to characterise acts of abortion performed after quickening, and 'wilfully and maliciously' for the offence committed before quickening. The 1828 Act used 'unlawfully and maliciously' for both cases. Neither of these Acts suggests when abortion could be lawful, and the 1837 Act is equally silent (as indeed is the current statute, passed in 1861). However, although one may dismiss the use of the formulae in early statutes as being part of the prolix style of draftsmanship then favoured, in 1837 the word may have had some distinctive purpose, however elusive. The Criminal Law Commissioners, commenting in 1846 that other countries' codes have this proviso, suggested the expediency of adding to the then existing law 'Provided that no act specified in the last preceding Article shall be punishable when such act is done in good faith with the intention of saving the life of the mother whose miscarriage is intended to be procured.' This proviso was later incorporated into the Infant Life (Preservation) Act, 1929 as a defence in child destruction prosecutions but regarding abortion, no guidance was given on the meaning of the word 'unlawfully' until nearly a century after this recommended proviso, in the leading case of *R v Bourne* in 1938.

Present law

1. THE CRIMES

The relevant Criminal Offences are contained in the following Statutory provisions.

OFFENCES AGAINST THE PERSON ACT 1861

58.—Every woman, being with child, who, with intent to procure her own miscarriage, shall unlawfully administer to herself any poison or other noxious thing, or shall unlawfully use any instrument or other means whatsoever with the like intent and whosoever, with intent to procure the miscarriage of any woman, whether she be or not with child, shall unlawfully administer to her or cause to be taken by her any poison or other noxious thing, or shall unlawfully use any instrument or other means whatsoever with the like intent, shall be guilty of an offence, and being convicted thereof shall be liable to imprisonment.

59.—Whosoever shall unlawfully supply or procure any poison or other noxious thing, or any instrument or thing whatsoever, knowing that the same is intended to be unlawfully used or employed with intent to procure the miscarriage of any woman, whether she be or not be with child, shall be guilty of an offence, and being convicted thereof shall be liable to imprisonment for a term not exceeding five years.

INFANT LIFE (PRESERVATION) ACT 1929

An Act to amend the law with regard to the destruction of children at or before birth.

1.—(1) Subject as hereinafter in this subsection provided, any person who, with intent to destroy the life of a child capable of being born alive, by any wilful act causes a child to die before it has an existence independent of its mother, shall be guilty of felony, to wit, of child destruction, and shall be liable on conviction thereof on indictment to penal servitude for life:

Provided that no person shall be found guilty of an offence under this section unless it is proved that the act which caused the death of the child was not done in good faith for the purpose only of preserving the life of the mother.

(2) For the purposes of this Act, evidence that a woman had at any material time been pregnant for a period of twenty-eight weeks or more shall be *prima facie* proof that she was at that time pregnant of a child capable of being born alive.

2. THE LAWFUL ABORTION

(a) At common law

R v Bourne
[1939] 1 KB 687, CCC

Macnaughten J: The evidence called on behalf of the Crown proved that on June 14, 1938, the defendant performed an operation on the girl in question at St. Mary's Hospital, and thereby procured her miscarriage. The following facts were also proved: On April 27, 1938, the girl, who was then under the age of fifteen, had been raped with great violence in circumstances which would have been most terrifying to any woman, let alone a child of fourteen, by a man who was in due course convicted of the crime. In consequence of the rape the girl became pregnant. Her case was brought to the attention of the defendant, who, after examination of the girl, performed the operation with the consent of her parents.

The defence put forward was that, in the circumstances of the case, the operation was not unlawful. The defendant was called as a witness on his own behalf and stated that, after he had made careful examination of the girl and had informed himself of all the relevant facts of the case, he had come to the conclusion that it was his duty to perform the operation. He had satisfied himself that the girl was in fact pregnant in consequence of the rape committed on her. He had also satisfied himself that she had not been infected with venereal disease; if he had found that she was so infected, he would not have performed the operation, since in that case there would have been a risk that the operation would cause a spread of the disease. Nor would he have performed the operation if he had found that the girl was either feeble-minded or had what he called a "prostitute mind", since in such cases pregnancy and child-birth would not be likely to affect a girl injuriously. He satisfied himself that she was a normal girl in every respect, though she was somewhat more mature than most girls of her age. In his opinion the continuance of the pregnancy would probably cause serious injury to the girl, injury so serious as to justify the removal of the pregnancy at a time when the operation could be performed without any risk to the girl and under favourable conditions.

The evidence of the defendant was supported and confirmed by Lord Horder, and also by Dr J R Rees, a specialist in medical psychology. Dr Rees expressed the view that, if the girl gave birth to a child, the consequence was likely to be that she would become a mental wreck.

. . .

The charge against Mr Bourne is made under s 58 of the Offences Against the Person Act 1861, that he unlawfully procured the miscarriage of the girl who was the first witness in the case. It is a very grave crime, and judging by the cases that come before the Court it is a crime by no means uncommon. This is the second case at the present session of this Court where a charge has been preferred of an offence against this section, and I only mention the other case to show you how different the case now before you is from the type of case which usually comes before a criminal court. In that other case a woman without any medical skill or medical qualifications did what is alleged against Mr Bourne here; she unlawfully used an instrument for the purpose of procuring the miscarriage of a pregnant girl; she did it for money; 2*l* 5*s* was her fee; a pound was paid on making the appointment, and she came from a distance to a place in London to perform the operation. She used her instrument, and, within an interval of time measured not by minutes but by seconds, the victim of her malpractice was dead on the floor. That is the class of case which usually comes before the Court.

The case here is very different. A man of the highest skill, openly, in one of our great hospitals, performs the operation. Whether it was legal or illegal you will have to determine, but he performs the operation as an act of charity, without fee or reward, and unquestionably believing that he was doing the right thing, and that he ought, in the performance of his duty as a member of a profession devoted to the alleviation of human suffering, to do it. That is the case that you have to try to-day.

Nine years ago Parliament passed an Act called the Infant Life (Preservation) Act 1929 (19 & 20 Geo 5, c 34). Sect 1, sub-s 1, of that Act provides that 'any person who, with intent to destroy the life of a child capable of being born alive, by any wilful act causes a child to die before it has an existence independent of its mother, shall be guilty of felony, to wit, of child destruction, and shall be liable on conviction thereof on indictment to penal servitude for life: Provided that no person shall be found guilty of an offence under this section unless it is proved that the act which caused the death of the child was not done in good faith for the purposes only of preserving the life of the mother.' It is true, as Mr Oliver has said, that [the 1929 Act] provides for the case where a child is killed by a wilful act at the time when it is being delivered in the ordinary course of nature; but in my view the proviso that it is necessary for the Crown to prove that the act was not done in good faith for the purpose only of preserving the life of the mother is in accordance with what has always been the common law of England with regard to the killing of an unborn child. No such proviso is in fact set out in s 58 of the Offences Against the Person Act 1861; but the words of that section are that any person who 'unlawfully' uses an instrument with intent to procure miscarriage shall be guilty of felony. In my opinion the word 'unlawfully' is not, in that section, a meaningless word. I think it imports the meaning expressed by the proviso in s 1, sub-s 1, of the Infant Life (Preservation) Act 1929, and that s 58 of the Offences Against the Person Act 1861, must be read as if the words making it an offence to use an instrument with intent to procure a miscarriage were qualified by a similar proviso.

In this case, therefore, my direction to you in law is this—that the burden rests on the Crown to satisfy you beyond reasonable doubt that the defendant did not procure the miscarriage of the girl in good faith for the purpose only of preserving her life. If the Crown fails to satisfy you of that, the defendant is entitled by the law of this land to a verdict of acquittal. If, on the other hand, you are satisfied that what the defendant did was not done by him in good faith for the purpose only of preserving the life of the girl, it is your duty to find him guilty. It is said, and I think said rightly, that this is a case of great importance to the public and, more especially, to the medical profession; but you will observe that it has nothing to do with the ordinary case of procuring abortion to which I have already referred. In those cases the operation is performed by a person of no skill, with no medical qualifications, and there is no pretence that it is done for the preservation of the mother's life. Cases of that sort are in no way affected by the consideration of the question which is put before you to-day.

What then is the meaning to be given to the words 'for the purpose of preserving the life of the mother'. There has been much discussion in this case as to the difference between danger to life and danger to health. It may be that you are more fortunate than I am, but I confess that I have found it difficult to understand what the discussion really meant, since life depends upon health, and it may be that health is so gravely impaired that death results. A question was asked by the learned Attorney-General in the course of his cross-examination of Mr Bourne. 'I suggest to you, Mr Bourne', said the Attorney-General, 'that there is a perfectly clear line—there may be border-line cases—there is a clear line of distinction between danger to health and danger to life'. The answer of Mr Bourne was: 'I cannot agree without qualifying it; I cannot say just yes or no. I can say there is a large group whose health may be damaged, but whose life almost certainly will not be sacrificed. There is another group at the other end whose life will be definitely in very great danger'. And then he adds: 'There is a large body of material between those two extremes in which it is not really possible to say how far life will be in danger, but we find, of course, that the health is depressed to such an extent that life is shortened, such as in cardiac cases, so that you may say that their life is in danger, because death might occur within measurable distance of the time of their labour'. If that view commends itself to you, you will not accept the suggestion that there is a clear line of distinction between danger to health and danger to life. Mr Oliver wanted you to give what he called a wide and liberal meaning to the words 'for the purpose of preserving the life of the mother'. I should prefer the word 'reasonable' to the words 'wide and liberal'. I think you should take a reasonable view of those words.

It is not contended that those words mean merely for the purpose of saving the mother from instant death. There are cases, we are told, where it is reasonably certain that a pregnant woman will not be able to deliver the child which is in her womb and survive. In such a case where the doctor anticipates, basing his opinion upon the experience of the profession, that the child cannot be delivered without the death of the mother, it is obvious that the sooner the operation is performed the better. The law does not require the doctor to wait until the unfortunate woman is in peril of immediate death. In such a case he is not only entitled, but it is his duty to perform the operation with a view to saving her life.

...

As I have said, I think those words ought to be construed in a reasonable sense, and, if the doctor is of opinion, on reasonable grounds and with adequate knowledge, that the probable consequence of the continuance of the pregnancy will be to make the woman a physical or mental wreck, the jury are quite entitled to take the view that the doctor who, under those circumstances and in that honest belief, operates, is operating for the purpose of preserving the life of the mother.

If the effect of *Bourne* is to make lawful a 'therapeutic' abortion, what were the limits at common law to this notion? As Glanville Williams wrote in his paper, 'The Law of Abortion' (1952) Current Legal Problems 128 at p 136:

The decision in *Bourne* has ameliorated the law but has not yet taken full practical effect. The medical practitioner is said to be still chary to act, except in the clearest cases, partly because he fears that public opinion may not be in favour and partly because he is not certain how far the *Bourne* decision protects him.

There were some further English cases which were considered in the New Zealand Case of *R v Woolnough* [1977] 2 NZLR 508 (Court of Appeal) where the court was asked to interpret section 183 of the Crimes Act 1961 which adopts, in essence, the language of section 58 of the English statute.

Richmond P: Since *Bourne* there have been two further cases spaced at intervals of 10 years in England to which we were referred by counsel. The first was *R v Bergmann* (unreported, UK, 1948, Morris J). In *Smith and Hogan's Criminal Law* (3rd ed) 273–274 the learned authors state that Morris J (as he then was) '... is reported to have said that the court will not look too narrowly into the question of danger to life where danger to health is anticipated'. The later case is *R v Newton* . . . In that case Ashworth J is reported as directing the jury in the following way:

The law about the use of instruments to procure miscarriage is this: 'Such use of an instrument is unlawful unless the use is made in good faith for the purpose of preserving the life or health of the woman'. When I say health I mean not only her physical health but also her mental health. But although I have said that 'it is unlawful unless', I must emphasise and add that the burden of proving that it was not used in good faith is on the Crown ([1958] Crim L Rev 469).

In New Zealand there is no real authority on the point. In *R v Anderson* [1951] NZLR 439 at 443, it appears to have been assumed that *Bourne's* case applied in New Zealand but the point was not really in issue. When the question arose for consideration at the first trial of Dr Woolnough, and again at the second trial, Speight J and Chilwell J accordingly had no New Zealand authority on which to found an opinion. In effect what they have done is to expand the *Bourne* test, in words at least, if not so greatly as a matter of substance, by accepting the preservation of the *health* of the mother as an alternative justification to preserving the *life* of the mother. This is the way the matter was put by Ashworth J in *R v Newton*, but Speight J and Chilwell J have in another respect qualified the test by stressing the need for an honest belief that the abortion was necessary to preserve the woman from *serious* danger to her life or physical or mental health, not being merely the normal dangers of pregnancy and childbirth. As earlier mentioned, the most fundamental criticism made by the Solicitor-General is to the effect that Speight J and Chilwell J went too far when they accepted that serious danger to the *health* of the mother could be a justification for an abortion irrespective of whether or not such danger to health carried with it a real threat to the mother's *life* . . .

In the present case the court is concerned only with the concept of the welfare of the mother as a justification for an abortion in the early stages of pregnancy. In that field we have the assistance of s 182(2), which at least shows that the legislature itself was positively of the view that a bona fide intention to preserve the *life* of the mother in the late stages of pregnancy would justify the procurement of her miscarriage. The narrow question, then, is whether the courts ought not, in the case of early pregnancy at least, to extend that concept to include a bona fide intention to preserve the *health* of the mother from serious harm.

I can see no sufficient reason why this should not be done. In the first place it seems to me that the 'reasonable' interpretation of preservation of the *life* of the mother which was accepted in *Bourne* is likely to be an artificial and perhaps difficult one in practice. That this is the view of some English judges appears from the gradual shift away in emphasis disclosed in the directions given to the jury by Morris J and Ashworth J in the two cases to which I have earlier referred. The textbooks favour the open acknowledgement of preservation of health as well as preservation of life as preventing an abortion from being unlawful. Reference may be made to *Glanville Williams* (op cit) 153–154 and to *Smith and Hogan* (op cit) 274. Moreover, it is important to remember that the function impliedly entrusted to the courts by s 183 is not to say who is right and who is wrong as between the extreme views held by different sections of the community as regards this highly controversial subject. Rather the courts have to do their best to draw a line at a point where the procuring of a miscarriage ceases to be merely a matter of debate, from a religious, moral or ethical point of view, and becomes activity of a kind which warrants its designation as criminal. Finally I remind myself that as at the time when the Crimes Act 1961 was enacted, after lengthy preliminary consideration by a committee and then by the late Sir George Finlay, Ashworth J's direction in *R v Newton* had not only been reported in the *Criminal Law Review* but had also been the subject of an extensive article in that same journal. All this affords some indication that our legislature was content to accept the developing views of the English judges as applicable in this country.

[Woodhouse J agreed. Wild CJ dissented.]

(b)   The Abortion Act 1967

Even after these cases, it could be said that the law remained sufficiently uncertain as to what was lawful. Professor Glanville Williams sets the scene for the 1967 Abortion Act as follows (*Textbook of Criminal Law* (2nd ed 1983), p 296; footnotes omitted):

Bourne's acquittal did not at once produce a large increase in medical abortions. The attitude of the medical profession in general was hostile, and tragic cases continued to occur. A girl of 12, pregnant by her father, was refused an abortion. Special boarding schools were opened for expectant mothers aged from 12 upwards, in order that they might continue with their lessons while looking after their babies. Women who had been raped, women deserted by their husbands, and overburdened mothers living in poverty with large families, also failed to get a medical abortion. One "liberal" hospital in London and one in Newcastle performed the operation comparatively freely, and abortions could be readily bought in Harley Street; but in general the mass of women could only go to a 'back-street abortionist', wielding a knitting needle, syringe or stick of slippery elm, or to a skilled operator acting illegally for large fees. Some unwilling mothers-to-be used dangerous methods on themselves, or occasionally committed suicide. Although illegal abortions ran into thousands each year, convictions were comparatively few (less than a hundred a year), largely because women who had sought the help of an abortionist were unwilling to give him away, but partly also because the police themselves tended not to look upon abortions as a real crime. The only people who were effectively deterred by the law were the doctors, who alone could operate safely. The problem was common to all Christian countries that started with an unqualified prohibition of abortion.

At the same time as these evils were beginning to be acknowledged, the opinion arose that a woman had the right to control her own fertility. But against the pro-abortionists was arrayed a powerful religious lobby basing itself upon the 'sanctity of life'.

The Abortion Act 1967 was a compromise measure which did not concede all the demands of the libertarians and feminists but substantially liberalised the law. In England and Scotland it supersedes the case law, including *Bourne*.

The Report of the Committee on the Working of the Abortion Act chaired by Mrs Justice Lane which reported in 1974 (Cmnd 5578) described the situation before the 1967 Act as follows (pp 197–8; footnotes omitted):

The Acts of 1861 and 1929, with the new and liberal interpretation given to them by Mr Justice Macnaghten remained the law of England and Wales until the passing of the Abortion Act 1967. The number of abortions performed in reliance upon that interpretation (as distinct from those which were certainly illegal) rose; eg in 1966 in NHS hospitals alone there were 6,100 recorded abortions. Nevertheless, it was felt by many, though by no means all, concerned with the problems that there was insufficient precision in the law and that doctors and patients alike ought to have a clearer indication of when abortion was permissible. This, quite apart from the views of those who advocated a more liberal law, was why a new Act was considered to be necessary.

In 1937, a year or so before the Bourne case was tried, a Home Office and Ministry of Health Inter-Departmental Committee, under the chairmanship of Mr Norman Birkett, KC (later Lord Birkett) was set up to 'enquire into the prevalence of abortion, and the law relating thereto, and to consider what steps might be taken by more effective enforcement of the law or otherwise to secure a reduction of the maternal mortality and morbidity arising therefrom'. The Committee of course considered the effect of the Bourne case before recommending, in 1939, that:—

the law should ... be amended to make unmistakably clear that a medical practitioner is acting legally, when in good faith he procures the abortion of a pregnant woman in circumstances which satisfy him that continuance of the pregnancy is likely to endanger her life or seriously to impair her health.

Neither the government of the day, nor any succeeding government, introduced any legislation to implement the recommendation. Various private members introduced Bills to amend the abortion law, including Mr Joseph Reeves in 1952, Mr Kenneth Robinson in 1961 and Lord Silkin in the House of Lords in 1965. Lord Silkin's measure was superseded in 1966 by Mr David Steel's 'Medical Termination Bill' which, after considerable amendment, was passed as the Abortion Act 1967, coming into force on the 27 April 1968.

Section 1 of the 1967 Abortion Act provides:

1.—(1) Subject to the provisions of this section, a person shall not be guilty of an offence under the law relating to abortion when a pregnancy is terminated by a registered medical practitioner if two registered medical practitioners are of the opinion, formed in good faith—

(a) that the continuance of the pregnancy would involve risk to the life of the pregnant woman, or of injury to the physical or mental health of the pregnant woman or any existing children of her family, greater than if the pregnancy were terminated; or

(b) that there is a substantial risk that if the child were born it would suffer from such physical or mental abnormalities as to be seriously handicapped.

(2) In determining whether the continuance of a pregnancy would involve such risk of injury to health as is mentioned in paragraph (a) of subsection (1) of this section, account may be taken of the pregnant woman's actual or reasonably foreseeable environment.

(3) Except as provided by subsection (4) of this section, any treatment for the termination of pregnancy must be carried out in a hospital vested in the Minister of Health or the Secretary of State under the National Health Service Acts, or in a place for the time being approved for the purposes of this section by the said Minister or the Secretary of State.

(4) Subsection (3) of this section, and so much of subsection (1) as relates to the opinion of two registered medical practitioners, shall not apply to the termination of a pregnancy by a registered medical practitioner in a case where he is of the opinion, formed in good faith, that the termination is immediately necessary to save the life or to prevent grave permanent injury to the physical or mental health of the pregnant woman.

The 1967 Act replaces the common law. Section 5(2) provides that:

(2) For the purposes of the law relating to abortion, anything done with intent to procure the miscarriage of a woman is unlawfully done unless authorised by section 1 of this Act.

3. THE OPERATION OF THE 1967 ACT

(a) The Regulations

By section 2 of the Abortion Act 1967, the Secretary of State is empowered to make regulations.

2.—(1) The Minister of Health in respect of England and Wales, and the Secretary of State in respect of Scotland, shall by statutory instrument make regulations to provide—

(a) for requiring any such opinion as is referred to in section 1 of this Act to be certified by the practitioners or practitioner concerned in such form and at such time as may be prescribed by the regulations, and for requiring the preservation and disposal of certificates made for the purposes of the regulations;

(b) for requiring any registered medical practitioner who terminates a pregnancy to give notice of the termination and such other information relating to the termination as may be so prescribed;

(c) for prohibiting the disclosure, except to such persons or for such purposes as may be so prescribed, of notices given or information furnished pursuant to the regulations.

Contravention of these regulations is, by virtue of s 2(3), a summary criminal offence. The Abortion Regulations 1968 (SI 1968 No 390, as amended) deal with two main areas.

(i) Certification of the necessary medical opinions under the Act

The Abortion Regulations 1968 (as amend), Reg 3 provide as follows:

Certificate of opinion

3.—(1) Any opinion to which section 1 of the Act refers shall be certified in the appropriate form set out in Schedule 1 to these regulations.

(2) Any certificate of an opinion referred to in section 1(1) of the Act shall be given before the commencement of the treatment for the termination of the pregnancy to which it relates.

(3) Any certificate of an opinion referred to in section 1(4) of the Act shall be given before the commencement of the treatment for the termination of the pregnancy to which it relates or, if that is not reasonably practicable, not later than 24 hours after such termination.

(4) Any such certificate as is referred to in paragraphs (2) and (3) of this regulation shall be preserved by the practitioner who terminated the pregnancy to which it relates for a period of three years beginning with the date of such termination and may then be destroyed.

The Abortion (Amendment) Regulations 1976 (SI 1976 No 15), Schedule sets out this form:

SCHEDULE 1   Regulation 4

IN CONFIDENCE   **Certificate A**

Not to be destroyed within three years of the date of operation

ABORTION ACT 1967

CERTIFICATE TO BE COMPLETED BEFORE AN ABORTION IS PERFORMED UNDER SECTION 1(1) OF THE ACT

I, ...
(Name and qualifications of practitioner in block capitals)

of ....
(Full address of practitioner)

Have/have not* seen/and examined* the pregnant woman to whom this certificate relates at ....

....
(Full address of place at which patient was seen or examined)

on ....

and I, ...
(Name and qualifications of practitioner in block capitals)

of ....
(Full address of practitioner)

Have/have not* seen/and examined* the pregnant woman to whom this certificate relates at ....
(Full address of place at which patient was seen or examined)

on ....

We hereby certify that we are of the opinion, formed in good faith, that in the case of ....
(Full name of pregnant woman in block capitals)

of ....
(Usual place of residence of pregnant woman in block capitals)

(Ring appropriate num-ber(s))

1. the continuance of the pregnancy would involve risk to the life of the pregnant woman greater than if the pregnancy were terminated;

2. the continuance of the pregnancy would involve risk of injury to the physical or mental health of the pregnant woman greater than if the pregnancy were terminated;

3. the continuance of the pregnancy would involve risk of injury to the physical or mental health of the existing child(ren) of the family of the pregnant woman greater than if the pregnancy were terminated;

4. there is substantial risk that if the child were born it would suffer from such physical or mental abnormalities as to be seriously handicapped.

This certificate of opinion is given before the commencement of the treatment for the termination of pregnancy to which it refers and relates to the circumstances of the pregnant woman's individual case.

Signed ....

Date ....

Signed ....

Date ....

* Delete as appropriate.

SCHEDULE 1

IN CONFIDENCE   **Certificate B**
Not to be destroyed within three years of the date of operation

ABORTION ACT 1967

CERTIFICATE TO BE COMPLETED IN RELATION TO ABORTION PERFORMED
IN EMERGENCY UNDER SECTION 1(4) OF THE ACT

I, ...

(Name and qualifications of practitioner in block capitals)

of ....

....

(Full address of practitioner)

hereby certify that I *am/was of the opinion formed in good faith that it *is/was necessary immediately to terminate the pregnancy of

....

(Full name of pregnant woman in block capitals)

of ....

....

(Usual place of residence of pregnant woman in block capitals)

(*Ring   in order 1.   to save the life of the pregnant woman; or
appropriate
number*)   2.   to prevent grave permanent injury to the physical or mental
                      health of the pregnant woman.

This certificate of opinion is given—

          A. before the commencement of the treatment for the termination of the
(*Ring   pregnancy to which it relates; or
appropriate
letter*)   if that is not reasonably practicable, then

          B. not later than 24 hours after such termination.

          Signed ....

                      Date ....

                      * Delete as appropriate

The only case dealing with the issue of certification is *R v Smith* [1974] 1 All
ER 376, CA. In that case, Scarman LJ said (footnote omitted):

> The Act, though it renders lawful abortions that before its enactment would have
> been unlawful, does not depart from the basic principle of the common law as
> declared in *R v Bourne*, namely that the legality of an abortion depends on the
> opinion of the doctor. It has introduced the safeguard of two opinions: but, if they
> are formed in good faith by the time the operation is undertaken, the abortion is
> lawful. Thus a great social responsibility is firmly placed by the law on the shoulders
> of the medical profession.
> On 28th April 1970 at the Hayward Nursing Home a Miss Rodgers underwent an
> operation performed by the appellant, the initial purpose of which was to terminate
> her pregnancy. The prosecution's case was that when he operated, the appellant was
> not acting in good faith; he had not formed a bona fide opinion as to the balance of
> risk between termination and continuation of her pregnancy, that is to say, that its
> continuance would involve risk to her physical or mental health greater than if it
> were terminated. The appellant's defence was twofold: he said that he formed an
> honest opinion as to the need for an abortion, but that when he had the girl on the
> operating table, he found she was starting an inevitable abortion. Thus, according
> to him, his operation became not a termination but a facilitating and tidying up of
> an inevitable abortion—a natural process which had already begun. If this be the
> truth, the prosecution concedes that the operation would be lawful without the need
> of recourse to the Abortion Act 1967.
>   . . . If the jury rejected, as they did, the tale of an inevitable abortion, the sequence
> of events was such as to call for very careful consideration whether it was possible
> to believe that the appellant had formed in good faith, or at all, the opinion necessary
> to give him the protection of the 1967 Act. Had he, or had he not, abused the trust
> reposed in him by the Act of Parliament? The burden was on the prosecution to
> prove beyond reasonable doubt that he had. All this was faithfully explained to the
> jury by the recorder. We quote only one passage towards the end of the summing-
> up:
> > '[The appellant] took the view that if any girl wanted her pregnancy terminated,
> > that of itself was, if not entirely sufficient, a very powerful indication of the risk
> > of injury to her mental health if the pregnancy continued being greater than if the
> > pregnancy was terminated. He told you that all his actions were within the Act,
> > so he was telling you that, though he took the view that really with every girl or

woman who wanted her pregnancy terminated that was a very powerful reason for terminating it, because it may involve risk to her mental health, he still acted within the Act and balanced the risks of termination against the risks of continuation. If two doctors genuinely form an opinion in each case that they deal with that the risk of continuance is more than the risk of termination, it does not matter whether they are right or wrong in that view. If they form that opinion genuinely and in good faith, that in fact comes within the Act, and there is no guilt attached to it. You have to wonder in the case of [the appellant] whether such a view could genuinely be held by a medical man, whether it was held in the case of Miss Rodgers in particular. The only indication on the case notes about any danger to her mental or physical health was the word 'depressed', 'not willing to marry and depressed'. Those are the only words about it on the case notes. You have to ask yourselves, was there any balancing of the risks involved in allowing the pregnancy to continue and allowing the pregnancy to be terminated, or was this a mere routine abortion for cash? That is what you have to consider. Was a second opinion even contemplated as a necessity in this case of Miss Rodgers? If, on the very first interview when the girl was seen by [the appellant], the very first interview he had with her, he offered to operate on her the next morning, was there any real contemplation or thought that a second opinion was necessary?'

These were the questions for the jury; and they have been answered adversely to the appellant. The view the jury took was one fully open to them on the evidence; and we can see no reason for the suggestion that their view was wrong or unsafe or unsatisfactory . . .

(ii) Collection of data

The 1968 Regulations require 'any practitioner' who terminates a pregnancy to notify the Chief Medical Officer (Regulation 4(1)). Significantly, the Regulations make particular provision for the observance of confidentiality except in eight specific circumstances. These are set out in Regulation 5 in Chapter 6 (*supra*). You are referred to them.

(b) Conscientious objection

The Abortion Act 1967, s 4 reads as follows:

4.—(1) Subject to subsection (2) of this section, no person shall be under any duty, whether by contract or by any statutory or other legal requirement, to participate in any treatment authorised by this Act to which he has a conscientious objection:
Provided that in any legal proceedings the burden of proof of conscientious objection shall rest on the person claiming to rely on it.

(2) Nothing in subsection (1) of this section shall affect any duty to participate in treatment which is necessary to save the life or to prevent grave permanent injury to the physical or mental health of a pregnant woman.

What is the effect of this provision on doctors? Mason and McCall Smith in *Law and Medical Ethics* (2nd ed 1987), at p 81, allege that:

. . . Of greater importance is the undeniable and unfortunate result of the 1967 Act that the profession of gynaecologist is now virtually closed to those who feel unable to accept its wide terms, whether this be on religious or on Hippocratic grounds. Even so, while a doctor may, in general, refuse to take part in the abortion procedure, he remains under an obligation to advise. Such advice is subject to the normal rules of medical negligence and the conscientious objector's only recourse is, therefore, to refer his patient to another practitioner, a practice which is only marginally compatible with a strong conscience and which must damage the essential bond of trust between doctor and patient. The doctor's conscience does not absolve him from treating a woman when the continuation of the pregnancy is life-threatening and there is, of course, no right to conscience in treating the *results* of a legal abortion; these considerations apply equally to the nursing staff.

In *Janaway v Salford Health Authority* [1988] 3 All ER 1079, the House of Lords construed the scope of s 4 of the Abortion Act.

Lord Keith: My Lords, the appellant, Mrs Janaway (the applicant), took up employment with the respondent health authority on 25 June 1984. She was engaged as a secretary/receptionist at Irlam Health Centre, working for a Dr Barooah. On 11 September 1984 she was asked by Dr Barooah to type a letter which had to do with referring a pregnant patient for an appointment with a consultant with a view to the latter forming an opinion as to whether the pregnancy should be terminated under the Abortion Act 1967. The applicant, a Roman Catholic holding the belief that abortion is morally wrong, refused to type the letter, which was eventually written by hand by another doctor at the health centre. On 31 October 1984 the applicant was interviewed by a personnel officer from the authority and told him that she felt entitled to refuse to type the letter, and any others concerned with termination of pregnancy, by virtue of the conscientious objection provision contained in s 4(1) of the 1967 Act, to which I shall refer later. On 7 November 1984 the personnel officer wrote to the applicant stating that her refusal to type correspondence of the kind in question amounted to a breach of the authority's disciplinary rules as being 'unjustified refusal of a lawful and reasonable instruction' and asking for a firm assurance that she would in future carry out any such instructions. The applicant sent in reply a letter dated 12 November 1984 which concluded:

'. . . except insofar as I stand by the protection afforded by S 4(1) of the Abortion Act [1967] I confirm that I will continue, as I have done in the past, to carry out my contractual duties as detailed in my job description.'

On 27 November 1984 the applicant had a meeting, at which she reaffirmed her position, with the personnel officer and the community services administrator. On 30 November the latter wrote to her saying that legal advice had been obtained to the effect that s 4(1) of the 1967 Act did not apply to her refusal, and that her employment had been terminated from 27 November on grounds of misconduct. The applicant appealed against her dismissal to the authority's appeal tribunal, but her appeal was dismissed, and the authority formally ratified the decision on 6 February 1985.

On 17 June the applicant applied, with leave, for judicial review in the shape of an order of certiorari to quash the authority's decision of 6 February 1985 and a declaration that, by reason of her conscientious objection to typing correspondence of the kind in question, she was not under any duty to carry out such work.

The application was dismissed by Nolan J on 12 February 1985, and his decision was affirmed by the Court of Appeal (Slade, Balcombe and Stocker LJJ) ([1988] 2 WLR 442) on 18 December 1987. The applicant now appeals, with leave granted by the Court of Appeal, to your Lordships' House. . . .

The applicant claims the protection of s 4(1). The issue in the case turns on the true construction of the words in that subsection 'participate in any treatment authorised by this Act'. For the applicant it is maintained that the words cover taking part in any arrangements preliminary to and intended to bring about medical or surgical measures aimed at terminating a pregnancy, including the typing of letters referring a patient to a consultant. The health authority argues that the meaning of the words is limited to taking part in the actual procedures undertaken at the hospital or other approved place with a view to the termination of a pregnancy.

The argument for the applicant proceeds on the lines that the acts attracting the protection afforded by s 4(1) are intended to be coextensive with those which are authorised by s 1(1) and which in the absence of that provision would be criminal. The criminal law about accessories treats one who aids and abets, counsels or procures a criminal act as liable to the same extent as a principal actor. In the absence of s 1(1) the applicant by typing a letter of referral would be counselling or procuring an abortion, or at least helping to do so, and subject to a possible defence on the principle of *R v Bourne* [1938] 3 All ER 615, [1939] 1 KB 687 would be criminally liable. Therefore any requirement to type such a letter is relieved, in the face of a conscientious objection, by s 4(1).

The majority of the Court of Appeal (Slade and Stocker LJJ) accepted the main thrust of the applicant's argument, to the effect that ss 1(1) and 4(1) are coextensive, but decided against her on the ground that her intention in typing a letter of referral would not be to assist in procuring an abortion but merely to carry out the obligations of her employment. In their view the typing of such a letter by the applicant would not be a criminal offence in the absence of s 1(1).

Nolan J, however, and Balcombe LJ in the Court of Appeal rejected the applicant's main argument. They accepted the argument for the health authority that on a proper construction the word 'participate' in s 4(1) did not import the whole concept of principal and accessory residing in the criminal law, but in its ordinary and natural meaning referred to actually taking part in treatment administered in a hospital or other approved place in accordance with s 1(3), for the purpose of terminating a pregnancy.

In my opinion Nolan J and Balcombe LJ were right to reach the conclusion they did. I agree entirely with their view about the natural meaning of the word 'participate' in this context. Although the word is commonly used to describe the activities of accessories in the criminal law field, it is not a term of art there. It is in any event not being used in a criminal context in s 4(1). Ex hypothesi treatment for termination of a pregnancy under s 1 is not criminal. I do not consider that Parliament can reasonably have intended by its use to import all the technicalities of the criminal law about principal and accessory, which can on occasion raise very nice questions about whether someone is guilty as an accessory. Such niceties would be very difficult of solution for an ordinary health authority. If Parliament had intended the result contended for by the applicant, it could have procured it very clearly and easily by referring to participation 'in anything authorised by this Act' instead of 'in any treatment [so] authorised'. It is to be observed that s 4 appears to represent something of a compromise in relation to conscientious objection. One who believes all abortion to be morally wrong would conscientiously object even to such treatment as is mentioned in sub-s (2), yet the subsection would not allow the objection to receive effect.

The applicant's argument placed some reliance on a passage in the speech of Lord Roskill in *Royal College of Nursing of the United Kingdom v Department of Health and Social Security* [1981] 1 All ER 545 at 577, [1981] AC 800 at 837–838:

'My Lords, I read and reread the 1967 Act to see if I can discern in its provisions any consistent pattern in the use of the phrase "a pregnancy is terminated" or "termination of a pregnancy" on the one hand and "treatment for the termination of a pregnancy" on the other hand. One finds the former phrase in s 1(1) and (1) (*a*), the latter in s 1(3), the former in ss 1(4) and 2(1)(*b*) and the latter in s 3(1)(*a*) and (*c*). Most important to my mind is s 4, which is the conscientious objection section. This section in two places refers to "participate in treatment" in the context of conscientious objection. If one construes s 4 in conjunction with s 1(1), as surely one should do in order to determine to what it is that conscientious objection is permitted, it seems to me that s 4 strongly supports the wider construction of s 1(1). It was suggested that acceptance of the department's submission involved rewriting that subsection so as to add words which are not to be found in the language of the subsection. My Lords, with great respect to that submission, I do not agree. If one construes the words "when a pregnancy is terminated by a registered medical practitioner" in s 1(1) as embracing the case where the "treatment for the termination of a pregnancy is carried out under the control of a doctor in accordance with ordinary current medical practice" I think one is reading "termination of pregnancy" and "treatment for termination of pregnancy" as virtually synonymous and as I think Parliament must have intended they should be read. Such a construction avoids a number of anomalies as, for example, where there is no pregnancy or where the extra-amniotic process fails to achieve its objective within the normal limits of time set for its operation.'

That case was concerned with a particular process of treatment for the termination of pregnancy carried out in hospital, important parts of which were performed not by a registered medical practitioner but by a nurse acting under his instructions.

The issue was whether the actions of the nurse were unlawful, and it was held that they were not, on the ground that what was authorised by the Act was the whole medical process resulting in termination of pregnancy and that the process was carried out by a registered medical practitioner when that was done under his supervision and in accordance with his instructions, notwithstanding that certain parts of the process were carried out by others. The House was not concerned with the meaning of the word 'participate' in s 4(1) in relation to anything other than the actual medical process carried out in the hospital, and then only indirectly. So Lord Roskill's words cannot be read as having any bearing on the decision of the present case.

In the Court of Appeal, Stocker LJ had raised the question of the extent to which a doctor employed by a health authority could rely on 'the conscience clause' which Slade LJ had noted was 'unique of its kind in English statute law'. 'It is clear', Stocker LJ stated ([1988] 2 WLR 442, 445):

'that in many, if not all cases a medical practitioner signing the form with the intention that an abortion will, in due course be carried out would, but for the Act, be criminally liable as counselling or procuring the resultant abortion and that section 1(1) by its terms removes such criminal liability. In my view, apart from section 4(1), a doctor employed by a health authority in the position of Dr Barooah, or any other employed doctor, would be under a duty in the performance of his professional duties to certify on the green form and to take such other steps as he might consider advisable in any case in which his medical and clinical opinion was that an abortion should be performed for any of the reasons set out in the Act, or in the green form itself. Apart from section 4(1) he would be in breach of his professional duty to his patient and of his duty to the employing authority if he refused to do so; he would also be in breach of his contract of employment and liable to the sanctions that such breach entailed'.

In the House of Lords, Lord Keith concluded his speech as follows:

A certain amount of argument was addressed to the Abortion Regulations 1968, SI 1968/390, which, inter alia, set out the form of certificate, known as 'the green form', to be signed by two registered medical practitioners in pursuance of s 1(1)(a) of the 1967 Act, and to the position in relation to s 4(1) of practitioners who might be required to sign such a certificate. The regulations do not appear to contemplate that the signing of the certificate would form part of treatment for the termination of pregnancy, since reg 3(2) provides:
   'Any certificate of an opinion referred to in section 1(1) of the Act shall be given before the commencement of the treatment for the termination of the pregnancy to which it relates.'
It does not appear whether or not there are any circumstances under which a doctor might be under any legal duty to sign a green form, so as to place in difficulties one who had a conscientious objection to doing so. The fact that during the 20 years that the 1967 Act has been in force no problem seems to have surfaced in this connection may indicate that in practice none exists. So I do not think it appropriate to express any opinion on the matter.

Do you think that the House of Lords should have expressed a view? If so, what should it have been?

4. THE GROUNDS

As we have seen, section 1(1) of the 1967 Abortion Act sets out the grounds for lawfully terminating a pregnancy. Professor Williams in his *Textbook of Criminal Law* (2nd ed 1983), pp 297–301, analyses these provisions as follows (footnotes omitted):

13.5. The fetal ground

The fetal ground (s 1(1)(*b*)) does not need extensive consideration. It is sometimes justified for eugenic reasons, but in fact the contribution that abortion is likely to make to the betterment of man's genetic inheritance is slight. No: the argument for abortion on the fetal indication relates to the welfare of the parents, whose lives may well be blighted by having to rear a grossly defective child, and perhaps secondarily by consideration for the public purse. That this is the philosophy of the Act is borne out by the fact that it allows termination only where the child if born would be seriously handicapped, not where it is merely carrying undesirable genes.

Whereas the health grounds recognised in the Act merely enlarge on the attitude of the judge in *Bourne*, that the health of full human beings is to be preferred to the interest of the fetus in being born where the two interests conflict, the fetal ground marks a new departure. The fetus is destroyed not necessarily in its own interest (the physician need make no judgment that life will be a burden for it), but in the interest either of the parents or of society at large, though of course only upon the request of the mother.

Although argument still rages on whether abortion should be permitted merely as a matter of convenience to the woman, the fetal ground is almost universally accepted. But it is of some interest to note that anyone who does accept the fetal ground for abortion commits himself to the view that the moral status of the fetus is not the same as that of a child. For we do not permit children to be killed because they are seriously handicapped.

Isn't the fetal ground abominably vague?

The physician must decide whether there is a 'substantial' risk that the child if born would be 'seriously' handicapped. Advances in knowledge and medical skills make it more and more possible to attach a precise mathematical weight to the chance of the fetus being affected by genetic defects or by what happens to it in the womb. But the doctor still has to decide whether the case is sufficiently grave to justify termination. He may, of course, take the view that a relatively low risk justifies termination if the risk is of a relatively serious handicap: in common sense, the two factors are inversely related. Even when the doctor thinks that the 'fetal indication' is not itself sufficiently present, the fact that the patient is extremely depressed by worry that the child may be affected can itself be a reason for termination on the health ground.

13.6. The health grounds

The health grounds subdivide in relation to the health of the woman and the health of existing children of her family.

Where a pregnancy is terminated on the ground of risk of injury to health, how great must the risk be to justify the termination?

When the Abortion Bill came before the House of Lords, much attention was given to this question. The adjectives 'serious', 'grave' and 'substantial' were considered, but their lordships finally adopted Lord Parker CJ's suggestion (moved in his absence by Lord Dilhorne, a strong opponent of relaxing the law), which now appears in the Act. The risk of injury feared from allowing the pregnancy to continue must be 'greater than if the pregnancy were terminated'. Lord Parker said of his amendment that the doctor's decision was to be arrived at by comparing one risk with another, and only if the risk in continuation were greater than the risk in termination would a defence be created under the Act. If that was the test, he said, it would be unnecessary and wrong to talk about risk as being 'serious' or 'substantial'.

In making this move some of the opponents of freer abortion were perhaps misled by propaganda emanating from their own side. It had been widely argued, against the practice of abortion, that it was a dangerous operation, and on this supposition the formula was a restrictive one. Even so, the formula was a doubtful advantage for the restrictionists, because no one knew how long it might be before the danger of the operation was reduced, thus extending its legality. But in any case the assumption that the operation was particularly dangerous was wrong even in 1967, at least in cases where the termination was performed early enough. Figures from

Eastern Europe indicated that the operation, properly performed within the first trimester (the first three months of pregnancy), was much safer (at least from the point of view of mortality) than normal childbirth. This has also been found in England, and experience in performing the operation has steadily increased its safety. There are, of course, other risks associated with medical termination of pregnancy besides death, just as there are other risks associated with childbirth.

The wording of the Act, then, suggests the argument that first-trimester abortions are now left to medical discretion in the sense that if the doctor comes to the conclusion that, as the figures firmly show, the general mortality risk of a first-trimester abortion is less than maternal mortality, and if he further believes that the morbidity risk does not affect the general conclusion that abortion is safer, and that there is nothing in his patient's condition to affect the application of the statistical argument to her case, he is entitled to terminate an early pregnancy without finding a more specific ground for termination. Although this argument has not been ventilated in court, and would doubtless be regarded with extreme reserve by the judges, there is no logical answer to it. The risks associated with normal maternity must be among the risks resulting from a decision not to terminate, so that they can enter into a calculation of the risks that are 'greater than if the pregnancy were terminated'; and if these risks by themselves are greater than the risks of termination, no other question need logically be asked.

But that would mean that we have abortion on demand, which Parliament never intended. So the Act ought not to be interpreted in that way
Some would say so. The opposing view is that Parliament consciously settled for a certain test for the legality of abortion; that test is acceptable to very many people, and the courts should apply it according to its wording. It is not for the courts to speculate whether Parliament made some mistake of fact, and how it would have worded the Act if it had not made that mistake.

Some doctors (including hospital doctors) accept the above argument and assume that the Act enables them to terminate on the ground of hardship and distress, provided that they act early enough. Others, however, who disapprove of abortion, construe the Act restrictively so that a great variation of practice is found between hospitals in different parts of the country.

The argument that abortion is safer than childbirth (or may be held so to be by the particular doctor) applies to vaginal terminations performed in the first two or three months of pregnancy, when the operation is done without incision, by curettage of the womb or by the vacuum aspiration method. Ideally it should be performed within six weeks of pregnancy. Mortality and morbidity begin to increase after the second month, and are particularly associated with termination by hysterotomy. Even the higher risk of a late termination can be medically justified in appropriate cases, but obviously it requires more serious grounds than does an early termination.

Can the doctor act at a very early stage, before it has been established whether the woman is pregnant?
No reason why not: the doctor may act on the ground that *if* the woman is pregnant it will be bad for the pregnancy to continue.

The point is important because of the practice of menstrual aspiration at an early date when the diagnosis of pregnancy may be uncertain. It may of course be argued, against the legality of operating, that the Abortion Act validates the proceeding only if the woman is in fact pregnant, because it supposes that 'a pregnancy is terminated'. But this would overlook the question of the *mens rea* required for an offence under section 58. Because of this consideration, the Law Officers of the Crown expressed the opinion in 1979 that menstrual aspiration is lawful.

Although the section makes it an offence to use means to procure the miscarriage of a woman who is in fact with child, it obviously supposes that the defendant believed that the woman was or might be with child. Now the attitude of the doctor in the case we are considering is this. If the woman is with child, then what he does will result in an abortion, and it will be lawful under the Abortion Act. If the woman is not with child, then there will be no abortion. Either there will be no abortion, or it will be a lawful abortion. The doctor's intention being not to procure any abortion except a lawful abortion, it cannot reasonably be argued that an offence is committed.

What is meant by 'the mental health of the pregnant woman'?
There is no case-law, but the phrase is capable of a wide interpretation.

Narrowly interpreted, it may require the doctor to fear that the patient will suffer from what is commonly called a mental illness, whether a psychosis or severe neurosis. This may include a depressive psychosis, and the British Medical Association recognises that termination may properly be advised on account of a 'reactive depression', which is a pathological state of hopeless despair resulting from circumstances. If the question is one of mental illness, the natural course would be to call in a psychiatrist, a specialist in mental disorder.

But 'mental health' is susceptible of a wider meaning. The definition of health advanced by the World Health Organisation is that it is 'the state of complete mental, physical and social well-being, and not merely an absence of disease or infirmity'. Gynaecologists who take this broad view do not insist upon a psychiatric opinion, but are ready to act on their own opinion of the case, backed by the family doctor.

Can the doctor take account of the fact that the woman is a suicide risk?
A serious threat of suicide can clearly be taken into account, because it indicates the depth of the woman's depression. The BMA memorandum states that 'the view that pregnant women never commit suicide is fallacious'.

Can the doctor take account of a risk to the health of the woman arising not during the pregnancy but as a consequence of her having to rear the child if it is born?
The words of the Act suggest answers both ways.

The Act refers to 'risk of injury to the health of the *pregnant* woman', and one may argue that when the child has been born the woman is no longer pregnant. Moreover, it must be 'the continuance of the pregnancy' that produces this risk, and it is perhaps slightly strange, though not impossible, to say that the burden on a mother of having to rear a child was a result of 'the continuance of the pregnancy'.

On the other hand there are two clues in the Act making it reasonably clear that the wider meaning was intended by Parliament.
1 The words just quoted are used with regard to both the health of the woman and the health of existing children of her family. If one pays regard to the health of existing children, as the Act allows, it would be illogical to do this only during the time of gestation of the new addition to the family. What was evidently intended was that existing children might be adversely affected by the extra child being born and having to be brought up by an already overburdened mother.
2 Subsection (2) provides that 'account may be taken of the pregnant woman's actual or reasonably foreseeable environment'. This is not, as has sometimes been thought, a purely 'social' ground for termination, since it is related to the question of health. It does not allow the operation merely because the patient will otherwise lose her job or her husband. Still, the statutory words make it clear that the question of health is to be considered broadly. There is not much point in directing the doctor to look ahead to the woman's future environment if he is to consider only the time of pregnancy. So it is really quite clear that the Act is intended to provide for the case of the overburdened mother.

The Act allows termination out of consideration for existing children of the family. How can existing children be affected in health by having another brother or sister?
Sometimes it may be reasonable to make this judgment. Consider the mother of a 'problem family'. She is living in poverty, with a large brood of children. Her husband has been in prison and has now been arrested again. Her existing children are badly cared for and play truant. Now she is pregnant once more. It may, confidently be predicted that if the pregnancy is allowed to go to term, matters will be worsened for the existing children to the extent that their health may be affected.

In practice, doctors who terminate on this ground generally tick it as an extra to the health of the woman.

Can the doctor take the poverty of the family into account?
Not directly, but he can if the woman's poverty, aggravated by the addition to her family, is likely to affect her health or that of her other children.

To what extent, if any, do you think the grounds for abortion in the 1967 Act place limitations upon a doctor who wishes to perform an abortion on a pregnant woman? Would he act lawfully, for example, if (a) the woman were diagnosed as HIV positive or (b) the woman discovered through tests the sex of her child but wants a child of the other sex and so seeks an abortion?

Problems arising from the present law

1. THE INTER-RELATIONSHIP BETWEEN THE ABORTION ACT 1967 AND THE INFANT LIFE (PRESERVATION) ACT 1929

Section 5(1) of the Abortion Act 1967 provides that:

5.—(1) Nothing in this Act shall affect the provisions of the Infant Life (Preservation) Act 1929 (protecting the life of the viable foetus).

You will recall Section 1 of the 1929 Act states:

1.—(1) Subject as hereinafter in this subsection provided, any person who, with intent to destroy the life of a child *capable of being born alive*, by any wilful act causes a child to die before it has an existence independent of its mother, shall be guilty of felony, to wit, of child destruction, and shall be liable on conviction thereof on indictment to penal servitude for life:
Provided that no person shall be found guilty of an offence under this section unless it is proved that the act which caused the death of the child was not done in good faith for the purpose only of preserving the life of the mother.
   (2) For the purposes of this Act, evidence that a woman had at any material time been pregnant for a period of twenty-eight weeks or more shall be *prima facie* proof that she was at that time pregnant of a child capable of being born alive.
(**our emphasis**)

Much, then, turns on the expression 'capable of being born alive'. What the Act provides is that a foetus will *prima facie* be so regarded if it has reached 28 weeks of gestational age. The Act does not, therefore preclude the possibility that a child may be *capable of being born alive* at an earlier gestational age. Thus, the issue is what is the precise meaning of the phrase 'capable of being born alive' and does this equate with a particular period of time? This critically important question fell to be considered in the case of *C v S* [1988] QB 135, [1987] 1 All ER 1230. The case concerned an application by C, the father of a child carried by S, his former girlfriend for an injunction to prevent her seeking or obtaining an abortion. At first instance, Heilbron J set out the facts, the medical testimony and the legal background:

When she[s] next saw the college doctor on 6 February she told him that she wanted a termination, and on 9 February he signed the certificate of opinion, having seen her and examined her on a number of occasions. This is the certificate required by the terms of the Abortion Regulations 1968, SI 1968/390, before an abortion can be performed. She saw a consultant at the hospital two days later, who also examined her, as he was required to do, and he signed the certificate. The ground was number 2 on the form, namely that the continuance of the pregnancy would involve risk of injury to her physical or mental health greater than if the pregnancy was terminated.

Miss S further stated in her affidavit that she believed her mental state was now precarious and that these proceedings have caused her more anxiety and distress, and no one has doubted that, except Mr C, for he asserted in his affidavit that she was healthy and would suffer no risk to her health, either mental or physical. That was directly contrary to the views of two doctors. It is not suggested that Mr C is possessed of any medical qualifications or that he has any medical knowledge as to Miss S's condition, which, on the evidence before me, indicates that her health has been adversely affected by a difficult and complicated pregnancy with all the attendant anxieties which she mentions. . . .

[Counsel for the applicant] . . . submits that . . . the doctor would be contravening the provisions of [the 1929 Act] and would be guilty, because he would be aborting a foetus of 18 weeks. Indeed, he further submitted that any doctor who has since 1967, or who proposed to, abort a foetus of that duration must be guilty of the offence.

Counsel did not resile from the implications of that assertion, relying for it on the terms of the 1929 Act and the statements of Mr Norris in his affidavits, particularly in that which stated that 'an unborn child of eighteen weeks gestation were it to be delivered by hysterotomy *would be* live born' (my emphasis).

The affidavits are important. They indicate very clearly the wide difference in thinking and interpretation between medical men, all of high reputation and great experience, in regard to the language used in the 1929 Act. I will now read the affidavits, so as to incorporate their explanation of certain phrases and terms into this judgment. I begin, because it was the first, with that of Mr Norris, emeritus consultant gynaecologist at St Peter's Hospital, Chertsey. He stated in para 2 of his first affidavit that 'an unborn child of eighteen weeks gestation were it to be delivered by hysterotomy would be live born'. He then went on to refer to a definition of this expression or condition by the World Health Assembly under art 23 of the Constitution of the World Health Organisation in 1976 (subsequent to both the Acts in this matter) as being—

the complete expulsion or extraction from its mother of a product of conception irrespective of the duration of pregnancy, which after such separation breathes or [and I emphasise the 'or' in his affidavit] shows any other evidence of life such as beating of the heart, pulsation of the umbilical cord or definite movement of voluntary muscle whether or not the umbilical cord has been cut or the placenta is attached.

To that affidavit Professor John Richard Newton replied. He did so, in his first affirmation, on 16 February. He said:

I am the Layson Tait Professor of Obstetrics and Gynaecology and Head of Department at the Birmingham University Medical School Queen Elizabeth Hospital Edgbaston Birmingham. I have been a Gynaecologist for twenty years and held my present position since 1979.

He had been shown a copy of Mr Norris's affidavit and asked to comment on it and in regard to para 2 he said:

I believe it confusing in the circumstances to use the words "live born" for a foetus of 18 weeks gestation. As Mr. Norris says the term has been defined by Article 23 of the World Health Assembly in 1976. There is now produced . . . a copy of a report known as "Report on Foetal Viability and Clinical Practice" which was prepared in August 1985 by a representative committee on behalf of the Royal College of Obstetricians and Gynaecologists, the British Paediatric Association, Royal College of General Practitioners, Royal College of Midwives, British Medical Association and the Department of Health and Social Security . . . I refer in particular to the twelfth page of that report in which reference is made to the recommendation of the World Health Organisation concerning perinatal statistics. The committee to which I have referred above was charged with the task of considering foetal viability and comparison is made between the World Health Organisation definition and the concept of foetal viability. As will be seen from the report the purpose behind the World Health Organisation definition was to standardise the perinatal statistics for member countries of births. The purpose behind the definition was specifically not to define independent foetal viability and the committee go on to consider that concept and I believe that to be the important concept in these circumstances. Foetal viability means that the foetus is capable of independent human existence separate from the mother.

He then refers to the contents of this report of the various prestigious colleges and associations of doctors and says:

It will be seen that in the survey of 29 neo-natal intensive care units in the United Kingdom during 1982 no foetus of less than 23 weeks survived after delivery. It is my conclusion therefore that a foetus of anything below 23 weeks cannot survive independent of its mother and has therefore no viability.

A few days later Mr Norris swore a second affidavit, in order to amplify the first. He then suggested that the period of gestation was 2, or possibly 3, weeks more than the 18 weeks which had been mentioned. He went on to explain the expression 'live born' which had been used in his first affidavit:

4 . . . In case there is any ambiguity I wish to assert that in so stating I mean that in my opinion any foetus of eighteen weeks or longer gestation is capable of being born alive and that by "alive" I mean showing real and discernible signs of life within the meaning of the World Health Organisation definition set out in my original Affidavit and of the Births and Deaths Registration Act 1926 current when the Infant Life (Preservation) Act 1929 was passed and also of the Births and Deaths Registration Act 1953 now current. Under the provisions of both these statutes such a child shall be registered as a live birth.

5. A child of eighteen or even twenty-one weeks gestational age although capable of being born alive and capable of surviving for some time outside the womb is not generally regarded by the medical profession as being viable because present paediatric skills are insufficient to assist it to remain alive for more than a limited time.

On the same day, 19 February, Professor Newton, having read the second affidavit of Mr Norris, stated in a further affidavit:

1 . . . Although he uses the expression "live born" in [his first] affidavit he does not mention, nor did I understand that he was specifically referring to the words actually appearing in an Act of Parliament namely the words "born alive" in Section 1 Infant Life (Preservation) Act 1929. This has now been drawn to my attention and I give my comments.

2. The expression "born alive" used in the Infant Life (Preservation) Act 1929 raises difficulties before the expiration of 28 weeks of gestation.

3. Although it is difficult to generalise, for reasons which I will refer to in paragraph 4 after 8 weeks of gestation some fetuses will exhibit some primitive fetal movement, have a primitive heart tube which contracts and the circulation has started to develop but these fetuses will be quite incapable of life separate from the mother.

4. Each individual fetus in each individual mother develops differently and at different rates . . .

He then refers to the difficulty of the medical assessment of the gestational period in any particular case, which must be approximate and which may be complicated, as indeed in this case, by irregular menstruation. However, there are some firm generalisations on development which could be made:

In a fetus of 18–21 weeks gestation the cardiac muscle is contracting and a primitive circulation is developing, but in my opinion lung development does not occur until after 24 weeks gestation; before this time the major air passages have been formed and there is gradual development of the bronchioles but these terminate in a blind sac incapable of gas exchange prior to 24 weeks.

He says that a fetus of 18 to 21 weeks gestation could be delivered by hysterotomy but that would not be routinely used on such a fetus, and he describes the type of operation:

Once placental separation occurs whether the delivery has been by hysterotomy or vaginally it will not be able to respirate . . . What constitutes "born alive" is controversial among the medical profession and often turns not only on medical knowledge but on the moral views of the person giving his opinion. I would mention that the development of each particular fetus in each particular mother is an individual process, the progress of which [at] any stage before 28 weeks can best be ascertained by an examination of the particular mother in question or at the very least detailed knowledge of that individual person.

With that I must entirely agree, and counsel for Mr C conceded that that must be so. It is an important aspect of this case, to which I will later refer. Professor Newton continued:

Whether or not a fetus up to 24 weeks of gestation is delivered by hysterotomy or vaginal delivery it will not be capable of surviving once the placental separation occurs. Up to 24 weeks in my opinion the lungs are incapable of sustaining life because they are not adequately developed. The development of other organs within the fetus is at an equally primitive stage incapable of sustaining life. I do not consider the indicia referred to in paragraph 3 hereof to equate with being "alive". I equate "alive" with being able to sustain a separate independent existence and in my opinion this a fetus is clearly not capable of being able to do until after 24 weeks of gestation.

Later Heilbron J reviewed the nineteenth century cases concerned with murder of 'a very young infant who died or was killed before or not long after separation of its mother at first'.

In *R v Handley* (1874) 13 Cox CC 79 Brett J, a very distinguished judge, directed the jury that a child was considered to have been 'born alive' when it existed as a live child, that is to say breathing and living by reason of its breathing through its own lungs alone, without deriving any of its living or power of living by or through any connection with its mother.

In *R v Poulton* (1832) 5 C & P 329, 172 ER 997 even the fact of the child having breathed was said not to be conclusive proof of it having been in 'a living state' after birth. In that case three doctors had given evidence and the judge told the jury (5 C & P 329 at 330, 172 ER 997 at 998):

. . . if there is all this uncertainty among these medical men, perhaps you would think it too much for you to say that you are satisfied that the child was born alive.

In *R v Enoch* (1833) 5 C & P 539, 172 ER 1089, and similarly in *R v Wright* (1841) 9 C & P 754, 173 ER 1039, the judge directed the jury that to be alive there must be, in addition to breathing, a circulation independent of the mother. The limited indicia of life which Mr Norris said was sufficient would not at any rate have accorded with those directions.

Counsel's case that Mr C was entitled to an injunction because a crime was threatened depended, it appears, partly, as counsel for Miss S submitted, on the extraordinary and dogmatic assertion with regard to the ability to be born alive of *every* 18-week fetus, without any personal knowledge or examination of any of these countless unborn children, partly on his interpretation of 'being born alive' and partly on the view adumbrated by counsel for Mr C that, if any doctor was intending to perform an abortion on an 18-week fetus, it would be perverse of him or her to assert other than that the fetus was capable of being born alive. Counsel, though not Mr Norris, submitted that no other interpretation of 'live born' than that of Mr Norris is within the words of the Act.

I disagree. Counsel for Mrs S pointed out that Mr Norris did not disagree with Professor Newton that an 18-week fetus cannot breathe and cannot even be mechanically ventilated. I would have thought that to say, as he has, that a child is live born or alive, even though it cannot breathe, would surprise not only doctors but many ordinary people.

The word 'viable' is, I believe from what I have heard in this case, sometimes used interchangeably and in a number of cases where others might use the words 'born alive'. In the United States of America, in the Supreme Court, in *Roe v Wade* 410 US 113 at 163 (1973) it was said:

With respect to the State's important and legitimate interest in potential life, the "compelling" point is at *viability*. This is so because the fetus then presumably has the capability of meaningful life outside the mother's womb. State regulation protective of fetal life after viability thus has both logical and biological justifications. (My emphasis.)

As far as the phrase in the 1929 Act is concerned, counsel for Mr C submits, it either contains an ambiguity or the phrase is a technical one. In my view, one or both of those submissions is or are correct. That expression, in my judgment, does not have a clear and plain meaning. It *is* ambiguous. It is a phrase which is capable of different interpretations, and probably for the reason that it is also a medical concept and, as with the example of earlier days, the expertise of doctors may well be required and gratefully received to assist the court.

Even distinguished medical men have found considerable difficulties but have discovered that it is more helpful to equate that phrase with viability, possibly with the example from the parliamentary draftsman in mind.

I cannot accept counsel for the plaintiff's submission that this is not, at any rate in this court, even partly a matter of expert opinion as to the meaning of 'alive', for I have to point out that the first expert, namely Mr Norris, who produced an affidavit on that very topic was introduced by him. Professor Newton replied later.

Counsel on behalf of the Official Solicitor, acting as amicus curiae, submitted that the alleged threatened criminality raised a difficult question of interpretation and pointed out that s 5(1) of the 1967 Act itself incorporates the word 'viable' in the phrase which refers to 'protecting the life of the viable foetus', a section to which I have already referred. By that date, he argued, Parliament would no doubt be aware of the controversies over the law on abortion and it is possible that the use of that word is some indication that Parliament thought it necessary to use that particular qualifying word. I think that that is possible too, though I would not attach too much weight to the parenthesis containing that word as an aid to construction.

Perhaps it is more significant that, though the reference to a fetus of 28 weeks or more being deemed 'capable of being born alive' is referable to the burden of proof, it is probably dealing with a fetus of an age that would be known or expected to be viable in 1929.

Mr Norris, of course, does not limit his statement to a question of presumption. He goes much further and in effect makes his 18 weeks an irrebuttable presumption, thus, at a stroke, as it were, reducing the 28 weeks to 18.

Counsel for the Official Solicitor submitted that the court should reject Mr Norris's interpretation of 'born alive' as the minimum indicia, without breathing, possibly without circulation and minus a number of indications referred to by Professor Newton.

In considering this submission, I find Mr Norris's statements as to the inevitability of every 18-week fetus being born alive unacceptable. It is not necessary for me, nor would I want, to try to decide on affidavit evidence in a somewhat limited sphere the answer, which baffles men and women with great scientific expertise, to a very profound question. I would, however, say that I am not greatly attracted to the very limited definition relied on by Mr Norris and I do not accept it as a realistic one.

Heilbron J, however, does not seem to reach a final view on this issue since she dismissed the plaintiff's application on other grounds.

On appeal [1987] 1 All ER 1230 at 1241, the Court of Appeal dealt squarely with the point. Sir John Donaldson MR stated that:

We have received affidavit evidence from three doctors, none of whom has examined Miss S. Their evidence is thus necessarily directed at the stage in the development of a fetus which can normally be expected to have been reached by the 18th to 21st week. On this, as one would expect, they are in substantial agreement. At that stage the cardiac muscle is contracting and a primitive circulation is developing. Thus the fetus could be said to demonstrate real and discernible signs of life. On the other hand, the fetus, even if then delivered by hysterotomy, would be incapable ever of breathing either naturally or with the aid of a ventilator. It is not a case of the fetus requiring a stimulus or assistance. It cannot and will never be able to breathe. Where the doctors disagree is as to whether a fetus, at this stage of development, can properly be described as 'a child capable of being born alive' within the meaning of the 1929 Act. That essentially depends on the interpretation of the statute and is a matter for the courts.

We have no evidence of the state of the fetus being carried by Miss S but, if it has reached the normal stage of development and so is incapable ever of breathing, it is not in our judgment 'a child capable of being born alive' within the meaning of the 1929 Act and accordingly the termination of this pregnancy would not constitute an offence under that Act.

Is it not the case that the Court of Appeal has interpreted the 1929 Act as protecting the 'viable foetus'?

Even if this is so, it still leaves the question of what 'viable' means? Does it mean 'capable of surviving'? If it does, even this needs further clarification. For how long must a foetus be capable of surviving to come within this definition? The rule in homicide cases is that it is immaterial how long the person (including the newborn child) would have lived. As Glanville Williams tells us: '. . ., every instance of killing is an instance of accelerating death; and even if death is hastened by as little as five minutes it is still a criminal homicide.' (*Textbook of Criminal Law*, *supra*, at p 378.)

Support for this wide view of 'the capacity to survive' is to be found in Heilbron J's tentative observation that 'viability . . . embraces not only being born alive but surviving, for however short a time . . .' (at p 1238). Would a court adopt this view when considering a foetus *in utero*? Or would a court determine that a crime was committed only where it could be shown that a foetus would have been capable of being born alive or surviving for a reasonable period of time?

2. INTERACTION WITH THE LAW OF HOMICIDE

The law is summarised by Professor Glanville Williams in his, *Textbook of Criminal Law* (2nd ed, 1983 p 289; footnotes omitted):

Homicide and the new-born

The law protecting neonates and the unborn is not ordinarily met with in legal practice; but it is of importance for obstetric surgeons and is a matter of philosophical and human interest. It is also the subject of strongly-felt differences of moral opinion.

The definition of homicide . . . requires the victim to be in *rerum natura* or 'in being', which means that he must be 'completely born alive.'

Although injuries to a fetus causing its death do not generally amount to homicide, there is a curious rule by which they can do so. If a fetus is injured in the womb and is subsequently born alive but dies as a result of the prenatal injury, this is murder or manslaughter according to the mental element. So whether the offender is guilty of the crime will sometimes depend upon whether a doctor is able to remove the fetus from the womb while it is still alive, even though it is so premature that it is doomed to die almost immediately.

In a New Jersey case, D shot a pregnant woman whose twin sons were then delivered by caesarean section (hysterotomy) but died a short time later. He was convicted of murder of the infants. Had they died in the womb it would not have been murder.

The rule also applies to illegal abortionists. In this it seems to be over-severe, for it makes what may be a purely accidental fact turn the abortionist into a murderer.

Two American cases directly raise this issue and represent English law. *Commonwealth v Edelin* (1976) 359 NE 2d 4 (Supreme Judicial Court of Massachusetts) (footnotes omitted).

Caplan J: *1. Basic circumstances.* Some days before September 30 1973, the patient appeared with her mother at the outpatient clinic in Boston City Hospital requesting an abortion. Dr H R Holtrop, chief of the outpatient OBS/GYN service, interviewed the patient and advised her about alternatives to abortion, which she did not accept. He then inquired about her last menstrual period. She placed it at a date which would indicate she was seventeen weeks gone. After physical examination, Dr

Holtrop concluded that the gestational age was twenty weeks. He then advised and approved abortion by the saline method (a common method in use for abortions in the second trimester), and introduced Dr Edelin as the surgeon who would carry out the procedure.

At the patient's admission to hospital on September 30, a student entering his third year at medical school worked up the history and examined the patient. He estimated a gestational age of twenty-four weeks but, because of his lack of clinical experience, he put that as only a guess. Dr Enrique Gimenez-Jimeno, a junior resident, also examined the patient and estimated twenty-four weeks; he recorded finding a fetal heartbeat. On October 1, Dr Holtrop, with the two estimates before him, reexamined the patient; he concluded that the period was twenty-one to twenty-two weeks.

On October 2 the patient was brought to the 'saline unit' for abortion by amniocentesis with saline infusion, a process of inducing fetal death and a miscarriage by introducing a salt solution into the amniotic sac containing the fetus. Dr Edelin, with all prior estimates before him, made his own measurement and estimated the gestational period as twenty to twenty-two weeks. Proceeding in the usual way, Dr Edelin inserted a long needle through the abdominal skin at a selected, locally anesthetized spot, hoping to reach into the amniotic sac and to drain off clear amniotic fluid; salt solution would then be let into the sac. The needle, however, recovered a bloody tap; and the result was the same on further tries. This indicated that the needle had not gone true into the amniotic sac. To introduce salt solution elsewhere than in the sac might endanger the patient. Dr Edelin surmised that he was dealing with an anterior placenta, ie, one connected to the front of the uterine wall, a condition that could account for his recovering the bloody taps.

Accordingly, Dr Edelin discontinued his probes and consulted Dr James F Penza who as associate director of the OBS/GYN department was his supervisor. It was agreed that Dr Penza would himself attempt amniocentesis the following morning and, if that failed, Dr Edelin would perform a hysterotomy. On October 3 Dr Penza made the further attempts but they failed. Thereupon Dr Edelin went forward with the other agreed procedure.

The abortion by hysterotomy involved incision of the uterus to reach and remove the products of conception. In about ten minutes' time after the patient received general anesthesia, Dr Edelin commenced incising through the abdominal wall to reach the uterus. As he had diagnosed an anterior placenta, he made a low transverse cut just above the pubic hairline. The process of incising, retracting, and so forth was laborious and took perhaps thirty minutes. Reaching the uterus, Dr Edelin made a transverse incision of about six to seven centimeters, a relatively small cut: the lower part of the uterus is thick at twenty to twenty-two weeks and excessive bleeding was to be avoided. Dr Edelin reached into the incision with the index and middle fingers of his left hand, steadying the uterus with his right hand. He swept the uterine cavity with his fingers to detach the placenta from the uterine wall; then he began to peel the amniotic sac, intending to recover the sac intact through the incision, the rest to follow. As he brought his fingers behind the sac and began to ease the sac through the incision, the sac ruptured. Dr Edelin then sought to take hold of a lower extremity of the fetus in order to draw the fetus through the uterine incision. This was difficult because of the size and location of that incision.

Upon removal of the fetus, Dr Edelin put his hand on its chest wall for a few seconds; finding no heartbeat or other sign of life, he placed the fetus in a stainless steel basin held for the purpose by an attending nurse. He turned his attention promptly to the patient with the open uterine incision. After removing any remaining material in the cavity, and swabbing the cavity and taking other indicated steps, he undertook the suturing process and concluded the procedure. The patient recovered without incident.

The fetus and placenta were transferred to the pathology laboratory according to usual practice on the morning of the operation. The resident pathologist weighed the fetus twice and recorded 600 grams (one pound, five ounces). For preservation, the fetus and cord were placed in formalin, a ten per cent solution of formaldehyde.

2. *The question of the condition and potentiality of the fetus.* A large amount of testimony was admitted on these subjects which on the part of the prosecution ran

thus. As against the pathologist's weigh-in of the fetus at 600 grams just after the operation, the medical examiner, Dr George W Curtis, at an autopsy on February 12, 1974, found a weight of 693 grams for the fetus, seven grams for the umbilical cord (one pound, eight and one-half ounces total), and it was his opinion that the fact that the fetus had been soaking for more than four months would not have increased the weight and might have reduced it. Individual organs were weighed separately. There was evidence also as to the crown-to-heel and crown-to-rump length of the fetus (respectively 33.5 and 21 centimeters). The weight and length figures were related to sundry published tables in order to support estimates about the gestational age of the fetus.

Evidence was admitted about the condition of the fetal lungs and the possibility of respiratory activity by the fetus. According to Dr Curtis, the lungs sank in water and had a solid appearance, indications of the absence of respiratory movement. Microscopic examination of lung tissue later fixed on slides, however, showed partial expansion of some of the alveoli. This suggested respiratory activity, but left the question where it had taken place. Dr Curtis's testimony is fairly read as allowing any of three possibilities: that the fetus had sucked amniotic fluid (as it might have done when distressed), or had taken in room air through the uterine incision, or had done so after delivery clear of the uterus. The last might be token postnatal 'life' in some sense.

Dr John F Ward, a pathologist testified on the basis of his microscopic examination of lung tissue that the fetus 'did breathe outside the uterus'. His adoption of the third alternative appears based at least in part on his skepticism about the phenomenon of respiratory movement in utero incident to the sucking of amniotic fluid; in this he seemed to stand somewhat apart from other experts.

Their analysis of post mortem materials or data led experts for the Commonwealth to put the gestational age at the time of the operation at twenty-four weeks, excepting Dr Ward who went somewhat higher to twenty-six weeks. All recognised that the figures were only estimates. Several prosecution experts would answer in the affirmative the inferential question of 'viability' of the fetus at the time of the operation. The exact import of such judgments turned on the meaning to be ascribed to that term. Here the testimony was diverse, with one Commonwealth witness going so far as to say that a fetus was to be considered viable if it had any chance of surviving, and another expert stating that a fetus was viable if it could survive for one moment outside the uterus, which might be the case with a fetus of twelve weeks' age. In this connection (as in other respects later mentioned) the judge allowed very considerable latitude for the expression by witnesses of medical ideas which did not relate or channel back to legal standards. For example, the judge did not bring to bear during trial (or, for that matter, in his charge to the jury) the Supreme Court's definition of viability in the relevant sense of the point at which the State might, if it chose, constitutionally assert its interest in bringing the fetus to full term.

3. *The question of homicidal conduct.* We can find no dispute in the testimony about the proposition that the established procedure ('protocol') for abortions by hysterotomy at Boston City Hospital accepted and envisaged detachment of the placenta as the first surgical move after completion of the uterine incision, with subsequent peeling of the amniotic sac. On the part of the prosecution there was testimony tending to show that a reverse procedure resembling Caesarean section performed when a fetus approached or reached term, was possible and might have been preferable, especially with a fetus of a gestational age approximating the present here: this procedure would involve first breaching the amniotic sac and removing the fetus, then separating the placenta. There was also testimony critical of the relatively small size of the uterine incision which may have caused the rupture of the amniotic sac.

Dr Gimènez testified that he walked into the operating room when the operation was under way. He said he saw Dr Edelin's sweeping motion, evidently the one detaching the placenta, after which, he said, Dr Edelin remained motionless for at least three minutes with his hand in the uterus, his eyes fixed on a clock on the wall. He said, further, that all others in the room—the anesthetist, student assistant, and nurses—also remained still with their eyes on the clock. Then Dr Edelin delivered the fetus from the uterus. The interval of immobility as testified to by Dr Gimènez appeared to start immediately after the detachment of the placenta and to end with the delivery of the fetus; the testimony did not refer to any space of time that might cover detachment of the amniotic sac, rupture of the sac with spill of fluid, and grappling for an extremity of the fetus in order to accomplish the withdrawal.

Dr Gimènez testified that the fetus appeared dead on delivery. With regard to the testing for heartbeat extra utero, an expert called by the defence stated his opinion that ten seconds would be required to reach certainty about the existence of a heartbeat.

C.   The accusation and theories of commonwealth and defense

We turn to the precise accusation. The short-form manslaughter indictment found by the grand jury on April 11, 1974, stated simply 'that [Dr Edelin] did assault and beat a certain person, to wit: a male child described to the . . . Jurors as Baby Boy and by such assault and beating did kill the said person.' The Commonwealth was required to respond to an order for particulars of the alleged manslaughter. First, as to when the death of the 'person' had supposedly taken place, the Commonwealth declined the tendered proposition that the death occurred 'when the fetus was totally expelled or removed from the body of the mother', and adopted the propositions that death occurred 'when Baby Boy was within the mother, albeit detached from the mother and independent of the mother, and [*sic*] . . . when Baby Boy was partially expelled or removed from the body of the mother'. As to the defendant's supposed act claimed to constitute the manslaughter, the Commonwealth particularised that Dr Edelin's 'act during the course of a hysterotomy, which act constituted manslaughter, was his waiting 3–5 minutes after he manually separated the placenta from the uterine wall and before he removed the person from the abdominal cavity of his mother'.

From the indictment as particularised, it appeared that the Commonwealth's theory was that, upon the detachment of the placenta, the fetus became a 'person' within the manslaughter statute, and was then killed by a wanton and reckless act of Dr Edelin, all before the birth of the fetus through its complete delivery clear of the mother's body. The defense asserted by repeated motions that such an accusation would be an untenable usage of the manslaughter statute and would, besides, enable the Commonwealth to evade or subvert the constitutional rule of *Wade-Bolton*. The defense contended that manslaughter could be made out, if at all, only where a fetus was born alive completely outside the mother's body and was homicidally destroyed by acts committed at that stage.

The defense did not persuade the trial judge to limit the case as just indicated and to confine the evidence accordingly. (How far the judge's ultimate instructions to the jury, which we proceed to describe, represented a shift of position, and whether such a shift was prejudicial, are questions considered in 'Additional Views of Three Justices', at p 16 *infra*.)

D.   The judge's instructions to the jury

. . .

The manslaughter statute could apply only as follows. Only when a fetus had been born alive outside its mother could it become a 'person' within the meaning of the statute. Thus, to be convicted of the crime, Dr Edelin must be found—by reckless or wanton acts— to have 'caused the death of a person who had been alive outside the body of his or her mother', 'caused the death of a person, once that person became such'. We set out this part of the charge in full text:

A fetus is not a person, and not the subject of an indictment of manslaughter. In order for a person to exist, he or she must be born. Unborn persons, as I said, are not the subject of the crime of manslaughter. Birth is the process which causes the emergence of a new individual from the body of its mother. Once outside the body of its mother, the child has been born within the commonly accepted meaning of that word.

Killing or causing the death of a person who is born alive and is outside the body of his or her mother may be the subject of manslaughter. In order for the defendant to be found guilty in this case, you must be satisfied beyond a reasonable doubt, as I have defined that term for you, that the defendant caused the death of a person who had been alive outside the body of his or her mother. If you believe beyond a reasonable doubt that the defendant, by his conduct, caused the death of a person, once that person became such as I have defined the word for you, you may find the defendant guilty of the crime of manslaughter, if that death was caused by wanton or reckless conduct on the part of the defendant. If, on the other hand, you do not find beyond a reasonable doubt that the defendant by his conduct caused the death of a person, then you must acquit him of the crime charged.

Two more points. 'Born alive': As to what birth meant, the judge said it was 'the process which causes the emergence of a new individual from the body of its mother'. The judge, however, did not discuss the meaning of 'alive'—how far this connoted an ability to survive, under what conditions, for what length of time.

'Viability'; The judge left it to the jury in their 'consideration of the facts of this case' to 'determine' whether viability had 'any applicability.' If they determine that it did, it should be taken to mean 'the ability to live postnatally'. The judge however, did not discuss what the chances, conditions, or duration of survival must be.

After receiving the charge, the jury returned a verdict of guilty. Dr Edelin was sentenced by the judge to one year's probation, execution of the sentences being stayed pending appeal.

. . .

Manslaughter assumes that the victim was a live and independent person. This is well understood, and the judge so charged. Destruction of a fetus in utero is not a manslaughter. The further question was debated at common law, whether manslaughter might rest on a defendant's injuring a fetus in utero, where the fetus was later born alive, and then died of the injury without futher guilty intervention by the defendant. In this Commonwealth, Holmes J. seems to intimate a preference for the view that the prenatal acts could not ground a manslaughter despite the later live birth and death. *Dietrich v Northamptonshire*, 138 Mass 14 & 15, 17 (1884). (Common sense, besides common law, tended to support this position, for if a contrary rule were adopted, a putative defendant might be encouraged to make sure he extinguished the fetus while still in utero.) The effect, be it noted, was not to let the defendant off, but to subject him to the typical criminal abortion statute. . . .

But if acts of a defendant during the prenatal period could ever be availed of in obtaining a conviction of manslaughter, that was a legal impossibility in the circumstances of this case after the *Wade-Bolton* decisions. (Thus our reading of the Judge's charge is actually required to keep it within constitutional bounds.) Under *Wade-Bolton*, the State's regulation of abortions after viability to promote its interest 'in the potentiality of human life' is expected to be expressed in 'tailored' legislation. See *Wade*, 410 US at 164–165, 93 S Ct 705. The detail that may be involved, representing an adjustment and accommodation of many considerations, is exemplified by the comprehensive legislation in fact adopted by our Legislature in August, 1974. The manslaughter statute is flat and contains no such detail, and it would be not only incongruous but, we think, unconstitutional to attempt to bring it to bear on a physician as he went about the predelivery process of peforming an abortion. After *Wade-Bolton*, even if not before, the manslaughter statute could take hold only after a live birth and only with respect to acts of the physician in the postnatal period.

If the manslaughter statute conceivably could be utilized to control and punish a physician's conduct in the prenatal period, then the judge would be bound to say just how the statute should be applied consistently with *Wade-Bolton*. The most obvious of the several matters calling for guidance by the trial judge would be a definition or description of viability marking the stage at which a physician would begin to owe a duty to the 'potentiality of human life' inherent in the fetus. On this point, as our digest of the judge's charge indicates, the instructions were uninstructive and left a wide-open option to the members of the jury.

However, that omission from the charge does not embarrass a decision to reverse and acquit because, on any view of viability tenable under *Wade-Bolton*, there was no sufficient showing of recklessness in Dr Edelin's prenatal conduct—any more than in his postnatal conduct—to permit reference of the question to a jury. His 'quo animo' turned on whether he believed in good faith that the fetus was not viable at the time of the operation and was not palpably unreasonable in this belief—a combination of an internal and an external standard of criminality. See *Commonwealth v Welansky* 316 Mass at 398–399, 55 N E 2d 902, referring to *Commonwealth v Pierce*, 138 Mass 165 (1884). Of course manslaughter could not be supported by proof merely of a mistake of judgment, even if that was the result of negligence or gross negligence.

[Subsequently, the Massachusetts' Supreme Judicial Court has held that the intentional killing of a *viable* fetus *in utero* could be murder: *Commonwealth v Laurence* (1989) 404 Mass 378, applying *Commonwealth v Cass* (1984) 467 NE 2d 1324—neither case involved an abortion and these cases represent a minority view in America.]

In California, the Supreme Court took a similar view to the *Edein* court when interpreting the provisions of the California Code in *Keeler v Superior Court of Amador County* 470 P 2d 617 (1970).

Mosk J: On February 23, 1969, Mrs Keeler was driving on a narrow mountain road in Amador County after delivering the girls to their home. She met petitioner driving in the opposite direction; he blocked the road with his car, and she pulled over to the side. He walked to her vehicle and began speaking to her. He seemed calm, and she rolled down her window to hear him. He said, 'I hear you're pregnant. If you are you had better stay away from the girls and from here.' She did not reply, and he opened the car door; as she later testified, 'He assisted me out of the car . . . [I]t wasn't roughly at this time.' Petitioner then looked at her abdomen and became 'extremely upset.' He said, 'You sure are. I'm going to stomp it out of you.' He pushed her against the car, shoved his knee in her abdomen, and struck her in the face with several blows. She fainted, and when she regained consciousness petitioner had departed.

Mrs Keeler drove back to Stockton, and the police and medical assistance were summoned. She had suffered substantial facial injuries, as well as extensive bruising of the abdominal wall. A Caesarian section was performed and the fetus was examined *in utero*. Its head was found to be severely fractured, and it was delivered stillborn. The pathologist gave as his opinion that the cause of death was skull fracture with consequent cerebral hemorrhaging, that death would have been immediate, and that the injury could have been the result of force applied to the mother's abdomen. There was no air in the fetus' lungs, and the umbilical cord was intact.

Upon delivery the fetus weighed five pounds and was 18 inches in length. Both Mrs Keeler and her obstetrician testified that fetal movements had been observed prior to February 23, 1969. The evidence was in conflict as to the estimated age of the fetus; the expert testimony on the point, however, concluded 'with reasonable medical certainty' that the fetus had developed to the stage of viability, ie, that in the event of premature birth on the date in question it would have had a 75 percent to 96 percent chance of survival.

An information was filed charging petitioner, in Count I, with committing the crime of murder (Pen Code, § 187) in that he did 'unlawfully kill a human being, to wit Baby Girl VOGT, with malice aforethought'.
. . .
Penal Code section 187 provides: 'Murder is the unlawful killing of a human being, with malice aforethought'. The dispositive question is whether the fetus which petitioner is accused of killing was, on February 23, 1969, a 'human being' within the meaning of this statute. If it was not, petitioner cannot be charged with its 'murder' and prohibition will lie.

Section 187 was enacted as part of the Penal Code of 1872. Inasmuch as the provision has not been amended since that date, we must determine the intent of the Legislature at the time of its enactment. But section 187 was, in turn, taken verbatim from the first California statute defining murder, part of the Crimes and Punishments Act of 1850. (Stats 1850, ch 99, § 19, p 231.) Penal Code section 5 (also enacted in 1872) declares: 'The provisions of this Code, so far as they are substantially the same as existing statutes, must be construed as continuations thereof, and not as new enactments'. We begin, accordingly, by inquiring into the intent of the Legislature in 1850 when it first defined murder as the unlawful and malicious killing of a 'human being'.

It will be presumed, of course, that in enacting a statute the Legislature was familiar with the relevant rules of the common law, and, when it couches its enactment in common law language, that its intent was to continue those rules in statutory form. (*Baker v Baker* 13 Cal 87, 95–96 (1859); *Morris v Oney* 217 Cal App 2d 864 at 870, 32 Cal Rptr 88 (1963).) This is particularly appropriate in considering the work of the first session of our Legislature: its precedents were necessarily drawn from the common law, as modified in certain respects by the Constitution and by legislation of our sister states.

We therefore undertake a brief review of the origins and development of the common law of abortional homicide. (For a more detailed treatment, see Means, The Law of New York concerning Abortion and the Status of the Foetus, 1664–1968: A Case of Cessation of Constitutionality (1968) 14 NYLF 411 [hereinafter cited as Means]; Stern, Abortion: Reform and the Law (1968) 59 J Crim L, C & PS 84; Quay, Justifiable Abortion—Medical and Legal Foundations II (1961) 49 Geo LJ 395.) From that inquiry it appears that by the year 1850—the date with which we are concerned—an infant could not be the subject of homicide at common law *unless it had been born alive*. Perhaps the must influential statement of the 'born alive' rule is that of Coke, in mid-17th century: '[If a woman be quick with childe, and by a potion or otherwise killeth it in her wombe, or if a man beat her, whereby the childe dyeth in her body, and she is delivered of a dead childe, this is a great misprision [ie, misdemeanor], and no murder; but if the childe be born alive and dyeth of the potion, battery, or other cause, this is murder; for in law it is accounted a reasonable creature, *in rerum natura*, when it is born alive.]'(3 Coke, Institutes *58 (1648).) In short, 'By Coke's time, the common law regarded abortion as murder only if the foetus is (1) quickened, (2) born alive, (3) lives for a brief interval, and (4) then dies'. (Means, at p 420.) Whatever intrinsic defects there may have been in Coke's work (see 3 Stephen, A History of the Criminal Law of England (1883) pp 52–60), the common law accepted his views as authoritative. In the 18th century, for example, Coke's requirement that an infant be born alive in order to be the subject of homicide was reiterated and expanded by both Blackstone and Hale....

We conclude that in declaring murder to be the unlawful and malicious killing of a 'human being' the Legislature of 1850 intended that term to have the settled common law meaning of a person who had been born alive, and did not intend the act of feticide—as distinguished from abortion—to be an offense under the laws of California....

Notes to extract
[a] Aftermath Cal Pen Code § 187. 'Murder is the unlawful killing of a human being, *or a fetus*, with malice aforethought. . . .' The words in italics were added by amendment in 1970, 'triggered' by *Keeler*.

The word 'fetus' in section 187 is interpreted to mean 'a viable unborn child'. *People v Smith*—Cal App 3d —, 129 Cal Rptr 498 (1976).

Do you think the English common law would consider that abortion amounted to homicide? What if, however, the abortion procedure leads to the death of the fetus *outside* the mother's body? Is it relevant whether or not the fetus is sufficiently mature to be considered 'viable'? Does compliance with the Abortion Act 1967 provide the doctor with a defence to homicide?

3. THE CLAIMS OF OTHERS

(a) To prevent

(i) The father qua father

Paton v Trustees of British Pregnancy Advisory Service
[1978] 2 All ER 987 (footnotes omitted)

Sir George Baker P: . . . the plaintiff, who is the husband of the second defendant, seeks an injunction in effect to restrain the first defendants, a charitable organisation, and particularly his wife, the second defendant, from causing or permitting an abortion to be carried out on his wife without his consent . . .

The husband's case must therefore depend on a right which he has himself. I would say a word about the illegitimate, usually called the putative, but I prefer myself to refer to the illegitimate, father. Although American decisions to which I have been referred concern illegitimate fathers, and statutory provisions about them, it seems to me that in this country the illegitimate father can have no rights whatsoever except those given to him by statute. That was clearly the common law. One provision which makes an inroad into this is s 14 of the Guardianship of Minors Act 1971, and s 9(1) and some other sections of that Act applicable to illegitimate children, giving the illegitimate father or mother the right to apply for the custody of or access to an illegitimate child. But the equality of parental rights provision in s 1(1) of the Guardianship Act 1973 expressly does not apply in relation to a minor who is illegitimate: see s 1(7).

So this plaintiff must, in my opinion, bring his case, if he can, squarely within the framework of the fact that he is a husband. It is, of course, very common for spouses to seek injunctions for personal protection in the matrimonial courts during the pendency of or, indeed, after divorce actions, but the basic reason for the non-molestation injunction often granted in the family courts is to protect the other spouse or the living children, and to ensure that no undue pressure is put on one or other of the spouses during the pendency of the case and during the breaking-up of the marriage.

There was, of course, the action for restitution of conjugal rights, a proceeding which always belied its name and was abolished in 1970. It arose because in ecclesiastical law the parties could not end the consortium by agreement. In a sense the action for restitution was something of a fiction. The court ordered the spouse to return to cohabitation. If the spouse did not return then that spouse was held to be in desertion. No more could happen. The court could not compel matrimonial intercourse: *Forster v Forster*. So matrimonial courts have never attempted the enforcement of matrimonial obligations by injunction.

The law is that the court cannot and would not seek to enforce or restrain by injunction matrimonial obligations, if they be obligations such as sexual intercourse or contraception (a non-molestation injunction given during the pendency of divorce proceedings could, of course, cover attempted intercourse). No court would even grant an injunction to stop sterilisation or vasectomy. Personal family relationships in marriage cannot be enforced by the order of a court. An injunction in such circumstances was described by Judge Mager in *Jones v Smith* in the District Court of Appeal of Florida as 'ludicrous'.

I ask the question 'If an injunction were ordered, what could be the remedy?' and I do not think I need say any more than that no judge could even consider sending a husband or wife to prison for breaking such an order. That, of itself, seems to me to cover the application here; this husband cannot by law by injunction stop his wife having what is now accepted to be a lawful abortion within the terms of the Abortion Act 1967.

The case which was first put forward to me a week ago, and indeed is to be found in the writ, is that the wife had no proper legal grounds for seeking a termination of her pregnancy and that, not to mince words, she was being spiteful, vindictive and utterly unreasonable in seeking so to do. It now appears I need not go into the evidence in the affidavits because it is accepted and common ground that the provisions of the 1967 Act have been complied with, the necessary certificate has been given by two doctors and everything is lawfully set for the abortion.

. . . The two doctors have given a certificate. It is not and cannot be suggested that that certificate was given in other than good faith and it seems to me that there is the end of the matter in English law. The 1967 Act gives no right to a father to be consulted in respect of the termination of a pregnancy. True, it gives no right to the mother either, but obviously the mother is going to be right at the heart of the matter consulting with the doctors if they are to arrive at a decision in good faith, unless, of course, she is mentally incapacitated or physically incapacitated (unable to make any decision or give any help) as, for example, in consequence of an accident. The

husband, therefore, in my view, has no legal right enforceable at law or in equity to stop his wife having this abortion or to stop the doctors from carrying out the abortion.
. . .

Very helpfully I have been referred to American authorities. The Supreme Court of the United States has reached the same conclusion, that a husband, or an illegitimate father, has no right to stop his wife, or the woman who is pregnant by him, from having a legal abortion. In *Planned Parenthood of Central Missouri v Danforth, Attorney-General of Missouri* the Supreme Court by a majority held that the State of Missouri

> may not constitutionally require the consent of the spouse, as is specified under § 3(3) of the Missouri Act, as a condition for abortion during the first 12 weeks of pregnancy . . . clearly since the State cannot regulate or proscribe abortion during the first stage when the physician and his patient make that decision, the State cannot delegate authority to any particular person, even the spouse, to prevent abortion during that same period.

It is interesting to note that the Missouri spousal consent provision would have required the husband's consent even if he was not the father.

A spousal consent provision in an English Act could not of course be challenged as unconstitutional but there is no such provision in the 1967 Act or in the Abortion Regulations 1968 to which a challenge of ultra vires could be made. There is no provision even for consultation with the spouse and reg 5 prohibits disclosure except in specified instances, of which disclosure to the spouse is not one.

Counsel have been unable to discover any extant decision in those countries whose laws derive from the common law that the consent of the husband is required before an otherwise legal abortion can be performed on the wife. Counsel for the husband's researches show that in Roman law, centuries ago, the father's consent was required or otherwise abortion was a crime, but today the only way he can put the case is that the husband has a right to have a say in the destiny of the child he has conceived. The law of England gives him no such right; the 1967 Act contains no such provision. It follows, therefore, that in my opinion this claim for an injunction is completely misconceived and must be dismissed.

In *C v S* (*op cit*), the *Paton* case was applied where the father was not married to the mother. At first instance, Heilbron J said:

> Counsel's case on behalf of Mr C is that he has the locus standi to bring these proceedings, based on his personal interest, which he does not put as high as a legal right, and because the proposed termination encompasses, he submits, a threatened crime concerning the life of his child.
> If it were to be decided that there was no such threat, he concedes that he has no standing qua father, for he does not contend that as a father he has any special rights. He concedes too that a husband has no special rights qua husband, and he accepts the correctness of the decision in *Paton v Trustees of BPAS* [1978] 2 All ER 987, [1979] QB 276 in that regard.

In the Court of Appeal the Master of the Rolls said the following:

> **Sir John Donaldson MR:** . . . Technically, and now in substance in the light of what counsel for Mr C has said, the questions whether a putative father has any right to be heard on an application of this nature and whether a fetus is a legal person in law capable of suing do not arise, and of course we do not rule on them. But I have also to say that, if we had been in favour of Mr C on all other points, we should have had to have given very considerable thought to the words of Baker P in *Paton v Trustees of BPAS* [1978] 2 All ER 987 at 992, [1979] QB 276 at 282 where he said:
> . . . not only would it be a bold and brave judge . . . who would seek to interfere with the discretion of doctors acting under the [Abortion Act 1967], but I think he would really be a foolish judge who would try to do any such thing, unless possibly, there is clear bad faith and an obvious attempt to perpetrate a criminal offence.

Even then, of course, the question is whether that is a matter which should be left to the Director of Public Prosecutions and the Attorney-General.

So, with that addendum on behalf of the court, we dismiss the appeal.

These cases conclude the matter in English law.

(ii) The father qua guardian

Even if the father cannot rely upon any right of his own to seek an injunction, can he act on behalf of the unborn child to enforce its rights? The following cases answer that question in the negative.

Paton v Trustees of BPAS (supra) (footnotes omitted)

Sir George Baker P: The foetus cannot, in English law, in my view, have any right of its own at least until it is born and has a separate existence from the mother. That permeates the whole of the civil law of this country (I except the criminal law, which is now irrelevant), and is, indeed, the basis of the decisions in those countries where law is founded on the common law, that is to say, in America, Canada, Australia, and, I have no doubt, in others.

For a long time there was great controversy whether after birth a child could have a right of action in respect of pre-natal injury. The Law Commission considered that and produced a working paper in 1973, followed by a final report, but it was universally accepted, and has since been accepted, that in order to have a right the foetus must be born and be a child. There was only one known possible exception which is referred to in the working paper, an American case, *White v Yup*, where the wrongful death of an eight month viable foetus, stillborn as a consequence of injury, led an American court to allow a cause of action, but there can be no doubt, in my view, that in England and Wales, the foetus has no right of action, no right at all, until birth. The succession cases have been mentioned. There is no difference. From conception the child may have succession rights by what has been called a 'fictional construction' but the child must be subsequently born alive. See per Lord Russell of Killowen in *Elliot v Joicey*.

The point was further elaborated by Heilbron J in *C v S (supra)*:

As to the position of the second plaintiff and his claim that the unborn child has the locus standi to make this application, counsel produced a wealth of authorities from far and wide, some of which he cited. His research and that of his junior was extensive, but it would serve no useful purpose, nor do I propose, to refer to most of them, for they did appear to be somewhat remote from the issue whether or not the unborn child could be a party to this motion. Counsel indeed referred me to *Mullick v Mullick* (1925) LR 52 Ind App 245, a Privy Council case relating to the right of an Indian idol to participate in legal proceedings. The facts of that case were so exceptional and so far removed from anything I have to decide as to be of little assistance.

The authorities, it seems to me, show that a child, after it has been born, and only then in certain circumstances based on his or her having a legal right, may be a party to an action brought with regard to such matters as the right to take, on a will or intestacy, or for damages for injuries suffered before birth. In other words, the claim crystallises on the birth, at which date, but not before, the child attains the status of a legal persona, and thereupon can then exercise that legal right.

This also appears to be the law in a number of Commonwealth countries. In *Medhurst v Medhurst* (1984) 46 OR (2d) 263 Reid J held in the Ontario High Court that an unborn child was not a person and that any rights accorded to the fetus are held contingent on a legal personality being acquired by the fetus on its subsequent birth alive. Nor could its father, the husband in that case, act as the fetus's next friend.

A similar decision was taken in *Dehler v Ottawa Civil Hospital* (1979) 25 OR (2d) 748, quoted with approval by Reid J, and affirmed by the Ontario Court of Appeal (see (1980) 29 OR (2d) 677n).

(Having cited *Paton*, the judge continued:)

I agree entirely.

In his reply, counsel's final position was summarised in this way: (1) he no longer relied on the numerous succession cases but he wished to retain some reliance on the position of the unborn child in *Thellusson v Woodford* (1979) 4 Ves 227, 31 ER 117; (2) he did not claim that a child had either a right to be born or a right to life in view of the terms of the 1967 Act; but (3) he maintained that the unborn child had a right to be a party because it was the subject of a threatened crime, that is to say that of child destruction. If there was no such threat, then this claim too failed.

In my judgment, there is no basis for the claim that the fetus can be a party, whether or not there is any foundation for the contention with regard to the alleged threatened crime, and I would dismiss the second plaintiff from this suit and the first plaintiff in his capacity as next friend.

The common law was also tested against principles of human rights in Canada (in relation to the Charter of Rights and Freedoms) and in Europe (by reference to the European Convention on Human Rights).

Paton v United Kingdom

(1980) 3 EHRR 408, (European Commission of Human Rights) (footnotes omitted)

4. The Commission, therefore, has to examine whether this application discloses any appearance of a violation of the provisions of the Convention invoked by the applicant, in particular Articles 2 and 8. It here recalls that the abortion law of High Contracting Parties to the Convention has so far been the subject of several applications under Article 25. The applicants either alleged that the legislation concerned violated the (unborn child's) right to life (Article 2) or they claimed that it constituted an unjustified interference with the (parents') right to respect for private life (Article 8). Two applications invoking Article 2 were declared inadmissible by the Commission on the ground that the applicants—in the absence of any measure of abortion directly affecting them by reason of a close link with the foetus—could not claim to be 'victims' of the abortion laws complained of. One application, invoking Article 8, was declared admissible by the Commission, in so far as it had been brought by two women. The Commission, and subsequently the Committee of Ministers, concluded that there was no breach of Article 8. That conclusion was based on an interpretation of Article 8 which, *inter alia*, took into account the High Contracting Parties' law on abortion as applied at the time when the Convention entered into force.

The question whether the unborn child is covered by Article 2 was expressly left open in Application No 6959/75 and has not yet been considered by the Commission in any other case. It has, however, been the subject of proceedings before the Constitutional Court of Austria, a High Contracting State in which the Convention has the rank of constitutional law. In those proceedings the Austrian Constitutional Court, noting the different view expressed on this question in legal writings, found that Article 2(1), first sentence, interpreted in the context of Article 2, paras (1) and (2), does not cover the unborn life.

6. Article 2(1), first sentence, provides: 'Everyone's right to life shall be protected by law' (in the French text: '*Le droit de toute personne à la vie est protégé parn la loi*'). The Commission, in its interpretation of this clause and, in particular, of the terms 'everyone' and 'life', has examined the ordinary meaning of the provision in the context both of Article 2 and of the Convention as a whole, taking into account the object and purpose of the Convention.

7. The Commission first notes that the term 'everyone' ('toute personne') is not defined in the Convention. It appears in Article 1 and in Section I, apart from Article 2(1), in Articles 5, 6, 8 to 11 and 13. In nearly all these instances the use of the word is such that it can apply only postnatally. None indicates clearly that it has any possible prenatal application, although such application in a rare case—eg under Article 6(1)—cannot be entirely excluded.

8. As regards, more particularly, Article 2, it contains the following limitations of 'everyone's' right to life enounced in the first sentence of paragraph (1):

—a clause permitting the death penalty in paragraph (1), second sentence: 'No one shall be deprived of his life intentionally save in the execution of a sentence of a court following his conviction of a crime for which this penalty is provided by law'; and

—the provision, in paragraph (2), that deprivation of life shall not be regarded as inflicted in contravention of Article 2 when it results from 'the use of force which is no more than absolutely necessary' in the following three cases: 'In defence of any person from unlawful violence'; 'in order to effect a lawful arrest or to prevent the escape of a person lawfully detained'; 'in action lawfully taken for the purpose of quelling a riot or insurrection'.

All the above limitations, by their nature, concern persons already born and cannot be applied to the foetus.

9. Thus both the general usage of the term 'everyone' ('toute personne') of the Convention (para 7 above) and the context in which this term is employed in Article 2 (para 8 above) tend to support the view that it does not include the unborn.

10. The Commission has next examined, in the light of the above considerations, whether the term 'life' in Article 2(1), first sentence, is to be interpreted as covering only the life of persons already born or also the 'unborn life' of the foetus. The Commission notes that the term 'life', too, is not defined in the Convention.

11. It further observes that another, more recent international instrument for the protection of human rights, the American Convention on Human Rights of 1969, contains in Article 4(1), first and second sentences, the following provisions expressly extending the right to life to the unborn:

Every person has the right to have his life respected. This right shall be protected by law and, in general, from the moment of conception.

12. The Commission is aware of the wide divergence of thinking on the question of where life begins. While some believe that it starts already with conception others tend to focus upon the moment of nidation, upon the point that the foetus becomes 'viable', or upon live birth.

13. The German Federal Constitutional Court, when interpreting the provision 'everyone has a right to life' in Article 2(2) of the Basic Law, stated as follows:

Life in the sense of the historical existence of a human individual exists according to established biological and physiological knowledge at least from the 14th day after conception (Nidation, Individuation) ... The process of development beginning from this point is a continuous one so that no sharp divisions or exact distinction between the various stages of development of human life can be made. It does not end at birth: for example, the particular type of consciousness peculiar to the human personality only appears a considerable time after the birth. The protection conferred by Article 2(2) first sentence of the Basic Law can therefore be limited neither to the 'complete' person after birth nor to the foetus capable of independent existence prior to birth. The right to life is guaranteed to every one who 'lives'; in this context no distinction can be made between the various stages of developing life before birth or between born and unborn children. 'Everyone' in the meaning of Article 2(2) of the Basic Law is 'every living human being', in other words: every human individual possessing life; 'everyone' therefore includes unborn human beings.

14. The Commission also notes that, in a case arising under the Constitution of the United States, the State of Texas argued before the Surpeme Court that, in general, life begins at conception and is present throughout pregnancy. The Court, while not resolving the difficult question where life begins, found that, 'with respect to the State's important and legitimate interest in potential life, the "compelling" point is at viability'.

15. The Commission finally recalls the decision of the Austrian Constitutional Court mentioned in paragraph 6 above which, while also given in the framework of constitutional litigation, had to apply, like the Commission in the present case, Article 2 of the European Convention on Human Rights.

16. The Commission considers with the Austrian Constitutional Court that, in interpreting the scope of the term 'life' in Article 2(1), first sentence, of the Convention, particular regard must be had to the context of the Article as a whole. It also observes that the term 'life' may be subject to different interpretations in different legal instruments, depending on the context in which it is used in the instrument concerned.

17. The Commission has already noted, when discussing the meaning of the term 'everyone' in Article 2 (para 8 above), that the limitations, in paragraphs (1) and (2) of the Article, of 'everyone's' right to 'life', by their nature, concern persons already born and cannot be applied to the foetus. The Commission must therefore examine whether Article 2, in the absence of any express limitation concerning the foetus, is to be interpreted:
—as not covering the foetus at all;
—as recognising a 'right to life' of the foetus with certain implied limitations; or
—as recognising an absolute 'right to life' of the foetus.

18. The Commission has first considered whether Article 2 is to be construed as recognising an absolute 'right to life' of the foetus and has excluded such an interpretation on the following grounds.

19. The 'life' of the foetus is intimately connected with, and cannot be regarded in isolation from, the life of the pregnant woman. If Article 2 were held to cover the foetus and its protection under this Article were, in the absence of any express limitation, seen as absolute, an abortion would have to be considered as prohibited even where the continuance of the pregnancy would involve a serious risk to the life of the pregnant woman. This would mean that the 'unborn life' of the foetus would be regarded as being of a higher value than the life of the pregnant woman. The 'right to life' of a person already born would thus be considered as subject not only to the express limitations mentioned in paragraph 8 above but also to a further, implied limitation.

20. The Commission finds that such an interpretation would be contrary to the object and purpose of the Convention. It notes that, already at the time of the signature of the Convention (4 November 1950), all High Contracting Parties, with one possible exception, permitted abortion when necessary to save the life of the mother and that, in the meanwhile, the national law on termination of pregnancy has shown a tendency towards further liberalisation.

21. Having thus excluded, as being incompatible with the object and purpose of the Convention, one of the three different constructions of Article 2 mentioned in paragraph 17 above, the Commission has next considered which of the two remaining interpretations is to be regarded as the correct one—ie whether Article 2 does not cover the foetus at all or whether it recognises a 'right to life' of the foetus with certain implied limitations.

22. The Commission here notes that the abortion complained of was carried out at the initial stage of the pregnancy—the applicant's wife was ten weeks pregnant— under section 1(1)(*a*) of the Abortion Act 1967 in order to avert the risk of injury to the physical or mental health of the pregnant woman. It follows that, as regards the second of the two remaining interpretations, the Commission is in the present case not concerned with the broad question whether Article 2 recognises a 'right to life' of the foetus during the whole period of the pregnancy but only with the narrower issue whether such a right is to be assumed for the initial stage of the pregnancy. Moreover, as regards implied limitations of a 'right to life' of the foetus at the initial stage, only the limitation protecting the life and health of the pregnant woman, the so-called 'medical indication', is relevant for the determination of the present case and the question of other possible limitations (ethic indication, eugenic indication, social indication, time limitation) does not arise.

23. The Commission considers that it is not in these circumstances called upon to decide whether Article 2 does not cover the foetus at all or whether it recognises a 'right to life' of the foetus with implied limitations. It finds that the authorisation, by the United Kingdom authorities, of the abortion complained of is compatible with Article 2(1), first sentence because, if one assumes that this provision applies

at the initial stage of the pregnancy, the abortion is covered by an implied limitation, protecting the life and health of the woman at that stage, of the 'right to life' of the foetus.

24. The Commission concludes that the applicant's complaint under Article 2 is inadmissible as being manifestly ill-founded within the meaning of Article 27(2).

Borowski v A.G. of Canada
[1987] 4 WWR 385 (Saskatchewan Court of Appeal)

Gerwing JA: Section 7 of the Canadian Charter of Rights and Freedoms provides that:

7. Everyone has the right to life, liberty and security of the person and the right not be deprived thereof except in accordance with the principles of fundamental justice.

The rights guaranteed by this section are subject, as are all of the rights and freedoms of the Charter, to limitation as provided for in s 1 which reads thus:

1. The *Canadian Charter of Rights and Freedoms* guarantees the rights and freedoms set out in it subject only to such reasonable limits prescribed by law as can be demonstrably justified in a free and democratic society.

The appellant's position is that the word 'everyone' in s 7 includes the foetus; that s 251(4) and (6) of the Criminal Code allows for the deprivation of the life, liberty and security of the person of the foetus, in violation of the principles of fundamental justice; . . .

Among other things, s 7 of the Charter guarantees the fundamental physical integrity and freedom of the person which is the base for, and a prerequisite to, the meaningful exercise of all other rights and freedoms. The 'right to life' is so clear with respect to autonomous human beings that not much need be said of its purpose, and to deprive a person of his life is the most radical deprivation of rights and the most flagrant violation, absent adherence to the fundamental principles of justice, of the values and traditions of our society.

However, as noted by Dickson J in *R v Big M Drug Mart Ltd*, *supra*, part of the investigation of the purpose requires that we consider that the Charter was not 'enacted in a vacuum'. Before concluding that the right to 'life' was intended to be extended by the Charter to a foetus, the history of the treatment of a foetus at law must be considered. 'Everyone' is an undefined term and therefore resort must be had to, inter alia, historical treatment at common law of a foetus in determining whether it can come within this term.

. . .

Rights of a foetus in civil law

It has been urged upon us that other branches of the common law than the criminal law surrounding abortions should be considered in the historic treatment of the foetus and its rights. Again I am of the view that such an examination is indeed appropriate in light of the comments in *R v Big M Drug Mart Ltd*.

The appellant contends that the treatment of the foetus in civil law, especially in the areas of tort, family law and inheritance of property, shows a status equivalent to that of a person historically which, he contends, supports his view that a foetus is within 'everyone' in s 7.

Tort

In this field of tort, the appellant relied upon *Montreal Tramways Co v Léveillé* [1933] SCR 456, 41 CRC 291, [1933] 4 DLR 337 [Que], and the cases following it. In that case an infant, born with club feet as a result of an incident when it was a foetus, was permitted following birth to claim for damages. Thus the civil law recognised a duty of care owing by third persons to the foetus, and a corresponding but inchoate right in the foetus to recover damages consequent on the breach of that duty.

It is, however, significant that the court in interpreting the term 'another' in the Code Civil of Quebec said [at 463–64]:

To the Company's contention that an unborn child being merely a part of its mother had no separate existence and, therefore, could not maintain an action under article 1053 CC, the answer, in my opinion, is that, although the child was not actually born at the time the Company by its fault created the conditions which brought about the deformity to its feet, yet, under the civil law, it is deemed to be so if for its advantage. Therefore when it was subsequently born alive and viable it was clothed with all the rights of action which it would have had if actually in existence at the date of the accident. The wrongful act of the Company produced its damage on the birth of the child and the right of action was then complete. *The separate existence of an unborn child is recognised even at common law, for it is well established that if a person wrongfully causes injury to a child before its birth which results in [the child's] death after it has been born alive, such person will be guilty of a criminal offence although the wrongful act was directed solely against the mother. R v Senior* [(1832) 1 Mood CC 346, 168 ER 1298]; Russel on Crimes, 8th ed, vol 1, p 622 [emphasis added].

It is significant that in this, as in all other cases following it which were cited by the appellant (*Duval v Seguin; Seguin v Duval; Blais v Duval* [1972] 2 OR 686, 26 DLR (3d) 418 (HC); *Watt v Rama* [1972] VR 353 (Sup Ct FC); and *Steeves v Fitzsimmons* (1975) 11 OR (2d) 387, 66 DLR (3d) 203 (HC)) the child was born live and appeared in the pleadings as a person in the usual sense.

The fact that the child always was born and had become a viable adult when the action was commenced precludes this area of law being seen as conclusive of the view that a foetus per se was treated as a person. A foetus which had become a person has been awarded damages for harm preceding its arrival at this point of autonomous existence. For the appellant's arguments to be conclusive, there would have to have been recognition that a foetus which had not attained viability had been accorded such status either before birth or after its destruction.

Property law

Similar arguments were made by the appellant based on the laws relating to inheritance of property and titles.

There are instances where, for example, if a gift is made to surviving children, it must be determined whether or not to include the foetus of a mother pregnant at the material time.

In English history from 1586 (see *The Earl of Bedford's Case* (1586) 7 Co Rep 7b, 77 ER 421), there has been a tradition of considering such a foetus, but again in result only if it is born viable.

In the case often cited as the locus classicus, and heavily relied upon by the appellant, *Thellusson v Woodford* (1805) 11 Ves 112, 32 ER 1030 (HL), Macdonald CB said [at 1042]:

It is, however, observable, that this question may never arise, if it shall so happen, that the children *in ventre matris* at the death of the testator shall not survive those, who were then born.

This followed a lengthy analysis of cases on inheritance of property and titles in English law to that date, in all of which the 'status' of the foetus was activated and accepted, as it were retroactively, after its birth.

This treatment is consistent with the description of the recognition of the status of the foetus as a 'legal fiction' by the Alberta Court of Appeal (see *Fitzsimonds v Royal Ins Co of Can* [1984] 2 WWR 762, 29 Alta LR (2d) 394, 4 CCLI 214, 28 CCLT 187, 7 DLR (4th) 406, [1984] ILR 1-1780, 51 AR 368), rather than with the recognition of the rights of the foetus qua foetus, as endowed with the status of personhood, as urged upon us by the appellant.

The appellant was unable to point to any case where a foetus which did not attain viable life after birth affected the succession of title or property rights.

The respondent, however, drew our attention to a case, albeit in the United States of America, *Re Roberts* 286 NYS 476 (1963), where a New York court concluded that a stillborn child had no rights in an estate, its property interests never having been perfected.

Family law

Similarly, suggestions that maintenance and custody cases in the Anglo-Canadian tradition have accorded status of personhood to a foetus are equally incorrect. The cases referred to us in fact dealt with rights which took effect and were perfected by birth: see, for example, *K v K* 41 Man R 504, [1933] 3 WWR 351 (KB), and *Solowon v Solowon* (1953) 8 WWR (NS) 288 (Alta SC).

In summary there are no cases in Anglo-Canadian law giving the foetus qua foetus status; the cases in these various branches of the civil law have, in my view, merely dealt with fully capacitated persons before the court, giving some effect to matters which had affected them before they attained that status. While it may be suggested that it would be rare to make such orders in tort or in family law in any event, it would be much more common in an estate and property law where property could be passed to the heirs of a stillborn or aborted foetus. However, no instance of this, as noted, has been referred to us.

III   Treatment outside of Anglo-Canadian law
United States of America

It is of some interest as well in considering the status of a foetus to consider what treatment it has been accorded in other countries.

The majority opinion of the United States Supreme Court in *Roe v Wade* 410 US 113, 35 L Ed 2d 147, 93 S Ct 705 (1973), is instructive. It provides the following useful review of the American historical position [at 138–41]:

. . . In this country, the law in effect in all but a few States until mid-19th century was the pre-existing English common law. Connecticut, the first State to enact abortion legislation, adopted in 1821 that part of Lord Ellenborough's Act that related to a woman 'quick with child'. The death penalty was not imposed, abortion before quickening was made a crime in that State only in 1860. In 1828, New York enacted legislation that, in two aspects, was to serve as a model for early anti-abortion statutes. First, while barring destruction of an unquickened fetus as well as a quick fetus, it made the former only a misdemeanor, but the latter second-degree manslaughter. Second, it incorporated a concept of therapeutic abortion by providing that an abortion was excused if it 'shall have been necessary to preserve the life of such mother, or shall have been advised by two physicians to be necessary for such purpose.' By 1840, when Texas had received the common law, only eight American States had statutes dealing with abortion. It was not until after the War Between the States that legislation began generally to replace the common law. Most of these initial statutes dealt severely with abortion after quickening but were lenient with it before quickening. Most punished attempts equally with completed abortions. While many statutes included the exception for an abortion thought by one or more physicians to be necessary to save the mother's life, that provision soon disappeared and the typical law required that the procedure actually be necessary for that purpose.

Gradually, in the middle and late 19th century the quickening distinction disappeared from the statutory law of most States and the degree of the offense and the penalties were increased. By the end of the 1950's, a large majority in the jurisdiction banned abortion, however and whenever performed, unless done to save or preserve the life of the mother. The exceptions, Alabama and the District of Columbia, permitted abortion to preserve the mother's health. Three States permitted abortions that were not 'unlawfully' performed or that were not 'without lawful justification', leaving interpretation of those standards to the courts. In the past several years, however, a trend toward liberalisation of abortion statutes has resulted in adoption, by about one-third of the States, of less stringent laws, most of them patterned after the ALI Model Penal Code, § 230.3. . . .

It is thus apparent that at common law, at the time of the adoption of our Constitution, and throughout the major portion of the 19th century, abortion was viewed with less disfavor than under most American statutes currently in effect. Phrasing it another way, a woman enjoyed a substantially broader right to terminate a pregnancy than she does in most States today. At least with respect to the early stage of pregnancy, and very possibly without such a limitation, the opportunity to make this choice was present in this country well into the 19th century. Even later, the law continued for some time to treat less punitively an abortion procured in early pregnancy.

The majority opinion then concludes [at 161–62]:

In areas other than criminal abortion, the law has been reluctant to endorse any theory that life, as we recognise it, begins before live birth or to accord legal rights to the unborn except in narrowly defined situations and except when the rights are contingent upon live birth. For example, the traditional rule of tort law denied recovery for prenatal injuries even though the child was born alive. That rule has been changed in almost every jurisdiction. In most States, recovery is said to be permitted only if the fetus was viable, or at least quick, when the injuries were sustained, though few courts have squarely so held. In a recent development, generally opposed by the commentators, some States permit the parents of a stillborn child to maintain an action for wrongful death because of prenatal injuries. Such an action, however, would appear to be one to vindicate the parents' interest and is thus consistent with the view that the fetus, at most, represents only the potentiality of life. Similarly, unborn children have been recognised as acquiring rights or interests by way of inheritance or other devolution of property, and have been represented by guardians ad litem. Perfection of the interests involved, again, has generally been contingent upon live birth. In short, the unborn have never been recognised in the law as persons in the whole sense.

This is a position which is consistent in principle, if not in detail, with the treatment accorded to the foetus to date in Anglo-Canadian law. The United States Supreme Court has twice reaffirmed *Roe v Wade* in *Thornburgh v Amer College of Obstetricians & Gynecologists* 90 L Ed 2d 779, 106 S Ct 2169 (1986), and in *Akron v Akron Center for Reproductive Health Inc* 462 US 416, 76 L Ed 2d 687, 103 S Ct 2481 (1983).

The court then examined the *Paton* case, both in the English court and the European Commission of Human Rights, before turning to West German law.

West Germany
The majority of the West German Constitutional Court, alone among the European and North American decisions referred to us, found the foetus to have an independent right to life within the context of the provision of the West German Constitution that 'everyone has the right to life'. (It should be noted that this decision was included in the survey of opinions by the European Economic Community Court in *Paton, supra*, and not accepted as governing the interpretation of its convention.)

It should, however, be noted that this decision on its face accepts that it is novel. Further, the legislative history of the Constitution of Germany and of the country itself were called in to aid to arrive at this interpretation. In the John Marshall Journal of Practice and Procedure, vol 9, No 3, in an introduction to the text of the West German decision, the author notes:

Unlike the legislative history of the US Constitution which, as far as can be determined, made no mention of the scope of constitutionality as it relates to the prenatal stage of human existence, the legislative history of the Basic Law shows that the drafters discussed the problem of the constitutional status of the unborn.

Thus the legislative history of the Basic Law gave support to the conclusion of the Federal Constitutional Court. After considerable debate and parliamentary maneuvering, it was concluded:

With the guaranteeing of the right to life, germinating life should also be protected. The motions introduced by the German Party in the Main Committee to attach a particular sentence about the protection of germinating life did not attain a majority only because, according to the view prevailing in the Committee, the value to be protected was already secured through the present version.

The Federal Constitutional Court also noted that the principles of the Basic Law are to 'be understood only in light of the historical experience and the spiritual-moral confrontation with the previous system of National Socialism'.

The Canadian Bill of Rights
The learned trial judge referred himself to *Morgentaler* and *Dehler* [*Morgentaler v R* [1976] 1 SCR 616, 30 CRNS 209, 20 CCC (2d) 449, 53 DLR (3d) 161, 4 NR 277

[Que], and *Dehler v Ottawa Civic Hospital* (1980) 25 OR (2d) 748, 14 CPC 4, 101 DLR (3d) 686, 3 L Med Q 141; affd 29 OR (2d) 677, 117 DLR (3d) 512, leave to appeal to SCC refused [1981] 1 SCR viii], Bill of Rights cases, as follows [at 24–25]:

The *Morgentaler* case entailed an attack on s 251 of the Criminal Code by those who were desirous of avoiding the prescribed procedures whereby unlawful abortions became lawful—by those who advocated abortions without the intervention of therapeutic abortion committees. In *Dehler v Ottawa Civic Hosp* (1980) 25 OR (2d) 748, 14 CPC 4, 101 DLR (3d) 686, 3 L Med Q 141; affd 29 OR (2d) 677, 117 DLR (3d) 512, leave to appeal to SCC refused [1981] 1 SCR viii, however, the attack on s 251 was virtually identical to that by the plantiff. It was alleged in *Dehler* that an unborn person is a human being from the moment of conception, or shortly thereafter, and that abortions result in the killing of innocent human beings without the process of law and the benefit of equality before the law and the full protection of the law. It was also alleged that subss (4), (5) and (6) of s 251 of the Criminal Code are ultra vires the Parliament of Canada as being inconsistent with the Canadian Bill of Rights in depriving unborn persons of the benefit and protection of the fundamental rights of that statute. An attempt was made to distinguish these claims from those considered in *Morgentaler*, but Robins J noted that the social values adopted by Parliament must be accepted, and that the wisdom of the legislation is not a matter into which the judiciary may intrude.

The *Dehler* decision resulted from an application by the defendants to dismiss the action. The plaintiff's claim was dismissed without any evidence ever being adduced, and the decision of Robins J was affirmed by the Ontario Court of Appeal without reasons and an application for leave to appeal to the Supreme Court of Canada was refused.

It is not possible to distinguish the plaintiff's claim, insofar as it relates to the Canadian Bill of Rights, from that asserted in *Dehler*, and on the basis of *Morgentaler* and *Dehler* no other conclusion is permissible but that the plaintiff's attack on subss (4), (5) and (6) of s 251 of the Criminal Code, on the ground that those subsections violate the provisions of the Canadian Bill of Rights, must fail.

As noted in *R v Therens* [1985] 1 SCR 613, [1985] 4 WWR 286, 45 CR (3d) 97, 32 MVR 153, 18 CCC (3d) 481, 18 DLR (4th) 655, 13 CRR 193, 40 Sask R 122, 59 NR 122, such Bill of Rights decisions may be used to assist in interpreting the Charter, although they are of course not determinative.

The learned trial judge, in my view correctly, looked to these decisions for some assistance. They, in my respectful view, point to the same conclusion as an analysis of the history of the rights of the foetus at common law, and suggest also that an interpretation of the Charter which gave independent rights to a foetus would be a major departure from tradition. This is not of course to suggest that such a radical step in recognition of rights could not have been taken. However, since it is so novel, it would suggest that clear and unambiguous wording should have been used to enshrine such rights.

The Supreme Court of Canada is to hear an appeal brought by Mr Borowski. The same court has held that the Canadian abortion legislation (s 251 Criminal Code) is unconstitutional because it offends the Canadian Charter of Rights and Freedoms (*Morgentaler v R* [1988] 1 SCR 30). The court did not deal with the status of the foetus. Instead, the court held that the woman's rights under the Charter were infringed—in particular her right to 'life, liberty and security of the person' (section 7).

Notice that the European Commission in the *Paton* case also considered the father's claim *qua* father under the Convention (footnotes omitted):

25. In its examination of the applicant's complaints concerning the Abortion Act 1967 and its application in this case, the Commission has next had regard to Article 8 of the Convention which, in paragraph (1), guarantees to everyone the right to

respect for his family life. The Commission here notes, apart from his principal complaint concerning the permission of the abortion, the applicant's ancillary submission that the 1967 Act denies the father of the foetus a right to be consulted, and to make applications, about the proposed abortion.

The Commission also observes that the applicant, who under Article 2 claims to be the victim of a violation of the right to life of the foetus of which he was the potential father, under Article 8 invokes a right of his own.

26. As regards the principal complaint concerning the permission of the abortion, the Commission recalls that the pregnancy of the applicant's wife was terminated in accordance with her wish and in order to avert the risk of injury to her physical or mental health. The Commission therefore finds that this decision, in so far as it interfered in itself with the applicant's right to respect for his family life, was justified under paragraph (2) of Article 8 as being necessary for the protection of the rights of another person. It follows that this complaint is also manifestly ill-founded within the meaning of Article 27(2).

27. The Commission has next considered the applicant's ancillary complaint that the Abortion Act 1967 denies the father of the foetus a right to be consulted, and to make applications, about the proposed abortion. It observes that any interpretation of the husband's and potential father's right, under Article 8 of the Convention, to respect for his private and family life, as regards an abortion which his wife intends to have performed on her, must first of all take into account the right of the pregnant woman, being the person primarily concerned in the pregnancy and its continuation or termination, to respect for her private life. The pregnant woman's right to respect for her private life, as affected by the developing foetus, has been examined by the Commission in its Report in the *Brüggemann and Scheuten* case. In the present case the Commission, having regard to the right of the pregnant woman, does not find that the husband's and potential father's right to respect for his private and family life can be interpreted so widely as to embrace such procedural rights as claimed by the applicant, ie a right to be consulted, or a right to make applications, about an abortion which his wife intends to have performed on her. The Commission concludes that this complaint is incompatible *ratione materiae* with the provisions of the Convention within the meaning of Article 27(2).

If it be correct that in law no rights vest in the father or the unborn child, what *locus standi* can a father claim to prevent an abortion? If the abortion is lawful, would he have none? However, what if the claim is based on the assertion that the abortion, if carried out, would be illegal?
League for Life in Manitoba Inc v Morgentaler
[1985] 4 WWR 633 (Manitoba Queens Bench)

Kroft J: The plaintiffs, the League For Life in Manitoba Inc and Patricia Frances Soenen, are proponents of the pro-life position. I do not question that their concern is honest and deeply felt. They have, through the civil process, sued Dr Morgentaler as well as the owners and lessees of the clinic from which he operates in the city of Winnipeg, seeking first a temporary and ultimately a permanent injunction restraining them from procuring or allowing the procuring of the miscarriage of female persons in contravention of s 251 of the Criminal Code.

The right of an attorney general as chief law officer of the Crown to bring proceedings for enforcement of the criminal law, either on his own initiative or ex relatione at the initiative of others, is of course not at issue (although, as will be indicated, the use of the civil injunction, even by an attorney-general, is open to some question). The position of a citizen or group whose interests and status are no different than any other member of the general public is much different and much more difficult.

The motion to strike out the statement of claim is first and foremost an attack on the status of the plaintiffs. Simply put, the defendants say that on the face of the material filed the plaintiffs as private citizens have no standing, and that without standing they have no right to seek injunctive or any other relief.

The question of standing in the present proceedings has two components. Firstly, it must be determined whether the nature of the interest claimed by these particular plaintiffs gives them any right to be parties to these proceedings. Secondly, it must be decided if the statement of claim reveals a justiciable or triable issue. Unless there is an interest which the court recognises, and an issue to be tried, then the defendants are correct in saying that the statement of claim and the entire proceedings should be struck out.

. . .

There is no difficulty in defining the rules that have been traditionally applied to determine whether a citizen, on his own, has sufficient standing and sufficient cause of action to permit him, through a private action, to enforce the public criminal law. Those rules were acknowledged even by counsel for the plaintiff to be quite stringent. There has, however, in recent years, been a trend toward relaxation or liberalisation. Notwithstanding the efforts of Lord Denning, the trend is less marked in Britain than in Canada, probably because we are a federal state, and now because we have the Charter of Rights.

The argument advanced on behalf of the plaintiffs was that the rules in Canada have been, by court decisions, sufficiently changed to justify a conclusion that they have standing and have a good cause of action.

When I speak of traditional rules I do not imply that they are outmoded. They have received recognition by courts of the highest level in Britain, in Canada, and elsewhere. For convenience I will list what I think to be an accurate statement of the criteria to be considered when a member of the public claims that there is a justiciable issue to be tried, and that he is entitled to a restraining order to prevent an anticipated breach of the criminal law.

1. The criminal law creates public not private rights.
2. Public rights can, in appropriate circumstances, be asserted in a civil action by the Attorney General, as the Crown officer who represents the public; or alternatively, by an individual acting with the consent of the Attorney General in a relator action.
3. A private individual may sue in his own name in respect of public rights if he can show that he faces the infringement of some personal right, or that he will suffer special and personal damages.

These principles were recognised in 1977 by the House of Lords in the *Gouriet* case . . .

The *Gouriet* decision ([1978] AC 435) was one in which the British Postal Union threatened to break the law and to impose an embargo on mail to South Africa. The Attorney General refused to take action and Mr Gouriet proceeded on his own. At the Appeal Court level all three judges would have granted an interim injunction while the justiciable issue was being determined; that is, while a declaration with respect to the role of the Attorney General was under consideration. Lord Denning, in a far more forceful way than his colleagues, was prepared to say that when an attorney-general refuses to take action, or delays in respect to a request for a relator action, the court, in an appropriate case, can in effect overrule him, thereby giving the right to any citizen to come directly to court and ask that the criminal law be enforced. That view was explicitly overruled by the House of Lords; and it is the House of Lords which has been followed in the Canadian cases which I mentioned.

It should be noted as well that there are important distinctions between *Gouriet* and the case before us now, so that even the Court of Appeal decisions might not necessarily be applicable here. To begin with, the Attorney General of England had refused to lay charges. In our case two sets of criminal charges have already been laid. Secondly, the majority of the English Court of Appeal, although allowing the interim injunction, did so because there was a separate issue to be tried. There is no such issue here.

Procuring an abortion contrary to s 251 of the Code is a crime in Canada, It has been declared to be such by Parliament and does not require my declaration to confirm it.

It is interesting to note that when the *Island Records* case . . . came before the court in England, one year after *Gouriet*, the same Lord Denning acknowledged the general law to be as I have stated it. He held that a private citizen can enforce the criminal law only where the criminal act is both an offence against the public at large, and also where, at the same time, it causes or threatens to cause special damage to a private individual. No such allegation appears in the statement of claim of the League and Ms Soenen.

. . .

I have given serious consideration and weight to the arguments advanced on behalf of the plaintiffs. Nonetheless, I have reached the conclusion that they do not have the status or standing to maintain their action.

In *Paton*, Sir George Baker P referred to this point (footnotes omitted):

The law relating to injunctions has been considered recently in the House of Lords, in *Gouriet v Union of Post Office Workers*. Many passages from their Lordships' speeches have been cited. I do not propose to go through them because it is now as clear as possible that there must be, first, a legal right in an individual to found an injunction and, second, that the enforcement of the criminal law is a matter for the authorities and for the Attorney-General. As counsel for the husband concedes, any process for the enforcement of the criminal law in a civil suit must be used with great caution, if at all. The private individual may have the right only if his right is greater than the public right, that is to say, that he would suffer personally and more than the general public unless he could restrain this offence. That proposition is not accepted by counsel for the first defendants or by counsel for the wife, and in any event it is not now suggested that the proposed abortion on the wife will be other than lawful. So, it is not necessary for me to decide that question or to consider *Gouriet v Union of Post Office Workers* further.

(See also *Wall v Livingston* [1982] 1 NZLR 734 (NZCA), where it was held that a doctor who was not treating the pregnant woman lacked *locus standi* to challenge the decision of two consultants to authorise an abortion on a teenage girl.)

Given that the whole force of the argument in *C v S* was the alleged illegality of the proposed abortion, how was it that the court was prepared to hear the plaintiff's arguments? All Heilbron J had to say on the matter was:

. . . I have not thought it necessary to add to this already long judgment by considering another hurdle that counsel might have encountered by reason of the decisions with regard to a private individual seeking to prevent the commission of an offence by way of an injunction, following the *Gouriet* line of cases.

Is it not even more intriguing that the Court of Appeal felt inclined to hear argument (and dispose of the case) on the assumption that the father had *locus standi* with not a single reference being made to *Gouriet*?

Was it one of those occasions when the Court of Appeal was tempted to issue a declaratory judgment without wishing to appear to do so?

(b)   To be consulted

There is no English law which precisely covers the question of whether a woman can be obliged in law to consult another, usually identified as her husband or the father of the child (if they be different), before undergoing an abortion.

The American case of *Schienberg v Smith* S D Florida 482 F Supp 529 (1979)) is a rare example of the courts confronting the question (footnotes omitted):

Aronovitz J: Section 458.505(4)(b) seeks to regulate the intrafamial exchange of information on questions relating to childbearing. Specifically, it requires that a married woman, who intends to seek an abortion, give her husband 'notice of the proposed termination of pregnancy and an opportunity to consult ... concerning the procedure.' Furthermore, as a precondition to actually securing the abortion, the wife must provide her attending physician with either:

1) a written statement that such notice and opportunity have been given; or
2) the written consent of her husband.

These requirements apply without regard to the point during the gestation period that the abortion would occur; in other words, they are equally applicable to first, second or third trimester abortions. If the husband and wife are 'separated or estranged', however, the statute contains an express exception rendering the notice requirement inapplicable.
. . .
Specific instances where a woman might desire or choose not to communicate with her husband concerning an impending termination of pregnancy include:

1) where the husband is not the father of the fetus; for instance, where the fetus is the product of an extramarital affair;
2) where the wife has been a rape victim, has not disclosed the incident to her husband, and has subsequently become pregnant;
3) where the husband, because of strong religious or moral precepts, would strenuously object;
4) where the husband is seriously ill or emotionally unstable and is unable to participate in any abortion decision; and
5) where the woman is a 'battered wife' and fears that discussion concerning an abortion may precipitate physical violence.

Dr Good also testified as to what he termed 'skewed relationships.' In such marriages, which Dr Good characterised as not uncommon, the power of the husband is so overwhelming that he will, if consulted, obstruct, or altogether prevent, a woman from freely deciding to secure an abortion. To obviate this possibility, Dr Good testified, many women in these relationships consciously choose not to consult with their spouse.

The testimony further indicated that in instances like those outlined above, the requirement of compulsory notification and consultation will, at the least, produce anxiety and stress for the woman and her marriage. Moreover, where a woman is forced to notify and consult with her husband against her will in order to obtain a legal abortion, she may choose less desirable alternatives. She may delay seeking an abortion, self-abort, or secure an illegal abortion, thereby risking serious, perhaps irreversible consequences.

Based upon the foregoing, the Court concludes that the record from the September 14, 1979 hearing supports a finding that mandatory spousal notice and consultation, with only a limited exception for 'separated or estranged' couples, *places an undue burden* on the right of a substantial number of pregnant women to decide to terminate their pregnancies.

B.

Defendants seek to justify this burden, arguing that the spousal notice and consultation requirement furthers two 'compelling' interests:

1) the state's interest in promoting the marital relationship; and,
2) the husband's interest in the procreative potential of the marriage.

Indeed, both interests are significant. In *Planned Parenthood v Danforth, supra,* the Supreme Court explicitly recognised the legitimacy of a husband's interest in his wife's pregnancy, the state's interest in protecting the marital relationship and the potential impact of an abortion decision on that relationship:

We are not unaware of the deep and proper concern and interest that a devoted and protective husband has in his wife's pregnancy and in the growth and development of the fetus she is carrying. Neither has this Court failed to appreciate the importance of the marital relationship in our society. See, eg,

Griswold v Connecticut, 381 US 479, 486 [85 S Ct 1678, 1682, 14 L Ed 2d 510] (1965); ... Moreover, we recognise that the decision whether to undergo or to forego an abortion may have profound effects on the future of any marriage, effects that are both physical and mental, and possibly deleterious.

Notwithstanding the significance of these interests, the Court in *Danforth* and the Fifth Circuit in *Poe v Gerstein*, found them insufficiently compelling to justify allowing a husband to have an absolute, unilateral veto over the wife's abortion decision. However, neither *Danforth* nor *Poe* considered whether less intrusive measures designed to insure a husband's participation in the abortion decision could, within constitutional contours, be predicated on these interests.

Defendants' reliance upon *Poe* in its effort to elevate a husband's procreative potential in a marriage to a 'compelling' interest is misplaced. As *Poe* points out, *Skinner v Oklahoma*, the seminal case on the fundamentality of procreational rights, 'did not guarantee the individual a procreative opportunity, it merely safeguarded *his* procreative potential from state infringement' by sterilization (emphasis supplied). Since abortion poses no physical threat to a man's personal ability to procreate, there is no fundamental constitutional interest which is safeguarded by the notification and consultation requirement.

The most Defendants can glean from *Poe* is recognition of the husband's 'strong interest' in the potential for having children with his wife. Where, as here, a statute imposes an undue burden upon a woman's constitutional right to choose to terminate her pregnancy, a 'strong' countervailing interest is insufficient justification.

Moreover, the Court questions whether the notice and consultation requirement furthers a husband's interest in the procreative potential of his marriage. The parties presented conflicting expert testimony concerning whether a first trimester abortion creates a substantial risk of loss of fertility in women. However, the testimony uniformly reflected that the consultation requirement might result in weeks of delay which, in turn, might substantially increase the risk of diminished marital procreative potential. Similarly, it should be noted that § 458.505(4)(b), at least in regard to the objective of preserving marital procreative potential, is grossly underinclusive because it does not require that a married woman notify and consult with her husband about an impending hysterectomy or tubal ligation—operations which altogether foreclose marital procreative potential according to expert testimony.

Whether the remaining interest asserted by Defendants would be sufficiently 'compelling' to justify the unduly burdensome nature of § 458.505(4)(b) need not be decided. As laudable as the state's goal of furthering the marital relationship may be, the Court seriously questions whether the mandatory spousal notice and consultation requirement does so and, even assuming it does in a generalised way, § 458.505(4)(b) is not drawn with sufficient particularity 'to express *only* the legitimate state [interest] at stake.'

Most notably, the statute makes no exception for a married woman carrying the child of someone other than her husband (notice is predicated upon husbandry rather than fatherhood). As the uncontroverted expert testimony emphasised, compelling a wife to disclose this fact against her will is a perverse way of promoting marital harmony. Thus, insofar as the statute seeks to promote marital harmony it is overinclusive because it includes husbands who may not have sired the fetus; in short, it 'sweeps too broadly.'

For the reasons elaborated above, the Court finds that Defendants have failed to justify the unduly burdensome nature of § 458.505(4)(b) insofar as it applies to first trimester abortions. The Court emphasises that it does not hold mandatory spousal notice and consultation *per se* unconstitutional. As presently drafted, however, § 458.505(4)(b) fails to conform to constitutional limitations.

If the court considered that there may be circumstances in which a woman *may* notify her husband, what do you think these circumstances can be as a matter of first principle? In a comment which reviews the case and its subsequent fate on appeal and retrial, the author notes that the Court of Appeal for the 5th

Circuit determined that if an abortion presents more than a *de minimis* risk to the procreative capacities of women, the spousal notification statute was constitutional. At the retrial, the judge held that abortion poses less than a *de minimis* risk to the procreative capabilities of women and so held the statute unconstitutional because there was no compelling State interest which justified an interference with the mother's right to an abortion ('Spousal Notification: An Unconstitutional Limitation on A Woman's Right to Privacy in the Abortion Decision', (1984) 12 Hofstra Law Review 531.)

In English law, if there were legislation as there was in Florida, this could only be challenged at one remove before the European Court of Human Rights. Which, if any, article of the Convention could be played in aid?

Alternatively, an English court could be asked to grant an injunction or other remedy at the suit of a husband or father who claims he has a right in law to be *notified* prior to an abortion? How would a court respond?

4.   INVOLVEMENT OF OTHERS IN THE MEDICAL PROCEDURE

The Abortion Act 1967 only applies 'when a pregnancy is terminated by a registered medical practitioner . . .' (section 1(1)). In *Royal College of Nursing of United Kingdom v Department of Health and Social Security* [1981] AC 800, [1981] 1 All ER 545, the House of Lords interpreted this provision. Although dissenting (along with Lord Edmund-Davies) Lord Wilberforce, sets out the medical background to the case.

> There is an agreed statement as to the nature of this treatment and the part in it played by the doctors and the nurses or midwives. Naturally this may vary somewhat from hospital to hospital, but, for the purpose of the present proceedings, the assumption has to be made of maximum nurse participation, ie that the nurse does everything which the doctor is not required to do. If that is not illegal, participation of a lesser degree must be permissible.
>
> 1. The first step is for a thin catheter to be inserted via the cervix into the womb so as to arrive at, or create, a space between the wall of the womb and the amniotic sac containing the fetus. This is necessarily done by a doctor. It may, sometimes, of itself bring an abortion, in which case no problem arises: the pregnancy will have been terminated by the doctor. If it does not, all subsequent steps except no 4 may be carried out by a nurse or midwife. The significant steps are as follows (I am indebted to Brightman LJ for their presentation):
>
> 2. The catheter (ie the end emerging from the vagina) is attached, probably via another tube, to a pump or to a gravity feed apparatus. The function of the pump or apparatus is to propel or feed the prostaglandin through the catheter into the womb. The necessary prostaglandin infusion is provided and put into the apparatus.
>
> *3. The pump is switched on, or the drip valve is turned, thus causing the prostaglandin to enter the womb.
>
> 4. The doctor inserts a cannula into a vein.
>
> *5. An oxytocin drip feed is linked up with the cannula. The necessary oxytocin (a drug designed to help the contractions) is supplied for the feed.
>
> 6. The patient's vital signs are monitored; so is the rate of drip or flow.
>
> *7. The flow rates of both infusions are, as necessary, adjusted.
>
> *8. Fresh supplies of both infusions are added as necessary.
>
> 9. The treatment is discontinued after discharge of the fetus, or expiry of a fixed period (normally 30 hours) after which the operation is considered to have failed.
>
> The only steps in this process which can be considered to have a direct effect leading to abortion (abortifacient steps) are those asterisked. They are all carried out by the nurse, or midwife. As the agreed statement records 'the causative factor in inducing . . . the termination of pregnancy is the effect of the administration of prostaglandin and/or oxytocin and not any mechanical effect from the insertion of the catheter or cannula'.

All the above steps 2 to 9 are carried out in accordance with the doctor's instructions, which should, as regards important matters, be in writing. The doctor will moreover be on call, but may in fact never be called.

On these facts the question has to be answered: has the pregnancy been terminated by the doctor; or has it been terminated by the nurse; or has it been terminated by doctor and nurse? I am not surprised that the nurses feel anxiety as to this.

The majority's view is stated in the speeches of Lords Diplock and Roskill.

Lord Diplock: My Lords, the wording and structure of [section 1 of the Abortion Act 1967] are far from elegant, but the policy of the Act, it seems to me, is clear. There are two aspects to it: the first is to broaden the grounds on which abortions may be lawfully obtained; the second is to ensure that the abortion is carried out with all proper skill and in hygienic conditions. Subsection (1) which deals with the termination of pregnancies other than in cases of dire emergency consists of a conditional sentence of which a protasis, which is a condition precedent to be satisfied in order to make the abortion lawful at all, is stated last: 'if two registered medical practitioners are of the opinion etc'. It is this part of the subsection which defines the circumstances which qualify a woman to have pregnancy terminated lawfully. . . .

The requirement of the Act as to the way in which the treatment be carried out, which in my view throws most light on the second aspect of its policy and the true construction of the phrase in sub-s (1) of s 1 which lies at the root of the dispute between the parties to this appeal, is the requirement in sub-s (3) that, except in cases of dire emergency, the treatment must be carried out in a national health service hospital (or private clinic specifically approved for that purpose by the minister). It is in my view evident that, in providing that treatment for termination of pregnancies should take place in ordinary hospitals Parliament contemplated that (conscientious objections apart) like other hospital treatment, it would be undertaken as a team effort in which, acting on the instructions of the doctor in charge of the treatment, junior doctors, nurses, paramedical and other members of the hospital staff would each do those things forming part of the whole treatment which it would be in accordance with accepted medical practice to entrust to a member of the staff possessed of their respective qualifications and experience.

Subsection (1) although it is expressed to apply only 'when a pregnancy is terminated by a registered medical practitioner' (the subordinate clause that although introduced by 'when' is another protasis and has caused the differences of judicial opinion in the instant case) also appears to contemplate treatment that is in the nature of a team effort and to extend its protection to all those who play a part in it. The exoneration from guilt is not confined to the registered medical practitioner by whom a pregnancy is terminated, it extends to any person who takes part in the treatment for its termination.

What limitation on this exoneration is imposed by the qualifying phrase, 'when a pregnancy is terminated by a registered medical practitioner'? In my opinion, in the context of the Act, what it requires is that a registered medical practitioner, whom I will refer to as a doctor, should accept responsibility for all stages of the treatment for the termination of the pregnancy. The particular method to be used should be decided by the doctor in charge of the treatment for termination of the pregnancy; he should carry out any physical acts, forming part of the treatment, that in accordance with accepted medical practice are done only by qualified medical practitioners, and should give specific instructions as to the carrying out of such parts of the treatment as in accordance with accepted medical practice are carried out by nurses or other members of the hospital staff without medical qualifications. To each of them, the doctor, or his substitute, should be available to be consulted or called on for assistance from beginning to end of the treatment, In other words, the doctor need not do everything with his own hands; the requirements of the subsection are satisfied when the treatment for termination of a pregnancy is one prescribed by a registered medical practitioner carried out in accordance with his directions and of which a registered medical practitioner remains in charge throughout.

My noble and learned friend Lord Wilberforce has described the successive steps taken in the treatment for termination of pregnancies in the third trimester by medical induction; and the parts played by registered medical practitioners and nurses respectively in the carrying out of the treatment. This treatment satisfies the interpretation that I have placed on the requirements of s 1 of the Act. I would accordingly allow the appeal and restore the declaration made by Woolf J.

Lord Roskill: . . . the crucial issue is whether 'a pregnancy is terminated by a registered medical practitioner' assuming, as of course I do for present purposes, that the other prerequisites of s 1(1) of the 1967 Act are also satisfied. If a narrow meaning is given to the phrase I have just quoted, then it is the nurse and not the doctor who terminates the pregnancy. If that be right the doctor and the nurse are each guilty of a separate offence against the 1861 Act, the nurse because she is carrying out an abortion when she is not a doctor and the doctor because he is attempting to carry out an abortion when he engages in the first step which is not authorised by the 1967 Act. In addition, he is aiding and abetting the nurse's offence and both, and maybe others as well, are guilty of conspiracy to infringe the 1861 Act. This is the position which the Royal College of Nursing feared might arise and which led them to institute the present proceedings on behalf of the nursing profession in order that the question whether or not their profession are, in these circumstances, entitled to the protection of the 1967 Act might be finally determined.
. . .

My Lords, I read and reread the 1967 Act to see if I can discern in its provisions any consistent pattern in the use of the phrase 'a pregnancy is terminated' or 'termination of a pregnancy' on the one hand and 'treatment for the termination of a pregnancy' on the other hand. One finds the former phrase in s 1(1) and (1)(*a*), the latter in s 1(3), the former in ss 1(4) and 2(1)(*b*) and the latter in s 3(1)(*a*) and (*c*). Most important to my mind is s 4, which is the conscientious objection section. This section in two places refers to 'participate in treatment' in the context of conscientious objection. If one construes s 4 in conjunction with s 1(1), as surely one should do in order to determine to what it is that conscientious objection is permitted, it seems to me that s 4 strongly supports the wider construction of s 1(1). It was suggested that acceptance of the department's submission involved rewriting that subsection so as to add words which are not to be found in the language of the subsection. My Lords, with great respect to that submission. I do not agree. If one construes the words 'when a pregnancy is terminated by a registered medical practitioner' in s 1(1) as embracing the case where the 'treatment for the termination of a pregnancy is carried out under the control of a doctor in accordance with ordinary current medical practice' I think one is reading 'termination of pregnancy' and 'treatment for termination of pregnancy' as virtually synonymous and as I think Parliament must have intended they should be read. Such a construction avoids a number of anomalies as, for example, where there is no pregnancy or where the extra-amniotic process fails to achieve its objective within the normal limits of time set for its operation. . . . I think that the successive steps taken by a nurse in carrying out the extra-amniotic process are fully protected provided that the entirety of the treatment for the termination of the pregnancy and her participation in it is at all times under the control of the doctor even though the doctor is not present throughout the entirety of the treatment.

5. ABORTION AND YOUNG GIRLS

The issues raised here are: (i) at what age may a young girl validly consent to an abortion?; (ii) is such consent both necessary and sufficient for a lawful abortion to be carried out, provided it would otherwise be within the Abortion Act?; (iii) to what extent may others, whether as parents, guardians or the court in wardship, have authority to consent to an abortion?

If abortion is no different from other forms of medical treatment in principle, then we have considered these issues in Chapter 4. [For cases dealing specifically with abortion, see: *C v Wren* (1987) 35 DLR (4th) 419 (Alberta CA); *Re P* (*a minor*) (1981) 80 LGR 301 (Butler-Sloss J)].

6. ABORTION PROCEDURES RAISING SPECIAL PROBLEMS

As we saw earlier, post-coital birth control by recourse to the 'morning after pill' or an IUD (an intra-uterine device) can only be regarded in law as birth control rather than abortion provided that the procedure is carried out before a fertilised egg is implanted in the uterus and not done with the intent to procure a miscarriage. (See the discussion *ante*, Ch 7.)

(a) Early abortions?

More problematical for our purposes is the procedure known as menstrual extraction or aspiration. As regards this procedure, Tunkel writes ((1979) BMJ 'Abortion: how early, how late and how legal?', footnotes omitted):

> ... In view of the legal uncertainties, a doctor who regularly performed menstrual extraction (a convenient but question-begging euphemism) might until recently have thought it best to play safe by complying hypothetically with the Abortion Act, although the girl's pregnancy, if any, cannot at such an early stage be diagnosed, it would be prudent to certify as for a termination, and certainly to notify if the pregnancy was subsequently confirmed histologically.

The DPP and Mr Goldthorp

One such practitioner was Mr W O Goldthorp, the Manchester consultant gynaecologist, who in an article in the *BMJ* described how he performed menstrual extractions from 10 to 18 days after a missed period. The Chief Constable of Manchester referred the matter to the Director of Public Prosecutions. Early in 1978 the DPP expressed the opinion that menstrual extraction in these circumstances was illegal, and that purported compliance with the Abortion Act made no difference. Mr Goldthorp thereupon ceased these extractions.

The DPP's opinion was based on his understanding of the Abortion Act, which gives protection to doctors 'when a pregnancy is terminated'. This was understood by the Lane Committee to exclude 'speculative' operations, done before the existence of a pregnancy could be known. To fill this gap the committee proposed that the Act be amended by adding a new subsection: 'In this Act references to termination of pregnancy include acts done with intent to terminate a pregnancy if such exists', but there has been no legislation to implement this. And since the Act in s 5(2) states categorically that 'anything done with intent to procure the miscarriage of a woman is unlawfully done unless authorised by section 1 of this Act', it seems to be a simple either/or choice. The DPP gave a further reason for his opinion: no doctor could hold the opinion in good faith, as required by the Act, that there was a risk to the woman or the child in the continuance of the pregnancy if he did not know that she was in fact pregnant.

If to some medical readers there seems an excessive literalism in these reasons it would be as well for them to realise that this is for better or worse part of our legal tradition in the interpretation of statutes. It serves to emphasise the importance of focusing on the actual words used by Parliament and not accepting some widely repeated paraphrase or believed meaning. We return to this point below. But on the question of menstrual extraction there is now further news: the DPP subsequently had his mind changed by his superiors, the Law Officers (the Attorney-General and Solicitor-General). In March 1979 they expressed the opinion (giving no reasons) that what Mr Goldthorp described in his article was protected by the Abortion Act; and that the Act's references to termination of pregnancy should be understood as including steps taken to terminate a pregnancy which two practitioners in good faith believe to exist.

In this unsatisfactory state of affairs it is difficult to say with confidence what the law is. If Mr Goldthorp or others have resumed these extractions there could be a test case, as the Lane Committee suggested. For the present we have the reasoned opinion of the DPP that the operations are illegal in all circumstances and the later bald statement of the Law Officers that words may be read into the Abortion Act, which would make them legal. (It is perhaps worth adding that the words suggested by the Law Officers might in any event still not confer protection, since the two practitioners do not positively 'believe a pregnancy to exist' if they merely think that there is a chance it might. The Lane Committee's amendment is much clearer; but it would take a bold judge to read that into the unamended Act.)

Would a criminal court today adopt the DPP's opinion or the Law Officers' second thoughts? The answer—or rather the question—is complicated by the fact that, although anyone may bring a prosecution for abortion, the police have to inform the DPP. He is thus given an opportunity to intervene, but he is subject to the control of the Law Officers. And, while the DPP who gave the anti-Goldthorp opinion is still in the saddle, the Law Officers who overrode him changed with the Government in May. Here, then, is rich material—medical, legal, and political—for those who enjoy speculating on current affairs. But it would be well to keep in mind what we are pondering: the prospect of prosecuting highly respected medical men. Their crime (maximum penalty, life imprisonment) is their open and ethical performance, with skill and success, of routine procedures at just the time when these are medically most desirable. Should there be even a shadow of criminality over this situation?

This is not all. Even given that the Law Officers were right and there is no longer any question of these early postcoital extractions being regarded as criminal, this exemption is achieved only by complying with the Abortion Act. The effect of this is to declare all non-statutory extraction criminal where the operator thinks, even erroneously, that the woman might be pregnant. Now however satisfied he may be with his diagnosis of, say, amenorrhoea, would not an honest practitioner admit that there is almost always a chance that he may be mistaken, may perhaps have been misled by his patient, and that possibly she has a very early pregnancy? If he thinks that this is a possibility then even though he does not believe it to be so, he extracts intending to remove the contents of the uterus, including any conception that may be present. It would seem odd (and perhaps even insulting to the patient) to insist on certifying under the Abortion Act in such a case. But if he does not, s 58 is inescapable: '. . .whosoever, with intent to procure the miscarriage of any woman, whether she be or be not with child, shall unlawfully use any instrument . . . shall be guilty . . .'. Perhaps the ultimate irony is that it is immaterial that she was never in fact pregnant at all. The crime is committed because of his conditional intent.

To summarise: if this account of the present law is correct, it follows that in all cases where very early, undiagnosable, pregnancy is a possibility, (1) no doctor is safe to perform a menstrual extraction, for whatever reason, without complying with the Abortion Act; and possibly also—(2) even with such compliance there may still be an offence.

Which view better reflects the law: that of the (then) DPP and the Lane Committee or the (then) Law Officers? Since then, the House of Lords in the *Royal College of Nursing* case (*supra*) has given its mind to the central question which is the meaning of the words in the Abortion Act of 'when a pregnancy is terminated'. Lord Wilberforce (who dissented in the final decision) stated that:

The argument for the department is carried even further than this, for it is said that the words 'when a pregnancy is terminated by a registered medical practitioner' mean 'when treatment for the termination of pregnancy is carried out by a registered medical practitioner'. This is said to be necessary in order to cover the supposed cases where the treatment is unsuccessful, or where there is no pregnancy at all. The latter hypothesis I regard as fanciful; the former, if it was Parliament's contemplation at all in 1967 (for failures under post-1967 methods are not in point), cannot be covered by any reasonable reading of the words. Termination is one thing; attempted and unsuccessful termination wholly another. I cannot be persuaded to embark on a radical reconstruction of the Act by reference to a fanciful hypothesis or an improbable casus omissus.

Lord Diplock, on the other hand, took a different view:

> . . .[I]f 'termination' or 'terminated' meant only the event of miscarriage and not the whole treatment undertaken with that object in mind, lack of success, which apparently occurs in 1% to 2% of cases, would make all who had taken part in the unsuccessful treatment guilty of an offence under s 58 or s 59 of the Offences against the Person Act 1861. This cannot have been the intention of Parliament.

Lord Edmund-Davies, while agreeing with Lord Diplock in his conclusion, took a somewhat different line:

> In the foreground was the submission that, were a termination of pregnancy embarked on when (as it turned out) the woman was not pregnant, the Act would afford no defence to a doctor prosecuted under the 1861 Act. And it was secondly urged that he would be equally defenceless even where he personally treated a pregnant woman throughout if, for some reason, the procedure was interrupted and the pregnancy not terminated. I have respectfully to say that in my judgment it is these objections which are themselves absurd. Lawful termination under the Act predicates the personal services of a doctor operating in s 1(3) premises and armed with the opinion of two medical practitioners. But where termination is nevertheless not achieved the appellants invite this House to contemplate the doctor and his nursing staff being prosecuted under s 58 of the 1861 Act, the charge being, of course, not the unlawful termination of pregnancy (for *ex hypothesi* there was *no* termination) but one of unlawfully administering a noxious thing or unlawfully using an instrument with intent to procure miscarriage. And on *that* charge unlawfulness has still to be established and the prosecution would assuredly fail. For the circumstances predicated themselves establish the absence of any mens rea in instituting the abortive treatment, and its initial lawfulness could not be rendered unlawful either by the discovery that the woman was not in fact pregnant or by non-completion of the abortive treatment. Were it otherwise, the unavoidable conclusion is that doctors and nurses could in such cases be convicted of what in essence would be the extraordinary crime of attempting to do a *lawful* act.
>
> My Lords, it was after drafting the foregoing that I happened on the following passage in Smith and Hogan's Criminal Law (4th Edn, 1978, p 346) which I now gratefully adopt, for it could not be more apposite:
>
> > . . . the legalisation of an abortion must include the steps which are taken towards it. Are we really to say that these are criminal until the operation is complete, when they are retrospectively authorised, or alternatively that they are lawful until the operation is discontinued or the woman is discovered not to be pregnant when, retrospectively, they become unlawful? When the conditions of the Act are otherwise satisfied, it is submitted that [the doctor] is not unlawfully administering, etc., and that this is so whether the pregnancy be actually terminated or not.

Which of their Lordships' views do you think represents the law?

(b) Selective reduction

Another procedure, which may arguably be an abortion, has caused controversy. This is the procedure known as 'selective reduction'. This, to quote the description of the Voluntary Licensing Authority in its 3rd Report (April 1988), in Annex 5:

> . . . is the term used to describe the procedure whereby one or more embryos in a multiple pregnancy are selectively killed to allow others to develop. In multiple pregnancies resulting from infertility treatment the procedure is used to avoid large multiple births though the technique was originated to stop the development of abnormal embryos in a multiple pregnancy where the remainder were normal.

The potentially crucial factual distinction between this procedure and other abortions is that when selective reduction is performed the destroyed foetus is absorbed into the mother's body and is not expelled. Is selective reduction lawful? This requires us to consider two questions: (1) does the procedure come within the offence under s 58 of the Offences Against the Person Act 1861 of acting 'with intent to procure a miscarriage'?; and, if it does, (2) would compliance with the terms of the Abortion Act 1967 render it lawful?

(i) The s 58 argument

Two inter-related arguments are put here to determine whether the procedure falls within s 58. First, is the medical practitioner acting with intent to procure a *miscarriage*, and secondly, is he terminating a pregnancy?

One commentator has taken the view that the procedure may come within s 58, namely I J Keown in 'Selective Reduction of Multiple Pregnancy' (1987) NLJ 1165.

> The first argument is that there is no need to invoke the protection of the Abortion Act since selective reduction is not prohibited by s 58. The argument runs that s 58 prohibits acts done with intent to procure miscarriage; that the word 'miscarriage' presupposes the expulsion of the fetus from the uterus, and that since selective reduction, which is performed in early pregnancy, results not in the expulsion of the fetus but in its absorption by the uterus, the procedure is not caught by the section.
>
> In support of this line of argument could be cited the many definitions of 'miscarriage', both medical and legal, which refer to the expulsion[1] of the fetus from the uterus or to the emptying[2] of the uterus. Against this, it may be argued that such definitions are sufficiently broad to include cases of termination of pregnancy followed by fetal absorption. In any event there is no evidence (either from medical practice or from the conduct of prosecutions for criminal abortion) that these definitions exclude such cases, nor is there any reason why they should do so. On the contrary, it has long been accepted by both medical and legal authorities that 'miscarriage' pertains not to the destination of the fetal remains but to the failure of gestation.
>
> **Defining miscarriage**
> In 1882, for example, a leading medical dictionary defined 'miscarriage' as the 'Interruption of gestation before the fetus has become viable'.[3] More significantly, legal authorities have defined the word sufficiently broadly to include the failure of gestation without subsequent fetal expulsion. In the Australian case of *R v Trim*, a case on s 62 of the Crimes Act 1928—the equivalent of s 58—decided by the Full Court of the Supreme Court of Victoria, Marfarlan J stated that s 62 merely required 'an intent to cause in the case of the woman in question the event of birth, carriage or bearing which would take place in the ordinary course of nature to go amiss—go wrong or fail'.[4]
>
> Again, Professor Glanville Williams defines the offence of abortion as follows: 'Abortion (or miscarriage) . . . may be deliberately induced, when it is a serious crime. For legal purposes, abortion means feticide: the *intentional* destruction of the fetus in the womb, or any untimely delivery brought about with intent to cause the death of the fetus'.[5]
>
> In addition to these broad definitions of miscarriage, which indicate that s 58 prohibits the termination of pregnancy even if the fetus is not thereafter expelled, it is relevant to point to the mischief against which the section is directed, namely, the destruction of the unborn child. As Professor Williams wrote in 1958:
>> both English law and the law of the great majority of the United States regard any interference with pregnancy, however early it may take place, as criminal, unless for therapeutic reasons. The fetus is a human life to be protected by the criminal law from the moment when the ovum is fertilised.[6]
>
> It is also possible that a subsidiary purpose of s 58 was to protect women from the dangers of attempted abortion.[7] Clearly, both purposes would be frustrated by an interpretation of 'miscarriage' which would allow anyone to attempt abortion provided the intention was to cause the fetus to be absorbed and not expelled.
>
> A second argument against the need to comply with the Abortion Act 1967 is that in aborting a fetus in a multiple pregnancy the intention of the operator is not to

cause the miscarriage of the woman but to ensure the better carriage of the remaining fetuses. With respect, this argument too founders on the established meaning of 'miscarriage' and on the mischief against which s 58 is directed. The section is infringed whether the woman miscarries of all the fetuses or only of one.

Notes to extract

[1] See eg John Ramsbotham *Practical Observations in Midwifery* (2nd ed, 1842) 376; *Queen-Empress v Ademma [1886] ILR IX Mad 369, 370*, cited in I J Keown, '"*Miscarriage': A Medico-Legal Analysis' [1984] Crim LR 604, 609*, an article which considers the definition of 'miscarriage' in relation to the use of pre-implantation methods of fertility control.

[2] See eg *Taylor's Principles and Practice of Medical Jurisprudence* (6th ed, 1910, ed Fred J Smith) II, 142; *R v Trim* [1943] VLR 109, 116.

[3] Richard Quain (ed), *A Dictionary of Medicine* (1882) Pt III, 992.

[4] [1943] VLR 109, 112. See also *Munah binti Ali v Public Prosecutor* (1958) 24 MLR 159, 160, CA ('causes a woman with child to miscarry' means to cause her to lose from the womb prematurely the products of conception').

[5] *Textbook of Criminal Law* (2nd ed, 1983) 292. (Emphasis in original) See also *ibid*, 290; 'Abortion' in *Black's Law Dictionary* (5th ed, 1979) 7. Similarly, Victor Tunkel has written, 'the use of the word "miscarriage" has always been understood to include any fatal interference with the fertilised ovum'. 'Modern Anti-Pregnancy Techniques and the Criminal Law' [1974] Crim LR 461, 465. See also the Report of the Peel Advisory Group on the Use of Fetuses and Fetal Material for Research, (1972) 4 para 21(a).

[6] *The Sanctity of Life and the Criminal Law* (1958) 141. See generally Keown, *loc cit* n 1, *supra*, 613.

[7] See generally I J Keown, *Abortion, Doctors and the Law* (Cambridge University Press, forthcoming) ch 2.

D P T Price in 'Selective Reduction and Feticide: The Parameters of Abortion' [1988] Criminal Law Review 199, explains (only to reject) another argument:

The other argument put forward by fertility specialists in favour of the legality of selective reduction *per se* is that they have not by their action terminated the pregnancy. It still continues by virtue of the fact that one or more foetuses still survive. Admittedly on one interpretation of that phrase this does appear to be true, although it might be countered that the expressions multiple pregnancy and multipregnancy themselves admit the existence of more than one pregnancy. However, one should bear in mind that the words 'termination of pregnancy' do not in fact appear in the 1861 Act but only in the Abortion Act 1967, ie not in the statute creating the offence but only in the statute containing an exclusion of liability. It cannot be supposed that it was the intention of Parliament when passing either Act that it should be lawful to terminate the development of a foetus or foetuses forming part of a multiple pregnancy, especially as techniques for selective termination of pregnancy are of such recent origin. Such foetuses not 'capable of being born alive' would then be denied any protection whatsoever under the criminal law. Whether the purpose of the law is seen as the protection of the mother, the protection of the foetus, or both, there can be no justification for drawing a distinction between single pregnancies and multipregnancies. The potential for life has equally been taken away, and there has additionally been a physical intrusion upon the mother.

(ii) The Abortion Act 1967 argument

The arguments of Keown and Price are compelling. However, Price's argument has further implications. If selective reduction falls within s 58 then it may only be carried out lawfully if done in compliance with the terms of the Abortion Act 1967. But, Price's argument would lead to the conclusion that the 1967 Act does not apply. If this is so, then the procedure can never be performed, since 'anything done with intent to procure the miscarriage of a woman is unlawfully done unless authorised by' the 1967 Act (section 5(2)).

In an opinion appended to the Voluntary Licensing Authority's 3rd Report, John Keown puts this point as follows:

As the better view is therefore that selective reduction is caught by section 58, the doctor would be well advised to comply with the requirements of the Abortion Act 1967 to render the procedure lawful. Compliance with the Abortion Act may, however, be ineffective. This is because the Act only affords protection when, in the words of section 1(1) 'a pregnancy is terminated'. As selective reduction results in the destruction of one or more but not all the fetuses, a court might rule that it does not terminate a pregnancy, and that compliance with the Abortion Act is ineffective.

Do you think a court would interpret s 1(1) of the 1967 Act in the way John Keown suggests, bearing in mind the words of Lord Diplock in the *Royal College of Nursing* case (*supra*) that the Act: 'started its parliamentary life as a private member's Bill and, maybe for that reason, it lacks the style and consistency of draftsmanship both internal to the Act itself and in relation to other statutes which one would expect to find in legislation that had its origin in the office of parliamentary counsel'?

Equally is Keown's view consistent with the approval of the majority of the judges in the Court of Appeal in *R v Salford Area Health Authority, ex p Janaway* [1988] 2 WLR 442 that section 1(1) of the 1967 Act creates a defence whenever an offence would have been committed under section 58 of the 1861 Act but for the existence of the 1967 Act? Do you think that the House of Lords' decision in the *Janaway* case (*supra* at p 754) rejecting this view of the proper interpretation of the Act makes Keown's argument more likely to succeed in a court?

7. PROPOSALS FOR REFORM

Proposals for reforms have concentrated on two areas: the grounds on which an abortion may lawfully be carried out and the time limit beyond which an abortion may not lawfully be carried out, save where the mother's life is in immediate danger—an exception which meets with general approval.

(a) The grounds

The following passage from the Lane Committee Report of 1974 (paras 200–211; footnote omitted) sets the scene for us:

The majority of notified abortions in England and Wales are carried out on the grounds of risk of injury to the mental or physical health of the mother. In 1971 these amounted to 76.4 per cent of all abortions: only 2 per cent were on the grounds of risk to life. The next largest single category was that of risk of injury to the physical or mental health of existing children: this was 3.3 per cent of the total number of abortions, but in combination with other grounds accounted for 16.3 per cent of the total. Only 1.1 per cent of all abortions were performed upon the ground of risk of the child being seriously handicapped . . .

There is no categorisation of the nature of the injury of which there is a risk. A few of our correspondents have suggested that there should be such categorisation in order, on the one hand, to assist doctors in the difficult task of decision-making and, on the other hand, to check the activities of some doctors who perform abortions without due regard to the requirements of the Act. A larger number of those who have sent us their views consider that such categorisation would be undesirable and unworkable. They point out the great detail which would be necessary, especially in psychiatric disorders, if cases appropriate for abortion were not to be excluded; the likelihood of repeated alteration being required as medical knowledge advanced and the fact that a particular condition may be of greater gravity and significance in one patient than in another. We accept this view and consider that allowing the exercise of wide medical discretion is the only practicable way of working the Act. But this is not to say that the problems mentioned by the former correspondents do not exist: they do.

201. As to the risk of death of the pregnant woman, there are official statistics which show that proportionately more maternal deaths occur from childbirth than from first-trimester abortion (both figures being low and decreasing over the last 40 or so years in this country) . . . This is seen by some doctors and others as justifying early abortion in every case in which it is sought. It has been suggested that there is no such thing as an abortion which is illegal for lack of grounds, since the published mortality figures show that early abortion is the lesser risk. We do not accept this argument. The statistically established risk must be taken into account, but the decision must be made on the facts and probabilities in the individual case. We regard as wholly unethical the practice, which we have been told exists among a few doctors, of signing Certificate A without even seeing the patient, in reliance on the statistical argument to justify doing so. . . . Further we consider it improper, when making decisions as to abortion to rely solely upon the maternal mortality statistics, which are in any case based on very small numbers of deaths, and to disregard the risks of morbidity. . . . Moreover some practitioners interpret the Act to mean that, because a pregnancy which is unwanted can cause injury to the health of the mother such as is not caused when a pregnancy is accepted, and because termination will eliminate any risk of injury to health arising during the continuance of the pregnancy or at or after child-birth, the risk of continuance must be greater than the risk of termination and therefore termination is permissible in every case. In our view this again is an unacceptable argument. What we understand the Act to intend, and what we consider to be essential, is an evaluation of the comparative risks of termination and non-termination in each individual case, taking into account the woman's age, parity and length of gestation, and other relevant factors. It is difficult in many cases to estimate the likelihood of ill-health arising as a result of the continuance of a pregnancy or of the birth of a child, whether the woman is seeking abortion or not, but it seems to us that some positive indication of such a likelihood should be found before any decision to terminate is taken.

202. We have received many criticisms of the wording in section 1(1)(*a*) of the Act "risk . . . greater than if the pregnancy were terminated'. It has been attacked as being vague and meaningless and as providing an excuse for the arguments mentioned in the preceding paragraph: it is said to have defeated the very purpose for which it was introduced, by amendment of the Bill when it was before Parliament, which purpose we understand to have been to quantify the degree of risk justifying abortion. Some of those who have expressed such views have suggested the deletion of the words '. . . greater than if the pregnancy were terminated' and the addition of adjectives describing the risk, such as 'substantial' (which appears in section 1(2)) or 'grave' (which appears in section 1(4)) or 'serious'; others have urged that the wording be left as it is. We do not consider that any such alterations in the wording would result in a better implementation of the intention of Parliament as we understand it to have been. Prosecution for breaches of the Act based upon an absence of medical 'opinion formed in good faith' would hardly be rendered any less difficult than it is now if other limiting words were substituted. Accordingly, we do not recommend any relevant amendment of the Act.

203. A provision of the Act which has come in for criticism is section 1(2), which provides that:

> In determining whether the continuance of pregnancy would involve such risk of injury to health as is mentioned in paragraph (*a*) of subsection (1) of this section, account may be taken of the pregnant woman's actual or reasonably foreseeable environment.

The opening words make it clear that the relevance of environment is for the purpose of ascertaining the risk of injury to health and we cannot suggest any alternative wording which would make the meaning plainer. But there is no doubt that, as the critics point out, the subsection is regarded by many people within, as well as outside, the medical profession as meaning that an undesirable environmental situation of the mother of itself suffices to justify abortion. In some instances, evidence we have received, while not critical of the subsection, differentiates between medical grounds and 'social grounds' in such a way as to show that both 'grounds' are considered to be valid.

204. One of the main difficulties in applying the statutory criteria for abortion under section 1(1) of the Act is to decide whether bearing an unwanted child is of itself likely to cause ill-health or not. So far as we can determine, in a large proportion of the abortions performed, the seriousness of the situation is such that the woman's health would probably be affected if the pregnancy were allowed to continue; affected, that is, by her distress rather than by any immediate physical consequences of the pregnancy. We are not referring here to cases where, due to heart or kidney conditions or other physical diseases or disabilities, injury is ascertainably likely to result and which are so obviously cases for abortion that they not do need discussion in this context.

205. The birth of an additional child to a woman afflicted by ill-health, or living in conditions of poverty or bad housing, may cause such a deterioration in her situation that not only her health but that of any existing children is likely to be injured. . . . There are undoubtedly many cases in which mothers in difficult circumstances manage to struggle along more or less successfully with their existing children but where a further child would cause disaster.

206. On the other hand, investigation of a pregnant woman's circumstances may reveal that although there would be some deterioration in her situation or that of any existing children she may have, no resultant ill-health is likely. Continuing with an unwanted pregnancy may interfere with a woman's present or future career, or way of life, whether she be married or single, but her physical and mental health may be unaffected. Not every threat of suicide or forecast of disaster has to be taken at its face value. There are patients who may exaggerate their symptoms and make threats and forecasts of disaster, the effect of which may draw attention to real problems which they have.

207. The point we desire to emphasise here, as elsewhere, is the need for investigation and evaluation of the attendant risks of the individual pregnancy. There is no justification for performing abortions merely because inconvenience would otherwise result. . . .

208. We have heard of occasional requests being made for cytological examination to determine the sex of the fetus and for abortion to be performed if the fetus is not of the desired sex, there being no question of a sex-linked defect. The making of such requests is perhaps an example of ignorance or disregard of the terms of the Act on the part of some members of the public. We have no evidence of such a request being granted. Plainly, in such circumstances and in the absence of grounds under the Act, abortion would be illegal and could not be too strongly condemned.

209. Finally, we refer to section 1(1)(b) of the Act which legalises abortion where there is 'a substantial risk that if the child were born it would suffer from such physical or mental abnormalities as to be seriously handicapped'. We have received some evidence and some comment upon this subsection, including in relation to a small number of tragic cases, particularly those of older women, where a seriously handicapped child has been born after a mother's request for abortion has been refused.

210. Research has been, and is being, undertaken into the antenatal diagnosis of fetal abnormalities, but it is as yet possible to diagnose only a small number of these abnormalities early enough in pregnancy to perform an abortion. With advances in the techniques of amniotic cell culture and of examination of the chromosomes and biochemical properties of the cells, it is hoped that more of these conditions will be detected at an earlier stage. Other genetic conditions which are not detectable by these methods, are known to have certain hereditary patterns and it is possible, with a knowledge of the family history, to calculate the chance of such a condition occurring. There are now about 35 Genetic Advisory Centres in Great Britain, available for consultation by doctors and by parents, this being a highly specialised area of advancing medical and scientific expertise.

211. The decision to be made as to abortion under section 1(1)(b) by the mother and father and the medical advisers may be among the most difficult under the Act,

for example where it is known that there is a risk but that it is not of a high order. We do not think that it would be appropriate to try to define this statutory ground more precisely and we make no recommendation with regard to the wording of the subsection.

Recommendations
(1) That the wording of the Act laying down the criteria for abortion be left unamended.
(2) That the criteria be applied and the risks to health weighed in each individual case and that the decision be not made in reliance solely upon generalisations, theories or statistics.

One legislative proposal directed to amending the grounds was the private member's Bill introduced by John Corrie MP in 1979 (the 'Corrie Bill'). The Abortion Act 1967 would have read as follows *if the Bill had been passed* (proposed amendments shown in italics).

1.—(1) Subject to the provisions of this section, a person shall not be guilty of an offence under the law relating to abortion when a pregnancy is terminated by a registered medical practitioner if two registered medical practitioners are of the opinion, formed in good faith, *that the pregnancy has lasted for less than twenty weeks and—*
    (a) *that the continuance of the pregnancy involves:—*
        (i) *grave risk to the life of the pregnant woman; or*
        (ii) *substantial risk of serious injury to the physical or mental health of the pregnant woman or any existing children of her family; or*
    (b) *that there is a substantial risk that if the child were born it would suffer from such physical or mental abnormalities as to be seriously handicapped.*
(2) In determining whether the continuance of a pregnancy would involve such risk of injury to health as is mentioned in paragraph (*a*) of subsection (1) of this section, account may be taken of the pregnant woman's actual or reasonably foreseeable environment.
(3) Except as provided by subsection (4) of this section, any treatment for the termination of pregnancy must be carried out in a hospital vested in the Minister of Health or the Secretary of State under the National Health Service Acts, or in a place for the time being approved for the purposes of this section by the said Minister or the Secretary of State.
(4) Subsection (3) of this section, and so much of subsection (1) as relates to the opinion of two registered medical practitioners, shall not apply to the termination of a pregnancy by a registered medical practitioner in a case where he is of the opinion, formed in good faith, that the termination is immediately necessary to save the life or to prevent grave permanent injury to the physical or mental health of the pregnant woman.

4.—(1) Subject to subsection (2) of this section, no person shall be under any duty, whether by contract or by any statutory or other legal requirement, to participate in any treatment authorised by this Act to which he has a conscientious objection *on religious, ethical or any other grounds.*
(2) Nothing in subsection (1) of this section shall affect any duty to participate in treatment which is necessary to save the life or to prevent grave permanent injury to the physical or mental health of a pregnant woman.

Questions

(i) How would you evaluate this proposed reform? In what ways would the amended section 1 of the Act have restricted the availability of abortions?
(ii) Do you think the amendment to the 'conscience' clause in s 4(1) would have broadened its scope? Notice that the Bill would have repealed s 4(3) which

places the burden of proof upon the individual claiming to have a conscientious objection.

(b) Time limits

Perhaps, for many anti-abortion campaigners, the primary target for reform is the time limit within which a lawful abortion may be performed. We turn to the Lane Committee Report again (paras 274–282; footnotes omitted):

An upper time limit for abortion

274. Numerous organisations and individuals have recommended an upper limit on the period of gestation at which abortion may lawfully take place. Their principal reasons for so doing may be summarised as follows:

(1) To encourage early application for, and performance of, abortion and thus to avoid or minimise the risks of the operation, which increase substantially after the first trimester of pregnancy.
(2) To spare the patient and the medical and nursing staff the revulsion and distress occasioned by later abortions, such reactions becoming progressively more severe as the fetus assumes an increasingly human form and movements may be seen.
(3) To avoid the destruction of a well-developed fetus and particularly one which might survive termination of pregnancy.

Some, but not all, of these recommendations included suggested exceptions to the proposed limit, such as in cases of grave danger to the mother's life or health, or where the child is deemed to be incapable of surviving. Other suggestions were that all late terminations should be performed in National Health Service hospitals or by National Health Service practitioners.

275. The recommendations we have received may be divided into two main categories:

(*a*) Those relating to an early upper limit of the 12th, 13th or 16th week of gestation. Mostly the 12th week was advocated.
(*b*) Those relating to a later limit of the 20th, 22nd, 24th or 26th week of gestation.

In referring to these time limits, it should be borne in mind that there is often extreme difficulty in calculating gestational age with accuracy; many women seeking abortion claim that their pregnancy is at an earlier stage than in fact it is.

276. (*a*) As to an early upper limit, some recommendations were coupled with a suggestion that abortion should be easier to obtain, or be obtainable on demand or request, up to the twelfth or thirteenth week of pregnancy. We approach the problem bearing in mind that abortion should only be obtainable on the health grounds laid down in the Act and that if it is to take place, it should desirably be performed early. ... We further bear in mind the desirability of avoiding distress to those who operate on and nurse abortion patients, but our conclusion is that there should be no early limit on abortion. ...

Our main reasons for this conclusion are, to begin with, that statistics show that at present numerous abortions are performed after the 12th week of pregnancy, for example, in 1971 the proportion was 22.3 per cent of all abortions performed. Although this percentage is falling it is likely that a considerable time will elapse before the number can be substantially reduced, as desirably it should be. Many women, particularly young ones, do not seek abortion until near, or after, the end of the first trimester. Further, there are and will probably continue to be, at any rate for the near future, delays in obtaining abortion until well into the second trimester, even when it has been sought within the first. Such an early restriction as has been suggested, while no doubt encouraging women to make early application for abortion, would operate unfairly and deprive many of them of a proper opportunity of obtaining it.

277. (*b*) As to a later limit, this has been one of the most frequently made of the recommendations we have received. Many responsible medical, nursing and other organisations and individuals support it. So far as statistics show, since the Abortion Act came into force there has been a gradual decline in the numbers of abortions performed after the 24th week of pregnancy; eg in 1969 the figure was 195, in 1970 it was 171, in 1971 it was 139, of which [the] last 114 cases were of resident women, 92 of whom were operated on in the NHS. Nevertheless, the fact remains that there is widespread anxiety concerning late abortions.

278. . . . The Peel Report on the Use of Fetuses and Fetal Material for Research defines a viable fetus as:

one which has reached the stage of maintaining the co-ordinated operation of its component parts so that it is capable of functioning as a self-sustaining whole independently of any connection with the mother.

A pre-viable fetus is defined as:

one which, although it may show some but not all signs of life, has not yet reached the stage at which it is able, and is incapable of being made able, to function as a self-sustaining whole independently of any connection with the mother.

The report recommended that:

The minimal limit of viability for human fetuses should be regarded as twenty weeks' gestational age. This corresponds to a weight of approximately 400–500 grammes.

We understand that at the time when the Peel Report was published, it was expected that the World Health Organisation would make a similar recommendation, but it has not yet made any recommendation on this matter. We further understand that if and when it does so, the favoured recommendation may be that a fetus weighing 500 grammes or more should be regarded as potentially viable. Birth-weight cannot be relevant to the working of the Abortion Act as the weight cannot be determined before termination of the pregnancy, but 500 grammes would correspond to a gestational age of approximately twenty-two weeks. The British Medical Association has supported the Peel Report recommendation. On the other hand, the Broderick Report on Death Certification and Coroners did not recommend any alteration in the definition of a stillbirth.

It may be remarked here that in most of those parts of the United States of America where abortion has been permitted, there has been an upper time limit of twenty-four weeks' gestational age, and this may also have been accepted as the lower limit of viability: gestational age, however, is often calculated from the assumed date of conception and not, as in this country, from the first day of the last menstruation, giving rise to a discrepancy of approximately two weeks. Thus in many cases a gestational age of twenty-four weeks in the USA would be reckoned as twenty-six in this and most other countries.

279. *Matters which have principally influenced the Committee*

(1) Informed opinion is, and the Committee agrees, that a maximum gestational age of twenty-eight weeks for abortion is too high, having regard to modern methods of sustaining prematurely-born infants. Viability must be a question of fact in each case but, while it may be theoretically possible for a fetus to survive at twenty-four weeks' gestation, in practice there is little hope of survival at a gestational age of less than twenty-six weeks. An upper limit of twenty-four weeks' gestation for abortion should afford protection for any fetus with a real chance of survival independently of its mother. Further research may justify a reduction of this period, but we foresee no likelihood of this for the immediate or near future. We have given anxious consideration to the evidence as to aborted fetuses having manifested movement or other signs of life. But we know of no case in this country in which anyone has been able to say that a fetus of less than 24 weeks' gestation was viable in the sense that it could have survived even the perinatal period. Much publicity was attracted by a tragic case in Scotland, but there the fetus was thought to be of about 30 weeks' gestation and for that reason might have had a chance of survival.

(2) According to evidence received from those concerned with a diagnostic

amniocentesis, the diagnosis of chromosomal abnormalities in the fetus, although often possible by eighteen or nineteen weeks' gestation, may in some cases not be made until the end of the twenty-second week. Further, in the detection of bio-chemical abnormalities diagnosis may not be made until twenty-four weeks' gestation. Nevertheless, the Committee would not be prepared to recommend an exception to the upper limit for abortion on the sole ground of diagnosis of fetal abnormality and we consider that such an exception would be unacceptable to the medical and nursing professions. . . . Further research into prenatal diagnosis of abnormality may necessitate re-consideration of the upper time limit we recommend, but we are concerned with the present and the immediately foreseeable future.

(3) There is a number, albeit small, of cases of women presenting for abortion between the twentieth and twenty-fourth weeks of pregnancy who nevertheless have compelling grounds for termination and should not be precluded from obtaining it. These include women who develop or manifest a serious medical or obstetric condition and a few with a serious mental condition.

(4) We do not consider that, as between the twentieth or twenty-second week on the one hand and the twenty-fourth week on the other, there is such an increase in the distress and revulsion of those concerned that this ought to outweigh the matters referred to in (1) to (3) above.

Recommendations of the committee

280. We recommend that the Abortion Act should be amended to authorise abortion up to the twenty-fourth week of pregnancy and not thereafter.

281. In order to preserve the life or health of the mother, or the child, termination of a pregnancy may be medically necessary in some cases after the twenty-fourth week of gestation and up to, or beyond, the normal date for delivery of the child. In this event, termination should be treated as induction of labour; every effort should be made to preserve the life of the child and all the statutory requirements as to obstetric care, notification and registration of the birth as a live-birth or as a still-birth, must be observed. We consider that this should afford appropriate protection for a viable fetus.

282. *Recommendations as to consequential statutory and administrative changes*
(a) Although the Infant Life (Preservation) Act 1929 should otherwise continue to be of full force and effect, section 1(2) (which makes evidence of twenty-eight weeks' pregnancy *prima facie* proof that the child was capable of being born alive) should be repealed. We suggest this, rather than amending the relevant period to twenty-four weeks, because this subsection has given rise to misunderstanding in the past and has been, we think, misinterpreted to mean that the offence of child-destruction cannot be committed or proved before the specified length of pregnancy.

More recently a Working Party set up jointly by the Royal College of Obstetricians and Gynaecologists and others recommended in their Report on Fetal Viability and Clinical Practice (1984), pp 10–15 (footnotes omitted) that the time limit for a lawful abortion should be reduced to 24 weeks.

The most compelling argument for change is the now well established fact that many babies of less than 28 completed weeks gestational age have a good chance of surviving if they are given appropriate care (see Table 1). A survey of 595 babies of less than 28 weeks gestational age in 29 neonatal intensive care units in Britain in 1982, revealed that the chances of survival for babies of 26 and 27 weeks was greater than fifty per cent. These babies are presently within the age range for legal abortion.

The arguments for maintaining the present figure of 28 weeks are—
(i) women, often for reasons beyond their control, continue to present late in pregnancy requesting legal abortion. More specifically some malformations and metabolic diseases can only be diagnosed between 20–28 weeks of gestation.
(ii) some individuals fear that change will encourage legislation which will restrict the terms of the 1967 Abortion Act.

(iii) any change in the age of viability is liable to make perinatal mortality statistics incompatible with previous years.

However, the Committee considered that, with the considerably improved prognosis for survival without handicap of babies of less than 28 completed weeks, retention of this gestational age as the time below which the fetus is implicitly regarded as being non-viable, is likely to have an adverse effect on obstetric practice. It is our view that the reasons for a change in the law are even more compelling than they were 11 years ago when the Lane Committee made its recommendation, and have no hesitation in recommending a lower gestational age. What is more difficult, is to determine what this figure should be.

Table 1
Number of babies of gestational age of less than 28 weeks admitted to 29 Neonatal Intensive Care Units in the UK during 1982 showing survival rates at 7 and 28 days of age. Figures in brackets are for comparison from the Australian study of Yu *et al*.

Gestational age	Admissions		Survival		
(in weeks)	Number	%	7 days	28 days	%
27	237(48)	40	158	136	57(70)
26	165(36)	28	105	93	56(57)
25	116(23)	19	57	44	38(32)
24	58(22)	10	12	9	16(36)
23	13	2	1	0	
22	5		0	0	0
<22	1	1	0	0	
Totals	595	100	333	282	47.4

Viability at 22 completed weeks (154 days from the first day of the LNMP).
There are valid arguments for adopting a 22 weeks or even a 20 weeks period of gestation. It represents the lowest period of gestation after which lung development could, in some cases, be sufficient to allow mechanical ventilation to support life until the baby is mature enough to survive on his or her own. It could also be argued that if a change in the gestational age of viability is to be made it is preferable to make a major change downwards to include all babies who are capable of surviving extrauterine life. The World Health Organisation (WHO) in 1977 recommended that, all infants weighing 500 gm or more (22 weeks gestation), whether liveborn or deadborn, should be registered as 'births'. We recognise the advantages of conforming with this figure with regard to comparability of perinatal statistics but would point out that their recommendation was chiefly designed to standardise perinatal statistics of member countries as is shown by the priority given to birthweight over gestational age. The issue of fetal viability addressed by the Committee in this paper is somewhat different. The gestational age to be selected is not one that should be regarded as a limit below which survival is unlikely and above which it is probable. In addition, birthweight is of little value to the clinician who cannot weigh the baby *in utero* and who has to make a reasoned decision on available knowledge of the possibility of survival after delivery relative to gestational age. Thus, we do not think that the WHO recommendation should weigh heavily in the making of the decision on an appropriate gestational age of fetal viability.

The Committee was also concerned about the effects of a gestational age that is set too low. They took note of the evidence of Table 1 that no baby less than 24 completed weeks of gestational age survived beyond the first week of life. (We recognise that the data relates to 1982, since when, technology has improved; survivors of 23 weeks of age have now been occasionally reported.)

Table 2 summarises some of the most recent national statistics and those from an RCOG study on late legal abortion in the first six months of 1982.

Table 2

Gestational age distribution of women in England and Wales having a legal abortion in the first six months of 1984 (figures obtained from Office of Population Censuses and Surveys).

Gestational age in weeks

	–12	13–14	15–16	17–19	20–21	22–23	24–27	Total
Number	58,533	4,172	2,376	2,091	589	287	139	68,187
%—Total	85.8	6.1	3.5	3.1	0.9	0.4	0.2	100

Percentage of legal abortions done for suspected and/or confirmed malformations relative to gestational age groups (RCOG Survey 1984)

Total abortions	364	217	381	793	591	258	124	26

Suspected and/or confirmed malformations (%)	1.9	1.9	4.2	9.6	19.3	7.7

It can be seen that while only 1.5 per cent of the total women resident in the UK who had a legal abortion reported in 1982 were more than 19 completed weeks of gestation, 19.3% of all abortions done for fetal abnormality were performed at this time.

Figures for 1982 from 26 of the 34 laboratories involved in the diagnosis of fetal neural tube, chromosome and metabolic abnormalities (Table 3) show that 14.5 per cent of the 17,878 amniocenteses were reported after 22 weeks gestation.

Table 3

Duration of pregnancy when the results of amniocenteses were reported

Total Amniocenteses	17,878
Known duration of pregnancy at report	12,744
Report at 22–33 weeks of pregnancy	11.5%
Report at 24 weeks of pregnancy or later	3.0%

(Unpublished data collected from 26 laboratories by Professor R Harris for 1982.)

There is no doubt that a proportion of late diagnoses of fetal malformation is due to a delay in attendance (whether for medical or personal reasons) and that the number would decrease if greater urgency of earlier attendance and diagnosis were emphasised by a lower gestational age of viability. The figures on structural abnormalities of the fetus diagnosed by ultrasound scan shown in Table 4 lend support to the view that a reduction of the gestational age of viability to below 24 weeks would interfere with attempts to reduce the number of babies born with severe malformations.

It is also likely that there will be a small decrease in late abortions for fetal malformation if chorion biopsy fulfils its promise of enabling the diagnosis of a number of disorders to be made during the first three months of pregnancy, but it should be recognised that neural defects, which currently represent the majority of detectable malformations, cannot be diagnosed in this way.

With improvements in technology it is probable that the diagnosis of even more disorders which are only detectable late in pregnancy will be possible.

Finally, a strong argument which persuaded the Committee against recommending a gestational age that is set too low, is the certainty that fear, ignorance and administrative delays will continue to be a major reason for late attendance for termination of pregnancy. These late attenders are usually the women in greatest need of help—the very young and socially deprived.

Table 4

Distribution of abnormalities and type of malformation relative to gestational age terminated amongst 174 late terminations of pregnancy from 447 scanned by ultrasound at King's College Hospital, London, between 1978–80. Figures in brackets refer to abnormalities such as polycystic kidneys, microcephaly and absent cerebellum where diagnosis could not have been made at an earlier gestational age. (Campbell—personal communication).

	Weeks of gestational age							
	20	21	22	23	24	25	26	
Abnormalities diagnosed	59	42	21	17	24	16	11	190
Pregnancies continuing	5	4	0	1	4	2	0	16
anecephaly	12	5	2	0	1	1	0	21
spina bifida	20	12	5	4	6	3	2	52
other NTD	6	4	5(2)	5(1)	2	4(2)	4(1)	30
GIT	7	4	1	0	1	0	0	13
renal	4	9(1)	4(1)	3	4	2(1)	4	30
hydrops	4	2	0	2	1	2	0	11
limbs	1	0	1	2	3(2)	0	1	8
other	0	2(1)	3	0	2	2	0	9
Total								174
Incidence								100%

Viability at 24 completed weeks (168 days from the first day of the LNMP)
The results of the survey of 29 neonatal intensive care units in Britain (Table 1) show that there is a sharp demarcation, in terms of survival, before and after 24 completed weeks of gestation. Amongst babies of 24–27 completed weeks gestation, survival at 28 days after birth was nearly fifty per cent. Although only 16 per cent of 24 week babies survived in our survey, it is noteworthy that 36 per cent survived in the Australian series reported by Yu *et al*. These findings support the view of the RCOG expressed in 1980 in a letter from the President at that time, Sir Anthony Alment, to the DHSS that '24 weeks does, at present and in the foreseeable future, represent the stage of pregnancy at which an expelled fetus might have a prospect of survival.'

National figures for legal abortions done for women resident in England and Wales, in 1982 show that whereas 1,490 were between 20 to 23 completed weeks of gestation inclusive, at the time of the abortion, only 198 were 24 weeks or more. Table 5 shows the results obtained from 12 laboratories that were able to provide information on legal abortions done for the major malformations (chromosome defects and neural tube abnormalities) 12 per cent were done between 22–23 weeks and 4.7 per cent at 24 weeks or later.

Table 5
Duration of pregnancy when legal termination of pregnancy (TOP) was done as a result of amniocenteses

Total amniocenteses	10,270
Total TOP	321
TOP at 22–23 weeks	39(12.1%)
TOP at 24 weeks and later	15(4.7%)

(Unpublished data collected from 12 laboratories by Professor R Harris for 1982.)

Adoption of 24 rather than 22 completed weeks as the age of viability seems reasonable to us because it represents a balance between conflicting interests. On the one hand, the great majority of fetuses that are capable of surviving extrauterine life would be protected, while on the other hand, it would ensure that, with few exceptions, women with currently accepted reasons for a legal abortion would still have time to obtain one. Such a definition does not preclude the registration of a live born infant at an earlier gestation.

The Corrie Bill also included a provision to reduce the time limit to 20 weeks. Corrie sought to do this by amending the 1967 Act and the 1929 Act (clauses 3 and 7 of the Bill).

Amendment and extension of Infant Life (Preservation) Act 1929
   3. The Infant Life (Preservation) Act 1929 shall be amer. led—
   (*a*) in subsection (2) of section 1, by leaving out the word 'twenty-eight' and
       substituting therefor the word 'twenty'; and
   (*b*) in subsection (2) of section 3 by leaving out the words 'Scotland or'.

Severely handicapped children
   7. Notwithstanding anything in section 1 of the Infant Life (Preservation) Act
1929, where two medical practitioners certify in good faith that from the evidence
of tests it appears to them that the child will be born severely handicapped then the
pregnancy may be terminated at any time until the twenty-eighth week of the
pregnancy and so much of section 1 of the principal Act as refers to twenty weeks
shall not apply.

In 1987 the Bishop of Birmingham, the Rt Rev Hugh Montiefiore
(concentrating only on the 1929 Act) introduced his Infant Life (Preservation)
Amendment Bill. He sought to replace 28 weeks with 24 weeks in s 1(2) of that
Act:

Amendment of s 1(2) of Infant Life (Preservation) Act 1929
1. In section 1(2) of the Infant Life (Preservation) Act 1929 (length of pregnancy
which is evidence under that Act that a woman was pregnant of a child capable of
being born alive) for the words 'twenty-eight weeks' there shall be substituted the
words 'twenty-four weeks'.

David Alton MP chose to concentrate only on amending the 1967 Act when
he introduced his Abortion (Amendment) Bill 1987, by which it was provided
that:

1.—(1) A woman's pregnancy may be terminated in accordance with section 1 of
the Abortion Act 1967 at any time up to the beginning of the 18th week of gestation.
   (2) Thereafter, up to the end of the 28th week of gestation, the pregnancy may be
terminated by a registered medical practitioner in a public hospital or on a consultant
gynaecologist's recommendation, in an approved place if, and only if, it is certified—
   (*a*) that the termination is necessary in order to save the woman's life, or
   (*b*) that it is likely that if the child were born it would suffer from severe
       physical or mental disability (the nature of the disability to be identified
       in the certificate), or
   (*c*) that the pregnancy appears to be due to an act of rape or incest committed
       against the woman at a time when she was under the age of 18, or
   (*d*) that the termination is immediately necessary to save the woman's life or
       to prevent grave permanent injury to her physical health.
   (3) Nothing in subsection (1) or (2) above shall make it unlawful for a woman's
pregnancy to be terminated by a medical practitioner in a public hospital or
approved place after the end of the 28th week of gestation if the practitioner carrying
out the termination is of the opinion, formed in good faith, that it is immediately
necessary to save the woman's life or to prevent grave injury to her physical health.

Questions

(i) Are you persuaded of the need to alter the time limit by legislation and, if
so, which approach commends itself to you?
(ii) Is any amendment in fact required in the light of the Court of Appeal's
decision in *C v S*?
(iii) Do you think the Alton Bill is less or more restrictive in the circumstances
that it would make abortions legal than the earlier Corrie Bill?
(iv) To what extent would the Alton Bill change the law for abortions to be
performed after the beginning of the 18th week of pregnancy and before the
end of the 28th week?

(v) Would a doctor act lawfully under the Alton proposals if he believed that one of the grounds in clause 1(2) existed but subsequently, after the abortion was performed, it transpired that he had been wrong?

(vi) What in the logic for the introduction of a distinct set of grounds for abortion performed after the beginning of the 18th week of pregnancy?

Finally, notice that in December 1988 a Bill (co-sponsored by David Alton) was introduced into the House of Commons. The Bill repeats the earlier Bill sponsored by David Alton.

Chapter 10

Pre-natal injury and actions for wrongful life and wrongful birth

Pre-natal injury

(i) COMMON LAW BACKGROUND

Pace, 'Civil Liability for Pre-Natal Injuries' (1977) 40 MLR 141 at 141–7 explains the law:

Although Blackstone was able to assert confidently that in criminal law 'Life is the immediate gift of God, a right inherent by nature in every individual, and it begins in contemplation of the law as soon as an infant is able to stir in the mother's womb',[1] subsequent legal development in relation to the unborn child in a civil context does not wholly endorse this view. The rights of such a child are recognised at law for certain limited purposes only, eg in connection with succession to property, the Fatal Accidents Acts and certain crimes, and there was an apparent hiatus in the law which was highlighted by the national tragedy caused by the devastating effects of the drug thalidomide. This apparent gap, which the Law Commission, in August 1974, proposed should be filled by the Congenital Disabilities (Civil Liability) Bill,[2] was suggested by the absence of any English decision on whether a tortious action would subsist at the suit of a plaintiff in respect of post-natal damage suffered as a result of pre-natal fault.

. . .

If the point had fallen to be decided [an English] court would doubtless have been swayed by the words of Lamont J spoken some six years earlier in the Canadian case of *Montreal Tramways v Leveille*[7]: 'the great weight of judicial opinion in the common law courts denies the right of a child when born to maintain an action for pre-natal injuries'. This was a reflection of various American authorities[8] and of the Irish case of *Walker v Great Northern Rly Co of Ireland*.[9] . . . In *Montreal Tramways*, a post-*Donoghue v Stevenson* case, the court had concluded in favour of liability but this would have been of little help to an English court. There the Supreme Court of Canada had to decide whether the defendant company was liable in respect of its negligence which, the majority of the court accepted, caused a pregnant woman passenger to give birth to a child with club-feet. The action was brought under a provision of the Quebec Civil Code whereby 'Every person . . . is responsible for the damage caused by his fault to another. . . .' . . . This case was not . . . directly in point on the question of whether a duty of care was owed in the situation under consideration[14]; it merely decided that in the circumstances of that case an unborn child, through the application of a fiction, was deemed to exist and so was "another" for the purposes of the Quebec Civil Code.

An inherent and perennial difficulty in claims for pre-natal injuries, and one which was largely the reason for the one-time refusal of a right of recovery by the American courts,[15] is the ascertainment of a causal *nexus* between the pre-natal negligence of the defendant and the post-natal harm to the child. Though Smith J's first reason for his dissent in *Montreal Tramways* was his view that the civil law fiction favoured by the majority was restricted to property questions, his second was that he doubted whether the medical evidence adduced would allow the reasonable inference that the plaintiff's club-feet resulted from the injury to the mother. Furthermore, in *Walker* a subsidiary ground advanced by O'Brien J for denying the claim was that it would be difficult to 'trace a hare lip to nervous shock, or a bunch of grapes on the face to the fright.'[16] Obviously the difficulty of establishing a connection between the defendant's conduct and the plaintiff's injury is not a sufficient reason for denying a right of action, though, on the state of medical knowledge at the time of *Walker*, difficulties in establishing a connection would in many cases have proved insurmountable. Advances in medical science will more often show the required connection without resort to mere speculation and conjecture,[17] although the difficulty of establishing such a connection will increase the more removed in time is the wrongful act from the accrual of the cause of action.

In *Watt v Rama*,[18] the Full Court of the Supreme Court of Victoria had to decide certain preliminary points of law which arose out of a car crash in which a pregnant woman driver had been injured by the faulty driving of the defendant. The woman driver had subsequently given birth to the plaintiff who suffered from brain damage, epilepsy and paralysis from the neck downwards. The questions which fell to be determined were whether (1) the defendant owed a duty of care not to cause injury to the unborn plaintiff; (2) he owed a duty of care to the infant plaintiff not to injure her mother; and (3) whether the damage complained of was in law too remote. For the purposes only of the determination of those questions it was *assumed* in the plaintiff's favour that the injuries sustained by her were caused by the defendant's faulty driving. Thus, at the subsequent trial of the action the ascertainment of a connection might well produce difficulties.

All three members of the court, after a comprehensive investigation of judicial and academic authorities, resorted to basic tort principles, in particular the statement of the 'neighbour principle' by Lord Atkin in *Donoghue v Stevenson*. Winneke CJ and Pape J held that it was reasonably foreseeable at the time of the collision that the defendant's conduct might cause injury to a pregnant woman in the car with which he collided. Therefore, the possibility of injury on birth to the child she was carrying must also be reasonably foreseeable. This gave rise to a potential relationship capable of imposing a duty on the defendant *vis-à-vis* the child if, and when, born alive. On such birth this relationship crystallised, since it was then that the child suffered injuries as a living person and there arose a duty on the defendant to take reasonable care in relation to the child. They concluded that the answers to the questions posed by the preliminary determination they were called upon to make were: (1) yes; (2) an answer was unnecessary; and (3) no.

The third member of the court, Gillard J reached the same conclusions but by a somewhat different route. The application of the 'neighbour principle' resulted in the finding that, on the assumed facts, the plaintiff was a member of a class which might reasonably and probably be affected by the defendant's carelessness:

> The unborn child should be included in the class of persons likely to be affected by [the driver's] carelessness since the regeneration of the human species implies the presence on the highway of many pregnant women.[19]

Furthermore, the defendant as a reasonable driver should have foreseen the presence of such a woman and the risk to her child, if his failure to reach the standard of a reasonably careful driver caused him to collide with and injure the mother.

All three judges emphasised that there was nothing unusual in there being a time-lag between the defendant's careless driving and the consequential damage suffered by the plaintiff, since, particularly in cases under *Donoghue v Stevenson*, the duty of care was not dependent on the existence, at the time of the defendant's fault, of a person with the right correlative to the defendant's duty to take care.[20] This lapse of time was relevant only in relation to the child's capacity to sue.

In *Duval v Seguin*,[21] the High Court of Ontario recognised that there were no authorities binding upon it and, as above, Fraser J had recourse to fundamental principles of tort. . . . He took the view that, applying *Donoghue v Stevenson*, an unborn child was:

> within the foreseeable risk incurred by a negligent motorist. When the unborn child becomes a living person and suffers damages [sic] as a result of pre-natal injuries caused by the negligent motorist the cause of action is completed. A tortfeasor is as liable to a child who has suffered pre-natal injury as to the victim with a thin skull or other physical defect.[22]

It is to be noted that, save for Gillard J who was prepared to deem an unborn child a person in being at the time of the defendant's negligence,[23] the judges in these cases avoided the question of whether legal status should be accorded to a foetus.[24] The approach adopted was basically that, since damage is essential to the tort of negligence, that tort is not completed until the damage is suffered. As the damage was not suffered in both cases until the birth of the plaintiff the tort was completed at birth, at which time there was no difficulty in attributing legal personality to the live plaintiff. On this view, according to *Watt v Rama*, pre-natal damage to the foetus is merely an evidentiary fact in relation to the issue of the causation of damage at birth.

This solution requires the establishment of a causal *nexus* between the defendant's wrongful act and the plaintiff's defective condition on birth. It is a *sine qua non* of this view that there is a birth and that that birth is a live one. The factual situation in these Commonwealth cases was such that it did not require the courts to discuss the problem of the point in time at which there is a live birth and consequent legal personality.

Notes to extract

[1] *Commentaries* (15th ed), Vol 1, p 129, *Cf Roe v Wade*, 35 L Ed 2d 147, 93 S Ct (1973), *per* Blackmun J at p 181: 'We need not resolve the difficult question of when life begins. When those trained in the respective disciplines of medicine, philosophy and theology are unable to arrive at any consensus the judiciary, at this point in the development of man's knowledge, is not in a position to speculate as to the answer.'

[2] Law Com No 60; Cmnd 5709: *Report on Injuries to Unborn Children*. See also Working Paper No 47: *Injuries to Unborn Children*. The Law Commission's recommendations were given effect by the Congenital Disabilities (Civil Liability) Bill, which was introduced by Mr Ray Carter MP on December 17, 1975, and which received its second reading in the House of Commons on February 6, 1976 (see HC Deb, February 6, 1976, Vol 904, col 1589 *et seq*). The amended Bill received the Royal Assent on July 22, 1976, and became the Congenital Disabilities (Civil Liability) Act 1976 (c 28). The Scottish Law Commission No 30, Cmnd 537: *Liability for Antenatal Injury*, thought the present law would enable a child, born alive, to recover for antenatal injuries. If legislation was necessary to avoid doubt 'it should do no more than provide . . . that if a person who is born alive sustains damage as a result of injuries suffered at or before birth, or as a result of the death before his birth of anyone in respect of whose death he would ordinarily have a right to sue, he should be entitled to recover reparation as if the damage had been sustained after his birth.': para 29.

. . .

[7] [1933] 4 DLR 339 at 340. This situation may well have prompted counsel's comment in *Dulieu v White & Sons* [1901] 85 LT 126 at 127, that he did not rely on the injury to a child, born prematurely as a result of its mother's nervous shock, as a cause of action.

[8] In America it was not until 1946 that the courts began to resile from their generally steadfast denial of a right of action.

[9] (1891) 28 LR Ir. 69.

. . .

[14] In most civil law systems there is no such concept as the common law duty of care—merely an approximation to it.

[15] In 1971 Alabama was the only State which denied a right of recovery. As this State has not adjudicated on the matter since 1926 it is likely that any future adjudication will result in a reversal of attitude.

[16] (1891) 28 LR Ir 69 at 81.

[17] For a useful, though dated, summary of the medical aspects of the problem, see Gordon, *The Unborn Plaintiff* (1965) 63 Mich LR 579, 603–627. For a vivid illustration of the difficulties of proof which can arise, see *Puhl v Milwaukee Auto Ins Co*, 8 Wis 2d 343 (1959), a case concerning mongolism, on which see Reed, *Pre-Natal Injuries: Development of the Right of Recovery* (1961) 10 *Defense Law Journal* 29, 46–48. Even today it should be noted that the aetiology of deformity, particularly in relation to teratogenic drugs, is a matter of some controversy. See also Edwards, 'The Problem of Compensation for Antenatal Injuries' (1973) 246 *Nature* 54.

[18] [1972] VR 353. The proposed appeal to the Privy Council was abandoned.
[19] *Ibid* at p 374. See also Fraser J in *Duval v Seguin* at 433, *infra*. The Law Commission recommended that the tortfeasor should take his victim as he finds her and a woman's pregnancy should be treated as one of her 'characteristics and constitution,' *op cit* para 74.
[20] This conclusion had been foreshadowed by the House of Lords in *Watson v Fram Reinforced Concrete Co (Scotland) Ltd and Winget Ltd* 1960 SC (HL) 92 at 109–110, 112, 115.
[21] [1972] 26 DLR (3d) 418.
[22] *Ibid* at p 434.
[23] *Ibid* at p 376. Though there was no entitlement to compensation until a live birth—at p 377.
[24] See, e g Fraser J at pp 433, 434. It seems that in so far as negligence is concerned 'the child could not in the very nature of things acquire rights correlative to a duty until it became by birth a living person,' *per* Winneke CJ and Pape J at 360.

(ii) CONGENITAL DISABILITIES (CIVIL LIABILITY) ACT 1976

Pace refers to the 1976 Act which replaces the common law for events arising after July 21, 1976. For our purposes, the relevant provisions of the Act are as follows:

1.—(1) If a child is born disabled as the result of such an occurrence before its birth as is mentioned in subsection (2) below, and a person (other than the child's own mother) is under this section answerable to the child in respect of the occurrence, the child's disabilities are to be regarded as damage resulting from the wrongful act of that person and actionable accordingly at the suit of the child.

(2) An occurrence to which this section applies is one which—

(a) affected either parent of the child in his or her ability to have a normal, healthy child; or

(b) affected the mother during her pregnancy, or affected her or the child in the course of its birth, so that the child is born with disabilities which would not otherwise have been present.

(3) Subject to the following subsections, a person (here referred to as 'the defendant') is answerable to the child if he was liable in tort to the parent or would, if sued in due time, have been so; and it is no answer that there could not have been such liability because the parent suffered no action-able injury, if there was a breach of legal duty which, accompanied by injury, would have given rise to the liability.

. . .

(5) The defendant is not answerable to the child, for anything he did or omitted to do when responsible in a professional capacity for treating or advising the parent, if he took reasonable care having due regard to then received professional opinion applicable to the particular class of case; but this does not mean that he is answerable only because he departed from received opinion.

. . .

4.—(1) Reference in this Act to a child being born disabled or with disabilities are to its being born with any deformity, disease or abnormality, including predisposition (whether or not susceptible of immediate prognosis) to physical or mental defect in the future.

(2) In this Act—

(a) 'born' means born alive (the moment of a child's birth being when it first has a life separate from its mother), and 'birth' has a corresponding meaning;

. . .

(5) This Act applies in respect of births after (but not before) its passing, and in respect of any such birth it replaces any law in force before its passing, whereby a person could be liable to a child in respect of disabilities with which it might be born; but in section 1(3) of this Act the expression 'liable in tort' does not include any reference to liability by virtue of this Act, or to liability by virtue of any such law.

The Act is of general application but in the context of medical law it is important to develop two issues: the first concerns negligent conduct before conception producing injury to a child conceived thereafter; and the second concerns a child who is negligently injured *en ventre sa mère*.

(a) Pre-conception

In its Report No 60 (1974) on 'Injuries on Unborn Children', the Law Commission sets out the following view (footnotes omitted):

76. As we have pointed out in paragraph 33 above, one of the differences between pre-natal injury and other personal injury is that the event or occurrence resulting from a negligent act or omission happens, in the case of pre-natal injury, at a time when the plaintiff is not in existence and to someone other than himself, namely his mother, or, exceptionally and, of course, only prior to conception, his father. So far as the negligent act or omission itself is concerned, it is of no consequence that it may happen before the plaintiff exists; the present common law rules easily comprehend this possibility. If a manufacturer negligently manufactures and markets a pram it is no answer to the claim of the child under whom it collapses that he was not alive at the date of its manufacture. In the case of pre-natal injuries, however, the equivalent of the pram's 'collapse' necessarily also occurs before the plaintiff is in existence and may occur even before the plaintiff is conceived. It is this latter possibility which has caused great concern amongst those whom we have consulted.

77. We have been given examples of cases where something happening to a child's parents before its conception can lead to its being born with disabilities. An obvious example is physical injury to a woman's pelvis causing injury to a child subsequently conceived and born. It is known that radiation of the reproductive organs of animals causes gene mutations and it can almost certainly do so also in man. The exposure of mother or father to radiation could cause gene mutations which might not become manifest for several generations. A claim has succeeded before the German Supreme Court for damages for pre-natal injury in the form of congenital syphilis caused by a blood transfusion given negligently to the mother before conception, the blood donor having suffered from the illness. The negligent supply of male sperm for artificial insemination would seem to be another possible source of pre-natal injury. The possibility that a contraceptive pill might prove both ineffective and damaging to the child born because of its ineffectiveness was not ruled out by our consultation with the medical profession. There are, no doubt, a number of other possible fact situations where pre-natal injury could be caused by an event happening before conception.

The 1976 Act, which seeks to implement their views, is discussed by Pace in his 'Civil Liability For Pre-Natal Injuries' *op cit* (pp 152–3) (footnotes omitted).

Although it is a considerable extension of the existing Commonwealth and American authorities, the Act provides that pre-conception occurrences may found a cause of action. This situation could arise when negligent X-ray treatment or defective birth-control substances affected a parent's reproductive system to such an extent that the child subsequently conceived was born disabled. The child has no right of action if at the time of the occurrence either parent knew of the risk of the child being born disabled, though this does not apply if the father is the defendant or where the occurrence is coincident with or *post* conception. This poses problems since 'new embryological data . . . purport to indicate that conception is a "process" over time, rather than an event'. Apart from this difficulty, the point has been made that to allow recovery for pre-conception negligence would be to recognise a legal interest in *not* being conceived. If this analysis is correct then English law will recognise the validity of 'wrongful life' actions and, indeed, Tedeschi would argue that pre-conception negligence does give rise to a 'wrongful life' action:

When a person fathers a child and infects it with a disease by one and the same act, then either the semen was already infected when it came into contact with the ovum, so that the new entity created is diseased from its conception (and this is the true meaning of congenital disease), or the single act results in paternity and in the infection of the mother, which will be transmitted from her to the infant. In the first case it is obvious that there was only one alternative to the new being, either not to exist or to exist with the disease. But in the second case as well no separation can be made between the act of the parent causing paternity and that causing the infection, as we are faced with a single act.

The Law Commission, favouring an action in such circumstances, approached the situation on the basis that, if a child has a legal right to begin life with a sound mind and body, and this is the effect of the proposed legislation, there is a correlative duty on its parents and others to avoid producing conception where the circumstances are likely to result in the birth of a disabled child. In other words, the remedy is sought not for being born but 'for compensation for the disability resulting from the sexual intercourse'. It should also be noted that in pre-conception cases compensation would not, without the help of the fiction provided by the Act, fulfil the function, as in other areas of tort, of restoring, as far as money can, the *status quo*. The fiction is contained in section 4(3) which states that 'Liability under this Act is to be regarded . . . as liability for personal injuries sustained by the child immediately after its birth'.

Pace, you will notice, refers to a 'wrongful life' action; we shall return to this later. For the medical lawyer, perhaps the most relevant context for consideration of this action is in the area of negligently performed IVF treatment, as we saw earlier, *supra* ch 8.)

(b) Damage caused *in utero*

Again, Pace (*op cit*) at pp 150–2 explains the law:

It will be noted that at the heart of the legislation lies the requirement of a live birth. As already stated, this could give rise to problems similar to those which have arisen in criminal law. If, in fact, a court concludes that the child, when born, was dead, the Law Reform (Miscellaneous Provisions) Act 1934 would be inapplicable since there would be no cause of action vested in the still-born child. It would be otherwise if the child was quick-born and survived for a short time only,[42] . . . .[43] Furthermore, an action could theoretically be brought under the Fatal Accidents Acts 1846–1959 [now Fatal Accidents Act 1976], because section 1 of the 1846 Act requires that the deceased would have been able to maintain an action if death had not ensued. Clearly this would be so in the case of a quick-born, though short-lived child but, since any estimate of pecuniary loss suffered as a result of the death of a newly-born child would be merely speculative, damages would be irrecoverable[44] although funeral expenses incurred by the parties for whom the action was brought might be recovered.[45] This is an area in which the English law of damages is arguably deficient and the practical result is tantamount to saying that the life of a newly-born child in these circumstances has no value. Admittedly there is a difficulty in the computation of damages owing to the lack of elements upon which damages are usually assessed. It can, however, hardly be denied that a newly-born child has a value and, perhaps, a basis for assessment could be found in the loss of the child's society and companionship.[46]

. . .

The Act requires that the child should be born alive disabled or with disabilities. According to section 4(1) this means that the child must be born with 'any deformity, disease or abnormality, including predisposition (whether or not susceptible of immediate prognosis) to physical or mental defect in the future'. This obviously limits the operation of the Act to damage which is capable of being assessed in pecuniary terms, so that the courts will not be faced with the novel situation in the American case of *Williams v State of New York*.[50] There an illegitimate child was born to her mentally deficient mother as a result of a sexual assault upon her mother, then a mental patient in a State institution. The plaintiff alleged that the State had been negligent in failing to provide proper supervision and protection for her mother, and that this alleged negligence had caused her (the plaintiff) to bear the stigma of illegitimacy and to be prejudiced in her property rights. The court dismissed the claim because it found it impossible to decide whether non-existence was preferable to existence as an illegitimate child. Such a disability would not fall within the definition of 'disability' proposed by the Act. The Law Commission disapproved of the approach in *Williams* and differentiated between the situation in which, eg the child's disability was caused by syphilitic intercourse when an action would lie, and the situation where, eg negligent treatment of a pregnant woman prevented spontaneous abortion,[51] when no action would lie. This difference is attributable, according to the Law Commission, to the fact that, in the latter case only, logic dictates that the child's claim must be based on the contention that he would have been better off had the spontaneous abortion succeeded and he had never been born. To guard against the possibility of so-called 'wrongful life' actions, section 1(2) (*b*) states that an action lies only where, but for the conduct giving rise to the disabled birth, the child would have been born normal—not that it would not have been born at all. There is, however, a difficulty in not treating the former case as a 'wrongful life' claim. As Tedeschi has pointed out[52]:

> How could the Manhattan hospital have prevented the unlawful birth and the mental heredity of Christine Williams without preventing her conception as well? And even assuming, for the sake of argument, that it could have been possible to create that life without those adverse circumstances—the fact remains that a single act had been committed, an act on which the plaintiff relied as her cause of action without it being open artificially to a split so as to advance the plaintiff's case.

Notes to extract

[42] See eg *Davies v British Picture Corporation Ltd*. . . . The position is similar in America under the wrongful death legislation.

[43] Statistical evidence suggests that a child born with a major disability is likely to die within 48 hours.

[44] See *Barnett v Cohen* [1921] 2 KB 461.

[45] Law Reform (Miscellaneous Provisions) Act 1934, s 2(3).

[46] See Michigan Public Act No 65, 1971, referred to in Mich LR 70, 1, 745. Note that Law Com No 56 (*Report on Personal Injury Litigation—Assessment of Damages*) recommended in para 177 that 'the parents of an unmarried minor child who is killed by another's wrong should be entitled to recover the sum of £1,000 from the wrongdoer in an action under the Fatal Accidents Acts'.

. . .

[50] 18 NY 2d 481 (1966). The Act would presumably cover injuries causing traumatic nymphomania, see *Gloria Sykes v San Francisco Municipal Ry*, 11 Med Sci & Law 51 (1971).

[51] See *Gleitman v Cosgrove*, 49 NJ 22 (1967).

[52] I Tedeschi, 'On tort liability for "wrongful life"' [1966] Israel LR 513 at 531.

Two further points, applicable to both types of action for pre-natal injury, are of interest to the medical lawyer. First, interestingly the Act sets out the standard of care in s 1(5) applicable when determining liability. Is this a statutory recital of the *Bolam* test? Or does it leave the court the power to decide what is proper professional conduct? If so, whither *Bolam*? What if the conduct complained of consisted of the doctor's failure to warn of certain risks to her child if she becomes pregnant, she becomes pregnant and the risks materialised? What test in assessing liability does the Act require the court to employ in determining whether the doctor was careless?

Secondly, the child's course of action is a derivative one, dependent upon a breach of the duty owed to the parent although no injury need be suffered by the parent. Being derivative it also follows that defences may be mounted based upon the conduct of the parent, such that, for example by s 1(4), any voluntary assumption of risk by a parent would provide a defence to the doctor (subject to the Unfair Contract Terms Act 1977 preventing this). Section 1(7) provides in relation to the defence of contributory negligence:

> (7) If in the child's action under this section it is shown that the parent affected shared the responsibility for the child being born disabled, the damages are to be reduced to such extent as the court thinks just and equitable having regard to the extent of the parent's responsibility.

John Eekelaar and Robert Dingwell raise, as yet, unanswered questions for medical law arising from the derivative nature of the action under the Act in 'Some Legal Issues in Obstetric Practice' [1984] JSWL 258, 265.

> ... If a child is to recover compensation, it is now necessary to show that the defendant was 'liable in tort' to a parent of the child, although this requirement has the modification that the parent does not have to have suffered some 'actionable injury.'[31] Nevertheless, there must still have been some breach of legal duty towards the parent.
>
> What difference does this make to the position of a child who has been injured by negligent delivery procedures? The answer would seem to be that unless the culpable acts or omissions can also be construed as breaching a legal duty to the mother, the child has lost its remedy. It is by no means clear that all such failures can be so construed. Inexpert manipulation of forceps, inadequate use of available monitoring equipment or a failure to make a Caesarean incision at an appropriate time all appear to be wrongs which primarily affect the child's well-being rather than the mother's and outside the scope of any duty to her. It is possible that the child's position could be saved by treating any default as a breach of duty towards the mother on the grounds that injury to the child is foreseeably likely to cause her consequential emotional distress.[32] The child's action would then be parasitic upon her actual or potential claim.
>
> This circuitous reasoning breaks down, however, if the attendant's default is the result of undue consideration for the mother or, particularly, if it was at her insistence by rejecting available and offered treatments. It is hard to see how the attendant could be in breach of a legal duty towards the mother when he is doing what she demands. Indeed, the Act itself compels a child's claim to be reduced by the extent to which the parent had contributed to the disability and, even, to be totally excluded if this has been done in respect to the parents' own case.[33] If a woman, for example, refuses a Caesarean section when indicated on sound professional grounds, or rejects the application of foetal monitoring, and the child subsequently goes into distress and sustains brain damage as a result of protracted labour, the child has no claim, either against the attendant (who will have committed no tort against the mother) or against the woman herself (since the 1976 Act disallows any claim by the child against its mother for ante-natal injuries unless they were incurred while she was driving).[34]
>
> Moreover, the abolition of an independent duty of care towards the child makes it harder for an attendant to resist a possible claim in assault if, in the child's interests, he disregards the mother's wishes in respect of procedures involving her person. The presence of such a duty would fortify any defence to such a claim founded on the principle of necessity or of using reasonable force to prevent a crime, viz negligent manslaughter of the child.[35] Its absence may call into question the application of the law of manslaughter for grossly negligent delivery procedures.
>
> Women's groups have shown an increasing interest in adopting the tactic of legal action as a way of enforcing demands for alternative childbirth.[36] With the weakening of the common law defence, obstetric attendants now find themselves caught between their long-established child protection duties and a statute which appears to give greater weight to the wishes of mothers. This unenviable position for obstetric attendants does not seem to have been created intentionally. There is

no indication that the Law Commission recognised the possible consequences when they recommended the reforms represented by the 1976 Act. With the agreement of the medical bodies which they consulted, the Commission accepted the proposition that 'a child born fully alive should have a right of action, accruing at birth, in respect of injury either sustained by it after conception and before birth, or resulting from injury sustained by its mother during pregnancy due to the fault of a third party'.[37] The technique which they adopted for translating this right into a legal form was, however, determined largely by 'the fact of physical identification of mother and foetus'.[38] It was thought that this could give rise to special legal problems.

The first of these was to do with the ascertainment of prospective liability. Lawyers have long considered it desirable that people entering into contractual or other relationships should be able to be reasonably confident of the possible extent of their duties. Pregnancy complicates that. Over a wide range of legal relationships, it was thought that, if potential defendants could not regulate their liability by contract with the mother, they would simply refuse to deal with women.[39] By making the child's action derivative from the mother's, third parties could be assured of the extent of their liability. This point does not, however, have any bearing on the problem under discussion. . . . Until the passage of the Congenital Disabilities (Civil Liability) Act 1976 . . . it seems that the combination of their statutory monopoly and the common law rules allowed obstetric attendants to balance the interests of mothers and children . . . gave them protection if they felt it necessary to defer to the latter. The monopoly shared by obstetricians and midwives was granted as a licence to represent the state as the ultimate guardian of the nation's children. Thus, while the wishes of mothers could never be lightly disregarded, they could not have the power of veto. Under the Midwives Act, this duty began with the commencement of professional attendance at any particular labour. The Congenital Disabilities (Civil Liability) Act 1976 only recognises a separate duty to the child after the moment of birth, defined as the point when the child has a life 'separate from its mother'.[41] Both medically and legally this is not a clear-cut concept, but obviously relates to a point later than the onset of labour.[42] Before that, the attendant's first duty appears to be the care of the mother in which, clearly, deference to her wishes will be a significant feature. If, in deferring to her and giving her correct professional attention, the child is injured, the law appears to hold that this is just too bad. On the other hand, if the attendant overrides the mother's wishes in attending to the child, he would seem to be at risk of litigation. . . .

Such arguments lead us towards concluding that the balance of policy was more or less properly struck before 1976. At the end of the day, parents should not ultimately be free to dictate the terms under which their children are born. An obstetric attendant would be well advised to listen carefully to their requests and to consider how far they could be followed consistently with sound professional practice and the child's well-being. The child is entitled to the benefits of available technological resources and professional expertise to minimise the risks of being severely prejudiced at the outset of his life. The risks of obstetric dictatorship are partially reduced by the freedom of parents to shop around licensed attendants and influence obstetric practice. The interests of the child are protected by the basic standards represented by the monopoly.

The attenuation of the attendant's duty of care by the Congenital Disabilities (Civil Liability) Act 1976 seems to run contrary to the spirit of legislative developments in the twentieth century. No convincing arguments have been produced for abrogating the common law rights of children . . . We believe that this aspect of the statute should be reviewed as a matter of some urgency. In the process, however, we would also draw attention to the emerging problem of the point at which child protection duties should properly begin. The new technologies of pre-natal intervention raise issues which could not have been foreseen by the drafters of the present statutes. It is important not to confound these with the perennial disputes about abortion or the relative priority of preserving the life of mother or child in extreme cases. We do not think that these have much to contribute to the circumstances we are addressing here, of routine childbirth and regularly available pre-natal intervention.

Notes to extract

[31] *Ibid* s 1(3).

[32] *McLoughlin v O'Brian* [1982] 2 WLR 982.

[33] Congenital Disabilities (Civil Liability) Act 1976, s 1(6).

[34] Congenital Disabilities (Civil Liability) Act 1976, ss 1(1) and 2. Cases where women refused Caesarean section despite the risks to the foetus are reported by Leiberman and Chaim, (1979) 53 *Obstetrics and Gynecology* 515–517 and Bowes and Selgestad, (1981) 58 *Obstetrics and Gynecology* 209–214. It has been suggested that the rising rate of Caesarean sections represents defensive medical practice in the wake of *Whitehouse v Jordan*. This has attracted criticism from feminist circles. If the doctors are defensively foisting Caesarean births on unwilling women, however, this almost certainly reflects a misunderstanding of their current legal position. Boyd and Francome, *One Birth in Nine—Trends in Caesarean Sections since 1978* (1983) and 'The most unnecessary cut of all', *The Health Services*, June 17, 1983.

[35] Criminal Law Act 1967, s 3(1). If no duty is owed to the child it is arguable that acts causing his death could never amount to negligent manslaughter. Similarly, the defence of necessity may be confined to protecting oneself or others to whom the defendant owes a duty: see *Loughnan* [1981] VR 443 (discussed in Grubb (1983) 3 OJLS 146).

[36] See, for instance, the articles by Robinson and Finch in *Nursing Mirror*, September 8, 1982.

[37] Law Commission, *Report on Injuries to Unborn Children*, Law Com No 60 (1974), paras 31–32.

[38] *Ibid* para 33.

[39] *Ibid* para 68.

. . .

[41] Congenital Disabilities (Civil Liability) Act 1976, s 4(2)(a).

[42] Pace, 'Civil Liability for Pre-natal Injuries' (1977) 40 MLR 141, 147.

Peter Cane offers another troublesome example for the medical lawyer in 'Injuries to Unborn Children' (1977) 51 ALJ 704, 707–8 (footnotes omitted).

The theoretical framework

The basic theoretical difficulty involved in compensating for pre-natal injuries is that at the time of the injuries the plaintiff is not a legal person. The position at common law has always been that legal personality begins at birth. It follows that until birth the child cannot possess legal rights or be owed legal duties, including a duty to take reasonable care. Thus, it is argued, a child cannot recover for injuries suffered before its birth. Various lines of reasoning have been used to overcome this difficulty. The richest source of material in this area is the American case-law. In American cases on negligence the framework of duty, breach and damage does not dominate the reasoning in the way it does in English and Australian cases. As a result, greatest attention has been directed by the American courts to the issue of legal personality.

The most influential approach has been a biological one which seeks to argue, with the aid of biological and medical data, that the unborn child at a given stage of its development either is or is not 'in fact' a live human being separate in some sense at least from its mother and so a legal person. This approach has been used both to allow and to deny recovery; sometimes both in the same case. At first, birth or viability was treated as a proper dividing line between recovery and non-recovery but these have since been abandoned by some courts in favour of the stage of quickening, or even conception. The crux of biological arguments is reliance on scientific facts as the basis of legal liability. The approach is open to two criticisms.

First, however important medical knowledge may be to questions of causation and proof it is of little help in deciding whether or not a defendant ought to be held liable for pre-natal injuries caused by him. No conclusion as to the proper limits of the defendant's liability can be drawn directly from evidence as to the stage reached in the physiological development of the embryo or foetus at the time of its injuries. One must supply a minor premise to the argument to the effect that legal personality begins at a particular point in the development of the unborn child. This premise is not a factual one; it cannot be simply asserted but must be justified in terms of the policy of the law.

Second, courts have been led by the approach into placing greater weight on the significance of conception, quickening or viability than is warranted. It is true that there is a point, called viability, at which a foetus acquires the ability to live separately from its mother, but it is also true that this point is difficult to fix accurately and that injuries suffered in the first three months of pregnancy are more likely to have serious consequences than those suffered later in the term. It is true that from conception itself an unborn child is in one sense separate from its mother, but it is also true that pre-natal events can cause miscarriage, and death or injury due to premature birth, even if the embryo or foetus itself is not directly injured by the defendant's act, simply because of the immaturity of the unborn child. The question which must be answered is whether it is thought proper to deny to a child the right to claim damages for injuries received at any particular stage of its pre-natal development.

The difficulties of the biological approach have led some courts to adopt a sudden approach—a causal approach which supposedly neither involves questions of legal personality nor calls medical knowledge in aid on questions of liability. In *Hornbuckle v Plantation Pipe Line Co*, Hawkins J said: 'At what particular moment after conception . . . the injury was inflicted is not controlling. . . . If a child born after an injury sustained at any period of its pre-natal life can prove the effect on it of a tort, it would have a right to recover'. Although the emphasis in this statement is on proof of causation, what is effectively being said is that legal personality begins at conception, and it is this coupled with the elements of the particular tort in question which gives causation its legal significance.

Third, general arguments about the harshness of the opposite result and the requirements of fairness and justice are frequently used in the American cases to attach legal consequences to the facts of biology or causation. These themes found their most influential expression in the words of Lamont J in the Canadian case of *Montreal Tramways v Leveille*: 'To my mind it is but natural justice that a child if born alive and viable, should be allowed to maintain an action in the courts for injuries wrongfully committed upon its person while in the womb of its mother'. The trouble with this approach is that "it points rather to what the law ought to be than to what it is' and so 'little assistance can be derived from such an appeal when one is searching for the answer to the vital question on the basis of principle. Further, the statement sees the matter solely from the child's point of view. . . .

Suppose the manufacturer of a drug warns: 'This drug may have such and such side effects on the mother but it is safe for the child'. The mother takes the drug and suffers no damage, but the child is born injured as a result. The manufacturer has failed to fulfil its duty to warn *vis-à-vis* the child but not the mother. Though it owes a duty to the mother, not only has it caused no damage to her, but also it has committed no breach of duty against her. The Act is not wide enough to impose liability to the child in such a case, which is unfortunate.

Drugs are not normally now prescribed during pregnancy which somewhat weakens the factual basis of this example. But what if the drugs were prescribed before conception with a warning that the mother's health would be at risk if she became pregnant but with no reference to the risk to the child?

Wrongful life

(i) AT COMMON LAW

The English common law was discussed by the Court of Appeal in *McKay v Essex Area Health Authority* [1982] QB 1166, [1982] 2 All ER 771.

Ackner LJ: Mary McKay was born on 15 August 1975 and is therefore 6½ years old. Whilst in her mother's womb she was infected with rubella (German measles) and as a result she is partly blind and deaf and is apparently disabled in other respects, the details of which have not been provided to us. She alleges in her statement of claim that Dr Gower-Davies, the second defendant, owed her a duty of care when she was *in utero*. She claims that he was negligent in that he failed to treat the rubella infection, after being told that it was suspected by her mother, the second plaintiff. She contends that this can be arrested by the injection of globulins in to the mother which, although it cannot reverse or ameliorate damage already done to the unborn child, can reduce the likelihood of further damage. . . . in addition to the claims referred to above, Mary seeks to add an additional claim against the doctor. Quite apart from his alleged failure to arrest the progress of the rubella infection by a process of injections, she claims that the duty of care which the doctor owed her when she was *in utero* involved advising her mother of the desirability of an abortion, which advice, as previously stated, the mother alleges she would have accepted. She accordingly claims that she has suffered damage by 'entry into a life in which her injuries are highly debilitating, and distress, loss and damage'. She makes a similar claim, *mutatis mutandis*, against the Essex Area Health Authority by reason of their alleged negligence in relation to their handling and testing of the samples and their failure to advise the doctor of the results of any such tests as they may have performed. . . .

(1) *The duty.* I can consider this in relation to the claim against the doctor, since what can be said in relation to the claim made against him applies, *mutatis mutandis*, to the claim against the area health authority.

The duty alleged is the duty to take care in relation to the unborn child. Hence the first claim for failing to treat the suspected rubella by injection, so as to reduce the likelihood of further damage. Thus, the selfsame duty is relied on for prenatal injuries as would be relied on postnatally, if there was a failure to give proper treatment after the child had been born. The embryo, or fetus, is in a comparable position to the child and adult which it may ultimately become. However, in stark contrast to the plea that the doctor should have advanced the prospect of a healthy birth of the child, the additional plea, which is still based on the same duty of care to the unborn child, relies on a negligent failure to prevent its birth. The basis of this additional claim is that, had the doctor properly discharged his obligation of care *towards the unborn child*, he would have advised the mother 'of the desirability of an abortion' (para 13), which advice the mother would have accepted (para 9). Accordingly, the fetus's existence *in utero* would have been terminated. Thus, the duty of care is said to involve a duty *to the fetus*, albeit indirectly, by advice to the mother to cause its death.

I cannot accept that the common law duty of care to a person can involve, without specific legislation to achieve this end, the legal obligation to that person, whether or not *in utero*, to terminate his existence. Such a proposition runs wholly contrary to the concept of the sanctity of human life.

Counsel for the plaintiffs contends that, where it can be established that a child's disabilities are so severe that it can be properly stated that she would be better off dead, the duty of care involves the duty to terminate its life. He seeks to support this proposition by reference to *Re B (a minor) (wardship: medical treatment)* [1981] 1 WLR 1421. As Griffiths LJ has pointed out, this was an urgent application made to the Court of Appeal in vacation and the two judgments were extempore. I am quite satisfied that Templeman LJ was saying no more than that, conceding for the purpose of argument that where the life of a child is so bound to be full of pain and suffering that it could be contended that the court could, in the exercise of its wardship jurisdiction, refuse to sanction an operation to prolong its life, the case before it clearly was not such a case. I do not consider that *Re B* provides any support to counsel for the plaintiffs' contention.

Counsel for the plaintiffs was constrained to concede that, if his submission was correct, then a child born with a very minor disability, such as a squint, would be entitled to sue the doctor for not advising an abortion, which advice would have been accepted, given that the risk (which fortunately did not eventuate) of serious disabilities was due to some infection which the doctor should have diagnosed. This would indeed be an odd position. Moreover, he accepted that, if the duty of care to the fetus involved a duty on the doctor, albeit indirectly, to prevent its birth, the child would have a cause of action against its mother who had unreasonably refused to have an abortion. Apart from the complicated religious and philosophical points that such an action would raise, the social implications in the potential disruption of family life and bitterness which it would cause between parent and child led the Royal Commission to conclude that such a right of action would be against public policy (see Cmnd 7054–I, para 1465).

Of course, the doctor, in accordance with his duty of care *to the mother*, owes her a duty to advise her of the rubella infection and its potential serious and irreversible effects and on the advisability of an abortion, such an operation having in such circumstances been legalised by the Abortion Act 1967. This is, however, *nihil ad rem*.

(2) *The injury and the damages.* The disabilities were caused by the rubella and not by the doctor (I ignore whether their extent could have been reduced through injections, because that is the subject of the infant's first claim). What then are her injuries, which the doctor's negligence has caused? The answer must be that there are none in any accepted sense. Her complaint is that she was allowed to be born at all, given the existence of her prenatal injuries. How then are her damages to be assessed? Not by awarding compensation for her pain, suffering and loss of amenities attributable to the disabilities, since these were already in existence before the doctor was consulted. She cannot say that, but for his negligence, she would have been born without her disabilities. What the doctor is blamed for is causing or permitting her to be born at all. Thus, the compensation must be based on a comparison between the value of non-existence (the doctor's alleged negligence having deprived her of this) and the value of her existence in a disabled state.

But how can a court begin to evaluate non-existence, 'The undiscover'd country from whose bourn No traveller returns'? No comparison is possible and therefore no damage can be established which a court could recognise. This goes to the root of the whole cause of action.

Counsel for the plaintiffs has provided no answer to the damage problem. His suggestion that you assess the compensation on the basis that the doctor had caused the disabilities and then you make some discount on a basis which he could not particularise because the doctor did not cause the disabilities does not, in my judgment, advance the matter, except to tend to confirm the impossibility of making such an assessment.

. . .

Stephenson LJ: The importance of this cause of action to this child is somewhat reduced by the existence of her other claim and the mother's claims, which, if successful, will give her some compensation in money or in care.

However, this is the first occasion on which the courts of this country or the Commonwealth have had to consider this cause of action, and I shall give my reasons for holding that it should be struck out.

If, as is conceded, any duty is owed to an unborn child, the authority's hospital laboratory and the doctor looking after the mother during her pregnancy undoubtedly owed the child a duty not to injure it, and, if she had been injured as a result of lack of reasonable care and skill on their part after birth, she could have sued them (as she is suing the doctor) for damages to compensate her for the injury they had caused her in the womb. (Cf the thalidomide cases, where it was assumed that such an action might lie: eg *Distillers Co (Biochemicals) Ltd v Thompson* [1971] 1 All ER 694, [1971] AC 458.) But this child has not been injured by either defendant, but by the rubella which has infected the mother without fault on anybody's part. Her right not to be injured before birth by the carelessness of others has not been infringed by either defendant, any more than it would have been if she had been disabled by disease after birth. Neither defendant has broken any duty to take reasonable care not to injure her. The only right on which she can rely as having been infringed is a right not to be born deformed or disabled, which means, for a child deformed or disabled before birth by nature or disease, a right to be aborted or killed; or, if that last plain word is thought dangerously emotive, deprived of the opportunity to live after being delivered from the body of her mother. The only duty which either defendant can owe to the unborn child infected with disabling rubella is a duty to abort or kill her or deprive her of that opportunity.

It is said that the duty does not go as far as that, but only as far as a duty to give the mother an opportunity to choose her abortion and death. That is true as far as it goes. The doctor's alleged negligence is in misleading the mother as to the advisability of an abortion, failing to inform or advise her of its advisability or desirability; the laboratory's alleged negligence is not so pleaded in terms but the negligence pleaded against them in failing to make or interpret the tests of the mother's blood samples or to inform the doctor of their results must, like the doctor's negligence, be a breach of their duty to give the doctor an opportunity to advise the mother of the risks in continuing to let the fetus live in the womb and be born alive. But the complaint of the child, as of the mother, against the health authority, as against the doctor, is that their negligence burdened her (and her mother) with her injuries. That is another way of saying that the defendants' breaches of their duties resulted not just in the child's being born but in her being born injured or, as the judge put it, with deformities. But, as the injuries or deformities were not the result of any act or omission of the defendants, the only result for which they were responsible was her being born. For that they were responsible because if they had exercised due care the mother would have known that the child might be born injured or deformed, and the plaintiffs' pleaded case is that, if the mother had known that, she would have been willing to undergo an abortion, which must mean she would have undergone one or she could not claim that the defendants were responsible for burdening her with an injured child. If she would not have undergone an abortion had she known the risk of the child being born injured, any negligence on the defendants' part could not give either plaintiff a cause of action in respect of the child being born injured.

I am accordingly of opinion that, though the judge was right in saying that the child's complaint is that she was born with deformities without which she would have suffered no damage and have no complaint, her claim against the defendants is a claim that they were negligent in allowing her, injured as she was in the womb, to be born at all, a claim for 'wrongful entry into life' or 'wrongful life'.

This analysis leads inexorably on to the question: how can there be a duty to take away life? How indeed can it be lawful? It is still the law that it is unlawful to take away the life of a born child or of any living person after birth. But the Abortion Act 1967 has given mothers a right to terminate the lives of their unborn children and made it lawful for doctors to help to abort them.

That statute (on which counsel for the plaintiffs relies) permits abortion in specified cases of risks to the mother and the child. I need not read those provisions which are enacted in the mother's interests, but there is one provision relevant to the interests of the child. Section 1(1) provides:

Subject to the provisions of this section, a person shall not be guilty of an offence under the law relating to abortion when a pregnancy is terminated by a registered medical practitioner if two registered medical practitioners are of the opinion, formed in good faith . . . (b) that there is a substantial risk that if the child were born it would suffer from such physical or mental abnormalities as to be seriously handicapped.

That paragraph may have been passed in the interests of the mother, the family and the general public, but I would prefer to believe that its main purpose, if not its sole purpose, was to benefit the unborn child; and, if and in so far as that was the intention of the legislature, the legislature did make a notable inroad on the sanctity of human life by recognising that it would be better for a child, born to suffer from such abnormalities as to be seriously handicapped, not to have been born at all.

That inroad, however, seems to stop short of a child capable of being born alive, because the sanctity of the life of a viable fetus is preserved by the enactment of s 5(1) that 'Nothing in this Act shall affect the provisions of the Infant Life (Preservation) Act 1929 (protecting the life of the viable foetus)'.

Another notable feature of the 1967 Act is that it does not directly impose any duty on a medical practitioner or anyone else to terminate a pregnancy, though it relieves conscientious objectors of a duty to participate in any treatment authorised by the Act in all cases with one exception: see s 4 of the Act. It is, however, conceded in this case that a medical practitioner is under a duty to the mother to advise her of her right under the Act to have her pregnancy terminated in cases such as the present. There was, on the pleaded facts of this case, a substantial risk that if the child were born it would suffer from such physical or mental abnormalities as to be seriously handicapped. And, from what we have been told without objection of her present mental and physical condition, that risk has become tragically actual.

There is no doubt that this child could legally have been deprived of life by the mother's undergoing an abortion with the doctor's advice and help. So the law recognises a difference between the life of a fetus and the life of those who have been born. But, because a doctor can lawfully by statute do to a fetus what he cannot lawfully do to a person who has been born, it does not follow that he is under a legal obligation to a fetus to do it and terminate its life, or that the fetus has a legal right to die.

Like this court when it had to consider the interests of a child born with Down's syndrome in *Re B (a minor) (wardship: medical treatment)* [1981] 1 WLR 1421, I would not answer until it is necessary to do so the question whether the life of a child could be so certainly 'awful' and 'intolerable' that it would be in its best interests to end it and it might be considered that it had a right to be put to death. But that is not this case. We have no exact information about the extent of this child's serious and highly debilitating congenital injuries; the judge was told that she is partly blind and deaf, but it is not and could not be suggested that the quality of her life is such that she is certainly better dead, or would herself wish that she had not been born or should now die.

I am therefore compelled to hold that neither defendant was under any duty to the child to give the child's mother an opportunity to terminate the child's life. That duty may be owed to the mother, but it cannot be owed to the child.

To impose such a duty towards the child would, in my opinion, make a further inroad on the sanctity of human life which would be contrary to public policy. It would mean regarding the life of a handicapped child as not only less valuable than the life of a normal child, but so much less valuable that it was not worth preserving, and it would even mean that a doctor would be obliged to pay damages to a child infected with rubella before birth who was in fact born with some mercifully trivial abnormality. These are the consequences of the necessary basic assumption that a child has a right to be born whole or not at all, not to be born unless it can be born perfect or 'normal', whatever that may mean.

Added to that objection must be the opening of the courts to claims by children born handicapped against their mothers for not having an abortion. For the reasons given by the Royal Commission on Civil Liability and Compensation for Personal Injury (report, vol 1; Cmnd 7054–I), cited by Ackner LJ, that is, to my mind, a graver objection than the extra burden on doctors already open to actions for negligent treatment of a fetus, which weighed with the Law Commission.

Finally, there is the nature of the injury and damage which the court is being asked to ascertain and evaluate.

The only duty of care which courts of law can recognise and enforce are duties owed to those who can be compensated for loss by those who owe the duties, in most cases, including cases of personal injury, by money damages which will as far as possible put the injured party in the condition in which he or she was before being injured. The only way in which a child injured in the womb can be compensated in damages is by measuring what it has lost, which is the difference between the value of its life as a whole and healthy normal child and the value of its life as an injured child. But to make those who have not injured the child pay for that difference is to treat them as if they injured the child, when all they have done is not taken steps to prevent its being born injured by another cause.

The only loss for which those who have not injured the child can be held liable to compensate the child is the difference between its condition as a result of their allowing it to be born alive and injured and its condition if its embryonic life had been ended before its life in the world had begun. But how can a court of law evaluate that second condition and so measure the loss to the child? Even if a court were competent to decide between the conflicting views of theologians and philosophers and to assume an 'afterlife' or non-existence as the basis for the comparison, how can a judge put a value on the one or the other, compare either alternative with the injured child's life in this world and determine that the child has lost anything, without the means of knowing what, if anything, it has gained?

Judges have to pluck figures from the air in putting many imponderables into pounds and pence. Loss of expectation of life, for instance, has been held so difficult that the courts have been driven to fix for it a constant and arbitrary figure. Counsel for the plaintiffs referred us to what judges have said on that topic in *Rose v Ford* [1937] 3 All ER 359, [1937] AC 826 and *Benham v Gambling* [1941] 1 All ER 7, [1941] AC 157. But, in measuring the loss caused by shortened life, courts are dealing with a thing, human life, of which they have some experience; here the court is being asked to deal with the consequences of death for the dead, a thing of which it has none. And the statements of judges on the necessity for juries to assess damages and their ability to do so in cases of extreme difficulty do not touch the problem presented by the assessment of the claims we are considering. To measure loss of expectation of death would require a value judgment where a crucial factor lies altogether outside the range of human knowledge and could only be achieved, if at all, by resorting to the personal beliefs of the judge who has the misfortune to attempt the task. If difficulty in assessing damages is a bad reason for refusing the task, impossibility of assessing them is a good one. A court must have a starting point for giving damages for a breach of duty. The only means of giving a starting point to a court asked to hold that there is the duty on a doctor or a hospital which this child alleges is to require the court to measure injured life against uninjured life, and that is to treat the doctor and the hospital as responsible not for the child's birth but for its injuries. That is what in effect counsel for the plaintiffs suggests that the court should do, tempering the injustice to the defendants by some unspecified discount. This seems almost as desperate an expedient as an American judge's suggestion that the measure of damages should be the 'diminished childhood' resulting from the substantial diminution of the parents' capacity to give the child special care: see the dissenting judgment of Handler J in *Berman v Allan* 404 A 2d 8 at 15, 19, 21 (1979). If there is no measure of damage which is not unjustified and indeed unjust, courts of law cannot entertain claims by a child affected with prenatal damage against those who fail to provide its mother with the opportunity to end its damaged life, however careless and unskilful they may have been and however liable they may be to the mother for that negligent failure.

If a court had to decide whether it were better to enter into life maimed or halt than not to enter it at all, it would, I think, be bound to say it was better in all cases of mental and physical disability, except possibly those extreme cases already mentioned, of which perhaps the recent case of *Croke v Wiseman* [1981] 3 All ER 852, [1982] 1 WLR 71 is an example, but certainly not excepting such a case as the present. However that may be, it is not for the courts to take such a decision by weighing life against death or to take cognisance of a claim like this child's. I would regard it on principle as disclosing no reasonable cause of action and would accordingly prefer the master's decision to the judge's.

I am happy to find support for this view of the matter in the Law Commission's Report and the Congenital Disabilities (Civil Liability) Act 1976, to which I have already referred, and in the strong current of American authority, to which we have been referred. Direct decisions of courts in the United States of America on the same topic are of no more than persuasive authority but contain valuable material and with one exception would rule out the infant plaintiff's claims in our case.

The first of the American cases is a decision of the Supreme Court of New Jersey in 1967: *Gleitman v Cosgrove* 227 A 2d 689. It was preceded by an article by G Tedeschi, 'On Tort Liability for Wrongful Life' (1966) Israel LR 513. That article treated . . . earlier cases mainly concerned with illegitimate children and of the acts of parents in producing a child likely to be diseased, but concentrated on the impossibility of comparing the two alternatives of non-existence and existence with the disease. *Gleitman*'s case has been followed in New Jersey and in other jurisdictions of the United States of America, all but one finally approving the decision on this point that the child has no claim for wrongful life against medical advisers for incompetent advice about the risks of being born severely disabled.

The facts in *Gleitman*'s case are very like the facts of this case. The infant plaintiff was born handicapped as a result of the mother's 'German measles' during pregnancy. Dr Cosgrove and another doctor, who was also a defendant, had advised the mother (though they denied it) that the disease would have no effect on her unborn child. The doctor agreed that, if the mother had told him of the disease, his duty as a physician required him to inform her of the possibility of birth defects. The boy sued the doctors for his birth defects, the mother for the effects on her emotional state caused by her son's condition, the father for the costs incurred in caring for him. The trial judge dismissed the boy's complaint at the close of the plaintiff's case and the parents' complaint after all the evidence was heard. The Supreme Court, by a majority, affirmed the judge's decision. Proctor J, delivering the judgment of the court, held that the boy's complaint was not actionable because the conduct complained of, even if true, did not give rise to damages cognisable at law (see 227 A 2d 689 at 692). Both Proctor J and Weintraub CJ, assenting on this point, stated that the boy's complaint involved saying that he would have been better off not to have been born at all. 'Man, who knows nothing of death or nothingness, cannot possibly know whether that is so.' (See 227 A 2d 689 at 711.)

Between 1977 and 1981 are to be found other reported decisions on claims by handicapped children and their parents against medical men and hospital authorities. In the earliest of them the Appeals Court of New York upheld motions to dismiss complaints by children suffering from Down's syndrome (mongolism) and polycystic kidney disease: see *Becker v Schwartz, Park v Chessin* 413 NYS 2d 895 (1978). Judge Jasen regarded the complaints as failing to state 'legally cognizable causes of action' (at 901), Judge Fuchsberg as 'not justiciable' (at 903).

These and later cases are helpfully reviewed by District Judge Blatt in dismissing another mongol child's claim for wrongful life in a South Carolina District Court: see *Phillips v USA* 508 F Supp 537 (1980), where he points out that the decision of the Court of Appeal in California in *Curlender v Bio-Science Laboratories* 165 Cal 477 (1980) is the only case recognising such a cause of action.

I have not found in the judgment of Presiding Justice Jefferson in the *Curlender* case any answer to the reasoned objections to this cause of action which are to be found in *Gleitman*'s case and those cases which have followed it.

. . .

Judicial opinion expressed in the American decisions can, I think, be summarised in the following propositions: (1) though what gives rise to the cause of action is not just life but life with defects, the real cause of action is negligence in causing life; (2) negligent advice or failure to advise is the proximate cause of the child's life (though not of its defects); (3) a child has no right to be born as a whole, functional being (without defects); (4) it is contrary to public policy, which is to preserve human life, to give a child a right not to be born except as a whole, functional being, and to impose on another a corresponding duty to prevent a child being born except without defects, that is, a duty to cause the death of an unborn child with defects; (5) it is impossible to measure the damages for being born with defects because it is impossible to compare the life of a child born with defects and non-existence as a human being; (6) accordingly, by being born with defects a child has suffered no injury cognisable by law and if it is to have a claim for being so born the law must be reformed by legislation.

The current of opinion has run in favour of the fourth consideration and against the fifth consideration even to the point of dismissing it altogether. Authority for that, and for the consideration which I have formulated, is to be found in particular in the judgment of the Supreme Court of New Jersey given by Pashman J in *Berman v Allan* 404 A 2d 8 at 11–13 (1979), in the judgments of Presiding Judge Cercone and Judge Spaeth in *Speck v Finegold* 408 A 2d 496 at 508, 512 (1979) and in the judgment of District Judge Blatt in *Phillips v USA* 508 F Supp 537 at 543 (1980), which I have already mentioned.

There are indications, to which counsel for the plaintiffs called our attention, that some of the judges' opinions on the sanctity of human life were influenced by the illegality of abortion in some states; but those indications do not, in my opinion, play a decisive part in their decisions or weaken their persuasive force in considering the right answer to the same question in a jurisdiction where abortion has some statutory sanction.

I do not think it matters whether the injury is not an injury recognised by the law or the damages are not damages which the law can award. Whichever way it is put, the objection means that the cause of action is not cognisable or justiciable or 'reasonable', and I can draw no distinction between the first two terms and the third as it is rather artificially used in RSC Ord 18, r 19.

The defendants must be assumed to have been careless. The child suffers from serious disabilities. If the defendants had not been careless, the child would not be suffering now because it would not be alive. Why should the defendants not pay the child for its suffering? The answer lies in the implications and consequences of holding that they should. If public policy favoured the introduction of this novel cause of action, I would not let the strict application of logic or the absence of precedent defeat it. But, as it would be, in my judgment, against public policy for the courts to entertain claims like those which are the subject of this appeal, I would for this reason, and for the other reasons which I have given, allow the appeal . . .

Griffiths LJ: The child's claim for 'wrongful life' is put against the hospital by the following steps. (1) The hospital when analysing the mother's blood owed a duty of care to the fetus in her womb. This point is conceded by the hospital for the purposes of this appeal. (2) The hospital discharge that duty of care by correctly advising whether the analysis shows that the mother has been infected. (3) In breach of that duty the hospital negligently advised that the analysis showed that the mother was not infected. (4) That breach of duty caused the birth of the child because, if the hospital had correctly advised that the mother was infected, she would have decided to have an abortion. (5) As a result of being born the child has to bear the afflictions of deafness, partial blindness and some degree of mental retardation, which society and the law should concur in treating as something that should not have happened to the child and for which she should be compensated by the negligent hospital.

It can thus be seen that the child's allegation is that but for the negligence of the hospital she would not have been born; it is a result of their wrong that she has been born; hence the term 'wrongful life'. The claim is put in a similar manner against the doctor.

Whether the law should give a remedy in such circumstances has been considered by the Law Commission. They concluded that there should be no liability for wrongful life and deliberately drafted cl 1 of the Congenital Disabilities (Civil Liability) Bill to exclude any such liability. Parliament accepted that advice and enacted the material part of the Congenital Disabilities (Civil Liability) Act 1976 in precisely the same language as the Law Commission's Bill. I am unable to accept the submission of counsel for the plaintiffs that the language of s 1 does not exclude the action for wrongful life; I have no doubt that it achieves its objective.

We have referred to seven decisions of courts in the United States of America; all save one of those courts have denied a remedy for wrongful life.

The remedy has been denied on a variety of different grounds. The Law Commission were of the opinion that it would impose an intolerable burden on the medical profession because of a subconscious pressure to advise abortions in doubtful cases for fear of actions for damages. I do not myself find this a convincing reason for denying the action if it would otherwise lie. The decision whether or not to have an abortion must always be the mother's; the duty of the medical profession can be no more than to advise her of her right to have an abortion and of the pros and cons of doing so. If there is a risk that the child will be born deformed, that risk must be explained to the mother, but it surely cannot be asserted that the doctor owes a duty to the fetus to urge its destruction. Provided the doctor gives a balanced explanation of the risks involved in continuing the pregnancy, including the risk of injury to the fetus, he cannot be expected to do more, and need have no fear of an action being brought against him.

To my mind, the most compelling reason to reject this cause of action is the intolerable and insoluble problem it would create in the assessment of damage. The basis of damages for personal injury is the comparison between the state of the plaintiff before he was injured and his condition after he was injured. This is often a hard enough task in all conscience and it has an element of artificiality about it, for who can say that there is any sensible correlation between pain and money? Nevertheless, the courts have been able to produce a broad tariff that appears at the moment to be acceptable to society as doing rough justice. But the whole exercise, difficult as it is, is anchored in the first place to the condition of the plaintiff before the injury which the court can comprehend and evaluate. In a claim for wrongful life how does the court begin to make an assessment? The plaintiff does not say, 'But for your negligence I would have been born uninjured'; the plaintiff says, 'But for your negligence I would never have been born.' The court then has to compare the state of the plaintiff with non-existence, of which the court can know nothing; this I regard as an impossible task. Counsel for the plaintiffs suggested that the court should assess the damages on the assumption that the plaintiff's injury had been caused by the hospital, and then discount the damages because it had not been so caused. But he was quite unable, and I do not blame him, to suggest any principle on which the discount should be calculated.

Again, suppose by some happy chance the child is born with only a slight deformity, can it bring an action on the basis that it would have been killed in the womb if the mother had been told of the risk of greater deformity? Such a claim seems utterly offensive; there should be rejoicing that the hospital's mistake bestowed the gift of life on the child. If such claims are rejected, on what basis could a claim be brought for a more serious injury? Only, it would seem, on the basis that the state of the child is such that it were better dead than alive. But, knowing nothing of death, who is to answer this question, and what two minds will approach the answer by the same route? I regard the question as wholly outside the competence of judicial determination.

I would reject this novel cause of action because I see no way of determining which plaintiffs can claim, that is, how gravely deformed must the child be before a claim will lie? and secondly because of the impossibility of assessing the damage it has suffered.

The common law does not have the tools to fashion a remedy in these cases. If society feels that such cases are deserving of compensation, some entirely novel and arbitrary measure of damage is called for, which I agree with the American judge would be better introduced by legislation than by judges striving to solve the insoluble.

The position at common law is by no means straightforward, as these judgments make clear. We would suggest the following analysis:

1. The action is by the child.
2. In analysing the action three issues have to be considered:

   (a) what is the doctor's *duty* to the child?
   (b) what *damage* known to the law does the child suffer?
   (c) what *damages*, if any, should be recoverable?

3. *Duty*. Is the doctor's duty to prevent the birth of the child *or* simply to inform

about the risk of handicap? This latter duty raises the question of 'Who should be informed?'. Since you cannot inform a foetus, it may be that the duty is to inform the mother, but since the duty is owed to the child, the mother is being informed *qua* agent.

4. Since the first duty (ie to prevent birth), as the Court of Appeal recognised in *McKay*, cannot be part of English law, there can be no action based upon any alleged breach of duty.

5. The duty should, therefore, be the second one stated above ie to inform about the risk of handicap. The Court of Appeal, in our view, were wrong to see this as a duty owed *only* to the mother, so that the child could not sue. There is no reason why the duty cannot be owed *to the child* through the agency of its mother and hence an action brought by the child for breach of a duty owed to it.

6. *Damage*. If the duty is to inform the child through its mother of the risk of handicap, what harm recognised in law does the child suffer as a consequence of breach of this duty? There are two possibilities: either it could be damaged in the form of *being born handicapped*, or in the form of *economic loss* arising from being born with a handicap (or *quaere*, for just being born at all?).

7. Is this a distinction without a difference? Is not the economic loss recoverable only if the birth is an injury? Since the argument has it that birth is not an injury, no economic loss can be recovered since it is not consequent upon any physical injury. The fallacy of this argument is to fail to recognise that in some circumstances economic loss arising from a breach of duty is recoverable in its own right. Could this situation be seen as such a case?

8. *Damages*. These would then be calculated either (i) on the basis of the totality of the child's costs of living or (ii) on the basis of the additional costs incurred by the child throughout its life because of its handicap. Which of these, do you think, is the more accurate measure?

9. If this were accepted, and economic loss were recoverable, is this not, *in effect*, merely another way of achieving what some might see as the just result, namely the provision of compensation? If this is so, why would a court stop at compensating merely for the consequence of being handicapped as opposed to the cost of being alive? The answer must lie in the limitless nature of the latter.

10. Support for the above analysis can be seen in the developing American law (for a most thorough discussion see A Capron, 'Genetic Counselling and the Law' (1979) 79 Columbia LR 619). We now set out some of the American case law whose analysis of this area deserves study.

We should first notice the decision of the Californian Court of Appeals in *Curlender v Bio-Science Laboratories*, referred to by Stephenson LJ in *McKay* as unhelpful but seen in the United States at the time as representing a breakthrough.

Curlender v Bio-Science Laboratories
165 Cal 477 (1980) (California Court of Appeals; footnotes omitted)

Jefferson J: The appeal presents an issue of first impression in California: What remedy, if any, is available in this state to a severely impaired child—genetically defective—born as the result of defendants' negligence in conducting certain genetic tests of the child's parents—tests which, if properly done, would have disclosed the high probability that the actual, catastrophic result would occur?

In the first cause of action against the named defendants, plaintiff Shauna alleged that on January 15, 1977, her parents, Phillis and Hyam Curlender, retained defendant laboratories to administer certain tests designed to reveal whether either of the parents were carriers of genes which would result in the conception and birth of a child with Tay-Sachs disease, medically defined as 'amaurotic familial idiocy'. The tests on plaintiff's parents were performed on January 21, 1977, and, it was alleged, due to defendants' negligence, 'incorrect and inaccurate' information was disseminated to plaintiff's parents concerning their status as carriers.

The complaint did not allege the date of plaintiff's birth, so we do not know whether the parents relied upon the test results in conceiving plaintiff, or, as parents-to-be when the tests were made, relied upon the results in failing to avail themselves of amniocentesis and an abortion. In any event, on May 10, 1978, plaintiff's parents were informed that plaintiff had Tay-Sachs disease.

As the result of the disease, plaintiff Shauna suffers from 'mental retardation, susceptibility to other diseases, convulsions, sluggishness, apathy, failure to fix objects with her eyes, inability to take an interest in her surroundings, loss of motor reactions, inability to sit up or hold her head up, loss of weight, muscle atrophy, blindness, pseudobulper palsy, inability to feed orally, decerebrate rigidity and gross physical deformity'. It was alleged that Shauna's life expectancy is estimated to be four years. The complaint also contained allegations that plaintiff suffers 'pain, physical and emotional distress, fear, anxiety, despair, loss of enjoyment of life, and frustration. . . .'

The complaint sought costs of plaintiff's care as damages and also damages for emotional distress and the deprivation of '72.6 years of her life'. In addition, punitive damages of three million dollars were sought, on the ground that '[a]t the time that Defendants . . . [tested the parents] Defendants, and each of them, had been expressly informed by the nation's leading authority on Tay-Sachs disease that said test procedures were substantially inaccurate and would likely result in disasterous [sic] and catastrophic consequences to the patients, and Defendants knew that said procedures were improper, inadequate and with insufficient controls and that the results of such testing were likely to be inaccurate and that a false negative result would have disasterous [sic] and catastrophic consequences to the Plaintiff, all in conscious disregard of the health, safety and well-being of Plaintiff. . . .'

. . .

A major (and much cited) opinion considering a claim for damages by an impaired infant plaintiff and his parents is *Gleitman v Cosgrove* 49 NJ 22, 227 A 2d 689 (1967) from the New Jersey Supreme Court. The Gleitmans brought a malpractice action against Mrs Gleitman's physician for damages because the Gleitman child, Jeffrey, had been born with serious impairments of sight, speech, and hearing. Mrs Gleitman had contracted rubella (measles) during the first trimester of pregnancy (the first three months). Defendant was made aware of this fact, but failed to inform the mother-to-be of any potentially harmful consequences to her child; Mrs Gleitman was assured by him that such consequences would not occur, although it was common medical knowledge that rubella, contracted during early pregnancy, often causes the type of defects suffered by Jeffrey, who was also mentally retarded.

The majority of the *Gleitman* court barred recovery by *either* the parents or the child on two grounds: (1) the perceived impossibility of computing damages and (2) public policy. With respect to the computation of damages, the court explained that '[t]he normal measure of damages in tort actions is compensatory. Damages are measured by comparing the condition plaintiff would have been in, had the defendants not been negligent, with plaintiff's impaired condition as a result of the negligence. The infant plaintiff would have us measure the difference between his life with defects against the utter void of nonexistence, but it is impossible to make such a determination. This Court cannot weigh the value of life with impairments against the nonexistence of life itself. By asserting that he should not have been born, the infant plaintiff makes it logically impossible for a court to measure his alleged damages because of the impossibility of making the comparison required by compensatory remedies'. (*Gleitman, supra,* 227 A 2d 689, 692).

Any decision negating the value of life directly or by implication was seen by the majority in *Gleitman* as an impermissible expression of public policy. There was considerable discussion of the legality of any abortion which would have been undertaken to prevent Jeffrey's birth. The majority referred with approval to the analysis presented in 1 Israel Law Review 513 (1966) by Tedeschi, entitled 'On Tort Liability for "Wrongful Life".'

A vastly different view was expressed by a dissenting opinion in *Gleitman*. It was there declared that the majority 'permits a wrong with serious consequential injury to go wholly unredressed. That provides no deterrent to professional irresponsibility and is neither just nor compatible with expanding principles of liability in the field of torts'. (*Gleitman, supra,* 227 A 2d 689, 703 (dis opn).) As to the impossibility of computing damages, reference was made to a statement by the United States Supreme Court in *Story Parchment Co v Paterson Co* 282 US 555, 563, 51 S Ct 248, 250, 75 L Ed 544 (1931), that difficulties encountered in computing damages cannot be permitted to justify a denial of liability. However, the reasoning and result in *Gleitman's* majority opinion have been, in the main, followed (albeit blindly in our opinion) in other jurisdictions. (See *Stewart v Long Island College Hospital* 58 Misc 2d 432, 296 NYS 2d 41 (1968) and *Dumer v St Michael's Hospital* 69 Wis 2d 766, 233 NW 2d 372 (1975).) It has also been analysed and criticised. (See Note, 55 Minn L Rev 58 (1971).)

Of some significance with respect to this question is the fact that in 1973, *Roe v Wade*, 410 US 113, 93 S Ct 705, 35 L Ed 2d 147, was decided by the United States Supreme Court. The nation's high court determined that parents have a *constitutionally protected right* to obtain an abortion during the first trimester of pregnancy, free of state interference. We deem this decision to be of considerable importance in defining the parameters of 'wrongful-life' litigation.

The *Roe v Wade* case played a rather substantial part in the partial retreat from the *Gleitman* holding by the New Jersey Supreme Court majority in *Berman v Allan* 80 NJ 421, 404 A 2d 8 (1979). The Bermans, parents and child, brought suit for medical malpractice. Mrs. Berman had become pregnant in her late thirties, a circumstance involving a substantial risk that the child would be born with Down's syndrome (mongolism), one of the major characteristics of which is mental retardation. Sharon Berman, the child, was so afflicted. Amniocentesis—by that time a well established technique for discerning birth defects *in utero*—had not been suggested to the Bermans. The majority in the *Berman* court held that the *parents* had stated a cause of action, and that they could recover damages for emotional distress, but that lifetime support for Sharon could not be awarded.

But the *Berman* court rejected the concept that the infant Sharon possessed an independent cause of action. Referring to the difficulty of measuring damages in such a case, the court declared that '[n]onetheless, were the *measure* of damages our sole concern, it is possible that some judicial remedy could be fashioned which would redress plaintiff, if only in part, for injuries suffered'. Here, the majority chose to rely on public policy considerations. The *Berman* court considered that Sharon had not suffered any damage cognisable at law by being brought into existence. It was explained that '[o]ne of the most deeply held beliefs of our society is that life—whether experienced with or without a major physical handicap—is more precious than nonlife. . . . Sharon, by virtue of her birth, will be able to love and be loved and to experience happiness and pleasure—emotions which are truly the essence of life and which are far more valuable than the suffering she may endure. To rule otherwise would require us to disavow the basic assumption upon which our society is based. This we cannot do.' (*Berman, supra,* 404 A 2d 8, 12–13.)

The dissenting opinion in *Berman*, noting that the majority had in effect partially overruled *Gleitman*, urged complete rejection of the majority view on the ground that '[t]he child . . . was owed directly, during its gestation, a duty of reasonable care from the same physicians who undertook to care for its mother—then expectant—and that duty, to render complete and competent medical advice, was seriously breached'. (*Berman, supra,* 404 A 2d 8, 15 (dis opn).) Taking cognisance of the present legality of abortions in the first trimester, the dissent perceived a duty on the part of medical practitioners to ensure that, under certain circumstances, parents-to-be had the opportunity to decide the future of their child—its existence or nonexistence. 'To be denied the opportunity—indeed, the right—to apply one's own moral values in reaching that decision [concerning the child's future], is a serious, irreversible wrong.' (*Id* 404 A 2d at p 18.)

The dissenting opinion in *Berman* expressed the cogent observation that, as for the child, '[a]n adequate comprehension of the infant's claims under these circumstances *starts with the realisation that the infant has come into this world and is here*, encumbered by an injury attributable to the malpractice of the doctors'. (*Berman, supra*, 404 A 2d 8, 19.) (Emphasis added.)

In New York . . . there have been a series of decisions wrestling with 'wrongful-life' problems with the quite predictable divergent expressions by the judiciary. In only one case, however (overruled by a higher court) did the court grant recognition to a cause of action by a child so born.

In *Park v Chessin* 60 AD 80, 400 NYS 2d 110 (1977), an intermediate New York appellate court considered the following facts. The Parks had had one child born with polycystic kidney disease, a fatal hereditary ailment. The baby died. The parents consulted defendant doctors and informed them of this; assured that the condition would not reoccur, the Parks had a second child, who also had the disease but survived for a short life span of 2 and ½ years. The court held that these facts gave both the parents and child causes of action, that 'decisional law must keep pace with expanding technological, economic and social change. Inherent in the abolition of the statutory ban on abortion . . . is a public policy consideration which gives potential parents the right, within certain statutory and case law limitations, *not* to have a child. This right extends to instances in which it can be determined with reasonable medical certainty that the child would be born deformed. *The breach of this right may also be said to be tortious to the fundamental right of a child to be born as a whole, functional human being.*' (*Park, supra*, 400 NYS 2d 110, 114.) (Emphasis added.)

But this view of the law also had a short life span. This decision was reviewed in *Becker v Schwartz* 46 NY 2d 401, 413 NYS 2d 895, 386 NE 2d 807 (1978) (as a companion case) and overruled. The Beckers and their mongoloid infant sought damages from medical doctors who had not, despite the mother's age when she became pregnant, warned of the danger or informed the Beckers of amniocentesis. The parents, declared *Becker*, had stated a cause of action and could recover their pecuniary loss but *not* damages for emotional distress, as the latter recovery would offend public policy. The infant plaintiffs in both *Becker* and *Park* were held to be barred from recovery because of the inability of the law to make a comparison between human existence with handicaps and no life at all. The court particularly rejected the idea that a child may expect life without deformity: 'There is no precedent for recognition at the Appellate Division of "the fundamental right of a child to be born as a whole, functional human being". . . .' (*Becker, supra*, 413 NYS 2d 895 at 900, 386 NE 2d 807 at 812.)

The high court in Pennsylvania issued an exhaustive opinion in 1979 concerning the various aspects of the 'wrongful-life' problem. The case was *Speck v Finegold*,— Pa Super—, 408 A 2d 496, a malpractice suit by parents and child occasioned by the birth of the child with neurofibromatosis, a seriously crippling condition already evidenced in the child's siblings. Overruling the trial court, *Speck* recognised the parents' cause of action but not that of the infant plaintiff.

We quote at length from the *Speck* court's opinion: 'In the instant case, we deny Francine's [infant plaintiff] claim to be made whole. When we examine Francine's claim, we find regardless of whether her claim is based on 'wrongful life' or otherwise, there is a failure to state a legally cognisable cause of action even though, admittedly, the defendants' actions of negligence were the proximate cause of her defective birth. Her claims to be whole have two fatal weaknesses. First, there is no precedent in appellate judicial pronouncements that holds a child has a fundamental right to be born as a whole, functional human being. Whether it is better to have never been born at all rather than to have been born with serious mental defects is a mystery more properly left to the philosophers and theologians, a mystery which would lead us into the field of metaphysics, beyond the realm of our understanding or ability to solve. . . . [This] cause of action . . . demands a calculation of damages dependent on a comparison between Hobson's choice of life in an impaired state and nonexistence. This the law is incapable of doing. [Fn omitted.] . . . unfortunately, . . . this is not an action cognisable in law. Thus, the recognised principle, not peculiar to traditional tort law alone, that it would be a denial of justice to deny all relief where a wrong is of such a nature as to preclude certain ascertained damages, is inapposite and inapplicable here.' (*Speck, supra,* 408 A 2d 496, 508.)

Other jurisdictions, following the lead of the New Jersey and New York cases, have rejected the concept of an infant's cause of action for 'wrongful life'. (See *Elliott v Brown* 361 So 2d 546 (Ala 1978), rejecting the 'wrongful life' cause of action in that jurisdiction; see also *Jacobs v Theimer* 519 SW 2d 846 (Tex 1975), holding that the mother of a defective child had stated a cause of action for failure of the defendant physician to diagnose rubella during early pregnancy and counsel accordingly; also, recovery was allowed for those costs reasonably related to caring for the child's physical defects. The court declared that '[n]o public policy obstacle should be interposed to that recovery'. (519 SW 2d 846, 849).)

Two decisions of note have involved Tay-Sachs impairment—the condition involved in the case before us. In *Howard v Lecher* 42 NY 2d 109, 397 NYS 2d 363, 366 NE 2d 64 (1977), an intermediate appellate court in New York considered an action brought by the parents to recover damages for emotional distress from the consulting physicians. In *Howard,* the child died. Denying recovery, the *Howard* majority reasoned that recognition of the parents' cause of action 'would require the extension of traditional tort concepts beyond manageable bounds'. (397 NYS 2d at 364, 366 NE 2d at 65.)

A dissenting judge in *Howard* expostulated that the issue was simply whether a patient and parent-to-be, the mother, may recover damages from her physician for the latter's negligence. He found it not unreasonable, given the present state of medical knowledge concerning genetically caused birth deformities and the procedures available for avoiding such deformities, for the law to require an attending physician to take a genealogical history of the parents, to perform any available appropriate tests indicated by such history, and inform the parents of any potential dangers so that they would be able to make an informed decision concerning continuation of pregnancy.

In *Gildiner v Thomas Jefferson Univ Hospital* 451 F Supp 692 (ED Pa 1978), the parents had been tested for Tay-Sachs; the tests indicated that amniocentesis should be performed; it was performed, but negligently; the parents were both carriers, and the infant born to them suffered from Tay-Sachs. Relying on *Gleitman v Cosgrove, supra,* 49 NJ 22, 227 A 2d 689, the federal district court held that the parents could recover damages, but the child could not. A strong public policy was perceived in allowing parental recovery: 'Tay-Sachs disease can be prevented only by accurate genetic testing combined with the right of parents to abort afflicted fetuses within appropriate time limitations. [¶] *Society has an interest in insuring that genetic testing is properly performed and interpreted*'. (*Gildiner, supra,* 451 F Supp 692, 696.) (Emphasis added.)

. . .

From our analysis and study, we conclude that certain general observations are appropriate concerning the decisional law in this country to date with respect to the 'wrongful life' problem.

First. For clear analysis it is important to recognise certain distinctions among the cases purportedly dealing with the 'wrongful-life' concept. One such distinction is that concerning the condition of the child involved. Surely there is a world of difference between an unwanted healthy child who is illegitimate (*Stills v Gratton, supra*), the unwanted tenth child of a marriage (*Custodio v Bauer* 251 Cal App 2d 303, 59 Cal Rptr 463 (1967)) and the severely deformed infant plaintiff, Shauna, in the case at bench. Illegitimacy is a status which may or may not prove to be a hindrance to one so born, depending on a multitude of other facts; it cannot be disputed that in present society such a circumstance, both socially and legally, no longer need present an overwhelming obstacle. The same is true for the simply unwanted child. We agree with the reasoning of *Zepeda* and *Stills* that a cause of action based upon impairment of status—illegitimacy contrasted with legitimacy— should not be recognisable at law *because* a necessary element for the establishment of any cause of action in tort is missing, *injury* and damages consequential to that injury. A child born with severe impairment, however, presents an entirely different situation because the necessary element of *injury* is present.

Second. The decisional law of other jurisdictions, while not dispositive of Shauna's claim pursuant to California law, is of considerable significance in defining the basic issues underlying the true 'wrongful-life' action—one brought by the infant whose painful existence is a direct and proximate result of negligence by others. That decisional law demonstrates some measure of progression in our law. Confronted with the fact that the births of these infants may be directly traced to the negligent conduct of others, and that the result of that negligence is palpable injury, involving not only pecuniary loss but untold anguish on the part of all concerned, the courts in our sister states have progressed from a stance of barring all recovery to a recognition that, at least, the parents of such a child may state a cause of action founded on negligence.

We note that there has been a gradual retreat from the position of accepting 'impossibility of measuring damages' as the sole ground for barring the infant's right of recovery, although the courts continue to express divergent views on how the parents' damages should be measured, in terms of allowing recovery for both pecuniary loss and damages for emotional distress, or, in recognising one element of recovery only, but not the other.

The concept of public policy has played an important role in this developing field of law. Public policy, as perceived by most courts, has been utilised as the basis for denying recovery; in some fashion, a deeply held belief in the sanctity of life has compelled some courts to deny recovery to those among us who have been born with serious impairment. But the dissents, written along the way, demonstrate that there is not universal acceptance of the notion that 'metaphysics' or 'religious beliefs', rather than law, should govern the situation; the dissents have emphasised that considerations of public policy should include regard for social welfare as affected by careful genetic counseling and medical procedures.

We have alluded to the monumental implications of *Roe v Wade*, *supra*, 410 US 113, 93 S Ct 705, 35 L Ed 2d 147, one of which is the present legality of, and availability of, eugenic abortion in the proper case. Another factor of substantial proportions in 'wrongful-life' litigation is the dramatic increase, in the last few decades, of the medical knowledge and skill needed to avoid genetic disaster. As the author of the article in the Yale Law Journal points out (see fn. 8): 'Genetic defects represent an increasingly large part of the overall national health care burden.' (87 Yale Law Journal 1496.) The writer concluded that the law indeed has an appropriate function in encouraging adequate and careful medical practice in the field of genetic counseling, observing that '[t]ort law, a well-recognised means of regulating the practice of medicine, can be used both to establish and to limit the duty of physicians to fulfil this [genetic counseling] function'. (87 Yale Law Journal 1499.)

Third. Despite the cool reception accorded such 'wrongful-life' litigation, both parents and their children have continued to seek redress for the wrongs committed, presumably for a number of reasons: (1) the serious nature of the wrong; (2) increasing sophistication as to the causes, which may not with present knowledge be attributed to the fine hand of providence but rather to lack of care; and (3) the understanding that the law reflects, perhaps later than sooner, basic changes in the way society views such matters.

. . . We have no difficulty in ascertaining and finding the existence of a duty owed by medical laboratories engaged in genetic testing to parents and their as yet unborn children to use ordinary care in administration of available tests for the purpose of providing information concerning potential genetic defects in the unborn. The public policy considerations with respect to the individuals involved and to society as a whole dictate recognition of such a duty, and it is of significance that in no decision that has come to our attention which has dealt with the 'wrongful-life' concept has it been suggested that public policy considerations negate the existence of such a duty. Nor have other jurisdictions had any difficulty in finding a breach of duty under appropriate circumstances or in finding the existence of the requisite proximate causal link between the breach and the claimed injury; we find no bar to a holding that the defendants owed a duty to the child plaintiff before us and breached that duty.

The real crux of the problem is whether the breach of duty was the proximate cause of *an injury cognisable at law*. The injury, of course, is not the particular defect with which a plaintiff is afflicted—considered in the abstract—but it is the birth of plaintiff with such defect.

The circumstance that the birth and injury have come hand in hand has caused other courts to deal with the problem by barring recovery. The reality of the 'wrongful-life' concept is that such a plaintiff both *exists* and *suffers*, due to the negligence of others. It is neither necessary nor just to retreat into meditation on the mysteries of life. We need not be concerned with the fact that had defendants not been negligent, the plaintiff might not have come into existence at all. The certainty of genetic impairment is no longer a mystery. In addition, a reverent appreciation of life compels recognition that plaintiff, however impaired she may be, has come into existence as a living person with certain rights.

One of the fears expressed in the decisional law is that, once it is determined that such infants have rights cognisable at law, nothing would prevent such a plaintiff from bringing suit against its own parents for allowing plaintiff to be born. In our view, the fear is groundless. The 'wrongful-life' cause of action with which we are concerned is based upon negligently caused failure by someone under a duty to do so to inform the prospective parents of facts needed by them to make a conscious choice *not* to become parents. If a case arose where, despite due care by the medical profession in transmitting the necessary warnings, parents made a conscious choice to proceed with a pregnancy, with full knowledge that a seriously impaired infant would be born, that conscious choice would provide an intervening act of proximate cause to preclude liability insofar as defendants other than the parents were concerned. Under such circumstances, we see no sound public policy which should protect those parents from being answerable for the pain, suffering and misery which they have wrought upon their offspring.

In our consideration of whether the child plaintiff has stated a cause of action, we find it instructive to look first to the statutory law of this state. Our Civil Code section 3281 provides that '*[e]very person* who suffers detriment from the unlawful act or omission of another, may recover from the person in fault a compensation therefor in money, which is called damages'. Civil Code section 3282 defines detriment as 'a loss or harm suffered in person or property'. Civil Code section 3333 provides: 'For the breach of an obligation not arising from contract, the measure of damages, except where otherwise expressly provided by this Code, is the amount which will compensate for all the detriment proximately caused thereby, whether it could have been anticipated or not'.

In addition, we have long adhered to the principle that there should be a remedy for every wrong committed. 'Fundamental in our jurisprudence is the principle that for every wrong there is a remedy and that an injured party should be compensated for all damage proximately caused by the wrongdoer. Although we recognise exceptions from these fundamental principles, no departure should be sanctioned unless there is a strong necessity therefor. [¶] The general rule of damages in tort is that the injured party may recover for all detriment caused whether it could have been anticipated or not.' (*Crisci v Security Ins Co* 66 Cal 2d 425 at 433, 58 Cal Rptr 13 at 18, 426 P 2d 173 at 178 (1967).)

We have concluded that it is clearly consistent with the applicable principles of the statutory and decisional tort law in this state to recognise a cause of action stated by plaintiff against the defendants. . . . the extent of recovery, however, is subject to certain limitations due to the nature of the tort involved. While ordinarily a defendant is liable for all consequences flowing from the injury (*Custodia v Bauer, supra*), it is appropriate in the case before us to tailor the elements of recovery, taking into account particular circumstances involved (as was done in *Stills v Gratton, supra*).

The complaint seeks damages based upon an actuarial life expectancy of plaintiff of more than 70 years—the life expectancy if plaintiff had been born without the Tay-Sachs disease. The complaint sets forth that plaintiff's actual life expectancy, because of the disease, is only four years. We reject as untenable the claim that plaintiff is entitled to damages as if plaintiff had been born without defects and would have had a normal life expectancy. Plaintiff's right to damages must be considered on the basis of plaintiff's mental and physical condition at birth and her expected condition during the short life span (four years according to the complaint) anticipated for one with her impaired condition. In similar fashion, we reject the notion that a 'wrongful-life' cause of action involves any attempted evaluation of a claimed right *not* to be born. In essence, we construe the 'wrongful-life' cause of action by the defective child as the right of such child to recover damages for the pain and suffering to be endured during the limited life span available to such a child and any special pecuniary loss resulting from the impaired condition.

Do you find the reasoning of the court persuasive? Remember Stephenson LJ in *McKay* thought *Curlender* did not provide 'any answer to the reasoned objections to this cause of action.' Does *Curlender* satisfactorily overcome the problems of *duty*, *damage* and *damages*? The California Supreme Court denied cert (ie refused leave to appeal) and, therefore, it might be thought that the Supreme Court had endorsed the views expressed in *Curlender*. But this was not so, as the subsequent decision of the Supreme Court in *Turpin v Sortini* shows.

Turpin v Sortini
643 P 2d 954 (1978) (Supreme Court of California; footnotes omitted)

Kaus J: The allegations of the complaint disclose the following facts. On September 24, 1976, James and Donna Turpin, acting on the advice of their pediatrician, brought their first—and at that time their only—daughter, Hope, to the Leon S Peters Rehabilitation Center at the Fresno Community Hospital for evaluation of a possible hearing defect. Hope was examined and tested by Adam J Sortini, a licensed professional specialising in the diagnosis and treatment of speech and hearing defects.

The complaint alleges that Sortini and other persons at the hospital negligently examined, tested and evaluated Hope and incorrectly advised her pediatrician that her hearing was within normal limits when, in reality, she was 'stone deaf' as a result of an hereditary ailment. Hope's parents did not learn of her condition until October 15, 1977 when it was diagnosed by other specialists. According to the complaint, the nature of the condition is such that there is a 'reasonable degree of medical probability' that the hearing defect would be inherited by any offspring of James and Donna.

The complaint further alleges that in December 1976, before learning of Hope's true condition and relying on defendant's diagnosis, James and Donna conceived a second child, Joy. The complaint avers that had the Turpins known of Hope's hereditary deafness they would not have conceived Joy. Joy was born August 23, 1977, and suffers from the same total deafness as Hope.

On the basis of these facts, James, Donna, Hope and Joy filed a complaint setting forth four causes of action against defendants Sortini, the hospital, the rehabilitation center and various Does. The first cause of action, brought on behalf of Hope, seeks damages for the harm Hope has allegedly suffered as a result of the delay in the diagnosis of her condition. The second cause of action—the only cause before us on this appeal—was brought on behalf of Joy and seeks (1) general damages for being 'deprived of the fundamental right of a child to be born as a whole, functional human being without total deafness' and (2) special damages for the 'extraordinary expenses for specialised teaching, training and hearing equipment' which she will incur during her lifetime as a result of her hearing impairment. The third and fourth causes of action, brought on behalf of James and Donna, seek, respectively, special damages relating to the support and medical care of Joy to the age of majority, and general damages for emotional distress sustained by James and Donna 'attendant to the raising and caring of a totally deaf child.'

The explanation for the divergent results [in other jurisdictions] is that while courts have been willing to permit parents to recover for medical costs or—in some cases—other harms which the parents would not have incurred 'but for' the defendants' negligence, they have been reluctant to permit the child to complain when, but for the defendant's negligence, he or she would not have been born at all.

In this context the recent decisions have either concluded that the child has sustained no 'legally cognisable injury' or that appropriate damages are impossible to ascertain.

. . . defendants' basic position—supported by the numerous out-of-state authorities—is that Joy has suffered no legally cognisable injury or rationally ascertainable damages as a result of their alleged negligence. Although the issues of 'legally cognisable injury' and 'damages' are intimately related and in some sense inseparable, past cases have generally treated the two as distinct matters and, for purposes of analysis, it seems useful to follow that approach.

With respect to the issue of legally cognisable injury, the parties agree that the difficult question here does not stem from the fact that defendants' allegedly negligent act and plaintiff's asserted injury occurred before plaintiff's birth. Although at one time the common law denied recovery for injuries inflicted before birth, California—in tune with other American jurisdictions—has long abandoned that arbitrary limitation. (See Civ Code, § 29; *Scott v McPheeters* 33 Cal App 2d 629, 92 P 2d 678 (1939). See generally Robertson, *Toward Rational Boundaries of Tort Liability for Injury to the Unborn: Prenatal Injuries, Preconception Injuries and Wrongful Life*, 1978 Duke LJ 1401, 1402–1413.) Thus, if Joy's deafness was caused by negligent treatment of her mother during pregnancy, or if it resulted from a tort committed upon her mother before conception (see, e g, *Renslow v Mennonite Hospital* (1977) 67 Ill 2d 348 [10 Ill Dec 484, 367 NE 2d 1250]; *Bergstresser v Mitchell* (8th Cir 1978) 577 F 2d 22; Annot (1979) 91 ALR 3d 316), it is clear that she would be entitled to recover against the negligent party.

Joy's complaint attempts, in effect, to bring her action within the scope of the foregoing line of cases, asserting that as a result of defendants' negligence she was 'deprived of the fundamental right of a child to be born as a whole, functional human being without total deafness. . . .' While the *Curlender* decision did not embrace this approach to 'injury' completely—refusing to permit the plaintiff to recover for a reduced lifespan—it too maintained that the proper point of reference for measuring defendant's liability was simply plaintiff's condition after birth, insisting that '[w]e need not be concerned with the fact that had defendants not been negligent, the plaintiff might not have come into existence at all' (106 Cal App 3d at 829), and rejecting 'the notion that a "wrongful life" cause of action involves any attempted evaluation of a claimed right *not* to be born.' (Original italics.) (*Id*, at pp 830–831, 165 Cal Rptr 477.)

The basic fallacy of the *Curlender* analysis is that it ignores the essential nature of the defendants' alleged wrong and obscures a critical difference between wrongful life actions and the ordinary prenatal injury cases noted above. In an ordinary prenatal injury case, if the defendant had not been negligent, the child would have been born healthy; thus, as in a typical personal injury case, the defendant in such a case has interfered with the child's basic right to be free from physical injury caused by the negligence of others. In this case, by contrast, the obvious tragic fact is that plaintiff never had a chance 'to be born as a whole, functional human being without total deafness'; if defendants had performed their jobs properly, she would not have been born with hearing intact, but—according to the complaint—would not have been born at all.

A plaintiff's remedy in tort is compensatory in nature and damages are generally intended not to punish a negligent defendant but to restore an injured person as nearly as possible to the position he or she would have been in had the wrong not been done. (See generally Rest 2d Torts, § 901, com a; *Stills v Gratton, supra*, 55 Cal App 3d at 706, 127 Cal Rptr 652; 4 Witkin, Summary of Cal Law (8th ed 1974) Torts, § 842, p 3137 and cases cited.) Because nothing defendants could have done would have given plaintiff an unimpaired life, it appears inconsistent with basic tort principles to view the injury for which defendants are legally responsible solely by reference to plaintiff's present condition without taking into consideration the fact that if defendants had not been negligent she would not have been born at all. (See Capron, *Tort Liability and Genetic Counseling* (1979) 79 Colum L Rev 619, 654–657; Comment *'Wrongful Life': The Right Not to be Born* (1980) 54 Tulane L Rev 480, 494–497.)

If the relevant injury in this case is the change in the plaintiff's position attributable to the tortfeasor's actions, then the injury which plaintiff has suffered is that, as a result of defendants' negligence, she has been born with an hereditary ailment rather than not being born at all. Although plaintiff has not phrased her claim for general damages in these terms, most courts and commentators have recognised that the basic claim of 'injury' in wrongful life cases is '[i]n essence . . . that [defendants], through their negligence, [have] forced upon [the child] the worse of . . . two alternatives[,] . . . that nonexistence—never being born—would have been preferable to existence in [the] diseased state.' (*Speck v Finegold* 268 Pa Super 342, 408 A 2d 496, 511–512 (1979) (conc & dis opn by Spaeth J), affd (1981) 439 A 2d 110.)

Given this view of the relevant injury which the plaintiff has sustained at the defendant's hands, some courts have concluded that the plaintiff has suffered no legally cognisable injury on the ground that considerations of public policy dictate a conclusion that life—even with the most severe of impairments—is, as a matter of law, always preferable to nonlife. The decisions frequently suggest that a contrary conclusion would 'disavow' the sanctity and value of less-than-perfect human life. (See, eg, *Berman v Allan*, *supra*, 404 A 2d at 12–13; *Phillips v United States*, *supra*, 508 F Supp at 543.)

Although it is easy to understand and to endorse these decisions' desire to affirm the worth and sanctity of less-than-perfect life, we question whether these considerations alone provide a sound basis for rejecting the child's tort action. To begin with, it is hard to see how an award of damages to a severely handicapped or suffering child would 'disavow' the value of life or in any way suggest that the child is not entitled to the full measure of legal and nonlegal rights and privileges according to all members of society.

Moreover, while our society and our legal system unquestionably place the highest value on all human life, we do not think that it is accurate to suggest that this state's public policy establishes—as a matter of law—that under all circumstances 'impaired life' is 'preferable' to 'nonlife.' For example, Health and Safety Code section 7186, enacted in 1976, provides in part: 'The Legislature finds that adult persons have the fundamental right to control the decisions relating to the rendering of their own medical care, including the decision to have life-sustaining procedures withheld or withdrawn in instances of a terminal condition. [¶] . . . The Legislature further finds that, in the interest of protecting individual autonomy, such prolongation of life for persons with a terminal condition may cause loss of patient dignity and unnecessary pain and suffering, while providing nothing medically necessary or beneficial to the patient.' This statute recognises that—at least in some situations—public policy supports the right of each individual to make his or her own determination as to the relative value of life and death. (Cf *Matter of Quinlan* (1976) 70 NJ 10 [355 A 2d 647, 662–664]; *Superintendent of Belchertown v Saikewicz* (1977) 373 Mass 728 [370 NE 2d 417, 423–427].)

Of course, in the wrongful life context, the unborn child cannot personally make any choice as to the relative value of life or death. At that stage, however, just as in the case of an infant after birth, the law generally accords the parents the right to act to protect the child's interests. As the wrongful birth decisions recognise, when a doctor or other medical care provider negligently fails to diagnose an hereditary problem, parents are deprived of the opportunity to make an informed and meaningful decision whether to conceive and bear a handicapped child. (See, eg, *Robak v United States*, *supra*, 658 F 2d 471 at 476; *Berman v Allan*, *supra*, 404 A 2d 8 at 14; *Jacobs v Theimer*, *supra*, 519 SW 2d 846 at 849; cf *Cobbs v Grant* (1972) 8 Cal 3d 229 at 242–243, 104 Cal Rptr 505, 502 P 2d 1.) Although in deciding whether or not to bear such a child parents may properly, and undoubtedly do, take into account their own interests, parents also presumptively consider the interests of their future child. Thus, when a defendant negligently fails to diagnose an hereditary ailment, he harms the potential child as well as the parents by depriving the parents of information which may be necessary to determine whether it is in the child's own interest to be born with defects or not to be born at all.

In this case, in which the plaintiff's only affliction is deafness, it seems quite unlikely that a jury would ever conclude that life with such a condition is worse than not being born at all. Other wrongful life cases, however, have involved children with much more serious, debilitating and painful conditions, and the academic literature refers to still other, extremely severe hereditary diseases. Considering the short life span of many of these children and their frequently very limited ability to perceive or enjoy the benefits of life, we cannot assert with confidence that in every situation there would be a societal consensus that life is preferable to never having been born at all.

While it thus seems doubtful that a child's claim for general damages should properly be denied on the rationale that the value of impaired life, as a matter of law, always exceeds the value of nonlife, we believe that the out-of-state decisions are on sounder grounds in holding that—with respect to the child's claim for pain and suffering or other general damages—recovery should be denied because (1) it is simply impossible to determine in any rational or reasoned fashion whether the plaintiff has in fact suffered an injury in being born impaired rather than not being born, and (2) even if it were possible to overcome the first hurdle, it would be impossible to assess general damages in any fair, nonspeculative manner.

Although we have determined that the trial court properly rejected plaintiff's claim for general damages, we conclude that her claim for the 'extraordinary expenses for specialised teaching, training and hearing equipment' that she will incur during her lifetime because of her deafness stands on a different footing.

Although the parents and child cannot, of course, both recover for the same medical expenses, we believe it would be illogical and anomalous to permit only parents, and not the child, to recover for the cost of the child's own medical care. If such a distinction were established, the afflicted child's receipt of necessary medical expenses might well depend on the wholly fortuitous circumstance of whether the parents are available to sue and recover such damages or whether the medical expenses are incurred at a time when the parents remain legally responsible for providing such care.

Realistically, a defendant's negligence in failing to diagnose an hereditary ailment places a significant medical and financial burden on the whole family unit. Unlike the child's claim for general damages, the damage here is both certain and readily measurable. Furthermore, in many instances these expenses will be vital not only to the child's well-being but to his or her very survival. (See *Schroeder v Perkel, supra*, 432 A 2d 834 at 841.) If, as alleged, defendants' negligence was in fact a proximate cause of the child's present and continuing need for such special, extraordinary medical care and training, we believe that it is consistent with the basic liability principles of Civil Code section 1714 to hold defendants liable for the cost of such care, whether the expense is to be borne by the parents or by the child. As Justice Jacobs of the New Jersey Supreme Court observed in his dissenting opinion in *Gleitman v Cosgrove, supra*, 227 A 2d at 703: 'While the law cannot remove the heartache or undo the harm, it can afford some reasonable measure of compensation toward alleviating the financial burdens'.

Moreover, permitting plaintiff to recover the extraordinary, additional medical expenses that are occasioned by the hereditary ailment is also consistent with the established parameters of the general tort 'benefit' doctrine discussed above. As we have seen, under that doctrine an offset is appropriate only insofar as the defendant's conduct has conferred a special benefit 'to the interest of the plaintiff that was harmed'. Here, the harm for which plaintiff seeks recompense is an economic loss, the extraordinary, out-of-pocket expenses that she will have to bear because of her hereditary ailment. Unlike the claim for general damages, defendants' negligence has conferred no incidental, offsetting benefit to this interest of plaintiff. (Cf *Schroeder v Perkel, supra*, 432 A 2d at 842.) Accordingly, assessment of these special damages should pose no unusual or insoluble problems.

In sum, we conclude that while a plaintiff-child in a wrongful life action may not recover general damages for being born impaired as opposed to not being born at all, the child—like his or her parents—may recover special damages for the extraordinary expenses necessary to treat the hereditary ailment.

Mosk, Justice, dissenting: I dissent.

An order is internally inconsistent which permits a child to recover special damages for a so-called wrongful life action, but denies all general damages for the very same tort. While the modest compassion of the majority may be commendable, they suggest no principle of law that justifies so neatly circumscribing the nature of damages suffered as a result of a defendant's negligence.

As recently as 1980, the Court of Appeal unanimously decided in *Curlender v Bio-Science Laboratories* 106 Cal App 3d 811, 165 Cal Rptr 477 (1980) that a cause of action exists for a wrongful-life tort. This court subsequently denied a petition for hearing. Thus *Curlender* was, and remains, the prevailing law of California. I see no persuasive reason to either abandon its doctrine, or to dilute its effectiveness by limiting recovery to special damages.

Do you agree with Mosk J that the majority of the court does not satisfactorily explain why special damages (for economic loss) are recoverable whilst general damages (for pain and suffering etc) are not? This revised approach has been taken up by other jurisdictions most notably by the distinguished Supreme Court of New Jersey in *Procanik v Cillo* (1984) 478 A 2d 755. In doing so, the New Jersey court, like the California Supreme Court before it, modified its earlier view, though on this occasion expanded liability by departing from the decisions in *Berman v Allan* 404 A 2d 8 (1979) and *Gleitman v Cosgrove* 227 A 2d 689 (1967) which we have already seen in the extracts above have been relied upon consistently by other courts to deny recovery (see, Teff 'The Action for "Wrongful Life" In England and the United States' (1985) 34 ICLQ 423).

So far we have been concerned with cases about children born disabled or diseased. Would the common law allow any action if the complaint is that the child has been born into circumstances that are alleged to be disadvantaged but the child is otherwise whole and healthy? Early in the development of this area of tort law, the American courts rejected claims of this kind.

Williams v State of New York
223 NE 2d 343 (1966) (NY Court of Appeals).

Desmond, Chief Judge: We are to decide whether the infant claimant Christine Williams (the claim of her mother Lorene Williams is not before us now) has alleged a sufficient cause of action against the State of New York. The claim asserts negligence of the State in the care and custody of the infant's mother while the latter was a patient at a State hospital for the mentally ill 'and more particularly in failing to provide adequate, sufficient and proper care and supervision over her while she was in the custody of the State and in negligently failing to protect and safeguard her health and physical body from attack and harm from others, which negligence resulted in the infant Christine Williams being conceived, being born and being born out of wedlock to a mentally deficient mother'. The theory of suit becomes clearer when we examine the paragraph where the particulars of claimant's damage are set out thus: as a result of this neglect of the State, the child has been 'deprived of property rights; deprived of a normal childhood and home life; deprived of proper parental care, support and rearing; caused to bear the stigma of illegitimacy'.

No such theory of suit has ever before, it seems, been put forward in any court anywhere (the closest being *Zepeda v Zepeda*, 41 Ill App 2d 240, 190 NE 2d 849, cert den 379 US 945, 85 S Ct 444, 13 L Ed 2d 545, of which more will be said hereafter). The Court of Claims Judge who heard the motion thought that this lack of precedent was not fatal, and that recovery of damages was possible since there had been a wrong by the State with resulting and reasonably to be anticipated harm to the child. The Appellate Division, reversing the Court of Claims and dismissing the claim, rejected the idea that there could be an obligation of the State to a person not yet conceived and, secondly, the Appellate Division held that the 'damages' are not susceptible of ascertainment, resting as they do 'upon the very fact of conception'.

Impossibility of entertaining this suit comes not so much from difficulty in measuring the alleged 'damages' as from the absence from our legal concepts of any such idea as a 'wrong' to a later-born child caused by permitting a woman to be violated and to bear an out-of-wedlock infant. If the pleaded facts are true, the State was grievously neglectful as to the mother, and as a result the child may have to bear unfair burdens as have many other sons and daughters of shame and sorrow. But the law knows no cure or compensation for it, and the policy and social reasons against providing such compensation are at least as strong as those which might be thought to favor it. Being born under one set of circumstance rather than another or to one pair of parents rather than another is not a suable wrong that is cognisable in court. The farthest reach of our law is to paternity proceedings (see Family Ct Act) and that was accomplished by statute.

Of interest on this general subject is *Zepeda v Zepeda*, 41 Ill App 2d 240, 190 NE 2d 849, cert den 379 US 945, 85 S Ct 444, 13 L Ed 2d 545, *supra*, where an illegitimate child sued his father because the father had by a fraud on the mother caused his birth. The Illinois courts dismissed the suit.

In *Williams* the court relied on the following case:

Zepeda v Zepeda
190 NE 2d 849 (1963) (Appellate Court of Illinois)

Dempsey, Presiding Justice: The plaintiff is the infant son of the defendant. He seeks damages from his father because he is an illegitimate child . . . the defendant is the plaintiff's father; the defendant induced the plaintiff's mother to have sexual relations by promising to marry her; this promise was not kept and could not be kept because, unbeknown to the mother, the defendant was already married. The complaint charges that the promise was fraudulent, that the acts of the defendant were wilful and that the defendant injured the plaintiff in his person, property and reputation by causing him to be born an adulterine bastard. The plaintiff seeks damages for the deprivation of his right to be a legitimate child, to have a normal home, to have a legal father, to inherit from his father, to inherit from his paternal ancestors and for being stigmatised as a bastard.

. . . An illegitimate's very birth places him under a disability.

It is of this that the plaintiff complains. His adulterine birth has placed him under a permanent disability. He protests not only the act which caused to him to be born but birth itself. Love of life being what it is, one may conjecture whether, if he were older, he would feel the same way. As he grows from infancy to maturity the natural instinct to preserve life may cause him to cherish his existence as much as, through his next friend, he now deplores it. Be that as it may, the quintessence of his complaint is that he was born and that he is. Herein lies the intrinsic difficulty of this case, a difficulty which gives rise to this question: are there overriding legal, social, judicial or other considerations which should preclude recognition of a cause of action?

Bearing in mind that an action for damages is implicit in any wrong that is called a tort (Prosser, Law of Torts, 2d ed, sec 1, pp 2–4) it may be inconsistent to say, as we do, that the plaintiff has been injured by a tortious act and then to question, as we do, his right to maintain an action to recover for this act. This is done deliberately, however, because on the one hand, we believe that the elements of a wilful tort are presented by the allegations of the complaint and, on the other hand, we approach with restraint the creation, by judicial sanction, of the new action required by the complaint.

Recognition of the plaintiff's claim means creation of a new tort: a cause of action for wrongful life. The legal implications of such a tort are vast, the social impact could be staggering. If the new litigation were confined just to illegitimates it would be formidable. In 1960 there were 224,330 illegitimate births in the United States, 14,262 in Illinois and 10,182 in Chicago. Vital Statistics of the United States 1960, Vol 1, secs 1, 2 (1962). Not only are there more such births year after year (in Illinois and Chicago the number in 1960 was twice that of 1950) but the ratio between illegitimate and legitimate births is increasing. This increase is attested by a report of the Illinois Department of Public Health, released in July, 1962. This report revealed that in Chicago in 1961, of the 87,989 live births 11,021 were illegitimate, a ratio of eight to one. In 1951 out of 81,801 births, 5,212 were illegitimate, a ratio of fifteen to one. The present Chicago ratio is twice that of the State and more than three times that of the Nation. The number of children who remain illegitimate is also of importance in estimating possible litigation. Accurate figures are not available, but a report made in October 1962 by the Illinois Public Aid Commission disclosed that in Cook County as of December 1961 there were 54,984 illegitimate children participating in the Aid to Department Children program. How many of these were born under circumstances making legitimation impossible, the report does not reveal.

That the doors of litigation would be opened wider might make us proceed cautiously in approving a new action, but it would not deter us. The plaintiff's claim cannot be rejected because there may be others of equal merit. It is not the suits of illegitimates which give us concern, great in numbers as these may be. What does disturb us is the nature of the new action and the related suits which would be encouraged. Encouragement would extend to all others born into the world under conditions they might regard as adverse. One might seek damages for being born of a certain color, another because of race; one for being born with a hereditary disease, another for inheriting unfortunate family characteristics; one for being born into a large and destitute family, another because a parent has an unsavory reputation.

The English courts did not consider this issue before the enactment of the Congenital Disabilities (Civil Liability) Act 1976. We turn now to consider the effect in general of that Act. We have already seen what would be the fate of a claim, such as was made in *Williams* and *Zepeda*, under the Act (see Pace, cited *supra* at p 813).

(ii) THE CONGENITAL DISABILITIES (CIVIL LIABILITY) ACT 1976

Section 1(2)(b) provides:

> (2) An occurrence to which this section applies is one which—
> . . .
> (b) affected the mother during her pregnancy, or affected her or the child in the course of its birth, so that the child is born with disabilities which would not otherwise have been present.

Ackner LJ in *McKay* states that:

> Subsection (2)(*b*) is so worded as to import the assumption that, but for the occurrence giving rise to a disabled birth, the child would have been born normal and healthy, not that it would not have been born at all. Thus, the object of the Law Commission that the child should have no right of action for 'wrongful life' is achieved. In para 89 of the report the commission stated that they were clear in their opinion that no cause of action should lie:
>> Such a cause of action, if it existed, would place an almost intolerable burden on medical advisers in their socially and morally exacting role. The danger that doctors would be under subconscious pressures to advise abortions in doubtful cases through fear of an action of damages, is, we think, a real one.
> This view was adopted by the Royal Commission on Civil Liability and Compensation for Personal Injury (report vol 1; Cmnd 7054–I, para 1485). (4) Section 4(5) of the 1976 Act provides as follows:
>> This Act applies in respect of births after (but not before) its passing, and in respect of any such birth it replaces any law in force before its passing, whereby a

person could be liable to a child in respect of disabilities with which it might be born . . .

Thus, there can be no question of such a cause of action arising in respect of births after 22 July 1976.

Stephenson and Griffiths LJJ agreed with this. Consequently, on facts which arise after 21 July 1976 no action for 'wrongful life' can lie. Do you agree? Is it absolutely clear that section 4(5) abolishes the common law? If the court were to recognise a claim of the sort in *McKay* would it be 'in respect of disabilities with which it might be born'?

Wrongful birth

This claim, brought by the parents of a handicapped child, has arisen in the two English cases of *Scuriaga v Powell* (1979) 123 Sol Jo 406 and *McKay v Essex Area Health Authority supra*, both of which we have already seen.

In *McKay*, Ackner LJ set out the claim of the mother as follows:

. . . [s]he alleges that within two months of the conception of the child, she told the doctor she thought she had been in contact with rubella. He therefore took a blood sample from her with a view to its being tested for infection. He negligently mislaid this sample and the further sample provided by her; alternatively he failed to interpret the results of such tests that may have been carried out by the first defendants, the Essex Area Health Authority. In the result, the doctor informed Mrs McKay that she and her unborn child had not been affected by rubella during the pregnancy and that she need not consider an abortion. Mrs McKay claims that if she had been properly advised by the doctor she would have decided to undergo an abortion and thus Mary would never have been born. She therefore claims damages on the basis that she has been 'burdened with a child with serious congenital disabilities', and accordingly claims cost of medical treatment and care and any other expense which would not have been required had the child been born without deformities. She makes a similar claim against the Essex Area Health Authority for their alleged negligence in failing to perform the appropriate tests on any samples provided to them by the doctor, in failing to inform the doctor properly or at all of the results of the tests, and in losing or confusing the blood samples.

Again, there was no suggestion that if Mrs McKay established the facts referred to above she would nevertheless fail to recover damages.

Here, you will notice that the claim alleges a negligent failure to provide information so as to give the mother an opportunity of abortion. The action may arise, also, from a negligent performance of a procedure such as an abortion. These were the facts of *Scuriaga v Powell*. In neither of these cases did the court analyse the nature of the claim. It seems to us that the action falls to be analysed in the way in which we have analysed the action for 'wrongful conception' (see *supra* ch 7). Here, of course, the parents allege that the doctors' negligence caused the birth of a *handicapped* child. In a 'wrongful conception' case the parents allege that the doctors' negligence caused them to conceive and give birth to a *healthy but unwanted* child.

A model for analysis which an English court might well adopt is provided by the Washington Supreme Court decision in *Harbeson v Parke-Davis* 656 P 2d 483 (1983) (footnotes omitted).

Pearson J: Plaintiff Leonard Harbeson has at all material times been a member of the United States Air Force. In 1970, while Mr Harbeson was stationed at Malstrom Air Force Base, his wife Jean conceived their first child. In December 1970, Mrs Harbeson learned, after suffering a grand mal seizure , that she was an epileptic. To control Mrs Harbeson's seizures, physicians at the Air Force Base prescribed

Dilantin, an anticonvulsant drug, which was the first choice of doctors in the treatment of epilepsy. Mrs Harbeson took Dilantin during the remainder of her pregnancy and in March 1971 gave birth to Michael, a healthy and intelligent child.

After Michael's birth, Mr Harbeson was transferred to McChord Air Force Base, near Tacoma. The medical facility serving the base was Madigan Army Medical Center. In May 1972, Mrs Harbeson went to Madigan for evaluation and treatment of her epilepsy. A neurologist at Madigan prescribed Dilantin to control her seizures. Between November 1972 and July 1973, the Harbesons informed three doctors at Madigan that they were considering having other children, and inquired about the risks of Mrs Harbeson's taking Dilantin during pregnancy. Each of the three doctors responded that Dilantin could cause cleft palate and temporary hirsutism. None of the doctors conducted literature searches or consulted other sources for specific information regarding the correlation between Dilantin and birth defects. The Harbesons relied on the assurances of the Madigan doctors and thereafter Mrs Harbeson became pregnant twice, giving birth to Elizabeth in April 1974, and Christine in May 1975. Throughout these pregnancies, Mrs Harbeson continued to take Dilantin as prescribed by the Madigan doctors. . . . Elizabeth and Christine have been diagnosed as suffering from 'fetal hydantoin syndrome'. They suffer from mild to moderate growth deficiencies, mild to moderate developmental retardation, wide-set eyes, lateral ptosis (drooping eyelids), hypoplasia of the fingers, small nails, low-set hairline, broad nasal ridge, and other physical and developmental defects. Had Mr and Mrs Harbeson been informed of the potential birth defects associated with the use of Dilantin during pregnancy, they would not have had any other children.

. . .

Wrongful birth

The epithet wrongful birth has been used to describe several fundamentally different types of action. See Annot, *Tort Liability For Wrongfully Causing One To Be Born*, 83 ALR 3d 15 (1978). Many of the actions once entitled wrongful birth are now referred to as wrongful conception and wrongful pregnancy actions. *Phillips v United States*, 508 F Supp 544, 545 n 1 (DSC 1981); Rogers, *Wrongful Life and Wrongful Birth: Medical Malpractice In Genetic Counseling and Prenatal Testing*, 33 SCL Rev 713, 739–41 (1982). A recent definition of a wrongful birth action is an action brought by parents against

> a physician [who] failed to inform [them] of the increased possibility that the mother would give birth to a child suffering from birth defects . . . [thereby precluding] an informed decision about whether to have the child.

(Footnotes omitted.) Comment, *Berman v Allan*, 8 Hofstra L Rev 257, 258 (1979), cited in *Phillips*, at 545 n 1.

Such an action was recognised by the New Jersey Supreme Court in *Schroeder v Perkel*, 87 NJ 53, 432 A 2d 834 (1981). Mr and Mrs Schroeder had two children, both of whom suffered from cystic fibrosis, a fatal genetic disorder. It was not until Mrs Schroeder was 8 months pregnant with their second child that the Schroeders learned they were carriers of the recessive gene which causes the disorder. They claimed that defendant pediatricians were negligent in failing to make an earlier diagnosis of cystic fibrosis in their first child. Had they known earlier of the condition, the Schroeders would have either avoided the conception of their second child, or terminated the pregnancy. The basis of their claim, therefore, was that 'they were deprived of an informed choice of whether to assume the risk of a second child'. 87 NJ at 57, 432 A 2d 834. The New Jersey Supreme Court recognised the cause of action and held that the parents could recover extraordinary medical expenses of raising the second child.

Schroeder is a paradigm wrongful birth case. The parents brought an action for the birth of a defective child. They claimed that defendant physicians had breached a duty to inform them of the risk of the child's being born defective. They claimed that had they known of this risk they would have prevented the birth of the child by contraception or abortion. They claimed that defendants' failure to inform was a proximate cause of the birth of the child and that the birth was an injury compensable in damages.

Although the definition we refer to above comprehends the *Schroeder* action, it excludes the cause of action recognised in a similar case, *Speck v Finegold*, 497 Pa 77, 439 A 2d 110 (1981). Mr Speck suffered from neurofibromatosis, a disorder caused by a genetic defect. After having two children who suffered from the disorder, Mr Speck decided to undergo a vasectomy. The vasectomy was unsuccessful, and Mrs Speck became pregnant. Mr and Mrs Speck decided to terminate the pregnancy. The abortion was unsuccessful, and Mrs Speck gave birth to a daughter who suffered from neurofibromatosis.

The court allowed the parents a cause of action to recover expenses attributable to the birth and rearing of their daughter. There appears to be no reason to exclude the action in *Speck* from the definition of wrongful birth. Like *Schroeder*, it is founded upon the birth of a defective child. The parents of the child alleged defendants breached a duty of care in performing the vasectomy and abortion procedures. Had these procedures been successful, they would have prevented conception or birth of the child. The parents alleged defendant's breach was a proximate cause of the birth of the child, and that birth was an injury to the parents, compensable in damages.

Both *Schroeder* and *Speck* recognise the right of parents to prevent the conception or birth of children suffering defects. They recognise that physicians owe a duty to parents to preserve that right. Physicians may breach this duty either by failure to impart material information or by negligent performance of a procedure to prevent the birth of a defective child. The parents' right to prevent a defective child and the correlative duty flowing from that right is the heart of the wrongful birth action.

For the purposes of the analysis which follows, therefore, wrongful birth will refer to an action based on an alleged breach of the duty of a health care provider to impart information or perform medical procedures with due care, where the breach is a proximate cause of the birth of a defective child. We do not in this opinion address issues which may arise where the birth of a healthy child is allegedly caused by a breach of duty owed to the parents. Such actions are referred to as wrongful conception or wrongful pregnancy, rather than wrongful birth. See generally, *Phillips*, at 545 n 1. Other jurisdictions have consistently treated such actions as different from, although related to, wrongful birth. We do likewise.

Having defined the scope of our inquiry, we now consider whether the wrongful birth action should be allowed in this state.

First, we measure the proposed wrongful birth action against the traditional concepts of duty, breach, injury, and proximate cause. The critical concept is duty. The core of our decision is whether we should impose upon health care providers a duty correlative to parents' right to prevent the birth of defective children.

Until recently, medical science was unable to provide parents with the means of predicting the birth of a defective child. Now, however, the ability to predict the occurrence and recurrence of defects attributable to genetic disorders has improved significantly. Parents can determine before conceiving a child whether their genetic traits increase the risk of that child's suffering from a genetic disorder such as Tay-Sachs disease or cystic fibrosis. After conception, new diagnostic techniques such as amniocentesis and ultrasonography can reveal defects in the unborn fetus. See generally, Peters and Peters, *Wrongful Life: Recognising the Defective Child's Right to a Cause of Action*, 18 Duq L Rev 857, 873–75 (1980). Parents may avoid the birth of the defective child by aborting the fetus. The difficult moral choice is theirs. *Roe v Wade*, 410 US 113, 93 S Ct 705, 35 L Ed 2d 147 (1973). We must decide, therefore, whether these developments confer upon potential parents the right to prevent, either before or after conception, the birth of a defective child. Are these developments the first steps towards a 'Fascist-Orwellian societal attitude of genetic purity', *Gildiner v Thomas Jefferson Univ Hosp*, 451 F Supp 692, 695 (EDPa 1978), or Huxley's brave new world? Or do they provide positive benefits to individual families and to all society by avoiding the vast emotional and economic cost of defective children?

We believe we must recognise the benefits of these medical developments and therefore we hold that parents have a right to prevent the birth of a defective child and health care providers a duty correlative to that right. This duty requires health care providers to impart to their patients material information as to the likelihood of future children being born defective, to enable the potential parents to decide whether to avoid the conception or birth of such children. If medical procedures are undertaken to avoid the conception or birth of defective children, the duty also requires that these procedures be performed with due care. This duty includes, therefore, the requirement that a health care provider who undertakes to perform an abortion use reasonable care in doing so. The duty does not, however, affect in any way the right of a physician to refuse on moral or religious grounds to perform an abortion. Recognition of the duty will 'promote societal interests in genetic counseling and prenatal testing, deter medical malpractice, and at least partially redress a clear and undeniable wrong'. (Footnotes omitted.) Rogers, *Wrongful Life and Wrongful Birth: Medical Malpractice in Genetic Counseling and Prenatal Testing*, 33 SCL Rev 713, 757 (1982) (hereinafter cited as Rogers).

We find persuasive the fact that all other jurisdictions to have considered this issue have recognised such a duty. These decisions are conveniently collected in Rogers, at 739–52, and we need not list them here.

Having recognised that a duty exists, we have taken the major step toward recognising the wrongful birth action. The second element of the traditional tort analysis is more straightforward. Breach will be measured by failure to conform to the appropriate standard of skill, care, or learning. RCW 4 24 290; RCW 7 70 040. *Gates v Jensen*, 92 Wash 2d 246, 595 P 2d 919 (1979).

More problematical is the question of whether the birth of a defective child represents an injury to the parents. The only case to touch on this question in this state did not resolve it. *Ball v Mudge*, 64 Wash 2d 247, 250, 391 P 2d 201 (1964). However, it is an inevitable consequence of recognising the parents' right to avoid the birth of a defective child that we recognise that the birth of such a child is an actionable injury. The real question as to injury, therefore, is not the existence of the injury, but the extent of that injury. In other words, having recognised that the birth of the child represents an injury, how do we measure damages? Other courts to have considered the issue have found this question troublesome. In particular, the New Jersey Supreme Court has taken a different approach to the question on each of the three occasions it has confronted it. In *Gleitman v Cosgrove*, 49 NJ 22, 227 A 2d 689 (1967), the court rejected the wrongful birth action altogether. One of the reasons for the rejection was the difficulty of measuring damages. When the court next considered the issue in *Berman v Allan*, 80 NJ 421, 404 A 2d 8 (1979), it upheld an action for wrongful birth and permitted damages for mental anguish. However, the court refused to allow damages to compensate for the medical and other costs incurred in raising, educating, and supervising the child. The court retreated from this position in the third case, *Schroeder v Perkel*, 87 NJ 53, 432 A 2d 834 (1981), and allowed the parents damages for certain medical expenses related to the child's affliction.

Other courts to have considered the issue exhibit widely divergent approaches. Comment, *Wrongful Birth Damages: Mandate and Mishandling by Judicial Fiat*, 13 Val U L Rev 127 (1978); Rogers, at 750–51.

More certain guidance than that provided by decisions of other jurisdictions on the issue of damages is provided by the Legislature in RCW 4 24 010. This statute provides that, in an action by parents for injury to a child, compensation may be recovered for four types of damages: medical, hospital, and medication expenses, loss of the child's services and support, loss of the child's love and companionship, and injury to the parent-child relationship. Recovery of damages for loss of companionship of the child, or injury or destruction of the parent-child relationship is not limited to the period of the child's minority. *Balmer v Dilley*, 81 Wash 2d 367, 502 P 2d 456 (1972). We have held that this section allows recovery for parental grief, mental anguish and suffering. *Hinzman v Palmanteer*, 81 Wash 2d 327, 501 P 2d 1228 (1972). The statute is not directly in point because a wrongful birth claim does not allege injury to the child as the cause of the parents' injury; rather it alleges the birth of the child is the cause of the injury. Nevertheless, the statute reflects a policy to compensate parents not only for pecuniary loss but also for emotional injury. There appears to be no compelling reason that policy should not apply in wrongful birth actions. Accordingly, we hold that recovery may include the medical, hospital, and medication expenses attributable to the child's birth and to its defective condition, and in addition damages for the parents' emotional injury caused by the birth of the defective child. In considering damages for emotional injury, the jury should be entitled to consider the countervailing emotional benefits attributable to the birth of the child. Restatement (Second) of Torts § 920 (1977). Rogers, at 751–52; *Eisbrenner v Stanley*, 106 Mich App 357, 308 NW 2d 209 (1981); *Kingsbury v Smith*, NH 442 A 2d 1003 (1982).

The final element to be considered is whether a breach of duty can be a proximate cause of the birth of the child. Proximate cause must be established by, first, a showing that the breach of duty was a cause in fact of the injury, and, second, a showing that as a matter of law liability should attach. *King v Seattle*, 84 Wash 2d 239, 249, 525 P 2d 228 (1974). Cause in fact can be established by proving that but for the breach of duty, the injury would not have occurred. *King v Seattle, supra.* The legal question whether liability should attach is essentially another aspect of the policy decision which we confronted in deciding whether the duty exists. We therefore hold that, as a matter of law in wrongful birth cases, if cause in fact is established, the proximate cause element is satisfied. This conclusion is consistent with the decisions of those other jurisdictions which have accepted wrongful birth actions, eg, *Robak v United States*, 658 F 2d 471 (7th Cir 1981).

The action for wrongful birth, therefore, fits within the conceptual framework of our law of negligence. An action in negligence claiming damages for the birth of a child suffering congenital defects may be brought in this state.

The parents may therefore recover damages for the wrongful births of Elizabeth and Christine. These damages may include pecuniary damages for extraordinary medical, educational, and similar expenses attributable to the defective condition of the children. In other words, the parents should recover those expenses in excess of the cost of the birth and rearing of two normal children. In addition, the damages may compensate for mental anguish and emotional stress suffered by the parents during each child's life as a proximate result of the physicians' negligence. Any emotional benefits to the parents resulting from the birth of the child should be considered in setting the damages. (Implicit in this conclusion, in response to the District Court's question 2a, is that neither RCW 4 24 290 nor RCW 4 24 010 applies directly to the claims of the Harbesons.)

Do you agree with the court's analysis of the problematic issues of *duty*, *damage* and *damages* which we encountered when considering the child's companion claim for 'wrongful life'? In particular, do you think the court properly analyses the type of 'injury' suffered by the parents in these cases? Two further points ought briefly to be considered. First, can there be any argument on grounds of public policy that if a child were born disabled, in the context of a 'wrongful birth' action, a court would not award damages for the upkeep of the child to its majority (or its lifetime if shorter)? If it is accepted that damages are to be recovered, ought the damages to be limited to the task of compensating for the difference between being normal and being handicapped? If this were right would it not put the parents of a handicapped child in a worse position than if their child was healthy? (For a discussion of the public policy issues involved in determining the appropriate measure of damages, see, Symmons' Policy Factors in Wrongful Birth (1987) 50 MLR 269.)

Second, some jurisdictions in the United States have been asked to admit the claim of siblings in a 'wrongful birth' case who allege that the birth has caused them 'loss of a portion of the family's wealth and parental attention, especially if the child's condition requires expensive treatment or a heavy expenditure of parental time'. (Wadlington, Waltz and Dworkin, *Cases and Materials on Medical Law* at p 832.) But these claims have been rejected on the whole (*Cox v Stretton* 352 NYS 2d 834 (1984); *Coleman v Garrison* 349 A 2d 8 (1975)), though not in every jurisdiction (*Custodio v Bauer* 59 Cal Rptr 463 (1967)).

Part III

B: During life

Chapter 11

Research

Background

It is a truism that for medical practice to develop and improve in any systematic and ordered way research must be carried out. It is equally a truism that such research must include research on human beings whether they are patients or are healthy human beings.

When we speak of research we adopt the analysis set out in Nicholson (ed), *Medical Research with Children* (1986) at pp 24–26:

> *Research* may be defined as in the *Shorter Oxford English Dictionary:* 'An investigation directed to the discovery of some fact by careful study of a subject; a course of critical or scientific inquiry'. The second part of that definition is more useful when considering medical research, because of the potential confusion, caused by the use of the word 'investigation' in the first part. 'Investigation' tends to be used more specifically in medical practice to denote the ascertainment of a particular anatomical, biochemical, or physiological value in a patient. Examples of such 'investigations' are a chest X-ray, the measurement of the haemoglobin level in blood, or lung function tests. In our discussions, however, 'research' was seldom used by itself, without some other word attached. Phrases such as 'research project', 'research procedure', or 'therapeutic research' were used more frequently.
>
> A *research project* is a systematic enquiry designed to contribute to generalisable knowledge. It is important to emphasise that it is systematic in design and execution, and requires honest and accurate recording of all information obtained. A speculative or haphazard attempt at a new therapy, for instance, cannot be regarded as a research project.
>
> A *research intervention* is a specific act performed on a research subject during the course of a research project. Such an intervention may involve the performance of an investigation, used in the medical sense noted above, such as the taking of a blood sample or the measurement of lung function tests, or even simply weighing the subject. Alternatively, an intervention might be manipulation of the subject's diet, or the giving of a substance.
>
> Research interventions may be either *invasive* or *non-invasive*. Essentially, any activity, part or all of which involves an entrance of any sort into a subject's body, is invasive. For instance, urine may be collected by both invasive and non-invasive techniques. If a urine bag is attached to an infant to collect urine voided normally, that is a non-invasive intervention, even though it may cause the infant some discomfort. If on the other hand the urine is collected by supra-pubic aspiration— that is, by passing a needle through the abdominal wall into the bladder and withdrawing some urine—the intervention is invasive. The borderline between invasive and non-invasive may sometimes be difficult to ascertain. Swabbing the skin so as to obtain a sample of bacteria growing thereon is a non-invasive intervention; swabbing the throat for similar purposes, while not involving the breaking of any skin or tegument, should be regarded as an invasive intervention.
>
> Some research projects do not involve any interventions and consist only in *observation*. The *Concise Oxford Dictionary* defines an observation as 'accurate watching and noting of phenomena as they occur in nature with regard to cause and effect or mutual relations', and it is in that sense that 'observation' has been used in this report. In medical research such 'accurate watching' might just be of the colour

of a subject's skin, or the size of the pupils of his eyes. Were the pulse to be measured by feeling it at the wrist, that would constitute an intervention rather than an observation. Pure observation is an activity more commonly found in psychological research, particularly that undertaken by human ethologists, when the behaviour of one or more subjects is observed and recorded.

Our concern here is with research interventions as defined. As the law stands, no legal complaint can arise from observational research as described.

Research on human beings has undoubtedly been carried out in one way or another as long as there has been medicine. As Caroline Faulder, in her book *Whose Body Is It?*, puts it (pp 64–65):

Few people would seriously argue that doctors are wrong to want to increase their understanding of the human body and the ills to which it is prone. Doctors want to be able to do the best they can for their present patients and they would like to do even better for future patients. *We* want them to find the cure for cancer and other serious diseases and to help us to live longer and healthier lives. *We* expect them to give us the best available treatment. *We* want to feel safe in their hands, reassured that whatever they suggest to us is backed by sound scientific knowledge and that our welfare is their first consideration. We want it all, but medical advance is impossible without research and experimentation—and some of that experimentation must be done on human beings.

In a sense all medical treatment is experimental. However well tried a particular therapy may be, the doctor can never be entirely sure how the individual patient will respond. Far more experimental is any treatment which is offered to patients simply because the doctor believes it works, even though it may never have been put to the test in a comparison with a control group of patients who either are not getting the treatment or are being offered an alternative.

By the end of the nineteenth century, as Faulder (*op cit*) writes (pp 62–64):

New treatments were proliferating and it became increasingly apparent to the more scientifically minded members of the profession that clinical observation and judgement, although valuable, was too easily distorted by prejudice and personal bias to be reliable. What was needed was some more objective method of verification. The first trial by numbers was done in the early nineteenth century by a Frenchman, Professor Pierre-Charles-Alexandre Louis, who was able to demonstrate the uselessness of blood-letting by comparing the results of large numbers of cases.

However, it was not until well into this century that controlled clinical trials began to be accepted as a method of scientific evaluation. And it was not until after the Second World War that the principle of randomisation was introduced into clinical research. This concept of random allocation was described by its innovator, the statistician Sir Ronald Fisher, who first used it in studies of agricultural crop production, as the primary principle of experimental design. It was another eminent statistician, Sir Austin Bradford Hill, who initiated its use in medical research with the historic trial in 1946 of the antibiotic Streptomycin for tuberculosis. Very simply, randomisation operates on the 'toss of a coin' principle: subjects suffering from a particular illness at the same stage are randomly allocated to different groups for different treatments and then carefully observed and followed up to compare the results. Its purpose is to eliminate any element of human or accidental bias in selecting patients for treatment which would distort the assessment of the results. Clinical trials using this principle of randomisation are called randomised controlled trials [RCT] . . .

That RCTs have become so widely used is probably due as much as anything to the pithy monograph extolling their virtues written by Dr Archibald Cochrane in the early seventies. He advocated not merely that they were efficient for testing new treatments but that they provided a cost-effective method for testing traditional procedures, many of them outdated and illogical, which the NHS was finding difficulty in discarding. He urged that even simple measures, like when a patient should be got out of bed after surgery, should be put to the test by this rigorous method.

Since then RCTs have been considerably developed and refined and they are now extensively used to test new drugs, surgical techniques, radiotherapy, screening procedures, alternative methods of delivering medical care and a host of other medical interventions.

Faulder asserts that (p 64):

This means that although only a relatively small percentage of patients actually receiving medical treatment are doing so in a trial (approximately 10 per cent), there are many more of us drawn from the so-called healthy population who may be involved in a trial, with or without our knowledge. For example, a trial testing different methods of counteracting hypertension or a new way of offering a screening service, say for cervical cancer, can be done on a regional basis throughout the community. Very often in such trials neither of the comparison groups taken out of a selected population will be aware that they are being monitored in a study.

Faulder goes on to identify types of research on humans as follows (pp 65–6):

... there is the non-therapeutic trial which is carried out on healthy volunteers who will get no personal benefit from the experiment but who offer their bodies, or their minds, to test a hypothesis, the effects of a drug or perhaps a psychological theory. The second form of human experimentation, or study, as doctors prefer to call it, is that done on patients with a particular illness or condition in clinical trials to compare the merits of different treatments. This type of clinical research combined with professional care enables doctors who are genuinely uncertain about which treatment they should be offering to their patients to feel secure that those who get the new treatment will be carefully monitored and that the final judgment of the results does not rely on their opinion alone.

Both forms of research contemplate the use of controls, that is, as Nicholson in *Medical Research With Children* (1986) (p 31) explains, 'controls are subjects who are used for the purposes of comparison. In a trial of a new drug, for instance, the subjects may ... receive either the drug or an inert substance, a placebo. Those receiving the placebo act as controls, since they will come under all the same influences—whether pathological, environmental or psychological—on the subjects, except for the influence of the drug that is on trial'.

In the case of *clinical* trials as Faulder adds (p 66): 'A control group of patients in a clinical trial receives the "best standard therapy" and is used as a measure of comparison with another group of patients allotted to the new treatment under study.'

Finally, Faulder identifies (p 66):

... three provisos [which] are fundamentally important in the ethical conduct of any trial using human subjects and they should be equally well understood by both categories of participants—patients/volunteers and doctors.

These are:

• Provided that the patients or volunteers who participate in all these types of experiments are fully informed and freely give their consent, they are not being used as guinea pigs.
• Provided that the trials are well designed and conform to the conditions prescribed in the Declaration of Helsinki, they are a reliable and ethical way of conducting medical research.
• Provided that the doctors who participate in a trial always put the welfare of their individual patients before the interests of science and society, they can be sure that they are caring for their patients according to the highest medical and ethical standards.

Undoubtedly, the greatest incentive to regulate research on human beings was the awareness of, and revulsion at, what had been done in the name of medical research during World War II. Jay Katz in his book *Experimentation with Human Beings* (1972) sets out the major elements of the trial of Dr Karl Brandt and others before the Nuremberg Military Tribunals (pp 292–306).

1. Indictment

The United States of America, by the undersigned Telford Taylor, Chief of Counsel for War Crimes, duly appointed to represent said Government in the prosecution of war criminals, charges that the defendants herein participated in a common design or conspiracy to commit and did commit war crimes and crimes against humanity, as defined in Control Council Law No 10, duly enacted by the Allied Control Council on 20 December 1945. . . .

. . .

Count Two [and Three]—War Crimes [and Crimes against Humanity]

Between September 1939 and April 1945 all of the defendants herein unlawfully, wilfully, and knowingly committed war crimes [and crimes against humanity], as defined by Article II of Control Council Law No 10, in that they were principals in, accessories to, ordered, abetted, took a consenting part in, and were connected with plans and enterprises involving medical experiments without the subjects' consent, upon [German civilians and] civilians and members of the armed forces of nations then at war with the German Reich . . . in the course of which experiments the defendants committed murders, brutalities, cruelties, tortures, atrocities, and other inhuman acts. Such experiments included, but were not limited to the following:

High-altitude experiments. From about March 1942 to about August 1942 experiments were conducted at the Dachau concentration camp, for the benefit of the German Air Force, to investigate the limits of human endurance and existence at extremely high altitudes. The experiments were carried out in a low-pressure chamber in which the atmospheric conditions and pressures prevailing at high altitude (up to 68,000 feet) could be duplicated. The experimental subjects were placed in the low-pressure chamber and thereafter the simulated altitude therein was raised. Many victims died as a result of these experiments and others suffered grave injury, torture, and ill-treatment. . . .

Freezing experiments. From about August 1942 to about May 1943 experiments were conducted at the Dachau concentration camp, primarily for the benefit of the German Air Force, to investigate the most effective means of treating persons who had been severely chilled or frozen. In one series of experiments the subjects were forced to remain in a tank of ice water for periods up to 3 hours. Extreme rigor developed in a short time. Numerous victims died in the course of these experiments. After the survivors were severely chilled, rewarming was attempted by various means. In another series of experiments, the subjects were kept naked outdoors for many hours at temperatures below freezing. The victims screamed with pain as parts of their bodies froze. . . .

Malaria experiments. From about February 1942 to about April 1945 experiments were conducted at the Dachau concentration camp in order to investigate immunisation for and treatment of malaria. Healthy concentration-camp inmates were infected by mosquitoes or by injections of extracts of the mucous glands of mosquitoes. After having contracted malaria the subjects were treated with various drugs to test their relative efficacy. Over 1,000 involuntary subjects were used in these experiments. Many of the victims died and others suffered severe pain and permanent disability. . . .

. . .

Sulfanilamide experiments. From about July 1942 to about September 1943 experiments to investigate the effectiveness of sulfanilamide were conducted at the

Ravensbrueck concentration camp for the benefit of the German Armed Forces. Wounds deliberately inflicted on the experimental subjects were infected with bacteria such as streptococcus, gas gangrene, and tetanus. Circulation of blood was interrupted by tying off blood vessels at both ends of the wound to create a condition similar to that of a battlefield wound. Infection was aggravated by forcing wood shavings and ground glass into the wounds. The infection was treated with sulfanilamide and other drugs to determine their effectiveness. Some subjects died as a result of these experiments and others suffered serious injury and intense agony. . . .

. . .

Epidemic jaundice experiments. From about June 1943 to about January 1945 experiments were conducted at the Sachsenhausen and Natzweiler concentration camps, for the benefit of the German Armed Forces, to investigate the causes of, and inoculations against, epidemic jaundice. Experimental subjects were deliberately infected with epidemic jaundice, some of whom died as a result, and others were caused great pain and suffering. . . .

. . .

Spotted fever [typhus] experiments. From about December 1941 to about February 1945 experiments were conducted at the Buchenwald and Natzweiler concentration camps, for the benefit of the German Armed Forces, to investigate the effectiveness of spotted fever and other vaccines. At Buchenwald numerous healthy inmates were deliberately infected with spotted fever virus in order to keep the virus alive; over 90 percent of the victims died as a result. Other healthy inmates were used to determine the effectiveness of different spotted fever vaccines and of various chemical substances. In the course of these experiments 75 percent of the selected number of inmates were vaccinated with one of the vaccines or nourished with one of the chemical substances and, after a period of 3 to 4 weeks, were infected with spotted fever germs. The remaining 25 percent were infected without any previous protection in order to compare the effectiveness of the vaccines and the chemical substances. As a result, hundreds of the persons experimented upon died. . . .

Experiments with poison. In or about December 1943, and in or about October 1944, experiments were conducted at the Buchenwald concentration camp to investigate the effect of various poisons upon human beings. The poisons were secretly administered to experimental subjects in their food. The victims died as a result of the poison or were killed immediately in order to permit autopsies. In or about September 1944 experimental subjects were shot with poison bullets and suffered torture and death. . . .

. . .

Between June 1943 and September 1944 the defendants Rudolf Brandt and Sievers . . . were principals in, accessories to, ordered, abetted, took a consenting part in, and were connected with plans and enterprises involving the murder of civilians and members of the armed forces of nations then at war with the German Reich and who were in the custody of the German Reich in exercise of belligerent control. One hundred [and] twelve Jews were selected for the purpose of completing a skeleton collection for the Reich University of Strasbourg. Their photographs and anthropological measurements were taken. Then they were killed. Thereafter, comparison tests, anatomical research, studies regarding race, pathological features of the body, form and size of the brain, and other tests, were made. The bodies were sent to Strasbourg and defleshed.

. . .

Opening statement of the prosecution by Brigadier General Telford Taylor

I turn now to the main part of the indictment and will outline at this point the prosecution's case relating to those crimes alleged to have been committed in the name of medical or scientific research. . . . What I will cover now comprehends all in the experiments charged as war crimes . . . and as crimes against humanity in . . . the indictment. . . .

. . .

A sort of rough pattern is apparent on the face of the indictment. Experiments concerning high altitude, the effect of cold, and the potability of processed sea water have an obvious relation to aeronautical and naval combat and rescue problems. The mustard gas and phosphorous burn experiments, as well as those relating to the healing value of sulfanilamide for wounds, can be related to air-raid and battlefield medical problems. It is well known that malaria, epidemic jaundice, and typhus were among the principal diseases which had to be combated by the German Armed Forces and by German authorities in occupied territories.

To some degree, the therapeutic pattern outlined above is undoubtedly a valid one, and explains why the Wehrmacht, and especially the German Air Force, participated in these experiments. Fanatically bent upon conquest, utterly ruthless as to the means or instruments to be used in achieving victory, and callous to the sufferings of people whom they regarded as inferior, the German militarists were willing to gather whatever scientifc fruit these experiments might yield.

But our proof will show that a quite different and even more sinister objective runs like a red thread through these hideous researches. We will show that in some instances the true object of these experiments was not how to rescue or to cure, but how to destroy and kill. The sterilisation experiments were, it is clear, purely destructive in purpose. The prisoners at Buchenwald who were shot with poisoned bullets were not guinea pigs to test an antidote for the poison; their murderers really wanted to know how quickly the poison would kill. This destructive object is not superficially as apparent in the other experiments, but we will show that it was often there.

Mankind has not heretofore felt the need of a word to denominate the science of how to kill prisoners most rapidly and subjugated people in large numbers. This case and these defendants have created this gruesome question for the lexicographer. For the moment we will christen this macabre science 'thanatology', the science of producing death. The thanatological knowledge, derived in part from these experiments, supplied the techniques for genocide, a policy of the Third Reich, exemplified in the 'euthanasia' program and in the widespread slaughter of Jews, gypsies, Poles, and Russians. This policy of mass extermination could not have been so effectively carried out without the active participation of German medical scientists.

. . .

The experiments known as 'high-altitude' or 'low-pressure' experiments were carried out at the Dachau concentration camp in 1942. According to the proof, the original proposal that such experiments be carried out on human beings originated in the spring of 1941 with a Dr Sigmund Rascher. Rascher was at that time a captain in the medical service of the German Air Force, and also held officer rank in the SS. He is believed now to be dead.

The origin of the idea is revealed in a letter which Rascher wrote to Himmler in May 1941 at which time Rascher was taking a course in aviation medicine at a German Air Force headquarters in Munich. According to the letter, this course included researches into high-altitude flying and

> considerable regret was expressed at the fact that no tests with human material had yet been possible for us, as such experiments are very dangerous and nobody volunteers for them. (1602-PS.)

Rascher, in this letter, went on to ask Himmler to put human subjects at his disposal and baldly stated that the experiments might result in death to the subjects but that the tests theretofore made with monkeys had not been satisfactory.

Rascher's letter was answered by Himmler's adjutant, the defendant, Rudolf Brandt, who informed Rascher that—'. . . Prisoners will, of course, gladly be made available for the high-flight researches'.

. . . The tests themselves were carried out in the spring and summer of 1942, using the pressure chamber which the German Air Force had provided. The victims were locked in the low-pressure chamber, which was an airtight ball-like compartment, and then the pressure in the chamber was altered to simulate the atmospheric conditions prevailing at extremely high altitudes. The pressure in the chamber could be varied with great rapidity, which permitted the defendants to duplicate the atmospheric conditions which an aviator might encounter in falling great distances through space without a parachute and without oxygen.

. . . The first report by Rascher was made in April 1942, and contains a description of the effect of the low-pressure chamber on a 37-year-old Jew. (1971-A-PS.) I quote:

The third experiment of this type took such an extraordinary course that I called an SS physician of the camp as witness, since I had worked on these experiments all by myself. It was a continuous experiment without oxygen at a height of 12 kilometers conducted on a 37-year-old Jew in good general condition. Breathing continued up to 30 minutes. After 4 minutes the experimental subject began to perspire and wiggle his head, after 5 minutes cramps occurred, between 6 and 10 minutes breathing increased in speed and the experimental subject became unconscious; from 11 to 30 minutes breathing slowed down to three breaths per minute, finally stopping altogether.

Severest cyanosis developed in between and foam appeared at the mouth.

At 5 minute intervals electrocardiograms from three leads were written. After breathing had stopped Ekg (electrocardiogram) was continuously written until the action of the heart had come to a complete standstill. About ½ hour after breathing had stopped, dissection was started.

. . .

Another series of experiments carried out at the Dachau concentration camp concerned immunisation for and treatment of malaria. Over 1,200 inmates of practically every nationality were experimented upon. Many persons who participated in these experiments have already been tried before a general military court held at Dachau, and the findings of that court will be laid before this Tribunal. The malaria experiments were carried out under the general supervision of a Dr Schilling, with whom the defendant Sievers and others in the box collaborated. The evidence will show that healthy persons were infected by mosquitoes or by injections from the glands of mosquitoes. Catholic priests were among the subjects. The defendant Gebhardt kept Himmler informed of the progress of these experiments. Rose furnished Schilling with fly eggs for them, and others of the defendants participated in various ways which the evidence will demonstrate.

After the victims had been infected they were variously treated with quinine, neosalvarsan, pyramidon, antipyrin, and several combinations of these drugs. Many deaths occurred from excessive doses of neosalvarsan and pyramidon. According to the findings of the Dachau court, malaria was the direct cause of 30 deaths and 300 to 400 others died as the result of subsequent complications.

. . .

From December 1941, until near the end of the war, a large program of medical experimentation was carried out upon concentration camp inmates at Buchenwald and Natzweiler to investigate the value of various vaccines. This research involved a variety of diseases—typhus, yellow fever, smallpox, paratyphoid A and B, cholera, and diphtheria. . . .

. . .

The general pattern of these typhus experiments was as follows. A group of concentration camp inmates, selected from the healthier ones who had some resistance to disease, were injected with an anti-typhus vaccine, the efficacy of which was to be tested. Thereafter, all the persons in the group would be infected with typhus. At the same time, other inmates who had not been vaccinated were also infected for purposes of comparison—these unvaccinated victims were called the 'control' group. But perhaps the most wicked and murderous circumstances in this whole case is that still other inmates were deliberately infected with typhus with the sole purpose of keeping the typhus virus alive and generally available in the bloodstream of the inmates.

. . .

The 20 physicians in the dock range from leaders of German scientific medicine, with excellent international reputations, down to the dregs of the German medical profession. All of them have in common a callous lack of consideration and human regard for, and an unprincipled willingness to abuse their power over the poor, unfortunate, defenseless creatures who had been deprived of their rights by a ruthless and criminal government. All of them violated the Hippocratic commandments which they had solemnly sworn to uphold and abide by, including the fundamental principle never to do harm—'*primum non nocere*'.

Outstanding men of science, distinguished for their scientific ability in Germany and abroad, are the defendants Rostock and Rose. Both exemplify, in their training and practice alike, the highest traditions of German medicine. Rostock headed the Department of Surgery at the University of Berlin and served as dean of its medical school. Rose studied under the famous surgeon, Enderlen, at Heidelberg and then became a distinguished specialist in the fields of public health and tropical diseases. Handloser and Schroeder are outstanding medical administrators. Both of them made their careers in military medicine and reached the peak of their profession. Five more defendants are much younger men who are nevertheless already known as the possessors of considerable scientific ability, or capacity in medical administration. These include the defendants Karl Brandt, Ruff, Beiglboeck, Schaefer, and Becker-Freyseng.

A number of the others such as Romberg and Fischer are well trained, and several of them attained high professional position. But among the remainder few were known as outstanding scientific men. Among them at the foot of the list is Blome who has published his autobiography entitled 'Embattled Doctor' in which he sets forth that he eventually decided to become a doctor because a medical career would enable him to become 'master over life and death'.

. . .

I intend to pass very briefly over matters of medical ethics, such as the conditions under which a physician may lawfully perform a medical experiment upon a person who has voluntarily subjected himself to it, or whether experiments may lawfully be performed upon criminals who have been condemned to death. This case does not present such problems. No refined questions confront us here.

None of the victims of the atrocities perpetrated by these defendants were volunteers, and this is true regardless of what these unfortunate people may have said or signed before their tortures began. Most of the victims had not been condemned to death, and those who had been were not criminals, unless it be a crime to be a Jew, or a Pole, or a gypsy, or a Russian prisoner of war.

. . .

Were it necessary, one could make a long list of the respects in which the experiments which these defendants performed departed from every known standard of medical ethics. But the gulf between these atrocities and serious research in the healing art is so patent that such a tabulation would be cynical.

. . .

These experiments revealed nothing which civilised medicine can use. It was, indeed, ascertained that phenol or gasoline injected intravenously will kill a man inexpensively and within 60 seconds. This and a few other 'advances' are all in the field of thanatology. . . .

Apart from these deadly fruits, the experiments were not only criminal but a scientific failure. It is indeed as if a just deity had shrouded the solutions which they attempted to reach with murderous means. The moral shortcomings of the defendants and the precipitous ease with which they decided to commit murder in quest of 'scientific results', dulled also that scientific hesitancy, that thorough thinking-through, that responsible weighing of every single step which alone can insure scientifically valid results. Even if they had merely been forced to pay as little as two dollars for human experimental subjects, such as American investigators may have to pay for a cat, they might have thought twice before wasting unnecessary numbers, and thought of simpler and better ways to solve their problems. The fact that these investigators had free and unrestricted access to human beings to be experimented upon misled them to the dangerous and fallacious conclusion that the results would thus be better and more quickly obtainable than if they had gone through the labor of preparation, thinking, and meticulous preinvestigation.

A particularly striking example is the sea-water experiment. I believe that three of the accused . . . will today admit that this problem could have been solved simply and definitively within the space of one afternoon. On 20 May 1944 when these accused convened to discuss the problem, a thinking chemist could have solved it right in the presence of the assembly within the space of a few hours by the use of nothing more gruesome than a piece of jelly, a semipermeable membrane and a salt solution, and the German Armed Forces would have had the answer on 21 May 1944. But what happened instead? The vast armies of the disenfranchised slaves were at the beck and call of this sinister assembly; and instead of thinking, they simply relied on their power over human beings rendered rightless by a criminal state and government. . . .

. . .

. . . Who could German medicine look to to keep the profession true to its traditions and protect it from the ravaging inroads of Nazi pseudo-science? This was the supreme responsibility of the leaders of German medicine—men like Rostock and Rose and Schroeder and Handloser. That is why their guilt is greater than that of any of the other defendants in the dock. They are the men who utterly failed their country and their profession, who showed neither courage nor wisdom nor the vestiges of moral character. . . .

. . .

3.   Extracts from argumentation and evidence of prosecution and defense

a.   Testimony of defense expert witness Dr Franz Vollhardt
Direct examination.

. . .

Dr Marx: Please, would you briefly tell the Tribunal what your scientific activities have been and in what special field you have taken a particularly great interest, and since when?
Witness Vollhardt: I am Professor of Internal Medicine at Frankfurt and predominantly I have dealt with the questions of circulation, metabolism, blood pressure, and kidney diseases.

. . .

Q: Which foreign academies and foreign societies have you been a member of? . . .
A: I am Honorary Doctor of the Sorbonne, Paris, of Goettingen and Freiburg; and, as far as societies are concerned, there are a lot of them, Medical Society of Edinburgh, at Geneva, at Luxembourg. I am an Honorary Member of the University at Santiago, and so on and so forth.

. . .

Q: Now, Professor, have you sufficient insight into the planning and carrying out of the so-called sea-water experiments to give an expert opinion on that subject?

. . .

A: I think that scientifically speaking the planning was excellent and I have no objection to the entire plan. It was good to add a hunger-and-thirst group because we know by experience that thirst can be borne less well than hunger, and if people are suffering from hunger and thirst too, they do not suffer from hunger, but do suffer from thirst; and that resembles what shipwrecked persons would be subjected to because they only suffer from thirst. It was excellent that Wofatit was to be introduced into the experiments too, although it was expected from the beginning that this wonderful discovery would show its value. . . .

. . .

Q: Could the aim of these experiments have been achieved with a semipermeable membrane?
A: I don't understand how one can imagine this. What we are concerned with is the question of how long the human body can survive without water and under the excess quantity of salt. Now, that is subject to the water content of the body and it depends first of all, upon whether water is only used by the intermediary tissues or whether the cell liquid too is being used up. In the latter case, there is a danger which becomes apparent through excess potassium quantities, and this was also

continuously observed and checked during such experiments, and there were no excess potassium quantities such as can be expected after 6 days.

Q: Nor would it be right to say that these experiments were not planned scientifically and medically, is that correct?

A: Absolutely not.

Q: Could they have been planned differently?

A: I couldn't imagine how.

Q: Were these experiments in the interests of active warfare, or in the interests of the care of shipwrecked sailors or soldiers?

A: The latter.

Q: In other words, for aviators and sailors who were shipwrecked or might be shipwrecked?

A: Towards the end of the war there was an increase in the number of pilots shot down as well as of shipwrecked personnel, and it was, therefore, the duty of the hygiene department concerned to consider the question of how one could best deal with such cases of shipwrecked personnel. . . .

. . .

Q: Now, Professor, the experiments we were talking about; did they have a practical valuable aim and did they show a corresponding result?

A: Yes, that is correct. For instance an important observation was made which Eppinger had expected; he wanted to see if the kidneys did concentrate salt under such extreme conditions to an even higher extent than one expected previously. One thought that it would be something like 2.0 percent but 2.6 or 2.7 percent and record figures of 3.0, 3.5, 3.6 and 4 percent are shown, so that the fortunate man who is in a position to concentrate 3.6 percent or 4 percent of salt would be able to live on sea water for quite a long period.

. . .

Finally, one unsuspected fact was shown which may be connected with this, and that is that the drinking of small quantities of sea water up to 500 cc given over a lengthy period turned out to be better than unalleviated thirst.

. . .

Q: So, you think that the result of these experiments is not only of importance in war-time, but is also of importance for the problems of seafaring nations?

A: Quite right, it is a wonderful thing for all seafaring nations.

. . .

b. Final plea for defendant Joachim Mrugowsky

. . .

The case with the typhus experiments is different. No order was given to kill a man in order to obtain knowledge. But the typhus experiments were dangerous experiments. Out of 724 experimental persons, 154 died. But these 154 deaths from the typhus experiments have to be compared with the 15,000 who died of typhus every day in the camps for Soviet prisoners of war, and the innumerable deaths from typhus among the civilian population of the occupied eastern territories and the German troops. This enormous number of deaths led to the absolute necessity of having effective vaccines against typhus in sufficient quantity. The newly developed vaccines had been tested in the animal experiments as to their compatibility.

. . .

The Tribunal will have to decide whether, in view of the enormous extent of epidemic typhus, in view of the 15,000 deaths it was causing daily in the camps for Russian prisoners of war alone, the order given by the government authorities to test the typhus vaccines was justified or not. If the answer is in the affirmative, then the typhus experiments at Buchenwald were not criminal, since the prosecution did not contest that they were carried out according to the rules of medical science.

. . .

c. Testimony of defendant Gerhard Rose
Direct examination.

. . .

Dr Fritz: What do you know about the reasons for this protest (against experiments) being ignored and the typhus experiments being carried out in spite of it?

. . .

Defendant Rose: The Buchenwald experiments (with typhus vaccine) had four main results. First of all, they showed that belief in the protective effect of Weigl vaccine was a mistake, although this belief seemed to be based on long observation. Secondly, they showed that the useful vaccines did not protect against infection, but almost certainly prevented death, under the conditions of the Buchenwald experiments. Thirdly, they showed that the objections of the biological experts to the vitelline membrane vaccines and to the lice vaccines were unjustified, and that vitelline membrane, rabbit lungs, and lice intestines were of equal value. We learned this only through the Buchenwald experiments. This left the way open to mass production of typhus vaccines.

The Buchenwald experiments showed in time that several vaccines were useless: First, the process according to Otto and Wohlrab, the process according to Cox, the process of Rickettsia Prowazeki and Rickettsia murina, that is, vaccine from egg cultures; secondly, the vaccines of the Behring works which were produced according to the Otto process, but with other concentrations; finally the Ipsen vaccines from mouse liver. The vaccines of the Behring works were in actual use at that time in thousands of doses. They always represented a danger to health. Without these experiments the vaccines, which were recognised as useless, would have been produced in large quantities because they all had one thing in common: their technical production was much simpler and cheaper than that of the useful vaccines. In any case, one thing is certain, that the victims of this Buchenwald typhus test did not suffer in vain and did not die in vain. There was only one choice, the sacrifice of human lives, of persons determined for that purpose, or to let things run their course, to endanger the lives of innumerable human beings who would be selected not by the Reich Criminal Police Office but by blind fate.

. . .

d.   Testimony of prosecution expert witness Dr Andrew C Ivy
Direct examination.

. . .

Mr Hardy: It is your opinion, then, that the state cannot assume the moral responsibility of a physician to his patient or experimental subject?
Witness Dr Ivy: That is my opinion.
Q: On what do you base your opinion? What is the reason for that opinion?
A: I base that opinion on the principles of ethics and morals contained in the oath of Hippocrates. I think it should be obvious that a state cannot follow a physician around in his daily administration to see that the moral responsibility inherent therein is properly carried out. This moral responsibility that controls or should control the conduct of a physician should be inculcated into the minds of physicians just as moral responsibility of other sorts, and those principles are clearly depicted or enunciated in the oath of Hippocrates with which every physician should be acquainted.
Q: Is the oath of Hippocrates the Golden Rule in the United States and to your knowledge throughout the world?
A: According to my knowledge it represents the Golden Rule of the medical profession. It states how one doctor would like to be treated by another doctor in case he were ill. And in that way how a doctor should treat his patients or experimental subjects. He should treat them as though he were serving as a subject.
Q: Several of the defendants have pointed out in this case that the oath of Hippocrates is obsolete today. Do you follow that opinion?
A: I do not. The moral imperative of the oath of Hippocrates I believe is necessary for the survival of the scientific and technical philosophy of medicine.

. . .

e.   Closing brief for defendant Siegfried Ruff

. . .

Experiments which time and again have been described in international literature without meeting any opposition do not constitute a crime from the medical point of view. For nowhere did a plaintiff arise from the side of the responsible professional organisation, or from that of the administration of justice, to denounce as criminal the experiments described in literature. On the contrary, the authors of those reports on their human experiments gained general recognition and fame; they were awarded the highest honors; they gained historical importance. And in spite of all this, are they supposed to have been criminals? No! In view of the complete lack of written legal norms, the physician, who generally knows only little about the law, has to rely on and refer to the admissibility of what is generally recognised to be admissible all over the world.

The defense is convinced that the Tribunal, when deciding this problem without prejudice, will first study the many experiments performed all over the world on healthy and sick persons, on prisoners and free people, on criminals and on the poor, even on children and mentally ill persons, in order to see how the medical profession in its international totality answers the question of the admissibility of human experiments, not only in theory but also in practice.

It is psychologically understandable that German research workers today will, if possible, have nothing to do with human experiments and will try to avoid them, or would like to describe them as inadmissible even if before 1933 they were perhaps of the opposite opinion. However, experiments performed in 1905–1912 by a highly respected American in Asia for the fight against the plague, which made him famous all over the world, cannot and ought not to be labelled as criminal because a Blome is supposed to have performed the same experiments during the Hitler period (which, in fact, however, were not performed at all); and experiments for which, before 1933, a foreign research worker, the Englishman Ross, was awarded the Nobel Prize for his malaria experiments, do not deserve to be condemned only because a German physician performed similar experiments during the Hitler regime. . . .

f. Testimony of prosecution expert witness Dr Andrew C Ivy
Cross-examination.
. . .

Dr Sauter: Witness, you spoke yesterday of a number of experiments carried out in the United States and in other countries outside of Germany. For example, pellagra, swamp fever, beri-beri, plague, etc. Now, I should like to have a very clear answer from you to the following question. In these experiments which you heard of partly from persons involved in them and partly from international literature, did deaths occur during the experiments and as a result of the experiments or not? Professor, I ask you this question because you said yesterday that you examined all international literature concerning this question and, therefore, have a certain specialized knowledge on this question.

Witness Dr Ivy: I also said that when one reviews the literature, he cannot be sure that he has done a complete or perfect job.

So far as the reports I have read and presented yesterday are concerned, there were no deaths in trench fever. There were no deaths mentioned, to my knowledge, in the article on pellagra. There were no deaths mentioned, to my knowledge, in the article on beri-beri, and there were no deaths in the article, according to my knowledge, in Colonel Strong's article on plague. I would not testify that I have read all the articles in the medical literature involving the use of human beings as subjects in medical experiments.

Q: And, in the literature which you have read, Witness, there was not a single case where deaths occurred? Did I understand you correctly?

A: Yes, in the yellow fever experiments I indicated that Dr Carroll and Dr Lazare died.

Q: That is the only case you know of?

A: That's all that I know of.
. . .

g.   Testimony of defendant Gerhard Rose
Cross-examination.

. . .

Mr McHaney: Now, would the extreme necessity for the large-scale production of typhus vaccines and the resultant experiments on human beings in concentration camps have arisen had not Germany been engaged in a war?

Defendant Rose: That question cannot simply be answered with 'yes' or 'no'. It is, on the whole, not very probable that without the war typhus would have broken out in the German camps, but it is not altogether beyond the bounds of possibility because in times of peace too typhus has broken out in individual cases from time to time. The primary danger in the camps is the louse danger, and infection by lice also occurs in times of peace. If typhus breaks out in a camp that is infected with lice, a typhus epidemic can arise in peacetime too, of course.

Q: But Germany had never experienced any difficulty with typhus before the war. Isn't that right?

A: Not for many decades, no.

Q: You stated that nine hundred persons were used in Dr Strong's plague experiments?

A: Yes, I know that number from the literature on the subject.

Q: What is the usual mortality in plague?

A: That depends on whether it is bubonic plague or lung pest. In one, namely, bubonic plague, the mortality can be as high as sixty or seventy percent. It also can be lower. In lung pest, the mortality is just about one hundred.

Q: How many people died in Dr Strong's plague experiments?

A: According to what his reports say, none of them died, but this result could not have been anticipated because this was the first time that anyone had attempted to innoculate living plague virus into human beings, and Strong said in his first publication in 1905 that he himself was surprised that no unpleasant incidents occurred and that there was only severe fever reaction. That despite this unexpectedly favorable outcome of Strong's experiments the specialists had considerable misgivings about this procedure can be seen first of all from publications where that is explicitly stated; for example, two Englishmen say that, contrary to expectations, these experiments went off well but nevertheless this process cannot be used for general vaccination because there is always the danger that, through some unexpected event, this strain again becomes virulent. Moreover, from other works that Strong later published it can be seen that guinea pigs and monkeys that he vaccinated with this vaccine died not of the plague, but of the toxic effects of the vaccine. All these difficulties are the reason why this enormously important discovery, which Koller and Otto made in 1903, and Strong in 1905, has only been generally applied, for all practical purposes, since 1926. That is an indication of the care and fear with which this whole matter was first approached, and Strong could not know ahead of time that his experiments would turn out well. I described here the enormous concern that Strong felt during all these months regarding the fact that that might happen which every specialist feared, viz, that the virus would become virulent again. That is an enormous responsibility.

Q: Be that as it may, nobody died. That is a fact, isn't it?

A: If anyone did die, the publications say nothing about it. There were deaths only among the monkeys and guinea pigs that are mentioned in the publication. If human beings died, there is no mention in the publication. It is generally known that if there are serious accidents in such experiments as this, they are only most reluctantly made public.

. . .

NOTE

Leo Alexander, 'Medical Science under Dictatorship'

. . .

[A] series of experiments gave results that might have been an important medical contribution if an important lead had not been ignored. The efficacy of various vaccines and drugs against typhus was tested at the Buchenwald and Natzweiler concentration camps. Prevaccinated persons and non-vaccinated controls were injected with live typhus rickettsias, and the death rates of the two series compared. After a certain number of passages, the Matelska strain of typhus rickettsia proved to become avirulent for man. Instead of seizing upon this as a possibility to develop a live vaccine, the experimenters, including the chief consultant, Professor Gerhard Rose, who should have known better, were merely annoyed at the fact that the controls did not die either, discarded this strain and continued testing their relatively ineffective dead vaccines against a new virulent strain. This incident shows that the basic unconscious motivation and attitude has a great influence in determining the scientist's awareness of the phenomena that pass through his vision.

* 241 *New England Journal of Medicine* 39, 43 (1949).

. . .

4. Final plea for defendant Karl Brandt by Dr Robert Servatius

. . .

It is contended that the state finds its limits in the eternal basic elements of law, which are said to be so clear that anyone could discern their violation as a crime, and that loyalty to the state beyond these limits is therefore a crime. One forgets that eternal law, the law of nature, is but a guiding principle for the state and the legislator and not a counter-code of law which the subject might use as a support against the state. It is emphasised that no other state had made such decisions up to now. This is true only to a certain extent. It is no proof, however, that such decisions were not necessary and admissible now. There is no prohibition against daring to progress.

The progress of medical science opened up the problem of experiments on human beings already in the past century, and eventually made it ripe for decision. It is not the first time that a state has adopted a certain attitude with regard to euthanasia with a change of ideology.

Only the statesmen decide what is to be done in the interests of the community, and they have never hesitated to issue such a decision whenever they deemed it necessary in the interest of their people. Thereupon their rules and orders were carried through under the authority of the state, which is the basis of society.

Inquisition, witch trials, and revolutionary tribunals have existed in the name of the state and eternal justice, and the executive participants did not consider themselves criminals but servants of their community. They would have been killed if they had stood up against what was believed to be newly discovered eternal justice. What is the subject to do if the orders of the state exceed the customary limits which the individual himself took for inviolable according to tradition.

What did the airman think who dropped the first atomic bomb on Hiroshima? Did he consider himself a criminal? What did the statesmen think who ordered this atomic bomb to be used. We know from the history of this event that the motive was patriotism, based on the harsh necessity of sacrificing hundreds of thousands to save their own soldiers' lives. This motive was stronger than the prohibition of the Hague Convention, under which belligerents have no unlimited right in the choice of methods for inflicting damage on the enemy.

'My cause is just and my quarrel honorable', says the king. And Shakespeare's soldier answers him: 'That's more than we know.' Another soldier adds: 'Ay, or more than we should seek after; for we know enough if we know we are the king's subjects; if his cause be wrong, our obedience to the king wipes the crime out of us.'

It is the hard necessity of the state on which the defense for Karl Brandt is based against the charge of having performed criminal experiments on human beings.

Here also—in addition to the care for the population—the lives of soldiers were at stake, soldiers who had to be protected from death and epidemics. In Professor Bickenbach's experiment, the issue was the lives of women and children who without 45 million gas masks would have been as unprotected against the expected gas attack as the Japanese were against the atomic bomb. Biological warfare was imminent, even praised abroad as cheaper and more effective than the atomic bomb.

The prosecution opposes to this necessity the condition of absolute voluntariness. It was a surprise to hear from the expert Professor Ivy that in the penitentiaries many hundreds of volunteers were pressing for admission to experiments, and that more volunteered than could be used. I do not want to dispose of this phenomenon with irony and sarcasm. There may be people who realise that the community has the right to ask them for a sacrifice. Their feeling of justice may tell them that insistence on humanity has its limits. If humanity means the appeal to the strong not to forget the weak in the abundance of might and wealth, the weak should also make their contribution when all are in need.

But what if in the emergency of war the convicts, and those declared to be unworthy to serve in the armed forces, refuse to accept such a sacrifice voluntarily, and only prove an asocial burden to state and community and bring about the downfall of the community? Is not compulsion by the state then admissible as an additional expiation?

The prosecution says 'No.' According to this, human rights demand the downfall of human beings.

But there is a mixture of voluntariness and compulsory expiation, 'purchased voluntariness'. Here the experimental subject does not make a sacrifice out of conviction for the good of the community but for his own good. The subject gives his consent because he is to receive money, cigarettes, a mitigation of punishment, etc. There may be isolated cases of this nature where the person is really a volunteer, but as a rule it is not so.

If one compares the actual risk with the advantage granted, one cannot admit the consent of these 'voluntary prisoners' as legal, in spite of all the protective forms they have to sign, for these can only have been obtained by taking advantage of inexperience, imprudence, or distress.

Looking through medical literature, one cannot escape the growing conviction that the word 'volunteer', where it appears at all, is used only as a word of protection and camouflage; it is hardly ever missing since the struggle over this problem became acute.

I will touch only briefly on what I have explained in detail in my closing brief. No one will contend that human beings really allowed themselves to be infected voluntarily with venereal disease; this has nowhere been stated explicitly in literature. Cholera and plague are also not minor inconveniences one is likely to undergo voluntarily for a trifle in the interest of science. Above all, it is not customary to hand over children for experimental purposes, and I cannot believe that in the 13 experiments carried out on a total of 223 children, as stated in Document Karl Brandt 117, ... the mothers gave their consent. Would not the mothers have deserved the praise of the scientist for the sacrifice they trustfully made in the interest of science, praise which is otherwise liberally granted to real volunteers in reports on experiments?

Is it not likely to have been similar to the experiments carried out by Professor McCance? The German authorities who condemn the defendants in a particularly violent form have no objection to raise here against the order to hand over weakling children to a research commission for experimental purposes. The questionnaires which the Tribunal approved for me in order to get further information about this matter have not been answered as the higher authorities did not give permission for such statements to be made. This silence says enough; it is proof of what is supposed to be legal today in the line of 'voluntariness'.

It is repeatedly shown that the experiments for which no consent was given were permitted with the full knowledge of the government authorities. It is further shown that these experiments were published in professional literature without meeting any objection, and that they were even accepted by the public without concern as a normal phenomenon when reports about them appeared in popular magazines.

This happens at a time when the same press is stigmatising as crimes against humanity the German experiments which were necessary in the interests of the state. Voluntariness is a fiction; the emergency of the state hard reality.

In all countries experiments on human beings have been performed by doctors, certainly not because they took pleasure in killing or tormenting, but only at the instigation and under the protection of their state, and in accordance with their own conviction of the necessity for these experiments in the struggle for the existence of the people.

. . .

5. Final statements of the defendants

. . .

a. Final statement of defendant Siegfried Handloser

. . .

More than 150 years ago, the motto and guiding principle created for German military doctors and their successors was 'Scientiae, Humanitati, Patriae' (For Science, Humanity, and Fatherland). Like the medical officers in their entirety I also have remained true to that guiding principle in thought and in deed. Realising the outcome of the events of these recent times, may the joint endeavors of all the nations succeed in avoiding in future the immeasurable misfortune of war, the dreadful side of which nobody knows better than the military doctor.

b. Final statement of defendant Gerhard Rose

. . .

. . . Everyone who, as a scientist, has an insight into the history of dangerous medical experiments, knows with certainty the following fact. Aside from the self-experiments of doctors, which represent a very small minority of such experiments, the extent to which subjects are volunteers is often deceptive. At the very best they amount to self-deceit on the part of the physician who conducts the experiment, but very frequently to a deliberate misleading of the public. In the majority of such cases, if we ethically examine facts, we find an exploitation of the ignorance, the frivolity, the economic distress, or other emergency on the part of the experimental subjects. I may only refer to the example which was presented to the Tribunal by Dr Ivy when he presented the forms for the American malaria experiments.

You yourselves, gentlemen of the Tribunal, are in a position to examine whether, on the basis of the information contained in these forms, individuals of the average education of an inmate of a prison can form a sufficiently clear opinion of the risks of an experiment made with pernicious malaria. These facts will be confirmed by any sincere and decent scientist in a personal conversation, though he would not like to make such a statement in public. . . .

. . .

6. Judgment

. . .

Beals, Sebring, Crawford, JJ : . . . Judged by any standard of proof the record clearly shows the commission of war crimes and crimes against humanity substantially as alleged in counts two and three of the indictment. Beginning with the outbreak of World War II criminal medical experiments on non-German nationals, both prisoners of war and civilians, including Jews and 'asocial' persons, were carried out on a large scale in Germany and the occupied countries. These experiments were not the isolated and casual acts of individual doctors and scientists working solely on their own responsibility, but were the product of coordinated policy-making and planning at high governmental, military, and Nazi Party levels, conducted as an integral part of the total war effort. They were ordered, sanctioned, permitted, or approved by persons in positions of authority who under all principles of law were under the duty to know about these things and to take steps to terminate or prevent them.

The great weight of the evidence before us is to the effect that certain types of medical experiments on human beings, when kept within reasonably well-defined bounds, conform to the ethics of the medical profession generally. The protagonists of the practice of human experimentation justify their views on the basis that such experiments yield results for the good of society that are unprocurable by other methods or means of study. All agree, however, that certain basic principles must be observed in order to satisfy moral, ethical, and legal concepts :

1. The voluntary consent of the human subject is absolutely essential.

This means that the person involved should have legal capacity to give consent; should be so situated as to be able to exercise free power of choice, without the intervention of any element of force, fraud, deceit, duress, over-reaching, or other ulterior form of constraint or coercion; and should have sufficient knowledge and comprehension of the elements of the subject matter involved as to enable him to make an understanding and enlightened decision. This latter element requires that before the acceptance of an affirmative decision by the experimental subject there should be made known to him the nature, duration, and purpose of the experiment; the method and means by which it is to be conducted; all inconveniences and hazards reasonably to be expected; and the effects upon his health or person which may possibly come from his participation in the experiment.

The duty and responsibility for ascertaining the quality of the consent rests upon each individual who initiates, directs, or engages in the experiment. It is a personal duty and responsibility which may not be delegated to another with impunity.

2. The experiment should be such as to yield fruitful results for the good of society, unprocurable by other methods or means of study, and not random and unnecessary in nature.

3. The experiment should be so designed and based on the results of animal experimentation and a knowledge of the natural history of the disease or other problem under study that the anticipated results will justify the performance of the experiment.

4. The experiment should be so conducted as to avoid all unnecessary physical and mental suffering and injury.

5. No experiment should be conducted where there is an *a priori* reason to believe that death or disabling injury will occur; except, perhaps, in those experiments where the experimental physicians also serve as subjects.

6. The degree of risk to be taken should never exceed that determined by the humanitarian importance of the problem to be solved by the experiment.

7. Proper preparations should be made and adequate facilities provided to protect the experimental subject against even remote possibilities of injury, disability, or death.

8. The experiment should be conducted only by scientifically qualified persons. The highest degree of skill and care should be required through all stages of the experiment of those who conduct or engage in the experiment.

9. During the course of the experiment the human subject should be at liberty to bring the experiment to an end if he has reached the physical or mental state where continuation of the experiment seems to him to be impossible.

10. During the course of the experiment the scientist in charge must be prepared to terminate the experiment at any stage, if he has probable cause to believe, in the exercise of the good faith, superior skill, and careful judgment required of him that a continuation of the experiment is likely to result in injury, disability, or death to the experimental subject.

Of the ten principles which have been enumerated our judicial concern, of course, is with those requirements which are purely legal in nature—or which at least are so clearly related to matters legal that they assist us in determining criminal culpability and punishment. To go beyond that point would lead us into a field that would be beyond our sphere of competence. However, the point need not be labored. We find from the evidence that in the medical experiments which have been proved, these ten principles were much more frequently honored in their breach than in their observance. Many of the concentration camp inmates who were the victims of these atrocities were citizens of countries other than the German Reich. They were non-German nationals, including Jews and 'asocial persons', both prisoners of war and civilians, who had been imprisoned and forced to submit to these tortures and barbarities without so much as a semblance of trial. In every single instance appearing in the record, subjects were used who did not consent to the experiments; indeed, as to some of the experiments, it is not even contended by the defendants that the subjects occupied the status of volunteers. In no case was the experimental subject at liberty of his own free choice to withdraw from any experiment. In many cases experiments were performed by unqualified persons; were conducted at random for no adequate scientific reason, and under revolting physical conditions. All of the experiments were conducted with unnecessary suffering and injury, and but very little, if any, precautions were taken to protect or safeguard the human subjects from the possibilities of injury, disability, or death. In every one of the experiments the subjects experienced extreme pain or torture, and in most of them they suffered permanent injury, mutilation, or death, either as a direct result of the experiments or because of lack of adequate follow-up care.

Obviously all of these experiments involving brutalities, tortures, disabling injury, and death were performed in complete disregard of international conventions, the laws and customs of war [and] the general principles of criminal law as derived from the criminal laws of all civilized nations . . . Manifestly human experiments under such conditions are contrary to 'the principles of the law of nations as they result from the usages established among civilized peoples, from the laws of humanity, and from the dictates of public conscience'.

. . .

There is some evidence to the effect that the camp inmates used as subjects in the first series submitted to being used as experimental subjects after being told that the experiments were harmless and that additional food would be given to volunteers. But these victims were not informed that they would be artificially infected with a highly virulent virus nor that they might die as a result. Certainly no one would seriously suggest that under the circumstances these men gave their legal consent to act as subjects. One does not ordinarily consent to be the special object of a murder, and if one did, such consent would not absolve his slayer.

. . .

[Sixteen of the twenty-three defendants were found guilty of war crimes and crimes against humanity. Seven, including Karl Brandt, Rudolf Brandt, and Joachim Mrugowsky, were sentenced to death by hanging; the other nine, including Siegfried Handloser and Gerhard Rose, to imprisonment varying from ten years to life.]

The ten principles set out in the above judgment have become known as the Nuremberg Code. It is sometimes thought that they constitute the first modern attempt to lay down the principles upon which research is to be conducted. Nicholson, however, points out in *Medical Research with Children* (1986) that (p 154):

The first modern guidelines for the conduct of clinical research were produced by the German Ministry of the Interior in 1931;[3] . . . They were produced in response to frequent allegations, in both the German Press and Parliament, of unethical conduct by doctors during the previous decade. At that time Germany had a thriving chemical industry, collaboration with which had enabled researchers to develop the first chemotherapeutic agents for infections such as malaria, trypanosomiasis, and leishmaniasis, and led to animal trials of Prontosil, the first sulphonamide, in 1933. Howard-Jones[4] suggests that doctors may well not have been 'sufficiently critical in exploiting the multiplicity of new remedies' placed at their disposal. In the midst of the public debate, the Berlin Medical Board suggested that there should be an official body to regulate all proposed experiments on humans: it seems likely that this was the first time that peer review of modern clinical research had been suggested. Little came of the suggestion, however.

Notes to extract
3. German Reich. Circular of the Ministry of the Interior on directives concerning new medical treatments and scientific experiments on man (1931). Translated in *Int Dig Hlth Legisl (Geneva)* **31**, 408–11 (1980).
4. Howard-Jones, N Human experimentation in historical and ethical perspectives. In *Human experimentation and medical ethics* (eds Z Bankowski and N Howard-Jones) pp 453–95. CIOMS, Geneva (1982).

Obviously, these earlier guidelines proved irrelevant once the Nazis embarked upon the kind of investigation mentioned in the *Brandt* trial.

The Nuremberg Code represented the basis on which civilised society was expected to conduct itself until it was supplemented by the Declaration of Helsinki of the World Health Organisation in 1964 (as amended in 1975 and 1983).

It is the mission of the medical doctor to safeguard the health of the people. His or her knowledge and conscience are dedicated to the fulfilment of this mission.

The Declaration of Geneva of the World Medical Association binds the physician with the words, 'The health of my patient will be my first consideration', and the International Code of Medical Ethics declares that 'A physician shall act only in the patient's interest when providing medical care which might have the effect of weakening the physical and mental condition of the patient'.

The purpose of biomedical research involving human subjects must be to improve diagnostic, therapeutic and prophylactic procedures and the understanding of the aetiology and pathogenesis of disease.

In current medical practice most diagnostic, therapeutic or prophylactic procedures involve hazards. This applies especially to biomedical research.

Medical progress is based on research which ultimately must rest in part on experimentation involving human subjects.

In the field of biomedical research a fundamental distinction must be recognised between medical research in which the aim is essentially diagnostic or therapeutic for a patient, and medical research, the essential object of which is purely scientific and without implying direct diagnostic or therapeutic value to the person subjected to the research.

Special caution must be exercised in the conduct of research which may affect the environment, and the welfare of animals used for research must be respected.

Because it is essential that the results of laboratory experiments be applied to human beings to further scientific knowledge and to help suffering humanity, the World Medical Association has prepared the following recommendations as a guide to every physician in biomedical research involving human subjects. They should be kept under review in the future. It must be stressed that the standards as drafted are only a guide to physicians all over the world. Physicians are not relieved from criminal, civil and ethical responsibilities under the laws of their own countries.

I   Basic principles
(1) Biomedical research involving human subjects must conform to generally accepted scientific principles and should be based on adequately performed laboratory and animal experimentation and on a thorough knowledge of the scientific literature.
(2) The design and performance of each experimental procedure involving human subjects should be clearly formulated in an experimental protocol which should be transmitted to a specially appointed independent committee for consideration, comment and guidance.
(3) Biomedical research involving human subjects should be conducted only by scientific qualified persons and under the supervision of a clinically competent medical person. The responsibility for the human subject must always rest with the medically qualified person and never rest on the subject of the research, even though the subject has given his or her consent.
(4) Biomedical research involving human subjects cannot legitimately be carried out unless the importance of the objective is in proportion to the inherent risk to the subject.
(5) Every biomedical research project involving human subjects should be preceded by careful assessment of predictable risks in comparison with foreseeable benefits to the subject or to others. Concern for the interests of the subject must always prevail over the interests of science and society.
(6) The right of the research subject to safeguard his or her integrity must always be

respected. Every precaution should be taken to respect the privacy of the subject and to minimize the impact of the study on the subject's physical and mental integrity and on the personality of the subject.

(7) Physicians should abstain from engaging in research projects involving human subjects unless they are satisfied that the hazards involved are believed to be predictable. Physicians should cease any investigation if the hazards are found to outweigh the potential benefits.

(8) In publication of the results of his or her research, the physician is obliged to preserve the accuracy of the results. Reports of experimentation not in accordance with the principles laid down in this Declaration should not be accepted for publication.

(9) In any research on human beings, each potential subject must be adequately informed of the aims, methods, anticipated benefits and potential hazards of the study and the discomfort it may entail. He or she should be informed that he or she is at liberty to abstain from participation in the study and that he or she is free to withdraw his or her consent to participation at any time. The physician should then obtain the subject's freely-given informed consent, preferably in writing.

(10) When obtaining informed consent for the research project the physician should be particularly cautious if the subject is in a dependent relationship to him or her or may consent under duress. In that case the informed consent should be obtained by a physician who is not engaged in the investigation and who is completely independent of this official relationship.

(11) In case of legal incompetence, informed consent should be obtained from the legal guardian in accordance with national legislation. Where physical or mental incapacity makes it impossible to obtain informed consent, or when the subject is a minor, permission from the responsible relative replaces that of the subject in accordance with national legislation.

Whenever the minor child is in fact able to give a consent, the minor's consent must be obtained in addition to the consent of the minor's legal guardian.

(12) The research protocol should always contain a statement of the ethical considerations involved and should indicate that the principles enunciated in the present Declaration are complied with.

II Medical research combined with professional care
(Clinical research)

(1) In the treatment of the sick person, the physician must be free to use a new diagnostic and therapeutic measure, if in his or her judgment it offers hope of saving life, re-establishing health or alleviating suffering.

(2) The potential benefits, hazards and discomfort of a new method should be weighed against the advantages of the best current diagnostic and therapeutic methods.

(3) In any medical study, every patient—including those of a control group, if any—should be assured of the best proven diagnostic and therapeutic method.

(4) The refusal of the patient to participate in a study must never interfere with the physician-patient relationship.

(5) If the physician considers it essential not to obtain informed consent, the specific reasons for this proposal should be stated in the experimental protocol for transmission to the independent committee (I.2).

(6) The physician can combine medical research with professional care, the objective being the acquisition of new medical knowledge, only to the extent that medical research is justified by its potential diagnostic or therapeutic value for the patient.

III Non-therapeutic biomedical research involving human subjects
(Non-clinical biomedical research)

(1) In the purely scientific application of medical research carried out on a human being, it is the duty of the physician to remain the protector of the life and health of that person on whom biomedical research is being carried out.

(2) The subjects should be volunteers—either healthy persons or patients for whom the experimental design is not related to the patient's illness.

(3) The investigator or the investigating team should discontinue the research if in his/her or their judgment it may, if continued, be harmful to the individual.

(4) In research on man, the interest of science and society should never take precedence over considerations related to the well-being of the subject.

Despite the Declaration of Helsinki in 1964, Beecher could still write his seminal paper entitled *Ethics and Clinical Research* in the New England Journal of Medicine (274 New Eng J Med 1354 (1966)) (footnotes omitted):

Nearly everyone agrees that ethical violations do occur. The practical question is, how often? A preliminary examination of the matter was based on 17 examples, which were easily increased to 50. These 50 studies contained references to 186 further likely examples, on the average 3.7 leads per study; they at times overlapped from paper to paper, but this figure indicates how conveniently one can proceed in a search for such material. The data are suggestive of widespread problems, but there is need for another kind of information, which was obtained by examination of 100 consecutive human studies published in 1964, in an excellent journal; 12 of these seemed to be unethical. If only one quarter of them is truly unethical, this still indicates the existence of a serious situation. Pappworth, in England, has collected, he says, more than 500 papers based upon unethical experimentation. It is evident from such observations that unethical or questionably ethical procedures are not uncommon.
. . .

Known effective treatment withheld

Example 1.   It is known that rheumatic fever can usually be prevented by adequate treatment of streptococcal respiratory infections by the parenteral administration of penicillin. Nevertheless, definitive treatment was withheld, and placebos were given to a group of 109 men in service, while benzathine penicillin G was given to others.

The therapy that each patient received was determined automatically by his military serial number arranged so that more men received penicillin than received placebo. In the small group of patients studied 2 cases of acute rheumatic fever and 1 of acute nephritis developed in the control of patients, whereas these complications did not occur among those who received benzathine penicillin G.

Example 2.   The sulfonamides were for many years the only antibacterial drugs effective in shortening the duration of acute streptococcal pharyngitis and in reducing its suppurative complications. The investigators in this study undertook to determine if the occurrence of the serious nonsuppurative complications, rheumatic fever and acute glomerulonephritis, would be reduced by this treatment. This study was made despite the general experience that certain antibiotics, including penicillin, will prevent the development of rheumatic fever.

The subjects were a large group of hospital patients; a control group of approximately the same size, also with exudative Group A streptococcus, was included. The latter group received only non-specific therapy (no sulfadiazine). The total group denied the effective penicillin comprised over 500 men.

Rheumatic fever was diagnosed in 5.4 per cent of those treated with sulfadiazine. In the control group rheumatic fever developed in 4.2 per cent.

In reference to this study a medical officer stated in writing that the subjects were not informed, did not consent and were not aware that they had been involved in an experiment, and yet admittedly 25 acquired rheumatic fever. According to this same medical officer *more than 70* who had had known definitive treatment withheld were on the wards with rheumatic fever when he was there.

Example 3.   This involved a study of the relapse rate in typhoid fever treated in two ways. In an earlier study by the present investigators chloramphenicol had been recognized as an effective treatment for typhoid fever, being attended by half the mortality that was experienced when this agent was not used. Others had made the same observations, indicating that to withhold this effective remedy can be a life-

or-death decision. The present study was carried out to determine the relapse rate under the two methods of treatment; of 408 charity patients 251 were treated with chloramphenicol, of whom 20, or 7.97 per cent, died. Symptomatic treatment was given, but chloramphenicol was withheld in 157, of whom 36, or 22.9 per cent died. According to the data presented, 23 patients died in the course of this study who would not have been expected to succumb if they had received therapy.
. . .

Physiologic studies
Example 5. In this controlled, double-blind study of the hematologic toxicity of chloramphenicol, it was recognised that chloramphenicol is 'well known as a cause of aplastic anemia' and that there is a 'prolonged morbidity and high mortality of aplastic anemia' and that 'chloramphenicol-induced aplastic anemia can be related to dose . . .' The aim of the study was 'further definition of the toxicology of the drug
. . .'

Forty-one randomly chosen patients were given either 2 or 6 gm of chloramphenicol per day; 12 control patients were used. 'Toxic bone-marrow depression, predominantly affecting erythropoiesis, developed in 2 of 20 patients given 2.0 gm and in 18 of 21 given 6 gm of chloramphenicol daily'. The smaller dose is recommended for routine use.

Example 6. In a study of the effect of thymectomy on the survival of skin homografts 18 children, three and a half months to eighteen years of age, about to undergo surgery for congenital heart disease, were selected. Eleven were to have total thymectomy as part of the operation, and 7 were to serve as controls. As part of the experiment, full-thickness skin homografts from an unrelated adult donor were sutured to the chest wall in each case. (Total thymectomy is occasionally, although not usually part of the primary cardiovascular surgery involved, and whereas it may not greatly add to the hazards of the necessary operation, its eventual effects in children are not known.) This work was proposed as part of a long-range study of 'the growth and development of these children over the years'. No difference in the survival of the skin homograft was observed in the 2 groups.
. . .

Example 8. Since the minimum blood-flow requirements of the cerebral circulation are not accurately known, this study was carried out to determine 'cerebral hemodynamic and metabolic changes . . . before and during acute reductions in arterial pressure induced by drug administration and/or postural adjustments'. Forty-four patients whose ages varied from the second to the tenth decade were involved. They included normotensive subjects, those with essential hypertension and finally a group with malignant hypertension. Fifteen had abnormal electrocardiograms. Few details about the reasons for hospitalization are given.

Signs of cerebral circulatory insufficiency, which were easily recognized, included confusion and in some cases a nonresponsive state. By alteration in the tilt of the patient 'the clinical state of the subject could be changed in a matter of seconds from one of alertness to confusion, and for the remainder of the flow, the subject was maintained in the latter state'. The femoral arteries were cannulated in all subjects, and the internal jugular veins in 14.

The mean arterial pressure fell in 37 subjects from 109 to 48 mm of mercury, with signs of cerebral ischemia. 'With the onset of collapse, cardiac output and right ventricular pressures decreased sharply'.

Since signs of cerebral insufficiency developed without evidence of coronary insufficiency the authors concluded that 'the brain may be more sensitive to acute hypotension than is the heart'.

Studies to improve the understanding of disease
Example 14. In this study of the syndrome of empending hepatic coma in patients with cirrhosis of the liver certain nitrogenous substances were administered to 9 patients with chronic alcoholism and advanced cirrhosis: ammonium chloride, di-ammonium citrate, urea or dietary protein. In all patients a reaction that included mental disturbances, a 'flapping tremor', and electroencephalographic changes

developed. Similarly signs had occurred in only 1 of the patients before these substances were administered:

The first sign noted was usually clouding of the consciousness. Three patients had a second or a third course of administration of a nitrogenous substance with the same results. It was concluded that marked resemblance between this reaction and impending hepatic coma implied that the administration of these [nitrogenous] substances to patients with cirrhosis may be hazardous.

Example 18. Melanoma was transplanted from a daughter to her volunteering and informed mother, 'in the hope of gaining a little better understanding of cancer immunity and in the hope that the production of tumour antibodies might be helpful in the treatment of the cancer patient'. Since the daughter died on the day after the transplantation of the tumour into her mother, the hope expressed seems to have been more theoretical than practical, and the daughter's condition was described as 'terminal' at the time the mother volunteered to be a recipient. The primary implant was widely excised on the twenty-fourth day after it had been placed in the mother. She died from metastatic melanoma on the four hundred and fifty-first day after transplantation. The evidence that this patient died of diffuse melanoma that metastasised from a small piece of transplanted tumour was considered conclusive.

Technical study of disease

Example 19. During bronchoscopy a special needle was inserted through a bronchus into the left atrium of the heart. This was done in an unspecified number of subjects, both with cardiac disease and with normal hearts.

The technique was a new approach whose hazards were at the beginning quite unknown. The subjects with normal hearts were used, not for their possible benefit but for that of patients in general.

. . .

Example 21. This was a study of the effect of exercise on cardiac output and pulmonary-artery pressure in 8 'normal' persons (that is, patients whose diseases were not related to the cardiovascular system), in 8 with congestive heart failure severe enough to have recently required complete bed rest, in 6 with hypertension, in 2 with aortic insufficiency, in 7 with mitral stenosis, and in 5 with pulmonary emphysema.

Intracardiac catheterisation was carried out, and the catheter then inserted into the right or left main branch of the pulmonary artery. The brachial artery was usually catheterised; sometimes, the radial or femoral arteries were catheterised. The subjects exercised in a supine position by pushing their feet against weighted pedals. 'The ability of these patients to carry on sustained work was severely limited by weakness and dyspnea'. Several were in severe failure. This was not a therapeutic attempt but rather a physiologic study.

Bizarre study

Example 22. There is a question whether ureteral reflux can occur in the normal bladder. With this in mind, vesicourethrography was carried out on 26 normal babies less than forty-eight hours old. The infants were exposed to x-rays while the bladder was filling and during voiding. Multiple spot films were made to record the presence or absence of ureteral reflux. None was found in this group, and fortunately no infection followed the catheterisation. What the results of the extensive x-ray exposure may be, no one can yet say.

Comment on death rates

In the foregoing examples a number of procedures, some with their own demonstrated death rates, were carried out. The following data were provided by 3 distinguished investigators in the field and respresent widely held views.

Cardiac catheterisation: right side of the heart, about 1 death per 1,000 cases; left side, 5 deaths per 1,000 cases. 'Probably considerably higher in some places, depending on the portal of entry'. (One investigator had 15 deaths in his first 150 cases.) It is possible that catheterisation of a hepatic vein or the renal vein would have a lower death rate than that of catheterisation of the right side of the heart, for if it is properly carried out, only the atrium is entered en route to the liver or the kidney, not the right ventricle, which can lead to serious cardiac irregularities. There is always the possibility, however, that the ventricle will be entered inadvertently. This occurs in at least half the cases, according to 1 expert—'but if properly done is too transient to be of importance'.

Liver biopsy: the death rate here is estimated at 2 to 3 per 1,000, depending in considerable part on the condition of the subject.

Anesthesia: the anesthesia death rate can be placed in general at about 1 death per 2,000 cases. The hazard is doubtless higher when certain practices such as deliberate evocation of ventricular extrasystoles under cyclopropane are involved.

. . .

In England, as Nicholson points out in *Medical Research with Children* (p 4):

. . . 1967, saw the publication of the first report of the Royal College of Physicians 'Committee on the supervision of the ethics of clinical investigations in institutions', which also recommended that every hospital or institution in which clinical research was undertaken should have a group of doctors that 'should satisfy itself of the ethics of all proposed investigations'. In the same year, M H Pappworth published his book *Human guinea pigs*,[9] which detailed several hundred reports of medical experiments that he considered unethical, most of which had been carried out either in the United Kingdom or in the United States of America. He proposed that 'research committees', each with at least one lay member, should be established in every region to review the ethics of proposed investigations, and that, by law, they should be responsible to the General Medical Council.

Over the next few years many hospitals in the United Kingdom did establish ethics committees to review proposed clinical research investigations. Even to this day, however, there is no statutory duty on health authorities, board of governors, or other hospital managers to set up such research ethics committees and, indeed, some have not yet done so. At the request of the Chief Medical Officer of the Department of Health and Social Security (DHSS) in 1973, the Royal College of Physicians committee again made recommendations,[2] suggesting principally (1) that all proposals for clinical research investigations should be referred to the appropriate ethics committee for approval, and (2) that there should be a lay member on each research ethics committee. The DHSS finally published an advisory circular in 1975[3] confirming the 1967 and 1973 recommendations of the Royal College of Physicians, but without giving them the force of statute.

Notes to extract
9. Pappworth, M H, *Human guinea pigs*. Routledge & Kegan Paul, London (1976).
2. Royal College of Physicians. *Supervision of the ethics of clinical research investigations in institutions*. Royal College of Physicians, London (1973).
3. Department of Health and Social Security. *Supervision of the ethics of clinical research investigations and fetal research*. HSC(IS)153. DHSS, London (1975).

The law relating to research in England

Research on animals has been regulated by law since the Cruelty to Animals Act 1876. (The current law is contained in the Animals (Scientific Procedure) Act 1986.) In contrast, there has never been any statute specifically regulating the conduct of research on human beings. You may think this is not atypical of the state of affairs in England. In the absence of any specific statutory framework we must look to the common law and, perhaps, analogous statutes.

(i) TERMINOLOGY

Traditionally, any analysis of the law and ethics concerning research on human beings has drawn a distinction between therapeutic and non-therapeutic research. Unless carefully analysed these terms may lead to confusion. Thus, it is important at the outset to understand what is meant by them before embarking on any examination of the law.

The Institute of Medical Ethics in its Working Party Report, *Medical Research with Children* (1986) defines the distinction between these terms and illustrates it as follows (pp 33–36; footnote omitted):

> The central point is that since therapy is distinguished from research by the intention of the person doing it, research can never be, in itself, therapy.
>
> Therefore the distinction has to be that *therapeutic research* is research consisting in an activity which has also a therapeutic intention, as well as a research intention, towards the subjects of the research, and *non-therapeutic research* is research activity which has not also a therapeutic intention.
>
> A therapeutic intention is to have as one's purpose therapy . . .
>
> This definition of the distinction between therapeutic and non-therapeutic research was approved by the working group because it makes clear the dual intent of therapeutic research. It was also argued, however, that such dual intent was unlikely or even impossible; a researcher would always have the primary intent of gaining new knowledge. Such a suggestion seems improbable, however: in reality, a researcher would be using his clinical and therapeutic acumen in the interests of the research element of his activity, at the same time as using his research skills for the clinical benefit of his research subject. If one invites friends round for dinner, one has the dual intent of feeding them and talking with them: it would indeed be a strange occasion if one fed them only without saying a word the whole evening; or vice versa!
>
> One research proposal examined by the working group illustrates both the need in some circumstances to decide whether a project is therapeutic or non-therapeutic, and the difficulties that may be met in so deciding. The proposal had been submitted to the working group by the chairman of a research ethics committee which had been in difficulty when trying to decide whether or not to approve the proposal.
>
> The purpose of the project was to study water fluxes in sick pre-term infants and to assess in particular the insensible water gain from humidifiers attached to artificial ventilators, and the insensible water loss from the lungs and skin. Ten infants requiring artificial ventilation for hyaline membrane disease would be studied. In such infants, water balance is very important in determining the development of several potentially fatal complications, but little is known about insensible water gain or loss from the expiratory tract in particular. In the study, deuterium oxide, heavy water or D_2O, would be added to the humidifier water in the artificial ventilator. Its accumulation in the neonate could then be followed by measuring the proportion of D_2O to ordinary water, H_2O, in blood samples taken sequentially. These blood samples would be very small, since only five microlitres (about one-twentieth of a drop) of blood would be required in order to measure D_2O by mass spectrometry; they would be taken—over a period of three days, and with no discomfort—from an umbilical arterial catheter, which is usually inserted when infants are artificially ventilated.
>
> The problem that has arisen with this proposal concerned the obtaining of parental consent. The policy in the special care baby unit where the proposed project would be undertaken was not to obtain informed consent for this type of study. The researchers therefore proposed to dispense with informed consent, while the research ethics committee thought that it should be obtained.
>
> One reason why it is necessary to establish whether such a project is therapeutic or non-therapeutic is a legal one. The removal of blood samples from the infants would be an assault unless consent had been given. Although there is no specific statement of the law in such circumstances, it is likely that the courts would always regard unconsented invasive non-therapeutic research as unlawful. They might take a somewhat more lenient view of unconsented therapeutic research, though not necessarily.
>
> The basic difficulty in considering whether or not this project is therapeutic

research is to decide whether there is a therapeutic intention towards the infant subjects. It is essential to provide humidified air to infants on artificial ventilators: one argument therefore states that the addition of D_2O to humidifier water merely alters slightly one therapeutic activity without in any way altering the therapeutic intention. It is a necessary part of medical practice to examine the results of therapies that are used in order that they may be improved: such assessment of a therapy is inevitably therapeutic research.

Another view would suggest that the addition of D_2O to humidifier water is not a necessary part of therapy, and is not intended, in itself, to be therapy. The taking of additional blood samples—even though they amount to a very small total quantity— is not a therapeutic activity; the researchers have not stated how soon the measurements of D_2O might be made, and nowhere in their protocol have they suggested that the measurements might be used to improve the control of water balance in the infant subjects. The project is therefore designed to gain physiological knowledge, and there is no therapeutic intention towards the infant subjects in the proposed activities that are additional to standard therapy.

The problem of deciding which argument is correct seems finally to be insoluble. In terms of the definitions adopted by the working group . . . it is possible, however, to conclude that this is a therapeutic research project since the researchers have both a therapeutic intention, in humidifying the air supplied by the ventilators, and a research intention. It is not suggested that the definitions adopted by the working group will solve all the problems with which research ethics committees are in practice faced. The researchers in the anorectal manometry project, for instance, had no therapeutic intention towards the controls that they used. To identify the controls as taking part in therapeutic research because there was a therapeutic intention towards the subjects of the research project seems invidious and inherently inequitable. In some circumstances it may then be important to abandon attempts to describe a whole research project as either therapeutic or non-therapeutic, and to consider instead the nature of the actual procedures undertaken. In this case, the subjects had therapeutic interventions performed on them, while the controls had non-therapeutic interventions performed.

The definitions adopted by the working group allow firm conclusions to be reached about some other projects mentioned earlier. When the Willowbrook experiments started, there was no therapeutic intention in them towards the handicapped subjects, although some benefits may have accrued to them incidentally. By the working group's definitions, they were therefore non-therapeutic research projects. On the other hand, the comparative trials of treatment regimes for leukaemia and other malignancies were and are therapeutic research, since there has always been a therapeutic intention towards each of the subjects, even when the major benefits would probably fall to later cohorts. The definitions also obviate the need for such complicating expressions as 'partly therapeutic', that have been suggested to describe an intervention such as the taking of an additional two millilitres of blood for a research purpose, when a blood specimen is to be taken anyway as part of therapy. Since the act of taking the blood sample has both a therapeutic and a research intention, the act is therapeutic—by definition.

Professor Richard Hare, a member of the Working Party, put it succinctly in his paper 'Little Human Guinea Pigs', in *Moral Dilemmas in Modern Medicine* (1985) (ed M Lockwood): 'therapeutic research is thus an activity which has both aims [therapy and research]; non-therapeutic research is an activity which has only a research and not a therapeutic aim'. We will adopt this understanding of the distinction between the two types of research.

The Institute's Working Party drew attention to one further term which warrants consideration in any examination of the regulations of research, namely, *innovative therapy* (pp 36–7).

Innovative therapy consists in the performance of a new or non-standard intervention as all or part of a therapeutic activity and not as part of a formal research project.

Innovative therapy may therefore be quite haphazard, starting just when a doctor has a bright idea that he wants to try out. If the bright idea seems to be any good, then innovative therapy can become research as soon as the bright idea is examined in a systematic manner. Much innovative therapy is surgical in nature, since surgeons often try out modifications to existing surgical procedures and occasionally try out new operations. It is rare for these modifications or new operations to be undertaken as part of a formal research project and they have not in general been subject first to peer review or review by a research ethics committee. Another sort of innovative therapy would be the introduction of new instruments, if these were not formally compared with existing ones. Innovative therapy is comparatively rare in the use of medicines, but it can still occur. A doctor may decide that a drug that is already available for the treatment of one disease might be useful in the treatment of another, and he is at liberty within the limits of his professional expertise to go ahead and try it. One example a few years ago was the use of injectable phenothiazine drugs. These were introduced to help in the treatment of schizophrenia, their value being that a schizophrenic could have his illness controlled by a monthly injection. Doctors looking after mentally handicapped children with severe behaviour disturbances realized that these drugs might help: it was found that monthly injections of quite small doses produced considerable improvement in the behaviour of the few children in whom the drugs were tried. It was then decided to set up a controlled trial to discover whether the results were real: ie what started as innovative therapy became therapeutic research as the trial was set up, and the haphazard procedures became formalised.

In our view, the Working Party was right to draw attention to innovative therapy and highlight the fact that it may consist in doing the same things with the same intentions as researchers may do, but without any of the constraints associated with the proper conduct of research. To the extent that the intention is to acquire knowledge and not merely to care for the patient, and that the procedure carries no more than a minimal risk of harm, it is our view that innovative therapy should be subject to the same regime of control that attends research properly so-called.

(ii) THERAPEUTIC RESEARCH

There are at least three situations in which therapeutic research may be carried out:

(1) a doctor tests the efficacy of a new treatment where none had previously been available and the patient would receive ordinary nursing care, symptomatic relief but nothing else.
(2) a doctor tests the efficacy of a new treatment as against other established forms of treatment.
(3) a doctor tests treatments A, B and C (all of which are established) because it has not been established which is the most efficacious.

All of these types of research can be generically described as 'clinical trials'. They can be carried out in a variety of ways which are the subject of considerable scientific dispute, for example the allocation of the patient to one treatment or another may, or may not, be *random*. As we shall see, the use of randomisation calls for particular examination.

Before considering in detail the law applicable to clinical trials, it is important to make a general point. Since clinical trials entail a doctor/patient relationship, the general law concerning the duty of the doctor to act in the best interests of his patient and not to harm him applies. This has certain consequences for the conduct of trials.

First, if the trial consists in testing a new treatment, the doctor must have reasonable grounds for believing that the new treatment may be efficacious. For example, all necessary and appropriate research on animals and other studies must have been carried out.

Secondly, patients not receiving any new treatment which is the subject of the trial, must receive the best available established treatment.

Thirdly, the trial must contain an appropriate mechanism (a 'stopping rule') whereby it may be discontinued if (a) a new treatment proves less beneficial than established treatment; or (b) a new treatment proves more beneficial than existing therapies or the best available other; or (c) therapy A shows a marked benefit over therapies B and C or vice versa (see for a description, W A Silverman, *Human Experimentation* (1986), ch 9).

In addition to these general propositions derived from the doctor's general duty to his patient, the law relating to the conduct of clinical trials is, in effect, the law relating to consent.

(a) The competent patient

We have already analysed the meaning of 'competence'. The only additional point which needs to be made here relates to the applicability of s 8(1) of the Family Law Reform Act 1969. This provision, you will recall, states that:

> the consent of a minor who has attained the age of 16 to any surgical, medical or dental treatment which, in the absence of consent, would constitute a trespass to his person, shall be as effective as it would be if he were of full age . . .

The question to be considered is whether therapeutic research is 'treatment' within the Act, so that a person over the age of 16 is *prima facie* competent. If therapeutic research, because it entails two intentions—to treat and to do research, is more than 'treatment' within the Act, then the power to consent would remain with the proxy until the minor reaches majority, ie 18, unless found to be competent as explained in the *Gillick* decision. On this analysis, a minor between 16 and 18 years of age would not *prima facie* be competent to consent to therapeutic research. Furthermore in applying *Gillick*, a relatively high standard of comprehension by the minor would have to be shown since therapeutic research entails research on a *sick* minor. It could be said that the law would protect such a minor from consenting save when the illness and the research were trivial because a court might well find any given minor lacked the necessary maturity to consent. This analysis would apply, perhaps, with even greater force, to a minor under 16.

The concern for the competence of the patient is not, of course, limited to the minor. Therapeutic research on adults equally contemplates research on a sick person. The law would insist that those contemplating research satisfy themselves that in assessing a patient's competence to volunteer they have taken account of the possible effect and pressure of such factors as pain, other medication and other therapies.

1. Voluntariness

We have seen before the law concerning voluntariness (*supra* ch 4). It is easy to state that the law requires that a patient truly must volunteer his consent. It is quite another thing to ensure that the consent is so volunteered.

The point is well put by the President's Commission in its 1982 Report 'Making Health Care Decisions' (pp 66–68; footnotes omitted).

> . . . Blatant coercion may be of so little concern in professional-patient relationships

because, as physicians so often proclaim, it is so easy for health professionals to elicit a desired decision through more subtle means. Indeed, some physicians are critical of the legal requirement for informed consent on the grounds that it must be mere window dressing since 'patients will, if they trust their doctor, accede to almost any request he cares to make'. On some occasions, to be sure, this result can be achieved by rational persuasion, since the professional presumably has good reasons for preferring a recommended course of action. But the tone of such critics suggests thay have something else in mind: an ability to package and present the facts in a way that leaves the patient with no real choice. Such conduct, capitalising on disparities in knowledge, position, and influence, is manipulative in character and impairs the voluntariness of the patient's choice.

Manipulation has more and less extreme forms. At one end of the spectrum is behaviour amounting to misrepresentation or fraud. Of particular concern in health care contexts is the withholding or distortion of information in order to affect the patient's beliefs and decisions. The patient might not be told about alternatives to the recommended course of action, for example, or the risks or other negative characteristics of the recommended treatment might be minimised. Such behaviour is justly criticised on two grounds: first, that it interferes with the patient's voluntary choice (and thus negates consent) and, second, that it interferes with the patient's ability to make an informed decision. At the other end of the spectrum are far more subtle instances: a professional's careful choice of words or nuances of tone and emphasis might present the situation in a manner calculated to heighten the appeal of a particular course of action.

It is well known that the way information is presented can powerfully affect the recipient's response to it. The tone of voice and other aspects of the practitioner's manner of presentation can indicate whether a risk of a particular kind with a particular incidence should be considered serious. Information can be emphasised or played down without altering the content. And it can be framed in a way that affects the listener—for example, 'this procedure succeeds most of the time' versus 'this procedure has a 40 percent failure rate'. Health professionals who are aware of the effects of such minor variations can choose their language with care; if, during discussion with a patient, they sense any unintended or confused impressions being created, they can adjust their presentation of information accordingly.

Because many patients are often fearful and unequal to their physicians in status, knowledge, and power, they may be particularly susceptible to manipulations of this type. Health care professionals should, therefore, present information in a form that fosters understanding. Patients should be helped to understand the prognosis for their situation and the implications of different courses of treatment. The difficult distinction, both in theory and in practice, is between acceptable forms of informing, discussion, and rational persuasion on the one hand, and objectionable forms of influence or manipulation on the other.

Since voluntariness is one of the foundation stones of informed consent, professionals have a high ethical obligation to avoid coercion and manipulation of their patients. The law penalises those who ignore the requirements of consent or who directly coerce it. But it can do little about subtle manipulations without incurring severe disruptions of private relationships by intrusive policing, and so the duty is best thought of primarily in ethical terms.

An English court would approach the issue as did the Court of Appeal in *Freeman v Home Office (No 2)* [1984] 1 All ER 1036 at 1044–5, as a matter of fact rather than a matter of law. Sir John Donaldson MR said:

Legal inability to consent
Counsel for the plaintiff submitted that such were the pressures of prison life and discipline that a prisoner could not, as a matter of law, give an effective consent to treatment in any circumstances. This is a somewhat surprising proposition since it would mean that, in the absence of statutory authority, no prison medical officer could ever treat a prisoner. The answer of counsel for the plaintiff was in part that

outside medical officers could be brought in, but I am not persuaded that this would reduce the pressures, whatever they may be.

In support of this proposition, we were referred to the judgment of Scott LJ in *Bowater v Rowley Regis BC* [1944] 1 All ER 465, [1944] 1 KB 476 at 479. Scott LJ there said:

> In regard to the doctrine *volenti non fit injuria*, I would add one reflection of a general kind. That general maxim has to be applied with especially careful regard to the varying facts of human affairs and human nature in any particular case, just because it is concerned with the intangible factors of mind and will. For the purpose of the rule, if it be a rule, a man cannot be said to be truly 'willing', unless he is in a position to choose freely; and freedom of choice predicates, not only full knowledge of the circumstances upon which the exercise of choice is conditioned, in order that he may be able to choose wisely, but the absence from his mind of any feeling of constraint, in order that nothing shall interfere with the freedom of his will.
>
> . . .

The judge expressed his view on this aspect of the argument by saying ([1983] 3 All ER 589 at 597, [1984] 2 WLR 130 at 145):

> The right approach, in my judgment, is to say that where, in a prison setting, a doctor has the power to influence a prisoner's situation and prospects a court must be alive to the risk that what may appear, on the face of it, to be a real consent is not in fact so.

I would accept that as a wholly accurate statement of the law. The judge said that he had borne this in mind throughout the case. The sole question is therefore whether, on the evidence, there was a real consent.

2. Information

The proposition that the patient must be adequately informed to make any consent to therapeutic research valid poses the question, what legal action would lie if the patient was not so informed? We have discussed already the relationship between the torts of battery and negligence and adequacy of information given to patients (*supra* ch 4). We will not rehearse the general points here. We must, however, ask whether in the specific context of therapeutic research any failure adequately to inform a patient would render the doctor liable to an action in battery or negligence.

Battery. One view, and it is ours, is that where there is a dual intention on the part of the doctor, i e to treat *and* to conduct research, any failure to inform the patient concerning *both* of these intentions and their possible consequences would amount in law to a battery. This is because in the absence of such knowledge the patient will have assented to a procedure which is materially different in its nature from that which the doctor intends to carry out. To put it another way, research adds a further component to the quality of the consent that the law requires.

The law does not require people to volunteer and will provide a remedy to the patient against the doctor who conscripts him, the remedy being in battery to demonstrate the law's concern for the rights of the patient.

Indeed, do you think that, in any event, the failure to disclose amounts to fraud so as to vitiate any consent which might otherwise be valid?

If this is the law, that failure properly to inform is a battery, then what must the doctor do to act lawfully? In short, the answer must be that the doctor must make explicit his intention to carry out research.

A court may insist on the patient being informed of three particular matters in addition to this generalised intention. Each of them is an aspect of the interests of the patient which the law of battery seeks to protect. The patient must be informed: (1) that he may at any time withdraw from the research and that if he does so he will suffer no adverse consequences in terms of the treatment he will then receive; (2) that the nature of the research may be such that he may be a member of a controlled group in a trial which is intended to evaluate the efficacy of a new therapy; (3) that the trial is a randomised controlled trial (RCT).

As regards (2), one consequence of being a member of a controlled group could be that the patient does not receive the form of treatment which subsequently proves to be more efficacious. To meet this ethical difficulty researchers ordinarily would be expected to provide for periodic examination of the emerging data. It is our view that a patient's consent is not informed for the purpose of the tort of battery unless made aware of this.

As regards (3), randomisation means that a treatment regime is assigned to a patient randomly without regard to the particular circumstances of that patient, his needs, his preferences or the preferences of his doctor. Again, it is our view that a patient may volunteer for such a trial but only lawfully so, if he knows it is randomised and he is aware of what this means.

Negligence. Putting aside the question of whether a battery action would lie, what is the duty of the doctor, looking now to the tort of negligence. Is the doctor merely obliged to conform with what we have seen to be his duty of care as regards information in pure treatment cases? Or are there additional obligations placed upon him by virtue of his dual intentions?

If the general duty were all that was required it would mean that in undertaking clinical trials a doctor would be held to the duty as explained in *Sidaway*. We have seen that this gives considerable weight to the views of the medical profession (*supra* ch 4). Does *Sidaway* apply to clinical trials?

One view is that *Sidaway* is limited to circumstances in which the doctor's only intention is to treat the patient and does not extend to cases of dual intention. This is because if we look to the majority views in *Sidaway*, the primary reliance on what doctors would do as a professional body has no relevance when what is being considered is research. Whether or not it is proper to engage in research is a matter of public policy and not professional opinion. That being so, what amounts to proper disclosure is a matter of law for the courts.

If we look at Lord Scarman's speech, as perhaps we would be entitled to in this context, we would say that ordinarily the doctor must advise the patient that he is involved in a clinical trial and what this entails. We would further say that Lord Scarman's recourse to the 'therapeutic privilege' as justifying non-disclosure of certain information is unavailable in the context of research. To argue that a doctor need not tell a patient that he is in a clinical trial since this would mean he had to be told of other things concerning his condition, would be to use one justifiable non-disclosure as support for an entirely distinct non-disclosure. Arguably this puts the cart before the horse! If the patient's interests require that he not be informed of certain matters concerning his condition for the purposes of his treatment, this is an argument against using him in a clinical trial rather than serving to justify his use and the subsequent non-disclosure of this to him.

If the above view that *Sidaway* and its reliance upon professional opinion does not govern in the conduct of clinical trials is right, what does the law of negligence say is the doctor's duty as regards disclosing information?

In our view, the law would demand disclosure of the following (bearing in mind that the term 'disclosure' refers not only to the volunteering of information but also to the truthful answering of any questions asked):

1. The information which we earlier considered essential so as to avoid a claim in battery;

2. The information which apprises the patient of the *material risks* associated with the research.

What does 'material' mean in this context? The meaning given to it in cases of informed consent having to do with treatment in North America is, that a risk is material if it would be judged to be so by a *reasonable patient*. Here, where we are discussing an intention to carry out research, a good argument may exist for saying that it should be those risks of which the *particular patient* volunteering for the research would wish to be informed.

In *Halushka v University of Saskatchewan* (1965) 52 WWR 608 at 616, Hall JA said:

> There can be no exceptions to the ordinary requirements of disclosure in the case of research as there may well be in ordinary medical practice. The researcher does not have to balance the probable effect of lack of treatment against the risk involved in the treatment itself. The example of risks being properly hidden from a patient when it is important that he should not worry can have no application in the field of research. The subject of medical experimentation is entitled to a full and frank disclosure of all the facts, probabilities and opinions which a reasonable man might be expected to consider before giving his consent.

Picard in *Legal Liability of Doctors and Hospitals in Canada* (2nd ed 1984) comments;'[a] point of concern about the test he [Hall JA] used is its use of the objective reasonable patient test when the more pro-patient subjective test would be more appropriate to the research setting . . .' (p 118). Do you agree?

3. The information must also be disclosed, in addition to any risks, which is material to allow the patient to make an informed decision.

Here we have in mind such information as the fact that the patient may have to undergo additional (and perhaps discomforting) tests; may have to stay in hospital when otherwise he would be at home; may have to visit the hospital more frequently for tests and other such inconveniencing circumstances associated with the research.

In the United States the disclosure of malpractice in the conduct of research highlighted by Beecher (*supra*), led to the consideration of whether there should be an institutionalised response to research, whether therapeutic or non-therapeutic and whether on the competent or incompetent. Areen, King, Goldberg and Capron in *Law, Science and Medicine* (1984) explain the US situation (pp 956–60; footnotes omitted):

> In 1972, the national press reported on the Tuskegee Syphilis Study. Congress became increasingly active as well, holding hearings on Tuskegee and other controversial areas of research, including psychosurgery and fetal research. The result was the National Research Act of 1974, Pub L No 93–348, 88 Stat 342, which established the National Commission for the Protection of Human Subjects of Biomedical and Behavioral Research. The Act also imposed a moratorium on non-therapeutic research conducted or funded by HEW on any living human fetus. The moratorium was to remain in effect until the National Commission recommended whether and under what circumstances research on fetuses should be conducted. The Commission was directed by the Act to make its report on fetal research within four months after the members took office.
>
> The mandated report was submitted to the Secretary of HEW on July 25, 1975. It was the first of a series of reports submitted by the Commission covering such related topics as research on children and research on prisoners, all of which played a very influential role both in shaping later federal regulations and in justifying the

establishment in 1978 of a second national commission, entitled the President's Commission for the Study of Ethical Problems in Medicine and Biomedical and Behavioral Research.

The spurt of congressional activity in 1974 coincided with the release by HEW [Dept of Health, Education and Welfare] of its first regulations governing research involving human subjects. The regulations provided that HEW would fund no research involving human subjects unless an appropriate committee of the sponsoring institution had approved the research as being in accordance with relevant federal regulations designed to ensure that informed consent would be obtained from all participants.

. . .

A number of changes have been made in the HHS [Dept of Health and Human Services] (formerly HEW) regulations since they were first promulgated in 1974. Most were directed at providing additional protection for particularly vulnerable subjects. Thus, regulations providing additional protection for fetuses and pregnant women and for children have been promulgated. Regulations governing research on the institutionalised mentally disabled have been proposed but never finalised.

On August 8, 1978, FDA [Food and Drugs Administration] proposed more detailed standards for the institutional review committees, now termed Institutional Review Boards (IRBs). On January 26, 1981, HHS published the current regulations with the intent of providing a common regulatory framework for IRBs whether they are reviewing research conducted or funded by HHS or within the jurisdiction of FDA. The current regulations, reflecting the general trend toward deregulation, also exempt from their requirements certain kinds of research that normally present little or no risk of harm to subjects, such as surveys, interviews, or observations of public behavior, and studies of data or documents.

In the context of therapeutic research the Regulations on 'Protection of Human Subjects' (1983) 45 CFR 46 provide as follows:

46.102

(e) 'Research' means a systematic investigation designed to develop or contribute to generalisable knowledge. Activities which meet this definition constitute 'research' for purposes of these regulations, whether or not they are supported or funded under a program which is considered research for other purposes. For example, some 'demonstration' and 'service' programs may include research activities.

(f) 'Human subject' means a living individual about whom an investigator (whether professional or student) conducting research obtains (1) data through intervention or interaction with the individual, or (2) identifiable private information. 'Intervention' includes both physical procedures by which data are gathered (for example, venipuncture) and manipulations of the subject or the subject's environment that are performed for research purposes. 'Interaction' includes communication or inter-personal contact between investigator and subject. 'Private information' includes information about behavior that occurs in a context in which an individual can reasonably expect that no observation or recording is taking place, and information which has been provided for specific purposes by an individual and which the individual can reasonably expect will not be made public (for example, a medical record). Private information must be individually indentifiable (ie, the identity of the subject is or may readily be ascertained by the investigator or associated with the information) in order for obtaining the information to constitute research involving human subjects.

46.116   General requirements for informed consent

Except as provided elsewhere in this or other subparts, no investigator may involve a human being as a subject in research covered by these regulations unless the investigator has obtained the legally effective informed consent of the subject . . . An investigator shall seek such consent only under circumstances that provide the prospective subject . . . sufficient opportunity to consider whether or not to participate and that minimise the possibility of coercion or undue influence. The information that is given to the subject . . . shall be in language understandable to the subject ... No informed consent, whether oral or written, may include any exculpatory language through which the subject ... is made to waive or appear to waive any of the subject's legal rights, or releases or appears to release the investigator, the sponsor, the institution or its agents from liability for negligence.

(a) Basic elements of informed consent. Except as provided in paragraph (c) or (d) of this section, in seeking informed consent the following information shall be provided to each subject:

(1) A statement that the study involves research, an explanation of the purposes of the research and the expected duration of the subject's participation, a description of the procedures to be followed, and identification of any procedures which are experimental;

(2) A description of any reasonably foreseeable risks or discomforts to the subject;

(3) A description of any benefits to the subject or to others which may reasonably be expected from the research;

(4) A disclosure of appropriate alternative procedures or courses of treatment, if any, that might be advantageous to the subject;

(5) A statement describing the extent, if any, to which confidentiality of records identifying the subject will be maintained;

(6) For research involving more than minimal risk, an explanation as to whether any compensation and an explanation as to whether any medical treatments are available if injury occurs and, if so, what they consist of, or where further information may be obtained;

(7) An explanation of whom to contact for answers to pertinent questions about the research and research subjects' rights, and whom to contact in the event of a research-related injury to the subject; and

(8) A statement that participation is voluntary, refusal to participate will involve no penalty or loss of benefits to which the subject is otherwise entitled, and the subject may discontinue participation at any time without penalty or loss of benefits to which the subject is otherwise entitled.

(b) Additional elements of informed consent. When appropriate, one or more of the following elements of information shall also be provided to each subject:

(1) A statement that the particular treatment or procedure may involve risks to the subject (or in the embryo or fetus, if the subject is or may become pregnant) which are currently unforeseeable;

(2) Anticipated circumstances under which the subject's participation may be terminated by the investigator without regard to the subject's consent;

(3) Any additional costs to the subject that may result from participation in the research;

(4) The consequences of a subject's decision to withdraw from the research and procedures for orderly termination of participation by the subject;

(5) A statement that significant new findings developed during the course of the research which may relate to the subject's willingness to continue participation will be provided to the subject; and

(6) The appropriate number of subjects in the study.

(c) An IRB may approve a consent procedure which does not include, or alters, some or all of the elements of informed consent set forth above, or waive the requirement to obtain informed consent provided the IRB finds and documents that:

(1) The research is to be conducted for the purpose of demonstrating or evaluating: (i) Federal, State or local benefit or service programs which are not themselves research programs, (ii) procedures for obtaining benefits or services under these programs, or (iii) possible changes in or alternatives to these programs or procedures; and

(2) The research could not practicably be carried out without the waiver or alteration.

(d) An IRB may approve a consent procedure which does not include, or which alters, some or all of the elements of informed consent set forth above, or waive the requirements to obtain informed consent provided the IRB finds and documents that:

(1) The research involves no more than minimal risk to the subjects;
(2) The waiver or alteration will not adversely affect the rights and welfare of the subjects;
(3) The research could not practicably be carried out without the waiver or alteration; and
(4) Wherever appropriate, the subjects will be provided with additional pertinent information after participation . . .

(f) Nothing in these regulations is intended to limit the authority of a physician to provide emergency medical care . . .

Do you think that these Regulations approximate to what a court would say was English law?

3. Limits of research

As with treatment, the permissible limits of therapeutic research are measured in law by reference to a risk-benefit ratio. A patient may only be exposed in the course of treatment to risks which can be demonstrated to bring with them the likelihood of greater benefit. Clearly, the more severe the patient's illness the greater are the risks which can lawfully be taken in treating him if a real probability of benefiting him exists. Similarly, in the context of therapeutic research the risks which research might expose the patient to (even without his knowledge) must be demonstrably outweighed by the expected benefits.

Prima facie, however, concern for the relationship between risk and benefit is of greater concern in the regulation of research which is non-therapeutic or which involves those who are incompetent to consent. We will consider this in greater detail later. When the research is therapeutic it will ordinarily be left to the patient to determine the risk-benefit ratio for himself—having, of course, been properly informed.

A further question needs to be examined. Is the doctor limited in the form of research to be employed in that he may not involve his patient in a *randomised* controlled trial? The question arises because randomisation, as we have seen, entails assigning a patient to a treatment category without reference to the patient's particular circumstances or preferences or, indeed, the doctor's preferences. The doctor may prefer one form of treatment rather than another when two are being compared but may as a consequence of the trial have to offer what, to him, is less preferable. The simple answer is that if the patient is apprised of all that is involved in being in a randomised controlled trial then his consent is properly informed. The law may not, however, be so simple. It will be clear from the brief description of randomisation that it may involve the patient waiving the doctor's duty to act in his best medical interests. It is undoubtedly in the patient's best medical interests to have a doctor who is confident that the treatment he is offering is the best for the patient. If he does not believe this (*a fortiori* he cannot know it if the trial is 'double blind') the patient may become aware of his doctor's lack of confidence and consequently lose confidence in his treatment himself. This is an illustration of what a number of commentators identify as an inevitable conflict of loyalties intrinsic, in particular, in RCTs. The doctor's duty to his patient is to carry out the trial with appropriate scientific rigour (Schafer, A 'The ethics of the randomised clinical trial', (1982) 307 New Eng J Med 719).

Even if such a conflict is not *inevitable* in RCTs the possibility nevertheless exists. This being so, the argument is that in law a patient who is ill should as a matter of public policy be prevented from absolving the doctor from his duty to do his best for the patient. How do you think an English court would resolve this?

(b) The incompetent patient

1. Adults

Any valid consent in the case of an incompetent adult must come from someone other than the patient. We have seen, however, in the context of treatment that without specific statutory authority the law does not empower anyone as a proxy even to consent to treatment. The case of *T v T* [1988] 1 All ER 613, has, as we have seen, provided a workable, though not wholly satisfactory, solution in the case of treatment. You will recall that Wood J decided that (p 625):

> I am content to rely on the principle that in these exceptional circumstances where there is no provision in law for consent to be given and therefore there is no one who can give the consent, and where the patient is suffering from such mental abnormality as never to be able to give such consent, a medical adviser is justified in taking such steps as good medical practice 'demands' . . .

Earlier in his judgment Wood J explained what he meant by 'demands' (p 621):

> What does medical practice demand? I use the word 'demand' because I envisage a situation where based on good medical practice there are really no two views of what course is for the best.

Does this judicial authorisation extend to therapeutic research? In the absence of authority it may help to analyse the problem in stages.

1. Wood J refers to treatment being lawful without the need for consent when it is 'medically demanded'. Research is, of course, never demanded as regards a particular patient—though it might be *desirable*. This would suggest that the answer to our question is no.

2. Such an answer would produce a curious result. We shall see that it is lawful for a proxy to consent to therapeutic research on a child. Obviously, the proxy must act in the best interests of the child and be satisfied that the risk-benefit ratio is in the child's favour. If it were unlawful to conduct therapeutic research on an incompetent adult, the adult would be in a worse position as a matter of law than a child. This is because any proposed therapeutic research though it carries risks, must, to be lawful, also carry an expected benefit. The adult would, consequently, be denied by law this chance of a benefit.

3. Therefore, in our view a court would decide that the law is as follows: an incompetent adult may be the subject of therapeutic research where that research would be justified in the case of a competent adult provided that the researcher has satisfied an appropriately constituted 'research ethics committee' as to the scientific validity of the proposed research and the need for, and the ethical propriety of, such research.

   In other words, a court would give effect to the public policy concern of protecting the vulnerable and not leaving the ultimate decision wholly to the medical profession by insisting on external review.

4. Do you think the House of Lords' reliance in *re F* (1989) (*supra* postscript to ch 7) on the *Bolam* test, to define the scope of permissible interventions without an individual's consent, affects the argument?

Since we are here talking about the incompetent adult, no issue of voluntariness or adequate disclosure of information arises. There remains, however, the issue of the appropriate limits of any permissible research. We have already discussed this issue in relation to the competent adult. Here, the solution to the problem of the legality of randomisation may be easier. If, as we argue, randomisation may be legally permissible only if the patient knowingly agrees to take part in such a trial, it follows that in the case of an incompetent patient, randomisation would be illegal.

2. Children

Can a proxy, who will usually be a parent, consent to therapeutic research on a child?

If we address the three issues which we have identified as significant, it goes without saying first of all that the consent of the proxy must be voluntarily given. A court would, of course, be vigilant to ensure that consent by, for example, a parent was not obtained by improper pressure. An example of this could be where a child would only receive otherwise available treatment *if* it was entered into a clinical trial. There may be circumstances where treatment is *only* available as part of a trial, ie when no accepted treatment currently exists. In such a case the offering of treatment only on terms would not amount to unlawful pressure.

As regards the information which (now) the proxy and not the patient must be given, the doctor must make *at least* as full a disclosure as the law would require him to give to the competent patient. Arguably, the law would also require the doctor to disclose to the proxy that information which materially affects the proxy in his continued care of the child, for example the consequences for the proxy of the participation of the child in the trial and also of the occurrence of a risk entailed in the trial *for the proxy*.

Finally, as regards the limits of the proxy's authority to consent, since we are considering *therapeutic* research these must fundamentally reflect the risk-benefit ratio of participation in the trial. The proxy must be satisfied that on a reasonable assessment of this ratio, it is in the best interests of the child to participate.

In essence, the proxy's authority in relation to a child is no different from the doctor's authority in relation to an incompetent adult. Is there, however, a difference for participation in a trial which involves randomisation? *Prima facie* it would appear that randomisation would be legally acceptable because the proxy can be informed of what it involves. But, since randomisation entails a possible conflict of loyalties for the doctor it could be said that a proxy was not acting in the child's best interests in consenting to a child's participation in an RCT. Indeed, can it *ever* be in a child's best interests to waive the doctor's duty to do his best for his patient? One further point is worth noting. Clearly as a matter of considerate decision-making by the proxy and good medical practice, the *assent* of the child should be sought and obtained when it can be meaningfully given. What if the child refuses the assent, on the assumption that the child can assent? Would a court find that involvement of the child was nonetheless unlawful?

(iii) NON-THERAPEUTIC RESEARCH

You will recall that here we are concerned with research where the researcher has only one intention, ie to obtain information through systematic enquiry so as to contribute to generalisable knowledge. There is no intention to treat the person who is the subject of the research.

There are two categories of persons upon whom non-therapeutic research may be carried out: patients and the healthy.

(a) Patients

We can perhaps deal shortly with patients. Ordinarily, a doctor's duty to care for his patient would preclude his engaging in non-therapeutic research on such a person. This is because it would ordinarily be difficult to show that it was in the best medical interests of the patient—who is by definition, ill—to be exposed to additional interventions which carry risks and which are not designed to aid in his treatment.

There may be, of course, circumstances in which a patient with a minor illness may volunteer to take part in non-therapeutic research. If the proposed research carries no demonstrable risk of harm to the patient nor will it affect deleteriously the patient's condition, then it may be that the patient may lawfully be party to non-therapeutic research. In our view, however, the evidence of absence of risk would have to be clear and compelling. In such a (rare) case the legal position of the patient will be the same as that of the healthy volunteer which we now turn to consider.

(b) Healthy volunteers

We noticed in the context of therapeutic research that there are some basic conditions to be met in any clinical trial. Equally, this is so in the conduct of non-therapeutic research. In addition to those points made earlier (see *supra* at pp 872-3) which are relevant here also, the following conditions must be observed:

1. the doctor must obtain an appropriate medical history from the patient so as to ensure that the proposed procedure carries no increased risk;
2. the doctor must obtain the permission of the volunteer to inform his family doctor that he is participating in a trial and to obtain from that doctor any relevant medical details about the volunteer;
3. the doctor must satisfy himself that the volunteer is not participating in any other trial contemporaneously nor engaging in other conduct, e g an intention to drive home in certain circumstances, whereby the volunteer's health may be put at risk;
4. the doctor must have available all appropriate medical equipment to meet any foreseeable eventuality arising out of the trial, e g in appropriate circumstances resuscitation equipment.

A failure to fulfil any of these obligations could well expose the doctor to liability in negligence if any harm ensues.

Beyond these general points, as with therapeutic research, the central legal issue warranting analysis is consent. If a valid consent is not obtained then liability in battery or negligence may arise.

1. The competent volunteer

As we have seen before, the common law looks to the understanding and maturity of an individual in determining competence. Just as with therapy, an adult would *prima facie* be presumed competent to volunteer for non-therapeutic research.

In the case of children, we have seen that s 8(1) of the Family Law Reform Act 1969 deems children between the ages of 16 and 18 to be competent to consent to treatment to the same extent as an adult. The Act has no application to non-therapeutic research since it is limited to 'surgical, medical or dental *treatment*' (our emphasis). The capacity of a child under 18 to consent to non-therapeutic research is, therefore, governed by the common law.

As we saw earlier, it is our view that the approach of the House of Lords in *Gillick* is applicable to therapeutic research. In our view this is equally true of non-therapeutic research. A child (under the age of 18) who has the capacity to understand what is involved in the research may be able to give a valid consent. The capacity of a child will, therefore, depend upon his or her understanding and maturity.

As we saw in relation to therapeutic research, this is likely to be a relatively high standard of comprehension. Since non-therapeutic research lacks any potentially beneficial consequences for the child and may indeed carry a risk of harm, in our view the law, arguably, would require an even greater level of comprehension for this type of research. Much may depend upon the seriousness (and likelihood of occurrence) of any risks to the child volunteer. The greater the risks or the more serious the consequences for the child, the more likely it is that a court would decide that a child lacked the capacity to give a valid consent in law.

Voluntariness. A court would analyse the voluntariness or otherwise of a healthy volunteer in accordance with the principles we have already seen in the context of therapeutic research, relying principally on the dictum of Lord Donaldson MR in *Freeman v Home Office (No 2) (supra* at pp 874–5). In short, it will be a matter of fact not of law. The matter which may be of primary concern is the possibility of exploitation of persons who may 'volunteer' for research because of some felt pressure. Pressure can come in a number of forms. There is the obvious case of financial inducements and the effect they may have on the financially disadvantaged. The less obvious case, perhaps, is what some have called 'contextual duress' when, for example, a student 'volunteers' to participate in research at the 'invitation' of his teacher, or an employee at the behest of his employer or a junior colleague at the behest of the leader of the research team 'volunteers'. As Gerald Dworkin points out in 'Law and Medical Experimentation' (1987) 13 Monash ULR 189, 204:

> It does not follow that financial inducements should destroy the voluntary n :ure of all responses, yet where students and out of work youths are offered significant sums of money to test new drugs, as happened in London recently, the nature of consents and inducements should be examined very carefully. In defending the use of such volunteers it was argued that there was nothing unethical in paying volunteers to test new drugs so long as they were fully informed of any possible risks; and a further justification was put forward that there was a no-fault compensation scheme in case anything went wrong. This does seem to miss the point: volunteers certainly can give informed consent to properly conducted research procedures, but even informed consent can be involuntary.

Particularly problematical is the position of prisoners who may have been told repeatedly that their sentence or conditions of imprisonment will not be affected but may nonetheless volunteer because (they think) their chances of parole, for example, may be improved.

In all such cases the law will begin with the premise that a competent adult is free to do what he wishes and must be assumed to have acted voluntarily if he participates. Thus, these particular examples and classes of person will not be treated any differently by the law.

Margaret Somerville weighs the arguments well concerning the use of prisoners in research in *Consent to Medical Care* (1980), pp 96–98:

> ... there is at least one commentator who believes that one is never, under any

conditions, justified in using these persons as research subjects. Bronstein[622] argues that the distinguishing and prohibitive element in the use of prisoners as subjects, is the involvement of the state and the necessary rights it has over the prisoners' bodies simply by virtue of the fact of imprisonment. He makes the thought-provoking statement that '[i]t is not so much the actual, occasional abuse of captive human subjects, but the potential for abuse which concerns [him]'.[623] Thus it is not necessary to show abuses to invalidate experimentation in prisons, because the 'potential for abuse' is sufficient to do this. It is important to consider these matters because it makes one realise that a discussion of 'informed' consent in relation to the use of prisoners as research subjects is not enough, as there may be a duty to not even request the prisoner's consent to participation in the experiment.[624] Kilbrandon[625] states this in a very effective way when he says that to put a man in prison is to deprive him of a large number of consents, therefore it is distasteful to confer on him a consent which is not for his own benefit.

An argument contrary to the above views advocating prohibition of medical experiments on prisoners, or only allowing it under much more restrictive conditions than apply to the unconfined population, is that prisoners should not be deprived of any more rights than accrue to other members of society, than absolutely necessary. One such right is that of personal inviolability of both mind and body, any exceptions normally depending on consent. And thus the corollary, the right to consent and the right not to consent. For reasons quite apart from medical experimentation, for instance to give a legal right of action against brutality in prisons it may be important to retain for prisoners these rights to inviolability, and to consent, and not to consent. Therefore, in the context of medical treatment or research, the right to consent should not be abrogated for fear that the rights associated with it, that of inviolability and the right not to consent, will also be affected. Rather its exercise must be safeguarded. This is expressed by Ramsey in the following words: 'I am one who happens to believe that prisoners have not been and should not be drummed out of the human race. They ought, therefore, not to be excluded in principle from the community of risk-filled human consent to good purposes, even if the needed practical protections for them are so formidable as to prohibit the general use of prisoners in medical research.'[626]

It may be that if research participation is seen as a privilege, it should not be allowed because distribution of this privilege can become a coercive tool in the hands of wardens and prison authorities, thus affecting the voluntariness of prisoners' consent. This is related to another reason for not allowing research on prisoners. It is that the attitude of prison staff towards prisoners often leaves much to be desired and may amount to coercion to consent, or even ignores, in all but theory, the necessity for free and informed consent. For instance, with respect to prisoner experimentation, a warden at Montana State Prison stated: 'we want our prison to be a living laboratory for the people of Montana . . . There should be no conflict in offering *our* physical and human resources [prisoners] to other disciplines . . .'[627]

Further, some arguments put forward in support of prison experimentation rely on the *control factor* inherent in imprisonment, as an advantage justifying research on prisoners taking place. But these arguments themselves provide further arguments *against* using prisoners, because they raise serious doubts about the validity of the consent given. Examples of such reasoning are that it is beneficial for experimental purposes to be able to totally control the subjects,[628] and the experimentation and the rewards it offers may themselves augment the effective power of the prison authorities over prisoners. Newman[629] found a reason given to justify the use of prisoner subjects was the doubtful altruism that wardens, as public officials, were interested in promoting science and, perhaps more realistically if still not acceptable, in promoting a research program which helps the training and education of prisoners. Both these words, training and education, may be used in their genuine sense, but may also be euphemisms for establishing and justifying a more effective system of control of prisoners, without corresponding educative benefit to them. Thus the very advantages of using prisoners—their availability, the convenience they offer as subjects, the ease with which they can be controlled—are precisely the factors throwing doubt on the validity of their consent and weighing against their participation in medical research.

Notes to extract

622 AB Sabin, AJ Bronstein, WN Hubbard, 'The Military/The Prisoner', in 'Experiments and Research with Humans: Values in Conflict', National Academy of Sciences, Academy Forum, Washington, 1975, (hereafter referred to as 'National Academy of Sciences Forum') p 127, per Bronstein, at pp 130–5.

623 *Ibid.*, at p 131.

624 See S Spicker, 'Inquiry and Commentary', part of the discussion led by AB Sabin *et al*, *ibid.*, at p 145.

625 Lord Kilbrandon, 'Final Discussion', in 'Wolstenholme and O'Connor eds'', [CIBA Foundation symposium, 'Ethics in Medical Progress: with special reference to transplantation'] p 202 at 205.

626 P Ramsey, ['The Ethics of a Cottage Industry in An Age of Community and Research Medicine' NEJM 284 (13) 700 (1971)] at 705.

627 WJ Estelle, 'The Changing Profile and Conditions Surrounding Clinical Research in Prisons', Clin Pharm & Therap 13(5) 831 (1972) (emphasis added).

Note the use of the possessive pronoun when describing prisoners and also the way in which they are seen as commodities rather than persons.

628 JD Moore, 'The Deer Lodge Research Unit', Clin Pharm & Therap 13(5) 833 (1972), at p 834.

629 RW Newman, 'The Participation of Prisoners in Clinical Research', in 'Ladimer and Newman eds' ['Clinical Investigation in Medicine: Legal Ethical and Moral aspects'] at 467.

Information. We set out all the relevant legal points relating to the duty to disclose when we considered therapeutic research (*supra* at pp 875–7): that research is being carried out; that the volunteer may withdraw at any time without adverse consequences; the form of the research, e g that it is an RCT; the need for the disclosure of material risks and information; answering any questions truthfully. We would only add one point, in the context of research on healthy volunteers we have no doubt that the courts would adopt a subjective test of materiality which would require disclosure of all information which *this* volunteer would want to know.

Contrast the decision of the Saskatchewan Court of Appeal in *Halushka v University of Saskatchewan* (1965) 52 WWR 608 (Saskatchewan Court of Appeal).

Hall JA: The appellants, Wyant and Merriman, were medical practitioners employed by the appellant, University of Saskatchewan. . . .

The respondent, a student at the University of Saskatchewan, had attended summer school in 1961. On August 21, 1961, he went to the employment office to find a job. At the employment office he was advised that there were no jobs available but that he could earn $50 by being the subject of a test at the University Hospital. The respondent said that he was told that the test would last a couple of hours and that it was a 'safe test and there was nothing to worry about'.

The respondent reported to the anaesthesia department at the University Hospital and there saw the appellant, Wyant. The conversation which ensued concerning the proposed test was related by the respondent as follows:

Dr Wyant explained to me that a new drug was to be tried out on the Wednesday following. He told me that electrodes would be put in both my arms, legs and head and that he assured me that it was a perfectly safe test it had been conducted many times before. He told me that I was not to eat anything on Wednesday morning that I was to report at approximately nine o'clock, then he said it would take about an hour to hook me up and the test itself would last approximately two hours, after the time I would be given fifty dollars, pardon me, I would be allowed to sleep first, fed and then given fifty dollars and driven home on the same day.

The appellant, Wyant, also told the respondent that an incision would be made in his left arm and that a catheter or tube would be inserted into his vein.

The respondent agreed to undergo the test and was asked by the appellant, Wyant, to sign a form of consent. This form, entered as Ex D1, reads as follows:

'Intensive Care
460-57-2

Halushka, Walter
72756 Jan 2'40 MR.
Dr. Nanson

Consent for tests on volunteers

I, Walter Halushka, age 21 of 236 – 3rd Street Saskatoon hereby state that I have volunteered for tests upon my person for the purpose of study of

Heart & Blood Circulation Response under General Anaesthesia

The tests to be undertaken in connection with this study have been explained to me and I understand fully what is proposed to be done. I agree of my own free will to submit to these tests, and in consideration of the remuneration hereafter set forth, I do release the chief investigators, *Drs G M Wyant and J E Merriman* their associates, technicians, and each thereof, other personnel involved in these studies, the University Hospital Board, and the University of Saskatchewan from all responsibility and claims whatsoever, for any untoward effects or accidents due to or arising out of said tests, either directly or indirectly.

I understand that I shall receive a remuneration of $50.00 for each test a series of *One* tests.

Witness my hand and seal.
[Sgd.] WALTER HALUSHKA
[Sgd.] IRIS ZAECHTOWSKI (Witness)
Date: Aug 22/61'

The respondent described the circumstances surrounding the signing of D1, saying:

He then gave me a consent form, I skimmed through it and picked out the word 'accident' on the consent form and asked Doctor Wyant what accidents were referred to, and he gave me an example of me falling down the stairs at home after the test and then trying to sue the University Hospital as a result. Being assured that any accident that would happen to me would be at home and not in the Hospital I signed the form.

The test contemplated was known as 'The Heart and Blood Circulation Response under General Anaesthesia', and was to be conducted jointly by the appellants, Wyant and Merriman, using a new anaesthetic agent known commercially as 'Fiuoromar'. This agent had not been previously used or tested by the appellants in any way.

The respondent returned to the University Hospital on August 23, 1961, to undergo the test. The procedure followed was that which had been described to the respondent and expected by him, with the exception that the catheter, after being inserted in the vein in the respondent's arm, was advanced towards his heart. When the catheter reached the vicinity of the heart, the respondent felt some discomfort. The anaesthetic agent was then administered to him. The time was then 11:32 am. Eventually the catheter tip was advanced through the various heart chambers out into the pulmonary artery where it was positioned.

The appellants, Wyant and Merriman, intended to have the respondent reach medium depth of surgical anaesthesia. However, an endotracheal tube which had been inserted to assist the respondent in breathing caused some coughing. In the opinion of the appellant, Wyant, the coughing indicated that the respondent was in the upper half of a light anaesthesia—on the verge of waking up. At 12:16 pm, therefore, the concentration of the mixture of the anaesthetic was increased. The respondent then descended into deeper surgical anaesthesia.

At about 12:20 pm there were changes in the respondent's cardiac rhythm which suggested to the appellants, Wyant and Merriman, that the level of the anaesthetic was too deep. The amount of anaesthetic was then decreased, or lightened.

At 12:25 pm the respondent suffered a complete cardiac arrest.

The appellants, Wyant and Merriman, and their assistants took immediate steps to resuscitate the respondent's heart by manual massage. To reach the heart, an incision was made from the breastbone to the line of the arm-pit and two of the ribs were pulled apart. A vasopressor was administered as well as urea, a drug used to combat swelling of the brain. After one minute and 30 seconds the respondent's heart began to function again.

The respondent was unconscious for a period of four days. He remained in the University Hospital as a patient until discharged 10 days later. On the day before he was discharged, the respondent was given $50 by the appellant, Wyant. At that time the respondent asked the appellant, Wyant, if that was all he was going to get for all he went through. The appellant said that $50 was all that they had bargained for but that he could give a larger sum in return for a complete release executed by the respondent's mother or elder sister.

As a result of the experiment, the appellants concluded that as an anaesthetic agent 'Fluoromar' had too narrow a margin of safety and it was withdrawn from clinical use in the University Hospital.

The respondent brought action against the appellants, basing his claim for damages on two grounds, namely, trespass to the person and negligence. . . .

The main issue before the jury concerning the respondent's claim of trespass to the person was that of consent. . . .

It was on the basis of the ordinary physician-patient relationship that the learned trial judge charged the jury on the matter of consent. In dealing with this part of the case he said:

In the circumstances of this case I will say that before signing such a document the plaintiff was entitled to a reasonably clear explanation of the proposed test and of the natural and expected results from it.

In my opinion, the duty imposed upon those engaged in medical research, as were the appellants, Wyant and Merriman, to those who offer themselves as subjects for experimentation, as the respondent did here, is at least as great as, if not greater than, the duty owed by the ordinary physician or surgeon to his patient. There can be no exceptions to the ordinary requirements of disclosure in the case of research as there may well be in ordinary medical practice. The researcher does not have to balance the probable effect of lack of treatment against the risk involved in the treatment itself. The example of risks being properly hidden from a patient when it is important that he should not worry can have no application in the field of research. The subject of medical experimentation is entitled to a full and frank disclosure of all the facts, probabilities and opinions which a reasonable man might be expected to consider before giving his consent. . . .   The respondent was not informed that the catheter would be advanced to and through his heart but was admittedly given to understand that it would be merely inserted in the vein in his arm. While it may be correct to say that the advancement of the catheter to the heart was not in itself dangerous and did not cause or contribute to the cause of the cardiac arrest, it was a circumstance which, if known, might very well have prompted the respondent to withhold his consent. The undisclosed or misrepresented facts need not concern matters which directly cause the ultimate damage if they are of a nature which might influence the judgment upon which the consent is based.

The court dismissed the appeal.

Which view would an English court prefer?

Limits. We are considering here the limits imposed by law to that which a healthy volunteer may consent, such that any consent given thereafter is invalid.

A competent person may, of course, agree to expose himself to a variety of risks. Indeed, society approves of this, eg by encouraging sport. But the example of sport is informative, for boxing matches which are inevitably risky encounters may lawfully be engaged in; prize fights, however, are unlawful despite the apparent consent of the participants. So it is with non-therapeutic risk. A person *can* lawfully take some risks with his body by volunteering for non-therapeutic research but the law would impose certain limits as a matter of public policy.

Nicholson (*op cit*) sets out in table form risk equivalents, ie an 'attempt to find equivalence between different scales of risks and the statistical probabilities of certain adverse events' (p 119; footnotes omitted).

Table 5.6   Risk equivalents

British definition	Negligible	Minimal	More than minimal.
American definition	Minimal	Minor increase over minimal	Greater than minor increase over minimal.
Risk of death	less than 1 per million	1 to 100 per million	Greater than 100 per million.
Risk of major complication	less than 10 per million	10 to 1000 per million	Greater than 1000 per million.
Risk of minor complication	less than 1 per thousand	1 to 100 per thousand	Greater than 100 per thousand.

Referring to this table he states that (p 120):

> . . . the overall risks of non-therapeutic research . . . would lie in the category 'minor increase over minimal' for both major and minor complications. It seems perfectly acceptable to subject adults, who have given informed consent, to such a level of risk.

The American term 'minimal risk' equivalent to the British term 'negligible risk' is defined in the HHS Regulations on the Protection of Human Subjects in 1983 as (para 46.102 (g)):

> (g) 'Minimal risk' means that the risks of harm anticipated in the proposed research are not greater, considering probability and magnitude, than those ordinarily encountered in daily life or during the performance of routine physical or psychological examinations or tests.

We agree that the limit suggested by Nicholson is probably that which a court would endorse. The implication of such a view is, of course, that any research on a healthy volunteer which on the basis of existing knowledge properly analysed poses a risk which is more than a 'minor increase over minimal' would in law amount to a battery and even, possibly, the crime of maim in appropriate circumstances.

2.   The incompetent volunteer

Here, we are considering the circumstances under which an incompetent individual may be lawfully volunteered for non-therapeutic research.

Adults. The first criterion which must be satisfied in law must be that there is a real and justified need for research on *incompetent* adults, ie that the knowledge sought may not be discovered from research on competent consenting adults. This is only a particular illustration of the general legal principle that the law seeks to protect the vulnerable.

Satisfying this criterion by no means implies that it is lawful thereafter to carry out non-therapeutic research. Indeed, it would appear that such research cannot lawfully be carried out. There is no one who, in law, can authorise it as a proxy. Even the court if it were to have a *parens patriae* power could not authorise such research since the power exists specifically for cases where 'some care should be thrown round [the ward]' (*Wellesley v Duke of Beaufort* (1827) 38 ER 236 at 243). Nor does the case of *T v T* assist, in which you will recall, Wood J held that the legal requirement for consent could be dispensed with if a particular intervention was 'medically demanded'. Non-therapeutic research is never 'medically demanded' or even 'demanded'. Thus, the need for consent could not be dispensed with in law.

The upshot of this analysis is that it would be unlawful to carry out non-therapeutic research on, eg the incompetent mentally ill or disabled, the unconscious and the senile incompetent.

Children. There are two issues which need to be considered: who, if anyone, can lawfully volunteer a child for non-therapeutic research and if anyone can, what are the limits to that for which the child can be volunteered? We will consider these issues together.

In a seminal article in 1978, 'Legality of Consent to Nontherapeutic Medical Research on Infants and Young Children' (1978) 53 Archives of Disease in Childhood 443, Professor Gerald Dworkin wrote that:

> For some years the view of lawyers advising the medical profession has been that such clinical research is unlawful. This is a view expressed, for example, by Speller,[2] the Medical Research Council,[3] the Medical Protection Society,[4] the Medical Defence Union,[5] Sir Harvey Druitt (a former Treasury Solicitor),[6] Sir George Godber (a former Chief Medical Officer to the Department of Health and Social Security (DHSS))[7] and to the DHSS itself. The authority for this view rests on general legal principle rather than on any specific rule or ruling. Thus, the general philosophy of the law is that parents are under a duty to look after a child's interests and so any nontherapeutic procedures cannot be justified.

> *Notes to extract*
> [2] Speller, S R (1971). *Law Relating to Hospitals and Kindred Institutions*, 5th ed, pp 144–145. H K Lewis, London.
> [3] Medical Research Council (1964). Responsibility in investigations on human subjects. *British Medical Journal*, **2**, 178–180.
> [4] Leahy Taylor, J (1975). Ethical and legal aspects of non-therapeutic clinical investigation. *Medico-Legal Journal*, **43**, 53–68.
> [5] Pratt, H (1977). Research on infants. *Lancet*, **1**, 699; 1052.
> [6] Curran, W J, and Beecher, H K (1969). Experimentation in children; a reexamination of legal ethical principles. *Journal of the American Medical Association*, **210**, 77–83.
> [7] Godber, G (1974). Discussion. Symposium on Constraints on the Advance of Medicine. *Proceedings of the Royal Society of Medicine*, **67**, 1311.

He ended his article with the following bold conclusion (at p 445):

> It is submitted that it is quite proper for those medical bodies which give guidance to the profession to change their present uncertain statements as to the law and replace them with a much clearer guide to the effect that 'although there is as yet no clear legal authority, it appears that it is lawful to conduct nontherapeutic research procedures on infants and young children provided the following requirements are strictly observed:
>
> (a) the design, details, and ethical criteria of the research are approved by the appropriate ethical committee;
> (b) there is voluntary, informed, parental consent; and
> (c) there is no, or a minimal, risk.

By 1987 when Professor Dworkin wrote his paper 'Law and Medical Experimentation' (1987) 13 Monash ULR 189, there had grown up a considerable volume of scholarship which tended to support his previous view. For example, we have referred on several occasions to the Working Group set up by the Institute of Medical Ethics whose report was published in 1986 entitled *Medical Research with Children*. In the chapter on 'risks and benefits on research on children', Nicholson writes (p 120):

> After a long debate, the working group agreed unanimously, however, that it was not acceptable to subject children, for whom only a proxy consent was available, to even a minor increase over minimal risk in non-therapeutic research. In other words, non-therapeutic research on children, regardless of possible benefits, can only be undertaken ethically if the risks of the procedures involved are in the 'minimal' category.

Furthermore, the climate of opinion and the popular understanding of what was involved had changed. Still Professor Dworkin (*ibid*) was cautious in analysing the law (pp 198–203):

> There is a widespread agreement that it is ethical, in some circumstances, to carry out non-therapeutic research with children.[35] The fourth International Summit Conference on Bioethics, held in Canada in April 1987, summarised the generally accepted controlling conditions: 'The specific project must be approved by a research ethics committee; all needed knowledge must have been obtained through research with adults or animals; there must be no valid alternative to the use of children in the research; a valid proxy consent (by family, guardians, ombudsman, those with power of attorney or others) must have been obtained for each research subject; and to the extent possible, the child should have given assent.'[35a] Is this ethical statement, however, reflected in the law?

(c) The 'best interests' of the child approach

For a long time, in England, the advice given to the medical profession was that non-therapeutic research upon young children was unlawful. The Medical Research Council stated that '. . . in the strict view of the law parents and guardians of minors cannot give consent on their behalf to any procedures which are of no particular benefit to them and which may carry some risk of harm'.[36] The authority for all this rested on general legal principle, rather than on any specific rule or ruling. Since the general philosophy of the law is that parents and guardians are under a duty to look after a child's interests, it seems to follow that non-therapeutic procedures cannot be justified.

Thus, in the well known case of *Wellesley v Duke of Beaufort*,[37] Lord Eldon, when exercising the Crown's power as *parens patriae*, showed that: 'it has always been the principle of this Court not to risk the incurring of damage to children . . . which it cannot repair, but rather to prevent the damage being done'.[38] The American Supreme Court, admittedly in a different context, expressed the view that:

> parents may be free to become martyrs themselves. But it does not follow [that] they are free, in identical circumstances, to make martyrs of their children before they have reached the age of full and legal discretion when they can make that choice for themselves.[39]

Recent developments in the law relating to sterilisation emphasise the courts' concern to safeguard the 'best interests' of incompetent subjects, although the extent to which courts should go in giving effect to those interests has varied in different jurisdictions. Thus, the Supreme Court of Canada refused to sanction a 'non-therapeutic' sterilisation of a mentally retarded girl even though it was said to be in her best interests, because it felt that the legislature was better equipped to decide such an important policy matter[40] whereas the House of Lords, scorning the value of the therapeutic/non-therapeutic distinction in this context, took a more robust view of its role and authorised the sterilisation of a 17 year old girl 'in her best interests'.[41] It would not have acted on a lower criterion than the best interests of the child; and other dicta also emphasise the parental duty to apply this standard.[42]

Thus, there is at least an arguable case in favour of the view that proxy consent cannot be given for non-therapeutic research. But a total ban would be Draconian and certainly out of line with national and international ethical codes. Accordingly, it becomes necessary to look for an alternative view of the law.

3.   Alternative views

(a)   Distorting the concepts of 'therapy'

Some of the views advanced have been unprepossessing. One extreme approach turned on the therapeutic/non-therapeutic distinction. If the concept of 'therapeutic' could be widened, then the scope for proxy consent would be increased. For example, the World Health Organisation defines 'health' as a state of complete physical, mental and *social* well-being and not merely the absence of disease or infirmity. Accordingly, it could be argued that carefully considered proxy consents for clinical research are exercises in social responsibility which could benefit the future well-being of the volunteered subject since one can reasonably expect a child in later life to identify with the objects of the research. This smacks very much of the 'ends justifying the means';[43] and is not attractive as a legal argument. Yet similar semantic arguments have been upheld.

For example, the early kidney transplantations could only be effected between very close relatives and American courts were asked to consider the legality of such transplantations from infant donors to twin donees, in cases where the ages of the sets of twins ranged from 14 to 19. Evidence was advanced that each donor twin and the parents had been fully informed of the nature of the operation and had given voluntary informed consents, and psychiatrists testified that if the operations were not performed and the sick twins were to die, the healthy potential donor twins could suffer 'grave emotional impact' for the remainder of their lives. The operations were accordingly adjudged 'therapeutic': they were necessary for the continued good health and future well-being of, and conferred benefits upon, the donors as well as upon the donees.[44]

Understandably, there are many who view such artificial attempts to distort descriptive terminology with distaste. For example, one Canadian court which was looking for a 'therapeutic' reason for ordering a hysterectomy to be performed on a seriously retarded child, found that reason in the child's alleged phobic aversion to blood which, it was feared, would seriously affect her when her menstrual period began. Accordingly, sterilisation was authorised. The Supreme Court of Canada stated that whilst sterilisation may, on occasion, be necessary as an adjunct to treatment of a serious malady, there was no room for subterfuge and that decision was, at best, dangerously close to the limits of the permissible.[45]

(b)   The concept of 'substituted judgment'

Another concept which is creeping into American case-law in contrast to the traditional 'best interests' approach to proxy consent is that of 'substituted judgment'. The proxy, or court, does not attempt to decide what is in the 'best interests' of the patient, but rather what decision would be made by the individual if he were competent. The court 'dons the mental mantle of the incompetent and substitutes itself as nearly as possible for the individual in the decision-making process'.[46] It is one of those strange doctrines which was used in England in the early nineteenth century in connection with the administration of the estates of incompetent persons,[47] forgotten, and then rediscovered recently by American courts. It has been raised in cases involving incompetent persons to help establish whether, for example, to consent to the withdrawal of life support systems or to certain unusual or controversial types of medical treatment, such as shock therapy or psychosurgery.[48]

It is a controversial concept, not the least because of the inherent difficulties of attempting to assess what an incompetent patient would have decided were he competent, whether that assessment should be subjective or objective and, if objective, how it can really differ from a 'best interests' approach. No court has yet been called upon to authorise its use in connection with clinical research, although it was raised in *Kaimowitz v Michigan Dept of Mental Health*[49] where it was held, understandably, that no proxy consent could be given for experimental psychosurgery. It is unlikely to be of much help in the current debate.

(c) The 'not against the interests of the child' approach

The most likely approach is to reconsider more carefully the emphasis which the legislature and the courts understandably place upon the need for proxies only to act in the best interests of the child or other incompetent person.

Most of these statements have been made in contexts quite different to those of non-therapeutic clinical research. Although much welfare legislation does stress that the welfare of a child is 'paramount', other provisions refer to the welfare of a child being the *first* consideration.[50] 'First consideration', of course, suggests that there are other considerations which can be balanced by a parent against the best interests of the child, and indeed override it. And where a court has to carry out these tasks it usually has to act as a 'judicial reasonable parent'.

The balancing of various interests can best be seen in ward of court cases. For example, in *Re X (a Minor)*[51] the defendants proposed to publish a book describing the depraved behaviour of the deceased father of a 14 year old girl. It was accepted that if she were to read the book or hear about it from others, it would be *psychologically* grossly damaging to her. The Court of Appeal, in exercising its wardship jurisdiction, was not prepared to allow the interests of the child to prevail over the wider interest of freedom of publication. It is not correct to say 'that in every case where a minor's interests are involved, those interests are always paramount and must prevail . . . The court is required to do a difficult balancing act'.[52] Here the court found the scale tipped heavily in favour of publication and against the minor.

Perhaps the most relevant analogy, however, concerns the power to take blood tests from children in paternity actions. Here, the conflict is between the interests of the child and that of doing justice. In 1970 the House of Lords considered a case[53] where an official guardian had objected to a blood test on a child in paternity proceedings on the ground that this intrusive procedure was not for the child's benefit. This argument was not accepted by the court, and statements abound in the judgments that the benefit of the child is not always an adequate criterion. Lord Reid analysed the situation clearly: first, he proclaimed the principle of physical integrity as: 'There is no doubt that a person of full age and capacity cannot be ordered to undergo a blood test against his will. . . . The real reason is that English law goes to great lengths to protect a person of full age and capacity from interference with his personal liberty.'[54] Secondly, he struck a blow against one modern theory of children's rights by denying them an absolute right to physical integrity as against their parents: 'But the position is very different with regard to young children. It is a legal wrong to use constraint on an adult beyond what is authorised by statute or ancient common law powers connected with crime and the like. But it is not and could not be a legal wrong for a parent or person authorised by him to use constraint to his young child provided it is not cruel or excessive.'[55] Thirdly, such a power goes beyond simple domestic situations such as chastisement: 'It seems to me to be impossible to deny that a parent can lawfully require that his young child should submit to a blood test. And if a parent can require that, why not the court?'[56] And fourthly, a move away from the 'best interests' approach:

> Surely a reasonable parent would have some regard to the general public interest and would not refuse a blood test unless he thought that would clearly be against the interests of the child?[57] . . . I would hold that the court ought to permit a blood test of a young child to be taken unless satisfied that this would be against the child's interest.[58]

Thus, there seems to be strong authority for saying that in some cases the 'best interests of the child' approach can give way to a rule that a parent should not do anything 'clearly against the interests' of the child. This certainly makes sense. In real life, reasonable parents cannot, and should not, always opt for that activity which presents the least physical risk to the child. Children must be allowed to run risks: climbing trees, riding bicycles, playing 'rough' sports, where the statistical risks may far outweigh anything involved in properly conducted clinical research. Medical procedures involving slight risks, for example vaccinations, occur daily where the benefit may be primarily for other children and the community. Thus, a reasonable and socially responsible parent might think that there was merit in taking the social interest into account and contributing to medical research, provided always that the risk to the child was 'minimal'.

This view of the law accords with the ethical codes and is now being acted upon by the medical profession.[59] Unfortunately, however, the law is not clear beyond all reasonable doubt. A blind development of the 'best interests' approach could box the law into an inflexible position. This appears to have happened in South Australia. The *Consent to Medical and Dental Procedures Act* 1985, which was passed presumably to clarify the law relating to teenage girls receiving contraceptive help from doctors, follows the *Gillick* line in providing that a minor under 16 has full capacity to consent to medical procedures if two practitioners are of the opinion first, that the minor is capable of understanding the nature and consequences of the procedure; and secondly, that 'the procedure is in the best interests of the health *and* well-being of the minor'.[60] It also provides for parental proxy consent, which presumably must be exercised subject to similar restraints. This would seem to authorise a 'medical procedure', which is defined as 'any procedure carried out by, or pursuant to directions given by, a medical practitioner'[60a] only if it complies with the best interests rule; in which case it would be difficult to argue that the scope for non-therapeutic research can be wider. Does that mean that, inadvertently, all clinical research on children under 16 has been ruled out?

There seems to be a strong case for general legislative consideration, and clarification, of the power to give proxy consent for the purposes of research on children.

Notes to extract

[35] For a deontological argument in favour see R B Redmon, 'How Children can be Respected as "Ends" Yet Still be Used as Subjects in Non-Therapeutic Research' (1986) 12 *Journal of Medical Ethics* 77.

[35a] At the time of going to press, the papers had not been published.

[36] Medical Research Council, 'Responsibilities in investigations on human subjects' in *Report of the Medical Research Council for the year* 1962–63 (London, HMSO, 1964); G Godber, 'Constraints Upon the Application of Medical Advances' (1974) 67 *Proceedings of Royal Soc of Med* 1273, 1311.

[37] (1827) 2 Russ 1; 38 ER 236.

[38] (1827) 2 Russ 1 at 18; 38 ER 236 at 242.

[39] *Prince v Massachusetts*, 328 US 158 at 170; 64 S Ct 438 at 444 (1944).

[40] *Re Eve* (1987) 31 DLR (4th) 1.

[41] *Re B (a minor)* [1987] 2 All ER 206.

[42] *Gillick v West Norfolk and Wisbech Area Health Authority* [1985] 3 All ER 432, per Lord Templeman; though dissenting on the main issue in the case.

[43] Although this deontological reasoning is designed to achieve the precise opposite. See Redmon, loc cit.

[44] Such transplantations from infant donors would not be considered ethical today. See also *Strunk v Strunk*, 445 SW 2d 145 (Ky 1969).

[45] See *Re K and Public Trustee* (1985) 19 DLR (4th) 255 (Court of Appeal of British Columbia) and *Re Eve* (1987) 31 DLR (4th) 1 at 22, 34 (Supreme Court of Canada).

[46] *Superintendent of Belchertown State School v Saikewicz*, 370 NE 2d 417 (1977).

[47] *Ex p Whitbread* (1816) 2 Mer 99; 35 ER 878.

[48] H W Classen, 'The Doctrine of Substituted Judgment in its Medicolegal Context' (1985) 31 *Med Trial Technique Q* 451.

[49] 42 USLW 2063 (1973).

[50] E g *Children Act* 1975 (UK) ss 3, 59.

[51] [1975] 1 All ER 697.

[52] Id 706 per Roskill LJ.

[53] *S v S* [1970] 3 All ER 107.

54 Id 111.
55 Ibid.
56 Ibid.
57 Id 112.
58 Id 113. There are now statutory provisions relating to blood testing in these situations eg *Family Law Reform Act* 1969 (UK) s 21; *Children (Equality of Status) Act* 1976 (NSW) s 19; *Status of Children Act* 1974 (Tas) s 10; *Community Welfare Act* 1972 (SA) s 112.
59 E g 'Research on Healthy Volunteers' *Journal of Royal College of Physicians of London*, A Report of the Royal College of Physicians (1986) 20 (Oct) 243.
60 Paragraph 6(2)(b) (emphasis added).
60a Section 4.

Questions

(i) Do you agree with Professor Dworkin's analysis of the English Law?

(ii) Do you think it is curious that non-therapeutic research may be performed on the incompetent child but not, on our view of the law, on the incompetent adult?

(c) Some institutional responses

In March 1988, reflecting the changed perception concerning the permissibility and propriety of carrying out non-therapeutic research on healthy volunteers, the Association of the British Pharmaceutical Industry (ABPI) published its 'Guidelines for Medical Experiments in Non-Patient Human Volunteers'. To these Guidelines are appended (i) an 'Outline Protocol for a Non-Patient Volunteer Study'; (ii) a 'Volunteer Agreement and Consent Form'; and (iii) a 'Model Information Document'. We also include these below.

GUIDELINES FOR MEDICAL EXPERIMENTS IN NON-PATIENT HUMAN VOLUNTEERS

1 Introduction

1.1 The Association of the British Pharmaceutical Industry (ABPI) established a committee in 1969, under the Chairmanship of Sir Charles Stuart-Harris, to investigate and advise on medical experiments involving pharmaceutical company staff volunteers. The report of this Committee, issued in 1970, set a standard of practice for member companies to provide safeguards for staff volunteers in drug studies. These published guidelines also acted as a basis for volunteer studies organised outside the pharmaceutical industry. However, research practices and opinions have inevitably changed during the past eighteen years, and these are not fully reflected in the 1984 updated commentary on the 1970 Stuart-Harris report.

1.2 In October 1986 the Royal College of Physicians published a report entitled 'Research on Healthy Volunteers'. The Association subsequently set up a Working Party to reconsider its own position, to review current guidelines related to volunteer studies, and to draft new ones. These guidelines take account of the conclusions reached by the Royal College of Physicians. The membership of the Working Party is shown in Appendix D.

1.3 In its 1970 report and the 1984 Update, the ABPI referred to staff and human volunteers, but did not define the term volunteer. Key elements in the definition of a non-patient volunteer are that the individual cannot be expected to derive therapeutic benefits from the proposed study, is not known to suffer any significant illness relevant to the proposed study, and whose mental state is such that he is able to understand and freely give valid consent to the study. This definition embraces the term 'healthy volunteer'.

1.4 Volunteer studies must only be undertaken when the appropriate aims, objectives, and methodologies are clearly defined and set out in a written, approved protocol.

1.5   No reference was made in the 1970 or 1984 documents to the payment which may be required by investigators in non-patient volunteer studies. That was because the previous guidelines referred exclusively to medical experiments on staff volunteers. It is recognised that volunteer studies sponsored by industry are conducted outside the premises of member companies, and a statement is therefore included on payment to investigators. (6.3).

1.6   The previous ABPI guidelines (1970 and 1984) stated that only new experimental designs such as the administration of a new chemical entity required the programme of work envisaged to be submitted to and approved by an independent and properly constituted Ethics Committee. It is now strongly recommended that all volunteer study protocols be submitted to and approved by an independent and properly constituted Ethics Committee. The definitive report on Ethics Committees, supported by the ABPI, is the 1984 document entitled 'Guidelines on the Practice of Ethics Committees in Medical Research' published by the Royal College of Physicians of London.

1.7   Companies conducting in-house volunteer studies should follow these ABPI guidelines, and should require that all volunteer studies conducted on their behalf should also follow the guidelines.

2   Justification for volunteer studies, and the assessment of risk

2.1   Medical experiments on human subjects are necessary to obtain information on the effects of substances intended to be used for diagnostic, prophylactic or therapeutic purposes. The justification for testing any agent in healthy individuals depends upon not only the importance of the information that can be obtained by this means but also the risks involved in obtaining it.

2.2   The acquisition of knowledge of the safety, pharmacokinetics and pharmaco-dynamics of a new medicine in man is important for the design of clinical trials in patients. While tests on volunteers may be desirable at any stage in the development of a medicinal product and the elucidation of its mode of action, they are of particular importance during the initial stages of investigation in man. Prophylactic agents such as vaccines must be entirely evaluated in people who are apparently healthy, so the use of volunteers for such studies is unavoidable and the justification depends upon laboratory evidence of potential efficacy and safety. Different considerations arise with respect to therapeutic agents, the efficacy and related safety of which can only be evaluated in patients. Human volunteer studies nevertheless enable those responsible for the development of a new medicine to understand better the way it is absorbed and metabolised before beginning to study its clinical effect in patients.

2.3   Volunteer studies should only be conducted after appropriate pre-clinical biological studies (toxicology, pharmacology, and drug metabolism) and chemistry and pharmaceutical development have been undertaken. Where a new chemical entity is involved the toxicological work should normally be equivalent to that which would be undertaken in support of a CTX or CTC for studies involving patients at the same stage of a medicine's development (Ref: Guidelines on Data Needed to Support the Administration of New Chemical Entities to Non-Patient Volunteers, ABPI, May, 1985).

2.4   The value of pharmacological studies in healthy volunteers justifies their acceptance as a normal phase in the investigation of a medicine prior to its use in patients. Such studies are not mandatory and volunteer studies should not be performed if they involve medicines whose identifiable toxicity or lack of safety is only compensated for by their potential unique efficacy. Such substances must be evaluated after their initial pre-clinical pharmacological evaluation by observations on their therapeutic activity in patients.

3   Recruitment of volunteers

3.1   Volunteers must be recruited of their own free will. They should initially be made aware of the possibility of volunteering by means of a general notice, rather than by direct approach, so that the initiative for volunteering rests entirely with the individual. Widespread or public advertising, especially if it is aimed at the poor, needy or socially disadvantaged, is unacceptable. Neither payment, nor the level thereof, should be mentioned in a public notice. This principle should apply wherever studies are conducted. No member of staff, student or other persons should be made to feel under obligation to volunteer, nor should they be disadvantaged in any way by not volunteering. The principles enshrined in the WMA Declaration of Helsinki as revised in 1975 (Tokyo) and 1983 (Venice) should be upheld.

3.2   No volunteer should be recruited unless capable of giving legally valid consent. All volunteers must be fully and properly informed so as to allow clear understanding of the nature and purpose of the proposed study. Any risks, either known or suspected, and any inconvenience, discomfort or pain likely to be experienced should be made clear to prospective volunteers, who must make their own decision on whether to participate or not. Volunteers should be informed verbally and in writing that they are free to withdraw from a study at any time and without explanation or reason, and that the registered medical practitioner in charge of the trial may withdraw them at any time if he considers it appropriate.

3.3   All establishments conducting volunteer studies must keep accurate records and avoid the excessive use of any volunteer. It is difficult to stipulate the maximum participation for any individual volunteer because of the variety of procedures and medicines involved; however, no person should take part in more than one study at a time, nor should any person receive a new chemical entity administered systemically at study intervals of less than four months. Account should be taken of such facts as the total exposure to test substances in any one year, and the total volume of blood taken in the year.

4   Monitoring exposure
4.1   There are three ways in which study participation may be monitored and excess participation prevented: by contact with the general practitioner (in the United Kingdom); by counselling the volunteer and supplying the volunteer with a record card; and by maintaining a register within a department conducting volunteer studies.

4.2   Potential volunteers should sign a form prior to each study giving the name and address of their general practitioner consenting to any approach which is made and consenting to the provision of relevant information by the general practitioner. If contact is made by a pharmaceutical company it should be the registered medical practitioner responsible for the study who contacts the general practitioner.

4.3   Volunteers should themselves be given a record card which gives relevant details of the studies in which they have taken part and dosages of drugs and details of radioactive exposure for which there are safety limits which should be recorded. They should be counselled appropriately on the potential dangers of excessive volunteering.

4.4   It is the responsibility of the establishment to maintain its own register of volunteers who have participated in studies. The volunteer establishment should maintain full records of studies and volunteers for a minimum of five years after the study is completed.

5   Special groups

Pregnancy
5.1   Women of childbearing potential should not normally be accepted as volunteers in early studies. In studies which involve drugs likely to be used in the treatment of women, volunteers who are women of childbearing potential may be accepted subject to the approval of an independent Ethics Committee. In this situation adequate safeguards must be taken to ensure absence of conception or a pre-existing pregnancy. Satisfactory reproductive toxicology studies must have been performed.

Children

5.2   Children should not normally be used in volunteer studies of pharmaceutically active substances.

Elderly

5.3   As the elderly may be at special risk their use in volunteer studies should be generally avoided. When it is likely that a substance will be used extensively in elderly patients, however, or where the effects of a medicine and its metabolism may be different in the elderly, then the use of elderly volunteers may be justified.

Mentally handicapped

5.4   Volunteer studies in the mentally handicapped cannot be justified.

Prisoners

5.5   Prisoners should never be used in volunteer studies.

6   Financial and other inducements

Reward

6.1   Volunteers may be rewarded in cash or in kind, but the amount should be reasonable and related to the nature and degree of inconvenience and discomfort involved. Payment should never be offered for undergoing risk. Payment of excessive amounts is discouraged especially as this may lead to inappropriate repeated volunteering solely for financial gain. Attention is therefore drawn to paragraph 3.3 regarding the maximum participation by an individual.

Withdrawal

6.2   When a volunteer withdraws or is withdrawn from a study for medical reasons related to the study, full payment should be made. If the volunteer withdraws for other reasons, including non-related medical reasons, a proportional payment may be made at the discretion of the investigator.

Investigators

6.3   Payments to investigators and institutions must be seen to be at a reasonable level for the work involved.

7   Safeguards

7.1   Great care and precautions must be taken before experiments on volunteers are commenced. It is the responsibility of the investigator to confirm that a volunteer is healthy, and suitable for inclusion in the study against carefully pre-determined criteria.

7.2   Volunteers for studies should be screened by a clinician who should take an appropriate medical history, including reference to allergies, smoking, alcohol or consumption of other medically active substances. This screening must take place shortly before the study begins. The medical examination should be appropriate to the study proposed including relevant blood, urine or other tests. If the history, examination, or tests show any abnormality that could be associated with an increased risk for the individual if he or she participated in the study, the volunteer should not take part. Any evidence of drug abuse including alcohol, should also preclude acceptance of the volunteer into the study.

7.3   All volunteer studies must be supervised by a medical practitioner fully registered in the United Kingdom, who is a fully paid up member of a recognised medical defence body. This practitioner should have appropriate facilities and experience to cope with any foreseeable medical contingency, should sign each protocol and consent form, and should be familiar with resuscitation techniques and capable of using the available equipment. He also has responsibility for the well being of the volunteers and may withdraw them at any time during the study.

7.4   All volunteers should be supervised during the administration of a medicine and for an appropriate period thereafter and advised to take appropriate precautions should the known or suspected effects of the medicine so demand. For example, any volunteer taking a medicine which is likely to cause drowsiness should not be allowed to drive or work with dangerous machinery or chemicals. (The volunteer should be advised of this in advance.) Details of any drug given to a volunteer must be recorded on a document to be carried by the volunteer, and this document must also give the telephone number(s) of the medical staff who can be contacted on a 24 hours a day basis in an emergency.

7.5   The initial dose in the first study of a new chemical entity should be well below the amount indicated as pharmacologically active in humans by previous animal studies, and only a small percentage of the no-toxic effect in animals.

7.6   Safeguards regarding communicable diseases must be taken to protect the volunteer, the investigator and all other staff involved including remote laboratory staff. Investigators should refer to the guidelines prepared by the ABPI Working Party on the handling of blood samples (1987). Volunteers found on initial examination to have medical contra-indications against participation in the study should be clearly advised of the reasons for their exclusion, and appropriately counselled. This will usually be by informing the volunteer's own general practitioner, with the consent of the volunteer.

7.7   Any adverse events occurring during a volunteer study should be followed up as appropriate.

7.8   The supervising doctor should pay particular regard to the possible need to follow up volunteers who withdraw from a study.

8   Suitability of facilities

8.1   Premises in which non-patient volunteer studies are conducted should be custom equipped and designed and be adequate for the purpose, including the provision of appropriate resuscitation equipment. Staff must have been properly trained in the use of this equipment. The facilities should be of the high standard expected for the involvement of healthy persons in experiments, and should be open to scrutiny by members of the independent Ethics Committee which considers the protocols for the studies conducted in each specific centre.

8.2   Member companies should satisfy themselves that studies conducted on their behalf by other establishments are conducted in premises which at minimum fulfil the above criteria.

8.3   Consideration will be given by the ABPI to the compilation of a directory of centres conducting studies on volunteers, listing all the facilities available within each centre, as suggested by the Medicines Commission (advice to Health Ministers on Healthy Volunteer Studies, DHSS, June 1987).

8.4   This directory should include pharmaceutical companies, contract houses, academic departments, medical schools, and any hospitals conducting volunteer studies.

9   Design and protocol

9.1   Research involving non-patient volunteers should conform to the highest ethical and scientific standards which apply to all clinical research. Ethical standards should apply in accordance with the Guidelines on the Practice of Ethics Committees in Medical Research published by the Royal College of Physicians of London in 1984.

9.2   The protocol should define the experiment, and contain an account of the information that will be provided to the volunteer. References should also be made to the provision of a formal agreement and consent form. A model outline protocol is detailed in Appendix A. Every volunteer study protocol must be submitted to and approved by an independent Ethics Committee prior to the administration of the test substances.

9.3   Animal studies must have been carried out appropriate to the particular pharmaceutical form to be used in the volunteer study, except where the test substance is already a licensed product. These will be referred to in the protocol and have the following objectives:

i) to determine the target organ and toxic effects in animals of relatively large doses, repeated at intervals depending on the test substance's biological and toxicological properties and the proposed human dosage and usage

ii) to demonstrate that the preparation elicits the required pharmacological responses in experimental animals that are likely to be analogous to the desired effects in man

iii) to attempt to define the absorption, distribution, metabolism and excretion of the test compound.

10   Ethics committees

10.1   All studies involving the administration of substances to non-patient volunteers, must have a written protocol submitted to and approved in writing by an appropriate independent Ethics Committee before the study begins.

10.2   Pharmaceutical companies contracting outside establishments to conduct volunteer studies on their behalf must ensure that protocols have been submitted to and approved by an independent Ethics Committee.

10.3   Once ethical approval has been given for the study, the supervision of the study becomes the sole responsibility of the named registered medical practitioners sponsoring and supervising the study. However, major protocol amendments should be referred to the Committee or its Chairman, and no further test substances should be administered before approval is received.

11   Consent and study administration

11.1   All volunteers participating in a clinical study must sign a simple form of agreement that records the basis upon which they have agreed to participate in the study. This agreement may be either with the sponsoring pharmaceutical company or the outside research establishment depending upon which is primarily responsible for recruitment and supervision of the study. The sponsoring company should ensure that it is fully satisfied with any agreements to be used by the outside research establishment.

11.2   The agreement should

i) evidence the fact that the volunteer has consented to participate in the light of proper explanation from the investigator of the nature and purpose of the study and any foreseeable risks attaching to participation.

ii) record that the volunteer has been told he is free to withdraw without need to justify that decision.

iii) deal with the issue of confidentiality and the agreement of the volunteer to disclosure of information generated by the study.

iv) if the investigator deems it appropriate to do so, authorise the investigator to contact the volunteer's general practitioner and authorise the general practitioner to disclose any information concerning the volunteer's health relevant to participation in the study.

Any information arising during the course of the study which the investigator wishes to be conveyed to the general practitioner or occupational physician should be the subject of further authorisation by the volunteer.

All records containing information about volunteers should be treated as confidential and, for staff volunteers, should be kept separate from other personnel records (preferably in the Medical Department). It must be recognised that they may become subject to disclosure in any legal proceedings where they are relevant to the issues in those proceedings.

11.4   It is good practice for the investigator to sign a corresponding statement, incorporated into the agreement or attached to it, to the effect that he has counselled the volunteer on the study and given the volunteer the opportunity to question him on any points felt by the volunteer to require clarification.

11.5   The explanation given by the investigator to the volunteer should be witnessed and the witness may reasonably be asked to sign a statement confirming this fact.

11.6   The information document, provided to the volunteer in connection with the study, should be referred to in the agreement and a copy attached. Companies should make every effort to ensure that the information document is comprehensible to the volunteer. The following points should be considered for inclusion in that document:

a.   confirmation of the principal features of the study;
b.   procedures to be used if assistance or advice is required;
c.   that the volunteer should at all times carry the personal record card giving details of the study;
d.   that the implications of his agreement to participate, in terms of any insurance cover that he may already have or may happen to be negotiating at the time, have been drawn to the volunteer's attention;
e.   that the study has been subject to review by an independent Ethics Committee; and
f.   that the volunteer will disclose relevant medical information during the course of the study;

A model information document appears as Appendix C.

11.7 and 11.8 are omitted. They deal with compensation payable to injured volunteers. We will return to this shortly.

11.9   It is recommended that a simple arbitration clause is included as part of the provisions concerning compensation for injury, whereby any difference or dispute in relation to the implementation of the compensation provisions may be resolved with a minimum of formality.

11.10   A model agreement, which is drawn on the basis that the pharmaceutical company is conducting the research in-house, appears as Appendix B. Where the research is performed elsewhere two documents may need preparation, the first dealing with the provisions relating to compensation for injury and the second dealing with all other matters relevant to the contractual relationship with the volunteer.

12   Conclusion
12.1   Medical experiments on non-patient volunteers constitute an essential step towards the development of many medicinal products. Information from such experiments is indispensable for the scientific assessment and development of most new medicines. These guidelines aim to provide a framework within which these studies can be conducted.

Appendix A

OUTLINE PROTOCOL FOR A NON-PATIENT VOLUNTEER STUDY

Contents
Summary
1.   INTRODUCTION AND RATIONALE FOR THIS STUDY
2.   OBJECTIVES
3.   PREVIOUS EVALUATION PROGRAMME
3.1   Animal toxicity programme
3.2   Summary of toxicity evaluation studies
3.3   Summary of animal pharmacology studies
3.4   Summary of previous human data
3.5   Non-interference of trial drug with haematology and clinical chemistry
3.6   Regulatory status
4.   STUDY DESIGN
4.1   Randomisation details
5.   SELECTION OF STUDY VOLUNTEERS
5.1   Number of volunteers
5.2   Inclusion criteria

Appendix B

DRAFT PROVISIONS FOR VOLUNTEER AGREEMENT AND CONSENT FORM

1. I, the undersigned voluntarily agree to take part in [named study].

2. I have been given a full explanation by the supervising doctor, Dr [name of supervising doctor] of the nature, purpose and likely duration of the study and what I will be expected to do and I have been advised about any discomfort and possible ill-effects on my health or well-being which he believes may result. The information document given to me is attached.

3. I have been given the opportunity to question Dr [　　　　] on all aspects of the study and have understood the advice and information given as a result.

4. I agree to Dr [　　　　] contacting my general practitioner [and teaching or university authority if appropriate] to make known my participation in the study and I authorise my general practitioner to disclose details of my relevant medical or drug history, in confidence.

5. I agree to comply with any instruction given during the study and to co-operate faithfully with Dr [　　　　] and to tell him immediately if I suffer any deterioration of any kind in my health or well-being or any unexpected or unusual symptoms however they may have arisen.

6. I agree that I will not seek to restrict the use to which the results of the study may

be put and, in particular, I accept that they may be disclosed to regulatory authorities for medicines in the UK and elsewhere.

7. I understand that I am free to withdraw from the study at any time without needing to justify my decision.

8. The company sponsoring the study confirms that:

i) I shall receive, in consideration for completing the study, the sum of £ _____ and that I shall receive the sum in full if it is necessary for me to withdraw from the study for medical reasons associated with participation in it. If I withdraw from the study for medical reasons not associated with the study a payment will be made to me proportional to the length of the period of participation, but if I withdraw for any other reason, the payment to be made, if any, shall be at the discretion of the supervising doctor;

ii) Subject to any overriding requirement of law necessitating the disclosure of documents relating to the study, the volunteer will not be referred to by name in any document concerning the study disclosed to any person not under the direct control of the supervising doctor;

iii) In the event of my suffering any significant deterioration in health or well-being caused directly by my participation in the study, compensation will be paid to me by the company.

iv) The amount of such compensation shall be calculated by reference to the amount of damages commonly awarded for similar injuries by an English court if liability is admitted, provided that such compensation may be reduced to the extent that I, by reason of contributory fault, am partly responsible for the injury (or where I have received equivalent payment for such injury under any policy of insurance effected by the company for my benefit);

v) Any dispute or disagreement as to the application of clause 8(iii) shall be referred to an arbitrator to be agreed between myself and the company, or in the absence of agreement, to be appointed by the President of the Royal College of Physicians of London with power in the arbitrator to consult a barrister of 10 years' standing in respect of any issue of law including the amount of damages to be awarded as payment of compensation.

9. The agreement shall be construed in accordance with English law and subject to clause 8(iii), (iv) and (v) above the English courts shall have sole jurisdiction over any dispute which may arise out of it.

Signed by the volunteer   . . . .

Dated: . . . .

Signed for and on behalf of   . . . .
the company by [   ]
its duly authorised
representative

Dated   . . . .

I confirm that I have explained the nature, purpose and possible hazards of
the above trial to   . . . .

Signed   . . . .

[I confirm that I have witnessed the above explanation

Signed   . . . .
                                                        Witness signature]

(NB   It may be appropriate for the supervising doctor to fulfil the obligations of the duly authorised representative of the company.)

Appendix C

MODEL INFORMATION DOCUMENT

1. The company sponsoring the study is [   ].
2. The supervising doctor is Dr [   ] of [   ].
3. The principal features of the study are:

4. If assistance or advice is required in emergency please use the following contact telephone numbers:

5. Some insurers treat participation in medical studies as a material fact which should be mentioned when making any proposal for health-related insurance and that accordingly participation in the study should be disclosed if the volunteer is in the process of seeking or renewing any such insurance and the volunteer should check that participation does not affect any existing policies held by the volunteer.

6. The study has been subject to review by an independent ethics committee which has not objected to its taking place.

7. The volunteer must inform the supervising doctor of the following:

i) All or any medication or drugs of whatever nature taken by him/her in the last 28 days or which he/she is planning to take [as follows]
   The volunteer must make known to the supervising doctor any changes to this information during the course of the study.
ii) Whether any of the criteria for exclusion from the study described by the supervising doctor apply to him/her.
iii) Any significant illnesses, past or present, including any consultation he/she has had with any doctor during the last 6 months, whether or not that resulted in medication or drug treatment.
iv) His/her history of drug, alcohol and tobacco intake.
v) His/her participation in other volunteer studies during the last 12 months.

These Guidelines relate only to research concerning drugs. The principles would appear to be applicable in other contexts. Furthermore, they purport to be concerned with the ethics of conducting such research. You may wish to consider the following questions.

Questions

(i) Do the purportedly ethical Guidelines give more or less protection to the healthy volunteer than the law as we have stated it? If the latter, what then is the standing of the Guidelines?
(ii) Do the Guidelines call for changes or additions in the light of the law as we have stated it? If so, how would you draft them?
(iii) Is there any unifying principle connecting the categories of persons identified as special groups in paragraph 5? What do pregnant women have in common with prisoners?
(iv) Does paragraph 6.1 make sense when it says 'payment should never be offered for undergoing risk'?
(v) Will the protection in paragraph 6.1 against volunteering for financial gain be assured by paragraphs 3.3 and 4.3? In particular, if volunteers are given a 'record card' (para 4.3), will they not just throw it away if they wish to participate for financial gain in another study?
(vi) Are the 'safeguards' in paragraph 7 (particularly para 7.4) adequate?
(vii) Is the approach of regarding the volunteer as contracting with the researcher an appropriate mechanism for properly protecting the interests of the volunteer?

At the request of the Minister of Health, the Medicines Commission submitted its advice to the Health Ministers in pursuance of its statutory obligations. The Medicines Commission's conclusions and recommendations *Advice to Health Ministers on Healthy Volunteer Studies* (June 1987) were as follows:

6.1 The fact that the licensing authority does not require HV studies to be undertaken should be publicised in clear and forthright terms. . . .

6.2 There should be no prohibition of HV studies. Such a measure would be neither desirable nor practicable. HV studies have a contribution to make in medical research and in the development of new treatments and thus, further 'downstream', to the general well-being of the nation and to its economic prosperity. The point at issue must be that of providing appropriate safeguards for individuals' interests to enable the broader public interest to continue to be served. From this all else follows.

6.3 The Commission considered carefully whether HV studies should be brought under statutory control, which would require primary legislation.

They concluded that there is inadequate reason on the basis of presently available information, to recommend this course of action. There is, however, a strong case for

—a better system of self-regulation;
—systematic collection of relevant data and;
—the careful monitoring of both the present position and of future developments.

6.4 Therefore the Commission recommended that organisations, University departments or individuals conducting HV studies in the UK should be invited to make appropriate entries to a voluntary list to be maintained by a central body. Arrangements for this list should be on the following lines:

6.4.1 Application for inclusion on the list should be supported by sufficient detail to identify the organisation and activity—ie official name or title, registered address (in the case of commercial concerns) or equivalent, names and qualifications of relevant employees carrying out HV tests, locations of tests, the nature of the premises, the medical support and other facilities (eg for resuscitation), available at these locations, and the procedures to be used at them with respect to volunteers, and should include a statement of compliance with any approved guidelines (such as the ABPI Code). The application form should incorporate a checklist, devised by the central body.

It is not envisaged that, in the first instance, inclusion in the list should be regarded as an indication of approved status, although this might be a later development. It might in any case be necessary from the outset for those compiling the list to indicate to applicants instances where their practices appeared to be markedly at variance with approved guidelines. This basic information should be updated annually or whenever major changes occur.

6.4.2 Annual returns should be made of

—number and duration of subject exposures to HV studies
—number of projects
—number of volunteers involved
—number of adverse events, their severity and outcome.

Organisations would need to maintain a register of participants for the purpose of compiling these returns.

6.4.3 Pharmaceutical companies should apply for listing for 'in-house' HV studies and be encouraged to contract for such studies only with listed organisations. Similarly the NHS and universities and other bodies should arrange that all premises in which tests are carried out by them, or on their behalf, should be included in the lists.

6.4.4 Relevant information derived from entry to these lists should be collected and made available for publication, with, of course, necessary safeguards for commercially confidential information.

It would be necessary to consider further

—how these lists should be drawn up

—who should do this work

—whether, with increasing information, the list might develop into a register of approved premises

—whether the list should be supported by an inspection facility in the interests of compliance.

In the Commission's view this can probably best be carried out by, or on behalf of, the DHSS.

6.5   Guidelines should be drawn up and publicised for the conduct of HV studies.

6.6   All HV studies should be submitted to a properly constituted ethics committee for prior approval. The role and constitution of ethics committees should be codified and elaborated by those concerned, and the DHSS should communicate appropriate guidance after consulting interested bodies.

6.7   Ethics committees should make clear, if it is not already clear, that they

—require from applicants a certified statement that pre-clinical investigations from which data have been submitted for their consideration have been carried out to a standard no less than that required by DHSS under the clinical trial exemption scheme; and in particular, because of the relevance to safety, that the quality and stability of the substance to be administered is assured.

—require, in submissions involving complex data, a succinct statement and/or an expert summary

—seek outside expert opinion if necessary (for example because there was no member of the ethics committee who could guide the committee on the particular field of medicine to be covered in the HV study)

—refuse applications which make inadequate provision for compensation for injury due to participation (see below).

6.8   No HV should be recruited for participation in a study without his valid consent having been obtained beforehand. No approach should be made to those incapable of giving such valid consent such as mentally handicapped people, nor to people detained under the Mental Health Act, or prisoners, nor to people under the age of 18. Special care is needed to ensure that valid consent can be obtained for instance when considering studies in people with any form of mental illness.

6.9   Every HV should be informed of any consequence for his employment or insurance status which may result from participation in a study.

6.10   Those conducting tests should be punctilious to avoid any suggestion of exercising undue influence on a person to take part in an HV test. Approaches made to subordinates or those who might be regarded as being in any dependent relationship to researchers or to their organisation (eg company employees, students, junior hospital staff) should make it clear that participation was entirely voluntary and that refusal would attract no sanction.

6.11   Every care should be taken to ascertain the state of health of the volunteer during approaches and any question of his condition being adversely affected by the test should be a matter for careful clinical consideration. A declaration about the state of health and any current medication should be required for all HVs recruited. Permission should be sought of HVs for notice to be sent to their own general practitioners of participation in the study; refusal to permit such communication should invariably lead to rejection as a participant.

6.12   Specific provision should be made during the test for medical support, and other facilities, eg for resuscitation, appropriate to the studies.

6.13   It is not necessary to exclude as participants people who are not in perfect health, provided the ill-health is irrelevant to the study (eg a previous hip replacement). It should be exceptional to use women of child-bearing potential and special care should be taken in considering tests in the elderly; in particular, renal or liver malfunction or anaemia should be a contraindication unless the ethics committee accepts that there are exceptional circumstances.

(Paragraphs 6.14–6.17 relate to compensation and are set out *infra* at p 914.)

Does this advice meet any of the points raised in the questions we posed earlier?

(iv) COMPENSATION

We are not concerned here with legal actions brought by participants in research who have been injured through some fault or misdeed on the part of the researcher. Instead, we are concerned with the question that has increasingly occupied the attention of medical researchers, commentators and the Government: if a participant in a trial, whether patient or healthy volunteer, suffers harm in some way related to the trial and has need for compensation, should he have to rely on a civil action in negligence or strict liability under the Consumer Protection Act 1987, or should there be some other method of compensation available to him? The Government's involvement in this question arises from the public concern following the deaths of two students (one in Cardiff and the other in Dublin) in 1985 who were healthy volunteers in drug trials.

The argument raised is that society gains through the willingness of some to participate in research and society should be prepared, therefore, to provide for any casualties of such research rather than leave them to the vagaries of litigation and the existing social security system. This argument was put by the Royal Commission on Civil Liability and Compensation for Personal Injury (Cmnd 7054) in 1978 and is reflected in their recommendation (paras 1339–1341).

Volunteers for medical research

1339   People may volunteer to take part in research or clinical trials of new forms of treatment or new drugs. Strict precautions are imposed, including the screening of experiments by medical ethical committees. Nevertheless the Medical Research Council stated in their evidence to us:

despite the exercise of the highest degree of care and skill by the medical investigator concerned, death or a personal injury which was quite unforeseen and indeed quite unforeseeable might be suffered by a person who volunteers to participate in such an investigation. For example, a volunteer taking part in a recent trial of live attenuated influenza vaccine developed a neurological lesion shortly after the administration of the vaccine—the first known neurological sequela to any attenuated influenza virus despite the fact that many hundreds of thousands of such inoculations had been given during the preceding ten years; a causal connection between the administration of the vaccine and the neurological lesion could neither be proved nor disproved. In such a situation, the Medical Research Council would seek authority to make an *ex gratia* payment from public funds to the volunteer or his dependants and such a payment has been approved for the volunteer who developed the lesion in question.

Patients undergoing clinical trials

1340   Patients as well as healthy volunteers may be asked if they will agree to accept a new form of treatment in the interests of research. If a patient is given such treatment, and through it suffers injury, or a worsening of his condition which would not have been expected with conventional treatment, he is in the same position as a healthy person volunteering to take part in research.

1341   We think that it is wrong that a person who exposes himself to some medical risk in the interests of the community should have to rely on *ex gratia* compensation in the event of injury. **We recommend** that any volunteer for medical research or clinical trials who suffers severe damage as a result should have a cause of action, on the basis of strict liability, against the authority to whom he has consented to make himself available.

Subsequently, the CIBA Foundation set up a Study Group to consider the appropriate means of compensating participants in medical research who are harmed. Their conclusions are published in the British Medical Journal (10 May 1980).

Methods of compensation

The study group began its work in broad sympathy with the objective of the royal commission's recommendation. The royal commission thought it wrong that those who expose themselves to some risk in the interests of the community should have to rely on ex gratia compensation in the event of injury. The recommendation was intended to give volunteers for medical research a legal right to compensation. In seeking to attain this objective the study group considered three possible ways of providing compensation: (a) negligence; (b) strict liability; (c) a 'no-fault' scheme.

Negligence is the basis of the present law of compensation for medical accidents. To receive compensation the injured person must show a failure to take reasonable care or exercise reasonable skill on the part of someone doing the research. The standard by which care and skill are judged is that of the reasonably competent person having the experience and qualifications that the person in the research team has or ought to have. It is for the injured person to prove negligence. If the accident occurred without negligence on anyone's part, or if it resulted from an error of judgment that anyone could have made despite the use of reasonable care and skill, no compensation will be legally payable.

Strict liability may be defined as liability, irrespective of negligence of the defendant or of someone for whom he is responsible, based solely on proof that he caused the injury in respect of which the claim is made. This is the mechanism of compensation that was favoured by the royal commission's report. The important elements of claims made on the basis of strict liability are that the claimant must seek redress through the courts against a named defendant and that the burden of proof of causation falls upon the claimant.

No-fault compensation—The royal commission used the term no-fault compensation to refer to 'compensation which is obtainable without proving fault and is provided outside the tort system'. No-fault compensation is a system of obtaining payment from a fund instead of taking proceedings against the person responsible for the injury. Compensation which is paid on a no-fault basis is therefore similar to an insurance system. Claims under such a system would be made to a board or some other body, which would determine whether, on the balance of probability, the injury had been caused by the medical research procedure and would decide on the level of compensation. Schemes of this nature currently operate in Sweden and New Zealand. The Swedish scheme is part of the patient insurance scheme introduced by an agreement between the Federation of Swedish County Councils and the main insurance companies. The New Zealand scheme applies to all injuries resulting from an accident and has by statute replaced the tort action for death or personal injury. Under a no-fault scheme neither the research organisation nor people engaged in the research would directly be parties to the claim.

The alternative modes of compensation

Each of the three methods of compensating persons injured in the course of medical research has its advocates. The main consequences of each appear to be as follows:

NEGLIGENCE

The Pearson Commission thought that liability based on negligence was unsatisfactory. Unforeseen injury or even death could occur during the course of a medical experiment despite the exercise of the highest degree of skill and care by the investigator. In these circumstances the injured person would not be legally entitled to compensation, though (as the Medical Research Council stated in its evidence to the royal commission) authority to make an ex gratia payment from public funds would be sought. 'We think that it is wrong,' said the Royal Commission, 'that a person who exposes himself to some medical risk in the interests of the community should have to rely on ex gratia compensation in the event of injury'. The study group is in complete agreement with this. Moreover, the community would be the poorer if individuals ceased to participate in medical research.

A further consideration arises from the possibility of legal proceedings based on an allegation of negligence. Proceedings lie against any one or more individuals undertaking the research claiming that he, she, or they had been negligent. Thus both plaintiff and defendant are personally involved in the anxiety, inconvenience, and delays of litigation.

STRICT LIABILITY

The recommendation of the royal commission on strict liability suffers from some of the disadvantages of claims based on negligence.

Firstly, the recommendation is that a cause of action should lie against 'the authority to whom he has consented to make himself available'. Although this would not, it seems, affect the researcher in the litigation personally, court proceedings against the authority employing the researcher would inevitably concern him and it is undesirable that the participant in the research who is making a claim and the researcher should be in the position of adversaries.

Secondly, claims on the basis of strict liability against the authority would almost certainly lead to authorities seeking insurance against this eventuality. (Medically qualified research workers are at present insured against liability for negligence through the medical defence societies; non-medically qualified researchers are not.) The cost of obtaining such insurance is unknown, but, as insurers do not yet have claims experience in strict liability cases on which to base their premiums, preliminary inquiries suggest that it could be substantial, at least in the early years. The cost would probably be particularly high in the case of therapeutic research which is carried out as part of the treatment of patients who are already sick.

Thirdly, it is not clear what the royal commission meant by the 'authority to whom he had consented to make himself available,' which would be the defendant in a strict liability claim. It could mean the body funding the research, in which case the cost of the insurance premiums would reduce the funds available for research, or it could mean the body employing the investigator, in which case the proposed liability would certainly lead to undesirable restrictions on investigators, an increasing administrative burden, and judgments on the desirability of medical research being made on financial rather than scientific and ethical grounds.

Finally, the proposal is that strict liability should be applied only for the benefit of those who suffer 'severe damage'. It is not known what precisely this is intended to mean, but, subject to an exclusion of small claims in the interests of economy of administration, it is not clear why the liability should be limited in this way.

In the light of these considerations the study group has concluded that a scheme based on strict liability would not adequately provide justice for those injured during the course of medical research and could well lead to restrictions that would impede socially beneficial research.

NO-FAULT COMPENSATION

Compared with litigation a no-fault compensation scheme would have the advantage of administrative simplicity. Claims can generally be handled quickly, and, since the claimant would not be seeking redress from the researcher, his employer, or the funding agency, it would be proper for the researcher to assist the claimant in preparing his claim. The researcher and the participant in the research would therefore not be adversaries, as would be inevitable in any scheme based on litigation. It is in the public interest that all participants in medical research should · appreciate that their wellbeing, and the public interest, are overriding considerations in the mind of the investigator.

Conclusions

The study group considered these three possible ways of providing compensation for those injured during the course of medical research and concluded that the present system based on negligence and supplemented by ex gratia payments from research-funding bodies is unsatisfactory. The group does, however, consider that whatever system of compensation is adopted, it should always be open to the participant in research to seek redress through the courts on the basis of negligence if it is suspected that this has occurred. The group considers that a scheme based on strict liability, while being an improvement on the present situation, would not meet the objectives of providing participants in medical research with the sure knowledge that they would receive a quick and just response to their quest for compensation. The group has, therefore, concluded that a no-fault scheme would provide the most satisfactory means for compensating participants (or their relatives) for injuries received during the course of medical research.

The study group considers that a fund should be established, administered by a board, to provide compensation on a no-fault basis and to which those injured (or their dependants) could apply direct. The pattern of operation of the Criminal Injuries Compensation Board would seem to be a suitable model. The fund could operate along the following lines.

NON-THERAPEUTIC RESEARCH

Non-therapeutic research is research in which the participant, whether healthy or sick, submits to investigation designed to contribute to the advancement of human knowledge, clearly understanding that he can expect no personal benefit.

Compensation should be available to participants injured as a consequence of non-therapeutic research. Injuries occurring during such research are rare and problems of causation are unlikely to be substantial. Any deterioration in health that occurs within a short time of the experiment, in the absence of any other evident explanation, can reasonably be assumed to be attributable to the experiment and should be compensated. Levels of compensation could relate to those awarded by the courts for similar disabilities in tort actions. The fund could be given the power to recover sums awarded from an individual—for example, in the event of negligence on the part of the experimenter—or producer—for example, if a chemical or other agent is used—where appropriate.

THERAPEUTIC RESEARCH

Therapeutic research is research in which the sick participant, usually after givir.g fully informed individual consent, submits to research into the treatment of disease from which he may directly or indirectly gain personal benefit. In some cases there may not be full consent—for example, children or patients who are mentally subnormal or have psychiatric diseases.

Therapeutic research not involving drugs (such as surgery and radiotherapy) which leads to injury could be compensated in the same way as non-therapeutic research. The fund would have to consider two factors in assessing compensation: (*a*) the probability of a causal relationship between the treatment and the event (see below); (*b*) the severity of the injury in relation to the natural history of the disease, since many surgical and radiotherapeutic treatments are applied in serious diseases with a high mortality—for example, cancer.

Therapeutic research on drugs—The following proposals do not cover cases in which the drug is incorrectly formulated, compounded, or labelled or contaminated during manufacture. Injury occurring as a result of such defects would be compensated under the law relating to product liability. These proposals relate to injury occurring during the course of therapeutic research on drugs where there is no defect in the manufacturing process. Such therapeutic research should be considered in two stages: before a product licence has been granted for the drug and after the licence has been granted. Injuries occurring during therapeutic research done before a product licence has been granted could be compensated in the same way as non-therapeutic research. The fund should subsequently recover the cost of the award from the pharmaceutical company concerned. Many large-scale or comparative studies of medicines are carried out after a product licence has been granted. Some minor and low-frequency major adverse drug reactions will be recognised at this stage. Particular problems may arise in relation to assessing risk and causation (see below), and the fund would have to make judgments on the balance of probabilities in each individual case. It would be reasonable to expect that minor adverse effects should properly be considered as part of the usual risk-benefit calculations of medical treatment and that small claims should, therefore, be excluded. Funds for compensation for injury as a consequence of therapeutic research should be provided by the pharmaceutical industry. There is also an associated problem not directly related to the conduct of therapeutic research. Drugs become available for general prescribing after a product licence has been granted, and thus compensation for adverse drug reactions occurring as a result of drug trials would pose a problem of natural justice since these reactions would also occur in patients not participating in trials who have received the same drug at the same time for therapeutic purposes.

CAUSATION

The fund would have to consider the question of causation. This is unlikely to be a problem for injuries that follow non-therapeutic research. The problem is much larger, however, in therapeutic research, especially in patients with serious illnesses which have a high short-term mortality and may have serious complications—for example, coronary thrombosis, leukaemia—in conditions which may produce widespread clinical manifestations or have an unpredictable course—for example, many rheumatic diseases—and in surgical procedures which may give imperfect results—for example, high bile duct strictures, resections for some gastrointestinal tumours. In the early stages of investigation of a new drug, on relatively small numbers of patients, it would be reasonable to consider that almost any unexpected event which cannot be readily explained in some other way should, in ordinary justice, be attributed to the treatment. Detailed consideration of the probability of a causal relationship between therapy and event would, however, be unavoidable particularly when larger-scale and prolonged studies are carried out.

There are two problems which are particularly relevant to large-scale therapeutic research on drugs. Firstly, several adverse drug reactions are indistinguishable from naturally occurring diseases—for example, strokes occurring in patients taking an oral contraceptive. This is not merely a question of difficulty in distinguishing such serious incidents from spontaneous disease: it is impossible to say whether a particular case is drug-related or not. The most that can be stated is that the risk of such phenomena is higher among people treated with a drug than among those not treated with it. Compensation for all such events occurring during treatment would again pose problems of natural justice since these same diseases occur in the (untreated) community at large. Secondly, many low-frequency adverse drug reactions are not due to side effects (undesirable but unavoidable actions of the drug) but to idiosyncrasy in the patient, because genetic or environmental factors in an individual may differ greatly from those affecting the rest of the community—for example, differences in drug metabolising or immune systems or even major differences in dietary habits. Inevitably difficult decisions will have to be made and each individual case will have to be considered on the balance of probabilities.

FINANCIAL CONSIDERATIONS

The study group has given considerable thought to the financial considerations. It suggests that the fund should be set up and financed by bodies with an interest in promoting medical research and organisations which provide professional indemnity for those who conduct research. The fund could be established with moneys provided by the Medical Research Council, the universities, the Department of Health and Social Security, the pharmaceutical industry, the medical protection societies, and private organisations funding research. These contributions would be equivalent to insurance premiums. The major advantage of operating such a scheme through a central fund would be that all who finance and conduct human experiments would contribute and thus the insurance cover could be provided much more economically than if individuals and organisations were left to make independent arrangements with insurance companies. The proportion from each of these bodies should be adjusted in the light of experience of the claims made. The fund should use as its guideline in determining compensation the levels of compensation paid for similar disabilities in the courts. The costs of such a scheme cannot be predicted, although information from Sweden suggests that they are unlikely to be very great.

In 1983 the ABPI published the following Guidelines in respect of injuries resulting to *patients* who are used in drug research.

GUIDELINES

Clinical trials—compensation for medicine-induced injury

It is becoming common practice for ethical committees to expect assurance that patients participating in clinical trials will be appropriately compensated, by a simple procedure, should they be adversely affected by reason of their involvement in the trial. While such adverse effects are very uncommon, the Association of the British Pharmaceutical Industry (ABPI) accepts this as a guiding principle and has noted that quite different considerations apply to medicines undergoing clinical trial compared to medicines generally available on prescription.

Consequently, in cases where injury is attributable to a medicine in clinical trial, the ABPI recommends to its member companies that the following guidelines should be accepted without legal commitment on the part of the member companies:

(a)   The company should favourably consider the provision of compensation for personal injury, including death, in accordance with these guidelines but without the requirement for negligence to be proved against the company.

(b)   Compensation should only be paid when there is a balance of probabilities that the injury (including exacerbation of an existing condition) was attributable to the company's medicine under trial.

(c)   Compensation should only be paid for the more serious injury of an enduring and disabling character, and not for temporary pain or discomfort or less serious or curable complaints such as skin rashes.

(d)   These guidelines only apply to injuries to patients involved in clinical trials, conventionally known as Phase II or Phase III trials, that is to say, patients under treatment and surveillance (usually in hospital) and suffering from the ailment which the medicine under trial is intended to treat. These guidelines do not apply to injuries arising from studies on healthy volunteers (Phase I), whether or not they are in hospital, for which separate guidelines for compensation already exist. These guidelines also do not apply to injuries arising from clinical trials on marketed products, except when the trial is on a marketed medicinal product being tested for a prospective indication not yet authorised by inclusion in a product licence.

(e)   These guidelines apply to an injury whether or not the adverse reaction causing the injury was foreseeable or predictable although compensation may be abated or excluded in the light of the factors mentioned in paragraph (j) below.

(f)   Compensation should not be payable (or should be abated, as the case may be) (i) when there has been a significant departure from the agreed protocol, (ii) where the injury was attributable to the wrongful act or default of a third party, including a doctor's failure to deal adequately with an adverse reaction, or (iii) when there has been contributory negligence by a patient.

(g)   Compensation should only be payable to patients receiving the medicine under trial and, therefore, not to control patients not receiving the trial medicine, nor to patients receiving placebos, nor to patients receiving other non-trial drugs or medicines for the purpose of comparison with the medicine under trial.

(h)   The giving of consents to participate in a clinical trial, whether in writing or otherwise, should not exclude a patient from the benefits of compensation or in any way prejudice his position under the guidelines, although compensation may be abated or excluded in the light of the factors mentioned in paragraph (j) below.

(i)   No compensation should be paid for the failure of a medicine to have its intended effect or to provide any other benefit to the patient. This includes the failure of any vaccine or other preparation to provide the preventive or prophylactic effect for which it is under trial, and the failure of any contraceptive preparation or device to prevent pregnancy.

(j)   The amount of any compensation paid by the company should be appropriate to the nature, severity and persistence of the injury. However, such compensation may be abated, or in certain circumstances excluded, in the light of the following factors (on which will depend the kind of risk the patient should be expected to accept):

(i) the seriousness of the disease being treated, the degree of probability that adverse reactions will occur and any warnings given;
(ii) the hazards of established treatments relative to those known or suspected of the trial medicine, and
(iii) the availability and relative efficacy of alternative treatments that the patient could have had if he had not volunteered for the trial.

Note: This guideline assumes that the level of any compensation paid will depend upon the circumstances in the light of the factors mentioned above. As an extreme example, there may be a patient suffering from serious or mortal disease such as cancer who is warned of a certain defined risk of adverse reaction. Participation in the trial is then based on an expectation that the benefit/risk ratio associated with participation is better than that associated with alternative treatment. It is, therefore, reasonable that the patient accepts the high risk and should not expect compensation for the occurrence of the adverse reaction of which he or she was told.

We have already seen the bulk of the ABPI's 1988 Guidelines in relation to healthy volunteers. Paragraphs 11.7–11.9 deal with compensation.

11.7 The agreement should clearly record the obligation the pharmaceutical company or research establishment has accepted in terms of financial rewards for participation and compensation in the event of injury. In particular, the volunteer should be given a clear commitment that in the event of bodily injury he will receive appropriate compensation without having to prove either that such injury arose through negligence or that the product was defective in the sense that it did not fulfil a reasonable expectation of safety. The agreement should not seek to remove that right of the volunteer, as an alternative, to pursue a claim on the basis of either negligence or strict liability if he is so minded.

11.8 Where pharmaceutical companies sponsor studies to be performed in outside research establishments, the responsibility for paying compensation should be clarified and reflected in the contractual documentation with the volunteer. Where the sponsor company is to provide the undertaking regarding compensation, it is recommended that the sponsor company enters into an unqualified obligation to pay compensation to the volunteer on proof of causation, having previously protected its rights to recourse against the research establishment in its agreement with that establishment, to cover the position where the negligence of its contractor may have caused or contributed to the injury suffered by the volunteer. A volunteer can reasonably expect that compensation will be paid quickly and that any dispute regarding who will finally bear the cost of the compensation paid to him will be resolved separately by the other parties to the research.

11.9 It is recommended that a simple arbitration clause is included as part of the provisions concerning compensation for injury, whereby any difference or dispute in relation to the implementation of the compensation provisions may be resolved with a minimum of formality.

Which of these Guidelines provides the best protection to those injured by drugs which are being tested?

Questions

(i) In guideline (a) of the 1983 ABPI Guidelines, is the use of the word 'attributable' intended to mean that the patient must prove that his injury was *caused* by the drug being tested? If so, as is the case for healthy volunteers (para 11.7: 1988 Guidelines), do you think a patient or a healthy volunteer should have to prove causation on a balance of probabilities? (Compare the Medicines Commission advice paras 6.17, *infra.*)

(ii) Do you think guideline (f) of the 1983 ABPI Guidelines is unfair in that it purports to prevent compensation being paid by the pharmaceutical company if the doctor is at fault?

(iii) Does guideline (c) of the 1983 ABPI Guidelines unduly restrict the types of injury for which compensation will be paid?

(iv) Does paragraph 11.7 of the 1988 ABPI Guidelines make it clear what, if any, test of causation is to be adopted in meeting a claim for compensation, who bears the burden of demonstrating causation and what that burden is? Notice the terms of clause 8(iii) of the draft agreement: 'in the event of my suffering any significant deterioration in health or well-being *caused directly* by my participation in the study, compensation will be paid to me by the company'. (Our emphasis.)

(v) Do you think the 1988 ABPI Guidelines indulge in naivety or wishful thinking in paragraphs 11.8 and 11.9? Will an insurer be willing to 'play the game'?

Consider the Medicines Commission's advice to the Health Ministers of June 1987 (*op cit*) in relation to compensation.

> 6.14   The question of payment to volunteers raises difficult issues. The Commission noted the view held by some that there should be no payments (other than expenses incurred) to healthy volunteers but did not consider that this should be adopted as a general principle. They recommend however that payment should be for expense, time, and inconvenience and should not be at a level of inducement which would encourage people to take part in studies against their better judgment, or which would encourage them to take part in multiple studies, or which might discourage them from giving truthful information about their health or their participation in previous studies. It should be made clear to the individual that he can withdraw from the study at any time without forfeiting payments made up to that point. Withdrawal from a test before completion should always attract payment pro rata to the period of participation.
>
> 6.15   The Commission considered at length the question of compensation for injury due to participation. They recognised that significant adverse effects from HV studies had been exceptionally rare in the United Kingdom. They nonetheless considered that it was essential that, for these rare occasions, there should be assurance in advance that there would be adequate compensation without the need for the volunteer to show negligence.
>
> 6.16   Effective provision should therefore be made in all HV tests to ensure that any volunteer who may be affected in health by tests should receive adequate compensation. To this end
>
> — all companies conducting HV studies should be expected to accept responsibility for 'no fault' compensation and to provide evidence of their ability to fulfil it
> — ethics committees should not approve tests in the private sector without satisfying themselves that such cover has been provided
> — Government (which does not insure on the principle of carrying its own risk) should indicate that sympathetic and comparable consideration would be given to the position of any HVs for injury due to participation in studies carried out by publicly funded bodies.
>
> 6.17   The Commission also recommend that further study should be given to the feasibility of new ways of funding these compensation arrangements, whether through statutory or non-statutory means, including the possibility of one or more central funds to which companies, universities or others conducting HV studies, or benefiting from them, might contribute. These further studies should *not* however delay the implementation of the steps set out in para 6.16 above.

Does the Commission's use of the word 'affected' in paragraph 6.16 indicate that a healthy volunteer would not have to establish a causal link between his injury and the trial? Does this advice, in fact, meet any of the points made in the above questions? Could an individual who is injured by a drug (whether as a patient or a healthy volunteer) pursue an action under the Consumer Protection Act 1987?

(v) INNOVATIVE THERAPY

We have already commented upon the notion of 'innovative therapy' and its relationship with research. We reached the conclusion (*supra* at pp 871–2) that where the doctor's intention is to acquire knowledge and not merely to care for his patient, the constraints normally associated with the conduct of research should apply whenever the patient might be exposed to more than a minimal risk of harm. There is, of course, a scientific as well as a moral and legal basis for this view. The pursuit of knowledge is best conducted in a systematic fashion. Bad science is bad ethics. Innovative therapy should properly be regarded as one of two things: *research* with all that flows therefrom, or *therapy*, in which case the sole intention is to care for the particular patient involved. Consequently, the law does not inhibit the development of therapy but it says either you defend it as research or you stand prepared to justify it in any action in negligence should harm result.

Pursuing the point concerning a claim in negligence relating to the performance of the procedure, we must take as our point of departure *Hunter v Hanley* 1955 SC 200. In that case, you will recall, Lord Clyde said:

> It follows from what I have said that in regard to allegations of deviation from ordinary professional practice . . . such a deviation is not necessarily evidence of negligence. Indeed it would be disastrous if this were so, for all inducement to progress in medical science would then be destroyed. Even a substantial deviation from normal practice may be warranted by the particular circumstances. To establish liability by a doctor where deviation from normal practice is alleged, three facts require to be established. First of all it must be proved that there is a usual and normal practice; secondly it must be proved that the defender has not adopted that practice; and thirdly (and this is of crucial importance) it must be established that the course the doctor adopted is one which no professional man of ordinary skill would have taken if he had been acting with ordinary care.

In the later case of *Landau v Werner* (1961) 105 Sol Jo 1008, CA, Sellers LJ stated that:

> A doctor might not be negligent if he tried a new technique but if he did he must justify it before the Court. If his novel or exceptional treatment had failed disastrously he could not complain if it was held that he went beyond the bounds of due care and skill as recognised generally.

These cases illustrate the desire of the courts to allow doctors some discretion so as to develop medical practice while wishing to set proper limits of the extent to which they may go. Notice the following words of Hunter J in *Brook v St John's Hickey Memorial Hospital* 380 NE 2d 72 (1978) (Supreme Court of Indiana):

> Too often courts have confused judgmental decisions and experimentation. Therapeutic innovation has long been recognised as permissible to avoid serious consequences. The everyday practice of medicine involves constant judgmental decisions by physicians as they move from one patient to another in the conscious

institution of procedures, special tests, trials and observations recognised generally by their profession as effective in treating the patient or providing a diagnosis of a diseased condition. Each patient presents a slightly different problem to the doctor. A physician is presumed to have the knowledge and skill necessary to use some innovation to fit the peculiar circumstances of each case.

If doctors are to be given some leeway but not encouraged to leap too far into the dark there must be some criterion in law to which the doctor can refer. What criterion would you suggest? Is the notion of 'minimal risk' of assistance, or would such a criterion unnecessarily inhibit the doctor from trying new techniques outside the ambit of systematic research?

Consider the following case which arose in the United States (footnotes omitted):

Karp v Cooley
493 F 2d 408 (1974) (United States Court of Appeals, Fifth Circuit)

Circuit Judge Bell: Medical history was made in 1969 when Dr Denton A Cooley, a thoracic surgeon, implanted the first totally mechanical heart in 47-year-old Haskell Karp. This threshold orthotopic cardiac prosthesis also spawned this medical malpractice suit by Mr Karp's wife, individually and as executrix of Mr Karp's estate, and his children, for the patient's wrongful death. . . .

There is no dispute that prior to entering St Luke's Episcopal Hospital in Houston on March 5, 1969, Haskell Karp had a long and difficult ten-year history of cardiac problems. He suffered a serious heart attack in 1959 and was hospitalised approximately two months because of diffuse anterior myocardial infarction. He had incurred four heart attacks, thirteen cardiac hospitalisations and considerable medical care culminating in the insertion of an electronic demand pacemaker in May, 1968. Subsequent hospitalisation in September and October, 1968 occurred, and finally the decision was made to seek the assistance of Dr Cooley. . . .
[Dr Cooley testified]:

I told [Mr Karp] we had no heart donor available, had no prospect of one . . . I told him that there was a possibility that we had a device which would sustain his life in the event that he would die on the operating table. We had a device which would sustain his life, hopefully, until we could get a suitable donor. I had told him that I did not know whether it would take a matter of hours or days, weeks, or maybe not at all, but it would sustain his life and give us another possibility of salvaging him through heart transplantation.

Dr Cooley said he did not recall who was present when these discussions began. Dr Cooley described his discussion of this device:

I told him that it was a heart pump similar to the one that we used in open-heart surgery; that it was a reciprocating-type pump with the membrane, in which the pumping element never became in contact with the bloodstream; that it was designed in such a manner that it would not damage the bloodstream or it would cause minimal damage to the bloodstream; that it would be placed in his body to take over the function of the dead heart and to propel blood throughout his body during this interim until we could have a heart transplant. . . . I told him this device had not been used in human beings; that it had been used in the laboratory; that we had been able to sustain the circulation in calves and that it had not been used in human beings. It had been used on the bench in what we call *in vitro* experiments, *in vitro* as opposed to *in vivo*. . . . I told him it had been tested in the laboratory, it had not been used in a human being, but I was confident that it would support his circulation. . . . I told him that we had been successful in keeping an animal alive for more than forty hours with the device, but that this was a calf. It was a 300-pound animal in which the demands on the pump were far greater than would be in the human body, and that I was reasonably confident that this device would sustain his life until we could get a heart transplant. But no guarantees were made at all.

Dr Cooley admitted he and Mr Karp did not discuss the number of animals in which the device had been tested, nor whether the animals sustained damage to their bodies by the use of this pump.

Asked by appellants' counsel whether he described it as a heart-lung pump similar to that used in other open heart surgeries, Dr Cooley said, 'I told him it was a pump. I didn't tell him it was a lung. I told him it was an artificial heart, that it was a pump which would replace temporarily the heart.'

. . .

According to the anesthesia record, . . . Mr Karp was brought into the operating room at about 1:15 pm. When Dr Keats saw Mr Karp at that time he believed Mr Karp's death to be imminent. Dr Keats said Mr Karp was in great distress; he was having difficulty breathing, shortness of breath and he was pale and sweating. Dr Keats said he hurriedly got Mr Karp on the operating table, started giving him oxygen, and put him to sleep as rapidly as possible so that they could put a tube in his windpipe to assist his breathing. Dr Keats then sent word to Dr Cooley that they 'had better go ahead with the operation as expeditiously as possible, otherwise the patient may not last long enough to have the operation'. . . . Dr Cooley says Mr Karp was near death when he entered the operating room, 'mottled and blue'. He said he felt Mr Karp was 'virtually moribund' at that time.

The operation was then begun with Dr Cooley as chief surgeon, Dr Liotta as first assistant, Dr Grady Hallman as second assistant, and Dr Keats as anesthesiologist. [Dr Cooley] said that he opened the pericardium and that as a result of very feeble heart action the heart pump was started as quickly as possible. Dr Keats remembers that as Mr Karp's heart became visible 'it was a very large heart that filled the entire surgical field'. Dr Cooley said that the heart was functioning very feebly, was virtually noncontractile and could not support Mr Karp. After Mr Karp had been on the heart-lung or heart oxygenator a sufficient time to get his heart going again an incision was made in the left ventricle. Dr Cooley said that Mr Karp had scar tissue circumferentially around the inside of his left ventricle, that his entire interventricular septum was one solid piece of scar tissue, the anterior ventricle was almost completely displaced by scar tissue, and there was an aneurysm on the posterior aspect of the ventricle. . . .

Although Dr Cooley said the situation was then 'virtually hopeless', he began to do what he could with the resection procedure. He excised the most severely damaged part of the ventricular myocardium in his repair of the left ventricle. Because of the extensive scarring it was necessary to excise part of the right ventricle. In completing this complicated repair it was then necessary to sew the partition back to the right ventricle, and sew the left ventricle back to them. Dr Cooley said that Mr Karp did not have an anterior aneurysm but that the anterior myocardium was diffusely dilated. He added that it was very difficult to differentiate between a dilated scarred heart and an aneurysm. He described the nonfunctioning large area on the left ventricle as having a paradoxical motion and a ballooning out effect. He compared the size of the balloon to a cantaloupe. He said there was no threat of break or rupture in lesions like this; that he had never seen one rupture; and that he never told a patient a ventricular aneurysm would burst.

It is to be noted here that although Mrs Karp testified her husband had appeared normal on the day of the surgery, there is no lay or expert testimony other than that Mr Karp was near death at the time of the operation.

According to Dr Hallman, the repair described above was done in the manner that cardiovascular surgeons normally go about performing this operation. However, Dr Hallman said that due to the extensive scarring of the heart, there simply was not sufficient healthy heart muscle remaining to form an efficient pump to support Mr Karp's life. Dr Hallman, Dr Keats and Dr Cooley all testified that at this point, that is after the attempted resection, Mr Karp was again faced with imminent death.

Dr Cooley said that it took about 20 minutes to make the resection repair. He said that after the repair the clamp was taken off the ascending aorta to attempt to restart the myocardium. He stated that there was fibrillation and that he attempted an electrical countershock at least once. He stated that there was a sinus type or nodal rhythm at that point but that the rhythm contraction was too weak to support life due to the fact that there simply was too much scar tissue in the heart. Dr Hallman testified that some thirty minutes elapsed between the end of the repair and the decision to remove the heart. Mr Karp's heart was then removed and the mechanical device was inserted. Dr Cooley said that the mechanical heart functioned very well and Mr Karp responded to stimulation within 15 or 20 minutes after the incision was closed. His blood pressure was well sustained according to Dr Cooley and he showed signs of cerebral activity. Dr Keats said that Mr Karp was amazingly well following the operation, that the records reflect that he was responding reasonably to commands within 20 minutes post-operatively. Dr Keats testified that the endocracheal [sic] tube was removed about 1:20 am, and that he saw Mr Karp some time the next morning at which time he was responsive and could communicate.

After the mechanical heart had been inserted, Dr Cooley said he went to Mrs Karp and told her that the wedge procedure had been unsuccessful; that he had proceeded with the use of the mechanical device and that they were going to try to get a donor. The transplant operation was performed on the morning of April 7, 1969, approximately 64 hours after the mechanical device had been implanted in Mr Karp. He died the next day, April 8, 1969, some 32 hours after the transplant surgery.

. . .

Suits charging failure by a physician adequately to disclose the risks and alternatives of proposed treatment are not innovations in American law. They date back a good half-century, and in the last decade have increased in number.

. . . Physicians and surgeons have a duty to make a reasonable disclosure to a patient of risks that are incident to medical diagnosis and treatment. True consent to what happens to one's self is the informed exercise of a choice, and that entails an opportunity to evaluate knowledgeably the options available and the risks attendant upon each. From these general principles, however, the focus in each individual case must necessarily relate back to what the physician said or failed to say and what the law requires him to say.

The Texas standard against which a physician's disclosure or lack of disclosure is tested is a medical one which must be proved by expert medical evidence of what a reasonable practitioner of the same school of practice and the same or similar locality would have advised a patient under similar circumstances. . . . As we understand appellants' contention, it is that Mr Karp was not told about the number of animals tested or the results of those tests; that he was not told there was a chance of permanent injury to his body by the mechanical heart, that complete renal shutdown could result from the use of the prosthesis, that the device was 'completely experimental'; and that Dr Cooley failed to tell Mr Karp that Dr Beazley had said Mr Karp was not a suitable candidate for surgery. Nine physicians testified, but none suggested a standard of disclosure required by Texas law under these circumstances. Appellants argue Dr Cooley himself set the standard requiring the disclosure of Dr Beazley's evaluation. Texas law does permit the defendant doctor to establish the standard of disclosure, but Dr Cooley's testimony says no more than that what is a reasonable medical practice is a question of medical judgment. Dr Cooley's admitted failure to tell Mr Karp of Dr Beazley's March 6 notation is of no import; Dr Leachman testified he did not think the notation made any difference, the March 6 notation, made during the course of an initial evaluation, was in Dr Beazley's view not a medical opinion but a reservation about the psychological or emotional acceptance of less than a perfect result.

What is missing from the evidence presented is the requisite expert testimony as to *what* risks under these circumstances a physician should disclose.

. . . What is significant then is what Mr Karp was told, and Mrs Karp's testimony is relevant only to the extent that it evidences what Mr Karp was told when she was present. Dr Cooley's undisputed testimony is that he began discussing with Mr Karp the proposed wedge excision and the alternative procedure of a mechanical heart as a stop-gap to a transplant about a week before the April 4 operation. He said he next talked with Mr Karp the evening of April 2. The consent form was prepared on April 3 and although there is a dispute as to *when* it was signed, there is no question it was signed by Mr Karp. Thus it was against the backdrop of at least two conversations with Dr Cooley, at which Mrs Karp was not present, that Mr Karp was presented and signed the consent document. The consent form is consistent with Dr Cooley's testimony of what he told Mr Karp. Although not necessarily conclusive, what Haskell Karp consented to and was told is best evidenced by this document. It is of considerable import that each step of the three-stage operation, objected to due to an alleged lack of informed consent, was specifically set out in the consent document signed by the patient. . . .

Appellants have not introduced evidence required by Texas law to show a lack of Karp's informed consent or of breach of Dr Cooley's duty to adequately apprise Karp of the nature and risks of the operation that warrant . . . submission of this issue to the jury.

. . .

To meet the proper standard of medical care, the physician must possess a reasonable degree of skill and exercise this skill with ordinary care and diligence. A specialist like Dr Cooley is bound to exercise the degree of skill and knowledge that is ordinarily possessed by similar specialists. As with the doctrine of informed consent, supra, plaintiffs are obligated under Texas law to produce expert medical testimony to establish a medical standard of conduct, deviation from that standard and proximate cause. Appellants again assert Dr Cooley testified to the established standard and that he did not meet it. The apparent theory is that Dr Cooley was negligent in proceeding with the wedge resection when he said it could not be beneficial. This language, however, cannot be considered alone as a standard, even if it were construed to be one; rather, it must be read in the context of his total testimony, which in no wise establishes negligence. Appellants also failed to raise a fact issue on the proximate cause question. . . . Since the expert testimony failed to evidence that there were negligent acts or omissions by defendants or that any of their acts or omissions were a proximate cause of Mr Karp's death, a directed verdict for both defendants was proper.

. . .

Appellants contend that the trial court erred in directing a verdict on the issue of experimentation. They acknowledge that no Texas case has expressly dealt with a cause of action based on experimentation, but assert that our court's decision in *Bender v Dingwerth* suggests that the decision as to what is actionable experimentation should be left to a jury. We do not agree.

A Texas court bound in traditional malpractice actions to expert medical testimony to determine how a reasonably careful and prudent physician would have acted under the same or similar circumstances would not likely vary that evidentiary requirement for an experimentation charge. This conclusion is also suggested by the few reported cases where experimentation has been recognised as a separate basis of liability. The record contains no evidence that Mr Karp's treatment was other than therapeutic and we agree that in this context an action for experimentation must be measured by traditional malpractice evidentiary standards. Whether there was informed consent is necessarily linked to the charge of experimentation, and Mr Karp's consent was expressly to all three stages of the operation actually performed—each an alternative in the event of a preceding failure. As previously discussed, appellants have not shown an absence of Mr Karp's informed consent. Causation and proximate cause are also requisite to an actionable claim of experimentation. Even if Dr DeBakey's testimony, as discussed subsequently, were admitted and did establish a standard and a departure from that standard in using this prosthetic device, substantial evidence . . . on causation and proximate cause simply is not reflected in the record. That alone would warrant the directed verdict on this issue.

. . .

We cannot conclude that the trial court's decision to exclude Dr DeBakey's testimony was clearly erroneous. His testimony would have shown at most that, in his opinion, *the* pump tested under his supervision was not ready for use in humans and that he would not have recommended its use. He may have demonstrated that the animals tested with a prosthetic device at Baylor died of renal failure, but he refused to state that the prosthetic heart used in those experiments was the reasonable medical probable cause of the renal failure. He repeatedly declined to give an opinion regarding *the* pump used in Mr Karp stating only that the Karp pump was similar to the ones developed under his supervision. He declined to answer the only hypothetical question propounded, even though he had examined at the court's request Karp's medical records, since he had not personally examined Mr Karp. While it is conceivable that relevance *might* have been established between Dr DeBakey's experiments and conclusions regarding his mechanical heart and the Karp device and its use, the record does not supply the link. Further, because of the absence of evidence on proximate cause on the informed consent and experimentation issues, Dr DeBakey's testimony, even if admitted, would not change the requirement . . . to direct a verdict for defendants. We therefore do not disturb the trial court's determination.

As you can see, this case also points us to another aspect of liability in negligence which warrants analysis in the context of innovative therapy. What must the doctor disclose to the patient so as to comply with his legal duty and thereby obtain a valid consent?

In the Canadian case of *Zimmer v Ringrose* (1981) 124 DLR (3d) 215 (Alberta Court of Appeal), Prowse JA appears to draw a distinction between the information which must be disclosed on the one hand if the case is one of research and on the other, if it is a case of innovative therapy. The plaintiff underwent an ineffective silver nitrate sterilisation operation. The defendant did not indicate to her that the procedure was not generally accepted in the medical community. The plaintiff subsequently became pregnant and underwent an abortion. The plaintiff sued the defendant, *inter alia*, in negligence for damages to compensate her for her injuries.

Prowse JA: I would not impose upon the appellant the duty of disclosure owed by a medical researcher to the subject of his experiment. The scope of this duty was described by Hall JA in *Halushka v University of Saskatchewan et al.* (1965) 53 DLR (2d) 436 at 443–4, 52 WWR 608 at 616:

> . . . the duty imposed upon those engaged in medical research . . . to those who offer themselves as subjects for experimentation . . . is at least as great as, if not greater than, the duty owed by the ordinary physician or surgeon to his patient. . . . The subject of medical experimentation is entitled to a full and frank disclosure of all the facts, probabilities and opinions which a reasonable man might be expected to consider before giving his consent.

In the case of a truly 'experimental' procedure, like the one conducted in *Halushka v University of Saskatchewan*, no therapeutic benefit is intended to accrue to the participant. The subject is simply part of a scientific investigation designed to enhance human knowledge. By contrast, the sterilisation procedure performed by the appellant in this case was directed towards achieving a therapeutic end. By means of a successful sterilisation, the respondent could avoid the occurrence of an unwanted pregnancy and the adverse health problems associated with it. In my opinion, the silver nitrate method was experimental only in the sense that it represented an innovation in sterilisation techniques which were relatively untried. According to the testimony of the respondent's expert witness, the procedure itself could not be dismissed out of hand as being medically untenable. Indeed, his primary criticism of the method appears to have been the absence of adequate clinical evaluation. To hold that every new development in medical methodology was 'experimental' in the sense outlined in *Halushka v University of Saskatchewan* would be to discourage advances in the field of medicine. In view of these considerations, the application of the standard of disclosure stated in the *Halushka* case would be inappropriate in this instance.

In the case at bar, the medical procedure performed was one to which the respondent had consented. Mrs Zimmer understood the nature of the silver nitrate technique and agreed to undergo that method of sterilisation. Consequently, the appellant is not liable for battery. However, the evidence does raise the question of negligence.

At trial, Macdonald, J found that there was no comparison given by the appellant between his method and other methods of effecting sterilisation. As a result, the respondent had no opportunity to measure the risks involved in the silver nitrate method against those involved in other forms of sterilisation. Furthermore, the appellant failed to apprise Mrs Zimmer of the fact that the silver nitrate technique had not been approved by the medical profession. A reasonable practitioner would have made such a disclosure for he would have realised that this information would likely influence his patient's decision whether to undergo the procedure. In view of his failure to satisfy this duty of care, I must conclude that the appellant's conduct was indeed negligent.

It should be emphasised that the problem here was not that the doctor was utilising an innovative technique but rather that he breached the duty of care imposed upon him by the doctor-patient relationship. A physician is entitled to decide that the situation dictates the adoption of an innovative course of treatment. As long as he discharges his duty of disclosure, and is not otherwise in breach of his duties of skill and care, eg, has not negligently adopted the procedure given the circumstances, the doctor will not be held liable for implementing such a course of treatment.

What distinction in the duty to disclose can you identify?

There is no English case which has yet specifically addressed this issue. Were it to do so, of course, unlike the Canadian case it would not have the decision in *Reibl v Hughes* as a background. It might be expected, therefore, that a court would begin with the House of Lords decision in *Sidaway*. There is one case, however, which may be instructive—*R v Mental Health Commission, ex p W* (1988) Times, 27 May (Divisional Court). As it happens, *Sidaway* did not serve as the basis for the court's analysis. This may be explicable, however, on the ground that the court is considering a statutory provision which seems to contemplate an action in battery in the case of non-compliance with the Act. The following extract is taken from the Lexis transcript.

Stuart-Smith LJ: The applicant is a young man of 27. Unhappily he is a compulsive paedophile. This had led him into trouble with the courts, such that over the past ten years or so he has been convicted of 16 offences of indecency or indecent assault on young boys under the age of 16. On three occasions he has served custodial sentences. He was released from a two year sentence on 19th September 1986. His evidence is that while in prison he had determined to try and change his ways; but he realised that he needed medical help in doing so. Within days of his release he consulted Dr Silverman, who is a consultant psychiatrist at Ealing Hospital and has had considerable experience in dealing with sexual deviation and sex offenders. Dr Silverman prescribed treatment by means of Cyproterone acetate which is an antiandrogen. Despite increasing doses the drug was not successful in suppressing the applicant's sexual urges.

. . . The applicant was afraid that he might re-offend again and also afraid about the high dosage he was receiving. He was therefore anxious to see if Dr Silverman could prescribe some more effective drug. Dr Silverman made enquiries both from a distinguished endocrinologist and ICI, the manufacturers of a drug, Goserelin, which they manufactured under the trade name Zoladex.

Goserelin is manufactured for the treatment of cancer of the prostate, but it operates by reducing the testosterone to castrate levels, which apparently allows a tumour to regress. As a result of his enquiries Dr Silverman concluded that Goserelin might be a suitable and safer treatment for the applicant. He explained to the applicant how it worked and gave him the ICI data sheet. The applicant was enthusiastic to receive it.

The treatment consists of a monthly subcutaneous injection of an implant into the abdomen. The implant is a small solid cylindrical depot 1 cm long and 1 mm in diameter. The cylinder is composed of polymer and degrades over the ensuing month, gradually releasing the drug. The applicant received the first injection on 8th July 1987. Within a short time the applicant found that he was no longer having sexual urges and was very pleased with the result. A second injection was given on about 8th August.

Meanwhile Dr Silverman had contacted the Mental Health Act Commissioners and told them that he was treating the applicant with Goserelin and that the applicant suffered from mental disorder within the meaning of the Mental Health Act 1983. He was unsure if the treatment came within the purview of section 57 of the Mental Health Act 1983.

On 18th August three Commissioners visited Ealing Hospital and interviewed the applicant. It is clear that the Commissioners concluded that the treatment was governed by section 57 of the Mental Health Act 1983 and the applicant was capable of understanding the nature, purpose and likely effects of it and had consented to it. . . .

A further injection was given on 8th September 1987, but it was made clear by the Commission that no further treatment could be given . . . The applicant consulted his solicitors who by letter of 30th September 1987 protested that the treatment did not fall within section 57 of the Mental Health Act 1983 and that therefore the Commission had no jurisdiction in the matter.
. . .

Section 57(2)(a) of the Mental Health Act 1983 provides: 'a registered medical practitioner appointed for the purposes of this Part of this Act by the Secretary of State (not being the responsible medical officer) and two other persons appointed for the purposes of this paragraph by the Secretary of State (not being registered medical practitioners) have certified in writing that the patient is capable of understanding the nature, purpose and likely effects of the treatment in question and has consented to it'.

A number of points should be made. . . . The subsection is concerned both with capacity and consent, and the Commissioners have to be satisfied on both heads. . . . [T]he words are 'capable of understanding' and not 'understands'. Thus the question is capacity and not actual understanding. . . . [I]t is capacity to understand the likely effects of the treatment and not possible side effects, however remote.

But there is a dispute between the parties as to the concept of consent and the proper test to be applied. [Counsel for the applicant] submits that this part of the Mental Health Act 1983 was passed to deal with the difficult problem when a mental patient does not have the capacity to understand the nature and likely effects of treatment, which in some cases may be irreversible, and therefore may not be able to consent as a matter of law, so that such treatment, if given, would amount to an assault. He therefore submits that the provisions of Section 57(2)(a) of the Mental Health Act 1983 are designed to meet this problem and that accordingly the question of consent should be approached in the same way that the Court considers this problem when deciding if a normal patient has consented to medical treatment. The question therefore is whether, as a matter of fact, the patient has consented or agreed to the treatment. An apparent consent will not be a true consent if it has been obtained by fraud, misrepresentation, duress or fundamental mistake; but that is the extent of the enquiry.

In support of this proposition [counsel for the applicant] relies upon *Chatterton v Gerson* [1981] QB 432, [1981] 1 All ER 257, at 442 of the former report where Bristow J said: 'In my judgment what the court has to do in each case is to look at all the circumstances and say "Was there a real consent?" I think justice requires that in order to vitiate the reality of consent there must be a greater failure of communication between doctor and patient than that involved in a breach of duty if the claim is based on negligence. When the claim is based on negligence the plaintiff must prove not only the breach of duty to inform, but that had the duty not been broken she would not have chosen to have the operation. Where the claim is based on trespass to the person, once it is shown that the consent is unreal, then what the plaintiff would have decided if she had been given the information which would have prevented vitiation of the reality of her consent is irrelevant. In my judgment once the patient is informed in broad terms of the nature of the procedure which is intended, and gives her consent, that consent is real, and the cause of the action on which to base a claim for failure to go into risks and implications is negligence, not trespass. Of course if information is withheld in bad faith, the consent will be vitiated by fraud'.

[Counsel for the Commission], on the other hand, submits that this test is not appropriate in a public law setting; I confess I do not follow this distinction. He submits that whether or not a patient consents is a matter for the subjective judgment of the Commissioners and they can apply any test which in their discretion they think fit. I cannot accept this. No doubt the consent has to be an informed consent in that he knows the nature and likely effect of the treatment. There can be no doubt that the applicant knew this. So too in this case, where the treatment was not routinely used for control of sexual urges and was not sold for this purpose, it was important that the applicant should realise that the use on him was a novel one and the full implications with use on young men had not been studied, since trials had only been involved with animals and older men.

The Court held that the Regulations made under section 57 of the Mental Health Act 1983 only applied to 'the surgical implantation of hormones for the purposes of reducing male sexual drive' and the synthetic compound 'Goserelin' given to the applicant was neither a 'hormone' nor was it given by 'surgical implantation'. (On these issues see P Fennell, 'Sexual Suppressants and the Mental Health Act' [1988] Crim LR 660.)

Questions

(i) Do you think that in a case which did not involve the Mental Health Act or some such statute, the court would use an analysis based upon battery? Is it not more likely that where there is no intention to carry out research, whether systematic or otherwise, an analysis based upon the tort of negligence (and thus on the case of *Sidaway*) is more likely?

(ii) You will notice that we draw a distinction between research which is *systematic* and, by implication, that which is *unsystematic*. In the case of the latter, though it be called innovative *therapy*, would not a battery action be held to lie if the patient remained uninformed of the innovative nature of the intervention?

Chapter 12

Selective treatment of neonates

Setting the scene

(i) ETHICS

Let us consider from the outset the most well-known English case concerned with the selective treatment of a handicapped neonate which resulted in the neonate's death. The case is *R v (Leonard) Arthur* (1981) Times, 6 November. The issues raised by this case (especially the ethical ones) are discussed by Dr R Gillon in his book, *Philosophical Medical Ethics* (1987) pp 1 and 175–183 (footnotes omitted).

> In November 1981 a respected paediatrician, the late Dr Leonard Arthur, was acquitted of the attempted murder of a newborn infant with Down's syndrome for whom he had prescribed dihydrocodeine and 'nursing care only' after the baby had been rejected by his mother. . . . In the Arthur case it seems to me that the crucial first moral question is indeed a question of scope: Do the same moral obligations that we have to our other patients extend to newborn infants with Down's syndrome? If the answer is yes our moral analysis will travel down the same path as in any moral dilemma concerning our patients—we will have the same sort of moral obligations to that newborn baby as we have to any other temporarily or permanently non-autonomous patient. If, on the other hand, the answer is no we do not have the same moral obligations to that baby as we have to our patients in general—suppose, for example, we have obligations more stringent than we have to a fetus but less stringent than we have to a young child—then our analysis will follow a different path, more like that followed when we consider our moral obligations to fetuses.
>
> **Moral decisions imposed by the nature of things**
> It seems that the scope of our moral obligations may be determined in several ways. Sometimes it is determined by individual and morally optional decisions; thus we can create self imposed moral obligations to some people and not others—for example, I may take on a previously non-existent moral obligation by promising one or more people that I will do something. Sometimes the scope of a moral obligation is determined by the morally optional decisions of a group of people. Such are the special moral obligations taken on by doctors, nurses and lifeboatmen (and possibly clergy?). Sometimes the scope of a moral obligation is determined by the laws or customs of a particular society. One society may require its members to help the sick and poor, another may leave this to individual charity. One society may require children to look after their ageing or sick parents, another may regard this as morally optional. I assume that the special moral obligations that we owe our family, neighbours, community, tribe, group, and nation are of this variable and socially determined kind.
>
> Sometimes, however, the scope of our moral obligations seems not to be optional. Instead these obligations derive from the nature of certain sorts of entity. I take it that there is something about the nature of other people (including our patients) that we recognise to impose on us certain sorts of moral obligations, to require from us a certain sort of moral respect. We recognise, moreover, that we have no moral option

about acknowledging these obligations. I take it that there is something different about the nature of waxworks, statues, or even dead bodies that allows us not to have the same moral obligations to them that we would acknowledge to the people they resemble (and, in the case of the bodies, were). Similarly, there is a morally relevant difference between pheasants and peasants which allows us to shoot one but not the other. Conversely, if there is no such difference then we are morally obliged to eschew such discrimination and be ready to shoot both or neither.

Which properties of things are morally relevant?
Such questions are crucial to discussion of a wide variety of medicomoral issues, including contraception, postcoital contraception, research on embryos, abortion, severe brain damage, persistent vegetative state, brain stem death, and traditional cardiorespiratory death. Characteristics of things that have been plausibly argued to be criteria for moral categorisation include membership of particular species, notably the human species, possession of the capacity to experience pain (sentience), and possession of the capacities of being a person, whatever those might be, but perhaps including the capacity of self awareness as a necessary condition. 'Viability', arbitrary dates of gestation, and passage through the birth canal and its associated physiological changes are, like quickening, implausible criteria on which to base fundamental moral distinctions.

These are complex and contentious issues. Perhaps seeking to avoid becoming embroiled in them, doctors sometimes think that unless they confront a particular medicomoral problem in their practice—for example, abortion—they do not need to bother too much about the moral arguments concerning it. But is it not obvious that any doctor who ever accepts the moral legitimacy of abortion as a bona fide medical practice—and most do—really needs to work out why he can justify abortion but not killing his adult patients? In particular, ought he not to work out what morally relevant characteristics the abortable fetus lacks that are present in his adult patients, lack of which justifies the deliberate medical killing of the fetus when there is deep moral and legal opprobrium for the deliberate medical killing of adult patients? A very similar question applies to any doctor who supports what Dr Arthur did or, more generally, who believes that newly born severely handicapped infants may in some circumstances be killed or actively 'allowed to die'. What morally relevant characteristics are lacking in such infants that are present in adult patients? Alternatively, what morally relevant characteristics are present in such infants that require us to treat them differently from fetuses at various stages of their development?

Handicapped neonates and handicapped adults
One sort of answer to the first question is that there is no morally relevant difference between newborn infants with serious handicaps and adults with similar handicaps and that both groups should be treated similarly. What is morally permissible treatment for handicapped newborn infants is morally permissible for similarly handicapped adults and vice versa, and what is morally impermissible for handicapped adults is morally impermissible for similarly handicapped newborn infants, and vice versa. The first thing to note is that this leaves the abortion question unanswered: if the newly born handicapped infant ought to be treated in the same way as any other patient with an equivalent handicap, how has it changed since it was an abortable handicapped fetus? Secondly, this position rules out medical management of severely diseased or handicapped newborn infants that would be unjustifiable in similarly diseased or handicapped adults or older children. Thus a doctor who held this line and believed that the prescribing of dihydrocodeine and nursing care only would be wrong for an adult or older child with Down's syndrome would also have to reject Dr Arthur's action, as the 'moral prosecution' argued. (To avoid this conclusion it might be argued that in fact Dr Arthur believed in those first few days that the infant had various probably fatal and untreatable cardiac and other abnormalities in addition to Down's syndrome, as the pathologist eventually showed. I know of no reason to make such an assumption, and no evidence was given at the trial to support it.)

Standards of medical care

To avoid the conclusion that management such as Dr Arthur's of an infant with uncomplicated Down's syndrome is morally wrong it might be argued that similar management would be justifiable with an older child or adult with uncomplicated Down's syndrome. How could such a line be sustained when it would allow a doctor, when faced with a patient with uncomplicated Down's syndrome whose parents do not wish it to live, to keep the patient in hospital; withhold any medical care he would normally be given; administer large doses of dihydrocodeine, knowing its depressive effects on respiration and appetite; and feed and hydrate the patient only on demand? Surely that would not be morally acceptable in an adult or older child with uncomplicated Down's syndrome? Why not? Because it would be widely agreed by doctors and society that having Down's syndrome does not in itself justify a reduction in the standards of medical care that patients in general are owed and which are not met by this hypothetical management of 'nursing care only', large doses of dihydrocodeine, and feeding and hydration only on demand.

That is not to argue that if one believes that the newly born infant with Down's syndrome should be treated like any other patient then he or she has to be treated with the most effective available medical treatment in all circumstances. Ex hypothesi the same sort of moral assessment would apply to proposed treatments for the infant as for any other patient. What treatment would the patient choose if he could deliberate about it (proxy respect for autonomy)? How much net benefit over harm can reasonably be expected for the patient (beneficence and non-maleficence)? Here the precise nature of the medical condition, the degree of handicap, the expected effects on the patient of the management proposed, and the probability of achieving for the patient a substantial net benefit over harm are crucial moral issues and will all vary according to the circumstances. Finally, would the proposed treatment be just or fair to the patient and to others, both in the burdens it imposes on all concerned and in the benefits it offers to the patient and any other beneficiaries in comparison with the resources it removes from others (justice)? These, I have suggested, are standard moral questions that should apply to all medical care and use of medical resources, but the important thing is that they would apply no more and no less when considering the newly born infant with Down's syndrome than in any other allocation of lifesaving medical resources, if doctors owe the newly born infant with Down's syndrome the same moral obligations that they owe to all their patients.

Down's syndrome and moral rights

But perhaps they don't. One possible line of argument supporting a distinction between the moral obligations of doctors to patients with Down's syndrome and to patients in general might be that having Down's syndrome gives people fewer moral rights against doctors than they would otherwise have. Expressed in terms of doctors' duties, the claim would be that if a patient has Down's syndrome doctors have less stringent moral obligations towards him or her than they would normally have. But how could such a claim be justified? Without a rationale it is no more convincing than a similar claim about patients with Gilbert's syndrome or those who happen to have blue eyes. Perhaps the justification offered would be that Down's syndrome results in such a low quality of life compared with normal human flourishing that doctors are not morally obliged to treat patients with Down's syndrome? This is an argument that the right to life organisations and many others find particularly objectionable—rightly so.

Its implications are that people with Down's syndrome of any age and development, and any degree of handicap, are morally second class and can be 'allowed to die' when those in the first class would be kept alive. Moreover, it implies that the same sort of moral discrimination is justified against anyone else with a similar quality of life to that of the least impaired person with Down's syndrome. Given the varying degrees of quality of life and the wide range of flourishing that older children and adults with Down's syndrome manifest, the argument that any person with Down's syndrome may be denied lifesaving medical care, let alone that such people may be actively 'allowed to die', is clearly morally unacceptable. But why is it morally unacceptable? The answer is surely that there is something about the nature of older children and adults with Down's syndrome that makes us recognise a moral obligation to treat them as we treat each other. But what is different about them (*a*) compared with newborn infants with Down's syndrome, if we believe that we can treat the latter in lifethreatening ways that we find morally unacceptable in relation to other patients, including older patients with Down's syndrome; and (*b*) compared with embryos and fetuses with Down's syndrome, if we believe that we may justifiably kill (abort) these?

What is a person?
One radical and contentious answer is that fetuses and newly born humans, whether they have Down's syndrome or not, are not people, whereas older children and adults, including those with Down's syndrome, are. According to this line of argument the 'right to life' is a right of people or persons; the moral obligation not to kill others is a duty not to kill other people or persons. What is meant by "a person" and "people" in this context is inadequately worked out and a subject of vigorous philosophical debate. One line of argument is that a necessary condition for being a person, and thus for being owed the moral respect due to persons, including an intrinsic (though prima facie) moral right not to be intentionally killed by others, is awareness of oneself or self consciousness. (This line of argument stems from a discussion about the nature of persons by the physician-philosopher John Locke.) It seems plausible that the morally special attributes that distinguish people from animals and other entities to which we do not accord an intrinsic right to life require a capacity for self consciousness. According to this argument self consciousness is not morally important in itself but is a necessary condition of all the remarkable and distinguishing characteristics that endow people with special moral importance and thus special moral rights. This argument supposes that all newborn infants, like all fetuses, are not self conscious and therefore cannot be people and therefore do not have an intrinsic moral right to life. Clearly part of the argument rests on empirical claims and requires appropriate empirical support, but there seems little doubt that newly fertilised ova are not self conscious and equally little doubt that adults are, therefore somewhere along the developmental line, perhaps gradually rather than suddenly, self consciousness must develop.

The right to life and newborn infants
Of course, even if this argument were accepted it does not imply that fetuses and babies should not in most cases be carefully protected. There are several justifications for such protection other than an intrinsic right to life. The first is that the development from newly fertilised ovum to self conscious human being is gradual, and there are plausible consequentialist reasons for reflecting such development by according gradually increasing moral protection to the developing embryo, fetus, and newly born infant. Secondly, in most cases mothers, fathers, families, and societies put enormous value on newly born babies—much greater value than, in our society, they typically put on the embryo and fetus—and thus there are important consequentialist reasons for reflecting this distinction in our social institutions. Thirdly, in most cases great personal and social anguish and disruption would result if newly born babies were not given very careful protection, especially by doctors.

None the less, if it is true that newly born infants have not yet developed into people and therefore do not yet have the full moral rights of people, including the 'right to life,' then it becomes justifiable for societies to determine that in certain circumstances the protection that should normally be extended to newly born infants may be withdrawn. In cases where an intrinsic right to life did not exist to function as a moral 'trump card' such circumstances would be determined by considerations of overall harm and benefit, which took into account both the moral repugnance normally evinced at infanticide and also the harm to families and society of keeping alive unwanted severely handicapped infants. Given the great social disagreement over these issues it would, of course, be intolerable—even in merely consequentialist terms—to impose any such withdrawal of protection or 'allowing to die.' If the parents of severely handicapped newborn infants want them to be medically sustained then their wishes should if possible be respected—but if, having considered the matter, the parents want the infant to be painlessly 'allowed to die' then according to this argument their wishes too can legitimately be respected.

The question of acts and omissions

Many doctors would support active 'allowing to die' of the sort carried out by Dr Arthur but would reject any active killing of such infants. I believe I have shown that it is difficult to justify even active 'allowing to die' unless it is also agreed that severely handicapped newborn infants are not owed the same moral duties, especially the duty to preserve their lives, that doctors owe to their patients in general. I have also argued previously, however, against the customary medical assumption that the distinction between acts and omissions can justify a moral distinction between withdrawal of medical treatment and active killing. A moral question has to be answered first—namely, which medical acts and omissions to act are morally justifiable and which are not? Knowingly causing conditions in which an infant is likely to die when it is otherwise unlikely to do so, and where there is no intention of benefiting the infant by doing so, is normally regarded as morally culpable, as murder or manslaughter. The father who killed baby Brown, also an infant with Down's syndrome, was jailed for manslaughter. What are the morally important differences between what he did and what Dr Arthur did? There is no reason to suppose that the verdict on baby Brown's father would have been ameliorated had his baby died because the father gave dihydrocodeine, fed and hydrated it only on demand, and then did not obtain medical care when it became ill. Such treatment could only be justified if (*a*) the newborn infant, like the fetus, does not have an intrinsic right to life and (*b*) there is sufficient justification in terms of overall benefit over harm (in this context restriction of such treatments to doctors and parents acting together may help to minimise the harm).

A radical challenge

Here, then, is a radical challenge to those who would support Dr Arthur's action. If they believe that they owe the same duty to respect the lives of newborn infants with Down's syndrome as they owe to all their other patients how do they justify their support of actions that they would almost certainly reject in older patients with Down's syndrome? (And if they also defend abortion—for example, of fetuses with Down's syndrome—how do they justify their different attitudes to the fetus and to the newborn infant?) If, on the other hand, they believe that they do not owe the same duty to newborn infants with Down's syndrome that they owe to their other patients, how do they justify this position without falling into the trap of denying all patients with Down's syndrome the moral protection they afford to their patients in general? I believe that the issue turns on the question of personhood and that it is because the newly born infant is not a person that it is justifiable in cases of severe handicap to 'allow it to die' in the way Dr Arthur allowed baby Pearson to die. But while there may be some social benefits in distinguishing between actively 'allowing to die' and painlessly killing such infants, there is, I believe, no other moral difference, and doctors who accept such 'allowing to die' of severely handicapped newborn infants should not deceive themselves into believing that there is such a difference. Those who do not accept these radical claims yet wish to support action like Dr Arthur's need to cudgel their brains for a rationale, one that is consistent with their attitudes to abortion, the 'morning after pill,' embryo research, and the treatment of newborn infants with spina bifida or anencephaly, of patients with severe dementia, of patients in persistent vegetative state, and of those with 'brain stem death.' Such are the widespread ramifications of questions about the scope of our moral obligations to human beings at different stages of their lives.

(ii)   THE INVOLVEMENT OF THE LAW

Some have said that there is 'a strong argument for keeping the law out of these cases . . . when the good order of society in general is not at stake, the criminal law should stay its hand'. (Glanville Williams, *Textbook of Criminal Law* (2nd ed) 1983, at p 285.)

Leaving aside the question of whether the life or death of a young child is of little concern to 'the good order of society', how can the law, whether criminal or civil, be kept out? It is already involved whenever a doctor undertakes the care of a patient and whenever a parent has a child. The legal questions arising are as follows. First, in relation to the doctors:

1. Under what circumstances, if any, may a doctor be guilty of murder or manslaughter (criminal law)?

2. Under what circumstances, if any, may the doctor be liable in the torts of negligence or battery (civil law)? Secondly, in relation to the parents:

1. Under what circumstances, if any, may the parents be guilty of murder or manslaughter or be accomplices to such an offence by another. Similarly may the parents be guilty of the offence of 'wilful neglect' under s 1 of the Children and Young Persons Act 1933 (criminal law)?

2. Under what circumstances, if any, may a parent be judged to be failing in his parental obligations owed to his child or be otherwise liable in tort (civil law)?

(iii) THE CASES

We shall concentrate here on the two English authorities and the subsequent Canadian case. The numerous cases decided in the United States, though instructive, rely heavily upon constitutional theory and, therefore, are of limited assistance in understanding the development of English law although where relevant we will discuss them.

R v Arthur

(6 Nov 1981), (Leicester Crown Court, Farquharson J and a jury; the following is taken from a transcript of the judge's summing up)

Farquharson J: In this case the act, or acts if you like, upon which the prosecution rely to say this was an attempt to kill on the part of Dr Arthur is the preparation of those two documents, that is to say, the case notes and the treatment chart. It was his endorsement on the case notes to the effect that the child should receive nursing care only, coupled with the prescription he wrote into the treatment chart, that the child should have 5 milligrammes of dihydrocodeine not less than every four hours and at the discretion of the nurse in charge of the child; that is to say, it was under the general heading 'as required'. The prosecution contend before you that those acts were set into train—the course of events—which could only have resulted in the child's death and therefore, they say, that that must have amounted—the preparation and endorsement of those treatment charts and case notes—to an attempt to kill. Whether it does or not is one of the important and vital questions that you have got to decide. As I have already indicated to you, the prosecution must prove not only an act which you as a jury decide is an attempt to cause the death of John Pearson, but an act accompanied by an intent that the child should die at the time the act was carried out.

. . .

The defence, of course, contend that this does not amount to an act that could properly be described as an attempt. They point out the act was revocable: it could have been stopped, halted and reversed because at any time the mother could have changed the opinion which in the agony of giving birth she had already expressed. The fact that it can be recalled, or revoked, members of the jury,—that is to say, the treatment prescribed by Dr Arthur—does not in itself mean that it could not be an attempt, but it is something that you should take very carefully into account.

. . . the defence do not rest their case there. They go further into what I might describe as the wider field with which we are concerned here and say, What is more, Dr Arthur was not committing an act, a positive act, at all; he was simply prescribing a treatment which involved the creation of a set of circumstances whereby the child would peacefully die, and that there is all the difference in the world between the one and the other. . . . The prosecution contend that the nurses were acting as the doctors' agents, in carrying out that task . . .

. . . However serious the case may be; however much the disadvantage of a mongol or, indeed, any other handicapped child, no doctor has the right to kill it. There is no special law in this country that places doctors in a separate category and gives them extra protection over the rest of us. It is undoubtedly the case that doctors are, of course, the only profession who have to deal with these terrible problems. But notwithstanding that they are given no special power, members of the jury, to commit an act which causes death, which is another way of saying killing. Neither in law is there any special power, facility or licence to kill children who are handicapped or seriously disadvantaged in an irreversible way. There is no special law of that kind at all. May I hasten to add—and in the same breath—that none of the eminent practitioners who have come before this court has sought to suggest that there is or should be. They have recognised the limitations which the law has placed upon their profession and, indeed, it is the same as the limitation placed upon everybody else.

But that does not mean that any profession can set out a code of ethics and say that the law must accept it and take notice of it. It may be that in any particular feature the ethic is wrong.

. . .

If a child is born with a serious handicap—the instance we have been given is duodenal atresia where a mongol has an ill-formed intestine whereby that child will die of the ailment if he is not operated on—a surgeon may say: as this child is a mongol, handicapped in the way I have already been discussing with you, I do not propose to operate; I shall allow (and you have heard this expression several times) nature to take its course.

No one could say that that surgeon was committing an act of murder by declining to take a course which would save the child.

Equally, if a child not otherwise going to die, who is severely handicapped, is given a drug in such an excessive amount by the doctor that the drug itself will cause his death and the doctor does that intentionally it would be open to the jury to say: yes, he was killing, he was murdering that child.

It is very easy, is not it, to draw the line between those two examples. They are opposite ends of the spectrum.

It is very much more difficult, on the other hand, to say where the line should be drawn in relation to this case and you have got to draw it.

Another instance was given by counsel—not in the case of a child—where perhaps somebody is suffering from the agonies of terminal cancer and the doctor is obliged to give increasing dosages of a pain killer (an analgesic) to relieve the pain. There comes such a point that the amounts of those doses are such that in themselves they will kill off the patient, but he is driven to it on medical grounds.

There again you will undoubtedly say that that could never be murder. That was a proper practice of medicine.

The example also given by [counsel for Dr Arthur] is that where a child gets pneumonia and, as in this case, no treatment is given it in the way of antibiotics. Dealing, as we still are, with children with irreversible handicaps who their mothers have rejected, if the doctor said: 'I am not going to give it antibiotics', and by a merciful dispensation of providence he dies, once again it would be very unlikely, I would suggest, that you (or any other jury) would say that that doctor was committing murder.

Both those two further examples that I have just cited to you may be put at opposite ends of the same spectrum. Easy to recognise; easy to categorise.

But what is the position here? Was what Dr Arthur did in setting out that course of management, prescribing that drug, in the way of a holding operation, in the nature of setting conditions where the child could, if it happened, if it contracted pneumonia, die peacefully? Or if it revealed any other organic defect die peacefully? Or was it a positive act on the part of Dr Arthur which was likely to kill the child and represented an attempt, within the definition I have given you, accompanied by an intent on his part that it should as a result of the treatment that he prescribed die?

If the prosecution have proved the latter, members of the jury, and you draw the line, so to speak, at that point, well, then he would be guilty of murder or attempted murder as the position now is.

If, on the other hand, they have not been able to do so and what Dr Arthur here prescribed and arranged, if you like, comes into that first category of a management that represents a holding operation but not in the nature of a positive act, why then he would be not guilty.

. . . [I]t appears there was a discussion as to whether the mother should or should not keep the child. But the result of that discussion is shown in the middle of that page 3, 'Parents do not wish the baby to survive. Nursing care only.' . . . [T]he houseman who was the specialist in gynaecology although he had done his paediatric work previously, said that: 'Nursing care only involves dealing with the bodily functions; the child must be kept warm, fed and cherished. I mean fed with an ordinary feed. One has to consider all the options. If pneumonia developed I would understand this—that is nursing care only—to mean that the baby should not be treated but kept comfortable, warm and cherished.'

. . . By the time the nurses were in fact looking after the child it had plainly developed pneumonia, and by that stage, whichever side is right about the legal effect of what happened, by that stage at all events it was accepted that the child had reached a stage where, if infection overcame it, it was going to be left to die . . .

In his statement to the police Dr Arthur said 'If a non-treatment course of conduct with mongol children is adopted, it is in accordance with my own practice, which is accepted by modern paediatric thought. If non-treatment is elected it means it would be wrong to treat infection with antibiotics. The withholding of food is accepted by many doctors as part of non-treatment. Some lay people feel that this is distasteful. Sometimes we do feed babies, even if non-treatment is decided upon, if the parents or nurses wish it. But our major aim is to relieve distress in the child. The baby will take water or water and sugar. If it is fed milk it may be that it will inhale it and suffer a distressing condition. Paediatricians may use any of these foods or water. It really contributes little to the ultimate outcome. When non-treatment is decided upon the paediatrician may hope that parents will change their mind after the immediate shock of the birth. If they do not do so the course is continued in the hope that the baby will die peacefully from infection.'

As a matter of legal analysis, the summing-up of Farquharson J raises the following difficulties:

1. the distinction drawn between acts and omissions for the purposes of homicide and the assumption that liability only attaches to the former.
2. another way of looking at the above is to ask 'what should be the proper understanding of the doctor's duty to his patient?'—in particular, the notion

that he may 'let nature take its course', or engage in a 'holding operation' may be difficult to sustain without further clarification.

3. to what extent evidence of practice of some (or even all) members of the medical profession assists in determining what is a doctor's legal duty in this context.

4. what significance, if any, should be attached to the fact that the parents did not wish the child to survive.

5. following on from 4 above, how can Farquharson J's direction to the jury be reconciled with the earlier wardship case of *Re B (a Minor)*, decided by the Court of Appeal, in which the court unanimously authorised that surgery be carried out to relieve an otherwise fatal obstruction in the stomach of a baby suffering from Down's Syndrome?

We should now turn to consider the Court of Appeal's decision in *re B*.

Re B (a Minor)
[1981] 1 WLR 1421 (Court of Appeal)

Templeman LJ: This is a very poignantly sad case. Although we sit in public, for reasons which I think will be obvious to everybody in court, and if not will be obvious in the course of this judgment, it would be lamentable if the names of the parents of the child concerned were revealed in any way to the general public. The press and people who frequent these courts are usually very helpful in referring to names by initials, and this is a case where nothing ought to be leaked out to identify those concerned with the case.

It concerns a little girl who was born on July 28, 1981. She was born suffering from Down's syndrome, which means that she will be a mongol. She was also born with an intestinal blockage which will be fatal unless it is operated upon. When the parents were informed of the condition of the child they took the view that it would be unkind to this child to operate upon her, and that the best thing to do was for her not to have the operation, in which case she would die within a few days. During those few days she could be kept from pain and suffering by sedation. They took the view that would be the kindest thing in the interests of the child. They so informed the doctors at the hospital, and refused to consent to the operation taking place. It is agreed on all hands that the parents came to that decision with great sorrow. It was a firm decision: they genuinely believed that it was in the best interests of this child. At the same time, it is of course impossible for parents in the unfortunate position of these parents to be certain that their present view should prevail. The shock to caring parents finding that they have given birth to a child who is a mongol is very great indeed, and therefore while great weight ought to be given to the views of the parents they are not views which necessarily must prevail.

What happened then was that the doctors being informed that the parents would not consent to the operation contacted the local authority who very properly made the child a ward of court and asked the judge to give care and control to the local authority and to authorise them to direct that the operation be carried out, and the judge did so direct. But when the child was moved from the hospital where it was born to another hospital for the purposes of the operation a difference of medical opinion developed. The surgeon who was to perform the operation declined to do so when he was informed that the parents objected. In a statement he said that when the child was referred to him for the operation he decided he wished to speak to the parents of the child personally and he spoke to them on the telephone and they stated that in view of the fact that the child was mongoloid they did not wish to have the operation performed. He further stated:

> I decided therefore to respect the wishes of the parents and not to perform the operation, a decision which would, I believe (after about 20 years in the medical profession), be taken by the great majority of surgeons faced with a similar situation.

Therefore the local authority came back to the judge. The parents were served in due course and appeared and made their submissions to the judge, and in addition inquiries were made and it was discovered that the surgeon in the hospital where the child was born and another surgeon in a neighbouring hospital were prepared and advised that the operation should be carried out. So there is a difference of medical opinion.

This morning the judge was asked to decide whether to continue his order that the operation should be performed or whether to revoke that order, and the position now is stark. The evidence, as I have said, is that if this little girl does not have this operation she will die within a matter of days. If she has the operation there is a possibility that she will suffer heart trouble as a result and that she may die within two or three months. But if she has the operation and it is successful, she has Down's syndrome, she is mongoloid, and the present evidence is that her life expectancy is short, about 20 to 30 years.

The parents say that no one can tell what will be the life of a mongoloid child who survives during that 20 or 30 years, but one thing is certain. She will be very handicapped mentally and physically and no one can expect that she will have anything like a normal existence. They make that point not because of the difficulties which will be occasioned to them but in the child's interest. This is not a case in which the court is concerned with whether arrangements could or could not be made for the care of this child, if she lives, during the next 20 or 30 years; the local authority is confident that the parents having for good reason decided that it is in the child's best interests that the operation should not be performed, nevertheless good adoption arrangements could be made and that in so far as any mongol child can be provided with a happy life then such a happy life can be provided.

The question which this court has to determine is whether it is in the interests of this child to be allowed to die within the next week or to have the operation in which case if she lives she will be a mongoloid child, but no one can say to what extent her mental or physical defects will be apparent. No one can say whether she will suffer or whether she will be happy in part. On the one hand the probability is that she will not be a cabbage as it is called when people's faculties are entirely destroyed. On the other hand it is certain that she will be very severely mentally and physically handicapped.

On behalf of the parents, Mr Gray has submitted very movingly, if I may say so, that this is a case where nature has made its own arrangements to terminate a life which would not be fruitful and nature should not be interfered with. He has also submitted that in this kind of decision the views of responsible and caring parents, as these are, should be respected, and that their decision that it is better for the child to be allowed to die should be respected. Fortunately or unfortunately, in this particular case the decision no longer lies with the parents or with the doctors, but lies with the court. It is a decision which of course must be made in the light of the evidence and views expressed by the parents and the doctors, but at the end of the day it devolves on this court in this particular instance to decide whether the life of this child is demonstrably going to be so awful that in effect the child must be condemned to die, or whether the life of this child is still so imponderable that it would be wrong for her to be condemned to die. There may be cases, I know not, of severe proved damage where the future is so certain and where the life of the child is so bound to be full of pain and suffering that the court might be driven to a different conclusion, but in the present case the choice which lies before the court is this: whether to allow an operation to take place which may result in the child living for 20 or 30 years as a mongoloid or whether (and I think this must be brutally the result) to terminate the life of a mongoloid child because she also has an intestinal complaint. Faced with that choice I have no doubt that it is the duty of this court to decide that the child must live. The judge was much affected by the reasons given by the parents and came to the conclusion that their wishes ought to be respected. In my judgment he erred in that the duty of the court is to decide whether it is in the interests of the child that an operation should take place. The evidence in this case only goes to show that if the operation takes place and is successful then the child may live the normal span of a mongoloid child with the handicaps and defects and life of a mongol child, and it is not for this court to say that life of that description ought to be extinguished.

Accordingly the appeal must be allowed and the local authority must be authorised themselves to authorise and direct the operation to be carried out on the little girl.

Dunn LJ: I agree, and as we are differing from the view expressed by the judge I would say a few words of my own. I have great sympathy for the parents in the agonising decision to which they came. As they put it themselves, 'God or nature has given the child a way out.' But the child now being a ward of court, although due weight must be given to the decision of the parents which everybody accepts was an entirely responsible one, doing what they considered was the best, the fact of the matter is that this court now has to make the decision. It cannot hide behind the decision of the parents or the decision of the doctors; and in making the decision this court's first and paramount consideration is the welfare of this unhappy little baby.

One of the difficulties in the case is that there is no prognosis as to the child's future, except that as a mongol her expectation of life is confined to 20 to 30 years. We were told that no reliable prognosis can be made until probably she is about two years old. That in itself leads me to the route by which the court should make its decision, because there is no evidence that this child's short life is likely to be an intolerable one. There is no evidence at all as to the quality of life which the child may expect. As Mr Turcan on behalf of the Official Solicitor said, the child should be put into the same position as any other mongol child and must be given the chance to live an existence. I accept that way of putting it.

I agree with Templeman LJ that the court must step in to preserve this mongol baby's life.

As a matter of legal analysis, the judgments raise the following difficulties:

1. The nature of the doctor's responsibility to the child patient. What is the extent of his duty? What are the criteria of a life 'demonstrably going to be so awful'? And, who sets these criteria and who adjudicates upon them in a particular case? In answering such questions can it be assumed that the law permits those caring for babies to allow some to die through a policy of benign neglect?

2. What is the responsibility of the parents? Is it to act in 'the best interests of the child'? If so, how are 'best interests' determined, and by whom?

3. What is the power of the court in such cases? What significance should be attached by the court to the wishes of the parents?

4. Generally, can it ever legally be permissible to withhold treatment that would ordinarily be given to any other patient solely because this patient is mentally handicapped?

Consider now the following Canadian decision which relies upon the *re B* case. Keep in mind these questions of legal analysis as you do.

Re Superintendent of Family and Child Service and Dawson
(1983) 145 DLR (3d) 610 (British Columbia, Supreme Court).

McKenzie J: The subject of these proceedings is a severely retarded boy approaching seven years, who shortly after birth suffered profound brain damage through meningitis which inflamed the lining of his brain and left him with no control over his faculties, limbs or bodily functions. At the age of five months life-support surgery was performed by implanting a shunt which is a plastic tube which drains excess cerebrospinal fluid from the head to another body cavity from which it is expelled or absorbed.

As perceived by his parents the boy is legally blind, with atrophied optic nerves, partly deaf, incontinent, cannot hold a spoon to feed himself, cannot stand, walk, talk, or hold objects. They say that he has no method of communicating with his environment and think he is in pain. The sounds he makes are too soft to be heard from any distance. He is subject to seizures despite anticonvulsant medication. He is restrained by splints which are bandages on his arms to keep his elbows straight so that he cannot chew on his hands and roughly handle his face. Staff carry him from bed to wheelchair, which has a moulded 'insert' to ensure he is held securely and he is belted in with a hip belt.

This description applies to his condition as it existed when he was a patient in Sunnyhill Hospital before the shunt stopped operating. About six weeks ago a blockage in the shunt was detected and the parents gave their consent to remedial surgery but, after a day's reflection, withdrew their consent on the ground that the boy should be allowed to die with dignity rather than continue to endure a life of suffering. They continued to maintain that position . . .

Having cited and adopted the reasoning of Templeman LJ in *Re B* McKenzie J continues:

I respect and have given anxious consideration to the views of the parents. In so doing I must give some weight to the fact that they were divorced in mid-1980 after extended matrimonial discord. Also I must give weight to my conclusion based on the evidence that they thought Stephen better dead long before the need for the critical decision arose about replacement of the shunt. Despite the evidence of highly qualified professionals, in whom I place great reliance, they are satisfied Stephen will promptly die if treatment is denied. My finding is that it is by no means a certainty that death will soon follow and a real possibility exists that his life will go on indefinitely but in pain and progressive deterioration. I must reject their assertion that they would consent to the operation if they could be assured that he would thereafter be comfortable and free of pain when at the same time they reject the opinions of competent professionals that such will probably be the case. I believe that their minds are firmly made up and closed shut.

I regret having to make such findings. . . .

I cannot accept their view that Stephen would be better off dead. If it is to be decided that 'it is in the best interests of Stephen Dawson that his existence cease', then it must be decided that, for him, non-existence is the better alternative. This would mean regarding the life of a handicapped child as not only less valuable than the life of a normal child, but so much less valuable that it is not worth preserving. I tremble at contemplating the consequences if the lives of disabled persons are dependent upon such judgments.

To refer back to the words of Templeman LJ I cannot in conscience find that this is a case of severe proved damage 'where the future is so certain and where the life of the child is so bound to be full of pain and suffering that the court might be driven to a different conclusion'. I am not satisfied that 'the life of this child is demonstrably going to be so awful that in effect the child must be condemned to die'. Rather I believe that 'the life of this child is still so imponderable that it would be wrong for her to be condemned to die'.

There is not a simple choice here of allowing the child to live or die according to whether the shunt is implanted or not. There looms the awful possibility that without the shunt the child will endure in a state of progressing disability and pain. It is too simplistic to say that the child should be allowed to die in peace.

The *Dawson* case raises the same difficulties as *Re B*, upon which the judge relied even though the case concerned a boy of six and not a neonate.

The legal position

There are three areas of law which are important: the *criminal law*, in particular, homicide and wilful neglect of a child; *tort*, in particular, negligence and battery; and *family law*.

As you would expect, the importance of the issues raised has meant that they have primarily been regarded as matters for the criminal law. Thus, the criminal law has set the agenda and an analysis of it will, for the most part, provide a mode of resolving the issues which arise in tort and family law concerning the respective legal duties of the doctors, parents and others.

Thus, we will concentrate on the law of homicide, making reference where necessary to, for example, family law, particularly as regards the notion of acting in the 'best interests' of the child.

(i) THE ACTS/OMISSIONS SAGA

Traditionally, the criminal law has drawn a distinction between acts and omissions. Criminal liability has ordinarily depended upon there being *an act* done by the defendant. Given the difficulties involved in determining precisely what conduct amounts to an act or an omission, it will come as no surprise that this distinction has bedevilled medical law just as it has created problems elsewhere. Before trying to find a way out of the problem, it is important to take note of what the traditional approach consists of.

(a) Acts

Although positive conduct in the form of an act is required for there to be criminal liability, it does not follow that every positive act by a doctor in caring for a neonate will be unlawful. Some obviously are unlawful; some may not be.

Professor Skegg in his book *Law, Ethics and Medicine*, analyses this issue at pp 128–131 (footnotes omitted).

> The fact that a patient would be severely handicapped if he were to live, or would find life a burden, does not affect the general principle that it is murder to kill a person by doing some positive act, with the intention of hastening death. There were several statements to this effect in Farquharson J's direction to the jury in *R v Arthur*. . . .
>
> As the consent of the patient or others, or the patient's medical condition, will not provide a doctor with a defence if he administers a drug for the purpose of ending the patient's life, it is as well to consider whether the doctor's exemplary motive, medical qualifications, or compliance with medical ethics, would provide him with a defence. . . . However, it is clear that the motive of alleviating suffering will not provide a legal justification for a doctor who intentionally administers what he knows to be a lethal dose of drug. In *R v Arthur* Farquharson J said that it was accepted that the doctor had acted from the highest of motives, but directed the jury that 'however noble his motives were . . . that is irrelevant to the question of your deciding what his intent was'. . . . If a doctor acts with the intention of bringing about the death of a patient, the fact that he was acting to alleviate suffering, or for some other exemplary motive, would not at present provide him with a defence to a charge of murder.
>
> In some circumstances the fact that a person has particular medical qualifications will affect that person's liability for murder or manslaughter. If a patient died in the course of a heart transplant operation, performed by a doctor with appropriate qualifications and experience, the doctor would not normally be liable. But if the operation were performed by a layman it would be very difficult to resist the conclusion that he exposed the patient to an unjustified risk, and that he was grossly negligent in attempting the operation. However, the fact that someone was medically qualified would make no difference if he administered a drug—or took any other action—for the purpose of hastening the death of a patient. In the few cases in which doctors have been prosecuted for murder or attempted murder in consequence

of things done in the course of medical practice, trial judges have stressed that the law does not place doctors in any special position. In *R v Adams* Devlin J said that the law was the same for all: there was not any special defence for medical men. And in *R v Arthur* Farquharson J said there 'is no special law . . . that places doctors in a separate category and gives them extra protection over the rest of us'. They are, he said, 'given no special power . . . to commit an act which causes death'.

Even if a doctor acted in compliance with statements on medical ethics propounded by the British Medical Association, or any other organisation, this would not of itself provide a doctor with a defence if he administered a drug—or did any other act—for the purpose of hastening the death of a patient. In *R v Arthur* Farquharson J commented that it was customary for a profession to agree on rules of conduct for its members but instructed the jury that 'that does not mean that any profession can set out a code of ethics and say that the law must accept it and take notice of it. It may be that in any particular feature the ethic is wrong.' He said that 'whatever a profession may evolve as a system of standards of ethics, cannot stand on its own, and cannot survive if it is in conflict with the law'. It would therefore be open to a jury to find a doctor guilty of murder even though they believed that he acted in accordance with the ethical standards currently accepted by the medical profession.

The conclusion must be that neither the consent of the patient or anyone else, nor the condition of the patient, nor the doctor's exemplary motive, professional qualifications, or compliance with accepted standards of medical ethics, would provide any defence for a doctor who prescribed or administered a drug—or did any other act—for the purpose of hastening the death of the patient.

Some acts, however, are lawful even though they may hasten death. As ever, intention is the key. Devlin J summing up in *R v Bodkin Adams* [1957] CLR 365, said:

But that does not mean that a doctor who is aiding the sick and the dying has to calculate in minutes, or even in hours, and perhaps not in days or weeks, the effect upon a patient's life of the medicines which he administers or else be in peril of a charge of murder. If the first purpose of medicine, the restoration of health, can no longer be achieved there is still much for a doctor to do, and he is entitled to do all that is proper and necessary to relieve pain and suffering, even if the measures he takes may incidentally shorten life. That is not because there is any special defence for medical men; it is not because doctors are put into any category from other citizens for this purpose. The law is the same for all, and what I have said to you rests simply upon this: no act is murder which does not cause death. 'Cause' means nothing philosophical or technical or scientific. It means what you twelve men and women sitting as a jury in the jury box would regard in a common-sense way as the cause. . . . If, for example, because a doctor has done something or has omitted to do something death occurs, it can be scientifically proved—if it could—at eleven o'clock instead of twelve o'clock, or even on Monday instead of Tuesday, no people of common sense would say, 'Oh, the doctor caused her death'. They would say the cause of her death was the illness or the injury, or whatever it was, which brought her into hospital, and the proper medical treatment that is administered and that has an incidental effect of determining the exact moment of death, or may have, is not the cause of death in any sensible use of the term. But it remains the fact, and it remains the law, that no doctor, nor any man, no more in the case of the dying than of the healthy, has the right deliberately to cut the thread of life.

We must be very clear what Devlin J means, because it must be clear that we are on the edge of a discussion about euthanasia, voluntary or otherwise. The mere mention of the word 'euthanasia' is instantly a recipe for confused (and emotive) thinking. Devlin J may be resting his analysis on either of two legal grounds.

1.   No intention

Devlin J may have been saying that although the doctor did an act which 'played some part in' the death of the patient, the doctor should not be liable, unless he intended to bring about the death. Devlin J must have meant that the doctor should not be held to have intended the death because of the theory of 'double effect', if the jury found that his primary intention was to relieve the pain of his patient.

The theory of 'double effect' which Devlin J introduces into English criminal law purports to be a theory about intention. It seems to say that if an act may have two effects and the actor *desires* only one of them, which is considered a *good* effect, then he should be regarded as blameless even though his act also produces a bad effect. The words 'primary' and 'secondary' are used to describe the intention concerning the good and the bad effect.

For the lawyer, this theory is not without difficulties; see, for example, Glanville Williams, *The Sanctity of Life and the Criminal Law*, (1957) at p 286:

> ... When you know that your conduct will have two consequences, one in itself good and one in itself evil, you are compelled as a moral agent to choose between acting and not acting by making a judgment of value, that is to say by deciding whether the good is more to be desired than the evil is to be avoided. If this is what the principle of double effect means, well and good; but if it means that the necessity of making a choice of values can be avoided merely by keeping your mind off one of the consequences, it can only encourage a hypocritical attitude towards moral problems.
>
> What is true of morals is true of the law. There is no legal difference between desiring or intending a consequence as following from your conduct, and persisting in your conduct with a knowledge that the consequence will inevitably follow from it, though not desiring that consequence. When a result is foreseen as certain, it is the same as if it were desired or intended. It would be an undue refinement to distinguish between the two.

Professor Williams must be right on the law when he makes clear that the consequence that is undesired may nevertheless be intended in law (*R v Moloney* [1985] AC 905 and *R v Nedrick* [1986] 3 All ER 1). Thus for the lawyer, if not for the moral philosopher, the judgment that an act is blameless cannot analytically rest on a theory of intention as expressed in the 'double-effect' theory. It must rest, if anywhere, on a judgment that acts (though intended) ought as a matter of moral judgment and public policy to be regarded as attracting no blame because of their social worth. This, of course, raises its own problems; what is the principle which underlies any specific determination that a particular cause of conduct is blameless?

2.   No causation

Devlin J may, in the alternative, have meant to rely on causation: that a doctor's act in such circumstances would not be regarded in law as the cause of the patient's death.

Again, Glanville Williams addresses the issue as follows in his book (*op cit*), at pp 289–290:

> ... While I am reluctant to criticise a legal doctrine that gives a beneficial result, the use of the language of causation seems here to conceal rather than to reveal the valuation that is being made. To take an example, suppose that it were shown that the administration of morphine in regular medical practice caused a patient to die of respiratory failure or pneumonia. Medically speaking, this death would not be caused by the disease: it would be caused by the administration of morphine. There seems to be some difficulty in asserting that for legal purposes the causation is precisely the opposite.

Lord Devlin responded to this observation in a lecture in 1960 later published in *Samples of Law Making*. Having referred to his direction to the jury concerned with double-effect, the judge went on, at p 95 (footnote omitted):

> This direction was not, however, given on the basis that the relief of pain justified an act that would otherwise be murder in law. Before a man can be convicted of murder, it must be proved that his act was the cause of the death. That does not invariably, or even frequently, mean the medical cause of death. Medicine is concerned with the immediate physical cause and the criminal law with the guilty cause. On a death certificate no one would put dangerous driving, for example, as a cause of death; but there is an offence known to the law of causing death by dangerous driving. If a man injured in a road crash by dangerous driving was taken to hospital and there died, the driver could not escape conviction unless he could show that there was improper treatment in the hospital of a man who would otherwise have lived. The law might regard negligent treatment as a new and supervening cause of death, but proper medical treatment consequent upon illness or injury plays no part in legal causation; and to relieve the pains of death is undoubtedly proper medical treatment.

Attractive as Lord Devlin's response may be, is it not somewhat question-begging to say that the criminal law is concerned with the 'guilty' cause? Surely our problem is to determine which cause *is* the guilty cause? Has not Lord Devlin in fact conceded Professor Williams's point and admitted that the doctor by his acts does cause the death of the patient but now seeks to rely on another ground? Is not this other ground the same as that which was hinted at in our discussion of intention? It is suggested that the more appropriate analysis is as follows:

the doctor by his act *intends* (on any proper understanding of the term) the death of his patient and by his act *causes* (on any proper understanding of the term) the death of his patient, but the intention is not culpable and the cause is not blameworthy because the law permits the doctor to do the act in question.

On what basis, as a matter of principle, does the law permit this sort of treatment?

Professor Skegg suggests the interesting notion that, as far as the law is concerned, when the patient is near death anyway the doctor's conduct is *de minimis* (*op cit* at pp 135–136). The difficulty with such an analysis is that it too is question begging—why is it *de minimis*? The better response must be that the law permits this kind of treatment because the law recognises that it is socially desirable to allow doctors who care for patients who are in distress and have no prospect of relief to do that which offers relief. Of course, this still leaves open the circumstances under which such relief is given and any limits to it. Must the patient be dying? Skegg observes in *Law, Ethics and Medicine* (at p 135) that:

> ... Although the courts would have the last word on the propriety of the treatment, [where death was imminent] there could here be no doubt what their view would be.

In a footnote to his text (note 55) Skegg continues:

> But there is no similar consensus that it would be proper to administer pain-killing drugs which may lead to the death of a patient who would otherwise be expected to live for years. Some risk would sometimes be justifiable, but not nearly as great a risk as in those cases where death is imminent in any event. Professor Glanville Williams's argument which leads to the conclusion that 'a physician may give any amount of drug necessary to deaden pain, even though he knows that that amount will bring about speedy or indeed immediate death' (Williams *Sanctity*, 288) goes beyond *Adams*, and the current consensus.

(b) Omissions

Let us now consider the other half of the traditional analysis—omissions. Glanville Williams writes, in his *Textbook of Criminal Law* (2nd ed), at pp 148–149:

> A crime can be committed by omission, but there can be no omission in law in the absence of a duty to act. The reason is obvious. If there is an act, someone acts; but if there is an omission, everyone (in a sense) omits. We omit to do everything in the world that is not done. Only those of us omit in law who are under a duty to act.

Ordinarily there is no liability under the criminal law if a person omits to act to save life. An exception to this proposition exists where the law imposes an obligation to act. Two problems arise. First, what amounts to an omission and how can it be distinguished from an act? Secondly, when in law is a duty to act recognised?

As to the first: the difficulty in defining what is an omission does not lie in saying what it is, that much is clear; it is a non-action or failure to act. Rather, the difficulty lies in saying whether in any particular set of circumstances there is, in a person's behaviour (the propriety of which is under scrutiny), something that can be called an act rather than omission since the former more readily attracts liability. If, for example, the facts are that 'X' has suffered harm and 'Y' appears responsible, a court may set out on a voyage of discovery to find some act by 'Y' on which to base liability. That the voyage may lead to the land of 'Humpty Dumpty' can be seen in the following analysis by Professor Williams, of a doctor who turns off the respirator of a patient who is not dead. For Professor Williams, a traditionalist in his analysis here, the issue can be put as follows (*Textbook of Criminal Law* (1st ed), p 237, footnote omitted):

> The question then arises whether stopping a respirator is an act of killing or a decision to let nature take its course. Common sense suggests it is the latter. Suppose that the respirator worked only as long as the doctor turned a handle. If he stopped turning, he would be regarded as merely commencing to omit to save the patient's life. Suppose, alternatively, that the respirator worked electrically but was made to shut itself off every 24 hours. Then the deliberate failure to restart it would be an omission. It can make no moral difference that the respirator is constructed to run continuously and has to be stopped. Stopping the respirator is not a positive act of killing the patient, but a decision not to strive any longer to save him.

Another commentator suggests the following, Leng, 'Death and the Criminal Law' (1982) 45 MLR 206, at 208–9, (footnotes omitted):

> It is submitted that it is correct to characterise termination as an omission. This entails recognition that the act/omission distinction does not rest upon what is done, or upon a concept of willed muscular contraction, but upon the impact of what is done on the victim. The *provision* of life support is in fact a series of acts (albeit accomplished mechanically): termination of support is an omission to continue such acts which has no positive effect on the patient but merely fails to avert the natural cessation of vital functions.
>
> If this characterisation and the general proposition that the doctor/patient relationship imports a duty recognised by the criminal law are accepted, a doctor deliberately discontinuing support to a patient who is not legally dead escapes liability only if it is further accepted that sometimes *it lies within a doctor's duty to allow a patient to die*.
>
> This proposition may not be as problematic as first appears. Whereas the jurisprudence of duty relationships is well developed there has been relatively little consideration of the scope of a duty once found. Where duty and breach have been established the act required has not been onerous: eg alerting a doctor or social worker, provision of food at no personal expense or performing one's contract of

employment. The law clearly allows some balancing of the interests of the person under the duty as against those of the person to whom it is owed. Stated briefly the doctor's duty is to preserve life and health. This is an unreal oversimplification. The doctor (with the policeman and judge) implements the state's broad duty to preserve the life and health of citizens. The state does not take every measure to preserve life but must balance competing calls upon its resources. The doctor gives practical effect to this balance. He must take decisions on allocation of skilled attention, drugs, blood and equipment, involving qualitative judgments of cost-effectiveness, likelihood of survival, and the value of the life involved. Some such decisions will adversely affect chances of survival. From this broad perspective, a responsible and procedurally correct decision to terminate life-support to a brain-dead patient may fall within a doctor's duty although it leads to immediate death as traditionally defined.

You may well feel that this approach is unhelpful. Indeed, you may wonder whether such a complicated question of responsibility can be resolved by being encapsulated in one word. It is even more unhelpful when it is recalled that the act/omission distinction, whatever it is, ceases to be of legal significance where there is a duty to act. Doctors caring for patients are under a *duty* to care for their patients; any liability for their conduct will turn on whether they have breached this duty, whether by act or omission. Perhaps the crucial question, thereafter, is 'when is a doctor in breach of his duty?'.

As to the second question of when a duty to care for a patient arises, we have seen (*supra* ch 2) that when there is a relationship of doctor and patient the doctor is fixed with a duty in law. This does not, of course, tell us what the *content* of that duty may be in any case, and it is to this that we must turn next.

(ii) THE DOCTOR'S DUTY

What duty does a doctor owe in caring for his newborn baby patient? The complementary question which we must address is whether the doctor owes a *different* duty to neonates who are physically or mentally handicapped.

Notice that we are concerned with neonates who are handicapped and not neonates who are dying. This distinction is clearly very important. The duties owed to a dying patient, whether neonate or not, may, as we shall see, be different from the duty owed to the neonate being considered here (*infra* ch 14 and see now *re C* (1989) Times April 21, discussed in *postscript infra*). Nonetheless, not all of the traditional analysis has always reflected this distinction.

(a) Some unhelpful arguments

More generally, the traditional analysis of the doctor's duty here has often rested on one or the other of two unhelpful arguments. Before we proceed with our analysis it would be as well to dispose of these here. They are: the distinction drawn between *ordinary* and *extraordinary treatment* and the argument which relies on an absolutist understanding of the *principle of the sanctity of life*.

1. Sanctity of life

Helga Kuhse and Peter Singer put (without accepting) the argument of those who would rely upon an absolutist view of the sanctity of human life, in their book, *Should the Baby Live?* (1985) (at pp 18–20) (footnotes omitted).

...[A]ll human life is of equal worth. According to this view, the life a Down's syndrome baby is no less valuable than the life of a normal baby, or of any other patient. Since all human life is of equal worth, it is as wrong to let a Down's syndrome baby die, when it could be kept alive, as it would be to let any other patients die when they could be kept alive.

The sanctity of human life

The simple answer gains support from two quite distinct sources. One is the traditional doctrine of the sanctity of human life. Those who speak of 'the sanctity of life' hold a cluster of related ideas, rather than a single doctrine; nevertheless they agree in rejecting claims that one human life is more valuable than another. . . . For the moment it is enough to note that it has had a dominant influence on both morality and law in Western civilisation. The central idea is well expressed by Sanford Kadish, writing on the view of human life taken by Anglo-American law:

> all human lives must be regarded as having an equal claim to preservation simply because life is an irreducible value. Therefore, the value of a particular life, over and above the value of life itself, may not be taken into account.

Here the key claim is that life is an irreducible value—that is, the value of life cannot be reduced to anything else, such as the happiness, self-consciousness, rationality, autonomy, or even simple consciousness, that life makes possible. Life is not valuable because of the qualities it may possess; it is valuable in itself. It is easy to see how this claim leads to the conclusion that all human life is of equal value.

The traditional sanctity of life doctrine is also sometimes supported by the claim that human life is of *infinite* value. The Chief Rabbi of Great Britain, Rabbi Immanuel Jakobovits, has referred to this idea as the ground for opposition to euthanasia:

> The basic reasoning behind the firm opposition of Judaism to any form of euthanasia proper is the attribution of *infinite* value to every human life. Since infinity is, by definition, indivisible, it follows that every fraction of life, however small, remains equally infinite so that it makes morally no difference whether one shortens life by seventy years or by only a few hours, or whether the victim of murder was young and robust or aged and physically or mentally debilitated.

Dr Moshe Tendler, a professor of Talmudic law, confirms this position:

> human life is of infinite value. This in turn means that a piece of infinity is also infinity, and a person who has but a few moments to live is no less of value than a person who has 60 years to live . . . a handicapped individual is a perfect specimen when viewed in an ethical context. The value is an absolute value. It is not relative to life expectancy, to state of health, or to usefulness to society.

The Protestant theologian Paul Ramsey, Professor of Religion at Princeton University, takes a similar view:

> there is no reason for saying that [six months in the life of a baby born with the invariably fatal Tay Sachs disease] are a life span of lesser worth to God than living seventy years before the onset of irreversible degeneration. A genuine humanism would say the same thing in other language. It is only a reductive naturalism or social utilitarianism that would regard those months of infant life as worthless because they lead to nothing on a time line of earthly achievement. All our days and years are of equal worth whatever the consequence; death is no more a tragedy at one time than at another time.

A value might be irreducible without being infinite, and if human life is of irreducible rather than infinite value, there may not be great value in prolonging human existence by a few moments. On the other hand, if human life is of infinite value, every second of prolonged life would be as valuable as a lifetime. This is, on the face of it, implausible; most of us are indifferent to the prospect of our life being shortened by one second, but we are very far from indifferent to the thought that our life might be cut short by thirty years. As far as the treatment of John Pearson [in the *Arthur* case] and Baby Doe [a similar case in the USA] is concerned, however, the difference between irreducible value and infinite value does not matter. Both babies could, with appropriate care, have lived for many years, possibly a near-normal lifespan. (The life expectancy of people with Down's syndrome is less than normal, but some do live into their forties or even fifties.) So if human life is in itself a value, irrespective of the quality of the particular life, the presence of Down's syndrome is not relevant to the value a life has.

Gordon Dunstan in *The Dictionary of Medical Ethics* also gives us a helpful explanation (pp384–5):

Sanctity or sacredness of human life. Phrases, having overtones taken from religious terminology, used to express the presumptive inviolability of the human person, his right to life, with its attendant right to protection in the enjoyment of his total integrity. The principle is implicit in the Hippocratic tradition . . . and was heavily reinforced by Jewish and Christian theology. It finds modern expression in the Geneva Declaration of the World Medical Association, 'I will maintain the utmost respect for human life from the time of conception, even under threat. I will not use my medical knowledge contrary to the laws of humanity'. In Judaism, every moment of life is infinitely precious, and has therefore an inviolable claim to protection. The words 'sanctity' and 'sacredness' imply—indeed, taken literally, they assert—a divine sanction for this inviolability as in itself divinely willed for man, proper to the created nature of man and the divine purpose of his existence. *Sanctity* (from the Latin *sanctus*) denotes 'holiness', a word which, in its historic evolution, denoted the numinous separateness of God, then his ethical purity, then the ethical purity, or saintliness, of those 'separated' or dedicated to God; thence a claim to religious reverence and protection, inviolability. *Sacredness* (from the Latin *sacer*) has a similar meaning: set apart, dedicated to religious use; holy by association; and therefore to be respected, protected.

The words are sometimes used in controversy, eg about abortion . . ., as though they self-evidently gave *absolute* protection, or imposed *absolute* prohibitions on the taking of life. The supposition cannot be supported from the moral tradition in which the concepts themselves have been preserved. The Jewish Law, for instance, which forbade murder in the Sixth (Fifth) Commandment (Exodus 20: 13), also enjoined capital punishment for a number of crimes. The principle, properly used, asserts a human right to enjoy protection in life and bodily integrity; that right may be violated only for just cause approved by the general moral sense and by public authority. It is for society itself to work out and maintain the second-order conventions and rules by means of which the principle can operate in professional practice as in the other activities of ordered human life.

Finally, consider the following account by S McLean and G Maher in *Medicine, Morals and the Law*, pp 1 *et seq* (footnotes omitted):

. . . [I]t is often said that the value of life permeates all medical practice and is the focal point of proper medical ethics. Thus the Geneva Convention Code of Medical Ethics (1949) includes the vow that:

I will maintain the utmost respect for human life from the time of conception; even under threat. I will not use my medical knowledge contrary to the laws of humanity.

However despite the evident stress on the value of life, it is obvious that in fact we do not place as much value on life as we appear to, and that we certainly do not treat life as 'sacred' or absolute in the sense that life is treated as completely inviolable. Many societies which proffer a belief in the sanctity of life also accept capital punishment and war.

This gap between our easy acceptance of the supreme importance of life in theory and our willingness to compromise this value in practice is disadvantageous in two ways. One is that this inconsistency is no mere mistake or misapprehension of some factual situation, but is rather a device for making moral choices without openly considering the issues (this might be called the ideological function of the belief in the sanctity of life since it serves to divert our attention from difficult choices). Secondly, and following on from this point, many difficult but important moral issues are left undiscussed or inconsistently resolved. To raise explicitly the actual value which we are prepared to give to life opens up many issues in medical practice which need to be identified and tackled directly.

On deeper reflection it should not come as any great surprise to discover that what passes for the sanctity of life does not really mean taking life as an ultimate value in the sense that it overrides all other possible moral considerations.

. . .

What we see then is that the broad idea of the sanctity of life is open to a variety of interpretations which need to be kept distinct and which the notion of 'sanctity' does not by itself make clear. It is one thing to say that life, simply as life, has some value but another to assert that life is the paramount factor in any set of moral considerations. Or take the idea of sanctity of life as meaning that it is always wrong to kill. Does this principle apply without exception, or may we take life when to do so results in other lives being saved? Again, if life is sacred, does it follow that it is always right to save life, and, if this is the case, is the duty to save life the highest moral duty? It is evident that the doctrine of sanctity of life can be applied to many different types of situation, any discussion of the doctrine must make clear those various distinctions ... What is it about human life that we value? The central question in the theoretical debate on the 'sacredness' of life must surely be this one, and its centrality stems not only from the nature of theoretical arguments but also from its implications for practical action. Indeed if we had a clearer notion as to why and to what extent life is of value and what special considerations affect the value of human life, then we would be several steps nearer to a fuller understanding of several of the complex ethical issues of modern medical practice.

This is not to say that we cannot give reasons for placing value on human life; on the contrary, it is more likely that we will be faced with a number of arguments, many of them mutually inconsistent. Historically (as we noted earlier) the traditional reason given for the special value of human life is the possession of an immortal soul by all humans, and only by them. But we have noted that this belief in itself is not sufficient to support the doctrine of sanctity of life (in the sense of mortal life). More to the point, whatever the extent of religious belief today (and it should not be underestimated) religious doctrines can contribute to moral argument only by abandoning any special claim to unchallengeable and intrinsic correctness. In other words, we still need rational and logically consistent supporting arguments in order to provide acceptable moral standards in respect of the question of the value of human life...

... [W]e find some writers advancing the argument that both utilitarianism and autonomy-based ethics can throw light on the problem of the value of human life. What we need to note, however, are the differing reasons for valuing life and to attend to distinctions about the meaning of human life. For example, Singer draws a distinction between what he sees as two distinct meanings of 'human life'. One meaning is membership of the species homo sapiens but, argues Singer, in itself such a biological classification has no special moral significance. That we should have ever considered it to be so is probably a carry-over from the Christian doctrine of ensoulation. Secondly, what is of special moral significance is the idea of human life as a 'person', or in other words the possession of certain special characteristics, the most significant being rationality and awareness of oneself as a continuing entity. Singer's argument is that what is morally wrong about the taking of the life of a 'person' is the disrespect shown for his or her autonomy. But why should we place value on 'conscious' life, a category which would include the cases of 'mere' membership of the species homo sapiens (such as infants and foetuses) as well as animals? *Ex hypothesi* it cannot be because such life-forms enjoy autonomy, though in some cases it makes sense to talk of the potential for autonomy. In this category we can find good reasons for valuing merely 'conscious' life in utilitarian considerations, for these life-forms can themselves experience pain and pleasure, and the continuation or termination of their existence can lead to the increase or decrease in the happiness of others.

A similar general argument has been presented by Glover [in *Causing Death and Saving Lives* (1977)], who points to a distinction between life as 'mere' consciousness (awareness, or the having of experiences) and life at a higher level of consciousness, which includes certain emotional and cognitive experiences. This second state is of importance, in that it is an aspect of a life worth living whereas mere consciousness has no value in itself but is valuable only as a means to a worthwhile life. Glover notes that there can be many proposed candidates for what constitutes a life worth living and he does not attempt to list all of these (though he does stress that his concept of a life worth living is not necessarily identical with that of a morally virtuous life). But the lack of the ability to specify the ingredients of a worthwhile life has some significance for Glover's general argument, for he is led on to argue that the best judge of the worth of a life, at least as regards the continuation of that life, is the person living it; or in other words, the crucial criterion here is that of autonomy.

Thus we find Glover advancing the argument that, whereas the only relevant moral considerations in cases of 'mere' life are those based on consequences or side-effects, in the case of worthwhile lives there are direct reasons for not killing, that is reasons based on the particular life itself (or the person whose life it is).

We should make clear a distinction to be drawn in claims based on autonomy which stress the need to allow a worthwhile life to continue or develop. These arguments need not pre-suppose any particular form of the good life (such as may have been argued for in ancient philosophy). Some theories do perhaps point to a particular form of life as *the* good form but use the argument from the necessary incompleteness of knowledge or from relativism to argue that these are matters for the individual. What such theories are saying, accordingly, is that although there may be such things as morally good life-styles, there is a practical difficulty in knowing precisely what these are, and that the value of autonomy is that it leaves decisions as to what is morally good to the person or persons directly concerned. However, other theories look to autonomy as necessarily a central feature of moral life; these take the value of autonomy as something independent of the particular type of life which the autonomous person chooses. In other words, autonomy is itself a moral good, and is to be treated as such.

We can then note the general argument about the value of human life. Simply as life, there are good reasons for respecting life, such as the capacity to feel pain (and pleasure) enjoyed by the particular life-form, the possible and actual contribution of that life-form to general social welfare, and other considerations of a similar utilitarian nature. But because of the possession of certain crucial moral characteristics human life has a special value over and above its value as 'mere' life . . .

Later, (pp 64–66), McLean and Maher return to the arguments:

. . .[T]here remains the further problem that the decision taken may be more of a moral than a scientific nature, in which case there is no clear reason why it should be taken by doctors as seemed to be the suggestion. Thus, the decision to remove an intestinal blockage or to perform other relatively minor surgery on a Mongol baby may lead to the use of this distinction in an attempt to justify not performing it, whereas if the child was otherwise normal then we might see the intervention as perfectly ordinary. The decision, then, is not simply about matters which are capable of scientific regulation but is more fundamentally one which is tied up with other notions, such as quality of life, prognosis of improvement in health and so on.

Thus, the sanctity of life argument, with its traditional corresponding theories, can give us no clear answers to the question of life and death since implicit in this modified version is the acceptance that not all life will be allowed or helped to survive. . . . [Glover's] worthwhile life is a matter of potential. Therefore, the argument would run, even if it is wrong to kill a potentially worthwhile life, it is less wrong to do so when the alternative is a life with the same potential or greater potential for worthwhile life. This type of argument may be used to justify terminating a pregnancy where the baby is known to be damaged, on the grounds that nothing is lost if the following child is normal or has equal potential.

Another argument against killing is the so-called autonomy argument which renders it wrong to override the preference of a person for staying alive, even in circumstances where we might believe it to be in his interests not to stay alive. However, it is argued, babies do not have preferences and therefore they have no autonomy to be overridden. Babies may have desires, eg, to be fed or changed, but this is not to be equated with a preference of life over death since it is no more than a basic instinct for survival. Thus, Glover argues that there is a difference between having biological instinctive behaviour and actually having desires because, 'Desires . . . presuppose concepts'. It is not necessary that these concepts can be verbalised, but it is necessary that they are understood and experienced by the person. The argument for personal autonomy would not therefore provide a convincing argument against infanticide.

The worthwhile life argument brings us squarely to the issue of the quality of life, a concept much employed by those seeking to support the humaneness of killing or letting die. Glover for example suggests that in the absence of a convincing reason against infanticide, and in the absence of clear criteria to determine when it may be carried out, the best alternative is for us to take decisions about the quality of life of a given child by considering whether or not we would consider such a life worth living. Not that he, or any other supporters of this line, would claim that this is an easy decision, nor would they claim that there would be consensus readily available on which to base our decisions. Nonetheless, given our attitudes to, eg gross deformities, and our conviction that some forms of life are not worth living, then in their view the quality of life argument 'either ceases to be an objection to killing or else becomes a positive argument in favour of it'. Thus, it is argued, the direct arguments against killing are unsatisfactory when we are talking of killing a baby.

2. Ordinary/extraordinary

The argument concerning ordinary and extraordinary treatment, accepting as it does the moral propriety of withholding treatment in some cases, can, of course, only be advanced once an absolutist view of the sanctity of life is rejected. An outstanding analysis, pinpointing the deficiencies of this new argument, can be found in the President's Commission for the Study of Ethical Problems in Medical and Biomedical and Behavioural Research, Report of 1983 *Deciding to Forego Life-Sustaining Treatment* (pp 82–88) (footnotes omitted).

Ordinary versus extraordinary treatment. In many discussions and decisions about life-sustaining treatment, the distinction between ordinary and extraordinary (also termed 'heroic' or 'artificial') treatment plays an important role. In its origins within moral theology, the distinction was used to mark the difference between obligatory and nonobligatory care—ordinary care being obligatory for the patient to accept and others to provide, and extraordinary care being optional. It has also played a role in professional policy statements and recent judicial decisions about life-sustaining treatment for incompetent patients. As with the other terms discussed, defining and applying a distinction between ordinary and extraordinary treatment is both difficult and controversial and can lead to inconsistent results, which makes the terms of questionable value in the formulation of public policy in this area.

The meaning of the distinction. 'Extraordinary' treatment has an unfortunate array of alternative meanings, as became obvious in an exchange that took place at a Commission hearing concerning a Florida case [*Satz v Perlmutter* 379 So 2d 358 (1980)] involving the cessation of life-sustaining treatment at the request of a 76-year-old man dying of amyotrophic lateral sclerosis. The attending physician testified:

I deal with respirators every day of my life. To me, this is not heroic. This is standard procedure . . . I have other patients who have run large corporations who have been on portable respirators. Other people who have been on them and have done quite well for as long as possible.

By contrast, the trial judge who had decided that the respirator could be withdrawn told the Commission:

Certainly there is no question legally that putting a hole in a man's trachea and inserting a mechanical respirator is extraordinary life-preserving means. I do not think that the doctor would in candor allow that that is not an extraordinary means of preserving life. I understand that he deals with them every day, but in the sense of ordinary as against extraordinary, I believe it to be extraordinary.

There was no question in this case, nobody ever raised the question that this mechanical respirator was not an extraordinary means of preserving life.

The most natural understanding of the ordinary/extraordinary distinction is as the difference between common and unusual care, with those terms understood as applying to a patient in a particular condition. This interprets the distinction in a literal, statistical sense and, no doubt, is what some of its users intend. Related, though different, is the idea that ordinary care is simple and that extraordinary care is complex, elaborate, or artificial, or that it employs elaborate technology and/or great efforts or expense. With either of these interpretations, for example, the use of antibiotics to fight a life-threatening infection would be considered ordinary treatment. On the statistical interpretation, a complex of resuscitation measures (including physical, chemical, and electrical means) might well be ordinary for a hospital patient, whereas on the technological interpretation, resuscitation would probably be considered extraordinary. Since both common/unusual and simple/complex exist on continuums with no precise dividing line, on either interpretation there will be borderline cases engendering disagreement about whether a particular treatment is ordinary or extraordinary.

A different understanding of the distinction, one that has its origins in moral theology, inquires into the usefulness and burdensomeness of a treatment. Here, too, disagreement persists about which outcomes are considered useful or burdensome. Without entering into the complexity of these debates, the Commission notes that any interpretation of the ordinary/extraordinary distinction in terms of usefulness and burdensomeness to an individual patient has an important advantage over the common/unusual or simple/complex interpretations in that judgments about usefulness and burdensomeness rest on morally important differences.

Despite the fact that the distinction between what is ordinary and what is extraordinary is hazy and variably defined, several courts have employed the terms in discussing cases involving the cessation of life-sustaining treatment of incompetent patients. In some cases, the courts used these terms because they were part of the patient's religious tradition. In other cases, the terms have been used to characterise treatments as being required or permissibly foregone. For example, the New Jersey Supreme Court in the *Quinlan* case [*re Quinlan* 355 A 2d 647 (1976)] recognised a distinction based on the possible benefit to the individual patient:

> One would have to think that the use of the same respirator or life support could be considered 'ordinary' in the context of the possibly curable patient but 'extraordinary' in the context of the forced sustaining by cardio-respiratory processes of an irreversibly doomed patient.

Likewise, the Massachusetts Supreme Judicial Court [*Superintendent of Belchertown State School v Saikewicz* 370 NE 2d 417 (1977)] quoted an article in a medical journal concerning the proposition that ordinary treatment could become extraordinary when applied in the context of a patient for whom there is no hope:

> We should not use *extraordinary* means of prolonging life or its semblance when, after careful consideration, consultation and application of the most well conceived therapy it becomes apparent that there is no hope for the recovery of the patient. Recovery should not be defined simply as the ability to remain alive; it should mean life without intolerable suffering.

Even if the patient or a designated surrogate is held to be under no obligation to accept 'extraordinary' care, there still remains the perplexing issue about what constitutes the dividing line between the two. The courts have most often faced the question of what constitutes 'ordinary' care in cases when the respirator was the medical intervention at issue. Generally the courts have recognised, in the words of one judge, that 'the act of turning off the respirator is the termination of an optional, extraordinary medical procedure which will allow nature to take its course.'

For many, the harder questions lie in less dramatic interventions, including the use of artificial feeding and antibiotics. In one criminal case involving whether the defendant's robbery and assault killed his victim or whether she died because life-supporting treatments were later withdrawn after severe brain injury was confirmed, the court held that 'heroic' (and unnecessary) measures included 'infusion of drugs in order to reduce the pressure in the head when there was no obvious response to those measures of therapy'. In another case, in which a patient's refusal of an amputation to prevent death from gangrene was overridden, antibiotics were described by the physician 'as heroic measures, meaning quantities in highly unusual amounts risking iatrogenic disease in treating gangrene'. Here the assessment, in addition to relying on 'benefits', also seems to rely to some degree upon the risk and invasiveness of the intervention. One court did begin to get at the scope of the questions underlying the ordinary/extraordinary distinction. Faced with the question of treatment withdrawal for a permanently unconscious automobile accident victim, the Delaware Supreme Court [*Severns v Wilmington Medical Center* 421 A 2d 1334 (1980)] asked what might constitute life-sustaining measures for a person who has been comatose for many months:

Are 'medicines' a part of such life-sustaining systems? If so, which medicines? Is food or nourishment a part of such life-sustaining systems? If so, to what extent? What extraordinary measures (or equipment) are a part of such systems? What measures (or equipment) are regarded by the medical profession as not extraordinary under the circumstances? What ordinary equipment is used? How is a respirator regarded in this context?

The moral significance of the distinction. Because of the varied meanings of the distinction, whether or not it has moral significance depends upon the specific meaning assigned to it. The Commission believes there is no basis for holding that whether a treatment is common or unusual, or whether it is simple or complex, is in itself significant to a moral analysis of whether the treatment is warranted or obligatory. An unusual treatment may have a lower success rate than a common one; if so, it is the lower success rate rather than the unusualness of the procedure that is relevant to evaluating the therapy. Likewise, a complex, technological treatment may be costlier than a simple one, and this difference may be relevant to the desirability of the therapy. A patient may choose a complex therapy and shun a simple one, and the patient's choice is always relevant to the moral obligation to provide the therapy.

If the ordinary/extraordinary distinction is understood in terms of the usefulness and burdensomeness of a particular therapy, however, the distinction does have moral significance. When a treatment is deemed extraordinary because it is too burdensome for a particular patient, the individual (or a surrogate) may appropriately decided not to undertake it. The reasonableness of this is evident—a patient should not have to undergo life-prolonging treatment without consideration of the burdens that the treatment would impose. Of course, whether a treatment is warranted depends on its usefulness or benefits as well. Whether serious burdens of treatment (for example, the side effects of chemotherapy treatments for cancer) are worth enduring obviously depends on the expected benefits—how long the treatment will extend life, and under what conditions. Usefulness might be understood as mere extension of life, no matter what the conditions of that life. But so long as mere biological existence is not considered the *only* value, patients may want to take the nature of that additional life into account as well.

This line of reasoning suggests that extraordinary treatment is that which, in the patient's view, entails significantly greater burdens than benefits and is therefore undesirable and not obligatory, while ordinary treatment is that which, in the patient's view, produces greater benefits than burdens and is therefore reasonably desirable and undertaken. The claim, then, that the treatment is extraordinary is more of an expression of the conclusion than a justification for it.

Gillon, in an editorial in (1981) 7 Medical Ethics 56, confirms the view of the President's Commission:

. . . [T]houghtful proponents of the use of the distinction between ordinary and extraordinary means agree with opponents that the moral assessment of any individual's case must properly come *before* it is decided whether any particular treatment is to be classified as ordinary or extraordinary; moreover not only the 'means' (ie the proposed means of treatment) but also the patient's particular circumstances and the anticipated harms and benefits to him in those circumstances of those means of treatment must be assessed before the means can be classified as being either ordinary or extraordinary. Thus there is no question of observing whether some proposed means of treatment X is, as a matter of non-evaluative fact, ordinary or extraordinary and then using this observation or 'fact' to decide whether or not patient Y in circumstances Z should be treated with X; rather it is a matter of first deciding whether or not it would be *right* to treat patient Y in context Z with treatment X and then, depending on that decision, classifying X as ordinary or extraordinary means of treatment.

Non-Catholics are often—perhaps always—surprised at this revelation when first they meet it, supposing reasonably enough that 'ordinary' means 'usual, common-place, not exceptional' (to quote the Oxford English Dictionary) and conversely that 'extraordinary' means 'unusual, uncommon, exceptional.' However, although these concepts may obliquely enter the analysis of specific cases it is clear that, as Strong explicitly states, the conflation of 'ordinary' with 'customary' and of 'extraordinary' with 'unusual' must be rejected; he indeed goes further and suggests that for the purpose of medical ethics 'perhaps we would avoid confusion if we used the terms "ethically indicated," and "ethically non-indicated" in place of the terms "ordinary" and "extraordinary".' Of course once we accept such an understanding of the distinction it remains open to ask what are the criteria upon which it should be made—what are the substantive moral principles upon which we can decide whether treatment X is or is not 'ethically indicated' (ie indicated by some process of ethical analysis) for patient Y in circumstances Z.

Roman Catholic authorities have proposed excessive expense, excessive pain, excessive difficulty or other inconvenience, and no reasonable or 'proportionate' hope of benefit as criteria for deciding that a treatment is 'extraordinary' in the context of a particular patient in particular circumstances. This approach is reflected by the Church of England. Thus the moral theologian Professor G R Dunstan in an article on this subject in the *Dictionary of Medical Ethics* suggests that the distinction has different connotations for moralists and for doctors but is used by both with the same intention, notably 'to insist that it is the patient's ultimate interest which should determine the treatment he receives, that interest being seen in relation to his unique being and his unique human and social environment'. Dunstan states that ordinary (and hence morally obligatory) procedures are for the moralist those which, when relativised to a particular patient in a particular context offer the patient 'a reasonable hope of benefit, without excessive expense, pain or other serious inconvenience'. Similarly in medical usage 'ordinary' would indicate 'what is normal, established, well-tried; of known effectiveness, within the resources and skills available; of calculable and acceptable risk; of generally low mortality; involving pain, disturbance, inconvenience, all within predictable limits of acceptability and control; and all proportionate to an expected and lasting benefit to the patient'.

Conversely 'extraordinary' (and hence morally optional) means are for the moralist those means which, when relativised to a particular patient in a particular context, do not satisfy the criteria for being 'ordinary' and which would impose on the patient 'undue suffering or expense, or, it may be, an undue distortion of his personality or a barrier in his relationships with his kin, a lessening of his human capacity, and all without a reasonable hope of benefit'. In the medical connotation extraordinary procedures would be those which in relation to a particular patient in a particular context would fail to meet the criteria for being ordinary—they would include for instance 'investigatory and experimental procedures of uncertain efficacy, or even carrying a high mortality rate; those involving a heavy disproportion between the pain, mutilation, disfigurement or psychological disruption of the patient and any immediate or long-term benefit reasonably predictable; or of disproportionate cost'.

There can be few people involved in making medical-ethical decisions, whether in practice or merely in theory, who would disagree with the general principles of assessment proposed in either the Roman Catholic or Church of England positions as outlined above. Both, however, knowingly leave many important moral questions unanswered. What is to count as 'excessive' expense, pain, difficulty or other inconvenience; what is a 'reasonable' or 'proportionate' hope of benefit; what indeed is to count as a 'benefit'; and who should decide these weighty matters? No attempt is made to answer such questions here. Rather, the crucial point for health workers not versed in Christian theology to appreciate is that an appeal to the ordinary/extraordinary means distinction cannot help them to answer these questions, for the distinction itself can only be made *after* the questions have been answered.

The distinction between ordinary means and extraordinary means has a dangerously deceptive appearance of simplicity. It appears to be a distinction made by assessing means of treatment, whereas in fact, as Dunstan puts it 'the criteria for decision relate primarily to the patient not to the remedy'. It appears to be a distinction made by determining whether particular means of treatment are usual or unusual, and again this is not the case. It appears to give a single *criterion* for making a moral decision whereas in fact it is only a label for a decision making process which uses a cluster of different moral criteria: above all it appears to be a distinction based upon a simple, uncontroversial, morally non-evaluative assessment, whereas in fact it is based upon complex potentially controversial and essentially moral assessments.

Those who are motivated by their religious orientations to use the distinction between ordinary and extraordinary means in the context of medical ethics may be expected to be aware of all this; those who are not so motivated need to appreciate these complexities before using the distinction at all. However all health workers will risk less confusion, if not for themselves then at least for their patients and for their patients' relatives, if they specify the moral criteria which they believe should be used when deciding whether or not to undertake particular treatments for particular patients in particular circumstances. Specifying the criteria, which may well relate to the risks, costs, pain, likelihood of success, anticipated results and side effects, both physical and psychological of a proposed treatment, will not only reduce confusion but will also provide an opportunity for discussion of the complex issues, both among staff involved and also with patients and/or their relatives. Moreover once the actual criteria of decision are specified the misleading labels 'ordinary means' and 'extraordinary means' become superfluous and may be safely allowed to 'drop out of the picture' by those who have no special reason to retain them.

In short, the distinction is unhelpful in that the words represent a conclusion having evaluated several factors. It is upon these factors, and the relative weights to be given to them, which any proper analysis should concentrate, as we shall see.

(b)   The better view

It is worth noting at the outset that one of the most distinguished criminal lawyers takes a somewhat heretical stand. Professor Williams in his discussion of *Arthur* concludes in his *Textbook of Criminal Law* (2nd ed 1983), at p 285:

> It may be thought to be wrong that doctors who have to take these difficult decisions, often in circumstances in which they must act quickly if they are to act effectively, should be subject to the law of murder if they are subsequently held to have broken the nebulous rules. . . . There is, surely, a strong argument for keeping the law out of these cases. When a question is so much a matter of opinion, and when the good order of society in general is not at stake, the criminal law should stay its hand. Even if wardship proceedings are taken, the decision of the parents that a defective child should be allowed to die should prevail; and doctors generally recognise this.

We would respectfully demur from Professor Williams's position that the law has no place in this area (we will discuss later the separate issue of the role of the parents). We take the view that in a matter of such importance affecting as it does the further existence of a child, the criminal law is necessarily involved and rightly should be so. It does not follow, of course, that the verdict of the criminal law will always be that it is homicide to allow a child to die.

The only statements in English law of the doctor's duty are those in *Re B* and *Arthur (supra)* (and see now *re C* (1989) Times, 21 April discussed in postscript). We have already suggested that the directions in *Arthur* do not properly represent the law. Thus, we are left with the brief statement of Templeman LJ in *Re B* (a civil case). Being a civil case, it uses the language of family law that the doctor's duty was to act in the best interests of the child which, as we have seen, contemplates in theory that some children may be allowed to die.

The task for the law (ie the courts) is, therefore, twofold: first to decide whether it is necessary to articulate formally what 'best interests' means and secondly, if so, then to spell out the legal parameters of this generalised notion. This must be our next task.

1. What is the test?

'Best interests'. The prime judicial candidate as a test to describe a doctor's duty is that he must act in the best interests of the child. This would be entirely in keeping with the wealth of authority and tradition of family law. The difficulties it presents for a lawyer are that it provides no guidance as to the law to respond to the facts of any particular case. It necessarily regards each decision, whether or not to treat, as an individual decision to be made on the particular facts of the case. The analytical flaw in this approach is that it is unprincipled: the criteria for decisions are normative and not factual. Because of this, it would appear to leave such responses to those caring for the baby. This has the double disadvantage of leaving them without any real help and also thereby leaving them with a virtually unfettered discretion. The poverty of this analysis can be seen in *Re B (A Minor) (Sterilisation: Wardship)* [1988] AC 199, [1987] 2 All ER 206, where the House of Lords applied the 'best interests' (so-called) test so as to decide a most complicated issue on what many would regard as, in effect, a rudimentary enquiry of fact. (See *supra* chs 4 and 7 for a discussion of this case.) Clearly the interests of those with whose particular interests the law is concerned, can only be served if some better guidance is offered by the courts. Do you agree?

It can be argued, as we have seen, that the courts in *Re B* and in *Dawson* have in fact provided some (albeit very limited) guidance. In *Re B*, Templeman LJ talked in terms of a 'demonstrably awful' life which might absolve the doctor of his duty to sustain it. McKenzie J approved this in *Dawson* but it is worth noting that in *McKay v Essex Area Health Authority* [1982] 2 All ER 771, Ackner LJ, in a reserved judgment, cast some doubt on the authority of Templeman LJ's *ex tempore* proposition (at 787; see also Stephenson LJ at 781).

'Quality of life'. So, this seems to mean that 'best interests' becomes, for the judiciary in this context, 'quality of life'; another general (and in itself, meaningless) test; but one which offers some hope for further analysis and articulation. Also, if 'quality of life' is the test this serves to highlight two further critical points. First, the test is not factual but *normative*. Secondly, being normative, it has to be *established* as a matter of principle through some institutional process (though it may ordinarily be *applied* in particular cases by those caring for the patient).

The vagueness and imprecision involved in recourse to the 'quality of life' test is well-put by Larry Gostin in his article 'A Moment in Human Development: Legal Protection, Ethical Standards and Social Policy on the Selective Non-Treatment of Handicapped Neonates', (1985) 11 American Journal of Law and Medicine, 32 at pp 39–41.

The term 'quality of life' has been introduced into Anglo-American jurisprudence[24] and by commentators[25] to justify the withholding of medically indicated treatment for severely handicapped infants whose life would be so bereft of enjoyment as not to be worth living. As under social utilitarian thought, medically effective treatment, even if available and efficacious for an otherwise normal infant, could be withheld based upon broader consideration of the infant's handicaps. The relevant factors under a 'quality of life' assessment relate not to social worth or to economic cost, but to the infant's potential for human contentment.

It is difficult to argue with the premise underlying the 'quality of life' position, for there must come a point for most of us where life is so devoid of meaning and contentment that it is not worth living. As a philosophic position, its weakness is that the factors which would justify forsaking continued life are seldom, if ever, specified. If one accepts that continued life is not in the infant's interests, then those who make this decision must be clear about the criteria to be adopted. Yet the basis for identifying and measuring those interests under a 'quality of life' standard is unclear.

In practice, the term 'quality of life' often is not used as a coherent moral theory which defines with any certainty which handicapping conditions should or should not be treated. Rather, the term is employed as a signal by those who believe that selective non-treatment decisions are too delicate and complex to be governed by any coherent legal or ethical standard. Accordingly, most of those who advocate a 'quality of life' assessment seek to maintain the decision-making process within a confidential doctor/patient framework.

Notes to extract

[24] Courts have been reluctant expressly to adopt a 'quality of life' criterion and have been careful not to demarcate a class of individuals, such as the mentally retarded or senile, as deserving a lower standard of legal protection. Yet several courts have made implicit assessments of personal quality of life and normalcy in coming to their decisions. It is helpful to distinguish between two groupings of cases to determine whether a court is actually employing a "quality of life' standard. The first are cases which are decided principally by an assessment of the medical benefits, risks and adverse effects of the treatment in question. (Is there a 'substantial chance for cure?' Are there 'medically effective alternative treatments?') Here, the court's decision follows directly from the medical assessment. The principal finding is factual, ie, whether a medical consensus exists that the treatment is indicated and that there are no medically recognised alternatives. Given this finding of fact courts will usually come to the same decision, irrespective of the legal standard applied. See, eg *Custody of a Minor*, 375 Mass 733, 379 NE 2d 1053 (1978), *affd*, 378 Mass 732, 393 NE 2d 836 (1979) (order permitting chemotherapy for minor patient suffering from acute lymphocytic leukemia over parental objection; court found chemotherapy offered a 'substantial chance for cure' and the alternative treatment of metabolic therapy was medically ineffective and poisonous); ie *Hofbauer*, 65 AD 2d 108, 411 NYS 2d 416 (1978), affd, 47 NY 2d 648, 393 NE 2d 1009, 419 NYS 2d 936 (1979) (a child suffering from Hodgkins Disease whose parents failed to follow attending physician's recommendation for treatment by radiation and chemotherapy, but rather placed child under care of licensed physician advocating nutritional or metabolic therapy, was not a neglected child; court found parents had justifiable concerns about deleterious effects of radiation and chemotherapy, that alternative treatments were controlling child's condition, and that conventional treatments would be administered if child's condition so warranted); *Ex rel Cicero*, 101 Misc 2d 699, 421 NYS 2d 965 (Sup Ct 1979) (guardian appointed to consent to corrective surgery for infant born with meningomyelocele. The court found child unlikely to live beyond 24 months without surgery and that surgery would permit child to walk with leg braces and to have 'normal intellectual development' with little future risk of mental retardation.).

The cases cited above should be distinguished from those where the court is influenced not only by its findings of fact as to the choices of treatment, but also by the person's wider characteristics, including his or her potential for intellectual and social functioning. See, eg *Re Phillip B*, 92 Cal App 3d 796, 156 Cal Rptr 48 (1979), cert denied sub nom 445 US 949 (1980) (court declined to order life-prolonging heart surgery for minor suffering from congenital ventricular septal heart defect. The trial court found corrective surgery to be medically indicated with 5 to 10 per cent mortality rate but noted that the child had Down's Syndrome; the judge commented that he personally could not handle it 'if it happened to me.'); *Infant Doe, [in re the Treatment and Care of Infant Doe*, No GU 8204–004A (Ind Cir Ct, April 12, 1982)] (court order barring doctors from providing nourishment or treatment for Downs Syndrome infant born with a deformity in the stomach wall which prevented food being digested; the condition could have been corrected by surgery which was serious but considered within the range of standard medical practice); *Re Spring*, 380 Mass 629, 405 NE 2d 115 (1980) (court approval for removal of 78 year old patient from kidney dialysis, probate court found patient to be senile and incapable of restoration to a 'normal, cognitive, integrated functioning existence'); *Superintendent of Belchertown State School v Saikewicz*, 373 Mass 728, 370 NE 2d 417 (1977) (authorisation for non-treatment of 67 year old mentally retarded ward suffering from acute myeloblastic monocytic leukemia; probate court found chemotherapy was life-prolonging and was treatment of choice, but patient's profound retardation was a significant issue in the case); *Re Conroy* 98 NJ 321, 486 A 2d 1209 (1985) (nursing home resident with severe and permanent mental and physical defects and limited life expectancy could have life-sustaining treatment withdrawn in certain circumstances).

If one were to remove the wider 'quality of life' element from the facts of these cases the results would appear anomalous and, in some instances, clearly erroneous. It is highly probable that the court in each of these cases would have opted to prolong a life it considered worth living. See Annas, *Quality of Life in the Courts: Early Spring in Fantasyland*, 10 Hast Cen Rpt 9 (Aug 1980). A further, albeit less apparent, instance of a quality of life assessment occurred in *Re Quinlan*, 70 NJ 10, 355 A 2d 647, cert denied, 429 US 922 (1976) and its progeny. . . . See also, Annas, *Reconciling Quinlan and Saikewicz: Decision-Making for the Terminally Ill Incompetent*, 4 Am JL & Med 367 (1979).

[25] See, eg, Goldstein, ['Medical Care for the Child at Risk: On State Supervention of Parental Autonomy' 86 Yale LJ 645 (1977)], at 651–61; Williams, ['Down's Syndrome and the Duty to Preserve Life' 131 New LJ 1020 (1981)], at 1020–21.

The American approach to 'best interests' is helpfully set out in the President's Commission Report (*op cit*), *Deciding to Forego Life-Sustaining Treatment*, at pp 217–223 (footnotes omitted).

Best interests of the infant. In most circumstances, people agree on whether a proposed course of therapy is in a patient's best interests. Even with seriously ill newborns, quite often there is no issue—either a particular therapy plainly offers net benefits or no effective therapy is available. Sometimes, however, the right outcome will be unclear because the child's 'best interests' are difficult to assess.

The Commission believes that decisionmaking will be improved if an attempt is made to decide which of three situations applies in a particular case—(1) a treatment is available that would clearly benefit the infant, (2) all treatment is expected to be futile, or (3) the probable benefits to an infant from different choices are quite uncertain (see Table 1 . . .). The three situations need to be considered separately, since they demand differing responses.

Clearly beneficial therapies. The Commission's inquiries indicate that treatments are rarely withheld when there is a medical consensus that they would provide a net benefit to a child. Parents naturally want to provide necessary medical care in most circumstances, and parents who are hesitant at first about having treatment administered usually come to recognise the desirability of providing treatment after discussions with physicians, nurses, and others. Parents should be able to choose among alternative treatments with similarly beneficial results and among providers,

Table 1:

Treatment options for seriously ill newborns—physician's assessment in relation to parent's preference

Physician's Assessment of Treatment Options*	Parents Prefer to Accept Treatment**	Parents Prefer to Forego Treatment**
Clearly beneficial	Provide treatment	Provide treatment during review process
Ambiguous or uncertain	Provide treatment	Forego treatment
Futile	Provide treatment unless provider declines to do so	Forego treatment

* The assessment of the value to the infant of the treatments available will initially be by the attending physician. Both when this assessment is unclear and when the joint decision between parents and physician is to forego treatment, this assessment would be reviewed by intra-institutional mechanisms and possibly thereafter by court.
** The choice made by the infant's parents or other duly authorised surrogate who has adequate decisionmaking capacity and has been adequately informed, based on their assessment of the infant's best interests.

. . .

but not to reject treatment that is reliably expected to benefit a seriously ill newborn substantially, as is usually true if life can be saved.

Many therapies undertaken to save the lives of seriously ill newborns will leave the survivors with permanent handicaps, either from the underlying defect (such as heart surgery not affecting the retardation of a Down's Syndrome infant) or from the therapy itself (as when mechanical ventilation for a premature baby results in blindness or a scarred trachea). One of the most troubling and persistent issues in this entire area is whether, or to what extent, the expectation of such handicaps should be considered in deciding to treat or not to treat a seriously ill newborn. The Commission has concluded that a very restrictive standard is appropriate: such permanent handicaps justify a decision not to provide life-sustaining treatment only when they are so severe that continued existence would not be a net benefit to the infant. Though inevitably somewhat subjective and imprecise in actual application, the concept of 'benefit' excludes honoring idiosyncratic views that might be allowed if a person were deciding about his or her own treatment. Rather, net benefit is absent only if the burdens imposed on the patient by the disability or its treatment would lead a competent decisionmaker to choose to forego the treatment. As in all surrogate decisionmaking, the surrogate is obligated to try to evaluate benefits and burdens from the infant's own perspective. The Commission believes that the handicaps of Down's Syndrome, for example, are not in themselves of this magnitude and do not justify failing to provide medically proven treatment, such as surgical correction of a blocked intestinal tract.

This is a very strict standard in that it excludes consideration of the negative effects of an impaired child's life on other persons, including parents, siblings, and society. Although abiding by this standard may be difficult in specific cases, it is all too easy to undervalue the lives of handicapped infants; the Commission finds it imperative to counteract this by treating them no less vigorously than their healthy peers or than older children with similar handicaps would be treated.

Clearly futile therapies. When there is no therapy that can benefit an infant, as in anencephaly or certain severe cardiac deformities, a decision by surrogates and providers not to try predictably futile endeavors is ethically and legally justifiable. Such therapies do not help the child, are sometimes painful for the infant (and probably distressing to the parents), and offer no reasonable probability of saving life for a substantial period. The moment of death for these infants might be delayed for a short time—perhaps as long as a few weeks—by vigorous therapy. Of course, the prolongation of life—and hope against hope—may be enough to lead some parents to want to try a therapy believed by physicians to be futile. As long as this choice does not cause substantial suffering for the child, providers should accept it, although individual health care professionals who find it personally offensive to engage in futile treatment may arrange to withdraw from the case.

Just as with older patients, even when cure or saving of life are out of reach, obligations to comfort and respect a dying person remain. Thus infants whose lives are destined to be brief are owed whatever relief from suffering and enhancement of life can be provided, including feeding, medication for pain, and sedation, as appropriate. Moreover, it may be possible for parents to hold and comfort the child once the elaborate means of life-support are withdrawn, which can be very important to all concerned in symbolic and existential as well as physical terms.

Ambiguous cases. Although for most seriously ill infants there will be either a clearly beneficial option or no beneficial therapeutic options at all, hard questions are raised by the smaller number for whom it is very difficult to assess whether the treatments available offer prospects of benefit—for example, a child with a debilitating and painful disease who might live with therapy, but only for a year or so, or a respirator-dependent premature infant whose long-term prognosis becomes bleaker with each passing day.

Much of the difficulty in these cases arises from factual uncertainty. For the many infants born prematurely, and sometimes for those with serious congenital defects, the only certainty is that without intensive care they are unlikely to survive; very little is known about how each individual will fare with treatment. Neonatology is too new a field to allow accurate predictions of which babies will survive and of the complications, handicaps, and potentials that the survivors might have.

The longer some of these babies survive, the more reliable the prognosis for the infant becomes and the clearer parents and professionals can be on whether further treatment is warranted or futile. Frequently, however, the prospect of long-term survival and the quality of that survival remain unclear for days, weeks, and months, during which time the infants may have an unpredictable and fluctuating course of advances and setbacks.

One way to avoid confronting anew the difficulties involved in evaluating each case is to adopt objective criteria to distinguish newborns who will receive life-sustaining treatment from those who will not. Such criteria would be justified if there were evidence that their adoption would lead to decisions more often being made correctly.

Strict treatment criteria proposed in the 1970s by a British physician for deciding which newborns with spina bifida should receive treatment rested upon the location of the lesion (which influences degree of paralysis), the presence of hydrocephalus (fluid in the brain, which influences degree of retardation), and the likelihood of an infection. Some critics of this proposal argued with it on scientific grounds, such as objecting that long-term effects of spina bifida cannot be predicted with sufficient accuracy at birth. Other critics, however, claimed this whole approach to ambiguous cases exhibited the 'technical criteria fallacy'. They contended that an infant's future life—and hence the treatment decisions based on it—involves value considerations that are ignored when physicians focus solely on medical prognosis.

The decision [to treat or not] must also include evaluation of the meaning of existence with varying impairments. Great variation exists about these essentially evaluative elements among parents, physicians, and policy makers. It must be an open question whether these variations in evaluation are among the relevant factors to consider in making a treatment decision. When Lorber uses the phrase 'contraindications to active therapy', he is medicalising what are really value choices.

The Commission agrees that such criteria necessarily include value considerations. Supposedly objective criteria such as birth weight limits or checklists for severity of spina bifida have not been shown to improve the quality of decisionmaking in ambiguous and complex cases. Instead, their use seems to remove the weight of responsibility too readily from those who should have to face the value questions—parents and health care providers.

Furthermore, any set of standards, when honestly applied, leaves some difficult or uncertain cases. When a child's best interests are ambiguous, a decision based upon them will require prudent and discerning judgment. Defining the category of cases in a way that appropriately protects and encourages the exercise of parental judgment will sometimes be difficult. The procedures the Commission puts forward in the remainder of this chapter are intended to assist in differentiating between the infants whose interests are in fact uncertain and for whom surrogates' decisions (whether for or against therapy) should be honored, and those infants who would clearly benefit from a certain course of action, which, if not chosen by the parents and providers, ought to be authorised by persons acting for the state as *parens patriae*.

2. Who establishes the test?

There is considerable confusion in analytical terms between decisions taken concerning the treatment of a particular patient and decisions taken concerning the principles or rules which should govern the management of a particular case. As a matter of legal analysis the principles or rules come first; attention should then be directed towards their application.

So, what we are concerned with here is *who sets* the criteria by reference to which a decision is taken concerning the management and care of a baby? If it is thought that these principles must be principles of law, then we must identify the relevant law-making institution and see whether anything has been established, or we must argue by analogy from existing law not specific to the case but sufficiently similar to be thought to be relevant. If, however, we think that the rules are not a matter of law, then we may have to look to other sources. But we may be able to dispose of this alternative immediately. Can it be argued that the law has no concern for, indeed has nothing to say about, the care of a child when that care may involve its death? To assert that the law is not involved is to assert something strange, namely that the management of the care of handicapped babies is outside the law: it can be neither lawful nor unlawful. But, English law conceives of no 'legal vacuum'; that which is not unlawful must be lawful. You will understand that, if it is being asserted that letting babies die at the say so of parents, doctors or others is lawful, reference must be made to some legal authority. This calls for an analysis of the law which, *ex hypothesi*, concedes the first of the propositions advanced earlier, namely, that the question of who sets the criteria is a legal one.

The alternative position is not without its adherents. Professor Glanville Williams argues: '. . . The criminal law should stay its hand . . . The decision of the parents should prevail . . .' (Correspondence, *The Times*, 13 August 1981). We submit, however, that Professor Williams cannot be understood as saying the law is not involved. Rather, he must mean that there is law and the law grants a discretion (*quaere*, an unlimited one) to the parents to decide on the management of the care of their child.

Thus, we must now turn to the law. Ordinarily law is derived from statute or case law. There is no statute directly governing the management of the care of handicapped babies in England (nor is there likely to be, given the controversial nature of the problem; but see D Brahams and M Brahams, '*R v Arthur*—Is Legislation Appropriate?' (1981) 78 LSG 1342). The US experience is different. The Federal Administration attempted to introduce in 1982, Regulations dealing with the non-treatment of handicapped babies. The interim Regulations were struck down on procedural grounds: *American Academy of Paediatrics v Heckler* 561 F Supp 395 (1983, DDC). The final Rules were similarly struck down by the Supreme Court in *Bowen v American Hospital Association* 106 S Ct 2101 (1986). See also Annas 'Checkmating the Baby Doe Regulations' (1986) Hastings Center Report, 29 August (see now Child Abuse Amendments 1984).

Let us now turn to the English cases. What do they tell us about who sets the criteria? In *Arthur* one thing does appear clear from Farquharson J's direction to the jury. He recognises that it is for the court ultimately to prescribe what doctors and parents may do. It may be, however, that the rule enunciated by the judge is one which grants almost complete discretion to doctors and parents.

In *Re B*, however, Templeman LJ, while confirming the involvement of the law, insisted on a test which gave less scope to the discretion of the doctors and parents. Dunn LJ is curiously ambivalent. He agrees with Templeman LJ but goes on to suggest that the parents' wishes might have lawfully prevailed had the matter not been brought to the court's attention. In other words, the court grants a very great discretion to the parents and doctors. Accepting then that the law is the appropriate mechanism for defining principles and rules applicable in this area, we next have to consider the content of these legal rules. As we have argued, English law applies a 'best interests' test which, in this context calls for an evaluation of the neonate's 'quality of life'.

3. What does the test mean?

We have already seen the 'quality of life' test in some of the material which has gone before. We now consider further analysis of it. In a study written for the Law Reform Commission of Canada, 'Sanctity of Life or Quality of Life', it is stated that (pp 50–51; footnotes omitted):

> The answer of course depends upon what is meant, or what meaning we give to 'quality of life'. What makes the question one of practical relevance and not just academic interest is that quality of life concerns are already and long have been influencing medical decisions. But what makes the question an urgent and somewhat worrisome one for society, medicine and law is that quality of life can and does mean many very different things, has no single, generally accepted meaning, and some of its connotations and the uses to which the concept is put are definitely opposed to and in conflict with the sanctity of life principle as outlined earlier.
>
> It is probably its very elusiveness which makes the concept so attractive to media and public. It is so vague and glibly used in such quite different contexts (environmental and medical for instance) and in support of such quite different positions (for instance to improve the quality of air, or to cease medical treatment) that the concept seems to commit one to nothing specific, and is seldom given tangible content.
>
> But its very elusiveness encourages as well the polarised, extreme and hostile views about its moral legitimacy and usefulness. There are those who think it answers all questions, and those who think it answers none. There are those who would welcome the replacement of the 'traditional' ethic of the absolute value of human life by an ethic of its relative value. There are others who see any recognition of quality of life factors as a danger to be resisted at all costs.
>
> But it is also possible, and in my view legitimate and preferable, to see no need to choose between an old ethic and a new one. Instead, to recognise an urgent need to on the one hand articulate and refine the 'old' ethic, and on the other hand to propose

a carefully delineated and restricted meaning and purpose for quality of life. The purpose of such an exercise would be to encourage both medical decision-making and (perhaps) law-making to more formally recognise an interest in considering and protecting *both* the intrinsic value of each human life, *and* the quality of those lives, even when this involves a decision to cease or not initiate treatment or life support.

But to make this case successfully depends first of all of course on the meaning we intend for quality of life. . . .

Later, the study continues (at pp 57–60):

Quality is a comparative property, an evaluative property. And it is true that quality of life used in environmental/social contexts does essentially involve a comparison with other things—a ranking of the conditions which maximise optimal human life or general happiness requirements of a region. Implicit in the comparison is a readiness to discard or improve certain conditions because of where they rank on the scale.

But in the medical/health context, quality of life *need* not involve a comparison of *different human lives* as the basis for decisions to treat some and not others. Ideally, at the heart of quality of life concerns in this context should be only a comparison of the qualities *this patient* now has with the qualities deemed by *this patient* (or, if incompetent or irreversibly comatose, by the patient's agents) to be normative and desirable, and either still or no longer present actually or potentially.

The real comparison in question is in a sense one between what the patient is and was, is and can or cannot be in the future. The quality of life comparison or evaluation in the medical context need not be a comparison *with others* or a relativising of persons' lives. And the quality of life norm and decision need not be arbitrary or based upon how treatment or non-treatment will relieve or burden others or society. The norm can and must include whatever the value sciences, medicine and public policy agree upon concerning the essential quality or qualities of a human person; and the decision can and must be in the first instance by, and for the benefit of the patient and no one else.

To include quality of life considerations in life saving or life support decision-making by no means must imply *harm* rather than improvement or benefit to the patients. If quality of life is limited only to what is intended here, then quite the contrary is the case and must be the case if the concept is to have any justifiably normative value.

In the first place, investigations, prognoses and conclusions arrived at concerning a patient's actual or potential level of function or degree of suffering, need not inevitably and exclusively lead to decisions *to cease* or *not initiate* life supporting treatment. Given that the sanctity of life principle imposes the burden of proof on those who would cease to support life, the consideration of quality of life factors should more often lead to the opposite decision—to initiate or continue that treatment if there is any realistic hope of minimal human function and controllable pain and suffering.

Secondly, even when quality of life factors do contribute to a decision to cease or not initiate life saving or supporting treatment, there remains the continuing obligation to seek to improve the newborn's or the patient's *care and comfort*. Neither physician nor patient are usually faced with only two options—to continue or discontinue life support treatment. The third option and continuing responsibility of health care professionals and families, no matter how damaged the patient's condition, is to seek to improve the level of care and comfort of the dying, including being physically present to them. The sanctity of life surely calls for at least the same respect and consideration for dying life as for healthy life. And if greater needs call for greater care and concern, then the dying deserve more, not less of it, than the healthy.

Thirdly, even decisions to cease or not initiate life saving treatments, based partly on quality of life considerations, can and must offer a reasonable hope of *benefit* to the patient. In other words, death should not always be resisted at any cost in terms of present and future suffering and damage, as if anything is an improvement over death. It is an integral part of my thesis that this is not so, that some conditions of human life are so damaged, and will likely remain so or become worse if treatment is continued or initiated, that death can reasonably be seen as beneficial, as an improvement for that patient.

The final weighing and balancing of reasons and criteria normally belongs to the patient, and within morally acceptable parameters different patients may and will weigh the criteria differently and come to different decisions. For the incompetent, the determination of benefit to patient or newborn must be made by proxies. While it remains enormously difficult to make such decisions in the interests and for the benefit of others, it is my contention that they must sometimes be made, and that reasonable and morally justifiable decisions for the benefit of others, based partially at least on quality of life matters, are possible. There will be occasion to come back to the 'who decides' question and the other points in more detail as the argument unfolds.

In the light of the above, quality of life in the medical context need not come out the loser when compared to quality of life in the environmental/social context. As noted, there are of course great differences in the contexts and the functions within them of quality of life criteria. But in both contexts the ultimate aim of these criteria is objective improvement and benefit, even if in the medical context that will often be limited to reducing rather than eliminating the patient's discomfort and indignity. In claiming this, the medical cases envisioned are primarily those in which the quality of life criteria are used in decisions made *by others* for the incompetent patient. In such cases the use of these criteria for the patient's objective improvement or reduction of discomfort or some other benefit is a realistic aim. Obviously it may be otherwise for patients able to *themselves* accept or refuse treatment. Since, as I shall argue below, competent patients have the right to refuse treatment on any grounds at all, whether they seem reasonable or foolish to others, there can be no guarantee at all of objective improvement and benefit in the decisions made and criteria used by competent patients for themselves.

Just before attempting to put flesh on the dry bones, to offer more argument for the claims made, the thesis of this quality of life section of the paper should be summarised.

Quality of life need not mean the 'relativising of lives'. Excluded here in this paper from that concept and its criteria are considerations such as social worth, social utility, social status or relative worth. The sanctity of life principle rightly insists on the intrinsic worth and equal value of every life. In excluding these elements from the meaning intended for quality of life, one need not of course deny that they can be ingredients of quality of life in wider contexts than our own. At least some of them are factors which a 'general' quality of life theory must consider and weigh in other contexts. I am only excluding these factors from this particular context of medical decision-making in life and death matters, and primarily when such decisions are made by proxies or patients' agents for patients or newborns unable to make these decisions themselves. Whatever the merits and realities of characteristics such as social status in other areas of concern, here I do not believe they should have determinative weight.

New circumstances such as increasingly sophisticated life support systems and treatment have challenged us to recognise in human life a distinction between mere existence and quality with more clarity than previously needed. But that does not mean that in our context the shifting sands of new medical technology, evolving social realities or subjective preferences comprise an adequate source for the meaning and criteria of a quality of life concept, or in themselves validly answer our questions. What is involved here, or should be, is a search for and a weighing of the *inherent features* of human life. That is an objective meaning of "quality" light years away from mere considerations of relative and changing circumstances, facts and values. It does not make the task easier, or ensure an immediate consensus but at least the task is defensible.

In this sense, meaning and criteria for quality of life in life or death decision-making, should focus not on features or conditions which permit patients to act comfortably, well and without burdening others or society, but rather on features and conditions which allow them to act *at all*, even to a minimal extent. The real question and issue raised by considerations of quality of life is not about the value of this patient's *life*—it is about the value of this patient's *treatment*.

The meaning and criteria of quality of life should focus on *benefit to the patient*, and in some circumstances to initiate treatment or prolong or postpone death can reasonably be seen as non-beneficial to the patient. One such circumstance is *excruciating, intractable and prolonged pain and suffering*. Another is the lack of capacity for what can be considered an inherent feature of human life, namely a *minimal capacity to experience, to relate with other human beings*. In such instances to preserve life could in some cases be a dishonouring of the sanctity of life itself, and allowing even death could be a demonstration of respect for the individual and for human life in general.

Later, the study continues (at pp 70–72):

In particular there are two such quality of life criteria relevant to decisions to treat, or to continue treatment or to stop treatment. The first considers the capacity to experience, to relate. The second considers the intensity and susceptibility to control of the patient's pain and suffering. If despite treatment there is not and cannot be even a minimal capacity to experience, and to relate, or if the level of pain and suffering will be prolonged, excruciating and intractable, then a decision to cease or not initiate treatment (of for instance a comatose patient) can be preferable to treatment.

The word 'life' can mean two things in this context. It can mean vital or metabolic processes alone, a life incapable of experiencing or communicating and one which therefore could be called 'human biological life'. Or it could mean a level or quality of life which includes *both* metabolic functions and at least a minimal capacity to experience or communicate, which together could be called 'human personal life'. . . .

Given that the sanctity of life principle imposes the burden of proof on those who would cease to support the lives of others, the consideration of quality of life criteria should not inevitably and exclusively lead to decisions to cease or not initiate life supporting or saving treatment. Quite the opposite should just as often or more often be the case.

While a degree of 'indignity' is an inescapable element of death and dying, and while not every instance of a patient's life being externally supported is thereby undignified, there are cases in which the refusal to consider and weigh the patient's quality of life can result in a prolongation of treatment to the point that a real and further indignity is being done.

Both medical decision-making and law should continue to protect the intrinsic sanctity and value of each human life. But medicine (and perhaps law as well) should formally acknowledge that in some cases the quality or conditions of a patient's life can be so damaged and minimal that treatment or further treatment could be a violation precisely of that life's sanctity and value.

Even in those cases for which it is decided to cease or not initiate external life supporting *treatment*, there always remains a continuing obligation no matter how damaged the patient's condition, to provide whatever amount of *care and comfort* is needed and possible.

The elusiveness of the concept of 'quality of life' leading, perhaps, to confusion, is well illustrated by the judgment of Liacos J in the well-known case of *Superintendent of Belchertown v Saikewicz* 370 NE 2d 417 (1976). Liacos J appeared to want to take advantage of the concept and yet not be seen to be engaging in the calculation that the concept necessarily entails. When discussing whether a mentally retarded person suffering from acute myeloblastic monocytic leukaemia, who was adult but incompetent to consent, should have chemotherapy, he said:

The sixth factor identified by the judge as weighing against chemotherapy was 'the quality of life possible for him even if the treatment does bring about remission'. To the extent that this formulation equates the value of life with any measure of the quality of life, we firmly reject it. A reading of the entire record clearly reveals, however, the judge's concern that special care be taken to respect the dignity and worth of Saikewicz's life precisely because of his vulnerable position. The judge, as well as all the parties, were keenly aware that the supposed ability of Saikewicz, by virtue of his mental retardation, to appreciate or experience life had no place in the decision before them. Rather than reading the judge's formulation in a manner that demeans the value of the life of one who is mentally retarded, the vague, and perhaps ill-chosen term 'quality of life' should be understood as a reference to the continuing state of pain and disorientation precipitated by the chemotherapy treatment.

Clearly, since the test is an evaluative one, the law calls for the exercise of discretion. What, as a matter of law, is the nature of this discretion?

Is the discretion unlimited? To argue that parents or doctors have an unlimited discretion is to state that a court would not seek to intervene in, or impose sanction for, *any* decision whatever it may be. This only has to be stated to be seen to be untenable in the light of *Arthur* since, if there were an unlimited discretion, no prosecution could sensibly have been brought and once it had been the judge would have directed the jury to acquit. Similarly, the decision in *Re B* would be a curious one.

Is the discretion limited? If, as we argue, there is a *limited* discretion granted by the law, the question is what is the nature of the limitation? The only response which conforms with the traditional approach of the law can be that any decision made should be in the best interests of the child. Any other test would subjugate the interests of the child to those of others. There is no authority in English law that the interests of those who have the care of a child may give second place to the child's interests. This, of course, is a formal test which does not give substance to the notion of 'best interests' but we have already given substance to it in our discussion of 'quality of life'.

Authority to support our conclusion can be found in the *Gillick* case in which the House of Lords makes clear that parents have 'duties' to their children rather than 'rights' over them and that the primary duty is to act in the child's best interests, reflected also in the child care legislation of this century which stresses the paramount nature of the child's welfare.

Some also would pray in aid the Children and Young Persons Act 1933, s 1, which creates the offence of 'wilful neglect' of a child. This provision does not, however, clinch any argument, since it begs the central question of whether to adopt a new regime of management which allows a baby to die is necessarily 'wilful neglect'. A parent *can* be guilty under s 1 for failing to provide adequate medical treatment (e g *R v Senior* [1899] 1 QB 283; *R v Lowe* [1973] QB 702; *Oakey v Jackson* [1914] 1 KB 216). The law was stated by the House of Lords in *R v Sheppard* [1981] AC 394, [1980] 3 All ER 899. Notice that the failure to provide must be 'wilful' and the failure must be to provide 'adequate medical aid' so as to cause the child unnecessary suffering or injury to health. Lord Diplock said:

Such a failure as it seems to me could not be properly described as 'wilful' unless the parent *either* (1) had directed his mind to the question whether there was some risk (though it might fall far short of a probability) that the child's health might suffer unless he were examined by a doctor and provided with such curative treatment as the examination might reveal as necessary, and had made a conscious decision, for whatever reason, to refrain from arranging for such medical examination, *or* (2) had so refrained because he did not care whether the child might be in need of medical treatment or not.

  ... I have referred to the parent's knowledge of the existence of some risk of injury to health rather than of a probability. The section speaks of an act or omission that is 'likely' to cause unnecessary suffering or injury to health. This word is imprecise. It is capable of covering a whole range of possibilities from 'it's on the cards' to 'it's more probable than not'; but, having regard to the ordinary parent's lack of skill in diagnosis and to the very serious consequences which may result from failure to provide a child with timely medical attention, it should in my view be understood as excluding only what would fairly be described as highly unlikely . . .

Lord Edmund-Davies added:

The justice (and, with respect, the common sense) of the matter is surely that, as Professor Glanville Williams has put it in his Textbook of Criminal Law (1978, p 88):

We do not run to a doctor whenever a child is a little unwell. We invoke medical aid only when we think that a doctor is reasonably necessary and may do some good. The requirement of wilfulness means, or should mean, that a parent who omits to call in the doctor to his child is not guilty of the offence if he does not know that the child needs this assistance.

But to that must be added that a parent reckless about the state of his child's health, not caring whether or not he is at risk, cannot be heard to say that he never gave the matter a thought and was therefore not wilful in not calling in a doctor. In such circumstances recklessness constitutes mens rea no less than positive awareness of the risk involved in failure to act. . . .

Lord Keith added:

This appeal is concerned solely with a failure to provide adequate medical care. The word 'adequate', as applied to medical care, may mean no more than 'ordinarily competent'. If it is related to anything, I think it is related to the prevention of unnecessary suffering or injury to health, as mentioned in s 1(1), where in my view the adjective 'unnecessary' qualifies both 'suffering' and 'injury to health'. There could be no question of a finding of neglect against a parent who provided ordinarily competent medical care, but whose child nevertheless suffered further injury to its health, for example paralysis in a case of poliomyelitis, because the injury to health would not in the circumstances have been unnecessary, in the sense that it could have been prevented through the provision by the parent of adequate medical care. Failure to provide adequate medical care may be deliberate, as when the child's need for it is perceived yet nothing is done, negligent, as when the need ought reasonably to have been perceived but was not, or entirely blameless, as when the need was not perceived but was not such as ought to have been perceived by an ordinary reasonable parent. I would say that in all three cases the parent has neglected the child in the sense of the statute, since I am of opinion that in a proper construction of s 1(2)(a) it is to be ascertained objectively and in the light of events whether the parent failed to provide ordinarily competent medical care which as a matter of fact the child needed in order to prevent unnecessary suffering or injury to its health.

Do you agree with Lord Keith's analysis of the word 'adequate'? Is this not the nub of the issue in these non-treatment cases? Lord Keith might be said to have considered 'adequate' to be a matter of fact. Is it not, however, really a matter of judgment based on normative criteria? In other words, does not 'adequate' also connote 'appropriate'? If this is so, are we any further in determining the extent of parental duty after reading Lord Keith's speech?

  The cases of *Senior, Lowe* and *Oakey v Jackson* (mentioned above), though establishing potential parental liability, throw little light on the problem we are considering since they are all cases where medical treatment was called for on any reasonable view of the facts.

But what of the doctor? The test of limited discretion of acting in the 'best interests' must be the same for him. For if the parents, acting in the 'best interests' of the child (as understood above), withhold consent to a particular treatment aimed at preserving life, the doctor *must* lawfully respect their decision. If the parents are not acting in the 'best interests' of the child (as understood above), he *may* act on his own judgment relying on the defence of necessity or set in motion an application to the court to ward the child to obtain authoritative guidance. It is then for the *court* to determine the 'best interests' of the child.

In the case of newborns, the courts have accepted an objective test of 'best interests', ie that which is in the child's best interests must be determined by reference to what a *reasonable person* would think was in the child's 'best interests'; in other words, 'quality of life' as seen through the eyes of the reasonable person.

There is another approach whereby the court seeks to give effect to what it presumes would be the decision of the disabled person if they had been able to express a view. This more subjective approach has become known in the US as the test of 'substituted judgment' (see *supra* ch 4 for a discussion). Clearly, it ought to have no place in the case of a newborn child who has, as yet, no preferences. As the child grows older, however, this approach may come into play (see *Dawson*). It is most relevant in the case of the adult incompetent (see *infra* ch 14).

4. Who applies the test?

Having determined what test is to be applied?, who decides what the test means? and what is to decide these questions?, the final question is who applies the test? There are four candidates: (i) the court or other institutional body; (ii) the doctor(s); (iii) the parent(s); (iv) a combination of (ii) and (iii).

Institutional decision making. Let us consider three decisions of the American courts. Each concerned an adult incompetent, but they will help the analysis for us in relation to neonates.

Re Karen Quinlan
355 A 2d 647 (1976) (Supreme Court of New Jersey)

Hughes CJ: If a putative decision by Karen to permit this non-cognitive, vegetative existence to terminate by natural forces is regarded as a valuable incident of her right of privacy, as we believe it to be, then it should not be discarded solely on the basis that her condition prevents her conscious exercise of the choice. The only practical way to prevent destruction of the right is to permit the guardian and family of Karen to render their best judgment, subject to the qualifications hereinafter stated as to whether she would exercise it in these circumstances. If their conclusion is in the affirmative this decision should be accepted by a society the overwhelming majority of whose members would, we think, in similar circumstances, exercise such a choice in the same way for themselves or for those closest to them. It is for this reason that we determine that Karen's right of privacy may be asserted in her behalf, in this respect, by her guardian and family under the particular circumstances presented by this record.

. . .

I suggest that it would be more appropriate to provide a regular forum for more input and dialogue in individual situations and to allow the responsibility of these judgments to be shared. Many hospitals have established an Ethics Committee composed of physicians, social workers, attorneys and theologians, . . . which serves to review the individual circumstances of ethical dilemma and which has provided much in the way of assistance and safeguards for patients and their medical caretakers. Generally, the authority of these committees is primarily restricted to the hospital setting and their official status is more that of an advisory body than of an enforcing body.

The concept of an Ethics Committee which has this kind of organisation and is readily accessible to those persons rendering medical care to patients, would be, I think, the most promising direction for further study at this point. . . . [This would allow] some much needed dialogue regarding these issues and [force] the point of exploring all of the options for a particular patient. It diffuses the responsibility for making these judgments. Many physicians, in many circumstances, would welcome this sharing of responsibility. I believe that such an entity could lend itself well to an assumption of a legal status which would allow courses of action not now undertaken because of the concern for liability. [27 Baylor L Rev 6, 8–9 (1975)].

The most appealing factor in the technique suggested by Dr Teel seems to us to be the diffusion of professional responsibility for decision, comparable in a way to the value of multi-judge courts in finally resolving on appeal difficult questions of law. Moreover, such a system would be protective to the hospital as well as the doctor in screening out, so to speak, a case which might be contaminated by less than worthy motivations of family or physician. In the real world and in relationship to the momentous decision contemplated, the value of additional views and diverse knowledge is apparent.

We consider that a practice of applying to a court to confirm such decisions would generally be inappropriate, not only because that would be a gratuitous encroachment upon the medical profession's field of competence, but because it would be impossibly cumbersome. Such a requirement is distinguishable from the judicial overview traditionally required in other matters such as the adjudication and commitment of mental incompetents. This is not to say that in the case of an otherwise justiciable controversy access to the courts would be foreclosed; we speak rather of a general practice and procedure.

And although the deliberations and decisions which we describe would be professional in nature they should obviously include at some stage the feelings of the family of an incompetent relative. Decision-making within health care if it is considered as an expression of a primary obligation of the physician, primum non nocere, should be controlled primarily within the patient-doctor-family relationship, as indeed was recognised by Judge Muir in his supplemental opinion of November 12, 1975.

If there could be created not necessarily this particular system but some reasonable counterpart, we would have no doubt that such decisions, thus determined to be in accordance with medical practice and prevailing standards, would be accepted by society and by the courts, at least in cases comparable to that of Karen Quinlan.

Superintendent of Belchertown v Saikewicz
370 NE 2d 417 (1976) (Supreme Judicial Court of Massachusetts) (footnotes omitted)

Liacos J: We think it appropriate, and highly desirable, in cases such as the one before us to charge the guardian *ad litem* with an additional responsibility to be discharged if there is a finding of incompetency. This will be the responsibility of presenting to the judge, after as thorough an investigation as time will permit, all reasonable arguments in favour of administering treatment to prolong the life of the individual involved. This will ensure that all viewpoints and alternatives will be aggressively pursued and examined at the subsequent hearing where it will be determined whether treatment should or should not be allowed. The report of the guardian or temporary guardian will, of course, also be available to the judge at this hearing on the ultimate issue of treatment. Should the probate judge then be satisfied that the incompetent individual would, as determined by the standards previously set forth, have chosen to forego potentially life-prolonging treatment, the judge shall issue the appropriate order. If the judge is not so persuaded, or finds that the interests of the State require it, then treatment shall be ordered.

Commensurate with the powers of the Probate Court already described, the probate judge may, at any step in these proceedings, avail himself or herself of the additional advice or knowledge of any person or group. We note here that many health care institutions have developed medical ethics committees or panels to consider many of the issues touched on here. Consideration of the findings and advice of such groups as well as the testimony of the attending physicians and other medical experts ordinarily would be of great assistance to a probate judge faced with such a difficult decision. We believe it desirable for a judge to consider such views wherever available and useful to the court. We do not believe, however, that this option should be transformed by us into a required procedure. We take a dim view of any attempt to shift the ultimate decision-making responsibility away from the duly established courts of proper jurisdiction to any committee, panel or group, ad hoc or permanent. Thus, we reject the approach adopted by the New Jersey Supreme Court in the *Quinlan* case of entrusting the decision whether to continue artificial life support to the patient's guardian, family, attending doctors, and hospital 'ethics committee', 70 NJ at 55, 355 A 2d 647 at 671. One rationale for such a delegation was expressed by the lower court judge in the *Quinlan* case, and quoted by the New Jersey Supreme Court: 'The nature, extent and duration of care by societal standards is the responsibility of a physician. The morality and conscience of our society places this responsibility in the hands of the physician. What justification is there to remove it from the control of the medical profession and place it in the hands of the courts?' *Id*, at 44, 355 A 2d at 665. For its part, the New Jersey Supreme Court concluded that 'a practice of applying to a court to confirm such decisions would generally be inappropriate, not only because that would be a gratuitous encroachment upon the medical profession's field of competence, but because it would be impossibly cumbersome. Such a requirement is distinguishable from the judicial overview traditionally required in other matters such as the adjudication and commitment of mental incompetents. This is not to say that in the case of an otherwise justiciable controversy access to the courts would be foreclosed; we speak rather of a general practice and procedure.' *Id* at 50, 355 A 2d at 669.

We do not view the judicial resolution of the most difficult and awesome question—whether potentially life-prolonging treatment should be withheld from a person incapable of making his own decision—as constituting a 'gratuitous encroachment' on the domain of medical expertise. Rather, such questions of life and death seem to us to require the process of detached but passionate investigation and decision that forms the ideal on which the judicial branch of government was created. Achieving this ideal is our responsibility and that of the lower court, and is not to be entrusted to any other group purporting to represent the 'morality and conscience of our society', no matter how highly motivated or impressively constituted.

Eichner v Dillon
42 NYS 2d 517 (1980) (Supreme Court, Appellate Division of New York, on appeal; see 438 NYS 2d 266) (footnotes omitted)

Mollen PJ: The final problem concerns the actual implementation of the right of the terminally ill but comatose patient to refuse extraordinary medical treatment. *Quinlan* and *Saikewicz* present two divergent models of implementation. *Quinlan* provided that:

> Upon the concurrence of the guardian and family of Karen, should the responsible attending physicians conclude that there is no reasonable possibility of Karen's ever emerging from her present comatose condition to a cognitive, sapient state and that the life-support apparatus now being administered to Karen should be discontinued, they shall consult with the hospital 'Ethics Committee' or like body of the institution in which Karen is then hospitalised. If that consultative body agrees that there is no reasonable possibility of Karen's ever emerging from her present comatose condition to a cognitive, sapient state, the present life-support

system may be withdrawn and said action shall be without any civil or criminal liability therefor on the part of any participant, whether guardian, physician, hospital or others. (*Matter of Quinlan*, 355 A 2d at 671 *supra*.)

In the view of the *Quinlan* court, the decision to terminate was, in the final analysis, a purely medical one: the injection of the judicial process would constitute a 'gratuitous encroachment upon the medical profession's field of competence' (*Matter of Quinlan*, 355 A 2d at 669 *supra*).

This approach has been criticised, not only because it arguably constitutes an improper shifting of 'the ultimate decision-making responsibility away from the duly established courts of proper jurisdiction' to the Ethics Committee of the hospital (*Superintendent of Belchertown State School v Saikewicz*, 370 NE 2d at 434, *supra*), but more significantly because the Ethics Committee, as an *institution*, is an ill-defined, amorphous body, which in some hospitals may not even exist (see, eg, Hirsch & Donovan, The Right to Die: Medico-Legal Implications of *Re Quinlan*, 30 Rutgers L Rev 267, 276, 280–285). Hence, uniformity of the decision-making process could never be guaranteed under the *Quinlan* model, and for these reasons, the *Saikewicz* court rejected it (see *Superintendent of Belchertown State School v Saikewicz*, 370 NE 2d at 434, *supra*). Instead, *Saikewicz* provided that final decision making must reside with the judicial process and the judicial process alone (*Superintendent of Belchertown State School v Saikewicz*, 370 NE 2d at 434–435). This alternate implementation model has, in turn, engendered criticism that the judicial process is wrongfully injecting itself into what is essentially a medical decision (see Relman, The Saikewicz Decision: A Medical Viewpoint, 4 Amer JL & Med 233, 234; Relman, The Saikewicz Decision: Judges as Physicians, 298 NEJ Med 508, 509; Dunn, Who 'Pulls the Plug': The Practical Effect of the Saikewicz Decision, Medicolegal News [Winter, 1978]; see also, Annas, Reconciling Quinlan and Saikewicz: Decision Making for the Terminally Ill Incompetent, 4 Amer JL & Med 367, 369–371, 395). Contrary to the opinion expressed in some circles, we do not view the *Saikewicz* decision as evincing a 'total distrust of physicians' judgments' or a 'resounding vote of "no confidence" in the ability of physicians and families to act in the best interests of the incapable patient suffering from a terminal illness' (Relman, The Saikewicz Decision: Judges as Physicians, 298 NEJ Med 508). The judicial process is neither ignorant of nor insensitive to the needs and expertise of the medical community on intersecting issues. In reaching a determination the courts *must* rely upon the medical profession in deciding the medical aspects of the problem; we recognise the primacy of the medical profession as to those aspects. But, there are other significant considerations involved, such as the wishes of the patient to the extent ascertainable, religious factors where present, the views of the family, and the concerns of society. We agree with the *Saikewicz* court that the neutral presence of the law is necessary to weigh these factors, and, thus, judicial intervention is required before any life-support system can be withdrawn. We are convinced that 'questions of life and death . . . require the process of detached but passionate investigation and decision that forms the ideal on which the judicial branch of government was created' (*Superintendent of Belchertown State School v Saikewicz*, 370 NE 2d at 435, *supra*). Certainly, this bespeaks no distrust of the good faith or competence of the physician, for courts inevitably must trust the doctor's judgment as to medical prognosis. Rather, our decision recognises that the societal interests to be safeguarded are so great that the courts have no choice but to intervene and examine each case on an *individual* patient-to-patient basis. Just as a hospital or physician must seek a court order prior to giving a blood transfusion to a child over the religious objections of his parents, we believe that the hospital or physician must seek a court order in situations such as the one at bar.

Are any of these suggested mechanisms satisfactory? Are not the courts in the United States over-concerned to lay down some institutional device? Is not the proper role of the court that of *reviewing* decisions having laid down the criteria for others to make them, rather than trying to make every decision itself or to create some *ad hoc* body to do so?

Incidentally, it is now not only the courts in the United States which are concerned to create some appropriate institutional body; as a consequence of the Federal Government's involvement in the *Baby Doe* saga, Congress has passed the Child Abuse Amendments 1984 to the Child Abuse Prevention and Treatment Act 1974. In accordance with the Act and implementing Regulations, the Secretary of Health and Human Sciences published Model Guidelines to encourage the establishment of Infant Care Review Committees (ICRCs) within health care facilities. (For an analysis of them and a consideration of their effect, see L Gostin, 'A Moment in Human Development' (1985) 11 Am JL Med 32.)

It will come as no surprise that there is no English case on this point. It is probable, however, that the English courts would favour a more pragmatic approach whereby those having care of the child are left to make decisions within stated boundaries (see, for example, *re C* (1989) *postscript infra*).

Parents and/or doctors. As we saw earlier, the approach of the English courts is to recognise a limited discretion in parents and doctors to act in what is, at least in their view, the best interests of the child. There is a concomitant legal assumption that *prima facie* this view will prevail. It is, however, subject to review by the court since ultimately their decision must conform with the standard laid down by the law. (See Templeman LJ in *Re B* [1981] 1 WLR 1421.) The view of Dunn LJ in *Re B* raises the only doubt. You will recall that he said (at 1424): 'But the child now being a ward of court, although due weight must be given to the decision of the parents which *everybody accepts was an entirely responsible one, doing what they considered was the best*, the fact of the matter is that this court now has to make the decision' (emphasis added).

If by this Dunn LJ meant that a parent has a free hand to decide whatever he wishes unless the court is involved, we would respectfully demur. Since analytically the decision is for the parents, as it is the parents who are legally entitled to give or withhold consent, the doctor must comply with their wishes *or*, if it is thought that the parents are not acting in the best interests of the child, apply to the court for an authoritative ruling. Lord Templeman in *Gillick* explained the legal position as follows ([1985] 3 All ER 402 at 432).

> A doctor tenders advice and offers treatment which the doctor considers to be in the best interests of the patient. A patient is free to reject the advice and refuse the treatment: see *Sidaway v Bethlem Royal Hospital Governors* [1985] 1 All ER 643 at 665, [1985] 2 WLR 480 at 508. Where the patient is an infant, the medical profession accepts that a parent having custody and being responsible for the infant is entitled on behalf of the infant to consent to or reject treatment if the parent considers that the best interests of the infant so require. Where doctor and parent disagree, the court can decide and is not slow to act. I accept that if there is no time to obtain a decision from the court, a doctor may safely carry out treatment in an emergency if the doctor believes the treatment to be vital to the survival or health of an infant and notwithstanding the opposition of a parent or the impossibility of alerting the parent before the treatment is carried out. In such a case the doctor must have the courage of his convictions that the treatment is necessary and urgent in the interests of the patient and the court will, if necessary, approve after the event treatment which the court would have authorised in advance, even if the treatment proves to be unsuccessful.

Because of the speed with which the wardship jurisdiction may be invoked, will such an 'emergency' situation often arise?

One other question warrants attention. What if a parent demands that his or her child continues to receive treatment when in the doctor's view such treatment can no longer be justified? Is this a situation where, subject to the court's intervention, the parental view of 'best interests' prevails, or could it be seen as the converse of Lord Templeman's doctor acting in an 'emergency', when 'the doctor must have the courage of his convictions' and rely upon the doctrine of necessity with the knowledge that his conduct is always subject to review by the courts?

Professor Skegg would appear to agree with Lord Templeman's view. In *Law, Ethics and Medicine* (at pp 107–8) he states:

> If criminal proceedings were brought as a result of a doctor overriding a parent's refusal of consent, and thereby saving a child's life, the courts could be relied on to make an order of absolute discharge.[36] The medical defence societies have assured doctors of their full support in such cases,[37] and in civil proceedings any award of damages would be unlikely to be more than nominal. However, these considerations do not do away with the need for a justification. Once it is accepted that a doctor should act in a particular manner then, in the absence of a good reason to the contrary, the law should provide a justification. In some cases the difficulties of providing a justification which permits the approved conduct, but not other conduct also, may count against doing so. But this factor can only be determined after the possible justifications have been examined. The case for providing a justification is here supported by other considerations. One is that because of their uncertainty about the law, some doctors have been hesitant to act, with the result that lives have been lost which could otherwise have been saved.[38] Another is that very occasionally the doctor's intervention may not have the desired effect, and may even hasten the patient's death. It would be unreasonable to require a doctor to risk incurring liability in these cases.
>
> Doctors have frequently proceeded without consent where parents have refused consent. The courts have yet to deal with this situation, but Ormrod LJ has said, extrajudicially, that where parents have religious or cultural objections 'to various forms of treatment, such as blood transfusion or operation', the doctor 'is entitled to act on his clinical judgment of the child's best interests'. But added that the doctor would be unwise to follow this course 'except in urgent cases'.[39]

Later (at p 109), he continues:

> A doctor should not be justified in proceeding without consent wherever failure to treat would cause 'unnecessary suffering or injury to health',[42] for this would enable a doctor to bypass the parent altogether in a great many circumstances. But a justification which was restricted to circumstances in which the parent was risking criminal liability by wilfully neglecting the child, in a manner likely to cause unnecessary suffering or injury to its health, would not be adequate. It would not apply to cases where the patent's neglect was not wilful,[43] yet the need for treatment was no less urgent.

Notes to extract
  [36] Powers of Criminal Courts Act 1973, s 7(1).
  [37] See eg S Cochrane Shanks, reported in [1961] 1 *Br Med J* Suppl *292*; J Leahy Taylor, Letter, 'Thou shalt not strive officiously', (1982) 285 *Br Med J* 1743.
  [38] For examples, see *Taylor's Principles and Practice of Medical Jurisprudence* (12th edn, 1965, ed K Simpson), vol i, 67; Note, 'Parent's Refusal of Consent' [1960] 1 *Br Med J* 1371.
  [39] Ormrod, ['A Lawyer Looks at Medical Ethics' (1978) 46 Medico-Leg J 18], 25.
  [42] Cf Children and Young Persons Act 1933, s 1.
  [43] See *R v Sheppard* [1981] AC 394, [1980] 3 All ER 899, HL.

Professor Skegg goes on to offer the following three pre-conditions before a doctor may disregard parental views.'

> First, that in the circumstances it is not reasonable, or in the time available practicable, to take action so that someone else is empowered to authorise the performance of the procedure. Secondly, that the procedure is necessary to save the

life of the child, to prevent permanent injury to its health, or to prevent prolonged pain and suffering.[44] And thirdly, that despite the making of all reasonable efforts to obtain consent, consent has been unreasonably refused.[45]

Notes to extract
[44] Cf Health Amendment Act 1961 (NZ), s 2. For another formulation, see S R Speller, *Law of Doctor and Patient* (1973), 30, and generally ibid 31–5.
[45] Or, where the person authorised to consent is unavailable, but is known to object to the procedure in question, it would have been unreasonable for that person to have withheld consent.

You may think that Skegg has failed to square the circle since he still leaves open the question of how the doctor judges whether a parent's refusal to consent is unreasonable.

In the United States, the courts have, by and large, regarded the parental view of 'best interests' as prevailing. Areen, King, Goldberg and Capron in *Law, Science and Medicine* (at pp 1223–1224), state:

Traditionally, the law has presumed that parents act with the best interests of their children in mind; consequently, we are very deferential to parental decisions about children and are reluctant to intervene. See, eg, *Wisconsin v Yoder* 406 US 205, 92 S Ct 1526, 32 L Ed 2d 15 (1972); *Pierce v Society of Sisters* 268 US 510, 45 S Ct 571, 69 L Ed 1070 (1925); *Meyer v Nebraska* 262 US 390, 43 S Ct 625, 67 L Ed 1042 (1923). This deference, however, has never been absolute. *Prince v Massachusetts* 321 US 158, 64 S Ct 438, 88 L Ed 2d 645 (1944). Where it can be shown that parents have abused or neglected their children or where there is substantial reason to believe that they will do so, the state acting under its *parens patriae* powers can intervene.

With respect to health care matters, courts have intervened and ordered life-saving treatment over parental objection. See, eg, *Re Hamilton* 657 SW 2d 425 (Tenn App 1983); *State v Perricone* 37 NJ 463, 181 A 2d 751, certiorari denied 371 US 890, 83 S Ct 189, 9 L Ed 2d 124 (1962); *People ex rel Wallace v Labrenz*, 411 Ill 618, 104 NE 2d 769, certiorari denied 344 US 824, 73 S Ct 24, 97 L Ed 642 (1952); *Maine Medical Center v Houle* No 74–145 (Super Ct, Cumberland Cty, Me, Feb 14 1974). Courts traditionally have been reluctant, however, to intervene where life is not in imminent danger. See, eg *Re Seiferth* 309 NY 80, 127 NE 2d 820 (1955); *Re Phillip B* 92 Cal App 3d 796, 156 Cal Rptr 48 (1979); *Re Hofbauer* 65 AD 2d 108, 411 NYS 2d 416 (1978); affd 47 NY 2d 648, 419 NYS 2d 936 NE 2d 1009 (1979). This reluctance is perhaps explained by the fact that it has been difficult to distinguish these parental decisions from a number of other decisions parents are allowed to make about education, religion and discipline which may also adversely affect the future growth and development of the child.

This is not to suggest that the traditional legal line has always been a satisfactory one. In those instances where the judgment of the relevant medical community is that a child's physical health will be seriously impaired and cannot be satisfactorily treated at a later time, courts have increasingly intervened to order treatment even where life is not in imminent danger. See, eg *Re Sampson* 65 Misc 2d 658, 317 NYS 2d 641 (1970); affd 29 NY 2d 900, 328 NYS 2d 686, 278 NE 2d 918 (1972)) *Custody of a minor* 375 Mass 733, 379 NE 2d 1053 (1978); *Re Jensen* 54 Or App 1, 633 P 2d 1302 (1981).

If courts have been so consistent in ordering lifesaving for children over parental objection, why then have we spent the last decade or more debating questions concerning appropriate care for newborns with congenital disabilities who need lifesaving treatment? One explanation is that the behaviour of health care professionals and parents at times has been at odds with legal standards and not subject to judicial review. Several surveys of physicians have indicated their willingness to withhold treatment in accordance with parental wishes where children suffering from Down's syndrome needed operative care. See, eg, Treating the Defective Newborn: A Survey of Physicians' Attitudes, 6 Hastings Ctr Rep 2

(1976); Shaw, Randolph, and Manard, Ethical Issues in Pediatric Surgery: A National Survey of Pediatricians and Pediatric Surgeons, 60 Pediatrics 588 (1977); Todres *et al*, Pediatricians' Attitudes Affecting Decisionmaking in Defective Newborns, 60 Pediatrics 197 (1977).

In addition, we have come to realise that decisions about appropriate medical care for the majority of disabled newborns, particularly those born prematurely, involve more than the issue of whether lifesaving operative treatment should be given. The decisions are extremely complex because prognosis is uncertain and adverse consequences may result from the treatment as well as the underlying condition.

In such circumstances who makes decisions for the child is of great importance. Are parents best situated to make medical care decisions about newborns? Will they be able to disregard conditions such as costs, concerns for family stability and impact on siblings? Should they? Will they be able to overcome their own sense of guilt or loss that the birth of a seriously ill infant may cause when they expected a normal child? Should we favour parental decisionmaking but make the decisions subject to review and careful monitoring? If review is desirable, what form should it take? Should monitoring be done at an institutional level or is governmental involvement desirable?

Two cases concerned with recourse to the controversial treatment involving the use of laetrile (a chemical compound occurring naturally in, for example, apricot pits and containing cyanide), illustrate the difficulties that can be faced by a court in setting the limits of parental discretion to consent to (or refuse) treatment on their child.

In *Custody of a Minor* 393 NE 2d 836 (1979) (Supreme Judicial Court of Massachusetts), Hennessey J sets out the relevant principles.

The principles governing this case are set out fully in our prior opinion concerning this child. *Custody of a Minor*, —— Mass ——, 379 NE 2d 1053 (1978). We summarise those principles below. Basically they place three sets of interests in competition: the natural rights of the parents, the responsibilities of the State, and the best interests of the child.

While recognising that there exists a private realm of family life which the State cannot enter, *Prince v Massachusetts* 321 US 158, 166, 64 S Ct 438, 88 L Ed 645 (1944), we think that family autonomy is not absolute, and may be limited where, as here, it appears that parental decisions will jeopardise the health or safety of a child. *Custody of Minor* —— Mass ——, 389 NE 2d 68 (1979). *Wisconsin v Yoder* 406 US 205, 234, 92 S Ct 1526, 32 L Ed 15 (1972).

It is well settled that parents are the 'natural guardians of their children . . . [with] the legal as well as the moral obligation to support . . . educate' and care for their children's development and well-being. *Richards v Forrest* 278 Mass 547 at 553, 180 NE 508 at 511 (1932). See *Purinton v Jamrock* 195 Mass 187 at 199, 80 NE 802 (1907). As such, it is they who have the primary right to raise their children according to the dictates of their own consciences. See *Quilloin v Walcott* 434 US 246 at 255, 98 S Ct 549 (1978), quoting from *Prince v Massachusetts* 321 US 158 at 166, 64 S Ct 438, 88 L Ed 645 (1944). *Pierce v Society of Sisters* 268 US 510 at 535, 45 S Ct 571, 69 L Ed 1970 (1925). *Meyer v Nebraska* 262 US 390 at 399, 43 S Ct 625, 67 L Ed 1042 (1923). Indeed, these 'natural rights' of parents have been recognised as encompassing an entire private realm of family life which must be afforded protection from unwarranted State interference. *Quilloin v Walcott* supra. *Smith v Organization of Foster Families for Equality & Reform* 431 US 816 at 842, 97 S Ct 2094, 53 L Ed 2d 14 (1977), and cases cited. In light of these principles, this court and others have sought to treat the exercise of parental prerogative with great deference. See, e g, *Richards v Forrest* supra 278 Mass at 556, 180 NE 802; *Wisconsin v Yoder* 406 US 205, 92 S Ct 1526, 32 L Ed 2d 15 (1972).

It is also well established, however, that the parental rights described above do not clothe parents with life and death authority over their children. See *Prince v*

Massachusetts 321 US 158 at 166–167, 64 S Ct 438, 88 L Ed 645 (1944). This court has stated that the parental right to control a child's nurture is grounded not in any absolute property right which can be enforced to the detriment of the child, but rather is akin to a trust, subject to a correlative duty to care for and protect the child, and terminable by the parents' failure to discharge their obligations. *Richards v Forrest* supra 278 Mass at 553, 1980 NE 508. *Purinton v Jamrock* supra 195 Mass at 201,80 NE 802. *Donnelly v Donnelly* 4 Mass App 162 at 164, 344 NE 2d 195 (1976). Thus we have stated that where a child's well-being is placed in issue, it is not the rights of parents that are chiefly to be considered. The first and paramount duty is to consult the welfare of the child. *Purinton v Jamrock* supra 195 Mass at 199, 80 NE 802.

The standard to be applied in such circumstances is articulated in GL c 119, s 24. Pursuant to this provision, a child may be taken from the custody of his parents on a showing that the child is without necessary and proper physical care and that the parents are unwilling to provide such care. The essential inquiry involves application of the 'substituted judgment' or 'best interests of the child' principles, as more fully dicussed infra. On a proper showing that parental conduct threatens a child's well-being, the interests of the State and of the individual child may mandate intervention.

Because we are dealing with a child, we find little relevance in arguments which posit the existence of a fundamental right in competent adults to make personal health care decisions and to choose or reject medical treatment, whether orthodox or unorthodox, rational or foolish. We appreciate that the law presently appears to impose certain limitations on such rights in competent adults, and express no opinion as to whether there is such unfettered freedom of choice arising from the constitutional right of privacy and the right of bodily integrity (compare *Roe v Wade* 410 US 113 at 153, 93 S Ct 705, 35 L Ed 2d 147 (1973); *Eisenstadt v Baird* 405 US 438 at 453, 92 S Ct 1029, 31 L Ed 2d 349 (1972); *Skinner v Oklahoma* 316 US 535 at 541, 62 S Ct 1110, 86 L Ed 1655 (1942)), or whether such freedom of choice might be deemed a logical extention of the right to refuse life-prolonging and life-saving medical care in appropriate circumstances. Cf *Superintendent of Belchertown State School v Saikewicz* 373 Mass 728, 370 NE 2d 417 (1977); *Lane v Candura* 376 NE 2d 1232 (1978).

Even were we to assume that competent adults have the right to use controversial treatments without limitation, we are dealing here with a three year old child. The parents do not—and indeed cannot—assert on their own behalf the privacy rights of their child. *Custody of a Minor* 379 NE 2d 1053 (1978). On the other hand, the child's own rights of privacy and bodily integrity are fully recognised in principles set out in this opinion. '[T]he State must recognise the dignity and worth of [an incompetent] person and afford to that person the same panoply of rights and choices it recognises in competent persons.' *Saikewicz* supra, 370 NE 2d at 428. Such respect is manifested by use of the 'substituted judgment' doctrine, according to which a court must seek to identify and effectuate the actual values and preferences of the incompetent individual. Id at 370 NE 2d 417. In the case of a child, however, the substituted judgment doctrine and the 'best interests of the child' test are essentially coextensive, involving examination of the same criteria and application of the same basic reasoning. *Custody of a Minor*, supra, 379 NE 2d 1053.

In applying these principles, the court found that the parents in opting for treatment involving laetrile, albeit in conjunction with chemotherapy, were failing to provide appropriate care for their child suffering from acute lymph cytic leukaemia.

By contrast in the same year in the New York case of *Re Hofbauer* 393 NE 2d 1009 (1979) (New York, Court of Appeals), Jasen J took a somewhat different view of the discretion of the parent (footnote omitted).

. . . [I]t is important to stress that a parent, in making the sensitive decision as to how the child should be treated, may rely upon the recommendations and competency of the attending physician if he or she is duly licensed to practise medicine in this State, for '[i]f a physician is licensed by the State, he is recognised by the State as capable of exercising acceptable clinical judgment.' (*Doe v Bolton* 410 US 179 at 199, 93 S Ct 739 at 751, 35 L Ed 2d 201 at 217, reh den 410 US 959, 93 S Ct 1410, 35 L Ed 2d 694.) Obviously, for all practical purposes, the average parent must rely upon the recommendations and competency of the attending physician since the physician is both trained and in the best position to evaluate the medical needs of the child.

Ultimately, however, the most significant factor in determining whether a child is being deprived of adequate medical care, and, thus, a neglected child within the meaning of the statute, is whether the parents have provided an acceptable course of medical treatment for their child in light of all the surrounding circumstances. This inquiry cannot be posed in terms of whether the parent has made a 'right' or a 'wrong' decision, for the present state of the practice of medicine, despite its vast advances, very seldom permits such definitive conclusions. Nor can a court assume the role of surrogate parent and establish as the objective criteria with which to evaluate a parent's decision its own judgment as to the exact method or degree of medical treatment which should be provided, for such standard is fraught with subjectivity. Rather, in our view, the court's inquiry should be whether the parents, once having sought accredited medical assistance and having been made aware of the seriousness of their child's affliction and the possibility of cure if a certain mode of treatment is undertaken, have provided for their child a treatment which is recommended by their physician and which has not been totally rejected by all responsible medical authority.

With these considerations in mind and cognisant that the State has the burden of demonstrating neglect (see *Re C Children* 55 AD 2d 646, 390 NYS 2d 10), we now examine the facts of this case. It is abundantly clear that this is not a case where the parents, for religious reasons, refused necessary medical procedures for their child (eg *Re Sampson* 37 AD 2d 668, 323 NE 2d 253; affd 29 NY 2d 900, 326 NYS 2d 398; *Re Gregory S* 85 Misc 2d 846, 380 NE 2d 620), nor is this a case where the parents have made an irreversible decision to deprive their child of a certain mode of treatment (*Custody of a Minor* 379 NE 2d 1053 [Mass]). Indeed, this is not a case where the child is receiving no medical treatment, for the record discloses that Joseph's mother and father were concerned and loving parents who sought qualified medical assistance for their child.

Rather, appellants predicate their charge of neglect upon the basis that Joseph's parents have selected for their child a mode of treatment which is inadequate and ineffective. Both courts below found, however—and we conclude that these findings are supported by the record—that numerous qualified doctors have been consulted by Dr Schachter and have contributed to the child's care; that the parents have both serious and justifiable concerns about the deleterious effects of radiation treatments and chemotherapy; that there is medical proof that the nutritional treatment being administered Joseph was controlling his condition and that such treatment is not as toxic as is the conventional treatment; and that conventional treatments will be administered to the child if his condition so warrants. In light of these affirmed findings of fact, we are unable to conclude, as a matter of law, that Joseph's parents have not undertaken reasonable efforts to ensure that acceptable medical treatment is being provided their child.

Is Jasen J saying that, as a matter of law, parents need only seek the views of doctors but then have an unlimited discretion to ignore what the doctors advise? Had he misunderstood *Custody of a Minor*? Which of the two cases is to be preferred?

Re Hamilton (1983) 657 SW 2d 425 (Court of Appeals of Tennessee), illustrates the difficulties the US courts have encountered in attempting to strike a balance between two deeply felt and constitutionally protected convictions, that the family as a unit should be free to determine its own destiny, including the pursuit of religious belief, and that the state has an interest in the protection of children. The following is the opinion of the court (footnote omitted):

Per curiam: Following an evidentiary hearing, the trial court determined:

The Court finds that Pamela Hamilton is a dependent and neglected child under Tennessee Code Annotated 37–202(6)(iv) and that her legal guardian, her father, has refused to provide necessary medical care for his child, Pamela.

In the Court's opinion, the medical proof shown through the witnesses, the depositions, is that Ewing's Sarcoma will spread when untreated, that there is a twenty-five (25%) to fifty (50%) percent chance to successfully deal with the Ewing's Sarcoma on a long-term basis when localised, as I believe the evidence indicates Pamela's presently is; that there is less than twenty-five (25%) percent chance of living with treatment when cancer has spread. . . .

(T)here is undisputed and uncontradicted testimony that without treatment Pamela will die within six (6) to nine (9) months. That is to say that medical care is necessary and available which can deal within certain bounds with Ewing's Sarcoma and that medicines are available and are necessary for her pain. . . .

The evidence does not preponderate against the trial court's fact finding; however, where the State undertakes to deny the rights of parents and their children, due process requires that the State support its charges by clear and convincing evidence. *Santosky v Kramer* 455 US 745, 102 S Ct 1388, 71 L Ed 2d 599 (1982). The findings of the trial court are supported by clear and convincing evidence except his conclusion that the sarcoma has not metastasised.

Dr Elizabeth I Thompson, an examining physician and member of the staff of St Jude Children's Research Hospital furnished the court with a concise summary of Pamela's prognosis with treatment:

Because of the site, interval progression of this tumor since diagnosis and questionable bone scale the long-term prognosis for this patient is very guarded. If she truly has tumor in the vertebral body, her chances of long-term remission with chemotherapy and radiation are less than 25%. If the vertebral lesion on bone scan is not tumor, the best estimate I could give of long-term remission is 25–50%. Her chance of temporary response and pain relief is, of course, much higher—at least 80%.

Appellants, however, do not seriously question the medical evidence but base their objections to medical treatment, including medication to combat pain, on religious grounds, relying on the First Amendment to the Constitution of the United States for the protection of the free exercise of their religious convictions. The members of the appellant's family are members of a Protestant religious sect, The Church of God of the Union Assembly, Incorporated, which, according to the father, himself a lay minister, has churches in Arizona, Texas, Mississippi, Alabama, Ohio, Illinois, Kentucky, North Carolina, South Carolina, Tennessee and Georgia. A tenet of the church is:

All members of the church are forbidden to use medicine, vaccinations or shots of any kind but are taught by the church to live by faith.

Apparently, medical treatment such as suturing wounds, extracting teeth, and setting fractured bones does not fall within the prohibition; indeed, Pamela was treated by an orthopedic surgeon for a fracture of her femur which led to the discovery of the affliction, Ewing's Sarcoma. The father, despite his protestations, is pragmatic if not enlightened in his approach to medical treatment. His expressions to the trial court are revealing. In response to questions about reaching his decision to forego medical treatment for his daughter, he said:

Q. Will you tell us what kind of soul searching you've gone through in reaching your decision?
A. She does not want it . . .
Q. . . . Do you have an opinion yourself in terms of the medical treatment?
A. Well, if they're going to give you something to make you sick and your hair come out, it must not be too good for you. If they can't guarantee it to heal you, why do it, because if a doctor were to tell me he had a medicine that would heal me I'd go right there in just a minute, but there ain't none.

The beneficial effects of modern medicine are beyond serious enlightened dispute. Beginning around 1970 noted cancer treatment centers, such as Memorial Sloan-Kettering, Duke, Anderson, and Saint Jude, employing combined radiation and chemotherapy treatments, have succeeded in establishing long term remission of tumors in a significant number of patients suffering from Ewing's Sarcoma.

While the prognosis with treatment in Pamela's case is guarded, the consequence of no treatment is certain, painful death in six to nine months according to medical opinion.

Accordingly, the issue thus becomes whether the father may refuse to procure recognised, and widely accepted medical treatment which has proven effective in numerous cases for this affliction on religious grounds.

Appellant cites *Superintendent of Belchertown v Saikewicz* 373 Mass 728, 370 NE 2d 417 (1977), as authority for an incompetent individual not being subjected to medical treatment involving chemotherapy. The case is not applicable. In *Saikewicz* all of the attending physicians recommended against this form of treatment for the patient.

Appellee cites four cases in which the Court ordered treatment despite the resistance of the child's parents to the treatment. In *Mitchell v Davis* 205 SW 2d 812 (Tex Civ App 1947), the mother was charged with criminal neglect for failure to provide treatment for her son's arthritic knee condition, a non-life-threatening ailment. The mother defended on the ground that she considered healing only possible through prayer. The Court held that this religious belief of the mother did not constitute a defense to the charge of neglect.

In *Custody of a Minor* 375 Mass 733, 379 NE 2d 1053 (1978), the parents stopped the treatment of their two-year-old daughter suffering from leukemia because of the adverse side effects of the treatment. No religious argument was raised. The Court ordered the treatments to resume. The court balanced the interests of (1) the natural rights of parenthood; (2) the responsibility of the state; and (3) the needs of the child. The Court then reached the conclusion that when the child's life is endangered, the state's interest in protecting the life of the child always outweighs the parental interests.

In *Re Jensen* 54 Or App 1, 633 P 2d 1302 (1981), the parents refused treatment on religious grounds of the child's condition of hydrocephalus. The child faced the possibility of severe brain damage, but her life was not in immediate danger. The Court ordered treatment for the child, holding that, although the parents are free to provide religious training to their child, that right does not include the right to jeopardise the child's health.

In the case of *People In Interest of DLE* 645 P 2d 271 (Colo 1982), a 14-year-old's life was in danger because of failure to treat a grand mal epileptic condition. A Colorado statute prohibited a finding of neglect if the child was in good faith 'under treatment solely by spiritual means through prayer'. The parents objected to treatment on religious grounds. The Colorado Supreme Court found that in a life-threatening situation the child was dependent and neglected, despite the statute.

Pamela has not reached the age of accountability and it is well-settled that the state as *parens patriae* has a special duty to protect minors and, if necessary, make vital decisions as to whether to submit a minor to necessary treatment where the condition is life threatening, as wrenching and distasteful as such actions may be. See *State Dept of Human Services v Northern* 563 SW 2d 197 (Tenn App 1978). A state may reasonably limit the free exercise of religion in such cases. 16 CJS, Constitutional Law s 206(2), p 1031.

Our Constitution guarantees Americans more personal freedom than enjoyed by any other civilised society, but there are times when the freedom of the individual must yield. Where a child is dying with cancer and experiencing pain which will surely become more excruciating as the disease progresses, as in Pamela's circumstance, we believe, is one of those times when humane considerations and life-saving attempts outweigh unlimited practices of religious beliefs. We, therefore, designate the Director of the Office of Human Services in Knoxville or his successor in said office to act for and on behalf of Pamela in consenting to necessary treatment, which treatment shall be at the direction and under the supervision of St Jude Children's Research Hospital and its staff. The Director will accede to and respect the wishes of the parents regarding Pamela to the extent that the treatment recommended by the physicians is not interfered with or impaired.

Question

Which judicial approach, whether in England or America, most respects both what justice demands and a coherent set of legal rules and principles?

Postscript

In *Re C (a minor)* (1989) Times, 21 April, the Court of Appeal (Lord Donaldson MR, Balcolmbe and Nicholls LJJ) authorised the non-treatment of a severely handicapped baby. Baby C was born prematurely suffering from hydrocephalus. C suffered from damage to the cortex of the brain, which the judge (Ward J), described as 'gross and abnormally severe.' The damage was irreparable and the prognosis for the child's life was 'hopeless' and death was inevitable. Before her death there was 'no prospect of a happy life for this child' (per Ward J). She was blind, probably deaf and suffered from generalised spastic cerebral palsy of all four limbs. Mentally, her intellectual capacity was negligible if it existed at all. The hospital sought the permission of the court—the child being a ward of court—not to treat C (including the provision of naso-gastric feeding and hydration) if any condition developed which called for medical intervention.

The Court of Appeal approved that part of the trial judge's order which stated that 'the hospital authority [should] continue to treat the minor within the parameters of the opinion' of an expert paediatrician whose report had been sought by the Official Solicitor. That report stated:

> In the event of [C] acquiring a serious infection, or being unable to take feeds normally by mouth I do not think it would be correct to give antibiotics, to set up intravenous fusions or nasal-gastric feeding regimes ... the opinion of the local nurses and carers should be taken into account ... if they believed she was in pain or would suffer less by a particular course of action, it would be correct to consider that course of action, always bearing in mind the balance between short-term gain and needless prolongation of suffering.

In relation to the obligations to treat a handicapped neonate, what does this case tell us about (i) what is the test to determine this issue?; (ii) who establishes the test?; (iii) what the test means?; and (iv) who applies the test?

Notice the following points:

(i) C was a ward of court and, therefore, as we saw in *Re B*, the decision was for the court to make acting in C's 'best interests.'

(ii) However, Lord Donaldson MR said that had this not been the case the decision would 'have been solely a matter for the parents.' Does this not remind you of Dunn LJ's view in *Re B*? Is it consistent with our view of the law? Does it assume an *unlimited* or *limited* discretion in the parents (usually) to determine where their child's 'best interests' lie?

(iii) The court relied heavily upon (indeed it simply adopted) the independent expert's view of the best course for C. Does this suggest that here, again, the courts may be paying *undue* regard to professional opinion? Was the expert's view one based upon medical criteria or did it involve questions of values, which, in our view, are not the exclusive domain of the medical profession?

(iv) The court distinguished *Re B* and the *Dawson* case from Canada. How do you think *Re C* differs from these cases? Could it be that (a) C was dying in any event; B and Stephen Dawson were not in immediate danger apart from the supervening condition; or (b) the difference in C's quality of life which appears to have been considerably lower than that of B and Stephen Dawson? In fact, the Court of Appeal relied heavily on the fact that C was terminally ill. Do you think this should be an important factor (see chapter 14 for a discussion in the context of adults)?

(v) Notice the Court of Appeal's specific approval of the expert's view that the opinions of the local nurses and carers would be relevant (quaere determinative?) if they thought that C would suffer if a particular procedure were not performed. A procedure would then be performed because it would provide symptomatic relief (ie overcome pain, suffering and discomfort) even though if there was no pain etc, the expert was of the view that, in principle, the procedure should not be performed to prolong C's life (see also the *Dawson* case on symptomatic relief as a relevant criterion in determining 'best interests').

Chapter 13

Donation and transplant of human tissue and fluids

The living donor: the common law

(a) CONSENT

(i) Adults

The first issue that we should consider is whether an adult may, as a matter of law, validly consent to the removal of one of his organs for transplantation. The following quote, setting the scene, is from Jesse Dukeminier 'Supplying Organs for Transplantation' (1970) 68 Michigan Law Review 811, at pp 853–4 (footnotes omitted).

> Mayhem is the crime of intentionally and maliciously maiming or disfiguring a person. At common law, mayhem was limited only to deprivation of such of a man's organs 'as may render him the less able, in fighting, either to defend himself or to annoy his adversary'. Included were a man's hand, his finger, his foot, his testicle, or his eye. The significance of the organs in fighting is irrelevant today, and modern statutes have extended the crime of mayhem to disfigurings in general and to the disfiguring of women as well as of men. Under modern law, it is possible to contend that surgically removing an internal organ from a person constitutes mayhem.
>
> Again the question arises whether, if removing a kidney for transplantation is mayhem, consent by the donor is a defense to the charge. Only two cases are even remotely relevant, and in both of those the victim's consent had no effect. In *Wright's Case*, recorded by Lord Coke in 1603, 'a strong and lustie rogue' directed his companion to cut off the rogue's left hand so that he might get out of work and beg more effectively. Both the rogue and his companion were convicted of mayhem; consent was held to be no defense to the crime. In *State v Bass*, a man wanted his fingers cut off so that he could collect insurance money. With full knowledge of the purpose, a physician deadened four fingers of the man's left hand, which were then cut off by another man using an electric saw. The physician was convicted of being an accessory to mayhem. The court held that consent of the person was no defense to the charge. Although the opinion of the court in *State v Bass* was extremely vague, the court apparently thought that cutting off the fingers was no 'benefit' to the man and that the conduct was 'antisocial'. The court did not indicate what policy propositions it assumed in its determinations that insurance proceeds provided no offsetting benefits for the loss of the fingers and that the conduct was antisocial.

The Law Reform Commission of Australia Report No 7 (1977) on 'Human Tissue Transplants' (pp 22–24, footnotes omitted) states as follows:

> The common law of . . . England, offers no rule or principle dealing with human tissue transplants as such, nor, for that matter, with surgery as such. There is a lack of case law, and in the rare decisions when judges have spoken on the common law principles applicable to surgery, the central issues have not involved the lawfulness of the surgery, but other legal questions such as divorce, or injury during a sporting event. This has caused resort to analogy and rationalisation by some legal writers, resulting in suggestions that common law principles applicable to transplantation

may be derived from consideration of recondite legal rules such as the ancient common law offence of 'maim'. More accepted and authoritative (but in the opinion of some hardly less bizarre) has been the suggestion that surgery amounts in law to 'assault and battery' (hereafter called assault), thus falling under the law of trespass 'based on the inviolability of the person'. In extra-curial analyses of the common law both Lord Devlin and Lord Justice Edmund Davies have taken this view of surgery. The opinions of such judges as these, and the lack of judicial precedent, expose the failure of the common law to provide acceptable answers to the modern medical practice of transplantation. There is little prospect of a constructive reply to the plea for reform made by Professor Daube in 1966:

> An operation should be treated as a positive, beneficent, admirable action from the outset, not as a lawful infliction of harm. It is a cure, and only where essential elements are lacking in a situation does it become wrongful. After all, we do not construe marital . . . intercourse as rape licensed by virtue of consent . . .

Briefly, the common law principles of assault, in their application to the transplantation of human tissue (and to surgery generally) may be seen from the following summary. First, assault amounts to a tort, or civil wrong, giving rise to a private claim for damages enforceable in the courts. Assault is also a crime, punishable by criminal process. Secondly, the common law regards all surgery as a trespass to the person but one which can be justified or defended, in the case of the tort of assault, on the basis of consent given by the patient. Thus, it will be a defence to a claim for damages for assault if the surgeon proves that the patient consented to the operation. This defence, unfortunately, may not extend to the case of the emergency-unconscious patient, or the patient who lacks legal capacity (a small child or a mental patient). Worse, it may have no application at all in the case of a live donor of tissue, because, despite his consent, it cannot be said that the surgery on him is for his benefit. Thirdly, in the case of the crime of assault, at least, occasioning 'grievous bodily harm', consent of the patient or victim is no defence to a charge. . . .

. . . However, the proposition that consent is no defence to a criminal charge is the general rule, and exceptions have been made to it. Presumably normal surgery would be an exception, but there is no decided case directly in point. The consent should be free and informed. The surgeon should advise the patient of all material facts relevant to the operation so that the patient may balance risk and benefit. Deception or even failure to make full disclosure may vitiate consent. The law and literature on 'consent' is extensive, requiring separate consideration of the adult patient, the child, the mentally incompetent, and the patient who is unconscious or an emergency case . . .

Consent to assault: What does the common law have to say to a 'normal' donor, that is to say an adult, with mental competence, properly advised, and anxious to give tissue for transplant, for example, one of two healthy kidneys? At first sight it may seem that removal of the tissue would not offend any legal principle. However, the criminal law is not entirely sympathetic to the defence of 'consent'. In addition, it cannot be said in any normal sense, that the removal of the tissue is for the benefit of the donor. It follows that the surgeon's legal position is not easily determined.

Professor Dworkin, writing in 1970, states the following in 'The Law Relating to Organ Transplantation in England' (1970) 33 MLR 353 at 355–9 (footnotes omitted):

> To determine the legality of live donor transplantations it is first necessary to examine the legal basis for surgical operations generally. Under medieval law, a person committed the crime of mayhem (maim) if he so injured another as to make him less able to fight or to defend himself or to annoy an adversary. To amputate a limb, even with the victim's consent was, on the face of it, an unlawful act, since it deprived the king of a fighting man. In early Victorian times when soldiers, as part of their training, had to bite cartridges, a soldier got a dentist to pull out his front teeth to enable him to avoid training and it was thought that both were guilty of a crime. The modern law is obscure but the crime, to some extent, turns on two

interconnected factors. The first is the nature of the physical harm: one person does not have a licence to mutilate or cause bodily harm to another for any purpose merely because that person has consented. The degree of bodily harm is, of course, important: the test is no longer whether it impairs or may impair the victim's ability to fight for his country, but presumably the seriousness of the harm must be of that order. 'Bodily harm . . . includes any hurt or injury calculated to interfere with the health or comfort of the prosecutor. Such hurt or injury need not be permanent, but must, no doubt, be more than merely transient or trifling' The second factor involves questions of public policy. The law may permit some kinds of assault and battery but not others: the dividing line between the permissible and the impermissible is not clear but the courts have accepted and still accept the burden of safeguarding individuals even against themselves.

The relevance of this aspect of the criminal law is that it provides a basis for saying that many surgical operations are *prima facie* unlawful. Without further justification not only would operations be criminal acts, but they would also be unlawful in the civil law and surgeons might be liable to pay compensation for the consequences of their acts, even though they had exercised all reasonable care. What are the criteria, then, which convert unlawful acts into lawful surgical operations? In some countries the criminal codes absolve from responsibility persons who perform in good faith and with reasonable care and skill a surgical operation upon another person, with his consent and for his benefit, if the performance of the operation is reasonable in the circumstances. No such provision appears in any United Kingdom legislation but it is clear, of course, that surgery, within limits, is a perfectly legal activity. Sir James Fitzjames Stephen formulated the general proposition that 'everyone has a right to consent to the infliction of any bodily injury in the nature of a surgical operation upon himself' and stated that although he knew of no authority for this, the existence of surgery as a profession assumed its truth. . . .

Professor Dworkin then identified four conditions to be satisfied:

(i)   *The patient must give a full, free and informed consent. . . .*

(ii)   *The operation must be therapeutic: it must be expressly for the patient's benefit.* The major distinguishing feature between surgical operations and unlawful mutilation is, of course, that all surgical operations are allegedly in the medical interests of the patient. Coke refers to a case in 1603 where 'a young and lustie rogue prevailed upon a friend to cut off his left hand, so that he might be better able to beg'. Both were found guilty of the crime of maim; today, they would also be criminally liable. In the criminal codes of some countries, the provisions concerning surgical operations expressly state that they must be for the patient's benefit; in other countries this, until recently, has been accepted as being obvious.

(iii) *There must be lawful justification.* This is a relatively unexplored and open-ended requirement. Ethical and social questions are more relevant here and the courts may occasionally use this rubric to extend the law to meet new circumstances. Most surgical operations are lawful. The most obvious example of an unlawful operation is that of abortion because, apart from those cases where abortion is permissible under the Abortion Act 1967, abortions are statutory criminal offences, whether performed by doctors or unqualified persons. . . . It is unlikely that the courts would condemn circumcision as unlawful. No doubt the ritual circumcision of Jewish infants could be upheld on grounds of religious toleration, although circumcision for non-religious reasons would have to be accepted on wider public policy grounds.

(iv)   *Generally, the operation must be performed by a person with appropriate medical skills.*

Professor Dworkin went on to examine the legality of transplantation in the context of kidney transplants.

Is it lawful to remove a kidney from a live donor?
The legality of live donor transplants turns upon whether or not the first three conditions for lawful surgical operations are satisfied.

× R v. Donovan 1934 2 KB 498 at p 509.

First, is the operation therapeutic? There is no doubt that the purpose of a kidney transplant is to benefit the donee. It seems equally clear that to take a kidney from a living donor can rarely be of any benefit to him. It is arguable that the donor who is left with one healthy kidney may be in no worse position than he is with two, since after a time the remaining kidney apparently does the work of two. Indeed, it may be that life insurance companies would accept an otherwise healthy donor as a normal risk. The difficulty, however, arises should anything happen to the solitary kidney: a kidney illness to a person with only one kidney is generally far more serious than to a person with two. A kidney transplant, then, in most cases can be of no therapeutic value to the donor.

Secondly, is there lawful justification for the surgical procedure? It has been suggested that the removal of a kidney from a healthy donor is not a maiming in the accepted sense because it is no great disability in most cases to lose one kidney. One calculation suggests that the total risk involved to the donor is 0.12 per cent, divided into an immediate risk of 0.05 per cent as a post-operative accidental risk, and 0.07 per cent as the risk of any kind of accident occurring later to affect the remaining kidney. Whether or not this can be said to be a maiming, it is most certainly the infliction of bodily harm which is capable of being more than transient or trifling.

Arguments, of varying force, can be put forward to support the view that such transplants are lawfully justified. Thus, the courts have by implication recognised the legality of some kinds of homografts; for example, the practice of taking blood from donors for the purposes of blood transfusions is incapable, without more, of being legally challenged today. The position of a blood donor and a kidney donor, although in some ways similar in kind, is, however, clearly different in degree. It is difficult to categorise the blood transfusion procedure as the infliction of bodily harm of more than a trifling or transient nature.

Perhaps a closer, though by no means close, analogy is that of skin-grafting. In an American case, *Bonner v Moran*, a court held a surgeon liable for trespass when a fifteen-year-old boy consented to skin grafts being taken from his body for the benefit of his badly burned cousin. The basis of the decision was that the boy was not old enough to give his consent, and his parents should have done so for him. By implication, it can be argued that the court would have allowed a non-therapeutic skin-graft had the proper consent been obtained.

Another argument is that the courts should treat a volunteer in this situation in the same favourable way as rescuers. A volunteer who risks his life or exposes himself to injury, for example, in rescuing a person from a fire, is not condemned for his actions if he has acted reasonably, nor are they regarded as unlawful; instead, he may be entitled to recover damages for any injury he suffers from the person whose negligence created the dangerous situation. The courts treat rescuers favourably: 'danger invites rescue' is now an accepted phrase. If this is so, the law should look favourably on a volunteer donor so that the act would not be categorised as unlawful.

These are merely some arguments which a willing court might use if it was prepared to restate the existing law to meet new medical trends. Speaking extra-judicially, Edmund Davies LJ has said that he would

be surprised if a surgeon were successfully sued for trespass to the person or convicted of causing bodily harm to one of full age and intelligence who freely consented to act as donor—always provided that the operation did not present unreasonable risk to the donor's life or health. That proviso is essential. A man may declare himself ready to die for another, but the surgeon must not take him at his word.

Until this issue is judicially or legislatively resolved, however, it is arguable in legal theory that the taking of a kidney from a healthy donor is normally an unlawful operation.

Thirdly, is there an informed voluntary consent? Even if the courts were to decide that live donor transplants were, within limits, lawfully justified, problems could arise in connection with the donor's consent to the removal of a kidney. In addition to all the strict requirements that the donor must be fully informed of all the relevant facts and risks, so that he can make up his own mind, difficulties may arise in those situations where the donor and donee are related. The relationship between donor and donee may be, for example, that of twins or parent and child: in these family situations the social and psychological pressures upon a person who knows that his failure to give consent will result in the death of the sick person must be very strong indeed. It may often be difficult to decide whether a consent in this situation is truly voluntary. It is true that where doctors are in doubt whether the donor's consent is in fact voluntary they may solve the problem (for the donor, at least, and his family, though not for the potential donee) by saying that the donor is medically unsuitable. Although the medical prospects are better where the blood relationship is closest, the chances of a truly voluntary consent are greater where the relationship is distant or non-existent.

Thus, in principle, can an adult give valid consent to the removal of an organ or other tissue for the purposes of transplantation? What more is relevant before we can answer this question? Which, if any, of the following do you consider to be of legal significance:

1. that the tissue is regenerative (eg blood or bone marrow) or is non-regenerative (eg a kidney)? (See Dukeminier and Sanders 'Medical Advances and Legal Lag: Hemodialysis and Kidney Transplantation' (1968) 15 UCLA Law Review 357.) The distinction is a factual one. Its relevance in law arguably lies in the fact that in the case of non-regenerative tissue the risks to the donor's health will ordinarily be greater (even in the case of twinned organs such as kidneys) such that the law will scrutinise more carefully the benefit/burden ratio and the reality of the donor's consent.
2. that the tissue is not only non-regenerative but is also vital for life, eg a liver or heart? Would this not be murder?
3. that the donation is beneficial to the donor in that it is in his medical interests? Or is it enough that it does not harm him? If the former, how can this benefit be demonstrated?

Skegg comments, in *Law, Ethics and Medicine*, on the legality of consent regardless of apparent competence. He states at p 36 (footnotes omitted):

... Indeed, sometimes a procedure is performed on a person in the knowledge that it will certainly be to that person's bodily detriment. This is the case when a kidney is removed from a healthy person, for transplantation into someone who is in need of it. The operation is a major one, and is not without risks. But it is not unreasonably dangerous, and the probable benefit to the recipient far outweighs the probable detriment to the donor. Hence, if called upon to deal with a case in which a kidney had been removed from a consenting adult, for transplantation into someone in need of it, the courts may confidently be expected to take the view that the operation did not amount to the offence of battery. Even though the operation causes serious bodily harm, there is clearly a good reason for it. ...

He continues (p 37):

... A court is not likely to inquire closely into whether there are good reasons for a particular intervention. There is no danger of a court attempting to decide whether there were good reasons for removing a kidney from a living donor, instead of keeping the patient on dialysis in the hope that a suitable cadaver kidney would become available. ...

He continues (p 43):

To revert to the example of the removal of a kidney from a living person for transplantation to another: as there is a shortage of kidneys for transplantation, and as transplants from living donors are at least as successful as those from cadavers, the courts may be expected to accept that there is a 'just cause or excuse', or 'good reason', for such operations. Where consent is also present, such operations will not amount to the offence of causing grievous bodily harm.

Notice the Human Organ Transplants Bill (discussed *infra*) would make it a criminal offence to transplant an organ from a living donor who was not closely related to the donee (ie a cousin or closer relative). The Government, who introduced the Bill proposed that there would be exceptions to this but these are, as yet, unspecified. In addition to these issues concerning general capacity to consent, a donor must clearly be capable in fact (generally see *supra* ch 4). Dworkin (*supra*) alerted us to a particular problem in this context, namely, the risk of consent being given which, in reality, is a grudging consent as a consequence of perceived or real family pressure (contrast the effect of the Human Organ Transplants Bill *requiring* a close familial connection). This problem also, and perhaps more critically arises in the case of donors who are children, to which we now turn.

(ii)   Children

Can a child in his own right ever in law consent to donate an organ or tissue to another? In the absence of any statutory guidance, two views of the common law may be advanced. The first would mirror the analysis in *Gillick*; the second would suggest that there are some things to which a child may not in law consent and thereby equates competence with majority or some other particular cut-off point.

If we take the second view first, not only does this apparently fly in the face of *Gillick* but it also poses problems for a traditional common law approach which does not rely on particular cut-off points. Granted that there may be a distinction between the situation of transplantation and *Gillick* in that here the intervention may not be 'treatment' in the narrow sense of *obviously* benefiting the child; nonetheless there seems no reason to limit *Gillick* to that sort of procedure. Furthermore, it leaves unclear what the particular cut-off point would be. The age of 16 seems to have no particular relevance because section 8(1) of the Family Law Reform Act 1969 would only put the matter beyond doubt if every donation by a child was indisputably seen as 'treatment'.

In fact, very few donations can be seen as treatment even given a liberal interpretation of that term. But yet, can it be said that a donation of blood by a $17\frac{1}{2}$ year old highly intelligent person, which is unlikely to attract the description 'treatment', is unlawful in every case? If our legal instinct leads us to answer no, then we must look elsewhere for a guiding principle. What of the attainment of the age of 18, the only other candidate? Why should the attaining of majority be relevant? Can it be the case that, until majority, every donation is unlawful? Our example of the $17\frac{1}{2}$-year-old blood donor, which admittedly is proposed without authority, suggests otherwise.

This takes us back to our first view that the *Gillick* decision would also be relevant in this context, ie that the competence in law of a child must turn on the child's capacity to understand or comprehend the proposed procedure. This would produce the conclusion that the validity of the child's consent will turn on such factual questions as the seriousness of the intervention, the degree of risk intrinsic in the procedure, the long-term implications for the donor and so on. It may be, therefore, that it would be a rare child whom the law would find competent to consent to the donation of a kidney as against the donation of blood. But the law has no hard and fast rule.

(iii)   Parents, the court and others

The question here is the extent in law to which a proxy, usually a parent, can volunteer a child as the donor of an organ or other tissue. In analysing the legal regime regulating the proxy's authority, a significant factor must be the seriousness of the procedure involved and its consequences. Removal of a kidney calls for more careful deliberation than perhaps the removal of a small quantity of skin or blood. Removal of bone marrow, which may be a painful process carrying certain risks but is less serious in its consequences than the removal of a kidney since it is regenerative, falls somewhere between these.

We have already seen the general approach adopted by the law in analysing the authority of the proxy (*supra* ch 4) in our discussion of the general law of consent, specifically in cases such as *Bonner v Moran* 126 F 2d 121; *Hart v Brown* 289 A 2d 386 and *Strunk v Strunk* 445 SW 2d 145. These cases make two points. First, if the legal test is 'best interests' of the incompetent donor, then they appear to identify a doubtful notion of benefit, ie the psychological and emotional benefits derived from altruism. Secondly, if the courts are not adopting this approach then are they introducing another test, that the proxy may consent to that which is 'not against the interests' of the incompetent donor? This would allow the proxy to consent to a wider range of interventions, including some tissue donations. But, *quaere* whether this would be so where the procedure involves other than minimal risk, eg blood donation?

Where an incompetent person is an adult, we have seen that the law does not empower anyone to make decisions regarding the treatment of that adult. Therefore, *a fortiori*, this would apply to decisions regarding the removal of healthy tissue.

We have already noted the dispute concerning the existence (and scope of) the court's power as *parens patriae*. If such a power were effective, would it permit the court to consent to the removal of healthy tissue? May it depend on the seriousness of the invasion and its consequences?

A doctor's power lawfully to treat an incompetent adult was, as we have seen, stated by Wood J in *T v T* (*supra* ch 4) as restricted to those circumstances where it was medically 'demanded'. Would such a test not rule out the removal of healthy tissue? Is the answer affected by the House of Lords decision in *re F* (1989)? Furthermore, would a court regard this criterion as relevant in the exercise of any *parens patriae* power it may have?

(b) DISPENSING WITH CONSENT

The question of whether a court will order a person to donate tissue to another in the face of his refusal was considered by a Pennsylvanian court in *McFall v Shimp* in 1978. Russell Scott discusses the case in his book, *The Body as Property* (pp 127–129).

Robert McFall of Pittsburgh, Pennsylvania, was overwhelmed by the symptoms of aplastic anaemia in June 1978. A nightmare began for the thirty-nine-year-old bachelor when he began to develop bruises after bumping into objects during his work installing insulation materials in confined spaces in buildings. The bruises would not go away, and soon he began to have nosebleeds that continued for hours at a time. He went to a local hospital in suburban Pittsburgh, where the doctors diagnosed aplastic anaemia, a rare, almost certainly fatal disease of the bone marrow and blood. The prospects of death after contracting this disease have been put by some medical studies at 90 percent, with an average survival period somewhere between three and four months. There is only one real source of cure, and that is a transplant of compatible bone marrow. This transplant gives a good expectation of complete recovery. Without it, the patient must expect to die.

The statistical likelihood of finding compatible bone marrow is almost one in sixty thousand. In practice, the prospect is hopeless, because no means exist for testing the community. There are as yet no computerised banks containing comprehensive national tissue information (though in some parts of the world, for example, at Westminster Hospital in London, computerised tissue banks are being built up and already contain information about thousands of prospective donors). On the other hand, the prospect of finding tissue compatibility inside a family is far higher, and increases with the closeness of the relationship.

Robert McFall had three brothers and three sisters. They had all gone their separate ways following their mother's death in 1949, and there had been little family communication after that time. By means of computer checks through driver's licence records, they were all traced, and agreed to submit to tissue-typing tests. None of them turned out to be a compatible donor. It was then decided to enquire whether a first cousin of McFall, David Shimp, a crane operator in a steel mill, would agree to be tested. Shimp was aged forty-three and married. When both men were younger they had gone to camps together and had shared many experiences.

Shimp agreed to undergo a preliminary test but did not bother to tell his wife. The test proved to be positive, suggesting that Shimp's bone marrow would be a perfect match for Robert McFall. A second test was arranged, but Shimp cancelled the appointment. He had changed his mind, and from that time onward refused to have anything more to do with the affair. According to reports, Shimp said his wife was angry that he had taken the test without discussing it with her, and wanted him to discontinue his participation. His mother had expressed the same wish. One report said that Shimp had been influenced by a dream that if he went into hospital for the bone marrow removal, he would never come out. Friends and other relatives put great pressure on him to proceed with the tests, but he would not budge. It was even said that he considered bringing legal proceedings to stop harassment, because the story had gotten into the hands of the media, which gave it considerable publicity. However, it was Robert McFall who first resorted to the courts.

In the last week of July, McFall sued David Shimp in Allegheny County Court, Pennsylvania, asking for an order that would compel Shimp to submit to further tests, and eventually to the removal of a quantity of his bone marrow for transplant to McFall. Time was now all-important for McFall, and the normal delays of court hearings too risky. His lawyers asked for an urgent preliminary injunction, which, if granted, would direct Shimp forthwith to undergo the further tests. In this atmosphere events moved rapidly, and *McFall v Shimp* was dealt with and disposed of on July 25 and 26 by the Civil Division of the Allegheny County Court, Judge John P Flaherty, Jr, presiding.

The plaintiff's brief was a document of originality and persuasion, skilfully prepared by his attorney, John W Murtagh, Jr. Its opening words went straight to the heart of the matter, posing for determination an issue as profound as any that could be put to a court of law. The judge was asked, in so many words, to determine whether society may overrule a citizen's claim to an absolute right to his bodily security in order to save the life of one of its members. The brief submitted, for reasons it set out in detail, that the answer 'is and must be "yes"'. It then tackled some of the medical questions, asserting that the removal procedure was medically safe, would at most result in minor and temporary discomfort, and would deprive the defendant of nothing but his time because bone marrow is a regenerative tissue that promptly replaces itself.

McFall's lawyers had found no precedent or comparable case that could directly assist the court, and the judge himself later commented that 'a diligent search has produced no authority'. Accordingly, the claim for legal relief was put in fundamental terms, based on morality, ethics, custom, scholarly legal pronouncements, and judicial opinion. . . .

McFall's case then cited some well-known circumstances in which bodily integrity is lawfully disregarded because of overriding social considerations: public health requirements for vaccination and quarantine; criminal law powers to take hair, blood, clothes, and semen; marriage law requirements of blood tests; defence law requirements of military service; and compulsory assistance to law enforcement officers in emergencies. To these McFall sought to add his own case as representing a new category. To demonstrate that the court could, by reference to principle and precedent, extend the law in this fashion if it wished, the plaintiff produced the fruits of some extremely original research.

Power to make an order of the kind requested was traced back some seven hundred years from the Allegheny County Court, through the Pennsylvanian and United States legal systems, to the ancient English Courts of Chancery and the powers to dispense justice granted to those courts in the reign of King Edward I. This English king ascended his throne in the year 1272, and in the thirteenth year of his reign, Parliament passed the statute now known as the second Statute of Westminster. It contained the following provision: 'Whensoever from thenceforth a writ shall be found in the Chancery, and in a like case falling under the same right and requiring a like remedy, no precedent of a writ can be produced, the Clerks in Chancery shall agree in forming a new one; lest it happen for the future that the Court of our lord the king be deficient in doing justice to the suitors'. . . .

The question was whether Robert McFall's claim should be recognised by the courts, and whether the law should regard David Shimp as having a duty toward him. 'Has the duty the Plaintiff seeks to impose upon the Defendant ever been recognised in law or equity?' asked the brief. In support of an affirmative answer, reliance was next placed upon the so-called Rescue Cases.

The legal principle of rescue recognises the social duty of a citizen to act positively to attempt to rescue another who is in personal danger. A yachtsman may be found to have a positive duty to try to save a drowning man. American and British laws have not favoured the rescue concept and have been reluctant to equate moral with legal obligation. Generally speaking, their approach has been to recognise that certain relationships should produce legal duties and obligations, for example, the relationship of doctor and patient. They have been slow to build specific legal duties on the foundation of general moral concepts, particularly when this might result in conflict with 'individualist' philosophy. In the words of one American judge, 'common law courts have been reluctant to impose affirmative duties on individuals even in situations in which most people would feel under a moral obligation to act'.

McFall's lawyer claimed that in recent years American and English lawmakers had undergone some change of heart. Examples were provided of the 'ebbing of the strongly individualist philosophy of the early common law', and of cases in which courts had countenanced exceptions to the general rule that refuses to impose a duty to rescue. On the subject of yachtsmen, he was able to point to a decision in which a court held that a yacht owner whose guest fell overboard was under a positive duty to rescue the guest. He put to the court that it was possible to detect a growing Anglo-American acceptance of the principle that legal consequences should attach to conduct that displays indifference to the peril of a stranger. On McFall's behalf, he also put forward and supported a model set of standards proposed in 1965 by a prominent advocate of the rescue principle. These standards, which did not reach the statute book, contained specific suggestions for the provision of medical aid by means of blood transfusion. The basic proposal was that a person should have a legal duty to attempt rescue whenever another was in imminent danger and the first person was the only practical source of help. The duty would apply only if the danger would lead to substantial harm to person or property, and the risk to the rescuer would be 'disproportionately' less than the prospective harm. On the subject of blood transfusion, no objection was seen to a general rule that citizens should be placed under a community duty to give blood. The drafter urged that, at the very least, any blood donor could logically be placed under a duty to continue to give blood, for by giving his tissue in the first place, he indicated that his bodily security was 'subordinated to some other interest'; it was accepted, however, that a person opposed to blood transfusion should not normally be held liable for failure to give blood even if it resulted in loss of life. When these standards were formulated in 1965, the safe removal of bone marrow had not appeared as a lifesaving procedure, but presumably the same philosophy of compulsory donation could be applied to bone marrow donation, and to any other body tissue or organ which, as medicine develops, may be removed without impairing a person's health or well-being. It should not be forgotten in considering this argument that right now a person with one healthy kidney is as acceptable to life insurance companies as a person with two.

The plaintiff's brief argued that Shimp's behaviour in undergoing the first test had placed him in the same position as the blood donor who has previously given blood. By permitting himself to be tissue-typed and by demonstrating a four-tissue match with his cousin, he had obligated himself to continue. The brief claimed that Shimp had 'cruelly abandoned the Plaintiff after the Plaintiff was allowed to hope for a successful end to his ordeal', and should be compelled to continue to offer aid because the plaintiff had thereby been exposed to the risk of greater harm: McFall's chances of cure had been diminished due to the delays caused by Shimp's initial embarkation on a programme of assistance and his later refusal to proceed.

The brief ended with the plea that the court, as the voice of society, should not in the name of the defendant's bodily security abandon Robert McFall to a short, medically dominated life and certain death. 'Our noblest tradition as a free people and our common sense of decency, society and morality all point to the proper result in this case. We respectfully suggest that it is time our law did likewise.'

On July 25, 1978, in a preliminary hearing, Judge Flaherty had to decide whether Robert McFall had disclosed any kind of legal case at all and whether David Shimp had an obligation even to offer a defence. He considered the matter and heard medical evidence of the plaintiff's low chance of survival, the 'minimal risks' in bone marrow removal, and the fact that the plaintiff would have at least a 50 percent chance of cure after a transplant from the defendant. The judge then directed that Shimp's attorney file a brief setting out the reasons why he should not be ordered to give the bone marrow. A hearing was fixed for the next day. McFall had negotiated his first legal hurdle.

The essence of Shimp's defence was contained in his attorney's argument that the law of Pennsylvania did not impose upon him any duty to help his cousin. Whatever had been said about 'minimal risks' of bone marrow donation, the fact remained that the risks existed, and it could be dangerous. Though it is regarded medically as safe, bone marrow removal involves general anaesthetic and extraction of the marrow from the pelvic bone by means of a specially designed needle, which may be inserted as many as two hundred times in order to obtain the required quantity. This process can have a strong psychological effect upon the donor, particularly if he has a fear of surgery, or a fear of losing part of his body, and can cause him to develop hostility toward the recipient.

Even if no risk existed, his client was still under no legal obligation to come to anybody's aid, said Shimp's attorney. Finally, he said, McFall's claim was suspect because it rested upon a view of what the law ought to be, not upon the reality of the law as it then was.

Judge Flaherty delivered his final opinion on July 26, 1978. He accepted the evidence that Shimp was the only suitable donor and that McFall was unlikely to survive without the transplant. He also agreed that the Allegheny County Court is a successor to the English Courts of Chancery and derives power from the second Statute of Westminster.

The judge analysed the American common law attitude to the rescue principle and noted that the common law had consistently adhered to the rule that one human being is under no legal compulsion to aid another who is in distress or danger. He said that 'on the surface' the rule 'appears to be revolting in a moral sense'. However, he felt that mature reflection would demonstrate that it is of 'the very essence of our free society', which takes respect for the individual and his protection as its first principle. The judge contrasted this philosophy with that of societies which hold that the individual exists to serve the community as a whole. On the other hand, in a free society like the United States, moral conflicts such as that raised by Robert McFall are bound to happen. The judge considered that the true decision in this case was a moral one, and rested upon the defendant Shimp, adding that in the view of the court his refusal was 'morally indefensible'. He was, however, not prepared to compel Shimp to submit to bodily intrusion. 'To do so would defeat the sanctity of the individual and would impose a rule that would know no limits and one could not

imagine where the line would be drawn. . . . Forcible extraction of living body tissue causes revulsion to the judicial mind. Such would raise the spectre of the Swastika and the Inquisition, reminiscent of the horrors this portends.'
Robert McFall lost the case. About three weeks later he died.

Do you agree with the judge's views in this case? Was the plaintiff's counsel correct to distinguish his case from a case where a 'stranger' refused to donate an organ on the basis that Shimp had undertaken an obligation to donate by submitting to the tissue-typing tests? Even if this argument were correct, do you think an English court would *enforce* such an obligation against an unwilling donor?

The living donor: liability in tort

(a) NEGLIGENCE

(i) Action by donee

When, if ever, can the donor of tissue or an organ, or a doctor or procurement agency, be liable to the donee who suffers harm as a consequence of the donation?

The ordinary principles of negligence apply in any possible action brought by a donee of tissue or an organ. What may be helpful here is to notice the sorts of particular problems which arise in any possible negligence action (see generally, Kusanovich, 'Medical Malpractice Liability and the Organ Transplant' (1971) 5 USFL Rev 223).

1. An action versus the donor

The donor's potential liability will most probably arise from allegations of non-disclosure of a known (or knowable?) genetic problem or other relevant history which could cause injury to the donee. The question is what is the donor's duty in such circumstances?

There is a growing body of law in the United States which may help us to deal with this question. It concerns the liability of a sexual partner for a sexually transmitted disease. In the 1989 Supplement to *Law, Science and Medicine*, Areen, King, Goldberg and Capron write at pp 129–30:

> . . . A legal basis for such a suit can be found in earlier cases involving nondisclosure of venereal disease, such as *Kathleen K v Robert B* 150 Cal App 3d 992, 198 Cal Rptr 273 (1984), in which a woman sued her former boyfriend for infecting her with genital herpes. In reversing the trial court's summary judgment for defendant, a District Court of Appeal observed that the defendant's constitutional right of privacy is overcome both by the allegedly tortious nature of his conduct, and by the state's interest 'in the prevention and control of contagious and dangerous disease'. *Id* at 996, 198 Cal Rptr at 276. Noting that herpes is not listed among the venereal diseases in the California Health and Safety Code, the court stated:
>> [T]hat section was enacted in 1957, long before herpes achieved its present notoriety. We are not inclined to bar appellant's cause of action on the basis that genital herpes is not a venereal disease. It is a disease that can be propagated by sexual contact. Like AIDS it is now known by the public to be a contagious and dreadful disease. At the core of this action is the misrepresentation of defendant that he did not have a contagious disease that could be passed to his partner. If a person knowingly has genital herpes, AIDS or some other contagious and serious disease, a limited representation that he or she does not have venereal disease is no defense to this type of action.
> *Id* at 996–997, n 3, 198 Cal Rptr at 276, n 3. The court went on to say that consent to sexual intercourse was vitiated by one partner's concealment of the risk of infecting

the other with a contagious disease. *Id* at 997, 198 Cal Rptr at 276. A Georgia court has allowed a man to use a negligence theory in suing his former girlfriend for infecting him with herpes. The court ruled that whether an infected person exercised due care is a jury question, and declined to impose a specific duty to warn in all herpes cases. *Long v Adams*, 175 Ga App 538, 333 SE 2d 852 (1985). See also Note, Liability in Tort for the Sexual Transmission of Disease: Genital Herpes and the Law, 70 Cornell L Rev 101 (1984) (discussing recovery based on theories of negligence and battery).

The English courts could well reach a similar conclusion to the California decision. The duty of the donor might well turn on such factors as (i) knowledge that he was a carrier; (ii) knowledge that he belongs to a high risk group (eg in the context of infection with HIV).

This body of law, important as it is, does not, however, really help us in analysing the liability of a donor to a donee in the context of the donation of body tissue or an organ. This is because what we have in mind here differs in one significant respect from sexually transmitted disease: the tissue and organ donation in which we are interested takes place in circumstances of anonymity. The donee simply cannot trace who the donor was. And, when a donee attempted to do so, the Florida court in the following case refused his application.

Rasmussen v South Florida Blood Service
(1987) 500 So 2d 533 (Supreme Court of Florida; footnotes omitted)

Barkett, Justice: We have for review *South Florida Blood Service, Inc v Rasmussen*, 467 So 2d 798 (Fla 3d DCA 1985). In that decision, the district court certified the following as a question of great public importance:

Do privacy interests of volunteer blood donors and a blood service's and society's interest in maintaining a strong volunteer blood donation system outweigh a plaintiff's interest in discovering the names and addresses of the blood donors in the hope that further discovery will provide some evidence that he contracted AIDS from transfusions necessitated by injuries which are the subject of his suit?

We answer the question in the affirmative.

On May 24, 1982, petitioner, Donald Rasmussen, was sitting on a park bench when he was struck by an automobile. He sued the driver and alleged owner of the automobile for personal injuries he sustained in the accident. While hospitalised as a result of his injuries, Rasmussen received fifty-one units of blood via transfusion. In July of 1983, he was diagnosed as having 'Acquired Immune Deficiency Syndrome' (AIDS) and died of that disease one year later. In an attempt to prove that the source of his AIDS was the necessary medical treatment he received because of injuries sustained in the accident, Rasmussen served respondent, South Florida Blood Service (Blood Service), with a *subpoena duces tecum* requesting 'any and all records, documents and other material indicating the names and addresses of the [51] blood donors'. (South Florida Blood Service is not a party to the underlying personal injury litigation, and there has been no allegation of negligence on the part of the Blood Service.)

The Blood Service moved the trial court to either quash the *subpoena* or issue a protective order barring disclosure.

. . .

It is now known that AIDS is a major health problem with calamitous potential. At present, there is no known cure and the mortality rate is high. As noted by the court below, medical researchers have identified a number of groups which have a high incidence of the disease and are labelled 'high risk' groups. . . .

As the district court recognised, petitioner needs more than just the names and addresses of the donors. His interest is in establishing that one or more of the donors has AIDS or is in a high risk group. Petitioner argues that his inquiry *may* never go beyond comparing the donors' names against a list of known AIDS victims, or against other public records (e g, conviction records in order to determine whether any of the donors is a known drug user). He contends that because a limited inquiry *may* reveal the information he seeks, with no invasion of privacy, the donors' privacy rights are not yet at issue. We find this argument disingenuous. As we have already noted, the discovery rules allow a trial judge upon good cause shown to set conditions under which discovery will be given. Some method could be formulated to verify the Blood Service's report that none of the donors is a known AIDS victim while preserving the confidentiality of the donors' identities. However, the *subpoena* in question gives petitioner access to the names and addresses of the blood donors with no restrictions on their use. There is nothing to prohibit petitioner from conducting an investigation without the knowledge of the persons in question. We cannot ignore, therefore, the consequences of disclosure to nonparties, including the possibility that a donor's coworkers, friends, employers, and others may be queried as to the donor's sexual preferences, drug use, or general life-style.

The threat posed by the disclosure of the donors' identities goes far beyond the immediate discomfort occasioned by third party probing into sensitive areas of the donors' lives. Disclosure of donor identities in any context involving AIDS could be extremely disruptive and even devastating to the individual donor. If the requested information is released, and petitioner queries the donors' friends and fellow employees, it will be functionally impossible to prevent occasional references to AIDS. As the district court recognised:

AIDS is the modern day equivalent of leprosy. AIDS, or a suspicion of AIDS, can lead to discrimination in employment, education, housing and even medical treatment.

We wish to emphasise that although the importance of protecting the privacy of donor information does not depend on the special stigma associated with AIDS, public response to the disease does make this a more critical matter. By the very nature of this case, disclosure of donor identities is disclosure in a damaging context'. We conclude, therefore, that the disclosure sought here implicates constitutionally protected privacy interests.

Our analysis of the interests to be served by denying discovery does not end with the effects of disclosure on the private lives of the fifty-one donors implicated in this case. Society has a vital interest in maintaining a strong volunteer blood supply, a task that has become more difficult with the emergence of AIDS. The donor population has been reduced by the necessary exclusion of potential blood donors through AIDS screening and testing procedures as well as by the unnecessary reduction in the donor population as a result of the widespread fear that donation itself can transmit the disease. In light of this, it is clearly 'in the public interest to discourage any serious disincentive to volunteer blood donation'. Because there is little doubt that the prospect of inquiry into one's private life and potential association with AIDS will deter blood donation, we conclude that society's interest in a strong and healthy blood supply will be furthered by the denial of discovery in this case.

In balancing the competing interests involved, we do not ignore Rasmussen's interest in obtaining the requested information in order to prove aggregation of his injuries and obtain full recovery. We recognise that petitioner's interest parallels the state's interest in ensuring full compensation for victims of negligence. However, we find that the discovery order requested here would do little to advance that interest. The probative value of the discovery sought by Rasmussen is dubious at best. The potential of significant harm to most, if not all, of the fifty-one unsuspecting donors in permitting such a fishing expedition is great and far outweighs the plaintiff's need under these circumstances. . . .

We think that this would reflect what an English court would decide. (For an analogous example of the balancing of the factors of public policy, see *D v National Society for the Prevention of Cruelty to Children* [1978] AC 171, [1977] 1 All ER 589).

Do you agree with the court's view of the demands of public policy?

2.   An action versus the doctor or procurement agency

Here the donee will be alleging incompetence in carrying out the particular procedure, a failure to discover relevant medical information from the donor or the donee, not carrying out proper tests or failing to inform a donee of the risks and alternatives, in breach of the doctor's legal duty.

Norrie illustrates some of these situations in 'Human Tissue Transplants: Legal Liability in Different Jurisdictions', (1985) International and Comparative Law Quarterly 442 at pp 445–6 (footnotes omitted):

> ... For example, to transfer blood taken from a hepatitis sufferer to a recipient would surely suggest liability in damages for the person responsible to ensure that the blood was uninfected. In *Ravenis v Detroit General Hospital* [234 NW 2d 411 (1975)], a claim was held competent where it was alleged that the hospital was negligent in the selection of cornea donors who were not fit within the medical standard of care of the community. Similarly, concern has lately been expressed about patients receiving blood transfusions from donors who suffer from acquired immunodeficiency syndrome (AIDS) [*semble* infected with HIV]. Since the person actually performing the operation is ultimately responsible for the recipient's health, it is with him that liability must eventually rest, though he may also share it with the physician responsible for the extraction of the donation if he is different. Giesen cites a French case in which a surgeon was held liable for transplanting a cornea into a recipient, having taken it from a donor who had died from rabies. The recipient shortly afterwards also died from rabies. In this case it would appear that the transplanting surgeon was responsible not only for the transplantation, but also for the wrongful diagnosis of the donor's death as being from brain-fever. Difficulties as to who is liable to the recipient may arise if the person performing the transplant into the recipient is different from the person extracting the organ from the donor (as will generally be the case, for example, with blood transfusions). It is submitted that the determination of the person liable in such circumstances shall depend upon the extent to which the surgeon performing the transplant is entitled to rely on what he is told by the person extracting the donation. While the transplanting surgeon, being ultimately responsible for the patient's welfare, must in the general case be held liable for failing personally to ensure the suitability of the donation (just as a surgeon, being ultimately responsible for the procedure in any operation, is not entitled to rely on a swab count reported correct to him by a nurse), it is nevertheless possible to envisage circumstances in which he may escape liability. In, for example, the case of blood transfusions, it is suggested that the doctor performing the transfusion is entitled to rely on the information concerning the blood which he is given from the blood bank or persons responsible for taking the donation, because it would be unreasonable to expect him to carry out his own (repeat) tests to determine the blood group etc of the donation.

(For a discussion of the law in the United States, see Annotation 'Liability of hospital, physician, or other individual medical practitioner for injury or death resulting from blood transfusion' 20 ALR 4th 129.)

In the early days of heart transplants the Texas courts had to consider the extent of the doctor's duty to disclose information to a patient already *in extremis*.

Karp v Cooley
493 F 2d 408 (1974) (United States Court of Appeals; footnotes omitted)

Bell, Circuit Judge: Medical history was made in 1969 when Dr Denton A Cooley, a thoracic surgeon, implanted the first totally mechanical heart in 47-year-old Haskell Karp. This threshold orthotopic cardiac prosthesis also spawned this medical malpractice suit by Mr Karp's wife, individually and as executrix of Mr Karp's estate, and his children, for the patient's wrongful death. . . .

Suits charging failure by a physician adequately to disclose the risks and alternatives of proposed treatment are not innovations in American law. They date back a good half-century, and in the last decade have increased in number. . . . Physicians and surgeons have a duty to make a reasonable disclosure to a patient of risks that are incident to medical diagnosis and treatment. True consent to what happens to one's self is the informed exercise of a choice, and that entails an opportunity to evaluate knowledgeably the options available and the risks attendant upon each. From these general principles, however, the focus in each individual case must necessarily relate back to what the physician said or failed to say and what the law requires him to say.

The Texas standard against which a physician's disclosure or lack of disclosure is tested is a medical one which must be proved by expert medical evidence of what a reasonable practitioner of the same school of practice and the same or similar locality would have advised a patient under similar circumstances. . . .

As we understand appellants' contention, it is that Mr Karp was not told about the number of animals tested or the results of those tests; that he was not told there was a chance of permanent injury to his body by the mechanical heart, that complete renal shutdown could result from the use of the prosthesis, that the device was 'completely experimental'; and that Dr Cooley failed to tell Mr Karp that Dr Beazley had said Mr Karp was not a suitable candidate for surgery. Nine physicians testified, but none suggested a standard of disclosure required by Texas law under these circumstances. Appellants argue Dr Cooley himself set the standard requiring the disclosure of Dr Beazley's evaluation. Texas law does permit the defendant doctor to establish the standard of disclosure, but Dr Cooley's testimony says no more than that what is a reasonable medical practice is a question of medical judgment. Dr Cooley's admitted failure to tell Mr Karp of Dr Beazley's March 6 notation is of no import; Dr Leachman testified he did not think the notation made any difference, the March 6 notation, made during the course of an initial evaluation, was in Dr Beazley's view not a medical opinion but a reservation about the psychological or emotional acceptance of less than a perfect result.

What is missing from the evidence presented is the requisite expert testimony as to *what* risks under these circumstances a physician should disclose. . . . What is significant then is what Mr Karp was told, and Mrs Karp's testimony is relevant only to the extent that it evidences what Mr Karp was told when she was present. Dr Cooley's undisputed testimony is that he began discussing with Mr Karp the proposed wedge excision and the alternative procedure of a mechanical heart as a stop-gap to a transplant about a week before the April 4 operation. He said he next talked with Mr Karp the evening of April 2. The consent form was prepared on April 3 and although there is a dispute as to *when* it was signed, there is no question it was signed by Mr Karp. Thus it was against the backdrop of at least two conversations with Dr Cooley, at which Mrs Karp was not present, that Mr Karp was presented and signed the consent document. The consent form is consistent with Dr Cooley's testimony of what he told Mr Karp. Although not necessarily conclusive, what Haskell Karp consented to and was told is best evidenced by this document. It is of considerable import that each step of the three-stage operation, objected to due to an alleged lack of informed consent, was specifically set out in the consent document signed by the patient. . . .

Appellants have not introduced evidence required by Texas law to show a lack of Karp's informed consent or of breach of Dr Cooley's duty to adequately apprise Karp of the nature and risks of the operation that warrant . . . submission of this issue to the jury.

To what extent would an English court follow the reasoning in this decision?

(ii)   Action by donor

1.   An action versus the doctor

Is the extent of the doctor's duty to disclose the same when the doctor is advising the donor? After all, the donor is a healthy person who is being subjected to procedures of varying degrees of risk. Is there any room here for the doctrine of the 'therapeutic privilege'?

Another aspect of the duty may be a doctor's obligation to counsel a donor prior to the procedure. The duty encompasses a obligation to explain not only the alternatives, consequences and risks but also, importantly, to advise about the possible psychological, as well as physical, reactions he may develop after the donation.

In addition to actions based upon a failure to inform the donor, a doctor might, of course, be sued for the negligent performance of the procedure whereby he injures the donor, or for performing the procedure negligently in circumstances where it should not have occurred at all because, for example, the donor is unreasonably exposed to risk. We are here in the realm of medical malpractice law which we have already considered in chapter 5.

2.   An action versus a third party

Urbanski v Patel
(1978) 84 DLR (3d) 650 (Manitoba Queen's Bench)

Wilson, J:—These two suits for medical malpractice were consolidated for trial. Plaintiffs Shirley and Stanley Firman, husband and wife, claim damages caused by defendants' negligence in mistakenly removing Mrs Firman's one and only kidney, whereby both their lives have been seriously disrupted. Plaintiff Urbanski, Mrs Firman's father, donated one of his own kidneys (as what father would not?) for transplant, in a vain effort to ease the disaster, and claims his own costs and other expenses associated with that operation. . . .

. . . Patel admits negligence, and concedes liability to the Firmans, but denies any responsibility to Urbanski as a result of his negligent treatment of Mrs Firman. . . .

. . . Shirley Firman and her doctor decided that, all things considered, it would be just as well if there were no more children. And so, it was arranged she would undergo a tubal ligation. And, because for some time she had felt occasional abdominal discomfort (nothing specific or disabling and perhaps caused, thought her doctor, by an ovarian cyst) her operation was to include exploration for and, if found, removal of that offender.

Otherwise in good health, on April 17th Mrs Firman submitted to this procedure when, by mistake, defendant incorrectly identified a body found in the lower left quadrant of her abdomen and excised this, believing it to be an ovarian cyst.

But, it was a kidney, out of place indeed (ectopic) but a kidney none the less. Indeed, her only kidney, this being a congenital accident hitherto unknown, or even suspected. And while seemingly one can get along quite well—as had this plaintiff—with only half the normal complement of two kidneys, the situation is altogether different if the patient has none at all.

Within two days of the operation Mrs Firman had been admitted to the emergency department of the Health Sciences Centre in Winnipeg. By that time, the material removed had been correctly identified, and the total absence of any renal function was confirmed. On the day following, April 20th, significance of this irreversible disaster was explained to the plaintiff husband and wife, and Mrs Firman was put on peritoneal dialysis. . . .

. . . [A] suitable candidate may be invited to surrender one of his two kidneys to someone else who has none at all, the risk to the donor, seemingly not that great in any event, being entirely overborne by the desperate condition of the other, and the expected improvement in life-style for the donee.

Search elsewhere was finally abandoned, and in the spring of 1976 Shirley's father, the plaintiff Urbanski, volunteered one of his kidneys, implanted May 8th. Unhappily, this was not a success, and it had to be removed three days later, when of course she went back to the machine. On May 31st a cadaveric transplant was attempted, with no more success, and this was removed on June 4, 1976.

. . . Victor Urbanski, in its simplest terms this plaintiff says that he did no more than would any other father, faced with the obvious distress of his daughter, namely, donated one of his own kidneys so that she—who had none—may have a better chance of survival.

Defendant's plea is that this act, and the expenses attendant thereon, may not be looked upon as a foreseeable consequence of the wrong done to Shirley Firman.

That argument prevailed in *Sirianni v Anna* 285 NYS 2d 709 (1967). In that case, because of the acute infection which set in after a routine hernia repair, an exploratory operation was done to see if, perhaps, the patient's condition was caused by a wound abscess or by appendicitis. In the course of this surgery a kidney was removed. And, as with Mrs Firman, that was the patient's only kidney. Dialysis was not a full answer, and his mother donated one of her kidneys, and sued for her expense and general damages.

Her action failed, Ward, J, considering (p 712) that:

The premeditated, knowledgeable and purposeful act of this plaintiff in donating one of her kidneys to preserve the life of her son did not extend or reactivate the consummated negligence of these defendants. The conduct of the plaintiff herein is a clearly defined, independent, intervening act with full knowledge of the consequences.

Mrs Sirianni's decision to give up one of her kidneys he thought was wilful, intentional, voluntary, free from accident, and could not be laid at defendant's door. The classical tests of foreseeability and proximate cause, thought the learned Judge, precluded recovery, because plaintiff's conduct was a clearly defined, independent, intervening act. And, since that act was independent, as well as unforeseeable, it broke the causation, and superseded defendant's negligence in removing the kidney.

But in 1963, when Mrs Sirianni's son lost his kidney, indeed in 1967 when her case was decided, the notion of organ transplant was in its infancy. We all know that not until December, 1967, did Dr Christiaan Barnard accomplish the first heart transplant in man. So then, Ward, J, could well comment, as he did (p 713) that, 'The miracle of modern medical science seems now to be on the threshold of successfully transferring many organs from one human body to another'.

Sirianni, of course, is not binding on me. Apart from that, in studying that case one should read, too, the commentary thereon included in the very useful article 'Medical Malpractice Liability and the Organ Transplant', published with the April, 1971 issue, 5 USFL Rev 223, by Mark Kusanovich, who wrote, at pp 258-9:

Kidney transplantation is of recent origin. Thus, the date on which Sirianni's kidney was negligently removed is relevant to determine whether a contingency of transplant from a live donor was foreseeable. Apparently, the first successful human kidney transplant was performed in 1954. By 1963, 244 kidney transplants had involved live donors. But at that time the field was still very new with live donors coming from close members of the family and with some physicians discouraging donation except from identical twins. Thus, in 1963, the date of the Sirianni transplant, the question whether it was foreseeable that Sirianni, who had no twin, would receive a live organ donation was debatable. Since 1963, kidney transplantation has progressed rapidly. The statistics up to 1970 indicate that approximately 4,000 kidney transplants have been performed and registered. Therefore, it is arguable in the future that whenever disease or removal of kidneys is foreseeable, human donation will likewise be foreseeable.

In testifying before me, Dr Thomson spoke of 123 kidney transplants in Winnipeg alone; both he and Dr Fenton spoke of the many thousands performed in the United States and Europe. If not routine—because of the danger of rejection, and so worsening of the patient's chance for a successful operation by risking the build-up of antibodies—certainly I think it can fairly be said, in light of today's medicine, kidney transplant is an accepted remedy in renal failure. Certainly defendant here can hardly be heard to deny its 'foreseeability', in the dictionary sense of that word.

In other terms, the transplant, surely, must be viewed as an expected result, something to be anticipated, as a consequence of the loss of normal kidney function.

The world of medicine has progressed beyond the *ratio* in *Sirianni*, so that, given the disaster which befell Shirley Firman, it was entirely foreseeable that one of her family would be invited, and would agree, to donate a kidney for transplant, an act which accords, too, with the principle developed in the many 'rescue' cases.

American jurisprudence perhaps anticipated our own in this field, Mr Justice Cardozo's classic remarks in *Wagner v International Railway Co* 232 NY 176 (1921), being penned in 1921. From that judgment, p 180:

Danger invites rescue. The cry of distress is the summons to relief. The law does not ignore these reactions of the mind in tracing conduct to its consequences. It recognises them as normal. It places their effects within the range of the natural and probable. The wrong that imperils life is a wrong to the imperilled victim; it is a wrong also to his rescuer ... The risk of rescue, if only it be not wanton, is born of the occasion. The emergency begets the man. The wrongdoer may not have foreseen the coming of a deliverer. He is accountable as if he had ...

In 1935, with *Haynes v Harwood* [1935] 1 KB 146 at 156–7, Greer, LJ, accepted the American rule as stated by Professor Goodhart in the Cambridge Law Journal, vol V (1935), p 132:

In accurately summing up the American authorities ... the learned author says this (at p 196): 'The American rule is that the doctrine of the assumption of risk does not apply where the plaintiff has, under an exigency caused by the defendant's wrongful misconduct, consciously and deliberately faced a risk, even of death, to rescue another from imminent danger of personal injury or death, whether the person endangered is one to whom he owes a duty of protection, as a member of his family, or is a mere stranger to whom he owes no such special duty.' In my judgment that passage not only represents the law of the United States, but I think it also accurately represents the law of this country.

Both pronouncements were adopted by our own Supreme Court in *Corothers v Slobodian* (1974) 51 DLR (3d) 1, [1975] 2 SCR 633, [1975] 3 WWR 142, wherein Ritchie, J, disposed of the notion of *novus actus*, or 'independent' act by the rescuer, so long as the one imperilled continues in the situation which prompts rescue.

And so, defendant, I find, is answerable to Victor Urbanski.

Technical considerations behind the decision to invite him to undergo such an operation are adequately reviewed in Dr Thomson's letter of March 30, 1976, ex 20, wherein the doctor presents the primacy of the woman's father as most likely source for the attempt, and the very significant advantages to Mrs Firman in the event of success. Given the situation so outlined, and the relationship between the proposed donor and donee, the man's response to the invitation is not surprising.

Following an extensive series of tests and examinations, for which he was obliged to attend the Health Sciences Centre, on May 5, 1976, Victor Urbanski was admitted to hospital, and his left kidney was removed the day following. Up and around within a day or so, he was discharged from hospital on May 14th. No involvement or abnormalities were noted on his post-operative examinations, May 31 and November 16, 1976, with the exception of some hernia problems, present before the event. Removal of the left kidney does not affect his life expectancy, and apart from the anual medical examination recommended in such cases, his life-style should not be changed by what he has undergone, and see the medical reports, ex 28.

For all that, this plaintiff now has but one kidney, and stands in some prejudice, should his kidney function suffer distress by reason of illness or trauma.

For the operation itself, loss of his kidney and post-operative recovery (for which the doctors thought six weeks would suffice, although his discomfort, perhaps loss of confidence, persisted somewhat beyond that period) I would allow $5,000.

Although he operates a farm, Victor Urbanski's principal income is from his trade as a carpenter, seasonal work done in the local district. I am not persuaded there was any serious disruption of the farm; on the other hand, he lost the best part of the building season. For loss of income $3,500 is not unreasonable. Adding $150 for the cost of his several trips into Winnipeg for tests, etc, his claim is allowed at $8,650.

And finally, for Manitoba Hospital Services Commission as to medical and hospital services, drugs, etc, related to Victor Urbanski's operation, $1,906.26.

The approach of the court in *Urbanski* is not without its critics. G Robertson in 'A New Application of the Rescue Principle' (1980) 96 LQR 19, 20 writes:

[The] treatment of the foreseeability question is, however, open to criticism. In regarding the issue of foreseeability as being relevant only to the question of remoteness, the court failed to consider *whether or not the defendant owed the plaintiff a duty of care.* The defendant was unaware, until after the operation, that the patient had only one kidney, and thus he could not be expected to have foreseen, at the time of the operation, that removal of the patient's kidney would result in the need for transplantation. It follows, therefore, that since injury to the plaintiff was not reasonably foreseeable at the time of the negligent act, no duty of care was owed to him by the defendant. (Our emphasis.)

Perhaps, the most important aspect of *Urbanski* is the way in which the court treated the plaintiff's conduct as not amounting to a voluntary assumption of the risk of injury. Again, Robertson explains.

The significance of *Urbanski* lies in the fact that it extends the basis for recovery in rescue cases to an entirely new type of situation. In previous cases, the rescue attempt has involved a *risk* of physical injury to the rescuer, which he has chosen, either consciously or instinctively, to ignore in going to the assistance of the person in danger. In the *Urbanski* situation, physical injury is inevitable, and it is the rescuer's conscious decision to submit to such injury that forms the basis of the rescue attempt.

Despite this distinction, the court regarded the plaintiff's claim as falling within the established 'rescue principle', and it is submitted that an English court would be likely to do the same. There is no reason why the plaintiff's claim should be prejudiced merely because the sustaining of physical injury is a necessary part, and not merely an incidental consequence, of the rescue attempt. Moreover, it is now clear ... that the law affords as much protection to the rescuer who stops for reflection before making his attempt, as it does to the person who rescues on impulse: *Haynes v Harwood* [1935] 1 KB 146 at 159.

The court also concluded that the defence of *volenti* should be rejected, ... The plaintiff in *Urbanski* can scarcely be said to have *voluntarily* assumed the risk of injury, notwithstanding that he realised that such injury was inevitable, given the dilemma in which he had been placed by the defendant's negligent act. The plaintiff's parental feelings towards his daughter, coupled with an understandable sense of moral obligation, left him without any real choice in the matter.

The case has not been followed in the United States of America. In four decisions (*Sirianni v Anna* 285 NYS 2d 709 (1967); *Moore v Shah* 458 NYS 2d 33 (1982); *Ornelas v Fry* 727 P 2d 819 (1986) and *Petersen v Farberman* 736 SW 2d 441 (1987)), courts have refused to apply the 'rescue doctrine' in this type of situation.

Moore v Shah
458 NYS 2d 33 (1982) (Supreme Court NY, Appellate Division)

Weiss, Justice: In what appears to be a case of first impression for an appellate court, we are called upon today to determine whether the donor for a kidney transplant has a cause of action against a physician who was allegedly guilty of negligence in the diagnosis and prescribed treatment of his patient, the donee, in this case the donor's father. The complaint alleges that the negligent diagnosis and treatment caused the father's kidney failure, necessitating later transplantation. Plaintiffs would have this court extend the well-defined principles of the rescue doctrine to one whose decision to come to the aid of his father was deliberate and reflective, not made under the pressures and exigencies of an emergency situation, and significantly, at a time after defendant's alleged negligent acts. For the reasons stated, we decline to do so and affirm the order at Special Term which granted defendant's motion to dismiss the third cause of action asserted in the complaint by plaintiff Marvin Richard Moore.

The predicate for holding a defendant liable must be that a duty is owed the plaintiff, the breach of which duty is the proximate cause of plaintiff's injury (*Palsgraf v Long Is RR Co,* 248 NY 339, 162 NE 99). In order to establish the existence of such duty, a defendant must foresee that his negligence could cause injury, in this case not only to his patient, but to the patient's son as well. While questions concerning what is foreseeable are generally issues for resolution by the finder of fact, there are certain instances where only one conclusion may be drawn from the established facts and where the question of legal cause may be decided as a matter of law (*Derdiarian v Felix Contr Corp*, 51 NY 2d 308 at 315, 434 NYS 2d 166, 414 NE 2d 666). Plaintiff contends, however, that the rescue doctrine serves to establish the requisite foreseeability between the doctor's negligence in treatment of his father and injury to himself as the rescuer (see Prosser, Torts [4th ed], § 44, p 277; see, also, *Gibney v State of New York*, 137 NY 1, 6, 33 NE 142; *Eckert v Long Is RR Co*, 43 NY 502), arguing that defendant knew or should have known plaintiff would logically be the first person to donate a kidney to his father. It is true that a wrong perpetrated upon a victim is also a wrong to his rescuer (*Wagner v International Ry Co*, 232 NY 176, 180, 133 NE 437), and that so long as the rescue is not a rash or wanton act, the rescue doctrine extends a defendant's liability to the rescuer (*Provenzo v Sam*, NY 2d 256, 296 NYS 2d 322, 244 NE 2d 26; *Wagner v International Ry Co*, 232 NY 176, 180–181, 133 NE 437, *supra*; *Lafferty v Manhasset Med Center Hosp*, 79 AD 2d 996, 1000, 435 NYS 2d 307; affd 54 NY 2d 277, 445 NYS 2d 111, 429 NE 2d 789). While plaintiff did not act compulsively or instinctively under pressures of emergency requiring the immediate action usually attendant rescues, there are authorities which have applied the doctrine in other than spontaneous reaction situations (see *Guarina v Mine Safety Appliance Co*, 25 NY 2d 460, 306 NYS 2d 942, 255 NE 2d 173; *Rucker v Andress*, 38 AD 2d 684, 327 NYS 2d 848; *Keith v Payne*, 164 App Div 642, 150 NYS 37). However, we find that foreseeability alone is not enough to impose liability. Since plaintiff was never defendant's patient, no duty to him originally existed. Therefore, we are here involved with a question of whether foreseeability should be employed as the sole means to create a duty where none existed before (see 2 Harper & James, Torts, § 18.2, particularly p 1027; see, generally, §§ 18.3–18.5). It is obvious that extension of liability of a physician to every person who conceivably might come forward as a kidney donor could create a group beyond manageable limits. Then Associate Judge Cooke, writing for the Court of Appeals in *Pulka v Edelman*, 40 NY 2d 781, 390 NYS 2d 393, 358 NE 2d 1019, said:

> If a rule of law were established so that liability would be imposed in an instance such as this, it is difficult to conceive of the bounds to which liability logically would flow. The liability potential would be all but limitless and the outside boundaries of that liability, both in respect to space and the extent of care to be exercised, particularly in the absence of control, would be difficult of definition. (*Id* at 786, 390 NYS 2d 393, 358 NE 2d 1019.)

We agree. In order to recover, a plaintiff must be one within the 'zone of danger' (*Tobin v Grossman*, 24 NY 2d 609, 616, 301 NYS 2d 554, 249 NE 2d 419; *Palsgraf v Long Is RR Co*, 248 NY 339, 162 NE 99, *supra*). It is difficult to charge a physician with the responsibility to foresee each and every person other than his patient who might conceivably be affected by his negligence.

> A duty arises when the relationship between individuals, the asserted plaintiff and defendant, is such as to impose upon the latter a legal obligation for the benefit of the former. . . . 'While a court might impose a legal duty where none existed before . . . such an imposition must be exercised with extreme care. . . .' In the absence of duty, there is no breach and therefore no liability . . . (*De Angelis v Lutheran Med Center*, 84 AD 2d 17, 22, 445 NYS 2d 188).

Our research has disclosed but one reported case in which the plaintiff was an actual organ donor. In *Sirianni v Anna* 55 Misc 2d 553, 285 NYS 2d 709, where a similar factual pattern to the instant case existed, Special Term granted defendant's motion to dismiss the complaint. While this court is not bound by *stare decisis* to follow that decision, we are persuaded by subsequent cases that it was correct. Only one year ago, the Court of Appeals held that where there is no allegation that the defendant was negligent with respect to the plaintiff as opposed to the patient, the case does not fall within recognised limits to the rescue doctrine and it declined to extend existing principles of law so as to include third parties who suffer (shock) as a result of direct injury to others (*Lafferty v Manhasset Med Center Hosp* 54 NY 2d 277, 445 NYS 2d 111, 429 NE 2d 789, citing *Tobin v Grossman* 24 NY 2d 609, 301 NYS 2d 544, 249 NE 2d 419, *supra*; *Vaccaro v Squibb Corp* 52 NY 2d 809, 436

NYS 2d 871, 418 NE 2d 386; *Becker v Schwartz* 46 NY 2d 401, NYS 2d 895, 386 NE 2d 807; *Howard v Lecher* 42 NY 2d 109, 397 NYS 2d 363, 366 NE 2d 64). We agree with the opinion of the Appellate Division, Second Department, 'that courts should not shirk their duty to overturn unsound precedent and should strive to continually develop the common law in accordance with our changing society. . . . Yet, the mere potential ability to change the common law is not the same as the desirability of making a particular change . . .'. (*DeAngelis v Lutheran Med Center*, 84 AD 2d 17, 24, 445 NYS 2d 188, *supra*). There are serious policy considerations which militate against the recovery sought here. Our decision may best be summarised in the words of then Associate Judge Breitel in *Tobin v Grossman*, 24 NY 2d 609, 301 NYS 2d 554, 249 NE 2d 419, *supra*: 'Every injury has ramifying consequences, like the ripplings of the waters, without end. The problem for the law is to limit the legal consequences of wrongs to a controllable degree' (*id* at 619, 301 NYS 2d 554, 249 NE 2d 419). We decline here to extend the common law to create a remedy for these plaintiffs.

Questions

(i) Which decision do you think an English court would be more likely to follow? Notice the remarks of John Spencer in 'Tissue Donors: Are they Rescuers, or Merely Volunteers?' [1979] CLJ 45, 46–7 that:

. . . what are the unspoken factors in cases such as these which influence judges to find that consequences are or are not reasonably foreseeable? To a large extent, they are how badly the defendant has behaved, and how meritoriously the plaintiff. It is hard to think of a more striking piece of medical negligence than removing a kidney in mistake for an ovarian cyst. And it is hard to think of a more meritorious plaintiff than the altruistic Mr Urbanski who, in the face of pain, risk and personal inconvenience, volunteered his vital organs in an attempt to repair the mistake.

Do you agree? (*Urbanski* was followed in a decision of the German Federal Supreme Court on 30 June 1987, JZ 1988, 150.)
(ii) If an English court did follow *Urbanski*, what implications might this have for future cases? Robertson, *op cit*, considers three possible developments.

. . . [I]f the plaintiff in *Urbanski* had had only one kidney, would it have been 'reasonable' for him to offer this for transplantation? (a hypothetical situation, given that the medical profession would almost certainly refuse such an offer). There must come a point in such cases at which the extent of the proposed injury to the rescuer is so great as to make it unreasonable for him to decide to submit to such injury. . . .
The *Urbanski* decision also leaves other interesting questions unanswered. For example, as mentioned above, the transplant of the plaintiff's kidney proved to be unsuccessful. What if the patient's husband had then agreed to donate one of *his* kidneys, would he have been able to recover damages from the defendant as well? If there had been several unsuccessful transplants from members of the patient's family before success was finally achieved, would all the donors have had a cause of action against the defendant? Although one might instinctively answer this question in the negative, it is difficult to see the legal grounds on which such an answer could be substantiated. Surely it is reasonably foreseeable that a kidney transplant, even successive transplants, may be unsuccessful; and that suitable members of the patient's family will continue to come forward as donors until success is achieved. Moreover, the mere fact that previous transplants have been unsuccessful does not *necessarily* mean that transplants from other donors will also fail. Thus, it may be as reasonable for the last in the succession of donors, as it is for the first, to come to the assistance of the patient.
Secondly, the court in *Urbanski* was obviously influenced by the father/daughter relationship that existed between rescuer and rescuee. Would the court's decision have been the same if the rescuer had been a complete stranger, inspired by altruistic rather than parental sentiment? Although such transplants are presently uncommon in most countries, the point is not without legal significance. It would seem

unreasonable to make the outcome of the plaintiff's claim depend on the existence of a special relationship between himself and the rescuee. Whether the rescuer is a relation of the rescuee or a mere stranger, he should be entitled to compensation if he acts reasonably, out of a genuine desire to assist a person who has been placed in danger due to the defendant's negligence. Certainly, this has been the approach adopted in previous rescue cases: see, for example, *Chadwick v British Railways Board* [1967] 2 All ER 945, [1967] 1 WLR 912. However, it is thought unlikely that courts would be willing to extend this approach to the *Urbanski* situation. One suspects that policy considerations, possibly couched in terms of the defence of *volenti*, would weigh heavily against the plaintiff. In a country which frowns upon payment even to blood donors, the possibility of a non-relative receiving compensation, albeit from a negligent defendant, for the voluntary act of donating a kidney is one which courts would be unlikely to encourage.

Do you agree with Robertson's final point? Spencer, *op cit*, does not. He states:

It is inconceivable that anyone not closely connected with Mrs Firman would have succeeded in a claim. Perhaps the decision can be seen as part of a general recognition by the courts that members of a family feel morally obliged to do more for each other than they are legally required to do, and a consequential willingness to compensate them, directly or indirectly, when they do it . . .

(iii)   Action by third party

We can return to the analogy with sexually transmitted diseases to illustrate the questions which could arise here. Areen *et al op cit*, ask the following:

. . . Would the physicians for Robert B . . . be liable to sexual partners who contract AIDS from their patients? See Mills, Special Report: The Acquired Immunodeficiency Syndrome, 314 New Eng J Med 931 (1986). What if the patient is married? See LA Times, May 21, 1986, at 6, col 3 (Association of State and Territorial Health Officials recommends notifying sexual contacts of those who test positive for AIDS antibodies). What if the person contracting the disease is the child of the patient? (AIDS is an especially serious condition for an infant who contracts the disease from its mother before birth.) If the law imposes liability on physicians in these circumstances, what are the implications for access to medical care for people in high-risk populations?

Areen *et al* in posing their questions draw on the line of authority which began with the landmark decision of *Tarasoff* (see *supra* Ch 6). Rosencrantz and Lavey in 'Treating Patients with Communicable Diseases: Limiting Liability for Physicians and Safeguarding the Public Health', (1987) 32 St Louis ULJ 75, 88 after discussing *Tarasoff*, go on to argue that:

The theories of tort liability applied . . . involved a . . . duty to third persons from general principles of negligence and medical malpractice. The theory of tort liability applied in cases such as *Fosgate* [*Fosgate v Corona* 330 A 2d 355 (1974)] establishes potential tort liability for physicians who discharge infectious TB patients without adequate warnings to identifiable at-risk persons. TB patients with poor medication compliance records may pose an especially high risk of tort liability because of the foreseeable possibility that the patient will again become infectious.

Moreover, the same tort principles may apply when physicians discharge AIDS patients with no attempt to identify and counsel specific at-risk people. Proving causation between the physician's conduct and the disease of a nonpatient may be a difficult, but not insurmountable burden for the plaintiff.

Question

Do you think that there are any material differences between the position of the doctor in Areen's questions and his (or a procurement agency's) position in the context of the donation of tissue or an organ? Do you think that an English court would find a doctor or a procurement agency liable?

D Pearl and S Pearl in 'AIDS—An Overview of the Legal Implications' (1989) 86 Law Soc Gaz 28, write:

> *Gammill v United States* 727 F 2d 950 (1984) recognises that a doctor may owe a duty to report that he has diagnosed a patient suffering from an infectious disease in order that third parties at risk of infection from a patient may be informed and protected. The case limits the doctor's duty of care to 'a patient's family, treating attendants, or other persons likely to be exposed' who are specifically known to the doctor in question. Since USA courts are as a rule more rigorous in holding doctors liable in negligence than UK courts, it is unlikely that a UK court would hold that doctors owed any wider duty to inform third parties than this. We can anticipate that a doctor would certainly be under a duty, despite the confidentiality principle, to a wife or sexual partner of a patient or, in the case of an organ donor who is HIV positive, he would be clearly obliged to provide information to protect the donee.

Do you agree with the conclusion reached?

(b) THE CONSUMER PROTECTION ACT 1987

We have seen the Consumer Protection Act 1987 earlier (see Ch 7). The issue for us here is whether the strict liability regime of that Act could be applied to tissue or an organ which subsequently caused harm to the donee. Could the donor, the doctor or the procurement agency be liable for such harm? The Act concerns itself, you will recall, with defective products. Thus, we must ask two questions. First, and fundamentally, is tissue or an organ properly to be described as a 'product' within the meaning of the Act? B Werthmann in *Medical Malpractice Law* describes the approach of the American courts in relation to strict product liability in tort (pp 31–2):

> Whether blood used in a transfusion is such a 'product' has been the subject of considerable debate. In *Cunningham v MacNeil Memorial Hospital*,[17] the Illinois Supreme Court held that whole blood used in a transfusion is a product for purposes of products liability. Subsequently, however, the Illinois legislature passed legislation providing that the furnishing of blood, blood products, and other human tissues is a service, not a product, for purposes of liability in tort or contract. Ultimately, all jurisdictions, either by decisional law or by legislative enactment, have decreed blood transfusions performed in a hospital to be a service incident to treatment and not a product.[18]
>
> Some courts have, however, distinguished between blood furnished by a blood bank and blood furnished by a hospital. Reasoning that the sale of blood is incidental to the function of a hospital, whose primary purpose is to provide a service, whereas provision of blood is itself the primary function of a blood bank, the Supreme Court of Colorado ruled in *Belle Bonfils Memorial Blood Bank v Hansen*[19] that a patient could maintain an action for strict liability and breach of warranty against a blood bank.

Notes to extract
17. *Cunningham v MacNeal Mem Hosp* 266 NE 2d 897 (Ill 1970).
18. See, for example, Okla Stat tit 63, § 2151, which provides in pertinent part:
    The procurement, processing, distribution, or use of whole blood, plasma, blood products, blood derivatives . . . shall be deemed a transaction. . . . No such transaction shall give rise to any implied warranty of fitness, quality, suitability of purpose . . . in the absence of negligence.
    See also *Fisher v Sibley Mem Hosp*, 403 A 2d 1130 (DC 1979).
19. *Belle Bonfils Mem Blood Bank v Hansen*, 579 P 2d 1158 (Colo 1978). After Hansen's suit was filed, Colorado enacted § 13–22–104, CRS 1973, which immunises

blood banks as well as hospitals from liability for all damages other than those caused by negligence or wilful misconduct in carrying out blood transfusions. Section 13–22–104 does not have retroactive application.

Werthmann is concerned only with blood. Do you think in terms of the relevant legal analysis that the English courts would find that there is any difference between blood and other tissue and organs? We doubt it. Would an English court draw the distinction referred to by Werthmann between a hospital and a blood bank? The key may be commerce. There is (as yet) no commerce in blood or other tissues or other organs in the UK, as we shall see.

The second question we must consider is whether, on the assumption that the tissue or organ is a product within the Act, it is *defective* in any particular case. This is obviously a question of fact, ie whether the product meets the definition of 'defective' contained in s 3. Ordinarily, there will be no real issue here. The only significant circumstance in which a matter of legal argument will arise is when the argument is advanced (s 4(1)(e)): 'that the state of scientific and technical knowledge at the relevant time was not such that a producer of products of the same description as the product in question might be expected to have discovered the defect if it had existed in his products while they were under his control'. This is the so-called 'state of the art defence'. An example in our context would be if at the time the tissue or organ was donated (in the case of a donor) or supplied or implanted (in the case of a doctor or procurement agency), there was no test which would allow the discovery of what subsequently proved to be harmful (see, for example, *Dwan v Farquhar* 1 Qd R 234 (1988), which makes the same point but in an action in negligence).

The living donor: agreements to donate

(a) THE AGREEMENTS

Ordinarily, there will be two distinct agreements. The first will be between the donor and a doctor or other agency involved in the removal and storage of the tissue or organ ('the donation agreement'). Rarely, there will not be a doctor or other agency involved as in the case of sperm donation.

The second agreement will be between the doctor or storing institution and the donee ('the transfer agreement').

(b) THE VALIDITY OF THE AGREEMENTS

(i)   The donation agreement

The agreement can take one of two forms: a gift or a contract. Whichever of the two it is, its validity will depend upon considerations of public policy which involve consideration of those questions of consent, maim etc which we explored earlier in this Chapter and more generally in Chapter 4. If the agreement amounts to a contract and the donor is paid, then, the public policy issues of sale and commercialism which we discuss below will also arise.

(ii) The transfer agreement

If the transfer agreement is in the form of a gift then there would seem to be no reason why such an agreement would not be valid if it is intended for the treatment of the patient (donee). If, on the other hand, the agreement purports to be a contract, it may be found to be invalid on grounds of public policy.

1. Introduction

The following is from J Dukeminier 'Supplying Organs for Transplantation' (1970) 68 Michigan Law Review 811, 857–861 (footnotes omitted).

Is the sale of a spare organ against public policy?

There are at least four basic positions from which one may approach the problem of organ sale. The first is founded upon an acceptance of the general ethical principle of preservation of life. That principle, simply stated, is that an individual should not endanger his life except for the love of another or in a case such that the danger is an indirect consequence of the activity. This position has deep roots in Judaeo-Christian, and even earlier, teachings that man should not seek his own destruction. Unlike the Eskimos, who encourage suicide by the elderly when they can no longer contribute to the family larder, most western societies have long condemned taking one's own life. In ancient Athens a man who unsuccessfully attempted suicide was punished by the cutting off of his hand. In medieval England a stake was driven through the heart of a man who committed suicide and all his property was forfeited to the crown; Christians who committed suicide could not be buried in consecrated ground. Remnants of this attitude can still be found in laws against abetting and, in some places, attempting suicide.

However, the principle of preserving life does permit some exceptions. Society condones, and even praises, some acts of heroism and self-sacrifice, such as that of the man who gives up his seat in the lifeboat, the passerby who enters a burning building to save the occupants, or the mother who jumps into the rapids to save her child. These are heroic acts motivated by the desire to help others. Under this view, the sole motivation for risking one's life by giving up an organ must be the love of one's fellow man, and a gift of a spare organ to a specific donee is permissible so long as such a motivation exists. Otherwise, allowing the removal of an organ for transplantation is condemned.

Yet if a charitable motive is so important in judging conduct in situations involving a risking of one's life, how can we permit men to risk their lives in driving racing cars, in entering boxing contests, and in pursuing all kinds of paid risky occupations and still object to the paid kidney donor? When confronted with this question many moral theologians draw a line between direct and indirect effects. For race car drivers and others in risky occupations, dying or being functionally impaired is an indirect consequence, which is foreseen as only possible. In the transplantation case, they argue, removal of the organ from the donor is a life-risking procedure which is the necessary means to the end. If, however, the direct-indirect distinction is accepted, the conclusion that it is unethical to pay a man for a kidney to save life, even though the risks to him are small, but ethical to pay a race car driver at the Indianapolis 500 for entertainment, even though the risks to him are great, can hardly be avoided. Such a principle is troubling indeed.

The second position from which the problem of organ sale can be approached may be characterised as one of 'free will'. This position is based upon the principle that a person should be able to do whatever he chooses, so long as he does not harm another. Particularly among the young, this position is now much in vogue. It underlies much of the current trend to liberate 'sins', such as private deviate sexual conduct and fornication by the unmarried, from criminal sanction. Undoubtedly this principle has also influenced the judicial decisions which have relaxed old proscriptions against obscenity, and it is the base of the recent decisions holding that statutes requiring motorcyclists to wear helmets are unconstitutional since the state may not require a citizen to protect his health alone. As applied to organ sales, the argument would be that an individual has the right to decide for himself whether to sell an organ.

A principal difficulty with this view is that in harming himself a person may harm society; a person who gives or sells a kidney might, if his other kidney fails, have to be maintained by the government on an artificial kidney machine. If he gives or sells other spare organs, the risk that he will disable himself is greater and the resulting harm to society may be substantial. To represent society's interest, a person other than the donor, such as a judge or a physician, must appraise the possible harm to society at large.

A variation of the free-will view is that free will, or informed consent as it is known in medico-legal terminology, should be the ethical criterion, but that a monetary payment for an organ would constitute economic coercion so that the consent would not really represent an act of free will. This is merely a conclusion, however, and is not a reason. What is really at issue is the determination of criteria by which to measure 'unfair inducement' or 'economic coercion' in situations involving the risking of life. Why is it unfair to induce a man to sell a kidney and not unfair to induce him into the boxing ring or into a coal mine?

The third way of evaluating the propriety of permitting organ sale is not to start from any general ethical rule of human conduct but to narrow the problem to the context of the physician-patient relationship. Professor Paul Freund has pointed out that '[t]he great traditional safeguard in the field of medical experimentation is the disciplined fidelity of the physician to his patient: *primum non nocere*. First of all, do not do injury.' From this viewpoint the basic question is not the donor's motivation or free will; the issue is whether buying this particular organ from this individual patient is for his welfare. If the principle of totality permits sacrificing a part of the body for the good of the whole—which includes spiritual gain and the avoidance of psychological trauma—it is not difficult to conceive of situations in which a physician could ethically conclude that the sale is for the patient's welfare. Suppose, for example, that a very rich man needs a kidney and the closest tissue match is his sister, who is poor. While the sister is thinking about offering a kidney, her brother lets her know that he will accept it only in exchange for 100,000 dollars—an exchange which may have income and estate tax advantages for him. If the sister decides to sell the kidney, her knowledge of forthcoming remuneration makes it impossible to conclude that she acts solely for spiritual gain, and yet it does not seem unethical to allow her to sell the kidney. Under the principle of totality, the surgeon must conclude that the donor benefits by removal of his kidney. To arrive at that conclusion the surgeon may have to inquire as to how the donor proposes to use any monetary payment and may then have to decide for himself whether the donor will benefit physically or mentally from that particular use.

Finally, the question of organ sale can be probed by disregarding ethical positions and analysing only the consequences of permitting such sales. Sales will have some impact both on the total amount of economic resources which are to be allocated to medicine and on the selection of recipients, but the precise nature of that impact is not clear. The nature of the impact will depend upon the manner in which two distinguishable problems are approached: (1) creating an adequate quantity of organs supplied and (2) selecting the persons to receive them. The quantity of organs supplied could be increased by buying them, and they could then be allocated among recipients by some method other than sale. For example, a third party, such as the government or a hospital, might absorb the cost. But the consequence of the government's purchase of organs for recipients might be that the government's economic resources which are committed to medicine would be used for the purchase of organs rather than for other medical needs. To achieve the best use of the resources available for medical purposes, other ways of securing a satisfactory quantity of organs should first be exhausted. If the cost of buying organs is passed on to the recipient, life-saving resources would be distributed on the basis of ability to pay. The use of wealth as a means of selecting who shall be saved among the dying raises immensely troublesome ethical and legal quandaries.

Under some approaches to the problem the procedure of buying organs may be thought to be impermissible in some or all circumstances. The sounder arguments, however, appear to permit a surgeon to offer remuneration if, acting in accordance with contemporary ethical standards and with the permission of a hospital review committee, he concludes that in a particular case the operation will promote the physical or mental health of the donor. In arriving at that conclusion, the surgeon and the review committee must balance various interests, but the most important is the doctor's duty to his patient.

Having seen the arguments, consider now the following material presented on both sides for and against sale.

2. Anti-sale

The Australian Law Reform Commission (Report No 7) 'Human Tissue Transplants' (1977) states (paras 176–7):

176. Payment for human tissue could take many forms, apart from cash. For example, for live donors, it could include free medical care, life insurance, and waiver of medical bills. For cadaver donations it could include payment of funeral expenses, or priority for relatives if they need a future transplant. A number of views have been put to the Commission by way of comment on payment or remuneration. These include the views that payment would cause unfair or undesirable encouragement of donation from persons who are poor or, worse, unhealthy; that payment could cause deterioration in standards of testing with increase of health danger to recipients; that payment would increase the possibility of donors lying or concealing health defects, thus increasing danger to recipients. Some assert that traffic in 'human spare parts' is objectionable in itself, and that payment will encourage blackmail, coercion, or duress, particularly by stronger or older members of families in relation to weaker or younger members. Commerce it is said, will lead to pressure for the introduction of legal notions of warranties and conditions of fitness, with the consequent growth of law suits concerning defective or diseased tissue.

177. On the other hand there are those who take the view that sale and payment may be the only means of obtaining an adequate supply of tissues for community needs, and should not be prohibited. Others submit that prohibition should be limited to the 'donor', or in the case of a dead body, to the person entitled to authorise removal of tissue, the person lawfully in possession, the executor, administrator and relatives. On this view, there is no reason to forbid sale of all human tissues in all circumstances, for example the sale of treated and sterile human blood vessels by a reputable medical supply company which may have lawfully acquired the tissue in Australia or elsewhere. It is understood that tissue of this kind is currently on sale in Australia. Another view in support of commerce suggests that a law which prohibits the sale by a person of his tissues, could unreasonably hold back medical advances in the field of bone marrow transplantation. Bone marrow, a regenerative tissue, may be transplanted in children, in cases involving the rare disease aplastic anaemia, with a high prospect of success (a 50 per cent–70 per cent prospect of being alive at the end of twelve months, as opposed to a 90 per cent prospect of death without the transplant). It has been put to the Commission that the process of bone marrow removal and 'follow up' in relation to aplastic anaemia, can be traumatic for a donor, and that the fairest way of obtaining such tissue would be by purchase from willing sellers of their own tissue.

Consider now, the following report of The Transplantation Society entitled 'Commercialisation in Transplantation: the Problems and some Guidelines for Practice', published in *The Lancet*, 28 September 1985, at pp 715–716.

Within three decades, treatment of end-stage renal failure has evolved from a few desperate attempts to prolong life by whatever means available to a large multidisciplinary effort sustaining tens of thousands of individuals by chronic dialysis and/or kidney transplantation. Particularly in the past few years, both therapies have increased in scope, and effectiveness, with rising rates of success. These, in turn, have broadened the criteria for acceptance of patients for treatment.

The results of transplantation especially have improved during recent years, both in regard to patient survival and to graft function, owing to a sustained effort by clinicians and scientists working in many different disciplines. As a result, progressively increasing numbers of patients with end-stage renal disease have sought available care in the hope of returning toward normal health; in parallel, there has been increasing government responsibility toward the provision of the cost of treatment. Similarly the increasing success of heart and liver transplantation has led to an explosion in the number of these transplants in the past two years.

However, with success have come problems. The patients presenting themselves for help include not only individuals from societies with the means, facilities, and expertise to provide such help for their own citizens, but also persons from less medically advanced societies (both able to pay and not) who desperately seek aid from those most able to provide it. As new units open in response to such pleas, competition for both patients and organs grows, particularly as the supply of not only kidneys but also hearts and livers has failed to meet the demand. On the one hand, such competition sharpens the skills of those already in the field and forces rapid acquisition of skills and knowledge by those entering it; on the other, the increasing success and apparent 'ease' of transplantation may encourage false hopes and expectations among patients and among those delivering their care, as well as among state or government agencies sponsoring such treatment.

Thus, kidney transplantation in some Western countries is beginning to shift from university centres to private care; certainly private insurance companies now insure graft recipients with greater enthusiasm than in prior years. However, with this shift may come growing pains. For example, in the United States, some who perform renal transplants have advertised for patients from other countries (who can pay), guaranteeing rapid and successful transplantation using cadaver kidneys, while local patients wait for months in the belief that the system is equitable and they will receive a kidney 'in their turn'. Similarly, wealthy individuals from other countries are placed on transplant lists where they compete with local patients for scarce cadaver kidneys; indeed, the spectre of favouritism has recently been raised in the public press in the USA. The public outcry in response has been predictable. Furthermore, private hospitals in Europe now perform kidney transplants for foreigners who can afford the substantial fees. Such hospitals have assured patients of a cadaver graft within a brief period, as little as two weeks. The unacceptable consequence of this is that the kidneys go only to patients who can pay. The cadaver kidneys used are imported from the United States. Indeed, kidneys from the United States have been exported to several distant countries; in 1984, this figure may have been as high as 600 kidneys. With as many as 20 000 dialysis patients awaiting transplantation in the United States alone, foreign distribution of kidneys that might have been used in the USA, particularly when it gives an advantage to patients with money or to for-profit centres, does not seem reasonable. It certainly does not seem fair nor in keeping with the philosophy by which organ distribution was originally initiated. Although such activities are, theoretically at least, well within the spirit of 'free enterprise', it would not be surprising if the bereaved families of kidney donors would be less anxious to donate their gift if they thought the organ would be used in these ways. Indeed, a recent law enacted in 1984 in the United States has expressly forbidden acquisition or transfer of human organs for 'valuable consideration' (Public Law 98-507, Oct 19, 1984). In 1972, the Ontario Human Tissues Gift Act made commerce in human tissue a crime, and in 1978, the Council of Europe, in Resolution (78) 29 concerning the harmonisation of legislations of member states relating to removal, grafting, and transplantation of human substances, resolved that 'no substance may be offered for profit'.

Beginning with transplantation between identical twins, kidneys from living related sources have been used successfully for many years, particularly in the United States, as both short-term and long-term functional results were consistently superior to those of cadaver organs. Ethical doubts about such a step, although still debated, have generally been resolved. The spectrum of immunological and psychosocial barriers including the HLA match and personal and social motivation have been important determinants in the choice of such donors. However, since the advent of more effective immunosuppressive agents, particularly cyclosporine, the success of cadaver transplantation has improved to such an extent as to rival that of haplo-identical related donor-recipient combinations. As a result, two questions are being asked increasingly; first, should living related sources be used at all?; secondly, should kidneys from living unrelated ('emotionally related') sources be used? The answer to the first question is dependent basically upon the supply and demand of cadaver kidneys. A patient can generally receive a kidney from a motivated related donor with reasonable expectation of good graft function without waiting often for prolonged periods for a cadaver organ. The answer to the second question is more difficult, although again based primarily upon organ supply. With the assurance of relative success, it does not seem unreasonable that in selected instances, donation from unrelated persons, particularly a spouse or individual with a close relationship and intense interest in the welfare of the recipient, should be permitted. Indeed, several experienced centres are beginning to consider (and undertake) such donations.

However, in the current climate of commercialisation, instances of brokerage of kidneys from living unrelated donors have begun to emerge. In a South American country, for instance, advertisements from desperate individuals have appeared in newspapers offering a kidney or even an eye (for corneal transplantation) for money. In this regard, many of us receive occasional pathetic appeals from people in disadvantaged countries offering to sell a kidney to get money, often for care of an ill relative. Besides being an eloquent comment on the social inequalities of our society in general, such appeals raise unsettling ethical questions of a more specific nature. The concept of buying and selling organs in general has been deplored by the transplant community. It does not seem unlikely that a few of the unscrupulous will acquiesce to the profit motive; indeed such brokerage has already been seriously suggested in the United States before being quashed by law, and even more recently in Europe. Furthermore, an active market of living unrelated kidney transplantation with payment to donors is occurring in at least one city in India; some of these donors make their way, with the potential recipient and 'proof' of consanguinity, to the west. Thus recently, a major newspaper has described the buying of kidneys from impoverished donors for transplantation in private hospitals in Western countries. Some donations were coerced, some for meagre fees; and allegedly there was no follow-up of the donors after surgery. Again, public outrage was palpable. A similar situation exists in other countries where kidneys are bought from destitute living donors in surrounding regions. It seems clear that when patient care is relegated to the laws of the market place, particularly when the less privileged can be exploited to improve the health of the more privileged, all in society are diminished.

Specific arguments against the sale of organs from unrelated and emotionally disinterested living donors can be made. Normal safeguards which protect family donors and recipients are threatened by brokerage arrangements, when otherwise unacceptable donors may become acceptable if the price is right. Similarly, one can argue that less than ideal kidneys could be sold more cheaply than organs of good quality. Even if motivation of both donor and recipient is correct, the sale of organs essentially forces the donor to have an operation; bribery before the procedure, blackmail and extortion after it, are possibilities both for the donor and the recipient. Indeed, as a practical example, it could be argued that the buying and selling of blood for transfusion in those countries where this is permitted has led to a less safe and more expensive service; similar commercialisation of organs for transplantation may lead to the same thing.

The Council of The Transplantation Society takes the view that the donation of an organ is a gift of extraordinary magnitude and that transplant surgeons hold a donated organ in trust for society. Thus the Council and its ethics subcommittee on examining data collected on these subjects and considering their ramifications for transplantation as a whole, proposes the following guidelines for the distribution and the use of organs from cadaver sources and from living unrelated donors.

Guidelines for cadaver organ distribution
1. The best possible use must be made of the donor gift.
2. Organs should be transplanted to the most appropriate recipient on the basis of medical and immunological criteria.
3. Usable organs should never be wasted. In the majority of cases, an organ will be used within an established regional or national organ sharing network, and only if it cannot be placed should it be offered to other recognised networks, and then only to non-profit centres.
4. Sharing of organs should only be arranged via national and/or regional organ sharing networks.
5. Priorities in the assignment of organs cannot be influenced by political considerations, gifts, special payments or by favouritism to special groups.
6. Transplant surgeons/physicians should not advertise regionally, nationally, or internationally.

Guidelines for the donation of kidneys by unrelated living donors
1. Living unrelated donors (ie, not first-degree relatives) should be used exceptionally when a satisfactory cadaver or living related donor cannot be found.
2. It must be established by the patient and transplant team alike that the motives of the donor are altruistic and in the best interest of the recipient and not self serving or for profit. In the best interests of all concerned, the motivation and medical suitability of the donor should be evaluated by physicians independently of the potential recipient, the recipient's physicians, and the transplant team. An independent donor advocate should be assigned to the unrelated donor to ensure that informed consent is made without pressure, to enhance personal attention given to the donor throughout the entire donation period, to ensure official expressions of gratitude, and to aid with subsequent problems or difficulties. In all instances, and especially in the exceptional case where the emotionally related donor is not a spouse or second degree relative, the donor advocate would ensure and document that the donation was one of true altruism and not self serving or for profit.
3. Active solicitation of living unrelated donors for profit is unacceptable.
4. Living unrelated donors must be of legal age.
5. The living unrelated donor must satisfy the same ethical, medical, and psychiatric criteria used in the selection of living related donors.
6. It should be clearly understood that no payment to the donor by the recipient, the recipient's relatives or any other supporting organisation, can be allowed. However, reimbursement of loss of work earnings and any other expenses related to the donation is acceptable.
7. The diagnostic and operative procedures on the donor and recipient must be performed only in recognised institutions whose staff are experienced in living related and cadaveric transplantation. It would be expected that the donor advocate should be a member of the same institution but not a member of the transplant team.

Special resolution
No transplant surgeon/team shall be involved directly or indirectly in the buying or selling of organs/tissues or in any transplant activity aimed at commercial gain to himself/herself or an associated hospital or institute. Violation of these guidelines by any member of The Transplantation Society may be cause for expulsion from the Society.

Article 9 of Resolution (78) 29 of the Council of Ministers of the European Communities on 'Harmonisation of Legislations of Member States Relating to Removal, Grafting and Transplantation of Human Substances', provides:

No substance may be offered for profit. However, loss of earnings and any expenses caused by the removal or preceding examination may be refunded. The donor, or potential donor, must be compensated, independently of any possible medical responsibility, for any damage sustained as a result of a removal procedure or preceding examination, under a social security or other insurance scheme.

The Standards Committee of the General Medical Council considered the issue of the 'Transplantation of Non-Regenerative Tissue' in 1985 and the Council endorsed its Report in a published statement on 6 November 1985 as follows:

Sale of anatomical organs by live donors
The Committee have considered a dossier of evidence, compiled by the 'Mail on Sunday' newspaper, which supports allegations that in India poor people are recruited for money to become living donors in kidney transplant operations, some of which have taken place in the United Kingdom. The Committee have embarked on a thorough review of the ethical and legal implications of all operations which involve the transplantation of non-regenerative organs from living donors. Meanwhile, the Committee recommend that as an interim measure the Council should issue advice to the profession that it is unethical and improper for a registered medical practitioner, wittingly or unwittingly, to encourage or to take part in any way in the development of such trafficking in the sale of human organs; and that, accordingly, no surgeon should undertake the transplantation of a non-regenerative organ from a living donor without first making due inquiry to establish beyond reasonable doubt that the donor's consent has not been given as a result of any form of undue influence.

3. Pro-sale

Lori Andrews 'My Body, My Property', Hastings Center Report, Volume 16, October 1986, 28 at pp 31–38, writes:

The market's effect on donors
The property approach requires the individual's consent before her body parts can be used by others. But in some instances body parts—such as kidneys or corneas—may be in such short supply or a particular patient may have such a rare tissue or fluid type that the issue of payment to donors will arise, as it did in the Moore and Hagiwara cases.

The criticisms of a market for body parts focus on potential harms to the donor, the recipient, and society. In organ transplantation, Congress and some state legislatures have already decided to prohibit payment out of fear that poor, minority, or otherwise vulnerable people will be coerced to exchange body parts for money. Is this prohibition justified? And should it apply to the sale of bodily materials in other circumstances?

In its harshest form, allowing payment to living persons who donate solid organs could lead society to view poor people as suddenly having capital and consequently being ineligible for welfare benefits.[31] (A man with a $50,000 kidney, like a man with $50,000 in the bank, would not qualify for welfare.[32]) Such a society would include among its citizens walking human carcasses whose need for money has led them to go under the knife. These individuals would be doubly cursed. Not only would they have to give up precious body parts but, to the extent that the operations left them physically disabled or different looking (sans eye or limb, for example), they might be shunned.[33] Given society's deplorable track record in caring for the disabled, creating more disabled individuals seems immoral.

Suppose a person's body parts were not taken into account in determining his or her net worth. Even then there is concern that allowing payment for body parts could unduly coerce the poor to donate. The strongest argument against paying donors is that people in dire straits will consent to debilitating surgeries out of a desperate need for money. But banning payment on ethical grounds to prevent such scenarios overlooks one important fact: to the person who needs money to feed his children or to purchase medical care for her parent, the option of not selling a body part is worse than the option of selling it. Society has not benefited individuals by banning organ sales unless it also provides a means to escape desperate conditions.

Naturally, the need for money is not a justification for any action (we would not want the person to become a contract killer for a fee). But it is difficult to justify a prohibition on payment for what otherwise would be a legal and ethical act—giving up body parts for someone else's valid use. Similarly, the analogy to slavery is inapposite. We do not want people to sell themselves into slavery *nor* do we want them to 'give' themselves into slavery without pay. In contrast, with respect to organ donation or the development of a diagnostic or therapeutic product from bodily materials, the underlying activity is one we want to encourage.

Where regenerative bodily products are concerned—blood, sweat, and semen or, arguably, embryos—the criticism is even less justified, assuming that the product can be removed safely. In any paid labor, we are giving our body. For example, in response to the idea that a poor woman may be coerced into serving as a surrogate mother despite the risks due to the fee, Laurence Karp and Roger Donahue point out that 'it seems inconsistent to categorically deny such women this kind of livelihood while we permit and even encourage people to earn money by such dangerous means as coal mining, or racing little cars around a track at 200 miles per hour'.[34] In some instances—professional boxing—the assaults to the body are obvious. In others they may be more subtle. The scholar chugging coffee in front of a glowering word processor is damaging her body as well.

It is not the payment that harms the body, but the physical risk to the person of removing the body part or the subsequent risk of living without it. Neither of these risks is present where the sale of a body part becomes effective on the person's death. And when a person donates a body part while alive, the physical risks vary considerably depending on what the part is and how it is removed.

How much risk should a paid donor be allowed to run? One way of deciding would be to compare the level of risk people face when they donate organs with the risk of selling another product of their body, their labor. Along those lines, sales of regenerative body parts seem to present less potential physical harm than do many jobs (such as firefighting).

Giving up a heart or other nonregenerative body part that invariably causes death goes beyond the types of sacrifices that paid labor may demand. Arguably, such sacrifices should be prevented, whether for fee or for free. But an intermediary case—giving up kidneys or other nonregenerative body parts, which does not cause death—does not on its face justify such a drastic prohibition. The risk to a healthy thirty-five-year-old in donating a kidney is the same as the risk in driving a car sixteen miles every working day.[35] Moreover, allowing a market in body parts could reduce the use of (and thus the physical harms to) living donors, since more people may decide to sell their body parts upon death than currently donate them.

Physicians have adopted an odd view of risks to organ donors. Transplant surgeons traditionally have maintained that removing a kidney from a live donor presents minimal health risks. 'However', Arthur Caplan points out, 'when the proposal was made to buy and sell kidneys what had historically been deemed 'minimal risks' suddenly escalated into intolerable dangers when profit became an obvious motive!'[36] I have found a similar shift in perspective among infertility specialists, who describe as safe the ovarian stimulation, laparoscopy, and anesthesia used to harvest eggs from patients undergoing *in vitro* fertilisation. Yet they say that same process is too dangerous to be undertaken by a woman who wishes to be a paid egg donor.

Guarding against coercion

Part of the concern with selling body parts or doing risky paid labor rests on the belief that people should enter into these transactions voluntarily. Courts do not order specific performance when an individual, such as an opera singer, reneges on a job. Voluntariness should have its counterpart in body part donation as well. In 1890 a man sold the Royal Caroline Institute in Sweden the rights to his body after death. Later, he tried to refund the money and cancel the contract. In the subsequent lawsuit, the court held that he must turn his body over to the Institute and also ordered him to pay damages for diminishing the worth of his body by having two teeth removed.[37] In contrast, in the US, under the Uniform Anatomical Gift Act, promises to donate body parts upon death are revocable. With living donors, revocation should be allowed up until the time the transfer is made.

Just as we would not condone a labor system that did not allow people to choose their own employers, we should insist that paid donations from living people be voluntary: that is, made by the person himself or herself. It is one thing for people to have the right to treat their own bodies as property, quite another to allow others to treat a person as property. A hospital should not be allowed to take, sell, and use blood or eggs from a comatose woman to help pay her costs of hospitalisation. People should be prohibited from selling their relative's body parts when the relative dies (unless the deceased left orders to that effect). Nor should judges be allowed to sentence offenders to pay their fines in body product donations (once the property approach has established a market value for them). If this seems farfetched, consider that there already have been instances in which judges sentenced defendants to give blood transfusions. Similarly, an eighteenth-century British statute allowed judges to order anatomical dissection of hanged murderers.[38] It is possible to maintain that people are priceless by not allowing others to treat a person's body commercially either before or after death and by giving people the power to refuse to sell their body parts.

A decision to sell certain types of body parts—nonregenerative ones (such as a kidney) or parts that could give rise to offspring (sperm, eggs, and embryos)—has lifelong implications. With respect to other decisions of long-lasting consequences (such as marriage), society has sometimes adopted added protections to assure that the decision has been carefully made. A similar approach might be used with regard to body parts. In this area, only competent adults should be allowed to decide to sell. There should be a short waiting period (like the cooling-off period that protects consumers from door-to-door salesmen) between the agreement to sell an organ and its removal, and the donor should be required to observe certain formalities (such as signing a witnessed consent form).

Only the person who owns the body part should be allowed to sell it. This approach has two goals. The first is to assure that others do not treat one's body as property. For example, it will prevent the harms associated with holding the body as security until funeral costs are paid.[39] The second is to attempt to assure that the individual is adequately compensated for the body part by limiting the amount any middleman receives. If the middleman cannot 'sell' the part, but can only be compensated for bringing together the donor and recipient, the donor may more likely receive adequate compensation and the transaction will less likely be viewed as excessively commercial. There might even be limitations on what the middleman (physician or entrepreneur) receives, similar to the statutory limitation in some states of 'reasonableness' in the amount of money an attorney receives in connection with arranging a private adoption.

One state already has adopted an approach similar to the one I am advocating here. A California statute prohibits a person from knowingly acquiring, receiving, selling, or promoting the transfer or otherwise transferring any organ for transplantation for valuable consideration. The law is directed against brokering organs rather than the direct selling from a donor to a recipient. There is an exception to the ban on selling and buying for 'the person from whom the organ is removed, [or] . . . the person who receives the transplant, or those persons' next-of-kin who assisted in obtaining the organ for purposes of transplantation'.[40]

This approach may also have the additional benefit in rare instances of preventing crimes. Much of the original horror with recognising commercial value in the body or its parts resulted from cases in which people fell prey to murderers who sold their bodies to medical schools for research. Even in the past decade, there have been cases where mortuary technicians have illicitly sold tissues and organs of corpses.[41] Limiting some parties' ability to sell the body parts does not undermine the property approach. Zoning laws restrict the uses that can be made of land, yet it is still considered property. Similarly, restrictions in a closed corporation on who may buy shares of stock or in a cooperative apartment or who may buy a unit do not undermine their status as property.

Giving an individual sole rights over his or her body parts is in keeping with attitudes toward the body held in other areas of law. Attempted suicide and suicide are no longer considered crimes.[42] However, aiding and abetting a suicide is a crime. Competent individuals can refuse a readily available lifesaving treatment, but their physicians cannot withhold it. Thus, people are allowed to control what is done to their bodies (even to the point of physical damage) in ways that other individuals are not.

Ironically, our current policy is just the reverse. Other people seem to have property rights in our body parts, but we do not. In a British case, an accused man who poured his urine sample down the sink was found guilty of stealing it from the police department.[43] And although an individual has no property interest in his or her cell lines, scientists are quick to claim a property interest in those cell lines. Such a claim was the basis of a six-year conflict between microbiologist Leonard Hayflick and the National Institutes of Health. The conflict was over which side owned a cell line that Hayflick had developed with embryonic living tissue under NIH funding and then sold to scientists around the world.[44]

The notion that other people may own our body parts while we may not has an historical basis. In England, even though courts said people had no property rights in their body, until 1804 creditors apparently had such rights since they could arrest dead bodies for a debt. For example, the poet Dryden's body was arrested as it was being transported for burial.[45] And in feudal times, it was a crime to maim oneself because this rendered one less able to fight for the king.[46] Thus, the common law basis for preventing people from voluntarily transferring their body parts (which was later interpreted to prohibit even gratuitous organ donation) may not have its roots in the view that the body is sacred and that people should not be objectified as property. Rather, it may arise from the notion that people were the property of the Crown.

The market's effect on recipients

We can protect potential donors from the market's effect by attempting to assure that donations are voluntary and by limiting donations to body parts that do not unreasonably affect the person's ability to function. But how does a market affect potential recipients? The policy of prohibiting payment for body parts and products has been justified as protecting potential recipients by raising the quality of donations and preventing a situation in which body parts are affordable only by the rich.

The work of Richard Titmuss on policies governing blood donation raised serious questions of quality control, when blood is sold.[47] Among other things, he argued that paid donors have an incentive not to disclose illnesses or characteristics that might make their blood of dubious quality. Subsequent work by Harvey Sapolsky and Stan Finkelstein[48] challenged Titmuss's conclusions. They pointed to a Government Accounting Office study in which some voluntary groups in the United States reported hepatitis rates as high as the worst paid groups; and some commercially collected blood was nearly as good as the best of the volunteer blood.

Even if paid donors are more likely to misrepresent their condition than are volunteer donors, payment need not be banned on quality control grounds since tests are available to assess the fitness of the donor. In this country [ie the USA] we allow payment for blood and sperm, although it is easy to lie about their quality; yet we do not allow payment for body organs such as kidneys, although organ transplantation offers more independent checks on quality. Nor is banning payment the only mechanism to enhance quality, since if known risks are not disclosed, liability may follow. While this may not offer sufficient protection to the recipients of blood (since donors may not be solvent), organ donors would be better paid and a portion of that money could be used to buy insurance. When a person sells organs contingent on death, payment to an estate could be withheld if it was clear that he failed to disclose a known harmful condition. Already, the Ontario Law Reform Commission has recommended enacting a criminal law prohibiting people selling their gametes from knowingly concealing infectious and genetic disorders.

A market in solid organs is also thought harmful to potential recipients because of the possibility that only the rich will be able to afford organs. On the issue of the poor selling and the rich buying body parts, Thomas Murray says, 'Our consciences can tolerate considerable injustice, but such naked, undisguised profiteering in life would be too much for us'.[49] Yet other equally troublesome but less visible inequities are already occurring in allocating other kinds of medical care. When a drug company prices a medication necessary for someone's life beyond a person's reach or a physician with unique skills refuses to accept patients who receive Medicare, that is also profiteering in life, but the injustice may be overlooked. Currently at least fifty different types of artificial body parts (such as artificial blood vessels and joints) have been designed to substitute for human ones.[50] It is as important ethically to address discrimination between rich and poor recipients with respect to those products as it is with respect to human body parts. A visible market in body parts may lull people out of complacency to address more general issues of allocation in health care.

If we were to ban payment for all body parts (including blood) in this country, we could not sit back, assured that we had eliminated coercion of the poor. Even today, American drug companies undertake plasma collection in Third World countries throughout Latin America and Asia to meet the needs for plasma products here. People in poor countries are giving of their bodies for people in rich countries. Perhaps we should struggle to assure noncommercialisation of human body products in all countries. But if this reduced the blood supply, doctors might have to turn down some patients who needed surgery. Would proponents of total market bans support that outcome?

Quality and cost issues raised by the sale of body parts are similar to issues raised by other medical treatments. Thus they should be handled in the same way with attempts to enhance the quality of care, the informed consent process, access to medical services, and so forth. A market for solid organs may even diminish risks to the recipient. If more organs were available, it would become easier to avoid rejection and recipients who would have died for lack of an organ might gain a chance to live.

The market's effect on society
Will a market in body parts harm society by creating an attitude that people are commodities? The body is a symbol of the whole person and degrading it can be viewed as an assault to the whole person. Our distaste with viewing the body as property is, in part, a reaction to our belief that human beings should have no price.

Certainly people are more than the sum of their parts.[51] But treating the body as property does not mean it is a person's only property. Cognitive functions can be included within the property characterisation. Indeed, they already are, for example, under the legal doctrine of copyright, patent, and other so-called 'intellectual property' rights. I view my uniqueness as a person as more related to my intellectual products than my bodily products. (Definitions of personhood, for example, rarely revolve around the possession of body parts, but rather focus on sentience or other cognitive traits.) Arguably it commercialises me less as a person to sell my bone marrow than to sell my intellectual products. Thus, I do not view payment for body parts as commercialising people. The danger I see in the sale of a physical (as opposed to a mental) bodily product comes from the potential for physical harm in removing the bodily material or living without it. This danger can be handled by limiting the types of body parts that can be sold and the circumstances under which they can be sold.

Selling body parts has also been criticised as harmful to society because it could diminish altruism. But in our society, the basics of life—food, shelter, health care—are already sold. Nevertheless, many people continue to act altruistically, devoting time, money, or goods to provide needy people with those basics. The possibility of selling tissue or organs seems only a modest further step toward a market, unlikely to change vastly the impulse toward altruism. Even people who take advantage of the market may engage in altruistic behavior. One patient, Ted Slavin, received up to $10.00 per millilitre from commercial enterprises for his blood, which was used in manufacturing diagnostic kits for hepatitis B virus. At the same time, he provided additional blood—at no charge—to a research project at the Fox Chase Cancer Center, which used it to develop a vaccine against hepatitis B.[52]

Where a family member or friend is concerned, donation is likely to remain purely voluntary even if payment is allowed; thus the ban on payment cannot be justified as promoting personal altruism based on family or friendship ties. In contrast, donation to strangers is, as Kenneth Arrow notes, a 'diffuse expression of confidence by individuals in the workings of society as a whole'. Arrow questions whether there is merit to advancing that form of giving since 'such an expression of impersonal altruism is as far removed from the feelings of personal altruism as any market place'.[53]

Moreover, an argument can be made that neither personal nor social altruism is furthered by a ban on payment. Are people really more virtuous when they perform a particular act once the temptation to perform a contrary act has been removed by law? As Milton wrote in *Areopagitica*, 'I cannot praise a fugitive and cloistered virtue . . . that never sallies out and sees her adversary'.

Allowing individuals to treat parts of their bodies as property is also said to be conducive to allowing others to treat them as property. According to this argument, if we view the primary object, the body part, as marketable, this will lead us to treat the secondary object, the individual person, as a commodity. As Joel Feinberg points out, however, 'The weakness of the argument consists in the difficulty of showing that the alleged coarsening effects really do transfer from primary to secondary objects'.

The issue of commodification goes far beyond the question of payment for human organs, tissues, and waste products. A variety of components of our social and legal structure have been criticised as commodifying people. The idea that biological parents have a greater right to control over their children than do other members of the community has been criticised by some feminists as treating children as property. Richard Abel, in a far-ranging critique of the American tort system, has argued that damages should not be allowed for pain and suffering because that inappropriately commodifies our emotions.[54]

To guard against the appearance that people are commodities we must not let other people treat one's body parts as property. Body parts will thus not be saleable in the sense of cars, farm animals, or baseball cards. There will be no means for a tax man or physician to put a lien against a person's body parts. Nor can relatives choose to sell a person's parts after his or her death. This might better be called a quasi-property approach. However, it differs from previous notions of quasi-property by recognising the right of an individual to compensation for certain types of body parts. Under this approach human beings have the right to treat certain physical parts of their bodies as objects for possession, gift, and trade, but they do not become objects so long as others cannot treat them as property.

The market's effect on the doctor/patient relationship

The treatment of body parts as property will help curtail activities by physicians, researchers, and their attorneys that deny individuals information about or control over body parts that will be removed.

Implicit in many arguments made by physician/researchers is that the removed body part belongs to the doctor, not the patient. Why do physicians feel that way? I can only speculate that it is because society allows medical practitioners to do things to a patient's body (for example, cut it up) that no one else (other than the patient) is allowed to do. Perhaps this gives physicians the feeling that the patient's body belongs in some sense to them.

Physicians argue that getting patients' permission to use their body parts and products would change the relationship between patients and physicians or researchers. Some argue that discussing the research with the patient may imply that a patient has a right to direct the scope or direction of the study. But that is absurd. Just because IBM is required to make certain disclosures to me when I buy a share of stock does not mean that I can set policy for the operation of the company. Related to this is an argument that paying for the patient's cells, tissue, fluids, or organs would tie up physicians in endless negotiation with their patients. But when payment for human biological material is required, it is no more disastrous to the research enterprise than payment for pipettes, microscopes, animals, or laboratory equipment. It may represent a modest increase in the cost of doing business (just as an increase in fuel prices would raise the costs of lighting the laboratory). But the money paid would go to a good cause, slightly enhancing the resources of medical patients at a time when they need money to pay for medical care. If the patient is unwilling to sell rights to the biological materials, the physician need not barter; she can simply avoid using that specimen and approach other patients. Moreover, we allow the patient to pay the physician for services without being concerned that it will lead to endless negotiations.

Just as physicians raise the price of their services to cover rising malpractice insurance rates, so they will charge slightly more for the right to use the specimens of some patients for research. If it strikes you as unfair (it does me) to force patients to pay for the research by increasing medical costs, consider that under the current system the 'cost' of the human specimens is borne entirely by the patients who own them and who do not even get in return a right to refuse to participate.

Another reason has been advanced against disclosure: it would decrease patient-physician trust if the patient were aware that the physician might develop a commercial product from the patient's body parts. Yet this begs the question of whether the information is relevant. It might diminish the patient's trust to know the success rate and unnecessary surgery rates of a practitioner or health care facility; yet this information is clearly relevant to patient decision making.

There is a similar concern that disclosing the commercial potential of human body parts may tarnish the image of the researchers by making it appear that profit rather than scientific knowledge is their goal. However, the media is already informing the public about the relationship between researchers and the corporate sector. 'The public cannot help but see that the goals of some scientists—clinical or basic—are different than in the past,' says Leon Rosenberg, dean of the Yale University School of Medicine. 'The biotechnology revolution has moved us, literally or figuratively, from the class room to the board room and from the *New England Journal* to the *Wall Street Journal*.'[55]

Finally, people point to the difficulty of assigning values to body parts as an implicit barrier to the property approach. But the value of many items that are currently bought and sold (such as paintings or jewels) is difficult to assess. This is no reason to prohibit the market from developing a particular price.

Arguments about the difficulty in assessing the value of a patient's contribution to research take a variety of forms. Some argue that the patient's contribution is too small to warrant compensation compared to the contribution of researchers and other participants. Yet if a person designs and makes a car, she expects to have to pay for even the smallest screw she uses—though her contribution and the contribution of the other materials vastly overwhelms the role of the screw. Others argue that so many people contribute to a particular advance (for example, 7,000 pituitary glands were used to research the molecular structure of ACTH[56]) that it would be difficult to compensate all of them. Yet large companies have little trouble devising a means to allocate payment among thousands of employees, suppliers, and stockholders. It is also argued that it may be unfair to compensate the patient whose bodily material is used to make a commercially exploitable product, since many other patients' materials were used in research leading up to this advance (and thus it is difficult to measure that particular patient's contribution). That criticism has no more merit than claiming that a scientist should not be paid since he or she is building upon work done by previous researchers.

In fact, determining worth is problematic only when the contribution is evaluated after the fact. There is no compelling reason why before-the-fact contracts should not be made in which the buyer and seller themselves agree on a price (as they do in many other market transactions). Unless the contract involves unconscionable coercion, there is no ethical reason to intervene in the bargain struck between them. Nor does it seem appropriate for policy makers to grapple around in advance for a formula by which to set the price (such as a formula based on how much the bodily material had been altered by the scientist).

In a variation on the value argument physician/researchers seem to imply that the patient has already been paid for the body part by receiving the benefits of the surgery. John Moore, for example, was allegedly helped by his treatment at UCLA. (This argument is harder to make when the patient dies or otherwise does not recover.) But patients may feel they have already paid for their health benefits in the price of the surgery. The patient has a right to know about the research so that she can choose the 'price' she is willing to pay for the surgery. Perhaps she would rather choose a surgeon whose price is set solely in terms of dollars and insurance coverage rather than one who commercially exploits, say, her ovaries.

The future of the body as property

Some of the finest advances in society have resulted from a refusal to characterise human beings (blacks, women, children) as property. Why, then, am I arguing for a property approach here? Let me emphasise that I am advocating not that people be treated by others as property, but only that they have the autonomy to treat their own parts as property, particularly their regenerative parts. Such an approach is helpful, rather than harmful, to people's well-being. It offers potential psychological, physical, and economic benefits to individuals and provides a framework for handling evolving issues regarding the control of extracorporeal biological materials.

It is time to start acknowledging that people's body parts are their personal property. This is distinguishable from the past characterisations of people as property, which were immoral because they failed to take into account the nonbodily aspects of the individual (blacks and women were deemed incapable of rational thought) and they created the rights of ownership by others (masters, husbands, parents). Allowing people to transfer and sell their own body parts, while protecting them from coercion, does not present those dangers.

References

[31] [footnote omitted]

[32] One commentator has suggested that if the body has a market value, all decedents would have to include that value in their gross estate for tax purposes. See 'Tax Consequences of Transfers of Bodily Parts', *Columbia Law Review* 73 (1973), 842, 862.

[33] See Sam Gorovitz, 'Will We Still Be "Human" If We Have Engineered Genes And Animal Organs?' *The Washington Post*, December 9, 1984, p C1.

[34] Laurence E Karp and Roger P Donahue, 'Preimplantation Ectogenesis: Science and Speculation Concerning *In Vitro* Fertilisation and Related Procedures', *Western Journal of Medicine* 12 (1976), 295.

[35] Jean Hamburger and Jean Crosnier, 'Moral and Ethical Problems in Transplantation', in Felix Rapaport and Jean Dausset, eds, *Human Transplantation* (New York: Grune and Stratton, 1968), p 38.

[36] Arthur L Caplan, 'Blood, Sweat, Tears, and Profits: The Ethics of the Sale and Use of Patient Derived Materials in Biomedicine', *Clinical Research* 33:4 (October 1985), 448–450.

[37] Scott [*The Body as Property* (1981)], pp 185–86.

[38] Matthews ['Whose Body? People as Property' (1983) 36 Current Legal Problems 193], p 205.

[39] Such practices are described in *Jefferson County Burial Soc v Scott*, 218 Ala 354, 118 S 644 (1928).

[40] Cal. Penal Code §367f (e) (West 1986).

[41] Scott, p 181.

[42] A 1975 law review article, 'Criminal Aspects of Suicide in the United States', 7 *North Carolina Central Law Journal* 156, 158 n 19–21 (1975) listed only three states (Oklahoma, Texas, and Washington) which still had laws against attempted suicide. Those statutes have since been repealed.

[43] *R v Welsh* [1974] RTR 478, reported in Matthews, pp 223–24.

44 Constance Holden, 'Hayflick Case Settled', *Science* 215 (1982), 271.
45 See Note, 'The Sale of Human Body Parts', *Michigan Law Review* 72 (1974), 1182, 1243, n 409.
46 Bernard Dickens, 'The Control of Living Body Materials', *University of Toronto Law Journal* 27 (1977), 142, 164.
47 Richard Titmuss, *The Gift Relationship: From Human Blood to Special Policy* (New York: Vintage, 1972).
48 Harvey M Sapolsky and Stan N Finkelstein, 'Blood Policy Revisited—A New Look at "The Gift Relationship",' *Public Interest*, 46 (1977), 15.
49 Thomas H Murray, 'The Gift of Life Must Always Remain a Gift', *Discover* 7:3 (March 1986), 90.
50 See, e g, L L Hench, 'Biomaterials', *Science* 208 (1980), 826.
51 See Leon R. Kass, 'Thinking About the Body', *Hastings Center Report*, 15:1 (February 1985), 20.
52 Baruch S Blumberg, Irving Millman, W Thomas London, *et al*, 'Ted Slavin's Blood and the Development of HBV Vaccine', *New England Journal of Medicine* 312 (1985), 189 (letter).
53 Kenneth J Arrow, 'Gifts and Exchanges', *Philosophy & Public Affairs* 1 343, (1972), 360.
54 Richard L Abel, 'A Critique of American Tort Law', *British Journal of Law & Society* 8 (1981), 199, 200, 210.
55 Leon E Rosenberg, 'Using Patient Materials for Production Development: A Dean's Perspective', *Clinical Research* 33:4 (October 1985), 452–54.
56 Angela R Holder and Robert J Levine, 'Informed Consent for Research on Specimens Obtained At Autopsy or Surgery: A Case Study in the Overprotection of Human Subjects', 24(2) *Clinical Research* (February 1976), 68, 75.

Consider, finally, the following description of the position in the United States of America. Note, 'Sale of Human Organs' (1985) 71 Virginia Law Review 1015 at 1020–1; 1024; 1026–9; 1032–7 (footnotes omitted).

The problem of scarcity has engendered widespread debate on methods of increasing organ supply. Several commentators have argued that the most effective solution is to create a commercial market in transplantable organs. These commentators have offered different proposals ranging from permitting organ sales in limited circumstances, to supporting their legalisation, to encouraging their sale. Another proposal suggests that state law should establish a combined altruistic-market system of organ procurement. A final commentator would provide financial incentives for organ donation by requiring private and government health insurance agencies to pay $2500 to the closest relative of an organ donor.

The argument that permitting sales will encourage organ donations is plausible considering that various individuals have actually attempted to sell their organs. According to news reports, poor people in Brazil, through newspaper advertisements, have offered to sell their kidneys or corneas. Although there have been no confirmed sales of organs in the United States, the House Subcommittee on Health and the Environment has received letters from individuals desiring to sell their organs. One individual wanted to sell a kidney to finance an education and another offered to sell an organ to pay for her daughter's medical treatment.

H Barry Jacobs formulated the first serious proposal to buy and sell human organs, and his plan generated a great deal of publicity. According to initial reports, Jacobs established a company to broker human kidneys. Unlike an earlier proposal by another entrepreneur in which people could contract to sell their organs after death, Jacobs intended to broker kidneys from healthy live donors. Under this brokering arrangement, the donor would set a price for his kidney, and Jacobs would collect $2000 to $5000 for his brokerage services. The buyer would normally pay these charges, unless the recipient were entitled to Medicare benefits. Jacobs also planned to bring Third World indigents to the United States so that they could sell one of their kidneys for a nominal price. Jacobs maintained that the indigents could give informed consent, despite their inability to read, through tape recorded conversations. . . .

In response to the issues raised by the Jacobs proposal, the federal law [National Organ Transplant Act 1984] prohibits organ sales by providing, in part:

(a) Prohibition

It shall be unlawful for any person to knowingly acquire, receive, or otherwise transfer any human organ for valuable consideration for use in human transplantation if the transfer affects interstate commerce.

(b) Penalties

Any person who violates subsection (a) of this section shall be fined not more than $50,000 or imprisoned not more than five years, or both.

(c) Definitions

For purposes of subsection (a) of this section:

(1) The term 'human organ' means the human kidney, liver, heart, lung, pancreas, bone marrow, cornea, eye, bone, and skin, and any other human organ specified by the Secretary of Health and Human Services by regulation.

(2) The term 'valuable consideration' does not include the reasonable payments associated with the removal, transportation, implantation, processing, preservation, quality control, and storage of a human organ or the expenses of travel, housing, and lost wages incurred by the donor of a human organ in connection with the donation of the organ.

. . .

Shortly after Jacobs announced his proposal, Virginia Delegate Mary Marshall, the future sponsor of the Virginia legislation, vowed to make it illegal. Marshall was disturbed at the prospect of Jacobs' profiting from organ shortages and was especially concerned about his intention to buy kidneys primarily from Third World indigents. In March 1984, the Virginia legislature responded to Jacobs' proposal by passing the following statute:

With the exception of hair, blood and other self-replicating body fluids, it shall be unlawful for any person to sell, to offer to sell, to buy, to offer to buy or to procure through purchase any natural body part for any reason including, but not limited to, medical and scientific uses such as transplantation, implantation, infusion or injection. Nothing in this section shall prohibit the reimbursement of expenses associated with the removal and preservation of any natural body parts for medical and scientific purposes.

The legislature needed to act because prior Virginia law prohibited only the sale of organs from dead bodies; consequently, Jacobs could legally solicit kidneys from live donors. By prohibiting the buying and selling of 'any natural body part', the new legislation forbids the sale of organs from both live persons and dead bodies.

Maryland also enacted legislation prohibiting the sale of human organs. The Maryland prohibition provides in relevant part:

Except for a nonprofit organisation that qualifies under § 501(c)(3) of the Internal Revenue Code, a person may not sell, buy, or act as a broker for a profit in the transfer of any human organ that:

(i) Is removed from a human body which is alive or dead at the time of removal; and

(ii) Is not under the exclusive control of the [State Anatomy] Board.

The statute defines 'human organ' to include all organs except plasma and blood. This legislation, like its Virginia counterpart, was most likely a response to Jacobs' proposal. The bill was requested one month after Jacobs announced his plan and was introduced in January 1984, the same month as the Virginia bill. Maryland's reaction to Jacobs' proposal is not surprising, given its geographical proximity to Virginia. Senator Julian Lapides, the bill's sponsor, told the Maryland Senate Finance Committee that although he knew of no proposals to market organs in Maryland, the issue was becoming a national concern.

Although this bill encountered little opposition, a Maryland Senate Finance Committee member did note that the prohibition of organ sales might abolish a potentially effective system of organ procurement. He also claimed that people in need of transplants might be desperate enough to ignore any prohibition on the purchase of organs. Additionally, the State Medical Society requested that an organ recipient be allowed to pay for the donor's medical and legal expenses. The legislature enacted the bill without this requested exception.

California also enacted a statute to regulate the sale of human organs. The statute makes it a felony for 'any person to knowingly acquire, receive, sell, promote the transfer of, or otherwise transfer any human organ, for purposes of transplantation, for valuable consideration'. Various exceptions, however, show that the California statute is specifically designed to eliminate the brokering of organs rather than prohibiting two-party sales.

The statute allows individuals to purchase an organ for their own transplant or to sell an organ to a recipient. Moreover, the statute's proscription on organ sales does not apply to a recipient's next-of-kin who assists in obtaining the needed organ. Finally, a physician or surgeon who transplants a brokered organ is not liable if the transplant was performed under life threatening or emergency conditions. Because of these exceptions, the statute applies only to a middleman who brokers an organ sale or to a doctor who transplants a brokered organ in a nonemergency situation.

Two additional California laws deal with the sale of organs and tissues. The first law is of limited application and makes it a misdemeanor to sell unlawfully the body, and presumably the organs, of an unclaimed dead person. The second law makes it illegal for a physician to perform a transfusion using blood obtained from a paid donor. Although this statute does not prohibit the buying and selling of human blood, it does inhibit a commercial blood market by discouraging physicians from using purchased blood. . . .

In reaction to Jacobs' proposal, the various legislatures prohibited all organ sales. This broad prohibition may have been a hasty and inappropriate response. The legislatures could have responded by regulating the market in human organs to eliminate the most undesirable elements of Jacobs' proposal. This section reviews the arguments both for and against the complete prohibition of all organ sales.

A frequently cited virtue of a commercial organ market is its potential to save thousands of lives by generating a sufficient supply of organs. The effect, however, of an organ market on the supply of available organs is uncertain. The supporters of organ sales argue that if organs could be sold, more organs would become available for use in transplants. One commentator asserts that common sense, supported by economic theory, suggests that people who do not want to donate their organs may be willing to sell them.

The opponents of organ sales dispute a commercial market's ability to increase the supply of organs. They argue that commercial sales may lead to a collapse of the voluntary donation system and result in an overall decrease in available organs. To support this conclusion, opponents refer to the effect on supply of the commercial blood market. When the states first permitted the sale of blood, the overall blood supply dropped sharply because the decrease in voluntary donations was larger than the increase in paid donations.

In addition to disputing the impact of a commercial market on organ supply, commentators disagree over the appropriateness of distributing organs based on the recipient's ability to pay. According to the opponents of organ sales, a commercial market would wrongly discriminate against individuals who were unable to pay for the needed organ. Supporters of the market respond that individuals may not be required to purchase an organ with their personal wealth. The government could subsidise the cost of organs, or Medicare and private insurance companies could pay for the transplanted organ as a cost of surgery. Moreover, discrimination already exists in the present medical care system. The wealth discrimination argument logically applies to all medical care allocated by market forces and would thus prohibit any life-saving health care from being bought or sold.

The foregoing arguments analysed the effects of a commercial organ market from a broad societal viewpoint. Commentators have also examined the organ market from an individual seller's perspective, focusing on the risks of donating a kidney and the coercive effect of a monetary payment. The removal of an organ is not without risk; at least sixteen people have died while donating a kidney to a relative. According to some opponents of organ sales, a monetary inducement to donate is so coercive that it deprives some sellers of the ability to give informed consent to this potentially risky operation. Supporters of an organ market respond by noting that society often allows individuals to risk their lives for money by engaging in high-paying, hazardous occupations. For example, the issue of informed consent does not arise when coal miners and racecar drivers receive a monetary premium for the risks they undertake.

One response to this argument is that existing evidence shows that individuals who 'voluntarily' donate a kidney to a relative may be subject to greater coercion than those who sell their organs. People often decide to donate a kidney to a needy relative before they have been informed of the potential risks. Donors often describe their choice as 'necessary' and family members may even openly pressure them to donate. Because of this subtle coercion, doctors occasionally provide bogus medical excuses for reluctant potential donors. Thus, a market system may actually be less coercive than the present voluntary system.

In addition to addressing the societal and individual effects of an organ market, commentators have raised ethical objections to organ sales. Congressman Gore, the House sponsor of the National Organ Transplant Act, has argued that '[i]t is against our system of values to buy and sell parts of human beings'. Another commentator argues that monetary considerations should play no role in life and death decisions. This second argument suggests, however, abolishing all market allocation decisions in medicine, meaning that no life-saving health care should be bought or sold.

Supporters of organ sales have made strong ethical arguments for a commercial market. One ethicist asserted that any system that alleviates human suffering and death is acceptable, regardless of the participants' underlying motivations. He further noted that the medical profession is humanely oriented even though doctors receive high fees for their services. Another philosopher found no 'morally relevant' difference between organ donations and organ sales or between compensating the doctor, but not the donor, for his contribution. Thus, the ethical arguments, like the previous arguments, support both sides of the issue.

Finally, transplant surgeons have addressed the propriety of a commercial organ market. Three medical transplant associations recently adopted a resolution calling for the expulsion of any member who participates in a commercial organ market. The resolution also condemned the 'recent scheme' as 'abhorrent' and 'completely morally and ethically irresponsible'.

In sum, although most commentators agree that Jacobs' proposal was inappropriate, they disagree on the desirability of prohibiting all organ sales. The next section suggests some alternatives to an unrestrained organ market or to a complete ban on organ sales. These suggestions are designed to increase the supply of organs and avoid the undesirable effects of an unregulated organ market.

B. Alternatives to a complete prohibition of organ sales

Rather than responding to Jacobs' proposal by banning all organ sales, the legislatures could have regulated the commercial organ market. Many observers believed that this approach would have increased the availability of organs while minimising the problems associated with organ sales. Commentators have posed a number of regulatory alternatives that include permitting individuals to sell organs without a broker, permitting the sale of cadaveric organs, providing noncash incentives to those who donate organs, and allowing monetary payments to family donors.

The first alternative to the wholesale prohibition of organ sales is to allow sales between the donor and recipient but to forbid organ 'brokering' by third parties. This regulation has the advantage of responding directly to the situation that the legislatures apparently tried to prevent—the exploitive brokering of human organs. The limited prohibition eliminates the major problems of a commercial organ market, while allowing individuals to buy or to sell organs legally.

A second regulatory alternative is to allow only the sale of cadaveric organs. If this solution substantially increased the supply of organs, it might eliminate the need for live donations. A cadaveric organ market would thus have several advantages. It would eliminate the risk, however slight, that accompanies the removal of kidneys from live donors. Moreover, the market would avoid the coercion caused by family members and monetary inducement. This limited market is not permitted by any of the present statutes because the statutes are written broadly enough to prohibit organ sales from cadavers.

A third possible regulation would limit the compensation for an organ donation to specific noncash options. This regulation may be appropriate because nonpecuniary payment for an organ might be ethically justifiable even though a direct cash payment might not. A good example of a noncash payment is an unenacted congressional tax bill that would have provided income and estate tax deductions for decedents who donated organs for transplantation. In essence, the bill attempted to reduce the need for living donors and to increase the supply of organs by providing an incentive to donate organs posthumously. Other alternatives to a direct cash payment include providing the donor with free life insurance or medicial care, giving his relatives transplant priority, or cancelling or reducing his hospital bill if the donation is made after a long hospital stay.

A system of organ 'trading' is an additional form of noncash payment. Under this system, if a donor's organ is incompatible with the recipient, the donor could trade his organ for a suitable match. An opponent of organ sales has supported this trading system because '[i]f we permit a father to donate his kidney to his wife or child, however, it is difficult to justify not permitting him to at least trade his kidney for another (directly or through a brokerage firm) in the event that his tissue is not a close enough match'. An organ trading system is justified because the quality of consent, the risks undertaken, and the donor's motivation are the same as in a direct intrafamily donation.

A fourth alternative to a complete prohibition of sales is to allow the recipient to purchase an organ from a family member. A wealthy individual in need of a kidney might prefer to pay a relative for donating the needed organ. A donee should be allowed to express his appreciation by a monetary gift; those not wanting to buy or sell an organ can engage in a purely donative transaction. This alternative of allowing intrafamily sales is consistent with the usual legal and medical views on intrafamily affairs. The law has traditionally respected private family decisions, and the medical profession has stopped long ago analysing the motives behind intrafamily donations.

Who do you think has the better of the argument? You will have noticed that the statutory prohibition of organ sales has occurred in the USA. In England, as yet there is no legislation. However, as a consequence of a recent highly publicised instance of the sale of kidneys by Turkish donors for transplantation in England, in April 1989 the Government introduced into Parliament the Human Organ Transplants Bill. The Bill seeks to ban the sale of human organs derived either from a live or dead donor. The Bill would create a criminal offence, punishable with up to three months' imprisonment, for anyone to make or receive payment for the supply of an organ or to act as a broker for such an arrangement or to advertise an organ for sale.

The Bill would criminalise all the participants in a commercial donation— the donor, the doctor, the donee and any broker that might exist. In this respect, its scope contrasts starkly with that of the Surrogacy Arrangements Act 1985, which only criminalises the broker in a surrogate arrangement. What is the difference between using your body to produce a child for another and using (by giving away) a part of your body to enhance the health (perhaps even save the life) of another? Only the former would be lawful if the Bill becomes law.

The Bill deals only with 'organs'. Is there anything intrinsically different between selling 'organs' and selling tissue or other body products, e g skin, blood or semen? Could the difference, if any, be only in the fact that 'organs' are non-regenerative? But why should this be relevant if the vice of donation, attacked by the Bill, is *commerce* and not the fact of donation itself? Do you think the Bill should, therefore, extend to tissue and other body products?

(c) TERMS OF THE AGREEMENTS

If the agreements amount to a gift then the only question that has to be asked is 'to what did the parties agree?'. For example, were a donor of tissue to impose a condition to further a legitimate object (such as, that the tissue be transplanted into a particular person or in specific circumstances), then use of the tissue in non-compliance with that term would be unlawful.

If the agreements were contracts, on the assumption that such a contract was otherwise lawful, then terms may be implied by law as well as being expressly agreed between the parties. Consideration of implied terms, of course, only becomes important as regards the *transfer agreement*.

Here it may be asked whether, all things being equal, the provisions of the Sale of Goods Act 1979 and of the Supply of Goods and Services Act 1982 apply? Both the 1979 and 1982 Acts apply only where the supplier of the goods or service acts 'in the course of a business'. It seems clear that the activities of a private hospital, blood bank, semen bank or the like would constitute a 'business'. (So, too, would the activities of an NHS hospital were it to contract with the donee: see s 18(1) of the 1982 Act.) If so, should the transfer agreement be categorised as a contract for the supply of *goods* or *services*?

Matthews in 'The Body as Property' (1983) 36 Current Legal Problems 193 writes (pp 225–6):

> More problematic is the potential application of the Sale of Goods Act 1979, with its terms regarding quality implied into contracts of sale. If a private hospital sells blood to a patient which turns out not to be fit for its purpose (eg because contaminated by hepatitis), is there a breach of section 14 of the Act?[43] The American courts, as one might expect, have long had to grapple with this kind of question. Broadly, cases have fallen into two categories: first, where the court has held the supply of blood to constitute a *service* rather than a *sale of goods*,[44] and secondly, where the court has held the supply to be a sale of goods.[45] Which way the courts have decided has been influenced by a number of factors, such as whether the defendant was a hospital or a blood bank, whether either was profit-making or non profit-making, and so on. In any case, the American law of product liability[46] and general negligence is now so highly developed there is no longer a substantial difference between supplying a service badly and selling faulty goods, but the American experience has (as always) proved instructive. On principle, it is submitted that blood ought to be 'goods' within the 1979 Act wherever it is dealt with commercially.
>
> *Notes to extract*
> [43] ie implied terms as to merchantable quality (s 14(2)) and fitness for purpose (s 14(3)).
> [44] eg *Perlmutter v Beth David Hospital* 308 NY 100, 123 NE (2d) 792 (1954).
> [45] eg *Belle Bonfils Memorial Blood Bank v Hansen* 579 P 2d 1158 (1978).
> [46] See, eg Frumer and Friedman, *Products Liability*, para 19.02 [1] n 2.

Since the 1982 Act, the point that Matthews argues has become irrelevant since identical terms will be implied however the contract is categorised. Though not a matter of contract law, it is worth noting the possible effect of the Consumer Protection Act 1987. Assuming that a donee is a consumer for the purposes of the Act, it remains important to determine the precise nature of the transfer agreement, since the 1987 Act only imposes strict liability for the provision of defective *goods*. Would the supply of tissue be held by a court to be the supply of *goods* within the meaning of the Act? Given the existence of the defence of 'state of the art' in section 5 of the 1987 Act, can one think of a case in which a successful action could be brought based upon strict liability but not in negligence? Is this not important in determining a court's attitude to whether an action can be brought at all under the Act?

(d) ENFORCEABILITY

McFall v Shimp
(The Court of Common Pleas, Allegheny County, Pennsylvania, Order, 26 July 1978)

Flaherty J: The plaintiff, Robert McFall, suffers from a rare bone marrow disease and the prognosis for his survival is very dim, unless he receives a bone marrow transplant from a compatible donor. Finding a compatible donor is a very difficult task, and limited to a selection among close relatives. After a search and certain tests, it has been determined that only the defendant is suitable as a donor. The defendant refuses to submit to the necessary transplant, and before the Court is a request for a preliminary injunction which seeks to compel the defendant to submit to further tests, and, eventually, the bone marrow transplant.

Although a diligent search has produced no authority, the plaintiff cites the ancient statute of King Edward I, *St Westminster 2, 13 Ed 1, c 24*, pointing out, as is the case, that this Court is a successor to the English Courts of Chancery and derives power from this statute, almost 700 years old. The question posed by the plaintiff is that, in order to save the life of one of its members by the only means available, may society infringe upon one's absolute right to his 'bodily security'?

The common law has consistently held to a rule which provides that one human being is under no legal compulsion to give aid or to take action to save that human being or to rescue. A great deal has been written regarding this rule which, on the surface, appears to be revolting in a moral sense. Introspection, however, will demonstrate that the rule is founded upon the very essence of our free society. It is noteworthy that counsel for the plaintiff has cited authority which has developed in other societies in support of the plaintiff's request in this instance. Our society, contrary to many others, has as its first principle, the respect for the individual, and that society and government exist to protect the individual from being invaded and hurt by another. Many societies adopt a contrary view which has the individual existing to serve the society as a whole. In preserving such a society as we have it is bound to happen that great moral conflicts will arise, and will appear harsh in a given instance. In this case, the Chancellor is being asked to force one member of society to undergo a medical procedure which would provide that part of that individual's body would be removed from him and given to another so that the other could live. Morally, this decision rests with the defendant, and, in the view of the Court, the refusal of the defendant is morally indefensible. For our law to *compel* the defendant to submit to an intrusion of his body would change every concept and principle upon which our society is founded. To do so would defeat the sanctity of the individual, and would impose a rule which would know no limits, and one could not imagine where the line would be drawn.

This request is not to be compared with an action at law for damages, but rather is an action in equity before a chancellor, which in the ultimate, if granted, would require the forcible submission to the medical procedure. For a society, which respects the rights of *one* individual, to sink its teeth into the jugular vein or neck of one of its members and suck from it sustenance for *another* member, is revolting to our hard-wrought concepts of jurisprudence. Forcible extraction of living body tissue causes revulsion to the judicial mind. Such would raise the spectre of the swastika and the Inquisition, reminiscent of the horrors this portends.

This Court makes no comment on the law regarding the plaintiff's rights in an action at law for damages, but has no alternative but to deny the requested equitable relief. An Order will be entered denying the request for a preliminary injunction.

Scott, in his book *The Body as Property*, comments on this case as follows (p 136):

> . . . [T]here are other notable aspects of *McFall v Shimp*; the facts that the proceeding itself was readily entertained by the court, that Robert McFall was accorded *locus standi* (standing to sue) and that the 'cause of action' upon which it was based did not offend either the procedural or substantive requirements of Pennsylvania law.

In other words, there is no reason why the submissions in the brief filed by McFall's attorney may not survive to be considered and accepted by another court on another day.

Of course, if the doctor were to suffer loss either because as a private doctor he had been put to expense or because he had failed to make the profit which would flow from the opportunity to transplant the organ in someone else, damages would be recoverable.

The above concerns the enforcement of the *donation agreement*. As far as the *transfer agreement* is concerned, there can be no question of the law specifically enforcing an agreement to transplant tissue or an organ into a patient on the traditional ground that equity will not enforce a contract for personal services. If, however, the refusal to carry out the agreement constitutes a breach because the doctor refuses for reasons other than medical ones, then a patient would have a remedy in damages.

The Dead Donor

(a) INTRODUCTION

Gerald Dworkin, in 'The Law Relating to Organ Tra. plantation in England' (1970) 33 MLR 353, 364–5 (footnotes omitted), writes as follows:

Because of the practical difficulties of obtaining organs from live donors, medical attention was directed to the possibility of obtaining organs from the bodies of dead donors. The practical advantages are obvious: the donor, once pronounced dead, is not exposed to any of the hazards which face the live donor; in some cases, such as heart or liver transplants, it is not possible to take organs from live donors; and the potential supply of organs from cadavers is much greater than from live volunteers. Practical difficulties also exist: until recently, although eyes could be 'kept' for several hours after death all other organs had to be taken and used within an hour of death; even with rapid medical progress it will be desirable for some time to come to perform the operation as soon as possible after the death of the donor.

2. The existing law
(a) *Common law.* The common law position concerning corpses is curious but relatively well established. A corpse cannot ordinarily be the subject of ownership. Usually the executor or next-of-kin will have lawful possession of the body and there is a duty to arrange for burial at the earliest opportunity. It follows that, at common law, a man cannot by his will, or otherwise, legally determine what shall happen with his body after his death, although in most cases his wishes concerning the disposal of his body will be observed. That does not, of itself, authorise organs to be taken from corpses for the purpose of transplantation.
(b) *Statute.* The need for human bodies for medical purposes is not new: bodies have always been required for anatomical teaching and research. But any attempt on the part of persons in possession of a body to sell it, even for the purpose of dissection, was unlawful; the bodies of persons convicted of murder were alone capable of being used for dissection. The scandals of body-snatching and the publicity of the murder trial of Burke and Hare led to the passing of the Anatomy Act 1832, which enabled bodies to be supplied legally to medical schools for the purpose of anatomical examination. The demand for corpses was then successfully met for over a century.

It is only in recent times that the medical profession realised that the law relating to cadavers was far too restrictive. The successful development of the corneal graft operation focused attention on the lack of supply of eyes and the inability of potential donors to bequeath their eyes for such purposes. In a little debated, but carefully prepared, piece of legislation the Corneal Grafting Act 1952 (the wording of which to some extent followed the Anatomy Act 1832) was passed authorising the use of eyes of deceased persons for therapeutic purposes. This Act quickly proved to be too narrow, for it did not enable any other part of the body to be removed. However, once this kind of provision was on the statute book, it was much easier to extend it. The Human Tissue Act 1961 at present governs the English law relating to cadaver transplantation.

(b) THE HUMAN TISSUE ACT 1961

The Human Tissue Act 1961, s 1 (as amended) provides:

1.—(1) If any person, either in writing at any time or orally in the presence of two or more witnesses during his last illness, has expressed a request that his body or any specified part of his body be used after his death for therapeutic purposes or for purposes of medical education or research, the person lawfully in possession of his body after his death may, unless he has reason to believe that the request was subsequently withdrawn, authorise the removal from the body of any part or, as the case may be, the specified part, for use in accordance with the request.

(2) Without prejudice to the foregoing subsection, the person lawfully in possession of the body of a deceased person may authorise the removal of any part from the body for use for the said purposes if, having made such reasonable enquiry as may be practicable, he has no reason to believe—

(a) that the deceased had expressed an objection to his body being so dealt with after his death, and had not withdrawn it; or

(b) that the surviving spouse or any surviving relative of the deceased objects to the body being so dealt with.

(3) Subject to subsections (4) and (5) of this section, the removal and use of any part of a body in accordance with an authority given in pursuance of this section shall be lawful.

(4) No such removal shall be effected except by a fully registered medical practitioner, who must have satisfied himself by personal examination of the body that life is extinct.

(4A) No such removal of an eye or part of an eye shall be effected except by—

(a) a registered medical practitioner, who must have satisfied himself by personal examination of the body that life is extinct; or

(b) a person in the employment of a health authority acting on the instructions of a registered medical practitioner who must, before giving those instructions, be satisfied that the person in question is sufficiently qualified and trained to perform the removal competently and must also either—

(i) have satisfied himself by personal examination of the body that life is extinct, or

(ii) be satisfied that life is extinct on the basis of a statement to that effect by a registered medical practitioner who has satisfied himself by personal examination of the body that life is extinct. [Inserted by Corneal Tissue Act 1986.]

(5) Where a person has reason to believe that an inquest may be required to be held on any body or that a post-mortem examination of any body may be required by the coroner, he shall not, except with the consent of the coroner,—

(a) give an authority under this section in respect of the body; or

(b) act on such an authority given by any other person.

(6) No authority shall be given under this section in respect of any body by a person entrusted with the body for the purpose only of its interment or cremation.

(7) In the case of a body lying in a hospital, nursing home or other institution, any authority under this section may be given on behalf of the person having the control and management thereof by any officer or person designated for that purpose by the first-mentioned person.

(8) Nothing in this section shall be construed as rendering unlawful any dealing with, or with any part of, the body of a deceased person which is lawful apart from this Act.

(9) In the application of this section to Scotland, for subsection (5) there shall be substituted the following subsection:—

'(5) Nothing in this section shall authorise the removal of any part from a body in any case where the procurator fiscal has objected to such removal.'

(i)   Authorisation of removal

1.   Donation under section 1(1)

The requirements to be satisfied are as follows:

(1) request by deceased prior to death;
(2) in the appropriate form;
(3) no withdrawal of request;
(4) life is extinct;
(5) an authorisation within s 1(1):
  (a) by a person lawfully in possession;
  (b) concerning the removal of that specified in s 1(1).

In considering these requirements it is important to notice that the drafting of the Act gives rise to a number of problems of interpretation but there are no cases to assist us.

Request by deceased. To be valid the request must have been made by a competent person. The precise nature of competence is not specified in the Act. An analogy may be drawn with capacity to make a valid will.

Cockburn CJ put it as follows in *Banks v Goodfellow* (1870) LR 5 QB 549 at 567:

> . . . [H]e ought to be capable of making his will with an understanding of the nature of the business in which he is engaged, a recollection of the property he means to dispose of, of the persons who are the objects of his bounty, and the manner in which it is to be distributed between them. It is not necessary that he should view his will with the eye of a lawyer, and comprehend its provisions in their legal form. It is sufficient if he has such a mind and memory as will enable him to understand the elements of which it is composed, and the disposition of his property in its simple forms.

Do you think that an English court would insist upon this level of comprehension? Or do you think the approach would be the same as we suggested for making a valid request under the Data Protection Act 1984? (*supra* Ch 6). (See also *Re K* [1988] Ch 310, [1988] 1 All ER 358.)

A related question is whether the provisions of the Wills Act 1831, s 7 requiring that the testator be 18 or over, would be applicable by analogy here? Lanham argues otherwise, and we agree:

David Lanham, 'Transplants and the Human Tissue Act 1961' (1971) 11 Med Sci Law 16, 17:

> There is no mention in the Act of any age limit within which it is possible to make a request. At the committee stage in the House of Commons Mr Page raised the problem of the age of consent. He asked whether a request by a teenager would be sufficient under the section and suggested a provision that a request could be made on behalf of very young children by the guardian. (HC Deb, Vol 643, col 839). The Ministry of Health in a brief reply (*ibid*, col 846) said that there was no age limit. No special provision was made to cover the position of very young children. The solution is probably that if a child is old enough to understand the position sufficiently to make the request, the request is valid for section 1(1). If the child is not old enough, section 1(1) will not be applicable and authorisation will have to be made under section 1(2).

Appropriate form. Given that the request may be made in writing, some concern has been expressed as to whether a printed card (a donor card) comes within the terms of the Act. The British Transplant Society took the view that in addition to amending s 1(2) of the Act (on which see *infra*), the following new subsection should be added:

> For the avoidance of doubt in the interpretation of this section it is hereby declared:
> (b) that a printed but personally signed donor card or other document, is 'in writing' for the purpose of subsection 1 of this section.

A further question is whether the request in writing must be signed. Again the statute is silent on the matter. Do you think the purpose of the statute would be defeated if a court interpreted 'in writing' as demanding a signature?

Finally, if the request is made orally it must be made in the 'last illness'. Ordinarily this would pose problems of interpretation but since the request only falls to be considered after death, hindsight resolves the question.

Withdrawal of request. Lanham, *op cit*, at p 7, writes as follows:

> If the person who is lawfully in possession of the body has reason to believe that the request has been withdrawn, he is not permitted to authorise the removal and use of the body in accordance with the request. No form of withdrawal is specified, so that the request can be withdrawn orally even if it was given in writing. Nor if the withdrawal is oral need it be made in the presence of two witnesses. It will only operate, however, if it is communicated in some way to the person who becomes the person lawfully in possession of the body, since the original request is effective unless the person lawfully in possession does have reason to believe that the request has been withdrawn. If the patient changes his mind again after withdrawing the request, he must presumably renew his request in writing or in the presence of two or more witnesses. There appears, however, to be no duty upon the person lawfully in possession to make inquiries about whether a request once given had been withdrawn. ... It is presumably for any person knowing of the withdrawal to acquaint the person lawfully in possession of the body with the fact of withdrawal.

Life is extinct. The obvious importance of this is reflected in the fact that there is a further specific provision in s 1(4) that death be established by personal examination by the transplant surgeon.

Prima facie this means that the death of the donor should first be established by those caring for the patient/donor using the established criteria and procedures for determining death (see *infra*, Ch 15). Then, for a second time, death must be determined to have occurred by the transplant surgeon. Because of the development of ventilators and artificial support, the determining of death is not incompatible with the continued presence of heartbeat and respiration (see *infra*, Ch 15). This gives rise to the so-called 'beating heart cadaver' whereby an organ can be removed from a corpse, the heart and respiration of which is artificially maintained after the declaration of death so as to preserve the organs' viability prior to transplant.

An authorisation within s1(1)

A. 'LAWFULLY IN POSSESSION'

The authorisation for the removal of an organ must be given by a person lawfully in possession of the corpse. The meaning of this phrase is explained by Lanham in his article, *op cit*, (pp 18–20):

> It is almost commonplace knowledge that in general a dead body cannot be owned. This means that at common law a body cannot be stolen. The law does, however, recognise a right to possession of a dead body and is prepared to protect that possession. Possession is one of the most difficult concepts of the law and it is perhaps not surprising that there has been some doubt as to its meaning under the Human Tissue Act 1961.

The leading case of possession of a dead body is *Williams v Williams* (1881) 20 Ch D 659 where Kay J held that the deceased's executors were lawfully entitled to the possession of his body. If the deceased has died intestate, his administrators will then be entitled to possession. In *R v Fox* (1841) 2 QB 246 the executors were able to enforce their right to possession against a gaoler who refused to deliver up the body of a deceased prisoner unless the executors first satisfied certain claims made by the gaoler against the deceased. But the fact that the executors or administrators have a better right than the person in whose custody the body is does not mean that the latter person is not lawfully in possession until the executors claim their right.

That persons other than the executors or administrators might lawfully be in possession of the body was recognised in *R v Feist* (1858) D & B 590 where it was held that the master of a workhouse was a person having lawful possession of the body of a deceased pauper for the purposes of permitting the body to undergo anatomical examination under the Anatomy Act 1832. The case has been criticised (see *Russell on Crime*, 12th ed, p 1419) on the ground that the master of the workhouse was merely the servant of the poor law authority and that possession of the workhouse was in the latter body. Even if the criticism is valid it does not affect the principle that a person other than the executor or administrator may be lawfully in possession of a dead body.

If it be accepted that a person other than the executor may be lawfully in possession of a dead body certain cases at common law indicate the persons who are in possession in different circumstances. In *Williams v Williams (supra)* the executors' right to possession of the body was linked with the responsibility for its burial. In the cases below responsibility for burial was established, and by parity of reasoning those under the duty to bury must have had the right to possession of the body.

In *Ambrose v Kerrison* (1851) 10 CB 776 it was held that a husband was under a duty to dispose of the body of his deceased wife even though he was separated from her. Jervis CJ expressly likened the position of the husband to that of an executor. The case was followed in *Bradshaw v Beard* (1862) 12 CBNS 344. It was held in *R v Vann* (1851) 2 Den 325 that a father was under a duty to dispose of the body of his deceased child if he had the means to do so, and in *R v Stewart* (1840) 12 Ad & El 773 it was said that every householder in whose house a person died was bound to arrange for the burial of the body.

As might be expected, any statement of general principles is lacking in the cases referred to above. It is submitted, however, that the person who has actual physical custody of the body has lawful possession (and the duty of disposal) of it until someone with a higher right (eg an executor or parent) claims the body. Though in no way authoritative in court, the following statement in *Hansard*, HC Deb Vol 643, col 835, seems to represent the law; 'In the absence of executors there is a common law duty to see that the body is buried and the person lawfully in possession is normally the occupier of the premises where the body lies, or the person who has the body'.

One particular aspect of very great importance in the present context is the legal position when a person dies in hospital. When the Human Tissue Bill was passing through Parliament it was said that 50 per cent of the deaths in this country occur in hospital. It would appear on the general principles discussed above that where a person dies in hospital the hospital management committee or board of governors are legally in possession of the body until someone with a better title to possession (eg an executor) claims it. When the Bill was in committee in the House of Commons, an amendment was moved to make it clear beyond any doubt that where a body lay in a hospital the person having control of the management of the hospital was lawfully in possession. The Government resisted the amendment on the ground that it might be interpreted as giving the hospital authorities a right to possession enforceable against executors. (HC Deb, Vol 643, col 836.) Nonetheless it seems clear at common law that the hospital authorities are lawfully in possession of the body and this position is impliedly confirmed by section 1(7) of the 1961 Act—'In the case of a body lying in a hospital, nursing home or other institution, any authority under this section may be given on behalf of the person having the control and management thereof by any officer or person designated for that purpose by the first-mentioned person'. This provision clearly assumes that the hospital authorities are normally in possession of a body lying in hospital and provides a convenient system whereby a designated person (eg the medical superintendent) may carry out the function of the person lawfully in possession.

. . .

Despite the seemingly overwhelming case for arguing that the hospital authority is capable of being lawfully in possession of the deceased's body, Doctor Addison, in his letter to the *British Medical Journal* [(1968) 1 Br Med J 516] says that the Medical Defence Union has been advised by leading counsel that, save in the exceptional case, the hospital where a patient died is not lawfully in possession of the body for the purposes of the Act. It is respectfully suggested that, at least in the context of the road accident victim, counsel is wrong.

The strongest case is one in which the person who dies in hospital dies intestate and without a spouse or relatives. In such a case there is no one at the time of death with a better right to possession than the hospital and it cannot be doubted that the hospital is lawfully in possession of the body. But even if there is someone with a better right to possession than the hospital, it does not follow that he is in possession as soon as the patient dies. Suppose the patient has made a will naming executors. The executors will have a better right to possession than the hospital, but at the time of the patient's death they may not even know that there is a body over which they have a right to possession. Without knowledge they cannot have the intention to possess and so one of the elements normally required for the acquisition of possession is missing. The same holds true if the person leaves a widow or other surviving relatives. The cases where a person possesses objects of which he has no knowledge but which are contained in his property (eg *Elwes v Brigg Gas Co* (1886) Ch D 562) are not in point and do not invalidate the general rule requiring *animus possidendi*. If Professor Woodruff's statement that many grafts are lost because next-of-kin cannot be contacted in time is right, cases in which the executors or relatives cannot be found in time can hardly be regarded as 'exceptional'. At the very least until the executors or relatives know about the death, the hospital must be regarded as lawfully in possession of the body.

In other cases there is more room for argument. Presumably the mere fact that the executors or relatives know about the death is not enough to vest possession in them. There must be an intention to possess. Furthermore that intention must presumably be communicated to the hospital, since intention by itself does not constitute possession: see *Salmond on Jurisprudence* (11th ed, p 322).

But once a person with a better right of possession communicates his intention to possess to the hospital, the hospital's authority under the 1961 Act ceases. If, as is almost certainly the case, the hospital recognises that person's right to possession, the latter becomes the possessor. While the body remains in the hospital, the hospital may also be in possession but since there will be another person lawfully in possession, his consent will be a necessary condition to the giving of authority under the Act. If on the other hand the hospital were to refuse to recognise the executor's or relative's rights (a situation which seems most unlikely), the hospital and not the executors or relatives would remain in possession, but the hospital would not then be lawfully in possession, and once again the hospital's powers under the Act would cease.

Finally, one class of person who might be regarded as lawfully in possession of the body is specifically denied the right of granting authority under the Act. Section 1(6) provides that: 'No authority shall be given under this section in respect of any body by a person entrusted with the body for the purposes only of its interment or cremation'. Accordingly, a funeral undertaker is not able to give authority as a person lawfully in possession of the body.

It will be noticed that the statute states that the person 'lawfully in possession' *may* authorise. It is clear, therefore, that the donor's expressed request need not necessarily be complied with, since the person lawfully in possession retains an absolute discretion. This must be right since there will be circumstances in which it would be undesirable to remove any tissue, whatever the donor's wishes.

B.   REMOVAL OF THAT SPECIFIED IN S 1(1)

It will be noted that there is a discrepancy in the wording of s 1(1) between what the donor may have requested and what the person 'lawfully in possession' may authorise. The Human Tissue Act 1961, s 1(1) states (our emphasis):

> **1.**—(1) If any person, either in writing at any time or orally in the presence of two or more witnesses during his last illness has expressed a request that *his body or any specified part of his body* be used after his death for therapeutic purposes or for purposes of medical education or research, the person lawfully in possession of his body after his death may, unless he has reason to believe that the request was subsequently withdrawn, authorise the removal from the body of *any part or, as the case may be the specified part*, for use in accordance with the request.

The upshot would appear to be that, although no problems arise in relation to transplantation, the donor may not, under s 1(1), leave 'his body' for purposes of medical education and research.

Consent of the coroner. Lanham, *op cit*, writes at pp 21–22:

> An inquest may be required where there is reasonable cause to suspect that the deceased died either a violent or unnatural death or a sudden death of which the cause is unknown or died in prison or in such place or circumstances as to require an inquest in pursuance of any Act: Coroners Act 1887, s 3(1). In the case of a sudden death of which the cause is unknown the coroner may, as an alternative, order a post mortem examination: Coroners (Amendment) Act 1926, s 21. Except in the circumstances mentioned above, the coroner has no right to require an inquest. *R v Price* (1884) 12 QBD 247 at 248, and, except as provided by section 21 of the 1926 Act, no power to order a post mortem unless an inquest is to be held (see Henslowe Wellington, *The King's Coroner* (1906) Vol II, p 25).
>
> The importance of these provisions in relation to organ transplants is that in practice the victims of motoring accidents may constitute an important category of potential donors and that this is the kind of case in which the coroner's consent is necessary. The attitude of coroners is therefore of great significance. In the nature of things there is no reported case giving guidance on how coroners ought to exercise their discretion.
>
> . . . First, the Act itself does not state any absolute bars to the coroner's granting consent. It may be that for practical reasons it will not be possible to obtain organs from a victim of homicide in time for transplantation because of the desirability of preserving the body so far as possible intact for the post mortem examination. But there may be cases where the investigation of the causation of the injuries would in no way be impeded by the removal of organs unconnected with the injuries (e g, where the kidneys are removed in the case of fatal head injuries) and in such circumstances a coroner might be prepared to give consent. Secondly, the meaning of 'consent' is not entirely clear. An express prior consent to the removal of organs from a specified dead body is obviously adequate. But can the coroner give a general consent in advance? Can he, for instance, notify the hospitals in his area that 'in the following circumstances ————— I consent to the removal of the following organs ————— from any dead body over which I have jurisdiction'. Alternatively, can he delegate to his pathologist the power to give consent in certain defined circumstances? Generally when a statute confers on a public officer or body a discretion to consent to a certain course of action the discretion must be exercised on a specific application for consent and a general statement of policy is not regarded as an exercise of the discretion. . . .
>
> . . . Again, a person or body given discretionary powers by Parliament is generally

expected to exercise those powers himself and not to delegate their exercise. But neither of these rules is absolute. A body given a discretion may sometimes 'in the honest exercise of its discretion, adopt a policy and announce it to those concerned, so long as it is ready to listen to reason why, in an exceptional case, that policy should not be applied' see *Schmidt v Secretary of State* [1969] 2 Ch 149 at 169. Furthermore, in one of the leading cases on delegation, *Vine v National Dock Labour Board* [1957] AC 488, Lord Somervell, far from stating an absolute rule against delegation said (at p 512) 'In deciding whether a "person" has power to delegate one has to consider the nature of the duty and the character of the person'. For a case which illustrates the fact that the rule against delegation is not absolute see *Osgood v Nelson* (1872) LR 5 HL 636. These cases are, like those in which the general rules about fettering discretion and non-delegation, far removed from the question of the coroner's jurisdiction but it is thought they may be used to support the very beneficial practice whereby coroners give general advance consent. Provided that the coroner's policy clearly achieves the purpose of section 1(5)—to preserve relevant evidence—there is every reason the law should recognise the legality of the practice.

Brazier in her book, *Medicine, Patients and the Law* at 279–80 (footnote omitted), argues that the obtaining of authority from the coroner:

> . . . could have the effect of delaying for an unacceptably long period the opportunity to remove organs. This may be the case particularly where a coroner regards his duty to act as coroner as being of greater importance than the secondary power which he has to authorise the use of organs before his coroner's duties are complete. In a controversial case in Leicester in 1980, the father of a girl who had died in a road accident had given surgeons permission to use any of her organs, including her heart, which had been removed by surgeons. At a subsequent inquest, the coroner complained that he had not given permission for the heart to be removed since permission had been sought from him only for the removal of a kidney. He therefore directed that in future written permission would have to be obtained from him and countersigned by a pathologist. This incident highlighted the problem that coroners, acting in pursuance of what they regarded as their legal duties, could adversely restrict the use of organs even where parents or other relatives had consented. It was for such reasons that the Home Secretary circularised coroners, stressing that it was not part of a coroner's function to place obstacles in the way of the development of medical science or to take moral or ethical decisions in this matter, and that the coroners should assist rather than hinder the procedure for organ removal. A coroner should refuse his consent only where there might be later criminal proceedings in which the organ might be required as evidence, or if the organ itself might be the cause or partial cause of the death, or where its removal might impede further inquiries [HC (77) 28 August (1975)].

2. Donation under section 1(2)

The Human Tissue Act 1961, s 1(2) provides:

> Without prejudice to the foregoing subsection, the person lawfully in possession of the body of a deceased person may authorise the removal of any part from the body for use for the said purposes if, having made such reasonable enquiry as may be practicable, he has no reason to believe—
> (a) that the deceased had expressed an objection to his body being so dealt with after his death, and had not withdrawn it; or
> (b) that the surviving spouse or any surviving relative of the deceased objects to the body being so dealt with.

The requirements to be satisfied under s 1(2) are largely those already considered, ie the requirements relating to (a) the persons lawfully in possession; (b) the need for a deceased person; (c) removal of only a part or parts of the body.

There are, in addition, other requirements which only arise in s 1(2). These relate to the following statutory words:

(1) 'having made such reasonable enquiry as may be practicable';
(2) 'the person lawfully in possession has no reason to believe . . .';
(3) 'that the deceased has (not) expressed an objection';
(4) 'that the surviving spouse or any surviving relative . . .';
(5) 'that the surviving spouse or any surviving relative "*objects*" '.

These are considered separately below.

'*Having made such reasonable enquiry as may be practicable*'. PDG Skegg in 'Human Tissue Act 1961' (1976) 16 Med Sci Law pp 197–199, examines this requirement.

Had it been so desired, s 1(2) could easily have specified that the person lawfully in possession of the body should never authorise the removal of parts of it unless the surviving spouse, and any relatives of the deceased, had agreed to this being done. But s 1(2) imposes no such requirement. Nor does it require the person lawfully in possession of the body to make all possible enquiries whether there is a relevant objection. He need only make 'such reasonable enquiry as may be practicable'.

If the requirement of reasonable enquiries stood on its own, there could clearly be considerable discussion of the extent to which the impracticability of an enquiry should be given weight in determining whether that enquiry was 'reasonable'. However, as s 1(2) requires, not the making of all reasonable enquiries, but only 'such reasonable enquiry as may be practicable', that consideration need not be pursued at this stage. Putting aside the issue of practicability, what enquiries are reasonable?

In determining whether the person lawfully in possession of the body has made reasonable enquiries, some weight must clearly be given to the resources—both in terms of finance and manpower—available to him, and to the other claims on those resources. Where a hospital authority is the person lawfully in possession of a body, it is clearly not reasonable for all other administrative activities to cease for a day, while staff assist in an enquiry as to whether any one of the dozens of traceable relatives of the deceased has any objection to the removal of a pituitary gland for research purposes, or an eye for corneal transplantation. Where the newly bereft spouse or parent is the person lawfully in possession of the body, he or she can hardly be expected to spend many hours telephoning distant relatives, with whom they may have had no contact for years, enquiring whether they have any objection to the removal of a specimen from the body of the deceased spouse or child.

Another factor which should be taken into account in determining the reasonableness of an enquiry is its likely utility. An enquiry would not be unreasonable because every available colleague or friend of the deceased has not been contacted, to enquire whether the deceased ever expressed an objection to the use of his body for the envisaged purpose. Although it is possible that any one of them may recall some relevant statement of the deceased, the likelihood of the enquiry producing relevant information would normally be so slight that it would not be unreasonable to omit to make it.

A third consideration in determining whether it is reasonable to enquire of a particular person is that person's age and his physical and emotional condition. It would surely be unreasonable to enquire of young children, or of someone who was critically ill as a result of the accident in which the potential donor died. It would probably also be considered unreasonable to approach a severely distressed spouse or relative, whose health could be detrimentally affected in consequence of an enquiry.

In determining what amounts to a reasonable enquiry, a court would undoubtedly give considerable weight to accepted attitudes concerning what is a reasonable enquiry. In practice, it is widely accepted that a reasonable enquiry normally requires no more than enquiring of either the spouse or a close relative whether he or she has reason to believe that the deceased had expressed an objection, or whether some other person, whose objection is relevant, objects. Even where a more extensive enquiry is practicable, this enquiry is generally regarded as reasonable (see eg HSC (IS) 156, para 11). Given this consensus, it is unlikely that a court would take a different view.

As already stressed, s 1(2) does not require the making of all reasonable enquiries. It requires only 'such reasonable enquiry as may be practicable'. The crucial issue is whether, in determining the practicability of an enquiry, it is permissible to take account of the time within which the part must be removed if it is to be of use for the desired purpose. The Long Title of the Act indicates that the main purpose of s 1 was 'to make provision with respect to the use of parts of bodies of deceased persons for therapeutic purposes and purposes of medical education and research'. The purpose of s 1(2) is not simply to allow the relative to object if he so wishes . . . If it was, it would require that the person lawfully in possession of the body contact every relative and enquire whether he or she objects. As it stands, s 1(2) attempts a compromise between the interests of the parties specified and the interests of those who may benefit from the use of parts of the body. For this reason, it requires only 'such reasonable enquiry as may be practicable'. In determining the practicability of an enquiry, there is no warrant for excluding from consideration the time within which a part must be removed if it is to be of use for the intended and approved purpose. Indeed, this factor will sometimes be crucial. For example, when it is desired to remove a kidney for transplantation from a body which is not being maintained on a ventilator, it will not be practicable to make as extensive enquiries as when it is desired to remove a bone for the purpose of medical education. This is because a kidney which is left in a body for more than an hour after the cessation of respiration and circulation becomes irreversibly damaged.

The issue of whether it is permissible to take account of the time available in determining the practicability of an enquiry is closely related to, but distinct from, one other issue. This is whether the person lawfully in possession may ever give his authority without making any enquiry, on the grounds that no enquiry was both reasonable and practicable. On one view, s 1(2) requires that at least some enquiry always be made before the person lawfully in possession of the body may authorise the removal. But on another view, an enquiry need only be made if it is both reasonable and practicable to make one. On this interpretation, if no enquiry was both reasonable and practicable the person lawfully in possession of the body could still give his authority, if he had no reason to believe that there was a relevant objection. In such circumstances, s 1(2) would operate like its predecessor in the Corneal Grafting Act 1952, where there was no obligation to make an enquiry in any circumstances. If a choice must be made between these two approaches, the second seems preferable. But it may be questioned whether in practice any choice is necessary. It is difficult to envisage a situation where at least some enquiry is not both reasonable and practicable. Extensive enquiries are clearly impracticable in the case of an accident victim who is brought into hospital dead, and whose kidneys must be removed within a very short time if they are to be of use for transplantation. However, at the very least, it is always both reasonable and practicable to enquire whether the deceased is carrying on his person any indication that he expressed an objection to the proposed use of his body.

Notice the interpretation given to the important word 'practicable'. Dworkin argues otherwise in 'The Law Relating to Organ Transplantation in England', *op cit*, pp 367–8:

. . . The only guidance given to the hospital is that it may act provided it has made such reasonable inquiry as may be practicable. . . . [The argument that] it would not be practicable to spend too long trying to trace relatives since the body must be used within a short time after the death would not be decisive. The practicability of the inquiry must relate to the steps taken to trace the relatives not to the practicability of using the body, since the basis of the provision is to allow the relative to object if he so wishes. Where a close relative is available and does not object then the medical authorities are on slightly safer ground in proceeding in spite of the possibility that other relatives who were within the range of immediate contact and who were not consulted might object and claim that the use of the body was unlawful. It is clear, however, that a hospital will rarely be in a position to guarantee that it has made all reasonable inquiries if the body is used within a few hours of death.

Do you accept Dworkin's interpretation of the word 'practicable'? Do you agree with the conclusions he arrives at?

'The person lawfully in possession has no reason to believe'. These words may call for a somewhat different interpretation in subsection (2) than in subsection (1). Here, subsection (2), there can be no doubt that the person lawfully in possession is under a duty to enquire so as to enable him to conclude that there is no reason to believe that an objection has not been made. Subsection (1) makes no specific reference to an 'enquiry' such that it is less clear there that having 'a reason to believe' involves the obligation to seek out information. It is our view that, under s 1(1), the person lawfully in possession of a body can act provided he does not have actual (or possibly, constructive) knowledge that a request has been withdrawn from the information already available to him.

'That the deceased has (not) expressed an objection'. The short point here is that the statute is silent as to the form in which the objection must be expressed. It could be argued that a written objection is required for the sake of certainty. However, as we have seen, wherever writing was thought necessary by Parliament it has been stated, e g written request in s 1(1).

'That the surviving spouse or any surviving relative (has not objected)
PDG Skegg, 'Human Tissue Act 1961' (1976) 16 Med Sci Law (*op cit*), writes:

> . . . The Act does not provide any definition of 'relative', but the separate reference to 'any surviving spouse' lends support to the view that in this context 'relative' does not include persons to whom the deceased was related only by marriage. The courts have given a restrictive interpretation to 'relative' or 'relation' when used by a testator in his will (see e g *Anon* (1716) 1 P Wms 327; *Eagles v Le Breton* (1873) 42 LJ Ch 362 at 363; *Re Bridgen, Chaytor v Edwin* [1938] Ch 205 at 208–210). However, this is because 'else it would be uncertain; for the relation may be infinite' (*Anon, supra*), and it would be unwise to assume that 'relative' would be interpreted in a limited sense in this context. The original Memorandum on the Act advised hospital authorities of the Minister's opinion that the word should be interpreted in its widest sense, to include those who claim quite a distant relationship with the deceased (HM (61)98, para 8). The recent Guidance Circular was more equivocal. It simply advised that there are 'some circumstances' in which 'relative' should be interpreted 'in the widest sense, e g to include those who although claiming only a distant relationship are nevertheless closely connected with the deceased' (HSC (IS) 156, para 11). In fact, there is no warrant for interpreting the word differently according to the circumstances. The Circular appears to confuse the issue of who is a relative with the issue of whether it is reasonable and practicable to enquire of a particular relative.

The precise words of the Health Service Circular to which Skegg referred are: 'In most instances it will be sufficient to discuss the matter with any one relative who had been in close contact with the deceased, asking him his own views, the views of the deceased and also if he has any reason to believe that any other relative would be likely to object.' (Set out in the DHSS Working Party Report (1983) 'Cadaveric Organs for Transplantation. Code of Practice'.)

'Objects'. PDG Skegg, *op cit*, analyses this requirement.

It has been said that, 'You cannot consent to a thing unless you have knowledge of it' (*Re Caughey, ex p Ford* (1876) 1 ChD 521 at 528 per Jessel MR). Similarly, it could be said that a person cannot object to something being done unless he is aware of the proposal to do it (cf. *R v Feist, supra*). But it may also be argued that a person can have a sufficiently clear and consistent attitude to certain conduct for it to be said that he 'objects' to it, even though he is ignorant of a particular proposal to act. Even on this broader interpretation of 'objects', there would still be many people who could not be said to object, even though on being informed of a particular proposal they might well object. The problem in practice is that the person lawfully in possession of the body could not know into which category of actual or potential objector a spouse or relative came. At present, it would be wise to act as if s 1(2)(b) read 'objects *or* would object', rather than simply 'objects'.

Do you agree that the section contemplates *potential* objectors, particularly in the light of Skegg's more narrow reading of the words of the statute in other contexts?

(ii) Failure to comply with the Human Tissue Act 1961

All that has gone before on our analysis of the Human Tissue Act 1961 rests in part, at least, on the assumption that someone aggrieved at a failure properly to comply with the terms of the Act can in law do something about it. Curiously, this is at the same time the most important question and yet the most neglected. It is commonly assumed that if the Act is not complied with 'something can be done', but we must examine this premise closely.

1. Criminal law

The common law. PDG Skegg writes in 'Liability for the Unauthorized Removal of Cadaveric Transplant Material', (1974) 14 Med Sci Law 53, 55–56:

> It has long been established that it is a common law crime to prevent the disposal of a corpse by detaining it for a claim upon a debt (*R v Scott* (1842) 2 QB 248 n) or by selling it when retained and employed to bury it (*R v Cundick* (1822) Dow & Ry NP 13). As it seems that there is a more general offence of preventing the lawful disposal of the body (see *R v Young* (1784) 4 Wentworth's System of Pleading 219, which appears to be the case referred to in *R v Lynn*; *R v Hunter* [1973] 3 WLR 374) the question arises whether, by removing transplant material, a doctor could be said to prevent the disposal of the body. If the removal involved the retention of the whole body, despite the request of the person entitled to possession that the body be delivered up to him, then the doctor would almost certainly incur liability. However, so long as that which was available for disposal was recognizable as the body of the deceased it is doubtful whether the unauthorized retention of internal parts of the body could be said to prevent the disposal of the body. Doctors often retain parts of bodies after post-mortem examinations—indeed, where sufficient material is retained after an official post-mortem examination, coroners sometimes permit the disposal of the corpse before inquiries into the death are completed. It does not appear to have been suggested that by retaining parts of a body a doctor prevents the disposal of the corpse. The unauthorized removal and retention of transplant material would, therefore, be unlikely to amount to a common law crime of preventing disposal of the body, much less to the narrower statutory crime of wilfully obstructing a burial (Burial Laws Amendment Act 1880, s 7).
>
> There are *dicta* to the effect that the common law will not allow any indecent interference with the bodies of the dead (eg, *Foster v Dodd* (1866) LR 1 QB 475 at 485). The cases along these lines have all concerned interferences with bodies after burial, but the courts might well hold that certain interferences with dead bodies at any earlier stage also constitute a common law crime. Touchings of a sexual nature and pointless mutilation might be held to amount to such a crime. For the present purpose, the important question is whether unauthorized interferences with an

unburied corpse for medical purposes would amount to a common law crime. Although the means by which bodies used to be acquired for the practice of anatomy were sometimes unlawful, there is reason to believe that the practice of anatomy was itself perfectly lawful at common law (Anatomy Act 1832, Preamble; *R v Price* (1884) 12 QBD 251 at 252, 253; *R v Feist* (1858) Dears & B, 590 at 594–5, *in arguendo*). This being so, the very much more limited interference with a body involved in the removal of organs or tissues for transplantation, should not amount to any common law crime of indecent or improper interference with a corpse.

Do you not think that the last suggestion of Professor Skegg can more properly be dealt with by noticing that the transplant doctor will lack the necessary intention to act indecently for the offence?

Under the Act. The Act itself does not provide for any sanction for failure to comply with its requirements. However, the suggestion has been put that the ancient crime of disobedience of a statute may be relevant, which is a common law crime.

R v Lennox-Wright
[1973] Criminal LR 529 (Central Criminal Court)

HH Judge Lawson, QC: The defendant, who had taken and failed two medical examinations abroad, gained admission to the ophthalmic department of an English hospital by means of false representations, and a forged document which purported to show that he had qualified as an MD of Louvain University in Belgium.

In the course of his work at the hospital, he removed the eyes from a dead body for their further use in a different hospital. He was charged *inter alia*, with (after amendment): 'Doing an act in disobedience of a statute by removing parts of a dead body, contrary to section 1(4) of the Human Tissue Act 1961'.

The Human Tissue Act 1961, makes provision for the use of parts of bodies of deceased persons for therapeutic purposes and purposes of medical education and research and with respect to the circumstances in which the removal of parts of a body may be carried out. Section 1(4) of the Act provides that: 'No such removal shall be effected except by a fully registered medical practitioner, who must have satisfied himself by personal examination of the body that life is extinct'.

On a motion to quash the count it was contended by the defence that the Act was merely regulatory and created no offence; and that the Act provided no punishment for contravening section 1(4).

Held, (1) The law was well settled that if a statute prohibits a matter of public grievance to the liberties and securities of the subject or commands a matter of public convenience (such as repairing of highways or the like) all acts or omissions contrary to the prohibitions or command of the statute are misdemeanours at common law punishable by indictment unless such method manifestly appears to be excluded by statute. (2 Hawkins, c 25, s 4; *R v Hall* [1891] 1 QB 747; *R v Wright*, (1841) 1 Burr 543.) See paragraph 6 of *Archbold*.

(2) It followed that the punishment was governed by the common law and therefore an unlimited term of imprisonment or an unlimited fine could apply.

Commentary. According to Stephen, *Digest of the Criminal Law*, Art 152: 'Every one commits a misdemeanour who wilfully disobeys any statute of the realm by doing any act which it forbids, or by omitting to do any act which it requires to be done, and which concerns the public or any part of the public, unless it appears from the statute that it was the intention of the Legislature to provide some other penalty for such disobedience'.

It is usual at the present day for Parliament, when it intends to create a criminal offence, expressly so to provide and to lay down a maximum punishment for the offence. So common is this practice that it might be thought that, when Parliament does not provide in express terms for a criminal sanction at the present day, none is intended. This is particularly so since the effect of applying the principle stated above is that the offence is a misdemeanour triable on indictment and punishable with fine and imprisonment at the discretion of the court.

Section 1(8) of the Human Tissue Act provides:

(8) Nothing in this section shall be construed as rendering unlawful any dealing with, or with any part of, the body of a deceased person which is lawful apart from this Act.

Is the effect of s 1(8) that even if *R v Lennox-Wright* is correct, it has no application to the Human Tissue Act? Now the matter seems beyond dispute since the case of *R v Horseferry Road Justices, ex p Independent Broadcasting Authority* [1987] QB 54, [1986] 2 All ER 666 shows that the ancient crime does not have much life, if any, left in it and certainly does not apply in the case of the Human Tissue Act.

R v Horseferry Road Justices, ex p Independent Broadcasting Authority [1987] QB 54, [1986] 2 All ER 666 (Divisional Court, QBD)

Lloyd LJ: In 1976 the Law Commission in their Report on Conspiracy and Criminal Law Reform (HC Paper (1975–76) no 176) p 140 para 6.1 described the 'doctrine' of contempt of statute as obsolete, but not dead. They recommended that the doctrine be abolished (p 142, para 6.5):

In essence [they said] this is a matter of statutory construction; and the modern approach would, we think, be to ask whether, in the absence of an express provision making particular conduct an offence, there was any intent by Parliament to penalise that conduct. The answer today, we suggest, would always be in the negative . . .

In *Maxwell on the Interpretation of Statutes* (12th edn, 1969) pp 334–335 it is said that the procedure by way of indictment for breach of a statutory duty is never used today.

How then does the matter stand? The one thing which to my mind emerges clearly from all the authorities to which I have referred and in particular from the qualification in *Hawkins*, 'unless such method of proceeding do manifestly appear to be excluded', is that it is a question of construction in each case whether a breach of statutory duty for which Parliament has provided no remedy creates an offence or not. Among the factors which will have to be considered are: (i) whether the duty is mandatory or prohibitory; (ii) whether the statute is ancient or modern; for in ancient statutes it was far more common than it is today for no offence to be defined, but to leave enforcement, for example, to a common informer; and (iii) whether there are any other means of enforcing the duty. In the case of mandatory duty imposed by a modern statute, enforceable by way of judicial review, the inference that Parliament did *not* intend to create an offence in the absence of an express provision to that effect is, nowadays, almost irresistible.

Counsel for the IBA urged us to hold that *R v Price* (1840) 11 Ad & El 727, 113 ER 590, *Rathbone v Bundock* [1962] 2 All ER 257, [1962] 2 QB 260 and *R v Lennox-Wright* [1973] Crim LR 529 were wrongly decided, if they cannot be distinguished. He argued that the rule as stated in *Hawkins* has ceased to exist: cessante ratione legis, cessat lex ipsa. I do not find it necessary to go that far; for, as I have said, the 'rule' or 'doctrine' never was more than a rule of construction. It is not a substantive rule of law. The only difference between today and 1716, when *Hawkins* was first published, is that it is easier to infer in the case of a modern statute that Parliament does not intend to create an offence unless it says so. There is no longer any presumption, if indeed there ever were, that a breach of duty imposed by statute is indictable. Nowadays the presumption, if any, is the other way; although I would prefer to say that it requires clear language, or a very clear inference, to create a crime.

2. *Tort liability*

Professor Skegg examines this again in his article 'Liability for the Unauthorized Removal of Cadaveric Transplant Material' (1974) 14 Med Sci Law 53.

There do not appear to be any reported English cases in which a plaintiff has recovered damages for an unauthorized interference with a corpse. Nor are there any established torts which are obviously applicable to such conduct.

The English courts have not recognized any property interest in a corpse (*Dr Handasyde's* case (C 18), 1 Hawk. PC 148, n 8, 2 East PC 652; *R v Sharpe* (1857) Dears & B 160 at 163; *Williams v Williams* (1882) 20 ChD 659 at 662–3, 665; *R v Price* (1884) 12 QBD 247 at 252); so the unauthorized removal of cadaveric transplant material would not give rise to an action in trespass to goods, conversion, or detinue (see, eg, *Dr Handasyde's* case, also *Hamps v Darby* [1948] 2 KB 311 at 319, 320, 322, 328). The tort of negligence would very rarely be applicable, for the doctor would not normally owe a duty of care to the person aggrieved by the unauthorized removal (see the comments on *Owens v Liverpool Corpn* [1939] 1 KB 394 in *Bourhill v Young* [1943] AC 92 at 100, 105, 110, 116). In the rare cases where the doctor did owe such a duty, knowledge of the unauthorized removal would be unlikely to cause nervous shock, or to harm health. The innominate tort of intentional acts calculated to cause bodily injury (see *Wilkinson v Downton* [1897] 2 QB 57; *Janvier v Sweeney* [1919] 2 KB 316) would rarely, if ever, apply.

Although the courts have not recognized any property interest in the corpse of a human being, they have recognised that the person under a duty to dispose of the body has a right to possession for that purpose (eg, *R v Fox* (1841) 2 QB 246). On the principle *ubi jus ibi remedium*, an intentional and unauthorized interference with this right should render the interferer liable, at the suit of the person entitled to possession. Recovery was permitted in one Canadian case (*Edmonds v Armstrong Funeral Home Ltd* [1931] 1 DLR 676), where a doctor had made an unauthorized post-mortem examination of the corpse. The unauthorized removal of transplant material would probably also be actionable. There would not be any need to prove actual damage, although the measure of damages would obviously be greater if the plaintiff could show that he suffered in consequence of the interference. Of course, in many cases the unauthorized interference would not come to the notice of the potential plaintiff and, even if it did, it might be difficult for him to establish that he was the person entitled to possession of the corpse. If the potential plaintiff has consented to the removal of the transplant material, and the doctor had complied with any conditions he expressly or impliedly laid down, it would not be open to him to recover damages on the ground of interference with his right to possession. The fact that the doctor did not comply with the provisions of the Human Tissue Act 1961 would be irrelevant.

Subsequently, Skegg considered whether an action in negligence for nervous shock would lie. He concluded (in 'Liability for the Unauthorized Removal of Cadaveric Transplant Material: Some Further Comments' (1977) 17 Med Sci Law 123, p 124) that:

> There is, at present sic (1977) however, an important restriction on recovery for nervous shock . . . This is the principle in *Hambrook v Stokes Bros* ([1925] 1 KB 141 at 152, 159, 165), which could be held to preclude the recovery of damages for nervous shock where the potential plaintiff learnt of the unauthorized removal from others after the event, rather than witnessed the removal or its consequences for himself.

Do you think this limitation has survived *McLoughlin v O'Brian* [1983] 1 AC 410, [1982] 2 All ER 298, HL (see Norrie (1985) 34 ICLQ 442, 463)?

Reform of the law

(a)   INTRODUCTION

The following is taken from the Report of the Working Party on the 'Supply of Donor Organs for Transplantation' (1987), chaired by Sir Raymond Hoffenberg (footnotes omitted):

Transplantation of the kidneys and other organs has been one of the great advances of the last quarter of a century. There is much public interest and support. Most people are prepared to give organs in appropriate circumstances, yet there is a shortfall in organ supply and a growing waiting list for transplants. For kidneys this has risen from 2,500 to 3,500 in the last five years. The waiting lists for heart transplants, liver transplants and corneal grafts have doubled in the last two years. We, a working party from the Conference of Medical Royal Colleges and their Faculties in the UK, have been asked by the Department of Health and Social Security to find out why there is a shortfall and to make recommendations to remedy this.

. . .

It has been estimated that about 4,000 brain stem deaths occur each year in the United Kingdom. In 1986, 800 donors provided 1,600 kidneys and in the same year there were 200 heart, 120 liver and about 1,500 corneal donations. In the first quarter of 1987 kidney donation fell by 19.1% in comparison with the same period in 1986. Heart donations increased by 37% and liver donations by 10% showing that there were more multiple donations from a smaller number of donors.

There are insufficient kidneys to meet the needs of those waiting for renal transplantation and for those who in succeeding years will develop renal failure. About 2,500 people start dialysis each year and this could rise to around 4,000. The projected need for kidneys, therefore, is at least 2,500 and might be as high as 4,000 each year. This could be achieved if a higher proportion of those with brain stem death were to become donors. The cost savings to the health service of a kidney transplant have recently been estimated at £30,000, this being the amount that would otherwise be spent on chronic dialysis.

. . .

Reasons for the shortfall

1)   Lack of medical experience and knowledge

Most doctors will have little experience of brain stem death and of requesting organ donation. Knowledge of the criteria for brain stem death, of the arrangements for transplantation and of the benefit of transplantation is not universal. Skill and sensitivity in the approach to bereaved relatives is variable. As a result there may be a reluctance to diagnose brain stem death and a failure to ask for organ donation. Some hospitals seldom provide organs for transplantation, yet when a sympathetic and experienced person talks with the relatives, permission is likely to be granted. Some hospitals have obtained 90% agreement to donation.

2)   Doubts about the success of the transplant programme

This should no longer be entertained since the benefits of transplantation to the majority of recipients are proven. The three-year survival rate of kidney transplants is now commonly in excess of 75%, for hearts about 75% at one year and for livers 70% at one year. The actuarial patient survival statistics for kidney recipients show a better prognosis than is experienced by patients with gastrointestinal cancer, stage II carcinoma of the breast and carcinoma of the prostate, for example. Patients with kidney transplants have been recorded to survive in good health for 25 years, liver transplants for 16 years, heart transplants for 15 years and pancreas transplants for 8 years. Lung transplants have survived up to 3 years. With improvements in tissue matching and immunosuppression in more recent years, more patients with organ transplants can be expected to survive with their transplant for long periods of time, if not for the term of their natural life. For the failing heart, liver and lung, transplantation may be the only option. For the failing kidney, transplantation provides a better quality of life at lower cost than dialysis. The public is well aware of the benefits of transplantation in adults and in children.

3)   Doubts about the criteria for brain stem death

The BBC Panorama programme of 1980 which cast doubt on the criteria was followed by a fall in the number of organ donations, but this has since risen and an increase of about a third followed the BBC 'That's Life' programme in 1985. In the three months since the publication of articles on brain stem death in the Sunday

Times at the end of 1986, there has been a 19.1% fall in the number of kidney donations.

We have taken evidence from a physician and from an anaesthetist who are opposed to the removal of organs from heart-beating donors. They accept that the fulfilment of the criteria for brain stem death does permit withdrawal of ventilation but they believe that death only occurs when circulation and respiration cease. Further refinement of tests of brain stem function would not satisfy them that death had occurred before the heart stops beating. The difference between our views and theirs is in the concept of when death occurs.

We are convinced that the criteria for brain stem death are adequate and believe that once the brain stem is dead, sentient existence is no longer possible and that the person is dead. We do not think that electro-encephalography, four-vessel arteriography, doppler or isotope studies of cerebral blood flow would give further useful information.

We accept that a small minority of doctors and some members of the public have reservations about the concept of brain stem death despite full explanation, and that patients and their relatives must always be free to decline consent to organ donation.

The Society of British Neurological Surgeons at its meeting in April 1987 unanimously supported the view that the clinical criteria for the diagnosis of brain stem death were entirely satisfactory. There is overwhelming informed professional opinion that ventilation after death does no more than allow the heart to beat, so maintaining circulation. This makes possible the donation in good condition of kidneys, heart, lung, liver and pancreas.

4)   Demand for intensive care beds
It is not possible to transfer to intensive care units all those who might become brain stem dead. Transfer and treatment should be in the interest of the patient. A possible exception is when relatives have particularly requested organ donation. If there is an insufficient number of staffed intensive care beds for all those who require intensive care, organ donation will be reduced. Many clinicians in charge of intensive care units agree that given more beds, equipment and staff, more potential donors could be managed.

5)   Constraints of time
It may take several hours to discuss matters with bereaved relatives and to make the arrangements for organ donation with a transplant team.

6)   Limited theatre time
Because of pressure on operating theatres for other emergencies, there may be reluctance to embark upon organ removal, especially more lengthy multiple organ retrieval, which may occupy a theatre for several hours. The disruption to the donor hospitals' routine has been a significant disincentive to further referral of donors in some hospitals.

7)   Cost
There is no rational basis for financial arguments against procurement. As clinical budgeting takes hold, there will be greater awareness both of the costs of removing organs and the cost savings to the health service of a successful transplant.

8)   Medico-legal constraints
We have found general praise for the attitude and helpfulness of coroners. Seldom has the need for a coroner's post mortem examination prevented the donation of organs.

Caplan reviewed the situation in the US and Europe in a seminal article in 1984 'Organ Procurement: It's Not in the Cards' (1984) 14 Hastings Center Report 9 (number 5) (footnotes omitted).

Not so long ago the distinguished Senator from Vermont, George Aiken, proposed a novel solution to the problem of ending the Vietnam War. He wryly observed that the fastest way to stop that conflict was simply to declare ourselves the winners and go home.

Defenders of the philosophy of voluntarism in the procurement of cadaver organs for transplantation seem to have taken to heart Aiken's ironic proposal for resolving an apparently intractable problem. Alfred and Blair Sadler declare that they are unable to see 'any significant developments in transplantation [that] would justify discarding the principles of informed consent and encouraged voluntarism embodied in the Uniform Anatomical Gift Act'. They are not looking carefully enough. The facts about both the supply of and the demand for cadaver organs do not support their decision to solve the crisis in organ procurement by declaring the system a success. Our society's decision in the late 1960s to rely on a public policy of voluntarism as the primary means for assuring an adequate supply of organs for transplantation is no longer tenable. Perhaps such a system was appropriate when organ transplantation was in its infancy, but this is no longer the case.

The Center for Disease Control estimates that about 20,000 persons die each year under circumstances that would make them suitable for cadaver organ donation. This number should provide a maximum possible pool of 40,000 kidneys for transplant. Yet in 1982 only 3,691 cadaver kidney transplants were performed. The best estimates are that less than 15 percent of potential donors are utilised under the present policy.

Recent studies estimate that between 6,000 and 10,000 persons on hemodialysis are waiting for kidney transplants. Some believe the number of possible recipients in the United States would be as high as 22,500 per year if transplant surgeons were not forced by the severe inadequacy of the present supply of cadaver kidneys to be so conservative in formulating criteria for eligibility for renal transplantation. Similar statistics exist concerning the shortfall of tissues for corneal transplants, hearts, lungs and, as the media remind us every day, livers. And unless something is done to modify the present reliance on a voluntary system, the shortage in cadaver organs will continue to worsen. Rapid progress in the development of surgical techniques, tissue matching, and immunosuppressive drugs will lead to incessant demands for more cadaver organs in the years ahead.

Transplantation may be, as the Sadlers observe, a 'halfway' solution to the problem of organ failure. But for those suffering from renal failure, kidney transplants afford a better quality of life than dialysis, and they are far cheaper. Medicare's End-Stage Renal Disease Program has passed the $2 billion mark in reimbursing the costs of more than 70,000 dialysis patients. How can anyone possibly conclude that the present approach to procurement is adequate, acceptable, or working well?

Nor is it at all evident that donor cards have played a significant role in helping to produce even the small degree of procurement success that has been attained in the United States. Less than 15 percent of the population carry donor cards. Transplant coordinators estimate that less than 3 percent of donors have cards in their possession at the time of death. Where data are available on the number of drivers designated as donors in states where organ donation boxes are provided on licenses the compliance rate is not impressive.

Three possible alternatives

What then are the possible policy alternatives to the present system of voluntarism and donor cards? And more important, which of these alternatives is most consistent with the values of individual choice, altruism, and freedom?

One possible public policy alternative is to allow the creation of a market in cadaver organs. There are two variants of this approach. The 'strong market approach' would allow individuals or, after death, their next of kin to auction organs for sale to the highest bidder. The 'weak market approach', on the other hand, would discourage direct compensation of donors by recipients but would allow for the creation of various tax incentives or in-kind reimbursements (those who donate could guarantee their loved ones or friends priority for future transplants) to encourage donation.

A second approach—that of 'presumed consent'—would grant medical personnel the authority to remove organs from cadavers for transplantation whenever usable organs were available at the time of death. Again, there are two variants. In 'strong presumed consent' the state would grant physicians complete authority to remove usable tissues regardless of the wishes of the deceased or family members. In 'weak presumed consent' the law would presume that organ procurement can be undertaken in the absence of some form of objection from the deceased or family members. Weak consent places the burden of opting out of organ donation on those who have objections to this procedure rather than, as is the case under the present system of voluntarism, upon those who wish to opt for organ donation.

A third approach, which has not been widely discussed in the current debate about organ procurement policies, is what I have termed 'required request'. In the strong version, every citizen would be asked to indicate his or her willingness to participate in organ donation, perhaps by means of a mandatory check-off on applications for a driver's license, a social security card, or on tax returns.

In the weak version, current legislation pertaining to the definition of death might be modified to state that at the time death is declared a person who has no connection to the process of determining death would be required to ask family members about the possibility of organ donation.

What the public thinks

There has been a good deal of public debate about the moral acceptability of the strong market approach to procuring cadaver organs. Near unanimity of public opinion has emerged about the unacceptability of an open market in cadaver organs. At least one state, Virginia, banned the sale of organs for transplantation. Other states are considering such bans, as is the United States Congress [this, as we have seen, subsequently occurred in the National Organ Transplant Act 1984]. Transplant surgeons have repeatedly stated their adamant opposition to market solutions. The moral revulsion that has characterised discussions in the popular press and in professional journals about the spectacle of the desperately ill furiously bidding against one another for a kidney or a liver has, at least for the present, rendered both versions of this policy academic.

Similarly, little public enthusiasm has emerged for a system of strong presumed consent. In a recent survey the Battelle National Heart Transplantation Study found that less than 8 percent of those interviewed felt that 'doctors should have the power to remove organs from people who died recently but have not signed an organ donor card without consulting the next-of-kin'.

Public opinion aside, the Sadlers argue that any form of presumed consent would have a corrosive effect on the trust that exists between the medical community and the public. They also note that presumed consent would not necessarily lead to an increase in the supply of cadaver organs for transplant. But those European nations that have adopted versions of presumed consent lack evidence to determine whether these concerns are justified.

The European experience

Various European nations, including Austria, Denmark, Poland, Switzerland, and France, have legislation mandating a policy of strong presumed consent. Other nations such as Finland, Greece, Italy, Norway, Spain, and Sweden have adopted versions of weak presumed consent. However, as the Sadlers correctly observe, the available empirical data does not show that these countries have dramatically increased their supply of cadaver organs.

The Swedes, for example, transplant nearly as many patients suffering from kidney failure as they maintain on hemodialysis. This compares quite favorably with the one-to-nine ratio that prevails in the United States. However, statistics on the rates of organ procurement in Sweden and other European countries are not readily available. Indeed, all these countries still have waiting lists for those needing kidney transplants.

In June 1984 I visited France to discuss organ procurement with a number of transplant surgeons and nurses. Organ transplantation in France has been confined almost exclusively to corneas and kidneys. French physicians and government officials estimated that approximately 800 kidney transplants were performed in 1982. This suggests a rate that is only slightly higher than the rate of kidney transplantation in the United States. There are indeed waiting lists for those on hemodialysis who hope for a transplant.

Why should this be so, given that France has a policy of strong presumed consent? French physicians offer two explanations. First, though the law has resulted in an increase in the number of cadaver organs available for transplant, this increase is not reflected in the overall rates because the additional organs have been utilised to decrease the numbers of live donors. Whereas live donors have provided about a third of the kidneys available for transplant in France in the late 1970s, today live donors make up less than 10 percent of the donor pool. (Live donors constitute nearly a third of the donor pool in the United States, Britain, and other nations with public policies of voluntarism based upon donor cards.)

Second, French physicians note that, despite a public policy allowing strong presumed consent, doctors are not willing to remove organs from cadavers without the consent of family members. Strong presumed consent exists only on paper in France. In practice French physicians find it psychologically intolerable to remove tissues from a body without obtaining the permission of next-of-kin.

In the view of both physicians and nurses, however, the French public strongly supports organ transplantation. The physicians I spoke with reported consent rates of between 90 and 95 percent when permission was sought to remove solid organs. In practice French physicians believe strongly in allowing family members to retain the right to object to organ removal. But few family members actually do object, indicating that a public policy of weak presumed consent is compatible with the moral values of both health professionals and the public in France.

Even if French physicians are only willing to participate in a system whose governing philosophy is one of weak presumed consent, why, given the low rate of refusal, are a larger number of organs not available for transplant? The answer is illuminating for its policy implications for the United States.

France, unlike the United States, does not have a cadre of highly trained personnel to handle the process of organ procurement. Health professionals, usually nurses, must bear the burdens of inquiring about objections to organ removal, locating a suitable recipient, and arranging the removal of organs. French hospital administrators, physicians, and nurses all reported that this process was both time-consuming and costly. Given the growing concern in France over the rising costs of health care there is a reluctance to devote scarce medical resources to organ procurement. French transplant surgeons also noted that, at present, there were severe limits both in terms of personnel and hospital space on the number of transplants of all types that can now be performed. One surgeon noted that 'if we had your resources and facilities for transplantation we would be much more aggressive in pursuing organ donors'. Limits on the availability of transplant services in France seem to dampen the ardor with which organ procurement is undertaken.

Moreover, the French, like their American counterparts, find it psychologically difficult to approach grieving family members about the prospect of organ procurement even if only to ascertain whether the family objects to what is usually described in the consent process as a routine, customary, and legally sanctioned practice. Busy emergency room personnel are loath to take the time necessary to fully discuss the subject of transplantation with distraught family members. In sum, despite the existence on paper of a strong version of presumed consent, health care professionals in France are only willing to operate within the boundaries of weak presumed consent. And while this approach has helped to increase the supply of available cadaver kidneys to the point where few live donations are utilised, economic, organisational, and psychological factors limit the willingness of French medical personnel to ask about objections to removing kidneys and other solid organs for transplantation.

The French experience with strong presumed consent legislation holds important lessons for those, such as myself, who believe that our system of organ procurement must be changed. The French physicians' unwillingness to act upon the authority granted them by the state to remove organs regardless of the wishes of family members parallels the unwillingness of American physicians to remove organs solely on the basis of the legal authority granted by donor cards. As organ procurement specialists know all too well, donor cards are almost never viewed by hospital administrators and physicians as adequate authorisation for allowing organ retrieval. The permission of family members is always sought prior to organ removal whether or not a donor card or other legal document can be found.

On the other hand, the practical experience obtained by the French with a version of weak presumed consent does not support the sorts of concerns raised by the Sadlers about presumed consent. French physicians are impressed with the fact that objections have been raised by less than 10 percent of the families who have been given the opportunity to refuse consent. The French press has not reported any dissatisfaction on the part of the public with presumed consent. And French physicians were uniformly relieved to be able to decrease their earlier dependence on live donors. A policy of weak presumed consent appears to have produced a significant amount of social good while allowing for family choice and autonomy in an atmosphere of mutual respect.

The organisational, financial, and psychological factors at work in the French system of organ procurement are also present in the United States. Unlike the French, we have a large number of highly trained and proficient specialists available in the field of organ procurement, but constant pressures to reduce costs in combination with an increasingly litigious atmosphere in medicine make it unlikely that the modest reforms of the present voluntary system proposed by the Sadlers and others will lead to significant improvement in the supply of cadaver organs.

The existing legal arrangements for obtaining organs from cadavers has come to be known as a system of 'opting in', ie the donor or relative has to opt to donate. To the extent that the law may be responsible for the under-supply of organs (as mentioned above), apart from a programme of public education which seems to have produced little over the last decade or so two proposals for reform have been advanced in England – a system of 'opting out' and the principle of 'required request'.

(b) 'OPTING OUT'

Consider, first, the article by Jesse Dukeminier 'Supplying Organs for Transplantation', (1970) 68 Michigan Law Review 811 at pp 837–842.

Routine salvaging of cadaver organs unless there is objection
A significant increase in the supply of organs for transplantation would result if usable organs were removed from cadavers routinely unless, before the time of removal, an objection had been entered, either by the decedent during his life or by his next of kin after the decedent's death. This approach is not as extreme as the proposal to salvage useful organs without regard to objection, since under this approach persons who do not wish to make their organs available may object and opt out.[95] Nor is this approach as radical a departure from traditional humanist values as the Uniform Anatomical Gift Act, for, by making the basic presumption one which favors life, and by thus putting the burden of objecting upon persons who would deny life to another, the policy of saving human life is given first priority and the wishes of persons to preserve a corpse inviolate are also accommodated. This method would produce far more organs for transplantation than are produced by statutes permitting organ donation by the decedent.

Some time ago Dr David Sanders and the author proposed legislation to make removal of usable cadaver organs routine unless the decedent or his next of kin instructed otherwise.[96] In light of the 1967 Gallup poll results,[97] it appears that a carefully drawn statute embodying such an approach would be acceptable to a majority of people in this country. Indeed, in a recent questionnaire submitted to physicians, Dr Robert Williams found that the Dukeminier-Sanders proposal was favored by seventy-one percent of those responding.[98] Similar figures from Britain indicate that two-thirds of the British people favor routine removal of cadaver kidneys.[99] A leading kidney transplant surgeon from England, Professor Roy Calne, writes that in his experience most relatives would prefer not to be asked for the kidneys but would rather that the kidneys be removed routinely.[100]

Perhaps the simplest way to provide for routine salvaging of cadaver organs would be to enact a statute permitting prompt autopsies for organ removal on all persons who die in authorised hospitals, unless objection is first entered. In many countries the public already accepts routine autopsies. In France, for example, cadaver organs may be removed without permission of the family if the person dies in a hospital approved by the Minister of Public Health.[101] In several European countries, autopsies are performed on all persons who die in hospitals unless some objection is made.[102] In Israel the Anatomy and Pathology Act, passed in 1953, permits an autopsy without consent so long as three physicians formally attest in writing that the autopsy may help the lives of other existing patients;[103] and ninety percent of all persons who die in hospitals in Israel are subjected to autopsies.[104] In the United States, where consent for an autopsy must always be secured before such an operation may be performed, the autopsy rate in those hospitals approved for internships and residencies by the Council on Medical Education varies from twenty-five per cent to one hundred per cent of the persons who die within the hospital. The average autopsy rate is approximately fifty per cent.[105]

If a broad autopsy statute is unacceptable, the best substitute is a statute dealing solely with removal of organs for transplantation. The details of such a statute need to be carefully considered. There are at least four major problems. First, what organs may be routinely removed? The legislative draftsman might conclude that only those organs with a high degree of transplantation success could be removed—at the present time, corneas and kidneys. In England a Renal Transplantation Bill was introduced in Parliament on November 27, 1968; section 2 of the bill provided:

It shall be lawful to remove from the body of a human person, duly certified as dead, any kidney or kidneys required for the direct purpose of saving the life of another sick human being, unless there is reason to believe that the deceased during his lifetime had instructed otherwise.[106]

The bill failed on second reading because, among other things, the Minister of Health objected to legislation for a single organ.[107] Since each new successful development in transplantation would require an amendment to the statute, the legislature might appropriately conclude that the more useful statute would permit the removal of all organs usable in transplantation.

A middle position might be taken between permitting only specified organs to be removed and permitting all usable organs to be removed. For example, a medical board or the state director of public health could be empowered to promulgate administrative regulations specifying the organs that could be removed routinely; the statute could provide a general guideline, such as a provision that the list be limited to organs which can be transplanted with a good chance of success when transplantation is recognised by the medical profession as appropriate therapy. Such an approach, however, would prevent routine removal of organs for experimental purposes, including experiments to save life; and such a limitation on experimentation might be felt to be too restrictive.

The second problem to be solved in drafting an organ removal statute is the determination of which persons are to be authorised to remove organs routinely. This problem is probably best solved by administrative regulations that enumerate the capabilities and qualifications that are required of the medical staff, and the supporting equipment and facilities that must be available, before organs may be removed routinely. Again, these regulations could be drawn up by an authorised medical board or a state health official. In France, for example, the Minister of Public Health approves hospitals at which autopsies may be performed without permission of the family.[108] The regulations could license hospitals, qualified surgeons, or both.

The third problem which must be faced in drafting an appropriate statute is whether any bodies should be excluded from routine removal of organs. Section 3 of the British Renal Transplantation Bill provided an exclusion for any person who, at the time of his death, was

- (a) mentally insane, or
- (b) mentally handicapped, or
- (c) below the age of 18, or
- (d) 65 years old or more than that age, or
- (e) deprived of his liberty by the conviction and judgment of a court, or
- (f) a permanent resident of a hostel, home or institution for the aged, the disabled, or the handicapped.[109]

The primary purpose of these exclusions was to ensure that only those who are free to object fall within the terms of the bill. A secondary purpose was to set at ease the minds of older persons, who might fear that doctors would hasten their demise in order to transplant their organs into a younger person.

The fourth drafting problem concerns the method of registering objections so that organs cannot be removed at death. There are various possible methods: a card could be carried by the person, a statement could be made to the hospital upon entering, a statement could be made to the physician, or a central computer registry could be established. One of the problems discussed previously in connection with organ donation statutes reappears in another form here. That problem was how to provide a means to aid the surgeon in finding out quickly and conclusively that he has a valid consent.[110] The problem under the approach being examined here is determining how the surgeon can find out quickly and conclusively that there is no objection. Fortunately, the latter is more readily soluble than the former and does not contain within it any many subsidiary problems. The presumption is that there is no objection which the surgeon knew or ought to have known from the next of kin. Hence the problem is narrowed to the detemination of what inquiry the surgeon ought to be required to make. The statute could provide that a valid objection must be entered in a specific way, such as through registration with a national computer system. For instance, section 7 of the British Renal Transplantation Bill provided for a central renal registry in the Ministry of Health in which any person might register his objection to the transplantation of his kidneys.[111] With such a provision, the only inquiry the surgeon would have to make would be to the computer, and it would be possible for surgeons to ascertain within minutes whether the donor had entered any objection. If a computer error occurs, the next of kin would have a cause of action against the organisation responsible for the computer, not against the surgeon. Alternatively, a statute might contain a provision for a compensation fund for the next of kin in cases involving a decedent who had filed an objection but whose objection had been ignored by mistake. As a practical matter, few suits would probably be brought as a result of computer malfunction, because if organ removal becomes routine, the practice will become part of the expectations of the next of kin and of the public, just as routine autopsies are part of the expectations of persons in some European countries. If a surgeon removes an organ, not knowing that a valid objection has been filed, the damages would be measured by the mental pain and suffering of the next of kin; if the public accepts routine organ removal, the damages awarded by a jury for unauthorised removal are not likely to be great. Hence there would be little incentive to sue either a computer organisation or a surgeon in case of an error.

A final question which pertains to the filing of objections is whether the next of kin, as well as the decedent, should have the power to object and thereby to prevent removal of organs. The British bill permitted only the decedent to object, but the next of kin could bring the decedent's objection to attention of the surgeons. In any event, the question is not very important, because if the next of kin objects, either on the ground that the decedent instructed otherwise or for his own personal reasons, it is unlikely that a surgeon will remove the organs. A tug of war for organs with the next of kin would be most unseemly. Nonetheless, a statute in the United States should expressly permit the next of kin to object, since such a provision would help to avoid first amendment difficulties.

Notes to extract

95. Analogies to this approach may be found in the practice of routinely giving vaccinations to school children unless there is objection, and in the requiring of certain medical procedures upon birth unless there is objection. E g, Mass Gen Laws Ann ch 111, § 110A (1967), which provides that every newborn child shall be subjected to a pheynlketonuria test unless the parents object that the test conflicts with their religious tenets and practices.

96. Sanders & Dukeminier, [*Medical Advance and Legal Lag: Hemodialysis and Kidney Transplantation* (1968) 15 UCLA L Rev 357] at 410–13; Dukeminier & Sanders, *Organ Transplantation: A Proposal for Routine Salvaging of Cadaver Organs*, 279 New England J Medicine 413 (1968).

For similar proposals, see CIBA Foundation Symposium, [Ethics in Medical Progress, Wolstenholme and O'Connor eds 1966], at 213 (remarks of Lord Kilbrandon); *id* at 191–92 (remarks of D Daube). See also Kennedy, *Alive or Dead?*, in Current Legal Problems 102, 120–22 (G Keeton & G Schwarzenburger ed 1969).

97. [footnote omitted]

98. *Our Role in the Generation, Modification and Termination of Life*, 124 Archives of Internal Medicine 215, 230, 233 (1969). The greatest approval came from Roman Catholics (88%) and the lowest from those with no religion (60%). The Dukeminier-Sanders proposal is favored by Castel, *Some Legal Aspects of Human Organ Transplantation*, 46 Can B Rev 345, 402 (1968); Randall & Randall, *The Developing Field of Human Organ Transplantation*, 5 Gonzaga L Rev 20, 31 (1969); and Richards, *Medical-Legal Problems of Organ Transplantation*, 21 Hastings LJ 77, 99 (1969).

99. 762 Parl Deb, HC (5th ser) 826 (1968).

100. Renal Transplantation 154 (1967).

101. Decree No 47-2057 of Oct 20, 1947, 1 Intl Digest of Health Legislation 95 (1948). In such a case, death must be determined by two doctors applying procedures recognised by the Minister of Public Health. Victims of crimes or of accidents occurring at work, persons who commit suicide, and Moslems are excluded from the reach of the decree. See also French Minister of Social Affairs, Circular No 62, April 24, 1968, 19 Intl Digest of Health Legislation 628 (1968).

102. Decree of Sept 13, 1960, Bulletin du Service fédéral de l'hygiène publique, Supp A, Nov 12, 1960, at 58, 12 Intl Digest of Health Legislation 565 (1961) (Switzerland); Law No 246 of June 9, 1967, Intl Digest of Health Legislation 950 (1968) (Denmark); Law No 260 of July 8, 1957, 9 Intl Digest of Health Legislation 485 (1958) (Finland). Law No 104 of March 14, 1958, 10 Intl Digest of Health Legislation 541 (1959) (Sweden). The Swiss Canton of Vaud permits the removal of cadaver tissue for transplantation when two physicians authorise it. Order of Sept 13, 1960, 12 Intl Digest of Health Legislation 565 (1961). Section 7 of Decree-Law No 45,683 of April 25, 1964, 16 Intl Digest of Health Legislation 394 (1965) (Portugal), provides that if the decedent neither prohibited nor consented to removal of his cadaver organs, and if no objection by the family is made within four hours of death, the organs may be removed for transplantation. Ministry of Health Order No 47, June 13, 1966, 18 Intl Digest of Health Legislation 370 (1967) (Czechoslovakia), provides for routine removal of cadaver organs unless the deceased declared his objection in writing during life. See also Ministry of Health Instruction No 5, March 1, 1968, 20 Intl Digest of Health Legislation 427 (1969).

103. I Jakobovitz, Jewish Medical Ethics 150 (1959).

104. *Id* at 152. The removed organs cannot be transplanted, however. They must be delivered for burial in order to comply with the rule of Judaism that all parts of the deceased must be buried. See 3 Tradition: A Journal of Orthodox Thought 75 (1960); 4 *id* 97 (1961). It might be argued that this rule is not violated by transplantation because the organ will eventually come to rest, even though it will be in a different body.

105. Council on Medical Education of the AMA & the Assn of American Medical Colleges, Directory of Approved Internships and Residencies 1967–68, Consolidated List of Hospitals 31–76 (1967).

106. Renal Transplantation Bill, introduced in the House of Commons on Nov 27, 1968, Bill 41 ; see 774 Parl Deb, HC (5th ser) 511 (1968).
107. 776 Parl Deb, HC (5th ser) 1797 (1969).
108. See note 101 *supra*.
109. Renal Transplantation Bill, introduced in the House of Commons on Nov 27, 1968, Bill 41.
110. . . . If a choice must be made between the carrying of donation cards and the carrying of objection cards, it would be far more sensible to require that objection cards be carried. Such a requirement would lessen the psychological disincentives to donations and would aid significantly in attaining the goal of an adequate supply of organs.
111. For a discussion of how the registry would work, see Parliamentary Debates, House of Commons Official Report, Standing Comm C, Renal Transplantation Bill, June 26, 1968, 34–39.
112. [footnote omitted].

Despite numerous attempts, no Bill has reached the statute book in England. The latest dismissal of the idea is contained in the Report of the Working Party on the Supply of Organs for Transplantation, chaired by Sir Raymond Hoffenberg, (*op cit*) p 6 :

We have been told that an *Opting Out* Scheme might increase donations by allowing organs to be removed after brain stem death from those who had not recorded an objection, but we do not recommend this. There would be a risk that organs might be removed when this had not been the wish of the person or their relatives. It does not in itself enlist the co-operation of doctors. We would prefer organ donation to be seen as a positive gift with the consent of relatives who in practice would always be approached.

The French law, which has developed since Dukeminier was writing in 1970, is discussed by Redmond-Cooper in 'Transplants Opting Out or In—the Implications' (1984) 134 New Law Journal 648 (footnotes omitted).

In France the contracting out system was introduced by a Law of December 22, 1976, article 2(i) of which provides that organs may be removed from a body for therapeutic or scientific ends where the deceased had not, during his lifetime, made known his objection to such a removal. The implementing *décret* of the Conseil d'Etat was passed on March 31, 1978, and prescribes the conditions under which removal of organs may be effected. Objections to removal may be general or limited to particular organs and can be expressed by any means. If a person is hospitalised immediately before death, any indication of objection, coming either from the victim himself or from statements made by his family (relating to the *deceased's* objection, not that of the relatives) and supported by necessary evidence must be entered on a special register.

In practice, however, French doctors prefer to obtain the consent of the next of kin (although in a recent decision the Conseil d'Etat held that the *décret* was correct in not providing a right of refusal for relatives), possibly since the majority of French people would seem to be unaware of the provisions of the Law of 1976. The result of this is that the number of transplants performed in France is lower than in the UK.

Any opting out system introduced in the UK would therefore need to be different in both conception and implementation from the French Law of 1976. It is clear that if relatives are asked at the time of death whether they wish to exercise a veto over the removal of organs, a great many, through grief and shock, will refuse permission. By placing the onus of objection on the individual and removing all rights from the next of kin, the problem becomes an ethical one: who has the ultimate moral right to decide on the disposal of a dead body? A possible solution might be to permit next of kin to register a binding objection at the time of death, but not to require formal consultation by surgeons. In any event, an opting out system would need to be accompanied by adequate publicity in order to avoid the situation which has arisen in France and also to protect the rights and beliefs of individuals and their families.

In the event of a sudden death of a non-hospitalised person, it is standard medical procedure to perform a post mortem before removing body organs for transplantation. If an opting out system is introduced this practice should become mandatory. In France the Law of 1976 makes no provision for a post mortem examination, although the Law of 1949 relating to corneal grafts refers specifically to the necessity for such an examination. Without a post mortem there is a very real possibility that a latent disease in the deceased may be passed on to the recipient of an organ.

In October 1979 a woman died suddenly in France and her eyes were immediately used to provide a corneal transplant. The operation was successful and the recipient was allowed to return home, but he died soon after from rabies. At a subsequent enquiry the dead woman's family revealed that she had been in Egypt immediately before her death where she had been bitten by a dog. As a result of this incident the director of the eye bank involved was charged with manslaughter. The case is still pending before the French courts.

Difficulties of opting out

The difficulties raised by a system of opting out may therefore be summarised as follows: in order to avoid the risk of large numbers of people opting out through fear or misunderstanding, great care must be exercised in the installation of the system; there should be a statutory definition of what constitutes death and this should be in line with the popular notion of death; adequate publicity is essential in order to ensure that anyone who wishes to opt out may do so on the basis of an informed decision; a post mortem examination should be a statutory requirement.

However, it may not be necessary to take the radical step of introducing an opting out system. A better solution might consist in maintaining a revised form of opting in. This could be implemented, not through the use of cards as at present, but through a centralised computer. Consent could be given at the level of the local GP who would be available to advise potential donors and to ask all patients coming to the surgery whether they would be willing to donate their organs. The names of all those in agreement could then be placed by the GP on a national register, together with details of relevant illnesses and drug treatment, and possibly, consent of next of kin. The information contained in this register would be available only in the event of the death of the individual and the possibility of his body being used for a transplant.

The solution to the shortage of body organs available for transplant does not therefore necessarily reside in the introduction of a system of opting out: a similar result could be achieved through a revised form of opting in.

Recently, Belgium enacted legislation adopting an 'opting out' system, the Law of 13 June 1986 on the removal and transplantation of organs (*Moniteur belge*, 14 February 1987, No 32, pp 2129–2132).

CHAPTER III
Removal after death

10. (1) Organs and tissues for transplantation, and for the preparation of therapeutic substances in accordance with the conditions laid down in Section 2, may be removed from the body of any person recorded in the Register of the Population or any person recorded for more than six months in the Aliens Register, unless it is established that an objection to such a removal has been expressed.

It shall be a requirement, in the case of persons other than those mentioned above, that they have explicitly expressed their consent to the removal.

(2) Only a person who has attained 18 years of age and is capable of making known his wishes may express the objection provided for in subsection 1.

If a person has not attained 18 years of age but is capable of making known his wishes, the objection may be expressed either by him or, during his lifetime, by his close relatives living with him.

If a person has not attained 18 years of age and is incapable of making known his wishes, the objection may be expressed during his lifetime by his close relatives living with him.

If a person is incapable of making known his wishes by reason of his mental condition, the objection may be expressed during his lifetime by any legal representative or guardian for the time being he may have, failing which, by his closest relative.

(3) The Crown shall make provision for a method of expressing an objection to the removal for the donor or the persons referred to in subsection 2.

For this purpose, the Crown shall be empowered, under the conditions and in accordance with the rules laid down by it:

(a) at the request of the person concerned, to have the objection made known through the Services of the National Register;

(b) to regulate access to this information, so that the physicians carrying out the removal can be informed of the objection.

(4) A physician may not proceed to carry out the removal:

1.   if an objection has been expressed in the manner provided for by the Crown;

2.   if an objection has been expressed by the donor in another manner that has nevertheless been communicated to the physician; or

3.   if a close relative has communicated his objection to the physician. This objection may not override the expressed wishes of the donor.

'Close relative' means a relative up to the first degree of, or the spouse residing with, the donor.

Do you think the case for 'opting out' has been made?

(c)   REQUIRED REQUEST

Note the following from 'Organ Procurement: It's Not in the Cards', by Caplan (1984) 14 Hastings Center Report 9 (number 5).

One key factor emerges from both the French and the American experience: the major obstacle to organ procurement is the failure to ask family members about organ donation. French physicians are entitled by law to take tissues without asking anyone but are unwilling to do so. American physicians are entitled by the Uniform Anatomical Gift Act to take tissues from those who sign donor cards but they are unwilling to do so. Whether or not one believes that the wishes of the family should supersede either the wishes of the public, as in France, or the wishes of the individual, as in the United States, in fact both countries always treat the family as the final authority insofar as the disposition of the dead is concerned.

The respect accorded family members' wishes in these two large and medically sophisticated nations would seem to dictate the kind of public policy change that has the greatest chance of alleviating the shortage in cadaver donors. The French experience indicates that the only practical policy options are those that recognise and respect the role of family members in participating in decisions about cadaver donation. The weak version of required request acknowledges the role of family members, while at the same time ensuring that an optimal environment exists for eliciting organ donations.

Physicians, nurses, or other hospital personnel should be required to inquire whether available family members will give their consent to organ donation. This could be accomplished by modifying the current legal process for declaring death in all states to include a provision requiring that a request concerning organ donation be made to available family members by a party not connected with the determination of death. When family members are not available, organs would be removed only if a donor card or other legal document were present. Or, hospital accreditation requirements could be revised to include a provision mandating that at death the families of potential donors be approached about their willingness to consent.

. . . People must be asked to act if their altruistic motivations are to make a significant difference in helping those in need.

Cadaver organ donation is, whether we like it or not, a family matter. Families should be given every opportunity to act upon their desire to transform the tragedy of death into the gift of life. But they must be asked. If our society were to institute a policy of weak required request, those who are, according to the public opinion polls, willing to give would have a maximal opportunity to do so. We should not allow our concern for the rights and values of the individual to blind us to policy options that can accommodate both individual autonomy and community good.

An example of the legislation in the United States can be seen in a 1985 amendment to the New York Public Health Law.

4351. 1. Where, based on accepted medical standards, a patient is a suitable candidate for organ or tissue donation, the person in charge of such hospital, or his designated representative, other than a person connected with the determination of death, shall at the time of death request any of the following persons, in the order or priority stated, when persons in prior classes are not available and in the absence of (1) actual notice of contrary intentions by the decedent, or (2) actual notice of opposition by a member of any of the classes specified in paragraph (a), (b), (c), (d), or (e) hereof or (3) other reason to believe that an anatomical gift is contrary to the decedent's religious beliefs, to consent to the gift of all or any part of the decedent's body for any purpose specified in article forty-three of this chapter:
(a) the spouse;
(b) a son or daughter twenty-one years of age or older;
(c) either parent;
(d) a brother or sister twenty-one years of age or older;
(e) a guardian of the person of the decedent at the time of his death.
Where said hospital administrator or his designee shall have received actual notice of opposition from any of the persons named in this subdivision or where there is otherwise reason to believe that an anatomical gift is contrary to the decedent's religious beliefs, such gift of all or any part of the decedent's body shall not be requested. Where a donation is requested, consent or refusal need only be obtained from the person or persons in the highest priority class available.
2. Where a donation is requested, said person in charge of such hospital or his designated representative shall complete a certificate of request for an anatomical gift, on a form supplied by the commissioner [of Health]. Said certificate shall include a statement to the effect that a request for consent to an anatomical gift has been made, and shall further indicate thereupon whether or not consent was granted, the name of the person granting or refusing the consent, and his or her relationship to the decedent. Upon completion of the certificate, said person shall attach the certificate of request for an anatomical gift to the death certificate required by this chapter or, in the city of New York, to the death certificate required by the administrative code of the city of New York.
3. A gift made pursuant to the request required by this section shall be executed pursuant to applicable provisions of article forty-three of this chapter.
4. The commissioner shall establish regulations concerning the training of hospital employees who may be designated to perform the request, and the procedures to be employed in making it.
5. The commissioner shall establish such additional regulations as are necessary for the implementation of this section.

Daphne Sipes examines the position in the US in 'Requesting Organ Donations: A New State Approach to Organ Transplants' (1987) Health Law in Canada, as follows:

Comparison of inquiry statutes

1. Type of inquiry
The present 32 states' 'required request/routine inquiry' statutes[37] can be organised into three general types of mandates. The first type requires that the hospital administrator or his designee shall request consent to donate all or part of the deceased's body as an anatomical gift from the decedent's appropriate next of kin. In this category are the laws of Alabama, Arizona, Delaware, Florida, Georgia[38], Illinois, Louisiana, Maine[39], Maryland, Michigan, Missouri, New Hampshire, New

York, Ohio, Oregon, Pennsylvania, West Virginia, and Wisconsin. For example, the Alabama statute requires that '[w]hen death occurs in a hospital to a patient who has not made an anatomical gift to take effect upon death, the hospital administrator, or designated representative, shall request the person described . . . to consent to the gift of organs of the decedent's body as an anatomical gift'.[40]

Maryland has enacted two statutes in the organ procurement area.[41] The first statute parallels the Alabama statute, but it requires requests for consents only of minor decedents' organs.[42] The Wisconsin statute varies by requiring that the next of kin 'be requested to consider consenting to the gift'.[43]

Arizona's Act probably belongs to this group, although its statute should be construed as allowing the hospital to develop protocol designating an OPA [Organ Procurement Agency] to be the requester.[44] The Arizona statute is also interesting because it specifies that the requester 'shall . . . attempt to obtain consent to donate'.[45]

The second group of statutes also requires affirmative action be taken. In this class, either a hospital administrator or a person appointed through hospital protocol is required to inform about (instead of request) organ donation. California, Delaware, Kansas, Minnesota, Pennsylvania, and Texas require every hospital to develop a protocol that shall require that the appropriate next of kin be asked whether the decedent/patient was a donor, and if not, that the family be informed of the option of giving all or part of the deceased's body as an anatomical gift.

The laws of Indiana, Massachusetts, Rhode Island, and Tennessee can also be generally classified with this group. The Indiana and Massachusetts statutes do not mandate the development of a protocol and do not require specific inquiry about whether the patient was a donor, but they do require that the hospital administrator inform the family of the opportunity or procedures for making an organ donation of the deceased's body. There are some ambiguous terms in the Rhode Island law. Although the Act requires that each Rhode Island hospital develop a protocol that 'shall require that any deceased individual's next of kin . . . shall be informed of the option to donate organs',[46] the statute also refers to the making of a 'request'.[47]

The Tennessee statute is very different in comparison to all of the other 37 Acts, because of its specificity. It requires that every hospital 'develop and implement an organ and tissue donation policy and procedure to assist the physicians in identifying and evaluating terminal patients who may be suitable organ or tissue donors'.[48] The policy is required to contain, among other points, 'mechanisms for informing the next of kin of the potential donor about organ and tissue donation options'.[49] Every Tennessee hospital policy must also include provisions for the identification of potential donors who 'shall be notified' to the appropriate OPA.[50] Nowhere in the Act is the hospital or others required to obtain consent; however, the Act does order all health care people to make every effort to identify potential donors and to inform the appropriate OPA.[51]

The Delaware, Ohio and Pennsylvania Acts combine the first and second categories. The Delaware law mandates the hospital to request consent from the decedent's family, as in category one. The Delaware statute also requires the development of protocol for identifying terminally ill patients and for inquiring whether they are a donor and, if they are not, of informing the appropriate person of the option to donate. The Ohio statute tracks the Federal law by requiring every hospital to develop a protocol that will require an OPA (not the hospital) to inform families of donation procedures, when consistent with hospital protocol.

The third classification includes the state statutes of Connecticut, Hawaii, Kentucky, New Jersey, and Virginia. The Connecticut and Hawaii statutes do not require affirmative inquiry, but permit inquiry or discussion about organ donation. The Connecticut statute mandates the development of protocol, which is permissive, 'whereby families of deceased patients or patients whose death is imminent *may* under circumstances set forth in such protocol be made aware of the option' to donate.[52] The Hawaii law, a very short Act, simply states that the hospital administrator *may* request consent for organ donations from the appropriate family member. New Jersey's Act requires affirmative action by the hospital to ascertain only at the time of admission whether a patient is a donor and to record his response.[53]

The Kentucky Act does not specifically require that anyone request consent for organ donation or even that a decedent's family be informed of the option to donate. The law does require that as a condition of licensure each hospital shall establish an 'organ procurement for transplant protocol, in consultation with a federally certified' OPA.[54] The statute further specifies that when an individual has died and/or meets the criteria as a potential donor, the hospital administrator shall notify the federally certified OPA 'of the potential availability of the organ'.[55] The Virginia Act only requires, as a hospital regulation, that each hospital establish an organ procurement protocol.

As a proposal for uniform legislation, every hospital should have a policy that directs the timely and routine inquiry of patients and of their families about the possibility of organ donation. In addition, a uniform Act should include the characteristics of the Connecticut, Georgia, Kentucky, New Jersey, Maryland, Minnesota and Tennessee laws that promote a systems approach to identifying both adult and minor potential donors not only at the time of a hospital admission, but also at other appropriate times in advance of the time of death.

2. *Exceptions*

Most of the statutes excuse an inquiry for certain reasons. The exceptions are expressed either as condition precedents to the inquiry or as specific exemptions. The usual exemption is based upon the actual notice of contrary indications of the donor-patient or of his family in the order of their statutory, priority status. For example, the Alabama statute states that the request shall be made 'in the absence of actual notice of contrary indication by the decedent or one in a prior class'.[56] Alabama, Delaware, Florida, Georgia, Illinois, New York, Oregon, West Virginia follow this type of condition precedent.[57]

In addition, Delaware, Louisiana, Illinois, Maryland, Massachusetts, Michigan, and Missouri also specifically direct that no inquiry is to be made if there is actual notice of contrary intention by a donor-patient or by his family members according to their priority. The Florida, New York, Ohio and West Virginia Acts ignore priority and specify that no inquiry is to be made if there is a contrary indication by the donor-patient or any family member. Pennsylvania's Act ignores priority to a certain extent and directs that no request shall be made if there is no valid donor card to be found and if any family member has objected. Wisconsin's statute varies by stating that the request 'does not have' to be made if there are contrary indications by the decedent or a priority member.[58]

Inquiry may also be excused if a potential donor is not a medically suitable candidate. Nonsuitability appears as a condition precedent in most of the statutes.[59] Georgia, Indiana, Kentucky, Louisiana, Maryland, Massachusetts, Michigan, Missouri, New Hampshire, New York, Ohio, West Virginia, and Wisconsin follow this approach. Kentucky and Ohio generally require that the patient be identified as a potential donor who meets the criteria of the hospital protocol. Alabama, Delaware, Oregon, and Pennsylvania state that non-suitability is an authorised exception. The Connecticut, Pennsylvania, and Texas Acts require that protocol shall take non-suitability into account, whereas the protocol in the California, Kansas, Rhode Island, and Washington statutes merely permits non-suitability to be considered.

Several of the statutes also regard the decedent's religious belief to be a factor in determining whether to make an inquiry. Connecticut is the only state with a law that requires not only the decedent's, but also the family's, known religious belief to be considered. The California, Kansas, Rhode Island, and Washington statutes provide that protocol may take the decedent's religious belief into account. Illinois, Louisiana, Michigan, New York, Ohio, and West Virginia specify that no inquiry shall be made if there is actual notice or reason to believe that the decedent's religious belief is contrary to an anatomical gift. Maryland states that in all discussions with the family, the requester shall take into account the religious belief of the decedent.

There are other miscellaneous exceptions in several of the statutes. For example, the Alabama Act provides that the attending physician may in his sole judgment determine that inquiry shall not be made because of his 'special and peculiar knowledge of the decedent and/or the circumstances surrounding the death of the patient'.[60] In the Georgia statute, a will instrument may prevent the organ donation of a minor patient. In the Kansas Act, hospital protocol may take into account the ability of the hospital to maintain the donor. Maryland, Ohio, Pennsylvania, and Texas dictate that sensitivity to the family's 'circumstances' shall be observed in all donation discussions.[61] The Massachusetts statute specifically excuses a discussion when it would cause the family 'undue emotional stress'.[62] The Illinois Director of Public Health may terminate mandatory requests by a rule signifying that the need for donations has been met. Texas does not allow inquiry unless the hospital has been notified by an OPA that it is available for retrieval and that there is a need for the donation.

In formulating uniform legislation, it would be preferable that all of the above factors be regarded in routine requests. Although statutes similar to that of West Virginia are praiseworthy in considering any family member's objections, the wording should be avoided as it thwarts organ giving and could present even more family dissension when a priority family member is allowed by law to be overruled by a lower priority member.[63] Also, it could conflict with the UAGA's [Uniform Anatomical Gift Act] order of the next of kin, depending upon the wording adopted. Another reason that the wording should be avoided is that it eliminates any opportunity for an organ donation discussion and that could frustrate a priority class member who may have welcomed the opportunity to discuss the subject with the family as a unit. Moreover, the statutory language should affirmatively encourage health professionals to participate in the organ donation process, instead of avoiding what will inevitably be a stressful time for the family.[64]

Despite the type of statute adopted, the obvious contradictions of a potential donation could be eliminated in advance by determining a person's intention to donate at the time of admission and at other times, as appropriate. It should be noted that pursuant to the UAGA, the prior indication of a person to donate cannot be subsequently cancelled by a family member.[65] A patient's previously documented intention to donate could be tactfully discussed with the family to reiterate the donor's decision, to prevent family surprise, and to reinforce the intent of the UAGA and of the common law, which allow a person to have the first decision of whether to donate his own body.

No request should be made and no gift should be accepted if the patient-donor is an obviously unsuitable candidate or, as the Kansas statute points out,[66] would become unsuitable if the hospital could not maintain the body. Various phrases from the Georgia statute resolve some of these issues and comport with the intent of both the UAGA and the Task Force studies:

Upon the admission of a person to any hospital, the hospital shall inquire about the person's desire to donate any or all of his body. His expression shall be recorded in a book kept for such purposes and shall also be recorded in his permanent medical record. His expression shall be deemed to be sufficient notice under this act and under the UAGA not to be contravened by any persons. Unless a gift of any or all of a person's body is deemed to be medically unsuitable, the gift, whether made before the death of the person who is giving his organs, tissues, or other parts, or whether made by a priority member in the order as specified by law, becomes effective and irrevocable upon the death of the person whose organs or body is being donated. Delivery of the document executing the anatomical gift during the donor's lifetime is not necessary to make the gift valid.[67]

To provide uniformity, a hospital's protocol should take into account all of the excuses from inquiry as would be appropriate, but the ultimate decision about whether to request a donation or to initiate an organ donation discussion with the family should be left to the discretion of trained transplant coordinators who may be approaching the family at an awkward time. It is preferable that any inquiry statute set the framework for the hospital's organ procurement protocol by specifying the obvious factors that procurement personnel must consider. The legislation mandating the development of protocol should be neither vague, as by allowing the protocol to be determined, nor inflexible. Specifying a minimum of conditions in the statute to be included in the organ procurement protocol will provide certainty for legislative purposes and flexibility for enforcement purposes.

3. Designated requesters

Most of the states specifically designate the hospital, the hospital administrator, or designee to inquire about organ donation. These include Alabama, Delaware, Florida, Hawaii, Indiana, Illinois, Louisiana, Maryland, Missouri, Massachusetts, New Hampshire, New Jersey, New York, Oregon, Pennsylvania, and West Virginia. [Some states include amongst those designated to inquire] the 'physician responsible for the care of the patient'.[68] Several of the statutes provide only for the development of protocol and therefore do not specify who is to be responsible for an inquiry.[69] In either type of statute, someone with an OPA could be the designated requester. In fact, the Missouri Act specifically allows the hospital official to designate an OPA and the Georgia statute requires that an OPA shall request the consent. Maine orders the attending physician to request, unless he is unable or is connected with the determination of death, then the hospital administrator or his designee shall request the consent. The Ohio statute specifies that notification to the family about organ donation procedures shall be the responsibility of the OPA, unless otherwise designated. However, the Ohio statute also directs that the requesters of consent shall be the OPA, the hospital administrator, or his designee. Arizona, Florida, Hawaii, New York, Maine, Missouri, and West Virginia all specify that the requester shall not be a person connected with the determination of death.[70]

Most of the thirty-two statutes are activated when a death occurs in a hospital. Therefore, it is preferable that the statute designate the hospital administrator or his designee to enforce the hospital's organ procurement protocol. The statute should also require that protocol specify the titles or positions of requesters and whether and when attending physicians or OPA personnel should be requesters.

4. Potential donors

According to the UAGA, a person has the statutory right to donate all or a part of his body.[71] Such a gift takes effect at death.[72] Under the UAGA, the rights of a donee are paramount to the rights of all others, except the coroner's. This provision 'recognises and gives legal effect to the right of the individual to dispose of his own body without subsequent veto by others'.[73] Thus, the routine inquiry statutes shall not apply unless a person has failed to execute an anatomical gift or has failed to indicate his contrary intention. The Illinois, Minnesota, and Pennsylvania Acts contain some interesting features. With a valid donation card of the decedent, the Illinois law allows a decedent's body to be used for an anatomical gift, if the hospital administrator is unable to obtain consent from the next-of-kin. Thus, the decedent's desire to donate may not be overridden in such a case. It is really not clear from the Illinois Act if the inability to obtain consent, rather than the unavailability of the appropriate kin, is what the law intends. At first glance, it appears that the Minnesota Act provides a similar respect for a person's donor card. However, the card constitutes consent if there is no objection from a relative or if no relative can be located. The Pennsylvania law provides for a two-part limitation. In the face of a family objection, a valid donor card controls as the necessary consent. Thus, clearly a person's already executed intent to donate cannot be subsequently vetoed by a family member. However, if a person has no card, then opposition by any family member, regardless of priority, prohibits a request.[74]

The majority of the inquiry statutes parallel the UAGA in terms of the order of priority of family members who may donate when a person has died, but has not previously executed an anatomical gift of his organs. The UAGA specifies the order of priority to be '(1) the spouse, (2) an adult son or daughter, (3) either parent, (4) an adult brother or sister, (5) a guardian of the person of the decedent at the time of his death, (6) any other person authorised or under obligation to dispose of the body'.[75] The following routine inquiry states either refer to their particular UAGA statute for reference to the priority order or specify an order that adheres to the UAGA scheme: Alabama, Arizona, California, Connecticut, Delaware, Florida, Georgia, Hawaii, Indiana, Illinois, Kansas, Louisiana, Maine, Massachusetts, Michigan, Minnesota, Missouri, New York, Ohio, Oregon, Pennsylvania, Rhode Island, Texas, West Virginia, Washington, and Wisconsin.[76]

In the UAGA, the word 'decedent' is defined as 'a deceased individual and includes a stillborn infant or fetus'.[77] Thus, the priority classes in the UAGA presume the next of kin's authority to donate the organs of any aged decedent.[78] The Georgia and the Maryland statutes specifically refer to required requests in the case of minor decedents. These two statutes set out a scheme of priority that differs from the UAGA's order of priority. Georgia provides the order of priority to be: '(1) Both parents; (2) If both parents are not readily available . . ., one parent; (3) If the parents are divorced or legally separated, the custodial parent; (4) . . . the noncustodial parent; (5) . . . the legal guardian; (6) Any other person authorised or obligated to dispose of the body'.[79] This scheme is not advisable because it conflicts with the usual scheme of priority provided by the UAGA; it presents potential conflicts between divorced parents; and it unnecessarily contradicts the definition of decedent in the UAGA. As an alternative, divorcing parents could specify their desires about their children's organ donation in their divorce decrees as they do when deciding who will take the tax exemption for children. Maryland's statute also sets out a priority order for pediatric decedents.[80] Although the Maryland statute more closely follows the UAGA scheme, its version is not advisable for the same reasons that the Georgia version is not.

Several of the statutes state that consent will be obtained in the order of priority specified when prior members are not available at or near the time of death or at the time of the request. For instance, both Illinois and Texas detail concepts of the 'availability' of family members to be questioned. In fact, the Texas immunity clause defines 'good faith' in terms of reasonable attempts to locate the appropriate family member. Many specify also that consent or denial controls in order of priority members who are available. There could conceivably be a situation when the request occurs at a time different than the time of death. Since the gift is not effective until death, there may be a time lag between when a lower class member, who was available, has consented to the anatomical gift and when a higher priority class member subsequently appears and disagrees with the consent. Two of the statutes resolve this conflict by borrowing from the UAGA, which specifies that '[i]f the donee has actual notice of contrary indications by the decedent or that a gift by a member of a class is opposed by a member of the same or a prior class, the donee shall not accept the gift'.[81] Within a particular class, all of the members must consent, because one denial within the class will control.

A few of the laws allow any member's objection to donation to override the mandate of a statute to request.[82] Although the Florida Act states that the known contrary intention of any member shall prevent a request for donation to be made, regardless of the priority status of the objector, the statute also provides that the consent or the denial need only be obtained from the highest available priority class. Thus, a lower priority class member, who could prevent a request from being made, is unable to override a priority class's consent.

Priority classes should be respected in all cases and a statute should not track the language of those Acts that allow inquiries to be excused because of any family member's objection. Despite the grief or the family dissension that could be caused by allowing a higher priority member to override a lower priority member, a systematic approach provides less confusion and delay and accounts for the presumption that the higher the priority member, the more probable he knew the decedent's wishes.

5. Time of request

Most of the timings of the requests or discussions in the inquiry statutes are linked to the time at or immediately preceding death.[83] The other state laws are connected to the time 'on or before the occurrence of death'.[84] Other statutes also recognise the identification of potential donors at other times. Delaware specifically states that organ donation may be discussed when a patient's death is imminent, a person is in a terminal condition, or a person is incompetent. The Connecticut law uses the language 'imminent'.[85] The Kentucky and Minnesota statutes include the time when a patient has been identified as having a terminal condition. Inquiries in the Missouri and the New Hampshire laws are timed to the existence of a 'suitable candidate'.[86] The Tennessee statute is by comparison the most inclusive in terms of specifying the timing of consultation, determination or death, evaluation for donation, and organ procurements. The statute also specifies that patients eligible for declaration of brain death be evaluated for possible organ donation. Uniform legislation should borrow from the Tennessee law, which particularises the co-ordination of timing for donation procedures.

While it is understandable that the time at or after death presents the final opportunity for a possible organ donation, the goal of legislation in this area should be to encourage education about donation prior to one's death. Therefore, the period at or after death should not be the only time when inquiries are activated. As the Georgia, New Jersey, and Maryland statutes provide, admission into a hospital is a convenient opportunity to decide about organ donation. With a statute that requires routine inquiry at the time of admission, the hospital staff could be relieved from dealing with hurried discussions during a family's grief and would be legally protected in carrying out the decedent's intention to donate his body. The inquiries should begin at and prior to admission, perhaps in physicians' offices where discussions can be more personal, less pressured, and where literature may be available.

Notes to extract

37. [footnote omitted]
38. Georgia's Act requires the request be made by an OPA, who shall have been notified by the hospital administrator. Ga Code Ann, §§ 44-5-143(c)(1), 44-5-143.1(b).
39. Maine's law requires that the attending physician be the first to make the request, unless he is unable or he determined death, in which case, the obligation passes to the hospital administrator. Ch 574, § 3, 1986 Me Laws 107, 109.
40. Ala Code § 22-19-142(a).
41. . . . Both Acts were passed on May 27, 1986.
42. Ch 764, § (B)(1), 1986 Md Laws 3111, 3112. Another part of the Act requires that all hospitals routinely inquire at the time of admission whether a patient is an organ donor and note the information in his admission form. *Id* at § A. The Georgia and New Jersey laws also require a hospital to inquire at the time of admission and to document a patient's expression of intent to donate. Massachusetts enacted a substantially similar provision in 1971 with the adoption of the UAGA. . . .

The second Maryland law requires that '[a]s a condition to licensure, each . . . hospital shall develop a protocol for the procurement of organ and tissues'. Ch 673, § 1, 1986 Md Laws 3513, 3513. It would appear that the second statute could implement required requests of all patients, not only minor patients. However, the first statute, as originally proposed, substituted 'minor patient' for 'an individual', resulting in the inference that the Maryland legislature may not have intended to mandate the request in all cases. Ch 764, House Bill 1027, 1986 Md Laws 3111.
43. Wis Stat Ann § 155.06(2m)(a).
44. Ch 261, § 4(A), 1986 Ari Sess Laws 857, 859. . . .
45. *Id*, § 4(C).
46. Ch 226, 1986 RI Pub Laws 437, 437.
47. *Id*, This may present a contradictory intent, since the statute directs that information be given to the family, not that a request be made.
48. Ch 885, § 2(c), 1986 Tenn Pub Acts 1015, 1015.
49. *Id*, § 2(d).
50. *Id*, § 2(e), at 1015–16. The Minnesota Act contains this idea, generally.
51. *Id*, § 2(g), at 1016. New sections in Kentucky law mandate a similar obligation

to all hospital and allied health personnel and penalties for non-compliance. Ky Rev Stat § 216B.990(4)–(5) (Supp 1986).

52. Pub Act 86–88, 1986 Conn Acts 235, 235 [emphasis added]. The New Jersey Act is reported to be under amendment. Davis, *Legal-Ethics Committee Report*, NATCO, vol *III*, No 3, at p 5. (Feb. 1987) (North American Transplant Coordinators Organisation newsletter).

53. *See supra*, note 42, and accompanying text.

54. Sec 311.241(1).

55. *Id*, at § 311.241(2).

56. Sec 22-19-142(a). This language parallels the UAGA . . . at § 2(b).

57. Florida, New York, Ohio, and West Virginia, however, also excuse inquiry if any family member objects, regardless of his priority status.

58. Sec 155.06(2m)(b).

59. The Florida Act provides only general direction for excusing requests by permitting its department of health to set procedures.

60. Sec 22-19-142(d).

61. This is the requirement now specified by federal law. . . .

62. Ch 360, §§ 2, 8(b), 1986 Mass Acts 527, 528.

63. *See, supra*, note 57.

64. (footnote omitted)

65. UAGA . . . at § 2(e). *See also, infra*, note 74 and accompanying text.

66. Ch 227, § 1(a), 1986 Kan Sess Laws 1029, 1029.

67. *See*, eg, Ga Code Ann § 44-4-143(d), (f); § 44-5-145(b); UAGA at § 2(c)–(e) and § 4(b).

68. Ch 360. §§ 2, 8(b), 1986 Mass Acts 527, 528.

69. Ariz, Cal, Conn, Kan, Ky, Minne, Mo, RI, Tenn, Tex, Va, Wash, Wis.

70. Section 4(c) of the UAGA also provides that the donee physician shall not participate in the removal or transplantation of the donated parts. The UAGA further provides that the time of death shall be determined by the attending physician of the donor or else the physician who certifies death. The physician who determines the time of death shall not participate in the removal or transplanting procedures. *Id.* § 7(b).

71. UAGA . . . at § 2(a).

72. *Id*.

73. *Id*, 2(e) Comment.

74. The Illinois, Minnesota, and Pennsylvania statutes are merely following what is already the principle in the Uniform Anatomical Gift Act. A person has the right to decide whether his body organs and tissues shall be donated, without a family members subsequently vetoing that decision. *See supra*, notes 65 and 73 and accompanying text.

75. *Id*, § 2(b)(1)–(6).

76. Del, Ill, NY, Minne, Ohio, & W Va omit class (6). NY requires the next of kin to be 21 years of age. *See generally*, UAGA at § 2 (citing jurisdictional differences).

77. Sec. 1(b).

78. *See generally*, § 2(a)–(b) and Comment (explaining the age requirements under the UAGA).

79. Sec 44-5-143.1(b)(1)–(6).

80. Ch 764, § 1(B)(I)–(IV), 1986 Md Laws 3111, 3112–3.

81. UAGA § 2(c). Persons authorised may make the gift after or immediately before death. *Id*, § 2(c). The section authorises the survivors to execute the necessary documents even prior to death. *Id* § 2(c) at Comment.

82. *See supra*, note 63, and accompanying text.

83. Ala, Cal, Fla, Ind, Kan, Ky, La, Me, Md, Mich, NY, Penn, Or, RI, Tex, W Va, Wash, Wis. Illinois' statute says 'at or after notification of death'.

84. Ariz, Del, Ga (also at the time of admission), Mass.

85. Conn requires protocol to identify potential donors. Pub Act 86–88, 1986 Conn Acts 235.

86. Ch 194, § 1(1), 1986 Mo Laws 905; ch 191, § 3(1), 1986 NH Laws 531, 532.

In England, not only legislation but even the idea of 'required request' has been rejected by the Hoffenberg Working Party.

> We have considered *legally required request*. In the USA, 30 States have in the past two years enacted legislation requiring either that the hospital administrator or his designee should ask for the gift of organs, or that protocols are established for requesting the gift. In a smaller number of States there are penalties for non-compliance by fine or loss of licence. We agree with the Society of British Neurological Surgeons and with some others who have given evidence to us that the establishment of the above procedures for referral with an effective audit would be preferable to legally required request.

Do you agree with this rather perfunctory rejection of the notion of 'required request'? Is the Working Party's fear simply one of legal sanction against doctors who do not 'request' as the statute would require?

(d) OTHER REFORMS

(i) Clarifying the 1961 Act

The most extensive review of the Human Tissue Act with a view to clarifying its provisions within the framework of a system of 'opting in' was attempted by the British Transplantation Society in the Committee Report in 1975.

> The Committee agreed that, in view of the unhelpful interpretations of the Human Tissue Act which persist in some quarters, statutory clarification of the Act was desirable.
> The existing S.1 (2). . . should be repealed, and the following provision substituted:
> 'Without prejudice to the foregoing subsection, the person lawfully in possession of the body of a deceased person may authorise the removal of any part from the body for use for the said purposes if, *having made such inquiry as is both reasonable and practicable in the time available,* he has no reason to believe that the deceased had expressed an objection (which he was not known to have withdrawn) to his body being so dealt with after his death.
> *Provided that authorisation shall not be given under this subsection if the person lawfully in possession of the body has reason to believe that the surviving spouse or any surviving relative of the deceased objects to the body being so dealt with.'*
> In addition there should be a new subsection, providing that
> 'For the avoidance of doubt in the interpretation of this section, it is hereby declared:
> (a) That the hospital authority is the person in possession of the body of a deceased person lying in the hospital, and that this possession is lawful until such time as the hospital authority fails to comply with a request for possession of the body, made by the person who has the right to immediate possession of it.
> (b) That a printed but personally signed "donor card", or other document, is "in writing" for the purpose of subsection 1 of this section.
> (c) The "time available", for the purpose of an inquiry under subsection 2 of this section, extends only until the moment at which steps must be taken to remove the part of the body, if it is to be suitable for the therapeutic or other purpose in question.'
> The effect of these provisions would be to overcome the unfortunate (and, it is thought, unjustified) doubts concerning the interpretation of 'such reasonable inquiry as may be practicable' and 'person lawfully in possession of the body' under the present law, and to prevent any doubts arising over the interpretation of 'in writing'.
> Only in one respect does the suggested amendment seek to alter what the Committee understands to be the current legal position. Though authorisation could not be given under the proposed S. 1 (2) if the person lawfully in possession of the body had reason to believe that the spouse or any relative of the deceased objected,

he would no longer be under a duty to make inquiries as to whether they did object. He would, however, invariably approach the closest available relatives, in the course of making 'such inquiry as is both reasonable and practicable' to determine whether the deceased had expressed an objection. They would thus have the opportunity of making known their own (or others') objections. This change would represent a reversion to the legal position of the spouse and relatives under the Corneal Grafting Act, 1952, which was very much more satisfactory in this respect.

Some members of the Committee favoured a more radical amendment of the Human Tissue Act. But in view of the failure of more radical proposals to make progress through Parliament, and in view of the general consensus among surgeons that it would be undesirable to remove organs for transplantation in the face of objections from the spouse or relatives, it was decided to press for a limited amendment.

(ii)   Without permission and ignoring objections

J Dukeminier writes in 'Supplying Organs for Transplantation', Michigan Law Review *op cit* (at pp 831–835):

Removal of cadaver organs regardless of objection

A recent analysis of the problem of supplying organs resulted in the suggestion that legislation be enacted to authorise the removal, with or without consent, of cadaver organs useful for transplantation.[65] The ethical basis for this solution to the problem of organ supply is that saving human life is paramount to all other policies and that no one has the right to deny another the chance to live.

Today, in disposing of the dead, the principle of protecting life requires that a coroner perform an autopsy on a body when homicidal behavior is suspected, even though the next of kin objects. Courts have uniformly held that the rights of the decedent and next of kin are subordinate to the paramount public interest in apprehending killers.[66] In these circumstances the autopsy may be held without the consent of the next of kin or even over his positive objection.[67] Catching a murderer both prevents further homicidal behavior by the man apprehended and deters homicidal behavior by others. The overriding principle is protecting the lives of the survivors.

. . .

If one accepts the view that saving human life requires the removal of useful cadaver organs regardless of the wishes of the decedent or next of kin the question arises whether a statute effectuating that policy would run foul of any constitutional provisions prohibiting the taking of property without compensation. One recent study concludes that such a statute would constitute a taking of the property of the next of kin, who would have to be paid just compensation for the cadaver organs.[75] That conclusion, however, is erroneous. Even accepting the highly questionable assumption that it is appropriate to classify the next of kin's interest in a cadaver as a property right, the next of kin's claim does not become an 'interest' in property until the death of the decedent. At any time prior to the occurrence of that event, the potential interest may be abolished without paying compensation, as may be seen by an analysis of the law relating to the closely analogous cases of a right of dower or an expectancy of an heir. While the decedent is alive, these rights are contingent upon surviving the decedent; in legal parlance, dower remains inchoate, and the expectancy of an heir is not recognised as an interest or right at all. Inchoate dower may be abolished without violating the Constitution.[76] Indeed almost a hundred years ago the Supreme Court declared:

[Dower] is wholly given by law and the power that gave it may increase, diminish, or otherwise alter it, or wholly take it away. It is upon the same footing with the expectancy of heirs, apparent or presumptive, before the death of the ancestor. Until that event occurs the law of descent and distribution may be moulded according to the will of the legislature.[77]

Thus, by analogy to inchoate dower or to the expectancy of an heir, it may be concluded that the rights of the next of kin to control the cadavers of persons living can be changed or abolished without paying any compensation.

It might also be thought that the decedent has an interest in what is done with his body, but the common-law rule is that there is no property in a dead body and that consequently a man cannot by will dispose of his body.[78] If, however, cadaver organs are deemed to be property,[79] compensation for their taking is not required, since succession to a man's property at death can be changed, and perhaps even abolished, by a legislature without violating the Constitution:

Rights of succession to the property of a deceased, whether by will or by intestacy, are of statutory creation, and the dead hand rules succession only by sufferance. Nothing in the Federal Constitution forbids the legislature of a state to limit, condition, or even abolish the power of testamentary disposition over property within its jurisdiction.[80]

State supreme courts, with the exception of that of Wisconsin,[81] agree that the power to dispose of property by will may be controlled by the legislature,[82] subject only to the constitutional guarantees of equal protection and due process of law. These broad statements may not be wholly reliable, inasmuch as the power of the legislature to abolish testation has never been directly tested.[83] Yet if the state can take by taxation a percentage of a man's property at death in order to raise revenue and to break up great fortunes, it is difficult to find any reason why the state cannot constitutionally take a specific item, such as a kidney, to save a human life.

Moreover, if organs are treated as property of the decedent, the decedent may have no power to order destruction of his organs by burial or cremation so long as the organs have value. It has been held in a number of cases that a direction to destroy one's own property at death is against public policy and is therefore void.[84] Although these cases could provide the basis for an argument that permitting the destruction of valuable human organs to satisfy a decedent's wish is against public policy, courts today probably would not accept such an argument. Thinking of a cadaver as a valuable resource is still too startling; but as organ transplants become very successful courts may become more receptive to the argument.

It is, however, extremely troublesome to use property terms in the litany of justification for the taking of cadaver organs, for cadaver organs are not property in any conventional sense. Under modern law the next of kin is given a cause of action for unauthorised dissection, and courts have sometimes characterised this right in the next of kin as a property[85] or a quasi-property right.[86] But as Dean Prosser points out, 'it is in reality the personal feelings of the survivors which are being protected under a fiction likely to deceive no one but a lawyer'.[87] Even if the fiction is accepted for purposes of unauthorised dissection cases, the answer to the question whether the rights are property rights for purposes of the Constitution should not turn upon a characterisation made by state courts in such an entirely different context. In determining the constitutionality of legislation authorising the removal of cadaver organs regardless of objection it is inappropriate to begin the analysis by accepting a characterization of cadaver organs as property. As Justice Jackson said some years ago with reference to another claim of a constitutionally protected 'property right': 'We cannot start the process of decision by calling such a claim as we have here a "property right"; whether it is a property right is really the question to be answered'.[88]

In striking a balance between the interests of the public and the desires of the decedent and the survivors, legislatures have already subordinated the interests of the decedent and survivors to the public interest in saving human life, to interests of public health and convenience, and to the economic welfare of undertakers, employers, and insurers.[89] In view of that background, it would surely be odd to find that the fourteenth amendment forbids subordinating the interest of the decedent and next of kin to the public interest in saving the life of a human being.

Notes to extract
65. Note, *Compulsory Removal of Cadaver Organs*, 69 Colum L Rev 693 (1969).
66. *Gahn v Leary*, 318 Mass 425, 61 NE 2d 844 (1945); *Kingsley v Forsyth* 192 Minn 468, 257 NW 95 (1934); *Hirko v Reese* 351 Pa 238, 40 A 2d 408 (1945).

67. *Young v College of Physicians & Surgeons*, 81 Md 358, 32 A 177 (1895); *Sturgeon v Crosby Mortuary, Inc* 140 Neb 82, 299 NW 378 (1941).
. . .

75. Note, *supra* note 65, at 697.

76. *Ferry v Spokane*, P & S Ry, 258 US 314 (1922); Opinion of the Justices, 337 Mass 786, 151 NE 2d 475 (1958).

77. *Randall v Kreiger*, 90 US (23 Wall) 137, 148 (1874).

78. *Williams v Williams* (1881) 20 ChD 659.

79. In *Re Johnson's Estate* 169 Misc 215, 7 NYS 2d 81 (Sur Ct 1938), a will provided that the decedent's body was to be used for medical research; there were no other provisions. Nonetheless, the will was probated. Since an instrument that does not dispose of property or appoint an executor is not testamentary in character and is not entitled to probate, the body must have been treated as property.

80. *Irving Trust Co v Day*, 314 US 556, 562 (1942).

81. *Nunnemacher v State*, 129 Wis 190, 108 NW 627 (1906).

82. See 1 W Page, Law of Wills § 3.1 (Bowe-Parker ed 1960, Supp 1967).

83. See J Scurlock, Retroactive Legislation Affecting Interests in land 90–105 (1953).

84. Eg, *Brown v Burdett* (1882) 21 ChD 667 in which a devise of a house in trust to brick up the windows and doors for twenty years was held invalid. See also *Colonial Trust Co v Brown*, 105 Conn 261, 135 A 555 (1926), in which a trustee was directed not to erect a downtown building more than three stories in height—a directive which would have substantially decreased the value of the property. The provision was held invalid. In *M'Caig v University of Glasgow* 1907 SC 231 at 242 (Scotland), Lord Kyllachy said a direction to lay waste the testator's estate or to turn the property into money and throw it into the sea is invalid. Similarly, in *Board of County Commrs v Scott*, 88 Minn 386, 93 NW 109 (1903), the court assumed that a testator's direction to destroy all his money and evidence of credit was void.

85. *Bogert v Indianapolis*, 13 Ind 134 (1859). See Note, *Property in Corpses*, 5 St Louis LJ 280 (1958).

86. *Pierce v Proprietors of Swan Point Cemetery*, 10 RI 227 (1872); *cf Cohen v Groman Mortuary*, 231 Cal App 2d 1, 41 Cal Rptr 481 (1964).

87. W Prosser, The Law of Torts 51 (3d ed 1964).

88. *United States v Willow River Power Co*, 324 US 499 at 502 (1945).

89. See notes 66–74 *supra*.

Question

Dukeminier refers to constitutional objections. In the absence of any statutory provision allowing or forbidding this, what legal objections might there be in English law?

Use of fetal tissue

(a) THE BACKGROUND

The following article by Raanan Gillon from (1988) 296 British Medical Journal, (footnotes omitted) sets the scene:

Ethics of fetal brain cell transplants

In analysing the ethical issues provoked by the technique of transplanting fetal brain cells into the brains of patients with Parkinson's disease . . . it may be helpful to consider the various affected parties within the framework of four widely acceptable moral considerations: respect for people and their autonomy, beneficence (doing good), non-maleficence (avoiding doing harm), and justice (fairness in distribution of resources, in respect for rights, and in respect for morally acceptable laws). Such analysis is benefited by discussions on this subject at Britain's first multidisciplinary conference on philosophy and ethics in reproductive medicine, which was held [in April 1988] in Leeds.

Obligations to the recipients of the fetal brain cells seem well met. Thus, as the conference heard from Dr Richard West, chairman of the ethics committee that approved the research, the committee followed the standard research ethics committee guidelines of the Royal College of Physicians. Theoretical considerations, animal research, and preliminary results of clinical research abroad had shown a reasonable prospect of benefiting the severely affected patients (beneficence) with an acceptably low risk of harming them (non-maleficence). The requirement of adequately informed consent respected their autonomy, and no justice considerations were infringed either in terms of fair distribution of resources or infringement of the subject's rights; and the procedures were legally acceptable.

Moral qualms were expressed at the conference about the women whose aborted fetuses were used. Although such women signed consent forms disclaiming any views on the disposal of the fetus, some participants vigorously argued that the women concerned ought to be given more explicit information if the fetal tissues might be used for transplantation or other research and their specific unpressured consent obtained. On the other hand, a woman lawyer argued that not to be satisfied with an adult woman's signature disclaiming views on disposal of the fetus smacked of patronising sexism. In addition, such women might be benefited by being told the outcome, where successful, of any use made of fetal tissues, as proposed by the Conference of Medical Royal Colleges for transplantation.

The women's welfare might be adversely affected if special and more risky abortion techniques were used in order to preserve the fetal brains for transplantation. Furthermore, if such use became widespread women might be increasingly exploited by commercial or other pressures to become pregnant to provide aborted tissues. But given suitable controls to prevent such problems no insuperable moral objections seemed to arise from the perspective of the pregnant women. Their autonomy could be respected, they could be benefited with low probability of harm, their rights could be respected, and they could actually contribute to greater distributive justice by permitting their fetuses to be used to benefit others medically; and provided the abortions are carried out according to the requirements of the Abortion Act the procedures are lawful.

But is the Abortion Act a morally acceptable law? The main ethical objections offered at the conference concerned precisely that question in relation to the third affected party, the aborted fetuses. One of the main speakers, Miss Pamela Sims, a consultant obstetrician and gynaecologist and moral opponent of abortion, argued that, since abortion and the Abortion Act were morally unacceptable, using fetal parts for transplantation after abortion was also morally unacceptable—'the end cannot justify the means'.

Clearly if the fetus is to be accorded full moral status destroying it for the benefit of others would be unacceptable: but, as the ethics committee reportedly reasoned, it was not for its members to deploy their personal moral reservations about abortions in coming to their decisions. It, like the Peel committee, to whose advice it had scrupulously adhered, started from the presumption that abortions were to be carried out. The moral question then becomes: *given* that abortions have been carried out is it morally acceptable to use fetal tissues to benefit others? The relevant means here, as philosopher Jenifer Jackson pointed out, was the transplantation of tissues from already aborted fetuses, and those means could be morally acceptable even to those who believed the abortions themselves and the Abortion Act to be morally wrong. Dr Wendy Greengross, general practitioner and member of the Warnock Committee, illustrated the point succinctly—the fact that a brain dead man on a respirator had been murdered would not morally prohibit using his organs for transplantation.

Finally, are the interests of society threatened by this development? Some concern was expressed at the conference that ethics committees were able locally to make socially controversial decisions including decisions about 'human brain transplants' with only one lay member on the committee and without any of the members having had any formal training in ethical analysis. Ms Jean Robinson, a lay member of the General Medical Council, vigorously argued that there should be a minimum of two lay members on an ethics committee, which should always be prepared to justify its decisions to the public (as it had in this case). Several of the foreign visitors found it peculiar that no national bioethics committee had been established, at least to provide analysis and advice on particularly contentious or difficult medicomoral issues. Such a committee, if also charged to anticipate developments in bioethics, would provide a foothold on the 'slippery slope' about which Miss Sims warned the conference.

This recent controversy permitted the BMA to offer the following Guidelines on the use of fetal tissue.

Guidelines

1 Tissue may be obtained only from dead fetuses resulting from therapeutic or spontaneous abortion. Death of the fetus is defined as an irreversible loss of function of the organism as a whole.

2 United Kingdom laws on transplantation must be followed. The woman from whom the fetal material is obtained must consent to the use of the fetal material for research and/or therapeutic purposes.

3 Transplantation activity must not interfere with the method of performing abortions, nor the timing of abortions, or influence the routine abortion procedure of the hospital in any way. Abortions must be performed subject to the Abortion Act, and any subsequent amendments thereof, uninfluenced by the fate of the fetal tissue. The anonymity of the donor should be maintained.

4 The generation or termination of a pregnancy solely to produce suitable material is unethical. There should be no link between the donor and the recipient.

5 There must be no financial reward for the donation of fetal material or a fetus.

6 Nervous tissue may only be used as isolated neurones or tissue fragments for transplantation. Other fetal organs may be used as either complete or partial organs for transplantation.

7 All hospital staff directly involved in the procedures—including the abortion—must be informed about the procedures involved.

8 Every project involving transplantation of fetal tissue must be approved by the local ethical research committee.

(Note that the Secretary of State has set up a Working Party to advise on what action, if any, should be taken.)

(b)   IS IT LAWFUL?

We would offer the following analysis:

(i) Obviously, the foetus must be dead. The current therapeutic techniques which call for transplant of fetal tissue into patients whose illness may be ameliorated or cured as a consequence, contemplate the use of tissue for fetuses of 6–8 weeks gestational age. Such a fetus cannot survive *ex utero*.

Since the tissue is harvested only when the fetus is *ex utero*, and since when it is *ex utero* at that age of gestation it will die immediately, the legal problem only concerns the 'legality of the means' whereby the death was brought about. It would be otherwise if it were proposed to use tissue from a fetus which would be capable of surviving *ex utero*. In such a case, no tissue could be used until the fetus died naturally and clearly any attempts to bring about its death would be either child destruction or homicide depending upon whether the fetus yet had an 'existence independent of its mother'.

(ii) Assuming again that the tissue is from an early fetus, the death may only lawfully be brought about if the death is a consequence of a lawfully produced abortion. If the tissue is from a fetus where death was as a consequence of a late abortion, it will be a matter of whether the fetus was 'capable of being born alive' and if it was, whether the abortion was performed so as to preserve the life of the mother so as to comply with the Infant Life (Preservation) Act 1929.

(iii) Some objections have been raised against the possibility of a woman becoming pregnant by her spouse or partner solely with the intention of aborting the fetus and thereby providing tissue for transplant into the spouse or partner. Apart from possible ethical objections, are there legal objections to this? There may be, of course; principally objections under the Abortion Act properly applied. In addition, there may be an argument that their conduct so offends against public policy as to amount to a crime, ie conduct calculated to corrupt public morals—if this be a crime in itself. If, however, as may be the case, the crime consists only in conspiracy to corrupt public morals, a charge could only be brought if the couple were not married (see G Williams, *Textbook of Criminal Law* (2nd ed) at p 432).

(iv) On the assumption that the above legal conditions are satisfied, it has been argued that the consent of the mother is required before the fetal tissue may be used. Is this a legal requirement? As we saw earlier in the discussion concerning control of eggs, sperm and embryos, consent can only be a legal requirement if the fetus is regarded as a chattel owned by the mother.

If it be good law that there is no property in a dead body, there can be no question of ownership and thus no requirement for consent. This proposition of law in all probability only applies, however, to dead bodies, a term which may only embrace fetuses of such gestational age that their death has to be registered as a 'still birth' under the Births and Deaths Registration Act 1953, ie on reaching 28 weeks' gestational age.

Does this mean, therefore, that below this age a dead fetus is amenable to ownership? If so, who owns it? If the mother is the most obvious candidate *prima facie* for ownership, can it be said that undergoing an abortion entails abandonment of her property? Can the mother rebut the presumption of abandonment by expressly reserving the right to be consulted over the disposition of the aborted fetus? Would such an express reservation (which, in practice, would mean that she did not sign the standard consent form to an abortion) have any legal effect?

Part III

C: The end of life

Chapter 14

Treatment of the dying and treatment for dying

In this chapter we are concerned with patients who fall into three types of situation:

(a) the patient who is dying and whose condition is fatal when the patient has reached that point at which there is no longer any treatment which will cure him or prevent the continued progress of his disease to death—category A.

(b) the patient who is not dying as defined in (a), but who will die if not given life-sustaining treatment—category B.

(c) the patient who wishes to die whatever his condition and asks to be assisted to die—category C.

We should observe at this point that there is little, if any, English case law to assist us in this area. Instead, to help and illustrate our analysis we rely on a number of the American cases concerned with the issues we discuss. While many American cases raise constitutional law issues, we will see that the common law is also often developed in the case law. In any event, we would argue that the values reflected in the constitutional arguments assist us because they may equally be reflected in the common law. Given medical law's commitment to respect for a patient's autonomy, the most fruitful analysis in terms of principles may be to divide patients into the *competent* and the *incompetent* patient, and then take each of the above categories in turn.

The competent patient

We have seen earlier that respect for autonomy is translated in law into the proposition that, ordinarily, a patient remains the master of his own fate even if that be death (see *supra* ch 4: *Bouvia v Superior Court* (1986) 225 Cal Rptr 297).

Before considering the application of this principle in the factual circumstances set out above as (a), (b) and (c), it is as well to dispose of analytical approaches which prove on close scrutiny to be unhelpful. We examined these approaches earlier when considering the treatment of neonates and found them wanting (*supra* ch 12); this concerned the law of murder and the distinction sometimes drawn between *acts* and *omissions* and also between, *extraordinary* and *ordinary* treatment. We saw that the lawfulness of conduct could not be determined solely by reference to whether it was an act or omission even if these terms were (which we doubt) clearly definable. Not every act causing death is unlawful: concomitantly not every omission when death results is lawful. The real issue, as we saw and will see again, is the extent of the doctor's duty to his patient. This duty will vary depending upon the circumstances and, in particular, the category into which the patient falls.

One further mode of analysis which is largely unhelpful but is relevant here (though not before in the case of neonates), concerns the law of suicide. It is largely unhelpful because in situations (a) and (b) which we contemplate, the better view is that the patient does not commit suicide. In any event, even if he were considered to be doing so, the doctor would not in all probability be regarded as 'aiding and abetting suicide' within s 2(1) of the Suicide Act 1961.

In the President's Commission Report 'Deciding to Forego Life-Sustaining Treatment' in 1983 (hereafter in this chapter called 'the President's Commission'), the legal position is explained (pp 38–39).

> . . . [I]n recent years judges have consistently distinguished between suicide and the refusal of treatment by, or on behalf of, terminally ill patients.[77] Some courts did so by treating the earlier cases as examples of incompetent or unreasonable refusals of 'life-saving' treatments (refusals that can legitimately be prevented), as distinct from competent refusals of treatments that are at best 'life-prolonging' but not curative. Furthermore, in cases in which treatment refusal has been found to be acceptable, courts have held that death resulted from a 'natural cause'—the patient's illness— which means that the patient's death was not considered to result from suicide, since it was neither self-inflicted nor 'caused' by health professionals who honored the patient's decision to refuse treatment.[78] The Commission has not found any instances in which criminal or civil liability has been imposed upon health professionals or others (such as family members) for acquiescing in a patient's refusal of life-sustaining treatment.

> *Notes to extract*
> [77] 'There is a real and in this case determinative distinction between the unlawful taking of the life of another and the ending of artificial life support systems as a matter of self-determination.' *In Re Quinlan* 70 NJ 10, 355 A 2d 647. 670, cert denied, 429 US 922 (1976).
> [78] In the case of the competent adult's refusing medical treatment such an act does not necessarily constitute suicide since (1) in refusing treatment the patient may not have the specific intent to die, and (2) even if he did, to the extent that the cause of death was from natural causes the patient did not set the death producing agent in motion with the intent of causing his own death. Furthermore, the underlying state interest in this area lies in the prevention of irrational self-destruction. What we consider here is a competent, rational decision to refuse treatment when death is inevitable and the treatment offers no hope of cure or preservation of life. There is no connection between the conduct here in issue and any State concern to prevent suicide.
> *Superintendent of Belchertown State School v Saikewicz* 370 NE 2d 417, 426 n 11 (1977) (citations omitted); see also *Satz v Perlmutter* 362 So 2d 160 (Fla App 1978); affd 379 So 2d 359 (Fla 1980).
> Since a patient has a right to refuse life-saving treatment, that right necessarily entails a right on the part of others to effectuate the patient's refusal, and no prosecution could occur for aiding an act that is not itself a crime. 'The constitutional protection extends to third parties whose action is necessary to effectuate the exercise of that right'. *Re Quinlan* 70 NJ 10, 355 A 2d 647, 670; cert denied 429 US 922 (1976). . . .

You will notice from the reference to 'terminally ill' patients (which corresponds roughly to our category A), that the law is not different in the United States. As regards patients in category B, the New Jersey Supreme Court adopted the same view in *Re Conroy* 486 A 2d 1209 (1985) at 1224.

> **Schrieber J:** . . . In any event, declining life-sustaining medical treatment may not properly be viewed as an attempt to commit suicide. Refusing medical intervention merely allows the disease to take its natural course; if death were eventually to occur, it would be the result, primarily, of the underlying disease, and not the result of a self-inflicted injury. See *Satz v Perlmutter, supra* 362 *So* 2d at 162; *Saikewicz, supra* 373 *Mass* at 743 n 11, 370 *NE* 2d at 426 n 11; *Colyer, supra* 99 *Wash* 2d at 121, 660 *P* 2d at 743; see also *President's Commission Report, supra,* at 38 (summarising case law on the subject). But cf *In Re Caulk* NH, 480 A 2d 93 at 96–97 (1984) (stating

that attempt of an otherwise healthy prisoner to starve himself to death because he preferred death to life in prison was tantamount to attempted suicide, and that the state, to prevent such suicide, could force him to eat). In addition, people who refuse life-sustaining medical treatment may not harbor a specific intent to die, *Saikewicz, supra,* 373 *Mass* at 743, n 11, 370 *NE* 2d at 426 n 11; rather, they may fervently wish to live, but to do so free of unwanted medical technology, surgery, or drugs, and without protracted suffering, see *Satz v Perlmutter, supra,* 362 *So* 2d at 162–63 ('The testimony of Mr Perlmutter ... is that he really wants to live, but [to] do so, God and Mother Nature willing, under his own power.').

Recognising the right of a terminally ill person to reject medical treatment respects that person's intent, not to die, but to suspend medical intervention at a point consonant with the 'individual's view respecting a personally preferred manner of concluding life'. Note, 'The Tragic Choice: Termination of Care for Patients in a Permanent Vegetative State', 51 *NYUL Rev* 285, 310 (1976). The difference is between self-infliction or self-destruction and self-determination. See Byrn, 'Compulsory Lifesaving Treatment for the Competent Adult', 44 *Fordham L Rev* 1, 16–23 (1975). To the extent that our decision in *John F Kennedy Memorial Hosp v Heston,* 58 *NJ* 576, 581–82, 279 *A* 2d 670 (1971), implies the contrary, we now overrule it.

Obviously on the other hand, patients in category C would raise the suggestion that the doctor was 'aiding and abetting' suicide.

Let us now return to the relevant analaysis.

(a) CATEGORY A—THE DYING PATIENT

We are concerned with the dying. We use this description conscious of its limitations, as expressed by the President's Commission *op cit* (pp 24–26).

Other phrases—though useful as general descriptions—are similarly unacceptable when an unambiguous definition is required. For example, attempts—such as those in several statutes[43]—to make the obligations of patients and providers different when a patient is 'terminally ill' are dubious for several reasons. First, although a decision to undertake a life-sustaining treatment will frequently depend on whether the patient believes the treatment is likely to extend life substantially enough to be worth its burdens, patients with similar prognoses evaluate relevant facts very differently. The closeness of death may be strongly felt by someone who has only a remote chance of dying soon, while for another person it may not seem imminent until his or her organs have nearly ceased to function. Moreover, prognostication near the end of life is notoriously uncertain.[44] At best, confidence in predicting death is possible only in the final few hours. Patients with the same stage of a disease but with different family settings, personalities, and 'things to live for' actually do live for strikingly varied periods of time. It seems difficult to devise or to justify policies that restrict people's discretion to make appropriate decisions by allowing some choices only to 'terminally ill' patients or by denying them other choices.

Although the Commission has attempted to avoid rhetorical slogans so as to escape the ambiguities and misunderstandings that often accompany them, it uses 'dying' and 'terminally ill' as descriptive terms for certain patients, not as ironclad categories. There seem to be no other terms to use for a patient whose illness is likely to cause death within what is to that person a very short time. Of course, the word 'dying' is in some ways an unilluminating modifier for 'patient'—since life is always a 'terminal' condition—and further refinements, such as 'imminently', do little to clarify the situation. Therefore, words like 'dying' are used in this Report in their colloquial sense and with a caution against regarding them as a source of precision that is not theirs to bestow.

Notes to extract
[43] Natural Death Acts have usually tried to define a class of patients who have 'incurable injury, diseases, or illness ... where the application of life-sustaining

procedures would serve only to prolong the dying process'. Medical Treatment Decision Act. . . . The 1982 amendments to the Medicare program provide much more substantial reimbursement for 'palliation and management' of 'terminally ill' patients (defined as those for whom death is expected within six months) than for treatment of disease for these patients or for any treatment of other patients. § 122, Part II, Tax Equity and Fiscal Responsibility Act, Pub L No 97–248 (1982). . . . See also Paul Ramsey, The Patient as Person, Yale Univ Press, New Haven, Conn (1970) at 113.

[44] 'Physicians' predictions of prognosis were relatively inaccurate, with actual survival plus or minus one month coinciding with that predicted in only 16% of patients. Except in patients who were very ill and had short prognosis of three to four months, survival was consistently underestimated.' Linda J Aiken and Martita M Marx, *Hospices: Perspectives on the Public Policy Debate*, 37 Am Psychologist 1271, 1275 (1982) (reporting data from JW Yates, FP McKegney, and LE Kun, *A Comparative Study of Home Nursing Care of Patients with Advanced Cancer*, Proceedings of the Third National Conference on Human Values of Cancer, American Cancer Society, New York, 1982).

The subjective nature of prognoses affects the types of treatment that are encouraged, which in turn affects patients' outcome. In one study, physicians who preferred to intubate and artificially ventilate a patient with severe chronic lung disease projected that the patient would survive about 15 months; other physicians who decided against artificial ventilation when presented with the same case predicted that, even with artificial life support, the patient had only 6 months to live. Pearlman, Inui, and Carter, [*Variability in Physician Bioethical Decision making: A Case Study of Euthanasia*, 97 Annals Int Med 420 (1982)]. See also J Englebert Dunphy, *Annual Discourse—On Caring for the Patient with Cancer*, 295 New Eng J Med 313, 314 (1976); Mark Siegler, *Pascal's Wager and the Hanging of Crepe*, 293 New Eng J Med 853 (1985); cf Arno G Motulsky, *Biased Ascertainment and the Natural History of Disease*, 298 New Eng J Med 1196 (1978).

(i) The patient who says 'leave me alone'

1. Respecting the patient's wishes

First, we should consider the influential *Conroy* decision from New Jersey. While this case actually concerned an *incompetent* patient, the court helpfully analysed the legal issues relevant for us here in the case of a *competent* patient.

Re Conroy
486 A 2d 1209 (1985) (New Jersey Supreme Court)

Schrieber J: At issue here are the circumstances under which life-sustaining treatment may be withheld or withdrawn from incompetent, institutionalised, elderly patients with severe and permanent mental and physical impairments and a limited life expectancy. . . .

At the time of trial, Ms Conroy was no longer ambulatory and was confined to bed, unable to move from a semi-fetal position. She suffered from arteriosclerotic heart disease, hypertension, and diabetes mellitus; her left leg was gangrenous to her knee; she had several necrotic decubitus ulcers (bed sores) on her left foot, leg, and hip; an eye problem required irrigation; she had a urinary catheter in place and could not control her bowels; she could not speak; and her ability to swallow was very limited. On the other hand, she interacted with her environment in some limited ways: she could move her head, neck, hands, and arms to a minor extent; she was able to scratch herself, and had pulled at her bandages, tube, and catheter; she moaned occasionally when moved or fed through the tube, or when her bandages were changed; her eyes sometimes followed individuals in the room; her facial expressions were different when she was awake from when she was asleep; and she smiled on occasion when her hair was combed, or when she received a comforting rub.

Dr Kazemi and Dr Davidoff, a specialist in internal medicine who observed Ms Conroy before testifying as an expert on behalf of the guardian, testified that Ms Conroy was not brain dead, comatose, or in a chronic vegetative state. They stated, however, that her intellectual capacity was very limited, and that her mental condition probably would never improve. Dr Davidoff characterised her as awake, but said that she was severely demented, was unable to respond to verbal stimuli, and, as far as he could tell, had no higher functioning or consciousness. Dr Kazemi, in contrast, said that although she was confused and unaware, 'she responds somehow'.

...

The starting point in analysing whether life-sustaining treatment may be withheld or withdrawn from an incompetent patient is to determine what rights a competent patient has to accept or reject medical care. It is therefore necessary at the outset of this discussion to identify the nature and extent of a patient's rights that are implicated by such decisions.

The right of a person to control his own body is a basic societal concept, long recognised in the common law:

No right is held more sacred, or is more carefully guarded by the common law, than the right of every individual to the possession and control of his own person, free from all restraint or interference of others, unless by clear and unquestionable authority of law. As well said by Judge Cooley, 'The right to one's person may be said to be a right of complete immunity: to be let alone'. Cooley on Torts, 29. [*Union Pac Rly Co v Botsford* 141 *US* 250 at 251, 11 *S Ct* 1000 at 1001, 35 *L Ed* 734, 737 (1891) (refusing to compel personal injury plaintiff to undergo pretrial medical examination).]

Accord Perna v Pirozzi, 92 *NJ* 446 at 459–65, 457, *A* 2d 431 (1983). Judge Cardozo succinctly captured the essence of this theory as follows: 'Every human being of adult years and sound mind has a right to determine what shall be done with his own body; and a surgeon who performs an operation without his patient's consent commits an assault, for which he is liable in damages'. *Schloendorff v Society of New York Hosp* 211 *NY* 125 at 129–30, 105 *NE* 92 at 93 (1914).

The doctrine of informed consent is a primary means developed in the law to protect this personal interest in the integrity of one's body. 'Under this doctrine, no medical procedure may be performed without a patient's consent, obtained after explanation of the nature of the treatment, substantial risks, and alternative therapies.' Cantor, 'A Patient's Decision to Decline Life-Saving Medical Treatment: Bodily Integrity Versus the Preservation of Life,' 26 *Rutgers L Rev* 228, 237 (1973) (footnote omitted); see also *Perna v Pirozzi, supra*, 92 *NJ* at 461, 457 *A* 2d 431 ('Absent an emergency, patients have the right to determine not only whether surgery is to be performed on them, but who shall perform it.').

The doctrine of informed consent presupposes that the patient has the information necessary to evaluate the risks and benefits of all the available options and is competent to do so. Cf Wanzer, Adelstein, Cranford, Federman, Hook, Moertel, Safar, Stone, Taussig & Van Eys, 'The Physician's Responsibility Toward Hopelessly Ill Patients', 310 *New Eng J Med* 955, 957 (1984) ('There are three basic prerequisites for informed consent: the patient must have the capacity to reason and make judgments, the decision must be made voluntarily and without coercion, and the patient must have a clear understanding of the risks and benefits of the proposed treatment alternatives or nontreatment, along with a full understanding of the nature of the disease and the prognosis.'). In general, it is the doctor's role to provide the necessary medical facts and the patient's role to make the subjective treatment decision based on his understanding of those facts. Cf Hilfiker, *supra*, 308 *New Eng J Med* at 718 (acknowledging that 'our ability [as doctors] to phrase options, stress information, and present our own advice gives us tremendous power').

The patient's ability to control his bodily integrity through informed consent is significant only when one recognises that this right also encompasses a right to informed refusal. Note, 'Informed Consent and the Dying Patient', 83 *Yale LJ* 1632, 1648 (1974). Thus, a competent adult person generally has the right to decline to have any medical treatment initiated or continued. See *Superintendent of Belchertown*

State School v Saikewicz 373 *Mass* 728 at 738, 370 *NE* 2d 417 at 424 (1977); In *Re Quackenbush*, 156 *NJ super* 282 at 290, 383 *A* 2d 785 (Cty Ct 1978); cf *Bennan v Parsonnet*, 83 *NJL* 20 at 22–23, 26–27, 83 *A* 948 (Sup Ct 1912) (acknowledging common-law rule that patient is 'the final arbiter as to whether he shall take his chances with the operation or take his chances of living without it', but holding that surgeon had implied consent while patient was unconscious to perform necessary surgical operation).

The right to make certain decisions concerning one's body is also protected by the federal constitutional right of privacy. The Supreme Court first articulated the right of privacy in *Griswold v Connecticut*, 381 *US* 479, 85 *S Ct* 1678, 14 *L Ed* 2d 510 (1965), which held that married couples have a constitutional right to use contraceptives. The Court in *Roe v Wade*, 410 *US* 113, 93 *S Ct* 705, 35 *L Ed* 2d 147 (1973), further extended its recognition of the privacy right to protect a woman's decision to abort a pregnancy although the woman's right to choose abortion directly conflicted with the state's legitimate and important interest in preserving the potentiality of fetal life. Finally, in *Quinlan, supra* 70 *NJ* at 40, 355 *A* 2d 647, we indicated that the right of privacy enunciated by the Supreme Court 'is broad enough to encompass a patient's decision to decline medical treatment under certain circumstances', even if that decision might lead to the patient's death. *Accord Saikewicz, supra*, 373 *Mass* at 738, 370 *NE* 2d at 424; *Quackenbush, supra*, 156 *NJ Super* at 289–90, 383 *A* 2d 785. While this right of privacy might apply in a case such as this, we need not decide that issue since the right to decline medical treatment is, in any event, embraced within the common-law right to self-determination. *Accord In Re Storar* 52 *NY* 2d 363 at 376–77, 420 *NE* 2d 64 at 70, 438 *NYS* 2d 266 at 272–73; *cert* denied, 454 *US* 858, 102 *S Ct* 309, 70 *L Ed* 2d 153 (1981); Note, 'Live or Let Die; Who Decides an Incompetent's Fate? *In Re Storar* and *Eichner', 1982 BYUL Rev* 387, 390–92.

. . . In view of the case law, we have no doubt that Ms Conroy, if competent to make the decision and if resolute in her determination, could have chosen to have her nasogastric tube withdrawn. Her interest in freedom from nonconsensual invasion of her bodily integrity would outweigh any state interest in preserving life or in safeguarding the integrity of the medical profession. In addition, rejecting her artificial means of feeding would not constitute attempted suicide, as the decision would probably be based on a wish to be free of medical intervention rather than a specific intent to die, and her death would result, if at all, from her underlying medical condition, which included her inability to swallow. Finally, removal of her feeding tube would not create a public health or safety hazard, nor would her death leave any minor dependents without care or support.

Although *Conroy* is an American case, we are confident that it reflects the English common law (see *R v Blaue* [1975] 3 All ER 466, [1975] 1 WLR 1411).

You will have noticed that Schrieber J refers to the fact that the patient should be adequately informed of the available treatment options. This is to ensure that the patient in opting to forgo further treatment is made aware of what may be done for him, eg by way of symptomatic relief. Treatment, even involving surgery, may be desirable and the patient might well wish to consent to it, if aware that it could alleviate unpleasant symptoms, although it would have no effect on the underlying condition.

Clare Conroy was not competent to make a treatment decision. The principle that the court accepted was being used as a basis for recognising an *incompetent* patient's right to refuse treatment. The New Jersey Supreme Court in its subsequent decision of *Re Farrell* 529 A 2d 404 (1987), applied the principle expressed by Schrieber J in the case of a competent patient (footnotes omitted).

Garibaldi J: Kathleen [Farrell] married Francis Farrell in 1969. They had two children. Prior to her illness, Mrs Farrell worked as a keypunch operator. In November 1982, she began to experience symptoms associated with ALS [amyotrophic lateral sclerosis], a disorder of the nervous system that results in degeneration of the victim's muscles. Although it eventually renders a patient incapable of movement, ALS does not impair the patient's mental faculties. The cause of the disease is unknown and there is no available treatment or cure. At the time of diagnosis, a victim's life expectancy even with life-sustaining treatment is usually one to three years.

After she became ill, Mrs. Farrell was admitted to a Philadelphia hospital where she underwent a tracheotomy and was connected to a respirator. In the autumn of 1983, she was released from the hospital because it could provide no further help for her condition. She returned home to live with her husband and their two teenage sons. Thereafter Mrs Farrell was paralysed and confined to bed in need of around-the-clock nursing care. Insurance covered all the expenses of this care.

In November 1985, after an experimental program that her husband characterised as 'their last hope' had failed, Mrs Farrell told him that she wanted to be disconnected from the respirator that sustained her breathing. Mr Farrell told her doctor, John Pino, of her decision. The doctor advised Mrs Farrell that she would die if her respirator were removed. Dr Pino arranged for a psychologist, Dr Jean Orost, to interview Mrs Farrell. Dr Orost determined that Mrs Farrell was not clinically depressed and needed no psychiatric treatment. She concluded that Mrs Farrell had made an informed, voluntary, and competent decision to remove the respirator. Dr Orost continued to see Mrs Farrell on a weekly basis from the time of their first interview in January 1986 until her death the following June.

. . .

In resolving this case, as well as the two other cases we decide today, we build on the principles established in *Quinlan* and *Conroy*. Hence, we start by affirming the well-recognised common-law right of self-determination that '[e]very human being of adult years and sound mind has a right to determine what shall be done with his own body . . .' *Schloendorff v Society of New York Hosp*, 211 *NY* 125, 129–30, 105 *NE* 92 at 93 (1914) (Cardozo, J). In *Conroy*, we stated that '[t]he right of a person to control his own body is a basic societal concept, long recognised in the common law.' 98 *NJ* at 346, 486 *A* 2d 1209. We explained that the doctrine of 'informed consent' was developed to protect the right to self-determination in matters of medical treatment. *Id* at 346–48, 486 *A* 2d 1209. This doctrine prescribes the 'duty of a physician to disclose to a patient information that will enable him to evaluate knowledgeably the options available and the risks attendant upon each before subjecting that patient to a course of treatment'. *Perna v Pirozzi*, 92 *NJ* 446 at 459, 457 *A* 2d 431 (1983) (citations omitted); see *Conroy, supra*, 98 *NJ* at 346, 486 *A* 2d 1209.

. . .

[I]n *Conroy* we recognised the patient's right to give an informed refusal to medical treatment as the logical correlative of the right to give informed consent. We stated that 'a competent adult person generally has the right to decline to have any medical treatment initiated or continued'. *Conroy, supra*, 98 *NJ* at 347, 486 *A* 2d 1209.

While we held that a patient's right to refuse medical treatment even at the risk of personal injury or death is primarily protected by the common law, we recognised that it is also protected by the federal and state constitutional right of privacy. See *id* at 348, 486 *A* 2d 1209; *Quinlan supra*, 70 *NJ* at 38–42, 355 *A* 2d 647.

. . .

The general rule that guides us today is that the patient, his or her loved ones, and his or her doctor are the people most properly involved in medical decisions. And in the case of a competent adult patient, it is primarily that person who should make the decision. A competent person's interest in her or his self-determination generally outweighs any countervailing interest the state might have. The requirements set forth in this opinion adequately protect the competent patient without unduly restricting the patient's right to determine his or her own medical treatment.

Hence, we conclude that a competent patient like Kathleen Farrell can choose to have her life-supporting treatment discontinued. Mrs Farrell's right to live the remaining days of her life as she chose outweighed any interests the state had in compelling her to accept treatment.

2. Limits to the extent to which the patient's refusal must be respected

The court in *Conroy* was anxious to make the point that the patient's freedom to control his own fate by refusing treatment is subject to certain necessary limits. Schrieber J said:

Whether based on common-law doctrines or on constitutional theory, the right to decline life-sustaining medical treatment is not absolute. In some cases, it may yield to countervailing societal interests in sustaining the person's life. Courts and commentators have commonly identified four state interests that may limit a person's right to refuse medical treatment: preserving life, preventing suicide, safeguarding the integrity of the medical profession, and protecting innocent third parties.

We have already considered three of these interests (*supra* chs 4 and 12). Here, it may be worthwhile to examine the only interest we haven't considered namely, 'safeguarding the integrity of the medical profession'. Insofar as this goes beyond asking them to be involved in suicide and act illegally, the New Jersey Supreme Court in the subsequent case to *Conroy* of *Re Farrell (supra)*, stated:

Even as patients enjoy control over their medical treatment, health-care professionals remain bound to act in consonance with specific ethical criteria. We realise that these criteria may conflict with some concepts of self-determination. In the case of such a conflict, a patient has no right to compel a health-care provider to violate generally accepted professional standards. Cf *President's Commission Report, supra*, at 44. ('A health care professional has an obligation to allow a patient to choose from among medically accepted treatment options . . . or to reject all options. No one, however, has an obligation to provide interventions that would, in his or her judgment, be countertherapeutic.')

What sort of circumstances do you think the court has in mind?

Do you think the court in the next case correctly dealt with this issue? In *Brophy v New England Sinai Hospital* 497 NE 2d 626 (1986), the Supreme Judicial Court of Massachusetts recognised the right of an incompetent patient in a persistent vegetative state (on which see *infra*) to refuse artificial hydration and nutrition. However, the court did not require the hospital in which Brophy was, to desist from these interventions. Liacos J said:

The hospital argues that it has no constitutional, statutory, or common law right to deny nutrition and hydration to Brophy so as to bring about his death.[39] The probate judge held that the hospital and its medical staff 'should not be compelled to withhold food and water to a patient, contrary to its moral and ethical principles, when such principles are recognised and accepted within a significant segment of the medical profession and the hospital community'. We agree. Neither GL c 111, §70E (1984 ed), the Massachusetts patients' rights statute, the doctrine of informed consent, nor any other provision of law requires the hospital to cease hydration and nutrition upon request of the guardian. There is nothing in *Superintendent of Belchertown State School v Saikewicz*, 373 Mass 728, 370 NE 2d 417 (1977), and its progeny which would justify compelling medical professionals, in a case such as this, to take active measures which are contrary to their view of the ethical duty toward their patients. See *Brandt v St Vincent Infirmary*, 287 Ark 431, 701 SW 2d 103, 106–107 (1985). There is substantial disagreement in the medical community over the appropriate medical action. It would be particularly inappropriate to force the hospital, which is willing to assist in a transfer of the patient, to take affirmative steps to end the provision of nutrition and hydration to him. A patient's right to refuse medical treatment does not warrant such an unnecessary intrusion upon the hospital's ethical integrity in this case.[40]

Notes to extract

39. No one cites us any authority to the contrary. Normally, the interest in preserving the integrity of the medical profession is discussed in terms of the impact

that court authorised removal or abstention from treatment will have on the medical profession and on medical ethics generally. *Saikewicz, supra*, 373 Mass at 743–744, 370 NE 2d 417. *Re Conroy, supra*, 98 NJ at 351–353, 486 A 2d 1209. In particular, in *Saikewicz, supra*, 373 Mass at 744, 370 NE 2d 417, we noted that it was 'not necessary to deny a right of self-determination to a patient in order to recognise [such] interest'. Whatever effect our decision will generally have on medical ethics, see *supra* at 638, it is clear in this case that we can preserve the ethical integrity of the hospital and its staff without impact upon any patient right of self-determination.
40.   [footnote omitted].

Questions

(i) Do you agree with this? Should a patient's right to refuse an offer of treatment be subject to him finding a doctor who is prepared to comply with the patient's request? There was another hospital willing to accept Brophy on his terms. What would have been the position if there had not been?
(ii) Brophy was already receiving treatment. Does the decision mean that he could not have refused it *before* it had begun? If not, why should the patient subsequently be unable to require a doctor to desist from an intervention?

There is one further question concerning the limits of a patient's refusal: can it in law extend to forbidding nurses to carry out the regular activities of washing and changing and otherwise supervising the patient's general hygiene (ie 'nursing care')? In the unlikely event a patient 'turns his head to the wall' and forbids anyone to have anything to do with him, are the nurses so bound? Would this not be a clear example of a situation where the interests of others, whether health care professionals or other patients whose health might be compromised by complying with the request, would prevail over the patient's? This would mean that the patient could be bathed, cleaned and looked after against his wishes. The justification in law would rest in public policy.

The same arguments would not apply, however, where what was being considered was not 'nursing care'. Interventions, the purpose of which is not to safeguard the interests of others but to sustain the patient, call for separate analysis. Examples of such interventions are artificial hydration and nutrition. These fall to be considered within the more general question of the extent of a doctor's duty to his dying patient, to be examined next.

(ii) The patient who says 'I'm in your hands'

What is the scope and extent of the doctor's duty to care for his dying patient?

As we saw in the case of neonates, the doctor faced with a dying patient should change his treatment from treatment for living to treatment for dying. The primary duty is to comfort the patient by symptomatic relief and other appropriate care (see *re C (a minor)* (1989) discussed in postscript to ch 12). We have seen that it may include the administration of drugs which may hasten death if the primary intention is the relief of pain. In his summing up to the jury in *R v Bodkin Adams* [1957] CLR 365 (discussed *supra* ch 12), Devlin J said:

> If the first purpose of medicine, the restoration of health, can no longer be achieved there is still much for a doctor to do, and he is entitled to do all that is proper and necessary to relieve pain and suffering, even if the measures he takes may incidentally shorten life.

The obligation is discussed by the President's Commission (*op cit*) in their 1983 Report (pp 78–81).

> . . . [A]lthough medication is commonly used to relieve the suffering of dying patients (even when it causes or risks causing death), physicians are not held to have violated the law. How can this failure to prosecute be explained, since it does not rest on an explicit waiver of the usual legal rule?

The explanation lies in the importance of defining physicians' responsibilities regarding these choices and of developing an accepted and well-regulated social role that allows the choices to be made with due care. The search for medical treatments that will benefit a patient often involves risk, sometimes great risk, for the patient: for example, some surgery still carries a sizeable risk of mortality, as does much of cancer therapy. Furthermore, seeking to cure disease and to prolong life is only a part of the physician's traditional role in caring for patients; another important part is to comfort patients and relieve their suffering.[105] Sometimes these goals conflict, and a physician and patient (or patient's surrogate) have the authority to decide which goal has priority. Medicine's role in relieving suffering is especially important when a patient is going to die soon, since the suffering of such a patient is not an unavoidable aspect of treatment that might restore health, as it might be for a patient with a curable condition.

Consequently, the use of pain-relieving medications is distinguished from the use of poisons, though both may result in death, and society places the former into the category of acceptable treatment while continuing the traditional prohibition against the latter.[106] Indeed, in the Commission's view it is not only possible but desirable to draw this distinction. If physicians (and other health professionals) became the dispensers of 'treatments' that could only be understood as deliberate killing of patients, patients' trust in them might be seriously undermined.[107] And irreparable damage could be done to health care professionals' self-image and to their ability to devote themselves wholeheartedly to the often arduous task of treating gravely ill patients. Moreover, whether or not one believes there are some instances in which giving a poison might be morally permissible, the Commission considers that the obvious potential for abuse of a public, legal policy condoning such action argues strongly against it.[108]

For the use of morphine or other pain-relieving medication that can lead to death to be socially and legally acceptable, physicians must act within the socially defined bounds of their role.[109] This means that they are not only proceeding with the necessary agreement of the patient (or surrogate) and in a professionally skilful fashion (for example, by not taking a step that is riskier than necessary), but that there are sufficiently weighty reasons to run the risk of the patient dying.[110] For example, were a person experiencing great pain from a condition that will be cured in a few days, use of morphine at doses that would probably lead to death by inducing respiratory depression would usually be unacceptable. On the other hand, for a patient in great pain—especially from a condition that has proved to be untreatable and that is expected to be rapidly fatal—morphine can be both morally and legally acceptable if pain relief cannot be achieved by less risky means.

This analysis rests on the special role of physicians and on particular professional norms of acceptability that have gained social sanction (such as the difference between morphine, which can relieve pain, and strychnine, which can only cause death).[111] Part of acceptable behaviour—from the medical as well as the ethical and legal standpoints—is for the physician to take into account all the foreseeable effects, not just the intended goals, in making recommendations and in administering treatment.[112] The degree of care and judgment exercised by the physician should therefore be guided not only by the technical question of whether pain can be relieved but also by the broader question of whether care providers are certain enough of the facts in this case, including the patient's priorities and subjective experience, to risk death in order to relieve suffering. If this can be answered affirmatively, there is no moral or legal objection to using the kinds and amounts of drugs necessary to relieve the patient's pain.

Notes to extract

[105] Judicial Council, Current Opinions of the Judicial Council of the American Medical Association, American Medical Association, Chicago (1982) at 9, . . .
[106] 'Neither will I administer a poison to anybody when asked to do so, nor will I suggest such a course.' *Selections from the Hippocratic Corpus: Oath*, in Stanley Joel Reiser, Arthur J Dyck, and William J Curran, eds, Ethics in Medicine, MIT Press, Cambridge, Mass (1977) at 5.

[107] 'Euthanasia would threaten the patient-physician relationship; confidence might give way to suspicion ... Can the physician, historic battler for life, become an affirmative agent of death without jeopardising the trust of his dependants?' David W Louisell, *Euthanasia and Biathanasia: On Dying and Killing*, 40 Linacre Q 234, 243 (1973).

[108] Yale Kamisar, *Some Non-Religious Views Against Proposed 'Mercy-Killing' Legislation*, 42 Minn L Rev 696 (1958); Beauchamp, ... *John C Fletcher, Is Euthanasia Ever Justifiable?*, in Peter H Wiernik, ed, Controveries in Oncology, John Wiley & Sons, Inc, New York (1982) at 297.

[109] See Dennis Horan, *Euthanasia and Brain Death*, 35 Annals NY Acad Sci 363, 374 (1978). *Cf* Tamar Lewin, *Execution by Injection: A Dilemma for Prison Doctors*, NY Times, Dec 12, 1982, at E-20; Norman St John-Stevas, Life, Death and the Law, World Publishing Co, New York (1961) at 276–77.

[110] This consideration plays a prominent part in what is known in Catholic medical ethics as the 'doctrine of double effect'. This doctrine, which is designed to provide moral guidance for an action that could have at least one bad and one good effect, holds that such an action is permissible if it satisfies these four conditions: (1) the act itself must be morally good or neutral (for example, administering a pain-killer); (2) only the good consequences of the action must be intended (relief of the patient's suffering); (3) the good effect must not be produced by means of the evil effect (the relief of suffering must not be produced by the patient's death); and (4) there must be some weighty reason for permitting the evil (the relief of great suffering, which can only be achieved through a high risk of death). The Commission makes use of many of the moral considerations found in this doctrine, but endorses the conclusion that people are equally responsible for all of the foreseeable effects of their actions, thereby having no need for a policy that separates 'means' from 'merely foreseen consequences'. See e g, William E May, *Double Effect*, in 1 Encyclopedia of Bioethics, ... at 316; Joseph T Mangan, SJ, *An Historical Analysis of the Principle of Double Effect*, 10 Theological Stud 4 (1949); Donagan, ... Richard A McCormick, SJ, Ambiguity in Moral Choice, Marguette Univ Press, Milwaukee, Wisc (1973); J M Boyle, *Toward Understanding the Principle of Double Effect*, 90 Ethics 527 (1980).

[111] These issues were addressed in a national survey conducted for the Commission by Louis Harris and Associates. Physicians, especially, distinguished between administering drugs to relieve pain, knowing that the dose might be lethal, and complying with a patient's wish to have his or her life ended. In the case of a patient in severe pain who had no hope of recovery and who asked to have the pain eased, knowing it might shorten life, 79% of the public and 82% of the physicians said it would be ethically permissible to administer drugs to relieve the pain even at the risk of shortening life. Furthermore, 84% of physicians said they would be likely to administer such drugs under these circumstances. When asked whether the law should allow such treatment, assuming the patient has requested the drug and understands the consequences, 71% of the public and 53% of the physicians said yes. When asked whether a physician would be right or wrong to comply with the wishes of a dying patient in severe pain who directly asks to have his or her life ended, 45% of the public said it would be right. Among physicians, however just 5% thought such compliance was ethically permissible, and a mere 2% said they would comply with such a request. 52% of the public thought the law should allow physicians to comply with a request for mercy killing, but only 26% of physicians thought so. Harris ... at 217–62.

See also, John M Ostheimer, *The Polls: Changing Attitudes Toward Euthanasia*, 44 Pub Opinion Q 123 (1980).

[112] This is a weighty responsibility, and one that correctly entails serious liabilities for the physician if wrongly carried out. Society does want risky treatments to be offered and suffering to be relieved but wants to circumscribe the authority to risk life or to relieve suffering in ways expected to shorten life. One way to do so is to impose penalties for negligent or otherwise unjustified actions that lead to death, and this is the role of legal proceedings for homicide and wrongful death.

You will notice that the President's Commission refer to the need for the doctor to have the consent and co-operation of the patient and to have explained the various treatment options. In the case of a competent patient this, of course, is ordinarily a prerequisite for lawful care.

There is little English authority or writing on this subject. What writing exists mainly contents itself with an analysis of whether the doctor's conduct amounts to an act or omission for the purposes of legal analysis. We have already suggested that this is a somewhat arid approach (*supra* ch 12). It could be said, however, that much of the American case law and writing on this subject was, until *Conroy*, no more helpful since it focuses upon discrete forms of medical intervention such as nutrition or hydration. Arguably, the better analysis to adopt is to determine by way of general principle the scope and extent of the doctor's duty and then apply such principles to particular circumstances. If such an approach is adopted it will be seen immediately that hydration or nutrition or some other form of intervention *may* or *may not* be called for in a particular context, depending upon the application of the general relevant legal principle to that situation.

By contrast, to debate whether hydration or nutrition is called for as a general rule loses sight of this more principled approach. Indeed, it may be said that the true reason why American cases and scholarship are preoccupied with such questions as whether hydration is legally required is because the preoccupation is not with the doctor's duty as a matter of general principle. Rather it is with the spectre of suicide and with certain perceived state interests in preserving life. *Conroy* finally rejected what the court saw as a number of untenable approaches and adopted what we have called 'the more principled approach'.

Re Conroy 486 A 2d 1209 (1985) (Supreme Court of New Jersey)

Schrieber J: . . . [W]e reject the distinction that some have made between actively hastening death by terminating treatment and passively allowing a person to die of a disease as one of limited use in a legal analysis of such a decision-making situation.
. . . [W]e also reject any distinction between withholding and withdrawing life-sustaining treatment. . . . We also find unpersuasive the distinction relied upon by some courts, commentators, and theologians between 'ordinary' treatment, which they would always require, and 'extraordinary' treatment, which they deem optional.
. . .
Some commentators, as indeed did the Appellate Division here, 190 *NJ Super*. at 473, 464 *A*2d 303, have made yet a fourth distinction, between the termination of artificial feedings and the termination of other forms of life-sustaining medical treatment. See eg, *E. Healy, Medical Ethics* 66 (1956); *J. Piccione, Last Rights: Treatment and Care Issues in Medical Ethics* 23, 38 (1984). According to the Appellate Division:

If, as here, the patient is not comatose and does not face imminent and inevitable death, nourishment accomplishes the substantial benefit of sustaining life until the illness takes its natural course. Under such circumstances nourishment always will be an essential element of ordinary care which physicians are ethically obligated to provide. [190 *NJ Super*. at 473, 464 *A*2d 303.]

Certainly, feeding has an emotional significance. As infants we could breathe without assistance, but we were dependent on others for our lifeline of nourishment. Even more, feeding is an expression of nurturing and caring, certainly for infants and children, and in many cases for adults as well.

Once one enters the realm of complex, high-technology medical care, it is hard to shed the 'emotional symbolism' of food. See *Barber, supra*, 147 *Cal.App* 3d at 1016, 195 *Cal.Rptr*. at 490. However, artificial feedings such as nasogastric tubes, gastrostomies, and intravenous infusions are significantly different from bottle-feeding or spoonfeeding—they are medical procedures with inherent risks and possible side effects, instituted by skilled health-care providers to compensate for impaired physical functioning. Analytically, artificial feeding by means of a nasogastric tube or intravenous infusion can be seen as equivalent to artificial breathing by means of a respirator. Both prolong life through mechanical means when the body is no longer able to perform a vital bodily function on its own. *Ibid.*

Furthermore, while nasogastric feeding and other medical procedures to ensure nutrition and hydration are usually well tolerated, they are not free from risks or burdens; they have complications that are sometimes serious and distressing to the patient. *Caulk, supra*, 480 *A*2d at 99 (Douglas, J., dissenting); Lo & Dornbrand, 'Sounding Board: Guiding the Hand that Feeds: Caring for the Demented Elderly', 311 *New Eng J Med* 402, 403 (1984); Lynn & Childress, *supra*, 13 *Hastings Center Rep* at 18, 20; Paris & Fletcher, 'Infant Doe Regulations and the Absolute Requirement to Use Nourishment and Fluids for the Dying Infant', 11 *Law Med & Health Care* 210, 211–13 (1983); Zerwekh, 'The Dehydration Question', 13 *Nursing 83* 47, 49 (1983). Nasogastric tubes may lead to pneumonia, cause irritation and discomfort, and require arm restraints for an incompetent patient. Lo & Dornbrand, *supra*, 311 *New Eng J Med* at 403; Lynn & Childress, *supra*, 13 *Hastings Center Rep* at 17–18. The volume of fluid needed to carry nutrients itself is sometimes harmful. Zerwekh, *supra*, 13 *Nursing 83* at 51.

Finally, dehydration may well not be distressing or painful to a dying patient. For patients who are unable to sense hunger and thirst, withholding of feeding devices such as nasogastric tubes may not result in more pain than the termination of any other medical treatment. See Lynn & Childress, *supra*, 13 *Hastings Center Rep* at 19, 20; Paris & Fletcher, *supra*, 11 *Law Med & Health Care* at 211. Indeed, it has been observed that patients near death who are not receiving nourishment may be more comfortable than patients in comparable conditions who are being fed and hydrated artificially. See Zerwekh, *supra*, 13 *Nursing 83* at 51; Lynn & Childress, *supra*, 13 *Hastings Center Rep* at 19. Thus, it cannot be assumed that it will always be beneficial for an incompetent patient to receive artificial feeding or harmful for him not to receive it. See Wanzer, Adelstein, Cranford, Federman, Hook, Moertel, Safar, Stone, Taussig & Van Eys, *supra*, 310 *New Eng J Med* at 959 ('if [a severely and irreversibly demented] patient rejects food and water by mouth, it is ethically permissible to withhold nutrition and hydration artificially administered by vein or gastric tube. Spoon feeding should be continued if needed for comfort.')

Under the analysis articulated above, withdrawal or withholding of artificial feeding, like any other medical treatment, would be permissible if there is sufficient proof to satisfy the subjective, limited-objective, or pure-objective test [we discuss these later in this chapter]. A competent patient has the right to decline any medical treatment, including artificial feeding, and should retain that right when and if he becomes incompetent. In addition, in the case of an incompetent patient who has given little or no trustworthy indication of an intent to decline treatment and for whom it becomes necessary to engage in balancing under the limited-objective or pure-objective test, the pain and invasiveness of an artificial feeding device, and the pain of withdrawing that device, should be treated just like the results of administering or withholding any other medical treatment.

(iii)   The patient who says 'I demand . . .'

The patient, as we have seen, may absolve the doctor from his duty to provide any particular treatment by refusing that treatment. The question which remains is whether the patient may demand that the doctor exceed what would ordinarily be regarded as his duty. Admittedly, the doctor's duty contemplates the exercise of appropriate discretion, but is there a point at which the doctor is not obliged to comply with the requests or demands of his patient?

There are three issues which come to mind. The first is when the patient requests or demands a form of care which the doctor in the exercise of reasonable medical judgment determines is futile, in that it will be of no benefit of any kind to the patient. Of course, if there is some element of benefit but only at considerable cost, it is for the competent patient to be given the choice whether to opt for it or not, but this is not what we are considering here.

The second issue is more problematical. Some would argue that a doctor's duty to his patient is circumscribed by his duty to society. They would draw the implication that a doctor, in deciding whether to offer or provide a particular treatment, should consider the effect that his decision will have on overall resources. The Archbishop of Canterbury, in his Edwin Stevens lecture at the Royal Society of Medicine in 1976 (70 Proc Roy Soc Med 80), wrote:

> The doctor has a responsibility—an accountability—to the patient and the patient's family under his immediate care. But he has also a responsibility to the other patients in the long waiting queue. He has a further responsibility—to the Government, or, to put it more personally but none the less accurately, to his fellow tax-payers who provide the resources to keep the National Health Service going. The question arises as to whether some kind of consensus—I had almost said some kind of ethic—can emerge on the distribution of resources as between one part of the Health Service and another. A free-for-all could be disastrous.

What view would a court take? In our view, a court would decide that it is not the responsibility of a doctor caring for a particular patient to consider the interests of others. The fact that the patient is dying is of no consequence here. Only if the treatment is otherwise uncalled for, as being futile, would the doctor be justified in ignoring the patient's request or demand. As Robert Veatch has pointed out in his book *A Theory of Medical Ethics*, it is not for the doctor to do other than care for his patient's interests (see eg pp 281–287). To ask him to do so is to ask him to adopt an impossibly bifurcated moral position.

The third issue concerns the patient who demands that the doctor put an end to his suffering, ie kill him. Since the criminal law categorises such conduct as murder and since no one can consent to being killed, the doctor is under no duty to comply with such a demand.

(b) CATEGORY B—THE PATIENT WHO WILL DIE IF NOT GIVEN LIFE-SUSTAINING TREATMENT

(i) The patient who says 'leave me alone'

You will remember the *Bouvia* decision ((1986) 225 Cal Rptr 297 supra ch 4). The court emphasised that:

> '[A] person of adult years and in sound mind has the right, in the exercise of control over his own body, to determine whether or not to submit to lawful medical treatment.' (*Cobbs v Grant* 8 Cal 3d 229 at 242, 104 Cal Rptr 505 at 502 P.2d 1 (1972).) It follows that such a patient has the right to refuse *any* medical treatment, even that which may save or prolong her life.

As a result, you will remember the court upheld Elizabeth Bouvia's right to refuse medical intervention. The court described what would be her existence if the court were to refuse her application.

> Here, if force fed, petitioner faces 15 to 20 years of a painful existence, endurable only by the constant administrations of morphine. Her condition is irreversible. There is no cure for her palsy or arthritis. Petitioner would have to be fed, cleaned, turned, bedded, toileted by others for 15 to 20 years! Although alert, bright, sensitive, perhaps even brave and feisty, she must lie immobile, unable to exist except through physical acts of others. Her mind and spirit may be free to take great flights but she herself is imprisoned and must lie physically helpless subject to the ignominy, embarrassment, humiliation and dehumanising aspects created by her helplessness. We do not believe it is the policy of this State that all and every life must be preserved against the will of the sufferer. It is incongruous, if not monstrous, for medical practitioners to assert their right to preserve a life that someone else must

live, or, more accurately, endure, for '15 to 20 years'. We cannot conceive it to be the policy of this State to inflict such an ordeal upon anyone.

This case, therefore, makes it clear that a competent patient may refuse life-sustaining treatment even though she is not dying. It also makes it clear that the doctor still has a duty to comfort her by providing appropriate treatment for symptomatic relief unless this is also refused.

> Petitioner is without means to go to a private hospital and, apparently . . . hospital as a public facility was required to accept her. Having done so it may not deny her relief from pain and suffering merely because she has chosen to exercise her fundamental right to protect what little privacy remains to her.

The President's Commission had previously identified the principle stated in *Bouvia* as being the law in its 1983 Report (p 3):

> The voluntary choice of a competent and informed patient should determine whether or not life-sustaining therapy will be undertaken, just as such choices provide the basis for other decisions about medical treatment. Health care institutions and professionals should try to enhance patients' abilities to make decisions on their own behalf and to promote understanding of the available treatment options.
> . . . Health care professionals serve patients best by maintaining a presumption in favor of sustaining life, while recognising that competent patients are entitled to choose to forego any treatments, including those that sustain life.

The position in English law is the same. Professor Skegg in *Law, Ethics and Medicine* (1984) states the law thus (pp 156–7):

> Where the need for treatment does not result from some act of the patient's, taken with the intention of ending his own life, a doctor is rarely if ever entitled to override a patient's wishes. As the doctor is not entitled to administer treatment against the patient's wishes, there is clearly no question of his being under a duty to do so.[57] Hence in *R v Blaue*[58]—where a Jehovah's Witness refused to consent to a blood transfusion even though she knew that she would die without one—there was no hint of criticism of the doctor who respected her wishes.[59] Had she been willing to consent, the doctor would have been under a duty to provide a blood transfusion to save her life. As she refused consent the doctor was not entitled, much less obliged, to do so.[60]
> . . . [A]n adult patient's refusal of consent releases a doctor from any obligation he would otherwise be under, to save the patient's life. The doctor will not be in breach of his duty in allowing the patient to die.

Notes to extract
[57] He may, however, be under a duty to inform the patient of the likely consequences of his refusal.
[58] [1975] 3 All ER 466, [1975] 1 WLR 1411.
[59] Blaue was the original assailant, who was indicted for murder. Had there been grounds for criticising the doctor's omission to act, Blaue's counsel could have been expected to suggest that the doctor's conduct contributed to a break in the chain of causation between Blaue's acts and the girl's death.
[60] This point appears to have been overlooked in *R v Stone* [1977] QB 354, [1977] 2 All ER 341—although see National Assistance Act 1948, s 47.

The California Court of Appeal in *Bartling v Superior Court* 209 Cal Rptr 220 (1984) in affirming the approach of the law set out above, also confirmed the view expressed earlier as regards patients in category A that the patient's conduct does not amount to suicide in these circumstances.

Hastings, Associate Justice: In this case we are called upon to decide whether a competent adult patient, with serious illnesses which are probably incurable but have not been diagnosed as terminal, has the right, over the objection of his physicians and the hospital, to have life-support equipment disconnected despite the fact that withdrawal of such devices will surely hasten his death.

... Mr. Bartling was 70-years-old and suffered from emphysema, chronic respiratory failure, arteriosclerosis, an abdominal aneurysm (abnormal ballooning of the main artery passing through the abdomen to the legs), and a malignant tumor of the lung. Mr. Bartling also had a history of what real parties term 'chronic acute anxiety/depression' and alcoholism.

Mr. Bartling entered Glendale Adventist on April 8, 1984, for treatment of his depression. A routine physical examination, including a chest x-ray, was performed, and a tumor was discovered on Mr. Bartling's lung. A biopsy of the tumor was performed by inserting a needle in the lung, which caused the lung to collapse. Tubes were inserted in Mr. Bartling's chest and through his nasal passage and throat in order to reinflate his lung. Because of his emphysema, the hole made by the biopsy needle did not heal properly and the lung did not reinflate. While Mr. Bartling was being treated with antibiotics to promote healing of the lung, a tracheotomy was performed and he was placed on a ventilator . . .

Several doctors also expressed the view that disconnecting Mr. Bartling's ventilator would have been tantamount to aiding a suicide. This is not a case, however, where real parties would have brought about Mr. Bartling's death by unnatural means by disconnecting the ventilator. Rather, they would merely have hastened his inevitable death by natural causes. (*Satz v Perlmutter, supra*, 362 So2d 160, 162–163). Several cases have, to our satisfaction, placed this issue to rest. In *Re Quinlan, supra*, 70 NJ 10, 355 A2d 647 (1976), the court stated: 'We would see, however, a real distinction between the self-infliction of deadly harm and a self-determination against artificial life-support or radical surgery, for instance, in the face of irreversible, painful and certain imminent death.' (355 A2d at p 665.) And in *Superintendent of Belchertown v Saikewicz, supra*, 370 NE2d 417, the court succinctly answers this argument as follows: 'The interest in protecting against suicide seems to require little if any discussion. In the case of the competent adult's refusing medical treatment such an act does not necessarily constitute suicide since (1) in refusing treatment the patient may not have the specific intent to die, and (2) even if he did, to the extent that the cause of death was from natural causes the patient did not set the death producing agent in motion with the intent of causing his own death . . . Furthermore, the underlying State interest in this area lies in the prevention of irrational self-destruction. What we consider here is a competent, rational decision to refuse treatment when death is inevitable and the treatment offers no hope of cure or preservation of life. There is no connection between the conduct here in issue and any State concern to prevent suicide.' (370 NE2d at p 426, fn 11.)

The court upheld Bartling's right to refuse medical treatment. This, in our view, also represents the law for a patient in our category B.

2. The patient who says 'I'm in your hands'

The issue which arises here is what is the duty of a doctor when caring for a patient who comes within category B in the absence of any specified instructions from the patient? Apart from the obligation to seek to consult his patient, the doctor will ordinarily be held to the duty of care which applies generally in the care of any patient. The particular circumstances of a patient in this category may, however, give rise to a variation in the doctor's duty. The patient may be suffering from an underlying condition which, though not fatal, condemns him to a life which on an objective standard would be regarded as insufferable or intolerable.

Here, the doctor may have to consider whether further treatment including life-sustaining treatment is called for or whether it would be classified as 'extraordinary' or not morally obligatory. If, for example, the life-sustaining treatment could at best only succeed in returning the patient to a life of suffering or worse, we have seen already (*supra*) that the doctor may be under no duty to provide the treatment. In essence, the analysis here is no different from that which applies to the case of the incompetent patient in this category which we will examine more fully shortly. We leave the detailed analysis until then.

(iii)　The patient who says 'I demand . . .'

As we have seen, there are no circumstances here (as elsewhere) in which a patient may *insist* that a doctor goes beyond that which in objective terms is seen to be the extent of the doctor's legal duty. We have seen, however, that the doctor may retain a discretion to do so in certain circumstances, subject to available resources.

(c)　CATEGORY C—THE PATIENT WHO WISHES TO DIE WHATEVER HIS CONDITION AND ASKS TO BE ASSISTED TO DIE.

The legal position is explained by Professor Glanville Williams in his *Textbook of Criminal Law* (2nd ed 1983, pp 579–80).

A person cannot consent to his own death. The rule is not based upon utilitarian considerations even though these may sometimes buttress it. It is a theocratic survival in our predominantly secular law; and religious ('transcendental') arguments are still its main support.

What is the difference between killing a person with his consent and assisting his suicide?

The first is generally murder, while the second is the statutory offence just considered. The distinction between them is the distinction between perpetrators and accessories. If a doctor, to speed his dying patient's passing, injects poison with the patient's consent, this will be murder; but if the doctor places the poison by the patient's side, and the patient takes it, this will be suicide in the patient and the doctor's guilt will be of the abetment offence under the Suicide Act (not abetment in murder). Although this is the theoretical distinction, a case of consent-killing is occasionally reduced to one of assisting suicide.[1]

The distinction may be thought to have no moral relevance, since the doctor assists the patient's death in both cases. But one or two points may be made. If V asks D to help him to die, D may reasonably say: 'I do not approve of what you propose, and will not do the job for you. But you are entitled to act on your own responsibility; and since you are ill and cannot obtain the means of suicide yourself. I do not mind supplying them to you.' Besides this, the fact that the patient takes the poison with his own hand helps to allay fears that perhaps he did not really consent. Suicide is more clearly an act of self-determination than consent to be killed, and requires greater strength of purpose.[2]

The question may again be asked whether there is any social value in denying the doctor's right to help his patient in this way in terminal cases. Several unsuccessful attempts have been made to change the law, but they have foundered because of the united opposition of the churches and of the medical profession itself. Doctors fear that if they were given the legal power to terminate their patient's lives, although with consent, they would lose the confidence of their patients.[3]

Notes to extract
[1] Eg *Robey* (1971) 1 CAR(S) 127.
[2] On the ethics of the matter see Glover, [*Causing Death and Saving Lives* (1977)] 183–184.
[3] The third Bill introduced by Lady Wootton in the House of Lords on behalf of the Voluntary Euthanasia Society in 1975 provided that 'an incurable patient who

causes his own death by overdosing or other intentional action shall be deemed to have died by misadventure'. This would allow recovery on a policy of life insurance, and a physician who knowingly provided the overdose would not be guilty of assisting suicide. The Bill was rejected.

The German code establishes a compromise offence of killing on request, punishable with 5 years' imprisonment (Fletcher, *Rethinking Criminal Law* 332). The CLRC in its Working Paper on OAP tentatively proposed an offence of mercy-killing punishable with 2 years' imprisonment, but this modest suggestion for an alleviation of the law (which would not have gone so far in leniency as the present practice of the courts) met with immense opposition from Christian bodies and societies, and the committee became fearful that continuing it would imperil the larger reform. So the proposal disappeared without trace in the final Report.

There is now a large literature on the legislation of voluntary death. My own views and suggestions will be found in my book *The Sanctity of Life and the Criminal Law*, Chap 8 and in 63 Proc Roy Soc Med 663 and 41 Medico-Legal Journal 14 (reprinted in part in *Beneficent Euthanasia*, ed M Kohl (Buffalo, NY 1975) 145). The opposing views were debated by Kamisar and myself in 42 Minn LRev 969; 43 *ibid* 1 (reprinted in part in *Euthanasia and the Right to Death*, ed A B Downing (London 1969) 85, in *Social Ethics*, ed Mappes and Zembaty (New York 1977) 44, in *Contemporary Issues in Bioethics*, ed Tom L Beauchamp and LeRoy Walters (Encino, Calif 1978) 308, in *Ethical Issues in Death and Dying*, ed Beauchamp and Perlin (Englewood Cliffs, NJ 1978) 2201, and in *Applying Ethics*, ed Vincent Barry (Belmont, Calif 1981) 239. See also J Glover, *op cit* Chaps 3.14. A full presentation of the case against is *Your Death Warrant?* ed J Gould and Lord Craigmyle (London 1971).

The Archbishop of Canterbury, Dr Coggan, in his Stevens Memorial Lecture, quoted writings against the legislation of euthanasia and said: 'The warnings given in these books seem to me to be so weighty as to make the case very strong indeed for leaving the issues much as they now are in the hands of doctors' (70 Proc Roy Soc Med 80). The lawyer must, however, comment that at present the law does not leave the issue in the hands of doctors: it treats euthanasia as murder.

You will notice that in footnote 3 Professor Williams refers to the deliberations of the Criminal Law Revision Committee. Roger Leng discusses these, and the present law, in further detail in his article 'Mercy Killing and the CLRC' (1982) NLJ 76.

Recent history of the problem

Prior to 1957 cases of compassionate killing were in theory murder and subject to the death penalty. The rigidity of this position was in a number of ways modified, making it very unlikely that a genuine 'mercy killer' would actually suffer the ultimate penalty. First the mercy killer might benefit from the exercise of prosecutorial discretion. In giving evidence to the Royal Commission on Capital Punishment 1949–53 (The Gowers Commission) the then Director of Public Prosecutions stated that in cases of doubt as between murder and manslaughter his instinct was to choose the lesser charge. Many mercy killings, committed in private with resort to less violent means of death, would fall into this doubtful category. However, the DPP's decision might always be overridden by the magistrates choosing to commit for murder in appropriate cases. Secondly, the Gowers Commission recognised the existence of a significant number of verdicts of acquittal which might be characterised as sympathetic or perverse depending upon one's view of the role of the jury. Thirdly, mercy-killings which in fact resulted in murder convictions would almost invariably be subject to commutation of sentence by the Home Secretary, frequently following a recommendation to that effect from the jury. In evidence to the Gowers Commission the Home Office attempted to explain jury recommendations of mercy and concluded that 1071 cases in the period 1900–1949 could be attributed to the 'pitiable circumstances' of the case. It is likely that this figure contained a high proportion of mercy-killings. The commutation of the death sentence to 'life' would frequently be followed by early release.

Many bodies and individuals giving evidence to the Gowers Commission favoured legal recognition of the practical position that mercy killers were not dealt with as murderers. The Society of Labour Lawyers (supported by Lord Denning) recommended a provision on the following lines:

If a person who has killed another proves that he killed that person with the compassionate intention of saving him physical or mental suffering, he shall not be guilty of murder.

The Commission foresaw difficulties in proving or disproving the necessary motive in court and consequently considered that the provision might be open to abuse. Moreover, the courts would have great difficulty in dealing with cases of actual or potential mixed motive, such as the daughter who killed an invalid father where the motive might be compassion, gain or removal of inconvenience.

The Commission 'reluctantly' rejected the proposal but nevertheless considered that true mercy killers should be excepted from the penalty for murder. This would be accomplished either by the exercise of executive discretion by the Home Secretary or (its preferred alternative) by a binding recommendation from the jury. The proposal was not really coherent. If the mitigation of sentence were to be achieved by Home Secretary's licence he would be faced with precisely the same problem in determining motive but without the jury's advantages in hearing the evidence, observing the demeanour of the defendant, etc. If the decision were to be taken by the jury they would have to apply some criteria, and would surely have to be guided by the judge. Again precisely the same problems of definition and proof would arise.

No change in law or practice directly relating to mercy killing resulted from the Gowers Report. However, as it turned out, the enactment of another of its recommendations, the creation of diminished responsibility by s 2 of the Homicide Act 1957, achieved by a back door what it has declined to recommend openly. . . .

In 1970 the Home Secretary referred the whole of the law concerning offences against the person, including homicide, to the Criminal Law Revision Committee and it became pertinent to consider whether the practice of the Courts in dealing with the compassionate killer under s 2 should be regularised by the creation of a specific category of homicide. In the CLRC's twelfth report on the *Penalty for Murder*, published in 1972, mention was made of certain tragic cases including compassionate killing where special considerations applied and where it should be made possible by means of a special provision for the judge to make a hospital or probation order or even, where appropriate, to grant a conditional discharge (para 42). This provisional conclusion was prompted by a recognition that whereas some such cases might be dealt with satisfactorily under s 2, in others there might be insufficient evidence of mental abnormality to found that defence but nevertheless the objective circumstances of the victim and the motive of the killer would justify disposal other than as for murder.

This realistic switch of emphasis away from the accused's state of mind to the circumstances and related motives involved in the case was reflected in the bold provisional proposal in the CLRC's 1976 *Working Paper on Offences Against the Person* of a new offence of mercy killing, subject to a maximum sentence of two years' imprisonment. The proposed offence would have applied where a person from compassion unlawfully killed another where the accused with reasonable cause believed that the victim was (i) permanently subject to great bodily pain or suffering, or (ii) permanently helpless from bodily or mental incapacity or (iii) subject to rapid and incurable bodily or mental degeneration.

The CLRC's fourteenth report (1980)

In the Committee's final report on *Offences Against the Person* (1980, para 115) the mercy killing proposal was summarily dropped on the ground that it was too controversial for the exercise in law reform on which the Committee was engaged. This conclusion sits very uneasily with comments made in the same paragraph describing compassionate killing as giving rise to a sentencing problem and pointing out that when an actual case of this nature arises 'no one connected with the case wishes to see the defendant convicted of murder'. . . .

A number of issues require examination. What is the ethical position entailed in recommending a mercy killing defence? Is the CLRC an appropriate body to make such a proposal? How controversial would it be? Is the diminished responsibility defence in present or amended form capable of accommodating the range of killings which by virtue of compassionate motive require to be treated as something less than murder?

The major argument addressed to the CLRC against its original 1976 proposal was that it would mean that the sick and the handicapped would receive less protection from the law than the well and the able-bodied. This is an argument about degrees not absolutes since whether a killing is treated as murder or mercy killing it would remain a serious criminal offence and subject to punishment. Further the objection rests upon an assumption that the potential mercy killer will be deterred more or less according to the punishment which he anticipates. Although the psychological effects of formal deterrents are not susceptible to empirical research the traditional view is that deterrence is more effective in relation to crimes rationally designed to improve the position of the wrong-doer (eg theft) but less effective where the criminal act is prompted by some strong emotion which cannot be rationally suppressed. It is submitted that in true cases of mercy killing the prospect of a particular type of punishment is unlikely to govern the degree of deterrence.

If this is right the major ethical question is not whether killing in certain circumstances should be allowed or partially justified. Rather the real ethical problem focuses on the killer. Having done the totally prohibited act how should he be dealt with?

The Committee was impressed by representations to the effect that as lawyers they had no special qualifications for solving fundamental ethical problems. As a basis for proposing no change this is open to a number of objections. First it was not its task to decide to whom the fundamental ethical question should be addressed. Rightly or wrongly the question of the appropriate legal response to the compassionate killer fell within its general remit. It was its task to answer it within the limits of its own competence. In refusing, it implicitly misstated its own role, which in fact was to propose reform, for which the final responsibility for enactment or non-enactment would rest with Parliament. If Parliament is to fulfil its function of resolving difficult ethical dilemmas it cannot work in a vacuum but must be provided with foundations on which to build a structure of discussion. If the CLRC considered that mercy killing posed problems of sentencing which could not be resolved within the conceptual and practical framework of murder, it was its duty to say so and propose reform leaving it to Parliament to temper the lawyers' view with broader considerations and perhaps reject the proposal.

In stating that the original proposal would be too 'controversial' to be included in its final Report, the CLRC is using 'controversial' in a very limited sense. It clearly does not mean that the actual practice of treating mercy killers as other than murderers is open to such grave objections that it should not be proposed, for this is the very practice which it hopes will continue. What it actually means is that to embody the practice in an unequivocal legal provision would create a terrible fuss and might cause more trouble than it is worth. This hypocrisy will remain politically sensible while it is assumed that in all appropriate cases mercy killers can be dealt with under diminished responsibility. Is this assumption sound?

Mercy killers are not all alike: they occupy a continuum which stretches from the mother, so deranged by constant reminders of her child's suffering that she cannot control her desire to end the child's misery, to the parents who, having rationally weighed up all factors, consider that it is their responsibility to the child to end the suffering. The former clearly falls within the terms of s 2, the latter, on strict application of that provision, does not. Many would consider that the formal legal response to each case should be flexible to allow the judge to sentence in an appropriate manner. The CLRC fondly hopes that the connivances of psychiatrists and judges will continue to accommodate the latter case without the need for legislative change. This hope may be fulfilled but there is evidence that the appeal judges are losing patience with pleas of diminished responsibility in their more extravagant and less legally justified forms. As Lawton LJ [the chairman of the CLRC in 1980] said in *Vinagre* (1979) 69 Cr App R 104 'it was never intended that pleas should be introduced on such flimsy grounds . . . cases are tried by the court not by psychiatrists . . . pleas to manslaughter on the ground of diminished responsibility should only be accepted where there is clear evidence of mental imbalance'. Those words were spoken in a different context, and even if applied to a mercy killing would perhaps only entail a shift from plea acceptance to a similar jury verdict. Nevertheless, the statement indicates the strain placed upon the Courts, psychiatrists and the substance of the law by present practice in mercy killing cases and might suggest that it is time that this 'fundamental ethical issue' should cease to be dealt with in an *ad hoc* fashion by the Courts and be resolved by a general statutory provision recognising mercy killing as a ground for mitigation in its own right.

Do you agree? Would doctors be comfortable with (and accept) the role of the 'mercy killer'? (For a discussion see Wanzer *et al*, 'The Physician's Responsibility Towards Hopelessly Ill Patients' (1989) 320 New Eng J Med 844—favouring assisting suicide but more circumspect concerning active killing).

The incompetent patient

We assume here that the patient will have been found incompetent by reference to the relevant legal tests discussed at length earlier (*supra* ch 4). Further, we have seen that the law provides a justification for the doctor to treat the incompetent patient who, by definition, is unable to consent to such treatment (recently accepted by the House of Lords in *re F* (1989) discussed in *postscript* to ch 7). This may be subject to what we say later concerning any directive made prior to the onset of incompetence.

(a) CATEGORY A—THE DYING PATIENT

If the doctor's duty is to care for his dying patient, the problem is one of determining which treatment option is appropriate in the absence of being able to consult the patient. The law here is the same as we have already seen in the context of the competent dying patient. The doctor's duty is to comfort the patient, relieve symptoms but not to engage in that which is futile.

The American jurisprudence on the treatment of the incompetent tends to confuse the patient who is dying, for whom there is no prospect of cure or prevention of the continued progress of the disease to death (our category A), with those patients who are very ill and may be dying but for whom treatment holds out some hope of remission, if not cure, albeit not without burdening the patient.

We take the view that this latter group should be properly considered in our category B, since the American jurisprudence is concerned with the debate about which *treatment* option should be chosen and who should make the choice. Implicit in those questions is the assumption that the choice will materially affect the progress and the eventual fate of the patient.

(b) CATEGORY B—THE PATIENT WHO IS NOT DYING (AS DEFINED IN A) BUT WHO WILL DO SO IF NOT GIVEN LIFE-SUSTAINING TREATMENT

(i) Factual situations

Factually, within this category, there may be three groups of patient as reflected in the American case law. The law applicable to them, as we shall discover, may be the same.

Group 1. The patient who is ill and may be dying but for whom there is some therapy available. The therapy offers the possibility of benefit to the patient but is accompanied by very considerable risks of harm. The patient, by virtue of being incompetent, cannot evaluate the relevant factors and make a choice whether to have the therapy. Indeed, the choice may be between competing therapies.

The paradigm case is *Superintendent of Belchertown State School v Saikewicz* 307 NE 2d 417 (1976).

Group 2. The patient who is ill and falls victim to a supervening illness which is life threatening. An example would be a patient suffering from senile dementia who falls victim of 'end-stage' renal failure.

Illustrative cases of this group of patients are *Re Spring* 405 NE 2d 115 (1980) and *Re Dinnerstein* 380 NE 2d 134 (1978).

Group 3. The patient who is in a 'persistent vegetative state'. This is the patient who has suffered irreversible loss of higher brain function (see *infra* ch 15) but continues to breathe (without necessarily requiring recourse to a respirator) and, if appropriately cared for, may survive for an extended period of time.

The paradigm case is *Re Quinlan* 355 A 2d 647 (1976).

(ii) Legal themes

In analysing the law as it applies to these groups of patients, the question to be kept in mind, as we have seen, is: how does the doctor decide what to do when he cannot ask the patient? Does he apply (a) 'substituted judgment' which we saw earlier (*supra* chs 4 and 12)? As a criterion its aim is to apply a more or less subjective test so as to give effect to what the patient would have wished. Or does he apply (b) some form of more objective judgment whereby a view is arrived at as to what is in the patient's best interests. (We will return to this tentative explanation of 'substituted judgment' later.)

Depending upon the test used by the doctor, it is clear that he may have to refer to others, whether relatives, friends or even the court. A final question then arises. Having decided what he thinks is right in law, does the doctor have to go to court to confirm his decision or if he properly applies the relevant legal criteria, can he make the decision himself? Of course, in this latter case it would always be open to a court to review the propriety of his action. We saw this issue arise in our discussion of treating handicapped neonates in chapter 12.

(iii) The law

There is again a complete absence of English case law to guide us to the English law. Again, therefore, we must look to other common law jurisdictions. In effect, this means we must look to the United States since only there have the relevant issues been litigated. Our view is that an English court with a case of the type described would reflect the analysis contained in the United States cases.

1. Group 1 patients

Superintendent of Belchertown v Saikewicz 370 NE 2d 417 (1976) (Supreme Judicial Court of Massachusetts) (footnotes omitted)

Liacos J: . . . Joseph Saikewicz, at the time the matter arose, was sixty-seven years old, with an IQ of ten and a mental age of approximately two years and eight months. He was profoundly mentally retarded. The record discloses that, apart from his leukemic condition, Saikewicz enjoyed generally good health. He was physically strong and well built, nutritionally nourished, and ambulatory. He was not, however, able to communicate verbally—resorting to gestures and grunts to make his wishes known to others and responding only to gestures or physical contacts. In the course of treatment for various medical conditions arising during Saikewicz's residency at the school, he had been unable to respond intelligibly to inquiries such as whether he was experiencing pain. It was the opinion of a consulting psychologist, not contested by the other experts relied on the judge below, the Saikewicz was not aware of dangers and was disoriented outside his immediate environment. As a result of his condition, Saikewicz had lived in State institutions since 1923 and had resided at the Belchertown State School since 1928. Two of his sisters, the only members of his family who could be located, were notified of his condition and of the hearing, but they preferred not to attend or otherwise become involved.

On April 19, 1976, Saikewicz was diagnosed as suffering from acute myeloblastic monocytic leukemia . . .

Chemotherapy, as was testified to at the hearing in the Probate Court, involves the administration of drugs over several weeks, the purpose of which is to kill the leukemia cells. This treatment unfortunately affects normal cells as well. . . . Estimates of the effectiveness of chemotherapy are complicated in cases, such as the one presented here, in which the patient's age becomes a factor. According to the medical testimony before the court below, persons over age sixty have more difficulty tolerating chemotherapy and the treatment is likely to be less successful than in younger patients. This prognosis may be compared with the doctor's estimates that, left untreated, a patient in Saikewicz's condition would live for a matter of weeks or, perhaps, several months. According to the testimony, a decision to allow the disease to run its natural course would not result in pain for the patient, and death would probably come without discomfort.

An important facet of the chemotherapy process, to which the judge below directed careful attention, is the problem of serious adverse side effects caused by the treating drugs. Among these side effects are severe nausea, bladder irritation, numbness and tingling of the extremities, and loss of hair. The bladder irritation can be avoided, however, if the patient drinks fluids, and the nausea can be treated by drugs. It was the opinion of the guardian *ad litem*, as well as the doctors who testified before the probate judge, that most people elect to suffer the side effects of chemotherapy rather than to allow their leukemia to run its natural course.

Drawing on the evidence before him including the testimony of the medical experts, and the report of the guardian *ad litem*, the probate judge issued detailed findings with regard to the costs and benefits of allowing Saikewicz to undergo chemotherapy. The judge's findings are reproduced in part here because of the importance of clearly delimiting the issues presented in this case. The judge below found:

5. That the majority of persons suffering from leukemia who are faced with a choice of receiving or foregoing such chemotherapy, and who are able to make an informed judgment thereon, choose to receive treatment in spite of its toxic side effects and risks of failure.

6. That such toxic side effects of chemotherapy include pain and discomfort, depressed bone marrow, pronounced anemia, increased chance of infection, possible bladder irritation, and possible loss of hair.

7. That administration of such chemotherapy requires cooperation from the patient over several weeks of time, which cooperation said Joseph Saikewicz is unable to give due to his profound retardation.

8. That, considering the age and general state of health of said Joseph Saikewicz, there is only a 30–40 percent chance that chemotherapy will produce a remission of said leukemia, which remission would probably be for a period of time of from 2 to 13 months, but that said chemotherapy will certainly not completely cure such leukemia.

9. That if such chemotherapy is to be administered at all it should be administered immediately, inasmuch as the risks involved will increase and the chances of successfully bringing about remission will decrease as time goes by.

10. That, at present, said Joseph Saikewicz's leukemia condition is stable and is not deteriorating.

11. That said Joseph Saikewicz is not now in pain and will probably die within a matter of weeks or months a relatively painless death due to the leukemia unless other factors should intervene to themselves cause death.

12. That it is impossible to predict how long said Joseph Saikewicz will probably live without chemotherapy or how long he will probably live with chemotherapy, but it is to a very high degree medically likely that he will die sooner, without treatment than with it.

Balancing these various factors, the judge concluded that the following considerations weighed *against* administering chemotherapy to Saikewicz: '(1) his age, (2) his inability to cooperate with the treatment, (3) probable adverse side effects of treatment, (4) low chance of producing remission, (5) the certainty that treatment will cause immediate suffering, and (6) the quality of life possible for him even if the treatment does bring about remission.'

The following considerations were determined to weigh in *favor* of chemotherapy: '(1) the chance that his life may be lengthened thereby; and (2) the fact that most people in his situation when given a chance to do so elect to take the gamble of treatment.'

Concluding that, in this case, the negative factors of treatment exceeded the benefits, the probate judge ordered on May 13, 1976, that no treatment be administered to Saikewicz for his condition of acute myeloblastic monocytic leukemia except by further order of the court. The judge further ordered that all reasonable and necessary supportive measures be taken, medical or otherwise, to safeguard the well-being of Saikewicz in all other respects and to reduce as far as possible any suffering or discomfort which he might experience.

. . .

Saikewicz died on September 4, 1976, at the Belchertown State School hospital. Death was due to bronchial pneumonia, a complication of the leukemia. Saikewicz died without pain or discomfort.

. . .

The question what legal standards govern the decision whether to administer potentially life-prolonging treatment to an incompetent person encompasses two distinct and important subissues. First, does a choice exist? That is, is it the unvarying responsibility of the State to order medical treatment in all circumstances involving the care of an incompetent person? Second, if a choice does exist under certain conditions, what considerations enter into the decision-making process?

We think that principles of equality and respect for all individuals require the conclusion that a choice exists. . . . we recognise a general right in all persons to refuse medical treatment in appropriate circumstances. The recognition of that right must extend to the case of an incompetent, as well as a competent, patient because the value of human dignity extends to both.

This is not to deny that the State has a traditional power and responsibility, under the doctrine of *parens patriae*, to care for and protect the 'best interests' of the incompetent person. Indeed, the existence of this power and responsibility has impelled a number of courts to hold that the 'best interests' of such a person mandate an unvarying responsibility by the courts to order necessary medical treatment for an incompetent person facing an immediate and severe danger to life. *Application of the President & Directors of Georgetown College, Inc*, 118 US App DC 80, 331 F 2d 1000; cert denied 377 US 978, 84 S Ct 1883, 12 L Ed 2d 746 (1964). *Long Island Jewish-Hillside Medical Center v Levitt*, 73 Misc 2d 395, 342 NYS 2d 356 (NY Sup Ct 1973). Cf *In Re Weberlist*, 79 Misc 2d 753, 360 NYS 2d 783 (NY Sup Ct 1974). Whatever the merits of such a policy where life-saving treatment is available—a situation unfortunately not presented by this case—a more flexible view of the 'best interests' of the incompetent patient is not precluded under other conditions. For example, other courts have refused to take it on themselves to order certain forms of treatment or therapy which are not immediately required although concededly beneficial to the innocent person. *In Re CFB*, 497 SW 2d 831 (Mo App 1973). *Green's*

Appeal, 448 Pa 338, 292 A 2d 387 (1972). *In Re Frank*, 41 Wash 2d 294, 248 P 2d 553 (1952). Cf *In Re Rotkowitz*, 175 Misc 948, 25 NYS 2d 624 (NY Dom Rel Ct 1941); *Mitchell v Davis*, 205 SW 2d 812 (Tex App 1947). While some of these cases involved children who might eventually be competent to make the necessary decisions without judicial interference, it is also clear that the additional period of waiting might make the task of correction more difficult. See, e g, *In Re Frank, supra*. These cases stand for the proposition that, even in the exercise of the *parens patriae* power, there must be respect for the bodily integrity of the child or respect for the rational decision of those parties, usually the parents, who for one reason or another are seeking to protect the bodily integrity or other personal interest of the child. See *In Re Hudson*, 13 Wash 2d 673, 126 P 2d 765 (1942).

The 'best interests' of an incompetent person are not necessarily served by imposing on such persons results not mandated as to competent persons similarly situated. It does not advance the interest of the State or the ward to treat the ward as a person of lesser status or dignity than others. To protect the incompetent person within its power, the State must recognise the dignity and worth of such a person and afford to that person the same panoply of rights and choices it recognises in competent persons. If a competent person faced with death may choose to decline treatment which not only will not cure the person but which substantially may increase suffering in exchange for a possible yet brief prolongation of life, then it cannot be said that it is always in the 'best interests' of the ward to require submission to such treatment. Nor do statistical factors indicating that a majority of competent persons similarly situated choose treatment resolve the issue. The significant decisions of life are more complex than statistical determinations. Individual choice is determined not by the vote of the majority but by the complexities of the singular situation viewed from the unique perspective of the person called on to make the decision. To presume that the incompetent person must always be subjected to what many rational and intelligent persons may decline is to downgrade the status of the incompetent person by placing a lesser value on his intrinsic human worth and vitality.

The trend in the law has been to give incompetent persons the same rights as other individuals. *Boyd v Registrars of Voters of Belchertown*, 368 Mass ——c, 334 NE 2d 629 (1975). Recognition of this principle of equality requires understanding that in certain circumstances it may be appropriate for a court to consent to the withholding of treatment from an incompetent individual. This leads us to the question of how the right of an incompetent person to decline treatment might best be exercised so as to give the fullest possible expression to the character and circumstances of that individual.

The problem of decision-making presented in this case is one of first impression before this court, and we know of no decision in other jurisdictions squarely on point. The well publicised decision of the New Jersey Supreme Court in *Re Quinlan*, 70 NJ 10, 355 A 2d 647 (1976), provides a helpful starting point for analysis, however.

Liacos J then set out the facts of *Quinlan* (for this case see *infra*) and continued:

The exposition by the New Jersey court of the principle of substituted judgment, and of the legal standards that were to be applied by the guardian in making this decision, bears repetition here.

If a putative decision by Karen to permit this non-cognitive, vegetative existence to terminate by natural forces is regarded as a valuable incident of her right of privacy, as we believe it to be, then it should not be discarded solely on the basis that her condition prevents her conscious exercise of the choice. The only practical way to prevent destruction of the right is to *permit the guardian and family of Karen to render their best judgment*, subject to the qualifications [regarding consultation with attending physicians and hospital 'Ethics Committee'] hereinafter stated, *as to whether she would exercise it in these circumstances*. If their conclusion is in the affirmative this decision should be accepted by a society the overwhelming majority of whose members would, we think, in similar circumstances, exercise such a choice in the same way for themselves or for those closest to them. It is for this reason that we determine that Karen's right of privacy may be asserted in her behalf, in this respect, by her guardian and family under the particular circumstances presented by this record (emphasis supplied). *Id* at 41–42, 355 A 2d 647.

The court's observation that most people in like circumstances would choose a natural death does not, we believe, detract from or modify the central concern that the guardian's decision conform, to the extent possible, to the decision that would have been made by Karen Quinlan herself. Evidence that most people would or would not act in a certain way is certainly an important consideration in attempting to ascertain the predilections of any individual, but care must be taken, as in any analogy, to ensure that operative factors are similar or at least to take notice of the dissimilarities. With this in mind, it is profitable to compare the situations presented in the *Quinlan* case and the case presently before us. Karen Quinlan, subsequent to her accident, was totally incapable of knowing or appreciating life, was physically debilitated, and was pathetically reliant on sophisticated machinery to nourish and clean her body. Any other person suffering from similar massive brain damage would be in a similar state of total incapacity, and thus it is not unreasonable to give weight to a supposed general, and widespread, response to the situation.

Karen Quinlan's situation, however, must be distinguished from that of Joseph Saikewicz. Saikewicz was profoundly mentally retarded. His mental state was a cognitive one but limited in his capacity to comprehend and communicate. Evidence that most people choose to accept the rigors of chemotherapy has no direct bearing on the likely choice that Joseph Saikewicz would have made. Unlike most people, Saikewicz had no capacity to understand his present situation or his prognosis. The guardian *ad litem* gave expression to this important distinction in coming to grips with this 'most troubling aspect' of withholding treatment from Saikewicz. 'If he is treated with toxic drugs he will be involuntarily immersed in a state of painful suffering, the reason for which he will never understand. Patients who request treatment know the risks involved and can appreciate the painful side-effects when they arrive. They know the reason for the pain and their hope makes it tolerable.' To make a worthwhile comparison, one would have to ask whether a majority of people would choose chemotherapy if they were told merely that something outside of their previous experience was going to be done to them, that this something would cause them pain and discomfort, that they would be removed to strange surroundings and possibly restrained for extended periods of time, and that the advantages of this course of action were measured by concepts of time and mortality beyond their ability to comprehend.

To put the above discussion in proper perspective, we realise that an inquiry into what a majority of people would do in circumstances that truly were similar assumes an objective viewpoint not far removed from a 'reasonable person' inquiry. While we recognise the value of this kind of indirect evidence, we should make it plain that the primary test is subjective in nature—that is, the goal is to determine with as much accuracy as possible the wants and needs of the individual involved. This may or may not conform to what is thought wise or prudent by most people. The problems of arriving at an accurate substituted judgment in matters of life and death vary greatly in degree, if not in kind, in different circumstances. For example, the responsibility of Karen Quinlan's father to act as she would have wanted could be discharged by drawing on many years of what was apparently an affectionate and close relationship. In contrast, Joseph Saikewicz was profoundly retarded and noncommunicative his entire life, which was spent largely in the highly restrictive atmosphere of an institution. While it may thus be necessary to rely to a greater degree on objective criteria, such as the supposed inability of profoundly retarded persons to conceptualise or fear death, the effort to bring the substituted judgment into step with the values and desires of the affected individual must not, and need not, be abandoned.

The 'substituted judgment' standard which we have described commends itself simply because of its straightforward respect for the integrity and autonomy of the individual. . . . [W]e now reiterate the substituted judgment doctrine as we apply it in the instant case. We believe that both the guardian *ad litem* in his recommendation and the judge in his decision should have attempted (as they did) to ascertain the incompetent person's actual interests and preferences. In short, the decision in cases such as this should be that which would be made by the incompetent person, if that person were competent, but taking into account the present and future incompetency of the individual as one of the factors which would necessarily enter into the decision-making process of the competent person. Having recognised the right of a competent person to make for himself the same decision as the court made in this case, the question is, do the facts on the record support the proposition that Saikewicz himself would have made the decision under the standard set forth. We believe they do.

The two factors considered by the probate judge to weigh in favor of administering chemotherapy were: (1) the fact that most people elect chemotherapy and (2) the chance of a longer life. Both are appropriate indicators of what Saikewicz himself would have wanted, provided that due allowance is taken for this individual's present and future incompetency. We have already discussed the perspective this brings to the fact that most people choose to undergo chemotherapy. With regard to the second factor, the chance of a longer life carries the same weight for Saikewicz as for any other person, the value of life under the law having no relation to intelligence or social position. Intertwined with this consideration is the hope that a cure, temporary or permanent, will be discovered during the period of extra weeks or months potentially made available by chemotherapy. The guardian *ad litem* investigated this possibility and found no reason to hope for a dramatic breakthrough in the time frame relevant to the decision.

The probate judge identified six factors weighing against administration of chemotherapy. Four of these—Saikewicz's age, the probable side effects of treatment, the low chance of producing remission, and the certainty that treatment will cause immediate suffering—were clearly established by the medical testimony to be considerations that any individual would weigh carefully. A fifth factor—Saikewicz's inability to cooperate with the treatment—introduces those considerations that are unique to this individual and which therefore are essential to the proper exercise of substituted judgment. The judge heard testimony that Saikewicz would have no comprehension of the reasons for the severe disruption of his formerly secure and stable environment occasioned by the chemotherapy. He therefore would experience fear without the understanding from which other patients draw strength. The inability to anticipate and prepare for the severe side effects of the drugs leaves room only for confusion and disorientation. The possibility that such a naturally uncooperative patient would have to be physically restrained to allow the slow intravenous administration of drugs could only compound his pain and fear, as well as possibly jeopardise the ability of his body to withstand the toxic effects of the drugs.

The sixth factor identified by the judge as weighing against chemotherapy was 'the quality of life possible for him even if the treatment does bring about remission'. To the extent that this formulation equates the value of life with any measure of the quality of life, we firmly reject it. A reading of the entire record clearly reveals, however, the judge's concern that special care be taken to respect the dignity and worth of Saikewicz's life precisely because of his vulnerable position. The judge, as well as all the parties, were keenly aware that the supposed ability of Saikewicz, by virtue of his mental retardation, to appreciate or experience life had no place in the decision before them. Rather than reading the judge's formulation in a manner that demeans the value of the life of one who is mentally retarded, the vague, and perhaps ill-chosen, term 'quality of life' should be understood as a reference to the continuing state of pain and disorientation precipitated by the chemotherapy treatment. Viewing the term in this manner, together with the other factors properly considered by the judge, we are satisfied that the decision to withhold treatment from Saikewicz was based on a regard for his actual interests and preferences and that the facts supported this decision.

. . .

In this case, a ward of a State institution was discovered to have an invariably fatal illness, the only effective—in the sense of life-prolonging—treatment for which involved serious and painful intrusions on the patient's body. While an emergency existed with regard to taking action to begin treatment, it was not a case in which immediate action was required. Nor was this a case in which life-saving, as distinguished from life-prolonging, procedures were available. Because the individual involved was thought to be incompetent to make the necessary decisions, the officials of the State institutions properly initiated proceedings in the Probate Court.

. . . We note here that many health care institutions have developed medical ethics committees or panels to consider many of the issues touched on here. Consideration of the findings and advice of such groups as well as the testimony of the attending physicians and other medical experts ordinarily would be of great assistance to a probate judge faced with such a difficult decision. We believe it desirable for a judge to consider such views wherever available and useful to the court. We do not believe, however, that this option should be transformed by us into a required procedure. We take a dim view of any attempt to shift the ultimate decision-making responsibility away from the duly established courts of proper jurisdiction to any committee, panel or group, ad hoc or permanent. Thus, we reject the approach adopted by the New Jersey Supreme Court in the *Quinlan* case of entrusting the decision whether to continue artificial life support to the patient's guardian, family, attending doctors, and hospital 'ethics committee'. 70 NJ at 55, 355 A 2d 647, 671. One rationale for such a delegation was expressed by the lower court judge in the *Quinlan* case, and quoted by the New Jersey Supreme Court: 'The nature, extent and duration of care by societal standards is the responsibility of a physician. The morality and conscience of our society places this responsibility in the hands of the physician. What justification is there to remove it from the control of the medical profession and place it in the hands of the courts?' *Id* at 44, 355 A 2d at 665. For its part, the New Jersey Supreme Court concluded that 'a practice of applying to a court to confirm such decisions would generally be inappropriate, not only because that would be a gratuitous encroachment upon the medical profession's field of competence, but because it would be impossibly cumbersome. Such a requirement is distinguishable from the judicial overview traditionally required in other matters such as the adjudication and commitment of mental incompetents. This is not to say that in the case of an otherwise justiciable controversy access to the courts would be foreclosed; we speak rather of a general practice and procedure'. *Id* at 50, 355 A 2d at 669.

We do not view the judicial resolution of this most difficult and awesome question—whether potentially life-prolonging treatment should be withheld from a person incapable of making his own decision—as constituting a 'gratuitous encroachment' on the domain of medical expertise. Rather, such questions of life and death seem to us to require the process of detached but passionate investigation and decision that forms the ideal on which the judicial branch of government was created. Achieving this ideal is our responsibility and that of the lower court, and is not to be entrusted to any other group purporting to represent the 'morality and conscience of our society', no matter how highly motivated or impressively constituted.

The Supreme Court in New Jersey in *Re Conroy* 486 A 2d 1209 (1985) analysed the law as follows (footnotes omitted):

Since the condition of an incompetent patient makes it impossible to ascertain definitively his present desires, a third party acting on the patient's behalf often cannot say with confidence that his treatment decision for the patient will further rather than frustrate the patient's right to control his own body. Cf Smith, '*In Re Quinlan*: Defining the Basis for Terminating Life Support Under the Right of Privacy', 12 *Tulsa LJ* 150, 161 (1976) (arguing that permitting a guardian to make personal medical decisions for an incompetent patient actually interferes with the patient's right of privacy). Nevertheless, the goal of decision-making for incompetent patients should be to determine and effectuate, insofar as possible, the decision that the patient would have made if competent. Ideally, both aspects of the patient's right to bodily integrity—the right to consent to medical intervention and the right to refuse it—should be respected.

In light of these rights and concerns, we hold that life-sustaining treatment may be withheld or withdrawn from an incompetent patient when it is clear that the particular patient would have refused the treatment under the circumstances involved. The standard we are enunciating is a subjective one, consistent with the notion that the right that we are seeking to effectuate is a very personal right to control one's own life. The question is not what a reasonable or average person would have chosen to do under the circumstances but what the particular patient would have done if able to choose for himself.

The patient may have expressed, in one or more ways, an intent not to have life-sustaining medical intervention. Such an intent might be embodied in a written document, or 'living will', stating the person's desire not to have certain types of life-sustaining treatment administered under certain circumstances. It might also be evidenced in an oral directive that the patient gave to a family member friend, or health care provider. It might consist of a durable power of attorney or appointment of a proxy authorising a particular person to make the decisions on the patient's behalf if he is no longer capable of making them for himself. See *NJSA* 46: 2B–8 (providing that principal may confer authority on agent that is to be exercisable 'notwithstanding later disability or incapacity of the principal at law or later uncertainty as to whether the principal is dead or alive'). It might take the form of reactions that the patient voiced regarding medical treatment administered to others. See, eg, *Storar, supra*, 52 *NY* 2d 363, 420 *NE* 2d 64, 438 *NYS* 2d 266 (withdrawal of respirator was justified as an effectuation of patient's stated wishes when patient, as member of Catholic religious order, had stated more than once in formal discussions concerning the moral implications of the *Quinlan* case, most recently two months before he suffered cardiac arrest that left him in an irreversible coma, that he would not want extraordinary means used to keep him alive under similar circumstances). It might also be deduced from a person's religious beliefs and the tenets of that religion, *id* at 378, 420 *NE* 2d at 72, 438 *NYS* 2d at 274, or from the patient's consistent pattern of conduct with respect to prior decisions about his own medical care. Of course, dealing with the matter in advance in some sort of thoughtful and explicit way is best for all concerned.

Any of the above types of evidence, and any other information bearing on the person's intent, may be appropriate aids in determining what course of treatment the patient would have wished to pursue. In this respect, we now believe that we were in error in *Quinlan, supra*, 70 *NJ* at 21, 41, 355 *A* 2d 647, to disregard evidence of statements that Ms Quinlan made to friends concerning artificial prolongation of the lives of others who were terminally ill. See criticism of this portion of *Quinlan* opinion in Collester, *supra*, 30 *Rutgers L Rev* at 318; Smith, *supra*, 12 *Tulsa LJ* at 163; and *D. Meyers, supra*, at 282 n 65. Such evidence is certainly relevant to shed light on whether the patient would have consented to the treatment if competent to make the decision.

Although all evidence tending to demonstrate a person's intent with respect to medical treatment should properly be considered by surrogate decision-makers, or by a court in the event of any judicial proceedings, the probative value of such evidence may vary depending on the remoteness, consistency, and thoughtfulness of the prior statements or actions and the maturity of the person at the time of the statements or acts. *Colyer, supra*, 99 *Wash* 2d at 131, 660 *P* 2d at 748. Thus, for example, an offhand remark about not wanting to live under certain circumstances made by a person when young and in the peak of health would not in itself constitute clear proof twenty years later that he would want life-sustaining treatment withheld under those circumstances. In contrast, a carefully considered position, especially if written, that a person had maintained over a number of years or that he had acted upon in comparable circumstances might be clear evidence of his intent.

Another factor that would affect the probative value of a person's prior statements of intent would be their specificity. Of course, no one can predict with accuracy the precise circumstances with which he ultimately might be faced. Nevertheless, any details about the level of impaired functioning and the forms of medical treatment that one would find tolerable should be incorporated into advance directives to enhance their later usefulness as evidence.

Medical evidence bearing on the patient's condition, treatment, and prognosis, like evidence of the patient's wishes, is an essential prerequisite to decision-making under the subjective test. The medical evidence must establish that the patient fits within the Claire Conroy pattern: an elderly, incompetent nursing-home resident with severe and permanent mental and physical impairments and a life expectancy of approximately one year or less. In addition, since the goal is to effectuate the patient's right of informed consent, the surrogate decision-maker must have at least as much medical information upon which to base his decision about what the patient would have chosen as one would expect a competent patient to have before consenting to or rejecting treatment. Such information might include evidence about the patient's present level of physical, sensory, emotional, and cognitive functioning; the degree of physical pain resulting from the medical condition, treatment, and termination of treatment, respectively; the degree of humiliation, dependence, and loss of dignity probably resulting from the condition and treatment; the life expectancy and prognosis for recovery with and without treatment; the various treatment options; and the risks, side effects, and benefits of each of those options. Particular care should be taken not to base a decision on a premature diagnosis or prognosis. See *Colyer, supra*, 99 *Wash* 2d at 143–45, 660 *P* 2d at 754–55 (Dore, J, dissenting).

We recognise that for some incompetent patients it might be impossible to be clearly satisfied as to the patient's intent either to accept or reject the life-sustaining treatment. Many people may have spoken of their desires in general or casual terms, or, indeed, never considered or resolved the issue at all. In such cases, a surrogate decision-maker cannot presume that treatment decisions made by a third party on the patient's behalf will further the patient's right to self-determination, since effectuating another person's right to self-determination presupposes that the substitute decision-maker knows what the person would have wanted. Thus, in the absence of adequate proof of the patient's wishes, it is naive to pretend that the right to self-determination serves as the basis for substituted decision-making. See *Storar, supra*, 52 *NY* 2d at 378–380, 420 *NE* 2d at 72–73, 438 *NYS* 2d at 274–75; Veatch, 'An Ethical Framework for Terminal Care Decisions: A New Classification of Patients', 32(9) *J Am Geriatrics Soc'y* 665, 666 (1984).

We hesitate, however, to foreclose the possibility of humane actions, which may involve termination of life-sustaining treatment, for persons who never clearly expressed their desires about life-sustaining treatment but who are now suffering a prolonged and painful death. An incompetent, like a minor child, is a ward of the state, and the state's *parens patriae* power supports the authority of its courts to allow decisions to be made for an incompetent that serve the incompetent's best interests, even if the person's wishes cannot be clearly established. This authority permits the state to authorise guardians to withhold or withdraw life-sustaining treatment from an incompetent patient if it is manifest that such action would further the patient's best interests in a narrow sense of the phrase, even though the subjective test that we articulated above may not be satisfied. We therefore hold that life-sustaining treatment may also be withheld or withdrawn from a patient in Claire Conroy's situation if either of two 'best interests' tests—a limited-objective or a pure-objective test—is satisfied.

Under the limited-objective test, life-sustaining treatment may be withheld or withdrawn from a patient in Claire Conroy's situation when there is some trustworthy evidence that the patient would have refused the treatment, and the decision-maker is satisfied that it is clear that the burdens of the patient's continued life with the treatment outweigh the benefits of that life for him. By this we mean that the patient is suffering, and will continue to suffer throughout the expected duration of his life, unavoidable pain, and that the net burdens of his prolonged life (the pain and suffering of his life with the treatment less the amount and duration of pain that the patient would likely experience if the treatment were withdrawn) markedly outweigh any physical pleasure, emotional enjoyment, or intellectual satisfaction that the patient may still be able to derive from life. This limited-objective standard permits the termination of treatment for a patient who had not unequivocally expressed his desires before becoming incompetent, when it is clear that the treatment in question would merely prolong the patient's suffering.

Medical evidence will be essential to establish that the burdens of the treatment to the patient in terms of pain and suffering outweigh the benefits that the patient is experiencing. The medical evidence should make it clear that the treatment would merely prolong the patient's suffering and not provide him with any net benefit. Information is particularly important with respect to the degree, expected duration, and constancy of pain with and without treatment, and the possibility that the pain could be reduced by drugs or other means short of terminating the life-sustaining treatment. The same types of medical evidence that are relevant to the subjective analysis, such as the patient's life expectancy, prognosis, level of functioning, degree of humiliation and dependency, and treatment options, should also be considered.

This limited-objective test also requires some trustworthy evidence that the patient would have wanted the treatment terminated. This evidence could take any one or more of the various forms appropriate to prove the patient's intent under the subjective test. Evidence that, taken as a whole, would be too vague, casual, or remote to constitute the clear proof of the patient's subjective intent that is necessary to satisfy the subjective test—for example, informally expressed reactions to other people's medical conditions and treatment—might be sufficient to satisfy this prong of the limited-objective test.

In the absence of trustworthy evidence, or indeed any evidence at all, that the patient would have declined the treatment, life-sustaining treatment may still be withheld or withdrawn from a formerly competent person like Claire Conroy if a third, pure-objective test is satisfied. Under that test, as under the limited-objective test, the net burdens of the patient's life with the treatment should clearly and markedly outweigh the benefits that the patient derives from life. Further, the recurring, unavoidable and severe pain of the patient's life with the treatment should be such that the effect of administering life-sustaining treatment would be inhumane. Subjective evidence that the patient would not have wanted the treatment is not necessary under this pure-objective standard. Nevertheless, even in the context of severe pain, life-sustaining treatment should not be withdrawn from an incompetent patient who had previously expressed a wish to be kept alive in spite of any pain that he might experience.

Although we are condoning a restricted evaluation of the nature of a patient's life in terms of pain, suffering, and possible enjoyment under the limited-objective and pure-objective tests, we expressly decline to authorise decision-making based on assessments of the personal worth or social utility of another's life, or the value of that life to others. We do not believe that it would be appropriate for a court to designate a person with the authority to determine that someone else's life is not worth living simply because, to that person, the patient's 'quality of life' or value to society seems negligible. The mere fact that a patient's functioning is limited or his prognosis dim does not mean that he is not enjoying what remains of his life or that it is in his best interests to die. But cf *In Re Dinnerstein*, 6 *Mass App Ct* 466 at 473, 380 *NE* 2d 134 at 138 (1978) (indicating, in reference to possible resuscitation of half-paralysed, elderly victim of Alzheimer's disease, that prolongation of life is not required if there is no hope to return to a 'normal, integrated, functioning, cognitive existence'); see also *President's Commission Report, supra,* at 135 (endorsing termination of treatment whenever surrogate decision-maker in his discretion believes it is in the patient's best interests, defined broadly to 'take into account such factors as the relief of suffering, the preservation or restoration of functioning, and the quality as well as the extent of life sustained'). More wide-ranging powers to make decisions about other people's lives, in our view, would create an intolerable risk for socially isolated and defenseless people suffering from physical or mental handicaps.

We are aware that it will frequently be difficult to conclude that the evidence is sufficient to justify termination of treatment under either of the 'best interests' tests that we have described. Often, it is unclear whether and to what extent a patient such as Claire Conroy is capable of, or is in fact, experiencing pain. Similarly, medical experts are often unable to determine with any degree of certainty the extent of a nonverbal person's intellectual functioning or the depth of his emotional life. When the evidence is insufficient to satisfy either the limited-objective or pure-objective standard, however, we cannot justify the termination of life-sustaining treatment as clearly furthering the best interests of a patient like Ms Conroy.

The surrogate decision-maker should exercise extreme caution in determining the patient's intent and in evaluating medical evidence of the patient's pain and possible enjoyment, and should not approve withholding or withdrawing life-sustaining treatment unless he is manifestly satisfied that one of the three tests that we have outlined has been met. Cf *In Re Grady*, 85 *NJ* 235 at 266, 426 *A* 2d 467 (1981) (requiring that evidence be clear and convincing before a court would approve sterilisation of an incompetent, mentally retarded adult). When evidence of a person's wishes or physical or mental condition is equivocal, it is best to err, if at all, in favor of preserving life. See *Osborne, supra*, 294 *A* 2d at 374 (stating in dictum that when a patient is 'suffering impairment of capacity for choice, it may be better to give weight to the known instinct for survival'); Dyck, 'Ethical Aspects of Care for the Dying Incompetent', 32(9) *J Am Geriatrics Soc'y* 661, 663 (1984) ('[S]ituations in which [decision-makers] are uncertain about what is best should be resolved in favor of extending life where possible.'). Or, as one writer has said as a justification for requiring a high degree of safety and certainty of diagnosis in the determination of brain death: '[I]f there is a lot to lose by being wrong, it is generally better to stick to the safer, known way in the absence of the highest probability for proceeding otherwise.' D Walton, *Ethics of Withdrawal of Life-Support Systems: Case Studies on Decision Making in Intensive Care* 82 (1983).

A number of comments can be made.

1. You will notice that *Conroy* enlarges on the test suggested by *Saikewicz* by making it clear that there are in fact three tests. Do you think that this is justified and represents an improvement in the law?

2. Is there a confusion here in the use of the term 'substituted judgment'? Can it be said that any of the *Conroy* tests are examples of substituted judgment? (See our discussion *supra* ch 4.)

Substituted judgment is here used as a technical term. It is not a term which is synonymous with proxy-decision making. Instead, it is a term intending to state the criteria to be employed by a proxy in reaching a decision. Its meaning is best stated by the New Jersey Supreme Court in *Re Jobes* 529 A 2d 434 (1987)—a case we will return to later. Garibaldi J said (footnote omitted):

> [Substituted judgment] is intended to ensure that the surrogate decisionmaker effectuates as much as possible the decision that the incompetent patient would make if he or she were competent. Under the substituted judgment doctrine, where an incompetent's wishes are not clearly expressed, a surrogate decisionmaker considers the patient's personal value system for guidance. The surrogate considers the patient's prior statements about and reactions to medical issues, and all the facets of the patient's personality that the surrogate is familiar with—with, of course, particular reference to his or her relevant philosophical, theological, and ethical values—in order to extrapolate what course of medical treatment the patient would choose. See *Re Roe*, 383 *Mass* 415 at 442, 421 *NE* 2d 40 at 56–59 (1981).

Garibaldi J talks of the 'decision that the incompetent *would* make' (our emphasis). The first test in *Conroy*—the 'subjective test'—asks the proxy to decide what decision the incompetent *did* make. The law then requires that the patient's earlier wishes are complied with. This is not strictly speaking, in our view, substituted judgment at all. Equally, the third test in *Conroy*—the 'objective test'—is not substituted judgment, but an expression of the 'best interests' test with which English law is very familiar. The second *Conroy* test— 'the limited-objective test'—is, however, an expression of the substituted judgment test in our view, even if the objective element limits the emphasis placed on the incompetent's views and enjoins the proxy to find a 'middle-ground . . . which combined elements of both self-determination and objective physical factors' (*per* Handler J in *Re Jobes* 529 A 2d 434 at 458 (1987)).

3. Does the *Conroy* court define the limited-objective test too narrowly by considering the only burdens to be pain and suffering? Could not the burden of a particular treatment be seen in a more general way? Equally, should this argument be applied to the 'objective' test? In *Conroy*, Handler J in a concurring opinion put the arguments for a wider appreciation of relevant factors (footnotes omitted):

> **Handler J:** In my opinion, the Court's objective tests too narrowly define the interests of people like Miss Conroy. While the basic standard purports to account for several concerns, it ultimately focuses on pain as the critical factor. The presence of significant pain in effect becomes the sole measure of such a person's best interests. 'Pain' thus eclipses a whole cluster of other human values that have a proper place in the subtle weighing that will ultimately determine how life should end.
>
> The Court's concentration on pain as the exclusive criterion in reaching the life-or-death decision in reality transmutes the best-interests determination into an exercise of avoidance and nullification rather than confrontation and fulfillment. In most cases the pain criterion will dictate that the decision be one not to withdraw life-prolonging treatment and not to allow death to occur naturally. First, pain will not be an operative factor in a great many cases. '[P]resently available drugs and techniques allow pain to be reduced to a level acceptable to virtually every patient, usually without unacceptable sedation.' *President's Commission Report, supra*, at 50–51. See *id* at 19 n 19 *citing* Saunders, 'Current Views on Pain Relief and Terminal Care' in *The Therapy of Pain* 215 (Swerdlow, ed 1981) (a hospice reports complete control of pain in over 99% of its dying patients). See generally *id* at 277–95. See also generally *The Management of Terminal Disease* (Saunders, ed 1978); *The Experience of Dying* (Pattison, ed 1977); *Psychopharmacologic Agents for the Terminally Ill and Bereaved* (Goldberg *et al*, eds 1973). Further, as was true in Miss Conroy's case, health care providers frequently encounter difficulty in evaluating the degree of pain experienced by a patient. Finally, '[o]nly a minority of patients—fewer than half of those with malignancies, for example—have substantial problems with pain. . . .' *President's Commission Report, supra* at 278, *citing* Twycross, 'Relief of Pain' in *The Management of Terminal Disease, supra*, at 66. Thus, in a great many cases, the pain test will become an absolute bar to the withdrawal of life-support therapy.
>
> The pain requirement, as applied by the Court in its objective tests, effectively negates other highly relevant considerations that should appropriately bear on the decision to maintain or to withdraw life-prolonging treatment. The pain standard may dictate the decision to prolong life despite the presence of other factors that reasonably militate in favor of the termination of such procedures to allow a natural death. The exclusive pain criterion denies relief to that class of people who, at the very end of life, might strongly disapprove of an artificially extended existence in spite of the absence of pain. See *Re Torres*, 357 *NW* 332 at 340 (Minn 1984) (although a patient 'cannot feel pain', that patient may have a guardian petition to forego life-sustaining treatment). Thus, some people abhor dependence on others as much, or more, than they fear pain. Other individuals value personal privacy and dignity, and prise independence from others when their personal needs and bodily functions are involved. Finally, the ideal of bodily integrity may become more important than simply prolonging life at its most rudimentary level. Persons, like Miss Conroy, 'may well have wished to avoid . . . "[t]he ultimate horror [not of] death but the possibility of being maintained in limbo, in a sterile room, by machines controlled by strangers."' In *Re Torres, supra*, 357 *NW* 2d at 340, quoting Steel, 'The Right to Die: New Options in California', 93 *Christian Century* [July–Dec 1976].
>
> Clearly, a decision to focus exclusively on pain as the single criterion ignores and devalues other important ideals regarding life and death. Consequently, a pain

standard cannot serve as an indirect proxy for additional and significant concerns that bear on the decision to forego life-prolonging treatments.

. . .

I would therefore have the Court adopt a test that does not rely exclusively on pain as the ultimately determinative criterion. Rather, the standard should consist of an array of factors to be medically established and then evaluated by the decision-maker both singly and collectively to reach a balance that will justify the determination whether to withdraw or to continue life-prolonging treatment. The withdrawal of life-prolonging treatment from an unconscious or comatose, terminally ill individual near death, whose personal views concerning life-ending treatment cannot be ascertained, should be governed by such a standard.

Several important criteria bear on this critical determination. The person should be terminally ill and facing imminent death. There should also be present the permanent loss of conscious thought processes in the form of a comatose state or profound unconsciousness. Further, there should be the irreparable failure of at least one major and essential bodily organ or system. See, e g, *Re Quinlan*, 70 *NJ* 10, 355 *A* 2d 647 (1976) (respiratory system); *Barber, supra* (same); *Re Dinnerstein*, 6 *Mass App* 466, 380 *NE* 2d 134 (1978) (heart); *Saikewicz, supra* (circulatory system); *Conroy, supra* (swallowing reflex); *Torres, supra* (cerebral cortex and brain-stem); *Re Hamlin*, 102 *Wash* 2d 810, 689 *P* 2d 1372 (1984) (cerebral cortex). Obviously the presence or absence of significant pain is highly relevant.

In addition, the person's general physical condition must be of great concern. The presence of progressive, irreversible, extensive, and extreme physical deterioration, such as ulcers, lesions, gangrene, infection, incontinence and the like, which frequently afflict the bed-ridden, terminally ill, should be considered in the formulation of an appropriate standard. The medical and nursing treatment of individuals in *extremis* and suffering from these conditions entails the constant and extensive handling and manipulation of the body. At some point, such a course of treatment upon the insensate patient is bound to touch the sensibilities of even the most detached observer. Eventually, pervasive bodily intrusions, even for the best motives, will arouse feelings akin to humiliation and mortification for the helpless patient. When cherished values of human dignity and personal privacy, which belong to every person living or dying, are sufficiently transgressed by what is being done to the individual, we should be ready to say: enough.

Do you agree with Handler J's criticism of the majority in *Conroy*? If you do, do you think the factors he considers relevant are satisfactory or exhaustive? (See also in *Re Jobes infra, per* Handler and Pollock JJ.)

If the court applies a 'pain-orientated' test, then it would be inapplicable in the case of a patient in a persistent vegetative state (*infra*).

4. Do you think that *Saikewicz* was an appropriate case for the use of substituted judgment? *Saikewicz*, you will recall, had an 'IQ of ten and a mental age of approximately two years and eight months'. Compare the approach of the New York Court of Appeals in *Re John Storar* 420 NE 2d 64 (1981).

Wachtler Justice: John Storar was profoundly retarded with a mental age of about eighteen months. At the time of this proceeding he was fifty-two years old and a resident of the Newark Development Center, a state facility, which had been his home since the age of five. His closest relative was his mother, a seventy-seven-year-old widow who resided near the facility. He was her only child and she visited him almost daily.

In 1979 physicians at the Center noticed blood in his urine and asked his mother for permission to conduct diagnostic tests. She initially refused but after discussions with the Center's staff gave her consent. The tests, completed in July 1979, revealed that he had cancer of the bladder. It was recommended that he receive radiation therapy at a hospital in Rochester. When the hospital refused to administer the treatment without the consent of a legal guardian, Mrs Storar applied to the court and was appointed guardian of her son's person and property in August, 1979. With her consent he received radiation therapy for six weeks, after which the disease was found to be in remission.

However in March, 1980 blood was again observed in his urine. The lesions in his bladder were cauterised in an unsuccessful effort to stop the bleeding. At that point his physician diagnosed the cancer as terminal, concluding that after using all medical and surgical means then available, the patient would nevertheless die from the disease.

In May the physicians at the Center asked his mother for permission to administer blood transfusions. She initially refused but the following day withdrew her objection. For several weeks John Storar received blood transfusions when needed. However, on June 19 his mother requested that the transfusions be discontinued.

The Director of the Center then brought this proceeding, pursuant to Section 33.03 of the Mental Health Law, seeking authorisation to continue the transfusions, claiming that without them 'death would occur within weeks'. Mrs Storar cross petitioned for an order prohibiting the transfusions, and named the district attorney as a party. The court appointed a guardian *ad litem* and signed an order temporarily permitting the transfusions to continue, pending the determination of the proceeding.

At the hearing in September the court heard testimony from various witnesses including Mrs Storar, several employees at the Center, and seven medical experts. All the experts concurred that John Storar had irreversible cancer of the bladder, which by then had spread to his lungs and perhaps other organs, with a very limited life span, generally estimated to be between three and six months. They also agreed that he had an infant's mentality and was unable to comprehend his predicament or to make a reasoned choice of treatment. In addition, there was no dispute over the fact that he was continuously losing blood.

The medical records show that at the time of the hearing, he required two units of blood every eight to fifteen days. The staff physicians explained that the transfusions were necessary to replace the blood lost. Without them there would be insufficient oxygen in the patient's blood stream. To compensate for this loss, his heart would have to work harder and he would breathe more rapidly, which created a strain and was very tiresome. He became lethargic and they feared he would eventually bleed to death. They observed that after the transfusions he had more energy. He was able to resume most of his usual activities—feeding himself, showering, taking walks and running—including some mischievous ones, such as stealing cigarette butts and attempting to eat them.

It was conceded that John Storar found the transfusions disagreeable. He was also distressed by the blood and blood clots in his urine which apparently increased immediately after a transfusion. He could not comprehend the purpose of the transfusions and on one or two occasions had displayed some initial resistance. To eliminate his apprehension he was given a sedative approximately one hour before a transfusion. He also received regular doses of narcotics to alleviate the pain associated with the disease.

On the other hand several experts testified that there was support in the medical community for the view that, at this stage, transfusions may only prolong suffering and that treatment could properly be limited to administering pain killers. Mrs Storar testified that she wanted the transfusions discontinued because she only wanted her son to be comfortable. She admitted that no one had ever explained to her what might happen to him if the transfusions were stopped. She also stated that she was not 'sure' whether he might die sooner if the blood was not replaced and was unable to determine whether he wanted to live. However, in view of the fact that he obviously disliked the transfusions and tried to avoid them, she believed that he would want them discontinued.

The court held that the Center's application for permission to continue the transfusions should be denied. It was noted that John Storar's fatal illness had not affected his limited mental ability. He remained alert and carried on many of his usual activities. However, the court emphasised that the transfusions could not cure the disease, involved some pain and that the patient submitted to them reluctantly.

The court held that a person has a right to determine what will be done with his own body and, when he is incompetent, this right may be exercised by another on his behalf. In this case, the court found that John Storar's mother was the person in the best position to determine what he would want and that she 'wants his suffering to stop and believes that he would want this also'.

The Appellate Division affirmed in a brief memorandum.

. . . John Storar was never competent at any time in his life. He was always totally incapable of understanding or making a reasoned decision about medical treatment. Thus it is unrealistic to attempt to determine whether he would want to continue potentially life prolonging treatment if he were competent. As one of the experts testified at the hearing, that would be similar to asking whether 'if it snowed all summer would it then be winter?' Mentally John Storar was an infant and that is the only realistic way to assess his rights in this litigation (see, Bryn, *op cit* p 24 n 107). . . . [T]here is the additional complication of two threats to his life. There was cancer of the bladder which was incurable and would in all probability claim his life. There was also the related loss of blood which posed the risk of an earlier death, but which, at least at the time of the hearing, could be replaced by transfusions. Thus, as one of the experts noted, the transfusions were analogous to food—they would not cure the cancer, but they could eliminate the risk of death from another treatable cause. Of course, John Storar did not like them, as might be expected of one with an infant's mentality. But the evidence convincingly shows that the transfusions did not involve excessive pain and that without them his mental and physical abilities would not be maintained at the usual level. With the transfusions on the other hand, he was essentially the same as he was before except of course he had a fatal illness which would ultimately claim his life. Thus, on the record, we have concluded that the application for permission to continue the transfusions should have been granted. Although we understand and respect his mother's despair, as we respect the beliefs of those who oppose transfusions on religious grounds, a court should not in the circumstances of this case allow an incompetent patient to bleed to death because someone, even someone as close as a parent or sibling, feels that this is best for one with an incurable disease.

. . . Neither the common law nor existing statutes require persons generally to seek prior court assessment of conduct which may subject them to civil and criminal liability. If it is desirable to enlarge the role of the courts in cases involving discontinuance of life sustaining treatment for incompetents by establishing, as the Appellate Division suggested in the *Eichner* case [a case heard contemporaneously by the court], a mandatory procedure of successive approvals by physicians, hospital personnel, relatives and the courts, the change should come from the Legislature.

Is it not, therefore, better law to have a rule which says that substituted judgment can only be resorted to when the patient was at some point competent and, thus, had been able to express his view? (See the President's Commission, p 133.) The point was well made by the Canadian Supreme Court in *Re Eve* (1981) 115 DLR (3d) 283 (a case concerned with the court's jurisdiction to authorise a sterilisation operation on an incompetent adult, *supra* ch 4). You will recall that Eve had always been mentally incompetent.

La Forest J: . . . [I]t is obviously fiction to suggest that a decision so made [ie applying the 'substituted judgment' test] is that of the mental incompetent, however much the court may try to put itself in her place. What the incompetent would do if she or he could make the choice is simply a matter of speculation. The sophistry embodied in the argument favouring substituted judgment has been fully revealed in *Eberhardy, supra*, at p 893 where in discussing *Grady, supra*, the court stated:

The fault we find in the New Jersey case is the *ratio decidendi* of first concluding, correctly we believe, that the right to sterilisation is a personal choice, but then equating a decision made by others with the choice of the person to be sterilised. It clearly is not a personal choice, and no amount of legal legerdemain can make it so.

. . .

We conclude that the question is not choice because it is sophistry to refer to it as such, but rather the question is whether there is a method by which others, acting in behalf of the person's best interests and in the interests, such as they may be, of the state, can exercise the decision. Any governmentally sanctioned (or ordered) procedure to sterilise a person who is incapable of giving consent must be denominated for what it is, that is, the state's intrusion into the determination of whether or not a person who makes no choice shall be allowed to procreate.

5. Do you regard substituted judgment, at least in the 'limited-objective' form described in *Conroy*, as entailing any risks for the patient? Is there not some considerable danger involved in allowing others to claim knowledge of what the patient may have wished, particularly if those others may at the same time be potential beneficiaries of the patient's estate? Could it be that this fear motivated the *Conroy* court to introduce an 'objective' element into the substituted judgment test? What level of proof would you think an English court would require if it adopted this approach? For an early example of looking to relatives as authorities on the wishes of an incompetent patient, see *Re Quinlan* 355 A 2d 647 at 664 (1976) (See also *Re Jobes, infra*).

> Our affirmation of Karen's independent right of choice, however, would ordinarily be based upon her competency to assert it. The sad truth, however, is that she is grossly incompetent and we cannot discern her supposed choice based on the testimony of her previous conversations with friends, where such testimony is without sufficient probative weight. . . . Nevertheless we have concluded that Karen's right of privacy may be asserted on her behalf by her guardian under the peculiar circumstances here present.
>   If a putative decision by Karen to permit this non-cognitive, vegetative existence to terminate by natural forces is regarded as a valuable incident of her right of privacy, as we believe it to be, then it should not be discarded solely on the basis that her condition prevents her conscious exercise of the choice. The only practical way to prevent destruction of the right is to permit the guardian and family of Karen to render their best judgment, subject to the qualifications hereinafter stated, as to whether she would exercise it in these circumstances. If their conclusion is in the affirmative this decision should be accepted by a society the overwhelming majority of whose members would, we think, in similar circumstances, exercise such a choice in the same way for themselves or for those closest to them. It is for this reason that we determine that Karen's right of privacy may be asserted in her behalf, in this respect, by her guardian and family under the particular circumstances presented by this record.

6. Did the *Conroy* court intend to restrict their decision to patients such as Claire Conroy who had 'a life expectancy of approximately one year or less'? Should it make any difference that a patient has a better prognosis? Is a different legal approach necessary in such a case?

7. Does the doctor need to go to court to confirm his decision? Immediately after *Saikewicz* it was thought by some that doctors had lost the capacity to make decisions concerning this group of patients because, instead, they must go to the court with the facts and let the court decide. Note the following quote from G Annas, 'Reconciling Quinlan and Saikewicz: Decision Making for the Terminally Ill Incompetent' (1979) 4 Am JL Med 367 at 386–7:

> On March 2, 1978, the legal columnist of *The New England Journal of Medicine* wrote that physicians and news reporters were correct in concluding that in *Saikewicz*, the Massachusetts Supreme Judicial Court 'really did mean that all decisions on either removal of life-support systems or continuation of life-extending therapy in otherwise dying patients who are incompetent . . . must go before a Probate Court for

approval'.[48] With this encouragement, Dr Relman wrote an accompanying editorial which concluded that the justices had a 'total distrust of physicians' judgments' and that their 'astonishing opinion can only be viewed as a resounding vote of "no confidence" in the ability of physicians and families to act in the best interests of the incapable patient suffering from a terminal illness'. As previously noted, Relman urged judges in other jurisdictions to adopt the *Quinlan* approach instead, and suggested additionally that all those who did not agree with him take a 'guided visit to a large acute-care hospital'.[49]

Notes to extract
[48] Curran, *Law-Medicine Notes: The Saikewicz Decision*, 298 New England J Med 499 (1978). Professor Curran reaffirmed his views in a reply to letters addressing his initial column:

> The courts have never before been so universally intrusive as to demand that *every decision either to continue or not to continue* life-sustaining medical efforts in mentally incompetent persons must go to court for determination. . . .
>
> . . .
>
> . . . The issue is clear. The Supreme Judicial Court does not trust any part of the private community except the probate court to decide these matters.

298 New England J Med 1209 (1978) (emphasis added). While the distinction between removal and continuance of treatment is literally true, the decision to continue treatment is trivial insofar as potential liability goes, since the suit would not be for negligence or homicide, but would allege a battery. The physician's defense would be privilege, that is, that he was doing his best to save the patient's life, and the likelihood that he would lose such a suit, so long as he was acting in good faith, approaches zero.

It is, however, possible that some day there will be a successful battery suit by the patient's guardian or the administrator of his or her estate against a physician who continued treatment even though the patient had signed a living will and the patient's guardian had demanded that treatment be halted. A successful suit of this type might be more effective than legislation in encouraging physicians to take 'living wills' seriously.
[49] Relman, 'The Saikewicz Decision: Judges as Physicians,' 298 New England J Med 508, 508-9 (1978).

The court in *Quinlan* had anticipated this point.

> We consider that a practice of applying to a court to confirm such decisions would generally be inappropriate, not only because that would be a gratuitous encroachment upon the medical profession's field of competence, but because it would be impossibly cumbersome. Such a requirement is distinguishable from the judicial overview traditionally required in other matters such as the adjudication and commitment of mental incompetents. This is not to say that in the case of an otherwise justiciable controversy access to the courts would be foreclosed; we speak rather of a general practice and procedure.

The court concluded:

> [W]e do not intend to be understood as implying that a proceeding for judicial declaratory relief is necessarily required for the implementation of comparable decisions in the field of medical practice.

The Massachusetts Supreme Judicial Court always asserted that the conclusion drawn from *Saikewicz* by some was unwarranted. In *Re Spring* 405 NE 2d 115 (1980) the court was able to put the matter beyond dispute. Writing for the court Braucher J held, *inter alia*:

> . . . It is reported that our *Saikewicz* decision was interpreted by some as requiring judicial approval before life-prolonging treatment could be withheld from an incompetent patient, even in cases of 'brain death'. See Annas, *supra* at 387. We therefore take this occasion to point out that neither the *Saikewicz* case nor the

present case presented any issue as to the legal consequences of action taken without court approval. . . . Neither the present case nor the *Saikewicz* case involved the legality of action taken without judicial authority, and our opinions should not be taken to establish any requirement of prior judicial approval that would not otherwise exist. . . . [P]rivate medical decisions must be made responsibly, subject to judicial scrutiny if good faith or due care is brought into question in subsequent litigation, although the concurrence of qualified consultants may be highly persuasive on issues of good faith and good medical practice. This is true of medical decisions generally, and is no less true of a decision to withhold medical treatment from an incompetent patient. When a court is properly presented with the legal question, whether treatment may be withheld, it must decide that question and not delegate it to some private person or group. Subsidiary questions as to how to carry out the decision, particularly purely medical questions, must almost inevitably be left to private decision, but with no immunity for action taken in bad faith or action that is grievously unreasonable.

2.   Group 2 patients

The relevant law was stated by the Supreme Judicial Court in *Re Spring* 405 NE 2d 115 (1980) (footnote omitted).

Braucher J: . . . The ward was born in 1901, had been married for fifty-five years at the time of the hearing, and had one son, the temporary guardian. The ward was suffering from 'end-stage kidney disease', which required him to undergo hemodialysis treatment (filtering of the blood) three days a week, five hours a day. He also suffered from 'chronic organic brain syndrome', or senility, and was completely confused and disoriented. Both the kidney disease and the senility were permanent and irreversible; there was no prospect of a medical breakthrough that would provide a cure for either disease. Apart from the kidney disease and senility the ward's health was good.

Without the dialysis treatment the ward would die; with it he might survive for months. Survival for five years would be not probable, but conceivable. The treatment did not cuase a remission of the disease or restore him even temporarily to a normal, cognitive, integrated, functioning existence, but simply kept him alive. He experienced unpleasant side effects such as dizziness, leg cramps, and headaches; on occasion he kicked nurses, resisted transportation for dialysis, and pulled the dialysis needles out of his arm. His disruptive behavior was controlled through heavy sedation. He would not have suffered any discomfort if the dialysis had been terminated. There was no evidence that while competent he had expressed any wish or desire as to the continuation or withdrawal of treatment in such circumstances, but his wife and son were of the opinion that if competent he would request withdrawal of treatment.

. . . [T]here is something approaching consensus in support of some of the principles elaborated in the *Saikewicz* opinion. A person has a strong interest in being free from nonconsensual invasion of his bodily integrity, and a constitutional right of privacy that may be asserted to prevent unwanted infringements of bodily integrity. Thus a competent person has a general right to refuse medical treatment in appropriate circumstances, to be determined by balancing the individual interest against countervailing State interests, particularly the State interest in the preservation of life. In striking that balance, account is to be taken of the prognosis and of the magnitude of the proposed invasion. The same right is also extended to an incompetent person, to be exercised through a 'substituted judgment' on his behalf. The decision should be that which would be made by the incompetent person, if he were competent, taking into account his actual interests and preferences and also his present and future incompetency. . . .

The present case does not involve State action in the same sense as the *Saikewicz* case, since the patient here was not in State custody. While apparently competent, the patient had acquiesced in hemodialysis treatment, and had received such treatments for several months before his incompetence became apparent. His wife and son filed a petition for the appointment of a guardian and for an order that the treatments be discontinued. Again we hold that the proceeding was properly initiated, and that the judge appropriately decided that the treatments in question should be withheld. Again we disapprove shifting of the ultimate decision-making responsibility away from the duly established courts of proper jurisdiction.

. . . We have pointed out the similarities between the present case and the *Saikewicz* case, which are quite sufficient to bring into play the 'substituted judgment' standard applied in that case. Thus the judge's finding that the ward 'would, if competent, choose not to receive the life-prolonging treatment' was critical. An expression of intent by the ward while competent was not essential. The judge properly relied in part on the opinion of the ward's wife of fifty-five years. That opinion was corroborated by that of the son, and there was every indication that there was a close relationship within the family group, that the wife and son had only the best interests of the ward at heart, and that they were best informed as to his likely attitude. There was no evidence that financial considerations were involved.

You will notice that *Spring* does appear to be an appropriate case for substituted judgment since Earle Spring had been competent before the onset of senility. One important point to notice from *Spring* is that the lower courts found that 'the ward's attending physician together with the ward's wife and son are to make the decision with reference to the continuance or determination of the dialysis treatment'. This finding was rejected by the Supreme Judicial Court. Although it is by no means clear, it appears that the court thought that the decision must be for the doctor having properly directed himself as to the relevant law. However, the court insisted that it retained ultimate responsibility to review the decision to ensure that it complied with the law.

In *Re Dinnerstein* 380 NE 2d 134 (1978) (Appeal Court of Massachusetts) is one of the few other cases which touch on the law relating to patients in group 2—at least that is how we interpret the case although, as you will see, the court seems to have treated the case (somewhat confusingly) as not within our category B at all, but within our earlier category A (the 'dying patient').

Justice Armstrong: . . . The patient is a sixty-seven year old woman who suffers from a condition known as Alzheimer's disease. It is a degenerative disease of the brain of unknown origin, described as presenile dementia, and results in destruction of brain tissue and, consequently deterioration in brain function. The condition is progressive and unremitting, leading in stages to disorientation, loss of memory, personality disorganisation, loss of intellectual function, and ultimate loss of all motor function. The disease typically leads to a vegetative or comatose condition and then to death. The course of the disease may be gradual or precipitous, averaging five to seven years. At this time medical science knows of no cure for the disease and no treatment which can slow or arrest its course. No medical breakthrough is anticipated.

The patient's condition was diagnosed as Alzheimer's disease in July, 1975, although the initial symptoms of the disease were observed as early as 1972. She entered a nursing home in November, 1975, where her (by that time) complete disorientation, frequent psychotic outbursts, and deteriorating ability to control elementary bodily functions made her dependent on intensive nursing care. In February, 1978, she suffered a massive stroke, which left her totally paralysed on her left side. At the present time she is confined to a hospital bed, in an essentially vegetative state, immobile, speechless, unable to swallow without choking, and barely able to cough. Her eyes occasionally open and from time to time appear to fix on or follow an object briefly; otherwise she appears to be unaware of her environment. She is fed through a naso-gastric tube, intravenous feeding having been abandoned because it came to cause her pain. It is probable that she is experiencing some discomfort from the naso-gastric tube, which can cause irritation, ulceration, and infection in her throat and esophageal tract, and which must be removed from time to time, and that procedure itself causes discomfort. She is catheterised and also, of course, requires bowel care. Apart from her Alzheimer's disease and paralysis, she suffers from high blood pressure which is difficult to control; there is risk in lowering it due to a constriction in an artery leading to a kidney. She has a serious, life-threatening coronary artery disease, due to arteriosclerosis. Her condition is hopeless, but it is difficult to predict exactly when she will die. Her life expectancy is no more than a year, but she could go into cardiac or respiratory arrest at any time. One of these, or another stroke, is most likely to be the immediate cause of her death.

In this situation her attending physician has recommended that, when (and if) cardiac or respiratory arrest occurs, resuscitation efforts should not be undertaken. Such efforts typically involve the use of cardiac massage or chest compression and delivery of oxygen under compression through an endotracheal tube into the lungs. An electrocardiogram is connected to guide the efforts of the resuscitation team and to monitor the patient's progress. Various plastic tubes are usually inserted intravenously to supply medications or stimulants directly to the heart. Such medications may also be supplied by direct injection into the heart by means of a long needle. A defibrillator may be used, applying electric shock to the heart to induce contractions. A pacemaker, in the form of an electrical conducting wire, may be fed through a large blood vessel directly to the heart's surface to stimulate contractions and to regulate beat. These procedures, to be effective, must be initiated with a minimum of delay as cerebral anoxia, due to a cutoff of oxygen to the brain, will normally produce irreversible brain damage within three to five minutes and total brain death within fifteen minutes. Many of these procedures are obviously highly intrusive, and some are violent in nature. The defibrillator, for example, causes violent (and painful) muscle contractions which, in a patient suffering (as this patient is) from osteoporosis, may cause fracture of vertebrae or other bones. Such fractures, in turn, cause pain, which may be extreme.

The patient's family, consisting of a son, who is a physician practicing in New York City, and a daughter, with whom the patient lived prior to her admission to the nursing home in 1975, concur in the doctor's recommendation that resuscitation should not be attempted in the event of cardiac or respiratory arrest. They have joined with the doctor and the hospital in bringing the instant action for declaratory relief, asking for a determination that the doctor may enter a 'no-code' order[3] on the patient's medical record without judicial authorisation or, alternatively, if such authorisation is a legal prerequisite to the validity of a 'no-code' order, that that authorisation be given. The probate judge appointed a guardian *ad litem*, who has taken a position in opposition to the prayers of the complaint.

... This case does not offer a life-saving or life-prolonging treatment alternative within the meaning of the *Saikewicz* case. It presents a question peculiarly within the competence of the medical profession of what measures are appropriate to ease the imminent passing of an irreversibly, terminally ill patient in light of the patient's history and condition and the wishes of her family. That question is not one for judicial decision, but one for the attending physician, in keeping with the highest traditions of his profession, and subject to court review only to the extent that it may be contended that he has failed to exercise 'the degree of care and skill of the average qualified practitioner, taking into account the advances in the profession'.

The case is remanded to the Probate Court, where a judgment is to enter in accordance with the prayers of the complaint for declaratory relief, declaring that on the findings made by the judge the law does not prohibit a course of medical treatment which excludes attempts at resuscitation in the event of cardiac or respiratory arrest and that the validity of an order to that effect does not depend on prior judicial approval.

Note to extract

3. The terminology derives from the development in recent years, in acute care hospitals, of specialised 'teams' of doctors and nurses trained in the administration of cardiopulmonary resuscitative measures. If a patient goes into cardiac or respiratory arrest, the nurse in attendance causes a notice to be broadcast on the hospital's intercommunications system giving a code word and the room number. The members of the code team converge on the room immediately from other parts

of the hospital. In the hospital in question, if the code is broadcast at night, all doctors then in the hospital for whatever reason are expected to respond to the code. A 'no-code' order entered in a patient's medical record instructs the nursing staff, as part of the attending physician's ongoing instructions to the nursing staff for the care of the patient, not to summon the code team in the event of cardiac or respiratory arrest. A no-code order is sometimes called ONTR (order not to resuscitate); (Rabkin, Gillerman, & Rice, Orders Not to Resuscitate, 295 New Eng J Med 364 [1976]) or DNR (do not resuscitate) (*Re Quinlan*, 70 NJ 10, 29, 355 A 2d 647; cert denied sub nom *Garger v New Jersey*, 429 US 922, 97 S Ct 319, 50 L Ed 2d 289 (1976)).

Do you agree with our view that this is really a case within category B and, in particular, group 2 and was misanalysed by the court? There is a problem, however. You will see that the court's approach is not consistent with that adopted in *Spring* because the court in *Dinnerstein* held that only *if* a patient fell within category A (as we have defined it) could recourse to the court be dispensed with. The court went on to hold that if there was some possibility of benefit to the patient, in the sense of a chance of cure or remission, then the court must be consulted, at least when it was proposed not to offer the treatment. The consultation is intended to allow the court to make the ultimate decision. Is this reconcilable with the subsequent decision of the higher court, the Supreme Judicial Court of Massachusetts, in *Re Spring* (1980)?

3. Group 3 patients

This group of patients was helpfully defined by Dr Fred Plum, a leading academic neurologist in the *Quinlan* case, as a person: 'who remains with the capacity to maintain the vegetative parts of neurological function but who ... no longer has any cognitive function'. (For our discussion of this sort of person in the context of the definition of death, see *infra* ch 15.)

The law begins with what has become one of the most famous of all medical-legal cases—In *Re Quinlan* 355 A 2d 647 (1976), a decision of the New Jersey Supreme Court. The case captured the attention of the world, both because of its tragic facts and because it caused the highest court in a leading jurisdiction in America to wrestle for the first time with the questions of the definition of death and the doctor's duty to the dying and the comatose.

Hughes CJ: *The litigation*

The central figure in this tragic case is Karen Ann Quinlan, a New Jersey resident. At the age of 22, she lies in a debilitated and allegedly moribund state at Saint Clare's Hospital in Denville, New Jersey. The litigation has to do, in final analysis, with her life,—its continuance or cessation,—and the responsibilities, rights and duties, with regard to any fateful decision concerning it, of her family, her guardian, her doctors, the hospital, the State through its law enforcement authorities, and finally the courts of justice.

. . .

The factual base

. . .

On the night of April 15, 1975, for reasons still unclear, Karen Quinlan ceased breathing for at least two 15 minute periods. She received some ineffectual mouth-to-mouth resuscitation from friends. She was taken by ambulance to Newton Memorial Hospital. There she had a temperature of 100 degrees, her pupils were unreactive and she was unresponsive even to deep pain. The history at the time of her admission to that hospital was essentially incomplete and uninformative.

Three days later, Dr Morse examined Karen at the request of the Newton admitting physician, Dr McGee. He found her comatose with evidence of decortication, a condition relating to derangement of the cortex of the brain causing a physical posture in which the upper extremities are flexed and the lower extremities are extended. She required a respirator to assist her breathing. Dr Morse was unable to obtain an adequate account of the circumstances and events leading up to Karen's admission to the Newton Hospital. Such initial history or etiology is crucial in neurological diagnosis. Relying as he did upon the Newton Memorial records and his own examination, he concluded that prolonged lack of oxygen in the bloodstream, anoxia, was identified with her condition as he saw it upon first observation. When she was later transferred to Saint Clare's Hospital she was still unconscious, still on a respirator and a tracheotomy had been performed. On her arrival Dr Morse conducted extensive and detailed examinations. An electroencephalogram (EEG) measuring electrical rhythm of the brain was performed and Dr Morse characterised the result as 'abnormal but it showed some activity and was consistent with her clinical state'. Other significant neurological tests, including a brain scan, an angiogram, and a lumbar puncture were normal in result. Dr Morse testified that Karen has been in a state of coma, lack of consciousness, since the began treating her. He explained that there are basically two types of coma, sleep-like unresponsiveness and awake unresponsiveness. Karen was originally in a sleep-like unresponsive condition but soon developed 'sleep-wake' cycles, apparently a normal improvement for comatose patients occurring wtihin three to four weeks. In the awake cycle she blinks, cries out and does things of that sort but is still totally unaware of anyone or anything around her.

Dr Morse and other expert physicians who examined her characterised Karen as being in a 'chronic persistent vegetative state'. . . .

The further medical consensus was that Karen in addition to being comatose is in a chronic and persistent 'vegetative' state, having no awareness of anything or anyone around her and existing at a primitive reflex level. Although she does have some brain stem function (ineffective for respiration) and has other reactions one normally associates with being alive, such as moving, reacting to light, sound and noxious stimuli, blinking her eyes, and the like, the quality of her feeling impulses is unknown. She grimaces, makes stereotyped cries and sounds and has chewing motions. Her blood pressure is normal.

Karen remains in the intensive care unit at Saint Clare's Hospital, receiving 24-hour care by a team of four nurses characterised, as was the medical attention, as 'excellent'. She is nourished by feeding by way of a nasal-gastro tube and is routinely examined for infection, which under these circumstances is a serious life threat. The result is that her condition is considered remarkable under the unhappy circumstances involved.

Karen is described as emaciated; having suffered a weight loss of at least 40 pounds, and undergoing a continuing deteriorative process. Her posture is described as fetal-like and grotesque; there is extreme flexion-rigidity of the arms, legs and related muscles and her joints are severely rigid and deformed.

From all of this evidence, and including the whole testimonial record, several basic findings in the physical area are mandated. Severe brain and associated damage, albeit of uncertain etiology, has left Karen in a chronic and persistent vegetative state. No form of treatment which can cure or improve that condition is known or available. As nearly as may be determined, considering the guarded area of remote uncertainties characteristic of most medical science predictions, she can *never* be restored to cognitive or sapient life. Even with regard to the vegetative level and improvement therein (if such it may be called) the prognosis is extremely poor and the extent unknown if it should in fact occur.

She is debilitated and moribund and although fairly stable at the time of argument before us (no new information having been filed in the meanwhile in expansion of the record), no physician risked the opinion that she could live more than a year and indeed she may die much earlier. Excellent medical and nursing care so far has been able to ward off the constant threat of infection, to which she is peculiarly susceptible because of the respirator, the tracheal tube and other incidents of care in her vulnerable condition. Her life accordingly is sustained by the respirator and tubal feeding, and removal from the respirator would cause her death soon, although the time cannot be stated with more precision.

The court opted for its own (and an early) variant of 'substituted judgment':

Our affirmation of Karen's independent right of choice, however, would ordinarily be based upon her competency to assert it. The sad truth, however, is that she is grossly incompetent and we cannot discern her supposed choice based on the testimony of her previous conversations with friends, where such testimony is without sufficient probative weight. Nevertheless we have concluded that Karen's right of privacy may be asserted on her behalf by her guardian under the peculiar circumstances here present.

If a putative decision by Karen to permit this non-cognitive, vegetative existence to terminate by natural forces is regarded as a valuable incident of her right of privacy, as we believe it to be, then it should not be discarded solely on the basis that her condition prevents her conscious exercise of the choice. The only practical way to prevent destruction of the right is to permit the guardian and family of Karen to render their best judgment, subject to the qualifications hereinafter stated, as to whether she would exercise it in these circumstances. If their conclusion is in the affirmative this decision should be accepted by a society the overwhelming majority of whose members would, we think, in similar circumstances, exercise such a choice in the same way for themselves or for those closest to them. It is for this reason that we determine that Karen's right of privacy may be asserted in her behalf, in this respect, by her guardian and family under the particular circumstances presented by this record.

As a consequence, the court afforded to the plaintiff (Quinlan's father) the following relief (footnote omitted):

Upon the concurrence of the guardian and family of Karen, should the responsible attending physicians conclude that there is no reasonable possibility of Karen's ever emerging from her present comatose condition to a cognitive, sapient state and that the life-support apparatus now being administered to Karen should be discontinued, they shall consult with the hospital 'Ethics Committee' or like body of the institution in which Karen is then hospitalised. If that consultative body agrees that there is no reasonable possibility of Karen's ever emerging from her present comatose condition to a cognitive, sapient state, the present life-support system may be withdrawn and said action shall be without any civil or criminal liability therefor on the part of any participant, whether guardian, physician, hospital or others.

The reference by Hughes CJ to the hospital's Ethics Committee reflects his approval of a proposal made in an article by Dr Karen Teel cited to the court. In 'The Physician's Dilemma: A Doctor's View: What the Law Should Be?' 27 Baylor Law Review 6 (1975), Dr Teel argued (as we have seen earlier) that:

Many hospitals have established an Ethics Committee composed of physicians, social workers, attorneys, and theologians, . . . which serves to review the individual circumstances of ethical dilemma and which has provided much in the way of assistance and safeguards for patients and their medical caretakers. Generally, the authority of these committees is primarily restricted to the hospital setting and their official status is more that of an advisory body than of an enforcing body.

The concept of an Ethics Committee which has this kind of organisation and is readily accessible to those persons rendering medical care to patients, would be, I think, the most promising direction for further study at this point. . . . [This would allow] some much needed dialogue regarding these issues and [force] the point of exploring all of the options for a particular patient. It diffuses the responsibility for making these judgments. Many physicians, in many circumstances, would welcome this sharing of responsibility. I believe that such an entity could lend itself well to an assumption of a legal status which would allow courses of action not now undertaken because of the concern for liability.

Before examining what subsequent courts have made of the *Quinlan* decision, there is a central question which needs to be considered.

In laying down a procedure for decision-making in the case of this adult incompetent, what task was given by the court to:

(a) the doctor?
(b) the guardian—Quinlan's father, appointed under the New Jersey statute?
(c) the hospital Ethics Committee?

Arguably, the court confused the various responsibilities of these and in its declaration does not really provide for the application of substituted judgment. Indeed, it could be said that the court was generally confused concerning the various strands of analysis, although it may be forgiven for this since it was breaking new ground.

What the court seems to do is as follows:

(i) the court says that the decision concerning Quinlan's further treatment is for the guardian based upon his understanding of what she would wish, ie a form of substituted judgment.
(ii) but, the guardian's authority was to be exercised only if Karen Quinlan's case was hopeless such that further treatment could be regarded as 'extraordinary'.
(iii) whether Quinlan's condition was hopeless was a medical matter (rather than as it should be understood, a normative issue): being a medical matter, it was for the doctors to confirm.
(iv) but, this medical condition also had to be confirmed by the Ethics Committee—thereby transforming the Committee into a group concerned only with medical facts rather the normative response to those facts.

So, *Quinlan* seems to be a case, albeit less than clearly expressed, of substituted judgment because the court (a) heard evidence of Karen Quinlan's alleged stated wishes which she had not expressly written down, and (b) heard evidence of what her guardian thought she would have wanted. It was on this basis that the court purported to give authority to the guardian. The declaration issued by the court, however, confuses the issue by assigning to the various parties peculiar roles rather of a fact-finding nature and setting up a cumbersome procedure.

We have already seen how the New Jersey Supreme Court in the subsequent case of *Conroy* seemed to lay down general principles to be applied when determining what, if any, treatment to offer a patient in our category B. In two further cases the New Jersey Supreme Court considered the relationship between *Conroy* and *Quinlan* in the case of a patient in group 3, ie one who is in a persistent vegetative state. While content to apply, if possible, the subjective test of *Conroy* (see *Re Peter* 529 A 2d 419 (1987)), ie when there is clear and convincing evidence of the patient's real wishes, the court refused to apply the limited-objective and objective tests of *Conroy* in this situation, looking instead to the *Quinlan* decision (in *Re Jobes* A 2d 434 (1987)).

Re Peter
529 A 2d 419 (New Jersey Supreme Court (1987); footnotes omitted)

Garibaldi J: This appeal requires us to set forth the guidelines under which a life-sustaining nasogastric tube may be withdrawn from a sixty-five-year-old nursing home patient who is in a persistent vegetative state with no hope of recovery, but is not expected to die in the near future.

Hilda Peter was a secretary at Irvington General Hospital. From 1982 until she became incapacitated, she lived with her close friend, Eberhard Johanning. In

October 1984, he found her collapsed on their kitchen floor. She was resuscitated by paramedics but has remained comatose in a persistent vegetative state. Her body can maintain only the vegetative parts of neurological functions. There is no reasonable hope that she will ever regain any cognitive capacity. Since January 1985, she has been sustained by a nasogastric tube in a nursing home.

. . .

The cornerstone of our analysis of any request to decline life-sustaining medical treatment on behalf of an incompetent patient is our holding today in *Farrell*, 108 *NJ* 335, 529 *A* 2d 404 (1987), that a competent patient has the right to refuse life-sustaining medical treatment. That right is not lost because of incompetency. See *Conroy, supra*, 98 *NJ* at 356, 359–60, 486 *A* 2d 1209; *Re Quinlan* 70 *NJ* 10, 41, 355 *A* 2d 647; *cert* denied *sub nom Garger v New Jersey* 429 *US* 922, 97 *S Ct* 319, 50 *L Ed* 2d 289 (1976). All patients, competent or incompetent, with some limited cognitive ability or in a persistent vegetative state, terminally ill or not terminally ill, are entitled to choose whether or not they want life-sustaining medical treatment. We have previously explained that a surrogate decisionmaker may assert an incompetent patient's rights to self-determination and privacy. See *Conroy, supra*, 98 *NJ* at 356, 486 *A* 2d 1209; *Quinlan, supra*, 70 *NJ* at 41, 355 *A* 2d 647. In order truly to preserve those rights, 'the goal of decisionmaking for incompetent patients should be to determine and effectuate, insofar as possible, the decision that the patient would have made if competent'. *Conroy, supra*, 98 *NJ* at 360, 486 *A* 2d 1209; see *Quinlan, supra*, 70 *NJ* at 41, 355 *A* 2d 647.

Medical choices are private, regardless of whether a patient is able to make them personally or must rely on a surrogate. They are not to be decided by societal standards of reasonableness or normalcy. Rather, it is the patient's preferences—formed by his or her unique personal experiences—that should control.

The privacy that we accord medical decisions does not vary with the patient's condition or prognosis. The patient's medical condition is generally relevant only to determine whether the patient is or is not competent, and if incompetent, how the patient, in view of that condition, would choose to treat it were she or he competent.

. . . *Conroy* was specifically concerned with 'elderly, formerly competent patients' like Claire Conroy, 'who, *unlike Karen Quinlan*, are awake and conscious and can interact with their environment to a limited extent. . . . The capacities of such people, while significantly diminished, are not as limited as those of irreversibly comatose persons. . . .' *Id* at 359, 486 *A* 2d 1209. Ms Peter is not a Claire Conroy-type patient. Rather, like Karen Quinlan, she is in a persistent vegetative state. In the cases of such patients, the one-year life-expectancy test and the limited-objective and objective tests set forth in *Conroy* are inapplicable, and we look instead primarily to *Quinlan* for guidance).

Under *Quinlan*, the life-expectancy of a patient in a persistent vegetative state is not an important criterion in determining whether life-sustaining treatment may be withdrawn. For this kind of patient, our 'focal point . . . should be the prognosis as to the reasonable possibility of return to cognitive and sapient life, as distinguished from the forced continuance of . . . biological vegetative existence'. 70 *NJ* at 51, 355 *A* 2d 647. See generally Note, *The 'Terminal Condition' Condition in Virginia's Natural Death Act*, 73 *Va L Rev* 749, 771 (1987) (contrasting *Quinlan's* 'prognosis-based approach' with the approach of statutes that condition the right to decline treatment on the patient's life-expectancy.

Life-expectancy analyses assume that there are at least some benefits to be derived from the continued sustenance of an incompetent patient. That assumption, which is usually valid, see *President's Commission For the Study of Ethical Problems in Medicine and Biomedical Research, Deciding to Forego Life-Sustaining Treatment* 3 (hereinafter *President's Commission Report*), quoted in *In re Farrell, supra*, 108 *NJ* at 351, 529 *A* 2d 412, is not appropriate in the case of persistently vegetative patients such as Karen Quinlan or Ms Peter. See *infra* at 424–425. In *Quinlan*, we recognised that most people would consider an artificially-prolonged vegetative existence 'unendurable'. 70 *NJ* at 39–40, 355 *A* 2d 647. Since then other courts have similarly appreciated the special situation of surrogate decisionmakers for irreversibly vegetative patients, and have not made their option to choose among courses of medical treatment contingent on any life-expectancy test. See, eg *Corbett v D'Alessandro* 487 *So* 2d 368 (Fla Dist Ct App), review denied, 492 *So* 2d 1331 (Fla 1986) (deciding that husband of persistently vegetative patient could cause removal of her life-sustaining nasogastric tube); *Re Torres*, 357 *NW* 2d 332 (Minn 1984) (allowing conservator to cause life-sustaining respirator to be withdrawn from persistently vegetative patient); *Re Colyer*, 99 *Wash* 2d 114, 660 *P* 2d 738 (1983) (allowing husband to discontinue life-support system sustaining his wife in persistent vegetative state); see also *Brophy v New England Sinai Hosp*, 398 *Mass* 417 at 435–36, 497 *NE* 2d 626 at 636 (Mass 1986) (condemning long-term artificial sustenance of vegetative patients). Accordingly, we hold that the *Conroy* life-expectancy test is inapplicable in determining whether life-sustaining treatment may be withdrawn or withheld from a patient in a persistent vegetative state.

. . .

The limited-objective and objective tests that we established for patients like Claire Conroy balance the benefits that a patient would experience by having his or her life extended by medical treatment against the 'unavoidable pain' and suffering that he or she would feel as a result of the treatment. *Conroy, supra*, 98 *NJ* at 365–67, 486 *A* 2d 1209. Even in the case of a patient like Claire Conroy—the type of patient for whom the balancing tests were created—it can be difficult or impossible to measure the burdens of embarrassment, frustration, helplessness, rage, and other emotional pain, or the benefits or enjoyable feelings like contentment, joy, satisfaction, gratitude, and well-being that the patient experiences as a result of life-sustaining treatment. '[M]edical experts are often unable to determine with any degree of medical certainty the extent of a non-verbal person's intellectual functioning or the depth of his emotional life.' *Conroy, supra*, 98 *NJ* at 368, 486 *A* 2d 1209. Likewise, it is often 'unclear whether and to what extent a patient such as Claire Conroy is capable of, or is in fact, experiencing [physical] pain.' *Id* at 367–68, 486 *A* 2d 1209. For a perceptive analysis, see Cantor, *Conroy: Best Interests and the Handling of Dying Patients*, 37 *Rutgers L Rev* 543, 569 (1985).

While a benefits-burdens analysis is difficult with marginally cognitive patients like Claire Conroy, it is essentially impossible with patients in a persistent vegetative state. By definition such patients, like Ms Peter, do not experience any of the benefits or burdens that the *Conroy* balancing tests are intended or able to appraise. Therefore, we hold that these tests should not be applied to patients in the persistent vegetative state.

Rather, for those patients we look to *Quinlan* for guidance. Under *Quinlan,* if the guardian and family of a patient in a persistent vegetative state conclude that the patient would not want to be sustained by life-supporting treatment, and the attending physician agrees that the life-support apparatus should be discontinued, and both the attending physician and hospital prognosis committee verify the patient's medical condition, then the guardian can refuse such treatment on the patient's behalf. *Quinlan, supra*, 70 *NY* at 41, 355 *A* 2d 647. The interested parties need not have clear and convincing evidence of the patient's intentions; they need only 'render their best judgment' as to what medical decision the patient would want them to make. *Id*. In the present case, however, Ms Peter did leave clear and convincing evidence of her desire not to be sustained in her present condition. Therefore, we apply the *Conroy* subjective test in this case. . . .

Our constant goal is to insure that patients' medical preferences are respected. Therefore, the *Conroy* subjective test is applicable in every surrogate-refusal-of-treatment case, regardless of the patient's medical condition or life-expectancy. Under this test, life-sustaining treatment may be withdrawn or withheld whenever there is clear and convincing proof that if the patient were competent, he or she would decline the treatment. Once the subjective test is met, the patient's life expectancy and the balance between the benefits and burdens of continued treatment are no longer important. The patient's right to self-determination simply overrides these objective standards.

In applying the subjective test, we consider an exceptionally broad range of evidence. For a discussion of the various kinds of proof that may establish a patient's intent under the subjective test, see *Conroy, supra*, 98 *NJ* at 362, 486, *A* 2d 1209. Of course, some types of evidence are more helpful than others. Clearly, the best evidence is a 'living will', a written statement that specifically explains the patient's preferences about life-sustaining treatment. Some states have statutes that recognise the validity of living wills and prescribe procedures for their execution. See *Re Farrell, supra*, 108 *NJ* at 342—343 n 2, 529 *A* 2d at 407 n 2 (1987) (detailing relevant statutes). Unfortunately, the New Jersey Legislature has not enacted such a law. 'Whether or not they are legally binding, however, such advance directives are relevant evidence of the patient's intent.' *Conroy, supra*, 98 *NJ* at 361 n 5, 486 *A* 2d 1209.

The court in *Peter* did not determine what test should be applied when the subjective test is inapplicable. The court did resolve this in *Re Jobes* 529 A 2d 434 (1987) (New Jersey Supreme Court). In this case, the court concluded that there was no evidence which was sufficiently 'clear and convincing' to satisfy the subjective test so as to decide whether to remove the feeding tube from Mrs Jobes. The court went on to hold that in such a case the court should approach the problem as follows:

Garibaldi J: Because of the unique problems involved in decisionmaking for any patient in the persistent vegetative state, we necessarily distinguish their cases from cases involving other patients. Accordingly, in *Peter* we held that neither the life-expectancy test nor the balancing tests set forth in *Conroy* are appropriate in the case of a persistently vegetative patient. See *Peter, supra*, 108 *NJ* at 374–376, 529 *A* 2d at 423–425. Those holdings are equally relevant in this case. In any case involving a patient in the persistent vegetative state, 'we look instead primarily to *Quinlan* for guidance'. *Id* at 376, 529 *A* 2d at 425.

. . .

Where an irreversibly vegetative patient like Mrs Jobes has not clearly expressed her intentions with respect to medical treatment, the *Quinlan* 'substituted judgment' approach best accomplishes the goal of having the patient make her own decision. In most cases in which the 'substituted judgment' doctrine is applied, the surrogate decisionmaker will be a family member or close friend of the patient. Generally it is the patient's family or other loved ones who support and care for the patient, and who best understand the patient's personal values and beliefs. Hence they will be best able to make a substituted medical judgment for the patient.

The location of the patient should occasion minimal interference with the patient's right, expressed either directly or through a surrogate decisionmaker, to determine his or her treatment. Particularly at the present time—when terminal and vegetative patients are not permitted to remain in hospitals—we prefer not to impose extra restrictions on the withdrawal of treatment because the patient is at home or in a nursing home. Nevertheless, we recognise that generally, because of the presence of attending physicians and prognosis committees, hospitals afford greater protection against the premature termination or undue prolongation of life-support measures. We believe that the procedures of independent medical verification that we establish today adequately protect patients, without unduly burdening their rights to self-determination and privacy.

If a disagreement arises among the patient, family, guardian, or doctors, or if there is evidence of improper motives or malpractice, judicial intervention will be required. We expect, however, that disagreements will be rare and that intervention seldom will be necessary. We emphasise that even in those few cases in which the courts may have to intervene, they will not be making the ultimate decision whether to terminate medical treatment. Rather, they will be acting to insure that all the guidelines and procedures that we have set forth are properly followed.

Courts are not the proper place to resolve the agonizing personal problems that underlie these cases. Our legal system cannot replace the more intimate struggle that must be borne by the patient, those caring for the patient, and those who care about the patient.

The challenge for the courts will be to evolve innovative and flexible processes by which affected individuals can participate comfortably and confidently to secure the vindication of the interests we all seek to protect. [Chief Justice Joseph Weintraub Lecture by Justice Alan B Handler at Rutgers Law School (March 11, 1987), 119 *NJLJ* 482 (March 19, 1987).]

Ideally, each person should set forth his or her intentions with respect to life-supporting treatment. This insures that the patient's own resolution of this extraordinarily personal issue will be honored. Failure to express one's intentions imposes an awesome and painful responsibility on the surrogate decisionmaker.

Handler J (concurring) added:

Today this Court holds that though Mrs Jobes' intention to accept or refuse life-sustaining treatment has not been clearly established by clear and convincing evidence, the Court will uphold the decision of close family members who made the treatment determination based on what they believe Mrs Jobes would have decided. *Ante* at 446–447. The court is satisfied to effectuate the decision of the patient's family. It has in these circumstances adopted the individual right of self-determination reflected by the substituted judgment of a surrogate decisionmaker as the standard for resolving the fundamental issue of whether to terminate life-sustaining treatment.

While this 'substituted judgment' standard fits well the facts of this case, the Court notes that in many cases this standard will not be workable, e g, in cases where the patient has always been incompetent or when there is no one sufficiently familiar with the patient to be able to know how the patient would have decided. *Ante* at 449–450. The Court does not suggest standards for how treatment decisions should be made in such cases. *Id*. I would add that there will be difficult cases in which the relationship of family members or putative friends of the patient may not be close enough for them to be an appropriate source for the awesome decision of whether to discontinue life-perpetuating treatment.

In the cases now before the Court, the decision to discontinue or to refuse treatment was either made by the patient herself or made by the patient's guardian on the basis of trustworthy evidence of what the patient would have decided.

So, New Jersey law has arrived at the position in which 'substituted judgment' is capable of two meanings. The first is in the case of the patient in a persistent vegetative state, and in such a case it means that which the court in *Quinlan* decided. The second meaning applies in the case of a patient who is still able to interact with the environment, or will be able to do so having received the proposed treatment, albeit that the level of interaction is extremely limited as in *Conroy* itself. The meaning here of 'substituted judgment' is the 'limited-objective' test. As the word 'objective' implies, it is a test which combines the concern of the court in *Quinlan* for the views and preferences of the patient as expressed to others, with an objective assessment of whether the proposed procedure will bring greater benefit than burden to the patient. The consideration of benefits and burdens is ignored as regards the patient in the persistent vegetative state since the court assumes that the patient is beyond benefit or burden. Indeed, given the objective element employed in *Conroy*, is it right to call the limited-objective test an example of substituted judgment at all?

In addition to the drawback already expressed concerning *Quinlan*—that there is always a risk of placing decision-making power in the hands of relatives—are there any other drawbacks in the approach of the New Jersey courts?

Would an English court, given its ever ready recourse to the best interests test and its reluctance to become involved in what it regards as questions of medical judgment, be prepared to engage in the level of detailed analysis represented by the New Jersey cases? But, is such an approach necessary to establish the legal nature of the doctor's duty with any certainty? In part, English law would say 'no' because it does not recognise any authority in the patient's relatives.

On the other hand, the doctor does need some legal test in reaching decisions about treatment and there is no reason in principle why the New Jersey approach could not be incorporated into English law including the recognition of the role of relatives as providing evidence of the wishes and preferences of the patient. If such a development occurred in English law, the courts would also have to address the question of what, if any, checks should be placed upon the role to be played by the relatives. As we have seen, Garibaldi J considered this problem in some detail in *Jobes*. In addition to what we have already seen, he said (footnotes omitted):

Garibaldi J: Normally those family members close enough to make a substituted judgment would be a spouse, parents, adult children, or siblings. Generally in the absence of such a close degree of kinship, we would not countenance health care professionals deferring to the relatives of a patient, and a guardian would have to be appointed. However, if the attending health care professionals determine that another relative, eg, a cousin, aunt, uncle, niece, or nephew, functions in the role of the patient's nuclear family, then that relative can and should be treated as a close and caring family member. See *Re Farrell, supra*, 108 *NJ* at 355, 529 *A* 2d at 414 (noting the conspicuous presence of family members vis-a-vis health care professionals).

There will, of course, be some unfortunate situations in which family members will not act to protect a patient. We anticipate that such cases will be exceptional. Whenever a health-care professional becomes uncertain about whether family members are properly protecting a patient's interests, termination of life-sustaining treatment should not occur without the appointment of a guardian.

We realise that there may be rare situations where a health-care professional's assessment of a family situation proves to be wrong. In such a case, if the professional has made a good faith determination in this regard, he or she will not be subject to any criminal or civil liability.

Mrs Jobes is blessed with warm, close, and loving family members. It is entirely proper to assume that they are best qualified to determine the medical decisions she would make. Moreover, there is some trustworthy evidence that supports their judgment of Mrs Jobes' personal inclinations. Therefore, we will not presume to disturb their decision.

Thus, we hold that the right of a patient in an irreversibly vegetative state to determine whether to refuse life-sustaining medical treatment may be exercised by the patient's family or close friend. If there are close and caring family members who are willing to make this decision there is no need to have a guardian appointed. We require merely that the responsible relatives comply with the medical confirmation procedures that we henceforth establish. . . . If there are no close family members, and the patient has not left clear and convincing evidence that he or she intended another relative or a nonrelative friend to make surrogate medical decisions in the case of his or her incompetency, see, eg, *Peter, supra*, 108 *NJ* at 370, 529 *A* 2d at 422 (where patient gave her friend durable power of attorney to make medical decisions), then a guardian must be appointed and comply with the following procedural requirements. Cf *id* at 384, 529 *A* 2d at 429.

. . .

In *Quinlan*, we realised that in the absence of legislation, the responsibility of establishing procedural guidelines for the effectuation of decisions to withdraw life-support is incumbent upon the court. Therefore, we held that when the guardian, the family, and the attending physician concur that life support should be withdrawn from a hospital patient in a persistent vegetative state, they must secure the confirmation of a hospital prognosis committee that there is no reasonable possibility that the patient might recover to a cognitive sapient state. See *Quinlan, supra*, 70 *NJ* at 50, 355 *A* 2d 647. Once such a confirmation is secured, the life-supporting treatment may be withdrawn. *Id Quinlan* specifically rejected any provision for judicial review of this procedure as unnecessary and 'impossibly cumbersome'. See *Id*.

Amicus New Jersey Hospital Association has informed us that since *Quinlan* was decided, approximately eighty-five percent of New Jersey's acute-care hospitals have established prognosis committees that check the attending physician's prognosis when withdrawal of life support from a vegetative patient is under consideration. Thus it appears that the *Quinlan* procedure is functioning in the setting for which it was intended.

Mrs Jobes, of course, is in a nursing home rather than a hospital. We believe, however, that the processes of surrogate decisionmaking should be substantially the same regardless of where the patient is located. Otherwise, the patient's right to determine his or her medical treatment could be frustrated by an irrelevant factor. Nevertheless, we recognise there are safeguards in a hospital that are usually not present in a nursing home, ie, the hospital patient normally has his or her own attending physician and, as noted above, many hospitals have prognosis committees. The lack of these safeguards was among the reasons that we developed the Ombudsman procedures that protect elderly nursing home patients. See *Conroy, supra*, 98 *NJ* at 375–76, 486 *A* 2d 1209; *Peter, supra*, 108 *NJ* at 383, 529 *A* 2d at 428.

Because Mrs Jobes is not elderly, the Ombudsman does not have jurisdiction over her case. See *NJSA* 52:27G-1, 2(i) (Ombudsman has jurisdiction only in cases where the patient is at least sixty years old). Fortunately, Mrs Jobes is not in the vulnerable predicament that so many elderly nursing home patients are in because she has a caring and responsible family. For non-elderly non-hospitalised patients in a persistent vegetative state who, like Mrs Jobes, have a caring family or close friend, or a court-appointed guardian in attendance, we hold that the surrogate decisionmaker who declines life-sustaining medical treatment must secure statements from at least two independent physicians knowledgeable in neurology that the patient is in a persistent vegetative state and that there is no reasonable possibility that the patient will ever recover to a cognitive, sapient state. If the patient has an attending physician, then that physician likewise must submit such a statement. These independent neurological confirmations will substitute for the concurrence of the prognosis committee for patients who are not in a hospital setting and thereby prevent inappropriate withdrawal of treatment. In a proper case, however, they should not be difficult to obtain, and this requirement should not subject the patient to undesired treatment.

As long as the guidelines we hereby establish are followed in good faith, no criminal or civil liability will attach to anyone involved in the implementation of a surrogate decision to decline medical treatment. Accordingly, judicial review of such decisions is not necessary or appropriate. As we have explained, patients and their families may suffer when the courts become involved in their sensitive and personal medical decisions:

No matter how expedited, judicial intervention in this complex and sensitive area may take too long. Thus, it could infringe the very rights that we want to protect. The mere prospect of a cumbersome, intrusive and expensive court proceeding, during such an emotional and upsetting period in the lives of a patient and his or her loved ones, would undoubtedly deter many persons from deciding to discontinue treatment. And even if the patient or the family were willing to submit to such a proceeding, it is likely that the patient's rights would nevertheless be frustrated by judicial deliberation. Too many patients have died before their right to reject treatment was vindicated in court. . . . Of course, if there is a dispute among the members of a patient's family, the guardian and the physicians, any interested party can invoke judicial aid to insure that the guidelines we have established are properly followed and that the patient is protected.

Do you think an English court would adopt this procedural scheme?

Advance directives

We have seen that some of the American cases considered above refer to the fact that the patient had made an 'advance directive', such as a 'living will'. Such directives constitute attempts by a person to stipulate what treatment he should receive should he ever become incompetent and is unable to make his intentions known. They are, therefore, attempts to define the doctor's duty in terms of the patient's expressed wishes, rather than in terms of the general law.

The President's Commission (*op cit*) in its 1983 Report (pp 136–9) describes the basis of an advanced directive and the situation in the United States at the time of the Report. By the end of 1987, 38 states and the District of Columbia had enacted living will statutes. Every state now has a durable power of attorney statute, although only some (e g California) make specific provision for health care decisions.

Advance directives

An 'advance directive' lets people anticipate that they may be unable to participate in future decisions about their own health care—an 'instruction directive' specifies the types of care a person wants (or does not want) to receive; a 'proxy directive' specifies the surrogate a person wants to make such decisions if the person is ever unable to do so; and the two forms may be combined. Honoring such a directive shows respect for self-determination in that it fulfils two of the three values that underlie self-determination. First, following a directive, particularly one that gives specific instructions about types of acceptable and unacceptable interventions, fulfils the instrumental role of self-determination by promoting the patient's subjective, individual evaluation of well-being. Second, honoring the directive shows respect for the patient as a person.

An advance directive does not, however, provide self-determination in the sense of active moral agency by the patient on his or her own behalf. The discussion between patient and health care professional leading up to a directive would involve active participation and shared decisionmaking, but at the point of actual decision the patient is incapable of participating. Consequently, although self-determination is involved when a patient establishes a way to project his or her wishes into a time of anticipated incapacity, it is a sense of self-determination lacking in one important attribute: active, contemporaneous personal choice. Hence a decision not to follow an advance directive may sometimes be justified even when it would not be acceptable to disregard a competent patient's contemporaneous choice. Such a decision would most often rest on a finding that the patient did not adequately envision and consider the particular situation within which the actual medical decision must be made.

Advance directives are not confined to decisions to forego life-sustaining treatment but may be drafted for use in any health care situation in which people anticipate they will lack capacity to make decisions for themselves. However, the best-known type of directive—formulated pursuant to a 'natural death' act—does deal with decisions to forego life-sustaining treatment. Beginning with the passage in 1976 of the California Natural Death Act, 14 states and the District of Columbia have enacted statutory authorisation for the formulation of advance directives to forego life-sustaining treatment. . . . In addition, 42 states have enacted 'durable power of attorney' statutes; though developed in the context of law concerning property, these statutes may be used to provide a legal authority for an advance directive. . . .

Despite a number of unresolved issues about how advance directives should be drafted, given legal effect, and used in clinical practice, the Commission recommends that advance directives should expressly be endowed with legal effect under state law. For such documents to assist decisionmaking, however, people must be encouraged to develop them for their individual use, and health care professionals should be encouraged to respect and abide by advance directives whenever reasonably possible, even without specific legislative authority.

Existing alternative documents. Several forms of advance directives are currently used. 'Living wills' were initially developed as documents without any binding legal effects; they are ordinarily instruction directives. The intent behind the original 'natural death' act was simply to give legal recognition to living wills drafted according to certain established requirements. They are primarily instruction directives, although their terms are poorly enough defined that the physician and surrogate who will carry them out will have to make substantial interpretations. 'Durable power of attorney' statutes are primarily proxy directives, although by limiting or describing the circumstances in which they are to operate they also contain elements of instruction directives. Furthermore, durable powers of attorney may incorporate extensive personal instructions.

Two preliminary points are worth noting here, both of which will be developed later. You will notice that the President's Commission refer to the wishes of the patient sometimes running the risk of being frustrated by an advance directive 'when the patient did not adequately envisage and consider the particular situation'. This overlooks the development mentioned in the next paragraph of the Report of the 'enduring power of attorney' whereby a proxy may be empowered to decide on behalf of the patient. The other matter is one which bedevilled American thinking and practice concerning advance directives and concerns what we call the 'triggering event', considered *infra*, ie the event which brings into operation the advance directive. You will notice that the President's Commission say that these directives 'are not confined to decisions to forego *life-sustaining* treatment' (our emphasis). This implies that the onset of incompetence would be enough of itself to trigger the provisions of an advance directive whatever these directions might be and whether or not the patient was dying. In fact, however, as we will see, everywhere in the United States there has been insistence on terminal illness or imminent death or some such expression.

Before noticing in outline the development in the United States we must consider what, if any, validity advance directives have in English law.

(a) THE VALIDITY OF ADVANCE DIRECTIVES IN ENGLISH LAW

(i) The living will

The President's Commission discussed the 'living will' in its 1983 Report (pp 139–141).

Living wills. People's concerns about the loss of ability to direct care at the end of their lives have led a number of commentators as well as religious, educational, and professional groups to promulgate documents, usually refered to as living wills,[49] by which individuals can indicate their preference not to be given 'heroic' or 'extraordinary' treatments. There have been many versions proposed, varying widely in their specificity. Some explicitly detailed directives have been drafted by physicians—outlining a litany of treatments to be foregone or disabilities they would not wish to suffer in their final days.[50] The model living wills proposed by educational groups have somewhat more general language[51]; they typically mention 'life-sustaining procedures which would serve only to artificially prolong the dying process'. One New York group has distributed millions of living wills.[52] The columnist who writes 'Dear Abby' reports receiving tens of thousands of requests for copies each time she deals with the subject.[53] Despite their popularity, their legal force and effect is uncertain.[54] The absence of explicit statutory authorisation in most jurisdictions raises a number of important issues that patients and their lawyers or other advisors should keep in mind when drafting living wills.

First, it is uncertain whether health care personnel are required to carry out the terms of a living will; conversely, those who, in good faith, act in accordance with living wills are not assured immunity from civil or criminal prosecution. No penalties are provided for the destruction, concealment, forgery or other misuse of living wills, which leaves them somewhat vulnerable to abuse. The question of whether a refusal of life-sustaining therapy constitutes suicide is unresolved,as are the insurance implications of a patient's having died as a result of a physician's withholding treatment pursuant to a living will.

Yet even in states that have not enacted legislation to recognise and implement advance directives, living wills may still have some legal effect.[55] For example, should a practitioner be threatened with civil liability or criminal prosecution for having acted in accord with such a document, it should at least serve as evidence of a patient's wishes and assessment of benefit when he or she was competent.[56] Indeed, no practitioner has been successfully subjected to civil liability or criminal prosecution for having followed the provisions in a living will, nor do there appear to be any cases brought for having acted against one.[57]

Notes to extract
[49] *Questions and Answers About the Living Wills* (pamphlet), Concern for Dying, New York (nd).
[50] Walter Modell, *A 'Will' to Live* (Sounding Board), 290 New Eng J Med 907 (1974); *Last Rights* (Letters), 295 New Eng J Med 1139 (1976); See also Sissela Bok, *Personal Directions for Care at the End of Life*, 295 New Eng J Med 367 (1976).
[51] Among the groups that have promulgated living wills are the Society for the Right to Die, the Euthanasia Education Council, the American Protestant Hospital Association, the American Catholic Hospital Association, and the American Public Health Association.
[52] See note 49 *supra*.
[53] Letter from Abigail van Buren to Joanne Lynn (Sept 10, 1981). Ann Landers reports similar public enthusiasm. Letter from Ann Landers to Joanne Lynn (Sept 16, 1981).
[54] For a discussion of the legal effects of living wills, see Luis Kutner, *Due Process of Euthanasia: The Living Will, A Proposal*, 44 Ind LJ 539, 552 (1969); Michael T Sullivan, *The Dying Person—His Plight and His Right*, 8 New Eng L Rev 197, 215 (1973); Comment, *Antidysthanasia Contracts: A Proposal for Legalising Death With Dignity*, 5 Pac LJ 738, 739–40 (1974); Note, *The 'Living Will': The Right to Death With Dignity?*, 26 Case W Res L Rev 485, 509–526 (1976); Note, *Informed Consent and the Dying Patient*, 83 Yale LJ 1632, 1663–64 (1974); Note, *The Right to Die*, 10 Cal WL Rev 613, 625 (1974).
[55] See Note, *Living Wills—Need for Legal Recognition*, 78 W Va L Rev 370 (1976); See also, *Re Storar* 52 NY 2d 363, 420 NE 2d 64 (1981) (on reliance on oral advance directives with burden of proof being clear and convincing evidence).
[56] See Kutner, *supra* note 54; Note, *The 'Living Will': The Right to Death with Dignity?*, *supra* note 54; David J Sharpe and Robert F Hargest, *Lifesaving Treatment for Unwilling Patients*, 36 Fordham L Rev 695, 702 (1968).
[57] A UPI study, reported in *The Right to Die*, 12 Trial (Jan 1976), stated that no living will had been tested in the courts. None since has come to the Commission's attention.

Since the Report, American courts have dealt with cases in which the patient had made a living will. We have already seen that the New Jersey case of *Conroy* determines that under the subjective test a patient's wishes, clearly and compellingly stated, are to determine the treatment, if any, he should receive— otherwise the doctor would commit a battery. In *Conroy*, the court considered that a living will could be evidence of a patient's wishes at common law (footnote omitted).

Garibaldi J: The patient may have expressed, in one or more ways, an intent not to have life-sustaining medical intervention. Such an intent might be embodied in a written document, or "living will", stating the person's desire not to have certain types of life-sustaining treatment administered under certain circumstances. It might also be evidenced in an oral directive that the patient gave to a family member, friend, or health care provider.

The court, in a footnote, approved the earlier Florida Supreme Court case of *John F Kennedy Memorial Hospital v Bludworth* 452 So 2d 921 (1984) where it was said:

> **Alderman CJ:** We have recognised that terminally ill incompetent persons being sustained only through use of extraordinary artificial means have the same right to refuse to be held on the threshold of death as terminally ill competent persons. Since incompetent persons may not exercise this right while they are incompetent, there must be a means by which this right may be exercised on their behalf, otherwise it will be lost. The means developed by the courts to afford this right to incompetent persons is the doctrine of 'substituted judgment'. Under this doctrine close family members or legal guardians substitute their judgment for what they believe the terminally ill incompetent persons, if competent, would have done under these circumstances. If such a person, while competent, had executed a so-called 'living' or 'mercy' will, that will would be persuasive evidence of that incompetent person's intention and it should be given great weight by the person or persons who substitute their judgment on behalf of the terminally ill incompetent.

Question

Would an English court take the same view of the common law?

In similar circumstances, the Ontario High Court in 1987 held a doctor liable in battery for ignoring an incompetent patient's expression of her wishes, written before the onset of incompetence.

Malette v Shulman
(1988) 63 OR (2d) 243 (Ontario High Court)

> **Donnelly J:** Dr Shulman, on being confronted with an unconscious patient in a life threatening situation in whose possession was found a card refusing blood as a Jehovah's Witness, faced a dilemma of dreadful finality. An immediate decision was required, either to follow the instruction given by the card or to administer the blood transfusion which he regarded as medically essential. He squarely faced the fundamental issue of the conflict between the patient's right over her own body and society's interest in preserving life.
>
> Dr Shulman acknowledged an awareness of the patient's right to make a decision against a certain treatment in favour of alternative treatment and of his ethical obligation to abide by that decision. However, upon considering the validity of the card, he was not reasonably satisfied that it constituted an adequate instruction because there was no evidence that (1) it represented the plaintiff's current intent; (2) the instruction applied to the present life threatening circumstances; (3) at the time the plaintiff made the decision and signed the card she was fully informed of risk of refusal of treatment and accordingly that this was a rational and informed decision.
>
> Since there was a 'shadow of doubt' regarding 'informed' rejection of treatment, Dr Shulman regarded himself as obliged to treat to the best of his ability and administered blood.
> . . .
> The 'card' was subject to attack by the defence on the basis of its inherent frailties—that it may have been signed because of religious peer pressure, under medical misinformation, not in contemplation of life threatening circumstances, or that it may not represent current instructions.
> . . .
> Mrs Bisson's participation has the effect of rendering unlikely these speculative frailties. It confirms the card and signature as her mother's, her mother's current status as a Jehovah's Witness and her mother's wish not to have blood. It raises nothing inconsistent with the card representing the mother's current intent applying to life threatening situations. The card itself presents a clear, concise statement, essentially stating, 'As a Jehovah's Witness, I refuse blood'. That message is

unqualified. It does not exempt life threatening perils. On the face of the card, its message is seen to be rooted in religious conviction. Its obvious purpose as a card is as protection to speak in circumstances where the card carrier cannot (presumably because of illness or injury). There is no basis in evidence to indicate that the card may not represent the current intention and instruction of the card holder.

I therefore find that the card is a written declaration of a valid position which the card carrier may legitimately take in imposing a written restriction on her contract with the doctor. Dr Shulman's doubt about the validity of the card, although honest, was not rationally founded on the evidence before him. Accordingly, but for the issue of informed refusal, there was no rationally founded basis for the doctor to ignore that restriction.

Informed Refusal
A conscious, rational patient is entitled to refuse any medical treatment and the doctor must comply, no matter how ill advised he may believe that instruction to be. The doctor lawfully invades the patient's body for the purpose of treatment only after he has fully communicated to the patient the risks of treatment and the patient makes the affirmative decision, premised on a reasonable appreciation and awareness of the risks, to permit that treatment for his body. Otherwise such treatment is a battery with liability consequences.

. . .

The defence contended that the Doctrine of Informed Consent should be extended to Informed Refusal on the following analysis. Since there is an obligation on the doctor recommending treatment to advise as to the risks, it must logically follow there is a higher duty where the patient proposes a course of action that the doctor believes to be prejudicial. Thus Dr Shulman was obliged in law to advise the refusing patient of the attendant risks. Only then could he be satisfied that the refusal was based on a proper understanding of risks. There was no opportunity to fulfil his obligation to ensure there was an opportunity for an informed choice and so he was not bound by the refusal of treatment.

No case has been cited supporting this concept of Informed Refusal of Treatment.

. . .

The Doctrine of Informed Consent does not extend to Informed Refusal. The written direction contained in the card was not properly disregarded on the basis that circumstances prohibited verification of that decision as an informed choice. The card constituted a valid restriction of Dr Shulman's right to treat the patient and the administration of blood by Dr Shulman did constitute battery.

(In *Re Saunders* 492 NYS 2d 510 (1985) a New York Court declared the patient's living will to have the following effect):

McCaffrey J: Thus, in the absence of the Legislature to adopt or enact a statute that would otherwise recognise the validity of a living will, . . . the court declares the following:
(1) The court deems the document executed by the petitioner to be in the nature of an informed medical consent statement by her authorising the refusal or discontinuance of further medical treatment by artificial means or devices when or if she is terminally ill, with death imminent and suffers irreversible brain damage and becomes comatose and no longer able to express her wishes (hereinafter, the 'stated condition').
(2) The document executed by the petitioner is evidence of the most persuasive quality and is a clear and convincing demonstration that while competent the petitioner clearly and explicitly expressed an informed, rational and knowing decision to decline certain medical treatment by artificial means and devices while in a terminally ill state or condition and it should be given great weight by the hospital authorities and treating physicians attending her.
(3) That the right to discontinue medical treatment by means of artificial means and devices is not lost when and if the petitioner is found to be in the 'stated condition' specified in (1) above and is no longer able to personally express her wishes to refuse or discontinue medical treatment by use of artificial means or devices.

(4) No further judicial proceedings or court order is required for the discontinuance of medical treatment by artificial means or devices if such discontinuance is in accordance with accepted medical practices said petitioner is found to be in the 'stated condition' specified in (1) above.

. . .

(ii)   The enduring power of attorney

In its 1988 Report, the Working Party on *The Living Will* (King's College, London/Age Concern) discussed the validity of enduring powers of attorney in relation to health care decisions under the existing English law (at 48–9; footnotes omitted).

. . .

Powers of attorney

As regards powers of attorney, under the Common Law it is arguable that an adult patient could nominate another as his agent so that the other may take decisions concerning the patient's health. There seems, however, to be no reported case in which this has occurred. In any event, any agency would (in the absence of any statutory provision) terminate on the incompetence of the patient.

As for statute law, the agency which a person may create for the management of his affairs under the Powers of Attorney Act 1971, terminates on the incompetence of that person. The Enduring Powers of Attorney Act 1985, however, permits the creation of a power of attorney which, providing certain statutory conditions are met, continues after the creator has become incompetent. Although the Act was designed to give power to deal specifically with the financial affairs of the individual, the question arises whether section 3(1) of the Act, which states that the scope of the general authority of an enduring power of attorney extends to an incompetent's 'property or affairs', thereby covers health care decisions, specifically about treatment. It is most unlikely that a court would so construe the statute in the light of the treatment of what is now Section 95 of the Mental Health Act, 1983 in *re W (EEM)* [1971]. When interpreting the Court of Protection's powers 'with respect to the property and affairs of a patient' in relation to this case Ungoed-Thomas J stated that the court did not have jurisdiction over 'the management or care of the patient's person', . . .

It seems, therefore, that without a specific statutory provision creating an enduring power of attorney in relation to health care decisions, this form of advance directive has no legal validity, unlike for example in California, since the Durable Power of Attorney Health Care Act, 1983.

Even when their state has not enacted an enduring power of attorney Act specially in relation to health care decisions the courts have been prepared to interpret a general statutory provision as extending to include health care decision. In *Re Jobes (supra)* Schrieber J said:

Hilda Peter did not leave a living will, but she did execute a durable power of attorney, which specifically authorises Eberhard Johanning to make 'all medical decisions' for her and 'to be given full and complete authority to manage and direct her medical care'. New Jersey's Powers of Attorney statute provides that a 'principal may confer authority on an agent that is to be exercisable notwithstanding later disability or incapacity of the principal at law or later uncertainty as to whether the principal is dead or alive.' *NJSA* 46:2B–8(a). Although the statute does not specifically authorise conveyance of durable authority to make medical decisions, it should be interpreted that way. *See Conroy, supra,* 98, *NJ* at 361, 486 *A* 2d 1209. *See generally President's Commission Report, supra,* at 146–47; Note, *Appointing An Agent to Make Medical Treatment Choices,* 84 *Colum L Rev* 985, 1015–20 (1984) (recommending that durable powers of attorney statutes be construed to empower conveyance of authority to make medical decisions).

It would have been better if Ms Peter had specifically provided in her power of attorney that Mr Johanning had authority to terminate life-sustaining treatment.

Nonetheless, that instrument, which she executed shortly before she became incompetent; Mr. Johanning's explanation that Ms Peter directed him to refuse life-sustaining treatment on her behalf in a situation like this; and nine reliable hearsay accounts of her disinclination for the kind of treatment that Mr Johanning seeks to discontinue establish clearly and convincingly that Hilda Peter would, if competent, choose to withdraw the nasogastric tube that is sustaining her.

Question

Do you think that in the absence of any specific statutory provision an English court is likely to take the approach adopted in *Re Jobes*?

(b) DEVELOPMENTS IN THE UNITED STATES

We take the view that the interest in advance directives is likely to increase in the United Kingdom with consequent pressure to clarify their legal status or enact appropriate legislation. For this reason, it may be instructive to examine briefly the current state of the law in the United States.

(i) The early living will statutes

The first living will statute in the United States was the California Natural Death Act 1976.

7186. Legislative findings and declarations

The Legislature finds that adult persons have the fundamental right to control the decisions relating to the rendering of their own medical care, including the decision to have life-sustaining procedures withheld or withdrawn in instances of a terminal condition.

The Legislature further finds that modern medical technology has made possible the artificial prolongation of human life beyond natural limits.

The Legislature further finds that, in the interest of protecting individual autonomy, such prolongation of life for persons with a terminal condition may cause loss of patient dignity and unnecessary pain and suffering, while providing nothing medically necessary or beneficial to the patient.

The Legislature further finds that there exists considerable uncertainty in the medical and legal professions as to the legality of terminating the use or application of life-sustaining procedures where the patient has voluntarily and in sound mind evidenced a desire that such procedures be withheld or withdrawn.

In recognition of the dignity and privacy which patients have a right to expect, the Legislature hereby declares that the laws of the State of California shall recognise the right of an adult person to make a written directive instructing his physician to withhold or withdraw life-sustaining procedures in the event of a terminal condition.

7187. Definitions

The following definitions shall govern the construction of this chapter.

(a) . . .

(b) 'Directive' means a written document voluntarily executed by the declarant in accordance with the requirements of section 7188. The directive, or a copy of the directive, shall be made part of the patient's medical records.

(c) 'Life-sustaining procedures' means any medical procedure or intervention which utilises mechanical or other artificial means to sustain, restore, or supplant a vital function, which, when applied to a qualified patient, would serve only to artificially prolong the moment of death and where, in the judgment of the attending physician, death is imminent whether or not such procedures are utilised. 'Life-sustaining procedure' shall not include the administration of medication or the performance of any medical procedure deemed necessary to alleviate pain.

(d) . . .

(e) 'Qualified patient' means a patient diagnosed and certified in writing to be afflicted with a terminal condition by two physicians, one of whom shall be the attending physician, who have personally examined the patient.

(f) 'Terminal condition' means an incurable condition caused by injury, disease, or illness, which, regardless of the application of life-sustaining procedures, would, within reasonable medical judgment, produce death, and where the application of life-sustaining procedures serves only to postpone the moment of death of the patient.

7188. Directive to physicians

Any adult person may execute a directive directing the withholding or withdrawal of life-sustaining procedures in a terminal condition. The directive shall be signed by the declarant in the presence of two witnesses not related to the declarant by blood or marriage and who would not be entitled to any portion of the estate of the declarant upon his decease under any will of the declarant or codicil thereto then existing or, at the time of the directive, by operation of law then existing. In addition, a witness to a directive shall not be the attending physician, an employee of the attending physician or a health facility in which the declarant is a patient, or any person who has a claim against any portion of the estate of the declarant upon his decease at the time of the execution of the directive. The directive shall be in the following form.:

DIRECTIVE TO PHYSICIANS

Directive made this _____ day of _____ (month, year). I _____, being of sound mind, willfully, and voluntarily make known my desire that my life shall not be artificially prolonged under the circumstances set forth below, do hereby declare:
1. If at any time I should have an incurable injury, disease, or illness certified to be a terminal condition by two physicians, and where the application of life-sustaining procedures would serve only to artificially prolong the moment of my death and where my physician determines that my death is imminent whether or not life-sustaining procedures are utilised, I direct that such procedures be withheld or withdrawn, and that I be permitted to die naturally.
2. In the absence of my ability to give directions regarding the use of such life-sustaining procedures, it is my intention that this directive shall be honored by my family and physician(s) as the final expression of my legal right to refuse medical or surgical treatment and accept the consequences from such refusal.
3. If I have been diagnosed as pregnant and that diagnosis is known to my physician, this directive shall have no force or effect during the course of my pregnancy.
4. I have been diagnosed and notified at least 14 days ago as having a terminal condition by _____, MD, whose address is _____, and whose telephone number is _____. I understand that if I have not filled in the physician's name and address, it shall be presumed that I did not have a terminal condition when I made out this directive.
5. This directive shall have no force or effect five years from the date filled in above.
6. I understand the full import of this directive and I am emotionally and mentally competent to make this directive.

Signed _____
City, County and State of Residence _____

The declarant has been personally known to me and I believe him or her to be of sound mind.

Witness_____
Witness_____

7188.5. Directive to physicians: patient in skilled nursing facility

A directive shall have no force or effect if the declarant is a patient in a skilled nursing facility as defined in subdivision (c) of Section 1250 at the time the directive is executed unless one of the two witnesses to the directive is a patient advocate or ombudsman as may be designated by the State Department of Aging for this purpose pursuant to any other applicable provision of law. The patient advocate or ombudsman shall have the same qualifications as a witness under Section 7188.

The intent of this section is to recognise that some patients in skilled nursing facilities may be so insulated from a voluntary decisionmaking role, by virtue of the custodial nature of their care, as to require special assurance that they are capable of willfully and voluntarily executing a directive.

7189. Revocation of directive

(a) A directive may be revoked at any time by the declarant, without regard to his mental state or competency, by any of the following methods:

(1) By being canceled, defaced, obliterated, or burnt, torn, or otherwise destroyed by the declarant or by some person in his presence and by his direction.

(2) By a written revocation of the declarant expressing his intent to revoke, signed and dated by the declarant. Such revocation shall become effective only upon communication to the attending physician by the declarant or by a person acting on behalf of the declarant. The attending physician shall record in the patient's medical record the time and date when he received notification of the written revocation.

(3) By a verbal expression by the declarant of his intent to revoke the directive. Such revocation shall become effective only upon communication to the attending physician by the declarant or by a person acting on behalf of the declarant. The attending physician shall record in the patient's medical record the time, date, and place of the revocation and the time, date, and place, if different, of when he received notification of the revocation.

(b) There shall be no criminal or civil liability on the part of any person for failure to act upon a revocation made pursuant to this section unless that person has actual knowledge of the revocation.

7189.5. Term of directive

A directive shall be effective for five years from the date of execution thereof, unless sooner revoked in a manner prescribed in Section 7189. Nothing in this chapter shall be construed to prevent a declarant from reexecuting a directive at any time in accordance with the formalities of Section 7188, including reexecution subsequent to a diagnosis of a terminal condition. If the declarant has executed more than one directive, such time shall be determined from the date of execution of the last directive known to the attending physician. If the declarant becomes comatose or is rendered incapable of communicating with the attending physician, the directive shall remain in effect for the duration of the comatose condition or until such time as the declarant's condition renders him or her able to communicate with the attending physician.

7190. Immunity from civil or criminal liability

No physician or health facility which, acting in accordance with the requirements of this chapter, causes the withholding or withdrawal of life-sustaining procedures from a qualified patient, shall be subject to civil liability therefrom. No licensed health professional, acting under the direction of a physician, who participates in the withholding or withdrawal of life-sustaining procedures in accordance with the provisions of this chapter shall be subject to any civil liability. No physician, or licensed health professional acting under the direction of a physician, who participates in the withholding or withdrawal of life-sustaining procedures in accordance with the provisions of this chapter shall be guilty of any criminal act or of unprofessional conduct.

7191. Duties of physician

(a) Prior to effecting a withholding or withdrawal of life-sustaining procedures from a qualified patient pursuant to the directive, the attending physician shall determine that the directive complies with Section 7188, and, if the patient is mentally competent, that the directive and all steps proposed by the attending physician to be undertaken are in accord with the desires of the qualified patient.

(b) If the declarant was a qualified patient at least 14 days prior to executing or reexecuting the directive, the directive shall be conclusively presumed, unless revoked, to be the directions of the patient regarding the withholding or withdrawal of life-sustaining procedures. No physician, and no licensed health professional acting under the direction of a physician, shall be criminally or civilly liable for failing to effectuate the directive of the qualified patient pursuant to this subdivision. A failure by a physician to effectuate the directive of a qualified patient pursuant to this division shall constitute unprofessional conduct if the physician refuses to make the necessary arrangements, or fails to take the necessary steps, to effect the transfer of the qualified patient to another physician who will effectuate the directive of the qualified patient.

(c) If the declarant becomes a qualified patient subsequent to executing the directive, and has not subsequently reexecuted the directive, the attending physician may give weight to the directive as evidence of the patient's directions regarding the withholding or withdrawal of life-sustaining procedures and may consider other factors, such as information from the affected family or the nature of the patient's illness, or injury, or disease, in determining whether the totality of circumstances known to the attending physician justify effectuating the directive. No physician, and no licensed health professional acting under the direction of a physician, shall be criminally or civilly liable for failing to effectuate the directive of the qualified patient pursuant to this subdivision.

7192. Suicide: insurance

(a) The withholding or withdrawal of life-sustaining procedures from a qualified patient in accordance with the provisions of this chapter shall not, for any purpose, constitute a suicide.

(b) The making of a directive pursuant to Section 7188 shall not restrict, inhibit, or impair in any manner the sale, procurement, or issuance of any policy of life insurance, nor shall it be deemed to modify the terms of an existing policy of life insurance. No policy of life insurance shall be legally impaired or invalidated in any manner by the withholding or withdrawal of life-sustaining procedures from an insured qualified patient, notwithstanding any term of the policy to the contrary.

(c) No physician, health facility, or other health provider, and no health care service plan, insurer issuing disability insurance, self-insured employee welfare benefit plan, or nonprofit hospital service plan, shall require any person to execute a directive as a condition, for being insured for, or receiving, health care services.

7193. Rights as cumulative

Nothing in this chapter shall impair or supersede any legal right or legal responsibility which any person may have to effect the withholding or withdrawal of life-sustaining procedures in any lawful manner. In such respect the provisions of this chapter are cumulative.

7194. Criminal penalties

Any person who wilfully conceals, cancels, defaces, obliterates, or damages the directive of another without such declarant's consent shall be guilty of a misdemeanor. Any person who, except where justified or excused by law, falsifies or forges the directive of another, or wilfully conceals or withholds personal knowledge of a revocation as provided in Section 7189, with the intent to cause a withholding or withdrawal of life-sustaining procedures contrary to the wishes of the declarant, and thereby, because of any such act, directly causes life-sustaining procedures to be withheld or withdrawn and death to thereby be hastened, shall be subject to prosecution for unlawful homicide as provided in Chapter 1 (commencing with Section 187) of Title 8 of Part 1 of the Penal Code.

7195. Construction of chapter

Nothing in this chapter shall be construed to condone, authorise, or approve mercy killing, or to permit any affirmative or deliberate act or omission to end life other than to permit the natural process of dying as provided in this chapter.

The President's Commission *op cit* (pp 141–5) (footnotes omitted) discussed critically this and other early Natural Death Acts.

Natural death acts. To overcome the uncertain legal status of living wills, 13 states and the District of Columbia have followed the lead set by California in 1976 and enacted statutes that formally establish the requirements for a 'directive to physicians'. The California statute was labeled a 'natural death' act and this term is now used generically to refer to other state statutes. Although well-intended, these acts raise a great many new problems without solving many of the old ones.

No natural death act yet deals with all the issues raised when living wills are used without specific statutory sanction. For instance, the acts differ considerably in their treatment of penalties for failing to act in accord with a properly executed directive or to transfer the patient to a physician who will follow the directive. In some jurisdictions, the statutes consider these failures to be unprofessional conduct and therefore grounds for professional discipline, including the suspension of a license to practice medicine. Other statutes fail to address the issue, presumably, however, existing remedies such as injunctions or suits for breach of contract or for battery are available to patients or their heirs, although there do not appear to be any instances of such penalties being sought.

Some of the statutes attempt to provide patients with adequate opportunity to reconsider their decision by imposing a waiting period between the time when a patient decides that further treatment is unwanted and the time when the directive becomes effective. Under the California statute, for example, a directive is binding only if it is signed by a 'qualified patient', technically defined as someone who has been diagnosed as having a 'terminal condition'. This is defined as an incurable condition that means death is 'imminent' regardless of the 'life-sustaining procedures' used. A patient must wait 14 days after being told of the diagnosis before he or she can sign a directive, which would require a miraculous cure, a misdiagnosis, or a very loose interpretation of the word 'imminent' in order for the directive to be of any use to a patient. The statute requires that when a directive is signed, the patient must be fully competent and not overwhelmed by disease or by the effects of treatment, but a study of California physicians one year after the new law was enacted found that only about half the patients diagnosed as terminally ill even remain conscious for 14 days. There is an inherent tension between ensuring that dying patients have a means of expressing their wishes about treatment termination before they are overcome by incompetence and ensuring that people do not make binding choices about treatment on the basis of hypothetical rather than real facts about their illness and dying process. If a waiting period is deemed necessary to resolve this tension the time should be defined in a way that does not substantially undercut the objective of encouraging advance directives by people who are at risk of becoming incapacitated.

Although the California statute was inspired in part by the situation of Karen Quinlan, whose father had to pursue judicial relief for a year in order to authorise the removal of her respirator, it would not apply in a case like hers.

> The only patients covered by this statute are those who are on the edge of death *despite the doctors' efforts*. The very people for whom the greatest concern is expressed about a prolonged and undignified dying process are unaffected by the statute because their deaths are not imminent.

The class of persons thus defined by many of the statutes, if it indeed contains any members, at most constitutes a small percentage of those incapacitated individuals for whom decisions about life-sustaining treatment must be made. Although some statutes have not explicitly adopted the requirement that treatments may be withheld or withdrawn only if death is imminent whether or not they are used, this requirement is still found in one of the most recently passed natural death acts. Such a limitation greatly reduces an act's potential.

Some of the patients for whom decisions to forego life-sustaining treatment need to be made are residents of nursing homes rather than hospitals. Concerned that they might be under undue pressure to sign a directive, the California legislature provided additional safeguards for the voluntariness of their directives by requiring that a patient advocate or ombudsman serve as a witness. The Commission believes that health care providers should make reasonable efforts to involve disinterested parties, not only as witnesses to the signing of a directive under a natural death act, but also as counselors to patients who request such a directive to ensure that they are acting as voluntarily and competently as possible. Yet statutory requirements of this sort may have the effect of precluding use of advance directives by long-term care residents, even though some residents of these facilities might be as capable as any other person of using the procedure in a free and knowing fashion.

Paradoxically, natural death acts may restrict patients' ability to have their wishes about life-sustaining treatment respected. If health care providers view these as the exclusive means for making and implementing a decision to forego treatment and, worse, if they believe that such a decision cannot be made by a surrogate on behalf of another but only in accordance with an advance directive properly executed by a patient, some dying patients may be subject to treatment that is neither desired nor beneficial. In fact, although 6.5% of the physicians surveyed in California reported that during the first year after passage of the act there they withheld or withdrew procedures they previously would have administered. 10% of the physicians reported that they provided treatment they formerly would have withheld.

In addition there is the danger that people will infer that a patient who has not executed a directive in accordance with the natural death act does not desire life-sustaining treatment to be ended under any circumstances. Yet the person may fail to sign a directive because of ignorance of its existence, inattention to its significance, uncertainty about how to execute one, or failure to foresee the kind of medical circumstances that in fact develop. Unfortunately, even the explicit disclaimer contained in many of these laws—that the act is not intended to impair or supersede any preexisting common-law legal rights or responsibilities that patients and practitioners may have with respect to the withholding or withdrawing of life-sustaining procedures—does not in itself correct this difficulty.

First, the declarations about the right of competent patients to refuse 'life-sustaining procedures' take on a rather pale appearance since such procedures are defined by the statutes as those that cannot stop an imminent death. (In other words, competent patients may refuse futile treatments.) Second, it is hard to place great reliance on preexisting common law rights, since had the common law established such rights there would have been no real need for the statutes. Thus, if health care providers are to treat patients appropriately in states that have adopted natural death acts, they will need the encouragement of their attorneys—backed by sensible judicial interpretation of the statutes—to read the acts as authorising a new, additional means for patients to exercise 'informed consent' regarding life-saving treatment, but not as a means that limits decisionmaking of patients who have not executed binding directives pursuant to the act.

The greatest value of the natural death acts is the impetus they provide for discussions between patients and practitioners about decisions to forego life-sustaining treatment. This educational effect might be obtained, however, without making the documents binding by statute and without enforcement and punishment provisions.

You will remember we mentioned earlier the difficulties concerning the 'triggering event'. This features in the comments of the President's Commission above and is discussed more fully by G Gelfand 'Living Will Statutes: The First Decade' (1987) Wisconsin LR 737, 740–744 and 746–7.

Every existing living will act requires that the patient's physical condition or prognosis be 'terminal' or sufficiently poor in order to bring the provisions of a living will into effect.[8] Subtle differences in the way the various statutes define this requirement are crucial because medical treatments may not be withheld unless the declarant's condition qualifies under the statute.

The most significant difference among the various statutory definitions concerns whether the patient's terminal status must be determined irrespective of the effect of the life-supporting treatments. Surprisingly, half of the current living will statutes require that the patient be in a condition where death will occur shortly *whether or not* life-supporting treatments are employed.[9] If the patient will die shortly with or without life-supporting treatment, there is little reason to engage in euthanasia.[10]

Further, if the intent of living will statutes was to permit the 'natural death' of persons who would otherwise linger for years maintained by modern machinery in a vegetative but 'alive' state,[11] then the requirement that death be imminent whether or not treatment is withdrawn nullifies the purpose of such statutes. Even states that have repeatedly 'fine-tuned' their living will statutes through amendments, however, continue to define the necessary patient prognosis as requiring imminent death even with medical treatment.[12] This contradiction between legislative intent and action almost certainly occurs by oversight, as many such statutes are internally inconsistent with regard to this point.[13] In jurisdictions with such inconsistent statutes, a physician presented with a typical and seemingly proper case for the application of a living will—that is, a comatose, terminal individual who can be mechanically maintained with no change in prognosis for years—would have to seek judicial clarification of the statutory definition[14] or risk a homicide prosecution for ending the life of such a patient.[15]

A related question involves the timing of death generally for the purposes of defining a qualified terminally ill patient. A number of statutes require that the patient's condition be such that medical treatments serve only to postpone the moment of dying.[16] This may be the best definition possible, for it conveys more of a sense of the futility of treatment than a time frame for death. Yet such a provision would be far too broad if taken literally. Most medical interventions serve only to postpone the moment of death, even in an otherwise healthy patient.

Other statutes require that death be 'imminent',[17] or that it will occur within a 'short time'.[18] These provisions seem to contain the most appropriate standard[19] since the objective of living will statutes was to allow for the euthanatising of patients with little or no remaining life. However, this standard substitutes a time measure for what is really a more profound question about the futility of medical treatment.[20] If a patient will linger, even for a considerable time, in a vegetative state which medical treatment cannot improve, the intent of living will statutes arguably should be to allow such a patient to die.[21] Perhaps the most satisfactory codification of this intent is found in Alabama's living will statute which allows discontinuance of treatment where 'death is imminent or [the patient's] condition is hopeless'.[22]

. . .

Perhaps the most important question, however, concerns the need for such a definition of any kind in the statutes. Political compromise has produced the present requirement that the patient's prognosis be terminal. Yet there may be many cases in which a patient could live for a substantial period, but only if he endures great pain, total physical incapacity, or drastic treatment such as amputation. Since living will statutes reflect a dramatic step toward the recognition of patient autonomy, it can be expected that future provisions will permit the decision to decline treatment in such non-terminal cases.

Notes to extract
8. Every living will act requires that the patient's prognosis be 'terminal' or the like. Thirty-two states and the Uniform Act, while attaching varying meanings to the term, require that the patient be in a 'terminal condition'. See Cal Health & Safety Code § 7187(f) (West Supp 1976); Tex Rev Civ Stat Ann art 4590h, § 2(7) (Vernon 1977, 1979, 1983, 1985); 1987 Ark Act 713 § 1(7) (1977, 1987) ('terminal condition or in a permanently unconscious state'); Or Rev Stat § 97.050(6) (1977, 1983, 1987); Nev Rev Stat § 449.590 (1977, 1985); Kan Stat Ann § 65-28, 102(e) (1979); Wash Rev Code Ann § 70-122.020(7) (1979); D C Code Ann 6-2421(6) (1981); Del Code Ann tit 16, § 2501(e) (1982, 1983); Wis Stat Ann § 154.01(8) (West 1983, 1986); Ill Ann Stat ch 110½, § 702(h) (Smith-Hurd 1983, 1987); Va Code Ann § 54-325.8:2 (1983, 1984); Wyo Stat § 32-36-144(a)(vi) (1984, 1985); W Va Code § 16-30-2(6) (1984); Ga Code Ann § 31-32-2(10) (1984, 1986, 1987); Fla Stat Ann § 765.03(6) (West 1984, 1985); La Rev Stat Ann § 40:1299.58.2(8) (West 1984, 1985); Mo Ann Stat § 459.010(6) (Vernon 1985); Tenn Code Ann § 32-11-103(9) (1985); Mont Code Ann § 50-9.102(7) (1985); Colo Rev Stat § 15-18-103(10) (1985); Okla Stat Ann tit

63, § 3102(8) (West 1985, 1987); Iowa Code Ann § 144A.2(8) (West 1985, 1987); Ind Code Ann § 16-8-11-9 (Burns 1985); Md Health-Gen Code Ann §5-601(g) (1985, 1987); Me Rev Stat Ann tit 22, § 2921(8) (1985); N H Rev Stat Ann § 137-H:2(VI) (1985); Ariz Rev Stat Ann § 36-3201(6) (1985); Conn Gen Stat § 19a570(3) (1985); Utah Code Ann § 75-2-1103(7) (1985); Alaska Stat § 18.12.100(7) (1986); S C Code Ann § 44-77-20(d) (Law Co-op 1986); Haw Rev Stat § 327D-2 (1986). See also Uniform Act § 1(9) (1985); N M Stat Ann § 24-7-2(F) (1977, 1984) ('terminal illness'); Vt Stat Ann tit 18, § 5252(5) (1981) (patient must be in a 'terminal state'); Ala Code § 22-8A-3(6) (1981) (patient must be 'terminally ill or injured'). Two other statutes have similar requirements that are left unnamed. See NC Gen Stat § 90-321(b) (1977, 1979, 1981, 1983); Miss Code Ann § 41-41-107 [in official form] (1984). Idaho had such a requirement in 1977 (Idaho Code § 39-4503(2) (1977)), but this definition was deleted in the 1986 amendments, as was the word 'terminal' in every place where that term had previously appeared in the statute. The Idaho Legislature's intention in making this change is not clear.

The judicially created rights, on the other hand, do not depend on the patient being in such a terminal condition. Notably, the California and Georgia courts have essentially held their states' 'terminal condition' requirements unconstitutional. See *Bouvia v Superior Court*, 179 Cal App 3d 1127, 225 Cal Rptr 297 (1986); *Bartling v Superior Court*, 163 Cal App 3d 186, 209 Cal Rptr 220 (1984); *Zant v Prevatte*, 248 Ga 832, 286 SE 2d 715 (1982). The Model Act set out in Section V of this Article, following the logic of these decisions, and the eloquent dissent of Justice Douglas of the New Hampshire Supreme Court, does not require that a declarant be in a 'terminal condition'. See Model Act, § IC3; *Re Caulk*, 125 NH 226, 232, 480 A 2d 93, 97 (1984); see also Note, *Re Caulk: A Prisoner's Right to Die—the Factor of Intent*, 37 Me L Rev 447 (1985).

9. See, eg, Del Code Ann tit 16, § 2501(e) (1982, 1983) (emphasis added): '"Terminal condition" shall mean any disease, illness or condition sustained by any human being from which there is no reasonable medical expectation of recovery and which, as a medical probability, will result in the death of such human being *regardless of the use or discontinuance* of medical treatment implemented for the purpose of sustaining life, or the life processes.' Prior to 'fine-tuning' by amendment in 1983, this section had required that 'death [be] imminent, whether or not such procedures are utilised'. See *infra* notes 12–13 and accompanying text.

For similar provisions, see Cal Health & Safety Code § 7187(f) (West Supp 1976); N M Stat Ann § 24-7-2(F) (1977, 1984); Tex Rev Civ Stat Ann art 4590h, § 2(4) (Vernon 1977, 1979, 1983, 1985); Or Rev Stat § 97.050(6) (1977, 1983, 1985, 1987); Idaho Code § 39-4503(3) (1977, 1986); Kan Stat Ann § 65-28, 102(c) (1979); Wash Rev Code Ann § 70.122.020(4), (7) (1979); Vt Stat Ann tit 18, § 5252(5) (1981); Ala Code § 22-8A-3(3) (1981); D C Code Ann § 6-2421(6) (1981); Del Code Ann tit 16, § 2501(e) (1982, 1983); Wyo Stat § 33-26-144(a)(iii), (vi) (1984, 1985); W Va Code § 16-30-2(3), (6) (1984); Ga Code Ann § 31-32-2(10) (1984, 1986, 1987); Mo Ann Stat § 459.010(3), (6) (Vernon 1985); Tenn Code Ann § 32-11-103(9) (1985); Okla Stat Ann tit 63, § 3102(4), (8) (West 1985, 1987); Utah Code Ann § 75-2-1103(7) (1985). The Louisiana statute contained this language in 1984, but it was deleted by amendment in 1985. The same language, however, still appears in the 1985 version of the official form. La Rev Stat Ann § 40:1299.58.3(c) (West 1984, 1985).

Further, the provisions of the living will acts of Alabama, Maryland and South Carolina are internally inconsistent with regard to whether the terminal condition is determined with or without regard to continued use of life-supporting treatments.

See also Wash Rev Code Ann § 70.122.020(4) (1979): '"Life sustaining procedure" means any medical or surgical procedure or intervention which ... would serve only to artificially prolong the moment of death and where, in the judgment of the attending physician, death is imminent whether or not such procedures are utilised.' The Georgia, California, Texas, Oklahoma, Idaho, Oregon, and Wyoming provisions, *supra*, are similar.

The Wisconsin Act once contained the most implausible of these provisions: '"Terminal Condition" means an incurable condition caused by injury or illness that reasonable medical judgment finds would cause death within 30 days, regardless of the application of life-sustaining procedures, so that the application of life-sustaining procedures serves only to postpone the moment of death.' The words 'within 30 days' were changed to 'imminently' by the 1986 amendment. Wis Stat Ann § 154.01(8) (West 1983, 1986).

10. See 9B ULA 609, § 1 comment at 612–13 (1985).

11. See, eg, the legislative findings accompanying the California Natural Death Act:

The Legislature . . . finds that modern medical technology has made possible the artificial prolongation of human life beyond natural limits.

The Legislature further finds that, in the interest of protecting individual autonomy, such prolongation of life for persons . . . may cause a loss of patient dignity and unnecessary pain and suffering, while providing nothing medically necessary or beneficial to the patient.

Cal Health & Safety Code § 7186 (West Supp 1976). About half of the statutes have similar legislative declarations.

12. The most notable example is Delaware's provision. See Del Code Ann tit 16, § 2501(e) (1982, 1983). The provision in question was drafted in 1982. That particular provision was amended and improved by the deletion of an 'imminency' requirement in 1983, yet the crucial inappropriate language remains. See also Wisconsin's statute, discussed *supra* note 9. The Texas, New Mexico, Oregon, Idaho, Wyoming, and Georgia provisions have likewise been amended over the past few years, yet they continue to have the inappropriate provision requiring that death be imminent even with the use of life-prolonging treatments.

13. The provisions on this point of the Alabama, South Carolina and Maryland acts are most likely the product of oversight because these acts are internally inconsistent. Alabama's Act, § 22-8A-3(3), requires that 'death will occur *whether or not* [life-sustaining procedures are] utilised'. Section 22-8A-3(6), however, requires that the patient be in a condition such that 'death is imminent or [his] condition is hopeless *unless* he or she is artificially supported through [life-sustaining procedures]' (emphasis added).

Maryland's comparable section, 5-601, is internally inconsistent. Sections 5-601(e) and (g) define both 'life-sustaining procedure' and 'terminal condition' in a manner that assumes that the patient could be kept 'alive' by such procedures. Indeed, subsection (e) stresses that such procedures 'would serve to secure only a precarious and burdensome *prolongation* of life' (emphasis added). Thus, it is clear that the Maryland legislature realised that the patient could live for a 'prolong[ed]' period. Yet, the official form of Declaration, provided in section 5-602(c), states 'If at any time . . . the physicians have determined that my death is imminent and will occur *whether or not* life-sustaining procedures are utilised' (emphasis added). Subsequent terminology within the same declaration reverses course again and suggests that the life-sustaining procedures could 'artificially prolong' the patient's life.

The recently enacted South Carolina statute is also internally inconsistent. Section 44-77-20(b) defines 'life-sustaining procedures' as those where death will occur '*whether or not*' they are used (emphasis added). However, subsection (d) defines a 'terminal condition' as one where 'death is imminent *without* the use of life-sustaining procedures' (emphasis added). The official form employs the latter language. See § 44-77-50.

It must be noted, however, that the Oklahoma and Missouri provisions, which contain the 'death is imminent regardless of medical procedures' language, might reflect an intentional choice by the respective legislatures. Both statutes are patterned after the Uniform Act which explicitly rejects such language in its definition. Thus, the Oklahoma and Missouri legislatures would have had to affirmatively change the language to obtain the provisions found in their statutes. No reason for doing so is apparent.

14. An alternative would be to proceed outside the statute, as such statutes do not provide the exclusive course of action. . . .

15. The 'good faith' immunity may not apply to a physician's error of law. . . .

16. See Cal Health & Safety Code § 7187(f) (West Supp 1976); Tex Rev Civ Stat Ann § 4590h, 2(7) (Vernon 1977, 1979, 1983, 1985); N C Gen Stat § 90-321(a)(2) (1977, 1979, 1981, 1983); 1987 Ark Act 713 § 1(4) (1977, 1987); Or Rev Stat § 97.050(6) (1977, 1983, 1985, 1987); Idaho Code § 39-4503(3) (1977, 1986); Nev Rev Stat § 449.590 (1977, 1985); Kan Stat Ann § 65-28, 102(c) (1979); Wash Rev Code Ann § 70.122.020(7) (1979); Vt Stat Ann tit 18, § 5252(5) (1981); Ala Code § 22-8A-3(3) (1981); D C Code Ann § 6-2421(6) (1981); Del Code Ann tit 16, § 2501(d) (1981, 1983); Wis Stat Ann § 154.01(8) (West 1983, 1986); Ill Ann Stat ch 110½, § 702(h) (Smith-Hurd 1983); Va Code Ann § 54.325.8:2 (1983, 1984); W Va Code § 16-30-2(6) (1984); Wyo Stat § 33-26-144(a)(iii) (1984, 1985); Ga Code Ann § 31-32-2(5) (1984, 1986, 1987); Fla Stat Ann § 765.03(3)(b) (West 1984, 1985); La Rev Stat Ann § 40:1299.58.2(8) (West 1984, 1985); Mo Ann Stat § 459.010(3) (Vernon 1985); Mont Code Ann § 50-9-102(4) (1985); Colo Rev Stat § 15-18-103(10) (1985); Okla Stat Ann tit 63, § 3102(8) (West 1985, 1987); Iowa Code Ann § 144A.2(5)(b) (West 1985, 1987); Ind Code Ann § 16-8-11-4(2) (Burns 1985); Me Rev Stat Ann tit 22, § 2921(4) (1985); N H Rev Stat Ann § 137-H:2(VI) (1985); Ariz Rev Stat Ann § 36-3201(4) (1985); Conn Gen Stat § 19a-570(1) (1985); Utah Code Ann § 75-2-1103(6)(a) (1985); Alaska Stat § 18.12.100(4) (1986); S C Code Ann § 44-77-20(b) (Law Co-op 1986); Haw Rev Stat § 327D-2 (1986); Uniform Act § 1(4) (1985).

17. The eight statutes cited *supra* note 9 require that death be 'imminent' regardless of whether or not medical treatment is employed. In addition, the following eight statutes simply require that death be 'imminent' (unless medical treatments are employed): Wis Stat Ann § 154.01(8) (West 1983, 1986); Ill Ann Stat ch 110½, § 702(h) (Smith-Hurd 1983); Va Code Ann § 54-325.8:2 (1983, 1984); Wyo Stat § 33-26 144(a)(vi) (1984, 1985); Fla Stat Ann § 765.03(6) (West 1984); Md Health-Gen Code Ann § 5-601(g) (1985, 1987); N H Rev Stat Ann § 137-H:2(VI) (1985); S C Code Ann § 44-77-20(d)(ii) (Law Co-op 1986).

18. The statutes of four states require that death will occur within a 'short time'. See Mo Ann Stat § 459.010(3), (6) (Vernon 1985); Tenn Code Ann § 32-11-103(9) (1985); Ind Code Ann § 16-8-11-9(2) (Burns 1985); Me Rev Stat Ann tit 22, § 2921(8) (1985). Further, the statutes of five states and the Uniform Act specify a 'relatively short time'. See Mont Code Ann § 50-9-102(7) (1985); Iowa Code Ann § 144A.2(8) (West 1985, 1987); Alaska Stat § 18.12.100(7) (1986); Haw Rev Stat § 327D-2 (1986); 1987 Ark Act 713 § (9) (1977, 1987); Uniform Act § 1(9) (1985).

19. Notably, all eight ('short time' and 'relatively short time') provisions discussed *supra* note 18 are among the most recent and may indicate a trend.

20. A patient like Karen Quinlan, who lingered in a coma (unaided by the life-prolonging treatments that living will acts would allow to be discontinued) during virtually the entire first decade of living will statutes, could not be terminated under any of these provisions. See *Re Quinlan*, 70 NJ 10, 355 A 2d 647; *cert denied*, 429 US 922 (1976). But see 1987 Ark Act 713 (1977, 1987) (special provisions throughout the Act dealing with patients who are 'permanently unconscious').

Compare Del Code Ann tit 16, § 2501(e) (1982, 1983) ('will result in the death'); N M Stat Ann § 24-7-2(F) (1977, 1984) (same); Conn Gen Stat § 19a-570(3) (1985) (same); Or Rev Stat § 97.050(6) (1977, 1983, 1985, 1987) (will 'produce death'); Vt Stat Ann tit 18, § 5252(5) (1981) (same); La Rev Stat Ann § 40:1299.58.2(8) (West 1984, 1985) (same); Utah Code Ann § 75-2-1103(7) (1985) (same); Ala Code § 22-8A-3(3) (1981) ('death will occur'); W Va Code § 16-30-2(3) (1984) (same); Ariz Rev Stat Ann § 36-3201(6) (1985) (same); D C Code Ann § 6-2421(3), (6) (1981) ((3) same as Alabama; (6) same as Oregon); Ga Code Ann § 31-32-2(5), (10) (1984, 1986, 1987) ((5) same as Alabama; (10) same as Oregon).

21. See, eg, *supra* note 11 (quoting from the legislative findings accompanying the California Act). On the other hand, since most living will statutes do not allow death by starvation or active euthanasia, some cases will occur where the patient simply will not die even though treatment is withdrawn or withheld.

22. Ala Code § 22-8A-3(6) (1981). In suggesting the Alabama statute as a model, however, the contradictory provision in section 22-8A-3(3) should not be included. See *supra* note 13.

A further limitation concerns the types of treatment that a patient may require a doctor not to offer. Gelfand (pp 750–3) discusses this also:

In defining the types of treatments which may be withheld, the vast majority of living will statutes specifically exempt nutrition, hydration, comfort care, and the alleviation of pain.[49] Many other statutes which do not discuss the point probably were not intended to differ in substance.[50] Under such statutes, food, water, comfort care, and pain reduction techniques cannot be withdrawn.[51] These restrictions produce a dilemma in cases where the techniques necessary to reduce pain or maintain nutrition and hydration also prolong the life (and misery) of the patient.

... [A]n ... approach to this problem would be to modify the existing living will forms, as Alaska's and Utah's very recent statutes do, to permit the declarant to specify his individual wishes with regard to such treatments.[54]

The reluctance of most states to permit such a choice is undoubtedly the result of the none-too-merciful image of a patient slowly and painfully starving to death.[55] This problem, of course, would not arise if living will statutes permitted active euthanasia.

A number of states further require that the only types of treatments which may be withheld are those that are 'mechanical' and 'artificial'.[56] Delaware's statute in particular goes to some lengths to emphasise this requirement.[57] Such a requirement probably stems from the image of 'natural' death that was employed to generate legislative support for living will statutes. But the terms 'mechanical' and 'artificial' may prove unduly restrictive. For example, while some treatments may be artificial in some sense, they may not be mechanical if performed by a person such as a physician, nurse, or respiratory therapist, acting without the aid of any machines.

The requirement that only mechanical and artificial treatments may be withdrawn or withheld is probably intended to distinguish between services such as natural feeding and 'artificial' means of feeding—ie, intravenous feeding or feeding through a nasogastric tube.[58] Alaska explicitly draws this distinction by allowing the withholding of nutrition or hydration which is 'provided by gastric tube or intravenously'.[59]

Emotional considerations aside, it is not clear why a legal distinction should turn on the use of a tube. It may be argued that the artificial methods are more invasive. The concern about invasiveness, however, would have to be viewed only in a very short-term sense to justify such a distinction. If the less invasive treatment is keeping the patient alive, it is, in a larger sense, causing the patient's continued exposure to other invasive treatments and to the suffering and indignity of a life of greatly diminished value. Keeping such a patient alive against his wishes is at least as invasive to his right to self-determination as the tube is to his (often insensate) body.

Similar requirements that such treatments be 'extraordinary'[60] suffer from a lack of any useful analytical content. References to the 'extraordinary' or 'heroic'[61] nature of treatments convey little more than a conclusion that the particular treatment should be withdrawn.[62] If the word extraordinary is given its commonly understood meaning, today's extraordinary treatment will be tomorrow's ordinary treatment as its use becomes accepted. The patient's choice should depend instead on the success or futility of the treatment's application.

Notes to extract
49. See the following statutes exempting nutrition, hydration, and treatments to reduce pain: 1987 Ark Act 713 § 6(b) (1977, 1987); Idaho Code § 39-4503(3) (1977, 1986); Wis Stat Ann § 154.01(5)(a), (b) (West 1983, 1986); Ga Code Ann § 31-32-2(5)(A), (B) (1984, 1986, 1987); Fla Stat Ann § 765.03(3) (West 1984, 1985); Mo Ann Stat § 459.010(3) (Vernon 1985); Tenn Code Ann § 32-11-103(5), (6) (1985); Mont Code Ann § 50-9-202(2) (1985); Colo Rev Stat § 15-18-103(7) (1985); Okla Stat Ann tit 63, § 3102(4) (West 1985, 1987); Iowa Code Ann § 144A.2(5) (West 1985, 1987); Ind Code Ann § 16-8-11-4 (Burns 1985); Md Health-Gen Code Ann § 5-605(1) (1985, 1987); N H Rev Stat Ann § 137-H·2(II) (1985); Me Rev Stat Ann tit 22 § 2921(4) (1985); Ariz Rev Stat Ann § 36-3201(4) (1985); Conn Gen Stat §§ 19a-570(1), 19a-573 (1985); S C Code Ann § 44-77-20(b) (Law Co-op 1986); Haw Rev Stat § 327D-2 (1986).

The following statutes expressly exempt only pain medication and comfort care: Cal Health & Safety Code § 7187(c) (West Supp 1976); Tex Rev Civ Stat Ann art 4590h, § 2(4) (Vernon 1977, 1979, 1983, 1985); Nev Rev Stat § 449.570 (1977, 1985); Kan Stat Ann § 65-28, 102(c) (1979); Wash Rev Code Ann § 70.122.020(4) (1979); Vt Stat Ann tit 18, § 5253 (in official form) (1981); Ala Code § 22-8A-3(3) (1981); D C Code Ann § 6-2421(3) (1981); Del Code Ann tit 16, § 2501(d) (1982, 1983); Ill Ann Stat ch 110½, § 702(d) (Smith-Hurd 1983, 1987); Va Code Ann § 54-325.8:2 (1983, 1984); W Va Code § 16-30-2(3) (1984); Wyo Stat § 33-26-144(a)(iii) (1984, 1985). Notably, this second group of statutes is comprised of earlier versions than the first group with statutory coverage of nutrition and hydration, and the first group probably reflects the future trend. In addition, Maine exempts nutrition and hydration only. See Me Rev Stat Ann tit 22, § 2921(4) (1985). Oregon's statute exempts comfort care, pain medication and nutrition (and probably hydration, as part of nutrition), but subjects this exemption to the phrase 'which in the medical judgment of the attending physician a patient can tolerate', and other restrictions. Or Rev State § 97.050(3) (1977, 1983, 1985, 1987). Louisiana exempts only comfort care. La Rev Stat Ann § 40:1209.58.2(4) (West 1984, 1985). The Florida, Georgia, and California courts have implicitly held these restrictions unconstitutional. See *Bouvia v Superior Court*, 179 Cal App 3d 1127, 225 Cal Rptr 297 (1986); *Corbett v D'Allessandro*, 487 So 2d 368 (Fla App 1986); *Zant v Prevatte*, 248 Ga 832, 286 SE 2d 715 (1982). . . . No court has upheld such restrictions. Further, the New Jersey and Massachusetts courts have also held the right to have food and water withdrawn to be constitutional in nature, although these two states have no living will statutes. See *Re Conroy*, 98 NJ 321, 486 A 2d 1209 (1983); *Brophy v New England Sinai Hosp*, 398 Mass 417, 497 NE 2d 626 (1986). Accordingly, it appears extremely likely that these provisions are void.

In a poorly worded 1987 amendment, Illinois changed a blanket prohibition on withdrawing food, hydration, and comfort care into a blanket prohibition on withdrawing comfort care and a prohibition on withdrawing food and hydration in certain circumstances only. As to this latter point, the Act now states, '[n]utrition and hydration shall not be withdrawn or withheld from a qualified patient if the withdrawal or withholding would result in death solely from dehydration or starvation rather than from the existing terminal condition'. Ill Ann Stat ch 110½ § 702(d) (Smith-Hurd 1983, 1987). This provision is apparently intended to permit the withdrawal of food and hydration in virtually all relevant cases, yet its language actually states that neither can ever be withdrawn. The difficulty is a product of the Illinois Legislature's reliance upon an intentionally myopic view of causation. . . .

50. No explicit provision is found in the Acts of New Mexico, North Carolina, or Mississippi (which is unduly brief). From the more general terms in these Acts, it appears that the drafters most likely did not intend to approve of the withholding of food or other basic needs. For example, New Mexico's Act defines the treatments to be withdrawn as those 'designed *solely* to sustain the life processes'. N M Stat Ann § 24-7-2(C) (1977, 1984) (emphasis added).

51. It may, however, be possible for a declarant to vary this term in some states but not in others. For example, compare Montana and Vermont provisions, *supra* note 49, with Maryland provisions, *supra* note 49.

. . .

54. [footnote omitted]

55. Many patients, of course, will be comatose and unable to feel starvation. In those cases where the patient can feel pain, however, such a death is an extremely cruel one. So much pain is quite a price to pay for an emotional desire to avoid active euthanasia.

56. Sixteen statutes employ both terms: Cal Health & Safety Code § 7187(c) (West Supp 1976); Text Rev Civ Stat Ann art 4590h, § 2(4) (Vernon 1977, 1979, 1983, 1985); Or Rev Stat § 97.050(3) (1977, 1983, 1985, 1987); Idaho Code § 39-4503(3) (1977, 1986); Nev Rev Stat § 449.570 (1977, 1985); Wash Rev Code Ann § 70.122.020(4) (1979); Vt Stat Ann tit 18, § 5252(2) (1981); Del Code Ann tit 16, § 2501(d) (1982, 1983); Va Code Ann § 54-325.8:2 (1983, 1984); Fla Stat Ann

§ 765.03(3)(a) (West 1984, 1985); Miss Code Ann § 41-41-103(b) (1984); Okla Stat Ann tit 63, § 3102(4) (West 1985, 1987); Iowa Code Ann § 144A.2(5)(a) (West 1985, 1987); Ind Code Ann § 16-8-11-4(1) (Burns 1985); Md Health-Gen Code Ann § 5.601(e) (1985, 1987); N H Rev Stat Ann § 137-H:2(II) (1985). Connecticut uses the phrase 'mechanical or electronic'. See Conn Gen Stat § 19a-570(1) (1985). Four states employ only the term 'artificial'. See N C Gen Stat § 90-321(a)(2) (1977, 1979, 1981, 1983); D C Code Ann § 6-2421(3) (1981); W Va Code § 16-30-2(3) (1984); Mo Ann Stat § 459.010(3) (Vernon 1985). Further, Illinois provides a listing of treatments which serve the same purpose. See Ill Ann Stat ch 110½ § 702(d) (Smith-Hurd 1985, 1987).

57. See Del Code Ann tit 16, § 2501(a), (d) (1982, 1983).

58. See Tenn Code Ann § 32-11-103(6) (1985) (specifically prohibiting withdrawal of 'nonartificial oral feeding').

59. Alaska Stat § 18.12.010(c) (official form). See also Alaska Stat § 18.12.040(b) (1986).

60. Four statutes employ the term 'extraordinary measures'. See N C Gen Stat § 90-321(a)(2) (1977, 1979, 1981, 1983); Vt Stat Ann tit 18, § 5252(2) (1981); Miss Code Ann § 41-41-103(b) (1984); Okla Stat Ann tit 63, § 3102(4) (West 1985, 1987).

61. Despite its widespread use in the context of euthanasia decisions, the term 'heroic' is not found in any living will statute.

62. See *Re Conroy*, 98 NJ at 372, 486 A 2d at 1235.

(ii) Subsequent 'living will' statutes

The Society for the Right to Die in its Handbook of 1985 on 'Living Will Laws' (pp 5–7) describes the evolution in the legislative responses which has taken place subsequently.

The new legislation

The year 1985 saw an acceleration in lawmaking that exceeded any other period in the history of 'living will' legislation. Where enactment of the first 23 statutes had been spread over eight years (ten between 1976 and 1980, and 13 between 1981 and 1984), an additional 13 were adopted in just four months in 1985, between March 4 and July 1: in Arizona, Colorado, Connecticut, Indiana, Iowa, Maine, Maryland, Missouri, Montana, New Hampshire, Oklahoma, Tennessee, and Utah. Also, one of the earliest statutes, the 1977 Texas Natural Death Act, was significantly amended during the same period, eliminating its hampering limitations and bringing it into line with the best in living will legislation.

With 36 living will laws now in place, in terms of overall US population, 2 out of every 3 citizens have access to a recognised means of refusing in advance futile prolongation of dying if they become terminally ill with no hope of recovery. Their rights are further strengthened by the fact that the legislation reduces a pervasive concern of physicians in today's litigious climate: it provides health caregivers with immunity from liability for carrying out patients' wishes under the circumstances specified in their living wills.

No two statutes are alike in every detail. In August 1985 the National Conference of Commissioners on Uniform State Laws, whose role it is to develop model legislation when the commissioners see a need for nationwide uniformity, approved a 'Uniform Rights of the Terminally Ill Act' recommending it for adoption throughout the United States [set out *infra*]. . . . Three of the 1985 state statutes (Iowa's, Maine's and Montana's) have certain provisions drawn from the NCCUSL Act before its formal adoption in August.

The recent extraordinary gains in acceptance of the living will concept may be attributed to a number of developments. Primary among them is the continuing advance of medical technology and the acquisition of sophisticated life-prolonging 'machinery' by more and more hospitals throughout the country. Many more people have become aware of the issues surrounding the right to die, both through personal experience with the final illness of a friend or relative and through growing exposure via the media; court cases have proliferated, and with them, newspaper coverage and televised panel discussions. Some of the traditional opposition to living will legislation has softened, as pro and con groups have sought mutually acceptable compromises in the course of the legislative process.

One evidence of compromise is apparent in a legislative trend that appeared first in five of the statutes enacted in 1984 (Florida's, Georgia's, Illinois's, Wisconsin's, and Wyoming's) and is confirmed by all 13 of the laws adopted in 1985: a statement on artificial feeding. A common feature in living will legislation is a section defining terms used; for example, 'terminal condition', 'qualified patient'—and 'life-sustaining procedures' which can be withheld or withdrawn. In connection with the third phrase, 'life-sustaining procedures', the newest laws consistently make mention of sustenance or nourishment or food and fluids in their 'definitions' sections. Some of these state that under no circumstances whatsoever can tubal feeding and hydration be counted among the treatments that may be withheld or withdrawn from the terminally ill patient under the statute. Others suggest that sustenance must be given only if it is necessary for the patient's comfort. . . . Ambiguity in the way these sections are worded may in some states lead to inconsistency of interpretation and/or controversy—but experience with this aspect of the new statutes is as yet too limited to show just how great a problem the ambiguity will cause. In view of the fact that the majority of statutes contain a suggested declaration form that need be only 'substantially' followed, presumably permitting the addition of personal instructions, the Society for the Right to Die suggests that the declarant include his or her wishes with regard to tubally administered sustenance as well as other life-prolonging treatment; one cannot predict for certain whether or not this specific request will be honored without question, but it will nevertheless constitute a clear documentation of the declarant's intent. Furthermore, even in states where the statute appears unequivocally to exclude artificial feeding from the procedures that can be withheld from the qualified patient, the provision may be challenged on the grounds that it violates the individual's constitutional right of privacy.

Whatever else may be said of it, it is clear that artificial feeding has become the major right-to-die issue of the '80s and the specific procedure being challenged in several of the cases currently in the courts. . . . Withholding artificially administered feeding from the hopelessly ill and from permanently unconscious patients is a sensitive subject, widely debated by ethicists, theologians, and the medical community. The American Medical Association, and two state medical societies, recently addressed the issue and concluded that withholding it is ethically permissible. . . .

Among those who oppose withdrawing sustenance by tube under any circumstances are members of the Catholic community. It was at least partly to assuage opposition to living will legislation on the part of the Catholic Conference of Bishops in several states that law drafters specifically excluded this procedure from the definition of life support that could be withheld from dying patients. As a further result of compromise, all but three of the new statutes contain a 'pregnancy' clause invalidating the living will of an otherwise qualified patient who is pregnant. (Four of them—Arizona's, Colorado's, Iowa's, and Montana's—qualify this point by adding that the declaration is invalid if the fetus 'could develop to the point of live birth with continued application of life-sustaining procedures'.)

In one of the three that lack the pregnancy clause, Maine's, it was dropped from the bill after 'serious debate'. Even though excluding pregnant women from qualified patients is unlikely to affect nearly as many terminally ill women as prohibiting the withdrawal of food and fluids, there are those—and the Society for the Right to Die is among them—who protest the pregnancy clause (unless it is qualified as above) on grounds of the constitutional right of privacy.

In presumably the same spirit of conciliation, lawmakers in Indiana and Maryland saw fit to authorise not only the customary advance document rejecting life support in the event of a terminal condition but an alternative declaration as well: one in which the declarant specifically requests that all possible measures be taken to *extend* life, no matter how hopeless the prognosis may be. Many physicians are likely to view this request as a potential problem, entailing inappropriate or even unavailable medical measures.

The National Conference of Commissioners on Uniform State Laws approved in 1985 a Uniform Rights of the Terminally Ill Act (discussed in the above extract) which sets out a model Act on living wills. We set below both the Act and the accompanying commentary. In a prefatory note to the Act, the Commissioners explain its purposes and approach.

Prefatory note

The Rights of the Terminally Ill Act authorises an adult person to control decisions regarding administration of life-sustaining treatment by executing a declaration instructing a physician to withhold or withdraw life-sustaining treatment in the event the person is in a terminal condition and is unable to participate in medical treatment decisions. As the preceding sentence indicates, the scope of the Act is narrow. It does not address treatment of persons who have not executed such a declaration; it does not cover treatment of minors; and it does not address treatment decisions by proxy. Its impact is limited to treatment that is merely life prolonging, and to patients whose terminal condition is incurable and/or irreversible, whose death will soon occur, and who are unable to participate in treatment decisions. Beyond its narrow scope, the Act is not intended to affect any existing rights and responsibilities of persons to make medical treatment decisions. The Act merely provides *one* way by which a terminally-ill patient's desires regarding the use of life-sustaining procedures can be legally implemented.

The purposes of the Act are (1) to present an Act which is simple, effective, and acceptable to persons desiring to execute a declaration and to physicians and health-care facilities whose conduct will be affected, (2) to provide for the effectiveness of a declaration in states other than the state in which it is executed through uniformity of scope and procedure, and (3) to avoid the inconsistency in approach which has characterised the early statutes.

The Act's basic structure and substance are similar to that found in most of the existing legislation. The Act has drawn upon existing legislation in order to avoid further complexity and to permit its effective operation in light of prior enactments. Departures from existing statutes have been made, however, in order to simplify procedures, improve drafting, and clarify language. Selected provisions have been reworked to express more adequately a specific concept (ie, life-sustaining treatment, terminal condition) or to reflect changes in established procedure (ie, the qualifications of witnesses). The Act's stylistic and substantive departures from existing legislation were pursued for the purposes of clarity and simplicity.

UNIFORM RIGHTS OF THE TERMINALLY ILL ACT

Section 1. Definitions

As used in the [Act], unless the context otherwise requires:

(1) 'Attending physician' means the physician who has primary responsibility for the treatment and care of the patient.

(2) 'Declaration' means a writing executed in accordance with the requirements of Section 2(a).

(3) 'Health-care provider' means a person who is licensed, certified, or otherwise authorised by the law of this State to administer health care in the ordinary course of business or practice of a profession.

(4) 'Life-sustaining treatment' means any medical procedure or intervention that, when administered to a qualified patient, will serve only to prolong the process of dying.

(5) 'Person' means an individual, corporation, business trust, estate, trust, partnership, association, joint venture, government, governmental subdivision or agency, or any other legal or commercial entity.

(6) 'Physician' means an individual [licensed to practice medicine in this State].

(7) 'Qualified patient' means a patient [18] or more years of age who has executed a

declaration and who has been determined by the attending physician to be in a terminal condition.

(8) 'State' means a state, territory, or possession of the United States, the District of Columbia, or the Commonwealth of Puerto Rico.

(9) 'Terminal condition' means an incurable or irreversible condition that, without the administration of life-sustaining treatment, will, in the opinion of the attending physician, result in death within a relatively short time.

Comment

The Act's definitions of 'life-sustaining treatment' and 'terminal condition' are interdependent and must be read together. This has caused drafting problems in many existing acts, and the Act has been drafted to avoid the problems detected in existing legislation.

Most of the 'life-sustaining treatment' and 'terminal condition' definitions in existing statutes were considered problematical in that they (1) were tautological, defining 'terminal condition' with respect to 'life-sustaining treatment' and vice versa, and (2) defined terminal condition as requiring 'imminent' death 'whether or not' or 'regardless of' the application of life-sustaining treatment. Strictly speaking, if death is 'imminent' even with the full application of life-sustaining treatment, there is little point in having a statute permitting withdrawal of such procedures. The Act's definitions have attempted to avoid these problems.

The 'life-sustaining treatment' definition found in many statutes inserts the clause 'and when, in the judgment of the attending physician, death will occur whether or not such procedure or intervention is utilised', after the phrase 'will serve only to prolong the dying process' found in the Act's provision. Because the Act's life-sustaining treatment definition concerns only those procedures or interventions applied to 'qualified patients' (ie, those who have been determined to be in a terminal condition), and because a terminal condition is defined as 'incurable or irreversible' with death resulting 'in a relatively short time', the requirement that death be 'inevitable' has been satisfied by the presence of 'qualified patient' in the life-sustaining treatment definition. Therefore, this additional clause was excluded because it was considered repetitious and possibly confusing.

The Act defines 'life-sustaining treatment' in an all-inclusive manner, dealing with those procedures necessary for comfort care or alleviation of pain separately in Section 6(b), where it is provided that such procedures need not be withdrawn or withheld pursuant to a declaration. Most existing statutes incorporate 'comfort care' as an exclusion from the definition of life-sustaining treatment. Because many such procedures *are* life-sustaining, however, the Act avoids definitional confusion by treating them in a separate provision that reflects the Act's policy more clearly, and better reflects the fact that comfort care does not involve a fixed group of procedures applicable in all instances.

Subsection (9) of Section 1 is the 'terminal condition' definition. The difficulty of trying to express such a condition in precise, accurate, but not unduly restricting language is obvious. A definition must preserve the physicians' professional discretion in making such determinations. Consequently, the Act's definition of terminal condition incorporates not only selected language from various state acts, but also suggestions from medical literature in the field.

The Act employs the term 'terminal condition' rather than terminal illness, and it is important that these two different concepts be distinguished. Terminal illness, as generally understood, is both broader and narrower than terminal condition. Terminal illness connotes a disease process that will lead to death; 'terminal condition' is not limited to disease. 'Terminal illness' also connotes an inevitable process leading to death, but does not contain limitations as to the time period prior to death, or potential for nonreversibility, as does 'terminal condition'.

The terminal condition definition requires that the condition be 'incurable or irreversible'. These adjectives were chosen over the similar phrase, 'no possibility of recovery', because of possible ambiguity in the term 'recovery' (ie, recovery to 'normal' or to some other stage). A number of state statutes now use 'incurable' and/or 'irreversible', and the terms appear to comport with the criteria applied by physicians in terminal care situations. The phrase 'incurable *or* irreversible' is to be read conjunctively when the circumstances warrant. A condition which is reversible but incurable is *not* a terminal condition.

Subsection (9) also requires that the condition result in the death of the patient within a 'relatively short time ... without the administration of life-sustaining treatment'. This requirement differs to some degree from the language employed in most of the statutes. First, the decision that death will occur in a relatively short time is to be made without considering the possibilities of extending life with life-sustaining treatment. The alternative is that required by a number of states—that death be imminent whether or not life-sustaining procedures are applied. The President's Commission for the Study of Ethical Problems in Medicine and Biomedical Research has noted that such a definition severely limits the group of terminally-ill patients able to qualify under these acts. It is precisely because life can be prolonged indefinitely by new medical technology that these acts have come into existence. Though the Act intends to err on the side of prolonging life, it should not be made wholly ineffective as to the actual situation it purports to address. The provisions which require that death be imminent regardless of the application of life-sustaining procedures appear to have that effect. Therefore, such provisions have been excluded in the Act.

The terminal condition definition of subsection (9) requires that death result 'in a relatively short time'. Rejecting the 'imminency' language employed in a number of statutes, this alternative was chosen because it provides needed flexibility and reflects the balancing character of the time frame judgment. Though the phrase, 'relatively short time', does not eliminate the need for judgment, it focuses the physician's medical judgment and avoids the narrowing implications of the word 'imminent'.

The 'relatively short time' formulation is employed to avoid both the unduly constricting meaning of 'imminent' and the artificiality of another alternative— fixed time periods, such as six months, one year, or the like. The circumstances and inevitable variations in disorder and diagnosis make unrealistic a fixed time period. Physicians may be hesitant to make predictions under a fixed time period standard unless the standard of physician judgment is so loose as to be unenforceable. Under the Act's standard, considerations such as the strength of the diagnosis, the type of disorder, and the like can be reflected in the judgment that death will result within a relatively short time, as they are now reflected in judgments physicians must and do make.

The life-sustaining treatment and terminal condition definitions exclude certain types of disorders, such as kidney disease requiring dialysis, and diabetes requiring continued use of insulin. This is accomplished in the requirement that terminal conditions be 'irreversible', and that life-sustaining procedures serve '*only* to prolong the dying process'. For purposes of the Act, diabetes treatable with insulin is 'reversible', a diabetic person so treatable is not in the 'dying process', and insulin is a treatment the benefits of which foreclose it serving '*only*' to prolong the dying process.

Section 2. Declaration relating to use of life-sustaining treatment

(a) An individual of sound mind and [18] or more years of age may execute at any time a declaration governing the withholding or withdrawal of life-sustaining treatment. The declaration must be signed by the declarant, or another at the declarant's direction, and witnessed by two individuals.

(b) A declaration may, but need not, be in the following form:

DECLARATION

If I should have an incurable or irreversible condition that will cause my death within a relatively short time, and I am no longer able to make decisions regarding my medical treatment, I direct my attending physicians, pursuant to the Uniform Rights of the Terminally Ill Act of this State, to withhold or withdraw treatment that only prolongs the process of dying and is not necessary to my comfort or to alleviate pain.

Signed this_____day of_____, _____.

    Signature _____

    Address _____

The declarant voluntarily signed this writing in my presence.

    Witness _____

    Address _____

    Witness _____

    Address _____

(c) A physician or other health-care provider who is furnished a copy of the declaration shall make it a part of the declarant's medical record and, if unwilling to comply with the declaration, promptly so advise the declarant.

Comment
Section 2 sets out the minimal requirements regarding the making and execution of a valid declaration. A 'sample' declaration form is offered in this section. The form is not mandatory, as some acts require; it 'may, but need not, be' followed. The form provided also is not as elaborate as others. The drafters rejected a more detailed declaration for two reasons. First, the form is to serve only as an example of a valid declaration. A more elaborate form may have erroneously implied that a declaration more simply constructed would not be legally sufficient. Second, the sample form's simple structure and specific language attempts to provide notice of exactly what is to be effectuated through these documents to those persons desiring to execute a declaration and the physicians who are to honor it.

The Act's provisions governing witnesses to a declaration have also been simplified. Section 2 provides only that the declaration be signed by the declarant in the presence of two witnesses. The Act does not require witnesses to meet any specific qualifications for two primary reasons. First, the interest in simplicity mandates as uncomplicated a procedure as possible. It is intended that the Act present a viable alternative for those persons interested in participating in their medical treatment decisions in the event of a terminal condition.

Second, the absence of more elaborate witness requirements relieves physicians of the inappropriate and perhaps impossible burden of determining whether the legalities of the witness requirements have been met. Many physicians understandably and rightly would be hesitant to make such decisions and, therefore, the effectiveness of the declaration might be jeopardised. It should be noted, as well, that protection against abuse in these situations is provided by the criminal penalties in Section 9. The attending physicians and other health-care professionals will be able, in most circumstances, to discuss the declaration with the patient and family and any suspicion of duress or wrongdoing can be discovered and handled by established hospital procedures.

Section 2(c) requires that a physician or health-care provider who is given a copy of the declaration record it in the declarant's medical records. This step is critical to the effectuation of the declaration, and the duty applies regardless of the time of receipt. If a copy of the same declaration is already in the record, its re-recording would not be necessary, but its receipt should be noted as evidence of its continued force. Section 2(c) is not duplicative of Section 5 which requires recording the terms of the declaration (or the document itself, when available, in the event of telephonic communication to the physician by another physician, for example) at the time the physician makes a determination of terminal condition. It was deemed important that knowledge of the declaration and its continued force be specifically noted at this critical juncture.

Section 2(c) imposes a duty on the physician or other health-care provider to inform the declarant of his or her unwillingness to comply with the provisions of the declaration. This will provide notice to the declarant that certain terms may be deemed medically unreasonable (Section 10(f)), or that a different provider who is willing to carry out the Act (Section 7) should be informed of the declaration.

Section 3. When declaration operative
A declaration becomes operative when (i) it is communicated to the attending physician and (ii) the declarant is determined by the attending physician to be in a terminal condition and no longer able to make decisions regarding administration of life-sustaining treatment. When the declaration becomes operative, the attending physician and other health-care providers shall act in accordance with its provisions or comply with the transfer provisions of Section 7.

Comment
Section 3 establishes the preconditions to the declaration becoming operative. Once operative, Section 3 provides that the attending physician shall act in accordance with the provisions of the declaration or transfer care of the patient under Section 7. This provision is not intended to eliminate the physician's need to evaluate particular requests in terms of reasonable medical practice under Section 10(f), nor to relieve the physician from carrying out the declaration except for any specific unreasonable or unlawful request in the declaration. Transfer of the patient under Section 7 is to occur if the physician, for reasons of conscience, for example, is unwilling to carry out the Act or to follow medically reasonable requests in the declaration.

Section 4. Revocation of declaration
(a) A declaration may be revoked at any time and in any manner by the declarant, without regard to the declarant's mental or physical condition. A revocation is effective upon communication to the attending physician or other health-care provider by the declarant or a witness to the revocation.
(b) The attending physician or other health-care provider shall make the revocation a part of the declarant's medical record.

Comment
Section 4 provides for revocation of a declaration and is modeled after North Carolina's similar provision. Virtually every other statute sets out specific examples of how a declaration can be revoked—by physical destruction, by a signed, dated writing, or by a verbal expression of revocation. A provision that freely allowed revocation and avoided procedural complications was desired. The simple language of Section 4 appears to meet these qualifications. It should be noted that the revocation is, of course, not effective until communicated to the attending physician or another health-care provider working under a physician's guidance, such as nursing facility or hospice staff. The Act, unlike many statutes, also does not explicitly require that a person relaying the revocation be acting on the declarant's behalf. Such a requirement could impose an unreasonable burden on the attending physician. The communication is assumed to be in good faith, and the physician may rely on it.

In employing a general revocation provision, it was intended to permit revocation by the broadest range of means. Therefore, for example, it is intended that a revocation can be effected in writing, orally, by physical defacement or destruction of a declaration, and by physical sign communicating intention to revoke.

Section 5. Recording determination of terminal condition and declaration
Upon determining that the declarant is in a terminal condition, the attending physician who knows of a declaration shall record the determination and the terms of the declaration in the declarant's medical record.

Comment
Section 5 of the Act requires that an attending physician record the determination that the patient is in a terminal condition in the patient's medical records. The section provides that an attending physician must know of the declaration's existence. It is anticipated that knowledge may in some instances occur through oral

communication between physicians. If the attending physician determines that the patient is in a terminal condition, and has been notified of the declaration, the physician is to make the determination of terminal condition, as defined in Section 1(9), part of the patient's medical records. There is no explicit requirement that the physician inform the patient of the terminal condition. That decision is to be left to the physician's professional discretion under existing standards of care. The Act also does not require, as do many statutes, that a physician other than the attending physician concur in the terminal condition determination. It appears to be the established practice of most physicians to request a second opinion or, more often, review by a panel or committee established as a matter of hospital procedure, and the Act is not intended to discourage such a practice. Requiring it, however, would almost inevitably freeze in a single process or set of processes for review in this evolving area of medicine. Because existing policies and regulations typically address the review issue, requiring a specific form of review in the Act was viewed as an unnecessary regulation of normal hospital procedures. Moreover, in smaller or rural health facilities a second qualified physician or review mechanism may not be readily available to confirm the attending physician's determination.

The physician must record the terms of the declaration in the medical record so that its specific language or any special provisions are known at later stages of treatment. It is assumed that 'terms' of the declaration will be a copy of the declaration itself in most instances, although cases of an emergency character may arise, for example, in which the contents of a declaration can be reliably conveyed, and where obtaining a copy of the declaration prior to making decisions governed by it will be impracticable. In such cases, the terms of the declaration will suffice for recording purposes under Section 5.

Section 6. Treatment of qualified patient

(a) A qualified patient may make decisions regarding life-sustaining treatment as long as the patient is able to do so.

(b) This [Act] does not affect the responsibility of the attending physician or other health-care provider to provide treatment, including nutrition and hydration, for a patient's comfort care or alleviation of pain.

(c) Unless the declaration otherwise provides, the declaration of a qualified patient known to the attending physician to be pregnant must not be given effect as long as it is probable that the fetus could develop to the point of live birth with continued application of life-sustaining treatment.

Comment

Section 6(a) recognises the right of patients who have made a declaration and are determined to be in a terminal condition to make decisions regarding use of life-sustaining procedures. Until unable to do so, such patients have the right to make such decisions independently of the terms of the declaration. In affording patients a 'right to make decisions regarding use of life-sustaining procedures', the Act is intended to reflect existing law pertaining to this issue. As Sections 10(e) and (f) indicate, qualifications on a patient's right to force the carrying out of those decisions in a manner contrary to law or accepted standards of medical practice, for example, are not intended to be overridden.

In Section 6(b) the Act uses the term 'comfort care' in defining procedures that may be applied notwithstanding a declaration instructing withdrawal or withholding of life-sustaining treatment. The purpose of permitting continuation of life-sustaining treatment deemed necessary for comfort care or alleviation of pain is to allow the physician to take appropriate steps to insure comfort and freedom from pain, as dictated by reasonable medical standards. Many existing statutes employ the term 'comfort care' in connection with the alleviation of pain, and the Act follows this example. Although the phrase 'to alleviate pain' arguably is subsumed within the term comfort care, the additional specificity was considered helpful for both the doctor and layperson.

Section 6(b) does not set out a separate rule governing the provision of nutrition and hydration. Instead, each is subject to the same considerations of necessity for comfort care and alleviation of pain as are all other forms of life-sustaining treatment. If nutrition and hydration are not necessary for comfort care or alleviation of pain, they may be withdrawn. This approach was deemed preferable to the approach in a few existing statutes, which treat nutrition and hydration as comfort care in all cases, regardless of circumstances, and exclude comfort care from the life-sustaining treatment definition.

It is debatable whether physicians or other professionals perceive the providing of nourishment through intravenous feeding apparatus or nasogastric tubes as comfort care *in all cases* or whether such procedures at times merely prolong the dying process. Whether procedures to provide nourishment should be considered life-sustaining treatment or comfort care appears to depend on the factual circumstances of each case and, therefore, such decisions should be left to the physician, exercising reasonable medical judgment. Declarants may, however, specifically express their views regarding continuation or noncontinuation of such procedures in the declaration, and those views will control.

Section 6(c) addresses the problem of a qualified patient who is pregnant. The states which address this issue typically require that the declaration be given no force or effect during the pregnancy. Because this requirement inadvertently may do more harm than good to the fetus, Section 6(c) provides a more suitable, if more complicated standard. It is possible to hypothesise a situation in which life-sustaining treatment, such as medication, may prove possibly fatal to a fetus which is at or near the point of viability outside the womb. In such cases, the Act's provision would permit the life-sustaining treatment to be withdrawn or withheld as appropriate in order best to assure survival of the fetus. Also, for example, if the qualified patient is only a few weeks pregnant and the physician, pursuant to reasonable medical judgment, determines that it is not probable that the fetus could develop to a point of viability outside the womb even with application of life-sustaining treatment, such treatment may also be withheld or withdrawn. Thus, the pregnancy provision attempts to honor the terminally-ill patient's right to refuse life-sustaining treatment without jeopardizing in any respect the likelihood of life for the fetus. The declaration can, however, specifically address this issue, and should control the treatment provided, whether it calls for continuation of life-sustaining treatment in all cases, or in none.

Section 7. Transfer of patients
An attending physician or other health-care provider who is unwilling to comply with this [Act] shall as promptly as practicable take all reasonable steps to transfer care of the declarant to another physician or health-care provider.

Comment
Section 7 is designed to address situations in which a physician or health-care provider is unwilling to make and record a determination of terminal condition, or to respect the medically reasonable decisions of the patient regarding withholding or withdrawal of life-sustaining procedures, due to personal convictions or policies unrelated to medical judgment called for under the Act. In such instances, the physician or health-care provider must promptly take all reasonable steps to transfer the patient to another physician or health-care provider who will comply with the applicable provisions of the Act.

Section 8. Immunities
(a) in the absence of knowledge of the revocation of a declaration, a person is not subject to civil or criminal liability or discipline for unprofessional conduct for carrying out the declaration pursuant to the requirements of this [Act].
(b) A physician or other health-care provider, whose actions under this [Act] are in accord with reasonable medical standards, is not subject to criminal or civil liability or discipline for unprofessional conduct with respect to those actions.

Comment
Section 8 provides immunities for persons acting pursuant to the declaration and in accordance with the Act. Immunities are extended in Section 8(a) to physicians as

well as persons operating under the physician's direction or with the physician's authorisation, and to facilities in which the withholding or withdrawal of life sustaining procedures occurs. Section 8(b) serves both to immunise physicians from liability as long as reasonable medical judgment is exercised, and to impose 'reasonable medical standards' as the criterion that should govern all of the specific medical decisions called for throughout the Act. Section 8(b), in conjunction with Section 10(f), therefore, avoids the need to restate the medical standard in each section of the Act requiring a medical judgment.

Section 9 of the Act creates criminal penalties for conduct that violates the Act.

Section 10. Miscellaneous provisions
(a) Death resulting from the withholding or withdrawal of life-sustaining treatment pursuant to a declaration and in accordance with this [Act] does not constitute, for any purpose, a suicide or homicide.

(c) The making of a declaration pursuant to Section 2 does not affect in any manner the sale, procurement, or issuance of any policy of life insurance or annuity, nor does it affect, impair, or modify the terms of an existing policy of life insurance or annuity. A policy of life insurance or annuity is not legally impaired or invalidated in any manner by the withholding or withdrawal of life-sustaining treatment from an insured qualified patient, notwithstanding any term to the contrary.

(c) A person may not prohibit or require the execution of a declaration as a condition for being insured for, or receiving, health-care services.

(d) This [Act] creates no presumption concerning the intention of an individual who has revoked or has not executed a declaration with respect to the use, withholding, or withdrawal of life-sustaining treatment in the event of a terminal condition.

(e) This [Act] does not affect the right of a patient to make decisions regarding use of life-sustaining treatment, so long as the patient is able to do so, or impair or supersede any right or responsibility that a person has to effect the withholding or withdrawal of medical care.

(f) This [Act] does not require any physician or other health-care provider to take any action contrary to reasonable medical standards.

(g) This [Act] does not condone, authorise, or approve mercy-killing or euthanasia.

Section 11. When health-care provider may presume validity of declaration
In the absence of knowledge to the contrary, a physician or other health-care provider may presume that a declaration complies with this [Act] and is valid.

Section 12 deals with declarations executed in another state.

Section 13. Effect of previous declaration
An instrument executed before the effective date of this [Act] which substantially complies with Section 2(a) must be given effect pursuant to the provisions of this [Act].

Section 14 (omitted).

Section 15 (omitted).

Section 16. Severability
If any provision of this [Act] or its application to any person or circumstance is held invalid, the invalidity does not affect other provisions or applications of this [Act] which can be given effect without the invalid provision or application, and to this end the provisions of this [Act] are severable.

Question

As you will notice, the Uniform Act deals with many of the difficulties we discuss. Does it satisfactorily deal with all of them? Would the Act apply to patients such as *Quinlan, Jobes* and *Peter*?

(iii) Enduring powers of attorney statutes

'Living will' Acts represent the first generation of statutes dealing with the rights of the dying to refuse medical treatment. The second generation of statutes are the enduring power of attorney Acts. Five states have enacted such legislation—California, Illinois, Maine, Nevada and Rhode Island—specifically authorising an agent to consent to or refuse medical treatment on behalf of the other. Three others—Colorado, North Carolina and Pennsylvania—allow the agent to consent to treatment only on behalf of the other. It is likely that the power to consent to treatment will be interpreted as including the power to refuse treatment also, even though the statute makes no explicit provision for this.

As regards enduring powers of attorney, the first and best known example is the Californian Durable Power of Attorney Health Care Act 1983.

2430 Definitions
As used in this article:

(a) 'Durable power of attorney for health care' means a durable power of attorney to the extent that it authorises an attorney in fact to make health care decisions for the principal.

(b) 'Health care' means any care, treatment, service, or procedure to maintain, diagnose, or treat an individuals physical or mental condition.

(c) 'Health care decision' means consent, refusal of consent, or withdrawal of consent to health care.

(d) 'Health care provider' means a person who is licensed, certified, or otherwise authorised or permitted by the law of this state to administer health care in the ordinary course of business or practice of a profession.

(e) . . .

(f) . . .

2431 (omitted).

2432 Attorney in fact: health care decisions: requirements: restrictions on parties designated as attorney in fact: patient advocates or ombudsman

(a) An attorney in fact under a durable power of attorney may not make health care decisions unless both of the following requirements are satisfied:

(1) The durable power of attorney specifically authorises the attorney in fact to make health care decisions.

(2) The durable power of attorney contains the date of its execution and is witnessed by one of the following methods:

(A) Be signed by at least two persons each of whom witnessed either the signing of the instrument by the principal or the principal's acknowledgment of the signature or of the instrument, each witness making the following declaration in substance: 'I declare under penalty of perjury under the laws of California that the principal is personally known to me, that the principal signed or acknowledged this durable power of attorney in my presence, that the principal appears to be of sound mind and under no duress, fraud, or undue influence, that I am not the person appointed as attorney in fact by this document, and that I am not a health care provider, an employee of a health care provider, the operator of a community care facility, . . . an employee of an operator of a community care facility, the operator of a residential care facility for the elderly, nor an employee of an operator of a residential care facility for the elderly.' In addition, the declaration of at least one of the witnesses must include the following: 'I am not related to the principal by blood, marriage, or adoption, and to the best of my knowledge I am not entitled to any part of the estate of the principal upon the death of the principal under a will now existing or by operation of law.'.

(B) Be acknowledged before a notary public at any place within this state, the notary public certifying to the substance of the following:

State of California
County of _____ } ss

On this _____ day of _____, in the year _____
before me, _____
(here insert name of notary public)
NOTARY SEAL _____
(Signature of Notary Public)

personally appeared _____, personally known to me (or proved to me on the basis of satisfactory evidence) to be the person whose name is subscribed to this instrument, and acknowledged that he or she executed it. I declare under penalty of perjury that the person whose name is subscribed to this instrument appears to be of sound mind and under no duress, fraud, or undue influence.

(b) Except as provided in section 2432.5:

(1) Neither the treating health care provider nor an employee of the treating health care provider, nor an operator of a community care facility or residential care facility for the elderly nor an employee of an operator of a community care facility or residential care facility for the elderly, may be designated as the attorney in fact to make health care decisions under a durable power of attorney.
(2) A health care provider or employee of a health care provider may not act as an attorney in fact to make health care decisions if the health care provider becomes the principal's treating health care provider.
(c) A conservator may not be designated as the attorney in fact to make health care decisions under a durable power of attorney for health care executed by a person who is a conservatee under the Lanterman-Petris-Short Act, Part 1 (commencing with Section 5000) of Division 5 of the Welfare and Institutions Code, unless (1) the power of attorney is otherwise valid, (2) the conservatee is represented by legal counsel, and (3) the lawyer representing the conservatee signs a certificate stating: 'I have advised my client concerning his or her rights in connection with this matter and the consequences of signing or not signing this durable power of attorney and my client, after being so advised, has executed this durable power of attorney.'
(d) None of the following may be used as a witness under subdivision (a):

(1) A health care provider.
(2) An employee of a health care provider.
(3) The attorney in fact.
(4) The operator of a community care facility.
(5) An employee of an operator of a community care facility.
(6) The operator of a residential care facility for the elderly.
(7) An employee of an operator of a residential care facility for the elderly.

(e) At least one of the persons used as a witness under subdivision (a) shall be a person who is not one of the following:

(1) A relative of the principal by blood, marriage, or adoption.
(2) A person who would be entitled to any portion of the estate of the principal upon his or her death under any will or codicil thereto of the principal existing at the time of execution of the durable power of attorney or by operation of law then existing.

(f) A durable power of attorney for health care is not effective if the principal is a patient in a skilled nursing facility as defined in subdivision (c) of Section 1250 of the Health and Safety Code at the time of its execution unless one of the witnesses is a patient advocate or ombudsman as may be designated by the State Department of Aging for this purpose pursuant to any other applicable provision of law. The patient advocate or ombudsman shall include in the declaration required by subdivision (a)(2)(A) a declaration that he or she is serving as a witness as required by this subdivision. It is the intent of this subdivision to recognise that some patients in skilled nursing facilities are insulated from a voluntary decisionmaking role, by virtue of the custodial nature of their care, so as to require special assurance that they are capable of willfully and voluntarily executing a durable power of attorney for health care.

2432.5 Health care provider or community care facility employees; designation as attorney in fact; conditions

. . . An employee of the treating health care provider or an employee of an operator of a community care facility or an employee of a residential care facility for the elderly may be designated as the attorney in fact to make health care decisions under a durable power of attorney if (a) the employee so designated is a relative of the principal by blood, marriage, or adoption, and (b) the other requirements of this article are satisfied.

2433. Notice: warning to person executing document; form

(a) A printed form of a durable power of attorney for health care that is sold or otherwise distributed in this state for use by a person who does not have the advice of legal counsel shall provide no other authority than the authority to make health care decisions on behalf of the principal and shall contain in not less than 10-point boldface type or a reasonable equivalent thereof, the following warning statement:

WARNING TO PERSON EXECUTING THIS DOCUMENT

This is an important legal document. Before executing this document, you should know these important facts:

This document gives the person you designate as your agent (the attorney in fact) the power to make health care decisions for you. Your agent must act consistently with your desires as stated in this document or otherwise made known.

Except as you otherwise specify in this document, this document gives your agent the power to consent to your doctor not giving treatment or stopping treatment necessary to keep you alive.

Notwithstanding this document, you have the right to make medical and other health care decisions for yourself so long as you can give informed consent with respect to the particular decision. In addition, no treatment may be given to you over your objection, and health care necessary to keep you alive may not be stopped or withheld if you object at the time.

This document gives your agent authority to consent, to refuse to consent, or to withdraw consent to any care, treatment, service, or procedure to maintain, diagnose, or treat a physical or mental condition. This power is subject to any statement of your desires and any limitations that you include in this document. You may state in this document any types of treatment that you do not desire. In addition, a court can take away the power of your agent to make health care decisions for you if your agent (1) authorizes anything that is illegal, (2) acts contrary to your known desires, or (3) where your desires are not known, does anything that is clearly contrary to your best interests.

Unless you specify a shorter period in this document, this power will exist for seven years from the date you execute this document and, if you are unable to make health care decisions for yourself at the time when this seven-year period ends, this power will continue to exist until the time when you become able to make health care decisions for yourself.

You have the right to revoke the authority of your agent by notifying your agent or your treating doctor, hospital, or other health care provider orally or in writing of the revocation.

Your agent has the right to examine your medical records and to consent to their disclosure unless you limit this right in this document.

Unless you otherwise specify in this document, this document gives your agent the power after you die to (1) authorize an autopsy, (2) donate your body or parts thereof for transplant or therapeutic or educational or scientific purposes, and (3) direct the disposition of your remains.

If there is anything in this document that you do not understand, you should ask a lawyer to explain it to you.

(b) The printed form described in subdivision (a) shall also include the following notice: 'This power of attorney will not be valid for making health care decisions unless it is either (1) signed by two qualified adult witnesses who are personally known to you and who are present when you sign or acknowledge your signature or (2) acknowledged before a notary public in California.'

(c) A durable power of attorney prepared for execution by a person resident in this state that permits the attorney in fact to make health care decisions and that is not a printed form shall include one of the following:

(1) The substance of the statements provided for in subdivision (a) in capital letters.

(2) A certificate signed by the principal's lawyer stating: 'I am a lawyer authorized to practice law in the state where this power was executed, and the principal was my client at the time this power of attorney was executed. I have advised my client concerning his or her rights in connection with this power of attorney and the applicable law and the consequences of signing or not signing this power of attorney, and my client, after being so advised, has executed this power of attorney.'

(d) If a durable power of attorney includes the certificate provided for in paragraph (2) of subdivision (c) and permits the attorney in fact to make health care decisions for the principal, the applicable law of which the client is to be advised by the lawyer signing the certificate includes, but is not limited to, the matters listed in subdivision (a).

2434. Attorney in fact; health care decisions; priority

(a) Unless the durable power of attorney provides otherwise, the attorney in fact designated in a durable power of attorney for health care who is known to the health care provider to be available and willing to make health care decisions has priority over any other person to act for the principal in all matters of health care decisions, but the attorney in fact does not have authority to make a particular health care decision if the principal is able to give informed consent with respect to that decision.

(b) Subject to any limitations in the durable power of attorney, the attorney in fact designated in a durable power of attorney for health care may make health care decisions for the principal, before or after the death of the principal, to the same extent as the principal could make health care decisions for himself or herself if the principal had the capacity to do so, including a disposition under the Uniform Anatomical Gift Act, Chapter 3.5 (commencing with Section 7150.5) of Part 1 of Division 7 of the Health and Safety Code. In exercising the authority under the durable power of attorney for health care, the attorney in fact has a duty to act consistent with the desires of the principal as expressed in the durable power of attorney or otherwise made known to the attorney in fact at any time or, if the principal's desires are unknown, to act in the best interests of the principal.

(c) Nothing in this article affects any right the person designated as attorney in fact may have, apart from the durable power of attorney for health care, to make or participate in the making of health care decisions on behalf of the principal.

2435. Attorney in fact; authority to consent

A durable power of attorney may not authorise the attorney in fact to consent to any of the following on behalf of the principal:

(a) Commitment to or placement in a mental health treatment facility.

(b) Convulsive treatment (as defined in Section 5325 of the Welfare and Institutions Code).

(c) Psychosurgery (as defined in Section 5325 of the Welfare and Institutions Code).

(d) Sterilisation.

(e) Abortion.

2436. Attorney in fact; information regarding proposed health care: reception, review and consent to disclosure of medical records.

Except to the extent the right is limited by the durable power of attorney, an attorney in fact designated to make health care decisions under a durable power of attorney has the same right as the principal to receive information regarding the proposed health care, to receive and review medical records, and to consent to the disclosure of medical records.

2436.5. Expiration of durable power of attorney

Unless a shorter period is provided in the durable power of attorney for health care, a durable power of attorney for health care executed after January 1, 1984, expires seven years after the date of its execution unless at the end of the seven-year period the principal lacks the capacity to make health care decisions for himself or herself, in which case the durable power of attorney for health care continues in effect until the time when the principal regains the capacity to make health care decisions for himself or herself.

2437. Principal's powers: revocation of attorney in fact or durable power of attorney; dissolution or annulment of marriage

(1) Revoke the appointment of the attorney in fact under the durable power of attorney for health care by notifying the attorney in fact orally or in writing.

(2) Revoke the authority granted to the attorney in fact to make health care decisions by notifying the health care provider orally or in writing.

(b) If the principal notifies the health care provider orally or in writing that the authority granted to the attorney in fact to make health care decisions is revoked, the health care provider shall make the notification a part of the principal's medical records and shall make a reasonable effort to notify the attorney in fact of the revocation.

(c) It is presumed that the principal has the capacity to revoke a durable power of attorney for health care. This presumption is a presumption affecting the burden of proof.

(d) Unless it provides otherwise, a valid durable power of attorney for health care revokes any prior durable power of attorney for health care.

(e) Unless the durable power of attorney expressly provides otherwise, if after executing a durable power of attorney for health care the principal's marriage is dissolved or annulled, the dissolution or annulment revokes any designation of the former spouse as an attorney in fact to make health care decisions for the principal. If any designation is revoked solely by this subdivision, it is revived by the principal's remarriage to the former spouse.

2438. Immunities of health care provider

(a) Subject to any limitations stated in the durable power of attorney and to subdivision (b) and to Sections 2435, 2440, 2441, 2442, and 2443, a health care provider is not subject to criminal prosecution, civil liability, or professional disciplinary action except to the same extent as would be the case if the principal, having had the capacity to give informed consent, had made the health care decision on his or her own behalf under like circumstances, if the health care provider relies on a health care decision and both of the following requirements are satisfied:

(1) The decision is made by an attorney in fact who the health care provider believes in good faith is authorised under this article to make the decision.

(2) The health care provider believes in good faith that the decision is not inconsistent with the desires of the principal as expressed in the durable power of attorney or otherwise made known to the health care provider, and, if the decision is to withhold or withdraw health care necessary to keep the principal alive, the health care provider has made a good faith effort to determine the desires of the principal to the extent that the principal is able to convey those desires to the health care provider and the results of the effort are made a part of the principal's medical records.

(b) Nothing in this article authorises a health care provider to do anything illegal.

(c) Notwithstanding the health care decision of the attorney in fact designated by a durable power of attorney for health care, the health care provider is not subject to criminal prosecution, civil liability, or professional disciplinary action for failing to withdraw health care necessary to keep the principal alive.

2439. Health care decisions on behalf of another: emergency treatment
(a) Subject to Section 2434, nothing in this article affects any right a person may have to make health care decisions on behalf of another.
(b) This article does not affect the law governing health care treatment in an emergency.

2440. Principal's objections: governing law
Nothing in this article authorises an attorney in fact to consent to health care, or to consent to the withholding or withdrawal of health care necessary to keep the principal alive, if the principal objects to the health care or to the withholding or withdrawal of the health care. In such a case, the case is governed by the law that would apply if there were no durable power of attorney for health care.

2441. Restriction on execution of durable power of attorney for health care as condition for admission, treatment or insurance
No health care provider, health care service plan, insurer issuing disability insurance, self-insured employee welfare plan, or nonprofit hospital plan or similar insurance plan, may condition admission to a facility, or the providing of treatment, or insurance, on the requirement that a patient execute a durable power of attorney for health care.

2442. Alteration or forgery of durable power of attorney; withholding or withdrawing health care necessary to keep the principal alive; unlawful homicide
Any person who, except where justified or excused by law, alters or forges a durable power of attorney for health care of another, or wilfully conceals or withholds personal knowledge of a revocation as provided under Section 2437, with the intent to cause a withholding or withdrawal of health care necessary to keep the principal alive contrary to the desires of the principal, and thereby, because of such act, directly causes health care necessary to keep the principal alive to be withheld or withdrawn and the death of the principal thereby to be hastened, is subject to prosecution for unlawful homicide as provided in Chapter 1 (commencing with Section 187) of Title 8 of Part 1 of the Penal Code.

2443. Mercy killings: natural process of dying; attempted suicide
Nothing in this article shall be constructed to condone, authorise, or approve mercy killing, or to permit any affirmative or deliberate act or omission to end life other than the withholding or withdrawal of health care pursuant to a durable power of attorney for health care so as to permit the natural process of dying. In making health care decisions under a durable power of attorney health care, an attempted suicide by the principal shall not be constructed to indicate a desire of the principal that health care treatment be restricted or inhibited.

The Californian Act is clearly complex. It is discussed by S Martyn and L Jacobs in 'Legislating Advance Directives for the Terminally Ill: The Living Will and Durable Power of Attorney' (1984) 63 Nebraska LR 779, 797–802 (footnotes omitted).

Key provisions of the California Act
Under the California Durable Power of Attorney for Health Care Decisions Act, in order to appoint an attorney-in-fact for medical decisionmaking, the patient (or principal) must specify that his trusted relative, friend, or other surrogate is empowered to make health care decisions on his behalf. The attorney-in-fact must be a California citizen who, under this specified designation of authority, may not combine medical decisionmaking with other authority granted him by a general durable power of attorney. Restrictions on who may serve as agent protect the principal from conflicts of interest. An attorney-in-fact may not be the principal's treating health care provider or one of its employees, nor may he be the operator or employee of a community care facility. [Notice this is now subject to section

2432.5—for relatives.] The agent's decisionmaking power is limited only by the principal's own ability to give informed consent.

A valid document must follow one of two prescribed methods of execution: (1) at least two 'qualified' witnesses must attest to the principal's signature or must acknowledge his signature; or (2) the document must be acknowledged by the principal before a notary public in California. If the patient is confined to a community care facility, the Act requires one witness to be a patient advocate or an ombudsman so designated by the State Department of Aging for that purpose. The *caveat* 'Warning to [the] Person Executing This Document' must appear in ten point boldface type if the document is printed, or all capital letters if it is typed. This serves to further alert the principal to the significance of the document he has created. Alternatively, the drafting attorney may sign a statement certifying that he has informed his client of the legal consequences of signing the document. These provisions have been incorporated into a statutory form that becomes effective Jan 1, 1985.

Finally, the durable power of attorney is invalid if it has been allowed to expire. Section 2436.5 states that it expires seven years after the date of execution, unless the principal lacks the capacity to make health care decisions for himself, in which case the document remains valid until the principal regains the capacity to make health care decisions. Of course, the principal retains power to revoke the document at any time prior to the statutory limit. His competence to revoke is presumed. This power of revocation extends both to the removal of the attorney-in-fact (either orally or by writing) and to his authority for health care decisionmaking, through notification of the health care provider. Once notified, the provider must add the revocation to the patient's medical records and must make a reasonable effort to notify the attorney-in-fact. Unless otherwise stated, a valid durable power of attorney for health care revokes any prior version.

C. Legal effects of the California Act

Under the Durable Power of Attorney for Health Care Decisions Act, the attorney-in-fact exercises broad health care decisionmaking power encompassing both the administration and termination of medical treatment for the unconscious patient. Unlike a Living Will that is catalysed by a diagnosis of terminal illness and imminent death, the agent appointed under this Act may give 'consent, refusal of consent, or withdrawal of consent to health care', which includes 'any care, treatment, service, or procedure to maintain, diagnose, or treat an individual's physical or mental condition'. For example, the attorney-in-fact may make a disposition under the Uniform Anatomical Gift Act, receive information regarding proposed treatment, and review and release information found in medical records. In short, any decisionmaking power that the principal himself might have exerted, including the power to demand the termination of life-supports, is within the purview of the attorney-in-fact's authority, absent an expression of contrary intent by the principal. Despite this broad grant of power, the statute places certain absolute limitations on the agent's decisionmaking authority. The attorney-in-fact may not commit the principal to a mental institution, and may not authorise psychosurgery, electroconvulsive treatment, sterilisation, or abortion.

D. The limits of health care decisionmaking power

Under the California Statute, the attorney-in-fact is prohibited from exercising his statutory authority: (1) after expiration of the seven-year statute of limitations, (2) to revoke the agent's authority; (3) where he lacks the capacity to give informed consent on the part of the principal; (4) in dereliction of his duty to act consistent with the principal's expressed desires; or (5) in a manner clearly contrary to the principal's best interests, if his desires are unknown. Section 2411 sets up elaborate procedures whereby interested parties (including both principal and agent) can petition the probate court for determination of these issues.

Nowhere does the Durable Power of Attorney for Health Care Decisions Act define the best interests of the principal. The common law standard of 'best interests', which relies heavily on prior expressed intentions, was recommended for use in durable power statutes by the President's Commission. Under the common law 'best interests' standard, the principal may choose to communicate his express desires privately to his chosen surrogate or more formally through a Living Will or express language in the durable power of attorney document. The attorney-in-fact would then have a duty to act in accordance with the principal's wishes, as expressed in the Durable Power of Attorney, Living will, or otherwise. If the principal's wishes are not known, the agent must act in the best interests of the principal, with knowledge that his decision, whether to act by affirmation or omission, will be subject to the scrutiny of the probate court through the petition process initiated by interested parties who challenge the attorney-in-fact's interpretation of the best interests of the principal. Emergency treatment, however, may be provided without the attorney-in-fact's authorisation if unavailable because of time restraints.

The physician immunity provision of the Durable Power of Attorney for Health Care Decisions Act is a source of added concern. Section 2438 states that there shall be immunity from civil and criminal liability as well as from professional censure for health care providers who act on the basis of a good faith belief that the attorney-in-fact is authorised by the statute to make a health care decision. The Act imposes additional duties on the health care provider: (1) the provider must believe, in good faith, that the decision is not inconsistent with the principal's wishes; and, (2) if the decision is to withhold or withdraw health care necessary to keep the principal alive, the provider must make a 'good faith' effort to determine the desires of the principal (to the extent that the principal is able to convey those desires to the health care provider) and log those desires in the principal's medical records.

Despite frequent statutory references to 'good faith', health care provider immunity appears to be based on a higher standard. Good faith efforts, as previously discussed, are valid only if the health care provider *relies* on a health care decision made by the attorney-in-fact pursuant to the statute. In other words, the physician is granted immunity only if he agrees to subordinate his own judgment to that of the surrogate decisionmaker.

Like the Natural Death Act, the Durable Power of Attorney for Health Care Decisions Act's immunity provision frees health care providers from the vague restrictions of civil, criminal, and professional sanctions. Unlike similar Living Will immunity provisions, however, the scope of immunity is not limited to terminal illness and imminent death. As long as the decisionmaker acts within the scope of delegated authority, the number of occasions and kinds of decisions that can be ruled on are unlimited.

Extended immunity solves the twofold problem of Living Will immunity provisions. Extending the scope of physician immunity gives health care personnel more incentive to discuss and listen to patient and surrogate decisionmakers. Patient autonomy is also reinforced by allowing principals to delegate decisionmaking to the entire range of decisions while incompetent. Thus, patient and physician are encouraged to act in tandem, rather than concerning themselves with conflicting personal or legal obligations. The Durable Power of Attorney Act resolves legal conflicts by clarifying and focusing on the primary moral right—personal autonomy in decisionmaking.

(iv)   A new hybrid statute

A third generation of statutes is emerging in the United States which combine provisions relating to living wills with the option of appointing a proxy to decide on behalf of the patient. Eight states now have this—Arkansas, Delaware, Florida, Louisiana, Texas, Utah, Virginia and Wyoming. The Texas Natural Death Act of 1977 was amended in 1985 to include, *inter alia*, the following provisions:

Sec 3(e): The directive may include other directions, including a designation of another person to make a treatment decision in accordance with Section 4A of this Act for the declarant if the declarant is comatose, incompetent, or otherwise mentally or physically incapable of communication.

Sec 4A: ... The desire of a qualified patient who is competent shall at all times supersede the effect of a directive. If an adult qualified patient is comatose, incompetent, or otherwise mentally or physically incapable of communication and has issued a directive under this Act without designating a person to make a treatment decision, the attending physician shall comply with the directive unless the physician believes that the directive does not reflect the present desire of the patient.

You may think that in the absence of recourse to a proxy s 4A is at best equivocal in its commitment to respect for the patient's autonomy. Even in the case where a proxy is appointed, section 4B seems to limit the powers of the proxy.

Sec 4B: If an adult qualified patient who has designated a person to make a treatment decision as authorised by Section 3(e) of this Act is comatose, incompetent, or otherwise mentally or physically incapable of communication, the attending physician and the person designated by the patient *may* make a treatment decision to withhold or withdraw life-sustaining procedures from the patient. [Our emphasis.]

(Contrast the Californian 'pure' enduring power of attorney legislation.)

Thus, the Texas statute may be a model of the principle of combining the two forms of directive, but its wording falls somewhat short of the ideal. Which form of advance directive best furthers the autonomy of the incompetent patient?

(c) ENGLISH LAW IN THE FUTURE

If it is thought desirable that advance directives should have legal effect in England, the following points should be borne in mind:

1. We have seen that a court could find that a living will couched in appropriate terms, has legal effect. To put the matter beyond doubt, however, legislation would be called for.
2. We have seen that an enduring power of attorney in relation to decisions about health care has no legal effect. Thus, legislation is essential to introduce these.
3. If legislation concerning living wills and enduring powers of attorney were contemplated, there are a number of problematic issues which would have to be resolved.

(i) The triggering event

Should this be the onset of incompetence or should there be a further requirement, as a matter of law, so that the advance directive would come into operation only when the patient is *both* incompetent and dying (however defined)? We have seen that in the US the latter has been the approach adopted. Arguably, such a position is too restrictive if the purpose of the advanced directive is truly to facilitate the expression of autonomy by the patient.

Opting for the former alternative does of course bring its own problems. The person may direct, for example, that with the onset of a condition rendering him irretrievably incompetent he should not receive ever again any form of medical intervention but merely be allowed to die. This would place any doctor caring for him in a most difficult position. What would you advise a doctor to do in such a position?

(ii)   Exclusion of certain treatments and conditions

In the United States, statutes on advance directives have typically excluded, as we have seen, hydration and feeding as treatments which can be covered by any advance directive. In other words, a doctor would remain the final judge of whether to continue with these interventions by reference to general principles, whatever the patient stipulated. Earlier we have taken the view that hydration and feeding are no different in principle from any other intervention. Thus an exception, on the US model, would not be appropriate.

Statutes in the US have also excluded the operation of advance directives if executed by a woman who proves to be pregnant at the time the directive would otherwise come into effect. The reason is clear—namely the concern for the unborn child and the possibility of ensuring its survival even at the expense of ignoring the wishes of the mother. Can you think of other circumstances in which the interests of the unborn child are put before those of the mother? Would any statute, to be defensible, have to stipulate that the unborn child would have to be viable or have a reasonable prospect of reaching the stage of gestation at which it could be viable? (The problem of the pregnant woman who is in a 'persistent vegetative state' or who is even 'brain dead' has already arisen in the US in cases where it has been thought right that treatment, if it can properly be called that here, should be continued in an attempt to allow the fetus to develop sufficiently to reach viability and so have the chance of survival. How do you think the law should respond to this situation? (See Note, 'Incubating for the State: The Precarious Autonomy of Persistently Vegetative and Brain-Dead Pregnant Women' (1988) 22 Georgia LR 1103)).

(iii)   Living wills, durable powers—or both?

A disadvantage associated with the living will is that it may suffer from one or two faults. It may be drafted in general terms. If so, it will require interpretation to determine whether the patient's condition warrants its implementation. The interpretation would have to be made by the doctor, perhaps advised by others. This could result in the denial of the very purpose of the living will as a vehicle facilitating respect for the autonomy of the patient. If, on the other hand, the patient, foreseeing the above danger, draws up a living will with great precision as to the conditions under which it will come into operation there is, of course, a considerable risk of its failing to take effect since the patient's condition may not be one contemplated by the living will. Thus, again the patient's will may be frustrated.

The advantage of including an enduring power of attorney is that discretion can be granted, within the general parameters of a living will-type document, to a proxy who will exercise the choice that the patient would have wished to make in the light of all the prevailing circumstances.

A combination of the two types of document may, therefore, be the most desirable solution. This would, of course, require legislation in England.

(iv) Formalities

It goes without saying that any statute giving legal force to advance directives must provide numerous safeguards to protect the interests of the patient. The American statutes demonstrate a punctilious concern for these: who may be a witness, provisions for any change of mind, the need for writing, a maximum term of validity, are some of the central issues that would have to be addressed.

Chapter 15

Death

Introduction

We start with a quote from Christopher Pallis, *ABC of Brain Stem Death* (pp 1–4; footnotes omitted):

Reappraising death

People have been alarmed for centuries at the prospect of being declared dead when they were still living. There was generalised anxiety about the subject 140 years ago, after Edgar Allan Poe had published various short stories, such as *Premature Burial*, in which people had been interred alive. Towards the end of the last century Count Karnice-Karnicki of Berlin patented a coffin of a particular type. If the 'corpse' regained consciousness after burial he or she could summon help from the surface by a system of flags and bells. Recent controversies have revived this longstanding fear of premature or mistaken diagnosis of death.

The need to reappraise death

A dead brain in a body whose heart is still beating is one of the more macabre products of modern technology. During the past 30 years techniques have developed that can artificially maintain ventilation, circulation, and elimination of waste products of metabolism in a body whose brain has irreversibly ceased to function. Such cases begin to appear in all countries as their intensive care facilities reach a certain standard. What we do when confronted with such circumstances raises important question. Brain death compels doctors (and society as a whole) to re-evaluate assumptions that go back for millennia.

Brain death was described as early as 1959. Renal transplantation was then in its infancy, whole-body irradiation being the only means of modifying the immune response. It is important to emphasise this, because some critics seem to believe that brain death was invented by neurologists to satisfy the demands of transplant surgeons. If transplantation were superseded tomorrow by better methods of treating end-stage renal failure brain dead patients would still be produced in large numbers in well run intensive care units in many parts of the world.

Over half a million people die each year in Great Britain. Whether at home or in hospital, they 'die their own death'. No machines are concerned. Their heart stops and that is the beginning and end of it. Epidemiological data suggest that brain death relates to perhaps 4000 deaths a year—well under 1% of all deaths. These people have sustained acute, irreparable, structural brain damage, which has plunged them into the deepest coma. The brain damage includes permanent loss of the capacity to breathe. But prompt action by doctors has ensured that ventilation is taken over by a machine before the resulting anoxia can stop the heart.

. . .

Concepts and criteria

All talk of the criteria of death—and ipso facto all arguments about better criteria—must be related to some overall concept of what death means. When we consider death the tests we carry out and the decisions we make should be logically derived from conceptual and philosophical premises. There can be no free-floating criteria, unrelated to such premises.

The box [over the page] lists several concepts that have prevailed from time to time. In the middle ages, if one entered certain monasteries one ceased to enjoy the limited rights and heavy duties of the outside world. One would be considered 'dead' by civil society. The appropriate criterion for such a concept of death would presumably be a certificate from the father superior of the monastery confirming that one had entered it. Esoteric concepts may be met by esoteric criteria.

Both Hellenic and Judaeo-Christian cultures identified death with the departure of the soul from the body. In 1957 Pope Pius XII, speaking to an international congress of anaesthetists, raised the question of whether one should 'continue the resuscitation process despite the fact that the soul may already have left the body'. I would find it difficult to identify this particular state or to formulate relevant criteria.

Some people have held that the surest notion of death is the biblical one: 'Ashes to ashes, dust to dust'. The appropriate criterion for such a concept would be putrefaction, but no one would argue today that this is necessary before a person can be pronounced dead. We all readily grasp the difference between 'Is this woman dead?' and 'Has every enzyme stopped working, in every cell of her body?' The controversy is between those who think of death as 'dissolution of the organism as a whole' and those who insist that it can mean only 'dissolution of the whole organism'.

Asked what they mean by death, most people will probably talk about the heart 'having stopped for good'. This is indeed a mechanism of death (and, until brain death appeared on the scene, it was also a universal attribute of a cadaver) but is it really a concept of death? When asked whether an individual is dead whose cardiac function has been permanently taken over by a machine many people begin to realise that a beating heart is not an end in itself but a means to another end: the preservation of the brain. This has been unconsciously perceived by people with little or no knowledge of physiology: we have been hanging and decapitating for centuries.

I conceive of human death as a state in which there is irreversible loss of the capacity for consciousness combined with irreversible loss of the capacity to breathe (and hence to maintain a heart beat). Alone, neither would be sufficient. Both are essentially brain stem functions (predominantly represented, incidentally, at different ends of the brain stem). The concept is admittedly a hybrid one, expressing both philosophical and physiological attributes. It corresponds perhaps to an intermediate stage of current concerns, seeking to maintain a footing on both types of ground. Although seldom explicitly formulated, this view of death is, I believe, widely shared in the West. It is the implicit basis for British practice in diagnosing 'brain death'.

Some people, particularly in the USA, have gone further and proposed a concept of death that would equate it with the loss of personal identity, or with the 'irreversible loss of that which is essentially significant to the nature of man'. 'Cognitive death' is already being evaluated as part of the 'next generation of problems'. I am opposed to 'higher brain' formulations of death because they are the first step along a slippery slope. If one starts equating the loss of higher functions with death, then, which higher functions? Damage to one hemisphere or to both? If to one hemisphere, to the 'verbalising' dominant one, or to the 'attentive' non-dominant one? One soon starts arguing frontal versus parietal lobes.

Concepts

- Entering certain monastic orders in the Middle Ages

- The soul leaving the body

- 'Ashes to ashes; dust to dust'

- Irreversible loss of capacity for consciousness and of capacity to breathe

- Loss of personal identity (the 'higher brain' formulation)

Over the past 100 years modern man has 'secularised his philosophical understanding of his nature' and has sought to find 'more biological formulations of what it meant to be dead'. When we strike these existential chords, however, the responses are likely to be implicitly philosophical. If we understand this we will be more tolerant of the diversity of answers people will give when asked, 'What is it that is so central to your humanity that when you lose it you are dead?'

Death: an event or a process?

In 1968 the 22nd World Medical Assembly in Sydney stated: 'Death is a gradual process at the cellular level, with tissues varying in their ability to withstand deprivation of oxygen. But clinical interest lies not in the state of preservation of isolated cells but in the fate of a person. Here the point of death of the different cells and organs is not so important as the certainty that the process has become irreversible, whatever techniques of resuscitation may be employed.' In thus defining death the delegates in Sydney were endorsing—whether they knew it or not—one of the options offered by the *Concise Oxford Dictionary*, which describes death both as 'dying' (a process) and 'being dead' (a state).

It has, of course, been thought for centuries that growth of the hair and nails might continue after the heart had stopped. Surgeons discovered years ago that they could harvest skin 24 hours after irreversible asystole and transplant it. A bone graft or an arterial graft would 'take' even if the tissue had been collected 48 hours after death. In the light of such observations, the classical signs of death (permanent cessation of breathing and of the heartbeat) will be perceived rather differently: they will be seen as major and easily detectable events, triggering a final, rapid sequence of biological changes. They are the usual points of no return in the dissolution of the organism as a whole and proof positive that the process leading to death of the whole organism has indeed become irreversible.

Legal constraints and dictionary definitions have probably delayed acceptance of the notion of death as a process. Fifteen years ago the editorial of a leading American journal talked of the 'end point' of existence 'which ought to be as clear and sharp as in a chemical titration'. In fact the simultaneous destruction of all tissues—death as an event—is rare indeed. The sudden carbonisation of the whole body by a nuclear explosion is the only example that readily comes to mind.

In the heat of the public controversy about brain death two years ago a limerick was written which summed up the simple wisdom that death is a process:

In our graveyards with winter winds blowing
There's a great deal of to-ing and fro-ing
But can it be said
That the buried are dead
When their nails and their hair are still growing?

I think all cultures capable of asking such a question would answer it with an unequivocal 'yes'—whether the premises were true or not.

But there are other points of no return. One type of event epitomises the fact that these may in fact precede cessation of the heart beat—decapitation. Once the head has been severed from the neck the heart continues to beat. Is that individual alive or dead? If those who hold that a person can be truly dead only when the heart has stopped believe that a decapitated individual is still alive, simply because his heart is still beating, they have a concept of life so different from mine that I doubt if bridges could be built. If, however, they accept that such an individual is dead they should extrapolate this awareness to a similar situation, extended over hours or days (because of a closed circulation). They will be thinking about brain death.

The vegetative state, whole brain death, and death of the brain stem

About 10 years ago [a] picture of an unsuccessfully decapitated chicken appeared in a leading magazine. The forebrain ha[d] been amputated and [lay] on the ground. The brain stem [was] still in situ. The bird, still breathing, was fed with a dropper for several weeks. Was it alive or dead?

The chicken must be considered alive so long as its brain stem is functioning. Let us transfer the argument to a child with hydranencephaly. There is a spinal cord, a brain stem, and perhaps some diencephalic structures but certainly no cerebral hemispheres. The cranial cavity is full of cerebrospinal fluid and transilluminates when a light is applied to it. The child can breathe spontaneously, swallow, and grimace in response to painful stimuli. Its eyes are open. The heart can beat normally for months. No culture would declare that child dead. This emphasises the certainty we instinctively allocate to persisting brain stem function, even in the absence of anything we could describe as cerebration.

These examples may help one grasp the essence of a much more common and important condition: the vegetative state. This is a chronic condition, the result of either cerebral anoxia (which may devastate the cortical mantle of the brain) or of impact injury to the head (which may massively shear the subcortical white matter, disconnecting the cortex from underlying structures). Other pathological processes may also on occasion be responsible. Affected individuals, if adequately nursed, may survive for years. They open their eyes, so that by definition they cannot be described as comatose. But, although awake, they show no behavioural evidence of awareness. Conjugate roving movements of the eyes are common, orientating movements rare. The patients do not speak or initiate purposeful movement of their limbs. Abnormal motor responses to stimulation may often be seen. Like the hydranencephalic child, the patients grimace, swallow, and breathe spontaneously. Their pupillary and corneal reflexes are usually preserved. They have a working brain stem, but show no evidence of meaningful function above the level of the tentorium.

I have described the vegetative state so that I can contrast it with whole brain death. Brain dead individuals show no signs of neural function above the level of the foramen magnum. Even homoeostatic functions, dependent on central neural mechanisms, are affected. The patients are in deep irreversible coma, and have irreversibly lost the capacity to breathe. Brain stem death is the physiological kernel of brain death, the anatomical substratum of its cardinal signs (apnoeic coma with absent brain stem reflexes) and the main determinant of its invariable cardiac prognosis: asystole within hours or days.

[A controversy has developed] in the United States between those who have accepted death as synonymous with 'death of all structures above the foramen magnum', and others tentatively suggesting that death of large parts of both cerebral hemispheres (the vegetative state) might be enough. Very few informed physicians in the United States, it must be emphasised, subscribe to the latter view. A different disagreement smoulders on, meanwhile, both within the United Kingdom and to some extent between British and American neurologists, about whether we can clinically identify death of the brain stem and about what flows from such an identification. When people engaged in one discussion are suddenly parachuted into the other communication is bound, for a while, to be difficult.

Understanding death

Next consider the following from *Death, Dying, and the Biological Revolution*, by Robert H Veatch (pp 24–25; footnotes omitted):

Four separate levels in the definition of death debate must be distinguished. First, there is the purely formal analysis of the term *death*, an analysis that gives the structure and specifies the framework that must be filled in with content. Second, the *concept* of death is considered, attempting to fill the content of the formal definition. At this level the question is, What is so essentially significant about life that its loss is termed *death*? Third, there is the question of the locus of death: where in the organism ought one to look to determine whether death has occurred? Fourth, one must ask the question of the criteria of death: what technical tests must be applied at the locus to determine if an individual is living or dead?

Serious mistakes have been made in slipping from one level of the debate to another and in presuming that expertise on one level necessarily implies expertise on another. For instance, the Report of the Ad Hoc Committee of the Harvard Medical School to Examine the Definition of Brain Death is titled 'A Definition of Irreversible Coma'. The report makes clear that the committee members are simply reporting empirical measures which are criteria for predicting an irreversible coma. Yet the name of the committee seems to point more to the question of locus, where to look for measurement of death. The committee was established to examine the death of the brain. The implication is that the empirical indications of irreversible coma are also indications of 'brain death'. But by the first sentence of the report the committee claims that 'Our primary purpose is to define irreversible coma as a new criterion for death'. They have now shifted so that they are interested in 'death'. They must be presuming a philosophical concept of death—that a person in irreversible coma should be considered dead—but they nowhere argue this or even state it as a presumption.

Even the composition of the Harvard committee membership signals some uncertainty of purpose. If empirical criteria were their concern, the inclusion of nonscientists on the panel was strange. If the philosophical concept of death was their concern, medically trained people were overrepresented. As it happened, the committee did not deal at all with conceptual matters. The committee and its interpreters have confused the question at different levels.

As for the formal analysis of the term, Veatch offers the following (p 25):

A strictly formal definition of death might be the following:
Death means a complete change in the status of a living entity characterised by the irreversible loss of those characteristics that are essentially significant to it.

He points out, however, that (p 26):

Such a definition would apply equally well to a human being, a nonhuman animal, a plant, an organ, a cell, or even metaphorically to a social phenomenon like a society or to any temporally limited entity like a research project, a sports event, or a language. To define the death of a human being, we must recognise the characteristics that are essential to humanness. It is quite inadequate to limit the discussion to the death of the heart or the brain.

(a) THE CONCEPT

See again Veatch, *op cit* (pp 29–42; footnotes omitted):

To ask what is essentially significant to a human being is a philosophical question—a question of ethical and other values. Many elements make human beings unique—their opposing thumbs, their possession of rational souls, their ability to form cultures and manipulate symbol systems, their upright postures, their being created in the image of God, and so on. Any concept of death will depend directly upon how one evaluates these qualities. Four choices seem to me to cover the most plausible approaches.

Irreversible loss of flow of vital fluids
At first it would appear that the irreversible cessation of heart and lung activity would represent a simple and straightforward statement of the traditional understanding of the concept of death in Western culture. Yet upon reflection this proves otherwise. If patients simply lose control of their lungs and have to be permanently supported by a mechanical respirator, they are still living persons as long as they continue to get oxygen. If modern technology produces an efficient,

compact heart-lung machine capable of being carried on the back or in a pocket, people using such devices would not be considered dead, even though both heart and lungs were permanently nonfunctioning. Some might consider such a technological man an affront to human dignity; some might argue that such a device should never be connected to a human; but even they would, in all likelihood, agree that such people are alive.

. . .

Irreversible loss of the soul from the body

There is a longstanding tradition, sometimes called vitalism, that holds the essence of man to be independent of the chemical reactions and electrical forces that account for the flow of the bodily fluids . . .

The departure of the soul might be seen by believers as occurring at about the time that the fluids stop flowing. But it would be a mistake to equate these two concepts of death, as according to the first fluid stops from natural, if unexplained, causes, and death means nothing more than that stopping of the flow which is essential to life. According to the second view, the fluid stops flowing at the time the soul departs, and it stops because the soul is no longer present. Here the essential thing is the loss of the soul, not the loss of the fluid flow.

The irreversible loss of the capacity for bodily integration

In the debate between those who held a traditional religious notion of the animating force of the soul and those who had the more naturalistic concept of the irreversible loss of the flow of bodily fluids, the trend to secularism and empiricism made the loss of fluid flow more and more the operative concept of death in society. But man's intervention in the dying process through cardiac pacemakers, respirators, intravenous medication and feeding, and extravenous purification of the blood has forced a sharper examination of the naturalistic concept of death. It is now possible to manipulate the dying process so that some parts of the body cease to function while other parts are maintained indefinitely . . .

We now must consider whether concepts of death that focus on the flow of fluids or the departure of the soul are philosophically appropriate. The reason that the question arises as a practical matter is fear of a 'false positive' determination that human life is present. There are several ways of handling doubtful cases. Many would argue that when there is moral or philosophical doubt about whether someone is dead, it would be (morally) safer to act as if the person were alive. At the most rigorous extreme of this course, those advocating a position called tutiorism say that if there is any question at all that an action may be morally wrong, it should be avoided. In this case, the presence of any doubt about whether a person is dead would lead us to err on the safe side and consider the person to be living. An intermediate position, called probabiliorism, is that when there is moral doubt, we may follow a course of action whose morality is in doubt if (and only if) the probability that it is moral is more likely than that it is not. Another position, called probabilism, offers the most leeway, holding that a 'probable opinion' may be followed even though the contrary opinion is also probable or even more probable. In the case under consideration, the probabilist could consider the individual dead even though moral doubt, even perhaps serious doubt, remained; while holders of the more rigorous positions would argue that we should take the morally safer course and consider the person alive even though the heart and lungs had permanently stopped functioning and fluid flow could never be restored.

Even the probabilist, however, traditionally has placed restrictions on legitimizing actions supported by a probable opinion—for instance, when a life may be saved by taking one of the probable courses of action. This is clearly the sort of case involved in trying to decide whether to treat an individual as dead.

Thus, when modifying our traditional concept of death to pronounce dead some individuals who would under older concepts be considered alive (that is, those with heart and lung but no brain function), the problem of moral doubt must be resolved . . . The most plausible [solution is]: to treat the real situation as one of perplexed conscience. There are two relevant and important moral principles at stake—

preservation of an individual life and preservation of the dignity of an individual by being able to distinguish a dead person from a living one. The introduction of a moral obligation to treat the dead as dead leaves one perplexed. It creates moral pressures in each direction. The defenders of the older concepts, which may lead to false pronouncements of living, must defend their action as well. It seems to me that only when such positive moral pressure is introduced on both sides of the argument can we plausibly overcome the claim that we must take the morally safer course. We must consider that it may be not only right to call persons dead, but also wrong to call them alive. This will still mean minimising the life-saving exception, but at least at this point there will be a positive moral argument for doing so. It can be seen that it is quite difficult to justify any divergence from the older, more traditional concepts of death. Nevertheless, the case is being made for a neurologically centered concept.

At first it would appear that the irreversible loss of brain activity is the concept of death held by those no longer satisfied with the vitalistic concept of the departure of the soul or the animalistic concept of the irreversible cessation of fluid flow. This is why the name *brain death* is frequently given to the new proposals, but the term is unfortunate for two reasons.

First, as we have seen, it is not the heart and lungs as such that are essentially significant but rather the vital functions—the flow of fluids—which we believe according to the best empirical human physiology to be associated with these organs. An 'artificial brain' is not a present-day possibility but a walking, talking, thinking individual who had one would certainly be considered living. It is not the collection of physical tissues called the brain, but rather their functions—consciousness; motor control; sensory feeling; ability to reason; control over bodily functions including respiration and circulation; major integrating reflexes controlling blood pressure, ion levels, and pupil size; and so forth—which are given essential significance by those who advocate adoption of a new concept of death or clarification of the old one. In short they see the body's capacity for integrating its functions as the essentially significant indication of life.

Second, as suggested earlier, we are not interested in the death of particular cells, organs, or organ systems, but in the death of the person as a whole—the point at which the person as a whole undergoes a quantum change through the loss of characteristics held to be essentially significant, the point at which 'death behaviour' becomes appropriate. Terms such as *brain death* or *heart death* should be avoided because they tend to obscure the fact that we are searching for the meaning of the death of the person as a whole. At the public policy level, this has very practical consequences. A statute adopted in Kansas specifically refers to 'alternative definitions of death' and says that they are 'to be used for all purposes in this state. . . .' According to this language, which has resulted from talking of brain and heart death, a person in Kansas may be simultaneously dead according to one definition and alive according to another. When a distinction must be made, it should be made directly on the basis of the philosophical significance of the functions mentioned above rather than on the importance of the tissue collection called the brain. For purposes of simplicity we shall use the phrase *the capacity for bodily integration* to refer to the total list of integrating mechanisms possessed by the body. The case for these mechanisms being the ones that are essential to humanness can indeed be made. Man is more than the flowing of fluids. He is a complex, integrated organism with capacities for internal regulation. With and only with these integrating mechanisms is homo sapiens really a human person.

There appear to be two general aspects to this concept of what is essentially significant: first, a capacity for integrating one's internal bodily environment (which is done for the most part unconsciously through highly complex homeostatic, feedback mechanisms) and, secondly, a capacity for integrating one's self, including one's body, with the social environment through consciousness which permits interaction with other persons. Clearly these taken together offer a more profound understanding of the nature of man than does the simple flow of bodily fluids. Whether or not it is more a profound concept of man than that which focuses simply on the presence or absence of the soul, it is clearly a very different one. The ultimate

test between the two is that of meaningfulness and plausibility. For many in the modern secular society, the concept of loss of capacity for bodily integration seems much more meaningful and plausible, that is, we see it as a much more accurate description of the essential significance of man and of what is lost at the time of death. According to this view, when individuals lose all of these 'truly vital' capacities we should call them dead and behave accordingly.
. . .

The irreversible loss of the capacity for social interaction
The fourth major alternative for a concept of death draws on the characteristics of the third concept and has often been confused with it. Henry Beecher offers a summary of what he considers to be essential to man's nature:

the individual's personality, his conscious life, his uniqueness, his capacity for remembering, judging, reasoning, acting, enjoying, worrying, and so on . . .

Beecher goes on immediately to ask the anatomical question of locus. He concludes that these functions reside in the brain and that when the brain no longer functions, the individual is dead. . . . What is remarkable is that Beecher's list, with the possible exception of 'uniqueness', is composed entirely of functions explicitly related to consciousness and the capacity to relate to one's social environment through interaction with others. All the functions which give the capacity to integrate one's internal bodily environment through unconscious, complex, homeostatic reflex mechanisms—respiration, circulation, and major integrating reflexes—are omitted. In fact, when asked what was essentially significant to man's living, Beecher replied simply, 'Consciousness'.

Thus a fourth concept of death is the irreversible loss of the capacity for consciousness or social integration. This view of the nature of man places even more emphasis on social character. Even, given a hypothetical human being with the full capacity for integration of bodily function, if he had irreversibly lost the capacity for consciousness and social interaction, he would have lost the essential character of humanness and, according to this definition, the person would be dead.

Even if one moves to the so-called higher functions and away from the mere capacity to integrate bodily functions through reflex mechanisms, it is still not clear precisely what is ultimately valued. We must have a more careful specification of 'consciousness or the capacity for social integration'. Are these two capacities synonymous and, if not, what is the relationship between them? Before taking up that question, we must first make clear what is meant by capacity.

Holders of this concept of death and related concepts of the essence of man specifically do not say that individuals must be valued by others in order to be human. This would place life at the mercy of other human beings who may well be cruel or insensitive. Nor does this concept imply that the essence of man is the fact of social interaction with others, as this would also place a person at the mercy of others. The infant raised in complete isolation from other human contact would still be human, provided that the child retained the mere capacity for some form of social interaction. This view of what is essentially significant to the nature of man makes no quantitative or qualitative judgments. It need not, and for me could not, lead to the view that those who have more capacity for social integration are more human. The concepts of life and death are essentially bipolar, threshold concepts. Either one has life or one does not. Either a particular type of death behaviour is called for or it is not. One does not pronounce death half-way or read a will half-way or become elevated from the vice presidency to the presidency half-way.
. . .

Precisely what are the functions considered to be ultimately significant to human life according to this concept: There are several possibilities.

The capacity for rationality is one candidate. Homo sapiens is a rational animal, as suggested by the name. The human capacity for reasoning is so unique and so important that some would suggest that it is the critical element in man's nature. But certainly infants lack any such capacity and they are considered living human beings. Nor is possession of the potential for reasoning what is important. Including potential might resolve the problem of infants, but does not explain why those who have no potential for rationality (such as the apparently permanent back ward psychotic or the senile individual) are considered to be humanly living in a real if not full sense and to be entitled to the protection of civil and moral law.

Consciousness is a second candidate that dominates much of the medical and biological literature. If the rationalist tradition is reflected in the previous notion, then the empiricalist philosophical tradition seems to be represented in the emphasis on consciousness. What may be of central significance is the capacity for experience. This would include the infant and the individual who lacks the capacity for rationality, and focuses attention on the ability for sensory activity summarised as consciousness. Yet, this is a very individualistic understanding of man's nature. It describes what is essentially significant to the human life without any reference to other human beings.

Social interaction is a third candidate. At least in the Western tradition, man is seen as an essentially social animal. Perhaps it is man's capacity or potential for social interaction that has such ultimate significance that its loss is considered death. Is this in any sense different from the capacity for experience? Certainly it is conceptually different and places a very different emphasis on man's essential role. Yet it may well be that the two functions, experience and social interaction, are completely coterminous. It is difficult to conceive a case where the two could be separated, at least if social interaction is understood in its most elementary form. While it may be important for a philosophical understanding of man's nature to distinguish between these two functions, it may not be necessary for deciding when a person has died. Thus, for our purposes we can say that the fourth concept of death is one in which the essential element that is lost is the capacity for consciousness or social interaction or both.

The concept presents one further problem. The Western tradition which emphasises social interaction also emphasises, as we have seen, the importance of the body. Consider the admittedly remote possibility that the electrical impulses of the brain could be transferred by recording devices onto magnetic computer tape. Would that tape together with some kind of minimum sensory device be a living human being and would erasure of the tape be considered murder? If the body is really essential to man, then we might well decide that such a creature would not be a living human being.

Where does this leave us? . . . The earlier concepts of death—the irreversible loss of the soul and the irreversible stopping of the flow of vital body fluids—strike me as quite implausible. The soul as an independent nonphysical entity that is necessary and sufficient for a person to be considered alive is a relic from the era of dichotomised anthropologies. Animalistic fluid flow is simply too base a function to be the human essence. The capacity for bodily integration is more plausible, but I suspect it is attractive primarily because it includes those higher functions that we normally take to be central—consciousness, the ability to think and feel and relate to others. When the reflex networks that regulate such things as blood pressure and respiration are separated from the higher functions, I am led to conclude that it is the higher functions which are so essential that their loss ought to be taken as the death of the person. While consciousness is certainly important, man's social nature and embodiment seem to me to be the truly essential characteristics. I therefore believe that death is most appropriately thought of as the irreversible loss of the embodied capacity for social interaction.

Veatch favours the 'irreversible loss of the capacity for social interaction' as the most appropriate concept of death. Are you persuaded, particularly in the light of the implications of such a view (see *infra*)?

Lamb's analysis in his book *Death, Brain Death and Ethics* leads to a somewhat different conclusion (pp 11–16).

[W]hilst it is important to separate the sphere of the philosophical from the medical, it is equally important to stress that in any discussion of death neither party can afford to ignore the contributions of the other. Medical judgments are informed by philosophical presuppositions, whether or not the latter are explicitly formulated. The diagnosis of any illness may be clinical and empirical, but it would be lacking in significance if there were no underlying concepts of health and disease. Whether a patient is classified as dead or alive depends on our understanding of the relevant concept of death. According to Capron and Kass ... the departure from the traditional concept of death manifest in the employment of brain-related criteria has brought these extra-medical concepts to the forefront of concern. Whilst traditional criteria, based on the cessation of cardio-respiratory functions, remained congruent with public conceptions of death, the phenomenon of death remained exclusively a matter of medical concern. But once medicine appeared to depart from traditional criteria for determining death, clarification of these extra-medical concepts of death became a matter of urgent concern for those responsible for the management of death. In view of the importance attached to a diagnosis of death in terms of the social, religious, political and ethical consequences, it is essential that this challenge be met and that the concept of death be made explicit. Furthermore, it is essential that criteria and tests for death should be logically derived from the appropriate concept of death.

The concept of death involves a philosophical judgment that a significant change has taken place, which presupposes an idea of the necessary conditions of life. These may range from the faculties involved in social interaction to the capacity to maintain bodily integration. Concepts of death may vary according to cultural patterns, religious traditions and scientific practice. ... They may include such distinct formulations as 'the separation of soul and body', 'destruction of all physical structures', 'loss of the capacity for social interaction', 'irreversible loss of consciousness', 'loss of bodily integration', and many others. Related to these concepts are appropriate criteria, and tests to ascertain that the criteria have been met. It follows that any shift in the concept of death will necessitate corresponding changes in the criteria and tests for death. However, it does not follow that new criteria and tests mean that a change of concept has taken place. They may indicate nothing more than refinements of previous criteria and tests. For example, the employment of stethoscopes and cardiograms constituted technically better tests for death which did not entail any departure from the traditional cardio-respiratory-based concept of death.

Criteria for death only have meaning if they can be shown to be logically derived from the appropriate concept of death. It is therefore meaningless to use 'free-floating criteria' which are not derived from a clearly-determined concept of death. ... Clarity concerning the concept of death provides a point of reference when deciding upon criteria, but some definitions of death are philosophically inadequate despite the fact that criteria can be logically derived from them. ... Concepts of death, such as 'entering a monastery' or exclusion from the family, tribe or clan, are widely used and yield appropriate criteria. But they can refer to death only in a metaphorical sense.

The essential point here is that some concepts are more relevant than others. The requirement for a definition of death is a demand for the selection of a concept that is superior to others. For this reason vaguely formulated and indeterminate concepts should be eschewed. Thus a concept of death as 'the loss of that which is essentially significant to the nature of man' is unsatisfactory, since we can say that a patient has lost what is essentially significant but is still alive. This is because concepts like 'essentially significant' are by their very nature undetermined. For if by 'the loss of what is essentially significant' is meant 'the loss of the capacity for social interaction' then various interpretations are possible, from loss of libido to blindness, from senility to dementia, which will provide appropriate criteria. But the question of which, if any, of these states might best fulfil the requirements of the definition cannot be answered without further conceptual guidelines. On what grounds can it be inferred that 'massive brain damage', or 'loss of reproductive function' and so on amount to the 'loss of what is essentially significant'? Furthermore, all of the fore-mentioned criteria may be fulfilled when it is patently obvious that the patient is alive and, in some cases, that his situation is even reversible. If the 'loss of that

which is essentially significant' is to have any meaning as a concept of death, then it must be framed so that it involves an irreversible state where the organism as a whole cannot function. Only a concept which specifies the irreversible loss of specified functions (due to the destruction of their anatomical substratum) can avoid the anomalous situation where a patient is said to be alive according to one concept but dead according to another. The only wholly satisfactory concept of death is that which trumps other concepts of death in so far as it yields a diagnosis of death which is beyond dispute. It follows that any criterion which, when fulfilled, leaves it possible for someone to say that the patient is still alive, is unsatisfactory. For this reason concepts relating specifically to psychological functions or moral qualities are wholly inadequate. In fact any criterion which, when fulfilled, leaves it possible for the organism as a whole to continue to function is inadequate. It should not be possible to say that the person is still alive although the criterion has been met, nor to say that the person is dead although the criterion has not been met.
. . .

The concept of death that will be proposed and defended in this chapter is the '*irreversible loss of function of the organism as a whole*'. There is confusion between this and 'death of the whole organism'. This is often present—although unformulated—in arguments which maintain that the concept of death should be left undetermined, or that death is a process with no special point at which a non-arbitrary diagnosis can be factually ascertained. . . . Criteria for the 'death of the whole organism' could only be met by tests for putrefaction, since cellular life in certain tissues can continue long after it has ceased in others, and long past the point where the organism as a whole has ceased to function. However, putrefaction has never been seriously advanced as a definition of death by either physicians or philosophers. Consequently, the argument that the concept of death should remain undetermined has no place in a world where practical decisions regarding the criteria of death necessitate an acceptable concept. In contrast criteria for 'irreversible loss of function of the organism as a whole' can be determined with precision, and appropriate diagnostic tests are constantly being developed. . . . The 'irreversible loss of function of the organism as a whole' is a biological concept which yields clinical criteria and tests. It presupposes the irreversible loss of the capacity for consciousness and the irreversible loss of the capacity to breathe, and hence sustain a spontaneous heart-beat. It supersedes ethical and religious-based concepts and its appropriate criterion is the death of the critical system as measured by tests for the irreversible cessation of brainstem function.

Failure to understand the relationship between the concept and criteria for death may lead to serious errors of judgement in practical matters. A patient in a vegetative state, it is argued, may meet a concept of death as 'a worthless existence' but, unless the individual's critical system is dead, it will not satisfy the concept of death formulated above as the 'irreversible loss of function of the organism as a whole'. The latter concept is currently employed in medical practice, if not explicitly formulated. It explains why an anencephalic infant would not be regarded as dead as long as its brainstem remained intact. . . .

For the above reasons it has become commonplace in the literature on brain death to describe the concept of death as a philosophical matter and the development of diagnostic criteria as a task for medical expertise and to warn against conflating definitions of what death is with the problem of when death occurs. The philosophical analysis of death is held to identify what it is that the diagnostic criteria are supposed to determine. . . .

Whilst this distinction is important, it is nevertheless equally important that it should not be drawn too rigidly. Philosophical issues do not exist in complete isolation from technical and scientific issues; they interact and interpenetrate. For this reason a more flexible distinction has been formulated by Bernat, Culver and Gert. . . .

Providing a definition is primarily a philosophical task: the choice of the criteria is primarily medical: and the selection of tests to prove that the criterion is satisfied is solely a medical matter.

This formulation can be illustrated as follows: suppose the concept of death were 'absence of fluid flow', then the criteria would be based on cessation of pulse, heartbeat and respiration, and could be determined by relatively straightforward empirical tests. If, however, the concept were the 'integrated functioning of the organism as a whole', one would have to decide which organ has decisive responsibility for this. If it is a matter of general agreement that the brain has this responsibility, then tests for measuring brain functions will be important. The formulation proposed by Bernat *et al.* has the merit of maintaining the distinction between philosophical discourse regarding the concept of death and medical discourse. Yet it recognises that, whilst philosophical and practical issues can be distinguished at one level, they mutually interact at another level. It is therefore important to be wary of attempts to settle—at the outset of any discussion—which kinds of problems belong exclusively to philosophy and which belong exclusively to medicine. Whilst Veatch's and Korein's formulations correctly identify the concept of death as a philosophical issue and the criteria for death as a practical matter, the three-level distinction between concept, criteria and practical tests, which is proposed by Bernat *et al.*, is preferable because it acknowledges the interaction between conceptual issues and the application of criteria in a practical context.

Whether we subscribe to the Veatch or Lamb view, it is clear that we must look to the brain as the appropriate 'locus' (as Veatch puts it) and not to the heart and lungs.

Further we must remind ourselves of Lamb's observation (at p 13) that: 'Only a concept which specifies the irreversible loss of specified functions (due to the destruction of their anatomical substratum) can avoid the anomalous situation where a patient is said to be alive according to one concept but dead according to another'. This entails that the relevant locus chosen must be that which is physiologically responsible for the functions deemed critical to the relevant concept of brain death.

(b) THE CRITERIA

What we are concerned with here is the means of identifying the presence or absence of the relevant functions of the locus (ie the whole brain or a part thereof). If the appropriate concept of death is *loss of the capacity for social interaction* then the correct locus of death is the brain. The criteria will then be the permanent and irreversible loss of function of the *higher brain*.

The President's Commission for the Study of Ethical Problems in Medicine and Biomedical and Behavioural Research: 'Medical, Legal and Ethical Issues in the Determination of Death: *Defining Death*', states as follows (pp 38, 40; footnotes omitted):

The 'higher brain' formulations
When all brain processes cease, the patient loses two important sets of functions. One set encompasses the integrating and coordinating functions, carried out principally but not exclusively by the cerebellum and brainstem. The other set includes the psychological functions which make consciousness, thought, and feeling possible. These latter functions are located primarily but not exclusively in the cerebrum, especially the neocortex. The two 'higher brain' formulations of brain-oriented definitions of death discussed here are premised on the fact that loss of cerebral functions strips the patient of his psychological capacities and properties.

A patient whose brain has permanently stopped functioning will, by definition, have lost those brain functions which sponsor consciousness, feeling, and thought. Thus the higher brain rationales support classifying as dead bodies which meet 'whole brain' standards . . . The converse is not true, however. If there are parts of the brain which have no role in sponsoring consciousness, the higher brain formulation would regard their continued functioning as compatible with death.

The concepts: Philosophers and theologians have attempted to describe the attributes a living being must have to be a person. 'Personhood' consists of the complex of activities (or of capacities to engage in them) such as thinking, reasoning, feeling, human intercourse which make the human different from, or superior to, animals or things. One higher brain formulation would define death as the loss of what is essential to a person. Those advocating the personhood definition often relate these characteristics to brain functioning. Without brain activity, people are incapable of these essential activities. A breathing body, the argument goes, is not in itself a person; and, without functioning brains, patients are merely breathing bodies. Hence personhood ends when the brain suffers irreversible loss of function.

For other philosophers, a certain concept of 'personal identity' supports a brain-oriented definition of death. According to this argument, a patient literally ceases to exist as an individual when his or her brain ceases functioning, even if the patient's body is biologically alive. Actual decapitation creates a similar situation: the body might continue to function for a short time, but it would no longer be the 'same' person. The persistent identity of a person as an individual from one moment to the next is taken to be dependent on the continuation of certain mental processes which arise from brain functioning. When the brain processes cease (whether due to decapitation or to 'brain death') the person's identity also lapses. The mere continuation of biological activity in the body is irrelevant to the determination of death, it is argued, because after the brain has ceased functioning the body is no longer identical with the person.

Critique: Theoretical and practical objections to these arguments led the Commission to rely on them only as confirmatory of other views in formulating a definition of death. First, crucial to the personhood argument is acceptance of one particular concept of those things that are essential to being a person, while there is no general agreement on this very fundamental point among philosophers, much less physicians or the general public. Opinions about what is essential to personhood vary greatly from person to person in our society—to say nothing of intercultural variations.

The argument from personal identity does not rely on any particular conception of personhood, but it does require assent to a single solution to the philosophical problem of identity. Again, this problem has persisted for centuries despite the best attempts by philosophers to solve it. Regardless of the scholarly merits of the various philosophical solutions, their abstract technicality makes them less useful to public policy.

Further, applying either of these arguments in practice would give rise to additional important problems. Severely senile patients, for example, might not clearly be persons, let alone ones with continuing personal identities; the same might be true of the severely retarded. Any argument that classified these individuals as dead would not meet with public acceptance.

Equally problematic for the 'higher brain' formulations, patients in whom only the neocortex or subcortical areas have been damaged may retain or regain spontaneous respiration and circulation. Karen Quinlan is a well-known example of a person who apparently suffered permanent damage to the higher centers of the brain but whose lower brain continues to function. Five years after being removed from the respirator that supported her breathing for nearly a year, she remains in a persistent vegetative state but with heart and lungs that function without mechanical assistance. Yet the implication of the personhood and personal identity arguments is that Karen Quinlan, who retains brainstem function and breathes spontaneously, is just as dead as a corpse in the traditional sense. The Commission rejects this conclusion and the further implication that such patients could be buried or otherwise treated as dead persons.

If, however, the preferred concept of death is *loss of bodily integration*, then the correct locus is again the brain. However, here the criteria will be the permanent and irreversible loss of functions of the brain.

For some, particularly in the United States, this 'permanent and irreversible loss of function of the *brain* means: of the *usable brain*. The President's Commission (*op cit*) writes (pp 32 and 35–6):

One characteristic of living things which is absent in the dead is the body's capacity to organise and regulate itself. In animals, the neural apparatus is the dominant locus of these functions. In higher animals and man, regulation of both maintenance of the internal environment (homeostasis) and interaction with the external environment occurs primarily within the cranium.

External threats, such as heat or infection, or internal ones, such as liver failure or endogenous lung disease, can stress the body enough to overwhelm its ability to maintain organisation and regulation. If the stress passes a certain level, the organism as a whole is defeated and death occurs.

This process and its denouement are understood in two major ways. Although they are sometimes stated as alternative formulations of a 'whole brain definition' of death, they are actually mirror images of each other. The Commission has found them to be complementary; together they enrich one's understanding of the 'definition'. The first focuses on the integrated functioning of the body's major organ systems, while recognising the centrality of the whole brain, since it is neither revivable nor replaceable. The other identifies the functioning of the whole brain as the hallmark of life because the brain is the regulator of the body's integration. . . .

A (more) significant criticism shares the view that life consists of the coordinated functioning of the various bodily systems, in which process the whole brain plays a crucial role. At the same time, it notes that in some adult patients lacking all brain functions it is possible through intensive support to achieve constant temperature, metabolism, waste disposal, blood pressure, and other conditions typical of living organisms and not found in dead ones. Even with extraordinary medical care, these functions cannot be sustained indefinitely—typically, no longer than several days—but it is argued that this shows only that patients with nonfunctional brains are dying, not that they are dead. In this view, the respirator, drugs, and other resources of the modern intensive-care unit collectively substitute for the lower brain, just as a pump used in cardiac surgery takes over the heart's function.

This criticism rests, however, on a premise about the role of artificial support vis-a-vis the brainstem which the Commission believes is mistaken or at best incomplete. While the respirator and its associated medical techniques do substitute for the functions of the intercostal muscles and the diaphragm, which without neuronal stimulation from the brain cannot function spontaneously, they cannot replace the myriad functions of the brainstem or of the rest of the brain. The startling contrast between bodies lacking *all* brain functions and patients with intact brainstems (despite severe neocortical damage) manifests this. The former lie with fixed pupils, motionless except for the chest movements produced by their respirators. The latter can not only breathe, metabolise, maintain temperature and blood pressure, and so forth, *on their own* but also sigh, yawn, track light with their eyes, and react to pain or reflex stimulation.

It is not easy to discern precisely what it is about patients in this latter group that makes them alive while those in the other category are not. It is in part that in the case of the first category (ie, absence of all brain functions) when the mask created by the artificial medical support is stripped away what remains is not an integrated organism but 'merely a group of artificially maintained sub-systems'. Sometimes, of course, an artificial substitute can forge the link that restores the organism as a whole to unified functioning. Heart or kidney transplants, kidney dialysis, or an iron lung used to replace physically-impaired breathing ability in a polio victim, for example, restore the integrated functioning of the organism as they replace the failed function of a part. Contrast such situations, however, with the hypothetical one and of a decapitated body treated so as to prevent the outpouring of blood and to generate respiration: continuation of bodily functions in that case would not have restored the requisites of human life.

However, in the United Kingdom a different view is taken. Pallis, *op cit*, explains the English approach as follows (pp 5–9, 17):

From brain death to brain stem death

Historical background

Brain death was first described clinically in 1959 when two French physicians identified a condition they called 'coma dépassé'—literally, a state beyond coma. Twenty of their 23 patients were suffering from primary intracranial disorders and the other three from the cerebral sequelae of cardiorespiratory arrest. All the classic features of brain death are found in this early report. As well as obvious signs indicating death of the nervous system the authors mentioned poikilothermia, diabetes insipidus, a sustained hypotension which proves increasingly difficult to control with pressor amines, and progressive acidosis, initially respiratory and later metabolic. Awed by the potential of resuscitatory techniques the authors described the condition created as both 'une revelation et une rancon'. Those affected were said to have the appearance of 'corpses with a good volume pulse'. Articles published in the early 1960s already hinted that the cerebral circulation was 'blocked' by raised intracranial pressure in most of these cases. These early publications already hint at the presence of cerebral oedema and intracranial hypertension. Within a few years a 'blocked' cerebral circulation was to be recognised as a common concomitant of the condition.

In 1968 the report of the Ad Hoc Committee of the Harvard Medical School brought awareness of brain death to a much wider audience. (Influenced by the French, the committee initially used the term 'irreversible coma' to describe the condition; this has led to confusion as this term was later sometimes used to describe the vegetative state.) The Harvard criteria demanded that the patient should be unreceptive and unresponsive, the most intensely painful stimuli evoking 'no vocal or other response, not even a groan, withdrawal of a limb or quickening of respiration'. No movements were to occur during observation for one hour. Apnoea was to be confirmed by three minutes off the respirator (the centrality of apnoea, properly defined and tested for, had already been appreciated). The Harvard criteria also required that there should be 'no reflexes', the emphasis being on brain stem reflexes. A flat or isoelectric electroencephalogram at high gain was of 'great confirmatory value'. All the tests were to be repeated at least 24 hours later, with no change in the findings.

Harvard criteria

1   Unreceptivity and unresponsivity

2   No movements (observe for 1 h)

3   Apnoea (3 min off respirator)

4   Absence of elicitable reflexes

5   Isoelectric EEG 'of great confirmatory value' (at 5 μV/mm)

All of the above tests shall be repeated at least 24 hours later with no change

---

The report unambiguously proposed that this clinical state should be accepted as death, recognised the moral, ethical, religious, and legal implications, and boldly saw itself as preparing the way 'for better insight into all these matters as well as for better law than is currently applicable'. A year later Beecher, the chairman of the Harvard Committee, stated that this body was 'unanimous in its belief that an electroencephalogram was not essential to a diagnosis of irreversible coma', although it could provide 'valuable supporting data'.

Within three years of this radical yet humane proposal two neurosurgeons from Minneapolis made the challenging suggestion that 'in patients with known but irreparable intracranial lesions' irreversible damage to the brain stem was the 'point of no return'. The diagnosis 'could be based on clinical judgment'.

The Minnesota workers had introduced the notion of aetiological preconditions. (Twenty of their 25 patients has sustained massive craniocerebral trauma and the others were suffering from other primary intracranial disorders.) They emphasised the importance of apnoea to the determination of brain death; in fact they insisted on four minutes of disconnection from the respirator. (I will return to this later. One obviously does not want the tests for brain death, such as the demonstration of apnoea after disconnection, to produce the very brain death one is testing for.) They demanded absent brain stem reflexes, stated that the findings should not change for at least 12 hours, and emphasised that the electroencephalogram was not mandatory for the diagnosis. Their recommendations later became known as the Minnesota criteria, and were to influence thinking and practice in the UK considerably. I am emphasising this because it has been suggested that doctors in the UK have been overcritical of much American work on this subject.

Minnesota criteria

1 'Known but irreparable intracranial lesion'

2 No spontaneous movement

3 Apnoea (4 min)

4 Absent brain stem reflexes

5 'All findings unchanged for at least 12 hours'

EEG not mandatory

Since 1971 doctors have sought to identify the necessary and sufficient component (or physiological kernel) of brain death. It was soon realised that absent tendon reflexes (demanded in both the French and Harvard criteria) really implied loss of function of the spinal cord and that this was irrelevant to a diagnosis of brain death. The original insistence of the French on areflexia is strange, for the works of Babinski contain accounts of knee jerks persisting for up to eight minutes after decapitation on the guillotine. Death of the brain and death of the whole nervous system are not the same thing. If the heart beat continues for long enough many patients with dead brains will recover their tendon reflexes or show pathological limb reflexes. The presence or absence of such reflexes, while providing clues whether the spinal cord is alive or dead, tell us nothing about whether the brain stem is functioning or not. Spinal areflexia is in fact the exception in brain death (established by the angiographic demonstration of a non-perfused brain).

The limb reflexes in brain stem death

1   The tendon (stretch) reflexes of the limbs are segmental spinal reflexes

2   Brain stem death may be complicated by spinal shock, causing areflexia

3   After an interval, if the spinal cord is viable, abnormal reflexes will appear below the level of a dead brain stem

4   The reflex pattern in the limbs is of no prognostic value in cases of brain stem death

---

There has also been a systematic attempt to look critically at the meaning of minimal cellular activity above the level of a dead brain stem. It was gradually realised that the cardiac prognosis depended critically on whether the brain stem was functioning or not. If the brain stem was dead the heart would stop quite soon. The presence of very low voltage residual electroencephalographic activity—seen in a few cases— did not influence the outcome. Such activity usually subsided anyway before asystole supervened. Physicians have therefore been focusing on how to identify irreversible loss of brain stem function.

In retrospect it is interesting that insight into the importance of the brain stem had been achieved as early as 1964, when Professor Keith Simpson, asked by the Medical Protection Society for words to use in a test case, suggested that 'there is life so long as a circulation of oxygenated blood is maintained to live brain stem centers'.

Irreversible loss of brain stem function

The table [below] highlights the implications of the memoranda on brain death issued by the Conference of Medical Royal Colleges and their Faculties in the UK in 1976 and 1979. The first memorandum (which I will call the UK code) emphasises that 'permanent functional death of the brain stem constitutes brain death' and that this should be diagnosed only in a defined context (irremediable structural brain damage) and after certain specified conditions have been excluded. It shows how the permanent loss of brain stem function can be determined clinically and describes simple tests for recognising the condition. The second memorandum identifies brain stem death with death itself. These documents mark a milestone in thinking about brain death and have already influenced practice in most English-speaking countries and in many others.

The basic propositions

Irreversible loss of brain stem function is as valid a yardstick of death as cessation of the heart beat

The loss of brain stem function can be determined operationally (in clinical terms)

The irreversibility of the loss is determined by

● The exclusion of reversible causes of loss of brain stem function
● A context of irremediable structural brain damage

What the proposals imply

Two major strides are necessary before one can accept the propositions implicit in the conference memoranda. The first is the step from 'classical' death to whole brain death. In most countries medical opinion has accepted the basic concept of brain death, although there are still a few influenced by religious or other considerations who oppose it. Leading spokesmen of all the main Western religions have endorsed it, and publications on the subject are numerous.

Doctors were still taking this first step when they were faced with another challenge: that death of the brain stem was the necessary and sufficient component of whole brain death. It has already been explained . . . how death of the brain stem relates to a given philosophical concept of death (the irreversible loss of the capacity for consciousness and the capacity to breathe). The task is now to convince people that this condition can be identified clinically—and that it is not in conflict with more traditional notions of brain death or of death itself. If we accept the concept of brain stem death it might be wise to change the words we use and no longer speak of 'brain death' when what we mean is brain stem death.

Two important conceptual steps

1 From classical death
    → to total brain death

2 From total brain death
    → to brain stem death

Some neurologists—and many experts in electroencephalography—have been caught off balance by these essentially conceptual, rather than technological, developments. Some of the main proponents of the idea of whole brain death (their first battle won, the role of their electroencephalographs well defined, their areas of expertise widely accepted) have proved reluctant to move a little further.

Functions of the brain stem

As well as being essential for maintaining breathing the brain stem is necessary for the proper functioning of the cortex. It has long been known that small, strategically situated lesions of the brain stem, of acute onset and affecting the paramedian tegmental area bilaterally, might cause prolonged coma because they damage critical parts of the ascending reticular activating system.

The reticular formation constitutes the central core of the brain stem and projects to wide areas of the limbic system and neocortex. Projections from the upper part of the brain stem are responsible for alerting mechanisms. These can be thought of as generating the capacity for consciousness. The content of consciousness (what a person knows, thinks, or feels) is a function of activated cerebral hemispheres. But unless there is a functioning brain stem, 'switching on' the hemispheres, one cannot speak of such a content. There is evidence that brain stem injury in man may massively reduce cerebral oxidative metabolism, cerebral blood flow, or both. Apart from mechanisms essential for respiration, the brain stem contains others which contribute to maintaining blood pressure. All the motor outputs from the hemispheres have to travel through the brain stem, as do all the sensory inputs to the brain (other than sight and smell). . . .

Because the brain stem nuclei are so near one another brain stem function can be clinically evaluated in a unique way. Testing the various cranial nerve reflexes probes the brain stem slice by slice, as if it were salami. Respiratory function can also be assessed very accurately. An acute, massive, and irreversible brain stem lesion (primary or secondary) prevents meaningful functioning of the 'brain as a whole', even if isolated parts of the brain may, for a short while, still emit signals of biological activity.

The difference between functional death (death of the organism as a whole) and total cellular death (death of the whole organism) has already been emphasised. The table [below] summarises the parallel argument in relation to the brain as a whole and the whole brain.

> The irreversible cessation of heart beat and respiration implies death of *the patient as a whole*. It does not necessarily imply the immediate death of *every cell in the body*.
>
> The irreversible cessation of brain stem function implies death of *the brain as a whole*. It does not necessarily imply the immediate death of *every cell in the brain*

Mechanisms of brain stem death

The brain stem may be damaged by a primary lesion or because raised pressure in the supratentorial or infratentorial compartments of the skull has had catastrophic effects on its blood supply and structural integrity. Direct hypoxic damage affects the cortex more than the brain stem. Brain stem damage in hypoxic encephalopathy is often the result of coning due to cerebral oedema. Several factors may operate in any given case.

A severe head injury may be associated with a pronounced rise of intracranial pressure, even in the absence of a subdural or extradural haemorrhage. Similar rises may be seen after subarachnoid haemorrhage. Intracranial hypertension is also a feature of the cerebral oedema that almost invariably complicates acute anoxic insults to the brain. The initial effects, in such cases, are often complicated by the development of various intracranial 'shifts'. There may be downward-spreading oedema and caudal displacement of the diencephalon and brain stem with stretching of the perforating pontine branches of the basilar artery and secondary haemorrhages in their territory. Or the brain stem may be compressed from uncal herniation into the tentorial opening.

A pressure cone at the level of the foramen magnum may further damage the brain stem. Venous drainage may be compromised. Ischaemic changes may be striking. If ventilation is continued at room temperature in the presence of a dead brain autolysis will occur. The whole brain may liquefy. Fragments of the destroyed cerebella tonsils may become detached and be found even as far away as the roots of the cauda equina.

The severity of the pathological changes may vary widely. Among the factors responsible for such variations are the duration of ventilation after arrest of the cerebral circulation, and the proportion of cases, in some American series, which were not due to primary structural brain damage.

About half the patients in whom brain stem death is diagnosed in the United Kingdom have sustained a recent head injury. Another 30% have had a very recent intracranial haemorrhage (usually subarachnoid, from a ruptured aneurysm). Other primary intracranial conditions are abscess, meningitis, or encephalitis. In cases of cerebral tumour brain stem death may occur after operation or, rarely, when a prior decision has been taken, with the relatives' consent, to put the patient on a ventilator when in terminal coma (with the aim of making organs available for transplantation). Cardiac and respiratory arrest and hypoperfusion of the brain complicating profound shock) are relatively rare causes of brain stem death. They result more often in a vegetable state.

Primary lesions of the brain stem (haemorrhages or infarcts) seldom cause total loss of brain stem function. Restricted lesions (causing restricted deficits) are more common. Massive lesions may occur, however, and result in brain stem death.

Judicial hanging is another cause of lethal, primary brain stem injury. Death in such cases is widely believed to be due to a fracture-dislocation of the odontoid, with compression of the upper two segments of the spinal cord. Although such a lesion may be found in some cases. Professor Simpson, Home Office Pathologist when capital punishment was still resorted to in the UK, has informed me that a rupture of the brain stem (between pons and medulla) was more common.

In judicial hanging respiration stops immediately, because of the effect of the brain stem rupture on the respiratory centre. The carotid or vertebral arteries may remain patent. The heart may go on beating for 20 minutes. Circulation continues, and parts of the brain are probably irrigated with blood (of diminishing oxygen saturation) for several minutes. I would guess that an electroencephalogram might, for a short while, continue to show some activity, despite the mortal injury to the brain stem. Is such an individual alive or dead? The very posing of such a question forces one to focus attention on the reversibility or irreversibility of the brain stem lesion and away from extraneous considerations.

Like the stopping of the heart in classical death the irreversible loss of brain stem function is ascertained by simple bedside tests. Their very simplicity seems to render them suspect in a technological age. This is not the case in relation to 'cardiac' death. What is the rationality behind such a double standard?

A heart stops and its inability to function as a pump is diagnosed by an absent pulse, an unrecordable blood pressure, and the absence of audible contractions. McMichael has recently drawn attention to William Harvey's careful observations of what is happening as the hearts of many animals cease to beat. 'The ventricle ceases to beat before the auricles, so that the auricles may be said to outlive it. . . . With all other parts inactive and dead, the right auricle goes on beating, so that life appears to linger longest in this auricle.' But knowledge of this electrophysiological fact—namely, that death of the heart as a whole may in normal individuals without heart disease precede death of the whole heart—has never really altered clinical practice. After clinical asystole has been present for several minutes few doctors would ask for an electrocardiogram to confirm that every part of the heart has really ceased to generate electrical signals. Still fewer would request that the trace be recorded at maximum amplification, using intracardiac probes. And strictly no one would suggest that the clinical findings be corroborated by non-perfusion on coronary angiography, or by biopsy evidence of necrosed cardiac muscle. Yet equivalent procedures have been suggested in relation to brain death.

If the context is known doctors have never objected to equating permanent loss of function with death. 'To live is to function: that is all there is to living' Oliver Wendell Holmes said. The argument is about permanence more than about pathology. And here the evidence can only be empirical. The first patient to speak again after having shown unequivocal evidence of a dead brain stem will create as great a sensation as if the decapitated head of Louix XVI had started berating his executioners.

Aware of the different views held in the United States, Pallis goes on (p 23; footnotes omitted):

One of the main criticisms of codes based on the clinical identification of a dead brain stem is that they could result in diagnoses of death in some patients who might still show fragments of electroencephalographic activity at maximal amplification. It has been emphasised that 'the prediction of a fatal outcome is not a valid criterion for the accuracy of standards designed to determine that death has already occurred'. I take this to mean that predicting someone is going to die is not the same as saying he is already dead. Superficially, this sounds unexceptionable. But it has meaning only if the words 'fatal outcome', 'dead', and 'death' are unquestioningly (and perhaps even reflexly) used in a doubly traditional sense—that is, either as synonyms for 'asystole', or as shorthand for the eventual development of an electrocephalographic pattern characterised (in 1969) as 'no activity over $2 \mu V$ when recording from scalp electrode pairs 10 or more centimetres apart, with inter-electrode resistances of under 10,000 ohms (or impedances under 6000 ohms)'.

If one rejects these premises and believes that a person is dead when he has irreversibly lost the capacity for consciousness and the capacity to breathe (irrespective of whether the heart is beating or not, or of whether or not the electroencephalogram may still be showing a few flickers at extreme amplification) this kind of 'critique' assumes a different dimension. It is reduced to the trite conclusion that if a dead brain stem heralds asystole (or the imminent extinction of the electroencephalogram) the differing notions of death are doomed to converge. The words doctors use are indeed important.

How long in fact may cardiac action persist after a diagnosis of brain stem death? Published evidence suggests that in most cases asystole develops within days. Of the 63 patients diagnosed as brain dead in a large Danish series (and maintained on the ventilator) 29 developed asystole within 12 hours, 10 after 12–24 hours, 16 after 24–72 hours, and eight after 72–211 hours. Experience from Great Britain and elsewhere is in line with these observations. A recent case in the USA achieved wide publicity because asystole failed to develop during the two months that followed a diagnosis of brain death. The brain stem would not have been declared dead in this case as early as it was had UK-type criteria been used. Although the necropsy changes were striking it is impossible retrospectively to compute the duration of brain stem death from pathological data alone.

Which view of the concept of death, and all that follows therefrom, do you prefer? Do you think the American or English approach is more defenceable in determining the criteria for 'brain death'?

The Law

(a) ENGLAND

Black's Law Dictionary (at 360, Rev 5th ed 1979) defines death as follows:

> The cessation of life; permanent cessations of all vital functions and signs. Numerous states have enacted statutory definitions of death which include brain-related criteria.

This was judicially recognised in the following case:

Smith v Smith
317 SW 2d 275 (1958) (Supreme Court of Arkansas) (footnotes omitted)

This case raised the question of whose estate inherited Mr Smith's estate. In turn the court had to determine whether Mr and Mrs Smith died simultaneously in the accident.

Harris, Chief Justice: Hugh Smith and Lucy Coleman Smith, his wife, lived at Siloam Springs, Arkansas. They had no children. On April 22, 1947, Mrs Smith executed a will leaving all property to her husband. On November 3, 1952, Mr Smith executed a will leaving all property to his wife. On April 19, 1957, while riding together in an automobile, the Smiths had an accident. Hugh Smith was dead when assistance arrived at the scene, and Lucy Coleman Smith was unconscious, and remained so until her death seventeen days later on May 6th. . . . Let it first be observed that in reading appellant's petition, as a whole, the assertion of the death of Lucy Coleman Smith appears to be predicated on the theory that such demise occurred 'as a matter of medical science', and of course, appellant could not have meant otherwise, for he had already filed the petitions, heretofore mentioned, in the probate court, together with the physician's letter, stating that Mrs Smith was a patient in the hospital, and would be incapacitated for several months. Black's Law Dictionary, 4th Edition, page 488, defines death as follows:

> The cessation of life; the ceasing to exist; defined by physicians as a total stoppage of the circulation of the blood, and a cessation of the animal and vital functions consequent thereon, such as respiration, pulsation, etc.,

Admittedly, this condition did not exist, and as a matter of fact, it would be too much of a strain on credulity for us to believe any evidence offered to the effect that Mrs Smith was dead, scientifically or otherwise, unless the conditions set out in the definition existed. . . .

To summarize and conclude, this litigation is determined by two facts. First, Hugh Smith and Lucy Coleman Smith did not die simultaneously . . .

It may be against the background of philosophical argument and the realities generated by technological advance that this definition is not entirely satisfactory.

In England, there is no statute defining death. Also, there is little English case law concerning the definition of death. The English law, as one might expect, did not historically need to resolve the question of when someone was dead. The first case in which the issue arose was *R v Potter* in 1963 which is discussed by David Meyers in his book *The Human Body and the Law* (p 116–117, footnotes omitted).

In *Potter*, it seems, a man was admitted to the hospital with a severe head injury he had sustained in a fight with the named defendant. He stopped breathing after fourteen hours and was placed on an artificial respirator for twenty-four hours, at the end of which a kidney was removed for transplantation. After this nephrectomy the respirator was shut off and there was no spontaneous respiration or circulation.

Under traditional definitions of death, the victim in *Potter* was not dead until his breathing and circulation came to a persistent and complete halt when the respirator was finally turned off nearly two days after his admission to hospital. Yet if this were the case, was not the physician who removed the victim's kidney guilty of a crime (malicious wounding) and a civil wrong (battery), for the removal took place while the victim was still 'alive', without his consent and was not for his benefit. Furthermore, it would seem that the physician, in shutting off the respirator and allowing the patient-victim to die, serves to break the chain of causation between the original wrongful act (the assault in *Potter*) and the death that finally is allowed to occur; the physician constitutes a *novus actus interveniens* which releases the original wrongdoer from legal liability for homicide. It would seem that the judge considered such to be the case in *Potter*, for the defendant was committed for trial by the Coroner after a jury's finding of manslaughter, yet was convicted only of common assault by the court.

Potter illustrates the most usual circumstances under which this issue may, if at all, become relevant in law. Indeed, it was the circumstances of the most significant English case in which the court was given the opportunity to adopt brain death criteria in English law.

R v Malcherek, R v Steel
[1981] 2 All ER 422, [1981] 1 WLR 690, CA

Lord Lane CJ: I start with the applicant Steel. . . . It was on October 10 1977, at about 9 am, that Carol Wilkinson was walking to work from her home to the bakery. At some time on that morning between about nine o'clock and half-past-nine, she was savagely attacked by someone who stripped off the greater part of her clothing, and then battered her about the head with a 50 lb stone which was found nearby. She was found shortly afterwards, in a field by the road, unconscious. She was taken as rapidly as could be to hospital. She had multiple fractures of the skull and severe brain damage as well as a broken arm and other superficial injuries which need not concern us. She was put almost immediately on a life support machine in the shape of a ventilator. On 12th October the medical team in whose charge she was, after a number of tests, came to the conclusion that her brain had ceased to function and that, accordingly, the ventilator was in effect operating on a lifeless body. The life support machine was switched off and all bodily functions ceased shortly afterwards.

. . . Upon admission to the casualty department of the Bradford Royal Infirmary at about 10.15 a.m. on Monday, October 10, Carol was seen by Dr Nevelos, who found her to be deeply unconscious with no motor activity, her eyes open and the pupils fixed. She was breathing only with the aid of the ventilator. An hour later she was admitted to the intensive care unit of the Royal Infirmary and during the whole of that day she remained deeply unconscious and unresponsive. At 10.00 pm the consultant neuro-surgeon, a Mr Price, examined her. He found her to be in a deep coma, unresponding to any stimulus. He carried out a test for electrical activity in the brain which proved negative. The total absence of any motor activity since the girl had been admitted to hospital and the early fixation of the pupils, which I have already mentioned, led him to the conclusion that there had been a devastating impact injury to the brain. The cerebral function monitor showed no activity. Her eyes were too occluded, so it is said, to allow any caloric testing. The suggestion was made by Mr Price that her temperature should be raised and that if by the morning her cerebral function remained as it had been up to date, namely, zero, they should declare her brain to be dead. In fact, in the morning shortly after 10.00 a.m., a cerebral blood flow test was carried out which indicated that there was no blood circulating in the brain. Several electroencephalogram tests were made during that day. None of them had any positive result.

On Wednesday, October 12, two days after the injuries had been inflicted, another electroencephalogram test was made in the morning and another one at 6.00 pm but none of those tests showed any signs of electrical activity at all. After that there was a consultation between the doctors who were in charge of the patient, and it was agreed among them that the continued use of the ventilator was without any purpose. At 6.15 pm the patient was withdrawn from the ventilator, and at 6.40 pm she was declared to be dead. There is an indication, though we are told it was not part of the evidence at the trial, that on post-mortem 50 minutes later it was found that her brain was already in the process of decomposition.

Much of the cross-examination of the medical men was taken up with suggestions that they had failed to conform to certain criteria which have been laid down by the royal medical colleges on the subject of the ascertainment of brain death. The matter which Mr. Steer invites this court to take into consideration as possibly differentiating the case of [Steel] from that of [Malcherek] is that he says that two of the suggested tests were not carried out properly, namely the corneal reflex test and the vestibulo-ocular reflex test. The corneal reflex test consists of touching the cornea of the eye with a piece of cotton wool to see if that creates any reaction in the patient and, as we understand it, the vestibulo-ocular reflex test consists of putting ice cold water into the aperture of the ear, again to see if that produces any reflex in the patient. Reasons were given for neither of those tests having been carried out.

The court then discussed the facts of *Malcherek*, the second case

... The victim was Christina Malcherek, his wife, who was then aged 32. It seems that in November 1978 she left Malcherek in order to go and live with her daughters at Poole. There was a non-molestation order in force, directed at Malcherek, but on the evening of March 26 1979 he went to her flat where she was living. There was a quarrel and, to cut a long story short, he stabbed his wife nine times with a kitchen knife. One of the stabs resulted in a deep penetrating wound to Mrs Malcherek's abdomen.

She was taken to Poole General Hospital and there was preliminary treatment in order to try to rectify her very low blood pressure, which was ascertained on admission. The surgical registrar then performed a laparotomy and removed rather more than one and a half litres of blood from the abdomen. There was a section of the intestine which was damaged, and he excised that and joined up the two ends. For several days it seemed as though Mrs Malcherek was making an uneventful recovery. Indeed, she was clearly confidently expected to survive. However, on April 1 she collapsed and the preliminary diagnosis was that she had suffered a massive pulmonary embolism. She was resuscitated and arrangements were made for her admission to the Western Hospital at Southampton, which was equipped to deal with this type of emergency. She arrived there shortly before midnight. A couple of hours later her condition suddenly deteriorated and her heart stopped. She was taken straight away to the operating theatre and given cardiac massage. The surgeon then opened her chest. He found that her heart was distended and not beating. He made an incision into the pulmonary artery and extracted from the pulmonary artery a large clot of blood some twelve inches long, which had plainly formed in one of the veins of the leg (which, we are told, is a common complication of major abdominal surgery), and had then moved on from the leg to the pulmonary artery with the results already described. When the clot was removed the heart started again spontaneously. It will be appreciated that since the heart was not beating for a period of something like 30 minutes there was a grave danger of anoxic damage to the brain. She was returned to the ward and connected to a ventilator. Throughout the Monday she remained on that machine receiving intensive care, but in the afternoon an electroencephalogram showed that there were indeed symptoms of severe anoxic damage to the brain. The prognosis was poor.

The consultant neurologist saw her at 7.00 pm. She was unresponsive to any stimulus save that her pupils did react to light. He suggested a further electroencephalogram because at that stage it was not clear how much brain damage had been suffered. On the morning of Tuesday, Dr Manners decided to dispense with the ventilator if that could possibly be done. When that was done she was able, first of all, to breathe adequately by herself, but towards midday she suffered a sharp and marked deterioration and the diagnosis was that she had suffered a cerebral vascular accident—possibly a ruptured blood vessel, possibly a clot—causing further brain damage. In any event, by 1.45 pm her attempts to breathe were inadequate and she was put back onto the ventilator. There was a continued deterioration and by the following day she was deeply unconscious and seemed to have irreversible brain damage. There was less electrical activity than before when a further electroencephalogram was carried out.

On April 5 the situation had deteriorated still more, and it was quite obvious at 1.15 p.m. on that day, when Dr Lawton made an examination, that her brain was irretrievably damaged. He carried out five of the six royal medical colleges' confirmatory tests. The one he omitted was the 'gag reflex' test, again for reasons which he explained. The patient's relations were consulted and a decision was made to disconnect the ventilator, which was done at 4.30 pm. A supply of oxygen was fed to her lungs in case she should make spontaneous efforts to breathe but she did not, and shortly after 5.00 pm she was certified to be dead.

In these circumstances, as in the earlier case, the judge decided that the question of causation should not be left for the jury's consideration. Consequently, the only issue they had to decide was the one of intent, there being no argument but that Malcherek had in fact inflicted the knife wound or wounds on Mrs Malcherek. In this case the principal and, in effect, the only ground of appeal, as Mr Field-Fisher has told us, is that the judge should have left the issue of causation to the jury.

This is not the occasion for any decision as to what constitutes death. Modern techniques have undoubtedly resulted in the blurring of many of the conventional and traditional concepts of death. A person's heart can now be removed altogether without death supervening; machines can keep the blood circulating through the vessels of the body until a new heart can be implanted in the patient, and even though a person is no longer able to breathe spontaneously a ventilating machine can, so to speak, do his breathing for him, as is demonstrated in the two cases before us. There is, it seems, a body of opinion in the medical profession that there is only one true test of death and that is the irreversible death of the brain stem, which controls the basic functions of the body such as breathing. When that occurs it is said the body has died, even though by mechanical means the lungs are being caused to operate and some circulation of blood is taking place.

We have had placed before us, and have been asked to admit, evidence that in each of these two cases the medical men concerned did not comply with all the suggested criteria for establishing such brain death. Indeed, further evidence has been suggested and placed before us that those criteria or tests are not in themselves stringent enough. However, in each of these two cases there is no doubt that whatever test is applied the victim died; that is to say, applying the traditional test, all body functions, breathing and heartbeat and brain function came to an end, at the latest, soon after the ventilator was disconnected.

The question posed for answer to this court is simply whether the judge in each case was right in withdrawing from the jury the question of causation. Was he right to rule that there was no evidence on which the jury could come to the conclusion that the assailant did not cause the death of the victim? The way in which the submissions are put by Mr Field-Fisher on the one hand and Mr Wilfred Steer on the other is as follows: the doctors, by switching off the ventilator and the life support machine, were the cause of death or, to put it more accurately, there was evidence which the jury should have been allowed to consider that the doctors, and not the assailant, in each case may have been the cause of death.

In each case it is clear that the initial assault was the cause of the grave head injuries in the one case and of the massive abdominal haemorrhage in the other. In each case the initial assault was the reason for the medical treatment being necessary. In each case the medical treatment given was normal and conventional. At some stage the doctors must decide if and when treatment has become otiose. This decision was reached, in each of the two cases here, in circumstances which have already been set out in some detail. It is no part of the task of this court to inquire whether the criteria, the royal medical colleges' confirmatory tests, are a satisfactory code of practice. It is no part of the task of this court to decide whether the doctors were, in either of these two cases, justified in omitting one or more of the so called 'confirmatory tests'. The doctors are not on trial: the applicant and the appellant respectively were.

. . .

There is no evidence in the present case that at the time of conventional death, after the life support machinery was disconnected, the original wound or injury was other than a continuing, operating and indeed substantial cause of the death of the victim, although it need hardly be added that it need not be substantial to render the assailant guilty. There may be occasions, although they will be rare, when the original injury has ceased to operate as a cause at all, but in the ordinary case if the treatment is given bona fide by competent and careful medical practitioners, then evidence will not be admissible to show that the treatment would not have been administered in the same way by other medical practitioners. In other words, the fact that the victim has died, despite or because of medical treatment for the initial injury given by careful and skilled medical practitioners, will not exonerate the original assailant from responsibility for the death. It follows that so far as the ground of appeal in each of these cases relates to the direction given on causation, that ground fails. It also follows that the evidence which it is sought to adduce now, although we are prepared to assume that it is both credible and was not available properly at the trial—and a reasonable explanation for not calling it at the trial has been given—if received could, under no circumstances, afford any ground for allowing the appeal.

The reason is this. Nothing which any of the two or three medical men whose statements are before us could say would alter the fact that in each case the assailant's actions continued to be an operating cause of the death. Nothing the doctors could say would provide any ground for a jury coming to the conclusion that the assailant in either case might not have caused the death. The furthest to which their proposed evidence goes, as already stated, is to suggest, first, that the criteria or the confirmatory tests are not sufficiently stringent and, secondly, that in the present case they were in certain respects inadequately fulfilled or carried out. It is no part of this court's function in the present circumstances to pronounce upon this matter, nor was it a function of either of the juries at these trials. Where a medical practitioner adopting methods which are generally accepted comes bona fide and conscientiously to the conclusion that the patient is for practical purposes dead, and that such vital functions as exist—for example, circulation—are being maintained solely by mechanical means, and therefore discontinues treatment, that does not prevent the person who inflicted the initial injury from being responsible for the victim's death. Putting it in another way, the discontinuance of treatment in those circumstances does not break the chain of causation between the initial injury and the death.

Although it is unnecessary to go further than that for the purpose of deciding the present point, we wish to add this thought. Whatever the strict logic of the matter may be, it is perhaps somewhat bizarre to suggest, as counsel have impliedly done, that where a doctor tries his conscientious best to save the life of a patient brought to hospital in extremis, skilfully using sophisticated methods, drugs and machinery to do so, but fails in his attempt and therefore discontinues treatment, he can be said to have caused the death of the patient.

The Court of Appeal sidestepped the need to adopt brain death criteria, but as Skegg points out in his book *Law, Ethics and Medicine*, the trial judge in *Malcherek* seems to have gone further (at 196; footnotes omitted).

The judge at Malcherek's original trial was reported to have said, 'To have kept her on the respirator would have been, in effect, to ventilate a corpse'. This statement, and his ruling that there was no evidence to show that the victim was still alive when the doctors switched off the machine, indicated the trial judge's acceptance of the view that once brain death is established a person is dead for the purpose of the law of homicide, even though the heart continues to beat.

It should be noted that courts in a number of jurisdictions have in similar circumstances to *Malcherek and Steel* confirmed that court's view on causation without finding it necessary to determine whether the victim was already dead when the ventilator was turned off (*Finlayson v HM* Advocate 1978 SLT (Notes) 60 (Scotland); *R v Kitching and Adams* [1976] 6 WWR 697 (Manitoba)).

The third case in England where the issue was raised was curiously enough, a case in which an issue of copyright turned on whether one of the alleged copyright holders was dead.

Mail Newspapers plc v Express Newspapers plc [1987] FSR 90

Millett J: Mrs. B had suffered a brain hæmorrhage while 24 weeks pregnant. She was being kept on a life-support system in the hope that the baby could be born alive. The evidence suggested that Mrs. B was probably clinically dead, but tests had not been undertaken.

Seven national newspapers obtained and published, without any authority from Mr. B, photographs of the couple's wedding. Thereafter Mr. B entered into an agreement with the plaintiffs granting them exclusive rights to all his archive photographs and undertaking to pose exclusively for the plaintiffs for photographs with his baby within 24 hours of its birth, all rights to those photographs to be owned by the plaintiffs. The plaintiffs wrote to many national newspapers informing them that they held the exclusive rights to Mr. B's photographs and warning them not to publish these. The defendants replied that they intended to use the photographs. The plaintiffs therefore obtained *ex parte* injunctions restraining the defendants from publishing the photographs.

On the *inter partes* hearing of the motion, the defendants argued that the copyright in the photographs vested either in Mrs. B alone or in Mr. and Mrs. B together, and that Mr. B was unable to grant an exclusive licence since Mrs. B was still alive and had not consented. The evidence was that before the wedding Mr. B had asked his fiancée to arrange for the photographs to be taken, but that afterwards Mr. B paid the bill.

. . .

The evidence, such as it is, suggests that Mrs. Bell is probably clinically dead, that is to say, that her brain had ceased to function altogether, although she is breathing and her bodily functions are being kept going. Medical tests to determine whether or not Mrs. Bell is clinically dead have not been undertaken, and understandably no one has thought it appropriate to obtain a death certificate.

. . . [I]n submitting to me that the plaintiffs have no real prospect of succeeding at the trial Mr. Shaw was really submitting that Mrs. Bell is unarguably still alive. The evidence before me does not go nearly far enough to warrant any such conclusion. I have no doubt at all that there is at the very least a serious question to be tried whether Mrs. Bell is alive or dead. Indeed, so far as the evidence before me goes, it supports the conclusion that she is probably already legally dead.

Millett J does not seem to advance the cause of clarity, so necessary in this area, when he uses expressions such as Mrs Bell was 'clinically dead' and, a little later, that she was 'legally dead' implying as a consequence that there are different types of death.

(b)   UNITED STATES

In some, but a diminishing number of jurisdictions, the definition of death is a matter of common law for the courts. All jurisdictions which have considered the matter have adopted some form of 'brain death'. The President's Commission, *op cit*, explains as follows (pp 68–69; footnotes omitted):

Judicial developments: Over the past decade, courts as well as legislations have attempted to "redefine" death. While courts adhered for a time to the traditional cardiopulmonary standards, the recent trend has been to recognize the brain-based standard, even in the absence of an explicit statute. Nonetheless, the courts have not all been willing to 'update' the common law nor have their rulings established consistent standards of universal application. More fundamentally, the court cases that persistently arise hint at the uncertainty about legal standards that pervades the medical community in states without statutes.

Cases have also arisen in jurisdictions having a statute on death. The cases have mostly involved after-the-fact rulings concerning determinations of death. Generally, the statutes have been upheld by the courts, although in one case the ambiguity of the statutory language led to a 'hung jury' and in another the judge refused to apply an 'organ donor' statute in a nontransplant case.

The court cases have arisen in a variety of legal contexts. Some defendants charged with murder have argued that they could not be guilty of homicide because their victims were alive when physicians—who should bear the responsibility for the deaths—removed them from the respirators. Doctors have also been sued for removing organs for transplantation from a patient declared dead on the basis of brain-oriented criteria. A third category of cases has involved petitioning a court for permission to terminate life-support systems for bodies without functioning brains.

While the courts have generally recognized brain-oriented criteria, they have often limited their rulings to the context of the particular type of case before the court, (eg, explicitly stating that the precedential value of a decision is limited to criminal cases). Moreover, some of the most widely discussed cases did not reach the appellate level, limiting their actual impact to the particular court that decided them.

One case involving the question of whether a respirator-supported patient lacking all brain functions is dead or alive which reached the highest court of a state warrants particular mention because of the relationship of the court's ruling to the policy proposed in this Report. In the case of *Re Bowman* [(1980) 617 P 2d 731], the Washington Supreme Court late in 1980 affirmed a lower court ruling that a person without any brain function is dead. The trial court in *Bowman* had ruled that five-year-old Matthew Bowman was dead, having suffered massive physical injuries. The court enjoined the removal of the 'extraordinary measures' sustaining respiration and heartbeat, however, pending an appeal. The case was set for argument before the state's highest court a week later, but the day before the argument was scheduled, all of Matthew's bodily functions ceased irretrievably. Although this event made the case moot, the court decided to rule upon the case nonetheless. The Washington Supreme Court observed in its ruling:

An electroencephalogram (EEG) gave no reading and a radionucleide scan, which shows whether blood is getting to and through the brain, found a total absence of blood flow. No cornea reflex was present and Matthew's pupils were dilated and nonreactive to any stimuli. There were also no deep tendon reflexes or other signs of brain stem action, nor responses to deep pain or signs of spontaneous breathing. Body temperature and drug intake had been controlled to avoid adverse influence on these tests. The testifying physician indicated that he believed Matthew's brain was dead under the most rigid criteria available, called the 'Harvard criteria', and that his cardiovascular system would, despite the life support systems, fail in 14 to 60 days. [The physician] . . . recommended that he be removed from the ventilator, a recommendation consented to by his mother.

The case of *People v Eulo* 472 NE 2d 286 (1984) in New York's highest court, the Court of Appeals, is a good example of this sort of approach (footnotes omitted).

Cooke, Chief Justice: On the evening of July 19, 1981, defendant and his girlfriend attended a volunteer fireman's fair in Kings Park, Suffolk County. Not long after they arrived, the two began to argue, reportedly because defendant was jealous over one of her former suitors, whom they had seen at the fair. The argument continued through the evening; it became particularly heated as the two sat in defendant's pick-up truck, parked in front of the home of the girlfriend's parents. Around midnight, defendant shot her in the head with his unregistered handgun.

The victim was rushed by ambulance to the emergency room of St. John's Hospital. A gunshot wound to the left temple causing extreme hemorrhaging was apparent. A tube was placed in her windpipe to enable artificial respiration and intravenous medication was applied to stabilize her blood pressure.

Shortly before 2:00 a.m., the victim was examined by a neurosurgeon, who undertook various tests to evaluate damage done to the brain. Painful stimuli were applied and yielded no reaction. Various reflexes were tested and, again, there was no response. A further test determined that the victim was incapable of spontaneously maintaining respiration. An electroencephalogram (EEG) resulted in 'flat', or 'isoelectric', readings indicating no activity in the part of the brain tested.

Over the next two days, the victim's breathing was maintained solely by a mechanical respirator. Her heartbeat was sustained and regulated through medication. Faced with what was believed to be an imminent cessation of these two bodily functions notwithstanding the artificial maintenance, the victim's parents consented to the use of certain of her organs for transplantation.

On the afternoon of July 23, a second neurosurgeon was called in to evaluate whether the victim's brain continued to function in any manner. A repetition of all of the previously conducted tests led to the same diagnosis: the victim's entire brain had irreversibly ceased to function. This diagnosis was reviewed and confirmed by the Deputy Medical Examiner for Suffolk County and another physician.

The victim was pronounced dead at 2:20 p.m. on July 23, although at that time she was still attached to a respirator and her heart was still beating. Her body was taken to a surgical room where her kidneys, spleen, and lymph nodes were removed. The mechanical respirator was then disconnected, and her breathing immediately stopped, followed shortly by a cessation of the heartbeat.

Defendant was indicted for second degree murder. After a jury trial, he was convicted of manslaughter. . . .

Defendant's principal point . . . is that the respective Trial Judges failed to adequately instruct the juries as to what constitutes a person's death, the time at which criminal liability for a homicide would attach. It is claimed that in New York, the time of death has always been set by reference to the functioning of the heart and the lungs; that death does not occur until there has been an irreversible cessation of breathing and heartbeat.

There having been extensive testimony at both trials concerning each victim's diagnosis as 'brain dead', defendants argue that, in the absence of clear instruction, the juries may have erroneously concluded that defendants would be guilty of homicide if their conduct was the legal cause of the victims' 'brain death' rather than the victims' ultimate state of cardiorespiratory failure. . . .

Death has been conceptualized by the law as, simply, the absence of life: 'Death is the opposite of life; it is the termination of life' (*Evans v People*, 49 NY 86, 90). But, while erecting death as a critical milepost in a person's legal life, the law has had little occasion to consider the precise point at which a person ceases to live.

. . .

Within the past two decades, machines that artificially maintain cardiorespiratory functions have come into widespread use. This technical accomplishment has called into question the universal applicability of the traditional legal and medical criteria for determining when a person has died.

. . .

It became clear in medical practice that the traditional 'vital signs'—breathing and heartbeat—are not independent indicia of life, but are, instead, part of an integration of functions in which the brain is dominant. As a result, the medical community began to consider the cessation of brain activity as a measure of death.

The movement in law towards recognising cessation of brain functions as criteria for death followed this medical trend. The immediate motive for adopting this position was to ease and make more efficient the transfer of donated organs. Organ transfers, to be successful, require a 'viable, intact organ'. Once all of a person's vital functions have ceased, transferable organs swiftly deteriorate and lose their transplant value. The technical ability to artificially maintain respiration and heartbeat after the entire brain has ceased to function was sought to be applied in cases of organ transplant to preserve the viability of donated organs.

Thus, the first legal recognition of cessation of brain functions as a criterion for determining death came in the form of a Kansas statute enacted in 1970. Denominated '[a]n Act relating to and defining death', the statute states, in part, that death will be deemed to have occurred when a physician applying ordinary medical standards determines that there is an 'absence of spontaneous respiratory and cardiac functions and . . . attempts at resuscitation are considered hopeless . . . *or* . . . there is the absence of spontaneous brain function'.

In the years following enactment of this statute, a growing number of sister States enacted statutes of their own. Some opted for the Kansas approach. Others defined death solely in terms of brain-based criteria as determined by accepted methods of medical practice. And still others retain the cardiorespiratory yardstick, but provide that when artificial means of sustaining respiration and heartbeat preclude application of the traditional criteria, death may be determined according to brain-based criteria, namely the irreversible cessation of brain functions. In the absence of any statute defining death, some jurisdictions have judicially adopted brain-based criteria for determining death. Professional and quasi-governmental groups (including the American Bar Association, the American Medical Association, the President's Commission for the Study of Ethical Problems in Medicine and Biomedical and Behavioral Research, and the National Conference of Commissioners on Uniform State Laws) have jointly indorsed a single standard that includes both cardiorespiratory and brain-based criteria.

In New York, the term 'death', although used in many statutes, has not been expressly defined by the Legislature. This raises the question of how this court may construe these expressions of the term 'death' in the absence of clarification by the Legislature. . . .

We hold that a recognition of brain-based criteria for determining death is not unfaithful to prior judicial definitions of 'death', as presumptively adopted in the many statutes using that term. Close examination of the common-law conception of death and the traditional criteria used to determine when death has occurred leads inexorably to this conclusion.

Courts have not engaged in a metaphysical analysis of when life should be deemed to have passed from a person's body, leaving him or her dead. Rather, they have conceptualised death as the absence of life, unqualified and undefined (see *Evans v People*, 49 NY 86, 90, *supra*). On a practical level, this broad conception of death as 'the opposite of life' was substantially narrowed through recognition of the cardiorespiratory criteria for determining when death occurs. Under these criteria, the loci of life are the heart and the lungs; where there is no breath or heartbeat, there is no life. Cessation manifests death.

Considering death to have occurred when there is an irreversible and complete cessation of the functioning of the entire brain, including the brain stem, is consistent with the common-law conception of death (see *Commonwealth v Golston*, 373 Mass. 249, 254, 366 NE2d 744). Ordinarily, death will be determined according to the traditional criteria of irreversible cardiorespiratory repose. When, however, the respiratory and circulatory functions are maintained by mechanical means, their significance, as signs of life, is at best ambiguous. Under such circumstances, death may nevertheless be deemed to occur when, according to accepted medical practice, it is determined that the entire brain's function has irreversibly ceased.

Death remains the single phenomenon identified at common law; the supplemental criteria are merely adapted to account for the 'changed conditions' that a dead body may be attached to a machine so as to exhibit demonstrably false indicia of life. It reflects an improved understanding that in the complete and irreversible absence of a functioning brain, the traditional loci of life—the heart and the lungs—function only as a result of stimuli originating from outside of the body and will never again function as part of an integrated organism.

This court searches in vain for evidence that, apart from the concept of death, the Legislature intended to render immutable the criteria used to determine death. By extension, to hold to the contrary would be to say that the law could not recognize diagnostic equipment such as the stethoscope or more sensitive equipment even when it became clear that these instruments more accurately measured the presence of signs of life.

As you will have noticed in the Chief Judge's opinion, he refers to legislative definitions which have been enacted in the majority of US jurisdictions. We return to the President's Commission for a description of these (pp 62–67; footnotes omitted):

Legislative developments: The statutes proposed or adopted fall into seven basic groups.

The Kansas-inspired statutes: In 1970 the Kansas legislature took the first legal action in an American jurisdiction recognising brain-based criteria for the determination of death. The Kansas Supreme Court had shortly before then reiterated its adherence to the common law standard of 'complete cessation of *all* vital functions . . . even if artificially maintained'. The statute, proposed by a physician-legislator and adopted without substantial debate, provides alternative 'definitions' of death, one based upon traditional heart-lung functions and the other upon *brain* functions.

A person will be considered medically and legally dead if, in the opinion of a physician, based on ordinary standards of medical practice, there is the absence of spontaneous respiratory and cardiac function and, because of the disease or condition which caused, directly or indirectly, these functions to cease, or because of the passage of time since these functions ceased, attempts at resuscitation are considered hopeless; and, in this event, death will have occurred at the time these functions ceased; or

A person will be considered medically and legally dead if, in the opinion of a physician, based on ordinary standards of medical practice, there is the absence of spontaneous brain functions; and if based on ordinary standards of medical practice, during reasonable attempts to either maintain or restore spontaneous circulatory or respiratory function in the absence of aforesaid brain function, it appears that further attempts at resuscitation or supportive maintenance will not succeed, death will have occurred at the time when these conditions first coincide. Death is to be pronounced before artificial means of supporting respiratory and circulatory function are terminated and before any vital organ is removed for purposes of transplantation.

These alternative definitions of death are to be utilised for all purposes in this state, including the trials of civil and criminal cases, any laws to the contrary notwithstanding.

With slight variations, in 1972 Maryland, and in 1973 New Mexico and Virginia, enacted statutes patterned on the Kansas model. (In 1975 Oklahoma adopted a statute drawn solely from the second 'alternative definition' of the Kansas prototype.)

The dual nature of the Kansas statute is its most troublesome feature. The alternative standards are set forth in two separate, complex paragraphs without a description of how they were to be related to the single phenomenon, death. When the statute was enacted, transplantation was very much in the news. The two-pronged statute seems to create one definition of death for most people and another, apparently more lenient standard for 'harvesting' organs from potential donors.

The Capron-Kass proposal: To overcome the confusion of the 'two deaths' problem, Professor Alexander Morgan Capron and Dr Leon R. Kass proposed a model statute in a 1972 law review article. Substantially shorter than the Kansas version, it spelled out how the two standards for death were related. It also avoided language in the Kansas statute about 'hopeless' treatment that may have implied that the statute had to do with terminating treatment for dying patients rather than defining when death occurs. As subsequently revised by Professor Capron, it states:

A person will be considered dead if in the announced opinion of a physician, based on ordinary standards of medical practice, he has experienced an irreversible cessation of respiratory and circulatory functions, or in the event that artificial means of support preclude a determination that these functions have ceased, he has experienced an irreversible cessation of total brain functions. Death will have occurred at the time when the relevant functions ceased.

Seven states have adopted versions of the Capron-Kass model. Alaska, Iowa, Louisiana and Michigan enacted the statute with only minor modifications, while other states have made more substantial modifications. . . .

The American Bar Association proposal: The ABA proposed its own model statute in 1975. It resembled a California law enacted in the previous year. The ABA statute states:

For all legal purposes, a human body, with irreversible cessation of total brain function, according to usual and customary standards of medical practice, shall be considered dead.

Some version of the ABA model statute can be found on the books of five states. Montana and Tennessee adopted the proposal verbatim. Illinois employed largely the same language but, regrettably, inserted it as an amendment to the state's Uniform Anatomical Gift Act, thus creating the impression that it applies only to organ donors. Because it ignores determinations of death based on the traditional cardiopulmonary criteria, a 'single standard' statute of the ABA-type might appear to be irrelevant to most patients. To avoid this problem, several states, including California, amended the statute to permit determinations to be made based on 'other usual and customary procedures'—unfortunately, without explicating these terms or their relationship to the brain-based standards. The inclusion of this second undefined alternative resurrects—indeed, magnifies—the 'two (unrelated) deaths' problem of the Kansas statute.

The Uniform Brain Death Act: A third model statute received the approval in 1978 of the National Conference of Commissioners on Uniform State Laws. The Uniform Brain Death Act, adopted verbatim by Nevada, and in part by West Virginia, provides;

For legal and medical purposes, an individual who has sustained irreversible cessation of all functioning of the brain, including the brain stem, is dead. A determination under this section must be made in accordance with reasonable medical standards.

The American Medical Association proposal: Most recently, the American Medical Association proposed a model bill, which no jurisdiction has yet adopted. As amended at the December 1979 Interim Meeting of the AMA, the proposal incorporated cardiopulmonary and brain-based alternatives for declaring death. Unlike most other statutes, it contained extensive provisions to limit liability for people making or taking actions pursuant to declarations as authorised by the state.

Individual state statutes: Seven states have adopted statutes that do not closely track any of the model proposals. In 1975, Oklahoma adopted the 'brain death' half of the Kansas statute, as mentioned previously, and Oregon enacted a law with alternative definitions that is much shorter than the Kansas statute.

In recent years, states have turned increasingly to nonstandard statutes. North Carolina originally adopted a rather confusing statute in 1977 incorporating both 'brain-death' and 'living wills' provisions. It recently substituted a somewhat clearer statute, an amalgam of the American Bar Association and Capron-Kass approaches. Its central provision reads: 'Brain death may be used as the sole basis for the determination that a person has died, particularly when brain death occurs in the presence of artificially maintained respiratory and circulatory functions'.

In 1979, three states enacted idiosyncratic statutes. The provisions in Arkansas and Connecticut essentially elaborate a brain-only standard. Connecticut, like Illinois, placed its law as an amendment to the state's Uniform Anatomical Gift Act. Wyoming's law amalgamates the basic structure of the ABA model with several features of the Uniform Brain Death Act, specifically the inclusion of explicit reference to the brainstem and the replacement of 'shall be considered dead' by 'is dead'. Most unusually, Wyoming drew on the NCCUSL's 'Comment' for additional *statutory* language defining brain functions as 'purposeful activity of the brain as distinguished from random activity'.

Finally, Florida in 1980 became the twenty-sixth state with a statutory 'definition' of death. Its statute also draws on the ABA model and Uniform Brain Death Act in only explicitly recognising 'irreversible cessation of the functioning of the entire brain', but draws on the Capron-Kass approach by implicitly acknowledging the cardio-pulmonary standard. It provides that the brain-based standard is to be used 'where respiratory and circulatory functions are maintained by artificial means of support so as to preclude a determination that these functions have ceased'. The Florida statute also specifically requires that determinations of death be made by two physicians, including one specialist, and that the family be notified of the procedures used to determine death; the statute also draws on Sections 2 and 3 of the AMA model in insulating from liability those acting in accordance with its terms.

Uniform Determination of Death Act : Legislative response to the statute recommended in this Report began shortly after the President's Commission, the Uniform Law Commissioners and other sponsors of the proposal had officially acted. While this Report was being prepared, Colorado and Idaho (the latter in place of its existing statute) became the first states to enact the Uniform Determination of Death Act, bringing to 27 the states with statutory 'definitions' of death.

The Uniform Determination of Death Act recommended by the President's Commission has now become the standard model. Section 1 reads as follows:

1. Determination of death

An individual who has sustained either (1) irreversible cessation of circulatory and respiratory functions, or (2) irreversible cessation of all functions of the entire brain, including the brain stem, is dead. A determination of death must be made in accordance with accepted medical standards.

Pallis, *op cit*, comments on the problems of the Act, not only its terms but the underlying premise of 'whole brain death' upon which it is based (at pp 28–29, 30–32; footnotes omitted).

The "cessation of all functions of the entire brain" is—quite simply—something that is impossible to determine. No available technique or combination of techniques can ever hope to assess "all functions of the entire brain'. The commission's report correctly states that all functions cannot be taken to include 'electrical and metabolic activity at the level of individual cells or even groups of cells', but in the clinical context of suspected brain death there is a great deal more than this that simply cannot be evaluated. In a comatose patient there is no way of assessing such important functions as those of the thalmus, basal ganglia, or cerebellum, to mention but a few.

The proposed model statute will give the impression, at least to a lay public, of seeking to identify 'death of the whole brain' rather than 'death of the brain as a whole'. The medical guidelines accompanying the report make the disingenuous disclaimer that 'all functions of the entire brain' means only 'those functions that are clinically ascertainable'. But the introduction to the report states wisely that 'in language as well as content, any legislation ought to make personal sense to lay people'. The average layman does not know that many (if not most) cerebral functions cannot be clinically tested in the context under discussion. And, if someone in a glass house may be allowed to throw a pebble, our own code errs in much the same way when it states that in brain death '*all* functions of the brain have permanently and irreversibly ceased' (my emphasis). All functions are undoubtedly on the verge of ceasing. And all relevant—that is, brain stem—functions have certainly ceased. But neither of these statements is quite the same as asserting that all brain functions have actually ceased. This seems to be as untestable a proposition in London as it is in Washington. But this very untestability is less relevant to those who equate death with permanent loss of function of the brain stem (which can be shown) than to those who insist that the neurological deficit should include all the other intracranial systems (few of which can be tested).

The Uniform Determination of Death Act has also already encountered another type of criticism within the USA itself—namely, that 'it contains the most serious flaw that the Commission finds in previous statutes: it provides two independent standards of death without explaining the relationship between them'. The same point had been raised over a decade earlier in a detailed critique of the Kansas Statute (the first in the common law world seeking to define death). Kennedy had then shrewdly emphasised that it was 'in no way inspiring of confidence in one's doctor to learn that there are two types of death'. The new critics point out that 'irreversible cessation of circulatory and respiratory functions' works as a test of death (in the absence of cardiopulmonary support) only because it produces the true standard of death: the irreversible cessation of whole brain function. This approach incorporates the useful distinction between a standard (or concept) of death and a test for death. Their proposed alternative statute would define death in terms of 'irreversible cessation of all functions of the entire brain' and then show how such a state can be determined in one of two ways: either by prolonged absence of spontaneous circulation and respiration, or (in the presence of artificial means of cardiovascular support) by tests specifically directed at brain function. The alternative statute would seem to reconcile the claims of conceptual clarity and practical usefulness. All that would remain would be to amend this amendment, so that it read 'irreversible cessation of all brain stem functions' instead of 'all functions of the entire brain'. This would be more relevant because of the ease and thoroughness with which these functions can be tested, because of the prognostic implications of their loss, and because of the relation of this loss to an acceptable philosophical concept of death.

Pallis then goes on to discuss the use of the electroencephalogram.

The main argument about the electroencephalogram is conceptual, not technical. To what overall concept of death does the electroencephalographic criterion (of electrocerebral silence) relate? Whether they realise it or not the advocates and the detractors of the electroencephalogram are pursuing different objectives, related to different concepts of death. The former are seeking to diagnose the biological 'death of the whole brain'—that is, the death of most, if not all, brain cells. With this objective in mind the scalp electroencephalogram may be considered relevant (provided one keeps in mind that it is quite incapable of achieving the desired end). Those who claim that the electroencephalogram is irrelevant are seeking to diagnose death of the brain as a functional unit (death of the 'brain as a whole'). They do this by concentrating on what allows the brain to function as a unit: the brain stem. In pursuit of that objective the electroencephalogram is indeed irrelevant. Recording an electroencephalogram from the scalp is not testing a brain stem function.

How important, in practice, is the difference between the two approaches? An important study carried out at the Salpêtrière Hospital in Paris over 10 years ago showed that when apnoeic coma and absent brain stem reflexes occurred in a context of structural brain disease minor residual electroencephalographic activity was common but never persisted. In the vast majority of cases no electroencephalogram could be recorded after 48 hours.

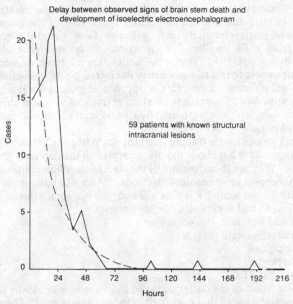

Delay between observed signs of brain stem death and development of isoelectric electroencephalogram

59 patients with known structural intracranial lesions

Prognostic significance of brain stem signs (Structural brain lesions. No drug induced cases)				
No of cases	Brain stem areflexia	Apnoea	EEG	Asystole within days
>1000	All	All	'Isoelectric'	All
147	All	All	Some residual activity	All
16	None	None	'Isoelectric'	None

The table above seeks to make a different, but equally relevant point. It too deals with patients suffering from structural brain disease, contrasting the prognostic implications of clinically dead brain stems (in patients with remnants of electroencephalographic activity) with the prognostic implications of 'isoelectric' electroencephalograms (in patients with residual clinical signs of brain stem function). All patients with potentially reversible causes of brain stem dysfunction (such as drugs and metabolic disturbances) were excluded in this survey. Over 1000 cases were identified who combined apnoeic coma, brain stem areflexia, and an 'isoelectric' electroencephalogram. All developed asystole within days. A further 147 cases were identified, with brain stem areflexia and apnoea, in whom there was some residual electroencephalographic activity. Again, all developed asystole within a few days. Like the first group, they also had dead brain stems. The conclusion seems to be that, irrespective of what the electroencephalogram may show, a clinically dead brain stem always heralds asystole. A further 16 well-documented case reports were found of patients who had isoelectric electroencephalograms (strictly defined) but some residual brain stem function. None of these developed astysole. Again this is not surprising: parts of their brain stems were still functioning.

The technical argument

The technical argument has centred on the fact that an intensive care unit is about the most hostile environment imaginable for trying to record 'electrocerebral silence'. Many encephalograms in these circumstances show multiple artefacts which may be bizarre and difficult to identify and locate. If the nurse is wearing nylon underwear static electricity may generate false signals. Electromagnetic disturbances from calls on the Tannoy system may also generate confusing information. But apart from artefacts, some experts have argued that it is intrinsically impossible to record a genuinely isoelectric electroencephalogram at an amplification of 2 μV/mm because this is approaching the noise level of even the most sensitive apparatus. To exclude cerebral activity of just over this magnitude (in a noisy trace inevitably contaminated by signals several times larger) is certainly a major demand not always achievable.

Anyway, does an isoelectric tracing from the scalp imply electrocerebral silence, as is so often implied? What about signals generated in the depths of the sulci or by the basal cortex? Why are the advocates of the electroencephalogram not requesting traces from pharyngeal or sphenoidal electrodes? And what about attentuation of signals en route to the scalp? Even at normal voltage such attenuation may be considered. These thoughts evoked a further limerick:

We sat back and watched with some glee
All these experts on death disagree
Are we all being dull
Or could a thick skull
Be a cause of a flat EEG?

But even if the whole of the cortex could be shown to be electrically silent (which is impossible) would it mean that every cell in the brain was dead? There have been cases where thalamic probing has shown persistent neuronal discharges in the presence of an isoelectric electroencephalogram. The electroencephalogram therefore does not test cerebral function with the rigour demanded by the concept of death of the whole brain. If those who accept this concept were logical they would have to drill burrholes and probe with depth electrodes before diagnosing a totally dead brain.

There is a final facet to the technical critique. The electroencephalogram is often said to be 'objective'. This is not so. In the American Collaborative Study special efforts were made to identify artefacts in the records, yet about 6% of 2256 electroencephalograms were classified as unsatisfactory because of technical difficulties. Discordance between those interpreting the records was put at only 3%, which is exceptionally good. There is no sharp end point, as recordable electroencephalographic activity gradually submerges into noise. These are not the hallmarks of an objective test.

The clinical argument

Those who argue that the electroencephalogram is irrelevant to establishing the presence of a dead brain stem are often misunderstood. They are not saying the electroencephalogram is irrelevant to the diagnosis of the condition causing the coma (it may be most useful, for instance, in establishing a diagnosis of hepatic encephalopathy or of herpes simplex encephalitis). Nor are they denying the prognostic value of the electroencephalogram after head injury or acute cerebral anoxia, although even here there is accumulating evidence that judiciously directed clinical assessments may provide very reliable prognostic data. There is even evidence that in patients rendered comatose after a cardiac arrest the clinical signs elicited within the first hour may indicate whether the electroencephalogram will remain isoelectric.

There seems to be a difference of opinion among the advocates of the electroencephalogram about its exact purpose. Some believe it to be necessary for ascertaining that unspecified preconditions have been met. Others consider it part of the final testing, an isoelectric trace being deemed the ultimate proof that the brain is dead. Neither attitude is warranted. In patients in deep coma the electroencephalogram may generate misleading data. To those unaware of the pitfalls it may suggest death in patients who may survive. There is a report of a patient being declared dead on the basis of a single electroencephalogram. Conversely, persistent electroencephalographic activity often generates false hope in relation to 'beating heart cadavers', doomed to develop asystole because their brain stems are already dead. It has been claimed that to do an electroencephalogram in the clinical context of brain stem death is 'reassuring' to the relatives. If the electroencephalogram is recorded in the knowledge (which the relatives do not share) that it is non-contributory this is manipulative behaviour.

Some electroencephalographic artefacts in suspected brain death

Idiomuscular potentials

People touching bed
People walking past bed
Fluid dripping from patient
Fluid dripping into patient
Sphygmomanometer

Pulse
Electrocardiogram
Ballistocardiogram
Pacemaker
Dialysis machine

Respiratory artefacts
    (a) ventilation tube vibrations (electrostatic artefacts)
    (b) head movement

Hiccup
Shivering

In summary, the electroencephalogram relates (inaccurately) to an unformulated (but unacceptable) concept of death. It provides answers of variable reliability to what is widely felt to be the wrong question. This should make its use questionable for anyone with any concern for intellectual clarity in this field. To the more pragmatically minded the capacity of the electroencephalogram to lead to wrong practical decisions should suggest caution in its use.

The argument about residual sentience
Is there more than atavistic mysticism in the essentially untestable supposition of residual sentience in the isolated forebrain, or in cell aggregates elsewhere in the cortex or deeper structures? Clinical experience offers no support for this notion. Really deep coma, as distinct from stupor or delirium, is always associated with an absence of purposeful response to stimuli, and is always followed by profound amnesia, no matter what the cause of the coma.

Confusion is engendered by including in discussions about residual sentience and the electroencephalogram a wide variety of different neurological conditions, ranging from the vegetative state to physiological sleep, and including such diverse entities as experiences during the induction and anaesthesia in a normal person and the locked-in syndrome in a fully conscious individual. The electroencephalographic correlates of such a miscellany will, of course, range from "electrocerebral silence' to normal activity.

The question is sometimes asked whether the small part of the reticular formation situated rostral to the brain stem proper could generate anything remotely resembling a capacity for consciousness? There is no anatomical basis for such an assumption. Current concepts of the reticular formation still emphasise the primacy of the brain stem nuclei. The reticular formation of the thalamus has purely internal connections. It has an important gating role, but there is nothing to suggest that it has global cerebral projections, as does the reticular formation of the brain stem.

I do not believe there could be residual sentience above a dead brain stem. But I would ask those who disagree—and who want to be logical about the conclusions to be drawn from their premises—to face up to the scenario of a patient with a dead brain stem, doomed to asystole within a few days, yet showing remnants of electroencephalographic activity (which they equate with residual sentience). Can they conceive of a greater hell than an isolated sentience, aware of its precarious existence, and with no means of expression? Would they anaesthetise such a preparation? Or just sedate it? And might not this further depression of cerebral function, in a patient already in 'coma dépassé', prove to be the last straw?

The problem has, of course, fascinated physiologists and philosophers for generations. With appropriate corrections of time scale, it is the problem of what happens, for a few seconds, in a decapitated head. The following limerick, which could have been written by one of the *tricoteuses* sitting at the foot of the guillotine, in Paris in 1793, puts the forbidden question:

We knit on, too *blasées* to ask it:
'Could the tetraparesis just mask it?
When the brain stem is dead
Can the cortex be said
to tick on, in the head, in the basket?"

The cultural argument

Electroencephalograms are nevertheless still widely resorted to in the USA in the diagnosis of brain death. Few people are prepared to discuss the cultural (rather than neurological) dimensions of this addiction. Our American colleagues practise in a litigious atmosphere in which 'a climate of general public unease about brain death exists, partly engendered by sensational fiction'. For good or ill, instrumental medicine has taken giant steps forward—often evicting good clinical practice in its wake. Many American jurors have a touchingly naive faith in the supremacy of machines such as the electroencephalograph, do not realise that there is at least a 3% variance in the reading of such records, and are blissfully unaware of the problems of obtaining artefact-free traces at high amplification.

Leading neurologists in the USA readily endorse these doubts about the scientific relevance of the electroencephalogram and emphasise that in the 'less legally demanding' conditions of the UK 'it is doubtful that the experienced physician needs the electroencephalogram to tell him that the brain is dead'. But, as an American colleague wrote to me, they 'have to protect the young people who are educated with them against the malevolent ravages of opportunistic lawyers'. They live 'in a climate where physicians have been brought to court as potential murderers for having killed an already dead patient'. Physicians resorted to electroencephalograms 'to save a great deal of later polemical accusation'.

It was suggested in the *Panorama* TV programme on brain death (13 October 1980), and is still believed in the USA, that our reluctance in the UK to use the electroencephalogram for diagnosing brain death is due to the paucity of such machines in our hospitals. Economics, it was claimed, was a consideration in formulating our code. The paucity of machines is admitted but the implication is unwarranted. As the question of economics has been raised, let me say that I believe it to be relevant to the continued advocacy of instrumental diagnosis in the USA. Vested interests should be openly declared. They rarely are, in either verbal or written discussions on the use of electroencephalography in the diagnosis of death.

Conclusions

Modern technology, in its desperate attempts to save human life, has produced an entity widely known as brain death. It has also generated a conceptual crisis: that of knowing—at the simplest, bedside level—whether a patient is alive or dead.

I have argued that the conceptual challenge can, and should, be met. We must evolve a concept of death that is in keeping with the cultural context of our age and which would in practice enable us to steer a course between 'treating the putrefying body as if it were alive, and treating patients who are mentally retarded as if they were dead'. The recognition of a dead brain stem is the first step along such a course. In these articles I have sought to show how such a state can be identified clinically and how it relates to an overall concept of death.

The lay public, however, is not on the whole interested in physiological argument about the reticular formation, or in philosophical controversies about the nature of death. People are concerned that their kidneys should not be removed while they are comatose from treatable conditions. The UK code can give the public absolute reassurance in this respect. It is scientifically sound and clinically foolproof (provided the necessary attention is given to preconditions and exclusions and provided the doctors carrying out the tests are reasonably competent and know what they are doing and why). The whole ethos subtending the code is humane. In practice it will be of· help to relatives, nursing staff, and doctors who 'may unintentionally find themselves caring for a biological preparation with no other humane attributes than physical form'.

As if anticipating later developments, Shakespeare had Macbeth proclaim (act III, scene IV) that there was once a time " that when the brains were out, the man would die'. The challenge today is a double one; to replace the words 'would die' by the words 'is dead'— and to be more specific about 'the brains being out'. The death of the brain stem would surely be enough.

Do Pallis' views about the relevance of higher brain function clinch the argument for you that the better criterion for determining death is an absence of functioning in the *brain stem*? We are convinced.

(c) OTHER JURISDICTIONS

The President's Commission, *op cit*, surveys the law in other countries as follows (pp 70–72; footnotes omitted):

The interference of increasingly sophisticated medical technology with determining death by traditional heart-lung criteria is also a matter of concern outside the United States as well. Indeed, an international body broached the issue as early as 1968 when, a few days after the publication of the seminal Harvard criteria, the 22nd Congress of the World Medical Assembly (WMA) adopted its 'Declaration of Sydney'. This statement, framed in general terms, recognised that, although physicians will usually be able to meet their legal responsibility in diagnosing death by relying on classical heart-lung criteria, artificial respirators and transplantation of cadaver organs posed problems for which these criteria seem insufficient. The WMA concluded that 'no single technological criterion is entirely satisfactory in the present state of medicine nor can any one technological procedure be substituted for the overall judgment of the physician'. A determination of death should, the WMA declared, 'be based on clinical judgment supplemented *if necessary* by a number of diagnostic aids of which the electroencephalograph is currently the most helpful'.

The Declaration of Sydney went on to recommend that, where transplantation is involved, the determination of death should be made by two or more physicians, who must not be 'immediately concerned with the performance of transplantation'. This recommendation remains the most frequent common denominator in statutes found in other countries, as death is most often defined in the context of rules relating to organ transplantation.

Questions raised by the new resuscitative technology have also received some, albeit not entirely satisfactory, attention in international legal bodies. In 1976 the Parliamentary Assembly of the Council of Europe issued a 'Report on the Rights of the Sick and Dying' which included a recommendation on the prolongation of life. Unfortunately, the report seems to confuse patient participation in decisions about medical care with legal rules on the irreversible cessation of brain function.

In model legislation on transplantation in 1978, the Council of Europe dealt obliquely with the 'definition' of death. Like the model American statute on transplantation (the Uniform Anatomical Gift Act), the European proposal did not state the basis on which death could be declared in so many words. It went somewhat further than the American provision, however, implying that cessation of brain functions is a ground for pronouncing death, at least when organs are to be removed. The 1978 Council of Europe proposal stated that "[d]eath having occurred, a removal [of organs or tissues for transplantation] may be effected even if the function of some organ other than the brain may be artificially preserved'.

A number of countries have taken up these issues through national medical societies or law reform commissions. As a result at least 13 countries have statutes of national force and effect that allow for the determination of death based on brain-oriented criteria. At least ten countries require specific tests (usually electroencephalography and/or cerebral angiography) as part of their statutes or regulations promulgated pursuant to statutory authority.

Two countries, Canada and Australia, have a legal situation that parallels the United States; a few provinces have enacted statutes, while the others have not. In 1977 the Law Reform Commission of Australia recommended, in the context of human tissue transplants, a statute declaring death to occur upon 'irreversible cessation of all functions of the brain' or 'irreversible cessation of blood in the body'. The Law Reform Commission of Canada recently proposed amending the federal 'Interpretation Act' to add a brain-based 'definition' to the law 'for all purposes within the jurisdiction of the Parliament of Canada'. Other countries, such as Great Britain, rely on codes of medical practice drafted by nationally recognised bodies with quasi-legal status and accepted by the relevant executive branch departments. A recently published survey of the international situation identifies fifteen countries where the medical profession has officially recognised brain-based criteria in determining death in the absence of statutory or case law, and five countries where it has not, although physicians in some of these countries may in fact employ the criteria in declaring death in appropriate cases.

The Canadian Model Statute referred to by the President's Commission is as follows:

(1) a person is dead when an irreversible cessation of all that person's brain functions has occurred.

(2) the irreversible cessation of brain functions can be determined by the prolonged absence of spontaneous circulatory and respiratory functions.

(3) when the determination of the prolonged circulatory and respiratory functions is made impossible by the use of artificial means of support, the irreversible cessation of brain functions can be determined by any means recognised by the ordinary standards of current medical practice.

To what extent, if at all, does this model statute differ from the US statutes?

(d)   ENGLAND AGAIN

(i)   the Code of Practice

You will have seen that the President's Commission referred to the Code of Practice called 'Diagnosis of Death'. The following is from this 1976 Code of Practice, (1976) 2 BMJ 1187–8:

I Diagnosis of brain death (October 1976)

With the development of intensive-care techniques and their wide availability in the United Kingdom it has become commonplace for hospitals to have deeply comatose and unresponsive patients with severe brain damage who are maintained on artificial respiration by means of mechanical ventilators. This state has been recognised for many years and it has been the concern of the medical profession to establish diagnostic criteria of such rigour that on their fulfilment the mechanical ventilator can be switched off, in the secure knowledge that there is no possible chance of recovery.

There has been much philosophical argument about the diagnosis of death which has throughout recorded history been accepted as having occurred when the vital functions of respiration and circulation have ceased. However, with the technical ability to maintain these functions artificially the dilemma of when to switch off the ventilator has been the subject of much public interest. It is agreed that permanent functional death of the brainstem constitutes brain death and that once this has occurred further artificial support is fruitless and should be withdrawn. It is good medical practice to recognise when brain death has occurred and to act accordingly, sparing relatives from the further emotional trauma of sterile hope.

Codes of practice, such as the Harvard criteria (1968),[1] have been devised to guide medical practitioners in the diagnosis of brain death. These have provided considerable help with the problem and they have been refined as the knowledge gained from experience has been collated.

More recently Forrester[2] has written on established practice in Scotland and Jennett[3] has made useful observations. The diagnostic criteria presented for brain death here have been written with the advice of the subcommittee of the Transplant Advisory Panel, the working-party of the Royal College of Physicians, the working-party of the Faculty of Anaesthetists, and the Royal College of Surgeons and have been approved by the Conference of Medical Royal Colleges and their Faculties in the United Kingdom. They are accepted as being sufficient to distinguish between those patients who retain the functional capacity to have a chance of even partial recovery and those where no such possibility exists.

Conditions under which the diagnosis of brain death should be considered

1. *The patient is deeply comatose.*
(a) There should be no suspicion that this state is due to depressant drugs.   *Note 1*
(b) Primary hypothermia as a cause of coma should have been excluded.
(c) Metabolic and endocrine disturbances which can be responsible for or can contribute to coma should have been excluded.   *Note 2*
2. *The patient is being maintained on a ventilator because spontaneous respiration had previously become inadequate or had ceased altogether.*
(a) Relaxants (neuromuscular blocking agents) and other drugs should have been excluded as a cause of respiratory inadequacy or failure   *Note 3*
3. *There should be no doubt that the patient's condition is due to irremediable structural brain damage. The diagnosis of a disorder which can lead to brain death should have been fully established.*   *Note 4*

Notes

Note 1

Narcotics, hypnotics, and tranquillisers may have prolonged duration of action particularly when some hypothermia exists. The benzodiazepines are markedly cumulative and persistent in their actions and are commonly used as anticonvulsants or to assist synchronisation with mechanical ventilators. It is therefore recommended that the drug history should be carefully reviewed and adequate intervals allowed for the persistence of drug effects to be excluded. This is of particular importance in patients where the primary cause of coma lies in the toxic effects of drugs followed by anoxic cerebral damage.

Note 2

Metabolic and endocrine factors contributing to the persistence of coma must be subject to careful assessment. There should be no profound abnormality of the serum-electrolytes, acid-base balance, or blood-glucose.

Note 3

Immobility, unresponsiveness, and lack of spontaneous respiration may be due to the use of neuromuscular blocking drugs and the persistence of their effects should be excluded by elicitation of spinal reflexes (flexion or stretch) or by the demonstration of adequate neuromuscular conduction with a conventional nerve stimulator. Equally, persistent effects of hypnotics and narcotics should be excluded as the cause of respiratory failure.

Note 4

It may be obvious within hours of a primary intra-cranial event such as severe head injury, spontaneous intra-cranial haemorrhage or following neurosurgery that the condition is irremediable. However, when a patient has suffered primarily from cardiac arrest, hypoxia or severe circulatory insufficiency with an indefinite period of cerebral anoxia, or is suspected of having cerebral air or fat embolism then it may take much longer to establish the diagnosis and to be confident of the prognosis. In some patients the primary pathology may be a matter of doubt and a confident diagnosis may only be reached by continuity of clinical observation and investigation.

Diagnostic tests for the confirmation of brain death

All brainstem reflexes are absent:

(i) The pupils are fixed in diameter and do not respond to sharp changes in the intensity of incident light.

(ii) There is no corneal reflex.

(iii) The vestibulo-ocular reflexes are absent. *Note (a)*

(iv) No motor responses within the cranial nerve distribution can be elicited by adequate stimulation of any somatic area.

(v) There is no gag reflex or reflex response to bronchial stimulation by a suction catheter passed down the trachea.

(vi) No respiratory movements occur when the patient is disconnected from the mechanical ventilator for long enough to ensure that the arterial carbon dioxide tension rises above the threshold for stimulation of respiration. *Note (b)*

Note (a)

Vestibulo-ocular reflexes.—These are absent when no eye movement occurs during or following the slow injection of 20 ml of ice-cold water into each external auditory meatus in turn, clear access to the tympanic membrane having been established by direct inspection. This test may be contra-indicated on one or other side by local trauma.

Note (b)

Disconnection from the ventilator.—During this test it is necessary for the arterial carbon-dioxide tension to exceed the threshold for respiratory stimulation—that is, the $PaCO_1$ should normally reach 50 mmHg (6.65 kPa). This is best achieved by measurement of the blood gases; if this facility is available it is recommended that the patient should be disconnected when the $PaCO_2$ reaches 40–45 mm Hg following administration of 5% CO_2 in oxygen through the ventilator. This starting level has been chosen because patients may be moderately hypothermic (35°C–37°C), flaccid, and with a depressed metabolic rate, so that arterial carbon-dioxide tension rises only slowly in apnoea (about 2 mm Hg/min). (Hypoxia during disconnection should be prevented by delivering oxygen at 6 litres/min through a catheter into the trachea.) If blood-gas analysis is not available to measure the $PaCO_2$ and PaO_2 the alternative procedure is to supply the ventilator with pure oxygen for ten minutes (pre-oxygenation), then with 5% CO_2 in oxygen for five minutes and to disconnect the ventilator for ten minutes, while delivering oxygen at 6 litres/minute by catheter into the trachea. This establishes diffusion oxygenation and ensures that during apnoea hypoxia will not occur even in ten or more minutes of respiratory arrest. Those patients with preexisting chronic respiratory insufficiency, who may be unresponsive to raised levels of carbon dioxide and who normally exist on an hypoxic drive, are special cases and should be expertly investigated with careful blood-gas monitoring.

Other considerations
1. Repetition of testing
It is customary to repeat the tests to ensure that there has been no observer error. The interval between tests must depend upon the primary pathology and the clinical course of the disease. Note 4 indicates some conditions where it would be unnecessary to repeat them since a prognosis of imminent brain death can be accepted as being obvious.

In some conditions the outcome is not so clear cut and in these it is recommended that the tests should be repeated. The interval between tests depends upon the progress of the patient and might be as long as 24 hours. This is a matter for medical judgement and repetition time must be related to the signs of improvement, stability, or deterioration which present themselves.

2. Integrity of spinal reflexes
It is well established that spinal-cord function can persist after insults which irretrievably destroy brainstem function. Reflexes of spinal origin may persist or return after an initial absence in brain dead patients.[4]

3. Confirmatory investigations
It is now widely accepted that electro-encephalography is not necessary for the diagnosis of brain death.[5-9] Indeed this view was expressed from Harvard in 1969[10] only a year after the publication of their original criteria.

Electroencephalography has its principal value at earlier stages in the care of patients, in whom the original diagnosis is in doubt. When electroencephalography is used, the strict criteria recommended by the Federation of EEG Societies[11] must be followed.

Other investigations such as cerebral angiography or cerebral blood-flow measurements are not required for the diagnosis of brain death.

4. Body temperature
The body temperature in these patients may be low because of depression of central temperature regulation by drugs or by brainstem damage and it is recommended that it should be not less than 35°C before the diagnostic tests are carried out. A low-reading thermometer should be used.

5. Specialist opinion and the status of the doctors concerned
Experienced clinicians in intensive-care units, acute medical wards, and accident and emergency departments should not normally require specialist advice. Only when the primary diagnosis is in doubt is it necessary to consult with a neurologist or neurosurgeon.

Decision to withdraw artificial support should be made after all the criteria presented above have been fulfilled and can be made by any one of the following combination of doctors:
(a) A consultant who is in charge of the case and one other doctor.
(b) In the absence of a consultant, his deputy, who should have been registered for 5 years or more *and* who should have had adequate previous experience in the care of such cases, and one other doctor.

References
[1] Report of the Ad Hoc Committee of Harvard Medical School to examine the definition of brain death. Definition of irreversible coma. *Journal of the American Medical Association*, 1968, **205**, 337.
[2] Forrester, A C Brain death and the donation of cadaver kidneys. *Health Bulletin*, 1976, **34**, 199.
[3] Jennett, B The donor doctor's dilemma: observations on the recognition and management of brain death. *Journal of Medical Ethics*, 1975, **1**, 63.
[4] Ivan, L P Spinal reflexes in cerebral death. *Neurology*, 1973, **23**, 650.
[5] Walker, A E The neurosurgeon's responsibility for organ procurement. *Journal of Neurosurgery*, 1976, **44**, 1.

[6] Mohandas, A and Chou S N Brain death. A clinical and pathological study. *Journal of Neurosurgery*, 1971, **35**, 211.

[7] Brain damage and brain death. *Lancet*, 1974, **1**, 341.

[8] Brain death. *British Medical Journal*, 1975, **1**, 356.

[9] MacGillivray, B. The diagnosis of cerebral death. In *Proceedings of the Tenth Congress of the European Dialysis and Transplant Association*, ed J F Moorhead. London, Pitman Medical, 1973.

[10] Beecher, H K After the 'definition of irreversible coma', *New England Journal of Medicine*, 1969, **281**, 1070.

[11] The International Federation of EEG Societies. Report. *Electroencephalography and Clinical Neurophysiology*, 1974, **37**, 430; 1975, **38**, 536.

An addendum was produced in 1979, set out below ((1979) 1 BMJ 332).

II   Memorandum on the diagnosis of death (January 1979)

1 In October 1976 the Conference of Royal Colleges and their Faculties (UK) published a report unanimously expressing the opinion that 'Brain Death', when it had occurred, could be diagnosed with certainty. The report has been widely accepted.

The Conference was not at that time asked whether or not it believed that death itself should be presumed to occur when brain death takes place or whether it would come to some other conclusion. The present report examines this point and should be considered as an addendum to the original report.

2 Exceptionally, as a result of massive trauma, death occurs instantaneously or near-instantaneously. Far more commonly, death is not an event, it is a process, the various organs and systems supporting the continuation of life failing and eventually ceasing altogether to function, successively and at different times.

3 Cessation of respiration and cessation of the heart beat are examples of organic failure occurring during the process of dying and since the moment that the heart beat ceases is usually detectable with simplicity by no more than clinical means, it has for many centuries been accepted as the moment of death itself, without any serious attempt being made to assess the validity of this assumption.

4 It is now universally accepted, by the lay public as well as by the medical profession, that it is not possible to equate death itself with cessation of the heart beat. Quite apart from the elective cardiac arrest of open-heart surgery, spontaneous cardiac arrest followed by successful resuscitation is today a commonplace and although the more sensational accounts of occurrences of this kind still refer to the patient being 'dead' until restoration of the heartbeat, the use of the quote marks usually demonstrates that this word is not to be taken literally, for to most people the one aspect of death that is beyond debate is its irreversibility.

5 In the majority of cases, in which a dying patient passes through the processes leading to the irreversible state we call death, successive organic failures eventually reach a point at which brain death occurs and this is the point of no return.

6 In a minority of cases, brain death does not occur as a result of the failure of other organs or systems but as a direct result of severe damage to the brain itself from, perhaps, a head injury or a spontaneous intracranial haemorrhage. Here the order of events is reversed; instead of the failure of such vital functions as heart beat and respiration eventually resulting in brain death, brain death results in the cessation of spontaneous respiration; this is normally followed within minutes by cardiac arrest due to hypoxia. If, however, oxygenation is maintained by artificial ventilation the heart beat can continue for some days, and haemoperfusion will for a time be adequate to maintain function in other organs, such as the liver and kidneys.

7 Whatever the mode of its production, brain death represents the stage at which a patient becomes truly dead, because by then all functions of the brain have permanently and irreversibly ceased. It is not difficult or illogical in any way to equate this with the concept in many religions of the departure of the spirit from the body.

8 In the majority of cases, since brain death is part of or the culmination of a failure of all vital functions, there is no necessity for a doctor specifically to identify brain death individually before concluding that the patient is dead. In a minority of cases in which it is brain death that causes failure of other organs and systems, the fact that these systems can be artificially maintained even after brain death has made it important to establish a diagnostic routine which will identify with certainty the existence of brain death.

Conclusion

9 It is the conclusion of the Conference that the identification of brain death means that the patient is dead, whether or not the function of some organs, such as a heart beat, is still maintained by artificial means.

Given the near universal acceptance of the approach adopted in this Code, we are confident that an English court would adopt as the concept of death that which is reflected, at least implicitly, in the Code; would adopt the locus (ie brain); and would adopt the criteria for determining the presence or absence of the relevant functions and the means of determining clinically these criteria.

A court would adopt the concept and, consequently, the locus as a matter of law on the grounds that it would be recognised that the historical definition was no more than a rudimentary attempt to identify the locus and criteria of what has always been the concept of death in English law.

(ii) Non-compliance with Code

Questions concerning compliance or non-compliance with the Code only arise, of course, in those circumstances in which the patient's vital functions are being artificially maintained.

Clearly if the patient dies in other circumstances the death will be recognised by the prolonged irreversible absence of vital functions. (Note s 2 of the Draft Canadian statute, *supra*.)

If the patient is receiving artificial life-support, will non-compliance with the Code have any legal consequences? There are two sets of problems:

1. the consequences as regards the definition of death.
2. the legality of the doctor's conduct.

It may be useful to divide non-compliance with the Code by looking at the three stages contemplated in the Code.

Stage 1 requires that the doctor exclude patients with certain conditions; see Code (1)(a), (b) and (c), and (2) and (3), *supra*.

Stage 2 requires that the doctor perform the specific clinical 'tests for confirming brain death', *supra*.

Stage 3 requires that the doctor repeat the testing.

1. For the determination of death

The question we are concerned with here is, would a court when presented with evidence of non-compliance with the Code determine that a patient was not dead when the doctor states that he was. Undoubtedly, whether a person is dead will always be a question of law for the court. A court in making a determination will make a finding that death occurred on the basis of medical evidence (save the most obvious circumstances with which we are by definition not concerned here). The medical evidence must *prima facie* include a demonstration that the doctor has complied with the Code. If the doctor's non-compliance occurs at *stage 1* it would be open to the court, on appropriate facts, to find that the patient was not dead at the time certified. If the non-compliance occurs at *stage 2*, what has to be tested is whether a court would decide that a patient was not dead because, for example, the doctor failed to carry out one or more of the stipulated tests. At first blush, this would seem to be a somewhat recondite point, but we are assuming here so as to test the analysis, that the precise moment of death is important legally. We take the view that a court would, in the absence of irresponsible behaviour by the doctor, be reluctant to find that the patient was not dead at the time asserted, but how can this conclusion be justified in the face of the fact that a person must be presumed to be living until shown to be dead? The justification may be that, although the determination of death is a matter of law, medical evidence is the only material upon which the court can act. We have no doubt that if responsible medical evidence were that the omission of the test(s) was irrelevant on the particular facts the court would not question this. (See *Malcherek*, where two tests were not carried out by the doctors and Lord Lane CJ stated: '[r]easons were given for neither of these tests having been carried out' and the court nevertheless did not cast doubt on the doctor's determination of death.) This would obviously be the case where the test could not physically be carried out but may also be the case in other circumstances where good medical reason exists for omitting it. Would this view prevail even if none of the prescribed tests had been carried out?

If the non-compliance occurs at *stage 3*, again the only relevant legal question is whether the patient was dead at the time the first set of tests was carried out. If the purpose of the repetition of the tests is *confirmatory*, in view of what has been said before, it must follow that a court would hold that death had occurred no later then the completion of the first set of tests. Of course, if the repeat tests were more than confirmatory, major problems arise not merely concerning repetition of the tests but concerning the validity of the tests themselves. Obviously if a second set of tests are called for why not a third and so on?

Pallis addressed this point in *ABC of Brain Stem Death*, (pp 16–17).

Virtually all codes urge that testing be carried out twice. The recommended intervals between the relevant tests have progressively shortened. There are several reasons why this has happened. Firstly, the objections to ventilating corpses have become more widely accepted. Secondly, when the first and second examinations for brain death were separated by as long as 24 hours several patients would develop asystole before the second examination. Finally, it became widely recognised that provided scrupulous attention was given to the preconditions and exclusions the second examination always confirmed the first. In other words, the more time spent in ascertaining the irremediable nature of the structural brain damage causing the coma the less important does the interval between tests become.

What is the purpose of retesting in a patient with a non-functioning brain stem due to well established, irremediable, structural brain damage? The UK code claims that it is to ensure that there has been no observer error. This is entirely praiseworthy, although no properly documented case has been published where the diagnosis of brain stem death has been revised after repeat testing. In my opinion retesting usually has a different purpose. It ensures that the non-functioning of the brain stem is not just a single observation at one point in time but that it has persisted. For how long? For a period several hundredfold that during which brain stem neurons could survive the total ischaemia of a non-perfused brain. At Hammersmith Hospital we like to separate our tests by two to three hours, which is more than enough to ensure that the findings are irreversible.

One further point which may be noted arises from the final paragraph of the 1976 Code. Although not entirely clearly drafted, the paragraph seems to contemplate that the determination should be made (or confirmed) by medical practitioners of appropriate standing and experience. If this procedure was not complied with, again would a court hold that the patient certified as dead was not dead? Provided the tests were carried out with appropriate skill and the results would not be doubted by informed medical opinion, we have no doubt that a court would find the patient dead despite imprecise compliance.

2. The legality of the doctor's conduct

The concern here is with the possible criminal liability of the doctor for homicide and civil liability in negligence for failing to carry out his duty.

Apart from the unique issue of the doctor's *mens rea* for the purposes of homicide (to which we shall return shortly), there seem to us to be two common features necessary to establish either civil or criminal liability. First, was the doctor's conduct in breach of his duty to his patient? Secondly, if it was, did the breach cause the patient's death?

It follows from this that the doctor's conduct will only be unlawful if the court has found that the patient is not dead either because there has been a failure to comply with the pre-conditions (at stage 1) or an irresponsible performance or failure to perform the tests (at stage 2). To make the issue abundantly clear, we are not here concerned with the doctor's decision in good faith to treat for dying even to the point of withdrawing a patient from a ventilator (see *infra*, ch 14). Here, instead we are concerned with the doctor who acts deliberately with an intention to bring about the death of the patient.

In these circumstances, we have no doubt that a court would decide that the doctor was both in breach of his legal duty to his patient and, that, his conduct in *bad faith* would be a legal cause of death. It follows, therefore, that a doctor could be guilty of murder or manslaughter and could be liable in negligence for the patient's death.

(e) THE NEED FOR LEGISLATION IN ENGLAND

The Criminal Law Reform Committee in 1980 in its 14th Report, 'Offences Against the Person' (Cmnd 7844), reported (para 37) that:

> We have considered whether there should be a statutory definition of death. A memorandum issued by the honorary secretary of the Conference of Medical Royal Colleges and Faculties in the United Kingdom on 15 January 1979[2] refers to an earlier report of the Conference which expressed their unanimous opinion that 'brain death' could be diagnosed with certainty. The memorandum states that the report published by the Conference has been widely accepted and says that the identification of brain death means that a patient is truly dead, whether or not the function of some organs, such as a heart beat, is still maintained by artificial means. Brain death is said to be when all the functions of the brain have permanently and irreversibly ceased. We are however extremely hesitant about embodying in a statute (which is not always susceptible of speedy amendment) an expression of present medical opinion and knowledge derived from a field of science which is continually progressing and inevitably altering its opinions in the light of new information. If a statutory definition of death were to be enacted there would, in our opinion, be a risk that further knowledge would cause it to lose the assent of the majority of the medical profession. In that event, far from assisting the medical profession, for example in cases of organ transplants, the definition might be a hindrance to them. Moreover, while there might be agreement that the statutory definition was defective, there might be differences of view about the proper content of any new definition. An additional reason for not recommending a definition of death is that such definition would have wide repercussions outside offences against

the person and the criminal law. A legal definition of death would also have to be applicable in the civil law. It would be undesirable to have a statutory definition confined only to offences against the person, which is the extent of our present remit. For these reasons therefore we are not recommending the enactment of a definition of death.[3]

Notes to extract
[2] Published in the British Medical Journal and the Lancet, 3rd February 1979.
[3] Professor Williams is of opinion that in any offences against the person legislation a clause should be included to declare that for the purposes of the Act a person shall be accounted dead if he has suffered brain death according to criteria accepted in standard medical practice.

Do you think they misunderstood the issue of what a statute would contain? Does not Professor Glanville Williams's recorded dissent show a greater understanding of how a statute would be framed?

The arguments for legislation are put by Professor Skegg in his article, 'The Case for a Statutory "Definition of Death" ' (1976) 2 J of Med Ethics 190:

An examination of the case against legislation

A great variety of objections have been put forward against the enactment of any provision dealing with the time of death. It has been said that death is a technical, clinical matter, and hence not the proper subject of a statutory provision; that the time of death is not subject to clear-cut definition; and that it would not be possible to provide a definition that would cover all contingencies and be suitable for inclusion in an Act. It has also been said that a statute would be too inflexible and would require amendment in a few years' time; that any statute must await a degree of unanimity on the part of the medical profession; and that independent certification of death provides an adequate safeguard in transplant cases.

A number of these objections result from a failure to recognise the possibility of distinguishing between the point at which death may be deemed to have occurred, and the criteria for determining whether that point has been reached ... For example, a statute could provide that a person shall be considered dead when all brain function has irreversibly ceased. Such a provision would cover all contingencies, and would be suitable for inclusion in an Act. It would be unlikely to require amendment in a few year's time, unless it was desired to commence considering as corpses persons whose total brain function had not irreversibly ceased. So fundamental a change would properly be the subject of new legislation. An enactment which equated the death of a human being with total brain death would leave room for the development of new or better criteria for determining when that stage had been reached.

The objection that a statutory enactment must await a degree of unanimity within the medical community is open to question. It could be argued that it is precisely because the medical profession and society at large are not generally agreed as to when death may be said to occur that legislation is needed. It is, of course, true that legislation should prescribe a stage which can be recognised by the medical profession. There would be no point in a statute which simply stated that death was the cessation of life. Equally, it would be undesirable for a statute to refer to irreversible loss of consciousness if there was disagreement as to what is meant by this term, or as to how accurately this state could be recognised. But subject to this, lack of unanimity on the part of the medical profession may be seen as a reason for, rather than against, legislation on this matter.

It is a mistake to think that independent certification of death is an adequate safeguard in transplant cases. Such certification is highly desirable. But it is important that there be agreement as to what it is that is to be certified, and such agreement is sometimes lacking at present. Doctors are not all agreed whether they may ever treat as dead a body in which the heart continues to beat without artificial means of support. This matter could be determined one way or the other by legislation.

The case for legislation

If the objections to a statutory provision are less than conclusive, what is the case for such legislation? Some of the relevant considerations have already been mentioned. The stage in the process of dying at which a person is to be regarded as dead for legal purposes is one of legitimate public interest. Yet at present there are divergent views and practices, and it seems likely that these differences will continue for some time to come.

If no action is taken uncertainty will continue, and doctors may treat as corpses bodies which many would regard as those of living human beings. At present such matters can only be resolved *ex post facto*. Even then, there is no guarantee that the matter will be clarified for the future. Given the current tendency of English judges to seek to avoid difficult issues by characterising them as ones of fact, they may simply leave the matter to the jury. Whichever way the jury resolved the matter, its decision would be of very little value for the future.

Whether the matter is treated as one of law or of fact, it is doubtful whether it is best dealt with in the course of a particular dispute. Neither the judge nor the jury is well placed to consider all the relevant considerations. The particular circumstances of the case, and the expert evidence adduced, may be given disproportionate weight. Furthermore, it is unfair to potential litigants that they must go to the expense and emotional exhaustion of court proceedings before they can discover whether a doctor was justified in treating a particular 'beating heart cadaver' as dead. The legitimate interests of both the medical profession and the public are such that there would seem to be a *prima facie* case for legislation.

An alternative to legislation

But are there any acceptable alternatives to legislation? It has been suggested . . . that what is needed is for 'the new concept of brain death to be incorporated into a code of practice', worked out by the medical profession after consultation with lawyers, theologians and other interested parties, and 'sanctioned by the Ministry of Health'. It was said that such a code would 'serve as an authoritative statement to be followed by doctors and courts alike', and could be kept under review by a permanent standing committee appointed by the Minister. There is much to be said for any attempt to reach an informed consensus of doctors and of the public at large. But unanimity seems unlikely to be achieved in the near future (see, eg, *Daily Mail*, 8 September 1976, p 1), and if achieved will not necessarily continue. Some writers are already arguing that a person is dead when capacity for consciousness has been irreversibly lost, even if brain stem activity continues. When the medical profession and the public are not of one mind as to when a person may properly be considered dead, there is no reason why the courts should feel obliged to treat as authoritative a statement by any committee which has not had law-making powers conferred on it by Parliament. Although it would be open to Parliament to confer on a committee the power to make regulations for determining when a person is to be regarded as dead for legal purposes, the matter would seem to be too important for Parliament simply to pass to some other body—unless, perhaps, strict guidelines had been imposed by Parliament, or the regulations were to require affirmative resolutions of both Houses of Parliament before coming into force.

A possible enactment

If there is to be legislation, what form should it take? Ideally, it would apply to all persons, for all purposes. It should not be too detailed, but should identify the common factor to which the different tests point.

The key provision could state simply that 'a person shall be regarded as dead for legal purposes when all brain activity (including brain stem activity) has irreversibly ceased'. This provision would leave the medical profession free to develop new and better criteria for determining when all brain activity had irreversibly ceased, and in this context committees of experts would undoubtedly have a part to play. If this approach were adopted, it might help to reassure some sections of the public if the statute added, *ex abundanti cautela*, that the person must be incapable of breathing again without artificial assistance.

If desired, there could be a further provision to the effect that 'the irreversible cessation of brain activity may be deduced from the absence of respiration or circulation for an appropriate period, or by any other means in accordance with good medical practice'. And in view of some of the evidential problems which could arise in litigation ... there might be advantages in also providing that 'where respiration continued with artificial assistance, the onus of establishing that the person was already dead lies on whoever wishes to rely on that fact'.

Has Professor Skegg made out his case in principle, leaving aside his particular proposal referring to absence of 'all brain activity'? Medical consensus has been reached since Skegg was writing, as we have seen.

(f) DEATH AND THE VEGETATIVE STATE

As we have seen, some may argue for a concept of death which consists in the loss of capacity for social interaction. The locus would remain the brain but the criteria for its determination would be the irreversible loss of functions of the higher brain. We have noticed already the rejection of this by the President's Commission in favour of the whole brain. We too would reject it, but in favour of the brain stem.

Skegg marshalls the arguments concerning death of the higher brain, which he calls 'cognitive death', in his book *Law, Ethics, and Medicine* (pp 213–223; footnotes omitted).

Many of the arguments for regarding as dead those patients whose hearts continue to beat, but who are brain dead, apply also to those who are in an irreversible non-cognitive condition. But the fundamental argument is that, once cognitive death has occurred, the person may be said to have ceased to exist, even if the body continues to breathe spontaneously. Doctors, as well as philosophers and theologians, have supported this approach. For example, one doctor (who uses 'cerebral death' to refer to what is here described as 'cognitive death') has written:

The personal, identifiable life of an individual human can be equated with the living function of that part of the brain called the cerebrum. Cerebral function is manifested in consciousness, awareness, memory, anticipation, recognition and emotions ... There is no human life in the [irreversible] absence of these. ...

I would emphasise ... that 'cerebral death' and 'brain death' are different things, and that the term 'cerebral death' expresses the medical concept which is equated with the death of the individual person.

If a doctor acted upon this view in practice, and removed a heart from a patient who had sustained cognitive death, but whose brain-stem was still functioning, the courts might be forced to consider the issue. It could come before the courts in other ways also. For example, the defendant in a personal injury claim could argue that as the plaintiff had sustained cognitive death he was no longer a living person, and hence not entitled to damages on the basis that he was still alive.

Were such a case to come before the courts, it would be particularly important that the courts make a clear distinction between the medical facts about the patient's condition and the separate issue of whether, given those facts, the patient was to be regarded as alive or dead. Whether the patient is in an irreversible non-cognitive condition is undoubtedly a medical question. But whether a patient in this condition is alive or dead, for the purpose of English law, is not a matter on which the courts should feel obliged to follow the views of the doctors who gave evidence, or even the views of the medical profession generally. ... For the foreseeable future, conventional usage will be so clear that patients in an irreversible non-cognitive state must be regarded as alive for the purpose of English law. But the currently accepted view is likely to come under increasing attack, and it is possible that opinion will become so divided that the courts will have to take account of other considerations. It is therefore as well to consider some of the arguments and considerations which might, in the event, influence the courts.

Many of the reasons which have been put forward for regarding as dead those patients who have sustained brain death apply also to those patients who have sustained cognitive death. For example, the first of the two reasons offered in the Harvard Report, in support of the 'new criterion for death', was that:

Improvements in resuscitative and supportive measures have led to increased efforts to save those who are desperately injured. Sometimes these efforts have only partial success so that the result is an individual whose heart continues to beat but whose brain is irreversibly damaged. The burden is great on patients who suffer permanent loss of intellect, on their families, on the hospitals, and on those in need of hospital beds already occupied by these comatose patients.

Although this consideration can hardly stand on its own as a sufficient reason for regarding anyone as dead, it has much greater application to those who have sustained cognitive death than to those who have sustained brain death. Even if doctors were not free to withdraw artificial ventilation when brain death was established, those bodies can rarely be kept functioning for more than a few days. By contrast, patients who have sustained cognitive death may continue in that state for months, and sometimes even years.

The other reason often given for regarding brain-dead patients as dead is the desirability of doctors being free to remove organs from such bodies for transplantation. Patients who have sustained cognitive death would be a particularly suitable source of organs for transplantation, as their hearts, livers, and kidneys will often be in excellent condition. But such patients would provide a very small proportion of the organs required for transplantation, so the possible benefit to transplantation if those patients were regarded as dead would not be comparable with the benefit which would accrue in the saving of medical resources.

The debate about cognitive death has been unlike much of that about brain death, for most of those who favour patients in an irreversibly non-cognitive condition being regarded as dead have not relied on the incidental advantages of such an approach. They have focused on more fundamental issues. Death being the cessation of life, many of them have sought to determine what is distinctive about the life of a human person, as opposed to other members of the animal kingdom. They argue that if a person's brain is damaged to such an extent that he can never return to consciousness, can never perform any cognitive function, then that person has died. The Co-ordinator of the Protection of Life Project of the Law Reform Commission of Canada, E. W. Keyserlingk, has taken this view. In a study written for the Commission, he stated:

In my view, if the medical tests have in fact determined that there is no potential for spontaneous cerebral brain function, even if spontaneous respiration continues, then the human person is dead. Obviously this view is based on the conviction that man is essentially more than a biological 'respiratory' being, and is essentially a rational, experiencing, communicating being. It is based as well on the strong medical evidence that the specific loci in the brain in which these latter functions reside are cerebral or higher brain centres.

. . .

If the courts were to hold that someone who was once a living person, but who had sustained cognitive death, was dead for legal purposes, it is difficult to see that there could be any legal objection to these spontaneously breathing bodies being cremated or buried.

Even if a judge did have freedom of decision in this matter he might consider that, although there are very significant differences between patients who have sustained cognitive death and patients who have not lost their cognitive faculties, there are also significant differences between patients who have sustained cognitive death but continue to breathe spontaneously and almost all corpses. He would be likely to recognise that a move to regard as dead all patients who have sustained cognitive death would be very controversial, and that a trial was a particularly unsuitable occasion to determine such an issue. Even if a judge was personally in favour of a statute providing that a person is dead once cognitive death occurs, considerations such as these could be expected to lead him to persist with the view that—in the absence of statutory intervention—a patient who is breathing spontaneously is not to be regarded as dead. He would not consider that it was for him to introduce a fundamental distinction between personal and bodily life.

Of course, it could be argued that acceptance of the view that a patient who has sustained brain death is dead, even though his heart continues to beat, has already involved acceptance of a distinction between human personal life, and human biological life, in relation to some bodies which would not in the past have been regarded as corpses. A patient who has sustained brain death may be maintained on a ventilator for some days before systemic death occurs. But the fact that there has been a relatively small departure from the traditional approach, whereby a person was not regarded as dead before his heart stopped pumping blood around his body, is not necessarily an argument for a much more striking departure. The argument may lead to doubt as to the wisdom of having taken the first step, rather than encourage the taking of the second or third.

... The conclusion, then is that while patients who have sustained brain death can now be regarded as dead for the purpose of English law, those who have merely sustained cognitive death will not now, or in the near future, be regarded as dead for the purpose of English law. Even if conventional usage becomes much less clear, and doctors come to favour reclassification, judges should be wary of giving effect to the new view in advance of its very widespread acceptance, or its adoption by statute.

Can Skegg's view really be challenged? You will recall our analysis in chapter 14 of a doctor's duty to a 'persistently vegetative patient'. Would that analysis have been necessary if these patients were dead in law? Would you consider Karen Quinlan dead? We would not.

(g)   A SPECIAL CASE—THE ANENCEPHALIC

The anencephalic is a baby born with a fatal neurological condition—anencephaly—involving the absence of all, or most of, the cerebral hemispheres, ie the higher brain.

The question how the law should respond to the anencephalic baby arises from proposals to harvest the organs of such a baby for another while the anencephalic was still breathing without support. G Annas writes in 'From Canada with Love: Anencephalic Newborns as Organ Donors' (1987) 17 Hastings Center Report 36 at 36–39; (footnotes omitted) as follows:

Determining death
The central issue in the debate about using anencephalic infants as organ sources is whether they must be dead, and if so, how death can be determined. Some have argued that since they lack higher brain function anencephalics should not be considered living human beings and thus their organs should be available for immediate use. Although almost all agree that anencephalic infants—unlike nearly every other handicapped newborn—need not be treated to prolong their lives, the majority believe that they are living human beings and that killing them would be murder.

In January 1987, transplant surgeon Calvin Stiller convened an international group, among them Leonard Bailey, in London, Ontario, to discuss this issue. Diverse views were expressed, including that anencephalic infants could be used as organ donors, but only upon pronouncement of death using classical brain death criteria. To utilise such criteria, it would be necessary to put the child on a mechanical ventilator, because simply permitting him or her to stop breathing naturally would normally result in organs that deteriorate as the child's breathing becomes more com romised. This intervention would likely prolong the child's life; in the most extreme (but unlikely) scenario, the child's brain-stem might become strong enough to sustain independent breathing for weeks, or even months or years.

Arthur Caplan presented the position to the London meeting that anencephalic infants should be considered a separate category of human ('living but brain absent') and that parents should be able to donate their newborns' organs prior to their death. He justifies this position on the basis that the anencephalic child can never develop even a 'semblance of personhood', that the 'need for these organs is real', and that (most convincing for Caplan), 'many parents are eager to have their dead or anencephalic child used as a donor in the hope that something good might come of a tragic situation'. He does not believe that existing brain death criteria can be applied, and so is content with less exacting criteria to determine if anencephalic newborns are eligible for organ donation.

Declaring brain death in children

Since the country's first human heart transplant—in which the donor was, in fact, an anecephalic infant—great strides have been made in the mechanics of determining death. There is now general medical, legal, and ethical agreement that an individual is dead either when he or she has irreversible cessation of circulation and respiration, or irreversible cessation 'of all functions of the entire brain, including the brain stem'. However, the medical consultants to the President's Commission concluded in 1981 that because of the 'increased resistance to damage' of their brains, 'physicians should be particularly cautious in applying neurologic criteria to determine death in children younger than five years'.

Responding to that challenge, a Task Force for the Determination of Brain Death in Children was established to develop guidelines for children under five. After years of study and deliberation, the group's report, which has been widely endorsed, was published in June, 1987. The guidelines provide accepted clinical criteria for determining brain death in three categories of children: those over one year of age; those aged two months to one year; and those aged seven days to two months. The criteria are inapplicable to infants under seven days of age; for infants less than two months, in addition to meeting strict clinical criteria, two electroencephalograms separated by at least forty-eight hours are recommended. The guidelines are recommendations only and are not meant as universal requirements. The group did not specifically deal with anencephalic infants, but the basic determination to be made is that the insult to the brain is 'irreversible'. Since anencephalic newborns have no higher brain function, different clinical criteria could be used to determine brain death for them.

New clinical criteria for anencephalics?

This leaves essentially two policy choices: we can abandon attempts to justify use of anencephalic infants as organ donors because there is currently no clinically accepted means to declare brain death in these infants; or we can carry out the research necessary to establish a clinically valid procedure for doing so. The Canadian group has decided to take the second route and experiment on methods to use as organ donors anencephalic newborns who can be validly declared brain-dead on classic criteria. The group has developed a basic protocol that calls for the parents to agree, prior to birth, that: (1) the infant will be resuscitated; (2) periodic testing will be done to determine brain death (removal from the ventilator at six-to-twelve-hour intervals for a ten-minute period to determine ability to breathe spontaneously); (3) organ donation is acceptable; and (4) a definite time limit (to be determined by the parents but not more than fourteen days) after which the infant will be removed from the ventilator and permitted to die. Low dose morphine is administered to prevent potential suffering on the part of the infant, although whether anencephalic newborns can suffer is unknown.

This is a true experiment in the sense that there has never been a clinical trial to determine how anencephalic infants do with full ventilator support. They have almost never been so supported, primarily because the condition is quickly and universally fatal. As one pediatric intensive care specialist put it, it would be 'futile and inhumane' to support respiration in these infants artificially. How can we determine if this research is legally and ethically proper?

First, we must determine if it is proper to use dying newborns to help others rather than as ends in themselves. Anencephalic infants differ from all other organ donors in that they are not placed on life-support systems initially for their own sake, but solely for the sake of others. Specifically, since anencephalic newborns are not routinely resuscitated, intubated, or placed on ventilators and given other support, we cannot justify these interventions as 'treatment' for these infants. Rather, these interventions can only be seen as treatment for the benefit of the ultimate organ recipient, and perhaps as treatment for the parents. If we determine that it is never ethically appropriate to prolong an unconsenting person's dying process for the sake of another, then our inquiry is at an end. If we conclude that it may be appropriate to do so (for example, if the harm to the dying child is trivial and the benefit to others is enormous), we can go on to the second step.

This second step would entail research, like that underway in Canada, to determine: how long anencephalic infants can survive with the support available in an intensive care unit; whether they feel pain or have other sensations; the state of their kidneys, liver, and heart, which will determine their general usefulness for transplantation; and whether it is true that the condition of anencephaly can be easily and accurately distinguished from all other abnormalities of infants.

Capron puts the argument against anencephalics being considered as dead in 'Anencephalic Donors: Separate the Dead From the Dying' (1987) 17 Hastings Center Report 5 (footnotes omitted):

Adding anencephalics to the category of dead persons would be a radical change, both in the social and medical understanding of what it means to be dead and in the social practices surrounding death. Anencephalic infants may be dying, but they are still alive and breathing. Calling them 'dead' will not change physiologic reality or otherwise cause them to resemble those (cold and nonrespirating) bodies that are considered appropriate for post-mortem examinations and burial. . . . Physicians do not consider anencephalic infants as dead, but as dying. Their perception is borne out by statistics. One study of liveborn infants with anecephaly, conducted over a thirty-year period, found an equal distribution among males and females. Significantly more males survived the first day of life, but none lived longer than seven days, while female survival was comparable to male after the first day. One female (1.1 percent) survived 14 days:

> The results of this study show that over 40 percent of anencephalic infants can be expected to survive longer than 24 hours (51% males; 34% females), and of these, 35 percent will still be alive on the third day and 5 percent on the seventh day.

For most of the infants in this study, anencephaly was the only neural tube defect, and most of these had no anomalies in other organ systems. Among those infants who also had spina bifida or encephalocele (a protrusion of the brain substance through an opening in the skull), one third had defects in another major organ system.

. . . Although the diagnosis is usually made accurately by neurologists, authors of the thirty-year study just mentioned found that in 'conducting this study, it became obvious that it is important to verify the diagnosis of anencephaly'. They describe several cases of long survival:

> One infant initially coded as anencephaly, who survived over 4 months, had hydranencephaly rather than anencephaly, and another who lived for 12 days actually had amniotic band syndrome mimicking anencephaly.

Misdiagnosis by itself would not appear to be a great enough risk to preclude the use of anencephaly as a category to trigger further action (such as declaration of 'death'). But the observed relationship to—or even overlapping with—other congenital neurological defects underlines the problems that the proposal would create. For example, hydranencephalics have normal brain development early in gestation; as a result of some event (such as an in utero infection) their cerebral hemispheres are destroyed and replaced with fluid. Like anencephalics, hydranencephalics survive depending upon the extent to which their brain stems are able to regulate vegetative functioning, but they usually survive somewhat longer because their skulls are intact and thus their brains are not open to infection.

To further complicate the picture, other neurological conditions, such as certain types of microcephaly, are also inconsistent with long-term survival. Microcephaly—literally, a small head—covers a spectrum of problems, including cases in which the hemispheres fail to form. Whatever their clinical differences from anencephalic babies, hydranencephalic and some microcephalic infants are *conceptually* indistinguishable if the characteristic separating anencephalics from normal children is their lethal neurological condition.

Because of the existence of these other diagnostic categories, decision makers will be pressured to expand the 'definition' to sweep in other similarly situated 'dead' neonates. Indeed, Dr Alan Shewmon, a pediatric neurologist at UCLA, has pointed out that babies—such as hydranencephalics—who typically live a little longer than anencephalics are actually likely to be *more* attractive sources of organs because of the extra time for development. At present, the regional organ procurement association for California does not accept organs from infants younger than two months of age because of physiologic difficulties (such as the tendency of vessels to clot).

More important, these other diagnostic categories serve as a reminder that the proposals involve a variety of infants who are going to die in a relatively short time. Distinguishing those who will die within a day or two from those (including *some* microcephalics and hydranencephalics as well as the remaining anencephalics) who will die over the following two weeks is inevitably imprecise. The distinctions rest on clinical judgment, not moral principle.

. . .

'Defining' anencephalics as dead would place these patients into the same category as patients who lack the capacity to breathe on their own, which has always been taken as a basic sign of life. Perhaps the proponents of this change do not see this as a major alteration because they think the law already lumps together some people who are 'more dead' (those whose hearts have stopped) with others who are merely 'brain dead'. But all persons found to meet the standards of the UDDA [the Uniform Determination of Death Act] are equally dead; it is merely the means of measuring the absence of the integrated functioning of heart, lungs, and brain that differs between those who are and those who are not being treated by methods that can induce breathing and heartbeat.

Defining anencephalics as dead so that they may be used as organ donors could, ironically, actually decrease organ donation. Imagine the effect of the law on the process of seeking organ donations from the relatives of a deceased person. At present, when that situation arises, the person seeking permission can explain that the patient is dead; despite the heaving chest and other appearances of life, if the physicians were to cease the mechanical interventions, it would immediately be apparent that the body is in the same state that we have always recognised as dead. The next-of-kin are told that they do not face a difficult decision over whether to let the patient die; instead they face the reality that their loved one is now a corpse—albeit a corpse with artificially generated heartbeat and breathing—whose organs are still being maintained in a way that would make them useful for transplants. (Remember that only a fraction of persons declared dead on the basis of absence of brain functions are candidates for organ donation.)

If anencephalic babies were also regarded as dead bodies suitable for organ donation, this certainty would be lost. For in these cases, decisions about the extent of treatment remain—indeed, some parents may even wish to try heroic or experimental means to lengthen their child's life. The message to those involved in organ transplantation—both as relatives of potential donors and as physicians, nurses, and others seeking permission for donation—is thus likely to introduce new elements of uncertainty. Is *any* particular patient—and not just an anencephalic baby—*really* dead? Or do the physicians mean only that the outlook for the patient's survival is poor, so why not allow the organs to be taken and bring about death in this (useful) fashion?

Alternatively, perhaps some who favor the anencephalic standard for death *do* mean to change the law radically. A few commentators have argued for many years that the statutes on death should move beyond new means for measuring the traditional state of death and should instead declare that persons who have lost only the higher (neocortical) functions of their brains are also dead. These suggestions have been uniformly rejected by legislators across the country—as well as by most medical, ethical, and legal writers. Yet the inclusion of anencephalics in the 'definition' of death would amount to the first recognition of a 'higher brain' standard—and a first step toward a broader use of this standard—because these babies, despite the massive deficit in their brains, still have some functions (principally at the brain stem level).

To state that such patients are dead would be equivalent to saying that the late Karen Quinlan was 'dead' for the more than ten years that she lived after her respirator was removed. Like the anencephalic babies, Ms. Quinlan and other patients in a persistent vegetative state lack the ability to think, to communicate, and probably even to process any sensations of pain and pleasure (at least in the way that we think of these phenomena). Some people may consider such a life as unrewarding, but that does not justify loose use of language about who is 'dead'. Emotionally, one may be tempted to say that a person in a permanent coma is 'as good as dead' because he or she cannot participate in any of the activities that give life meaning. But such a breathing, metabolising patient does not embody what we mean by dead and is not ready for burial—or organ donation.

A statute that labels anencephalics 'dead' is a bad idea because either it will treat differently another group that is identical on the relevant criteria (the permanently comatose, who are dying and lacking consciousness) or it will lead to a further revision in medical and legal standards under which the permanently comatose would also be regarded as 'dead' although many of them can survive for years with nothing more than ordinary nursing care.

For many people, the prospect of being in a permanent coma is unacceptable; if that occurred, they would want to be allowed to die without further treatment. But that is a separate problem to which society is already responding in other ways. It would be highly controversial—and, indeed, would be rejected by most people—to call people who are in a coma but who still breathe on their own 'dead', especially when the purpose is to allow removal of their vital organs, which *would* then cause their death as that term is now used. This was the nightmarish scenario that took place in the Jefferson Institute in Robin Cook's novel *Coma*.

In 1988, the Working Party of the Medical Royal Colleges on 'Organ Transplantation in Neonates', chaired by Sir Raymond Hoffenberg, considered this question.

5.1 It is understood that, providing there was professional confidence that brain stem death criteria could be applied to the neonate of a certain gestational age, then there could be no legal or ethical objection to the parents agreeing to, and a surgeon undertaking, organ retrieval.
5.2 There is little firm evidence that the well-established criteria used for diagnosing brain stem death in older children and adults can be applied to neonates with beating hearts in the first seven days of life for the purpose of organ removal. The ethics committee of the Child Neurology Society in the United States has concluded that there is insufficient information to diagnose brain death at this age and in that country a joint task force is investigating the matter further and will report soon.
5.3 Until acceptable criteria for brain stem death in the first seven days of life are agreed it is the view of the Working Party that the brain stem death criteria used in older children and adults cannot be used to justify the removal of organs from such neonates with beating hearts for transplantation.

Instead, the Working Party suggested the following (para 4.7.3):

. . . Tests of brain stem function are applied in adults because the absence of such function establishes that the brain is dead; they are clearly inapplicable when the forebrain itself is missing. Such infants clearly have a major neurological deficiency incompatible with life for longer than a few hours. A view which commended itself to the Working Party was that organs could be removed from an anencephalic infant when two doctors (who are not members of the transplant team) agreed that spontaneous respiration had ceased. In the adult the diagnosis of brain death plus apnoea is recognised as death. The Working Party felt by analogy that the absence of the forebrain in these infants plus apnoea would similarly be recognised as death.

Questions

(i) Do you agree with the Working Party's view that the tests for determining absence of 'brain stem' function are inapplicable to anencephalic children?

(ii) Is the Working Party rejecting 'brain stem' function as a criteria for determining death or merely the medical tests to determine its presence or absence? If it is the former, does the Working Party require us, as Capron predicts, to rethink our criteria more generally?

Index